KU-771-864

THE
NEW ENGLISH
BIBLE

THE BIBLE

A NEW ENGLISH TRANSLATION

Directed by Representatives of

THE BAPTIST UNION OF GREAT BRITAIN AND IRELAND

THE CHURCH OF ENGLAND

THE CHURCH OF SCOTLAND

THE COUNCIL OF CHURCHES FOR WALES

THE IRISH COUNCIL OF CHURCHES

THE LONDON YEARLY MEETING OF
THE SOCIETY OF FRIENDS

THE METHODIST CHURCH OF GREAT BRITAIN

THE ROMAN CATHOLIC CHURCH IN
ENGLAND AND WALES

THE ROMAN CATHOLIC CHURCH IN IRELAND

THE ROMAN CATHOLIC CHURCH
IN SCOTLAND

THE UNITED REFORMED CHURCH

THE BRITISH AND FOREIGN BIBLE SOCIETY

THE NATIONAL BIBLE SOCIETY OF SCOTLAND

THE
NEW ENGLISH
BIBLE

THE BIBLE SOCIETIES

in association with

OXFORD UNIVERSITY PRESS
CAMBRIDGE UNIVERSITY PRESS

Text and notes of The New English Bible

©

THE DELEGATES OF THE OXFORD UNIVERSITY PRESS
AND
THE SYNDICS OF THE CAMBRIDGE UNIVERSITY PRESS
1961, 1970

The New Testament
First edition 1961
Second edition 1970

The Old Testament
First published 1970

Bible Society edition first published 1972
Editorial arrangement, section headings
and illustrations
© The British and Foreign Bible Society 1972
This edition without illustrations
first published 1975

The British and Foreign Bible Society
146 Queen Victoria Street, London EC4V 4BX

The National Bible Society of Scotland
5 St. Andrew Square, Edinburgh EH2 2BL

Printed in Great Britain
at the University Press, Oxford
by Vivian Ridler
Printer to the University

BFBS–1975–100M–BN43   ISBN 0 564 00211 9

PREFACE

TO THE NEW ENGLISH BIBLE

IN May 1946 the General Assembly of the Church of Scotland received an overture from the Presbytery of Stirling and Dunblane, where it had been initiated by the Reverend G. S. Hendry, recommending that a translation of the Bible be made in the language of the present day, inasmuch as the language of the Authorized Version, already archaic when it was made, had now become even more definitely archaic and less generally understood. The General Assembly resolved to make an approach to other Churches, and, as a result, delegates of the Church of England, the Church of Scotland, and the Methodist, Baptist, and Congregational Churches met in conference in October. They recommended that the work should be undertaken; that a completely new translation should be made, rather than a revision, such as had earlier been contemplated by the University Presses of Oxford and Cambridge; and that the translators should be free to employ a contemporary idiom rather than reproduce the traditional 'biblical' English.

In January 1947 a second conference, held like the first in the Central Hall, Westminster, included representatives of the University Presses. At the request of this conference, the Churches named above appointed representatives to form the Joint Committee on the New Translation of the Bible. This Committee met for the first time in July of the same year. By January 1948, when its third meeting was held, invitations to be represented had been sent to the Presbyterian Church of England, the Society of Friends, the Churches in Wales, the Churches in Ireland, the British and Foreign Bible Society, and the National Bible Society of Scotland: these invitations were accepted. At a much later stage the hierarchies of the Roman Catholic Church in England and Scotland accepted an invitation to appoint representatives, and these attended as observers.

The Joint Committee provided for the actual work of translation from the original tongues by appointing three panels, to deal, respectively, with the Old Testament, the Apocrypha, and the New Testament. Their members were scholars drawn from various British universities, whom the Committee believed to be representative of competent biblical scholarship at the present time. Apprehending, however, that sound scholarship does not necessarily carry with it a delicate sense of English style, the Committee appointed a fourth panel, of trusted literary advisers, to whom all the work of the translating panels was to be submitted

for scrutiny. It should be said that denominational considerations
played no part in the appointment of the panels.

The Joint Committee issued general directions to the panels, in
pursuance of the aims which the enterprise had in view. The
translating panels adopted the following procedure. An individual
was invited to submit a draft translation of a particular book, or
group of books. Normally he would be a member of the panel
concerned. Very occasionally a draft translation was invited from
a scholar outside the panel, who was known to have worked
specially on the book in question. The draft was circulated in
typescript to members of the panel for their consideration. They
then met together and discussed the draft round a table, verse by
verse, sentence by sentence. Each member brought his view about
the meaning of the original to the judgement of his fellows, and
discussion went on until they reached a common mind. There are
passages where, in the present state of our knowledge, no one
could say with certainty which of two (or even more) possible
meanings is intended. In such cases, after careful discussion,
alternative meanings have been recorded in footnotes, but only
where they seemed of sufficient importance. There is probably no
member of a panel who has not found himself obliged to give up,
perhaps with lingering regret, a cherished view about the meaning
of this or that difficult passage, but in the end the panel accepted
corporate responsibility for the interpretation set forth in the
translation adopted.

The resultant draft was now remitted to the panel of literary
advisers. They scrutinized it, once again, verse by verse, sentence
by sentence, and took pains to secure, as best they could, the tone
and level of language appropriate to the different kinds of writing
to be found in the Bible, whether narrative, familiar discourse,
argument, law, rhetoric or poetry. The translation thus amended
was returned to the translating panel, who examined it to make
sure that the meaning intended had not been in any way misunder-
stood. Passages of peculiar difficulty might on occasion pass
repeatedly between the panels. The final form of the version was
reached by agreement between the translators concerned and the
literary advisers. It was then ready for submission to the Joint
Committee.

Since January 1948 the Joint Committee has met regularly
twice a year in the Jerusalem Chamber, Westminster Abbey, with
four exceptions during 1954–5 when the Langham Room in the
precincts of the Abbey was kindly made available. At these meetings the Committee has received reports on the progress of the work
from the Conveners of the four panels, and its members have had in
their hands typescripts of the books so far translated and revised.
They have made such comments and given such advice or
decisions as they judged to be necessary, and from time to time
they have met members of the panels in conference.

Of the original members of the panels most have happily been able to stay with the work all through, though some have been lost, through death or otherwise, and their places have been filled by fresh appointments.

The Committee has warmly appreciated the courteous hospitality of the Dean of Westminster and of the Trustees of the Central Hall. We owe a great debt to the support and the experienced counsel of the University Presses of Oxford and Cambridge. We recognize gratefully the service rendered to the enterprise by the Reverend Dr. G. S. Hendry and the Reverend Professor J. K. S. Reid, who have successively held the office of Secretary to the Committee. To those who have borne special responsibility, as Chairmen of the Joint Committee, we owe more than could readily be told. Dr. J. W. Hunkin, Bishop of Truro, our first Chairman, brought to the work an exuberant vigour and initiative without which the formidable project might hardly have got off the ground at all. On his lamented death in 1950 he was succeeded by Dr. A. T. P. Williams, then Bishop of Durham and subsequently Bishop of Winchester, who for eighteen years guided our enterprise with judicious wisdom, tact, and benign firmness, but who to our sorrow died when the end of the task was in sight. To both of these we would put on record the gratitude of the Committee and of all engaged in the enterprise.

If we embarked on mentioning the names of those who have served on the various committees and panels, the list would be a long one; and if we mentioned some and not others, the selection would be an invidious one. There are, nevertheless, three names the omission of which would be utterly wrong. As Vice-Chairman and Director, Dr. C. H. Dodd has from start to finish given outstanding leadership and guidance to the project, bringing to the work scholarship, sensitivity, and an ever watchful eye. Professor Sir Godfrey Driver, Joint Director since 1965, has also brought to the work a wealth of knowledge and wisdom; to his enthusiasm, tenacity of purpose, and unflagging devotion the whole enterprise is greatly indebted. Professor W. D. McHardy, Deputy Director since 1968, has made an invaluable contribution particularly, but by no means exclusively, in the sphere of the Apocrypha. It is right that the names of these three scholars should always be associated with The New English Bible. Our debt to them is incalculably great.

DONALD EBOR:
Chairman of the Joint Committee

1970

CONTENTS

THE NEW TESTAMENT

INTRODUCTION

TO THIS EDITION

THE Bible consists of a collection of books which were written over a very long period of time, in Hebrew, Aramaic, and Greek. The earliest parts of the Old Testament go back more than three thousand years, while the latest portions of it were written a thousand years later, some centuries before the New Testament.

The Bible here appears in a new translation, the New English Bible, which, as the Preface to this volume explains, is not a revision of any previous version, but was made direct from the original languages into contemporary English.

The two basic questions facing the translators were: 'What do we translate?' and 'How do we translate it?' In the first place, an attempt must be made to ensure that what is translated is what was intended by the first writer, in spite of the centuries of copying by hand that have intervened between his own time and the invention of printing.

The Old Testament

In the Old Testament the translators have used as the basis for their work the Hebrew text printed in the 1937 edition of R. Kittel's *Biblia Hebraica*. This is a standard printed edition of the Hebrew Scriptures regularly used by scholars in all countries. It reproduces the text of a Hebrew manuscript dated A.D. 1008, now in Leningrad, which is the earliest complete dated manuscript of the Hebrew Bible extant. A few undated manuscripts of portions of the Old Testament are a century or so older, and there are many fragments that are older still; but until modern times these were thought to be the oldest manuscripts of the Hebrew Bible in existence. In and since 1947, however, much older Hebrew manuscripts have been found in caves at Qumran, near the Dead Sea; they are commonly called the Dead Sea Scrolls. They include two copies of Isaiah and parts of all the other books of the Old Testament except Esther. Some of these Scrolls are up to two thousand years old, and so are much older than the Hebrew texts on which earlier translations of the Old Testament have been based. This recently discovered material has been referred to constantly in preparing the present translation.

At first, Hebrew was written with consonants only, but in course of time dots and strokes were added to indicate the pronunciation of the vowels. There are no such vowel-signs in the Dead Sea Scrolls, as the system was a later development. In this translation, and in most English Bibles, God is frequently referred to as 'the LORD'. This title (when printed thus in capitals) stands for the four Hebrew consonants YHWH which represent the name of the God of Israel. This name was considered too sacred to be pronounced, and the expression 'my Lord' was substituted for it in reading, though the consonants still had to be written. Along with these consonants the vowels for 'my Lord' were inserted. The mixture of the vowels of one word (which had to be read) and the consonants of another (which had to be written, but could not be read out) produced the word 'Jehovah'. This has been used in six places in Exodus, where a name for God, rather than a title, seems most appropriate and there is a footnote explaining why it occurs. It is also used in some footnotes and in combination with other words in some proper names. Elsewhere 'the LORD' is used, as in other English Bibles.

Even before the Scrolls were first copied out, the work of translating the Old Testament from Hebrew into other languages had already started. The Greek translation, known as the Septuagint, was begun in the third century B.C., for the benefit of Greek-speaking Jews in Egypt. Manuscripts of this translation still exist which are much earlier than any Hebrew manuscripts other than the Dead Sea Scrolls. The Greek translation was the first of many such 'ancient versions', which included the Old Latin, the Aramaic Targums, the Syriac (known as the Peshitta), and the Latin Vulgate. These versions provide the modern translator with hints which may help him to recover the early form of the Hebrew text from which the versions were made.

Sometimes, however, both Hebrew text and ancient versions are so obscure that the translators had to put what they supposed, to the best of their judgement, was originally written. Places where this occurs are indicated in the footnotes of this edition by the abbreviation 'Prob. rdg.' standing for 'Probable reading', but in all such cases the literal meaning of the Hebrew text is also given. Since footnotes in this edition are kept to a minimum, there is no indication of a departure from the traditional Hebrew text if the translators' reading has the support of a Dead Sea Scroll or of an ancient version, or if it involves an alteration only of the vowels of the Hebrew (which, as we have seen, were supplied later) but not the consonants. Here and there, the order of the verses has been changed, but the numbering of the verses will make it clear where such changes have taken place, and wherever necessary a footnote is given.

The headings of the Psalms, although forming part of the traditional text of the Old Testament and commonly printed in English Bibles, have been omitted; they are almost certainly not original. On the other hand, as a footnote explains, the identity of the speakers in the Song of Songs has been indicated.

The New Testament

The translators of the New Testament faced a complex situation with regard to the Greek original. No text today commands the same degree of general acceptance as did that underlying the Revised Version at the time of its appearance in 1881. The translators have assessed the evidence coming from three sources, (a) ancient manuscripts of the New Testament in Greek, (b) manuscripts of early translations into other languages, and (c) quotations from the New Testament by early Christian writers, and have in each passage selected for translation the reading which in their judgement seemed most likely to represent what the author wrote. In the footnotes they have recorded other readings which seemed to deserve consideration, referring to the three sources of evidence as 'witnesses'. The Greek text which they followed has since been published in The Greek New Testament, edited by R. V. G. Tasker (Oxford and Cambridge University Presses, 1964).

Since the revision of 1881 our knowledge of the Greek used in the New

Testament has been greatly enriched by the discovery of many thousands of papyrus documents in popular Greek of the New Testament period. These have given a better appreciation of the finer shades of idiom, which sometimes clarifies the meaning of passages in the New Testament.

The New Testament of the New English Bible was first published in 1961. In this second edition, embodied in the complete Bible in 1970, a number of modifications have been introduced, mostly in minor details. Old Testament passages quoted in the New have been harmonized with the present version of the Old Testament where this seemed desirable and practicable; but where the Greek is not an exact equivalent of the Hebrew, the translators have rendered the Greek that was before them.

The English of the N.E.B.

The second basic question facing the translators was how to express in English the meaning of the text. The translators of the New English Bible were under no such restrictions as earlier revisers had been in their choice of language. They were instructed to replace constructions and idioms of the biblical languages by those of contemporary English. It was not enough to substitute for Hebrew or Greek words English words more or less equivalent. Each word has its own area of meaning, and in different languages these rarely coincide exactly. Instead of trying to render the same word of the original everywhere by the same English word, the present translators were free to exploit a wide range of English words covering a similar area of meaning in order to carry over the meaning of the sentence as a whole. They have sought to say in their own native idiom what they believed the author to be saying in his, and to use the natural English of the present day, avoiding archaism, jargon, and stilted or slipshod speech.

The Present Edition

While the text used is that of the New English Bible, without change and with the footnotes of the Standard Edition, one new feature is the inclusion of more frequent section headings, to aid the reader in following the main themes and in finding some particular passage he may be looking for.

1972

THE
OLD TESTAMENT

GUIDE TO THE NOTES

THE footnotes in this edition of the Old Testament serve (a) to give cross-references to parallel passages, chiefly in the historical books, (b) to indicate where verses or parts of verses have been transposed, (c) to give the meaning of proper names where it appears to be reflected in the context, (d) to give an alternative interpretation where the Hebrew is capable of such, and (e) to indicate places where the translators have adopted what seemed to them the most probable correction of the text where the Hebrew and the ancient versions cannot be convincingly translated as they stand.

Unless otherwise indicated by its wording, a note refers to the single word against which the reference is placed.

ABBREVIATIONS, ETC.

I. GENERAL

Aram.	Aramaic (text or word)
ch(s).	chapter(s)
cp.	compare
Heb.	Hebrew (text or word)
mng.	meaning
MS(S).	manuscript(s)
om.	omit(s)
or	indicating an alternative interpretation
poss.	possible
prob.	probable
rdg.	reading
Sept.	Septuagint (Greek version of the Old Testament)
[. . .]	In the text itself square brackets are used to indicate words that are probably late additions to the Hebrew text.

II. BOOKS OF THE OLD TESTAMENT

Gen.	Genesis	*Ruth*	Ruth
Exod.	Exodus	*1 Sam.*	1 Samuel
Lev.	Leviticus	*2 Sam.*	2 Samuel
Num.	Numbers	*1 Kgs.*	1 Kings
Deut.	Deuteronomy	*2 Kgs.*	2 Kings
Josh.	Joshua	*1 Chr.*	1 Chronicles
Judg.	Judges	*2 Chr.*	2 Chronicles

Ezra	Ezra	*Hos.*	Hosea
Neh.	Nehemiah	*Joel*	Joel
Esther	Esther	*Amos*	Amos
Job	Job	*Obad.*	Obadiah
Ps(s).	Psalm(s)	*Jonah*	Jonah
Prov.	Proverbs	*Mic.*	Micah
Eccles.	Ecclesiastes	*Nahum*	Nahum
S. of S.	Song of Songs	*Hab.*	Habakkuk
Isa.	Isaiah	*Zeph.*	Zephaniah
Jer.	Jeremiah	*Hag.*	Haggai
Lam.	Lamentations	*Zech.*	Zechariah
Ezek.	Ezekiel	*Mal.*	Malachi
Dan.	Daniel		

MARGINAL NUMBERS

THE conventional verse divisions in the Old Testament are based on those in Hebrew manuscripts. Nevertheless any system of division into numbered verses is foreign to the spirit of this translation, which is intended to convey the meaning in natural English—the prose in paragraphs, the poetic passages in lines corresponding to the structure of the Hebrew.

For purposes of reference, and of comparison with other translations, verse numbers are placed in the margin opposite the line in which the first word belonging to the verse in question appears. Sometimes, however, successive verses are combined in a continuous translation, so that the precise point where a new verse begins cannot be fixed; in these cases the verse numbers, joined by a hyphen, are placed at the point where the passage begins.

GENESIS

God creates the world

1 IN THE BEGINNING of creation, when God made heaven and earth,[a] the earth was without form and void, with darkness over the face of the abyss, and a mighty wind that swept[b] over the surface of the waters. ³ God said, 'Let there be light', and ⁴ there was light; and God saw that the light was good, and he separated light ₅ from darkness. He called the light day, and the darkness night. So evening came, and morning came, the first day.

⁶ God said, 'Let there be a vault between the waters, to separate water ⁷ from water.' So God made the vault, and separated the water under the vault from the water above it, and ⁸ so it was; and God called the vault heaven. Evening came, and morning came, a second day.

⁹ God said, 'Let the waters under heaven be gathered into one place, so that dry land may appear'; and so it ¹⁰ was. God called the dry land earth, and the gathering of the waters he called seas; and God saw that it was ¹¹ good. Then God said, 'Let the earth produce fresh growth, let there be on the earth plants bearing seed, fruit-trees bearing fruit each with seed ¹² according to its kind.' So it was; the earth yielded fresh growth, plants bearing seed according to their kind and trees bearing fruit each with seed according to its kind; and God saw ¹³ that it was good. Evening came, and morning came, a third day.

¹⁴ God said, 'Let there be lights in the vault of heaven to separate day from night, and let them serve as signs both for festivals and for seasons and years. ¹⁵ Let them also shine in the vault of heaven to give light on earth.' So it ¹⁶ was; God made the two great lights, the greater to govern the day and the lesser to govern the night; and ¹⁷ with them he made the stars. God put these lights in the vault of heaven to ¹⁸ give light on earth, to govern day and night, and to separate light from darkness; and God saw that it was ¹⁹ good. Evening came, and morning came, a fourth day.

God said, 'Let the waters teem with ²⁰ countless living creatures, and let birds fly above the earth across the vault of heaven.' God then created the ²¹ great sea-monsters and all living creatures that move and swarm in the waters, according to their kind, and every kind of bird; and God saw that it was good. So he blessed them and ²² said, 'Be fruitful and increase, fill the waters of the seas; and let the birds increase on land.' Evening came, and ²³ morning came, a fifth day.

God said, 'Let the earth bring forth ²⁴ living creatures, according to their kind: cattle, reptiles, and wild animals, all according to their kind.' So it was; God made wild animals, cattle, and ²⁵ all reptiles, each according to its kind; and he saw that it was good. Then ²⁶ God said, 'Let us make man in our image and likeness to rule the fish in the sea, the birds of heaven, the cattle, all wild animals on earth, and all reptiles that crawl upon the earth.' So God created man in his own image; ²⁷ in the image of God he created him; male and female he created them. God blessed them and said to them, ²⁸ 'Be fruitful and increase, fill the earth and subdue it, rule over the fish in the sea, the birds of heaven, and every living thing that moves upon the earth.' God also said, 'I give you all ²⁹ plants that bear seed everywhere on earth, and every tree bearing fruit which yields seed: they shall be yours for food. All green plants I give for ³⁰ food to the wild animals, to all the birds of heaven, and to all reptiles on earth, every living creature.' So it was; and God saw all that he had made, ³¹ and it was very good. Evening came, and morning came, a sixth day.

Thus heaven and earth were com-**2** pleted with all their mighty throng. On the sixth day God completed ² all the work he had been doing, and on the seventh day he ceased from all his work. God blessed the seventh ³ day and made it holy, because on that day he ceased from all the work he had set himself to do.

This is the story of the making of ⁴ heaven and earth when they were created.

a Or In the beginning God created heaven and earth.   b Or and the spirit of God hovering.

A*

Garden of Eden

5 When the LORD God made earth and heaven, there was neither shrub nor plant growing wild upon the earth, because the LORD God had sent no rain on the earth; nor was there any 6 man to till the ground. A flood*c* used to rise out of the earth and water all 7 the surface of the ground. Then the LORD God formed a man*d* from the dust of the ground*e* and breathed into his nostrils the breath of life. Thus the man became a living creature. 8 Then the LORD God planted a garden in Eden away to the east, and there he put the man whom he had formed. 9 The LORD God made trees spring from the ground, all trees pleasant to look at and good for food; and in the middle of the garden he set the tree of life and the tree of the knowledge of good and evil. 10   There was a river flowing from Eden to water the garden, and when it left the garden it branched into 11 four streams. The name of the first is Pishon; that is the river which encircles all the land of Havilah, 12 where the gold*f* is. The gold*f* of that land is good; bdellium*g* and cornelians 13 are also to be found there. The name of the second river is Gihon; this is the one which encircles all the land of 14 Cush. The name of the third is Tigris; this is the river which runs east of Asshur. The fourth river is the Euphrates. 15   The LORD God took the man and put him in the garden of Eden to till 16 it and care for it. He told the man, 'You may eat from every tree in the 17 garden, but not from the tree of the knowledge of good and evil; for on the day that you eat from it, you will 18 certainly die.' Then the LORD God said, 'It is not good for the man to be alone. I will provide a partner for him.' 19 So God formed out of the ground all the wild animals and all the birds of heaven. He brought them to the man to see what he would call them, and whatever the man called each living 20 creature, that was its name. Thus the man gave names to all cattle, to the birds of heaven, and to every wild animal; but for the man himself no 21 partner had yet been found. And so the LORD God put the man into a trance, and while he slept, he took one of his ribs and closed the flesh 22 over the place. The LORD God then

built up the rib, which he had taken out of the man, into a woman. He brought her to the man, and the man 23 said:

'Now this, at last—
bone from my bones,
flesh from my flesh!—
this shall be called woman,*h*
for from man*i* was this taken.'

That is why a man leaves his father 24 and mother and is united to his wife, and the two become one flesh. Now 25 they were both naked, the man and his wife, but they had no feeling of shame towards one another.

Man's disobedience

The serpent was more crafty than any 3 wild creature that the LORD God had made. He said to the woman, 'Is it true that God has forbidden you to eat from any tree in the garden?' The 2 woman answered the serpent, 'We may eat the fruit of any tree in the garden, except for the tree in the 3 middle of the garden; God has forbidden us either to eat or to touch the fruit of that; if we do, we shall die.' The serpent said, 'Of course you will 4 not die. God knows that as soon as 5 you eat it, your eyes will be opened and you will be like gods*j* knowing both good and evil.' When the woman 6 saw that the fruit of the tree was good to eat, and that it was pleasing to the eye and tempting to contemplate, she took some and ate it. She also gave her husband some and he ate it. Then the 7 eyes of both of them were opened and they discovered that they were naked; so they stitched fig-leaves together and made themselves loincloths.

The man and his wife heard the 8 sound of the LORD God walking in the garden at the time of the evening breeze and hid from the LORD God among the trees of the garden. But 9 the LORD God called to the man and said to him, 'Where are you?' He 10 replied, 'I heard the sound as you were walking in the garden, and I was afraid because I was naked, and I hid myself.' God answered, 'Who told you 11 that you were naked? Have you eaten from the tree which I forbade you?' The man said, 'The woman you gave 12 me for a companion, she gave me fruit from the tree and I ate it.' Then the 13 LORD God said to the woman, 'What is this that you have done?' The woman said, 'The serpent tricked me,

c Or mist.   *d Heb.* adam.   *e Heb.* adamah.   *f Or* frankincense.   *g Or* gum resin.
h Heb. ishshah.   *i Heb.* ish.   *j Or* God.

14 and I ate.' Then the LORD God said to the serpent:

'Because you have done this you are accursed
more than all cattle and all wild creatures.
On your belly you shall crawl, and dust you shall eat
all the days of your life.

15 I will put enmity between you and the woman,
between your brood and hers.
They shall strike at your head,
and you shall strike at their heel.'

16 To the woman he said:

'I will increase your labour and your groaning,
and in labour you shall bear children.
You shall be eager[k] for your husband,
and he shall be your master.'

17 And to the man he said:

'Because you have listened to your wife
and have eaten from the tree which I forbade you,
accursed shall be the ground on your account.
With labour you shall win your food from it
all the days of your life.

18 It will grow thorns and thistles for you,
none but wild plants for you to eat.

19 You shall gain your bread by the sweat of your brow
until you return to the ground;
for from it you were taken.
Dust you are, to dust you shall return.'

20 The man called his wife Eve[l] because she was the mother of all who
21 live. The LORD God made tunics of skins for Adam and his wife and
22 clothed them. He said, 'The man has become like one of us, knowing good and evil; what if he now reaches out his hand and takes fruit from the tree of life also, eats it and lives for ever?'
23 So the LORD God drove him out of the garden of Eden to till the ground from
24 which he had been taken. He cast him out, and to the east of the garden of Eden he stationed the cherubim and a sword whirling and flashing to guard the way to the tree of life.

Cain and Abel

4 The man lay with his wife Eve, and she conceived and gave birth to Cain. She said, 'With the help of the LORD I have brought a man into
2 being.' Afterwards she had another child, his brother Abel. Abel was a shepherd and Cain a tiller of the soil.
3 The day came when Cain brought some of the produce of the soil as a
4 gift to the LORD; and Abel brought some of the first-born of his flock, the fat portions of them.[m] The LORD received Abel and his gift with favour;
5 but Cain and his gift he did not receive. Cain was very angry and his
6 face fell. Then the LORD said to Cain, 'Why are you so angry and cast down?
7 If you do well, you are accepted;[n] if not, sin is a demon crouching at the door.
It shall be eager for you, and you will be mastered by it.'[o]

8 Cain said to his brother Abel, 'Let us go into the open country.' While they were there, Cain attacked his brother Abel and murdered him. Then
9 the LORD said to Cain, 'Where is your brother Abel?' Cain answered, 'I do not know. Am I my brother's keeper?'
10 The LORD said, 'What have you done? Hark! your brother's blood that has been shed is crying out to me from
11 the ground. Now you are accursed, and banished from[p] the ground which has opened its mouth wide to receive your brother's blood, which
12 you have shed. When you till the ground, it will no longer yield you its wealth. You shall be a vagrant and
13 a wanderer on earth.' Cain said to the LORD, 'My punishment is heavier than
14 I can bear; thou hast driven me today from the ground, and I must hide myself from thy presence. I shall be a vagrant and a wanderer on earth, and anyone who meets me can kill me.' The LORD answered him, 'No:
15 if anyone kills Cain, Cain shall be avenged sevenfold.' So the LORD put a mark on Cain, in order that anyone meeting him should not kill him.
16 Then Cain went out from the LORD's presence and settled in the land of Nod[q] [r] to the east of Eden.

Cain's descendants

17 Then Cain lay with his wife; and she conceived and bore Enoch. Cain was then building a city, which he named
18 Enoch after his son. Enoch begot Irad; Irad begot Mehujael; Mehujael

k Or feel an urge.   l That is Life.   m Or some of the first-born, that is the sucklings, of his flock.   n Or you hold your head up.   o Or but you must master it.   p and banished from: or more than (cp. 3. 17).   q That is Wandering.   r and settled . . . Nod: or and he lived as a wanderer in the land.

begot Methushael; Methushael begot Lamech.

19 Lamech married two wives, one named Adah and the other Zillah. 20 Adah bore Jabal who was the ancestor of herdsmen who live in tents; 21 and his brother's name was Jubal; he was the ancestor of those who play 22 the harp and pipe. Zillah, the other wife, bore Tubal-cain, the master of all coppersmiths and blacksmiths, and Tubal-cain's sister was Naamah. 23 Lamech said to his wives:

'Adah and Zillah, listen to me;
wives of Lamech, mark what I say:
I kill a man for wounding me,
a young man for a blow.
24 Cain may be avenged seven times,
but Lamech seventy-seven.'

Seth

25 Adam lay with his wife again. She bore a son, and named him Seth,[s] 'for', she said, 'God has granted me another son in place of Abel, because Cain 26 killed him.' Seth too had a son, whom he named Enosh. At that time men began to invoke the LORD[t] by name.

Adam's descendants

5 This is the record of the descendants of Adam. On the day when God created man he made him in the like- 2 ness of God. He created them male and female, and on the day when he created them, he blessed them and called them man. 3 Adam was one hundred and thirty years old when he begot a son in his likeness and image, and named him 4 Seth. After the birth of Seth he lived eight hundred years, and had other 5 sons and daughters. He lived nine hundred and thirty years, and then he died.

6 Seth was one hundred and five 7 years old when he begot Enosh. After the birth of Enosh he lived eight hundred and seven years, and had 8 other sons and daughters. He lived nine hundred and twelve years, and then he died.

9[u] Enosh was ninety years old when 10 he begot Kenan. After the birth of Kenan he lived eight hundred and fifteen years, and had other sons and 11 daughters. He lived nine hundred and five years, and then he died.

12 Kenan was seventy years old when 13 he begot Mahalalel. After the birth of Mahalalel he lived eight hundred and forty years, and had other sons and 14 daughters. He lived nine hundred and ten years, and then he died.

15 Mahalalel was sixty-five years old 16 when he begot Jared. After the birth of Jared he lived eight hundred and thirty years, and had other sons and 17 daughters. He lived eight hundred and ninety-five years, and then he died.

18 Jared was one hundred and sixty-two years old when he begot Enoch. 19 After the birth of Enoch he lived eight hundred years, and had other 20 sons and daughters. He lived nine hundred and sixty-two years, and then he died.

21 Enoch was sixty-five years old when 22 he begot Methuselah. After the birth of Methuselah, Enoch walked with God for three hundred years, and had 23 other sons and daughters. He lived three hundred and sixty-five years. 24 Having walked with God, Enoch was seen no more, because God had taken him away.

25 Methuselah was one hundred and eighty-seven years old when he begot 26 Lamech. After the birth of Lamech he lived for seven hundred and eighty-two years, and had other sons and 27 daughters. He lived nine hundred and sixty-nine years, and then he died.

28 Lamech was one hundred and eighty-two years old when he begot 29 a son. He named him Noah, saying, 'This boy will bring us relief from our work, and from the hard labour that has come upon us because of the LORD's curse upon the ground.' After 30 the birth of Noah, he lived for five hundred and ninety-five years, and had other sons and daughters. La- 31 mech lived seven hundred and seventy-seven years, and then he died. Noah 32 was five hundred years old when he begot Shem, Ham and Japheth.

Man's wickedness

6 When mankind began to increase and to spread all over the earth and 2 daughters were born to them, the sons of the gods saw that the daughters of men were beautiful; so they took for themselves such women as 3 they chose. But the LORD said, 'My life-giving spirit shall not remain in man for ever; he for his part is mortal flesh: he shall live for a hundred and twenty years.'

In those days,[v] when the sons of the 4 gods had intercourse with the daughters

s *That is* Granted.   t *This represents the Hebrew consonants* YHWH, *probably pronounced* Yahweh, *but traditionally read as* Jehovah.   u *Verses 9–32: cp.* 1 Chr. 1. 2–4.   v *Prob. rdg.; Heb. adds* and also afterwards (*cp. Num. 13. 33*).

of men and got children by them, the Nephilim[w] were on earth. They were the heroes of old, men of renown.

5 When the LORD saw that man had done much evil on earth and that his thoughts and inclinations were always 6 evil, he was sorry that he had made man on earth, and he was grieved at 7 heart. He said, 'This race of men whom I have created, I will wipe them off the face of the earth—man and beast, reptiles and birds. I am sorry 8 that I ever made them.' But Noah had won the LORD's favour.

Noah builds an ark

9 This is the story of Noah. Noah was a righteous man, the one blameless man of his time; he walked with God. 10 He had three sons, Shem, Ham and 11 Japheth. Now God saw that the whole world was corrupt[x] and full of 12 violence. In his sight the world had become corrupted, for all men had 13 lived corrupt lives on earth. God said to Noah, 'The loathsomeness[y] of all mankind has become plain to me, for through them the earth is full of violence. I intend to destroy them, 14 and the earth with them. Make yourself an ark with ribs of cypress; cover it with reeds and coat it inside and 15 out with pitch. This is to be its plan: the length of the ark shall be three hundred cubits, its breadth fifty cubits, and its height thirty cubits. 16 You shall make a roof for the ark, giving it a fall of one cubit when complete; and put a door in the side of the ark, and build three decks, 17 upper, middle, and lower. I intend to bring the waters of the flood over the earth to destroy every human being under heaven that has the spirit of life; everything on earth shall perish. 18 But with you I will make a covenant, and you shall go into the ark, you and your sons, your wife and your sons' 19 wives with you. And you shall bring living creatures of every kind into the ark to keep them alive with you, two of each kind, a male and a female; 20 two of every kind of bird, beast, and reptile, shall come to you to be kept 21 alive. See that you take and store every kind of food that can be eaten; this shall be food for you and for them.' 22 Exactly as God had commanded him, so Noah did.

The flood

7 The LORD said to Noah, 'Go into the ark, you and all your household; for I have seen that you alone are righteous before me in this generation. Take with you seven pairs, male and 2 female, of all beasts that are ritually clean, and one pair, male and female, of all beasts that are not clean; also 3 seven pairs, male and female, of every bird—to ensure that life continues on earth. In seven days' time I will 4 send rain over the earth for forty days and forty nights, and I will wipe off the face of the earth every living thing that I have made.' Noah did all 5 that the LORD had commanded him. He was six hundred years old when 6 the waters of the flood came upon the earth.

And so, to escape the waters of the 7 flood, Noah went into the ark with his sons, his wife, and his sons' wives. And into the ark with Noah went one 8-9 pair, male and female, of all beasts, clean and unclean, of birds and of everything that crawls on the ground, two by two, as God had commanded. Towards the end of seven days the 10 waters of the flood came upon the earth. In the year when Noah was six 11 hundred years old, on the seventeenth day of the second month, on that very day, all the springs of the great abyss broke through, the windows of the sky were opened, and rain fell on the 12 earth for forty days and forty nights. On that very day Noah entered the 13 ark with his sons, Shem, Ham and Japheth, his own wife, and his three sons' wives. Wild animals of every 14 kind, cattle of every kind, reptiles of every kind that move upon the ground, and birds of every kind—all 15 came to Noah in the ark, two by two of all creatures that had life in them. Those which came were one male and 16 one female of all living things; they came in as God had commanded Noah, and the LORD closed the door on him. The flood continued upon the 17 earth for forty days, and the waters swelled and lifted up the ark so that it rose high above the ground. They 18 swelled and increased over the earth, and the ark floated on the surface of the waters. More and more the waters 19 increased over the earth until they covered all the high mountains everywhere under heaven. The waters 20 increased and the mountains were covered to a depth of fifteen cubits. Every living creature that moves 21 on earth perished, birds, cattle, wild animals, all reptiles, and all mankind. Everything died that had the breath 22

w Or giants.   x Or ripe for destruction.   y Or end.

of life in its nostrils, everything on
23 dry land. God wiped out every living
thing that existed on earth, man and
beast, reptile and bird; they were
all wiped out over the whole earth,
and only Noah and his company in
the ark survived.

After the flood

24 When the waters had increased over
the earth for a hundred and fifty days,
8 God thought of Noah and all the wild
animals and the cattle with him in
the ark, and he made a wind pass
over the earth, and the waters began
2 to subside. The springs of the abyss
were stopped up, and so were the
windows of the sky; the downpour
3 from the skies was checked. The water
gradually receded from the earth, and
by the end of a hundred and fifty
4 days it had disappeared. On the seventeenth day of the seventh month
the ark grounded on a mountain
5 in Ararat. The water continued to
recede until the tenth month, and on
the first day of the tenth month the
tops of the mountains could be seen.
6 After forty days Noah opened the
trap-door that he had made in the
7 ark, and released a raven to see
whether the water had subsided, but
the bird continued flying to and fro
until the water on the earth had dried
8 up. Noah waited for seven days,[z]
then he released a dove from the ark
to see whether the water on the earth
9 had subsided further. But the dove
found no place where she could settle,
and so she came back to him in the
ark, because there was water over the
whole surface of the earth. Noah
stretched out his hand, caught her
10 and took her into the ark. He waited
another seven days and again released
11 the dove from the ark. She came back
to him towards evening with a newly
plucked olive leaf in her beak. Then
Noah knew for certain that the water
on the earth had subsided still fur-
12 ther. He waited yet another seven
days and released the dove, but she
13 never came back. And so it came about
that, on the first day of the first
month of his six hundred and first
year, the water had dried up on the
earth, and Noah removed the hatch
and looked out of the ark. The surface
of the ground was dry.
14 By the twenty-seventh day of the
second month the whole earth was
15 16 dry. And God said to Noah, 'Come
out of the ark, you and your wife,

your sons and their wives. Bring out 17
every living creature that is with you,
live things of every kind, bird and
beast and every reptile that moves on
the ground, and let them swarm over
the earth and be fruitful and increase
there.' So Noah came out with his 18
sons, his wife, and his sons' wives.
Every wild animal, all cattle, every 19
bird, and every reptile that moves on
the ground, came out of the ark by
families. Then Noah built an altar 20
to the LORD. He took ritually clean
beasts and birds of every kind, and
offered whole-offerings on the altar.
When the LORD smelt the soothing 21
odour, he said within himself, 'Never
again will I curse the ground because
of man, however evil his inclinations
may be from his youth upwards. I will
never again kill every living creature,
as I have just done.

> While the earth lasts 22
> seedtime and harvest, cold and
> heat,
> summer and winter, day and night,
> shall never cease.'

God's covenant with Noah

God blessed Noah and his sons and 9
said to them, 'Be fruitful and increase,
and fill the earth. The fear and dread 2
of you shall fall upon all wild animals
on earth, on all birds of heaven, on
everything that moves upon the
ground and all fish in the sea; they are
given into your hands. Every creature 3
that lives and moves shall be food for
you; I give you them all, as once I
gave you all green plants. But you 4
must not eat the flesh with the life,
which is the blood, still in it. And 5
further, for your life-blood I will
demand satisfaction; from every
animal I will require it, and from a
man also I will require satisfaction
for the death of his fellow-man.

> He that sheds the blood of a man, 6
> for that man his blood shall be shed;
> for in the image of God
> has God made man.

But you must be fruitful and increase, 7
swarm throughout the earth and rule[a]
over it.'

God spoke to Noah and to his sons 8
with him: 'I now make my covenant 9
with you and with your descendants
after you, and with every living 10
creature that is with you, all birds
and cattle, all the wild animals with
you on earth, all that have come out

z Noah . . . days: *prob. rdg., cp. verse 10; Heb. om.*   a *Prob. rdg., cp. 1. 28; Heb. increase.*

11 of the ark. I will make my covenant
with you: never again shall all living
creatures be destroyed by the waters
of the flood, never again shall there
be a flood to lay waste the earth.'
12 God said, 'This is the sign of the
covenant which I establish between
myself and you and every living
creature with you, to endless generations:
13 My bow I set in the cloud,
sign of the covenant
between myself and earth.
14 When I cloud the sky over the
earth,
the bow shall be seen in the cloud.
15 Then will I remember the covenant
which I have made between myself
and you and living things of every
kind. Never again shall the waters
become a flood to destroy all living
16 creatures. The bow shall be in the
cloud; when I see it, it will remind me
of the everlasting covenant between
God and living things on earth of every
17 kind.' God said to Noah, 'This is the
sign of the covenant which I make
between myself and all that lives on
earth.'

Noah and his sons

18 The sons of Noah who came out of
the ark were Shem, Ham and Japheth;
19 Ham was the father of Canaan. These
three were the sons of Noah, and their
descendants spread over the whole
earth.
20 Noah, a man of the soil, began the
21 planting of vineyards. He drank some
of the wine, became drunk and lay
22 naked inside his tent. When Ham,
father of Canaan, saw his father
naked, he told his two brothers out-
23 side. So Shem and Japheth took a
cloak, put it on their shoulders and
walked backwards, and so covered
their father's naked body; their faces
were turned the other way, so that
they did not see their father naked.
24 When Noah woke from his drunken
sleep, he learnt what his youngest son
25 had done to him, and said:

'Cursed be Canaan,
slave of slaves
shall he be to his brothers.'

26 And he continued:

'Bless, O LORD,
the tents of Shem;[b]

may Canaan be his slave.
May God extend[c] Japheth's bounds, 27
let him dwell in the tents of Shem,
may Canaan be their slave.'

After the flood Noah lived for three 28
hundred and fifty years, and he was 29
nine hundred and fifty years old when
he died.

Noah's descendants

These are the descendants of the sons 10
of Noah, Shem, Ham and Japheth,
the sons born to them after the flood.
The sons of Japheth: Gomer, 2[d]
Magog, Madai, Javan,[e] Tubal, Me-
shech and Tiras. The sons of Gomer: 3
Ashkenaz, Riphath and Togarmah.
The sons of Javan: Elishah, Tarshish, 4
Kittim[f] and Rodanim. From these 5
the peoples of the coasts and islands
separated into their own countries,
each with their own language, family
by family, nation by nation.
The sons of Ham: Cush, Mizraim,[g] 6[h]
Put and Canaan. The sons of Cush: 7
Seba, Havilah, Sabtah, Raamah and
Sabtecha. The sons of Raamah:
Sheba and Dedan. Cush was the 8
father of Nimrod, who began to show
himself a man of might on earth; and 9
he was a mighty hunter before the
LORD, as the saying goes, 'Like
Nimrod, a mighty hunter before the
LORD.' His kingdom in the beginning 10
consisted of Babel, Erech, and Accad,
all of them in the land of Shinar. From 11
that land he migrated to Asshur and
built Nineveh, Rehoboth-Ir, Calah,
and Resen, a great city between 12
Nineveh and Calah. From Mizraim 13[i]
sprang the Lydians, Anamites, Lehabites, Naphtuhites, Pathrusites, 14
Casluhites, and the Caphtorites, from
whom the Philistines were descended.
Canaan was the father of Sidon, 15
who was his eldest son, and Heth,[j]
the Jebusites, the Amorites, the Gir- 16
gashites, the Hivites, the Arkites, the 17
Sinites, the Arvadites, the Zemarites, 18
and the Hamathites. Later the Canaanites spread, and then the Canaanite 19
border ran from Sidon towards Gerar
all the way to Gaza; then all the way
to Sodom and Gomorrah, Admah and
Zeboyim as far as Lasha. These were 20
the sons of Ham, by families and
languages with their countries and
nations.
Sons were born also to Shem, elder 21

---

b Bless . . . Shem: *prob. rdg.*; *Heb.* Blessed is the LORD the God of Shem.   c *Heb.* japht.
d *Verses 2–4: cp. 1 Chr. 1. 5–7.*   e *Or* Greece.   f *Or* Tarshish of the Kittians.
g *Or* Egypt.   h *Verses 6–8: cp. 1 Chr. 1. 8–10.*   i *Verses 13–18: cp. 1 Chr. 1. 11–16.*
j *Or* the Hittites.

brother of Japheth, the ancestor of all
22[k] the sons of Eber. The sons of Shem:
Elam, Asshur, Arphaxad, Lud[l] and
23 Aram. The sons of Aram: Uz, Hul,
24 Gether and Mash. Arphaxad was the
father of Shelah, and Shelah the
25 father of Eber. Eber had two sons:
one was named Peleg,[m] because in his
time the earth was divided; and his
26 brother's name was Joktan. Joktan
was the father of Almodad, Sheleph,
27 Hazarmoth, Jerah, Hadoram, Uzal,
28 29 Diklah, Obal, Abimael, Sheba, Ophir,
Havilah and Jobab. All these were sons
30 of Joktan. They lived in the eastern
hill-country, from Mesha all the way
31 to Sephar. These were the sons of
Shem, by families and languages with
their countries and nations.
32   These were the families of the sons
of Noah according to their genealogies,
nation by nation; and from them
came the separate nations on earth
after the flood.

The tower of Babel

11 Once upon a time all the world spoke
a single language and used the same[n]
2 words. As men journeyed in the east,
they came upon a plain in the land of
3 Shinar and settled there. They said to
one another, 'Come, let us make bricks
and bake them hard'; they used
bricks for stone and bitumen for
4 mortar. 'Come,' they said, 'let us
build ourselves a city and a tower
with its top in the heavens, and make
a name for ourselves; or we shall be
5 dispersed all over the earth.' Then
the LORD came down to see the city
and tower which mortal men had
6 built, and he said, 'Here they are, one
people with a single language, and
now they have started to do this;
henceforward nothing they have a
mind to do will be beyond their reach.
7 Come, let us go down there and confuse their speech, so that they will not
understand what they say to one
8 another.' So the LORD dispersed them
from there all over the earth, and they
9 left off building the city. That is why
it is called Babel,[o] because the LORD
there made a babble of the language
of all the world; from that place the
LORD scattered men all over the face
of the earth.

Shem's descendants

10[p] This is the table of the descendants of
Shem. Shem was a hundred years old
when he begot Arphaxad, two years

after the flood. After the birth of 11
Arphaxad he lived five hundred years,
and had other sons and daughters.
Arphaxad was thirty-five years old 12
when he begot Shelah. After the birth 13
of Shelah he lived four hundred and
three years, and had other sons and
daughters.
Shelah was thirty years old when 14
he begot Eber. After the birth of Eber 15
he lived four hundred and three years,
and had other sons and daughters.
Eber was thirty-four years old 16
when he begot Peleg. After the birth 17
of Peleg he lived four hundred and
thirty years, and had other sons and
daughters.
Peleg was thirty years old when he 18
begot Reu. After the birth of Reu he 19
lived two hundred and nine years,
and had other sons and daughters.
Reu was thirty-two years old when 20
he begot Serug. After the birth of Serug 21
he lived two hundred and seven years,
and had other sons and daughters.
Serug was thirty years old when he 22
begot Nahor. After the birth of Nahor 23
he lived two hundred years, and had
other sons and daughters.
Nahor was twenty-nine years old 24
when he begot Terah. After the birth 25
of Terah he lived a hundred and nineteen years, and had other sons and
daughters.
Terah was seventy years old when 26
he begot Abram, Nahor and Haran.

Terah's descendants

This is the table of the descendants of 27
Terah. Terah was the father of Abram,
Nahor and Haran. Haran was the
father of Lot. Haran died in the 28
presence of his father in the land of his
birth, Ur of the Chaldees. Abram and 29
Nahor married wives; Abram's wife
was called Sarai, and Nahor's Milcah.
She was Haran's daughter; and he was
also the father of Milcah and of Iscah.
Sarai was barren; she had no child. 30
Terah took his son Abram, his grand- 31
son Lot the son of Haran, and his
daughter-in-law Sarai Abram's wife,
and they set out from Ur of the Chaldees for the land of Canaan. But when
they reached Harran, they settled
there. Terah was two hundred and 32
five years old when he died in Harran.

The LORD calls Abram

The LORD said to Abram, 'Leave your 12
own country, your kinsmen, and your

---

k *Verses 22–9: cp. 1. Chr. 1. 17–23.*   l *Or the Lydians.*   m *That is Division.*
n *Or used few.*   o *That is Babylon.*   p *Verses 10–26: cp. 1 Chr. 1. 24–7.*

father's house, and go to a country
2 that I will show you. I will make you
into a great nation, I will bless you
and make your name so great that it
shall be used in blessings:

3   Those that bless you I will bless,
those that curse you, I will execrate.
All the families on earth
will pray to be blessed as you are
blessed.'

4 And so Abram set out as the LORD
had bidden him, and Lot went with
him. Abram was seventy-five years
5 old when he left Harran. He took his
wife Sarai, his nephew Lot, all the
property they had collected, and all
the dependants they had acquired in
Harran, and they started on their
journey to Canaan. When they
6 arrived, Abram passed through the
country to the sanctuary at Shechem,
the terebinth-tree of Moreh. At that
time the Canaanites lived in this land.
7 There the LORD appeared to Abram
and said, 'I give this land to your
descendants.' So Abram built an altar
there to the LORD who had appeared
8 to him. Thence he went on to the hill-
country east of Bethel and pitched
his tent between Bethel on the west
and Ai on the east. There he built an
altar to the LORD and invoked the
9 LORD by name. Thus Abram journeyed by stages towards the Negeb.

Abram in Egypt

10 There came a famine in the land, so
severe that Abram went down to
11 Egypt to live there for a while. When
he was approaching Egypt, he said to
his wife Sarai, 'I know very well that
12 you are a beautiful woman, and that
when the Egyptians see you, they will
say, "She is his wife"; then they will
13 kill me but let you live. Tell them that
you are my sister, so that all may go
well with me because of you and my
life may be spared on your account.'
14 When Abram arrived in Egypt, the
Egyptians saw that she was indeed
15 very beautiful. Pharaoh's courtiers
saw her and praised her to Pharaoh,
and she was taken into Pharaoh's
16 household. He treated Abram well
because of her, and Abram came to
possess sheep and cattle and asses,
male and female slaves, she-asses, and
17 camels. But the LORD struck Pharaoh
and his household with grave diseases
on account of Abram's wife Sarai.
18 Pharaoh summoned Abram and said
to him, 'Why have you treated me
like this? Why did you not tell me that

she is your wife? Why did you say that 19
she was your sister, so that I took her
as a wife? Here she is: take her and
be gone.' Then Pharaoh gave his men 20
orders, and they sent Abram away
with his wife and all that he had.

Abram and Lot part company

Abram went up from Egypt into the 13
Negeb, he and his wife and all that he
had, and Lot went with him. Abram 2
was now very rich in cattle and in
silver and gold. From the Negeb he 3
journeyed by stages to Bethel, to the
place between Bethel and Ai where he
had pitched his tent in the beginning,
where he had set up an altar on the 4
first occasion and had invoked the
LORD by name. Now Lot was travel- 5
ling with Abram, and he too possessed
sheep and cattle and tents. The land 6
could not support them both together;
for their livestock were so numerous
that they could not settle in the same
district, and there were quarrels be- 7
tween Abram's herdsmen and Lot's.
The Canaanites and the Perizzites
were then living in the land. So Abram 8
said to Lot, 'Let there be no quarrelling
between us, between my herdsmen
and yours; for we are close kinsmen.
The whole country is there in front of 9
you; let us part company. If you go
left, I will go right; if you go right, I
will go left.' Lot looked up and saw 10
how well-watered the whole Plain of
the Jordan was; all the way to Zoar
it was like the Garden of the LORD,
like the land of Egypt. This was before
the LORD had destroyed Sodom and
Gomorrah. So Lot chose all the Plain 11
of the Jordan and took the road on
the east side. Thus they parted
company. Abram settled in the land 12
of Canaan; but Lot settled among the
cities of the Plain and pitched his
tents near Sodom. Now the men of 13
Sodom were wicked, great sinners
against the LORD.

After Lot and Abram had parted, 14
the LORD said to Abram, 'Raise your
eyes and look into the distance from
the place where you are, north and
south, east and west. All the land you 15
can see I will give to you and to your
descendants for ever. I will make your 16
descendants countless as the dust of
the earth; if anyone could count the
dust upon the ground, then he could
count your descendants. Now go 17
through the length and breadth of
the land, for I give it to you.' So 18
Abram moved his tent and settled by
the terebinths of Mamre at Hebron;

and there he built an altar to the LORD.

Abram rescues Lot

14 It was in the time of Amraphel king of Shinar, Arioch king of Ellasar, Kedorlaomer king of Elam, and Tidal 2 king of Goyim. They went to war against Bera king of Sodom, Birsha king of Gomorrah, Shinab king of Admah, Shemeber king of Zeboyim, and the king of Bela, that is Zoar. 3 These kings joined forces in the valley of Siddim, which is now the Dead Sea. 4 They had been subject to Kedor-laomer for twelve years, but in the 5 thirteenth year they rebelled. Then in the fourteenth year Kedorlaomer and his confederate kings came and defeated the Rephaim in Ashteroth-karnaim, the Zuzim in Ham, the 6 Emim in Shaveh-kiriathaim, and the Horites in the hill-country from Seir^q as far as El-paran on the edge of the 7 wilderness. On their way back they came to En-mishpat, which is now Kadesh, and laid waste all the country of the Amalekites and also that of the Amorites who lived in Hazazon-8 tamar. Then the kings of Sodom, Gomorrah, Admah, Zeboyim, and Bela, which is now Zoar, marched out and drew up their forces against them 9 in the valley of Siddim, against Kedor-laomer king of Elam, Tidal king of Goyim, Amraphel king of Shinar, and Arioch king of Ellasar, four kings 10 against five. Now the valley of Siddim was full of bitumen pits; and when the kings of Sodom and Gomorrah fled, they fell into them, but the rest 11 escaped to the hill-country. The four kings captured all the flocks and herds of Sodom and Gomorrah and all their 12 provisions, and went away. They also carried off Lot, Abram's nephew, who was living in Sodom, and with him 13 his flocks and herds. But a fugitive came and told Abram the Hebrew, who at that time was dwelling in the terebinths of Mamre the Amorite. This Mamre was the brother of Eshcol and Aner, who were allies of Abram. 14 When Abram heard that his kinsman had been taken prisoner, he mustered his retainers, men born in his house-hold, three hundred and eighteen of them, and pursued as far as Dan. 15 Abram and his followers surrounded the enemy by night, attacked them and pursued them as far as Hobah, 16 north of Damascus; he then brought back all the flocks and herds and also his kinsman Lot with his flocks and herds, together with the women and the other captives. On his return from 17 this defeat of Kedorlaomer and his confederate kings, the king of Sodom came out to meet him in the valley of Shaveh, which is now the King's Valley.

Melchizedek blesses Abram

Then Melchizedek king of Salem 18 brought food and wine. He was priest of God Most High, and he pronounced 19 this blessing on Abram:

'Blessed be Abram
by God Most High,
creator^r of heaven and earth.
And blessed be God Most High,   20
who has delivered your enemies into
　　your power.'

Abram gave him a tithe of all the booty.

The king of Sodom said to Abram, 21 'Give me the people, and you can take the property'; but Abram said to the 22 king of Sodom, 'I lift my hand and swear by the LORD, God Most High, creator of heaven and earth: not a 23 thread or a shoe-string will I accept of anything that is yours. You shall never say, "I made Abram rich." I 24 will accept nothing but what the young men have eaten and the share of the men who went with me. Aner, Eshcol, and Mamre shall have their share.'

The LORD's covenant with Abram

After this the word of the LORD came **15** to Abram in a vision. He said, 'Do not be afraid, Abram, I am giving you a very great reward.'^{s} Abram replied, 2 'Lord GOD, what canst thou give me? I have no standing among men, for the heir to my household is Eliezer of Damascus.' Abram continued, 'Thou 3 hast given me no children, and so my heir must be a slave born in my house.' Then came the word of the LORD to 4 him: 'This man shall not be your heir; your heir shall be a child of your own body.' He took Abram outside and 5 said, 'Look up into the sky, and count the stars if you can. So many', he said, 'shall your descendants be.'

Abram put his faith in the LORD, 6 and the LORD counted that faith to him as righteousness; he said to him, 7 'I am the LORD who brought you out from Ur of the Chaldees to give you

q Prob. rdg.; Heb. in their hill-country, Seir.　　r Or owner.　　s I am giving . . . reward: or I am your shield, your very great reward.

8 this land to occupy.' Abram said, 'O
9 Lord GOD, how can I be sure that I shall occupy it?' The LORD answered, 'Bring me a heifer three years old, a she-goat three years old, a ram three years old, a turtle-dove, and a fledg-
10 ling.' He brought him all these, halved the animals down the middle and placed each piece opposite its corresponding piece, but he did not
11 halve the birds. When the birds of prey swooped down on the carcasses,
12 Abram scared them away. Then, as the sun was going down, a trance came over Abram and great fear came
13 upon him. The LORD said to Abram, 'Know this for certain, that your descendants will be aliens living in a land that is not theirs; they will be slaves, and will be held in oppression
14 there for four hundred years. But I will punish that nation whose slaves they are, and after that they shall come
15 out with great possessions. You yourself shall join your fathers in peace
16 and be buried in a good old age; and the fourth generation shall return here, for the Amorites will not be ripe for
17 punishment till then.' The sun went down and it was dusk, and there appeared a smoking brazier and a flaming torch passing between the
18 divided pieces. That very day the LORD made a covenant with Abram, and he said, 'To your descendants I give this land from the River of
19 Egypt to the Great River, the river
20 Euphrates, the territory of the Ken-
21 ites, Kenizzites, Kadmonites, Hittites, Perizzites, Rephaim, Amorites, Canaanites, Girgashites, Hivites, and Jebusites.'

Hagar and Ishmael

16 Abram's wife Sarai had borne him no children. Now she had an Egyptian
2 slave-girl whose name was Hagar, and she said to Abram, 'You see that the LORD has not allowed me to bear a child. Take my slave-girl; perhaps I shall found a family through her.' Abram agreed to what his wife said;
3 so Sarai, Abram's wife, brought her slave-girl, Hagar the Egyptian, and gave her to her husband Abram as a wife.[t] When this happened Abram
4 had been in Canaan for ten years. He lay with Hagar and she conceived; and when she knew that she was with
5 child, she despised her mistress. Sarai said to Abram, 'I have been wronged

and you must answer for it. It was I who gave my slave-girl into your arms, but since she has known that she is with child, she has despised me. May the LORD see justice done between
6 you and me.' Abram replied to Sarai, 'Your slave-girl is in your hands; deal with her as you will.' So Sarai ill-treated her and she ran away.
7 The angel of the LORD found her by a spring of water in the wilderness on
8 the way to Shur, and he said, 'Hagar, Sarai's slave-girl, where have you come from and where are you going?' She answered, 'I am running away
9 from Sarai my mistress.' The angel of the LORD said to her, 'Go back to your mistress and submit to her ill-treatment.' The angel also said, 'I
10 will make your descendants too many to be counted.' And the angel of the
11 LORD said to her:

'You are with child and will bear a son.
You shall name him Ishmael,[u]
because the LORD has heard of your
        ill-treatment.
He shall be a man like the wild ass,   12
his hand against every man
and every man's hand against him;
and he shall live at odds with[v] all his
        kinsmen.'

13 She called the LORD who was speaking to her by the name El-Roi,[w] for she said, 'Have I indeed seen God and
14 still live[x] after that vision?' That is why men call the well Beer-lahai-roi;[y] it lies between Kadesh and Bered.
15 Hagar bore Abram a son, and he named the child she bore him Ishmael.
16 Abram was eighty-six years old when Hagar bore Ishmael.

Abram's new name

17 When Abram was ninety-nine years old, the LORD appeared to him and said, 'I am God Almighty. Live always in my presence and be perfect,
2 so that I may set my covenant between myself and you and multiply your descendants.' Abram threw him-
3 self down on his face, and God spoke with him and said, 'I make this cove-
4 nant, and I make it with you: you shall be the father of a host of nations.
5 Your name shall no longer be Abram,[z] your name shall be Abraham,[a] for I make you father of a host of nations.
6 I will make you exceedingly fruitful; I will make nations out of you, and
7 kings shall spring from you. I will

t Or concubine.   u That is God heard.   v Or live to the east of . . .   w That is God of a
vision.   x God and still live: prob. rdg.; Heb. hither.   y That is the Well of the Living One of
Vision.   z That is High Father.   a That is Father of a Multitude.

fulfil my covenant between myself and you and your descendants after you, generation after generation, an everlasting covenant, to be your God, yours

8 and your descendants' after you. As an everlasting possession I will give you and your descendants after you the land in which you now are aliens, all the land of Canaan, and I will be God to your descendants.'

9 God said to Abraham, 'For your part, you must keep my covenant, you and your descendants after you,

10 generation by generation. This is how you shall keep my covenant between myself and you and your descendants after you: circumcise yourselves, every

11 male among you. You shall circumcise the flesh of your foreskin, and it shall be the sign of the covenant

12 between us. Every male among you in every generation shall be circumcised on the eighth day, both those born in your house and any foreigner, not of your blood but bought with

13 your money. Circumcise both those born in your house and those bought with your money; thus shall my covenant be marked in your flesh as

14 an everlasting covenant. Every uncircumcised male, everyone who has not had the flesh of his foreskin circumcised, shall be cut off from the kin of his father. He has broken my covenant.'

Isaac's birth foretold

15 God said to Abraham, 'As for Sarai your wife; you shall call her not Sarai,[b]

16 but Sarah.[c] I will bless her and give you a son by her. I will bless her and she shall be the mother of nations; the kings of many people shall spring

17 from her.' Abraham threw himself down on his face; he laughed and said to himself, 'Can a son be born to a man who is a hundred years old? Can Sarah bear a son when she is ninety?'

18 He said to God, 'If only Ishmael might live under thy special care!'

19 But God replied, 'No. Your wife Sarah shall bear you a son, and you shall call him Isaac.[d] With him I will fulfil my covenant, an everlasting covenant

20 with his descendants after him. I have heard your prayer for Ishmael. I have blessed him and will make him fruitful. I will multiply his descendants; he shall be father of twelve princes, and I will raise a great nation from him.

21 But my covenant I will fulfil with Isaac, whom Sarah will bear to you

22 at this season next year.' When he had finished talking with Abraham, God ascended and left him.

23 Then Abraham took Ishmael his son, everyone who had been born in his household and everyone bought with money, every male in his household, and he circumcised them that very same day in the flesh of their foreskins as God had told him to do.

24 Abraham was ninety-nine years old when he circumcised the flesh of his

25 foreskin. Ishmael was thirteen years old when he was circumcised in the

26 flesh of his foreskin. Both Abraham and Ishmael were circumcised on the

27 same day, and all the men of his household, born in the house or bought with money from foreigners, were circumcised with him.

18 The LORD appeared to Abraham by the terebinths of Mamre. As Abraham was sitting at the opening of his tent

2 in the heat of the day, he looked up and saw three men standing in front of him. When he saw them, he ran from the opening of his tent to meet them and bowed low to the ground.

3 'Sirs,' he said, 'if I have deserved your favour, do not pass by my humble self

4 without a visit. Let me send for some water so that you may wash your feet

5 and rest under a tree; and let me fetch a little food so that you may refresh yourselves. Afterwards you may continue the journey which has brought you my way.' They said, 'Do

6 by all means as you say.' So Abraham hurried into the tent to Sarah and said, 'Take three measures of flour quickly, knead it and make some

7 cakes.' Then Abraham ran to the cattle, chose a fine tender calf and gave it to a servant, who hurriedly prepared it.

8 He took curds and milk and the calf he had prepared, set it before them, and waited on them himself under the tree

9 while they ate. They asked him where Sarah his wife was, and he said, 'There, in the tent.' The stranger said, 'About

10 this time next year I will be sure to come back to you, and Sarah your wife shall have a son.' Now Sarah was listening at the opening of the tent,

11 and he was close beside it. Both Abraham and Sarah had grown very old, and Sarah was past the age of

12 child-bearing. So Sarah laughed to herself and said, 'I am past bearing children now that I am out of my time, and my husband is old.' The LORD

13 said to Abraham, 'Why did Sarah laugh and say, "Shall I indeed bear a

b That is Mockery.   *c That is* Princess.   *d That is* He laughed.

14 child when I am old?" Is anything impossible for the LORD? In due season I will come back to you, about this time next year, and Sarah shall have a son.'
15 Sarah lied because she was frightened, and denied that she had laughed; but he said, 'Yes, you did laugh.'

Abraham pleads for Sodom

16 The men set out and looked down towards Sodom, and Abraham went with them to start them on their way.
17 The LORD thought to himself, 'Shall I conceal from Abraham what I intend
18 to do? He will become a great and powerful nation, and all nations on earth will pray to be blessed as he is
19 blessed. I have taken care of him on purpose that he may charge his sons and family after him to conform to the way of the LORD and to do what is right and just; thus I shall fulfil all
20 that I have promised for him.' So the LORD said, 'There is a great outcry over Sodom and Gomorrah; their sin
21 is very grave. I must go down and see whether their deeds warrant the outcry which has reached me. I am re-
22 solved to know the truth.' When the men turned and went towards Sodom, Abraham remained standing before
23 the LORD. Abraham drew near him and said, 'Wilt thou really sweep away
24 good and bad together? Suppose there are fifty good men in the city; wilt thou really sweep it away, and not pardon the place because of the fifty
25 good men? Far be it from thee to do this—to kill good and bad together; for then the good would suffer with the bad. Far be it from thee. Shall not the judge of all the earth do what is
26 just?' The LORD said, 'If I find in the city of Sodom fifty good men, I will pardon the whole place for their sake.'
27 Abraham replied, 'May I presume to speak to the Lord, dust and ashes
28 that I am: suppose there are five short of the fifty good men? Wilt thou destroy the whole city for a mere five men?' He said, 'If I find forty-five
29 there I will not destroy it.' Abraham spoke again, 'Suppose forty can be found there?'; and he said, 'For the
30 sake of the forty I will not do it.' Then Abraham said, 'Please do not be angry, O Lord, if I speak again: suppose thirty can be found there?' He answered, 'If I find thirty there I
31 will not do it.' Abraham continued, 'May I presume to speak to the Lord: suppose twenty can be found there?' He replied, 'For the sake of the twenty

I will not destroy it.' Abraham said, 32 'I pray thee not to be angry, O Lord, if I speak just once more: suppose ten can be found there?' He said, 'For the sake of the ten I will not destroy it.' When the LORD had finished talk- 33 ing with Abraham, he left him, and Abraham returned home.

Destruction of Sodom and Gomorrah

The two angels came to Sodom in the **19** evening, and Lot was sitting in the gateway of the city. When he saw them he rose to meet them and bowed low with his face to the ground. He 2 said, 'I pray you, sirs, turn aside to my humble home, spend the night there and wash your feet; you can rise early and continue your journey.' 'No,' they answered, 'we will spend the night in the street.' But Lot was so 3 insistent that they did turn aside and enter his house. He prepared a meal for them, baking unleavened cakes, and they ate them. Before they lay 4 down to sleep, the men of Sodom, both young and old, surrounded the house —everyone without exception. They 5 called to Lot and asked him where the men were who had entered his house that night. 'Bring them out', they shouted, 'so that we can have intercourse with them.'

Lot went out into the doorway to 6 them, closed the door behind him and 7 said, 'No, my friends, do not be so wicked. Look, I have two daughters, 8 both virgins; let me bring them out to you, and you can do what you like with them; but do not touch these men, because they have come under the shelter of my roof.' They said, 'Out 9 of our way! This man has come and settled here as an alien, and does he now take it upon himself to judge us? We will treat you worse than them.' They crowded in on the man Lot and pressed close to smash in the door. But 10 the two men inside reached out, pulled Lot in, and closed the door. Then 11 they struck the men in the doorway with blindness, both small and great, so that they could not find the door.

The two men said to Lot, 'Have 12 you anyone else here, sons-in-law, sons, or daughters, or any who belong to you in the city? Get them out of this place, because we are going to destroy 13 it. The outcry against it has been so great that the LORD has sent us to destroy it.' So Lot went out and spoke 14 to his intended sons-in-law.[e] He said, 'Be quick and leave this place; the

e Or his sons-in-law, who had married his daughters.

LORD is going to destroy the city.' But they did not take him seriously.

15 As soon as it was dawn, the angels urged Lot to go, saying, 'Be quick, take your wife and your two daughters who are here, or you will be swept away when the city is punished.'
16 When he lingered, they took him by the hand, with his wife and his daughters, and, because the LORD had spared him, led him on until he was outside
17 the city. When they had brought them out, they said, 'Flee for your lives; do not look back and do not stop anywhere in the Plain. Flee to the hills or
18 you will be swept away.' Lot replied,
19 'No, sirs. You have shown your servant favour and you have added to your unfailing care for me by saving my life, but I cannot escape to the hills; I shall be overtaken by the
20 disaster, and die. Look, here is a town, only a small place, near enough for me to reach quickly. Let me escape to it —it is very small—and save my life.'
21 He said to him, 'I grant your request: I will not overthrow this town you
22 speak of. But flee there quickly, because I can do nothing until you are there.' That is why the place was
23 called Zoar.ᶠ The sun had risen over
24 the land as Lot entered Zoar; and then the LORD rained down fire and brimstone from the skies on Sodom and
25 Gomorrah. He overthrew those cities and destroyed all the Plain, with everyone living there and everything grow-
26 ing in the ground. But Lot's wife, behind him, looked back, and she turned into a pillar of salt.
27 Next morning Abraham rose early and went to the place where he had
28 stood in the presence of the LORD. He looked down towards Sodom and Gomorrah and all the wide extent of the Plain, and there he saw thick smoke rising high from the earth like
29 the smoke of a lime-kiln. Thus, when God destroyed the cities of the Plain, he thought of Abraham and rescued Lot from the disaster, the overthrow of the cities where he had been living.

Origin of Moab and Ammon

30 Lot went up from Zoar and settled in the hill-country with his two daughters, because he was afraid to stay in Zoar; he lived with his two daughters
31 in a cave. The elder daughter said to the younger, 'Our father is old and there is not a man in the country to
32 come to us in the usual way. Come now, let us make our father drink wine and then lie with him and in this way keep the family alive through our father.' So that night they gave 33 him wine to drink, and the elder daughter came and lay with him, and he did not know when she lay down and when she got up. Next day the 34 elder said to the younger, 'Last night I lay with my father. Let us give him wine to drink again tonight; then you go in and lie with him. So we shall keep the family alive through our father.' So they gave their father wine 35 to drink again that night, and the younger daughter went and lay with him, and he did not know when she lay down and when she got up. In this 36 way both Lot's daughters came to be with child by their father. The elder 37 daughter bore a son and called him Moab; he was the ancestor of the present Moabites. The younger also 38 bore a son, whom she called Ben-ammi; he was the ancestor of the present Ammonites.

Abraham and Abimelech

Abraham journeyed by stages from 20 there into the Negeb, and settled between Kadesh and Shur, living as an alien in Gerar. He said that Sarah 2 his wife was his sister, and Abimelech king of Gerar sent and took her. But 3 God came to Abimelech in a dream by night and said, 'You shall die because of this woman whom you have taken. She is a married woman.' Now 4 Abimelech had not gone near her; and he said, 'Lord, wilt thou destroy an innocent people? Did he not tell me 5 himself that she was his sister, and she herself said that he was her brother. It was with a clear conscience and in all innocence that I did this.' God said 6 to him in the dream, 'Yes: I know that you acted with a clear conscience. Moreover, it was I who held you back from committing a sin against me: that is why I did not let you touch her. Send back the man's wife now; he is 7 a prophet, and he will intercede on your behalf, and you shall live. But if you do not send her back, I tell you that you are doomed to die, you and all that is yours.' So Abimelech rose 8 early in the morning, summoned all his servants and told them the whole story; the men were terrified. Abi- 9 melech then summoned Abraham and said to him, 'Why have you treated us like this? What harm have I done to you that you should bring this great sin on me and my kingdom? You have

ᶠ That is Small.

done a thing that ought not to be done.'
10 And he asked Abraham, 'What was
11 your purpose in doing this?' Abraham
answered, 'I said to myself, There can
be no fear of God in this place, and
they will kill me for the sake of my
12 wife. She is in fact my sister, she is my
father's daughter though not by the
same mother; and she became my
13 wife. When God set me wandering
from my father's house, I said to her,
"There is a duty towards me which
you must loyally fulfil: wherever we
go, you must say that I am your
14 brother."' Then Abimelech took
sheep and cattle, and male and female
slaves, gave them to Abraham, and
15 returned his wife Sarah to him. Abimelech said, 'My country lies before
16 you; settle wherever you please.' To
Sarah he said, 'I have given your
brother a thousand pieces of silver, so
that your own people may turn a
blind eye on it all, and you will be
17 completely vindicated.' Then Abraham interceded with God, and God
healed Abimelech, his wife, and his
slave-girls, and they bore children;
18 for the LORD had made every woman
in Abimelech's household barren on
account of Abraham's wife Sarah.

The birth of Isaac

21 The LORD showed favour to Sarah as he
had promised, and made good what he
2 had said about her. She conceived and
bore a son to Abraham for his old age,
at the time which God had appointed.
3 The son whom Sarah bore to him,
4 Abraham named Isaac.*g* When Isaac
was eight days old Abraham circumcised him, as God had commanded.
5 Abraham was a hundred years old
6 when his son Isaac was born. Sarah
said, 'God has given me good reason
to laugh, and everybody who hears
7 will laugh with me.' She said, 'Whoever would have told Abraham that
Sarah would suckle children? Yet I
have borne him a son for his old age.'

Hagar and Ishmael sent away

8 The boy grew and was weaned, and on
the day of his weaning Abraham gave
9 a feast. Sarah saw the son whom
Hagar the Egyptian had borne to
10 Abraham laughing at him, and she
said to Abraham, 'Drive out this
slave-girl and her son; I will not have
this slave-girl's son sharing the inherit-
11 ance with my son Isaac.' Abraham
was vexed at this on his son Ishmael's
12 account, but God said to him, 'Do

not be vexed on account of the boy
and the slave-girl. Do what Sarah
says, because you shall have descendants through Isaac. I will make a 13
great nation of the slave-girl's son too,
because he is your own child.'
Abraham rose early in the morning, 14
took some food and a waterskin full
of water and gave it to Hagar; he set
the child on her shoulder and sent her
away, and she went and wandered in
the wilderness of Beersheba. When 15
the water in the skin was finished,
she thrust the child under a bush, and 16
went and sat down some way off,
about two bowshots away, for she
said, 'How can I watch the child die?'
So she sat some way off, weeping
bitterly. God heard the child crying, 17
and the*h* angel of God called from
heaven to Hagar, 'What is the matter,
Hagar? Do not be afraid: God has
heard the child crying where you laid
him. Get to your feet, lift the child 18
up and hold him in your arms,
because I will make of him a great
nation.' Then God opened her eyes 19
and she saw a well full of water; she
went to it, filled her waterskin and gave
the child a drink. God was with the 20-1
child, and he grew up and lived in the
wilderness of Paran. He became an
archer, and his mother found him a
wife from Egypt.

The pact between Abraham and Abimelech

Now about that time Abimelech, with 22
Phicol the commander of his army,
addressed Abraham in these terms:
'God is with you in all that you do.
Now swear an oath to me in the name 23
of God, that you will not break faith
with me, my offspring, or my descendants. As I have kept faith with you,
so shall you keep faith with me and
with the country where you have come
to live as an alien.' Abraham said, 'I 24
swear.' It happened that Abraham 25
had a complaint against Abimelech
about a well which Abimelech's men
had seized. Abimelech said, 'I do not 26
know who did this. You never told me,
and I have heard nothing about it till
now.' So Abraham took sheep and 27
cattle and gave them to Abimelech;
and the two of them made a pact.
Abraham set seven ewe-lambs apart, 28
and when Abimelech asked him why 29
he had set these lambs apart, he said, 30
'Accept these from me in token that
I dug this well.' Therefore that place 31
was called Beersheba,*i* because there

g That is He laughed.   *h Or* an.   *i That is* Well of Seven *and* Well of an Oath.

32 the two of them swore an oath. When they had made the pact at Beersheba, Abimelech and Phicol the commander of his army returned at once to the 33 country of the Philistines, and Abraham planted a strip of ground[j] at Beersheba. There he invoked the LORD, the everlasting God, by name, 34 and he lived as an alien in the country of the Philistines for many a year.

God tests Abraham

22 The time came when God put Abraham to the test. 'Abraham', he called, and Abraham replied, 'Here I am.' 2 God said, 'Take your son Isaac, your only son, whom you love, and go to the land of Moriah. There you shall offer him as a sacrifice on one of 3 the hills which I will show you.' So Abraham rose early in the morning and saddled his ass, and he took with him two of his men and his son Isaac; and he split the firewood for the sacrifice, and set out for the place of which 4 God had spoken. On the third day Abraham looked up and saw the place 5 in the distance. He said to his men, 'Stay here with the ass while I and the boy go over there; and when we have worshipped we will come back 6 to you.' So Abraham took the wood for the sacrifice and laid it on his son Isaac's shoulder; he himself carried the fire and the knife, and the two of 7 them went on together. Isaac said to Abraham, 'Father', and he answered, 'What is it, my son?' Isaac said, 'Here are the fire and the wood, but where is the young beast for the sacrifice?' 8 Abraham answered, 'God will provide himself with a young beast for a sacrifice, my son.' And the two of them 9 went on together and came to the place of which God had spoken. There Abraham built an altar and arranged the wood. He bound his son Isaac and laid him on the altar on top of the 10 wood. Then he stretched out his hand 11 and took the knife to kill his son; but the angel of the LORD called to him from heaven, 'Abraham, Abraham.' 12 He answered, 'Here I am.' The angel of the LORD said, 'Do not raise your hand against the boy; do not touch him. Now I know that you are a God-fearing man. You have not withheld from me your son, your only son.' 13 Abraham looked up, and there he saw a ram caught by its horns in a thicket. So he went and took the ram and offered it as a sacrifice instead of 14 his son. Abraham named that place

Jehovah-jireh;[k] and to this day the saying is: 'In the mountain of the LORD it was provided.' Then the angel 15 of the LORD called from heaven a second time to Abraham, 'This is 16 the word of the LORD: By my own self I swear: inasmuch as you have done this and have not withheld your son, your only son, I will bless you 17 abundantly and greatly multiply your descendants until they are as numerous as the stars in the sky and the grains of sand on the sea-shore. Your descendants shall possess the cities of their enemies. All nations on earth shall 18 pray to be blessed as your descendants are blessed, and this because you have obeyed me.'

Abraham went back to his men, 19 and together they returned to Beersheba; and there Abraham remained.

Nahor's descendants

After this Abraham was told, 'Milcah 20 has borne sons to your brother Nahor: Uz his first-born, then his brother 21 Buz, and Kemuel father of Aram, and Kesed, Hazo, Pildash, Jidlaph and 22 Bethuel; and a daughter, Rebecca, 23 has been born to Bethuel.' These eight Milcah bore to Abraham's brother Nahor. His concubine, whose 24 name was Reumah, also bore him sons: Tebah, Gaham, Tahash and Maacah.

The death and burial of Sarah

Sarah lived for a hundred and twenty- 23 seven years, and died in Kiriath-arba, 2 which is Hebron, in Canaan. Abraham went in to mourn over Sarah and to weep for her. At last he rose and 3 left the presence of the dead. He said to the Hittites, 'I am an alien and a 4 settler among you. Give me land enough for a burial-place, so that I can give my dead proper burial.' The Hit- 5 tites answered Abraham, 'Do, pray, 6 listen to what we have to say, sir. You are a mighty prince among us. Bury your dead in the best grave we have. There is not one of us who will deny you his grave or hinder you from burying your dead.' Abraham stood 7 up and then bowed low to the Hittites, the people of that country. He said to 8 them, 'If you are willing to let me give my dead proper burial, then listen to me and speak for me to Ephron son of Zohar, asking him to give me the 9 cave that belongs to him at Machpelah, at the far end of his land. Let him give

---

j Or planted a tamarisk.   *k* That is the LORD will provide.

it to me for the full price, so that I may take possession of it as a burial-place within your territory.' Ephron the Hittite was sitting with the others, and he gave Abraham this answer in the hearing of everyone as they came into the city gate: 'No, sir; hear what I have to say. I will make you a gift of the land and I will also give you the cave which is on it. In the presence of all my kinsmen I give it to you; so bury your dead.' Abraham bowed low before the people of the country and said to Ephron in their hearing, 'If you really mean it—but do listen to me! I give you the price of the land: take it and I will bury my dead there.' And Ephron answered, 'Do listen to me, sir: the land is worth four hundred shekels of silver. But what is that between you and me? There you may bury your dead.' Abraham came to an agreement with him and weighed out the amount that Ephron had named in the hearing of the Hittites, four hundred shekels of the standard recognized by merchants. Thus the plot of land belonging to Ephron at Machpelah to the east of Mamre, the plot, the cave that is on it, every tree on the plot, within the whole area, became the legal possession of Abraham, in the presence of all the Hittites as they came into the city gate. After this Abraham buried his wife Sarah in the cave on the plot of land at Machpelah to the east of Mamre, which is Hebron, in Canaan. Thus the plot and the cave on it became Abraham's possession as a burial-place, by purchase from the Hittites.

A wife for Isaac

24 By this time Abraham had become a very old man, and the LORD had blessed him in all that he did. Abraham said to his servant, who had been long in his service and was in charge of all his possessions, 'Put your hand under my thigh: I want you to swear by the LORD, the God of heaven and earth, that you will not take a wife for my son from the women of the Canaanites in whose land I dwell; you must go to my own country and to my own kindred to find a wife for my son Isaac.' The servant said to him, 'What if the woman is unwilling to come with me to this country? Must I in that event take your son back to the land from which you came?' Abraham said to him, 'On no account are you to take

my son back there. The LORD the God of heaven who took me from my father's house and the land of my birth, the LORD who swore to me that he would give this land to my descendants—he will send his angel before you, and from there you shall take a wife for my son. If the woman is unwilling to come with you, then you will be released from your oath to me; but you must not take my son back there.' So the servant put his hand under his master Abraham's thigh and swore an oath in those terms.

The servant took ten camels from his master's herds, and also all kinds of gifts from his master; he set out for Aram-naharaim*l* and arrived at the city where Nahor lived. Towards evening, the time when the women come out to draw water, he made the camels kneel down by the well outside the city. He said, 'O LORD God of my master Abraham, give me good fortune this day; keep faith with my master Abraham. Here I stand by the spring, and the women of the city are coming out to draw water. Let it be like this: I shall say to a girl, "Please lower your jar so that I may drink"; and if she answers, "Drink, and I will water your camels also", that will be the girl whom thou dost intend for thy servant Isaac. In this way I shall know that thou hast kept faith with my master.'

Before he had finished praying silently, he saw Rebecca coming out with her water-jug on her shoulder. She was the daughter of Bethuel son of Milcah, the wife of Abraham's brother Nahor. The girl was very beautiful, a virgin, who had had no intercourse with a man. She went down to the spring, filled her jar and came up again. Abraham's servant hurried to meet her and said, 'Give me a sip of water from your jar.' 'Drink, sir', she answered, and at once lowered her jar on to her hand to let him drink. When she had finished giving him a drink, she said, 'Now I will draw water for your camels until they have had enough.' So she quickly emptied her jar into the water-trough, hurried again to the well to draw water and watered all the camels. The man was watching quietly to see whether or not the LORD had made his journey successful. When the camels had finished drinking, the man took a gold nose-ring weighing half a shekel, and two

l That is Aram of Two Rivers.

bracelets for her wrists weighing ten 23 shekels, also of gold, and said, 'Tell me, please, whose daughter you are. Is there room in your father's house for 24 us to spend the night?' She answered, 'I am the daughter of Bethuel, the 25 son of Nahor and Milcah; and we have plenty of straw and fodder and also room for you to spend the night.' 26 So the man bowed down and pros- 27 trated himself to the LORD. He said, 'Blessed be the LORD the God of my master Abraham, who has not failed to keep faith and truth with my master; for I have been guided by the LORD to the house of my master's kinsman.'

28   The girl ran to her mother's house and told them what had happened. 29-30 Now Rebecca had a brother named Laban; and, when he saw the nose-ring, and also the bracelets on his sister's wrists, and heard his sister Rebecca tell what the man had said to her, he ran out to the man at the spring. When he came to him and found him still standing there by the 31 camels, he said, 'Come in, sir, whom the LORD has blessed. Why stay out-side? I have prepared the house, and 32 there is room for the camels.' So he brought the man into the house, un-loaded the camels and provided straw and fodder for them, and water for him and all his men to wash their feet. 33 Food was set before him, but he said, 'I will not eat until I have delivered my message.' Laban said, 'Let us hear 34 it.' He answered, 'I am the servant 35 of Abraham. The LORD has greatly blessed my master, and he has become a man of power. The LORD has given him flocks and herds, silver and gold, male and female slaves, camels and 36 asses. My master's wife Sarah in her old age bore him a son, to whom he 37 has given all that he has. So my master made me swear an oath, say-ing, "You shall not take a wife for my son from the women of the Canaanites 38 in whose land I dwell; but you shall go to my father's house and to my 39 family to find a wife for him." So I said to my master, "What if the 40 woman will not come with me?" He answered, "The LORD, in whose pres-ence I have lived, will send his angel with you and will make your journey successful. You shall take a wife for my son from my family and from my 41 father's house; then you shall be released from the charge I have laid upon you. But if, when you come to my family, they will not give her to

you, you shall still be released from the charge." So I came to the spring 42 today, and I said, "O LORD God of my master Abraham, if thou wilt make my journey successful, let it be like 43 this. Here I stand by the spring. When a young woman comes out to draw water, I shall say to her, 'Give me a little water to drink from your jar.' If 44 she answers, 'Yes, do drink, and I will draw water for your camels as well', she is the woman whom the LORD intends for my master's son." Before 45 I had finished praying silently, I saw Rebecca coming out with her water-jar on her shoulder. She went down to the spring and drew some water, and I said to her, "Please give me a drink." She quickly lowered her jar 46 from her shoulder and said, "Drink; and I will water your camels as well." So I drank, and she also gave my camels water. I asked her whose 47 daughter she was, and she said, "I am the daughter of Bethuel, the son of Nahor and Milcah." Then I put the ring in her nose and the bracelets on her wrists, and I bowed low and 48 prostrated myself before the LORD. I blessed the LORD the God of my master Abraham, who had led me by the right road to take my master's niece for his son. Now tell me if you 49 will keep faith and truth with |my master. If not, say so, and I will turn elsewhere.'

Laban and Bethuel answered, 'This 50 is from the LORD; we can say nothing for or against. Here is Rebecca her- 51 self; take her and go. She shall be the wife of your master's son, as the LORD has decreed.' When Abraham's ser- 52 vant heard what they said, he pros-trated himself on the ground before the LORD. Then he brought out gold 53 and silver ornaments, and robes, and gave them to Rebecca, and he gave costly gifts to her brother and her mother. He and his men then ate and 54 drank and spent the night there. When they rose in the morning, he said, 'Give me leave to go back to my master.' Her brother and her mother 55 said, 'Let the girl stay with us for a few days, say ten days, and then she shall go.' But he said to them, 'Do 56 not detain me, for the LORD has granted me success. Give me leave to return to my master.' They said, 'Let 57 us call the girl and see what she says.' They called Rebecca and asked her if 58 she would go with the man, and she said, 'Yes, I will go.' So they let their 59 sister Rebecca and her nurse go with

60 Abraham's servant and his men. They blessed Rebecca and said to her:

'You are our sister, may you be the mother of myriads;
may your sons possess the cities of their enemies.'

61 Then Rebecca and her companions mounted their camels at once and followed the man. So the servant took Rebecca and went his way.
62 Isaac meanwhile had moved on as far as Beer-lahai-roi and was living
63 in the Negeb. One evening when he had gone out into the open country hoping to meet them,[m] he looked up
64 and saw camels approaching. When Rebecca raised her eyes and saw Isaac, she slipped hastily from her camel,
65 saying to the servant, 'Who is that man walking across the open towards us?' The servant answered, 'It is my master.' So she took her veil and
66 covered herself. The servant related
67 to Isaac all that had happened. Isaac conducted her into the tent[n] and took her as his wife. So she became his wife, and he loved her and was consoled for the death of his mother.

Descendants of Abraham and Keturah

25 1[o] Abraham married another wife, whose
2 name was Keturah. She bore him Zimran, Jokshan, Medan, Midian,
3 Ishbak and Shuah. Jokshan became the father of Sheba and Dedan. The sons of Dedan were Asshurim, Le-
4 tushim and Leummim, and the sons of Midian were Ephah, Epher, Enoch, Abida and Eldaah. All these were descendants of Keturah.

The death of Abraham

5 Abraham had given all that he had to
6 Isaac; and he had already in his life-time given presents to the sons of his concubines, and had sent them away eastwards, to a land of the east, out
7 of his son Isaac's way. Abraham had lived for a hundred and seventy-five
8 years when he breathed his last. He died at a good old age, after a very long life, and was gathered to his
9 father's kin. His sons, Isaac and Ishmael, buried him in the cave at Machpelah, on the land of Ephron son of
10 Zohar the Hittite, east of Mamre, the plot which Abraham had bought from the Hittites. There Abraham was
11 buried with his wife Sarah. After the death of Abraham, God blessed his son Isaac, who settled close by Beer-lahai-roi.

Ishmael's descendants

This is the table of the descendants of 12 Abraham's son Ishmael, whom Hagar the Egyptian, Sarah's slave-girl, bore to him. These are the names of the 13[p] sons of Ishmael named in order of their birth: Nebaioth, Ishmael's eldest son, then Kedar, Adbeel, Mibsam, Mishma, Dumah, Massa, Hadad, 14 15 Teman, Jetur, Naphish and Kedemah. These are the sons of Ishmael, 16 after whom their hamlets and encampments were named, twelve princes according to their tribal groups. Ishmael had lived for a hundred and 17 thirty-seven years when he breathed his last. So he died and was gathered to his father's kin. Ishmael's sons in- 18 habited the land from Havilah to Shur, which is east of Egypt on the way to Asshur, having settled to the east of his brothers.

The birth of Esau and Jacob

This is the table of the descendants of 19 Abraham's son Isaac. Isaac's father was Abraham. When Isaac was forty 20 years old he married Rebecca the daughter of Bethuel the Aramaean from Paddan-aram and the sister of Laban the Aramaean. Isaac appealed 21 to the LORD on behalf of his wife because she was barren; the LORD yielded to his entreaty, and Rebecca conceived. The children pressed hard on 22 each other in her womb, and she said, 'If this is how it is with me, what does it mean?' So she went to seek guidance of the LORD. The LORD said to her: 23

'Two nations in your womb,
two peoples, going their own ways from birth!
One shall be stronger than the other;
the older shall be servant to the younger.'

When her time had come, there were 24 indeed twins in her womb. The first 25 came out red, hairy all over like a hair-cloak, and they named him Esau.[q] Immediately afterwards his brother 26 was born with his hand grasping Esau's heel, and they called him Jacob.[r] Isaac was sixty years old when they were born.

---

m hoping . . . them: or to relieve himself.   n Prob. rdg.; Heb. adds Sarah his mother.
o Verses 1–4: cp. 1 Chr. 1. 32, 33.   p Verses 13–16: cp. 1 Chr. 1. 29–31.   q That is Covering.
r That is He caught by the heel.

Esau sells his birthright

27 The boys grew up; and Esau became skilful in hunting, a man of the open plains, but Jacob led a settled life 28 and stayed among the tents. Isaac favoured Esau because he kept him supplied with venison, but Rebecca 29 favoured Jacob. One day Jacob prepared a broth and when Esau came in 30 from the country, exhausted, he said to Jacob, 'I am exhausted; let me swallow some of that red broth': this 31 is why he was called Edom.*s* Jacob said, 'Not till you sell me your rights 32 as the first-born.' Esau replied, 'I am at death's door; what use is my birth-33 right to me?' Jacob said, 'Not till you swear!'; so he swore an oath and sold 34 his birthright to Jacob. Then Jacob gave Esau bread and the lentil broth, and he ate and drank and went away without more ado. Thus Esau showed how little he valued his birthright.

Isaac at Gerar and Beersheba

26 There came a famine in the land—not the earlier famine in Abraham's time —and Isaac went to Abimelech the 2 Philistine king at Gerar. The LORD appeared to Isaac and said, 'Do not go down to Egypt, but stay in this country 3 as I bid you. Stay in this country and I will be with you and bless you, for to you and to your descendants I will give all these lands. Thus shall I fulfil the oath which I swore to your father 4 Abraham. I will make your descendants as many as the stars in the sky; I will give them all these lands, and all the nations of the earth will pray 5 to be blessed as they are blessed—all because Abraham obeyed me and kept my charge, my commandments, 6 my statutes, and my laws.' So Isaac lived in Gerar.

7   When the men of the place asked him about his wife, he told them that she was his sister; he was afraid to say that Rebecca was his wife, in case they killed him because of her; for 8 she was very beautiful. When they had been there for some considerable time, Abimelech the Philistine king looked down from his window and saw Isaac and his wife Rebecca 9 laughing together. He summoned Isaac and said, 'So she is your wife, is she? What made you say she was your sister?' Isaac answered, 'I thought I should be killed because of 10 her.' Abimelech said, 'Why have you

treated us like this? One of the people might easily have gone to bed with your wife, and then you would have made us liable to retribution.' So 11 Abimelech warned all the people, threatening that whoever touched this man or his wife would be put to death.

Isaac sowed seed in that land, and 12 that year he reaped a hundredfold, and the LORD blessed him. He became 13 more and more powerful, until he was very powerful indeed. He had flocks 14 and herds and many slaves, so that the Philistines were envious of him. They had stopped up all the wells dug 15 by the slaves in the days of Isaac's father Abraham, and filled them with earth. Isaac dug them again, all those 18 wells dug in his father Abraham's time, and stopped up by the Philistines after his death, and he called them by the names which his father had given them.

Then Abimelech said to him, 'Go 16 away from here; you are too strong for us.' So Isaac left that place and 17 encamped in the valley of Gerar, and stayed there. Then Isaac's slaves dug 19*t* in the valley and found a spring of running water, but the shepherds of 20 Gerar quarrelled with Isaac's shepherds, claiming the water as theirs. He called the well Esek,*u* because they made difficulties for him. His men 21 then dug another well, but the others quarrelled with him over that also, so he called it Sitnah.*v* He moved on 22 from there and dug another well, but there was no quarrel over that one, so he called it Rehoboth,*w* saying, 'Now the LORD has given us plenty of room and we shall be fruitful in the land.'

Isaac went up country from there to 23 Beersheba. That same night the LORD 24 appeared to him there and said, 'I am the God of your father Abraham. Fear nothing, for I am with you. I will bless you and give you many descendants for the sake of Abraham my servant.' So Isaac built an altar there 25 and invoked the LORD by name. Then he pitched his tent there, and there also his slaves dug a well. Abimelech came to him from Gerar 26 with Ahuzzath his friend and Phicol the commander of his army. Isaac 27 said to them, 'Why have you come here? You hate me and you sent me away.' They answered, 'We have seen 28 plainly that the LORD is with you, so we thought, "Let the two of us put

s That is Red.   *t Verse 18 transposed to follow 15.*   *u That is* Difficulty.   *v That is* Enmity.
w That is Plenty of room.

each other to the oath and make
29 a treaty that will bind us." We have
not attacked you, we have done you
nothing but good, and we let you go
away peaceably. Swear that you will
do us no harm, now that the LORD
30 has blessed you.' So Isaac gave a feast
31 and they ate and drank. They rose
early in the morning and exchanged
oaths. Then Isaac bade them farewell,
and they parted from him in peace.
32 The same day Isaac's slaves came and
told him about a well that they had
dug: 'We have found water', they
33 said. He named the well Shibah.*ᵡ This
is why the city is called Beersheba*ʸ to
this day.
34   When Esau was forty years old he
married Judith daughter of Beeri the
Hittite, and Basemath daughter of
35 Elon the Hittite; this was a bitter
grief to Isaac and Rebecca.

Jacob obtains Isaac's blessing

27 When Isaac grew old and his eyes
became so dim that he could not see,
he called his elder son Esau and said
to him, 'My son', and he answered,
2 'Here I am.' Isaac said, 'Listen now:
I am old and I do not know when I
3 may die. Take your hunting gear,
your quiver and your bow, and go out
into the country and get me some
4 venison. Then make me a savoury
dish of the kind I like, and bring it to
me to eat so that I may give you my
5 blessing before I die.' Now Rebecca
was listening as Isaac talked to his
son Esau. When Esau went off into
the country to find some venison and
6 bring it home, she said to her son
Jacob, 'I heard your father talking
to your brother Esau, and he said,
7 "Bring me some venison and make it
into a savoury dish so that I may eat
it and bless you in the presence of the
8 LORD before I die." Listen to me, my
9 son, and do what I tell you. Go to the
flock and pick me out two fine young
kids, and I will make them into a
savoury dish for your father, of the
10 kind he likes. Then take them in to
your father, and he will eat them so
that he may bless you before he dies.'
11 Jacob said to his mother Rebecca,
'But my brother Esau is a hairy man,
12 and my skin is smooth. Suppose my
father feels me, he will know I am
tricking him and I shall bring a curse
upon myself instead of a blessing.'
13 His mother answered him, 'Let the
curse fall on me, my son, but do as I
14 say; go and bring me the kids.' So

Jacob fetched them and brought them
to his mother, who made them into
a savoury dish of the kind that his
father liked. Then Rebecca took her 15
elder son's clothes, Esau's best clothes
which she kept by her in the house,
and put them on her younger son
Jacob. She put the goatskins on his 16
hands and on the smooth nape of his
neck; and she handed her son Jacob 17
the savoury dish and the bread she
had made. He came to his father and 18
said, 'Father.' He answered, 'Yes, my
son; who are you?' Jacob answered 19
his father, 'I am Esau, your elder son.
I have done as you told me. Come,
sit up and eat some of my venison, so
that you may give me your blessing.'
Isaac said to his son, 'What is this 20
that you found so quickly?', and
Jacob answered, 'It is what the LORD
your God put in my way.' Isaac then 21
said to Jacob, 'Come close and let me
feel you, my son, to see whether you
are really my son Esau.' When Jacob 22
came close to his father, Isaac felt him
and said, 'The voice is Jacob's voice,
but the hands are the hands of Esau.'
He did not recognize him because 23
his hands were hairy like Esau's, and
that is why he blessed him. He said, 24
'Are you really my son Esau?', and
he answered, 'Yes.' Then Isaac said, 25
'Bring me some of your venison to eat,
my son, so that I may give you my
blessing.' Then Jacob brought it to
him, and he ate it; he brought wine
also, and he drank it. Then his father 26
Isaac said to him, 'Come near, my
son, and kiss me.' So he came near and 27
kissed him, and when Isaac smelt the
smell of his clothes, he blessed him
and said:

'Ah! The smell of my son is like the
   smell of open country
   blessed by the LORD.
God give you dew from heaven   28
and the richness of the earth,
corn and new wine in plenty!
Peoples shall serve you,   29
nations bow down to you.
   Be lord over your brothers;
may your mother's sons bow down to
   you.
A curse upon those who curse you;
a blessing on those who bless you!'

   Isaac finished blessing Jacob; and 30
Jacob had scarcely left his father
Isaac's presence, when his brother
Esau came in from his hunting. He 31
too made a savoury dish and brought
it to his father. He said, 'Come, father,

x That is Oath.   *y That is* Well of an Oath.

and eat some of my venison, so that
32 you may give me your blessing.' His
father Isaac said, 'Who are you?' He
33 said, 'I am Esau, your elder son.' Then
Isaac became greatly agitated[z] and
said, 'Then who was it that hunted
and brought me venison? I ate it all
before you came in and I blessed him,
34 and the blessing will stand.' When
Esau heard what his father said, he
gave a loud and bitter cry and said,
35 'Bless me too, father.' But Isaac said,
'Your brother came treacherously
36 and took away your blessing.' Esau
said, 'He is rightly called Jacob.[a]
This is the second time he has supplanted me. He took away my right
as the first-born and now he has taken
away my blessing. Have you kept
37 back any blessing for me?' Isaac
answered, 'I have made him lord over
you, and I have given him all his
brothers as slaves. I have bestowed
upon him corn and new wine for his
sustenance. What is there left that
38 I can do for you, my son?' Esau asked
his father, 'Had you then only one
blessing, father? Bless me too, my
39 father.' And Esau cried bitterly. Then
his father Isaac answered:

'Your dwelling shall be far from the
  richness of the earth,
  far from the dew of heaven above.
40 By your sword shall you live,
  and you shall serve your brother;
  but the time will come when you
    grow restive
  and break off his yoke from your
    neck.'

Jacob escapes to Harran

41 Esau bore a grudge against Jacob
because of the blessing which his
father had given him, and he said to
himself, 'The time of mourning for
my father will soon be here; then I will
42 kill my brother Jacob.' When Rebecca
was told what her elder son Esau was
saying, she called her younger son
Jacob, and she said to him, 'Esau your
brother is threatening to kill you.
43 Now, my son, listen to me. Slip away
at once to my brother Laban in
44 Harran. Stay with him for a while
45 until your brother's anger cools. When
it has subsided and he forgets what
you have done to him, I will send and
fetch you back. Why should I lose
you both in one day?'
46 Rebecca said to Isaac, 'I am weary
to death of Hittite women! If Jacob
marries a Hittite woman like those
who live here, my life will not be worth

living.' Isaac called Jacob, blessed him 28
and gave him instructions. He said,
'You must not marry one of these
women of Canaan. Go at once to the 2
house of Bethuel, your mother's
father, in Paddan-aram, and there
find a wife, one of the daughters of
Laban, your mother's brother. God 3
Almighty bless you, make you fruitful and increase your descendants
until they become a host of nations.
May he bestow on you and your off- 4
spring the blessing of Abraham, and
may you thus possess the country
where you are now living, the land
which God gave to Abraham!' So 5
Isaac sent Jacob away, and he went
to Paddan-aram to Laban, son of
Bethuel the Aramaean, and brother
to Rebecca the mother of Jacob and
Esau. Esau discovered that Isaac had 6
given Jacob his blessing and had sent
him away to Paddan-aram to find a
wife there; and that when he blessed
him he had forbidden him to marry
a woman of Canaan, and that Jacob 7
had obeyed his father and mother
and gone to Paddan-aram. Then 8
Esau, seeing that his father disliked
the women of Canaan, went to Ish- 9
mael, and, in addition to his other
wives, he married Mahalath sister of
Nebaioth and daughter of Abraham's
son Ishmael.

Jacob's dream at Bethel

Jacob set out from Beersheba and 10
went on his way towards Harran. He 11
came to a certain place and stopped
there for the night, because the sun
had set; and, taking one of the stones
there, he made it a pillow for his
head and lay down to sleep. He dreamt 12
that he saw a ladder, which rested on
the ground with its top reaching to
heaven, and angels of God were going
up and down upon it. The LORD was 13
standing beside him[b] and said, 'I am
the LORD, the God of your father
Abraham and the God of Isaac. This
land on which you are lying I will give
to you and your descendants. They 14
shall be countless as the dust upon
the earth, and you shall spread far
and wide, to north and south, to
east and west. All the families of the
earth shall pray to be blessed as you
and your descendants are blessed.
I will be with you, and I will protect 15
you wherever you go and will bring
you back to this land; for I will not
leave you until I have done all that
I have promised.' Jacob woke from 16

z Or incensed.   a That is He supplanted.   b Or on it or by it.

his sleep and said, 'Truly the LORD is in this place, and I did not know it.'
17 Then he was afraid and said, 'How fearsome is this place! This is no other than the house of God, this is the gate
18 of heaven.' Jacob rose early in the morning, took the stone on which he had laid his head, set it up as a sacred pillar and poured oil on the top of it.
19 He named that place Beth-El;[c] but the earlier name of the city was Luz.
20 Thereupon Jacob made this vow: 'If God will be with me, if he will protect me on my journey and give me food to eat and clothes to wear,
21 and I come back safely to my father's house, then the LORD shall be my
22 God, and this stone which I have set up as a sacred pillar shall be a house of God. And of all that thou givest me, I will without fail allot a tenth part to thee.'

Jacob, Rachel, and Leah

29 Jacob continued his journey and came
2 to the land of the eastern tribes. There he saw a well in the open country and three flocks of sheep lying beside it, because the flocks were watered from that well. Over its mouth was a huge
3 stone, and all the herdsmen used to gather there and roll it off the mouth of the well and water the flocks; then they would put it back in its
4 place over the well. Jacob said to them, 'Where are you from, my friends?' 'We are from Harran', they replied.
5 He asked them if they knew Laban the grandson of Nahor. They answered,
6 'Yes, we do.' 'Is he well?' Jacob asked; and they answered, 'Yes, he is well, and here is his daughter Rachel
7 coming with the flock.' Jacob said, 'The sun is still high, and the time for folding the sheep has not yet come. Water the flocks and then go and
8 graze them.' But they replied, 'We cannot, until all the herdsmen have gathered together and the stone is rolled away from the mouth of the well; then we can water our flocks.'
9 While he was talking to them, Rachel came up with her father's flock, for
10 she was a shepherdess. When Jacob saw Rachel, the daughter of Laban his mother's brother, with Laban's flock, he stepped forward, rolled the stone off the mouth of the well and
11 watered Laban's sheep. He kissed
12 Rachel, and was moved to tears. He told her that he was her father's kinsman and Rebecca's son; so she ran
13 and told her father. When Laban

heard the news of his sister's son Jacob, he ran to meet him, embraced him, kissed him warmly and welcomed him to his home. Jacob told Laban everything, and Laban said, 'Yes, 14 you are my own flesh and blood.' So Jacob stayed with him for a whole month.

Laban said to Jacob, 'Why should 15 you work for me for nothing simply because you are my kinsman? Tell me what your wages ought to be.' Now Laban had two daughters: the 16 elder was called Leah, and the younger Rachel. Leah was dull-eyed, but 17 Rachel was graceful and beautiful. Jacob had fallen in love with Rachel 18 and he said, 'I will work seven years for your younger daughter Rachel.' Laban replied, 'It is better that I 19 should give her to you than to anyone else; stay with me.' So Jacob worked 20 seven years for Rachel, and they seemed like a few days because he loved her. Then Jacob said to Laban, 21 'I have served my time. Give me my wife so that we may sleep together.' So Laban gathered all the men of the 22 place together and gave a feast. In the 23 evening he took his daughter Leah and brought her to Jacob, and Jacob slept with her. At the same time 24 Laban gave his slave-girl Zilpah to his daughter Leah. But when morning 25 came, Jacob saw that it was Leah and said to Laban, 'What have you done to me? Did I not work for Rachel? Why have you deceived me?' Laban 26 answered, 'In our country it is not right to give the younger sister in marriage before the elder. Go through 27 with the seven days' feast for the elder, and the younger shall be given you in return for a further seven years' work.' Jacob agreed, and completed 28 the seven days for Leah.

Jacob's children

Then Laban gave Jacob his daughter Rachel as wife; and he gave his slave- 29 girl Bilhah to serve his daughter Rachel. Jacob slept with Rachel also; 30 he loved her rather than Leah, and he worked for Laban for a further seven years. When the LORD saw that Leah 31 was not loved, he granted her a child; but Rachel was childless. Leah con- 32 ceived and bore a son; and she called him Reuben,[d] for she said, 'The LORD has seen my humiliation; now my husband will love me.' Again she con- 33 ceived and bore a son and said, 'The LORD, hearing that I am not loved,

c _That is_ House of God.　　d _That is_ See, a son.

has given me this child also'; and she
34 called him Simeon.[e] She conceived
again and bore a son; and she said,
'Now that I have borne him three
sons my husband and I will surely be
35 united.' So she called him Levi.[f] Once
more she conceived and bore a son;
and she said, 'Now I will praise the
LORD'; therefore she named him
Judah.[g] Then for a while she bore no
more children.

30   When Rachel found that she bore
Jacob no children, she became jealous
of her sister and said to Jacob, 'Give
2 me sons, or I shall die.' Jacob said
angrily to Rachel, 'Can I take the
place of God, who has denied you
3 children?' She said, 'Here is my slave-
girl Bilhah. Lie with her, so that she
may bear sons to be laid upon my
knees, and through her I too may build
4 up a family.' So she gave him her
slave-girl Bilhah as a wife, and Jacob
5 lay with her. Bilhah conceived and
6 bore Jacob a son. Then Rachel said,
'God has given judgement for me; he
has indeed heard me and given me a
7 son', so she named him Dan.[h] Rachel's
slave-girl Bilhah again conceived and
8 bore Jacob another son. Rachel said,
'I have played a fine trick on my
sister, and it has succeeded'; so she
9 named him Naphtali.[i] When Leah
found that she was bearing no more
children, she took her slave-girl
Zilpah and gave her to Jacob as a
10 wife, and Zilpah bore Jacob a son.
11 Leah said, 'Good fortune has come',
12 and she named him Gad.[j] Zilpah,
Leah's slave-girl, bore Jacob another
13 son, and Leah said, 'Happiness has
come, for young women will call me
happy.' So she named him Asher.[k]
14   In the time of wheat-harvest Reuben went out and found some mandrakes in the open country and brought
them to his mother Leah. Then
Rachel asked Leah for some of her
15 son's mandrakes, but Leah said, 'Is it
so small a thing to have taken away
my husband, that you should take
my son's mandrakes as well?' But
Rachel said, 'Very well, let him sleep
with you tonight in exchange for your
16 son's mandrakes.' So when Jacob
came in from the country in the evening, Leah went out to meet him and
said, 'You are to sleep with me tonight;
I have hired you with my son's mandrakes.' That night he slept with her,

and God heard Leah's prayer, and she 17
conceived and bore a fifth son. Leah 18
said, 'God has rewarded me, because
I gave my slave-girl to my husband.'
So she named him Issachar.[l] Leah 19
again conceived and bore a sixth son.
She said, 'God has endowed me with 20
a noble dowry. Now my husband will
treat me in princely style, because I
have borne him six sons.' So she
named him Zebulun.[m] Later she bore 21
a daughter and named her Dinah.
Then God thought of Rachel; he 22
heard her prayer and gave her a child;
so she conceived and bore a son and 23
said, 'God has taken away my humiliation.' She named him Joseph,[n] say- 24
ing, 'May the LORD add another son!'

Jacob's bargain with Laban

When Rachel had given birth to 25
Joseph, Jacob said to Laban, 'Let me
go, for I wish to return to my own
home and country. Give me my wives 26
and my children for whom I have
served you, and I will go; for you
know what service I have done for
you.' Laban said to him, 'Let me have 27
my say, if you please. I have become
prosperous and the LORD has blessed
me for your sake. So now tell me what 28
I owe you in wages, and I will give
it you.' Jacob answered, 'You must 29
know how I have served you, and how
your herds have prospered under my
care. You had only a few when I came, 30
but now they have increased beyond
measure, and the LORD brought blessings to you wherever I went. But is
it not time for me to provide for my
family?' Laban said, 'Then what shall 31
I give you?', but Jacob answered,
'Give me nothing; I will mind your
flocks[o] as before, if you will do what I
suggest. Today I will go over your 32
flocks and pick out from them every
black lamb, and all the brindled and
the spotted goats, and they shall be
my wages. This is a fair offer, and it 33
will be to my own disadvantage later
on, when we come to settling my
wages: every goat amongst mine that
is not spotted or brindled and every
lamb that is not black will have been
stolen.' Laban said, 'Agreed; let it 34
be as you have said.' But that day 35
he removed the he-goats that were
striped and brindled and all the
spotted and brindled she-goats, all
that had any white on them, and every

---

e That is Hearing.   f That is Union.   g That is Praise.   h That is He has given judgement.
i That is Trickery.   j That is Good Fortune.   k That is Happy.   l That is Reward.
m That is Prince.   n The name may mean either He takes away or May he add.   o Prob. rdg.;
Heb. adds I will watch.

ram that was black, and he handed
36 them over to his own sons. Then he
put a distance of three days' journey
between himself and Jacob, while
Jacob was left tending those of La-
37 ban's flocks that remained. Thereupon Jacob took fresh rods of white
poplar, almond, and plane tree, and
peeled off strips of bark, exposing the
38 white of the rods. Then he fixed the
peeled rods upright in the troughs at
the watering-places where the flocks
came to drink; they faced the she-
goats that were on heat when they
39 came to drink. They felt a longing
for the rods and they gave birth to
young that were striped and spotted
40 and brindled. As for the rams, Jacob
divided them, and let the ewes run
only with such of the rams in Laban's
flock as were striped and black; and
thus he bred separate flocks for himself, which he did not add to Laban's
41 sheep. As for the goats, whenever the
more vigorous were on heat, he put
the rods in front of them at the
troughs so that they would long for the
42 rods; he did not put them there for
the weaker goats. Thus the weaker
came to be Laban's and the stronger
43 Jacob's. So Jacob increased in wealth
more and more until he possessed
great flocks, male and female slaves,
camels, and asses.

Jacob runs away from Laban

31 Jacob learnt that Laban's sons were
saying, 'Jacob has taken everything
that was our father's, and all his
wealth has come from our father's
2 property.' He also noticed that Laban was not so well disposed to him
3 as he had once been. Then the LORD
said to Jacob, 'Go back to the land
of your fathers and to your kindred.
4 I will be with you.' So Jacob sent to
fetch Rachel and Leah to his flocks
5 out in the country and said to them,
'I see that your father is not as well
disposed to me as once he was; yet
the God of my father has been with
6 me. You know how I have served
your father to the best of my power,
7 but he has cheated me and changed
my wages ten times over. Yet God did
8 not let him do me any harm. If Laban
said, "The spotted ones shall be your
wages", then all the flock bore spotted
young; and if he said, "The striped
ones shall be your wages", then all
9 the flock bore striped young. God has
taken away your father's property
10 and has given it to me. In the season
when the flocks were on heat, I had

a dream: I looked up and saw that
the he-goats mounting the flock were
striped and spotted and dappled. The 11
angel of God said to me in my dream,
"Jacob", and I replied, "Here I am",
and he said, "Look up and see: all 12
the he-goats mounting the flock are
striped and spotted and dappled. I
have seen all that Laban is doing to
you. I am the God who appeared to 13
you at Bethel where you anointed a
sacred pillar and where you made
your vow. Now leave this country at
once and return to the land of your
birth."' Rachel and Leah answered 14
him, 'We no longer have any part or
lot in our father's house. Does he not 15
look on us as foreigners, now that he
has sold us and spent on himself the
whole of the money paid for us? But 16
all the wealth which God has saved
from our father's clutches is ours and
our children's. Now do everything
that God has said.' Jacob at once set 17
his sons and his wives on camels, and 18
drove off all the herds and livestock
which he had acquired in Paddan-
aram, to go to his father Isaac in
Canaan.

When Laban the Aramaean had 19
gone to shear his sheep, Rachel stole
her father's household gods, and 20
Jacob deceived Laban, keeping his
departure secret. So Jacob ran away 21
with all that he had, crossed the
River and made for the hill-country
of Gilead. Three days later, when 22
Laban heard that Jacob had run
away, he took his kinsmen with him, 23
pursued Jacob for seven days and
caught up with him in the hill-
country of Gilead. But God came to 24
Laban in a dream by night and said
to him, 'Be careful to say nothing to
Jacob, either good or bad.'

Laban overtakes Jacob

When Laban overtook him, Jacob 25
had pitched his tent in the hill-
country of Gilead, and Laban pitched
his in the company of his kinsmen in
the same hill-country. Laban said to 26
Jacob, 'What have you done? You
have deceived me and carried off my
daughters as though they were captives taken in war. Why did you slip 27
away secretly without telling me? I
would have set you on your way
with songs and the music of tambourines and harps. You did not even 28
let me kiss my daughters and their
children. In this you were at fault. It 29
is in my power to do you an injury,

but yesterday the God of your father spoke to me; he told me to be careful to say nothing to you, either good or 30 bad. I know that you went away because you were homesick and pining for your father's house, but why did you steal my gods?'

31   Jacob answered, 'I was afraid; I thought you would take your daugh-32 ters from me by force. Whoever is found in possession of your gods shall die for it. Let our kinsmen here be witnesses: point out anything I have that is yours, and take it back.' Jacob did not know that Rachel had stolen 33 the gods. So Laban went into Jacob's tent and Leah's tent and that of the two slave-girls, but he found nothing. When he came out of Leah's tent he 34 went into Rachel's. Now she had taken the household gods and put them in the camel-bag and was sitting on them. Laban went through everything in the tent and found nothing. 35 Rachel said to her father, 'Do not take it amiss, sir, that I cannot rise in your presence: the common lot of woman is upon me.' So for all his search Laban did not find his household gods.

36   Jacob was angry, and he expostulated with Laban, exclaiming, 'What have I done wrong? What is my offence, that you have come after me 37 in hot pursuit and gone through all my possessions? Have you found anything belonging to your household? If so, set it here in front of my kinsmen and yours, and let them judge 38 between the two of us. In all the twenty years I have been with you, your ewes and she-goats have never miscarried; I have not eaten the rams 39 of your flocks; I have never brought to you the body of any animal mangled by wild beasts, but I bore the loss myself; you claimed compensation from me for anything stolen by day 40 or by night. This was the way of it: by day the heat consumed me and the frost by night, and sleep deserted 41 me. For twenty years I have been in your household. I worked for you fourteen years to win your two daughters and six years for your flocks, and you changed my wages ten times over. 42 If the God of my father, the God of Abraham and the Fear of Isaac, had not been with me, you would have sent me away empty-handed. But God saw my labour and my hardships, and last night he rebuked you.'

The agreement between Jacob and Laban

Laban answered Jacob, 'The daugh-43 ters are my daughters, the children are my children, the flocks are my flocks; all that you see is mine. But as for my daughters, what can I do today about them and the children they have borne? Come now, we will 44 make an agreement, you and I, and let it stand as a witness between us.' So Jacob chose a great stone and set 45 it upright as a sacred pillar. Then he 46 told his kinsmen to gather stones, and they took them and built a cairn, and there beside the cairn they ate together. Laban called it Jegar-saha-47 dutha,*p* and Jacob called it Gal-ed.*q* Laban said, 'This cairn is witness 48 today between you and me.' For this reason it was named Gal-ed; it was 49 also named Mizpah,*r* for Laban said, 'May the LORD watch between you and me, when we are parted from each other's sight. If you ill-treat my 50 daughters or take other wives beside them when no one is there to see, then God be witness between us.' Laban 51 said further to Jacob, 'Here is this cairn, and here the pillar which I have set up between us. This cairn is wit-52 ness and the pillar is witness: I for my part will not pass beyond this cairn to your side, and you for your part shall not pass beyond this cairn and this pillar to my side to do an injury, otherwise the God of Abraham 53 and the God of Nahor will judge between us.' And Jacob swore this oath in the name of the Fear of Isaac his father. He slaughtered an animal 54 for sacrifice, there in the hill-country, and summoned his kinsmen to the feast. So they ate together and spent the night there.

Laban rose early in the morning, 55 kissed his daughters and their children, blessed them and went home again. Then Jacob continued his **32** journey and was met by angels of God. When he saw them, Jacob said, 'This 2 is the company of God', and he called that place Mahanaim.*s*

Jacob prepares to meet Esau

Jacob sent messengers on ahead to 3 his brother Esau to the district of Seir in the Edomite country, and this is 4 what he told them to say to Esau, 'My lord, your servant Jacob says, I have been living with Laban and have

p Aramaic for Cairn of Witness.   *q Hebrew for* Cairn of Witness.   *r That is* Watch-tower.
s That is Two Companies.

5 stayed there till now. I have oxen, asses, and sheep, and male and female slaves, and I have sent to tell you this, my lord, so that I may win your 6 favour.' The messengers returned to Jacob and said, 'We met your brother Esau already on the way to meet you 7 with four hundred men.' Jacob, much afraid and distressed, divided the people with him, as well as the sheep, cattle, and camels, into two com- 8 panies, thinking that, if Esau should come upon one company and destroy it, the other company would survive. 9 Jacob said, 'O God of my father Abraham, God of my father Isaac, O LORD at whose bidding I came back to my own country and to my kindred, and who didst promise me pros- 10 perity, I am not worthy of all the true and steadfast love which thou hast shown to me thy servant. When I crossed the Jordan, I had nothing but the staff in my hand; now I have two 11 companies. Save me, I pray, from my brother Esau, for I am afraid that he may come and destroy me, sparing 12 neither mother nor child. But thou didst say, I will prosper you and will make your descendants like the sand of the sea, which is beyond all counting.' 13   Jacob spent that night there; and as a present for his brother Esau he chose from the herds he had with him 14 two hundred she-goats, twenty he-goats, two hundred ewes and twenty 15 rams, thirty milch-camels with their young, forty cows and ten young bulls, 16 twenty she-asses and ten he-asses. He put each herd separately into the care of a servant and said to each, 'Go on ahead of me, and leave gaps between 17 the herds.' Then he gave these instructions to the first: 'When my brother Esau meets you and asks you to whom you belong and where you are going and who owns these beasts you are 18 driving, you are to say, "They belong to your servant Jacob; he sends them as a present to my lord Esau, and he 19 is behind us."' He gave the same instructions to the second, to the third, and all the drovers, telling them to say the same thing to Esau when 20 they met him. And they were to add, 'Your servant Jacob is behind us'; for he thought, 'I will appease him with the present that I have sent on ahead, and afterwards, when I come into his presence, he will perhaps receive me 21 kindly.' So Jacob's present went on ahead of him, but he himself spent that night at Mahaneh.

Jacob wrestles at Peniel

During the night Jacob rose, took his 22 two wives, his two slave-girls, and his eleven sons, and crossed the ford of Jabbok. He took them and sent them 23 across the gorge with all that he had. So Jacob was left alone, and a man 24 wrestled with him there till^t daybreak. When the man saw that he 25 could not throw Jacob, he struck him in the hollow of his thigh, so that Jacob's hip was dislocated as they wrestled. The man said, 'Let me go, 26 for day is breaking', but Jacob replied, 'I will not let you go unless you bless me.' He said to Jacob, 'What is your 27 name?', and he answered, 'Jacob.' The man said, 'Your name shall no 28 longer be Jacob, but Israel,^{u} because you strove with God and with men, and prevailed.' Jacob said, 'Tell me, 29 I pray, your name.' He replied, 'Why do you ask my name?', but he gave him his blessing there. Jacob called 30 the place Peniel,^{v} 'because', he said, 'I have seen God face to face and my life is spared.' The sun rose as Jacob 31 passed through Penuel, limping because of his hip. This is why the Is- 32 raelites to this day do not eat the sinew of the nerve that runs in the hollow of the thigh; for the man had struck Jacob on that nerve in the hollow of the thigh.

Jacob and Esau reconciled

Jacob raised his eyes and saw Esau **33** coming towards him with four hundred men; so he divided the children between Leah and Rachel and the two slave-girls. He put the slave-girls with 2 their children in front, Leah with her children next, and Rachel with Joseph last. He then went on ahead of them, 3 bowing low to the ground seven times as he approached his brother. Esau 4 ran to meet him and embraced him; he threw his arms round him and kissed him, and they wept. When 5 Esau looked up and saw the women and children, he said, 'Who are these with you?' Jacob replied, 'The children whom God has graciously given to your servant.' The slave-girls came 6 near, each with her children, and they bowed low. Then Leah with her chil- 7 dren came near and bowed low, and afterwards Joseph and Rachel came near and bowed low also. Esau said, 8 'What was all that company of yours that I met?' And he answered, 'It was meant to win favour with you,

---

t Or at.   *u* *That is* God strove.   *v* *That is* Face of God (*elsewhere* Penuel).

9 my lord.' Esau answered, 'I have more
than enough. Keep what is yours,
10 my brother.' But Jacob said, 'On no
account: if I have won your favour,
then, I pray, accept this gift from me;
for, you see, I come into your presence
as into that of a god, and you receive
11 me favourably. Accept this gift which
I bring you; for God has been gracious
to me, and I have all I want.' So he
urged him, and he accepted it.
12   Then Esau said, 'Let us set out, and
13 I will go at your pace.' But Jacob
answered him, 'You must know, my
lord, that the children are small; the
flocks and herds are suckling their
young and I am concerned for them,
and if the men overdrive them for a
14 single day, all my beasts will die. I beg
you, my lord, to go on ahead, and I
will go by easy stages at the pace of
the children and of the livestock that
I am driving, until I come to my lord
15 in Seir.' Esau said, 'Let me detail
some of my own men to escort you',
but he replied, 'Why should my lord
16 be so kind to me?' That day Esau
17 turned back towards Seir, but Jacob
set out for Succoth; and there he built
himself a house and made shelters
for his cattle. Therefore he named that
place Succoth.[w]
18   On his journey from Paddan-aram,
Jacob came safely to the city of
Shechem in Canaan and pitched his
19 tent to the east of it. The strip of
country where he had pitched his tent
he bought from the sons of Hamor
father of Shechem for a hundred
20 sheep.[x] There he set up an altar and
called it El-Elohey-Israel.[y]

Dinah's dishonour avenged

34 Dinah, the daughter whom Leah had
borne to Jacob, went out to visit the
2 women of the country, and Shechem,
son of Hamor the Hivite the local
prince, saw her; he took her, lay with
3 her and dishonoured her. But he
remained true to Jacob's daughter
Dinah; he loved the girl and com-
4 forted her. So Shechem said to his
father Hamor, 'Get me this girl for a
5 wife.' When Jacob heard that Shechem
had violated his daughter Dinah, his
sons were with the herds in the open
country, so he said nothing until they
6 came home. Meanwhile Shechem's
father Hamor came out to Jacob to
7 discuss it with him. When Jacob's
sons came in from the country and
heard, they were grieved and angry,

because in lying with Jacob's daughter he had done what the Israelites
held to be an outrage, an intolerable
thing. Hamor appealed to them in 8
these terms: 'My son Shechem is in
love with this girl; I beg you to let him
have her as his wife. Let us ally our- 9
selves in marriage; you shall give us
your daughters, and you shall take
ours in exchange. You must settle 10
among us. The country is open to you;
make your home in it, move about
freely and acquire land of your own.'
And Shechem said to the girl's father 11
and brothers, 'I am eager to win your
favour and I will give whatever you
ask. Fix the bride-price and the gift as 12
high as you like, and I will give whatever you ask; but you must give me
the girl in marriage.'
    Jacob's sons gave a dishonest reply 13
to Shechem and his father Hamor,
laying a trap for them because
Shechem had violated their sister
Dinah: 'We cannot do this,' they said; 14
'we cannot give our sister to a man
who is uncircumcised; for we look on
that as a disgrace. There is one condi- 15
tion on which we will consent: if you
will follow our example and have
every male among you circumcised,
we will give you our daughters and 16
take yours for ourselves. Then we can
live among you, and we shall all
become one people. But if you refuse 17
to listen to us and be circumcised, we
will take the girl and go away.' Their 18
proposal pleased Hamor and his son
Shechem; and the young man, who 19
was held in respect above anyone in
his father's house, did not hesitate to
do what they had said, because his
heart was taken by Jacob's daughter.
    So Hamor and Shechem went back 20
to the city gate and addressed their
fellow-citizens: 'These men are friend- 21
ly to us; let them live in our country
and move freely in it. The land has
room enough for them. Let us marry
their daughters and give them ours.
But these men will agree to live with 22
us and become one people on this one
condition only: every male among us
must be circumcised as they have been.
Will not their herds, their livestock, 23
and all their chattels then be ours?
We need only consent to their condition, and then they are free to live
with us.' All the able-bodied men 24
agreed with Hamor and Shechem,
and every single one of them was circumcised, every able-bodied male.

w *That is* Shelters.   x *Or* pieces of money (*cp. Josh. 24. 32; Job 42. 11*).   y *That is* God
the God of Israel.

25 Then two days later, while they were still in great pain, Jacob's two sons Simeon and Levi, full brothers to Dinah, armed themselves with swords, boldly entered the city and killed 26 every male. They cut down Hamor and his son Shechem and took Dinah from Shechem's house and went off 27 with her. Then Jacob's other sons came in over the dead bodies and plundered the city, to avenge their 28 sister's dishonour. They seized flocks, cattle, asses, and everything, both inside the city and outside in the open 29 country; they also carried off all their possessions, their dependants, and their women, and plundered everything in the houses.

30 Jacob said to Simeon and Levi, 'You have brought trouble on me, you have made my name stink among the people of the country, the Canaanites and the Perizzites. My numbers are few; if they muster against me and attack me, I shall be destroyed, I and 31 my household with me.' They answered, 'Is our sister to be treated as a common whore?'

God blesses Jacob at Bethel

35 God said to Jacob, 'Go up to Bethel and settle there; build an altar there to the God who appeared to you when you were running away from your 2 brother Esau.' So Jacob said to his household and to all who were with him, 'Rid yourselves of the foreign gods which you have among you, purify yourselves, and see your clothes 3 are mended.[z] We are going to Bethel, so that I can set up an altar there to the God who answered me in the day of my distress, and who has been with 4 me all the way that I have come.' So they handed over to Jacob all the foreign gods in their possession and the rings from their ears, and he buried them under the terebinth-tree 5 near Shechem. Then they set out, and the cities round about were panic-stricken, and the inhabitants dared 6 not pursue the sons of Jacob. Jacob and all the people with him came to 7 Luz, that is Bethel, in Canaan. There he built an altar, and he called the place El-bethel, because it was there that God had revealed himself to him when he was running away from his 8 brother. Rebecca's nurse Deborah died and was buried under the oak below Bethel, and he named it Allon-bakuth.[a] 9 God appeared again to Jacob when he came back from Paddan-aram and blessed him. God said to him: 10

'Jacob is your name,
but your name shall no longer be Jacob:
Israel shall be your name.'

So he named him Israel. And God said 11 to him:

'I am God Almighty.
Be fruitful and increase as a nation;
a host of nations shall come from you,
and kings shall spring from your body.
The land which I gave to Abra- 12 ham and Isaac I give to you;
and to your descendants after you I give this land.'

God then left him, and Jacob erected 13 14 a sacred pillar in the place where God had spoken with him, a pillar of stone, and he offered a drink-offering over it and poured oil on it. Jacob called the 15 place where God had spoken with him Bethel.

The death of Rachel

They set out from Bethel, and when 16 there was still some distance to go to Ephrathah, Rachel was in labour and her pains were severe. While her pains 17 were upon her, the midwife said, 'Do not be afraid, this is another son for you.' Then with her last breath, as she 18 was dying, she named him Ben-oni,[b] but his father called him Benjamin.[c] So Rachel died and was buried by the 19 side of the road to Ephrathah, that is Bethlehem. Jacob set up a sacred 20 pillar over her grave; it is known to this day as the Pillar of Rachel's Grave. Then Israel journeyed on and 21 pitched his tent on the other side of Migdal-eder. While Israel was living 22 in that district, Reuben went and lay with his father's concubine Bilhah, and Israel came to hear of it.

Jacob's sons

The sons of Jacob were twelve. The 23 sons of Leah: Jacob's first-born Reuben, then Simeon, Levi, Judah, Issachar and Zebulun. The sons of 24 Rachel: Joseph and Benjamin. The 25 sons of Rachel's slave-girl Bilhah: Dan and Naphtali. The sons of Leah's 26 slave-girl Zilpah: Gad and Asher. These were Jacob's sons, born to him in Paddan-aram.

[z] Or change your clothes.   [a] That is Oak of Weeping.   [b] That is Son of my ill luck.
[c] That is Son of good luck or Son of the right hand.

The death of Isaac

27 Jacob came to his father Isaac at Mamre by Kiriath-arba, that is Hebron, where Abraham and Isaac had 28 dwelt. Isaac had lived for a hundred and eighty years when he breathed 29 his last. He died and was gathered to his father's kin at a very great age, and his sons Esau and Jacob buried him.

Esau's descendants

36 This is the table of the descendants of 2 Esau: that is Edom. Esau took Canaanite women in marriage, Adah daughter of Elon the Hittite and Oholibamah daughter of Anah son of 3 Zibeon the Horite,[d] and Basemath, Ishmael's daughter, sister of Nebaioth. 4[e] Adah bore Eliphaz to Esau; Ba- 5 semath bore Reuel, and Oholibamah bore Jeush, Jalam and Korah. These were Esau's sons, born to him in 6 Canaan. Esau took his wives, his sons and daughters and everyone in his household, his herds, his cattle, and all the chattels that he had acquired in Canaan, and went to the district of Seir out of the way of his brother 7 Jacob, because they had so much stock that they could not live together; the land where they were staying could not support them because of 8 their herds. So Esau lived in the hill-country of Seir. Esau is Edom. 9 This is the table of the descendants of Esau father of the Edomites in the hill-country of Seir.

10 These are the names of the sons of Esau: Eliphaz was the son of Esau's wife Adah. Reuel was the son of 11 Esau's wife Basemath. The sons of Eliphaz were Teman, Omar, Zepho, 12 Gatam and Kenaz. Timna was concubine to Esau son Eliphaz, and she bore Amalek to him. These are the descendants of Esau's wife Adah. 13 These are the sons of Reuel: Nahath, Zerah, Shammah and Mizzah. These were the descendants of Esau's wife 14 Basemath. These were the sons of Esau's wife Oholibamah daughter of Anah son of Zibeon. She bore him Jeush, Jalam and Korah.

15 These are the chiefs descended from Esau. The sons of Esau's eldest son Eliphaz: chief Teman, chief Omar, 16 chief Zepho, chief Kenaz, chief Korah, chief Gatam, chief Amalek. These are the chiefs descended from Eliphaz in Edom. These are the descendants of Adah.

These are the sons of Esau's son 17 Reuel: chief Nahath, chief Zerah, chief Shammah, chief Mizzah. These are the chiefs descended from Reuel in Edom. These are the descendants of Esau's wife Basemath.

These are the sons of Esau's wife 18 Oholibamah: chief Jeush, chief Jalam, chief Korah. These are the chiefs born to Oholibamah daughter of Anah wife of Esau.

These are the sons of Esau, that 19 is Edom, and these are their chiefs.

Seir's descendants

These are the sons of Seir the Horite, 20[f] the original inhabitants of the land: Lotan, Shobal, Zibeon, Anah, Dishon, 21 Ezer and Dishan. These are the chiefs of the Horites, the sons of Seir in Edom. The sons of Lotan were Hori 22 and Hemam, and Lotan had a sister named Timna.

These are the sons of Shobal: 23 Alvan, Manahath, Ebal, Shepho and Onam.

These are the sons of Zibeon: Aiah 24 and Anah. This is the Anah who found some mules in the wilderness while he was tending the asses of his father Zibeon. These are the children 25 of Anah: Dishon and Oholibamah daughter of Anah.

These are the children of Dishon: 26 Hemdan, Eshban, Ithran and Cheran.

These are the sons of Ezer: Bilhan, 27 Zavan and Akan. These are the sons 28 of Dishan: Uz and Aran.

These are the chiefs descended from 29 the Horites: chief Lotan, chief Shobal, chief Zibeon, chief Anah, chief Di- 30 shon, chief Ezer, chief Dishan. These are the chiefs that were descended from the Horites according to their clans in the district of Seir.

The kings of Edom

These are the kings who ruled over 31[g] Edom before there were kings in Israel: Bela son of Beor became king 32 in Edom, and his city was named Dinhabah; when he died, he was 33 succeeded by Jobab son of Zerah of Bozrah. When Jobab died, he 34 was succeeded by Husham of Teman. When Husham died, he was succeeded 35 by Hadad son of Bedad, who defeated Midian in Moabite country. His city was named Avith. When Hadad died, 36 he was succeeded by Samlah of Masrekah. When Samlah died, he was 37

---

d Prob. rdg. (cp. verses 20, 21); Heb. Hivite.   e Verses 4, 5, 9–13; cp. 1 Chr. 1. 35–7.   f Verses 20–8: cp. 1 Chr. 1. 38–42.   g Verses 31–43: cp. 1 Chr. 1. 43–54.

succeeded by Saul of Rehoboth on
38 the River. When Saul died, he was
succeeded by Baal-hanan son of
39 Akbor. When Baal-hanan died, he
was succeeded by Hadar.[h] His city
was named Pau; his wife's name was
Mehetabel daughter of Matred a woman of Me-zahab.[i]

40 These are the names of the chiefs
descended from Esau, according to
their families, their places, by name:
chief Timna, chief Alvah, chief Je-
41 theth, chief Oholibamah, chief Elah,
42 chief Pinon, chief Kenaz, chief Te-
43 man, chief Mibzar, chief Magdiel,
and chief Iram: all chiefs of Edom
according to their settlements in the
land which they possessed. (Esau is
the father of the Edomites.)

Joseph and his brothers

37 So Jacob lived in Canaan, the country
2 in which his father had settled. And
this is the story of the descendants of
Jacob.

When Joseph was a boy of seventeen, he used to accompany his
brothers, the sons of Bilhah and
Zilpah, his father's wives, when they
were in charge of the flock; and he
brought their father a bad report of
3 them. Now Israel loved Joseph more
than any other of his sons, because he
was a child of his old age, and he made
4 him a long, sleeved robe. When his
brothers saw that their father loved
him more than any of them, they
hated him and could not say a kind
word to him.

5 Joseph had a dream; and when he
told it to his brothers, they hated him
6 still more. He said to them, 'Listen to
7 this dream I have had. We were in
the field binding sheaves, and my
sheaf rose on end and stood upright,
and your sheaves gathered round
and bowed low before my sheaf.'
8 His brothers answered him, 'Do you
think you will one day be a king and
lord it over us?' and they hated him
still more because of his dreams and
9 what he said. He had another dream,
which he told to his father and his
brothers. He said, 'Listen: I have had
another dream. The sun and moon
and eleven stars were bowing down
10 to me.' When he told it to his father
and his brothers, his father took him
to task: 'What is this dream of yours?'
he said. 'Must we come and bow low
to the ground before you, I and your
11 mother and your brothers?' His

brothers were jealous of him, but his
father did not forget.

Joseph sold into Egypt

Joseph's brothers went to mind their 12
father's flocks in Shechem. Israel said 13
to him, 'Your brothers are minding
the flocks in Shechem; come, I will
send you to them', and he said, 'I am
ready.' He said to him, 'Go and see if 14
all is well with your brothers and the
sheep, and bring me back word.' So
he sent off Joseph from the vale of
Hebron and he came to Shechem. A 15
man met him wandering in the open
country and asked him what he was
looking for. He replied, 'I am looking 16
for my brothers. Tell me, please,
where they are minding the flocks.'
The man said, 'They have gone away 17
from here; I heard them speak of
going to Dothan.' So Joseph followed
his brothers and he found them in
Dothan. They saw him in the distance, 18
and before he reached them, they
plotted to kill him. They said to each 19
other, 'Here comes that dreamer. Now 20
is our chance; let us kill him and throw
him into one of these pits and say
that a wild beast has devoured him.
Then we shall see what will come of
his dreams.' When Reuben heard, he 21
came to his rescue, urging them not
to take his life. 'Let us have no blood- 22
shed', he said. 'Throw him into this
pit in the wilderness, but do him no
bodily harm.' He meant to save him
from them so as to restore him to his
father. When Joseph came up to his 23
brothers, they stripped him of the
long, sleeved robe which he was
wearing, took him and threw him into 24
the pit. The pit was empty and had no
water in it.

Then they sat down to eat some 25
food and, looking up, they saw an
Ishmaelite caravan coming in from
Gilead on the way down to Egypt,
with camels carrying gum tragacanth
and balm and myrrh. Judah said to 26
his brothers, 'What shall we gain by
killing our brother and concealing
his death? Why not sell him to the 27
Ishmaelites? Let us do him no harm,
for he is our brother, our own flesh
and blood'; and his brothers agreed
with him. Meanwhile some Midianite 28
merchants passed by and drew Joseph
up out of the pit. They sold him for
twenty pieces of silver to the Ishmaelites, and they brought Joseph to
Egypt. When Reuben went back to 29
the pit, Joseph was not there. He rent

h Or Hadad; cp. 1 Chr. 1. 50.   i Or daughter of Mezahab.

30 his clothes and went back to his brothers and said, 'The boy is not there. Where can I go?'

31 Joseph's brothers took his robe, killed a goat and dipped it in the goat's

32 blood. Then they tore the robe, the long, sleeved robe, brought it to their father and said, 'Look what we have found. Do you recognize it? Is this

33 your son's robe or not?' Jacob did recognize it, and he replied, 'It is my son's robe. A wild beast has devoured him. Joseph has been torn to pieces.'

34 Jacob rent his clothes, put on sack-cloth and mourned his son for a long

35 time. His sons and daughters all tried to comfort him, but he refused to be comforted. He said, 'I will go to my grave mourning for my son.' Thus

36 Joseph's father wept for him. Mean-while the Midianites had sold Joseph in Egypt to Potiphar, one of Pharaoh's eunuchs, the captain of the guard.[j]

Judah and Tamar

38 About that time Judah left his brothers and went south and pitched his tent in company with an Adul-

2 lamite named Hirah. There he saw Bathshua the daughter of a Canaanite and married her. He slept with her,

3 and she conceived and bore a son,

4 whom he called Er. She conceived again and bore a son whom she called

5 Onan. Once more she conceived and bore a son whom she called Shelah, and she ceased to bear children[k]

6 she had given birth to him. Judah found a wife for his eldest son Er; her

7 name was Tamar. But Judah's eldest son Er was wicked in the LORD's

8 sight, and the LORD took his life. Then Judah told Onan to sleep with his brother's wife, to do his duty as the husband's brother and raise up issue

9 for his brother. But Onan knew that the issue would not be his; so when-ever he slept with his brother's wife, he spilled his seed on the ground so as not to raise up issue for his brother.

10 What he did was wicked in the LORD's sight, and the LORD took his life.

11 Judah said to his daughter-in-law Tamar, 'Remain as a widow in your father's house until my son Shelah grows up'; for he was afraid that he too would die like his brothers. So Tamar went and stayed in her father's house.

12 Time passed, and Judah's wife Bathshua died. When he had finished mourning, he and his friend Hirah the Adullamite went up to Timnath

at sheep-shearing. When Tamar was 13 told that her father-in-law was on his way to shear his sheep at Timnath, she took off her widow's weeds, veiled 14 her face, perfumed herself and sat where the road forks in two directions on the way to Timnath. She did this because she knew that Shelah had grown up and she had not been given to him as a wife. When Judah saw her, 15 he thought she was a prostitute, although she had veiled her face. He 16 turned to her where she sat by the roadside and said, 'Let me lie with you', not knowing that she was his daughter-in-law. She said 'What will you give me to lie with me?' He 17 answered, 'I will send you a kid from my flock', but she said, 'Will you give me a pledge until you send it?' He 18 asked what pledge he should give her, and she replied, 'Your seal and its cord, and the staff which you hold in your hand.' So he gave them to her and lay with her, and she conceived. She 19 then rose and went home, took off her veil and resumed her widow's weeds. Judah sent the kid by his 20 friend the Adullamite in order to recover the pledge from the woman, but he could not find her. He asked 21 the men of that place, 'Where is that temple-prostitute, the one who was sitting where the road forks?', but they answered, 'There is no temple-prostitute here.' So he went back to 22 Judah and told him that he had not found her and that the men of the place had said there was no such prostitute here. Judah said, 'Let her 23 keep my pledge, or we shall get a bad name. I did send a kid, but you could not find her.' About three months later 24 Judah was told that his daughter-in-law Tamar had behaved like a common prostitute and through her wanton conduct was with child. Judah said, 'Bring her out so that she may be burnt.' But when she was 25 brought out, she sent to her father-in-law and said, 'The father of my child is the man to whom these things belong. See if you recognize whose they are, the engraving on the seal, the pattern of the cord, and the staff.' Judah recognized them and said, 'She 26 is more in the right than I am, because I did not give her to my son Shelah.' He did not have intercourse with her again. When her time was 27 come, there were twins in her womb, and while she was in labour one of 28 them put out a hand. The midwife

j Or executioner.　　k ceased . . . children: or was at Kezib.

took a scarlet thread and fastened it round the wrist, saying, 'This one
29 appeared first.' No sooner had he drawn back his hand, than his brother came out and the midwife said, 'What! you have broken out first!'
30 So he was named Perez.*l* Soon afterwards his brother was born with the scarlet thread on his wrist, and he was named Zerah.*m*

Joseph and Potiphar's wife

39 When Joseph was taken down to Egypt, he was bought by Potiphar, one of Pharaoh's eunuchs, the captain of the guard, an Egyptian. Potiphar bought him from the Ishmaelites who
2 had brought him there. The LORD was with Joseph and he prospered. He lived in the house of his Egyptian
3 master, who saw that the LORD was with him and was giving him success
4 in all that he undertook. Thus Joseph found favour with his master, and he became his personal servant. Indeed, his master put him in charge of his household and entrusted him with all
5 that he had. From the time that he put him in charge of his household and all his property, the LORD blessed the Egyptian's household for Joseph's sake. The blessing of the LORD was on all that was his in house and field.
6 He left everything he possessed in Joseph's care, and concerned himself with nothing but the food he ate.

Now Joseph was handsome and
7 good-looking, and a time came when his master's wife took notice of him and said, 'Come and lie with me.'
8 But he refused and said to her, 'Think of my master. He does not know as much as I do about his own house, and he has entrusted me with all he
9 has. He has given me authority in this house second only to his own, and has withheld nothing from me except you, because you are his wife. How can I do anything so wicked, and sin against
10 God?' She kept asking Joseph day after day, but he refused to lie with
11 her and be in her company. One day he came into the house as usual to do his work, when none of the men of the household were there indoors.
12 She caught him by his cloak, saying, 'Come and lie with me', but he left the cloak in her hands and ran out of the
13 house. When she saw that he had left his cloak in her hands and had run out
14 of the house, she called out to the men of the household, 'Look at this! My husband has brought in a Hebrew to

make a mockery of us. He came in here to lie with me, but I gave a loud scream. When he heard me scream 15 and call out, he left his cloak in my hand and ran off.' She kept his cloak 16 with her until his master came home, and then she repeated her tale. She 17 said, 'That Hebrew slave whom you brought in to make a mockery of me, has been here with me. But when I 18 screamed for help and called out, he left his cloak in my hands and ran off.' When Joseph's master heard his 19 wife's story of what his slave had done to her, he was furious. He took Joseph 20 and put him in the Round Tower, where the king's prisoners were kept; and there he stayed in the Round Tower. But the LORD was with Jo- 21 seph and kept faith with him, so that he won the favour of the governor of the Round Tower. He put 22 Joseph in charge of all the prisoners in the tower and of all their work. He 23 ceased to concern himself with anything entrusted to Joseph, because the LORD was with Joseph and gave him success in everything.

Joseph interprets the prisoners' dreams

It happened later that the king's **40** butler and his baker offended their master the king of Egypt. Pharaoh 2 was angry with these two eunuchs, the chief butler and the chief baker, and he put them in custody in the 3 house of the captain of the guard, in the Round Tower where Joseph was imprisoned. The captain of the guard 4 appointed Joseph as their attendant, and he waited on them. One night, 5 when they had been in prison for some time, they both had dreams, each needing its own interpretation—the king of Egypt's butler and his baker who were imprisoned in the Round Tower. When Joseph came to them 6 in the morning, he saw that they looked dejected. So he asked these 7 eunuchs, who were in custody with him in his master's house, why they were so downcast that day. They 8 replied, 'We have each had a dream and there is no one to interpret it for us.' Joseph said to them, 'Does not interpretation belong to God? Tell me your dreams.' So the chief butler 9 told Joseph his dream: 'In my dream', he said, 'there was a vine in front of me. On the vine there were three 10 branches, and as soon as it budded, it blossomed and its clusters ripened into grapes. Now I had Pharaoh's cup in 11

l That is Breaking out.   *m That is* Redness.

my hand, and I plucked the grapes, crushed them into Pharaoh's cup and put the cup into Pharaoh's hand.'

12 Joseph said to him, 'This is the interpretation. The three branches are three
13 days: within three days Pharaoh will raise you and restore you to your post, and then you will put the cup into Pharaoh's hand as you used to do
14 when you were his butler. But when things go well with you, if you think of me, keep faith with me and bring my case to Pharaoh's notice and help
15 me to get out of this house. By force I was carried off[n] from the land of the Hebrews, and I have done nothing here to deserve being put in this dungeon.'

16 When the chief baker saw that Joseph had given a favourable interpretation, he said to him, 'I too had a dream, and in my dream there were three baskets of white bread on my
17 head. In the top basket there was every kind of food which the baker prepares for Pharaoh, and the birds were eating out of the top basket on
18 my head.' Joseph answered, 'This is the interpretation. The three baskets
19 are three days: within three days Pharaoh will raise you and hang you up on a tree, and the birds of the air will eat your flesh.'

20 The third day was Pharaoh's birthday and he gave a feast for all his servants. He raised the chief butler and the chief baker in the presence of
21 his court. He restored the chief butler to his post, and the butler put the
22 cup into Pharaoh's hand; but he hanged the chief baker. All went as Joseph had said in interpreting the
23 dreams for them. Even so the chief butler did not remember Joseph, but forgot him.

Joseph interprets Pharaoh's dreams

41 Nearly two years later Pharaoh had a dream: he was standing by the Nile,
2 and there came up from the river seven cows, sleek and fat, and they
3 grazed on the reeds. After them seven other cows came up from the river, gaunt and lean, and stood on the river-bank beside the first cows.
4 The cows that were gaunt and lean devoured the cows that were sleek
5 and fat. Then Pharaoh woke up. He fell asleep again and had a second
6 dream: he saw seven ears of corn, full and ripe, growing on one stalk. Growing up after them were seven other ears, thin and shrivelled by the east

wind. The thin ears swallowed up the 7 ears that were full and ripe. Then Pharaoh woke up and knew that it was a dream. When morning came, 8 Pharaoh was troubled in mind; so he summoned all the magicians and sages of Egypt. He told them his dreams, but there was no one who could interpret them for him. Then 9 Pharaoh's chief butler spoke up and said, 'It is time for me to recall my faults. Once Pharaoh was angry with 10 his servants, and he imprisoned me and the chief baker in the house of the captain of the guard. One night we 11 both had dreams, each needing its own interpretation. We had with us a young 12 Hebrew, a slave of the captain of the guard, and we told him our dreams and he interpreted them for us, giving each man's dream its own interpretation. Each dream came true as it had 13 been interpreted to us: I was restored to my position, and he was hanged.'

Pharaoh thereupon sent for Joseph, 14 and they hurriedly brought him out of the dungeon. He shaved and changed his clothes, and came in to Pharaoh. Pharaoh said to him, 'I have 15 had a dream, and no one can interpret it to me. I have heard it said that you can understand and interpret dreams.' Joseph answered, 'Not I, but God, 16 will answer for Pharaoh's welfare.' Then Pharaoh said to Joseph, 'In my 17 dream I was standing on the bank of the Nile, and there came up from the 18 river seven cows, fat and sleek, and they grazed on the reeds. After them 19 seven other cows came up that were poor, very gaunt and lean; I have never seen such gaunt creatures in all Egypt. These lean, gaunt cows de- 20 voured the first cows, the fat ones. They 21 were swallowed up, but no one could have guessed that they were in the bellies of the others, which looked as gaunt as before. Then I woke up. After 22 I had fallen asleep again, I saw in a dream seven ears of corn, full and ripe, growing on one stalk. Growing 23 up after them were seven other ears, shrivelled, thin, and blighted by the east wind. The thin ears swallowed 24 up the seven ripe ears. When I told all this to the magicians, no one could explain it to me.'

Joseph said to Pharaoh, 'Pharaoh's 25 dreams are one dream. God has told Pharaoh what he is going to do. The 26 seven good cows are seven years, and the seven good ears of corn are seven years. It is all one dream. The seven 27

n *Or* stolen.

lean and gaunt cows that came up after them are seven years, and the empty ears of corn blighted by the east wind will be seven years of

28 famine. It is as I have said to Pharaoh: God has let Pharaoh see what he is

29 going to do. There are to be seven years of great plenty throughout the

30 land. After them will come seven years of famine; all the years of plenty in Egypt will be forgotten, and the

31 famine will ruin the country. The good years will not be remembered in the land because of the famine that

32 follows; for it will be very severe. The doubling of Pharaoh's dream means that God is already resolved to do this, and he will very soon put it into effect.

33 Pharaoh should now look for a shrewd and intelligent man, and put him in

34 charge of the country. This is what Pharaoh should do: appoint controllers over the land, and take one fifth of the produce of Egypt during

35 the seven years of plenty. They should collect all this food produced in the good years that are coming and put the corn under Pharaoh's control in store in the cities, and keep it under

36 guard. This food will be a reserve for the country against the seven years of famine which will come upon Egypt. Thus the country will not be devastated by the famine.'

Joseph made ruler over Egypt

37 The plan pleased Pharaoh and all his

38 courtiers, and he said to them, 'Can we find a man like this man, one who

39 has the spirit of a god^o in him?' He said to Joseph, 'Since a god^p has made all this known to you, there is no one

40 so shrewd and intelligent as you. You shall be in charge of my household, and all my people will depend on your every word. Only my royal throne shall make me greater than you.'

41 Pharaoh said to Joseph, 'I hereby give you authority over the whole

42 land of Egypt.' He took off his signet-ring and put it on Joseph's finger, had him dressed in fine linen, and

43 hung a gold chain round his neck. He mounted him in his viceroy's chariot and men cried 'Make way!' before him. Thus Pharaoh made him ruler over all

44 Egypt and said to him, 'I am the Pharaoh. Without your consent no man shall lift hand or foot through-

45 out Egypt.' Pharaoh named him Zaphenath-paneah, and he gave him as wife Asenath the daughter of Potiphera priest of On. And Joseph's

authority extended over the whole of Egypt.

46 Joseph was thirty years old when he entered the service of Pharaoh king of Egypt. When he took his leave of the king, he made a tour of inspec-

47 tion through the country. During the seven years of plenty there were abun-

48 dant harvests, and Joseph gathered all the food produced in Egypt during those years and stored it in the cities, putting in each the food from the surrounding country. He

49 stored the grain in huge quantities; it was like the sand of the sea, so much that he stopped measuring: it was beyond all measure.

50 Before the years of famine came, two sons were born to Joseph by Asenath the daughter of Potiphera

51 priest of On. He named the elder Manasseh,^{q} 'for', he said, 'God has caused me to forget all my troubles

52 and my father's family.' He named the second Ephraim,^{r} 'for', he said, 'God has made me fruitful in the land

53 of my hardships.' When the seven years of plenty in Egypt came to an

54 end, seven years of famine began, as Joseph had foretold. There was famine

55 in every country, but throughout Egypt there was bread. So when the famine spread through all Egypt, the people appealed to Pharaoh for bread, and he ordered them to go to

56 Joseph and do as he told them. In every region there was famine, and Joseph opened all the granaries and sold corn to the Egyptians, for the

57 famine was severe. The whole world came to Egypt to buy corn from Joseph, so severe was the famine everywhere.

Joseph's brothers come to Egypt for corn

42 When Jacob saw that there was corn in Egypt, he said to his sons, 'Why do you stand staring at each other?

2 I have heard that there is corn in Egypt. Go down and buy some so that we may keep ourselves alive and not

3 starve.' So Joseph's brothers, ten of them, went down to buy grain from

4 Egypt, but Jacob did not let Joseph's brother Benjamin go with them, for fear that he might come to harm.

5 So the sons of Israel came down with everyone else to buy corn, because of the famine in Canaan.

6 Now Joseph was governor of all Egypt, and it was he who sold the

o Or of God.   p Or God.   q That is Causing to forget.   r That is Fruit.

corn to all the people of the land. Joseph's brothers came and bowed to 7 the ground before him, and when he saw his brothers, he recognized them but pretended not to know them and spoke harshly to them. 'Where do you come from?' he asked. 'From Canaan,' 8 they answered, 'to buy food.' Although Joseph had recognized his brothers, 9 they did not recognize him. He remembered also the dreams he had had about them; so he said to them, 'You are spies; you have come to spy out the weak points in our defences.' 10 They answered, 'No, sir: your servants 11 have come to buy food. We are all sons of one man. Your humble servants are honest men, we are not spies.' 12 'No,' he insisted, 'it is to spy out our weaknesses that you have come.' 13 They answered him, 'Sir, there are twelve of us, all brothers, sons of one man in Canaan. The youngest is still with our father, and one has dis- 14 appeared.' But Joseph said again to them, 'No, as I said before, you are 15 spies. This is how you shall be put to the proof: unless your youngest brother comes here, by the life of Pharaoh, you shall not leave this 16 place. Send one of your number to bring your brother; the rest will be kept in prison. Thus your story will be tested, and we shall see whether you are telling the truth. If not, then, by the life of Pharaoh, you must be 17 spies.' So he kept them in prison for three days.

Joseph's brothers go back to Canaan

18 On the third day Joseph said to the brothers, 'Do what I say and your lives will be spared; for I am a God- 19 fearing man: if you are honest men, your brother there shall be kept in prison, and the rest of you shall take 20 corn for your hungry households and bring your youngest brother to me; thus your words will be proved true, and you will not die.'*s* 21   They said to one another, 'No doubt we deserve to be punished because of our brother, whose suffering we saw; for when he pleaded with us we refused to listen. That is why these 22 sufferings have come upon us.' But Reuben said, 'Did I not tell you not to do the boy a wrong? But you would not listen, and his blood is on our 23 heads, and we must pay.' They did not know that Joseph understood, because he had used an interpreter.

Joseph turned away from them and 24 wept. Then, turning back, he played a trick on them. First he took Simeon and bound him before their eyes; then he gave orders to fill their bags 25 with grain, to return each man's silver, putting it in his sack, and to give them supplies for the journey. All this was done; and they loaded the 26 corn on to their asses and went away. When they stopped for the night, one 27 of them opened his sack to give fodder to his ass, and there he saw his silver at the top of the pack. He said to his 28 brothers, 'My silver has been returned to me, and here it is in my pack.' Bewildered and trembling, they said to each other, 'What is this that God has done to us?'

When they came to their father 29 Jacob in Canaan, they told him all that had happened to them. They said, 'The man who is lord of the country 30 spoke harshly to us and made out that we were spies. We said to him, 31 "We are honest men, we are not spies. There are twelve of us, all brothers, 32 sons of one father. One has disappeared, and the youngest is with our father in Canaan." This man, the lord of the 33 country, said to us, "This is how I shall find out if you are honest men. Leave one of your brothers with me, take food for your hungry households and go. Bring your youngest brother 34 to me, and I shall know that you are not spies, but honest men. Then I will restore your brother to you, and you can move about the country freely."' But on emptying their sacks, each of 35 them found his silver inside, and when they and their father saw the bundles of silver, they were afraid. Their father Jacob said to them, 'You 36 have robbed me of my children. Joseph has disappeared; Simeon has disappeared; and now you are taking Benjamin. Everything is against me.' Reuben said to his father, 'You may 37 kill both my sons if I do not bring him back to you. Put him in my charge, and I shall bring him back.' But 38 Jacob said, 'My son shall not go with you, for his brother is dead and he alone is left. If he comes to any harm on the journey, you will bring down my grey hairs in sorrow to the grave.'

Joseph's brothers return with Benjamin

The famine was still severe in the 43 country. When they had used up the 2 corn they had brought from Egypt,

s Prob. rdg.; Heb. adds and they did so.

their father said to them, 'Go back and buy a little more corn for us to 3 eat.' But Judah replied, 'The man plainly warned us that we must not go into his presence unless our brother 4 was with us. If you let our brother go with us, we will go down and buy 5 food for you. But if you will not let him, we will not go; for the man said to us, "You shall not come into my presence, unless your brother is with 6 you."' Israel said, 'Why have you treated me so badly? Why did you tell the man that you had yet another 7 brother?' They answered, 'He questioned us closely about ourselves and our family: "Is your father still alive?" he asked, "Have you a brother?", and we answered his questions. How could we possibly know that he would tell us to bring our brother to 8 Egypt?' Judah said to his father Israel, 'Send the boy with me; then we can start at once. By doing this we shall save our lives, ours, yours, and our dependants', and none of us will 9 starve. I will go surety for him and you may hold me responsible. If I do not bring him back and restore him to you, you shall hold me guilty all 10 my life. If we had not wasted all this time, by now we could have gone back twice over.'

11 Their father Israel said to them, 'If it must be so, then do this: take in your baggage, as a gift for the man, some of the produce for which our country is famous: a little balsam, a little honey, gum tragacanth, myrrh, 12 pistachio nuts, and almonds. Take double the amount of silver, and restore what was returned to you in your packs; perhaps it was a mistake. 13 Take your brother with you and go 14 straight back to the man. May God Almighty make him kindly disposed to you, and may he send back the one whom you left behind, and Benjamin too. As for me, if I am bereaved, then 15 I am bereaved.' So they took the gift and double the amount of silver, and with Benjamin they started at once for Egypt, where they presented themselves to Joseph.

16 When Joseph saw Benjamin with them, he said to his steward, 'Bring these men indoors, kill a beast and make dinner ready, for they will eat 17 with me at noon.' He did as Joseph told him and brought the men into 18 the house. When they came in they were afraid, for they thought, 'We have been brought in here because of that affair of the silver which was replaced in our packs the first time. He means to trump up some charge against us and victimize us, seize our asses and make us his slaves.' So 19 they approached Joseph's steward and spoke to him at the door of the house. They said, 'Please listen, my lord. 20 After our first visit to buy food, when 21 we reached the place where we were to spend the night, we opened our packs and each of us found his silver in full weight at the top of his pack. We have brought it back with us, and have added other silver to buy 22 food. We do not know who put the silver in our packs.' He answered, 'Set 23 your minds at rest; do not be afraid. It was your God, the God of your father, who hid treasure for you in your packs. I did receive the silver.' Then he brought Simeon out to them.

The steward brought them into 24 Joseph's house and gave them water to wash their feet, and provided fodder for their asses. They had their 25 gifts ready when Joseph arrived at noon, for they had heard that they were to eat there. When Joseph came 26 into the house, they presented him with the gifts which they had brought, bowing to the ground before him. He asked them how they were and 27 said, 'Is your father well, the old man of whom you spoke? Is he still alive?' They answered, 'Yes, my lord, our 28 father is still alive and well.' And they bowed low and prostrated themselves. Joseph looked and saw his own 29 mother's son, his brother Benjamin, and asked, 'Is this your youngest brother, of whom you told me?', and to Benjamin he said, 'May God be gracious to you, my son!' Joseph was 30 overcome; his feelings for his brother mastered him, and he was near to tears. So he went into the inner room and wept. Then he washed his face 31 and came out; and, holding back his feelings, he ordered the meal to be served. They served him by himself, 32 and the brothers by themselves, and the Egyptians who were at dinner were also served separately; for Egyptians hold it an abomination to eat with Hebrews. The brothers were 33 seated in his presence, the eldest first according to his age and so on down to the youngest: they looked at one another in astonishment. Joseph sent 34 them each a portion from what was before him, but Benjamin's was five times larger than any of the other portions. Thus they drank with him and all grew merry.

The missing goblet

44 Joseph gave his steward this order:
'Fill the men's packs with as much
food as they can carry and put each
man's silver at the top of his pack.
2 And put my goblet, my silver goblet,
at the top of the youngest brother's
pack with the silver for the corn.' He
3 did as Joseph said. At daybreak the
brothers were allowed to take their
4 asses and go on their journey; but
before they had gone very far from
the city, Joseph said to his steward,
'Go after those men at once, and when
you catch up with them, say, "Why
5 have you repaid good with evil? Why
have you stolen the silver goblet? It is
the one from which my lord drinks,
and which he uses for divination. You
6 have done a wicked thing."' When he
caught up with them, he repeated all
7 this to them, but they replied, 'My
lord, how can you say such things?
No, sir, God forbid that we should do
8 any such thing! You remember the
silver we found at the top of our packs?
We brought it back to you from
Canaan. Why should we steal silver
9 or gold from your master's house? If
any one of us is found with the goblet,
he shall die; and, what is more, my
lord, we will all become your slaves.'
10 He said, 'Very well, then; I accept
what you say. The man in whose
possession it is found shall be my
slave, but the rest of you shall go
11 free.' Each man quickly lowered his
pack to the ground and opened it.
12 The steward searched them, beginning
with the eldest and finishing with the
youngest, and the goblet was found
in Benjamin's pack.
13   At this they rent their clothes; then
each man loaded his ass and they
14 returned to the city. Joseph was still
in the house when Judah and his
brothers came in. They threw them-
15 selves on the ground before him, and
Joseph said, 'What have you done?
You might have known that a man
like myself would practise divination.'
16 Judah said, 'What shall we say, my
lord? What can we say to prove our
innocence? God has found out our
sin. Here we are, my lord, ready to be
made your slaves, we ourselves as well
as the one who was found with the
17 goblet.' Joseph answered, 'God forbid
that I should do such a thing! The
one who was found with the goblet
shall become my slave, but the rest of
you can go home to your father in
peace.'

Judah pleads for Benjamin

Then Judah went up to him and said, 18
'Please listen, my lord. Let me say a
word to your lordship, I beg. Do not
be angry with me, for you are as
great as Pharaoh. You, my lord, 19
asked us whether we had a father or
a brother. We answered, "We have 20
an aged father, and he has a young
son born in his old age; this boy's full
brother is dead and he alone is left of
his mother's children, he alone, and
his father loves him." Your lordship 21
answered, "Bring him down to me so
that I may set eyes on him." We told 22
you, my lord, that the boy could not
leave his father, and that his father
would die if he left him. But you 23
answered, "Unless your youngest brother comes here with you, you shall
not enter my presence again." We 24
went back to your servant our father,
and told him what your lordship had
said. When our father told us to go 25
and buy food, we answered, "We 26
cannot go down; for without our
youngest brother we cannot enter the
man's presence; but if our brother is
with us, we will go." Our father, my 27
lord, then said to us, "You know that
my wife bore me two sons. One left 28
me, and I said, 'He must have been
torn to pieces.' I have not seen him to
this day. If you take this one from me 29
as well, and he comes to any harm,
then you will bring down my grey
hairs in trouble to the grave." Now, 30
my lord, when I return to my father
without the boy—and remember, his
life is bound up with the boy's—what 31
will happen is this: he will see that
the boy is not with us and will die,
and your servants will have brought
down our father's grey hairs in
sorrow to the grave. Indeed, my lord, 32
it was I who went surety for the boy
to my father. I said, "If I do not
bring him back to you, then you shall
hold me guilty all my life." Now, my 33
lord, let me remain in place of the boy
as your lordship's slave, and let him
go with his brothers. How can I 34
return to my father without the boy?
I could not bear to see the misery
which my father would suffer.'

*Joseph makes himself known to his
      brothers*

Joseph could no longer control his **45**
feelings in front of his attendants, and
he called out, 'Let everyone leave my
presence.' So there was nobody present
when Joseph made himself known to

2 his brothers, but so loudly did he weep that the Egyptians and Phar-
3 aoh's household heard him. Joseph said to his brothers, 'I am Joseph; can my father be still alive?' His brothers were so dumbfounded at finding themselves face to face with Joseph that they could not answer.
4 Then Joseph said to his brothers, 'Come closer', and so they came close. He said, 'I am your brother Joseph
5 whom you sold into Egypt. Now do not be distressed or take it amiss that you sold me into slavery here; it was God who sent me ahead of you to save
6 men's lives. For there have now been two years of famine in the country, and there will be another five years with neither ploughing nor harvest.
7 God sent me ahead of you to ensure that you will have descendants on earth, and to preserve you all, a great
8 band of survivors. So it was not you who sent me here, but God, and he has made me a father^t to Pharaoh, and lord over all his household and ruler
9 of all Egypt. Make haste and go back to my father and give him this message from his son Joseph: "God
10 has made me lord of all Egypt. Come down to me; do not delay. You shall live in the land of Goshen and be near me, you, your sons and your grand-sons, your flocks and herds and all
11 that you have. I will take care of you there, you and your household and all that you have, and see that you are not reduced to poverty; there are still
12 five years of famine to come." You can see for yourselves, and so can my brother Benjamin, that it is Joseph himself who
13 is speaking to you. Tell my father of all the honour which I enjoy in Egypt, tell him all you have seen, and make
14 haste to bring him down here.' Then he threw his arms round his brother Benjamin and wept, and Benjamin too em-
15 braced him weeping. He kissed all his brothers and wept over them, and after-wards his brothers talked with him.
16   When the report that Joseph's brothers had come reached Pharaoh's house, he and all his courtiers were
17 pleased. Pharaoh said to Joseph, 'Say to your brothers: "This is what you are to do. Load your beasts and go to
18 Canaan. Fetch your father and your households and bring them to me. I will give you the best that there is in Egypt, and you shall enjoy the fat of
19 the land." You shall also tell them: "Take wagons from Egypt for your

dependants and your wives and fetch your father and come. Have no 20 regrets at leaving your possessions, for all the best that there is in Egypt is yours."' The sons of Israel did as 21 they were told, and Joseph gave them wagons, according to Pharaoh's orders, and food for the journey. He provided 22 each of them with a change of cloth-ing, but to Benjamin he gave three hundred pieces of silver and five changes of clothing. Moreover he sent 23 his father ten asses carrying the best that there was in Egypt, and ten she-asses loaded with grain, bread, and provisions for his journey. So he 24 dismissed his brothers, telling them not to quarrel among themselves on the road, and they set out. Thus they 25 went up from Egypt and came to their father Jacob in Canaan. There they 26 gave him the news that Joseph was still alive and that he was ruler of all Egypt. He was stunned and could not believe it, but they told him all 27 that Joseph had said; and when he saw the wagons which Joseph had sent to take him away, his spirit revived. Israel said, 'It is enough. Joseph my 28 son is still alive; I will go and see him before I die.'

Jacob and his family journey to Egypt

So Israel set out with all that he had **46** and came to Beersheba where he offered sacrifices to the God of his father Isaac. God said to Israel in a 2 vision by night, 'Jacob, Jacob', and he answered, 'I am here.' God said, 3 'I am God, the God of your father. Do not be afraid to go down to Egypt, for there I will make you a great nation. I will go down with you to 4 Egypt, and I myself will bring you back again without fail; and Joseph shall close your eyes.' So Jacob set out 5 from Beersheba. Israel's sons con-veyed their father Jacob, their depen-dants, and their wives in the wagons which Pharaoh had sent to carry them. They took the herds and the 6 stock which they had acquired in Canaan and came to Egypt, Jacob and all his descendants with him, his 7 sons and their sons, his daughters and his sons' daughters: he brought all his descendants to Egypt.

Israelites who entered Egypt

  These are the names of the Israelites 8^u who entered Egypt: Jacob and his sons, as follows: Reuben, Jacob's

t Or counsellor. u Verses 8–25: cp. Exod. 6. 14–16; Num. 26. 5–50; 1 Chr. 4. 1, 24; 5. 3; 6. 1; 7. 1, 6, 13, 30; 8. 1–5.

9 eldest son. The sons of Reuben: Enoch, Pallu, Hezron and Carmi.
10 The sons of Simeon: Jemuel, Jamin, Ohad, Jachin, Zohar, and Saul, who was the son of a Canaanite woman.
11 The sons of Levi: Gershon, Kohath
12 and Merari. The sons of Judah: Er, Onan, Shelah, Perez and Zerah; of these Er and Onan died in Canaan. The sons of Perez were Hezron and
13 Hamul. The sons of Issachar: Tola,
14 Pua, Iob and Shimron. The sons of Zebulun: Sered, Elon and Jahleel.
15 These are the sons of Leah whom she bore to Jacob in Paddan-aram, and there was also his daughter Dinah. His sons and daughters numbered thirty-three in all.
16 The sons of Gad: Ziphion, Haggi, Shuni, Ezbon, Eri, Arodi and Areli.
17 The sons of Asher: Imnah, Ishvah, Ishvi, Beriah, and their sister Serah. The sons of Beriah: Heber and Mal-
18 chiel. These are the descendants of Zilpah whom Laban gave to his daughter Leah; sixteen in all, born to Jacob.
19 The sons of Jacob's wife Rachel:
20 Joseph and Benjamin. Manasseh and Ephraim were born to Joseph in Egypt. Asenath daughter of Poti-phera priest of On bore them to him.
21 The sons of Benjamin: Bela, Becher and Ashbel; and the sons of Bela: Gera, Naaman, Ehi, Rosh, Muppim,
22 Huppim and Ard. These are the descendants of Rachel; fourteen in all, born to Jacob.
23 24 The son[v] of Dan: Hushim. The sons of Naphtali: Jahzeel, Guni, Jezer and
25 Shillem. These are the descendants of Bilhah whom Laban gave to his daughter Rachel; seven in all, born to Jacob.
26 The persons belonging to Jacob who came to Egypt, all his direct descendants, not counting the wives
27 of his sons, were sixty-six in all. Two sons were born to Joseph in Egypt. Thus the house of Jacob numbered seventy when it entered Egypt.

Jacob and his family in Egypt

28 Judah was sent ahead that he might appear before Joseph in Goshen, and
29 so they entered Goshen. Joseph had his chariot made ready and went up to meet his father Israel in Goshen. When they met, he threw his arms round him and wept, and embraced
30 him for a long time, weeping. Israel said to Joseph, 'I have seen your face again, and you are still alive. Now I
31 am ready to die.' Joseph said to his brothers and to his father's household,

'I will go and tell Pharaoh; I will say to him, "My brothers and my father's household who were in Canaan have
32 come to me."' Now his brothers were shepherds, men with their own flocks and herds, and they had brought them with them, their flocks and herds and
33 all that they possessed. So Joseph said, 'When Pharaoh summons you and asks you what your occupation is,
34 you must say, "My lord, we have been herdsmen all our lives, as our fathers were before us." You must say this if you are to settle in the land of Goshen, because all shepherds are an abomination to the Egyptians.'

47 Joseph came and told Pharaoh, 'My father and my brothers have arrived from Canaan, with their flocks and their cattle and all that they have, and they are now in
2 Goshen.' Then he chose five of his brothers and presented them to
3 Pharaoh, who asked them what their occupation was, and they answered,
4 'My lord, we are shepherds, we and our fathers before us, and we have come to stay in this land; for there is no pasture in Canaan for our sheep, because the famine there is so severe. We beg you, my lord, to let us settle
5 now in Goshen.' Pharaoh said to Joseph, 'So your father and your
6 brothers have come to you. The land of Egypt is yours; settle them in the best part of it. Let them live in Goshen, and if you know of any capable men among them, make them chief herdsmen over my cattle.'
7 Then Joseph brought his father in and presented him to Pharaoh, and Jacob gave Pharaoh his blessing.
8 9 Pharaoh asked Jacob his age, and he answered, 'The years of my earthly sojourn are one hundred and thirty; hard years they have been and few, not equal to the years that my fathers
10 lived in their time.' Jacob then blessed Pharaoh and went out from
11 his presence. So Joseph settled his father and his brothers, and gave them lands in Egypt, in the best part of the country, in the district of Rameses, as
12 Pharaoh had ordered. He supported his father, his brothers, and all his father's household with all the food they needed.

Joseph's administration

13 There was no bread in the whole country, so very severe was the famine, and Egypt and Canaan were
14 laid low by it. Joseph collected all

v Prob. rdg.; Heb. sons.

the silver in Egypt and Canaan in return for the corn which the people bought, and deposited it in Pharaoh's 15 treasury. When all the silver in Egypt and Canaan had been used up, the Egyptians came to Joseph and said, 'Give us bread, or we shall die before your eyes. Our silver is all 16 spent.' Joseph said, 'If your silver is spent, give me your herds and I will 17 give you bread in return.' So they brought their herds to Joseph, who gave them bread in exchange for their horses, their flocks of sheep and herds of cattle, and their asses. He main- tained them that year with bread in 18 exchange for their herds. The year came to an end, and the following year they came to him again and said, 'My lord, we cannot conceal it from you: our silver is all gone and our herds of cattle are yours. Nothing is left for your lordship but our bodies 19 and our lands. Why should we perish before your eyes, we and our land as well? Take us and our land in payment for bread, and we and our land alike will be in bondage to Pharaoh. Give us seed-corn to keep us alive, or we shall die and our land will become 20 desert.' So Joseph bought all the land in Egypt for Pharaoh, because the Egyptians sold all their fields, so severe was the famine; the land be- 21 came Pharaoh's. As for the people, Pharaoh set them to work as slaves from one end of the territory of 22 Egypt to the other. But Joseph did not buy the land which belonged to the priests; they had a fixed allowance from Pharaoh and lived on this, so that they had no need to sell their land.

23 Joseph said to the people, 'Listen; I have today bought you and your land for Pharaoh. Here is seed-corn 24 for you. Sow the land, and give one fifth of the crop to Pharaoh. Four fifths shall be yours to provide seed for your fields and food for yourselves, your households, and your dependants.' 25 The people said, 'You have saved our lives. If it please your lordship, we 26 will be Pharaoh's slaves.' Joseph es- tablished it as a law in Egypt that one fifth should belong to Pharaoh, and this is still in force. It was only the priests' land that did not pass into Pharaoh's hands.

Jacob's last will

27 Thus Israel settled in Egypt, in Goshen; there they acquired land,

and were fruitful and increased greatly. Jacob stayed in Egypt for 28 seventeen years and lived to be a hundred and forty-seven years old. When the time of his death drew near, 29 he summoned his son Joseph and said to him, 'If I may now claim this fa- vour from you, put your hand under my thigh and swear by the LORD that you will deal loyally and truly with me and not bury me in Egypt. When 30 I die like my forefathers, you shall carry me from Egypt and bury me in their grave.' He answered, 'I will do as you say'; but Jacob said, 'Swear it.' 31 So he swore the oath, and Israel sank down over the end of the bed.

Jacob blesses Ephraim and Manasseh

The time came when Joseph was told **48** that his father was ill, so he took with him his two sons, Manasseh and Ephraim. Jacob heard that his son 2 Joseph was coming to him, and he summoned his strength and sat up on the bed. Jacob said to Joseph, 'God 3 Almighty appeared to me at Luz in Canaan and blessed me. He said to 4 me, "I will make you fruitful and increase your descendants until they become a host of nations. I will give this land to your descendants after you as a perpetual possession." Now, 5 your two sons, who were born to you in Egypt before I came here, shall be counted as my sons; Ephraim and Manasseh shall be mine as Reuben and Simeon are. Any children born 6 to you after them shall be counted as yours, but in respect of their tribal territory they shall be reckoned under their elder brothers' names. As I was 7 coming from Paddan-aram I was bereaved of Rachel your mother on the way, in Canaan, whilst there was still some distance to go to Ephrath, and I buried her there by the road to Ephrath, that is Bethlehem.'

When Israel saw Joseph's sons, he 8 said, 'Who are these?' Joseph replied 9 to his father, 'They are my sons whom God has given me here.' Israel said, 'Bring them to me, I beg you, so that I may take them on my knees.'[w] Now 10 Israel's eyes were dim with age, and he could not see; so Joseph brought the boys close to his father, and he kissed them and embraced them. He 11 said to Joseph, 'I had not expected to see your face again, and now God has granted me to see your sons also.' Joseph took them from his father's 12 knees and bowed to the ground. Then 13

w Or may bless them.

he took the two of them, Ephraim on his right at Israel's left and Manasseh on his left at Israel's right, and brought 14 them close to him. Israel stretched out his right hand and laid it on Ephraim's head, although he was the younger, and, crossing his hands, laid his left hand on Manasseh's head; but 15 Manasseh was the elder. He blessed Joseph and said:

'The God in whose presence my forefathers lived,
my forefathers Abraham and Isaac,
the God who has been my shepherd all my life until this day,
16 the angel who ransomed me from all misfortune,
may he bless these boys;
they shall be called by my name,
and by that of my forefathers, Abraham and Isaac;
may they grow into a great people on earth.'

17 When Joseph saw that his father was laying his right hand on Ephraim's head, he was displeased; so he took hold of his father's hand to move it from Ephraim's head to Manasseh's.
18 He said, 'That is not right, my father. This is the elder; lay your right hand 19 on his head.' But his father refused; he said, 'I know, my son, I know. He too shall become a people; he too shall become great, but his younger brother shall be greater than he, and his descendants shall be a whole nation 20 in themselves.' That day he blessed them and said:

'When a blessing is pronounced in Israel,
men shall use your names and say,
God make you like Ephraim and Manasseh',

thus setting Ephraim before Manasseh.
21 Then Israel said to Joseph, 'I am dying. God will be with you and will bring you back to the land of your 22 fathers. I give you one ridge of land more than your brothers: I took it from the Amorites with my sword and my bow.'

Jacob's prophecy concerning his sons

49 Jacob summoned his sons and said, 'Come near, and I will tell you what will happen to you in days to come.

2 Gather round me and listen, you sons of Jacob;
listen to Israel your father.
3 Reuben, you are my first-born,

my strength and the first fruit of my vigour,
excelling in pride, excelling in might,
turbulent as a flood, you shall not 4 excel;
because you climbed into your father's bed;
then you defiled his concubine's couch.
Simeon and Levi are brothers, 5
their spades became weapons of violence.
My soul shall not enter their council, 6
my heart shall not join their company;
for in their anger they killed men,
wantonly they hamstrung oxen.
A curse be on their anger because it 7 was fierce;
a curse on their wrath because it was ruthless!
I will scatter them in Jacob,
I will disperse them in Israel.
Judah, your brothers shall praise you, 8
your hand is on the neck of your enemies.
Your father's sons shall do you homage.
Judah, you lion's whelp, 9
you have returned from the kill, my son,
and crouch and stretch like a lion;
and, like a lion,*x* who dare rouse you?
The sceptre shall not pass from 10 Judah,
nor the staff from his descendants,
so long as tribute is brought to him
and the obedience of the nations is his.
To the vine he tethers his ass, 11
and the colt of his ass to the red vine;
he washes his cloak in wine,
his robes in the blood of grapes.
Darker than wine are his eyes, 12
his teeth whiter than milk.
Zebulun dwells by the sea-shore, 13
his shore is a haven for ships,
and his frontier rests on Sidon.
Issachar, a gelded ass 14
lying down in the cattle-pens,
saw that a settled home was good 15
and that the land was pleasant,
so he bent his back to the burden
and submitted to perpetual forced labour.
Dan—how insignificant his people, 16
lowly as any tribe in Israel!*y*
Let Dan be a viper on the road, 17
a horned snake on the path,
who bites the horse's fetlock
so that the rider tumbles backwards.

x Or lioness.   y Or Dan shall judge his people as one of the tribes of Israel.

18 For thy salvation I wait in hope,
O LORD.

19 Gad is raided by raiders,
and he raids them from the rear.

20 Asher shall have rich food as daily
fare,
and provide dishes fit for a king.

21 Naphtali is a spreading terebinth
putting forth lovely boughs.

22 Joseph is a fruitful tree[z] by a spring
with branches climbing over the
wall.

23 The archers savagely attacked him,
they shot at him and pressed him
hard,

24 but their bow was splintered by the
Eternal
and the sinews of their arms were
torn apart
by the power of the Strong One of
Jacob,
by the name of the Shepherd[a] of
Israel,

25 by the God of your father—so may
he help you,
by God Almighty—so may he bless
you
with the blessings of heaven above,
the blessings of the deep that lurks
below.
The blessings of breast and womb

26 and the blessings of your father are
stronger
than the blessings of the everlasting
pools[b]
and the bounty of the eternal hills.
They shall be on the head of
Joseph,
on the brow of the prince among[c]
his brothers.

27 Benjamin is a ravening wolf:
in the morning he devours the prey,
in the evening he snatches a share
of the spoil.'

The death and burial of Jacob

28 These, then, are the twelve tribes of
Israel, and this is what their father
Jacob said to them, when he blessed

29 them each in turn. He gave them his
last charge and said, 'I shall soon be
gathered to my father's kin; bury me
with my forefathers in the cave on
the plot of land which belonged to

30 Ephron the Hittite, that is the cave
on the plot of land at Machpelah
east of Mamre in Canaan, the field
which Abraham bought from Ephron

31 the Hittite for a burial-place. There
Abraham was buried with his wife

Sarah; there Isaac and his wife
Rebecca were buried; and there I
buried Leah. The land and the cave 32
on it were bought from the Hittites.'
When Jacob had finished giving 33
his last charge to his sons, he drew his
feet up on to the bed, breathed his
last, and was gathered to his father's
kin.

Then Joseph threw himself upon his 50
father, weeping and kissing his face.
He ordered the physicians in his 2
service to embalm his father Israel,
and they did so, finishing the task 3
in forty days, which was the usual
time for embalming. The Egyptians
mourned him for seventy days; and 4
then, when the days of mourning for
Israel were over, Joseph approached
members of Pharaoh's household and
said, 'If I can count on your goodwill,
then speak for me to Pharaoh; tell him
that my father made me take an oath, 5
saying, "I am dying. Bury me in the
grave that I bought[d] for myself in
Canaan." Ask him to let me go up and
bury my father, and afterwards I will
return.' Pharaoh answered, 'Go and 6
bury your father, as he has made
you swear to do.' So Joseph went to 7
bury his father, accompanied by all
Pharaoh's courtiers, the elders of his
household, and all the elders of Egypt,
together with all Joseph's own house- 8
hold, his brothers, and his father's
household; only their dependants,
with the flocks and herds, were left in
Goshen. He took with him chariots 9
and horsemen; they were a very great
company. When they came to the 10
threshing-floor of Atad beside the
river Jordan, they raised a loud and
bitter lament; and there Joseph
observed seven days' mourning for
his father. When the Canaanites who 11
lived there saw this mourning at the
threshing-floor of Atad, they said,
'How bitterly the Egyptians are
mourning!'; accordingly they named
the place beside the Jordan Abel-
mizraim.[e]

Thus Jacob's sons did what he had 12
told them to do. They took him to 13
Canaan and buried him in the cave
on the plot of land at Machpelah,
the land which Abraham had bought
as a burial-place from Ephron the
Hittite, to the east of Mamre. Then, 14
after he had buried his father, Joseph returned to Egypt with his brothers and all who had gone up with
him.

z Or a fruitful ben-tree.   a Prob. rdg.; Heb. adds stone.   b Or hills.   c the prince among: or
the one cursed by.   d Or dug.   e That is Mourning (or Meadow) of Egypt.

Joseph reassures his brothers

15 When their father was dead Joseph's brothers were afraid and said, 'What if Joseph should bear a grudge against us and pay us out for all the harm 16 that we did to him?' They therefore approached Joseph with these words: 'In his last words to us before he died, 17 your father gave us this message for you: "I ask you to forgive your brothers' crime and wickedness; I know they did you harm." So now forgive our crime, we beg; for we are servants of your father's God.' When they said this to him, Joseph wept. 18 His brothers also wept[f] and prostrated themselves before him; they said, 'You see, we are your slaves.' 19 But Joseph said to them, 'Do not be 20 afraid. Am I in the place of God? You meant to do me harm; but God meant to bring good out of it by preserving the lives of many people, as we see 21 today. Do not be afraid. I will provide for you and your dependants.' Thus he comforted them and set their minds at rest.

The death of Joseph

Joseph remained in Egypt, he and 22 his father's household. He lived there to be a hundred and ten years old and 23 saw Ephraim's children to the third generation; he also recognized as his the children of Manasseh's son Ma-chir. He said to his brothers, 'I am 24 dying; but God will not fail to come to your aid and take you from here to the land which he promised on oath to Abraham, Isaac and Jacob.' He 25 made the sons of Israel take an oath, saying, 'When God thus comes to your aid, you must take my bones with you from here.' So Joseph died 26 at the age of a hundred and ten. He was embalmed and laid in a coffin in Egypt.

f Prob. rdg.; Heb. came.

EXODUS

The suffering of the Israelites

1 THESE ARE THE NAMES of the Israelites who entered Egypt with Jacob, each with his household: 2 Reuben, Simeon, Levi and Judah; 3 4 Issachar, Zebulun and Benjamin; Dan 5 and Naphtali, Gad and Asher. There were seventy of them all told, all direct descendants of Jacob. Joseph was already in Egypt. 6 In course of time Joseph died, he and all his brothers and that whole 7 generation. Now the Israelites were fruitful and prolific; they increased in numbers and became very power-ful,[a] so that the country was overrun 8 by them. Then a new king ascended the throne of Egypt, one who knew 9 nothing of Joseph. He said to his people, 'These Israelites have become 10 too many and too strong for us. We must take precautions to see that they do not increase any further; or we shall find that, if war breaks out, they will join the enemy and fight against us, and they will become masters of the 11 country.' So they were made to work in gangs with officers set over them, to break their spirit with heavy labour. This is how Pharaoh's store-cities, Pithom and Rameses, were built. But the more harshly they were 12 treated, the more their numbers increased beyond all bounds, until the Egyptians came to loathe the sight of them. So they treated their 13 Israelite slaves with ruthless severity, and made life bitter for them with 14 cruel servitude, setting them to work on clay and brick-making, and all sorts of work in the fields. In short they made ruthless use of them as slaves in every kind of hard labour.

Then the king of Egypt spoke to 15 the Hebrew midwives, whose names were Shiphrah and Puah. 'When you 16 are attending the Hebrew women in childbirth,' he told them, 'watch as the child is delivered and if it is a boy, kill him; if it is a girl, let her live.' But they were God-fearing women. 17 They did not do what the king of Egypt had told them to do, but let the boys live. So he summoned those 18 Hebrew midwives and asked them

a Or numerous.

why they had done this and let
19 the boys live. They told Pharaoh
that Hebrew women were not like
Egyptian women. When they were in
labour they gave birth before the mid-
20 wife could get to them. So God made
the midwives prosper, and the people
increased in numbers and in strength.
21 God gave the midwives homes and
families of their own, because they
22 feared him. Pharaoh then ordered all
his people to throw every new-born
Hebrew boy into the Nile, but to let
the girls live.

The birth of Moses

2 A descendant of Levi married a
2 Levite woman who conceived and
bore a son. When she saw what a
fine child he was, she hid him for
3 three months, but she could conceal
him no longer. So she got a rush
basket for him, made it watertight
with clay and tar, laid him in it, and
put it among the reeds by the bank of
4 the Nile. The child's sister took her
stand at a distance to see what would
5 happen to him. Pharaoh's daughter
came down to bathe in the river,
while her ladies-in-waiting walked
along the bank. She noticed the basket
among the reeds and sent her slave-
6 girl for it. She took it from her and
when she opened it, she saw the child.
It was crying, and she was filled with
pity for it. 'Why,' she said, 'it is a
7 little Hebrew boy.' Thereupon the
sister said to Pharaoh's daughter,
'Shall I go and fetch one of the
Hebrew women as a wet-nurse to
8 suckle the child for you?' Pharaoh's
daughter told her to go; so the girl
went and called the baby's mother.
9 Then Pharaoh's daughter said to
her, 'Here is the child, suckle him
for me, and I will pay you for it myself.' So the woman took the child and
10 suckled him. When the child was old
enough, she brought him to Pharaoh's
daughter, who adopted him and called
him Moses,[b] 'because', she said, 'I
drew[c] him out of the water.'

Moses escapes to Midian

11 One day when Moses was grown up,
he went out to his own kinsmen and
saw them at their heavy labour. He
saw an Egyptian strike one of his
12 fellow-Hebrews. He looked this way
and that, and, seeing there was no
one about, he struck the Egyptian
down and hid his body in the sand.
13 When he went out next day, two

Hebrews were fighting together. He
asked the man who was in the wrong,
'Why are you striking him?' 'Who 14
set you up as an officer and judge
over us?' the man replied. 'Do you
mean to murder me as you murdered
the Egyptian?' Moses was alarmed.
'The thing must have become known',
he said to himself. When Pharaoh 15
heard of it, he tried to put Moses to
death, but Moses made good his escape
and settled in the land of Midian.

Now the priest of Midian had seven 16
daughters. One day as Moses sat by
a well, they came to draw water and
filled the troughs to water their
father's sheep. Some shepherds came 17
and drove them away; but Moses got
up, took the girls' part and watered
their sheep himself. When the girls 18
came back to their father Reuel, he
asked, 'How is it that you are back
so quickly today?' 'An Egyptian 19
rescued us from the shepherds,' they
answered; 'and he even drew the
water for us and watered the sheep.'
'But where is he then?' he said to his 20
daughters. 'Why did you leave him
behind? Go and invite him to eat with
us.' So it came about that Moses 21
agreed to live with the man, and he
gave Moses his daughter Zipporah in
marriage. She bore him a son, and 22
Moses called him Gershom, 'because',
he said, 'I have become an alien[d]
living in a foreign land.'

Years passed, and the king of Egypt 23
died, but the Israelites still groaned
in slavery. They cried out, and their
appeal for rescue from their slavery
rose up to God. He heard their groan- 24
ing, and remembered his covenant
with Abraham, Isaac and Jacob; he 25
saw the plight of Israel, and he took
heed of it.

The call of Moses

Moses was minding the flock of his **3**
father-in-law Jethro, priest of Midian.
He led the flock along the side of the
wilderness and came to Horeb, the
mountain of God. There the angel of 2
the LORD appeared to him in the
flame of a burning bush. Moses noticed
that, although the bush was on fire,
it was not being burnt up; so he said 3
to himself, 'I must go across to see this
wonderful sight. Why does not the
bush burn away?' When the LORD 4
saw that Moses had turned aside to
look, he called to him out of the bush,
'Moses, Moses.' And Moses answered,

b Heb. Mosheh.   *c Heb. verb mashah.*   *d Heb. ger.*

5 'Yes, I am here.' God said, 'Come no nearer; take off your sandals; the place where you are standing is 6 holy ground.' Then he said, 'I am the God of your forefathers, the God of Abraham, the God of Isaac, the God of Jacob.' Moses covered his face, for he was afraid to gaze on God.

7   The LORD said, 'I have indeed seen the misery of my people in Egypt. I have heard their outcry against their slave-masters. I have taken heed of 8 their sufferings, and have come down to rescue them from the power of Egypt, and to bring them up out of that country into a fine, broad land; it is a land flowing with milk and honey, the home of Canaanites, Hittites, Amorites, Perizzites, Hivites, 9 and Jebusites. The outcry of the Israelites has now reached me; yes, I have seen the brutality of the Egyp- 10 tians towards them. Come now; I will send you to Pharaoh and you shall bring my people Israel out of Egypt.' 11 'But who am I,' Moses said to God, 'that I should go to Pharaoh, and that I should bring the Israelites out of 12 Egypt?' God answered, 'I am*e* with you. This shall be the proof that it is I who have sent you: when you have brought the people out of Egypt, you shall all worship God here on this mountain.'

13   Then Moses said to God, 'If I go to the Israelites and tell them that the God of their forefathers has sent me to them, and they ask me his name, 14 what shall I say?' God answered, 'I AM; that is who I am.*f* Tell them that 15 I AM has sent you to them.' And God said further, 'You must tell the Israelites this, that it is JEHOVAH*g* the God of their forefathers, the God of Abraham, the God of Isaac, the God of Jacob, who has sent you to them. This is my name for ever; this 16 is my title in every generation. Go and assemble the elders of Israel and tell them that JEHOVAH the God of their forefathers, the God of Abraham, Isaac and Jacob, has appeared to me and has said, "I have indeed turned my eyes towards you; I have marked all that has been done to you in 17 Egypt, and I am resolved to bring you up out of your misery in Egypt, into the country of the Canaanites, Hittites, Amorites, Perizzites, Hivites, and Jebusites, a land flowing with 18 milk and honey." They will listen to you, and then you and the elders of

Israel must go to the king of Egypt. Tell him, "It has happened that the LORD the God of the Hebrews met us. So now give us leave to go a three days' journey into the wilderness to offer sacrifice to the LORD our God." I know well that the king of Egypt 19 will not give you leave unless he is compelled. I shall then stretch out my 20 hand and assail the Egyptians with all the miracles I shall work among them. After that he will send you away. Further, I will bring this 21 people into such favour with the Egyptians that, when you go, you will not go empty-handed. Every 22 woman shall ask her neighbour or any woman who lives in her house for jewellery of silver and gold and for clothing. Load your sons and daughters with them, and plunder Egypt.'

Moses answered, 'But they will 4 never believe me or listen to me; they will say, "The LORD did not appear to you."' The LORD said, 'What have 2 you there in your hand?' 'A staff', Moses answered. The LORD said, 3 'Throw it on the ground.' Moses threw it down and it turned into a snake. He ran away from it, but the LORD 4 said, 'Put your hand out and seize it by the tail.' He did so and gripped it firmly, and it turned back into a staff in his hand. 'This is to convince the 5 people that the LORD the God of their forefathers, the God of Abraham, the God of Isaac, the God of Jacob, has appeared to you.' Then the LORD said, 6 'Put your hand inside the fold of your cloak.' He did so, and when he drew it out the skin was diseased, white as snow. The LORD said, 'Put it back 7 again', and he did so. When he drew it out this time it was as healthy as the rest of his body. 'Now,' said the 8 LORD, 'if they do not believe you and do not accept the evidence of the first sign, they may accept the evidence of the second. But if they are not con- 9 vinced even by these two signs, and will not accept what you say, then fetch some water from the Nile and pour it out on the dry ground, and the water you take from the Nile will turn to blood on the ground.'

But Moses said, 'O LORD, I have 10 never been a man of ready speech, never in my life, not even now that thou hast spoken to me; I am slow and hesitant of speech.' The LORD 11 said to him, 'Who is it that gives man speech? Who makes him dumb or

e Or I will be; *Heb.* ehyeh.   *f* I AM . . . I am: *or* I will be what I will be.   *g The Hebrew consonants are* YHWH, *probably pronounced* Yahweh, *but traditionally read* Jehovah.

deaf? Who makes him clear-sighted
12 or blind? Is it not I, the LORD? Go
now; I will help your speech and tell
13 you what to say.' But Moses still
protested, 'No, Lord, send whom thou
14 wilt.' At this the LORD grew angry
with Moses and said, 'Have you not
a brother, Aaron the Levite? He, I
know, will do all the speaking. He is
already on his way out to meet you,
and he will be glad indeed to see you.
15 You shall speak to him and put the
words in his mouth; I will help both
of you to speak and tell you both what
16 to do. He will do all the speaking to
the people for you, he will be the
mouthpiece, and you will be the god
17 he speaks for. But take this staff, for
with it you are to work the signs.'
18   At length Moses went back to
Jethro his father-in-law and said, 'Let
me return to my kinsfolk in Egypt
and see if they are still alive.' Jethro
told him to go and wished him well.

Moses returns to Egypt

19 The LORD spoke to Moses in Midian
and said to him, 'Go back to Egypt,
for all those who wished to kill you
20 are dead.' So Moses took his wife and
children, mounted them on an ass and
set out for Egypt with the staff of
21 God in his hand. The LORD said to
Moses, 'While you are on your way
back to Egypt, keep in mind all the
portents I have given you power
to show. You shall display these before Pharaoh, but I will make him
obstinate and he will not let the people
22 go. Then tell Pharaoh that these are
the words of the LORD: "Israel is my
23 first-born son. I have told you to let
my son go, so that he may worship
me. You have refused to let him go,
so I will kill your first-born son."'
24   During the journey, while they were
encamped for the night, the LORD met
25 Moses, meaning to kill him, but Zipporah picked up a sharp flint, cut off
her son's foreskin, and touched him
with it, saying, 'You are my blood-
26 bridegroom.' So the LORD let Moses
alone. Then she said,[h] 'Blood-bride-
groom by circumcision.'
27   Meanwhile the LORD had ordered
Aaron to go and meet Moses in the
wilderness. Aaron went and met him
at the mountain of God, and he kissed
28 him. Then Moses told Aaron everything, the words the LORD had sent
him to say and the signs he had
29 commanded him to perform. Moses
and Aaron went and assembled all

the elders of Israel. Aaron told them 30
everything that the LORD had said to
Moses; he performed the signs before
the people, and they were convinced. 31
They heard that the LORD had shown
his concern for the Israelites and seen
their misery; and they bowed themselves to the ground in worship.

Pharaoh's disobedience

After this, Moses and Aaron came to 5
Pharaoh and said, 'These are the
words of the LORD the God of Israel:
"Let my people go so that they may
keep my pilgrim-feast in the wilderness."' 'Who is the LORD,' asked 2
Pharaoh, 'that I should obey him
and let Israel go? I care nothing for
the LORD: and I tell you I will not
let Israel go.' They replied, 'It has 3
happened that the God of the
Hebrews met us. So let us go three
days' journey into the wilderness to
offer sacrifice to the LORD our God,
or else he will attack us with pestilence
or sword.' But the king of Egypt said, 4
'Moses and Aaron, what do you mean
by distracting the people from their
work? Back to your labours! Your 5
people already outnumber the native
Egyptians; yet you would have them
stop working!'
   That very day Pharaoh ordered the 6
people's overseers and their foremen
not to supply the people with the 7
straw used in making bricks, as they
had done hitherto. 'Let them go and
collect their own straw, but see that 8
they produce the same tally of bricks
as before. On no account reduce it.
They are a lazy people, and that is
why they are clamouring to go and
offer sacrifice to their god. Keep the 9
men hard at work; let them attend
to that and take no notice of a pack
of lies.' The overseers and foremen 10
went out and said to the people,
'Pharaoh's orders are that no more
straw is to be supplied. Go and get it 11
for yourselves wherever you can find
it; but there will be no reduction
in your daily task.' So the people 12
scattered all over Egypt to gather
stubble for straw, while the overseers 13
kept urging them on, bidding them
complete, day after day, the same
quantity as when straw was supplied.
Then the Israelite foremen were flogged 14
because they were held responsible by
Pharaoh's overseers, who asked them,
'Why did you not complete the usual
number of bricks yesterday or today?'
So the foremen came and appealed to 15

h Or Therefore women say.

Pharaoh: 'Why do you treat your
16 servants like this?' they said. 'We are
given no straw, yet they keep on
telling us to make bricks. Here are we
being flogged, but it is your people's
17 fault.' But Pharaoh replied, 'You are
lazy, you are lazy. That is why you
talk about going to offer sacrifice to
18 the LORD. Now go; get on with your
work. You will be given no straw, but
you must produce the tally of bricks.'
19 When they were told that they must
not let the daily tally of bricks fall
short, the Israelite foremen saw that
20 they were in trouble. As they came
out from Pharaoh's presence they
found Moses and Aaron waiting to
21 meet them, and said, 'May this bring
the LORD's judgement down upon
you: you have made us stink in the
nostrils of Pharaoh and his subjects;
you have put a sword in their hands to
kill us.'

The call of Moses repeated

22 Moses went back to the LORD, and
said, 'Why, O Lord, hast thou brought
misfortune on this people? And why
23 didst thou ever send me? Since I first
went to Pharaoh to speak in thy name
he has heaped misfortune on thy people, and thou hast done nothing at all
6 to rescue them.' The LORD answered,
'Now you shall see what I will do to
Pharaoh. In the end Pharaoh will let
them go with a strong hand, nay,
will drive them from his country with
an outstretched arm.'
2   God spoke to Moses and said, 'I am
3 the LORD. I appeared to Abraham,
Isaac, and Jacob as God Almighty.
But I did not let myself be known to
4 them by my name JEHOVAH.[i] Moreover, I made a covenant with them
to give them Canaan, the land where
they settled for a time as foreigners.
5 And now I have heard the groaning
of the Israelites, enslaved by the
Egyptians, and I have called my
6 covenant to mind. Say therefore to
the Israelites, "I am the LORD. I will
release you from your labours in
Egypt. I will rescue you from slavery
there. I will redeem you with arm
outstretched and with mighty acts of
7 judgement. I will adopt you as my
people, and I will become your God.
You shall know that I, the LORD, am
your God, the God who releases you
8 from your labours in Egypt. I will
lead you to the land which I swore
with uplifted hand to give to Abraham, to Isaac and to Jacob. I will

give it you for your possession. I am
the LORD."'
Moses repeated these words to the 9
Israelites, but they did not listen to
him; they had become impatient
because of their cruel slavery.
Then the LORD spoke to Moses 10
and said, 'Go and tell Pharaoh king 11
of Egypt to set the Israelites free
to leave his country.' Moses made 12
answer in the presence of the LORD,
'If the Israelites do not listen to me,
how will Pharaoh listen to such a
halting speaker as I am?'
Thus the LORD spoke to Moses and 13
Aaron and gave them their commission to the Israelites and to Pharaoh,
namely that they should bring the
Israelites out of Egypt.

Genealogy of Moses and Aaron

These were the heads of fathers' 14
families:
Sons of Reuben, Israel's eldest son:
Enoch, Pallu, Hezron and Carmi;
these were the families of Reuben.
Sons of Simeon: Jemuel, Jamin, 15
Ohad, Jachin, Zohar, and Saul, who
was the son of a Canaanite woman;
these were the families of Simeon.
These were the names of the sons 16
of Levi in order of seniority: Gershon,
Kohath and Merari. Levi lived to be
a hundred and thirty-seven.
Sons of Gershon, family by family: 17
Libni and Shimei.
Sons of Kohath: Amram, Izhar, 18
Hebron and Uzziel. Kohath lived to
be a hundred and thirty-three.
Sons of Merari: Mahli and Mushi. 19
These were the families of Levi in
order of seniority. Amram married his 20
father's sister Jochebed, and she bore
him Aaron and Moses. Amram lived
to be a hundred and thirty-seven.
Sons of Izhar: Korah, Nepheg and 21
Zichri.
Sons of Uzziel: Mishael, Elzaphan 22
and Sithri.
Aaron married Elisheba, who was 23
the daughter of Amminadab and the
sister of Nahshon, and she bore him
Nadab, Abihu, Eleazar and Ithamar.
Sons of Korah: Assir, Elkanah and 24
Abiasaph; these were the Korahite
families.
Eleazar son of Aaron married one 25
of the daughters of Putiel, and she
bore him Phinehas. These were the
heads of the Levite families, family
by family.
It was this Aaron, together with 26
Moses, to whom the LORD said, 'Bring

i See note on 3. 15.   *j Verses 14–16: cp. Gen. 46. 8–11; Num. 26. 5, 6, 12, 13.*

the Israelites out of Egypt, mustered
27 in their tribal hosts.' These were the
men who told Pharaoh king of Egypt
to let the Israelites leave Egypt. It
was this same Moses and Aaron.

The LORD promises deliverance

28 When the LORD spoke to Moses in
29 Egypt he said, 'I am the LORD. Tell
Pharaoh king of Egypt all that I say
30 to you.' Moses made answer in the
presence of the LORD, 'I am a halting
speaker; how will Pharaoh listen to
7 me?' The LORD answered Moses, 'See
now, I have made you like a god for
Pharaoh, with your brother Aaron as
2 your spokesman. You must tell your
brother Aaron all I bid you say, and
he will tell Pharaoh, and Pharaoh will
let the Israelites go out of his country;
3 but I will make him stubborn. Then
will I show sign after sign and portent
after portent in the land of Egypt.
4 But Pharaoh will not listen to you, so
I will assert my power in Egypt, and
with mighty acts of judgement I will
bring my people, the Israelites, out
5 of Egypt in their tribal hosts. When
I put forth my power against the
Egyptians and bring the Israelites
out from them, then Egypt will know
6 that I am the LORD.' So Moses and
Aaron did exactly as the LORD had
7 commanded. At the time when they
spoke to Pharaoh, Moses was eighty
years old and Aaron eighty-three.

Aaron's staff

8 9 The LORD said to Moses and Aaron, 'If
Pharaoh demands some portent from
you, then you, Moses, must say to
Aaron, "Take your staff and throw it
down in front of Pharaoh, and it will
10 turn into a serpent." When Moses
and Aaron came to Pharaoh, they did
as the LORD had told them. Aaron
threw down his staff in front of
Pharaoh and his courtiers, and it
11 turned into a serpent. At this, Pharaoh summoned the wise men and the
sorcerers, and the Egyptian magicians too did the same thing by their
12 spells. Every man threw his staff
down, and each staff turned into a
serpent; but Aaron's staff swallowed
13 up theirs. Pharaoh, however, was
obstinate; as the LORD had foretold,
he would not listen to Moses and
Aaron.

The plague of blood

14 Then the LORD said to Moses, 'Pharaoh
is obdurate: he has refused to set the
15 people free. Go to him in the morning

on his way out to the river. Stand and
wait on the bank of the Nile to meet
him, and take with you the staff that
turned into a snake. Say this to him: 16
"The LORD the God of the Hebrews
sent me to bid you let his people go in
order to worship him in the wilderness. So far you have not listened to
his words; so now the LORD says, 'By 17
this you shall know that I am the
LORD.' With this rod that I have in
my hand, I shall now strike the water
in the Nile and it will be changed into
blood. The fish will die and the river 18
will stink, and the Egyptians will be
unable to drink water from the Nile."'
The LORD then told Moses to say to 19
Aaron, 'Take your staff and stretch
your hand out over the waters of
Egypt, its rivers and its streams, and
over every pool and cistern, to turn
them into blood. There shall be blood
throughout the whole of Egypt, blood
even in their wooden bowls and jars
of stone.' So Moses and Aaron did as 20
the LORD had commanded. He lifted
up his staff and struck the water of
the Nile in the sight of Pharaoh and
his courtiers, and all the water was
changed into blood. The fish died 21
and the river stank, and the Egyptians could not drink water from the
Nile. There was blood everywhere in
Egypt. But the Egyptian magicians 22
did the same thing by their spells;
and still Pharaoh remained obstinate,
as the LORD had foretold, and did not
listen to Moses and Aaron. He turned 23
away, went into his house and dismissed the matter from his mind.
Then the Egyptians all dug for drinking 24
water round about the river, because
they could not drink from the waters
of the Nile itself. This lasted for 25
seven days from the time when the
LORD struck the Nile.

The plague of frogs

The LORD then told Moses to go into 8
Pharaoh's presence and say to him,
'These are the words of the LORD: "Let
my people go in order to worship me.
If you refuse to let them go, I will 2
plague the whole of your territory
with frogs. The Nile shall swarm with 3
them. They shall come up from the
river into your house, into your bedroom and on to your bed, into the
houses of your courtiers and your
people, into your ovens and your
kneading-troughs. The frogs shall 4
clamber over you, your people, and
your courtiers."' Then the LORD told 5
Moses to say to Aaron, 'Take your

B

staff in your hand and stretch it out over the rivers, streams, and pools, to bring up frogs upon the land of
6 Egypt.' So Aaron stretched out his hand over the waters of Egypt, and the frogs came up and covered all the
7 land. The magicians did the same thing by their spells: they too brought
8 up frogs upon the land of Egypt. Then Pharaoh summoned Moses and Aaron. 'Pray to the LORD', he said, 'to take the frogs away from me and my people, and I will let the people go to
9 sacrifice to the LORD.' Moses said, 'Of your royal favour, appoint a time when I may intercede for you and your courtiers and people, so that you and your houses may be rid of the frogs, and none be left except in the
10 Nile.' 'Tomorrow', Pharaoh said. 'It shall be as you say,' replied Moses, 'so that you may know there is no one
11 like our God, the LORD. The frogs shall depart from you, from your houses, your courtiers, and your people: none shall be left except in the Nile.'
12 Moses and Aaron left Pharaoh's presence, and Moses appealed to the LORD to remove the frogs which he
13 had brought on Pharaoh. The LORD did as Moses had asked, and in house and courtyard and in the open the
14 frogs all perished. They piled them into countless heaps and the land
15 stank; but when Pharaoh found that he was given relief he became obdurate; as the LORD had foretold, he did not listen to Moses and Aaron.

The plague of maggots

16 The LORD then told Moses to say to Aaron, 'Stretch out your staff and strike the dust on the ground, and it will turn into maggots throughout
17 the land of Egypt', and they obeyed. Aaron stretched out his staff and struck the dust, and it turned into maggots on man and beast. All the
18 dust turned into maggots throughout the land of Egypt. The magicians tried to produce maggots in the same way by their spells, but they failed. The
19 maggots were everywhere, on man and beast. 'It is the finger of God', said the magicians to Pharaoh, but Pharaoh remained obstinate; as the LORD had foretold, he did not listen to them.

The plague of flies

20 The LORD told Moses to rise early in the morning and stand in Pharaoh's path as he went out to the river and to say to him, 'These are the words of

the LORD: "Let my people go in order
21 to worship me. If you do not let my people go, I will send swarms of flies upon you, your courtiers, your people, and your houses. The houses of the Egyptians shall be filled with the swarms and so shall all the land they
22 live in, but on that day I will make an exception of Goshen, the land where my people live: there shall be no swarms there. Thus you shall know that I, the LORD, am here in the land.
23 I will make a distinction between my people and yours. Tomorrow this
24 sign shall appear."' The LORD did this; dense swarms of flies infested Pharaoh's house and those of his courtiers; throughout Egypt the land was threatened with ruin by the
25 swarms. Pharaoh summoned Moses and Aaron and said to them, 'Go and sacrifice to your God, but in this
26 country.' 'That we cannot do,' replied Moses, 'because the victim we shall sacrifice to the LORD our God is an abomination to the Egyptians. If the Egyptians see us offer such an animal, will they not stone us to
27 death? We must go a three days' journey into the wilderness to sacrifice to the LORD our God, as he com-
28 mands us.' 'I will let you go,' said Pharaoh, 'and you shall sacrifice to your God in the wilderness; only do not go far. Now intercede for me.'
29 Moses answered, 'As soon as I leave you I will intercede with the LORD. Tomorrow the swarms will depart from Pharaoh, his courtiers, and his people. Only let not Pharaoh trifle any more with the people by prevent-ing them from going to sacrifice to
30 the LORD.' Then Moses left Pharaoh
31 and interceded with the LORD. The LORD did as Moses had said; he removed the swarms from Pharaoh, his courtiers, and his people; not one
32 was left. But once again Pharaoh became obdurate and did not let the people go.

The plague on the cattle

9 The LORD said to Moses, 'Go into Pharaoh's presence and say to him, "These are the words of the LORD the God of the Hebrews: 'Let my people
2 go in order to worship me.' If you refuse to let them go and still keep your hold on them, the LORD will
3 strike your grazing herds, your horses and asses, your camels, cattle, and sheep with a terrible pestilence. But
4 the LORD will make a distinction between Israel's herds and those of

the Egyptians. Of all that belong to Israel not a single one shall die.'''

5 The LORD fixed a time and said, 'Tomorrow I will do this throughout
6 the land.' The next day the LORD struck. All the herds of Egypt died, but from the herds of the Israelites
7 not one single beast died. Pharaoh inquired and was told that not a beast from the herds of Israel had died; and yet he remained obdurate and did not let the people go.

The plague of boils

8 The LORD said to Moses and Aaron, 'Take handfuls of soot from a kiln. Moses shall toss it into the air in
9 Pharaoh's sight, and it will turn into a fine dust over the whole of Egypt. All over Egypt it will become fester-
10 ing boils on man and beast.' They took the soot from the kiln and stood before Pharaoh. Moses tossed it into the air and it produced festering boils
11 on man and beast. The magicians were no match for Moses because of the boils, which attacked them and
12 all the Egyptians. But the LORD made Pharaoh obstinate; as the LORD had foretold to Moses, he did not listen to Moses and Aaron.

The plague of hail

13 The LORD then told Moses to rise early in the morning, present himself before Pharaoh, and say to him, 'These are the words of the LORD the God of the Hebrews: "Let my people go in
14 order to worship me. This time I will strike home with all my plagues against you, your courtiers, and your people, so that you may know that there is none like me in all the earth.
15 By now I could have stretched out my hand, and struck you and your people with pestilence, and you would have
16 vanished from the earth. I have let you live only to show you my power and to spread my fame throughout
17 the land. Since you still obstruct my people and will not let them go,
18 tomorrow at this time I will send a violent hailstorm, such as has never been in Egypt from its first beginnings
19 until now. Send now and bring your herds under cover, and everything you have out in the open field. If anything, whether man or beast, which happens to be in the open, is not brought in, the hail will fall on it,
20 and it will die."'' Those of Pharaoh's subjects who feared the word of the LORD hurried their slaves and cattle
21 into their houses. But those who did not take to heart the word of the LORD left their slaves and cattle in the open.

22 The LORD said to Moses, 'Stretch out your hand towards the sky to bring down hail on the whole land of Egypt, on man and beast and every growing thing throughout the land.'
23 Moses stretched out his staff towards the sky, and the LORD sent thunder and hail, with fire flashing down to the ground. The LORD rained down
24 hail on the land of Egypt, hail and fiery flashes through the hail, so heavy that there had been nothing like it in all Egypt from the time that Egypt became a nation. Throughout
25 Egypt the hail struck everything in the fields, both man and beast; it beat down every growing thing and
26 shattered every tree. Only in the land of Goshen, where the Israelites lived, was there no hail.

27 Pharaoh sent and summoned Moses and Aaron. 'This time I have sinned,' he said; 'the LORD is in the right; I and my people are in the wrong.
28 Intercede with the LORD, for we can bear no more of this thunder and hail. I will let you go; you need wait no
29 longer.' Moses said, 'When I leave the city I will spread out my hands in prayer to the LORD. The thunder shall cease, and there shall be no more hail, so that you may know that the earth
30 is the LORD's. But you and your subjects—I know that you do not yet
31 fear the LORD God.' (The flax and barley were destroyed because the barley was in the ear and the flax in
32 bud, but the wheat and spelt were not destroyed because they come later.)
33 Moses left Pharaoh's presence, went out of the city and lifted up his hands to the LORD in prayer: the thunder and hail ceased, and no more rain fell.
34 When Pharaoh saw that the downpour, the hail, and the thunder had ceased, he sinned again, he and his
35 courtiers, and became obdurate. So Pharaoh remained obstinate; as the LORD had foretold through Moses, he did not let the people go.

The plague of locusts

10 Then the LORD said to Moses, 'Go into Pharaoh's presence. I have made him and his courtiers obdurate, so that I may show these my signs
2 among them, and so that you can tell your children and grandchildren the story: how I made sport of the Egyptians, and what signs I showed among them. Thus you will know

3 that I am the LORD.' Moses and Aaron went in to Pharaoh and said to him, 'These are the words of the LORD the God of the Hebrews: "How long will you refuse to humble yourself before me? Let my people go in order to 4 worship me. If you refuse to let my people go, tomorrow I will bring 5 locusts into your country. They shall cover the face of the land so that it cannot be seen. They shall eat up the last remnant left you by the hail. They shall devour every tree that grows in 6 your country-side. Your houses and your courtiers' houses, every house in Egypt, shall be full of them; your fathers never saw the like nor their fathers before them; such a thing has not happened from their time until now."' He turned and left Pharaoh's 7 presence. Pharaoh's courtiers said to him, 'How long must we be caught in this man's toils? Let their menfolk go and worship the LORD their God. Do you not know by now that Egypt is 8 ruined?' So Moses and Aaron were brought back to Pharaoh, and he said to them, 'You may go and worship the LORD your God; but who exactly is 9 to go?' 'All,' said Moses, 'young and old, boys and girls, sheep and cattle; for we have to keep the LORD's 10 pilgrim-feast.' Pharaoh replied, 'Very well then; take your dependants with you when you go; and the LORD be with you. But beware, there is 11 trouble in store for you. No, your menfolk may go and worship the LORD, for that is all you asked.' So they were driven out from Pharaoh's presence.

12   Then the LORD said to Moses, 'Stretch out your hand over Egypt so that the locusts may come and invade the land and devour all the vegetation in it, everything the hail has left.' 13 Moses stretched out his staff over the land of Egypt, and the LORD sent a wind roaring in from the east all that day and all that night. When morning came, the east wind had brought 14 the locusts. They invaded the whole land of Egypt, and settled on all its territory in swarms so dense that the like of them had never been seen 15 before, nor ever will be again. They covered the surface of the whole land till it was black with them. They devoured all the vegetation and all the fruit of the trees that the hail had spared. There was no green left on tree or plant throughout all Egypt. 16 Pharaoh hastily summoned Moses

and Aaron. 'I have sinned against the LORD your God and against you', he said. 'Forgive my sin, I pray, just this 17 once. Intercede with the LORD your God and beg him only to remove this deadly plague from me.' Moses left 18 Pharaoh and interceded with the LORD. The LORD changed the wind 19 into a westerly gale, which carried the locusts away and swept them into the Red Sea.[k] There was not a single locust left in all the territory of Egypt. But the LORD made Pharaoh obstinate, 20 and he did not let the Israelites go.

The plague of darkness

Then the LORD said to Moses, 'Stretch 21 out your hand towards the sky so that there may be darkness over the land of Egypt, darkness that can be felt.' Moses stretched out his hand towards 22 the sky, and it became pitch dark throughout the land of Egypt for three days. Men could not see one another; 23 for three days no one stirred from where he was. But there was no darkness wherever the Israelites lived. Pharaoh summoned Moses. 'Go', he 24 said, 'and worship the LORD. Your dependants may go with you; but your flocks and herds must be left with us.' But Moses said, 'No, you 25 must yourself supply us with animals for sacrifice and whole-offering to the LORD our God; and our own flocks 26 must go with us too—not a hoof must be left behind. We may need animals from our own flocks to worship the LORD our God; we ourselves cannot tell until we are there how we are to worship the LORD.' The LORD made 27 Pharaoh obstinate, and he refused to let them go. 'Out! Pester me no more!' 28 he said to Moses. 'Take care you do not see my face again, for on the day you do, you die.' 'You are right,' 29 said Moses; 'I shall never see your face again.'

Death of the first-born foretold

Then the LORD said to Moses, 'One 11 last plague I will bring upon Pharaoh and Egypt.[j] After that he will let you go; he will send you packing, as a man dismisses a rejected bride. Let the 2 people be told that men and women alike should ask their neighbours for jewellery of silver and gold.' The LORD 3 made the Egyptians well-disposed towards them, and, moreover, Moses was a very great man in Egypt in the eyes of Pharaoh's courtiers and of the people.

k Or the Sea of Reeds.

4 Moses then said, 'These are the words of the LORD: "At midnight I will go out among the Egyptians. 5 Every first-born creature in the land of Egypt shall die: the first-born of Pharaoh who sits on his throne, the first-born of the slave-girl at the hand-mill, and all the first-born of the cattle. 6 All Egypt will send up a great cry of anguish, a cry the like of which has never been heard before, nor ever will 7 be again. But among all Israel not a dog's tongue shall be so much as scratched, no man or beast be hurt." Thus you shall know that the LORD does make a distinction between 8 Egypt and Israel. Then all these courtiers of yours will come down to me, prostrate themselves and cry, "Go away, you and all the people who follow at your heels." After that I will go away.' Then Moses left Pharaoh's presence hot with anger.

9 The LORD said to Moses, 'Pharaoh will not listen to you; I will there-fore show still more portents in the 10 land of Egypt.' All these portents had Moses and Aaron shown in the presence of Pharaoh, and yet the LORD made him obstinate, and he did not let the Israelites leave the country.

Institution of the Passover

12 The LORD said to Moses and Aaron 2 in Egypt: This month is for you the first of months; you shall make it the 3 first month of the year. Speak to the whole community of Israel and say to them: On the tenth day of this month let each man take a lamb or a kid for his family, one for each household, 4 but if a household is too small for one lamb or one kid, then the man and his nearest neighbour may take one between them. They shall share the cost, taking into account both the number of persons and the amount 5 each of them eats. Your lamb or kid must be without blemish, a yearling male. You may take equally a sheep 6 or a goat. You must have it in safe keeping until the fourteenth day of this month, and then all the assembled community of Israel shall slaughter the victim between dusk and dark. 7 They must take some of the blood and smear it on the two door-posts and on the lintel of every house in which they 8 eat the lamb. On that night they shall eat the flesh roast on the fire; they shall eat it with unleavened cakes and 9 bitter herbs. You are not to eat any

of it raw or even boiled in water, but roasted, head, shins, and entrails. You 10 shall not leave any of it till morning; if anything is left over until morning, it must be destroyed by fire.

This is the way in which you must 11 eat it: you shall have your belt fastened, your sandals on your feet and your staff in your hand, and you must eat in urgent haste. It is the LORD's Passover. On that night I 12 shall pass through the land of Egypt and kill every first-born of man and beast. Thus will I execute judgement, I the LORD, against all the gods of Egypt. And as for you, the blood will 13 be a sign on the houses in which you are: when I see the blood I will pass over[l] you; the mortal blow shall not touch you, when I strike the land of Egypt.

You shall keep this day as a day of 14 remembrance, and make it a pilgrim-feast, a festival of the LORD; you shall keep it generation after generation as a rule for all time. For seven days you 15 shall eat unleavened cakes. On the very first day you shall rid your houses of leaven; from the first day to the seventh anyone who eats leavened bread shall be outlawed from Israel. On the first day there shall be a 16 sacred assembly and on the seventh day there shall be a sacred assembly: on these days no work shall be done, except what must be done to provide food for everyone; and that will be allowed. You shall observe these com- 17 mandments because this was the very day on which I brought you out of Egypt in your tribal hosts. You shall observe this day from generation to generation as a rule for all time.

You shall eat unleavened cakes in 18 the first month from the evening which begins the fourteenth day until the evening which begins the twenty-first day. For seven days no leaven 19 may be found in your houses, for anyone who eats anything fermented shall be outlawed from the com-munity of Israel, be he foreigner or native. You must eat nothing fer- 20 mented. Wherever you live you must eat your cakes unleavened.

Moses summoned all the elders of 21 Israel and said to them, 'Go at once and get sheep for your families and slaughter the Passover. Then take a 22 bunch of marjoram,[m] dip it in the blood in the basin[n] and smear some blood from the basin[o] on the lintel and the two door-posts. Nobody may

l Or stand guard over.   *m* Or hyssop.   *n* Or on the threshold.   *o* Or from the threshold.

go out through the door of his house
23 till morning. The LORD will go through
Egypt and strike it, but when he sees
the blood on the lintel and the two
door-posts, he will pass over that door
and will not let the destroyer enter
24 your houses to strike you. You shall
keep this as a rule for you and your
25 children for all time. When you enter
the land which the LORD will give you
as he promised, you shall observe this
26 rite. Then, when your children ask
you, "What is the meaning of this
27 rite?" you shall say, "It is the LORD'S
Passover, for he passed over the
houses of the Israelites in Egypt but
spared our houses.''' The people
bowed down and prostrated themselves.

The death of the first-born

28 The Israelites went and did all that
the LORD had commanded Moses and
29 Aaron; and by midnight the LORD had
struck down every first-born in Egypt,
from the first-born of Pharaoh on his
throne to the first-born of the captive
in the dungeon, and the first-born of
30 cattle. Before night was over Pharaoh
rose, he and all his courtiers and all
the Egyptians, and a great cry of
anguish went up, because not a house
31 in Egypt was without its dead. Pharaoh'summoned Moses and Aaron while
it was still night and said, 'Up with
you! Be off, and leave my people,
you and your Israelites. Go and
32 worship the LORD, as you ask; take
your sheep and cattle, and go; and
33 ask God's blessing on me also.' The
Egyptians urged on the people and
hurried them out of the country, 'or
else', they said, 'we shall all be dead.'
34 The people picked up their dough
before it was leavened, wrapped their
kneading-troughs in their cloaks, and
35 slung them on their shoulders. Meanwhile the Israelites had done as
Moses had told them, asking the
Egyptians for jewellery of silver and
36 gold and for clothing. As the LORD
had made the Egyptians well-disposed
towards them, they let them have
what they asked; in this way they
plundered the Egyptians.

The exodus from Egypt

37 The Israelites set out from Rameses
on the way to Succoth, about six
hundred thousand men on foot, not
38 counting dependants. And with them
too went a large company of every
kind, and cattle in great numbers,
both flocks and herds. The dough they 39
had brought from Egypt they baked
into unleavened cakes, because there
was no leaven; for they had been
driven out of Egypt and allowed no
time even to get food ready for themselves.

The Israelites had been settled in 40
Egypt for four hundred and thirty
years. At the end of four hundred and 41
thirty years, on this very day, all the
tribes of the LORD came out of Egypt.
This was a night of vigil as the LORD 42
waited to bring them out of Egypt.
It is the LORD'S night; all Israelites
keep their vigil generation after generation.

Rules for the Passover

The LORD said to Moses and Aaron: 43
These are the rules for the Passover.
No foreigner may partake of it; any 44
bought slave may eat it if you have
circumcised him; no stranger or hired 45
man may eat it. Each lamb must be 46
eaten inside the one house, and you
must not take any of the flesh outside
the house. You must not break a
single bone of it. The whole commu- 47
nity of Israel shall keep this feast. If 48
there are aliens living with you and
they are to keep the Passover to the
LORD, every male of them must be
circumcised, and then he can take
part; he shall rank as native-born. No
one who is uncircumcised may eat of
it. The same law shall apply both to 49
the native-born and to the alien who
is living among you.

The Israelites did all that the LORD 50
had commanded Moses and Aaron;
and on this very day the LORD brought 51
the Israelites out of Egypt mustered
in their tribal hosts.

Dedication of the first-born

The LORD spoke to Moses and said, 13
'Every first-born, the first birth of 2
every womb among the Israelites, you
must dedicate to me, both man and
beast; it is mine.'

Pilgrim-feast of unleavened bread

Then Moses said to the people, 3
'Remember this day, the day on
which you have come out of Egypt,
the land of slavery, because the LORD
by the strength of his hand has brought
you out. No leaven may be eaten this
day, for today, in the month of Abib, 4
is the day of your exodus; and when 5
the LORD has brought you into the
country of the Canaanites, Hittites,
Amorites, Hivites, and Jebusites, the

land which he swore to your fore-fathers to give you, a land flowing with milk and honey, then you must observe this rite in this same month.

6 For seven days you shall eat un-leavened cakes, and on the seventh day there shall be a pilgrim-feast of 7 the LORD. Only unleavened cakes shall be eaten during the seven days; nothing fermented and no leaven shall be seen throughout your territory.

8 On that day you shall tell your son, "This commemorates what the LORD did for me when I came out of Egypt."

9 You shall have the record of it as a sign upon your hand, and upon your forehead as a reminder, to make sure that the law of the LORD is always on your lips, because the LORD with a strong hand brought you out of 10 Egypt. This is a rule, and you shall keep it at the appointed time from year to year.

First-born belong to the LORD

11 'When the LORD has brought you into the land of the Canaanites as he swore to you and to your forefathers, and 12 given it to you, you shall surrender to the LORD the first birth of every womb; and of all first-born offspring of your cattle the males belong to the 13 LORD. Every first-born male ass you may redeem with a kid or lamb, but if you do not redeem it, you must break its neck. Every first-born among your sons you must redeem. 14 When in time to come your son asks you what this means, you shall say to him, "By the strength of his hand the LORD brought us out of Egypt, out of 15 the land of slavery. When Pharaoh proved stubborn and refused to let us go, the LORD killed all the first-born in Egypt both man and beast. That is why I sacrifice to the LORD the first birth of every womb if it is a male and redeem every first-born of my sons. 16 You shall have the record of it as a sign upon your hand, and upon your forehead as a phylactery, because by the strength of his hand the LORD brought us out of Egypt." '

The cloud and the fire

17 Now when Pharaoh let the people go, God did not guide them by the road towards the Philistines, although that was the shortest; for he said, 'The people may change their minds when they see war before them, and turn 18 back to Egypt.' So God made them go round by way of the wilderness

towards the Red Sea; and the fifth generation of Israelites departed from Egypt.

Moses took the bones of Joseph 19 with him, because Joseph had exacted an oath from the Israelites: 'Some day', he said, 'God will show his care for you, and then, as you go, you must take my bones with you.'

They set out from Succoth and 20 encamped at Etham on the edge of the wilderness. And all the time the 21 LORD went before them, by day a pillar of cloud to guide them on their journey, by night a pillar of fire to give them light, so that they could travel night and day. The pillar of 22 cloud never left its place in front of the people by day, nor the pillar of fire by night.

Crossing the Red Sea

The LORD spoke to Moses and said, **14** 'Speak to the Israelites: they are to 2 turn back and encamp before Pi-hahiroth,*p* between Migdol and the sea to the east of Baal-zephon; your camp shall be opposite, by the sea. Pharaoh will then think that the 3 Israelites are finding themselves in difficult country, and are hemmed in by the wilderness. I will make 4 Pharaoh obstinate, and he will pursue them, so that I may win glory for my-self at the expense of Pharaoh and all his army; and the Egyptians shall know that I am the LORD.' The Israelites did as they were bidden.

When the king of Egypt was told 5 that the Israelites had slipped away, he and his courtiers changed their minds completely, and said, 'What have we done? We have let our Israel-ite slaves go free!' So Pharaoh put 6 horses to his chariot, and took his troops with him. He took six hundred 7 picked chariots and all the other chariots of Egypt, with a commander in each. Then Pharaoh king of Egypt, 8 made obstinate by the LORD, pursued the Israelites as they marched de-fiantly away. The Egyptians, all Phar- 9 aoh's chariots and horses, cavalry and infantry, pursued them and over-took them encamped beside the sea by Pi-hahiroth to the east of Baal-zephon. Pharaoh was almost upon 10 them when the Israelites looked up and saw the Egyptians close behind. In their terror they clamoured to the LORD for help and said to Moses, 11 'Were there no graves in Egypt, that you should have brought us here to

p Or where the desert tracks begin.

die in the wilderness? See what you
have done to us by bringing us out
12 of Egypt! Is not this just what we
meant when we said in Egypt, "Leave
us alone; let us be slaves to the
Egyptians"? We would rather be
slaves to the Egyptians than die here
13 in the wilderness.' 'Have no fear,'
Moses answered; 'stand firm and see
the deliverance that the LORD will
bring you this day; for as sure as you
see the Egyptians now, you will never
14 see them again. The LORD will fight
for you; so hold your peace.'
15 The LORD said to Moses, 'What is
the meaning of this clamour? Tell the
16 Israelites to strike camp. And you
shall raise high your staff, stretch out
your hand over the sea and cleave it
in two, so that the Israelites can pass
17 through the sea on dry ground. For
my part I will make the Egyptians
obstinate and they will come after
you; thus will I win glory for myself
at the expense of Pharaoh and his
army, chariots and cavalry all to-
18 gether. The Egyptians will know that
I am the LORD when I win glory for
myself at the expense of their Pharaoh,
his chariots and cavalry.'
19 The angel of God, who had kept in
front of the Israelites, moved away
to the rear. The pillar of cloud moved
from the front and took its place
20 behind them and so came between
the Egyptians and the Israelites. And
the cloud brought on darkness and
early nightfall, so that contact was
lost throughout the night.
21 Then Moses stretched out his hand
over the sea, and the LORD drove the
sea away all night with a strong east
wind and turned the sea-bed into dry
22 land. The waters were torn apart, and
the Israelites went through the sea on
the dry ground, while the waters made
a wall for them to right and to left.
23 The Egyptians went in pursuit of
them far into the sea, all Pharaoh's
24 horse, his chariots, and his cavalry. In
the morning watch the LORD looked
down on the Egyptian army through
the pillar of fire and cloud, and he
25 threw them into a panic. He clogged
their chariot wheels and made them
lumber along heavily, so that the
Egyptians said, 'It is the LORD
fighting for Israel against Egypt; let
26 us flee.' Then the LORD said to Moses,
'Stretch out your hand over the sea,
and let the water flow back over the
Egyptians, their chariots and their
27 cavalry.' So Moses stretched out his
hand over the sea, and at daybreak

the water returned to its accustomed
place; but the Egyptians were in
flight as it advanced, and the LORD
swept them out into the sea. The water 28
flowed back and covered all Pharaoh's
army, the chariots and the cavalry,
which had pressed the pursuit into
the sea. Not one man was left alive.
Meanwhile the Israelites had passed 29
along the dry ground through the sea,
with the water making a wall for them
to right and to left. That day the 30
LORD saved Israel from the power of
Egypt, and the Israelites saw the
Egyptians lying dead on the sea-
shore. When Israel saw the great 31
power which the LORD had put forth
against Egypt, all the people feared
the LORD, and they put their faith in
him and in Moses his servant.

The song of Moses

Then Moses and the Israelites sang 15
this song to the LORD:

I will sing to the LORD, for he has
    risen up in triumph;
the horse and his rider he has hurled
    into the sea.
    The LORD is my refuge and my 2
    defence,
    he has shown himself my deliverer.
    He is my God, and I will glorify
    him;
    he is my father's God, and I will
    exalt him.
    The LORD is a warrior: the LORD is 3
    his name.
    The chariots of Pharaoh and his 4
    army
    he has cast into the sea;
    the flower of his officers
    are engulfed in the Red Sea.
    The watery abyss has covered them, 5
    they sank into the depths like a
    stone.
Thy right hand, O LORD, is majestic 6
    in strength:
thy right hand, O LORD, shattered the
    enemy.
    In the fullness of thy triumph   7
    thou didst cast the rebels down:
    thou didst let loose thy fury;
    it consumed them like chaff.
At the blast of thy anger the sea 8
    piled up:
    the waters stood up like a bank:
    out at sea the great deep congealed.
The enemy said, 'I will pursue, I will 9
    overtake;
    I will divide the spoil,
    I will glut my appetite upon them;
    I will draw my sword,
    I will rid myself of them.'

10 Thou didst blow with thy blast; the
   sea covered them.
   They sank like lead in the swelling
   waves.
11 Who is like thee, O LORD, among
   the gods*q*?
   Who is like thee, majestic in holiness,
   worthy of awe and praise, who
   workest wonders?
12 Thou didst stretch out thy right
   hand,
   earth engulfed them.
13 In thy constant love thou hast led the
   people
   whom thou didst ransom:
   thou hast guided them by thy
   strength
   to thy holy dwelling-place.
14 Nations heard and trembled;
   agony seized the dwellers in Philistia.
15 Then the chieftains of Edom were
   dismayed,
   trembling seized the leaders of
   Moab,
   all the inhabitants of Canaan were in
   turmoil;
16 terror and dread fell upon them:
   through the might of thy arm they
   stayed stone-still,
   while thy people passed, O LORD,
   while the people whom thou madest
   thy own*r* passed by.
17 Thou broughtest them in and didst
   plant them
   in the mount that is thy possession,
   the dwelling-place, O LORD, of thy
   own making,
   the sanctuary, O LORD, which thy
   own hands prepared.
18 The LORD shall reign for ever and
   for ever.

19 For Pharaoh's horse, both chariots
   and cavalry, went into the sea, and
   the LORD brought back the waters
20 over them, but Israel had passed
   through the sea on dry ground. And
   Miriam the prophetess, Aaron's sister,
   took up her tambourine, and all the
   women followed her, dancing to the
21 sound of tambourines; and Miriam
   sang them this refrain:

   Sing to the LORD, for he has risen up
   in triumph;
   the horse and his rider he has hurled
   into the sea.

   ### Bitter water at Marah

22 Moses led Israel from the Red Sea out
   into the wilderness of Shur. For three
   days they travelled through the wilder-
23 ness without finding water. They came

to Marah, but could not drink the
Marah water because it was bitter;
that is why the place was called Marah. The people complained to Moses 24
and asked, 'What are we to drink?'
Moses cried to the LORD, and the 25
LORD showed him a log which he
threw into the water, and then the
water became sweet.
   It was there that the LORD laid
down a precept and rule of life; there
he put them to the test. He said, 'If 26
only you will obey the LORD your God,
if you will do what is right in his eyes,
if you will listen to his commands and
keep all his statutes, then I will never
bring upon you any of the sufferings
which I brought on the Egyptians;
for I the LORD am your healer.'
   They came to Elim, where there 27
were twelve springs and seventy palm-
trees, and there they encamped beside
the water.

The LORD gives manna

The whole community of the Israelites 16
set out from Elim and came into the
wilderness of Sin, which lies between
Elim and Sinai. This was on the
fifteenth day of the second month after
they had left Egypt.
   The Israelites complained to Moses 2
and Aaron in the wilderness and said, 3
'If only we had died at the LORD's
hand in Egypt, where we sat round
the fleshpots and had plenty of bread
to eat! But you have brought us out
into this wilderness to let this whole
assembly starve to death.' The LORD 4
said to Moses, 'I will rain down bread
from heaven for you. Each day the
people shall go out and gather a day's
supply, so that I can put them to the
test and see whether they will follow
my instructions or not. But on the 5
sixth day, when they prepare what
they bring in, it shall be twice as
much as they have gathered on other
days.' Moses and Aaron then said to 6
all the Israelites, 'In the evening you
will know that it was the LORD who
brought you out of Egypt, and in the 7
morning you will see the glory of the
LORD, because he has heeded your
complaints against him; it is not
against us that you bring your complaints; we are nothing.' 'You shall 8
know this', Moses said, 'when the
LORD, in answer to your complaints,
gives you flesh to eat in the evening,
and in the morning bread in plenty.
What are we? It is against the LORD

q Or in might.   r madest thy own: or didst create.

that you bring your complaints, and not against us.'

9 Moses told Aaron to say to the whole community of Israel, 'Come into the presence of the LORD, for he 10 has heeded your complaints.' While Aaron was speaking to the community of the Israelites, they looked towards the wilderness, and there was the glory of the LORD appearing in the 11 cloud. The LORD spoke to Moses and 12 said, 'I have heard the complaints of the Israelites. Say to them, "Between dusk and dark you will have flesh to eat and in the morning bread in plenty. You shall know that I the LORD am your God."'

13 That evening a flock of quails flew in and settled all over the camp, and in the morning a fall of dew lay all 14 around it. When the dew was gone, there in the wilderness, fine flakes appeared, fine as hoar-frost on the 15 ground. When the Israelites saw it, they said to one another, 'What is that?',[s] because they did not know what it was. Moses said to them, 'That is the bread which the LORD has 16 given you to eat. This is the command the LORD has given: "Each of you is to gather as much as he can eat: let every man take an omer a head 17 for every person in his tent."' The Israelites did this, and they gathered, 18 some more, some less, but when they measured it by the omer, those who had gathered more had not too much, and those who had gathered less had not too little. Each had just as much 19 as he could eat. Moses said, 'No one 20 may keep any of it till morning.' Some, however, did not listen to Moses; they kept part of it till morning, and it became full of maggots and stank, 21 and Moses was angry with them. Each morning every man gathered as much as he could eat, and when the sun 22 grew hot, it melted away. On the sixth day they gathered twice as much food, two omers each. All the chiefs of the community came and told 23 Moses. 'This', he answered, 'is what the LORD has said: "Tomorrow is a day of sacred rest, a sabbath holy to the LORD." So bake what you want to bake now, and boil what you want to boil; put aside what remains over 24 and keep it safe till morning.' So they put it aside till morning as Moses had commanded, and it did not stink, nor 25 did maggots appear in it. 'Eat it today,' said Moses, 'because today is a sabbath of the LORD. Today you will find none outside. For six days 26 you may gather it, but on the seventh day, the sabbath, there will be none.'

27 Some of the people did go out to gather it on the seventh day, but they 28 found none. The LORD said to Moses, 'How long will you refuse to obey 29 my commands and instructions? The LORD has given you the sabbath, and so he gives you two days' food every sixth day. Let each man stay where he is; no one may stir from his home 30 on the seventh day.' And the people kept the sabbath on the seventh day.

31 Israel called the food manna; it was white, like coriander seed, and it tasted like a wafer made with honey.

32 'This', said Moses, 'is the command which the LORD has given: "Take a full omer of it to be kept for future generations, so that they may see the bread with which I fed you in the wilderness when I brought you out 33 of Egypt."' So Moses said to Aaron, 'Take a jar and fill it with an omer of manna, and store it in the presence of the LORD to be kept for future ge-34 nerations.' Aaron did as the LORD had commanded Moses, and stored it before the Testimony for safe keep-35 ing. The Israelites ate the manna for forty years until they came to a land where they could settle; they ate it until they came to the border of 36 Canaan. (An omer is one tenth of an ephah.)

Water from the rock

17 The whole community of Israel set out from the wilderness of Sin and travelled by stages as the LORD told them. They encamped at Rephidim, where there was no water for the 2 people to drink, and a dispute arose between them and Moses. When they said, 'Give us water to drink', Moses said, 'Why do you dispute with me? Why do you challenge the LORD?' 3 There the people became so thirsty that they raised an outcry against Moses: 'Why have you brought us out of Egypt with our children and our 4 herds to let us all die of thirst?' Moses cried to the LORD, 'What shall I do with these people? In a moment 5 they will be stoning me.' The LORD answered, 'Go forward ahead of the people; take with you some of the elders of Israel and the staff with which you struck the Nile, and go. 6 You will find me waiting for you there, by a rock in Horeb. Strike the rock; water will pour out of it, and the

s Heb. man-hu (cp. verse 31).

people shall drink.' Moses did this in
7 the sight of the elders of Israel. He
named the place Massah[t] and Meribah,[u] because the Israelites had
disputed with him and challenged the
LORD with their question, 'Is the
LORD in our midst or not?'

War with Amalek

8 The Amalekites came and attacked
9 Israel at Rephidim. Moses said to
Joshua, 'Pick your men, and march
out tomorrow to fight for us against
Amalek; and I will take my stand
on the hill-top with the staff of God
10 in my hand.' Joshua carried out his
orders and fought against Amalek
while Moses, Aaron and Hur climbed
11 to the top of the hill. Whenever Moses
raised his hands Israel had the advantage, and when he lowered his hands
12 Amalek had the advantage. But when
his arms grew heavy they took a stone
and put it under him and, as he sat,
Aaron and Hur held up his hands,
one on each side, so that his hands
13 remained steady till sunset. Thus
Joshua defeated Amalek and put
its people to the sword.
14 The LORD said to Moses, 'Record
this in writing, and tell it to Joshua
in these words: "I am resolved to blot
out all memory of Amalek from under
15 heaven."' Moses built an altar, and
16 named it Jehovah-nissi and said, 'My
oath upon it: the LORD is at war with
Amalek generation after generation.'

Jethro visits Moses

18 Jethro priest of Midian, father-in-law
of Moses, heard all that God had done
for Moses and Israel his people, and
how the LORD had brought Israel out
2 of Egypt. When Moses had dismissed
his wife Zipporah, Jethro his father-
3 in-law had received her and her two
sons. The name of the one was Gershom, 'for', said Moses, 'I have become
4 an alien[v] living in a foreign land'; the
other's name was Eliezer,[w] 'for', he
said, 'the God of my father was my
help and saved me from Pharaoh's
sword.'
5 Jethro, Moses' father-in-law, now
came to him with his sons and his
wife, to the wilderness where he was
encamped at the mountain of God.
6 Moses was told, 'Here is Jethro, your
father-in-law, coming to you with
7 your wife and her two sons.' Moses
went out to meet his father-in-law,
bowed low to him and kissed him, and
they greeted one another. When they

came into the tent Moses told him all 8
that the LORD had done to Pharaoh
and to Egypt for Israel's sake, and
about all their hardships on the
journey, and how the LORD had
saved them. Jethro rejoiced at all the 9
good the LORD had done for Israel in
saving them from the power of Egypt.
He said, 'Blessed be the LORD who 10-11
has saved you from the power of
Egypt and of Pharaoh. Now I know
that the LORD is the greatest of all
gods, because he has delivered the
people from the power of the Egyptians who dealt so arrogantly with
them.' Jethro, Moses' father-in-law, 12
brought a whole-offering and sacrifices for God; and Aaron and all the
elders of Israel came and shared the
meal with Jethro in the presence of
God.

Moses sets up a court of law

The next day Moses took his seat to 13
settle disputes among the people, and
they were standing round him from
morning till evening. When Jethro 14
saw all that he was doing for the
people, he said, 'What are you doing
for all these people? Why do you sit
alone with all of them standing round
you from morning till evening?' 'The 15
people come to me', Moses answered,
'to seek God's guidance. Whenever 16
there is a dispute among them, they
come to me, and I decide between
man and man. I declare the statutes
and laws of God.' But his father-in- 17
law said to Moses, 'This is not the best
way to do it. You will only wear your- 18
self out and wear out all the people
who are here. The task is too heavy
for you; you cannot do it by yourself.
Now listen to me: take my advice, and 19
God be with you. It is for you to be
the people's representative before God,
and bring their disputes to him. You 20
must instruct them in the statutes
and laws, and teach them how they
must behave and what they must do.
But you must yourself search for 21
capable, God-fearing men among all
the people, honest and incorruptible
men, and appoint them over units of a
thousand, of a hundred, of fifty or of
ten. They shall sit as a permanent 22
court for the people; they must refer
difficult cases to you but decide simple
cases themselves. In this way your
burden will be lightened, and they will
share it with you. If you do this, God 23
will give you strength, and you will be

---

t That is Challenge.   *u That is* Dispute.   *v Cp. 2. 22.*   *w That is* God my help.

able to go on. And, moreover, this whole people will here and now regain 24 peace and harmony.' Moses listened to his father-in-law and did all he had 25 suggested. He chose capable men from all Israel and appointed them leaders of the people, officers over units of a thousand, of a hundred, of fifty or of 26 ten. They sat as a permanent court, bringing the difficult cases to Moses but deciding simple cases themselves. 27 Moses set his father-in-law on his way, and he went back to his own country.

Israel at Mount Sinai

19 In the third month after Israel had left Egypt,[x] they came to the wilder- 2 ness of Sinai. They set out from Rephidim and entered the wilderness of Sinai, where they encamped, pitching their tents opposite the mountain. 3 Moses went up the mountain of God, and the LORD called to him from the mountain and said, 'Speak thus to the house of Jacob, and tell this to 4 the sons of Israel: You have seen with your own eyes what I did to Egypt, and how I have carried you on eagles' wings and brought you here 5 to me. If only you will now listen to me and keep my covenant, then out of all peoples you shall become my special possession; for the whole earth is 6 mine. You shall be my kingdom of priests, my holy nation. These are the words you shall speak to the Israelites.' 7 Moses came and summoned the elders of the people and set before them all these commands which the LORD 8 had laid upon him. The people all answered together, 'Whatever the LORD has said we will do.' Moses brought this answer back to the LORD. 9 The LORD said to Moses, 'I am now coming to you in a thick cloud, so that I may speak to you in the hearing of the people, and their faith in you may never fail.' Moses told the 10 LORD what the people had said, and the LORD said to him, 'Go to the people and hallow them today and tomorrow and make them wash their 11 clothes. They must be ready by the third day, because on the third day the LORD will descend upon Mount Sinai in the sight of all the people. 12 You must put barriers round the mountain and say, "Take care not to go up the mountain or even to touch the edge of it." Any man who touches the mountain must be put to death.

No hand shall touch him;[y] he shall 13 be stoned or shot dead:[z] neither man nor beast may live. But when the ram's horn sounds, they may go up the mountain.' Moses came down 14 from the mountain to the people. He hallowed them and they washed their clothes. He said to the people, 'Be 15 ready by the third day; do not go near a woman.' On the third day, 16 when morning came, there were peals of thunder and flashes of lightning, dense cloud on the mountain and a loud trumpet blast; the people in the camp were all terrified.

Moses brought the people out from 17 the camp to meet God, and they took their stand at the foot of the mountain. Mount Sinai was all smoking because 18 the LORD had come down upon it in fire; the smoke went up like the smoke of a kiln; all the people were terrified, and the sound of the trumpet grew 19 ever louder. Whenever Moses spoke, God answered him in a peal of thunder.[a] The LORD came down upon the 20 top of Mount Sinai and summoned Moses to the mountain-top, and Moses went up. The LORD said to Moses, 21 'Go down; warn the people solemnly that they must not force their way through to the LORD to see him, or many of them will perish. Even the 22 priests, who have access to the LORD, must hallow themselves, for fear that the LORD may break out against them.' Moses answered the LORD, 23 'The people cannot come up Mount Sinai, because thou thyself didst solemnly warn us to set a barrier to the mountain and so to keep it holy.' The LORD therefore said to him, 'Go 24 down; then come up and bring Aaron with you, but let neither priests nor people force their way up to the LORD, for fear that he may break out against them.' So Moses went down to the 25 people and spoke to them.

The Ten Commandments

God spoke, and these were his words: **20** I am the LORD your God who 2 brought you out of Egypt, out of the land of slavery.

You shall have no other god[b] to set 3 against me.

You shall not make a carved image 4 for yourself nor the likeness of anything in the heavens above, or on the earth below, or in the waters under the earth.

You shall not bow down to them or 5

---

x *Prob. rdg.; Heb. adds* on this day.   y *Or* it. *or* by voice.   b *Or* gods.

z *Or* hurled to his death.   a in . . . thunder:

worship[c] them; for I, the LORD your God, am a jealous god. I punish the children for the sins of the fathers to the third and fourth generations of

6 those who hate me. But I keep faith with thousands, with[d] those who love me and keep my commandments.

7 You shall not make wrong use of the name of the LORD your God; the LORD will not leave unpunished the man who misuses his name.

8 Remember to keep the sabbath day
9 holy. You have six days to labour and
10 do all your work. But the seventh day is a sabbath of the LORD your God; that day you shall not do any work, you, your son or your daughter, your slave or your slave-girl, your cattle or
11 the alien within your gates; for in six days the LORD made heaven and earth, the sea, and all that is in them, and on the seventh day he rested. Therefore the LORD blessed the sabbath day and declared it holy.

12 Honour your father and your mother, that you may live long in the land which the LORD your God is giving you.

13 You shall not commit murder.
14 You shall not commit adultery.
15 You shall not steal.
16 You shall not give false evidence against your neighbour.
17 You shall not covet your neighbour's house; you shall not covet your neighbour's wife, his slave, his slave-girl, his ox, his ass, or anything that belongs to him.

God tests the people

18 When all the people saw how it thundered and the lightning flashed, when they heard the trumpet sound and saw the mountain smoking, they trembled and stood at a distance.
19 'Speak to us yourself,' they said to Moses, 'and we will listen; but if God
20 speaks to us we shall die.' Moses answered, 'Do not be afraid. God has come only to test you, so that the fear of him may remain with you and keep
21 you from sin.' So the people stood at a distance, while Moses approached the dark cloud where God was.

Laws concerning altars

22 The LORD said to Moses, Say this to the Israelites: You know now that I
23 have spoken to you from heaven. You shall not make gods of silver to be worshipped as well as me, nor shall you make yourselves gods of gold.
24 You shall make an altar of earth for

me, and you shall sacrifice on it both your whole-offerings and your shared-offerings, your sheep and your cattle. Wherever I cause my name to be invoked, I will come to you and bless you. If you make an altar of stones for 25 me, you must not build it of hewn stones, for if you use a chisel on it, you will profane it. You must not 26 mount up to my altar by steps, in case your private parts be exposed on it.

Laws concerning slaves

These are the laws you shall set before 21 them:

When you buy a Hebrew slave, he 2 shall be your slave for six years, but in the seventh year he shall go free and pay nothing.

If he comes to you alone, he shall 3 go away alone; but if he is married, his wife shall go away with him.

If his master gives him a wife, and 4 she bears him sons or daughters, the woman and her children shall belong to her master, and the man shall go away alone. But if the slave should 5 say, 'I love my master, my wife, and my children; I will not go free', then 6 his master shall bring him to God: he shall bring him to the door or the door-post, and his master shall pierce his ear with an awl, and the man shall be his slave for life.

When a man sells his daughter into 7 slavery, she shall not go free as a male slave may. If her master has not had 8 intercourse with her and she does not please him, he shall let her be ransomed. He has treated her unfairly and therefore has no right to sell her to strangers. If he assigns her to his 9 son, he shall allow her the rights of a daughter. If he takes another woman, 10 he shall not deprive the first of meat, clothes, and conjugal rights. If he 11 does not provide her with these three things, she shall go free without any payment.

Laws concerning acts of violence

Whoever strikes another man and 12 kills him shall be put to death. But if 13 he did not act with intent, but they met by act of God, the slayer may flee to a place which I will appoint for you. But if a man has the presump- 14 tion to kill another by treachery, you shall take him even from my altar to be put to death.

Whoever strikes his father or mother 15 shall be put to death.

Whoever kidnaps a man shall be 16

c Or or be led to worship.   d with . . . with: or for a thousand generations with . . .

put to death, whether he has sold him, or the man is found in his possession.

17 Whoever reviles his father or mother shall be put to death.

18 When men quarrel and one hits another with a stone or with a spade,[e] and the man is not killed but takes to

19 his bed; if he recovers so as to walk about outside with a stick, then the one who struck him has no liability, except that he shall pay for loss of time and shall see that he is cured.

20 When a man strikes his slave or his slave-girl with a stick and the slave dies on the spot, he must be punished.

21 But he shall not be punished if the slave survives for one day or two, because he is worth money to his master.

22 When, in the course of a brawl, a man knocks against a pregnant woman so that she has a miscarriage but suffers no further hurt, then the offender must pay whatever fine the woman's husband demands after assessment.

23 Wherever hurt is done, you shall
24 give life for life, eye for eye, tooth for
25 tooth, hand for hand, foot for foot, burn for burn, bruise for bruise, wound for wound.

26 When a man strikes his slave or slave-girl in the eye and destroys it, he shall let the slave go free in com-
27 pensation for the eye. When he knocks out the tooth of a slave or a slave-girl, he shall let the slave go free in compensation for the tooth.

Owners' liability

28 When an ox gores a man or a woman to death, the ox shall be stoned, and its flesh may not be eaten; the owner of the ox shall be free from liability.

29 If, however, the ox has for some time past been a vicious animal, and the owner has been duly warned but has not kept it under control, and the ox kills a man or a woman, then the ox shall be stoned, and the owner shall

30 be put to death as well. If, however, the penalty is commuted for a money payment, he shall pay in redemption of his life whatever is imposed upon

31 him. If the ox gores a son or a daugh-
32 ter, the same rule shall apply. If the ox gores a slave or slave-girl, its owner shall pay thirty shekels of silver to their master, and the ox shall be stoned.

33 When a man removes the cover of

a well[f] or digs a well[f] and leaves it uncovered, then if an ox or an ass falls into it, the owner of the well shall 34 make good the loss. He shall repay the owner of the beast in silver, and the dead beast shall be his.

When one man's ox butts another's 35 and kills it, they shall sell the live ox, share the price and also share the dead beast. But if it is known that 36 the ox has for some time past been vicious and the owner has not kept it under control, he shall make good the loss, ox for ox, but the dead beast is his.

Laws concerning restitution

When a man steals an ox or a sheep 22 and slaughters or sells it, he shall repay five beasts for the ox and four sheep for the sheep. He shall pay in 2–4[g] full; if he has no means, he shall be sold to pay for the theft. But if the animal is found alive in his possession, be it ox, ass, or sheep, he shall repay two.

If a burglar is caught in the act and is fatally injured, it is not murder; but if he breaks in after sunrise and is fatally injured, then it is murder.

When a man burns off a field or a 5 vineyard and lets the fire spread so that it burns another man's field,[h] he shall make restitution from his own field according to the yield expected; and if the whole field is laid waste, he shall make restitution from the best part of his own field or vineyard.

When a fire starts and spreads to a 6 heap of brushwood, so that sheaves, or standing corn, or a whole field is destroyed, he who started the fire shall make full restitution.

When one man gives another silver 7 or chattels for safe keeping, and they are stolen from that man's house, the thief, if he is found, shall restore two-fold. But if the thief is not found, the 8 owner of the house shall appear before God, to make a declaration that he has not touched his neighbour's property. In every case of law-breaking involv- 9 ing an ox, an ass, or a sheep, a cloak, or any lost property which may be claimed, each party shall bring his case before God; he whom God declares to be in the wrong shall restore two-fold to his neighbour.

When a man gives an ass, an ox, a 10 sheep or any beast into his neigh-bour's keeping, and it dies or is

e Or fist.   f Or cistern.   g Verses 2–4 rearranged thus: 3b, 4, 2, 3a.   h Or When a man uses his field or vineyard for grazing, and lets his beast loose, and it feeds in another man's field.

injured or is carried off, there being
11 no witness, the neighbour shall swear
by the LORD that he has not touched
the man's property. The owner shall
accept this, and no restitution shall
12 be made. If it has been stolen from
him, he shall make restitution to the
13 owner. If it has been mauled by a wild
beast, he shall bring it in as evidence;
he shall not make restitution for what
has been mauled.

14 When a man borrows a beast from
his neighbour and it is injured or dies
while its owner is not with it, the
borrower shall make full restitution;
15 but if the owner is with it, the borrower shall not make restitution. If it
was hired, only the hire shall be due.

Various laws

16 When a man seduces a virgin who is
not yet betrothed, he shall pay the
17 bride-price for her to be his wife. If
her father refuses to give her to him,
the seducer shall pay in silver a sum
equal to the bride-price for virgins.
18 You shall not allow a witch to live.
19 Whoever has unnatural connection
with a beast shall be put to death.
20 Whoever sacrifices to any god but
the LORD shall be put to death under
solemn ban.
21 You shall not wrong an alien, or be
hard upon him; you were yourselves
22 aliens in Egypt. You shall not ill-
treat any widow or fatherless child.
23 If you do, be sure that I will listen if
24 they appeal to me; my anger will be
roused and I will kill you with the
sword; your own wives shall become
widows and your children fatherless.
25 If you advance money to any poor
man amongst my people, you shall
not act like a money-lender: you must
not exact interest in advance from
him.
26 If you take your neighbour's cloak
in pawn, you shall return it to him by
27 sunset, because it is his only covering.
It is the cloak in which he wraps his
body; in what else can he sleep? If he
appeals to me, I will listen, for I am
full of compassion.
28 You shall not revile God, nor curse
a chief of your own people.
29 You shall not hold back the first of
your harvest, whether corn or wine.
You shall give me your first-born sons.
30 You shall do the same with your oxen
and your sheep. They shall stay with
the mother for seven days; on the
eighth day you shall give them to me.
31 You shall be holy to me: you shall
not eat the flesh of anything in the
open country killed by beasts, but you
shall throw it to the dogs.

Justice and equity

You shall not spread a baseless rumour. **23**
You shall not make common cause
with a wicked man by giving malicious evidence.

You shall not be led into wrong- 2
doing by the majority, nor, when you
give evidence in a lawsuit, shall you
side with the majority to pervert
justice; nor shall you favour the poor 3
man in his suit.

When you come upon your enemy's 4
ox or ass straying, you shall take it
back to him. When you see the ass of 5
someone who hates you lying helpless
under its load, however unwilling you
may be to help it, you must give him
a hand with it.

You shall not deprive the poor man 6
of justice in his suit. Avoid all lies, and 7
do not cause the death of the innocent
and the guiltless; for I the LORD will
never acquit the guilty. You shall not 8
accept a bribe, for bribery makes the
discerning man blind and the just man
give a crooked answer.

You shall not oppress the alien, for 9
you know how it feels to be an alien;
you were aliens yourselves in Egypt.

Sabbath years and days

For six years you may sow your land 10
and gather its produce; but in the 11
seventh year you shall let it lie fallow
and leave it alone. It shall provide
food for the poor of your people, and
what they leave the wild animals may
eat. You shall do likewise with your
vineyard and your olive-grove.

For six days you may do your work, 12
but on the seventh day you shall
abstain from work, so that your ox and
your ass may rest, and your home-
born slave and the alien may refresh
themselves.

Be attentive to every word of mine. 13
You shall not invoke other gods: your
lips shall not speak their names.

Three pilgrim-feasts

Three times a year you shall keep a 14
pilgrim-feast to me. You shall cele- 15
brate the pilgrim-feast of Unleavened
Bread for seven days; you shall eat
unleavened cakes as I have commanded you, at the appointed time in the
month of Abib, for in that month you
came out of Egypt.

No one shall come into my presence 16
empty-handed. You shall celebrate
the pilgrim-feast of Harvest, with the

firstfruits of your work in sowing the land, and the pilgrim-feast of In-gathering at the end[i] of the year, when you bring in the fruits of all your

17 work on the land. These three times a year shall all your males come into the presence of the Lord GOD.

18   You shall not offer the blood of my sacrifice at the same time as anything leavened.

The fat of my festal offering shall not remain overnight till morning.

19   You shall bring the choicest first-fruits of your soil to the house of the LORD your God.

You shall not boil a kid in its mother's milk.

The LORD promises success

20 And now I send an angel before you to guard you on your way and to bring you to the place I have prepared.

21 Take heed of him and listen to his voice. Do not defy him; he will not pardon your rebelliousness, for my

22 authority rests in him. If you will only listen to his voice and do all I tell you, then I will be an enemy to your enemies, and I will harass those who

23 harass you. My angel will go before you and bring you to the Amorites, the Hittites, the Perizzites, the Ca-naanites, the Hivites, and the Jebusites,

24 and I will make an end of them. You are not to bow down to their gods, nor worship them, nor observe their rites, but you shall tear down all their images and smash their sacred pillars.

25 Worship the LORD your God, and he will bless your bread and your water. I will take away all sickness out of

26 your midst. None shall miscarry or be barren in your land. I will grant you a full span of life.

27   I will send my terror before you and throw into confusion all the peo-ples whom you find in your path. I will make all your enemies turn their

28 backs. I will spread panic before you to drive out in front of you the Hivites,

29 the Canaanites and the Hittites. I will not drive them out all in one year, or the land would become waste and the

30 wild beasts too many for you. I will drive them out little by little until your numbers have grown enough to take possession of the whole country.

31 I will establish your frontiers from the Red Sea to the sea of the Phil-istines, and from the wilderness to the River. I will give the inhabitants of the country into your power, and you

shall drive them out before you. You 32 shall make no covenant with them 33 and their gods. They shall not stay in your land for fear they make you sin against me; for then you would wor-ship their gods, and in this way you would be ensnared.

Moses on Mount Sinai

Then he said to Moses, 'Come up to 24 the LORD, you and Aaron, Nadab and Abihu, and seventy of the elders of Israel. While you are still at a distance, you are to bow down; and then Moses 2 shall approach the LORD by himself, but not the others. The people may not go up with him at all.'

Moses came and told the people all 3 the words of the LORD, all his laws. The whole people answered with one voice and said, 'We will do all that the LORD has told us.' Moses wrote 4 down all the words of the LORD. He rose early in the morning and built an altar at the foot of the mountain, and put up twelve sacred pillars, one for each of the twelve tribes of Israel. He 5 then sent the young men of Israel and they sacrificed bulls to the LORD as whole-offerings and shared-offerings. Moses took half the blood and put it 6 in basins and the other half he flung against[j] the altar. Then he took the 7 book of the covenant and read it aloud for all the people to hear. They said, 'We will obey, and do all that the LORD has said.' Moses then took 8 the blood and flung it over the people, saying, 'This is the blood of the cove-nant which the LORD has made with you on the terms of this book.'

Moses went up with Aaron, Nadab 9 and Abihu, and seventy of the elders of Israel, and they saw[k] the God of 10 Israel. Under his feet there was, as it were, a pavement of sapphire,[l] clear blue as the very heavens; but the 11 LORD did not stretch out his hand towards the leaders of Israel. They stayed there before God;[m] they ate and they drank. The LORD said to 12 Moses, 'Come up to me on the moun-tain, stay there and let me give you the tablets of stone, the law and the commandment, which I have written down that you may teach them.' Moses arose with Joshua his assistant 13 and went up the mountain of God; he 14 said to the elders, 'Wait for us here until we come back to you. You have Aaron and Hur; if anyone has a dis-pute, let him go to them.' So Moses 15

i Or beginning.   j Or upon.   k Or they were afraid of . . .   l Or lapis lazuli.   m Or They saw God; and . . .

went up the mountain and a cloud
16 covered it. The glory of the LORD
rested upon Mount Sinai, and the
cloud covered the mountain for six
days; on the seventh day he called to
17 Moses out of the cloud. The glory of
the LORD looked to the Israelites like
a devouring fire on the mountain-top.
18 Moses entered the cloud and went up
the mountain; there he stayed forty
days and forty nights.

Contributions for the sanctuary

25 The LORD spoke to Moses and said:
2 Tell the Israelites to set aside a contribution for me; you shall accept
whatever contribution each man shall
3 freely offer. This is what you shall
4 accept: gold, silver, copper; violet,
purple, and scarlet yarn; fine linen
5 and goats' hair; tanned rams' skins,
6 porpoise[n]-hides, and acacia-wood; oil
for the lamp, balsam for the anointing oil and for the fragrant incense;
7 cornelian and other stones ready for
setting in the ephod and the breast-
8 piece.[o] Make me a sanctuary, and
9 I will dwell among them. Make it
exactly according to the design I show
you, the design for the Tabernacle
and for all its furniture. This is how
you must make it:

The Ark of the Tokens

10 Make an Ark, a chest of acacia-wood,
two and a half cubits long, one cubit
and a half wide, and one cubit and a
11 half high. Overlay it with pure gold
both inside and out, and put a band
12 of gold all round it. Cast four gold
rings for it, and fasten them to its
four feet, two rings on each side.
13 Make poles of acacia-wood and plate
14 them with gold, and insert the poles
in the rings at the sides of the Ark to
15 lift it. The poles shall remain in the
rings of the Ark and never be re-
16 moved. Put into the Ark the Tokens
of the Covenant,[p] which I shall give
17 you. Make a cover of pure gold, two
and a half cubits long and one cubit
18 and a half wide. Make two gold
cherubim of beaten work at the ends
19 of the cover, one at each end; make
each cherub of one piece with the
20 cover. They shall be made with wings
outspread and pointing upwards, and
shall screen the cover with their wings.
They shall be face to face, looking
21 inwards over the cover. Put the cover
above the Ark, and put into the Ark
22 the Tokens that I shall give you. It is

there that I shall meet you, and from
above the cover, between the two
cherubim over the Ark of the Tokens,
I shall deliver to you all my commands for the Israelites.

The table for the Bread

Make a table of acacia-wood, two 23
cubits long, one cubit wide, and one
cubit and a half high. Overlay it with 24
pure gold, and put a band of gold all
round it. Make a rim round it a hand's 25
breadth wide, and a gold band round
the rim. Make four gold rings for the 26
table, and put the rings at the four
corners by the legs. The rings, which 27
are to receive the poles for carrying
the table, must be adjacent to the rim.
Make the poles of acacia-wood and 28
plate them with gold; they are to be
used for carrying the table. Make its 29
dishes and saucers, and its flagons
and bowls from which drink-offerings
may be poured: make them of pure
gold. Put the Bread of the Presence[q] 30
on the table, to be always before me.

The golden lamp-stand

Make a lamp-stand of pure gold. The 31
lamp-stand, stem and branches, shall
be of beaten work, its cups, both
calyxes and petals, shall be of one
piece with it. There are to be six 32
branches springing from its sides;
three branches of the lamp-stand shall
spring from the one side and three
branches from the other side. There 33
shall be three cups shaped like
almond blossoms, with calyx and
petals, on the first branch, three cups
shaped like almond blossoms, with
calyx and petals, on the next branch,
and similarly for all six branches
springing from the lamp-stand. On 34
the main stem of the lamp-stand there
are to be four cups shaped like almond blossoms, with calyx and petals,
and there shall be calyxes of one 35
piece with it under the six branches
which spring from the lamp-stand,
a single calyx under each pair of
branches. The calyxes and the bran- 36
ches are to be of one piece with it,
all a single piece of beaten work of
pure gold. Make seven lamps for this 37
and mount them to shed light over
the space in front of it. Its tongs and 38
firepans shall be of pure gold. The 39
lamp-stand and all these fittings shall
be made from one talent of pure gold.
See that you work to the design which 40
you were shown on the mountain.

n _Strictly_ sea-cow.   o _Or_ pouch.   p Tokens of the Covenant: _or_ Testimony.   q _Or_ Shewbread.

B*

The Tabernacle

26 Make the Tabernacle of ten hangings of finely woven linen, and violet, purple, and scarlet yarn, with cherubim worked on them, all made by a 2 seamster. The length of each hanging shall be twenty-eight cubits and the breadth four cubits; all are to be of 3 the same size. Five of the hangings shall be joined together, and similarly 4 the other five. Make violet loops along the edge of the last hanging in 5 each set, fifty for each set; they must 6 be opposite one another. Make fifty gold fasteners, join the hangings one to another with them, and the Tabernacle will be a single whole.

7 Make hangings of goats' hair, eleven in all, to form a tent over the 8 Tabernacle; each hanging is to be thirty cubits long and four wide; all 9 eleven are to be of the same size. Join five of the hangings together, and similarly the other six; then fold the sixth hanging double at the front of 10 the tent. Make fifty loops on the edge of the last hanging in the first set and make fifty loops on the joining edge 11 of the second set. Make fifty bronze[r] fasteners, insert them into the loops and join up the tent to make it a 12 single whole. The additional length of the tent hanging[s] is to fall over the 13 back of the Tabernacle. On each side there will be an additional cubit in the length of the tent hangings; this shall fall over the two sides of the 14 Tabernacle to cover it. Make for the tent a cover of tanned rams' skins and an outer covering of porpoise-hides.

15 Make for the Tabernacle planks of 16 acacia-wood as uprights, each plank ten cubits long and a cubit and a half 17 wide, and two tenons for each plank joined to each other. You shall do the same for all the planks of the Taber-18 nacle. Arrange the planks thus: twenty planks for the south side, 19 facing southwards, with forty silver sockets under them, two sockets under each plank for its two tenons; 20 and for the second or northern side of 21 the Tabernacle, twenty planks, with forty silver sockets, two under each 22 plank. Make six planks for the far end 23 of the Tabernacle on the west. Make two planks for the corners of the 24 Tabernacle at the far end; at the bottom they shall be alike, and at the top, both alike, they shall fit into a single ring. Do the same for both of them; they shall be for the two corners. There shall be eight planks with their 25 silver sockets, sixteen sockets in all, two sockets under each plank severally.

Make bars of acacia-wood: five for 26 the planks on the one side of the Tabernacle, five for the planks on the 27 other side and five for the planks on the far end of the Tabernacle on the west. The middle bar is to run along 28 from end to end half-way up the planks. Overlay the planks with gold, 29 make rings of gold on them to hold the bars, and plate the bars with gold. Set up the Tabernacle according to 30 the design you were shown on the mountain.

Make a Veil of finely woven linen 31 and violet, purple, and scarlet yarn, with cherubim worked on it, all made by a seamster. Fasten it with hooks 32 of gold to four posts of acacia-wood overlaid with gold, standing in four silver sockets. Hang the Veil below 33 the fasteners and bring the Ark of the Tokens inside the Veil. Thus the Veil will make a clear separation for you between the Holy Place and the Holy of Holies. Place the cover over the 34 Ark of the Tokens in the Holy of Holies. Put the table outside the Veil 35 and the lamp-stand at the south side of the Tabernacle, opposite the table which you shall put at the north side. For the entrance of the tent make a 36 screen of finely woven linen, embroidered with violet, purple, and scarlet. Make five posts of acacia-wood for the 37 screen and overlay them with gold; make golden hooks for them and cast five bronze sockets for them.

The altar

Make the altar of acacia-wood; it shall 27 be square, five cubits long by five cubits broad and three cubits high. Let its horns at the four corners be of 2 one piece with it, and overlay it with bronze. Make for it pots to take away 3 the fat and the ashes, with shovels, tossing bowls, forks, and firepans, all of bronze. Make a grating for it of 4 bronze network, and fit four bronze rings on the network at its four corners. Put it below the ledge of the 5 altar, so that the network comes half-way up the altar. Make poles of 6 acacia-wood for the altar and overlay them with bronze. They shall be 7 inserted in the rings at both sides of

r Or copper and so throughout the description of the Tabernacle.   *s Prob. rdg.; Heb. adds* half the *hanging which remains over.*

8 the altar to carry it. Leave the altar a hollow shell. As you were shown on the mountain, so shall it be made.

Court of the Tabernacle

9 Make the court of the Tabernacle. For the one side, the south side facing southwards, the court shall have hangings of finely woven linen a
10 hundred cubits long, with twenty posts and twenty sockets of bronze; the hooks and bands on the posts shall
11 be of silver. Similarly all along the north side there shall be hangings a hundred cubits long, with twenty posts and twenty sockets of bronze; the hooks and bands on the posts shall
12 be of silver. For the breadth of the court, on the west side, there shall be hangings fifty cubits long, with ten
13 posts and ten sockets. On the east side, towards the sunrise, which was
14 fifty cubits, hangings shall extend fifteen cubits from one corner, with
15 three posts and three sockets, and hangings shall extend fifteen cubits from the other corner, with three posts
16 and three sockets. At the gateway of the court, there shall be a screen twenty cubits long of finely woven linen embroidered with violet, purple, and scarlet, with four posts and four
17 sockets. The posts all round the court shall have bands of silver, with hooks
18 of silver, and sockets of bronze. The length of the court shall be a hundred cubits, and the breadth fifty, and the height five cubits, with finely woven linen and bronze sockets throughout.
19 All the equipment needed for serving the Tabernacle, all its pegs and those of the court, shall be of bronze.

Tending the lamp

20 You yourself are to command the Israelites to bring you pure oil of pounded olives ready for the regular
21 mounting of the lamp. In the Tent of the Presence[t] outside the Veil that hides the Tokens, Aaron and his sons shall keep the lamp in trim from dusk to dawn before the LORD. This is a rule binding on their descendants among the Israelites for all time.

The priests' vestments

28 You yourself are to summon to your presence your brother Aaron and his sons out of all the Israelites to serve as my priests: Aaron and his sons Nadab and Abihu, Eleazar and Itha-
2 mar. For your brother Aaron make sacred vestments, to give him dignity and grandeur. Tell all the craftsmen 3 whom I have endowed with skill to make the vestments for the consecration of Aaron as my priest. These are 4 the vestments they shall make: a breast-piece, an ephod, a mantle, a chequered tunic, a turban, and a sash. They shall make sacred vestments for Aaron your brother and his sons to wear when they serve as my priests, using gold; violet, purple, and scarlet 5 yarn; and fine linen.

The ephod shall be made of gold, 6 and with violet, purple, and scarlet yarn, and with finely woven linen worked by a seamster. It shall have two 7 shoulder-pieces joined back and front. The waist-band on it shall be of the 8 same workmanship and material as the fabric of the ephod, and shall be of gold, with violet, purple, and scarlet yarn, and finely woven linen. You 9 shall take two cornelians and engrave on them the names of the sons of Israel: six of their names on the one 10 stone, and the six other names on the second, all in order of seniority. With 11 the skill of a craftsman, a seal-cutter, you shall engrave the two stones with the names of the sons of Israel; you shall set them in gold rosettes, and 12 fasten them on the shoulders of the ephod, as reminders of the sons of Israel. Aaron shall bear their names on his two shoulders as a reminder before the LORD.

Make gold rosettes and two chains 13 14 of pure gold worked into the form of ropes, and fix them on the rosettes. Make the breast-piece of judgement; 15 it shall be made, like the ephod, by a seamster in gold, with violet, purple, and scarlet yarn, and finely woven linen. It shall be a square folded, a 16 span long and a span wide. Set in it 17 four rows of precious stones: the first row, sardin, chrysolite and green fel-spar; the second row, purple gar- 18 net, lapis lazuli and jade; the third 19 row, turquoise, agate and jasper; the 20 fourth row, topaz, cornelian and green jasper, all set in gold rosettes. The 21 stones shall correspond to the twelve sons of Israel name by name; each stone shall bear the name of one of the twelve tribes engraved as on a seal.

Make for the breast-piece chains of 22 pure gold worked into a rope. Make 23 two gold rings, and fix them on the two upper corners of the breast-piece. Fasten the two gold ropes to the two 24 rings at those corners of the breast-piece, and the other ends of the ropes 25

[t] Or Tent of Meeting.

to the two rosettes, thus binding the breast-piece to the shoulder-pieces on
26 the front of the ephod. Make two gold rings and put them at the two lower corners of the breast-piece on the
27 inner side next to the ephod. Make two gold rings and fix them on the two shoulder-pieces of the ephod, low down in front, along its seam above
28 the waist-band of the ephod. Then the breast-piece shall be bound by its rings to the rings of the ephod with violet braid, just above the waist-band of the ephod, so that the breast-piece will not be detached from the ephod.
29 Thus, when Aaron enters the Holy Place, he shall carry over his heart in the breast-piece of judgement the names of the sons of Israel, as a constant reminder before the LORD.
30 Finally, put the Urim and the Thummim into the breast-piece of judgement, and they will be over Aaron's heart when he enters the presence of the LORD. So shall Aaron bear these symbols of judgement upon the sons of Israel over his heart constantly before the LORD.
31 Make the mantle of the ephod a
32 single piece of violet stuff. There shall be a hole for the head in the middle of it. All round the hole there shall be a hem of woven work, with an oversewn edge, so that it cannot be torn.
33 All round its skirts make pomegranates of violet, purple, and scarlet stuff, with golden bells between them,
34 a golden bell and a pomegranate alternately the whole way round the
35 skirts of the mantle. Aaron shall wear it when he ministers, and the sound of it shall be heard when he enters the Holy Place before the LORD and when he comes out; and so he shall not die.
36 Make a rosette of pure gold and engrave on it as on a seal, 'Holy to
37 the LORD'.[u] Fasten it on a violet braid and set it on the very front of
38 the turban. It shall be on Aaron's forehead; he has to bear the blame for shortcomings in the rites with which the Israelites offer their sacred gifts, and the rosette shall be always on his forehead so that they may be acceptable to the LORD.
39 Make the chequered tunic and the turban of fine linen, but the sash of
40 embroidered work. For Aaron's sons make tunics and sashes; and make tall head-dresses to give them dignity
41 and grandeur. With these invest your brother Aaron and his sons, anoint them, install them and consecrate

them; so shall they serve me as priests. Make for them linen drawers 42 reaching to the thighs to cover their private parts; and Aaron and his sons 43 shall wear them when they enter the Tent of the Presence or approach the altar to minister in the Holy Place. Thus they will not incur guilt and die. This is a rule binding on him and his descendants for all time.

Consecration of the priests

In consecrating them to be my priests 29 this is the rite to be observed. Take a young bull and two rams without blemish. Take unleavened loaves, un- 2 leavened cakes mixed with oil, and unleavened wafers smeared with oil, all made of wheaten flour; put them 3 in a single basket and bring them in it. Bring also the bull and the two rams. Bring Aaron and his sons to the 4 entrance of the Tent of the Presence, and wash them with water. Take the 5 vestments and invest Aaron with the tunic, the mantle of the ephod, the ephod itself and the breast-piece, and fasten the ephod to him with its waist-band. Set the turban on his 6 head, and the symbol of holy dedication on the turban. Take the anoint- 7 ing oil, pour it on his head and anoint him. Then bring his sons forward, 8 invest them with tunics, gird them 9 with the sashes and tie their tall head-dresses on them. They shall hold the priesthood by a rule binding for all time.

Next you shall install Aaron and his sons. Bring the bull to the front 10 of the Tent of the Presence, and they shall lay their hands on its head. Slaughter the bull before the LORD 11 at the entrance to the Tent of the Presence. Take some of its blood, and 12 put it with your finger on the horns of the altar. Pour all the rest of it at the base of the altar. Then take the fat 13 covering the entrails, the long lobe of the liver, and the two kidneys with the fat upon them, and burn it on the altar; but the flesh of the bull, and its 14 skin and offal, you shall destroy by fire outside the camp. It is a sin-offering.

Take one of the rams, and Aaron 15 and his sons shall lay their hands on its head. Then slaughter it, take its 16 blood and fling it against the sides of the altar. Cut the ram up; wash its 17 entrails and its shins, lay them with the pieces and the head, and burn the 18 whole ram on the altar: it is a whole-offering to the LORD; it is a soothing odour, a food-offering to the LORD.

19 Take the second ram, and let Aaron and his sons lay their hands on its 20 head. Then slaughter it, take some of its blood, and put it on the lobes of the right ears of Aaron and his sons, and on their right thumbs and big toes. Fling the rest of the blood 21 against the sides of the altar. Take some of the blood which is on the altar and some of the anointing oil, and sprinkle it on Aaron and his vestments, and on his sons and their vestments. So shall he and his vestments, and his sons and their vest- 22 ments become holy. Take the fat from the ram, the fat-tail, the fat covering the entrails, the long lobe of the liver, the two kidneys with the fat upon them, and the right leg: for 23 it is a ram of installation. Take also one round loaf of bread, one cake cooked with oil, and one wafer from the basket of unleavened bread that 24 is before the LORD. Set all these on the hands of Aaron and of his sons and present them as a special gift before 25 the LORD. Then take them out of their hands, and burn them on the altar with the whole-offering for a soothing odour to the LORD: it is a food- 26 offering to the LORD. Take the breast of Aaron's ram of installation, present it as a special gift before the LORD, and it shall be your perquisite.

27 Hallow the breast of the special gift and the leg of the contribution, that which is presented and that which is set aside from the ram of installation, that which is for Aaron and that which 28 is for his sons; and they shall belong to Aaron and his sons, by a rule binding for all time, as a gift from the Israelites, for it is a contribution, set aside from their shared-offerings, their contribution to the LORD.

29 Aaron's sacred vestments shall be kept for the anointing and installa- 30 tion of his sons after him. The priest appointed in his stead from among his sons, the one who enters[v] the Tent of the Presence to minister in the Holy Place, shall wear them for seven days. 31 Take the ram of installation, and 32 boil its flesh in a sacred place; Aaron and his sons shall eat the ram's flesh and the bread left in the basket, at the entrance to the Tent of the Presence. 33 They shall eat the things with which expiation was made at their installa-tion and their consecration. No un-qualified person may eat them, for

they are holy. If any of the flesh of 34 the installation, or any of the bread, is left over till morning, you shall destroy it by fire; it shall not be eaten, for it is holy.

Do this with Aaron and his sons 35 as I have commanded you, spending seven days over their installation.

Offer a bull daily, a sin-offering 36 as expiation for sin; offer the sin-offering on the altar when you make expiation for it, and consecrate it by anointing. For seven days you shall 37 make expiation for the altar, and consecrate it, and it shall be most holy. Whatever touches the altar shall be forfeit as sacred.

Daily sacrifices

This is what you shall offer on the 38 altar: two yearling rams regularly every day. You shall offer the one 39 ram at dawn, and the second between dusk and dark, a tenth of an ephah 40 of flour mixed with a quarter of a hin of pure oil of pounded olives, and a drink-offering of a quarter of a hin of wine for the first ram. You shall offer 41 the second ram between dusk and dark, and with it the same grain-offering and drink-offering as at dawn, for a soothing odour: it is a food-offering to the LORD, a regular whole- 42 offering in every generation; you shall make the offering at the entrance to the Tent of the Presence before the LORD, where I meet you and speak to you. I shall meet the Israelites there, 43 and the place will be hallowed by my glory. I shall hallow the Tent of the 44 Presence and the altar; and Aaron and his sons I shall consecrate to serve me as priests. I shall dwell in 45 the midst of the Israelites, I shall become their God, and by my dwelling 46 among them they will know that I am the LORD their God who brought them out of Egypt. I am the LORD their God.

Altar of incense

Make an altar on which to burn **30** incense; make it of acacia-wood. It 2 shall be square, a cubit long by a cubit broad and two cubits high; the horns of one piece with it. Overlay it 3 with pure gold, the top, the sides all round, and the horns; and put round it a band of gold. Make pairs of gold 4 rings for it; put them under the band at the two corners on both sides to receive the poles by which it is to be carried. Make the poles of acacia-wood 5

v Or when he enters.

6 and overlay them with gold. Put it
7 before the Veil in front of the Ark of
the Tokens where I will meet you. On
it Aaron shall burn fragrant incense;
every morning when he tends the
8 lamps he shall burn the incense, and
when he mounts the lamps between
dusk and dark, he shall burn the
incense; so there shall be a regular
burning of incense before the LORD
9 for all time. You shall not offer on it
any unauthorized incense, nor any
whole-offering or grain-offering; and
you shall not pour a drink-offering
10 over it. Aaron shall make expiation
with blood on its horns once a year;
with blood from the sin-offering of
the yearly Expiation[w] he shall do this
for all time. It is most holy to the
LORD.

Expiation money

11 The LORD spoke to Moses and said:
12 When you number the Israelites for
the purpose of registration, each man
shall give a ransom for his life to the
LORD, to avert plague among them
13 during the registration. As each man
crosses over to those already counted
he shall give half a shekel by the
sacred standard (twenty gerahs to the
shekel) as a contribution to the LORD.
14 Everyone from twenty years old and
upwards who has crossed over to those
already counted shall give a con-
15 tribution to the LORD. The rich man
shall give no more than the half-
shekel, and the poor man shall give
no less, when you give the contribution
to the LORD to make expiation for
16 your lives. The money received from
the Israelites for expiation you shall
apply to the service of the Tent of the
Presence. The expiation for your lives
shall be a reminder of the Israelites
to the LORD.

The bronze basin

17 The LORD spoke to Moses and said:
18 Make a bronze basin for ablution with
its stand of bronze; put it between
the Tent of the Presence and the
19 altar, and fill it with water with which
Aaron and his sons shall wash their
20 hands and feet. When they enter the
Tent of the Presence they shall wash
with water, lest they die. So also when
they approach the altar to minister,
to burn a food-offering to the LORD,
21 they shall wash their hands and feet,
lest they die. It shall be a rule for all
time binding on him and his descendants in every generation.

The anointing oil and the incense

22 The LORD spoke to Moses and said:
23 You yourself shall take spices as
follows: five hundred shekels of sticks
of myrrh, half that amount (two
hundred and fifty shekels) of fragrant
cinnamon, two hundred and fifty
shekels of aromatic cane, five hundred
24 shekels of cassia by the sacred standard, and a hin of olive oil. From
25 these prepare sacred anointing oil,
a perfume compounded by the perfumer's art. This shall be the sacred
anointing oil. Anoint with it the Tent
26 of the Presence and the Ark of the
Tokens, the table and all its vessels,
27 the lamp-stand and its fittings, the
altar of incense, the altar of whole-
28 offering and all its vessels, the basin
and its stand. You shall consecrate
29 them, and they shall be most holy;
whatever touches them shall be forfeit
as sacred. Anoint Aaron and his sons,
30 and consecrate them to be my priests.
Speak to the Israelites and say: This
31 shall be the holy anointing oil for my
service in every generation. It shall
32 not be used for anointing the human
body, and you must not prepare any
oil like it after the same prescription.
It is holy, and you shall treat it as
holy. The man who compounds per-
33 fume like it, or who puts any of it on
any unqualified person, shall be cut
off from his father's kin.

The LORD said to Moses, Take
34 fragrant spices: gum resin,[x] aromatic
shell, galbanum; add pure frankincense to the spices in equal propor-
tions. Make it into incense, perfume
35 made by the perfumer's craft, salted
and pure, a holy thing. Pound some
36 of it into fine powder, and put it in
front of the Tokens in the Tent of the
Presence, where I shall meet you; you
shall treat it as most holy. The incense
37 prepared according to this prescription you shall not make for your own
use. You shall treat it as holy to the
LORD. The man who makes any like
38 it for his own pleasure shall be cut off
from his father's kin.

The master craftsmen

31 The LORD spoke to Moses and said,
2 Mark this: I have specially chosen
Bezalel son of Uri, son of Hur, of the
3 tribe of Judah. I have filled him with
divine spirit, making him skilful and
4 ingenious, expert in every craft, and
a master of design, whether in gold,
5 silver, copper, or cutting stones to be

w Or Atonement.   x Or mastic.

set, or carving wood, for workman-
6 ship of every kind. Further, I have
appointed Aholiab[y] son of Ahisamach
of the tribe of Dan to help him, and I
have endowed every skilled craftsman
with the skill which he has. They shall
make everything that I have com-
7 manded you: the Tent of the Presence,
the Ark for the Tokens, the cover over
it, and all the furnishings of the tent;
8 the table and its vessels, the pure
lamp-stand and all its fittings, the
9 altar of incense, the altar of whole-
offering and all its vessels, the basin
10 and its stand; the stitched vestments,
that is the sacred vestments for
Aaron the priest and the vestments
for his sons when they minister as
11 priests, the anointing oil and the
fragrant incense for the Holy Place.
They shall carry out all I have commanded you.

Sabbath observance

12 The LORD spoke to Moses and said,
13 Speak to the Israelites, you yourself,
and say to them: Above all you shall
observe my sabbaths, for the sabbath
is a sign between me and you in every
generation that you may know that I
14 am the LORD who hallows you. You
shall keep the sabbath, because it is
a holy day for you. If anyone profanes
it he must be put to death. Anyone
who does work on it shall be cut off
15 from his father's kin. Work may be
done on six days, but on the seventh
day there is a sabbath of sacred rest,
holy to the LORD. Whoever does work
on the sabbath day must be put to
16 death. The Israelites shall keep the
sabbath, they shall keep it in every
17 generation as a covenant for ever. It is
a sign for ever between me and the
Israelites, for in six days the LORD
made the heavens and the earth, but
on the seventh day he ceased work
and refreshed himself.

18 When he had finished speaking
with Moses on Mount Sinai, the LORD
gave him the two tablets of the
Tokens, tablets of stone written with
the finger of God.

The golden calf

32 When the people saw that Moses was
so long in coming down from the
mountain, they confronted Aaron and
said to him, 'Come, make us gods to
go ahead of us. As for this fellow
Moses, who brought us up from Egypt,
we do not know what has become of

him.' Aaron answered them, 'Strip 2
the gold rings from the ears of your
wives and daughters, and bring them
to me.' So all the people stripped 3
themselves of their gold earrings
and brought them to Aaron. He took 4
them out of their hands, cast the
metal in a mould, and made it into the
image of a bull-calf. 'These', he said,
'are your gods, O Israel, that brought
you up from Egypt.' Then Aaron was 5
afraid and built an altar in front
of it and issued this proclamation,
'Tomorrow there is to be a pilgrim-
feast to the LORD.' Next day the 6
people rose early, offered whole-
offerings, and brought shared-offerings. After this they sat down to eat
and drink and then gave themselves
up to revelry. But the LORD said to Mo- 7
ses, 'Go down at once, for your people, the people you brought up from
Egypt, have done a disgraceful thing;
so quickly have they turned aside 8
from the way I commanded them.
They have made themselves an image of a bull-calf, they have prostrated themselves before it, sacrificed
to it and said, "These are your gods,
O Israel, that brought you up from
Egypt."' So the LORD said to Moses, 9
'I have considered this people, and
I see that they are a stubborn people.
Now, let me alone to vent my anger 10
upon them, so that I may put an end
to them and make a great nation
spring from you.' But Moses set him- 11
self to placate the LORD his God: 'O
LORD,' he said, 'why shouldst thou
vent thy anger upon thy people,
whom thou didst bring out of Egypt
with great power and a strong hand?
Why let the Egyptians say, "So he 12
meant evil when he took them out,
to kill them in the mountains and
wipe them off the face of the earth"?
Turn from thy anger, and think better
of the evil thou dost intend against
thy people. Remember Abraham, Isaac 13
and Israel, thy servants, to whom
thou didst swear by thy own self:
"I will make your posterity countless as the stars in the sky, and all
this land, of which I have spoken,
I will give to them, and they shall
possess it for ever."' So the LORD 14
relented, and spared his people the
evil with which he had threatened
them.

Moses turned and went down the 15
mountain with the two tablets of the
Tokens in his hands, inscribed on both
sides; on the front and on the back

y Or Oholiab.

16 they were inscribed. The tablets were the handiwork of God, and the writing was God's writing, engraved 17 on the tablets. Joshua, hearing the uproar the people were making, said to Moses, 'Listen! There is fighting in 18 the camp.' Moses replied,

'This is not the clamour of warriors, nor the clamour of a defeated people;
it is the sound of singing that I hear.'

19 As he approached the camp, Moses saw the bull-calf and the dancing, and he was angry; he flung the tablets down, and they were shattered to pieces at the foot of the mountain. 20 Then he took the calf they had made and burnt it; he ground it to powder, sprinkled it on water, and made the 21 Israelites drink it. He demanded of Aaron, 'What did this people do to you that you should have brought 22 such great guilt upon them?' Aaron replied, 'Do not be angry, sir. The people were deeply troubled; that 23 you well know. And they said to me, "Make us gods to go ahead of us, because, as for this fellow Moses, who brought us up from Egypt, we do not 24 know what has become of him." So I said to them, "Those of you who have any gold, strip it off." They gave it me, I threw it in the fire, and out 25 came this bull-calf.' Moses saw that the people were out of control and that Aaron had laid them open to the 26 secret malice of their enemies. He took his place at the gate of the camp and said, 'Who is on the LORD's side? Come here to me'; and the Levites all 27 rallied to him. He said to them, 'These are the words of the LORD the God of Israel: 'Arm yourselves, each of you, with his sword. Go through the camp from gate to gate and back again. Each of you kill his brother, his friend, 28 his neighbour.'' The Levites obeyed, and about three thousand of the peo-29 ple died that day. Moses then said, 'Today you have consecrated yourselves to the LORD completely, because you have turned each against his own son and his own brother and so have this day brought a blessing upon yourselves.'
30 The next day Moses said to the people, 'You have committed a great sin. I shall now go up to the LORD; perhaps I may be able to secure 31 pardon for your sin.' So Moses returned to the LORD and said, 'O hear me! This people has committed a great sin: they have made themselves gods of gold. If thou wilt 32 forgive them, forgive. But if not, blot out my name, I pray, from thy book which thou hast written.' The LORD 33 answered Moses, 'It is the man who has sinned against me that I will blot out from my book. But go now, lead 34 the people to the place which I have told you of. My angel shall go ahead of you, but a day will come when I shall punish them for their sin.' And 35 the LORD smote the people for worshipping the bull-calf which Aaron had made.

Onwards to Canaan

The LORD spoke to Moses: 'Come, go 33 up from here, you and the people you have brought up from Egypt, to the land which I swore to Abraham, Isaac, and Jacob that I would give to their posterity. I will send an angel 2 ahead of you, and will drive out the Canaanites, the Amorites and the Hittites and the Perizzites, the Hivites and the Jebusites. I will bring you to 3 a land flowing with milk and honey, but I will not journey in your company, for fear that I annihilate you on the way; for you are a stubborn people.' When the people heard this 4 harsh sentence they went about like mourners, and no man put on his ornaments. The LORD said to Moses, 5 'Tell the Israelites, "You are a stubborn people: at any moment, if I journey in your company, I may annihilate you. Put away your ornaments now, and I will determine what to do to you."' And so the Is-6 raelites stripped off their ornaments, and wore them no more from Mount Horeb onwards.

The Tent of the Presence

Moses used to take a[z] tent and pitch it 7 at a distance outside the camp. He called it the Tent of the Presence, and everyone who sought the LORD would go out to the Tent of the Presence outside the camp. Whenever Moses went 8 out to the tent, all the people would rise and stand, each at the entrance to his tent, and follow Moses with their eyes until he entered the tent. When Moses entered it, the pillar of 9 cloud came down, and stayed at the entrance to the tent while the LORD spoke with Moses. As soon as the 10 people saw the pillar of cloud standing at the entrance to the tent, they would all prostrate themselves, every man

z Or the.

11 at the entrance to his tent. The LORD would speak with Moses face to face, as one man speaks to another. Then Moses would return to the camp, but his young assistant, Joshua son of Nun, never moved from inside the tent.

The LORD's promise

12 Moses said to the LORD, 'Thou bidst me lead this people up, but thou hast not told me whom thou wilt send with me. Thou hast said to me, "I know you by name, and, further, you have 13 found favour with me." If I have indeed won thy favour, then teach me to know thy way, so that I can know thee and continue in favour with thee, for this nation is thy own people.'
14 The LORD answered, 'I will go with you in person and set your mind at 15 rest.' Moses said to him, 'Indeed if thou dost not go in person, do not send 16 us up from here; for how can it ever be known that I and thy people have found favour with thee, except by thy going with us? So shall we be distinct, I and thy people, from all the peoples 17 on earth.' The LORD said to Moses, 'I will do this thing that you have asked, because you have found favour with me, and I know you by name.'
18   And Moses prayed, 'Show me thy 19 glory.' The LORD answered, 'I will make all my goodness*a* pass before you, and I will pronounce in your hearing the Name JEHOVAH.*b* I will be gracious to whom I will be gracious, and I will have compassion on whom 20 I will have compassion.' But he added, 'My face you cannot see, for no mortal man may see me and live.'
21 The LORD said, 'Here is a place beside me. Take your stand on the 22 rock and when my glory passes by, I will put you in a crevice of the rock and cover you with my hand until I 23 have passed by. Then I will take away my hand, and you shall see my back, but my face shall not be seen.'

The Covenant

34 The LORD said to Moses, 'Cut two stone tablets like the first, and I will write on the tablets the words which were on the first tablets, which you 2 broke in pieces. Be ready by morning. Then in the morning go up Mount Sinai; stand and wait for me there on 3 the top. No man shall go up with you, no man shall even be seen anywhere on the mountain, nor shall flocks or herds

graze within sight of that mountain.'
So Moses cut two stone tablets like 4 the first, and he rose early in the morning and went up Mount Sinai as the LORD had commanded him, taking the two stone tablets in his hands. And the LORD came down in the 5 cloud and took his place beside him and pronounced the Name JEHOVAH. Then the LORD passed in front of 6 him and called aloud, 'JEHOVAH, the LORD, a god compassionate and gracious, long-suffering, ever constant and true, maintaining constancy to 7 thousands, forgiving iniquity, rebellion, and sin, and not sweeping the guilty clean away; but one who punishes sons and grandsons to the third and fourth generation for the iniquity of their fathers!' Moses made 8 haste, bowed to the ground and prostrated himself. He said, 'If I have 9 indeed won thy favour, O Lord, then may the Lord go in our company. However stubborn a people they are, forgive our iniquity and our sin and take us as thy own possession.'
The LORD said, Here and now I 10 make a covenant. In full view of all your people I will do such miracles as have never been performed in all the world or in any nation. All the surrounding peoples shall see the work of the LORD, for fearful is that which I will do for you.*c* Observe all I com- 11 mand you this day; and I for my part will drive out before you the Amorites and the Canaanites and the Hittites and the Perizzites and the Hivites and the Jebusites. Be careful not to make 12 a covenant with the natives of the land against which you are going, or they will prove a snare in your midst. No: you shall demolish their 13 altars, smash their sacred pillars and cut down their sacred poles. You shall 14 not prostrate yourselves to any other god. For the LORD's name is the Jealous God, and a jealous god he is. Be careful not to make a covenant 15 with the natives of the land, or, when they go wantonly after their gods and sacrifice to them, you may be invited, any one of you, to partake of their sacrifices, and marry your sons to their 16 daughters, and when their daughters go wantonly after their gods, they may lead your sons astray too.
You shall not make yourselves gods 17 of cast metal.
You shall observe the pilgrim-feast 18 of Unleavened Bread: for seven days,

a Or character.   *b See note on 3. 15.*   *c* for fearful . . . for you: *or* (for he is to be feared) which I will do for you.

as I have commanded you, you shall eat unleavened cakes at the appointed time, in the month of Abib, because in the month of Abib you went out from Egypt.

19 Every first birth of the womb belongs to me, and the males of all your herds, both cattle and sheep.

20 You may buy back the first birth of an ass by giving a sheep instead, but if you do not buy it, you must break its neck. You shall buy back all the first-born of your sons, and no one shall come into my presence empty-handed.

21 For six days you shall work, but on the seventh day you shall cease work; even at ploughing time and harvest you shall cease work.

22 You shall observe the pilgrim-feast of Weeks, the firstfruits of the wheat harvest, and the pilgrim-feast of Ingathering at the turn of the year.

23 Three times a year all your males shall come into the presence of the Lord,

24 the LORD the God of Israel; for after I have driven out the nations before you and extended your frontiers, there will be no danger from covetous neighbours when you go up these three times to enter the presence of the LORD your God.

25 You shall not offer the blood of my sacrifice at the same time as anything leavened, nor shall any portion of the victim of the pilgrim-feast of Passover remain overnight till morning.

26 You shall bring the choicest first-fruits of your soil to the house of the LORD your God.

You shall not boil a kid in its mother's milk.

Moses descends from Mount Sinai

27 The LORD said to Moses, 'Write these words down, because the covenant I make with you and with Israel is in

28 these words.' So Moses stayed there with the LORD forty days and forty nights, neither eating nor drinking, and wrote down the words of the covenant, the Ten Words,[d] on the

29 tablets. At length Moses came down from Mount Sinai with the two stone tablets of the Tokens in his hands, and when he descended, he did not know that the skin of his face shone because he had been speaking with the

30 LORD. When Aaron and the Israelites saw how the skin of Moses' face shone, they were afraid to approach him.

31 He called out to them, and Aaron and all the chiefs in the congregation

turned towards him. Moses spoke to them, and afterwards all the Israelites 32 drew near. He gave them all the commands with which the LORD had charged him on Mount Sinai, and 33 finished what he had to say.

Then Moses put a veil over his face, and whenever he went in before the 34 LORD to speak with him, he removed the veil until he came out. Then he would go out and tell the Israelites all the commands he had received. When- 35 ever the skin of Moses' face shone in the sight of the Israelites, he would put the veil back over his face until he went in again to speak with the LORD.

Commands for the sabbath

Moses called the whole community of 35 Israelites together and thus addressed them: These are the LORD's commands to you: On six days you may 2 work, but the seventh you are to keep as a sabbath of sacred rest, holy to the LORD. Whoever works on that day shall be put to death. You are not 3 even to light your fire at home on the sabbath day.

Commands for the Tabernacle

These words Moses spoke to all the 4 community of Israelites: This is the command the LORD has given: Each 5 of you set aside a contribution to the LORD. Let all who wish, bring a contribution to the LORD: gold, silver, copper; violet, purple, and 6 scarlet yarn; fine linen and goats' hair; tanned rams' skins, porpoise- 7 hides, and acacia-wood; oil for the 8 lamp, perfume for the anointing oil and for the fragrant incense; corne- 9 lians and other stones ready for setting in the ephod and the breast-piece. Let every craftsman among 10 you come and make everything the LORD has commanded. The Taber- 11 nacle, its tent and covering, fasteners, planks, bars, posts, and sockets, the 12 Ark and its poles, the cover and the Veil of the screen, the table, its poles, 13 and all its vessels, and the Bread of the Presence, the lamp-stand for the 14 light, its fittings, lamps and the lamp oil; the altar of incense and its poles, 15 the anointing oil, the fragrant incense, and the screen for the entrance of the Tabernacle, the altar of whole- 16 offering, its bronze grating, poles, and all appurtenances, the basin and its 17 stand; the hangings of the court, its posts and sockets, and the screen for the gateway of the court; the pegs of 18

d Or Ten Commandments.

19 the Tabernacle and court and their cords, the stitched vestments for ministering in the Holy Place, that is the sacred vestments for Aaron the priest and the vestments for his sons when they minister as priests.

The people bring their offerings

20 The whole community of the Israelites went out from Moses' presence,
21 and everyone who was so minded brought of his own free will a contribution to the LORD for the making of the Tent of the Presence and all its service, and for the sacred vestments.
22 Men and women alike came and freely brought clasps, earrings, finger-rings, and pendants, gold ornaments of every kind, every one of them presenting a special gift of gold to the LORD.
23 And every man brought what he possessed of violet, purple, and scarlet yarn, fine linen and goats' hair, tanned rams' skins and porpoise-
24 hides. Every man, setting aside a contribution of silver or copper, brought it as a contribution to the LORD, and all who had acacia-wood suitable for any part of the work brought it.
25 Every woman with the skill spun and brought the violet, purple, and
26 scarlet yarn, and fine linen. All the women whose skill moved them spun
27 the goats' hair. The chiefs brought cornelians and other stones ready for setting in the ephod and the breast-
28 piece, the perfume and oil for the light, for the anointing oil, and for the
29 fragrant incense. Every Israelite man and woman who was minded to bring offerings to the LORD for all the work which he had commanded through Moses did so freely.

The craftsmen receive the contributions

30 Moses said to the Israelites, 'Mark this: the LORD has specially chosen Bezalel son of Uri, son of Hur, of
31 the tribe of Judah. He has filled him with divine spirit, making him skilful and ingenious, expert in every craft,
32 and a master of design, whether in
33 gold, silver, and copper, or cutting precious stones for setting, or carving
34 wood, in every kind of design. He has inspired both him and Aholiab son of Ahisamach of the tribe of Dan
35 to instruct workers and designers of every kind, engravers, seamsters, embroiderers in violet, purple, and scarlet yarn and fine linen, and weavers, fully endowing them with skill to
36 execute all kinds of work. Bezalel and

Aholiab shall work exactly as the LORD has commanded, and so also shall every craftsman whom the LORD has made skilful and ingenious in these matters, to know how to execute every kind of work for the service of the sanctuary.'

2 Moses summoned Bezalel, Aholiab, and every craftsman to whom the LORD had given skill and who was willing, to come forward and set to
3 work. They received from Moses every contribution which the Israelites had brought for the work of the service of the sanctuary, but the people still brought freewill offerings morning
4 after morning, so that the craftsmen at work on the sanctuary left what they were doing, every one of them,
5 and came to Moses and said, 'The people are bringing much more than we need for doing the work which the LORD has commanded.' So Moses sent
6 word round the camp that no man or woman should prepare anything more as a contribution for the sanctuary. So the people stopped bringing gifts;
7 what was there already was more than enough for all the work they had to do.

Making the Tabernacle

8 Then all the craftsmen among the workers made the Tabernacle of ten hangings of finely woven linen, and violet, purple, and scarlet yarn, with cherubim worked on them, all made by a seamster. The length of each hang-
9 ing was twenty-eight cubits and the breadth four cubits, all of the same size. They joined five of the hang-
10 ings together, and similarly the other five. They made violet loops on the
11 outer edge of the one set of hangings and they did the same for the outer edge of the other set of hangings.
12 They made fifty loops for each hanging; they made also fifty loops for the end hanging in the second set, the
13 loops being opposite each other. They made fifty gold fasteners, with which they joined the hangings one to another, and the Tabernacle became a single whole.

14 They made hangings of goats' hair, eleven in all, to form a tent over the
15 Tabernacle; each hanging was thirty cubits long and four cubits wide, all
16 eleven of the same size. They joined five of the hangings together, and
17 similarly the other six. They made fifty loops on the edge of the outer hanging in the first set and fifty loops on the joining edge of the second set,

18 and fifty bronze fasteners to join up the tent and make it a single whole.
19 They made for the tent a cover of tanned rams' skins and an outer covering of porpoise-hides.
20 They made for the Tabernacle planks of acacia-wood as uprights,
21 each plank ten cubits long and a cubit
22 and a half wide, and two tenons for each plank joined to each other. They did the same for all the planks of the
23 Tabernacle. They arranged the planks thus: twenty planks for the south
24 side, facing southwards, with forty silver sockets under them, two sockets under each plank for its two tenons;
25 and for the second or northern side
26 of the Tabernacle twenty planks with forty silver sockets, two under each
27 plank. They made six planks for the far end of the Tabernacle on the west.
28 They made two planks for the corners
29 of the Tabernacle at the far end; at the bottom they were alike, and at the top, both alike, they fitted into a single ring. They did the same for both of them at the two corners.
30 There were eight planks with their silver sockets, sixteen sockets in all, two sockets under each plank.
31 They made bars of acacia-wood: five for the planks on the one side
32 of the Tabernacle, five bars for the planks on the second side of the Tabernacle, and five bars for the planks on the far end of the Tabernacle on
33 the west. They made the middle bar to run along from end to end half-way
34 up the frames. They overlaid the frames with gold, made rings of gold on them to hold the bars and plated the bars with gold.
35 They made the Veil of finely woven linen and violet, purple, and scarlet yarn, with cherubim worked on it,
36 all made by a seamster. And they made for it four posts of acacia-wood overlaid with gold, with gold hooks, and cast four silver sockets for them.
37 For the entrance of the tent a screen of finely woven linen was made, embroidered with violet, purple, and
38 scarlet, and five posts of acacia-wood with their hooks. They overlaid the tops of the posts and the bands round them with gold; the five sockets for them were of bronze.

Making the Ark

37 Bezalel then made the Ark, a chest of acacia-wood, two and a half cubits long, one cubit and a half wide, and
2 one cubit and a half high. He overlaid it with pure gold, both inside and

out, and put a band of gold all round it. He cast four gold rings to be on its 3 four feet, two rings on each side of it. He made poles of acacia-wood and 4 plated them with gold, and inserted 5 the poles in the rings at the sides of the Ark to lift it. He made a cover of 6 pure gold, two and a half cubits long and one cubit and a half wide. He 7 made two gold cherubim of beaten work at the ends of the cover, one at 8 each end; he made each cherub of one piece with the cover. They had 9 wings outspread and pointing upwards, screening the cover with their wings; they stood face to face, looking inwards over the cover.

Making the table

He made the table of acacia-wood, 10 two cubits long, one cubit wide, and one cubit and a half high. He over- 11 laid it with pure gold and put a band of gold all round it. He made a rim 12 round it a hand's breadth wide, and a gold band round the rim. He cast 13 four gold rings for it, and put the rings at the four corners by the four legs. The rings, which were to receive 14 the poles for carrying the table, were close to the rim. These carrying-poles 15 he made of acacia-wood and plated them with gold. He made the vessels 16 for the table, its dishes and saucers, and its flagons and bowls from which drink-offerings were to be poured; he made them of pure gold.

Making the lamp-stand

He made the lamp-stand of pure gold. 17 The lamp-stand, stem, and branches, were of beaten work, its cups, both calyxes and petals, were of one piece with it. There were six branches spring- 18 ing from its sides; three branches of the lamp-stand sprang from one side and three branches from the other side. There were three cups shaped 19 like almond blossoms, with calyx and petals, on the first branch, three cups shaped like almond blossoms, with calyx and petals, on the next branch, and similarly for all six branches springing from the lamp-stand. On 20 the main stem of the lamp-stand there were four cups shaped like almond blossoms, with calyx and petals, and 21 there were calyxes of one piece with it under the six branches which sprang from the lamp-stand, a single calyx under each pair of branches. The calyxes and the branches were of 22 one piece with it, all a single piece of beaten work of pure gold. He made 23

its seven lamps, its tongs and fire-
24 pans of pure gold. The lamp-stand
and all these fittings were made from
one talent of pure gold.

Making the altar of incense

25 He made the altar of incense of
acacia-wood, square, a cubit long by
a cubit broad and two cubits high,
26 the horns of one piece with it. He
overlaid it with pure gold, the top,
the sides all round, and the horns, and
27 he put round it a band of gold. He
made pairs of gold rings for it; he put
them under the band at the two
corners on both sides to receive the
poles by which it was to be carried.
28 He made the poles of acacia-wood
and overlaid them with gold.

Making the anointing oil and the incense

29 He prepared the sacred anointing oil
and the fragrant incense, pure, compounded by the perfumer's art.

Making the altar of whole-offering

38 He made the altar of whole-offering
of acacia-wood, square, five cubits
long by five cubits broad and three
2 cubits high. Its horns at the four
corners were of one piece with it, and
3 he overlaid it with bronze. He made
all the vessels for the altar, its pots,
shovels, tossing bowls, forks, and fire-
4 pans, all of bronze. He made for the
altar a grating of bronze network
under the ledge, coming half-way up.
5 He cast four rings for the four corners
of the bronze grating to receive the
6 poles, and he made the poles of
acacia-wood and overlaid them with
7 bronze. He inserted the poles in the
rings at the sides of the altar to carry
it. He left the altar a hollow shell.

Making the bronze basin

8 The basin and its stand of bronze he
made out of the bronze mirrors of
the women who were on duty at the
entrance to the Tent of the Presence.

Court of the Tabernacle

9 He made the court. For the south side
facing southwards the hangings of
the court were of finely woven linen
10 a hundred cubits long, with twenty
posts and twenty sockets of bronze;
the hooks and bands on the posts were
11 of silver. Along the north side there
were hangings of a hundred cubits,

with twenty posts and twenty sockets
of bronze; the hooks and bands on
the posts were of silver. On the west 12
side there were hangings fifty cubits long, with ten posts and ten
sockets; the hooks and bands on
the posts were of silver. On the east 13
side, towards the sunrise, fifty cubits,
there were hangings on either side 14–15
of the gateway of the court; they
extended fifteen cubits to one corner,
with their three posts and their three
sockets, and fifteen cubits to the
second corner, with their three posts
and their three sockets. The hangings 16
of the court all round were of finely
woven linen. The sockets for the posts 17
were of bronze, the hooks and bands
on the posts of silver, the tops of them
overlaid with silver, and all the posts
of the court were bound with silver.
The screen at the gateway of the 18
court was of finely woven linen,
embroidered with violet, purple, and
scarlet, twenty cubits long and five
cubits high to correspond to the hangings of the court, with four posts and 19
four sockets of bronze, their hooks of
silver, and the tops of them and their
bands overlaid with silver. All the 20
pegs for the Tabernacle and those for
the court were of bronze.

These were the appointments of the 21
Tabernacle, that is the Tabernacle of
the Tokens which was assigned by
Moses to the charge of the Levites
under Ithamar son of Aaron the priest.
Bezalel son of Uri, son of Hur, of the 22
tribe of Judah made everything the
LORD had commanded Moses. He was 23
assisted by Aholiab son of Ahisamach
of the tribe of Dan, an engraver, a
seamster, and an embroiderer in fine
linen with violet, purple, and scarlet
yarn.

Metals for the sanctuary

The gold of the special gift used for 24
the work of the sanctuary amounted
in all to twenty-nine talents seven
hundred and thirty shekels, by the
sacred standard. The silver contributed 25
by the community when registered
was one hundred talents one thousand seven hundred and seventy-five
shekels, by the sacred standard.

This amounted to a beka a head, 26
that is half a shekel by the sacred
standard, for every man from twenty
years old and upwards, who had been
registered, a total of six hundred and
three thousand five hundred and fifty
men. The hundred talents of silver 27
were for casting the sockets for the

sanctuary and for the Veil, a hundred sockets to a hundred talents,
28 a talent to a socket. With the one thousand seven hundred and seventy-five shekels he made hooks for the posts, overlaid the tops of the posts
29 and put bands round them. The bronze of the special gift came to seventy talents two thousand four
30 hundred shekels; with this he made sockets for the entrance to the Tent of the Presence, the bronze altar and its bronze grating, all the vessels for
31 the altar, the sockets all round the court, the sockets for the posts at the gateway of the court, all the pegs for the Tabernacle, and the pegs all round the court.

Making the priests' vestments

39 They used violet, purple, and scarlet yarn in making the stitched vestments for ministering in the sanctuary and in making the sacred vestments for Aaron, as the LORD had commanded Moses.
2 They made the ephod of gold, with violet, purple, and scarlet yarn, and
3 finely woven linen. The gold was beaten into thin plates, cut and twisted into braid to be worked in by a seamster with the violet, purple,
4 and scarlet yarn, and fine linen. They made shoulder-pieces for it, joined
5 back and front. The waist-band on it was of the same workmanship and material as the fabric of the ephod; it was gold, with violet, purple, and scarlet yarn, and finely woven linen, as the LORD commanded Moses.
6 They prepared the cornelians, fixed in gold rosettes, engraved by the art of a seal-cutter with the names of
7 the sons of Israel, and fastened them on the shoulders of the ephod as reminders of the sons of Israel, as the LORD had commanded Moses.
8 They made the breast-piece; it was worked like the ephod by a seamster, in gold, with violet, purple, and scarlet yarn, and finely woven linen.
9 They made the breast-piece square, folded, a span long and a span wide.
10 They set in it four rows of precious stones: the first row, sardin, chrysolite
11 and green felspar; the second row, purple garnet, lapis lazuli and jade;
12 the third row, turquoise, agate and
13 jasper; the fourth row, topaz, cornelian and green jasper, all set in gold
14 rosettes. The stones corresponded to the twelve sons of Israel, name by name, each bearing the name of one of the twelve tribes engraved as on a seal. They made for the breast-15 piece twisted cords of pure gold worked into a rope. They made two 16 gold rosettes and two gold rings, and they fixed the two rings on the two corners of the breast-piece. They 17 fastened the two gold ropes to the two rings at those corners of the breast-piece, and the other ends of 18 the two ropes to the two rosettes, thus binding them to the shoulder-pieces on the front of the ephod. They 19 made two gold rings and put them at the two corners of the breast-piece on the inner side next to the ephod. They made two gold rings and fixed 20 them on the two shoulder-pieces of the ephod, low down and in front, close to its seam above the waist-band on the ephod. They bound the 21 breast-piece by its rings to the rings of the ephod with a violet braid, just above the waist-band on the ephod, so that the breast-piece would not become detached from the ephod; so the LORD had commanded Moses. They made the mantle of the ephod a 22 single piece of woven violet stuff, with 23 a hole in the middle of it which had a hem round it, with an oversewn edge so that it could not be torn. All round 24 its skirts they made pomegranates of violet, purple, and scarlet stuff, and finely woven linen. They made 25 bells of pure gold and put them all round the skirts of the mantle between the pomegranates, a bell and a pome-26 granate alternately the whole way round the skirts of the mantle, to be worn when ministering, as the LORD commanded Moses.

They made the tunics of fine linen, 27 woven work, for Aaron and his sons, the turban of fine linen, the tall head-28 dresses and their bands all of fine linen, the drawers of finely woven linen, and the sash of finely woven linen, 29 embroidered in violet, purple, and scarlet, as the LORD had commanded Moses.

They made a rosette of pure gold as 30 the symbol of their holy dedication and inscribed on it as the engraving on a seal, 'Holy to the LORD',*e* and 31 they fastened on it a violet braid to fix it on the turban at the top, as the LORD had commanded Moses.

The Tabernacle completed

Thus all the work of the Tabernacle 32 of the Tent of the Presence was completed, and the Israelites did

e on it ... LORD: *or* 'JEHOVAH' on it in sacred characters as engraved on a seal.

everything exactly as the LORD had
33 commanded Moses. They brought the
Tabernacle to Moses, the tent and all
its furnishings, its fasteners, planks,
34 bars, posts and sockets, the covering
of tanned rams' skins and the outer
covering of porpoise-hides, the Veil of
35 the screen, the Ark of the Tokens and
36 its poles, the cover, the table and its
vessels, and the Bread of the Presence,
37 the pure lamp-stand with its lamps
in a row and all its fittings, and the
38 lamp oil, the gold altar, the anointing oil, the fragrant incense, and the
screen at the entrance of the tent,
39 the bronze altar, the bronze grating
attached to it, its poles and all its
furnishings, the basin and its stand,
40 the hangings of the court, its posts and
sockets, the screen for the gateway
of the court, its cords and pegs, and
all the equipment for the service of
the Tabernacle for the Tent of the
41 Presence, the stitched vestments for
ministering in the sanctuary, that is
the sacred vestments for Aaron the
priest and the vestments for his sons
42 when they minister as priests. As the
LORD had commanded Moses, so the
Israelites carried out the whole work.
43 Moses inspected all the work, and
saw that they had carried it out
according to the command of the
LORD; and he blessed them.

The Tabernacle consecrated

40 The LORD spoke to Moses and said:
2 On the first day of the first month you
shall set up the Tabernacle, the Tent
3 of the Presence. You shall put the Ark
of the Tokens in it and screen the Ark
4 with the Veil. You shall bring in the
table and lay it; then you shall bring
in the lamp-stand and mount its
5 lamps. You shall then set the gold
altar of incense in front of the Ark of
the Tokens and put the screen of the
entrance of the Tabernacle in place.
6 You shall put the altar of whole-
offering in front of the entrance of
the Tabernacle, the Tent of the
7 Presence. You shall put the basin
between the Tent of the Presence and
8 the altar and put water in it. You
shall set up the court all round and
put in place the screen of the gate-
9 way of the court. You shall take the
anointing oil and anoint the Tabernacle and everything in it; thus you
shall consecrate it and all its furnish-
10 ings, and it shall be holy. You shall
anoint the altar of whole-offering and
all its vessels; thus shall you consecrate it, and it shall be most holy.

You shall anoint the basin and its 11
stand and consecrate it. You shall 12
bring Aaron and his sons to the
entrance of the Tent of the Presence
and wash them with the water. Then 13
you shall clothe Aaron with the sacred
vestments, anoint him and consecrate
him; so shall he be my priest. You 14
shall then bring forward his sons,
clothe them in tunics, anoint them 15
as you anointed their father, and they
shall be my priests. Their anointing
shall inaugurate a hereditary priesthood for all time.

Exactly as the LORD had com- 16
manded him, so Moses did. In the first 17
month of the second year, on the first
day of that month, the Tabernacle
was set up.

Moses set up the Tabernacle. He 18
put the sockets in place, inserted the
planks, fixed the crossbars and set up
the posts. He spread the tent over the 19
Tabernacle and fixed the covering of
the tent above it, as the LORD had
commanded him. He took the Tokens 20
and put them in the Ark, inserted
the poles in the Ark, and put the
cover over the top of the Ark. He 21
brought the Ark into the Tabernacle,
set up the Veil of the screen and so
screened the Ark of the Tokens, as
the LORD had commanded him. He 22
put the table in the Tent of the
Presence on the north side of the
Tabernacle outside the Veil and 23
arranged bread on it before the LORD,
as the LORD had commanded him.
He set the lamp-stand in the Tent of 24
the Presence opposite the table at the
south side of the Tabernacle and 25
mounted the lamps before the LORD,
as the LORD had commanded him.
He set up the gold altar in the Tent of 26
the Presence in front of the Veil and 27
burnt fragrant incense on it, as the
LORD had commanded him. He set up 28
the screen at the entrance of the
Tabernacle, fixed the altar of whole-
offering at the entrance of the
Tabernacle, the Tent of the Presence,
and offered on it whole-offerings and
grain-offerings, as the LORD had commanded him. He set up the basin 30
between the Tent of the Presence and
the altar and put water there for
washing, and Moses and Aaron and 31
his sons used to wash their hands and
feet when they entered the Tent of 32
the Presence or approached the altar,
as the LORD had commanded Moses.
He set up the court all round the 33
Tabernacle and the altar, and put a
screen at the gateway of the court.

The cloud over the Tabernacle

34 Thus Moses completed the work, and the cloud covered the Tent of the Presence, and the glory of the LORD
35 filled the Tabernacle. Moses was unable to enter the Tent of the Presence, because the cloud had settled on it and the glory of the LORD filled the
36 Tabernacle. At every stage of their journey, when the cloud lifted from the Tabernacle, the Israelites broke camp;
37 but if the cloud did not lift from the Tabernacle, they did not break camp until the day it lifted. For the cloud of
38 the LORD hovered over the Tabernacle by day, and there was fire in the cloud by night, and the Israelites could see it at every stage of their journey.

LEVITICUS

Whole-offerings

1 THE LORD SUMMONED MOSES and spoke to him from the
2 Tent of the Presence, and said, Say this to the Israelites: When any man among you presents an animal as an offering to the LORD, the offering may be presented either from the herd or from the flock.
3 If his offering is a whole-offering from the cattle, he shall present a male without blemish; he shall present it at the entrance to the Tent of the Presence before the LORD so as to
4 secure acceptance for himself. He shall lay his hand on the head of the victim and it will be accepted on his behalf[a]
5 to make expiation for him. He shall slaughter the bull before the LORD, and the Aaronite priests shall present the blood and fling it against the altar all round at the entrance of the Tent
6 of the Presence. He shall then flay the
7 victim and cut it up. The sons of Aaron the priest shall kindle a fire on the altar and arrange wood on the
8 fire. The Aaronite priests shall arrange the pieces, including the head and the suet, on the wood on the altar-fire,
9 the entrails and shins shall be washed in water, and the priest shall burn it all on the altar as a whole-offering, a food-offering of soothing odour to the LORD.
10 If the man's whole-offering is from the flock, either from the rams or from the goats, he shall present a
11 male without blemish. He shall slaughter it before the LORD at the north side of the altar, and the Aaronite priests shall fling the blood
12 against the altar all round. He shall cut it up, and the priest shall arrange the pieces, together with the head and the suet, on the wood on the altar-fire,
13 the entrails and shins shall be washed in water, and the priest shall present and burn it all on the altar: it is a whole-offering, a food-offering of soothing odour to the LORD.
14 If a man's offering to the LORD is a whole-offering of birds, he shall present turtle-doves or young pigeons
15 as his offering. The priest shall present it at the altar, and shall wrench off the head and burn it on the altar; and the blood shall be drained out
16 against the side of the altar. He shall take away the crop and its contents in one piece, and throw it to the east side of the altar where the ashes are.
17 He shall tear it by its wings without severing them completely, and shall burn it on the altar, on top of the wood of the altar-fire: it is a whole-offering, a food-offering of soothing odour to the LORD.

Grain-offerings

2 When any person presents a grain-offering to the LORD, his offering shall be of flour. He shall pour oil on it and
2 add frankincense to it. He shall bring it to the Aaronite priests, one of whom shall scoop up a handful of the flour and oil with all the frankincense. The priest shall burn this as a token on the altar, a food-offering of soothing odour to the LORD. The remainder of
3 the grain-offering belongs to Aaron and his sons: it is most sacred, it is taken from the food-offerings of the LORD.
4 When you present as a grain-offering something baked in an oven,

a Or by him (the LORD).

it shall consist of unleavened cakes of flour mixed with oil and unleavened 5 wafers smeared with oil. If your offering is a grain-offering cooked on a griddle, it shall be an unleavened 6 cake of flour mixed with oil. Crumble it in pieces and pour oil on it. This is a grain-offering. 7 If your offering is a grain-offering cooked in a pan, it shall be made of 8 flour with oil. Bring an offering made up in this way to the LORD and present it to the priest, who shall bring it to 9 the altar; then he shall set aside part of the grain-offering as a token and burn it on the altar, a food-offering 10 of soothing odour to the LORD. The remainder of the grain-offering belongs to Aaron and his sons: it is most sacred, it is taken from the food-offerings of the LORD. 11 No grain-offering which you present to the LORD shall be made of anything that ferments; you shall not burn any leaven or any honey as 12 a food-offering to the LORD. As for your offering of firstfruits, you shall present them to the LORD, but they shall not be offered up at the altar as 13 a soothing odour. Every offering of yours which is a grain-offering shall be salted; you shall not fail to put the salt of your covenant with God on your grain-offering. Salt shall accompany all offerings. 14 If you present to the LORD a grain-offering of first-ripe grain, you must present fresh corn roasted, crushed 15 meal from fully ripened corn. You shall add oil to it and put frankincense 16 upon it. This is a grain-offering. The priest shall burn as its token some of the crushed meal, some of the oil, and all the frankincense as a food-offering to the LORD.

Shared-offerings

3 If a man's offering is a shared-offering from the cattle, male or female, he shall present it without 2 blemish before the LORD. He shall lay his hand on the head of the victim and slaughter it at the entrance to the Tent of the Presence. The Aaronite priests shall fling the blood against the 3 altar all round. One of them shall present part of the shared-offering as a food-offering to the LORD: he shall remove the fat covering the entrails 4 and all the fat upon the entrails, the two kidneys with the fat on them beside the haunches, and the long lobe of the liver with the kidneys.

The Aaronites shall burn it on the 5 altar on top of the whole-offering which is upon the wood on the fire, a food-offering of soothing odour to the LORD.

If a man's offering as a shared- 6 offering to the LORD is from the flock, male or female, he shall present it without blemish. If he is presenting a 7 ram as his offering, he shall present it before the LORD, lay his hand on the 8 head of the victim and slaughter it in front of the Tent of the Presence. The Aaronites shall then fling its blood 9 against the altar all round. He shall present part of the shared-offering as a food-offering to the LORD; he shall remove its fat, the entire fat-tail cut off close by the spine, the fat covering the entrails and all the fat upon the entrails, the two kidneys with the 10 fat on them beside the haunches, and the long lobe of the liver with the kidneys. The priest shall burn it at 11 the altar, as food offered to the LORD.

If the man's offering is a goat, he 12 shall present it before the LORD, lay 13 his hand on its head and slaughter it in front of the Tent of the Presence. The Aaronites shall then fling its blood against the altar all round. He 14 shall present part of the victim as a food-offering to the LORD; he shall remove the fat covering the entrails and all the fat upon the entrails, the 15 two kidneys with the fat on them beside the haunches, and the long lobe of the liver with the kidneys. The 16 priest shall burn this at the altar, as a food-offering of soothing odour. All fat belongs to the LORD. This is a rule 17 for all time from generation to generation wherever you live: you shall not eat any fat or any blood.

Sin-offerings

The LORD spoke to Moses and said, 4 Say this to the Israelites: These are 2 the rules for any man who inadvertently transgresses any of the commandments of the LORD and does anything prohibited by them:

If the anointed priest sins so as to 3 bring guilt on the people, for the sin he has committed he shall present to the LORD a young bull without blemish as a sin-offering. He shall bring the 4 bull to the entrance of the Tent of the Presence before the LORD, lay his hand on its head and slaughter it before the LORD. The anointed 5 priest shall then take some of its blood and bring it to the Tent of the

6 Presence. He shall dip his finger in the blood and sprinkle some of the blood in front of the sacred Veil 7 seven times before the LORD. The priest shall then put some of the blood before the LORD in the Tent of the Presence on the horns of the altar where fragrant incense is burnt, and he shall pour the rest of the bull's blood at the base of the altar of whole-offering at the entrance of the 8 Tent of the Presence. He shall set aside all the fat from the bull of the sin-offering; he shall set aside the fat covering the entrails and all the fat 9 upon the entrails, the two kidneys with the fat on them beside the haunches, and the long lobe of the 10 liver with the kidneys. It shall be set aside as the fat from the ox at the shared-offering is set aside. The priest shall burn the pieces of fat on the 11 altar of whole-offering. But the skin of the bull and all its flesh, including head and shins, its entrails and offal, 12 the whole of it, he shall take away outside the camp to a place ritually clean, where the ash-heap is, and destroy it on a wood-fire on top of the ash-heap.

13   If the whole community of Israel sins inadvertently and the matter is not known to the assembly, if they do what is forbidden in any commandment of the LORD and so incur 14 guilt, then, when the sin they have committed is notified to them, the assembly shall present a young bull as a sin-offering and shall bring it in 15 front of the Tent of the Presence. The elders of the community shall lay their hands on the victim's head before the LORD, and it shall be slaughtered 16 before the LORD. The anointed priest shall then bring some of the blood to 17 the Tent of the Presence, dip his finger in it and sprinkle it in front of the Veil seven times before the LORD. 18 He shall put some of the blood on the horns of the altar before the LORD in the Tent of the Presence and pour all the rest at the base of the altar of whole-offering at the entrance of the 19 Tent of the Presence. He shall then set aside all the fat from the bull and 20 burn it on the altar. He shall deal with this bull as he deals with the bull of the sin-offering, and in this way the priest shall make expiation for their guilt and they shall be for- 21 given. He shall take the bull outside the camp and burn it as the other bull was burnt. This is a sin-offering for the assembly.

22   When a man of standing sins by doing inadvertently what is forbidden in any commandment of the LORD his God, thereby incurring guilt, and 23 the sin he has committed is made known to him, he shall bring as his offering a he-goat without blemish. 24 He shall lay his hand on the goat's head and shall slaughter it before the LORD in the place where the whole-offering is slaughtered. It is a sin-offering. The priest shall then take 25 some of the blood of the victim with his finger and put it on the horns of the altar of whole-offering. He shall pour out the rest of the blood at the base of the altar of whole-offering. He shall burn all the fat at the altar 26 in the same way as the fat of the shared-offering. Thus the priest shall make expiation for that man's sin, and it shall be forgiven him.

If any person among the common 27 people sins inadvertently and does what is forbidden in any command- ment of the LORD, thereby incurring guilt, and the sin he has committed 28 is made known to him, he shall bring as his offering for the sin which he has committed a she-goat without blemish. He shall lay his hand on the 29 head of the victim and slaughter it in the place where the whole-offering is slaughtered. The priest shall then 30 take some of its blood with his finger and put it on the horns of the altar of whole-offering. All the rest of the blood he shall pour at the base of the altar. He shall remove all its fat as 31 the fat of the shared-offering is re- moved, and the priest shall burn it on the altar as a soothing odour to the LORD. So the priest shall make expia- tion for that person's guilt, and it shall be forgiven him.

If the man brings a sheep as his 32 offering for sin, it shall be a ewe without blemish. He shall lay his 33 hand on the head of the victim and slaughter it as a sin-offering in the place where the whole-offering is slaughtered. The priest shall then take some of the 34 blood of the victim with his finger and put it on the horns of the altar of whole-offering. All the rest of the blood he shall pour out at the base of the altar. He shall remove all the fat, 35 as the fat of the sheep is removed from the shared-offering. The priest shall burn the pieces of fat at the altar on top of the food-offerings to the LORD, and shall make expia- tion for the sin that the man has committed, and it shall be forgiven him.

5 If a person hears a solemn adjuration to give evidence as a witness to something he has seen or heard and does not declare what he knows, he commits a sin and must accept responsibility.

2 If a person touches anything unclean, such as the dead body of an unclean animal, whether wild or domestic, or of an unclean reptile, or

3 if he touches anything unclean in a man, whatever that uncleanness may be, and it is concealed by him although he is aware of it, he shall

4 incur guilt. Or if a person rashly utters an oath to do something evil or good, in any matter in which such a man may swear a rash oath, and it is concealed by him although he is aware of it, he shall in either case

5 incur guilt. Whenever a man incurs guilt in any of these cases and confesses

6 how he has sinned therein, he shall bring to the LORD, as his penalty for the sin that he has committed, a female of the flock, either a ewe or a she-goat, as a sin-offering, and the priest shall make expiation for him on account of his sin which he has committed, and he shall be pardoned.

7 But if he cannot afford as much as a young animal, he shall bring to the LORD for the sin he has committed two turtle-doves or two young pigeons, one for a sin-offering and the

8 other for a whole-offering. He shall bring them to the priest, and present first the one intended for the sin-offering. He shall wrench its head back

9 without severing it. He shall sprinkle some of the blood of the victim against the side of the altar, and what is left of the blood shall be drained out at the base of the altar: it is a sin-

10 offering. He shall deal with the second bird as a whole-offering according to custom, and the priest shall make expiation for the sin the man has committed, and it shall be forgiven him.

11 If the man cannot afford two turtle-doves or two young pigeons, for his sin he shall bring as his offering a tenth of an ephah of flour, as a sin-offering. He shall add no oil to it nor put frankincense on it, be-

12 cause it is a sin-offering. He shall bring it to the priest, who shall scoop up a handful from it as a token and burn it on the altar on the food-offerings to the LORD: it is a sin-

13 offering. The priest shall make expiation for the sin the man has committed in any one of these cases, and it shall be forgiven him. The remainder belongs to the priest, as with the grain-offering.

Guilt-offerings

14 The LORD spoke to Moses and said:

15 When any person commits an offence by inadvertently defaulting in dues sacred to the LORD, he shall bring as his guilt-offering to the LORD a ram without blemish from the flock, the value to be determined by you in silver shekels according to the sacred standard, for a guilt-offering; he shall

16 make good his default in sacred dues, adding one fifth. He shall give it to the priest, who shall make expiation for his sin with the ram of the guilt-offering, and it shall be forgiven him.

17 If and when any person sins unwittingly and does what is forbidden by any commandment of the LORD, thereby incurring guilt, he must accept responsibility. He shall bring to

18 the priest as a guilt-offering a ram without blemish from the flock, valued by you, and the priest shall make expiation for the error into which he has unwittingly fallen, and it shall be forgiven him. It is a guilt-

19 offering; he has been guilty of an offence against the LORD.

6 The LORD spoke to Moses and said:

2 When any person sins and commits a grievous fault against the LORD, whether he lies to a fellow-countryman about a deposit or contract, or a

3 theft, or wrongs him by extortion, or finds lost property and then lies about it, and swears a false oath in regard to any sin of this sort that he com-

4 mits—if he does this, thereby incurring guilt, he shall restore what he has stolen or gained by extortion, or the deposit left with him or the lost prop-

5 erty which he found, or anything at all concerning which he swore a false oath. He shall make full restitution, adding one fifth to it, and give it back to the aggrieved party on the day

6 when he offers his guilt-offering. He shall bring to the LORD as his guilt-offering a ram without blemish from the flock, valued by you, as a guilt-offering. The priest shall make expia-

7 tion for his guilt before the LORD, and he shall be forgiven for any act which has brought guilt upon him.

Further laws concerning offerings

8 The LORD spoke to Moses and said,

9 Give this command to Aaron and his sons: This is the law of the whole-offering. The whole-offering shall remain on the altar-hearth all night

till morning, and the altar-fire shall
10 be kept burning there. Then the priest,
having donned his linen robe and put
on linen drawers to cover himself, shall
remove the ashes to which the fire
reduces the whole-offering on the
altar and put them beside the altar.
11 He shall then change into other
garments and take the ashes outside
the camp to a ritually clean place.
12 The fire shall be kept burning on the
altar; it shall never go out. Every
morning the priest shall have fresh
wood burning thereon, arrange the
whole-offering on it, and on top burn
13 the fat from the shared-offerings. Fire
shall always be kept burning on the
altar; it shall not go out.

14   This is the law of the grain-offering.
The Aaronites shall present it before
15 the LORD in front of the altar. The
priest shall set aside a handful of
the flour from it, with the oil of the
grain-offering, and all the frankincense on it. He shall burn this token
of it on the altar as a soothing odour
16 to the LORD. The remainder Aaron
and his sons shall eat. It shall be
eaten in the form of unleavened cakes
and in a holy place. They shall eat
it in the court of the Tent of the
17 Presence. It shall not be baked with
leaven. I have allotted this to them as
their share of my food-offerings. Like
the sin-offering and the guilt-offering
18 it is most sacred. Any male descendant of Aaron may eat it, as a due
from the food-offerings to the LORD,
for generation after generation for all
time. Whatever touches them is to be
forfeit as sacred.

19   The LORD spoke to Moses and said:
20 This is the offering which Aaron and
his sons shall present to the LORD:[b]
one tenth of an ephah of flour, the
usual grain-offering, half of it in the
21 morning and half in the evening, it
shall be cooked with oil on a griddle;
you shall bring it well-mixed, and so
present it crumbled in small pieces
as a grain-offering, a soothing odour
22 to the LORD. The anointed priest in
the line of Aaron shall offer it. This
is a rule binding for all time. It shall
be burnt in sacrifice to the LORD
23 as a complete offering. Every grain-
offering of a priest shall be a complete offering; it shall not be eaten.

24   The LORD spoke to Moses and said,
25 Speak to Aaron and his sons in these
words: This is the law of the sin-
offering. The sin-offering shall be
slaughtered before the LORD in the
place where the whole-offering is
slaughtered; it is most sacred. The 26
priest who officiates shall eat of the
flesh; it shall be eaten in a sacred
place, in the court of the Tent of the
Presence. Whatever touches its flesh 27
is to be forfeit as sacred. If any of the
blood is splashed on a garment, that
shall be washed in a sacred place. An 28
earthenware vessel in which the sin-
offering is boiled shall be smashed. If
it has been boiled in a copper vessel,
that shall be scoured and rinsed with
water. Any male of priestly family 29
may eat of this offering; it is most
sacred. If, however, part of the blood 30
is brought to the Tent of the Presence
to make expiation in the holy place,
the sin-offering shall not be eaten; it
shall be destroyed by fire.

This is the law of the guilt-offering: 7
it is most sacred. The guilt-offering 2
shall be slaughtered in the place where
the whole-offering is slaughtered, and
its blood shall be flung against the
altar all round. The priest shall set 3
aside and present all the fat from it:
the fat-tail and the fat covering the
entrails, the two kidneys with the fat 4
on them beside the haunches, and the
long lobe of the liver with the kidneys.
The priest shall burn these pieces on 5
the altar as a food-offering to the
LORD; it is a guilt-offering. Any male 6
of priestly family may eat it. It shall
be eaten in a sacred place; it is most
sacred. There is one law for both sin- 7
offering and guilt-offering: they shall
belong to the priest who performs
the rite of expiation. The skin of any 8
man's whole-offering shall belong
to the priest who presents it. Every 9
grain-offering baked in an oven and
everything that is cooked in a pan or
on a griddle shall belong to the priest
who presents it. Every grain-offering, 10
whether mixed with oil or dry, shall
be shared equally among all the
Aaronites.

This is the law of the shared- 11
offering presented to the LORD. If a 12
man presents it as a thank-offering,
then, in addition to the thank-
offering, he shall present unleavened
cakes mixed with oil, wafers of unleavened flour smeared with oil, and
well-mixed flour and flat cakes mixed
with oil. He shall present flat cakes 13
of leavened bread in addition to his
shared thank-offering. One part of 14
every offering he shall present as a
contribution for the LORD: it shall
belong to the priest who flings the

b Prob. rdg.; Heb. adds on the day when he is anointed.

blood of the shared-offering against
5 the altar. The flesh shall be eaten on
the day of its presentation; none of it
shall be put aside till morning.
6 If a man's sacrifice is a votive
offering or a freewill offering, it may
be eaten on the day it is presented or
7 on the next day. Any flesh left over on
the third day shall be destroyed by
8 fire. If any flesh of his shared-offering
is eaten on the third day, the man who
has presented it shall not be accepted.
It will not be counted to his credit, it
shall be reckoned as tainted and the
person who eats any of it shall accept
9 responsibility. No flesh which comes
into contact with anything unclean
shall be eaten; it shall be destroyed by
fire.
10 The flesh may be eaten by anyone
who is clean, but the person who, while
unclean, eats flesh from a shared-
offering presented to the LORD shall
be cut off from his father's kin.
11 When any person is contaminated by
contact with anything unclean, be it
man, beast, or reptile, and then eats
any of the flesh from the shared-
offerings presented to the LORD, that
person shall be cut off from his father's
kin.
12 The LORD spoke to Moses and said,
13 Speak to the Israelites in these words:
You shall not eat the fat of any ox,
14 sheep, or goat. The fat of an animal
that has died a natural death or has
been mauled by wild beasts may be
put to any other use, but you shall
15 not eat it. Every man who eats fat
from a beast of which he has presented
any part as a food-offering to the
LORD shall be cut off from his father's
kin.
16 You shall eat none of the blood,
whether of bird or of beast, wherever
17 you may live. Every person who eats
any of the blood shall be cut off from
his father's kin.
18 The LORD spoke to Moses and said,
19 Speak to the Israelites in these words:
Whoever comes to present a shared-
offering shall set aside part of it as
20 an offering to the LORD. With his
own hands he shall bring the food-
offerings to the LORD. He shall also
bring the fat together with the breast
which is to be presented as a special
21 gift before the LORD; the priest shall
burn the fat on the altar, but the
breast shall belong to Aaron and his
22 descendants. You shall give the right
hind-leg of your shared-offerings as a
23 contribution for the priest; it shall be

the perquisite of the Aaronite who
presents the blood and the fat of the
shared-offering. I have taken from 34
the Israelites the breast of the special
gift and the leg of the contribution
made out of the shared-offerings, and
have given them as a due from the
Israelites to Aaron the priest and his
descendants for all time. This is the 35
portion prescribed for Aaron and his
descendants out of the LORD's food-
offerings, appointed on the day when
they were presented as priests to the
LORD; and on the day when they were 36
anointed, the LORD commanded that
these prescribed portions should be
given to them by the Israelites. This
is a rule binding on their descendants
for all time.
This, then, is the law of the 37
whole-offering, the grain-offering, the
sin-offering, the guilt-offering, the in-
stallation-offerings, and the shared-
offerings, with which the LORD charged 38
Moses on Mount Sinai on the day
when he commanded the Israelites to
present their offerings to the LORD in
the wilderness of Sinai.

Consecrating the priests
The LORD spoke to Moses and said, 8
'Take Aaron and his sons with him, 2
the vestments, the anointing oil, the
ox for a sin-offering, the two rams, and
the basket of unleavened cakes, and 3
assemble all the community at the
entrance to the Tent of the Presence.'
Moses did as the LORD had com- 4
manded him, and the community assembled at the entrance to the Tent of
the Presence. He told the community 5
that this was what the LORD had commanded. He presented Aaron and 6
his sons and washed them in water.
He invested Aaron with the tunic, 7
girded him with the sash, robed him
with the mantle, put the ephod on
him, tied it with its waist-band and
fastened the ephod to him with the
band. He put the breast-piece*c* on him 8
and set the Urim and Thummim in
it. He then put the turban upon his 9
head and set the gold rosette as a
symbol of holy dedication on the front
of the turban, as the LORD had commanded him. Moses then took the 10
anointing oil, anointed the Tabernacle and all that was within it and
consecrated them. He sprinkled some 11
of the oil seven times on the altar,
anointing the altar, all its vessels, the
basin and its stand, to consecrate them.
He poured some of the anointing oil 12

c Or pouch.

on Aaron's head and so consecrated
13 him. Moses then brought the sons
of Aaron forward, invested them
with tunics, girded them with sashes
and tied their tall head-dresses on
them, as the LORD had commanded
him.
14 He then brought up the ox for
the sin-offering; Aaron and his sons
15 laid their hands on its head, and he
slaughtered it. Moses took some of the
blood and put it with his finger on
the horns round the altar. Thus he
purified the altar, and when he had
poured out the rest of the blood at the
base of the altar, he consecrated it by
16 making expiation for it. He took all
the fat upon the entrails, the long lobe
of the liver, and the two kidneys with
their fat, and burnt them on the altar,
17 but the ox, its skin, its flesh, and its
offal, he destroyed by fire outside the
camp, as the LORD had commanded
him.
18 Moses then brought forward the
ram of the whole-offering; Aaron and
his sons laid their hands on the ram's
19 head, and he slaughtered it. Moses
flung its blood against the altar all
20 round. He cut the ram up and burnt
21 the head, the pieces, and the suet. He
washed the entrails and the shins in
water and burnt the whole on the
altar. This was a whole-offering, a
food-offering of soothing odour to the
LORD, as the LORD had commanded
Moses.
22 Moses then brought forward the
second ram, the ram for the installation of priests. Aaron and his sons laid
23 their hands upon its head, and he
slaughtered it. Moses took some of its
blood and put it on the lobe of Aaron's
right ear, on his right thumb, and on
24 the big toe of his right foot. He then
brought forward the sons of Aaron,
put some of the blood on the lobes of
their right ears, on their right thumbs,
and on the big toes of their right feet.
He flung the rest of the blood against
25 the altar all round; he took the fat,
the fat-tail, the fat covering the entrails, the long lobe of the liver, and the
two kidneys with their fat, and the
26 right leg. Then from the basket of unleavened cakes before the LORD he
took one unleavened cake, one cake
of bread made with oil, and one wafer,
and laid them on the fatty parts and
27 the right leg. He put the whole on the
hands of Aaron and of his sons, and he
presented it as a special gift before
28 the LORD. He took it from their hands
and burnt it on the altar on top of the

whole-offering. This was an installa-
tion-offering, it was a food-offering of
soothing odour to the LORD.
Moses then took the breast and pre- 29
sented it as a special gift before the
LORD; it was his portion of the ram of
installation, as the LORD had commanded him. He took some of the 30
anointing oil and some of the blood
on the altar and sprinkled it on Aaron
and his vestments, and on his sons
and their vestments with him. Thus
he consecrated Aaron and his vestments, and with him his sons and
their vestments.
Moses said to Aaron and his sons, 31
'Boil the flesh of the ram at the
entrance to the Tent of the Presence,
and eat it there, together with the
bread in the installation-basket, in
accordance with the command: "Aaron and his sons shall eat it." The re- 32
mainder of the flesh and bread you
shall destroy by fire. You shall not 33
leave the entrance to the Tent of the
Presence for seven days, until the day
which completes the period of your
installation, for it lasts seven days.
What was done this day followed the 34
LORD's command to make expiation
for you. You shall stay at the entrance 35
to the Tent of the Presence day and
night for seven days, keeping vigil to
the LORD, so that you do not die, for so
I was commanded.'
Aaron and his sons did everything 36
that the LORD had commanded through
Moses.

Aaron offers sacrifices

On the eighth day Moses summoned 9
Aaron and his sons and the Israelite
elders. He said to Aaron, 'Take for 2
yourself a bull-calf for a sin-offering
and a ram for a whole-offering, both
without blemish, and present them
before the LORD. Then bid the Israel- 3
ites take a he-goat for a sin-offering,
a calf and a lamb, both yearlings
without blemish, for a whole-offering,
and a bull and a ram for shared- 4
offerings to be sacrificed before the
LORD, together with a grain-offering
mixed with oil. This day the LORD will
appear to you.'
They brought what Moses had com- 5
manded to the front of the Tent of
the Presence, and all the community
approached and stood before the
LORD. Moses said, 'This is what the 6
LORD has commanded you to do, so
that the glory of the LORD may appear
to you. Come near to the altar,' he said 7
to Aaron; 'prepare your sin-offering

and your whole-offering and make expiation for yourself and for your household. Then prepare the offering of the people and make expiation for them, as the LORD has commanded.'

8 So Aaron came near to the altar and slaughtered the calf, which was 9 his sin-offering. The sons of Aaron presented the blood to him, and he dipped his finger in the blood and put it on the horns of the altar. The rest of the blood he poured out at the base of the altar. Part of the sin-offering, the fat, the kidneys, and the long lobe of the liver, he burnt on the altar as the LORD had commanded Moses, but the flesh and the skin he destroyed by fire outside the camp. Then he slaughtered the whole-offering; his sons handed him the blood, and he flung it against the altar all round. They handed him the pieces of the whole-offering and the head, and he burnt them on the altar. He washed the entrails and the shins and burnt them on the altar, on top of the whole-offering.

5 He then brought forward the offering of the people. He took the he-goat, the people's sin-offering, slaughtered it and performed the rite of the sin-offering as he had previously done for himself. He presented the whole-offering and prepared it in the manner prescribed. He brought forward the grain-offering, took a handful of it and burnt it on the altar, in addition to the morning whole-offering. He slaughtered the bull and the ram, the shared-offerings of the people. His sons handed him the blood, and he flung it against the altar all round. But the fatty parts of the bull, the fat-tail of the ram, the fat covering the entrails, and the two kidneys with the fat upon them, and the long lobe of the liver, all this fat they first put on the breasts of the animals and then burnt it on the altar. Aaron presented the breasts and the right leg as a special gift before the LORD, as Moses had commanded. Then Aaron lifted up his hands towards the people and pronounced the blessing over them. He came down from performing the rites of the sin-offering, the whole-offering, and the shared-offerings. Moses and Aaron entered the Tent of the Presence, and when they came out, they blessed the people, and the glory of the LORD appeared to all the people. Fire came out from before the LORD and consumed the whole-offering and the fatty parts on the altar. All the people saw, and they shouted and fell on their faces.

The sin of Nadab and Abihu

Now Nadab and Abihu, sons of 10 Aaron, took their firepans, put fire in them, threw incense on the fire and presented before the LORD illicit fire which he had not commanded. Fire 2 came out from before the LORD and destroyed them; and so they died in the presence of the LORD. Then Moses 3 said to Aaron, 'This is what the LORD meant when he said: Among those who approach me, I must be treated as holy; in the presence of all the people I must be given honour.' Aaron was dumbfounded. Moses sent 4 for Mishael and Elzaphan, the sons of Aaron's uncle Uzziel, and said to them, 'Come and carry your cousins outside the camp away from the holy place.' They came and carried them 5 away in their tunics outside the camp, as Moses had told them. Moses then 6 said to Aaron and to his sons Eleazar and Ithamar, 'You shall not leave your hair dishevelled or tear your clothes in mourning, lest you die and the LORD be angry with the whole community. Your kinsmen, all the house of Israel, shall weep for the destruction by fire which the LORD has kindled. You shall not leave the 7 entrance to the Tent of the Presence lest you die, because the LORD's anointing oil is on you.' They did as Moses had said.

Laws concerning priests

The LORD spoke to Aaron and said: 8 You and your sons with you shall not 9 drink wine or strong drink when you are to enter the Tent of the Presence, lest you die. This is a rule binding on your descendants for all time, to make 10 a distinction between sacred and profane, between clean and unclean, and 11 to teach the Israelites all the decrees which the LORD has spoken to them through Moses.

Moses said to Aaron and his survi- 12 ving sons Eleazar and Ithamar, 'Take what is left over of the grain-offering out of the food-offerings of the LORD, and eat it without leaven beside the altar; it is most sacred. You shall 13 eat it in a sacred place; it is your due and that of your sons out of the LORD's food-offerings, for so I was

14 commanded. You shall eat the breast of the special gift and the leg of the contribution in a clean place, you and your sons and daughters; for they have been given to you and your children as your due out of the shared-

15 offerings of the Israelites. The leg of the contribution and the breast of the special gift shall be brought, along with the food-offerings of fat, to be presented as a special gift before the LORD, and it shall belong to you and your children together, a due for all time; for so the LORD has commanded.'

16 Moses made searching inquiry about the goat of the sin-offering and found that it had been burnt. He was angry with Eleazar and Ithamar, Aaron's

17 surviving sons, and said, 'Why did you not eat the sin-offering in the sacred place? It is most sacred. It was given to you to take away the guilt of the community by making expia-

18 tion for them before the LORD. If the blood is not brought within the sacred precincts, you shall eat the sin-offering there as I was commanded.'

19 But Aaron replied to Moses, 'See, they have today presented their sin-offering and their whole-offering before the LORD, and this is what has befallen me; if I eat a sin-offering today, will it be right in the eyes of

20 the LORD?' When Moses heard this, he deemed it right.

Clean and unclean creatures

11 The LORD spoke to Moses and Aaron
2 and said, Speak to the Israelites in these words: Of all animals on land these are the creatures you may eat:
3 you may eat any animal which has a parted foot or a cloven hoof and also
4 chews the cud; those which have only a cloven hoof or only chew the cud you may not eat. These are: the camel, because it chews the cud but has not a cloven hoof; you shall regard it as
5 unclean; the rock-badger,*d* because it chews the cud but has not a parted foot; you shall regard it as unclean;
6 the hare, because it chews the cud but has not a parted foot; you shall
7 regard it as unclean; the pig, because it has a parted foot and a cloven hoof but does not chew the cud; you shall
8 regard it as unclean. You shall not eat their flesh or even touch their dead bodies; you shall regard them as unclean.
9 Of creatures that live in water these

you may eat: all those that have fins and scales, whether in salt water or fresh; but all that have neither fins 10 nor scales, whether in salt or fresh water, including both small creatures in shoals and larger creatures, you shall regard as vermin. They shall be 11 vermin to you; you shall not eat their flesh, and their dead bodies you shall treat as those of vermin. Every crea- 12 ture in the water that has neither fins nor scales shall be vermin to you.

These are the birds you shall regard 13 as vermin, and for this reason they shall not be eaten: the griffon-vulture,*e* the black vulture, and the bearded vulture;*f* the kite and every kind of 14 falcon; every kind of crow,*g* the desert- 15 owl, the short-eared owl, the long-eared owl, and every kind of hawk; the tawny owl, the fisher-owl, and 17 the screech-owl; the little owl, the 18 horned owl, the osprey, the stork,*h* 19 every kind of cormorant, the hoopoe, and the bat.

All teeming winged creatures that 20 go on four legs shall be vermin to you, except those which have legs jointed 21 above their feet for leaping on the ground. Of these you may eat every 22 kind of great locust, every kind of long-headed locust, every kind of green locust, and every kind of desert locust. Every other teeming winged 23 creature that has four legs you shall regard as vermin; you would make 24 yourselves unclean with them: who-ever*i* touches their dead bodies shall 25 be unclean till evening. Whoever picks 25 up their dead bodies shall wash his clothes but remain unclean till evening.

You shall regard as unclean every 26 animal which has a parted foot but has not a cloven hoof and does not chew the cud: whoever*i* touches them shall be unclean. You shall regard as 27 unclean all four-footed wild animals that go on flat paws; whoever*i* touches their dead bodies shall be unclean till evening. Whoever takes 28 up their dead bodies shall wash his clothes but remain unclean till evening. You shall regard them as unclean.

You shall regard these as unclean 29 among creatures that teem on the ground: the mole-rat,*j* the jerboa, and every kind of thorn-tailed lizard; the 30 gecko, the sand-gecko, the wall-gecko, the great lizard, and the chameleon. You shall regard these as unclean 31 among teeming creatures; whoever*i*

d Or rock-rabbit.   *e* Or eagle.   *f* Or ossifrage.
g Or raven.   *h* Or heron.   *i* Or whatever.
j Or weasel.

32 touches them when they are dead shall be unclean till evening. Anything on which any of them falls when they are dead shall be unclean, any article of wood or garment or skin or sacking, any article in regular use; it shall be plunged into water but shall remain unclean till evening, when it shall be 33 clean. If any of these falls into an earthenware vessel, its contents shall be unclean and it shall be smashed. 34 Any food on which water from such a vessel is poured shall be unclean, and any drink in such a vessel shall be 35 unclean. Anything on which the dead body of such a creature falls shall be unclean; an oven or a stove shall be broken, and they are unclean and you 36 shall treat them as such; but a spring or a cistern where water collects shall remain clean, though whatever[k] touches 37 the dead body shall be unclean. When any of their dead bodies falls on seed intended for sowing, it remains clean; 38 but if the seed has been soaked in water and any dead body falls on it, you shall treat it as unclean.

39 When any animal allowed as food dies, all that touch the carcass shall be 40 unclean till evening. Whoever eats any of the carcass shall wash his clothes but remain unclean till evening; whoever takes up the carcass shall wash his clothes and be unclean till 41 evening. All creatures that teem on the ground are vermin; they shall not 42 be eaten. All creatures that teem on the ground, crawl on their bellies, go on all fours or have many legs, you shall not eat, because they are vermin 43 which contaminate. You shall not contaminate yourselves through any teeming creature. You shall not defile yourselves with them and make your- 44 selves unclean by them. For I am the LORD your God; you shall make yourselves holy and keep yourselves holy, because I am holy. You shall not defile yourselves with any teeming creature that creeps on the ground. 45 I am the LORD who brought you up from Egypt to become your God. You shall keep yourselves holy, because I am holy.

46 This, then, is the law concerning beast and bird, every living creature that swims in the water and every living creature that teems on the land. 47 It is to make a distinction between the unclean and the clean, between living creatures that may be eaten and living creatures that may not be eaten.

Purification after childbirth

The LORD spoke to Moses and said, 12 Speak to the Israelites in these words: 2 When a woman conceives and bears a male child, she shall be unclean for seven days, as in the period of her impurity through menstruation. On 3 the eighth day, the child shall have the flesh of his foreskin circumcised. The woman shall wait for thirty-three 4 days because her blood requires purification; she shall touch nothing that is holy, and shall not enter the sanctuary till her days of purification are completed. If she bears a female child, 5 she shall be unclean for fourteen days as for her menstruation and shall wait for sixty-six days because her blood requires purification. When her days 6 of purification are completed for a son or a daughter, she shall bring a yearling ram for a whole-offering and a young pigeon or a turtle-dove for a sin-offering to the priest at the entrance to the Tent of the Presence. He shall 7 present it before the LORD and make expiation for her, and she shall be clean from the issue of her blood. This is the law for the woman who bears a child, whether male or female. If she 8 cannot afford a ram, she shall bring two turtle-doves or two young pigeons, one for a whole-offering and the other for a sin-offering. The priest shall make expiation for her and she shall be clean.

Laws concerning ritual uncleanness

The LORD spoke to Moses and Aaron 13 and said: When any man has a dis- 2 coloration on the skin of his body, a pustule or inflammation, and it may develop into the sores of a malignant skin-disease, he shall be brought to the priest, either to Aaron or to one of his sons. The priest shall examine 3 the sore on the skin; if the hairs on the sore have turned white and it appears to be deeper than the skin, it shall be considered the sore of a malignant skin-disease, and the priest, after examination, shall pronounce him ritually unclean. But if the inflam- 4 mation on his skin is white and seems no deeper than the skin, and the hairs have not turned white, the priest shall isolate the affected person for seven days. If, when he examines him on 5 the seventh day, the sore remains as it was and has not spread in the skin, he shall keep him in isolation for another seven days. When the priest 6

---

k Or whoever.

examines him again on the seventh day, if the sore has faded and has not spread in the skin, the priest shall pronounce him ritually clean. It is only a scab; the man shall wash his 7 clothes and so be clean. But if the scab spreads on the skin after he has been to the priest to be pronounced ritually clean, the man shall show himself a second time to the priest. 8 The priest shall examine him again, and if it continues to spread, he shall pronounce him ritually unclean; it is a malignant skin-disease.

9 When anyone has the sores of a malignant skin-disease, he shall be 10 brought to the priest, and the priest shall examine him. If there is a white mark on the skin, turning the hairs white, and an ulceration appears in 11 the mark, it is a chronic skin-disease on the body, and the priest shall pronounce him ritually unclean; there is no need for isolation because he is 12 unclean already. If the skin-disease breaks out and covers the affected person from head to foot as far as the 13 priest can see, the priest shall examine him, and if he finds the condition spread all over the body, he shall pronounce him ritually clean. It has all 14 gone white; he is clean. But from the moment when raw flesh appears, the man shall be considered unclean. 15 When the priest sees it, he shall pronounce him unclean. Raw flesh is to be considered unclean; it is a malig-16 nant skin-disease. On the other hand, when the raw flesh heals and turns white, the man shall go to the priest, 17 who shall examine him, and if the sores have gone white, he shall pronounce him clean. He is ritually clean.

18 When a fester appears on the skin 19 and heals up, but is followed by a white mark or reddish-white inflammation on the site of the fester, the man shall show himself to the priest. 20 The priest shall examine him; if it seems to be beneath the skin and the hairs have turned white, the priest shall pronounce him ritually unclean. It is a malignant skin-disease which has broken out on the site of the 21 fester. But if the priest on examination finds that it has no white hairs, is not beneath the skin and has faded, he 22 shall isolate him for seven days. If the affection has spread at all in the skin, then the priest shall pronounce him unclean; for it is a malignant skin-23 disease. But if the inflammation is no worse and has not spread, it is only

the scar of the fester, and the priest shall pronounce him ritually clean.

24 Again, in the case of a burn on the skin, if the raw spot left by the burn becomes a reddish-white or white 25 inflammation, the priest shall examine it. If the hairs on the inflammation have turned white and it is deeper than the skin, it is a malignant skin-disease which has broken out at the site of the burn. The priest shall pronounce the man ritually unclean; it is 26 a malignant skin-disease. But if the priest on examination finds that there is no white hair on the inflammation and it is not beneath the skin and has faded, he shall keep him in isolation for seven days. When the priest ex-27 amines him on the seventh day, if the inflammation has spread at all in the skin, the priest shall pronounce him unclean; it is a malignant skin-28 disease. But if the inflammation is no worse, has not spread and has faded, it is only a mark from the burn. The priest shall pronounce him ritually clean because it is the scar of the burn.

29 When a man, or woman, has a sore 30 on the head or chin, the priest shall examine it; and if it seems deeper than the skin and the hair is yellow and sparse, the priest shall pronounce him ritually unclean; it is a scurf, a malignant skin-disease of the head or chin. 31 But when the priest sees the sore, if it appears to be no deeper than the skin and yet there is no yellow hair on the place, the priest shall isolate the 32 affected person for seven days. He shall examine the sore on the seventh day: if the scurf has not spread and there are no yellow hairs on it and it 33 seems no deeper than the skin, the man shall get himself shaved except for the scurfy part, and the priest shall keep him in isolation for another 34 seven days. The priest shall examine it again on the seventh day, and if the scurf has not spread on the skin and appears to be no deeper than the skin, the priest shall pronounce him clean. The man shall wash his clothes 35 and so be ritually clean. But if the scurf spreads at all in the skin after the man has been pronounced clean, 36 the priest shall examine him again. If it has spread in the skin, the priest need not even look for yellow hair; 37 the man is unclean. If, however, the scurf remains as it was but black hair has begun to grow on it, it has healed. The man is ritually clean and the priest shall pronounce him so.

38 When a man, or woman, has inflamed patches on the skin and they 39 are white, the priest shall examine them. If they are white and fading, it is dull-white leprosy that has broken out on the skin. The man is ritually clean.

40 When a man's hair falls out from his head, he is bald behind but not 41 ritually unclean. If the hair falls out from the front of the scalp, he is bald 42 on the forehead but clean. But if on the bald patch behind or on the forehead there is a reddish-white sore, it is a malignant skin-disease breaking 43 out on those parts. The priest shall examine him, and if the discoloured sore on the bald patch behind or on the forehead is reddish-white, similar in appearance to a malignant skin-44 disease on the body, the man is suffering from such a disease; he is ritually unclean and the priest must not fail to pronounce him so. The symptoms are in this case on his head.

45 One who suffers from a malignant skin-disease shall wear his clothes torn, leave his hair dishevelled, conceal his upper lip, and cry, 'Unclean, 46 unclean.' So long as the sore persists, he shall be considered ritually unclean. The man is unclean: he shall live apart and must stay outside the settlement.

47 When there is a stain of mould, whether in a garment of wool or linen, 48 or in the warp or weft of linen or wool, or in a skin or anything made of skin; 49 if the stain is greenish or reddish in the garment or skin, or in the warp or weft, or in anything made of skin, it is a stain of mould which must be 50 shown to the priest. The priest shall examine it and put the stained 51 material aside for seven days. On the seventh day he shall examine it again. If the stain has spread in the garment, warp, weft, or anything, whatever the use of the skin, the stain is a rotting 52 mould: it is ritually unclean. He shall burn the garment or the warp or weft, whether wool or linen, or anything of skin which is stained; because it is a rotting mould, it must be destroyed 53 by fire. But if the priest sees that the stain has not spread in the garment, warp or weft, or anything made of 54 skin, he shall give orders for the stained material to be washed, and then he shall put it aside for another 55 seven days. After it has been washed the priest shall examine the stain; if it has not changed its appearance,

although it has not spread, it is unclean and you shall destroy it by fire, whether the rot is on the right side or the wrong. If the priest examines it 56 and finds the stain faded after being washed, he shall tear it out of the garment, skin, warp, or weft. If, however, 57 the stain reappears in the garment, warp or weft, or in anything of skin, it is breaking out afresh and you shall destroy by fire whatever is stained. If 58 you wash the garment, warp, weft, or anything of skin and the stain disappears, it shall be washed a second time and then it shall be ritually clean.

This is the law concerning stain of 59 mould in a garment of wool or linen, in warp or weft, or in anything made of skin; by it they shall be pronounced clean or unclean.

The Lord spoke to Moses and said: 14 This is the law concerning a man 2 suffering from a malignant skin-disease. On the day when he is to be cleansed he shall be brought to the priest. The priest shall go outside the 3 camp and examine him. If the man is healed of his disease, then the priest 4 shall order two clean small birds to be brought alive for the man who is to be cleansed, together with cedar-wood, scarlet thread, and marjoram.[l] He shall order one of the birds to be 5 killed over an earthenware bowl containing fresh water. He shall then take 6 the living bird and the cedar-wood, scarlet thread, and marjoram and dip them and the living bird in the blood of the bird that has been killed over the fresh water. He shall sprinkle the 7 blood seven times on the man who is to be cleansed from his skin-disease and so cleanse him; the living bird he shall release to fly away over the open country. The man to be cleansed 8 shall wash off his clothes, shave off all his hair, bathe in water and so be ritually clean. He may then enter the camp but must stay outside his tent for seven days. On the seventh day he 9 shall shave off all the hair on his head, his beard, and his eyebrows, and then shave the rest of his hair, wash his clothes and bathe in water; then he shall be ritually clean.

On the eighth day he shall bring 10 two yearling rams and one yearling ewe, all three without blemish, a grain-offering of three tenths of an ephah of flour mixed with oil, and one log of oil. The officiating priest shall place the 11 man to be cleansed and his offerings

l Or hyssop.

before the LORD at the entrance to
12 the Tent of the Presence. He shall
then take one of the rams and offer it
with the log of oil as a guilt-offering,
presenting them as a special gift
13 before the LORD. The ram shall be
slaughtered where the sin-offerings
and the whole-offerings are slaughtered, within the sacred precincts, because the guilt-offering, like the sin-
offering, belongs to the priest. It is
14 most sacred. The priest shall then take
some of the blood of the guilt-offering
and put it on the lobe of the right ear
of the man to be cleansed, and on his
right thumb and the big toe of his
15 right foot. He shall next take the log
of oil and pour some of it on the palm
16 of his own left hand, dip his right
forefinger into the oil on his left palm
and sprinkle some of it with his finger
17 seven times before the LORD. He shall
then put some of the oil remaining on
his palm on the lobe of the right ear
of the man to be cleansed, on his
right thumb and on the big toe of his
right foot, on top of the blood of the
18 guilt-offering. The remainder of the
oil on the priest's palm shall be put
upon the head of the man to be
cleansed, and thus the priest shall
make expiation for him before the
19 LORD. The priest shall then perform
the sin-offering and make expiation
for the uncleanness of the man who
is to be cleansed. After this he shall
20 slaughter the whole-offering and offer
it and the grain-offering on the altar.
Thus the priest shall make expiation
for him, and then he shall be clean.
21   If the man is poor and cannot afford
these offerings, he shall bring one
young ram as a guilt-offering to be a
special gift making expiation for him,
and a grain-offering of a tenth of an
ephah of flour mixed with oil, and
22 a log of oil, also two turtle-doves or
two young pigeons, whichever he can
afford, one for a sin-offering and the
23 other for a whole-offering. He shall
bring them to the priest for his cleansing on the eighth day, at the entrance
to the Tent of the Presence before the
24 LORD. The priest shall take the ram
for the guilt-offering and the log of
oil, and shall present them as a
25 special gift before the LORD. The ram
for the guilt-offering shall then be
slaughtered, and the priest shall take
some of the blood of the guilt-offering,
and put it on the lobe of the right ear
of the man to be cleansed and on his
right thumb and on the big toe of his

right foot. He shall pour some of the 26
oil on the palm of his own left hand
and sprinkle some of it with his 27
right forefinger seven times before the
LORD. He shall then put some of the 28
oil remaining on his palm on the lobe
of the right ear of the man to be
cleansed, and on his right thumb and
on the big toe of his right foot exactly
where the blood of the guilt-offering
was put. The remainder of the oil on 29
the priest's palm shall be put upon
the head of the man to be cleansed to
make expiation for him before the
LORD. Of the birds which the man has 30
been able to afford, turtle-doves or
young pigeons, whichever it may be,
the priest shall deal with one as a 31
sin-offering and with the other as a
whole-offering and shall make the
grain-offering with them. Thus the priest
shall make expiation before the LORD
for the man who is to be cleansed.
This is the law for the man with a 32
malignant skin-disease who cannot
afford the regular offering for his
cleansing.

The LORD spoke to Moses and 33
Aaron and said: When you have 34
entered the land of Canaan which
I give you to occupy, if I inflict a
fungous infection upon a house in the
land you have occupied, its owner 35
shall come and report to the priest
that there appears to him to be a
patch of infection in his house. The 36
priest shall order the house to be
cleared before he goes in to examine
the infection, or everything in it will
become unclean. After this the priest
shall go in to inspect the house. If on 37
inspection he finds the patch on the
walls consists of greenish or reddish
depressions, apparently going deeper
than the surface, he shall go out of the 38
house and, standing at the entrance,
shall put it in quarantine for seven
days. On the seventh day he shall 39
come back and inspect the house, and
if the patch has spread in the walls,
he shall order the infected stones to 40
be pulled out and thrown away outside the city in an unclean place. He 41
shall then have the house scraped inside throughout, and all the daub*m*
they have scraped off shall be tipped
outside the city in an unclean place.
They shall take fresh stones to replace 42
the others and replaster the house
with fresh daub.

If the infection reappears in the 43
house and spreads after the stones
have been pulled out and the house

m Or mud.

44 scraped and redaubed, the priest shall come and inspect it. If the infection has spread in the house, it is a corro-
45 sive growth; the house is unclean. The house shall be demolished, stones, timber, and daub, and it shall all be taken away outside the city to
46 an unclean place. Anyone who has entered the house during the time it has been in quarantine shall be un-
47 clean till evening. Anyone who has slept or eaten a meal in the house
48 shall wash his clothes. But if, when the priest goes into the house and inspects it, he finds that the infection has not spread after the redaubing, then he shall pronounce the house ritually clean, because the infection has been cured.

49 In order to rid the house of impurity, he shall take two small birds, cedar-wood, scarlet thread, and mar-
50 joram. He shall kill one of the birds over an earthenware bowl containing
51 fresh water. He shall then take the cedar-wood, marjoram, and scarlet thread, together with the living bird, dip them in the blood of the bird that has been killed and in the fresh water, and sprinkle the house seven times.
52 Thus he shall purify the house, using the blood of the bird, the fresh water, the living bird, the cedar-wood, the
53 marjoram, and the scarlet thread. He shall set the living bird free outside the city to fly away over the open country, and make expiation for the house; and then it shall be clean.

54 This is the law for all malignant
55 skin-diseases, and for scurf, for mould
56 in clothes and fungus in houses, for a discoloration of the skin, scab, and
57 inflammation, to declare when these are pronounced unclean and when clean. This is the law for skin-disease, mould, and fungus.

15 The LORD spoke to Moses and Aaron
2 and said, Speak to the Israelites and say to them: When any man has a discharge from his body, the discharge
3 is ritually unclean. This is the law concerning the uncleanness due to his discharge whether it continues or has been stopped; in either case he is unclean.
4 Every bed on which the man with a discharge lies down shall be ritually unclean, and everything on which he
5 sits shall be unclean. Any man who touches the bed shall wash his clothes, bathe in water and remain unclean
6 till evening. Whoever sits on anything on which the man with a discharge

has sat shall wash his clothes, bathe in water and remain unclean till eve-
7 ning. Whoever touches the body of the man with a discharge shall wash his clothes, bathe in water and remain
8 unclean till evening. If the man spits on one who is ritually clean, the latter shall wash his clothes, bathe in water and remain unclean till evening.
9 Everything on which the man sits when riding shall be unclean. Who-
10 ever touches anything that has been under him shall be unclean till evening, and whoever handles such things shall wash his clothes, bathe in water and remain unclean till evening. Any-
11 one whom the man with a discharge touches without having rinsed his hands in water shall wash his clothes, bathe in water and remain unclean
12 till evening. Any earthenware bowl touched by the man shall be smashed, and every wooden bowl shall be rinsed with water.

13 When the man is cleansed from his discharge, he shall reckon seven days to his cleansing, wash his clothes, bathe his body in fresh water and be
14 ritually clean. On the eighth day he shall obtain two turtle-doves or two young pigeons and, coming before the LORD at the entrance to the Tent of the Presence, shall give them to the
15 priest. The priest shall deal with one as a sin-offering and the other as a whole-offering, and shall make for him before the LORD the expiation required by the discharge.

16 When a man has emitted semen, he shall bathe his whole body in water and be unclean till evening. Every
17 piece of clothing or skin on which there is any semen shall be washed and remain unclean till evening. This
18 applies also to the woman with whom a man has had intercourse; they shall both bathe themselves in water and remain unclean till evening.

19 When a woman has a discharge of blood, her impurity shall last for seven days; anyone who touches her shall be unclean till evening. Every-
20 thing on which she lies or sits during her impurity shall be unclean. Any-
21 one who touches her bed shall wash his clothes, bathe in water and remain unclean till evening. Whoever touches
22 anything on which she sits shall wash his clothes, bathe in water and remain unclean till evening. If he is on the
23 bed or seat where she is sitting, by touching it he shall become unclean till evening. If a man goes so far as to
24 have intercourse with her and any of

her discharge gets on to him, then he shall be unclean for seven days, and every bed on which he lies down shall be unclean.

25 When a woman has a prolonged discharge of blood not at the time of her menstruation, or when her discharge continues beyond the period of menstruation, her impurity shall last all the time of her discharge; she shall be unclean as during the period of her

26 menstruation. Any bed on which she lies during the time of her discharge shall be like that which she used during menstruation, and everything on which she sits shall be unclean as

27 in her menstrual uncleanness. Every person who touches them shall be unclean; he shall wash his clothes, bathe in water and remain unclean till even-

28 ing. If she is cleansed from her discharge, she shall reckon seven days and after that she shall be ritually

29 clean. On the eighth day she shall obtain two turtle-doves or two young pigeons and bring them to the priest at the entrance to the Tent of

30 Presence. The priest shall deal with one as a sin-offering and with the other as a whole-offering, and make for her before the LORD the expiation required by her unclean discharge.

31 In this way you shall warn the Israelites against uncleanness, in order that they may not bring uncleanness upon the Tabernacle where I dwell among them, and so die.

32 This is the law for the man who has a discharge, or who has an emission

33 of semen and is thereby unclean, and for the woman who is suffering her menstruation—for everyone, male or female, who has a discharge, and for the man who has intercourse with a woman who is unclean.

The Day of Atonement

16 The LORD spoke to Moses after the death of Aaron's two sons, who died when they offered illicit fire before

2 the LORD. He said to him: Tell your brother Aaron that he must not enter the sanctuary within the Veil, in front of the cover over the Ark, except at the appointed time, on pain of death; for I appear in the cloud above the

3 cover. When Aaron enters the sanctuary, this is what he shall do. He shall bring a young bull for a sin-offering

4 and a ram for a whole-offering. He shall wear a sacred linen tunic and linen drawers to cover himself, and he shall put a linen sash round his waist

and wind a linen turban round his head; all these are sacred vestments, and he shall bathe in water before putting them on. He shall take from 5 the community of the Israelites two he-goats for a sin-offering and a ram for a whole-offering. He shall present 6 the bull as a sin-offering and make expiation for himself and his household. Then he shall take the two he- 7 goats and set them before the LORD at the entrance to the Tent of the Presence. He shall cast lots over the 8 two goats, one to be for the LORD and the other for the Precipice.[n] He shall 9 present the goat on which the lot for the LORD has fallen and deal with it as a sin-offering; but the goat on which 10 the lot for the Precipice has fallen shall be made to stand alive before the LORD, for expiation to be made over it before it is driven away into the wilderness to the Precipice.

Aaron shall present his bull as 11 a sin-offering, making expiation for himself and his household, and then slaughter the bull as a sin-offering. He shall take a firepan full of glow- 12 ing embers from the altar before the LORD, and two handfuls of powdered fragrant incense, and bring them within the Veil. He shall put the incense on 13 the fire before the LORD, and the cloud of incense will hide the cover over the Tokens so that he shall not die. He 14 shall take some of the bull's blood and sprinkle it with his finger both on the surface of the cover, eastwards, and seven times in front of the cover.

He shall then slaughter the people's 15 goat as a sin-offering, bring its blood within the Veil and do with its blood as he did with the bull's blood, sprinkling it on the cover and in front of it. He shall make for the sanctuary the 16 expiation required by the ritual uncleanness of the Israelites and their acts of rebellion, that is by all their sins; and he shall do the same for the Tent of the Presence, which dwells among them in the midst of all their uncleanness. No other man shall be 17 within the Tent of the Presence from the time when he enters the sanctuary to make expiation until he comes out, and he shall make expiation for himself, his household, and the whole assembly of Israel.

He shall then come out to the altar 18 which is before the LORD and make expiation for it. He shall take some of the bull's blood and some of the goat's blood and put it all over the

n Or for Azazel.

9 horns of the altar; he shall sprinkle some of the blood on the altar with his finger seven times. So he shall purify it from all the uncleanness of the Israelites and hallow it.

20 When Aaron has finished making expiation for the sanctuary, for the Tent of the Presence, and for the altar, he shall bring forward the live goat.

21 He shall lay both his hands on its head and confess over it all the iniquities of the Israelites and all their acts of rebellion, that is all their sins; he shall lay them on the head of the goat and send it away into the wilderness in charge of a man who is waiting ready.

22 The goat shall carry all their iniquities upon itself into some barren waste and the man shall let it go, there in the wilderness.

23 Aaron shall then enter the Tent of the Presence, take off the linen clothes which he had put on when he entered the sanctuary, and leave them there.

24 He shall bathe in water in a consecrated place and put on his vestments; then he shall go out and perform his own whole-offering and that of the people, thus making expiation for him-

25 self and for the people. He shall burn the fat of the sin-offering upon the

26 altar. The man who drove the goat away to the Precipice shall wash his clothes and bathe in water, and not

27 till then may he enter the camp. The two sin-offerings, the bull and the goat, the blood of which was brought within the Veil to make expiation in the sanctuary, shall be taken outside the camp and destroyed by fire—

28 skin, flesh, and offal. The man who burns them shall wash his clothes and bathe in water, and not till then may he enter the camp.

29 This shall become a rule binding on you for all time. On the tenth day of the seventh month you shall mortify yourselves; you shall do no work, whether native Israelite or alien settler,

30 because on this day expiation shall be made on your behalf to cleanse you, and so make you clean before the

31 LORD from all your sins. This is a sabbath of sacred rest for you, and you shall mortify yourselves; it is a rule

32 binding for all time. Expiation shall be made by the priest duly anointed and installed to serve in succession to his father; he shall put on the sacred

33 linen clothes and shall make expiation for the holy sanctuary, the Tent of the Presence, and the altar, on behalf of the priests and the whole

assembly of the people. This shall 34 become a rule binding on you for all time, to make for the Israelites once a year the expiation required by all their sins.

And Moses carried out the LORD's commands.

The one place of sacrifice

The LORD spoke to Moses and said, 17 Speak to Aaron, his sons, and all the 2 Israelites in these words: This is what the LORD has commanded. Any Is- 3 raelite who slaughters an ox, a sheep, or a goat, either inside or outside the camp, and does not bring it to the 4 entrance of the Tent of the Presence to present it as an offering to the LORD before the Tabernacle of the LORD shall be held guilty of bloodshed: that man has shed blood and shall be cut off from his people. The purpose 5 is that the Israelites should bring to the LORD the animals which they slaughter in the open country; they shall bring them to the priest at the entrance to the Tent of the Presence and sacrifice them as shared-offerings to the LORD. The priest shall fling the 6 blood against the altar of the LORD at the entrance to the Tent of the Presence, and burn the fat as a soothing odour to the LORD. They shall no 7 longer sacrifice their slaughtered beasts to the demons[o] whom they wantonly follow. This shall be a rule binding on them and their descendants for all time.

You shall say to them: Any Is- 8 raelite or alien settled in Israel who offers a whole-offering or a sacrifice and 9 does not bring it to the entrance of the Tent of the Presence to sacrifice it to the LORD shall be cut off from his father's kin.

Eating blood forbidden

If any Israelite or alien settled in 10 Israel eats any blood, I will set my face against the eater and cut him off from his people, because the life of a 11 creature is the blood, and I appoint it to make expiation on the altar for yourselves: it is the blood, that is the life, that makes expiation. Therefore 12 I have told the Israelites that neither you, nor any alien settled among you, shall eat blood.

Any Israelite or alien settled in 13 Israel who hunts beasts or birds that may lawfully be eaten shall drain out the blood and cover it with earth, be- 14 cause the life of every living creature

o Or satyrs.

is the blood, and I have forbidden the Israelites to eat the blood of any creature, because the life of every creature is its blood: every man who eats it shall be cut off.

15 Every person, native or alien, who eats that which has died a natural death or has been mauled by wild beasts shall wash his clothes and bathe in water, and remain ritually unclean till evening; then he shall be 16 clean. If he does not wash his clothes and bathe his body, he must accept responsibility.

Immorality forbidden

18 The LORD spoke to Moses and said, 2 Speak to the Israelites in these words: 3 I am the LORD your God. You shall not do as they do in Egypt where you once dwelt, nor shall you do as they do in the land of Canaan to which I am bringing you; you shall not con- 4 form to their institutions. You must keep my laws and conform to my institutions without fail: I am the 5 LORD your God. You shall observe my institutions and my laws: the man who keeps them shall have life through them. I am the LORD.

6 No man shall approach a blood-relation for intercourse. I am the 7 LORD. You shall not bring shame on your father by intercourse with your mother: she is your mother; you shall 8 not bring shame upon her. You shall not have intercourse with your father's wife: that is to bring shame upon 9 your father. You shall not have inter-course with your sister, your father's daughter, or your mother's daughter, whether brought up in the family or in another home; you shall not bring 10 shame upon them. You shall not have intercourse with your son's daughter or your daughter's daughter: that is 11 to bring shame upon yourself. You shall not have intercourse with a daughter of your father's wife, begot-ten by your father: she is your sister, and you shall not bring shame upon 12 her. You shall not have intercourse with your father's sister: she is a 13 blood-relation of your father. You shall not have intercourse with your mother's sister: she is a blood-relation 14 of your mother. You shall not bring shame upon your father's brother by approaching his wife: she is your 15 aunt. You shall not have intercourse with your daughter-in-law: she is your son's wife; you shall not bring 16 shame upon her. You shall not have intercourse with your brother's wife:

that is to bring shame upon him. You 17 shall not have intercourse with both a woman and her daughter, nor shall you take her son's daughter or her daughter's daughter to have inter-course with them: they are her blood-relations, and such conduct is lewdness. You shall not take a woman who is 18 your wife's sister to make her a rival-wife, and to have intercourse with her during her sister's lifetime.

You shall not approach a woman to 19 have intercourse with her during her period of menstruation. You shall not 20 have sexual intercourse with the wife of your fellow-countryman and so make yourself unclean with her. You 21 shall not surrender any of your chil-dren to Molech and thus profane the name of your God: I am the LORD. You shall not lie with a man as with a 22 woman: that is an abomination. You 23 shall not have sexual intercourse with any beast to make yourself unclean with it, nor shall a woman submit her-self to intercourse with a beast: that is a violation of nature. You shall not 24 make yourselves unclean in any of these ways; for in these ways the heathen, whom I am driving out before you, made themselves unclean. This is how the land became unclean, 25 and I punished it for its iniquity so that it spewed out its inhabitants. You, unlike them, shall keep my laws 26 and my rules: none of you, whether natives or aliens settled among you, shall do any of these abominable things. The people who were there 27 before you did these abominable things and the land became unclean. So the land will not spew you out for 28 making it unclean as it spewed them out; for anyone who does any of these 29 abominable things shall be cut off from his people. Observe my charge, 30 therefore, and follow none of the abominable institutions customary be-fore your time; do not make your-selves unclean with them. I am the LORD your God.

Rules about conduct

The LORD spoke to Moses and said, 19 Speak to all the community of the 2 Israelites in these words: You shall be holy, because I, the LORD your God, am holy. You shall revere, every man 3 of you, his mother and his father. You shall keep my sabbaths. I am the LORD your God. Do not resort to idols; 4 you shall not make gods of cast metal for yourselves. I am the LORD your God.

5 When you sacrifice a shared-offering to the LORD, you shall slaughter it so as to win acceptance 6 for yourselves. It must be eaten on the day of your sacrifice or the next day. Whatever is left over till the third day shall be destroyed by fire; 7 it is tainted, and if any of it is eaten on the third day, it will not be ac-8 ceptable. He who eats it must accept responsibility, because he has profaned the holy-gift to the LORD: that person shall be cut off from his father's kin.

9 When you reap the harvest of your land, you shall not reap right into the edges of your field; neither shall you 10 glean the loose ears of your crop; you shall not completely strip your vineyard nor glean the fallen grapes. You shall leave them for the poor and the alien. I am the LORD your God.

11 You shall not steal; you shall not cheat or deceive a fellow-countryman. 12 You shall not swear in my name with intent to deceive and thus profane the name of your God. I am the LORD.

13 You shall not oppress your neighbour, nor rob him. You shall not keep back a hired man's wages till next morning. 14 You shall not treat the deaf with contempt, nor put an obstruction in the way of the blind. You shall fear your God. I am the LORD.

15 You shall not pervert justice, either by favouring the poor or by subservience to the great. You shall judge your fellow-countryman with strict 16 justice. You shall not go about spreading slander among your father's kin, nor take sides against your neighbour on a capital charge. I am the LORD. 17 You shall not nurse hatred against your brother. You shall reprove your fellow-countryman frankly and so you 18 will have no share in his guilt.[p] You shall not seek revenge, or cherish anger towards your kinsfolk; you shall love your neighbour as a man like yourself. I am the LORD.

19 You shall keep my rules. You shall not allow two different kinds of beast to mate together. You shall not plant your field with two kinds of seed. You shall not put on a garment woven with two kinds of yarn.

20 When a man has intercourse with a slave-girl who has been assigned to another man and neither ransomed nor given her freedom, inquiry shall be made. They shall not be put to death, because she has not been freed.

The man shall bring his guilt-offering, 21 a ram, to the LORD to the entrance of the Tent of the Presence, and with it 22 the priest shall make expiation for him before the LORD for his sin, and he shall be forgiven the sin he has committed.

When you enter the land, and plant 23 any kind of tree for food, you shall treat it as bearing forbidden fruit. For three years it shall be forbidden and may not be eaten. In the fourth year 24 all its fruit shall be a holy-gift to the LORD, and this releases it for use. In 25 the fifth year you may eat its fruit, and thus the yield it gives you shall be increased. I am the LORD your God.

You shall not eat meat with the 26 blood in it. You shall not practise divination or soothsaying. You shall 27 not round off your hair from side to side, and you shall not shave the edge of your beards. You shall not gash 28 yourselves in mourning for the dead; you shall not tattoo yourselves. I am the LORD.

Do not prostitute your daughter 29 and so make her a whore; thus the land shall not play the prostitute and be full of lewdness. You shall keep my 30 sabbaths, and revere my sanctuary. I am the LORD.

Do not resort to ghosts and spirits, 31 nor make yourselves unclean by seeking them out. I am the LORD your God.

You shall rise in the presence of 32 grey hairs, give honour to the aged, and fear your God. I am the LORD.

When an alien settles with you in 33 your land, you shall not oppress him. He shall be treated as a native born 34 among you, and you shall love him as a man like yourself, because you were aliens in Egypt. I am the LORD your God.

You shall not pervert justice in 35 measurement of length, weight, or quantity. You shall have true scales, 36 true weights, true measures dry and liquid. I am the LORD your God who brought you out of Egypt. You shall 37 observe all my rules and laws and carry them out. I am the LORD.

Penalties for disobedience

The LORD spoke to Moses and said, 20 Say to the Israelites: Any Israelite or 2 alien settled in Israel who gives any of his children to Molech shall be put to death: the common people shall stone him. I, for my part, set my face 3

[p] Or and for that you will incur no blame.

against that man and cut him off from his people, because he has given a child of his to Molech, thus making my sanctuary unclean and profaning 4 my holy name. If the common people connive at it when a man has given a child of his to Molech and do not put 5 him to death, I will set my face against man and family, and both him and all who follow him in his wanton following after Molech,[q] I will cut off from their people.

6 I will set my face against the man who wantonly resorts to ghosts and spirits, and I will cut that person off 7 from his people. Hallow yourselves and be holy, because I the LORD your 8 God am holy. You shall keep my rules and obey them: I am the LORD who hallows you.

9 When any man reviles his father and his mother, he shall be put to death. He has reviled his father and his mother; his blood shall be on his 10 own head. If a man commits adultery with his neighbour's wife, both adulterer and adulteress shall be put to 11 death. The man who has intercourse with his father's wife has brought shame on his father. They shall both be put to death; their blood shall be 12 on their own heads. If a man has intercourse with his daughter-in-law, they shall both be put to death. Their deed is a violation of nature; their 13 blood shall be on their own heads. If a man has intercourse with a man as with a woman, they both commit an abomination. They shall be put to death; their blood shall be on their 14 own heads. If a man takes both a woman and her mother, that is lewdness. Both he and they shall be burnt; thus there shall be no lewdness in 15 your midst. A man who has sexual intercourse with any beast shall be 16 put to death, and you shall kill the beast. If a woman approaches any animal to have intercourse with it, you shall kill both woman and beast. They shall be put to death; their 17 blood shall be on their own heads. If a man takes his sister, his father's daughter or his mother's daughter, and they see one another naked, it is a scandalous disgrace. They shall be cut off in the presence of their people. The man has had intercourse with his sister and he shall accept 18 responsibility. If a man lies with a woman during her monthly period and brings shame upon her, he has exposed her discharge and she has

uncovered the source of her discharge; they shall both be cut off from their people. You shall not have intercourse 19 with your mother's sister or your father's sister: it is the exposure of a blood-relation. They shall accept responsibility. A man who has inter- 20 course with his uncle's wife has brought shame upon his uncle. They shall accept responsibility for their sin and shall be proscribed and put to death. If a man takes his brother's wife, it 21 is impurity. He has brought shame upon his brother; they shall be proscribed.

You shall keep all my rules and my 22 laws and carry them out, that the land into which I am bringing you to live may not spew you out. You shall 23 not conform to the institutions of the nations whom I am driving out before you: they did all these things and I abhorred them, and I told you that 24 you should occupy their land, and I would give you possession of it, a land flowing with milk and honey. I am the LORD your God: I have made a clear separation between you and the nations, and you shall make a clear 25 separation between clean beasts and unclean beasts and between unclean and clean birds. You shall not make yourselves vile through beast or bird or anything that creeps on the ground, for I have made a clear separation between them and you, declaring them unclean. You shall be holy to me, 26 because I the LORD am holy. I have made a clear separation between you and the heathen, that you may belong to me. Any man or woman among you 27 who calls up ghosts or spirits shall be put to death. The people shall stone them; their blood shall be on their own heads.

Holiness of the priests

The LORD said to Moses, Say to the 21 priests, the sons of Aaron: A priest shall not render himself unclean for the death of any of his kin except 2 for a near blood-relation, that is for mother, father, son, daughter, brother, or full sister who is unmarried and a 3 virgin; nor shall he make himself un- 4 clean for any married woman[r] among his father's kin, and so profane himself.

Priests shall not make bald patches 5 on their heads as a sign of mourning, nor cut the edges of their beards, nor gash their bodies. They shall be holy 6

q Or in his lusting after human sacrifice.　　r for any married woman: prob. rdg.; Heb. husband.

to their God, and they shall not profane the name of their God, because they present the food-offerings of the LORD, the food of their God, and they
7 shall be holy. A priest shall not marry a prostitute or a girl who has lost her virginity, nor shall he marry a woman divorced from her husband; for he is
8 holy to his God. You shall keep him holy because he presents the food of your God; you shall regard him as holy because I the LORD, I who hallow them,
9 am holy. When a priest's daughter profanes herself by becoming a prostitute, she profanes her father. She shall be burnt to death.

10 The high priest, the one among his fellows who has had the anointing oil poured on his head and has been consecrated to wear the vestments, shall neither leave his hair dishevelled nor
11 tear his clothes. He shall not enter the place where any man's dead body lies; not even for his father or his mother
12 shall he render himself unclean. He shall not go out of the sanctuary for fear that he dishonour the sanctuary of his God, because the consecration of the anointing oil of his God is upon
13 him. I am the LORD. He shall marry a
14 woman who is still a virgin. He shall not marry a widow, a divorced woman, a woman who has lost her virginity, or a prostitute, but only a virgin from
15 his father's kin; he shall not dishonour his descendants among his father's kin, for I am the LORD who hallows him.

16 The LORD spoke to Moses and said,
17 Speak to Aaron in these words: No man among your descendants for all time who has any physical defect shall come and present the food of his God.
18 No man with a defect shall come, whether a blind man, a lame man, a
19 man stunted or overgrown, a man de-
20 formed in foot or hand, or with misshapen brows or a film over his eye or a discharge from it, a man who has a scab or eruption or has had a
21 testicle ruptured. No descendant of Aaron the priest who has any defect in his body shall approach to present the food-offerings of the LORD; because he has a defect he shall not approach to present the food of his
22 God. He may eat the bread of God both from the holy-gifts and from the
23 holiest of holy-gifts, but he shall not come up to the Veil nor approach the altar, because he has a defect in his body. Thus he shall not profane my sanctuaries, because I am the LORD who hallows them.

Thus did Moses speak to Aaron and 24 his sons and to all the Israelites.

Holiness of offerings

The LORD spoke to Moses and said, 22
Tell Aaron and his sons that they must 2 be careful in the handling of the holy-gifts of the Israelites which they hallow to me, lest they profane my holy name. I am the LORD. Say to 3 them: Any man of your descent for all time who while unclean approaches the holy-gifts which the Israelites hallow to the LORD shall be cut off from my presence. I am the LORD. No man descended from Aaron who 4 suffers from a malignant skin-disease, or has a discharge, shall eat of the holy-gifts until he is cleansed. A man who touches anything which makes him unclean or who has an emission of semen, a man who touches any ver- 5 min which makes him unclean or any human being who makes him unclean: any person who touches such 6 a thing shall be unclean till sunset and unless he washes his body shall not eat of the holy-gifts. When the 7 sun goes down, he shall be clean, and after that he may eat from the holy-gifts, because they are his food. He 8 shall not eat an animal that has died a natural death or has been mauled by wild beasts, thereby making himself unclean. I am the LORD. The 9 priests shall observe my charge, lest they make themselves guilty and die for profaning my name. I am the LORD who hallows them. No unquali- 10 fied person may eat any holy-gift; nor may a stranger lodging with a priest or a hired man eat a holy-gift. A slave bought by a priest with his 11 own money may do so, and slaves born in his household may also share his food. When a priest's daughter 12 marries an unqualified person, she shall not eat any of the contributions of holy-gifts; but if she is widowed or 13 divorced and is childless and comes back to her father's house as in her childhood, she shall share her father's food. No unqualified person may eat any of it.

When a man inadvertently eats a 14 holy-gift, he shall make good the holy-gift to the priest, adding a fifth to its value. The priests shall not profane 15 the holy-gifts of the Israelites which they set aside for the LORD; they shall 16 not let men eat their holy-gifts and so incur guilt and its penalty, because I am the LORD who hallows them.

The LORD spoke to Moses and said, 17

18 Speak to Aaron and his sons and to all the Israelites in these words: When any man of the house of Israel or any alien in Israel presents, whether in fulfilment of a vow or for a freewill offering, such an offering as is presented to the LORD for a whole-offering
19 so as to win acceptance for yourselves, it shall be a male without defect, of
20 cattle, sheep, or goats. You shall not present anything which is defective, because it will not be acceptable on
21 your behalf. When a man presents a shared-offering to the LORD, whether cattle or sheep, to fulfil a special[s] vow or as a freewill offering, if it is to be acceptable it must be perfect;
22 there shall be no defect in it. You shall present to the LORD nothing blind, disabled, mutilated, with running sore, scab, or eruption, nor set any such creature on the altar as a food-
23 offering to the LORD. If a bull or a sheep is overgrown or stunted, you may make of it a freewill offering, but it will not be acceptable in fulfilment
24 of a vow. If its testicles have been crushed or bruised, torn or cut, you shall not present it to the LORD; this is forbidden in your land.
25 You shall not procure any such creature from a foreigner and present it as food for your God. Their deformity is inherent in them, a permanent defect, and they will not be acceptable on your behalf.
26 The LORD spoke to Moses and said:
27 When a calf, a lamb, or a kid is born, it must not be taken from its mother for seven days. From the eighth day onwards it will be acceptable when offered as a food-offering to the LORD.
28 You shall not slaughter a cow or sheep at the same time as its young.
29 When you make a thank-offering to the LORD, you shall sacrifice it so as
30 to win acceptance for yourselves; it shall be eaten that same day, and none be left till morning. I am the LORD.
31 You shall observe my commandments and perform them. I am the
32 LORD. You shall not profane my holy name; I will be hallowed among the Israelites. I am the LORD who hallows
33 you, who brought you out of Egypt to become your God. I am the LORD.

The appointed seasons

23 The LORD spoke to Moses and said,
2 Speak to the Israelites in these words: These are the appointed seasons of the LORD, and you shall proclaim them as sacred assemblies; these are my appointed seasons. On six days work 3 may be done, but every seventh day is a sabbath of sacred rest, a day of sacred assembly, on which you shall do no work. Wherever you live, it is the LORD's sabbath.

These are the appointed seasons of 4 the LORD, the sacred assemblies which you shall proclaim in their appointed order. In the first month on the four- 5 teenth day between dusk and dark is the LORD's Passover. On the fifteenth 6 day of this month begins the LORD's pilgrim-feast of Unleavened Bread; for seven days you shall eat unleavened cakes. On the first day there shall be 7 a sacred assembly; you shall not do your daily work. For seven days you 8 shall present your food-offerings to the LORD. On the seventh day also there shall be a sacred assembly; you shall not do your daily work.

The LORD spoke to Moses and said, 9 Speak to the Israelites in these words: 10 When you enter the land which I give you, and you reap its harvest, you shall bring the first sheaf of your harvest to the priest. He shall present 11 the sheaf as a special gift before the LORD on[t] the day after the sabbath, so as to gain acceptance for yourselves. On the day you present the sheaf, you 12 shall prepare a perfect yearling ram for a whole-offering to the LORD, with the proper grain-offering, two 13 tenths of an ephah of flour mixed with oil, as a food-offering to the LORD, of soothing odour, and also with the proper drink-offering, a quarter of a hin of wine. You shall eat neither 14 bread, nor grain, parched or fully ripened, during that day, the day on which you bring your God his offering; this is a rule binding on your descendants for all time wherever you live.

From the day after the sabbath, the 15 day on which you bring your sheaf as a special gift, you shall count seven full weeks. The day after the seventh 16 sabbath will make fifty days, and then you shall present to the LORD a grain-offering from the new crop. You 17 shall bring from your homes two loaves as a special gift; they shall contain two tenths of an ephah of flour and shall be baked with leaven. They are the LORD's firstfruits. In 18 addition to the bread you shall present seven perfect yearling sheep, one young bull, and two rams. They shall be a whole-offering to the LORD with the proper grain-offering and the proper drink-offering, a food-offering of

s fulfil a special: *or* discharge a . . .   *t* Or from.

19 soothing odour to the LORD. You shall also prepare one he-goat for a sin-offering and two yearling sheep for a 20 shared-offering, and the priest shall present them in addition to the bread of the firstfruits as a special gift before the LORD. They shall be a holy-21 gift to the LORD for the priest. On that same day you shall proclaim a sacred assembly for yourselves; you shall not do your daily work. This is a rule binding on your descendants for all time wherever you live.

22 When you reap the harvest in your land, you shall not reap right into the edges of your field, neither shall you glean the fallen ears. You shall leave them for the poor and for the alien. I am the LORD your God.

23 The LORD spoke to Moses and said, 24 Speak to the Israelites in these words: In the seventh month you shall keep the first day as a sacred rest, a day of remembrance and acclamation, a day 25 of sacred assembly. You shall not do your daily work; you shall present a food-offering to the LORD.

26 The LORD spoke to Moses and said: 27 Further, the tenth day of this seventh month is the Day of Atonement. There shall be a sacred assembly; you shall mortify yourselves and present 28 a food-offering to the LORD. On that same day you shall do no work be-cause it is a day of expiation, to make expiation for you before the LORD 29 your God. Therefore every person who does not mortify himself on that day shall be cut off from his father's 30 kin. I will extirpate any person who 31 does any work on that day. You shall do no work; it is a rule binding on your descendants for all time wherever 32 you live. It is for you a sabbath of sacred rest, and you shall mortify yourselves. From the evening of the ninth day to the following evening you shall keep your sabbath-rest.

33 The LORD spoke to Moses and said, 34 Speak to the Israelites in these words: On the fifteenth day of this seventh month the LORD's pilgrim-feast of Tabernacles[u] begins, and it lasts for 35 seven days. On the first day there shall be a sacred assembly; you shall not 36 do your daily work. For seven days you shall present a food-offering to the LORD; and on the eighth day there shall be a sacred assembly, and you shall present a food-offering to the LORD. It is the closing ceremony; you shall not do your daily work.

37 These are the appointed seasons of the LORD which you shall proclaim as sacred assemblies for presenting food-offerings to the LORD, whole-offerings and grain-offerings, shared-offerings and drink-offerings, each on its day, besides the LORD's sabbaths and all 38 your gifts, your vows, and your free-will offerings to the LORD.

Further, from the fifteenth day of 39 the seventh month, when the harvest has been gathered, you shall keep the LORD's pilgrim-feast for seven days. The first day is a sacred rest and so is the eighth day. On the first day you 40 shall take the fruit of citrus-trees, palm fronds, and leafy branches, and willows[v] from the riverside, and you shall rejoice before the LORD your God for seven days. You shall keep this as 41 a pilgrim-feast in the LORD's honour for seven days every year. It is a rule binding for all time on your descen-dants; in the seventh month you shall hold this pilgrim-feast. You shall live 42 in arbours for seven days, all who are native Israelites, so that your descen-43 dants may be reminded how I made the Israelites live in arbours when I brought them out of Egypt. I am the LORD your God.

Thus Moses announced to the Is-44 raelites the appointed seasons of the LORD.

Tending the lamps

The LORD spoke to Moses and said: **24** Command the Israelites to take pure 2 oil of pounded olives ready for the regular mounting of the lamp outside 3 the Veil of the Tokens in the Tent of the Presence. Aaron shall keep the lamp in trim regularly from dusk to dawn before the LORD: this is a rule binding on your descendants for all time. The lamps on the lamp-stand, 4 ritually clean, shall be regularly kept in trim by him before the LORD.

Bread of the Presence

You shall take flour and bake it into 5 twelve loaves, two tenths of an ephah to each. You shall arrange them in 6 two rows, six to a row on the table, ritually clean, before the LORD. You 7 shall sprinkle pure frankincense on the rows, and this shall be a token of the bread, offered to the LORD as a food-offering. Sabbath after sabbath 8 he shall arrange it regularly before the LORD as a gift from the Israelites. This is a covenant for ever; it is the 9 privilege of Aaron and his sons, and they shall eat the bread in a holy

u Or Booths or Arbours.   v Or poplars.

place, because it is the holiest of holy-gifts. It is his due out of the food-offerings of the LORD for all time.

Various penalties

10-11 Now there was in the Israelite camp a man whose mother was an Israel-ite and his father an Egyptian; his mother's name was Shelomith daugh-ter of Dibri of the tribe of Dan; and he went out and became involved in a brawl with an Israelite of pure descent. He uttered the Holy Name in blasphemy, so they brought him to

12 Moses; and they kept him in custody until the LORD's will should be clearly made known to them.

13   The LORD spoke to Moses and said,
14 Take the man who blasphemed out of the camp. Everyone who heard him shall put a hand[w] on his head, and then all the community shall stone

15 him to death. You shall say to the Israelites: When any man whatever blasphemes his God, he shall accept

16 responsibility for his sin. Whoever utters the Name of the LORD shall be put to death: all the community shall stone him; alien or native, if he utters the Name, he shall be put to death.

17   When one man strikes another and kills him, he shall be put to death.

18 Whoever strikes a beast and kills it shall make restitution, life for life.

19 When one man injures and disfigures his fellow-countryman, it shall be

20 done to him as he has done; fracture for fracture, eye for eye, tooth for tooth; the injury and disfigurement that he has inflicted upon another shall in turn be inflicted upon him.

21   Whoever strikes a beast and kills it shall make restitution, but whoever strikes a man and kills him shall be

22 put to death. You shall have one penalty for alien and native alike. For I am the LORD your God.

23   Thus did Moses speak to the Israelites, and they took the man who blasphemed out of the camp and stoned him to death. The Israelites did as the LORD had commanded Moses.

Sabbath years and the year of jubilee

25 The LORD spoke to Moses on Mount
2 Sinai and said, Speak to the Israelites in these words: When you enter the land which I give you, the land shall
3 keep sabbaths to the LORD. For six years you may sow your fields and for six years prune your vineyards and

gather the harvest, but in the seventh 4 year the land shall keep a sabbath of sacred rest, a sabbath to the LORD. You shall not sow your field nor prune your vineyard. You shall not harvest 5 the crop that grows from fallen grain, nor gather in the grapes from the unpruned vines. It shall be a year of sacred rest for the land. Yet what the 6 land itself produces in the sabbath year shall be food for you, for your male and female slaves, for your hired man, and for the stranger lodging under your roof, for your cattle and 7 for the wild animals in your country. Everything it produces may be used for food.

You shall count seven sabbaths of 8 years, that is seven times seven years, forty-nine years, and in the seventh 9 month on the tenth day of the month, on the Day of Atonement, you shall send the ram's horn round. You shall send it through all your land to sound a blast, and so you shall hallow the 10 fiftieth year and proclaim liberation in the land for all its inhabitants. You shall make this your year of jubilee. Every man of you shall return to his patrimony, every man to his family. The fiftieth year shall be your jubilee. 11 You shall not sow, and you shall not harvest the self-sown crop, nor shall you gather in the grapes from the unpruned vines, because it is a jubilee, 12 to be kept holy by you. You shall eat the produce direct from the land.

In this year of jubilee you shall 13 return, every one of you, to his patri-mony. When you sell or buy land 14 amongst yourselves, neither party shall drive a hard bargain. You shall 15 pay your fellow-countryman accord-ing to the number of years since the jubilee, and he shall sell to you accord-ing to the number of annual crops. The more years there are to run, the 16 higher the price, the fewer the years, the lower, because he is selling you a series of crops. You must not victimize 17 one another, but you shall fear your God, because I am the LORD your God. Observe my statutes, keep my judge- 18 ments and carry them out; and you shall live in the land in security. The 19 land shall yield its harvest; you shall eat your fill and live there secure. If 20 you ask what you are to eat during the seventh year, seeing that you will neither sow nor gather the harvest, I 21 will ordain my blessing for you in the sixth year and the land shall produce a crop to carry over three years. When 22

w Or their hands.

you sow in the eighth year, you will still be eating from the earlier crop; you shall eat the old until the new crop is gathered in the ninth year.

23 No land shall be sold outright, because the land is mine, and you are coming into it as aliens and settlers. 24 Throughout the whole land of your patrimony, you shall allow land which has been sold to be redeemed.

25 When one of you is reduced to poverty and sells part of his patrimony, his next-of-kin who has the duty of redemption shall come and redeem what his kinsman has sold. 26 When a man has no such next-of-kin and himself becomes able to afford its 27 redemption, he shall take into account the years since the sale and pay the purchaser the balance up to the jubilee. Then he may return to his patrimony. 28 But if the man cannot afford to buy back the property, it shall remain in the hands of the purchaser till the year of jubilee. It shall then revert to the original owner, and he shall return to his patrimony.

29 When a man sells a dwelling-house in a walled town, he shall retain the right of redemption till the end of the year of the sale; for a time he shall 30 have the right of redemption. If it is not redeemed before a full year is out, the house in the walled town shall vest in perpetuity in the buyer and his descendants; it shall not revert at the 31 jubilee. Houses in unwalled hamlets shall be treated as property in the open country: the right of redemption shall hold good, and in any case the house shall revert at the jubilee. 32 Levites shall have the perpetual right to redeem houses of their own patrimony in towns belonging to 33 them. If one of the Levites does not redeem his house in such a town, then it shall still revert to him at the jubilee, because the houses in Levite towns are their patrimony in Israel. 34 The common land surrounding their towns shall not be sold, because it is their property in perpetuity.

35 When your brother-Israelite is reduced to poverty and cannot support himself in the community, you shall assist him as you would an alien or a stranger, and he shall live with you. 36 You shall not charge him interest on a loan, either by deducting it in advance from the capital sum, or by adding it on repayment. You shall fear your God, and your brother shall 37 live with you; you shall not deduct interest when advancing him money

nor add interest to the payment due for food supplied on credit. I am the 38 LORD your God who brought you out of Egypt to give you the land of Canaan and to become your God.

When your brother is reduced to 39 poverty and sells himself to you, you shall not use him to work for you as a slave. His status shall be that of a 40 hired man or a stranger lodging with you; he shall work for you until the year of jubilee. He shall then leave 41 your service, with his children, and go back to his family and to his ancestral property: because they are my slaves 42 whom I brought out of Egypt, they shall not be sold as slaves are sold. You shall not drive him with ruthless 43 severity, but you shall fear your God. Such slaves as you have, male or 44 female, shall come from the nations round about you; from them you may buy slaves. You may also buy the chil- 45 dren of those who have settled and lodge with you and such of their family as are born in the land. These may become your property, and you may leave 46 them to your sons after you; you may use them as slaves permanently. But your fellow-Israelites you shall not drive with ruthless severity.

When an alien or a stranger living 47 with you becomes rich, and your brother becomes poor and sells himself to the alien or stranger or to a member of some alien family, he shall 48 have the right of redemption after he has sold himself. One of his brothers may redeem him, or his uncle, his 49 cousin, or any blood-relation of his family, or, if he can afford it, he may redeem himself. He and his purchaser 50 together shall reckon from the year when he sold himself to the year of jubilee, and the price shall be adjusted to the number of years. His period of service with his owner shall be reckoned at the rate of a hired man. If there are still many years to run to 51 the year of jubilee, he must repay for his redemption a proportionate amount of the sum for which he sold himself; if there are few, he shall reckon and 52 repay accordingly. He shall have the 53 status of a labourer hired from year to year, and you shall not let him be driven with ruthless severity by his owner. If the man is not redeemed in 54 the intervening years, he and his children shall be released in the year of jubilee; for it is to me that the 55 Israelites are slaves, my slaves whom I brought out of Egypt. I am the LORD your God.

Blessings for obedience

26 You shall not make idols for yourselves; you shall not erect a carved image or a sacred pillar; you shall not put a figured stone on your land to prostrate yourselves upon, because I
2 am the LORD your God. You shall keep my sabbaths and revere my sanctuary. I am the LORD.

3 If you conform to my statutes, if you observe my commandments and
4 carry them out, I will give you rain at the proper time; the land shall yield its produce and the trees of the
5 country-side their fruit. Threshing shall last till vintage and vintage till sowing; you shall eat your fill and live
6 secure in your land. I will give peace in the land, and you shall lie down to sleep with no one to terrify you. I will rid your land of dangerous beasts and
7 it shall not be ravaged by war. You shall put your enemies to flight and they shall fall in battle before you.
8 Five of you shall pursue a hundred and a hundred of you ten thousand; so shall your enemies fall in battle
9 before you. I will look upon you with favour, I will make you fruitful and increase your numbers: I will give my
10 covenant with you its full effect. Your old harvest shall last you in store until you have to clear out the old to
11 make room for the new. I will establish my Tabernacle among you and
12 will not spurn you. I will walk to and fro among you; I will become your God and you shall become my people.
13 I am the LORD your God who brought you out of Egypt and let you be their slaves no longer; I broke the bars of your yoke and enabled you to walk upright.

Punishments for disobedience

14 But if you do not listen to me, if you fail to keep all these commandments
15 of mine, if you reject my statutes, if you spurn my judgements, and do not obey all my commandments, but
16 break my covenant, then be sure that this is what I will do: I will bring upon you sudden terror, wasting disease, recurrent fever, and plagues that dim the sight and cause the appetite to fail. You shall sow your seed to no purpose, for your enemies
17 shall eat the crop. I will set my face against you, and you shall be routed by your enemies. Those that hate you shall hound you on until you run when there is no pursuit.

18 If after all this you do not listen to me, I will go on to punish you seven
19 times over for your sins. I will break down your stubborn pride. I will make the sky above you like iron and the
20 earth beneath you like bronze. Your strength shall be spent in vain; your land shall not yield its produce nor the trees of the land their fruit.

21 If you still defy me and refuse to listen, I will multiply your calamities
22 seven times, as your sins deserve. I will send wild beasts among you; they shall tear your children from you, destroy your cattle and bring your numbers low; and your roads shall be
23 deserted. If after all this you have not
24 learnt discipline but still defy me, I in turn will defy you and scourge you
25 seven times over for your sins. I will bring war in vengeance upon you, vengeance irrevocable under covenant; you shall be herded into your cities, I will send pestilence among you, and you shall be given over to the enemy.
26 I will cut short your daily bread until ten women can bake your bread in a single oven; they shall dole it out by weight, and though you eat, you shall not be satisfied.

27 If in spite of this you do not listen
28 to me and still defy me, I will defy you in anger, and I myself will punish you seven times over for your sins.
29 Instead of meat you shall eat your
30 sons and your daughters. I will destroy your hill-shrines and demolish your incense-altars. I will pile your rotting carcasses on the rotting logs*x* that were your idols, and I will spurn
31 you. I will make your cities desolate and destroy your sanctuaries; the soothing odour of your offerings I will
32 not accept. I will destroy your land, and the enemies who occupy it shall
33 be appalled. I will scatter you among the heathen, and I will pursue you with the naked sword; your land shall be desolate and your cities heaps of
34 rubble. Then, all the time that it lies desolate, while you are in exile in the land of your enemies, your land shall
35 enjoy its sabbaths to the full. All the time of its desolation it shall have the sabbath rest which it did not have
36 when you lived there. And I will make those of you who are left in the land of your enemies so ridden with fear that, when a leaf flutters behind them in the wind, they shall run as if it were the sword behind them; they shall fall with no one in pursuit. Though no
37 one pursues them they shall stumble

x rotting logs: or effigies.

over one another, as if the sword were behind them, and there shall be no 38 stand made against the enemy. You shall meet your end among the heathen, and your enemies' land shall 39 swallow you up. Those who are left shall pine away in an enemy land under their own iniquities; and with their fathers' iniquities upon them too, they shall pine away as they did. 40 But though they confess their iniquity, their own and their fathers', their treachery, and even their de- 41 fiance of me, I will defy them in my turn and carry them off into their enemies' land. Yet if then their stubborn spirit is broken and they accept 42 their punishment in full, I will remember my covenant with Jacob and my covenant with Isaac, yes, and my covenant with Abraham, and I will 43 remember the land. The land shall be rid of its people and enjoy in full its sabbaths while it lies desolate, and they shall pay in full the penalty because they rejected my judgements 44 and spurned my statutes. Yet even then, in their enemies' land, I shall not have rejected nor spurned them, bringing them to an end and so breaking my covenant with them, because 45 I am the LORD their God. I will remember on their behalf the covenant with the men of former times whom I brought out of Egypt in full sight of all the nations, that I might be their God. I am the LORD.

46 These are the statutes, the judgements, and the laws which the LORD established between himself and the Israelites on Mount Sinai through Moses.

Laws concerning dedications

27 The LORD spoke to Moses and said, 2 Speak to the Israelites in these words: When a man makes a special[y] vow to the LORD which requires your valua- 3 tion of living persons, a male between twenty and sixty years old shall be valued at fifty silver shekels, that is 4 shekels by the sacred standard. If it is a female, she shall be valued at 5 thirty shekels. If the person is between five years old and twenty, the valuation shall be twenty shekels for a male 6 and ten for a female. If the person is between a month and five years old, the valuation shall be five shekels for 7 a male and three for a female. If the person is over sixty and a male, the valuation shall be fifteen shekels, but 8 if a female, ten shekels. If the man is

too poor to pay the amount of your valuation, the person shall be set before the priest, and the priest shall value him according to the sum which the man who makes the vow can afford: the priest shall make the valuation.

If the vow concerns a beast such as 9 may be offered as an offering to the LORD, then every gift shall be holy to the LORD. He shall not change it for 10 another, or substitute good for bad or bad for good. But if a substitution is in fact made of one beast for another, then both the original beast and its substitute shall be holy to the LORD. If the vow concerns any unclean beast 11 such as may not be offered as an offering to the LORD, then the animal shall be brought before the priest, and 12 he shall value it whether good or bad. The priest's valuation shall be decisive; in case of redemption the pay- 13 ment shall be increased by one fifth.

When a man dedicates his house 14 as holy to the LORD, the priest shall value it whether good or bad, and the priest's valuation shall be decisive. If 15 the donor redeems his house, he shall pay the amount of the valuation increased by one fifth, and the house shall be his.

If a man dedicates to the LORD part 16 of his ancestral land, you shall value it according to the amount of seedcorn it can carry, at the rate of fifty shekels of silver for a homer of barley seed. If he dedicates his land from the 17 year of jubilee, it shall stand at your valuation; but if he dedicates it after 18 the year of jubilee, the priest shall estimate the price in silver according to the number of years remaining till the next year of jubilee, and this shall be deducted from your valuation. If 19 the man who dedicates his field should redeem it, he shall pay the amount of your valuation in silver, increased by one fifth, and it shall be his. If he does 20 not redeem it but sells the land to another man, it shall no longer be redeemable; when the land reverts at 21 the year of jubilee, it shall be like land that has been devoted, holy to the LORD. It shall belong to the priest as his patrimony.

If a man dedicates to the LORD 22 land which he has bought, land which is not part of his ancestral land, the 23 priest shall estimate the amount of the value for the period until the year of jubilee, and the man shall give the amount fixed as at that day; it is

y makes a special: or discharges a . . .

24 holy to the LORD. At the year of jubilee the land shall revert to the man from whom he bought it, whose 25 patrimony it is. Every valuation you make shall be made by the sacred standard (twenty gerahs to the shekel). 26 Notwithstanding, no man may dedicate to the LORD the first-born of a beast which in any case has to be offered as a first-born, whether an ox 27 or a sheep. It is the LORD's. If it is any unclean beast, he may redeem it at your valuation and shall add one fifth; but if it is not redeemed, it shall 28 be sold at your valuation. Notwithstanding, nothing which a man devotes to the LORD irredeemably from his own property, whether man or beast or ancestral land, may be sold or redeemed. Everything so devoted is most 29 holy to the LORD. No human being thus devoted may be redeemed, but he shall be put to death.

30 Every tithe on land, whether from grain or from the fruit of a tree, belongs to the LORD; it is holy to the LORD. If a man wishes to redeem any 31 of his tithe, he shall pay its value increased by one fifth. Every tenth 32 creature that passes under the counting rod shall be holy to the LORD; this applies to all tithes of cattle and sheep. There shall be no inquiry 33 whether it is good or bad, and no substitution. If any substitution is made, then both the tithe-animal and its substitute shall be forfeit as holy; it shall not be redeemed.

34 These are the commandments which the LORD gave Moses for the Israelites on Mount Sinai.

NUMBERS

Numbering Israel at Sinai

1 ON THE FIRST DAY of the second month in the second year after the Israelites came out of Egypt, the LORD spoke to Moses at the Tent of the Presence in the wilderness of 2 Sinai in these words: 'Number the whole community of Israel by families in the father's line, recording the name 3 of every male person aged twenty years and upwards fit for military service. You and Aaron are to make a detailed list of them by their tribal 4 hosts, and you shall have to assist you one head of family from each tribe. 5 These are their names:

6 of Reuben, Elizur son of Shedeur;
of Simeon, Shelumiel son of Zurishaddai;
7 of Judah, Nahshon son of Amminadab;
8 of Issachar, Nethaneel son of Zuar;
9 of Zebulun, Eliab son of Helon;
10 of Joseph: of Ephraim, Elishama son of Ammihud;
of Manasseh, Gamaliel son of Pedahzur;
11 of Benjamin, Abidan son of Gideoni;
12 of Dan, Ahiezer son of Ammishaddai;
13 of Asher, Pagiel son of Ocran;
14 of Gad, Eliasaph son of Reuel;
15 of Naphtali, Ahira son of Enan.'

16 These were the conveners of the whole community, chiefs of their fathers' tribes and heads of Israelite clans. So Moses and Aaron took these 17 men who had been indicated by name. They summoned the whole com- 18 munity on the first day of the second month, and they registered their descent by families in the father's line, recording every male person aged 19 twenty years and upwards, as the LORD had told Moses to do. Thus it was that he drew up the detailed lists in the wilderness of Sinai:

20 The tribal list of Reuben, Israel's eldest son, by families in the father's line, with the name of every male person aged twenty years and upwards 21 fit for service, the number in the list of the tribe of Reuben being forty-six thousand five hundred.

22 The tribal list of Simeon, by families in the father's line, with the name of every male person aged twenty years and upwards fit for service, the 23 number in the list of the tribe of Simeon being fifty-nine thousand three hundred.

24 The tribal list of Gad, by families in the father's line, with the names of all men aged twenty years and upwards fit for service, the number in 25 the list of the tribe of Gad being

forty-five thousand six hundred and fifty.

6 The tribal list of Judah, by families in the father's line, with the names of all men aged twenty years and up-27 wards fit for service, the number in the list of the tribe of Judah being seventy-four thousand six hundred.

28 The tribal list of Issachar, by families in the father's line, with the names of all men aged twenty years 29 and upwards fit for service, the number in the list of the tribe of Issachar being fifty-four thousand four hundred.

30 The tribal list of Zebulun, by families in the father's line, with the names of all men aged twenty years 31 and upwards fit for service, the number in the list of the tribe of Zebulun being fifty-seven thousand four hundred.

32 The tribal lists of Joseph: that of Ephraim, by families in the father's line, with the names of all men aged twenty years and upwards fit for 33 service, the number in the list of the tribe of Ephraim being forty thousand 34 five hundred; that of Manasseh, by families in the father's line, with the names of all men aged twenty years 35 and upwards fit for service, the number in the list of the tribe of Manasseh being thirty-two thousand two hundred.

36 The tribal list of Benjamin, by families in the father's line, with the names of all men aged twenty years 37 and upwards fit for service, the number in the list of the tribe of Benjamin being thirty-five thousand four hundred.

38 The tribal list of Dan, by families in the father's line, with the names of all men aged twenty years and up-39 wards fit for service, the number in the list of the tribe of Dan being sixty-two thousand seven hundred.

40 The tribal list of Asher, by families in the father's line, with the names of all men aged twenty years and up-41 wards fit for service, the number in the list of the tribe of Asher being forty-one thousand five hundred.

42 The tribal list of Naphtali, by families in the father's line, with the names of all men aged twenty years 43 and upwards fit for service, the number in the list of the tribe of Naphtali being fifty-three thousand four hundred.

44 These were the numbers recorded in the detailed lists by Moses and Aaron and the twelve chiefs of Israel,

each representing one tribe and being the head of a family. The total number 45 of Israelites aged twenty years and upwards fit for service, recorded in the lists of fathers' families, was six 46 hundred and three thousand five hundred and fifty. A list of the Levites 47 by their fathers' families was not made.

The Levites appointed over the Tabernacle

The LORD spoke to Moses and said, 48 'You shall not record the total num- 49 ber of the Levites or make a detailed list of them among the Israelites. You 50 shall put the Levites in charge of the Tabernacle of the Tokens, with its equipment and everything in it. They shall carry the Tabernacle and all its equipment; they alone shall be its attendants and shall pitch their tents round it. The Levites shall take the 51 Tabernacle down when it is due to move and shall put it up when it halts; any unqualified person who comes near it shall be put to death. All other 52 Israelites shall pitch their tents, each tribal host in its proper camp and under its own standard. But the Le- 53 vites shall encamp round the Tabernacle of the Tokens, so that divine wrath may not follow the whole community of Israel; the Tabernacle of the Tokens shall be in their keeping.' The Israelites did exactly as the 54 LORD had told Moses to do.

Plan of the camp

The LORD spoke to Moses and Aaron 2 and said, 'The Israelites shall encamp 2 each under his own standard by the emblems of his father's family; they shall pitch their tents round the Tent of the Presence, facing it.

'In front of it, on the east, the 3 division of Judah shall be stationed under the standard of its camp by tribal hosts. The chief of Judah shall be Nahshon son of Amminadab. His 4 host, with its members as detailed, numbers seventy-four thousand six hundred men. Next to Judah the tribe 5 of Issachar shall be stationed. Its chief shall be Nethaneel son of Zuar; his host, with its members as detailed, 6 numbers fifty-four thousand four hundred. Then the tribe of Zebulun: 7 its chief shall be Eliab son of Helon; his host, with its members as detailed, 8 numbers fifty-seven thousand four hundred. The number listed in the 9 camp of Judah, by hosts, is one hundred and eighty-six thousand four

hundred. They shall be the first to
march.

10   'To the south the division of Reuben shall be stationed under the
standard of its camp by tribal hosts.
The chief of Reuben shall be Elizur
11 son of Shedeur; his host, with its
members as detailed, numbers forty-
12 six thousand five hundred. Next to
him the tribe of Simeon shall be
stationed. Its chief shall be Shelumiel
13 son of Zurishaddai; his host, with its
members as detailed, numbers fifty-
14 nine thousand three hundred. Then
the tribe of Gad: its chief shall be
15 Eliasaph son of Reuel; his host, with
its members as detailed, numbers
forty-five thousand six hundred and
16 fifty. The number listed in the camp
of Reuben, by hosts, is one hundred
and fifty-one thousand four hundred
and fifty. They shall be the second to
march.

17   'When the Tent of the Presence
moves, the camp of the Levites shall
keep its station in the centre of the
other camps; they shall all move in
the order of their encamping, each
man in his proper place under his
standard.

18   'To the west the division of Ephraim shall be stationed under the
standard of its camp by tribal hosts.
The chief of Ephraim shall be Elisha-
19 ma son of Ammihud; his host, with
its members as detailed, numbers
20 forty thousand five hundred. Next to
him the tribe of Manasseh shall be
stationed. Its chief shall be Gamaliel
21 son of Pedahzur; his host, with its
members as detailed, numbers thirty-
22 two thousand two hundred. Then the
tribe of Benjamin: its chief shall be
23 Abidan son of Gideoni; his host, with
its members as detailed, numbers
thirty-five thousand four hundred.
24 The number listed in the camp of
Ephraim, by hosts, is one hundred and
eight thousand one hundred. They
shall be the third to march.

25   'To the north the division of Dan
shall be stationed under the standard
of its camp by tribal hosts. The chief
of Dan shall be Ahiezer son of Am-
26 mishaddai; his host, with its members
as detailed, numbers sixty-two thou-
27 sand seven hundred. Next to him the
tribe of Asher shall be stationed. Its
28 chief shall be Pagiel son of Ocran; his
host, with its members as detailed,
numbers forty-one thousand five hun-
29 dred. Then the tribe of Naphtali:
its chief shall be Ahira son of Enan;
30 his host, with its members as detailed,

numbers fifty-three thousand four
hundred. The number listed in the 31
camp of Dan is a hundred and fifty-
seven thousand six hundred. They
shall march, under their standards,
last.'

These were the Israelites listed by 32
their fathers' families. The total number in the camp, recorded by tribal
hosts, was six hundred and three
thousand five hundred and fifty.
The Levites were not included in 33
the detailed lists with their fellow-
Israelites, for so the LORD had commanded Moses. The Israelites did 34
exactly as the LORD had commanded
Moses, pitching and breaking camp
standard by standard, each man according to his family in his father's
line.

Concerning the Levites

These were the descendants of Aaron 3
and Moses at the time when the LORD
spoke to Moses on Mount Sinai. The 2
names of the sons of Aaron were
Nadab the eldest, Abihu, Eleazar and
Ithamar. These were the names of 3
Aaron's sons, the anointed priests who
had been installed in the priestly
office. Nadab and Abihu fell dead be- 4
fore the LORD because they had presented illicit fire before the LORD in
the wilderness of Sinai. They left no
sons; Eleazar and Ithamar continued
to perform the priestly office in their
father's presence.

The LORD spoke to Moses and said, 5
'Bring forward the tribe of Levi and 6
appoint them to serve Aaron the
priest and to minister to him. They 7
shall be in attendance on him and on
the whole community before the Tent
of the Presence, undertaking the
service of the Tabernacle. They shall 8
be in charge of all the equipment in
the Tent of the Presence, and be in
attendance on the Israelites, undertaking the service of the Tabernacle.
You shall assign the Levites to Aa- 9
ron and his sons as especially dedicated to him out of all the Israelites.
To Aaron and his line you shall com- 10
mit the priestly office and they shall
perform its duties; any unqualified
person who intrudes upon it shall be
put to death.'

The LORD spoke to Moses and said, 11
'I take the Levites for myself out of 12
all the Israelites as a substitute for
the eldest male child of every woman;
the Levites shall be mine. For every 13
eldest child, if a boy, became mine
when I destroyed all the eldest sons in

Egypt. So I have consecrated to myself all the first-born in Israel, both man and beast. They shall be mine. I am the LORD.'

14 The LORD spoke to Moses in the
15 wilderness of Sinai and said, 'Make a detailed list of all the Levites by their families in the father's line, every male from the age of one month and upwards.'
16 Moses made a detailed list of them in accordance with the command
17 given him by the LORD. Now these were the names of the sons of Levi:

Gershon, Kohath and Merari.
18 Descendants of Gershon, by families: Libni and Shimei.
19 Descendants of Kohath, by families: Amram, Izhar, Hebron and Uzziel.
20 Descendants of Merari, by families: Mahli and Mushi.

These were the families of Levi, by fathers' families:
21 Gershon: the family of Libni and the family of Shimei. These were the
22 families of Gershon, and the number of males in their list as detailed, from the age of one month and upwards,
23 was seven thousand five hundred. The families of Gershon were stationed on
24 the west, behind the Tabernacle. Their
25 chief was Eliasaph son of Lael, and in the service of the Tent of the Presence they were in charge of the Tabernacle and its coverings, of the screen at the entrance to the Tent of the
26 Presence, the hangings of the court, the screen at the entrance to the court all round the Tabernacle and the altar, and of all else needed for its maintenance.
27 Kohath: the family of Amram, the family of Izhar, the family of Hebron, the family of Uzziel. These were the
28 families of Kohath, and the number of males, from the age of one month and upwards, was eight thousand six hundred. They were the guardians of
29 the holy things. The families of Kohath were stationed on the south, at
30 the side of the Tabernacle. Their chief
31 was Elizaphan son of Uzziel; they were in charge of the Ark, the table, the lamp-stands and the altars, together with the sacred vessels used in their service, and the screen with everything needed for its mainte-
32 nance. The chief over all the chiefs of the Levites was Eleazar son of Aaron the priest, who was appointed overseer of those in charge of the sanctuary.

Merari: the family of Mahli, the 33 family of Mushi. These were the families of Merari, and the number of 34 males in their list as detailed from the age of one month and upwards was six thousand two hundred. Their 35 chief was Zuriel son of Abihail; they were stationed on the north, at the side of the Tabernacle. The Merarites 36 were in charge of the planks, bars, posts, and sockets of the Tabernacle, together with its vessels and all the equipment needed for its maintenance, the posts, sockets, pegs, and cords of 37 the surrounding court.

In front of the Tabernacle on the 38 east, Moses was stationed, with Aaron and his sons, in front of the Tent of the Presence eastwards. They were in charge of the sanctuary on behalf of the Israelites; any unqualified person who came near would be put to death.

The number of Levites recorded by 39 Moses on the detailed list by families at the command of the LORD was twenty-two thousand males aged one month and upwards.

Ransoming the first-born

The LORD said to Moses, 'Make a 40 detailed list of all the male first-born in Israel aged one month and upwards, and count the number of persons. You shall reserve the Levites for 41 me—I am the LORD—in substitution for the eldest sons of the Israelites, and in the same way the Levites' cattle in substitution for the first-born cattle of the Israelites.' As the 42 LORD had told him to do, Moses made a list of all the eldest sons of the Israelites, and the total number of 43 first-born males recorded by name in the register, aged one month and upwards, was twenty-two thousand two hundred and seventy-three.

The LORD spoke to Moses and said, 44 'Take the Levites as a substitute for 45 all the eldest sons in Israel and the cattle of the Levites as a substitute for their cattle. The Levites shall be mine. I am the LORD. The eldest sons 46 in Israel will outnumber the Levites by two hundred and seventy-three. This remainder must be ransomed, 47 and you shall accept five shekels for each of them, taking the sacred shekel and reckoning twenty gerahs to the shekel; you shall give the money with 48 which they are ransomed to Aaron and his sons.'

Moses took the money paid as ran- 49 som for those who remained over when the substitution of Levites was 50 complete. The amount received was one thousand three hundred and sixty-five shekels of silver by the 51 sacred standard. In accordance with what the LORD had said, he gave the money to Aaron and his sons, doing what the LORD had told him to do.

The Levites' duties

4 The LORD spoke to Moses and Aaron 2 and said, 'Among the Levites, make a count of the descendants of Kohath 3 between the ages of thirty and fifty, by families in the father's line, comprising everyone who comes to take duty in the service of the Tent of the Presence.

4 'This is the service to be rendered by the Kohathites in the Tent of 5 the Presence; it is most sacred. When the camp is due to move, Aaron and his sons shall come and take down the Veil of the screen and cover the 6 Ark of the Tokens with it; over this they shall put a covering of porpoise-hide[a] and over that again a violet cloth all of one piece; they shall then put 7 its poles in place. Over the Table of the Presence they shall spread a violet cloth and lay on it the dishes, saucers, and flagons, and the bowls for drink-offerings; the Bread regularly presented shall also lie upon it; 8 then they shall spread over them a scarlet cloth and over that a covering of porpoise-hide, and put the poles in 9 place. They shall take a violet cloth and cover the lamp-stand, its lamps, tongs, firepans, and all the containers 10 for the oil used in its service; they shall put it with all its equipment in a sheet of porpoise-hide slung from a 11 pole. Over the gold altar they shall spread a violet cloth, cover it with a porpoise-hide covering, and put its 12 poles in place. They shall take all the articles used for the service of the sanctuary, put them on a violet cloth, cover them with a porpoise-hide covering, and sling them from a pole. 13 They shall clear the altar of the fat and ashes, spread a purple cloth over 14 it, and then lay on it all the equipment used in its service, the firepans, forks, shovels, tossing-bowls, and all the equipment of the altar, spread a covering of porpoise-hide over it and 15 put the poles in place. Once Aaron and his sons have finished covering the sanctuary and all the sacred equipment, when the camp is due to move, the Kohathites shall come to carry it;

they must not touch it on pain of death. All these things are the load to be carried by the Kohathites, the things connected with the Tent of the Presence. Eleazar son of Aaron the 16 priest shall have charge of the lamp-oil, the fragrant incense, the regular grain-offering, and the anointing oil, with the general oversight of the whole Tabernacle and its contents, the sanctuary and its equipment.'

The LORD spoke to Moses and 17 Aaron and said, 'You must not let 18 the families of Kohath be extirpated, and lost to the tribe of Levi. If they 19 are to live and not die when they approach the most holy things, this is what you must do: Aaron and his sons shall come and set each man to his appointed task and to his load, and the Kohathites themselves shall 20 not enter to cast even a passing glance on the sanctuary, on pain of death.'

The LORD spoke to Moses and said, 21 'Number the Gershonites by families 22 in the father's line. Make a detailed 23 list of all those between the ages of thirty and fifty who come on duty to perform service in the Tent of the Presence.

'This is the service to be rendered 24 by the Gershonite families, comprising their general duty and their loads. They shall carry the hangings of the 25 Tabernacle, the Tent of the Presence, its covering, that is the covering of porpoise-hide which is over it, the screen at the entrance to the Tent of the Presence, the hangings of the 26 court, the screen at the entrance to the court surrounding the Tabernacle and the altar, their cords and all the equipment for their service; and they shall perform all the tasks connected with them. These are the acts of service they shall render. All the 27 service of the Gershonites, their loads and their other duties, shall be directed by Aaron and his sons; you shall assign them the loads for which they shall be responsible. This is the service 28 assigned to the Gershonite families in connection with the Tent of the Presence; Ithamar son of Aaron shall be in charge of them.

'You shall make a detailed list of 29 the Merarites by families in the father's line, all those between the 30 ages of thirty and fifty, who come on duty to perform service in the Tent of the Presence.

'These are the loads for which they 31 shall be responsible in virtue of their

a Strictly hide of sea-cow.

service in the Tent of the Presence: the planks of the Tabernacle with its 32 bars, posts, and sockets, the posts of the surrounding court with their sockets, pegs, and cords, and all that is needed for the maintenance of them; you shall assign to each man by name the load for which he is responsible. 33 These are the duties of the Merarite families in virtue of their service in the Tent of the Presence. Ithamar son of Aaron the priest shall be in charge of them.'

34   Moses and Aaron and the chiefs of the community made a detailed list of the Kohathites by families in the 35 father's line, taking all between the ages of thirty and fifty who came on duty to perform service in the Tent of 36 the Presence. The number recorded by families in the detailed lists was two thousand seven hundred and fifty. 37 This was the total number in the detailed lists of the Kohathite families who did duty in the Tent of the Presence; they were recorded by Moses and Aaron as the LORD had told them to do through Moses.

-9   The Gershonites between the ages of thirty and fifty, who came on duty for service in the Tent of the Presence, were recorded in detailed lists by 40 families in the father's line. Their number, by families in the father's line, was two thousand six hundred and 41 thirty. This was the total recorded in the lists of the Gershonite families who came on duty in the Tent of the Presence, and were recorded by Moses and Aaron as the LORD had told them to do.

-3   The families of Merari, between the ages of thirty and fifty, who came on duty to perform service in the Tent of the Presence, were recorded in detailed lists by families in the father's line. 44 Their number by families was three 45 thousand two hundred. These were recorded in the Merarite families by Moses and Aaron as the LORD had told them to do through Moses.

46   Thus Moses and Aaron and the chiefs of Israel made a detailed list of all the Levites by families in the 47 father's line, between the ages of thirty and fifty years; these were all who came to perform their various duties and carry their loads in the service of the Tent of the Presence. 48 Their number was eight thousand 49 five hundred and eighty. They were recorded one by one by Moses at the command of the LORD, according to

their general duty and the loads they carried.[b] For so the LORD had told Moses to do.

Safeguard against defilement

The LORD spoke to Moses and said: 5 Command the Israelites to expel from 2 the camp everyone who suffers from a malignant skin-disease or a discharge, and everyone ritually unclean from contact with a corpse. You shall 3 put them outside the camp, both male and female, so that they will not defile your camps in which I dwell among you. The Israelites did this: 4 they put them outside the camp. As the LORD had said when he spoke to Moses, so the Israelites did.

Law of restitution

The LORD spoke to Moses and said, 5 Say to the Israelites: When anyone, 6 man or woman, wrongs another and thereby breaks faith with the LORD, that person has incurred guilt which demands reparation. He shall confess 7 the sin he has committed, make restitution in full with the addition of one fifth, and give it to the man to whom compensation is due. If there is no 8 next-of-kin to whom compensation can be paid, the compensation payable in that case shall be the LORD's, for the use of the priest, in addition to the ram of expiation with which the priest makes expiation for him.

Every contribution made by way of 9 holy-gift which the Israelites bring to the priest shall be the priest's. The 10 priest shall have the holy-gifts which a man gives; whatever is given to him shall be his.

Law concerning jealousy

The LORD spoke to Moses and said, 11 Speak to the Israelites in these words: 12 When a married woman goes astray, is unfaithful to her husband, and has 13 sexual intercourse with another man, and this happens without the husband's knowledge, and the crime is undetected, because, though she has been defiled, there is no direct evidence against her and she was not caught in the act, but when in such 14 a case a fit of jealousy comes over the husband which causes him to suspect his wife, she being in fact defiled; or when, on the other hand, a fit of jealousy comes over a husband which causes him to suspect his wife, when she is not in fact defiled; then in 15 either case, the husband shall bring

his wife to the priest together with the prescribed offering for her, a tenth of an ephah of barley meal. He shall not pour oil on it nor put frankincense on it, because it is a grain-offering for jealousy, a grain-offering of protestation conveying an imputation of guilt.
16 The priest shall bring her forward and
17 set her before the LORD. He shall take clean^c water in an earthenware vessel, and shall take dust from the floor of the Tabernacle and add it to the
18 water. He shall set the woman before the LORD, uncover her head, and place the grain-offering of protestation in her hands; it is a grain-offering for jealousy. The priest shall hold in his own hand the water of contention
19 which brings out the truth. He shall then put the woman on oath and say to her, 'If no man has had intercourse with you, if you have not gone astray and let yourself become defiled while owing obedience to your husband, then may your innocence be established by the water of contention
20 which brings out the truth. But if, while owing him obedience, you have gone astray and let yourself become defiled, if any man other than your husband has had intercourse with
21 you' (the priest shall here put the woman on oath with an adjuration, and shall continue), 'may the LORD make an example of you among your people in adjurations and in swearing of oaths by bringing upon you mis-
22 carriage and untimely birth; and this water that brings out the truth shall enter your body, bringing upon you miscarriage and untimely birth.' The woman shall respond, 'Amen, Amen.'
23 The priest shall write these curses on a scroll and wash them off into the
24 water of contention; he shall make the woman drink the water that brings out the truth, and the water
25 shall enter her body. The priest shall take the grain-offering for jealousy from the woman's hand, present it as a special gift before the LORD, and
26 offer it at the altar. He shall take a handful from the grain-offering by way of token, and burn it at the altar; after this he shall make the woman
27 drink the water. If she has let herself become defiled and has been unfaithful to her husband, then when the priest makes her drink the water that brings out the truth and the water has entered her body, she will suffer a miscarriage or untimely birth, and her name will become an example in

adjuration among her kin. But if the 28 woman has not let herself become defiled and is pure, then her innocence is established and she will bear her child.

Such is the law for cases of jealousy, 29 where a woman, owing obedience to her husband, goes astray and lets herself become defiled, or where a fit of 30 jealousy comes over a man which causes him to suspect his wife. He shall set her before the LORD, and the priest shall deal with her as this law prescribes. No guilt will attach to the 31 husband, but the woman shall bear the penalty of her guilt.

Law for the Nazirite

The LORD spoke to Moses and said, 6 Speak to the Israelites in these words: 2 When anyone, man or woman, makes a special^d vow dedicating himself to the LORD as a Nazirite,^e he shall 3 abstain from wine and strong drink. These he shall not drink, nor anything made from the juice of grapes; nor shall he eat grapes, fresh or dried. During the whole term of his vow he 4 shall eat nothing that comes from the vine, nothing whatever, shoot or berry. During the whole term of his 5 vow no razor shall touch his head; he shall let his hair grow long and plait it until he has completed the term of his dedication: he shall keep himself holy to the LORD. During the whole 6 term of his vow he shall not go near a corpse, not even when his father or 7 mother, brother or sister, dies; he shall not make himself ritually unclean for them, because the Nazirite vow to his God is on his head. He shall 8 keep himself holy to the LORD during the whole term of his Nazirite vow.

If someone suddenly falls dead by 9 his side touching him and thereby making his hair, which has been dedicated, ritually unclean, he shall shave his head seven days later, on the day appointed for his ritual cleansing. On 10 the eighth day he shall bring two turtle-doves or two young pigeons to the priest at the entrance to the Tent of the Presence. The priest shall offer 11 one as a sin-offering and the other as a whole-offering and shall make expiation for him for the sin he has incurred through contact with the dead body; and he shall consecrate his head afresh on that day. The man 12 shall re-dedicate himself to the LORD for the term of his vow and bring

c Or holy.　　　|d makes a special: or performs a . . .　　　e That is separated one or dedicated one.

a yearling ram as a guilt-offering. The previous period shall not be reckoned, because the hair which he dedicated became unclean.

13 The law for the Nazirite, when the term of his dedication is completed, shall be this. He shall be brought to the entrance to the Tent of the Pres-
14 ence and shall present his offering to the LORD: one yearling ram without blemish as a whole-offering, one yearling ewe without blemish as a sin-offering, one ram without blemish as
15 a shared-offering, and a basket of cakes made of flour mixed with oil, and of wafers smeared with oil, both unleavened, together with the proper grain-offerings and drink-offerings.
16 The priest shall present all these before the LORD and offer the man's
17 sin-offering and whole-offering; the ram he shall offer as a shared-offering to the LORD, together with the basket of unleavened cakes and the proper
18 grain-offering and drink-offering. The Nazirite shall shave his head at the entrance to the Tent of the Presence, take the hair which had been dedicated and put it on the fire where the
19 shared-offering is burning. The priest shall take the shoulder of the ram, after boiling it, and take also one unleavened cake from the basket and one unleavened wafer, and put them on the palms of the Nazirite's hands, his hair which had been dedicated
20 having been shaved. The priest shall then present them as a special gift before the LORD; these, together with the breast of the special gift and the leg of the contribution, are holy and belong to the priest. When this has been done, the Nazirite is again free to drink wine.
21 Such is the law for the Nazirite who has made his vow. Such is the offering he must make to the LORD for his dedication, apart from anything else that he can afford. He must carry out his vow in full according to the law governing his dedication.

The priests' blessing

22 The LORD spoke to Moses and said,
23 Speak to Aaron and his sons in these words: These are the words with which you shall bless the Israelites:

24 The LORD bless you and watch over you;
25 the LORD make his face shine upon*f* you
and be gracious to you;

f Or to.

the LORD look kindly on you and give 26 you peace.

They shall pronounce my name over 27 the Israelites, and I will bless them.

Offerings for the dedication of the altar

On the day that Moses completed the 7 setting up of the Tabernacle, he anointed and consecrated it; he also anointed and consecrated its equipment, and the altar and its vessels. The chief men of Israel, heads of 2 families—that is the chiefs of the tribes, who had assisted in preparing the detailed lists—came forward and 3 brought their offering before the LORD, six covered wagons and twelve oxen, one wagon from every two chiefs and from each one an ox.*g* These they brought forward before the Tabernacle; and the LORD spoke to 4 Moses and said, 'Accept these from 5 them: they shall be used for the service of the Tent of the Presence. Assign them to the Levites as their several duties require.'

So Moses accepted the wagons and 6 oxen and assigned them to the Levites. He gave two wagons and four oxen to 7 the Gershonites as required for their service; four wagons and eight oxen 8 to the Merarites as required for their service, in charge of Ithamar the son of Aaron the priest. He gave none to 9 the Kohathites because the service laid upon them was that of the holy things: these they had to carry themselves on their shoulders.

When the altar was anointed, the 10 chiefs brought their gift for its dedication and presented their offering before it. The LORD said to Moses, 11 'Let the chiefs present their offering for the dedication of the altar one by one, on consecutive days.'

The chief who presented his offer- 12 ing on the first day was Nahshon son of Amminadab of the tribe of Judah. His offering was one silver dish weigh- 13 ing a hundred and thirty shekels by the sacred standard and one silver tossing-bowl weighing seventy, both full of flour mixed with oil as a grain-offering; one saucer weighing ten gold 14 shekels, full of incense; one young bull, 15 one full-grown ram, and one yearling ram, as a whole-offering; one he-goat 16 as a sin-offering; and two bulls, five 17 full-grown rams, five he-goats, and five yearling rams, as a shared-offering.

g Or a bull.

c

This was the offering of Nahshon son of Amminadab.

18 On the second day Nethaneel son of Zuar, chief of Issachar, brought
19 his offering. He brought one silver dish weighing a hundred and thirty shekels by the sacred standard and one silver tossing-bowl weighing sev-
20 enty, both full of flour mixed with oil as a grain-offering; one saucer weighing ten gold shekels, full of
21 incense; one young bull, one full-grown ram, and one yearling ram, as a
22 whole-offering; one he-goat as a sin-
23 offering; and two bulls, five full-grown rams, five he-goats, and five yearling rams, as a shared-offering. This was the offering of Nethaneel son of Zuar.

24 On the third day the chief of the Zebulunites, Eliab son of Helon, came.
25 His offering was one silver dish weighing a hundred and thirty shekels by the sacred standard and one silver tossing-bowl weighing seventy, both full of flour mixed with oil as a
26 grain-offering; one saucer weighing
27 ten gold shekels, full of incense; one young bull, one full-grown ram, and one yearling ram, as a whole-offering;
28 29 one he-goat as a sin-offering; and two bulls, five full-grown rams, five he-goats, and five yearling rams, as a shared-offering. This was the offering of Eliab son of Helon.

30 On the fourth day the chief of the Reubenites, Elizur son of Shedeur,
31 came. His offering was one silver dish weighing a hundred and thirty shekels by the sacred standard and one silver tossing-bowl weighing seventy, both full of flour mixed with oil as a grain-
32 offering; one saucer weighing ten gold
33 shekels, full of incense; one young bull, one full-grown ram, and one yearling
34 ram, as a whole-offering; one he-goat
35 as a sin-offering; and two bulls, five full-grown rams, five he-goats, and five yearling rams, as a shared-offering. This was the offering of Elizur son of Shedeur.

36 On the fifth day the chief of the Simeonites, Shelumiel son of Zuri-
37 shaddai, came. His offering was one silver dish weighing a hundred and thirty shekels by the sacred standard and one silver tossing-bowl weighing seventy, both full of flour mixed with
38 oil as a grain-offering; one saucer weighing ten gold shekels, full of
39 incense; one young bull, one full-grown ram, and one yearling ram, as
40 a whole-offering; one he-goat as a sin-
41 offering; and two bulls, five full-grown rams, five he-goats, and five yearling rams, as a shared-offering. This was the offering of Shelumiel son of Zuri-shaddai.

On the sixth day the chief of the 42 Gadites, Eliasaph son of Reuel, came. His offering was one silver dish weigh- 43 ing a hundred and thirty shekels by the sacred standard and one silver tossing-bowl weighing seventy, both full of flour mixed with oil as a grain-offering; one saucer weighing ten 44 gold shekels, full of incense; one 45 young bull, one full-grown ram, and one yearling ram, as a whole-offering; one he-goat as a sin-offering; and two 46 bulls, five full-grown rams, five he-goats, and five yearling rams, as a shared-offering. This was the offering of Eliasaph son of Reuel.

On the seventh day the chief of the 48 Ephraimites, Elishama son of Am-mihud, came. His offering was one 49 silver dish weighing a hundred and thirty shekels by the sacred standard and one silver tossing-bowl weighing seventy, both full of flour mixed with oil as a grain-offering; one saucer 50 weighing ten gold shekels, full of incense; one young bull, one full- 51 grown ram, and one yearling ram, as a whole-offering; one he-goat as a 52 sin-offering; and two bulls, five full- 53 grown rams, five he-goats, and five year-ling rams, as a shared-offering. This was the offering of Elishama son of Ammihud.

On the eighth day the chief of the 54 Manassites, Gamaliel son of Pedah-zur, came. His offering was one 55 silver dish weighing a hundred and thirty shekels by the sacred standard and one silver tossing-bowl weighing seventy, both full of flour mixed with oil as a grain-offering; one saucer 56 weighing ten gold shekels, full of incense; one young bull, one full- 57 grown ram, and one yearling ram, as a whole-offering; one he-goat as a sin- 58 offering; and two bulls, five full- 59 grown rams, five he-goats, and five yearling rams, as a shared-offering. This was the offering of Gamaliel son of Pedahzur.

On the ninth day the chief of the 60 Benjamites, Abidan son of Gideoni, came. His offering was one silver 61 dish weighing a hundred and thirty shekels by the sacred standard and one silver tossing-bowl weighing seventy, both full of flour mixed with oil as a grain-offering; one 62 saucer weighing ten gold shekels, full of incense; one young bull, one 63

full-grown ram, and one yearling ram,
64 as a whole-offering; one he-goat as a
65 sin-offering; and two bulls, five full-
grown rams, five he-goats, and five
yearling rams, as a shared-offering.
This was the offering of Abidan son of
Gideoni.
66   On the tenth day the chief of the
Danites, Ahiezer son of Ammishaddai,
67 came. His offering was one silver
dish weighing a hundred and thirty
shekels by the sacred standard and
one silver tossing-bowl weighing seventy, both full of flour mixed with
68 oil as a grain-offering; one saucer
weighing ten gold shekels, full of
69 incense; one young bull, one full-grown
ram, and one yearling ram, as a
70 whole-offering; one he-goat as a sin-
71 offering; and two bulls, five full-
grown rams, five he-goats, and five
yearling rams, as a shared-offering.
This was the offering of Ahiezer son of
Ammishaddai.
72   On the eleventh day the chief of
the Asherites, Pagiel son of Ocran,
73 came. His offering was one silver dish
weighing a hundred and thirty shekels
by the sacred standard and one silver
tossing-bowl weighing seventy, both
full of flour mixed with oil as a grain-
74 offering; one saucer weighing ten gold
75 shekels, full of incense; one young
bull, one full-grown ram, and one
76 yearling ram, as a whole-offering; one
77 he-goat as a sin-offering; and two
bulls, five full-grown rams, five he-
goats, and five yearling rams, as a
shared-offering. This was the offering
of Pagiel son of Ocran.
78   On the twelfth day the chief of the
Naphtalites, Ahira son of Enan, came.
79 His offering was one silver dish weighing a hundred and thirty shekels by
the sacred standard and one silver
tossing-bowl weighing seventy, both
full of flour mixed with oil as a grain-
80 offering; one saucer weighing ten gold
81 shekels, full of incense; one young
bull, one full-grown ram, and one
82 yearling ram, as a whole-offering; one
83 he-goat as a sin-offering; and two bulls,
five full-grown rams, five he-goats,
and five yearling rams, as a shared-
offering. This was the offering of
Ahira son of Enan.
84   This was the gift from the chiefs of
Israel for the dedication of the altar
when it was anointed: twelve silver
dishes, twelve silver tossing-bowls,
85 and twelve golden saucers; each
silver dish weighed a hundred and
thirty shekels, each silver tossing-bowl

seventy shekels. The total weight of
the silver vessels was two thousand
four hundred shekels by the sacred
standard. There were twelve golden 86
saucers full of incense, ten shekels
each by the sacred standard: the total
weight of the gold of the saucers was
a hundred and twenty shekels. The 87
number of beasts for the whole-
offering was twelve bulls, twelve full-
grown rams, and twelve yearling
rams, with the prescribed grain-
offerings, and twelve he-goats for the
sin-offering. The number of beasts for 88
the shared-offering was twenty-four
bulls, sixty full-grown rams, sixty he-
goats, and sixty yearling rams. This
was the gift for the dedication of the
altar when it was anointed. And when 89
Moses entered the Tent of the Presence to speak with God, he heard the
Voice speaking from above the cover
over the Ark of the Tokens from
between the two cherubim: the Voice
spoke to him.

Aaron sets up the lamps

The LORD spoke to Moses and said, 8
'Speak to Aaron in these words: 2
"When you mount the seven lamps,
see that they shed their light forwards
in front of the lamp-stand."' Aaron 3
did this: he mounted the lamps, so
as to shed light forwards in front of
the lamp-stand, as the LORD had instructed Moses. The lamp-stand was 4
made of beaten-work in gold, as well
as the stem and the petals. Moses
made it to match the pattern which
the LORD had shown him.

Levites belong to the LORD

The LORD spoke to Moses and said: 5
Take the Levites apart from the rest 6
of the Israelites and cleanse them
ritually. This is what you shall do to 7
cleanse them. Sprinkle lustral water
over them; they shall then shave their
whole bodies, wash their clothes, and
so be cleansed. Next, they shall take 8
a young bull as a whole-offering[h] with
its prescribed grain-offering, flour
mixed with oil; and you shall take
a second young bull as a sin-offering.
Bring the Levites before the Tent of 9
the Presence and call the whole community of Israelites together. Bring 10
the Levites before the LORD, and let
the Israelites lay their hands on their
heads. Aaron shall present the Levites 11
before the LORD as a special gift
from the Israelites, and they shall be

h as a whole-offering: *prob. rdg.; Heb. om.*

dedicated to the service of the LORD.

12 The Levites shall lay their hands on the heads of the bulls; one bull shall be offered as a sin-offering and the other as a whole-offering to the LORD, to make expiation for the Levites.

13 Then you shall set the Levites before Aaron and his sons, presenting them

14 to the LORD as a special gift. You shall thus separate the Levites from the rest of the Israelites, and they shall be mine.

15 After this, the Levites shall enter the Tent of the Presence to serve in it, ritually cleansed and presented as a

16 special gift; for they are given and dedicated to me, out of all the Israelites. I have accepted them as mine in place of all that comes first from the womb, every first child among the

17 Israelites; for every first-born male creature, man or beast, among the Israelites is mine. On the day when I struck down every first-born creature in Egypt, I hallowed all the first-born

18 of the Israelites to myself, and I have accepted the Levites in their place.

19 I have given the Levites to Aaron and his sons, dedicated among the Israelites to perform the service of the Israelites in the Tent of the Presence and to make expiation for them, and then no calamity will befall them when they come close to the sanctuary.

20 Moses and Aaron and the whole community of Israelites carried out all the commands the LORD had given to Moses for the dedication of the

21 Levites. The Levites purified themselves of sin and washed their clothes, and Aaron presented them as a special gift before the LORD and made expiation for them, to cleanse them.

22 Then at last they went in to perform their service in the Tent of the Presence, before Aaron and his sons. Thus the commands the LORD had given to Moses concerning the Levites were all carried out.

The Levites' periods of service

23 The LORD spoke to Moses and said:

24 Touching the Levites: they shall begin their active work in the service of the Tent of the Presence at the age of

25 twenty-five. At the age of fifty a Levite shall retire from regular service

26 and shall serve no longer. He may continue to assist his colleagues in attendance in the Tent of the Presence but shall perform no regular service. This is how you shall arrange the attendance of the Levites.

Keeping the Passover

9 In the first month of the second year after they came out of Egypt, the LORD spoke to Moses in the wilderness of Sinai and said, 'Let the Israelites

2 prepare the Passover at the time appointed for it. This shall be between

3 dusk and dark on the fourteenth day of this month, and you shall keep it at this appointed time, observing every rule and custom proper to it.' So

4 Moses told the Israelites to prepare the Passover, and they prepared it on

5 the fourteenth day of the first month, between dusk and dark, in the wilderness of Sinai. The Israelites did exactly as the LORD had instructed Moses.

6 It happened that some men were ritually unclean through contact with a corpse and so could not keep the Passover on the right day. They came before Moses and Aaron that same

7 day and said, 'We are unclean through contact with a corpse. Must we therefore be debarred from presenting the LORD's offering at its appointed time with the rest of the Israelites?' Moses

8 answered, 'Wait, and let me hear what commands the LORD has for you.'

9 The LORD spoke to Moses and said,

10 Tell the Israelites: If any one of you or of your descendants is ritually unclean through contact with a corpse, or if he is away on a long journey, he shall keep a Passover to the LORD

11 none the less. But in that case he shall prepare the victim in the second month, between dusk and dark on the fourteenth day. It shall be eaten with unleavened cakes and bitter

12 herbs; nothing shall be left over till morning, and no bone of it shall be broken. The Passover shall be kept

13 exactly as the law prescribes. The man who, being ritually clean and not absent on a journey, neglects to keep the Passover, shall be cut off from his father's kin, because he has not presented the LORD's offering at its appointed time. That man shall accept responsibility for his sin.

14 When an alien is settled among you, he also shall keep the Passover to the LORD, observing every rule and custom proper to it. The same law is binding on you all, alien and native alike.

The cloud over the Tabernacle

15 On the day when they set up the Tabernacle, that is the Tent of the Tokens, cloud covered it, and in the evening a brightness like fire appeared

16 over it till morning. So it continued: the cloud covered it by day and a 17 brightness like fire by night. Whenever the cloud lifted from the tent, the Israelites struck camp, and at the place where the cloud settled, there 18 they pitched their camp. At the command of the LORD they struck camp, and at the command of the LORD they encamped again, and continued in camp as long as the cloud rested 19 over the Tabernacle. When the cloud stayed long over the Tabernacle, the Israelites remained in attendance on 20 the LORD and did not move on; and it was the same when the cloud continued over the Tabernacle only a few days: at the command of the LORD they remained in camp, and at the command of the LORD they struck 21 camp. There were also times when the cloud continued only from evening till morning, and in the morning, when the cloud lifted, they moved on. Whether by day or by night, they moved as soon as the cloud lifted. 22 Whether it was for a day or two, for a month or a year, whenever the cloud stayed long over the Tabernacle, the Israelites remained where they were and did not move on; they did so only 23 when the cloud lifted. At the command of the LORD they encamped, and at his command they struck camp. At the LORD's command, given through Moses, they remained in attendance on the LORD.

The silver trumpets

10 The LORD spoke to Moses and said: 2 Make two trumpets of beaten silver and use them for summoning the community and for breaking camp. 3 When both are sounded, the whole community shall muster before you at the entrance to the Tent of the 4 Presence. If a single trumpet is sounded, the chiefs who are heads of 5 the Israelite clans shall muster. When you give the signal for a shout, those encamped on the east side are to move 6 off. When the signal is given for a second shout those encamped to the south are to move off. A signal to 7 shout is the signal to move off. When you convene the assembly, you shall sound a trumpet but not raise a shout. 8 This sounding of the trumpets is the duty of the Aaronite priests and shall be a rule binding for all time on your descendants. 9 When you go into battle against an invader and you are hard pressed by him, you shall raise a cheer when the trumpets sound, and this will serve as a reminder of you before the LORD your God and you will be delivered from your enemies. On your festal 10 days and at your appointed seasons and on the first day of every month, you shall sound the trumpets over your whole-offerings and your shared-offerings, and the trumpets shall be a reminder on your behalf before the LORD your God. I am the LORD your God.

The Israelites depart from Sinai

In the second year, on the twentieth 11 day of the second month, the cloud lifted from the Tabernacle of the Tokens, and the Israelites moved by 12 stages from the wilderness of Sinai, until the cloud came to rest in the wilderness of Paran. The first time 13 that they broke camp at the command of the LORD given through Moses, the standard of the division of 14 Judah moved off first with its tribal hosts: the host of Judah under Nahshon son of Amminadab, the host 15 of Issachar under Nethaneel son of Zuar, and the host of Zebulun under 16 Eliab son of Helon. Then the Taber- 17 nacle was taken down, and its bearers, the sons of Gershon and Merari, moved off.

Secondly, the standard of the divi- 18 sion of Reuben moved off with its tribal hosts: the host of Reuben under Elizur son of Shedeur, the host of 19 Simeon under Shelumiel son of Zurishaddai, and the host of Gad under 20 Eliasaph son of Reuel. The Kohath- 21 ites, the bearers of the holy things, moved off next, and on their arrival found the Tabernacle set up.

Thirdly, the standard of the divi- 22 sion of Ephraim moved off with its tribal hosts: the host of Ephraim under Elishama son of Ammihud, the 23 host of Manasseh under Gamaliel son of Pedahzur, and the host of Benjamin 24 under Abidan son of Gideoni.

Lastly, the standard of the division 25 of Dan, the rearguard of all the divisions, moved off with its tribal hosts: the host of Dan under Ahiezer son of Ammishaddai, the host of Asher under 26 Pagiel son of Ocran, and the host of 27 Naphtali under Ahira son of Enan.

This was the order of march for the 28 Israelites, mustered in their hosts, and in this order they broke camp.

And Moses said to Hobab son of 29 Reuel the Midianite, his brother-in-law, 'We are setting out for the place which the LORD promised to give us.

Come with us, and we will deal generously with you, for the LORD has given an assurance of good for-
30 tune for Israel.' But he replied, 'No, I will not; I would rather go to my own
31 country and my own people.' Moses said, 'Do not desert us, I beg you; for you know where we ought to camp in the wilderness, and you will be our
32 guide. If you will go with us, then all the good fortune with which the LORD favours us we will share with you.'
33 Then they moved off from the mountain of the LORD and journeyed for three days, and the Ark of the Covenant of the LORD kept a day's journey ahead of them to find them a
34 place to rest. The cloud of the LORD hung over them by day when they
35 moved camp. Whenever the Ark began to move, Moses said,

'Up, LORD, and may thy enemies be scattered
and those that hate thee flee before thee.'

36 When it halted, he said,

'Rest, LORD of the countless thousands of Israel.'

The people cry for meat

11 There came a time when the people complained to the LORD of their hardships. When he heard, he became angry and fire from the LORD broke out among them, and was raging at one end
2 of the camp, when the people appealed to Moses. He interceded with the
3 LORD, and the fire died down. Then they named that place Taberah,[i] because the fire of the LORD had burned among them there.
4 Now there was a mixed company of strangers who had joined the Israelites. These people began to be greedy for better things, and the Israelites themselves wept once again and cried, 'Will no one give us meat?
5 Think of it! In Egypt we had fish for the asking, cucumbers and water-melons, leeks and onions and garlic.
6 Now our throats are parched; there is nothing wherever we look except
7 this manna.' (The manna looked like coriander seed, the colour of gum
8 resin. The people went about collecting it, ground it up in hand-mills or pounded it in mortars, then boiled it in the pot and made it into cakes. It
9 tasted like butter-cakes. When dew fell on the camp at night, the manna

fell with it.) Moses heard the people 10 wailing, all of them in their families at the opening of their tents. Then the LORD became very angry, and Moses was troubled. He said to the LORD, 11 'Why hast thou brought trouble on thy servant? How have I displeased the LORD that I am burdened with the care of this whole people? Am I their 12 mother? Have I brought them into the world, and am I called upon to carry them in my bosom, like a nurse with her babies, to the land promised by thee on oath to their fathers? Where 13 am I to find meat to give them all? They pester me with their wailing and their "Give us meat to eat." This 14 whole people is a burden too heavy for me; I cannot carry it alone. If that 15 is thy purpose for me, then kill me outright. But if I have won thy favour, let me suffer this trouble at thy hands[j] no longer.'
The LORD answered Moses, 'As- 16 semble seventy elders from Israel, men known to you as elders and officers in the community; bring them to me at the Tent of the Presence, and there let them take their stand with you. I will come down and speak with you 17 there. I will take back part of that same spirit which has been conferred on you and confer it on them, and they will share with you the burden of taking care for the people; then you will not have to bear it alone. And 18 to the people you shall say this: "Hallow yourselves in readiness for tomorrow; you shall have meat to eat. You wailed in the LORD's hearing; you said, 'Will no one give us meat? In Egypt we lived well.' The LORD will give you meat and you shall eat it. Not for one day only, nor for two days, 19 nor five, nor ten, nor twenty, but for a 20 whole month you shall eat it until it comes out at your nostrils and makes you sick; because you have rejected the LORD who dwells in your midst, wailing in his presence and saying, 'Why did we ever come out of Egypt?'"'
Moses replied, 'Here am I with six 21 hundred thousand men on the march around me, and thou dost promise them meat to eat for a whole month. How can the sheep and oxen be 22 slaughtered that would be enough for them? If all the fish in the sea could be caught, would they be enough?' The LORD said to Moses, 'Is there a 23 limit to the power of the LORD? You will see this very day whether or not my words come true.'

---

i That is Burning.   *j* this trouble . . . hands: *prob. original rdg., altered in Heb. to* my trouble.

The elders prophesy

24 Moses came out and told the people what the LORD had said. He assembled seventy men from the elders of the people and stationed them round the 25 Tent. Then the LORD descended in the cloud and spoke to him. He took back part of that same spirit which he had conferred on Moses and conferred it on the seventy elders; as the spirit alighted on them, they fell into a prophetic ecstasy, for the first and only time.

26 Now two men named Eldad and Medad, who had been enrolled with the seventy, were left behind in the camp. But, though they had not gone out to the Tent, the spirit alighted on them none the less, and they fell into 27 an ecstasy there in the camp. A young man ran and told Moses that Eldad and Medad were in an ecstasy in the 28 camp, whereupon Joshua son of Nun, who had served with Moses since he was a boy, broke in, 'My lord Moses, 29 stop them!' But Moses said to him, 'Are you jealous on my account? I wish that all the LORD's people were prophets and that the LORD would 30 confer his spirit on them all!' And Moses rejoined the camp with the elders of Israel.

The LORD sends quails

31 Then a wind from the LORD sprang up; it drove quails in from the west, and they were flying all round the camp for the distance of a day's journey, three feet above the ground. 32 The people were busy gathering quails all that day, all night, and all next day, and even the man who got least gathered ten homers. They spread them out to dry all about the camp. 33 But the meat was scarcely between their teeth, and they had not so much as bitten it, when the LORD's anger broke out against the people and he 34 struck them with a deadly plague. That place was called Kibroth-hattaavah[k] because there they buried the people who had been greedy for meat.

Miriam and Aaron speak against Moses

35 From Kibroth-hattaavah the Israelites went on to Hazeroth, and while they 12 were at Hazeroth, Miriam and Aaron began to speak against Moses. They blamed him for his Cushite wife (for he had married a Cushite woman), 2 and they said, 'Is Moses the only one with[l] whom the LORD has spoken? Has he not spoken with[l] us as well?' Moses was in fact a man of great 3 humility, the most humble man on earth. But the LORD heard them and 4 suddenly he said to Moses, Aaron and Miriam, 'Go out all three of you to the Tent of the Presence.' So the three went out, and the LORD descended in 5 a pillar of cloud; he stood at the entrance to the tent and summoned Aaron and Miriam. The two of them went forward, and he said, 6

'Listen to my words.
If he[m] were your prophet and nothing more,
I would make myself known to him in a vision,
I would speak with him in a dream.
But my servant Moses is not such a 7 prophet;
he alone is faithful[n] of all my household.
With him I speak face to face, 8
openly and not in riddles.
He shall see the very form of the LORD.
How do you dare speak against my servant Moses?'

Thus the anger of the LORD was 9 roused against them, and he left them; and as the cloud moved from the tent, 10 there was Miriam, her skin diseased and white as snow. Aaron turned towards her and saw her skin diseased. Then he said to Moses, 'Pray, my 11 lord, do not make us pay the penalty of sin, foolish and wicked though we have been. Let her not be like some- 12 thing still-born, whose flesh is half eaten away when it comes from the womb.' So Moses cried, 'Not this, O 13 LORD! Heal her, I pray.' The LORD 14 replied, 'Suppose her father had spat in her face, would she not have to remain in disgrace for seven days? Let her be kept for seven days in confinement outside the camp and then be brought back.' So Miriam was 15 kept outside for seven days, and the people did not strike camp until she was brought back. After this they set 16 out from Hazeroth and pitched camp in the wilderness of Paran.

The spies report on Canaan

The LORD spoke to Moses and said, **13** 'Send men out to explore the land 2 of Canaan which I am giving to the Israelites; from each of their fathers' tribes send one man, and let him be a man of high rank.' So Moses sent 3

---

k *That is* the Graves of Greed. l *Or* by. m *Prob. rdg.; Heb.* the LORD. n *Or* to be trusted.

them from the wilderness of Paran at the command of the LORD, all of them leading men among the Israelites. 4 These were their names:

from the tribe of Reuben, Shammua son of Zaccur;
5 from the tribe of Simeon, Shaphat son of Hori;
6 from the tribe of Judah, Caleb son of Jephunneh;
7 from the tribe of Issachar, Igal son of Joseph;
8 from the tribe of Ephraim, Hoshea son of Nun;
9 from the tribe of Benjamin, Palti son of Raphu;
10 from the tribe of Zebulun, Gaddiel son of Sodi;
11 from the tribe of Joseph (that is from the tribe of Manasseh), Gaddi son of Susi;
12 from the tribe of Dan, Ammiel son of Gemalli;
13 from the tribe of Asher, Sethur son of Michael;
14 from the tribe of Naphtali, Nahbi son of Vophsi;
15 from the tribe of Gad, Geuel son of Machi.

16 These are the names of the men whom Moses sent to explore the land. But Moses called the son of Nun Joshua, not Hoshea.
17 When Moses sent them to explore the land of Canaan, he said to them, 'Make your way up by the Negeb, and 18 go on into the hill-country. See what the land is like, and whether the people who live there are strong or 19 weak, few or many. See whether it is easy or difficult country in which they live, and whether the cities in which they live are weakly defended or well 20 fortified; is the land fertile or barren, and does it grow trees or not? Go boldly in and take some of its fruit.' It was the season when the first grapes were ripe.
21 They went up and explored the country from the wilderness of Zin as 22 far as Rehob by Lebo-hamath. They went up by the Negeb and came to Hebron, where Ahiman, Sheshai and Talmai, the descendants of Anak,⁰ were living. (Hebron was built seven 23 years before Zoan in Egypt.) They came to the gorge of Eshcol,ᵖ and there they cut a branch with a single bunch of grapes, and they carried it on a pole two at a time; they also 24 picked pomegranates and figs. It was

from the bunch of grapes which the Israelites cut there that that place was named the gorge of Eshcol. After 25 forty days they returned from exploring the country, and came back to 26 Moses and Aaron and the whole community of Israelites at Kadesh in the wilderness of Paran. They made their report to them and to the whole community, and showed them the fruit of the country. And this was the story 27 they told Moses: 'We made our way into the land to which you sent us. It is flowing with milk and honey, and here is the fruit it grows; but its 28 inhabitants are sturdy, and the cities are very strongly fortified; indeed, we saw there the descendants of Anak. We also saw the Amalekites 29 who live in the Negeb, Hittites, Jebusites, and Amorites who live in the hill-country, and the Canaanites who live by the sea and along the Jordan.'

Then Caleb called for silence before 30 Moses and said, 'Let us go up at once and occupy the country; we are well able to conquer it.' But the men who 31 had gone with him said, 'No, we cannot attack these people; they are stronger than we are.' Thus their 32 report to the Israelites about the land which they had explored was discouraging: 'The country we explored', they said, 'will swallow up any who go to live in it. All the people we saw there are men of gigantic size. When 33 we set eyes on the Nephilimᵠ (the sons of Anakʳ belong to the Nephilim) we felt no bigger than grasshoppers; and that is how we looked to them.'

The people rebel against the LORD

Then the whole Israelite community 14 cried out in dismay; all night long they wept. One and all they made 2 complaints against Moses and Aaron: 'If only we had died in Egypt or in the wilderness!' they said. 'Far happier if we had! Why should the LORD 3 bring us to this land, to die in battle and leave our wives and our dependants to become the spoils of war? To go back to Egypt would be better than this.' And they began to talk of 4 choosing someone to lead them back.

Then Moses and Aaron flung them- 5 selves on the ground before the assembled community of the Israelites, and two of those who had 6 explored the land, Joshua son of Nun and Caleb son of Jephunneh, rent

o descendants of Anak: or tall men.   p Eshcol: *that is* Bunch of Grapes.   q Or giants.
r sons of Anak: or tall men.

7 their clothes and addressed the whole community: 'The country we penetrated and explored', they said, 'is 8 very good land indeed. If the LORD is pleased with us, he will bring us into this land which flows with milk and 9 honey, and give it to us. But you must not rebel against the LORD. You need not fear the people of the land; for there we shall find food. They have lost the protection that they had: the LORD is with us. You have nothing to 10 fear from them.' But by way of answer the assembled Israelites threatened to stone them, when suddenly the glory of the LORD appeared to them all in the Tent of the Presence.

11 Then the LORD said to Moses, 'How much longer will this people treat me with contempt? How much longer will they refuse to trust me in spite of all the signs I have shown among them? 12 I will strike them with pestilence. I will deny them their heritage, and you and your descendants I will make into a nation greater and more numerous 13 than they.' But Moses answered the LORD, 'What if the Egyptians hear of it? It was thou who didst bring this people out of Egypt by thy strength. 14 What if they tell the inhabitants of this land? They too have heard of thee, LORD, that thou art with this people, and art seen face to face, that thy cloud stays over them, and thou goest before them in a pillar of cloud by day and in a pillar of fire by night. 15 If then thou dost put them all to death at one blow, the nations who have heard these tales of thee will say, 16 "The LORD could not bring this people into the land which he promised them by oath; and so he destroyed them in the wilderness."

17 'Now let the LORD's might be shown in its greatness, true to thy proclama-18 tion of thyself—"The LORD, long-suffering, ever constant, who forgives iniquity and rebellion, and punishes sons to the third and fourth generation for the iniquity of their fathers, though he does not sweep them clean 19 away." Thou hast borne with this people from Egypt all the way here; forgive their iniquity, I beseech thee, as befits thy great and constant love.'

The LORD pronounces punishment

20 The LORD said, 'Your prayer is an-21 swered; I pardon them. But as I live, in very truth the glory of the LORD 22-3 shall fill the earth. Not one of all those who have seen my glory and the signs which I wrought in Egypt and in the wilderness shall see the country which I promised on oath to their fathers. Ten times they have challenged me and not obeyed my voice. None of those who have flouted me shall see this land. But my servant Caleb 24-5 showed a different spirit: he followed me with his whole heart. Because of this, I will bring him into the land in which he has already set foot, the territory of the Amalekites and the Canaanites who dwell in the Vale, and put his descendants in possession of it. Tomorrow you must turn back and set out for the wilderness by way of the Red Sea.'*

The LORD spoke to Moses and Aaron 26 and said, 'How long must I tolerate*t* 27 the complaints of this wicked community? I have heard the Israelites making complaints against me. Tell 28 them that this is the very word of the LORD: As I live, I will bring home to you the words I have heard you utter. Here in this wilderness your bones 29 shall lie, every man of you on the register from twenty years old and upwards, because you have made these complaints against me. Not one of you 30 shall enter the land which I swore with uplifted hand should be your home, except only Caleb son of Jephunneh and Joshua son of Nun. As for your 31 dependants, those dependants who, you said, would become the spoils of war, I will bring them in to the land you have rejected, and they shall enjoy it. But as for the rest of you, 32 your bones shall lie in this wilderness; your sons shall be wanderers in the 33 wilderness forty years, paying the penalty of your wanton disloyalty till the last man of you dies there. Forty 34 days you spent exploring the country, and forty years you shall spend—a year for each day—paying the penalty of your iniquities. You shall know what it means to have me against you.*u* I, the LORD, have spoken. This 35 I swear to do to all this wicked community who have combined against me. There shall be an end of them here in this wilderness; here they shall die.' But the men whom Moses 36 had sent to explore the land, and who came back and by their report set all the community complaining against him, died of the plague 37 before the LORD; they died of the plague because they had made a bad report. Of those who went to explore 38 the land, Joshua son of Nun and Caleb

s Or the Sea of Reeds.   t must I tolerate: prob. rdg.; Heb. for.   u Or to thwart me.

son of Jephunneh alone remained alive.

Israel defeated at Hormah

39 When Moses reported the LORD's words to all the Israelites, the people
40 were plunged in grief. They set out early next morning and made for the heights of the hill-country, saying, 'Look, we are on our way up to the place the LORD spoke of. We admit
41 that we have been wrong.' But Moses replied, 'Must you persist in disobeying the LORD's command? No good
42 will come of this. Go no further; you will not have the LORD with you, and
43 your enemies will defeat you. For in front of you are the Amalekites and Canaanites, and you will die by the sword, because you have ceased to follow the LORD, and he will no longer
44 be with you.' But they went recklessly on their way towards the heights of the hill-country, though neither the Ark of the Covenant of the LORD nor Moses moved with them out of the
45 camp; and the Amalekites and Canaanites from those hills came down and fell upon them, and crushed them at Hormah.

Laws concerning offerings

15 The LORD spoke to Moses and said,
2 Speak to the Israelites in these words: When you enter the land where you are to live, the land I am giving
3 you, you will make food-offerings to the LORD; they may be whole-offerings or any sacrifice made in fulfilment of a special[v] vow or by way of free-will offering or at one of the appointed seasons. When you thus make an offering of soothing odour from herd
4 or flock to the LORD, the man who offers, in presenting it, shall add a grain-offering of a tenth of an ephah of flour mixed with a quarter of a hin
5 of oil. You shall also add to the whole-offering or shared-offering a quarter of a hin of wine as a drink-offering with each lamb sacrificed.
6 If the animal is a ram, the grain-offering shall be two tenths of an ephah of flour mixed with a third of a
7 hin of oil, and the wine for the drink-offering shall be a third of a hin; in this way you will make an offering of soothing odour to the LORD.
8 When you offer to the LORD a young bull, whether as a whole-offering or as a sacrifice to fulfil a special[w] vow, or as a shared-offering,
9 you shall add a grain-offering of three

tenths of an ephah of flour mixed with half a hin of oil, and for the drink- 10 offering, half a hin of wine; the whole will thus be a food-offering of soothing odour to the LORD. This is what must 11 be done in each case, for every bull or ram, lamb or kid, whatever the 12 number of each that you offer. Every 13 native Israelite shall observe these rules in each case when he offers a food-offering of soothing odour to the LORD.

When an alien residing with you or 14 permanently settled among you offers a food-offering of soothing odour to the LORD, he shall do as you do. There 15 is one and the same rule for you and for the resident alien, a rule binding for all time on your descendants; you and the alien are alike before the LORD. There shall be one law and one 16 custom for you and for the alien residing with you.

The LORD spoke to Moses and said, 17 Speak to the Israelites in these words: 18 After you have entered the land into which I am bringing you, whenever 19 you eat the bread of the country, you shall set aside a contribution for the LORD. You shall set aside a cake made 20 of your first kneading of dough, as you set aside the contribution from the threshing-floor. You must give a 21 contribution to the LORD from your first kneading of dough; this rule is binding on your descendants.

When through inadvertence you 22 omit to carry out any of these commands which the LORD gave to Moses —any command whatever that the 23 LORD gave you through Moses on that first day and thereafter and made binding on your descendants—if it 24 be done inadvertently, unnoticed by the community, then the whole community shall offer one young bull as a whole-offering, a soothing odour to the LORD, with its proper grain-offering and drink-offering according to custom; and they shall add one he-goat as a sin-offering. The priest 25 shall make expiation for the whole community of Israelites, and they shall be forgiven. The omission was inadvertent; and they have brought their offering, a food-offering to the LORD; they have made their sin-offering before the LORD for their inadvertence; the whole community 26 of Israelites and the aliens residing among you shall be forgiven. The inadvertence was shared by the whole people.

v in fulfilment of a special: or to discharge a . . .   w fulfil a special: or discharge a . . .

27 If any individual sins inadvertently, he shall present a yearling she-goat as 28 a sin-offering, and the priest shall make expiation before the LORD for the said individual, and he shall be for- 29 given. For anyone who sins inadvertently, there shall be one law for all, whether native Israelite or resident 30 alien. But the person who sins presumptuously, native or alien, insults the LORD. He shall be cut off from his 31 people, because he has brought the word of the LORD into contempt and violated his command. That person shall be wholly cut off; the guilt shall be on his head alone.

A sabbath-breaker stoned

32 During the time that the Israelites were in the wilderness, a man was found gathering sticks on the sabbath 33 day. Those who had caught him in the act brought him to Moses and Aaron 34 and all the community, and they kept him in custody, because it was not clearly known what was to be done 35 with him. The LORD said to Moses, 'The man must be put to death; he must be stoned by all the community 36 outside the camp.' So they took him outside the camp and all stoned him to death, as the LORD had commanded Moses.

Tassels on garments

37 The LORD spoke to Moses and said, 38 Speak to the Israelites in these words: You must make tassels like flowers on the corners of your garments, you and your children's children. Into this tassel you shall work a violet thread, 39 and whenever you see this in the tassel, you shall remember all the LORD's commands and obey them, and not go your own wanton ways, led astray by your own eyes and 40 hearts. This token is to ensure that you remember all my commands and obey them, and keep yourselves holy, consecrated to your God. 41 I am the LORD your God who brought you out of Egypt to become your God. I am the LORD your God.

The authority of Moses challenged

16 Now Korah son of Izhar, son of Kohath, son of Levi, with the Reubenites Dathan and Abiram sons of 2 Eliab and On son of Peleth, challenged the authority of Moses. With them in their revolt were two hundred and fifty Israelites, all men of rank in the community, conveners of assembly 3 and men of good standing. They con-

fronted Moses and Aaron and said to them, 'You take too much upon yourselves. Every member of the community is holy and the LORD is among them all. Why do you set yourselves up above the assembly of the LORD?' When Moses heard this, he prostrated 4 himself, and he said to Korah and all 5 his company, 'Tomorrow morning the LORD shall declare who is his, who is holy and may present offerings to him. The man whom the LORD chooses shall present them. This is what you must 6 do, you, Korah, and all your company: you must take censers and put fire in 7 them, and then place incense on them before the LORD tomorrow. The man whom the LORD then chooses is the man who is holy. You take too much upon yourselves, you sons of Levi.' Moses said to Korah, 'Now listen, 8 you sons of Levi. Is it not enough for 9 you that the God of Israel has set you apart from the community of Israel, bringing you near him to maintain the service of the Tabernacle of the LORD and to stand before the community as their ministers? He has 10 brought you near him and your brother Levites with you; now you seek the priesthood as well. That is 11 why you and all your company have combined together against the LORD. What is Aaron that you should make these complaints against him?' Moses sent to fetch Dathan and Abi- 12 ram sons of Eliab, but they answered, 'We are not coming. Is it a small 13 thing that you have brought us away from a land flowing with milk and honey to let us die in the wilderness? Must you also set yourself up as prince over us? What is more, you 14 have not brought us into a land flowing with milk and honey, nor have you given us fields and vineyards to inherit. Do you think you can hoodwink men like us? We are not coming.' This answer made Moses very angry, 15 and he said to the LORD, 'Take no notice of their murmuring. I have not taken from them so much as a single ass; I have done no wrong to any of them.' Moses said to Korah, 'Present your- 16 selves before the LORD tomorrow, you and all your company, you and they and Aaron. Each man of you is to 17 take his censer and put incense on it. Then you shall present them before the LORD with their two hundred and fifty censers, and you and Aaron shall also bring your censers.' So each man 18 took his censer and put fire in it and placed incense on it; Moses and Aaron took their stand at the entrance 19 to the Tent of the Presence, and Korah gathered his whole company together and faced them at the entrance to the Tent of the Presence.

Then the glory of the LORD appeared 20 to the whole community. And the LORD spoke to Moses and Aaron and 21 said, 'Stand apart from this company, so that I may make an end of them in 22 a single instant.' But they prostrated themselves and said, 'O God, God of the spirits of all mankind, if one man sins, wilt thou be angry with the 23 whole community?' But the LORD 24 said to Moses, 'Tell them to stand back from the dwellings of Korah, Dathan and Abiram.'

25 So Moses rose and went to Dathan and Abiram, and the elders of Israel 26 followed him. He said to the whole community, 'Stand well away from the tents of these wicked men; touch nothing of theirs, or you will be swept 27 away because of all their sins.' So they moved away from the places occupied by Korah, Dathan and Abiram. Now Dathan and Abiram, holding themselves erect, had come out to the entrance of their tents with their wives, their sons, and their 28 dependants. Then Moses said, 'This shall prove to you that it is the LORD who sent me to do all these things, and it was not my own heart that 29 prompted me. If these men die a natural death and share the common fate of man, then the LORD has not 30 sent me; but if the LORD makes a great chasm, and the ground opens its mouth and swallows them and all that is theirs, and they go down alive to Sheol, then you will know that these men have held the LORD in contempt.'

31 Hardly had Moses spoken when the 32 ground beneath them split; the earth opened its mouth and swallowed them and their homes—all the followers of 33 Korah and all their property. They went down alive into Sheol with all that they had; the earth closed over them, and they vanished from the 34 assembly. At their cries all the Israelites round them fled, shouting, 'Look to yourselves! the earth will swallow 35 us up.' Meanwhile fire had come out from the LORD and burnt up the two hundred and fifty men who were presenting the incense.

36 Then the LORD spoke to Moses and 37 said, 'Bid Eleazar son of Aaron the priest set aside the censers from the burnt remains, and scatter the fire from them far and wide, because they are holy. And the censers of these men 38 who sinned at the cost of their lives you shall make into beaten plates to cover the altar; they are holy, because they have been presented before the LORD. Let them be a sign to the Israelites.' So Eleazar the priest took 39 the bronze^x censers which the victims of the fire had presented, and they were beaten into plates to make a covering for the altar, as a reminder 40 to the Israelites that no person unqualified, not descended from Aaron, should come forward to burn incense before the LORD, or his fate would be that of Korah and his company. All this was done as the LORD commanded Eleazar through Moses.

Next day all the community of the 41 Israelites raised complaints against Moses and Aaron and taxed them with causing the death of some of the LORD's people. As they gathered 42 against Moses and Aaron, they turned towards the Tent of the Presence and saw that the cloud covered it, and the glory of the LORD appeared. Moses 43 and Aaron came to the front of the Tent of the Presence, and the LORD 44 spoke to Moses and Aaron and said, 'Stand well clear of this community, 45 so that in a single instant I may make an end of them.' Then they prostrated themselves, and Moses said to Aaron, 46 'Take your censer, put fire from the altar in it, set incense on it, and go with it quickly to the assembled community to make expiation for them. Wrath has gone forth already from the presence of the LORD. The plague has begun.' So Aaron took his censer, 47 as Moses had said, ran into the midst of the assembly and found that the plague had begun among the people. He put incense on the censer and made expiation for the people, standing between the dead and the living, 48 and the plague stopped. Fourteen 49 thousand seven hundred died of it, in addition to those who had died for the offence of Korah. When Aaron came 50 back to Moses at the entrance to the Tent of the Presence, the plague had stopped.

Aaron's staff

The LORD spoke to Moses and said, 1 'Speak to the Israelites and tell them 2 to give you a staff for each tribe, one from every tribal chief, twelve in all,

x Or copper.

and write each man's name on his
3 staff. On Levi's staff write the name
of Aaron, for there shall be one staff
4 for each head of a tribe. You shall put
them all in the Tent of the Presence
before the Tokens, where I meet you,
5 and the staff of the man I choose shall
sprout. I will rid myself of the complaints of these Israelites, who keep
on complaining against you.'
6   Moses thereupon spoke to the
Israelites, and each of their chiefs
handed him a staff, each of them one
for his tribe, twelve in all, and Aa-
7 ron's staff among them. Moses put
them before the LORD in the Tent
8 of the Tokens, and next day when
he entered the tent, he found that
Aaron's staff, the staff for the tribe of
Levi, had sprouted. Indeed, it had
sprouted, blossomed, and produced
9 ripe almonds. Moses then brought out
the staffs from before the LORD and
showed them to all the Israelites; they
saw for themselves, and each man
10 took his own staff. The LORD said to
Moses, 'Put back Aaron's staff in
front of the Tokens to be kept as a
warning to all rebels, so that you may
rid me once and for all of their complaints, and then they shall not die.'
11 Moses did this; as the LORD had
commanded him, so he did.
12   The Israelites said to Moses, 'This
is the end of us! We perish, one and
13 all! Every single person who goes near
the Tabernacle of the LORD dies. Is
this to be our final end?'

Priests and Levites

18 The LORD said to Aaron: You and your
sons, together with the members of
your father's tribe, shall be fully
answerable for the sanctuary. You and
your sons alone shall be answerable
2 for your priestly office; but you shall
admit your kinsmen of Levi, your
father's tribe, to be attached to you
and assist you while you and your
sons are before the Tent of the
3 Tokens. They shall be in attendance
on you and fulfil all the duties of the
Tent, but shall not go near the holy
vessels and the altar, or they will die
4 and you with them. They shall be
attached to you and be responsible
for the maintenance of the Tent of the
Presence in every detail; no unquali-
5 fied person shall come near you. You
yourselves shall be responsible for the
sanctuary and the altar, so that wrath
may no more fall on the Israelites.
6 I have myself taken the Levites your
kinsmen out of all the Israelites as a

gift for you, given to the LORD for
the maintenance of the Tent of the
Presence. But only you and your sons 7
may fulfil the duties of your priestly
office that concern the altar or lie
within the Veil. This duty is yours;
I bestow on you this gift of priestly
service. The unqualified person who
intrudes on it shall be put to death.
  The LORD said to Aaron: I, the 8
LORD, commit to your control the
contributions made to me, that is all
the holy-gifts of the Israelites. I give
them to you and to your sons for your
allotted portion due to you in perpetuity. Out of the most holy gifts kept 9
back from the altar-fire this part shall
belong to you: every offering, whether
grain-offering, sin-offering, or guilt-
offering, rendered to me as a most holy
gift, belongs to you and to your sons.
You shall eat it as befits most holy 10
gifts; every male may eat it. You shall
regard it as holy.
  This also is yours: the contribution 11
from all such of their gifts as are
presented as special gifts by the
Israelites. I give them to you and to
your sons and daughters with you as
a due in perpetuity. Every person in
your household who is ritually clean
may eat them.
  I give you all the choicest of the oil, 12
the choicest of the new wine and the
corn, the firstfruits which are given to
the LORD. The first-ripe fruits of all 13
produce in the land which are brought
to the LORD shall be yours. Everyone
in your household who is clean may
eat them.
  Everything in Israel which has 14
been devoted to God shall be yours.
  All the first-born of man or beast 15
which are brought to the LORD shall
be yours. Notwithstanding, you must
accept payment in redemption of any
first-born of man and of unclean
beasts: at the end of one month you 16
shall redeem it at the fixed price of
five shekels of silver by the sacred
standard (twenty gerahs to the shekel). You must not, however, allow 17
the redemption of the first-born of a
cow, sheep, or goat; they are holy.
You shall fling their blood against the
altar and burn their fat in sacrifice as
a food-offering of soothing odour to
the LORD; their flesh shall be yours, 18
as are the breast of the special gift
and the right leg.
  All the contributions from holy- 19
gifts, which the Israelites set aside for
the LORD, I give to you and to your
sons and daughters with you as a due

in perpetuity. This is a perpetual covenant of salt before the LORD with you and your descendants also.

20 The LORD said to Aaron: You shall have no patrimony in the land of Israel, no holding among them; I am your holding in Israel, I am your patrimony.

21 To the Levites I give every tithe in Israel to be their patrimony, in return for the service they render in main-

22 taining the Tent of the Presence. In order that the Israelites may not henceforth approach the Tent and

23 thus incur the penalty of death, the Levites alone shall perform the service of the Tent, and they shall accept the full responsibility for it. This rule is binding on your descendants for all time. They shall have no patrimony

24 among the Israelites, because I give them as their patrimony the tithe which the Israelites set aside as a contribution to the LORD. Therefore I say to them: You shall have no patrimony among the Israelites.

25 The LORD spoke to Moses and said,

26 Speak to the Levites in these words: When you receive from the Israelites the tithe which I give you from them as your patrimony, you shall set aside from it the contribution to the LORD,

27 a tithe of the tithe. Your contribution shall count for you as if it were corn from the threshing-floor and juice

28 from the vat. In this way you too shall set aside the contribution due to the LORD out of all tithes which you receive from the Israelites and shall give the LORD's contribution to

29 Aaron the priest. Out of all the gifts you receive you shall set aside the contribution due to the LORD; and the gift which you hallow[y] must be taken from the choicest of them.

30 You shall say to the Levites: When you have set aside the choicest part of your portion, the remainder shall count for you as the produce of the

31 threshing-floor and the winepress, and you may eat it anywhere, you and your households. It is your payment for service in the Tent of the Presence.

32 When you have set aside its choicest part, you will incur no penalty in respect of it, and you will not be pro-faning the holy-gifts of the Israelites; so you will not die.

Purification from uncleanness

19 The LORD spoke to Moses and Aaron
2 and said: This is a law and a statute which the LORD has ordained. Tell the Israelites to bring you a red cow without blemish or defect, which has never borne the yoke. You shall give 3 it to Eleazar the priest, and it shall be taken outside the camp and slaugh-tered[z] to the east of it. Eleazar the 4 priest shall take some of the blood on his finger and sprinkle it seven times towards the front of the Tent of the Presence. The cow shall be burnt in 5 his sight, skin, flesh, and blood, to-gether with the offal. The priest shall 6 then take cedar-wood, marjoram, and scarlet thread, and throw them into the heart of the fire in which the cow is burning. He shall wash his clothes 7 and bathe his body in water; after which he may enter the camp, but he remains ritually unclean till sunset. The man who burnt the cow shall wash 8 his clothes and bathe his body in water, but he also remains unclean till sunset. Then a man who is clean shall 9 collect the ashes of the cow and deposit them outside the camp in a clean place. They shall be reserved for use by the Israelite community in the water of ritual purification; for the cow is a sin-offering. The man who 10 collected the ashes of the cow shall wash his clothes, but he remains un-clean till sunset. This rule shall be binding for all time on the Israelites and on the alien who is living with them.

Whoever touches a corpse shall be 11 ritually unclean for seven days. He 12 shall get himself purified with the water of ritual purification on the third day and on the seventh day, and then he shall be clean. If he is not purified both on the third day and on the seventh, he shall not be clean. Everyone who touches a corpse, that 13 is the body of a man who has died, and does not purify himself, defiles the Tabernacle of the LORD. That person shall be cut off from Israel. The water of purification has not been flung over him; he remains unclean, and his impurity is still upon him.

When a man dies in a tent, this is 14 the law: everyone who goes into the tent and everyone who was inside the tent shall be ritually unclean for seven days, and every open vessel 15 which has no covering tied over it shall also be unclean. In the open, anyone 16 who touches a man killed with a weapon or one who has died naturally, or who touches a human bone or a

y you hallow: prob. rdg.; Heb. obscure. it . . .

z Or he shall take it outside the camp and slaughter

grave, shall be unclean for seven days.
17 For such uncleanness, they shall take some of the ash from the burnt mass of the sin-offering and add fresh water
18 to it in a vessel. Then a man who is clean shall take marjoram, dip it in the water, and sprinkle the tent with all the vessels in it and all the people who were there, or the man who has touched a human bone, a corpse (whether the man was killed or died
19 naturally), or a grave. The man who is clean shall sprinkle the unclean man on the third day and on the seventh; on the seventh day he shall purify him; then the man shall wash his clothes and bathe in water, and at sunset he
20 shall be clean. If a man who is unclean does not get himself purified, that person shall be cut off from the assembly, because he has defiled the sanctuary of the LORD. The water of purification has not been flung over
21 him: he is unclean. This rule shall be binding on you for all time. The man who sprinkles the water of purification shall also wash his clothes, and whoever touches the water shall be
22 unclean till sunset. Whatever the unclean man touches shall be unclean, and any person who touches that shall be unclean till sunset.

Water from the rock

20 In the first month the whole community of Israel reached the wilderness of Zin and stayed some time at Kadesh; there Miriam died and was buried.
2   There was no water for the community; so they gathered against
3 Moses and Aaron. The people disputed with Moses and said, 'If only we had perished when our brothers perished in the presence of the LORD!
4 Why have you brought the assembly of the LORD into this wilderness for
5 us and our beasts to die here? Why did you fetch us up from Egypt to bring us to this vile place, where nothing will grow, neither corn nor figs, vines nor pomegranates? There is
6 not even any water to drink.' Moses and Aaron came forward in front of the assembly to the entrance of the Tent of the Presence. There they fell prostrate, and the glory of the LORD appeared to them.
7   The LORD spoke to Moses and said,
8 'Take a^a staff, and then with Aaron your brother assemble all the community, and, in front of them all, speak to the rock and it will yield its

water. Thus you will produce water for the community out of the rock, for them and their beasts to drink.'
9 Moses left the presence of the LORD with the staff, as he had commanded
10 him. Then he and Aaron gathered the assembly together in front of the rock, and he said to them, 'Listen to me, you rebels. Must we get water out of
11 this rock for you?' Moses raised his hand and struck the rock twice with his staff. Water gushed out in abundance and they all drank, men and
12 beasts. But the LORD said to Moses and Aaron, 'You did not trust me so far as to uphold my holiness in the sight of the Israelites; therefore you shall not lead this assembly into the land which I promised to give them.'
13 Such were the waters of Meribah,^{b} where the people disputed with the LORD and through which his holiness was upheld.

The Edomites refuse passage to Israel

14 From Kadesh Moses sent envoys to the king of Edom: 'This is a message from your brother Israel. You know all the hardships we have encountered,
15 how our fathers went down to Egypt, and we lived there for many years. The Egyptians ill-treated us and our
16 fathers before us, and we cried to the LORD for help. He listened to us and sent an angel, and he brought us out of Egypt; and now we are here at Kadesh, a town on your frontier.
17 Grant us passage through your country. We will not trespass on field or vineyard, or drink from your wells. We will keep to the king's highway; we will not turn off to right or left until we have crossed your territory.'
18 But the Edomites answered, 'You shall not cross our land. If you do, we will march out and attack you in
19 force.' The Israelites said, 'But we will keep to the main road. If we and our flocks drink your water, we will pay you for it; we will simply cross
20 your land on foot.' But the Edomites said, 'No, you shall not', and took the field against them with a large army
21 in full strength. Thus the Edomites refused to allow Israel to cross their frontier, and Israel went a different way to avoid a conflict.

The death of Aaron

22 The whole community of Israel set out from Kadesh and came to Mount Hor.
23 At Mount Hor, near the frontier of

a Or the. b That is Dispute.

Edom, the LORD said to Moses and
24 Aaron, 'Aaron shall be gathered to
his father's kin. He shall not enter the
land which I promised to give the
Israelites, because over the waters
of Meribah you rebelled against my
25 command. Take Aaron and his son
26 Eleazar, and go up Mount Hor. Strip
Aaron of his robes and invest Eleazar
his son with them, for Aaron shall be
taken from you: he shall die there.'
27 Moses did as the LORD had commanded him: they went up Mount Hor
28 in sight of the whole community, and
Moses stripped Aaron of his robes and
invested his son Eleazar with them.
There Aaron died on the mountain-
top, and Moses and Eleazar came
29 down from the mountain. So the
whole community saw that Aaron
had died, and all Israel mourned him
for thirty days.

The Canaanites attack Israel

21 When the Canaanite king of Arad who
lived in the Negeb heard that the
Israelites were coming by way of
Atharim, he attacked them and took
2 some of them prisoners. Israel thereupon made a vow to the LORD and
said, 'If thou wilt deliver this people
into my power, I will destroy their
3 cities.' The LORD listened to Israel
and delivered the Canaanites into their
power. Israel destroyed them and
their cities and called the place
Hormah.[c]

A plague of snakes

4 Then they left Mount Hor by way of
the Red Sea to march round the
flank of Edom. But on the way they
5 grew impatient and spoke against
God and Moses. 'Why have you
brought us up from Egypt', they said,
'to die in the desert where there is
neither food nor water? We are
heartily sick of this miserable fare.'
6 Then the LORD sent poisonous snakes
among the people, and they bit the
Israelites so that many of them died.
7 The people came to Moses and said,
'We sinned when we spoke against
the LORD and you. Plead with the
LORD to rid us of the snakes.' Moses
therefore pleaded with the LORD for
8 the people; and the LORD told Moses
to make a serpent[d] of bronze and
erect it as a standard, so that anyone who had been bitten could look
9 at it and recover. So Moses made
a bronze serpent and erected it as a
standard, so that when a snake had
bitten a man, he could look at the
bronze serpent and recover.

The Israelites journey around Moab

The Israelites went on and encamped 10
at Oboth. They moved on from Oboth 11
and encamped at Iye-abarim in the
wilderness on the eastern frontier of
Moab. From there they moved and 12
encamped by the gorge of the Zared.
They moved on from the Zared and 13
encamped by the farther side of the
Arnon in the wilderness which extends
into Amorite territory, for the Arnon
was the Moabite frontier; it lies between Moab and the Amorites. That 14
is why the Book of the Wars of the
LORD speaks of Vaheb[e] in Suphah and
the gorges:

Arnon and the watershed of the gorges 15
that falls away towards the dwellings
          at Ar
and slopes towards the frontier of
          Moab.

From there they moved on to Beer:[f] 16
this is the water-hole where the LORD
said to Moses, 'Gather the people
together and I will give them water.'
It was then that Israel sang this 17
song:

Well up, spring water! Greet it with
          song,
the spring unearthed by the princes, 18
laid open by the leaders of the people
with sceptre and with mace,
a gift from the wilderness.

And they proceeded from Beer[g] to Na- 19
haliel, and from Nahaliel to Bamoth;
then from Bamoth to the valley in 20
the Moabite country below the summit
of Pisgah overlooking the desert.

Israel conquers Sihon

Then Israel sent envoys to the Amor- 21
ite king Sihon and said, 'Grant us 22
passage through your country. We
will not trespass on field or vineyard,
nor will we drink from your wells. We
will travel by the king's highway till
we have crossed your territory.' But 23
Sihon would not grant Israel passage
through his territory; he mustered
all his people and came out against
Israel in the wilderness. He advanced
as far as Jahaz and attacked Israel,
but only put them to the sword, 24
giving no quarter, and occupied their
land from the Arnon to the Jabbok,
the territory of the Ammonites, where

c That is Destruction.   d Or snake.   e Name meaning Watershed.   f Name meaning
Water-hole.   g Prob. rdg.; Heb. from a gift.

25 the country became difficult. So Israel took all these Amorite cities and settled in them, that is in Heshbon and
26 all its dependent villages. Heshbon was the capital of the Amorite king Sihon, who had fought against the former king of Moab and taken from him
27 all his territory as far as the Arnon. Therefore the bards say:

Come to Heshbon, come!
Let us see the city of Sihon rebuilt and restored!
28 For fire blazed out from Heshbon,
and flames from Sihon's city.
It devoured Ar of Moab,
and swept the high ground at Arnon head.

29 Woe to you, Moab;
it is the end of you, you people of Kemosh.
He has made his sons fugitives
and his daughters the prisoners of Sihon the Amorite king.
30 From Heshbon to Dibon their very embers are burnt out
and they are extinct,
while the fire spreads onward to Medeba.

31 Thus Israel occupied the territory of the Amorites.

Israel conquers Og

32 Moses then sent men to explore Jazer; the Israelites captured it together with its dependent villages and drove
33 out the Amorites living there. Then they turned and advanced along the road to Bashan. Og king of Bashan, with all his people, took the field
34 against them at Edrei. The LORD said to Moses, 'Do not be afraid of him. I have delivered him into your hands, with all his people and his land. Deal with him as you dealt with Sihon the Amorite king who lived in Heshbon.'
35 So they put him to the sword with his sons and all his people, until there was no survivor left, and they occupied his land.

Balak sends for Balaam

22 The Israelites went forward and encamped in the lowlands of Moab on the farther side of the Jordan from Jericho.
2 Balak son of Zippor saw what Israel
3 had done to the Amorites, and Moab was in terror of the people because there were so many of them. The Moabites were sick with fear at the sight
4 of them; and they said to the elders

of Midian, 'This horde will soon lick up everything round us as a bull crops the spring grass.' Balak son of Zippor was at that time king of Moab. He sent a deputation to summon 5 Balaam son of Beor, who was at Pethor by the Euphrates in the land of the Amavites, with this message, 'Look, an entire nation has come out of Egypt; they cover the face of the country and are settling at my very door. Come at once and lay a curse on 6 them, because they are too many for me; then I may be able to defeat them and drive them from the country. I know that those whom you bless are blessed, and those whom you curse are cursed.'

The elders of Moab and Midian 7 took the fees for augury with them, and they came to Balaam and told him what Balak had said. 'Spend this 8 night here,' he said, 'and I will give you whatever answer the LORD gives to me.' So the Moabite chiefs stayed with Balaam. God came to Balaam 9 and asked him, 'Who are these men with you?' Balaam replied, 'Balak 10 son of Zippor king of Moab has sent them to me and he says, "Look, a 11 people newly come out of Egypt is covering the face of the country. Come at once and denounce them for me; then I may be able to fight them and drive them away." ' God said to 12 Balaam, 'You are not to go with them or curse the people, because they are to be blessed.'[h] So Balaam rose in the 13 morning and said to Balak's chiefs, 'Go back to your own country; the LORD has refused to let me go with you.' Then the Moabite chiefs took 14 their leave and went back to Balak, and told him that Balaam had refused to come with them; whereupon 15 Balak sent a second and larger embassy of higher rank than the first. They came to Balaam and told him, 16 'This is the message from Balak son of Zippor: "Let nothing stand in the way of your coming. I will confer 17 great honour upon you; I will do whatever you ask me. But you must come and denounce this people for me." ' Balaam gave this answer to 18 Balak's messengers: 'Even if Balak were to give me all the silver and gold in his house, I could not disobey the command of the LORD my God in anything, small or great. But stay here 19 for this night, as the others did, that I may learn what more the LORD has to say to me.' During the night God 20

[h] *Or* are blessed.

C*

came to Balaam and said to him, 'If these men have come to summon you, then rise and go with them, but do only
21 what I tell you.' So in the morning Balaam rose, saddled his ass and went with the Moabite chiefs.

Balaam's ass

22 But God was angry because Balaam was going, and as he came riding on his ass, accompanied by his two servants, the angel of the LORD took his stand in the road to bar his way.
23 When the ass saw the angel standing in the road with his sword drawn, she turned off the road into the fields, and Balaam beat the ass to bring her
24 back on to the road. Then the angel of the LORD stood where the road ran through a hollow, with fenced vine-
25 yards on either side. The ass saw the angel and, crushing herself against the wall, crushed Balaam's foot against
26 it, and he beat her again. The angel of the LORD moved on further and stood in a narrow place where there was no room to turn either to right or left.
27 When the ass saw the angel, she lay down under Balaam. At that Balaam lost his temper and beat the ass with
28 his stick. The LORD then made the ass speak, and she said to Balaam, 'What have I done? This is the third
29 time you have beaten me.' Balaam answered the ass, 'You have been making a fool of me. If I had had a sword here, I should have killed you on
30 the spot.' But the ass answered, 'Am I not still the ass which you have ridden all your life? Have I ever taken such a liberty with you before?' He said,
31 'No.' Then the LORD opened Balaam's eyes: he saw the angel of the LORD standing in the road with his sword drawn, and he bowed down and fell
32 flat on his face before him. The angel said to him, 'What do you mean by beating your ass three times like this? I came out to bar your way but you
33 made straight for me, and three times your ass saw me and turned aside. If she had not turned aside, I should by now have killed you and spared her.'
34 Balaam replied to the angel of the LORD, 'I have done wrong. I did not know that you stood in the road con-fronting me. But now, if my journey displeases you, I am ready to go back.'
35 The angel of the LORD said to Balaam, 'Go on with these men; but say only what I tell you.' So Balaam went on with Balak's chiefs.

Balaam and Balak

When Balak heard that Balaam was 36 coming, he came out to meet him as far as Ar of Moab by the Arnon on his frontier. Balak said to Balaam, 37 'Did I not send time and again to summon you? Why did you not come? Did you think that I could not do you honour?' Balaam replied, 'I have 38 come, as you see. But now that I am here, what power have I of myself to say anything? Whatever is the word God puts into my mouth, that is what I will say.' So Balaam went with Balak 39 till they came to Kiriath-huzoth, and 40 Balak slaughtered cattle and sheep and sent them to Balaam and to the chiefs who were with him.

In the morning Balak took Balaam 41 and led him up to the Heights of Baal, from where he could see the full extent of the Israelite host. Then Balaam 2 said to Balak, 'Build me here seven altars and prepare for me seven bulls and seven rams.' Balak did as he 2 asked and offered a bull and a ram on each altar. Then he said to him, 'I 3– have prepared the seven altars, and I have offered the bull and the ram on each altar.' Balaam said to Balak, 'Take your stand beside your sacrifice, and let me go off by myself. It may happen that the LORD will meet me. Whatever he reveals to me, I will tell you.' So he went forthwith, and God met him. The LORD put words into 5 Balaam's mouth and said, 'Go back to Balak, and speak as I tell you.' So he went back, and found Balak 6 standing by his sacrifice, and with him all the Moabite chiefs. And Balaam 7 uttered his oracle:

From Aram,^{i} from the mountains of
    the east,
Balak king of Moab has brought me:
'Come, lay a curse for me on Jacob,
come, execrate Israel.'
How can I denounce whom God has 8
    not denounced?
How can I execrate whom the LORD
    has not execrated?
From the rocky heights I see them, 9
I watch them from the rounded hills.
I see a people that dwells alone,
that has not made itself one with the
    nations.
Who can count the host^j of Jacob 10
or number the hordes^k of Israel?
Let me die as men die who are
    righteous,
grant that my end may be as theirs!

Then Balak said to Balaam, 'What is 11

---

i Or Syria.   *j* Or dust.   *k* Or quarter *or* sands.

this you have done? I sent for you to denounce my enemies, and what you 12 have done is to bless them.' But he replied, 'Must I not keep to the words that the LORD puts into my mouth?'

13 Balak then said to him, 'Come with me now to another place from which you will see them, though not the full extent of them; you will not see them all. Denounce them for me from there.'

14 So he took him to the Field of the Watchers[l] on the summit of Pisgah, where he built seven altars and offered a bull and a ram on each altar. 15 Balaam said to Balak, 'Take your stand beside your sacrifice, and I will 16 meet God over there.' The LORD met Balaam and put words into his mouth, and said, 'Go back to Balak, and 17 speak as I tell you.' So he went back, and found him standing beside his sacrifice, with the Moabite chiefs. Balak asked what the LORD had said, 18 and Balaam uttered his oracle:

Up, Balak, and listen:
hear what I am charged to say, son of Zippor.
19 God is not a mortal that he should lie, not a man that he should change his mind.[m]
Has he not spoken, and will he not make it good?
What he has proclaimed, he will surely fulfil.
20 I have received command to bless; I will bless and I cannot gainsay it.
21 He has discovered no iniquity in Jacob
and has seen no mischief in Israel.[n]
The LORD their God is with them, acclaimed among them as king.[o]
22 What its curving horns are to the wild ox,
God is to them, who brought them out of Egypt.
23 Surely there is no divination in[p] Jacob,
and no augury in[p] Israel;
now is the time to say of Jacob and of Israel, 'See what God has wrought!'
24 Behold a people rearing up like a lioness,
rampant like a lion;
he will not couch till he devours the prey
and drinks the blood of the slain.

25 Then Balak said to Balaam, 'You will not denounce them; then at least do 26 not bless them'; and he answered, 'Did I not warn you that I must do

all the LORD tells me?' Balak replied, 27 'Come, let me take you to another place; perhaps God will be pleased to let you denounce them for me from there.' So he took Balaam to the 28 summit of Peor overlooking Jeshimon, and Balaam told him to build 29 seven altars for him there and prepare seven bulls and seven rams. Balak did 30 as Balaam had said, and he offered a bull and a ram on each altar.

But now that Balaam knew that 24 the LORD wished him to bless Israel, he did not go and resort to divination as before. He turned towards the desert; and as he looked, he saw Israel 2 encamped tribe by tribe. The spirit of God came upon him, and he uttered 3 his oracle:

The very word of Balaam son of Beor, the very word of the man whose sight is clear,
the very word of him who hears the 4 words of God,
who with staring eyes sees in a trance the vision from the Almighty:
how goodly are your tents, O Jacob, 5 your dwelling-places, Israel,
like long rows of palms,   6
like gardens by a river,
like lign-aloes planted by the LORD,
like cedars beside the water!
The water in his vessels shall over- 7 flow,
and his seed shall be like great waters
so that his king may be taller than Agag,
and his kingdom lifted high.
What its curving horns are to the wild 8 ox,
God is to him, who brought him out of Egypt;
he shall devour his adversaries the nations,
crunch their bones, and smash their limbs in pieces.
When he reclines he couches like a 9 lion,
like a lioness, and no one dares rouse him.
Blessed be they that bless you,
and they that curse you be accursed!

Balaam's oracle

At that Balak was very angry with 10 Balaam, beat his hands together and said, 'I summoned you to denounce my enemies, and three times you have persisted in blessing them. Off with 11 you to your own place! I promised to confer great honour upon you, but

l Or Field of Zophim.   m Or feel regret.   n Or None can discover calamity in Jacob nor see trouble in Israel.   o Or royal care is bestowed on them.   p Or against.

now the LORD has kept this honour
12 from you.' Balaam answered, 'But I
told your own messengers whom you
13 sent: "If Balak gives me all the silver
and gold in his house, I cannot disobey
the command of the LORD by doing
anything of my own will, good or bad.
What the LORD speaks to me, that is
14 what I will say." Now I am going to
my own people; but first, I will warn
you what this people will do to yours
15 in the days to come.' So he uttered
his oracle:

The very word of Balaam son of Beor,
  the very word of the man whose sight
    is clear,
16 the very word of him who hears the
    words of God,
who shares the knowledge of the Most
    High,
who with staring eyes sees in a trance
  the vision from the Almighty:
17   I see him, but not now;
I behold him, but not near:
a star shall come forth out of Jacob,
a comet arise from Israel.
He shall smite the squadrons*q* of
    Moab,
and beat down all the sons of strife.
18 Edom shall be his by conquest
  and Seir, his enemy, shall be his.
Israel shall do valiant deeds;
19 Jacob shall trample them down,
  the last survivor from Ar shall he
    destroy.

20 He saw Amalek and uttered his
oracle:

First of all the nations was Amalek,
but his end shall be utter destruction.

21 He saw the Kenites and uttered his
oracle:

Your refuge, though it seems secure,
  your nest, though set on the mountain
    crag,
22 is doomed to burning, O Cain.
How long must you dwell there in my
    sight?

23 He uttered his oracle:

Ah, who are these assembling in the
  north,
24 invaders from the region of Kittim?
They will lay waste Assyria; they will
    lay Eber waste:
he too shall perish utterly.

25 Then Balaam arose and returned home,
and Balak also went on his way.

Israel worships the Baal of Peor

When the Israelites were in Shittim, 25
the people began to have intercourse
with Moabite women, who invited 2
them to the sacrifices offered to their
gods; and they ate the sacrificial food
and prostrated themselves before the
gods of Moab. The Israelites joined 3
in the worship of the Baal of Peor,
and the LORD was angry with them.
He said to Moses, 'Take all the leaders 4
of the people and hurl them down to
their death before the LORD in the full
light of day, that the fury of his anger
may turn away from Israel.' So Moses 5
said to the judges of Israel, 'Put to
death, each one of you, those of his
tribe who have joined in the worship
of the Baal of Peor.'

One of the Israelites brought a 6
Midianite woman into his family in
open defiance of Moses and all the
community of Israel, while they were
weeping by the entrance of the Tent of
the Presence. Phinehas son of Eleazar, 7
son of Aaron the priest, saw him. He
stepped out from the crowd and took
up a spear, and he went into the inner 8
room after the Israelite and trans-
fixed the two of them, the Israelite
and the woman, pinning them together. Thus the plague which had
attacked the Israelites was brought
to a stop; but twenty-four thousand 9
had already died.

The LORD spoke to Moses and 10
said, 'Phinehas son of Eleazar, son 11
of Aaron the priest, has turned my
wrath away from the Israelites; he
displayed among them the same jealous anger that moved me, and therefore in my jealousy I did not exterminate the Israelites. Tell him that 12
I hereby grant him my covenant of
security of tenure. He and his descen- 13
dants after him shall enjoy the priesthood under a covenant for all time,
because he showed his zeal for his God
and made expiation for the Israelites.'
The name of the Israelite struck down 14
with the Midianite woman was Zimri
son of Salu, a chief in a Simeonite
family, and the Midianite woman's 15
name was Cozbi daughter of Zur, who
was the head of a group of fathers'
families in Midian.

The LORD spoke to Moses and said, 16
'Make the Midianites suffer as they 17-
made you suffer with their crafty
tricks, and strike them down; their
craftiness was your undoing at Peor
and in the affair of Cozbi their sister,

q Or heads.

the daughter of a Midianite chief, who was struck down at the time of the plague that followed Peor.'

The numbering of Israel

1 After the plague the LORD said to Moses and Eleazar the priest, son of 2 Aaron, 'Number the whole community of Israel by fathers' families, recording everyone in Israel aged twenty years and upwards fit for military 3 service.' Moses and Eleazar collected them in the lowlands of Moab by the 4 Jordan near Jericho,*r* all who were twenty years of age and upwards, as the LORD had commanded Moses.

These were the Israelites who came out of Egypt:

5*s* Reubenites (Reuben was Israel's eldest son): Enoch, the Enochite family; Pallu, the Palluite family; 6 Hezron, the Hezronite family; Carmi, 7 the Carmite family. These were the Reubenite families; the number in their detailed list was forty-three thousand seven hundred and thirty. 9 Son of Pallu: Eliab. Sons of Eliab: Nemuel, Dathan and Abiram. These were the same Dathan and Abiram, conveners of the community, who defied Moses and Aaron and joined the company of Korah in defying 10 the LORD. Then the earth opened its mouth and swallowed them up with Korah, and so their company died, while fire burnt up the two hundred and fifty men, and they became a 11 warning sign. The Korahites, however, did not die.

12 Simeonites, by their families: Nemuel, the Nemuelite family; Jamin, the Jaminite family; Jachin, the 13 Jachinite family; Zerah, the Zarhite family; Saul, the Saulite family. 14 These were the Simeonite families; the number in their detailed list was twenty-two thousand two hundred.

15 Gadites, by their families: Zephon, the Zephonite family; Haggi, the Haggite family; Shuni, the Shunite 16 family; Ozni, the Oznite family; Eri, 17 the Erite family; Arod, the Arodite family; Areli, the Arelite family. 18 These were the Gadite families; the number in their detailed list was forty thousand five hundred.

19 The sons of Judah were Er, Onan, Shelah, Perez and Zerah; Er and 20 Onan died in Canaan. Judahites, by their families: Shelah, the Shelanite family; Perez, the Perezite family; 21 Zerah, the Zarhite family. Perezites: Hezron, the Hezronite family; Hamul,

the Hamulite family. These were the 22 families of Judah; the number in their detailed list was seventy-six thousand five hundred.

Issacharites, by their families: 23 Tola, the Tolaite family; Pua, the Puite family; Jashub, the Jashubite 24 family; Shimron, the Shimronite family. These were the families of 25 Issachar; the number in their detailed list was sixty-four thousand three hundred.

Zebulunites, by their families: 26 Sered, the Sardite family; Elon, the Elonite family; Jahleel, the Jahleelite family. These were the Zebulunite 27 families; the number in their detailed list was sixty thousand five hundred.

Josephites, by their families: Ma- 28 nasseh and Ephraim. Manassites: 29 Machir, the Machirite family. Machir was the father of Gilead: Gilead, the Gileadite family. Gileadites: Jeezer, 30 the Jeezerite family; Helek, the Helekite family; Asriel, the Asrielite 31 family; Shechem, the Shechemite family; Shemida, the Shemidaite 32 family; Hepher, the Hepherite family. Zelophehad son of Hepher had no 33 sons, only daughters; their names were Mahlah, Noah, Hoglah, Milcah and Tirzah. These were the families 34 of Manasseh; the number in their detailed list was fifty-two thousand seven hundred.

Ephraimites, by their families: 35 Shuthelah, the Shuthalhite family; Becher, the Bachrite family; Tahan, the Tahanite family. Shuthalhites: 36 Eran, the Eranite family. These were 37 the Ephraimite families; the number in their detailed list was thirty-two thousand five hundred. These were the Josephites, by families.

Benjamites, by their families: Bela, 38 the Balaite family; Ashbel, the Ashbelite family; Ahiram, the Ahiramite family; Shupham, the Shupham- 39 ite family; Hupham, the Huphamite family. Belaites: Ard and Naaman. 40 Ard, the Ardite family; Naaman, the Naamite family. These were the 41 Benjamite families; the number in their detailed list was forty-five thousand six hundred.

Danites, by their families: Shuham, 42 the Shuhamite family. These were the families of Dan by their families; the number in the detailed list of the 43 Shuhamite family was sixty-four thousand four hundred.

Asherites, by their families: Imna, 44 the Imnite family; Ishvi, the Ishvite

r Prob. rdg.; Heb. adds saying. *s Verses 5–50: cp. Gen. 46. 8–25; Exod. 6. 14, 15; 1 Chr. chs. 4–8.*

family; Beriah, the Beriite family.
45 Beriite families: Heber, the Heber-
ite family; Malchiel, the Malchielite
46 family. The daughter of Asher was
47 named Serah. These were the Asherite
families; the number in their detailed
list was fifty-three thousand four hundred.
48 Naphtalites, by their families: Jahzeel, the Jahzeelite family; Guni, the
49 Gunite family; Jezer, the Jezerite
family; Shillem, the Shillemite family.
50 These were the Naphtalite families
by their families; the number in their
detailed list was forty-five thousand
four hundred.
51 The total in the Israelite lists was
six hundred and one thousand seven
hundred and thirty.

The land to be apportioned by lot

52 The LORD spoke to Moses and said,
53 'The land shall be apportioned among
these tribes according to the number
54 of names recorded. To the larger
group you shall give a larger property
and to the smaller a smaller; a property shall be given to each in proportion to its size as shown in the
55 detailed lists. The land, however, shall
be apportioned by lot; the lots shall
be cast for the properties by families
56 in the father's line. Properties shall
be apportioned by lot between the
larger families and the smaller.'

The tribe of Levi

57 The detailed lists of Levi, by families:
Gershon, the Gershonite family; Kohath, the Kohathite family; Merari,
the Merarite family.
58 These were the families of Levi: the
Libnite, Hebronite, Mahlite, Mushite,
and Korahite families.
Kohath was the father of Amram;
59 Amram's wife was named Jochebed
daughter of Levi, born to him in
Egypt. She bore to Amram Aaron,
60 Moses, and their sister Miriam. Aaron's
sons were Nadab, Abihu, Eleazar and
61 Ithamar. Nadab and Abihu died
because they presented illicit fire
before the LORD.
62 In the detailed lists of Levi the
number of males, aged one month and
upwards, was twenty-three thousand.
They were recorded separately from
the other Israelites because no property was allotted to them among the
Israelites.

Caleb and Joshua

63 These were the detailed lists prepared
by Moses and Eleazar the priest when
they numbered the Israelites in the
lowlands of Moab by the Jordan near
Jericho. Among them there was not 64
a single one of the Israelites whom
Moses and Aaron the priest had
recorded in the wilderness of Sinai;
for the LORD had said they should all 65
die in the wilderness. None of them
was still living except Caleb son of
Jephunneh and Joshua son of Nun.

When daughters inherit

A claim was presented by the daugh- 2
ters of Zelophehad son of Hepher,
son of Gilead, son of Machir, son of
Manasseh, son of Joseph. Their names
were Mahlah, Noah, Hoglah, Milcah
and Tirzah. They appeared at the 2
entrance of the Tent of the Presence
before Moses, Eleazar the priest, the
chiefs, and all the community, and
spoke as follows: 'Our father died in 3
the wilderness. He was not among the
company of Korah which combined
together against the LORD; he died for
his own sin and left no sons. Is it right 4
that, because he had no son, our
father's name should disappear from
his family? Give us our property on
the same footing as our father's
brothers.'
So Moses brought their case before 5
the LORD, and the LORD spoke to 6
Moses and said, 'The claim of the 7
daughters of Zelophehad is good. You
must allow them to inherit on the
same footing as their father's brothers.
Let their father's patrimony pass to
them. Then say this to the Israelites:
"When a man dies leaving no son, his 8
patrimony shall pass to his daughter.
If he has no daughter, you shall give 9
it to his brothers. If he has no brothers, 10
you shall give it to his father's brothers. If his father has no brothers, 11
then you shall give possession to the
nearest survivor in his family, and
he shall inherit. This shall be a legal
precedent for the Israelites, as the
LORD has commanded Moses."'

Joshua succeeds Moses

The LORD said to Moses, 'Go up this 12
mountain, Mount Abarim, and look
out over the land which I have given
to the Israelites. Then, when you 13
have looked out over it, you shall be
gathered to your father's kin like your
brother Aaron; for you and Aaron 14
disobeyed my command when the
community disputed with me in the
wilderness of Zin: you did not uphold
my holiness before them at the waters.'

These were the waters of Meribah-by-Kadesh in the wilderness of Zin.

16 Then Moses said, 'Let the LORD, the God of the spirits of all mankind, appoint a man over the community 17 to go out and come in at their head, to lead them out and bring them home, so that the community of the LORD may not be like sheep without a shep-18 herd.' The LORD answered Moses, 'Take Joshua son of Nun, a man endowed with spirit; lay your hand 19 on him and set him before Eleazar the priest and all the community. Give him his commission in their 20 presence, and delegate some of your authority to him, so that all the community of the Israelites may obey 21 him. He must appear before Eleazar the priest, who will obtain a decision for him by consulting the Urim before the LORD; at his word they shall go out and shall come home, both Joshua and the whole community of the Israelites.'

22 Moses did as the LORD had commanded him. He took Joshua, presented him to Eleazar the priest and 23 the whole community, laid his hands on him and gave him his commission, as the LORD had instructed him.

Daily sacrifices

28 The LORD spoke to Moses and said, 2 Give this command to the Israelites: See that you present my offerings, the food for the food-offering of soothing odour, to me at the appointed time. 3 Tell them: This is the food-offering which you shall present to the LORD: the regular daily whole-offering of two yearling rams without blemish. 4 One you shall sacrifice in the morning and the second between dusk and 5 dark. The grain-offering shall be a tenth of an ephah of flour mixed with a quarter of a hin of oil of pounded 6 olives. (This was the regular whole-offering made at Mount Sinai, a sooth-ing odour, a food-offering to the 7 LORD.) The wine for the proper drink-offering shall be a quarter of a hin to each ram; you are to pour out this strong drink in the holy place as an 8 offering to the LORD. You shall sacri-fice the second ram between dusk and dark, with the same grain-offering as at the morning sacrifice and with the proper drink-offering; it is a food-offering of soothing odour to the LORD.

The sabbath, and monthly offerings

9 For the sabbath day: two yearling rams without blemish, a grain-offering of two tenths of an ephah of flour mixed with oil, and the proper drink-offering. This whole-offering, presen-10 ted every sabbath, is in addition to the regular whole-offering and the proper drink-offering.

11 On the first day of every month you shall present a whole-offering to the LORD, consisting of two young bulls, one ram and seven yearling rams 12 without blemish. The grain-offering shall be three tenths of flour mixed with oil for each bull, two tenths of flour mixed with oil for the full-grown 13 ram, and one tenth of flour mixed with oil for each young ram. This is a whole-offering, a food-offering of 14 soothing odour to the LORD. The proper drink-offering shall be half a hin of wine for each bull, a third for the full-grown ram and a quarter for each young ram. This is the whole-offering to be made, month by month, 15 throughout the year. Further, one he-goat shall be sacrificed as a sin-offering to the LORD, in addition to the regular whole-offering and the proper drink-offering.

Sacrifices at the appointed seasons

16 The Passover of the LORD shall be held on the fourteenth day of the first 17 month, and on the fifteenth day there shall be a pilgrim-feast; for seven days you must eat only unleavened cakes. 18 On the first day there shall be a sacred assembly; you shall not do your daily 19 work. As a food-offering, a whole-offering to the LORD, you shall present two young bulls, one ram, and seven yearling rams, all without blemish. 20 You shall offer the proper grain-offerings of flour mixed with oil, three tenths for each bull, two tenths for 21 the ram, and one tenth for each of the 22 seven young rams; and as a sin-offer-ing, one he-goat to make expiation for you. All these you shall offer in 23 addition to the morning whole-offering, which is the regular sacrifice. 24 You shall repeat this daily till the seventh day, presenting food as a food-offering of soothing odour to the LORD, in addition to the regular whole-offering and the proper drink-offering. 25 On the seventh day there shall be a sacred assembly; you shall not do your daily work.

26 On the day of Firstfruits, when you bring to the LORD your grain-offering from the new crop at your Feast of Weeks, there shall be a sacred assem-bly; you shall not do your daily work. 27 You shall bring a whole-offering as

a soothing odour to the LORD: two young bulls, one full-grown ram, and 28 seven yearling rams. The proper grain-offering shall be of flour mixed with oil, three tenths for each bull, 29 two tenths for the one ram, and a tenth for each of the seven young rams, 30 and there shall be one he-goat as a sin-offering to make expiation for you; 31 they shall all be without blemish. All these you shall offer in addition to the regular whole-offering with the proper grain-offering and drink-offering.

29 On the first day of the seventh month there shall be a sacred assembly; you shall not do your daily work. It shall be a day of acclamation. 2 You shall sacrifice a whole-offering as a soothing-odour to the LORD: one young bull, one full-grown ram, and seven yearling rams, without blemish. 3 Their proper grain-offering shall be of flour mixed with oil, three tenths for the bull, two tenths for the one ram, 4 and one tenth for each of the seven 5 young rams, and there shall be one he-goat as a sin-offering to make 6 expiation for you. This is in addition to the monthly whole-offering and the regular whole-offering with their proper grain-offerings and drink-offerings according to custom; it is a food-offering of soothing odour to the LORD.

7 On the tenth day of this seventh month there shall be a sacred assembly, and you shall mortify your- 8 selves; you shall not do any work. You shall bring a whole-offering to the LORD as a soothing odour: one young bull, one full-grown ram, and seven yearling rams; they shall all be without blem- 9 ish. The proper grain-offering shall be of flour mixed with oil, three tenths for the bull, two tenths for the one 10 ram, and one tenth for each of the 11 seven young rams, and there shall be one he-goat as a sin-offering, in addition to the expiatory sin-offering and the regular whole-offering, with the proper grain-offering and drink-offering.

12 On the fifteenth day of the seventh month there shall be a sacred assembly. You shall not do your daily work, but shall keep a pilgrim-feast to 13 the LORD for seven days. As a whole-offering, a food-offering of soothing odour to the LORD, you shall bring thirteen young bulls, two full-grown rams, and fourteen yearling rams; 14 they shall all be without blemish. The proper grain-offering shall be of flour mixed with oil, three tenths for each

of the thirteen bulls, two tenths for each of the two rams, and one tenth 15 for each of the fourteen young rams, and there shall be one he-goat as a 16 sin-offering, in addition to the regular whole-offering with the proper grain-offering and drink-offering.

On the second day: twelve young 17 bulls, two full-grown rams, and fourteen yearling rams, without blemish, together with the proper grain- 18 offerings and drink-offerings for bulls, full-grown rams, and young rams, as prescribed according to their number, and there shall be one he-goat as a sin- 19 offering, in addition to the regular whole-offering with the proper grain-offering and drink-offering.

On the third day: eleven bulls, two 20 full-grown rams, and fourteen yearling rams, without blemish, together 21 with the proper grain-offerings and drink-offerings for bulls, full-grown rams, and young rams, as prescribed according to their number, and there 22 shall be one he-goat as a sin-offering, in addition to the regular whole-offering, with the proper grain-offering and drink-offering.

On the fourth day: ten bulls, two 23 full-grown rams, and fourteen yearling rams, without blemish, together 24 with the proper grain-offerings and drink-offerings for bulls, full-grown rams, and young rams, as prescribed according to their number, and there 25 shall be one he-goat as a sin-offering, in addition to the regular whole-offering with the proper grain-offering and drink-offering.

On the fifth day: nine bulls, two 26 full-grown rams, and fourteen yearling rams, without blemish, together 27 with the proper grain-offerings and drink-offerings for bulls, full-grown rams, and young rams, as prescribed according to their number, and there 28 shall be one he-goat as a sin-offering, in addition to the regular whole-offering with the proper grain-offering and drink-offering.

On the sixth day: eight bulls, two 29 full-grown rams, and fourteen yearling rams, without blemish, together 30 with the proper grain-offerings and drink-offerings for bulls, full-grown rams, and young rams, as prescribed according to their number, and there 31 shall be one he-goat as a sin-offering, in addition to the regular whole-offering with the proper grain-offering and drink-offering.

On the seventh day: seven bulls, 32 two full-grown rams, and fourteen

33 yearling rams, without blemish, together with the proper grain-offerings and drink-offerings for bulls, full-grown rams, and young rams, as prescribed according to their number, 34 and there shall be one he-goat as a sin-offering, in addition to the regular whole-offering with the proper grain-offering and drink-offering.

35 The eighth day you shall keep as a closing ceremony; you shall not do 36 your daily work. As a whole-offering, a food-offering of soothing odour to the LORD, you shall bring one bull, one full-grown ram, and seven year-37 ling rams, without blemish, together with the proper grain-offerings and drink-offerings for bulls, full-grown rams, and young rams, as prescribed 38 according to their number, and there shall be one he-goat as a sin-offering, in addition to the regular whole-offering with the proper grain-offering and drink-offering.

39 These are the sacrifices which you shall offer to the LORD at the appointed seasons, in addition to the votive offerings, the freewill offerings, the whole-offerings, the grain-offerings, the drink-offerings, and the shared-offerings.

40 Moses told the Israelites exactly what the LORD had commanded him.

Decrees concerning women's vows

30 Then Moses spoke to the heads of the Israelite tribes and said, This is the 2 LORD's command: When a man makes a vow to the LORD or swears an oath and so puts himself under a binding obligation, he must not break his word. Every word he has spoken, he 3 must make good. When a woman, still young and living in her father's house, makes a vow to the LORD or puts her-4 self under a binding obligation, if her father hears of it and keeps silence, then any such vow or obligation shall 5 be valid. But if her father disallows it when he hears of it, none of her vows or obligations shall be valid; the LORD will absolve her, because her father 6 has disallowed it. If the woman is married when she is under a vow or a binding obligation rashly uttered, 7 then if her husband hears of it and keeps silence when he hears, her vow or obligation by which she has bound 8 herself shall be valid. If, however, her husband disallows it when he hears of it and repudiates the vow which she has taken upon herself or the rash utterance with which she has bound herself, then the LORD will absolve

her. Every vow by which a widow 9 or a divorced woman has bound herself shall be valid. But if it is in her 10 husband's house that a woman makes a vow or puts herself under a binding obligation by an oath, and her hus-11 band, hearing of it, keeps silence and does not disallow it, then every vow and obligation under which she has put herself shall be valid; but if her 12 husband clearly repudiates them when he hears of them, then nothing that she has uttered, whether vow or obligation, shall be valid. Her husband has repudiated them, and the LORD will absolve her.

The husband can confirm or repu-13 diate any vow or oath by which a woman binds herself to mortification. If he maintains silence day after day, 14 he thereby confirms every vow or obligation under which she has put herself: he confirms them, because he kept silence at the time when he heard them. If he repudiates them some 15 time after he has heard them, he shall be responsible for her default.

Such are the decrees which the 16 LORD gave to Moses concerning a husband and his wife and a father and his daughter, still young and living in her father's house.

Vengeance on the Midianites

The LORD spoke to Moses and said, **31** 'You are to exact vengeance for Israel 2 on the Midianites and then you will be gathered to your father's kin.'

Then Moses spoke to the people in 3 these words: 'Let some men among you be drafted for active service. They shall fall upon Midian and exact vengeance in the LORD's name. You 4 shall send out a thousand men from each of the tribes of Israel.' So the 5 men were called up from the clans of Israel, a thousand from each tribe, twelve thousand in all, drafted for active service. Moses sent out this 6 force, a thousand from each tribe, with Phinehas son of Eleazar the priest, who was in charge of the holy vessels and of the trumpets to give the signal for the battle-cry. They made war on 7 Midian as the LORD had commanded Moses, and slew all the men. In addi-8 tion to those slain in battle they killed the kings of Midian—Evi, Rekem, Zur, Hur, and Reba, the five kings of Midian—and they put to death also Balaam son of Beor. The Israelites 9 took captive the Midianite women and their dependants, and carried off all their beasts, their flocks, and their

10 property. They burnt all their cities, in which they had settled, and all their
11 encampments. They took all the spoil and plunder, both man and beast,
12 and brought them—captives, plunder, and spoil—to Moses and Eleazar the priest and to all the community of the Israelites, to the camp in the lowlands of Moab by the Jordan at Jericho.

Purifying the spoil

13 Moses and Eleazar the priest and all the leaders of the community went to
14 meet them outside the camp. Moses spoke angrily to the officers of the army, the commanders of units of a thousand and of a hundred, who were
15 returning from the campaign: 'Have you spared all the women?' he said.
16 'Remember, it was they who, on Balaam's departure, set about seducing the Israelites into disloyalty to the LORD that day at Peor, so that the plague struck the community of the
17 LORD. Now kill every male dependant, and kill every woman who has had
18 intercourse with a man, but spare for yourselves every woman among them
19 who has not had intercourse. You yourselves, every one of you who has taken life and every one who has touched the dead, must remain outside the camp for seven days. Purify yourselves and your captives on the
20 third day and on the seventh day, and purify also every piece of clothing, every article made of skin, everything woven of goat's hair, and everything made of wood.'
21   Eleazar the priest said to the soldiers returning from battle, 'This is a law and statute which the LORD has or-
22-3 dained through Moses. Anything which will stand fire, whether gold, silver, copper, iron, tin, or lead, you shall pass through fire and then it will be clean. Other things shall be purified by the water of ritual purification; whatever cannot stand fire shall be
24 passed through the water. On the seventh day you shall wash your clothes, and then be clean; after this you may re-enter the camp.'

Dividing the spoil

25 The LORD spoke to Moses and said,
26 'Count all that has been captured, man or beast, you and Eleazar the priest and the heads of families in the
27 community, and divide it equally between the fighting men who went on the campaign and the whole com-
28 munity. You shall levy a tax for the LORD: from the combatants it shall

be one out of every five hundred, whether men, cattle, asses, or sheep,
29 to be taken out of their share and given to Eleazar the priest as a con-
30 tribution for the LORD. Out of the share of the Israelites it shall be one out of every fifty taken, whether man or beast, cattle, asses, or sheep, to be given to the Levites who are in charge of the LORD's Tabernacle.'
31 Moses and Eleazar the priest did as the LORD had commanded Moses.
32 These were the spoils, over and above the plunder taken by the fighting men: six hundred and seventy-five thou-
33 sand sheep, seventy-two thousand cattle, sixty-one thousand asses; and
34 3 of persons, thirty-two thousand girls who had had no intercourse with a man.
36 The half-share of those who took part in the campaign was thus three hundred and thirty-seven thousand five hundred sheep, the tax for the
37 LORD from these being six hundred and seventy-five; thirty-six thousand
38 cattle, the tax being seventy-two; thirty thousand five hundred asses,
39 the tax being sixty-one; and sixteen
40 thousand persons, the tax being thirty-two. Moses gave Eleazar the priest
41 the tax levied for the LORD, as the LORD had commanded him.
42-3 The share of the community, being the half-share for the Israelites which Moses divided off from that of the combatants, was three hundred and thirty-seven thousand five hundred sheep, thirty-six thousand cattle,
44 thirty thousand five hundred asses,
45 and sixteen thousand persons. Moses
46 4 took one out of every fifty, whether man or beast, from the half-share of the Israelites, and gave it to the Levites who were in charge of the LORD's Tabernacle, as the LORD had commanded him.
48 Then the officers who had commanded the forces on the campaign, the commanders of units of a thousand
49 and of a hundred, came to Moses and said to him, 'Sir, we have checked the roll of the fighting men who were under our command, and not one of
50 them is missing. So we have brought the gold ornaments, the armlets, bracelets, finger-rings, earrings, and pendants that each man has found, to offer them before the LORD as a ransom for our lives.'
51 Moses and Eleazar the priest received this gold from the commanders of units of a thousand and of a hun-
52 dred, all of it craftsman's work, and

the gold thus levied as a contribution to the LORD weighed sixteen thousand 53 seven hundred and fifty shekels; for every man in the army had taken 54 plunder. So Moses and Eleazar the priest received the gold from the commanders of units of a thousand and of a hundred, and brought it to the Tent of the Presence that the LORD might remember Israel.

The tribes east of Jordan

32 Now the Reubenites and the Gadites had large and very numerous flocks, and when they saw that the land of Jazer and Gilead was good grazing 2 country, they came and said to Moses and Eleazar the priest and to the 3 leaders of the community, 'Ataroth, Dibon, Jazer, Nimrah, Heshbon, Ele- 4 aleh, Sebam, Nebo, and Beon, the region which the LORD has subdued before the advance of the Israelite community, is grazing country, and 5 our flocks are our livelihood. If', they said, 'we have found favour with you, sir, then let this country be given to us as our possession, and do not make 6 us cross the Jordan.' Moses replied to the Gadites and the Reubenites, 'Are your kinsmen to go into battle while 7 you stay here? How dare you discourage the Israelites from crossing over to the land which the LORD has 8 given them? This is what your fathers did when I sent them out from Kadesh- 9 barnea to view the land. They went up as far as the gorge of Eshcol and viewed the land, and on their return so discouraged the Israelites that they would not enter the land which the 10 LORD had given them. The LORD became angry that day, and he 11 solemnly swore: "Because they have not followed me with their whole heart, none of the men who came out of Egypt, from twenty years old and upwards, shall see the land which I promised on oath to Abraham, Isaac 12 and Jacob." This meant all except Caleb son of Jephunneh the Kenizzite and Joshua son of Nun, who followed 13 the LORD with their whole heart. The LORD became angry with Israel, and he made them wander in the wilderness for forty years until that whole generation was dead which had done 14 what was wrong in his eyes. And now you are following in your fathers' footsteps, a fresh brood of sinful men to fire the LORD's anger once more 15 against Israel; for if you refuse to follow him, he will again abandon this whole people in the wilderness and

you will be the cause of their destruction.'

Presently they came forward with 16 this offer: 'We will build folds for our sheep here and towns for our dependants. Then we can be drafted as a 17 fighting force to go at the head of the Israelites until we have brought them to the lands that will be theirs. Meanwhile our dependants can live in the walled towns, safe from the people of the country. We will not return until 18 every Israelite is settled in possession of his patrimony; we will claim no 19 share of the land with them over the Jordan and beyond, because our patrimony has already been allotted to us east of the Jordan.' Moses answered, 20 'If you stand by your promise, if in the presence of the LORD you are drafted for battle, and the whole draft 21 crosses the Jordan in front of the LORD and remains there until the LORD has driven out his enemies, and 22 the land falls before him, then you may come back and be quit of your obligation to the LORD and to Israel; and this land shall be your possession in the sight of the LORD. But I warn 23 you, if you fail to do all this, you will have sinned against the LORD, and your sin will find you out. So build 24 towns for your dependants and folds for your sheep; but carry out your promise.'

The Gadites and Reubenites ans- 25 wered Moses, 'Sir, we are your servants and will do as you command. Our 26 dependants and wives, our flocks and all our beasts shall remain here in the cities of Gilead; but we, all who have 27 been drafted for active service with the LORD, will cross the river and fight, according to your command.'

Accordingly Moses gave these in- 28 structions to Eleazar the priest and Joshua son of Nun and to the heads of the families in the Israelite tribes: 'If the Gadites and Reubenites, all 29 who have been drafted for battle before the LORD, cross the Jordan with you, and if the land falls into your hands, then you shall give them Gilead for their possession. But if, thus 30 drafted, they fail to cross with you, then they shall acquire land alongside you in Canaan.' The Gadites and 31 Reubenites said in response, 'Sir, the LORD has spoken, and we will obey. Once we have been drafted, we will 32 cross over before the LORD into Canaan; then we shall have our patrimony here beyond the Jordan.'

So to the Gadites, the Reubenites, 33

and half the tribe of Manasseh son of Joseph, Moses gave the kingdoms of Sihon king of the Amorites and Og king of Bashan, the whole land with its towns and the country round them.
34 The Gadites built Dibon, Ataroth,
35 Aroer, Atroth-shophan, Jazer, Jog-
36 behah, Beth-nimrah, and Beth-haran, all of them walled towns with folds
37 for their sheep. The Reubenites built
38 Heshbon, Elealeh, Kiriathaim, Nebo, Baal-meon (whose name was changed), and Sibmah; these were the names they gave to the towns they built.
39 The sons of Machir son of Manasseh invaded Gilead, took it and drove out
40 the Amorite inhabitants; Moses then assigned Gilead to Machir son of Manasseh, and he made his home
41 there. Jair son of Manasseh attacked and took the tent-villages of Ham[t]
42 and called them Havvoth-jair.[u] No-bah attacked and took Kenath and its villages and gave it his own name, Nobah.

The stages of Israel's journey

33 These are the stages in the journey of the Israelites, when they were led by Moses and Aaron in their tribal hosts
2 out of Egypt. Moses recorded their starting-points stage by stage as the Lord commanded him. These are their stages from one starting-point to the next:
3   The Israelites left Rameses on the fifteenth day of the first month, the day after the Passover; they marched out defiantly in full view of all the
4 Egyptians, while the Egyptians were burying all the first-born struck down by the Lord as a judgement on their gods.
5   The Israelites left Rameses and encamped at Succoth.
6   They left Succoth and encamped at Etham on the edge of the wilderness.
7   They left Etham, turned back near Pi-hahiroth[v] on the east of Baal-zephon, and encamped before Migdol.
8   They left Pi-hahiroth, passed through the Sea into the wilderness, marched for three days through the wilderness of Etham, and encamped at Marah.
9   They left Marah and came to Elim, where there were twelve springs of water and seventy palm-trees, and encamped there.
10   They left Elim and encamped by the Red Sea.

They left the Red Sea and encamped 11 in the wilderness of Sin.
They left the wilderness of Sin and 12 encamped at Dophkah.
They left Dophkah and encamped 13 at Alush.
They left Alush and encamped at 14 Rephidim, where there was no water for the people to drink.
They left Rephidim and encamped 15 in the wilderness of Sinai.
They left the wilderness of Sinai 16 and encamped at Kibroth-hattaa-vah.
They left Kibroth-hattaavah and 17 encamped at Hazeroth.
They left Hazeroth and encamped 18 at Rithmah.
They left Rithmah and encamped 19 at Rimmon-parez.
They left Rimmon-parez and en- 20 camped at Libnah.
They left Libnah and encamped at 21 Rissah.
They left Rissah and encamped at 22 Kehelathah.
They left Kehelathah and encamped 23 at Mount Shapher.
They left Mount Shapher and en- 24 camped at Haradah.
They left Haradah and encamped at 25 Makheloth.
They left Makheloth and encamped 26 at Tahath.
They left Tahath and encamped at 27 Tarah.
They left Tarah and encamped at 28 Mithcah.
They left Mithcah and encamped at 29 Hashmonah.
They left Hashmonah and encamped 30 at Moseroth.
They left Moseroth and encamped 31 at Bene-jaakan.
They left Bene-jaakan and en- 32 camped at Hor-haggidgad.
They left Hor-haggidgad and en- 33 camped at Jotbathah.
They left Jotbathah and encamped 34 at Ebronah.[w]
They left Ebronah and encamped 35 at Ezion-geber.
They left Ezion-geber and encamped 36 in the wilderness of Zin, that is of Kadesh.
They left Kadesh and encamped on 37 Mount Hor on the frontier of Edom.
Aaron the priest went up Mount 38 Hor at the command of the Lord and there he died, on the first day of the fifth month in the fortieth year after the Israelites came out of Egypt; he 39

---

t Prob. rdg.; Heb. their tent-villages.   *u That is* Tent-villages of Jair.   *v See Exod. 14. 2.*
w Or Abronah.

was a hundred and twenty-three years old when he died there.

40 The Canaanite king of Arad, who lived in the Canaanite Negeb, heard that the Israelites were coming.

41 They left Mount Hor and encamped at Zalmonah.

42 They left Zalmonah and encamped at Punon.

43 They left Punon and encamped at Oboth.

44 They left Oboth and encamped at Iye-abarim on the frontier of Moab.

45 They left Iyim and encamped at Dibon-gad.

46 They left Dibon-gad and encamped at Almon-diblathaim.

47 They left Almon-diblathaim and encamped in the mountains of Abarim east of Nebo.

Canaan's frontiers and territories

48 They left the mountains of Abarim and encamped in the lowlands of Moab by the Jordan near Jericho.

49 Their camp beside the Jordan extended from Beth-jeshimoth to Abel-

50 shittim in the lowlands of Moab. In the lowlands of Moab by the Jordan near Jericho the LORD spoke to Moses

51 and said, Speak to the Israelites in these words: You will soon be cross-

52 ing the Jordan to enter Canaan. You must drive out all its inhabitants as you advance, destroy all their carved figures and their images of cast metal,

53 and lay their hill-shrines in ruins. You must take possession of the land and settle there, for to you I have given

54 the land to occupy. You must divide it by lot among your families, each taking its own territory, the large family a large territory and the small family a small. It shall be assigned to them according to the fall of the lot, each tribe and family taking its own

55 territory. If you do not drive out the inhabitants of the land as you advance, any whom you leave in possession will become like a barbed hook in your eye and a thorn in your side. They shall continually dispute your posses-

56 sion of the land, and what I meant to do to them I will do to you.

34 The LORD spoke to Moses and said,

2 Give these instructions to the Israelites: Soon you will be entering Canaan. This is the land assigned to you as a perpetual patrimony, the land of Canaan thus defined by its

3 frontiers. Your southern border shall start from the wilderness of Zin, where it marches with Edom, and run southwards from the end of the Dead Sea on its eastern side. It shall

4 then turn from the south up the ascent of Akrabbim and pass by Zin, and its southern limit shall be Kadesh-barnea. It shall proceed by Hazar-

5 addar to Azmon and from Azmon turn towards the Torrent of Egypt,

6 and its limit shall be the sea. Your western frontier shall be the Great Sea and the seaboard; this shall be your frontier to the west. This shall

7 be your northern frontier: you shall draw a line from the Great Sea to Mount Hor and from Mount Hor to

8 Lebo-hamath, and the limit of the frontier shall be Zedad. From there

9 it shall run to Ziphron, and its limit shall be Hazar-enan; this shall be your frontier to the north. To the

10 east you shall draw a line from Hazar-enan to Shepham; it shall run down

11 from Shepham to Riblah east of Ain, continuing until it strikes the ridge east of the sea of Kinnereth. The

12 frontier shall then run down to the Jordan and its limit shall be the Dead Sea. The land defined by these frontiers shall be your land.

13 Moses gave these instructions to the Israelites: This is the land which you shall assign by lot, each taking your own territory; it is the land which the LORD has ordered to be given to nine tribes and a half tribe.

14 For the Reubenites, the Gadites, and the half tribe of Manasseh have already occupied their territories, family by

15 family. These two and a half tribes have received their territory here beyond the Jordan, east of Jericho, towards the sunrise.

16 The LORD spoke to Moses and said,

17 These are the men who shall assign the land for you: Eleazar the priest

18 and Joshua son of Nun. You shall also take one chief from each tribe to

19 assign the land. These are their names:

from the tribe of Judah: Caleb son of Jephunneh;

20 from the tribe of Simeon: Samuel son of Ammihud;

21 from the tribe of Benjamin: Elidad son of Kislon;

22 from the tribe of Dan: the chief Bukki son of Jogli;

23 from the Josephites: from Manasseh, the chief Hanniel son of Ephod; and

24 from Ephraim, the chief Kemuel son of Shiphtan;

25 from Zebulun: the chief Elizaphan son of Parnach;

26 from Issachar: the chief Paltiel son of Azzan;

27 from Asher: the chief Ahihud son of Shelomi;
28 from Naphtali: the chief Pedahel son of Ammihud.
29 These were the men whom the LORD appointed to assign the territories in the land of Canaan.

The Levites' towns

35 The LORD spoke to Moses in the low-
2 lands of Moab by the Jordan near Jericho and said: Tell the Israelites to set aside towns in their patrimony as homes for the Levites, and give them also the common land surrounding
3 the towns. They shall live in the towns, and keep their beasts, their herds, and all their livestock on the common
4 land. The land of the towns which you give the Levites shall extend from the centre of the town outwards for a thousand cubits in each direc-
5 tion. Starting from the town the eastern boundary shall measure two thousand cubits, the southern two thousand, the western two thousand, and the northern two thousand, with the town in the centre. They shall have this as the common land adjoining their towns.
6 When you give the Levites their towns, six of them shall be cities of refuge, in which the homicide may take sanctuary; and you shall give
7 them forty-two other towns. The total number of towns to be given to the Levites, each with its common land,
8 is forty-eight. When you set aside these towns out of the territory of the Israelites, you shall allot more from the larger tribe and less from the smaller; each tribe shall give towns to the Levites in proportion to the patrimony assigned to it.

Cities of refuge

9 The LORD spoke to Moses and said,
10 Speak to the Israelites in these words: You are crossing the Jordan to the
11 land of Canaan. You shall designate certain cities to be places of refuge, in which the homicide who has killed a man by accident may take sanctuary.
12 These cities shall be places of refuge from the vengeance of the dead man's next-of-kin, so that the homicide shall not be put to death without standing
13 his trial before the community. The cities appointed as places of refuge
14 shall be six in number, three east of
15 the Jordan and three in Canaan. These six cities shall be places of refuge, so that any man who has taken life inadvertently, whether he be Israelite,

resident alien, or temporary settler, may take sanctuary in one of them.
16 If the man strikes his victim with anything made of iron and he dies, then he is a murderer: the murderer
17 must be put to death. If a man has a stone in his hand capable of causing death and strikes another man and he dies, he is a murderer: the murderer
18 must be put to death. If a man has a wooden thing in his hand capable of causing death, and strikes another man and he dies, he is a murderer: the murderer must be put to death.
19 The dead man's next-of-kin shall put the murderer to death; he shall put him to death because he had attacked
20 his victim. If the homicide sets upon a man openly of malice aforethought or aims a missile at him of set purpose
21 and he dies, or if in enmity he falls upon him with his bare hands and he dies, then the assailant must be put to death; he is a murderer. His next-of-kin shall put the murderer to death because he had attacked his victim.
22 If he attacks a man on the spur of the moment, not being his enemy, or hurls a missile at him not of set pur-
23 pose, or if without looking he throws a stone capable of causing death and it hits a man, then if the man dies, provided he was not the man's enemy and was not harming him of set purpose,
24 the community shall judge between the striker and the next-of-kin accord-
25 ing to these rules. The community shall protect the homicide from the vengeance of the kinsman and take him back to the city of refuge where he had taken sanctuary. He must stay there till the death of the duly
26 anointed high priest. If the homicide ever goes beyond the boundaries of the city where he has taken sanctuary,
27 and the next-of-kin finds him outside
28 and kills him, then the next-of-kin shall not be guilty of murder. The homicide must remain in the city of refuge till the death of the high priest; after the death of the high priest he
29 may go back to his property. These shall be legal precedents for you for all time wherever you live.

Laws concerning homicide

30 The homicide shall be put to death as a murderer only on the testimony of witnesses; the testimony of a single witness shall not be enough to bring
31 him to his death. You shall not accept payment for the life of a homicide guilty of a capital offence; he must
32 be put to death. You shall not accept

a payment from a man who has taken sanctuary in a city of refuge, allowing him to go back before the death of the 33 high priest and live at large. You shall not defile your land by bloodshed. Blood defiles the land, and expiation cannot be made on behalf of the land for blood shed on it except by the 34 blood of the man that shed it. You shall not make the land which you inhabit unclean, the land in which I dwell; for I, the LORD, dwell among the Israelites.

Law concerning marriage of heiresses

36 The heads of the fathers' families of Gilead son of Machir, son of Manasseh, one of the families of the sons of Joseph, approached Moses and the chiefs, heads of families in Israel, and 2 addressed them. 'Sir,' they said, 'the LORD commanded you to distribute the land by lot to the Israelites, and you were also commanded to give the patrimony of our brother Zelophehad 3 to his daughters. Now if any of them shall be married to a husband from another Israelite tribe, her patrimony will be lost to the patrimony of our fathers and be added to that of the tribe into which she is married, and so part of our allotted patrimony will 4 be lost. Then, when the jubilee year comes round in Israel, her patrimony would be added to the patrimony of the tribe into which she is married,

and it would be permanently lost to the patrimony of our fathers' tribe.'

So Moses, instructed by the LORD, 5 gave the Israelites this ruling: 'The tribe of the sons of Joseph is right. This is the LORD's command for the 6 daughters of Zelophehad: They may marry whom they please, but only within a family of their father's tribe. No patrimony in Israel shall pass 7 from tribe to tribe, but every Israelite shall retain his father's patrimony. Any woman of an Israelite tribe who 8 is an heiress may marry a man from any family in her father's tribe. Thus the Israelites shall retain each one the patrimony of his forefathers. No 9 patrimony shall pass from one tribe to another, but every tribe in Israel shall retain its own patrimony.'

The daughters of Zelophehad acted 10 in accordance with the LORD's command to Moses; Mahlah, Tirzah, 11 Hoglah, Milcah and Noah, the daughters of Zelophehad, married sons of their father's brothers. They married 12 within the families of the sons of Manasseh son of Joseph, and their patrimony remained with the tribe of their father's family.

These are the commandments and 13 the decrees which the LORD issued to the Israelites through Moses in the lowlands of Moab by the Jordan near Jericho.

DEUTERONOMY

Moses explains the law

1 THESE ARE THE WORDS that Moses spoke to all Israel in Transjordan, in the wilderness, that is to say in the Arabah opposite Suph, between Paran on the one side and Tophel, Laban, Hazeroth, and Diza- 2 hab on the other. (The journey from Horeb through the hill-country of Seir to Kadesh-barnea takes eleven days.)

3–4 On the first day of the eleventh month of the fortieth year, after the defeat of Sihon king of the Amorites who ruled in Heshbon, and the defeat at Edrei of Og king of Bashan who ruled in Ashtaroth, Moses repeated to

the Israelites all the commands that the LORD had given him for them. It 5 was in Transjordan, in Moab, that Moses resolved to promulgate this law. These were his words: The LORD 6 our God spoke to us at Horeb and said, 'You have stayed on this mountain long enough; go now, make for 7 the hill-country of the Amorites, and pass on to all their neighbours in the Arabah, in the hill-country, in the Shephelah, in the Negeb, and on the coast, in short, all Canaan and the Lebanon as far as the great river, the Euphrates. I have laid the land open 8 before you; go in and occupy it, the land which the LORD swore to give to your forefathers Abraham, Isaac and

Jacob, and to their descendants after them.'

The court of law

9 At that time I said to you, 'You are a burden too heavy for me to carry 10 unaided. The LORD your God has increased you so that today you are as numerous as the stars in the sky. 11 May the LORD the God of your fathers increase your number a thousand times and may he bless you as he 12 promised. How can I bear unaided the heavy burden you are to me, and put 13 up with your complaints? Choose men of wisdom, understanding, and repute for each of your tribes, and I will set them in authority over you.' 14 Your answer was, 'What you have 15 told us to do is right.' So I took men of wisdom and repute and set them in authority over you, some as commanders over units of a thousand, of a hundred, of fifty or of ten, and others as officers, for each of your 16 tribes. And at that time I gave your judges this command: 'You are to hear the cases that arise among your kinsmen and judge fairly between man and man, whether fellow-countryman 17 or resident alien. You must be impartial and listen to high and low alike: have no fear of man, for judgement belongs to God. If any case is too difficult for you, bring it before 18 me and I will hear it.' At the same time I instructed you in all these duties.

Spies sent out

19 Then we set out from Horeb, in obedience to the orders of the LORD our God, and marched through that vast and terrible wilderness, as you found it to be, on the way to the hill-country of the Amorites; and so we 20 came to Kadesh-barnea. Then I said to you, 'You have reached the hill-country of the Amorites which the 21 LORD our God is giving us. The LORD your God has indeed now laid the land open before you. Go forward and occupy it in fulfilment of the promise which the LORD the God of your fathers made you; do not be dis-22 couraged or afraid.' But you all came to me and said, 'Let us send men ahead to spy out the country and report back to us about the route we should take and the cities we shall 23 find.' I approved this plan and picked twelve of you, one from each tribe.

They set out and made their way up 24 into the hill-country as far as the gorge of Eshcol, which they explored. They took samples of the fruit of the 25 country and brought them back to us, and made their report: 'It is a rich land that the LORD our God is giving us.'

But you refused to go up and 26 rebelled against the command of the LORD your God. You muttered trea-27 son in your tents and said, 'It was because the LORD hated us that he brought us out of Egypt to hand us over to the Amorites to be wiped out. What shall we find up there? Our 28 kinsmen have discouraged us by their report of a people bigger and taller than we are, and of great cities with fortifications towering to the sky. And they told us they saw there the descendants of the Anakim.'[a]

Then I said to you, 'You must not 29 dread them nor be afraid of them. The 30 LORD your God who goes at your head will fight for you and he will do again what you saw him do for you in Egypt and in the wilderness. You saw there 31 how the LORD your God carried you all the way to this place, as a father carries his son.' In spite of this you 32 did not trust the LORD your God, who 33 went ahead on the journey to find a place for your camp. He went in fire by night to show you the way you should take, and in a cloud by day.

Caleb and Joshua rewarded

When the LORD heard your com-34 plaints, he was indignant and solemn-35 ly swore: 'Not one of these men, this wicked generation, shall see the rich land which I swore to give your fore-fathers, except Caleb son of Jephun-36 neh. He shall see it, and to him and his descendants I will give the land on which he has set foot, because he followed the LORD with his whole heart.' On your account the LORD was 37 angry with me also and said, 'You yourself shall never enter it, but 38 Joshua son of Nun, who is in attendance on you, shall enter it. Encourage him, for he shall put Israel in possession of that land. Your depen-39 dants who, you thought, would become spoils of war, and your children who do not yet know good and evil, they shall enter; I will give it to them, and they shall occupy it. You must 40 turn back and set out for the wilderness by way of the Red Sea.'[b]

---

a the descendants . . . Anakim: *or* the tall men.   *b* Or the Sea of Reeds.

Israel defeated at Hormah

41 You answered me, 'We have sinned against the LORD; we will now go up and attack just as the LORD our God commanded us.' And each of you fastened on his weapons, thinking it an easy thing to invade the hill- 42 country. But the LORD said to me, 'Tell them not to go up and not to fight; for I will not be with them, and 43 their enemies will defeat them.' And I told you this, but you did not listen; you rebelled against the LORD's command and defiantly went up to the 44 hill-country. The Amorites living in the hills came out against you and like bees they chased you; they 45 crushed you at Hormah in Seir. Then you came back and wept before the LORD, but he would not hear you or 46 listen to you. That is why you remained in Kadesh as long as you did.

The years in the wilderness

2 So we turned and set out for the wilderness by way of the Red Sea as the LORD had told us we must do, and we spent many days marching round 2 the hill-country of Seir. Then the LORD 3 said to me, 'You have been long enough marching round these hills; 4 turn towards the north. And give the people this charge: "You are about to go through the territory of your kinsmen the descendants of Esau who live in Seir. Although they are afraid of 5 you, be on your guard and do not provoke them; for I shall not give you any of their land, not so much as a foot's-breadth: I have given the hill-country 6 of Seir to Esau as a possession. You may purchase food from them for silver, and eat it, and you may buy[c] 7 water to drink."' The LORD your God has blessed you in everything you have undertaken; he has watched your journey through this great wilderness; these forty years the LORD your God has been with you and you 8 have gone short of nothing. So we went on past our kinsmen, the descendants of Esau who live in Seir, and along the road of the Arabah which comes from Elath and Ezion-geber, and we turned and followed the road 9 to the wilderness of Moab. There the LORD said to me, 'Do not harass the Moabites nor provoke them to battle, for I will not give you any of their land as a possession. I have given Ar to the descendants of Lot as a posses- 10 sion.' (The Emim once lived there—

a great and numerous people, as tall as the Anakim. The Rephaim also 11 were reckoned as Anakim; but the Moabites called them Emim. The 12 Horites lived in Seir at one time, but the descendants of Esau occupied their territory: they destroyed them as they advanced and then settled in the land instead of them, just as Israel did in their own territory which the LORD gave them.) 'Come now, cross 13 the gorge of the Zared.' So we went across. The journey from Kadesh- 14 barnea to the crossing of the Zared took us thirty-eight years, until the whole generation of fighting men had passed away as the LORD had sworn that they would. The LORD's hand was 15 raised against them, and he rooted them out of the camp to the last man.

When the last of the fighting men 16 among the people had died, the LORD 17 spoke to me, 'Today', he said, 'you 18 are to cross by Ar[d] which lies on the frontier of Moab, and when you reach 19 the territory of the Ammonites, you must not harass them or provoke them to battle, for I will not give you any Ammonite land as a possession; I have assigned it to the descendants of Lot.' (This also is reckoned as the 20 territory of the Rephaim, who lived there at one time; but the Ammonites called them Zamzummim. They were 21 a great and numerous people, as tall as the Anakim, but the LORD destroyed them as the Ammonites advanced and occupied their territory instead of them, just as he had done for the 22 descendants of Esau who lived in Seir. As they advanced, he destroyed the Horites so that they occupied their territory and took possession instead of them: so it is to this day. It was 23 Caphtorites from Caphtor who destroyed the Avvim who lived in the hamlets near Gaza, and settled in the land instead of them.) 'Come, set out 24 on your journey and cross the gorge of the Arnon, for I have put Sihon the Amorite, king of Heshbon, and his territory into your hands. Begin to occupy it and provoke him to battle. Today I will begin to put the fear and 25 dread of you upon all the peoples under heaven; if they so much as hear a rumour of you, they will quake and tremble before you.'

Israel conquers Sihon

Then I sent messengers from the 26 wilderness of Kedemoth to Sihon

c Or dig for.   d by Ar: or the gully.

27 king of Heshbon with these peaceful overtures: 'Grant us passage through your country by the highway: we will keep to the highway, trespassing 28 neither to right nor to left, and we will pay you the full price for the food 29 we eat and the water we drink. The descendants of Esau who live in Seir granted us passage, and so did the Moabites who live in Ar. We will simply pass through your land on foot, until we cross the Jordan to the land which the LORD our God is giving us.' 30 But Sihon king of Heshbon refused to grant us passage; for the LORD your God had made him stubborn and obstinate, in order that he and his land might become subject to you, as 31 it still is. So the LORD said to me, 'Come, I have begun to deliver Sihon and his territory into your hands. 32 Begin now to occupy his land.' Then Sihon with all his people came out to 33 meet us in battle at Jahaz, and the LORD our God delivered him into our hands; we killed him with his sons 34 and all his people. We captured all his cities at that time and put to death everyone in the cities, men, women, and dependants; we left no 35 survivor. We took the cattle as booty and plundered the cities we captured. 36 From Aroer on the edge of the gorge of the Arnon and the level land of the gorge, as far as Gilead, no city walls were too lofty for us; the LORD our 37 God laid them all open to us. But you avoided the territory of the Ammonites, both the parts along the gorge of the Jabbok and their cities in the hills, thus fulfilling all that the LORD our God had commanded.

Israel conquers Og

3 Next we turned and advanced along the road to Bashan. Og king of Bashan, with all his people, came out against 2 us at Edrei. The LORD said to me, 'Do not be afraid of him, for I have delivered him into your hands, with all his people and his land. Deal with him as you dealt with Sihon the king of the Amorites who lived in Heshbon.' 3 So the LORD our God also delivered Og king of Bashan into our hands, with all his people. We slaughtered 4 them and left no survivor, and at the same time we captured all his cities; there was not a single town that we did not take from them. In all we took sixty cities, the whole region of Argob, the kingdom of Og in Bashan;

5 all these were fortified cities with high walls, gates, and bars, apart from a great many open settlements. Thus 6 we put to death all the men, women, and dependants in every city, as we did to Sihon king of Heshbon. All the 7 cattle and the spoil from the cities we took as booty for ourselves.

At that time we took from these 8 two Amorite kings in Transjordan the territory that runs from the gorge of the Arnon to Mount Hermon 9 (the mountain that the Sidonians call Sirion and the Amorites Senir), all 10 the cities of the tableland, and the whole of Gilead and Bashan as far as Salcah and Edrei, cities in the kingdom of Og king in Bashan. (Only Og 11 of Bashan remained as the sole survivor of the Rephaim. His sarcophagus of basalt[e] was nearly fourteen feet long and six feet wide, and it may still be seen in the Ammonite city of Rabbah.)

The tribes east of Jordan

At that time, when we occupied this 12 territory, I assigned to the Reubenites and Gadites the land beyond Aroer on the gorge of the Arnon and half the hill-country of Gilead with its towns. The rest of Gilead and the 13 whole of Bashan the kingdom of Og, all the region of Argob, I assigned to half the tribe of Manasseh. (All Bashan used to be called the land of the Rephaim. Jair son of Manasseh 14 took all the region of Argob as far as the Geshurite and Maacathite border. There are tent-villages in Bashan still called by his name, Havvoth-jair.[f]) To Machir I assigned Gilead, and to 15 the Reubenites and the Gadites I assigned land from Gilead to the gorge of the Arnon, that is to the middle of the gorge; and its territory ran[gh] to the gorge of the Jabbok, the Ammonite frontier, and included the 17 Arabah, with the Jordan and adjacent land, from Kinnereth to the Sea of the Arabah, that is the Dead Sea, below the watershed of Pisgah on the east. At that time I gave you this 18 command: 'The LORD your God has given you this land to occupy; let all your fighting men be drafted and cross at the head of their fellow-Israelites. Only your wives and dependants and 19 your livestock—I know you have much livestock—shall stay in the towns I have given you. This you 20 shall do until the LORD gives your kinsmen security as he has given it to

---

e Or iron.   f That is Tent-villages of Jair.   g that is ... ran: or including the bed of the gorge and the adjacent strip of land ...   h and its territory ran: prob. rdg.; Heb. and territory and ...

you, and until they too occupy the land which the LORD your God is giving them on the other side of the Jordan; then you may return to the possession which I have given you, every man to his own.'

21 At that time also I gave Joshua this charge: 'You have seen with your own eyes all that the LORD your God has done to these two kings; he will do the same to all the kingdoms into

22 which you will cross over. Do not be afraid of them, for the LORD your God himself will fight for you.'

Moses not to enter Canaan

23 At that same time I pleaded with the

24 LORD, 'O Lord GOD, thou hast begun to show to thy servant thy greatness and thy strong hand: what god is there in heaven or on earth who can match thy works and mighty deeds?

25 Let me cross over and see that rich land which lies beyond the Jordan, and the fine hill-country and the

26 Lebanon.' But because of you the LORD brushed me aside and would not listen. 'Enough!' he answered. 'Say

27 no more about this. Go to the top of Pisgah and look west and north, south and east; look well at what you see, for you shall not cross this river

28 Jordan. Give Joshua his commission, encourage him and strengthen him; for he will lead this people across, and he will put them in possession of the land you see before you.'

29 So we remained in the valley opposite Beth-peor.

Moses exhorts Israel to obey

4 Now, Israel, listen to the statutes and laws which I am teaching you, and obey them; then you will live, and go in and occupy the land which the LORD the God of your fathers is

2 giving you. You must not add anything to my charge, nor take anything away from it. You must carry out all the commandments of the LORD your God which I lay upon you.

3 You saw with your own eyes what the LORD did at Baal-peor; the LORD your God destroyed among you every man who went over to the Baal of

4 Peor, but you who held fast to the LORD your God are all alive today.

5 I have taught you statutes and laws, as the LORD my God commanded me; these you must duly keep when you

6 enter the land and occupy it. You must observe them carefully, and thereby you will display your wisdom

and understanding to other peoples. When they hear about these statutes, they will say, 'What a wise and understanding people this great nation is!' What great nation has a god[i] close 7 at hand as the LORD our God is close to us whenever we call to him? What 8 great nation is there whose statutes and laws are just, as is all this law which I am setting before you today? But 9 take good care: be on the watch not to forget the things that you have seen with your own eyes, and do not let them pass from your minds as long as you live, but teach them to your sons and to your sons' sons. You must 10 never forget that day when you stood before the LORD your God at Horeb, and the LORD said to me, 'Assemble the people before me; I will make them hear my words and they shall learn to fear me all their lives on earth, and they shall teach their sons to do so.' Then 11 you came near and stood at the foot of the mountain. The mountain was ablaze with fire to the very skies: there was darkness, cloud, and thick mist. When the LORD spoke to you from 12 the fire you heard a voice speaking, but you saw no figure; there was only a voice. He announced the terms of 13 his covenant to you, bidding you observe the Ten Words,[j] and he wrote them on two tablets of stone. At that 14 time the LORD charged me to teach you statutes and laws which you should observe in the land into which you are passing to occupy it.

Warning against idolatry

On the day when the LORD spoke to 15 you out of the fire on Horeb, you saw no figure of any kind; so take good care not to fall into the degrading 16 practice of making figures carved in relief, in the form of a man or a woman, or of any animal on earth or bird 17 that flies in the air, or of any reptile 18 on the ground or fish in the waters under the earth. Nor must you raise 19 your eyes to the heavens and look up to the sun, the moon, and the stars, all the host of heaven, and be led on to bow down to them and worship them; the LORD your God assigned these for the worship of[k] the various peoples under heaven. But you are the 20 people whom the LORD brought out of Egypt, from the smelting-furnace, and took for his own possession, as you are to this day. The LORD was 21 angry with me on your account and swore that I should not cross the

i Or gods.   j Or Ten Commandments.   k assigned . . . worship of: or created these for.

Jordan nor enter the rich land which the LORD your God is giving you for 22 your possession. I shall die in this country; I shall not cross the Jordan, but you are about to cross and occupy 23 that rich land. Be careful not to forget the covenant which the LORD your God made with you, and do not make yourselves a carved figure of anything which the LORD your God has 24 forbidden. For the LORD your God is a devouring fire, a jealous god.

25 When you have children and grandchildren and grow old in the land, if you then fall into the degrading practice of making any kind of carved figure, doing what is wrong in the eyes of the LORD your God and provoking 26 him to anger, I summon heaven and earth to witness against you this day: you will soon vanish from the land which you are to occupy after crossing the Jordan. You will not live long 27 in it; you will be swept away. The LORD will disperse you among the peoples, and you will be left few in number among the nations to which 28 the LORD will lead you. There you will worship gods made by human hands out of wood and stone, gods that can neither see nor hear, neither eat nor 29 smell. But if from there you seek the LORD your God, you will find him, if indeed you search with all your 30 heart and soul. When you are in distress and all these things come upon you, you will in days to come turn back to the LORD your God and obey 31 him. The LORD your God is a merciful god; he will never fail you nor destroy you, nor will he forget the covenant guaranteed by oath with your forefathers.

32 Search into days gone by, long before your time, beginning at the day when God created man on earth; search from one end of heaven to the other, and ask if any deed as mighty 33 as this has been seen or heard. Did any people ever hear the voice of God speaking out of the fire, as you heard 34 it, and remain alive? Or did ever a god attempt to come and take a nation for himself away from another nation, with a challenge, and with signs, portents, and wars, with a strong hand and an outstretched arm, and with great deeds of terror, as the LORD your God did for you in Egypt 35 in the sight of you all? You have had sure proof that the LORD is God; 36 there is no other. From heaven he let you hear his voice for your instruction, and on earth he let you see his great fire, and out of the fire you heard his words. Because he loved your fa- 37 thers and chose their children after them, he in his own person brought you out of Egypt by his great strength, so that he might drive out before you 38 nations greater and more powerful than you and bring you in to give you their land in possession as it is today. This day, then, be sure and take to 39 heart that the LORD is God in heaven above and on earth below; there is no other. You shall keep his statutes and 40 his commandments which I give you today; then all will be well with you and with your children after you, and you will live long in the land which the LORD your God is giving you for all time.

Some cities of refuge

Then Moses set apart three cities in 41 the east, in Transjordan, to be places 42 of refuge for the homicide who kills a man without intent, with no previous enmity between them. If he takes sanctuary in one of these cities his life shall be safe. The cities were: 43 Bezer-in-the-Wilderness on the tableland for the Reubenites, Ramoth in Gilead for the Gadites, and Golan in Bashan for the Manassites.

Introduction to the Commandments

This is the law which Moses laid down 44 for the Israelites. These are the pre- 45 cepts, the statutes, and the laws which Moses proclaimed to the Israelites, when they came out of Egypt and 46 were in Transjordan in the valley opposite Beth-peor in the land of Sihon king of the Amorites who lived in Heshbon. Moses and the Israelites had defeated him when they came out of Egypt and had occupied his terri- 47 tory and the territory of Og king of Bashan, the two Amorite kings in the east, in Transjordan. The territory 48 ran from Aroer on the gorge of the Arnon to Mount Sirion, that is Hermon; and all the Arabah on the east, 49 in Transjordan, as far as the Sea of the Arabah below the watershed of Pisgah.

Moses summoned all Israel and said 5 to them: Listen, O Israel, to the statutes and the laws which I proclaim in your hearing today. Learn them and be careful to observe them. The 2 LORD our God made a covenant with us at Horeb. It was not with our fore- 3 fathers that the LORD made this covenant, but with us, all of us who are alive and are here this day. The 4

LORD spoke with you face to face on
5 the mountain out of the fire. I stood
between the LORD and you at that
time to report the words of the LORD;
for you were afraid of the fire and
did not go up the mountain. And the
LORD said:

The Ten Commandments

6 I am the LORD your God who brought
you out of Egypt, out of the land of
slavery.
7   You shall have no other god[l] to set
against me.
8   You shall not make a carved image
for yourself nor the likeness of anything in the heavens above, or on the
earth below, or in the waters under
the earth.
9   You shall not bow down to them or
worship[m] them; for I, the LORD your
God, am a jealous god. I punish the
children for the sins of the fathers to
the third and fourth generations of
10 those who hate me. But I keep faith
with thousands, with[n] those who love
me and keep my commandments.
11   You shall not make wrong use of the
name of the LORD your God; the LORD
will not leave unpunished the man who
misuses his name.
12   Keep the sabbath day holy as the
13 LORD your God commanded you. You
have six days to labour and do all
14 your work. But the seventh day is a
sabbath of the LORD your God; that
day you shall not do any work, neither
you, your son or your daughter, your
slave or your slave-girl, your ox, your
ass, or any of your cattle, nor the
alien within your gates, so that your
slaves and slave-girls may rest as you
15 do. Remember that you were slaves
in Egypt and the LORD your God
brought you out with a strong hand
and an outstretched arm, and for that
reason the LORD your God commanded
you to keep the sabbath day.
16   Honour your father and your mother,
as the LORD your God commanded
you, so that you may live long, and
that it may be well with you in the land
which the LORD your God is giving
you.
17   You shall not commit murder.
18   You shall not commit adultery.
19   You shall not steal.
20   You shall not give false evidence
against your neighbour.
21   You shall not covet your neighbour's wife; you shall not set your
heart on your neighbour's house, his

land, his slave, his slave-girl, his ox,
his ass, or on anything that belongs
to him.

The people promise to obey

These Commandments the LORD spoke 22
in a great voice to your whole assembly on the mountain out of the fire,
the cloud, and the thick mist; then
he said no more. He wrote them on
two tablets of stone and gave them
to me. When you heard the voice out 23
of the darkness, while the mountain
was ablaze with fire, all the heads of
your tribes and the elders came to
me and said, 'The LORD our God has 24
shown us his glory and his greatness,
and we have heard his voice out of
the fire: today we have seen that God
may speak with men and they may
still live. Why should we now risk 25
death? for this great fire will devour
us. If we hear the voice of the LORD
our God again, we shall die. Is there 26
any mortal man who has heard the
voice of the living God speaking out
of the fire, as we have, and has lived?
You shall go near and listen to all 27
that the LORD our God says, and
report to us all that the LORD our God
has said to you; we will listen and
obey.'

When the LORD heard these words 28
which you spoke to me, he said, 'I
have heard what this people has said
to you; every word they have spoken
is right. Would that they always had 29
such a heart to fear me and to observe
all my commandments, so that all
might be well with them and their
children for ever! Go, and tell them 30
to return to their tents, but you your- 31
self stand here beside me, and I will
set forth to you all the commandments,
the statutes and laws which you shall
teach them to observe in the land
which I am giving them to occupy.'

You shall be careful to do as the 32
LORD your God has commanded you;
do not turn from it to right or to left.
You must conform to all the LORD 33
your God commands you, if you would
live and prosper and remain long in
the land you are to occupy.

The greatest commandment

These are the commandments, sta- 6
tutes, and laws which the LORD your
God commanded me to teach you to
observe in the land into which you
are passing to occupy it, a land flowing with milk and honey, so that you 2

l Or gods.   m Or or be led to worship . . .
with . . .

n with . . . with: or for a thousand generations

may fear the LORD your God and keep all his statutes and commandments which I am giving you, both you, your sons, and your descendants all your lives, and so that you may live long.

3 If you listen, O Israel, and are careful to observe them, you will prosper and increase greatly as the LORD the God of your fathers promised you.

4 Hear, O Israel, the LORD[o] is our
5 God, one LORD, and you must love the LORD your God with all your heart
6 and soul and strength. These commandments which I give you this day
7 are to be kept in your heart; you shall repeat them to your sons, and speak of them indoors and out of doors, when you lie down and when you
8 rise. Bind them as a sign on the hand and wear them as a phylactery on the
9 forehead; write them up on the doorposts of your houses and on your gates.

Warnings against disobedience

10 The LORD your God will bring you into the land which he swore to your forefathers Abraham, Isaac and Jacob that he would give you, a land of great and fine cities which you did
11 not build, houses full of good things which you did not provide, rock-hewn cisterns which you did not hew, and vineyards and olive-groves which you did not plant. When you eat your
12 fill there, be careful not to forget the LORD who brought you out of Egypt,
13 out of the land of slavery. You shall fear the LORD your God, serve him alone and take your oaths in his name.
14 You must not follow other gods, gods of the nations that are around you;
15 if you do, the LORD your God who is in your midst will be angry with you, and he will sweep you away off the face of the earth, for the LORD your God is a jealous god.
16 You must not challenge the LORD your God as you challenged him at
17 Massah.[p] You must diligently keep the commandments of the LORD your God as well as the precepts and statutes
18 which he gave you. You must do what is right and good in the LORD's eyes so that all may go well with you, and you may enter and occupy the rich land which the LORD promised by
19 oath to your forefathers; then you shall drive out all your enemies before you, as the LORD promised.

20 When your son asks you in time to come, 'What is the meaning of the precepts, statutes, and laws which

the LORD our God gave you?', you 21 shall say to him, 'We were Pharaoh's slaves in Egypt, and the LORD brought us out of Egypt with his strong hand, sending great disasters, signs, and 22 portents against the Egyptians and against Pharaoh and all his family, as we saw for ourselves. But he led us 23 out from there to bring us into the land and give it to us as he had promised to our forefathers. The LORD 24 commanded us to observe all these statutes and to fear the LORD our God; it will be for our own good at all times, and he will continue to preserve our lives. It will be counted to our 25 credit if we keep all these commandments in the sight of the LORD our God, as he has bidden us.'

Israel's relationship with other nations

When the LORD your God brings you 7 into the land which you are entering to occupy and drives out many nations before you—Hittites, Girgashites, Amorites, Canaanites, Perizzites, Hivites, and Jebusites, seven nations more numerous and powerful than you—when the LORD your God delivers 2 them into your power and you defeat them, you must put them to death. You must not make a treaty with them or spare them. You must not intermarry 3 with them, neither giving your daughters to their sons nor taking their daughters for your sons; if you do, they 4 will draw your sons away from the LORD[q] and make them worship other gods. Then the LORD will be angry with you and will quickly destroy you. But 5 this is what you must do to them: pull down their altars, break their sacred pillars, hack down their sacred poles and destroy their idols by fire, for you are 6 a people holy to the LORD your God; the LORD your God chose you out of all nations on earth to be his special possession.

It was not because you were more 7 numerous than any other nation that the LORD cared for you and chose you, for you were the smallest of all nations; it was because the LORD loved you 8 and stood by his oath to your forefathers, that he brought you out with his strong hand and redeemed you from the land of slavery, from the power of Pharaoh king of Egypt. Know then that the LORD your God 9 is God, the faithful God; with those who love him and keep his commandments he keeps covenant and faith

o See note on Exod. 3. 15.   *p That is Challenge.*   *q Prob. rdg.; Heb. me.*

10 for a thousand generations, but those who defy him and show their hatred for him he repays with destruction: he will not be slow to requite any who so hate him.

11 You are to observe these commandments, statutes, and laws which I give you this day, and keep them.

Blessings for obedience

12 If you listen to these laws and are careful to observe them, then the LORD your God will observe the sworn covenant he made with your forefathers and will keep faith with you.

13 He will love you, bless you and cause you to increase. He will bless the fruit of your body and the fruit of your land, your corn and new wine and oil, the offspring of your herds, and of your lambing flocks, in the land which he swore to your forefathers to give

14 you. You shall be blessed above every other nation; neither among your people nor among your cattle shall there be impotent male or barren

15 female. The LORD will take away all sickness from you; he will not bring upon you any of the foul diseases of Egypt which you know so well, but will bring them upon all your enemies.

16 You shall devour all the nations which the LORD your God is giving over to you. Spare none of them, and do not worship their gods; that is the snare which awaits you.

17 You may say to yourselves, 'These nations outnumber us, how can we

18 drive them out?' But you need have no fear of them; only remember what the LORD your God did to Pharaoh

19 and to the whole of Egypt, the great challenge which you yourselves witnessed, the signs and portents, the strong hand and the outstretched arm by which the LORD your God brought you out. He will deal thus with all the

20 nations of whom you are afraid. He will also spread panic among them until all who are left or have gone into

21 hiding perish before you. Be in no dread of them, for the LORD your God is in your midst, a great and terrible

22 god. He will drive out these nations before you little by little. You will not be able to exterminate them quickly, for fear the wild beasts become too

23 numerous for you. The LORD your God will deliver these nations over to you and will throw them into great panic

24 in the hour of their destruction. He will put their kings into your hands, and you shall wipe out their name from under heaven. When you destroy them,

no man will be able to withstand you. Their idols you shall destroy by fire; 25 you must not covet the silver and gold on them and take it for yourselves, or you will be ensnared by it; for these things are abominable to the LORD your God. You must not intro- 26 duce any abominable idol into your houses and thus bring yourselves under solemn ban along with it. You shall hold it loathsome and abominable, for it is forbidden under the ban.

A rich land to be possessed

You must carefully observe every- **8** thing that I command you this day so that you may live and increase and may enter and occupy the land which the LORD promised to your forefathers upon oath. You must remem- 2 ber all that road by which the LORD your God has led you these forty years in the wilderness to humble you, to test you and to discover whether or no it was in your heart to keep his commandments. He humbled you 3 and made you hungry; then he fed you on manna which neither you nor your fathers had known before, to teach you that man cannot live on bread alone but lives by every word that comes from the mouth of the LORD. The clothes on your backs did 4 not wear out nor did your feet swell all these forty years. Take this lesson 5 to heart: that the LORD your God was disciplining you as a father disciplines his son; and keep the com- 6 mandments of the LORD your God, conforming to his ways and fearing him. For the LORD your God is bring- 7 ing you to a rich land, a land of streams, of springs and underground waters gushing out in hill and valley, a land of 8 wheat and barley, of vines, fig-trees, and pomegranates, a land of olives, oil, and honey. It is a land where you 9 will never live in poverty nor want for anything, a land whose stones are iron-ore and from whose hills you will dig copper. You will have plenty to 10 eat and will bless the LORD your God for the rich land that he has given you.

Warning against forgetting the LORD

Take care not to forget the LORD your 11 God and do not fail to keep his commandments, laws, and statutes which I give you this day. When you have 12 plenty to eat and live in fine houses of your own building, when your herds 13 and flocks increase, and your silver and gold and all your possessions

14 increase too, do not become proud
and forget the LORD your God who
brought you out of Egypt, out of the
15 land of slavery; he led you through
the vast and terrible wilderness infested with poisonous snakes and
scorpions, a thirsty, waterless land,
where he caused water to flow from
16 the hard rock; he fed you in the wilderness on manna which your fathers
did not know, to humble you and test
you, and in the end to make you
17 prosper. Nor must you say to yourselves, 'My own strength and energy
18 have gained me this wealth', but
remember the LORD your God; it is
he that gives you strength to become
prosperous, so fulfilling the covenant
guaranteed by oath with your forefathers, as he is doing now.
19   If you forget the LORD your God
and adhere to other gods, worshipping
them and bowing down to them, I
give you a solemn warning this day
that you will certainly be destroyed.
20 You will be destroyed because of your
disobedience to the LORD your God,
as surely as were the nations whom
the LORD destroyed at your coming.

The LORD's promise

9 Listen, O Israel; this day you will
cross the Jordan to occupy the territory of nations greater and more
powerful than you, and great cities
2 with walls towering to the sky. They
are great and tall people, the descendants of the Anakim, of whom you
know, for you have heard it said, 'Who
can withstand the sons of Anak?'
3 Know then this day that it is the
LORD your God himself who goes at
your head as a devouring fire; he will
subdue them and destroy them at
your approach; you shall drive them
out and overwhelm them, as he promised you.
4   When the LORD your God drives
them out before you, do not say to
yourselves, 'It is because of my own
merit that the LORD has brought me
5 in to occupy this land.' It is not because
of your merit or your integrity that
you are entering their land to occupy
it; it is because of the wickedness of
these nations that the LORD your God
is driving them out before you, and
to fulfil the promise which the LORD
made to your forefathers, Abraham,
Isaac and Jacob.

Rebellion at Horeb

6 Know then that it is not because of
any merit of yours that the LORD your

God is giving you this rich land to
occupy; indeed, you are a stubborn
people. Remember and never forget, 7
how you angered the LORD your God
in the wilderness: from the day when
you left Egypt until you came to this
place you have defied the LORD. In 8
Horeb you roused the LORD's anger,
and the LORD in his wrath was on the
point of destroying you. When I went 9
up the mountain to receive the tablets
of stone, the tablets of the covenant
which the LORD made with you, I
remained on the mountain forty days
and forty nights without food or drink.
Then the LORD gave me the two 10
tablets of stone written with the finger
of God, and upon them were all the
words the LORD spoke to you out of
the fire, upon the mountain on the
day of the assembly. At the end of 11
forty days and forty nights the LORD
gave me the two tablets of stone,
the tablets of the covenant, and said 12
to me, 'Make haste down from the
mountain because your people whom
you brought out of Egypt have done
a disgraceful thing. They have already
turned aside from the way which I
told them to follow and have cast for
themselves an image of metal.'
Then the LORD said to me, 'I have 13
considered this people and I find them
a stubborn people. Let me be, and I 14
will destroy them and blot out their
name from under heaven; and of you
alone I will make a nation more powerful and numerous than they.' So I 15
turned and went down the mountain,
and it was ablaze; and I had the two
tablets of the covenant in my hands.
When I saw that you had sinned 16
against the LORD your God and had
cast for yourselves an image of a bull-
calf, and had already turned aside
from the way the LORD had told you
to follow, I took the two tablets and 17
flung them down and shattered them
in the sight of you all. Then once again 18
I lay prostrate before the LORD, forty
days and forty nights without food
or drink, on account of all the sins
that you had committed, and because
you had done what was wrong in the
eyes of the LORD and provoked him
to anger. I dreaded the LORD's anger 19
and his wrath which threatened to
destroy you; and once again the LORD
listened to me. The LORD was greatly 20
incensed with Aaron also and would
have killed him; so I prayed for him
as well at that same time. I took the 21
calf, that sinful thing that you had
made, and burnt it and pounded it,

grinding it until it was as fine as dust; then I flung its dust into the torrent that flowed down the mountain. 22 You also roused the LORD's anger at Taberah, and at Massah, and at 23 Kibroth-hattaavah. Again, when the LORD sent you from Kadesh-barnea with orders to advance and occupy the land which he was giving you, you defied the LORD your God and did 24 not trust him or obey him. You were defiant from the day that the LORD 25 first knew you. Forty days and forty nights I lay prostrate before the LORD because he had threatened to destroy 26 you, and I prayed to the LORD and said, 'O Lord GOD, do not destroy thy people, thy own possession, whom thou didst redeem by thy great power and bring out of Egypt by thy strong 27 hand. Remember thy servants, Abraham, Isaac and Jacob, and overlook the stubbornness of this people, their 28 wickedness and their sin; otherwise the people in the land out of which thou didst lead us will say, "It is because the LORD was not able to bring them into the land which he promised them and because he hated them, that he has led them out to kill 29 them in the wilderness." But they are thy people, thy own possession, whom thou didst bring out by thy great strength and by thy outstretched arm.'

The Covenant

10 At that time the LORD said to me, 'Cut two tablets of stone like the first, and make also a wooden chest, an Ark. Come to me on the mountain, 2 and I will write on the tablets the words that were on the first tablets which you broke in pieces, and you 3 shall put them into the Ark.' So I made the Ark of acacia-wood and cut two tablets of stone like the first, and went up the mountain taking the 4 tablets with me. Then in the same writing as before, the LORD wrote down the Ten Words[r] which he had spoken to you out of the fire, upon the mountain on the day of the assembly, and the LORD gave them to me. 5 I turned and came down the mountain, and I put the tablets in the Ark that I had made, as the LORD had commanded me, and there they have remained ever since.

6[s] (The Israelites journeyed by stages from Beeroth-bene-jaakan to Moserah. There Aaron died and was buried; and his son Eleazar succeeded him in the 7 priesthood. From there they came to

Gudgodah and from Gudgodah to Jotbathah, a land of many ravines. At that time the LORD set apart the 8 tribe of Levi to carry the Ark of the Covenant of the LORD, to attend on the LORD and minister to him, and to give the blessing in his name, as they have done to this day. That is why 9 the Levites have no holding or patrimony with their kinsmen; the LORD is their patrimony, as he promised them.)

I stayed on the mountain forty days 10 and forty nights, as I did before, and once again the LORD listened to me; he consented not to destroy you. The LORD said to me, 'Set out now 11 at the head of the people so that they may enter and occupy the land which I swore to give to their forefathers.'

The LORD demands obedience

What then, O Israel, does the LORD 12 your God ask of you? Only to fear the LORD your God, to conform to all his ways, to love him and to serve him with all your heart and soul. This you 13 will do by keeping the commandments of the LORD and his statutes which I give you this day for your good. To 14 the LORD your God belong heaven itself, the highest heaven, the earth and everything in it; yet the LORD cared 15 for your forefathers in his love for them and chose their descendants after them. Out of all nations you were his chosen people as you are this day. So now you must circumcise the 16 foreskin of your hearts and not be stubborn any more, for the LORD 17 your God is God of gods and Lord of lords, the great, mighty, and terrible God. He is no respecter of persons and is not to be bribed; he secures justice 18 for widows and orphans, and loves the alien who lives among you, giving him food and clothing. You too must 19 love the alien, for you once lived as aliens in Egypt. You must fear the 20 LORD your God, serve him, hold fast to him and take your oaths in his name. He is your praise, your God 21 who has done for you these great and terrible things which you have seen with your own eyes. When your fore- 22 fathers went down into Egypt they were only seventy strong, but now the LORD your God has made you countless as the stars in the sky.

The greatness of the LORD

You shall love the LORD your God and 11 keep for all time the charge he laid

r Or Ten Commandments.   s Verses 6, 7: cp. Num. 33. 31, 32.

upon you, the statutes, the laws, and
2 the commandments. This day you
know the discipline of the LORD,
though your children who have neither
known nor experienced it do not; you
know his greatness, his strong hand
3 and outstretched arm, the signs he
worked and his acts in Egypt against
Pharaoh the king and his country,
4 and all that he did to the Egyptian
army, its horses and chariots, when he
caused the waters of the Red Sea to
flow over them as they pursued you.
In this way the LORD destroyed them,
and so things remain to this day.
5 You know what he did for you in the
wilderness as you journeyed to this
6 place, and what he did to Dathan and
Abiram sons of Eliab, son of Reuben,
when the earth opened its mouth and
swallowed them in the sight of all
Israel, together with their households
and their tents and every living thing
7 in their company. With your own eyes
you have seen the mighty work that
the LORD did.

The blessings of the promised land

8 You shall observe all that I command
you this day, so that you may have
strength to enter and occupy the land
9 into which you are crossing, and so
that you may live long in the land
which the LORD swore to your forefathers to give them and their descendants, a land flowing with milk and
10 honey. The land which you are entering to occupy is not like the land of
Egypt from which you have come,
where, after sowing your seed, you
irrigated it by foot like a vegetable
11 garden. But the land into which you
are crossing to occupy is a land of
mountains and valleys watered by the
12 rain of heaven. It is a land which the
LORD your God tends[t] and on which
his eye rests from year's end to year's
13 end. If you pay heed to the commandments which I give you this day, and
love the LORD your God and serve
14 him with all your heart and soul, then
I will send rain for your land in season,
both autumn and spring rains, and
you will gather your corn and new
15 wine and oil, and I will provide pasture in the fields for your cattle: you
16 shall eat your fill. Take good care not
to be led astray in your hearts nor to
turn aside and serve other gods and
17 prostrate yourselves to them, or the
LORD will become angry with you:
he will shut up the skies and there will

be no rain, your ground will not yield
its harvest, and you will soon vanish
from the rich land which the LORD
is giving you. You shall take these 18
words of mine to heart and keep them
in mind; you shall bind them as a
sign on the hand and wear them as
a phylactery on the forehead. Teach 19
them to your children, and speak of
them indoors and out of doors, when
you lie down and when you rise. Write 20
them up on the door-posts of your
houses and on your gates. Then you 21
will live long, you and your children,
in the land which the LORD swore to
your forefathers to give them, for as
long as the heavens are above the
earth.

If you diligently keep all these 22
commandments that I now charge
you to observe, by loving the LORD
your God, by conforming to his ways
and by holding fast to him, the LORD 23
will drive out all these nations before
you and you shall occupy the territory of nations greater and more
powerful than you. Every place where 24
you set the soles of your feet shall be
yours. Your borders shall run from
the wilderness to[u] the Lebanon and
from the River, the river Euphrates,
to the western sea. No man will be 25
able to withstand you; the LORD
your God will put the fear and dread
of you upon the whole land on which
you set foot, as he promised you.
Understand that this day I offer you 26
the choice of a blessing and a curse.
The blessing will come if you listen 27
to the commandments of the LORD
your God which I give you this day,
and the curse if you do not listen to 28
the commandments of the LORD your
God but turn aside from the way that
I command you this day and follow
other gods whom you do not know.

When the LORD your God brings 29
you into the land which you are
entering to occupy, there on Mount
Gerizim you shall pronounce the blessing and on Mount Ebal the curse.
(These mountains are on the other 30
side of the Jordan, close to Gilgal beside the terebinth of Moreh, beyond
the road to the west which lies in
the territory of the Canaanites of the
Arabah.) You are about to cross the 31
Jordan to enter and occupy the land
which the LORD your God is giving
you; you shall occupy it and settle in
it, and you shall be careful to observe 32
all the statutes and laws which I set
before you this day.

t which ... tends: or whose soil the LORD your God has made firm.   u Prob. rdg.; Heb. and.

The one place of worship

12 These are the statutes and laws that you shall be careful to observe in the land which the LORD the God of your fathers is giving you to occupy as long 2 as you live on earth. You shall demolish all the sanctuaries where the nations whose place you are taking worship their gods, on mountain-tops and hills and under every spreading 3 tree. You shall pull down their altars and break their sacred pillars, burn their sacred poles and hack down the idols of their gods and thus blot out the name of them from that place.

4 You shall not follow such practices in the worship of the LORD your 5 God, but you shall resort to the place which the LORD your God will choose out of all your tribes to receive his Name that it may dwell there. There 6 you shall come and bring your whole-offerings and sacrifices, your tithes and contributions, your vows and freewill offerings, and the first-born 7 of your herds and flocks. There you shall eat before the LORD your God; so you shall find joy in whatever you undertake, you and your families, because the LORD your God has blessed you.

8 You shall not act as we act here today, each of us doing what he 9 pleases, for till now you have not reached the place of rest, the patrimony which the LORD your God is 10 giving you. You shall cross the Jordan and settle in the land which the LORD your God allots you as your patrimony; he will grant you peace from all your enemies on every side, and 11 you will live in security. Then you shall bring everything that I command you to the place which the LORD your God will choose as a dwelling for his Name—your whole-offerings and sacrifices, your tithes and contributions, and all the choice gifts that you have vowed to the 12 LORD. You shall rejoice before the LORD your God with your sons and daughters, your male and female slaves, and the Levites who live in your settlements because they have no holding or patrimony among you. 13 See that you do not offer your whole-offerings in any place at ran-14 dom, but offer them only at the place which the LORD will choose in one of your tribes, and there you must do 15 all I command you. On the other hand, you may freely kill for food in all your settlements, as the LORD your God blesses you. Clean and unclean alike may eat it, as they would eat the meat of gazelle or buck. But on no 16 account must you eat the blood; pour it out on the ground like water. In all 17 your settlements you may not eat any of the tithe of your corn and new wine and oil, or any of the first-born of your cattle and sheep, or any of the gifts that you vow, or any of your freewill offerings and contributions; but you shall eat it before the LORD 18 your God in the place that the LORD your God will choose—you, your sons and daughters, your male and female slaves, and the Levites in your settlements; so you shall find joy before the LORD your God in all that you undertake. Be careful not to neglect the 19 Levites in your land as long as you live.

When the LORD your God extends 20 your boundaries, as he has promised you, and you say to yourselves, 'I would like to eat meat', because you have a craving for it, then you may freely eat it. If the place that the LORD 21 your God will choose to receive his Name is far away, then you may slaughter a beast from the herds or flocks which the LORD has given you and freely eat it in your own settlements as I command you. You may 22 eat it as you would the meat of gazelle or buck; both clean and unclean alike may eat it. But you must strictly re- 23 frain from eating the blood, because the blood is the life; you must not eat the life with the flesh. You must 24 not eat it, you must pour it out on the ground like water. If you do not 25 eat it, all will be well with you and your children after you; for you will be doing what is right in the eyes of the LORD. But such holy-gifts as you 26 may have and the gifts you have vowed, you must bring to the place which the LORD will choose. You must 27 present your whole-offerings, both the flesh and the blood, on the altar of the LORD your God; but of your shared-offerings you shall eat the flesh, while the blood is to be poured on the altar of the LORD your God. See that you listen and do all that 28 I command you, and then it will go well with you and your children after you for ever; for you will be doing what is good and right in the eyes of the LORD your God.

Warning against idolatry

When the LORD your God extermin- 29 ates, as you advance, the nations

whose country you are entering to occupy, you shall take their place and
30 settle in their land. After they have been destroyed, take care that you are not ensnared into their ways. Do not inquire about their gods and say, 'How do these nations worship their
31 gods? I too will do the same.' You must not do for the LORD your God what they do, for all that they do for their gods is hateful and abominable to the LORD. As sacrifices for their gods they even burn their sons and their daughters.
32 See that you observe everything I command you: you must not add anything to it, nor take anything away from it.
13 When a prophet or dreamer appears among you and offers you a sign or
2 a portent and calls on you to follow other gods whom you have not known and worship them, even if the sign
3 or portent should come true, do not listen to the words of that prophet or that dreamer. God is testing you through him to discover whether you love the LORD your God with all your
4 heart and soul. You must follow the LORD your God and fear him; you must keep his commandments and obey him, serve him and hold fast to
5 him. That prophet or that dreamer shall be put to death, for he has preached rebellion against the LORD your God who brought you out of Egypt and redeemed you from that land of slavery; he has tried to lead you astray from the path which the LORD your God commanded you to take. You must rid yourselves of this wickedness.
6 If your brother, your father's son or your mother's son, or your son or daughter, or the wife of your bosom or your dearest friend should entice you secretly to go and worship other gods—gods whom neither you nor
7 your fathers have known, gods of the people round about you, near or far, at one end of the land or the other—
8 then you shall not consent or listen. You shall have no pity on him, you shall not spare him nor shield him,
9 you shall put him to death; your own hand shall be the first to be raised against him and then all the people
10 shall follow. You shall stone him to death, because he tried to lead you astray from the LORD your God who brought you out of Egypt, out of the
11 land of slavery. All Israel shall hear of it and be afraid; never again will any-

thing as wicked as this be done among you.
12– When you hear that miscreants have appeared in any of the cities which the LORD your God is giving you to occupy, and have led its inhabitants astray by calling on them to serve other gods whom you have not known, then you shall investigate 14 the matter carefully. If, after diligent examination, the report proves to be true and it is shown that this abominable thing has been done among you, you shall put the inhabitants of that 15 city to the sword; you shall lay the city under solemn ban together with everything in it. You shall gather all 16 its goods into the square and burn both city and goods as a complete offering to the LORD your God; and it shall remain a mound of ruins, never to be rebuilt. Let nothing out 17 of all that has been laid under the ban be found in your possession, so that the LORD may turn from his anger and show you compassion; and in his compassion he will increase you as he swore to your forefathers, provided 18 that you obey the LORD your God and keep all his commandments which I give you this day, doing only what is right in the eyes of the LORD your God.

A forbidden mourning practice

You are the sons of the LORD your **14** God: you shall not gash yourselves nor shave your forelocks in mourning for the dead. You are a people holy 2 to the LORD your God, and the LORD has chosen you out of all peoples on earth to be his special possession.

Clean and unclean creatures

You shall not eat any abominable 3 thing. These are the animals you may 4 eat: ox, sheep, goat, buck, gazelle, 5 roebuck, wild-goat, white-rumped deer, long-horned antelope, and rock-goat. You may eat any animal which has 6 a parted foot or a cloven hoof and also chews the cud; those which only 7 chew the cud or only have a parted or cloven hoof you may not eat. These are: the camel, the hare, and the rock-badger,*v* because they chew the cud but do not have cloven hoofs; you shall regard them as unclean; and the 8 pig, because it has a cloven hoof but does not chew the cud, you shall regard as unclean. You shall not eat their flesh or even touch their dead carcasses. Of creatures that live in 9

v Or rock-rabbit.

water you may eat all those that have
10 fins and scales, but you may not eat
any that have neither fins nor scales;
you shall regard them as unclean.
12 You may eat all clean birds. These
are the birds you may not eat: the
griffon-vulture,[w] the black vulture, the
13 bearded vulture,[x] the kite, every kind
15 of falcon, every kind of crow,[y] the
desert-owl, the short-eared owl, the
long-eared owl, every kind of hawk,
16 the tawny owl, the screech-owl, the
17 little owl, the horned owl, the osprey,
18 the fisher-owl, the stork,[z] every kind of
cormorant, the hoopoe, and the bat.
19 All teeming winged creatures you
shall regard as unclean; they may not
20 be eaten. You may eat every clean
insect.
21 You shall not eat anything that has
died a natural death. You shall give
it to the aliens who live in your settlements, and they may eat it, or you
may sell it to a foreigner; for you are
a people holy to the LORD your God.
You shall not boil a kid in its
mother's milk.

Law of the tithe

22 Year by year you shall set aside a
tithe of all the produce of your seed,
of everything that grows on the land.
23 You shall eat it in the presence of the
LORD your God in the place which he
will choose as a dwelling for his Name
—the tithe of your corn and new wine
and oil, and the first-born of your
cattle and sheep, so that for all time
you may learn to fear the LORD your
24 God. When the LORD your God has
blessed you with prosperity, and the
place which he will choose to receive
his Name is far from you and the
journey too great for you to be able
25 to carry your tithe, then you may
exchange it for silver. You shall tie up
the silver and take it with you to the
place which the LORD your God will
26 choose. There you shall spend it as
you will on cattle or sheep, wine or
strong drink, or whatever you desire;
you shall consume it there with rejoicing, both you and your family, in the
27 presence of the LORD your God. You
must not neglect the Levites who live
in your settlements; for they have no
holding or patrimony among you.
28 At the end of every third year you
shall bring out all the tithe of your
produce for that year and leave it in
29 your settlements so that the Levites,
who have no holding or patrimony
among you, and the aliens, orphans,

and widows in your settlements may
come and eat their fill. If you do this
the LORD your God will bless you in
everything to which you set your hand.

The year of remission

At the end of every seventh year you 15
shall make a remission of debts. This 2
is how the remission shall be made:
everyone who holds a pledge shall
remit the pledge of anyone indebted
to him. He shall not press a fellow-
countryman for repayment, for the
LORD's year of remission has been
declared.[a] You may press foreigners; 3
but if it is a fellow-countryman that
holds anything of yours, you must
remit all claim upon it. There will 4–5
never be any poor among you if only
you obey the LORD your God by carefully keeping these commandments
which I lay upon you this day; for the
LORD your God will bless you with
great prosperity in the land which
he is giving you to occupy as your
patrimony. When the LORD your God 6
blesses you, as he promised, you will
lend to men of many nations, but you
yourselves will not borrow; you will
rule many nations, but they will not
rule you.
When one of your fellow-country- 7
men in any of your settlements in the
land which the LORD your God is
giving you becomes poor, do not be
hard-hearted or close-fisted with your
countryman in his need. Be open- 8
handed towards him and lend him
on pledge as much as he needs. See 9
that you do not harbour iniquitous
thoughts when you find that the
seventh year, the year of remission, is
near, and look askance at your needy
countryman and give him nothing. If
you do, he will appeal to the LORD
against you, and you will be found
guilty of sin. Give freely to him and do 10
not begrudge him your bounty, because it is for this very bounty that
the LORD your God will bless you in
everything that you do or undertake.
The poor will always be with you in 11
the land, and for that reason I command you to be open-handed with
your countrymen, both poor and distressed, in your own land.

Treatment of slaves

When a fellow-Hebrew, man or wo- 12
man, sells himself to you as a slave,
he shall serve you for six years and in
the seventh year you shall set him
free. But when you set him free, do 13

w Or eagle.   x Or ossifrage.   y Or raven.   z Or heron.   a Or has come.

14 not let him go empty-handed. Give to him lavishly from your flock, from your threshing-floor and your wine-press. Be generous to him, because the
18 LORD your God has blessed you. Do not take it amiss when you have to set him free, for his six years' service to you has been worth twice[b] the wage of a hired man. Then the LORD your God will bless you in everything you
15 do. Remember that you were slaves in Egypt and the LORD your God redeemed you; that is why I am giving you this command today.

16 If, however, a slave is content to be with you and says, 'I will not leave
17 you, I love you and your family', then you shall take an awl and pierce through his ear to the door, and he will be your slave for life. You shall treat a slave-girl in the same way.

Dedicating the first-born

19[c] You shall dedicate to the LORD your God every male first-born of your herds and flocks. You shall not plough with the first-born of your cattle, nor shall you shear the first-born of your
20 sheep. Year by year you and your family shall eat them in the presence of the LORD your God, in the place
21 which the LORD will choose. If any animal is defective, if it is lame or blind, or has any other serious defect, you must not sacrifice it to the LORD
22 your God. Eat it in your settlements; both clean and unclean alike may eat it as they would the meat of gazelle
23 or buck. But you must not eat the blood; pour it out on the ground like water.

Three pilgrim-feasts

16 Observe the month of Abib and keep the Passover to the LORD your God, for it was in that month that the LORD your God brought you out of Egypt
2 by night. You shall slaughter a lamb, a kid, or a calf as a Passover victim to the LORD your God in the place which he will choose as a dwelling for his
3 Name. You shall eat nothing leavened with it. For seven days you shall eat unleavened cakes, the bread of affliction. In urgent haste you came out of Egypt, and thus as long as you live you shall commemorate the day of
4 your coming out of Egypt. No leaven shall be seen in all your territory for seven days, nor shall any of the flesh which you have slaughtered in the evening of the first day remain over-

night till morning. You may not 5 slaughter the Passover victim in any of the settlements which the LORD your God is giving you, but only in 6 the place which he will choose as a dwelling for his Name; you shall slaughter the Passover victim in the evening as the sun goes down, the time of your coming out of Egypt. You shall boil it and eat it in the place 7 which the LORD your God will choose, and then next morning you shall turn and go to your tents. For six days you 8 shall eat unleavened cakes, and on the seventh day there shall be a closing ceremony in honour of the LORD your God; you shall do no work.

Seven weeks shall be counted: start 9 counting the seven weeks from the time when the sickle is put to the standing corn; then you shall keep 10 the pilgrim-feast of Weeks to the LORD your God and offer a freewill offering in proportion to the blessing that the LORD your God has given you. You 11 shall rejoice before the LORD your God, with your sons and daughters, your male and female slaves, the Levites who live in your settlements, and the aliens, orphans, and widows among you. You shall rejoice in the place which the LORD your God will choose as a dwelling for his Name and 12 remember that you were slaves in Egypt. You shall keep and observe all these statutes.

You shall keep the pilgrim-feast of 13 Tabernacles[d] for seven days, when you bring in the produce from your threshing-floor and winepress. You 14 shall rejoice in your feast, with your sons and daughters, your male and female slaves, the Levites, aliens, orphans, and widows who live in your settlements. For seven days you shall 15 keep this feast to the LORD your God in the place which he will choose, when the LORD your God gives you his blessing in all your harvest and in all your work; you shall keep the feast with joy.

Three times a year all your males 16 shall come into the presence of the LORD your God in the place which he will choose: at the pilgrim-feasts of Unleavened Bread, of Weeks, and of Tabernacles. No one shall come into the presence of the LORD empty-handed. Each of you shall bring such 17 a gift as he can in proportion to the blessing which the LORD your God has given you.

---

b worth twice: or equivalent to. Arbours.   c Verse 18 transposed to follow verse 14.   d Or Booths or

Justice

18 You shall appoint for yourselves judges and officers, tribe by tribe, in every settlement which the LORD your God is giving you, and they shall dispense true justice to the people.
19 You shall not pervert the course of justice or show favour, nor shall you accept a bribe; for bribery makes the wise man blind and the just man give
20 a crooked answer. Justice, and justice alone, you shall pursue, so that you may live and occupy the land which the LORD your God is giving you.
21 You shall not plant any kind of tree as a sacred pole beside the altar of the LORD your God which you shall
22 build. You shall not set up a sacred pillar, for the LORD your God hates them.

17 You shall not sacrifice to the LORD your God a bull or sheep that has any defect or serious blemish, for that would be abominable to the LORD your God.
2 If so be that, in any one of the settlements which the LORD your God is giving you, a man or woman is found among you who does what is wrong in the eyes of the LORD your God, by
3 breaking his covenant and going to worship other gods and prostrating himself before them or before the sun and moon and all the host of heaven —a thing that I have forbidden—
4 then, if it is reported to you or you hear of it, make thorough inquiry. If the report proves to be true, and it is shown that this abominable thing has
5 been done in Israel, then bring the man or woman who has done this wicked deed to the city gate and stone
6 him to death. Sentence of death shall be carried out on the testimony of two or of three witnesses: no one shall be put to death on the testimony of a
7 single witness. The first stones shall be thrown by the witnesses and then all the people shall follow; thus you shall rid yourselves of this wickedness.
8 When the issue in any lawsuit is beyond your competence, whether it be a case of blood against blood, plea against plea, or blow against blow, that is disputed in your courts, then go up without delay to the place which the LORD your God will choose.
9 There you must go to the levitical priests or to the judge then in office; seek their guidance, and they will
10 pronounce the sentence. You shall act on the pronouncement which they make from the place which the LORD will choose. See that you carry out all their instructions. Act on the instruc-
11 tion which they give you, or on the precedent that they cite; do not swerve from what they tell you, either to right or to left. Anyone who presumes
12 to reject the decision either of the priest who ministers there to the LORD your God, or of the judge, shall die; thus you will rid Israel of wicked-
13 ness. Then all the people will hear of it and be afraid, and will never again show such presumption.

Instructions concerning a king

When you come into the land which
14 the LORD your God is giving you, and occupy it and settle in it, and you then say, 'Let us appoint over us a king, as all the surrounding nations
15 do', you shall appoint as king the man whom the LORD your God will choose. You shall appoint over you a man of your own race; you must not appoint a foreigner, one who is not of your
16 own race. He shall not acquire many horses, nor, to add to his horses, shall he cause the people to go back to Egypt, for this is what the LORD said to you, 'You shall never go back that
17 way.' He shall not acquire many wives and so be led astray; nor shall he acquire great quantities of silver
18 and gold for himself. When he has ascended the throne of the kingdom, he shall make a copy of this law in a book at the dictation of the levitical
19 priests. He shall keep it by him and read from it all his life, so that he may learn to fear the LORD his God and keep all the words of this law and
20 observe these statutes. In this way he shall not become prouder than his fellow-countrymen, nor shall he turn from these commandments to right or to left; then he and his sons will reign long over his kingdom in Israel.

Provision for the priests and Levites

The levitical priests, the whole tribe 18 of Levi, shall have no holding or patri- mony in Israel; they shall eat the food-offerings of the LORD, their patri- mony. They shall have no patrimony 2 among their fellow-countrymen; the LORD is their patrimony, as he pro- mised them.
This shall be the customary due of 3 the priests from those of the people who offer sacrifice, whether a bull or a sheep: the shoulders, the cheeks, and the stomach shall be given to the priest. You shall give him also the 4 firstfruits of your corn and new wine

and oil, and the first fleeces at the
5 shearing of your flocks. For it was he
whom the LORD your God chose from
all your tribes to attend on the LORD
and to minister in the name of the
LORD, both he and his sons for all
time.
6   When a Levite comes from any
settlement in Israel where he may be
lodging to the place which the LORD
will choose, if he comes in the eager-
7 ness of his heart and ministers in the
name of the LORD his God, like all
his fellow-Levites who attend on the
8 LORD there, he shall have an equal
share of food with them, besides
what he may inherit from his father's family.

Against sorcery

9 When you come into the land which
the LORD your God is giving you, do
not learn to imitate the abominable
10 customs of those other nations. Let
no one be found among you who
makes his son or daughter pass
through fire, no augur or soothsayer
11 or diviner or sorcerer, no one who
casts spells or traffics with ghosts
and spirits, and no necromancer.
12 Those who do these things are abominable to the LORD, and it is because
of these abominable practices that
the LORD your God is driving them
13 out before you. You shall be whole-
hearted in your service of the LORD
your God.

The LORD promises a prophet like Moses

14 These nations whose place you are
taking listen to soothsayers and augurs,
but the LORD your God does not per-
15 mit you to do this. The LORD your
God will raise up a prophet from
among you like myself, and you shall
16 listen to him. All this follows from
your request to the LORD your God
on Horeb on the day of the assembly.
There you said, 'Let us not hear again
the voice of the LORD our God, nor
see this great fire again, or we shall
17 die.' Then the LORD said to me, 'What
18 they have said is right. I will raise up
for them a prophet like you, one of
their own race, and I will put my
words into his mouth. He shall convey
19 all my commands to them, and if anyone does not listen to the words which
he will speak in my name I will require
20 satisfaction from him. But the prophet who presumes to utter in my
name what I have not commanded

him or who speaks in the name of
other gods—that prophet shall die.'
If you ask yourselves, 'How shall we 21
recognize a word that the LORD has
not uttered?', this is the answer: When 22
the word spoken by the prophet in
the name of the LORD is not fulfilled
and does not come true, it is not a
word spoken by the LORD. The prophet has spoken presumptuously; do
not hold him[e] in awe.

More cities of refuge

When the LORD your God exter- 19
minates the nations whose land he is
giving you, and you take their place
and settle in their cities and houses, you 2
shall set apart three cities in the land
which he is giving you to occupy.
Divide into three districts the terri- 3
tory which the LORD your God is
giving you as patrimony, and determine where each city shall lie. These
shall be places in which homicides
may take sanctuary.
    This is the kind of homicide who 4
may take sanctuary there and save
his life: the man who strikes another
without intent and with no previous
enmity between them; for instance, 5
the man who goes into a wood with
his mate to fell trees, and, when cutting a tree, he relaxes his grip on the
axe,[f] the head glances off the tree,
hits the other man and kills him. The
homicide may take sanctuary in any
one of these cities, and his life shall be
safe. Otherwise, when the dead man's 6
next-of-kin who had the duty of
vengeance pursued him in the heat of
passion, he might overtake him if the
distance were great, and take his life,
although the homicide was not liable
to the death-penalty because there had
been no previous enmity on his part.
That is why I command you to set 7
apart these cities.
    If the LORD your God extends your 8
boundaries, as he swore to your forefathers, and gives you the whole land
which he promised to them, because 9
you keep all the commandments that
I am laying down today and carry
them out by loving the LORD your
God and by conforming to his ways
for all time, then you shall add three
more cities of refuge to these three.
Let no innocent blood be shed in the 10
land which the LORD your God is
giving you as your patrimony, or
blood-guilt will fall on you.
    When one man is the enemy of 11
another, and he lies in wait for him,

e Or it.   f when . . . axe: or as he swings the axe to cut a tree.

attacks him and strikes him a blow so that he dies, and then takes sanc-12 tuary in one of these cities, the elders of his own city shall send to fetch him; they shall hand him over to the next-13 of-kin, and he shall die. You shall show him no mercy, but shall rid Israel of the guilt of innocent blood; then all will be well with you.

14 Do not move your neighbour's boundary stone, fixed by the men of former times in the patrimony which you shall occupy in the land the LORD your God gives you for your possession.

Laws concerning witnesses

15 A single witness may not give evidence against a man in the matter of any crime or sin which he commits: a charge must be established on the evidence of two or three witnesses.
16 When a malicious witness comes forward to give false evidence against 17 a man, and the two disputants stand before the LORD, before the priests 18 and the judges then in office, if, after careful examination by the judges, he be proved to be a false witness giving 19 false evidence against his fellow, you shall treat him as he intended to treat his fellow, and thus rid your-20 selves of this wickedness. The rest of the people when they hear of it will be afraid: never again will anything as wicked as this be done among you. 21 You shall show no mercy: life for life, eye for eye, tooth for tooth, hand for hand, foot for foot.

Laws concerning warfare

20 When you take the field against an enemy and are faced by horses and chariots and an army greater than yours, do not be afraid of them; for the LORD your God, who brought you 2 out of Egypt, will be with you. When you are about to join battle, the priest shall come forward and address 3 the army in these words: 'Hear, O Israel, this day you are joining battle with the enemy; do not lose heart, or be afraid, or give way to panic in face 4 of them; for the LORD your God will go with you to fight your enemy for 5 you and give you the victory.' Then the officers shall address the army in these words: 'Any man who has built a new house and has not dedicated it shall go back to his house; or he may die in battle and another man dedi-6 cate it. Any man who has planted a vineyard and has not begun to use

it shall go back home; or he may die in battle and another man use it. Any 7 man who has pledged himself to take a woman in marriage and has not taken her shall go back home; or he may die in battle and another man take her.' The officers shall further 8 address the army: 'Any man who is afraid and has lost heart shall go back home; or his comrades will be dis-couraged as he is.' When these officers 9 have finished addressing the army, commanders shall be appointed to lead it.

When you advance on a city to 10 attack it, make an offer of peace. If 11 the city accepts the offer and opens its gates to you, than all the people in it shall be put to forced labour and shall serve you. If it does not make 12 peace with you but offers battle, you shall besiege it, and the LORD your 13 God will deliver it into your hands. You shall put all its males to the sword, but you may take the women, 14 the dependants, and the cattle for yourselves, and plunder everything else in the city. You may enjoy the use of the spoil of your enemies which the LORD your God gives you. That is 15 what you shall do to cities at a great distance, as opposed to those which belong to nations near at hand. In the 16 cities of these nations whose land the LORD your God is giving you as a patrimony, you shall not leave any creature alive. You shall annihilate 17 them—Hittites, Amorites, Canaanites, Perizzites, Hivites, Jebusites—as the LORD your God commanded you, so 18 that they may not teach you to imi-tate all the abominable things that they have done for their gods and so cause you to sin against the LORD your God.

When you are at war, and lay siege 19 to a city for a long time in order to take it, do not destroy its trees by taking the axe to them, for they provide you with food; you shall not cut them down. The trees of the field are not men that you should besiege them. But you may destroy or cut 20 down any trees that you know do not yield food, and use them in siege-works against the city that is at war with you, until it falls.

Undetected murder

When a dead body is found lying 21 in open country, in the land which the LORD your God is giving you to occupy, and it is not known who struck the blow, your elders and your judges 2

shall come out and measure the distance to the surrounding towns to
3 find which is nearest. The elders of that town shall take a heifer that has never been mated[g] or worn a yoke,
4 and bring it down to a ravine where there is a stream that never runs dry and the ground is never tilled or sown, and there in the ravine they shall
5 break its neck. The priests, the sons of Levi, shall then come forward; for the LORD your God has chosen them to minister to him and to bless in the name of the LORD, and their voice shall be decisive in all cases of dispute
6 and assault. Then all the elders of the town nearest to the dead body shall wash their hands over the heifer whose neck has been broken in the
7 ravine. They shall solemnly declare: 'Our hands did not shed this blood, nor did we witness the bloodshed.
8 Accept expiation, O LORD, for thy people Israel whom thou hast redeemed, and do not let the guilt of innocent blood rest upon thy people Israel: let this bloodshed be expiated
9 on their behalf.' Thus, by doing what is right in the eyes of the LORD, you shall rid yourselves of the guilt of innocent blood.

Law concerning women captives

10 When you wage war against your enemy and the LORD your God delivers them into your hands and you take
11 some of them captive, then if you see a comely woman among the captives and take a liking to her, you may
12 marry her. You shall bring her into your house, where she shall shave her
13 head, pare her nails, and discard the clothes which she had when captured. Then she shall stay in your house and mourn for her father and mother for a full month. After that you may have intercourse with her; you shall be her
14 husband and she your wife. But if you no longer find her pleasing, let her go free. You must not sell her, nor treat her harshly, since you have had your will with her.

Law of the first-born

15 When a man has two wives, one loved and the other unloved, if they both bear him sons, and the son of the un-
16 loved wife is the elder, then, when the day comes for him to divide his property among his sons, he shall not treat the son of the loved wife as his first-born in contempt of his true

first-born, the son of the unloved wife.
17 He shall recognize the rights of his first-born, the son of the unloved wife, and give him a double share of all that he possesses; for he was the first-fruits of his manhood, and the right of the first-born is his.

Law concerning a disobedient son

18 When a man has a son who is disobedient and out of control, and will not obey his father or his mother, or pay attention when they punish him,
19 then his father and mother shall take hold of him and bring him out to the elders of the town, at the town gate.
20 They shall say to the elders of the town, 'This son of ours is disobedient and out of control; he will not obey us, he is a wastrel and a drunkard.'
21 Then all the men of the town shall stone him to death, and you will thereby rid yourselves of this wickedness. All Israel will hear of it and be afraid.

Various laws

22 When a man is convicted of a capital offence and is put to death, you shall
23 hang him on a gibbet; but his body shall not remain on the gibbet overnight; you shall bury it on the same day, for a hanged man is offensive[h] in the sight of God. You shall not pollute the land which the LORD your God is giving you as your patrimony.

22 When you see a fellow-country-man's ox or sheep straying, do not
2 ignore it but take it back to him. If the owner is not a near neighbour and you do not know who he is, take the animal into your own house and keep it with you until he claims it,
3 and then give it back to him. Do the same with his ass or his cloak or anything else that your fellow-country-man has lost, if you find it. You may not ignore it.

4 When you see your fellow-country-man's ass or ox lying on the road, do not ignore it; you must help him to lift it to its feet again.

5 No woman shall wear an article of man's clothing, nor shall a man put on woman's dress; for those who do these things are abominable to the LORD your God.

6 When you come across a bird's nest by the road, in a tree or on the ground, with fledglings or eggs in it and the mother-bird on the nest, do not take both mother and young. Let the
7

g Prob. rdg.; Heb. put to work.　　h Or accursed.

mother-bird go free, and take only the young; then you will prosper and live long.

8 When you build a new house, put a parapet along the roof, or you will bring the guilt of bloodshed on your house if anyone should fall from it.

9 You shall not sow your vineyard with a second crop, or the full yield will be forfeit, both the yield of the seed you sow and the fruit of the vineyard.

10 You shall not plough with an ox and an ass yoked together.

11 You shall not wear clothes woven with two kinds of yarn, wool and flax together.

12 You shall make twisted tassels on the four corners of your cloaks which you wrap round you.

Laws concerning chastity

13 When a man takes a wife and after having intercourse with her turns

14 against her and brings trumped-up charges against her, giving her a bad name and saying, 'I took this woman and slept with her and did not find

15 proof of virginity in her', then the girl's father and mother shall take the proof of her virginity to the elders of

16 the town, at the town gate. The girl's father shall say to the elders, 'I gave my daughter in marriage to this man,

17 and he has turned against her. He has trumped up a charge and said, "I have not found proofs of virginity in your daughter." Here are the proofs.' They shall then spread the garment

18 before the elders of the town. The elders shall take the man and punish

19 him: they shall fine him a hundred pieces of silver because he has given a bad name to a virgin of Israel, and hand them to the girl's father. She shall be his wife: he is not free to

20 divorce her all his life long. If, on the other hand, the accusation is true and no proof of the girl's virginity is

21 found, then they shall bring her out to the door of her father's house and the men of her town shall stone her to death. She has committed an outrage in Israel by playing the prostitute in her father's house: you shall rid yourselves of this wickedness.

22 When a man is discovered lying with a married woman, they shall both die, the woman as well as the man who lay with her: you shall rid Israel of this wickedness.

23 When a virgin is pledged in marriage to a man and another man comes upon

her in the town and lies with her, you 24 shall bring both of them out to the gate of that town and stone them to death; the girl because, although in the town, she did not cry for help, and the man because he dishonoured another man's wife: you shall rid yourselves of this wickedness. If the man 25 comes upon such a girl in the country and rapes her, then the man alone shall die because he lay with her. You 26 shall do nothing to the girl, she has done nothing worthy of death: this deed is like that of a man who attacks another and murders him, for the man 27 came upon her in the country and, though the girl cried for help, there was no one to rescue her.

When a man comes upon a virgin 28 who is not pledged in marriage and forces her to lie with him, and they are discovered, then the man who lies 29 with her shall give the girl's father fifty pieces of silver, and she shall be his wife because he has dishonoured her. He is not free to divorce her all his life long.

A man shall not take his father's 30 wife: he shall not bring shame on his father.

Those excluded from the assembly

No man whose testicles have been **23** crushed or whose organ has been severed shall become a member of the assembly of the LORD.

No descendant of an irregular union, 2 even down to the tenth generation, shall become a member of the assembly of the LORD.

No Ammonite or Moabite, even 3 down to the tenth generation, shall become a member of the assembly of the LORD. They shall never become members of the assembly of the LORD, because they did not meet you with 4 food and water on your way out of Egypt, and because they hired Balaam son of Beor from Pethor in Aram-naharaim[i] to revile you. The 5 LORD your God refused to listen to Balaam and turned his denunciation into a blessing, because the LORD your God loved you. You shall never 6 seek their welfare or their good all your life long.

You shall not regard an Edomite 7 as an abomination, for he is your own kin; nor an Egyptian, for you were aliens in his land. The third genera- 8 tion of children born to them may become members of the assembly of the LORD.

i That is Aram of Two Rivers.

Holiness of war camps

9 When you are encamped against an enemy, you shall be careful to avoid 10 any foulness. When one of your number is unclean because of an emission of seed at night, he must go outside the camp; he may not come within it. 11 Towards evening he shall wash himself in water, and at sunset he may 12 come back into the camp. You shall have a sign outside the camp showing 13 where you can withdraw. With your equipment you will have a trowel, and when you squat outside, you shall scrape a hole with it and then turn 14 and cover your excrement. For the LORD your God goes about in your camp, to keep you safe and to hand over your enemies as you advance, and your camp must be kept holy for fear that he should see something indecent and go with you no further.

Various laws

15 You shall not surrender to his master a slave who has taken refuge 16 with you. Let him stay with you anywhere he chooses in any one of your settlements, wherever suits him best; you shall not force him.

17 No Israelite woman shall become a temple-prostitute, and no Israelite man shall prostitute himself in this way.

18 You shall not allow a common prostitute's fee, or the pay of a male prostitute, to be brought into the house of the LORD your God in fulfilment of any vow, for both of them are abominable to the LORD your God.

19 You shall not charge interest on anything you lend to a fellow-countryman, money or food or anything else 20 on which interest can be charged. You may charge interest on a loan to a foreigner but not on a loan to a fellow-countryman, for then the LORD your God will bless you in all you undertake in the land which you are entering to occupy.

21 When you make a vow to the LORD your God, do not put off its fulfilment; otherwise the LORD your God will require satisfaction of you and you 22 will be guilty of sin. If you choose not to make a vow, you will not be guilty 23 of sin; but if you voluntarily make a vow to the LORD your God, mind what you say and do what you have promised.

24 When you go into another man's vineyard, you may eat as many grapes as you wish to satisfy your hunger, but you may not put any into your basket.

25 When you go into another man's standing corn, you may pluck ears to rub in your hands, but you may not put a sickle to his standing corn.

Law of divorce

When a man has married a wife, but 24 she does not win his favour because he finds something shameful in her, and he writes her a note of divorce, gives it to her and dismisses her; and 2 suppose after leaving his house she goes off to become the wife of another man, and this next husband turns 3 against her and writes her a note of divorce which he gives her and dismisses her, or dies after making her his wife—then in that case her first 4 husband who dismissed her is not free to take her back to be his wife again after she has become for him unclean. This is abominable to the LORD; you must not bring sin upon the land which the LORD your God is giving you as your patrimony.

When a man is newly married, he 5 shall not be liable for military service or any other public duty. He shall remain at home exempt from service for one year and enjoy the wife he has taken.

Various laws

No man shall take millstones, or even 6 the upper one alone, in pledge; that would be taking a life in pledge.

When a man is found to have kid- 7 napped a fellow-countryman, an Israelite, and to have treated him harshly and sold him, he shall die: you shall rid yourselves of this wickedness.

Be careful how you act in all cases 8 of malignant skin-disease; be careful to observe all that the levitical priests tell you; I gave them my commands which you must obey. Remember what 9 the LORD your God did to Miriam, on your way out of Egypt.

When you make a loan to another 10 man, do not enter his house to take a pledge from him. Wait outside, and 11 the man whose creditor you are shall bring the pledge out to you. If he is a 12 poor man, you shall not sleep in the cloak he has pledged. Give it back to 13 him at sunset so that he may sleep in it and bless you; then it will be counted to your credit in the sight of the LORD your God.

You shall not keep back the wages 14

of a man who is poor and needy, whether a fellow-countryman or an alien living in your country in one of 15 your settlements. Pay him his wages on the same day before sunset, for he is poor and his heart is set on them: he may appeal to the LORD against you, and you will be guilty of sin.

16 Fathers shall not be put to death for their children, nor children for their fathers; a man shall be put to death only for his own sin.

17 You shall not deprive aliens and orphans of justice nor take a widow's 18 cloak in pledge. Remember that you were slaves in Egypt and the LORD your God redeemed you from there; that is why I command you to do this.

19 When you reap the harvest in your field and forget a swathe, do not go back to pick it up; it shall be left for the alien, the orphan, and the widow, in order that the LORD your God may bless you in all that you undertake.

20 When you beat your olive-trees, do not strip them afterwards; what is left shall be for the alien, the orphan, and the widow.

21 When you gather the grapes from your vineyard, do not glean afterwards; what is left shall be for the alien, the orphan, and the widow.

22 Remember that you were slaves in Egypt; that is why I command you to do this.

25 When two men go to law and present themselves for judgement, the judges shall try the case; they shall acquit the innocent and condemn the 2 guilty. If the guilty man is sentenced to be flogged, the judge shall cause him to lie down and be beaten in his presence; the number of strokes shall correspond to the gravity of the 3 offence. They may give him forty strokes, but not more; otherwise, if they go further and exceed this number, your fellow-countryman will have been publicly degraded.

4 You shall not muzzle an ox while it is treading out the corn.

A brother-in-law's duty

5 When brothers live together and one of them dies without leaving a son, his widow shall not marry outside the family. Her husband's brother shall have intercourse with her; he shall take her in marriage and do his duty 6 by her as her husband's brother. The first son she bears shall perpetuate the dead brother's name so that it may 7 not be blotted out from Israel. But

if the man is unwilling to take his brother's wife, she shall go to the elders at the town gate and say, 'My husband's brother refuses to perpetuate his brother's name in Israel; he will not do his duty by me.' At this the 8 elders of the town shall summon him and reason with him. If he still stands his ground and says, 'I will not take her', his brother's widow shall go up 9 to him in the presence of the elders; she shall pull his sandal off his foot and spit in his face and declare: 'Thus we requite the man who will not build up his brother's family.' His 10 family shall be known in Israel as the House of the Unsandalled Man.

Other laws

When two men are fighting and the 11 wife of one of them comes near to drag her husband clear of his opponent, if she puts out her hand and catches hold of the man's genitals, you shall cut off her hand and show 12 her no mercy.

You shall not have unequal weights 13 in your bag, one heavy, the other light. You shall not have unequal 14 measures in your house, one large, the other small. You shall have true and 15 correct weights and true and correct measures, so that you may live long in the land which the LORD your God is giving you. All who commit these 16 offences, all who deal dishonestly, are abominable to the LORD.

The Amalekites to be destroyed

Remember what the Amalekites did 17 to you on your way out of Egypt, how 18 they met you on the road when you were faint and weary and cut off your rear, which was lagging behind exhausted: they showed no fear of God. When the LORD your God gives you 19 peace from your enemies on every side, in the land which he is giving you to occupy as your patrimony, you shall not fail to blot out the memory of the Amalekites from under heaven.

Law of the firstfruits

When you come into the land which 26 the LORD your God is giving you to occupy as your patrimony and settle in it, you shall take the firstfruits of 2 all the produce of the soil, which you gather in from the land which the LORD your God is giving you, and put them in a basket. Then you shall go to the place which the LORD your

God will choose as a dwelling for his
3 Name and come to the priest, whoever he shall be in those days. You
shall say to him, 'I declare this day
to the LORD your God that I have
entered the land which the LORD
swore to our forefathers to give us.'
4 The priest shall take the basket from
your hand and set it down before the
5 altar of the LORD your God. Then you
shall solemnly recite before the LORD
your God: 'My father was a homeless[j]
Aramaean who went down to Egypt
with a small company and lived there
until they became a great, powerful,
6 and numerous nation. But the Egyptians ill-treated us, humiliated us and
7 imposed cruel slavery upon us. Then
we cried to the LORD the God of our
fathers for help, and he listened to us
and saw our humiliation, our hard-
8 ship and distress; and so the LORD
brought us out of Egypt with a strong
hand and outstretched arm, with
terrifying deeds, and with signs and
9 portents. He brought us to this place
and gave us this land, a land flowing
10 with milk and honey. And now I have
brought the firstfruits of the soil
which thou, O LORD, hast given me.'
You shall then set the basket before
the LORD your God and bow down in
11 worship before him. You shall all
rejoice, you and the Levites and the
aliens living among you, for all the
good things which the LORD your God
has given to you and to your family.
12 When you have finished taking a
tithe of your produce in the third year,
the tithe-year, you shall give it to the
Levites and to the aliens, the orphans,
and the widows. They shall eat it in
your settlements and be well fed.
13 Then you shall declare before the
LORD your God: 'I have rid my house
of the tithe that was holy to thee and
given it to the Levites, to the aliens,
the orphans, and the widows, according to all the commandments which
thou didst lay upon me. I have not
broken or forgotten any of thy com-
14 mandments. I have not eaten any of
the tithe while in mourning, nor have
I rid myself of it for unclean purposes,
nor offered any of it to[k] the dead. I
have obeyed the LORD my God: I have
done all that thou didst command me.
15 Look down from heaven, thy holy
dwelling-place, and bless thy people
Israel and the ground which thou
hast given to us as thou didst swear
to our forefathers, a land flowing with
milk and honey.'

A holy people

16 This day the LORD your God commands you to keep these statutes and
laws: be careful to observe them with
17 all your heart and soul. You have
recognized the LORD this day as your
God; you are to conform to his ways,
to keep his statutes, his commandments, and his laws, and to obey him.
18 The LORD has recognized you this day
as his special possession, as he promised you, and to keep his command-
19 ments; he will raise you high above all
the nations which he has made, to
bring him praise and fame and glory,
and to be a people holy to the LORD
your God, according to his promise.

Recording the law

27 Moses, with the elders of Israel, gave
the people this charge: 'Keep all the
commandments that I lay upon you
2 this day. On the day that you cross the
Jordan to the land which the LORD
your God is giving you, you shall set
up great stones and plaster them over.
3 You shall inscribe on them all the
words of this law, when you have
crossed over to enter the land which
the LORD your God is giving you, a
land flowing with milk and honey, as
the LORD the God of your fathers
promised you. When you have crossed
4 the Jordan you shall set up these
stones on Mount Ebal, as I command
you this day, and cover them with
5 plaster. You shall build an altar there
to the LORD your God: it shall be an
altar of stones on which you shall use
6 no tool of iron. You shall build the
altar of the LORD your God with blocks
of undressed stone, and you shall
offer whole-offerings upon it to the
LORD your God. You shall slaughter
7 shared-offerings and eat them there,
and rejoice before the LORD your
God. You shall inscribe on the stones
8 all the words of this law, engraving
them with care.'

9 Moses and the levitical priests
spoke to all Israel, 'Be silent, Israel,
and listen; this day you have become a people belonging to the LORD
your God. Obey the LORD your God,
10 and observe his commandments and
statutes which I lay upon you this
day.'

Curses for disobedience

11 That day Moses gave the people this
12 command: 'Those who shall stand for
the blessing of the people on Mount

j Or wandering.   *k Or for.*

Gerizim when you have crossed the Jordan are these: Simeon, Levi, Judah, Issachar, Joseph, and Benjamin. 13 Those who shall stand on Mount Ebal for the curse are these: Reuben, Gad, Asher, Zebulun, Dan, and Naphtali.'

14 The Levites, in the hearing of all Israel, shall intone these words:

15 'A curse upon the man who carves an idol or casts an image, anything abominable to the LORD that craftsmen make, and sets it up in secret': the people shall all respond and say, 'Amen.'

16 'A curse upon him who slights his father or his mother': the people shall all say, 'Amen.'

17 'A curse upon him who moves his neighbour's boundary stone': the people shall all say, 'Amen.'

18 'A curse upon him who misdirects a blind man': the people shall all say, 'Amen.'

19 'A curse upon him who withholds justice from the alien, the orphan, and the widow': the people shall all say, 'Amen.'

20 'A curse upon him who lies with his father's wife, for he brings shame upon his father': the people shall all say, 'Amen.'

21 'A curse upon him who lies with any animal': the people shall all say, 'Amen.'

22 'A curse upon him who lies with his sister, his father's daughter or his mother's daughter': the people shall all say, 'Amen.'

23 'A curse upon him who lies with his wife's mother': the people shall all say, 'Amen.'

24 'A curse upon him who strikes another man in secret': the people shall all say, 'Amen.'

25 'A curse upon him who takes reward to kill a man with whom he has no feud': the people shall all say, 'Amen.'

26 'A curse upon any man who does not fulfil this law by doing all that it prescribes': the people shall all say, 'Amen.'

Blessings for obedience

28 If you will obey the LORD your God by diligently observing all his commandments which I lay upon you this day, then the LORD your God will raise you high above all nations of the 2 earth, and all these blessings shall come to you and light upon you, because you obey the LORD your God:

A blessing on you in the city; a 3 blessing on you in the country.

A blessing on the fruit of your 4 body, the fruit of your land and of your cattle, the offspring of your herds and of your lambing flocks.

A blessing on your basket and your 5 kneading-trough.

A blessing on you as you come in; 6 and a blessing on you as you go out.

May the LORD deliver up the ene- 7 mies who attack you and let them be put to rout before you. Though they come out against you by one way, they shall flee before you by seven ways.

May the LORD grant you a blessing 8 in your granaries and in all your labours; may the LORD your God bless you in the land which he is giving you.

The LORD will set you up as his 9 own holy people, as he swore to you, if you keep the commandments of the LORD your God and conform to his ways. Then all people on earth shall 10 see that the LORD has named you as his very own, and they shall go in fear of you. The LORD will make you 11 prosper greatly in the fruit of your body and of your cattle, and in the fruit of the ground in the land which he swore to your forefathers to give you. May the LORD open the heavens 12 for you, his rich treasure house, to give rain upon your land at the proper time and bless everything to which you turn your hand. You shall lend to many nations, but you shall not borrow; the LORD will make you 13 the head and not the tail: you shall be always at the top and never at the bottom, when you listen to the commandments of the LORD your God, which I give you this day to keep and to fulfil. You shall turn neither to 14 the right nor to the left from all the things which I command you this day nor shall you follow after and worship other gods.

The consequences of disobedience

But if you do not obey the LORD your 15 God by diligently observing all his commandments and statutes which I lay upon you this day, then all these maledictions shall come to you and light upon you:

A curse upon you in the city; a curse 16 upon you in the country.

A curse upon your basket and your 17 kneading-trough.

A curse upon the fruit of your body, 18 the fruit of your land, the offspring of your herds and of your lambing flocks.

19 A curse upon you as you come in; and a curse upon you as you go out.

20 May the LORD send upon you starvation, burning thirst, and dysentery,*l* whatever you are about, until you are destroyed and quickly perish for your evil doings, because you have forsaken me.

21 May the LORD cause pestilence to haunt you until he has exterminated you out of the land which you are

22 entering to occupy; may the LORD afflict you with wasting disease and recurrent fever, ague and eruptions; with drought, black blight and red; and may these plague you until you

23 perish. May the skies above you be bronze, and the earth beneath you

24 iron. May the LORD turn the rain upon your country into fine sand, and may dust come down upon you from the sky until you are blotted out.

25 May the LORD put you to rout before the enemy. Though you go out against them by one way, you shall flee before them by seven ways. May you be repugnant to all the kingdoms

26 on earth. May your bodies become food for the birds of the air and the wild beasts, with no man to scare them away.

27 May the LORD strike you with Egyptian boils and with tumours, scabs, and itches, for which you will

28 find no cure. May the LORD strike you with madness, blindness, and bewilder-

29 ment; so that you will grope about in broad daylight, just as a blind man gropes in darkness, and you will fail to find your way. You will also be oppressed and robbed, day in, day

30 out, with no one to save you. A woman will be pledged to you, but another shall ravish her; you will build a house but not live in it; you will plant a vineyard but not enjoy

31 its fruit. Your ox will be slaughtered before your eyes, but you will not eat any of it; and before your eyes your ass will be stolen and will not come back to you; your sheep will be given to the enemy, and there will be no

32 one to recover them. Your sons and daughters will be given to another people while you look on; your eyes will strain after them all day long,

33 and you will be powerless. A nation whom you do not know shall eat the fruit of your land and all your toil, and your lot will be nothing but brutal

34 oppression. The sights you see will

drive you mad. May the LORD strike 35 you on knee and leg with malignant boils for which you will find no cure; they will spread from the sole of your foot to the crown of your head. May 36 the LORD give you up, you and the king whom you have appointed, to a nation whom neither you nor your fathers have known, and there you will worship other gods, gods of wood and stone. You will become a horror, 37 a byword, and an object-lesson to all the peoples amongst whom the LORD disperses you.

You will carry out seed for your 38 fields in plenty, but you will harvest little; for the locusts will devour it. You will plant vineyards and cultivate 39 them, but you will not drink the wine or gather the grapes; for the grub will eat them. You will have olive-trees 40 all over your territory, but you will not anoint yourselves with their oil; for your olives will drop off. You will 41 bear sons and daughters, but they will not remain yours because they will be taken into captivity. All your 42 trees and the fruit of the ground will be infested with the mole-cricket. The 43 alien who lives with you will raise himself higher and higher, and you will sink lower and lower. He will lend 44 to you but you will not lend to him: he will be the head and you the tail.

All these maledictions will come 45 upon you; they will pursue you and overtake you until you are destroyed because you did not obey the LORD your God by keeping the commandments and statutes which he gave you. They shall be a sign and a portent to 46 you and your descendants for ever, because you did not serve the LORD 47 your God with joy and with a glad heart for all your blessings. Then in 48 hunger and thirst, in nakedness and extreme want, you shall serve your enemies whom the LORD will send against you, and they will put a yoke of iron on your neck when they have subdued you. May the LORD raise 49 against you a nation from afar, from the other end of the earth, who will swoop upon you like a vulture, a nation whose language you will not understand, a nation of grim aspect 50 with no reverence for age and no pity for the young. They will devour the 51 young of your cattle and the fruit of your land, when you have been subdued. They will leave you neither corn, nor new wine nor oil, neither the offspring of your herds nor of your

l Or cursing, confusion, and rebuke.

lambing flocks, until you are annihi-
2 lated. They will besiege you in all your
cities until they bring down your
lofty impregnable walls, those city
walls throughout your land in which
you trust. They will besiege you
within all your cities, throughout the
land which the LORD your God has
53 given you. Then you will eat your own
children, the flesh of your sons and
daughters whom the LORD your God
has given you, because of the dire
straits to which you will be reduced
54 when your enemy besieges you. The
pampered, delicate man will not
share with his brother, or the wife
of his bosom, or his own remaining
55 children, any of the meat which he is
eating, the flesh of his own children.
He is left with nothing else because
of the dire straits to which you will
be reduced when your enemy besieges
56 you within your cities. The pampered,
delicate woman, the woman who has
never even tried to put a foot to the
ground, so delicate and pampered she
is, will not share with her own hus-
57 band or her son or her daughter the
afterbirth which she expels, or any
boy or girl that she may bear. She
will herself eat them secretly in her
extreme want, because of the dire
straits to which you will be reduced
when your enemy besieges you within
your cities.
58 If you do not observe and fulfil all
the law written down in this book, if
you do not revere this honoured and
dreaded name, this name 'the LORD[m]
59 your God', then the LORD will strike
you and your descendants with unima-
ginable plagues, malignant and persistent, and with sickness, persistent
60 and severe. He will bring upon you
once again all the diseases of Egypt
which you dread, and they will cling
61 to you. The LORD will bring upon you
sickness and plague of every kind not
written down in this book of the law,
62 until you are destroyed. Then you
who were countless as the stars in
the sky will be left few in number,
because you did not obey the LORD
63 your God. Just as the LORD took
delight in you, prospering and increasing you, so now it will be his delight
to destroy and exterminate you, and
you will be uprooted from the land
which you are entering to occupy.
64 The LORD will scatter you among all
peoples from one end of the earth to
the other, and there you will worship
other gods whom neither you have

known nor your forefathers, gods of
wood and stone. Among those nations 65
you will find no peace, no rest for
the sole of your foot. Then the LORD
will give you an unquiet mind, dim
eyes, and failing appetite. Your life 66
will hang continually in suspense,
fear will beset you night and day, and
you will find no security all your life
long. Every morning you will say, 67
'Would God it were evening!', and
every evening, 'Would God it were
morning!', for the fear that lives in
your heart and the sights that you
see. The LORD will bring you sorrow- 68
ing back to Egypt by that very road
of which I said to you, 'You shall not
see that road again'; and there you
will offer to sell yourselves to your
enemies as slaves and slave-girls, but
there will be no buyer.

These are the words of the covenant 29
which the LORD commanded Moses
to make with the Israelites in Moab,
in addition to the covenant which he
made with them on Horeb.

The covenant with Israel in Moab

Moses summoned all the Israelites 2
and said to them: 'You have seen with
your own eyes all that the LORD did
in Egypt to Pharaoh, to all his servants, and to the whole land, the 3
great challenge which you yourselves
witnessed, those great signs and portents, but to this day the LORD has 4
not given you a mind to learn, or eyes
to see, or ears to hear. I led you for 5
forty years in the wilderness; your
clothes did not wear out on you, nor
did your sandals wear out and fall off
your feet; you ate no bread and drank 6
no wine or strong drink, in order that
you might learn that I am the LORD
your God. You came to this place 7
where Sihon king of Heshbon and Og
king of Bashan came to attack us, and
we defeated them. We took their land 8
and gave it as patrimony to the
Reubenites, the Gadites, and half the
tribe of Manasseh. You shall observe 9
the provisions of this covenant and
keep them so that you may be successful in all you do.

'You all stand here today before 10
the LORD your God, tribal chiefs,
elders, and officers, all the men of
Israel, with your dependants, your 11
wives, the aliens who live in your
camp—all of them, from those who
chop wood to those who draw water
—and you are ready to accept the 12
oath and enter into the covenant which

the LORD your God is making with
13 you today. The covenant is to consti-
tute you his people this day, and he
will be your God, as he promised you
and as he swore to your forefathers,
14 Abraham, Isaac and Jacob. It is not
with you alone that I am making this
15 covenant and this oath, but with all
those who stand here with us today
before the LORD our God and also with
those who are not here with us today.
16 For you know how we lived in Egypt
and how we and you, as we passed
17 through the nations, saw their loathsome idols and the false gods they had,
the gods of wood and stone, of silver
18 and gold. If there should be among
you a man or woman, family or tribe,
who is moved today to turn from the
LORD our God and to go worshipping
the gods of those nations—if there is
among you such a root from which
19 springs gall and wormwood, then
when he hears the terms of this oath,
he may inwardly flatter himself and
think, "All will be well with me even
if I follow the promptings of my stubborn heart"; but this will bring every-
20 thing to ruin. The LORD will not be
willing to forgive him; for then his
anger and resentment will overwhelm
this man, and the denunciations prescribed in this book will fall heavily on
him, and the LORD will blot out his
21 name from under heaven. The LORD
will single him out from all the tribes
of Israel for disaster to fall upon him,
according to the oath required by the
covenant and prescribed in this book
of the law.
22 'The next generation, your sons
who follow you and the foreigners who
come from distant countries, will see
the plagues of this land and the ulcers
which the LORD has brought upon its
23 people, the whole land burnt up with
brimstone and salt, so that it cannot
be sown, or yield herb or green plant.
It will be as desolate as were Sodom
and Gomorrah, Admah and Zeboyim,
when the LORD overthrew them in his
24 anger and rage. Then they, and all
the nations with them, will ask, "Why
has the LORD so afflicted this land?
Why has there been this great out-
25 burst of wrath?" The answer will be:
"Because they forsook the covenant
of the LORD the God of their fathers
which he made with them when he
26 brought them out of Egypt. They
began to worship other gods and to
bow down to them, gods whom they
had not known and whom the LORD

had not assigned to them. The anger 27
of the LORD was roused against that
land, so that he brought upon it all
the maledictions written in this book.
The LORD uprooted them from their 28
soil in anger, in wrath and great fury,
and banished them to another land,
where they are to this day."
'There are things hidden, and they 29
belong to the LORD our God, but
what is revealed belongs to us and
our children for ever; it is for us to
observe all that is prescribed in this
law.

Choice of life or death

'When these things have befallen you, 30
the blessing and the curse of which I
have offered you the choice, if you
and your sons take them to heart
there in all the countries to which the
LORD your God has banished you,
if you turn back to him and obey him 2
heart and soul in all that I command
you this day, then the LORD your God 3
will show you compassion and restore
your fortunes. He will gather you
again from all the countries to which
he has scattered you. Even though 4
he were to banish you to the four
corners of the world, the LORD your
God will gather you from there, from
there he will fetch you home. The 5
LORD your God will bring you into the
land which your forefathers occupied,
and you will occupy it again; then he
will bring you prosperity and make
you more numerous than your forefathers were. The LORD your God will 6
circumcise^n your hearts and the hearts
of your descendants, so that you will
love him with all your heart and soul
and you will live. Then the LORD your 7
God will turn all these denunciations
against your enemies and the foes
who persecute you. You will then 8
again obey the LORD and keep all his
commandments which I give you this
day. The LORD your God will make 9
you more than prosperous in all that
you do, in the fruit of your body and
of your cattle and in the fruits of the
earth; for, when you obey the LORD
your God by keeping his commandments and statutes, as they are written
in this book of the law, and when you
turn back to the LORD your God with
all your heart and soul, he will again
rejoice over you and be good to you,
as he rejoiced over your forefathers.

'The commandment that I lay on 11
you this day is not too difficult for
you, it is not too remote. It is not in 12

n Or incline.

heaven, that you should say, "Who will go up to heaven for us to fetch it and tell it to us, so that we can keep 3 it?" Nor is it beyond the sea, that you should say, "Who will cross the sea for us to fetch it and tell it to us, so 4 that we can keep it?" It is a thing very near to you, upon your lips and in your heart ready to be kept.

5 'Today I offer you the choice of life 6 and good, or death and evil. If you obey the commandments of the LORD your God which I give you this day, by loving the LORD your God, by conforming to his ways and by keeping his commandments, statutes, and laws, then you will live and increase, and the LORD your God will bless you in the land which you are entering to 7 occupy. But if your heart turns away and you do not listen and you are led on to bow down to other gods and 8 worship them, I tell you this day that you will perish; you will not live long in the land which you will enter to 9 occupy after crossing the Jordan. I summon heaven and earth to witness against you this day: I offer you the choice of life or death, blessing or curse. Choose life and then you and 10 your descendants will live; love the LORD your God, obey him and hold fast to him: that is life for you and length of days in the land which the LORD swore to give to your forefathers, Abraham, Isaac and Jacob.'

Moses addresses Joshua

1 Moses finished speaking these words 2 to all Israel, and then he said, 'I am now a hundred and twenty years old, and I can no longer move about as I please; and the LORD has told me that 3 I may not cross the Jordan. The LORD your God will cross over at your head and destroy these nations before your advance, and you shall occupy their lands; and, as he directed, Joshua 4 will lead you across. The LORD will do to these nations as he did to Sihon and Og, kings of the Amorites, and to their 5 lands; he will destroy them. The LORD will deliver them into your power, and you shall do to them as I com- 6 manded you. Be strong, be resolute; you must not dread them or be afraid, for the LORD your God himself goes with you; he will not fail you or forsake you.'

7 Moses summoned Joshua and said to him in the presence of all Israel, 'Be strong, be resolute; for it is you who are to lead this people into the land which the LORD swore to give their forefathers, and you are to bring them into possession of it. The LORD 8 himself goes at your head; he will be with you; he will not fail you or forsake you. Do not be discouraged or afraid.'

The law to be read every seven years

Moses wrote down this law and gave 9 it to the priests, the sons of Levi, who carried the Ark of the Covenant of the LORD, and to all the elders of Israel. Moses gave them this command: 'At 10 the end of every seven years, at the appointed time for the year of remission, at the pilgrim-feast of Tabernacles, when all Israel comes to enter 11 the presence of the LORD your God in the place which he will choose, you shall read this law publicly in the hearing of all Israel. Assemble the 12 people, men, women, and dependants, together with the aliens who live in your settlements, so that they may listen, and learn to fear the LORD your God and observe all these laws with care. Their children, too, who do not 13 know them, shall hear them, and learn to fear the LORD your God all their lives in the land which you will occupy after crossing the Jordan.'

The LORD's last instructions to Moses

The LORD said to Moses, 'The time 14 of your death is drawing near; call Joshua, and then come and stand in the Tent of the Presence so that I may give him his commission.' So Moses and Joshua went and took their stand in the Tent of the Presence; and the 15 LORD appeared in the tent in a pillar of cloud, and the pillar of cloud stood at the entrance of the tent.

The LORD said to Moses, 'You are 16 about to die like your forefathers, and this people, when they come into the land and live among foreigners, will go wantonly after their gods; they will abandon me and break the covenant which I have made with them. Then my anger will be roused against 17 them, and I will abandon them and hide my face from them. They will be an easy prey, and many terrible disasters will come upon them. They will say on that day, "These disasters have come because our God is not among us." On that day I will hide 18 my face because of all the evil they have done in turning to other gods.

'Now write down this rule of life[o] 19

o *rule of life: or* song.

and teach it to the Israelites; make them repeat it, so that it may be on
20 record against them. When I have brought them into the land which I swore to give to their forefathers, a land flowing with milk and honey, and they have plenty to eat and grow fat, they will turn to other gods and worship them, they will spurn me and
21 break my covenant; and many calamities and disasters will follow. Then this rule of life will confront them as a record, for it will not be forgotten by their descendants. For even before I bring them into the land which I swore to give them, I know which way their thoughts incline already.'
22 That day Moses wrote down this rule of life and taught it to the Israel-
23 ites. The LORD[p] gave Joshua son of Nun his commission in these words: 'Be strong, be resolute; for you shall bring the Israelites into the land which I swore to give them, and I will be with you.'
24 When Moses had finished writing down these laws in a book, from
25 beginning to end, he gave this command to the Levites who carried the Ark of the Covenant of the LORD:
26 'Take this book of the law and put it beside the Ark of the Covenant of the LORD your God to be a witness
27 against you. For I know how defiant and stubborn you are; even during my lifetime you have defied the LORD; how much more, then, will you do so
28 when I am dead? Assemble all the elders of your tribes and your officers; I will say all these things in their hearing and will summon heaven and
29 earth to witness against them. For I know that after my death you will take to degrading practices and turn aside from the way which I told you to follow, and in days to come disaster will come upon you, because you are doing what is wrong in the eyes of the LORD and so provoking him to anger.'

The Song of Moses

30 Moses recited this song from beginning to end in the hearing of the whole assembly of Israel:

32 Give ear to what I say, O heavens, earth, listen to my words;
2 my teaching shall fall like drops of rain,
my words shall distil like dew,
like fine rain upon the grass
and like the showers on young plants.

When I call aloud the name of the 3
LORD,[q]
you shall respond, 'Great is our God,
the creator[r] whose work is perfect, 4
and all his ways are just,
a faithful god, who does no wrong,
righteous and true is He!'

Perverse and crooked generation 5
whose faults have proved you no
children of his,
is this how you repay the LORD, 6
you brutish and stupid people?
Is he not your father who formed you?
Did he not make you and establish
you?
Remember the days of old, 7
think of the generations long ago;
ask your father to recount it
and your elders to tell you the tale.

When the Most High parcelled out the 8
nations,
when he dispersed all mankind,
he laid down the boundaries of every
people
according to the number of the sons of
God;
but the LORD's share was his own peo- 9
ple,
Jacob was his allotted portion.
He found him in a desert land, 10
in a waste and howling void.
He protected and trained him,
he guarded him as the apple of his eye,
as an eagle watches over its nest, 11
hovers above its young,
spreads its pinions and takes them up,
and carries them upon its wings.
The LORD alone led him, 12
no alien god at his side.
He made him ride on the heights of 13
the earth
and fed him on the harvest of the
fields;
he satisfied him with honey from the
crags
and oil from the flinty rock,
curds from the cattle, milk from the 14
ewes,
the fat of lambs' kidneys,
of rams, the breed of Bashan, and of
goats,
with the finest flour of wheat;
and he drank wine from the blood of
the grape.
Jacob ate and was well fed, 15
Jeshurun grew fat and unruly,[s]
he grew fat, he grew bloated and sleek.
He forsook God who made him
and dishonoured the Rock of his salvation.
They roused his jealousy with foreign 16
gods

p Prob. rdg.; Heb. He.   q Or the name JEHOVAH.   *r Or rock.   s Or and kicked.*

and provoked him with abominable
practices.
17 They sacrificed to foreign demons that
are no gods,
gods who were strangers to them;
they took up with new gods from their
neighbours,
gods whom your fathers did not acknowledge.
18 You forsook the creator[t] who begot you
and cared nothing for God who brought
you to birth.
19 The LORD saw and spurned them;
his own sons and daughters provoked
him.
20 'I will hide my face from them,' he
said;
'let me see what their end will be,
for they are a mutinous generation,
sons who are not to be trusted.
21 They roused my jealousy with a god
of no account,
with their false gods they provoked
me;
so I will rouse their jealousy with a
people of no account,
with a brutish nation I will provoke
them.
22 For fire is kindled by my anger,
it burns to the depths of Sheol;
it devours earth and its harvest
and sets fire to the very roots of the
mountains.
23 I will heap on them one disaster after
another,
I will use up all my arrows on them:
24 pangs of hunger, ravages of plague,
and bitter pestilence.
I will harry them with the fangs of
wild beasts
and the poison of creatures that crawl
in the dust.
25 The sword will make orphans in the
streets
and widows in their own homes;
it will take toll of young man and
maid,
of babes in arms and old men.
26 I had resolved to strike them down
and to destroy all memory of them,
27 but I feared that I should be provoked
by their foes,
that their enemies would take the
credit
and say, "It was not the LORD,
it was we who raised the hand that
did this."'
28 They are a nation that lacks good
counsel,
devoid of understanding.
29 If only they had the wisdom to understand this

and give thought to their end!
How could one man pursue a thousand 30
of them,
how could two put ten thousand to
flight,
if their Rock had not sold them to
their enemies,
if the LORD had not handed them
over?
For the enemy have no Rock like ours, 31
in themselves they are mere fools.
Their vines are vines of Sodom, 32
grown on the terraces of Gomorrah;
their grapes are poisonous,
the clusters bitter to the taste.
Their wine is the venom of serpents, 33
the cruel poison of asps;
all this I have in reserve, 34
sealed up in my storehouses
till the day of punishment and ven- 35
geance,
till the moment when they slip and
fall;
for the day of their downfall is near,
their doom is fast approaching.
The LORD will give his people justice 36
and have compassion on his servants;
for he will see that their strength is
gone:
alone, or defended by his clan, no one
is left.

He will say, 'Where are your gods, 37
the rock in which you sought shelter,
the gods who ate the fat of your 38
sacrifices
and drank the wine of your drink-
offerings?
Let them rise to help you!
Let them give you shelter!
See now that I, I am He, 39
and there is no god beside me:
I put to death and I keep alive,
I wound and I heal;
there is no rescue from my grasp.
I lift my hand to heaven 40
and swear: As I live for ever,
when I have whetted my flashing 41
sword,
when I have set my hand to judgement,
then I will punish my adversaries
and take vengeance on my enemies.
I will make my arrows drunk with 42
blood,
my sword shall devour flesh,
blood of slain and captives,
the heads of the enemy princes.'
Rejoice with him, you heavens, 43
bow down, all you gods, before him;
for he will avenge the blood of his
sons
and take vengeance on his adversaries;

[t] Or rock.

he will punish those who hate him
and make expiation for his people's
land.

44 This is the song that Moses came
and recited in the hearing of the
people, he and Joshua son of Nun.
45 Moses finished speaking to all Israel,
46 and then he said, 'Take to heart all
these warnings which I solemnly give
you this day: command your children
to be careful to observe all the words
47 of this law. For you they are no empty
words; they are your very life, and
by them you shall live long in the
land which you are to occupy after
crossing the Jordan.'

Moses allowed to see Canaan

48 That same day the Lord spoke to
49 Moses and said, 'Go up this mount
Abarim, Mount Nebo in Moab, to the
east of Jericho, and look out over the
land of Canaan that I am giving to
50 the Israelites for their possession. On
this mountain you shall die and be
gathered to your father's kin, just as
Aaron your brother died on Mount
Hor and was gathered to his father's
51 kin. This is because both of you were
unfaithful to me at the waters of
Meribah-by-Kadesh in the wilderness
of Zin, when you did not uphold my
52 holiness among the Israelites. You
shall see the land from a distance but
you may not enter the land I am
giving to the Israelites.'

Moses blesses the tribes of Israel

33 This is the blessing that Moses the man
of God pronounced upon the Israelites
before his death:

2 The Lord came from Sinai
and shone forth from Seir.
He showed himself from Mount Paran,
and with him were myriads of holy
ones[u]
streaming along at his right hand.
3 Truly he loves his people
and blesses his saints.[v]
They sit at his feet
and receive his instruction,
4 the law which Moses laid upon us,
as a possession for the assembly of
Jacob.
5 Then a king arose[w] in Jeshurun,
when the chiefs of the people were
assembled
together with all the tribes of Israel.

Of Reuben he said:[x]   6
May Reuben live and not die out,
but may he be few in number.

And of Judah he said this: 7
Hear, O Lord, the cry of Judah
and join him to his people,
thou whose hands fight for him,
who art his helper against his foes.

Of Levi he said: 8
Thou didst give thy Thummim to
Levi,
thy Urim to thy loyal servant
whom thou didst prove at Massah,
for whom thou didst plead at the
waters of Meribah,
who said of his parents, I do not know 9
them,
who did not acknowledge his brothers,
nor recognize his children.
They observe thy word
and keep thy covenant;
they teach thy precepts to Jacob,   10
thy law to Israel.
They offer thee the smoke of sacrifice
and offerings on thy altar.
Bless all his powers,[y] O Lord,   11
and accept the work of his hands.
Strike his adversaries hip and thigh,
and may his enemies rise no more.

Of Benjamin he said: 12

The Lord's beloved dwells in security,
the High God[z] shields him all the day
long,
and he dwells under his protection.

Of Joseph he said: 13

The Lord's blessing is on his land
with precious fruit watered from
heaven above
and from the deep that lurks below,
with precious fruit ripened by the sun, 14
precious fruit, the produce of the
months,
with all good things from the ancient 15
mountains,
the precious fruit of the everlasting
hills,
the precious fruits of earth and all its 16
store,
by the favour of him who dwells in the
burning bush.
This shall rest[a] upon the head of
Joseph,
on the brow of him who was prince
among[b] his brothers.
In majesty he shall be like a first-born 17
ox,

u and with . . . holy ones: prob. rdg.; Heb. and he came from myriads of holiness.   v Or holy ones.
w Or Then there was a king . . .   x Of Reuben he said: prob. rdg.; Heb. om.   y Or skill.
z the High God: prob. rdg.; Heb. upon him.   a Prob. rdg., cp. Gen. 49. 26; Heb. has an unintelligible
form.   b him . . . among: or the one cursed by.

his horns those of a wild ox
with which he will gore nations
and drive[c] them to the ends of earth.
Such will be the myriads of Ephraim,
and such the thousands of Manasseh.

18 Of Zebulun he said:

Rejoice, Zebulun, when you sally
    forth,
rejoice in your tents, Issachar.

19 They shall summon nations to the
    mountain,
there they will offer true sacrifices,
for they shall suck the abundance of
    the seas
and draw out[d] the hidden wealth of
    the sand.

20 Of Gad he said:

Blessed be Gad, in his wide domain;
he couches like a lion
tearing an arm or a scalp.

21 He chose the best for himself,
for to him was allotted a ruler's
    portion,
when the chiefs of the people were
    assembled together.
He did what the LORD deemed right,
observing his ordinances for Israel.

22 Of Dan he said:

Dan is a lion's cub
springing out from Bashan.

23 Of Naphtali he said:

Naphtali is richly favoured
and full of the blessings of the LORD;
his patrimony stretches to the sea and
    southward.

24 Of Asher he said:

Asher is most blest of sons,
may he be the favourite among[e] his
    brothers
and bathe his feet in oil.

25 May your bolts be of iron and bronze,
and your strength last as long as you
    live.

26 There is none like the God of Jeshurun
who rides the heavens to your help,
riding the clouds in his glory,

27 who humbled the gods of old
and subdued[f] the ancient powers;
who drove out the enemy before you
and gave the word to destroy.

Israel lives in security,   28
the tribes of Jacob by themselves,
in a land of corn and wine[g]
where the skies drip with dew.
Happy are you, people of Israel, peer- 29
    less, set free;
the LORD is the shield that guards you,
the Blessed One is your glorious sword.
Your enemies come cringing to you,
and you shall trample their bodies
    under foot.

The death of Moses

Then Moses went up from the lowlands 34
of Moab to Mount Nebo, to the top of
Pisgah, eastwards from Jericho, and
the LORD showed him the whole land:
Gilead as far as Dan; the whole of 2
Naphtali; the territory of Ephraim
and Manasseh, and all Judah as far
as the western sea; the Negeb and the 3
Plain; the valley of Jericho, the Vale
of Palm Trees, as far as Zoar. The 4
LORD said to him, 'This is the land
which I swore to Abraham, Isaac and
Jacob that I would give to their
descendants. I have let you see it with
your own eyes, but you shall not cross
over into it.'

There in the land of Moab Moses 5
the servant of the LORD died, as the
LORD had said. He was buried in a 6
valley in Moab opposite Beth-peor, but
to this day no one knows his burial-
place. Moses was a hundred and 7
twenty years old when he died; his
sight was not dimmed nor had his
vigour failed. The Israelites wept for 8
Moses in the lowlands of Moab for
thirty days; then the time of mourning for Moses was ended. And Joshua 9
son of Nun was filled with the spirit
of wisdom, for Moses had laid his
hands on him, and the Israelites
listened to him and did what the
LORD had commanded Moses.

There has never yet risen in Israel 10
a prophet like Moses, whom the LORD
knew face to face: remember all the 11
signs and portents which the LORD
sent him to show in Egypt to Pharaoh
and all his servants and the whole land;
remember the strong hand of Moses 12
and the terrible deeds which he did in
the sight of all Israel.

c and drive: *prob. rdg.*; *Heb.* together.   d draw out: *prob. rdg.*; *Heb. obscure.*   e Or of.
f *Prob. rdg.*; *Heb.* under.   g Or new wine.

THE BOOK OF
JOSHUA

Israel prepares to occupy Canaan

1 AFTER THE DEATH of Moses the servant of the LORD, the LORD said to Joshua son of Nun, his assis- 2 tant, 'My servant Moses is dead; now it is for you to cross the Jordan, you and this whole people of Israel, to the 3 land which I am giving them. Every place where you set foot is yours: I have given it to you, as I promised 4 Moses. From the desert and the Lebanon to the great river, the river Euphrates, and across all the Hittite country westwards to the Great Sea,*a* 5 all this shall be your land. No one will ever be able to stand against you: as I was with Moses, so will I be with you; I will not fail you or forsake you. 6 Be strong, be resolute; it is you who are to put this people in possession of the land which I swore to give to their 7 fathers. Only be strong and resolute; observe diligently all the law which my servant Moses has given you. You must not turn from it to right or left, if you would prosper wherever you 8 go. This book of the law must ever be on your lips; you must keep it in mind day and night so that you may diligently observe all that is written in it. Then you will prosper and be 9 successful in all that you do. This is my command: be strong, be resolute; do not be fearful or dismayed, for the LORD your God is with you wherever 10 you go.' Then Joshua told the officers 11 to pass through the camp and give this order to the people: 'Get food ready to take with you; for within three days you will be crossing the Jordan to occupy the country which the LORD your God is giving you to 12 possess.' To the Reubenites, the Gadites, and the half tribe of Manasseh, 13 Joshua said, 'Remember the command which Moses the servant of the LORD gave you when he said, "The LORD your God will grant you security here and will give you this territory." 14 Your wives and dependants and your herds may stay east of the Jordan in the territory which Moses has given

you, but for yourselves, all the warriors among you must cross over as a fighting force at the head of your kinsmen. You must help them, until 15 the LORD grants them security like you and they too take possession of the land which the LORD your God is giving them. You may then return to the land which is your own possession, the territory which Moses the servant of the LORD has given you east of the Jordan.' They answered 16 Joshua, 'Whatever you tell us, we will do; wherever you send us, we will go. As we obeyed Moses, so will we obey 17 you; and may the LORD your God be with you as he was with Moses! Who- 18 ever rebels against your authority, and fails to carry out all your orders, shall be put to death. Only be strong and resolute.'

Rahab and the spies

Joshua son of Nun sent two spies **2** out from Shittim secretly with orders to reconnoitre the country. The two men came to Jericho and went to the house of a prostitute named Rahab, and spent the night there. It was 2 reported to the king of Jericho that some Israelites had arrived that night to explore the country. So the king 3 sent to Rahab and said, 'Bring out the men who have come to you and are now in your house; they are here to explore the whole country.' The wo- 4 man, who had taken the two men and hidden them,*b* 'Yes, the men did come to me, but I did not know where they came from; and when it 5 was time to shut the gate at nightfall, they had gone. I do not know where they were going, but if you hurry after them, you will catch them up.' In fact, she had taken them up on to 6 the roof and concealed them among the stalks of flax which she had laid out there in rows. The messengers 7 went in pursuit of them down the road to the fords of the Jordan, and the gate was closed as soon as they had gone out. The men had not yet 8 settled down, when Rahab came up

a Or the Mediterranean Sea.   *b* Prob. rdg.; Heb. him.

9 to them on the roof and said to them, 'I know that the LORD has given this land to you, that terror of you has descended upon us all, and that because of you the whole country is 10 panic-stricken. For we have heard how the LORD dried up the water of the Red Sea[c] before you when you came out of Egypt, and what you did to Sihon and Og, the two Amorite kings beyond the Jordan, whom you put 11 to death. When we heard this, our courage failed us; your coming has left no spirit in any of us; for the LORD your God is God in heaven above and 12 on earth below. Swear to me now by the LORD that you will keep faith with my family, as I have kept faith with you. Give me a token of good 13 faith; promise that you will spare the lives of my father and mother, my brothers and sisters and all who belong to them, and save us from 14 death.' The men replied, 'Our lives for yours, so long as you do not betray our business. When the LORD gives us the country, we will deal honestly 15 and faithfully by you.' She then let them down through an opening by a rope; for the house where she lived 16 was on an angle of the wall. 'Take to the hills,' she said, 'or the pursuers will come upon you. Hide yourselves there for three days until they come 17 back, and then go on your way.' The men warned her that they would be released from the oath she had made 18 them take unless she did what they told her. 'When we enter the land,' they said, 'you must fasten this strand of scarlet cord in the opening through which you have lowered us, and get everybody together here in the house, your father and mother, your brothers 19 and all your family. If anybody goes out of doors into the street, his blood shall be on his own head; we shall be quit of the oath. But if a hand is laid on anyone who stays indoors with you, his blood shall be on our heads. 20 Remember too that, if you betray our business, then we shall be quit of 21 the oath you have made us take.' She replied, 'It shall be as you say', and sent them away. They set off, and she fastened the strand of scarlet cord in 22 the opening. The men made their way into the hills and stayed there three days until the pursuers returned. They had searched all along the road, 23 but had not found them.[d] The two

men then turned and came down from the hills, crossed the river and returned to Joshua son of Nun. They told him all that had happened to them and said to him, 'The LORD has 24 put the whole country into our hands, and now all its people are panic-stricken at our approach.'

Israel crosses the Jordan

Joshua rose early in the morning, and 3 he and all the Israelites set out from Shittim and came to the Jordan, where they encamped before crossing the river. At the end of three days the 2 officers passed through the camp, and 3 gave this order to the people: 'When you see the Ark of the Covenant of the LORD your God being carried forward by the levitical priests, then you too shall leave your positions and set out. Follow it, but do not go close 4 to it; keep some distance behind, about a thousand yards. This will show you the way you are to go, for you have not travelled this way before.' Joshua then said to the peo- 5 ple, 'Hallow yourselves, for tomorrow the LORD will do a great miracle among you.' To the priests he said, 6 'Lift up the Ark of the Covenant and pass in front of the people.' So they lifted up the Ark of the Covenant and went in front of the people. Then the 7 LORD said to Joshua, 'Today I will begin to make you stand high in the eyes of all Israel, and they shall know that I will be with you as I was with Moses. Give orders to the priests who 8 carry the Ark of the Covenant, and tell them that when they come to the edge of the waters of the Jordan, they are to take their stand in the river.'

Then Joshua said to the Israelites, 9 'Come here and listen to the words of the LORD your God. By this you shall 10 know that the living God is among you and that he will drive out before you the Canaanites, the Hittites, the Hivites, the Perizzites, the Girgash-ites, the Amorites, and the Jebusites: the Ark of the Covenant of the LORD,[e] 11 the lord of all the earth, is to cross the Jordan at your head. Choose twelve 12 men from the tribes of Israel, one man from each tribe. When the priests 13 carrying the Ark of the LORD, the lord of all the earth, set foot in the waters of the Jordan, then the waters of the Jordan will be cut off; the water coming down from upstream will

---

c Or the Sea of Reeds.   d three days . . . found them: or three days while the pursuers scoured the land and searched all along the road, but did not find them.   e of the LORD: prob. rdg., cp. verse 17; Heb. om.

D

14 stand piled up like a bank.' So the people set out from their tents to cross the Jordan, with the priests in front of them carrying the Ark of the Cove-
15 nant. Now the Jordan is in full flood in all its reaches throughout the time of harvest. When the priests reached the Jordan and dipped their feet in
16 the water at the edge, the water coming down from upstream was brought to a standstill; it piled up like a bank for a long way back, as far as Adam, a town near Zarethan. The waters coming down to the Sea of the Arabah, the Dead Sea, were completely cut off, and the people crossed
17 over opposite Jericho. The priests carrying the Ark of the Covenant of the LORD stood firm on the dry bed in the middle of the Jordan; and all Israel passed over on dry ground until the whole nation had crossed the river.

The twelve memorial stones

4 When the whole nation had finished crossing the Jordan, the LORD said to
2 Joshua, 'Take twelve men from the
3 people, one from each tribe, and order them to lift up twelve stones from this place, out of the middle of the Jordan, where the feet of the priests stood firm. They are to carry them across and set them down in the camp
4 where you spend the night.' Joshua summoned the twelve men whom he had chosen out of the Israelites, one
5 man from each tribe, and said to them, 'Cross over in front of the Ark of the LORD your God as far as the middle of the Jordan, and let each of you take a stone and hoist it on his shoulder, one
6 for each of the tribes of Israel. These stones are to stand as a memorial among you; and in days to come, when your children ask you what
7 these stones mean, you shall tell them how the waters of the Jordan were cut off before the Ark of the Covenant of the LORD when it crossed the Jordan. Thus these stones will always
8 be a reminder to the Israelites.' The Israelites did as Joshua had commanded: they lifted up twelve stones from the middle of the Jordan, as the LORD had instructed Joshua, one for each of the tribes of Israel, carried them across to the camp and set them down there.
9 Joshua set up twelve stones in the middle of the Jordan at the place where the priests stood who carried the Ark of the Covenant, and there

they are to this day. The priests carry-10 ing the Ark remained standing in the middle of the Jordan until every command which the LORD had told Joshua to give to the people was fulfilled, and the people had made good speed across. When all the people 11 had finished crossing, then the Ark of the LORD crossed, and the priests with it.*f* At the head of the Israelites, 12 there crossed over the Reubenites, the Gadites, and the half tribe of Manasseh, as a fighting force, as Moses had told them to do; about forty thousand 13 strong, drafted for active service, they crossed over to the lowlands of Jericho in the presence of the LORD to do battle.

That day the LORD made Joshua 14 stand very high in the eyes of all Israel, and the people revered him, as they had revered Moses all his life.

The LORD said to Joshua, 'Com-15 ⲓ mand the priests carrying the Ark of the Tokens to come up from the Jordan.' So Joshua commanded the 17 priests to come up from the Jordan; and when the priests carrying the Ark 18 of the Covenant of the LORD came up from the river-bed, they had no sooner set foot on dry land than the waters of the Jordan came back to their place and filled up all its reaches as before. On the tenth day of the first month 19 the people came up out of the Jordan and camped in Gilgal in the district east of Jericho, and there Joshua set 20 up the twelve stones which they had taken from the Jordan. He said to the 21 Israelites, 'In days to come, when your descendants ask their fathers what these stones mean, you shall explain 22 that the Jordan was dry when Israel crossed over, and that the LORD your 23 God dried up the waters of the Jordan in front of you until you had gone across, just as the LORD your God did at the Red Sea when ⁺he dried it up for us until we had crossed. Thus 24 all people on earth will know how strong is the hand of the LORD; and thus they will stand in awe of the LORD your God for ever.'

Israel at Gilgal

When all the Amorite kings to the 5 west of the Jordan and all the Canaanite kings by the sea-coast heard that the LORD had dried up the waters before the advance of the Israelites until they had crossed, their courage melted away and there was no more

f Prob. rdg.; Heb. adds before the people.

spirit left in them for fear of the Israelites.

2 At that time the LORD said to Joshua, 'Make knives of flint, seat yourself, and make Israel a circum-
3 cised people again.' Joshua thereupon made knives of flint and circumcised the Israelites at Gibeath-haaraloth.*g*
4 This is why Joshua circumcised them: all the males who came out of Egypt, all the fighting men, had died in the wilderness on the journey from Egypt.
5 The people who came out of Egypt had all been circumcised, but not those who had been born in the wil-
6 derness during the journey. For the Israelites travelled in the wilderness for forty years, until the whole nation, all the fighting men among them, had passed away, all who came out of Egypt and had disobeyed the voice of the LORD. The LORD swore that he would not allow any of these to see the land which he had sworn to their fathers to give us, a land flowing with
7 milk and honey. So it was their sons, whom he had raised up in their place, that Joshua circumcised; they were uncircumcised because they had not been circumcised on the journey.
8 When the circumcision of the whole nation was complete, they stayed where they were in camp until they
9 had recovered. The LORD then said to Joshua, 'Today I have rolled away from you the reproaches of the Egyptians.' Therefore the place is called Gilgal*h* to this very day.
10 The Israelites encamped in Gilgal, and at sunset on the fourteenth day of the month they kept the Passover
11 in the lowlands of Jericho. On the day after the Passover, they ate their un-leavened cakes and parched grain, and that day it was the produce of
12 the country. It was from that day, when they first ate the produce of the country, that the manna ceased. The Israelites received no more manna; and that year they ate what had grown in the land of Canaan.

The captain of the LORD's army

13 When Joshua came near Jericho he looked up and saw a man standing in front of him with a drawn sword in his hand. Joshua went up to him and said, 'Are you for us or for our ene-
14 mies?' And the man said to him, 'I am here as captain of the army of the LORD.' Joshua fell down before him, face to the ground, and said, 'What

have you to say to your servant, my lord?' The captain of the LORD's army 15 said to him, 'Take off your sandals; the place where you are standing is holy'; and Joshua did so.

Destruction of Jericho

Jericho was bolted and barred against 6 the Israelites; no one went out, no one came in. The LORD said to Joshua, 2 'Look, I have delivered Jericho and her king*i* into your hands. You shall 3 march round the city with all your fighting men, making the circuit of it once, for six days running. Seven 4 priests shall go in front of the Ark carrying seven trumpets made from rams' horns. On the seventh day you shall march round the city seven times and the priests shall blow their trumpets. At the blast of the rams' 5 horns, when you hear the trumpet sound, the whole army shall raise a great shout; the wall of the city will collapse and the army shall advance, every man straight ahead.' So Joshua 6 son of Nun summoned the priests and gave them their orders: 'Take up the Ark of the Covenant; let seven priests with seven trumpets of ram's horn go in front of the Ark of the LORD.' Then he said to the army, 'March on 7 and make the circuit of the city, and let the men drafted from the two and a half tribes go in front of the Ark of the LORD.' When Joshua had spoken 8 to the army, the seven priests carrying the seven trumpets of ram's horn before the LORD passed on and blew the trumpets, with the Ark of the Covenant of the LORD following them. The drafted men marched in front of 9 the priests who blew the trumpets, and the rearguard followed the Ark, the trumpets sounding as they marched. But Joshua ordered the army not 10 to shout, or to raise their voices or utter a word, till the day came when he would tell them to shout; then they were to give a loud shout. Thus 11 he caused the Ark of the LORD to go round the city, making the circuit of it once, and then they went back to the camp and spent the night there. Joshua rose early in the morning and 12 the priests took up the Ark of the LORD. The seven priests carrying the 13 seven trumpets of ram's horn went marching in front of the Ark of the LORD, blowing the trumpets as they went, with the drafted men in front of them and the rearguard following

g That is the Hill of Foreskins.   *h That is* Rolling Stones.   *i Prob. rdg.; Heb. adds* the fighting men.

the Ark of the LORD, the trumpets
14 sounding as they marched. They
marched round the city once on the
second day and returned to the camp;
15 this they did for six days. But on the
seventh day they rose at dawn and
marched seven times round the city
in the same way; that was the only
day on which they marched round
16 seven times. The seventh time the
priests blew the trumpets and Joshua
said to the army, 'Shout! The LORD
17 has given you the city. The city shall
be under solemn ban: everything in
it belongs to the LORD. No one is to
be spared except the prostitute Rahab and everyone who is with her in
the house, because she hid the men
18 whom we sent. And you must beware
of coveting anything that is forbidden
under the ban; you must take none of
it for yourselves; this would put the
Israelite camp itself under the ban
19 and bring trouble on it. All the silver
and gold, all the vessels of copper and
iron, shall be holy; they belong to
the LORD and they must go into the
20 LORD's treasury.' So they blew the
trumpets, and when the army heard
the trumpet sound, they raised a great
shout, and down fell the walls, every man
21 straight ahead, and took it. Under
the ban they destroyed everything
in the city; they put everyone to the
sword, men and women, young and
old, and also cattle, sheep, and asses.
22   But the two men who had been
sent out as spies were told by Joshua
to go into the prostitute's house and
bring out her and all who belonged
23 to her, as they had sworn to do. So the
young men went and brought out
Rahab, her father and mother, her
brothers and all who belonged to her.
They brought out the whole family
and left them outside the Israelite
24 camp. They then set fire to the city
and everything in it, except that they
deposited the silver and gold and the
vessels of copper and iron in the
25 treasury of the LORD's house. Thus
Joshua spared the lives of Rahab the
prostitute, her household and all who
belonged to her, because she had
hidden the men whom Joshua had
sent to Jericho as spies; she and her
family settled permanently among the
26 Israelites. It was then that Joshua laid
this curse on Jericho:

May the LORD's curse light on the man
    who comes forward

to rebuild this city of Jericho:
the laying of its foundations shall cost
    him his eldest son,
the setting up of its gates shall cost
    him his youngest.

Thus the LORD was with Joshua, 27
and his fame spread throughout the
country.

Achan's sin

But the Israelites defied the ban: 7
Achan son of Carmi, son of Zabdi,
son of Zerah, of the tribe of Judah,
took some of the forbidden things,
and the LORD was angry with the
Israelites.
Joshua sent men from Jericho with 2
orders to go up to Ai, near Beth-aven,
east of Bethel, and see how the land
lay; so the men went up and explored
Ai. They returned to Joshua and 3
reported that there was no need for
the whole army to move: 'Let some
two or three thousand men go forward to attack Ai. Do not make the
whole army toil up there; the population is small.' And so about three 4
thousand men went up, but they
turned tail before the men of Ai, who 5
killed some thirty-six of them; they
chased them all the way from the
gate to the Quarries[j] and killed them
on the pass. At this the courage of the
people melted and flowed away like
water. Joshua and the elders of Israel 6
rent their clothes and flung themselves
face downwards to the ground; they
lay before the Ark of the LORD till
evening and threw dust on their heads.
Joshua said, 'Alas, O Lord GOD, why 7
didst thou bring this people across
the Jordan only to hand us over to
the Amorites to be destroyed? If only
we had been content to settle on the
other side of the Jordan! I beseech 8
thee, O Lord; what can I say, now
that Israel has been routed by the
enemy? When the Canaanites and all 9
the natives of the country hear of this,
they will come swarming around us
and wipe us off the face of the earth.
What wilt thou do then for the honour
of thy great name?'
The LORD said to Joshua, 'Stand 10
up; why lie prostrate on your face?
Israel has sinned: they have broken 11
the covenant which I laid upon them,
by taking forbidden things for themselves. They have stolen them, and
concealed it by mingling them with
their own possessions. That is why the 12
Israelites cannot stand against their

j Or to Shebarim.

enemies: they are put to flight because they have brought themselves under the ban. Unless they destroy every single thing among them that is forbidden under the ban, I will be 13 with them no longer. Stand up; you must hallow the people; tell them they must hallow themselves for tomorrow. Tell them, These are the words of the LORD the God of Israel: You have forbidden things among you, Israel; you cannot stand against your enemies un- 14 til you have rid yourselves of them. In the morning come forward tribe by tribe, and the tribe which the LORD chooses shall come forward clan by clan; the clan which the LORD chooses shall come forward family by family; and the family which the LORD chooses 15 shall come forward man by man. The man who is chosen as the harbourer of forbidden things shall be burnt, he and all that is his, because he has broken the covenant of the LORD and 16 committed outrage in Israel.' Early in the morning Joshua rose and brought Israel forward tribe by tribe, and the tribe of Judah was chosen. 17 He brought forward the clans of Judah, and the clan of Zerah was chosen; then the clan of Zerah family by family, and the family of Zabdi 18 was chosen. He brought that family forward man by man, and Achan son of Carmi, son of Zabdi, son of Zerah, of the tribe of Judah, was chosen. 19 Then Joshua said to Achan, 'My son, give honour to the LORD the God of Israel and make your confession to him: tell me what you have 20 done, hide nothing from me.' Achan answered Joshua, 'I confess, I have sinned against the LORD the God of 21 Israel. This is what I did: among the booty I caught sight of a fine mantle from Shinar, two hundred shekels of silver, and a bar of gold weighing fifty shekels. I coveted them and I took them. You will find them hidden in the ground inside my tent, with the 22 silver underneath.' So Joshua sent messengers, who ran to the tent, and there was the stuff[k] hidden in the tent 23 with the silver underneath. They took the things from the tent, brought them to Joshua and all the Israelites, and spread them out before the LORD. 24 Then Joshua took Achan son of Zerah, with the silver, the mantle, and the bar of gold, together with his sons and daughters, his oxen, his asses, and his sheep, his tent, and everything he had,

and he and all Israel brought them up to the Vale of Achor.[l] Joshua said, 25 'What trouble you have brought on us! Now the LORD will bring trouble on you.' Then all the Israelites stoned him to death; and they raised a great 26 pile of stones over him, which remains to this day. So the LORD's anger was abated. That is why to this day that place is called the Vale of Achor.

Destruction of Ai

The LORD said to Joshua, 'Do not be 8 fearful or dismayed; take the whole army and attack Ai. I deliver the king of Ai into your hands, him and his people, his city and his country. Deal 2 with Ai and her king as you dealt with Jericho and her king; but you may keep for yourselves the cattle and any other spoil that you may take. Set an ambush for the city to the west of it.' So Joshua and all the army prepared 3 for the assault on Ai. He chose thirty thousand fighting men and dispatched them by night, with these orders: 'Lie 4 in ambush to the west of the city, not far from it, and all of you hold yourselves in readiness. I myself will 5 approach the city with the rest of the army, and when the enemy come out to meet us as they did last time, we shall take to flight before them. Then 6 they will come out and pursue us until we have drawn them away from the city, thinking that we have taken to flight as we did last time. While we are in flight, come out from your ambush 7 and occupy the city; the LORD your God will deliver it into your hands. When you have taken it, set it on fire. 8 Thus you will do what the LORD commands. These are your orders.' So 9 Joshua sent them off, and they went to the place of ambush and waited between Bethel and Ai to the west of Ai, while Joshua spent the night with the army.

Early in the morning Joshua rose, 10 mustered the army and marched against Ai, he himself and the elders of Israel at its head. All the armed 11 forces with him marched on until they came within sight of the city. They encamped north of Ai, with the valley between them and the city; but Joshua 12 took some five thousand men and set them in ambush between Bethel and Ai to the west of the city.[m] When the 14 king of Ai saw them, he and the citizens rose with all speed that morning and marched out to do battle against

---

k Or the mantle.   l That is Trouble.   m So Sept.; Heb. adds (13) So the army pitched camp to the north of the city, and the rearguard to the west, while Joshua went that night into the valley.

Israel; he did not know that there was an ambush set for him to the
15 west of the city. Joshua and all the Israelites made as if they were routed by them and fled towards the wilder-
16 ness, and all the people in the city were called out in pursuit. So they pursued Joshua and were drawn away
17 from the city. Not a man was left in Ai; they had all gone out in pursuit of the Israelites and during the pursuit had left the city undefended.
18 Then the LORD said to Joshua, 'Point towards Ai with the dagger you are holding, for I will deliver the city into your hands.' So Joshua pointed with his dagger towards Ai.
19 At his signal, the men in ambush rose quickly from their places and, entering the city at a run, took it and
20 promptly set fire to it. The men of Ai looked back and saw the smoke from the city already going up to the sky; they were powerless to make their escape in any direction, and the Israelites who had feigned flight towards the wilderness turned on their
21 pursuers. For when Joshua and all the Israelites saw that the ambush had seized the city and that smoke was already going up from it, they turned
22 and fell upon the men of Ai. Those who had come out to meet the Israelites were now hemmed in with Israelites on both sides of them, and the Israelites cut them down until there was not a single survivor, nor
23 had any escaped. The king of Ai was taken alive and brought to Joshua.
24 When the Israelites had cut down to the last man all the citizens of Ai who were in the open country or in the wilderness to which they had pursued them, and the massacre was complete, they all turned back to Ai and put it
25 to the sword. The number who were killed that day, men and women, was twelve thousand, the whole popula-
26 tion of Ai. Joshua held out his dagger and did not draw back his hand until he had put to death all who lived in
27 Ai; but the Israelites kept for themselves the cattle and any other spoil that they took, following the word
28 of the LORD spoken to Joshua. So Joshua burnt Ai to the ground, and left it the desolate ruined mound it
29 remains to this day. He hanged the king of Ai on a tree and left him there till sunset; and when the sun had set, he gave the order and they cut him down and flung down his body at the entrance of the city gate. Over the body

they raised a great pile of stones, which is there to this day.

Joshua records the law at Mount Ebal

30 At that time Joshua built an altar
31 to the LORD the God of Israel on Mount Ebal. The altar was of blocks of undressed stone on which no tool of iron had been used, following the commands given to the Israelites by Moses the servant of the LORD, as is described in the book of the law of Moses. At the altar they offered whole-offerings to the LORD, and
32 slaughtered shared-offerings. There in the presence of the Israelites he engraved on blocks[n] of stone a copy of
33 the law of Moses. And all Israel, elders, officers, and judges, took their stand on either side of the Ark, facing the levitical priests who carried the Ark of the Covenant of the LORD—all Israel, native and alien alike. Half of them stood facing Mount Gerizim and half facing Mount Ebal, to fulfil the command of Moses the servant of the LORD that the blessing should be pro-
34 nounced first. Then Joshua recited the whole of the blessing and the cursing word by word, as they are
35 written in the book of the law. There was not a single word of all that Moses had commanded which he did not read aloud before the whole congregation of Israel, including the women and dependants and the aliens resident in their company.

The Gibeonites' ruse

9 When the news of these happenings reached all the kings west of the Jordan, in the hill-country, the Shephelah, and all the coast of the Great Sea running up to the Lebanon, the kings of the Hittites, Amorites, Canaanites,
2 Perizzites, Hivites, and Jebusites agreed to join forces and fight against Joshua and Israel.
3 When the inhabitants of Gibeon heard how Joshua had dealt with
4 Jericho and Ai, they adopted a ruse of their own. They went and disguised themselves, with old sacking for their asses, old wine-skins split and men-
5 ded, old and patched sandals for their feet, old clothing to wear, and by way of provisions nothing but dry and mouldy bread. They came to Joshua
6 in the camp at Gilgal and said to him and the Israelites, 'We have come from a distant country to ask you now to grant us a treaty.' The Israelites
7

n Or on the blocks.

said to the Hivites, 'But maybe you live in our neighbourhood: if so, how 8 can we grant you a treaty?' They said to Joshua, 'We are your slaves.' Joshua asked them who they were 9 and where they came from. 'Sir,' they replied, 'our country is very far away, and we have come because of the renown of the LORD your God. We have heard of his fame, of all that he 10 did to Egypt, and to the two Amorite kings east of the Jordan, Sihon king of Heshbon and Og king of Bashan 11 who lived at Ashtaroth. Our elders and all the people of our country told us to take provisions for the journey and come to meet you, and say, "We are your slaves; please grant us a 12 treaty." Look at our bread; it was hot from the oven when we packed it at home on the day we came away. 13 Now it is dry and mouldy. Look at the wine-skins; they were new when we filled them, and now they are all split; look at our clothes and our sandals, worn out by the long journey.' 14 The chief men of the community accepted some of their provisions, and did not at first seek guidance 15 from the LORD. So Joshua received them peaceably and granted them a treaty, promising to spare their lives, and the chiefs pledged their faith to them on oath.

16 Within three days of granting them the treaty, the Israelites learnt that they were in fact neighbours and 17 lived near by. So the Israelites set out and on the third day they reached their cities; these were Gibeon, Ke-phirah, Beeroth, and Kiriath-jearim. 18 The Israelites did not slaughter them, because of the oath which the chief men of the community had sworn to them by the LORD the God of Israel, but the people were all indignant with 19 their chiefs. The chiefs all replied to the assembled people, 'But we swore an oath to them by the LORD the God of Israel; we cannot touch them now. 20 What we will do is this: we will spare their lives so that the oath which we swore to them may bring no harm 21 upon us. But though their lives must be spared, they shall be set to chop wood and draw water for the community.' The people agreed to do as 22 their chiefs had said. Joshua summoned the Gibeonites and said, 'Why did you play this trick on us? You told us that you live a long way off, 23 when you are near neighbours. There is a curse upon you for this: for all time you shall provide us with slaves,

to chop wood and draw water for the house of my God.' They answered 24 Joshua, 'We were told, sir, that the LORD your God had commanded Moses his servant to give you the whole country and to exterminate all its inhabitants; so because of you we were in terror of our lives, and that is why we did this. We are in your power: 25 do with us whatever you think right and proper.' What he did was this: 26 he saved them from death at the hands of the Israelites, and they did not kill them; but thenceforward he 27 set them to chop wood and draw water for the community and for the altar of the LORD. And to this day they do it at the place which the LORD chose.

Joshua defeats the Amorites in Gibeon

When Adoni-zedek king of Jerusalem 10 heard that Joshua had captured Ai and destroyed it (for Joshua had dealt with Ai and her king as he had dealt with Jericho and her king), and that the inhabitants of Gibeon had made their peace with Israel and were living among them, he was greatly 2 alarmed; for Gibeon was a large place, like a royal city: it was larger than Ai, and its men were all good fighters. So Adoni-zedek king of Jerusalem 3 sent to Hoham king of Hebron, Pi-ram king of Jarmuth, Japhia king of Lachish, and Debir king of Eglon, and said, 'Come up and help me, and 4 we will attack the Gibeonites, because they have made their peace with Joshua and the Israelites.' So the five 5 Amorite kings, the kings of Jerusalem, Hebron, Jarmuth, Lachish, and Eglon, joined forces and advanced to take up their positions for the attack on Gibeon. But the men of Gibeon sent 6 this message to Joshua in the camp at Gilgal: 'We are your slaves, do not abandon us, come quickly to our relief. All the Amorite kings in the hill-country have joined forces against us; come and help us.' So Joshua 7 went up from Gilgal with all his forces and all his fighting men. The LORD 8 said to Joshua, 'Do not be afraid of them; I have delivered them into your hands, and not a man will be able to stand against you.' Joshua 9 came upon them suddenly, after marching all night from Gilgal. The 10 LORD threw them into confusion before the Israelites, and Joshua defeated them utterly in Gibeon; he pursued them down the pass of Beth-horon

and kept up the slaughter as far as
11 Azekah and Makkedah. As they were
fleeing from Israel down the pass, the
LORD hurled great hailstones at them
out of the sky all the way to Azekah:
more died from the hailstones than
the Israelites slew by the sword.

The sun stands still

12 On that day when the LORD delivered
the Amorites into the hands of Israel,
Joshua spoke with the LORD, and he
said in the presence of Israel:

Stand still, O Sun, in Gibeon;
stand, Moon, in the Vale of Aijalon.

13 So the sun stood still and the moon
halted until a nation had taken vengeance on its enemies, as indeed is
written in the Book of Jashar.[o] The
sun stayed in mid heaven and made
no haste to set for almost a whole day.
14 Never before or since has there been
such a day as this day on which the
LORD listened to the voice of a man;
15 for the LORD fought for Israel. So
Joshua and all the Israelites returned
to the camp at Gilgal.

Joshua advances into Canaan

16 The five kings fled and hid themselves
17 in a cave at Makkedah, and Joshua
was told that they had been found
18 hidden in this cave. Joshua replied,
'Roll some great stones to the mouth
of the cave and post men there to
19 keep watch over the kings. But you
must not stay; keep up the pursuit,
attack your enemies from the rear and
do not let them reach their cities; the
LORD your God has delivered them
20 into your hands.' When Joshua and
the Israelites had finished the work
of slaughter and all had been put to
the sword—except a few survivors
who escaped and entered the fortified
21 cities—the whole army rejoined Joshua
at Makkedah in peace; not a man
of the Israelites suffered so much
22 as a scratch on his tongue. Then
Joshua said, 'Open the mouth of the
cave, and bring me out those five
23 kings.' They did so; they brought the
five kings out of the cave, the kings of
Jerusalem, Hebron, Jarmuth, Lachish,
24 and Eglon. When they had brought
them to Joshua, he summoned all the
Israelites and said to the commanders
of the troops who had served with him,
'Come forward and put your feet on
the necks of these kings.' So they
came forward and put their feet on

their necks. Joshua said to them, 'Do 25
not be fearful or dismayed; be strong
and resolute; for the LORD will do
this to every enemy you fight against.'
And he struck down the kings and 26
slew them; then he hung their bodies
on five trees, where they remained
hanging till evening. At sunset, on 27
Joshua's orders they took them down
from the trees and threw them into
the cave in which they had hidden;
they piled great stones against its
mouth, and there the stones are to
this day.[p]

On that same day, Joshua captured 28
Makkedah and put both king and
people to the sword, destroying both
them and every living thing in the
city. He left no survivor, and he dealt
with the king of Makkedah as he had
dealt with the king of Jericho. Then 29
Joshua and all the Israelites marched
on from Makkedah to Libnah and
attacked it. The LORD delivered the 30
city and its king to the Israelites, and
they put its people and every living
thing in it to the sword; they left no
survivor there, and dealt with its king
as they had dealt with the king of
Jericho. From Libnah Joshua and all 31
the Israelites marched on to Lachish,
took up their positions and attacked
it. The LORD delivered Lachish into 32
their hands; they took it on the
second day and put every living thing
in it to the sword, as they had done at
Libnah.

Meanwhile Horam king of Gezer 33
had advanced to the relief of Lachish;
but Joshua struck him down, both
king and people, and not a man of
them survived. Then Joshua and all 34
the Israelites marched on from Lachish to Eglon, took up their positions
and attacked it; that same day they 35
captured it and put its inhabitants
to the sword, destroying every living
thing in it as they had done at Lachish. From Eglon Joshua and all the 36
Israelites advanced to Hebron and
attacked it. They captured it and put 37
its king to the sword together with
every living thing in it and in all its
villages; as at Eglon, he left no survivor, destroying it and every living
thing in it. Then Joshua and all the 38
Israelites wheeled round towards Debir and attacked it. They captured 39
the city with its king, and all its
villages, put them to the sword and
destroyed every living thing; they
left no survivor. They dealt with
Debir and its king as they had dealt

[o] Or the Book of the Upright.   [p] and there . . . day: or on this very day.

40 So Joshua massacred the population of the whole region—the hill-country, the Negeb, the Shephelah, the watersheds—and all their kings. He left no survivor, destroying everything that drew breath, as the Lord the God of Israel had commanded. 41 Joshua carried the slaughter from Kadesh-barnea to Gaza, over the whole land of Goshen and as far as 42 Gibeon. All these kings he captured at the same time, and their country with them, for the Lord the God of Israel 43 fought for Israel. And Joshua returned with all the Israelites to the camp at Gilgal.

Joshua defeats Jabin and his allies

11 When Jabin king of Hazor heard of all this, he sent to Jobab king of Madon, to the kings of Shimron and Akshaph, 2 to the northern kings in the hill-country, in the Arabah opposite Kinnereth, in the Shephelah, and in the 3 district of Dor on the west, the Canaanites to the east and the west, the Amorites, Hittites, Perizzites, and Jebusites in the hill-country, and the Hivites below Hermon in the land of 4 Mizpah. They took the field with all their forces, a great horde countless as the grains of sand on the sea-shore, among them a great number of horses 5 and chariots. All these kings made common cause, and came and encamped at the waters of Merom to 6 fight against Israel. The Lord said to Joshua, 'Do not be afraid of them, for at this time tomorrow I shall deliver them to Israel all dead men; you shall hamstring their horses 7 and burn their chariots.' So Joshua and his army surprised them by the waters of Merom and fell upon them. 8 The Lord delivered them into the hands of Israel; they struck them down and pursued them as far as Greater Sidon, Misrephoth on the west, and the Vale of Mizpah on the east. They struck them down until not a 9 man was left alive. Joshua dealt with them as the Lord had commanded: he hamstrung their horses and burnt their chariots. 10 At this point Joshua turned his forces against Hazor, formerly the head of all these kingdoms. He captured the city and put its king to 11 death with the sword. They killed every living thing in it and wiped them

all out; they spared nothing that drew breath, and Hazor itself they destroyed by fire. So Joshua captured 12 these kings and their cities and put them to the sword, destroying them all, as Moses the servant of the Lord had commanded. The cities whose ruined 13 mounds are still standing were not burnt by the Israelites; it was Hazor alone that Joshua burnt. The Israel- 14 ites plundered all these cities and kept for themselves the cattle and any other spoil they took; but they put every living soul to the sword until they had destroyed every one; they did not leave alive any one that drew breath. The Lord laid his commands 15 on his servant Moses, and Moses laid these same commands on Joshua, and Joshua carried them out. Not one of the commands laid on Moses by the Lord did he leave unfulfilled.

Joshua conquers the whole country

And so Joshua took the whole coun- 16 try, the hill-country, all the Negeb, all the land of Goshen, the Shephelah, the Arabah, and the Israelite hill-country with the adjoining lowlands. His conquests extended from the bare 17 mountain which leads up to Seir as far as Baal-gad in the Vale of Lebanon under Mount Hermon. He took prisoner all their kings, struck them down and put them to death. It was 18 a long war that he fought against all these kingdoms. Except for the Hi- 19 vites who lived in Gibeon, not one of their cities came to terms with the Israelites; all were taken by storm. It 20 was the Lord's purpose that they should offer an obstinate resistance to the Israelites in battle, and that thus they should be annihilated without mercy and utterly destroyed,[q] as the Lord had commanded Moses.

It was then that Joshua proceeded 21 to wipe out the Anakim from the hill-country, from Hebron, Debir, Anab, all the hill-country of Judah and all the hill-country of Israel, destroying both them and their cities. No Ana- 22 kim were left in the land taken by the Israelites; they survived only in Gaza, Gath, and Ashdod. Thus Joshua took the whole country, 23 fulfilling all the commands that the Lord had laid on Moses; he assigned it as Israel's patrimony, allotting to each tribe its share; and the land was at peace.

q offer . . . destroyed: or obstinately engage the Israelites in battle so that they should annihilate them without mercy, only that he might destroy them . . .

Kings defeated by Moses

12 These are the names of the kings of the land whom the Israelites slew, and whose territory they occupied beyond the Jordan towards the sunrise from the gorge of the Arnon as far as Mount Hermon and all the Arabah on 2 the east. Sihon the Amorite king who lived in Heshbon: his rule extended from Aroer, which is on the edge of the gorge of the Arnon, along the middle of the gorge and over half Gilead as far as the gorge of the Jab-3 bok, the Ammonite frontier; along the Arabah as far as the eastern side of the Sea of Kinnereth and as far as the eastern side of the Sea of the Arabah, the Dead Sea, by the road to Beth-jeshimoth and from Teman under 4 the watershed of Pisgah. Og king of Bashan, one of the survivors of the Rephaim, who lived in Ashtaroth and 5 Edrei: he ruled over Mount Hermon, Salcah, all Bashan as far as the Geshurite and Maacathite borders, and half Gilead as far as the boundary of Sihon 6 king of Heshbon. Moses the servant of the LORD put them to death, he and the Israelites, and he gave their land to the Reubenites, the Gadites, and half the tribe of Manasseh, as their possession.

Kings defeated by Joshua

7 These are the names of the kings whom Joshua and the Israelites put to death beyond the Jordan to the west, from Baal-gad in the Vale of Lebanon as far as the bare mountain that leads up to Seir. Joshua gave their land to the Israelite tribes to be their posses-sion according to their allotted shares, 8 in the hill-country, the Shephelah, the Arabah, the watersheds, the wilder-ness, and the Negeb; lands of the Hittites, Amorites, Canaanites, Periz-9 zites, Hivites, and Jebusites. The king of Jericho; the king of Ai which is 10 beside Bethel; the king of Jerusalem; 11 the king of Hebron; the king of Jar-12 muth; the king of Lachish; the king of 13 Eglon; the king of Gezer; the king of 14 Debir; the king of Geder; the king 15 of Hormah; the king of Arad; the king 16 of Libnah; the king of Adullam; the king of Makkedah; the king of Bethel; 17 the king of Tappuah; the king of 18 Hepher; the king of Aphek; the king 19 of Aphek*r*-in-Sharon; the king of 20 Madon; the king of Hazor; the king of Shimron-meron; the king of Akshaph; 21 the king of Taanach; the king of

Megiddo; the king of Kedesh; the 22 king of Jokneam-in-Carmel; the king 23 of Dor in the district of Dor; the king of Gaiam-in-Galilee; the king of Tirzah: 24 thirty-one kings in all, one of each town.

Districts still to be occupied

By this time Joshua had become very **13** old, and the LORD said to him, 'You are now a very old man, and much of the country remains to be occupied. The country which remains is this: all 2 the districts of the Philistines and all the Geshurite country (this is 3 reckoned as Canaanite territory from Shihor to the east of Egypt as far north as Ekron; and it belongs to the five lords of the Philistines, those of Gaza, Ashdod, Ashkelon, Gath, and Ekron); all the districts of the Av-vim on the south; all the Canaan-4 ite country from the low-lying land which belongs to the Sidonians as far as Aphek, the Amorite frontier; 5 the land of the Gebalites and all the Lebanon to the east from Baal-gad under Mount Hermon as far as Lebo-hamath. I will drive out in favour of 6 the Israelites all the inhabitants of the hill-country from the Lebanon as far as Misrephoth on the west, and all the Sidonians. In the mean time you are to allot all this to the Israelites for their patrimony, as I have comman-ded you. Distribute this land now to 7 the nine tribes and half the tribe of Manasseh for their patrimony.' For 8 half the tribe of Manasseh and*s* with them the Reubenites and the Gadites had each taken their patrimony which Moses gave them east of the Jordan, as Moses the servant of the LORD had ordained. It started from Aroer 9 which is by the edge of the gorge of the Arnon, and the level land half-way along the gorge, and included all the tableland from Medeba as far as Dibon; all the cities of Sihon, the 10 Amorite king who ruled in Heshbon, as far as the Ammonite frontier; and 11 it also included Gilead and the Ge-shurite and Maacathite territory, and all Mount Hermon and the whole of Bashan as far as Salcah, all the king-12 dom of Og which he ruled from both Ashtaroth and Edrei in Bashan. He was a survivor of the remnant of the Rephaim, but Moses put them both to death and occupied their lands. But the Israelites did not drive out 13 the Geshurites and the Maacathites; the Geshurites and the Maacathites

r of Aphek: prob. rdg.; Heb. om.   *s For half . . . Manasseh and: prob. rdg.; Heb. om.*

live among the Israelites to this day.
14 The tribe of Levi, however, received no patrimony; the LORD the God of Israel is their patrimony, as he promised them.

Territory allotted to the tribes east of Jordan

15 So Moses allotted territory to the tribe of the Reubenites family by
16 family. Their territory started from Aroer which is by the edge of the gorge of the Arnon, and the level land half-way along the gorge, and included all the tableland as far as Medeba;
17 Heshbon and all its cities on the tableland, Dibon, Bamoth-baal, Beth-baal-
18 meon, Jahaz, Kedemoth, Mephaath,
19 Kiriathaim, Sibmah, Zereth-shahar
20 on the hill in the Vale, Beth-peor, the watershed of Pisgah, and Beth-
21 jeshimoth, all the cities of the tableland, all the kingdom of Sihon the Amorite king who ruled in Heshbon, whom Moses put to death together with the princes of Midian, Evi, Rekem, Zur, Hur, and Reba, the vassals of Sihon who dwelt in the
22 country. Balaam son of Beor, who practised augury, was among those whom the Israelites put to the sword.
23 The boundary of the Reubenites was the Jordan and the adjacent land: this is the patrimony of the Reubenites family by family, both the cities and their hamlets.
24   Moses allotted territory to the Gad-
25 ites family by family. Their territory was Jazer, all the cities of Gilead and half the Ammonite country as far as
26 Aroer which is east of Rabbah. It reached from Heshbon as far as Ramoth-mizpeh and Betonim, and from Mahanaim as far as the boun-
27 dary of Lo-debar; it included in the valley Beth-haram, Beth-nimrah, Succoth, and Zaphon, the rest of the kingdom of Sihon king of Heshbon. The boundary was the Jordan and the adjacent land as far as the end of the Sea of Kinnereth east of the Jor-
28 dan. This is the patrimony of the Gadites family by family, both the cities and their hamlets.
29   Moses allotted territory to the half tribe of Manasseh: it was for half the tribe of the Manassites family by
30 family. Their territory ran from Mahanaim and included all Bashan, all the kingdom of Og king of Bashan and all Havvoth-jair in Bashan—
31 sixty cities. Half Gilead, and Ashtaroth and Edrei the royal cities of Og in Bashan, belong to the sons of

Machir son of Manasseh on behalf of half the Machirites family by family.
     These are the territories which 32 Moses allotted to the tribes as their patrimonies in the lowlands of Moab east of the Jordan. But to the tribe of 33 Levi he gave no patrimony: the LORD the God of Israel is their patrimony, as he promised them.

Canaan divided by lot

Now follow the possessions which the 14 Israelites acquired in the land of Canaan, as Eleazar the priest, Joshua son of Nun, and the heads of the families of the Israelite tribes allotted them. They were assigned by lot, 2 following the LORD's command given through Moses, to the nine and a half tribes. To two and a half tribes Moses 3 had given patrimonies beyond the Jordan; but he gave none to the Levites as he did to the others. The tribe 4 of Joseph formed the two tribes of Manasseh and Ephraim. The Levites were given no share in the land, only cities to dwell in, with their common land for flocks and herds. So the 5 Israelites, following the LORD's command given to Moses, assigned the land.

Joshua gives Hebron to Caleb

Now the tribe of Judah had come to 6 Joshua in Gilgal, and Caleb son of Jephunneh the Kenizzite said to him, 'You remember what the LORD said to Moses the man of God concerning you and me at Kadesh-barnea. I was forty 7 years old when Moses the servant of the LORD sent me from there to explore the land, and I brought back an honest report. The others who went 8 with me discouraged the people, but I loyally carried out the purpose of the LORD my God. Moses swore an 9 oath that day and said, "The land on which you have set foot shall be your patrimony and your sons' after you as a possession for ever; for you have loyally carried out the purpose of the LORD my God." Well, the LORD has 10 spared my life as he promised; it is now forty-five years since he made this promise to Moses, at the time when Israel was journeying in the wilderness. Today I am eighty-five years old. I am still as strong as I was 11 on the day when Moses sent me out; I am as fit now for war as I was then and am ready to take the field again. Give me today this hill-country which 12 the LORD then promised me. You heard on that day that the Anakim were there and their cities were large and well fortified. Perhaps the LORD will be with me and I shall dispossess 13 them as he promised.' Joshua blessed Caleb and gave him Hebron for his 14 patrimony, and that is why Hebron remains to this day in the patrimony of Caleb son of Jephunneh the Kenizzite. It is because he loyally carried out the purpose of the LORD the God 15 of Israel. Formerly the name of Hebron was Kiriath-arba. This Arba was the chief man of the Anakim. And the land was at peace.

Territory allotted to Judah

15 This is the territory allotted to the tribe of the sons of Judah family by family. It started from the Edomite frontier at the wilderness of Zin and ran as far as the Negeb at its southern end, 2 and it had a common border with the Negeb at the end of the Dead Sea, where an inlet of water bends towards the 3 Negeb. It continued from the south by the ascent of Akrabbim, passed by Zin, went up from the south of Kadeshbarnea, passed by Hezron, went on to 4 Addar and turned round to Karka. It then passed along to Azmon, reached the Torrent of Egypt, and its limit was the sea. This was their southern boundary.
5   The eastern boundary is the Dead Sea as far as the mouth of the Jordan and the adjacent land northwards from the inlet of the sea, at the mouth 6 of the Jordan. The boundary goes up to Beth-hoglah; it passes north of Beth-arabah and thence to the stone 7 of Bohan son of Reuben, thence to Debir from the Vale of Achor, and then turns north to the districts[*t*] in front of the ascent of Adummim south of the gorge. The boundary then passes the waters of En-shemesh and the 8 limit there is En-rogel. It then goes up by the Valley of Ben-hinnom to the southern slope of the Jebusites (that is Jerusalem). Thence it goes up to the top of the hill which faces the Valley of Hinnom on the west; this is at the northern end of the Vale of 9 Rephaim. The boundary then bends round from the top of the hill to the spring of the waters of Nephtoah, runs round to the cities of Mount Ephron and round to Baalah, that 10 is Kiriath-jearim. It then continues westwards from Baalah to Mount Seir, passes on to the north side of the slope of Mount Jearim, that is Kesalon, down to Beth-shemesh and on

to Timnah. The boundary then goes 11 north to the slope of Ekron, bends round to Shikkeron, crosses to Mount Baalah and reaches Jabneel; its limit is the sea. The western boundary is 12 the Great Sea and the land adjacent. This is the whole circuit of the boundary of the tribe of Judah family by family.

Caleb receives Hebron

Caleb son of Jephunneh received his 13 share of the land within the tribe of Judah as the LORD had said to Joshua. It was Kiriath-arba, that is Hebron. This Arba was the ancestor of the Anakim. Caleb drove out the three 14 Anakim: these were Sheshai, Ahiman and Talmai, descendants of Anak. From there he attacked the inhabi- 15 tants of Debir; the name of Debir was formerly Kiriath-sepher. Caleb an- 16 nounced that whoever should attack Kiriath-sepher and capture it would receive his daughter Achsah in marriage. Othniel, son of Caleb's brother 17 Kenaz, captured it, and Caleb gave him his daughter Achsah. When she 18 came to him, he incited her to ask her father for a piece of land. As she sat on the ass, she made a noise, and Caleb asked her, 'What did you mean by that?' She replied, 'I want a 19 favour from you. You have put me in this dry Negeb; you must give me pools of water as well.' So Caleb gave her the upper pool and the lower pool.

The cities of Judah

This is the patrimony of the tribe of 20 the sons of Judah family by family. These are the cities belonging to the 21 tribe of Judah, the full count. By the Edomite frontier in the Negeb: Kabzeel, Eder, Jagur, Kinah, Dimonah, 22 Ararah,[*u*] Kedesh, Hazor, Ithnan, 23 Ziph, Telem, Bealoth, Hazor-hadattah, 24 25 Kerioth-hezron, Amam, Shema, Mo- 26 ladah, Hazar-gaddah, Heshmon, Beth- 27 pelet, Hazar-shual, Beersheba and 28 its villages, Baalah, Iyim, Ezem, 29 Eltolad, Kesil, Hormah, Ziklag, Mad- 30 31 mannah, Sansannah, Lebaoth, Shil- 32 him, Ain, and Rimmon: in all, twentynine cities with their hamlets.
   In the Shephelah: Eshtaol, Zorah, 33 Ashnah, Zanoah, En-gannim, Tappu- 34 ah, Enam, Jarmuth, Adullam, Socoh, 35 Azekah, Shaaraim, Adithaim, Gede- 36 rah, namely both parts of Gederah: fourteen cities with their hamlets. Zenan, Hadashah, Migdal-gad, Dilan, 37 38 Mizpeh, Joktheel, Lachish, Bozkath, 39

t Prob. rdg., cp. 18. 17; Heb. to Gilgal.   u Prob. rdg.; Heb. Adadah.

40 Eglon, Cabbon, Lahmas, Kithlish,
41 Gederoth, Beth-dagon, Naamah, and
Makkedah: sixteen cities with their
42 43 hamlets. Libnah, Ether, Ashan, Jiph-
44 tah, Ashnah, Nezib, Keilah, Achzib,
and Mareshah: nine cities with their
45 hamlets. Ekron, with its villages and
46 hamlets, and from Ekron westwards,
all the cities near Ashdod and their
47 hamlets. Ashdod with its villages
and hamlets, Gaza with its villages
and hamlets as far as the Torrent of
Egypt and the Great Sea and the
land adjacent.
48 In the hill-country: Shamir, Jattir,
49 Socoh, Dannah, Kiriath-sannah, that
50 is Debir, Anab, Eshtemoh, Anim,
51 Goshen, Holon, and Giloh: eleven
52 cities in all with their hamlets. Arab,
53 Dumah, Eshan, Janim, Beth-tappuah,
54 Aphek,ᵛ Humtah, Kiriath-arba, that
is Hebron, and Zior: nine cities in
55 all with their hamlets. Maon, Car-
56 mel, Ziph, Juttah, Jezreel, Jokdeam,
57 Zanoah, Cain, Gibeah, and Timnah:
ten cities in all with their hamlets.
58 59 Halhul, Beth-zur, Gedor, Maarath,
Beth-anoth, and Eltekon: six cities in
all with their hamlets. Tekoa, Ephrathah, that is Bethlehem, Peor, Etam,
Culom, Tatam, Sores, Carem, Gallim,
Baither, and Manach: eleven cities in
60 all with their hamlets. Kiriath-baal,
that is Kiriath-jearim, and Rabbah:
two cities with their hamlets.
61 In the wilderness: Beth-arabah,
62 Middin, Secacah, Nibshan, Ir-melach,
and En-gedi: six cities with their
hamlets.
63 At Jerusalem, the men of Judah
were unable to drive out the Jebusites who lived there, and to this day
Jebusites and men of Judah live together in Jerusalem.

*Territory allotted to Ephraim and
Manasseh*

16 This is the lot that fell to the sons of
Joseph: the boundary runs from the
Jordan at Jericho, east of the waters of
Jericho by the wilderness, and goes
up from Jericho into the hill-country
2 to Bethel. It runs on from Bethel to
Luz and crosses the Archite border at
3 Ataroth.ʷ Westwards it descends to
the boundary of the Japhletites as far
as the boundary of Lower Beth-horon
4 and Gezer; its limit is the sea. Here
Manasseh and Ephraim the sons of
Joseph received their patrimony.
5 This was the boundary of the
Ephraimites family by family: their

eastern boundary ran from Ataroth-
addar up to Upper Beth-horon. It 6
continued westwards to Michmethath
on the north, going round by the east
of Taanath-shiloh and passing by it
on the east of Janoah. It descends 7
from Janoah to Ataroth and Naarath,
touches Jericho and continues to the
Jordan, and from Tappuah it goes 8
westwards by the gorge of Kanah;
and its limit is the sea. This is the
patrimony of the tribe of Ephraim
family by family. There were also 9
cities reserved for the Ephraimites
within the patrimony of the Manassites, each of these cities with its
hamlets. They did not however drive 10
out the Canaanites who dwelt in
Gezer; the Canaanites have lived
among the Ephraimites to the present
day but have been subject to forced
labour in perpetuity.
This is the territory allotted to the 17
tribe of Manasseh, Joseph's eldest
son. Machir was Manasseh's eldest
son and father of Gilead, a fighting
man; Gilead and Bashan were allotted
to him.
The rest of the Manassites family 2
by family were the sons of Abiezer,
the sons of Helek, the sons of Asriel,
the sons of Shechem, the sons of
Hepher, and the sons of Shemida;
these were the male offspring of Manasseh son of Joseph family by family.
Zelophehad son of Hepher, son of 3
Gilead, son of Machir, son of Manasseh,
had no sons but only daughters: their
names were Mahlah, Noah, Hoglah,
Milcah and Tirzah. They presented 4
themselves before Eleazar the priest
and Joshua son of Nun, and before
the chiefs, and they said, 'The LORD
commanded Moses to allow us to inherit on the same footing as our kinsmen.' They were therefore given a
patrimony on the same footing as their
father's brothers according to the
commandment of the LORD.
There fell to Manasseh's lot ten 5
shares, apart from the country of
Gilead and Bashan beyond the Jordan, because Manasseh's daughters 6
had received a patrimony on the same
footing as his sons. The country of
Gilead belonged to the rest of Manasseh's sons. The boundary of Manasseh 7
reached from Asher as far as Michmethath, which is to the east of
Shechem, and thence southwards towards Jashub byˣ En-tappuah. The 8
territory of Tappuah belonged to

v Or Aphekah.   w Ataroth-addar *in 16. 5; 18. 13.*   x Jashub by: *prob. rdg.; Heb. the* inhabitants of.

Manasseh, but Tappuah itself was on the border of Manasseh and be-
9 longed to Ephraim. The boundary then followed the gorge of Kanah to the south of the gorge (these cities*y* belong to Ephraim, although they lie among the cities of Manasseh), the boundary of Manasseh being on the north of
10 the gorge; its limit was the sea. The southern side belonged to Ephraim and the northern to Manasseh, and their boundary was the sea. They marched with Asher on the north and Issachar
11 on the east. But in Issachar and Asher, Manasseh possessed Beth-shean and its villages, Ibleam and its villages, the inhabitants of Dor and its villages, the inhabitants of En-dor and its villages, the inhabitants of Taanach and its villages, and the inhabitants of Megiddo and its villages. (The
12 third is the district of Dor.*z*) The Manassites were unable to occupy these cities; the Canaanites main-tained their hold on that part of the
13 country. When the Israelites grew stronger, they put the Canaanites to forced labour, but they did not drive them out.
14 The sons of Joseph appealed to Joshua and said, 'Why have you given us only one lot and one share as our patrimony? We are a numerous people; so far the LORD has blessed
15 us.' Joshua replied, 'If you are so numerous, go up into the forest in the territory of the Perizzites and the Rephaim and clear it for yourselves. You are their near neighbours*a* in the
16 hill-country of Ephraim.' The sons of Joseph said, 'The hill-country is not enough for us; besides, all the Cana-anites have chariots of iron, those who inhabit the valley beside Beth-shean and its villages and also those in
17 the Vale of Jezreel.' Joshua replied to the tribes of Joseph, that is Ephraim and Manasseh: 'You are a numerous people with great resources. You shall
18 not have one lot only. The hill-country is yours. It is forest land; clear it and it shall be yours to its furthest limits. The Canaanites may be powerful and equipped with chariots of iron, but you will be able to drive them out.'

Division of the land at Shiloh

18 The whole community of the Isra-elites met together at Shiloh and established the Tent of the Presence there. The country now lay subdued

at their feet, but there remained 2 seven tribes among the Israelites who had not yet taken possession of the patrimonies which would fall to them. Joshua therefore said to them, 'How 3 much longer will you neglect to take possession of the land which the LORD the God of your fathers has given you? Appoint three men from each 4 tribe whom I may send out to travel through the whole country. They shall make a register showing the patri-mony suitable for each tribe, and come back to me, and then it can be 5 shared out among you in seven por-tions. Judah shall retain his boundary in the south, and the house of Joseph their boundary in the north. You 6 shall register the land in seven por-tions, bring the lists here, and I will cast lots for you in the presence of the LORD our God. Levi has no share 7 among you, because his share is the priesthood of the LORD; and Gad, Reuben, and the half tribe of Manas-seh have each taken possession of their patrimony east of the Jordan, which Moses the servant of the LORD gave them.' So the men set out on their 8 journeys. Joshua ordered the emis-saries to survey the country: 'Go through the whole country,' he said, 'survey it and return to me, and I will cast lots for you here before the LORD in Shiloh.' So the men went and passed 9 through the country; they registered it on a scroll, city by city, in seven portions, and came to Joshua in the camp at Shiloh. Joshua cast lots for 10 them in Shiloh before the LORD, and distributed the land there to the Israelites in their proper shares.

Territory allotted to Benjamin

This is the lot which fell to the tribe of 11 the Benjamites family by family. The territory allotted to them lay between the territory of Judah and Joseph. Their boundary at its northern corner 12 starts from the Jordan; it goes up the slope on the north side of Jericho, continuing westwards into the hill-country, and its limit there is the wilderness of Beth-aven. From there 13 it runs on to Luz, to the southern slope of Luz, that is Bethel, and down to Ataroth-addar over the hill-country south of Lower Beth-horon. The boundary then bends round at the 14 west corner southwards from the hill-country above Beth-horon, and its limit is Kiriath-baal, that is Kiriath-

jearim, a city of Judah. This is the
15 western side. The southern side starts
from the edge of Kiriath-jearim and
ends[b] at the spring of the waters of
16 Nephtoah. It goes down to the edge
of the hill to the east of the Valley of
Ben-hinnom, north of the Vale of
Rephaim, down the Valley of Hinnom,
to the southern slope of the Jebusites
17 and so to En-rogel. It then bends
round north and comes out at En-
shemesh, goes on to the districts in
front of the ascent of Adummim and
thence down to the Stone of Bohan
18 son of Reuben. It passes to the
northern side of the slope facing the
Arabah and goes down to the Arabah,
19 passing the northern slope of Beth-
hoglah, and its limit is the northern
inlet of the Dead Sea, at the southern
mouth of the Jordan. This forms the
20 southern boundary. The Jordan is the
boundary on the east side. This is
the patrimony of the Benjamites, the
complete circuit of their boundaries
family by family.

21　　The cities belonging to the tribe
of the Benjamites family by family
are: Jericho, Beth-hoglah, Emek-
22 keziz, Beth-arabah, Zemaraim, Beth-
3 24 el, Avvim, Parah, Ophrah, Kephar-
ammoni, Ophni, and Geba: twelve
25 cities in all with their hamlets. Gibeon,
26 Ramah, Beeroth, Mizpah, Kephirah,
7 28 Mozah, Rekem, Irpeel, Taralah, Zela,
Eleph, Jebus, that is Jerusalem,
Gibeah, and Kiriath-jearim: fourteen
cities in all with their hamlets. This is
the patrimony of the Benjamites
family by family.

Territory allotted to Simeon

19　The second lot cast was for Simeon,
the tribe of the Simeonites family by
family. Their patrimony was included
2 in that of Judah. For their patrimony
3 they had Beersheba,[c] Moladah, Hazar-
4 shual, Balah, Ezem, Eltolad, Beth-
5 ul, Hormah, Ziklag, Beth-marcaboth,
6 Hazar-susah, Beth-lebaoth, and Sha-
ruhen: in all, thirteen cities and their
7 hamlets. They had Ain, Rimmon,
Ether, and Ashan: four cities and their
8 hamlets, all the hamlets round these
cities as far as Baalath-beer, Ramath-
negeb. This was the patrimony of the
9 tribe of Simeon family by family. The
patrimony of the Simeonites was part
of the land allotted to the men of
Judah, because their share was larger
than they needed. The Simeonites

therefore had their patrimony within
the territory of Judah.

Territory allotted to Zebulun

The third lot fell to the Zebulunites 10
family by family. The boundary of
their patrimony extended to Shadud.[d]
Their boundary went up westwards 11
as far as Maraiah and touched Dab-
besheth and the gorge east of Jokneam. It turned back from Shadud 12
eastwards towards the sunrise up to
the border of Kisloth-tabor, on to
Daberath and up to Japhia. From 13
there it crossed eastwards towards
the sunrise to Gath-hepher, to Ittah-
kazin, out to Rimmon, and bent
round[e] to Neah. The northern bound- 14
ary went round to Hannathon, and
its limits were the Valley of Jiphtah-
el, Kattath, Nahalal, Shimron, Idalah, 15
and Bethlehem: twelve cities in all
with their hamlets. These cities and 16
their hamlets were the patrimony of
Zebulun family by family.

Territory allotted to Issachar

The fourth lot cast was for the sons 17
of Issachar family by family. Their 18
boundary included Jezreel, Kesulloth,
Shunem, Hapharaim, Shion, Anaha- 19
rath, Rabbith, Kishion, Ebez, Rem- 20 21
eth, En-gannim, En-haddah, and
Beth-pazzez. The boundary touched 22
Tabor, Shahazumah, and Beth-shemesh, and its limit was the Jordan:
sixteen cities with their hamlets. This 23
was the patrimony of the tribe of the
sons of Issachar family by family,
both cities and hamlets.

Territory allotted to Asher

The fifth lot cast was for the tribe of 24
the Asherites family by family. Their 25
boundary included Helkath, Hali, Be-
ten, Akshaph, Alammelech, Amad, 26
and Mishal; it touched Carmel on the
west and the swamp of Libnath. It 27
then turned back towards the east
to Beth-dagon, touched Zebulun and
the Valley of Jiphtah-el on the north
at Beth-emek and Neiel, and reached
Cabul on its northern side, and Ab- 28
don, Rehob, Hammon, and Kanah as
far as Greater Sidon. The boundary 29
turned at Ramah, going as far as the
fortress city of Tyre, and then back
again to Hosah, and its limits to the
west were Mehalbeh, Achzib, Acco,[f] 30
Aphek, and Rehob: twenty-two cities

b Prob. rdg.; Heb. adds westwards and ends . . .　　c Prob. rdg., cp. 1 Chr. 4. 28; Heb. adds and
Sheba.　　d Prob. rdg.; Heb. Sarid (similarly in verse 12).　　e and bent round: prob. rdg.; Heb.
which stretched.　　f Mehalbeh . . . Acco: prob. rdg.; Heb. from the district of Achzib and Ummah.

81 in all with their hamlets. This was the patrimony of the tribe of Asher family by family, these cities and their hamlets.

Territory allotted to Naphtali

32 The sixth lot cast was for the sons
33 of Naphtali family by family. Their boundary started from Heleph and from Elon-bezaanannim and ran past Adami-nekeb and Jabneel as far as Lakkum, and its limit was the Jordan.
34 The boundary turned back westwards to Aznoth-tabor and from there on to Hukok. It touched Zebulun on the south, Asher on the west, and the low-lying land by the Jordan on the east.
35 Their fortified cities were Ziddim, Zer, Hammath, Rakkath, Kinnereth,
36 37 Adamah, Ramah, Hazor, Kedesh, Ed-
38 rei, En-hazor, Iron, Migdal-el, Horem, Beth-anath, and Beth-shemesh: nine-
39 teen cities with their hamlets. This was the patrimony of the tribe of Naphtali family by family, both cities and hamlets.

Territory allotted to Dan

40 The seventh lot cast was for the tribe of the sons of Dan family by family.
41 The boundary of their patrimony was
42 Zorah, Eshtaol, Ir-shemesh, Shaalab-
43 bin, Aijalon, Jithlah, Elon, Timnah,
44 Ekron, Eltekeh, Gibbethon, Baalath,
45 46 Jehud, Bene-berak, Gath-rimmon; and on the west Jarkon was the bound-
47 ary opposite Joppa. But the Danites, when they lost this territory, marched against Leshem, attacked it and cap-tured it. They put its people to the sword, occupied it and settled in it; and they renamed the place Dan after
48 their ancestor Dan. This was the patri-mony of the tribe of the sons of Dan family by family, these cities and their hamlets.

Joshua settles in Timnath-serah

49 So the Israelites finished allocating the land and marking out its frontiers; and they gave Joshua son of Nun a
50 patrimony within their territory. They followed the commands of the LORD and gave him the city for which he asked, Timnath-serah in the hill-country of Ephraim, and he rebuilt the city and settled in it.
51 These are the patrimonies which Eleazar the priest and Joshua son of Nun and the heads of families as-signed by lot to the Israelite tribes at Shiloh before the LORD at the entrance of the Tent of the Presence. Thus they completed the distribution of the land.

Cities of refuge appointed

20 The LORD spoke to Joshua and com-
2 manded him to say this to the Isra-elites: 'You must now appoint your cities of refuge, of which I spoke to
3 you through Moses. They are to be places where the homicide, the man who kills another inadvertently with-out intent, may take sanctuary. You shall single them out as cities of refuge from the vengeance of the dead man's
4 next-of-kin. When a man takes sanc-tuary in one of these cities, he shall halt at the entrance of the city gate and state his case in the hearing of the elders of that city; if they admit him into the city, they shall grant him a place where he may live as one of
5 themselves. When the next-of-kin comes in pursuit, they shall not sur-render him: he struck down his fellow without intent and had not previously
6 been at enmity with him. The homi-cide may stay in that city until he stands trial before the community. On the death of the ruling high priest, he may return to the city and home
7 from which he has fled.' They dedi-cated Kedesh in Galilee in the hill-country of Naphtali, Shechem in the hill-country of Ephraim, and Kiriath-arba, that is Hebron, in the hill-
8 country of Judah. Across the Jordan eastwards from Jericho they appointed these cities: from the tribe of Reuben, Bezer-in-the-wilderness on the table-land, from the tribe of Gad, Ramoth in Gilead, and from the tribe of Manas-seh, Golan in Bashan. These were the
9 appointed cities where any Israelite or any alien residing among them might take sanctuary. They were intended for any man who killed another inad-vertently, to ensure that no one should die at the hand of the next-of-kin until he had stood his trial before the community.

The Levites' cities

21 The heads of the Levite families approached Eleazar the priest and Joshua son of Nun and the heads of the families of the tribes of Israel.
2 They came before them at Shiloh in the land of Canaan and said, 'The LORD gave his command through Moses that we were to receive cities to live in, together with the common land belonging to them for our cattle.'
3 The Israelites therefore gave part of their patrimony to the Levites, the

following cities with their common land, according to the command of the Lord.

4 This is the territory allotted to the Kohathite family: those Levites who were descended from Aaron the priest received thirteen cities chosen by lot from the tribes of Judah, Simeon, and 5 Benjamin; the rest of the Kohathites were allotted family by family[g] ten cities from the tribes of Ephraim, Dan, and half Manasseh.

6 The Gershonites were allotted family by family thirteen cities from the tribes of Issachar, Asher, Naphtali, and the half tribe of Manasseh in Bashan.

7 The Merarites were allotted family by family twelve cities from the tribes of Reuben, Gad, and Zebulun.

8 So the Israelites gave the Levites these cities with their common land, allocating them by lot as the Lord had commanded through Moses.

9 The Israelites designated the follow-10 ing cities out of the tribes of Judah and Simeon for those sons of Aaron who were of the Kohathite families of the Levites, because their lot came 11 out first. They gave them Kiriath-arba (Arba was the father of Anak), that is Hebron, in the hill-country of Judah, and the common land round 12 it, but they gave the open country near the city, and its hamlets, to Caleb son of Jephunneh as his patri-mony.

13[h] To the sons of Aaron the priest they 14 gave Hebron, a city of refuge for the homicide, Libnah, Jattir, Eshtemoa, 16 Holon, Debir, Ashan,[i] Juttah, and Beth-shemesh, each with its common land: nine cities from these two tribes. 17 They also gave cities from the tribe 18 of Benjamin, Gibeon, Geba, Anathoth, 19 and Almon, each with its common land: four cities. The number of the cities with their common land given to the sons of Aaron the priest was thirteen.

20 The cities which the rest of the Kohathite families of the Levites received by lot were from the tribe of 21 Ephraim. They gave them Shechem, a city of refuge for the homicide, in the hill-country of Ephraim, Gezer, 22 Kibzaim, and Beth-horon, each with 23 its common land: four cities. From the tribe of Dan, they gave them 24 Eltekeh, Gibbethon, Aijalon, and Gath-rimmon, each with its common

land: four cities. From the half tribe 25 of Manasseh, they gave them Taanach and Gath-rimmon, each with its com-mon land: two cities. The number 26 of the cities belonging to the rest of the Kohathite families with their com-mon land was ten.

The Gershonite families of the Le- 27 vites received, out of the share of the half tribe of Manasseh, Golan in Bashan, a city of refuge for the homi-cide, and Be-ashtaroth,[j] each with its common land: two cities. From the 28 tribe of Issachar they received Kishon, Daberah, Jarmuth, and En-gannim, 29 each with its common land: four cities. From the tribe of Asher they 30 received Mishal, Abdon, Helkath, and 31 Rehob, each with its common land: four cities. From the tribe of Naphtali 32 they received Kedesh in Galilee, a city of refuge for the homicide, Ham-moth-dor, and Kartan, each with its common land: three cities. The num- 33 ber of the cities of the Gershonite families with their common land was thirteen.

From the tribe of Zebulun the rest 34 of the Merarite families of the Levites received Jokneam, Kartah, Rimmon,[k] 35 and Nahalal, each with its common land: four cities. East of the Jordan 36 at Jericho, from the tribe of Reuben they were given Bezer-in-the-wilder-ness on the tableland, a city of refuge for the homicide, Jahaz, Kedemoth, 37 and Mephaath, each with its common land: four cities. From the tribe of 38 Gad they received Ramoth in Gilead, a city of refuge for the homicide, Mahanaim, Heshbon, and Jazer, each 39 with its common land: four cities in all. Twelve cities in all fell by lot to 40 the rest of the Merarite families of the Levites.

The cities of the Levites within the 41 Israelite patrimonies numbered forty-eight in all, with their common land. Each city had its common land round 42 it, and it was the same for all of them.

The Lord fulfils his promise

Thus the Lord gave Israel all the 43 land which he had sworn to give to their forefathers; they occupied it and settled in it. The Lord gave them 44 security on every side as he had sworn to their forefathers. Of all their enemies not a man could withstand them; the Lord delivered all their enemies into their hands. Not a word 45

g family by family: prob. rdg.; Heb. from the families (similarly in verse 6).   h Verses 13–39: cp. 1 Chr. 6. 57–81.   i Prob. rdg., cp. 1 Chr. 6. 59; Heb. Ain.   j Prob. rdg.; Heb. Be-ashtarah. k Prob. rdg., cp. 19. 13; 1 Chr. 6. 77; Heb. Dimnah.

of the LORD's promises to the house of Israel went unfulfilled; they all came true.

The altar by the Jordan

22 At that time Joshua summoned the Reubenites, the Gadites, and the half 2 tribe of Manasseh, and said to them, 'You have observed all the commands of Moses the servant of the LORD, and you have obeyed me in all the commands that I too have laid upon you. 3 All this time you have not deserted your brothers; up to this day you have diligently observed the charge laid on you by the LORD your God. 4 And now that the LORD your God has given your brothers security as he promised them, you may turn now and go to your homes in your own land, the land which Moses the servant of the LORD gave you east of 5 the Jordan. But take good care to keep the commands and the law which Moses the servant of the LORD gave you: to love the LORD your God; to conform to his ways; to observe his commandments; to hold fast to him; to serve him with your 6 whole heart and soul.' Joshua blessed them and dismissed them; and they 7-8 went to their homes. He sent them home with his blessing, and with these words: 'Go to your homes richly laden, with great herds, with silver and gold, copper and iron, and with large stores of clothing. See that you share with your kinsmen the spoil you have taken from your enemies.'

Moses had given territory to one half of the tribe of Manasseh in Bashan, and Joshua gave territory to the other half west of the Jordan among their kinsmen.

9 So the Reubenites, the Gadites, and the half tribe of Manasseh left the rest of the Israelites and went from Shiloh in Canaan on their way into Gilead, the land which belonged to them according to the decree of the LORD 10 given through Moses. When these tribes came to Geliloth by the Jordan,[l] they built a great altar there by the 11 river for all to see. The Israelites heard that the Reubenites, the Gadites, and the half tribe of Manasseh had built the altar facing the land of Canaan, at Geliloth by the Jordan 12 opposite the Israelite side. When the news reached them, all the community of the Israelites assembled at Shiloh to advance against them with a dis- 13 play of force. At the same time the Israelites sent Phinehas son of Eleazar the priest into the land of Gilead, to the Reubenites, the Gadites, and the half tribe of Manasseh, and 14 ten leading men with him, one from each of the tribes of Israel, each of them the head of a household among the clans of Israel. They came to the 15 Reubenites, the Gadites, and the half tribe of Manasseh in the land of Gilead, and remonstrated with them in these words: 'We speak for the whole com- 16 munity of the LORD. What is this treachery you have committed against the God of Israel? Are you ceasing to follow the LORD and building your own altar this day in defiance of the LORD? Remember our offence at Peor, 17 for which a plague fell upon the community of the LORD; to this day we have not been purified from it. Was that offence so slight that you dare 18 cease to follow the LORD today? If you defy the LORD today, then tomorrow he will be angry with the whole community of Israel. If the land you 19 have taken is unclean, then cross over to the LORD's own land, where the Tabernacle of the LORD now rests, and take a share of it with us; but do not defy the LORD and involve us in your defiance by building an altar of your own apart from the altar of the LORD our God. Remember the 20 treachery of Achan son of Zerah, who defied the ban and the whole community of Israel suffered for it. He was not the only one who paid for that sin with his life.'

Then the Reubenites, the Gadites, 21 and the half tribe of Manasseh remonstrated with the heads of the clans of Israel: 'The LORD the God of gods, 22 the LORD the God of gods, he knows, and Israel must know: if this had been an act of defiance or treachery against the LORD, you could not save us today. If we had built ourselves an 23 altar meaning to forsake the LORD, or had offered whole-offerings and grain-offerings upon it, or had presented shared-offerings, the LORD himself would exact punishment. The truth 24 is that we have done this for fear that the day may come when your sons will say to ours, "What have you to do with the LORD, the God of Israel? The 25 LORD put the Jordan as a boundary between our sons and your sons. You have no share in the LORD, you men of Reuben and Gad." Thus your sons will prevent our sons from going in awe of the LORD. So we resolved to set 26

l Prob. rdg.; Heb. adds which was in Canaan.

ourselves to build an altar, not for
27 whole-offerings and sacrifices, but as
a witness between us and you, and
between our descendants after us.
Thus we shall be able to do service
before the LORD, as we do now, with
our whole-offerings, our sacrifices, and
our shared-offerings; and your sons
will never be able to say to our sons
that they have no share in the LORD.
28 And we thought, if ever they do say
this to us and our descendants, we
will point to this copy of the altar
of the LORD which we have made,
not for whole-offerings and not for
sacrifices, but as a witness between us
29 and you. God forbid that we should
defy the LORD and forsake him this
day by building another altar for
whole-offerings, grain-offerings, and
sacrifices, in addition to the altar of
the LORD our God which stands in
front of his Tabernacle.'
30   When Phinehas the priest and the
leaders of the community, the heads of
the Israelite clans, who were with him,
heard what the Reubenites, the Gadites, and the Manassites said, they
31 were satisfied. Phinehas son of Eleazar the priest said to the Reubenites,
Gadites, and Manassites, 'We know
now that the LORD is in our midst
today; you have not acted treacherously against the LORD, and thus you
have preserved all Israel from punish-
32 ment at his hand.' Then Phinehas
son of Eleazar the priest and the
leaders left the Reubenites and the
Gadites in Gilead and reported to
33 the Israelites in Canaan. The Israelites
were satisfied, and they blessed God
and thought no more of attacking
Reuben and Gad and ravaging their
34 land. The Reubenites and Gadites
said, 'The altar is a witness between
us that the LORD is God', and they
named it 'Witness'.

*Joshua exhorts the people to obey the
LORD*

23 A long time had passed since the LORD
had given Israel security from all the
enemies who surrounded them, and
2 Joshua was now a very old man. He
summoned all Israel, their elders and
heads of families, their judges and
officers, and said to them, 'I have
3 become a very old man. You have
seen for yourselves all that the LORD
our God has done to these peoples
for your sake; it was the LORD God
4 himself who fought for you. I have

allotted you your patrimony tribe by
tribe, the land of all the peoples that
I have wiped out and of all these that
remain between the Jordan and the
Great Sea which lies towards the setting sun. The LORD your God himself 5
drove them out for your sake; he
drove them out to make room for you,
and you occupied their land, as the
LORD your God had promised you.
Be resolute therefore: observe and 6
perform everything written in the
book of the law of Moses, without
swerving to right or to left. You must 7
not associate with the peoples that
are left among you; you must not call
upon their gods by name, nor[m] swear
by them nor prostrate yourselves in
worship before them. You must hold 8
fast to the LORD your God as you
have done down to this day. For your 9
sake the LORD has driven out great
and mighty nations; to this day not a
man of them has withstood you. One 10
of you can put to flight a thousand,
because the LORD your God fights for
you, as he promised. Be on your guard 11
then, love the LORD your God, for[n] if 12
you do turn away and attach yourselves to the peoples that still remain
among you, and intermarry with them
and associate with them and they
with you, then be sure that the LORD 13
will not continue to drive those
peoples out to make room for you.
They will be snares to entrap you,
whips for your backs and barbed
hooks in your eyes, until you vanish
from the good land which the LORD
your God has given you. And now I 14
am going the way of all mankind. You
know in your heart of hearts that
nothing that the LORD your God has
promised you has failed to come true,
every word of it. But the same LORD 15
God who has kept his word to you to
such good effect can equally bring
every kind of evil on you, until he has
rooted you out from this good land
which he has given you. If you break 16
the covenant which the LORD your
God has prescribed and prostrate
yourselves in worship before other
gods, then the LORD will be angry with
you and you will quickly vanish from
the good land he has given you.'

Joshua's farewell address

Joshua assembled all the tribes of 24
Israel at Shechem. He summoned the
elders of Israel, the heads of families,
the judges and officers; and they

m you must not call . . . nor: *or* the name of their gods shall not be your boast, nor must you . . .
n Be on . . . for: *or* Take very good care to love the LORD your God, but . . .

2 presented themselves before God. Joshua then said this to all the people: 'This is the word of the LORD the God of Israel: "Long ago your forefathers, Terah and his sons Abraham and Nahor, lived beside the Euphrates,

3 and they worshipped other gods. I took your father Abraham from beside the Euphrates and led him through the length and breadth of Canaan. I gave him many descendants: I gave

4 him Isaac, and to Isaac I gave Jacob and Esau. I put Esau in possession of the hill-country of Seir, but Jacob

5 and his sons went down to Egypt. I sent Moses and Aaron, and I struck the Egyptians with plagues—you know well what I did among them—

6 and after that I brought you out; I brought your fathers out of Egypt and you came to the Red Sea. The Egyptians sent their chariots and cavalry to pursue your fathers to the

7 sea. But when they appealed to the LORD, he put a screen of darkness between you and the Egyptians, and brought the sea down on them and it covered them; you saw for yourselves what I did to Egypt. For a long time

8 you lived in the wilderness. Then I brought you into the land of the Amorites who lived east of the Jordan; they fought against you, but I delivered them into your hands; you took possession of their country and

9 I destroyed them for your sake. The king of Moab, Balak son of Zippor, took the field against Israel. He sent for Balaam son of Beor to lay a curse

10 on you, but I would not listen to him. Instead of that he blessed you; and so I saved you from the power of Balak.

11 Then you crossed the Jordan and came to Jericho. The citizens of Jericho fought against you,[o] but I delivered

12 them into your hands. I spread panic before you, and it was this, not your sword or your bow, that drove out

13 the two kings of the Amorites. I gave you land on which you had not laboured, cities which you had never built; you have lived in those cities and you eat the produce of vineyards and olive-groves which you did not plant."

14 'Hold the LORD in awe then, and worship him in loyalty and truth. Banish the gods whom your fathers worshipped beside the Euphrates and

15 in Egypt, and worship the LORD. But if it does not please you to worship the LORD, choose here and now whom

you will worship: the gods whom your forefathers worshipped beside the Euphrates, or the gods of the Amorites in whose land you are living. But I and my family, we will worship the

16 LORD.' The people answered, 'God forbid that we should forsake the

17 LORD to worship other gods, for it was the LORD our God who brought us and our fathers up from Egypt, that land of slavery; it was he who displayed those great signs before our eyes and guarded us on all our wanderings among the many peoples through

18 whose lands we passed. The LORD drove out before us the Amorites and all the peoples who lived in that country. We too will worship the LORD; he is our God.' Joshua answered

19 the people, 'You cannot worship the LORD. He is a holy god, a jealous god, and he will not forgive your

20 rebellion and your sins. If you forsake the LORD and worship foreign gods, he will turn and bring adversity upon you and, although he once brought you prosperity, he will make an end

21 of you.' The people said to Joshua,

22 'No; we will worship the LORD.' He said to them, 'You are witnesses against yourselves that you have chosen the LORD and will worship him.' 'Yes,' they answered, 'we are witnesses.' He said to them, 'Then

23 here and now banish the foreign gods that are among you, and turn your hearts to the LORD the God of Israel.'

24 The people said to Joshua, 'The LORD our God we will worship and his voice

25 we will obey.' So Joshua made a covenant that day with[p] the people; he drew up a statute and an ordinance

26 for them in Shechem and wrote its terms in the book of the law of God. He took a great stone and set it up there under the terebinth[q] in the

27 sanctuary of the LORD, and said to all the people, 'This stone is a witness against us; for it has heard all the words which the LORD has spoken to us. If you renounce your God, it shall be a witness against you.' Then Joshua

28 dismissed the people, each man to his patrimony.

The death of Joshua

29 After these things, Joshua son of Nun the servant of the LORD died; he was

30 a hundred and ten years old. They buried him within the border of his own patrimony in Timnath-serah in the hill-country of Ephraim to the

o *Prob. rdg.; Heb. adds* Amorites, Perizzites, Canaanites, Hittites, Girgashites, Hivites, and Jebusites.
p *Or for.* q *Or pole.*

31 north of Mount Gaash. Israel served the LORD during the lifetime of Joshua and of the elders who outlived him and who well knew all that the LORD had done for Israel.

The death of Eleazar

32 The bones of Joseph, which the Israelites had brought up from Egypt, were buried in Shechem, in the plot of land which Jacob had bought from the sons of Hamor father of Shechem for a hundred sheep;*r* and they passed into the patrimony of the house of Joseph. Eleazar son of Aaron died and 33 was buried in the hill which had been given to Phinehas his son in the hill-country of Ephraim.

r Or pieces of money (cp. Gen. 33. 19; Job 42. 11).

THE BOOK OF
JUDGES

Conquests of Judah and Simeon

1 AFTER THE DEATH of Joshua the Israelites inquired of the LORD which tribe should attack the Ca-
2 naanites first. The LORD answered, 'Judah shall attack. I hereby deliver
3 the country into his power.' Judah said to his brother Simeon, 'Go forward with me into my allotted territory, and let us do battle with the Canaanites; then I in turn will go with you into your territory.' So Simeon
4 went with him; then Judah advanced to the attack, and the LORD delivered the Canaanites and Perizzites into their hands. They slaughtered ten
5 thousand of them at Bezek. There they came upon Adoni-bezek, engaged him in battle and defeated the
6 Canaanites and Perizzites. Adoni-bezek fled, but they pursued him, took him prisoner and cut off his
7 thumbs and his great toes. Adoni-bezek said, 'I once had seventy kings whose thumbs and great toes were cut off picking up the scraps from under my table. What I have done God has done to me.' He was brought to Jerusalem and died there.
8 The men of Judah made an assault on Jerusalem and captured it, put its people to the sword and set fire
9 to the city. Then they turned south to fight the Canaanites of the hill-country, the Negeb, and the Shephelah.
10 Judah attacked the Canaanites in Hebron, formerly called Kiriath-arba, and defeated Sheshai, Ahiman and
11 Talmai. From there they marched against the inhabitants of Debir, formerly called Kiriath-sepher. Caleb 12 said, 'Whoever attacks Kiriath-sepher and captures it, to him I will give my daughter Achsah in marriage.' Oth- 13 niel, son of Caleb's younger brother Kenaz, captured it, and Caleb gave him his daughter Achsah. When she 14 came to him, he incited her to ask her father for a piece of land. As she sat on the ass, she made a noise, and Caleb said, 'What did you mean by that?' She replied, 'I want to ask a 15 favour of you. You have put me in this dry Negeb; you must give me pools of water as well.' So Caleb gave her the upper pool and the lower pool.

The descendants of Moses' father- 16 in-law, the Kenite, went up with the men of Judah from the Vale of Palm Trees to the wilderness of Judah which is in the Negeb of Arad and settled among the Amalekites. Judah then 17 accompanied his brother Simeon, attacked the Canaanites in Zephath and destroyed it; hence the city was called Hormah.*a* Judah took Gaza, 18 Ashkelon, and Ekron, and the territory of each. The LORD was with 19 Judah and they occupied the hill-country, but they could not drive out the inhabitants of the Vale because they had chariots of iron. Hebron was 20 given to Caleb as Moses had directed, and he drove out the three sons of Anak. But the Benjamites did not 21 drive out the Jebusites of Jerusalem; and the Jebusites have lived on in Jerusalem with the Benjamites till the present day.

a That is Destruction.

Joseph captures Bethel

22 The tribes of Joseph attacked Bethel,
23 and the LORD was with them. They
sent spies to Bethel, formerly called
24 Luz. These spies saw a man coming
out of the city and said to him, 'Show
us how to enter the city, and we will
25 see that you come to no harm.' So he
showed them how to enter, and they
put the city to the sword, but let the
26 man and his family go free. He went
into Hittite country, built a city and
named it Luz, which is still its name
today.

*Conquests of Manasseh and
Ephraim*

27 Manasseh did not drive out the inhabitants of Beth-shean with its villages, nor of Taanach, Dor, Ibleam,
and Megiddo, with the villages of each
of them; the Canaanites held their
28 ground in that region. Later, when
Israel became strong, they put them
to forced labour, but they never completely drove them out.
29   Ephraim did not drive out the
Canaanites who lived in Gezer, but
the Canaanites lived among them
there.

Conquests of the other tribes

30 Zebulun did not drive out the inhabitants of Kitron and Nahalol, but
the Canaanites lived among them and
were put to forced labour.
31   Asher did not drive out the inhabitants of Acco and Sidon, of Ahlab,
Achzib, Helbah, Aphik and Rehob.
32 Thus the Asherites lived among the
Canaanite inhabitants and did not
drive them out.
33   Naphtali did not drive out the
inhabitants of Beth-shemesh and of
Beth-anath, but lived among the Canaanite inhabitants and put the inhabitants of Beth-shemesh and Beth-anath
to forced labour.
34   The Amorites pressed the Danites
back into the hill-country and did not
allow them to come down into the
35 Vale. The Amorites held their ground
in Mount Heres and in Aijalon and
Shaalbim, but the tribes of Joseph
increased their pressure on them until
they reduced them to forced labour.
36   The boundary of the Edomites ran
from the ascent of Akrabbim, upwards from Sela.

The angel of the LORD at Bokim

The angel of the LORD came up from **2**
Gilgal to Bokim, and said, 'I brought[b]
you up out of Egypt and into the
country which I vowed I would give
to your forefathers. I said, I will never
break my covenant with you, and **2**
you in turn must make no covenant
with the inhabitants of the country;
you must pull down their altars. But
you did not obey me, and look what you
have done! So I said, I will not drive **3**
them out before you; they will decoy
you, and their gods will shut you fast
in the trap.' When the angel of the **4**
LORD said this to the Israelites, they
all wept and wailed, and so the place **5**
was called Bokim;[c] and they offered
sacrifices there to the LORD.

*The new generation forsakes the
LORD*

Joshua dismissed the people, and the **6**
Israelites went off to occupy the
country, each man to his allotted
portion. As long as Joshua was alive **7**
and the elders who survived him—
everyone, that is, who had witnessed
the whole great work which the LORD
had done for Israel—the people worshipped the LORD. At the age of a **8**
hundred and ten Joshua son of Nun,
the servant of the LORD, died, and **9**
they buried him within the border of
his own property in Timnath-heres
north of Mount Gaash in the hill-
country of Ephraim. Of that whole **10**
generation, all were gathered to their
forefathers, and another generation
followed who did not acknowledge the
LORD and did not know what he had
done for Israel. Then the Israelites **11**
did what was wrong in the eyes of the
LORD, and worshipped the Baalim.[d]
They forsook the LORD, their fathers' **12**
God who had brought them out of
Egypt, and went after other gods,
gods of the races among whom they
lived; they bowed down before them
and provoked the LORD to anger; they **13**
forsook the LORD and worshipped the
Baal and the Ashtaroth.[e] The LORD **14**
in his anger made them the prey of
bands of raiders and plunderers; he
sold them to their enemies all around
them, and they could no longer make
a stand. Every time they went out to **15**
battle the LORD brought disaster upon
them, as he had said when he gave
them his solemn warning, and they
were in dire straits.

b Prob. rdg.; Heb. I will bring.   *c That is* Weepers.   *d* The Baalim *were Canaanite deities.*
e The Ashtaroth *were Canaanite deities.*

Israel's inconstancy

16 The LORD set judges over them, who
rescued them from the marauding
17 bands. Yet they did not listen even to
these judges, but turned wantonly to
worship other gods and bowed down
before them; all too soon they abandoned the path of obedience to the
LORD's commands which their forefathers had followed. They did not
18 obey the LORD. Whenever the LORD
set up a judge over them, he was with
that judge, and kept them safe from
their enemies so long as he lived. The
LORD would relent as often as he heard
them groaning under oppression and
19 ill-treatment. But as soon as the judge
was dead, they would relapse into
deeper corruption than their forefathers and give their allegiance to
other gods, worshipping them and
bowing down before them. They gave
up none of their evil practices and
20 their wilful ways. And the LORD was
angry with Israel and said, 'This
nation has broken the covenant which
I laid upon their forefathers and has
21 not obeyed me, and now, of all the
nations which Joshua left at his
death, I will not drive out to make
22 room for them one single man. By
their means I will test Israel, to see
whether or not they will keep strictly
to the way of the LORD as their fore-
23 fathers did.' So the LORD left those
nations alone and made no haste to
drive them out or give them into
Joshua's hands.

Nations left to test Israel

3 These are the nations which the LORD
left as a means of testing all the
Israelites who had not taken part in
2 the battles for Canaan, his purpose
being to teach succeeding generations
of Israel, or those at least who had not
learnt in former times, how to make
3 war. These were: the five lords of the
Philistines, all the Canaanites, the
Sidonians, and the Hivites who lived
in Mount Lebanon from Mount Baal-
4 hermon as far as Lebo-hamath. His
purpose also was to test whether the
Israelites would obey the commands
which the LORD had given to their
5 forefathers through Moses. Thus the
Israelites lived among the Canaanites,
the Hittites, the Amorites, the Perizzites, the Hivites, and the Jebusites.
6 They took their daughters in marriage
and gave their own daughters to their
sons; and they worshipped their gods.

*Othniel delivers Israel from Cushan-
rishathaim*

The Israelites did what was wrong in 7
the eyes of the LORD; they forgot the
LORD their God and worshipped the
Baalim and the Asheroth.*f* The LORD 8
was angry with Israel and he sold them
to Cushan-rishathaim, king of Aram-
naharaim,*g* who kept them in subjection for eight years. Then the Is- 9
raelites cried to the LORD for help and
he raised up a man to deliver them,
Othniel son of Caleb's younger brother
Kenaz, and he set them free. The 10
spirit of the LORD came upon him
and he became judge over Israel. He
took the field, and the LORD delivered
Cushan-rishathaim king of Aram into
his hands; Othniel was too strong for
him. Thus the land was at peace for 11
forty years until Othniel son of Kenaz
died.

Ehud delivers Israel from Moab

Once again the Israelites did what 12
was wrong in the eyes of the LORD,
and because of this he roused Eglon
king of Moab against Israel. Eglon 13
mustered the Ammonites and the
Amalekites, advanced to attack Israel
and took possession of the Vale of
Palm Trees. The Israelites were sub- 14
ject to Eglon king of Moab for eighteen years. When they cried to the 15
LORD for help, he raised up a man to
deliver them, Ehud son of Gera the
Benjamite, who was left-handed. The
Israelites sent him to pay their tribute to Eglon king of Moab. Ehud 16
made himself a two-edged sword, only
fifteen inches long, which he fastened
on his right side under his clothes, and 17
he brought the tribute to Eglon king
of Moab. Eglon was a very fat man.
When Ehud had finished presenting 18
the tribute, he sent on the men who
had carried it, and he himself turned 19
back from the Carved Stones at Gilgal. 'My lord king,' he said, 'I have a
word for you in private.' Eglon called
for silence and dismissed all his attendants. Ehud then came up to 20
him as he sat in the roof-chamber of
his summer palace and said, 'I have
a word from God for you.' So Eglon
rose from his seat, and Ehud reached 21
with his left hand, drew the sword from
his right side and drove it into his
belly. The hilt went in after the blade 22
and the fat closed over the blade; he
did not draw the sword out but left it
protruding behind. Ehud went out to 23

f Plural of Asherah, the name of a Canaanite goddess.   *g That is Aram of Two Rivers.*

the porch, shut the doors on him and
24 fastened them. When he had gone
away, Eglon's servants came and,
finding the doors fastened, they said,
'He must be relieving himself in the
25 closet of his summer palace.' They
waited until they were ashamed to
delay any longer, and still he did not
open the doors of the roof-chamber.
So they took the key and opened the
doors; and there was their master
26 lying on the floor dead. While they had
been waiting, Ehud made his escape;
he passed the Carved Stones and
27 escaped to Seirah. When he arrived
there, he sounded the trumpet in
the hill-country of Ephraim, and the
Israelites came down from the hills
28 with him at their head. He said to
them, 'Follow me, for the LORD has
delivered your enemy the Moabites
into your hands.' Down they came
after him, and they seized the fords of
the Jordan against the Moabites and
29 allowed no man to cross. They killed
that day some ten thousand Moabites,
all of them men of substance and all
30 fighting men; not one escaped. Thus
Moab on that day became subject to
Israel, and the land was at peace for
eighty years.

Shamgar delivers Israel from the Philistines

31 After Ehud there was Shamgar of
Beth-anath.[h] He killed six hundred
Philistines with an ox-goad, and he
too delivered Israel.

Deborah and Barak prepare for battle

4 After Ehud's death the Israelites once
again did what was wrong in the eyes
2 of the LORD, so he sold them to Jabin
the Canaanite king, who ruled in
Hazor. The commander of his forces
was Sisera, who lived in Harosheth-
3 of-the-Gentiles. The Israelites cried to
the LORD for help, because Sisera had
nine hundred chariots of iron and had
oppressed Israel harshly for twenty
4 years. At that time Deborah wife of
Lappidoth,[i] a prophetess, was judge
5 in Israel. It was her custom to sit
beneath the Palm-tree of Deborah
between Ramah and Bethel in the hill-
country of Ephraim, and the Israelites
6 went up to her for justice. She sent for
Barak son of Abinoam from Kedesh
in Naphtali and said to him, 'These
are the commands of the LORD the
God of Israel: "Go and draw ten
thousand men from Naphtali and

Zebulun and bring them with you to
Mount Tabor, and I will draw Sisera, 7
Jabin's commander, to the Torrent of
Kishon with his chariots and all his
rabble, and there I will deliver them
into your hands."' Barak answered 8
her, 'If you go with me, I will go; but
if you will not go, neither will I.'
'Certainly I will go with you,' she 9
said, 'but this venture will bring you
no glory, because the LORD will leave
Sisera to fall into the hands of a
woman.' So Deborah rose and went
with Barak to Kedesh. Barak sum- 10
moned Zebulun and Naphtali to
Kedesh and marched up with ten
thousand men, and Deborah went
with him.

Jael kills Sisera

Now Heber the Kenite had parted 11
company with the Kenites, the descendants of Hobab, Moses' brother-
in-law, and he had pitched his tent at
Elon-bezaanannim near Kedesh.
Word was brought to Sisera that 12
Barak son of Abinoam had gone up
to Mount Tabor; so he summoned all 13
his chariots, nine hundred chariots of
iron, and his troops, from Harosheth-
of-the-Gentiles to the Torrent of Kishon. Then Deborah said to Barak, 14
'Up! This day the LORD gives Sisera
into your hands. Already the LORD
has gone out to battle before you.'
So Barak came charging down from
Mount Tabor with ten thousand men
at his back. The LORD put Sisera to 15
rout with all his chariots and his army
before Barak's onslaught; but Sisera
himself dismounted from his chariot
and fled on foot. Barak pursued the 16
chariots and the army as far as Haro-
sheth, and the whole army was put to
the sword and perished; not a man
was left alive. Meanwhile Sisera fled 17
on foot to the tent of Jael wife of
Heber the Kenite, because Jabin king
of Hazor and the household of Heber
the Kenite were at peace. Jael came 18
out to meet Sisera and said to him,
'Come in here, my lord, come in; do
not be afraid.' So he went into the
tent, and she covered him with a rug.
He said to her, 'Give me some water 19
to drink; I am thirsty.' She opened a
skin full of milk, gave him a drink and
covered him up again. He said to her, 20
'Stand at the tent door, and if anybody comes and asks if someone is
here, say No.' But Jael, Heber's wife, 21
took a tent-peg, picked up a hammer,
crept up to him, and drove the peg

h of Beth-anath: or son of Anath.   i wife of Lappidoth: or a spirited woman.

into his skull as he lay sound asleep.
His brains oozed out on the ground,
22 his limbs twitched, and he died. When
Barak came up in pursuit of Sisera,
Jael went out to meet him and said to
him, 'Come, I will show you the man
you are looking for.' He went in with
her, and there was Sisera lying dead
23 with the tent-peg in his skull. That
day God gave victory to the Israelites
24 over Jabin king of Canaan, and they
pressed home their attacks upon that
king of Canaan until they had made
an end of him.

The song of Deborah and Barak

5 That day Deborah and Barak son of
Abinoam sang this song:

2 For the leaders, the leaders[j] in Israel,
for the people who answered the call,
bless ye the LORD.
3 Hear me, you kings; princes, give ear;
I will sing, I will sing to the LORD.
I will raise a psalm to the LORD the
God of Israel.
4 O LORD, at thy setting forth from Seir,
when thou camest marching out of the
plains of Edom,
earth trembled; heaven quaked;
the clouds streamed down in torrents.
5 Mountains shook in fear before the
LORD, the lord of Sinai,
before the LORD, the God of Israel.
6 In the days of Shamgar of Beth-
anath,[k]
in the days of Jael, caravans plied no
longer;
men who had followed the high roads
went round by devious paths.
7 Champions there were none,
none left in Israel,
until I,[l] Deborah, arose,
arose, a mother in Israel.
8 They chose new gods,
they consorted with demons.[m]
Not a shield, not a lance was to be
seen
in the forty thousand of Israel.
9 Be proud at heart, you marshals of
Israel;
you among the people that answered
the call,
bless ye the LORD.
10 You that ride your tawny she-asses,
that sit on saddle-cloths,
and you that take the road afoot,
ponder this well.
11 Hark, the sound of the players striking up

in the places where the women draw
water!
It is the victories of the LORD that
they commemorate there,
his triumphs as the champion of
Israel.
Down to the gates came the LORD's
people:
'Rouse, rouse yourself, Deborah, 12
rouse yourself, lead out the host.
Up, Barak! Take prisoners in plenty,
son of Abinoam.'
Then down marched the column[n] and 13
its chieftains,
the people of the LORD marched
down[o] like warriors.
The men of Ephraim showed a brave 14
front in the vale,
crying, 'With you, Benjamin! Your
clansmen are here!'
From Machir down came the marshals,
from Zebulun the bearers of the
musterer's staff.
Issachar joined with Deborah in the 15
uprising,[p]
Issachar stood by Barak;
down into the valley they rushed.
But Reuben, he was split into factions,
great were their heart-searchings.
What made you linger by the cattle- 16
pens
to listen to the shrill calling of the
shepherds?[q]
Gilead stayed beyond Jordan;   17
and Dan, why did he tarry by the
ships?
Asher lingered by the sea-shore,
by its creeks he stayed.
The people of Zebulun risked their 18
very lives,
so did Naphtali on the heights of the
battlefield.

Kings came, they fought;   19
then fought the kings of Canaan
at Taanach by the waters of Megiddo;
no plunder of silver did they take.
The stars fought from heaven,   20
the stars in their courses fought against
Sisera.
The Torrent of Kishon swept him 21
away,
the Torrent barred his flight, the Torrent of Kishon;
march on in might, my soul!
Then hammered the hooves of his 22
horses,
his chargers galloped, galloped away.

---

j Or For those who had flowing locks.   *k* of Beth-anath: *or* son of Anath.   *l* Or you.   *m* Or
satyrs.   *n* Prob. rdg.; Heb. survivor.   *o* Prob. rdg.; Heb. adds to me.   *p* in the uprising: *prob.
rdg.; Heb.* my officers.   *q* Prob. rdg.; Heb. adds Reuben was split into factions, great were their
heart-searchings.

23 A curse on Meroz, said the angel of the LORD;
a curse, a curse on its inhabitants,
because they brought no help to the LORD,
no help to the LORD and the fighting men.

24 Blest above women be Jael,
the wife of Heber the Kenite;
blest above all women in the tents.

25 He asked for water: she gave him milk,
she offered him curds in a bowl fit for a chieftain.

26 She stretched out her hand for the tent-peg,
her right hand to hammer the weary.
With the hammer she struck Sisera,
she crushed his head;
she struck and his brains ebbed out.

27 At her feet he sank down, he fell, he lay;
at her feet he sank down and fell.
Where he sank down, there he fell,
done to death.

28 The mother of Sisera peered through the lattice,
through the window she peered and shrilly cried,
'Why are his chariots so long coming?
Why is the clatter of his chariots so long delayed?'

29 The wisest of her princesses answered her,
yes, she found her own answer:

30 'They must be finding spoil, taking their shares,
a wench to each man, two wenches,
booty of dyed stuffs for Sisera,
booty of dyed stuffs,
dyed stuff, and striped, two lengths of striped stuff—
to grace the victor's neck.'

31 So perish all thine enemies, O LORD;
but let all who love thee be like the sun rising in strength.

The land was at peace for forty years.

The Midianites conquer Israel

6 The Israelites did what was wrong in the eyes of the LORD and he delivered them into the hands of Midian for 2 seven years. The Midianites were too strong for Israel, and the Israelites were forced to find themselves hollow places in the mountains, and caves 3 and strongholds. If the Israelites had sown their seed, the Midianites and the Amalekites and other eastern tribes would come up and attack 4 Israel. They then pitched their camps in the country and destroyed the crops as far as the outskirts of Gaza, leaving nothing to support life in Israel, sheep or ox or ass. They came 5 up with their herds and their tents, like a swarm of locusts; they and their camels were past counting. They had come into the land for its growing crop,*r* and so the Israelites were 6 brought to destitution by the Midianites, and they cried to the LORD for help. When the Israelites cried to the 7 LORD because of what they had suffered from the Midianites, he sent 8 them a prophet who said to them, 'These are the words of the LORD the God of Israel: I brought you up from Egypt, that land of slavery. I delivered 9 you from the Egyptians and from all your oppressors. I drove them out before you and gave you their lands. I said to you, "I am the LORD your 10 God: do not stand in awe of the gods of the Amorites in whose country you are settling." But you did not listen to me.'

The LORD visits Gideon

Now the angel of the LORD came and 11 sat under the terebinth at Ophrah which belonged to Joash the Abiezrite. His son Gideon was threshing wheat in the winepress, so that he might get it away quickly from the Midianites. The angel of the LORD 12 showed himself to Gideon and said, 'You are a brave man, and the LORD is with you.' Gideon said, 'But pray, 13 my lord, if the LORD really is with us, why has all this happened to us? What has become of all those wonderful deeds of his, of which we have heard from our fathers, when they told us how the LORD brought us out of Egypt? But now the LORD has cast us off and delivered us into the power of the Midianites.' The LORD turned 14 to him and said, 'Go and use this strength of yours to free Israel from the power of the Midianites. It is I that send you.' Gideon said, 'Pray, 15 my lord, how can I save Israel? Look at my clan: it is the weakest in Manasseh, and I am the least in my father's family.' The LORD answered, 'I will 16 be with you, and you shall lay low all Midian as one man.' He replied, 'If I 17 stand so well with you, give me a sign that it is you who speak to me. Please 18 do not leave this place until I come with my gift and lay it before you.' He answered, 'I will stay until you come back.' So Gideon went in, pre- 19 pared a kid and made an ephah of

r for its growing crop: *or* and laid it waste.

flour into unleavened cakes. He put the meat in a basket, poured the broth into a pot and brought it out to him under the terebinth. As he approached, 20 the angel of God said to him, 'Take the meat and the cakes, and put them here on the rock and pour out the 21 broth', and he did so. Then the angel of the LORD reached out the staff in his hand and touched the meat and the cakes with the tip of it. Fire sprang up from the rock and consumed the meat and the cakes; and the angel of the LORD was no more to be 22 seen. Then Gideon knew that it was the angel of the LORD and said, 'Alas, Lord GOD! Then it is true: I have seen the angel of the LORD face to face.' 23 But the LORD said to him, 'Peace be with you; do not be afraid, you shall 24 not die.' So Gideon built an altar there to the LORD and named it Jehovah-shalom.[s] It stands to this day at Ophrah-of-the-Abiezrites.

Gideon tears down the altar of Baal

25 That night the LORD said to Gideon, 'Take a young bull of your father's, the yearling bull,[t] tear down the altar of Baal which belongs to your father and cut down the sacred pole which 26 stands beside[u] it. Then build an altar of the proper pattern[v] to the LORD your God on the top of this earth-work;[w] take the yearling bull and offer it as a whole-offering with the wood of the sacred pole that you cut 27 down.' So Gideon took ten of his servants and did as the LORD had told him. He was afraid of his father's family and his fellow-citizens, and so he did it by night, and not by day. 28 When the citizens rose early in the morning, they found the altar of Baal overturned and the sacred pole which had stood beside it cut down and the yearling bull offered up as a whole-offering on the altar which he had 29 built. They asked each other who had done it, and, after searching inquiries, were told that it was Gideon son of 30 Joash. So the citizens said to Joash, 'Bring out your son. He has over-turned the altar of Baal and cut down the sacred pole beside it, and he must 31 die.' But as they crowded round him Joash retorted, 'Are you pleading Baal's cause then? Do you think that it is for you to save him? Whoever pleads his cause shall be put to death at dawn. If Baal is a god, and some-

one has torn down his altar, let him take up his own cause.' That day 32 Joash named Gideon Jerubbaal,[x] say-ing, 'Let Baal plead his cause against this man, for he has torn down his altar.'

Gideon's fleece

All the Midianites, the Amalekites, 33 and the eastern tribes joined forces, crossed the river and camped in the Vale of Jezreel. Then the spirit of the 34 LORD took possession of Gideon; he sounded the trumpet and the Abiez-rites were called out to follow him. He sent messengers all through Manas- 35 seh; and they too were called out. He sent messengers to Asher, Zebulun, and Naphtali, and they came up to meet the others. Gideon said to God, 36 'If thou wilt deliver Israel through me as thou hast promised—now, 37 look, I am putting a fleece of wool on the threshing-floor. If there is dew only on the fleece and all the ground is dry, then I shall be sure that thou wilt deliver Israel through me, as thou hast promised.' And that is 38 what happened. He rose early next day and wrung out the fleece, and he squeezed enough dew from it to fill a bowl with water. Gideon then said 39 to God, 'Do not be angry with me, but give me leave to speak once again. Let me, I pray thee, make one more test with the fleece. This time let the fleece alone be dry, and all the ground be covered with dew.' God let it be so 40 that night: the fleece alone was dry, and on all the ground there was dew.

Gideon selects his army

Jerubbaal, that is Gideon, and all the 7 people with him rose early and pitched camp at En-harod;[y] the Midianite camp was in the vale to the north of the hill of Moreh. The LORD said to 2 Gideon, 'The people with you are more than I need to deliver Midian into their hands: Israel will claim the glory for themselves and say that it is their own strength that has given them the victory. Now make a procla- 3 mation for all the people to hear, that anyone who is scared or fright-ened is to leave Mount Galud[z] at once and go back home.' Twenty-two thousand of them went, and ten thousand were left. The LORD then 4 said to Gideon, 'There are still too many. Bring them down to the water,

---

s That is the LORD is peace.   t the yearling bull: prob. rdg.; Heb. the second bull, seven years old.
u Or on.   v of . . . pattern: or with the stones in rows.   w Or stronghold or refuge.   x That
is Let Baal plead.   y That is Spring of Fright.   z Prob. rdg.; Heb. Mount Gilead.

and I will separate them for you there. When I say to you, "This man shall go with you", he shall go; and if I say, "This man shall not go with you", he 5 shall not go.' So Gideon brought the people down to the water and the LORD said to him, 'Make every man who laps the water with his tongue like a dog stand on one side, and on 6 the other every man who goes down on his knees and drinks.' The number of those who lapped was three hundred, and all the rest went down on their knees to drink, putting their 7 hands to their mouths. The LORD said to Gideon, 'With the three hundred men who lapped I will save you and deliver Midian into your hands, and 8 all the rest may go home.' So Gideon sent all these Israelites home, but he kept the three hundred, and they took with them the jars*a* and the trumpets which the people had. The Midianite camp was below him in the vale.

The Midianites are routed

9 That night the LORD said to him, 'Go down at once and attack the camp, for 10 I have delivered it into your hands. If you are afraid to do so, then go down 11 first with your servant Purah and listen to what they are saying. That will give you courage to go down and attack the camp.' So he and his servant Purah went down to the part of the camp where the fighting men lay. 12 Now the Midianites, the Amalekites, and the eastern tribes were so many that they lay there in the valley like a swarm of locusts; there was no counting their camels; in number they were like grains of sand on the sea-13 shore. When Gideon came close, there was a man telling his companion a dream. He said, 'I dreamt that I saw a hard, stale barley-cake rolling over and over through the Midianite camp; it came to a tent, hit it*b* and turned it upside down, and the tent collap-14 sed.' The other answered, 'Depend upon it, this is the sword of Gideon son of Joash the Israelite. God has delivered Midian and the whole army 15 into his hands.' When Gideon heard the story of the dream and its interpretation, he prostrated himself. Then he went back to the Israelite camp and said, 'Up! The LORD has delivered the camp of the Midianites into your 16 hands.' He divided the three hundred men into three companies, and gave every man a trumpet and an empty jar with a torch inside it. Then he said 17 to them, 'Watch me: when I come to the edge of the camp, do exactly as I do. When I and my men blow our 18 trumpets, you too all round the camp will blow your trumpets, and shout, "For the LORD and for Gideon!"'

Gideon and the hundred men who 19 were with him reached the outskirts of the camp at the beginning of the middle watch; the sentries had just been posted. They blew their trumpets and smashed their jars. The three 20 companies all blew their trumpets and smashed their jars, then grasped the torches in their left hands and the trumpets in their right, and shouted, 'A sword for the LORD and for Gideon!' Every man stood where he 21 was, all round the camp, and the whole camp leapt up in a panic and fled. The three hundred blew their 22 trumpets, and throughout the camp the LORD set every man against his neighbour. The army fled as far as Beth-shittah in Zererah, as far as the ridge of Abel-meholah by Tabbath. The Israelites from Naphtali and 23 Asher and all Manasseh were called out and they pursued the Midianites. Gideon sent men through all the hill-24 country of Ephraim with this message: 'Come down and cut off the Midianites. Hold the fords of the Jordan against them as far as Beth-barah.' So all the Ephraimites were called out and they held the fords of the Jordan as far as Beth-barah. They captured 25 the two Midianite princes, Oreb and Zeeb. Oreb they killed at the Rock of Oreb, and Zeeb by the Winepress of Zeeb, and they kept up the pursuit of the Midianites; afterwards they brought the heads of Oreb and Zeeb across the Jordan to Gideon.

The men of Ephraim said to Gideon, **8** 'Why have you treated us like this? Why did you not summon us when you went to fight Midian?'; and they reproached him violently. But he said 2 to them, 'What have I done compared with you? Are not Ephraim's gleanings better than the whole vintage of Abiezer? God has delivered Oreb and 3 Zeeb, the princes of Midian, into your hands. What have I done compared with you?' At these words of his, their anger died down.

Gideon captures the kings of Midian

Gideon came to the Jordan, and he 4 and his three hundred men crossed over to continue the pursuit, weary

---

a Prob. rdg.; Heb. provisions.   *b Prob. rdg.; Heb. adds and it fell.*

5 though they were. He said to the men of Succoth, 'Will you give these men of mine some bread, for they are weary, and I am pursuing Zebah and 6 Zalmunna, the kings of Midian?' But the chief men of Succoth replied, 'Are Zebah and Zalmunna already in your hands, that we should give your army 7 bread?' Gideon said, 'For that, when the LORD delivers Zebah and Zalmunna into my hands, I will thresh your bodies with desert thorns and 8 briars.' He went on from there to Penuel and made the same request; the men of Penuel answered like the 9 men of Succoth. He said to the men of Penuel, 'When I return safely, I will pull down your castle.'

10   Zebah and Zalmunna were in Karkor with their army of fifteen thousand men. These were all that remained of the whole host of the eastern tribes; a hundred and twenty thousand armed men had fallen in battle. 11 Gideon advanced along the track used by the tent-dwellers east of Nobah and Jogbehah, and his attack caught the army when they were off their 12 guard. Zebah and Zalmunna fled; but he went in pursuit of these Midianite kings and captured them both; and their whole army melted away.

13   As Gideon son of Joash was return-14 ing from the battle by the Ascent of Heres, he caught a young man from Succoth. He questioned him, and one by one he numbered off the names of the rulers of Succoth and its elders, 15 seventy-seven in all. Gideon then came to the men of Succoth and said, 'Here are Zebah and Zalmunna, about whom you taunted me. "Are Zebah and Zalmunna", you said, "already in your hands, that we should give 16 your weary men bread?"' Then he took the elders of the city and he disciplined those men of Succoth with 17 desert thorns and briars. He also pulled down the castle of Penuel and 18 put the men of the city to death. Then he said to Zebah and Zalmunna, 'What of the men you killed in Tabor?' They answered, 'They were like you, every one had the look of a king's son.' 19 'They were my brothers,' he said, 'my mother's sons. I swear by the LORD, if you had let them live I would not 20 have killed you'; and he said to his eldest son Jether, 'Up with you, and kill them.' But he was still only a lad, and did not draw his sword, because 21 he was afraid. So Zebah and Zalmunna said, 'Rise up yourself and dispatch us, for you have a man's

strength.' So Gideon rose and killed them both, and he took the crescents from the necks of their camels.

Gideon's golden ephod

After this the Israelites said to Gid- 22 eon, 'You have saved us from the Midianites; now you be our ruler, you and your son and your grandson.' Gideon replied, 'I will not rule over 23 you, nor shall my son; the LORD will rule over you.' Then he said, 'I have 24 a request to make: will every one of you give me the earrings from his booty?'—for the enemy wore golden earrings, being Ishmaelites. They said, 25 'Of course, we will give them.' So a cloak was spread out and every man threw on to it the golden earrings from his booty. The earrings for which 26 he asked weighed seventeen hundred shekels of gold; this was in addition to the crescents and pendants and the purple cloaks worn by the Midianite kings, not counting the chains on the necks of their camels. Gideon made it 27 into an ephod and he set it up in his own city of Ophrah. All the Israelites turned wantonly to its worship, and it became a trap to catch Gideon and his household.

The death of Gideon

Thus the Midianites were subdued by 28 the Israelites; they could no longer hold up their heads. For forty years the land was at peace, all the lifetime of Gideon, that is Jerubbaal son of 29 Joash; and he retired to his own home. Gideon had seventy sons, his own off- 30 spring, for he had many wives. He had 31 a concubine who lived in Shechem, and she also bore him a son, whom he named Abimelech. Gideon son of 32 Joash died at a ripe old age and was buried in his father's grave at Ophrah-of-the-Abiezrites. After his death, the 33 Israelites again went wantonly to the worship of the Baalim and made Baal-berith their god. They forgot 34 the LORD their God who had delivered them from their enemies on every side, and did not show to the family 35 of Jerubbaal, that is Gideon, the loyalty that was due to them for all the good he had done for Israel.

Abimelech's insurrection

Abimelech son of Jerubbaal went to 9 Shechem to his mother's brothers, and spoke with them and with all the clan of his mother's family. 'I beg you,' 2 he said, 'whisper a word in the ears of the chief citizens of Shechem. Ask them which is better for them: that seventy men, all the sons of Jerubbaal, should rule over them, or one man. Tell them to remember that I am their 3 own flesh and blood.' So his mother's brothers repeated all this to each of them on his behalf; and they were moved to come over to Abimelech's side, because, as they said, he was 4 their brother. They gave him seventy pieces of silver from the temple of Baal-berith, and with these he hired idle and reckless men, who followed 5 him. He came to his father's house in Ophrah and butchered his seventy brothers, the sons of Jerubbaal, on a single stone block, all but Jotham the youngest, who survived because he had 6 hidden himself. Then all the citizens of Shechem and all Beth-millo came together and made Abimelech king beside the old propped-up terebinth at Shechem.

Jotham's parable

7 When this was reported to Jotham, he went and stood on the summit of Mount Gerizim. He cried at the top of his voice: 'Listen to me, you citizens of Shechem, and may God listen to you:
8   'Once upon a time the trees came to anoint a king, and they said to the 9 olive-tree: Be king over us. But the olive-tree answered: What, leave my rich oil by which gods and men are honoured, to come and hold sway over the trees?
10   'So the trees said to the fig-tree: Then will you come and be king over 11 us? But the fig-tree answered: What, leave my good fruit and all its sweetness, to come and hold sway over the trees?
12   'So the trees said to the vine: Then will you come and be king over us? 13 But the vine answered: What, leave my new wine which gladdens gods and men, to come and hold sway over the trees?
14   'Then all the trees said to the thornbush: Will you then be king over us? 15 And the thorn said to the trees: If you really mean to anoint me as your king, then come under the protection of my shadow; if not, fire shall come out of the thorn and burn up the cedars of Lebanon.'
16   Then Jotham said, 'Now, have you acted fairly and honestly in making Abimelech king? Have you done the right thing by Jerubbaal and his household? Have you given my 17 father his due—who fought for you,

and threw himself into the forefront of the battle and delivered you from the Midianites? Today you have risen 18 against my father's family, butchered his seventy sons on a single stone block, and made Abimelech, the son of his slave-girl, king over the citizens of Shechem because he is your brother. In this day's work have you 19 acted fairly and honestly by Jerubbaal and his family? If so, I wish you joy in Abimelech and wish him joy in you! If not, may fire come out 20 of Abimelech and burn up the citizens of Shechem and all Beth-millo; may fire also come out from the citizens of Shechem and Beth-millo and burn up Abimelech.' After which Jotham slip- 21 ped away and made his escape; he came to Beer, and there he settled out of reach of his brother Abimelech.

Rise and fall of Abimelech

After Abimelech had been prince over 22 Israel for three years, God sent an 23 evil spirit to make a breach between Abimelech and the citizens of Shechem, and they played him false. This 24 was done on purpose, so that the violent murder of the seventy sons of Jerubbaal might recoil on their brother Abimelech who did the murder and on the citizens of Shechem who encouraged him to do it. The citizens 25 of Shechem set men to lie in wait for him on the hill-tops, but they robbed all who passed that way, and so the news reached Abimelech.

Now Gaal son of Ebed came with 26 his kinsmen to Shechem, and the citizens of Shechem transferred their allegiance to him. They went out into 27 the country-side, picked the early grapes in their vineyards, trod them in the winepress and held festival. They went into the temple of their god, where they ate and drank and reviled Abimelech. 'Who is Abimelech,' 28 said Gaal son of Ebed, 'and who are the Shechemites, that we should be his subjects? Have not this son of Jerubbaal and his lieutenant Zebul been subjects of the men of Hamor the father of Shechem? Why indeed should we be subject to him? If only 29 this people were in my charge I should know how to get rid of Abimelech! I would say to him, "Get your men together, and come out and fight."' When Zebul the governor of the city 30 heard what Gaal son of Ebed said, he was very angry. He resorted to a ruse 31 and sent messengers to Abimelech to say, 'Gaal son of Ebed and his kinsmen have come to Shechem and 32 are turning the city against you. Get up now in the night, you and the people with you, and lie in wait in the open 33 country. Then be up in the morning at sunrise, and advance rapidly against the city. When he and his people come out, do to him what the 34 situation demands.' So Abimelech and his people rose in the night, and lay in wait to attack Shechem, in four 35 companies. Gaal son of Ebed came out and stood in the entrance of the city gate, and Abimelech and his people rose from their hiding-place. 36 Gaal saw them and said to Zebul, 'There are people coming down from the tops of the hills', but Zebul replied, 'What you see is the shadow of the 37 hills, looking like men.' Once more Gaal said, 'There are people coming down from the central ridge of the hills, and one company is coming along the road of the Soothsayers' 38 Terebinth.' Then Zebul said to him, 'Where are your brave words now? You said, "Who is Abimelech that we should be subject to him?" Are not these the people you despised? Go out 39 and fight him.' Gaal led the citizens of Shechem out and attacked Abi- 40 melech, but Abimelech routed him and he fled. The ground was strewn with corpses all the way to the entrance 41 of the gate. Abimelech established himself in Arumah, and Zebul drove away Gaal and his kinsmen and allowed them no place in Shechem.

42 Next day the people came out into the open, and this was reported to 43 Abimelech. He on his side took his supporters, divided them into three companies and lay in wait in the open country; and when he saw the people coming out of the city, he rose and 44 attacked them. Abimelech and the company with him advanced rapidly and took up position at the entrance of the city gate, while the other two companies advanced against all those who were in the open and struck them 45 down. Abimelech kept up the attack on the city all that day and captured it; he killed the people in it, pulled the city down and sowed the site with 46 salt. When the occupants of the castle of Shechem heard of this, they went into the great hall[c] of the temple of 47 El-berith. It was reported to Abimelech that all the occupants of the castle of Shechem had collected to- 48 gether. So he and his people went up Mount Zalmon carrying axes; there

he cut brushwood, and took it and hoisted it on his shoulder. He said to his men, 'You see what I am doing; be quick and do the same.' So each 49 man cut brushwood; then they followed Abimelech and laid the brushwood against the hall, and burnt it over their heads. Thus all the occupants of the castle of Shechem died, about a thousand men and women.

Abimelech then went to Thebez, 50 besieged it and took it. There was a 51 strong castle in the middle of the city, and all the citizens, men and women, took refuge there. They shut themselves in and went on to the roof. Abimelech came up to the castle and 52 attacked it. As he approached the entrance to the castle to set fire to it, a woman threw a millstone down on 53 his head and fractured his skull. He 54 called hurriedly to his young armour-bearer and said, 'Draw your sword and dispatch me, or men will say of me: A woman killed him.' So the young man ran him through and he died. When the Israelites saw that 55 Abimelech was dead, they all went back to their homes. It was thus that 56 God requited the crime which Abimelech had committed against his father by the murder of his seventy brothers, and brought all the wicked- 57 ness of the men of Shechem on their own heads. The curse of Jotham son of Jerubbaal came home to them.

Tola and Jair judge Israel

After Abimelech, Tola son of Pua, **10** son of Dodo, a man of Issachar who lived in Shamir in the hill-country of Ephraim, came in his turn to deliver Israel. He was judge over Israel for **2** twenty-three years, and when he died he was buried in Shamir.

After him came Jair the Gileadite; **3** he was judge over Israel for twenty-two years. He had thirty sons, who **4** rode thirty asses; they had thirty towns in the land of Gilead, which to this day are called Havvoth-jair.[d] When Jair died, he was buried in **5** Kamon.

The Ammonites oppress Israel

Once more the Israelites did what was **6** wrong in the eyes of the LORD, worshipping the Baalim and the Ashtaroth, the deities of Aram and of Sidon and of Moab, of the Ammonites and of the Philistines. They forsook the LORD and did not worship him. The **7** LORD was angry with Israel, and he

c Or vault.   d That is Tent-villages of Jair.

sold them to the Philistines and the
8 Ammonites, who[e] for eighteen years
harassed and oppressed the Israelites
who lived beyond the Jordan in the
9 Amorite country in Gilead. Then the
Ammonites crossed the Jordan to
attack Judah, Benjamin, and Ephraim, so that Israel was in great dis-
10 tress. The Israelites cried to the LORD
for help and said, 'We have sinned
against thee; we have forsaken our
God and worshipped the Baalim.'
11 And the LORD said to the Israelites,
'The Egyptians, the Amorites, the
12 Ammonites, the Philistines; the Sidonians too and the Amalekites and
the Midianites—all these oppressed
you and you cried to me for help; and
13 did not I deliver you? But you forsook me and worshipped other gods;
therefore I will deliver you no more.
14 Go and cry for help to the gods you
have chosen, and let them save you
15 in the day of your distress.' But the
Israelites said to the LORD, 'We have
sinned. Deal with us as thou wilt; only
save us this day, we implore thee.'
16 They banished the foreign gods and
worshipped the LORD; and he could
endure no longer to see the plight of
Israel.
17 Then the Ammonites were called
to arms, and they encamped in Gilead, while the Israelites assembled and
18 encamped in Mizpah. The people of
Gilead and their chief men said to one
another, 'If any man will strike the
first blow at the Ammonites, he shall
be lord over the inhabitants of Gilead.'

Jephthah rules in Gilead

11 Jephthah the Gileadite was a great
warrior; he was the son of Gilead by
2 a prostitute. But Gilead had a wife
who bore him several sons, and when
they grew up they drove Jephthah
away; they said to him, 'You have no
inheritance in our father's house; you
3 are another woman's son.' So Jephthah, to escape his brothers, went
away and settled in the land of Tob,
and swept up a number of idle men
who followed him.
4 The time came when the Ammon-
5 ites made war on Israel, and when
the fighting began, the elders of Gilead
went to fetch Jephthah from the land
6 of Tob. They said to him, 'Come and
be our commander so that we can
7 fight the Ammonites.' But Jephthah
said to the elders of Gilead, 'You
drove me from my father's house in
hatred. Why come to me now when

you are in trouble?' 'It is because of 8
that', they replied, 'that we have
turned to you now. Come with us
and fight the Ammonites, and become
lord over all the inhabitants of Gilead.'
Jephthah said to them, 'If you ask 9
me back to fight the Ammonites and
if the LORD delivers them into my
hands, then I will be your lord.' The 10
elders of Gilead said again to Jephthah, 'We swear by the LORD, who
shall be witness between us, that we
will do what you say.' Jephthah then 11
went with the elders of Gilead, and the
people made him their lord and commander. And at Mizpah, in the presence of the LORD, Jephthah repeated
all that he had said.

Jephthah and the king of Ammon

Jephthah sent a mission to the king of 12
Ammon to ask what quarrel he had
with them that made him invade their
country. The king gave Jephthah's 13
men this answer: 'When the Israelites
came up from Egypt, they took our
land from the Arnon as far as the Jabbok and the Jordan. Give us back
these lands in peace.' Jephthah sent 14
a second mission to the king of Ammon, and they said, 'This is Jephthah's 15
answer: Israel did not take either the
Moabite country or the Ammonite
country. When they came up from 16
Egypt, the Israelites passed through
the wilderness to the Red Sea[f] and
came to Kadesh. They then sent 17
envoys to the king of Edom asking
him to grant them passage through
his country, but the king of Edom
would not hear of it. They sent also
to the king of Moab, but he was not
willing; so Israel remained in Kadesh.
They then passed through the wilder- 18
ness, skirting Edom and Moab, and
kept to the east of the Arnon. They encamped beside the Arnon, but they
did not enter Moabite territory, because the Arnon is the frontier of
Moab. Israel then sent envoys to the 19
king of the Amorites, Sihon king of
Heshbon, asking him to give them free
passage through his country to their
destination. But Sihon would not 20
grant Israel free passage through his
territory; he mustered all his people,
encamped in Jahaz and fought Israel.
But the LORD the God of Israel de- 21
livered Sihon and all his people into
the hands of Israel; they defeated
them and occupied all the territory of
the Amorites in that region. They took 22
all the Amorite territory from the

e Prob. rdg.; Heb. adds in that year.　　f Or the Sea of Reeds.

23 Arnon to the Jabbok and from the wilderness to the Jordan. The LORD the God of Israel drove out the Amorites for the benefit of his people Israel. And do you now propose to 24 take their place? It is for you to possess whatever Kemosh your god gives you; and all that the LORD our God 25 gave us as we advanced is ours. For that matter, are you any better than Balak son of Zippor, king of Moab? Did he ever quarrel with Israel or 26 attack them? For three hundred years Israelites have lived in Heshbon and its dependent villages, in Aroer and its villages, and in all the towns by the Arnon. Why did you not oust[g] them 27 during all that time? We have done you no wrong; it is you who are doing us wrong by attacking us. The LORD who is judge will judge this day between the 28 Israelites and the Ammonites.' But the king of the Ammonites would not listen to the message which Jephthah had sent him.

Jephthah's vow

29 Then the spirit of the LORD came upon Jephthah and he passed through Gilead and Manasseh, by Mizpeh of Gilead, and from Mizpeh over to the 30 Ammonites. Jephthah made this vow to the LORD: 'If thou wilt deliver 31 the Ammonites into my hands, then the first creature that comes out of the door of my house to meet me when I return from them in peace shall be the LORD's; I will offer that as a whole- 32 offering.' So Jephthah crossed over to attack the Ammonites, and the LORD 33 delivered them into his hands. He routed them with great slaughter all the way from Aroer to Minnith, taking twenty towns, and as far as Abel-keramim. Thus Israel crushed Ammon. 34 But when Jephthah came to his house in Mizpah, who should come out to meet him with tambourines and dances but his daughter, and she his only child; he had no other, neither son nor 35 daughter. When he saw her, he rent his clothes and said, 'Alas, my daughter, you have broken my heart, such trouble you have brought upon me. I have made a vow to the LORD and 36 I cannot go back.' She replied, 'Father, you have made a vow to the LORD; do to me what you have solemnly vowed, since the LORD has avenged you on the Ammonites, your enemies. 37 But, father, grant me this one favour. For two months let me be, that I may

roam[h] the hills with my companions and mourn that I must die a virgin.' 'Go', he said, and he let her depart for 38 two months. She went with her companions and mourned her virginity on the hills. At the end of two months 39 she came back to her father, and he fulfilled the vow he had made; she died a virgin. It became a tradition 40 that the daughters of Israel should go year by year and commemorate the fate of Jephthah's daughter, four days in every year.

The Gileadites defeat Ephraim

The Ephraimites mustered their forces 12 and crossed over to Zaphon. They said to Jephthah, 'Why did you march against the Ammonites and not summon us to go with you? We will burn your house over your head.' Jephthah answered, 'I and 2 my people had a feud with the Ammonites, and had I appealed to you for help, you would not have saved us[i] from them. When I saw that we were not to 3 look for help from you, I took my life in my hands and marched against the Ammonites, and the LORD delivered them into my power. Why then do you attack me today?' Jephthah then 4 mustered all the men of Gilead and fought Ephraim, and the Gileadites defeated them. The Gileadites seized 5 the fords of the Jordan and held them against Ephraim. When any Ephraimite who had escaped begged leave to cross, the men of Gilead asked him, 'Are you an Ephraimite?', and if he said, 'No', they would retort, 'Say 6 Shibboleth.' He would say 'Sibboleth', and because he could not pronounce the word properly, they seized him and killed him at the fords of the Jordan. At that time forty-two thousand men of Ephraim lost their lives.

Ibzan, Elon, and Abdon judge Israel

Jephthah was judge over Israel for 7 six years; when he died he was buried in his own city in Gilead. After him 8 Ibzan of Bethlehem was judge over Israel. He had thirty sons and thirty 9 daughters. He gave away the thirty daughters in marriage and brought in thirty girls for his sons. He was judge over Israel for seven years, and when 10 he died he was buried in Bethlehem. After him Elon the Zebulunite was 11 judge over Israel for ten years. When 12 he died, he was buried in Aijalon in the land of Zebulun. Next Abdon son 13 of Hillel the Pirathonite was judge

g *Or* recover.   h *Or that I may go down country to . . .* appeal to you for help, but you would not save us . . .   i *and had I . . . saved us: or* I did

14 over Israel. He had forty sons and thirty grandsons, who rode each on his own ass. He was judge over Israel 15 for eight years; and when he died he was buried in Pirathon in the land of Ephraim on the hill of the Amalekite.

The birth of Samson

13 Once more the Israelites did what was wrong in the eyes of the LORD, and he delivered them into the hands of the Philistines for forty years. 2 There was a man from Zorah of the tribe of Dan whose name was Manoah and whose wife was barren and child- 3 less. The angel of the LORD appeared to her and said, 'You are barren and have no child, but you shall conceive 4 and give birth to a son. Now you must do as I say: be careful to drink no wine or strong drink, and to eat no 5 forbidden food; you will conceive and give birth to a son, and no razor shall touch his head, for the boy is to be a Nazirite consecrated to God from the day of his birth. He will strike the first blow to deliver Israel from the 6 power of the Philistines.' The woman went and told her husband; she said to him, 'A man of God came to me; his appearance was that of an[j] angel of God, most terrible to see. I did not ask him where he came from nor did 7 he tell me his name. He said to me, "You shall conceive and give birth to a son. From this time onwards drink no wine or strong drink and eat no forbidden food, for the boy is to be a Nazirite consecrated to God from his birth to the day of his death."' 8 Manoah prayed to the LORD, 'If it please thee, O LORD, let the man of God whom thou didst send come again to tell us what we are to do with the 9 boy who is to be born.' God heard Manoah's prayer, and the angel of God came again to the woman, who was sitting in the fields; her husband 10 was not with her. The woman ran quickly and said to him, 'The man who came to me the other day has 11 appeared to me again.' Manoah went with her at once and approached the man and said, 'Was it you who talked with my wife?' He said, 'Yes, it was 12 I.' 'Now when your words come true,' Manoah said, 'what kind of boy will 13 he be and what will he do?' The angel of the LORD answered him, 'Your wife must be careful to do all 14 that I told her: she must not taste anything that comes from the vine. She must drink no wine or strong drink, and she must eat no forbidden food. She must do what I say.' Mano- 15 ah said to the angel of the LORD, 'May we urge you to stay? Let us prepare a kid for you.' The angel of 16 the LORD replied, 'Though you urge me to stay, I will not eat your food; but prepare a whole-offering if you will, and offer that to the LORD.' Manoah did not perceive that he was the angel of the LORD and said to him, 17 'What is your name? For we shall want to honour you when your words come true.' The angel of the LORD said to 18 him, 'How can you ask my name? It is a name of wonder.' Manoah took 19 a kid with the proper grain-offering, and offered it on the rock to the LORD, to him whose works are full of wonder. And while Manoah and his wife were watching, the flame went up from the 20 altar towards heaven, and the angel of the LORD went up in the flame; and seeing this, Manoah and his wife fell on their faces. The angel of the LORD 21 did not appear again to Manoah and his wife; and Manoah knew that he was the angel of the LORD. He said to 22 his wife, 'We are doomed to die, we have seen God',[k] but she replied, 'If 23 the LORD had wanted to kill us, he would not have accepted a whole-offering and a grain-offering at our hands; he would not now have let us see and hear all this.' The woman 24 gave birth to a son and named him Samson. The boy grew up in Ma-haneh-dan between Zorah and Esh-taol, and the LORD blessed him, and the spirit of the LORD began to drive him hard.

Samson's riddle

Samson went down to Timnath, and 14 there he saw a woman, one of the Philistines. When he came back, he 2 told his father and mother that he had seen a Philistine woman in Timnath and asked them to get her for him as 3 his wife. His father and mother said to him, 'Is there no woman among your cousins or in all our own people? Must you go and marry one of the un-circumcised Philistines?' But Samson said to his father, 'Get her for me, 4 because she pleases me.' His father and mother did not know that the LORD was at work in this, seeking an opportunity against the Philistines, who at that time were masters of Israel.[j]

Samson[l] went down to Timnath 5 and, when he reached the vineyards

j Or the.   k Or a god.   l Prob. rdg.; Heb. adds and his father and mother.

there, a young lion came at him
6 growling. The spirit of the LORD suddenly seized him and, having no weapon in his hand, he tore the lion in pieces as if it were a kid. He did not tell his parents what he had done.
7 Then he went down and spoke to the
8 woman, and she pleased him. After a time he went down again to take her to wife; he turned aside to look at the carcass of the lion, and he saw a swarm
9 of bees in it, and honey. He scraped the honey into his hands and went on, eating as he went. When he came to his father and mother, he gave them some and they ate it; but he did not tell them that he had scraped the
10 honey out of the lion's carcass. His father went down to see the woman, and Samson gave a feast there as the
11 custom of young men was. When the people saw him, they brought thirty
12 young men to be his escort. Samson said to them, 'Let me ask you a riddle. If you can guess it during the seven days of the feast, I will give you thirty lengths of linen and thirty
13 changes of clothing; but if you cannot guess the answer, then you shall give me thirty lengths of linen and thirty changes of clothing.' 'Tell us your
14 riddle,' they said; 'let us hear it.' So he said to them:

> Out of the eater came something to eat;
> out of the strong came something sweet.

At the end of three days they had
15 failed to guess the riddle. On the fourth day they said to Samson's wife, 'Coax your husband and make him tell you the riddle, or we shall burn you and your father's house. Did you invite us
16 here to beggar us?' So Samson's wife wept over him and said, 'You do not love me, you only hate me. You have asked my kinsfolk a riddle and you have not told it to me.' He said to her, 'I have not told it even to my father and mother; and am I to tell you?'
17 But she wept over him every day until the seven feast days were ended, and on the seventh day, because she pestered him, he told her, and she told
18 the riddle to her kinsfolk. So that same day the men of the city said to Samson before he entered the bridal chamber:[m]

> What is sweeter than honey?
> What is stronger than a lion?

and he replied, 'If you had not ploughed with my heifer, you would not have found out my riddle.' Then
19 the spirit of the LORD suddenly seized him. He went down to Ashkelon and there he killed thirty men, took their belts and gave their clothes to the men who had answered his riddle; but he was very angry and went off to his father's house. And
20 Samson's wife was given in marriage to the friend who had been his groomsman.

Samson burns the Philistines' corn

After a while, during the time of **15** wheat harvest, Samson went to visit his wife, taking a kid as a present for her. He said, 'I am going to my wife in our bridal chamber,' but her father would not let him in. He said, 'I was 2 sure that you hated her, so I gave her in marriage to your groomsman. Her young sister is better than she—take her instead.' But Samson said, 'This 3 time I will settle my score with the Philistines; I will do them some real harm.' So he went and caught three 4 hundred jackals and got some torches; he tied the jackals tail to tail and fastened a torch between each pair of tails. He then set the torches alight 5 and turned the jackals loose in the standing corn of the Philistines. He burnt up standing corn and stooks as well, vineyards and olive groves. The 6 Philistines said, 'Who has done this?' They were told that it was Samson, because the Timnite, his father-in-law, had taken his wife and given her to his groomsman. So the Philistines came and burnt her and her father. Samson said, 'If you do things like 7 this, I swear I will be revenged upon you before I have done.' He smote 8 them hip and thigh with great slaughter; and after that he went down to live in a cave in the Rock of Etam.

Samson defeats the Philistines at Lehi

The Philistines came up and pitched 9 camp in Judah, and overran Lehi. The 10 men of Judah said, 'Why have you attacked us?' They answered, 'We have come to take Samson prisoner and serve him as he served us.' So 11 three thousand men from Judah went down to the cave in the Rock of Etam. They said to Samson, 'Surely you know that the Philistines are our masters? Now see what you have brought upon us.' He answered, 'I only served them as they had served me.' They said to him, 'We have come 12

m he entered . . . chamber: *prob. rdg.; Heb.* the sun went down.

down to bind you and hand you over
to the Philistines.' 'Then you must
swear to me', he said, 'that you will
13 not set upon me yourselves.' They
answered, 'No; we will only bind you
and hand you over to us, we will
not kill you.' So they bound him with
two new ropes and brought him up
14 from the cave in the Rock. He came
to Lehi, and when they met him, the
Philistines shouted in triumph; but
the spirit of the LORD suddenly seized
him, the ropes on his arms became
like burnt tow and his bonds melted
15 away. He found the jaw-bone of an
ass, all raw, and picked it up and slew
16 a thousand men. He made this saying:

With the jaw-bone of an ass[n] I have
   flayed them like asses;[o]
with the jaw-bone of an ass I have
   slain a thousand men.

17 When he had said his say, he threw
away the jaw-bone; and he called that
18 place Ramath-lehi.[p] He began to feel
very thirsty and cried aloud to the
LORD, 'Thou hast let me, thy servant,
win this great victory, and must I now
die of thirst and fall into the hands of
19 the uncircumcised?' God split open
the Hollow of Lehi and water came
out of it. Samson drank, his strength
returned and he revived. This is why
the spring in Lehi is called En-hak-
kore[q] to this day.
20   Samson was judge over Israel for
twenty years in the days of the Philistines.

Samson at Gaza

16 Samson went to Gaza, and there he
saw a prostitute and went in to spend
2 the night with her. The people of
Gaza heard that Samson had come,
and they surrounded him and lay in
wait for him all that night at the city
gate. During the night, however, they
took no action, saying to themselves,
'When day breaks we shall kill him.'
3 Samson lay in bed till midnight; and
when midnight came he rose, seized
hold of the doors of the city gate and
the two posts, pulled them out, bar
and all, hoisted them on to his shoulders and carried them to the top of the
hill east of Hebron.

Samson and Delilah

4 After this Samson fell in love with a
woman named Delilah, who lived in
5 the valley of Sorek. The lords of the

Philistines went up country to see her
and said, 'Coax him and find out what
gives him his great strength, and how
we can master him, bind him and so
hold him captive; then we will each
give you eleven hundred pieces of
silver.' So Delilah said to Samson, 'Tell 6
me what gives you your great strength,
and how you can be bound and held
captive.' Samson replied, 'If they bind 7
me with seven fresh bowstrings not
yet dry, then I shall become as weak
as any other man.' So the lords of the 8
Philistines brought her seven fresh
bowstrings not yet dry, and she
bound him with them. She had men 9
already hidden in the inner room, and
she cried, 'The Philistines are upon
you, Samson!' But he snapped the
bowstrings as a strand of tow snaps
when it feels the fire, and his strength
was not tamed. Delilah said to Sam- 10
son, 'I see you have made a fool of me
and told me lies. Tell me this time
how you can be bound.' He said to 11
her, 'If you bind me tightly with new
ropes that have never been used, then
I shall become as weak as any other
man.' So Delilah took new ropes and 12
bound him with them. Then she cried,
'The Philistines are upon you, Samson!', while the men waited hidden in
the inner room. He snapped the ropes
off his arms like pack-thread. Delilah 13
said to him, 'You are still making a
fool of me and have told me lies. Tell
me: how can you be bound?' He said,
'Take the seven loose locks of my hair
and weave them into the warp, and
then drive them tight with the beater;
and I shall become as weak as any
other man.' So she lulled him to sleep,
wove the seven loose locks of his hair
into the warp, and drove them tight 14
with the beater, and cried, 'The Philistines are upon you, Samson!' He
woke from sleep and pulled away the
warp and the loom with it.[r] She said 15
to him, 'How can you say you love
me when you do not confide in me?
This is the third time you have made
a fool of me and have not told me
what gives you your great strength.'
She so pestered him with these words 16
day after day, pressing him hard and
wearying him to death, that he told 17
her his secret. 'No razor has touched
my head,' he said, 'because I am a
Nazirite, consecrated to God from the
day of my birth. If my head were
shaved, then my strength would leave

n ass: *Heb.* hamor.   o I have . . . asses: *or* I have reddened them blood-red, *or* I have heaped
them in heaps; *Heb.* hamor himmartim.   p *That is* Jaw-bone Hill.   q *That is* the Crier's
Spring.   r the warp . . . with it: *prob. rdg.; Heb. adds an unintelligible word.*

me, and I should become as weak as
8 any other man.' Delilah saw that he
had told her his secret; so she sent to
the lords of the Philistines and said,
'Come up at once, he has told me his
secret.' So the lords of the Philistines
came up and brought the money with
9 them. She lulled him to sleep on
her knees, summoned a man and he
shaved the seven locks of his hair for
her. She began to take him captive
10 and his strength left him. Then she
cried, 'The Philistines are upon you,
Samson!' He woke from his sleep and
said, 'I will go out as usual and shake
myself'; he did not know that the
11 LORD had left him. The Philistines
seized him, gouged out his eyes and
brought him down to Gaza. There
they bound him with fetters of bronze,
and he was set to grinding corn in the
12 prison. But his hair, after it had been
shaved, began to grow again.

The death of Samson

13 The lords of the Philistines assembled
together to offer a great sacrifice to
their god Dagon and to rejoice before
him. They said, 'Our god has delivered
Samson our enemy into our hands.'
14 The people, when they saw him,
praised their god, chanting:

Our god has delivered our enemy into
    our hands,
the scourge of our land who piled it
    with our dead.

25 When they grew merry, they said,
'Call Samson, and let him fight to
make sport for us.' So they summoned
Samson from prison and he made
sport before them all. They stood him
26 between the pillars, and Samson said
to the boy who held his hand, 'Put
me where I can feel the pillars which
support the temple, so that I may
27 lean against them.' The temple was
full of men and women, and all the
lords of the Philistines were there,
and there were about three thousand
men and women on the roof watching
28 Samson as he fought. Samson called
on the LORD and said, 'Remember me,
O Lord GOD, remember me: give me
strength only this once, O God, and
let me at one stroke be avenged on
29 the Philistines for my two eyes.' He
put his arms round the two central
pillars which supported the temple,
his right arm round one and his left
round the other, and braced himself

and said, 'Let me die with the 30
Philistines.' Then Samson leaned forward with all his might, and the
temple fell on the lords and on all the
people who were in it. So the dead
whom he killed at his death were
more than those he had killed in his
life. His brothers and all his father's 31
family came down, carried him up to
the grave of his father Manoah between Zorah and Eshtaol and buried
him there. He had been judge over
Israel for twenty years.

Micah and the Levite

There was once a man named Micah **17**
from the hill-country of Ephraim. He 2
said to his mother, 'You remember
the eleven hundred pieces of silver
which were taken from you, and how
you called down a curse on the thief
in my hearing? I have the money; I
took it and now I will give it back
to you.'[s] His mother said, 'May the
LORD bless you, my son.' So he gave 3
the eleven hundred pieces of silver
back to his mother, and she said, 'I
now solemnly dedicate this money of
mine to the LORD for the benefit of
my son, to make a carved idol and a
cast image.' He returned the money 4
to his mother, and she took two
hundred pieces of silver and handed
them to a silversmith, who made them
into an idol and an image, which stood
in Micah's house.

This man Micah had a shrine, and 5
he made an ephod and teraphim[t] and
installed one of his sons to be his
priest. In those days there was no 6
king in Israel and every man did
what was right in his own eyes. Now 7
there was a young man from Bethlehem in Judah, from the clan of Judah,
a Levite named Ben-gershom.[u] He had 8
left the city of Bethlehem to go and
find somewhere to live. On his way
he came to Micah's house in the hill-
country of Ephraim. Micah said to 9
him, 'Where have you come from?'
He replied, 'I am a Levite from Bethlehem in Judah, and I am looking for
somewhere to live.' Micah said to him, 10
'Stay with me and be priest and
father to me. I will give you ten pieces
of silver a year, and provide you with
food and clothes.' The Levite agreed 11
to stay with the man and was treated
as one of his own sons. Micah installed 12
the Levite, and the young man became his priest and a member of his
household. Micah said, 'Now I know 13

---

s and now . . . you: *transposed from verse 3.*
prob. rdg., cp. 18. 30; Heb. he lodged there.   *t* Or household gods.   *u* named Ben-gershom:

that the LORD will make me prosper, because I have a Levite for my priest.'

The Danites explore Laish

18 In those days there was no king in Israel and the tribe of the Danites was looking for territory to occupy, because they had not so far come into possession of the territory allotted to
2 them among the tribes of Israel. The Danites therefore sent out five fighting men of their clan from Zorah and Eshtaol to prospect, with instructions to go and explore the land. They came to Micah's house in the hill-country of Ephraim and spent the night there.
3 While they were there, they recognized the speech of the young Levite; they turned there and then and said to him, 'Who brought you here? What are you doing? What is your
4 business here?' He said, 'This is all Micah's doing: he has hired me and
5 I have become his priest.' They said to him, 'Then inquire of God on our behalf whether our mission will be
6 successful.' The priest replied, 'Go in peace. Your mission is in the LORD's
7 hands.' The five men went on their way and came to Laish. There they found the inhabitants living a care-free life, in the same way as the Sidonians, a quiet, carefree folk, with no hereditary king to keep the country under his thumb.[v] They were a long way from the Sidonians, and had no
8 contact with the Aramaeans. So the five men went back to Zorah and Eshtaol, and when their kinsmen
9 asked their news, they said, 'Come and attack them. It is an excellent country that we have seen. Will you hang back and do nothing about it? Start off now and take possession of
10 the land. When you get there, you will find a people living a carefree life in a wide expanse of open country. God has delivered it into your hands, a place where there is no lack of anything on earth.'

The Danites steal Micah's gods

11 And so six hundred armed men from the clan of the Danites set out from
12 Zorah and Eshtaol. They went up country and encamped in Kiriath-jearim in Judah: this is why that place to this day is called Mahaneh-dan;[w] it lies west of Kiriath-jearim.
13 From there they passed on to the hill-country of Ephraim and came to

Micah's house. The five men who had 14 been to explore the country round Laish spoke up and said to their kinsmen, 'Do you know that in one of these houses there are now an ephod and teraphim, an idol and an image? Now consider what you had best do.' So they turned aside to Micah's house 15 and greeted him. The six hundred 16 armed Danites took their stand at the entrance of the gate, and the five 17 men who had gone to explore the country went indoors to take the idol and the image, ephod and teraphim, while the priest was standing at the entrance with the six hundred armed men. The five men entered Micah's 18 house and took the idol and the image, ephod and teraphim.[x] The priest asked them what they were doing, but they 19 said to him, 'Be quiet; not a word. Come with us and be our priest and father. Which is better, to be priest in the household of one man or to be priest to a whole tribe and clan in Israel?' This pleased the priest; so 20 he took the ephod and teraphim, the idol and the image, and joined the company. They turned and went off, 21 putting the dependants, the herds, and the valuables in front. The Dan- 22 ites had gone some distance from Micah's house, when his neighbours were called out in pursuit and caught up with them. They shouted after 23 them, and the Danites turned round and said to Micah, 'What is the matter with you? Why have you come after us?' He said, 'You have taken my 24 gods which I made for myself, you have taken the priest, and you have gone off and left me nothing. How dare you say, "What is the matter with you?"' The Danites said to him, 25 'Do not shout at us. We are desperate men and if we fall upon you it will be the death of yourself and your family.' With that the Danites went on their 26 way and Micah, seeing that they were too strong for him, turned and went home.

Destruction of Laish

Thus they carried off the priest and 27 the things Micah had made for himself, and attacked Laish, whose people were quiet and carefree. They put them to the sword and set fire to their city. There was no one to save them, 28 for the city was a long way from Sidon and they had no contact with

v with no . . . thumb: prob. rdg.; Heb. and none authority.   w That is the Camp of Dan. phim and image.   humiliating anything in the land with inherited x Prob. rdg.; Heb. the idol of the ephod, and tera-

the Aramaeans,[y] although the city was in the vale near Beth-rehob. They rebuilt the city and settled in it, 29 naming it Dan after the name of their forefather Dan, a son of Israel; but 30 its original name was Laish. The Danites set up the idol, and Jonathan son of Gershom, son of Moses, and his sons were priests to the tribe of Dan 31 until the people went into exile. (They set up for themselves the idol which Micah had made, and it was there as long as the house of God was at Shiloh.)

A Levite and his concubine

19 In those days when no king ruled in Israel, a Levite was living in the heart of the hill-country of Ephraim. He had taken himself a concubine 2 from Bethlehem in Judah. In a fit of anger she had left him and had gone to her father's house in Bethlehem in Judah. When she had been there four 3 months, her husband set out after her with his servant and two asses to appeal to her and bring her back. She brought him in to the house of her father, who welcomed him when he 4 saw him. His father-in-law, the girl's father, pressed him and he stayed with him three days, and they were well 5 entertained during their visit. On the fourth day, they rose early in the morning, and he prepared to leave, but the girl's father said to his son-in-law, 'Have something to eat first, 6 before you go.' So the two of them sat down and ate and drank together. The girl's father said to the man, 'Why not spend the night and enjoy your-7 self?' When he rose to go, his father-in-law urged him to stay, and again he 8 stayed for the night. He rose early in the morning on the fifth day to depart, but the girl's father said, 'Have something to eat first.' So they lingered till late afternoon, eating and drinking 9 together. Then the man stood up to go with his concubine and servant, but his father-in-law said, 'See how the day wears on towards sunset. Spend the night here and enjoy yourself, and then rise early tomorrow 10 and set out for home.' But the man would not stay the night; he rose and left. He had reached a point opposite Jebus, that is Jerusalem, with his two laden asses and his concubine, 11 and when they were close to Jebus, the weather grew wild and stormy, and the young man said to his master, 'Come now, let us turn into this Jebusite

town and spend the night there.' But his master said to him, 'No, not 12 into a strange town where the people are not Israelites; let us go on to Gibeah. Come, we will go and find 13 some other place, and spend the night in Gibeah or Ramah.' So they went 14 on until sunset overtook them; they were then near Gibeah which belongs to Benjamin. They turned in to 15 spend the night there, and went and sat down in the open street of the town; but nobody took them into his house for the night.

Meanwhile an old man was coming 16 home in the evening from his work in the fields. He was from the hill-country of Ephraim, but he lived in Gibeah, where the people were Benjamites. He looked up, saw the travel-17 ler in the open street of the town, and asked him where he was going and where he came from. He answered, 18 'We are travelling from Bethlehem in Judah to the heart of the hill-country of Ephraim. I come from there; I have been to Bethlehem in Judah and I am going home, but nobody has taken me into his house. I have straw 19 and provender for the asses, food and wine for myself, the girl, and the young man; we have all we need, sir.' The old man said, 'You are welcome, 20 I will supply all your wants; you must not spend the night in the street.' So 21 he took him inside and provided fodder for the asses; they washed their feet, and ate and drank. While they 22 were enjoying themselves, some of the worst scoundrels in the town surrounded the house, hurling themselves against the door and shouting to the old man who owned the house, 'Bring out the man who has gone into your house, for us to have intercourse with him.' The owner of the house went 23 outside to them and said, 'No, my friends, do nothing so wicked. This man is my guest; do not commit this outrage. Here is my daughter, a vir-24 gin;[z] let me bring her[a] out to you. Rape her[a] and do to her[a] what you please; but you shall not commit such an outrage against this man.' But the 25 men refused to listen to him, so the Levite took hold of his concubine and thrust her outside for them. They assaulted her and abused her all night till the morning, and when dawn broke, they let her go. The girl came at day-26 break and fell down at the entrance of the man's house where her master was, and lay there until it was light.

y Prob. rdg., cp. verse 7; Heb. men.   z Prob. rdg.; Heb. adds and his concubine.   a Prob. rdg.; Heb. them.

27 Her master rose in the morning and opened the door of the house to set out on his journey, and there was his concubine lying at the door with her
28 hands on the threshold. He said to her, 'Get up and let us be off'; but there was no answer. So he lifted her on to
29 his ass and set off for home. When he arrived there, he picked up a knife, and he took hold of his concubine and cut her up limb by limb into twelve pieces; and he sent them through the
30 length and breadth of Israel. He told the men he sent with them to say to every Israelite, 'Has the like of this happened or been seen from the time the Israelites came up from Egypt till today? Consider this among yourselves and speak your minds.' So everyone who saw them said, 'No such thing has ever happened or been seen before.'

Preparing to attack Gibeah

20 All the Israelites, the whole community from Dan to Beersheba and out of Gilead also, left their homes and one man and assembled before the LORD
2 at Mizpah. The leaders of the people and all the tribes of Israel presented themselves in the general assembly of the people of God, four hundred thousand foot-soldiers armed with
3 swords; and the Benjamites heard that the Israelites had gone up to Mizpah. The Israelites asked how this
4 wicked thing had come about, and the Levite, to whom the murdered woman belonged, answered, 'I and my concubine came to Gibeah in Benjamin
5 to spend the night there. The citizens of Gibeah rose against me that night and surrounded the house where I was, intending to kill me; and they
6 raped my concubine and she died. I took her and cut her in pieces, and sent them through the length and breadth of Israel, because of the filthy outrage they had committed in Israel.
7 Now it is for you, the whole of Israel, to say here and now what you think
8 ought to be done.' All the people rose to their feet as one man and said, 'Not one of us shall go back to his tent,
9 not one shall return home. This is what we will now do to Gibeah. We
10 will draw lots for the attack: and we will take ten men out of every hundred in all the tribes of Israel, a hundred out of every thousand, and a thousand out of every ten thousand, to collect provisions from the people

for those who have taken the field against Gibeah in Benjamin to avenge the outrage committed in Israel.' Thus 11 all the Israelites to a man were massed against the town.

Israel defeats the Benjamites

The tribes of Israel sent men all 12 through the tribe of Benjamin saying, 'What is this wicked thing which has happened in your midst? Hand over 13 to us those scoundrels in Gibeah, and we will put them to death and purge Israel of this wickedness.' But the Benjamites refused to listen to their fellow-Israelites. They flocked from 14 their cities to Gibeah to go to war with the Israelites, and that day they 15 mustered out of their cities twenty-six thousand men armed with swords. There were also seven hundred picked men from Gibeah, left-handed men, 16 who could sling a stone and not miss by a hair's breadth. The Israelites, 17 without Benjamin, numbered four hundred thousand men armed with swords, every one a fighting man. The 18 Israelites at once moved on to Bethel, and there they sought an oracle from God, asking, 'Which of us shall attack Benjamin first?', and the LORD's answer was, 'Judah shall attack first.' So the Israelites set out at dawn and 19 encamped opposite Gibeah. They ad- 20 vanced to do battle with Benjamin and drew up their forces before the town. The Benjamites made a sally 21 from Gibeah and left twenty-two thousand of Israel dead on the field that day. The Israelites went up to 23 Bethel,[c] lamented before the LORD until evening and inquired whether they should again attack their brother Benjamin. The LORD said, 'Yes, attack him.' Then the Israelites took 22 fresh courage and again formed up on the same ground as the first day. So 24 the second day they advanced against the Benjamites, who sallied out from 25 Gibeah to meet them and laid another eighteen thousand armed men low. The Israelites, the whole people, went 26 back to Bethel, where they sat before the LORD lamenting and fasting until evening, and they offered whole-offerings and shared-offerings before the LORD. In those days the Ark of 27 the Covenant of God was there, and 28 Phinehas son of Eleazar, son of Aaron, served before the LORD.[d] The Israelites inquired of the LORD and said, 'Shall we again march out to battle

b Verses 22 and 23 transposed.   *c* to Bethel: *prob. rdg., cp. verses 18, 26; Heb. om.*   *d* Or before the Ark.

against Benjamin our brother or shall we desist?' The LORD answered, 'Attack him: tomorrow I will deliver him into your hands.' Israel then posted men in ambush all round Gibeah.

30 On the third day the Israelites advanced against the Benjamites and drew up their forces at Gibeah as **31** they had before; and the Benjamites sallied out to meet the army. They were drawn away from the town and began the attack as before by killing a few Israelites, about thirty,*e* on the highways which led across open country, one to Bethel and the other **32** to Gibeah. They thought they were defeating them once again, but the Israelites had planned a retreat to draw them away from the town out **33** on to the highways. Meanwhile the main body of Israelites left their positions and re-formed in Baal-tamar, while those in ambush, ten thousand picked men all told, burst out from their position in the neighbourhood **34** of Gibeah and came in on the east of the town. There was soon heavy fighting; yet the Benjamites did not suspect the disaster that was threaten**35**ing them. So the LORD put Benjamin to flight before Israel, and on that day the Israelites killed twenty-five thousand one hundred Benjamites, all armed men.

36 The men of Benjamin now saw that they had been defeated, for all that the Israelites, trusting in the ambush which they had set by Gibeah, had **37** given way before them. The men in ambush made a sudden dash on Gibeah, fell on the town from all sides and put all the inhabitants to the **38** sword. The agreed signal between the Israelites and those in ambush*f* was to be a column of smoke sent up from **39** the town. The Israelites then faced about in the battle; and Benjamin began to cut down the Israelites, killing about thirty of them,*g* in the belief that they were defeating them as they **40** had done in the first encounter. As the column of smoke began to go up from the town, the Benjamites looked back and thought the whole town was go**41**ing up in flames. When the Israelites faced about, the Benjamites saw that disaster had overtaken them and were **42** seized with panic. They turned and fled before the Israelites in the direction of the wilderness, but the fighting

caught up with them and soon those from the town were among them, cutting them down. They hemmed in the **43** Benjamites, pursuing them without respite,*h* and overtook them at a point to the east of Gibeah. Eighteen thou- **44** sand of the Benjamites fell, all of them fighting men. The survivors **45** turned and fled into the wilderness towards the Rock of Rimmon. The Israelites picked off the stragglers on the roads, five thousand of them, and chased them until they had cut down and killed two thousand more. Twenty-five thousand armed men of **46** Benjamin fell in battle that day, all fighting men. The six hundred who **47** survived turned and fled into the wilderness as far as the Rock of Rimmon, and there they remained for four months. The Israelites then turned **48** back to deal with the Benjamites, and put to the sword the people in the towns and the cattle, every creature that they found; they also set fire to every town within their reach.

Wives for the Benjamites

In Mizpah the Israelites had bound **21** themselves by oath that none of them would marry his daughter to a Benjamite. The people now came to **2** Bethel and remained there in God's presence till sunset, raising their voices in loud lamentation. They said, **3** 'O LORD God of Israel, why has it happened in Israel that one tribe should this day be lost to Israel?' Next day the people rose early, built **4** an altar there and offered whole-offerings and shared-offerings. At **5** that the Israelites asked themselves whether among all the tribes of Israel there was anyone who did not go up to the assembly before the LORD; for under the terms of the great oath anyone who had not gone up to the LORD at Mizpah was to be put to death. And **6** the Israelites felt remorse over their brother Benjamin, because, as they said, 'This day Israel has lost one whole tribe.' So they asked, 'What **7** shall we do for wives for those who are left? We have sworn to the LORD not to give any of our daughters to them in marriage. Is there anyone in **8** all the tribes of Israel who did not go up to the LORD at Mizpah?' Now it happened that no one from Jabesh-gilead had come to the camp for the assembly; so when they held a roll-call **9**

e Or about thirty wounded men.   *f Prob. rdg.; Heb. adds an unintelligible word.*   *g to cut . . . them: or to kill about thirty wounded men among the Israelites.*   *h without respite: or from Nohah.*

of the people, they found that no inhabitant of Jabesh-gilead was pres-
10 ent. Thereupon the community sent off twelve thousand fighting men with orders to go and put the inhabitants of Jabesh-gilead to the sword, men,
11 women, and dependants. 'This is what you shall do,' they said: 'put to death every male person, and every woman who has had intercourse with a man, but spare any who are virgins.' This
12 they did. Among the inhabitants of Jabesh-gilead they found four hundred young women who were virgins and had not had intercourse with a man, and they brought them to the
13 camp at Shiloh in Canaan. Then the whole community sent messengers to the Benjamites at the Rock of Rimmon to parley with them, and peace
14 was proclaimed. At this the Benjamites came back, and were given those of the women of Jabesh-gilead who had been spared; but these were not enough.
15 The people were still full of remorse over Benjamin because the LORD had made this gap in the tribes of Israel,
16 and the elders of the community said, 'What shall we do for wives for the rest? All the women in Benjamin have
17 been massacred.' They said, 'Heirs there must be for the remnant of Benjamin who have escaped! Then Israel will not see one of its tribes blotted
18 out. We cannot give them our own daughters in marriage because we have sworn that there shall be a curse on the man who gives a wife to a Benjamite.' Then they bethought
19 themselves of the pilgrimage in honour of the LORD, made every year to Shiloh, the place which lies to the north of Bethel, on the east side of the highway from Bethel to Shechem and to the south of Lebonah. They
20 said to the Benjamites, 'Go and hide
21 in the vineyards and keep watch. When the girls of Shiloh come out to dance, sally out of the vineyards, and each of you seize one of them for his wife; then make your way home to
22 the land of Benjamin. Then, if their fathers or brothers come and complain to you, say to them, "Let us keep them with your approval, for none of us has captured a wife in battle. Had you offered them to us, the guilt would be yours."'
23 All this the Benjamites did. They carried off as many wives as they needed, snatching them as they danced; then they went their way and returned to their patrimony, rebuilt their cities
24 and settled in them. The Israelites also dispersed by tribes and families, and every man went back to his own patrimony.
25 In those days there was no king in Israel and every man did what was right in his own eyes.

RUTH

Naomi and Ruth

1 LONG AGO, in the time of the Judges, there was a famine in the land, and a man from Bethlehem in Judah went to live in the Moabite country
2 with his wife and his two sons. The man's name was Elimelech, his wife's name was Naomi, and the names of his two sons Mahlon and Chilion. They were Ephrathites from Bethlehem in Judah. They arrived in the Moabite country and there they stayed.
3 Elimelech Naomi's husband died, so that she was left with her two sons.
4 These sons married Moabite women, one of whom was called Orpah and the other Ruth. They had lived there about ten years, when both Mahlon
5 and Chilion died, so that the woman was bereaved of her two sons as well as of her husband. Thereupon she set
6 out with her two daughters-in-law to return home, because she had heard while still in the Moabite country that the LORD had cared for his people and given them food. So with her two
7 daughters-in-law she left the place where she had been living, and took the road home to Judah. Then Naomi
8 said to her two daughters-in-law, 'Go back, both of you, to your mothers' homes. May the LORD keep faith with you, as you have kept faith with the

9 dead and with me; and may he grant each of you security in the home of a new husband.' She kissed them and 10 they wept aloud. Then they said to her, 'We will return with you to your 11 own people.' But Naomi said, 'Go back, my daughters. Why should you go with me? Am I likely to bear any more sons to be husbands for you? 12 Go back, my daughters, go. I am too old to marry again. But even if I could say that I had hope of a child, if I were to marry this night and if 13 I were to bear sons, would you then wait until they grew up? Would you then refrain from marrying? No, no, my daughters, my lot is more bitter than yours, because the LORD has been 14 against me.' At this they wept again. Then Orpah kissed her mother-in-law and returned to her people, but Ruth clung to her.

15 'You see,' said Naomi, 'your sister-in-law has gone gack to her people 16 and her gods;[a] go back with her.' 'Do not urge me to go back and desert you', Ruth answered. 'Where you go, I will go, and where you stay, I will stay. Your people shall be my people, 17 and your God my God. Where you die, I will die, and there I will be buried. I swear a solemn oath before the LORD your God: nothing but[b] 18 death shall divide us.' When Naomi saw that Ruth was determined to go 19 with her, she said no more, and the two of them went on until they came to Bethlehem. When they arrived in Bethlehem, the whole town was in great excitement about them, and the women said, 'Can this be Naomi?' 20 'Do not call me Naomi,'[c] she said, 'call me Mara,[d] for it is a bitter lot 21 that the Almighty has sent me. I went away full, and the LORD has brought me back empty. Why do you call me Naomi? The LORD has pronounced against me; the Almighty has brought 22 disaster on me.' This is how Naomi's daughter-in-law, Ruth the Moabitess, returned with her from the Moabite country. The barley harvest was beginning when they arrived in Bethlehem.

Ruth gleans in the field of Boaz

2 Now Naomi had a kinsman on her husband's side, a well-to-do man of the family of Elimelech; his name 2 was Boaz. Ruth the Moabitess said to Naomi, 'May I go out to the cornfields and glean behind anyone who will grant me that favour?' 'Yes, go, my daughter', she replied. So Ruth went 3 gleaning in the fields behind the reapers. As it happened, she was in that strip of the fields which belonged to Boaz of Elimelech's family, and 4 there was Boaz coming out from Bethlehem. He greeted the reapers, saying, 'The LORD be with you'; and they replied, 'The LORD bless you.' Then he asked his servant in charge 5 of the reapers, 'Whose girl is this?' 'She is a Moabite girl', the servant 6 answered, 'who has just come back with Naomi from the Moabite country. She asked if she might glean and 7 gather among the swathes behind the reapers. She came and has been on her feet with hardly a moment's rest[e] from daybreak till now.' Then Boaz said to 8 Ruth, 'Listen to me, my daughter: do not go and glean in any other field, and do not look any further, but keep close to my girls. Watch where the 9 men reap, and follow the gleaners; I have given them orders not to molest you. If you are thirsty, go and drink from the jars the men have filled.' She 10 fell prostrate before him and said, 'Why are you so kind as to take notice of me when I am only a foreigner?' Boaz answered, 'They have told me 11 all that you have done for your mother-in-law since your husband's death, how you left your father and mother and the land of your birth, and came to a people you did not know before. The LORD reward your 12 deed; may the LORD the God of Israel, under whose wings you have come to take refuge, give you all that you deserve.' 'Indeed, sir,' she said, 'you 13 have eased my mind and spoken kindly to me; may I ask you as a favour not to treat me only as one of your slave-girls?'[f] When meal-time 14 came round, Boaz said to her, 'Come here and have something to eat, and dip your bread into the sour wine.' So she sat beside the reapers, and he passed her some roasted grain. She ate all she wanted and still had some left over. When she got up to glean, Boaz 15 gave the men orders. 'She', he said, 'may glean even among the sheaves; do not scold her. Or you may even 16 pull out some corn from the bundles and leave it for her to glean, without reproving her.'

---

a Or god.   *b* I swear . . . nothing but: *or* The LORD your God do so to me and more if . . .
c *That is* Pleasure.   *d* *That is* Bitter.   *e* *Prob. rdg.; Heb. adds* in the house.   *f* may I . . .
slave-girls?: *or if you please, treat me as one of* your slave-girls.

Naomi's advice

17 So Ruth gleaned in the field till evening, and when she beat out what she had gleaned, it came to about a bushel
18 of barley. She took it up and went into the town, and her mother-in-law saw how much she had gleaned. Then Ruth brought out what she had saved
19 from her meal and gave it to her. Her mother-in-law asked her, 'Where did you glean today? Which way did you go? Blessings on the man who kindly took notice of you.' So she told her mother-in-law whom she had been working with. 'The man with whom I worked today', she said, 'is called
20 Boaz.' 'Blessings on him from the LORD', said Naomi. 'The LORD has kept faith with the living and the dead. For this man is related to us
21 and is our next-of-kin.' 'And what is more,' said Ruth the Moabitess, 'he told me to stay close to his men until they had finished all his harvest.'
22 'It is best for you, my daughter,' Naomi answered, 'to go out with his girls; let no one catch you in another
23 field.' So she kept close to his girls, gleaning with them till the end of both barley and wheat harvests; but she lived with her mother-in-law.

Ruth and Boaz at the threshing-floor

3 One day Ruth's mother-in-law Naomi said to her, 'My daughter, I want to
2 see you happily settled. Now there is our kinsman Boaz; you were with his girls. Tonight he is winnowing barley
3 at his threshing-floor. Wash and anoint yourself, put on your cloak and go down to the threshing-floor, but do not make yourself known to the man until he has finished eating and drink-
4 ing. But when he lies down, take note of the place where he lies. Then go in, turn back the covering at his feet and lie down. He will tell you what to do.'
5 'I will do whatever you tell me', Ruth
6 answered. So she went down to the threshing-floor and did exactly as her
7 mother-in-law had told her. When Boaz had eaten and drunk, he felt at peace with the world and went to lie down at the far end of the heap of grain. She came in quietly, turned back the covering at his feet and lay
8 down. About midnight something disturbed the man as he slept; he turned over and, lo and behold, there was
9 a woman lying at his feet. 'Who are you?' he asked. 'I am your servant, Ruth', she replied. 'Now spread your skirt over your servant, because you

are my next-of-kin.' He said, 'The 10 LORD has blessed you, my daughter. This last proof of your loyalty is greater than the first; you have not sought after any young man, rich or poor. Set your mind at rest, my 11 daughter. I will do whatever you ask; for, as the whole neighbourhood knows, you are a capable woman. Are 12 you sure that I am the next-of-kin? There is a kinsman even closer than I. Spend the night here and then in 13 the morning, if he is willing to act as your next-of-kin, well and good; but if he is not willing, I will do so; I swear it by the LORD. Now lie down till morning.' So she lay at his feet 14 till morning, but rose before one man could recognize another; and he said, 'It must not be known that a woman has been to the threshing-floor.' Then 15 he said, 'Bring me the cloak you have on, and hold it out.' So she held it out, and he put in six measures of barley and lifted it on her back, and she went to the town. When she came to her 16 mother-in-law, Naomi asked, 'How did things go with you, my daughter?' Ruth told her all that the man had done for her. 'He gave me these 17 six measures of barley,' she said; 'he would not let me come home to my mother-in-law empty-handed.' Naomi 18 answered, 'Wait, my daughter, until you see what will come of it. He will not rest until he has settled the matter today.'

Boaz acquires Elimelech's property

Now Boaz had gone up to the city 4 gate, and was sitting there; and, after a time, the next-of-kin of whom he had spoken passed by. 'Here,' he cried, calling him by name, 'come and sit down.' He came and sat down. Then 2 Boaz stopped ten elders of the town, and asked them to sit there, and they did so. Then he said to the next-of- 3 kin, 'You will remember the strip of field that belonged to our brother Elimelech. Naomi has returned from the Moabite country and is selling it. I 4 promised to open the matter with you, to ask you to acquire it in the presence of those who sit here, in the presence of the elders of my people. If you are going to do your duty as next-of-kin, then do so, but if not, someone must do it. So tell me, and then I shall know; for I come after you as next-of-kin.' He answered, 'I will act as next-of-kin.' Then Boaz said, 'On the 5 day when you acquire the field from Naomi, you also acquire Ruth the

Moabitess, the dead man's wife, so as to perpetuate the name of the dead man

6 with his patrimony.' Thereupon the next-of-kin said, 'I cannot act myself, for I should risk losing my own patrimony. You must therefore do my duty as next-of-kin. I cannot act.'

7 Now in those old days, when property was redeemed or exchanged, it was the custom for a man to pull off his sandal and give it to the other party. This was the form of attesta-

8 tion in Israel. So the next-of-kin said to Boaz, 'Acquire it for yourself', and

9 pulled off his sandal. Then Boaz declared to the elders and all the people, 'You are witnesses today that I have acquired from Naomi all that belonged to Elimelech and all that be-

10 longed to Mahlon and Chilion; and, further, that I have myself acquired Ruth the Moabitess, wife of Mahlon, to be my wife, to perpetuate the name of the deceased with his patrimony, so that his name may not be missing among his kindred and at the gate of his native place. You are witnesses this

11 day.' Then the elders and all who were at the gate said, 'We are witnesses. May the LORD make this woman, who has come to your home, like Rachel and Leah, the two who built up the house of Israel. May you do great things in Ephrathah and keep

a name alive in Bethlehem. May your 12 house be like the house of Perez, whom Tamar bore to Judah, through the offspring the LORD will give you by this girl.'

Boaz marries Ruth

So Boaz took Ruth and made her his 13 wife. When they came together, the LORD caused her to conceive and she bore Boaz a son. Then the women 14 said to Naomi, 'Blessed be the LORD today, for he has not left you without a next-of-kin. May the dead man's name be kept alive in Israel. The child 15 will give you new life and cherish you in your old age; for your daughter-in-law who loves you, who has proved better to you than seven sons, has borne him.' Naomi took the child and laid 16 him in her lap and became his nurse. Her neighbours gave him a name: 17 'Naomi has a son,' they said; 'we will call him Obed.' He was the father of Jesse, the father of David.

Genealogy from Perez to David

This is the genealogy of Perez: Perez 18 was the father of Hezron, Hezron of 19 Ram, Ram of Amminadab, Ammina- 20 dab of Nahshon, Nahshon of Salmon, Salmon of Boaz, Boaz of Obed, Obed 21 22 of Jesse, and Jesse of David.

THE FIRST BOOK OF
SAMUEL

The birth of Samuel

1 THERE WAS A MAN from Ramathaim, a Zuphite from the hillcountry of Ephraim, named Elkanah son of Jeroham, son of Elihu, son of Tohu, son of Zuph an Ephraimite;

2 and he had two wives named Hannah and Peninnah. Peninnah had children,

3 but Hannah was childless. This man used to go up from his own town every year to worship and to offer sacrifice to the LORD of Hosts in Shiloh. There Eli's two sons, Hophni and Phin-

4 ehas, were priests of the LORD. On the day when Elkanah sacrificed, he gave several shares of the meat to his wife

Peninnah with all her sons and daughters; but, although he loved Hannah, 5 he gave her only one share, because the LORD had not granted her children. Further, Hannah's rival used 6 to torment her and humiliate her because she had no children. Year after 7 year this happened when they went up to the house of the LORD; her rival used to torment her. Once when she was in tears and would not eat, her 8 husband Elkanah said to her, 'Hannah, why are you crying and eating nothing? Why are you so miserable? Am I not more to you than ten sons?' After they had finished eating and 9–10 drinking at the sacrifice at Shiloh,

Hannah rose in deep distress, and stood before the LORD and prayed to him, weeping bitterly. Meanwhile Eli the priest was sitting on his seat beside the door of the temple of the 11 LORD. Hannah made a vow in these words: 'O LORD of Hosts, if thou wilt deign to take notice of my trouble and remember me, if thou wilt not forget me but grant me offspring, then I will give the child to the LORD for his whole life, and no razor shall ever 12 touch his head.' For a long time she went on praying before the LORD, 13 while Eli watched her lips. Hannah was praying silently; but, although her voice could not be heard, her lips were moving and Eli took her for 14 a drunken woman. He said to her, 'Enough of this drunken behaviour! Go away till the wine has worn off.' 15 'No, sir,' she answered, 'I am a sober person, I have drunk no wine or strong drink, and I have been pouring 16 out my heart before the LORD. Do not think me so degraded, sir; all this time I have been speaking out of the fullness of my grief and misery.' 17 'Go in peace,' said Eli, 'and may the God of Israel answer the prayer you 18 have made to him.' Hannah said, 'May I be worthy of your kindness.' And she went away and took some- 19 thing to eat, no longer downcast. Next morning they were up early and, after prostrating themselves before the LORD, returned to their own home at Ramah. Elkanah had intercourse with his wife Hannah, and the LORD 20 remembered her. She conceived, and in due time bore a son, whom she named Samuel, 'because', she said, 'I asked the LORD for him.'

Samuel is lent to the LORD

21 Elkanah, with his whole household, went up to make the annual sacrifice to the LORD and to redeem his vow. 22 Hannah did not go with them, but said to her husband, 'When the child is weaned I will come up with him to enter the presence of the LORD, 23 and he shall[a] stay there always.' Her husband Elkanah said to her, 'Do what you think best; stay at home until you have weaned him. Only, may the LORD indeed see your vow fulfilled.' So the woman stayed and nursed her son until she had weaned 24 him; and when she had weaned him, she took him up with her. She took also a bull three years old, an ephah

of meal, and a flagon of wine, and she brought him, child as he was, into the house of the LORD at Shiloh. They 25 slaughtered the bull, and brought the boy to Eli. Hannah said to him, 'Sir, 26 as sure as you live, I am the woman who stood near you here praying to the LORD. It was this boy that I 27 prayed for and the LORD has given me what I asked. What I asked I have received; and now I lend him to the 28 LORD; for his whole life he is lent to the LORD.' And they prostrated themselves there before the LORD.

The song of Hannah

Then Hannah offered this prayer: 2

My heart rejoices in the LORD,
in the LORD I now hold my head high;
my mouth is full of derision of my foes,
exultant because thou hast saved me.
   There is none except thee,   2
   none so holy as the LORD,
   no rock like our God.
Cease your proud boasting,   3
let no word of arrogance pass your lips;
for the LORD is a god of all knowledge:
he governs all that men do.

Strong men stand in mute[b] dismay   4
but those who faltered put on new strength.
Those who had plenty sell themselves 5
for a crust,
and the hungry grow strong again.
The barren woman has seven children,
and the mother of many sons is left to languish.

The LORD kills and he gives life,   6
he sends down to Sheol, he can bring the dead up again.
The LORD makes a man poor, he 7 makes him rich,
he brings down and he raises up.
He lifts the weak out of the dust   8
and raises the poor from the dunghill;
to give them a place among the great,
to set them in seats of honour.

For the foundations of the earth are the LORD's,
he has built the world upon them.
He will guard the footsteps of his 9 saints,
while the wicked sink into silence and gloom;
not by mere strength shall a man prevail.

Those that stand against the LORD 10 will be terrified

a come up . . . he shall: or bring him up, and he shall come into the presence of the LORD and . . .
b in mute: prob. rdg.; Heb. obscure.

when the High God[c] thunders out of heaven.

The LORD is judge even to the ends of the earth,
he will give strength to his king
and raise high the head of his anointed prince.

11 Then Elkanah went to Ramah with his household, but the boy remained behind in the service of the LORD under Eli the priest.

Wickedness of Eli's sons

12 Now Eli's sons were scoundrels and 13 had no regard for the LORD. The custom of the priests in their dealings with the people was this: when a man offered a sacrifice, the priest's servant would come while the flesh was stew-
14 ing and would thrust a three-pronged fork into the cauldron or pan or kettle or pot; and the priest would take whatever the fork brought out. This should have been their practice whenever Israelites came to sacrifice
15 at Shiloh; but now under Eli's sons, even before the fat was burnt, the priest's servant came and said to the man who was sacrificing, 'Give me meat to roast for the priest; he will not accept what has been already
16 stewed, only raw meat.' And if the man answered 'Let them burn the fat first, and then take what you want', he said, 'No, give it to me now, or I
17 will take it by force.' The young men's sin was very great in the LORD's sight; for they brought the LORD's sacrifice into general contempt.
18 Samuel continued in the service of the LORD, a mere boy with a linen
19 ephod fastened round him. Every year his mother made him a little cloak and took it to him when she went up with her husband to offer
20 the annual sacrifice. Eli would give his blessing to Elkanah and his wife and say, 'The LORD grant you children by this woman in place of the one for which you asked him.'[d] Then they went home again.
21 The LORD showed his care for Hannah, and she conceived and gave birth to three sons and two daughters; meanwhile the boy Samuel grew up in the presence of the LORD.
22 Eli, now a very old man, had heard how his sons were treating all the Israelites, and how they lay with the women who were serving at the entrance to the Tent of the Presence.

So he said to them, 'Why do you do 23 such things? I hear from all the people how wickedly you behave. Have done 24 with it, my sons; for it is no good report that I hear spreading among the LORD's people. If a man sins a- 25 gainst another man, God will intervene; but if a man sins against the LORD, who can intercede for him?' For all this, they did not listen to their father's rebuke, for the LORD meant that they should die. But the 26 young Samuel, as he grew up, commended himself to the LORD and to men.

Eli and his family condemned

Now a man of God came to Eli and 27 said, 'This is the word of the LORD: You know that I revealed myself to your forefather when he and his family were in Egypt in slavery in the house of Pharaoh. You know that I 28 chose him from all the tribes of Israel to be my priest, to mount the steps of my altar, to burn sacrifices and to carry[e] the ephod before me; and that I assigned all the food-offerings of the Israelites to your family. Why then 29 do you show disrespect for my sacrifices and the offerings which I have ordained? What makes you resent them? Why do you honour your sons more than me by letting them batten on the choicest offerings of my people Israel? The LORD's word was, "I 30 promise that your house and your father's house shall serve before me for all time"; but now his word is, "I will have no such thing: I will honour those who honour me, and those who despise me shall meet with contempt. The time is coming when 31 I will lop off every limb of your own and of your father's family, so that no man in your house shall come to old age. You will even resent[f] the pros- 32 perity I give to Israel; never again shall there be an old man in your house. If I allow any to survive to 33 serve my altar, his eyes will grow dim and his appetite fail, his issue will be weaklings and die off. The fate of 34 your two sons shall be a sign to you: Hophni and Phinehas shall both die on the same day. I will appoint for 35 myself a priest who will be faithful, who will do what I have in my mind and in my heart. I will establish his family to serve in perpetual succession before my anointed king. Any of 36 your family that still live will come

---

c the High God: *prob. rdg.; Heb.* upon him.   d for which . . . him: *or* which you lent him.   e *Or* wear.   f You . . . resent: *prob. rdg.; Heb. obscure.*

and bow humbly before him to beg a fee, a piece of silver and a loaf, and will ask for a turn of priestly duty to earn a crust of bread."'

The LORD calls Samuel

3 So the child Samuel was in the LORD's service under his master Eli. Now in those days the word of the LORD was seldom heard, and no vision was **2** granted. But one night Eli, whose eyes were dim and his sight failing, was lying down in his usual place, **3** while Samuel slept in the temple of the LORD where the Ark of God was. Before the lamp of God had gone out, **4** the LORD called him, and Samuel **5** answered, 'Here I am', and ran to Eli saying, 'You called me: here I am.' 'No, I did not call you,' said Eli; 'lie down again.' So he went and lay **6** down. The LORD called Samuel again, and he got up and went to Eli. 'Here I am,' he said; 'surely you called me.' 'I did not call, my son,' he answered; **7** 'lie down again.' Now Samuel had not yet come to know the LORD, and the word of the LORD had not been **8** disclosed to him. When the LORD called him for the third time, he again went to Eli and said, 'Here I am; you did call me.' Then Eli understood that it was the LORD calling **9** the child; he told Samuel to go and lie down and said, 'If he calls again, say, "Speak, LORD; thy servant hears thee."' So Samuel went and lay down in his place.

10   The LORD came and stood there, and called, 'Samuel, Samuel', as before. Samuel answered, 'Speak; thy **11** servant hears thee.' The LORD said, 'Soon I shall do something in Israel which will ring in the ears of all who **12** hear it. When that day comes I will make good every word I have spoken against Eli and his family from be-**13** ginning to end. You are to[g] tell him that my judgement on his house shall stand for ever because[h] he knew of his sons' blasphemies against God[i] **14** and did not rebuke them. Therefore I have sworn to the family of Eli that their abuse of sacrifices and offerings shall never be expiated.'

15   Samuel lay down till morning and then opened the doors of the house of the LORD, but he was afraid to tell **16** Eli about the vision. Eli called Samuel: 'Samuel, my son', he said; and **17** he answered, 'Here I am.' Eli asked, 'What did the LORD say to you? Do not hide it from me. God forgive you if you hide one word of all that he said to you.' Then Samuel told him **18** everything and hid nothing. Eli said, 'The LORD must do what is good in his eyes.'

As Samuel grew up, the LORD was **19** with him, and none of his words went unfulfilled. From Dan to Beersheba, **20** all Israel recognized that Samuel was confirmed as a prophet of the LORD. So the LORD continued to appear in **21** Shiloh, because he had revealed himself there to Samuel.[j]

The Philistines capture the Ark

So Samuel's word had authority **4** throughout Israel. And the time came when the Philistines mustered for battle against Israel, and the Israelites went out to meet them. The Israelites encamped at Eben-ezer and the Philistines at Aphek. The Phil-**2** istines drew up their lines facing the Israelites, and when they joined battle the Israelites were routed by the Philistines, who killed about four thousand men on the field. When the **3** army got back to the camp, the elders of Israel asked, 'Why did the LORD let us be routed today by the Philistines? Let us fetch the Ark of the Covenant of the LORD from Shiloh to go with us and deliver us from the power of our enemies.' So the people **4** sent to Shiloh and fetched the Ark of the Covenant of the LORD of Hosts, who is enthroned upon the cherubim; Eli's two sons, Hophni and Phinehas, were there with the Ark. When the **5** Ark came into the camp all the Israelites greeted it with a great shout, and the earth rang with the shouting. The Philistines heard the **6** noise and asked, 'What is this great shouting in the camp of the Hebrews?' When they knew that the Ark of the LORD had come into the camp, they **7** were afraid and cried, 'A god has come into the camp. We are lost! No such thing has ever happened before. We are utterly lost! Who can deliver **8** us from the power of these mighty gods? These are the very gods who broke the Egyptians and crushed them in the wilderness. Courage, **9** Philistines, and act like men, or you will become slaves to the Hebrews as they were yours. Be men, and fight!' The Philistines then gave battle, and **10** the Israelites were defeated and fled to their homes. It was a great defeat,

---

g Prob. rdg.; Heb. I will.   h because: prob. rdg.; Heb. in guilt.   i against God: prob. original reading, altered in Heb. to to them.   j Prob. rdg.; Heb. adds according to the word of the LORD.

and thirty thousand Israelite foot-
11 soldiers perished. The Ark of God was
taken, and Eli's two sons, Hophni and
Phinehas, were killed.

The death of Eli and his sons

12 A Benjamite ran from the battlefield
and reached Shiloh on the same day,
his clothes rent and dust on his head.
13 When he arrived Eli was sitting on a
seat by the road to Mizpah, for he was
deeply troubled about the Ark of God.
The man entered the city with his
news, and all the people cried out in
14 horror. When Eli heard it, he asked,
'What does this uproar mean?' The
15 man hurried to Eli and told him. Eli
was ninety-eight years old and sat
16 staring with sightless eyes; so the man
said to him, 'I am the man who has
just arrived from the battle; this very
day I have escaped from the field.' Eli
asked, 'What is the news, my son?'
17 The runner answered, 'The Israelites
have fled from the Philistines; utter
panic has struck the army; your
two sons, Hophni and Phinehas, are
killed, and the Ark of God is taken.'
18 At the mention of the Ark of God,
Eli fell backwards from his seat by
the gate and broke his neck, for he
was old and heavy. So he died; he
had been judge over Israel for forty
19 years. His daughter-in-law, the wife
of Phinehas, was with child and near
her time, and when she heard of the
capture of the Ark and the deaths of
her father-in-law and her husband,
her labour suddenly began and she
20 crouched down and was delivered. As
she lay dying, the women who attended her said, 'Do not be afraid; you
have a son.' But she did not answer
21 or heed what they said. Then they
named the boy Ichabod,[k] saying,
'Glory has departed from Israel' (in
allusion to the capture of the Ark of
God and the death of her father-in-
22 law and her husband); 'Glory has
departed from Israel,' they said, 'because the Ark of God is taken.'

The Ark causes havoc

5 After the Philistines had captured the
Ark of God, they brought it from
2 Eben-ezer to Ashdod; and there they
carried it into the temple of Dagon
3 and set it beside Dagon himself. When
the people of Ashdod rose next morning, there was Dagon fallen face
downwards before the Ark of the
LORD; so they took him and put him
4 back in his place. Next morning when

they rose, Dagon had again fallen
face downwards before the Ark of
the LORD, with his head and his two
hands lying broken off beside his
platform; only Dagon's body remained
on it. This is why from that day to 5
this the priests of Dagon and all who
enter the temple of Dagon at Ashdod
do not set foot upon Dagon's platform.

Then the LORD laid a heavy hand 6
upon the people of Ashdod; he threw
them into distress and plagued them
with tumours, and their territory
swarmed with rats.[l] There was death
and destruction all through the city. 7
When the men of Ashdod saw this, they
said, 'The Ark of the God of Israel
shall not stay here, for he has laid a
heavy hand upon us and upon Dagon
our god.' So they sent and called all 8
the Philistine princes together to ask
what should be done with the Ark.
They said, 'Let the Ark of the God of
Israel be taken across to Gath.' They
took it there, and after its arrival the 9
hand of the LORD caused great havoc
in the city; he plagued everybody,
high and low alike, with the tumours
which broke out. Then they sent the 10
Ark of God on to Ekron. When the
Ark reached Ekron, the people cried,
'They have brought the Ark of the
God of Israel over to us, to kill us and
our families.' So they summoned all 11
the Philistine princes and said, 'Send
the Ark of the God of Israel away; let
it go back to its own place, or it will
be the death of us all.' There was
death and destruction all through the
city; for the hand of God lay heavy
upon it. Even those who did not die 12
were plagued with tumours; the cry
of the city went up to heaven.

The Philistines return the Ark

When the Ark of the LORD had been 6
in their territory for seven months,
the Philistines summoned the priests 2
and soothsayers and asked, 'What
shall we do with the Ark of the LORD?
Tell us how we ought to send it back
to its own place.' They answered, 'If 3
you send the Ark of the God of Israel
back, do not let it go without a gift,
but send it back with a gift for him by
way of indemnity; then you will be
healed and restored to favour; there
is no reason why his hand should not
be lifted from you.' When they were 4
asked, 'What gift shall we send back
to him?', they answered, 'Send five
tumours modelled in gold and five

---

k *That is* No-glory.   l *Or* mice.

gold rats, one for each of the Philistine princes, for the same plague afflicted 5 all of you and your princes. Make models of your tumours and of the rats which are ravaging the land, and give honour to the God of Israel; perhaps he will relax the pressure of his hand on you, on your god, and on 6 your land. Why should you be stubborn like Pharaoh and the Egyptians? Remember how this god made sport of them until they let Israel go. 7 Now make a new wagon ready with two milch-cows which have never been yoked; harness the cows to the wagon, and take their calves from them and drive them back to their 8 stalls. Then take the Ark of the LORD and put it on the wagon, place in a casket, beside it, the gold offerings that you are sending to him as an indemnity, and let it go where it will. 9 Watch it: if it goes up towards its own territory to Beth-shemesh, then it is the LORD who has done us this great injury; but if not, then we shall know that his hand has not touched us, but we have been the victims of chance.'

10 The men did this. They took two milch-cows and harnessed them to a wagon, shutting up their calves in 11 the stall, and they placed the Ark of the LORD on the wagon together with the casket, the gold rats, and the models 12 of their haemorrhoids. Then the cows went straight in the direction of Beth-shemesh; they kept to the same road, lowing as they went and turning neither right nor left, while the Philistine princes followed them as far as 13 the territory of Beth-shemesh. Now the people of Beth-shemesh were harvesting their wheat in the Vale, and when they looked up and saw the Ark they rejoiced at the sight of it. 14 The wagon came to the farm of Joshua of Beth-shemesh and halted there. Close by stood a great stone; so they chopped up the wood of the wagon and offered the cows as a 15 whole-offering to the LORD. Then the Levites lifted down the Ark of the LORD and the casket containing the gold offerings, and laid them on the great stone; and the men of Beth-shemesh offered whole-offerings and shared-offerings that day to the LORD. 16 The five princes of the Philistines watched all this, and returned to Ekron the same day.

17 These golden haemorrhoids which the Philistines sent back as a gift of indemnity to the LORD were for Ashdod, Gaza, Ashkelon, Gath, and Ekron, one for each city. The gold 18 rats were for all the towns of the Philistines governed by the five princes, both fortified towns and open settlements. The great stone where they deposited the Ark of the LORD stands witness on the farm of Joshua of Beth-shemesh to this very day.

But the sons of Jeconiah did not 19 rejoice with the rest of the men of Beth-shemesh when they welcomed the Ark of the LORD, and he struck down seventy of them. The people mourned because the LORD had struck them so heavy a blow, and the 20 men of Beth-shemesh said, 'No one is safe in the presence of the LORD, this holy God. To whom can we send it, to be rid of him?' So they sent this 21 message to the inhabitants of Kiriath-jearim: 'The Philistines have returned the Ark of the LORD; come down and take charge of it.' Then the men of 7 Kiriath-jearim came and took the Ark of the LORD away; they brought it into the house of Abinadab on the hill and consecrated his son Eleazar as its custodian.

Samuel judges Israel

So for a long while the Ark was 2 housed in Kiriath-jearim; and after some time, twenty years later, there was a movement throughout Israel to follow the LORD. So Samuel addressed 3 these words to the whole nation: 'If your return to the LORD is whole-hearted, banish the foreign gods and the Ashtaroth from your shrines; turn to the LORD with heart and mind, and worship him alone, and he will deliver you from the Philistines.' The Israel- 4 ites then banished the Baalim and the Ashtaroth, and worshipped the LORD alone.

Samuel summoned all Israel to an 5 assembly at Mizpah, so that he might intercede with the LORD for them. When they had assembled there, they 6 drew water and poured it out before the LORD and fasted all day, confessing that they had sinned against the LORD. It was at Mizpah that Samuel acted as judge over Israel.

When the Philistines heard that the 7 Israelites had assembled at Mizpah, their princes marched against them. The Israelites heard that the Philistines were advancing, and they were afraid. They said to Samuel, 'Do not 8 cease to pray for us to the LORD our God to save us from the power of the Philistines.' Thereupon Samuel took 9 a sucking lamb, offered it up complete as a whole-offering and prayed aloud to the LORD on behalf of Israel; and the LORD answered his prayer. 10 As Samuel was offering the sacrifice and the Philistines were advancing to battle with the Israelites, the LORD thundered loud and long over the Philistines and threw them into confusion. They fled in panic before the 11 Israelites, who set out from Mizpah in pursuit and kept up the slaughter of the Philistines till they reached a 12 point below Beth-car. There Samuel took a stone and set it up as a monument between Mizpah and Jeshanah,[m] naming it Eben-ezer,[n] 'for to this point', he said, 'the LORD has helped 13 us.' Thus the Philistines were subdued and no longer encroached on the territory of Israel; and the hand of the LORD was against them as long 14 as Samuel lived. The cities they had captured were restored to Israel, and from Ekron to Gath the borderland was freed from their control. Between Israel and the Amorites peace was 15 maintained. Samuel acted as judge in 16 Israel as long as he lived, and every year went on circuit to Bethel and Gilgal and Mizpah; he dispensed jus- 17 tice at all these places, returning always to Ramah. That was his home and the place from which he governed Israel, and there he built an altar to the LORD.

Israel demands a king

8 When Samuel grew old, he appointed 2 his sons to be judges in Israel. The eldest son was named Joel and the second Abiah; they acted as judges 3 in Beersheba. His sons did not follow in their father's footsteps but were intent on their own profit, taking bribes and perverting the course of 4 justice. So all the elders of Israel met, 5 and came to Samuel at Ramah and said to him, 'You are now old and your sons do not follow in your footsteps; appoint us a king to govern us, 6 like other nations.' But their request for a king to govern them displeased Samuel, and he prayed to the LORD. 7 The LORD answered Samuel, 'Listen to the people and all that they are saying; they have not rejected you, it is I whom they have rejected, I whom they will not have to be their king. 8 They are now doing to you just what they have done to me since I brought them up from Egypt: they have forsaken me and worshipped other gods.

Hear what they have to say now, but 9 give them a solemn warning and tell them what sort of king will govern them.' Samuel told the people who 10 were asking him for a king all that the LORD had said to him. 'This will 11 be the sort of king who will govern you', he said. 'He will take your sons and make them serve in his chariots and with his cavalry, and will make them run before his chariot. Some he 12 will appoint officers over units of a thousand and units of fifty. Others will plough his fields and reap his harvest; others again will make weapons of war and equipment for mounted troops. He will take your 13 daughters for perfumers, cooks, and confectioners, and will seize the best 14 of your cornfields, vineyards, and olive-yards, and give them to his lackeys. He will take a tenth of your 15 grain and your vintage to give to his eunuchs and lackeys. Your slaves, 16 both men and women, and the best of your cattle and your asses he will seize and put to his own use. He will 17 take a tenth of your flocks, and you yourselves will become his slaves. When that day comes, you will cry 18 out against the king whom you have chosen; but it will be too late, the LORD will not answer you.' The people 19 refused to listen to Samuel; 'No,' they said, 'we will have a king over us; then we shall be like other nations, 20 with a king to govern us, to lead us out to war and fight our battles.' So 21 Samuel, when he had heard what the people said, told the LORD; and he 22 answered, 'Take them at their word and appoint them a king.' Samuel then dismissed all the men of Israel to their homes.

Saul seeks the lost asses

There was a man from the district of 9 Benjamin, whose name was Kish son of Abiel, son of Zeror, son of Bechorath, son of Aphiah a Benjamite. He was a man of substance, and had a son 2 named Saul, a young man in his prime; there was no better man among the Israelites than he. He was a head taller than any of his fellows.

One day some asses belonging to 3 Saul's father Kish had strayed, so he said to his son Saul, 'Take one of the servants with you, and go and look for the asses.' They crossed the hill- 4 country of Ephraim and went through the district of Shalisha but did not find them; they passed through the

m *Prob. rdg. (cp. 2 Chr. 13. 19); Heb. the tooth.*   n *That is* Stone of Help.

district of Shaalim but they were not there; they passed through the district of Benjamin but again did not 5 find them. When they had entered the district of Zuph, Saul said to the servant with him, 'Come, we ought to turn back, or my father will stop thinking about the asses and begin 6 to worry about us.' The servant answered, 'There is a man of God in the city here, who has a great reputation, because everything he says comes true. Suppose we go there; he may tell us something about this errand of 7 ours.' Saul said, 'If we do go, what shall we offer him? There is no food left in our packs and we have no present for the man of God, nothing 8 at all.' The servant answered him again, 'Wait! I have here a quarter-shekel of silver. I can give that to the man, to tell us what we should do.' 10[o] Saul said, 'Good! let us go to him.' So they went to the city where the man 9 of God was. (In days gone by in Israel, when a man wished to consult God, he would say, 'Let us go to the seer.' For what is nowadays called a 11 prophet used to be called a seer.) As they were going up the hill to the city they met some girls coming out to draw water and asked, 'Shall we find 12 the seer there?' 'Yes,' they said, 'the seer is ahead of you now; he has just[p] arrived in the city because there is a 13 feast at the hill-shrine today. As you enter the city you will meet him before he goes up to the shrine to eat; the people will not start until he comes, for he has to bless the sacrifice before the company can eat. Go up now, and you will find him at once.' 14 So they went up to the city, and just as they were going in, there was Samuel coming towards them on his way up to the shrine.

Samuel and Saul

15 Now the day before Saul came, the LORD had disclosed his intention to 16 Samuel in these words: 'At this same time tomorrow I will send you a man from the land of Benjamin. Anoint him prince over my people Israel, and then he shall deliver my people from the Philistines. I have seen the sufferings of my people and their cry has 17 reached my ears.' The moment Saul appeared the LORD said to Samuel, 'Here is the man of whom I spoke to you. This man shall rule my people.' 18 Saul came up to Samuel in the gate-

way and said, 'Would you tell me where the seer lives?' Samuel replied, 19 'I am the seer. Go on ahead of me to the hill-shrine and you shall eat with me today; in the morning I will set you on your way, after telling you what you have on your mind. Trouble 20 yourself no more about the asses lost three days ago, for they have been found. But what is it that all Israel is wanting? It is you and your ancestral house.' 'But I am a Benjamite,' 21 said Saul, 'from the smallest of the tribes of Israel, and my family is the least important of all the families of the tribe of Benjamin. Why do you say this to me?' Samuel then brought 22 Saul and his servant into the dining-hall and gave them a place at the head of the company, which numbered about thirty. Then he said to the cook, 23 'Bring the portion that I gave you and told you to put on one side.' So 24 the cook took up the whole haunch and leg and put it before Saul; and Samuel said, 'Here is the portion of meat[q] kept for you. Eat it: it has been reserved for you at this feast to which I have invited the people.' So Saul dined with Samuel that day, and 25 when they came down from the hill-shrine to the city a bed was spread on the roof for Saul, and he stayed 26 there that night. At dawn Samuel called to Saul on the roof, 'Get up, and I will set you on your way.' When Saul rose, he and Samuel went out together into the street. As they came 27 to the end of the town, Samuel said to Saul, 'Tell the boy to go on.' He did so, and then Samuel said, 'Stay here a moment, and I will tell you the word of God.'

Saul is anointed king

Samuel took a flask of oil and poured 10 it over Saul's head, and he kissed him and said, 'The LORD anoints you prince over his people Israel; you shall rule the people of the LORD and deliver them from the enemies round about them. You shall have a sign that the LORD has anointed you prince to govern his inheritance: when you 2 leave me today, you will meet two men by the tomb of Rachel at Zelzah in the territory of Benjamin. They will tell you that the asses you are looking for have been found and that your father is concerned for them no longer; he is anxious about you and says again and again, "What shall I

3 do about my son?" From there go across country as far as the terebinth of Tabor, where three men going up to Bethel to worship God will meet you. One of them will be carrying three kids, the second three loaves, 4 and the third a flagon of wine. They will greet you and will offer you two loaves, which you will accept from 5 them. Then when you reach the Hill of God, where the Philistine governor[r] resides, you will meet a company of prophets coming down from the hill-shrine, led by lute, harp, fife, and drum, and filled with prophetic rap-6 ture. Then the spirit of the LORD will suddenly take possession of you, and you too will be rapt like a prophet 7 and become another man. When these signs happen, do whatever the occasion demands; God will be with you. 8 You shall go down to Gilgal ahead of me, and I will come to you to sacrifice whole-offerings and shared-offerings. Wait seven days until I join you; then 9 I will tell you what to do.' As Saul turned to leave Samuel, God gave him a new heart. On that same day all 10 these signs happened. When they reached the Hill there was a company of prophets coming to meet him, and the spirit of God suddenly took possession of him, so that he too was 11 filled with prophetic rapture. When people who had known him previously saw that he was rapt like the prophets, they said to one another, 'What can have happened to the son of Kish? Is Saul also among the prophets?' 12 One of the men of that place said, 'And whose sons are they?' Hence the proverb, 'Is Saul also among the 13 prophets?' When the prophetic rapture had passed, he went home.[s] 14 Saul's uncle said to him and the boy, 'Where have you been?' Saul answered, 'To look for the asses, and when we could not find them, we went to 15 Samuel.' His uncle said, 'Tell me what 16 Samuel said.' 'He told us that the asses had been found', said Saul; but he did not repeat what Samuel had said about his being king.

Samuel presents Saul to Israel

17 Meanwhile Samuel summoned the 18 Israelites to the LORD at Mizpah and said to the people, 'This is the word of the LORD the God of Israel: I brought Israel up from Egypt; I delivered you from the Egyptians and from all the kingdoms that oppressed 19 you; but today you have rejected your

God who saved you from all your misery and distress; you have said, "No, set up a king over us." Now therefore take up your positions before the LORD tribe by tribe and clan by clan.' 20 Samuel then presented all the tribes of Israel, and Benjamin was picked by lot. Then he presented the tribe 21 of Benjamin, family by family, and the family of Matri was picked. Then he presented the family of Matri, man by man, and Saul son of Kish was picked; but when they looked for him 22 he could not be found. They went on to ask the LORD, 'Will the man be coming back?' The LORD answered, 'There he is, hiding among the baggage.' So someone ran and fetched him out, 23 and as he took his stand among the people, he was a head taller than anyone else. Samuel said to the people, 24 'Look at the man whom the LORD has chosen; there is no one like him in this whole nation.' They all acclaimed him, shouting, 'Long live the king!' Samuel then explained to the people 25 the nature of a king, and made a written record of it on a scroll which he deposited before the LORD; he then dismissed them to their homes. Saul 26 too went home to Gibeah, and with him went some fighting men whose hearts God had moved. But there 27 were scoundrels who said, 'How can this fellow deliver us?' They thought nothing of him and brought him no gifts.

Saul defeats the Ammonites

About a month later Nahash the **11** Ammonite attacked and besieged Jabesh-gilead. The men of Jabesh said to Nahash, 'Come to terms with us and we will be your subjects.' Nahash answered them, 'On one con-2 dition only will I come to terms with you: that I gouge out your right eyes and bring disgrace on Israel.' The 3 elders of Jabesh-gilead then said, 'Give us seven days' respite to send messengers throughout Israel and then, if no one relieves us, we will surrender to you.' When the messengers 4 came to Gibeah, where Saul lived, and delivered their message, all the people broke into lamentation. Saul was just 5 coming from the field driving in the oxen, and asked why the people were lamenting; and they repeated what the men of Jabesh had said. When 6 Saul heard this, the spirit of God suddenly seized him. In his anger he took 7 a pair of oxen and cut them in pieces,

r Or garrison.   s Prob. rdg.; Heb. to the hill-shrine.

and sent messengers with the pieces all through Israel to proclaim that the same would be done to the oxen of any man who did not follow Saul and Samuel into battle. The fear of the LORD fell upon the people and they 8 came out, to a man. Saul mustered them in Bezek; there were three hundred thousand men from Israel 9 and thirty thousand from Judah. He said to the men who brought the message, 'Tell the men of Jabesh-gilead, "Victory will be yours tomorrow by the time the sun is hot."' The men of Jabesh heard what the mes- 10 sengers reported and took heart; and they said to Nahash, 'Tomorrow we will surrender to you, and then you may deal with us as you think fit.' 11 Next day Saul drew up his men in three columns; they forced their way right into the enemy camp during the morning watch and massacred the Ammonites while the day grew hot, after which the survivors scattered until no two men were left together.

Israel accepts Saul as king

12 Then the people said to Samuel, 'Who said that Saul should not reign over us? Hand the men over to us to be 13 put to death.' But Saul said, 'No man shall be put to death on a day when the LORD has won such a victory in 14 Israel.' Samuel said to the people, 'Let us now go to Gilgal and there renew 15 our allegiance to the kingdom.' So they all went to Gilgal and invested Saul there as king in the presence of the LORD, sacrificing shared-offerings before the LORD; and Saul and all the Israelites celebrated the occasion with great joy.

Samuel addresses the people

12 Then Samuel thus addressed the assembled Israelites: 'I have listened to your request and installed a king 2 to rule over you. And the king is now your leader, while I am old and white-haired and my sons are with you; but I have been your leader ever since I 3 was a child. Here I am. Lay your complaints against me in the presence of the LORD and of his anointed king. Whose ox have I taken, whose ass have I taken? Whom have I wronged, whom have I oppressed? From whom have I taken a bribe, to turn a blind eye? Tell me, and I will make restitu- 4 tion.' They answered, 'You have not wronged us, you have not oppressed us; you have not taken anything from

any man.' Samuel then said to them, 5 'This day the LORD is witness among you, his anointed king is witness, that you have found my hands empty.' They said, 'He is witness.' Samuel 6 said to the people, 'Yes, the LORD is witness, the LORD who gave you Moses and Aaron and brought your fathers out of Egypt. Now stand up, 7 and here in the presence of the LORD I will put the case against you and recite all the victories which he has won for you and for your fathers. After Jacob and his sons had come 8 down to Egypt and the Egyptians had made them suffer, your fathers cried to the LORD for help, and he sent Moses and Aaron, who brought them out of Egypt and settled them in this place. But they forgot the LORD their 9 God, and he abandoned them to Sisera, commander-in-chief of Jabin king of Hazor, to the Philistines, and to the king of Moab, and they had to fight against them. Then your fathers 10 cried to the LORD for help: "We have sinned, we have forsaken the LORD and we have worshipped the Baalim and the Ashtaroth. But now, if thou wilt deliver us from our enemies, we will worship thee." So the LORD sent 11 Jerubbaal and Barak, Jephthah and Samson, and delivered you from your enemies on every side; and you lived in peace and quiet.

'Then, when you saw Nahash king 12 of the Ammonites coming against you, although the LORD your God was your king, you said to me, "No, let us have a king to rule over us." Now, 13 here is the king you asked for; you chose him, and the LORD has set a king over you. If you will revere the 14 LORD and give true and loyal service, if you do not rebel against his commands, and if you and the king who reigns over you are faithful to the LORD your God, well and good; but 15 if you do not obey the LORD, and if you rebel against his commands, then he will set his face against you and against your king.

'Stand still, and see the great won- 16 der which the LORD will do before your eyes. It is now wheat harvest; 17 when I call upon the LORD and he sends thunder and rain, you will see and know how wicked it was in the LORD's eyes for you to ask for a king.' So Samuel called upon the LORD and 18 he sent thunder and rain that day; and all the people were in great fear of the LORD and of Samuel. They said to 19 Samuel, 'Pray for us your servants to the LORD your God, to save us from death; for we have added to all our other sins the great wickedness of asking for a king.' Samuel said to the people, 'Do not be afraid; although you have been so wicked, do not give up the worship of the LORD, but serve him with all your heart. Give up the worship of false gods which can neither help nor save, because they are false. For his name's sake the LORD will not cast you off, because he has resolved to make you his own people. As for me, God forbid that I should sin against the LORD and cease to pray for you. I will show you what is right and good: to revere the LORD and worship him faithfully with all your heart. Consider what great things he has done for you; but if you persist in wickedness, you shall be swept away, you and your king.'

Saul usurps the priest's office

Saul was fifty years[t] old when he became king, and he reigned over Israel for twenty-two[u] years. He picked three thousand men from Israel, two thousand to be with him in Michmash and the hill-country of Bethel and a thousand to be with Jonathan in Gibeah of Benjamin; and he sent the rest of the people home.

Jonathan killed the Philistine governor[v] in Geba, and the news spread among the Philistines that the Hebrews were in revolt.[w] Saul sounded the trumpet all through the land; and when the Israelites all heard that Saul had killed a Philistine governor and that the name of Israel stank among the Philistines, they answered the call to arms and came to join Saul at Gilgal.[x] The Philistines mustered to attack Israel; they had thirty thousand chariots and six thousand horse, with infantry as countless as sand on the sea-shore. They went up and camped at Michmash, to the east of Beth-aven. The Israelites found themselves in sore straits, for the army was hard pressed, so they hid themselves in caves and holes and among the rocks, in pits and cisterns. Some of them crossed the Jordan into the district of Gad and Gilead, but Saul remained at Gilgal, and all the people at his back were in alarm.[y] He waited seven days for his rendez-

with Samuel, but Samuel did not come to Gilgal; so the people began to drift away from Saul. He said therefore, 9 'Bring me the whole-offering and the shared-offerings', and he offered up the whole-offering. Saul had just 10 finished the sacrifice, when Samuel arrived, and he went out to greet him. Samuel said, 'What have you done?', 11 and Saul answered, 'I saw that the people were drifting away from me, and you yourself had not come as you had promised, and the Philistines were assembling at Michmash; and 12 I thought, "The Philistines will now move against me at Gilgal, and I have not placated the LORD"; so I felt compelled to make the whole-offering myself.' Samuel said to Saul, 'You have 13 behaved foolishly. You have not kept the command laid on you by the LORD your God; if you had, he would have established your dynasty over Israel for all time. But now your line will 14 not endure; the LORD will seek a man after his own heart, and will appoint him prince over his people, because you have not kept the LORD's command.'

Samuel left Gilgal without more 15 ado and went on his way. The rest of the people followed Saul, as he moved from Gilgal towards the enemy. At Gibeah of Benjamin he mustered the people who were with him; they were about six hundred men. Saul and his 16 son Jonathan and the men they had with them took up their quarters in Gibeah of Benjamin, while the Philistines were encamped in Michmash. Raiding parties went out from the 17 Philistine camp in three directions. One party turned towards Ophrah in the district of Shual, another towards 18 Beth-horon, and the third towards the range of hills overlooking the valley of Zeboim and the wilderness beyond.

No blacksmith was to be found in 19 the whole of Israel, for the Philistines were determined to prevent the Hebrews from making swords and spears. The Israelites had to go down to the 20 Philistines for their ploughshares, mattocks, axes, and sickles to be sharpened. The charge was two-thirds of a 21 shekel for ploughshares and mattocks, and one-third of a shekel for sharpening the axes and setting the goads.[z]

---

t fifty years: prob. rdg.; Heb. a year.   *u Prob. rdg.; Heb. two.*   *v Or garrison.*   *w that . . . revolt: prob. rdg.; Heb. has saying, Let the Hebrews hear after through the land.*   *x they answered . . . Gilgal: or they were summoned to follow Saul to Gilgal.*   *y but Saul . . . in alarm: or but Saul was still at Gilgal, and all the army joined him there.*   *z one-third . . . the goads: prob. rdg.; Heb. obscure.*

22 So when war broke out none of the followers of Saul and Jonathan had either sword or spear; only Saul and Jonathan carried arms.

War with the Philistines

23 Now the Philistines had posted a force to hold the pass of Michmash; 14 and one day Saul's son Jonathan said to his armour-bearer, 'Come, let us go over to the Philistine post beyond that ridge'; but he did not tell his 2 father. Saul, at the time, had his tent under the pomegranate-tree at Migron on the outskirts of Gibeah; and he had about six hundred men with him. 3 The ephod was carried by Ahijah son of Ahitub, Ichabod's brother, son of Phinehas son of Eli, the priest of the LORD at Shiloh. Nobody knew that 4 Jonathan had gone. On either side of the pass through which Jonathan tried to make his way over to the Philistine post stood two sharp columns of rock, called Bozez[a] and Seneh;[b] 5 one of them was on the north towards Michmash, and the other on the south 6 towards Geba. Jonathan said to his armour-bearer, 'Now we will visit the post of those uncircumcised rascals. Perhaps the LORD will take a hand in it, and if he will, nothing can stop him. He can bring us safe through, whether 7 we are few or many.' The young man answered, 'Do what you will, go forward; I am with you whatever you 8 do.' 'Good!' said Jonathan, 'we will 9 cross over and let them see us. If they say, "Stay where you are till we come to you", then we will stay where we 10 are and not go up to them. But if they say, "Come up to us", we will go up; this will be the sign that the LORD 11 has put them into our power.' So they showed themselves to the Philistines, and the Philistines said, 'Look! Hebrews coming out of the holes 12 where they have been hiding!' And they called across to Jonathan and the young man, 'Come up to us; we have something to show you.' Jonathan said to the young man, 'Come on, the LORD has put them into the 13 power of Israel.' Jonathan climbed up on hands and feet, and the young man followed him. The Philistines fell in front of Jonathan, and the young man, coming behind him, dispatched 14 them. In that first attack Jonathan and his armour-bearer killed about twenty of them, like men cutting a 15 furrow across a half-acre field. Terror

spread through the army in the field and through the whole people; the men at the post and the raiding parties were terrified; the very earth quaked, and there was panic.

16 Saul's men on the watch in Gibeah of Benjamin saw the mob of Philistines surging to and fro in confusion; so 17 he ordered the people to call the roll and find out who was missing; and they called the roll and found that Jonathan and his armour-bearer were 18 absent. Saul said to Ahijah, 'Bring forward the ephod', for it was he who carried the ephod at that time before 19 Israel. But while Saul was still speaking, the confusion in the Philistine camp was increasing more and more, and he said to the priest, 'Hold your 20 hand.' Then Saul and all his men with shouting made for the battlefield, where they found the enemy fighting 21 one another in complete disorder. The Hebrews who up to now had been under the Philistines, and had been with them in camp, changed sides and joined the Israelites under Saul and 22 Jonathan. All the Israelites in hiding in the hill-country of Ephraim heard that the Philistines were in flight, and they also joined in and set off in hot 23 pursuit. The LORD delivered Israel that day, and the fighting passed on beyond Beth-aven.

Jonathan's life in danger

24 Now the Israelites on that day had been driven to exhaustion. Saul had adjured the people in these words: 'A curse be on the man who eats any food before nightfall until I have taken vengeance on my enemies.' So 25 no one ate any food. Now there was honeycomb[c] in the country-side; but 26 when his men came upon it, dripping with honey though it was, not one of them put his hand to his mouth for 27 fear of the oath. But Jonathan had not heard his father lay this solemn prohibition on the people, and he stretched out the stick that was in his hand, dipped the end of it in the honeycomb, put it to his mouth and 28 was refreshed. One of the people said to him, 'Your father solemnly forbade this; he said, "A curse on the man who eats food today!"' Now the men 29 were faint with hunger. Jonathan said, 'My father has done the people nothing but harm; see how I am refreshed by this mere taste of honey. How much better if the people had

a *That is* Shining. b *That is* Bramble-bush. land went into the forest, and there was honey.

c Now . . . honeycomb: *prob. rdg.; Heb.* All the

eaten today whatever they took from their enemies by way of spoil! Then there would indeed have been a great slaughter of Philistines.'

31 They defeated the Philistines that day, and pursued them from Michmash to Aijalon. But the people were 32 so faint with hunger that they turned to plunder and seized sheep, cattle, and bullocks; they slaughtered them on the bare ground, and ate the meat 33 with the blood in it. Someone told Saul that the people were sinning against the LORD by eating their meat with the blood in it. 'This is treason!' cried Saul. 'Roll a great stone here at 34 once.' He then said, 'Go about among the people and tell them to bring their oxen and sheep, and let each man slaughter his here and eat it; and so they will not sin against the LORD by eating meat with the blood in it.' So as night fell each man came, driving his own ox, and slaughtered it there. 35 Thus Saul came to build an altar to the LORD, and this was the first altar to the LORD that Saul built.

36 Saul said, 'Let us go down and make a night attack on the Philistines and harry them till daylight; we will not spare a man of them.' The people answered, 'Do what you think best', but the priest said, 'Let us first con- 37 sult God.' So Saul inquired of God, 'Shall I pursue the Philistines? Wilt thou put them into Israel's power?'; but this time he received no answer. 38 So he said, 'Let all the leaders of the people come forward and let us find 39 out where the sin lies this day. As the LORD lives, the deliverer of Israel, even if it lies in my son Jonathan, he shall 40 die.' Not a soul answered him. Then he said to the Israelites, 'All of you stand on one side, and I and my son Jonathan will stand on the other.' The people answered, 'Do what you 41 think best.' Saul said to the LORD the God of Israel, 'Why hast thou not answered thy servant today? If this guilt lie in me or in my son Jonathan, O LORD God of Israel, let the lot be Urim; if it lie in thy people Israel, let it be Thummim.' Jonathan and Saul were taken, and the people were 42 cleared. Then Saul said, 'Cast lots 43 between me and my son Jonathan'; and Jonathan was taken. Saul said to Jonathan, 'Tell me what you have done.' Jonathan told him, 'True, I did taste a little honey on the tip of my stick. Here I am; I am ready to die.'

Then Saul swore a great oath that 44 Jonathan should die. But the peo- 45 ple said to Saul, 'Shall Jonathan die, Jonathan who has won this great victory in Israel? God forbid! As the LORD lives, not a hair of his head shall fall to the ground, for he has been at work with God today.' So the people ransomed Jonathan and he did not die. Saul broke off the pursuit of the 46 Philistines because they had made their way home.

Saul's conquests, and his descendants

When Saul had made his throne 47 secure in Israel, he fought against his enemies on every side, the Moabites, the Ammonites, the Edomites, the king of Zobah, and the Philistines; and wherever he turned he was successful.[d] He displayed his strength by 48 defeating the Amalekites and freeing Israel from hostile raids.

Saul's sons were: Jonathan, Ish- 49 yo and Malchishua. These were the names of his two daughters: Merab the elder and Michal the younger. His 50 wife was Ahinoam daughter of Ahimaaz, and his commander-in-chief was Abner son of his uncle Ner; Kish, Saul's 51 father, and Ner, Abner's father, were sons[e] of Abiel.

There was bitter warfare with the 52 Philistines throughout Saul's lifetime; any strong man and any brave man that he found he took into his own service.

Destruction of the Amalekites

Samuel said to Saul, 'The LORD sent 15 me to anoint you king over his people Israel. Now listen to the voice of the LORD. This is the very word of the 2 LORD of Hosts: "I am resolved to punish the Amalekites for what they did to Israel, how they attacked them on their way up from Egypt." Go now 3 and fall upon the Amalekites and destroy them, and put their property under ban. Spare no one; put them all to death, men and women, children and babes in arms, herds and flocks, camels and asses.' Thereupon Saul 4 called out the levy and mustered them in Telaim. There were two hundred thousand foot-soldiers and another ten thousand from Judah.[f] He came 5 to the Amalekite city and halted for a time in the gorge. Meanwhile he 6 sent word to the Kenites to leave the Amalekites and come down, 'or', he said, 'I shall destroy you as well as

d Or he found ample provision.   e Prob. rdg.; Heb. son.   f Prob. rdg.; Heb. ten thousand with the men of Judah.

them; but you were friendly to Israel when they came up from Egypt.' So 7 the Kenites left the Amalekites. Then Saul cut the Amalekites to pieces, all the way from Havilah to Shur on the 8 borders of Egypt. Agag the king of the Amelekites he took alive, but he destroyed all the people, putting them 9 to the sword. Saul and his army spared Agag and the best of the sheep and cattle, the fat beasts and the lambs and everything worth keeping; they were unwilling to destroy them, but anything that was useless and of no value they destroyed.

The LORD rejects Saul

10 Then the word of the LORD came to 11 Samuel: 'I repent of having made Saul king, for he has turned his back on me and has not obeyed my commands.' Samuel was angry; all night 12 he cried aloud to the LORD. Early next morning he went to meet Saul, but was told that he had gone to Carmel; Saul had set up a monument for himself there, and had then turned 13 and gone down to Gilgal. There Samuel found him, and Saul greeted him with the words, 'The LORD's blessing upon you! I have obeyed the 14 LORD's commands.' But Samuel said, 'What then is this bleating of sheep in my ears? Why do I hear the lowing 15 of cattle?' Saul answered, 'The people have taken them from the Amalekites. These are what they spared, the best of the sheep and cattle, to sacrifice to the LORD your God. The 16 rest we completely destroyed.' Samuel said to Saul, 'Let be, and I will tell you what the LORD said to me last 17 night.' 'Tell me', said Saul. So Samuel went on, 'Time was when you thought little of yourself, but now you are head of the tribes of Israel, and the LORD has anointed you king over 18 Israel. The LORD sent you with strict instructions to destroy that wicked nation, the Amalekites; you were to fight against them until you had wiped 19 them out. Why then did you not obey the LORD? Why did you pounce upon the spoil and do what was wrong in 20 the eyes of the LORD?' Saul answered Samuel, 'But I did obey the LORD; I went where the LORD sent me, and I have brought back Agag king of the Amalekites. The rest of them I de- 21 stroyed. Out of the spoil the people took sheep and oxen, the choicest of the animals laid under ban, to sacri-

fice to the LORD your God at Gilgal.' Samuel then said: 22

Does the LORD desire offerings and sacrifices as he desires obedience?
Obedience is better than sacrifice,
     and to listen to him than the fat of rams.
Defiance of him is sinful as witch- 23 craft,
     yielding to men*g* as evil as*h* idola- try.*i*
Because you have rejected the word of the LORD,
     the LORD has rejected you as king.

Saul said to Samuel, 'I have sinned. 24 I have ignored the LORD's command and your orders: I was afraid of the people and deferred to them. But 25 now forgive my sin, I implore you, and come back with me, and I will make my submission before the LORD.' Samuel answered, 'I will not come 26 back with you; you have rejected the word of the LORD and therefore the LORD has rejected you as king over Israel.' He turned to go, but Saul 27 caught the edge of his cloak and it tore. And Samuel said to him, 'The 28 LORD has torn the kingdom of Israel from your hand today and will give it to another, a better man than you. God who is the Splendour of Israel 29 does not deceive or change his mind; he is not a man that he should change his mind.' Saul said, 'I have sinned; 30 but honour me this once before the elders of my people and before Israel and come back with me, and I will make my submission to the LORD your God.' So Samuel went back with Saul, 31 and Saul made his submission to the LORD. Then Samuel said, 'Bring Agag 32 king of the Amalekites.' So Agag came to him with faltering step and said, 'Surely the bitterness of death has passed.' Samuel said, 'Your sword 33 has made women childless, and your mother of all women shall be childless too.' Then Samuel hewed Agag in pieces before the LORD at Gilgal.

Saul went to his own home at 34 Gibeah, and Samuel went to Ramah; and he never saw Saul again to his 35 dying day, but he mourned for him, because the LORD had repented of having made him king over Israel.

David anointed king

The LORD said to Samuel, 'How long 16 will you mourn for Saul because I have rejected him as king over Israel?

---

g yielding to men: *or* arrogance *or* obstinacy. household gods; *Heb.* teraphim.   *h* as evil as: *prob. rdg.; Heb.* evil and . . .   *i Or*

Fill your horn with oil and take it with you; I am sending you to Jesse of Bethlehem; for I have chosen my-
2 self a king among his sons.' Samuel answered, 'How can I go? Saul will hear of it and kill me.' 'Take a heifer with you,' said the Lord; 'say you have come to offer a sacrifice to the
3 Lord, and invite Jesse to the sacrifice; then I will let you know what you must do. You shall anoint for me
4 the man whom I show you.' Samuel did as the Lord had told him, and went to Bethlehem. The elders of the city came in haste to meet him, saying, 'Why have you come? Is all well?'
5 'All is well,' said Samuel; 'I have come to sacrifice to the Lord. Hallow yourselves and come with me to the sacrifice.' He himself hallowed Jesse and his sons and invited them to the
6 sacrifice also. They came, and when Samuel saw Eliab he thought, 'Here, before the Lord, is his anointed king.'
7 But the Lord said to him, 'Take no account of it if he is handsome and tall; I reject him. The Lord does not see as man sees; men judge by appearances but the Lord judges by the
8 heart.' Then Jesse called Abinadab and made him pass before Samuel, but he said, 'No, the Lord has not
9 chosen this one.' Then he presented Shammah, and Samuel said, 'Nor has
10 the Lord chosen him.' Seven of his sons Jesse presented to Samuel, but he said, 'The Lord has not chosen any
11 of these.' Then Samuel asked, 'Are these all?' Jesse answered, 'There is still the youngest, but he is looking after the sheep.' Samuel said to Jesse, 'Send and fetch him; we will not sit
12 down until he comes.' So he sent and fetched him. He was handsome, with ruddy cheeks and bright eyes.[j] The Lord said, 'Rise and anoint him:
13 this is the man.' Samuel took the horn of oil and anointed him in the presence of his brothers. Then the spirit of the Lord came upon David and was with him from that day onwards. And Samuel set out on his way back to Ramah.

David plays the harp for Saul

14 The spirit of the Lord had forsaken Saul, and at times an evil spirit from the Lord would seize him suddenly.
15 His servants said to him, 'You see, sir, how an evil spirit from God seizes
16 you; why do you not command your servants here to go and find some man who can play the harp?—then,

when an evil spirit from God comes on you, he can play and you will recover.' Saul said to his servants, 'Find me a 17 man who can play well and bring him to me.' One of his attendants said, 'I 18 have seen a son of Jesse of Bethlehem who can play; he is a brave man and a good fighter, wise in speech and handsome, and the Lord is with him.' Saul therefore sent messengers to 19 Jesse and asked him to send him his son David, who was with the sheep. Jesse took a homer of bread, a skin of 20 wine, and a kid, and sent them to Saul by his son David. David came 21 to Saul and entered his service; and Saul loved him dearly, and he became his armour-bearer. So Saul sent word 22 to Jesse: 'Let David stay in my service, for I am pleased with him.' And 23 whenever a spirit from God came upon Saul, David would take his harp and play on it, so that Saul found relief; he recovered and the evil spirit left him alone.

Goliath challenges Israel

The Philistines collected their forces 17 for war and massed at Socoh in Judah; they camped between Socoh and Aze- 2 kah at Ephes-dammim. Saul and the Israelites also massed, and camped in the Vale of Elah. They drew up 3 their lines facing the Philistines, the Philistines occupying a position on one hill and the Israelites on another, with a valley between them. A cham- 4 pion came out from the Philistine camp, a man named Goliath, from Gath; he was over nine feet in height. He had a bronze helmet on his head, 5 and he wore plate-armour of bronze, weighing five thousand shekels; on 6 his legs were bronze greaves, and one of his weapons was a dagger of bronze. The shaft of his spear was like a 7 weaver's beam, and its head, which was of iron, weighed six hundred shekels; and his shield-bearer marched ahead of him. The champion stood 8 and shouted to the ranks of Israel, 'Why do you come out to do battle, you slaves of Saul? I am the Philistine champion; choose your man to meet me. If he can kill me in fair fight, we 9 will become your slaves; but if I prove too strong for him and kill him, you shall be our slaves and serve us. Here and now I defy the ranks of 10 Israel. Give me a man,' said the Philistine, 'and we will fight it out.' When 11 Saul and the Israelites heard what

j and bright eyes: prob. rdg.; Heb. obscure.

the Philistine said, they were shaken and dismayed.

12 David was the son of an Ephrathite[k] called Jesse, who had eight sons. By Saul's time he had become
13 a feeble old man, and his three eldest sons had followed Saul to the war. The eldest was called Eliab, the next Abinadab, and the third Shammah;
14 David was the youngest. The three
15 eldest followed Saul, while David used to go to Saul's camp and back to Bethlehem to mind his father's flocks.
16 Morning and evening for forty days the Philistine came forward and took
17 up his position. Then one day Jesse said to his son David, 'Take your brothers an ephah of this parched grain and these ten loaves of bread,
18 and run with them to the camp. These ten cream-cheeses are for you to take to the commanding officer. See if your brothers are well and bring back some
19 token from them.' Saul and the brothers and all the Israelites were in the Vale of Elah, fighting the Philis-
20 tines. Early next morning David left someone in charge of the sheep, set out on his errand and went as Jesse had told him. He reached the lines just as the army was going out to take up position and was raising the
21 war-cry. The Israelites and the Philistines drew up their ranks opposite
22 each other. David left his things in charge of the quartermaster, ran to the line and went up to his brothers
23 to greet them. While he was talking to them the Philistine champion, Goliath, came out from the Philistine ranks and issued his challenge in the same words as before; and David heard him.
24 When the Israelites saw the man they
25 ran from him in fear. 'Look at this man who comes out day after day to defy Israel', they said. 'The king is to give a rich reward to the man who kills him; he will give him his daughter in marriage too and will exempt his family from service due in Israel.'
26 Then David turned to his neighbours and said, 'What is to be done for the man who kills this Philistine and wipes out our disgrace? And who is he, an uncircumcised Philistine, to defy
27 the army of the living God?' The people told him how the matter stood and what was to be done for the man
28 who killed him. His elder brother Eliab overheard David talking with the men and grew angry. 'What are you doing here?' he asked. 'And who

have you left to look after those few sheep in the wilderness? I know you, you impudent young rascal; you have only come to see the fighting.' David 29 answered, 'What have I done now? I only asked a question.' And he 30 turned away from him to someone else and repeated his question, but everybody gave him the same answer.

David kills Goliath

What David had said was overheard 31 and reported to Saul, who sent for him. David said to him, 'Do not lose 32 heart, sir. I will go and fight this Philistine.' Saul answered, 'You can- 33 not go and fight with this Philistine; you are only a lad, and he has been a fighting man all his life.' David said 34 to Saul, 'Sir, I am my father's shepherd; when a lion or bear comes and carries off a sheep from the flock, I go 35 after it and attack it and rescue the victim from its jaws. Then if it turns on me, I seize it by the beard and batter it to death. Lions I have killed 36 and bears, and this uncircumcised Philistine will fare no better than they; he has defied the army of the living God. The LORD who saved me 37 from the lion and the bear will save me from this Philistine.' 'Go then,' said Saul; 'and the LORD will be with you.' He put his own tunic on David, 38 placed a bronze helmet on his head and gave him a coat of mail to wear; he then fastened his sword on David 39 over his tunic. But David hesitated, because he had not tried them, and said to Saul, 'I cannot go with these, because I have not tried them.' So he took them off. Then he picked up his 40 stick, chose five smooth stones from the brook and put them in a shepherd's bag which served as his pouch. He walked out to meet the Philistine with his sling in his hand.

The Philistine came on towards 41 David, with his shield-bearer marching ahead; and he looked David up 42 and down and had nothing but contempt for this handsome lad with his ruddy cheeks and bright eyes.[l] He 43 said to David, 'Am I a dog that you come out against me with sticks?' And he swore at him in the name of his god. 'Come on,' he said, 'and I will give 44 your flesh to the birds and the beasts.' David answered, 'You have come 45 against me with sword and spear and dagger, but I have come against you in the name of the LORD of Hosts, the

---

k *Prob. rdg.; Heb. adds* Is this the man from Bethlehem in Judah? *prob. rdg.; Heb. obscure.*   l *handsome . . . bright eyes:*

God of the army of Israel which you
46 have defied. The LORD will put you
into my power this day; I will kill
you and cut your head off and leave
your carcass and the carcasses of the
Philistines to the birds and the wild
beasts; all the world shall know that
47 there is a God in Israel. All those who
are gathered here shall see that the
LORD saves neither by sword nor
spear; the battle is the LORD's, and he
will put you all into our power.'
48   When the Philistine began moving
towards him again, David ran quickly
49 to engage him. He put his hand into
his bag, took out a stone, slung it, and
struck the Philistine on the forehead.
The stone sank into his forehead, and
he fell flat on his face on the ground.
50 So David proved the victor with his
sling and stone; he struck Goliath
down and gave him a mortal wound,
51 though he had no sword. Then he ran
to the Philistine and stood over him,
and grasping his sword, he drew it
out of the scabbard, dispatched him
and cut off his head. The Philistines,
when they saw that their hero was
52 dead, turned and ran. The men of
Israel and Judah at once raised the
war-cry and hotly pursued them all
the way to Gath and even to the gates
of Ekron. The road that runs to Shaaraim, Gath, and Ekron was strewn
53 with their dead. On their return from
the pursuit of the Philistines, the Is-
54 raelites plundered their camp. David
took Goliath's head and carried it to
Jerusalem, leaving his weapons in his
tent.

Saul promotes David

55 Saul had said to Abner his commander-in-chief, when he saw David going
out against the Philistine, 'That boy
there, Abner, whose son is he?' 'By
your life, your majesty,' said Abner,
56 'I do not know.' The king said to
Abner, 'Go and find out whose son
57 the lad is.' When David came back
after killing the Philistine, Abner took
him and presented him to Saul with
the Philistine's head still in his hand.
58 Saul asked him, 'Whose son are you,
young man?', and David answered, 'I
am the son of your servant Jesse of
Bethlehem.'
1-2   That same day, when Saul had
finished talking with David, he kept
him and would not let him return any
more to his father's house, for he saw
that Jonathan had given his heart to
David and had grown to love him as

himself. So Jonathan and David made 3
a solemn compact because each loved
the other as dearly as himself. And 4
Jonathan stripped off the cloak he
was wearing and his tunic, and gave
them to David, together with his
sword, his bow, and his belt. David 5
succeeded so well in every venture
on which Saul sent him that he was
given a command in the army, and
his promotion pleased the ordinary
people, and even pleased Saul's officers.

Saul becomes jealous of David

At the home-coming of the army 6
when David returned from the slaughter of the Philistines, the women
came out from all the cities of Israel
to look on, and the dancers came out
to meet King Saul with tambourines,
singing, and dancing. The women as 7
they made merry sang to one another:

Saul made havoc among thousands
but David among tens of thousands.

Saul was furious, and the words 8
rankled. He said, 'They have given
David tens of thousands and me only
thousands; what more can they do
but make him king?' From that day 9
forward Saul kept a jealous eye on
David.

Next day an evil spirit from God 10
seized upon Saul; he fell into a
frenzy[m] in the house, and David
played the harp to him as he had
before. Saul had his spear in his hand,
and he hurled it at David, meaning 11
to pin him to the wall; but twice
David swerved aside. After this Saul 12
was afraid of David, because he saw
that the LORD had forsaken him and
was with David. He therefore re- 13
moved David from his household and
appointed him to the command of
a thousand men. David led his men
into action, and succeeded in every- 14
thing that he undertook, because the
LORD was with him. When Saul saw 15
how successful he was, he was more
afraid of him than ever; all Israel and 16
Judah loved him because he took the
field at their head.

Saul said to David, 'Here is my 17
elder daughter Merab; I will give her
to you in marriage, but in return
you must serve me valiantly and fight
the LORD's battles.' For Saul meant
David to meet his end at the hands of
the Philistines and not himself. David 18
answered Saul, 'Who am I and what
are my father's people, my kinsfolk,

m Or fell into prophetic rapture.

in Israel, that I should become the
19 king's son-in-law?' However, when
the time came for Saul's daughter
Merab to be married to David, she
had already been given to Adriel of
20 Meholah. But Michal, Saul's other
daughter, fell in love with David, and
when Saul was told of this, he saw
21 that it suited his plans. He said to himself, 'I will give her to him; let her be
the bait that lures him to his death at
the hands of the Philistines.' So Saul
proposed a second time to make David
22 his son-in-law, and ordered his courtiers to say to David privately, 'The
king is well disposed to you and you
are dear to us all; now is the time for
you to marry into the king's family.'
23 When Saul's people spoke in this
way to David, he said to them, 'Do
you think that marrying the king's
daughter is a matter of so little consequence that a poor man of no conse-
24 quence, like myself, can do it?' Saul's
courtiers reported what David had
25 said, and he replied, 'Tell David this:
all the king wants as the bride-price
is the foreskins of a hundred Philistines, by way of vengeance on his
enemies.' Saul was counting on David's
death at the hands of the Philis-
26 tines. The courtiers told David what
Saul had said, and marriage with
the king's daughter on these terms
pleased him well. Before the appoin-
27 ted time, David went out with his
men and slew two hundred Philistines; he brought their foreskins and
counted them out to the king in order
to be accepted as his son-in-law. So
Saul married his daughter Michal to
28 David. He saw clearly that the LORD
was with David, and knew that
Michal his daughter had fallen in love
29 with him; and so he grew more and
more afraid of David and was his
enemy for the rest of his life.
30 The Philistine officers used to come
out to offer single combat; and whenever they did, David had more success
against them than all the rest of Saul's
men, and he won a great name for
himself.

Saul tries to kill David

19 Saul spoke to Jonathan his son and
all his household about killing David.
But Jonathan was devoted to David
2 and told him that his father Saul was
looking for an opportunity to kill him.
'Be on your guard tomorrow morning,'
he said; 'conceal yourself, and remain
3 in hiding. Then I will come out and
join my father in the open country

where you are and speak to him about
you, and if I discover anything I will
tell you.' Jonathan spoke up for 4
David to his father Saul and said to
him, 'Sir, do not wrong your servant
David; he has not wronged you; his
conduct towards you has been beyond
reproach. Did he not take his life in 5
his hands when he killed the Philistine, and the LORD won a great victory
for Israel? You saw it, you shared in
the rejoicing; why should you wrong
an innocent man and put David to
death without cause?' Saul listened 6
to Jonathan and swore solemnly by
the LORD that David should not be
put to death. So Jonathan called 7
David and told him all this; then he
brought him to Saul, and he was in
attendance on the king as before.
War broke out again, and David 8
attacked the Philistines and dealt
them such a blow that they ran before him.
An evil spirit from the LORD came 9
upon Saul as he was sitting in the
house with his spear in his hand; and
David was playing the harp. Saul 10
tried to pin David to the wall with
the spear, but he avoided the king's
thrust so that Saul drove the spear
into the wall. David escaped and got
safely away. That night Saul sent 11
servants to keep watch on David's
house, intending to kill him in the
morning, but David's wife Michal
warned him to get away that night,
'or tomorrow', she said, 'you will be
a dead man.' She let David down 12
through a window, and he slipped
away and escaped. Michal took their 13
household gods and put them on the
bed; at its head she laid a goat's-hair
rug and covered it all with a cloak.
When the men arrived to arrest 14
David she told them he was ill. Saul 15
sent them back to see David for
themselves. 'Bring him to me, bed
and all,' he said, 'and I will kill him.'
When they came, there were the 16
household gods on the bed and the
goat's-hair rug at its head. Then Saul 17
said to Michal, 'Why have you played
this trick on me and let my enemy
get safe away?' And Michal answered,
'He said to me, "Help me to escape or
I will kill you."'
Meanwhile David made good his 18
escape and came to Samuel at Ramah, and told him how Saul had treated
him. Then he and Samuel went to
Naioth and stayed there. Saul was 19
told that David was there, and he 20
sent a party of men to seize him. When

they saw the company of prophets in rapture, with Samuel standing at their head, the spirit of God came upon them and they fell into prophetic
21 rapture. When this was reported to Saul he sent another party. These also fell into a rapture, and when he sent more men a third time, they did the
22 same. Saul himself then set out for Ramah and came to the great cistern in Secu. He asked where Samuel and David were and was told that they
23 were at Naioth in Ramah. On his way there the spirit of God came upon him too and he went on, in a rapture as he went, till he came to Naioth in
24 Ramah. There he too stripped off his clothes and like the rest fell into a rapture before Samuel and lay down naked all that day and all that night. That is why men say, 'Is Saul also among the prophets?'

Friendship of David and Jonathan

20 Then David made his escape from Naioth in Ramah and came to Jonathan. 'What have I done?' he asked. 'What is my offence? What does your father think I have done wrong, that
2 he seeks my life?' Jonathan answered him, 'God forbid! There is no thought of putting you to death. I am sure my father will not do anything whatever without telling me. Why should my father hide such a thing from me? I
3 cannot believe it!' David said, 'I am ready to swear to it: your father has said to himself, "Jonathan must not know this or he will resent it", because he knows that you have a high regard for me. As the LORD lives, your life upon it, there is only a step be-
4 tween me and death.' Jonathan said to David, 'What do you want me to do
5 for you?' David answered, 'It is new moon tomorrow, and I ought to dine with the king. Let me go and lie hidden in the fields until the third
6 evening. If your father happens to miss me, then say, "David asked me for leave to pay a rapid visit to his home in Bethlehem, for it is the annual sacrifice there for the whole
7 family." If he says, "Well and good", that will be a good sign for me; but if he flies into a rage, you will know that
8 he is set on doing me wrong. My lord, keep faith with me; for you and I have entered into a solemn compact before the LORD. Kill me yourself if I am guilty. Why let me fall into your
9 father's hands?' 'God forbid!' cried Jonathan. 'If I find my father set on doing you wrong I will tell you.'

David answered Jonathan. 'How will 10 you let me know if he answers harshly?' Jonathan said, 'Come with 11 me into the fields.' So they went together into the fields, and Jonathan 12 said to David, 'I promise you, David, in the sight of the LORD the God of Israel, this time tomorrow I will sound my father for the third time and, if he is well disposed to you, I will send and let you know. If my 13 father means mischief, the LORD do the same to me and more, if I do not let you know and get you safely away. The LORD be with you as he has been with my father! I know that as long 14 as I live you will show me faithful friendship, as the LORD requires; and if I should die, you will continue loyal 15 to my family for ever. When the LORD rids the earth of all David's enemies, may the LORD call him to account if 16 he and his house are no longer my friends.' Jonathan pledged himself 17 afresh to David because of his love for him, for he loved him as himself. Then he said to him, 'Tomorrow is the 18 new moon, and you will be missed when your place is empty. So go down 19 at nightfall for the third time to the place where you hid on the evening of the feast and stay by the mound there. Then I will shoot three arrows 20 towards it, as though I were aiming at a mark. Then I will send my boy 21 to find the arrows. If I say to him, "Look, the arrows are on this side of you, pick them up", then you can come out of hiding. You will be quite safe, I swear it; for there will be nothing amiss. But if I say to the lad, 22 "Look, the arrows are on the other side of you, further on", then the LORD has said that you must go; the LORD stand witness between us 23 for ever to the pledges we have exchanged.'

Jonathan gives David warning

So David hid in the fields. The new 24 moon came, the dinner was prepared, and the king sat down to eat. Saul 25 took his customary seat by the wall, and Abner sat beside him; Jonathan too was present, but David's place was empty. That day Saul said noth- 26 ing, for he thought that David was absent by some chance, perhaps because he was ritually unclean. But on 27 the second day, the day after the new moon, David's place was still empty, and Saul said to his son Jonathan, 'Why has not the son of Jesse come to the feast, either yesterday or today?'

28 Jonathan answered Saul, 'David asked permission to go to Bethlehem. 29 He asked my leave and said, "Our family is holding a sacrifice in the town and my brother himself has ordered me to be there. Now, if you have any regard for me, let me slip away to see my brothers." That is why he has not come to dine with the 30 king.' Saul was angry with Jonathan, 'You son of a crooked and unfaithful mother! You have made friends with the son of Jesse only to bring shame on yourself and dishonour on your 31 mother; I see how it will be. As long as Jesse's son remains alive on earth, neither you nor your crown will be safe. Send at once and fetch him; he 32 deserves to die.' Jonathan answered his father, 'Deserves to die! Why? 33 What has he done?' At that, Saul picked up his spear and threatened to kill him; and he knew that his father 34 was bent on David's death. Jonathan left the table in a rage and ate nothing on the second day of the festival; for he was indignant on David's behalf because his father had humiliated him.

35 Next morning, Jonathan went out into the fields to meet David at the appointed time, taking a young boy 36 with him. He said to the boy, 'Run and find the arrows; I am going to shoot.' The boy ran on, and he shot 37 the arrows over his head. When the boy reached the place where Jonathan's arrows had fallen, Jonathan called out after him, 'Look, the 38 arrows are beyond you. Hurry! No time to lose! Make haste!' The boy gathered up the arrows and brought 39 them to his master; but only Jonathan and David knew what this 40 meant; the boy knew nothing. Jonathan handed his weapons to the boy and told him to take them back to 41 the city. When the boy had gone, David got up from behind the mound and bowed humbly three times. Then they kissed one another and shed tears together, until David's grief was 42 even greater than Jonathan's. Jonathan said to David, 'Go in safety; we have pledged each other in the name of the LORD who is witness for ever between you and me and between your descendants and mine.'

David escapes to the cave of Adullam

21 David went off at once, while Jonathan returned to the city. David made his way to the priest Ahimelech at Nob, who hurried out to meet him and said, 'Why have you come alone and no one with you?' David answered 2 Ahimelech, 'I am under orders from the king: I was to let no one know about the mission on which he was sending me or what these orders were. When I took leave of my men I told them to meet me in such and such a place. Now, what have you 3 got by you? Let me have five loaves, or as many as you can find.' The priest 4 answered David, 'I have no ordinary bread available. There is only the sacred bread; but have the young men kept themselves from women?' David answered the priest, 'Women 5 have been denied us hitherto, when I have been on campaign, even an ordinary campaign, and the young men's bodies have remained holy; and how much more will they be holy today?' So, as there was no other 6 bread there, the priest gave him the sacred bread, the Bread of the Presence, which had just been taken from the presence of the LORD to be replaced by freshly baked bread on the day that the old was removed. One of Saul's servants happened to be 7 there that day, detained before the LORD; his name was Doeg the Edomite, and he was the strongest of all Saul's herdsmen. David said to Ahi- 8 melech, 'Have you a spear or sword here at hand? I have no sword or other weapon with me, because the king's business was urgent.' The priest 9 answered, 'There is the sword of Goliath the Philistine whom you slew in the Vale of Elah; it is wrapped up in a cloak behind the ephod. If you wish to take that, take it; there is no other weapon here.' David said, 'There is no sword like it; give it to me.'

That day, David went on his way, 10 eluding Saul, and came to Achish king of Gath. The servants of Achish 11 said to him, 'Surely this is David, the king of his country, the man of whom they sang as they danced:

Saul made havoc among thousands
but David among tens of thousands.'

These words were not lost on David, 12 and he became very much afraid of Achish king of Gath. So he altered his 13 behaviour in public and acted like a lunatic in front of them all, scrabbling on the double doors of the city gate and dribbling down his beard. Achish 14 said to his servants, 'The man is mad! Why bring him to me? Am I short of 15 madmen that you bring this one to plague me? Must I have this fellow in my house?'

2 David made his escape and went from there to the cave of Adullam. When his brothers and all his family heard that he was there, they joined

2 him. Men in any kind of distress or in debt or with a grievance gathered round him, about four hundred in number, and he became their chief.

3 From there David went to Mizpeh in Moab and said to the king of Moab, 'Let my father and mother come and take shelter with you until I know

4 what God will do for me.' So he left them at the court of the king of Moab, and they stayed there as long as David was in his stronghold.

Doeg kills the priests of Nob

5 The prophet Gad said to David, 'You must not stay in your stronghold; go at once into Judah.' So David went

6 as far as the forest of Hareth. News that David and his men had been seen reached Saul while he was in Gibeah, sitting under the tamarisk-tree on the hill-top with his spear in his hand and all his retainers standing

7 about him. He said to them, 'Listen to me, you Benjamites: do you expect the son of Jesse to give you all fields and vineyards, or make you all officers over units of a thousand and a hun-

8 dred? Is that why you have all conspired against me? Not one of you told me when my son made a compact with the son of Jesse; none of you spared a thought for me or told me that my son had set my own servant against me, who is lying in wait for me now.'

9 Then Doeg the Edomite, who was standing with the servants of Saul, spoke: 'I saw the son of Jesse coming to Nob, to Ahimelech son of Ahitub.

10 Ahimelech consulted the LORD on his behalf, then gave him food and handed over to him the sword of Goliath the

11 Philistine.' The king sent for Ahimelech the priest and his family, who were priests at Nob, and they all

12 came into his presence. Saul said, 'Now listen, you son of Ahitub', and the man answered, 'Yes, my lord?'

13 Then Saul said to him, 'Why have you and the son of Jesse plotted against me? You gave him food and the sword too, and consulted God on his behalf; and now he has risen against me and is at this moment

14 lying in wait for me.' 'And who among all your servants', answered Ahimelech, 'is like David, a man to be trusted,

the king's son-in-law, appointed to your staff and holding an honourable

15 place in your household? Have I on this occasion done something profane in consulting God on his behalf? God forbid! I trust that my lord the king will not accuse me or my family; for I know nothing whatever about it.'

16 But the king said, 'Ahimelech, you must die, you and all your family.'

17 He then turned to the bodyguard attending him and said, 'Go and kill the priests of the LORD; for they are in league with David, and, though they knew that he was a fugitive, they did not tell me.' The king's men, however, were unwilling to raise a hand

18 against the priests of the LORD. The king therefore said to Doeg the Edomite, 'You, Doeg, go and fall upon the priests'; so Doeg went and fell upon the priests, killing that day with his own hand eighty-five men

19 who could carry the ephod. He put to the sword every living thing in Nob, the city of priests: men and women, children and babes in arms, oxen,

20 asses, and sheep. One son of Ahimelech named Abiathar made his escape and

21 joined David. He told David how Saul had killed the priests of the

22 LORD. Then David said to him, 'When Doeg the Edomite was there that day, I knew that he would inform Saul. I have gambled with the lives of all

23 your father's family. Stay here with me, have no fear; he who seeks your life seeks mine, and you will be safe with me.'

David in Keilah

23 The Philistines were fighting against Keilah and plundering the threshing-floors; and when David heard this, he consulted the LORD and asked

2 whether he should go and attack the Philistines. The LORD answered, 'Go,

3 attack them, and relieve Keilah.' But David's men said to him, 'As we are now, we have enough to fear from Judah. How much worse if we challenge the Philistine forces at Keilah!'

4 David consulted the LORD once again and the LORD answered him, 'Go to Keilah; I will give the Philistines into

5 your hands.' So David and his men went to Keilah and fought the Philistines; they carried off their cattle, inflicted a heavy defeat on them and relieved the inhabitants. Abiathar

6 son of Ahimelech made good his escape and joined David at Keilah,

7 bringing the ephod with him. Saul was told that David had entered

E

Keilah, and he said, 'God has put him into my hands; for he has walked into a trap by entering a walled town with 8 gates and bars.' He called out the levy to march on Keilah and besiege 9 David and his men. When David learnt how Saul planned his undoing, he told Abiathar the priest to bring 10 the ephod, and then he prayed, 'O LORD God of Israel, I thy servant have heard news that Saul intends to come to Keilah and destroy the city be-11 cause of me. Will the citizens of Keilah surrender me to him? Will Saul come as I have heard? O LORD God of Israel, I pray thee, tell thy servant.' The LORD answered, 'He will come.' 12 Then David asked, 'Will the citizens of Keilah surrender me and my men to Saul?', and the LORD answered, 13 'They will.' Then David left Keilah at once with his men, who numbered about six hundred, and moved about from place to place. When the news reached Saul that David had escaped from Keilah, he made no further move.

David in the wilderness

14 While David was living in the fast-nesses of the wilderness of Ziph, in the hill-country, Saul searched for him day after day, but God did not 15 put him into his power. David well knew that Saul had come out to seek his life; and while he was at Horesh 16 in the wilderness of Ziph, Saul's son Jonathan came to him there and gave 17 him fresh courage in God's name: 'Do not be afraid,' he said; 'my father's hand shall not touch you. You will become king of Israel and I shall hold rank after you; and my father knows 18 it.' The two of them made a solemn compact before the LORD; then David remained in Horesh and Jonathan 19 went home. While Saul was at Gibeah the Ziphites brought him this news: 'David, we hear, is in hiding among us in the fastnesses of Horesh on the hill of Hachilah, south of Jeshimon. 20 Come down, your majesty, come whenever you will, and we are able to 21 surrender him to you.' Saul said, 'The LORD has indeed blessed you; you 22 have saved me a world of trouble. Go now and make further inquiry, and find out exactly where he is and who saw him there. They tell me that he by himself is crafty enough to outwit 23 me. Find out which of his hiding-places he is using; then come back to me at such and such a place, and I

will go along with you. So long as he stays in this country, I will hunt him down, if I have to go through all the clans of Judah one by one.' They set 24 out for Ziph without delay, ahead of Saul; David and his men were in the wilderness of Maon in the Arabah to the south of Jeshimon. Saul set off 25 with his men to look for him; but David got wind of it and went down to a refuge in the rocks, and there he stayed in the wilderness of Maon. Hearing of this, Saul went into the wilderness after him; he was on one 26 side of the hill, David and his men on the other. While David and his men were trying desperately to get away and Saul and his followers were closing in for the capture, a runner 27 brought a message to Saul: 'Come at once! the Philistines are harrying the land.' So Saul called off the pursuit 28 and turned back to face the Philis-tines. This is why that place is called the Dividing Rock. David went up 29 from there and lived in the fastnesses of En-gedi.

David spares Saul at En-gedi

When Saul returned from the pursuit 24 of the Philistines, he learnt that David was in the wilderness of En-gedi. So 2 he took three thousand men picked from the whole of Israel and went in search of David and his men to the east of the Rocks of the Wild Goats. There beside the road were some 3 sheepfolds, and near by was a cave, at the far end of which David and his men were sitting concealed. Saul came to the cave and went in to relieve himself. His men said to David, 'The 4 day has come: the LORD has put your enemy into your hands, as he pro-mised he would, and you may do what you please with him.' David said to his men, 'God forbid that I should harm my master, the LORD's anoin-ted, or lift a finger against him; he is the LORD's anointed.' So David re-proved his men severely and would not let them attack Saul. He himself got up stealthily and cut off a piece of Saul's cloak; but when he had cut it off, his conscience smote him. Saul rose, left the cave and went on his way; whereupon David also came out 8 of the cave and called after Saul, 'My lord the king!' When Saul looked round, David prostrated himself in obeisance and said to him, 'Why do 9 you listen when they say that David is out to do you harm? Today you can 10 see for yourself that the LORD put you into my power in the cave; I had a mind to kill you, but no, I spared your life and said, "I cannot lift a finger against my master, for he is the LORD's

11 anointed." Look, my dear lord, look at this piece of your cloak in my hand. I cut it off, but I did not kill you; this will show you that I have no thought of violence or treachery against you, and that I have done you no wrong; yet you are resolved to

12 take my life. May the LORD judge between us! but though he may take vengeance on you for my sake, I will

13 never lift my hand against you; "One wrong begets another", as the old saying goes, yet I will never lift my

14 hand against you. Who has the king of Israel come out against? What are you pursuing? A dead dog, a mere

15 flea. The LORD will be judge and decide between us; let him look into my cause, he will plead for me and will acquit me.'

16 When David had finished speaking, Saul said, 'Is that you, David my son?',

17 and he wept. Then he said, 'The right is on your side, not mine; you have treated me so well, I have treated

18 you so badly. Your goodness to me this day has passed all bounds: the LORD put me at your mercy but you

19 did not kill me. Not often does a man find his enemy and let him go safely on his way; so may the LORD reward you well for what you have done for

20 me today! I know now for certain that you will become king, and that the kingdom of Israel will flourish

21 under your rule. Swear to me by the LORD then that you will not exterminate my descendants and blot out my name from my father's house.'

22 David swore an oath to Saul; and Saul went back to his home, while David and his men went up to their fastness.

David greets Nabal

25 Samuel died, and all Israel came together to mourn for him, and he was buried in his house in Ramah. Afterwards David went down to the wilderness of Paran.

2 There was a man at Carmel in Maon, who had great influence and owned three thousand sheep and a thousand goats; and he was shearing

3 his flocks in Carmel. His name was Nabal and his wife's name Abigail; she was a beautiful and intelligent

woman, but her husband, a Calebite, was surly and mean. David heard in 4 the wilderness that Nabal was shearing his flocks, and sent ten of his men, 5 saying to them, 'Go up to Carmel, find Nabal and give him my greetings. You are to say, "All good wishes for 6 the year ahead! Prosperity to yourself, your household, and all that is yours! I hear that you are shearing. 7 Your shepherds have been with us lately and we did not molest them; nothing of theirs was missing all the time they were in Carmel. Ask your 8 own people and they will tell you. Receive my men kindly, for this is an auspicious day with us, and give what you can to David your son and your servant."' David's servants came and 9 delivered this message to Nabal in David's name. When they paused, Nabal answered, 'Who is David? Who 10 is this son of Jesse? In these days every slave who breaks away from his master sets himself up as a chief.[o] Am I to take my food and my wine 11 and the meat I have provided for my shearers and give it to men who come from I know not where?' David's men 12 turned and made their way back to him and told him all this. He said to 13 his men, 'Buckle on your swords, all of you.' So they buckled on their swords and followed David, four hundred of them, while two hundred stayed behind with the baggage.

Abigail appeases David

One of the young men said to Abigail, 14 Nabal's wife, 'David sent messengers from the wilderness to ask our master politely for a present, and he flew out[p] at them. The men have been very 15 good to us and have not molested us, nor did we miss anything all the time we were going about with them in the open country. They were as good as 16 a wall round us, night and day, while we were minding the flocks. Consider 17 carefully what you had better do, for it is certain ruin for our master and his whole family; he is such a good-for-nothing that it is no good talking to him.' So Abigail hastily collected 18 two hundred loaves and two skins of wine, five sheep ready dressed, five measures of parched grain, a hundred bunches of raisins, and two hundred cakes of dried figs, and loaded them on asses, but told her husband noth- 19 ing about it. Then she said to her servants, 'Go on ahead, I will follow you.'

o *Or* In these days there are many slaves who break away from their master. ‎ p flew out: *or* screamed.

20 As she made her way on her ass, hidden by the hill, there were David and his men coming down towards her, and 21 she met them. David had said, 'It was a waste of time to protect this fellow's property in the wilderness so well that nothing of his was missing. He has 22 repaid me evil for good.' David swore a great oath: 'God do the same to me and more if I leave him a single mother's son alive by morning!'

23   When Abigail saw David she dismounted in haste and prostrated her-24 self before him, bowing low to the ground at his feet, and said, 'Let me take the blame, my lord, but allow me, your humble servant, to speak out and let my lord give me a hearing. 25 How can you take any notice of this good-for-nothing? He is just what his name Nabal means: "Churl" is his name, and churlish his behaviour. I did not myself, sir, see the men you 26 sent. And now, sir, the LORD has restrained you from bloodshed and from giving vent to your anger. As the LORD lives, your life upon it, your enemies and all who want to see you 27 ruined will be like Nabal. Here is the present which I, your humble servant, have brought; give it to the young 28 men under your command. Forgive me, my lord, if I am presuming; for the LORD will establish your family for ever, because you have fought his wars. No calamity shall overtake you 29 as long as you live. If any man sets out to pursue you and take your life, the LORD your God will wrap your life up and put it with his own treasure, but the lives of your enemies he will hurl away like stones from a sling. 30 When the LORD has made good all his promises to you, and has made 31 you ruler of Israel, there will be no reason why you should stumble or your courage falter because you have shed innocent blood or given way to your anger. Then when the LORD makes all you do prosper, you will remember 32 me, your servant.' David said to Abigail, 'Blessed is the LORD the God of Israel who has sent you today to meet 33 me. A blessing on your good sense, a blessing on you because you have saved me today from the guilt of bloodshed and from giving way to my 34 anger. For I swear by the life of the LORD the God of Israel who has kept me from doing you wrong: if you had not come at once to meet me, not a man of Nabal's household, not a single mother's son, would have been 35 left alive by morning.' Then David

took from her what she had brought him and said, 'Go home in peace, I have listened to you and I grant your request.'

David marries Abigail

On her return she found Nabal hold-36 ing a banquet in his house, a banquet fit for a king. He grew merry and became very drunk, so drunk that his wife said nothing to him, trivial or serious, till daybreak. In the morning, 37 when the wine had worn off, she told him everything, and he had a seizure and lay there like a stone. Ten days 38 later the LORD struck him again and he died. When David heard that 39 Nabal was dead he said, 'Blessed be the LORD, who has himself punished Nabal for his insult, and has kept me his servant from doing wrong. The LORD has made Nabal's wrongdoing recoil on his own head.' David then sent to make proposals that Abigail should become his wife. And his ser-40 vants came to Abigail at Carmel and said to her, 'David has sent us to fetch you to be his wife.' She rose and 41 prostrated herself with her face to the ground, and said, 'I am his slave to command, I would wash the feet of my lord's servants.' So Abigail made 42 her preparations with all speed and, with her five maids in attendance, accompanied by David's messengers, rode away on an ass; and she became David's wife. David had also married 43 Ahinoam of Jezreel; both these women became his wives. Saul mean-44 while had given his daughter Michal, David's wife, to Palti son of Laish from Gallim.

David spares Saul at Ziph

The Ziphites came to Saul at Gibeah 26 to report that David was in hiding on the hill of Hachilah overlooking Jeshi-mon. Saul went down at once to the 2 wilderness of Ziph, taking with him three thousand picked men, to search for David there. He encamped beside 3 the road on the hill of Hachilah overlooking Jeshimon, while David was still in the wilderness. As soon as David knew that Saul had come to the wilderness in pursuit of him, he 4 sent out scouts and found that Saul had reached such and such a place. Without delay, he went to the place 5 where Saul had pitched his camp and observed where Saul and Abner son of Ner, the commander-in-chief, were lying. Saul lay within the lines with his troops encamped in a circle round

6 him. David turned to Ahimelech the Hittite and Abishai son of Zeruiah, Joab's brother, and said, 'Who will venture with me into the camp, to go to Saul?' Abishai answered, 'I will.'

7 David and Abishai entered the camp at night and found Saul lying asleep within the lines with his spear thrust into the ground by his head. Abner and the army were lying all round 8 him. Abishai said to David, 'God has put your enemy into your power to-day; let me strike him and pin him to the ground with one thrust of the spear; I shall not have to strike 9 twice.' David said to him, 'Do him no harm; who has ever lifted a finger against the LORD's anointed and gone 10 unpunished? As the LORD lives,' went on David, 'the LORD will strike him down; either his time will come and he will die, or he will go down to battle 11 and meet his end. God forbid that I should lift a finger against the LORD's anointed! But now let us take the spear which is by his head, and the 12 water-jar, and go.' So David took the spear and the water-jar from beside Saul's head and they went. The whole camp was asleep; no one saw him, no one knew anything, no one even woke up. A heavy sleep sent by the LORD had fallen on them.

13 Then David crossed over to the other side and stood on the top of a hill a long way off; there was no 14 little distance between them. David shouted across to the army and hailed Abner, 'Answer me, Abner!' He answered, 'Who are you to shout to the 15 king?' David said to Abner, 'Do you call yourself a man? Is there anyone like you in Israel? Why, then, did you not keep watch over your lord the king, when someone came to harm 16 your lord the king? This was not well done. As the LORD lives, you deserve to die, all of you, because you have not kept watch over your master the LORD's anointed. Look! Where are the king's spear and the water-jar that were by his head?'

17 Saul recognized David's voice and said, 'Is that you, David my son?' 18 'Yes, sir, it is', said David. 'Why must your majesty pursue me? What have I done? What mischief am I plotting? 19 Listen, my lord, to what I have to say. If it is the LORD who has set you against me, may an offering be acceptable to him; but if it is men, a curse on them in the LORD's name; for they have ousted me today from my share

in the LORD's inheritance and have banished me to serve other gods! Do 20 not let my blood be shed on foreign soil, far from the presence of the LORD, just because the king of Israel came out to look for a flea, as one might hunt a partridge over the hills.' Saul 21 answered, 'I have done wrong; come back, David my son. You have held my life precious this day, and I will never harm you again. I have been a fool, I have been sadly in the wrong.' David answered, 'Here is the king's 22 spear; let one of your men come across and fetch it. The LORD who rewards 23 uprightness and loyalty will reward the man into whose power he put you today, when I refused to lift a finger against the LORD's anointed. As I 24 held your life precious today, so may the LORD hold mine precious and deliver me from every distress.' Then 25 Saul said to David, 'A blessing is on you, David my son. You will do great things and be victorious.' So David went on his way and Saul returned home.

David lives among the Philistines

David thought, 'One of these days I **27** shall be killed by Saul. The best thing for me to do will be to escape into Philistine territory; then Saul will lose all further hope of finding me anywhere in Israel, search as he may, and I shall escape his clutches.' So David and his six hundred men 2 crossed the frontier forthwith to Achish son of Maoch king of Gath. David 3 settled in Gath with Achish, taking with him his men and their families and his two wives, Ahinoam of Jezreel and Abigail of Carmel, Nabal's widow. Saul was told that David had 4 escaped to Gath, and he gave up the search. David said to Achish, 'If I 5 stand well in your opinion, grant me a place in one of your country towns where I may settle. Why should I remain in the royal city with your majesty?' Achish granted him Ziklag 6 on that day: that is why Ziklag still belongs to the kings of Judah.

David spent a year and four months 7 in Philistine country. He and his men 8 would sally out and raid the Geshurites, the Gizrites, and the Amalekites, for it was they who inhabited the country from Telaim*q* all the way to Shur and Egypt. When David raided 9 the country he left no one alive, man or woman; he took flocks and herds, asses and camels, and clothes too,

q from Telaim: prob. rdg.; Heb. from of old.

and then came back again to Achish.
10 When Achish asked, 'Where was your
raid today?', David would answer,
'The Negeb of Judah' or 'The Negeb
of the Jerahmeelites' or 'The Negeb of
11 the Kenites'. Neither man nor woman
did David bring back alive to Gath,
for fear that they should denounce
him and his men for what they had
done. This was his practice as long
as he remained with the Philistines.
12 Achish trusted David, thinking that
he had won such a bad name among
his own people the Israelites that he
would remain his subject all his life.

28   In those days the Philistines mustered their army for an attack on Israel. Achish said to David, 'You know
that you and your men must take the
2 field with me.' David answered Achish,
'Good, you will learn what your servant can do.' And Achish said to
David, 'I will make you my bodyguard
for life.'

Saul and the medium at En-dor

3 By this time Samuel was dead, and
all Israel had mourned for him and
buried him in Ramah, his own city;
and Saul had banished from the land
all who trafficked with ghosts and
4 spirits. The Philistines mustered and
encamped at Shunem, and Saul
gathered all the Israelites and en-
5 camped on Gilboa; and when Saul saw
the Philistine force, fear struck him
6 to the heart. He inquired of the LORD,
but the LORD did not answer him,
whether by dreams or by Urim or by
7 prophets. So he said to his servants,
'Find me a woman who has a familiar
spirit, and I will go and inquire
through her.' His servants told him
that there was such a woman at En-
8 dor. Saul put on different clothes and
went in disguise with two of his men.
He came to the woman by night and
said, 'Tell me my fortunes by consulting the dead, and call up the man
9 I name to you.' But the woman
answered, 'Surely you know what Saul
has done, how he has made away with
those who call up ghosts and spirits;
why do you press me to do what will
10 lead to my death?' Saul swore her an
oath: 'As the LORD lives, no harm
11 shall come to you for this.' The woman asked whom she should call up,
12 and Saul answered, 'Samuel.' When
the woman saw Samuel appear, she
shrieked and said to Saul, 'Why have
13 you deceived me? You are Saul!' The
king said to her, 'Do not be afraid.

What do you see?' The woman
answered, 'I see a ghostly form coming
up from the earth.' 'What is it like?' 14
he asked; she answered, 'Like an old
man coming up, wrapped in a cloak.'
Then Saul knew it was Samuel, and he
bowed low with his face to the ground,
and prostrated himself. Samuel said 15
to Saul, 'Why have you disturbed me
and brought me up?' Saul answered,
'I am in great trouble; the Philistines
are pressing me and God has turned
away; he no longer answers me through
prophets or through dreams, and I
have summoned you to tell me what
I should do.' Samuel said, 'Why do 16
you ask me, now that the LORD has
turned from you and become your
adversary? He has done what he fore- 17
told through me. He has torn the
kingdom from your hand and given
it to another man, to David. You 18
have not obeyed the LORD, or executed the judgement of his fury against
the Amalekites; that is why he has
done this to you today. For the same 19
reason the LORD will let your people
Israel fall into the hands of the
Philistines and, what is more, tomorrow you and your sons shall be
with me. Yes, indeed, the LORD will
give the Israelite army into the hands
of the Philistines.' Saul was overcome 20
and fell his full length to the ground,
terrified by Samuel's words. He had
no strength left, for he had eaten
nothing all day and all night.

The woman went to Saul and saw 21
that he was much disturbed, and she
said to him, 'I listened to what you
said and I risked my life to obey you.
Now listen to me: let me set before 22
you a little food to give you strength
for your journey.' But he refused 23
to eat anything. When his servants
joined the woman in pressing him, he
yielded, rose from the ground and sat
on the couch. The woman had a fat- 24
ted calf at home, which she quickly
slaughtered. She took some meal,
kneaded it and baked unleavened
cakes, which she set before Saul and 25
his servants. They ate the food and
departed that same night.

The Philistines distrust David

The Philistines mustered all their 29
troops at Aphek, while the Israelites
encamped at En-harod[r] in Jezreel.
The Philistine princes were advancing 2
with their troops in units of a hundred
and a thousand; David and his men
were in the rear of the column with

r *Prob. rdg.; Heb.* at the spring.

3 Achish. The Philistine commanders asked, 'Why are those Hebrews there?' Achish answered, 'This is David, the servant of Saul king of Israel who has been with me now for a year or more. I have had no fault to find in him 4 ever since he came over to me.' The Philistine commanders were indignant and said to Achish, 'Send the man back to the town which you allotted to him. He shall not fight side by side with us, or he may turn traitor in the battle. What better way to buy his master's favour, than at the price 5 of our lives? This is that David of whom they sang, as they danced:

Saul made havoc among thousands but David among tens of thousands.'

6 Achish summoned David and said to him, 'As the LORD lives, you are an upright man and your service with my troops has well satisfied me. I have had no fault to find with you ever since you joined me, but the other princes are not willing to accept 7 you. Now go home in peace, and you will then be doing nothing that they 8 can regard as wrong.' David protested, 'What have I done, or what fault have you found in me from the day I first entered your service till now, that I should not come and fight against the 9 enemies of my lord the king?' Achish answered David, 'I agree that you have been as true to me as an angel of God, but the Philistine commanders insist that you shall not fight along-10 side them. Now rise early in the morning with those of your lord's subjects who have followed you, and go to the town which I allotted to you; harbour no evil thoughts, for I am well satisfied with you. Rise early and 11 start as soon as it is light.' So David and his men rose early to start that morning on their way back to the land of the Philistines, while the Philistines went on to Jezreel.

An Amalekite raid

30 On the third day David and his men reached Ziklag. Now the Amalekites had made a raid into the Negeb, attacked Ziklag and set fire to it; 2 they had carried off all the women, high and low, without putting one of them to death. These they drove with them and continued their march. 3 When David and his men approached the town, they found it destroyed by fire, and their wives, their sons, and 4 their daughters carried off. David and

the people with him wept aloud until they could weep no more. David's 5 two wives, Ahinoam of Jezreel and Abigail widow of Nabal of Carmel, were among the captives. David was 6 in a desperate position because the people, embittered by the loss of their sons and daughters, threatened to stone him. So David sought strength in the LORD his God. He told Abi-7 athar the priest, son of Ahimelech, to bring the ephod. When Abiathar had brought the ephod, David inquired 8 of the LORD, 'Shall I pursue these raiders? and shall I overtake them?' The answer came, 'Pursue them: you will overtake them and rescue everyone.' So David and his six hundred 9 men set out and reached the ravine of Besor.[s] Two hundred of them who 10 were too weary to cross the ravine stayed behind, and David with four hundred pressed on in pursuit.

In the open country they came 11 across an Egyptian and took him to David. They gave him food to eat and water to drink, also a lump of dried 12 figs and two bunches of raisins. When he had eaten these he revived; for he had had nothing to eat or drink for three days and nights. David 13 asked him, 'Whose slave are you? and where have you come from?' 'I am an Egyptian boy,' he answered, 'the slave of an Amalekite, but my master left me behind because I fell ill three days ago. We had raided the Negeb 14 of the Kerethites, part of Judah, and the Negeb of Caleb; we also set fire to Ziklag.' David asked, 'Can you guide 15 me to this band?' 'Swear to me by God', he answered, 'that you will not put me to death or hand me back to my master, and I will guide you to them.' So he led him down, and there 16 they were scattered everywhere, eating and drinking and celebrating the capture of the great mass of spoil taken from Philistine and Judaean territory.

David rescues the Amalekites' captives

David attacked from dawn till dusk 17 and continued till next day; only four hundred young men mounted on camels made good their escape. David rescued all those whom the 18 Amalekites had taken, including his two wives. No one was missing, high 19 or low, sons or daughters, and none of the spoil, nor anything they had taken for themselves: David recovered everything. They took all the 20

---

s *Prob. rdg.; Heb. adds* those who were left over remained.

flocks and herds, drove the cattle before him[t] and said, 'This is David's 21 spoil.' When David returned to the two hundred men who had been too weak to follow him and whom he had left behind at the ravine of Besor, they came forward to meet him and his men. David greeted them all, inquiring how things were with them. 22 But some of those who had gone with David, worthless men and scoundrels, broke in and said, 'These men did not go with us; we will not allot them any of the spoil that we have retrieved, except that each of them may take his own wife and children and then go.' 23 'That you shall never do,' said David, 'considering what the LORD has given us, and how he has kept us safe and given the raiding party into our 24 hands. Who could agree with what you propose? Those who stayed with the stores shall have the same share as those who went into battle. They 25 shall share and share alike.' From that time onwards, this has been the established custom in Israel down to this day.

26 When David reached Ziklag, he sent some of the spoil to the elders of Judah and to his friends, with this message: 'This is a present for you out of the spoil taken from the LORD's 27 enemies.' He sent to those in Beth-28 uel, in Ramoth-negeb, in Jattir, in Ararah,[u] in Siphmoth, in Eshtemoa, 29 in Rachal, in the cities of the Jerah-meelites, in the cities of the Kenites, 30 31 in Hormah, in Borashan, in Athak, in Hebron, and in all the places over which he and his men had ranged.

The death of Saul and his sons

31 1[v] The Philistines fought a battle against Israel, and the men of Israel were routed, leaving their dead on Mount 2 Gilboa. The Philistines hotly pursued

Saul and his sons and killed the three sons, Jonathan, Abinadab and Mal-chishua. The battle went hard for 3 Saul, for some archers came upon him and he was wounded in the belly by the archers. So he said to his armour-4 bearer, 'Draw your sword and run me through, so that these uncircumcised brutes may not come and taunt me and make sport of me.' But the armour-bearer refused, he dared not; whereupon Saul took his own sword and fell on it. When the armour-bearer 5 saw that Saul was dead, he too fell on his sword and died with him. Thus 6 they all died together on that day, Saul, his three sons, and his armour-bearer, as well as his men. And all the 7 Israelites in the district of the Vale and of the Jordan, when they saw that the other Israelites had fled and that Saul and his sons had perished, fled likewise, abandoning their cities, and the Philistines went in and occupied them.

Next day, when the Philistines 8 came to strip the slain, they found Saul and his three sons lying dead on Mount Gilboa. They cut off his head 9 and stripped him of his weapons; then they sent messengers through the length and breadth of their land to take the good news to idols and people alike. They deposited his armour in 10 the temple of Ashtoreth and nailed his body on the wall of Beth-shan. When the inhabitants of Jabesh- 11 gilead heard what the Philistines had done to Saul, the bravest of them 12 journeyed together all night long and recovered the bodies of Saul and his sons from the wall of Beth-shan; they brought them back to Jabesh and anointed them there with spices. Then 13 they took their bones and buried them under the tamarisk-tree in Jabesh, and fasted for seven days.

t They took . . . before him: *prob. rdg.*; Heb. David took all the flocks and herds; they drove before that cattle.   u *Prob. rdg.*; Heb. Aroer.   v Verses 1–13: cp. 1 Chr. 10. 1–12.

THE SECOND BOOK OF
SAMUEL

David learns of Saul's death

1 WHEN DAVID returned from his victory over the Amalekites, he spent
2 two days in Ziklag. And on the third day after Saul's death a man came from the army with his clothes rent and dust on his head. When he came into David's presence he fell to the
3 ground in obeisance, and David asked him where he had come from. He answered, 'I have escaped from the
4 army of Israel.' And David said to him, 'What news? Tell me.' 'The army has been driven from the field,' he answered, 'and many have fallen in
5 battle. Saul and Jonathan his son are dead.' David said to the young man who brought the news, 'How do you know that Saul and Jonathan are
6 dead?' The man answered, 'It so happened that I was on Mount Gilboa and saw Saul leaning on his spear with the chariots and horsemen closing in
7 upon him. He turned round and, seeing me, called to me. I said, "What is
8 it, sir?" He asked who I was, and I
9 said, "An Amalekite." Then he said to me, "Come and stand over me and dispatch me. I still live, but the
10 throes of death have seized me." So I stood over him and gave him the death-blow; for I knew that, broken as he was, he could not live. Then I took the crown from his head and the armlet from his arm, and I have
11 brought them here to you, sir.' At that David caught at his clothes and rent them, and so did all the men with
12 him. They beat their breasts and wept, because Saul and Jonathan his son and the people of the LORD, the house of Israel, had fallen in battle; and
13 they fasted till evening. David said to the young man who brought the news, 'Where do you come from?', and he answered, 'I am the son of an alien,
14 an Amalekite.' 'How is it', said David, 'that you were not afraid to raise your hand to slay the LORD's anoin-
15 ted?' And he summoned one of his own young men and ordered him to fall upon the man. So the young man

struck him down and killed him; and 16 David said, 'Your blood be on your own head; for out of your own mouth you condemned yourself when you said, "I killed the LORD's anointed."'

David laments over Saul and Jonathan

David made this lament over Saul 17 and Jonathan his son; and he ordered 18 that this dirge over them should be taught to the people of Judah. It was written down and may be found in the Book of Jashar:[a]

O prince of Israel, laid low in death! 19
How are the men of war fallen!

Tell it not in Gath, 20
proclaim it not in the streets of Ashkelon,
  lest the Philistine women rejoice,
  lest the daughters of the uncircumcised exult.

Hills of Gilboa, let no dew or rain fall 21
  on you,
  no showers on the uplands[b]!
For there the shields of the warriors
  lie tarnished,
  and the shield of Saul, no longer
  bright with oil.
The bow of Jonathan never held back 22
from the breast of the foeman, from
  the blood of the slain;
the sword of Saul never returned
  empty to the scabbard.

Delightful and dearly loved were Saul 23
  and Jonathan;
  in life, in death, they were not
  parted.
They were swifter than eagles,
  stronger than lions.

Weep for Saul, O daughters of Israel! 24
  who clothed you in scarlet and rich
  embroideries,
  who spangled your dress with jewels
  of gold.

How are the men of war fallen, fallen 25
  on the field!
  O Jonathan, laid low in death!
I grieve for you, Jonathan my bro- 26
  ther;
  dear and delightful you were to me;

---

a Or the Book of the Upright. *b* showers on the uplands: *prob. rdg.*; *Heb.* fields of offerings.

your love for me was wonderful,
  surpassing the love of women.
27 Fallen, fallen are the men of war;
  and their armour left on the field.

David made king of Judah

2 After this David inquired of the LORD,
'Shall I go up into one of the cities of
Judah?' The LORD answered, 'Go.'
David asked, 'To which city?', and
2 the answer came, 'To Hebron.' So
David went to Hebron with his two
wives, Ahinoam of Jezreel and Abi-
3 gail widow of Nabal of Carmel. David
also brought the men who had joined
him, with their families, and they
4 settled in the city*c* of Hebron. The
men of Judah came, and there they
anointed David king over the house
of Judah.
    Word came to David that the men
5 of Jabesh-gilead had buried Saul, and
he sent them this message: 'The LORD
bless you because you kept faith with
6 Saul your lord and buried him. For
this may the LORD keep faith and
truth with you, and I for my part will
show you favour too, because you
7 have done this. Be strong, be valiant,
now that Saul your lord is dead, and
the people of Judah have anointed
me to be king over them.'

Abner and Joab in conflict

8 Meanwhile Saul's commander-in-chief,
Abner son of Ner, had taken Saul's
son Ishbosheth, brought him across
9 the Jordan to Mahanaim, and made
him king over Gilead, the Asherites,
Jezreel, Ephraim, and Benjamin, and
10 all Israel. Ishbosheth was forty years
old when he became king over Israel,
and he reigned two years. The tribe
of Judah, however, followed David.
11 David's rule over Judah in Hebron
lasted seven years and a half.
12   Abner son of Ner, with the troops
of Saul's son Ishbosheth, marched out
13 from Mahanaim to Gibeon, and Joab
son of Zeruiah marched out with
David's troops from Hebron. They
met at the pool of Gibeon and took
up their positions one on one side of
the pool and the other on the other
14 side. Abner said to Joab, 'Let the young
men come forward and join in single
combat before us.' Joab answered,
15 'Yes, let them.' So they came up,
one by one, and took their places,
twelve for Benjamin and for Ishbosheth and twelve from David's men.

Each man seized his opponent by the 16
head and thrust his sword into his
side; and thus they fell together.
That is why that place, which lies
in Gibeon, was called the Field of
Blades.

Abner kills Asahel

There ensued a fierce battle that day, 17
and Abner and the men of Israel were
defeated by David's troops. All three 18
sons of Zeruiah were there, Joab,
Abishai and Asahel. Asahel, who was
swift as a gazelle on the plains, ran 19
straight after Abner, swerving neither
to right nor left in his pursuit. Abner 20
turned and asked, 'Is it you, Asahel?'
Asahel answered, 'It is.' Abner said, 21
'Turn aside to right or left, tackle one
of the young men and win his belt
for yourself.' But Asahel would not
abandon the pursuit. Abner again 22
urged him to give it up. 'Why should
I kill you?' he said. 'How could I look
Joab your brother in the face?' When 23
he still refused to turn aside, Abner
struck him in the belly with a back-
thrust of his spear*d* so that the spear
came out behind him, and he fell
dead in his tracks. All who came to
the place where Asahel lay dead
stopped there. But Joab and Abishai 24
kept up the pursuit of Abner, until,
at sunset, they reached the hill of
Ammah, opposite Giah on the road
leading to the pastures of Gibeon.

The fighting ceases

The Benjamites rallied to Abner and, 25
forming themselves into a single company, took up their stand on the
top of the hill of Ammah.*e* Abner 26
called to Joab, 'Must the slaughter go
on for ever? Can you not see that it
will be all the more bitter in the end?
Will you never recall the people from
the pursuit of their kinsmen?' Joab 27
answered, 'As God lives, if you had
not spoken, the people would not have
given up the pursuit till morning.'
Then Joab sounded the trumpet, and 28
all the people abandoned the pursuit
of the men of Israel and the fighting
ceased. Abner and his men moved 29
along the Arabah all that night,
crossed the Jordan and went on all
the morning till they reached Mahanaim. When Joab returned from the 30
pursuit of Abner, he assembled his
troops and found that, besides Asahel,
nineteen of David's men were missing. David's forces had routed the 31

---

*c Prob. rdg.; Heb. cities.   d a back-thrust of his spear: prob. rdg.; Heb. obscure.   e the hill of
Ammah: prob. rdg., cp. verse 24; Heb. a single hill.*

Benjamites and the followers of Abner, killing three hundred and sixty of
32 them. They took up Asahel and buried him in his father's tomb at Bethlehem. Joab and his men marched all night, and as day broke they reached Hebron.

3 The war between the houses of Saul and David was long drawn out, David growing steadily stronger while the house of Saul became weaker and weaker.

David's sons born at Hebron

2[f] Sons were born to David at Hebron. His eldest was Amnon, whose mother
3 was Ahinoam of Jezreel; his second Chileab, whose mother was Abigail widow of Nabal of Carmel; the third Absalom, whose mother was Maacah daughter of Talmai king of Geshur;
4 the fourth Adonijah, whose mother was Haggith; the fifth Shephatiah,
5 whose mother was Abital; and the sixth Ithream, whose mother was David's wife Eglah. These were all born to David at Hebron.

Abner plans a covenant with David

6 As the war between the houses of Saul and David went on, Abner made his position gradually stronger in the
7 house of Saul. Now Saul had had a concubine named Rizpah daughter of Aiah. Ishbosheth asked Abner, 'Why have you slept with my father's con-
8 cubine?' Abner was very angry at this and exclaimed, 'Am I a baboon in the pay of Judah? Up to now I have been loyal to the house of your father Saul, to his brothers and friends, and I have not betrayed you into David's hands; yet you choose this moment to charge me with disloyalty over this
9 woman. But now, so help me God, I will do all I can to bring about what
10 the LORD swore to do for David: I will set to work to bring down the house of Saul and to put David on the throne over Israel and Judah from
11 Dan to Beersheba.' Ishbosheth could not say another word; he was too
12 much afraid of Abner. Then Abner, seeking to make friends where he could, instead of going to David himself sent envoys with this message: 'Let us come to terms, and I will do all I can to bring the whole of Israel
13 over to you.' David sent answer: 'Good, I will come to terms with you, but on this one condition, that you do not come into my presence without bringing Saul's daughter Michal to

me.' David also sent messengers to 14 Saul's son Ishbosheth with the demand: 'Hand over to me my wife Michal to whom I was betrothed at the price of a hundred Philistine foreskins.' Thereupon Ishbosheth sent 15 and took her away from her husband, Paltiel son of Laish. Paltiel followed 16 her as far as Bahurim, weeping all the way, until Abner ordered him to go back home, and he went.

Abner now approached the elders 17 of Israel and said, 'For some time past you have wanted David for your king; now is the time to act, for this is 18 the word of the LORD about David: "By the hand of my servant David I will deliver my people Israel from the Philistines and from all their enemies."' Abner spoke also to the Ben- 19 jamites and then went on to report to David at Hebron all that the Israelites and the Benjamites had agreed. When Abner was admitted to David's 20 presence, there were twenty men with him and David gave a feast for them all. Then Abner said to David, 'I shall 21 now go and bring the whole of Israel over to your majesty, and they shall make a covenant with you. Then you will be king over a realm after your own heart.' David dismissed Abner, granting him safe conduct.

Joab kills Abner

David's men and Joab returned from 22 a raid bringing a great deal of plunder with them, and by this time Abner, after his dismissal, was no longer with David in Hebron. So when Joab and 23 his raiding party arrived, they were greeted with the news that Abner son of Ner had been with the king and had departed under safe conduct. Joab went in to the king and said, 24 'What have you done? Here you have had Abner with you. How could you let him go? He has got clean away! You know Abner son of Ner: he came 25 meaning to deceive you, to learn all about your movements and to find out what you are doing.' When he left 26 David's presence, Joab sent messengers after Abner and they brought him back from the Pool of Sirah; but David knew nothing of all this. On 27 Abner's return to Hebron, Joab drew him aside in the gateway, as though to speak privately with him, and there, in revenge for his brother Asahel, he stabbed him in the belly, and he died. When David heard the 28 news he said, 'I and my realm are for

f Verses 2–5: cp. 1 Chr. 3. 1–4.

ever innocent in the sight of the LORD
29 of the blood of Abner son of Ner. May
it recoil upon the head of Joab and
upon all his family! May the house of
Joab never be free from running sore
or foul disease, nor lack a son fit only
to ply the distaff or doomed to die by
30 the sword or beg his bread!' So Joab
and Abishai his brother slew Abner
because he had killed their brother
31 Asahel in battle at Gibeon. Then
David ordered Joab and all the people
with him to rend their clothes, put
on sackcloth and beat their breasts
for Abner, and the king himself walked
32 behind the bier. They buried Abner
in Hebron and the king wept aloud
at the tomb, while all the people wept
33 with him. The king made this lament
for Abner:

Must Abner die so base a death?
34 Your hands were not bound,
your feet not thrust into fetters;
you fell as one who falls at a ruffian's
hands.

And the people wept for him again.
35 They came to persuade David to
eat something; but it was still day
and he swore, 'So help me God! I will
not touch food of any kind before
36 sunset.' The people took note of
this and approved; indeed, everything
37 the king did pleased them. Everyone
throughout Israel knew on that day
that the king had had no hand in the
38 murder of Abner son of Ner. The king
said to his servants, 'Do you not
know that a warrior, a great man, has
39 fallen this day in Israel? King though
I am, I feel weak and powerless in
face of these ruthless sons of Zeruiah;
they are too much for me; the LORD
will requite the wrongdoer as he
deserves.'

The murder of Ishbosheth

4 When Saul's son Ishbosheth heard
that Abner had been killed in Hebron,
his courage failed him and all Israel
2 was dismayed. Now Ishbosheth had*g*
two officers, who were captains of
raiding parties, and whose names
were Baanah and Rechab; they were
Benjamites, sons of Rimmon of Beeroth, Beeroth being reckoned part of
3 Benjamin; but the Beerothites had
fled to Gittaim, where they have lived
ever since.
4 (Saul's son Jonathan had a son
lame in both feet. He was five years
old when word of the death of Saul
and Jonathan came from Jezreel. His

nurse had picked him up and fled,
but in her hurry to get away she fell
and was crippled. His name was
Mephibosheth.)
Rechab and Baanah, the sons of 5
Rimmon of Beeroth, came to the
house of Ishbosheth in the heat of the
day and went in, while he was taking his midday rest. Now the door- 6
keeper had been sifting wheat, but
she had grown drowsy and fallen
asleep, so Rechab and his brother
Baanah crept in, found their way to 7
the room where he was asleep on the
bed, and struck him dead. They cut
off his head and took it with them,
and, making their way along the
Arabah all night, came to Hebron.
They brought Ishbosheth's head to 8
David at Hebron and said to the king,
'Here is the head of Ishbosheth son
of Saul, your enemy, who sought your
life. The LORD has avenged your
majesty today on Saul and on his
family.' David answered Rechab and 9
his brother Baanah, the sons of Rimmon of Beeroth, with an oath: 'As the
LORD lives, who has rescued me from
all my troubles! I seized the man who 10
brought me word that Saul was dead
and thought it good news; I killed him
in Ziklag, and that was how I rewarded
him for his news. How much more 11
when ruffians have killed an innocent
man on his bed in his own house? Am
I not to take vengeance on you now
for the blood you have shed, and rid
the earth of you?' David gave the 12
word, and the young men killed them;
they cut off their hands and feet and
hung them up beside the pool in
Hebron, but the head of Ishbosheth
they took and buried in Abner's tomb
at Hebron.

David made king of all Israel

Now all the tribes of Israel came to 5 1*h*
David at Hebron and said to him, 'We
are your own flesh and blood. In the 2
past, while Saul was still king over us,
you led the forces of Israel to war and
you brought them home again. And
the LORD said to you, "You shall be
shepherd of my people Israel; you
shall be their prince."' All the elders 3
of Israel came to the king at Hebron;
there David made a covenant with
them before the LORD, and they anointed David king over Israel. David 4
came to the throne at the age of thirty
and reigned for forty years. In Hebron 5
he had ruled over Judah for seven
years and a half, and for thirty-three

g had: prob. rdg.; Heb. om.   h Verses 1–3, 6–10: cp. 1 Chr. 11. 1–9.

years he reigned in Jerusalem over Israel and Judah together.

David captures Zion

6 The king and his men went to Jerusalem to attack the Jebusites, whose land it was. The Jebusites said to David, 'Never shall you come in here; not till you have disposed of the blind and the lame', meaning that David
7 should never come in. None the less David did capture the stronghold of Zion, and it is now known as the City
8 of David. David said on that day, 'Everyone who would kill a Jebusite, let him use his grappling-iron to reach the lame and the blind, David's bitter enemies.' That is why they say, 'No blind or lame man shall come into the LORD's house.'
9 David took up his residence in the stronghold and called it the City of David. He built the city[i] round it, starting at the Millo and working inwards.
10 So David steadily grew stronger, for the LORD the God of Hosts was with him.

Hiram recognizes David's sovereignty

11[j] Hiram king of Tyre sent an embassy to David; he sent cedar logs, and with them carpenters and stonemasons,
12 who built David a house. David knew by now that the LORD had confirmed him as king over Israel and had made his royal power stand higher for the sake of his people Israel.

David's children born at Jerusalem

13 After he had moved from Hebron he took more concubines and wives from Jerusalem; and more sons and daugh-
14[k] ters were born to him. These are the names of the children born to him in Jerusalem: Shammua, Shobab,
15 Nathan, Solomon, Ibhar, Elishua,
16 Nepheg, Japhia, Elishama, Eliada and Eliphelet.

David routs the Philistines

17 When the Philistines learnt that David had been anointed king over Israel, they came up in force to seek him out. David, hearing of this, took refuge in
18 the stronghold. The Philistines had come and overrun the Vale of Reph-
19 aim. So David inquired of the LORD,

'If I attack the Philistines, wilt thou deliver them into my hands?' And the LORD answered, 'Go, I will deliver the Philistines into your hands.'
20 So he went up and attacked them at Baal-perazim and defeated them there. 'The LORD has broken through my enemies' lines,' David said, 'as a river breaks its banks.' That is why the place was named Baal-perazim.[l]
21 The Philistines left their idols behind them there, and David and his men carried them off.
22 The Philistines made another attack and overran the Vale of Rephaim.
23 David inquired of the LORD, who said, 'Do not attack now but wheel round and take them in the rear opposite the aspens. As soon as you hear
24 a rustling sound in the tree-tops, then act at once; for the LORD will have gone out before you to defeat the
25 Philistine army.' David did as the LORD had commanded, and drove the Philistines in flight all the way from Geba to Gezer.

David removes the Ark

6 After that David again summoned the picked men of Israel, thirty
2[m] thousand in all, and went with the whole army to Baalath-judah[n] to fetch the Ark of God which bears the name of the LORD of Hosts, who is
3 enthroned upon the cherubim. They mounted the Ark of God on a new cart and conveyed it from the house of Abinadab on the hill, with Uzzah and Ahio, sons of Abinadab, guiding
4 the cart. They took it with the Ark of God upon it from Abinadab's house on the hill, with Ahio walking
5 in front. David and all Israel danced for joy before the LORD without restraint to the sound of singing,[o] of harps and lutes, of tambourines and
6 castanets and cymbals. But when they came to a certain threshing-floor, the oxen stumbled, and Uzzah reached out to the Ark of God and took hold of it. The LORD was angry with Uzzah
7 and struck him down there for his rash act. So he died there beside the
8 Ark of God. David was vexed because the LORD's anger had broken out upon Uzzah, and he called the place Perez-uzzah,[p] the name it still
9 bears. David was afraid of the LORD that day and said, 'How can I harbour

---

i the city: prob. rdg., cp. 1 Chr. 11. 8; Heb. om.   j Verses 11–25: cp. 1 Chr. 14. 1–16.   k Verses 14–16: cp. 1 Chr. 3. 5–8; 14. 4–7.   l That is Baal of Break-through.   m Verses 2–11: cp. 1 Chr. 13. 6–14.   n to Baalath-judah: prob. rdg., cp. 1 Chr. 13. 6; Heb. from the lords of Judah.   o without . . . singing: prob. rdg., cp. 1 Chr. 13. 8; Heb. to the beating of batons.   p That is Outbreak on Uzzah.

10 the Ark of the LORD after this?' He felt he could not take the Ark of the LORD with him to the City of David, but turned aside and carried it to the
11 house of Obed-edom the Gittite. Thus the Ark of the LORD remained at Obed-edom's house for three months, and the LORD blessed Obed-edom and all his family.

David brings the Ark to Jerusalem

12[q] When they told David that the LORD had blessed Obed-edom's family and all that was his because of the Ark of God, he went and brought up the Ark of God from the house of Obed-edom to the City of David with much
13 rejoicing. When the bearers of the Ark of the LORD had gone six steps he
14 sacrificed an ox and a buffalo. David, wearing a linen ephod, danced with-
15 out restraint before the LORD. He and all the Israelites brought up the Ark of the LORD with shouting and blow-
16 ing of trumpets. But as the Ark of the LORD was entering the City of David, Saul's daughter Michal looked down through a window and saw King David leaping and capering before the LORD, and she despised him in her
17 heart. When they had brought in the Ark of the LORD, they put it in its place inside the tent that David had pitched for it, and David offered whole-offerings and shared-offerings
18 before the LORD. After David had completed these sacrifices, he blessed the people in the name of the LORD
19 of Hosts and gave food to all the people, a flat loaf of bread, a portion of meat, and a cake of raisins, to every man and woman in the whole gathering of the Israelites. Then all
20 the people went home. When David returned to greet his household, Michal, Saul's daughter, came out to meet him and said, 'What a glorious day for the king of Israel, when he exposed his person in the sight of his servants' slave-girls like any empty-
21 headed fool!' David answered Michal, 'But it was done in the presence of the LORD, who chose me instead of your father and his family and appointed me prince over Israel, the people of the LORD. Before the LORD I will
22 dance for joy, yes, and I will earn yet more disgrace and lower myself still more in your eyes. But those girls of whom you speak, they will honour me
23 for it.' Michal, Saul's daughter, had no child to her dying day.

The LORD's covenant with David

7 1[r] As soon as the king was established in his house and the LORD had given
2 him security from his enemies on all sides, he said to Nathan the prophet, 'Here I live in a house of cedar, while the Ark of God is housed in curtains.'
3 Nathan answered the king, 'Very well, do whatever you have in mind,
4 for the LORD is with you.' But that night the word of the LORD came to
5 Nathan: 'Go and say to David my servant, "This is the word of the LORD: Are you the man to build me
6 a house to dwell in? Down to this day I have never dwelt in a house since I brought Israel up from Egypt; I made my journey in a tent and a tabernacle.
7 Wherever I journeyed with Israel, did I ever ask any of the judges[s] whom I appointed shepherds of my people Israel why they had not built me a
8 house of cedar?" Then say this to my servant David: "This is the word of the LORD of Hosts: I took you from the pastures, and from following the sheep, to be prince over my people
9 Israel. I have been with you wherever you have gone, and have destroyed all the enemies in your path. I will make you a great name among the
10 great ones of the earth. I will assign a place for my people Israel; there I will plant them, and they shall dwell in their own land. They shall be disturbed no more, never again shall
11 wicked men oppress them as they did in the past, ever since the time when I appointed judges over Israel my people; and I will give you peace from all your enemies. The LORD has told you that he would build up your
12 royal house. When your life ends and you rest with your forefathers, I will set up one of your family, one of your own children, to succeed you and I
13 will establish his kingdom. It is he shall build a house in honour of my name, and I will establish his royal
14 throne for ever. I will be his father, and he shall be my son. When he does wrong, I will punish him as any father might, and not spare the rod.
15 My love will never be withdrawn from him as I withdrew it from Saul, whom I removed from your path.
16 Your family shall be established and your kingdom shall stand for all time in my sight, and your throne shall be established for ever."'
17 Nathan recounted to David all that

q Verses 12–19: cp. 1 Chr. 15. 25—16. 3.   r Verses 1–29: cp. 1 Chr. 17. 1–27.   s Prob. rdg., cp.
1 Chr. 17. 6; Heb. tribes.

had been said to him and all that had
18 been revealed. Then King David went
into the presence of the LORD and
took his place there and said, 'What
am I, Lord GOD, and what is my
family, that thou hast brought me
19 thus far? It was a small thing in thy
sight to have planned for thy servant's
house in days long past. But such, O
Lord GOD, is the lot of a man em-
20 barked on a high career.[t] And now
what more can I say? for well thou
knowest thy servant David, O Lord
21 GOD. Thou hast made good thy word;
it was thy purpose to spread thy
servant's fame, and so thou hast
22 raised me to this greatness. Great indeed art thou, O Lord GOD; we have
never heard of one like thee; there
23 is no god but thee. And thy people
Israel, to whom can they be compared? Is there any other nation on
earth whom thou, O God, hast set out
to redeem from slavery to be thy
people? Any other for whom thou hast
done great and terrible things to win
fame for thyself? Any other whom
thou hast redeemed for thyself from
Egypt by driving out other nations
and their gods to make way for them?
24 Thou hast established thy people Israel as thy own for ever, and thou,
25 O LORD, hast become their God. But
now, LORD God, perform what thou
hast promised for thy servant and
his house, and for all time; make good
26 what thou hast said. May thy fame
be great for evermore and let men
say, "The LORD of Hosts is God over
Israel." So shall the house of thy
servant David be established before
27 thee. O LORD of Hosts, God of Israel,
thou hast shown me thy purpose, in
saying to thy servant, "I will build
up your house"; and therefore I have
made bold to offer this prayer to thee.
28 Thou, O Lord GOD, art God; thou
hast made these noble promises to
thy servant, and thy promises come
29 true; be pleased now to bless thy
servant's house that it may continue
always before thee; thou, O Lord
GOD, hast promised, and thy blessing
shall rest upon thy servant's house for
evermore.'

David extends his kingdom

8 1[u] After this David defeated the Philistines and conquered them, and took
2 from them Metheg-ha-ammah. He defeated the Moabites, and he made
them lie along the ground and measured them off with a length of cord;
for every two lengths that were to
be put to death one full length was
spared. The Moabites became subject
to him and paid him tribute. David 3
also defeated Hadadezer the Rehobite,
king of Zobah, who was on his way
to re-erect his monument of victory
by[v] the river Euphrates. From him 4
David captured seventeen hundred
horse and twenty thousand foot; he
hamstrung all the chariot-horses, except a hundred which he retained.
When the Aramaeans of Damascus 5
came to the help of Hadadezer king
of Zobah, David destroyed twenty-
two thousand of them, and established 6
garrisons among these Aramaeans;
they became subject to him and
paid him tribute. Thus the LORD gave
David victory wherever he went.
David took the gold quivers borne 7
by Hadadezer's servants and brought
them to Jerusalem; and he also took 8
a great quantity of bronze[w] from
Hadadezer's cities, Betah and Bero-
thai.
When Toi king of Hamath heard 9
that David had defeated the entire
army of Hadadezer, he sent his son 10
Joram to King David to greet him
and to congratulate him on defeating
Hadadezer in battle (for Hadadezer
had been at war with Toi); and he
brought with him vessels of silver,
gold, and copper, which King David 11
dedicated to the LORD. He dedicated
also the silver and gold taken from
all the nations he had subdued, from 12
Edom and Moab, from the Ammonites, the Philistines, and Amalek, as
well as part of the spoil taken from
Hadadezer the Rehobite, king of
Zobah.
David made a great name for him- 13
self by the slaughter of eighteen
thousand Edomites in the Valley of
Salt, and on returning he stationed 14
garrisons throughout Edom, and all
the Edomites were subject to him.
Thus the LORD gave victory to David
wherever he went.

David's officers

David ruled over the whole of Israel 15[x]
and maintained law and justice
among all his people. Joab son of 16
Zeruiah was in command of the army;
Jehoshaphat son of Ahilud was secretary of state; Zadok and Abiathar 17

t embarked on a high career: prob. rdg., cp. 1 Chr. 17. 17; Heb. om.   u Verses 1–14: cp. 1 Chr. 18.
1–13.   v re-erect . . . victory by: or recover control of the crossings of . . .   w Or copper.
x Verses 15–18: cp. 20. 23–6; 1 Kgs. 4. 2–6; 1 Chr. 18. 14–17.

son of Ahimelech, son of Ahitub,[v] were priests; Seraiah was adjutant-
18 general; Benaiah son of Jehoiada commanded the Kerethite and Pele-thite guards. David's sons were priests.

David shows kindness to Mephibosheth

9 David asked, 'Is any member of Saul's family left, to whom I can show true kindness for Jonathan's sake?'
2 There was a servant of Saul's family named Ziba; and he was summoned to David. The king asked, 'Are you Ziba?', and he answered, 'Your ser-
3 vant, sir.' So the king said, 'Is no member of Saul's family still alive to whom I may show the kindness that God requires?' 'Yes,' said Ziba, 'there is a son of Jonathan still alive; he is
4 a cripple, lame in both feet.' 'Where is he?' said the king, and Ziba answered, 'He is staying with Machir son of Ammiel in Lo-debar.'
5 So the king sent and fetched him from Lo-debar, from the house of
6 Machir son of Ammiel, and when Mephibosheth, son of Jonathan and Saul's grandson, entered David's presence, he prostrated himself and did obeisance. David said to him, 'Mephibosheth', and he answered,
7 'Your servant, sir.' Then David said, 'Do not be afraid; I mean to show you kindness for your father Jon-athan's sake, and I will give you back the whole estate of your grandfather Saul; you shall have a place for your-
8 self at my table.' So Mephibosheth prostrated himself again and said, 'Who am I that you should spare a thought for a dead dog like me?'
9 Then David summoned Saul's servant Ziba to his presence and said to him, 'I assign to your master's grandson all the property that belonged to Saul
10 and his family. You and your sons and your slaves must cultivate the land and bring in the harvest to pro-vide for your master's household, but Mephibosheth your master's grand-son shall have a place at my table.' This man Ziba had fifteen sons and
11 twenty slaves. Then Ziba answered the king, 'I will do all that your majesty commands.' So Mephibosh-eth took his place in the royal house-
12 hold like one of the king's sons. He had a young son, named Mica; and the members of Ziba's household were all Mephibosheth's servants,
13 while Mephibosheth lived in Jeru-salem and had his regular place at the

king's table, crippled as he was in both feet.

David defeats the Ammonites and Aramaeans

10 Some time afterwards the king of the Ammonites died and was succeeded by
2 his son Hanun. David said, 'I must keep up the same loyal friendship with Hanun son of Nahash as his father showed me', and he sent a mission to condole with him on the death of his father. But when David's envoys entered the country of the Ammon-
3 ites, the Ammonite princes said to Hanun their lord, 'Do you suppose David means to do honour to your father when he sends you his con-dolences? These men of his are spies whom he has sent to find out how to
4 overthrow the city.' So Hanun took David's servants, and he shaved off half their beards, cut off half their garments up to the buttocks, and
5 dismissed them. When David heard how they had been treated, he sent to meet them, for they were deeply humi-liated, and ordered them to wait in Jericho and not to return until their
6 beards had grown again. The Am-monites knew that they had fallen into bad odour with David, so they hired the Aramaeans of Beth-rehob and of Zobah to come to their help with twenty thousand infantry; they also hired the king of Maacah with a thousand men, and twelve thousand
7 men from Tob. When David heard of it, he sent out Joab and all the fight-
8 ing men. The Ammonites came and took up their position at the entrance to the city, while the Aramaeans of Zobah and of Rehob and the men of Tob and Maacah took up theirs in the
9 open country. When Joab saw that he was threatened both front and rear, he detailed some picked Israelite troops and drew them up facing the
10 Aramaeans. The rest of his forces he put under his brother Abishai, who took up a position facing the Ammon-
11 ites. 'If the Aramaeans prove too strong for me,' he said, 'you must come to my relief; and if the Ammon-ites prove too strong for you, I will
12 come to yours. Courage! Let us fight bravely for our people and for the cities[a] of our God. And the LORD's
13 will be done.' But when Joab and his men came to close quarters with the Aramaeans, they put them to flight;
14 and when the Ammonites saw them

y *and Abiathar . . . Ahitub: prob. rdg., cp. 1 Sam. 22. 11, 20; 2 Sam. 20. 25; Heb. son of Ahitub and Ahimelech son of Abiathar.* z *Verses 1–19: cp. 1 Chr. 19. 1–19.* a *Or altars.*

in flight, they too fled before Abishai and entered the city. Then Joab returned from the battle against the Ammonites and came to Jerusalem.

15 The Aramaeans saw that they had been worsted by Israel; but they ral-
16 lied their forces, and Hadadezer sent to summon other Aramaeans from the Great Bend of the Euphrates, and they advanced to Helam under Shobach, commander of Hadadezer's
17 army. Their movement was reported to David, who immediately mustered all the forces of Israel, crossed the Jordan and advanced to meet them at Helam. There the Aramaeans took up positions facing David and en-
18 gaged him, but were put to flight by Israel. David slew seven hundred Aramaeans in chariots and forty thousand horsemen, mortally wounding Shobach, who died on the field.
19 When all the vassal kings of Hadadezer saw that they had been worsted by Israel, they sued for peace and submitted to the Israelites. The Aramaeans never dared help the Ammonites again.

David and Bathsheba

11 At the turn of the year, when kings take the field, David sent Joab out with his other officers and all the Israelite forces, and they ravaged Ammon and laid siege to Rabbah, while David remained in Jerusalem.
2 One evening David got up from his couch and, as he walked about on the roof of the palace, he saw from there a woman bathing, and she was very
3 beautiful. He sent to inquire who she was, and the answer came, 'It must be Bathsheba daughter of Eliam and
4 wife of Uriah the Hittite.' So he sent messengers to fetch her, and when she came to him, he had intercourse with her, though she was still being purified after her period, and then she
5 went home. She conceived, and sent word to David that she was pregnant.
6 David ordered Joab to send Uriah the Hittite to him. So Joab sent him
7 to David, and when he arrived, David asked him for news of Joab and the troops and how the campaign was
8 going; and then said to him, 'Go down to your house and wash your feet after your journey.' As he left the palace, a present from the king followed him.
9 But Uriah did not return to his house; he lay down by the palace gate with
10 the king's slaves. David heard that Uriah had not gone home, and said to

him, 'You have had a long journey, why did you not go home?' Uriah 11 answered David, 'Israel and Judah are under canvas,[b] and so is the Ark, and my lord Joab and your majesty's officers are camping in the open; how can I go home to eat and drink and to sleep with my wife? By your life, I cannot do this!' David then said to 12 Uriah, 'Stay here another day, and tomorrow I will let you go.' So Uriah stayed in Jerusalem that day. The next day David invited him to eat 13 and drink with him and made him drunk. But in the evening Uriah went out to lie down in his blanket[c] among the king's slaves and did not go home.

David plans Uriah's death

The following morning David wrote a 14 letter to Joab and sent Uriah with it. He wrote in the letter, 'Put Uriah 15 opposite the enemy where the fighting is fiercest and then fall back, and leave him to meet his death.' Joab 16 had been watching the city, and he stationed Uriah at a point where he knew they would put up a stout fight. The men of the city sallied out and 17 engaged Joab, and some of David's guards fell; Uriah the Hittite was also killed. Joab sent David a dis- 18 patch with all the news of the battle and gave the messenger these in- 19 structions: 'When you have finished your report to the king, if he is angry 20 and asks, "Why did you go so near the city during the fight? You must have known there would be shooting from the wall. Remember who killed 21 Abimelech son of Jerubbesheth. It was a woman who threw down an upper millstone on to him from the wall of Thebez and killed him! Why did you go so near the wall?"—if he asks this, then tell him, "Your servant Uriah the Hittite also is dead."'

So the messenger set out and, when 22 he came to David, he made his report as Joab had instructed. David was angry with Joab and said to the messenger, 'Why did you go so near the city during the fight? You must have known you would be struck down from the wall. Remember who killed Abimelech son of Jerubbesheth. Was it not a woman who threw down an upper millstone on to him from the wall of Thebez and killed him? Why did you go near the wall?' He 23 answered, 'The enemy massed against us and sallied out into the open; we pressed them back as far as the

b under canvas: or at Succoth.
c in his blanket: or on his pallet.

E*

24 gateway. There the archers shot down at us from the wall and some of your majesty's men fell; and your servant 25 Uriah the Hittite is dead.' David said to the man, 'Give Joab this message: "Do not let this distress you—there is no knowing where the sword will strike; press home your attack on the city, and you will take it and raze it to the ground"; and tell him to take heart.'

26 When Uriah's wife heard that her husband was dead, she mourned for 27 him; and when the period of mourning was over, David sent for her and brought her into his house. She became his wife and bore him a son. But what David had done was wrong in the eyes of the LORD.

Nathan's parable

12 The LORD sent Nathan the prophet to David, and when he entered his presence, he said to him, 'There were 2 once two men in the same city, one 3 rich and the other poor. The rich man had large flocks and herds, but the poor man had nothing of his own except one little ewe lamb. He reared it himself, and it grew up in his home with his own sons. It ate from his dish, drank from his cup and nestled in his arms; it was like a daughter to him. 4 One day a traveller came to the rich man's house, and he, too mean to take something from his own flocks and herds to serve to his guest, took the poor man's lamb and served up that.' 5 David was very angry, and burst out, 'As the LORD lives, the man who did 6 this deserves to die! He shall pay for the lamb four times over, because he has done this and shown no pity.' 7 Then Nathan said to David, 'You are the man. This is the word of the LORD the God of Israel to you: "I anointed you king over Israel, I rescued you 8 from the power of Saul, I gave you your master's daughter[d] and his wives to be your own, I gave you the daughters of Israel and Judah; and, had this not been enough, I would have 9 added other favours as great. Why then have you flouted the word of the LORD by doing what is wrong in my eyes? You have struck down Uriah the Hittite with the sword; the man himself you murdered by the sword of the Ammonites, and you have 10 stolen his wife. Now, therefore, since you have despised me and taken the wife of Uriah the Hittite to be your own wife, your family shall never again

have rest from the sword." This is the 11 word of the LORD: "I will bring trouble upon you from within your own family; I will take your wives and give them to another man before your eyes, and he will lie with them in broad daylight. What you did was done 12 in secret; but I will do this in the light of day for all Israel to see."' David said to Nathan, 'I have sinned 13 against the LORD.' Nathan answered him, 'The LORD has laid on another the consequences of your sin: you shall not die, but, because in this you 14 have shown your contempt for the LORD,[e] the boy that will be born to you shall die.'

The birth of Solomon

When Nathan had gone home, the 15 LORD struck the boy whom Uriah's wife had borne to David, and he was very ill. David prayed to God for the 16 child; he fasted and went in and spent the night fasting, lying on the ground. The older men of his house- 17 hold tried to get him to rise from the ground, but he refused and would eat no food with them. On the seventh 18 day the boy died, and David's servants were afraid to tell him. 'While the boy was alive,' they said, 'we spoke to him, and he did not listen to us; how can we now tell him that the boy is dead? He may do something desperate.' But David saw his ser- 19 vants whispering among themselves and guessed that the boy was dead. He asked, 'Is the boy dead?', and they answered, 'He is dead.' Then David 20 rose from the ground, washed and anointed himself, and put on fresh clothes; he entered the house of the LORD and prostrated himself there. Then he went home, asked for food to be brought, and when it was ready, he ate it. His servants asked him, 'What 21 is this? While the boy lived you fasted and wept for him, but now that he is dead you rise up and eat.' He answered, 22 'While the boy was still alive I fasted and wept, thinking, "It may be that the LORD will be gracious to me, and the boy may live." But now that he is 23 dead, why should I fast? Can I bring him back again? I shall go to him; he will not come back to me.' David 24 consoled Bathsheba his wife; he went to her and had intercourse with her, and she gave birth to a son and called him Solomon. And because the LORD loved him, he sent word through 25 Nathan the prophet that for the

d Prob. rdg.; Heb. house.   e the LORD: prob. rdg.; Heb. the enemies of the LORD.

LORD's sake he should be given the name Jedidiah.*j*

David captures Rabbah

26*g* Joab attacked the Ammonite city of
27 Rabbah and took the King's Pool. He sent messengers to David with this report: 'I have attacked Rabbah and
28 have taken the pool. You had better muster the rest of the army yourself, besiege the city and take it; otherwise I shall take the city and the name to be proclaimed over it will be
29 mine.' David accordingly mustered his whole forces, marched to Rabbah,
30 attacked it and took it. He took the crown from the head of Milcom, which weighed a talent of gold and was set with a precious stone, and this he placed on his own head. He also removed a great quantity of booty
31 from the city; he took its inhabitants and set them to work with saws and other iron tools, sharp and toothed, and made them work in the brick-kilns. David did this to all the cities of the Ammonites; then he and all his people returned to Jerusalem.

Amnon and Tamar

13 Now David's son Absalom had a beautiful sister named Tamar, and Amnon, another of David's sons, fell
2 in love with her. Amnon was so distressed that he fell sick with love for his half-sister; for he thought it an impossible thing to approach her
3 since she was a virgin. But he had a friend named Jonadab, son of David's brother Shimeah, who was a very
4 shrewd man. He said to Amnon, 'Why are you so low-spirited morning after morning, my lord? Will you not tell me?' So Amnon told him that he was in love with Tamar, his brother
5 Absalom's sister. Jonadab said to him, 'Take to your bed and pretend to be ill. When your father comes to visit you, say to him, "Please let my sister Tamar come and give me my food. Let her prepare it in front of me, so that I may watch her and then take
6 it from her own hands."' So Amnon lay down and pretended to be ill. When the king came to visit him, he said, 'Sir, let my sister Tamar come and make a few cakes in front of me, and serve them to me with her own
7 hands.' So David sent a message to Tamar in the palace: 'Go to your brother Amnon's quarters and pre-
8 pare a meal for him.' Tamar came to her brother and found him lying

down; she took some dough and kneaded it, made the cakes in front of him and baked them. Then she took
9 the pan and turned them out before him. But Amnon refused to eat and ordered everyone out of the room. When they had all left, he said to
10 Tamar, 'Bring the food over to the recess so that I may eat from your own hands.' Tamar took the cakes she had made and brought them to Amnon in the recess. But when she
11 offered them to him, he caught hold of her and said, 'Come to bed with me, sister.' But she answered, 'No,
12 brother, do not dishonour me, we do not do such things in Israel; do not behave like a beast. Where could I
13 go and hide my disgrace?—and you would sink as low as any beast in Israel. Why not speak to the king for me? He will not refuse you leave to marry me.' He would not listen, but
14 overpowered her, dishonoured her and raped her.

Then Amnon was filled with utter
15 hatred for her; his hatred was stronger than the love he had felt, and he said to her, 'Get up and go.' She
16 answered, 'No. It is wicked to send me away. This is harder to bear than all you have done to me.' He would
17 not listen to her, but summoned the boy who attended him and said, 'Get rid of this woman, put her out and bolt the door after her.' She had on
18 a long, sleeved robe, the usual dress of unmarried princesses; and the boy turned her out and bolted the door. Tamar threw ashes over her head,
19 rent the long, sleeved robe that she was wearing, put her hands on her head and went away, sobbing as she went. Her brother Absalom asked her,
20 'Has your brother Amnon been with you? Keep this to yourself, he is your brother; do not take it to heart.' So Tamar remained in her brother Absalom's house, desolate. When King
21 David heard the whole story he was very angry; but he would not hurt Amnon because he was his eldest son and he loved him. Absalom did
22 not speak a single word to Amnon, friendly or unfriendly; he hated him for having dishonoured his sister Tamar.

Absalom avenges Tamar

Two years later Absalom invited all
23 the king's sons to his sheep-shearing at Baal-hazor, near Ephron.*h* He
24 approached the king and said, 'Sir,

j That is Beloved of the LORD.   *g Verses 26–31: cp. 1 Chr. 20. 1–3.*   *h Prob. rdg.; Heb. Ephraim.*

I am shearing; will your majesty
25 and your servants come?' The king
answered, 'No, my son, we must not
all come and be a burden to you.'
Absalom pressed him, but David was
still unwilling to go and dismissed him
26 with his blessing. But Absalom said,
'If you cannot, may my brother Amnon come with us?' 'Why should he go
27 with you?' the king asked; but Absalom pressed him again, so he let
Amnon and all the other princes go
with him.
28 Then Absalom prepared a feast fit
for a king. He gave his servants these
orders: 'Bide your time, and when
Amnon is merry with wine I shall say
to you, "Strike." Then kill Amnon.
You have nothing to fear, these are
my orders; be bold and resolute.'
29 Absalom's servants did as he had told
them, whereupon all the king's sons
mounted their mules in haste and set
off for home.
30 While they were on their way, a
rumour reached David that Absalom
had murdered all the royal princes
31 and that not one was left alive. The
king stood up and rent his clothes and
then threw himself on the ground; all
his servants were standing round him
32 with their clothes rent. Then Jonadab,
son of David's brother Shimeah, said,
'Your majesty must not think that
they have killed all the young princes;
only Amnon is dead; Absalom has
looked black ever since Amnon ravished
33 his sister Tamar. Your majesty must
not pay attention to a mere rumour
that all the princes are dead; only
Amnon is dead.'

Absalom escapes

34 Absalom made good his escape. Meanwhile the sentry looked up and saw
a crowd of people coming down the
hill from the direction of Horonaim.[i]
He came and reported to the king,
'I see men coming down the hill from
35 Horonaim.' Then Jonadab said to the
king, 'Here come the royal princes,
36 just as I said they would.' As he
finished speaking, the princes came in
and broke into loud lamentations; the
king and all his servants also wept
bitterly.
37 But Absalom went to take refuge
with Talmai son of Ammihur king of
Geshur; and for a long while the king
38 mourned for Amnon. Absalom, having escaped to Geshur, stayed there
39 for three years; and David's heart
went out to him with longing, for he

became reconciled to the death of
Amnon.

Joab plans Absalom's return

14 Joab son of Zeruiah saw that the
2 king's heart was set on Absalom, so
he sent to Tekoah and fetched a wise
woman. He said to her, 'Pretend to be
a mourner; put on mourning, go without anointing yourself, and behave
like a bereaved woman who has been
3 long in mourning. Then go to the king
and repeat what I tell you.' He then
told her exactly what she was to say.
4 When the woman from Tekoah came
into the king's presence, she threw
herself, face downwards, on the ground
and did obeisance, and cried, 'Help,
5 your majesty!' The king asked, 'What
is it?' She answered, 'O sir, I am a
6 widow; my husband is dead. I had
two sons; they came to blows out in
the country where there was no one
to part them, and one of them struck
7 the other and killed him. Now, sir,
the kinsmen have risen against me
and they all cry, "Hand over the man
who has killed his brother, so that we
can put him to death for taking his
brother's life, and so cut off the succession." If they do this, they will
stamp out my last live ember and
leave my husband no name and no
descendant upon earth.' 'Go home,' said
8 the king to the woman, 'and I will
9 settle your case.' But the woman continued, 'The guilt be on me, your
majesty, and on my father's house;
let the king and his throne be blame-
10 less.' The king said, 'If anyone says
anything more to you, bring him to
me and he shall never molest you
11 again.' Then the woman went on, 'Let
your majesty call upon the LORD your
God, to prevent his kinsmen bound
to vengeance from doing their worst
and destroying my son.' The king
swore, 'As the LORD lives, not a hair
of your son's head shall fall to the
ground.'
12 The woman then said, 'May I add
one word more, your majesty?' 'Say
13 on', said the king. So she continued,
'How then could it enter your head to
do this same wrong to God's people?
Out of your own mouth, your majesty,
you condemn yourself: you have refused to bring back the man you have
14 banished. We shall all die; we shall be
like water that is spilt on the ground
and lost; but God will spare the man
who does not set himself to keep the
outlaw in banishment. I came to say 15

i *Prob. rdg.; Heb.* from a road behind him.

this to your majesty because the people have threatened me. I thought, "If I can only speak to the king, perhaps he will attend to my case; for he 16 will listen, and he will save me from the man who is seeking to cut off me and my son together from Israel, God's own possession." I thought too that 17 the words of my lord the king would be a comfort to me; for your majesty is like the angel of God and can decide between right and wrong. The LORD your God be with you!' Then the king 18 said to the woman, 'Tell me no lies: I shall now ask you a question.' 'Speak on, your majesty', she said. So he 19 asked, 'Is the hand of Joab behind you in all this?' 'Your life upon it, sir!' she answered; 'when your majesty asks a question, there is no way round it, right or left. Yes, your servant Joab did prompt me; it was he who put the whole story into my mouth. He did it to give a new turn 20 to this affair. Your majesty is as wise as the angel of God and knows all that goes on in the land.'

The king said to Joab, 'You have 21 my consent; go and fetch back the young man Absalom.' Then Joab 22 humbly prostrated himself, took leave of the king with a blessing and said, 'Now I know that I have found favour with your majesty, because you have granted my humble petition.' Joab went at once to Geshur 23 and brought Absalom to Jerusalem; but the king said, 'Let him go to his 24 own quarters; he shall not come into my presence.' So Absalom went to his own quarters and did not enter the king's presence.

No one in all Israel was so greatly 25 admired for his beauty as Absalom; he was without flaw from the crown of his head to the sole of his foot. His 26 hair, when he cut his hair (as he had to do every year, for he found it heavy), weighed two hundred shekels by the royal standard. Three sons 27 were born to Absalom, and a daughter named Tamar, who was a very beautiful woman.

David receives Absalom

Absalom remained in Jerusalem for 28 two whole years without entering the king's presence. He summoned Joab 29 to send a message by him to the king, but Joab refused to come; he sent for him a second time, but he still refused. Then Absalom said to his servants, 30 'You know that Joab has a field next to mine with barley growing in it;

go and set fire to it.' So Absalom's servants set fire to the field. Joab 31 promptly came to Absalom in his own quarters and said to him, 'Why have your servants set fire to my field?' Ab- 32 salom answered Joab, 'I had sent for you to come here, so that I could ask you to give the king this message from me: "Why did I leave Geshur? It would be better for me if I were still there. Let me now come into your majesty's presence and, if I have done any wrong, put me to death."' When 33 Joab went to the king and told him, he summoned Absalom, who came and prostrated himself humbly before the king; and he greeted Absalom with a kiss.

Absalom's conspiracy

After this, Absalom provided himself 15 with a chariot and horses and an escort of fifty men. He made it a 2 practice to rise early and stand beside the road which runs through the city gate. He would hail every man who had a case to bring before the king for judgement and would ask him what city he came from. When he answered, 'I come, sir, from such and such a tribe of Israel', Absalom would say 3 to him, 'I can see that you have a very good case, but you will get no hearing from the king.' And he would 4 add, 'If only I were appointed judge in the land, it would be my business to see that everyone who brought a suit or a claim got justice from me.' Whenever a man approached 5 to prostrate himself, Absalom would stretch out his hand, take hold of him and kiss him. By behaving like this to 6 every Israelite who sought the king's justice, Absalom stole the affections of the Israelites.

At the end of four years, Absalom 7 said to the king, 'May I have leave now to go to Hebron to fulfil a vow there that I made to the LORD? For 8 when I lived in Geshur, in Aram, I made this vow: "If the LORD brings me back to Jerusalem, I will become a worshipper of the LORD in Hebron."' The king answered, 'Certainly you 9 may go'; so he set off for Hebron at once. Absalom sent runners through 10 all the tribes of Israel with this message: 'As soon as you hear the sound of the trumpet, then say, "Absalom is king in Hebron."' Two hun- 11 dred men accompanied Absalom from Jerusalem; they were invited and went in all innocence, knowing nothing of the affair. Absalom also sent 12 to summon Ahithophel the Gilonite, David's counsellor, from Giloh his city, where he was offering the customary sacrifices. The conspiracy gathered strength, and Absalom's supporters increased in number.

David prepares his escape

13 When news reached David that the men of Israel had transferred their 14 allegiance to Absalom, he said to those who were with him in Jerusalem, 'We must get away at once; or there will be no escape from Absalom for any of us. Make haste, or else he will soon be upon us and bring disaster on us, showing no mercy to anyone in the 15 city.' The king's servants said to him, 'As your majesty thinks best; we are ready.'

16 When the king departed, all his household followed him except ten concubines, whom he left in charge of 17 the palace. At the Far House the king and all the people who were with him 18 halted. His own servants then stood[j] beside him, while the Kerethite and Pelethite guards and Ittai[k] with the six hundred Gittites under him marched 19 past the king. The king said to Ittai the Gittite, 'Are you here too? Why are you coming with us? Go back and stay with the new king, for you are a foreigner and, what is more, an 20 exile from your own country. You came only yesterday, and today must you be compelled to share my wanderings? I do not know where I am going. Go back home and take your countrymen with you; and may the LORD ever 21 be your steadfast friend.' Ittai swore to the king, 'As the LORD lives, your life upon it, wherever you may be, in life or in death, I, your servant, will 22 be there.' David said to Ittai, 'It is well, march on!' So Ittai the Gittite marched on with his whole company and all the dependants who were with 23 him. The whole country-side re-echoed with their weeping. And the king remained standing[l] while all the people crossed the gorge of the Kidron before him, by way of the olive-tree in the wilderness.[m]

The Ark is taken to Jerusalem

24 Zadok also was there with all the Levites; they were carrying the Ark of the Covenant of God, which they set down beside Abiathar[n] until all the people had passed out of the city.

But the king said to Zadok, 'Take the 25 Ark of God back to the city. If I find favour with the LORD, he will bring me back and will let me see the Ark and its dwelling-place again. But if 26 he says he does not want me, then here I am; let him do what he pleases with me.' The king went on to say 27 to Zadok the priest, 'Can you make good use of your eyes? You may safely go back to the city, you and Abiathar,[o] and take with you the two young men, Ahimaaz your son and Abiathar's son Jonathan. Do not forget: I will linger 28 at the Fords of the Wilderness until you can send word to me.' Then 29 Zadok and Abiathar took the Ark of God back to Jerusalem and stayed there.

David's counterplot

David wept as he went up the slope 30 of the Mount of Olives; he was bareheaded and went bare-foot. The people with him all had their heads uncovered and wept as they went. David had been 31 told that Ahithophel was among the conspirators with Absalom, and he prayed, 'Frustrate, O LORD, the counsel of Ahithophel.'

As David was approaching the top 32 of the ridge where it was the custom to prostrate oneself to God, Hushai the Archite was there to meet him with his tunic rent and earth on his head. David said to him, 'If you come 33 with me you will only be a hindrance; but you can help me to frustrate 34 Ahithophel's plans if you go back to the city and say to Absalom, "I will be your majesty's servant; up to now I have been your father's servant, and now I will be yours." You will 35 have with you, as you know, the priests Zadok and Abiathar; tell them everything that you hear in the king's household. They have with them 36 Zadok's son Ahimaaz and Abiathar's son Jonathan, and through them you may pass on to me everything you hear.' So Hushai, David's friend, 37 came to the city as Absalom was entering Jerusalem.

Ziba's treachery

When David had moved on a little 16 from the top of the ridge, he was met by Ziba the servant of Mephibosheth, who had with him a pair of asses saddled and loaded with two hundred loaves, a hundred clusters of raisins,

---

j Prob. rdg.; Heb. passed.   k and Ittai: prob. rdg.; Heb. om.   l Prob. rdg.; Heb. passing.
m by way . . . wilderness: prob. rdg.; Heb. obscure.   n beside Abiathar: prob. rdg.; Heb. and
Abiathar went up.   o you and Abiathar: prob. rdg., cp. verse 29; Heb. om.

a hundred bunches of summer fruit, 2 and a flagon of wine. The king said to him, 'What are you doing with these?' Ziba answered, 'The asses are for the king's family to ride on, the bread and the summer fruit are for the servants to eat, and the wine for anyone who becomes exhausted in the wilderness.' 3 The king asked, 'Where is your master's grandson?' 'He is staying in Jerusalem,' said Ziba, 'for he thought that the Israelites might now restore 4 to him his grandfather's throne.' The king said to Ziba, 'You shall have everything that belongs to Mephibosheth.' Ziba said, 'I am your humble servant, sir; may I continue to stand well with you.'

Shimei curses David

5 As King David approached Bahurim, a man of Saul's family, whose name was Shimei son of Gera, came out, 6 cursing as he came. He showered stones right and left on David and on all the king's servants and on every-7 one, soldiers and people alike. This is what Shimei said as he cursed him: 'Get out, get out, you scoundrel! you 8 man of blood! The LORD has taken vengeance on you for the blood of the house of Saul whose throne you stole, and he has given the kingdom to your son Absalom. You murderer, see how your crimes have overtaken you!' 9   Then Abishai son of Zeruiah said to the king, 'Why let this dead dog curse your majesty? I will go across 10 and knock off his head.' But the king said, 'What has this to do with you, you sons of Zeruiah? If he curses and if the LORD has told him to curse 11 David, who can question it?' David said to Abishai and to all his servants, 'If my son, my own son, is out to kill me, who can wonder at this Benjamite? Let him be, let him curse; let 12 the LORD has told him to do it. But perhaps the LORD will mark my sufferings and bestow a blessing on me in place of the curse laid on me this day.' 13 David and his men continued on their way, and Shimei moved along the ridge of the hill parallel to David's path, cursing as he went and hurling stones across the valley at him and 14 kicking up the dust. When the king and all the people with him reached the Jordan, they were worn out; and they refreshed themselves there.

Ahithophel advises Absalom

15 By now Absalom and all his Israelites had reached Jerusalem, and Ahitho-phel with him. When Hushai the 16 Archite, David's friend, met Absalom he said to him, 'Long live the king! Long live the king!' But Absalom re-17 torted, 'Is this your loyalty to your friend? Why did you not go with him?' Hushai answered Absalom, 'Because 18 I mean to attach myself to the man chosen by the LORD, by this people, and by all the men of Israel, and with him I will remain. After all, whom 19 ought I to serve? Should I not serve the son? I will serve you as I have served your father.' Then Absalom 20 said to Ahithophel, 'Give us your advice: how shall we act?' Ahitho-21 phel answered, 'Have intercourse with your father's concubines whom he left in charge of the palace. Then all Israel will come to hear that you have given great cause of offence to your father, and this will confirm the resolution of your followers.' So they set 22 up a tent for Absalom on the roof, and he lay with his father's concubines in the sight of all Israel. In 23 those days a man would seek counsel of Ahithophel as readily as he might make an inquiry of the word of God; that was how Ahithophel's counsel was esteemed by David and Absalom.

Ahithophel said to Absalom, 'Let **17** me pick twelve thousand men, and I will pursue David tonight. I shall 2 overtake him when he is tired and dispirited; I will cut him off from his 3 people and they will all scatter; and I shall kill no one but the king. I will 3 bring all the people over to you as a bride is brought to her husband. It is only one man's life that you are seeking; the rest of the people will be unharmed.' Absalom and all the elders 4 of Israel approved of Ahithophel's advice; but Absalom said, 'Summon 5 Hushai the Archite and let us hear what he too has to say.' Hushai came, 6 and Absalom told him all that Ahithophel had said and asked him, 'Shall we do what he says? If not, say what you think.'

Hushai advises Absalom

Hushai said to Absalom, 'For once 7 the counsel that Ahithophel has given is not good. You know', he went on, 8 'that your father and the men with him are hardened warriors and savage as a bear in the wilds robbed of her cubs. Your father is an old campaigner and will not spend the night with the main body; even now he will be 9 lying hidden in a pit or in some such place. Then if any of your men are

killed at the outset, anyone who hears the news will say, "Disaster has over-
10 taken the followers of Absalom." The courage of the most resolute and lion-hearted will melt away, for all Israel knows that your father is a man of war and has determined men with
11 him. My advice is this. Wait until the whole of Israel, from Dan to Beer-sheba, is gathered about you, count-less as grains of sand on the sea-shore, and then you shall march with them
12 in person. Then we shall come upon him somewhere, wherever he may be, and descend on him like dew falling on the ground, and not a man of his family or of his followers will be left
13 alive. If he retreats into a city, all Israel will bring ropes to that city, and we will drag it into a ravine until not a stone can be found on the site.'
14 Absalom and all the men of Israel said, 'Hushai the Archite gives us better advice than Ahithophel.' It was the LORD's purpose to frustrate Ahithophel's good advice and so bring disaster upon Absalom.

Leakages of information

15 Hushai told Zadok and Abiathar the priests all the advice that Ahithophel had given to Absalom and the elders
16 of Israel, and also his own. 'Now send quickly to David,' he said, 'and warn him not to spend the night at the Fords of the Wilderness but to cross the river at once, before a blow can be struck at the king and his followers.'
17 Jonathan and Ahimaaz were waiting at En-rogel, and a servant girl would go and tell them what happened and they would pass it on to King David; for they could not risk being seen
18 entering the city. But this time a lad saw them and told Absalom; so the two of them hurried to the house of a man in Bahurim. He had a pit in his courtyard, and they climbed down
19 into it. The man's wife took a cover-ing, spread it over the mouth of the pit and strewed grain over it, and no
20 one was any the wiser. Absalom's servants came to the house and asked the woman, 'Where are Ahimaaz and Jonathan?' She answered, 'They went beyond the pool.' The men searched but could not find them; so they went
21 back to Jerusalem. When they had gone the two climbed out of the pit and went off to report to King David and said, 'Over the water at once, make haste!', and they told him
22 Ahithophel's plan against him. So

David and all his company began at once to cross the Jordan; by day-break there was not one who had not reached the other bank.

Ahithophel takes his life

When Ahithophel saw that his advice 23 had not been taken he saddled his ass, went straight home to his own city, gave his last instructions to his house-hold, and hanged himself. So he died and was buried in his father's grave.

David's men rout the Israelites

By the time that Absalom had crossed 24 the Jordan with the Israelites, David was already at Mahanaim. Absalom 25 had appointed Amasa as commander-in-chief instead of Joab; he was the son of a man named Ithra, an Ish-maelite, by Abigal daughter of Na-hash and sister to Joab's mother Zeruiah. The Israelites and Absalom 26 camped in the district of Gilead. When David came to Mahanaim, he 27 was met by Shobi son of Nahash from the Ammonite town Rabbah, Machir son of Ammiel from Lo-debar, and Barzillai the Gileadite from Rogelim, bringing mattresses and blankets, 28 bowls and jugs.^{p} They brought also wheat and barley, meal and parched 29 grain, beans and lentils, honey and curds, sheep and fat cattle, and offered them to David and his people to eat, knowing that the people must be hungry and thirsty and weary in the wilderness.

David mustered the people who 18 were with him, and appointed officers over units of a thousand and a hun-dred. Then he divided the army in 2 three, one division under the com-mand of Joab, one under Joab's brother Abishai son of Zeruiah, and the third under Ittai the Gittite. The king announced to the army that he was coming out himself with them to battle. But they said, 'No, you must 3 not come out; if we turn and run, no one will take any notice, nor will they, even if half of us are killed; but you are worth ten thousand of us, and it would be better now for you to re-main in the city in support.' 'I will do 4 what you think best,' answered the king; and he then stood beside the gate, and the army marched past in their units of a thousand and a hun-dred. The king gave orders to Joab, 5 Abishai, and Ittai: 'Deal gently with the young man Absalom for my sake.'

p bringing . . . jugs: prob. rdg.; Heb. a couch, bowls and a potter's vessel.

The whole army heard the king giving all his officers this order to spare Absalom.

6 The army took the field against the Israelites and the battle was fought 7 in the forest of Ephron.[q] There the Israelites were routed before the onslaught of David's men; so great was the rout that twenty thousand men 8 fell that day. The fighting spread over the whole country-side, and the forest took toll of more people that day than the sword.

Joab kills Absalom

9 Now some of David's men caught sight of Absalom. He was riding a mule and, as it passed beneath a great oak,[r] his head was caught in its boughs; he found himself in mid air 10 and the mule went on from under him. One of the men who saw it went and told Joab, 'I saw Absalom hang-11 ing from an oak.' While the man was telling him, Joab broke in, 'You saw him? Why did you not strike him to the ground then and there? I would have given you ten pieces of silver 12 and a belt.' The man answered, 'If you were to put in my hands a thousand pieces of silver, I would not lift a finger against the king's son; for we all heard the king giving orders to you and Abishai and Ittai that whoever finds himself near the young man Absalom must take great care of him. 13 If I had dealt him a treacherous blow, the king would soon have known, and you would have kept well out of it.' 14 'That is a lie!' said Joab. 'I will make a start and show you.'[s] So he picked up three stout sticks and drove them against Absalom's chest while he was held fast in the tree and still alive. 15 Then ten young men who were Joab's armour-bearers closed in on Absalom, 16 struck at him and killed him. Joab sounded the trumpet, and the army came back from the pursuit of Israel 17 because he had called it off. They took Absalom's body and flung it into a great pit in the forest, and raised over it a huge pile of stones. The Israelites all fled to their homes.

18 The pillar in the King's Vale had been set up by Absalom in his lifetime, for he said, 'I have no son to carry on my name.' He had named the pillar after himself; and to this day it is called Absalom's Monument.

David grieves over Absalom

Ahimaaz son of Zadok said, 'Let me 19 run and take the news to the king that the LORD has avenged him and de-livered him from his enemies.' But Joab 20 replied, 'This is no day for you to be the bearer of news. Another day you may have news to carry, but not to-day, because the king's son is dead.' Joab told a Cushite to go and report 21 to the king what he had seen. The Cushite bowed low before Joab and set off running. Ahimaaz pleaded 22 again with Joab, 'Come what may,' he said, 'let me run after the Cushite.' 'Why should you, my son?' asked Joab. 'You will get no reward for your news.' 'Come what may,' he said, 'I 23 will run.' 'Go, then', said Joab. So Ahimaaz ran by the road through the Plain of the Jordan and outstripped the Cushite.

David was sitting between the two 24 gates when the watchman went up to the roof of the gatehouse by the wall and, looking out, saw a man running alone. The watchman called to the 25 king and told him. 'If he is alone,' said the king, 'then he has news.' The man came nearer and nearer. Then the 26 watchman saw another man running. He called down to the gate-keeper and said, 'Look, there is another man running alone.' The king said, 'He too brings news.' The watchman said, 'I 27 see by the way he runs that the first runner is Ahimaaz son of Zadok.' The king said, 'He is a good fellow and shall earn the reward for good news.' Ahimaaz called out to the king, 'All is 28 well!' He bowed low before him and said, 'Blessed be the LORD your God who has given into your hands the men who rebelled against your majesty.' The king asked, 'Is all well with 29 the young man Absalom?' Ahimaaz answered, 'Sir, your servant Joab sent me,[t] I saw a great commotion, but I did not know what had happened.' The king told him to stand on one 30 side; so he turned aside and stood there. Then the Cushite came in and 31 said, 'Good news, your majesty! The LORD has avenged you this day on all those who rebelled against you.' The 32 king said to the Cushite, 'Is all well with the young man Absalom?' The Cushite answered, 'May all the king's enemies and all rebels who would do you harm be as that young man is.'

q Prob. rdg.; Heb. Ephraim.   r Or terebinth.   s I will . . . show you: or I can waste no more time on you like this.   t Sir . . . sent me: prob. rdg.; Heb. At the sending of Joab the king's servant and your servant.

33 The king was deeply moved and went
up to the roof-chamber over the gate
and wept, crying out as he went, 'O,
my son! Absalom my son, my son
Absalom! If only I had died instead
of you! O Absalom, my son, my son.'

Joab's advice to David

19 Joab was told that the king was
weeping and mourning for Absalom;
2 and that day victory was turned to
mourning for the whole army, because
they heard how the king grieved for
3 his son; they stole into the city like
men ashamed to show their faces
4 after a defeat in battle. The king hid
his face and cried aloud, 'My son
Absalom; O Absalom, my son, my
5 son.' But Joab came into the king's
quarters and said to him, 'You have
put to shame this day all your servants, who have saved you and your
sons and daughters, your wives and
6 your concubines. You love those that
hate you and hate those that love you;
you have made us feel, officers and
men alike, that we are nothing to you;
for it is plain that if Absalom were
still alive and all of us dead, you
7 would be content. Now go at once and
give your servants some encouragement; if you refuse, I swear by the
LORD that not a man will stay with
you tonight, and that would be a
worse disaster than any you have suf-
8 fered since your earliest days.' Then
the king rose and took his seat in the
gate; and when the army was told
that the king was sitting in the gate,
they all appeared before him.

Judah is reconciled to David

Meanwhile the Israelites had all scat-
9 tered to their homes. Throughout all
the tribes of Israel people were discussing it among themselves and saying,
'The king has saved us from our enemies and freed us from the power of
the Philistines, and now he has fled
10 the country because of Absalom. But
Absalom, whom we anointed king,
has fallen in battle; so now why have
we no plans for bringing the king
back?'
11   What all Israel was saying came to
the king's ears.[u] So he sent word to
Zadok and Abiathar the priests: 'Ask
the elders of Judah why they should
be the last to bring the king back to
12 his palace. Tell them, "You are my
brothers, my flesh and my blood; why
13 are you last to bring me back?" And
tell Amasa, "You are my own flesh

and blood. You shall be my commander-in-chief, so help me God, for
the rest of your life in place of Joab."'
David's message won all hearts in 14
Judah, and they sent to the king,
urging him to return with all his
men.
    So the king came back to the Jordan; 15
and the men of Judah came to Gilgal
to meet him and escort him across the
river. Shimei son of Gera the Ben- 16
jamite from Bahurim hastened down
among the men of Judah to meet
King David with a thousand men 17
from Benjamin; Ziba was there too,
the servant of Saul's family, with his
fifteen sons and twenty servants.They
rushed into the Jordan under the
king's eyes and crossed to and fro 18
conveying his household in order to
win his favour. Shimei son of Gera,
when he had crossed the river, fell
down before the king and said to him, 19
'I beg your majesty not to remember
how disgracefully your servant behaved
when your majesty left Jerusalem;
do not hold it against me or take it
to heart. For I humbly acknowledge 20
that I did wrong, and today I am the
first of all the house of Joseph to come
down to meet your majesty.' But 21
Abishai son of Zeruiah objected,
'Ought not Shimei to be put to death
because he cursed the LORD's anointed prince?' David answered, 'What 22
right have you, you sons of Zeruiah,
to oppose me today? Why should any
man be put to death this day in Israel?
I know now that I am king of Israel.'
Then the king said to Shimei, 'You 23
shall not die', and confirmed it with an
oath.

Mephibosheth and Barzillai greet David

Saul's grandson Mephibosheth also 24
went down to meet the king. He had
not dressed his feet, combed his beard
or washed his clothes, from the day
the king went out until he returned
victorious. When he came from Jeru- 25
salem to meet the king, David said to
him, 'Why did you not go with me,
Mephibosheth?' He answered, 'Sir, my 26
servant deceived me; I did intend to
harness my ass and ride with the king
(for I am lame), but his stories set your 27
majesty against me. Your majesty
is like the angel of God; you must
do what you think right. My father's 28
whole family, one and all, deserved to
die at your majesty's hands, but you
gave me, your servant, my place at

u What . . . ears: prob. rdg.; Heb. has these words after back to his palace and adds to his palace.

your table. What further favour can
29 I expect of the king?' The king
answered, 'You have said enough. My
decision is that you and Ziba are to
30 share the estate.' Mephibosheth said,
'Let him have it all, now that your
majesty has come home victorious.'
31 Barzillai the Gileadite too had come
down from Rogelim, and he went as
far as the Jordan with the king to send
32 him on his way. Now Barzillai was
very old, eighty years of age; it was
he who had provided for the king
while he was at Mahanaim, for he was
33 a man of high standing. The king said
to Barzillai, 'Cross over with me and
I will provide for your old age in
34 my household in Jerusalem.' Barzillai
answered, 'Your servant is far too old
to go up with your majesty to Jeru-
35 salem. I am already eighty; and I cannot tell good from bad. I cannot taste
what I eat or drink; I cannot hear the
voices of men and women singing.
Why should I be a burden any longer
36 on your majesty? Your servant will
attend the king for a short way across
the Jordan; and why should the king
37 reward me so handsomely? Let me
go back and end my days in my own
city near the grave of my father and
mother. Here is my son Kimham; let
him cross over with your majesty,
and do for him what you think best.'
38 The king answered, 'Kimham shall
cross with me and I will do for him
whatever you think best; and I will do
for you whatever you ask.'
39 All the people crossed the Jordan
while the king waited. The king then
kissed Barzillai and gave him his
blessing. Barzillai went back to his
40 own home; the king crossed over to
Gilgal, Kimham with him. All the
people of Judah escorted the king
over the river, and so did half the
people of Israel.

Further disloyalty in Israel

41 The men of Israel came to the king in
a body and said, 'Why should our
brothers of Judah have got possession
of the king's person by joining King
David's own men and then escorting
him and his household across the Jor-
42 dan?' The men of Judah replied, 'Because his majesty is our near kinsman.
Why should you resent it? Have we
eaten at the king's expense? Have we
43 received any gifts?' The men of Israel
answered, 'We have ten times your
interest in the king and, what is more,
we are senior to you; why do you dis-

parage us? Were we not the first to
speak of bringing the king back?' The
men of Judah used language even
fiercer than the men of Israel.

There happened to be a man there, 20
a scoundrel named Sheba son of
Bichri, a man of Benjamin. He blew
the trumpet and cried out:

What share have we in David?
We have no lot in the son of Jesse.
Away to your homes, O Israel.

The men of Israel all left David, to 2
follow Sheba son of Bichri, but the
men of Judah stood by their king and
followed him from the Jordan to
Jerusalem.

When David came home to Jeru- 3
salem he took the ten concubines
whom he had left in charge of the
palace and put them under guard; he
maintained them but did not have
intercourse with them. They were kept
in confinement to the day of their
death, widowed in the prime of life.

The end of Sheba's revolt

The king said to Amasa, 'Call up the 4
men of Judah and appear before me
again in three days' time.' So Amasa 5
went to call up the men of Judah, but
it took longer than the time fixed
by the king. David said to Abishai, 6
'Sheba son of Bichri will give us more
trouble than Absalom; take the royal
bodyguard and follow him closely. If
he has occupied some fortified cities,
he may escape us.' Abishai was fol- 7
lowed by Joab[v] with the Kerethite and
Pelethite guards and all the fighting
men; they left Jerusalem in pursuit
of Sheba son of Bichri. When they 8
reached the great stone in Gibeon,
Amasa came towards them. Joab was
wearing his tunic and over it a belt
supporting a sword in its scabbard.
He came forward, concealing his
treachery, and said to Amasa, 'I hope 9
you are well, my brother', and with
his right hand he grasped Amasa's
beard to kiss him. Amasa was not on 10
his guard against the sword in Joab's
hand. Joab struck him with it in the
belly and his entrails poured out to
the ground; he did not strike a second
blow, for Amasa was dead. Joab and
his brother Abishai went on in pursuit of Sheba son of Bichri. One of 11
Joab's young men stood over Amasa
and called out, 'Follow Joab, all who
are for Joab and for David!' Ama- 12
sa's body lay soaked in blood in the
middle of the road, and when the man

v Abishai . . . Joab: prob. rdg.; Heb. Some men of Joab followed him.

saw how all the people stopped, he rolled him off the road into the field and threw a cloak over him; for everyone who came by saw the body and

13 stopped. When he had been dragged from the road, they all went on after Joab in pursuit of Sheba son of Bichri.

14 Sheba passed through all the tribes of Israel until he came to Abel-beth-maacah,[w] and all the clan of Bichri[x] rallied to him and followed him into

15 the city. Joab's forces came up and besieged him in Abel-beth-maacah, raised a siege-ramp against it and began undermining the wall to bring

16 it down. Then a wise woman stood on the rampart[y] and called from the city, 'Listen, listen! Tell Joab to step for-

17 ward and let me speak with him.' So he came forward and the woman said, 'Are you Joab?' He answered, 'I am.' 'Listen to what I have to say, sir', she went on, to which he replied, 'I am

18 listening.' 'In the old days', she said, 'there was a saying, "Go to Abel for the answer", and that settled the

19 matter. My city is known to be one of the most peaceable and loyal[z] in Israel; she is like a watchful mother in Israel, and you are seeking to kill her. Would you destroy the LORD's own

20 possession?' Joab answered, 'God forbid, far be it from me to ruin or de-

21 stroy! That is not our aim; but a man from the hill-country of Ephraim named Sheba son of Bichri has raised a revolt against King David; surrender this one man, and I will retire from the city.' The woman said to Joab, 'His head shall be thrown to

22 you over the wall.' Then the woman withdrew, and her wisdom won over the assembled people; they cut off Sheba's head and threw it to Joab. Then he sounded the trumpet and the whole army left the city and dispersed to their homes, while Joab went back to the king in Jerusalem.

David's officers

23[a] Joab was in command of the army,[b] and Benaiah son of Jehoiada commanded the Kerethite and Pelethite

24 guards. Adoram was in charge of the forced levy, and Jehoshaphat son of

25 Ahilud was secretary of state. Sheva was adjutant-general, and Zadok and

26 Abiathar were priests; Ira the Jairite was David's priest.

The Gibeonites avenged

In David's reign there was a famine 21 that lasted year after year for three years. So David consulted the LORD, and he answered, 'Blood-guilt rests on Saul and on his family because he put the Gibeonites to death.' (The Gib- 2 eonites were not of Israelite descent; they were a remnant of Amorite stock whom the Israelites had sworn that they would spare. Saul, however, had sought to exterminate them in his zeal for Israel and Judah.) King David summoned the Gibeonites, therefore, and said to them, 'What can be done 3 for you? How can I make expiation, so that you may have cause to bless the LORD's own people?' The Gib- 4 eonites answered, 'Our feud with Saul and his family cannot be settled in silver and gold, and there is no one man in Israel whose death would content us.' 'Then what do you want me to do for you?' asked David. They answered, 'Let us make an end 5 of the man who caused our undoing and ruined us, so that he shall never again have his place within the borders of Israel. Hand over to us seven 6 of that man's sons, and we will hurl them down to their death before[c] the LORD in Gibeah of Saul, the LORD's chosen king.' The king agreed to hand them over, but he spared Mephib- 7 osheth son of Jonathan, son of Saul, because of the oath that had been taken in the LORD's name by David and Saul's son Jonathan. The king 8 then took the two sons whom Rizpah daughter of Aiah had borne to Saul, Armoni and Mephibosheth, and the five sons whom Merab, Saul's daughter, had borne to Adriel son of Barzillai of Meholah. He handed them 9 over to the Gibeonites, and they flung them down from the mountain before the LORD; the seven of them fell together. They were put to death in the first days of harvest at the beginning of the barley harvest. Rizpah daugh- 10 ter of Aiah took sackcloth and spread it out as a bed for herself on the rock, from the beginning of harvest until the rains came and fell from heaven upon the bodies. She allowed no bird to set upon them by day nor any wild beast by night. When David was told 11 what Rizpah daughter of Aiah the concubine of Saul had done, he went 12

---

w Prob. rdg., cp. verse 15; Heb. Abel and Beth-maacah.   x Prob. rdg.; Heb. Beri.   y stood . . .
rampart: transposed from verse 15.   z My city . . . loyal: prob. rdg.; Heb. I am the requited ones
of the loyal ones.   a Verses 23–6: cp. 8. 16–18; 1 Kgs. 4. 2–6; 1 Chr. 18. 15–17.   b Prob. rdg.,
cp. 8. 16; Heb. adds Israel.   c Or for.

and took the bones of Saul and his son Jonathan from the citizens of Jabesh-gilead, who had stolen them from the public square at Beth-shan, where the Philistines had hung them on the day 13 they defeated Saul at Gilboa. He removed the bones of Saul and Jonathan from there and gathered up the bones of the men who had been hurled 14 to death. They buried the bones of Saul and his son Jonathan in the territory of Benjamin at Zela, in the grave of his father Kish. Everything was done as the king ordered, and thereafter the LORD was willing to accept prayers offered for the country.

Abishai rescues David

15 Once again war broke out between the Philistines and Israel. David and his men went down to the battle, but as he fought with the Philistines he fell 16 exhausted. Then Benob, one of the race of the Rephaim, whose bronze spear weighed three hundred shekels[d] and who wore a belt of honour, took David prisoner and was about to kill 17 him. But Abishai son of Zeruiah came to David's help, struck the Philistine down and killed him. Then David's officers took an oath that he should never again go out with them to war, for fear that the lamp of Israel might be extinguished.

More annals of war

18 Some time later war with the Philistines broke out again in Gob: it was then that Sibbechai of Hushah killed Saph, a descendant of the Rephaim. 19 In another war with the Philistines in Gob, Elhanan son of Jair[f] of Bethlehem killed Goliath of Gath, whose spear had a shaft like a weaver's beam. 20 In yet another war in Gath there appeared a giant with six fingers on each hand and six toes on each foot, twenty-four in all. He too was descended 21 from the Rephaim; and, when he defied Israel, Jonathan son of David's 22 brother Shimeai killed him. These four giants were the descendants of the Rephaim in Gath, and they all fell at the hands of David and his men.

David's song of deliverance

22 These are the words of the song David sang to the LORD on the day when the LORD delivered him from the power of all his enemies and from the power of Saul:

The LORD is my stronghold, my fort- 2[g]
    ress and my champion,
my God, my rock where I find safety; 3
my shield, my mountain fastness, my
    strong tower,
my refuge, my deliverer, who saves
    me from violence.
I will call on the LORD to whom all 4
    praise is due,
and I shall be delivered from my
    enemies.
When the waves of death swept round 5
    me,
and torrents of destruction overtook
    me,
the bonds of Sheol tightened about 6
    me,
the snares of death were set to catch
    me;
then in anguish of heart I cried to the 7
    LORD,
I called for help to my God;
he heard me from his temple,
and my cry rang in his ears.
The earth heaved and quaked, 8
heaven's foundations shook;
they heaved, because he was angry.
Smoke rose from his nostrils, 9
devouring fire came out of his mouth,
glowing coals and searing heat.
He swept the skies aside as he descen- 10
    ded,
thick darkness lay under his feet.
He rode on a cherub, he flew through 11
    the air;
he swooped[h] on the wings of the wind.
He curtained himself in darkness 12
and made dense vapour his canopy.
Thick clouds came out of the radiance 13
    before him;
glowing coals burned brightly.
The LORD thundered from the heavens 14
and the voice of the Most High spoke
    out.
He loosed his arrows, he sped them far 15
    and wide,
his lightning shafts, and sent them
    echoing.
The channels of the sea-bed were 16
    revealed,
the foundations of earth laid bare
at the LORD's rebuke,
at the blast of the breath of his
    nostrils.
He reached down from the height and 17
    took me,
he drew me out of mighty waters,
he rescued me from my enemies, strong 18
    as they were,
from my foes when they grew too
    powerful for me.

---

d shekels: *prob. rdg.*; *Heb.* weight.   e Verses 18–22: *cp.* 1 Chr. 20. 4–7.   f Jair: *prob. rdg., cp.* 1 Chr. 20. 5; *Heb.* Jaare-oregim.   g Verses 2–51: *cp.* Ps. 18. 2–50.   h *Prob. rdg., cp.* Ps. 18. 10; *Heb.* was seen.

19 They confronted me in the hour of my
peril,
but the LORD was my buttress.
20 He brought me out into an open place,
he rescued me because he delighted in
me.
21 The LORD rewarded me as my righteousness deserved;
my hands were clean, and he requited
me.
22 For I have followed the ways of the
LORD
and have not turned wickedly from
my God;
23 all his laws are before my eyes,
I have not failed to follow his decrees.
24 In his sight I was blameless
and kept myself from wilful sin;
25 the LORD requited me as my righteousness deserved
and my purity in his eyes.

26 With the loyal thou showest thyself
loyal
and with the blameless man blameless.
27 With the savage man thou showest
thyself savage,
and[i] tortuous with the perverse.
28 Thou deliverest humble folk,
thou lookest with contempt upon the
proud.
29 Thou, LORD, art my lamp,
and the LORD will lighten my darkness.
30 With thy help I leap over a bank,
by God's aid I spring over a wall.

31 The way of God is perfect,
the LORD's word has stood the test;
he is the shield of all who take refuge
in him.
32 What god is there but the LORD?
What rock but our God?—
33 the God who girds me[j] with strength
and makes my way blameless,[k]
34 who makes me swift as a hind
and sets me secure on the mountains;
35 who trains my hands for battle,
and my arms aim an arrow tipped with
bronze.

36 Thou hast given me the shield of thy
salvation,
in thy providence thou makest me
great.
37 Thou givest me room for my steps,
my feet have not faltered.
38 I pursue my enemies and destroy
them,

I do not return until I have made an
end of them.
39 I make an end of them, I strike them
down;
they rise no more, they fall beneath
my feet.
40 Thou dost arm me with strength for
the battle
and dost subdue my foes before me.
41 Thou settest[l] my foot on my enemies'
necks,
and I bring to nothing those that hate
me.
42 They cry out[m] and there is no one to
help them,
they cry to the LORD and he does not
answer.
43 I will pound them fine as dust on the
ground,
like mud in the streets will I trample
them.[n]
44 Thou dost deliver me from the clamour of the people,
and makest me master of the nations.
A people I never knew shall be my
subjects.
45 Foreigners shall come cringing to me;
as soon as they hear tell of me, they
shall obey me.
46 Foreigners shall be brought captive
to me,
and come limping from their strongholds.
47 The LORD lives, blessed is my rock,
high above all is God my rock and safe
refuge.

48 O God, who grantest me vengeance,
who dost subdue peoples under me,
49 who dost snatch me from my foes and
set me over my enemies,
thou dost deliver me from violent
men.
50 Therefore, LORD, I will praise thee
among the nations
and sing psalms to thy name,
51 to one who gives his king great
victories
and in all his acts keeps faith with his
anointed king,
with David and his descendants for
ever.

David's last words

23 These are the last words of David:

The very word of David son of Jesse,
the very word of the man whom the
High God raised up,

---

i With the savage . . . savage, and: *or* With the pure thou showest thyself pure, but . . .   *j* who
girds me: *prob. rdg., cp. Ps. 18. 32; Heb.* my refuge *or* my strength.   *k* and makes . . . blameless:
prob. rdg., cp. Ps. 18. 32; Heb. unintelligible.   *l Prob. rdg., cp. Ps. 18. 40; Heb. unintelligible.*
m cry out: *prob. rdg., cp. Ps. 18. 41; Heb.* look.   *n Prob. rdg., cp. Ps. 18. 42; Heb. adds* will I
stamp them down.

the anointed prince of the God of
Jacob,
and the singer of Israel's psalms:
2 the spirit of the LORD has spoken
through me,
and his word is on my lips.
3 The God of Israel spoke,
the Rock of Israel spoke of me:
'He who rules men in justice,
who rules in the fear of God,
4 is like the light of morning at sunrise,
a morning that is cloudless after rain
and makes the grass sparkle from the
earth.'
5 Surely, surely my house is true to God;
for he has made a pact with me for all
time,
its terms spelled out and faithfully
kept,
my whole salvation, all my[o] delight.
6 But the ungodly put forth no shoots,
they are all like briars tossed aside;
none dare put his hand to pick
them up,
7 none touch them but[p] with tool of
iron or of wood;
they are fit only for burning in the
fire.[q]

David's heroes

8[r] These are the names of David's
heroes. First came Ishbosheth the
Hachmonite,[s] chief of the three; it
was he who brandished his spear[t] over
eight hundred dead, all slain at one
9 time. Next to him was Eleazar son of
Dodo the Ahohite,[u] one of the heroic
three. He was with David at Pas-
dammim where the Philistines[v] had
gathered for battle. When the Israel-
10 ites fell back, he stood his ground and
rained blows on the Philistines until,
from sheer weariness, his hand stuck
fast to his sword; and so the LORD
brought about a great victory that
day. Afterwards the people rallied behind him, but it was only to strip the
11 dead. Next to him was Shammah son
of Agee a Hararite. The Philistines
had gathered at Lehi, where there was
a field with a fine crop of lentils; and,
when the Philistines put the people
12 to flight, he stood his ground in the
field, saved it[w] and defeated them.
So the LORD again brought about a
great victory.
13　　　Three of the thirty went down

towards the beginning of harvest to
join David at the cave of Adullam,
while a band of Philistines was encamped in the Vale of Rephaim. At 14
that time David was in the stronghold and a Philistine garrison held
Bethlehem. One day a longing came 15
over David, and he exclaimed, 'If
only I could have a drink of water
from the well[x] by the gate of Bethlehem!' At this the heroic three made 16
their way through the Philistine lines
and drew water from the well by the
gate of Bethlehem and brought it to
David. But David refused to drink it;
he poured it out to the LORD and said, 17
'God forbid that I should do such a
thing! Can I drink[y] the blood of these
men who risked their lives for it?' So
he would not drink it. Such were the
exploits of the heroic three.
　　Abishai the brother of Joab son of 18
Zeruiah was chief of the thirty. He
once brandished his spear over three
hundred dead, and he was famous
among the thirty. Some think he even 19
surpassed the rest of the thirty[z] in
reputation, and he became their captain, but he did not rival the three.
Benaiah son of Jehoiada, from Kab- 20
zeel, was a hero of many exploits. It
was he who smote the two champions
of Moab, and who went down into a
pit and killed a lion on a snowy day.
It was he who also killed the Egyp- 21
tian, a man of striking appearance
armed with a spear: he went to meet
him with a club, snatched the spear
out of the Egyptian's hand and killed
him with his own weapon. Such were 22
the exploits of Benaiah son of Jehoiada, famous among the heroic thirty.[z]
He was more famous than the rest of 23
the thirty, but he did not rival the
three. David appointed him to his
household.
　　Asahel the brother of Joab was 24
one of the thirty, and Elhanan son
of Dodo from Bethlehem; Shammah 25
from Harod, and Elika from Harod;
Helez from Beth-pelet,[a] and Ira son 26
of Ikkesh from Tekoa; Abiezer from 27
Anathoth, and Mebunnai from Hushah; Zalmon the Ahohite, and Ma- 28
harai from Netophah; Heled son of 29
Baanah from Netophah, and Ittai son
of Ribai from Gibeah of Benjamin;
Benaiah from Pirathon, and Hiddai 30

o Prob. rdg.; Heb. om.　　p but: prob. rdg.; Heb. he shall be filled.　　q Prob. rdg.; Heb. adds in
sitting.　　r Verses 8–39: cp. 1 Chr. 11. 10–41.　　s Prob. rdg.; Heb. Josheb-basshebeth a Tahche-
monite.　　t who . . . spear: prob. rdg., cp. 1 Chr. 11. 11; Heb. unintelligible.　　u the Ahohite:
prob. rdg., cp. 1 Chr. 11. 12; Heb. son of Ahohi.　　v He was . . . Philistines: prob. rdg., cp. 1 Chr.
11. 13; Heb. With David when they taunted them among the Philistines.　　w saved it: or cleared
it of the Philistines.　　x Or cistern.　　y I drink: prob. rdg., cp. 1 Chr. 11. 19; Heb. om.　　z Prob.
rdg.; Heb. three.　　a Prob. rdg., cp. Josh. 15. 27; Heb. from Pelet.

31 from the ravines of Gaash; Abi-albon
from Beth-arabah,[b] and Azmoth from
32 Bahurim;[c] Eliahba from Shaalbon,
and Hashem the Gizonite; Jonathan
33 son of[d] Shammah the Hararite, and
Ahiam son of Sharar the Hararite;[e]
34 Eliphelet son of Ahasbai son of the
Maacathite, and Eliam son of Ahith-
35 ophel the Gilonite; Hezrai from Car-
36 mel, and Paarai the Arbite; Igal son
of Nathan from Zobah, and Bani the
37 Gadite; Zelek the Ammonite, and
Naharai from Beeroth, armour-bearer
38 to Joab son of Zeruiah; Ira the Ith-
39 rite, Gareb the Ithrite, and Uriah
the Hittite: there were thirty-seven
in all.

David numbers Israel and Judah

24 1[f] Once again the Israelites felt the
LORD's anger, when he incited David
against them and gave him orders
that Israel and Judah should be
2 counted. So he instructed Joab and
the officers of the army[g] with him to
go round all the tribes of Israel, from
Dan to Beersheba, and make a record
of the people and report the number
3 to him. Joab answered, 'Even if the
LORD your God should increase the
people a hundredfold and your majesty
should live to see it, what pleasure
4 would that give your majesty?' But
Joab and the officers were overruled
by the king and they left his presence
5 in order to count the people. They
crossed the Jordan and began at
Aroer and the level land of the gorge,
proceeding towards Gad[h] and Jazer.
6 They came to Gilead and to the land
of the Hittites, to Kadesh, and then
to Dan and Iyyon[i] and so round to-
7 wards Sidon. They went as far as the
walled city of Tyre and all the towns
of the Hivites and Canaanites, and
then went on to the Negeb of Judah
8 at Beersheba. They covered the whole
country and arrived back at Jerusalem after nine months and twenty
9 days. Joab reported to the king the
total number of people: the number
of able-bodied men, capable of bearing
arms, was eight hundred thousand in
Israel and five hundred thousand in
Judah.

David chooses his punishment

10 After he had counted the people
David's conscience smote him, and

he said to the LORD, 'I have done a
very wicked thing: I pray thee, LORD,
remove thy servant's guilt, for I have
been very foolish.' He rose next morn- 11
ing, and meanwhile the command of
the LORD had come to the prophet
Gad, David's seer, to go and speak to 12
David: 'This is the word of the LORD:
I have three things in store for you;
choose one and I will bring it upon
you.' So Gad came to David and re- 13
peated this to him and said, 'Is it to
be three years of famine in your land,
or three months of flight with the
enemy at your heels, or three days
of pestilence in your land? Consider
carefully what answer I am to take
back to him who sent me.' Thereupon 14
David said to Gad, 'I am in a desperate
plight; let us fall into the hands of the
LORD, for his mercy is great; and let
me not fall into the hands of men.'
So the LORD sent a pestilence through- 15
out Israel from morning till the hour
of dinner, and from Dan to Beersheba
seventy thousand of the people died.
Then the angel stretched out his arm 16
towards Jerusalem to destroy it; but
the LORD repented of the evil and said
to the angel who was destroying
people, 'Enough! Stay your hand.' At
that moment the angel of the LORD
was standing by the threshing-floor of
Araunah the Jebusite.

When David saw the angel who was 17
striking down the people, he said to
the LORD, 'It is I who have done
wrong, the sin is mine; but these poor
sheep, what have they done? Let thy
hand fall upon me and upon my
family.' That same day Gad came to 18
David and said to him, 'Go and set up
an altar to the LORD on the threshing-
floor of Araunah the Jebusite.' David 19
did what Gad told him to do, and
went up as the LORD had commanded.
When Araunah looked down and saw 20
the king and his servants coming over
towards him, he went out, prostrated
himself low before the king and said, 21
'Why has your majesty come to visit
his servant?' David answered, 'To
buy the threshing-floor from you to
build an altar to the LORD, so that the
plague which has attacked the people
may be stopped.' Araunah answered 22
David, 'I beg your majesty to take it
and sacrifice what you think fit. I have
here the oxen for a whole-offering,

---

b Prob. rdg., cp. Josh. 18. 22; Heb. from Arabah.   c Prob. rdg., cp. 1 Chr. 11. 33; Heb. from
Bahurim.   d Hashem . . . son of: prob. rdg., cp. 1 Chr. 11. 34; Heb. the sons of Jashen, Jonathan.
e Prob. rdg., cp. 1 Chr. 11. 35; Heb. Ararite.   f Verses 1–25: cp. 1 Chr. 21. 1–27.   g Joab . . .
army: prob. rdg., cp. 1 Chr. 21. 2; Heb. Joab the officer of the army.   h began at . . . Gad: prob.
rdg.; Heb. encamped in Aroer on the right of the level land of the gorge Gad.   i Prob. rdg., cp.
1 Kgs. 15. 20; Heb. Yaan.

and their harness and the threshing-
23 sledges for the fuel.' Araunah[j] gave it
all to the king for his own use and said
to him, 'May the LORD your God accept
24 you.' But the king said to Araunah,
'No, I will buy it from you; I will
not offer to the LORD my God whole-
offerings that have cost me nothing.'

So David bought the threshing-floor
and the oxen for fifty shekels of silver.
He built an altar to the LORD there 25
and offered whole-offerings and shared-
offerings. Then the LORD yielded to his
prayer for the land; and the plague in
Israel stopped.

j Prob. rdg.; Heb. adds the king.

THE FIRST BOOK OF
KINGS

Abishag cares for David

1 KING DAVID was now a very
old man and, though they wrapped
clothes round him, he could not keep
2 warm. So his household said to him,
'Let us find a young virgin for your
majesty, to attend you and take care
of you; and let her lie in your bosom,
3 sir, and make you warm.' So they
searched all over Israel for a beautiful maiden and found Abishag, a
Shunammite, and brought her to the
4 king. She was a very beautiful girl,
and she took care of the king and
waited on him, but he had no intercourse with her.

Solomon to succeed David

5 Now Adonijah, whose mother was
Haggith, was boasting that he was to
be king; and he had already provided
himself with chariots and horsemen[a]
6 and fifty outrunners. Never in his
life had his father corrected him or
asked why he behaved as he did. He
was a very handsome man, too, and
7 was next in age to Absalom. He talked
with Joab son of Zeruiah and with
Abiathar the priest, and they gave
8 him their strong support; but Zadok
the priest, Benaiah son of Jehoiada,
Nathan the prophet, Shimei, Rei, and
David's bodyguard of heroes, did not
9 take his side. Adonijah then held a
sacrifice of sheep, oxen, and buffaloes
at the stone Zoheleth beside En-rogel,
and he invited all his royal brothers
and all those officers of the household
10 who were of the tribe of Judah. But
he did not invite Nathan the prophet,

Benaiah and the bodyguard, or Solomon his brother.

Then Nathan said to Bathsheba, 11
the mother of Solomon, 'Have you
not heard that Adonijah son of Haggith has become king, all unknown to
our lord David? Now come, let me 12
advise you what to do for your own
safety and for the safety of your son
Solomon. Go in and see King David 13
and say to him, "Did not your majesty swear to me, your servant, that
my son Solomon should succeed you
as king; that it was he who should sit
on your throne? Why then has Adonijah become king?" Then while you 14
are still speaking there with the king,
I will follow you in and tell the whole
story.'

So Bathsheba went to the king in 15
his private chamber; he was now very
old, and Abishag the Shunammite
was waiting on him. Bathsheba bowed 16
before the king and prostrated herself. 'What do you want?' said the
king. She answered, 'My lord, you 17
swore to me your servant, by the
LORD your God, that my son Solomon
should succeed you as king, and that
he should sit on your throne. But now, 18
here is Adonijah become king, all unknown to your majesty. He has sacri- 19
ficed great numbers of oxen, buffaloes,
and sheep, and has invited to the
feast all the king's sons, and Abiathar
the priest, and Joab the commander-
in-chief, but he has not invited your
servant Solomon. And now, your 20
majesty, all Israel is looking to you to
announce who is to succeed you on
the throne. Otherwise, when you, sir, 21

a Or a chariot and horses.

rest with your forefathers, my son Solomon and I shall be treated as 22 criminals.' She was still speaking to the king when Nathan the prophet 23 arrived. The king was told that Nathan was there; he came into the king's presence and prostrated himself 24 with his face to the ground. 'My lord,' he said, 'your majesty must, I suppose, have declared that Adonijah should succeed you and that he 25 should sit on your throne. He has today gone down and sacrificed great numbers of oxen, buffaloes, and sheep, and has invited to the feast all the king's sons, Joab the commander-in-chief, and Abiathar the priest; and at this very moment they are eating and drinking in his presence and shouting, "Long live King Adonijah!" 26 But he has not invited me your servant, Zadok the priest, Benaiah son of Jehoiada, or your servant Sol- 27 omon. Has this been done by your majesty's authority, while we[b] your servants have not been told who should succeed you on the throne?' 28 Thereupon King David said, 'Call Bathsheba', and she came into the king's presence and stood before him. 29 Then the king swore an oath to her: 'As the LORD lives, who has delivered 30 me from all my troubles: I swore by the LORD the God of Israel that Solomon your son should succeed me and that he should sit on my throne, and this day I give effect to my oath.' 31 Bathsheba bowed low to the king and prostrated herself; and she said, 'May my lord King David live for ever!'

Solomon is anointed king

32 Then King David said, 'Call Zadok the priest, Nathan the prophet, and Benaiah son of Jehoiada.' They came 33 into the king's presence and he gave them these orders: 'Take the officers of the household with you; mount my son Solomon on the king's mule and 34 escort him down to Gihon. There Zadok the priest and Nathan the prophet shall anoint him king over Israel. Sound the trumpet and shout, "Long 35 live King Solomon!" Then escort him home again, and he shall come and sit on my throne and reign in my place; for he is the man that I have appointed prince over Israel and Judah.' 36 Benaiah son of Jehoiada answered the king, 'It shall be done. And may the LORD, the God of my lord the king, 37 confirm it! As the LORD has been with your majesty, so may he be with

Solomon; may he make his throne even greater than the throne of my lord King David.' So Zadok the priest, 38 Nathan the prophet, and Benaiah son of Jehoiada, together with the Kerethite and Pelethite guards, went down and mounted Solomon on King David's mule and escorted him to Gihon. Zadok the priest took the 39 horn of oil from the Tent of the LORD and anointed Solomon; they sounded the trumpet and all the people shouted, 'Long live King Solomon!' Then all the 40 people escorted him home in procession, with great rejoicing and playing of pipes, so that the very earth split with the noise.

Adonijah's plot fails

Adonijah and his guests had finished 41 their banquet when the noise reached their ears. Joab, hearing the sound of the trumpet, exclaimed, 'What is all this uproar in the city? What has happened?' While he was still speak- 42 ing, Jonathan son of Abiathar the priest arrived. 'Come in', said Adonijah. 'You are an honourable man and bring good news.' 'Far otherwise,' 43 Jonathan replied; 'our lord King David has made Solomon king and 44 has sent with him Zadok the priest, Nathan the prophet, and Benaiah son of Jehoiada, together with the Kerethite and Pelethite guards; they have mounted him on the king's mule, and 45 Zadok the priest and Nathan the prophet have anointed him king at Gihon, and they have now escorted him home rejoicing, and the city is in an uproar. That was the noise you heard. More than that, Solomon has 46 taken his seat on the royal throne. Yes, and the officers of the household 47 have been to greet our lord King David with these words: "May your God make the name of Solomon your son more famous than your own and his throne even greater than yours", and the king bowed upon his couch. What 48 is more, he said this: "Blessed be the LORD the God of Israel who has set a successor on my throne this day while I am still alive to see it."' Then 49 Adonijah's guests all rose in panic and scattered. Adonijah himself, in 50 fear of Solomon, sprang up and went to the altar and caught hold of its horns. Then a message was sent to 51 Solomon: 'Adonijah is afraid of King Solomon; he has taken hold of the horns of the altar and has said, "Let King Solomon first swear to me that

b Has this . . . while we: *or* If this has been done by your majesty's authority, then we . . .

he will not put his servant to the
52 sword.''' Solomon said, 'If he proves
himself a man of worth, not a hair of
his head shall fall to the ground; but
if he is found to be troublesome, he
53 shall die.' Then King Solomon sent
and had him brought down from the
altar; he came in and prostrated himself before the king, and Solomon
ordered him home.

David's last words to Solomon

2 When the time of David's death drew
near, he gave this last charge to his
2 son Solomon: 'I am going the way of
all the earth. Be strong and show
3 yourself a man. Fulfil your duty to
the LORD your God; conform to his
ways, observe his statutes and his
commandments, his judgements and
his solemn precepts, as they are written in the law of Moses, so that you
may prosper in whatever you do and
4 whichever way you turn, and that
the LORD may fulfil this promise that
he made about me: "If your descendants take care to walk faithfully in
my sight with all their heart and with
all their soul, you shall never lack a
successor on the throne of Israel."
5 You know how Joab son of Zeruiah
treated me and what he did to two
commanders-in-chief in Israel, Abner
son of Ner and Amasa son of Jether.
He killed them both, breaking the
peace by bloody acts of war; and with
that blood he stained the belt about
my waist and the sandals on my feet.
6 Do as your wisdom prompts you, and
do not let his grey hairs go down to
7 the grave in peace. Show constant
friendship to the family of Barzillai of
Gilead; let them have their place at
your table; they befriended me when
I was a fugitive from your brother
8 Absalom. Do not forget Shimei son of
Gera, the Benjamite from Bahurim,
who cursed me bitterly the day I went
to Mahanaim. True, he came down to
meet me at the Jordan, and I swore by
the LORD that I would not put him to
9 death. But you do not need to let him
go unpunished now; you are a wise
man and will know how to deal with
him; bring down his grey hairs in
blood to the grave.'

The death of David

10 So David rested with his forefathers
and was buried in the city of David,
11 having reigned over Israel for forty
years, seven in Hebron and thirty-
12 three in Jerusalem; and Solomon suc-

ceeded his father David as king and
was firmly established on the throne.

Solomon puts Adonijah to death

Then Adonijah son of Haggith came 13
to Bathsheba, the mother of Solomon.
'Do you come as a friend?' she asked.
'As a friend,' he answered; 'I have 14
something to say to you.' 'Tell me',
she said. 'You know', he went on, 'that 15
the throne was mine and that all
Israel was looking to me to be king;
but I was passed over and the throne
has gone to my brother; it was his by
the LORD's will. And now I have one 16
request to make of you; do not refuse me.' 'What is it?' she said. He 17
answered, 'Will you ask King Solomon
(he will never refuse you) to give me
Abishag the Shunammite in marriage?'
'Very well,' said Bathsheba, 'I will 18
speak for you to the king.' So Bath- 19
sheba went in to King Solomon to
speak for Adonijah. The king rose to
meet her and kissed her, and seated
himself on his throne. A throne was
set for the king's mother and she sat
at his right hand. Then she said, 'I 20
have one small request to make of
you; do not refuse me.' 'What is it,
mother?' he replied; 'I will not refuse
you.' 'It is this, that Abishag the 21
Shunammite should be given to your
brother Adonijah in marriage.' At 22
that Solomon answered his mother,
'Why do you ask for Abishag the
Shunammite as wife for Adonijah?
you might as well ask for the throne,
for he is my elder brother and has
both Abiathar the priest and Joab
son of Zeruiah on his side.' Then 23
King Solomon swore by the LORD: 'So
help me God, Adonijah shall pay for
this with his life. As the LORD lives, 24
who has established me and set me
on the throne of David my father
and has founded a house for me as
he promised, this very day Adonijah
shall be put to death!' Thereupon 25
King Solomon gave Benaiah son of
Jehoiada his orders, and he struck
him down and he died.

Solomon dismisses Abiathar

Abiathar the priest was told by the 26
king to go off to Anathoth to his own
estate. 'You deserve to die,' he said,
'but in spite of this day's work I shall
not put you to death, for you carried
the Ark of the Lord GOD before my
father David, and you shared in all
the hardships that he endured.' So 27
Solomon dismissed Abiathar from his
office as priest of the LORD, and so

fulfilled the sentence that the LORD had pronounced against the house of Eli in Shiloh.

Solomon puts Joab to death

28 News of all this reached Joab, and he fled to the Tent of the LORD and caught hold of the horns of the altar; for he had sided with Adonijah,
29 though not with Absalom. When King Solomon learnt that Joab had fled to the Tent of the LORD and that he was by the altar, he sent Benaiah son of Jehoiada with orders to strike
30 him down. Benaiah came to the Tent of the LORD and ordered Joab in the king's name to come away; but he said, 'No; I will die here.' Benaiah re-
31 ported Joab's answer to the king, and the king said, 'Let him have his way; strike him down and bury him, and so rid me and my father's house of the guilt for the blood that he wantonly
32 shed. The LORD will hold him responsible for his own death, because he struck down two innocent men who were better men than he, Abner son of Ner, commander of the army of Israel, and Amasa son of Jether, commander of the army of Judah, and ran them through with the sword, without my father David's knowledge.
33 The guilt of their blood shall recoil on Joab and his descendants for all time; but David and his descendants, his house and his throne, will enjoy per-
34 petual prosperity from the LORD.' So Benaiah son of Jehoiada went up to the altar and struck Joab down and killed him, and he was buried in his house on the edge of the wilderness.
35 Thereafter the king appointed Benaiah son of Jehoiada to command the army in his place, and installed Zadok the priest in place of Abiathar.

Shimei forfeits his life

36 Next the king sent for Shimei and said to him, 'Build yourself a house in Jerusalem and stay there; you are not to leave the city for any other
37 place. If ever you leave it and cross the gorge of the Kidron, you shall die; make no mistake about that. Your
38 blood will be on your own head.' And Shimei said to the king, 'I accept your sentence; I will do as your majesty commands.' So for a long time Shimei
39 remained in Jerusalem; but three years later two of his slaves ran away to Achish son of Maacah, king of Gath. When Shimei heard that his slaves
40 were in Gath, he immediately saddled

his ass and went there to Achish in search of his slaves; he came to Gath and returned with them. When King 41 Solomon was told that Shimei had gone from Jerusalem to Gath and back, he sent for him and said, 'Did 42 I not require you to swear by the LORD? Did I not give you this solemn warning: "If ever you leave this city for any other place, you shall die; make no mistake about it"? And you said, "I accept your sentence; I obey." Why then have you not kept the oath 43 which you swore by the LORD, and the order which I gave you? Shimei, you 44 know in your own heart all the mischief you did to my father David; the LORD is now making that mischief recoil on your own head. But King 45 Solomon is blessed and the throne of David will be secure before the LORD for all time.' The king then gave orders 46 to Benaiah son of Jehoiada, and he went out and struck Shimei down; and he died. Thus Solomon's royal power was securely established.

Solomon marries Pharaoh's daughter

Solomon allied himself to Pharaoh 3 king of Egypt by marrying his daughter. He brought her to the City of David, until he had finished building his own house and the house of the LORD and the wall round Jerusalem. The people however continued to sa- 2 crifice at the hill-shrines, for till then no house had been built in honour of the name of the LORD. Solomon 3 himself loved the LORD, conforming to the precepts laid down by his father David; but he too slaughtered and burnt sacrifices at the hill-shrines.

Solomon asks the LORD for wisdom

Now King Solomon went to Gibeon 4 to offer a sacrifice, for that was the chief hill-shrine, and he used to offer a thousand whole-offerings on its altar. There that night the LORD God 5ᶜ appeared to him in a dream and said, 'What shall I give you? Tell me.' And 6 Solomon answered, 'Thou didst show great and constant love to thy servant David my father, because he walked before thee in loyalty, righteousness, and integrity of heart; and thou hast maintained this great and constant love towards him and hast now given him a son to succeed him on the throne. Now, O LORD my God, thou 7 hast made thy servant king in place of my father David, though I am a mere child, unskilled in leadership.

c Verses 5–14: cp. 2 Chr. 1. 7–12.

8 And I am here in the midst of thy people, the people of thy choice, too many to be numbered or counted.
9 Give thy servant, therefore, a heart with skill to listen, so that he may govern thy people justly and distinguish good from evil. For who is equal to the task of governing this
10 great people of thine?' The Lord was well pleased that Solomon had asked for
11 this, and he said to him, 'Because you have asked for this, and not for long life for yourself, or for wealth, or for the lives of your enemies, but have asked for discernment in administer-
12 ing justice, I grant your request; I give you a heart so wise and so understanding that there has been none like you before your time nor will
13 be after you. I give you furthermore those things for which you did not ask, such wealth and honour*d* as no
14 king of your time can match. And if you conform to my ways and observe my ordinances and commandments, as your father David did, I will give
15 you long life.' Then he awoke, and knew it was a dream.

Solomon came to Jerusalem and stood before the Ark of the Covenant of the Lord; there he sacrificed whole-offerings and brought shared-offerings, and gave a feast to all his household.

Solomon and the two mothers

16 Then there came into the king's presence two women who were prosti-
17 tutes and stood before him. The first said, 'My lord, this woman and I share the same house, and I gave birth to a child when she was there
18 with me. On the third day after my baby was born she too gave birth to a child. We were quite alone; no one else was with us in the house; only the
19 two of us were there. During the night
20 this woman's child died because she overlaid it, and she got up in the middle of the night, took my baby from my side while I, your servant, was asleep, and laid it in her bosom,
21 putting her dead child in mine. When I got up in the morning to feed my baby, I found him dead; but when I looked at him closely, I found that it was not the child that I had borne.'
22 The other woman broke in, 'No; the living child is mine; yours is the dead one', while the first retorted, 'No; the dead child is yours; mine is the living

one.' So they went on arguing in the king's presence. The king thought to 23 himself, 'One of them says, "This is my child, the living one; yours is the dead one." The other says, "No; it is your child that is dead and mine that is alive." ' Then he said, 'Fetch me a 24 sword.' They brought in a sword and 25 the king gave the order: 'Cut the living child in two and give half to one and half to the other.' At this the 26 woman who was the mother of the living child, moved with love for her child, said to the king, 'Oh! sir, let her have the baby; whatever you do, do not kill it.' The other said, 'Let neither of us have it; cut it in two.' Thereupon the king gave judgement: 27 'Give the living baby to the first woman; do not kill it. She is its mother.' When Israel heard the judge- 28 ment which the king had given, they all stood in awe of him; for they saw that he had the wisdom of God within him to administer justice.

Solomon's officers and governors

King Solomon reigned over Israel. 4 His officers were as follows: 2*e*

In charge of the calendar:*f* Azariah son of Zadok the priest.
Adjutant-general:*g* Ahijah son*h* of 3 Shisha.
Secretary of state: Jehoshaphat son of Ahilud.
Commander of the army: Benaiah 4 son of Jehoiada.
Priests: Zadok and Abiathar.
Superintendent of the regional 5 governors: Azariah son of Nathan.
King's Friend: Zabud son of Nathan.
Comptroller of the household: 6 Ahishar.
Superintendent of the forced levy: Adoniram son of Abda.

Solomon had twelve regional gover- 7 nors over Israel and they supplied the food for the king and the royal household, each being responsible for one month's provision in the year. These 8 were their names:

Ben-hur in the hill-country of Ephraim.
Ben-dekar in Makaz, Shaalbim, 9 Beth-shemesh, Elon, and Beth-hanan.
Ben-hesed in Aruboth; he had 10

---

d Or riches.   *e* Verses 2–6: cp. 2 Sam. 8. 16–18; 20. 23–6; 1 Chr. 18. 15–17.   *f* In . . . calendar: *prob. rdg.*; Heb. Elihoreph.   *g* Prob. rdg., cp. 1 Chr. 18. 16; Heb. Adjutants-general.
h Prob. rdg.; Heb. sons.

charge also of Socoh and all the land of Hepher.

11 Ben-abinadab, who had married Solomon's daughter Taphath, in all the district of Dor.

12 Baana son of Ahilud in Taanach and Megiddo, all Beth-shean as far as Abel-meholah beside Zartanah, and from Beth-shean below Jezreel as far as Jokmeam.

13 Ben-geber in Ramoth-gilead, including the tent-villages of Jair son of Manasseh in Gilead and the region of Argob in Bashan, sixty large walled cities with gate-bars of bronze.

14 Ahinadab son of Iddo in Mahanaim.

15 Ahimaaz in Naphtali; he also had married a daughter of Solomon, Basmath.

16 Baanah son of Hushai in Asher and Aloth.

17 Jehoshaphat son of Paruah in Issachar.

18 Shimei son of Elah in Benjamin.

19 Geber son of Uri in Gilead, the land of Sihon king of the Amorites and of Og king of Bashan.
In addition, one governor over all the governors[j] in the land.

Solomon's prosperity and wisdom increase

20 The people of Judah and Israel were countless as the sands of the sea; they ate and they drank, and enjoyed life.

21 Solomon ruled over all the kingdoms from the river Euphrates to Philistia and as far as the frontier of Egypt; they paid tribute and were subject to him all his life.

22 Solomon's provision for one day was thirty kor of flour and sixty kor

23 of meal, ten fat oxen and twenty oxen from the pastures and a hundred sheep, as well as stags, gazelles, roe-

24 bucks, and fattened fowl. For he was paramount over all the land west of the Euphrates from Tiphsah to Gaza, ruling all the kings west of the river;

25 and he enjoyed peace on all sides. All through his reign Judah and Israel continued at peace, every man under his own vine and fig-tree, from Dan to Beersheba.

26 Solomon had forty thousand chariot-horses in his stables and twelve thousand cavalry horses.

27 The regional governors, each for a month in turn, supplied provisions for King Solomon and for all who came to his table; they never fell

28 short in their deliveries. They provided also barley and straw, each according to his duty, for the horses and chariot-horses where it was required.

29 And God gave Solomon depth of wisdom and insight, and understanding as wide as the sand on the seashore,

30 so that Solomon's wisdom surpassed that of all the men of the east and of all Egypt. For he was wiser

31 than any man, wiser than Ethan the Ezrahite, and Heman, Kalcol, and Darda, the sons of Mahol; his fame spread among all the surrounding nations. He

32 uttered three thousand proverbs, and his songs numbered a thousand and five.

33 He discoursed of trees, from the cedar of Lebanon down to the marjoram that grows out of the wall, of beasts and birds, of reptiles and fishes. Men of

34 all races came to listen to the wisdom of Solomon, and from all the kings of the earth who had heard of his wisdom he received gifts.

Solomon's alliance with King Hiram

5 When Hiram king of Tyre heard that Solomon had been anointed king in his father's place, he sent envoys to him, because he had always been a friend of David.

2[j] Solomon sent this

3 answer to Hiram: 'You know that my father David could not build a house in honour of the name of the LORD his God, because he was surrounded by armed nations until the LORD made

4 them subject to him. But now on every side the LORD my God has given me peace; there is no one to oppose me, I fear no attack. So I propose to

5 build a house in honour of the name of the LORD my God, following the promise given by the LORD to my father David: "Your son whom I shall set on the throne in your place will build the house in honour of my name."

6 If therefore you will now give orders that cedars be felled and brought from Lebanon, my men will work with yours, and I will pay you for your men whatever sum you fix; for, as you know, we have none so skilled at felling timber as your Sidonians.'

7 When Hiram received Solomon's message, he was greatly pleased and said, 'Blessed be the LORD today who has given David a wise son to rule

8 over this great people.' And he sent this reply to Solomon: 'I have received your message. In this matter of timber, both cedar and pine, I will do

9 all you wish. My men shall bring down

i over . . . governors: prob. rdg.; Heb. om.   _j Verses 2–11: cp. 2 Chr. 2. 3–16._

the logs from Lebanon to the sea and I will make them up into rafts to be floated to the place you appoint; I will have them broken up there and you can remove them. You, on your part, will meet my wishes if you pro-10 vide the food for my household.' So Hiram kept Solomon supplied with all the cedar and pine that he wanted, 11 and Solomon supplied Hiram with twenty thousand kor of wheat as food for his household and twenty kor of oil of pounded olives; Solomon gave 12 this yearly to Hiram. (The LORD had given Solomon wisdom as he had promised him; there was peace be-13 tween Hiram and Solomon and they concluded an alliance.) King Solomon raised a forced levy from the whole of Israel amounting to thirty thousand 14 men. He sent them to Lebanon in monthly relays of ten thousand, so that the men spent one month in Lebanon and two at home; Adoniram was superintendent of the whole levy. 15 Solomon had also seventy thousand hauliers and eighty thousand quarry-16 men, apart from the three thousand three hundred foremen in charge of the work who superintended the 17 labourers. By the king's orders they quarried huge, massive blocks for laying the foundation of the LORD's 18 house in hewn stone. Solomon's and Hiram's builders and the Gebalites shaped the blocks and prepared both timber and stone for the building of the house.

6 1[k]   It was in the four hundred and eightieth year after the Israelites had come out of Egypt, in the fourth year of Solomon's reign over Israel, in the second month of that year, the month of Ziv, that he began to build the house of the LORD.

Solomon builds the Temple

2 The house which King Solomon built for the LORD was sixty cubits long by twenty cubits broad, and its height 3 was thirty cubits. The vestibule in front of the sanctuary was twenty cubits long, spanning the whole breadth of the house, while it projected ten 4 cubits in front of the house; and he furnished the house with em-5 brasures. Then he built a terrace a-gainst its wall round both the sanctuary and the inner shrine. He made 6 arcades all round: the lowest arcade was five cubits in depth, the middle six, and the highest seven; for he

made rebates all round the outside of the main wall so that the bearer beams might not be set into the walls. In the building of the house, only 7 blocks of undressed stone direct from the quarry were used; no hammer or axe or any iron tool whatever was heard in the house while it was being built.

The entrance to the lowest arcade 8 was in the right-hand corner of the house; there was access by a spiral stairway from that to the middle arcade, and from the middle arcade to the highest. So he built the house 9-10 and finished it, having constructed the terrace five cubits high against the whole building, braced the house with struts of cedar and roofed it with beams and coffering of cedar.

Then the word of the LORD came to 11 Solomon, saying, 'As for this house 12 which you are building, if you are obedient to my ordinances and con-form to my precepts and loyally observe all my commands, then I will fulfil my promise to you, the promise I gave to your father David, and I 13 will dwell among the Israelites and never forsake my people Israel.'

So Solomon built the LORD's 14 house and finished it. He lined the 15 inner walls of the house with cedar boards, covering the interior from floor to rafters with wood; the floor he laid with boards of pine. In the 16 innermost part of the house he parti-tioned off a space of twenty cubits with cedar boards from floor to rafters and made of it an inner shrine, to be the Most Holy Place. The sanctuary 17 in front of this was forty cubits long. The cedar inside the house was carved 18 with open flowers and gourds; all was cedar, no stone was left visible.

He prepared an inner shrine in the 19 furthest recesses of the house to receive the Ark of the Covenant of the LORD. This inner shrine was 20 twenty cubits square and it stood twenty cubits high; he overlaid it with red gold and made an altar of cedar. And Solomon overlaid the in-21 side of the house with red gold and drew a Veil[l] with golden chains across in front of the inner shrine.[m] The 22 whole house he overlaid with gold until it was all covered; and the whole of the altar by the inner shrine he overlaid with gold.

In the inner shrine he made two 23[n] cherubim of wild olive, each ten

k Verses 1–3: cp. 2 Chr. 3. 2–4.   l a Veil: prob. rdg.; Heb. om.   m Prob. rdg.; Heb. adds and overlaid it with gold.   n Verses 23–8: cp. 2 Chr. 3. 10–13.

24 cubits high. Each wing of the cherubim was five cubits long, and from
wing-tip to wing-tip was ten cubits.
25 Similarly the second cherub measured
ten cubits; the two cherubim were
26 alike in size and shape, and each ten
27 cubits high. He put the cherubim
within the shrine at the furthest recesses and their wings were outspread,
so that a wing of the one cherub
touched the wall on one side and a
wing of the other touched the wall on
the other side, and their other wings
28 met in the middle; and he overlaid
the cherubim with gold.
29 Round all the walls of the house
he carved figures of cherubim, palm-
trees, and open flowers, both in the
30 inner chamber and in the outer. The
floor of the house he overlaid with
gold, both in the inner chamber and
31 in the outer. At the entrance to the
inner shrine he made a double door
of wild olive; the pilasters and the[o]
32 door-posts were pentagonal. The doors
were of wild olive, and he carved
cherubim, palms, and open flowers on
them, overlaying them with gold and
hammering the gold upon the cheru-
33 bim and the palms. Similarly for the
doorway of the sanctuary he made a
34 square frame of wild olive and a
double door of pine, each leaf having
35 two swivel-pins. On them he carved
cherubim, palms, and open flowers,
overlaying them evenly with gold over
the carving.
36 He built the inner court with three
courses of dressed stone and one course
of lengths of cedar.
37 In the fourth year of Solomon's
reign the foundation of the house
of the LORD was laid, in the month of
38 Ziv; and in the eleventh year, in the
month of Bul, which is the eighth
month, the house was finished in all
its details according to the specifica-
tion. It had taken seven years to
build.

Solomon's other buildings

7 Solomon had been engaged on his
building for thirteen years by the
2 time he had finished it. He built the
House of the Forest of Lebanon, a
hundred cubits long, fifty broad, and
thirty high, constructed of four rows
of cedar columns, over which were
3 laid lengths of cedar. It had a cedar
roof, extending over the beams,
which rested on the columns, fifteen
in each row; and the number of the
beams was forty-five. There were 4
three rows of window-frames, and the
windows corresponded to each other
at three levels. All the doorways and 5
the windows had square frames, and
window corresponded to window at
three levels.
He made also the colonnade, fifty 6
cubits long and thirty broad,[p] with
a cornice above.
He built the Hall of Judgement, 7
the hall containing the throne where
he was to give judgement; this was
panelled in cedar from floor to rafters.
His own house where he was to 8
reside, in a court set back from the
colonnade, and the house he made
for Pharaoh's daughter whom he had
married, were constructed like the
hall.
All these were made of heavy 9
blocks of stone, hewn to measure and
trimmed with the saw on the inner
and outer sides, from foundation to
coping and from the court of the
house[q] as far as the great court. At 10
the base were heavy stones, massive
blocks, some ten and some eight
cubits in size, and above were heavy 11
stones dressed to measure, and cedar.
The great court had three courses of 12
dressed stone all around and a course
of lengths of cedar; so had the inner
court of the house of the LORD, and so
had the vestibule of the house.

Hiram the craftsman at work in the Temple

King Solomon fetched from Tyre 13
Hiram, the son of a widow of the 14
tribe of Naphtali. His father, a native
of Tyre, had been a worker in bronze,
and he himself was a man of great
skill and ingenuity, versed in every
kind of craftsmanship in bronze.
Hiram came to King Solomon and
executed all his works.
He cast in a mould the two bronze 15[r]
pillars. One stood eighteen cubits
high and it took a cord twelve cubits
long to go round it; it was hollow,
and the metal was four fingers thick.[s]
The second pillar was the same. He 16
made two capitals of solid copper to
set on the tops of the pillars, each
capital five cubits high. He made two 17
bands of ornamental network, in fes-
toons of chain-work, for the capitals
on the tops of the pillars, a band of
network for each capital. Then he 18

o and the: *prob. rdg.; Heb. om.* *p Prob. rdg.; Heb. adds* and a colonnade and pillars in front of them. *q Prob. rdg., cp. verse 12; Heb.* from outside. *r Verses 15–21: cp. 2 Chr. 3. 15–17.*
s it was . . . thick: *prob. rdg., cp. Jer. 52. 21; Heb. om.*

made pomegranates in two rows all round on top of the ornamental network of the one pillar; he did the same with the other capital. (The capitals at the tops of the pillars in the vestibule were shaped like lilies and were four cubits high.) Upon the capitals at the tops of the two pillars, immediately above the cushion, which was beyond the network upwards, were two hundred pomegranates in rows all round on the two capitals.[t] Then he erected the pillars at the vestibule of the sanctuary. When he had erected the pillar on the right side, he named it Jachin;[u] and when he had erected the one on the left side, he named it Boaz.[v] On the tops of the pillars was lily-work. Thus the work of the pillars was finished.

He then made the Sea of cast metal; it was round in shape, the diameter from rim to rim being ten cubits; it stood five cubits high, and it took a line thirty cubits long to go round it. All round the Sea on the outside under its rim, completely surrounding the thirty[x] cubits of its circumference, were two rows of gourds, cast in one piece with the Sea itself. It was mounted on twelve oxen, three facing north, three west, three south, and three east, their hind quarters turned inwards; the Sea rested on top of them. Its thickness was a hand-breadth; its rim was made like that of a cup, shaped like the calyx of a lily; it held two thousand bath of water.

He also made the ten trolleys of bronze; each trolley was four cubits long, four wide, and three high. This was the construction of the trolleys. They had panels set in frames; on these panels were portrayed lions, oxen, and cherubim, and similarly on the frames. Above and below the lions, oxen, and cherubim[y] were fillets of hammered work of spiral design. Each trolley had four bronze wheels with axles of bronze; it also had four flanges and handles beneath the laver, and these handles were of cast metal with a spiral design on their sides. The opening for the basin was set within a crown which projected one cubit; the opening was round with a level edge,[z] and it had decorations in relief. (The panels of the trolleys were square, not round.) The four wheels were beneath the panels, and the wheel-forks were made in one piece with the trolleys; the height of each wheel was a cubit and a half. The wheels were constructed like those of a chariot, their axles, hubs, spokes, and felloes being all of cast metal. The four handles were at the four corners of each trolley, of one piece with the trolley. At the top of the trolley there was a circular band half a cubit high; the struts and panels on[a] the trolley were of one piece with it. On the plates, that is on the panels,[b] he carved cherubim, lions, and palm-trees, wherever there was a blank space, with spiral work all round it. This is how the ten trolleys were made; all of them were cast alike, having the same size and the same shape.

He then made ten bronze basins, each holding forty bath and measuring four cubits; there was a basin for each of the ten trolleys. He put five trolleys on the right side of the house and five on the left side; and he put the Sea in the south-east corner of it.

Hiram made also the pots, the shovels, and the tossing-bowls. So he finished all the work which he had undertaken for King Solomon on the house of the LORD: the two pillars; the two bowl-shaped capitals on the tops of the pillars; the two ornamental networks to cover the two bowl-shaped capitals on the tops of the pillars; the four hundred pomegranates for the two networks, two rows of pomegranates for each network, to cover the bowl-shaped capitals on the two pillars; the ten trolleys and the ten basins on the trolleys; the one Sea and the twelve oxen which supported it; the pots, the shovels, and the tossing-bowls—all these objects in the house of the LORD which Hiram made for King Solomon being of bronze, burnished work. In the Plain of the Jordan the king cast them, in the foundry between Succoth and Zarethan.

Solomon put all these objects in their places; so great was the quantity of bronze used in their making that the weight of it was beyond all reckoning. He made also all the furnishings for the house of the LORD: the golden altar and the golden table

t the two capitals: prob. rdg.; Heb. the second capital.   u Or Jachun, meaning It shall stand.
v Or Booz, meaning In strength.   w Verses 23–6: cp. 2 Chr. 4. 2–5.   x Prob. rdg.; Heb. ten.
y and cherubim: prob. rdg.; Heb. om.   z Prob. rdg.; Heb. adds a cubit and a half (cp. verse 32).
a Prob. rdg.; Heb. adds the head of.   b Prob. rdg.; Heb. adds its struts.   c Verses 40–51: cp.
2 Chr. 4. 11—5. 1.

upon which was set the Bread of the
49 Presence; the lamp-stands of red gold,
five on the right side and five on the
left side of the inner shrine; the
flowers, lamps, and tongs, of gold;
50 the cups, snuffers, tossing-bowls, saucers, and firepans, of red gold; and
the panels for the doors of the inner
sanctuary, the Most Holy Place, and
for the doors of the house,[d] of gold.

The Ark brought into the Temple

51 When all the work which King Solomon did for the house of the LORD
was completed, he brought in the sacred treasures of his father David, the
silver, the gold, and the vessels, and
deposited them in the storehouses of
the house of the LORD.
8 1[e] Then Solomon summoned the
elders of Israel, all the heads of the
tribes who were chiefs of families in
Israel, to assemble in Jerusalem, in
order to bring up the Ark of the Covenant of the LORD from the City of
2 David, which is called Zion. All the
men of Israel assembled in King
Solomon's presence at the pilgrim-
feast in the month Ethanim, the
3 seventh month. When the elders of
Israel had all come, the priests took
4 the Ark of the LORD and carried it up
with the Tent of the Presence and all
the sacred furnishings of the Tent: it
was the priests and the Levites to-
5 gether who carried them up. King Solomon and the whole congregation of
Israel, assembled with him before the
Ark, sacrificed sheep and oxen in
numbers past counting or reckoning.
6 Then the priests brought in the Ark
of the Covenant of the LORD to its
place, the inner shrine of the house,
the Most Holy Place, beneath the
7 wings of the cherubim. The cherubim
spread their wings over the place of
the Ark; they formed a screen above
8 the Ark and its poles. The poles projected, and their ends could be seen
from the Holy Place immediately in
front of the inner shrine, but from
nowhere else outside; they are there
9 to this day. There was nothing inside
the Ark but the two tablets of stone
which Moses had deposited there at
Horeb, the tablets of the covenant
which the LORD made with the Israelites when they left Egypt.
10 Then the priests came out of the
Holy Place, since the cloud was filling
11 the house of the LORD, and they could
not continue to minister because of

it, for the glory of the LORD filled his
house. And Solomon said:

O LORD who hast set the sun in
heaven,
but hast chosen to dwell in thick
darkness,
here have I built thee a lofty house,
a habitation for thee to occupy for
ever.

Solomon blesses the people

And as they stood waiting, the king
turned round and blessed all the
assembly of Israel in these words:
'Blessed be the LORD the God of Israel
who spoke directly to my father David
and has himself fulfilled his promise.
For he said, "From the day when I
brought my people Israel out of
Egypt, I chose no city out of all the
tribes of Israel where I should build a
house for my Name to be there, but
I chose David to be over my people
Israel." My father David had in mind
to build a house in honour of the
name of the LORD the God of Israel,
but the LORD said to him, "You
purposed to build a house in honour
of my name; and your purpose was
good. Nevertheless, you shall not
build it; but the son who is to be
born to you, he shall build the house
in honour of my name." The LORD
has now fulfilled his promise: I have
succeeded my father David and taken
his place on the throne of Israel,
as the LORD promised; and I have built
the house in honour of the name of
the LORD the God of Israel. I have
assigned therein a place for the Ark
containing the Covenant of the LORD,
which he made with our forefathers
when he brought them out of Egypt.'

Solomon prays to the LORD

Then Solomon, standing in front of
the altar of the LORD in the presence
of the whole assembly of Israel, spread
out his hands towards heaven and
said, 'O LORD God of Israel, there is
no god like thee in heaven above or
on earth beneath, keeping covenant
with thy servants and showing them
constant love while they continue
faithful to thee in heart and soul.
Thou hast kept thy promise to thy
servant David my father; by thy
deeds this day thou hast fulfilled
what thou didst say to him in words.
Now therefore, O LORD God of Israel,
keep this promise of thine to thy

---

d *Prob. rdg.; Heb. adds* for the temple.   e *Verses 1–9: cp.* 2 *Chr.* 5. 2–10.   f *Verses 12–50: cp.*
2 *Chr.* 6. 1–39.

servant David my father: "You shall never want for a man appointed by me to sit on the throne of Israel, if only your sons look to their ways and walk before me as you have walked

5 before me." And now, O God of Israel, let the words which thou didst speak to thy servant David my father be confirmed.

7 'But can God indeed dwell on earth? Heaven itself, the highest heaven, cannot contain thee; how much less

8 this house that I have built! Yet attend to the prayer and the supplication of thy servant, O LORD my God, listen to the cry and the prayer which

9 thy servant utters this day, that thine eyes may ever be upon this house night and day, this place of which thou didst say, "My Name shall be there"; so mayest thou hear thy servant when he prays towards this

10 place. Hear the supplication of thy servant and of thy peole Israel when they pray towards this place. Hear thou in heaven thy dwelling and, when thou hearest, forgive.

11 'When a man wrongs his neighbour and he is adjured to take an oath, and the adjuration is made before thy

12 altar in this house, then do thou hear in heaven and act: be thou thy servants' judge, condemning the guilty man and bringing his deeds upon his own head, acquitting the innocent and rewarding him as his innocence may deserve.

13 'When thy people Israel are defeated by an enemy because they have sinned against thee, and they turn back to thee, confessing thy name and making their prayer and supplication to thee in this

14 house, do thou hear in heaven; forgive the sin of thy people Israel and restore them to the land which thou gavest to their forefathers.

15 'When the heavens are shut up and there is no rain because thy servant and thy people Israel have sinned against thee, and when they pray towards this place, confessing thy name and forsaking their sin when

16 they feel thy punishment, do thou hear in heaven and forgive their sin; so mayest thou teach them the good way which they should follow; and grant rain to thy land which thou hast given to thy people as their own possession.

17 'If there is famine in the land, or pestilence, or black blight or red, or locusts new-sloughed or fully grown; or if their enemies besiege them in any of their cities; or if plague or sickness

38 befall them, then hear the prayer or supplication of every man among thy people Israel, as each one, prompted by the remorse of his own heart, spreads out his hands towards this

39 house: hear it in heaven thy dwelling and forgive, and act. And, as thou knowest a man's heart, reward him according to his deeds, for thou alone knowest the hearts of all men;

40 and so they will fear thee all their lives in the land thou gavest to our forefathers.

41 'The foreigner too, the man who does not belong to thy people Israel, but has come from a distant land

42 because of thy fame (for men shall hear of thy great fame and thy strong hand and arm outstretched), when he comes and prays towards this

43 house, hear in heaven thy dwelling and respond to the call which the foreigner makes to thee, so that like thy people Israel all peoples of the earth may know thy fame and fear thee, and learn that this house which I have built bears thy name.

44 'When thy people go to war with an enemy, wherever thou dost send them, when they pray to the LORD, turning towards this city which thou hast chosen and towards this house which I have built in honour of thy name, do thou in heaven hear their

45 prayer and supplication, and grant them justice.

46 'Should they sin against thee (and what man is free from sin?) and shouldst thou in thy anger give them over to an enemy, who carries them captive to his own land, far or near; if in

47 the land of their captivity they learn their lesson and make supplication again to thee in that land and say, "We have sinned and acted perverse-

48 ly and wickedly", if they turn back to thee with heart and soul in the land of their captors, and pray to thee, turning towards their land which thou gavest to their forefathers and towards this city which thou didst choose and this house which I have built in honour of thy name; then in

49 heaven thy dwelling do thou hear their prayer and supplication, and grant them justice. Forgive thy

50 people their sins and transgressions against thee; put pity for them in their captors' hearts. For they are thy

51 possession, thy people whom thou didst bring out of Egypt, from the smelting-furnace, and so thine eyes

52 are ever open to the entreaty of thy servant and of thy people Israel, and

thou dost hear whenever they call to
53 thee. Thou thyself hast singled them
out from all the peoples of the earth
to be thy possession; so thou didst
promise through thy servant Moses
when thou didst bring our forefathers
from Egypt, O Lord GOD.'

Solomon again blesses Israel

54 When Solomon had finished this
prayer and supplication to the LORD,
he rose from before the altar of the
LORD, where he had been kneeling
with his hands spread out to heaven,
55 stood up and in a loud voice blessed
56 the whole assembly of Israel: 'Blessed
be the LORD who has given his people Israel rest, as he promised: not
one of the promises he made through
57 his servant Moses has failed. The
LORD our God be with us as he was
with our forefathers; may he never
58 leave us nor forsake us. May he turn
our hearts towards him, that we may
conform to all his ways, observing his
commandments, statutes, and judgements, as he commanded our fore-
59 fathers. And may the words of my
supplication to the LORD be with the
LORD our God day and night, that, as
the need arises day by day, he may
grant justice to his servant and jus-
60 tice to his people Israel. So all the
peoples of the earth will know that
61 the LORD is God, he and no other, and
you will be perfect in loyalty to the
LORD our God as you are this day,
conforming to his statutes and observing his commandments.'

Dedicating the Temple

62 When the king and all Israel came to
63 offer sacrifices before the LORD, Solomon offered as shared-offerings to
the LORD twenty-two thousand oxen
and a hundred and twenty thousand
sheep; thus it was that the king and
the Israelites dedicated the house of
64[g] the LORD. On that day also the king
consecrated the centre of the court
which lay in front[h] of the house of the
LORD; there he offered the whole-
offering, the grain-offering, and the
fat portions of the shared-offerings,
because the bronze altar which stood
before the LORD was too small to take
them all, the whole-offering, the grain-
offering, and the fat portions of the
shared-offerings.

65 So Solomon and all Israel with him,
a great assembly from Lebo-hamath
to the Torrent of Egypt, celebrated

the pilgrim-feast at that time before
the LORD our God for seven days. On the 66
eighth day he dismissed the people;
and they blessed the king, and went
home happy and glad at heart for all
the prosperity granted by the LORD
to his servant David and to his people
Israel.

The LORD appears again to Solomon

When Solomon had finished the house 9[i]
of the LORD and the royal palace and
all the plans for building on which
he had set his heart, the LORD ap- 2
peared to him a second time, as he
had appeared to him at Gibeon.
The LORD said to him, 'I have heard 3
the prayer and supplication which
you have offered me; I have consecrated this house which you have
built, to receive my Name for all
time, and my eyes and my heart shall
be fixed on it for ever. And if you, 4
on your part, live in my sight as your
father David lived, in integrity and
uprightness, doing all I command you
and observing my statutes and my
judgements, then I will establish your 5
royal throne over Israel for ever, as I
promised your father David when I
said, "You shall never want for a man
upon the throne of Israel." But if you 6
or your sons turn back from following
me and do not observe my commandments and my statutes which
I have set before you, and if you go
and serve other gods and prostrate
yourselves before them, then I will 7
cut off Israel from the land which I
gave them; I will renounce this house
which I have consecrated in honour
of my name, and Israel shall become
a byword and an object lesson among
all peoples. And this house will be- 8
come a ruin; every passer-by will be
appalled and gasp at the sight of it;
and they will ask, "Why has the
LORD so treated this land and this
house?" The answer will be, "Because 9
they forsook the LORD their God, who
brought their forefathers out of Egypt,
and clung to other gods, prostrating
themselves before them and serving
them; that is why the LORD has
brought this great evil on them."'

King Hiram is dissatisfied

Solomon had taken twenty years to 10[j]
build the two houses, the house of the
LORD and the royal palace. Hiram 11
king of Tyre had supplied him with
all the timber, both cedar and pine,

g Verses 64–6: cp. 2. Chr. 7. 7–10.   h Or to the east.   i Verses 1–9; cp. 2 Chr. 7. 11–22.
j Verses 10–28: cp. 2 Chr. 8. 1–18.

and all the gold, that he desired, and King Solomon gave Hiram twenty cities in the land of Galilee. But when Hiram went from Tyre to inspect the cities which Solomon had given him, they did not satisfy him, and he said, 'What kind of cities are these you have given me, my brother?' And so he called them the Land of Cabul,[k] the name they still bear. Hiram sent a hundred and twenty talents of gold to the king.

Solomon conscripts labour

This is the record of the forced labour which King Solomon conscripted to build the house of the LORD, his own palace, the Millo, the wall of Jerusalem, and Hazor, Megiddo, and Gezer. Gezer had been attacked and captured by Pharaoh king of Egypt, who had burnt it to the ground, put its Canaanite inhabitants to death, and given it as a marriage gift to his daughter, Solomon's wife; and Solomon rebuilt it. He also built Lower Beth-horon, Baalath, and Tamar in the wilderness, as well as all his store-cities, and the towns where he quartered his chariots and horses; and he carried out all his cherished plans for building in Jerusalem, in the Lebanon, and throughout his whole dominion. All the survivors of the Amorites, Hittites, Perizzites, Hivites, and Jebusites, who did not belong to Israel—that is their descendants who survived in the land, wherever the Israelites had been unable to annihilate them—were employed by Solomon on perpetual forced labour, as they still are. But Solomon put none of the Israelites to forced labour; they were his fighting men,[l] his captains and lieutenants, and the commanders of his chariots and of his cavalry. The number of officers in charge of the foremen over Solomon's work was five hundred and fifty; these superintended the people engaged on the work.

Then Solomon brought Pharaoh's daughter up from the City of David to her own house which he had built for her; later on he built the Millo.

Three times a year Solomon used to offer whole-offerings and shared-offerings on the altar which he had built to the LORD, making smoke-offerings before the LORD. So he completed the house.

Solomon's fleet

King Solomon built a fleet of ships 26 at Ezion-geber, near Eloth[m] on the shore of the Red Sea,[n] in Edom. Hiram sent men of his own to serve 27 with the fleet, experienced seamen, to work with Solomon's men; and they 28 went to Ophir and brought back four hundred and twenty talents of gold, which they delivered to King Solomon.

The queen of Sheba visits Solomon

The queen of Sheba heard of Sol- **10** 1[o] omon's fame[p] and came to test him with hard questions. She arrived in 2 Jerusalem with a very large retinue, camels laden with spices, gold in great quantity, and precious stones. When she came to Solomon, she told him everything she had in her mind, and Solomon answered all her ques- 3 tions; not one of them was too abstruse for the king to answer. When 4 the queen of Sheba saw all the wisdom of Solomon, the house which he had built, the food on his table, the 5 courtiers sitting round him, and his attendants standing behind in their livery, his cupbearers, and the whole-offerings which he used to offer in the house of the LORD, there was no more spirit left in her. Then she said to the 6 king, 'The report which I heard in my own country about you and your wisdom was true, but I did not believe 7 it until I came and saw for myself. Indeed I was not told half of it; your wisdom and your prosperity go far beyond the report which I had of them. Happy are your wives, happy 8 these courtiers of yours who wait on you every day and hear your wisdom! Blessed be the LORD your God who 9 has delighted in you and has set you on the throne of Israel; because he loves Israel for ever, he has made you their king to maintain law and justice.' Then she gave the king a hundred and 10 twenty talents of gold, spices in great abundance, and precious stones. Never again came such a quantity of spices as the queen of Sheba gave to King Solomon.

Solomon's wealth

Besides all this, Hiram's fleet of 11 ships, which had brought gold from Ophir, brought in also from Ophir cargoes of almug wood and precious stones. The king used the wood to 12

---

k *That is* Sterile Land.   l *Prob. rdg.; Heb. adds* and his servants.   m *Or* Elath.
n *Or the* Sea of Reeds.   o *Verses 1–25: cp.* 2 Chr. 9. 1–24.   p *Prob. rdg., cp.* 2 Chr. 9. 1; *Heb. adds* to the name of the LORD.

make stools for the house of the LORD and for the royal palace, as well as harps and lutes for the singers. No such almug wood has ever been imported or even seen since that time.

13 And King Solomon gave the queen of Sheba all she desired, whatever she asked, in addition to all that he gave her of his royal bounty. So she departed and returned with her retinue to her own land.

14 Now the weight of gold which Solomon received yearly was six hundred 15 and sixty-six talents, in addition to the tolls levied by the customs officers and profits on foreign trade, and the tribute of[q] the kings of Arabia and the regional governors.

16 King Solomon made two hundred shields of beaten gold, and six hundred shekels of gold went to the 17 making of each one; he also made three hundred bucklers of beaten gold, and three minas of gold went to the making of each buckler. The king put these into the House of the Forest of Lebanon.

18 The king also made a great throne of ivory and overlaid it with fine gold. 19 Six steps led up to the throne; at the back of the throne there was the head of a calf. There were arms on each side of the seat, with a lion standing 20 beside each of them, and twelve lions stood on the six steps, one at either end of each step. Nothing like it had 21 ever been made for any monarch. All Solomon's drinking vessels were of gold, and all the plate in the House of the Forest of Lebanon was of red gold; no silver was used, for it was reckoned of no value in the days of Solomon. 22 The king had a fleet of merchantmen at sea with Hiram's fleet; once every three years this fleet of merchantmen came home, bringing gold and silver, ivory, apes and monkeys.

Solomon's wisdom and fame

23 Thus King Solomon outdid all the kings of the earth in wealth and wis-24 dom, and all the world courted him, to hear the wisdom which God had 25 put in his heart. Each brought his gift with him, vessels of silver and gold, garments, perfumes and spices, horses and mules, so much year by year.

26[r] And Solomon got together many chariots and horses; he had fourteen hundred chariots and twelve thousand horses, and he stabled some in the chariot-towns and kept others at hand

in Jerusalem. The king made silver as 2 common in Jerusalem as stones, and cedar as plentiful as sycomore-fig in the Shephelah. Horses were imported 2 from Egypt and Coa for Solomon; the royal merchants obtained them from Coa by purchase. Chariots were im- 2 ported from Egypt for six hundred silver shekels each, and horses for a hundred and fifty; in the same way the merchants obtained them for export from all the kings of the Hittites and the kings of Aram.

Solomon defects from true worship

King Solomon was a lover of women, 1 and besides Pharaoh's daughter he married many foreign women, Moabite, Ammonite, Edomite, Sidonian, and Hittite, from the nations with 2 whom the LORD had forbidden the Israelites to intermarry, 'because', he said, 'they will entice you to serve their gods.' But Solomon was devoted to them and loved them dearly. He 3 had seven hundred wives, who were princesses, and three hundred concubines, and they turned his heart from the truth. When he grew old, 4 his wives turned his heart to follow other gods, and he did not remain wholly loyal to the LORD his God as his father David had been. He 5 followed Ashtoreth, goddess of the Sidonians, and Milcom, the loathsome god of the Ammonites. Thus Solomon 6 did what was wrong in the eyes of the LORD, and was not loyal to the LORD like his father David. He built a hill- 7 shrine for Kemosh, the loathsome god of Moab, on the height to the east of Jerusalem, and for Molech, the loathsome god of the Ammonites. Thus 8 he did for the gods to which all his foreign wives burnt offerings and made sacrifices. The LORD was angry 9 with Solomon because his heart was turned away from the LORD the God of Israel, who had appeared to him twice and had strictly commanded 1 him not to follow other gods; but he disobeyed the LORD's command. The LORD therefore said to Solomon, 1 'Because you have done this and have not kept my covenant and my statutes as I commanded you, I will tear the kingdom from you and give it to your servant. Nevertheless, for the sake of 1 your father David I will not do this in your day; I will tear it out of your son's hand. Even so not the whole 1 kingdom; I will leave him one tribe for the sake of my servant David and for the sake of Jerusalem, my chosen city.'

Two adversaries of Solomon

14 Then the LORD raised up an adversary for Solomon, Hadad the Edomite, of 15 the royal house of Edom. At the time when David reduced Edom, his commander-in-chief Joab had destroyed every male in the country when he 16 went into it to bury the slain. He and the armies of Israel remained there for six months, until he had destroyed 17 every male in Edom. Then Hadad, who was still a boy, fled the country with some of his father's Edomite servants, intending to enter Egypt. 18 They set out from Midian, made their way to Paran and, taking some men from there, came to Pharaoh king of Egypt, who assigned Hadad a house and maintenance and made him a 19 grant of land. Hadad found great favour with Pharaoh, who gave him in marriage a sister of Queen Tah- 20 penes his wife. She bore him his son Genubath; Tahpenes weaned the child in Pharaoh's house, and he lived there along with Pharaoh's 21 children. When Hadad heard in Egypt that David rested with his forefathers and that his commander-in-chief Joab was also dead, he said to Pharaoh, 'Let me go so that I may return to my 22 own country.' 'What is it that you find wanting in my country,' said Pharaoh, 'that you want to go back to your own?' 'Nothing,' said Hadad, 25 'but do, pray, let me go.' He remained an adversary for Israel all through Solomon's reign. This is the harm that Hadad caused: he maintained a stranglehold on Israel and became king of Edom.

23 Then God raised up another adversary against Solomon, Rezon son of Eliada, who had fled from his master 24 Hadadezer king of Zobah. He gathered men about him and became a captain of freebooters, who came to Damascus and occupied it; he became king there.

Ahijah prophesies to Jeroboam

26 Jeroboam son of Nebat, one of Solomon's courtiers, an Ephrathite from Zeredah, whose widowed mother was named Zeruah, rebelled against the 27 king. And this is the story of his rebellion. Solomon had built the Millo and closed the breach in the wall of the 28 city of his father David. Now this Jer-

oboam was a man of great energy; and Solomon, seeing how the young man worked, had put him in charge of all the labour-gangs in the tribal district of Joseph. On one occasion 29 Jeroboam had left Jerusalem, and the prophet Ahijah from Shiloh met him on the road. The prophet was wrapped in a new cloak, and the two of them were alone in the open country. Then 30 Ahijah took hold of the new cloak he was wearing, tore it into twelve pieces and said to Jeroboam, 'Take ten 31 pieces, for this is the word of the LORD the God of Israel: "I am going to tear the kingdom from the hand of Solomon and give you ten tribes. But 32 one tribe will remain his, for the sake of my servant David and for the sake of Jerusalem, the city I have chosen out of all the tribes of Israel. I have 33 done this because Solomon has forsaken me; he has prostrated himself before Ashtoreth goddess of the Sidonians, Kemosh god of Moab, and Milcom god of the Ammonites, and has not conformed to my ways. He has not done what is right in my eyes or observed my statutes and judgements as David his father did. Never- 34 theless I will not take the whole kingdom from him, but will maintain his rule as long as he lives, for the sake of my chosen servant David, who did observe my commandments and statutes. But I will take the kingdom, 35 that is the ten tribes, from his son and give it to you. One tribe I will give to 36 his son, that my servant David may always have a flame burning before me in Jerusalem, the city which I chose to receive my Name. But I will 37 appoint you to rule over all that you can desire, and to be king over Israel. If you pay heed to all my commands, 38 if you conform to my ways and do what is right in my eyes, observing my statutes and commandments as my servant David did, then I will be with you. I will establish your family for ever as I did for David; I will give Israel to you, and punish David's 39 descendants as they have deserved, but not for ever."'

After this Solomon sought to kill 40 Jeroboam, but he fled to King Shishak in Egypt and remained there till Solomon's death.

The death of Solomon

The other acts and events of Solomon's 41[t] reign, and all his wisdom, are recorded in the annals of Solomon. The reign 42

---

s Verse 25 transposed to follow verse 22.

t Verses 41–3: cp. 2 Chr. 9. 29–31.

of King Solomon in Jerusalem over the whole of Israel lasted forty years.

43 Then he rested with his forefathers and was buried in the city of David his father, and he was succeeded by his son Rehoboam.

Rehoboam's unwise decision

12 1ᵘ Rehoboam went to Shechem, for all Israel had gone there to make him 2 king. When Jeroboam son of Nebat, who was still in Egypt, heard of it, he remained there, having taken refuge 3 there to escape King Solomon. They now recalled him, and he and all the assembly of Israel came to Rehoboam 4 and said, 'Your father laid a cruel yoke upon us; but if you will now lighten the cruel slavery he imposed on us and the heavy yoke he laid on us, we 5 will serve you.' 'Give me three days,' he said, 'and come back again.' So the 6 people went away. King Rehoboam then consulted the elders who had been in attendance on his father Solomon while he lived: 'What answer do you advise me to give to this people?' 7 And they said, 'If today you are willing to serve this people, show yourself their servant now and speak kindly to them, and they will be your servants 8 ever after.' But he rejected the advice which the elders gave him. He next consulted those who had grown up with him, the young men in attend-9 ance, and asked them, 'What answer do you advise me to give to this people's request that I should lighten the yoke which my father laid on 10 them?' The young men replied, 'Give this answer to the people who say that your father made their yoke heavy and ask you to lighten it; tell them: "My little finger is thicker than 11 my father's loins. My father laid a heavy yoke on you; I will make it heavier. My father used the whip on 12 you; but I will use the lash."' Jeroboam and the people all came back to Rehoboam on the third day, as the 13 king had ordered. And the king gave them a harsh answer. He rejected the advice which the elders had given 14 him and spoke to the people as the young men had advised: 'My father made your yoke heavy; I will make it heavier. My father used the whip on 15 you; but I will use the lash.' So the king would not listen to the people; for the LORD had given this turn to the affair, in order that the word he had spoken by Ahijah of Shiloh to

ᵘ Verses 1–19: cp. 2 Chr. 10. 1–19.

Jeroboam son of Nebat might be fulfilled.

Israel secedes from Rehoboam

When all Israel saw that the king 16 would not listen to them, they answered:

What share have we in David?
We have no lot in the son of Jesse.
Away to your homes, O Israel;
now see to your own house, David.

So Israel went to their homes, and 17 Rehoboam ruled over those Israelites who lived in the cities of Judah.

Then King Rehoboam sent out 18 Adoram, the commander of the forced levies, but the Israelites stoned him to death; thereupon King Rehoboam mounted his chariot in haste and fled to Jerusalem. From that day to this, 19 the whole of Israel has been in rebellion against the house of David.

When the men of Israel heard that 20 Jeroboam had returned, they sent and called him to the assembly and made him king over the whole of Israel. The tribe of Judah alone followed the house of David.

When Rehoboam reached Jeru- 21 salem, he assembled all the house of Judah, the tribe of Benjamin also, a hundred and eighty thousand chosen warriors, to fight against the house of Israel and recover his kingdom. But the word of God came to Shem- 22 aiah the man of God: 'Say to Re- 23 hoboam son of Solomon, king of Judah, and to the house of Judah and to Benjamin and the rest of the people, "This is the word of the 24 LORD: You shall not go up to make war on your kinsmen the Israelites. Return to your homes, for this is my will."' So they listened to the word of the LORD and returned home, as the LORD had told them.

Jeroboam's rival religion

Then Jeroboam rebuilt Shechem in 25 the hill-country of Ephraim and took up residence there; from there he went out and built Penuel. 'As things now 26 stand,' he said to himself, 'the kingdom will revert to the house of David. If this people go up to sacrifice in the 27 house of the LORD in Jerusalem, it will revive their allegiance to their lord Rehoboam king of Judah, and they will kill me and return to King Rehoboam.' After giving thought to 28 the matter he made two calves of gold and said to the people, 'It is too

ᵛ Verses 21–4: cp. 2 Chr. 11. 1–4.

much trouble for you to go up to Jerusalem; here are your gods, Israel, that brought you up from Egypt.' 29 One he set up at Bethel and the other 30 he put at Dan, and this thing became a sin in Israel; the people went to Bethel to worship the one, and all the 31 way to Dan to worship the other. He set up shrines on the hill-tops also and appointed priests from every class of the people, who did not belong to the 32 Levites. He instituted a pilgrim-feast on the fifteenth day of the eighth month like that in Judah, and he offered sacrifices upon the altar. This he did at Bethel, sacrificing to the calves that he had made and compelling the priests of the hill-shrines, which he had set up, to serve at 33 Bethel. So he went up to the altar that he had made at Bethel on the fifteenth day of the eighth month; there, in a month of his own choosing, he instituted for the Israelites a pilgrim-feast and himself went up to the altar to burn the sacrifice.

The LORD shows disapproval

13 As Jeroboam stood by the altar to burn the sacrifice, a man of God from Judah, moved by the word of the 2 LORD, appeared at Bethel. He inveighed against the altar in the LORD's name, crying out, 'O altar, altar! This is the word of the LORD: "Listen! A child shall be born to the house of David, named Josiah. He will sacrifice upon you the priests of the hill-shrines who make offerings upon you, and he will burn human 3 bones upon you."' He gave a sign the same day: 'This is the sign which the LORD has ordained: This altar will be rent in pieces and the ashes upon it 4 will be spilt.' When King Jeroboam heard the sentence which the man of God pronounced against the altar at Bethel, he pointed to him from the altar and said, 'Seize that man!' Immediately the hand which he had pointed at him became paralysed, so 5 that he could not draw it back. The altar too was rent in pieces and the ashes were spilt, in fulfilment of the sign that the man of God had given at 6 the LORD's command. The king appealed to the man of God to pacify the LORD his God and pray for him that his hand might be restored. The man of God did as he asked; his hand was restored and became as it had 7 been before. Then the king said to the man of God, 'Come home and take refreshment at my table, and let me

give you a present.' But the man of 8 God answered, 'If you were to give me half your house, I would not enter it with you: I will eat and drink nothing in this place, for the LORD's command 9 to me was to eat and drink nothing, and not to go back by the way I came.' So he went back another way; 10 he did not return by the road he had taken to Bethel.

The prophet disobeys the LORD

At that time there was an aged pro- 11 phet living in Bethel. His sons came and recounted to him all that the man of God had done in Bethel that day; they also told their father what he had said to the king. Their father 12 said to them, 'Which road did he take?' They pointed out the road taken by the man of God who had come from Judah. He said to his sons, 'Saddle 13 an ass for me.' They saddled the ass, and he mounted it and went after the 14 man of God. He found him seated under a terebinth and said to him, 'Are you the man of God who came from Judah?' And he said, 'Yes, I am.' 'Come home and eat with me', said 15 the prophet. 'I cannot go back with 16 you or enter your house,' said the other; 'I can neither eat nor drink with you in this place, for it was told 17 me by the word of the LORD: "You shall eat and drink nothing there, nor shall you go back the way you came."' And the old man said to him, 'I also 18 am a prophet, as you are; and an angel commanded me by the word of the LORD to bring you home with me to eat and drink with me.' He was lying; but the man of Judah went 19 back with him and ate and drank in his house. While they were still 20 seated at table the word of the LORD came to the prophet who had brought him back, and he cried out to the man 21 of God from Judah, 'This is the word of the LORD: "You have defied the word of the LORD your God and have not obeyed his command; you have 22 come back to eat and to drink in the place where he forbade it; therefore your body shall not be laid in the grave of your forefathers."'

The prophet's death and burial

After they had eaten and drunk, he 23 saddled an ass for the prophet whom he had brought back. As he went on 24 his way a lion met him and killed him, and his body was left lying in the road, with the ass and the lion both standing beside it. Some passers-by 25 saw the body lying in the road and the lion standing beside it, and they brought the news to the city where the 26 old prophet lived. When the prophet who had caused him to break his journey heard it, he said, 'It is the man of God who defied the word of the LORD. The LORD has given him to the lion, and it has broken his neck and killed him in fulfilment of the word of the 27 LORD.' He told his sons to saddle an 28 ass and, when they had saddled it, he set out and found the body lying in the road with the ass and the lion standing beside it; the lion had neither devoured the body nor broken the 29 back of the ass. Then the prophet lifted the body of the man of God, laid it on the ass and brought it back to his own city to mourn over it and 30 bury it. He laid the body in his own grave and they mourned for him, say- 31 ing, 'My brother, my brother!' After burying him, he said to his sons, 'When I die, bury me in the grave where the man of God lies buried; 32 lay my bones beside his; for the sentence which he pronounced at the LORD's command against the altar in Bethel and all the hill-shrines of Samaria shall be carried out.'

Ahijah pronounces judgement on Jeroboam

33 After this Jeroboam still did not abandon his evil ways but went on appointing priests for the hill-shrines from all classes of the people; any man who offered himself he would consecrate to be priest of a hill-shrine. 34 By doing this he brought guilt upon his own house and doomed it to utter destruction.

14 At that time Jeroboam's son Abi- 2 jah fell ill, and Jeroboam said to his wife, 'Come now, disguise yourself so that people may not be able to recognize you as my wife, and go to Shiloh. Ahijah the prophet is there, the man who said I was to be king 3 over this people. Take with you ten loaves, some raisins, and a flask of syrup, and go to him; he will tell you what will happen to the child.' 4 Jeroboam's wife did so; she set off at once for Shiloh and came to Ahijah's house. Now Ahijah could not see, for his eyes were fixed in the blindness 5 of old age, and the LORD had said to him, 'The wife of Jeroboam is on her way to consult you about her son, who is ill; you shall give her such and such an answer.' When she came in, 6 concealing who she was, and Ahijah

heard her footsteps at the door, he said, 'Come in, wife of Jeroboam. Why conceal who you are? I have heavy news for you. Go and tell Jeroboam: 7 "This is the word of the LORD the God of Israel: I raised you out of the people and appointed you prince over my people Israel; I tore away the 8 kingdom from the house of David and gave it to you; but you have not been like my servant David, who kept my commands and followed me with his whole heart, doing only what was right in my eyes. You have 9 outdone all your predecessors in wickedness; you have provoked me to anger by making for yourself other gods and images of cast metal; and you have turned your back on me. For this I will bring disaster on the 10 house of Jeroboam and I will destroy them all, every mother's son, whether still under the protection of the family or not, and I will sweep away the house of Jeroboam in Israel, as a man sweeps up dung until none is left. Those of that house who die in the 11 city shall be food for the dogs, and those who die in the country shall be food for the birds. It is the word of the LORD."

'You must go home now; the mo- 12 ment you set foot in the city, the child will die. All Israel will mourn for 13 him and bury him; he alone of all Jeroboam's family will have proper burial, because in him alone could the LORD the God of Israel find anything good. Then the LORD will set up a 14 king over Israel who shall put an end to the house of Jeroboam. This first; and what next? The LORD will strike 15 Israel, till it trembles like a reed in the water; he will uproot its people from this good land which he gave to their forefathers and scatter them beyond the Euphrates, because they have made their sacred poles and provoked the LORD's anger. And he will aban- 16 don Israel for the sins that Jeroboam has committed and has led Israel to commit.' Jeroboam's wife went home 17 at once to Tirzah and, as she crossed the threshold of the house, the boy died. They buried him, and all Israel 18 mourned over him; and thus the word of the LORD was fulfilled which he had spoken through his servant Ahijah the prophet.

Other records of Jeroboam's reign

The other events of Jeroboam's reign, 19 in war and peace, are recorded in the annals of the kings of Israel. He 20 reigned twenty-two years; then he rested with his forefathers and was succeeded by his son Nadab.

Wickedness in Judah

21 In Judah Rehoboam son of Solomon had become king. He was forty-one years old when he came to the throne, and he reigned for seventeen years in Jerusalem, the city which the LORD had chosen out of all the tribes of Israel to receive his Name. Rehoboam's mother was a woman of
22 Ammon called Naamah. Judah did what was wrong in the eyes of the LORD, rousing his jealous indignation by the sins they committed, beyond anything that their forefathers had
23 done. They erected hill-shrines, sacred pillars, and sacred poles, on every high hill and under every spreading
24 tree. Worse still, all over the country there were male prostitutes attached to the shrines, and the people adopted all the abominable practices of the nations whom the LORD had dispossessed in favour of Israel.

The Temple is plundered

25 w In the fifth year of Rehoboam's reign Shishak king of Egypt attacked Jeru-
26 salem. He removed the treasures of the house of the LORD and of the royal palace, and seized everything, including all the shields of gold that
27 Solomon had made. King Rehoboam replaced them with bronze shields and entrusted them to the officers of the escort who guarded the entrance
28 of the royal palace. Whenever the king entered the house of the LORD, the escort carried them; afterwards they returned them to the guard-room.

Other records of Rehoboam's reign

29 x The other acts and events of Rehoboam's reign are recorded in the
30 annals of the kings of Judah. There was continual fighting between him
31 and Jeroboam. He rested with his forefathers and was buried with them in the city of David. (His mother was a woman of Ammon, whose name was Naamah.) He was succeeded by his son Abijam.

Abijam reigns over Judah

15 In the eighteenth year of the reign of Jeroboam son of Nebat, Abijam be-
2 came king of Judah. He reigned in Jerusalem for three years; his mother was Maacah granddaughter of Abi-
3 shalom. All the sins that his father had committed before him he committed too, nor was he faithful to the LORD his God as his ancestor David
4 had been. But for David's sake the LORD his God gave him a flame to burn in Jerusalem, by establishing his dynasty and making Jerusalem
5 secure, because David had done what was right in the eyes of the LORD and had not disobeyed any of his commandments all his life, except in the
7 matter of Uriah the Hittite. y The other acts and events of Abijam's reign are recorded in the annals of the kings of Judah. There was fighting
8 between Abijam and Jeroboam. And Abijam rested with his forefathers and was buried in the city of David; and he was succeeded by his son Asa.

Asa reigns over Judah

9 In the twentieth year of Jeroboam king of Israel, Asa became king of
10 Judah. He reigned in Jerusalem for forty-one years; his grandmother was Maacah granddaughter of Abishalom.
11 Asa did what was right in the eyes of
12 the LORD, like his ancestor David. He expelled from the land the male prostitutes attached to the shrines and did away with all the idols which his predecessors had made. He even de-
13 z prived his own grandmother Maacah of her rank as queen mother because she had an obscene object made for the worship of Asherah; Asa cut it down and burnt it in the gorge of the Ki-
14 dron. Although the hill-shrines were allowed to remain, Asa himself remained faithful to the LORD all his
15 life. He brought into the house of the LORD all his father's votive offerings and his own, gold and silver and sacred vessels.

Asa's alliance with Ben-hadad

16 Asa was at war with Baasha king of
17 a Israel all through their reigns. Baasha king of Israel invaded Judah and fortified Ramah to cut off all access to Asa
18 king of Judah. So Asa took all the gold and silver that remained in the treasuries of the house of the LORD and of the royal palace, and sent his servants with them to Ben-hadad son of Tabrimmon, son of Hezion, king of Aram, whose capital was Damascus,
19 with instructions to say, 'There is an

w Verses 25–8: cp. 2 Chr. 12. 9–11.   x Verses 29–31: cp. 2 Chr. 12. 13–16.   y Prob. rdg.; Heb. adds. (6) There was war between Rehoboam and Jeroboam all his days (cp. 14. 30).   z Verses 13–15: cp 2 Chr. 15. 16–18.   a Verses 17–22: cp 2 Chr. 16. 1–6.

alliance between us, as there was between our fathers. I now send you this present of silver and gold; break off your alliance with Baasha king of Israel, so that he may abandon 20 his campaign against me.' Ben-hadad listened willingly to King Asa; he ordered the commanders of his armies to move against the cities of Israel, and they attacked Iyyon, Dan, Abel-beth-maacah, and that part of Kin-nereth which marches with the land 21 of Naphtali. When Baasha heard of it, he stopped fortifying Ramah and 22 fell back on Tirzah. Then King Asa issued a proclamation requiring every man in Judah to join in removing the stones of Ramah and the timbers with which Baasha had fortified it; no one was exempted; and he used them to fortify Geba of Benjamin and Mizpah.

Other records of Asa's reign

23b All the other events of Asa's reign, his exploits and his achievements, and the cities he built, are recorded in the annals of the kings of Judah. But in his old age his feet were crippled by 24 disease. He rested with his forefathers and was buried with them in the city of his ancestor David; and he was suc-ceeded by his son Jehoshaphat.

Nadab reigns over Israel

25 Nadab son of Jeroboam became king of Israel in the second year of Asa king of Judah, and he reigned for two 26 years. He did what was wrong in the eyes of the LORD and followed in his father's footsteps, repeating the sin which he had led Israel to commit. 27 Baasha son of Ahijah, of the house of Issachar, conspired against him and attacked him at Gibbethon, a Philis-tine city, which Nadab was besieging 28 with all his forces. And Baasha slew him and usurped the throne in the 29 third year of Asa king of Judah. As soon as he became king, he struck down all the family of Jeroboam, des-troying every living soul and leaving not one survivor. Thus the word of the LORD was fulfilled which he spoke through his servant Ahijah the Shilo-30 nite. This happened because of the sins of Jeroboam and the sins which he led Israel to commit, and because he had provoked the anger of the LORD 31 God of Israel. The other events of Nadab's reign and all his acts are re-corded in the annals of the kings of 32 Israel. Asa was at war with Baasha king of Israel all through their reigns.

Baasha reigns over Israel

33 In the third year of Asa king of Judah, Baasha son of Ahijah became king of all Israel in Tirzah and reigned 34 twenty-four years. He did what was wrong in the eyes of the LORD and followed in Jeroboam's footsteps, re-peating the sin which he had led Israel to commit. Then the word of 16 the LORD came to Jehu son of Hanani 2 concerning Baasha: 'I raised you from the dust and made you a prince over my people Israel, but you have followed in the footsteps of Jeroboam and have led my people Israel into sin, and have provoked me to anger 3 with their sins. Therefore I will sweep away Baasha and his house and will deal with it as I dealt with the house 4 of Jeroboam son of Nebat. Those of Baasha's family who die in the city shall be food for the dogs, and those who die in the country shall be food 5 for the birds.' The other events of Baasha's reign, his achievements and his exploits, are recorded in the annals 6 of the kings of Israel. Baasha rested with his forefathers and was buried in Tirzah; and he was succeeded by his 7 son Elah. Moreover the word of the LORD concerning Baasha and his family came through the prophet Jehu son of Hanani, because of all the wrong that he had done in the eyes of the LORD, thereby provoking his anger: because he had not only sinned like the house of Jeroboam, but had also brought destruction upon it.

Elah reigns over Israel

8 In the twenty-sixth year of Asa king of Judah, Elah son of Baasha became king of Israel and he reigned in Tirzah 9 two years. Zimri, who was in his ser-vice commanding half the chariotry, plotted against him. The king was in Tirzah drinking himself drunk in the house of Arza, comptroller of the 10 household there, when Zimri broke in and attacked him, assassinated him and made himself king. This took place in the twenty-seventh year of 11 Asa king of Judah. As soon as he had become king and was enthroned, he struck down all the family of Baasha and left not a single mother's son 12 alive, kinsman or friend. He destroyed the whole family of Baasha, and thus fulfilled the word of the LORD con-cerning Baasha, spoken through the 13 prophet Jehu. This was what came of all the sins which Baasha and his son

b Verses 23, 24: cp. 2 Chr. 16. 11–14.

Elah had committed and the sins into which they had led Israel, provoking the anger of the LORD the God of 4 Israel with their worthless idols. The other events and acts of Elah's reign are recorded in the annals of the kings of Israel.

Rival factions in Israel

5 In the twenty-seventh year of Asa king of Judah, Zimri reigned in Tirzah for seven days. At the time the army was investing the Philistine city 6 of Gibbethon. When the Israelite troops in the field heard of Zimri's conspiracy and the murder of the king, there and then in the camp they made their commander Omri king 7 of Israel by common consent. Then Omri and his whole force withdrew from Gibbethon and laid siege to Tir-8 zah. Zimri, as soon as he saw that the city had fallen, retreated to the keep of the royal palace, set the whole of it on fire over his head and so perished. 9 This was what came of the sin he had committed by doing what was wrong in the eyes of the LORD and following in the footsteps of Jeroboam, repeating the sin into which he had led 10 Israel. The other events of Zimri's reign, and his conspiracy, are recorded in the annals of the kings of Israel.

11 Thereafter the people of Israel were split into two factions: one supported Tibni son of Ginath, determined to make him king; the other supported 12 Omri. Omri's party proved the stronger; Tibni lost his life and Omri became king.

Omri reigns over Israel

13 It was in the thirty-first year of Asa king of Judah that Omri became king of Israel and he reigned twelve years, 14 six of them in Tirzah. He bought the hill of Samaria from Shemer for two talents of silver and built a city on it which he named Samaria after She-15 mer the owner of the hill. Omri did what was wrong in the eyes of the LORD; he outdid all his predecessors 16 in wickedness. He followed in the footsteps of Jeroboam son of Nebat, repeating the sins which he had led Israel to commit, so that they provoked the anger of the LORD their 17 God with their worthless idols. The other events of Omri's reign, and his exploits, are recorded in the annals of 18 the kings of Israel. So Omri rested with his forefathers and was buried in Samaria; and he was succeeded by his son Ahab.

Ahab reigns over Israel

Ahab son of Omri became king of 29 Israel in the thirty-eighth year of Asa king of Judah, and he reigned over Israel in Samaria for twenty-two years. He did more that was wrong in 30 the eyes of the LORD than all his predecessors. As if it were not enough for 31 him to follow the sinful ways of Jeroboam son of Nebat, he contracted a marriage with Jezebel daughter of Ethbaal king of Sidon, and went and worshipped Baal; he prostrated himself before him and erected an altar to 32 him in the temple of Baal which he built in Samaria. He also set up a 33 sacred pole; indeed he did more to provoke the anger of the LORD the God of Israel than all the kings of Israel before him. In his days Hiel 34 of Bethel rebuilt Jericho; laying its foundations cost him his eldest son Abiram, and the setting up of its gates cost him Segub his youngest son. Thus was fulfilled what the LORD had spoken through Joshua son of Nun.

Food during famine

Elijah the Tishbite, of Tishbe in Gil- 17 ead, said to Ahab, 'I swear by the life of the LORD the God of Israel, whose servant I am, that there shall be neither dew nor rain these coming years unless I give the word.' Then 2 the word of the LORD came to him: 'Leave this place and turn eastwards; 3 and go into hiding in the ravine of Kerith east of the Jordan. You shall 4 drink from the stream, and I have commanded the ravens to feed you there.' He did as the LORD had told 5 him: he went and stayed in the ravine of Kerith east of the Jordan, and the 6 ravens brought him bread and meat morning and evening, and he drank from the stream. After a while the 7 stream dried up, for there had been no rain in the land. Then the word of the 8 LORD came to him: 'Go now to Zare- 9 phath, a village of Sidon, and stay there; I have commanded a widow there to feed you.' So he went off to 10 Zarephath. When he reached the entrance to the village, he saw a widow gathering sticks, and he called to her and said, 'Please bring me a little water in a pitcher to drink.' As she 11 went to fetch it, he called after her, 'Bring me, please, a piece of bread as well.' But she said, 'As the LORD your 12 God lives, I have no food to sustain me except a handful of flour in a jar and

a little oil in a flask. Here I am, gathering two or three sticks to go and cook something for my son and myself be-
13 fore we die.' 'Never fear,' said Elijah; 'go and do as you say; but first make me a small cake from what you have and bring it out to me; and after that make something for your son and
14 yourself. For this is the word of the LORD the God of Israel: "The jar of flour shall not give out nor the flask of oil fail, until the LORD sends rain
15 on the land."' She went and did as Elijah had said, and there was food for him and for her and her family for
16 a long time. The jar of flour did not give out nor did the flask of oil fail, as the word of the LORD foretold through Elijah.

Elijah revives the widow's son

17 Afterwards the son of this woman, the mistress of the house, fell ill and grew worse, until at last his
18 breathing ceased. Then she said to Elijah, 'What made you interfere, you man of God? You came here to bring my sins to light and kill my son!'
19 'Give me your son', he said. He took the boy from her arms and carried him up to the roof-chamber where his lodging was, and laid him on his own
20 bed. Then he called out to the LORD, 'O LORD my God, is this thy care for the widow with whom I lodge, that thou hast been so cruel to her son?'
21 Then he breathed deeply[c] upon the child three times and called on the LORD, 'O LORD my God, let the breath of life, I pray, return to the body of
22 this child.' The LORD listened to Elijah's cry, and the breath of life returned to the child's body, and he
23 revived; Elijah lifted him up and took him down from the roof into the house, gave him to his mother and said, 'Look,
24 your son is alive.' Then she said to Elijah, 'Now I know for certain that you are a man of God and that the word of the LORD on your lips is truth.'

Ahab searches for fodder

18 Time went by, and in the third year the word of the LORD came to Elijah: 'Go and show yourself to Ahab, and I
2 will send rain upon the land.' So he went to show himself to Ahab. At this time the famine in Samaria was at its
3 height, and Ahab summoned Obadiah, the comptroller of his household, a
4 devout worshipper of the LORD. When Jezebel massacred the prophets of the LORD, he had taken a hundred of

them and hidden them in caves, fifty by fifty, giving them food and drink
5 to keep them alive. Ahab said to Obadiah, 'Let us go through the land, both of us, to every spring and gully; if we can find enough grass we may keep the horses and mules alive and
6 lose none of our cattle.' They divided the land between them for their survey, Ahab going one way by himself and Obadiah another.

Obadiah encounters Elijah

7 As Obadiah was on his way, Elijah met him. Obadiah recognized him and fell prostrate before him and said, 'Can it be you, my lord Elijah?' 'Yes,'
8 he said, 'it is I; go and tell your master
9 that Elijah is here.' 'What wrong have I done?' said Obadiah. 'Why should you give me into Ahab's hands? He will put me to death. As
10 the LORD your God lives, there is no nation or kingdom to which my master has not sent in search of you. If they said, "He is not here", he made that kingdom or nation swear on oath
11 that they could not find you. Yet now you say, "Go and tell your master
12 that Elijah is here." What will happen? As soon as I leave you, the spirit of the LORD will carry you away, who knows where? I shall go and tell Ahab, and when he fails to find you, he will kill me. Yet I have been a worshipper of the LORD from boyhood.
13 Have you not been told, my lord, what I did when Jezebel put the LORD's prophets to death, how I hid a hundred of them in caves, fifty by fifty, and kept them alive with food
14 and drink? And now you say, "Go and tell your master that Elijah is here"! He will kill me.' Elijah an-
15 swered, 'As the LORD of Hosts lives, whose servant I am, I swear that I will show myself to him this very day.'
16 So Obadiah went to find Ahab and gave him the message, and Ahab went to meet Elijah.

Elijah confronts Ahab

17 As soon as Ahab saw Elijah, he said to him, 'Is it you, you troubler of
18 Israel?' 'It is not I who have troubled Israel,' he replied, 'but you and your father's family, by forsaking the commandments of the LORD and following Baal. But now, send and summon all
19 Israel to meet me on Mount Carmel, and the four hundred and fifty prophets of Baal with them and the four hundred prophets of the goddess

c *Or stretched himself.*

Asherah, who are Jezebel's pensioners.'
20 So Ahab sent out to all the Israelites and assembled the prophets on
21 Mount Carmel. Elijah stepped forward and said to the people, 'How long will you sit on the fence? If the LORD is God, follow him; but if Baal,
22 answer.' Then Elijah said to the people, 'I am the only prophet of the LORD still left, but there are four hundred
23 and fifty prophets of Baal. Bring two bulls; let them choose one for themselves, cut it up and lay it on the wood without setting fire to it, and I will prepare the other and lay it on the
24 wood without setting fire to it. You shall invoke your god by name and I will invoke the LORD by name; and the god who answers by fire, he is God.' And all the people shouted their approval.

No answer from Baal

25 Then Elijah said to the prophets of Baal, 'Choose one of the bulls and offer it first, for there are more of you; invoke your god by name, but do not
26 set fire to the wood.' So they took the bull provided for them and offered it, and they invoked Baal by name from morning until noon, crying, 'Baal, Baal, answer us'; but there was no sound, no answer. They danced wildly
27 beside the altar they had set up. At midday Elijah mocked them: 'Call louder, for he is a god; it may be he is deep in thought, or engaged, or on a journey; or he may have gone to
28 sleep and must be woken up.' They cried still louder and, as was their custom, gashed themselves with swords
29 and spears until the blood ran. All afternoon they raved and ranted till the hour of the regular sacrifice, but still there was no sound, no answer, no sign of attention.

The LORD answers by fire

30 Then Elijah said to all the people, 'Come here to me.' They all came, and he repaired the altar of the LORD
31 which had been torn down. He took twelve stones, one for each tribe of the sons of Jacob, the man named
32 Israel by the word of the LORD. With these stones he built an altar in the name of the LORD; he dug a trench round it big enough to hold two
33 measures of seed; he arranged the wood, cut up the bull and laid it on
34 the wood. Then he said, 'Fill four jars with water and pour it on the whole-

offering and on the wood.' They did so, and he said, 'Do it again.' They did it again, and he said, 'Do it a third time.'
35 They did it a third time, and the water ran all round the altar and even
36 filled the trench. At the hour of the regular sacrifice the prophet Elijah came forward and said, 'LORD God of Abraham, of Isaac, and of Israel, let it be known today that thou art God in Israel and that I am thy servant and have done all these things at thy
37 command. Answer me, O LORD, answer me and let this people know that thou, LORD, art God and that it is thou that hast caused them to be backsliders.'[d] Then the fire of the LORD
38 fell. It consumed the whole-offering, the wood, the stones, and the earth, and licked up the water in the trench.
39 When all the people saw it, they fell prostrate and cried, 'The LORD is God, the LORD is God.' Then Elijah said to
40 them, 'Seize the prophets of Baal; let not one of them escape.' They seized them, and Elijah took them down to the Kishon and slaughtered them there in the valley.

Elijah prays for rain

41 Elijah said to Ahab, 'Go back now, eat and drink, for I hear the sound of coming rain.' He did so, while Elijah
42 himself climbed to the crest of Carmel. There he crouched on the ground with his face between his knees. He
43 said to his servant, 'Go and look out to the west.' He went and looked; 'There is nothing to see', he said.
44 Seven times Elijah ordered him back, and seven times he went. The seventh time he said, 'I see a cloud no bigger than a man's hand, coming up from the west.' 'Now go', said Elijah, 'and tell Ahab to harness his chariot and be off, or the rain will stop him.'
45 Meanwhile the sky had grown black with clouds, the wind rose, and heavy rain began to fall. Ahab mounted his
46 chariot and set off for Jezreel; but the power of the LORD had come upon Elijah: he tucked up his robe and ran before Ahab all the way to Jezreel.

Elijah flies from Ahab

19 Ahab told Jezebel all that Elijah had done and how he had put all the prophets to death with the sword.
2 Jezebel then sent a messenger to Elijah to say, 'The gods do the same to me and more, unless by this time tomorrow I have taken your life as
3 you took theirs.' He was afraid and

d Or thou that dost bring them back to their allegiance.

fled for his life. When he reached Beersheba in Judah, he left his servant 4 there and himself went a day's journey into the wilderness. He came upon a broom-bush, and sat down under it and prayed for death: 'It is enough,' he said; 'now, LORD, take my life, for I am no better than my fathers 5 before me.' He lay down under the bush and, while he slept, an angel touched him and said, 'Rise and eat.' 6 He looked, and there at his head was a cake baked on hot stones, and a pitcher of water. He ate and drank 7 and lay down again. The angel of the LORD came again and touched him a second time, saying, 'Rise and eat; 8 the journey is too much for you.' He rose and ate and drank and, sustained by this food, he went on for forty days and forty nights to Horeb, the mount 9 of God. He entered a cave and there he spent the night.

The LORD encourages Elijah

Suddenly the word of the LORD came to him: 'Why are you here, Elijah?' 10 'Because of my great zeal for the LORD the God of Hosts', he said. 'The people of Israel have forsaken thy covenant, torn down thy altars and put thy prophets to death with the sword. I alone am left, and they seek 11 to take my life.' The answer came: 'Go and stand on the mount before the LORD.' For the LORD was passing by: a great and strong wind came rending mountains and shattering rocks before him, but the LORD was not in the wind; and after the wind there was an earthquake, but the 12 LORD was not in the earthquake; and after the earthquake fire, but the LORD was not in the fire; and after 13 the fire a low murmuring sound. When Elijah heard it, he muffled his face in his cloak and went out and stood at the entrance of the cave. Then there came a voice: 'Why are you here, 14 Elijah?' 'Because of my great zeal for the LORD the God of Hosts', he said. 'The people of Israel have forsaken thy covenant, torn down thy altars and put thy prophets to death with the sword. I alone am left, and they seek to take my life.' 15 The LORD said to him, 'Go back by way of the wilderness of Damascus, enter the city and anoint Hazael to 16 be king of Aram; anoint Jehu son[e] of Nimshi to be king of Israel, and Elisha son of Shaphat of Abel-meholah to be 17 prophet in your place. Anyone who

escapes the sword of Hazael Jehu will slay, and anyone who escapes the sword of Jehu Elisha will slay. But I 18 will leave seven thousand in Israel, all who have not bent the knee to Baal, all whose lips have not kissed him.'

The call of Elisha

Elijah departed and found Elisha son 19 of Shaphat ploughing; there were twelve pair of oxen ahead of him, and he himself was with the last of them. As Elijah passed, he threw his cloak over him, and Elisha, leaving his oxen, 20 ran after Elijah and said, 'Let me kiss my father and mother goodbye, and then I will follow you.' 'Go back,' he replied; 'what have I done to prevent you?' He followed him no further but 21 went home, took his pair of oxen, slaughtered them and burnt the wooden gear to cook the flesh, which he gave to the people to eat. Then he followed Elijah and became his disciple.

Ahab defeats the Aramaeans

Ben-hadad king of Aram, having 20 mustered all his forces, and taking with him thirty-two kings with their horses and chariots, marched against Samaria to take it by siege or assault. He sent envoys into the city to Ahab 2 king of Israel to say, 'Hear what Ben- 3 hadad says: Your silver and gold are mine, your wives and your splendid sons are mine.'[f] The king of Israel 4 answered, 'As you say, my lord king, I am yours and all that I have.' The 5 envoys came again and said, 'Hear what Ben-hadad says: I demand that you hand over your silver and gold, your wives and your sons. This time 6 tomorrow I will send my servants to search your house and your subjects' houses and to take possession of everything you prize, and remove it.' The king of Israel then summoned all 7 the elders of the land and said, 'You see this? The man is plainly picking a quarrel; for I did not demur when he sent to claim my wives and my sons, my silver and gold.' All the elders 8 and all the people answered, 'Do not listen to him; you must not consent.' So he gave this reply to Ben-hadad's 9 envoys: 'Say to my lord the king: I accepted your majesty's demands on the first occasion; but what you now ask I cannot do.' The envoys went away and reported to their master, and Ben-hadad sent back word: 'The 10 gods do the same to me and more, if

e Or grandson (cp. 2 Kgs. 9. 2).   *f Or are your wives and your sons any good to me?*

there is enough dust in Samaria to provide a handful for each of my men.'

11 The king of Israel made reply, 'Remind him of the saying: "The lame must not think himself a match for
12 the nimble."' This message reached Ben-hadad while he and the kings were drinking in their quarters.[g] At once he ordered his men to attack the city, and they did so.

13 Meanwhile a prophet had come to Ahab king of Israel and said to him, 'This is the word of the LORD: "You see this great rabble? Today I will give it into your hands and you shall
14 know that I am the LORD."' 'Whom will you use for that?' asked Ahab. 'The young men who serve the district officers', was the answer. 'Who will draw up the line of battle?' asked the
15 king. 'You', said the prophet. Then Ahab called up these young men, two hundred and thirty-two all told, and behind them the people of Israel,
16 seven thousand in all. They went out at midday, while Ben-hadad and his allies, those thirty-two kings, were drinking themselves drunk in their
17 quarters.[g] The young men sallied out first, and word was sent to Ben-hadad that a party had come out of
18 Samaria. 'If they have come out for peace,' he said, 'take them alive; if for battle, take them alive.'

19 So out of the city the young men
20 went, and the army behind them; each struck down his man, and the Aramaeans fled. The Israelites pursued them, but Ben-hadad king of Aram escaped on horseback with some of
21 the cavalry. Then the king of Israel advanced and captured the horses and chariots, inflicting a heavy defeat on the Aramaeans.

Ben-hadad prepares another attack

22 Then the prophet came to the king of Israel and said to him, 'Build up your forces; you know what you must do. At the turn of the year the king of
23 Aram will renew the attack.' But the king of Aram's ministers gave him this advice: 'Their gods are gods of the hills; that is why they defeated us. Let us fight them in the plain; and then we shall have the upper hand.
24 What you must do is to relieve the kings of their command and appoint
25 other officers in their place. Raise another army like the one you have lost. Bring your cavalry and chariots up to their former strength, and then let us fight them in the plain, and we

shall have the upper hand.' He listened to their advice and acted on it.

26 At the turn of the year Ben-hadad mustered the Aramaeans and ad-
27 vanced to Aphek to attack Israel. The Israelites too were mustered and formed into companies, and then went out to meet them and encamped opposite them. They seemed no better than a pair of new-born kids, while the Aramaeans covered the country-
28 side. The man of God came to the king of Israel and said, 'This is the word of the LORD: The Aramaeans may think that the LORD is a god of the hills and not a god of the valleys; but I will give all this great rabble into your hands and you shall know that I am the LORD.'

Ahab spares Ben-hadad

29 They lay in camp opposite one another for seven days; on the seventh day battle was joined and the Israelites destroyed a hundred thousand of the Aramaean infantry in one day. The
30 survivors fled to Aphek, into the citadel, and the city wall fell upon the twenty-seven thousand men who were left. Ben-hadad took refuge in the citadel, retreating into an inner room;
31 and his attendants said to him, 'Listen; we have heard that the kings of Israel are men to be trusted. Let us therefore put sackcloth round our waists and wind rough cord round our heads and go out to the king of Israel. It may be that he will spare your life.'
32 So they fastened on the sackcloth and the cord, and went to the king of Israel and said, 'Your servant Ben-hadad pleads for his life.' 'My royal
33 cousin,' he said, 'is he still alive?' The men, taking the word for a favourable omen, caught it up at once and said, 'Your cousin, yes, Ben-hadad.' 'Go and fetch him', he said. Then Ben-hadad came out and Ahab invited
34 him into his chariot. And Ben-hadad said to him, 'I will restore the cities which my father took from your father, and you may establish for yourself a trading quarter in Damascus, as my father did in Samaria.' 'On these terms', said Ahab, 'I will let you go.' So he granted him a treaty and let him go.

The LORD condemns Ahab

35 One of a company of prophets, at the command of the LORD, ordered a certain man to strike him, but the
36 man refused. 'Because you have not

g *in their quarters: or* at Succoth.

obeyed the LORD,' said the prophet, 'when you leave me, a lion will attack you.' When the man left, a lion did 37 meet him and attacked him. The prophet fell in with another man and ordered him to strike him. He struck 38 and wounded him. Then the prophet went off, with a bandage over his eyes, and thus disguised waited by the way- 39 side for the king. As the king was passing, he called out to him, 'Sir, I went into the thick of the battle, and a soldier came over to me with a prisoner and said, "Take charge of this fellow. If by any chance he gets away, your life shall be forfeit, or you 40 shall pay a talent of silver." As I was busy with one thing and another, sir, he disappeared.' The king of Israel said to him, 'You deserve to die.' And he said to the king of Israel,[h] 'You have passed sentence on yourself.' 41 Then he tore the bandage from his eyes, and the king of Israel saw that he 42 was one of the prophets. And he said to the king, 'This is the word of the LORD: "Because you let that man go when I had put him under a ban, your life shall be forfeit for his life, your 43 people for his people."' The king of Israel went home sullen and angry and entered Samaria.

Ahab and Naboth's vineyard

21 Naboth of Jezreel had a vineyard near the palace of Ahab king of 2 Samaria. One day Ahab made a proposal to Naboth: 'Your vineyard is close to my palace; let me have it for a garden; I will give you a better vineyard in exchange for it or, if you 3 prefer, its value in silver.' But Naboth answered, 'The LORD forbid that I should let you have land which has 4 always been in my family.' So Ahab went home sullen and angry because Naboth would not let him have his ancestral land. He lay down on his bed, covered his face and refused to 5 eat. His wife Jezebel came in to him and said, 'What makes you so sullen 6 and why do you refuse to eat?' He told her, 'I proposed to Naboth of Jezreel that he should let me have his vineyard at its value or, if he liked, in exchange for another; but he would 7 not let me have the vineyard.' 'Are you or are you not king in Israel?' said Jezebel. 'Come, eat and take heart; I will make you a gift of the 8 vineyard of Naboth of Jezreel.' So she wrote a letter in Ahab's name, sealed

it with his seal and sent it to the elders and notables of Naboth's city, who sat in council with him. She 9 wrote: 'Proclaim a fast and give Naboth the seat of honour among the people. And see that two scoundrels 10 are seated opposite him to charge him with cursing God and the king, then take him out and stone him to death.' So the elders and notables of Naboth's 11 city, who sat with him in council, carried out the instructions Jezebel had sent them in her letter: they pro- 12 claimed a fast and gave Naboth the seat of honour, and these two scoun- 13 drels came in, sat opposite him and charged him publicly with cursing God and the king. Then they took him outside the city and stoned him, and 14 sent word to Jezebel that Naboth had been stoned to death.

Elijah pronounces judgement on Ahab

As soon as Jezebel heard that Naboth 15 had been stoned and was dead, she said to Ahab, 'Get up and take possession of the vineyard which Naboth refused to sell you, for he is no longer alive; Naboth of Jezreel is dead.' When Ahab heard that Naboth was 16 dead, he got up and went to the vineyard to take possession. Then the 17 word of the LORD came to Elijah the Tishbite: 'Go down at once to Ahab 18 king of Israel, who is in Samaria; you will find him in Naboth's vineyard, where he has gone to take possession. Say to him, "This is the word of the 19 LORD: Have you killed your man, and taken his land as well?" Say to him, "This is the word of the LORD: Where dogs licked the blood of Naboth, there dogs shall lick your blood."' Ahab 20 said to Elijah, 'Have you found me, my enemy?' 'I have found you,' he said, 'because you have sold yourself to do what is wrong in the eyes of the LORD. I will bring[i] disaster upon you; 21 I will sweep you away and destroy every mother's son of the house of Ahab in Israel, whether under protection of the family or not. And I will 22 deal with your house as I did with the house of Jeroboam son of Nebat and of Baasha son of Ahijah, because you have provoked my anger and led Israel into sin.' And the LORD went on 23 to say of Jezebel, 'Jezebel shall be eaten by dogs by the rampart of Jezreel. Of the house of Ahab, those 24 who die in the city shall be food for

---

[h] You deserve . . . Israel: *prob. rdg.; Heb. om.* LORD, I am bringing . . .

[i] he said, . . . bring: *or* he said, 'Because you . . .

the dogs, and those who die in the country shall be food for the birds.' 25 (Never was a man who sold himself to do what is wrong in the LORD's eyes as Ahab did, and all at the prompting 26 of Jezebel his wife. He committed gross abominations in going after false gods, doing everything that the Amorites did, whom the LORD had dispossessed in favour of Israel.) 27 When Ahab heard this, he rent his clothes, put on sackcloth and fasted; he lay down in his sackcloth and went 28 about muttering to himself. Then the word of the LORD came to Elijah the 29 Tishbite: 'Have you seen how Ahab has humbled himself before me? Because he has thus humbled himself, I will not bring disaster upon his house in his own lifetime, but in his son's.'

Jehoshaphat allies himself with Ahab

22 For three years there was no war between the Aramaeans and the Israel 2[j] ites, but in the third year Jehosha phat king of Judah went down to visit 3 the king of Israel. The latter said to his courtiers, 'You know that Ramoth-gilead belongs to us, and yet we do nothing to recover it from the king of 4 Aram.' He said to Jehoshaphat, 'Will you join me in attacking Ramoth-gilead?' Jehoshaphat said to the king of Israel, 'What is mine is yours: my 5 self, my people, and my horses.' Then Jehoshaphat said to the king of Israel, 'First let us seek counsel from the 6 LORD.' The king of Israel assembled the prophets, some four hundred of them, and asked them, 'Shall I attack Ramoth-gilead or shall I refrain?' 'Attack,' they answered; 'the Lord will deliver it into your hands.' 7 Jehoshaphat asked, 'Is there no other prophet of the LORD here through 8 whom we may seek guidance?' 'There is one more', the king of Israel answered, 'through whom we may seek guidance of the LORD, but I hate the man, because he prophesies no good for me; never anything but evil. His name is Micaiah son of Imlah.' Jehoshaphat exclaimed, 'My lord king, 9 let no such word pass your lips!' So the king of Israel called one of his eunuchs and told him to fetch Micaiah son of Imlah with all speed.

The prophets promise success

10 The king of Israel and Jehoshaphat king of Judah were seated on their thrones, in shining armour, at the entrance to the gate of Samaria, and all the prophets were prophesying before them. One of them, Zedekiah 11 son of Kenaanah, made himself horns of iron and said, 'This is the word of the LORD: "With horns like these you shall gore the Aramaeans and make an end of them."' In the same vein 12 all the prophets prophesied, 'Attack Ramoth-gilead and win the day; the LORD will deliver it into your hands.' The messenger sent to fetch Micaiah 13 told him that the prophets had with one voice given the king a favourable answer. 'And mind you agree with them', he added. 'As the LORD lives,' 14 said Micaiah, 'I will say only what the LORD tells me to say.'

Micaiah prophesies defeat

When Micaiah came into the king's 15 presence, the king said to him, 'Micaiah, shall we attack Ramoth-gilead or shall we refrain?' 'Attack and win the day,' he said; 'the LORD will deliver it into your hands.' 'How 16 often must I adjure you', said the king, 'to tell me nothing but the truth in the name of the LORD?' Then 17 Micaiah said, 'I saw all Israel scattered on the mountains, like sheep without a shepherd; and I heard the LORD say, "They have no master, let them go home in peace."' The king of Israel 18 said to Jehoshaphat, 'Did I not tell you that he never prophesies good for me, nothing but evil?' Micaiah 19 went on, 'Listen now to the word of the LORD. I saw the LORD seated on his throne, with all the host of heaven in attendance on his right and on his left. The LORD said, "Who will entice 20 Ahab to attack and fall on[k] Ramoth-gilead?" One said one thing and one said another; then a spirit came for 21 ward and stood before the LORD and said, "I will entice him." "How?" said the LORD. "I will go out", he 22 said, "and be a lying spirit in the mouth of all his prophets." "You shall entice him," said the LORD, "and you shall succeed; go and do it." You see, then, 23 how the LORD has put a lying spirit in the mouth of all these prophets of yours, because he has decreed dis aster for you.' Then Zedekiah son of 24 Kenaanah came up to Micaiah and struck him in the face: 'And how did the spirit of the LORD pass from me to speak to you?' he said. Micaiah 25 answered, 'That you will find out on the day when you run into an inner room to hide yourself.' Then the king of 26

j Verses 2–35: cp. 2 Chr. 18. 2–34.   *k* Or at.

Israel ordered Micaiah to be arrested and committed to the custody of Amon the governor of the city and Joash 27 the king's son.[l] 'Lock this fellow up', he said, 'and give him prison diet of bread and water until I come home 28 in safety.' Micaiah retorted, 'If you do return in safety, the LORD has not spoken by me.'

Ahab dies in battle

29 So the king of Israel and Jehoshaphat king of Judah marched on Ramoth-30 gilead, and the king of Israel said to Jehoshaphat, 'I will disguise myself to go into battle, but you shall wear your royal robes.' So he went into 31 battle in disguise. Now the king of Aram had commanded the thirty-two captains of his chariots not to engage all and sundry but the king of 32 Israel alone. When the captains saw Jehoshaphat, they thought he was the king of Israel and turned to attack 33 him. But Jehoshaphat cried out and, when the captains saw that he was not the king of Israel, they broke off 34 the attack on him. But one man drew his bow at random and hit the king of Israel where the breastplate joins the plates of the armour. So he said to his driver, 'Wheel round and take me out of the line; I am wounded.' 35 When the day's fighting reached its height, the king was facing the Aramaeans propped up in his chariot, and the blood from his wound flowed down upon the floor of the chariot; and in 36 the evening he died. At sunset the herald went through the ranks, crying, 'Every man to his city, every man to 37 his country.' Thus died the king. He was brought to Samaria and they 38 buried him there. The chariot was swilled out at the pool of Samaria, and the dogs licked up the blood, and the prostitutes washed themselves in it, in fulfilment of the word the LORD had spoken.

Other records of Ahab's reign

39 Now the other acts and events of Ahab's reign, the ivory house and all the cities he built, are recorded in the annals of the kings of Israel. So Ahab 40 rested with his forefathers and was succeeded by his son Ahaziah.

Jehoshaphat reigns over Judah

Jehoshaphat son of Asa had become 41 king of Judah in the fourth year of Ahab king of Israel. He was thirty-42 five years old when he came to the throne, and he reigned in Jerusalem for twenty-five years; his mother was Azubah daughter of Shilhi. He follow-43 ed in the footsteps of Asa his father and did not swerve from them; he did what was right in the eyes of the LORD. But the hill-shrines were allowed to remain; the people continued to slaughter and burn sacrifices there. Jehoshaphat remained at peace with 44 the king of Israel. The other events of 45 Jehoshaphat's reign, his exploits and his wars, are recorded in the annals of the kings of Judah. But he did away 46 with such of the male prostitutes attached to the shrines as were still left over from the days of Asa his father.

There was no king in Edom, only[n] 47 a viceroy of Jehoshaphat; he built 48 merchantmen to sail to Ophir for gold, but they never made the journey because they were wrecked at Ezion-geber. Ahaziah son of Ahab proposed 49 to Jehoshaphat that his own men should go to sea with his; but Jehoshaphat would not consent.

Jehoshaphat rested with his fore-50 fathers and was buried with them in the city of David his father, and was succeeded by his son Joram.

Ahaziah reigns over Israel

Ahaziah son of Ahab became king of 51 Israel in Samaria in the seventeenth year of Jehoshaphat king of Judah, and reigned over Israel for two years. He did what was wrong in the eyes of 52 the LORD, following in the footsteps of his father and mother and in those of Jeroboam son of Nebat, who had led Israel into sin. He served Baal 53 and worshipped him, and provoked the anger of the LORD the God of Israel, as his father had done.

l son: or deputy.   m Verses 41–3: cp. 2 Chr. 20. 31–3.   n only: prob. rdg.; Heb. om.

THE SECOND BOOK OF
KINGS

Elijah foretells Ahaziah's death

1 AFTER AHAB'S DEATH Moab rebelled against Israel.
2 Ahaziah fell through a latticed window in his roof-chamber in Samaria and injured himself; he sent messengers to inquire of Baal-zebub the god of Ekron whether he would re-
3 cover from his illness. The angel of the LORD ordered Elijah the Tishbite to go and meet the messengers of the king of Samaria and say to them, 'Is there no god in Israel, that you go to inquire of Baal-zebub the god of
4 Ekron? This is the word of the LORD to your master: "You shall not rise from the bed where you are lying; you
5 will die."' Then Elijah departed. The messengers went back to the king. When asked why they had returned,
6 they answered that a man had come to meet them and had ordered them to return and say to the king who had sent them, 'This is the word of the LORD: "Is there no god in Israel, that you send to inquire of Baal-zebub the god of Ekron? In consequence, you shall not rise from the bed where
7 you are lying; you will die."' The king asked them what kind of man it was who had met them and said this.
8 'A hairy man', they answered, 'with a leather apron round his waist.' 'It is Elijah the Tishbite', said the king.

Fire falls from heaven

9 Then the king sent a captain to him with his company of fifty. He went up and found the prophet sitting on a hill-top and said to him, 'Man of God, the king orders you to come down.'
10 Elijah answered the captain, 'If I am a man of God, may fire fall from heaven and consume you and your company!' Fire fell from heaven and consumed the officer and his fifty men.
11 The king sent another captain of fifty with his company, and he went up and said to the prophet, 'Man of God, this is the king's command: Come down
12 at once.' Elijah answered, 'If I am a man of God, may fire fall from heaven

and consume you and your company!' God's fire fell from heaven and consumed the man and his company.
13 The king sent the captain of a third company with his fifty men, and this third captain went up the hill to Elijah and knelt down before him and pleaded with him: 'Man of God, consider me and these fifty servants of yours, and set some value on our lives. Fire fell from heaven and con-
14 sumed the other two captains of fifty and their companies; but let my life have some value in your eyes.' The
15 angel of the LORD said to Elijah, 'Go down with him. Do not be afraid.' So he rose and went down with him to
16 the king, and he said, 'This is the word of the LORD: "You have sent to inquire of Baal-zebub the god of Ekron, and therefore you shall not rise from the bed where you are lying;
17 you will die."' The word of the LORD which Elijah had spoken was fulfilled, and Ahaziah died; and because he had no son, his brother Jehoram succeeded him in the second year of Joram son of Jehoshaphat king of Judah.

Other records of Ahaziah's reign

18 The other events of Ahaziah's reign are recorded in the annals of the kings of Israel.

Elijah is taken up to heaven

2 The time came when the LORD would take Elijah up to heaven in a whirlwind. Elijah and Elisha left Gilgal,
2 and Elijah said to Elisha, 'Stay here; for the LORD has sent me to Bethel.' But Elisha said, 'As the LORD lives, your life upon it, I will not leave you.' So they went down country to Bethel.
3 There a company of prophets came out to Elisha and said to him, 'Do you know that the LORD is going to take your lord and master from you today?' 'I do know,' he replied; 'say no more.'
4 Then Elijah said to him, 'Stay here, Elisha; for the LORD has sent me to Jericho.' But he replied, 'As the LORD lives, your life upon it, I will not leave

5 you.' So they went to Jericho. There a company of prophets came up to Elisha and said to him, 'Do you know that the LORD is going to take your lord and master from you today?' 'I do
6 know,' he said; 'say no more.' Then Elijah said to him, 'Stay here; for the LORD has sent me to the Jordan.' The other replied, 'As the LORD lives, your life upon it, I will not leave you.' So the two of them went on.
7 Fifty of the prophets followed them, and stood watching from a distance as the two of them stopped by the
8 Jordan. Elijah took his cloak, rolled it up and struck the water with it. The water divided to right and left, and they both crossed over on dry ground.
9 While they were crossing, Elijah said to Elisha, 'Tell me what I can do for you before I am taken from you.' Elisha said, 'Let me inherit a double
10 share of your spirit.' 'You have asked a hard thing', said Elijah. 'If you see me taken from you, may your wish be granted; if you do not, it shall not be
11 granted.' They went on, talking as they went, and suddenly there appeared chariots of fire and horses of fire, which separated them one from the other, and Elijah was carried up
12 in the whirlwind to heaven. When Elisha saw it, he cried, 'My father, my father, the chariots and the horsemen of Israel!', and he saw him no more. Then he took hold of his
13 mantle and rent it in two, and he picked up the cloak which had fallen from Elijah, and came back and stood on the bank of the Jordan.
14 There he too struck the water with Elijah's cloak and said, 'Where is the LORD the God of Elijah?' When he struck the water, it was again divided to right and left, and he crossed over.
15 The prophets from Jericho, who were watching, saw him and said, 'The spirit of Elijah has settled on Elisha.' So they came to meet him, and fell on
16 their faces before him and said, 'Your servants have fifty stalwart men. Let them go and search for your master; perhaps the spirit of the LORD has lifted him up and cast him on some mountain or into some valley.' But he said, 'No, you must not send them.'
17 They pressed him, however, until he had not the heart to refuse. So they sent out the fifty men but, though they searched for three days, they did
18 not find him. When they came back to Elisha, who had remained at Jericho, he said to them, 'Did I not tell you not to go?'

Elisha purifies Jericho's water supply

The people of the city said to Elisha, 19 'You can see how pleasantly our city is situated, but the water is polluted and the country is troubled with miscarriages.' He said, 'Fetch me a new 20 bowl and put some salt in it.' When they had fetched it, he went out to 21 the spring and, throwing the salt into it, he said, 'This is the word of the LORD: "I purify this water. It shall cause no more death or miscarriage."' The water has remained pure till this 22 day, in fulfilment of Elisha's word.

Boys jeer at Elisha

He went up from there to Bethel and, 23 as he was on his way, some small boys came out of the city and jeered at him, saying, 'Get along with you, bald head, get along.' He turned round and 24 looked at them and he cursed them in the name of the LORD; and two she-bears came out of a wood and mauled forty-two of them. From there he 25 went on to Mount Carmel, and thence back to Samaria.

Jehoram reigns over Israel

In the eighteenth year of Jehoshaphat 3 king of Judah, Jehoram son of Ahab became king of Israel in Samaria, and he reigned for twelve years. He did 2 what was wrong in the eyes of the LORD, though not as his father and his mother had done; he did remove the sacred pillar of the Baal which his father had made. Yet he persisted in 3 the sins into which Jeroboam son of Nebat had led Israel, and did not give them up.

Elisha provides water for the army

Mesha king of Moab was a sheep- 4 breeder, and he used to supply the king of Israel regularly with the wool of a hundred thousand lambs and a hundred thousand rams. When Ahab 5 died, the king of Moab rebelled against the king of Israel. Then King Jehor- 6 am came from Samaria and mustered all Israel. He also sent this message to 7 Jehoshaphat king of Judah: 'The king of Moab has rebelled against me. Will you join me in attacking Moab?' 'I will,' he replied; 'what is mine is yours: myself, my people, and my horses.' 'From which direction shall we attack?' 8 Jehoram asked. 'Through the wilderness of Edom', replied the other. So 9 the king of Israel set out with the king of Judah and the king of Edom. When they had been seven days on the

march, they had no water left for
10 the army or the pack-animals. Then
the king of Israel said, 'Alas, the Lord
has brought together three kings,
only to put us at the mercy of the
11 Moabites.' But Jehoshaphat said, 'Is
there not a prophet of the Lord here
through whom we may seek guidance
of the Lord?' One of the officers of
the king of Israel answered, 'Elisha
son of Shaphat is here, the man who
12 poured water on Elijah's hands.' 'The
word of the Lord is with him', said
Jehoshaphat. So the king of Israel and
Jehoshaphat and the king of Edom
13 went down to Elisha. Elisha said to
the king of Israel, 'Why do you come
to me? Go to the prophets of your
father and your mother.' But the king
of Israel said to him, 'No; the Lord
has called us three kings out to put us
14 at the mercy of the Moabites.' 'As the
Lord of Hosts lives, whom I serve,'
said Elisha, 'I would not spare a look
or a glance for you, if it were not for
my regard for Jehoshaphat king of
15 Judah. But now, fetch me a minstrel.'
They fetched a minstrel, and while he
was playing, the power of the Lord
16 came upon Elisha and said, 'This
is the word of the Lord: "Pools will
17 form all over this ravine." The Lord
has decreed that you shall see neither
wind nor rain, yet this ravine shall be
filled with water for you and your
army and your pack-animals to drink.
18 But that is a mere trifle in the sight of
the Lord; what he will also do, is to
19 put Moab at your mercy. You will
raze to the ground every fortified town
and every noble city; you will cut
down all their fine trees; you will stop
up all the springs of water; and you
will spoil every good piece of land by
20 littering it with stones.' In the morning at the hour of the regular sacrifice
they saw water flowing in from the
direction of Edom, and the land was
flooded.

Destruction of Moab

21 Meanwhile all Moab had heard that
the kings had come up to fight against
them, and every man, young and old,
who could carry arms, was called out
22 and stationed on the frontier. When
they got up next morning and the sun
had risen over the water, the Moabites saw the water in front of them red
23 like blood and cried out, 'It is blood.
The kings must have quarrelled and
attacked one another. Now to the

plunder, Moab!' When they came 24
to the Israelite camp, the Israelites
turned out and attacked them and
drove the Moabites headlong in flight,
and themselves entered the land of
Moab, destroying as they went. They 25
razed the cities to the ground; they
littered every good piece of land with
stones, each man casting one stone on
to it; they stopped up every spring
of water; they cut down all their fine
trees; and they harried Moab until
only in Kir-hareseth were any buildings left standing, and even this city
the slingers surrounded and attacked.
When the king of Moab saw that 26
the war had gone against him, he took
seven hundred men with him, armed
with swords, to cut a way through to
the king of Aram, but they failed in
the attempt. Then he took his eldest 27
son, who would have succeeded him,
and offered him as a whole-offering
upon the city wall. The Israelites were
filled with such consternation at this
sight,[a] that they struck camp and
returned to their own land.

Elisha provides oil for a widow

The wife of a member of a company 4
of prophets appealed to Elisha. 'My
husband, your servant, has died', she
said. 'You know that he was a man
who feared the Lord; but a creditor
has come to take away my two boys
as his slaves.' Elisha said to her, 'How 2
can I help you? Tell me what you have
in the house.' 'Nothing at all', she
answered, 'except a flask of oil.' 'Go 3
out then', he said, 'and borrow vessels
from all your neighbours; get as many
empty ones as you can. Then, when 4
you come home, shut yourself in with
your sons, pour from the flask into all
these vessels and, as they are filled, set
them aside.' She left him and shut her- 5
self in with her sons. As they brought
her the vessels she filled them. When 6
they were all full, she said to one of
her sons, 'Bring me another.' 'There is
not one left', he said. Then the flow of
oil ceased. She came out and told the 7
man of God, and he said, 'Go and sell
the oil and redeem your boys who
are being taken as pledges,[b] and you
and they can live on what is left.'

Elisha rewards the Shunammite
woman

It happened once that Elisha went 8
over to Shunem. There was a great
lady there who pressed him to accept

a The Israelites . . . sight: or There was such great anger against the Israelites . . .   b redeem . . .
pledges: or pay off your debt.

her hospitality, and so, whenever he came that way, he stopped to take 9 food there. One day she said to her husband, 'I know that this man who comes here regularly is a holy man of 10 God. Why not build up the wall to make him a little roof-chamber, and put in it a bed, a table, a seat, and a lamp, and let him stay there whenever 11 he comes to us?' Once when he arrived and went to this roof-chamber and 12 lay down to rest, he said to Gehazi, his servant, 'Call this Shunammite woman.' He called her and, when she 13 appeared before the prophet, he said to his servant, 'Say to her, "You have taken all this trouble for us. What can I do for you? Shall I speak for you to the king or to the commander-in-chief?"' But she replied, 'I am content where I am, among my own people.' 14 He said, 'Then what can be done for her?' Gehazi said, 'There is only this: she has no child and her husband is 15 old.' 'Call her back', Elisha said. When she was called, she appeared in the 16 doorway, and he said, 'In due season, this time next year, you shall have a son in your arms.' But she said, 'No, no, my lord, you are a man of God and would not lie to your servant.' 17 Next year in due season the woman conceived and bore a son, as Elisha had foretold.

The Shunammite woman's son dies

18 When the child was old enough, he went out one day to the reapers where 19 his father was. All of a sudden he cried out to his father, 'O my head, my head!' His father told a servant to 20 carry him to his mother. He brought him to his mother; the boy sat on her 21 lap till midday, and then he died. She went up and laid him on the bed of the man of God, shut the door and went 22 out. She called her husband and said, 'Send me one of the servants and a she-ass, I must go to the man of God as fast as I can, and come straight 23 back.' 'Why go to him today?' he asked. 'It is neither new moon nor sabbath.'[c] 'Never mind that', she 24 answered. When the ass was saddled, she said to her servant, 'Lead on and do not slacken pace unless I tell you.' 25 So she set out and came to the man of God on Mount Carmel. The man of God spied her in the distance and said to Gehazi, his servant, 'That is the 26 Shunammite woman coming. Run and meet her, and ask, "Is all well

with you? Is all well with your husband? Is all well with the boy?"' She answered, 'All is well.' When she 27 reached the man of God on the hill, she clutched his feet. Gehazi came forward to push her away, but the man of God said, 'Let her alone; she is in great distress, and the LORD has concealed it from me and not told me.' 'My lord,' she said, 'did I ask for a 28 son? Did I not beg you not to raise my hopes and then dash them?' Then 29 he turned to Gehazi: 'Hitch up your cloak; take my staff with you and run. If you meet anyone on the way, do not stop to greet him; if anyone greets you, do not answer him. Lay my staff on the boy's face.' But the 30 mother cried, 'As the LORD lives, your life upon it, I will not leave you.' So he got up and followed her.[d]

Elisha revives the child

Gehazi went on ahead of them and 31 laid the staff on the boy's face, but there was no sound and no sign of life. So he went back to meet Elisha and told him that the boy had not roused. When Elisha entered the house, there 32 was the boy dead, on the bed where he had been laid. He went into the 33 room, and shut the door on the two of them and prayed to the LORD. Then, 34 getting on to the bed, he lay upon the child, put his mouth to the child's mouth, his eyes to his eyes and his hands to his hands; and, as he pressed[e] upon him, the child's body grew warm. Elisha got up and walked once up 35 and down the room; then, getting on to the bed again, he pressed[e] upon him and breathed into him[f] seven times; and the boy opened his eyes. The prophet summoned Gehazi and 36 said, 'Call this Shunammite woman.' She answered his call and the prophet said, 'Take your child.' She came in 37 and fell prostrate before him. Then she took up her son and went out.

Elisha provides an antidote

Elisha returned to Gilgal at a time 38 when there was a famine in the land. One day, when a group of prophets was sitting at his feet, he said to his servant, 'Set the big pot on the fire and prepare some broth for the company.' One of them went out into the 39 fields to gather herbs and found a wild vine, and filled the skirt of his garment with bitter-apples.[g] He came back and sliced them into the pot,

c Or full moon.　　d Or Went with her.　　e Prob. rdg.; Heb. crouched. 　　f and breathed into him: or and the boy sneezed.　　g Or poisonous wild gourds.

40 not knowing what they were. They poured it out for the men to eat, but, when they tasted it, they cried out, 'Man of God, there is death in the pot',
41 and they could not eat it. The prophet said, 'Fetch some meal.' He threw it into the pot and said, 'Now pour out for the men to eat.' This time there was no harm in the pot.

Elisha provides bread for the people

42 A man came from Baal-shalisha, bringing the man of God some of the new season's bread, twenty barley loaves, and fresh ripe ears of corn.[h] Elisha said, 'Give this to the people to
43 eat.' But his disciple protested, 'I cannot set this before a hundred men.' Still he repeated, 'Give it to the people to eat; for this is the word of the LORD: "They will eat and there
44 will be some left over."' So he set it before them, and they ate and left some over, as the LORD had said.

Elisha cures Naaman

5 Naaman, commander of the king of Aram's army, was a great man highly esteemed by his master, because by his means the LORD had given victory
2 to Aram; but he was a leper.[i] On one of their raids the Aramaeans brought back as a captive from the land of Israel a little girl, who became a servant to
3 Naaman's wife. She said to her mistress, 'If only my master could meet the prophet who lives in Samaria, he would get rid of the disease for him.'
4 Naaman went in and reported to his master word for word what the girl
5 from the land of Israel had said. 'Very well, you may go,' said the king of Aram, 'and I will send a letter to the king of Israel.' So Naaman went, taking with him ten talents of silver, six thousand shekels of gold, and ten
6 changes of clothing. He delivered the letter to the king of Israel, which read thus: 'This letter is to inform you that I am sending to you my servant Naaman, and I beg you to rid him of
7 his disease.' When the king of Israel read the letter, he rent his clothes and said, 'Am I a god[j] to kill and to make alive, that this fellow sends to me to cure a man of his disease? Surely you must see that he is picking
8 a quarrel with me.' When Elisha, the man of God, heard how the king of Israel had rent his clothes, he sent to him saying, 'Why did you rend your clothes? Let the man come to

me, and he will know that there is a prophet in Israel.' So Naaman came 9 with his horses and chariots and stood at the entrance to Elisha's house. Elisha sent out a messenger to say to 10 him, 'If you will go and wash seven times in the Jordan, your flesh will be restored and you will be clean.' Naaman was furious and went away, 11 saying, 'I thought he would at least have come out and stood, and invoked the LORD his God by name, waved his hand over the place and so rid me of the disease. Are not Abana and 12 Pharpar, rivers of Damascus, better than all the waters of Israel? Can I not wash in them and be clean?' So he turned and went off in a rage. But 13 his servants came up to him and said, 'If the prophet had bidden you do something difficult, would you not do it? How much more then, if he tells you to wash and be clean?' So he went 14 down and dipped himself in the Jordan seven times as the man of God had told him, and his flesh was restored as a little child's, and he was clean.

Naaman promises allegiance to the LORD

Then he and his retinue went back to 15 the man of God and stood before him; and he said, 'Now I know that there is no god anywhere on earth except in Israel. Will you accept a token of gratitude from your servant?' 'As the 16 LORD lives, whom I serve,' said the prophet, 'I will accept nothing.' He was pressed to accept, but he refused. 'Then if you will not,' said Naaman, 17 'let me, sir, have two mules' load of earth. For I will no longer offer whole-offering or sacrifice to any god but the LORD. In this one matter only may 18 the LORD pardon me: when my master goes to the temple of Rimmon to worship, leaning on my arm, and I worship in the temple of Rimmon when he worships there, for this let the LORD pardon me.' And Elisha 19 bade him farewell.

Naaman had gone only a short 20 distance on his way, when Gehazi, the servant of Elisha the man of God, said to himself, 'What? Has my master let this Aramaean, Naaman, go scot-free, and not accepted what he brought? As the LORD lives, I will run after him and get something from him.' So 21 Gehazi hurried after Naaman. When Naaman saw him running after him,

h fresh . . . corn: prob. rdg.; Heb. unintelligible.
j Or Am I God.

i he was a leper: or his skin was diseased.

F

he jumped down from his chariot to meet him and said, 'Is anything
22 wrong?' 'Nothing,' said Gehazi, 'but my master sent me to say that two young men of the company of prophets from the hill-country of Ephraim have just arrived. Could you provide them with a talent of silver and two
23 changes of clothing?' Naaman said, 'By all means; take two talents.' He pressed[k] him to take them; so he tied up the two talents of silver in two bags, and the two changes of clothing, and gave them to his two servants, and they walked ahead carrying them.
24 When Gehazi came to the citadel[l] he took them from the two servants, deposited them in the house and dismissed the men; and they departed.
25 When he went in and stood before his master, Elisha said, 'Where have you been, Gehazi?' 'Nowhere,' said Ge-
26 hazi. But he said to him, 'Was I not with you in spirit when the man turned back from his chariot to meet you? Is it not true that you have the money? You may buy gardens with it,[m][n] and olive-trees and vineyards, sheep and oxen, slaves and slave-
27 girls; but the disease of Naaman will fasten on you and on your descendants for ever.' Gehazi left his presence, his skin diseased, white as snow.

Elisha makes an axehead float

6 A company of prophets said to Elisha, 'You can see that this place where our community is living, under you as its
2 head, is too small for us. Let us go to the Jordan and each fetch a log, and make ourselves a place to live in.'
3 The prophet agreed. Then one of them said, 'Please, sir, come with us.' 'I
4 will', he said, and he went with them. When they reached the Jordan, they
5 began cutting down trees; but it chanced that, as one man was felling a trunk, the head of his axe flew off into the water. 'Oh, master!' he exclaimed,
6 'it was a borrowed one.' 'Where did it fall?' asked the man of God. When he was shown the place, he cut off a piece of wood and threw it in and
7 made the iron float. Then he said, 'There you are, lift it out.' So he stretched out his hand and took it.

Elisha discloses the king of Aram's plans

8 Once, when the king of Aram was making war on Israel, he held a con-

ference with his staff at which he said, 'I mean to attack in such and such a direction.' But the man of 9 God warned the king of Israel: 'Take care to avoid this place, for the Aramaeans are going down that way.'
So the king of Israel sent to the place 10 about which the man of God had given him this warning; and the king took special precautions every time he found himself near that place. The 11 king of Aram was greatly perturbed at this and, summoning his staff, he said to them, 'Tell me, one of you, who has betrayed us to the king of Israel?' 'None of us, my lord king,' 12 said one of his staff; 'but Elisha, the prophet in Israel, tells the king of Israel the very words you speak in your bedchamber.' 'Go and find out 13 where he is,' said the king, 'and I will send and seize him.' He was told that the prophet was at Dothan, and he 14 sent a strong force there with horses and chariots. They came by night and surrounded the city.

Elisha deceives the Aramaeans

When the disciple of the man of God 15 rose early in the morning and went out, he saw a force with horses and chariots surrounding the city. 'Oh, master,' he said, 'which way are we to turn?' He answered, 'Do not be 16 afraid, for those who are on our side are more than those on theirs.' Then 17 Elisha offered this prayer: 'O LORD, open his eyes and let him see.' And the LORD opened the young man's eyes, and he saw the hills covered with horses and chariots of fire all round Elisha. As they came down towards 18 him, Elisha prayed to the LORD: 'Strike this host, I pray thee, with blindness'; and he struck them blind as Elisha had asked. Then Elisha said 19 to them, 'You are on the wrong road; this is not the city. Follow me and I will lead you to the man you are looking for.' And he led them to Samaria. As soon as they had entered Samaria, 20 Elisha prayed, 'O LORD, open the eyes of these men and let them see again.' And he opened their eyes and they saw that they were inside Samaria. When the king of Israel saw them, he 21 said to Elisha, 'My father, am I to destroy them?' 'No, you must not do 22 that', he answered. 'You may destroy[o] those whom you have taken prisoner with your own sword and bow, but as

k Prob. rdg.; Heb. broke out on.　l Or hill.　m gardens with it: prob. rdg.; Heb. garments.
n Is it not . . . with it: or Was it a time to get the money and to get garments?　o Prob. rdg.;
Heb. Would you destroy.

for these men, give them food and water, and let them eat and drink, 23 and then go back to their master.' So he prepared a great feast for them, and they ate and drank and then went back to their master. And Aramaean raids on Israel ceased.

Ben-hadad besieges Samaria

24 But later, Ben-hadad king of Aram called up his entire army and marched 25 to the siege of Samaria. The city was near starvation, and they besieged it so closely that a donkey's head was sold for eighty shekels of silver, and a quarter of a kab of locust-beans for 26 five shekels. One day, as the king of Israel was walking along the city wall, a woman called to him, 'Help, my 27 lord king!' He said, 'If the LORD will not bring you help, where can I find any for you? From threshing-floor or 28 from winepress? What is your trouble?' She replied, 'This woman said to me, "Give up your child for us to eat today, 29 and we will eat mine tomorrow." So we cooked my son and ate him; but when I said to her the next day, "Now give up your child for us to eat", she 30 had hidden him.' When he heard the woman's story, the king rent his clothes. He was walking along the wall at the time, and when the people looked, they saw that he had sackcloth 31 underneath, next to his skin. Then he said, 'The LORD do the same to me and more, if the head of Elisha son of Shaphat stays on his shoulders today.'

Elisha promises relief from the famine

32 Elisha was sitting at home, the elders with him. The king had dispatched one of his retinue but, before the messenger arrived, Elisha said to the elders, 'See how this son of a murderer has sent to behead me! Take care, when the messenger comes, to shut the door and hold it fast against him. Can you not hear his master follow- 33 ing on his heels?' While he was still speaking, the king[p] arrived and said, 'Look at our plight! This is the LORD's doing. Why should I wait any longer 7 for him to help us?' But Elisha answered, 'Hear this word of the LORD: By this time tomorrow a shekel will buy a measure of flour or two measures of barley in the gateway of 2 Samaria.' Then the lieutenant on whose arm the king leaned said to the man of God, 'Even if the LORD were

to open windows in the sky, such a thing could not happen!' He answered, 'You will see it with your own eyes, but none of it will you eat.'

The Aramaeans abandon their camp

At the city gate were four lepers.[q] 3 They said to one another, 'Why should we stay here and wait for death? If we say we will go into the 4 city, there is famine there, and we shall die; if we say we will stay here, we shall die just the same. Well then, let us go to the camp of the Aramaeans and give ourselves up: if they spare us, we shall live; if they put us to death, we can but die.' And 5 so in the twilight they set out for the Aramaean camp; but when they reached the outskirts, they found no one there; for the Lord had caused 6 the Aramaean army to hear a sound like that of chariots and horses and of a great host, so that the word went round: 'The king of Israel has hired the kings of the Hittites and the kings of Egypt to attack us.' They had fled 7 at once in the twilight, abandoning their tents, their horses and asses, and leaving the camp as it stood, while they fled for their lives. When the 8 four men came to the outskirts of the camp, they went into a tent and ate and drank and looted silver and gold and clothing, and made off and hid them. Then they came back, went into another tent and rifled it, and made off and hid the loot. Then they said to 9 one another, 'What we are doing is not right. This is a day of good news and we are keeping it to ourselves. If we wait till morning, we shall be held to blame. We must go now and give the news to the king's household.' So 10 they came and called to the watch at the city gate and described how they had gone to the Aramaean camp and found not a single man in it and had heard no sound: nothing but horses and asses tethered, and the tents left as they were. Then the watch called 11 out and gave the news to the king's household in the palace. The king rose 12 in the night and said to his staff, 'I will tell you what the Aramaeans have done. They know that we are starving, and they have left their camp to go and hide in the open country, expecting us to come out, and then they can take us alive and enter the city.' One of his staff said, 'Send 13 out a party of men with some of the horses that are left; if they live, they

---

p Prob. rdg.; Heb. messenger.　　*q Or men suffering from skin-disease.*

will be as well off as all the other Israelites who are still left; if they die,[r] they will be no worse off than all those who have already perished. Let them go and see what has happened.'

14 So they picked two mounted men, and the king dispatched them in the track of the Aramaean army with the order to go and find out what had happened.

15 They followed as far as the Jordan and found the whole road littered with clothing and equipment which the Aramaeans had flung aside in their haste. The messengers returned

16 and reported this to the king. Then the people went out and plundered the Aramaean camp, and a measure of flour was sold for a shekel and two measures of barley for a shekel, so that the word of the LORD came true.

17 Now the king had appointed the lieutenant on whose arm he leaned to take charge of the gate, and the people trampled him to death there, just as the man of God had foretold

18 when the king visited him. For when the man of God said to the king, 'By this time tomorrow a shekel will buy two measures of barley or one measure of flour in the gateway of Sa-

19 maria', the lieutenant had answered, 'Even if the LORD were to open windows in the sky, such a thing could not happen!' And the man of God had said, 'You will see it with your own

20 eyes, but none of it will you eat.' And this is just what happened to him: the people trampled him to death at the gate.

The famine, and after

8 Elisha said to the woman whose son he had restored to life, 'Go away at once with your household and find lodging where you can, for the LORD has decreed a seven years' famine and it has already come upon the land.'

2 The woman acted at once on the word of the man of God and went away with her household; and she stayed in the Philistine country for seven years.

3 When she came back at the end of the seven years, she sought an audience of the king to appeal for the return of

4 her house and land. Now the king was questioning Gehazi, the servant of the man of God, about all the great

5 things Elisha had done; and, as he was describing to the king how he had brought the dead to life, the selfsame woman began appealing to the king for her house and her land. 'My lord king,' said Gehazi, 'this is the very

woman, and this is her son whom Elisha brought to life.' The king 6 asked the woman about it, and she told him. Then he entrusted the case to a eunuch and ordered him to restore all her property to her, with all the revenues from her land from the time she left the country till that day.

Hazael succeeds Ben-hadad

Elisha came to Damascus, at a time 7 when Ben-hadad king of Aram was ill; and when he was told that the man of God had arrived, he bade 8 Hazael take a gift with him and go to the man of God and inquire of the LORD through him whether he would recover from his illness. Hazael went, 9 taking with him as a gift all kinds of wares of Damascus, forty camel-loads. When he came into the prophet's presence, he said, 'Your son Ben-hadad king of Aram has sent me to you to ask whether he will recover from his illness.' 'Go and tell him that he will 10 recover,' he answered; 'but the LORD has revealed to me that in fact he will die.' The man of God stood there with 11 set face like a man stunned, until he could bear it no longer; then he wept. 'Why do you weep, my lord?' 12 said Hazael. He answered, 'Because I know the harm you will do to the Israelites: you will set their fortresses on fire and put their young men to the sword; you will dash their children to the ground and you will rip open their pregnant women.' But Hazael 13 said, 'I am a dog, a mere nobody; how can I do this great thing?' Elisha answered, 'The LORD has revealed to me that you will be king of Aram.' Hazael left Elisha and returned to his 14 master, who asked him what Elisha had said. 'He told me that you would recover', he replied. But the next day 15 he took a blanket and, after dipping it in water, laid it over the king's face, and he died; and Hazael succeeded him.

Joram reigns over Judah

In the fifth year of Jehoram son of 16 Ahab king of Israel, Joram son of Jehoshaphat king of Judah became king. He was thirty-two years old 17[s] when he came to the throne, and he reigned in Jerusalem for eight years. He followed the practices of the kings 18 of Israel as the house of Ahab had done, for he had married Ahab's daughter; and he did what was wrong

---

r *if they live . . . if they die:* prob. rdg.; Heb. obscure.   s *Verses 17–22: cp.* 2 Chr. 21. 5–10.

19 in the eyes of the LORD. But for his servant David's sake the LORD was unwilling to destroy Judah, since he had promised to give him and his sons a flame, to burn for all time.

Edom and Libnah revolt

20 During his reign Edom revolted against Judah and set up its own 21 king. Joram crossed over to Zair with all his chariots. He and his chariot-commanders set out by night, but they were surrounded by the Edom-ites and defeated,*t* whereupon the 22 people fled to their tents. So Edom has remained independent of Judah to this day; Libnah also revolted at the 23 same time. The other acts and events of Joram's reign are recorded in the 24 annals of the kings of Judah. So Joram rested with his forefathers and was buried with them in the city of David, and his son Ahaziah succeeded him.

Ahaziah reigns over Judah

25*u* In the twelfth year of Jehoram son of Ahab king of Israel, Ahaziah son of Joram king of Judah became king. 26 Ahaziah was twenty-two years old when he came to the throne, and he reigned in Jerusalem for one year; his mother was Athaliah grand-27 daughter of Omri king of Israel. He followed the practices of the house of Ahab and did what was wrong in the eyes of the LORD like the house of Ahab, for he was connected with that 28 house by marriage. He allied himself with Jehoram son of Ahab to fight against Hazael king of Aram at Ramoth-gilead; but King Jehoram 29 was wounded by the Aramaeans, and returned to Jezreel to recover from the wounds which were inflicted on him at Ramoth in battle with Hazael king of Aram; and because of his ill-ness Ahaziah son of Joram king of Judah went down to Jezreel to visit him.

Elisha anoints Jehu king of Israel

9 Elisha the prophet summoned one of the company of prophets and said to him, 'Hitch up your cloak, take this flask of oil with you and go to Ramoth-2 gilead. When you arrive, you will find Jehu son of Jehoshaphat, son of Nim-shi; go in and call him aside from his fellow-officers, and lead him through

to an inner room. Then take the 3 flask and pour the oil on his head and say, "This is the word of the LORD: I anoint you king over Israel"; then open the door and flee for your life.' So the young prophet went to 4 Ramoth-gilead. When he arrived, he 5 found the officers sitting together and said, 'Sir, I have a word for you.' 'For which of us?' asked Jehu. 'For you, sir', he said. He rose and went into 6 the house, and the prophet poured the oil on his head, saying, 'This is the word of the LORD the God of Israel: "I anoint you king over Israel, the people of the LORD. You shall strike 7 down the house of Ahab your master, and I will take vengeance on Jezebel for the blood of my servants the pro-phets and for the blood of all the LORD's servants. All the house of 8 Ahab shall perish and I will destroy every mother's son of his house in Israel, whether under the protection of the family or not. And I will make 9 the house of Ahab like the house of Jeroboam son of Nebat and the house of Baasha son of Ahijah. Jezebel shall 10 be devoured by dogs in the plot of ground at Jezreel and no one will bury her."' Then he opened the door and fled. When Jehu rejoined the king's 11 officers, they said to him, 'Is all well? What did this crazy fellow want with you?' 'You know him and the way his thoughts run', he said. 'Nonsense!' 12 they replied; 'tell us what happened.' 'I will tell you exactly what he said: "This is the word of the LORD: I anoint you king over Israel."' They 13 snatched up their cloaks and spread them under him on the stones*v* of the steps, and sounded the trumpet and shouted, 'Jehu is king.'

Jehu kills Jehoram and Ahaziah

Then Jehu son of Jehoshaphat, son of 14 Nimshi, laid his plans against Jehor-am, while Jehoram and the Israelites were defending Ramoth-gilead against Hazael king of Aram. King Jehoram 15 had returned to Jezreel to recover from the wounds inflicted on him by the Aramaeans when he fought against Hazael king of Aram. Jehu said to them, 'If you are on my side, see that no one escapes from the city to tell the news in Jezreel.' He mounted his 16 chariot and drove to Jezreel, for Jehor-am was laid up there, and Ahaziah king of Judah had gone down to visit him.

t and defeated: prob. rdg.; Heb. and he defeated Edom.   u Verses 25–9: cp. 2 Chr. 22. 1–6.
v Prob. rdg.; Heb. obscure.

17 The watchman standing on the watch-tower in Jezreel saw Jehu and his troop approaching and called out, 'I see a troop of men.' Then Jehoram said, 'Fetch a horseman and send to 18 find out if they come peaceably.' The horseman went to meet him and said, 'The king asks, "Is it peace?"' Jehu said, 'Peace? What is peace to you? Fall in behind me.' Thereupon the watchman reported, 'The messenger has met them but he is not coming 19 back.' A second horseman was sent; when he met them, he also said, 'The king asks, "Is it peace?"' 'Peace?' said Jehu. 'What is peace to you? Fall 20 in behind me.' Then the watchman reported, 'He has met them but he is not coming back. The driving is like the driving of Jehu son*w* of Nimshi, 21 for he drives furiously.' 'Harness my chariot', said Jehoram. They harnessed it, and Jehoram king of Israel and Ahaziah king of Judah went out each in his own chariot to meet Jehu, and met him by the plot of Naboth of 22 Jezreel. When Jehoram saw Jehu, he said, 'Is it peace, Jehu?' But he replied, 'Do you call it peace while your mother Jezebel keeps up her obscene idol-worship and monstrous sorcer- 23 ies?' Jehoram wheeled about and fled, crying out to Ahaziah, 'Treachery, 24 Ahaziah!' Jehu seized his bow and shot Jehoram between the shoulders; the arrow pierced his heart and he 25 sank down in his chariot. Then Jehu said to Bidkar, his lieutenant, 'Pick him up and throw him into the plot of land belonging to Naboth of Jezreel; remember how, when you and I were riding side by side behind Ahab his father, the Lord pronounced 26 this sentence against him: "It is the very word of the Lord: as surely as I saw yesterday the blood of Naboth and the blood of his sons, I will requite you in this plot." So pick him up and throw him into it and thus 27 fulfil the word of the Lord.' When Ahaziah king of Judah saw this, he fled by the road to Beth-haggan. Jehu went after him and said, 'Make sure of him too.' They shot him down in his chariot on the road up the valley*x* near Ibleam, but he escaped to Me- 28 giddo and died there. His servants conveyed his body to Jerusalem and buried him in his tomb with his fore-fathers in the city of David. 29 In the eleventh year of Jehoram son of Ahab, Ahaziah became king over Judah.

The death of Jezebel

Jehu came to Jezreel. Now Jezebel 30 had heard what had happened; she had painted her eyes and dressed her hair, and she stood looking down from a window. As Jehu entered the gate, 31 she said, 'Is it peace, you Zimri, you murderer of your master?' He looked 32 up at the window and said, 'Who is on my side, who?' Two or three eunuchs looked out, and he said, 'Throw her 33 down.' They threw her down, and some of her blood splashed on to the wall and the horses, which trampled her underfoot. Then he went in and 34 ate and drank. 'See to this accursed woman', he said, 'and bury her; for she is a king's daughter.' But when 35 they went to bury her they found nothing of her but the skull, the feet, and the palms of the hands; and they 36 went back and told him. Jehu said, 'It is the word of the Lord which his servant Elijah the Tishbite spoke, when he said, "In the plot of ground at Jezreel the dogs shall devour the flesh of Jezebel, and Jezebel's corpse 37 shall lie like dung upon the ground in the plot at Jezreel so that no one will be able to say: This is Jezebel."'

Jehu destroys the house of Ahab

Now seventy sons of Ahab were left **10** in Samaria. Jehu therefore sent a letter to Samaria, to the elders, the rulers of the city, and to the tutors of Ahab's children, in which he wrote: 'Now, when this letter reaches you, 2 since you have in your care your master's family as well as his chariots and horses, fortified cities and weapons, choose the best and the most 3 suitable of your master's family, set him on his father's throne, and fight for your master's house.' They were 4 panic-stricken and said, 'The two kings could not stand against him; what hope is there that we can?' Therefore the comptroller of the 5 household and the governor of the city, with the elders and the tutors, sent this message to Jehu: 'We are your servants. Whatever you tell us we will do; but we will not make any-one king. Do as you think fit.' Then 6 he wrote them a second letter: 'If you are on my side and will obey my orders, then bring the heads of your master's sons to me at Jezreel by this time tomorrow.' Now the royal princes, seventy in all, were with the nobles of the city who were bringing

w Or grandson (cp. verse 2).   *x the valley: prob. rdg.; Heb. to Gur.*

7 them up. When the letter reached them, they took the royal princes and killed all seventy; they put their heads in baskets and sent them to 8 Jehu in Jezreel. When the messenger came to him and reported that they had brought the heads of the royal princes, he ordered them to be put in two heaps and left at the entrance 9 of the city gate till morning. In the morning he went out, stood there and said to all the people, 'You are fair judges. If I conspired against my master and killed him, who put all 10 these to death? Be sure then that every word which the LORD has spoken against the house of Ahab shall be fulfilled, and that the LORD has now done what he spoke through 11 his servant Elijah.' So Jehu put to death all who were left of the house of Ahab in Jezreel, as well as all his nobles, his close friends, and his priests, until he had left not one survivor.

12 Then he set out for Samaria, and on the way there, when he had reached 13 a shepherds' shelter,[y] he came upon the kinsmen of Ahaziah king of Judah and said, 'Who are you?' 'We are kinsmen of Ahaziah,' they replied; 'and we have come down to greet the families of the king and of 14 the queen mother.' 'Take them alive', he said. So they took them alive; then they slew them and flung them into the pit that was there, forty-two of them; they did not leave a single survivor.

15 When he had left that place, he found Jehonadab son of Rechab coming to meet him. He greeted him and said, 'Are you with me heart and soul, as I am with you?' 'I am', said Jehonadab. 'Then if you are,' said Jehu, 'give me your hand.' He gave him his hand and Jehu helped him up into his 16 chariot. 'Come with me,' he said, 'and you will see my zeal for the LORD.' So he took him with him in his chariot. 17 When he came to Samaria, he put to death all of Ahab's house who were left there and so blotted it out, in fulfilment of the word which the LORD had spoken to Elijah.

Jehu stamps out Baal-worship

18 Then Jehu called all the people together and said to them, 'Ahab served the Baal a little; Jehu will serve him 19 much. Now, summon all the prophets of Baal, all his ministers and priests; not one must be missing. For I am holding a great sacrifice to Baal, and

no one who is missing from it shall live.' In this way Jehu outwitted the ministers of Baal in order to destroy them. So Jehu said, 'Let a sacred 20 ceremony for Baal be held.' They did so, and Jehu himself sent word 21 throughout Israel, and all the ministers of Baal came; there was not a man left who did not come. They went into the temple of Baal and it was filled from end to end. Then he said to the 22 person who had charge of the wardrobe, 'Bring out robes for all the ministers of Baal'; and he brought them out. Then Jehu and Jehonadab 23 son of Rechab went into the temple of Baal and said to the ministers of Baal, 'Look carefully and make sure that there are no servants of the LORD here with you, but only the ministers of Baal.' Then they went in to offer 24 sacrifices and whole-offerings. Now Jehu had stationed eighty men outside and said to them, 'I am putting these men in your charge, and any man who lets one escape shall answer for it with his life.' When he had finished offer- 25 ing the whole-offering, Jehu ordered the guards and the lieutenants to go and cut them all down, and let not one of them escape; so they slew them without quarter. The escort and the lieutenants then rushed into the keep of the temple of Baal and brought out 26 the sacred pole[z] from the temple of Baal and burnt it; and they pulled 27 down the sacred pillar of the Baal and the temple itself and made a privy of it—as it is today. Thus Jehu stamped 28 out the worship of Baal in Israel. He 29 did not however abandon the sins of Jeroboam son of Nebat who led Israel into sin, but he maintained the worship of the golden calves of Bethel and Dan.

The LORD commends Jehu

Then the LORD said to Jehu, 'You 30 have done well what is right in my eyes and have done to the house of Ahab all that it was in my mind to do. Therefore your sons to the fourth generation shall sit on the throne of Israel.' But Jehu was not careful to 31 follow the law of the LORD the God of Israel with all his heart; he did not abandon the sins of Jeroboam who led Israel into sin.

In those days the LORD began to 32 work havoc on Israel, and Hazael struck at them in every corner of their territory eastwards from the Jordan: 33 all the land of Gilead, Gad, Reuben, and Manasseh, from Aroer which is by the gorge of the Arnon, including Gilead and Bashan.

Other records of Jehu's reign

34 The other events of Jehu's reign, his achievements and his exploits, are recorded in the annals of the kings of 35 Israel. So Jehu rested with his forefathers and was buried in Samaria; and he was succeeded by his son 36 Jehoahaz. Jehu reigned over Israel in Samaria for twenty-eight years.

Athaliah seizes the throne

11 1[a] As soon as Athaliah mother of Ahaziah saw that her son was dead, she set out to destroy all the royal line. 2 But Jehosheba daughter of King Joram, sister of Ahaziah, took Ahaziah's son Joash and stole him away from among the princes who were being murdered; she put[b] him and his nurse in a bedchamber where he was hidden from Athaliah and was not 3 put to death. He remained concealed with her in the house of the LORD for six years, while Athaliah ruled the 4 country. In the seventh year Jehoiada sent for the captains of units of a hundred, both of the Carites and of the guards, and he brought them into the house of the LORD; he made an agreement with them and put them on their oath in the house of the LORD, 5 and showed them the king's son, and gave them the following orders: 'One third of you who are on duty on the sabbath are to be on guard in the 6 palace; the rest of you are to be on special duty in the house of the LORD, one third at the Sur Gate and the other third at the gate with[c] the out- 7 runners. Your two companies who are off duty on the sabbath shall be on duty for the king in the house of the 8 LORD. So you shall be on guard round the king, each man with his arms at the ready, and anyone who comes near the ranks is to be put to death; you must be with the king wherever he goes.'

Jehoiada anoints Joash king

9 The captains carried out the orders of Jehoiada the priest to the letter. Each took his men, both those who came on duty on the sabbath and those who came off, and came to 10 Jehoiada. The priest handed out to the captains King David's spears and shields, which were in the house of the LORD. Then the guards took up 11 their stations, each man carrying his arms at the ready, from corner to corner of the house to north and south,[d] surrounding the king. Then 12 he brought out the king's son, put the crown on his head, handed him the warrant and anointed him king. The people clapped their hands and shouted, 'Long live the king.' When 13 Athaliah heard the noise made by the guards and the people, she came into the house of the LORD where the people were and found the king 14 standing, as was the custom, on the dais,[e] amidst outbursts of song and fanfares of trumpets in his honour, and all the populace rejoicing and blowing trumpets. Then Athaliah rent her clothes and cried, 'Treason! Treason!' Jehoiada the priest gave orders 15 to the captains in command of the troops: 'Bring her outside the precincts and put to the sword anyone in attendance on her'; for the priest said, 'She shall not be put to death in the house of the LORD.' So 16 they laid hands on her and took her out by the entry for horses to the royal palace, and there she was put to death.

Jehoiada puts down idolatry

Then Jehoiada made a covenant be- 17 tween the LORD and the king and people that they should be the LORD's people, and also between the king and the people. And all the people went 18 into the temple of Baal and pulled it down; they smashed to pieces its altars and images, and they slew Mattan the priest of Baal before the altars. Then Jehoiada set a watch over the house of the LORD; he took the cap- 19 tains of units of a hundred, the Carites and the guards and all the people, and they escorted the king from the house of the LORD through the Gate of the Guards to the royal palace, and seated him on the royal throne. The whole people rejoiced and 20 the city was tranquil. That is how Athaliah was put to the sword in the royal palace.

Rebuilding the Temple

Joash was seven years old when he 21[f] became king. In the seventh year of 12 Jehu, Joash became king, and he reigned in Jerusalem for forty years;

---

a Verses 1–20: cp. 2 Chr. 22. 10–23. 21.   b she put: prob. rdg., cp. 2 Chr. 22. 11; Heb. om.
c Or behind.   d Prob. rdg.; Heb. adds of the altar and the house.   e Or by the pillar.
f 11. 21—12. 15: cp. 2 Chr. 24. 1–14.

his mother was Zibiah of Beersheba.
2 He did what was right in the eyes
of the LORD all his days, as Jehoiada
3 the priest had taught him. The hill-
shrines, however, were allowed to remain; the people still continued to
sacrifice and make smoke-offerings
there.

4 Then Joash ordered the priests to
take all the silver brought as holy-
gifts into the house of the LORD, the
silver for which each man was assessed,[g] the silver for the persons assessed under his name, and any silver
which any man brought voluntarily
5 to the house of the LORD. He ordered
the priests, also, each to make a contribution from his own funds, and to
repair the house wherever it was found
6 necessary. But in the twenty-third
year of the reign of Joash the priests
had still not carried out the repairs
7 to the house. King Joash summoned
Jehoiada the priest and the other
priests and said to them, 'Why are
you not repairing the house? Henceforth you need not contribute from
your own funds for the repair of the
8 house.' So the priests agreed neither
to receive money from the people nor
to undertake the repairs of the house.
9 Then Jehoiada the priest took a chest
and bored a hole in the lid and put it
beside the altar on the right side going
into the house of the LORD, and the
priests on duty at the entrance put
in it all the money brought into the
10 house of the LORD. And whenever they
saw that the chest was well filled, the
king's secretary and the high priest
came and melted down the silver
found in the house of the LORD and
11 weighed it. When it had been checked,
they gave the silver to the foremen
over the work in the house of the
LORD and they paid the carpenters
and the builders working on the
12 temple and the masons and the stone-
cutters; they used it also to buy timber and hewn stone for the repairs
and for all other expenses connected
13 with them. They did not use the silver
brought into the house of the LORD to
make silver cups, snuffers, tossing-
bowls, trumpets, or any gold or silver
14 vessels; but they paid it to the work-
15 men and used it for the repairs. No
account was demanded from the foremen to whom the money was given
for the payment of the workmen, for
16 they were acting on trust. Money
from guilt-offerings and sin-offerings

was not brought into the house of the
LORD: it belonged to the priests.

Hazael threatens Jerusalem

Then Hazael king of Aram came up 17
and attacked Gath and took it; and
he moved on against Jerusalem. But 18
Joash king of Judah took all the
holy-gifts that Jehoshaphat, Joram,
and Ahaziah his forefathers, kings of
Judah, had dedicated, and his own
holy-gifts, and all the gold that was
found in the treasuries of the house of
the LORD and in the royal palace, and
sent them to Hazael king of Aram;
and he withdrew from Jerusalem.

Other records of Joash's reign

The other acts and events of the reign 19
of Joash are recorded in the annals of
the kings of Judah. His servants re- 20[h]
volted against him and struck him
down in the house of Millo on the
descent to Silla. It was his servants 21
Jozachar son of Shimeath and Jehozabad son of Shomer who struck the
fatal blow; and he was buried with
his forefathers in the city of David.
He was succeeded by his son Amaziah.

Jehoahaz reigns over Israel

In the twenty-third year of Joash son 13
of Ahaziah king of Judah, Jehoahaz
son of Jehu became king over Israel
in Samaria and he reigned seventeen
years. He did what was wrong in the 2
eyes of the LORD and continued the
sinful practices of Jeroboam son of
Nebat who led Israel into sin, and did
not give them up. So the LORD was 3
roused to anger against Israel and he
made them subject for some years to
Hazael king of Aram and Ben-hadad
son of Hazael. Then Jehoahaz sought 4
to placate the LORD, and the LORD
heard his prayer, for he saw how the
king of Aram oppressed Israel. The 5
LORD appointed a deliverer for Israel,
who rescued them from the power of
Aram, and the Israelites settled down
again in their own homes. But they 6
did not give up the sinful practices of
the house of Jeroboam who led Israel
into sin, but continued in them; the
goddess Asherah[i] remained in Samaria. Hazael had left Jehoahaz no 7
armed force except fifty horsemen,
ten chariots, and ten thousand infantry; all the rest the king of Aram had
destroyed and made like dust under
foot.

---

g the silver . . . assessed: *prob. rdg.*; Heb. obscure.
goddess Asherah: *or* the sacred pole.

h *Verses 20, 21: cp.* 2 Chr. 24. 25–7.   i the

8 The other events of the reign of Jehoahaz, and all his achievements and his exploits, are recorded in the
9 annals of the kings of Israel. So Jehoahaz rested with his forefathers and was buried in Samaria; and he was succeeded by his son Jehoash.

Jehoash reigns over Israel

10 In the thirty-ninth year of Joash king of Judah, Jehoash son of Jehoahaz became king over Israel in Samaria
11 and reigned sixteen years. He did what was wrong in the eyes of the LORD; he did not give up any of the sinful practices of Jeroboam son of Nebat who led Israel into sin, but
12 continued in them. The other events of the reign of Jehoash, all his achievements, his exploits and his war with Amaziah king of Judah, are recorded
13 in the annals of the kings of Israel. So Jehoash rested with his forefathers and was buried in Samaria with the kings of Israel, and Jeroboam sat upon his throne.

Elisha's last words

14 Elisha fell ill and lay on his deathbed, and Jehoash king of Israel went down to him and wept over him and said, 'My father! My father, the chariots
15 and the horsemen of Israel!' 'Take bow and arrows', said Elisha, and he
16 took bow and arrows. 'Put your hand to the bow', said the prophet. He did so, and Elisha laid his hands on those
17 of the king. Then he said, 'Open the window toward the east'; he opened it and Elisha told him to shoot, and he shot. Then the prophet said, 'An arrow for the LORD's victory, an arrow for victory over Aram! You will
18 defeat Aram utterly at Aphek'; and he added, 'Now take up your arrows.' When the king had taken them, Elisha said, 'Strike the ground with them.' He struck three times and stopped.
19 The man of God was furious with him and said, 'You should have struck five or six times; then you would have defeated Aram utterly; as it is, you will strike Aram three times and no more.'
20 Then Elisha died and was buried.

A miracle at Elisha's grave

Year by year Moabite raiders used to
21 invade the land. Once some men were burying a dead man when they caught sight of the raiders. They threw the body into the grave of

Elisha and made off; when the body touched the prophet's bones, the man came to life and rose to his feet.
22 All through the reign of Jehoahaz, Hazael king of Aram oppressed Israel.
23 But the LORD was gracious and took pity on them; because of his covenant with Abraham, Isaac, and Jacob, he looked on them with favour and was unwilling to destroy them; nor has he even yet banished them from his sight.
24 When Hazael king of Aram died and was succeeded by his son Ben-hadad,
25 Jehoash son of Jehoahaz recaptured the cities which Ben-hadad had taken in war from Jehoahaz his father; three times Jehoash defeated him and recovered the cities of Israel.

Amaziah reigns over Judah

14 In the second year of Jehoash son of Jehoahaz king of Israel, Amaziah son of Joash king of Judah succeeded his
2 father. He was twenty-five years old when he came to the throne, and he reigned in Jerusalem for twenty-nine years; his mother was Jehoaddin of
3 Jerusalem. He did what was right in the eyes of the LORD, yet not as his forefather David had done; he followed his father Joash in everything.
4 The hill-shrines were allowed to remain; the people continued to slaughter and burn sacrifices there. When
5 the royal power was firmly in his grasp, he put to death those of his servants who had murdered the king
6 his father; but he spared the murderers' children in obedience to the LORD's command written in the law of Moses: 'Fathers shall not be put to death for their children, nor children for their fathers; a man shall be put to death only for his own sin.' He
7 defeated ten thousand Edomites in the Valley of Salt and captured Sela; he gave it the name Joktheel, which it still bears.

Judah and Israel in conflict

8 Then Amaziah sent messengers to Jehoash son of Jehoahaz, son of Jehu, king of Israel, to propose a meeting.
9 But Jehoash king of Israel sent this answer to Amaziah king of Judah: 'A thistle in Lebanon sent to a cedar in Lebanon to say, "Give your daughter in marriage to my son." But a wild beast in Lebanon, passing by, trampled
10 on the thistle. You have defeated Edom, it is true; and it has gone to your head. Stay at home and enjoy

j Verses 1–6: cp. 2 Chr. 25. 1–4.   k Verses 8–14: cp. 2. Chr. 25. 17–24.

your triumph. Why should you involve yourself in disaster and bring yourself to the ground, and Judah with you?'

11 But Amaziah would not listen; so Jehoash king of Israel marched out, and he and Amaziah king of Judah met one another at Beth-shemesh in 12 Judah. The men of Judah were routed by Israel and fled to their homes. 13 But Jehoash king of Israel captured Amaziah king of Judah, son of Joash, son of Ahaziah, at Beth-shemesh. He went to Jerusalem and broke down the city wall from the Gate of Ephraim to the Corner Gate, a distance of 14 four hundred cubits. He also took all the gold and silver and all the vessels found in the house of the LORD and in the treasuries of the royal palace, as well as hostages, and returned to Samaria.

Other records of Jehoash's reign

15 The other events of the reign of Jehoash, and all his achievements, his exploits and his wars with Amaziah king of Judah, are recorded in the 16 annals of the kings of Israel. So Jehoash rested with his forefathers and was buried in Samaria with the kings of Israel; and he was succeeded by his son Jeroboam.

The death of Amaziah

17[l] Amaziah son of Joash, king of Judah, outlived Jehoash son of Jehoahaz, 18 king of Israel, by fifteen years. The other events of Amaziah's reign are recorded in the annals of the kings 19 of Judah. A conspiracy was formed against him in Jerusalem and he fled to Lachish; but they sent after him to Lachish and put him to death 20 there. Then his body was conveyed on horseback to Jerusalem, and there he was buried with his forefathers in the 21 city of David. The people of Judah took Azariah, now sixteen years old, and made him king in succession to 22 his father Amaziah. It was he who built Elath and restored it to Judah after the king rested with his forefathers.

Jeroboam II reigns over Israel

23 In the fifteenth year of Amaziah son of Joash king of Judah, Jeroboam son of Jehoash king of Israel became king in Samaria and reigned for forty-nine

years. He did what was wrong in the 24 eyes of the LORD; he did not give up the sinful practices of Jeroboam son of Nebat who led Israel into sin. He 25 re-established the frontiers of Israel from Lebo-hamath to the Sea of the Arabah, in fulfilment of the word of the LORD the God of Israel spoken by his servant the prophet Jonah son of Amittai, of Gath-hepher. For the 26 LORD had seen how bitterly Israel had suffered; no one was safe, whether under the protection of his family or not, and Israel was left defenceless. But the LORD had made no threat 27 to blot out the name of Israel under heaven, and he saved them through Jeroboam son of Jehoash. The other 28 events of Jeroboam's reign, and all his achievements, his exploits, the wars he fought and how he recovered Damascus and Hamath in Jaudi for[m] Israel, are recorded in the annals of the kings of Israel. So Jeroboam rested with 29 his forefathers the kings of Israel; and he was succeeded by his son Zechariah.

Azariah reigns over Judah

In the twenty-seventh year of Jer- **15** oboam king of Israel, Azariah[n] son of Amaziah king of Judah became king. He was sixteen years old when he 2[o] came to the throne, and he reigned in Jerusalem for fifty-two years; his mother was Jecoliah of Jerusalem. He did what was right in the eyes 3 of the LORD, as Amaziah his father had done. But the hill-shrines were 4 allowed to remain; the people still continued to slaughter and burn sacrifices there. The LORD struck the king 5[p] with leprosy,[q] which he had till the day of his death; he was relieved of all duties and lived in his own house, while his son Jotham was comptroller of the household and regent. The 6 other acts and events of Azariah's reign are recorded in the annals of the kings of Judah. So he rested with his 7 forefathers and was buried with them in the city of David; and he was succeeded by his son Jotham.

Zechariah reigns over Israel

In the thirty-eighth year of Azariah 8 king of Judah, Zechariah son of Jeroboam became king over Israel in Samaria and reigned six months. He 9 did what was wrong in the eyes of the

---

l Verses 17–22: cp. 2 Chr. 25. 25—26. 2.   m in Jaudi for: prob. rdg.; Heb. to Judah in.   n Uzziah in verses 13, 30, 32, 34.   o Verses 2, 3: cp. 2 Chr. 26. 3, 4.   p Verses 5–7: cp. 2 Chr. 26. 21–3. q Or a skin-disease.

LORD, as his forefathers had done; he did not give up the sinful practices of Jeroboam son of Nebat who led Israel 10 into sin. Shallum son of Jabesh formed a conspiracy against him, attacked him in Ibleam, killed him and usurp- 11 ed the throne. The other events of Zechariah's reign are recorded in the 12 annals of the kings of Israel. Thus the word of the LORD spoken to Jehu was fulfilled: 'Your sons to the fourth generation shall sit on the throne of Israel.'

Shallum reigns over Israel

13 Shallum son of Jabesh became king in the thirty-ninth year of Uzziah king of Judah, and he reigned one full 14 month in Samaria. Then Menahem son of Gadi came up from Tirzah to Samaria, attacked Shallum son of Jabesh there, killed him and usurped 15 the throne. The other events of Shallum's reign and the conspiracy that he formed are recorded in the annals of the kings of Israel.

Menahem reigns over Israel

16 Then Menahem, starting out from Tirzah, destroyed Tappuah and everything in it and ravaged its territory; he ravaged it because it had not opened its gates to him, and he ripped open all the pregnant women.
17 In the thirty-ninth year of Azariah king of Judah, Menahem son of Gadi became king over Israel and he reigned 18 in Samaria for ten years. He did what was wrong in the eyes of the LORD; he did not give up the sinful practices of Jeroboam son of Nabat who led Israel 19 into sin. In his days Pul king of Assyria invaded the country, and Menahem gave him a thousand talents of silver to obtain his help in strengthening his 20 hold on the kingdom. Menahem laid a levy on all the men of wealth in Israel, and each had to give the king of Assyria fifty silver shekels. Then the king 21 of Assyria withdrew without occupying the country. The other acts and events of Menahem's reign are recorded in 22 the annals of the kings of Israel. So Menahem rested with his forefathers; and he was succeeded by his son Pekahiah.

Pekahiah reigns over Israel

23 In the fiftieth year of Azariah king of Judah, Pekahiah son of Menahem became king over Israel in Samaria and reigned for two years. He did what 24 was wrong in the eyes of the LORD; he did not give up the sinful practices of Jeroboam son of Nebat who led Israel into sin. Pekah son of Remaliah, 25 his lieutenant, formed a conspiracy against him and, with the help of fifty Gileadites, attacked him in Samaria in the citadel of the royal palace,[r] killed him and usurped the throne. The other acts and events of Pekahi- 26 ah's reign are recorded in the annals of the kings of Israel.

Pekah reigns over Israel

In the fifty-second year of Azariah 27 king of Judah, Pekah son of Remaliah became king over Israel in Samaria and reigned for twenty years. He 28 did what was wrong in the eyes of the LORD; he did not give up the sinful practices of Jeroboam son of Nebat who led Israel into sin. In the days of 29 Pekah king of Israel, Tiglath-pileser king of Assyria came and seized Iyon, Abel-beth-maacah, Janoah, Kedesh, Hazor, Gilead, and Galilee, with all the land of Naphtali, and deported the people to Assyria. Then Hoshea 30 son of Elah formed a conspiracy against Pekah son of Remaliah, attacked him, killed him and usurped the throne in the twentieth year of Jotham son of Uzziah. The other acts 31 and events of Pekah's reign are recorded in the annals of the kings of Israel.

Jotham reigns over Judah

In the second year of Pekah son of 32 Remaliah king of Israel, Jotham son of Uzziah king of Judah became king. He was twenty-five years old when he 33[s] came to the throne, and he reigned in Jerusalem for sixteen years; his mother was Jerusha daughter of Zadok. He did what was right in the eyes 34 of the LORD, as his father Uzziah had done; but the hill-shrines were 35 allowed to remain and the people continued to slaughter and burn sacrifices there. It was he who constructed the upper gate of the house of the LORD. The other acts and events of 36 Jotham's reign are recorded in the annals of the kings of Judah. In 37 those days the LORD began to make Rezin king of Aram and Pekah son of Remaliah attack Judah. And Jotham 38 rested with his forefathers and was buried with them in the city of David

---

r Prob. rdg.; Heb. adds Argob and Arieh.   s Verses 33–5: cp. 2 Chr. 27. 1–3.

his forefather; and he was succeeded by his son Ahaz.

Ahaz reigns over Judah

16 In the seventeenth year of Pekah son of Remaliah, Ahaz son of Jotham king 2[t] of Judah became king. Ahaz was twenty years old when he came to the throne, and he reigned in Jerusalem for sixteen years. He did not do what was right in the eyes of the LORD his God like his forefather David, 3 but followed in the footsteps of the kings of Israel; he even passed his son through the fire, adopting the abominable practice of the nations whom the LORD had dispossessed in favour 4 of the Israelites. He slaughtered and burnt sacrifices at the hill-shrines and on the hill-tops and under every spreading tree.

Assyria relieves Judah

5 Then Rezin king of Aram and Pekah son of Remaliah king of Israel attacked Jerusalem and besieged Ahaz but could 6 not bring him to battle. At that time the king of Edom[u] recovered Elath and drove the Judaeans out of it; so the Edomites entered the city and 7 have occupied it to this day. Ahaz sent messengers to Tiglath-pileser king of Assyria to say, 'I am your servant and your son. Come and save me from the king of Aram and from the king of Israel who are attacking me.' 8 Ahaz took the silver and gold found in the house of the LORD and in the treasuries of the royal palace and sent them to the king of Assyria as a bribe. 9 The king of Assyria listened to him; he advanced on Damascus, captured it, deported its inhabitants to Kir and put Rezin to death.

Ahaz rearranges the Temple

10 When King Ahaz went to meet Tiglath-pileser king of Assyria at Damascus, he saw there an altar of which he sent a sketch and a detailed plan to Uriah 11 the priest. Accordingly, Uriah built an altar, following all the instructions that the king had sent him from Damascus, and had it ready against the 12 king's return. When the king returned from Damascus, he saw the altar, approached it and mounted the steps; 13 there he burnt his whole-offering and his grain-offering and poured out his drink-offering, and he flung the blood of his shared-offerings against it. The 14 bronze altar that was before the LORD he removed from the front of the house, from between this altar and the house of the LORD, and put it on the north side of this altar. Then 15 King Ahaz gave these instructions to Uriah the priest: 'Burn on the great altar the morning whole-offering and the evening grain-offering, and the king's whole-offering and his grain-offering, and the whole-offering of all the people of the land, their grain-offering and their drink-offerings, and fling against it all the blood of the sacrifices. But the bronze altar shall be mine, to offer morning sacrifice.' Uriah the priest did all that the king 16 told him. Then King Ahaz broke up 17 the trolleys and removed the panels, and he took down the basin and the Sea of bronze from the oxen which supported it and put it on a stone base. In the house of the LORD he 18 turned round the structure they had erected for use on the sabbath, and the outer gate for the king, to satisfy the king of Assyria. The other acts 19[v] and events of the reign of Ahaz are recorded in the annals of the kings of Judah. So Ahaz rested with his fore- 20 fathers and was buried with them in the city of David; and he was succeeded by his son Hezekiah.

Samaria's inhabitants deported to Assyria

In the twelfth year of Ahaz king of **17** Judah, Hoshea son of Elah became king over Israel in Samaria and reigned nine years. He did what was 2 wrong in the eyes of the LORD, but not as the previous kings of Israel had done. Shalmaneser king of Assyria 3 made war upon him and Hoshea became tributary to him. But when the 4 king of Assyria discovered that Hoshea was being disloyal to him, sending messengers to the king of Egypt at So,[w] and withholding the tribute which he had been paying year by year, the king of Assyria arrested him and put him in prison. Then he in- 5 vaded the whole country and, reaching Samaria, besieged it for three years. In the ninth year of Hoshea he 6 captured Samaria and deported its people to Assyria and settled them in Halah and on the Habor, the river of Gozan, and in the cities of Media.

t Verses 2–4: cp. 2 Chr. 28. 1–4.
v Verses 19, 20: cp. 2 Chr. 28. 26, 27.
of Egypt.
u the king of Edom: prob. rdg.; Heb. Rezin king of Aram.
w to the king of Egypt at So: prob. rdg.; Heb. to So king

The reason for the deportation

7 All this happened to the Israelites because they had sinned against the LORD their God who brought them up from Egypt, from the rule of Pharaoh king of Egypt; they paid homage to 8 other gods and observed the laws and customs of the nations whom the LORD had dispossessed before them 9 and uttered blasphemies against the LORD their God; they built hill-shrines for themselves in all their settlements, from watch-tower to for-10 tified city, and set up sacred pillars and sacred poles on every high hill 11 and under every spreading tree, and burnt sacrifices at all the hill-shrines there, as the nations did whom the LORD had displaced before them. By this wickedness of theirs they pro-12 voked the LORD's anger. They wor-shipped idols, a thing which the LORD 13 had forbidden them to do. Still the LORD solemnly charged Israel and Judah by every prophet and seer, saying, 'Give up your evil ways; keep my commandments and statutes given in the law which I enjoined on your forefathers and delivered to you through my servants the prophets.' 14 They would not listen, however, but were as stubborn and rebellious as their forefathers had been, who refused to put their trust in the LORD their 15 God; they rejected his statutes and the covenant which he had made with their forefathers and the solemn warn-ings which he had given to them; they followed worthless idols and became worthless themselves; they imitated the nations round about them, a thing which the LORD had 16 forbidden them to do. Forsaking every commandment of the LORD their God, they made themselves images of cast metal, two calves, and also a sacred pole; they prostrated them-selves to all the host of heaven and 17 worshipped the Baal, and they made their sons and daughters pass through the fire. They practised augury and divination; they sold themselves to do what was wrong in the eyes of the LORD and so provoked his anger.
18   Thus it was that the LORD was in-censed against Israel and banished them from his presence; only the 19 tribe of Judah was left. Even Judah did not keep the commandments of the LORD their God but followed the 20 practices adopted by Israel; so the LORD rejected the whole race of Israel

and punished them and gave them over to plunderers and finally flung them out of his sight. When he tore 21 Israel from the house of David, they made Jeroboam son of Nebat king, who seduced Israel from their alle-giance to the LORD and led them into grave sin. The Israelites persisted in 22 all the sins that Jeroboam had com-mitted and did not give them up, until finally the LORD banished the 23 Israelites from his presence, as he had threatened through his servants the prophets, and they were carried into exile from their own land to Assyria; and there they are to this day.

Idolatry in Samaria

Then the king of Assyria brought 24 people from Babylon, Cuthah, Av-va, Hamath, and Sepharvaim, and settled them in the cities of Samaria in place of the Israelites; so they oc-cupied Samaria and lived in its cities. 25 In the early years of their settlement they did not pay homage to the LORD; and the LORD sent lions among them, and the lions preyed upon them. The 26 king was told that the deported peoples whom he had settled in the cities of Samaria did not know the es-tablished usage of the god of the country, and that he had sent lions among them which were preying up-on them because they did not know this. The king of Assyria, therefore, 27 gave orders that one of the priests deported from Samaria should be sent back to live there and teach the people the usage of the god of the country. So one of the deported priests came 28 and lived at Bethel, and taught them how they should pay their homage to the LORD. But each of the nations 29 made its own god, and they set them up within[x] the hill-shrines which the Samaritans had made, each nation in its own settlements. Succoth-benoth 30 was worshipped by the men of Bab-ylon, Nergal by the men of Cuth, Ashima by the men of Hamath, Nib- 31 haz and Tartak by the Avvites; and the Sepharvites burnt their children as offerings to Adrammelech and Anammelech, the gods of Sephar-vaim. While still paying homage to 32 the LORD, they appointed people from every class to act as priests of the hill-shrines and they resorted to them there. They paid homage to the 33 LORD while at the same time they served their own gods, according to

x Or in niches at.

the custom of the nations from which they had been carried into exile.

Israel continues disobedient

34 They keep up these old practices to this day; they do not pay homage to the LORD, for they do not keep his[y] statutes and his[y] judgements, the law and commandment, which he enjoined upon the descendants of Jacob 35 whom he named Israel. When the LORD made a covenant with them, he gave them this commandment: 'You shall not pay homage to other gods or bow down to them or serve them or 36 sacrifice to them, but you shall pay homage to the LORD who brought you up from Egypt with great power and with outstretched arm; to him you shall bow down, to him you shall 37 offer sacrifice. You shall faithfully keep the statutes, the judgements, the law, and the commandments which he wrote for you, and you shall 38 not pay homage to other gods. You shall not forget the covenant which I made with you; you shall not pay 39 homage to other gods. But to the LORD your God you shall pay homage, and he will preserve you from all 40 your enemies.' However, they would not listen but continued their former 41 practices. While these nations paid homage to the LORD they continued to serve their images, and their children and their children's children have maintained the practice of their forefathers to this day.

Hezekiah reigns over Judah

18 1[z] In the third year of Hoshea son of Elah king of Israel, Hezekiah son of 2 Ahaz king of Judah became king. He was twenty-five years old when he came to the throne, and he reigned in Jerusalem for twenty-nine years; his mother was Abi daughter of Zech-3 ariah. He did what was right in the eyes of the LORD, as David his fore-4 father had done. It was he who suppressed the hill-shrines, smashed the sacred pillars, cut down every sacred pole and broke up the bronze serpent that Moses had made; for up to that time the Israelites had been burning sacrifices to it; they called it Nehush-5 tan. He put his trust in the LORD the God of Israel; there was nobody like him among all the kings of Judah who succeeded him or among those who

had gone before him. He remained 6 loyal to the LORD and did not fail in his allegiance to him, and he kept the commandments which the LORD had given to Moses. So the LORD was with 7 him and he prospered in all that he undertook; he rebelled against the king of Assyria and was no longer subject to him. He conquered the 8 Philistine country as far as Gaza and its boundaries, alike the watch-tower and the fortified city.

Shalmaneser captures Samaria

In the fourth year of Hezekiah's reign 9 (that was the seventh year of Hoshea son of Elah king of Israel) Shalmaneser king of Assyria made an attack on Samaria, invested it and captured 10 it after a siege of three years; it was in the sixth year of Hezekiah (the ninth year of Hoshea king of Israel) that Samaria was captured. The king 11 of Assyria deported the Israelites to Assyria and settled them in Halah and on the Habor, the river of Gozan, and in the cities of Media, because 12 they did not obey the LORD their God but violated his covenant and every commandment that Moses the servant of the LORD had given them; they would not listen and they would not obey.

Sennacherib invades Judah

In the fourteenth year of the reign of 13[a] Hezekiah, Sennacherib king of Assyria attacked and took all the fortified cities of Judah. Hezekiah king 14 of Judah sent a message to the king of Assyria at Lachish: 'I have done wrong; withdraw from my land, and I will pay any penalty you impose upon me.' So the king of Assyria laid on Hezekiah king of Judah a penalty of three hundred talents of silver and thirty talents of gold; and Hezekiah 15 gave him all the silver found in the house of the LORD and in the treasuries of the royal palace. At that time 16 Hezekiah broke up the doors of the temple of the LORD and the doorframes which he himself had plated, and gave them to the king of Assyria.

Sennacherib presses for surrender

From Lachish the king of Assyria sent 17 the commander-in-chief, the chief eunuch, and the chief officer[b] with a strong force to King Hezekiah at

---

[y] Prob. rdg.; Heb. their.   [z] Verses 1–3: cp. 2 Chr. 29. 1, 2.   [a] Verses 13–37: cp. Isa. 36. 1–22; 2 Chr. 32. 1–19.   [b] the commander-in-chief, the chief eunuch, and the chief officer: or Tartan, Rab-saris, and Rab-shakeh.

Jerusalem, and they went up and came to Jerusalem and halted by the conduit of the Upper Pool on the causeway which leads to the Fuller's
18 Field. When they called for the king, Eliakim son of Hilkiah, the comptroller of the household, came out to them, with Shebna the adjutant-general and Joah son of Asaph, the
19 secretary of state. The chief officer said to them, 'Tell Hezekiah that this is the message of the Great King, the king of Assyria: "What ground have
20 you for this confidence of yours? Do you think fine words can take the place of skill and numbers? On whom then do you rely for support in your
21 rebellion against me? On Egypt? Egypt is a splintered cane that will run into a man's hand and pierce it if he leans on it. That is what Pharaoh king of Egypt proves to all who rely
22 on him. And if you tell me that you are relying on the LORD your God, is he not the god whose hill-shrines and altars Hezekiah has suppressed, telling Judah and Jerusalem that they must prostrate themselves before this altar in Jerusalem?"
23 'Now, make a bargain with my master the king of Assyria: I will give you two thousand horses if you can
24 find riders for them. Will you reject the authority of even the least of my master's servants and rely on Egypt
25 for chariots and horsemen? Do you think that I have come to attack this place and destroy it without the consent of the LORD? No; the LORD himself said to me, "Attack this land and destroy it."'
26 Eliakim son of Hilkiah, Shebna, and Joah said to the chief officer, 'Please speak to us in Aramaic, for we understand it; do not speak Hebrew to us within earshot of the people
27 on the city wall.' The chief officer answered, 'Is it to your master and to you that my master has sent me to say this? Is it not to the people sitting on the wall who, like you, will have to eat their own dung and drink their
28 own urine?' Then he stood and shouted in Hebrew, 'Hear the message of the Great King, the king of Assyria.
29 These are the king's words: "Do not be taken in by Hezekiah. He cannot
30 save you from me. Do not let him persuade you to rely on the LORD, and tell you that the LORD will save you and that this city will never be surrendered to the king of Assyria."
31 Do not listen to Hezekiah; these are

the words of the king of Assyria: "Make peace with me. Come out to me, and then you shall each eat the fruit of his own vine and his own fig-tree, and drink the water of his own cistern, until I come and take you to 32 a land like your own, a land of grain and new wine, of corn and vineyards, of olives, fine oil, and honey—life for you all, instead of death. Do not listen to Hezekiah; he will only mislead you by telling you that the LORD will save you. Did the god of any of these na- 33 tions save his land from the king of Assyria? Where are the gods of Ha- 34 math and Arpad? Where are the gods of Sepharvaim, Hena, and Ivvah? Where are the gods of Samaria? Did they save Samaria from me? Among 35 all the gods of the nations is there one who saved his land from me? And how is the LORD to save Jerusalem?"'

The people were silent and answered 36 not a word, for the king had given orders that no one was to answer him. Eliakim son of Hilkiah, comptroller 37 of the household, Shebna the adjutant-general, and Joah son of Asaph, secretary of state, came to Hezekiah with their clothes rent and reported what the chief officer had said.

Hezekiah seeks Isaiah's advice

When King Hezekiah heard their re- **19** 1 port, he rent his clothes and wrapped himself in sackcloth, and went into the house of the LORD. He sent Eli- 2 akim comptroller of the household, Shebna the adjutant-general, and the senior priests, all covered in sackcloth, to the prophet Isaiah son of Amoz, to 3 give him this message from the king: 'This day is a day of trouble for us, a day of reproof and contempt. We are like a woman who has no strength to bear the child that is coming to the birth. It may be that the LORD your 4 God heard all the words of the chief officer whom his master the king of Assyria sent to taunt the living God, and will confute what he, the LORD your God, heard. Offer a prayer for those who still survive.' King Hezeki- 5 ah's servants came to Isaiah, and he 6 told them to say this to their master: 'This is the word of the LORD: "Do not be alarmed at what you heard when the lackeys of the king of Assyria blasphemed me. I will put a spirit in 7 him and he shall hear a rumour and withdraw to his own country; and there I will make him fall by the sword."'

c Verses 1–37: cp. Isa. 37. 1–38; 2 Chr. 32. 20–2.

Hezekiah prays for help

8 So the chief officer withdrew. He heard that the king of Assyria had left Lachish, and he found him attack-
9 ing Libnah. But when the king learnt that Tirhakah king of Cush was on the way to make war on him, he sent messengers again to Hezekiah king of
10 Judah, to say to him, 'How can you be deluded by your god on whom you rely when he promises that Jerusalem shall not fall into the hands of the
11 king of Assyria? Surely you have heard what the kings of Assyria have done to all countries, exterminating their people; can you then hope to
12 escape? Did their gods save the nations which my forefathers destroyed, Gozan, Harran, Rezeph, and the people of Beth-eden living in Telassar?
13 Where are the kings of Hamath, of Arpad, and of Lahir, Sepharvaim, Hena, and Ivvah?'
14 Hezekiah took the letter from the messengers and read it; then he went up into the house of the LORD, spread
15 it out before the LORD and offered this prayer: 'O LORD God of Israel, enthroned on the cherubim, thou alone art God of all the kingdoms of the earth; thou hast made heaven and
16 earth. Turn thy ear to me, O LORD, and listen; open thine eyes, O LORD, and see; hear the message that Sennacherib has sent to taunt the living
17 God. It is true, O LORD, that the kings of Assyria have ravaged the
18 nations and their lands, that they have consigned their gods to the fire and destroyed them; for they were no gods but the work of men's hands, mere
19 wood and stone. But now, O LORD our God, save us from his power, so that all the kingdoms of the earth may know that thou, O LORD, alone art God.'

The LORD answers Hezekiah

20 Isaiah son of Amoz sent to Hezekiah and said, 'This is the word of the LORD the God of Israel: I have heard your prayer to me concerning Sen-
21 nacherib king of Assyria. This is the word which the LORD has spoken concerning him:

The virgin daughter of Zion disdains you,
    she laughs you to scorn;
the daughter of Jerusalem tosses her head

as you retreat.
Whom have you taunted and blas- 22
    phemed?
Against whom have you clamoured,
casting haughty glances at the Holy
    One of Israel?
You have sent your messengers to 23
    taunt the Lord,
    and said:
I have mounted my chariot and done
    mighty deeds:
I have gone high up in the mountains,
    into the recesses of Lebanon.
    I have cut down its tallest cedars,
    the best of its pines,
    I have reached its farthest corners,
    forest and meadow.
    I have dug wells   24
    and drunk the waters of a foreign
        land,
and with the soles of my feet I have
    dried up
    all the streams of Egypt.

Have you not heard long ago?   25
    I did it all.
In days gone by I planned it
    and now I have brought it about,
    making fortified cities tumble down
        into heaps of rubble.[d]
Their citizens, shorn of strength,   26
    disheartened and ashamed,
    were but as plants in the field, as
        green herbs,
    as grass on the roof-tops blasted be-
        fore the east wind.[e]
I know your rising up[f] and your 27
    sitting down,
    your going out and your coming in.
The frenzy of your rage against me[g] 28
    and your arrogance
    have come to my ears.
I will put a ring in your nose
    and a hook in your lips,
    and I will take you back by the road
        on which you have come.

This shall be the sign for you: this 29
year you shall eat shed grain and in the second year what is self-sown; but in the third year sow and reap, plant vineyards and eat their fruit. The survivors left in Judah shall strike 30 fresh root under ground and yield fruit above ground, for a remnant shall come 31 out of Jerusalem and survivors from Mount Zion. The zeal of the LORD will perform this.

'Therefore, this is the word of the 32 LORD concerning the king of Assyria:

He shall not enter this city

---

d heaps of rubble: *prob. rdg., cp. Isa. 37. 26; Heb. obscure.*   *e* the east wind: *prob. rdg., cp. Isa. 37. 27; Heb. it is mature.*   *f* your rising up: *prob. rdg., cp. Isa. 37. 28; Heb. om.*   *g* *Prob. rdg., cp. Isa. 37. 29; Heb. repeats* the frenzy of your rage against me.

F*

nor shoot an arrow there,
he shall not advance against it with
shield
nor cast up a siege-ramp against it.

33 By the way on which he came he shall
go back;
this city he shall not enter.
This is the very word of the LORD.

34 I will shield this city to deliver it,
for my own sake and for the sake of
my servant David.'

The LORD strikes down the Assyrians

35 That night the angel of the LORD went
out and struck down a hundred and
eighty-five thousand men in the Assyrian camp; when morning dawned,

36 they all lay dead. So Sennacherib king
of Assyria broke camp, went back to

37 Nineveh and stayed there. One day,
while he was worshipping in the
temple of his god Nisroch, Adrammelech and Sharezer his sons murdered
him and escaped to the land of Ararat. He was succeeded by his son
Esarhaddon.

Hezekiah falls ill

20 1 [h] At this time Hezekiah fell dangerously ill and the prophet Isaiah son of
Amoz came to him and said, 'This is
the word of the LORD: Give your last
instructions to your household, for
you are a dying man and will not

2 recover.' Hezekiah turned his face to
the wall and offered this prayer to the

3 LORD: 'O LORD, remember how I have
lived before thee, faithful and loyal
in thy service, always doing what
was good in thine eyes.' And he wept

4 bitterly. But before Isaiah had left the
citadel, the word of the LORD came to

5 him: 'Go back and say to Hezekiah,
the prince of my people: "This is the
word of the LORD the God of your
father David: I have heard your
prayer and seen your tears; I will heal
you and on the third day you shall go

6 up to the house of the LORD. I will add
fifteen years to your life and deliver
you and this city from the king of
Assyria, and I will protect this city
for my own sake and for my servant

7 David's sake."' Then Isaiah told
them to apply a fig-plaster; so they
made one and applied it to the boil,

8 and he recovered. Then Hezekiah asked Isaiah what sign the LORD would
give him that he would be cured and
would go up into the house of the

9 LORD on the third day. And Isaiah
said, 'This shall be your sign from the

LORD that he will do what he has
promised; shall the shadow go forward ten steps or back ten steps?'

10 Hezekiah answered, 'It is an easy
thing for the shadow to move forward
ten steps; rather let it go back ten

11 steps.' Isaiah the prophet called to the
LORD, and he made the shadow go
back ten steps where it had advanced
down the stairway of Ahaz.

Hezekiah receives Babylonian envoys

At this time Merodach-baladan son of

12 Baladan king of Babylon sent envoys
with a gift to Hezekiah; for he had
heard that he had been ill. Hezekiah

13 welcomed them and showed them all
his treasury, silver and gold, spices
and fragrant oil, his armoury and
everything to be found among his
treasures; there was nothing in his
house and in all his realm that Hezekiah did not show them. Then the

14 prophet Isaiah came to King Hezekiah and asked him, 'What did these
men say and where have they come
from?' 'They have come from a far-
off country,' Hezekiah answered, 'from

15 Babylon.' Then Isaiah asked, 'What
did they see in your house?' 'They
saw everything,' Hezekiah replied;
'there was nothing among my treasures that I did not show them.'

16 Then Isaiah said to Hezekiah, 'Hear

17 the word of the LORD: The time is
coming, says the LORD, when everything in your house, and all that your
forefathers have amassed till the
present day, will be carried away to
Babylon; not a thing shall be left.

18 And some of the sons who will be born
to you, sons of your own begetting,
shall be taken and shall be made
eunuchs in the palace of the king of

19 Babylon.' Hezekiah answered, 'The
word of the LORD which you have
spoken is good'; thinking to himself
that peace and security would last
out his lifetime.

Other records of Hezekiah's reign

The other events of Hezekiah's reign,

20 his exploits, and how he made the pool
and the conduit and brought water
into the city, are recorded in the
annals of the kings of Judah. So Hez-

21 ekiah rested with his forefathers and
was succeeded by his son Manasseh.

Manasseh revives idolatry

Manasseh was twelve years old when

21 he came to the throne, and he reigned

h Verses 1–11: cp. Isa. 38. 1–8, 21, 22.   i Verses 12–19: cp. Isa. 39. 1–8.   j Verses 1–9: cp.
2 Chr. 33. 1–9.

in Jerusalem for fifty-five years; his
2 mother was Hephzi-bah. He did what
was wrong in the eyes of the LORD, in
following the abominable practices of
the nations which the LORD had dispossessed in favour of the Israelites.
3 He rebuilt the hill-shrines which his
father Hezekiah had destroyed, he
erected altars to the Baal and made a
sacred pole as Ahab king of Israel had
done, and prostrated himself before all
the host of heaven and worshipped
4 them. He built altars in the house of
the LORD, that house of which the
LORD had said, 'Jerusalem shall re-
5 ceive my Name.' He built altars for all
the host of heaven in the two courts
6 of the house of the LORD; he made
his son pass through the fire, he
practised soothsaying and divination,
and dealt with ghosts and spirits. He
did much wrong in the eyes of the
7 LORD and provoked his anger; and
the image that he had made of the
goddess Asherah he put in the house,
the place of which the LORD had said
to David and Solomon his son, 'This
house and Jerusalem, which I chose
out of all the tribes of Israel, shall
8 receive my Name for all time. I will
not again make Israel outcasts from
the land which I gave to their forefathers, if only they will be careful to
observe all my commands and all the
law that my servant Moses gave them.'
9 But they did not obey, and Manasseh
misled them into wickedness far worse
than that of the nations which the
LORD had exterminated in favour of
the Israelites.

The LORD foretells Judah's destruction

10 Then the LORD spoke through his
11 servants the prophets: 'Because Manasseh king of Judah has done these
abominable things, outdoing the Amorites before him in wickedness, and
because he has led Judah into sin
12 with his idols, this is the word of the
LORD the God of Israel: I will bring
disaster on Jerusalem and Judah, disaster which will ring in the ears of all
13 who hear of it. I will mark down every
stone of Jerusalem with the plumb-
line of Samaria and the plummet of
the house of Ahab; I will wipe away
Jerusalem as when a man wipes his
14 plate and turns it upside down, and I
will cast off what is left of my people,
my own possession, and hand them
over to their enemies. They shall be
plundered and fall a prey to all their

enemies; for they have done what is 15
wrong in my eyes and have provoked
my anger from the day their forefathers left Egypt up to the present
day. And this Manasseh shed so much 16
innocent blood that he filled Jerusalem full to the brim, not to mention
the sin into which he led Judah by
doing what is wrong in my eyes.' The 17
other events and acts of Manasseh's
reign, and the sin that he committed,
are recorded in the annals of the kings
of Judah. So Manasseh rested with 18
his forefathers and was buried in the
garden-tomb of his family, in the
garden of Uzza; he was succeeded by
his son Amon.

Amon reigns over Judah

Amon was twenty-two years old when 19[k]
he came to the throne, and he reigned
in Jerusalem for two years; his mother was Meshullemeth daughter of
Haruz of Jotbah. He did what was 20
wrong in the eyes of the LORD as
his father Manasseh had done. He 21
followed in his father's footsteps and
served the idols that his father had
served and prostrated himself before
them. He forsook the LORD the God 22
of his fathers and did not conform to
his ways. King Amon's courtiers con- 23
spired against him and murdered him
in his house; but the people of the 24
land killed all the conspirators and
made his son Josiah king in his place.
The other events of Amon's reign are 25
recorded in the annals of the kings of
Judah. He was buried in his grave 26
in the garden of Uzza; he was succeeded by his son Josiah.

*Beginning of Josiah's reign over
    Judah*

Josiah was eight years old when he **22** 1[l]
came to the throne, and he reigned
in Jerusalem for thirty-one years; his
mother was Jedidah daughter of Adaiah of Bozkath. He did what was right 2
in the eyes of the LORD; he followed
closely in the footsteps of his forefather
David, swerving neither right nor
left.

Hilkiah discovers the book of the law

In the eighteenth year of his reign 3[m]
Josiah sent Shaphan son of Azaliah, son of Meshullam, the adjutant-
general, to the house of the LORD. 'Go 4
to the high priest Hilkiah,' he said,
'and tell him to melt down the silver
that has been brought into the house

k Verses 19–24: cp. 2 Chr. 33. 21–5.   l Verses 1, 2: cp. 2 Chr. 34. 1, 2.   m Verses 3–20:
cp. 2 Chr. 34. 8–28.

of the LORD, which those on duty at
the entrance have received from the
5 people, and to hand it over to the
foremen in the house of the LORD,
to pay the workmen who are carry-
6 ing out repairs in it, the carpenters,
builders, and masons, and to purchase timber and hewn stones for its
7 repair. They are not to be asked to
account for the money that has been
given them; they are acting on trust.'
8 The high priest Hilkiah told Shaphan
the adjutant-general that he had discovered the book of the law in the
house of the LORD, and he gave it
9 to him, and Shaphan read it. Then
Shaphan came to report to the king
and told him that his servants had
melted down the silver in the house
of the LORD and handed it over to
10 the foremen there. Then Shaphan the
adjutant-general told the king that
the high priest Hilkiah had given him
a book, and he read it out in the king's
11 presence. When the king heard what
was in the book of the law, he rent his
12 clothes, and ordered the priest Hilkiah, Ahikam son of Shaphan, Akbor
son of Micaiah, Shaphan the adjutant-
general, and Asaiah the king's atten-
13 dant, to go and seek guidance of
the LORD for himself, for the people,
and for all Judah, about what was
written in this book that had been
discovered. 'Great is the wrath of the
LORD', he said, 'that has been kindled
against us, because our forefathers did
not obey the commands in this book
and do all that is laid upon us.'
14 So Hilkiah the priest, Ahikam, Akbor, Shaphan, and Asaiah went to
Huldah the prophetess, wife of Shallum son of Tikvah, son of Harhas, the
keeper of the wardrobe, and consulted
her at her home in the second quarter
15 of Jerusalem. 'This is the word of the
LORD the God of Israel,' she answered:
'Say to the man who sent you to me,
16 "This is the word of the LORD: I am
bringing disaster on this place and its
inhabitants as foretold in the book
which the king of Judah has read,
17 because they have forsaken me and
burnt sacrifices to other gods, provoking my anger with all the idols they
have made with their own hands;
therefore, my wrath is kindled against
this place and will not be quenched."
18 This is what you shall say to the king
of Judah who sent you to seek guidance of the LORD: "This is the word of
the LORD the God of Israel: You have
listened to my words and shown a 1
willing heart, you humbled yourself
before the LORD when you heard me
say that this place and its inhabitants
would become objects of loathing and
scorn, you rent your clothes and wept
before me. Because of all this, I for my
part have heard you. This is the very
word of the LORD. Therefore, I will 2
gather you to your forefathers, and
you will be gathered to your grave in
peace; you will not live to see all the
disaster which I am bringing upon
this place."' So they brought back
word to the king.

Josiah reads the book to the people

Then the king sent and called all the **2**
elders of Judah and Jerusalem together, and went up to the house of 2
the LORD; he took with him the men
of Judah and the inhabitants of Jerusalem, the priests and the prophets,
the whole population, high and low.
There he read out to them all the
book of the covenant discovered in
the house of the LORD; and then, 3
standing on the dais,[o] the king made
a covenant before the LORD to obey
him and keep his commandments, his
testimonies, and his statutes, with all
his heart and soul, and so fulfil the
terms of the covenant written in this
book. And all the people pledged
themselves to the covenant.

Josiah puts down idolatrous worship

Next, the king ordered the high 4
priest Hilkiah, the deputy high priest,[p]
and those on duty at the entrance, to
remove from the house of the LORD all
the objects made for Baal and Asherah and all the host of heaven; he
burnt these outside Jerusalem, in the
open country by the Kidron, and
carried the ashes to Bethel. He sup- 5
pressed the heathen priests whom the
kings of Judah had appointed to burn
sacrifices at the hill-shrines in the
cities of Judah and in the neighbourhood of Jerusalem, as well as those
who burnt sacrifices to Baal, to the
sun and moon and planets and all the
host of heaven. He took the symbol of 6
Asherah[q] from the house of the LORD
to the gorge of the Kidron outside
Jerusalem, burnt it there and pounded
it to dust, which was then scattered
over the common burial-ground. He 7
also pulled down the houses of the
male prostitutes attached to the house

n Verses 1–3: cp. 2 Chr. 34. 29–32. *o Or* by the pillar. *p Prob. rdg.; Heb.* priests. *q* symbol of Asherah: *or* sacred pole.

of the LORD, where the women wove vestments in honour of Asherah.

8 He brought in all the priests from the cities of Judah and desecrated the hill-shrines where they had burnt sacrifices, from Geba to Beersheba, and dismantled the hill-shrines of the demons[r] in front of the gate of Joshua, the governor of the city, to the 9 left of the city gate. These priests, however, never came up to the altar of the LORD in Jerusalem but used to eat unleavened bread with the priests 10 of their clan. He desecrated Topheth in the Valley of Ben-hinnom, so that no one might make his son or daughter pass through the fire in honour 11 of Molech.[s] He destroyed the horses that the kings of Judah had set up in honour of the sun at the entrance to the house of the LORD, beside the room of Nathan-melek the eunuch in the colonnade, and he burnt the 12 chariots of the sun. He pulled down the altars made by the kings of Judah on the roof by the upper chamber of Ahaz and the altars made by Manasseh in the two courts of the house of the LORD; he pounded them to dust and threw it into the gorge of the 13 Kidron. Also, on the east of Jerusalem, to the south of the Mount of Olives, the king desecrated the hill-shrines which Solomon the king of Israel had built for Ashtoreth the loathsome goddess of the Sidonians, and for Kemosh the loathsome god of Moab, and for Milcom the abominable god 14 of the Ammonites; he broke down the sacred pillars and cut down the sacred poles and filled the places where they had stood with human bones.

15 At Bethel he dismantled the altar by[t] the hill-shrine made by Jeroboam son of Nebat who led Israel into sin, together with the hill-shrine itself; he broke its stones in pieces, crushed them to dust and burnt the sacred 16 pole. When Josiah set eyes on the graves which were there on the hill, he sent and took the bones from them and burnt them on the altar to desecrate it, thus fulfilling the word of the LORD announced by the man of God when Jeroboam stood by the altar at the feast. But when he caught sight of the grave of the man of God who 17 had foretold these things, he asked, 'What is that monument I see there?' The people of the city answered, 'The grave of the man of God who came from Judah and foretold all that you

have done to the altar at Bethel.' 'Leave it alone,' he said; 'let no one 18 disturb his bones.' So they spared his bones and also those of the prophet who came from Samaria. Further, 19 Josiah suppressed all the hill-shrines in the cities of Samaria, which the kings of Israel had set up and thereby provoked the LORD's anger, and he did to them what he had done at Bethel. He slaughtered on the altars 20 all the priests of the hill-shrines who were there, and he burnt human bones upon them. Then he went back to Jerusalem.

A memorable Passover

The king ordered all the people to 21 keep the Passover to the LORD their God, as this book of the covenant prescribed; no such Passover had been 22 kept either when the judges were ruling Israel or during the times of the kings of Israel and Judah. But in 23 the eighteenth year of Josiah's reign this Passover was kept to the LORD in Jerusalem. Further, Josiah got rid of 24 all who called up ghosts and spirits, of all household gods and idols and all the loathsome objects seen in the land of Judah and in Jerusalem, so that he might fulfil the requirements of the law written in the book which the priest Hilkiah had discovered in the house of the LORD. No king before 25 him had turned to the LORD as he did, with all his heart and soul and strength, following the whole law of Moses; nor did any king like him appear again.

Yet the LORD did not abate his 26 fierce anger; it still burned against Judah because of all the provocation which Manasseh had given him. 'Judah also I will banish from my 27 presence', he declared, 'as I banished Israel; and I will cast off this city of Jerusalem which once I chose, and the house where I promised that my Name should be.'

The death of Josiah

The other events and acts of Josiah's 28 reign are recorded in the annals of the kings of Judah. It was in his reign 29 that Pharaoh Necho king of Egypt set out for the river Euphrates to help the king of Assyria. King Josiah went to meet him; and when they met at Megiddo, Pharaoh Necho slew him. His attendants conveyed his body in 30[u]

r Or satyrs.   s in honour of Molech: or for an offering.   t Prob. rdg.; Heb. om.   u Verses
30–4: cp. 2 Chr. 36. 1–4.

a chariot from Megiddo to Jerusalem and buried him in his own burial place. Then the people of the land took Josiah's son Jehoahaz and anointed him king in place of his father.

Jehoahaz reigns over Judah

31 Jehoahaz was twenty-three years old when he came to the throne, and he reigned in Jerusalem for three months; his mother was Hamutal daughter of 32 Jeremiah of Libnah. He did what was wrong in the eyes of the LORD, as his 33 forefathers had done. Pharaoh Necho removed him from the throne[v] in Jerusalem, and imposed on the land a fine of a hundred talents of silver and 34 one talent of gold. Pharaoh Necho made Josiah's son Eliakim king in place of his father and changed his name to Jehoiakim. He took Jehoahaz and brought him to Egypt, where 35 he died. Jehoiakim paid the silver and gold to Pharaoh, taxing the country to meet Pharaoh's demands; he exacted it from the people, from every man according to his assessment, so that he could pay Pharaoh Necho.

Jehoiakim reigns over Judah

36 Jehoiakim was twenty-five years old when he came to the throne, and he reigned in Jerusalem for eleven years; his mother was Zebidah daughter of 37 Pedaiah of Rumah. He did what was wrong in the eyes of the LORD, as his 24 forefathers had done. During his reign Nebuchadnezzar king of Babylon took the field, and Jehoiakim became his vassal; but three years later he 2 broke with him and revolted. The LORD launched against him raiding-parties of Chaldaeans, Aramaeans, Moabites, and Ammonites, letting them range through Judah and ravage it, as the LORD had foretold through 3 his servants the prophets. All this happened to Judah in fulfilment of the LORD's purpose to banish them from his presence, because of all the sin that Manasseh had committed 4 and because of the innocent blood that he had shed; he had drenched Jerusalem with innocent blood, and the 5 LORD would not forgive him. The other events and acts of Jehoiakim's reign are recorded in the annals of the 6 kings of Judah. He rested with his forefathers, and was succeeded by his 7 son Jehoiachin. The king of Egypt

did not leave his own land again, because the king of Babylon had stripped him of all his possessions, from the Torrent of Egypt to the river Euphrates.

Nebuchadnezzar besieges Jerusalem

Jehoiachin was eighteen years old 8[w] when he came to the throne, and he reigned in Jerusalem for three months; his mother was Nehushta daughter of Elnathan of Jerusalem. He did what 9 was wrong in the eyes of the LORD, as his father had done. At that time 10 the troops of Nebuchadnezzar king of Babylon advanced on Jerusalem and besieged the city. Nebuchadnezzar 11 arrived while his troops were besieging it, and Jehoiachin king of Judah, 12 his mother, his courtiers, his officers, and his eunuchs, all surrendered to the king of Babylon. The king of Babylon, now in the eighth year of his reign, took him prisoner; and, as 13 the LORD had foretold, he carried off all the treasures of the house of the LORD and of the royal palace and broke up all the vessels of gold which Solomon king of Israel had made for the temple of the LORD. He carried 14 the people of Jerusalem into exile, the officers and the fighting men, ten thousand in number, together with all the craftsmen and smiths; only the weakest class of people were left. He 15 deported Jehoiachin to Babylon; he also took into exile from Jerusalem to Babylon the king's mother and his wives, his eunuchs and the foremost men of the land. He also deported to 16 Babylon all the men of substance, seven thousand in number, and a thousand craftsmen and smiths, all of them able-bodied men and skilled armourers. He made Mattaniah, uncle 17 of Jehoiachin, king in his place and changed his name to Zedekiah.

Zedekiah reigns over Judah

Zedekiah was twenty-one years old 18 when he came to the throne, and he reigned in Jerusalem for eleven years; his mother was Hamutal daughter of Jeremiah of Libnah. He did what was 19 wrong in the eyes of the LORD, as Jehoiakim had done. Jerusalem and 20 Judah so angered the LORD that in the end he banished them from his sight; and Zedekiah rebelled against the king of Babylon.

v removed . . . throne: prob. rdg., cp. 2 Chr. 36. 3; Heb. bound him at Riblah in the land of Hamath when he was king . . .   w Verses 8–17: cp. 2 Chr. 36. 9, 10.   x 24. 18—25. 21: cp. Jer. 52. 1–27.

Zedekiah is taken captive

1ʸ In the ninth year of his reign, in the tenth month, on the tenth day of the month, Nebuchadnezzar king of Babylon advanced with all his army against Jerusalem, invested it and erected watch-towers against it on 2 every side; the siege lasted till the 3 eleventh year of King Zedekiah. In the fourth month of that year,ᶻ on the ninth day of the month, when famine was severe in the city and there was 4 no food for the common people, the city was thrown open. When Zedekiah king of Judah saw this,ᵃ he and all his armed escort left the city and fled by night through the gate called Between the Two Walls, near the king's garden. They escaped towards the Arabah, although the Chaldaeans were surrounding the city. 5 But the Chaldaean army pursued the king and overtook him in the lowlands of Jericho; and all his company was 6 dispersed. The king was seized and brought before the king of Babylon at Riblah, where he pleaded his case 7 before him. Zedekiah's sons were slain before his eyes; then his eyes were put out, and he was brought to Babylon in fetters of bronze.

Destruction of Jerusalem

8 In the fifth month, on the seventh day of the month, in the nineteenth year of Nebuchadnezzar king of Babylon, Nebuzaradan, captain of the king's 9 bodyguard, came to Jerusalem and set fire to the house of the LORD and the royal palace; all the houses in the city, including the mansion of Ged- 10 aliah,ᵇ were burnt down. The Chaldaean forces with the captain of the guard pulled down the walls all 11 round Jerusalem. Nebuzaradan captain of the guard deported the rest of the people left in the city, those who had deserted to the king of Babylon 12 and any remaining artisans.ᶜ He left only the weakest class of people to be vine-dressers and labourers. 13 The Chaldaeans broke up the pillars of bronze in the house of the LORD, the trolleys, and the Sea of bronze, and took the metal to Bab- 14 ylon. They took also the pots, shovels, snuffers, saucers, and all the vessels of bronze used in the service of the 15 temple. The captain of the guard took away the precious metal, whether gold or silver, of which the firepans and the tossing-bowls were made. The bronze of the two pillars, the one 16 Sea, and the trolleys, which Solomon had made for the house of the LORD, was beyond weighing. The one pillar 17 was eighteen cubits high and its capital was bronze; the capital was three cubits high, and a decoration of network and pomegranates ran all round it, wholly of bronze. The other pillar, with its network, was exactly like it.

The captain of the guard took 18 Seraiah the chief priest and Zephaniah the deputy chief priest and the three on duty at the entrance; he took 19 also from the city a eunuch who was in charge of the fighting men, five of those with right of access to the king who were still in the city, the adjutant-generalᵈ whose duty was to muster the people for war, and sixty men of the people who were still there. These Nebuzaradan captain of the 20 guard brought to the king of Babylon at Riblah. There, in the land of 21 Hamath, the king of Babylon had them flogged and put to death. So Judah went into exile from their own land.

Gedaliah is murdered

Nebuchadnezzar king of Babylon ap- 22 pointed Gedaliah son of Ahikam, son of Shaphan, governor over the few people whom he had left in Judah. When the captains of the armed bands 23 and their men heard that the king of Babylon had appointed Gedaliah governor, they all came to him at Mizpah: Ishmael son of Nethaniah, Johanan son of Kareah, Seraiah son of Tanhumeth of Netophah, and Jaazaniah of Beth-maacah. Then Ged- 24 aliah gave them and their men this assurance: 'Have no fear of the Chaldaean officers. Settle down in the land and serve the king of Babylon; and then all will be well with you.' But in the seventh month Ishmael 25 son of Nethaniah, son of Elishama, who was a member of the royal house, came with ten men and murdered ⌈Gedaliah and the Jews and Chaldaeans who were with him at Mizpah. Thereupon all the people, 26 high and low, and the captains of the

---

ʸ Verses 1–12: cp. Jer. 39. 1–10; verses 1–17: cp. 2 Chr. 36. 17–20.   ᶻ In . . . year: prob. rdg., cp. Jer. 52. 6; Heb. om.   ᵃ When . . . this: prob. rdg., cp. Jer. 39. 4; Heb. om.   ᵇ Gedaliah: prob. rdg.; Heb. a great man.   ᶜ any remaining artisans: prob. rdg., cp. Jer. 52. 15; Heb. the remaining crowd.   ᵈ Prob. rdg.; Heb. adds commander-in-chief.

armed bands, fled to Egypt for fear of the Chaldaeans.

Jehoiachin released and honoured in Babylon

27[e] In the thirty-seventh year of the exile of Jehoiachin king of Judah, on the twenty-seventh day of the twelfth month, Evil-merodach[f] king of Babylon in the year of his acces-

sion showed favour to Jehoiachin king of Judah. He brought him out of prison, treated him kindly and gave 28 him a seat at table above the kings with him in Babylon. So Jehoiachin 29 discarded his prison clothes and lived as a pensioner of the king for the rest of his life. For his maintenance, a 30 regular daily allowance was given him by the king as long as he lived.

e *Verses 27–30: cp. Jer. 52. 31–4.*   f *Or Ewil-marduk.*

THE FIRST BOOK OF THE
CHRONICLES

Genealogies from Adam to Ishmael

1 1 2[a] ADAM, Seth, Enosh, Kenan, Ma-
3 halalel, Jared, Enoch, Methuselah,
4 Lamech, Noah.
   The sons of Noah: Shem, Ham and Japheth.
5[b] The sons of Japheth: Gomer, Magog, Madai, Javan,[c] Tubal, Meshech
6 and Tiras. The sons of Gomer: Ashkenaz, Diphath and Togarmah.
7 The sons of Javan: Elishah, Tarshish, Kittim[d] and Rodanim.
8[e] The sons of Ham: Cush, Mizraim,[f]
9 Put and Canaan. The sons of Cush: Seba, Havilah, Sabta, Raama and Sabtecha. The sons of Raama: Sheba
10 and Dedan. Cush was the father of Nimrod, who began to show himself
11[g] a man of might on earth. From Miz-
raim sprang the Lydians, Anamites,
12 Lehabites, Naphtuhites, Pathrusites, Casluhites, and the Caphtorites, from whom the Philistines were descended.
13 Canaan was the father of Sidon, who was his eldest son, and Heth,[h]
14 the Jebusites, the Amorites, the Gir-
15 gashites, the Hivites, the Arkites,
16 the Sinites, the Arvadites, the Zemarites, and the Hamathites.
17[i] The sons of Shem: Elam, Asshur, Arphaxad, Lud[j] and Aram. The sons of Aram: Uz, Hul, Gether and Mash.
18 Arphaxad was the father of Shelah,
19 and Shelah the father of Eber. Eber

had two sons: one was named Peleg,[k] because in his time the earth was divided, and his brother's name was Joktan. Joktan was the father of 20 Almodad, Sheleph, Hazarmoth, Jerah, Hadoram, Uzal, Diklah, Ebal,[l] Abi- 21 mael, Sheba, Ophir, Havilah and Jo- 23 bab. All these were sons of Joktan.
   The line of[n] Shem: Arphaxad, 24[m] Shelah, Eber, Peleg, Reu, Serug, Na- 25 hor, Terah, Abram, also known as 27 Abraham, whose sons were Isaac and 28 Ishmael.

Abraham's descendants

The sons of[p] Ishmael in the order 29[o] of their birth: Nebaioth the eldest, then Kedar, Adbeel, Mibsam, Mishma, 30 Dumah, Massa, Hadad, Teman, Jetur, 31 Naphish and Kedemah. These were Ishmael's sons.
   The sons of Keturah, Abraham's 32 concubine: she bore him Zimran, Jokshan, Medan, Midian, Ishbak and Shuah. The sons of Jokshan: Sheba and Dedan. The sons of Midian: 33 Ephah, Epher, Enoch, Abida and El-daah. All these were descendants of Keturah.

Esau's descendants

Abraham was the father of Isaac, and 34 Isaac's sons were Esau and Israel. The sons of Esau: Eliphaz, Reuel, 35[r] Jeush, Jalam, and Korah. The sons of 36

a *Verses 2–4: cp. Gen. 5. 9–32.*   b *Verses 5–7: cp. Gen. 10. 2–4.*   c *Or Greece.*   d *Or Tarshish of the Kittians.*   e *Verses 8–10: cp. Gen. 10. 6–8.*   f *Or Egypt.*   g *Verses 11–16: cp. Gen. 10. 13–18.*   h *Or the Hittites.*   i *Verses 17–23: cp. Gen. 10. 22–9.*   j *Or the Lydians.*   k *That is Division.*   l *Or Obal, cp. Gen. 10. 28.*   m *Verses 24–7: cp. Gen. 11. 10–26.*   n *The line of: prob. rdg.; Heb. om.*   o *Verses 29–31: cp. Gen. 25. 13–16.*   p *The sons of: prob. rdg., cp. Gen. 25. 13; Heb. om.*   q *Verses 32, 33: cp. Gen. 25. 1–4.*   r *Verses 35–7: cp. Gen. 36. 4, 5, 9–13.*

Eliphaz: Teman, Omar, Zephi, Ga-
37 tam, Kenaz, Timna and Amalek. The
sons of Reuel: Nahath, Zerah, Shammah and Mizzah.

Seir's descendants

38 The sons of Seir: Lotan, Shobal,
Zibeon, Anah, Dishon, Ezer and
39 Dishan. The sons of Lotan: Hori and
Homam; and Lotan had a sister
40 named Timna. The sons of Shobal:
Alvan, Manahath, Ebal, Shephi and
Onam. The sons of Zibeon: Aiah and
41 Anah. The sonᵗ of Anah: Dishon. The
sons of Dishon: Amram, Eshban,
42 Ithran and Cheran. The sons of Ezer:
Bilhan, Zavan and Akan. The sons of
Dishan: Uz and Aran.

Kings of Edom

43ᵘ These are the kings who ruled over
Edom before there were kings in
Israel: Bela son of Beor, whose city
44 was named Dinhabah. When he died,
he was succeeded by Jobab son of
45 Zerah of Bozrah. When Jobab died,
he was succeeded by Husham of Te-
46 man. When Husham died, he was
succeeded by Hadad son of Bedad,
who defeated Midian in Moabite
country. His city was named Avith.
47 When Hadad died, he was succeeded
48 by Samlah of Masrekah. When Samlah died, he was succeeded by Saul of
49 Rehoboth on the River. When Saul
died, he was succeeded by Baal-
50 hanan son of Akbor. When Baal-
hanan died, he was succeeded by
Hadad. His city was named Pai; his
wife's name was Mehetabel daughter
of Matred a woman of Me-zahab.ᵛ
51 After Hadad died the chiefs in
Edom were: chief Timna, chief Aliah,
52 chief Jetheth, chief Oholibamah, chief
53 Elah, chief Pinon, chief Kenaz, chief
54 Teman, chief Mibzar, chief Magdiel
and chief Iram. These were the chiefs
of Edom.

Israel's sons

2 These were the sons of Israel: Reuben, Simeon, Levi, Judah, Issachar,
2 Zebulun, Dan, Joseph, Benjamin,
Naphtali, Gad and Asher.

Judah's descendants

3 The sons of Judah: Er, Onan and
Shelah; the mother of these three was
a Canaanite woman, Bathshua.ʷ Er,

Judah's eldest son, displeased the
LORD and the LORD slew him. Then 4
Tamar, Judah's daughter-in-law, bore
him Perez and Zerah, making in all
five sons of Judah. The sons of Perez: 5
Hezron and Hamul. The sons of 6
Zerah: Zimri, Ethan, Heman, Calcol
and Darda, five in all. The son of 7
Zimri: Carmi.ˣ The son of Carmi:
Achar, who troubled Israel by his
violation of the sacred ban. The son of 8
Ethan: Azariah. The sons of Hezron: 9
Jerahmeel, Ram and Caleb. Ram was 10
the father of Amminadab, Ammina-
dab father of Nahshon prince of Judah.
Nahshon was the father of Salma, 11
Salma father of Boaz, Boaz father of 12
Obed, Obed father of Jesse. The eldest 13
son of Jesse was Eliab, the second
Abinadab, the third Shimea, the 14
fourth Nethaneel, the fifth Raddai,
the sixth Ozem, the seventh David; 15
their sisters were Zeruiah and Abigail. 16
The sons of Zeruiah: Abishai, Joab
and Asahel, three in all. Abigail was 17
the mother of Amasa; his father was
Jether the Ishmaelite.

Caleb son of Hezron had Jerioth by 18
Azubah his wife;ʸ these were her sons:
Jesher, Shobab and Ardon. When 19
Azubah died, Caleb married Ephrath,
who bore him Hur. Hur was the fa- 20
ther of Uri, and Uri father of Bezalel.
Later, Hezron, then sixty years of 21
age, had intercourse with the daughter of Machir father of Gilead, having
married her, and she bore Segub.
Segub was the father of Jair, who had 22
twenty-three cities in Gilead. Geshur 23
and Aram took from them Havvoth-
jair, and Kenath and its dependent
villages, a total of sixty towns. All
these were descendants of Machir
father of Gilead. After the death of 24
Hezron, Caleb had intercourse with
Ephrathah and she bore him Ashhur
the founder of Tekoa.

The sons of Jerahmeel eldest son 25
of Hezron byᶻ Ahijah were Ram the
eldest, Bunah, Oren and Ozem. Jerah- 26
meel had another wife, whose name
was Atarah; she was the mother of
Onam. The sons of Ram eldest son of 27
Jerahmeel: Maaz, Jamin and Eker.
The sons of Onam: Shammai and Jada. 28
The sons of Shammai: Nadab and
Abishur. The name of Abishur's wife 29
was Abihail; she bore him Ahban and
Molid. The sons of Nadab: Seled and 30
Ephraim; Seled died without children.

---

s Verses 38–42: cp. Gen. 36. 20–8.   t Prob. rdg.; Heb. sons; the same correction is made in several
other places in chs. 1–9.   u Verses 43–54: cp. Gen. 36. 31–43.   v Or daughter of Mezahab.
w Bathshua: or daughter of Shua.   x The son . . . Carmi: prob. rdg. (cp. Josh. 7. 1, 18); Heb. om.
y his wife: prob. rdg.; Heb. a woman and.   z by: prob. rdg.; Heb. om.

31 Ephraim's son was Ishi, Ishi's son
32 Sheshan, Sheshan's son Ahlai. The
sons of Jada brother of Shammai:
Jether and Jonathan; Jether died
33 without children. The sons of Jonathan: Peleth and Zaza. These were
the descendants of Jerahmeel.

34 Sheshan had daughters but no
sons. He had an Egyptian servant
35 named Jarha; he gave his daughter
in marriage to this Jarha, and she
36 bore him Attai. Attai was the father
of Nathan, Nathan father of Zabad,
37 Zabad father of Ephlal, Ephlal father
38 of Obed, Obed father of Jehu, Jehu
39 father of Azariah, Azariah father of
40 Helez, Helez father of Elasah, Elasah
father of Sisamai, Sisamai father of
41 Shallum, Shallum father of Jekamiah,
and Jekamiah father of Elishama.

42 The sons of Caleb brother of Jerahmeel: Mesha the eldest, founder of
Ziph, and[a] Mareshah founder of He-
43 bron. The sons of Hebron: Korah,
44 Tappuah, Rekem and Shema. Shema
was the father of Raham father of
Jorkoam, and Rekem was the father
45 of Shammai. The son of Shammai
was Maon, and Maon was the founder
46 of Beth-zur. Ephah, Caleb's concubine, was the mother of Haran, Moza
and Gazez; Haran was the father of
47 Gazez. The sons of Jahdai: Regem,
Jotham, Geshan, Pelet, Ephah and
48 Shaaph. Maacah, Caleb's concubine,
was the mother of Sheber and Tir-
49 hanah; she bore also Shaaph founder
of Madmannah, and Sheva founder of
Machbenah and Gibea. Caleb also had
a daughter named Achsah.

50 The descendants of Caleb: the sons
of Hur, the eldest son of Ephrathah:
Shobal the founder of Kiriath-jearim,
51 Salma the founder of Bethlehem, and
Hareph the founder of Beth-gader.
52 Shobal the founder of Kiriath-jearim
was the father of Reaiah[b] and the ancestor of half the Manahethites.[c]
53 The clans of Kiriath-jearim: Ith-
rites, Puhites, Shumathites, and Mish-
raites, from whom were descended
the Zareathites and the Eshtau-
lites.
54 The descendants of Salma: Bethlehem, the Netophathites, Ataroth, Beth-
joab, half the Manahethites, and the
Zorites.
55 The clans of Sophrites[d] living at
Jabez: Tirathites, Shimeathites, and
Suchathites. These were Kenites who
were connected by marriage with the
ancestor of the Rechabites.

David's descendants

These were the sons of David, born at 3
Hebron: the eldest Amnon, whose
mother was Ahinoam of Jezreel; the
second Daniel, whose mother was Abigail of Carmel; the third Absalom, 2
whose mother was Maacah daughter
of Talmai king of Geshur; the fourth
Adonijah, whose mother was Haggith; the fifth Shephatiah, whose 3
mother was Abital; the sixth Ithream,
whose mother was David's wife Eglah.
These six were born at Hebron, where 4
David reigned seven years and six
months. In Jerusalem he reigned
thirty-three years, and there the fol- 5[f]
lowing sons were born to him:
Shimea, Shobab, Nathan and Solomon; these four were sons of Bathsheba daughter of Ammiel. There 6
were nine others: Ibhar, Elishama,
Eliphelet, Nogah, Nepheg, Japhia, El- 7
ishama, Eliada and Eliphelet. These 8 9
were all the sons of David, with their
sister Tamar, in addition to his sons
by concubines.

Solomon's son was Rehoboam, his 10
son Abia, his son Asa, his son Jehoshaphat, his son Joram, his son 11
Ahaziah, his son Joash, his son Am- 12
aziah, his son Azariah, his son
Jotham, his son Ahaz, his son Hez- 13
ekiah, his son Manasseh, his son 14
Amon, and his son Josiah. The sons 15
of Josiah: the eldest was Johanan, the
second Jehoiakim, the third Zedekiah, the fourth Shallum. The sons of 16
Jehoiakim: Jeconiah and Zedekiah.
The sons of Jeconiah, a prisoner:[g] She- 17
altiel, Malchiram, Pedaiah, Shenazzar, 18
Jekamiah, Hoshama and Nedabiah.
The sons of Pedaiah: Zerubbabel 19
and Shimei. The sons of Zerubbabel: Meshullam and Hananiah;
they had a sister, Shelomith. There 20
were five others: Hashubah, Ohel,
Berechiah, Hasadiah and Jushab-
hesed. The sons of Hananiah: Pel- 21
atiah and Isaiah; his son was Rephaiah, his son Arnan, his son Obadiah,
his son Shecaniah. The sons of 22
Shecaniah: Shemaiah,[h] Hattush, Igeal,
Bariah, Neariah and Shaphat, six
in all. The sons of Neariah: Elioenai, 23
Hezekiah and Azrikam, three in
all. The sons of Elioenai: Hodaiah, 24

a Prob. rdg.; Heb. adds the sons of.   b Prob. rdg., cp. 4. 2; Heb. the seer.   c Prob. rdg., cp.
verse 54; Heb. Menuhoth.   d Or secretaries.   e Verses 1–4: cp. 2 Sam. 3. 2–5.   f Verses 5–8: cp.
14. 4–7; 2 Sam. 5. 14–16.   g Jeconiah, a prisoner: or Jeconiah; Assir, . . .   h Prob. rdg.; Heb.
adds and the sons of Shemaiah.

Eliashib, Pelaiah, Akkub, Johanan, Dalaiah and Anani, seven in all.

More of Judah's descendants

4 The sons of Judah: Perez, Hezron, 2 Carmi, Hur and Shobal. Reaiah son of Shobal was the father of Jahath, Jahath father of Ahumai and Lahad. These were the clans of the Zorathites.

3-4 The sons of Etam: Jezreel, Ishma, Idbash, Penuel the founder of Gedor, and Ezer the founder of Hushah; they had a sister named Hazelelponi. These were the sons of Hur: Ephrathah the eldest, the founder of Bethlehem.

5 Ashhur the founder of Tekoa had 6 two wives, Helah and Naarah. Naarah bore him Ahuzam, Hepher, Temeni and Haahashtari.[i] These were 7 the sons of Naarah. The sons of Helah: Zereth, Jezoar, Ethnan and 8 Coz. Coz was the father of Anub and Zobebah and the clans of Aharhel son of Harum.

9 Jabez ranked higher than his brothers; his mother called him Jabez because, as she said, she had borne 10 him in pain. Jabez called upon the God of Israel and said, 'I pray thee, bless me and grant me wide territories. May thy hand be with me, and do me no harm, I pray thee, and let me be free from pain'; and God granted his petition.

11 Kelub brother of Shuah was the father of Mehir the father of Eshton. 12 Eshton was the father of Beth-rapha, Paseah, and Tehinnah father of Irnahash. These were the men of Rechah.

13 The sons of Kenaz: Othniel and Seraiah. The sons of Othniel: Hathath and Meonothai.

14 Meonothai was the father of Ophrah.

Seraiah was the father of Joab founder of Ge-harashim,[j] for they were craftsmen.

15 The sons of Caleb son of Jephunneh: Iru, Elah and Naam. The son of Elah: Kenaz.

16 The sons of Jehaleleel: Ziph and Ziphah, Tiria and Asareel.

17-18 The sons of Ezra: Jether, Mered, Epher and Jalon. These were the sons of Bithiah daughter of Pharaoh, whom Mered had married; she conceived and gave birth to[k] Miriam, Shammai and Ishbah founder of

Eshtemoa. His Jewish wife was the mother of Jered founder of Gedor, Heber founder of Soco, and Jekuthiel founder of Zanoah. The sons of 19 his[l] wife Hodiah sister of Naham were Daliah father of Keilah the Garmite, and Eshtemoa the Maacathite.

The sons of Shimon: Amnon, Rinn- 20 ah, Ben-hanan and Tilon.

The sons of Ishi: Zoheth and Benzoheth.

The sons of Shelah son of Judah: 21 Er founder of Lecah, Laadah founder of Mareshah, the clans of the guild of linen-workers at Ashbea, Jokim, 22 the men of Kozeba, Joash, and Saraph who fell out with Moab and came back to Bethlehem.[m] (The records are ancient.) They were the potters, and 23 those who lived at Netaim and Gederah were there on the king's service.

Simeon's descendants

The sons of Simeon: Nemuel, Jamin, 24 Jarib, Zerah, Saul, his son Shallum, 25 his son Mibsam and his son Mishma. The sons of Mishma: his son Hamuel, 26 his son Zaccur and his son Shimei. Shimei had sixteen sons and six 27 daughters, but others of his family had fewer children, and the clan as a whole did not increase as much as the tribe of Judah. They lived at Beer- 28 sheba, Moladah, Hazar-shual, Bilhah, 29 Ezem, Tolad, Bethuel, Hormah, Zik- 30 lag, Beth-marcaboth, Hazar-susim, 31 Beth-birei, and Shaaraim. These were their cities until David came to the throne. Their settlements[n] were 32 Etam, Ain, Rimmon, Tochen, and Ashan, five cities in all. They had also 33 hamlets round these cities as far as Baal. These were the places where they lived.

The names on their register were: Meshobab, Jamlech, Joshah son of 34 Amaziah, Joel, Jehu son of Josibiah, 35 son of Seraiah, son of Asiel, Elioenai, 36 Jaakobah, Jeshohaiah, Asaiah, Adiel, Jesimiel, Benaiah, Ziza son of Shi- 37 phi, son of Allon, son of Jedaiah, son of Shimri, son of Shemaiah, whose 38 names are recorded as princes in their clans, and their families had greatly increased. They then went from the 39 approaches to Gedor east of the valley in search of pasture for their flocks. They found rich and good pasture in 40 a wide stretch of open country where everything was quiet and peaceful; before then it had been occupied by

---

i Temeni and Haahashtari: *or* the Temanite and the Ahashtarite.   *j* Or the Valley of Craftsmen.
k and gave birth to: *prob. rdg.; Heb. om.*   *l* his: *prob. rdg.; Heb. om.*   *m* and came . . . Bethlehem: *prob. rdg.; Heb. unintelligible.*   *n* Prob. rdg.; Heb. hamlets.

41 Hamites. During the reign of Hezekiah king of Judah these whose names are written above came and destroyed the tribes of Ham[o] and the Meunites whom they found there. They annihilated them so that no trace of them has remained to this day; and they occupied the land in their place, for there was pasture for their flocks.
42 Of their number five hundred Simeonites invaded the hill-country of Seir, led by Pelatiah, Neariah, Rephaiah,
43 and Uzziel, the sons of Ishi. They destroyed all who were left of the surviving Amalekites; and they live there still.

Reuben's descendants

5 The sons of Reuben, the eldest of Israel's sons. (He was, in fact, the first son born, but because he had committed incest with a wife of his father's the rank of the eldest was transferred to the sons of Joseph, Israel's son, who, however, could not be
2 registered as the eldest son. Judah held the leading place among his brothers because he fathered a ruler, and the rank of the eldest was his,
3 not[p] Joseph's.) The sons of Reuben, the eldest of Israel's sons: Enoch,
4 Pallu, Hezron and Carmi. The sons of Joel: his son Shemaiah, his son Gog,
5 his son Shimei, his son Micah, his son
6 Reaia, his son Baal, his son Beerah, whom Tiglath-pileser king of Assyria carried away into exile; he was a
7 prince of the Reubenites. His kinsmen, family by family, as registered in their tribal lists: Jeiel the chief,
8 Zechariah, Bela son of Azaz, son of Shema, son of Joel. They lived in Aroer, and their lands stretched as far
9 as Nebo and Baal-meon. Eastwards they occupied territory as far as the edge of the desert which stretches from the river Euphrates, for they had large numbers of cattle in Gilead.
10 During Saul's reign they made war on the Hagarites, whom they conquered, occupying their encampments over all the country east of Gilead.

Gad's descendants

11 Adjoining them were the Gadites, occupying the district of Bashan as
12 far as Salcah: Joel the chief; second in rank, Shapham; then Jaanai and
13 Shaphat in Bashan. Their fellow-tribesmen belonged to the families of Michael, Meshullam, Sheba, Jorai,

Jachan, Zia and Heber, seven in all.
These were the sons of Abihail son of 14 Huri, son of Jaroah, son of Gilead, son of Michael, son of Jeshishai, son of Jahdo, son of Buz. Ahi son of Abdiel, 15 son of Guni, was head of their family; they lived in Gilead, in Bashan and its 16 villages, and in all the common land of Sharon as far as it stretched. These 17 registers were all compiled in the reigns of Jotham king of Judah and Jeroboam king of Israel.

History of the tribes east of Jordan

The sons of Reuben, Gad, and half 18 the tribe of Manasseh: of their fighting men armed with shield and sword, their archers and their battle-trained soldiers, forty-four thousand seven hundred and sixty were ready for active service. They made war on 19 the Hagarites, Jetur, Nephish, and Nodab. They were given help against 20 them, for they cried to their God for help in the battle, and because they trusted him he listened to their prayer, and the Hagarites and all their allies surrendered to them.[q] They 21 drove off their cattle, fifty thousand camels, two hundred and fifty thousand sheep, and two thousand asses, and they took a hundred thousand captives. Many had been killed, for 22 the war was of God's making, and they occupied the land instead of them until the exile.

Half the tribe of Manasseh lived in 23 the land from Bashan to Baal-hermon, Senir, and Mount Hermon, and were numerous also in Lebanon. The heads 24 of their families were: Epher, Ishi, Eliel, Azriel, Jeremiah, Hodaviah, and Jahdiel, all men of ability and repute, heads of their families. But 25 they sinned against the God of their fathers, and turned wantonly to worship the gods of the peoples whom God had destroyed before them. So 26 the God of Israel stirred up Pul king of Assyria, that is Tiglath-pileser king of Assyria, and he carried into exile Reuben, Gad, and half the tribe of Manasseh. He took them to Halah, Habor, Hara, and the river Gozan, where they are to this day.

Levi's descendants

The sons of Levi: Gershon,[r] Kohath 6 and Merari. The sons of Kohath: 2 Amram, Izhar, Hebron and Uzziel. The children of Amram: Aaron, 3

---

o the tribes of Ham: prob. rdg., cp. verse 40; Heb. their tribes.　　p his, not: prob. rdg.; Heb. om.
q They were . . . surrendered to them: or They attacked them boldly, and the Hagarites and all their allies surrendered to them, for they cried . . . to their prayer.　　r Gershom in verses 16 and 17.

Moses and Miriam. The sons of Aaron: Nadab, Abihu, Eleazar and Ithamar. 4[8] Eleazar was the father of Phinehas, 5 Phinehas father of Abishua, Abishua father of Bukki, Bukki father of Uzzi, 6 Uzzi father of Zerahiah, Zerahiah 7 father of Meraioth, Meraioth father of Amariah, Amariah father of Ahi-8 tub, Ahitub father of Zadok, Zadok 9 father of Ahimaaz, Ahimaaz father of Azariah, Azariah father of Johanan, 10 and Johanan father of Azariah, the priest who officiated in the LORD's house which Solomon built at Jeru-11 salem. Azariah was the father of Amariah, Amariah father of Ahitub, 12 Ahitub father of Zadok, Zadok fa-13 ther of Shallum, Shallum father of Hilkiah, Hilkiah father of Azariah, 14 Azariah father of Seraiah, and Seraiah 15 father of Jehozadak. Jehozadak went into exile when the LORD sent Judah and Jerusalem into exile under Nebuchadnezzar.

16[t] The sons of Levi: Gershom, Kohath 17 and Merari. The sons of Gershom: 18 Libni and Shimei. The sons of Kohath: Amram, Izhar, Hebron and Uzziel. 19 The sons of Merari: Mahli and Mushi. The clans of Levi, family by family: 20[u] Gershom: his son Libni, his son Ja-21 hath, his son Zimmah, his son Joah, his son Iddo, his son Zerah, his son 22[v] Jeaterai. The sons of Kohath: his son Amminadab, his son Korah, his son 23 Assir, his son Elkanah, his son Ebi-24 asaph, his son Assir, his son Tahath, his son Uriel, his son Uzziah, his son 25 Saul. The sons of Elkanah: Amasai 26 and Ahimoth, his son Elkanah, his 27 son Zophai, his son Nahath, his son Eliab, his son Jeroham, his son El-28 kanah, his son Samuel: Joel the 29 eldest and Abiah the second. The sons of Merari: his son Mahli, his son Libni, 30 his son Shimei, his son Uzza, his son Shimea, his son Haggiah, his son Asaiah.

David's musicians

31 These are the men whom David appointed to take charge of the music in the house of the LORD when the Ark 32 should be deposited there. They performed their musical duties before the Tent of the Presence until Solomon built the house of the LORD in Jerusalem, and took their regular turns of 33 duty there. The following, with their descendants, took this duty. Of the line of Kohath: Heman the musician,

son of Joel, son of Samuel, son of 34 Elkanah, son of Jeroham, son of Eli-el, son of Toah, son of Zuph, son 35 of Elkanah, son of Mahath, son of Amasai, son of Elkanah, son of Joel, 36 son of Azariah, son of Zephaniah, son 37 of Tahath, son of Assir, son of Ebia-saph, son of Korah, son of Izhar, son 38 of Kohath, son of Levi, son of Israel. Heman's colleague Asaph stood at his 39 right hand. He was the son of Bera-chiah, son of Shimea, son of Michael, 40 son of Baaseiah, son of Malchiah, son 41[u] of Ethni, son of Zerah, son of Adaiah, son of Ethan, son of Zimmah, son of 42 Shimei, son of Jahath, son of Ger-43 shom, son of Levi. On their left stood 44 their colleague of the line of Merari: Ethan son of Kishi, son of Abdi, son of Malluch, son of Hashabiah, son of 45 Amaziah, son of Hilkiah, son of Amzi, 46 son of Bani, son of Shamer, son of 47 Mahli, son of Mushi, son of Merari, son of Levi. Their kinsmen the Levites 48 were dedicated to all the service of the Tabernacle, the house of God.

Aaron's descendants

But it was Aaron and his descendants 49 who burnt the sacrifices on the altar of whole-offering and the altar of incense, in fulfilment of all the duties connected with the most sacred gifts, and to make expiation for Israel, exactly as Moses the servant of God had commanded. The sons of Aaron: 50[x] his son Eleazar, his son Phinehas, his son Abishua, his son Bukki, his son 51 Uzzi, his son Zerahiah, his son Merai-52 oth, his son Amariah, his son Ahitub, his son Zadok, his son Ahimaaz. 53

Cities of the Levites

These are their settlements in en-54 campments in the districts assigned to the descendants of Aaron, to the clan of Kohath, for it was to them that the lot had fallen: they gave 55 them Hebron in Judah, with the common land round it, but they assigned 56 to Caleb son of Jephunneh the open country belonging to the town and its hamlets. They gave to the sons of 57[y] Aaron: Hebron the city[z] of refuge, Lib-nah, Jattir, Eshtemoa, Hilen, Debir, 58 Ashan, and Beth-shemesh, each with 59 its common land. And from the tribe of 60 Benjamin: Geba, Alemeth, and Anath-oth, each with its common land, making thirteen cities in all by their clans. They gave to the remaining clans 61

s Verses 4–8: cp. verses 50–3.   t Verses 16–19: cp. Exod. 6. 16–19.   u Verses 20, 21: cp. verses 41–3.   v Verses 22–8: cp. verses 33–8.   w Verses 41–3: cp. verses 20, 21.   x Verses 50–3: cp. verses 4–8.   y Verses 57–81: cp. Josh. 21. 13–39.   z Prob. rdg., cp. Josh 21. 13; Heb. cities.

of the sons of Kohath ten cities by lot
62 from the half tribe of Manasseh. To
the sons of Gershom according to their
clans they gave thirteen cities from
the tribes of Issachar, Asher, Naph-
63 tali, and Manasseh in Bashan. To the
sons of Merari according to their clans
they gave by lot twelve cities from
the tribes of Reuben, Gad, and Ze-
64 bulun. Israel gave these cities, each
with its common land, to the Levites.
65 (The cities mentioned above, from
the tribes of Judah, Simeon, and Benjamin, were assigned by lot.)
66	Some of the clans of Kohath had
67 cities allotted*a* to them. They gave
them the city*b* of refuge, Shechem in
the hill-country of Ephraim, Gezer,
68 69 Jokmeam, Beth-horon, Aijalon, and
Gath-rimmon, each with its common
70 land. From the half tribe of Manasseh,
Aner and Bileam, each with its common land, were given to the rest of the
clans of Kohath.
71	To the sons of Gershom they gave
from the half tribe of Manasseh: Golan
in Bashan, and Ashtaroth, each with
72 its common land. From the tribe of
73 Issachar: Kedesh, Daberath, Ramoth,
and Anem, each with its common
74 land. From the tribe of Asher: Ma-
75 shal, Abdon, Hukok, and Rehob,
76 each with its common land. From the
tribe of Naphtali: Kedesh in Galilee,
Hammon, and Kiriathaim, each with
its common land.
77	To the rest of the sons of Merari
they gave from the tribe of Zebulun:
Rimmon and Tabor, each with its
78 common land. On the east of Jordan,
opposite Jericho, from the tribe of
Reuben: Bezer-in-the-wilderness, Jah-
79 zah, Kedemoth, and Mephaath, each
80 with its common land. From the tribe
of Gad: Ramoth in Gilead, Mahanaim,
81 Heshbon, and Jazer, each with its common land.

Issachar's descendants

7 1*c* The sons of Issachar: Tola, Pua,
2 Jashub and Shimron, four. The sons
of Tola: Uzzi, Rephaiah, Jeriel, Jah-
mai, Jibsam, and Samuel, all able
men and heads of families by paternal
descent from Tola according to their
tribal lists; their number in David's
time was twenty-two thousand six
3 hundred. The son of Uzzi: Izrahiah. The sons of Izrahiah: Michael,

Obadiah, Joel and Isshiah, making a
total of five, all of them chiefs. In 4
addition there were bands of fighting men recorded by families according to the tribal lists to the number of thirty-six thousand, for they
had many wives and children. Their 5
fellow-tribesmen in all the clans of
Issachar were able men, eighty-seven
thousand; every one of them was
registered.

Benjamin's and Dan's descendants

The sons of Benjamin: Bela, Becher 6
and Jediael, three. The sons of Bela: 7
Ezbon, Uzzi, Uzziel, Jerimoth and Iri,
five. They were heads of their families
and able men; the number registered
was twenty-two thousand and thirty-
four. The sons of Becher: Zemira, 8
Joash, Eliezer, Elioenai, Omri, Jeremoth, Abiah, Anathoth and Alemeth;
all these were sons of Becher accord- 9
ing to their tribal lists, heads of their
families and able men; and the number registered was twenty thousand
two hundred. The son of Jediael: 10
Bilhan. The sons of Bilhan: Jeush,
Benjamin, Ehud, Kenaanah, Zethan,
Tarshish and Ahishahar. All these 11
were descendants of Jediael, heads
of*d* families and able men. The number was seventeen thousand two hundred men, fit for active service in war.
The sons of Dan:*e* Hushim and the 12
sons of Aher.*f*

Naphtali's descendants

The sons of Naphtali: Jahziel, Guni, 13
Jezer, Shallum. These were sons of
Bilhah.

Manasseh's descendants

The sons of Manasseh,*h* born of his 14*g*
concubine, an Aramaean: Machir
father of Gilead. Machir married a 15
woman whose name was*i* Maacah.
The second son was named Zelophehad, and Zelophehad had daughters.
Maacah wife of Machir had a son 16
whom she named Peresh. His brother's
name was Sheresh, and his sons were
Ulam and Rakem. The son of Ulam: 17
Bedan. These were the sons of Gilead
son of Machir, son of Manasseh. His 18
sister Hammoleketh was the mother
of Ishhod, Abiezer and Mahalah. The 19
sons of Shemida: Ahian, Shechem,
Likhi and Aniam.

a allotted: prob. rdg., cp. Josh. 21. 20; Heb. of their frontier.	*b* Prob. rdg., cp. Josh. 21. 21; Heb.
cities.	*c* Verses 1, 6, 13, 30 and 8. 1–5: cp. Gen. 46. 13, 17, 21–4.	*d* Prob. rdg.; Heb. to the
heads of.	*e* The sons of Dan: prob. rdg., cp. Gen. 46. 23; Heb. And Shuppim and Huppim, the
sons of Ir.	*f* Or another.	*g* Verses 14–19: cp. Num. 26. 29–33.	*h* Prob. rdg.; Heb. adds
Asriel.	*i* whose name was: prob. rdg.; Heb. to Huppim and Shuppim, and his sister's name
was . . .

Ephraim's descendants

20 The sons of Ephraim: Shuthelah, his son Bered, his son Tahath, his son
21 Eladah, his son Tahath, his son Zabad, his son Shuthelah. Ephraim's other sons Ezer and Elead were killed by the native Gittites when they came
22 down to lift their cattle. Their father Ephraim long mourned for them, and his kinsmen came to comfort him.
23 Then he had intercourse with his wife; she conceived and had a son whom he named Beriah (because disaster[j]
24 had come on his family). He had a daughter named Sherah; she built Lower and Upper Beth-horon and
25 Uzzen-sherah. He also had a son named Rephah; his son was Resheph,
26 his son Telah, his son Tahan, his son Laadan, his son Ammihud, his
27 son Elishama, his son Nun, his son Joshua.
28   Their lands and settlements were: Bethel and its dependent villages, to the east Naaran, to the west Gezer, Shechem, and Gaza, with their villages.
29 In the possession of Manasseh were Beth-shean, Taanach, Megiddo, and Dor, with their villages. In all of these lived the descendants of Joseph the son of Israel.

Asher's descendants

30 The sons of Asher: Imnah, Ishvah, Ishvi and Beriah, together with their
31 sister Serah. The sons of Beriah: Heber and Malchiel father of Birza-
32 vith. Heber was the father of Japhlet, Shomer, Hotham, and their sister
33 Shua. The sons of Japhlet: Pasach, Bimhal and Ashvath. These were the
34 sons of Japhlet. The sons of Shomer: Ahi, Rohgah, Jehubbah and Aram.
35 The sons of his brother Hotham:[k] Zophah, Imna, Shelesh and Amal.
36 The sons of Zophah: Suah, Harne-
37 pher, Shual, Beri, Imrah, Bezer, Hod, Shamma, Shilshah, Ithran and Beera.
38 The sons of Jether: Jephunneh, Pis-
39 pah and Ara. The sons of Ulla: Arah,
40 Haniel and Rezia. All these were descendants of Asher, heads of families, picked men of ability, leading princes. They were enrolled among the fighting troops; the total number was twenty-six thousand men.

Benjamin's descendants

8 The sons of Benjamin were: the eldest Bela, the second Ashbel, the third
2 Aharah, the fourth Nohah and the fifth Rapha. The sons of Bela: Addar, 3 Gera father of Ehud,[l] Abishua, Na- 4 aman, Ahoah, Gera, Shephuphan and 5 Huram. These were the sons of Ehud, 6 heads of families living in Geba, who were removed to Manahath: Naaman, 7 Ahiah, and Gera—he it was who removed them. He was the father of Uzza and Ahihud. Shaharaim had 8 sons born to him in Moabite country, after putting away his wives Mahasham and Baara. By his wife Hodesh 9 he had Jobab, Zibia, Mesha, Malcham, Jeuz, Shachia and Mirmah. 10 These were his sons, heads of families. By Mahasham he had had Abitub and 11 Elpaal. The sons of Elpaal: Eber, 12 Misham, Shamed who built Ono and Lod with its villages, also Beriah and 13 Shema who were heads of families living in Aijalon, having expelled the inhabitants of Gath. Ahio, Shashak, 14 Jeremoth, Zebadiah, Arad, Ader, Mi- 15 16 chael, Ispah, and Joha were sons of Beriah; Zebadiah, Meshullam, Hezeki, 17 Heber, Ishmerai, Jezliah, and Jobab 18 were sons of Elpaal; Jakim, Zichri, 19 Zabdi, Elienai, Zilthai, Eliel, Adaiah, 20 21 Beraiah, and Shimrath were sons of Shimei; Ishpan, Heber, Eliel, Abdon, 22 23 Zichri, Hanan, Hananiah, Elam, An- 24 tothiah, Iphedeiah, and Penuel were 25 sons of Shashak; Shamsherai, She- 26 hariah, Athaliah, Jaresiah, Eliah, and 27 Zichri were sons of Jeroham. These 28 were enrolled in the tribal lists as heads of families, chiefs living in Jerusalem.

Saul's family

Jehiel founder of Gibeon lived at 29[m] Gibeon; his wife's name was Maacah. His eldest son was Abdon, followed by 30 Zur, Kish, Baal, Nadab, Gedor, Ahio, 31 Zacher and Mikloth. Mikloth was the 32 father of Shimeah; they lived alongside their kinsmen in Jerusalem.
   Ner was the father of Kish, Kish 33 father of Saul, Saul father of Jonathan, Malchishua, Abinadab and Eshbaal. Jonathan's son was Merib- 34 baal, and he was the father of Micah. The sons of Micah: Pithon, Melech, 35 Tarea and Ahaz. Ahaz was the father 36 of Jehoaddah, Jehoaddah father of Alemeth, Azmoth and Zimri. Zimri was the father of Moza, and Moza 37 father of Binea; his son was Raphah, his son Elasah, and his son Azel. Azel 38 had six sons, whose names were Azrikam, Bocheru, Ishmael, Sheariah, Obadiah, and Hanan. All these

j Heb. beraah.   *k* Prob. rdg., cp. verse 32; Heb. Helem.   *l* father of Ehud: prob. rdg., cp. Judg.
3. 15; Heb. Abihud.   *m* Verses 29–38: cp. 9. 35–44.

39 were sons of Azel. The sons of his brother Eshek: the eldest Ulam, the
40 second Jeush, the third Eliphelet. The sons of Ulam were able men, archers, and had many sons and grandsons, a hundred and fifty. All these were descendants of Benjamin.

Repatriated Israelites

9 So all Israel were registered and recorded in the book of the kings of Israel; but Judah for their sins were
2[n] carried away to exile in Babylon. The first to occupy their ancestral land in their cities were lay Israelites, priests,
3 Levites, and temple-survitors. Jerusalem was occupied partly by Judahites, partly by Benjamites, and partly by men of Ephraim and Manasseh.
4 Judahites:[o] Uthai son of Ammihud, son of Omri, son of Imri, son of Bani, a descendant of Perez son of Judah.
5 Shelanites: Asaiah the eldest and his
6 sons. The sons of Zerah: Jeuel and six hundred and ninety of their kinsmen.
7 Benjamites: Sallu son of Meshullam, son of Hodaviah, son of Hassenuah,
8 Ibneiah son of Jeroham, Elah son of Uzzi, son of Micri, Meshullam son of Shephatiah, son of Reuel, son of
9 Ibniah, and their recorded kinsmen numbering nine hundred and fifty-six, all heads of families.
10 Priests: Jedaiah, Jehoiarib, Jachin,
11 Azariah son of Hilkiah, son of Meshullam, son of Zadok, son of Meraioth, son of Ahitub, the officer in charge
12 of the house of God, Adaiah son of Jeroham, son of Pashhur, son of Malchiah, Maasai son of Adiel, son of Jahzerah, son of Meshullam, son of
13 Meshillemith, son of Immer, and their colleagues, heads of families numbering one thousand seven hundred and sixty, men of substance and fit for the work connected with the service of the house of God.
14 Levites: Shemaiah son of Hasshub, son of Azrikam, son of Hashabiah,
15 a descendant of Merari, Bakbakkar, Heresh, Galal, Mattaniah son of Mica,
16 son of Zichri, son of Asaph, Obadiah son of Shemaiah, son of Galal, son of Jeduthun, and Berechiah son of Asa, son of Elkanah, who lived in the hamlets of the Netophathites.
17 The door-keepers were Shallum, Akkub, Talmon, and Ahiman; their
18 brother Shallum was the chief. Until then they had all been door-keepers in the quarters of the Levites at the king's
19 gate, on the east. Shallum son of

Kore, son of Ebiasaph, son of Korah, and his kinsmen of the Korahite family were responsible for service as guards of the thresholds of the Tabernacle; their ancestors had performed the duty of guarding the entrances to the camp of the LORD.
20 Phinehas son of Eleazar had been their overseer in the past—the LORD be with him! Zechariah son of Meshele-
21 miah was the door-keeper of the Tent of the Presence. Those picked to be
22 door-keepers numbered two hundred and twelve in all, registered in their hamlets. David and Samuel the seer had installed them because they were trustworthy. They and their sons had
23 charge, by watches, of the gates of the house, the tent-dwelling of the LORD.
24 The door-keepers were to be on four sides, east, west, north, and south.
25 Their kinsmen from their hamlets had to come on duty with them for seven
26 days at a time in turn. The four principal door-keepers were chosen for their trustworthiness; they were Levites and had charge of the rooms and
27 the stores in the house of God. They always slept in the precincts of the house of God (for the watch was their duty) and they had charge of the key for opening the gates every morning.
28 Some of them had charge of the vessels used in the service of the temple, keeping count of them as they were
29 brought in and taken out. Some of them were detailed to take charge of the furniture and all the sacred vessels, the flour, the wine, the oil, the incense, and the spices.
30 Some of the priests compounded
31 the ointment for the spices. Mattithiah the Levite, the eldest son of Shallum the Korahite, was in charge of the preparation of the wafers because
32 he was trustworthy. Some of their Kohathite kinsmen were in charge of setting out the rows of the Bread of the Presence every sabbath.
33 These, the musicians, heads of Levite families, were lodged in rooms set apart for them, because they were liable for duty by day and by night.
34 These are the heads of Levite families, chiefs according to their tribal lists, living in Jerusalem.

Saul's family

35[p] Jehiel founder of Gibeon lived at Gibeon; his wife's name was Maacah,
36 and his sons were Abdon the eldest,
37 Zur, Kish, Baal, Ner, Nadab, Gedor,

n Verses 2–22: cp. Neh. 11. 3–22.   o Prob. rdg.; Heb. om.   p Verses 35–44: cp. 8. 29–38.

48 Ahio, Zechariah and Mikloth. Mikloth
was the father of Shimeam; they
lived alongside their kinsmen in Jeru-
9 salem.*q* Ner was the father of Kish,
Kish father of Saul, Saul father of
Jonathan, Malchishua, Abinadab and
10 Eshbaal. The son of Jonathan was
Meribbaal, and Meribbaal was the
11 father of Micah: The sons of Micah: Pi-
12 thon, Melech, Tahrea and Ahaz. Ahaz
was the father of Jarah, Jarah father
of Alemeth, Azmoth, and Zimri; Zim-
13 ri father of Moza, and Moza father of
Binea; his son was Rephaiah, his son
14 Elasah, his son Azel. Azel had six
sons, whose names were Azrikam, Bocheru, Ishmael, Sheariah, Obadiah and
Hanan. These were the sons of Azel.

The death of Saul

17 The Philistines fought a battle against
Israel, and the men of Israel were
routed, leaving their dead on Mount
2 Gilboa. The Philistines hotly pursued
Saul and his sons and killed the three
sons, Jonathan, Abinadab and Malchi-
3 shua. The battle went hard for Saul,
for some archers came upon him and
4 he was wounded by them. So he said
to his armour-bearer, 'Draw your
sword and run me through, so that
these uncircumcised brutes may not
come and make sport of me.' But the
armour-bearer refused, he dared not;
whereupon Saul took his own sword
5 and fell on it. When the armour-
bearer saw that Saul was dead, he too
6 fell on his sword and died. Thus Saul
died and his three sons; his whole
house perished at one and the same
7 time. And all the Israelites in the Vale,
when they saw that their army had
fled and that Saul and his sons had
perished, fled likewise, abandoning
their cities, and the Philistines went
in and occupied them.
8 Next day, when the Philistines
came to strip the slain, they found
Saul and his sons lying dead on Mount
9 Gilboa. They stripped him, cut off his
head and took away his armour; then
they sent messengers through the
length and breadth of their land to
take the good news to idols and people
10 alike. They deposited his armour in
the temple of their god,*s* and nailed
up his skull in the temple of Dagon.
11 When the people of Jabesh-gilead
heard all that the Philistines had done
12 to Saul, the bravest of them set out
together to recover the bodies of Saul
and his sons; they brought them back
to Jabesh and buried their bones
under the oak-tree there, and fasted
for seven days. Thus Saul paid with 13
his life for his unfaithfulness: he had
disobeyed the word of the LORD and
had resorted to ghosts for guidance.
He had not sought guidance of the 14
LORD, who therefore destroyed him
and transferred the kingdom to David
son of Jesse.

David anointed king over Israel

Then all Israel assembled at Hebron 11 1*t*
to wait upon David. 'We are your own
flesh and blood', they said. 'In the 2
past, while Saul was still king, you
led the forces of Israel to war, and you
brought them home again. And the
LORD your God said to you, "You shall
be shepherd of my people Israel, you
shall be their prince."' All the elders 3
of Israel came to the king at Hebron;
there David made a covenant with
them before the LORD, and they anointed David king over Israel, as the
LORD had said through the lips of
Samuel.

David captures Zion

Then David and all Israel went to 4
Jerusalem (that is Jebus, where the
Jebusites, the inhabitants of the land,
lived). The people of Jebus said to 5
David, 'Never shall you come in
here'; none the less David did capture
the stronghold of Zion, and it is now
known as the City of David. David 6
said, 'The first man to kill a Jebusite
shall become a commander or an
officer', and the first man to go up was
Joab son of Zeruiah; so he was given
the command.
David took up his residence in the 7
stronghold: that is why they called
it the City of David. He built the city 8
round it, starting at the Millo and
including its neighbourhood, while
Joab reconstructed the rest of the
city. So David steadily grew stronger, 9
for the LORD of Hosts was with him.

David's chief men

Of David's heroes these were the 10*u*
chief, men who lent their full strength
to his government and, with all Israel,
joined in making him king; such was
the LORD's decree for Israel. First 11
came Jashoboam the Hachmonite,
chief of the three; he it was who
brandished his spear over three hundred, all slain at one time. Next to 12
him was Eleazar son of Dodo the

q Prob. rdg.; Heb. adds *with their kinsmen.*   *r* Verses 1–12: cp. 1 Sam. 31. 1–13.   *s* Or *gods.*
t Verses 1–9: cp. 2 Sam. 5. 1–3, 6–10.   *u* Verses 10–41: cp. 2 Sam. 23. 8–39.

13 Ahohite, one of the heroic three. He was with David at Pas-dammim where the Philistines had gathered for battle in a field carrying a good crop of barley; and when the people 14 had fled from the Philistines he stood his ground in the field, saved it*v* and defeated them. So the LORD brought about a great victory.

15 Three of the thirty chiefs went down to the rock to join David at the cave of Adullam, while the Philistines were encamped in the Vale of Re-16 phaim. At that time David was in the stronghold, and a Philistine garrison 17 held Bethlehem. One day a longing came over David, and he exclaimed, 'If only I could have a drink of water from the well*w* by the gate of Bethle-18 hem!' At this the three made their way through the Philistine lines and drew water from the well by the gate of Bethlehem, and brought it to David. But David refused to drink it; he 19 poured it out to the LORD and said, 'God forbid that I should do such a thing! Can I drink the blood of these men? They have brought it at the risk of their lives.' So he would not drink it. Such were the exploits of the heroic three.

20 Abishai the brother of Joab was chief of the thirty. He once brandished his spear over three hundred dead, and he was famous among the thirty. 21 He held higher rank than the rest of the thirty and became their captain, 22 but he did not rival the three. Benaiah son of Jehoiada, from Kabzeel, was a hero of many exploits. It was he who smote the two champions of Moab, and who went down into a pit 23 and killed a lion on a snowy day. It was he who also killed the Egyptian, a giant seven and a half feet high armed with a spear as big as the beam of a loom; he went to meet him with a club, snatched the spear out of the Egyptian's hand and killed him with 24 his own weapon. Such were the exploits of Benaiah son of Jehoiada, 25 famous among the heroic thirty.*x* He was more famous than the rest of the thirty, but did not rival the three. David appointed him to his household.

26 These were his valiant heroes: Asahel the brother of Joab, and El-hanan son of Dodo from Bethlehem; 27 Shammoth from Harod,*y* and Helez 28 from a place unknown; Ira son of Ikkesh from Tekoa, and Abiezer from

Anathoth; Sibbecai from Hushah, and 29 Ilai the Ahohite; Maharai from Net- 30 ophah, and Heled son of Baanah from Netophah; Ithai son of Ribai from 31 Gibeah of Benjamin, and Benaiah from Pirathon; Hurai from the ra- 32 vines of Gaash, and Abiel from Beth-arabah; Azmoth from Bahurim, and 33 Eliahba from Shaalbon; Hashem the 34 Gizonite, and Jonathan son of Shage the Hararite; Ahiam son of Sacar 35 the Hararite, and Eliphal son of Ur; Hepher from Mecherah, and Ahijah 36 from a place unknown; Hezro from 37 Carmel, and Naarai son of Ezbai; Joel 38 the brother of Nathan, and Mibhar the son of Haggeri; Zelek the Am- 39 monite, and Naharai from Beeroth, armour-bearer to Joab son of Zeruiah; Ira the Ithrite, and Gareb the Ithrite; 40 Uriah the Hittite, and Zabad son of 41 Ahlai. Adina son of Shiza the Reu- 42 benite, a chief of the Reubenites, was over these thirty. Also Hanan son 43 of Maacah, and Joshaphat the Mith-nite; Uzzia from Ashtaroth, Shama 44 and Jeiel the sons of Hotham from Aroer; Jediael son of Shimri, and Joha 45 his brother, the Tizite; Eliel the Ma- 46 havite, and Jeribai and Joshaviah sons of Elnaam, and Ithmah the Moabite; Eliel, Obed, and Jasiel, 47 from Zobah.*z*

David builds his army

These are the men who joined David 1 at Ziklag while he was banned from the presence of Saul son of Kish. They ranked among the warriors valiant in battle. They carried bows and could 2 sling stones or shoot arrows with the left hand or the right; they were Benjamites, kinsmen of Saul. The 3 foremost were Ahiezer and Joash, the sons of Shemaah the Gibeathite; Jeziel and Pelet, men of Beth-azmoth; Berachah and Jehu of Anathoth; Ish- 4 maiah the Gibeonite, a hero among the thirty and a chief among them; Jeremiah, Jahaziel, Johanan, and Josabad of Gederah; Eluzai, Jerimoth, 5 Bealiah, Shemariah, and Shephatiah the Haruphite; Elkanah, Isshiah, 6 Azareel, Joezer, Jashobeam, the Ko-rahites; and Joelah and Zebadiah 7 sons of Jeroham, of Gedor.

Some Gadites also joined David at 8 the stronghold in the wilderness, valiant men trained for war, who could handle the heavy shield and spear, grim as lions and swift as gazelles on the hills. Ezer was their 9

---

v saved it: or cleared it of the Philistines.   *w* Or cistern.   *x* Prob. rdg.; Heb. three.   *y* Prob. rdg., cp. 2 Sam. 23. 25; Heb. Haror.   *z* from Zobah: prob. rdg.; Heb. obscure.

chief, Obadiah the second, Eliab the third; Mishmannah the fourth and Jeremiah the fifth; Attai the sixth and Eliel the seventh; Johanan the eighth and Elzabad the ninth; Jeremiah the tenth and Machbanai the eleventh. These were chiefs of the Gadites in the army, the least of them a match for a hundred, the greatest a match for a thousand. These were the men who in the first month crossed the Jordan, which was in full flood in all its reaches, and wrought havoc in the valleys, east and west.

Some men of Benjamin and Judah came to David at the stronghold. David went out to them and said, 'If you come as friends to help me, join me and welcome; but if you come to betray me to my enemies, innocent though I am of any crime of violence, may the God of our fathers see and judge.' At that a spirit took possession of Amasai, the chief of the thirty, and he said:

We are on your side, David!
We are with you, son of Jesse!
Greetings, greetings to you
and greetings to your ally!
For your God is your ally.

So David welcomed them and attached them to the columns of his raiding parties.

Some men of Manasseh had deserted to David when he went with the Philistines to war against Saul, though he did not, in fact, fight on the side of the Philistines. Their princes brusquely dismissed him, saying to themselves that he would desert them for his master Saul, and that would cost them their heads. The men of Manasseh who deserted to him when he went to Ziklag were these: Adnah, Jozabad, Jediael, Michael, Jozabad, Elihu, and Zilthai, each commanding his thousand in Manasseh. It was they who stood valiantly by David against the raiders, for they were all good fighters, and they were given commands in his forces. From day to day men came in to help David, until he had gathered an immense army.

David's army at Hebron

These are the numbers of the armed bands which joined David at Hebron to transfer Saul's sovereignty to him, as the LORD had said: men of Judah, bearing heavy shield and spear, six thousand eight hundred, drafted for active service; of Simeon, fighting men drafted for active service, seven thousand one hundred; of Levi, four thousand six hundred, together with Jehoiada prince of the house of Aaron and three thousand seven hundred men, and Zadok a valiant fighter, with twenty-two officers of his own clan; of Benjamin, Saul's kinsmen, three thousand, though most of them had hitherto remained loyal to the house of Saul; of Ephraim, twenty thousand eight hundred, fighting men, famous in their own clans; of the half tribe of Manasseh, eighteen thousand, who had been nominated to come and make David king; of Issachar, whose tribesmen were skilled in reading the signs of the times to discover what course Israel should follow, two hundred chiefs, with all their kinsmen under their command; of Zebulun, fifty thousand troops well-drilled for battle, armed with every kind of weapon, bold and single-minded; of Naphtali, a thousand officers with thirty-seven thousand men bearing heavy shield and spear; of the Danites, twenty-eight thousand six hundred well-drilled for battle; of Asher, forty thousand troops well-drilled for battle; of the Reubenites and the Gadites and the half tribe of Manasseh east of Jordan, a hundred and twenty thousand, armed with every kind of weapon.

All these warriors, bold men in battle, came to Hebron, loyally determined to make David king over the whole of Israel; the rest of Israel, too, had but one thought, to make him king. They spent three days there with David, eating and drinking, for their kinsmen made provision for them. Their neighbours also round about, as far away as Issachar, Zebulun, and Naphtali, brought food on asses and camels, on mules and oxen, supplies of meal, fig-cakes, raisin-cakes, wine and oil, oxen and sheep, in plenty; for there was rejoicing in Israel.

David's intentions for the Ark

David consulted the officers over units of a thousand and a hundred on every matter brought forward. Then he said to the whole assembly of Israel, 'If you approve, and if the LORD our God opens a way, let us[a] send to our kinsmen who have stayed behind, in all the districts of Israel, and also to the priests and Levites in the cities where they have common lands,

_a_ and if . . . let us: _or_ and if it is from the LORD our God, let us seize the opportunity and . . .

3 bidding them join us. Let us fetch the
4 Ark of our God, for while Saul lived
we never resorted to it.' The whole
assembly resolved to do this; the
entire nation approved it.

David recovers the Ark

5 So David assembled all Israel from
the Shihor in Egypt to Lebo-hamath,
in order to fetch the Ark of God from
6[b] Kiriath-jearim. Then David and all
Israel went up to Baalah, to Kiriath-
jearim, which belonged to Judah, to
fetch the Ark of God, the LORD enthroned upon the cherubim, the Ark
7 which bore his name.[c] And they conveyed the Ark of God on a new cart
from the house of Abinadab, with
Uzza and Ahio guiding the cart.
8 David and all Israel danced for joy
before God without restraint to the
sound of singing, of harps and lutes,
of tambourines, and cymbals and
9 trumpets. But when they came to the
threshing-floor of Kidon, the oxen
stumbled, and Uzza put out his hand
10 to hold the Ark. The LORD was angry
with Uzza and struck him down because he had put out his hand to the
Ark. So he died there before God.
11 David was vexed because the LORD's
anger had broken out upon Uzza, and
he called the place Perez-uzza,[d] the
12 name it still bears. David was afraid
of God that day and said, 'How can
I harbour the Ark of God after this?'
13 So he did not take the Ark with him
into the City of David, but turned
aside and carried it to the house of
14 Obed-edom the Gittite. Thus the Ark
of God remained beside the house of
Obed-edom, in its tent,[e] for three
months, and the LORD blessed the
family of Obed-edom and all that he
had.

Hiram recognizes David's sovereignty

14 1[f] Hiram king of Tyre sent an embassy
to David; he sent cedar logs, and
masons and carpenters with them to
2 build him a house. David knew by
now that the LORD had confirmed him
as king over Israel and had made his
royal power stand higher for the sake
of his people Israel.

David's children born at Jerusalem

3 David married more wives in Jerusalem, and more sons and daughters

were born to him. These are the names 4
of the children born to him in Jerusalem: Shammua, Shobab, Nathan,
Solomon, Ibhar, Elishua, Elpelet, No- 5
gah, Nepheg, Japhia, Elishama, Bee- 7
liada and Eliphelet.

David defeats the Philistines

When the Philistines learnt that 8
David had been anointed king over
the whole of Israel, they came up in
force to seek him out. David, hearing
of this, went out to face them. Now the 9
Philistines had come and raided the
Vale of Rephaim. So David inquired 10
of God, 'If I attack the Philistines,
wilt thou deliver them into my hands?'
And the LORD answered, 'Go; I will
deliver them into your hands.' So he 11
went up and attacked them at Baal-
perazim and defeated them there.
'God has used me to break through
my enemies' lines,' David said, 'as a
river breaks its banks'; that is why
the place was named Baal-perazim.[h]
The Philistines left their gods behind 12
them there, and by David's orders
these were burnt.

The Philistines made another raid 13
on the Vale. Again David inquired of 14
God, and God said to him, 'No, you
must go up towards their rear; wheel
round without making contact and[i]
come upon them opposite the aspens.
Then, as soon as you hear a rustling 15
sound in the tree-tops, you shall give
battle, for God will have gone out
before you to defeat the Philistine
army.' David did as God commanded, 16
and they drove the Philistine army in
flight all the way from Gibeon to
Gezer. So David's fame spread through 17
every land, and the LORD inspired all
nations with dread of him.

David brings the Ark to Jerusalem

David built himself quarters in the 1
City of David, and prepared a place
for the Ark of God and pitched a tent
for it. Then he decreed that only 2
Levites should carry the Ark of God,
since they had been chosen by the
LORD to carry it and to serve him[j] for
ever. Next David assembled all Israel 3
at Jerusalem, to bring up the Ark of
the LORD to the place he had prepared
for it. He gathered together the sons 4
of Aaron and the Levites: of the sons 5
of Kohath, Uriel the chief with a
hundred and twenty of his kinsmen;

---

*b Verses 6–14: cp. 2 Sam. 6. 2–11.   c which bore his name: prob. rdg.; Heb. obscure.   d That is
Outbreak on Uzza.   e Or in his tent.   f Verses 1–16: cp. 2 Sam. 5. 11–25.   g Verses 4–7: cp.
3. 5–8.   h That is Baal of Break-through.   i No . . . contact and: or Do not go up to the
attack; withdraw from them and then . . .   j Or it.*

6 of the sons of Merari, Asaiah the chief with two hundred and twenty of his 7 kinsmen; of the sons of Gershom, Joel the chief with a hundred and 8 thirty of his kinsmen; of the sons of Elizaphan, Shemaiah the chief with 9 two hundred of his kinsmen; of the sons of Hebron, Eliel the chief with 10 eighty of his kinsmen; of the sons of Uzziel, Amminadab the chief with a hundred and twelve of his kins-11 men. And David summoned Zadok and Abiathar the priests, together with the Levites, Uriel, Asaiah, Joel, Shemaiah, Eliel, and Amminadab, 12 and said to them, 'You who are heads of families of the Levites, hallow yourselves, you and your kinsmen, and bring up the Ark of the LORD the God of Israel to the place which I have 13 prepared for it. It was because you were not present the first time, that the LORD our God broke out upon us. For we had not sought his guidance 14 as we should have done.' So the priests and the Levites hallowed themselves to bring up the Ark of the LORD the 15 God of Israel, and the Levites carried the Ark of God, bearing it on their shoulders with poles as Moses had prescribed at the command of the LORD.

16 David also ordered the chiefs of the Levites to install as musicians those of their kinsmen who were players skilled in making joyful music on their instruments, lutes and harps 17 and cymbals. So the Levites installed Heman of Joel and, from his kinsmen, Asaph son of Berechiah; and from their kinsmen the Merarites, 18 Ethan son of Kushaiah, together with their kinsmen of the second degree, Zechariah, Jaaziel, Shemiramoth, Jehiel, Unni, Eliab, Benaiah, Maaseiah, Mattithiah, Eliphelehu, and Mikneiah, and the door-keepers Obed-19 edom and Jeiel. They installed the musicians Heman, Asaph, and Ethen to sound the cymbals of bronze; 20 Zechariah, Jaaziel, Shemiramoth, Jehiel, Unni, Eliab, Maaseiah, and Benaiah to play on lutes;[k] Mattithiah, Eliphelehu, Mikneiah, Obed-edom, Jeiel, and Azaziah to play on harps.[l] 21 Kenaniah, officer of the Levites, was precentor in charge of the music because of his proficiency. Berechiah and Elkanah were door-keepers for the Ark, while the priests Shebaniah, Jehoshaphat, Nethaneel, Amasai,

Zechariah, Benaiah, and Eliezer sounded the trumpets before the Ark of God; and Obed-edom and Jehiah also were door-keepers for the Ark.

Then David and the elders of 25[m] Israel and the captains of units of a thousand went to bring up the Ark of the Covenant of the LORD with much rejoicing from the house of Obed-edom. Because God had helped the 26 Levites who carried the Ark of the Covenant of the LORD, they sacrificed seven bulls and seven rams.

Now David and all the Levites who 27 carried the Ark, and the musicians, and Kenaniah the precentor,[n] were arrayed in robes of fine linen; and David had on a linen ephod. All Israel 28 escorted the Ark of the Covenant of the LORD with shouts of acclamation, blowing on horns and trumpets, clashing cymbals and playing on lutes and harps. But as the Ark of the 29 Covenant of the LORD was entering the city of David, Saul's daughter Michal looked down through a window and saw King David dancing and making merry, and she despised him in her heart.

David gives thanks to the LORD

When they had brought in the Ark of 16 1[o] God, they put it inside the tent that David had pitched for it, and they offered whole-offerings and shared-offerings before God. After David had 2 completed these sacrifices, he blessed the people in the name of the LORD and gave food, a loaf of bread, a 3 portion of meat, and a cake of raisins, to each Israelite, man or woman. He 4 appointed certain Levites to serve before the Ark of the LORD, to repeat the Name, to confess and to praise the LORD the God of Israel. Their 5 leader was Asaph; second to him was Zechariah; then came Jaaziel,[p] Shemiramoth, Jehiel, Mattithiah, Eliab, Benaiah, Obed-edom, and Jeiel, with lutes and harps, Asaph, who sounded the cymbals; and Benaiah and Ja-6 haziel the priests, who blew the trumpets before the Ark of the Covenant of God continuously throughout that 7 day. It was then that David first ordained the offering of thanks to the LORD by Asaph and his kinsmen:

Give the LORD thanks and invoke him 8[q] by name,

---

k Prob. rdg.; Heb. adds al alamoth, possibly a musical term.   *l Prob. rdg.; Heb. adds al hashshemi-nith lenasseah, possibly musical terms.*   *m Verses 25–9: cp. 2 Sam. 6. 12–16.*   *n the precentor: prob. rdg.; Heb. obscure.*   *o Verses 1–3: cp. 2 Sam. 6. 17–19.*   *p Prob. rdg., cp. 15. 18, 20; Heb. Jeiel.*   *q Verses 8–22: cp. Ps. 105, 1–15.*

make his deeds known in the world around.

9 Pay him honour with song and psalm and think upon all his wonders.

10 Exult in his hallowed name;
let those who seek the LORD be joyful in heart.

11 Turn to the LORD, your strength,[r]
seek his presence always.

12 Remember the wonders that he has wrought,
his portents and the judgements he has given,

13 O offspring of Israel his servants, O chosen sons of Jacob.

14 He is the LORD our God;
his judgements fill the earth.

15 He called to mind his covenant from long ago,[s]
the promise he extended to a thousand generations—

16 the covenant made with Abraham, his oath given to Isaac,

17 the decree by which he bound himself for Jacob,
his everlasting covenant with Israel:

18 'I will give you the land of Canaan', he said,
'to be your possession, your patrimony.'

19 A small company it was,
few in number, strangers in that land,

20 roaming from nation to nation,
from one kingdom to another;

21 but he let no man ill-treat them,
for their sake he admonished kings:

22 'Touch not my anointed servants,
do my prophets no harm.'

23[t] Sing to the LORD, all men on earth,
proclaim his triumph day by day.

24 Declare his glory among the nations,
his marvellous deeds among all peoples.

25 Great is the LORD and worthy of all praise;
he is more to be feared than all gods.

26 For the gods of the nations are idols every one;
but the LORD made the heavens.

27 Majesty and splendour attend him,
might and joy are in his dwelling.

28 Ascribe to the LORD, you families of nations,

29 ascribe to the LORD glory and might;
ascribe to the LORD the glory due to his name,
bring a gift and come before him.

Bow down to the LORD in the splendour of holiness,[u]
and dance in his honour, all men on earth.

He has fixed the earth firm, immovable.

Let the heavens rejoice and the earth exult,
let men declare among the nations, 'The LORD is king.'
Let the sea roar and all the creatures in it,
let the fields exult and all that is in them;
then let the trees of the forest shout for joy
before the LORD when he comes to judge the earth.

It is good to give thanks to the LORD,
for his love endures for ever.

Cry, 'Deliver us, O God our saviour,
gather us in and save us from the nations
that we may give thanks to thy holy name
and make thy praise our pride.'

Blessed be the LORD the God of Israel
from everlasting to everlasting.

And all the people said 'Amen' and 'Praise the LORD.'

After the celebrations

David left Asaph and his kinsmen there before the Ark of the Covenant of the LORD, to perform regular service before the Ark as each day's duty required; as door-keepers he left Obed-edom son of Jeduthun, and Hosah. (Obed-edom and his kinsmen were sixty-eight in number.) He left Zadok the priest and his kinsmen the priests before the Tabernacle of the LORD at the hill-shrine in Gibeon, to make offerings there to the LORD upon the altar of whole-offering regularly morning and evening, exactly as it is written in the law enjoined by the LORD upon Israel. With them he left Heman and Jeduthun and the other men chosen and nominated to give thanks to the LORD, 'for his love endures for ever.' They had trumpets and cymbals for the players, and the instruments used for sacred song. The sons of Jeduthun kept the gate.
So all the people went home, and David returned to greet his household.

r your strength: *or* the symbol of his strength; *lit.* and his strength. *s* from long ago: *or* for ever.
t Verses 23–33: *cp.* Ps. 96. 1–13. *u* Or in holy vestments. *v* Verse 34: *cp.* Ps. 107. 1.
w Verses 35, 36: *cp.* Ps. 106. 47, 48.

The LORD's promise to David

17 As soon as David was established in his house, he said to Nathan the prophet, 'Here I live in a house of cedar, while the Ark of the Covenant of the LORD is housed in curtains.' 2 Nathan answered David, 'Do whatever you have in mind, for God is with you.' 3 But that night the word of God came 4 to Nathan: 'Go and say to David my servant, "This is the word of the LORD: It is not you who shall build 5 me a house to dwell in. Down to this day I have never dwelt in a house since I brought Israel up from Egypt; I lived in a tent and a tabernacle.*y* 6 Wherever I journeyed with Israel, did I ever ask any of the judges whom I appointed shepherds of my people why they had not built me a house of 7 cedar?" Then say this to my servant David: "This is the word of the LORD of Hosts: I took you from the pastures, and from following the sheep, to be 8 prince over my people Israel. I have been with you wherever you have gone, and have destroyed all the enemies in your path. I will make you as famous as the great ones of the 9 earth. I will assign a place for my people Israel; there I will plant them, and they shall dwell in their own land. They shall be disturbed no more, never again shall wicked men wear 10 them down as they did from the time when I first appointed judges over Israel my people, and I will subdue all your enemies. But I will make you great and the LORD shall build 11 up your royal house. When your life ends and you go to join your forefathers, I will set up one of your family, one of your own sons, to succeed you, and I will establish his kingdom. 12 It is he shall build me a house, and I will establish his throne for all time. 13 I will be his father, and he shall be my son. I will never withdraw my love from him as I withdrew it from your 14 predecessor. But I will give him a sure place in my house and kingdom for all time, and his throne shall be established for ever."'

David prays to the LORD

15 Nathan recounted to David all that had been said to him and all that had 16 been revealed. Then King David went into the presence of the LORD and took his place there and said, 'What am I, LORD God, and what is my family, that thou hast brought me thus far? It was a small thing in thy 17 sight, O God, to have planned for thy servant's house in days long past, and now thou lookest upon me as a man already embarked on a high career, O LORD God. What more can David 18 say to thee of the honour thou hast done thy servant, well though thou knowest him? For the sake of thy 19 servant, LORD, and according to thy purpose, thou hast brought me to all this greatness. O LORD, we have never 20 heard of one like thee; there is no god but thee. And thy people Israel, to 21 whom can they be compared? Is there any other nation on earth whom God has gone out to redeem from slavery, to make them his people? Thou hast won a name for thyself by great and terrible deeds, driving out nations before thy people whom thou didst redeem from Egypt. Thou hast made 22 thy people Israel thy own for ever, and thou, O LORD, hast become their God. But now, LORD, let what thou hast 23 promised for thy servant and his house stand fast for all time; make good what thou hast said. Let it stand fast, 24 that thy fame may be great for ever, and let men say, "The LORD of Hosts, the God of Israel, is Israel's God." So shall the house of thy servant David be established before thee. Thou, my 25 God, hast shown me thy purpose to build up thy servant's house; therefore I have been able to pray before thee. Thou, O LORD, art God, and 26 thou hast made these noble promises to thy servant; thou hast been pleased 27 to bless thy servant's house, that it may continue always before thee; thou it is who hast blessed it, and it shall be blessed for ever.'

David extends his kingdom

18 After this David defeated the Philistines and conquered them, and took from them Gath with its villages; he 2 defeated the Moabites, and they became subject to him and paid him tribute. He also defeated Hadadezer 3 king of Zobah-hamath, who was on his way to set up a monument of victory by the river Euphrates. From 4 him David captured a thousand chariots, seven thousand horsemen and twenty thousand foot; he hamstrung all the chariot-horses, except a hundred which he retained. When 5 the Aramaeans of Damascus came to the help of Hadadezer king of Zobah,

<hr>

x Verses 1–27: cp. 2 Sam. 7. 1–29.   *y I lived . . . tabernacle: prob. rdg.; Heb. I have been from*
tent to tent and from a tabernacle.   *z Verses 1–13: cp. 2 Sam. 8. 1–14.*

David destroyed twenty-two thousand
6 of them, and established garrisons among these Aramaeans; they became subject to him and paid him tribute. Thus the LORD gave David
7 victory wherever he went. David took the gold quivers borne by Hadadezer's servants and brought
8 them to Jerusalem. He also took a great quantity of bronze[a] from Hadadezer's cities, Tibhath and Kun; from this Solomon made the Sea of bronze,[a] the pillars, and the bronze[a] vessels.
9 When Tou king of Hamath heard that David had defeated the entire
10 army of Hadadezer king of Zobah, he sent his son Hadoram to King David to greet him and to congratulate him on defeating Hadadezer in battle (for Hadadezer had been at war with Tou); and he brought with him vessels of
11 gold, silver, and copper, which King David dedicated to the LORD. He dedicated also the silver and the gold which he had carried away from all the other nations, from Edom and Moab, from the Ammonites and the Philistines, and from Amalek.
12 Edom was defeated by Abishai son of Zeruiah, who destroyed eighteen thousand of them in the Valley of Salt
13 and stationed garrisons in the country. All the Edomites now became subject to David. Thus the LORD gave victory to David wherever he went.

David's government

14[b] David ruled over the whole of Israel and maintained law and justice among
15 all his people. Joab son of Zeruiah was in command of the army; Jehoshaphat son of Ahilud was secre-
16 tary of state; Zadok and Abiathar son of Ahimelech, son of Ahitub,[c] were priests; Shavsha was adjutant-
17 general; Benaiah son of Jehoiada commanded the Kerethite and Pelethite guards. The eldest sons of David were in attendance on the king.

Joab defeats the Aramaeans and Ammonites

19 1[d] Some time afterwards Nahash king of the Ammonites died and was suc-
2 ceeded by his son. David said, 'I must keep up the same loyal friendship with Hanun son of Nahash as his father showed me', and he sent a mission to condole with him on the death of his father. But when David's envoys entered the country of the Ammonites to condole with Hanun, the Ammonite princes said to Hanun, 3 'Do you suppose David means to do honour to your father when he sends you his condolences? These men of his are spies whom he has sent to find out how to overthrow the country.' So Hanun took David's servants, and 4 he shaved them, cut off half their garments up to the hips, and dismissed them. When David heard how 5 they had been treated, he sent to meet them, for they were deeply humiliated, and ordered them to wait in Jericho and not to return until their beards had grown again. The Am- 6 monites knew that they had brought themselves into bad odour with David, so Hanun and the Ammonites sent a thousand talents of silver to hire chariots and horsemen from Aram-naharaim,[e] Maacah, and Aram-zobah.[f] They hired thirty-two thou- 7 sand chariots and the king of Maacah and his people, who came and encamped before Medeba, while the Ammonites came from their cities and mustered for battle. When David 8 heard of it, he sent out Joab and all the fighting men. The Ammonites 9 came and took up their position at the entrance to the city, while the allied kings took up theirs in the open country. When Joab saw that he was 10 threatened both front and rear, he detailed some picked Israelite troops and drew them up facing the Aramaeans. The rest of his forces he put 11 under his brother Abishai, who took up a position facing the Ammonites. 'If the Aramaeans prove too strong 12 for me,' he said, 'you must come to my relief; and if the Ammonites prove too strong for you, I will relieve you. Courage! Let us fight bravely for our 13 people and for the cities[g] of our God. And the LORD's will be done.' But 14 when Joab and his men came to close quarters with the Aramaeans, they put them to flight; and when the 15 Ammonites saw them in flight, they too fled before his brother Abishai and entered the city. Then Joab came to Jerusalem. The Aramaeans saw 16 that they had been worsted by Israel, and they sent messengers to summon other Aramaeans from the Great

a Or copper.   b Verses 14–17: cp. 2 Sam. 8. 15–18; 20. 23–6; 1 Kgs. 4. 2–4.   c and Abiathar ... Ahitub: prob. rdg., cp. 2 Sam. 8. 17; Heb. son of Ahitub and Abimelech son of Abiathar. d Verses 1–19: cp. 2 Sam. 10. 1–19.   e That is Aram of Two Rivers.   f Maacah, and Aram-zobah: prob. rdg.; Heb. Aram-maacah, and Zobah.   g Or altars.

Bend of the Euphrates under Shophach, commander of Hadadezer's
17 army. Their movement was reported
to David, who immediately mustered
all the forces of Israel, crossed the
Jordan and advanced against them
and took up battle positions. The
Aramaeans likewise took up positions
18 facing David and engaged him, but
were put to flight by Israel. David
slew seven thousand Aramaeans in
chariots and forty thousand infantry,
killing Shophach the commander of
19 the army. When Hadadezer's men
saw that they had been worsted by
Israel, they sued for peace and submitted to David. The Aramaeans
were never again willing to give support to the Ammonites.

Joab destroys Rabbah

20 *h* At the turn of the year, when kings
take the field, Joab led the army out
and ravaged the Ammonite country.
He came to Rabbah and laid siege to
it, while David remained in Jerusalem;
he reduced the city and razed it to the
2 ground. David took the crown from
the head of Milcom and found that it
weighed a talent of gold and was set
with a precious stone, and this he
placed on his own head. He also removed a great quantity of booty from
3 the city; he took its inhabitants and
set them to work with saws and other
iron tools, sharp and toothed. David
did this to all the cities of the Ammonites; then he and all his people
returned to Jerusalem.

Three more victories

4 *i* Some time later war with the Philistines broke out in Gezer; it was then
that Sibbechai of Hushah killed Sip-
pai, a descendant of the Rephaim, and
the Philistines were reduced to sub-
5 mission. In another war with the
Philistines, Elhanan son of Jair killed
Lahmi brother of Goliath of Gath,
whose spear had a shaft like a weaver's
6 beam. In yet another war in Gath,
there appeared a giant with six
fingers on each hand and six toes on
each foot, twenty-four in all; he too
was descended from the Rephaim,
7 and, when he defied Israel, Jonathan
son of David's brother Shimea killed
8 him. These giants were the descendants of the Rephaim in Gath, and
they all fell at the hands of David and
his men.

David numbers Israel and Judah

21 Now Satan, setting himself against 21 1
Israel, incited David to count the
people. So he instructed Joab and his 2
public officers to go out and number
Israel, from Beersheba to Dan, and
to report the number to him. Joab 3
answered, 'Even if the LORD should
increase his people a hundredfold,
would not your majesty still be king
and all the people your slaves? Why
should your majesty want to do this?
It will only bring guilt on Israel.' But 4
Joab was overruled by the king; he
set out and went up and down the
whole country. He then came to
Jerusalem and reported to David the 5
numbers recorded: those capable of
bearing arms were one million one
hundred thousand in Israel, and four
hundred and seventy thousand in
Judah. Levi and Benjamin were not 6
counted by Joab, so deep was his
repugnance against the king's order.

David owns his guilt and makes an offering

God was displeased with all this and 7
proceeded to punish Israel. David 8
said to God, 'I have done a very
wicked thing: I pray thee remove thy
servant's guilt, for I have been very
foolish.' And the LORD said to Gad, 9
David's seer, 'Go and tell David, 10
"This is the word of the LORD: I have
three things to offer you; choose one
of them and I will bring it upon you."'
So Gad came to David and said to 11
him, 'This is the word of the LORD:
"Make your choice: three years of 12
famine, three months of harrying by
your foes and close pursuit by the
sword of your enemy, or three days
of the LORD's own sword, bringing
pestilence throughout the country,
and the LORD's angel working destruction in all the territory of Israel."
Consider now what answer I am to
take back to him who sent me.'
Thereupon David said to Gad, 'I am 13
in a desperate plight; let me fall into
the hands of the LORD, for his mercy
is very great; and let me not fall into
the hands of man.' So the LORD sent 14
a pestilence throughout Israel, and
seventy thousand men of Israel died.
And God sent an angel to Jerusalem 15
to destroy it; but, as he was destroying it, the LORD saw and repented of
the evil, and said to the destroying
angel at the moment when he was

h Verses 1–3: cp. 2 Sam. 12. 26–31.   *i Verses 4–7: cp. 2 Sam. 21. 18–22.*   *j Verses 1–27: cp.*
2 Sam. 24. 1–25.

standing beside the threshing-floor of
Ornan the Jebusite, 'Enough! Stay
your hand.'

16 When David looked up and saw the
angel of the LORD standing between
earth and heaven, with his sword
drawn in his hand and stretched
out over Jerusalem, he and the elders,
clothed in sackcloth, fell prostrate
17 to the ground; and David said to
God, 'It was I who gave the order
to count the people. It was I who sinned, I, the shepherd,[k] who did wrong.
But these poor sheep, what have they
done? O LORD my God, let thy hand
fall upon me and upon my family, but
check this plague on the people.'[l]

18 The angel of the LORD, speaking
through the lips of Gad, commanded
David to go to the threshing-floor of
Ornan the Jebusite and to set up there
19 an altar to the LORD. David went up
as Gad had bidden him in the LORD's
20 name. Ornan's four sons who were
with him hid themselves, but he was
busy threshing his wheat when he
21 turned and saw the angel. As David
approached, Ornan looked up and,
seeing the king, came out from the
threshing-floor and prostrated him-
22 self before him. David said to Ornan,
'Let me have the site of the threshing-
floor that I may build on it an altar to
the LORD; sell it me at the full price,
that the plague which has attacked
23 my people may be stopped.' Ornan
answered David, 'Take it and let your
majesty do as he thinks fit; see, here
are the oxen for whole-offerings, the
threshing-sledges for the fuel, and the
wheat for the grain-offering; I give
24 you everything.' But King David
said to Ornan, 'No, I will pay the full
price; I will not present to the LORD
what is yours, or offer a whole-offering
25 which has cost me nothing.' So David
gave Ornan six hundred shekels of gold
26 for the site, and built an altar to the
LORD there; on this he offered whole-
offerings and shared-offerings, and
called upon the LORD, who answered
him with fire falling from heaven on
27 the altar of whole-offering. Then, at
the LORD's command, the angel sheathed his sword.

The site for the Temple

28 It was when David saw that the LORD
had answered him at the threshing-
floor of Ornan the Jebusite that he
29 offered sacrifice there. The tabernacle of the LORD and the altar of
whole-offering which Moses had made
in the wilderness were then at the hill-
shrine in Gibeon; but David had been 30
unable to go there and seek God's
guidance, so shocked and shaken was
he at the sight of the angel's sword.
Then David said, 'This is to be the 22
house of the LORD God, and this is to
be an altar of whole-offering for
Israel.'

David prepares for building

David now gave orders to assemble 2
the aliens resident in Israel, and he
set them as masons to dress hewn
stones and to build the house of God.
He laid in a great store of iron to make 3
nails and clamps for the doors, more
bronze than could be weighed and 4
cedar-wood without limit; the men of
Sidon and Tyre brought David an
ample supply of cedar. David said, 5
'My son Solomon is a boy of tender
years, and the house that is to be built
to the LORD must be exceedingly
magnificent, renowned and celebrated
in every land; therefore I must make
preparations for it myself.' So David
made abundant preparation before
his death.

He sent for Solomon his son and 6
charged him to build a house for the
LORD the God of Israel. 'Solomon, my 7
son,' he said, 'I had intended to build
a house in honour of the name of the
LORD my God; but the LORD forbade 8
me and said, "You have shed much
blood in my sight and waged great
wars; for this reason you shall not
build a house in honour of my name.
But you shall have a son who shall be 9[m]
a man of peace; I will give him peace
from all his enemies on every side;
his name shall be Solomon, 'Man of
Peace', and I will grant peace and
quiet to Israel in his days. He shall 10
build a house in honour of my name;
he shall be my son and I will be a
father to him, and I will establish the
throne of his sovereignty over Israel
for ever." Now, Solomon my son, the 11
LORD be with you! May you prosper
and build the house of the LORD your
God, as he promised you should. But 12
may the LORD grant you wisdom and
discretion, so that when he gives you
authority in Israel you may keep the
law of the LORD your God. You will 13
prosper only if you are careful to
observe the decrees and ordinances
which the LORD enjoined upon Moses

---

k I, the shepherd: *prob. rdg.; Heb.* doing wrong.
people, not for a plague.   m *Verse 9: cp. 1 Kgs. 5. 4.*

l check . . . people: *prob. rdg.; Heb.* among thy

for Israel; be strong and resolute, neither faint-hearted nor dismayed.

14 'In spite of all my troubles, I have here ready for the house of the LORD a hundred thousand talents of gold and a million talents of silver, with great quantities of bronze and iron, more than can be weighed; timber and stone, too, I have got ready; and you 15 may add to them. Besides, you have a large force of workmen, masons, sculptors, and carpenters, and countless men skilled in work of every kind, 16 in gold and silver, bronze and iron. So now to work, and the LORD be with you!'

17 David ordered all the officers of 18 Israel to help Solomon his son: 'Is not the LORD your God with you? Will he not give you peace on every side? For he has given the inhabitants of the land into my power, and they will be subject to the LORD and his people. 19 Devote yourselves, therefore, heart and soul, to seeking guidance of the LORD your God, and set about building his sanctuary, so that the Ark of the Covenant of the LORD and God's holy vessels may be brought into a house built in honour of his name.'

Enrolling the Levites

23 David was now an old man, weighed down with years, and he appointed 2 Solomon his son king over Israel. He gathered together all the officers of Israel, the priests, and the Levites. 3 The Levites were enrolled from the age of thirty upwards, their males 4 being thirty-eight thousand in all. Of these, twenty-four thousand were to be responsible for the maintenance and service of the house of the LORD, six thousand to act as officers and 5 magistrates, four thousand to be doorkeepers, and four thousand to praise the LORD on the musical instruments which David had made for the service 6 of praise. David organized them in divisions, called after Gershon, Kohath, and Merari, the sons of Levi. 7 The sons of Gershon: Laadan and 8 Shimei. The sons of Laadan: Jehiel the chief, Zetham and Joel, three.[n] 9 These were the heads of the families 10 grouped under Laadan. The sons of Shimei: Jahath, Ziza, Jeush, and 11 Beriah, four. Jahath was the chief and Ziza the second, but Jeush and Beriah, having few children, were reckoned for duty as a single family. 12 The sons of Kohath: Amram, Izhar,

Hebron and Uzziel, four. The sons of 13 Amram: Aaron and Moses. Aaron was set apart, he and his sons in perpetuity, to dedicate the most holy gifts,[o] to burn sacrifices before the LORD, to serve him, and to give the blessing in his name for ever, but the sons of 14 Moses, the man of God, were to keep the name of Levite. The sons of 15 Moses: Gershom and Eliezer. The 16 sons of Gershom: Shubael the chief. The sons of Eliezer: Rehabiah the 17 chief. Eliezer had no other sons, but Rehabiah had very many. The sons 18 of Izhar: Shelomoth the chief. The 19 sons of Hebron: Jeriah the chief, Amariah the second, Jahaziel the third and Jekameam the fourth. The 20 sons of Uzziel: Micah the chief and Isshiah the second.

The sons of Merari: Mahli and 21 Mushi. The sons of Mahli: Eleazar and Kish. When Eleazar died, he left 22 daughters but no sons, and their cousins, the sons of Kish, married them. The sons of Mushi: Mahli, Eder 23 and Jeromoth, three.

Such were the Levites, grouped by 24 families in the father's line whose heads were entered in the detailed list; they performed duties in the service of the house of the LORD, from the age of twenty upwards. For David 25 said, 'The LORD the God of Israel has given his people peace and has made his abode in Jerusalem for ever. The 26 Levites will no longer have to carry the Tabernacle or any of the vessels for its service.' By these last words of 27 David the Levites were enrolled from the age of twenty upwards. Their 28 duty was to help the sons of Aaron in the service of the house of the LORD: they were responsible for the care of the courts and the rooms, for the cleansing of all holy things, and the general service of the house of God; for the rows of the Bread of the 29 Presence, the flour for the grain-offerings, unleavened wafers, cakes baked on the griddle, and pastry, and for the weights and measures. They 30 were to be on duty continually before the LORD every morning and evening, giving thanks and praise to him, and 31 at every offering of whole-offerings to the LORD, on sabbaths, new moons and at the appointed seasons, according to their prescribed number. The Levites were to have charge of 32 the Tent of the Presence and of the sanctuary, but the sons of Aaron their

n Prob. rdg.; Heb. adds The sons of Shimei: Shelomith, Haziel and Haran, three.   *o to dedicate . . . gifts: or* to be hallowed as most holy.

kinsmen were charged with the service of worship in the house of the LORD.

24 The divisions of the sons of Aaron: his sons were Nadab and Abihu, 2 Eleazar and Ithamar. Nadab and Abihu died before their father, leaving no sons; therefore Eleazar and Ithamar held the office of priest. 3 David, acting with Zadok of the sons of Eleazar and with Ahimelech of the sons of Ithamar, organized them in divisions for the discharge of the 4 duties of their office. The male heads of families proved to be more numerous in the line of Eleazar than in that of Ithamar, so that sixteen heads of families were grouped under the line of Eleazar and eight under that of 5 Ithamar. He organized them by drawing lots among them, for there were sacred officers*p* and officers of God in the line of Eleazar and in that of 6 Ithamar. Shemaiah the clerk, a Levite, son of Nethaneel, wrote down the names in the presence of the king, the officers, Zadok the priest, and Ahimelech son of Abiathar, and of the heads of the priestly and levitical families, one priestly family being taken from the line of Eleazar and one 7 from that of Ithamar. The first lot fell to Jehoiarib, the second to Jed-8 aiah, the third to Harim, the fourth 9 to Seorim, the fifth to Malchiah, the 10 sixth to Mijamin, the seventh to 11 Hakkoz, the eighth to Abiah, the ninth to Jeshua, the tenth to Shecan-12 iah, the eleventh to Eliashib, the 13 twelfth to Jakim, the thirteenth to Huppah, the fourteenth to Jeshebeab, 14 the fifteenth to Bilgah, the sixteenth 15 to Immer, the seventeenth to Hezir, 16 the eighteenth to Aphses, the nine-teenth to Pethahiah, the twentieth to 17 Jehezekel, the twenty-first to Jachin, 18 the twenty-second to Gamul, the twenty-third to Delaiah, and the 19 twenty-fourth to Maaziah. This was their order of duty for the discharge of their service when they entered the house of the LORD, according to the rule prescribed for them by their ancestor Aaron, who had received his instructions from the LORD the God of Israel.

20 Of the remaining Levites: of the sons of Amram: Shubael. Of the sons 21 of Shubael: Jehdeiah. Of Rehabiah: Isshiah, the chief of Rehabiah's sons. 22 Of the line of Izhar: Shelomoth. Of 23 the sons of Shelomoth: Jahath. The

sons of Hebron: Jeriah the chief, Amariah the second, Jahaziel the third and Jekameam the fourth. The 24 sons of Uzziel: Micah. Of the sons of Micah: Shamir; Micah's brother: 25 Isshiah. Of the sons of Isshiah: Zechariah. The sons of Merari: Mahli and 26 Mushi and also*q* Jaaziah his son. The 27 sons of Merari: of Jaaziah: Beno, Shoham, Zaccur and Ibri. Of Mahli: 28 Eleazar, who had no sons; of Kish: the 29 sons of Kish: Jerahmeel; and the sons 30 of Mushi: Mahli, Eder and Jerimoth. These were the Levites by families. These also, side by side with their 31 kinsmen the sons of Aaron, cast lots in the presence of King David, Zadok, Ahimelech, and the heads of the priestly and levitical families, the senior and junior houses casting lots side by side.

The singers

David and his chief officers assigned **25** special duties to the sons of Asaph, of Heman, and of Jeduthun, leaders in inspired prophecy to the accompaniment of harps, lutes, and cymbals; the number of the men who performed this work in the temple was as follows. Of the sons of Asaph: Zaccur, Joseph, 2 Nethaniah and Asarelah; these were under Asaph, a leader in inspired prophecy under the king. Of the sons 3 of Jeduthun: Gedaliah, Izri,*r* Isaiah, Shimei, Hashabiah, Mattithiah, these six under their father Jeduthun, a leader in inspired prophecy to the accompaniment of the harp, giving thanks and praise to the LORD. Of the 4 sons of Heman: Bukkiah, Mattaniah, Uzziel, Shubael, Jerimoth, Hananiah, Hanani, Eliathah, Giddalti, Romamti-ezer, Joshbekashah, Mallothi, Hothir, and Mahazioth; all these were sons of 5 Heman the king's seer, given to him through the promises of God for his greater glory. God had given Heman fourteen sons and three daughters, and they all served under their father 6 for the singing in the house of the LORD; they took part in the service of the house of God, with cymbals, lutes, and harps, while Asaph, Jeduthun, and Heman were under the king. Reckoned with their kinsmen, trained 7 singers of the LORD, they brought the total number of skilled musicians up to two hundred and eighty-eight. They 8 cast lots for their duties, young and old, master-singer and apprentice side by side.

---

p sacred officers: *or* officers of the sanctuary. *rdg.*, *cp.* *verse 11*; *Heb.* Zeri.   *q* and also: *prob. rdg.*; *Heb.* the sons of.   *r* Prob.

9 The first lot fell[s] to Joseph: he and his brothers and his sons, twelve.[t] The second to Gedaliah: he and his bro-
10 thers and his sons, twelve. The third to Zaccur: his sons and his brothers,
11 twelve. The fourth to Izri: his sons
12 and his brothers, twelve. The fifth to Nethaniah: his sons and his brothers,
13 twelve. The sixth to Bukkiah: his sons
14 and his brothers, twelve. The seventh to Asarelah: his sons and his brothers,
15 twelve. The eighth to Isaiah: his sons
16 and his brothers, twelve. The ninth to Mattaniah: his sons and his brothers,
17 twelve. The tenth to Shimei: his sons
18 and his brothers, twelve. The eleventh to Azareel: his sons and his brothers,
19 twelve. The twelfth to Hashabiah: his
20 sons and his brothers, twelve. The thir-
21 teenth to Shubael: his sons and his brothers, twelve. The fourteenth to
22 Mattithiah: his sons and his brothers, twelve. The fifteenth to Jeremoth: his
23 sons and his brothers, twelve. The sixteenth to Hananiah: his sons and
24 his brothers, twelve. The seventeenth to Joshbekashah: his sons and his
25 brothers, twelve. The eighteenth to Hanani: his sons and his brothers,
26 twelve. The nineteenth to Mallothi:
27 his sons and his brothers, twelve. The twentieth to Eliathah: his sons and
28 his brothers, twelve. The twenty-first to Hothir: his sons and his brothers,
29 twelve. The twenty-second to Gid-
30 dalti: his sons and his brothers, twelve. The twenty-third to Mahazioth: his sons and his brothers, twelve.
31 The twenty-fourth to Romamtiezer: his sons and his brothers, twelve.

Door-keepers

26 The divisions of the door-keepers: Korahites: Meshelemiah son of Kore,
2 son of Ebiasaph.[u] Sons of Meshel-emiah: Zechariah the eldest, Jedia-el the second, Zebediah the third,
3 Jathniel the fourth, Elam the fifth, Jehohanan the sixth, Elioenai the sev-
4 enth. Sons of Obed-edom: Shemai-ah the eldest, Jehozabad the second, Joah the third, Sacar the fourth,
5 Nethaneel the fifth, Ammiel the sixth, Issachar the seventh, Peulthai the eighth (for God had blessed him).
6 Shemaiah, his son, was the father of sons who had authority in their family, for they were men of great
7 ability. Sons of Shemaiah: Othni, Rephael, Obed, Elzabad and his bro-thers Elihu and Semachiah, men of

ability. All these belonged to the 8 family of Obed-edom; they, their sons and brothers, were men of ability, fit for service in the temple; total: sixty-two. Sons and brothers 9 of Meshelemiah, all men of ability, eighteen. Sons of Hosah, a Merarite: 10 Shimri the chief (he was not the eldest, but his father had made him chief), Hilkiah the second, Tebali- 11 ah the third, Zechariah the fourth. Total of Hosah's sons and brothers: thirteen.

The male heads of families con- 12 stituted the divisions of the door-keepers; their duty was to serve in the house of the LORD side by side with their kinsmen. Young and old, 13 family by family, they cast lots for the gates. The lot for the east gate fell to 14 Shelemiah; then lots were cast for his son Zechariah, a prudent counsellor, and he was allotted the north gate. To 15 Obed-edom was allotted the south gate, and the gatehouse to his sons. Hosah[v] was allotted the west gate, 16 together with the Shallecheth gate on the ascending causeway. Guard corre-sponded to guard. Six Levites were 17 on duty daily on the east side, four on the north and four on the south, and two at each gatehouse; at the 18 western colonnade there were four at the causeway and two at the colon-nade itself. These were the divisions 19 of the door-keepers, Korahites and Merarites.

Store-keepers

Fellow-Levites were in charge of the 20 stores of the house of God and of the stores of sacred gifts. Of the children 21 of Laadan, descendants of the Ger-shonite line through Laadan, heads of families in the group of Laadan the Gershonite, Jehiel[w] his brothers 22 Zetham and Joel were in charge of the stores of the house of the LORD. Of the families of Amram, Izhar, 23 Hebron and Uzziel, Shubael son of 24 Gershom, son of Moses, was overseer of the stores. The line of Eliezer his 25 brother: his son Rehabiah, his son Isaiah, his son Joram, his son Zichri, and his son Shelomoth. This Shelo- 26 moth and his kinsmen were in charge of all the stores of the sacred gifts dedicated by David the king, the heads of families, the officers over units of a thousand and a hundred, and other officers of the army. They 27

s Prob. rdg.; Heb. adds to Asaph.   t he . . . twelve: prob. rdg.; Heb. om.   u son of Ebiasaph: prob. rdg.; Heb. from the sons of Asaph.   v Hosah: prob. rdg.; Heb. Shuppim and Hosah. w Jehiel and: prob. rdg.; Heb. Jehieli. The sons of Jehieli . . .

had dedicated some of the spoils taken in the wars for the upkeep of 28 the house of the LORD. Everything which Samuel the seer, Saul son of Kish, Abner son of Ner, and Joab son of Zeruiah had dedicated, in short every sacred gift, was under the charge 29 of Shelomoth and his kinsmen. Of the family of Izhar, Kenaniah and his sons acted as clerks and magistrates 30 in the secular affairs of Israel. Of the family of Hebron, Hashabiah and his kinsmen, men of ability to the number of seventeen hundred, had the oversight of Israel west of the Jordan, both in the work of the LORD and in 31 the service of the king. Also of the family of Hebron, Jeriah was the chief. (In the fortieth year of David's reign search was made in the family histories of the Hebronites, and men of great ability were found among 32 them at Jazer in Gilead.) His kinsmen, all men of ability, two thousand seven hundred of them, heads of families, were charged by King David with the oversight of the Reubenites, the Gadites, and the half tribe of Manasseh, in religious and civil affairs alike.

Officers of the kingdom

27 The number of the Israelites—that is to say, of the heads of families, the officers over units of a thousand and a hundred, and the clerks who had their share in the king's service in the various divisions which took monthly turns of duty throughout the year— was twenty-four thousand in each division.

2   First, Jashobeam son of Zabdiel commanded the division for the first month with twenty-four thousand 3 in his division; a member of the house of Perez, he was chief officer of the temple staff for the first 4 month. Eleazar son of^x Dodai the Ahohite commanded the division for the second month with twenty-four 5 thousand in his division. Third, Benaiah son of Jehoiada the chief priest, commander of the army, was the officer for the third month with twenty-four thousand in his division 6 (he was the Benaiah who was one of the thirty warriors and was a chief among the thirty); but his son Ammi- 7 zabad commanded his division. Fourth, Asahel, the brother of Joab, was the officer commanding for the fourth month with twenty-four thousand in

his division; and his successor was Zebediah his son. Fifth, Shamhuth 8 the Zerahite^y was the officer commanding for the fifth month with twenty-four thousand in his division. Sixth, Ira son of Ikkesh, a man of 9 Tekoa, was the officer commanding for the sixth month with twenty-four thousand in his division. Seventh, 10 Helez an Ephraimite, from a place unknown, was the officer commanding for the seventh month with twenty-four thousand in his division. Eighth, 11 Sibbecai the Hushathite, of the family of Zerah, was the officer commanding for the eighth month with twenty-four thousand in his division. Ninth, 12 Abiezer, from Anathoth in Benjamin, was the officer commanding for the ninth month with twenty-four thousand in his division. Tenth, Maharai 13 the Netophathite, of the family of Zerah, was the officer commanding for the tenth month with twenty-four thousand in his division. Eleventh, 14 Benaiah the Pirathonite, from Ephraim, was the officer commanding for the eleventh month with twenty-four thousand in his division. Twelfth, 15 Heldai the Netophathite, of the family of Othniel, was the officer commanding for the twelfth month with twenty-four thousand in his division.

The following were the principal 16 officers in charge of the tribes of Israel: of Reuben, Eliezer son of Zichri; of Simeon, Shephatiah son of Maacah; of Levi, Hashabiah son of 17 Kemuel; of Aaron, Zadok; of Judah, 18 Elihu a kinsman of David; of Issachar, Omri son of Michael; of Zebulun, 19 Ishmaiah son of Obadiah; of Naphtali, Jerimoth son of Azriel; of Ephraim, 20 Hoshea son of Azaziah; of the half tribe of Manasseh, Joel son of Pedaiah; of the half of Manasseh in Gilead, Iddo 21 son of Zechariah; of Benjamin, Jaasiel son of Abner; of Dan, Azareel son 22 of Jeroham. These were the officers in charge of the tribes of Israel.

The abandoned census

David took no census of those under 23 twenty years of age, for the LORD had promised to make the Israelites as many as the stars in the heavens. Joab son of Zeruiah did begin to take 24 a census but he did not finish it; this brought harm upon Israel, and the census was not entered in the chronicle of King David's reign.

x Eleazar son of: prob. rdg., cp. 11. 12; Heb. om.   y the Zerahite: prob. rdg.; Heb. the Izrah.

The king's own officers

25 Azmoth son of Adiel was in charge of the king's stores; Jonathan son of Uzziah was in charge of the stores in the country, in the cities, in the vil-
26 lages and in the fortresses. Ezri son of Kelub had oversight of the workers
27 on the land; Shimei of Ramah was in charge of the vine-dressers, while Zabdi of Shephem had charge of the produce of the vineyards for the
28 wine-cellars. Baal-hanan the Gederite supervised the wild olives and the sycamore-figs in the Shephelah; Joash
29 was in charge of the oil-stores. Shitrai of Sharon was in charge of the herds grazing in Sharon, Shaphat son of
30 Adlai of the herds in the vales. Obil the Ishmaelite was in charge of the camels, Jehdeiah the Meronothite of
31 the asses. Jaziz the Hagerite was in charge of the flocks. All these were the officers in charge of King David's
32 possessions. David's favourite nephew Jonathan, a counsellor, a discreet and learned man, and Jehiel the Hach-monite, were tutors to the king's sons.
33 Ahithophel was a king's counsellor; Hushai the Archite was the King's
34 Friend. Ahithophel was succeeded by Jehoiada son of Benaiah, and Abiathar. Joab was commander of the army.

David addresses his people

28 David assembled at Jerusalem all the officers of Israel, the officers over the tribes, over the divisions engaged in the king's service, over the units of a thousand and a hundred, and those in charge of all the property and the cattle of the king and of his sons, as well as the eunuchs, the heroes and all
2 the men of ability. Then King David rose to his feet and said, 'Hear me, kinsmen and people. I had in mind to build a house as a resting-place for the Ark of the Covenant of the LORD which might serve as a footstool for the feet of our God, and I made
3 preparations to build it. But God said to me, "You shall not build a house in honour of my name, for you have been a fighting man and you have
4 shed blood." Nevertheless, the LORD the God of Israel chose me out of all my father's family to be king over Israel in perpetuity; for it was Judah that he chose as ruling tribe, and, out of the house of Judah, my father's family; and among my father's sons

it was I whom he was pleased to make king over all Israel. And out of all my 5 sons—for the LORD gave me many sons—he chose Solomon to sit upon the throne of the LORD's sovereignty over Israel; and he said to me, "It is 6 Solomon your son who shall build my house and my courts, for I have chosen him to be a son to me and I will be a father to him. I will establish his 7 sovereignty in perpetuity, if only he steadfastly obeys my commandments and my laws as they are now obeyed." Now therefore, in the presence of all 8 Israel, the assembly of the LORD, and within the hearing of our God, I bid you all study carefully the command-ments of the LORD your God, that you may possess this good land and hand it down as an inheritance for all time to your children after you. And 9 you, Solomon my son, acknowledge your father's God and serve him with whole heart and willing mind, for the LORD searches all hearts and discerns every invention of men's thoughts. If you search for him, he will let you find him, but if you forsake him, he will cast you off for ever. Remember, 10 then, that the LORD has chosen you to build a house for a sanctuary: be steadfast and do it.'

David gives the building plans to Solomon

David gave Solomon his son the plan 11 of the porch of the temple[z] and its buildings, strong-rooms, roof-chambers and inner courts, and the shrine of expiation;[a] also the plans of all he 12 had in mind for the courts of the house of the LORD and for all the rooms around it, for the stores of God's house and for the stores of the sacred gifts, for the divisions of the priests 13 and the Levites, for all the work con-nected with the service of the house of the LORD and for all the vessels used in its service. He prescribed the 14 weight of gold for all the gold vessels[b] used in the various services, and the weight of silver[c] for all the silver vessels used in the various services; and the weight of gold for the gold 15 lamp-stands and their lamps; and the weight of silver for the silver lamp-stands, the weight required for each lamp-stand and its lamps according to the use of each; and the weight 16 of gold for each of the tables for the rows of the Bread of the Presence, and of silver for the silver tables. He 17

z of the temple: *prob. rdg.; Heb. om.*   a the shrine . . . expiation: *or* the place for the Ark with its cover.   b for . . . vessels: *prob. rdg.; Heb.* for gold.   c of silver: *prob. rdg.; Heb. om.*

prescribed also the weight of pure gold for the forks, tossing-bowls and cups, the weight of gold for each of the golden dishes and of silver[c] for 18 each of the silver dishes; the weight also of refined gold for the altar of incense, and of gold for the model of the chariot, that is the cherubim with their wings outspread to screen the Ark 19 of the Covenant of the LORD. 'All this was drafted by the LORD's own hand,' said David; 'my part was to consider the detailed working out of the plan.' 20 Then David said to Solomon his son, 'Be steadfast and resolute and do it; be neither faint-hearted nor dismayed, for the LORD God, my God, will be with you; he will neither fail you nor forsake you, until you have finished all the work needed for the 21 service of the house of the LORD. Here are the divisions of the priests and the Levites, ready for all the service of the house of God. In all the work you will have the help of every willing craftsman for any task; and the officers and all the people will be entirely at your command.'

The people contribute willingly

29 King David then said to the whole assembly, 'My son Solomon is the one chosen by God, Solomon alone, a boy of tender years; and this is a great work, for it is a palace not for man 2 but for the LORD God. Now to the best of my strength I have made ready for the house of my God gold for the gold work, silver for the silver, bronze for the bronze, iron for the iron, and wood for the woodwork, together with cornelian and other gems for setting, stones for mosaic work, precious stones of every sort, and 3 marble in plenty. Further, because I delight in the house of my God, I give my own private store of gold and silver for the house of my God—over and above all the store which I have 4 collected for the sanctuary—namely three thousand talents of gold, gold from Ophir, and seven thousand talents of fine silver for overlaying 5 the walls of the buildings, for providing gold for the gold work, silver for the silver, and for any work to be done by skilled craftsmen. Now who is willing to give with open hand to the LORD today?' 6 Then the heads of families, the officers administering the tribes of Israel, the officers over units of a thousand and a hundred, and the

officers in charge of the king's service, responded willingly and gave for the 7 work of the house of God five thousand talents of gold, ten thousand darics, ten thousand talents of silver, eighteen thousand talents of bronze, and a hundred thousand talents of iron. Further, those who possessed 8 precious stones gave them to the treasury of the house of the LORD, into the charge of Jehiel the Gershonite. The people rejoiced at this 9 willing response, because in the loyalty of their hearts they had given willingly to the LORD; King David also was full of joy, and he blessed the LORD 10 in the presence of all the assembly and said, 'Blessed art thou, LORD God of our father Israel, from of old and for ever. Thine, O LORD, is the 11 greatness, the power, the glory, the splendour, and the majesty; for everything in heaven and on earth is thine;[d] thine, O LORD, is the sovereignty, and thou art exalted over all as head. Wealth and honour come 12 from thee; thou rulest over all; might and power are of thy disposing; thine it is to give power and strength to all. And now, we give thee thanks, our 13 God, and praise thy glorious name. 'But what am I, and what is my 14 people, that we should be able to give willingly like this? For everything comes from thee, and it is only of thy gifts that we give to thee. We are 15 aliens before thee and settlers, as were all our fathers; our days on earth are like a shadow, we have no abiding place. O LORD our God, from thee 16 comes all this wealth that we have laid up to build a house in honour of thy holy name, and everything is thine. I know, O my God, that thou 17 dost test the heart and that plain honesty pleases thee; with an honest heart I have given all these gifts willingly, and have rejoiced now to see thy people here present give willingly to thee. O LORD God of Abraham, 18 Isaac and Israel our fathers, maintain this purpose for ever in thy people's thoughts and direct their hearts toward thyself. Grant that 19 Solomon my son may loyally keep thy commandments, thy solemn charge, and thy statutes, that he may fulfil them all and build the palace for which I have prepared.'

Solomon is installed king

Then, turning to the whole assembly, 20 David said, 'Now bless the LORD your

c of silver: *prob. rdg.*; Heb. *om.*

d is thine: *prob. rdg.*; Heb. *om.*

God.' So all the assembly blessed the LORD the God of their fathers, bowing low and prostrating themselves before 21 the LORD and the king. The next day they sacrificed to the LORD and offered whole-offerings to him, a thousand oxen, a thousand rams, a thousand lambs, with the prescribed drink-offerings, and abundant sacrifices for 22 all Israel. So they ate and drank before the LORD that day with great rejoicing. They then appointed Solomon, David's son, king a second time and anointed him as the LORD's 23 prince, and Zadok as priest. So Solomon sat on the LORD's throne as king in place of his father David, and he prospered and all Israel obeyed 24 him. All the officers and the warriors, as well as all the sons of King David, 25 swore fealty to King Solomon. The LORD made Solomon stand very high

in the eyes of all Israel, and bestowed upon him sovereignty such as no king in Israel had had before him.

Other records of David's reign

David son of Jesse had ruled over the 26 whole of Israel, and the length of his 27 reign over Israel was forty years; he ruled for seven years in Hebron, and for thirty-three in Jerusalem. He died 28 in ripe old age, full of years, wealth, and honour; and Solomon his son ruled in his place. The events of King 29 David's reign from first to last are recorded in the books of Samuel the seer, of Nathan the prophet, and of Gad the seer, with a full account of 30 his reign, his prowess, and of the times through which he and Israel and all the kingdoms of the world had passed.

THE SECOND BOOK OF THE
CHRONICLES

Solomon prays for wisdom

1 KING SOLOMON, David's son, strengthened his hold on the kingdom, for the LORD his God was with him and made him very great. 2 Solomon spoke to all Israel, to the officers over units of a thousand and of a hundred, the judges and all the leading men of Israel, the heads of 3 families; and he, together with all the assembled people, went to the hill-shrine at Gibeon; for the Tent of God's Presence, which Moses the LORD's servant had made in the wilderness, 4 was there. (But David had brought up the Ark of God from Kiriath-jearim to the place which he had prepared for it, for he had pitched a tent 5 for it in Jerusalem.) The altar of bronze also, which Bezalel son of Uri, son of Hur, had made, was there in front of the Tabernacle of the LORD; and Solomon and the assembly re-6 sorted to it.[a] There Solomon went up to the altar of bronze before the LORD in the Tent of the Presence and offered 7[b] on it a thousand whole-offerings. That night God appeared to Solomon and

said, 'What shall I give you? Tell me.' Solomon answered, 'Thou didst show 8 great and constant love to David my father and thou hast made me king in his place. Now, O LORD God, let 9 thy word to David my father be confirmed, for thou hast made me king over a people as numerous as the dust on the earth. Give me now wisdom 10 and knowledge, that I may lead this people; for who is fit to govern this great people of thine?' God answered 11 Solomon, 'Because this is what you desire, because you have not asked for wealth or possessions or honour[c] or the lives of your enemies or even long life for yourself, but have asked for wisdom and knowledge to govern my people over whom I have made you king, wisdom and knowledge are 12 given to you; I shall also give you wealth and possessions and honour[c] such as no king has had before you and none shall have after you.' Then 13 Solomon returned from the hill-shrine at Gibeon, from before the Tent of the Presence, to Jerusalem and ruled over Israel.

a resorted to it: *or* worshipped him.   *b* Verses 7–12: *cp. 1 Kgs. 3. 5–14.*   *c* Or riches.

Solomon builds up his cavalry

14[d] Solomon got together many chariots and horses; he had fourteen hundred chariots and twelve thousand horses, and he stabled some in the chariot-towns and kept others at hand in
15 Jerusalem. The king made silver and gold as common in Jerusalem as stones, and cedar as plentiful as
16 sycomore-fig in the Shephelah. Horses were imported from Egypt and Coa for Solomon; the royal merchants obtained them from Coa by purchase.
17 Chariots were imported from Egypt for six hundred silver shekels each, and horses for a hundred and fifty; in the same way the merchants obtained them for export from all the kings of the Hittites and the kings of Aram.

Solomon negotiates with King Huram

2 1 Solomon resolved to build a house in honour of the name of the LORD, and
2 a royal palace for himself. He engaged seventy thousand hauliers and eighty thousand quarrymen, and three thousand six hundred men to superintend
3[e] them. Then Solomon sent this message to Huram king of Tyre: 'You were so good as to send my father David cedar-wood to build his royal resi-
4 dence. Now I am about to build a house in honour of the name of the LORD my God and to consecrate it to him, so that I may burn fragrant incense in it before him, and present the rows of the Bread of the Presence regularly, and whole-offerings morning and evening, on the sabbaths and the new moons and the appointed festivals of the LORD our God; for this is a duty laid upon Israel for ever.
5 The house I am about to build will be a great house, because our God is
6 greater than all gods. But who is able to build him a house when heaven itself, the highest heaven, cannot contain him? And who am I that I should build him a house, except that I may
7 burn sacrifices before him? Send me then a skilled craftsman, a man able to work in gold and silver, copper[f] and iron, and in purple, crimson, and violet yarn, who is also an expert engraver and will work with my skilled workmen in Judah and in Jerusalem who were provided by
8 David my father. Send me also cedar, pine, and algum timber from Lebanon, for I know that your men are expert at felling the trees of Lebanon; my

men will work with yours to get an 9 ample supply of timber ready for me, for the house which I shall build will be great and wonderful. I will supply 10 provisions for your servants, the wood-men who fell the trees: twenty thousand kor of wheat and twenty thousand kor of barley, with twenty thousand bath of wine and twenty thousand bath of oil.'

Huram king of Tyre sent this 11 answer by letter to Solomon: 'It is because of the love which the LORD has for his people that he has made you king over them.' The letter went 12 on to say, 'Blessed is the LORD the God of Israel, maker of heaven and earth, who has given to King David a wise son, endowed with intelligence and understanding, to build a house for the LORD and a royal palace for himself. I now send you a skilful 13 and experienced craftsman, master Huram. He is the son of a Danite 14 woman, his father a Tyrian; he is an experienced worker in gold and silver, copper[f] and iron, stone and wood, as well as in purple, violet, and crimson yarn, and in fine linen; he is also a trained engraver who will be able to work with your own skilled craftsmen and those of my lord David your father, to any design submitted to him. Now then, let my lord send his 15 servants the wheat and the barley, the oil and the wine, which he promised; we will fell all the timber in 16 Lebanon that you need and float it as rafts to the roadstead at Joppa, and you will convey it from there up to Jerusalem.'

Solomon takes a census

Solomon took a census of all the 17 aliens resident in Israel, similar to the census which David his father had taken; these were found to be a hundred and fifty-three thousand six hundred. He made seventy thousand 18 of them hauliers and eighty thousand quarrymen, and three thousand six hundred superintendents to make the people work.

Solomon builds the Temple

Then Solomon began to build the 3 house of the LORD in Jerusalem on Mount Moriah, where the LORD had appeared to his father David, on the site which David had prepared on the threshing-floor of Ornan the Jebusite. He began to build in the second month 2[g]

d Verses 14–17: cp. 9. 25–8; 1 Kgs. 10. 26–9.   e Verses 3–16: cp. 1 Kgs. 5. 2–11.   f Or bronze.
g Verses 2–4: cp. 1 Kgs. 6. 1–3.

3 of the fourth year of his reign. These are the foundations which Solomon laid for building the house of God: the length, according to the old standard of measurement, was sixty cubits and 4 the breadth twenty. The vestibule in front of the house[h] was twenty cubits long, spanning the whole breadth of the house, and its height was twenty; on the inside he overlaid it with pure 5 gold. He panelled the large chamber with pine, covered it with fine gold and carved on it palm-trees and chain- 6 work. He adorned the house with precious stones for decoration, and the 7 gold he used was from Parvaim. He covered the whole house with gold, its rafters and frames, its walls and doors; and he carved cherubim on the walls.

8 He made the Most Holy Place twenty cubits long, corresponding to the breadth of the house, and twenty cubits broad. He covered it all with 9 six hundred talents of fine gold, and the weight of the nails was fifty shekels of gold. He also covered the upper chambers with gold.

10[i] In the Most Holy Place he carved two images of cherubim and overlaid 11 them with gold. The total span of the wings of the cherubim was twenty cubits. A wing of the one cherub extended five cubits to reach the wall of the house, while its other wing reached out five cubits to meet a wing of the 12 other cherub. Similarly, a wing of the second cherub extended five cubits to reach the other wall of the house, while its other wing met a wing of 13 the first cherub. The wings of these cherubim extended twenty cubits; they stood with their feet on the 14 ground, facing the outer chamber. He made the Veil of violet, purple, and crimson yarn, and fine linen, and embroidered cherubim on it.

15[j] In front of the house he erected two pillars eighteen cubits high, with an architrave five cubits high on top of 16 each. He made chainwork like a neck-lace[k] and set it round the tops of the pillars, and he carved a hundred pomegranates and set them in the 17 chain-work. He erected the two pillars in front of the temple, one on the right and one on the left; the one on the right he named Jachin[l] and the one on the left Boaz.[m]

He then made an altar of bronze, 4 twenty cubits long, twenty cubits broad, and ten cubits high. He also 2[n] made the Sea of cast metal; it was round in shape, the diameter from rim to rim being ten cubits; it stood five cubits high, and it took a line thirty cubits long to go round it. Under the 3 Sea, on every side, completely sur-rounding the thirty[o] cubits of its circumference, were what looked like gourds,[p] two rows of them, cast in one piece with the Sea itself. It was 4 mounted on twelve oxen, three facing north, three west, three south, and three east, their hind quarters turned inwards; the Sea rested on top of them. Its thickness was a hand- 5 breadth; its rim was made like that of a cup, shaped like the calyx of a lily; when full it held three thousand bath. He also made ten basins for washing, 6 setting five on the left side and five on the right; in these they rinsed everything used for the whole-offering. The Sea was made for the priests to wash in.

He made ten golden lamp-stands 7 in the prescribed manner and set them in the temple, five on the right side and five on the left. He also made ten 8 tables and placed them in the temple, five on the right and five on the left; and he made a hundred golden tossing-bowls. He made the court of the 9 priests and the great precinct and the doors for it, and overlaid the doors of both with copper; he put the Sea at 10 the right side, at the south-east corner of the temple.

Huram made the pots, the shovels, 11[q] and the tossing-bowls. So he finished the work which he had undertaken for King Solomon on the house of God. The two pillars; the two bowl- 12 shaped capitals[r] on the tops of the pillars; the two ornamental networks to cover the two bowl-shaped capitals on the tops of the pillars; the four hun- 13 dred pomegranates for the two net-works, two rows of pomegranates for each network, to cover the two bowl-shaped capitals on the two[s] pillars; the ten[t] trolleys and the ten[t] basins on 14 the trolleys; the one Sea and the 15 twelve oxen which supported it; the 16 pots, the shovels, and the tossing-bowls[u]—all these[v] objects master

h house: prob. rdg.; Heb. length.   i Verses 10–13: cp. 1 Kgs. 6. 23–8.   j Verses 15–17: cp.
1 Kgs. 7. 15–21.   k necklace: prob. rdg.; Heb. obscure.   l Or Jachun, meaning It shall stand.
m Or Booz, meaning In strength.   n Verses 2–5: cp. 1 Kgs. 7. 23–6.   o Prob. rdg.; Heb. ten.
p Prob. rdg., cp. 1 Kgs. 7. 24; Heb. oxen.   q 4. 11—5. 1: cp. 1 Kgs. 7. 40–51.   r bowl-shaped
capitals: prob. rdg., cp. 1 Kgs. 7. 41; Heb. the bowls and the capitals.   s two: prob. rdg., cp.
1 Kgs. 7. 42; Heb. surface of the.   t the ten: prob. rdg., cp. 1 Kgs. 7. 43; Heb. he made the . . .
u tossing-bowls: prob. rdg., cp. 1 Kgs. 7. 45; Heb. forks.   v Prob. rdg., cp. 1 Kgs. 7. 45; Heb. their.

Huram made of bronze, burnished work for King Solomon for the house 17 of the LORD. In the Plain of the Jordan the king cast them, in the foundry between Succoth and Zere- 18 dah. Solomon made great quantities of all these objects; the weight of the copper[w] used was beyond reckoning. 19 Solomon made also all the furnishings for the house of God: the golden altar, the tables upon which was 20 set the Bread of the Presence, the lamp-stands of red gold whose lamps burned before the inner shrine in 21 the prescribed manner, the flowers and lamps and tongs of solid gold, 22 the snuffers, tossing-bowls, saucers, and firepans of red gold, and, at the entrance to the house, the inner doors leading to the Most Holy Place and those leading to the sanctuary, of gold.

5 When all the work which Solomon did for the house of the LORD was completed, he brought in the sacred treasures of his father David, the silver, the gold, and the vessels, and deposited them in the storehouses of the house of God.

Solomon installs the Ark

2[x] Then Solomon summoned the elders of Israel, and all the heads of the tribes who were chiefs of families in Israel, to assemble in Jerusalem, in order to bring up the Ark of the Covenant of the LORD from the City 3 of David, which is called Zion. All the men of Israel assembled in the king's presence at the pilgrim-feast in the 4 seventh month. When the elders of Israel had all come, the Levites took 5 the Ark and carried it up with the Tent of the Presence and all the sacred furnishings of the Tent: it was the priests and the Levites together 6 who carried them up. King Solomon and the whole congregation of Israel, assembled with him before the Ark, sacrificed sheep and oxen in numbers 7 past counting or reckoning. Then the priests brought in the Ark of the Covenant of the LORD to its place, the inner shrine of the house, the Most Holy Place, beneath the wings of the 8 cherubim. The cherubim spread their wings over the place of the Ark, and formed a covering above the Ark and 9 its poles. The poles projected, and their ends could be seen from the Holy Place immediately in front of the inner shrine, but from nowhere else outside; they are

there to this day. There was nothing in- 10 side the Ark but the two tablets which Moses had put there at Horeb, the tablets of the covenant[y] which the LORD made with the Israelites when they left Egypt.

Songs of praise

Now when the priests came out of 11 the Holy Place (for all the priests who were present had hallowed themselves without keeping to their divisions), all the levitical singers, Asaph, 12 Heman, and Jeduthun, their sons and their kinsmen, clothed in fine linen, stood with cymbals, lutes, and harps, to the east of the altar, together with a hundred and twenty priests who blew trumpets. Now the 13 trumpeters and the singers joined in unison to sound forth praise and thanksgiving to the LORD, and the song was raised with trumpets, cymbals, and musical instruments, in praise of the LORD, because 'that[z] is good, for his love endures for ever'; and the house was filled with the cloud of the glory of the LORD. The 14 priests could not continue to minister because of the cloud, for the glory of the LORD filled the house of God. Then 6 Solomon said:

O LORD who hast chosen to dwell in thick darkness,

here have I built thee a lofty house, 2 a habitation for thee to occupy for ever.

Solomon blesses Israel

And as they stood waiting, the king 3 turned round and blessed all the assembly of Israel in these words: 4 'Blessed be the LORD the God of Israel who spoke directly to my father David and has himself fulfilled his promise. For he said, "From the day 5 when I brought my people out of Egypt, I chose no city out of all the tribes of Israel where I should build a house for my Name to be there, nor did I choose any man to be prince over my people Israel. But I chose 6 Jerusalem for my Name to be there, and I chose David to be over my people Israel." My father David had 7 in mind to build a house in honour of the name of the LORD the God of Israel, but the LORD said to him, "You 8 purposed to build a house in honour of my name; and your purpose was good. Nevertheless, you shall not 9 build it; but the son who is to be born to you, he shall build the house in honour of my name." The LORD has now fulfilled his promise: I have succeeded my father David and taken his place on the throne of Israel, as the LORD promised; and I have built the house in honour of the name of the LORD the God of Israel. I have installed there the Ark containing the covenant of the LORD which he made with Israel.'

Solomon prays to the LORD

2 Then Solomon, standing in front of the altar of the LORD, in the presence of the whole assembly of Israel, 3 spread out his hands. He had made a bronze[b] platform, five cubits long, five cubits broad, and three cubits high, and had placed it in the centre of the precinct. He mounted it and knelt down in the presence of the assembly, and, spreading out his 4 hands towards heaven, he said, 'O LORD God of Israel, there is no god like thee in heaven or on earth, keeping covenant with thy servants and showing them constant love while they continue faithful to thee in heart and 5 soul. Thou hast kept thy promise to thy servant David my father; by thy deeds this day thou hast fulfilled what thou didst say to him in words. 6 Now, therefore, O LORD God of Israel, keep this promise of thine to thy servant David my father: "You shall never want for a man appointed by me to sit on the throne of Israel, if only your sons look to their ways and conform to my law, as you have done 7 in my sight." And now, O LORD God of Israel, let the word which thou didst speak to thy servant David be confirmed. 8 'But can God indeed dwell with man on the earth? Heaven itself, the highest heaven, cannot contain thee; how much less this house that I have 9 built? Yet attend to the prayer and the supplication of thy servant, O LORD my God; listen to the cry and the prayer which thy servant utters 10 before thee, that thine eyes may ever be upon this house day and night, this place of which thou didst say, "It shall receive my Name"; so mayest thou hear thy servant when he 11 prays towards this place. Hear the supplications of thy servant and of thy people Israel when they pray towards this place. Hear from heaven thy dwelling and, when thou hearest, forgive.

'When a man wrongs his neighbour 22 and he is adjured to take an oath, and the adjuration is made before thy altar in this house, then do thou hear 23 from heaven and act: be thou thy servants' judge, requiting the guilty man and bringing his deeds upon his own head, acquitting the innocent and rewarding him as his innocence may deserve.

'When thy people Israel are defeat- 24 ed by an enemy because they have sinned against thee, and they turn back to thee, confessing thy name and making their prayer and supplication before thee in this house, do thou 2 hear from heaven; forgive the sin of thy people Israel and restore them to the land which thou gavest to them and to their forefathers.

'When the heavens are shut up and 26 there is no rain, because thy servant and thy people Israel have sinned against thee, and when they pray towards this place, confessing thy name and forsaking their sin when they feel thy punishment, do thou 27 hear in heaven and forgive their sin; so mayest thou teach them the good way which they should follow, and grant rain to thy land which thou hast given to thy people as their own possession.

'If there is famine in the land, or 28 pestilence, or black blight or red, or locusts new-sloughed or fully grown, or if their enemies besiege them in any[c] of their cities, or if plague or sickness befall them, then hear the prayer or 29 supplication of every man among thy people Israel, as each one, prompted by his own suffering and misery, spreads out his hands towards this house; hear it from heaven thy dwell- 30 ing and forgive. And, as thou knowest a man's heart, reward him according to his deeds, for thou alone knowest the hearts of all men; and so they 31 will fear and obey thee all their lives in the land thou gavest to our forefathers.

'The foreigner too, the man who 32 does not belong to thy people Israel, but has come from a distant land because of thy great fame and thy strong hand and arm outstretched, when he comes and prays towards this house, hear from heaven thy 33 dwelling and respond to the call which like the foreigner makes to thee, so that like thy people Israel all peoples

b Or copper.   c in any: prob. rdg.; Heb. in the land.

of the earth may know thy fame and fear thee, and learn that this house which I have built bears thy name.

34 'When thy people go to war with their enemies, wherever thou dost send them, and they pray to thee, turning towards this city which thou hast chosen and towards this house which I have built in honour of thy 35 name, do thou from heaven hear their prayer and supplication, and grant them justice.

36 'Should they sin against thee (and what man is free from sin?) and shouldst thou in thy anger give them over to an enemy, who carries them 37 captive to a land far or near; if in the land of their captivity they learn their lesson and turn back and make supplication to thee in that land and say, "We have sinned and acted perversely 38 and wickedly", if they turn back to thee with heart and soul in the land of their captivity to which they have been taken, and pray, turning towards their land which thou gavest to their forefathers and towards this city which thou didst choose and this house which I have built in honour 39 of thy name; then from heaven thy dwelling do thou hear their prayer and supplications and grant them justice. Forgive thy people their sins 40 against thee. Now, O my God, let thine eyes be open and thy ears attentive to the prayer made in this 41 place. Arise now, O LORD God, and come to thy place of rest, thou and the Ark of thy might. Let thy priests, O LORD God, be clothed with salvation and thy saints rejoice in pros- 42 perity. O LORD God, reject not thy anointed prince; remember thy servant David's loyal service.'[d]

Fire from heaven

7 When Solomon had finished this prayer, fire came down from heaven and consumed the whole-offering and the sacrifices, while the glory of the 2 LORD filled the house. The priests were unable to enter the house of the LORD because the glory of the LORD 3 had filled it. All the Israelites were watching as the fire came down with the glory of the LORD on the house, and where they stood on the paved court they bowed low to the ground and worshipped and gave thanks to the LORD, because 'that[e] is good, for his love endures for ever.'

Celebrations

4 Then the king and all the people offered sacrifice before the LORD. 5 King Solomon offered a sacrifice of twenty-two thousand oxen and a hundred and twenty thousand sheep; in this way the king and all the peo- 6 ple dedicated the house of God. The priests stood at their appointed posts; so too the Levites with their musical instruments for the LORD's service, which King David had made for giving thanks to the LORD—'for his love endures for ever'—whenever he rendered praise with their help; opposite them, the priests sounded their trumpets; and all the Israelites were standing there.

7[f] Then Solomon consecrated the centre of the court which lay in front[g] of the house of the LORD; there he offered the whole-offerings and the fat portions of the shared-offerings, because the bronze altar which he had made could not take the whole-offering, the grain-offering, and the 8 fat portions. So Solomon and all Israel with him, a very great assembly from Lebo-hamath to the Torrent of Egypt, celebrated the pilgrim- 9 feast at that time for seven days. On the eighth day they held a closing ceremony; for they had celebrated the dedication of the altar for seven days; the pilgrim-feast lasted seven 10 days. On the twenty-third day of the seventh month he sent the people to their homes, happy and glad at heart for all the prosperity granted by the LORD to David and Solomon and to his people Israel.

The LORD appears again to Solomon

11 When Solomon had finished the house of the LORD and the royal palace and had successfully carried out all that he had planned for the house of the 12 LORD and the palace, the LORD appeared to him by night and said, 'I have heard your prayer and I have chosen this place to be my place of 13 sacrifice. When I shut up the heavens and there is no rain, or command the locusts to consume the land, or send 14 a pestilence against my people, if my people whom I have named my own submit and pray to me and seek me and turn back from their evil ways, I will hear from heaven and forgive 15 their sins and heal their land. Now my eyes will be open and my ears

---

d thy servant . . . service: or thy constant love for David thy servant.   e Or he.   f Verses 7–22: cp. 1 Kgs. 8. 64—9. 9.   g Or to the east.

attentive to the prayers which are 16 made in this place. I have chosen and consecrated this house, that my Name may be there for all time and my eyes and my heart be fixed on it 17 for ever. And if you, on your part, live in my sight as your father David lived, doing all I command you, and observing my statutes and my judgements, then I will establish your royal 18 throne, as I promised by a covenant granted to your father David when I said, "You shall never want for a man 19 to rule over Israel." But if you turn away and forsake my statutes and my commandments which I have set before you, and if you go and serve other gods and prostrate yourselves 20 before them, then I will uproot you from my land which I gave you, I will reject this house which I have consecrated in honour of my name, and make it a byword and an object-21 lesson among all peoples. And this house will become a ruin; every passer-by will be appalled at the sight of it, and they will ask, "Why has the LORD so treated this land and 22 this house?" The answer will be, "Because they forsook the LORD the God of their fathers, who brought them out of Egypt, and clung to other gods, prostrating themselves before them and serving them; that is why the LORD has brought this great evil on them."'

Solomon consolidates his kingdom

h Solomon had taken twenty years to build the house of the LORD and his 2 own palace, and he rebuilt the cities which Huram had given him and 3 settled Israelites in them. He went to 4 Hamath-zobah and seized it, and re-built Tadmor in the wilderness and all the store-cities which he had built 5 in Hamath. He also built Upper Beth-horon and Lower Beth-horon as fortified cities with walls and barred 6 gates, and Baalath, as well as all his store-cities, and all the towns where he quartered his chariots and horses; and he carried out all his cherished plans for building in Jerusalem, in the Lebanon, and throughout his whole 7 dominion. All the survivors of the Hittites, Amorites, Perizzites, Hivites, and Jebusites, who did not belong to 8 Israel—that is their descendants who survived in the land, wherever the Israelites had been unable to exter-minate them—were employed by Sol-

omon on forced labour, as they still are. He put none of the Israelites to 9 forced labour for his public works; they were his fighting men, his cap-tains and lieutenants, and the com-manders of his chariots and of his cavalry. These were King Solomon's 10 officers, two hundred and fifty of them, in charge of the foremen who superintended the people.

Solomon brought Pharaoh's daugh- 11 ter up from the City of David to the house he had built for her, for he said, 'No wife of mine shall live in the house of David king of Israel, be-cause this place which the Ark of the LORD has entered is[i] holy.'

Solomon completes the Temple

Then Solomon offered whole-offerings 12 to the LORD on the altar which he had built to the east of the vestibule, according to what was required for 13 each day, making offerings according to the law of Moses for the sabbaths, the new moons, and the three annual appointed feasts—the pilgrim-feasts of Unleavened Bread, of Weeks, and of Tabernacles.[j] Following the prac- 14 tice of his father David, he drew up the roster of service for the priests and that for the Levites for leading the praise and for waiting upon the priests, as each day required, and that for the door-keepers at each gate; for such was the instruction which David the man of God had given. The in- 15 structions which David had given concerning the priests and the Le-vites and concerning the treasuries were not forgotten.

By this time all Solomon's work 16 was achieved, from the foundation of the house of the LORD to its comple-tion; the house of the LORD was perfect. Then Solomon went to Ezion- 17 geber and to Eloth on the coast of Edom, and Huram sent ships under 18 the command of his own officers and manned by crews of experienced sea-men; and these, in company with Sol-omon's servants, went to Ophir and brought back four hundred and fifty talents of gold, which they delivered to King Solomon.

The queen of Sheba visits Solomon

The queen of Sheba heard of Sol- 9 1[k] omon's fame and came to test him with hard questions. She arrived in Jerusalem with a very large retinue, camels laden with spices, gold in

h Verses 1–18: cp. 1 Kgs. 9. 10–28.   i this place which . . . is: prob. rdg.; Heb. those which . . . are.   j Or Booths.   k Verses 1–24: cp. 1 Kgs. 10. 1–25.

abundance, and precious stones. When she came to Solomon, she told him 2 everything she had in her mind, and Solomon answered all her questions; not one of them was too abstruse for 3 him to answer. When the queen of Sheba saw the wisdom of Solomon, 4 the house which he had built, the food on his table, the courtiers sitting round him, his attendants and his cupbearers in their livery standing behind, and the stairs by which he went up to the house of the LORD, there was no more spirit left in her. 5 Then she said to the king, 'The report which I heard in my own country about you and your wisdom was true, 6 but I did not believe what they told me until I came and saw for myself. Indeed, I was not told half of the greatness of your wisdom; you surpass the report which I had of you. 7 Happy are your wives, happy these courtiers of yours who wait on you every day and hear your wisdom! 8 Blessed be the LORD your God who has delighted in you and has set you on his throne as his king; because in his love your God has elected Israel to make it endure for ever, he has made you king over it to maintain 9 law and justice.' Then she gave the king a hundred and twenty talents of gold, spices in great abundance, and precious stones. There had never been any spices to equal those which the queen of Sheba gave to King Solomon.

10 Besides all this, the servants of Huram and of Solomon, who had brought gold from Ophir, brought 11 also cargoes of algum wood and precious stones. The king used the wood to make stands for the house of the LORD and for the royal palace, as well as harps and lutes for the singers. The like of them had never before been seen in the land of Judah.

12 King Solomon gave the queen of Sheba all she desired, whatever she asked, besides his gifts in return for[l] what she had brought him. Then she departed and returned with her retinue to her own land.

Solomon's wealth and wisdom

13 Now the weight of gold which Solomon received yearly was six hundred 14 and sixty-six talents, in addition to the tolls levied on merchants and on traders who imported goods; all the

kings of Arabia and the regional governors also[m] brought gold and silver to the king.

15 King Solomon made two hundred shields of beaten gold, and six hundred shekels of gold went to the making of each one; he also made three 16 hundred bucklers of beaten gold, and three hundred shekels of gold went to the making of each buckler. The king put these into the House of the Forest of Lebanon.

17 The king also made a great throne of ivory and overlaid it with pure gold. Six steps and a footstool for the 18 throne were all encased in gold. There were arms on each side of the seat, with a lion standing beside each of them, and twelve lions stood on the 19 six steps, one at either end of each step. Nothing like it had ever been made for any monarch. All Solomon's 20 drinking vessels were of gold, and all the plate in the House of the Forest of Lebanon was of red gold; silver was reckoned of no value in the days of Solomon. The king had a fleet of 21 ships plying to Tarshish with Huram's men; once every three years this fleet of merchantmen came home, bringing gold and silver, ivory, apes, and monkeys.

22 Thus King Solomon outdid all the kings of the earth in wealth and wisdom, and all the kings of the earth 23 courted him, to hear the wisdom which God had put in his heart. Each 24 brought his gift with him, vessels of silver and gold, garments, perfumes and spices, horses and mules, so much year by year.

25 Solomon had standing for four thousand horses and chariots, and twelve thousand cavalry horses, and he stabled some in the chariot-towns and kept others at hand in Jerusalem. He ruled over all the kings from the 26 Euphrates to the land of the Philistines and the border of Egypt. He 27 made silver as common in Jerusalem as stones, and cedar as plentiful as sycomore-fig in the Shephelah. Horses 28 were imported from Egypt and from all countries for Solomon.

Other records of Solomon's reign

The rest of the acts of Solomon's reign, 29 from first to last, are recorded in the history of Nathan the prophet, in the prophecy of Ahijah of Shiloh, and in

l his gifts . . . for: prob. rdg.; Heb. om.　　m all . . . also: or and on all the kings of Arabia and the regional governors who . . .　　n Verses 25–8: cp. 1. 14–17; 1 Kgs. 10. 26–9.　　o Verses 29–31: cp. 1 Kgs. 11. 41–3.

the visions of Iddo the seer concerning Jeroboam son of Nebat. Solomon ruled in Jerusalem over the whole of Israel for forty years. Then he rested with his forefathers and was buried in the city of David his father, and he was succeeded by his son Rehoboam.

Rehoboam is made king

Rehoboam went to Shechem, for all Israel had gone there to make him king. When Jeroboam son of Nebat heard of it in Egypt, where he had taken refuge to escape Solomon, he returned from Egypt. They now recalled him, and he and all Israel came to Rehoboam and said, 'Your father laid a cruel yoke upon us; but if you will now lighten the cruel slavery he imposed on us and the heavy yoke he laid on us, we will serve you.' 'Give me three days,' he said, 'and come back again.' So the people went away. King Rehoboam then consulted the elders who had been in attendance on his father Solomon while he lived: 'What answer do you advise me to give to this people?' And they said, 'If you show yourself well-disposed to this people and gratify them by speaking kindly to them, they will be your servants ever after.' But he rejected the advice which the elders gave him. He next consulted those who had grown up with him, and asked them, 'What answer do you advise me to give to this people's request that I should lighten the yoke which my father laid on them?' The young men replied, 'Give this answer to the people who say that your father made their yoke heavy and ask you to lighten it; tell them: "My little finger is thicker than my father's loins. My father laid a heavy yoke on you; I will make it heavier. My father used the whip on you; but I will use the lash."' Jeroboam and the people all came back to Rehoboam on the third day, as the king had ordered. And the king gave them a harsh answer. He rejected the advice which the elders had given him and spoke to the people as the young men advised: 'My father made your yoke heavy; I will make it heavier. My father used the whip on you; but I will use the lash.' So the king would not listen to the people; for the LORD had given this turn to the affair, in order that the word he had spoken by Ahijah of Shiloh to Jeroboam son of Nebat might be fulfilled.

Israel rebels against Judah

When all Israel saw[q] that the king would not listen to them, they answered:

What share have we in David?
We have no lot in the son of Jesse.
Away to your homes, O Israel;
now see to your own house, David.

So all Israel went to their homes, and Rehoboam ruled over those Israelites who lived in the cities of Judah. Then king Rehoboam sent out Hadoram, the commander of the forced levies, but the Israelites stoned him to death; whereupon King Rehoboam mounted his chariot in haste and fled to Jerusalem. From that day to this, Israel has been in rebellion against the house of David.

Strengthening Judah

When Rehoboam reached Jerusalem, **11**[r] he assembled the tribes of Judah and Benjamin, a hundred and eighty thousand chosen warriors, to fight against Israel and recover his kingdom. But the word of the LORD came to Shemaiah the man of God: 'Say to Rehoboam son of Solomon, king of Judah, and to all the Israelites in Judah and Benjamin, "This is the word of the LORD: You shall not go up to make war on your kinsmen. Return to your homes, for this is my will."' So they listened to the word of the LORD and abandoned their campaign against Jeroboam.

Rehoboam resided in Jerusalem and built up the defences of certain cities in Judah. The cities in Judah and Benjamin which he fortified were Bethlehem, Etam, Tekoa, Beth-zur, Soco, Adullam, Gath, Mareshah, Ziph, Adoraim, Lachish, Azekah, Zorah, Aijalon, and Hebron. He strengthened the fortifications of these fortified cities, and put governors in them, as well as supplies of food, oil, and wine. Also he stored shields and spears in every one of the cities, and strengthened their fortifications. Thus he retained possession of Judah and Benjamin.

Now the priests and the Levites throughout the whole of Israel resorted to Rehoboam from all their territories; for the Levites had left all their common land and their own patrimony and had gone to Judah and Jerusalem, because Jeroboam and his successors rejected their services as 15 priests of the LORD, and he appointed his own priests for the hill-shrines, for the demons,[s] and for the calves which 16 he had made. Those, from all the tribes of Israel, who were resolved to seek the LORD the God of Israel followed the Levites to Jerusalem to sacrifice to the LORD the God of their 17 fathers. So they strengthened the kingdom of Judah and for three years made Rehoboam son of Solomon secure, because he followed the example of David and Solomon during that time.

Rehoboam's family

18 Rehoboam married Mahalath, whose father was Jerimoth son of David and whose mother was Abihail daughter 19 of Eliab son of Jesse. His sons by her were: Jeush, Shemariah and Zaham. 20 Next he married Maacah granddaughter of Absalom, who bore him 21 Abijah, Attai, Ziza and Shelomith. Of all his wives and concubines, Rehoboam loved Maacah most; he had in all eighteen wives and sixty concubines and became the father of twenty-eight sons and sixty daugh-22 ters. He appointed Abijah son of Maacah chief among his brothers, making him crown prince and planning to make him his successor on 23 the throne. He showed discretion in detailing his sons to take charge of all the fortified cities throughout the whole territory of Judah and Benjamin; he also made generous provision for them and procured them[t] wives.

Shishak invades Judah

12 When the kingdom of Rehoboam was on a firm footing and he became strong, he forsook the law of the LORD, he 2 and all Israel with him. In the fifth year of Rehoboam's reign, because of this disloyalty to the LORD, Shishak king 3 of Egypt attacked Jerusalem with twelve hundred chariots and sixty thousand horsemen, and brought with him from Egypt an innumerable following of Libyans, Sukkites, and 4 Cushites.[u] He captured the fortified cities of Judah and reached Jerusalem. 5 Then Shemaiah the prophet came to Rehoboam and the leading men of Judah, who had assembled in Jerusalem before the advance of Shishak,

and said to them, 'This is the word of the LORD: You have abandoned me; therefore I now abandon you to Shishak.' The princes of Israel and the 6 king submitted and said, 'The LORD is just.' When the LORD saw that they 7 had submitted, there came from him this word to Shemaiah: 'Because they have submitted I will not destroy them, I will let them barely escape; my wrath shall not be poured out on Jerusalem by means of Shishak, but 8 they shall become his servants; then they will know the difference between serving me and serving the rulers of other countries.' Shishak king of 9[v] Egypt in his attack on Jerusalem removed the treasures of the house of the LORD and of the royal palace. He seized everything, including the shields of gold that Solomon had made. King Rehoboam replaced them 10 with bronze shields and entrusted them to the officers of the escort who guarded the entrance of the royal palace. Whenever the king entered 11 the house of the LORD, the escort entered, carrying the shields; afterwards they returned them to the guard-room. Because Rehoboam sub- 12 mitted, the LORD's wrath was averted from him, and he was not utterly destroyed; Judah enjoyed prosperity.

A summary of Rehoboam's reign

Thus King Rehoboam increased his 13 power in Jerusalem. He was forty-one years old when he came to the throne, and he reigned for seventeen years in Jerusalem, the city which the LORD had chosen out of all the tribes of Israel as the place to receive his Name. Rehoboam's mother was a woman of Ammon called Naamah. He did what 14 was wrong, he did not make a practice of seeking guidance of the LORD. The 15 events of Rehoboam's reign, from first to last, are recorded in the histories of Shemaiah the prophet and Iddo the seer.[x] There was continual fighting between Rehoboam and Jeroboam. He rested with his forefathers and 16 was buried in the city of David; and he was succeeded by his son Abijah.

Abijah reigns over Judah

In the eighteenth year of King Jer- 13 oboam's reign Abijah became king of Judah. He reigned in Jerusalem 2 for three years; his mother was

---

s Or satyrs.   t procured them: prob. rdg.; Heb. asked for a multitude of . . .   u Or Nubians.
v Verses 9–11: cp. 1 Kgs. 14. 25–8.   w Verses 13–16: cp. 1 Kgs. 14. 29–31.   x Prob. rdg.; Heb.
adds to be enrolled by genealogy.

Maacah daughter of Uriel of Gibeah. There was fighting between Abijah 3 and Jeroboam. Abijah drew up his army of four hundred thousand picked troops in order of battle, while Jeroboam formed up against him with eight hundred thousand 4 picked troops. Abijah took up position on the slopes of Mount Zemaraim in the hill-country of Ephraim and called out, 'Hear me, Jeroboam and all 5 Israel: Ought you not to know that the LORD the God of Israel gave the kingship over Israel to David and his descendants in perpetuity by a cove- 6 nant of salt? Yet Jeroboam son of Nebat, the servant of Solomon son of David, rose in rebellion against his 7 lord, and certain worthless scoundrels gathered round him, who stubbornly opposed Solomon's son Rehoboam when he was young and inexperienced, 8 and he was no match for them. Now you propose to match yourselves against the kingdom of the LORD as ruled by David's sons, you and your mob of supporters and the golden calves which Jeroboam has made to 9 be your gods. Have you not dismissed from office the Aaronites, priests of the LORD, and the Levites, and followed the practice of other lands in appointing priests? Now, if any man comes for consecration with an offering of a young bull and seven rams, you accept him as a priest to a god 10 that is no god. But as for us, the LORD is our God and we have not forsaken him; we have Aaronites as priests ministering to the LORD with the Levites, duly discharging their office. 11 Morning and evening, these burn whole-offerings and fragrant incense to the LORD and offer the Bread of the Presence arranged in rows on a table ritually clean; they also kindle the lamps on the golden lamp-stand every evening. Thus we do indeed keep the charge of the LORD our God, 12 whereas you have forsaken him. God is with us at our head, and his priests stand there with trumpets to signal the battle-cry against you. Men of Israel, do not fight the LORD the God of your fathers; you will have no success.'

Judah defeats Israel

13 Jeroboam sent a detachment of his troops to go round and lay an ambush in the rear, so that his main body faced Judah while the ambush lay be- 14 hind them. The men of Judah turned to find that they were engaged front

and rear. Then they cried to the LORD for help. The priests sounded their trumpets, and the men of Judah raised 15 a shout, and when they did so, God put Jeroboam and all Israel to rout before Abijah and Judah. The Israel- 16 ites fled before the men of Judah, and God delivered them into their power. So Abijah and his men de- 17 feated them with very heavy losses, and five hundred thousand picked Israelites fell in the battle. After this, 18 the Israelites were reduced to submission, and Judah prevailed because they relied on the LORD the God of their fathers. Abijah followed up his 19 victory over Jeroboam and captured from him the cities of Bethel, Jeshanah, and Ephron, with their villages. Jeroboam did not regain his power 20 during the days of Abijah; finally the LORD struck him down and he died.

Other records of Abijah's reign

But Abijah established his position; 21 he married fourteen wives and became the father of twenty-two sons and sixteen daughters. The other events 22 of Abijah's reign, both what he said and what he did, are recorded in the story of the prophet Iddo. Abijah **14** rested with his forefathers and was buried in the city of David; and he was succeeded on the throne by his son Asa. In his days the land was at peace for ten years.

Asa reigns over Judah

Asa did what was good and right in 2 the eyes of the LORD his God. He sup- 3 pressed the foreign altars and the hillshrines, smashed the sacred pillars and hacked down the sacred poles, and 4 ordered Judah to seek guidance of the LORD the God of their fathers and to keep the law and the commandments. He also suppressed the hill-shrines 5 and the incense-altars in all the cities, and the kingdom was at peace under him. He built fortified cities in Judah, 6 for the land was at peace. He had no war to fight during those years, because the LORD had given him security. He said to the men of Judah, 'Let 7 us build these cities and fortify them, with walls round them, and towers and barred gates. The land still lies open before us. Because we have sought guidance of the LORD our God, he has sought us and given us security on every side.' So they built and prospered.

Judah defeats the Cushites

8 Asa had an army equipped with shields and spears; three hundred thousand men came from Judah, and two hundred and eighty thousand from Benjamin, shield-bearers and archers; all were valiant warriors.
9 Zerah the Cushite came out against them with an army a million strong and three hundred chariots. When he
10 reached Mareshah, Asa came out to meet him and they took up position in the valley of Zephathah at Mare-
11 shah. Asa called upon the LORD his God and said, 'There is none like thee, O LORD, to help men, whether strong or weak; help us, O LORD our God, for on thee we rely and in thy name we have come out against this horde. O LORD, thou art our God, how can
12 man vie with thee?' So the LORD gave Asa and Judah victory over the
13 Cushites and they fled, and Asa and his men pursued them as far as Gerar. The Cushites broke before the LORD and his army, and many of them fell mortally wounded; and Judah carried
14 off great loads of spoil. They destroyed all the cities around Gerar, for the LORD had struck the people with panic; and they plundered the cities,
15 finding rich spoil in them all. They also killed the herdsmen and seized many sheep and camels, and then they returned to Jerusalem.

Asa seeks the LORD's guidance

15 The spirit of God came upon Azariah
2 son of Oded, and he went out to meet Asa and said to him, 'Hear me, Asa and all Judah and Benjamin. The LORD is with you when you are with him; if you look for him, he will let himself be found; if you forsake him,
3 he will forsake you. For a long time Israel was without the true God, without a priest to interpret the law
4 and without law.[y] But when, in their distress, they turned to the LORD the God of Israel and sought him, he let
5 himself be found by them. At those times there was no safety for people as they went about their business; the inhabitants of every land had their fill of trouble; there was ruin on every
6 side, nation at odds with nation, city with city, for God harassed them with
7 every kind of distress. But now you must be strong and not let your courage fail; for your work will be

rewarded.' When Asa heard these 8 words,[z] he resolutely suppressed the loathsome idols in all Judah and Benjamin and in the cities which he had captured in the hill-country of Ephraim; and he repaired the altar of the LORD which stood before the vestibule of the LORD's house.[a] Then 9 he assembled all Judah and Benjamin and all who had come from Ephraim, Manasseh, and Simeon to reside among them; for great numbers had come over to him from Israel, when they saw that the LORD his God was with him. So they assembled at 10 Jerusalem in the third month of the fifteenth year of Asa's reign, and that 11 day they sacrificed to the LORD seven hundred oxen and seven thousand sheep from the spoil which they had brought. And they entered into a cove- 12 nant to seek guidance of the LORD the God of their fathers with all their heart and soul; all who would not seek 13 the LORD the God of Israel were to be put to death, young and old, men and women alike. Then they bound 14 themselves by an oath to the LORD, with loud shouts of acclamation while trumpets and horns sounded; and all 15 Judah rejoiced at the oath, because they had bound themselves with all their heart and had sought him earnestly, and he had let himself be found by them. So the LORD gave them security on every side. King Asa also 16[b] deprived Maacah his grandmother of her rank as queen mother because she had an obscene object made for the worship of Asherah; Asa cut it down, ground it to powder and burnt it in the gorge of the Kidron. Although the 17 hill-shrines were allowed to remain in Israel, Asa himself remained faithful all his life. He brought into the house 18 of God all his father's votive offerings and his own, gold and silver and sacred vessels. And there was no more 19 war until the thirty-fifth year of Asa's reign.

Asa buys Ben-hadad's assistance[c]

In the thirty-sixth year of the reign of 16 Asa, Baasha king of Israel invaded Judah and fortified Ramah to cut off all access to Asa king of Judah. So Asa 2 brought out silver and gold from the treasuries of the house of the LORD and the royal palace, and sent this request to Ben-hadad king of Aram,

y without law: or without the law.   z Prob. rdg.; Heb. adds and the prophecy, Oded the prophet.
a house: prob. rdg.; Heb. om.   b Verses 16–18: cp. 1 Kgs. 15. 13–15.   c Verses 1–6: cp. 1 Kgs.
15. 17–22.

3 whose capital was Damascus: 'There is an alliance between us, as there was between our fathers. I now send you herewith silver and gold; break off your alliance with Baasha king of Israel, so that he may abandon his 4 campaign against me.' Ben-hadad listened willingly to King Asa and ordered the commanders of his armies to move against the cities of Israel, and they attacked Iyyon, Dan, Abel-mayim, and all the store-cities of 5 Naphtali. When Baasha heard of it, he ceased fortifying Ramah and stopped 6 all work on it. Then King Asa took with him all the men of Judah and they carried away the stones of Ramah and the timbers with which Baasha had fortified it; and he used them to fortify Geba and Mizpah.

Hanani prophesies to Asa

7 At that time the seer Hanani came to Asa king of Judah and said to him, 'Because you relied on the king of Aram and not on the LORD your God, the army of the king of Israel has 8 escaped. The Cushites and the Libyans, were they not a great army with a vast number of chariots and horsemen? Yet, because you relied on the LORD, he delivered them into your 9 power. The eyes of the LORD range through the whole earth, to bring aid and comfort to those whose hearts are loyal to him. You have acted foolishly in this affair; you will have wars 10 from now on.' Asa was angry with the seer and put him in the stocks; for these words of his had made the king very indignant. At the same time he treated some of the people with great brutality.

Other records of Asa's reign

11[d] The events of Asa's reign, from first to last, are recorded in the annals of the 12 kings of Judah and Israel. In the thirty-ninth year of his reign Asa became gravely affected with gangrene in his feet; he did not seek guidance of the LORD but resorted to 13 physicians. He rested with his forefathers, in the forty-first year of his 14 reign, and was buried in the tomb which he had bought[e] for himself in the city of David, being laid on a bier[f] which had been heaped with all kinds of spices skilfully compounded; and they kindled a great fire in his honour.

Jehoshaphat reigns over Judah

17 Asa was succeeded by his son Jehoshaphat, who determined to resist Israel 2 by force. He posted troops in all the fortified cities of Judah and stationed officers[g] throughout Judah and in the cities of Ephraim which his father Asa 3 had captured. The LORD was with Jehoshaphat, for he followed the example his father had set in his early years and did not resort to the Baalim; 4 he sought guidance of the God of his father and obeyed his commandments and did not follow the practices of 5 Israel. So the LORD established the kingdom under his rule, and all Judah brought him gifts, and his wealth and 6 fame[h] became very great. He took pride in the service of the LORD; he also suppressed the hill-shrines and the sacred poles in Judah.

Teaching the people

7 In the third year of his reign he sent his officers, Ben-hayil, Obadiah, Zechariah, Nethaneel, and Micaiah, to 8 teach in the cities of Judah, together with the Levites, Shemaiah, Nethaniah, Zebadiah, Asahel, Shemiramoth, Jehonathan, Adonijah, Tobiah, and Tob-adonijah,[i] accompanied by the priests Elishama and Jehoram. 9 They taught in Judah, having with them the book of the law of the LORD; they went round the cities of Judah, teaching the people.

Jehoshaphat becomes ever more powerful

10 So the dread of the LORD fell upon all the rulers of the lands surrounding Judah, and they did not make war 11 on Jehoshaphat. Certain Philistines brought a gift, a great quantity of silver, to Jehoshaphat; the Arabs too brought him seven thousand seven hundred rams and seven thousand 12 seven hundred he-goats. Jehoshaphat became ever more powerful and built fortresses and store-cities in Judah; 13 and he had much work on hand in the cities of Judah. He had regular, 14 seasoned troops in Jerusalem, enrolled according to their clans in this way: of Judah, the officers over units of a thousand: Adnah the commander, together with three hundred thousand seasoned troops; and next to him the 15 commander Johanan, with two hundred and eighty thousand; and next 16 to him Amasiah son of Zichri, who

d Verses 11–14: cp. 1 Kgs. 15. 23, 24.   *e Or dug.*   *f Or in a niche.*   *g Or garrisons.*   *h Or*
riches.   *i Prob. rdg.; Heb. adds the Levites.*

had volunteered for the service of the LORD, with two hundred thousand 17 seasoned troops; and of Benjamin: an experienced soldier Eliada, with two hundred thousand men armed with 18 bows and shields; next to him Jehozabad, with a hundred and eighty thou- 19 sand fully-armed men. These were the men who served the king, apart from those whom the king had posted in the fortified cities throughout Judah.

Jehoshaphat visits Ahab

18 When Jehoshaphat had become very wealthy and famous,[j] he allied him- 2[k] self with Ahab by marriage. Some years afterwards he went down to visit Ahab in Samaria, and Ahab slaughtered many sheep and oxen for him and his retinue, and incited him to 3 attack Ramoth-gilead. What Ahab king of Israel said to Jehoshaphat king of Judah was this: 'Will you join me in attacking Ramoth-gilead?' And he answered, 'What is mine is yours, myself and my people; I will join with 4 you in the war.' Then Jehoshaphat said to the king of Israel, 'First let us 5 seek counsel from the LORD.' The king of Israel assembled the prophets, some four hundred of them, and asked them, 'Shall I attack Ramoth-gilead or shall I refrain?' 'Attack,' they answered, 'God will deliver it into your hands.' 6 Jehoshaphat asked, 'Is there no other prophet of the LORD here through 7 whom we may seek guidance?' 'There is one more', the king of Israel answered, 'through whom we may seek guidance of the LORD, but I hate the man, because he never prophesies any good for me; never anything but evil. His name is Micaiah son of Imla.' Jehoshaphat exclaimed, 'My lord king, 8 let no such word pass your lips!' So the king of Israel called one of his eunuchs and told him to fetch Micaiah son of Imla with all speed.

Conflicting prophecies

9 The king of Israel and Jehoshaphat king of Judah were seated on their thrones, clothed in their royal robes and in shining armour, at the entrance to the gate of Samaria, and all the prophets were prophesying before 10 them. One of them, Zedekiah son of Kenaanah, made himself horns of iron and said, 'This is the word of the LORD: "With horns like these you shall gore the Aramaeans and make 11 an end of them."' In the same vein

all the prophets prophesied, 'Attack Ramoth-gilead and win the day; the LORD will deliver it into your hands.' The messenger sent to fetch Micaiah 12 told him that the prophets had with one voice given the king a favourable answer. 'And mind you agree with them', he added. 'As the LORD lives,' 13 said Micaiah, 'I will say only what my God tells me to say.'

When Micaiah came into the king's 14 presence, the king said to him, 'Micaiah, shall I attack Ramoth-gilead or shall I refrain?' 'Attack and win the day,' he said, 'and it will fall into your hands.' 'How often must I ad- 15 jure you', said the king, 'to tell me nothing but the truth in the name of the LORD?' Then Micaiah said, 'I saw 16 all Israel scattered on the mountains, like sheep without a shepherd; and I heard the LORD say, "They have no master; let them go home in peace."' The king of Israel said to Jehoshaphat, 17 'Did I not tell you that he never prophesies good for me, nothing but evil?' Micaiah went on, 'Listen now 18 to the word of the LORD: I saw the LORD seated on his throne, with all the host of heaven in attendance on his right and on his left. The LORD 19 said, "Who will entice Ahab to attack and fall on[l] Ramoth-gilead?" One said one thing and one said another; then a spirit came forward and stood 20 before the LORD and said, "I will entice him." "How?" said the LORD. "I will go out", he said, "and be a 21 lying spirit in the mouth of all his prophets." "You shall entice him," said the LORD, "and you shall succeed; go and do it." You see, then, how the 22 LORD has put a lying spirit in the mouth of all these prophets of yours, because he has decreed disaster for you.' Then Zedekiah son of Kenaanah 23 came up to Micaiah and struck him in the face: 'And how did the spirit of the LORD pass from me to speak to you?' he said. Micaiah answered, 24 'That you will find out on the day when you run into an inner room to hide yourself.' Then the king of Israel 25 ordered Micaiah to be arrested and committed to the custody of Amon the governor of the city and Joash the king's son.[m] 'Lock this fellow up', he 26 said, 'and give him prison diet of bread and water until I come home in safety.' Micaiah retorted, 'If you do 27 return in safety, the LORD has not spoken by me.'[n]

j Or rich.   k Verses 2–34: cp. 1 Kgs. 22. 2–35.   l Or at.   m son: or deputy.   n Prob. rdg.; Heb. adds and he said, 'Listen, peoples, all together.'

Ahab dies in battle

28 So the king of Israel and Jehoshaphat king of Judah marched on Ramoth-
29 gilead, and the king of Israel said to Jehoshaphat, 'I will disguise myself to go into battle, but you shall wear your royal robes.' So he went into
30 battle in disguise. Now the king of Aram had commanded the captains of his chariots not to engage all and sundry but the king of Israel alone.
31 When the captains saw Jehoshaphat, they thought he was the king of Israel and wheeled to attack him. But Jehoshaphat cried out, and the LORD came to his help; and God drew them
32 away from him. When the captains saw that he was not the king of Israel,
33 they broke off the attack on him. But one man drew his bow at random and hit the king of Israel where the breast-plate joins the plates of the armour. So he said to his driver, 'Wheel round and take me out of the line; I am
34 wounded.' When the day's fighting reached its height, the king of Israel was facing the Aramaeans, propped up in his chariot; he remained so till evening, and at sunset he died.

The prophet Jehu rebukes Jehoshaphat

19 As Jehoshaphat king of Judah re-turned in safety to his home in Jeru-
2 salem, Jehu son of Hanani, the seer, went out to meet him and said, 'Do you take delight in helping the wicked and befriending the enemies of the LORD? The LORD will make you suffer for
3 this. Yet there is some good in you, for you have swept away the sacred poles from the land and have made a practice of seeking guidance of God.'

Jehoshaphat appoints judges

4 Jehoshaphat had his residence in Jerusalem, but he went out again among his people from Beersheba to the hill-country of Ephraim and brought them back to the LORD the
5 God of their fathers. He appointed judges throughout the land, one in each of the fortified cities of Judah,
6 and said to them, 'Be careful what you do; you are there as judges, to please not man but the LORD, who is
7 with you when you pass sentence. Let the dread of the LORD be upon you, then; take care what you do, for the LORD our God will not tolerate in-justice, partiality, or bribery.'
8 In Jerusalem Jehoshaphat appoint-ed some of the Levites and priests and some heads of families by paternal descent in Israel to administer the law of the LORD and to arbitrate in lawsuits among the inhabitants[o] of the city, and he gave them these
9 instructions: 'You must always act in the fear of the LORD, faithfully and with singleness of mind. In every suit
10 which comes before you from your kinsmen, in whatever city they live, whether cases of bloodshed or offences against the law or the commandments, against statutes or regulations, you shall warn them to commit no offence against the LORD; otherwise you and your kinsmen will suffer for it. If you act thus, you will be free of all offence.
11 Your authority in all matters which concern the LORD is Amariah the chief priest, and in those which concern the king it is Zebediah son of Ishmael, the prince of the house of Judah; the Levites are your officers. Be strong and resolute, and may the LORD be on the side of the good!'

Invasion from the east

20 It happened some time afterwards that the Moabites, the Ammonites, and some of the Meunites made war
2 on Jehoshaphat. News was brought to him that a great horde of them was attacking him from beyond the Dead Sea, from Edom, and was already at Hazazon-tamar, which is En-gedi.
3 Jehoshaphat in his alarm resolved to seek guidance of the LORD and pro-claimed a fast for all Judah. Judah
4 gathered together to ask counsel of the LORD; from every city of the land they came to consult him. Jehosh-
5 aphat stood up in the assembly of Judah and Jerusalem in the house of the LORD, in front of the New Court,
6 and said, 'O LORD God of our fathers, art not thou God in heaven? Thou rulest over all the kingdoms of the nations; in thy hand are strength and power, and there is none who can withstand thee. Didst not thou, O
7 God our God, dispossess the inhabit-ants of this land in favour of thy people Israel, and give it for ever to the descendants of Abraham thy
8 friend? So they lived in it and have built a sanctuary in it in honour of thy name and said, "Should evil come
9 upon us, war or flood,[p] pestilence or famine, we will stand before this house and before thee, for in this house is thy Name, and we will cry to thee in our distress and thou wilt hear
10 and save." Thou didst not allow

o in ... inhabitants: *prob. rdg.; Heb. obscure.*　p *Prob. rdg.; Heb.* judgement.

Israel, when they came out of Egypt, to enter the land of the Ammonites, the Moabites, and the people of the hill-country of Seir, so they turned aside and left them alone and did not 11 destroy them. Now see how these people repay us: they are coming to drive us out of thy possession which 12 thou didst give to us. Judge them, O God our God, for we have no strength to face this great horde which is invading our land; we know not what we ought to do; we lift our eyes to thee.'

Judah's victory is assured

13 So all Judah stood there before the LORD, with their dependants, their 14 wives and their children. Then, in the midst of the assembly, the spirit of the LORD came upon Jahaziel son of Zechariah, son of Benaiah, son of Jeiel, son of Mattaniah, a Levite of the line 15 of Asaph, and he said, 'Attend, all Judah, all inhabitants of Jerusalem, and King Jehoshaphat; this is the word of the LORD to you: "Have no fear; do not be dismayed by this great horde, for the battle is in God's 16 hands, not yours. Go down to meet them tomorrow; they will come up by the Ascent of Ziz. You will find them at the end of the valley, east of the 17 wilderness of Jeruel. It is not you who will fight this battle; stand firm and wait, and you will see the deliverance worked by the LORD: he is on your side, O Judah and Jerusalem. Do not fear or be dismayed; go out tomorrow 18 to face them; for the LORD is on your side."' Jehoshaphat bowed his face to the ground, and all Judah and the inhabitants of Jerusalem fell down before the LORD to make obeisance to 19 him. Then the Levites of the lines of Kohath and Korah stood up and praised the LORD the God of Israel with a mighty shout.

The LORD deludes the enemy

20 So they rose early in the morning and went out to the wilderness of Tekoa; and, as they were starting, Jehoshaphat took his stand and said, 'Hear me, O Judah and inhabitants of Jerusalem: hold firmly to your faith in the LORD your God and you will be upheld; have faith in his prophets 21 and you will prosper.' After consulting with the people, he appointed men to sing to the LORD and praise the splendour of his holiness*q* as they went before the armed troops, and they sang:

Give thanks to the LORD,
for his love endures for ever.

22 As soon as their loud shouts of praise were heard, the LORD deluded the Ammonites and Moabites and the men of the hill-country of Seir, who were invading Judah, and they were 23 defeated. It turned out that the Ammonites and Moabites had taken up a position against the men of the hill-country of Seir, and set themselves to annihilate and destroy them; and when they had exterminated the men of Seir, they savagely attacked one 24 another. So when Judah came to the watch-tower in the wilderness and looked towards the enemy horde, there they were all lying dead upon the ground; none had escaped. When 25 Jehoshaphat and his men came to collect the booty, they found a large number of cattle, goods, clothing, and precious things, which they plundered until they could carry away no more. They spent three days collecting the booty, there was so much of it. On 26 the fourth day they assembled in the Valley of Berakah,*r* the name that it bears to this day because they blessed the LORD there. Then all the men of 27 Judah and Jerusalem, with Jehoshaphat at their head, returned home to the city in triumph; for the LORD had given them cause to triumph over their enemies. They entered Jeru- 28 salem with lutes, harps, and trumpets playing, and went into the house of the LORD. So the dread of God fell 29 upon the rulers of every country, when they heard that the LORD had fought against the enemies of Israel; and the realm of Jehoshaphat was at 30 peace, God giving him security on all sides.

Other records of Jehoshaphat's reign

Thus Jehoshaphat reigned over Judah. 31*s* He was thirty-five years old when he came to the throne, and he reigned in Jerusalem for twenty-five years; his mother was Azubah daughter of Shilhi. He followed in the footsteps of 32 Asa his father and did not swerve from them; he did what was right in the eyes of the LORD. But the hill-shrines 33 were allowed to remain, and the people did not set their hearts upon the God of their fathers. The other 34 events of Jehoshaphat's reign, from first to last, are recorded in the history of Jehu son of Hanani, which is included in the annals of the kings of Israel.

Jehoshaphat's fleet is wrecked

35 Later Jehoshaphat king of Judah allied himself with Ahaziah king of
36 Israel; he did wrong in joining with him to build ships for trade with Tarshish; these were built in Ezion-
37 geber. But Eliezer son of Dodavahu of Mareshah denounced Jehoshaphat with this prophecy: 'Because you have joined with Ahaziah, the LORD will bring your work to nothing.' So the ships were wrecked and could not make the voyage to Tarshish.

Joram reigns over Judah

21 Jehoshaphat rested with his forefathers and was buried with them in the city of David. He was succeeded
2 by his son Joram, whose brothers were Azariah, Jehiel, Zechariah, Azariah, Michael, and Shephatiah, sons of Jehoshaphat. All of them were sons of
3 Jehoshaphat king of Judah, and their father gave them many gifts, silver and gold and other costly things, as well as fortified cities in Judah; but the kingship he gave to Joram because he was the eldest.
4 When Joram was firmly established on his father's throne, he put to the sword all his brothers and also some
5[t] of the princes of Israel. He was thirty-two years old when he came to the throne, and he reigned in Jeru-
6 salem for eight years. He followed the practices of the kings of Israel as the house of Ahab had done, for he had married Ahab's daughter; and he did what was wrong in the eyes of the
7 LORD. But for the sake of the covenant which he had made with David, the LORD was unwilling to destroy the house of David, since he had promised to give him and his sons a flame, to burn for all time.

Edom claims independence

8 During his reign Edom revolted against Judah and set up its own king.
9 Joram, with his commanders and all his chariots, advanced into Edom. He and his chariot-commanders set out by night, but they were surrounded
10 by the Edomites and defeated.[u] So Edom has remained independent of Judah to this day. Libnah revolted against him at the same time, because

he had forsaken the LORD the God of his fathers, and because he had built 11 hill-shrines in the hill-country of Judah and had seduced the inhabitants of Jerusalem into idolatrous practices and corrupted Judah.

The death of Joram

A letter reached Joram from Elijah 12 the prophet, which ran thus: 'This is the word of the LORD the God of David your father: "You have not followed in the footsteps of Jehoshaphat your father and of Asa king of Judah, but have followed the kings of 13 Israel and have seduced Judah and the inhabitants of Jerusalem, as the house of Ahab did; and you have put to death your own brothers, sons of your father's house, men better than yourself. Because of all this, the 14 LORD is about to strike a heavy blow at your people, your children, your wives, and all your possessions, and 15 you yourself will suffer from a chronic disease of the bowels, until they prolapse and become severely ulcerated."'
Then the LORD aroused against Joram 16 the anger of the Philistines and of the Arabs who live near the Cushites, and 17 they invaded Judah and made their way right through it, carrying off all the property which they found in the king's palace, as well as his sons and wives; not a son was left to him except the youngest, Jehoahaz. It was after 18 all this that the LORD struck down the king with an incurable disease of the bowels. It continued for some time, 19 and towards the end of the second year the disease caused his bowels to prolapse, and the painful ulceration brought on his death. But his people kindled no fire in his honour as they had done for his fathers. He was 20 thirty-two years old when he became king, and he reigned in Jerusalem for eight years. His passing went unsung, and he was buried in the city of David, but not in the burial-place of the kings.

Ahaziah reigns over Judah

Then the inhabitants of Jerusalem 22 1[v] made Ahaziah, his youngest son, king in his place, for the raiders who had joined the Arabs in the campaign had killed all the elder sons. So Ahaziah son of Joram became king of Judah. He was forty-two years old when he 2 came to the throne, and he reigned in Jerusalem for one year; his mother

t Verses 5–10: cp. 2 Kgs. 8. 17–22.
v Verses 1–6: cp. 2 Kgs. 8. 25–9.
u and defeated: prob. rdg.; Heb. and he defeated them.

G

was Athaliah granddaughter of Omri.
3 He too followed the practices of the
house of Ahab, for his mother was his
4 counsellor in wickedness. He did what
was wrong in the eyes of the LORD like
the house of Ahab, for they had been
his counsellors after his father's death,
5 to his undoing. He followed their
counsel also in the alliance he made
with Jehoram son of Ahab king of
Israel, to fight against Hazael king of
Aram at Ramoth-gilead. But Jehoram was wounded by the Aramaeans,
6 and returned to Jezreel to recover from
the wounds which were inflicted on him
at Ramoth in battle with Hazael king
of Aram.

Jehu kills Ahaziah

Because of Jehoram's illness Ahaziah
son of Joram king of Judah went
7 down to Jezreel to visit him. It was
God's will that the visit of Ahaziah to
Jehoram should be the occasion of his
downfall. During the visit he went
out with Jehoram to meet Jehu son of
Nimshi, whom the LORD had anointed
to bring the house of Ahab to an end.
8 So it came about that Jehu, who was
then at variance with the house of
Ahab, found the officers of Judah and
the kinsmen of Ahaziah who were his
9 attendants, and killed them. Then he
searched out Ahaziah himself, and his
men captured him in Samaria, where
he had gone into hiding. They brought
him to Jehu and put him to death;
they gave him burial, for they said,
'He was a son of Jehoshaphat who
sought the guidance of the LORD with
his whole heart.' Then the house of
Ahaziah had no one strong enough to
rule.

Athaliah seizes the throne

10[w] As soon as Athaliah mother of Ahaziah saw that her son was dead, she
set out to extirpate the royal line of
11 the house of Judah. But Jehosheba
daughter of King Joram took Ahaziah's son Joash and stole him away
from among the princes who were
being murdered; she put him and his
nurse in a bedchamber. Thus Jehosheba, daughter of King Joram and
wife of Jehoiada the priest, because
she was Ahaziah's sister, hid Joash
from Athaliah so that she did not put
12 him to death. He remained concealed
with them in the house of God for
six years, while Athaliah ruled the
country.

Joash is proclaimed king

In the seventh year Jehoiada felt him- 23
self strong enough to make an agreement with Azariah son of Jeroham,
Ishmael son of Jehohanan, Azariah
son of Obed, Maaseiah son of Adaiah,
and Elishaphat son of Zichri, all
captains of units of a hundred. They 2
went all through Judah and gathered
to Jerusalem the Levites from the
cities of Judah and the heads of clans
in Israel, and they came to Jerusalem.
All the assembly made a compact 3
with the king in the house of God,
and Jehoiada said to them, 'Here is
the king's son! He shall be king, as
the LORD promised that the sons of
David should be. This is what you 4
must do: a third of you, priests and
Levites, as you come on duty on the
sabbath, are to be on guard at the
threshold gates, another third are to 5
be in the royal palace, and another
third are to be at the Foundation
Gate, while all the people will be in
the courts of the house of the LORD.
Let no one enter the house of the 6
LORD except the priests and the attendant Levites; they may enter, for
they are holy, but all the people shall
continue to keep the LORD's charge.
The Levites shall mount guard round 7
the king, each with his weapons at the
ready; anyone who tries to enter the
house is to be put to death. They shall
stay with the king wherever he goes.'
The Levites and all Judah carried 8
out the orders of Jehoiada the priest
to the letter. Each captain took his
men, both those who came on duty on
the sabbath and those who came off,
for Jehoiada the priest had not released the outgoing divisions. And 9
Jehoiada the priest handed out to the
captains King David's spears, shields,
and bucklers, which were in the house
of God; and he posted all the people, 10
each man carrying his weapon at the
ready, from corner to corner of the
house to north and south,[x] surrounding the king. Then they brought out 11
the king's son, put the crown on his
head, handed him the warrant and
proclaimed him king, and Jehoiada
and his sons anointed him; and a
shout went up: 'Long live the king.'
When Athaliah heard the noise of the 12
people as they ran about cheering for
the king, she came into the house of
the LORD where the people were and 13
found the king standing on the dais[y]

w 22. 10—23. 21: *cp.* 2 *Kgs. 11. 1–20.*
y Prob. rdg., *cp.* 2 *Kgs. 11. 14; Heb.* by his pillar.

x Prob. rdg.; *Heb. adds* of the altar and the house.

at the entrance, amidst outbursts of song and fanfares of trumpets in his honour; all the populace were rejoicing and blowing trumpets, and singers with musical instruments were leading the celebrations. Athaliah rent her clothes and cried, 'Treason! Treason!' 14 Jehoiada the priest gave orders to[z] the captains in command of the troops: 'Bring her outside the precincts and let anyone in attendance on her be put to the sword'; for the priest said, 'Do not kill her in the house of the LORD.' 15 So they laid hands on her and took her to the royal palace and killed her there at the passage to the Horse Gate.

Jehoiada makes a covenant

16 Then Jehoiada made a covenant between the LORD[a] and the whole people and the king, that they should be the 17 LORD's people. And all the people went into the temple of Baal and pulled it down; they smashed its altars and images, and they slew Mattan the 18 priest of Baal before the altars. Then Jehoiada committed the supervision of the house of the LORD to the charge of the priests and the Levites whom David had allocated to the house of the LORD, to offer whole-offerings to the LORD as prescribed in the law of Moses, with the singing and rejoic-19 ing as handed down from David. He stationed the door-keepers at the gates of the house of the LORD, to prevent anyone entering who was in 20 any way unclean. Then he took the captains of units of a hundred, the nobles, and the governors of the people, and all the people of the land, and they escorted the king from the house of the LORD through the Upper Gate to the royal palace, and seated him on 21 the royal throne. The whole people rejoiced and the city was tranquil. That is how Athaliah was put to the sword.

Joash repairs the Temple

24 1[b] Joash was seven years old when he became king, and he reigned in Jerusalem for forty years; his mother 2 was Zibiah of Beersheba. He did what was right in the eyes of the LORD as long as Jehoiada the priest was alive. 3 Jehoiada chose him two wives, and he had a family of sons and daughters. 4 Some time after this, Joash decided 5 to repair the house of the LORD. So he

assembled the priests and the Levites and said to them, 'Go through the cities of Judah and collect the annual tax from all the Israelites for the restoration of the house of your God, and do it quickly.' But the Levites did not act quickly. The king then 6 called for Jehoiada the chief priest and said to him, 'Why have you not required the Levites to bring in from Judah and Jerusalem the tax imposed by Moses the servant of the LORD and by the assembly of Israel for the Tent of the Tokens?' For the wicked 7 Athaliah and her adherents had broken into the house of God and had devoted all its holy things to the service of the Baalim. So the king 8 ordered them to make a chest and to put it outside the gate of the house of the LORD; and proclamation was 9 made throughout Judah and Jerusalem that the people should bring to the LORD the tax imposed on Israel in the wilderness by Moses the servant of God. And all the leaders and all the 10 people gladly brought their taxes and cast them into the chest until it was full. Whenever the chest was brought 11 to the king's officers by the Levites and they saw that it was well filled, the king's secretary and the chief priest's officer would come to empty it, after which it was carried back to its place. This they did daily, and they collected a great sum of money. The king and 12 Jehoiada gave it to those responsible for carrying out the work in the house of the LORD, and they hired masons and carpenters to do the repairs, as well as craftsmen in iron and copper[c] to restore the house. So the work-13 men proceeded with their task and the new work progressed under their hands; they restored the house of God according to its original design and strengthened it. When they had 14 finished, they brought what was left of the money to the king and to Jehoiada, and it was made into vessels for the house of the LORD, both for service and for sacrificing, saucers and other vessels of gold and silver. While Jehoiada lived, whole-offerings were offered in the house of the LORD continually.

The death of Jehoiada

Jehoiada, now old and weighed down 15 with years, died at the age of a hundred and thirty and was buried 16 with the kings in the city of David,

---

z gave orders to: *prob. rdg., cp.* 2 Kgs. 11. 15; Heb. brought out.
2 Kgs. 11. 17; Heb. him.   b Verses 1–14: cp. 2 Kgs. 11. 21—12. 15.

a the LORD: *prob. rdg., cp.*
c Or bronze.

because he had done good in Israel and served God and his house.

Joash has Zechariah stoned

17 After the death of Jehoiada the leading men of Judah came and made obeisance to the king. He listened to 18 them, and they forsook the house of the LORD the God of their fathers and worshipped sacred poles and idols. And Judah and Jerusalem suffered 19 for this wickedness. But the LORD sent prophets to bring them back to himself, prophets who denounced 20 them and were not heeded. Then the spirit of God took possession of Zechariah son of Jehoiada the priest, and he stood looking down on the people and said to them, 'This is the word of God: "Why do you disobey the commands of the LORD and court disaster? Because you have forsaken the LORD, 21 he has forsaken you."' But they made common cause against him, and on orders from the king they stoned him to death in the court of the house of 22 the LORD. King Joash did not remember the loyalty of Zechariah's father Jehoiada but killed his son, who said as he was dying, 'May the LORD see this and exact the penalty.'

The death of Joash

23 At the turn of the year an Aramaean army advanced against Joash; they invaded Judah and Jerusalem and massacred all the officers, so that the army ceased to exist, and sent all their spoil to the king of Damascus. 24 Although the Aramaeans had invaded with a small force, the LORD delivered a very great army into their hands, because the people had forsaken the LORD the God of their fathers; and Joash suffered just punishment. 25[d] When the Aramaeans had withdrawn, leaving the king severely wounded, his servants conspired against him to avenge the death of the son of Jehoiada the priest; and they killed him on his bed. Thus he died and was buried in the city of David, but not in the burial-place 26 of the kings. The conspirators were Zabad son of Shimeath an Ammonite woman and Jehozabad son of Shimrith a Moabite woman. His children, 27 the many oracles about him, and his reconstruction of the house of God are all on record in the story given in the annals of the kings. He was succeeded by his son Amaziah.

Amaziah reigns over Judah

Amaziah was twenty-five years old 25 when he came to the throne, and he reigned in Jerusalem for twenty-nine years; his mother was Jehoaddan of Jerusalem. He did what was right in 2 the eyes of the LORD, but not wholeheartedly. When the royal power was 3 firmly in his grasp, he put to death those of his servants who had murdered the king his father; but he spared 4 their children, in obedience to the LORD's command written in the law of Moses: 'Fathers shall not die for their children, nor children for their fathers; a man shall die only for his own sin.'

Amaziah's victory in the Valley of Salt

Then Amaziah assembled the men of 5 Judah and drew them up by families, all Judah and Benjamin as well, under officers over units of a thousand and a hundred. He mustered those of twenty years old and upwards and found their number to be three hundred thousand, all picked troops ready for service, able to handle spear and shield. He also hired a 6 hundred thousand seasoned troops from Israel for a hundred talents of silver. But a man of God came to him 7 and said, 'My lord king, do not let the Israelite army march with you; the LORD is not with Israel—all these Ephraimites! For, if you make these 8 people[f] your allies in the war, God will overthrow you in battle; he has power to help or to overthrow.' Then 9 Amaziah said to the man of God, 'What am I to do about the hundred talents which I have spent on the Israelite army?' The man of God answered, 'It is in the LORD's power to give you much more than that.' So 10 Amaziah detached the troops which had come to him from Ephraim and sent them home; that infuriated them against Judah and they went home in a rage.

Then Amaziah took heart and led 11 his men to the Valley of Salt and there killed ten thousand men of Seir. The 12 men of Judah captured another ten thousand men alive, brought them to the top of a cliff[g] and hurled them over so that they were all dashed to pieces. Meanwhile the troops which 13 Amaziah had sent home without allowing them to take part in the battle

d Verses 25–7: cp. 2 Kgs. 12. 20, 21. rdg.; Heb. obscure.   e Verses 1–4: cp. 2 Kgs. 14. 1–6.   f these people: prob.   g a cliff: or Sela.

raided the cities of Judah from Samaria to Beth-horon, massacred three thousand people in them and carried off quantities of booty.

Israel attacks Judah

14 After Amaziah had returned from the defeat of the Edomites, he brought the gods of the people of Seir and, setting them up as his own gods, worshipped them and burnt sacrifices 15 to them. The LORD was angry with Amaziah for this and sent a prophet who said to him, 'Why have you resorted to gods who could not save 16 their own people from you?' But while he was speaking, the king said to him, 'Have we appointed you counsellor to the king? Stop! Why risk your life?' The prophet did stop, but first he said, 'I know that God has determined to destroy you because you have done this and have not listened to my counsel.'

17[h] Then Amaziah king of Judah, after consultation, sent messengers to Jehoash son of Jehoahaz, son of Jehu, king of Israel, to propose a meeting. 18 But Jehoash king of Israel sent this answer to Amaziah king of Judah: 'A thistle in Lebanon sent to a cedar in Lebanon to say, "Give your daughter in marriage to my son." But a wild beast in Lebanon, passing by, tram- 19 pled on the thistle. You have defeated Edom, you say, but it has gone to your head. Enjoy your glory at home and stay there. Why should you involve yourself in disaster and bring yourself to the ground, and Judah with you?'

20 But Amaziah would not listen; and this was God's doing in order to give Judah into the power of Jehoash, be- cause they had resorted to the gods 21 of Edom. So Jehoash king of Israel marched out, and he and Amaziah king of Judah met one another at 22 Beth-shemesh in Judah. The men of Judah were routed by Israel and fled 23 to their homes. But Jehoash king of Israel captured Amaziah king of Judah, son of Joash, son of Jehoahaz, at Beth-shemesh, and brought him to Jerusalem. There he broke down the city wall from the Gate of Ephraim to the Corner Gate, a distance of four 24 hundred cubits; he also took[i] all the gold and silver and all the vessels found in the house of God, in the care of Obed-edom, and the treasures of the royal palace, as well as hostages, and returned to Samaria.

Other records of Amaziah's reign

25[j] Amaziah son of Joash, king of Judah, outlived Jehoash son of Jehoahaz, king of Israel, by fifteen years. The 26 other events of Amaziah's reign, from first to last, are recorded in the annals of the kings of Judah and Israel. 27 From the time when he turned away from the LORD, there was conspiracy against him in Jerusalem and he fled to Lachish; but they sent after him to Lachish and put him to death there. 28 Then his body was conveyed on horse- back to Jerusalem, and there he was buried with his forefathers in the city of David.

Uzziah reigns over Judah

26 All the people of Judah took Uzziah, now sixteen years old, and made him king in succession to his father Amazi- 2 ah. It was he who built Eloth and restored it to Judah after the king rested with his forefathers.

3[k] Uzziah was sixteen years old when he came to the throne, and he reigned in Jerusalem for fifty-two years; his mother was Jecoliah of Jerusalem. 4 He did what was right in the eyes of the LORD, as Amaziah his father had 5 done. He set himself to seek the guidance of God in the days of Zechariah, who instructed him in the fear of God; as long as he sought guidance of the LORD, God caused him to prosper.

Uzziah's armaments

6 He took the field against the Philis- tines and broke down the walls of Gath, Jabneh, and Ashdod; and he built cities in the territory of Ashdod 7 and among the Philistines. God aided him against them, against the Arabs who lived in Gur-baal, and against the 8 Meunites. The Ammonites brought gifts to Uzziah and his fame spread to the borders of Egypt, for he had be- 9 come very powerful. Besides, he built towers in Jerusalem at the Corner Gate, at the Valley Gate, and at the 10 escarpment, and fortified them. He built other towers in the wilderness and dug many cisterns, for he had large herds of cattle both in the Shephelah and in the plain. He also had farmers and vine-dressers in the hill-country and in the fertile lands, for he loved the soil.

h Verses 17–24: cp. 2 Kgs. 14. 8–14.   i he also took: prob. rdg., cp. 2 Kgs. 14. 14; Heb. om.
j 25. 25—26. 2: cp. 2 Kgs. 14. 17–22.   k Verses 3, 4: cp. 2 Kgs. 15. 2, 3.

11 Uzziah had an army of soldiers trained and ready for service, grouped according to the census made by Jeiel the adjutant-general and Maaseiah the clerk under the direction of Hananiah, one of the king's commanders.
12 The total number of heads of families which supplied seasoned warriors was
13 two thousand six hundred. Under their command was an army of three hundred and seven thousand five hundred, a powerful fighting force to aid the king against his enemies.
14 Uzziah prepared for the whole army shields, spears, helmets, coats of mail,
15 bows, and[l] sling-stones. In Jerusalem he had machines designed by engineers for use upon towers and bastions, made to discharge arrows and large stones. His fame spread far and wide, for he was so wonderfully gifted that he became very powerful.

Uzziah's pride leads to his undoing

16 But when he grew powerful his pride led to his own undoing:[m] he offended against the LORD his God by entering the temple of the LORD to burn incense
17 on the altar of incense. Azariah the priest and eighty others of the LORD's priests, courageous men, went in after
18 King Uzziah, confronted him and said, 'It is not for you, Uzziah, to burn incense to the LORD, but for the Aaronite priests who have been consecrated for that office. Leave the sanctuary; for you have offended, and that will certainly bring you no
19 honour from the LORD God.' The king, who had a censer in his hand ready to burn incense, was indignant; and because of his indignation at the priests, leprosy broke out on his forehead in the presence of the priests, there in the house of the LORD, beside
20 the altar of incense. When Azariah the chief priest and the other priests looked towards him, they saw that he had leprosy on his forehead and they hurried him out of the temple, and indeed he himself hastened to leave, because the LORD had struck
21[n] him with the disease. And King Uzziah remained a leper till the day of his death; he lived in his own house as a leper, relieved of all duties and excluded from the house of the LORD, while his son Jotham was comptroller
22 of the household and regent. The other events of Uzziah's reign, from first to last, are recorded by the

prophet Isaiah son of Amoz. So he 23 rested with his forefathers and was buried in a burial-ground, but not that of the kings; for they said, 'He is a leper'; and he was succeeded by his son Jotham.

Jotham reigns over Judah

Jotham was twenty-five years old 27 when he came to the throne, and he reigned in Jerusalem for sixteen years; his mother was Jerushah daughter of Zadok. He did what was right in 2 the eyes of the LORD, as his father Uzziah had done, but unlike him he did not enter the temple of the LORD; the people, however, continued their corrupt practices. He constructed the 3 upper gate of the house of the LORD and built extensively on the wall at Ophel. He built cities in the hill- 4 country of Judah, and forts and towers on the wooded hills. He made 5 war on the king of the Ammonites and defeated him; and that year the Ammonites gave him a hundred talents of silver, ten thousand kor of wheat and ten thousand of barley. They paid him the same tribute in the second and third years. Jotham 6 became very powerful because he maintained a steady course of obedience to the LORD his God. The other 7 events of Jotham's reign, all that he did in war and in peace, are recorded in the annals of the kings of Israel and Judah. He was twenty-five years old 8 when he came to the throne, and he reigned in Jerusalem for sixteen years. He rested with his forefathers and 9 was buried in the city of David; and he was succeeded by his son Ahaz.

Ahaz reigns over Judah

Ahaz was twenty years old when he 28 came to the throne, and he reigned in Jerusalem for sixteen years. He did not do what was right in the eyes of the LORD like his forefather David, but followed in the footsteps of the 2 kings of Israel, and cast metal images for the Baalim. He also burnt sacri- 3 fices in the Valley of Ben-hinnom; he even burnt his sons in the fire according to the abominable practice of the nations whom the LORD had dispossessed in favour of the Israelites. He 4 slaughtered and burnt sacrifices at the hill-shrines and on the hill-tops and under every spreading tree.

l Prob. rdg.; Heb. adds for.   *m his pride . . . undoing: or he became so proud that he acted corruptly.*   *n Verses 21–3: cp. 2 Kgs. 15. 5–7.*   *o Verses 1–3: cp. 2 Kgs. 15. 33–5.*   *p Verses 1–4: cp. 2 Kgs. 16. 2–4.*

Ahaz suffers defeats

5 The LORD his God let him suffer at the hands of the king of Aram, and the Aramaeans defeated him, took many captives and brought them to Damascus; he was also made to suffer at the hands of the king of Israel, who 6 inflicted a severe defeat on him. This was Pekah son of Remaliah, who killed in one day a hundred and twenty thousand men of Judah, seasoned troops, because they had forsaken the 7 LORD the God of their fathers. And Zichri, an Ephraimite hero, killed Maaseiah the king's son[q] and Azrikam the comptroller of the household and Elkanah the king's chief minister. 8 The Israelites took captive from their kinsmen two hundred thousand women and children; they also took a large amount of booty and brought it to Samaria.

The Israelites surrender their captives

9 A prophet of the LORD was there, Oded by name; he went out to meet the army as it returned to Samaria and said to them, 'It is because the LORD the God of your fathers is angry with Judah that he has given them into your power; and you have massacred them in a rage that has 10 towered up to heaven. Now you propose to force the people of Judah and Jerusalem, male and female, into slavery. Are not you also guilty men 11 before the LORD your God? Now, listen to me. Send back those you have taken captive from your kinsmen, for the anger of the LORD is 12 roused against you.' Next, some Ephraimite chiefs, Azariah son of Jehohanan, Berechiah son of Meshillemoth, Hezekiah[r] son of Shallum, and Amasa son of Hadlai, met those 13 who were returning from the war and said to them, 'You must not bring these captives into our country; what you are proposing would make us guilty before the LORD and add to our sins and transgressions. We are guilty enough already, and there is 14 fierce anger against Israel.' So the armed men left the captives and the spoil with the officers and the as-15 sembled people. The captives were put in charge of men nominated for this duty, who found clothes from the spoil for all who were naked. They clothed them and shod them, gave them food and drink, and anointed them; those

who were tottering from exhaustion they conveyed on the backs of asses, and so brought them to their kinsmen in Jericho, in the Vale of Palm Trees. Then they themselves returned to Samaria.

Ahaz is unfaithful to the LORD

At that time King Ahaz sent to the 16 king of Assyria for help. The Edomites 17 had invaded again and defeated Judah and taken away prisoners; and 18 the Philistines had raided the cities of the Shephelah and of the Negeb of Judah and had captured Beth-shemesh, Aijalon, and Gederoth, as well as Soco, Timnah, and Gimzo with their villages, and occupied them. The 19 LORD had reduced Judah to submission because of Ahaz king of Judah; for his actions in Judah had been unbridled and he had been grossly unfaithful to the LORD. Then Tiglath- 20 pileser king of Assyria marched against him and, so far from assisting him, pressed him hard. Ahaz stripped 21 the house of the LORD, the king's palace and the houses of his officers, and gave the plunder to the king of Assyria; but all to no purpose. This King Ahaz, when hard pressed, 22 became more and more unfaithful to the LORD; he sacrificed to the gods of 23 Damascus who had defeated him and said, 'The gods of the kings of Aram helped them; I will sacrifice to them so that they may help me.' But in fact they caused his downfall and that of all Israel. Then Ahaz gathered to- 24 gether the vessels of the house of God and broke them up, and shut the doors of the house of the LORD; he made himself altars at every corner in Jerusalem, and at every single city of 25 Judah he made hill-shrines to burn sacrifices to other gods and provoked the anger of the LORD the God of his fathers.

Other records of the reign of Ahaz

The other acts and all the events of 26[s] his reign, from first to last, are recorded in the annals of the kings of Judah and Israel. So Ahaz rested with 27 his forefathers and was buried in the city of Jerusalem, but was not given burial with the kings of Judah. He was succeeded by his son Hezekiah.

Hezekiah calls for repentance

Hezekiah was twenty-five years old 29 1[t] when he came to the throne, and he

q son: or deputy.   r Or Jehizkiah.   s Verses 26, 27: cp. 2 Kgs. 16. 19, 20.   t Verses 1, 2: cp.
2 Kgs. 18. 1–3.

reigned in Jerusalem for twenty-nine years; his mother was Abijah daughter of Zechariah. He did what was right in the eyes of the LORD, as David his forefather had done.

3 In the first year of his reign, in the first month, he opened the gates of the house of the LORD and repaired them. 4 He brought in the priests and the Levites and gathered them together in the square on the east side, 5 and said to them, 'Levites, listen to me. Hallow yourselves now, hallow the house of the LORD the God of your fathers, and remove the pollution 6 from the sanctuary. For our forefathers were unfaithful and did what was wrong in the eyes of the LORD our God: they forsook him, they would have nothing to do with his dwelling-place, they turned their backs 7 on it. They shut the doors of the porch and extinguished the lamps, they ceased to burn incense and offer whole-offerings in the sanctuary to 8 the God of Israel. Therefore the anger of the LORD fell upon Judah and Jerusalem and he made them repugnant, an object of horror and derision, 9 as you see for yourselves. Hence it is that our fathers have fallen by the sword, our sons and daughters and 10 our wives are in captivity. Now I intend that we should pledge ourselves to the LORD the God of Israel, in order that his anger may be averted from 11 us. So, my sons, let no time be lost; for the LORD has chosen you to serve him and to minister to him, to be his ministers and to burn sacrifices.'

Worship is restored

12 Then the Levites set to work— Mahath son of Amasai and Joel son of Azariah of the family of Kohath; of the family of Merari, Kish son of Abdi and *Azariah* son of Jehalelel; of the family of Gershon, Joah son of 13 Zimmah and Eden son of Joah; of the family of Elizaphan, Shimri and Jeiel; of the family of Asaph, Zechariah and 14 Mattaniah; of the family of Heman, Jehiel and Shimei; and of the family of Jeduthun, Shemaiah and Uzziel. 15 They assembled their kinsmen and hallowed themselves, and then went in, as the king had instructed them at the LORD's command, to purify the 16 house of the LORD. The priests went inside to purify the house of the LORD; they removed all the pollution which they found in the temple into the court of the house of the LORD, and

the Levites took it from them and carried it outside to the gorge of the Kidron. 17 They began the rites on the first day of the first month, and on the eighth day they reached the porch; then for eight days they consecrated the house of the LORD, and on the sixteenth day of the first month they 18 finished. Then they went into the palace and said to King Hezekiah, 'We have purified the whole of the house of the LORD, the altar of whole-offering with all its vessels, and the table for the Bread of the Presence arranged in rows with all its vessels; 19 and we have put in order and consecrated all the vessels which King Ahaz cast aside during his reign, when he was unfaithful. They are now in place before the altar of the LORD.'

20 Then King Hezekiah rose early, assembled the officers of the city and went up to the house of the LORD. 21 They brought seven bulls, seven rams, and seven lambs for the whole-offering,[u] and seven he-goats as a sin-offering for the kingdom, for the sanctuary, and for Judah; these he commanded the priests of Aaron's line to offer on the altar of the LORD. 22 So the bulls were slaughtered, and the priests took their blood and flung it against the altar; the rams were slaughtered, and their blood was flung against the altar; the lambs were slaughtered, and their blood was flung against the altar. 23 Then the he-goats for the sin-offering were brought before the king and the assembly, who 24 laid their hands on them; and the priests slaughtered them and used their blood as a sin-offering on the altar to make expiation for all Israel. For the king had commanded that the whole-offering and the sin-offering should be made for all Israel.

25 He posted the Levites in the house of the LORD with cymbals, lutes, and harps, according to the rule prescribed by David, by Gad the king's seer and Nathan the prophet; for this rule had come from the LORD through 26 his prophets. The Levites stood ready with the instruments of David, and the priests with the trumpets. 27 Hezekiah gave the order that the whole-offering should be offered on the altar. At the moment when the whole-offering began, the song to the LORD began too, with the trumpets, led by the instruments of David king of Israel. 28 The whole assembly prostrated themselves, the singers sang

u for the whole-offering: prob. rdg.; Heb. om.

and the trumpeters sounded; all this continued until the whole-offering 29 was complete. When the offering was complete, the king and all his company bowed down and prostrated 30 themselves. And King Hezekiah and his officers commanded the Levites to praise the LORD in the words of David and of Asaph the seer. So they praised him most joyfully and bowed down and prostrated themselves.

The people bring their sacrifices

31 Then Hezekiah said, 'You have now given to the LORD with open hands; approach with your sacrifices and thank-offerings for the house of the LORD.' So the assembly brought sacrifices and thank-offerings; and every man of willing spirit brought whole-32 offerings. The number of whole-offerings which the assembly brought was seventy bulls, a hundred rams, and two hundred lambs; all these made a whole-offering to the LORD. 33 And the consecrated offerings were six hundred bulls and three thousand 34 sheep. But the priests were too few and could not flay all the whole-offerings; so their colleagues the Levites helped them until the work was completed and all the priests had hallowed themselves—for the Levites had been more scrupulous than the 35 priests in hallowing themselves. There were indeed whole-offerings in abundance, besides the fat of the shared-offerings and the drink-offerings for the whole-offerings. In this way the service of the house of the LORD was 36 restored; and Hezekiah and all the people rejoiced over what God had done for the people and because it had come about so suddenly.

Hezekiah appeals to Israel to repent

30 Then Hezekiah sent word to all Israel and Judah, and also wrote letters to Ephraim and Manasseh, inviting them to come to the house of the LORD in Jerusalem to keep the Passover of the LORD the God of Israel. 2 The king and his officers and all the assembly in Jerusalem had agreed to keep the Passover in the second 3 month, but they had not been able to keep it at that time, because not enough priests had hallowed themselves and the people had not as-4 sembled in Jerusalem. The proposal was acceptable to the king and the 5 whole assembly. So they resolved to make a proclamation throughout all Israel, from Beersheba to Dan, that

the people should come to Jerusalem to keep the Passover of the LORD the God of Israel. Never before had so many kept it according to the prescribed form. Couriers went through-6 out all Israel and Judah with letters from the king and his officers, proclaiming the royal command: 'Turn back, men of Israel, to the LORD the God of Abraham, Isaac, and Israel, so that he may turn back to those of you who escaped capture by the kings of Assyria. Do not be like your fore-7 fathers and your kinsmen, who were unfaithful to the LORD the God of their fathers, so that he made them an object of horror, as you yourselves saw. Do not be stubborn as your 8 forefathers were; submit yourselves to the LORD and enter his sanctuary which he has sanctified for ever, and worship the LORD your God, so that his anger may be averted from you. For when you turn back to the LORD, 9 your kinsmen and your children will win compassion from their captors and return to this land. The LORD your God is gracious and compassionate, and he will not turn away from you if you turn back to him.'

So the couriers passed from city to 10 city through the land of Ephraim and Manasseh and as far as Zebulun, but they were treated with scorn and ridicule. However, a few men of Asher, 11 Manasseh, and Zebulun submitted and came to Jerusalem. Further, the hand 12 of God moved the people in Judah with one accord to carry out what the king and his officers had ordered at the LORD's command.

Great rejoicing in Jerusalem

Many people, a very great assembly, 13 came together in Jerusalem to keep the pilgrim-feast of Unleavened Bread in the second month. They began by 14 removing the altars in Jerusalem; they removed the altars for burning sacrifices and threw them into the gorge of the Kidron. They killed the 15 passover lamb on the fourteenth day of the second month; and the priests and the Levites were bitterly ashamed. They hallowed themselves and brought whole-offerings to the house of the LORD. They took their accustomed 16 places, according to the direction laid down for them in the law of Moses the man of God; the priests flung against the altar the blood which they received from the Levites. But 17 many in the assembly had not hallowed themselves; therefore the Levites had to kill the passover lamb for every one who was unclean, in order 18 to hallow him to the LORD. For a majority of the people, many from Ephraim, Manasseh, Issachar, and Zebulun, had not kept themselves ritually clean, and therefore kept the Passover irregularly. But Hezekiah prayed for them, saying, 'May the 19 good LORD grant pardon to every one who makes a practice of seeking guidance of God, the LORD the God of his fathers, even if he has not observed the rules for the purification of the 20 sanctuary.' The LORD heard Hezeki-21 ah and healed the people. And the Israelites who were present in Jerusalem kept the feast of Unleavened Bread for seven days with great rejoicing, and the Levites and the priests praised the LORD every day with un-22 restrained fervour.[v] Hezekiah spoke encouragingly to all the Levites who had shown true understanding in the service of the LORD. So they spent the seven days of the festival sacrificing shared-offerings and making confession to[w] the LORD the God of their fathers.

23   Then the whole assembly agreed to keep the feast for another seven days; so they kept it for another seven days 24 with general rejoicing. For Hezekiah king of Judah set aside for the assembly a thousand bulls and seven thousand sheep, and his officers set aside for the assembly a thousand bulls and ten thousand sheep; and priests hallowed themselves in great 25 numbers. So the whole assembly of Judah, including the priests and the Levites, rejoiced, together with all the assembly which came out of Israel, and the resident aliens from Israel 26 and those who lived in Judah. There was great rejoicing in Jerusalem, the like of which had not been known there since the days of Solomon son 27 of David king of Israel. Then the priests and the Levites stood to bless the people; the LORD listened to their cry, and their prayer came to God's holy dwelling-place in heaven.

The people give willingly

31 When this was over, all the Israelites present went out to the cities of Judah and smashed the sacred pillars, hacked down the sacred poles and broke up the hill-shrines and the altars throughout Judah and Benjamin, Ephraim and Manasseh, until

they had made an end of them. That done, the Israelites returned, each to his own patrimony in his own city.

Then Hezekiah installed the priests 2 and the Levites in office, division by division, allotting to each priest or Levite his own particular duty, for whole-offerings or shared-offerings, to give thanks or to sing praise, or to serve in the gates of the several quarters in the LORD's house.

The king provided from his own 3 resources, as the share due from him, the whole-offerings for both morning and evening, and for sabbaths, new moons, and appointed seasons, as prescribed in the law of the LORD. He ordered the people living in Jeru-4 salem to provide the share due from the priests and the Levites, so that they might devote themselves entirely to the law of the LORD. As soon as the 5 king's order was issued to the Israelites, they gave generously from the firstfruits of their corn and new wine, oil and honey, all the produce of their land; they brought a full tithe of everything. The Israelites and the 6 Judaeans living in the cities of Judah also brought a tithe of cattle and sheep, and a tithe of all produce as offerings dedicated to the LORD their God, and they stacked the produce in heaps. They began to deposit the 7 heaps in the third month and completed them in the seventh. When 8 Hezekiah and his officers came and saw the heaps, they blessed the LORD and his people Israel. Hezekiah asked 9 the priests and the Levites about these heaps, and Azariah the chief 10 priest, who was of the line of Zadok, answered, 'From the time when the people began to bring their contribution into the house of the LORD, they have had enough to eat, enough and to spare; indeed, the LORD has so greatly blessed them that they have this great store left over.'

Providing for the Levites

Then Hezekiah ordered store-rooms 11 to be prepared in the house of the LORD, and this was done; and the 12 people honestly brought in their contributions, the tithe, and their dedicated gifts. The overseer in charge of them was Conaniah the Levite, with Shimei his brother as his deputy; Jehiel, Azaziah, Nahath, Asahel, Jeri-13 moth, Jozabad, Eliel, Ismachiah, Mahath, and Benaiah were appointed

[v] with unrestrained fervour: *prob. rdg.; Heb.* with powerful instruments.   [w] making confession to: *or* confessing.

by King Hezekiah and Azariah, the chief overseer of the house of God, to assist Conaniah and Shimei his 14 brother. And Kore son of Imnah the Levite, keeper of the East Gate, was in charge of the freewill offerings to God, to apportion the contributions made to the Lord and the most 15 sacred offerings. Eden, Miniamin, Jeshua, Shemaiah, Amariah, and Shecaniah in the priestly cities assisted him in the fair distribution of portions to their kinsmen, young and 16 old*x* alike, by divisions. Irrespective of their registration, shares were distributed to all males three years of age and upwards who entered the house of the Lord to take their daily part in the service, according to their divisions, 17 as their office demanded. The priests were registered by families, the Levites from twenty years of age and upwards by their offices in their divi-18 sions. They were registered with all their dependants, their wives, their sons, and their daughters, the whole company of them, because in virtue of their permanent standing they had 19 to keep themselves duly hallowed. As for the priests of Aaron's line in the common lands attached to their cities, in every city men were nominated to distribute portions to every male among the priests and to every one who was registered with the Levites.

20   Such was the action taken by Hezekiah throughout Judah; he did what was good and right and loyal in the 21 sight of the Lord his God. Whatever he undertook in the service of the house of God and in obedience to the law and the commandment to seek guidance of his God, he did with all his heart, and he prospered.

Sennacherib invades Judah

1*y* After these events and this example of loyal conduct, Sennacherib king of Assyria invaded Judah and encamped against the fortified cities, believing that he could attach them to himself. 2 When Hezekiah saw that he had come and was determined to attack Jeru-3 salem, he consulted his civil and military officers about blocking up the springs outside the city; and they 4 encouraged him. They gathered together a large number of people and blocked up all the springs and the stream which flowed through the land. 'Why', they said, 'should Assyrian kings come here and find plenty of 5 water?' Then the king acted boldly;

he made good every breach in the city wall and erected towers on it; he built another wall outside it and strengthened the Millo of the city of David; he also collected a great quantity of weapons and shields. He 6 appointed military commanders over the people and assembled them in the square by the city gate and spoke encouragingly to them in these words: 'Be strong; be brave. Do not let the 7 king of Assyria or the rabble he has brought with him strike terror or panic into your hearts. We have more on our side than he has. He has human 8 strength; but we have the Lord our God to help us and to fight our battles.' So spoke Hezekiah king of Judah, and the people were buoyed up by his words.

Sennacherib presses for surrender

After this, Sennacherib king of Assyria, 9 while he and his high command were at Lachish, sent envoys to Jerusalem to deliver this message to Hezekiah king of Judah and to all the Judaeans in Jerusalem: 'Sennacherib king of 10 Assyria says, "What gives you confidence to stay in Jerusalem under siege? Hezekiah is misleading you 11 into risking death by famine or thirst where you are, when he tells you that the Lord your God will save you from the grip of the Assyrian king. Was it not Hezekiah himself who sup-12 pressed the Lord's hill-shrines and altars and told the people of Judah and Jerusalem that they must prostrate themselves before one altar only and burn sacrifices there? You know 13 very well what I and my forefathers have done to all the peoples of the lands. Were the gods of these nations able to save their lands from me? Not one of the gods of these nations, 14 which my forefathers exterminated, was able to save his people from me. Much less will your god save you! How, 15 then, can Hezekiah deceive you or mislead you like this? How can you believe him, for no god of any nation or kingdom has been able to save his people from me or my forefathers? Much less will your gods save you!"'

The envoys of Sennacherib spoke 16 still more against the Lord God and against his servant Hezekiah. And 17 the king himself wrote a letter to defy the Lord the God of Israel, in these terms: 'Just as the gods of other nations could not save their people from me, so the god of Hezekiah will

x Or high and low.   *y Verses 1–19: cp. 2 Kgs. 18. 13–37; Isa. 36. 1–22.*

18 not save his people from me.' Then they shouted in Hebrew at the top of their voices at the people of Jerusalem on the wall, to strike them with fear and terror, hoping thus to cap-
19 ture the city. They described the god[z] of Jerusalem as being like the gods of the other peoples of the earth—things made by the hands of men.
20[a]   In this plight King Hezekiah and the prophet Isaiah son of Amoz cried
21 to heaven in prayer. So the LORD sent an angel who cut down all the fighting men, as well as the leaders and the commanders, in the camp of the king of Assyria, so that he went home disgraced to his own land. When he entered the temple of his god, certain of his own sons struck him down with their swords.
22   Thus the LORD saved Hezekiah and the inhabitants of Jerusalem from Sennacherib king of Assyria and all their enemies; and he gave them
23 respite on every side. Many people brought to Jerusalem offerings for the LORD and costly gifts for Hezekiah king of Judah. From then on he was held in high honour by all the nations.

Hezekiah falls ill

24 About this time Hezekiah fell dangerously ill and prayed to the LORD; the LORD said, 'I will heal you',[b] and
25 granted him a sign. But, being a proud man, he was not grateful for the good done to him, and Judah and
26 Jerusalem suffered for it. Then, proud as he was, Hezekiah submitted, and the people of Jerusalem with him, and the LORD's anger did not fall on them again in Hezekiah's time.

Events in Hezekiah's life

27 Hezekiah enjoyed great wealth and fame.[c] He built for himself treasuries for silver and gold, precious stones and spices, shields and other costly
28 things; and barns for the harvests of corn, new wine, and oil; and stalls for every kind of cattle, as well as sheep-
29 folds. He amassed[d] a great many flocks and herds; God had indeed
30 given him vast riches. It was this same Hezekiah who blocked the upper outflow of the waters of Gihon and directed them downwards and westwards to the city of David. In fact, Hezekiah was successful in every-

thing he attempted, even in the affair 31 of the envoys sent by the king[e] of Babylon—the envoys who came to inquire about the portent which had been seen in the land at the time when God left him to himself, to test him and to discover all that was in his heart.
    The other events of Hezekiah's 32 reign, and his works of piety, are recorded in the vision of the prophet Isaiah son of Amoz and in the annals of the kings of Judah and Israel. So 33 Hezekiah rested with his forefathers and was buried in the uppermost of the graves of David's sons; all Judah and the people of Jerusalem paid him honour when he died, and he was succeeded by his son Manasseh.

Manasseh reigns over Judah

Manasseh was twelve years old when 33 he came to the throne, and he reigned in Jerusalem for fifty-five years. He 2 did what was wrong in the eyes of the LORD, in following the abominable practices of the nations which the LORD had dispossessed in favour of the Israelites. He rebuilt the hill- 3 shrines which his father Hezekiah had dismantled, he erected altars to the Baalim and made sacred poles, he prostrated himself before all the host of heaven and worshipped them. He 4 built altars in the house of the LORD, that house of which the LORD had said, 'In Jerusalem shall my Name be for ever.' He built altars for all the 5 host of heaven in the two courts of the house of the LORD; he made his 6 sons pass through the fire in the Valley of Ben-hinnom, he practised soothsaying, divination, and sorcery, and dealt with ghosts and spirits. He did much wrong in the eyes of the LORD and provoked his anger; and 7 the image that he had had carved in relief he put in the house of God, the place of which God had said to David and Solomon his son, 'This house and Jerusalem, which I chose out of all the tribes of Israel, shall receive my Name for all time. I will not again 8 displace Israel from the land which I assigned to their forefathers, if only they will be careful to observe all that I commanded them through Moses, all the law, the statutes, and the rules.' But Manasseh misled Judah 9 and the inhabitants of Jerusalem into

z Or gods.   a Verses 20–2: cp. 2 Kgs. 19. 1–37; Isa. 37. 1–38.   b I will heal you: prob. rdg.,
cp. 2 Kgs. 20. 5; Heb. om.   c Or riches.   d Prob. rdg.; Heb. adds cities.   e Prob. rdg., cp.
2 Kgs. 20. 12; Heb. officers.   f Verses 1–9: cp. 2 Kgs. 21. 1–9.

wickedness far worse than that of the nations which the LORD had exterminated in favour of the Israelites.

Manasseh repents

10 The LORD spoke to Manasseh and to 11 his people, but they paid no heed. So the LORD brought against them the commanders of the army of the king of Assyria; they captured Manasseh with spiked weapons, and bound him with fetters, and brought him 12 to Babylon. In his distress he prayed to the LORD his God and sought to placate him, and made his humble submission before the God of his fa- 13 thers. He prayed, and God accepted his petition and heard his supplication. He brought him back to Jerusalem and restored him to the throne; and thus Manasseh learnt that the LORD was God.

14 After this he built an outer wall for the city of David, west of Gihon in the gorge, and extended it to the entrance by the Fish Gate, enclosing Ophel; and he raised it to a great height. He also put military commanders in all the fortified cities of 15 Judah. He removed the foreign gods and the carved image from the house of the LORD and all the altars which he had built on the temple mount and in Jerusalem, and threw them out of 16 the city. Moreover, he repaired the altar of the LORD and sacrificed at it shared-offerings and thank-offerings, and commanded Judah to serve the 17 LORD the God of Israel. But the people still continued to sacrifice at the hill-shrines, though only to the LORD their God.

Other records of Manasseh's reign

18 The rest of the acts of Manasseh, his prayer to his God, and the discourses of the seers who spoke to him in the name of the LORD the God of Israel, are recorded in the chronicles of the 19 kings of Israel. His prayer and the answer he received to it, and all his sin and unfaithfulness, and the places where he built hill-shrines and set up sacred poles and carved idols, before he submitted, are recorded in the 20 chronicles of the seers. So Manasseh rested with his forefathers and was buried in the garden-tomb of[g] his family; he was succeeded by his son Amon.

Amon reigns over Judah

Amon was twenty-two years old when 21[h] he came to the throne, and he reigned in Jerusalem for two years. He did 22 what was wrong in the eyes of the LORD as his father Manasseh had done. He sacrificed to all the images that his father Manasseh had made, and worshipped them. He was not sub- 23 missive before the LORD like his father Manasseh; his guilt was much greater. His courtiers conspired against 24 him and murdered him in his house; but the people of the land killed all 25 the conspirators and made his son Josiah king in his place.

Josiah's early reforms

Josiah was eight years old when he 34 1[i] came to the throne, and he reigned in Jerusalem for thirty-one years. He 2 did what was right in the eyes of the LORD; he followed in the footsteps of his forefather David, swerving neither right nor left. In the eighth year of 3 his reign, when he was still a boy, he began to seek guidance of the God of his forefather David; and in the twelfth year he began to purge Judah and Jerusalem of the hill-shrines and the sacred poles, and the carved idols and the images of metal. He saw 4 to it that the altars for the Baalim were destroyed and he hacked down the incense-altars which stood above them; he broke in pieces the sacred poles and the carved and metal images, grinding them to powder and scattering it on the graves of those who had sacrificed to them. He 5 also burnt the bones of the priests on their altars and purged Judah and Jerusalem. In the cities of Manasseh, 6 Ephraim, and Simeon, and as far as Naphtali, he burnt down their houses wherever he found them; he destroyed 7 the altars and the sacred poles, ground the idols to powder, and hacked down the incense-altars throughout the land of Israel. Then he returned to Jerusalem.

Hilkiah discovers the book of the law

In the eighteenth year of his reign, 8[j] after he had purified the land and the house, he sent Shaphan son of Azaliah and Maaseiah the governor of the city and Joah son of Joahaz the secretary of state to repair the house

g the garden-tomb of: prob. rdg., cp. 2 Kgs. 21. 18; Heb. om.   h Verses 21–5: cp. 2 Kgs. 21.
19–24.   i Verses 1, 2: cp. 2 Kgs. 22. 1, 2.   j Verses 8–32: cp. 2 Kgs. 22. 3—23. 3.

9 of the LORD his God. They came to Hilkiah the high priest and gave him the silver that had been brought to the house of God, the silver which the Levites, on duty at the threshold, had gathered from Manasseh, Ephraim, and all the rest of Israel, as well as from Judah and Benjamin and the 10 inhabitants of Jerusalem. It was then handed over to the foremen in charge of the work in the house of the LORD, and these men, working in the house, used it for repairing and strengthen-11 ing the fabric; they gave it also to the carpenters and builders to buy hewn stone, and timber for rafters and beams, for the buildings which the kings of Judah had allowed to fall 12–13 into ruin. The men did their work honestly under the direction of Jahath and Obadiah, Levites of the line of Merari, and Zechariah and Meshullam, members of the family of Kohath. These also had control of the porters and directed the workmen of every trade. The Levites were all skilled musicians, and some of them were secretaries, clerks, or door-keepers. 14 When they fetched the silver which had been brought to the house of the LORD, the priest Hilkiah discovered the book of the law of the LORD which 15 had been given through Moses. Then Hilkiah told Shaphan the adjutant-general, 'I have discovered the book of the law in the house of the LORD.' Hilkiah gave the book to Shaphan, 16 and he brought it to the king and reported to him: 'Your servants are doing all that was entrusted to them. 17 They have melted down the silver in the house of the LORD and have handed it over to the foremen and 18 the workmen.' Shaphan the adjutant-general also told the king that the priest Hilkiah had given him a book; and he read it out in the king's pres-19 ence. When the king heard what was in the book of the law, he rent his 20 clothes, and ordered Hilkiah, Ahikam son of Shaphan, Abdon son of Micah, Shaphan the adjutant-general, and 21 Asaiah the king's attendant, to go and seek guidance of the LORD, for himself and for all who still remained in Israel and Judah, about the contents of the book that had been discovered. 'Great is the wrath of the LORD,' he said, 'and it has been poured out upon us because our forefathers did not observe the command of the LORD and do all that is written in this book.'

Destruction of Jerusalem foretold

So Hilkiah and those whom the king 22 had instructed went to Huldah the prophetess, wife of Shallum son of Tikvah,[k] son of Hasrah, the keeper of the wardrobe, and consulted her at her home in the second quarter of Jerusalem. 'This is the word of the 23 LORD the God of Israel,' she answered: 'Say to the man who sent you to me, "This is the word of the LORD: I am 24 bringing disaster on this place and its inhabitants, fulfilling all the imprecations recorded in the book which was read in the presence of the king of Judah, because they have forsaken 25 me and burnt sacrifices to other gods, provoking my anger with all the idols they have made with their own hands; therefore my wrath is poured out upon this place and will not be quenched." This is what you shall say to 26 the king of Judah who sent you to seek guidance of the LORD: "This is the word of the LORD the God of Israel: You have listened to my words and shown a willing heart, you 27 humbled yourself before God when you heard what I said about this place and its inhabitants; you humbled yourself and rent your clothes and wept before me. Because of all this,[l] I for my part have heard you. This is the very word of the LORD. Therefore, I will gather you to your 28 forefathers, and you will be gathered to your grave in peace; you will not live to see all the disaster which I am bringing upon this place and upon its inhabitants."' So they brought back word to the king.

Josiah reads the book to the people

Then the king sent and called all the 29 elders of Judah and Jerusalem together, and went up to the house of the LORD; he took with him all the 30 men of Judah and the inhabitants of Jerusalem, the priests and the Levites, the whole population, high and low. There he read them the whole book of the covenant discovered in the house of the LORD; and then, standing on 31 the dais, the king made a covenant before the LORD to obey him and keep his commandments, his testimonies, and his statutes, with all his heart and soul, and so fulfil the terms of the covenant written in this book. Then he swore an oath with all who 32 were present in Jerusalem to keep

---

k Prob. rdg., cp. 2 Kgs. 22. 14; Heb. Tokhath.   *l Because of all this: prob. rdg.; Heb. om.*

the covenant.[m] Thereafter the inhabitants of Jerusalem did obey the covenant of God, the God of their fathers. 33 Josiah removed all abominable things from all the territories of the Israelites, so that everyone living in Israel might serve the LORD his God. As long as he lived they did not fail in their allegiance to the LORD the God of their fathers.

Josiah keeps the Passover

35 Josiah kept a Passover to the LORD in Jerusalem, and the passover lamb was killed on the fourteenth day of the 2 first month. He appointed the priests to their offices and encouraged them to perform the service of the house of 3 the LORD. He said to the Levites, the teachers of Israel, who were dedicated to the LORD, 'Put the holy Ark in the house which Solomon son of David king of Israel built; it is not to be carried about on your shoulders. Now is the time to serve the LORD your God 4 and his people Israel: prepare yourselves by families according to your divisions, following the written instructions of David king of Israel and 5 those of Solomon his son; and stand in the Holy Place as representatives of the family groups of the lay people, your brothers, one division of Levites 6 to each family group. Kill the passover lamb and hallow yourselves and prepare for your brothers to fulfil the word of the LORD given through Moses.' 7 Josiah contributed on behalf of all the lay people present thirty thousand small cattle, that is young rams and goats, for the Passover, in addition to three thousand bulls; all these were 8 from the king's own resources. And his officers contributed willingly for the people, the priests, and the Levites. Hilkiah, Zechariah, and Jehiel, the chief officers of the house of God, gave on behalf of the priests two thousand six hundred small cattle for the Passover, in addition to three hundred 9 bulls. And Conaniah, Shemaiah and Nethaneel his brothers, and Hashabiah, Jeiel, and Jozabad, the chiefs of the Levites, gave on behalf of the Levites for the Passover five thousand small cattle in addition to five hundred bulls. 10 When the service had been arranged, the priests stood in their places and the Levites in their divisions, according to the king's command. 11 They killed the passover victim, and

the priests flung the blood against the altar as the Levites flayed the animals. Then they removed the fat flesh,[n] 12 which they allocated to the people by groups of families for them to offer to the LORD, as prescribed in the book of Moses; and so with the bulls. They 13 cooked the passover victim over the fire according to custom, and boiled the holy offerings in pots, cauldrons, and pans, and served them quickly to all the people. After that they made 14 the necessary preparations for themselves and the priests, because the priests of Aaron's line were engaged till nightfall in offering whole-offerings and the fat portions; so the Levites made the necessary preparations for themselves and for the priests of Aaron's line. The singers, the sons 15 of Asaph, were in their places according to the rules laid down by David and by Asaph, Heman, and Jeduthun, the king's seers. The door-keepers stood, each at his gate; there was no need for them to leave their posts, because their kinsmen the Levites had made the preparations for them.

In this manner all the service of 16 the LORD was arranged that day, to keep the Passover and to offer whole-offerings on the altar of the LORD, according to the command of King Josiah. The people of Israel who were 17 present kept the Passover at that time and the pilgrim-feast of Unleavened Bread for seven days. No 18 Passover like it had been kept in Israel since the days of the prophet Samuel; none of the kings of Israel had ever kept such a Passover as Josiah kept, with the priests and Levites and all Judah and Israel who were present and the inhabitants of Jerusalem. In the eighteenth year of 19 Josiah's reign this Passover was kept.

Josiah dies in battle

After Josiah had thus organized all 20 the service of the house, Necho king of Egypt marched up to attack Carchemish on the Euphrates; and Josiah went out to confront him. But 21 Necho sent envoys to him, saying, 'What do you want with me, king of Judah? I have no quarrel with you today, only with those with whom I am at war. God has purposed to speed me on my way, and God is on my side; do not stand in his way, or he will destroy you.' Josiah would not be 22 deflected from his purpose but insisted

m to keep the covenant: *prob. rdg., cp. 2 Kgs. 23. 3; Heb.* and Benjamin.   n fat flesh: *or* whole-offering.

on fighting; he refused to listen to Necho's words spoken at God's command, and he sallied out to join battle 23 in the vale of Megiddo. The archers shot at him; he was severely wounded and told his bodyguard to carry him 24 off. They lifted him out of his chariot and carried him in his viceroy's chariot to Jerusalem. There he died and was buried among the tombs of his ancestors, and all Judah and Jeru-25 salem mourned for him. Jeremiah also made a lament for Josiah; and to this day the minstrels, both men and women, commemorate Josiah in their lamentations. Such laments have become traditional in Israel, and they are found in the written collections.

Other records of Josiah's reign

26 The other events of Josiah's reign, and his works of piety, all performed in accordance with what is laid down 27 in the law of the LORD, and his acts, from first to last, are recorded in the annals of the kings of Israel and Judah.

Reign and dethronement of Jehoahaz

36 1 [o] The people of the land took Josiah's son Jehoahaz and made him king in 2 place of his father in Jerusalem. He was twenty-three years old when he came to the throne, and he reigned 3 in Jerusalem for three months. Then Necho king of Egypt deposed him and fined the country a hundred talents of 4 silver and one talent of gold, and made his brother Eliakim king over Judah and Jerusalem in his place, changing his name to Jehoiakim; he also carried away his brother Jehoahaz to Egypt.

Jehoiakim reigns over Judah

5 Jehoiakim was twenty-five years old when he came to the throne, and he reigned in Jerusalem for eleven years. He did what was wrong in the eyes of 6 the LORD his God. So Nebuchadnezzar king of Babylon marched against him and put him in fetters and took 7 him to Babylon. He also removed to Babylon some of the vessels of the house of the LORD and put them 8 into his own palace there. The other events of Jehoiakim's reign, including the abominations he committed, and everything of which he was held guilty, are recorded in the annals of

the kings of Israel and Judah. He was succeeded by his son Jehoiachin.

Nebuchadnezzar takes Jehoiachin captive

Jehoiachin was eight years old when 9 [p] he came to the throne, and he reigned in Jerusalem for three months and ten days. He did what was wrong in the eyes of the LORD. At the turn of the 10 year King Nebuchadnezzar sent and brought him to Babylon, together with the choicest vessels of the house of the LORD, and made his father's brother Zedekiah king over Judah and Jerusalem.

Zedekiah reigns over Judah

Zedekiah was twenty-one years old 11 when he came to the throne, and he reigned in Jerusalem for eleven years. He did what was wrong in the eyes 12 of the LORD his God; he did not defer to the guidance of the prophet Jeremiah, the spokesman of the LORD. He also 13 rebelled against King Nebuchadnezzar, who had laid on him a solemn oath of allegiance. He was obstinate and stubborn and refused to return to the LORD the God of Israel.

Nebuchadnezzar destroys Jerusalem

All the chiefs of Judah and the priests 14 and the people became more and more unfaithful, following all the abominable practices of the other nations; and they defiled the house of the LORD which he had hallowed in Jerusalem. The LORD God of their fathers 15 had warned them betimes through his messengers, for he took pity on his people and on his dwelling-place; but they never ceased to deride his 16 messengers, scorn his words and scoff at his prophets, until the anger of the LORD burst out against his people and could not be appeased. So he brought 17 [q] against them the king of the Chaldaeans, who put their young men to the sword in the sanctuary and spared neither young man nor maiden, neither the old nor the weak; God gave them all into his power. And he brought all the 18 vessels of the house of God, great and small, and the treasures of the house of the LORD and of the king and his officers—all these he brought to Babylon. And they burnt down the house 19 of God, razed the city wall of Jerusalem and burnt down all its stately mansions and all their precious possessions until everything was destroyed.

---

[o] Verses 1–4: cp. 2 Kgs. 23. 30–4.   [p] Verses 9, 10: cp. 2 Kgs. 24. 8–17.   [q] Verses 17–20: cp. 2 Kgs. 25. 1–17.

20 Those who escaped the sword he took captive to Babylon, and they became slaves to him and his sons until the sovereignty passed to the 21 Persians, while the land of Israel ran the full term of its sabbaths. All the time that it lay desolate it kept the sabbath rest, to complete seventy years in fulfilment of the word of the LORD by the prophet Jeremiah.

Proclamation of Cyrus

22[r] Now in the first year of Cyrus king of Persia, so that the word of the LORD spoken through Jeremiah might be fulfilled, the LORD stirred up the heart of Cyrus king of Persia; and he issued a proclamation throughout his kingdom, both by word of mouth and in writing, to this effect:

This is the word of Cyrus king of 23 Persia: The LORD the God of heaven has given me all the kingdoms of the earth, and he himself has charged me to build him a house at Jerusalem in Judah. To every man of his people now among you I say, the LORD his God be[s] with him, and let him go up.

r Verses 22, 23: cp. Ezra 1. 1–3.   *s be: prob. rdg., cp. Ezra 1. 3; Heb. om.*

THE BOOK OF
EZRA

Proclamation of Cyrus

1 NOW in the first year of Cyrus king of Persia, so that the word of the LORD spoken through Jeremiah might be fulfilled, the LORD stirred up the heart of Cyrus king of Persia; and he issued a proclamation throughout his kingdom, both by word of mouth and in writing, to this effect:

2 This is the word of Cyrus king of Persia: The LORD the God of heaven has given me all the kingdoms of the earth, and he himself has charged me to build him a 3 house at Jerusalem in Judah. To every man of his people now among you I say, God be with him, and let him go up to Jerusalem in Judah, and rebuild the house of the LORD the God of Israel, the God whose 4 city is Jerusalem. And every remaining Jew, wherever he may be living, may claim aid from his neighbours in that place, silver and gold, goods[a] and cattle, in addition to the voluntary offerings for the house of God in Jerusalem.

Repatriating the Jews

5 Thereupon the heads of families of Judah and Benjamin, and the priests and the Levites, answered the summons, all whom God had moved to go up to rebuild the house of the LORD in Jerusalem. Their neighbours all 6 assisted them with gifts of every kind, silver[b] and gold, goods[a] and cattle and valuable gifts in abundance,[c] in addition to any voluntary service. More- 7 over, Cyrus king of Persia produced the vessels of the house of the LORD which Nebuchadnezzar had removed from Jerusalem and placed in the temple of his god; and he handed them 8 over into the charge of Mithredath the treasurer, who made an inventory of them for Sheshbazzar the ruler of Judah. This was the list: thirty 9 gold basins, a thousand silver basins, twenty-nine vessels of various kinds, thirty golden bowls, four hundred and 10 ten silver bowls of various types, and a thousand other vessels. The vessels 11 of gold and silver amounted in all to five thousand four hundred; and Sheshbazzar took them all up to Jerusalem, when the exiles were brought back from Babylon.

The roll of returning exiles

Of the captives whom Nebuchadnez- 2 1[d] zar king of Babylon had taken into exile in Babylon, these were the people of the province who returned to Jerusalem and Judah, each to his own

a Or pack-animals.   *b with gifts . . . silver: prob. rdg., cp. 1 Esdras 2. 9; Heb. with vessels of silver.*   *c in abundance: prob. rdg., cp. 1 Esdras 2. 9; Heb. apart.*   *d Verses 1–70: cp. Neh. 7. 6–73.*

G*

2 city, led by Zerubbabel, Jeshua,[e] Nehemiah, Seraiah, Reelaiah, Mordecai, Bilshan, Mispar, Bigvai, Rehum and Baanah.

The roll of the men of the people 3 of Israel: the family of Parosh, two thousand one hundred and seventy-4 two; the family of Shephatiah, three 5 hundred and seventy-two; the family of Arah, seven hundred and seventy-6 five; the family of Pahath-moab, namely the families of Jeshua and[f] Joab, two thousand eight hundred 7 and twelve; the family of Elam, one thousand two hundred and fifty-four; 8 the family of Zattu, nine hundred 9 and forty-five; the family of Zaccai, 10 seven hundred and sixty; the family of Bani, six hundred and forty-two; 11 the family of Bebai, six hundred and 12 twenty-three; the family of Azgad, one thousand two hundred and twenty-13 two; the family of Adonikam, six 14 hundred and sixty-six; the family of Bigvai, two thousand and fifty-six; 15 the family of Adin, four hundred and 16 fifty-four; the family of Ater, namely 17 that of Hezekiah, ninety-eight; the family of Bezai, three hundred and 18 twenty-three; the family of Jorah, one 19 hundred and twelve; the family of Hashum, two hundred and twenty-20 three; the family of Gibbar, ninety-21 five. The men[g] of Bethlehem, one 22 hundred and twenty-three; the men 23 of Netophah, fifty-six; the men of Anathoth, one hundred and twenty-24 eight; the men of Beth-azmoth,[h] forty-25 two; the men of Kiriath-jearim,[i] Kephirah, and Beeroth, seven hun-26 dred and forty-three; the men[j] of Ramah and Geba, six hundred and 27 twenty-one; the men of Michmas, one 28 hundred and twenty-two; the men of Bethel and Ai, two hundred and 29 twenty-three; the men[k] of Nebo, fifty-30 two; the men of Magbish, one hun-31 dred and fifty-six; the men of the other Elam, one thousand two hun-32 dred and fifty-four; the men of Harim, 33 three hundred and twenty; the men of Lod, Hadid, and Ono, seven hun-34 dred and twenty-five; the men of Jericho, three hundred and forty-five; 35 the men of Senaah, three thousand six hundred and thirty.

36 Priests: the family of Jedaiah, of the line of Jeshua, nine hundred and 37 seventy-three; the family of Immer,

one thousand and fifty-two; the fami-38 ly of Pashhur, one thousand two hundred and forty-seven; the family 39 of Harim, one thousand and seventeen.

Levites: the families of Jeshua and 40 Kadmiel, of the line of Hodaviah, seventy-four. Singers: the family of 41 Asaph, one hundred and twenty-eight. The guild of door-keepers: the family 42 of Shallum, the family of Ater, the family of Talmon, the family of Akkub, the family of Hatita, and the family of Shobai, one hundred and thirty-nine in all.

Temple-servitors: the family of Zi-43 ha, the family of Hasupha, the family of Tabbaoth, the family of Keros, the 44 family of Siaha, the family of Padon, the family of Lebanah, the family of 45 Hagabah, the family of Akkub, the 46 family of Hagab, the family of Shamlai,[l] the family of Hanan, the fami-47 ly of Giddel, the family of Gahar, the family of Reaiah, the family of 48 Rezin, the family of Nekoda, the family of Gazzam, the family of Uzza, the 49 family of Paseah, the family of Besai, the family of Asnah, the family 50 of the Meunim,[m] the family of the Nephusim,[n] the family of Bakbuk, the 51 family of Hakupha, the family of Harhur, the family of Bazluth, the fami-52 ly of Mehida, the family of Harsha, the family of Barkos, the family of Sis-53 era, the family of Temah, the fami-54 ly of Neziah, and the family of Hatipha.

Descendants of Solomon's servants: 55 the family of Sotai, the family of Hassophereth, the family of Peruda, the family of Jaalah, the family of 56 Darkon, the family of Giddel, the 57 family of Shephatiah, the family of Hattil, the family of Pochereth-hazzebaim, and the family of Ami.

The temple-servitors and the descen-58 dants of Solomon's servants amounted to three hundred and ninety-two in all.

The following were those who re-59 turned from Tel-melah, Tel-harsha, Kerub, Addan, and Immer, but could not establish their father's family nor whether by descent they belonged to Israel: the family of Delaiah, the 60 family of Tobiah, and the family of Nekoda, six hundred and fifty-two. Also of the priests: the family of 61

e Or Joshua (cp. Hag. 1. 1).   f and: prob. rdg., cp. Neh. 7. 11; Heb. om.   g Prob. rdg., cp. Neh. 7. 26; Heb. family.   h Prob. rdg., cp. Neh. 7. 28; Heb. the family of Azmoth.   i Prob. rdg., cp. Neh. 7. 29; Heb. the family of Kiriath-arim.   j Prob. rdg., cp. Neh. 7. 30; Heb. family. k Prob. rdg.; Heb. family (also in verses 30–5).   l Or Shalmai (cp. Neh. 7. 48).   m Or Meinim. n Or Nephisim.

Hobaiah, the family of Hakkoz, and the family of Barzillai who had married a daughter of Barzillai the Gileadite and went by his[o] name. These 62 searched for their names among those enrolled in the genealogies, but they could not be found; they were disqualified for the priesthood as unclean, and the governor forbade them to par- 63 take of the most sacred food until there should be a priest able to consult the Urim and the Thummim.

The whole assembled people num- 64 bered forty-two thousand three hundred and sixty, apart from their 65 slaves, male and female, of whom there were seven thousand three hundred and thirty-seven; and they had two hundred singers, men and women. Their horses numbered seven 66 hundred and thirty-six, their mules two hundred and forty-five, their 67 camels four hundred and thirty-five, and their asses six thousand seven hundred and twenty.

When they came to the house of the 68 LORD in Jerusalem, some of the heads of families volunteered to rebuild the house of God on its original site. According to their resources they gave 69 for the fabric fund a total of sixty-one thousand drachmas of gold, five thousand minas of silver, and one hundred priestly robes.

The priests, the Levites, and some 70 of the people lived in Jerusalem and its suburbs;[p] the singers, the doorkeepers, and temple-servitors,[q] and all other Israelites, lived in their own towns.

Building the altar

3 When the seventh month came, the Israelites now being settled in their towns, the people assembled as one man in Jerusalem. Then Jeshua son 2 of Jozadak and his fellow-priests, and Zerubbabel son of Shealtiel and his kinsmen, set to work and built the altar of the God of Israel, in order to offer upon it whole-offerings as prescribed in the law of Moses the man of God. They put the altar in place 3 first, because they lived in fear of the foreign population; and they offered upon it whole-offerings to the LORD, both morning and evening offerings. They kept the pilgrim-feast of Ta- 4 bernacles[r] as ordained, and offered

whole-offerings every day in the number prescribed for each day, and, 5 in addition to these, the regular whole-offerings and the offerings for sabbaths,[s] for new moons and for all the sacred seasons appointed by the LORD, and all voluntary offerings brought to the LORD. The offering of 6 whole-offerings began from the first day of the seventh month, although the foundation of the temple of the LORD had not yet been laid. They gave 7 money for the masons and carpenters, and food and drink and oil for the Sidonians and the Tyrians to fetch cedar-wood from the Lebanon to the roadstead at Joppa, by licence from Cyrus king of Persia.

Rebuilding the Temple

In the second year after their return 8 to the house of God in Jerusalem, and in the second month, Zerubbabel son of Shealtiel and Jeshua son of Jozadak started work, aided by all their fellow-Israelites, the priests and the Levites and all who had returned from captivity to Jerusalem. They appointed Levites from the age of twenty years and upwards to supervise the work of the house of the LORD. Jeshua with his sons and his 9 kinsmen, Kadmiel, Binnui, and Hodaviah,[t] together assumed control of those responsible for the work on the house of God.[u]

When the builders had laid the 10 foundation of the temple of the LORD, the priests in their robes took their places with their trumpets, and the Levites, the sons of Asaph, with their cymbals, to praise the LORD in the manner prescribed by David king of Israel; and they chanted praises and 11 thanksgiving to the LORD, singing, 'It is good to give thanks to the LORD,[v] for his love towards Israel endures for ever.' All the people raised a great shout of praise to the LORD because the foundation of the house of the LORD had been laid. But many of the 12 priests and Levites and heads of families, who were old enough to have seen the former house, wept and wailed aloud when they saw the foundation of this house laid, while many others shouted for joy at the top of their voice. The people could not 13 distinguish the sound of the shout of

o Prob. rdg., cp. 1 Esdras 5. 38; Heb. their.   p in Jerusalem and its suburbs: prob. rdg., cp. 1 Esdras 5. 46; Heb. om.   q Prob. rdg.; Heb. adds in their towns.   r Or Booths.   s for sabbaths:
prob. rdg., cp. 1 Esdras 5. 52; Heb. om.   t Binnui, and Hodaviah: prob. rdg.; Heb. and his sons the
family of Judah.   u Prob. rdg.; Heb. adds the family of Henadad, their family and their kinsmen
the Levites.   v to give thanks to the LORD: prob. rdg., cp. Ps. 106. 1; Heb. om.

joy from that of the weeping and wailing, so great was the shout which the people were raising, and the sound could be heard a long way off.

Work is halted

4 When the enemies of Judah and Benjamin heard that the returned exiles were building a temple to the

2 LORD the God of Israel, they approached Zerubbabel and Jeshua[w] and the heads of families and said to them, 'Let us join you in building, for like you we seek your God, and we have been sacrificing to him ever since the days of Esarhaddon king

3 of Assyria, who brought us here.' But Zerubbabel and Jeshua and the rest of the heads of families in Israel said to them, 'The house which we are building for our God is no concern of yours. We alone will build it for the LORD the God of Israel, as his majesty Cyrus king of Persia commanded us.'

4 Then the people of the land caused the Jews to lose heart and made them

5 afraid to continue building; and in order to defeat their purpose they bribed officials at court to act against them. This continued throughout the reign of Cyrus and into the reign of Darius king of Persia.

6 At the beginning of the reign of Ahasuerus, the people of the land brought a charge in writing against the inhabitants of Judah and Jerusalem.

7 And in the days of Artaxerxes king of Persia, with the agreement of Mithredath, Tabeel and all his colleagues wrote to him; the letter was written in Aramaic and read aloud in Aramaic.

8[x] Rehum the high commissioner and Shimshai the secretary wrote a letter to King Artaxerxes concerning Jerusalem in the following terms:

9 From Rehum the high commissioner, Shimshai the secretary, and all their colleagues, the judges, the commissioners, the overseers, and chief officers, the men of Erech and Babylon, and the Elamites in Susa,

10 and the other peoples whom the great and renowned Asnappar[y] deported and settled in the city of Samaria and in the rest of the province of Beyond-Euphrates.

11 Here follows the text of their letter:

To King Artaxerxes from his servants, the men of the province of Beyond-Euphrates:

Be it known to Your Majesty that 12 the Jews who left you and came to these parts have reached Jerusalem and are rebuilding that wicked and rebellious city; they have surveyed[z] the foundations and are completing the walls. Be it known to Your 13 Majesty that, if their city is rebuilt and the walls are completed, they will pay neither general levy, nor poll-tax, nor land-tax, and in the end[a] they will harm the monarchy. Now, because we eat the king's salt 14 and it is not right that we should witness the king's dishonour, therefore we have sent to inform Your Majesty, in order that search may 15 be made in the annals of your predecessors. You will discover by searching through the annals that this has been a rebellious city, harmful to the monarchy and its provinces, and that sedition has long been rife within its walls. That is why the city was laid waste. We 16 submit to Your Majesty that, if it is rebuilt and its walls are completed, the result will be that you will have no more footing in the province of Beyond-Euphrates.

The king sent this answer: 17

To Rehum the high commissioner, Shimshai the secretary, and all your colleagues resident in Samaria and in the rest of the province of Beyond-Euphrates, greeting. The 18 letter which you sent to me has now been read clearly in my presence. I have given orders and 19 search has been made, and it has been found that the city in question has a long history of revolt against the monarchy, and that rebellion and sedition have been rife in it. Powerful kings have ruled in Jeru- 20 salem, exercising authority over the whole province of Beyond-Euphrates, and general levy, poll-tax, and land-tax have been paid to them. Therefore, issue orders that these 21 men must desist. This city is not to be rebuilt until a decree to that effect is issued by me. See that you 22 do not neglect your duty in this matter, lest more damage and harm be done to the monarchy.

When the text of the letter from 23 King Artaxerxes was read before

---

w and Jeshua: *prob. rdg.*, *cp. 1 Esdras 5. 68*; *Heb. om.*   x *From 4. 8 to 6. 18 the text is in Aramaic.*
y Or Osnappar.   z have surveyed: *prob. rdg.*; *Aram.* are surveying.   a *in the end: or* certainly.

Rehum the high commissioner, Shimshai the secretary, and their colleagues, they hurried to Jerusalem and forcibly compelled the Jews to stop work. 24 From then onwards the work on the house of God in Jerusalem stopped; and it remained at a standstill till the second year of the reign of Darius king of Persia.

Work begins again

5 But the prophets Haggai[b] and Zechariah grandson of Iddo upbraided the Jews in Judah and Jerusalem, prophesying in the name of the God 2 of Israel. Then Zerubbabel son of Shealtiel and Jeshua son of Jozadak at once began to rebuild the house of God in Jerusalem, and the prophets of God were with them and supported 3 them. Tattenai, governor of the province of Beyond-Euphrates, Shethar-bozenai, and their colleagues promptly came to them and said, 'Who issued a decree permitting you to rebuild this house and complete its furnish- 4 ings?' They also asked them for the names of the men engaged in the 5 building. But the elders of the Jews were under God's watchful eye, and they were not prevented from continuing the work, until such time as a report should reach Darius and a royal letter should be received in answer.

A letter to Darius

6 Here follows the text of the letter sent by Tattenai, governor of the province of Beyond-Euphrates, Shethar-bozenai, and his colleagues, the inspectors in the province of Beyond-Euphrates, 7 to King Darius. This is the written report that they sent:

8   To King Darius, all greetings. Be it known to Your Majesty that we went to the province of Judah and found the house of the great God being rebuilt by the Jewish elders,[c] with massive stones and timbers laid in the walls. The work was being done thoroughly and was making good progress under their 9 direction. We asked these elders who had issued a decree for the rebuilding of this house and the 10 completion of the furnishings. We also asked them for their names, so that we might make a list of the 11 leaders for your information. This was their reply: 'We are the servants

of the God of heaven and earth, and we are rebuilding the house originally built many years ago; a great king of Israel built it and completed it. But because our fore- 12 fathers provoked the anger of the God of heaven, he put them into the power of Nebuchadnezzar the Chaldaean, king of Babylon, who pulled down this house and carried the people captive to Babylon. However, Cyrus king of Babylon 13 in the first year of his reign issued a decree that this house of God should be rebuilt. Moreover, there 14 were gold and silver vessels of the house of God, which Nebuchadnezzar had taken from the temple in Jerusalem and put in the temple in Babylon; and these King Cyrus took out of the temple in Babylon. He gave them to a man named Sheshbazzar, whom he had appointed governor, and said to him, "Take 15 these vessels; go and restore them to the temple in Jerusalem, and let the house of God there be rebuilt on its original site." Then this Sheshbaz- 16 zar came and laid the foundation of the house of God in Jerusalem; and from that time until now the rebuilding has continued, but it is not yet finished.' Now, therefore, 17 if it please Your Majesty, let search be made in the royal archives in Babylon, to discover whether a decree was issued by King Cyrus for the rebuilding of this house of God in Jerusalem. Then let the king send us his wishes in the matter.

Darius replies

Then King Darius issued an order, 6 and search was made in the archives where the treasures were deposited in Babylon. But it was in Ecbatana, 2 in the royal residence in the province of Media, that a scroll was found, on which was written the following memorandum:

In the first year of King Cyrus, 3 the king issued this decree concerning the house of God in Jerusalem: Let the house be rebuilt as a place where sacrifices are offered and fire-offerings brought. Its height shall be sixty cubits and its breadth sixty cubits, with three courses of 4 massive stones and one[d] course of timber, the cost to be defrayed

---

b Prob. rdg., cp. 1 Esdras 6. 1; Aram. adds the prophet.   c by . . . elders: prob. rdg., cp. 1 Esdras 6. 8; Aram. om.   d Prob. rdg., cp. 1 Esdras 6. 25; Aram. a new.

5 from the royal treasury. Also the gold and silver vessels of the house of God, which Nebuchadnezzar took out of the temple in Jerusalem and brought to Babylon, shall be restored; they shall all be taken back to the temple in Jerusalem, and restored each to its place in the house of God.

6 Then King Darius issued this order:[e]

Now, Tattenai, governor of the province of Beyond-Euphrates, Shethar-bozenai, and your colleagues, the inspectors in the province of Beyond-Euphrates, you are to keep away from the place, 7 and to leave the governor of the Jews and their elders free to re-build this house of God; let them 8 rebuild it on its original site. I also issue an order prescribing what you are to do for these elders of the Jews, so that the said house of God may be rebuilt. Their expenses are to be defrayed in full from the royal funds accruing from the taxes of the province of Beyond-Euphrates, so that the work may 9 not be brought to a standstill. And let them have daily without fail whatever they want, young bulls, rams, or lambs as whole-offerings for the God of heaven, or wheat, salt, wine, or oil, as the priests in 10 Jerusalem demand, so that they may offer soothing sacrifices to the God of heaven, and pray for the 11 life of the king and his sons. Furthermore, I decree that, if any man tampers with this edict, a beam shall be pulled out of his house and he shall be fastened erect to it and flogged; and, in addition, his house 12 shall be forfeit.[f] And may the God who made that place a dwelling for his Name overthrow any king or people that shall presume to tamper with this edict or to destroy this house of God in Jerusalem. I Darius have issued a decree; it is to be carried out to the letter.

The Temple is completed

13 Then Tattenai, governor of the province of Beyond-Euphrates, Shethar-bozenai, and their colleagues carried out to the letter the instructions which 14 King Darius had sent them, and the elders of the Jews went on with the rebuilding. As a result of the pro-

phecies of Haggai the prophet and Zechariah grandson of Iddo they had good success and finished the re-building as commanded by the God of Israel and according to the decrees of Cyrus and Darius;[g] and the house was 15 completed on the twenty-third[h] day of the month Adar, in the sixth year of King Darius.

Then the people of Israel, the priests 16 and the Levites and all the other exiles who had returned, celebrated the dedication of the house of God with great rejoicing. For its dedica- 17 tion they offered one hundred bulls, two hundred rams, and four hundred lambs, and as a sin-offering for all Israel twelve he-goats, corresponding to the number of the tribes of Israel. And they re-established the priests in 18 their groups and the Levites in their divisions for the service of God in Jerusalem, as prescribed in the book of Moses.

On the fourteenth day of the first 19 month the exiles who had returned kept the Passover. The priests and the 20 Levites, one and all, had purified themselves; all of them were ritually clean, and they killed the passover lamb for all the exiles who had re-turned, for their fellow-priests and for themselves. It was eaten by the 21 Israelites who had come back from exile and by all who had separated themselves from the peoples of the land and their uncleanness and sought the LORD the God of Israel. And they 22 kept the pilgrim-feast of Unleavened Bread for seven days with rejoicing; for the LORD had given them cause for joy by changing the disposition of the king of Assyria towards them, so that he encouraged them in the work of the house of God, the God of Israel.

Ezra surveys Jerusalem

Now after these events, in the reign of 7 Artaxerxes king of Persia, there came up from Babylon one Ezra son of Seraiah, son of Azariah, son of Hil-kiah, son of Shallum, son of Zadok, 2 son[i] of Ahitub, son of Amariah, son 3 of Azariah, son of Meraioth, son of 4 Zerahiah, son of Uzzi, son of Bukki, son of Abishua, son of Phinehas, son 5 of Eleazar, son of Aaron the chief priest. He was a scribe[j] learned in the 6 law of Moses which the LORD the God of Israel had given them; and the king granted him all that he asked,

for the hand of the LORD his God
7 was upon him. In the seventh year
of King Artaxerxes, other Israelites,
priests, Levites, singers, door-keepers,
and temple-servitors went up with
8 him to Jerusalem; and they reached
Jerusalem in the fifth month, in the
9 seventh year of the king. On the first
day of the first month Ezra fixed the
day for departure from Babylon, and
on the first day of the fifth month he
arrived at Jerusalem, for the gracious
10 hand of his God was upon him. For
Ezra had devoted himself to the
study and observance of the law of
the LORD and to teaching statute and
ordinance in Israel.

Artaxerxes writes to Ezra

11 This is a copy of the royal letter which
King Artaxerxes had given to Ezra
the priest and scribe, a scribe versed
in questions concerning the commandments and the statutes of the
LORD laid upon Israel:

12[k]   Artaxerxes, king of kings, to
Ezra the priest and scribe learned
in the law of the God of heaven:
13   This is my decision. I hereby
issue a decree that any of the people
of Israel or of its priests or Levites
in my kingdom who volunteer to go
14 to Jerusalem may go with you. You
are sent by the king and his seven
counsellors to find out how things
stand in Judah and Jerusalem with
regard to the law of your God with
15 which you are entrusted. You are
also to convey the silver and gold
which the king and his counsellors
have freely offered to the God of
Israel whose dwelling is in Jeru-
16 salem, together with any silver and
gold that you may find throughout the province of Babylon, and
the voluntary offerings of the people and of the priests which they
freely offer for the house of their
17 God in Jerusalem. In pursuance
of this decree you shall use the
money solely for the purchase of
bulls, rams, and lambs, and the
proper grain-offerings and drink-
offerings, to be offered on the altar
in the house of your God in Jeru-
18 salem. Further, should any silver
and gold be left over, you and your
colleagues may use it at your discretion according to the will of your
19 God. The vessels which have been

given you for the service of the
house of your God you shall hand
over to the God of Jerusalem; and 20
if anything else should be required
for the house of your God, which it
may fall to you to provide, you may
provide it out of the king's treasury.
And I, King Artaxerxes, issue an 21
order to all treasurers in the province of Beyond-Euphrates that
whatever is demanded of you by
Ezra the priest, a scribe learned in
the law of the God of heaven, is to
be supplied exactly, up to a hun- 22
dred talents of silver, a hundred kor
of wheat, a hundred bath of wine,
a hundred bath of oil, and salt
without reckoning. Whatever is de- 23
manded by the God of heaven, let
it be diligently carried out for the
house of the God of heaven; otherwise wrath may fall upon the realm
of the king and his sons. We also 24
make known to you that you have
no authority to impose general
levy, poll-tax, or land-tax on any
of the priests, Levites, musicians,
door-keepers, temple-servitors, or
other servants of this house of
God.
And you, Ezra, in accordance 25
with the wisdom of your God with
which you are entrusted, are to
appoint arbitrators and judges to
judge all your people in the province of Beyond-Euphrates, all who
acknowledge the laws of your God;[l]
and you and they are to instruct
those who do not acknowledge
them. Whoever will not obey the 26
law of your God and the law of the
king, let judgement be rigorously
executed upon him, be it death,
banishment, confiscation of property, or imprisonment.
Then Ezra said,[m] 'Blessed be the 27
LORD the God of our fathers who has
prompted the king thus to add glory to
the house of the LORD in Jerusalem, and 28
has made the king and his counsellors
and all his high officers well disposed
towards me!'
So, knowing that the hand of the
LORD my God was upon me, I took
courage and assembled leading men
out of Israel to go up with me.

Another register

These are the heads of families, as 8
registered, family by family, of those

k *The text of verses 12–26 is in Aramaic.*   l *to judge . . . your God: or all of them versed in the*
laws of your God, to judge all the people in the province of Beyond-Euphrates.   m *Then Ezra*
said: *prob. rdg., cp. 1 Esdras 8. 25; Heb. om.*

who went up with me from Babylon
2 in the reign of King Artaxerxes: of
the family of Phinehas, Gershom; of
the family of Ithamar, Daniel; of the
3 family of David, Hattush son of[n]
Shecaniah; of the family of Parosh,
Zechariah, and with him a hundred
4 and fifty males in the register; of
the family of Pahath-moab, Elihoenai
son of Zerahiah, and with him two
5 hundred males; of the family of
Zattu,[o] Shecaniah son of Jahaziel,
and with him three hundred males;
6 of the family of Adin, Ebed son of
Jonathan, and with him fifty males;
7 of the family of Elam, Isaiah son
of Athaliah, and with him seventy
8 males; of the family of Shephatiah,
Zebadiah son of Michael, and with
9 him eighty males; of the family of
Joab, Obadiah son of Jehiel, and with
him two hundred and eighteen males;
10 of the family of Bani,[p] Shelomith son
of Josiphiah, and with him a hundred
11 and sixty males; of the family of
Bebai, Zechariah son of Bebai, and
12 with him twenty-eight males; of the
family of Azgad, Johanan son of Hak-
katan, and with him a hundred and
13 ten males. The last were the family
of Adonikam, and these were their
names: Eliphelet, Jeiel, and Shemai-
14 ah, and with them sixty males; and
the family of Bigvai, Uthai and Zab-
bud, and with them seventy males.

Ezra reviews the people

15 I assembled them by the river which
flows toward Ahava; and we encamped there three days. When I
reviewed the people and the priests,
16 I found no Levite there. So I sent
Eliezer, Ariel, Shemaiah, Elnathan,
Jarib, Elnathan, Nathan, Zechariah,
and Meshullam, prominent men, and
Joiarib and Elnathan, men of discre-
17 tion, with instructions to go to Iddo,
the chief man of the settlement at
Casiphia; and I gave them a message
for him and his kinsmen, the temple-
servitors there, asking for servitors for
the house of our God to be sent to us.
18 And, because the gracious hand of our
God was upon us, they let us have
Sherebiah, a man of discretion, of the
family of Mahli son of Levi, son of
Israel, together with his sons and
19 kinsmen, eighteen men; also Hashabiah, together with Isaiah of the
family of Merari, his kinsmen and
20 their sons, twenty men; besides two

hundred and twenty temple-servitors
(this was an order instituted by
David and his officers to assist the
Levites). These were all indicated by
name.

Returning to Jerusalem

Then I proclaimed a fast there by the 21
river Ahava, so that we might mortify
ourselves before our God and ask from
him a safe journey for ourselves, our
dependants, and all our possessions.
For I was ashamed to ask the king for 22
an escort of soldiers and horsemen to
help us against enemies on the way,
because we had said to the king, 'The
hand of our God is upon all who seek
him, working their good; but his
fierce anger is on all who forsake him.'
So we fasted and asked our God for 23
a safe journey, and he answered our
prayer.
Then I separated twelve of the 24
chiefs of the priests, together with[q]
Sherebiah and Hashabiah and ten of
their kinsmen, and handed over to 25
them the silver and gold and the
vessels which had been set aside by
the king, his counsellors and his
officers and all the Israelites who were
present, as their contribution to the
house of our God. I handed over to 26
them six hundred and fifty talents
of silver, a hundred silver vessels
weighing two talents, a hundred
talents of gold, twenty golden bowls 27
worth a thousand drachmas, and two
vessels of a fine red copper,[r] precious
as gold. And I said to the men, 'You 28
are dedicated to the LORD, and the
vessels too are sacred; the silver and
gold are a voluntary offering to the
LORD the God of your fathers. Watch 29
over them and guard them, until
you hand them over in the presence
of the chiefs of the priests and the
Levites and the heads of families of
Israel in Jerusalem, in the rooms of
the house of the LORD.'
So the priests and Levites received 30
the consignment of silver and gold
and vessels, to be taken to the house
of our God in Jerusalem; and on the 31
twelfth day of the first month we left
the river Ahava bound for Jerusalem.
The hand of our God was upon us,
and he saved us from enemy attack
and from ambush on the way. When 32
we arrived at Jerusalem, we rested for
three days. And on the fourth day the 33
silver and gold and the vessels were

n son of: prob. rdg.; Heb. of the family of.
p of Bani: prob. rdg., cp. 1 Esdras 8. 36; Heb. om.
Heb. om.   r red copper: or orichalc.

o of Zattu: prob. rdg., cp. 1 Esdras 8. 32; Heb. om.
q together with: prob. rdg., cp. 1 Esdras 8. 54;

deposited in the house of our God in the charge of Meremoth son of Uriah the priest, who had with him Eleazar son of Phinehas, and they had with them the Levites Jozabad son of Jeshua and Noadiah son of Binnui. 34 Everything was checked as it was handed over, and at the same time a written record was made of the whole 35 consignment. Then those who had come home from captivity, the exiles who had returned, offered as whole-offerings to the God of Israel twelve bulls for all Israel, ninety-six rams and seventy-two[8] lambs, with twelve he-goats as a sin-offering; all these were offered as a whole-offering to the 36 LORD. They also delivered the king's commission to the royal satraps and governors in the province of Beyond-Euphrates; and these gave support to the people and the house of God.

Ezra receives bad news

9 When all this had been done, some of the leaders approached me and said, 'The people of Israel, including priests and Levites, have not kept themselves apart from the foreign population and from the abominable practices of the Canaanites, the Hittites, the Perizzites, the Jebusites, the Ammonites, the Moabites, the Egyptians, and the 2 Amorites. They have taken women of these nations as wives for themselves and their sons, so that the holy race has become mixed with the foreign population; and the leaders and magistrates have been the chief offenders.' 3 When I heard this news, I rent my robe and mantle, and tore my hair and my beard, and I sat dumbfounded; 4 and all who went in fear of the words of the God of Israel rallied to me because of the offence of these exiles. I sat there dumbfounded till the evening sacrifice.

Ezra pleads for mercy

5 Then, at the evening sacrifice, I rose from my humiliation and, in my rent robe and mantle, I knelt down and spread out my hands to the LORD my 6 God and said, 'O my God, I am humiliated, I am ashamed to lift my face to thee, my God; for we are sunk in our iniquities, and our guilt is so great 7 that it reaches high heaven. From the days of our fathers down to this present day our guilt has been great. For our iniquities we, our kings, and our priests have been subject to death,

captivity, pillage, and shameful humiliation at the hands of foreign kings, and such is our present plight. But 8 now, for a brief moment, the LORD our God has been gracious to us, leaving us some survivors and giving us a foothold in his holy place. He has brought light to our eyes again and given us some chance to renew our lives in our slavery. For slaves we are; 9 nevertheless, our God has not forsaken us in our slavery, but has made the kings of Persia so well disposed towards us as to give us the means of renewal, so that we may repair the house of our God and rebuild its ruins, and to give us a wall of defence in[t] Judah and Jerusalem. Now, O our 10 God, what are we to say after this? For we have neglected the commands 11 which thou gavest through thy servants the prophets, when thou saidst, "The land which you are entering and will possess is a polluted land, polluted by the foreign population with their abominable practices, which have made it unclean from end to end. Therefore, do not give your daughters 12 in marriage to their sons, and do not marry your sons to their daughters, and never seek their welfare or prosperity. Thus you will be strong and enjoy the good things of the land, and pass it on to your children as an everlasting possession." Now, after all 13 that we have suffered for our evil deeds and for our great guilt—although thou, our God, hast punished us less than our iniquities deserved and hast allowed us to survive as now we do—shall we again disobey thy commands 14 and join in marriage with peoples who indulge in such abominable practices? Would not thy anger against us be unrelenting, until no remnant, no survivor was left? O LORD God of 15 Israel, thou art righteous; now as before, we are only a remnant that has survived. Look upon us, guilty as we are in thy sight; for because of our guilt none of us can stand in thy presence.'

The people repent

While Ezra was praying and making 10 confession, prostrate in tears before the house of God, a very great crowd of Israelites assembled round him, men, women, and children, and they all wept bitterly. Then Shecaniah son 2 of Jehiel, one of the family of Elam, spoke up and said to Ezra, 'We have

s Prob. rdg., cp. 1 Esdras 8. 65; Heb. seventy-seven. for . . .

t Or thereby giving us a wall of defence

committed an offence against our God in marrying foreign wives, daughters of the foreign population. But in spite of this, there is still hope for 3 Israel. Now, therefore, let us pledge ourselves to our God to dismiss all these women and their brood, according to your advice, my lord, and the advice of those who go in fear of the command of our God; and let us act 4 as the law prescribes. Up now, the task is yours, and we will support you. Take courage and act.'

5 Ezra stood up and made the chiefs of the priests, the Levites, and all the Israelites swear to do as had been 6 said; and they took the oath. Then Ezra left his place in front of the house of God and went to the room of Jehohanan grandson of Eliashib and lodged[u] there; he neither ate bread nor drank water, for he was mourning for the offence committed by the 7 exiles who had returned. Next, there was issued throughout Judah and Jerusalem a proclamation that all the exiles should assemble in Jerusalem, 8 and that if anyone did not arrive within three days, it should be within the discretion of the chief officers and the elders to confiscate all his property and to exclude him from the com- 9 munity of the exiles. So all the men of Judah and Benjamin assembled in Jerusalem within the three days; and on the twentieth day of the ninth month the people all sat in the fore-court of the house of God, trembling with apprehension and shivering in 10 the heavy rain. Ezra the priest stood up and said, 'You have committed an offence in marrying foreign wives and 11 have added to Israel's guilt. Make your confession now to the LORD the God of your fathers and do his will, and separate yourselves from the foreign population and from your 12 foreign wives.' Then all the assembled people shouted in reply, 'Yes; we 13 must do what you say. But there is a great crowd of us here, and it is the rainy season; we cannot go on stand-ing out here in the open. Besides, this business will not be finished in one day or even two, because we have committed so grave an offence in this 14 matter. Let our leading men act for the whole assembly, and let all in our cities who have married foreign women present themselves at ap-pointed times, each man with the elders and judges of his own city, until

God's anger against us on this account is averted.' Only Jonathan son of 15 Asahel and Jahzeiah son of Tikvah, supported by Meshullam and Shab-bethai the Levite, opposed this.

So the exiles acted as agreed, and 16 Ezra the priest selected[v] certain men, heads of households representing their families, all of them designated by name. They began their formal in-quiry into the matter on the first day of the tenth month, and by the 17 first day of the first month they had finished their inquiry into all the marriages with foreign women.

A list of the offenders

Among the members of priestly fami- 18 lies who had married foreign women were found Maaseiah, Eliezer, Jarib, and Gedaliah of the family of Jeshua son of Jozadak and his brothers. They 19 pledged themselves to dismiss their wives, and they brought a ram from the flock as a guilt-offering for their sins. Of the family of Immer: Hanani 20 and Zebadiah. Of the family of Harim: 21 Maaseiah, Elijah, Shemaiah, Jehiel and Uzziah. Of the family of Pashhur: 22 Elioenai, Maaseiah, Ishmael, Neth-aneel, Jozabad and Elasah.

Of the Levites: Jozabad, Shimei, 23 Kelaiah (that is Kelita), Pethahiah, Judah and Eliezer. Of the singers: 24 Eliashib. Of the door-keepers: Shal-lum, Telem and Uri.

And of Israel: of the family of 25 Parosh: Ramiah, Izziah, Malchiah, Mijamin, Eleazar, Malchiah and Be-naiah. Of the family of Elam: Mat- 26 taniah, Zechariah, Jehiel, Abdi, Jer-emoth and Elijah. Of the family of 27 Zattu: Elioenai, Eliashib, Mattaniah, Jeremoth, Zabad and Aziza. Of the 28 family of Bebai: Jehohanan, Hanani-ah, Zabbai and Athlai. Of the family 29 of Bani: Meshullam, Malluch, Adaiah, Jashub, Sheal and Jeremoth. Of the 30 family of Pahath-moab: Adna, Kelal, Benaiah, Maaseiah, Mattaniah, Bez-alel, Binnui and Manasseh. Of the 31 family of Harim: Eliezer, Isshijah, Malchiah, Shemaiah, Simeon, Ben- 32 jamin, Malluch and Shemariah. Of the 33 family of Hashum: Mattenai, Mat-tattah, Zabad, Eliphelet, Jeremai, Manasseh and Shimei. Of the family 34 of Bani: Maadai, Amram and Uel, Benaiah, Bedeiah and Keluhi, Vani- 35 ah, Meremoth, Eliashib, Mattaniah, 37 Mattenai and Jaasau. Of the family 38 of[w] Binnui: Shimei, Shelemiah, Nathan 39

u Prob. rdg., cp. 1 Esdras 9. 2; Heb. went.   v and Ezra the priest selected: prob. rdg., cp. 1 Esdras 9. 16; Heb. obscure.   w Of the family of: prob. rdg., cp. 1 Esdras 9. 34; Heb. and Bani and.

40 and Adaiah, Maknadebai, Shashai
41 and Sharai, Azareel, Shelemiah and
42 Shemariah, Shallum, Amariah and
43 Joseph. Of the family of Nebo: Jeiel,

Mattithiah, Zabad, Zebina, Jaddai, Joel and Benaiah. All these had married 44
foreign women, and they dismissed
them, together with their children.*

x and they . . . children: *prob. rdg., cp. 1 Esdras 9. 36; Heb.* and some of them were women; and
they had borne sons.

THE BOOK OF
NEHEMIAH

Nehemiah prays for Jerusalem

1 THE NARRATIVE of Nehemiah
son of Hacaliah.
    In the month Kislev in the twen-
tieth year, when I was in Susa the
2 capital city, it happened that one of
my brothers, Hanani, arrived with
some others from Judah; and I asked
them about Jerusalem and about the
Jews, the families still remaining of
those who survived the captivity.
3 They told me that those still remaining in the province who had survived the captivity were facing great
trouble and reproach; the wall of
Jerusalem was broken down and the
gates had been destroyed by fire.
4 When I heard this news, I sat down
and wept; I mourned for some days,
fasting and praying to the God of
5 heaven. This was my prayer: 'O LORD
God of heaven, O great and terrible
God who faithfully keepest covenant
with those who love thee and observe
6 thy commandments, let thy ear be
attentive and thine eyes open, to hear
my humble prayer which I make to
thee day and night on behalf of thy
servants the sons of Israel. I confess
the sins which we Israelites have all
committed against thee, and of which
I and my father's house are also
7 guilty. We have wronged thee and
have not observed the commandments, statutes, and rules which thou
didst enjoin upon thy servant Moses.
8 Remember what thou didst impress
upon him in these words: "If you are
unfaithful, I will disperse you among
9 the nations; but if you return to me
and observe my commandments and
fulfil them, I will gather your children
who have been scattered to the ends
of the earth and will bring them home

to the place which I have chosen as a
dwelling for my Name." They are thy 10
servants and thy people, whom thou
hast redeemed with thy great might
and thy strong hand. O Lord, let thy 11
ear be attentive to my humble prayer,
and to the prayer of thy servants who
delight to revere thy name. Grant me
good success this day, and put it into
this man's heart to show me kindness.'

Nehemiah journeys to Jerusalem

Now I was the king's cupbearer, and 2
one day, in the month Nisan, in the
twentieth year of King Artaxerxes,
when his wine was ready, I took it up
and handed it to the king, and as I
stood before him I was feeling very
unhappy. He said to me, 'Why do you 2
look so unhappy? You are not ill; it
can be nothing but unhappiness.' I
was much afraid and answered, 'The 3
king will live for ever. But how can I
help looking unhappy when the city
where my forefathers are buried lies
waste and its gates are burnt?' 'What 4
are you asking of me?' said the king. I
prayed to the God of heaven, and then 5
I answered, 'If it please your majesty,
and if I enjoy your favour, I beg you
to send me to Judah, to the city where
my forefathers are buried, so that I
may rebuild it.' The king, with the 6
queen consort sitting beside him,
asked me, 'How long will the journey
last, and when will you return?' Then
the king approved the request and
let me go, and I told him how long I
should be. Then I said to the king, 7
'If it please your majesty, let letters
be given me for the governors in the
province of Beyond-Euphrates with
orders to grant me all the help I need
for my journey to Judah. Let me have 8
also a letter for Asaph, the keeper of

your royal forests, instructing him to supply me with timber to make beams for the gates of the citadel, which adjoins the palace, and for the city wall, and for the palace which I shall occupy.' The king granted my requests, for the gracious hand of my God was 9 upon me. I came in due course to the governors in the province of Beyond-Euphrates and presented to them the king's letters; the king had given me an escort of army officers with cavalry. 10 But when Sanballat the Horonite and the slave Tobiah, an Ammonite, heard this, they were much vexed that someone should have come to promote the interests of the Israelites.

Nehemiah surveys the walls

11 When I arrived in Jerusalem, I waited 12 three days. Then I set out by night, taking a few men with me; but I told no one what my God was prompting me to do for Jerusalem. I had no beast with me except the one on 13 which I myself rode. I went out by night through the Valley Gate towards the Dragon Spring and the Dung Gate, and I inspected the places where the walls of Jerusalem had been broken down and her gates 14 burnt. Then I passed on to the Fountain Gate and the King's Pool; but there was no room for me to ride 15 through. I went up the valley in the night and inspected the city wall; then I re-entered the city by the 16 Valley Gate. So I arrived back without the magistrates knowing where I had been or what I was doing. I had not yet told the Jews, the priests, the nobles, the magistrates, or any of those who would be responsible for the work.

Rebuilding begins

17 Then I said to them, 'You see our wretched plight. Jerusalem lies in ruins, its gates destroyed by fire. Come, let us rebuild the wall of Jeru-18 salem and be rid of the reproach.' I told them how the gracious hand of my God had been upon me and also what the king had said to me. They replied, 'Let us start the rebuilding.' So they set about the work vigorously and to good purpose.

19 But when Sanballat the Horonite, Tobiah the Ammonite slave, and Geshem the Arab heard of it, they jeered at us, asking contemptuously, 'What is this you are doing? Is this a rebellion against the king?' But I 20 answered them, 'The God of heaven will give us success. We, his servants, are making a start with the rebuilding. You have no stake, or claim, or traditional right in Jerusalem.'

Allocating the work

Eliashib the high priest and his fellow- 3 priests started work and rebuilt the Sheep Gate. They laid its beams[a] and set its doors in place; they carried the work as far as the Tower of the Hundred, as far as the Tower of Hananel, and consecrated it. Next to 2 Eliashib the men of Jericho worked; and next to them Zaccur son of Imri.

The Fish Gate was built by the sons 3 of Hassenaah; they laid its tie-beams and set its doors in place with their bolts and bars. Next to them Mere- 4 moth son of Uriah, son of Hakkoz, repaired his section; next to them Meshullam son of Berechiah, son of Meshezabel; next to them Zadok son of Baana did the repairs; and next 5 again the men of Tekoa did the repairs, but their nobles would not demean themselves to serve their governor.

The Jeshanah Gate[b] was repaired 6 by Joiada son of Paseah and Me-shullam son of Bosodeiah; they laid its tie-beams and set its doors in place with their bolts and bars. Next 7 to them Melatiah the Gibeonite and Jadon the Meronothite, the men of Gibeon and Mizpah, did the repairs as far as the seat of the governor of the province of Beyond-Euphrates. Next 8 to them Uzziel son of Harhaiah, a goldsmith, did the repairs, and next Hananiah, a perfumer; they reconstructed Jerusalem as far as the Broad Wall. Next to them Rephaiah son of 9 Hur, ruler of half the district of Jerusalem, did the repairs. Next to them 10 Jedaiah son of Harumaph did the repairs opposite his own house; and next Hattush son of Hashabniah. Malchiah son of Harim and Hasshub 11 son of Pahath-moab repaired a second section including the Tower of the Ovens.[c] Next to them Shallum son of 12 Hallohesh, ruler of half the district of Jerusalem, did the repairs with the help of his daughters.

The Valley Gate was repaired by 13 Hanun and the inhabitants of Zanoah; they rebuilt it and set its doors in place with their bolts and bars, and they repaired a thousand cubits of the

---

a laid its beams: *prob. rdg.*; *Heb.* consecrated it. City. c Or Furnaces.

b The Jeshanah Gate: *or* The gate of the Old

14 wall as far as the Dung Gate. The Dung Gate itself was repaired by Malchiah son of Rechab, ruler of the district of Beth-hakkerem; he rebuilt[d] it and set its doors in place with 15 their bolts and bars. The Fountain Gate was repaired by Shallun son of Col-hozeh, ruler of the district of Mizpah; he rebuilt[d] it and roofed it and set its doors in place with their bolts and bars; and he built the wall of the Pool of Shelah next to the king's garden and onwards as far as the steps leading down from the City of David.

16 After him Nehemiah son of Azbuk, ruler of half the district of Beth-zur, did the repairs as far as a point opposite the burial-place of David, as far as the artificial pool and the House 17 of the Heroes.[e] After him the Levites did the repairs: Rehum son of Bani and next to him Hashabiah, ruler of half the district of Keilah, did the re-18 pairs for his district. After him their kinsmen did the repairs: Binnui son of Henadad, ruler of half the district 19 of Keilah; next to him Ezer son of Jeshua, ruler of Mizpah, repaired a second section opposite the point at which the ascent meets the escarp-20 ment; after him Baruch son of Zabbai repaired a second section, from the escarpment to the door of the house 21 of Eliashib the high priest. After him Meremoth son of Uriah, son of Hakkoz, repaired a second section, from the door of the house of Eliashib to the end of the house of Eliashib.

22 After him the priests of the neighbourhood of Jerusalem did the re-23 pairs. Next Benjamin and Hasshub did the repairs opposite their own house; and next Azariah son of Maaseiah, son of Ananiah, did the repairs 24 beside his house. After him Binnui son of Henadad repaired a second section, from the house of Azariah as far as the escarpment and the corner. 25 Palal son of Uzai worked opposite the escarpment and the upper tower which projects from the king's house and belongs to the court of the guard. After him Pedaiah son of Parosh[f] 26 worked as far as a point on the east opposite the Water Gate and the 27 projecting tower. Next the men of Tekoa repaired a second section, from a point opposite the great projecting tower as far as the wall of Ophel.

28 Above the Horse Gate the priests did the repairs opposite their own houses. After them Zadok son of 29 Immer did the repairs opposite his own house; after him Shemaiah son of Shecaniah, the keeper of the East Gate, did the repairs. After him Han-30 aniah son of Shelemiah and Hanun, sixth son of Zalaph, repaired a second section. After him Meshullam son of Berechiah did the repairs opposite his room. After him Malchiah, a gold-31 smith, did the repairs as far as the house of the temple-servitors and the merchants, opposite the Mustering Gate, as far as the roof-chamber at the corner. Between the roof-chamber 32 at the corner and the Sheep Gate the goldsmiths and merchants did the repairs.

Overcoming opposition

When Sanballat heard that we were 4 rebuilding the wall, he was very indignant; in his anger he jeered at the Jews and said in front of his com-2 panions and of the garrison in Samaria, 'What do these feeble Jews think they are doing? Do they mean to reconstruct the place? Do they hope to offer sacrifice and finish the work in a day? Can they make stones again out of heaps of rubble, and burnt at that?' Tobiah the Ammonite, 3 who was beside him, said, 'Whatever it is they are building, if a fox climbs up their stone walls, it will break them down.'

Hear us, our God, for they treat us 4 with contempt. Turn back their reproach upon their own heads and let them become objects of contempt in a land of captivity. Do not condone 5 their guilt or let their sin be struck off the record, for they have openly provoked the builders.

We built up the wall until it was 6 continuous all round up to half its height; and the people worked with a will. But when Sanballat and Tobiah, 7 the Arabs and Ammonites and Ashdodites, heard that the new work on the walls of Jerusalem had made progress and that the filling of the breaches had begun, they were very angry; and they all banded together 8 to come and attack Jerusalem and to create confusion. So we prayed to our 9 God, and posted a guard day and night against them.

But the men of Judah said, 'The 10 labourers' strength has failed, and there is too much rubble; we shall never be able to rebuild the wall by

---

d *Prob. rdg.; Heb.* he will rebuild.   e *Or* and the barracks.   f *Prob. rdg.; Heb. adds* and the temple-servitors lodged on Ophel (*cp. 11. 21*).

11 ourselves.' And our adversaries said, 'Before they know it or see anything, we shall be upon them and kill them, 12 and so put an end to the work.' When the Jews who lived among them came in to the city, they warned us many times that they would gather from every place where they lived to attack 13 us, and that they would station themselves on the lowest levels below the wall, on patches of open ground. Accordingly I posted my people by families, armed with swords, spears, 14 and bows. Then I surveyed the position and at once addressed the nobles, the magistrates, and all the people. 'Do not be afraid of them', I said. 'Remember the Lord, great and terrible, and fight for your brothers, your sons and daughters, your wives and 15 your homes.' Our enemies heard that everything was known to us, and that God had frustrated their plans; and we all returned to our work on the wall.

Defending the working party

16 From that day forward half the men under me were engaged in the actual building, while the other half stood by holding their spears, shields, and bows, and wearing coats of mail; and officers supervised all the people of 17 Judah who were engaged on the wall. The porters carrying the loads had one hand on the load and a weapon 18 in the other. The builders had their swords attached to their belts as they built; the trumpeter was beside me. 19 I addressed the nobles, the magistrates, and all the people: 'The work is great and covers much ground', I said. 'We are isolated on the wall, each man at some distance from his neighbour. 20 Wherever the trumpet sounds, rally to us there, and our God will fight for 21 us.' So we continued with the work, half the men holding the spears, from 22 daybreak until the stars came out. At the same time I had said to the people, 'Let every man and his servant pass the night in Jerusalem, to act as a guard for us by night and a working 23 party by day.' So neither I nor my kinsmen nor the men under me nor my bodyguard ever took off our clothes, each keeping his right hand on[g] his weapon.

Nehemiah forbids enslaving fellow-countrymen

5 There came a time when the common people, both men and women, raised a great outcry against their fellow-Jews. Some complained that they 2 were giving their sons and daughters as pledges[h] for food to keep themselves alive; others that they were 3 mortgaging their fields, vineyards, and houses to buy corn in the famine; others again that they were borrowing 4 money on their fields and vineyards to pay the king's tax. 'But', they said, 5 'our bodily needs are the same as other people's, our children are as good as theirs; yet here we are, forcing our sons and daughters to become slaves. Some of our daughters are already enslaved, and there is nothing we can do, because our fields and vineyards now belong to others.' I was very angry 6 when I heard their outcry and the story they told. I mastered my feel- 7 ings and reasoned with the nobles and the magistrates. I said to them, 'You are holding your fellow-Jews as pledges for debt.' I rebuked them severely and said, 'As far as we have 8 been able, we have bought back our fellow-Jews who had been sold to other nations; but you are now selling your own fellow-countrymen, and they will have to be bought back by us!' They were silent and had not a word to say. I went on, 'What you 9 are doing is wrong. You ought to live so much in the fear of God that you are above reproach in the eyes of the nations who are our enemies. Speak- 10 ing for myself, I and my kinsmen are advancing them money and corn. Let us give up this taking of persons as pledges for debt. Give back today to your debtors 11 their fields and vineyards, their olive-groves and houses, as well as the income[i] in money, and in corn, new wine, and oil.' 'We will give them 12 back', they promised, 'and exact nothing more. We will do what you say.' So, summoning the priests, I put the offenders on oath to do as they had promised. Then I shook out the 13 fold of my robe and said, 'So may God shake out from his house and from his property every man who does not fulfil this promise. May he be shaken out like this and emptied!' And all the assembled people said 'Amen' and praised the LORD. And they did as they had promised.

Nehemiah forgoes his allowance

Moreover, from the time when I was 14 appointed governor in the land of

g keeping his right hand on: *prob. rdg.; Heb. obscure.* that they, their sons and daughters were many.   h that they . . . as pledges: *prob. rdg.; Heb. that they . . . as pledges were many.*   i *Prob. rdg.; Heb. hundredth.*

Judah, from the twentieth to the thirty-second year of King Artaxerxes, a period of twelve years, neither I 15 nor my kinsmen drew the governor's allowance of food. Former governors had laid a heavy burden on the people, exacting from them a daily toll[j] of bread and wine to the value of forty shekels of silver. Further, the men under them had tyrannized over the people; but, for fear of God, I did not 16 behave like this. I also put all my energy into the work on this wall, and I acquired no land; and all my men 17 were gathered there for the work. Also I had as guests at my table a hundred and fifty Jews, including the magistrates, as well as men who came to us 18 from the surrounding nations. The provision which had to be made each day was an ox and six prime sheep; fowls also were prepared for me, and every ten days skins of wine in abundance. Yet, in spite of all this, I did not draw the governor's allowance, because the people were so heavily 19 burdened. Remember for my good, O God, all that I have done for this people.

Further attempts to weaken Jerusalem

6 When the news came to Sanballat, Tobiah, Geshem the Arab, and the rest of our enemies, that I had rebuilt the wall and that not a single breach remained in it, although I had not yet set up the doors in the gates, 2 Sanballat and Geshem sent me an invitation to come and confer with them at Hakkephirim in the plain of Ono; this was a ruse on their part to 3 do me harm. So I sent messengers to them with this reply: 'I have important work on my hands at the moment; I cannot come down. Why should the work be brought to a standstill while I leave it and come 4 down to you?' They sent me a similar invitation four times, and each time 5 I gave them the same answer. On a fifth occasion Sanballat made a similar approach, but this time his mes- 6 senger came with an open letter. It ran as follows: 'It is reported among the nations—and Gashmu[k] confirms it—that you and the Jews are plotting rebellion, and it is for this reason that you are rebuilding the wall, and—so the report goes—that you yourself

want to be king. You are also said to 7 have put up prophets to proclaim in Jerusalem that Judah has a king, meaning yourself. The king will certainly hear of this. So come at once and let us talk the matter over.' Here 8 is the reply I sent: 'No such thing as you allege has taken place; you have made up the whole story.' They were 9 all trying to intimidate us, in the hope that we should then relax our efforts and that the work would never be finished. So I applied myself to it with greater energy.

One day I went to the house of 10 Shemaiah son of Delaiah, son of Mehetabel, for he was confined to his house. He said, 'Let us meet in the house of God, within the sanctuary, and let us shut the doors, for they are coming to kill you—they are coming to kill you by night.' But I said, 11 'Should a man like me run away? And can a man like me go into the sanctuary and survive[l]? I will not go in.' Then it dawned on me: God had not 12 sent him. His prophecy aimed at harm, ing me, and Tobiah and Sanballat had bribed him to utter it. He had been 13 bribed to frighten me into compliance and into committing sin; then they could give me a bad name and discredit me. Remember Tobiah and 14 Sanballat, O God, for what they have done, and also the prophetess Noadiah and all the other prophets who have tried to intimidate me.

The wall is finished

On the twenty-fifth day of the month 15 Elul the wall was finished; it had taken fifty-two days. When our ene- 16 mies heard of it, and all the surrounding nations saw it,[m] they thought it a very wonderful achievement,[n] and they recognized that this work had been accomplished by the help of our God.

All this time the nobles in Judah 17 were sending many letters to Tobiah, and receiving replies from him. For 18 many in Judah were in league with him, because he was a son-in-law of Shecaniah son of Arah, and his son Jehohanan had married a daughter of Meshullam son of Berechiah. They 19 were always praising[o] him in my presence and repeating to him what I said. Tobiah also wrote to me to intimidate me.

---

j a daily toll: *prob. rdg.; Heb. obscure.*   *k* Geshem *in 2. 19 and 6. 1, 2.*   *l* and survive: *or to save his life.*   *m Or* were afraid.   *n* they thought . . . achievement: *prob. rdg.; Heb.* they fell very much in their own eyes.   *o Or* repeating rumours about . . .

Nehemiah appoints guards for Jerusalem

7 Now when the wall had been rebuilt, and I had set the doors in place and the gate-keepers[p] had been appointed,
2 I gave the charge of Jerusalem to my brother Hanani, and to Hananiah, the governor of the citadel, for he was trustworthy and God-fearing above
3 other men. And I said to them, 'The entrances to Jerusalem are not to be left open during the heat of the day; the gates must be kept shut and barred while the gate-keepers are standing at ease. Appoint guards from among the inhabitants of Jerusalem, some on sentry-duty and others posted in front of their own homes.'

The roll of returning exiles

4 The city was large and spacious; there were few people in it and no houses
5 had yet been rebuilt. Then God prompted me to assemble the nobles, the magistrates, and the people, to be enrolled family by family. And I found the book of the genealogies of those who had been the first to come back. This is what I found written in
6[q] it: Of the captives whom Nebuchadnezzar king of Babylon had taken into exile, these are the people of the province who have returned to Jerusalem
7 and Judah, each to his own town, led by Zerubbabel, Jeshua,[r] Nehemiah, Azariah, Raamiah, Nahamani, Mordecai, Bilshan, Mispereth, Bigvai, Nehum and Baanah.

The roll of the men of the people
8 of Israel: the family of Parosh, two thousand one hundred and seventy-
9 two; the family of Shephatiah, three
10 hundred and seventy-two; the family of Arah, six hundred and fifty-two;
11 the family of Pahath-moab, namely the families of Jeshua and Joab, two thousand eight hundred and eighteen;
12 the family of Elam, one thousand two
13 hundred and fifty-four; the family of Zattu, eight hundred and forty-five;
14 the family of Zaccai, seven hundred
15 and sixty; the family of Binnui, six
16 hundred and forty-eight; the family of Bebai, six hundred and twenty-
17 eight; the family of Azgad, two thousand three hundred and twenty-two;
18 the family of Adonikam, six hundred
19 and sixty-seven; the family of Bigvai, two thousand and sixty-seven;
20 the family of Adin, six hundred and

fifty-five; the family of Ater, namely 21 that of Hezekiah, ninety-eight; the 22 family of Hashum, three hundred and twenty-eight; the family of Bezai, 23 three hundred and twenty-four; the 24 family of Harif, one hundred and twelve; the family of Gibeon, ninety- 25 five. The men of Bethlehem and 26 Netophah, one hundred and eighty-eight; the men of Anathoth, one 27 hundred and twenty-eight; the men 28 of Beth-azmoth, forty-two; the men 29 of Kiriath-jearim, Kephirah, and Beer-oth, seven hundred and forty-three; the men of Ramah and Geba, six 30 hundred and twenty-one; the men 31 of Michmas, one hundred and twenty-two; the men of Bethel and Ai, one 32 hundred and twenty-three; the men 33 of[s] Nebo, fifty-two; the men[t] of the 34 other Elam, one thousand two hundred and fifty-four; the men of 35 Harim, three hundred and twenty; the men of Jericho, three hundred 36 and forty-five; the men of Lod, Hadid, 37 and Ono, seven hundred and twenty-one; the men of Senaah, three thou- 38 sand nine hundred and thirty.

Priests: the family of Jedaiah, of 39 the line of Jeshua, nine hundred and seventy-three; the family of Immer, 40 one thousand and fifty-two; the 41 family of Pashhur, one thousand two hundred and forty-seven; the family 42 of Harim, one thousand and seventeen.

Levites: the families of Jeshua and[u] 43 Kadmiel, of the line of Hodvah, seventy-four. Singers: the family of 44 Asaph, one hundred and forty-eight. Door-keepers: the family of Shallum, 45 the family of Ater, the family of Talmon, the family of Akkub, the family of Hatita, and the family of Shobai, one hundred and thirty-eight in all.

Temple-servitors: the family of 46 Ziha, the family of Hasupha, the family of Tabbaoth, the family of 47 Keros, the family of Sia, the family of Padon, the family of Lebanah, the 48 family of Hagabah, the family of Shalmai, the family of Hanan, the 49 family of Giddel, the family of Gahar, the family of Reaiah, the family of 50 Rezin, the family of Nekoda, the 51 family of Gazzam, the family of Uzza, the family of Paseah, the family of 52 Besai, the family of the Meunim, the family of the Nephishesim,[v] the family 53 of Bakbuk, the family of Hakupha, the family of Harhur, the family of 54

p Prob. rdg.; Heb. adds the singers and the Levites.   q Verses 6–73: cp. Ezra 2. 1–70.   r Or Joshua (cp. Hag. 1. 1).   s Prob. rdg., cp. Ezra 2. 29; Heb. adds the other.   t Prob. rdg.; Heb. family (also in verses 35–8).   u and: prob. rdg., cp. Ezra 2. 40; Heb. to.   v Or Nephushesim.

Bazlith,[w] the family of Mehida, the
55 family of Harsha, the family of Barkos, the family of Sisera, the family of
56 Temah, the family of Neziah, and the
family of Hatipha.
57   Descendants of Solomon's servants:
the family of Sotai, the family of
58 Sophereth, the family of Perida, the
family of Jaalah, the family of Dar-
59 kon, the family of Giddel, the family
of Shephatiah, the family of Hattil,
the family of Pochereth-hazzebaim,
and the family of Amon.
60   The temple-servitors and the descendants of Solomon's servants amounted
to three hundred and ninety-two in
all.
61   The following were those who returned from Tel-melah, Tel-harsha,
Kerub, Addon, and Immer, but could
not establish their father's family nor
whether by descent they belonged to
62 Israel: the family of Delaiah, the
family of Tobiah, the family of Nek-
63 oda, six hundred and forty-two. Also
of the priests: the family of Hobaiah,
the family of Hakkoz, and the family of Barzillai who had married a
daughter of Barzillai the Gileadite
64 and went by his[x] name. These searched
for their names among those enrolled in the genealogies, but they
could not be found; they were disqualified for the priesthood as unclean,
65 and the governor forbade them to partake of the most sacred food until there
should be a priest able to consult
the Urim and the Thummim.
66   The whole assembled people numbered forty-two thousand three hun-
67 dred and sixty, apart from their
slaves, male and female, of whom there
were seven thousand three hundred
and thirty-seven; and they had two
hundred and forty-five singers, men
68 and women. Their horses numbered
seven hundred and thirty-six, their
mules two hundred and forty-five,
69 their camels four hundred and thirty-
five, and their asses six thousand
seven hundred and twenty.
70   Some of the heads of families gave
contributions for the work. The governor gave to the treasury a thousand drachmas of gold, fifty tossing-
bowls, and five hundred and thirty
71 priestly robes. Some of the heads of
families gave for the fabric fund
twenty thousand drachmas of gold
and two thousand two hundred minas

of silver. What the rest of the people 72
gave was twenty thousand drachmas
of gold, two thousand minas of silver,
and sixty-seven priestly robes.
    The priests, the Levites, and some 73
of the people lived in Jerusalem and
its suburbs;[y] the door-keepers, the
singers, the temple-servitors, and all
other Israelites, lived in their own
towns.

Ezra reads the law to the people

When the seventh month came, and
the Israelites were now settled in their
towns, the people assembled as one 8
man in the square in front of the
Water Gate, and Ezra the scribe[z] was
asked to bring the book of the law of
Moses, which the LORD had enjoined upon Israel. On the first day of 2
the seventh month, Ezra the priest
brought the law before the assembly,
every man and woman, and all who
were capable of understanding what
they heard.[a] He read from it, facing 3
the square in front of the Water Gate,
from early morning till noon, in the
presence of the men and the women,
and those who could understand;[b] all
the people listened attentively to the
book of the law. Ezra the scribe stood 4
on a wooden platform made for the
purpose,[c] and beside him stood Mattithiah, Shema, Anaiah, Uriah, Hilkiah, and Maaseiah on his right hand;
and on his left Pedaiah, Mishael,
Malchiah, Hashum, Hashbaddanah,
Zechariah and Meshullam. Ezra open- 5
ed the book in the sight of all the
people, for he was standing above
them; and when he opened it, they
all stood. Ezra blessed the LORD, the 6
great God, and all the people raised
their hands and answered, 'Amen,
Amen'; and they bowed their heads
and prostrated themselves humbly
before the LORD. Jeshua, Bani, Sher- 7
ebiah, Jamin, Akkub, Shabbethai,
Hodiah, Maaseiah, Kelita, Azariah,
Jozabad, Hanan, Pelaiah, the Levites,[d] expounded the law to the
people while they remained in their
places. They read from the book of 8
the law of God clearly, made its sense
plain and gave instruction in what
was read.
    Then Nehemiah the governor and 9
Ezra the priest and scribe, and the
Levites who instructed the people,
said to them all, 'This day is holy to

---

w Or Bazluth (cp. Ezra 2. 52).   x Prob. rdg., cp. 1 Esdras 5. 38; Heb. their.   y In Jerusalem
and its suburbs: prob. rdg., cp. 1 Esdras 5. 46; Heb. om.   z Or doctor of the law.   a were
capable . . . heard: or would teach them to understand.   b could understand: or were to instruct.
c Or for the address.   d Prob. rdg.; Heb. and the Levites.

the LORD your God; do not mourn or weep.' For all the people had been weeping while they listened to the
10 words of the law. Then he said to them, 'You may go now; refresh yourselves with rich food and sweet drinks, and send a share to all who cannot provide for themselves; for this day is holy to our Lord. Let there be no sadness, for joy in the LORD is
11 your strength.' The Levites silenced the people, saying, 'Be quiet, for this day is holy; let there be no sadness.'
12 So all the people went away to eat and to drink, to send shares to others and to celebrate the day with great rejoicing, because they had understood what had been explained to them.

Great rejoicing in Jerusalem

13 On the second day the heads of families of the whole people, with the priests and the Levites, assembled before Ezra the scribe to study the
14 law. And they found written in the law that the LORD had given commandment through Moses that the Israelites should live in arbours[e] during the feast of the seventh month,
15 and that they should make proclamation throughout all their cities and in Jerusalem: 'Go out into the hills and fetch branches of olive and wild olive, myrtle and palm, and other leafy boughs to make arbours, as pre-
16 scribed.' So the people went out and fetched them and made arbours for themselves, each on his own roof, and in their courts and in the courts of the house of God, and in the square at the Water Gate and the square at the
17 Ephraim Gate. And the whole community of those who had returned from the captivity made arbours and lived in them, a thing that the Israelites had not done from the days of Joshua son of Nun to that day; and
18 there was very great rejoicing. And day by day, from the first day to the last, the book of the law of God was read. They kept the feast for seven days, and on the eighth day there was a closing ceremony, according to the rule.

Recounting past mercies

9 On the twenty-fourth day of this month the Israelites assembled for a fast, clothed in sackcloth and with
2 earth on their heads. Those who were of Israelite descent separated themselves from all the foreigners; they took their places and confessed their sins and the iniquities of their fore-
3 fathers. Then they stood up in their places, and the book of the law of the LORD their God was read for one fourth of the day, and for another fourth they confessed and did obeis-
4 ance to the LORD their God. Upon the steps assigned to the Levites stood Jeshua, Bani, Kadmiel, Shebaniah, Bunni, Sherebiah, Bani, and Kenani, and they cried aloud to the LORD their
5 God. Then the Levites, Jeshua, Kadmiel, Bani, Hashabniah, Sherebiah, Hodiah, Shebaniah, and Pethahiah, said, 'Stand up and bless the LORD your God, saying: From everlasting to everlasting thy glorious name is blessed[f] and exalted above all blessing
6 and praise. Thou alone art the LORD; thou hast made heaven, the highest heaven with all its host, the earth and all that is on it, the seas and all that is in them. Thou preservest all of them, and the host of heaven worships thee.
7 Thou art the LORD, the God who chose Abram and brought him out of Ur of the Chaldees and named him Abra-
8 ham. Thou didst find him faithful to thee and didst make a covenant with him to give to him and to his descendants the land of the Canaanites, the Hittites, the Amorites, the Perizzites, the Jebusites, and the Girgashites; and thou didst fulfil thy promise, for thou art just.
9 'And thou didst see the misery of our forefathers in Egypt and didst hear their cry for help at the Red Sea,[g]
10 and didst work signs and portents against Pharaoh, all his courtiers and all the people of his land, knowing how arrogantly they treated our forefathers, and thou didst win for thyself a name that lives on to this day.
11 Thou didst tear the sea apart before them so that they went through the middle of it on dry ground; but thou didst cast their pursuers into the depths, like a stone cast into turbu-
12 lent waters. Thou didst guide them by a pillar of cloud in the day-time and by a pillar of fire at night to give them light on the road by which they
13 travelled. Thou didst descend upon Mount Sinai and speak with them from heaven, and give them right judgements and true laws, and statutes and commandments which were
14 good, and thou didst make known to them thy holy sabbath and give them

---

e *Or* tabernacles *or* booths.   f thy glorious name is blessed: *prob. rdg.*; *Heb.* and let them bless thy glorious name.   g *Or* the Sea of Reeds.

commandments, statutes, and laws 15 through thy servant Moses. Thou gavest them bread from heaven to stay their hunger and thou broughtest water out from a rock for them to quench their thirst, and thou didst bid them enter and take possession of the land which thou hadst solemnly 16 sworn to give them. But they, our forefathers, were arrogant and stubborn, and disobeyed thy command- 17 ments. They refused to obey and did not remember the miracles which thou didst accomplish among them; they remained stubborn, and they appointed a man to lead them back to slavery in Egypt. But thou art a forgiving god, gracious and compassionate, long-suffering and ever constant, and thou didst not forsake 18 them. Even when they made the image of a bull-calf in metal and said, "This is your god who brought you up from Egypt", and were guilty of 19 great blasphemies, thou in thy great compassion didst not forsake them in the wilderness. The pillar of cloud did not fail to guide them on their journey by day nor the pillar of fire by night to give them light on the road 20 by which they travelled. Thou gavest thy good spirit to instruct them; thy manna thou didst not withhold from them, and thou gavest them water to 21 quench their thirst. Forty years long thou didst sustain them in the wilderness, and they lacked nothing; their clothes did not wear out and their feet were not swollen.

22 'Thou gavest them kingdoms and peoples, allotting these to them as spoils of war. Thus they took possession of the land of Sihon king of Heshbon and the land of Og king of 23 Bashan. Thou didst multiply their descendants so that they became countless as the stars in the sky, bringing them into the land which thou didst promise to give to their forefathers 24 as their possession. When their descendants entered the land and took possession of it, thou didst subdue before them the Canaanites who inhabited it and gavest these, kings and peoples alike, into their hands to do with 25 them whatever they wished. They captured fortified cities and a fertile land and took possession of houses full of all good things, rock-hewn cisterns, vineyards, olive-trees, and fruit-trees in abundance; so they ate and were satisfied and grew fat and found 26 delight in thy great goodness. But they were defiant and rebelled against

thee; they turned their backs on thy law and killed thy prophets, who solemnly warned them to return to thee, and they were guilty of great blasphemies. Because of this thou 27 didst hand them over to their enemies who oppressed them. But when, in the time of their oppression, they cried to thee for help, thou heardest them from heaven and in thy great compassion didst send them saviours to save them from their enemies. But 28 when they had had a respite, they once more did what was wrong in thine eyes; and thou didst abandon them to their enemies who held them in subjection. But again they cried to thee for help, and many times over thou heardest them from heaven and in thy compassion didst save them. Thou 29 didst solemnly warn them to return to thy law, but they grew arrogant and did not heed thy commandments; they sinned against thy ordinances, which bring life to him who keeps them. Stubbornly they turned away in mulish obstinacy and would not obey. Many years thou wast 30 patient with them and didst warn them by thy spirit through thy prophets; but they would not listen. Therefore thou didst hand them over to foreign peoples. Yet in thy great 31 compassion thou didst not make an end of them nor forsake them; for thou art a gracious and compassionate god.

A binding declaration

'Now therefore, our God, thou great 32 and mighty and terrible God, who faithfully keepest covenant, do not make light of the hardships that have befallen us—our kings, our princes, our priests, our prophets, our forefathers, and all thy people—from the days of the kings of Assyria to this day. In all that has befallen us thou 33 hast been just, thou hast kept faith, but we have done wrong. Our kings, 34 our princes, our priests, and our forefathers did not keep thy law nor heed thy commandments and the warnings which thou gavest them. Even under 35 their own kings, while they were enjoying the great prosperity which thou gavest them and the broad and fertile land which thou didst bestow upon them, they did not serve thee; they did not abandon their evil ways. Today we are slaves, slaves here in 36 the land which thou gavest to our forefathers so that they might eat its fruits and enjoy its good things. All 37 its produce now goes to the kings whom thou hast set over us because of our sins. They have power over our bodies, and they do as they please with our beasts, while we are in dire distress.

38 'Because of all this we make a binding declaration in writing, and our princes, our Levites, and our priests witness the sealing.

The substance of the covenant

10 'Those who witness the sealing are Nehemiah the governor, son of Hac-
2 aliah, Zedekiah, Seraiah, Azariah,
3 Jeremiah, Pashhur, Amariah, Mal-
4 chiah, Hattush, Shebaniah, Malluch,
5 6 Harim, Meremoth, Obadiah, Daniel,
7 Ginnethon, Baruch, Meshullam, Abi-
8 ah, Mijamin, Maaziah, Bilgai, Shemai-
9 ah; these are the priests. The Levites: Jeshua[h] son of Azaniah, Binnui of
10 the family of Henadad, Kadmiel; and their brethren, Shebaniah, Hodiah,[i]
11 Kelita, Pelaiah, Hanan, Mica, Rehob,
12 Hashabiah, Zaccur, Sherebiah, Sheb-
13 14 aniah, Hodiah, Bani, Beninu. The chiefs of the people: Parosh, Pahath-
15 moab, Elam, Zattu, Bani, Bunni,
16 Azgad, Bebai, Adonijah, Bigvai, A-
17 18 din, Ater, Hezekiah, Azzur, Hodiah,
19 Hashum, Bezai, Hariph, Anathoth,
20 Nebai,[j] Magpiash, Meshullam, Hezir,
21 22 Meshezabel, Zadok, Jaddua, Pelatiah,
23 Hanan, Anaiah, Hoshea, Hananiah,
24 Hasshub, Hallohesh, Pilha, Shobek,
25 26 Rehum, Hashabnah, Maaseiah, Ahiah,
27 Hanan, Anan, Malluch, Harim, Ba-anah.

28 'The rest of the people, the priests, the Levites, the door-keepers, the singers, the temple-servitors, with their wives, their sons, and their daughters, all who are capable of understanding, all who for the sake of the law of God have kept themselves apart from the foreign population,
29 join with the leading brethren,[k] when the oath is put to them, in swearing to obey God's law given by Moses the servant of God, and to observe and fulfil all the commandments of the LORD our Lord, his rules and his statutes.

30 'We will not give our daughters in marriage to the foreign population or
31 take their daughters for our sons. If on the sabbath these people bring in merchandise, especially corn, for sale, we will not buy from them on the sabbath or on any holy day. We will forgo the crops of the seventh year

and release every person still held as a pledge for debt.

'We hereby undertake the duty of 32 giving yearly the third of a shekel for the service of the house of our God, for the Bread of the Presence, 33 the regular grain-offering and whole-offering, the sabbaths, the new moons, the appointed seasons, the holy-gifts, and the sin-offerings to make expiation on behalf of Israel, and for all else that has to be done in the house of our God. We, the priests, the Le- 34 vites, and the people, have cast lots for the wood-offering, so that it may be brought into the house of our God by each family in turn, at appointed times, year by year, to burn upon the altar of the LORD our God, as prescribed in the law. We under- 35 take to bring the firstfruits of our land and the firstfruits of every fruit-tree, year by year, to the house of the LORD; also to bring to the house of 36 our God, to the priests who minister in the house of our God, the first-born of our sons and of our cattle, as prescribed in the law, and the first-born of our herds and of our flocks; and to 37 bring to the priests the first kneading of our dough, and the first of the fruit of every tree, of the new wine and of the oil, to the store-rooms in the house of our God; and to bring to the Levites the tithes from our land, for it is the Levites who collect the tithes in all our farming villages. The 38 Aaronite priest shall be with the Levites when they collect the tithes; and the Levites shall bring up one tenth of the tithes to the house of our God, to the appropriate rooms in the storehouse. For the Israelites and the 39 Levites shall bring the contribution of corn, new wine, and oil to the rooms where the vessels of the sanctuary are kept, and where the ministering priests, the door-keepers, and the singers are lodged. We will not neglect the house of our God.'

Residents in Jerusalem

The leaders of the people settled in **11** Jerusalem; and the rest of the people cast lots to bring one in every ten to live in Jerusalem, the holy city, while the remaining nine lived in other towns. And the people were 2 grateful to all those who volunteered to live in Jerusalem.

These are the chiefs of the province 3 who lived in Jerusalem; but, in the

h Prob. rdg.; Heb. and Jeshua.   i Or, with Ezra 2. 40, Hodaviah.   j Or Nobai.   k the leading brethren: prob. rdg.; Heb. their brethren, their leading men.

towns of Judah, other Israelites, priests, Levites, temple-servitors, and descendants of Solomon's servants lived on their own property, in their 4 own towns. Some members of the tribes of Judah and Benjamin lived in Jerusalem. Of Judah: Athaiah son of Uzziah, son of Zechariah, son of Amariah, son of Shephatiah, son of 6 Mahalalel of the family of Perez, all of whose family, to the number of four hundred and sixty-eight men of 5 substance, lived in Jerusalem; and Maaseiah son of Baruch, son of Colhozeh, son of Hazaiah, son of Adaiah, son of Joiarib, son of Zechariah of the Shelanite family.

7 These were the Benjamites: Sallu son of Meshullam, son of Joed, son of Pedaiah, son of Kolaiah, son of Maa-8 seiah, son of Ithiel, son of Isaiah, and his kinsmen Gabbai and Sallai, nine 9 hundred and twenty-eight in all. Joel son of Zichri was their overseer, and Judah son of Hassenuah was second over the city.[l]

10 Of the priests: Jedaiah son of 11 Joiarib, son of[m] Seraiah, son of Hilkiah, son of Meshullam, son of Zadok, son of Meraioth, son of Ahitub, super-12 visor of the house of God, and his[n] brethren responsible for the work in the temple, eight hundred and twenty-two in all; and Adaiah son of Jeroham, son of Pelaliah, son of Amzi, son of Zechariah, son of Pashhur, son 13 of Malchiah, and his brethren, heads of fathers' houses, two hundred and forty-two in all; and Amasai[o] son of Azarel, son of Ahzai, son of Me-14 shillemoth, son of Immer, and his brethren, men of substance, a hundred and twenty-eight in all; their overseer was Zabdiel son of Haggedolim.

15 And of the Levites: Shemaiah son of Hasshub, son of Azrikam, son of 16 Hashabiah, son of Bunni; and Shabbethai and Jozabad of the chiefs of the Levites, who had charge of the external business of the house of God; 17 and Mattaniah son of Micah, son of Zabdi, son of Asaph, who as precentor led the prayer of thanksgiving, and Bakbukiah who held the second place among his brethren; and Abda son of Shammua, son of Galal, son of 18 Jeduthun. The number of Levites in the holy city was two hundred and eighty-four in all.

The gate-keepers who kept guard at 19 the gates were Akkub, Talmon, and their brethren, a hundred and seventy-two. The rest of the Israelites[p] were 20 in all the towns of Judah, each man on his own inherited property. But 21 the temple-servitors lodged on Ophel, and Ziha and Gishpa were in charge of them.

The overseer of the Levites in 22 Jerusalem was Uzzi son of Bani, son of Hashabiah, son of Mattaniah, son of Mica, of the family of Asaph the singers, for the supervision of the business of the house of God. For they 23 were under the king's orders, and there was obligatory duty for the singers every day. Pethahiah son of 24 Meshezabel, of the family of Zerah son of Judah, was the king's adviser on all matters affecting the people.

Settlements outside Jerusalem

As for the hamlets with their sur-25 rounding fields: some of the men of Judah lived in Kiriath-arba and its villages, in Dibon and its villages, and in Jekabzeel and its hamlets, in 26 Jeshua, Moladah, and Bethpelet, in 27 Hazar-shual, and in Beersheba and its villages, in Ziklag and in Meconah and 28 its villages, in Enrimmon, Zorah, 29 and Jarmuth, in Zanoah, Adullam, 30 and their hamlets, in Lachish and its fields and Azekah and its villages. Thus they occupied the country from Beersheba to the Valley of Hinnom.

The men of Benjamin lived in[q] 31 Geba, Michmash, Aiah, and Bethel with its villages, in Anathoth, Nob, 32 and Ananiah, in Hazor, Ramah, and 33 Gittaim, in Hadid, Zeboim, and Ne-34 ballat, in Lod, Ono, and[r] Ge-hara-35 shim.[s] And certain divisions of the 36 Levites in Judah were attached to Benjamin.

Priests and Levites

These are the priests and the Levites 12 who came back with Zerubbabel son of Shealtiel, and Jeshua:[t] Seraiah, Jeremiah, Ezra, Amariah, Malluch, 2 Hattush, Shecaniah, Rehum, Mere-3 moth, Iddo, Ginnethon, Abiah, Mi-4 5 jamin, Maadiah, Bilgah, Shemaiah, Joi-6 arib, Jedaiah, Sallu, Amok, Hilkiah, 7 Jedaiah. These were the chiefs of the priests and of their brethren in the days of Jeshua.

And the Levites: Jeshua, Binnui, 8

---

l second over the city: *or* over the second quarter of the city.   *m* son of: *prob. rdg.*; *Heb. obscure.*   *n* *Prob. rdg.*; *Heb. their.*   *o* *Prob. rdg.*; *Heb. Amashsai.*   *p* *Prob. rdg.*; *Heb. adds* the levitical priests.   *q* *Prob. rdg.*; *Heb. from.*   *r* and: *prob. rdg.*; *Heb. om.*   *s* Or and the Valley of Woods *or* and the Valley of Craftsmen.   *t* Or Joshua.

Kadmiel, Sherebiah, Judah, and Mattaniah, who with his brethren was in charge of the songs of thanksgiving.
9 And Bakbukiah and Unni their brethren stood opposite them in the ser-
10 vice. And Jeshua was the father of Joiakim, Joiakim the father of Eli-
11 ashib, Eliashib of Joiada, Joiada the father of Jonathan, and Jonathan the
12 father of Jaddua. And in the days of Joiakim the priests who were heads of families were: of Seraiah, Meraiah;
13 of Jeremiah, Hananiah; of Ezra, Me-
14 shullam; of Amariah, Jehohanan; of Malluch,[u] Jonathan; of Shebaniah,
15 Joseph; of Harim, Adna; of Meraioth,
16 Helkai; of Iddo, Zechariah; of Gin-
17 nethon, Meshullam; of Abiah, Zichri;
18 of Miniamin[v]; of Moadiah, Piltai; of Bilgah, Shammua; of Shemaiah, Je-
19 honathan; of Joiarib, Mattenai; of
20 Jedaiah, Uzzi; of Sallu,[w] Kallai; of
21 Amok, Eber; of Hilkiah, Hashabiah; of Jedaiah, Nethaneel.
22   [x]The heads of the priestly families[y] in the days of Eliashib, Joiada, Johanan, and Jaddua were recorded down to the reign of Darius the
23 Persian. The heads of the levitical families were recorded in the annals only down to the days of Johanan
24 the grandson of Eliashib. And the chiefs of the Levites: Hashabiah, Sherebiah, Jeshua, Binnui,[z] Kadmiel, with their brethren in the other turn of duty, to praise and to give thanks, according to the commandment of David the man of God, turn by turn.
25 Mattaniah, Bakbukiah, Obadiah, Meshullam, Talmon, and Akkub were gate-keepers standing guard at the
26 gatehouses. This was the arrangement in the days of Joiakim son of Jeshua, son of Jozadak, and in the days of Nehemiah the governor and of Ezra the priest and scribe.

Dedicating the wall

27 At the dedication of the wall of Jerusalem they sought out the Levites in all their settlements, and brought them to Jerusalem to celebrate the dedication with[a] rejoicing, with thanksgiving and song, to the accompaniment of cymbals, lutes, and
28 harps. And the Levites,[b] the singers, were assembled from the district

round Jerusalem and from the hamlets of the Netophathites; also from 29 Beth-gilgal and from the region of Geba and Beth-azmoth;[c] for the singers had built themselves hamlets in the neighbourhood of Jerusalem. The priests and the Levites purified 30 themselves; and they purified the people, the gates, and the wall. Then 31 I brought the leading men of Judah up on to the city wall, and appointed two great choirs to give thanks. One went in procession[d] to the right, going along the wall to the Dung Gate; and 32 after it went Hoshaiah with half the leading men of Judah, and Azariah, 33 Ezra, Meshullam, Judah, Benjamin, 34 Shemaiah, and Jeremiah; and certain 35 of the priests with trumpets: Zechariah son of Jonathan, son of Shemaiah, son of Mattanaiah, son of Micaiah, son of Zaccur, son of Asaph, and 36 his kinsmen, Shemaiah, Azarel, Milalai, Gilalai, Maai, Nethaneel, Judah, and Hanani, with the musical instruments of David the man of God; and Ezra the scribe led them. They went past the Fountain Gate 37 and thence straight forward by the steps up to the City of David, by the ascent to the city wall, past the house of David, and on to the Water Gate on the east. The other thanksgiving 38 choir went to the left,[e] and I followed it with half the leading men of[f] the people, continuing along the wall, past the Tower of the Ovens[g] to the Broad Wall, and past the Ephraim 39 Gate, and over the Jeshanah Gate,[h] and over the Fish Gate, taking in the Tower of Hananel and the Tower of the Hundred, as far as the Sheep Gate; and they halted at the Gate of the Guardhouse. So the two thanks- 40 giving choirs took their place in the house of God, and I and half the magistrates with me; and the priests 41 Eliakim, Maaseiah, Miniamin, Micaiah, Elioenai, Zechariah, and Hananiah, with trumpets; and Maaseiah, 42 Shemaiah, Eleazar, Uzzi, Jehohanan, Malchiah, Elam, and Ezer. The singers, led by Izrahiah, raised their voices. A great sacrifice was celebra- 43 ted that day, and they all rejoiced because God had given them great cause for rejoicing; the women and children rejoiced with them. And the

---

[u] Prob. rdg.; Heb. Malluchi, or Melichu.   [v] A name is missing here.   [w] Prob. rdg., cp. verse 7; Heb. Sallai.   [x] Prob. rdg.; Heb. prefixes The Levites.   [y] heads . . . families: prob. rdg.; Heb. heads of the families and the priests.   [z] Jeshua, Binnui: prob. rdg.; Heb. and Jeshua son of.   [a] Prob. rdg.; Heb. and.   [b] the Levites: prob. rdg.; Heb. the sons of.   [c] Beth-azmoth: prob. rdg., cp. 7. 28; Heb. Azmoth.   [d] One . . . procession: prob. rdg.; Heb. Processions.   [e] to the left: prob. rdg.; Heb. to the front.   [f] the leading men of: prob. rdg.; Heb. om.   [g] Or Furnaces.   [h] the Jeshanah Gate: or the gate of the Old City.

rejoicing in Jerusalem was heard a long way off.

Providing for the priests and Levites

44 On that day men were appointed to take charge of the store-rooms for the contributions, the firstfruits, and the tithes, to gather in the portions required by the law for the priests and Levites according to the extent of the farmlands round the towns; for all Judah was full of rejoicing at the ministry of the priests and Levites.
45 And they performed the service of their God and the service of purification, as did the singers and the door-keepers, according to the rules laid down by David and his son Solomon.
46 For it was in the days of David that Asaph took the lead as chief of the singers and director[i] of praise and
47 thanksgiving to God. And in the days of Zerubbabel and of Nehemiah all Israel gave the portions for the singers and the door-keepers as each day required; and they set apart the portion for the Levites, and the Levites set apart the portion for the Aaronites.

Nehemiah's reforms

13 On that day at the public reading from the book of Moses, it was found to be laid down that no Ammonite or Moabite should ever enter the
2 assembly of God, because they did not meet the Israelites with food and water but hired Balaam to curse them, though our God turned the
3 curse into a blessing. When the people heard the law, they separated from Israel all who were of mixed blood.

Nehemiah rebukes Eliashib

4 But before this, Eliashib the priest, who was appointed over the store-rooms of the house of our God, and who was connected by marriage with
5 Tobiah, had provided for his use a large room where formerly they had kept the grain-offering, the incense, the temple vessels, the tithes of corn, new wine, and oil prescribed for the Levites, singers, and door-keepers, and the contributions for the priests.
6 All this time I was not in Jerusalem because, in the thirty-second year of Artaxerxes king of Babylon, I had gone to the king. Some time later,
7 I asked permission from him and returned to Jerusalem. There I discovered the wicked thing that Eliashib had done for Tobiah's sake in providing him with a room in the courts of the house of God. I was 8 greatly displeased and threw all Tobiah's belongings out of the room. Then 9 I gave orders that the room should be purified, and that the vessels of the house of God, with the grain-offering and incense, should be put back into it.

Concerning the Levites

I also learnt that the Levites had not 10 been given their portions; both they and the singers, who were responsible for their respective duties, had made off to their farms. So I remonstrated 11 with the magistrates and said, 'Why is the house of God deserted?' And I recalled the men and restored them to their places. Then all Judah 12 brought the tithes of corn, new wine, and oil into the storehouses; and I 13 put in charge of them Shelemiah the priest, Zadok the accountant, and Pedaiah a Levite, with Hanan son of Zaccur, son of Mattaniah, as their assistant, for they were considered trustworthy men; their duty was the distribution of their shares to their brethren. Remember this, O God, to 14 my credit, and do not wipe out of thy memory the devotion which I have shown in the house of my God and in his service.

Concerning the sabbath

In those days I saw men in Judah 15 treading winepresses on the sabbath, collecting quantities of produce and piling it on asses—wine, grapes, figs, and every kind of load, which they brought into Jerusalem on the sabbath; and I protested to them about selling food on that day. Tyrians 16 living in Jerusalem also brought in fish and all kinds of merchandise and sold them on the sabbath to the people of Judah, even in Jerusalem. Then I complained to the nobles of 17 Judah and said to them, 'How dare you profane the sabbath in this wicked way? Is not this just what your fathers 18 did, so that our God has brought all this evil on us and on this city? Now you are bringing more wrath upon Israel by profaning the sabbath.' When the entrances to Jerusalem had 19 been cleared in preparation for the sabbath, I gave orders that the gates should be shut and not opened until after the sabbath. And I appointed some of the men under me to have charge of the gates so that no load might enter on the sabbath. Then on 20

i *Prob. rdg.; Heb. song.*

21 one or two occasions the merchants and all kinds of traders camped just outside Jerusalem, but I cautioned them. 'Why are you camping in front of the city wall?' I asked. 'If you do it again, I will take action against you.' After that they did not come on the 22 sabbath again. And I commanded the Levites who were to purify themselves and take up duty as guards at the gates, to ensure that the sabbath was kept holy. Remember this also to my credit, O God, and spare me in thy great love.

Concerning mixed marriages

23 In those days also I saw that some Jews had married women from Ash-24 dod, Ammon, and Moab. Half their children spoke the language of Ashdod or of the other peoples and could not speak the language of the Jews. 25 I argued with them and reviled them, I beat them and tore out their hair; and I made them swear in the name of God: 'We will not marry our daughters to their sons, or take any of their daughters in marriage for our sons or for ourselves.' 'Was it not for such 26 women', I said, 'that King Solomon of Israel sinned? Among all the nations there was no king like him; he was loved by his God, and God made him king over all Israel; nevertheless even he was led by foreign women into sin. Are we then to follow your 27 example and commit this grave offence, breaking faith with our God by marrying foreign women?'

Now one of the sons of Joiada son 28 of Eliashib the high priest had married a daughter of Sanballat the Horonite; therefore I drove him out of my presence. Remember, O God, 29 to their shame that they have defiled the priesthood and the covenant of the priests[j] and the Levites.

Thus I purified them from every-30 thing foreign, and I made the Levites and the priests resume the duties of their office; I also made provision for 31 the wood-offering at appointed times, and for the firstfruits. Remember me for my good, O God.

[j] *Or* priesthood.

ESTHER

A royal banquet

1 THE EVENTS here related happened in the days of Ahasuerus, the Ahasuerus who ruled from India to Ethiopia, a hundred and twenty-2 seven provinces. At this time he sat on his royal throne in Susa the capital 3 city. In the third year of his reign he gave a banquet for all his officers and his courtiers; and when his army of Persians and Medes, with his nobles and provincial governors, were in 4 attendance, he displayed the wealth of his kingdom and the pomp and splendour of his majesty for many days, a hundred and eighty in all. 5 When these days were over, the king gave a banquet for all the people present in Susa the capital city, both high and low; it was held in the garden court of the royal pavilion and 6 lasted seven days. There were white curtains and violet hangings fastened to silver rings with bands of fine linen and purple;[a] there were alabaster pillars and couches of gold and silver set on a mosaic pavement of malachite and alabaster, of mother-of-pearl and turquoise. Wine was served 7 in golden cups of various patterns: the king's wine flowed freely as befitted a king, and the law of the 8 drinking was that there should be no compulsion, for the king had laid it down that all the stewards of his palace should respect each man's wishes. In addition, Queen Vashti 9 gave a banquet for the women in the royal apartments of King Ahasuerus.

The queen refuses to obey the king

On the seventh day, when he was 10 merry with wine, the king ordered Mehuman, Biztha, Harbona, Bigtha, Abagtha, Zethar, and Carcas, the

[a] *bands . . . purple: or* white and purple cords.

1 seven eunuchs who were in attendance on the king's person, to bring Queen Vashti before him wearing her royal crown, in order to display her beauty to the people and the officers; for she was indeed a beautiful woman.

2 But Queen Vashti refused to come in answer to the royal command conveyed by the eunuchs. This greatly incensed the king, and he grew hot with anger.

3 Then the king conferred with his wise men versed in misdemeanours;[b] for it was his royal custom to consult all who were versed in law and religion,

4 those closest to him being Carshena, Shethar, Admatha, Tarshish, Meres, Marsena, and Memucan, the seven princes of Persia and Media who had access to the king and held

5 first place in the kingdom. He asked them, 'What does the law require to be done with Queen Vashti for disobeying the command of King Ahasuerus brought to her by the

6 eunuchs?' Then Memucan made answer before the king and the princes: 'Queen Vashti has done wrong, and not to the king alone, but also to all the officers and to all the peoples in all the provinces of King Ahasuerus.

7 Every woman will come to know what the queen has done, and this will make them treat their husbands with contempt; they will say, "King Ahasuerus ordered Queen Vashti to be brought before him and she did

8 not come." The great ladies of Persia and Media, who have heard of the queen's conduct, will tell all the king's officers about this day, and there will be endless disrespect and insolence!

9 If it please your majesty, let a royal decree go out from you and let it be inscribed in the laws of the Persians and Medes, never to be revoked, that Vashti shall not again appear before King Ahasuerus; and let the king give her place as queen to another woman who is more worthy of it than

20 she. Thus when this royal edict is heard through the length and breadth of the kingdom, all women will give honour to their husbands, high and

21 low alike.' Memucan's advice pleased the king and the princes, and the king

22 did as he had proposed. Letters were sent to all the royal provinces, to every province in its own script and to every people in their own language, in order that each man might be master in his own house and control all his own womenfolk.[c]

Esther is taken to the palace

2 Later, when the anger of King Ahasuerus had died down, he remembered Vashti and what she had done and what had been decreed against

2 her. So the king's attendants said, 'Let beautiful young virgins be

3 sought out for your majesty; and let your majesty appoint commissioners in all the provinces of your kingdom to bring all these beautiful young virgins into the women's quarters in Susa the capital city. Let them be committed to the care of Hegai, the king's eunuch in charge of the women, and let cosmetics be provided for them;

4 and let the one who is most acceptable to the king become queen in place of Vashti.' This idea pleased the king and he acted on it.

5 Now there was in Susa the capital city a Jew named Mordecai son of Jair, son of Shimei, son of Kish, a

6 Benjamite; he had been carried into exile from Jerusalem among those whom Nebuchadnezzar king of Babylon had carried away with Jeconiah king of Judah. He had a foster-child

7 Hadassah, that is Esther, his uncle's daughter, who had neither father nor mother. She was a beautiful and charming girl, and after the death of her father and mother Mordecai had adopted her as his own daughter.

8 When the king's order and his edict were published, and many girls were brought to Susa the capital city to be committed to the care of Hegai, Esther too was taken to the king's palace to be entrusted to Hegai, who had charge of the women. She attrac-

9 ted his notice and received his special favour: he readily provided her with her cosmetics and her allowance of food, and also with seven picked maids from the king's palace, and he gave her and her maids privileges in the women's quarters.

10 Esther had not disclosed her race or her family, because Mordecai had

11 forbidden her to do so. Every day Mordecai passed along by the forecourt of the women's quarters to learn how Esther was faring and what was happening to her.

Esther is made queen

12 The full period of preparation prescribed for the women was twelve months, six months with oil and myrrh and six months with perfumes and cosmetics. When the period was

b Or times.   _c and control . . . womenfolk: prob. rdg.; Heb. and speak in his own language._

complete, each girl's turn came to
13 go to King Ahasuerus, and she was
allowed to take with her whatever
she asked, when she went from the
women's quarters to the king's pal-
14 ace. She went into the palace in
the evening and returned in the
morning to another part of the women's quarters, to be under the care
of Shaashgaz, the king's eunuch in
charge of the concubines. She did
not again go to the king unless he expressed a wish for her; then she was
summoned by name.
15 When the turn came for Esther,
daughter of Abihail the uncle of
Mordecai her adoptive father, to go to
the king, she asked for nothing to take
with her except what was advised by
Hegai, the king's eunuch in charge of
the women; and Esther charmed all
16 who saw her. When she was taken to
King Ahasuerus in the royal palace,
in the seventh year of his reign, in
the tenth month, that is the month
17 Tebeth, the king loved her more than
any of his other women and treated
her with greater favour and kindness
than the rest of the virgins. He put a
royal crown on her head and made
18 her queen in place of Vashti. Then
the king gave a great banquet for all
his officers and courtiers, a banquet
in honour of Esther. He also proclaimed a holiday*d* throughout the
provinces and distributed gifts worthy
of a king.

Mordecai saves the king's life

19 Mordecai was in attendance at court;
20 on his instructions Esther had not
disclosed her family or her race, she
had done what Mordecai told her, as
21 she did when she was his ward. One
day when Mordecai was in attendance
at court, Bigthan and Teresh, two of
the king's eunuchs, keepers of the
threshold, who were disaffected, were
plotting to lay hands on King Ahasu-
22 erus. This became known to Mordecai,
who told Queen Esther; and she told
the king, mentioning Mordecai by
23 name. The affair was investigated and
the report confirmed; the two men
were hanged on the gallows. All this
was recorded in the royal chronicle in
the presence of the king.

Haman's plot against the Jews

3 After this, King Ahasuerus promoted Haman son of Hammedatha the
Agagite, advancing him and giving
him precedence above all his fellow-

officers. So the king's attendants at 2
court all bowed down to Haman and
did obeisance, for so the king had
commanded; but Mordecai did not
bow down to him or do obeisance.
Then the attendants at court said 3
to Mordecai, 'Why do you flout his
majesty's command?' Day by day 4
they challenged him, but he refused to
listen to them; so they informed
Haman, in order to discover if Mordecai's refusal would be tolerated,
for he had told them that he was a
Jew. When Haman saw that Morde- 5
cai was not bowing down to him or
doing obeisance, he was infuriated.
On learning who Mordecai's people 6
were, he scorned to lay hands on him
alone, and looked for a way to destroy all the Jews throughout the
whole kingdom of Ahasuerus, Mordecai and all his race.
In the twelfth year of King Ahas- 7
uerus, in the first month, Nisan,
they cast lots, Pur as it is called, in the
presence of Haman, taking day by
day and month by month, and the
lot fell on the thirteenth day of the
twelfth month,*e* the month Adar.
Then Haman said to King Ahasuerus, 8
'There is a certain people, dispersed
among the many peoples in all the
provinces of your kingdom, who keep
themselves apart. Their laws are
different from those of every other
people; they do not keep your
majesty's laws. It does not befit your
majesty to tolerate them. If it please 9
your majesty, let an order be made
in writing for their destruction; and
I will pay ten thousand talents of
silver to your majesty's officials, to be
deposited in the royal treasury.' So 10
the king took the signet-ring from his
hand and gave it to Haman son of
Hammedatha the Agagite, the enemy
of the Jews; and he said to him, 'The 11
money and the people are yours; deal
with them as you wish.'
On the thirteenth day of the first 12
month the king's secretaries were
summoned and, in accordance with
Haman's instructions, a writ was
issued to the king's satraps and the
governor of every province, and to the
officers over each separate people: for
each province in its own script and
for each people in their own language.
It was drawn up in the name of King
Ahasuerus and sealed with the king's
signet. Thus letters were sent by 13
courier to all the king's provinces
with orders to destroy, slay, and

d Or an amnesty.   e and the lot . . . twelfth month: prob. rdg., cp. verse 13; Heb. the twelfth.

exterminate all Jews, young and old, women and children, in one day, the thirteenth day of the twelfth month, the month Adar, and to plunder their

14 possessions. A copy of the writ was to be issued as a decree in every province and to be published to all the peoples, so that they might be ready

15 for that day. The couriers were dispatched post-haste at the king's command, and the decree was issued in Susa the capital city. The king and Haman sat down to drink; but the city of Susa was thrown into confusion.

Esther plans to save the Jews

4 When Mordecai learnt all that had been done, he rent his clothes, put on sackcloth and ashes, and went through the city crying loudly and bitterly.

2 He came within sight of the palace gate, because no one clothed with sackcloth was allowed to pass through

3 the gate. In every province reached by the royal command and decree there was great mourning among the Jews, with fasting and weeping and beating of the breast. Most of them made their beds of sackcloth and

4 ashes. When Queen Esther's maids and eunuchs came and told her, she was distraught, and sent garments for Mordecai, so that they might take off the sackcloth and clothe him with them; but he would not accept them.

5 Then Esther summoned Hathach, one of the king's eunuchs who had been appointed to wait upon her, and ordered him to find out from Mordecai what the trouble was and what it

6 meant. Hathach went to Mordecai in the city square in front of the palace

7 gate, and Mordecai told him all that had happened to him and how much money Haman had offered to pay into the royal treasury for the de-

8 struction of the Jews. He also gave him a copy of the writ for their destruction issued in Susa, so that he might show it to Esther and tell her about it, bidding her go to the king to plead for his favour and entreat

9 him for her people. Hathach went and told Esther what Mordecai had said,

10 and she sent him back with this

11 message: 'All the king's courtiers and the people of the provinces are aware that if any person, man or woman, enters the king's presence in the inner court unbidden, there is one law only: that person shall be put to death, unless the king stretches out to him the golden sceptre; then and

then only shall he live. It is now thirty days since I myself was called to go to the king.' But when they told 12 Mordecai what Esther had said, he 13 bade them go back to her and say, 'Do not imagine that you alone of all the Jews will escape because you are in the royal palace. If you remain 14 silent at such a time as this, relief and deliverance for the Jews will appear from another quarter, but you and your father's family will perish. Who knows whether it is not for such a time as this that you have come to royal estate?' Esther gave them this 15 answer to take back to Mordecai: 'Go 16 and assemble all the Jews to be found in Susa and fast for me; take neither food nor drink for three days, night or day, and I and my maids will fast as you do. After that I will go to the king, although it is against the law; and if I perish, I perish.' So Mordecai 17 went away and did exactly as Esther had bidden him.

Esther invites the king and Haman to a banquet

On the third day Esther put on her 5 royal robes and stood in the inner court of the king's palace, facing the palace itself; the king was seated on his royal throne in the palace, facing the entrance. When the king caught 2 sight of Queen Esther standing in the court, she won his favour and he stretched out to her the golden sceptre which he was holding. Thereupon Esther approached and touched the head of the sceptre. Then the king 3 said to her, 'What is it, Queen Esther? Whatever you ask of me, up to half my kingdom, shall be given to you.' 'If it please your majesty,' said 4 Esther, 'will you come today, sire, and Haman with you, to a banquet which I have made ready for you?' The king gave orders that Haman 5 should be fetched quickly, so that Esther's wish might be fulfilled; and the king and Haman went to the banquet which she had prepared. Over the wine the king said to Esther, 6 'Whatever you ask of me shall be given to you. Whatever you request of me, up to half my kingdom, it shall be done.' Esther said in answer, 7 'What I ask and request of you is this. If I have won your majesty's 8 favour, and if it please you, sire, to give me what I ask and to grant my request, will your majesty and Haman come tomorrow to the banquet which

I shall prepare for you both? Tomorrow I will do as your majesty has said.'

Haman sets up gallows for Mordecai

9 So Haman went away that day in good spirits and well pleased with himself. But when he saw Mordecai in attendance at court and how he did not rise nor defer to him, he was filled 10 with rage; but he kept control of himself and went home. Then he sent 11 for his friends and his wife Zeresh and held forth to them about the splendour of his wealth and his many sons, and how the king had promoted him and advanced him above the other 12 officers and courtiers. 'That is not all,' said Haman; 'Queen Esther invited no one but myself to accompany the king to the banquet which she had prepared; and she has invited me again 13 tomorrow with the king. Yet all this means nothing to me so long as I see that Jew Mordecai in attendance at 14 court.' Then his wife Zeresh and all his friends said to him, 'Let a gallows seventy-five feet high be set up, and recommend to the king in the morning to have Mordecai hanged upon it. Then go with the king to the banquet in good spirits.' Haman thought this an excellent plan, and he set up the gallows.

The king honours Mordecai

6 That night sleep eluded the king, so he ordered the chronicle of daily events to be brought; and it was read 2 to him. Therein was recorded that Mordecai had given information about Bigthana and Teresh, the two royal eunuchs among the keepers of the threshold who had plotted to lay 3 hands on King Ahasuerus. Whereupon the king said, 'What honour or dignity has been conferred on Mordecai for this?' The king's courtiers who were in attendance told him that nothing had been done for Mordecai. 4 The king asked, 'Who is that in the court?' Now Haman had just entered the outer court of the palace to recommend to the king that Mordecai should be hanged on the gallows 5 which he had prepared for him. The king's servants answered, 'It is Haman standing there'; and the king 6 bade him enter. He came in, and the king said to him, 'What should be done for the man whom the king wishes to honour?' Haman said to himself, 'Whom would the king wish 7 to honour more than me?' And he said to the king, 'For the man whom

the king wishes to honour, let there 8 be brought royal robes which the king himself wears, and a horse which the king rides, with a royal crown upon its head. And let the robes and 9 the horse be delivered to one of the king's most honourable officers, and let him attire the man whom the king wishes to honour and lead him mounted on the horse through the city square, calling out as he goes: "See what is done for the man whom the king wishes to honour."' Then 10 the king said to Haman, 'Fetch the robes and the horse at once, as you have said, and do all this for Mordecai the Jew who is in attendance at court. Leave nothing undone of all that you have said.' So Haman took the robes 11 and the horse, attired Mordecai, and led him mounted through the city square, calling out as he went: 'See what is done for the man whom the king wishes to honour.'

Then Mordecai returned to court 12 and Haman hurried off home mourning, with head uncovered. He told his 13 wife Zeresh and all his friends everything that had happened to him. And this was the reply of his friends and his wife Zeresh: 'If Mordecai, in face of whom your fortunes begin to fall, belongs to the Jewish race, you will not get the better of him; he will see your utter downfall.'

The king executes Haman

While they were still talking with 14 Haman, the king's eunuchs arrived and hurried him away to the banquet which Esther had prepared.

So the king and Haman went to 7 dine with Queen Esther. Again on 2 that second day, over the wine, the king said, 'Whatever you ask of me will be given to you, Queen Esther. Whatever you request of me, up to half my kingdom, it shall be done.' Queen Esther answered, 'If I have 3 found favour with your majesty, and if it please your majesty, my request and petition is that my own life and the lives of my people may be spared. For we have been sold, I and my 4 people, to be destroyed, slain, and exterminated. If it had been a matter of selling us, men and women alike, into slavery, I should have kept silence; for then our plight would not be such as to injure the king's interests.' Then 5 King Ahasuerus said to Queen Esther, 'Who is he, and where is he, who has presumed to do such a thing as this?' 'An adversary and an enemy,' said 6

Esther, 'this wicked Haman.' At that Haman was dumbfounded in the presence of the king and the queen. 7 The king rose from the banquet in a rage and went to the garden of the pavilion, while Haman remained where he was, to plead for his life with Queen Esther; for he saw that in the king's mind his fate was deter- 8 mined. When the king returned from the garden to the banqueting hall, Haman had flung himself across the couch on which Esther was reclining. The king exclaimed, 'Will he even assault the queen here in my presence?' No sooner had the words left the king's mouth than Haman hid his 9 face in despair.*f* Then Harbona, one of the eunuchs in attendance on the king, said, 'At Haman's house stands the gallows, seventy-five feet high, which he himself has prepared for Mordecai, who once served the king well.' 'Hang Haman on it', said the 10 king. So they hanged him on the gallows that he himself had prepared for Mordecai. After that the king's rage abated.

Esther pleads for the Jews

8 On that day King Ahasuerus gave Queen Esther the house of Haman, enemy of the Jews; and Mordecai came into the king's presence, for Esther had told him how he was 2 related to her. Then the king took off his signet-ring, which he had taken back from Haman, and gave it to Mordecai. And Esther put Mordecai in charge of Haman's house.
3 Once again Esther spoke before the king, falling at his feet in tears and pleading with him to avert the cala- mity planned by Haman the Agagite and to frustrate his plot against 4 the Jews. The king stretched out the golden sceptre to Esther, and she 5 rose and stood before the king, and said, 'May it please your majesty: if I have found favour with you, and if the proposal seems right to your majesty and I have won your approval, let a writ be issued to recall the letters which Haman son of Hammedatha the Agagite wrote in pursuance of his plan to destroy the Jews in all the 6 royal provinces. For how can I bear to see the calamity which is coming upon my race? Or how can I bear to see the destruction of my family?' 7 Then King Ahasuerus said to Queen Esther and to Mordecai the Jew, 'I have given Haman's house to Esther,

and he has been hanged on the gallows, because he threatened the lives of the Jews. Now you shall issue a writ 8 concerning the Jews in my name, in whatever terms you think fit, and seal it with the royal signet; for an order written in the name of the king and sealed with the royal signet can- not be revoked.'

The king issues a favourable decree

And so, on the twenty-third day of the 9 third month, the month Sivan, the king's secretaries were summoned; and a writ was issued to the Jews, exactly as Mordecai directed, and to the sat- raps, the governors, and the officers in the provinces from India to Ethio- pia, a hundred and twenty-seven provinces, for each province in its own script and for each people in their own language, and also for the Jews in their own script and language. The writ was drawn up in the name of 10 King Ahasuerus, and sealed with the royal signet, and letters were sent by mounted couriers riding on horses from the royal stables. By these 11 letters the king granted permission to the Jews in every city to unite and defend themselves, and to de- stroy, slay, and exterminate the whole strength of any people or province which might attack them, women and children too, and to plunder their possessions, throughout all the pro- 12 vinces of King Ahasuerus, in one day, the thirteenth day of the twelfth month, the month Adar. A copy of 13 the writ was to be issued as a decree in every province and published to all peoples, and the Jews were to be ready for that day, the day of vengeance on their enemies. So the 14 couriers, mounted on their royal hor- ses, were dispatched post-haste at the king's urgent command; and the decree was issued also in Susa the capital city.

Mordecai left the king's presence 15 in royal robes of violet and white, wearing a great golden crown and a cloak of fine linen and purple, and all the city of Susa shouted for joy. For 16 the Jews there was light and joy, gladness and honour. In every pro- 17 vince and every city reached by the royal command and decree, there was joy and gladness for the Jews, feasting and holiday. And many of the peoples of the land professed themselves Jews, because fear of the Jews had seized them.

f Haman . . . despair: *prob. rdg.*; *Heb.* they covered Haman's face.

The Jews destroy their enemies

9 On the thirteenth day of the twelfth month, the month Adar, the time came for the king's command and his edict to be carried out. The very day on which the enemies of the Jews had hoped to gain the upper hand over them was to become the day when the Jews should gain the upper hand over **2** those who hated them. On that day the Jews united in their cities in all the provinces of King Ahasuerus to fall upon those who had planned their ruin. No one could resist them, because fear of them had seized all **3** peoples. All the officers of the provinces, the satraps and the governors, and all the royal officials, aided the Jews, because fear of Mordecai **4** had seized them. Mordecai had become a great personage in the royal palace; his fame had spread throughout all the provinces as the power of the man grew steadily greater. **5** So the Jews put their enemies to the sword, with great slaughter and destruction; they worked their will on **6** those who hated them. In Susa, the capital city, the Jews killed five hundred men and destroyed them; **7** and they killed also Parshandatha, **8** Dalphon and Aspatha, Poratha, Ada- **9** lia and Aridatha, Parmashta, Arisai, **10** Aridai and Vaizatha, the ten sons of Haman son of Hammedatha, the enemy of the Jews; but they did not touch the plunder.

11 That day when the number of those killed in Susa the capital city came to **12** the notice of the king, he said to Queen Esther, 'In Susa, the capital city, the Jews have killed and destroyed five hundred men and the ten sons of Haman. What have they done in the rest of the king's provinces? Whatever you ask further will be given to you; whatever more you **13** seek shall be done.' Esther answered him, 'If it please your majesty, let tomorrow be granted to the Jews in Susa to do according to the edict for today; and let the bodies of Haman's ten sons be hung up on the gallows.' **14** The king gave orders for this to be done; the edict was issued in Susa and Haman's ten sons were hung up on **15** the gallows. The Jews in Susa united again on the fourteenth day of the month Adar and killed three hundred men in Susa; but they did not touch the plunder;

16 The rest of the Jews in the king's provinces had united to defend themselves; they took vengeance on[g] their enemies by killing seventy-five thousand of those who hated them; but they did not touch the plunder. This **17** was on the thirteenth day of the month Adar, and they rested on the fourteenth day and made that a day of feasting and joy. The Jews in Susa **18** had united on the thirteenth and fourteenth days of the month, and rested on the fifteenth day and made that a day of feasting and joy. This is **19** why isolated Jews who live in remote villages keep the fourteenth day of the month Adar in joy and feasting, as a holiday on which they send presents of food to one another.

The feast of Purim

Then Mordecai set these things on **20** record and sent letters to all the Jews in all the provinces of King Ahasuerus, far and near, binding them to **21** keep the fourteenth and fifteenth days of the month Adar, year by year, as **22** the days on which the Jews obtained relief from their enemies and as the month which was changed for them from sorrow into joy, from a time of mourning to a holiday. They were to keep them as days of feasting and joy, days for sending presents of food to one another and gifts to the poor.

So the Jews undertook to continue **23** the practice that they had begun in accordance with Mordecai's letter. This they did because Haman son of **24** Hammedatha the Agagite, the enemy of all the Jews, had plotted to destroy the Jews and had cast lots, Pur as it is called, with intent to crush and destroy them. But when the mat- **25** ter came before the king, he issued written orders that the wicked plot which Haman had devised against the Jews should recoil on his own head, and that he and his sons should be hanged on the gallows. Therefore, **26** these days were named Purim after the word Pur. Accordingly, because of all that was written in this letter, because of all they had seen and experienced in this affair, the Jews **27** resolved and undertook, on behalf of themselves, their descendants, and all who should join them, that they would without fail keep these two days as a yearly festival in the prescribed manner and at the appointed time; that **28** these days should be remembered and kept, generation after generation, in every family, province, and city,

---

g *Prob. rdg.; Heb.* got respite from.

that the days of Purim should always be observed among the Jews, and that the memory of them should never cease among their descendants.

29 Queen Esther daughter of Abihail gave full authority in writing to[h] Mordecai the Jew, to confirm this 30 second letter about Purim. Letters wishing peace and security were sent to all the Jews in the hundred and twenty-seven provinces of King A- 31 hasuerus, making the observance of these days of Purim at their appointed time binding on them, as Mordecai the Jew[i] had prescribed. In the same way they had prescribed regulations for fasts and lamentations for themselves and their descendants.

The command of Esther confirmed 32 these regulations for Purim, and the record is preserved in writing.

Other records concerning Mordecai

King Ahasuerus imposed forced la- **10** bour on the land and the coasts and islands. All the king's acts of au- **2** thority and power, and the dignities which he conferred on Mordecai, are written in the annals of the kings of Media and Persia. For Mordecai the **3** Jew was second only to King Ahasuerus; he was a great man among the Jews and was popular with the mass of his countrymen, for he sought the good of his people and promoted the welfare of all their descendants.[j]

h Prob. rdg.; Heb. and relations with all his race.   i Prob. rdg.; Heb. adds and Queen Esther.   j Or and was in friendly

THE BOOK OF
JOB

Prologue

1 THERE LIVED in the land of Uz a man of blameless and upright life named Job, who feared God and set 2 his face against wrongdoing. He had 3 seven sons and three daughters; and he owned seven thousand sheep and three thousand camels, five hundred yoke of oxen and five hundred asses, with a large number of slaves. Thus Job was the greatest man in all the East.

4 Now his sons used to foregather and give, each in turn, a feast in his own house; and they used to send and invite their three sisters to eat and 5 drink with them. Then, when a round of feasts was finished, Job sent for his children and sanctified them, rising early in the morning and sacrificing a whole-offering for each of them; for he thought that they might somehow have sinned against God and committed blasphemy in their hearts. This he always did.

The court of heaven

6 The day came when the members of the court of heaven took their places

in the presence of the LORD, and Satan[a] was there among them. The 7 LORD asked him where he had been. 'Ranging over the earth', he said, 'from end to end.' Then the LORD 8 asked Satan, 'Have you considered my servant Job? You will find no one like him on earth, a man of blameless and upright life, who fears God and sets his face against wrongdoing.' Satan answered the LORD, 'Has not 9 Job good reason to be God-fearing? Have you not hedged him round on 10 every side with your protection, him and his family and all his possessions? Whatever he does you have blessed, and his herds have increased beyond measure. But stretch out your hand 11 and touch all that he has, and then he will curse you to your face.' Then 12 the LORD said to Satan, 'So be it. All that he has is in your hands; only Job himself you must not touch.' And Satan left the LORD's presence.

Job's great loss

When the day came that Job's sons 13 and daughters were eating and drinking in the eldest brother's house, a 14 messenger came running to Job and

a Or the adversary.

said, 'The oxen were ploughing and the asses were grazing near them, 15 when the Sabaeans swooped down and carried them off, after putting the herdsmen to the sword; and I am the only one to escape and tell the tale.' 16 While he was still speaking, another messenger arrived and said, 'God's fire flashed from heaven. It struck the sheep and the shepherds and burnt them up; and I am the only one to 17 escape and tell the tale.' While he was still speaking, another arrived and said, 'The Chaldaeans, three bands of them, have made a raid on the camels and carried them off, after putting the drivers to the sword; and I am the only one to escape and tell the 18 tale.' While this man was speaking, yet another arrived and said, 'Your sons and daughters were eating and drinking in the eldest brother's house, 19 when suddenly a whirlwind swept across from the desert and struck the four corners of the house, and it fell on the young people and killed them; and I am the only one to 20 escape and tell the tale.' At this Job stood up and rent his cloak; then he shaved his head and fell prostrate on 21 the ground saying:

Naked I came from the womb,
naked I shall return whence I came.
The LORD gives and the LORD takes away;
blessed be the name of the LORD.

22 Throughout all this Job did not sin; he did not charge God with unreason.

Job's personal affliction

2 Once again the day came when the members of the court of heaven took their places in the presence of the LORD, and Satan was there among 2 them. The LORD asked him where he had been. 'Ranging over the earth', 3 he said, 'from end to end.' Then the LORD asked Satan, 'Have you considered my servant Job? You will find no one like him on earth, a man of blameless and upright life, who fears God and sets his face against wrongdoing. You incited me to ruin him without a cause, but his integrity 4 is still unshaken.' Satan answered the LORD, 'Skin for skin! There is nothing the man will grudge to save himself. 5 But stretch out your hand and touch his bone and his flesh, and see if he will not curse you to your face.' 6 Then the LORD said to Satan, 'So be it. He is in your hands; but spare 7 his life.' And Satan left the LORD's presence, and he smote Job with running sores from head to foot, so that 8 he took a piece of a broken pot to scratch himself as he sat among the ashes. Then his wife said to him, 'Are 9 you still unshaken in your integrity? Curse God and die!' But he answered, 10 'You talk as any wicked fool of a woman might talk. If we accept good from God, shall we not accept evil?' Throughout all this, Job did not utter one sinful word.

Job's friends sympathize

When Job's three friends, Eliphaz of 11 Teman, Bildad of Shuah, and Zophar of Naamah, heard of all these calamities which had overtaken him, they left their homes and arranged to come and condole with him and comfort him. But when they first saw him 12 from a distance, they did not recognize him; and they wept aloud, rent their cloaks and tossed dust into the air over their heads. For seven days 13 and seven nights they sat beside him on the ground, and none of them said a word to him; for they saw that his suffering was very great.

Job bewails his plight

After this Job broke silence and **3** 1 cursed the day of his birth:

Perish the day when I was born 3
and the night which said, 'A man is conceived'!
May that day turn to darkness; may 4
God above not look for it,
nor light of dawn shine on it.
May blackness sully it, and murk and 5
gloom,
cloud smother that day, swift darkness eclipse its sun.
Blind darkness swallow up that 6
night;
count it not among the days of the year,
reckon it not in the cycle of the months.
That night, may it be barren for ever, 7
no cry of joy be heard in it.
Cursed be it by those whose magic 8
binds even the monster of the deep,
who are ready to tame Leviathan himself with spells.
May no star shine out in its twilight; 9
may it wait for a dawn that never comes,
nor ever see the eyelids of the morning,
because it did not shut the doors of 10
the womb that bore me
and keep trouble away from my sight.

11 Why was I not still-born,
why did I not die when I came out of
the womb?
12 Why was I ever laid on my mother's
knees
or put to suck at her breasts?
16 Why was I not hidden like an untimely birth,
like an infant that has not lived to see
the light?
13 For then I should be lying in the
quiet grave,
asleep in death, at rest,
14 with kings and their ministers
who built themselves palaces,
15 with princes rich in gold
who filled their houses with silver.
17^b There the wicked man chafes no more,
there the tired labourer rests;
18 the captive too finds peace there
and hears no taskmaster's voice;
19 high and low are there,
even the slave, free from his master.

20 Why should the sufferer be born to
see the light?
Why is life given to men who find it so
bitter?
21 They wait for death but it does not
come,
they seek it more eagerly than^c hidden
treasure.
22 They are glad when they reach the
tomb,
and when they come to the grave they
exult.
23 Why should a man be born to wander
blindly,
hedged in by God on every side?
24 My sighing is all my food,
and groans pour from me in a torrent.
25 Every terror that haunted me has
caught up with me,
and all that I feared has come upon me.
26 There is no peace of mind nor quiet
for me;
I chafe in torment and have no rest.

First speech of Eliphaz

4 Then Eliphaz the Temanite began:

2 If one ventures to speak with you, will
you lose patience?
For who could hold his tongue any
longer?
3 Think how once you encouraged
those who faltered,
how you braced feeble arms,
4 how a word from you upheld the
stumblers
and put strength into weak knees.

But now that adversity comes upon 5
you, you lose patience;
it touches you, and you are unmanned.
Is your religion no comfort to you? 6
Does your blameless life give you no
hope?
For consider, what innocent man has 7
ever perished?
Where have you seen the upright
destroyed?
This I know, that those who plough 8
mischief and sow trouble
reap as they have sown;
they perish at the blast of God 9
and are shrivelled by the breath of his
nostrils.

The roar of the lion, the whimpering 10
of his cubs, fall silent;
the teeth of the young lions are broken;
the lion perishes for lack of prey 11
and the whelps of the lioness are
abandoned.

A word stole into my ears, 12
and they caught the whisper of it;
in the anxious visions of the night, 13
when a man sinks into deepest sleep,
terror seized me and shuddering; 14
the trembling of my body frightened me
A wind brushed my face 15
and made the hairs bristle on my
flesh;
and a figure stood there whose shape 16
I could not discern,
an apparition loomed before me,
and I heard the sound of a low voice:
'Can mortal man be more righteous 17
than God,
or the creature purer than his Maker?
If God mistrusts his own servants 18
and finds his messengers at fault,
how much more those that dwell in 19
houses whose walls are clay,
whose foundations are dust,
which can be crushed like a bird's nest
or torn down between dawn and dark, 20
how much more shall such men perish
outright and unheeded,
^ddie, without ever finding wisdom?' 21

Call if you will; is there any to answer 5
you?
To which of the holy ones will you
turn?
The fool is destroyed by his own 2
angry passions,
and the end of childish resentment is
death.
I have seen it for myself: a fool up- 3
rooted,

b Verse 16 transposed to follow verse 12. *c Or seek it among . . .* *d Prob. rdg.; transposing*
Their rich possessions are snatched from them *to follow 5. 4.*

his home in sudden ruin about him,[e]
4 his children past help,
  browbeaten in court with none to save
    them.
5 [f]Their rich possessions are snatched
    from them;
  what they have harvested others
    hungrily devour;
  the stronger man seizes it from the
    panniers,
  panting, thirsting for their wealth.
6 Mischief does not grow out of the soil
  nor trouble spring from the earth;
7 man is born to trouble,
  as surely as birds fly[g] upwards.

8 For my part, I would make my peti-
    tion to God
  and lay my cause before him,
9 who does great and unsearchable
    things,
  marvels without number.
10 He gives rain to the earth
  and sends water on the fields;
11 he raises the lowly to the heights,
  the mourners are uplifted by victory;
12 he frustrates the plots of the crafty,
  and they win no success,
13 he traps the cunning in their crafti-
    ness,
  and the schemers' plans are thrown
    into confusion.
14 In the daylight they run into darkness,
  and grope at midday as though it were
    night.
15 He saves the destitute from their
    greed,
  and the needy from the grip of the
    strong;
16 so the poor hope again,
  and the unjust are sickened.

17 Happy the man whom God rebukes!
  therefore do not reject the discipline
    of the Almighty.
18 For, though he wounds, he will bind
    up;
  the hands that smite will heal.
19 You may meet disaster six times, and
    he will save you;
  seven times, and no harm shall touch
    you.
20 In time of famine he will save you
    from death,
  in battle from the sword.
21 You will be shielded from the lash of
    slander,[h]
  and when violence comes you need
    not fear.
22 You will laugh at violence and starva-
    tion

and have no need to fear wild beasts;
for you have a covenant with the 23
  stones to spare your fields,
and the weeds have been constrained
  to leave you at peace.
You will know that all is well with 24
  your household,
you will look round your home and
  find nothing amiss;
you will know, too, that your descen- 25
  dants will be many
and your offspring like grass, thick
  upon the earth.
You will come in sturdy old age to the 26
  grave
as sheaves come in due season to the
  threshing-floor.

We have inquired into all this, and so 27
  it is;
this we have heard, and you may know
  it for the truth.

Job's reply

Then Job answered: 6

O that the grounds for my resentment 2
  might be weighed,
and my misfortunes set with them on
  the scales!
For they would outweigh the sands of 3
  the sea:
what wonder if my words are wild?[i]
The arrows of the Almighty find their 4
  mark in me,
and their poison soaks into my spirit;
God's onslaughts wear me away.
Does the wild ass bray when he has 5
  grass
or the ox low when he has fodder?
Can a man eat tasteless food un- 6
  seasoned with salt,
or find any flavour in the juice of
  mallows?
Food that should nourish me sticks in 7
  my throat,
and my bowels rumble with an
  echoing sound.

O that I might have my request,   8
that God would grant what I hope for:
that he would be pleased to crush me, 9
to snatch me away with his hand and
  cut me off!
For that would bring me relief,   10
and in the face of unsparing anguish I
  would leap for joy.[j]
Have I the strength to wait?   11
What end have I to expect, that I
  should be patient?
Is my strength the strength of stone, 12
or is my flesh bronze?

---

e ruin about him: *prob. rdg.; Heb. obscure.*   f *Line transposed from 4. 21.*   g *Or as sparks shoot.*
h from . . . slander: *or when slander is rife.*   i what . . . wild?: *or therefore words fail me.*
j *Prob. rdg.; Heb. adds* I have not denied the words of the Holy One.

13 Oh how shall I find help within myself?
The power to aid myself is put out of
my reach.

14 Devotion is due from his friends
to one who despairs and loses faith in
the Almighty;

15 but my brothers have been treacherous as a mountain stream,
like the channels of streams that run
dry,

16 which turn dark with ice
or are hidden with piled-up snow;

17 or they vanish the moment they are
in spate,
dwindle in the heat and are gone.

18 Then the caravans, winding hither
and thither,
go up into the wilderness and perish;[k]

19 the caravans of Tema look for their
waters,
travelling merchants of Sheba hope
for them;

20 but they are disappointed, for all
their confidence,
they reach them only to be balked.

21 So treacherous have you now been to
me:[l]
you felt dismay and were afraid.

22 Did I ever say, 'Give me this or that;
open your purses to save my life;

23 rescue me from my enemy;
ransom me out of the hands of ruthless
men'?

24 Tell me plainly, and I will listen in
silence;
show me where I have erred.

25 How harsh are the words of the upright man!
What do the arguments of wise men[m]
prove?

26 Do you mean to argue about words
or to sift the utterance of a man past
hope?

27 Would you assail an orphan[n]?
Would you hurl yourselves on a
friend?

28 So now, I beg you, turn and look at me:
am I likely to lie to your faces?

29 Think again, let me have no more
injustice;
think again, for my integrity is in
question.

30 Do I ever give voice to injustice?
Does my sense not warn me when my
words are wild?

7 Has not man hard service on earth,

and are not his days like those of a
hired labourer,
like those of a slave longing for the 2
shade
or a servant kept waiting for his
wages?
So months of futility are my portion, 3
troubled nights are my lot.
When I lie down, I think, 4
'When will it be day that I may rise?'
When the evening grows long and I
lie down,
I do nothing but toss till morning
twilight.
My body is infested with worms, 5
and scabs cover my skin.[o]
My days are swifter than a shuttle[p] 6
and come to an end as the thread runs
out.[q]

Remember, my life is but a breath of 7
wind;
I shall never again see good days.
Thou wilt behold me no more with a 8
seeing eye;
under thy very eyes I shall disappear.
As clouds break up and disperse, 9
so he that goes down to Sheol never
comes back;
he never returns home again, 10
and his place will know him no more.[r]

But I will not hold my peace; 11
I will speak out in the distress of my
mind
and complain in the bitterness of my
soul.
Am I the monster of the deep, am I 12
the sea-serpent,
that thou settest a watch over me?
When I think that my bed will com- 13
fort me,
that sleep will relieve my complaining,
thou dost terrify me with dreams 14
and affright me with visions.
I would rather be choked outright; 15
I would prefer death to all my sufferings.
I am in despair, I would not go on 16
living;
leave me alone, for my life is but a
vapour.
What is man that thou makest much 17
of him
and turnest thy thoughts towards
him,
only to punish him morning by morn- 18
ing
or to test him every hour of the day?
Wilt thou not look away from me for 19
an instant?

k Or and are lost.   l So . . . to me: prob. rdg.; Heb. obscure.   m wise men: prob. rdg.; Heb. unintelligible.   n Or a blameless man.   o Prob. rdg.; Heb. adds it is cracked and discharging.
p Or a fleeting odour.   q as . . . out: or without hope.   r Or and he will not be noticed any
more in his place.

Wilt thou not let me be while I swallow my spittle?

20 If I have sinned, how do I injure thee,
thou watcher of the hearts of men?
Why hast thou made me thy butt,
and why have I become thy target?

21 Why dost thou not pardon my offence
and take away my guilt?
But now I shall lie down in the grave;
seek me, and I shall not be.

First speech of Bildad

8 Then Bildad the Shuhite began:

2 How long will you say such things,
the long-winded ramblings of an old man?

3 Does God pervert judgement?
Does the Almighty pervert justice?

4 Your sons sinned against him,
so he left them to be victims of their own iniquity.

5 If only you will seek God betimes
and plead for the favour of the Almighty,

6 if you are innocent and upright,
then indeed will he watch over you
and see your just intent fulfilled.

7 Then, though your beginnings were humble,
your end will be great.

8 Inquire now of older generations
and consider the experience of their fathers;

9 for we ourselves are of yesterday and are transient;
our days on earth are a shadow.

10 Will not they speak to you and teach you
and pour out the wisdom of their hearts?

11 Can rushes grow where there is no marsh?
Can reeds flourish without water?

12 While they are still in flower and not ready to cut,^{s}
they wither earlier than^t any green plant.

13 Such is the fate of all who forget God;
the godless man's life-thread breaks off;

14 his confidence is gossamer,
and the ground of his trust a spider's web.

15 He leans against his house but it does not stand;
he clutches at it but it does not hold firm.

16 His is the lush growth of a plant in the sun,
pushing out shoots over the garden;

17 but its roots become entangled in a stony patch
and run against a bed of rock.

18 Then someone uproots it from its place,
which^u disowns it and says, 'I have never known you.'

19 That is how its life withers away,
and other plants spring up from the earth.

20 Be sure, God will not spurn the blameless man,
nor will he grasp the hand of the wrongdoer.

21 He will yet fill your mouth with laughter,
and shouts of joy will be on your lips;

22 your enemies shall be wrapped in confusion,
and the tents of the wicked shall vanish away.

Job's reply

Then Job answered: 9

2 Indeed this I know for the truth,
that no man can win his case against God.

3 If a man chooses to argue with him,
God will not answer one question in a thousand.^{v}

4 He is wise, he is powerful;
what man has stubbornly resisted him and survived?

5 It is God who moves mountains,
giving them no rest,
turning them over in his wrath;

6 who makes the earth start from its place
so that its pillars are convulsed;

7 who commands the sun's orb not to rise
and shuts up the stars under his seal;

8 who by himself spread out the heavens
and trod on the sea-monster's back;^{w}

9 who made Aldebaran and Orion,
the Pleiades and the circle of the southern stars;

10 who does great and unsearchable things,
marvels without number.

11 He passes by me, and I do not see him;
he moves on his way undiscerned by me;

12 if he hurries on, who can bring him back?
Who will ask him what he does?

13 God does not turn back his wrath;
the partisans of Rahab lie prostrate at his feet.

s and ... cut: *or* they are surely cut.   t *Or* wither like ...   u *Or* and.   v *If a man* ...
thousand: *or* If God is pleased to argue with him, man cannot answer one question in a thousand.
w *Or* on the crests of the waves.

14 How much less can I answer him
or find words to dispute with him?
15 Though I am right, I get no answer,
though I plead with my accuser for
mercy.
16 If I summoned him to court and he
responded,
I do not believe that he would listen
to my plea—
17 for he bears hard upon me for a
trifle
and rains blows on me without cause;
18 he leaves me no respite to recover my
breath
but fills me with bitter thoughts.
19 If the appeal is to force, see how strong
he is;
if to justice, who can compel him to
give me a hearing?
20 Though I am right, he condemns me
out of my own mouth;
though I am blameless, he twists my
words.
21 Blameless, I say; of myself
I reck nothing, I hold my life cheap.
22 But it is all one; therefore I say,
'He destroys blameless and wicked
alike.'
23 When a sudden flood brings death,
he mocks the plight of the innocent.
24 The land is given over to the power of
the wicked,
and the eyes of its judges are blind-
fold.*x*

25 My days have been swifter than a
runner,
they have slipped away and seen no
prosperity;
26 they have raced by like reed-built
skiffs,
swift as vultures swooping on carrion.
27 If I think, 'I will forget my griefs,
I will show a cheerful face and smile',
28 I tremble in every nerve;*y*
I know that thou wilt not hold me
innocent.
29 If I am to be accounted guilty,
why do I labour in vain?
30 Though I wash myself with soap
or cleanse my hands with lye,
31 thou wilt thrust me into the mud
and my clothes will make me loathsome.

32 He is not a man as I am, that I can
answer him
or that we can confront one another in
court.
33 If only there were one to arbitrate
between us
and impose his authority on us both,

so that God might take his rod from 34
my back,
and terror of him might not come on
me suddenly.
I would then speak without fear of 35
him;
for I know I am not what I am thought
to be.

I am sickened of life;   **10**
I will give free rein to my griefs,
I will speak out in bitterness of soul.
I will say to God, 'Do not condemn me, 2
but tell me the ground of thy complaint against me.
Dost thou find any advantage in 3
oppression,
in spurning the fruit of all thy labour
and smiling on the policy of wicked
men?
Hast thou eyes of flesh   4
or dost thou see as mortal man sees?
Are thy days as those of a mortal   5
or thy years as the life of a man,
that thou lookest for guilt in me   6
and dost seek in me for sin,
though thou knowest that I am 7
guiltless
and have none to save me from thee?

'Thy hands gave me shape and made 8
me;
and dost thou at once turn and destroy me?
Remember that thou didst knead me 9
like clay;
and wouldst thou turn me back into
dust?
Didst thou not pour me out like milk 10
and curdle me like cheese,
clothe me with skin and flesh   11
and knit me together with bones and
sinews?
Thou hast given me life and continu- 12
ing favour,
and thy providence has watched over
my spirit.
Yet this was the secret purpose of thy 13
heart,
and I know that this was thy intent:
that, if I sinned, thou wouldst be 14
watching me
and wouldst not acquit me of my
guilt.
If I indeed am wicked, the worse for 15
me!
If I am righteous, even so I may lift
up my head;*z*
if I am proud as a lion, thou dost hunt 16
me down
and dost confront me again with
marvellous power;

*x Prob. rdg.; Heb. adds if not he, then who?   y Or I am afraid of all that I must suffer.   z Prob.
rdg.; Heb. adds filled with shame and steeped in my affliction.*

17 thou dost renew thy onslaught upon me,
and with mounting anger against me
bringest fresh forces to the attack.
18 Why didst thou bring me out of the
womb?
O that I had ended there and no eye
had seen me,
19 that I had been carried from the womb
to the grave
and were as though I had not been
born.
20 Is not my life short and fleeting?
Let me be, that I may be happy for a
moment,
21 before I depart to a land of gloom,
a land of deep darkness, never to
return,
22 a land of gathering shadows, of deepen-
ing darkness,
lit by no ray of light,^{a} dark^b upon
dark.'

First speech of Zophar

11 Then Zophar the Naamathite began:

2 Should this spate of words not be
answered?
Must a man of ready tongue be always
right?
3 Is your endless talk to reduce men to
silence?
Are you to talk nonsense and no one
rebuke you?
4 You claim that your opinions are
sound;
you say to God, 'I am spotless in thy
sight.'
5 But if only he would speak
and open his lips to talk with you,
6 and expound to you the secrets of
wisdom,
for wonderful are its effects!
[Know then that God exacts from you
less than your sin deserves.]
7 Can you fathom the mystery of God,
can you fathom the perfection of the
Almighty?
8 It is higher than heaven; you can do
nothing.
It is deeper than Sheol; you can know
nothing.
9 Its measure is longer than the earth
and broader than the sea.
10 If he passes by, he may keep secret
his passing;
if he proclaims it, who can turn him
back?
11 He surely knows which men are false,
and when he sees iniquity, does he not
take note of it?^{c}

Can a fool grow wise?   12
can a wild ass's foal be born a man?
If only you had directed your heart 13
rightly
and spread out your hands to pray to
him!
If you have wrongdoing in hand, 14
thrust it away;
let no iniquity make its home with you.
Then you could hold up your head 15
without fault,
a man of iron, knowing no fear.
Then you will forget your trouble;   16
you will remember it only as flood-
waters that have passed;
life will be lasting, bright as noonday, 17
and darkness will be turned to morning.
You will be confident, because there is 18
hope;
sure of protection, you will lie down
in confidence;^{d}
great men will seek your favour.   19
Blindness will fall on the wicked;   20
the ways of escape are closed to them,
and their hope is despair.

Job's reply

Then Job answered: 12

No doubt you are perfect men^e 2
and absolute wisdom is yours!
But I have sense as well as you;   3
in nothing do I fall short of you;
what gifts indeed have you that others
have not?
Yet I am a laughing-stock to my 4
friend—
a laughing-stock, though I am innocent and blameless,
one that called upon God, and he
answered.^{f}
Prosperity and ease look down on mis- 5
fortune,
on the blow that fells the man who is
already reeling,
while the marauders' tents are left 6
undisturbed
and those who provoke God live safe
and sound.^{g}

Go and ask the cattle,   7
ask the birds of the air to inform you,
or tell the creatures that crawl to 8
teach you,
and the fishes of the sea to give you
instruction
Who cannot learn from all these   9
that the LORD's own hand has done
this?

---

a lit . . . light: *or* a place of disorder. b *Prob. rdg.; Heb.* obscure. c does . . . of it?: *or* he does
not stand aloof. d *Prob. rdg.; Heb. adds* and you will lie down unafraid. e *Prob. rdg.; Heb.*
No doubt you are people. f *Or* and he afflicted me. g *Prob. rdg.; Heb. adds* He brings it in
full measure to whom he will (*cp. 21. 17*).

¶1[h] (Does not the ear test what is spoken
  as the palate savours food?
12 There is wisdom, remember, in age,
   and long life brings understanding.)

10 In God's hand are the souls of all that
   live,
   the spirits of all human kind.
13 Wisdom and might are his,
   with him are firmness and understanding.
14 If he pulls down, there is no rebuilding;
   if he imprisons, there is no release.
15 If he holds up the waters, there is
   drought;
   if he lets them go, they turn the land
   upside down.
16 Strength and success belong to him,
   deceived and deceiver are his to use.
17 He makes counsellors behave like
   idiots
   and drives judges mad;
18 he looses the bonds imposed by kings
   and removes the girdle of office from
   their waists;
19 he makes priests behave like idiots
   and overthrows men long in office;
20 those who are trusted he strikes dumb,
   he takes away the judgement of old
   men;
21 he heaps scorn on princes
   and abates the arrogance of nobles.
23[i] He leads peoples astray and destroys
   them,
   he lays them low, and there they lie.
24 He takes away their wisdom from the
   rulers of the nations
   and leaves them wandering in a path-
   less wilderness;
25 they grope in the darkness without
   light
   and are left to wander like a drunkard.
22 He uncovers mysteries deep in obscurity
   and into thick darkness he brings
   light.

13 All this I have seen with my own eyes,
   with my own ears I have heard it, and
   understood it.
2 What you know, I also know;
   in nothing do I fall short of you.
3 But for my part I would speak with
   the Almighty
   and am ready to argue with God,
4 while you like fools are smearing
   truth with your falsehoods,
   stitching a patchwork of lies, one and
   all.
5 Ah, if you would only be silent

and let silence be your wisdom!
Now listen to my arguments   6
and attend while I put my case.
Is it on God's behalf that you speak 7
   so wickedly,
or in his defence that you allege what
   is false?
Must you take God's part,   8
or put his case for him?
Will all be well when he examines you? 9
Will you quibble with him as you
   quibble with a man?
He will most surely expose you   10
if you take his part by falsely accusing
   me.
Will not God's majesty strike you 11
   with dread,
and terror of him overwhelm you?
Your pompous talk is dust and ashes, 12
your defences will crumble like clay.
Be silent, leave me to speak my mind, 13
and let what may come upon me!
I will put my neck in the noose   14
and take my life in my hands.
If he would slay me, I should not 15
   hesitate;
I should still argue my cause to his
   face.
This at least assures my success, 16
that no godless man may appear
   before him.
Listen then, listen to my words,   17
and give a hearing to my exposition.
Be sure of this: once I have stated 18
   my case
I know that I shall be acquitted.
Who is there that can argue so forcibly 19
   with me
that he could reduce me straightway
   to silence and death?

Grant me these two conditions only, 20
and then I will not hide myself out of
   thy sight:
take thy heavy hand clean away from 21
   me
and let not the fear of thee strike me
   with dread.
Then summon me, and I will answer; 22
or I will speak first, and do thou
   answer me.
How many iniquities and sins are 23
   laid to my charge?
let me know my offences and my sin.
Why dost thou hide thy face   24
and treat me as thy enemy?
Wilt thou chase a driven leaf,   25
wilt thou pursue dry chaff,
prescribing punishment for me   26
and making me heir to the iniquities
   of my youth,
putting my feet in the stocks[j]   27

h *Verse 10 transposed to follow verse 12.*   i *Verse 22 transposed to follow verse 25.*   j *Prob. rdg.;*
Heb. adds keeping a close watch on all I do.

and setting a slave-mark on the arches of my feet?[k]

14 Man born of woman is short-lived and full of disquiet.

2 He blossoms like a flower and then he withers;
he slips away like a shadow and does not stay;
[l]he is like a wine-skin that perishes or a garment that moths have eaten.

3 Dost thou fix thine eyes on such a creature,
and wilt thou bring him into court to confront thee?[m]

5 The days of his life are determined, and the number of his months is known to thee;
thou hast laid down a limit, which he cannot pass.

6 Look away from him therefore and leave him alone
counting the hours day by day like a hired labourer.

7 If a tree is cut down,
there is hope that it will sprout again and fresh shoots will not fail.

8 Though its roots grow old in the earth, and its stump is dying in the ground,

9 if it scents water it may break into bud
and make new growth like a young plant.

10 But a man dies, and he disappears;[n]
man comes to his end, and where is he?

11 As the waters of a lake dwindle,
or as a river shrinks and runs dry,

12 so mortal man lies down, never to rise until the very sky splits open.
If a man dies, can he live again?[o]
He shall never be roused from his sleep.

13 If only thou wouldst hide me in Sheol and conceal me till thy anger turns aside,
if thou wouldst fix a limit for my time there, and then remember me!

14 [p]Then I would not lose hope, however long my service,
waiting for my relief to come.

15 Thou wouldst summon me, and I would answer thee;
thou wouldst long to see the creature thou hast made.

16 But now thou dost count every step I take,
watching all my course.

Every offence of mine is stored in thy 17 bag;
thou dost keep my iniquity under seal.

Yet as a falling mountain-side is 18 swept away,
and a rock is dislodged from its place, as water wears away stones, 19
and a rain-storm scours the soil from the land,
so thou hast wiped out the hope of frail man;
thou dost overpower him finally, and 20 he is gone;
his face is changed, and he is banished from thy sight.

His flesh upon him becomes black, 22[q] and his life-blood dries up within him.[r]
His sons rise to honour, and he sees 21 nothing of it;
they sink into obscurity, and he knows it not.

Second speech of Eliphaz

Then Eliphaz the Temanite answered: **15**

Would a man of sense give vent to 2 such foolish notions
and answer with a bellyful of wind?
Would he bandy useless words 3
and arguments so unprofitable?
Why! you even banish the fear of God 4 from your mind,
usurping the sole right to speak in his presence;
your iniquity dictates what you say, 5
and deceit is the language of your choice.

You are condemned out of your own 6 mouth, not by me;
your own lips give evidence against you.

Were you born first of mankind? 7
were you brought forth before the hills?
Do you listen in God's secret council 8
or usurp all wisdom for yourself alone?
What do you know that we do not 9 know?
What insight have you that we do not share?

We have age and white hairs in our 10 company,
men older than your father.

Does not the consolation of God suffice 11 you,
a word whispered quietly in your ear?
What makes you so bold at heart, 12
and why do your eyes flash,
that you vent your anger on God 13

k *Prob. rdg.; Heb. adds verse 28,* he is like ... have eaten, *now transposed to follow 14. 2.* l he is like ... have eaten: *13. 28 transposed here.* m *So one Heb. MS.; others add* (4) Who can produce pure out of unclean? No one. n *Or* and is powerless. o *Line transposed from beginning of verse 14.* p *See note on verse 12.* q *Verses 21 and 22 transposed.* r His flesh ... within him: *or* His own kin, maybe, regret him, and his slaves mourn his loss.

and pour out such a torrent of words?
4 What is frail man that he should be
innocent,
or any child of woman that he should
be justified?
5 If God puts no trust in his holy ones,
and the heavens are not innocent in
his sight,
6 how much less so is man, who is
loathsome and rotten
and laps up evil like water!

7 I will tell you, if only you will listen,
and I will describe what I have seen
8 [what has been handed down by wise
men
and was not concealed from them by
their fathers;
9 to them alone the land was given,
and no foreigner settled among them]:
10 the wicked are racked with anxiety
all their days,
the ruthless man for all the years in
store for him.
11 The noise of the hunter's scare rings
in his ears,
and in time of peace the raider falls on
him;
12 he cannot hope to escape from dark
death;
he is marked down for the sword;
13 he is flung out as food for vultures;
such a man knows that his destruction is certain.
14 Suddenly a black day comes upon him,
distress and anxiety overwhelm him
[like a king ready for battle];
15 for he has lifted his hand against God
and is pitting himself against the
Almighty,
16 charging him head down,
with the full weight of his bossed
shield.

27 Heavy though his jowl is and gross,
and though his sides bulge with fat,
28 the city where he lives will lie in ruins,
his house will be deserted;
it will soon become a heap of rubble.
29 He will no longer be rich, his wealth
will not last,
and he will strike no root in the earth;[s]
30 scorching heat will shrivel his shoots,
and his blossom will be shaken off by
the wind.
31 He deceives himself, trusting in his
high rank,
for all his dealings will come to nothing.
32 His palm-trees will wither unseason-
ably,
and his branches will not spread;
33 he will be like a vine that sheds its
unripe grapes,

like an olive-tree that drops its
blossom.
34 For the godless, one and all, are barren,
and their homes, enriched by bribery,
are destroyed by fire;
35 they conceive mischief and give birth
to trouble,
and the child of their womb is deceit.

Job's reply
Then Job answered: **16**
I have heard such things often before, 2
you who make trouble, all of you, with
every breath,
saying, 'Will this windbag never have 3
done?
What makes him so stubborn in
argument?'
If you and I were to change places,   4
I could talk like you;
how I could harangue you
and wag my head at you!
But no, I would speak words of 5
encouragement,
and then my condolences would flow
in streams.
If I speak, my pain is not eased;   6
if I am silent, it does not leave me.
Meanwhile, my friend wearies me with 7
false sympathy;
they tear me to pieces, he and his[t] 8
fellows.
He has come forward to give evidence
against me;
the liar testifies against me to my face,
in his wrath he wears me down, his 9
hatred is plain to see;
he grinds his teeth at me.

My enemies look daggers at me,
they bare their teeth to rend me,   10
they slash my cheeks with knives;
they are all in league against me.
God has left me at the mercy of 11
malefactors
and cast me into the clutches of
wicked men.
I was at ease, but he set upon me and 12
mauled me,
seized me by the neck and worried me.
He set me up as his target;
his arrows rained upon me from every 13
side;
pitiless, he cut deep into my vitals,
he spilt my gall on the ground.
He made breach after breach in my 14
defences;
he fell upon me like a fighting man.

I stitched sackcloth together to cover 15
my body
and I buried my forelock in the dust;

s Prob. rdg.; Heb. adds he will not escape from darkness.   *t Prob. rdg.; Heb.* my.

16 my cheeks were flushed with weeping
  and dark shadows were round my eyes,
17 yet my hands were free from violence
  and my prayer was sincere.

18 O earth, cover not my blood
  and let my cry for justice find no rest!
19 For look! my witness is in heaven;
  there is one on high ready to answer
    for me.
20 My appeal will come before God,
  while my eyes turn again and again to
    him.
21 If only there were one to arbitrate
    between man and God,
  as between a man and his neighbour!
22 For there are but few years to come
  before I take the road from which I
    shall not return.

17 My mind is distraught, my days are
    numbered,
  and the grave is waiting for me.
2 Wherever I turn, men taunt me,
  and my day is darkened by their
    sneers.
3 Be thou my surety with thyself,
  for who else can pledge himself for me?
4 Thou wilt not let those men triumph,
  whose minds thou hast sunk in
    ignorance;
5 if such a man denounces his friends to
    their ruin,
  his sons' eyes shall grow dim.

6 I am held up as a byword in every
    land,
  a portent for all to see;
7 my eyes are dim with grief,
  my limbs wasted to a shadow.
8 Honest men are bewildered at this,
  and the innocent are indignant at my
    plight.
9 In spite of all, the righteous man
    maintains his course,
  and he whose hands are clean grows
    strong again.

10 But come on, one and all, try again!
  I shall not find a wise man among you.
11 My days die away like an echo;
  my heart-strings*u* are snapped.
12 Day is turned into night,
  and morning*v* light is darkened before
    me.
13 If I measure Sheol for my house,
  if I spread my couch in the darkness,
14 if I call the grave my father
  and the worm my mother or my
    sister,
15 where, then, will my hope be,
  and who will take account of my piety?

I cannot take them down to Sheol 16
    with me,
  nor can they descend with me into the
    earth.

Second speech of Bildad
Then Bildad the Shuhite answered: 1
How soon will you bridle*w* your 2
    tongue?
  Do but think, and then we will talk.
What do you mean by treating us as 3
    cattle?
  Are we nothing but brute beasts to
    you?*x*
Is the earth to be deserted to prove 4
    you right,
  or the rocks to be moved from their
    place?

No, it is the wicked whose light is 5
    extinguished,
  from whose fire no flame will rekindle;
the light fades in his tent, 6
  and his lamp dies down and fails him.
In his iniquity his steps totter, 7
  and his disobedience trips him up;
he rushes headlong into a net 8
  and steps through the hurdle that
    covers a pit;
his heel is caught in a snare, 9
  the noose grips him tight;
a cord lies hidden in the ground for 10
    him
  and a trap in the path.
The terrors of death suddenly beset 11
    him
  and make him piss over his feet.
For all his vigour he is paralysed with 12
    fear;
  strong as he is, disaster awaits him.
Disease eats away his skin, 13
  Death's eldest child devours his limbs.
He is torn from the safety of his 14
    home,
  and Death's terrors escort him to
    their king.*y*
Magic herbs lie strewn about his tent, 15
  and his home is sprinkled with sulphur
    to protect it.
His roots beneath dry up, 16
  and above, his branches wither.
His memory vanishes from the face of 17
    the earth
  and he leaves no name in the world.
He is driven from light into darkness 18
  and banished from the land of the
    living.
He leaves no issue or offspring among 19
    his people,
  no survivor in his earthly home;

u Prob. rdg.; Heb. the desires of my heart.   *v* morning: prob. rdg.; Heb. near.   *w* bridle: prob.
rdg.; Heb. unintelligible.   *x* Prob. rdg.; Heb. adds rending himself in his anger.   *y* Or and you
conduct him to the king of terrors.

20 in the west men hear of his doom and
    are appalled;
  in the east they shudder with horror.
21 Such is the fate of the dwellings of
    evildoers,
  and of the homes of those who care
    nothing for God.

Job's reply

19 Then Job answered:

2 How long will you exhaust me
  and pulverize me with words?
3 Time and time again you have insul-
    ted me
  and shamelessly done me wrong.
4 If in fact I had erred,
  the error would still be mine.
5 But if indeed you lord it over me
  and try to justify the reproaches
    levelled at me,
6 I tell you, God himself has put me in
    the wrong,
  he has drawn the net round me.
7 If I cry 'Murder!' no one answers;
  if I appeal for help, I get no justice.
8 He has walled in my path so that I
    cannot break away,
  and he has hedged in the road before
    me.
9 He has stripped me of all honour
  and has taken the crown from my
    head.
10 On every side he beats me down and
    I am gone;
  he has pulled up my tent-rope^z like a
    tree.
11 His anger is hot against me
  and he counts me his enemy.
12 His raiders gather in force^a
  and encamp about my tent.
13 My brothers hold aloof from me,
  my friends are utterly estranged from
    me;
15 my kinsmen and intimates fall away,
  my retainers have forgotten me;
  my slave-girls treat me as a stranger,
  I have become an alien in their eyes.
16 I summon my slave, but he does not
    answer,
  though I entreat him as a favour.
17 My breath is noisome to my wife,
  and I stink in the nostrils of my own
    family.
18 Mere children despise me
  and, when I rise, turn their backs on
    me;
19 my intimate companions loathe me,
  and those whom I love have turned
    against me.
20 My bones stick out through my skin,^{b}

and I gnaw my under-lip with my
  teeth.

Pity me, pity me, you that are my 21
  friends;
for the hand of God has touched me.
Why do you pursue me as God pur- 22
  sues me?
Have you not had your teeth in me
  long enough?
O that my words might be inscribed, 23
O that they might be engraved in an
  inscription,
cut with an iron tool and filled with 24
  lead
to be a witness^c in hard rock!
But in my heart I know that my 25
  vindicator lives
and that he will rise last to speak in
  court;
and I shall discern my witness stand- 26
  ing at my side^d
and see my defending counsel, even
  God himself,
whom I shall see with my own eyes, 27
I myself and no other.

My heart failed me when you said,   28
'What a train of disaster he has
  brought on himself!
The root of the trouble lies in him.'
Beware of the sword that points at 29
  you,
the sword that sweeps away all
  iniquity;
then you will know that there is a
  judge.^{e}

Second speech of Zophar

Then Zophar the Naamathite an- **20**
swered:

My distress of mind forces me to reply, 2
  and this is why^f I hasten to speak:
I have heard arguments that are a 3
  reproach to me,
a spirit beyond my understanding
  gives me the answers.
Surely you know that this has been so 4
  since time began,
since man was first set on the earth:
the triumph of the wicked is short- 5
  lived,
the glee of the godless lasts but a
  moment?
Though he stands high as heaven,   6
  and his head touches the clouds,
he will be swept utterly away like his 7
  own dung,
and all that saw him will say, 'Where
  is he?'

z Or he has uprooted my hope. a *Prob. rdg.*; *Heb. adds* they raise an earthwork against me.
b *Prob. rdg.*; *Heb. adds* and my flesh. c to . . . witness: *or* for ever. d my witness . . . side:
prob. rdg.; *Heb. unintelligible.* e Or judgement. f this is why: *prob. rdg.*; *Heb. obscure.*

8 He will fly away like a dream and be
　lost,
　driven off like a vision of the night;
9 the eye which glimpsed him shall do
　so no more
　and shall never again see him in his
　place.
11*g* The youth and strength which filled
　his bones
　shall lie with him in the dust.
10 His sons will pay court to the poor,
　and their*h* hands will give back his
　wealth.
12 Though evil tastes sweet in his
　mouth,
　and he savours it, rolling it round his
　tongue,
13 though he lingers over it and will not
　let it go,
　and holds it back on his palate,
14 yet his food turns in his stomach,
　changing to asps' venom within him.
15 He gulps down wealth, then vomits it
　up,
　or God makes him discharge it.
16 He sucks the poison of asps,
　and the tongue of the viper kills him.
17 Not for him to swill down rivers of
　cream*i*
　or torrents of honey and curds;
18 he must give back his gains without
　swallowing them,
　and spew up his profit undigested;
19 for he has hounded and harassed the
　poor,
　he has seized houses which he did not
　build.
20 Because his appetite gave him no rest,
　and he cannot escape his own desires,
21 nothing is left for him to eat,
　and so his well-being does not last;
22 with every need satisfied his troubles
　begin,
　and the full force of hardship strikes
　him.
23 God vents his anger upon him
　and rains on him cruel blows.
24 He is wounded by weapons of iron
　and pierced by a bronze-tipped arrow;
25 out at his back the point comes,
　the gleaming tip from his gall-bladder.
26 Darkness unrelieved awaits him,
　a fire that needs no fanning will con-
　sume him.
　[Woe betide any survivor in his tent!]
27 The heavens will lay bare his guilt,
　and earth will rise up to condemn him.
28 A flood will sweep away his house,
　rushing waters on the day of wrath.
29 Such is God's reward for the wicked
　man

and the lot appointed for the rebel*j*
　by God.

Job's reply

Then Job answered:　　　　　　　**21**

Listen to me, do but listen,　　　2
and let that be the comfort you offer
　me.
Bear with me while I have my say;　3
when I have finished, you may mock.
May not I too voice*k* my thoughts?　4
Have not I as good cause to be im-
　patient?
Look at my plight, and be aghast;　5
clap your hand to your mouth.
When I stop to think, I am filled with 6
　horror,
and my whole body is convulsed.

Why do the wicked enjoy long life,　7
hale in old age, and great and power-
　ful?
They live to see their children settled, 8
their kinsfolk and descendants flourish-
　ing;
their families are secure and safe;　9
the rod of God's justice does not
　reach them.
Their bull mounts and fails not of its 10
　purpose;
their cow calves and does not miscarry.
Their children like lambs run out to 11
　play,
and their little ones skip and dance;
they rejoice with tambourine and harp 12
and make merry to the sound of the
　flute.
Their lives close in prosperity,　　13
and they go down to Sheol in peace.
To God they say, 'Leave us alone;　14
we do not want to know your ways.
What is the Almighty that we should 15
　worship him,
or what should we gain by seeking his
　favour?'

Is not the prosperity of the wicked in 16
　their own hands?
Are not their purposes very different
　from God's*l*?
How often is the lamp of the wicked 17
　snuffed out,
and how often does their ruin come
　upon them?
How often does God in his anger deal
　out suffering,
bringing it in full measure to whom
　he will?*m*
How often is that man like a wisp of 18
　straw before the wind,

*g Verses 10 and 11 transposed.　h Prob. rdg.; Heb. his.　i rivers of cream: prob. rdg.; Heb. ob-
scure.　j the rebel: prob. rdg.; Heb. his word.　k May . . . voice: prob. rdg.; Heb. obscure.
l God's: prob. rdg.; Heb. mine.　m Line transposed from 12. 6.*

like chaff which the storm-wind
whirls away?

19 You say, 'The trouble he has earned,
God will keep for his sons';
no, let him be paid for it in full and be
punished.

20 Let his own eyes see damnation come
upon him,
and the wrath of the Almighty be the
cup he drinks.

21 What joy shall he have in his children
after him,
if his very months and days are
numbered?

22 Can any man teach God,
God who judges even those in heaven
above?

23 One man, I tell you, dies crowned with
success,
lapped in security and comfort,

24 his loins full of vigour
and the marrow juicy in his bones;

25 another dies in bitterness of soul
and never tastes prosperity;

26 side by side they are laid in earth,
and worms are the shroud of both.

27 I know well what you are thinking
and the arguments you are marshall-
ing against me;

28 I know you will ask, 'Where is the
great man's home now,
what has become of the home of the
wicked?'

29 Have you never questioned travellers?
Can you not learn from the signs they
offer,

30 that the wicked is spared when disaster comes
and conveyed to safety before the day
of wrath?

31 No one denounces his conduct to his
face,
no one requites him for what he has
done.

2-3 When he is carried to the grave,
all the world escorts him, before and
behind;
the dust of earth is sweet to him,
and thousands keep watch at his
tomb.

34 How futile, then, is the comfort you
offer me!
How false your answers ring!

Third speech of Eliphaz

22 Then Eliphaz the Temanite answered:

2 Can man be any benefit to God?
Can even a wise man benefit him?

3 Is it an asset to the Almighty if you
are righteous?
Does he gain if your conduct is perfect?

Do not think that he reproves you 4
because you are pious,
that on this count he brings you to
trial.

No: it is because you are a very wicked 5
man,
and your depravity passes all bounds.

Without due cause you take a brother 6
in pledge,
you strip men of their clothes and
leave them naked.

When a man is weary, you give him no 7
water to drink
and you refuse bread to the hungry.

Is the earth, then, the preserve of the 8
strong
and a domain for the favoured few?

Widows you have sent away empty- 9
handed,
orphans you have struck defenceless.

No wonder that there are pitfalls in 10
your path,
that scares are set to fill you with
sudden fear.

The light is turned into darkness, and 11
you cannot see;
the flood-waters cover you.

Surely God is at the zenith of the 12
heavens
and looks down on all the stars, high
as they are.

But you say, 'What does God know? 13
Can he see through thick darkness to
judge?

His eyes cannot pierce the curtain of 14
the clouds
as he walks to and fro on the vault of
heaven.'

Consider the course of the wicked man, 15
the path the miscreant treads:

see how they are carried off before 16
their time,
their very foundation flowing away
like a river;

these men said to God, 'Leave us 17
alone;
what can the Almighty do to us?'

Yet it was he that filled their houses 18
with good things,
although their purposes and his were
very different.

The righteous see their fate and exult, 19
the innocent make game of them;

for their riches are swept away,   20
and the profusion of their wealth is
destroyed by fire.

Come to terms with God and you will 21
prosper;
that is the way to mend your fortune.

Take instruction from his mouth   22
and store his words in your heart.

If you come back to the Almighty in 23
true sincerity,

if you banish wrongdoing from your
home,

24 if you treat your precious metal as
dust[n]
and the gold of Ophir as stones from
the river-bed,

25 then the Almighty himself will be your
precious metal;
he will be your silver in double
measure.

26 Then, with sure trust in[o] the Almighty,
you will raise your face to God;

27 you will pray to him, and he will hear
you,
and you will have cause to fulfil your
vows.

28 In all your designs you will succeed,
and light will shine on your path;

29 but God brings down the pride of the
haughty[p]
and keeps safe the man of modest
looks.

30 He will deliver the innocent,[q]
and you will be delivered, because
your hands are clean.

Job's reply

23 Then Job answered:

2 My thoughts today are resentful,
for God's hand is heavy on me in my
trouble.

3 If only I knew how to find him,
how to enter his court,

4 I would state my case before him
and set out my arguments in full;

5 then I should learn what answer he
would give
and find out what he had to say.

6 Would he exert his great power to
browbeat me?
No; God himself would never bring a
charge against me.

7 There the upright are vindicated before him,
and I shall win from my judge an
absolute discharge.

8 If I go forward,[r] he is not there;
if backward,[s] I cannot find him;

9 when I turn[t] left,[u] I do not descry him;
I face right,[v] but I see him not.

10 But he knows me in action or at rest;
when he tests me, I prove to be gold.

11 My feet have kept to the path he has
set me,
I have followed his way and not
turned from it.

I do not ignore the commands that 12
come from his lips,
I have stored in my heart what he
says.

He decides,[w] and who can turn him 13
from his purpose?
He does what his own heart desires.

What he determines, that he carries 14
out;
his mind is full of plans like these.

Therefore I am fearful of meeting him; 15
when I think about him,[x] I am afraid;

it is God who makes me faint-hearted 16
and the Almighty who fills me with
fear,

yet I am not reduced to silence by the 17
darkness
nor[y] by the mystery which hides him.

[z] The day of reckoning is no secret to 24
the Almighty,
though those who know him have no
hint of its date.

Wicked men move boundary-stones 2
and carry away flocks and their
shepherds.

In the field they reap what is not theirs, 6[a]
and filch the late grapes from the
rich[b] man's vineyard.

They drive off the orphan's ass 3
and lead away the widow's ox with a
rope.

They snatch the fatherless infant from 9
the breast
and take the poor man's child in
pledge.

They jostle the poor out of the way; 4
the destitute huddle together, hiding
from them.

The poor rise early like the wild ass, 5
when it scours the wilderness for food;
but though they work till nightfall,[c]
their children go hungry.[d]

Naked and bare they pass the night; 7
in the cold they have nothing to cover
them.

They are drenched by rain-storms 8
from the hills
and hug the rock, their only shelter.

Naked and bare they go about their 10
work,
and hungry they carry the sheaves;

they press the oil in the shade where 11
two walls meet,
they tread the winepress but themselves go thirsty.

Far from the city, they groan like 12
dying men,

---

n *Prob. rdg.; Heb.* if you put your precious metal on dust.
p but . . . haughty: *prob. rdg.; Heb.* obscure.
s Or west.   t *Prob. rdg.; Heb.* he turns.   u Or north.
rdg.; *Heb.* He in one.   x when . . . him: *or* I stand aloof.
I am . . . and . . .   z *Prob. rdg.; Heb. prefixes* Why.
natural order.   b Or wicked.   c *Prob. rdg.; Heb.* Arabah.
food.

o with . . . in: *or* delighting in.
q *Prob. rdg.; Heb.* the not innocent.   r Or east.
v Or south.   w He decides: *prob.*
y yet I am not . . . nor: *or* indeed
a *Verses 3–9 re-arranged to restore the*
d go hungry: *prob. rdg.; Heb.* to it

and like wounded men they cry out;
but God pays no heed to their prayer.
13 Some there are who rebel against the
light of day,
who know nothing of its ways
and do not linger in the paths of light.
14 The murderer rises before daylight
to kill some miserable wretch.[e]
15 The seducer watches eagerly for twilight,
thinking, 'No eye will catch sight of
me.'
The thief prowls[f] by night,[g]
his face covered with a mask,
16 and in the darkness breaks into
houses
which he has marked down in the day.
One and all,[h] they are strangers to the
daylight,
17 but dark night is morning to them;
and in the welter of night they are at
home.
18 Such men are scum on the surface of
the water;
their fields have a bad name throughout the land,
and no labourer will go near their
vineyards.
19 As drought and heat make away with
snow,
so the waters of Sheol[i] make away
with the sinner.
20 The womb forgets him, the worm
sucks him dry;
he will not be remembered ever after.[j]
21 He may have wronged the barren
childless woman
and been no help to the widow;
22 yet God in his strength carries off even
the mighty;
they may rise, but they have no firm
hope of life.
23 He lulls them into security and confidence;
but his eyes are fixed on their ways.
24 For a moment they rise to the heights,
but are soon gone;
iniquity is snapped like a stick.[k]
They are laid low and wilt like a
mallow-flower;
they droop like an ear of corn on the
stalk.
25 If this is not so, who will prove me
wrong
and make nonsense of my argument?

Third speech of Bildad

5 Then Bildad the Shuhite answered:

Authority and awe rest with him   2
who has established peace in his
realm on high.
His squadrons are without number;   3
at whom will they not spring from
ambush?
How then can a man be justified in   4
God's sight,
or one born of woman be innocent?
If the circling moon is found wanting, 5
and the stars are not innocent in his
eyes,
much more so man who is but a   6
maggot,
mortal man who is only a worm.

Job's reply

Then Job answered: 26

What help you have given to the man 2
without resource,
what deliverance you have brought
to the powerless!
What counsel you offer to a man at   3
his wit's end,
what sound advice to the foolish!
Who has prompted you to say such   4
things,
and whose spirit is expressed in your
speech?

In the underworld the shades writhe 5
in fear,
the waters and all that live in them
are struck with terror.[l]
Sheol is laid bare,   6
and Abaddon uncovered before him.
God spreads the canopy of the sky   7
over chaos
and suspends earth in the void.
He keeps the waters penned in dense 8
cloud-masses,
and the clouds do not burst open
under their weight.
He covers the face of the full moon,[m] 9
unrolling his clouds across it.
He has fixed the horizon on the sur- 10
face of the waters
at the farthest limit of light and darkness.
The pillars of heaven quake   11
and are aghast at his rebuke.
With his strong arm he cleft the sea- 12
monster,
and struck down the Rahab by his
skill.
At his breath the skies are clear,   13
and his hand breaks the twisting[n]
sea-serpent.

---

e *See note on verse 15.*   f *The thief prowls: prob. rdg.; Heb.* Let him be like a thief.   g *Line transposed from end of verse 14.*   h *One and all: transposed from after* but *in next verse.*   i *snow . . . Sheol: prob. rdg.; Heb.* snow-water, Sheol.   j *Prob. rdg.; Heb. here adds* iniquity is snapped like a stick *(see note on verse 24).*   k *Line transposed from end of verse 20.*   l *are struck with terror: prob. rdg.; Heb. om.*   m *Or* He overlays the surface of his throne.   n *Or* primeval.

14 These are but the fringe of his power;
and how faint the whisper that we
hear of him!
[Who could fathom the thunder of
his might?]

27 Then Job resumed his discourse:

2 I swear by God, who has denied me
justice,
and by the Almighty, who has filled
me with bitterness:

3 so long as there is any life left in me
and God's breath is in my nostrils,

4 no untrue word shall pass my lips
and my tongue shall utter no falsehood.

5 God forbid that I should allow you to
be right;
till death, I will not abandon my
claim to innocence.

6 I will maintain the rightness of my
cause, I will never give up;
so long as I live, I will not change.

7 May my enemy meet the fate of the
wicked,
and my antagonist the doom of the
wrongdoer!

8 What hope has a godless man, when
he is cut off,[o]
when God takes away his life?

9 Will God listen to his cry
when trouble overtakes him?

10 Will he trust himself to the Almighty
and call upon God at all times?

11 I will teach you what is in God's
power,
I will not conceal the purpose of the
Almighty.

12 If all of you have seen these things,
why then do you talk such empty
nonsense?

13 This is the lot prescribed by God for
the wicked,
and the ruthless man's reward from
the Almighty.

14 He may have many sons, but they
will fall by the sword,
and his offspring will go hungry;

15 the survivors will be brought to the
grave by pestilence,
and no widows will weep for them.

16 He may heap up silver like dirt
and get himself piles of clothes;

17 he may get them, but the righteous
will wear them,
and his silver will be shared among
the innocent.

The house he builds is flimsy as a bird's **18**
nest
or a shelter put up by a watchman.

He may lie down rich one day, but **19**
never again;
he opens his eyes and all is gone.

Disaster overtakes him like a flood, **20**
and a storm snatches him away in the
night;

the east wind lifts him up and he is **21**
gone;
it whirls him far from home;

it flings itself on him without mercy, **22**
and he is battered and buffeted by its
force;

it snaps its fingers at him **23**
and whistles over him wherever he
may be.

God's unfathomable wisdom

There are mines for silver **28**
and places where men refine gold;

where iron is won from the earth **2**
and copper smelted from the ore;

the end of the seam lies in darkness, **3**
and it is followed to its farthest limit.[p]

Strangers cut the galleries;[q] **4**
they are forgotten as they drive forward far from men.[r]

While corn is springing from the earth **5**
above,
what lies beneath is raked over like a
fire,

and out of its rocks comes lapis lazuli, **6**
dusted with flecks of gold.

No bird of prey knows the way there, **7**
and the falcon's keen eye cannot descry it;

proud beasts do not set foot on it, **8**
and no serpent comes that way.

Man sets his hand to the granite rock **9**
and lays bare the roots of the mountains;

he cuts galleries in the rocks, **10**
and gems of every kind meet his eye;

he dams up the sources of the streams **11**
and brings the hidden riches of the
earth to light.

But where can wisdom be found? **12**
And where is the source of understanding?

No man knows the way to it; **13**
it is not found in the land of living men.

The depths of ocean say, 'It is not in us', **14**
and the sea says, 'It is not with me.'

Red gold cannot buy it, **15**
nor can its price be weighed out in
silver;

it cannot be set in the scales against **16**
gold of Ophir,
against precious cornelian or lapis lazuli;

o Or What is a godless man's thread of life when it is cut . . .   *p* Prob. rdg.; Heb. adds stones of
darkness and deep darkness.   *q* Strangers . . . galleries: prob. rdg.; Heb. obscure.   *r* Prob. rdg.;
Heb. adds languishing without foothold.

17 gold and crystal are not to be matched
   with it,
  no work in fine gold can be bartered
   for it;
18 black coral and alabaster are not
   worth mention,
  and a parcel of wisdom fetches more
   than red coral;
19 topaz[s] from Ethiopia is not to be
   matched with it,
  it cannot be set in the scales against
   pure gold.
20 Where then does wisdom come from,
  and where is the source of understanding?
21 No creature on earth can see it,
  and it is hidden from the birds of the
   air.
22 Destruction and death say,
   'We know of it only by report.'
23 But God understands the way to it,
  he alone knows its source;
24 for he can see to the ends of the earth
  and he surveys everything under
   heaven.
25 When he made a counterpoise for the
   wind
  and measured out the waters in proportion,
26 when he laid down a limit for the rain
  and a path for the thunderstorm,
27 even then he saw wisdom and took
   stock of it,
  he considered it and fathomed its very
   depths.
28 And he said to man:
    The fear of the Lord is wisdom,
    and to turn from evil is under-
    standing.

Job's final plea

29 Then Job resumed his discourse:
2 If I could only go back to the old days,
  to the time when God was watching
   over me,
3 when his lamp shone above my head,
  and by its light I walked through the
   darkness!
4 If I could be as in the days of my
   prime,
  when God protected my home,
5 while the Almighty was still there at
   my side,
  and my servants stood round me,
6 while my path flowed with milk,
  and the rocks streamed oil!
7 If I went through the gate out of the
   town
  to take my seat in the public square,
8 young men saw me and kept out of
   sight;

old men rose to their feet,
9 men in authority broke off their talk
  and put their hands to their lips;
10 the voices of the nobles died away,
  and every man held his tongue.
21[t] They listened to me expectantly
  and waited in silence for my opinion.
22 When I had spoken, no one spoke
   again;
  my words fell gently on them;
23 they waited for them as for rain
  and drank them in like showers in
   spring.
24 When I smiled on them, they took
   heart;
  when my face lit up, they lost their
   gloomy looks.
25 I presided over them, planning their
   course,
  like a king encamped with his troops.[u]

11 Whoever heard of me spoke in my
   favour,
  and those who saw me bore witness
   to my merit,
12 how I saved the poor man when he
   called for help
  and the orphan who had no protector.
13 The man threatened with ruin blessed
   me,
  and I made the widow's heart sing for
   joy.
14 I put on righteousness as a garment
   and it clothed me;
  justice, like a cloak or a turban, wrapped me round.
15 I was eyes to the blind
  and feet to the lame;
16 I was a father to the needy,
  and I took up the stranger's cause.
17 I broke the fangs of the miscreant
  and rescued the prey from his teeth.
18 I thought, 'I shall die with my powers
   unimpaired
  and my days uncounted as the grains
   of sand,[v]
19 with my roots spreading out to the
   water
  and the dew lying on my branches,
20 with the bow always new in my
   grasp
  and the arrow ever ready to my hand.'[w]

30 But now I am laughed to scorn
  by men of a younger generation,
  men whose fathers I would have disdained
  to put with the dogs who kept my
   flock.
2 What use were their strong arms to
   me,
  since their sturdy vigour had wasted
   away?

s Or chrysolite.   *t Verses 21–5 transposed to this point.*   *u Prob. rdg.;* Heb. adds *as when one*
comforts mourners.   *v Or as those of the phoenix.*   *w Verses 21–5 transposed to follow verse 10.*

H

3 They gnawed roots^x in the desert,
gaunt with want and hunger,^{y}
4 they plucked saltwort and wormwood
and root of broom^z for their food.
5 Driven out from the society of men,^{a}
pursued like thieves with hue and cry,
6 they lived in gullies and ravines,
holes in the earth and rocky clefts;
7 they howled like beasts among the
bushes,
huddled together beneath the scrub,
8 vile base-born wretches,
hounded from the haunts of men.
9 Now I have become the target of their
taunts,
my name is a byword among them.
10 They loathe me, they shrink from me,
they dare to spit in my face.
11 They run wild and savage^b me;
at sight of me they throw off all
restraint.
12 On my right flank they attack in a
mob;^{c}
they raise their siege-ramps against
me,
13 they tear down my crumbling defences
to my undoing,
and scramble up against me unhin-
dered;
14 they burst in through the gaping
breach;
at the moment of the crash they come
rolling in.
15 Terror upon terror overwhelms me,
it sweeps away my resolution like the
wind,
and my hope of victory vanishes like
a cloud.
16 So now my soul is in turmoil within
me,
and misery has me daily in its grip.
17 By night pain pierces my very bones,
and there is ceaseless throbbing in my
veins;
18 my garments are all bespattered with
my phlegm,
which chokes me like the collar of a
shirt.
19 God himself^d has flung me down in
the mud,
no better than dust or ashes.

20 I call for thy help, but thou dost not
answer;
I stand up to plead, but thou sittest
aloof;
21 thou hast turned cruelly against me
and with thy strong hand pursuest me
in hatred;

thou dost snatch me up and set me 22
astride the wind,
and the tempest^e tosses me up and
down.
I know that thou wilt hand me over to 23
death,
to the place appointed for all mortal
men.

Yet no beggar held out his hand 24
but was relieved^f by me in his distress.
Did I not weep for the man whose life 25
was hard?
Did not my heart grieve for the poor?
Evil has come though I expected good; 26
I looked for light but there came darkness.
My bowels are in ferment and know no 27
peace;
days of misery stretch out before me.
I go about dejected and friendless; 28
I rise in the assembly, only to appeal
for help.
The wolf is now my brother, 29
the owls of the desert have become my
companions.
My blackened skin peels off, 30
and my body is scorched by the heat.
My harp has been tuned for a dirge, 31
my flute to the voice of those who
weep.

What is the lot prescribed by God 31
above,
the reward from the Almighty on high?
Is not ruin prescribed for the mis- 3
creant
and calamity for the wrongdoer?
Yet does not God himself see my ways 4
and count my every step?

I swear I have had no dealings with 5
falsehood
and have not embarked on a course of
deceit.
I have come to terms with my eyes, 1
never to take notice of a girl.
Let God weigh me in the scales of 6
justice,
and he will know that I am innocent!
If my steps have wandered from the 7
way,
if my heart has followed my eyes,
or any dirt stuck to my hands,
may another eat what I sow, 8
and may my crops be pulled up by
the roots!
If my heart has been enticed by a 9
woman

x roots: prob. rdg.; Heb. om.   y Prob. rdg.; Heb. adds yesterday waste and derelict land.   z root
of broom: probably fungus on broom root.   a the society of men: prob. rdg.; Heb. obscure.
b They run . . . savage: prob. rdg.; Heb. He runs . . . savages.   c Prob. rdg.; Heb. adds they let
loose my feet.   d God himself: prob. rdg.; Heb. om.   e the tempest: prob. rdg.; Heb. unintelligible.
f was relieved: prob. rdg.; Heb. unintelligible.   g Verse 1 transposed to follow verse 5.

or I have lain in wait at my neighbour's door,

10 may my wife be another man's slave,
and may other men enjoy her.

11 [But that is a wicked act, an offence before the law;

12 it would be a consuming and destructive fire,
raging[h] among my crops.]

13 If I have ever rejected the plea of my slave
or of my slave-girl, when they brought their complaint to me,

14 what shall I do if God appears?
What shall I answer if he intervenes?

15 Did not he who made me in the womb make them?
Did not the same God create us in the belly?

16 If I have withheld their needs from the poor
or let the widow's eye grow dim with tears,

17 if I have eaten my crust alone,
and the orphan has not shared it with me—

18 the orphan who from boyhood honoured me like a father,
whom I guided from the day of his[i] birth—

19 if I have seen anyone perish for lack of clothing,
or a poor man with nothing to cover him,

20 if his body had no cause to bless me,
because he was not kept warm with a fleece from my flock,

21 if I have raised[j] my hand against the innocent,[k]
knowing that men would side with me in court,

22 then may my shoulder-blade be torn from my shoulder,
my arm be wrenched out of its socket!

23 But the terror of God was heavy upon me,[l]
and for fear of his majesty I could do none of these things.

24 If I have put my faith in gold
and my trust in the gold of Nubia,

25 if I have rejoiced in my great wealth
and in the increase of riches;

26 if I ever looked on the sun in splendour
or the moon moving in her glory,

27 and was led astray in my secret heart
and raised my hand in homage,

28 this would have been an offence before the law,

for I should have been unfaithful to God on high.

38[m] If my land has cried out in reproach at me,
and its furrows have joined in weeping,

39 if I have eaten its produce without payment
and have disappointed my creditors,

40 may thistles spring up instead of wheat,
and weeds instead of barley!

29 Have I rejoiced at the ruin of the man that hated me
or been filled with malice when trouble overtook him,

30 even though I did not allow my tongue to sin
by demanding his life with a curse?

31 Have the men of my household never said,
'Let none of us speak ill of him!

32 No stranger has spent the night in the street'?
For I have kept open house for the traveller.

33 Have I ever concealed my misdeeds as men do,
keeping my guilt to myself,

34 because I feared the gossip of the town
or dreaded the scorn of my fellow-citizens?

35 Let me but call a witness in my defence!
Let the Almighty state his case against me!
If my accuser had written out his indictment,
I would not keep silence and remain indoors.[n]

36 No! I would flaunt it on my shoulder and wear it like a crown on my head;

37 I would plead the whole record of my life
and present that in court as my defence.[o]

Job's speeches are finished.[p]

Elihu intervenes

32 So these three men gave up answering Job; for he continued to think himself righteous. Then Elihu son of 2 Barakel the Buzite, of the family of Ram, grew angry; angry because Job had made himself out more righteous than God,[q] and angry with the three 3 friends because they had found no answer to Job and had let God appear

h *Prob. rdg.; Heb.* uprooting.   i *Prob. rdg.; Heb.* my.   j *Or* waved.   k *Or* orphan.   l *Prob. rdg.; Heb.* A fear towards me is a disaster from God.   m *Verses 38–40 transposed (but see note p).*
n *Line transposed from verse 34.*   o *Verses 38–40 transposed to follow verse 28 (but see note p).*
p *The last line of verse 40 retained here.*   q *Or* had justified himself with God.

4 wrong.[r] Now Elihu had hung back
   while they were talking with Job
5 because they were older than he; but,
   when he saw that the three had no
   answer, he could no longer contain his
6 anger. So Elihu son of Barakel the
   Buzite began to speak:

   I am young in years,
   and you are old;
   that is why I held back and shrank
   from displaying my knowledge in
   front of you.
7 I said to myself, 'Let age speak,
   and length of years expound wisdom.'
8 But the spirit of God himself is in
   man,
   and the breath of the Almighty gives
   him understanding;
9 it is not only the old who are wise
   or the aged who understand what is
   right.
10 Therefore I say: Listen to me;
   I too will display my knowledge.
11 Look, I have been waiting upon your
   words,
   listening for the conclusions of your
   thoughts,
   while you sought for phrases;
12 I have been giving thought to your
   conclusions,
   but not one of you refutes Job or
   answers his arguments.
13 Take care then not to claim that you
   have found wisdom;
   God will rebut him, not man.
14 I will not string[s] words together like
   you[t]
   or answer him as you have done.

15 If these men are confounded and no
   longer answer,
   if words fail them,
16 am I to wait because they do not
   speak,
   because they stand there and no
   longer answer?
17 I, too, have a furrow to plough;
   I will express my opinion;
18 for I am bursting with words,
   a bellyful of wind gripes me.
19 My stomach is distended as if with
   wine,
   bulging like a blacksmith's bellows;
20 I must speak to find relief,
   I must open my mouth and answer;
21 I will show no favour to anyone,
   I will flatter no one, God or man;[u]
22 for I cannot use flattering titles,
   or my Maker would soon do away with
   me.

Elihu addresses Job

Come now, Job, listen to my words   33
and attend carefully to everything I
   say.
Look, I am ready to answer;   2
the words are on the tip of my tongue.
My heart assures me that I speak with 3
   knowledge,
and that my lips speak with sincerity.
For the spirit of God made me,   4
and the breath of the Almighty gave
   me life.
Answer me if you can,   5
marshal your arguments and confront
   me.
In God's sight[v] I am just what you 6
   are;
I too am only a handful of clay.
Fear of me need not abash you,   7
nor any pressure from me overawe you.
You have said your say and I heard   8
   you;
I have listened to the sound of your
   words:
'I am innocent', you said, 'and free 9
   from offence,
blameless and without guilt.
Yet God finds occasions to put me in 10
   the wrong
and counts me his enemy;
he puts my feet in the stocks   11
and keeps a close watch on all I do.'

Well, this is my answer: You are   12
   wrong.
God is greater than man;
why then plead your case with him?   13
for no one can answer his arguments.
Indeed, once God has spoken   14
he does not speak a second time to
   confirm it.
In dreams, in visions of the night,   15
when deepest sleep falls upon men,
while they sleep on their beds, God 16
   makes them listen,
and his correction strikes them with
   terror.
To turn a man from reckless conduct, 17
to check the pride[w] of mortal man,
at the edge of the pit he holds him 18
   back alive
and stops him from crossing the river
   of death.
Or again, man learns his lesson on a 19
   bed of pain,
tormented by a ceaseless ague in his
   bones;
he turns from his food with loathing 20
and has no relish for the choicest
   meats;

r *Prob. original rdg., altered in Heb. to* and had not proved Job wrong.   s *Prob. rdg.; Heb.* He has
not strung.   t *Prob. rdg.; Heb.* towards me.   u *Prob. rdg.; Heb.* I will not flatter man.   v *In
God's sight: or* In strength.   w *the pride: prob. rdg.; Heb. obscure.*

21 his flesh hangs loose upon him,
his bones are loosened and out of joint,

22 his soul draws near to the pit,
his life to the ministers of death.

23 Yet if an angel, one of thousands, stands by him,
a mediator between him and God,
to expound what he has done right
and to secure mortal man his due;[x]

24 if he speaks in the man's favour and says, 'Reprieve him,
let him not go down to the pit, I have the price of his release';

25 then that man will grow sturdier[y] than he was in youth,
he will return to the days of his prime.

26 If he entreats God to show him favour,
to let him see his face and shout for joy;[z]

27 if he declares before all men, 'I have sinned,
turned right into wrong and thought nothing of it';

28 then he saves himself from going down to the pit,
he lives and sees the light.

29 All these things God may do to a man, again and yet again,

30 bringing him back from the pit
to enjoy the full light of life.

31 Listen, Job, and attend to me;
be silent, and I myself will speak.

32 If you have any arguments, answer me;
speak, and I would gladly find you proved right;

33 but if you have none, listen to me:
keep silence, and I will teach you wisdom.

Elihu addresses Job's friends

34 Then Elihu went on to say:

2 Mark my words, you wise men;
you men of long experience, listen to me;

3 for the ear tests what is spoken
as the palate savours food.

4 Let us then examine for ourselves what is right;
let us together establish the true good.

5 Job has said, 'I am innocent,
but God has deprived me of justice,

6 he has falsified my case;
my state is desperate, yet I have done no wrong.'

7 Was there ever a man like Job
with his thirst for irreverent talk,

8 choosing bad company to share his journeys,
a fellow-traveller with wicked men?

9 For he says that it brings a man no profit
to find favour with God.

10 But listen to me, you men of good sense.
Far be it from God to do evil
or the Almighty to play false!

11 For he pays a man according to his work
and sees that he gets what his conduct deserves.

12 The truth is, God does no wrong,
the Almighty does not pervert justice.

13 Who committed the earth to his keeping?
Who but he established the whole world?

14 If he were to turn his thoughts inwards
and recall his life-giving spirit,

15 all that lives would perish on the instant,
and man return again to dust.

Elihu addresses Job

16 Now Job, if you have the wit, consider this;
listen to the words I speak.

17 Can it be that a hater of justice holds the reins?
18 Do you disparage a sovereign whose rule is so fair,
who will say to a prince, 'You scoundrel',
and call his magnates blackguards to their faces;

19 who does not show special favour to those in office
and thinks no more of rich than of poor?
All alike are God's creatures,

20 who may die in a moment, in the middle of the night;
at his touch the rich are no more,
and the mighty vanish though no hand is laid on them.

21 His eyes are on the ways of men,
and he sees every step they take;

22 there is nowhere so dark, so deep in shadow,
that wrongdoers may hide from him.

25 Therefore he repudiates all that they do;
he turns on them in the night, and they are crushed.

23 There are no appointed days for men
to appear before God for judgement.

24 He holds no inquiry, but breaks the powerful

and sets up others in their place.

26[a] For their crimes he strikes them down[b]
and makes them disgorge their bloated
wealth,[c]

27 because they have ceased to obey him
and pay no heed to his ways.

28 Then the cry of the poor reaches his
ears,
and he hears the cry of the distressed.

29–30 [Even if he is silent, who can condemn him?
If he looks away, who can find fault?
What though he makes a godless man
king
over a stubborn nation and all its
people?]

31 But suppose you were to say to God,
'I have overstepped the mark; I will
do no more[d] mischief.

32 Vile wretch that I am, be thou my
guide;
whatever wrong I have done, I will
do wrong no more.'

33 Will he, at these words, condone your
rejection of him?
It is for you to decide, not me:
but what can you answer?

34 Men of good sense will say,
any intelligent hearer will tell me,

35 'Job talks with no knowledge,
and there is no sense in what he says.

36 If only Job could be put to the test
once and for all
for answers that are meant to make
mischief!

37 He is a sinner and a rebel as well[e]
with his endless ranting against God.'

35 Then Elihu went on to say:

2 Do you think that this is a sound
plea
or maintain that you are in the right
against God?—

3 if you say, 'What would be the advantage to me?
how much should I gain from sinning?'

4 I will bring arguments myself against
you,
you and your three friends.

5 Look up at the sky and then consider,
observe the rain-clouds towering above
you.

6 How does it touch him if you have
sinned?
However many your misdeeds, what
does it mean to him?

7 If you do right, what good do you
bring him,

or what does he gain from you?

8 Your wickedness touches only men,
such as you are;
the right that you do affects none but
mortal man.

9 Men will cry out beneath the burdens
of oppression
and call for help against the power of
the great;

10 but none of them asks, 'Where is God
my Maker
who gives protection by night,

11 who grants us more knowledge than
the beasts of the earth
and makes us wiser than the birds of
the air?'

12 So, when they cry out, he does not
answer,
because they are self-willed and proud.

13 All to no purpose! God does not listen,
the Almighty does not see.

14 The worse for you when you say, 'He
does not see me'!
Humble yourself[f] in his presence and
wait for his word.

15 But now, because God does not grow
angry and punish
and because he lets folly pass unheeded,

16 Job gives vent to windy nonsense
and makes a parade of empty words.

36 Then Elihu went on to say:

2 Be patient a little longer, and let me
enlighten you;
there is still something more to be said
on God's side.

3 I will search far and wide to support
my conclusions,
as I defend the justice of my Maker.

4 There are no flaws in my reasoning;
before you stands one whose conclusions are sound.

5 God,[g] I say, repudiates the high and[h]
mighty

6 and does not let the wicked prosper,
but allows the just claims of the poor
and suffering;

7 he does not deprive the sufferer of his
due.[i]
Look at kings on their thrones:
when God gives them sovereign power,
they grow arrogant.

8 Next you may see them loaded with
fetters,
held fast in captives' chains:

9 he denounces their conduct to them,

a Verse 25 transposed to follow verse 22.　b he strikes them down: prob. rdg.; Heb. om.　c Or and chastises them where people see.　d more: prob. rdg.; Heb. obscure.　e Prob. rdg.; Heb. adds between us it is enough.　f Humble yourself: prob. rdg.; Heb. Judge.　g Prob. rdg.; Heb. adds a mighty one and not.　h and: prob. rdg.; Heb. om.　i deprive...due: or withdraw his gaze from the righteous.

showing how insolence and tyranny was their offence;

10 his warnings sound in their ears
and summon them to turn back from their evil courses.

11 If they listen to him, they spend[j] their days in prosperity
and their years in comfort.

12 But, if they do not listen, they die, their lesson unlearnt,
and cross the river of death.

13 Proud men rage against him
and do not cry to him for help when caught in his toils;

14 so they die in their prime,
like male prostitutes,[k] worn out.[l]

15 Those who suffer he rescues through suffering
and teaches them by the discipline of affliction.

16 Beware, if you are tempted to exchange hardship for comfort,[m]
for unlimited plenty spread before you, and a generous table;

17 if you eat your fill of a rich man's fare when you are occupied with the business of the law,

18 do not be led astray by lavish gifts of wine
and do not let bribery warp your judgement.

19 Will that wealth of yours, however great, avail you,
or all the resources of your high position?

21[n] Take care not to turn to mischief;
for that is why you are tried by affliction.

20 Have no fear if in the breathless terrors of the night
you see nations vanish where they stand.

22 God towers in majesty above us;
who wields such sovereign power as he?

23 Who has prescribed his course for him?
Who has said to him, 'Thou hast done wrong'?

24 Remember then to sing the praises of his work,
as men have always sung them.

25 All men stand back from[o] him;
the race of mortals look on from afar.

26 Consider; God is so great that we cannot know him;

the number of his years is beyond reckoning.

He draws up drops of water from the 27 sea[p]
and distils rain from the mist he has made;

the rain-clouds pour down in torrents,[q] 28
they descend in showers on mankind;

thus he sustains the nations 31
and gives them food in plenty.

Can any man read the secret of the 29 sailing clouds,
spread like a carpet under[r] his pavilion?

See how he unrolls the mist across the 30 waters,
and its streamers[s] cover the sea.

He charges the thunderbolts with 32[t] flame
and launches them straight[u] at the mark;

in his anger he calls up the tempest, 33
and the thunder is the herald of its coming.[v]

This too makes my heart beat wildly 37
and start from its place.

Listen, listen to the thunder of God's 2 voice
and the rumbling of his utterance.

Under the vault of heaven he lets it 3 roll,
and his lightning reaches the ends of the earth;

there follows a sound of roaring 4
as he thunders with the voice of majesty.[w]

God's voice is marvellous in its 5 working;[x]
he does great deeds that pass our knowledge.

For he says to the snow, 'Fall to 6 earth',
and to the rainstorms, 'Be fierce.'

And when his voice is heard,
the floods of rain pour down unchecked.[y]

He shuts every man fast indoors,[z] 7
and all men whom he has made must stand idle;

the beasts withdraw into their lairs 8
and take refuge in their dens.

The hurricane bursts from its prison, 9
and the rain-winds bring bitter cold;

at the breath of God the ice-sheet is 10 formed,
and the wide waters are frozen hard as iron.

---

j Prob. rdg.; Heb. adds they end.   *k* Cp. *Deut. 23. 17.*   *l* worn out: *prob. rdg.; Heb. unintelligible.* *m* for comfort: *prob. rdg.; Heb. om.*   *n* Verses 20 and 21 transposed.   *o* Or gaze at.   *p* from the sea: *prob. rdg.; Heb. om.*   *q* in torrents: *prob. rdg.; Heb. which.*   *r* spread . . . under: *prob. rdg.; Heb.* crashing noises.   *s* its streamers: *prob. rdg.; Heb.* the roots of.   *t* Verse 31 transposed to follow verse 28.   *u* and . . . straight: *prob. rdg.; Heb.* and gives orders concerning it.   *v* in his anger . . . coming: *prob. rdg.; Heb.* obscure.   *w* See note on verse 6.   *x* Prob. rdg.; Heb. thundering.   *y* And when . . . unchecked: *prob. rdg.; some words in these lines transposed from verse 4.* *z* indoors: *prob. rdg.; Heb. obscure.*

11 He gives the dense clouds their load
    of moisture,
   and the clouds spread his mist abroad,
12 as they travel round in their courses,
   steered by his guiding hand
   to do his bidding
   all over the habitable world.*a*

Elihu concludes his argument

14 Listen, Job, to this argument;
   stand still, and consider God's won-
    derful works.
15 Do you know how God assigns them
    their tasks,
   how he sends light flashing from his
    clouds?
16 Do you know why the clouds hang
    poised overhead,
   a wonderful work of his consummate
    skill,
17 sweating there in your stifling clothes,
   when the earth lies sultry under the
    south wind?
18 Can you beat out the vault of the
    skies, as he does,
   hard as a mirror of cast metal?
19 Teach us then what to say to him;
   for all is dark, and we cannot marshal
    our thoughts.
20 Can any man dictate to God when he
    is*b* to speak?
   or command him to make proclama-
    tion?
21 At one moment the light is not seen,
   it is overcast with clouds and rain;
   then the wind passes by and clears
    them away,
22 and a golden glow comes from the
    north.*c*
23 But the Almighty we cannot find; his
    power is beyond our ken,
   and his righteousness not slow to do
    justice.
24 Therefore mortal men pay him
    reverence,
   and all who are wise look to him.

The LORD speaks to Job

38 Then the LORD answered Job out of
   the tempest:
2 Who is this whose ignorant words
   cloud my design in darkness?
3 Brace yourself and stand up like a
   man;
   I will ask questions, and you shall
    answer.
4 Where were you when I laid the
    earth's foundations?
   Tell me, if you know and understand.

Who settled its dimensions? Surely 5
   you should know.
Who stretched his measuring-line
   over it?
On what do its supporting pillars rest? 6
Who set its corner-stone in place,
when the morning stars sang together 7
and all the sons of God shouted aloud?
Who watched over the birth of the 8
   sea,*d*
when it burst in flood from the
   womb?—
when I wrapped it in a blanket of 9
   cloud
and cradled it in fog,
when I established its bounds,   10
fixing its doors and bars in place,
and said, 'Thus far shall you come and 11
   no farther,
and here your surging waves shall
   halt.'*e*
In all your life have you ever called up 12
   the dawn
or shown the morning its place?
Have you taught it to grasp the 13
   fringes of the earth
and shake the Dog-star from its place;
to bring up the horizon in relief as 14
   clay under a seal,
until all things stand out like the folds
   of a cloak,
when the light of the Dog-star is 15
   dimmed
and the stars of the Navigator's Line
   go out one by one?
Have you descended to the springs of 16
   the sea
or walked in the unfathomable deep?
Have the gates of death been revealed 17
   to you?
Have you ever seen the door-keepers
   of the place of darkness?
Have you comprehended the vast 18
   expanse of the world?
Come, tell me all this, if you know.
Which is the way to the home of light 19
and where does darkness dwell?
And can you then take each to its 20
   appointed bound
and escort it on its homeward path?
Doubtless you know all this; for you 21
   were born already,
so long is the span of your life!

Have you visited the storehouse of 22
   the snow
or seen the arsenal where hail is
   stored,
which I have kept ready for the day of 23
   calamity,

a Prob. rdg.; Heb. adds (13) whether he makes him attain the rod, or his earth, or constant love.
b Prob. rdg.; Heb. I am.   *c Prob. rdg.; Heb. adds* this refers to God, terrible in majesty.   *d* Who
. . . *sea: prob. rdg.; Heb.* And he held back the sea with two doors.   *e Prob. rdg.; Heb.* here one
shall set on your surging waves.

for war and for the hour of battle?
24 By what paths is the heat spread
    abroad
    or the east wind carried far and wide
    over the earth?
25 Who has cut channels for the down-
    pour
    and cleared a passage for the thunder-
    storm,
26 for rain to fall on land where no man
    lives
    and on the deserted wilderness,
27 clothing lands waste and derelict with
    green
    and making grass grow on thirsty
    ground*f*?
28 Has the rain a father?
    Who sired the drops of dew?
29 Whose womb gave birth to the ice,
    and who was the mother of the frost
    from heaven,
30 which lays a stony cover over the
    waters
    and freezes the expanse of ocean?
31 Can you bind the cluster of the Plei-
    ades
    or loose Orion's belt?
32 Can you bring out the signs of the
    zodiac in their season
    or guide Aldebaran and its train?
33 Did you proclaim the rules that govern
    the heavens,
    or determine the laws of nature on
    earth?
34 Can you command the dense clouds
    to cover you with their weight of
    waters?
35 If you bid lightning speed on its way,
    will it say to you, 'I am ready'?
36 Who put wisdom in depths of dark-
    ness
    and veiled understanding in secrecy*g*?
37 Who is wise enough to marshal the
    rain-clouds
    and empty the cisterns of heaven,
38 when the dusty soil sets hard as iron,
    and the clods of earth cling together?
39 Do you hunt her prey for the lion-
    ess
    and satisfy the hunger of young lions,
40 as they crouch in the lair
    or lie in wait in the covert?
41 Who provides the raven with its
    quarry
    when its fledglings croak*h* for lack of
    food?
39 Do you know when the mountain-
    goats are born
    or attend the wild doe when she is in
    labour?

Do you count the months that they 2
    carry their young
or know the time of their delivery,
when they crouch down to open their 3
    wombs
and bring their offspring to the birth,
when the fawns grow and thrive in the 4
    open forest,
and go forth and do not return?
Who has let the wild ass of Syria 5
    range at will
and given the wild ass of Arabia its
    freedom?—
whose home I have made in the 6
    wilderness
and its lair in the saltings;
it disdains the noise of the city   7
and is deaf to the driver's shouting;
it roams the hills as its pasture   8
and searches for anything green.
Does the wild ox consent to serve you, 9
does it spend the night in your stall?
Can you harness its strength*i* with 10
    ropes,
or will it harrow the furrows*i* after you?
Can you depend on it, strong as it is, 11
or leave your labour to it?
Do you trust it to come back   12
and bring home your grain to the
    threshing-floor?

The wings of the ostrich are stunted;*j* 13
*k*her pinions and plumage are so
    scanty*l*
that she abandons her eggs to the 14
    ground,
letting them be kept warm by the sand.
She forgets that a foot may crush 15
    them,
or a wild beast trample on them;
she treats her chicks heartlessly as if 16
    they were not hers,
not caring if her labour is wasted
(for God has denied her wisdom   17
and left her without sense),
while like a cock she struts over the 18
    uplands,
scorning both horse and rider.

Did you give the horse his strength? 19
Did you clothe his neck with a mane?
Do you make him quiver like a locust's 20
    wings,
when his shrill neighing strikes terror?
He shows his mettle as he paws and 21
    prances;
he charges the armoured line with all
    his might.
He scorns alarms and knows no dismay; 22
he does not flinch before the sword.

f thirsty ground: *prob. rdg.; Heb.* source.   *g* secrecy: *prob. rdg.; Heb. word unknown.*   *h* Prob.
rdg.; Heb. adds they cry to God.   *i Prob. rdg.; Heb. transposes* strength *and* furrows.   *j* are
stunted: *prob. rdg.; Heb. unintelligible.*   *k Prob. rdg.; Heb. prefixes* if.   *l Prob. rdg.; Heb.* godly
or stork.

23 The quiver rattles at his side,
    the spear and sabre flash.
24 Trembling with eagerness, he devours
        the ground
    and cannot be held in when he hears
        the horn;
25 at the blast of the horn he cries 'Aha!'
    and from afar he scents the battle.[m]
26 Does your skill teach the hawk to use
        its pinions
    and spread its wings towards the
        south?
27 Do you instruct the vulture to fly high
    and build its nest aloft?
28 It dwells among the rocks and there it
        lodges;
    its station is a crevice in the rock;
29 from there it searches for food,
    keenly scanning the distance,
30 that its brood may be gorged with
        blood;
    and where the slain are, there the
        vulture is.

41 1[n] Can you pull out the whale[o] with a gaff
    or can you slip a noose round its
        tongue?
2 Can you pass a cord through its nose
    or put a hook through its jaw?
3 Will it plead with you for mercy
    or beg its life with soft words?
4 Will it enter into an agreement with
        you
    to become your slave for life?
5 Will you toy with it as with a bird
    or keep it on a string like a song-bird
        for your maidens?
6 Do trading-partners haggle over it
    or merchants share it out?

40 Then the LORD said to Job:

2 Is it for a man who disputes with the
        Almighty to be stubborn?
    Should he that argues with God
        answer back?

Job answers

3 And Job answered the LORD:
4 What reply can I give thee, I who
        carry no weight?
    I put my finger to my lips.
5 I have spoken once and now will not
        answer again;
    twice have I spoken, and I will do so
        no more.

The LORD speaks again

6 Then the LORD answered Job out of
    the tempest:

Brace yourself and stand up like a 7
    man;
I will ask questions, and you shall
    answer.
Dare you deny that I am just   8
or put me in the wrong that you may
    be right?
Have you an arm like God's arm,   9
can you thunder with a voice like his?
Deck yourself out, if you can, in 10
    pride and dignity,
array yourself in pomp and splendour;
unleash the fury of your wrath,   11
look upon the proud man and humble
    him;
look upon every proud man and bring 12
    him low,
throw down the wicked where they
    stand;
hide them in the dust together,   13
and shroud them in an unknown grave.
Then I in my turn will acknowledge   14
that your own right hand can save you.

Consider the chief of the beasts, the 15
    crocodile,[p]
who devours cattle as if they were
    grass:[q]
what strength is in his loins!   16
what power in the muscles of his belly!
His tail is rigid as[r] a cedar,   17
the sinews of his flanks are closely knit,
his bones are tubes of bronze,   18
and his limbs like bars of iron.
He is the chief of God's works,   19
made to be a tyrant over his peers;[s]
for he takes[t] the cattle of the hills for 20
    his prey
and in his jaws he crunches all wild
    beasts.
There under the thorny lotus he lies, 21
hidden in the reeds and the marsh;
the lotus conceals him in its shadow, 22
the poplars of the stream surround
    him.
If the river is in spate, he is not scared, 23
he sprawls at his ease though the
    stream is in flood.
Can a man blind[u] his eyes and take 24
    him
or pierce his nose with the teeth of a
    trap?
Can you fill his skin with harpoons   41 7[v]
or his head with fish-hooks?
If ever you lift your hand against him, 8
think of the struggle that awaits you,
    and let be.

No, such a man is in desperate case, 9

m *Prob. rdg.*; *Heb. adds* the thunder of the captains and the shouting.   n *41. 1–6 (in Heb.
40. 25–30) transposed to this point.   o Or* Leviathan.   p *chief . . . crocodile: prob. rdg.*; *Heb.* beasts
(behemoth) *which I have made with you.*   q *cattle . . . grass: prob. rdg.*; *Heb.* grass like cattle.
r Or *He bends his tail like . . .*   s *Prob. rdg.*; *Heb.* his sword.   t *Prob. rdg.*; *Heb.* they take.
u *Can a man blind: prob. rdg.*; *Heb. obscure.*   v *Verses 1–6 transposed to follow 39. 30.*

hurled headlong at the very sight of him.

10 How fierce he is when he is roused!
Who is there to stand up to him?
11 Who has ever attacked him[w] un-scathed?
Not a man[x] under the wide heaven.
12 I will not pass over in silence his limbs,
his prowess and the grace of his pro-portions.
13 Who has ever undone his outer gar-ment
or penetrated his doublet of hide?
14 Who has ever opened the portals of his face?
for there is terror in his arching teeth.
15 His back[y] is row upon row of shields,
enclosed in a wall[z] of flints;
16 one presses so close on the other
that air cannot pass between them,
17 each so firmly clamped to its neigh-bour
that they hold and cannot spring apart.
18 His sneezing sends out sprays of light,
and his eyes gleam like the shimmer of dawn.
19 Firebrands shoot from his mouth,
and sparks come streaming out;
20 his nostrils pour forth smoke
like a cauldron on a fire blown to full heat.
21 His breath sets burning coals ablaze,
and flames flash from his mouth.
22 Strength is lodged in his neck,
and untiring energy dances ahead of him.
23 Close knit is his underbelly,
no pressure will make it yield.
24 His heart is firm as a rock,
firm as the nether millstone.
25 When he raises himself, strong men[a] take fright,
bewildered at the lashings of his tail.
26 Sword or spear, dagger or javelin,
if they touch him, they have no effect.
27 Iron he counts as straw,
and bronze as rotting wood.
28 No arrow can pierce him,
and for him sling-stones are turned into chaff.
29 to him a club is a mere reed,
and he laughs at the swish of the sabre.
30 Armoured beneath with jagged sherds,
he sprawls on the mud like a threshing-sledge.
31 He makes the deep water boil like a cauldron,

he whips up the lake like ointment in a mixing-bowl.
32 He leaves a shining trail behind him,
and the great river is like white hair in his wake.
33 He has no equal on earth;
for he is made quite without fear.
34 He looks down on all creatures, even the highest;
he is king over all proud beasts.

Job repents

Then Job answered the LORD: 42

2 I know that thou canst do all things
and that no purpose is beyond thee.
3 But I have spoken of great things
which I have not understood,
things too wonderful for me to know.[b]
5 I knew of thee then only by report,
but now I see thee with my own eyes.
6 Therefore I melt away;[c]
I repent in dust and ashes.

Epilogue

7 When the LORD had finished speaking to Job, he said to Eliphaz the Teman-ite, 'I am angry with you and your two friends, because you have not spoken as you ought about me, as my servant Job has done. 8 So now take seven bulls and seven rams, go to my servant Job and offer a whole-offering for yourselves, and he will intercede for you; I will surely show him favour by not being harsh with you because you have not spoken as you ought about me, as he has done.' 9 Then Eli-phaz the Temanite and Bildad the Shuhite and Zophar the Naamathite went and carried out the LORD's com-mand, and the LORD showed favour to Job when he had interceded for his friends. 10 So the LORD restored Job's fortunes and doubled all his posses-sions.

11 Then all Job's brothers and sisters and his former acquaintance came and feasted with him in his home, and they consoled and comforted him for all the misfortunes which the LORD had brought on him; and each of them gave him a sheep[d] and a gold ring. 12 Furthermore, the LORD blessed the end of Job's life more than the begin-ning; and he had fourteen thousand head of small cattle and six thousand camels, a thousand yoke of oxen and

---

w Prob. rdg.; Heb. me.   x Prob. rdg.; Heb. He is mine.   y Prob. rdg.; Heb. pride.   z Prob. rdg.; Heb. seal.   a strong men: or leaders or gods.   b Prob. rdg.; Heb. adds (4) O listen, and let me speak; I will ask questions, and you shall answer.   c Or despise myself.   d Or piece of money.

13 as many she-asses. He had seven[e] sons
14 and three daughters; and he named
his eldest daughter Jemimah, the
second Keziah and the third Keren-
15 happuch. There were no women in all
the world so beautiful as Job's daughters; and their father gave them an
inheritance with their brothers.

Thereafter Job lived another hun- 16
dred and forty years, he saw his sons
and his grandsons to four generations,
and died at a very great age.   17

e Or fourteen.

PSALMS

BOOK 1

1

The source of happiness

1 Happy is the man
    who does not take the wicked for
      his guide
    nor walk the road that sinners tread
    nor take his seat among the scorn-
      ful;
2 the law of the LORD is his delight,
the law his meditation night and day.
3 He is like a tree
    planted beside a watercourse,
    which yields its fruit in season
    and its leaf never withers:
    in all that he does he prospers.
4 Wicked men are not like this;
    they are like chaff driven by the
      wind.
5 So when judgement comes the wicked
    shall not stand firm,
nor shall sinners stand in the assembly
    of the righteous.
6 The LORD watches over the way of
    the righteous,
    but the way of the wicked is
      doomed.

2

The LORD's anointed king

1 Why are the nations in turmoil?
    Why do the peoples hatch their
      futile plots?
2 The kings of the earth stand ready,
    and the rulers conspire together
    against the LORD and his anointed
      king.
3 'Let us break their fetters,' they cry,
    'let us throw off their chains!'
4 The Lord who sits enthroned in
    heaven
    laughs them to scorn;
5 then he rebukes them in anger,

    he threatens them in his wrath.
Of me he says, 'I have enthroned 6
    my king
    on Zion my holy mountain.'
I will repeat the LORD's decree: 7
'You are my son,' he said;
    'this day I become your father.
Ask of me what you will: 8
I will give you nations as your
    inheritance,
the ends of the earth as your pos-
    session.
You shall break them with a rod of 9
    iron,
you shall shatter them like a clay
    pot.'
Be mindful then, you kings;   10
learn your lesson, rulers of the
    earth:
worship the LORD with reverence; 11–12
tremble, and kiss the king,[a]
lest the LORD be angry and you are
    struck down in mid course;
for his anger flares up in a moment.
Happy are all who find refuge in
    him.

3

Confidence in adversity

    LORD, how my enemies have multi- 1
      plied!
Many rise up against me,
many there are who say of me,   2
    'God will not bring him victory.'
But thou, LORD, art a shield to cover 3
    me:
    thou art my glory, and thou dost
      raise my head high.
I cry aloud to the LORD,   4
and he answers me from his holy
    mountain.
I lie down and sleep,   5
and I wake again, for the LORD
    upholds me.

a tremble ... king: prob. rdg.; lit. tremble and kiss the mighty one; Heb. obscure.

6 I will not fear the nations in their myriads
who set on me from all sides.

7 Rise up, LORD; save me, O my God.
Thou dost strike all my foes across the face
and breakest the teeth of the wicked.

8 Thine is the victory, O LORD,
and may[b] thy blessing rest upon thy people.

4

Peace of heart

1 Answer me when I call, O God, maintainer of my right,
I was hard pressed, and thou didst set me at large;
be gracious to me now and hear my prayer.

2 Mortal men, how long will you pay me not honour but dishonour,
or set your heart on trifles and run after lies?

3 Know that the LORD has shown me[c] his marvellous love;
the LORD hears when I call to him.

4 However angry your hearts, do not do wrong;
though you lie abed resentful,[d] do not break silence:

5 pay your due of sacrifice, and trust in the LORD.

6 There are many who say, 'If only we might be prosperous again!
But the light of thy presence has fled from us, O LORD.'

7 Yet in my heart thou hast put more happiness
than they enjoyed when there was corn and wine in plenty.

8 Now I will lie down in peace, and sleep;
for thou alone, O LORD, makest me live unafraid.

5

Prayer for guidance

1 Listen to my words, O LORD,
consider my inmost thoughts;

2 heed my cry for help, my king and my God.

3 In the morning, when I say my prayers, thou wilt hear me.
I set out my morning sacrifice[e] and watch for thee, O LORD.

4 For thou art not a God who welcomes wickedness;
evil can be no guest of thine.[f]

There is no place for arrogance 5 before thee;
thou hatest evildoers,
thou makest an end of all liars. 6

The LORD detests traitors and men of blood.

But I, through thy great love, may 7 come into thy house,
and bow low toward thy holy temple in awe of thee.

Lead me, LORD, in thy righteous- 8 ness,
because my enemies are on the watch;
give me a straight path to follow.

There is no trusting what they say, 9 they are nothing but wind.
Their throats are an open[g] sepulchre;
smooth talk runs off their tongues.

Bring ruin on them, O God; 10
let them fall by their own devices.
Cast them out, after all their rebellions,
for they have defied thee.

But let all who take refuge in thee 11 rejoice,
let them for ever break into shouts of joy;
shelter those who love thy name,
that they may exult in thee.

For thou, O LORD, wilt bless the 12 righteous;
thou wilt hedge him round with favour as with a shield.

6

Prayer for help in time of trouble

O LORD, do not condemn me in thy 1 anger,
do not punish me in thy fury.

Be merciful to me, O LORD, for I am 2 weak;
heal me, my very bones are shaken;
my soul quivers in dismay. 3
And thou, O LORD—how long?

Come back, O LORD; set my soul free, 4
deliver me for thy love's sake.
None talk of thee among the dead; 5
who praises thee in Sheol?

I am wearied with groaning; 6
all night long my pillow is wet with tears,
I soak my bed with weeping.
Grief dims my eyes; 7
they are worn out with all my woes.
Away from me, all you evildoers, 8
for the LORD has heard the sound of my weeping.
The LORD has heard my entreaty; 9

b Thine . . . and may: *or* O LORD of salvation, may . . . resentful: *prob. rdg.; Heb.* say on your beds. *e Or* plea. protects a wicked man; an evil man cannot be thy guest.

c *Prob. rdg.; Heb.* him. d lie abed f who welcomes . . . thine: *or* who g *Or* inscribed.

the LORD will accept my prayer.
10 All my enemies shall be confounded
    and dismayed;
    they shall turn away in sudden con-
    fusion.

7

Prayer for justice

1 O LORD my God, in thee I find refuge;
    save me, rescue me from my pur-
    suers,
2   before they tear at my throat like
    a lion
    and carry me off beyond hope of
    rescue.
3 O LORD my God, if I have done any of
    these things—
    if I have stained my hands with
    guilt,
4   if I have repaid a friend evil for
    good
    or set free an enemy who attacked
    me without cause,
5 may my adversary come after me and
    overtake me,
    trample my life to the ground
    and lay my honour in the dust!

6   Arise, O LORD, in thy anger,
    rouse thyself in wrath against my
    foes.
    Awake, my God who hast ordered
    that justice be done;
7   let the peoples assemble around
    thee,
    and take thou thy seat on high above
    them.
8 O LORD, thou who dost pass sen-
    tence on the nations,
    O LORD, judge me as my righteous-
    ness deserves,
    for I am clearly innocent.
9 Let wicked men do no more harm,
    establish the reign of righteousness,[h]
    thou who examinest both heart and
    mind, thou righteous God.

10 God, the High God, is my shield
    who saves men of honest heart.
11 God is a just judge,
    every day he requites the raging
    enemy.

12 He sharpens his sword,
    strings his bow and makes it ready.
13 He has prepared his deadly shafts
    and tipped his arrows with fire.
14 But the enemy is in labour with
    iniquity;
    he conceives mischief, and his brood
    is lies.
15 He has made a pit and dug it deep,

and he himself shall fall into the
    hole that he has made.
His mischief shall recoil upon him- 16
    self,
and his violence fall on his own
    head.

I will praise the LORD for his 17
    righteousness
and sing a psalm to the name of the
    LORD Most High.

8

The LORD's glory and man's dignity

O LORD our sovereign, 1
    how glorious is thy name in all the
    earth!
Thy majesty is praised high as the
    heavens.
Out of the mouths of babes, of 2
    infants at the breast,
thou hast rebuked[i] the mighty,
silencing enmity and vengeance to
    teach thy foes a lesson.
When I look up at thy heavens, the 3
    work of thy fingers,
    the moon and the stars set in their
    place by thee,
what is man that thou shouldst 4
    remember him,
mortal man that thou shouldst care
    for him?
Yet thou hast made him little less 5
    than a god,
crowning him with glory and honour.
Thou makest him master over all 6
    thy creatures;
thou hast put everything under his
    feet:
all sheep and oxen, all the wild beasts, 7
    the birds in the air and the fish in 8
    the sea,
    and all that moves along the paths
    of ocean.
O LORD our sovereign, 9
    how glorious is thy name in all the
    earth!

9–10

Downfall of the godless

I will praise thee, O LORD, with all 1
    my heart,
I will tell the story of thy marvel-
    lous acts.
I will rejoice and exult in thee, 2
I will praise thy name in psalms, O
    thou Most High,
when my enemies turn back, 3
    when they fall headlong and perish
    at thy appearing;

[h] the reign of righteousness: *or* the cause of the righteous.   [i] *Prob. rdg.;* Heb. founded.

4 for thou hast upheld my right and my cause,
seated on thy throne, thou righteous judge.
5 Thou hast rebuked the nations and overwhelmed the ungodly,
thou hast blotted out their name for all time.
6 The strongholds of the enemy are thrown down for evermore;
thou hast laid their cities in ruins, all memory of them is lost.
7 The LORD thunders,[j] he sits enthroned for ever:
he has set up his throne, his judgement-seat.
8 He it is who will judge the world with justice
and try the cause of the peoples fairly.
9 So may the LORD be a tower of strength for the oppressed,
a tower of strength in time of need,
10 that those who acknowledge thy name may trust in thee;
for thou, LORD, dost not forsake those who seek thee.
11 Sing psalms to the LORD who dwells in Zion,
proclaim his deeds among the nations.
12 For the Avenger of blood has remembered men's desire,
and has not forgotten the cry of the poor.

13 Have pity on me, O LORD; look upon my affliction,
thou who hast lifted me up[k] and caught me back from the gates of death,
14 that I may repeat all thy praise and exult at this deliverance in the gates of Zion's city.

15 The nations have plunged into a pit of their own making;
their own feet are entangled in the net which they hid.
16 Now the LORD makes himself known. Justice is done:
the wicked man is trapped in his own devices.
17 They rush blindly down to Sheol, the wicked,
all the nations who are heedless of God.
18 But the poor shall not always be unheeded
nor the hope of the destitute be always vain.

19 Arise, LORD, give man no chance to boast his strength;
summon the nations before thee for judgement.
20 Strike them with fear, O LORD,
let the nations know that they are but men.

10
Why stand so far off, LORD,
hiding thyself in time of need?
2 The wicked man in his pride hunts down the poor:
may his crafty schemes be his own undoing!
3 The wicked man is obsessed with his own desires,
and in his greed gives wickedness his blessing;
4 arrogant as he is, he scorns the LORD
and leaves no place for God in all his schemes.
5 His ways are always devious;
thy judgements are beyond his grasp[l],
and he scoffs at all restraint.
6 He says to himself, 'I shall never be shaken;
no misfortune can check my course.'[m]
7 His mouth is full of lies and violence;
mischief and trouble lurk under his tongue.
8 He lies in ambush in the villages
and murders innocent men by stealth.
He is watching[n] intently for some poor wretch;
9 he seizes him and drags him away in his net;
he crouches stealthily, like a lion in its lair
crouching to seize its victim;
10 the good man[o] is struck down and sinks to the ground,
and poor wretches fall into his toils.
11 He says to himself, 'God has forgotten;
he has hidden his face and has seen nothing.'

12 Arise, LORD, set[p] thy hand to the task;
do not forget the poor, O God.
13 Why, O God, has the wicked man rejected thee
and said to himself that thou dost not care?
14 Thou seest that mischief and trouble are his companions,
thou takest the matter into thy own hands.
The poor victim commits himself to thee;

---

j thunders: *prob. rdg.*; *Heb. unintelligible.*   k thou ... me up: *prob. rdg.*; *Heb. from those who hate me.*   l beyond his grasp: *prob. rdg.*; *Heb. on high before him.*   m my course: *prob. rdg.*; *Heb. which.*   n *Prob. rdg.*; *Heb. storing up.*   o the good man: *prob. rdg.*; *Heb. om.*   p Or who settest.

fatherless, he finds in thee his helper.
15 Break the power of wickedness and wrong;
   hunt out all wickedness until thou canst find no more.

16 The LORD is king for ever and ever;
   the nations have vanished from his land.
17 Thou hast heard the lament of the humble, O LORD,
   and art attentive to their heart's desire,
18 bringing justice to the orphan and the downtrodden
   that fear may never drive men from their homes again.

11

A sure refuge

1 In the LORD I have found my refuge;
   why do you say to me,
   'Flee to the mountains like a bird';
2 see how the wicked string their bows
   and fit the arrow to the string,
   to shoot down honest men out of the darkness'?
3 When foundations are undermined,
   what can the good man do?
4 The LORD is in his holy temple,
   the LORD's throne is in heaven.
   His eye is upon mankind, he takes their measure at a glance.
5 The LORD weighs just and unjust
   and hates with all his soul the lover of violence.
6 He shall rain down red-hot coals upon the wicked;
   brimstone and scorching winds shall be the cup they drink.
7 For the LORD is just and loves just dealing;
   his face is turned towards the upright man.

12

When good faith is gone

1 Help, LORD, for loyalty is no more;
   good faith between man and man is over.
2 One man lies to another:
   they talk with smooth lip and double heart.
3 May the LORD make an end of such smooth lips
   and the tongue that talks so boastfully!
4 They said, 'Our tongue can win the day.

Words are our ally; who can muster us?'
'For the ruin of the poor, for the 5 groans of the needy,
now I will arise,' says the LORD,
   'I will place him in the safety for which he longs.'

The words of the LORD are pure 6 words:
silver refined in a crucible,
gold*q* seven times purified.
Do thou, LORD, protect us   7
and guard us from a profligate and evil generation.*r*
The wicked flaunt themselves on 8 every side,
while profligacy stands high among mankind.

13

Prayer of the oppressed

How long, O LORD, wilt thou quite 1 forget me?
How long wilt thou hide thy face from me?
How long must I suffer anguish in my 2 soul,
grief in my heart, day and night?
How long shall my enemy lord it over me?
Look now and answer me, O LORD 3 my God.
Give light to my eyes lest I sleep the sleep of death,
   lest my adversary say, 'I have 4 overthrown him',
   and my enemies rejoice at my downfall.
But for my part I trust in thy true 5 love.
My heart shall rejoice, for thou hast set me free.
I will sing to the LORD, who has 6 granted all my desire.

14

Man's wickedness

The impious fool says in his heart, 1*s*
'There is no God.'
How vile men are, how depraved and loathsome;
not one does anything good!
The LORD looks down from heaven 2 on all mankind
to see if any act wisely,
if any seek out God.
But all are disloyal, all are rotten to 3 the core;
not one does anything good,
no, not even one.

q gold: *prob. rdg.; Heb.* to the earth.   r a profligate and evil generation: *prob. rdg.; Heb.* the
generation which is for ever.   s *Verses 1–7: cp. Ps. 53. 1–6.*

4   Shall they not rue it,
    all evildoers who devour my people
    as men devour bread,
    and never call upon the LORD?
5   There they were in dire alarm;
  for God was in the brotherhood of the
    godly.
6   The resistance of their victim was
    too much for them,
    because the LORD was his refuge.
7 If only Israel's deliverance might come
    out of Zion!
    When the LORD restores his people's
    fortunes,
  let Jacob rejoice, let Israel be glad.

15

What the LORD requires

1   O LORD, who may lodge in thy
    tabernacle?
    Who may dwell on thy holy
    mountain?
2   The man of blameless life, who does
    what is right
    and speaks the truth from his heart;
3   who has no malice on his tongue,
    who never wrongs a friend
    and tells no tales against his
    neighbour;
4   the man who shows his scorn for
    the worthless
    and honours all who fear the LORD;
    who swears to his own hurt and
    does not retract;
5   who does not put his money out to
    usury
    and takes no bribe against an in-
    nocent man.
  He who does these things shall never
    be brought low.

16

Security and contentment

1 Keep me, O God, for in thee have I
    found refuge.
2   I have said to the LORD,
    'Thou, Lord, art my felicity.'
3   The gods whom earth holds sacred
    are all worthless,
    and cursed are all who make them
    their delight;[t]
4 those who run after them[u] find trouble
    without end.
    I will not offer them libations of
    blood
    nor take their names upon my lips.
5   Thou, LORD, my allotted portion,
    thou my cup,
    thou dost enlarge my boundaries:

    the lines fall for me in pleasant 6
    places,
  indeed I am well content with my
    inheritance.
I will bless the LORD who has given 7
  me counsel:
in the night-time wisdom comes to
  me in my inward parts.
I have set the LORD continually 8
  before me:
with him[v] at my right hand I cannot be shaken.
Therefore my heart exults   9
and my spirit rejoices,
my body too rests unafraid;
for thou wilt not abandon me to 10
  Sheol
nor suffer thy faithful servant to see
  the pit.
Thou wilt show me the path of life; 11
in thy presence is the fullness of joy,
in thy right hand pleasures for
  evermore.

17

Prayer for the LORD's help

  Hear, LORD, my plea for justice,   1
  give my cry a hearing,
  listen to my prayer,
  for it is innocent of all deceit.
  Let judgement in my cause issue 2
  from thy lips,
  let thine eyes be fixed on justice.
Thou hast tested my heart and watched 3
  me all night long;
  thou hast assayed me and found in
  me no mind to evil.
  I will not speak of the deeds of men; 4
  I have taken good note of all thy
  sayings.
I have not strayed from the course of 5
  duty;
  I have followed thy path and never
  stumbled.
I call upon thee, O God, for thou wilt 6
  answer me.
Bend down thy ear to me, listen to my
  words.
  Show me how marvellous thy true 7
  love can be,
  who with thy hand dost save
  all who seek sanctuary from their
  enemies.
  Keep me like the apple of thine eye; 8
  hide me in the shadow of thy wings
  from the wicked who obstruct me, 9
from deadly foes who throng round
  me.
  They have stifled all compassion; 10
  their mouths are full of pride;

t are all worthless . . . delight: prob. rdg.; Heb. obscure.   *u after them: prob. rdg.; Heb. obscure.*
v with him: prob. rdg.; Heb. om.

H*

11 they press me hard,^{w} now they hem
       me in,
   on the watch to bring me to the
       ground.
12 The enemy is like a lion eager for prey,
       like a young lion crouching in am-
       bush.
13 Arise, LORD, meet him face to face and
       bring him down.
   Save my life from the wicked;
14 make an end of them^x with thy
       sword.
   With thy hand, O LORD, make an
       end of them;^{x}
   thrust them out of this world in the
       prime of their life,
   gorged as they are with thy good
       things,
   blest with many sons
   and leaving their children wealth in
       plenty.
15 But my plea is just: I shall see thy
       face,
   and be blest with a vision of thee
       when I awake.

18

Song of deliverance

1   I love thee, O LORD my strength.
2^y The LORD is my stronghold, my fort-
       ress and my champion,
   my God, my rock where I find safety,
   my shield, my mountain refuge, my
       strong tower.
3 I will call on the LORD to whom all
       praise is due,
   and I shall be delivered from my
       enemies.
4 When the bonds of death held me fast,
   destructive torrents overtook me,
5 the bonds of Sheol tightened round
       me,
   the snares of death were set to catch
       me;
6 then in anguish of heart I cried to the
       LORD,
   I called for help to my God;
   he heard me from his temple,
   and my cry reached his ears.
7 The earth heaved and quaked,
   the foundations of the mountains
       shook;
   they heaved, because he was angry.
8 Smoke rose from his nostrils,
   devouring fire came out of his mouth,
   glowing coals and searing heat.
9 He swept the skies aside as he de-
       scended,

thick darkness lay under his feet.
He rode on a cherub, he flew through 10
   the air;
he swooped on the wings of the wind.
He made darkness around him his 11
   hiding-place
and dense^z vapour his canopy.^{a}
Thick clouds came out of the radiance 12
   before him,
hailstones and glowing coals.
The LORD thundered from the heavens 13
and the voice of the Most High spoke
   out.^{b}
He loosed his arrows, he sped them 14
   far and wide,
he shot forth lightning shafts and sent
   them echoing.
The channels of the sea-bed were 15
   revealed,
the foundations of earth laid bare
at the LORD's rebuke,
at the blast of the breath of his^a
   nostrils.
He reached down from the height and 16
   took me,
he drew me out of mighty waters,
he rescued me from my enemies, 17
   strong as they were,
from my foes when they grew too
   powerful for me.
They confronted me in the hour of my 18
   peril,
but the LORD was my buttress.
He brought me out into an open place, 19
he rescued me because he delighted in
   me.
The LORD rewarded me as my right- 20
   eousness deserved;
my hands were clean, and he requited
   me.
For I have followed the ways of the 21
   LORD
and have not turned wickedly from
   my God;
all his laws are before my eyes, 22
I have not failed to follow his decrees.
In his sight I was blameless 23
and kept myself from wilful sin;
the LORD requited me as my right- 24
   eousness deserved
and the purity of my life in his eyes.

With the loyal thou showest thyself 25
   loyal
and with the blameless man blameless.
With the savage man thou showest 26
   thyself savage,
and^d tortuous with the perverse.
Thou deliverest humble folk, 27

---

w they press me hard: *prob. rdg.*; *Heb.* our footsteps.   *x* make an end of them: *prob. rdg.*; *Heb.*
unintelligible.   *y* Verses 2–50: *cp.* 2 Sam. 22. 2–51.   *z Prob. rdg., cp.* 2 Sam. 22. 12; *Heb.*
dark.   *a Prob. rdg.*; *Heb. adds* thick clouds.   *b Prob. rdg.*; *Heb. adds* hailstones and glowing
coals.   *c Prob. rdg.*; *Heb.* thy.   *d* With the savage . . . savage, and: *or* With the pure thou
showest thyself pure, but . . .

and bringest proud looks down to
    earth.
28 Thou, LORD, dost make my lamp burn
    bright,
and my God will lighten my darkness.
29 With thy help I leap over a bank,
    by God's aid I spring over a wall.

30 The way of God is perfect,
    the LORD's word has stood the test;
    he is the shield of all who take refuge
        in him.
31 What god is there but the LORD?
    What rock but our God?—
32 the God who girds me with strength
    and makes my way blameless,
33 who makes me swift as a hind
    and sets me secure on the mountains;
34 who trains my hands for battle,
    and my arms aim an arrow tipped
        with bronze.

35 Thou hast given me the shield of thy
        salvation,
    thy hand sustains me, thy providence
        makes me great.
36 Thou givest me room for my steps,
    my feet have not faltered.
37 I pursue my enemies and overtake
        them,
    I do not return until I have made an
        end of them.
38 I strike them down and they will
        never rise again;
    they fall beneath my feet.
39 Thou dost arm me with strength for
        the battle
    and dost subdue my foes before me.
40 Thou settest my foot on my enemies'
        necks,
    and I bring to nothing those that hate
        me.
41 They cry out and there is no one to
        help them,
    they cry to the LORD and he does not
        answer.
42 I will pound them fine as dust before
        the wind,
    like mud in the streets will I trample
        them.[e]
43 Thou dost deliver me from the clam-
        our of the people,
    and makest me master of the nations.
    A people I never knew shall be my
        subjects;
44 as soon as they hear tell of me, they
        shall obey me,
    and foreigners shall come cringing to
        me.
45 Foreigners shall be brought captive to
        me,
    and emerge from their strongholds.

The LORD lives, blessed is my rock,   46
high above all is God who saves me.

O God, who grantest me vengeance,   47
who layest nations prostrate at my
        feet,
who dost rescue me from my foes and 48
        set me over my enemies,
thou dost deliver me from violent
        men.
Therefore, LORD, I will praise thee 49
        among the nations
and sing psalms to thy name,
to one who gives his king great vic- 50
        tories
and in all his acts keeps faith with his
        anointed king,
with David and his descendants for
        ever.

19

The LORD's works and words

The heavens tell out the glory of 1
        God,
    the vault of heaven reveals his
        handiwork.
One day speaks to another,   2
night with night shares its know-
        ledge,
    and this without speech or language 3
        or sound of any voice.
    Their music goes out through all 4
        the earth,
    their words reach to the end of the
        world.
In them a tent is fixed for the sun,
who comes out like a bridegroom from 5
        his wedding canopy,
rejoicing like a strong man to run his
        race.
    His rising is at one end of the 6
        heavens,
    his circuit touches their farthest
        ends;
    and nothing is hidden from his heat.

    The law of the LORD is perfect and 7
        revives the soul.
    The LORD's instruction never fails,
    and makes the simple wise.
The precepts of the LORD are right and 8
        rejoice the heart.
    The commandment of the LORD
        shines clear
    and gives light to the eyes.
    The fear of the LORD is pure and 9
        abides for ever.
The LORD's decrees are true and
        righteous every one,
more to be desired than gold, pure 10
        gold in plenty,
    sweeter than syrup or honey from
        the comb.

e Prob. rdg., cp. 2 Sam. 22. 43; Heb. will I empty them out.

11   It is these that give thy servant
        warning,
        and he who keeps them wins a
        great reward.
12   Who is aware of his unwitting sins?
        Cleanse me of any secret fault.
13   Hold back thy servant also from
        sins of self-will,
        lest they get the better of me.
        Then I shall be blameless
        and innocent of any great trans-
        gression.
14 May all that I say and think be ac-
        ceptable to thee,
        O Lord, my rock and my redeemer!

20

Victory to the Lord's anointed king

1   May the Lord answer you in the
        hour of trouble!
        The name of Jacob's God be your
        tower of strength,
2   give you help from the sanctuary
        and send you support from Zion!
3   May he remember all your offerings
        and look with favour on your rich
        sacrifices,
4   give you your heart's desire
        and grant success to all your plans!
5   Let us sing aloud in praise of your
        victory,
        let us do homage to the name of our
        God!
        The Lord grant all you ask!

6   Now I know
        that the Lord has given victory to
        his anointed king:
        he will answer him from his holy
        heaven
        with the victorious might of his
        right hand.
7 Some boast of chariots and some of
        horses,
        but our boast is the name of the Lord
        our God.
8   They totter and fall,
        but we rise up and are full of
        courage.
9   O Lord, save the king,
        and answer us in the hour of our
        calling.

21

Coming victory

1 The king rejoices in thy might, O
        Lord:
        well may he exult in thy victory,
2   for thou hast given him his heart's
        desire

and hast not refused him what he
        asked.
Thou dost welcome him with bless- 3
        ings and prosperity
        and set a crown of fine gold upon
        his head.
He asked of thee life, and thou didst 4
        give it him,
        length of days for ever and ever.
Thy salvation has brought him 5
        great glory;
thou dost invest him with majesty
        and honour,
        for thou bestowest blessings on him 6
        for evermore
        and dost make him glad with joy in
        thy presence.
The king puts his trust in the Lord; 7
        the loving care of the Most High
        holds him unshaken.

Your hand shall reach all your 8
        enemies:
your right hand shall reach those who
        hate you;
        at your coming you shall plunge 9
        them into a fiery furnace;
        the Lord in his anger will strike
        them down,
        and fire shall consume them.
It will exterminate their offspring 10
        from the earth
        and rid mankind of their posterity.
For they have aimed wicked blows 11
        at you,
        they have plotted mischief but
        could not prevail;
        but you will catch them round the 12
        shoulders
        and will aim with your bow-strings
        at their faces.

Be exalted, O Lord, in thy might; 13
        we will sing a psalm of praise to thy
        power.

22

Anguish and praise

My God, my God, why hast thou 1
        forsaken me
        and art so far from saving me, from
        heeding my groans?
O my God, I cry in the day-time but 2
        thou dost not answer,
        in the night I cry but get no respite.
And yet thou art enthroned in holi- 3
        ness,
        thou art he whose praises Israel
        sings.
In thee our fathers put their trust; 4
        they trusted, and thou didst rescue
        them.
Unto thee they cried and were de- 5
        livered;

in thee they trusted and were not
   put to shame.
6 But I am a worm, not a man,
   abused by all men, scorned by the
   people.
7 All who see me jeer at me,
make mouths at me and wag their
   heads:
8 'He threw himself on the LORD for
   rescue;
   let the LORD deliver him, for he
   holds him dear!'
9 But thou art he who drew me from
   the womb,
   who laid me at my mother's breast.
10 Upon thee was I cast at birth;
   from my mother's womb thou hast
   been my God.
11 Be not far from me,
for trouble is near, and I have no
   helper.
12 A herd of bulls surrounds me,
   great bulls of Bashan beset me.
13 Ravening and roaring lions
   open their mouths wide against
   me.
14 My strength drains away like water
   and all my bones are loose.
My heart has turned to wax and
   melts within me.
15 My mouth[f] is dry as a potsherd,
   and my tongue sticks to my jaw;
   I am laid[g] low in the dust of death.
16 The huntsmen are all about me;
   a band of ruffians rings me round,
   and they have hacked off[h] my
   hands and my feet.
17 I tell my tale of misery,
   while they look on and gloat.
18 They share out my garments among
   them
   and cast lots for my clothes.
19 But do not remain so far away,
   O LORD;
   O my help, hasten to my aid.
20 Deliver my very self from the
   sword,
   my precious life from the axe.
21 Save me from the lion's mouth,
   my poor body[i] from the horns of
   the wild ox.

22 I will declare thy fame to my
   brethren;
   I will praise thee in the midst of the
   assembly.
23 Praise him, you who fear the LORD;
   all you sons of Jacob, do him honour;
   stand in awe of him, all sons of
   Israel.

For he has not scorned the down- 24
   trodden,
   nor shrunk in loathing from his
   plight,
   nor hidden his face from him,
   but gave heed to him when he cried
   out.
Thou dost inspire my praise in the full 25
   assembly;
   and I will pay my vows before all
   who fear thee.
Let the humble eat and be satisfied. 26
Let those who seek the LORD praise
   him
   and be in good heart for ever.
Let all the ends of the earth remember 27
   and turn again to the LORD;
let all the families of the nations bow
   down before him.
For kingly power belongs to the 28
   LORD,
   and dominion over the nations is
   his.
How can those buried in the earth 29
   do him homage,
   how can those who go down to the
   grave bow before him?
But I shall live for his sake,
   my posterity[j] shall serve him.   30
This shall be told of the Lord to
   future generations;
   and they shall justify him,   31
   declaring to a people yet unborn
   that this was his doing.

23

The LORD my shepherd

The LORD is my shepherd; I shall 1
   want nothing.
He makes me lie down in green 2
   pastures,
   and leads me beside the waters of
   peace;
he renews life within me,   3
   and for his name's sake guides me
   in the right path.
Even though I walk through a valley 4
   dark as death
I fear no evil, for thou art with me,
thy staff and thy crook are my comfort.

Thou spreadest a table for me in the 5
   sight of my enemies;
   thou hast richly bathed my head
   with oil,
   and my cup runs over.
Goodness and love unfailing, these 6
   will follow me
   all the days of my life,

f Prob. rdg.; Heb. My strength.   *g* I am laid: *prob. rdg.; Heb.* thou wilt lay me.   *h* and they
have hacked off: *prob. rdg.; Heb.* like a lion.   *i* my poor body: *prob. rdg.; Heb.* thou hast
answered me.   *j* But I . . . posterity: *prob. rdg.; Heb. obscure.*

and I shall dwell in the house of the LORD
my whole life long.

24

Entrance of the king of glory

1 The earth is the LORD's and all that is in it,
the world and those who dwell therein.

2 For it was he who founded it upon the seas
and planted it firm upon the waters beneath.

3 Who may go up the mountain of the LORD?
And who may stand in his holy place?

4 He who has clean hands and a pure heart,
who has not set his mind on falsehood,
and has not committed perjury.

5 He shall receive a blessing from the LORD,
and justice from God his saviour.

6 Such is the fortune of those who seek him,
who seek the face of the God of Jacob.

7 Lift up your heads, you gates,
lift yourselves up, you everlasting doors,
that the king of glory may come in.

8 Who is the king of glory?
The LORD strong and mighty,
the LORD mighty in battle.

9 Lift up your heads, you gates,
lift them up, you everlasting doors,
that the king of glory may come in.

10 Who then is the king of glory?
The king of glory is the LORD of Hosts.

25

The source of lasting prosperity

1 Unto thee, O LORD my God, I lift up my heart.

2 In thee I trust: do not put me to shame,
let not my enemies exult over me.

3 No man who hopes in thee is put to shame;
but shame comes to all who break faith without cause.

4 Make thy paths known to me, O LORD;
teach me thy ways.

5 Lead me in thy truth and teach me;
thou art God my saviour.

For thee I have waited all the day long,
for the coming of thy goodness, LORD.[k]

6 Remember, LORD, thy tender care and thy love unfailing,
shown from ages past.

7 Do not remember the sins and offences of my youth,
but remember me in thy unfailing love.

8 The LORD is good and upright;
therefore he teaches sinners the way they should go.

9 He guides the humble man in doing right,
he teaches the humble his ways.

10 All the ways of the LORD are loving and sure
to men who keep his covenant and his charge.

11 For the honour of thy name, O LORD,
forgive my wickedness, great as it is.

12 If there is any man who fears the LORD,
he shall be shown the path that he should choose;

13 he shall enjoy lasting prosperity,
and his children after him shall inherit the land.

14 The LORD confides his purposes to those who fear him,
and his covenant is theirs to know.

15 My eyes are ever on the LORD,
who alone can free my feet from the net.

16 Turn to me and show me thy favour,
for I am lonely and oppressed.

17 Relieve the sorrows of my heart
and bring me out of my distress.

18 Look at my misery and my trouble
and forgive me every sin.

19 Look at my enemies, see how many they are
and how violent their hatred for me.

20 Defend me and deliver me,
do not put me to shame when I take refuge in thee.

21 Let integrity and uprightness protect me,
for I have waited for thee, O LORD.

22 O God, redeem Israel from all his sorrows.

26

Prayer for a firm footing

1 Give me justice, O LORD,
for I have lived my life without reproach,

k for the coming . . . LORD: transposed from end of verse 7.

and put unfaltering trust in the
LORD.

2 Test me, O LORD, and try me;
   put my heart and mind to the
   proof.

3 For thy constant love is before my
   eyes,
   and I live in thy truth.

4 I have not sat among worthless
   men,
   nor do I mix with hypocrites;

5 I hate the company of evildoers
   and will not sit among the ungodly.

6 I wash my hands in innocence
   to join in procession round thy
   altar, O LORD,

7 singing of thy marvellous acts,
   recounting them all with thankful
   voice.

8 O LORD, I love the beauty of thy
   house,
   the place where thy glory dwells.

9 Do not sweep me away with sinners,
   nor cast me out with men who thirst
   for blood,

10 whose fingers are active in mischief,
   and their hands are full of bribes.

11 But I live my life without reproach;
   redeem me, O LORD, and show me
   thy favour.

12 When once my feet are planted on
   firm ground,
   I will bless the LORD in the full
   assembly.

27

The cure for anxiety

1 The LORD is my light and my salvation;
   whom should I fear?
   The LORD is the refuge of my life;
   of whom then should I go in dread?

2 When evildoers close in on me to
   devour me,
   it is my enemies, my assailants,
   who stumble and fall.

3 If an army should encamp against
   me,
   my heart would feel no fear;
   if armed men should fall upon me,
   even then I should be undismayed.

4 One thing I ask of the LORD,
   one thing I seek:
   that I may be constant in the house
   of the LORD
   all the days of my life,
   to gaze upon the beauty of the
   LORD
   and to seek him*[l]* in his temple.

5 For he will keep me safe beneath
   his roof
   in the day of misfortune;

[l] Or and to pay my morning worship.

he will hide me under the cover of
his tent;
he will raise me beyond reach of
distress.

6 Now I can raise my head high
   above the enemy all about me;
   so will I acclaim him with sacrifice
   before his tent
   and sing a psalm of praise to the
   LORD.

7 Hear, O LORD, when I call aloud;
   show me favour and answer me.

8 'Come,' my heart has said,
   'seek his face.'*[m]*
   I will seek thy face, O LORD;

9 do not hide it from me,
   nor in thy anger turn away thy
   servant,
   whose help thou hast been;
   do not cast me off or forsake me,
   O God my saviour.

10 Though my father and my mother
   forsake me,
   the LORD will take me into his care.

11–12 Teach me thy way, O LORD;
   do not give me up to the greed of
   my enemies;
   lead me by a level path
   to escape my watchful foes;
   liars stand up to give evidence
   against me,
   breathing malice.

13 Well I know that I shall see the
   goodness of the LORD
   in the land of the living.

14 Wait for the LORD; be strong, take
   courage,
   and wait for the LORD.

28

Prayer for mercy and help

1 To thee, O LORD, I call;
   O my Rock, be not deaf to my cry,
   lest, if thou answer me with silence,
   I become like those who go down to
   the abyss.

2 Hear my cry for mercy
   when I call to thee for help,
   when I lift my hands to thy holy
   shrine.

3 Do not drag me away with the ungodly, with evildoers,
   who speak civilly to neighbours, with
   malice in their hearts.

4 Reward them for their works, their
   evil deeds;
   reward them for what their hands
   have done;
   give them their deserts.

5 Because they pay no heed to the
   works of the LORD

m seek his face: prob. rdg.; Heb. seek ye my face.

or to what his hands have done,
may he tear them down and never
build them up!

6 Blessed be the LORD,
for he has heard my cry for mercy.

7 The LORD is my strength, my shield,
in him my heart trusts;
so I am sustained, and my heart
leaps for joy,
and I praise him with my whole
body.[n]

8 The LORD is strength to his people,
a safe refuge for his anointed king.

9 O save thy people and bless thy own,
shepherd them, carry them for ever.

29

The LORD speaks in the storm

1 Ascribe to the LORD, you gods,
ascribe to the LORD glory and might.

2 Ascribe to the LORD the glory due
to his name;
bow down to the LORD in the splendour of holiness.[o]

3 The God of glory thunders:
the voice of the LORD echoes over
the waters,
the LORD is over the mighty waters.

4 The voice of the LORD is power.
The voice of the LORD is majesty.

5 The voice of the LORD breaks the
cedars,
the LORD splinters the cedars of
Lebanon.

6 He makes Lebanon skip like a calf,
Sirion like a young wild ox.

7 The voice of the LORD makes flames
of fire burst forth,

8 the voice of the LORD makes the
wilderness writhe in travail;
the LORD makes the wilderness of
Kadesh writhe.

9 The voice of the LORD makes the
hinds calve
and brings kids early to birth;
and in his temple all cry, 'Glory!'

10 The LORD is king above[p] the flood,
the LORD has taken his royal seat as
king for ever.

11 The LORD will give strength to his
people;
the LORD will bless his people with
peace.

30

Self-confidence shaken

1 I will exalt thee, O LORD;
thou hast lifted me up

and hast not let my enemies make
merry over me.

2 O LORD my God, I cried to thee and
thou didst heal me.

3 O LORD, thou hast brought me up
from Sheol
and saved my life as I was sinking
into the abyss.[q]

4 Sing a psalm to the LORD, all you
his loyal servants,
and give thanks to his holy name.

5 In his anger is disquiet, in his favour
there is life.
Tears may linger at nightfall,
but joy comes in the morning.

6 Carefree as I was, I had said,
'I can never be shaken.'

7 But, LORD, it was thy will to shake
my mountain refuge;
thou didst hide thy face, and I was
struck with dismay.

8 I called unto thee, O LORD,
and I pleaded with thee, Lord, for
mercy:

9 'What profit in my death if I go down
into the pit?
Can the dust confess thee or proclaim
thy truth?

10 Hear, O LORD, and be gracious to
me;
LORD, be my helper.'

11 Thou hast turned my laments into
dancing;
thou hast stripped off my sackcloth
and clothed me with joy,

12 that my spirit may sing psalms to
thee and never cease.
I will confess thee for ever, O LORD
my God.

31

The LORD's unfailing love

1 With thee, O LORD, I have sought
shelter,
let me never be put to shame.
Deliver me in thy righteousness;

2 bow down and hear me,
come quickly to my rescue;
be thou my rock of refuge,
a stronghold to keep me safe.

3 Thou art to me both rock and
stronghold;
lead me and guide me for the
honour of thy name.

4 Set me free from the net men have
hidden for me;
thou art my refuge,

5 into thy keeping I commit my
spirit.

n with my whole body: *prob. rdg.*; *Heb.* from my song.   o the splendour of holiness: *or* holy
vestments.   p *Or* since.   q and saved . . . abyss: *or* and rescued me alive from among those
who go down to the abyss.

17 When men cry for help, the LORD
hears them
and sets them free from all their
troubles.
18 The LORD is close to those whose
courage is broken
and he saves those whose spirit is
crushed.
19 The good man's misfortunes may
be many,
the LORD delivers him out of them
all.
20 He guards every bone of his body,
and not one of them is broken.
21 Their own misdeeds are death to
the wicked,
and those who hate the righteous
are brought to ruin.

22 The LORD ransoms the lives of his
servants,
and none who seek refuge in him
are brought to ruin.

35

Prayer for vindication

1 Strive, O LORD, with those who
strive against me;
fight against those who fight me.
2 Grasp shield and buckler,
and rise up to help me.
3 Uncover the spear and bar the way
against my pursuers.
Let me hear thee declare,
'I am your salvation.'
4 Shame and disgrace be on those who
seek my life;
and may those who plan to hurt me
retreat in dismay!
5 May they be like chaff before the
wind,
driven by the angel of the LORD!
6 Let their way be dark and slippery
as the angel of the LORD pursues
them!
7 For unprovoked they have hidden
a net[y] for me,
unprovoked they have dug a pit to
trap me.
8 May destruction unforeseen come
on him;
may the net which he hid catch
him;
may he crash headlong into it!
9 Then I shall rejoice in the LORD
and delight in his salvation.
10 My very bones cry out,
'LORD, who is like thee?—
thou saviour of the poor from those
too strong for them,

the poor and wretched from those who
prey on them.'
Malicious witnesses step forward;   11
they question me on matters of
which I know nothing.
They return me evil for good,   12
lying in wait[z] to take my life.
And yet when they were sick, I put on   13
sackcloth,
I mortified myself with fasting.
When my prayer came back unanswered,
I walked with head bowed in grief   14
as if for a brother;
as one in sorrow for his mother I lay
prostrate in mourning.
But when I stumbled, they crowded   15
round rejoicing,
they crowded about me;
nameless ruffians[a] jeered at me
and nothing would stop them.
When I slipped, brutes who would   16
mock even a hunchback
ground their teeth at me.
O Lord, how long wilt thou look on   17
at those who hate me for no reason[b]?
Rescue me out of their cruel grasp,
save my precious life from the unbelievers.
Then I will praise thee before a   18
great assembly,
I will extol thee where many people
meet.
Let no treacherous enemy gloat   19
over me
nor leer at me in triumph.[c]
No friendly greeting do they give   20
to peaceable folk.
They invent lie upon lie,
they open their mouths at me: 21
'Hurrah!' they shout in their joy,
feasting their eyes on me.
Thou hast seen all this, O LORD, do   22
not keep silence;
O Lord, be not far from me.
Awake, bestir thyself, to do me   23
justice,
to plead my cause, my Lord and
my God.
Judge me, O LORD my God, as thou   24
art true;
do not let them gloat over me.
Do not let them say to themselves,   25
'Hurrah!
We have swallowed him up at one
gulp.'
Let them all be disgraced and dis-   26
mayed
who rejoice at my fall;
let them be covered with shame and
dishonour

*y Prob. rdg., transposing a pit from this line to follow have dug.   z lying in wait: prob. rdg.; Heb.
bereavement.   a nameless ruffians: or ruffians who give me no rest.   b Line transposed
from verse 19.   c See note on verse 17.*

who glory over me.

27 But let all who would see me righted
    shout for joy,
  let them cry continually,
  'All glory to the LORD
  who would see his servant thrive!'

28 So shall I talk of thy justice
  and of thy praise all the day long.

36

*Man's sin and the LORD's righteous-
ness*

1 Deep in his heart, sin whispers to
    the wicked man
  who cherishes no fear of God.

2 For he flatters himself in his own
    opinion
  and, when he is found out, he does
    not mend his ways.[d]

3 All that he says is mischievous and
    false;
  he has turned his back on wisdom;

4 in his bed he plots how best to do
    mischief.
  So set is he on his wrong courses
  that he rejects nothing evil.

5 But thy unfailing love, O LORD,
    reaches to heaven,
  thy faithfulness to the skies.

6 Thy righteousness is like the lofty
    mountains,
  thy judgements are like the great
    abyss;
  O LORD, who savest man and beast,

7 how precious is thy unfailing love!
  Gods and men seek refuge in the
    shadow of thy wings.

8 They are filled with the rich plenty
    of thy house,
  and thou givest them water from
    the flowing stream of thy delights;

9 for with thee is the fountain of life,
  and in thy light we are bathed with
    light.

10 Maintain thy love unfailing over
    those who know thee,
  and thy justice toward men of
    honest heart.

11 Let not the foot of pride come near
    me,
  no wicked hand disturb me.

12 There they lie, the evildoers,
  they are hurled down and cannot
    rise.

37

Advice of an old man

1 Do not strive to outdo the evildoers
  or emulate those who do wrong.

For like grass they soon wither,   2
  and fade like the green of spring.
Trust in the LORD and do good;   3
  settle in the land and find safe pasture.
Depend upon the LORD,   4
  and he will grant you your heart's
    desire.
Commit your life to the LORD;   5
  trust in him and he will act.
  He will make your righteousness   6
    shine clear as the day
  and the justice of your cause like
    the sun at noon.
Wait quietly for the LORD, be   7
  patient till he comes;
  do not strive to outdo the success-
    ful
  nor envy him who gains his ends.
Be angry no more, have done with   8
    wrath;
  strive not to outdo in evildoing.
For evildoers will be destroyed,   9
  but they who hope in the LORD
    shall possess the land.
A little while, and the wicked will   10
  be no more;
  look well, and you will find their place
    is empty.
But the humble shall possess the   11
    land
  and enjoy untold prosperity.
The wicked mutter against the   12
    righteous man
  and grind their teeth at the sight of
    him;
  the Lord shall laugh at them,   13
  for he sees that their time is coming.
The wicked have drawn their   14
    swords
  and strung their bows
  to bring low the poor and needy
  and to slaughter honest men.
Their swords shall pierce their own   15
    hearts
  and their bows be broken.
Better is the little which the right-   16
    eous has
  than the great wealth of the wicked.
For the strong arm of the wicked   17
    shall be broken,
  but the LORD upholds the right-
    eous.
The LORD knows each day of the   18
    good man's life,
  and his inheritance shall last for
    ever.
When times are bad, he shall not be   19
    distressed,
  and in days of famine he shall have
    enough.
But the wicked shall perish,   20
  and their children shall beg their
    bread.[e]

---

d he does . . . ways: *prob. rdg.; Heb. unintelligible.*   *e Line transposed from verse 25.*

The enemies of the LORD, like fuel
in a furnace,[f]
are consumed in smoke.
21 The wicked man borrows and does
not pay back,
but the righteous is a generous
giver.
22 All whom the LORD has blessed shall
possess the land,
and all who are cursed by him shall
be destroyed.
23 It is the LORD who directs a man's
steps,
he holds him firm and watches over
his path.
24 Though he may fall, he will not go
headlong,
for the LORD grasps him by the
hand.
25 I have been young and am now
grown old,
and never have I seen a righteous
man forsaken.[g]
26 Day in, day out, he lends generously,
and his children become a blessing.
27 Turn from evil and do good,
and live at peace for ever;
28 for the LORD is a lover of justice
and will not forsake his loyal servants.
The lawless are banished for ever
and the children of the wicked
destroyed.
29 The righteous shall possess the land
and shall live there at peace for
ever.
30 The righteous man utters words of
wisdom
and justice is always on his lips.
31 The law of his God is in his heart,
his steps do not falter.
32 The wicked watch for the righteous man
and seek to take his life;
33 but the LORD will not leave him in
their power
nor let him be condemned before
his judges.
34 Wait for the LORD and hold to his
way;
he will keep you[h] safe from wicked
men[i]
and will raise you to be master of
the land.
When the wicked are destroyed, you
shall be there to see.
35 I have watched a wicked man at his
work,
rank as a spreading tree in its
native soil.

I passed by one day, and he was 36
gone;
I searched for him, but he could not
be found.
Now look at the good man, watch him 37
who is honest,
for the man of peace leaves descendants;
but transgressors are wiped out one 38
and all,
and the descendants of the wicked
are destroyed.
Deliverance for the righteous comes 39
from the LORD,
their refuge in time of trouble.
The LORD will help them and de- 40
liver them;[j]
he will save them because they seek
shelter with him.

38

Prayer in affliction

O LORD, do not rebuke me in thy 1
anger,
nor punish me in thy wrath.
For thou hast aimed thy arrows[k] at 2
me,
and thy hand weighs heavy upon
me.
Thy indignation has left no part of 3
my body unscarred;
there is no health in my whole
frame because of my sin.
For my iniquities have poured over 4
my head;
they are a load heavier than I can
bear.
My wounds fester and stink because 5
of my folly.
I am bowed down and utterly pros- 6
trate.
All day long I go about as if in
mourning,
for my loins burn with fever, 7
and there is no wholesome flesh in
me.
All battered and benumbed, 8
I groan aloud in my heart's longing.
O Lord, all my lament lies open 9
before thee
and my sighing is no secret to thee.
My heart beats fast, my strength has 10
ebbed away,
and the light has gone out of my
eyes.
My friends and my companions shun 11
me in my sickness,
and my kinsfolk keep far away.
Those who wish me dead defame 12
me,

---

f like . . . furnace: *prob. rdg.*; *Heb.* like the worth of rams.   g *See note on verse 20.*   h *Prob.*
rdg.; *Heb.* them.   i he will . . . wicked men: *transposed from verse 40.*   j *See note on verse 34.*
k thou . . . arrows: *prob. rdg.*; *Heb.* thy arrows have come down.

those who mean to injure me spread
    cruel gossip
and mutter slanders all day long.
13 But I am deaf, I do not listen;
    I am like a dumb man who cannot
        open his mouth.
14 I behave like a man who cannot
        hear
    and whose tongue offers no defence.
15 On thee, O LORD, I fix my hope;
    thou wilt answer, O Lord my God.
16 I said, 'Let them never rejoice over
        me
    who exult when my foot slips.'
17 I am indeed prone to stumble,
    and suffering is never far away.
18 I make no secret of my iniquity
    and am anxious at the thought of
        my sin.
19 But many are my enemies, all with-
        out cause,[l]
    and many those who hate me
        wrongfully.
20 Those who repay good with evil
    oppose me because my purpose is
        good.
21 But, LORD, do not thou forsake me;
    keep not far from me, my God.
22 Hasten to my help, O Lord my
        salvation.

39

The brevity of life

1   I said: I will keep close watch over
        myself
    that all I say may be free from sin.
    I will keep a muzzle on my mouth,
    so long as wicked men confront me.
2   In dumb silence I held my peace.
    So my agony was quickened,
3   and my heart burned within me.
    My mind wandered as the fever
        grew,
    and I began to speak:
4   LORD, let me know my end
    and the number of my days;
    tell me how short my life must be.
5   I know thou hast made my days a
        mere span long,
    and my whole life is nothing in thy
        sight.
    Man, though he stands upright, is
        but a puff of wind,
6   he moves like a phantom;
    the riches[m] he piles up are no more
        than vapour,
    he does not know who will enjoy
        them.
7   And now, Lord, what do I wait for?
    My hope is in thee.

Deliver me from all who do me   8
    wrong,
make me no longer the butt of fools.
I am dumb, I will not open my   9
    mouth,
because it is thy doing.
Plague me no more;   10
I am exhausted by thy blows.
When thou dost rebuke a man to   11
    punish his sin,
all his charm festers and drains
    away;
indeed man is only a puff of wind.
Hear my prayer, O LORD;   12
listen to my cry,
hold not thy peace at my tears;
for I find shelter with thee,
I am thy guest, as all my fathers
    were.
Frown on me no more and let me   13
    smile again,
before I go away and cease to be.

40

Thanksgiving and petition

I waited, waited for the LORD,   1
he bent down to me and heard my cry.
He brought me up out of the muddy   2
    pit,
out of the mire and the clay;
he set my feet on a rock
and gave me a firm footing;
and on my lips he put a new song,   3
a song of praise to our God.
Many when they see will be filled
    with awe
and will learn to trust in the LORD:
happy is the man   4
who makes the LORD his trust,
and does not look to brutal and
    treacherous men.
Great things thou hast done,   5
O LORD my God;
thy wonderful purposes are all for
    our good;
none can compare with thee;
I would proclaim them and speak of
    them,
but they are more than I can tell.
If thou hadst desired sacrifice and   6
    offering
thou wouldst have given me ears to
    hear.
If thou hadst asked for whole-
    offering and sin-offering
I would have said, 'Here I am.'[n]   7
My desire is to do thy will, O God,   8
and thy law is in my heart.
In the great assembly I have pro-   9
    claimed what is right,
I do not hold back my words,

l all . . . cause: *prob. rdg.*; *Heb. living.*   *m* the riches: *prob. rdg.*; *Heb. they murmur.*   *n Prob.*
rdg.; *Heb. adds* in a scroll of a book it is prescribed for me.

as thou knowest, O LORD.

10 I have not kept thy goodness hidden in my heart;
I have proclaimed thy faithfulness and saving power,
and not concealed thy unfailing love and truth
from the great assembly.

11 Thou, O LORD, dost not withhold thy tender care from me;
thy unfailing love and truth for ever guard me.

12 For misfortunes beyond counting press on me from all sides;
my iniquities have overtaken me, and my sight fails;
they are more than the hairs of my head,
and my courage forsakes me.

13[o] Show me favour, O LORD, and save me;
hasten to help me, O LORD.

14 Let those who seek to take my life be put to shame and dismayed one and all;
let all who love to hurt me shrink back disgraced;

15 let those who cry 'Hurrah!' at my downfall
be horrified at their reward of shame.

16 But let all those who seek thee be jubilant and rejoice in thee;
and let those who long for thy saving help ever cry,
'All glory to the LORD!'

17 But I am poor and needy;
O Lord, think of me.[p]
Thou art my help and my salvation;
O my God, make no delay.

41

Prayer for healing

1 Happy the man who has a concern for the helpless!
The LORD will save him in time of trouble.

2 The LORD protects him and gives him life,
making him secure in the land;
the LORD never leaves him[q] to the greed of his enemies.

3 He nurses him on his sick-bed;
he turns his bed when he is ill.

4 But I said, 'LORD, be gracious to me;
heal me, for I have sinned against thee.'

'His case is desperate,' my enemies 5 say;
'when will he die, and his line become extinct?'

All who visit me speak from an empty 6 heart,
alert to gather bad news;
then they go out to spread it abroad.

All who hate me whisper together 7 about me
and love to make the worst of everything:
'An evil spell is cast upon him; 8
he is laid on his bed, and will rise no more.'

Even the friend whom I trusted, who 9 ate at my table,[r]
exults over my misfortune.

O LORD, be gracious and restore me, 10 that I may pay them out to the full.[s]

Then I shall know that thou delight- 11 est in me
and that my enemy will not triumph over me.

But I am upheld by thee because of 12 my innocence;
thou keepest me for ever in thy sight.

Blessed be the LORD, the God of 13 Israel,
from everlasting to everlasting.

Amen, Amen.

BOOK 2
42–3

Thirsting for God

As a hind longs for the running 1 streams,
so do I long for thee, O God.

With my whole being I thirst for God, 2 the living God.
When shall I come to God and appear in his presence?

Day and night, tears are my food; 3
'Where is your God?' they ask me all day long.

As I pour out my soul in distress, I 4 call to mind
how I marched in the ranks of the great to the house of God,
among exultant shouts of praise, the clamour of the pilgrims.

How deep I am sunk in misery, 5
groaning in my distress;
yet I will wait for God;
I will praise him continually,
my deliverer, my God.

*o Verses 13–17: cp. Ps. 70. 1–5.   p O Lord . . . me: prob. rdg.; Heb. may the Lord think of me.
q never leaves him: prob. rdg.; Heb. do thou not give him up . . .   r who . . . table: or slanders me.
s to the full: transposed from end of verse 9.*

6 I am sunk in misery, therefore will I
      remember thee,
    though from the Hermons and the
      springs of Jordan,
    and from the hill of Mizar,
7 deep calls to deep in the roar of thy
      cataracts,
    and all thy waves, all thy breakers,
      pass over me.
8   The LORD makes his unfailing love
      shine forth*t*
    alike by day and night;
    his praise on my lips is a prayer
      to the God of my life.
9 I will say to God my rock, 'Why hast
      thou forgotten me?'
    Why must I go like a mourner because
      my foes oppress me?
10 My enemies taunt me, jeering*u* at my
      misfortunes,
    'Where is your God?' they ask me all
      day long.
11   How deep I am sunk in misery,
      groaning in my distress:
    yet I will wait for God;
    I will praise him continually,
      my deliverer, my God.
43 Plead my cause and give me judge-
      ment against an impious race;
    save me from malignant men and liars,
      O God.
2 Thou, O God, art my refuge; why hast
      thou rejected me?
    Why must I go like a mourner be-
      cause my foes oppress me?
3 Send forth thy light and thy truth to
      be my guide
    and lead me to thy holy hill, to thy
      tabernacle,
4 then shall I come to the altar of God,
      the God of my joy,
    and praise thee on the harp, O God,
      thou God of my delight.
5   How deep I am sunk in misery,
      groaning in my distress:
    yet I will wait for God;
    I will praise him continually,
      my deliverer, my God.

44

Perplexity in defeat

1   O God, we have heard for ourselves,
      our fathers have told us
    all the deeds which thou didst in their
      days,
2 all the work of thy hand in days of old.
    Thou didst plant them in the land and
      drive the nations out,
    thou didst make them strike root,
      breaking up the peoples;
3 it was not our fathers' swords won
      them the land,

nor their arm that gave them the
      victory,
    but thy right hand and thy arm
    and the light of thy presence; such
      was thy favour to them.
Thou art my king and my God;   4
at thy bidding Jacob is victorious.
By thy help we will throw back our   5
      enemies,
in thy name we will trample down our
      adversaries.
I will not trust in my bow,   6
nor will my sword win me the victory;
for thou dost deliver us from our foes 7
and put all our enemies to shame.
In God have we gloried all day long, 8
and we will praise thy name for ever.
But now thou hast rejected and hum-   9
      bled us
and dost no longer lead our armies
      into battle.
Thou hast hurled us back before the 10
      enemy,
and our foes plunder us as they will.
Thou hast given us up to be butchered 11
      like sheep
    and hast scattered us among the
      nations.
Thou hast sold thy people for next to 12
      nothing
and had no profit from the sale.
Thou hast exposed us to the taunts of 13
      our neighbours,
to the mockery and contempt of all
      around.
Thou hast made us a byword among   14
      the nations,
    and the peoples shake their heads at
      us;
so my disgrace confronts me all day   15
      long,
and I am covered with shame
    at the shouts of those who taunt   16
      and abuse me
    as the enemy takes his revenge.
All this has befallen us, but we do not 17
      forget thee
    and have not betrayed thy cove-
      nant;
we have not gone back on our pur-   18
      pose,
nor have our feet strayed from thy
      path.
Yet thou hast crushed us as the sea- 19
      serpent was crushed
and covered us with the darkness of
      death.
If we had forgotten the name of our 20
      God
and spread our hands in prayer to any
      other,
would not God find this out,   21
for he knows the secrets of the heart?

t makes . . . forth: *or* entrusts me to his unfailing love.   *u* jeering: *prob. rdg.; Heb. obscure.*

2 Because of thee we are done to death
all day long,
and are treated as sheep for
slaughter.
3 Bestir thyself, Lord; why dost thou
sleep?
Awake, do not reject us for ever.
4 Why dost thou hide thy face,
heedless of our misery and our
sufferings?
5 For we sink down to the dust
and lie prone on the earth.
6 Arise and come to our help;
for thy love's sake set us free.

45

Royal wedding song

1 My heart is stirred by a noble theme,
in a king's honour I utter the song I
have made,
and my tongue runs like the pen of
an expert scribe.
2 You surpass all mankind in beauty,
your lips are moulded in grace,
so you are blessed by God for ever.
3 With your sword ready at your side,
warrior king,
4 your limbs resplendent^v in their royal
armour,
ride on to execute true sentence and
just judgement.
Your right hand shall show you a
scene of terror:
5 your sharp arrows flying, nations
beneath your feet,
the courage of the king's foes melting away!^{w}
6 Your throne is like God's throne,
eternal,
your royal sceptre a sceptre of
righteousness.
7 You have loved right and hated wrong;
so God, your God, has anointed you
above your fellows with oil, the
token of joy.
8 Your robes are all fragrant with
myrrh and powder of aloes,
and the music of strings greets you
from a palace panelled with ivory.
9 A princess takes her place among the
noblest of your women,
a royal lady at your side in gold of
Ophir.

10 Listen, my daughter, hear my words
and consider them:
forget your own people and your
father's house;

and, when the king desires your 11
beauty,
remember that he is your lord.
Do him obeisance, daughter of 12
Tyre,
and the richest in the land will
court you with gifts.

In the palace honour awaits her;^{x} 13
she is a king's daughter,
arrayed in cloth-of-gold richly em- 14
broidered.
Virgins shall follow her into the
presence of the king;
her companions shall be brought to
her,
escorted with the noise of revels 15
and rejoicing
as they enter the king's palace.

You shall have sons, O king, in 16
place of your forefathers
and will make them rulers over all
the land.^{y}
I will declare your fame to all genera- 1
tions;
therefore the nations will praise you
for ever and ever.

46

The city of God

God is our shelter and our refuge,   1
a timely help in trouble;
so we are not afraid when the earth 2
heaves
and the mountains are hurled into
the sea,
when its waters seethe in tumult   3
and the mountains quake before
his majesty.
There is a river whose streams glad- 4
den the city of God,^{z}
which the Most High has made his
holy dwelling;
God is in that city; she will not be 5
overthrown,
and he will help her at the break of
day.
Nations are in tumult, kingdoms
hurled down;
when he thunders, the earth surges
like the sea.
The Lord of Hosts is with us,   7
the God of Jacob our high stronghold.

Come and see what the Lord has 8
done,
the devastation he has brought
upon earth,

---

v your limbs resplendent: *prob. rdg.*; *Heb.* and in your pomp prosper. w the courage . . . away:
prob. rdg.; *Heb.* obscure. x honour awaits her: *prob. rdg.*; *Heb.* all honoured. y over all the
land: *or* in all the earth. z the city of God: *or* a wondrous city.

9   from end to end of the earth he
      stamps out war:
    he breaks the bow, he snaps the spear
    and burns the shield in the fire.

10 Let be then: learn that I am God,
    high over the nations, high above
    earth.
11 The LORD of Hosts is with us,
    the God of Jacob our high strong-
    hold.

47

God is king of all

1   Clap your hands, all you nations;
    acclaim our God with shouts of joy.
2   How fearful is the LORD Most High,
    great sovereign over all the earth!
3   He lays the nations prostrate be-
    neath us,
    he lays peoples under our feet;
4   he chose our patrimony for us,
    the pride of Jacob whom he loved.

5   God has gone up with shouts of
    acclamation,
    the LORD has gone up with a fan-
    fare of trumpets.
6   Praise God,[a] praise him with psalms;
    praise our king, praise him with
    psalms.
7   God is king of all the earth;
    sing psalms with all your art.
8   God reigns over the nations,
    God is seated on his holy throne.
9   The princes of the nations assemble
    with the families of Abraham's
    line;[b]
    for the mighty ones of earth belong
    to God,
    and he is raised above them all.

48

Praise of Zion

1 The LORD is great and worthy of our
    praise
    in the city of our God, upon his
    holy hill.
2 Fair and lofty, the joy of the whole
    earth
    is Zion's hill, like the farthest
    reaches of the north,[c]
    the hill of the great King's city.
3 In her palaces God is known for a
    tower of strength.
4 See how the kings all gather round
    her,
    marching on in company.
5 They are struck with amazement when
    they see her,
    they are filled with alarm and panic;

    they are seized with trembling,   6
    they toss in pain like a woman in
    labour,
    like the ships of Tarshish   7
    when an east wind wrecks them.
All we had heard we saw with our 8
    own eyes
    in the city of the LORD of Hosts,
    in the city of our God,
    the city which God plants firm for
    evermore.
O God, we re-enact the story of thy 9
    true love
    within thy temple;
    the praise thy name deserves, O 10
    God,
    is heard at earth's farthest bounds.
    Thy hand is charged with justice,
    and the hill of Zion rejoices,   11
    Judah's daughter-cities exult
    in thy judgements.

    Make the round of Zion in proces- 12
    sion,
    count the number of her towers,
    take good note of her ramparts, 13
    pass her palaces in review,
    that you may tell generations yet
    to come:
    Such is God,   14
    our God for ever and ever;
    he shall be our guide eternally.

49

The common lot

    Hear this, all you nations;   1
    listen, all who inhabit this world,
    all mankind, every living man, 2
    rich and poor alike;
    for the words that I speak are wise, 3
    my thoughtful heart is full of under-
    standing.

    I will set my ear to catch the moral 4
    of the story
    and tell on the harp how I read the
    riddle:
    why should I be afraid in evil 5
    times,
    beset by the wickedness of treach-
    erous foes,
    who trust in their riches   6
    and boast of their great wealth?
Alas! no man can ever ransom him- 7
    self
    nor pay God the price of that re-
    lease;
    his ransom would cost too much, 8
    for ever beyond his power to pay,
    the ransom that would let him live 9
    on always
    and never see the pit of death.

a Praise God: *or* Praise, you gods.   *b* the families of Abraham's line: *prob. rdg.; Heb.* the God of
Abraham.   *c Or* of Zaphon.

10 But remember this:^d wise men must die;
stupid men, brutish men, all perish.^e
11 The grave is their eternal home,
their dwelling for all time to come;
they may give their own names to estates,
but they must leave their riches to others.^f
12 For men are like oxen whose life cannot last,
they are like cattle whose time is short.
13 Such is the fate of foolish men
and of all who seek to please them:
14 like sheep they run headlong into Sheol, the land of Death;
he is their shepherd and urges them on;
their flesh must rot away^g
and their bodies be wasted by Sheol,
stripped of all honour.
15 But God will ransom my life,
he will take me from the power of Sheol.
16 Do not envy a man when he grows rich,
when the wealth of his family increases;
17 for he will take nothing when he dies,
and his wealth will not go with him.
18 Though in his lifetime he counts himself happy
and men praise him in his^h prosperity,
19 heⁱ will go to join the company of his forefathers
who will never again see the light.
20 For men are like oxen whose life cannot last,
they are like cattle whose time is short.

50

God's basis of judgement

1 God, the LORD God, has spoken
and summoned the world from the rising to the setting sun.
2 God shines out from Zion, perfect n beauty.
3 Our God is coming and will not keep silence:
consuming fire runs before him
and wreathes him closely round.^j
4 He summons heaven on high and earth
to the judgement of his people:

'Gather to me my loyal servants, 5
all who by sacrifice have made a covenant with me.'
The heavens proclaim his justice, 6
for God himself is the judge.

Listen, my people, and I will speak; 7
I will bear witness against you, O Israel:
I am God, your God,
shall I not^k find fault with your 8 sacrifices,
though^l your offerings are before me always?
I need take no young bull from 9 your house,
no he-goat from your folds;
for all the beasts of the forest are 10 mine
and the cattle in thousands on my hills.
I know every bird on those hills, 11
the teeming life of the fields is my care.
If I were hungry, I would not tell 12 you,
for the world and all that is in it are mine.
Shall I eat the flesh of your bulls 13
or drink the blood of he-goats?
Offer to God the sacrifice of thanks- 14 giving
and pay your vows to the Most High.
If you call upon me in time of 15 trouble,
I will come to your rescue, and you shall honour me.

God's word to the wicked man is 16 this:
What right have you to recite my laws
and make so free with the words of my covenant,
you who hate correction 17
and turn your back when I am speaking?
If you meet a thief, you choose him 18 as your friend;
you make common cause with adulterers;
you charge your mouth with wick- 19 edness
and harness your tongue to slander.
You are for ever talking against 20 your brother,
stabbing your own mother's son in the back.
All this you have done, and shall 21 I keep silence?

d But remember this: *prob. rdg.; Heb.* But he will remember this.   *e Line transposed from here to follow verse 11.*   *f Line transposed from verse 10.*   *g* and urges . . . rot away: *prob. rdg.; Heb. obscure.*   *h* him . . . his: *prob. rdg.; Heb.* you . . . your.   *i* he: *prob. rdg.; Heb.* you. *j* and wreathes him closely round: *or* and rages round him.   *k Or* I will not.   *l Or* for.

You thought that I was another
like yourself,
but point by point I will rebuke you
to your face.
22 Think well on this, you who forget
God,
or I will tear you in pieces and no
one shall save you.
23 He who offers a sacrifice of thanksgiving
does me due honour,
and to him who follows my way[m]
I will show the salvation of God.

51

Prayer for forgiveness

1 Be gracious to me, O God, in thy
true love;
in the fullness of thy mercy blot out
my misdeeds.

2 Wash away all my guilt
and cleanse me from my sin.
3 For well I know my misdeeds,
and my sins confront me all the
day long.
4 Against thee, thee only, I have sinned
and done what displeases thee,
so that thou mayest be proved right
in thy charge
and just in passing sentence.

5 In iniquity I was brought to birth
and my mother conceived me in
sin;
6 yet, though thou hast hidden the
truth in darkness,
through this mystery thou dost
teach me wisdom.
7 Take hyssop[n] and sprinkle me,
that I may be clean;
wash me, that I may become whiter
than snow;
8 let me hear the sounds of joy and
gladness,
let the bones dance which thou hast
broken.
9 Turn away thy face from my sins
and blot out all my guilt.

10 Create a pure heart in me, O God,
and give me a new and steadfast
spirit;
11 do not drive me from thy presence
or take thy holy spirit from me;
12 revive in me the joy of thy deliverance
and grant me a willing spirit to
uphold me.

I will teach transgressors the ways 13
that lead to thee,
and sinners shall return to thee
again.
O LORD God, my deliverer, save me 14
from bloodshed,[o]
and I will sing the praises of thy
justice.
Open my lips, O Lord, 15
that my mouth may proclaim thy
praise.
Thou hast no delight in sacrifice; 16
if I brought thee an offering, thou
wouldst not accept it.
My sacrifice, O God, is a broken 17
spirit;
a wounded heart, O God, thou wilt
not despise.

Let it be thy pleasure to do good 18
to Zion,
to build anew the walls of Jerusalem.
Then only shalt thou delight in the 19
appointed sacrifices;[p]
then shall young bulls be offered on
thy altar.

52

Where wickedness leads

Why make your wickedness your 1-2
boast, you man of might,
forging wild lies all day against God's
loyal servant?
Your slanderous tongue is sharp as
a razor.
You love evil and not good, 3
falsehood, not speaking the truth;
cruel gossip you love and slanderous 4
talk.
So may God[q] pull you down to the 5
ground,
sweep you away, leave you ruined
and homeless,
uprooted from the land of the
living.
The righteous will look on, awe- 6
struck,
and laugh at his plight:
'This is the man', they say, 7
'who does not make God his refuge,
but trusts in his great wealth
and takes refuge in wild lies.'
But I am like a spreading olive-tree 8
in God's house;
for I trust in God's true love for ever
and ever.
I will praise thee for ever for what 9
thou hast done,

---

m him who follows my way: *prob. rdg.; Heb.* him who puts a way.   n *Or* marjoram.   o *Or*
from punishment by death.   p *Prob. rdg.; Heb. adds* a whole-offering and one wholly consumed.
q *Or* So God will.

and glorify thy name among thy loyal
    servants;
    for that is good.

53

Man's wickedness

    The impious fool says in his heart,
    'There is no God.'
    How vile men are, how depraved
      and loathsome;
    not one does anything good!
2 God looks down from heaven
    on all mankind
    to see if any act wisely,
    if any seek out God.
3 But all are unfaithful, all are rotten
      to the core;
    not one does anything good,
    no, not even one.

4 Shall they not rue it,
    these evildoers who devour my
      people
    as men devour bread,
    and never call upon God?
5 There they were in dire alarm
    when God scattered them.
    The crimes of the godless were
      frustrated;[s]
    for God had rejected them.
6 If only Israel's deliverance might come
    out of Zion!
    When God restores his people's for-
      tunes,
    let Jacob rejoice, let Israel be glad.

54

God is my helper

1 Save me, O God, by the power of
    thy name,
    and vindicate me through thy
      might.
2 O God, hear my prayer,
    listen to my supplication.
3 Insolent men rise to attack me,
    ruthless men seek my life;
    they give no thought to God.

4 But God is my helper,
    the Lord the mainstay of my life.
5 May their own malice recoil on my
    watchful foes;
    silence them by thy truth, O Lord.
6 I will offer thee a willing sacrifice
    and praise thy name, for that is
      good;
7 God has rescued me from every
    trouble,
    and I look on my enemies' downfall
    with delight.

55

A friend's disloyalty

    Listen, O God, to my pleading,   1
    do not hide thyself when I pray.
    Hear me and answer,   2
    for my cares give me no peace.
    I am panic-stricken at the shouts of 3
      my enemies,
    at the shrill clamour of the wicked;
    for they heap trouble on me
    and they revile me in their anger.
    My heart is torn with anguish   4
    and the terrors of death come upon
      me.
    Fear and trembling overwhelm me 5
    and I shudder from head to foot.
    [t]Oh that I had the wings of a dove 6
    to fly away and be at rest!
    I should escape far away   7
    and find a refuge in the wilderness;
    soon I should find myself a sanc- 8
      tuary
    from wind and storm,
    from the blasts of calumny, O 9
      Lord,
    from my enemies' contentious
      tongues.
I have seen violence and strife in the
    city;
    day and night they encircle it,   10
    all along its walls;
    it is filled with trouble and mischief,
    alive with rumour and scandal,   11
    and its public square is never free
    from violence and spite.
    It was no enemy that taunted me, 12
    or I should have avoided him;
    no adversary that treated me with
      scorn,
    or I should have kept out of his
      way.
    It was you, a man of my own sort, 13
    my comrade, my own dear friend,
    with whom I kept pleasant com- 14–15
      pany
    in the house of God.

    May death strike them,
    and may they[u] perish in confusion,
    may they go down alive into Sheol;
    for their homes are haunts of evil!

    But I will call upon God;   16
    the Lord will save me.
    Evening and morning and at noon 17
    I nurse my woes, and groan.
    He has heard my cry, he rescued 18
      me
    and gave me back my peace,
    when they beset me like archers,[v]

---

r Verses 1–6: cp. Ps. 14. 1–7.
rdg.; Heb. prefixes And I said.
obscure.
    s The crimes . . . frustrated: prob. rdg.; Heb. obscure.   *t Prob.*
    u Prob. rdg.; Heb. we.   *v when . . . archers: prob. rdg.; Heb.*

massing against me,
19 like Ishmael and the desert tribes
and those who dwell in the East,
who have no respect for an oath
nor any fear of God.
20 Such men do violence to those at
peace with them
and break their promised word;
21 their speech is smoother than butter
but their thoughts are of war;
their words are slippery as oil
but sharp as drawn swords.

22 Commit your fortunes to the LORD,
and he will sustain you;
he will never let the righteous be
shaken.
23 Cast them, O God, into the pit of
destruction;
bloodthirsty and treacherous,
they shall not live out half their
days;
but I will put my trust in thee.

56

In God I trust

1 Be gracious to me, O God, for the
enemy persecute me,
my assailants harass me all day long.
2 All the day long my watchful foes
persecute me;
countless are those who assail me.
3 Appear on high[w] in my day of fear;
I put my trust in thee.
4 With God to help me I will shout
defiance,
in God I trust and shall not be
afraid;
what can mortal men do to me?
5 All day long abuse of me is their
only theme,
all their thoughts are hostile.
6 In malice they are on the look-out,
and watch for me,
they dog my footsteps;
but, while they lie in wait for me,
7 it is they who will not[x] escape.
O God, in thy anger bring ruin on
the nations.

8 Enter my lament in thy book,[y]
store every tear in thy flask.[z]
9 Then my enemies will turn back
on the day when I call upon thee;[a]
for this I know, that God is on my
side,
10 with God to help me I will shout
defiance.[b]

In God I trust and shall not be 11
afraid;
what can man do to me?
I have bound myself with vows to 12
thee, O God,
and will redeem them with due
thank-offerings;
for thou hast rescued me from 13
death[c]
to walk in thy presence, in the light
of life.

57

Prayer for God to show himself

Be gracious to me, O God, be 1
gracious;
for I have made thee my refuge.
I will take refuge in the shadow of
thy wings
until the storms are past.
I will call upon God Most High, 2
on God who fulfils his purpose for
me.
He will send his truth and his love 3
that never fails,
he will send from heaven and save
me.
God himself will frustrate my persecutors;
for I lie down among lions, man- 4
eaters,
whose teeth are spears and arrows
and whose tongues are sharp swords.
Show thyself, O God, high above 5
the heavens;
let thy glory shine over all the
earth.
Men have prepared a net to catch 6
me as I walk,
but I bow my head to escape from
it;
they have dug a pit in my path
but have fallen into it themselves.

My heart is steadfast, O God, 7
my heart is steadfast.
I will sing and raise a psalm;
awake, my spirit, 8
awake, lute and harp,
I will awake at dawn of day.[e]
I will confess thee, O Lord, among 9
the peoples,
among the nations I will raise a
psalm to thee,
for thy unfailing love is wide as the 10
heavens
and thy truth reaches to the skies.

w Appear on high: *prob. rdg.*; *Heb.* Height.   x it is . . . not: *prob. rdg.*; *Heb.* for iniquity.
y Enter . . . book: *prob. rdg.*; *Heb.* obscure.   z *Prob. rdg.*; *Heb. adds* is it not in thy book?
a Enter . . . thee: *or* Thou hast entered my lament in thy book, my tears are put in thy flask. Then
my enemies turned back, when I called upon thee.   b *Prob. rdg.*; *Heb. adds* With the LORD to
help me I will shout defiance.   c *Prob. rdg.*; *Heb. adds* is it not my feet from stumbling (*cp.* Ps.
116. 8).   d *Verses 7–11: cp.* Ps. 108. 1–5.   e at dawn of day: *or* the dawn.

11 Show thyself, O God, high above
   the heavens;
  let thy glory shine over all the
   earth.

58

The triumph of righteousness

1 Answer, you rulers:[f] are your judgements just?
  Do you decide impartially between
   man and man?
2 Never! Your hearts devise all kinds
   of wickedness
  and survey the violence that you
   have done on earth.

3 Wicked men, from birth they have
   taken to devious ways;
  liars, no sooner born than they go
   astray,
4 venomous with the venom of serpents,
  of the deaf asp which stops its ears
5 and will not listen to the sound of
   the charmer,
  however skilful his spells may be.

6 O God, break the teeth in their
   mouths.
  Break, O LORD, the jaws of the unbelievers.[g]
7 May they melt, may they vanish like
   water,
  may they wither like trodden grass,[h]
8 like an abortive birth which melts
   away
  or a still-born child which never
   sees[i] the sun!
9 All unawares, may they be rooted up
   like[j] a thorn-bush,
  like weeds which a man angrily[k]
   clears away!

10 The righteous shall rejoice that he has
   seen vengeance done
  and shall wash his feet in the blood
   of the wicked,
11 and men shall say,
  'There is after all a reward for the
   righteous;
  after all, there is a God that judges on
   earth.'

59

God my strong tower

1 Rescue me from my enemies, O my
   God,

be my tower of strength against all
   who assail me,
rescue me from these evildoers, 2
deliver me from men of blood.
Savage men lie in wait for me, 3
they lie in ambush ready to attack
   me;
for no fault or guilt of mine, O
   LORD,
innocent as I am, they run to take 4-5
   post against me.
But thou, LORD God of Hosts, Israel's
   God,
do thou bestir thyself at my call,
   and look:
awake, and punish all the nations.
Have no mercy on villains and
   traitors,
who run wild at nightfall like dogs, 6
snarling and prowling round the
   city,
wandering to and fro in search of 15[l]
   food,
and howling if they are not satisfied.
From their mouths comes a stream 7
   of nonsense;
'But who will hear?' they murmur.
But thou, O LORD, dost laugh at 8
   them,
and deride all the nations.
O my strength,[m] to thee I turn in the 9
   night-watches;
for thou, O God, art my strong
   tower.
My God, in his true love, shall be 10
   my champion;
with God's help, I shall gloat over
   my watchful foes.
Wilt thou not kill them, lest my 11
   people forget?
Scatter them by thy might and
   bring them to ruin.
Deliver them,[n] O Lord, to be de- 12
   stroyed
by their own sinful words;
let what they have spoken entrap
   them in their pride.
Let them be cut off for their cursing
   and falsehood;
bring them to an end in thy wrath, 13
and they will be no more;
then they will know that God is
   ruler in Jacob,
even to earth's farthest limits.[o] [p]
But I will sing of thy strength, 16
and celebrate thy love when morning comes;
for thou hast been my strong tower

f Or *you gods.*   g *the jaws of the unbelievers: or* the lions' fangs.   h *like trodden grass: prob.*
rdg.; *Heb. obscure.*   i *sees: prob. rdg.; Heb.* they see.   j *may they be rooted up: prob. rdg.;*
Heb. your pots.   k *angrily: prob. rdg.; Heb.* like anger.   l *Verse transposed.*   m Or *refuge.*
n Deliver them: *prob. rdg.; Heb.* Our shield.   o *Prob. rdg.; Heb. adds* (14) who run wild at nightfall like dogs, snarling and prowling round the city (*cp. verse 6*).   p *Verse 15 transposed to follow*
verse 6.

and a sure retreat in days of trouble.
17   O thou my strength, I will raise a
     psalm to thee;
     for thou, O God, art my strong
     tower.

60

Help against enemies

1   O God, thou hast cast us off and
    broken us;
    thou hast been angry and rebuked
    us cruelly.
2   Thou hast made the land quake and
    torn it open;
    it gives way and crumbles into
    pieces.
3   Thou hast made thy people drunk
    with a bitter draught,
    thou hast given us wine that makes
    us stagger.
4   But thou hast given a warning to
    those who fear thee,
    to make their escape before the
    sentence falls.

5[q] Deliver those that are dear to thee;
     save them with thy right hand, and
     answer.
6 God has spoken from his sanctuary:[r]
     'I will go up now and measure out
     Shechem;
     I will divide the valley of Succoth
     into plots;
7 Gilead and Manasseh are mine;
     Ephraim is my helmet, Judah my
     sceptre;
8 Moab is my wash-bowl, I fling my
     shoes at Edom;
     Philistia is the target of my anger.'

9 Who can bring me to the fortified city,
     who can guide me to Edom,
10 since thou, O God, hast abandoned us
     and goest not forth with our armies?
11 Grant us help against the enemy,
     for deliverance by man is a vain
     hope.
12   With God's help we shall do vali-
     antly,
     and God himself will tread our
     enemies under foot.

61

Prayer for support

1   Hear my cry, O God, listen to my
    prayer.
2 From the end of the earth I call to
    thee with fainting heart;
    lift me up and set me upon a rock.
3   For thou hast been my shelter,
    a tower for refuge from the enemy.

In thy tent will I make my home 4
    for ever
    and find my shelter under the cover
    of thy wings.
For thou, O God, hast heard my vows 5
    and granted the wish[s] of all who
    revere thy name.

To the king's life add length of days, 6
    year upon year for many genera-
    tions;
    may he dwell in God's presence for 7
    ever,
    may true and constant love pre-
    serve him.

So will I ever sing psalms in honour 8
    of thy name
    as I fulfil my vows day after day.

62

Dependence on God

Truly my heart waits silently for God; 1
    my deliverance comes from him.
In truth he is my rock of deliverance, 2
    my tower of strength, so that I
    stand unshaken.
    How long will you assail a man with 3
    your threats,
    all battering on a leaning wall?
In truth men plan to topple him from 4
    his height,
    and stamp on the fallen stones.[t]
    With their lips they bless him, the
    hypocrites,
    but revile him in their hearts.
Truly my heart waits silently for God; 5
    my hope of deliverance comes from
    him.
In truth he is my rock of deliverance, 6
    my tower of strength, so that I am
    unshaken.
    My deliverance and my honour 7
    depend upon God,
    God who is my rock of refuge and
    my shelter.
Trust always in God, my people,   8
    pour out your hearts before him;
    God is our shelter.

    In very truth men are a puff of 9
    wind,
    all men are faithless;
    put them in the balance and they
    can only rise,
    all of them lighter than wind.

Put no trust in extortion,   10
    do not be proud of stolen goods;
    though wealth breeds wealth, set
    not your heart on it.
    One thing God has spoken,   11

q Verses 5–12: cp. Ps. 108. 6–13.   *r from his sanctuary: or in his holiness.*   *s Prob. rdg.; Heb.*
the inheritance.   *t the fallen stones: transposed from end of verse 3.*

two things I have learnt:
'Power belongs to God'

12 and 'True love, O Lord, is thine';
thou dost requite a man for his deeds.

63

Remembering God

1 O God, thou art my God, I seek thee
early
with a heart that thirsts for thee
and a body wasted with longing for
thee,
like a dry and thirsty land that has no
water.

2 So longing, I come before thee in
the sanctuary
to look upon thy power and glory.

3 Thy true love is better than life;
therefore I will sing thy praises.

4 And so I bless thee all my life
and in thy name lift my hands in
prayer.

5 I am satisfied as with a rich and sump-
tuous feast
and wake the echoes with thy praise.

6 When I call thee to mind upon my
bed
and think on thee in the watches of
the night,

7 remembering how thou hast been
my help
and that I am safe in the shadow of
thy wings,

8 then I humbly follow thee with all
my heart,
and thy right hand is my support.

9 Those who seek my life, bent on evil,
shall sink into the depths of the
earth;

10 they shall be given over to the
sword;
they shall be carrion for jackals.

11 The king shall rejoice in God,
and whoever swears by God's name
shall exult;
the voice of falsehood shall be
silenced.

64

God overthrows evildoers

1 Hear me, O God, hear my lament;
keep me safe from the threats of
the enemy.

2 Hide me from the factions of the
wicked,
from the turbulent mob of evildoers,

who sharpen their tongues like 3
swords
and wing their cruel words like
arrows,[u]
to shoot down the innocent from 4
cover,
shooting suddenly, themselves unseen.

They boldly[v] hide their snares, 5
sure that none will see them;
they hatch their secret plans[w] with 6
skill and cunning,
with evil[x] purpose and deep design.
But God with his arrow shoots 7
them down,
and sudden is their overthrow.

They may repeat their wicked tales,[y] 8
but their mischievous tongues[z] are
their undoing.
All who see their fate take fright at
it,
every man is afraid; 9
'This is God's work', they declare;
they learn their lesson from what he
has done.
The righteous rejoice and seek refuge 10
in the LORD
and all the upright exult.

65

Praise for God's abundant provision

We owe thee praise, O God, in Zion; 1-2
thou hearest prayer, vows shall be
paid to thee.
All men shall lay their guilt before 3
thee:
our sins are too heavy for us;
only thou canst blot them out.
Happy is the man of thy choice, whom 4
thou dost bring
to dwell in thy courts;
let us enjoy the blessing of thy
house,
thy holy temple.
By deeds of terror answer us with 5
victory,
O God of our deliverance,
in whom men trust from the ends of
the earth
and far-off seas;
thou art girded with strength, 6
and by thy might dost fix the mountains in their place,
dost calm the rage of the seas and their 7
raging waves.[a]
The dwellers at the ends of the 8
earth
hold thy signs in awe;

---

u and wing . . . arrows: *prob. rdg.*; Heb. they tread their arrow a cruel word.   *v See first note on
verse 8.*   *w* their secret plans: *prob. rdg.*; Heb. unintelligible.   *x* evil: *prob. rdg.*; Heb. man.
y They . . . tales: *transposed from after* boldly *in verse 5.*   *z* their mischievous tongues: *prob. rdg.*;
Heb. against them their tongues.   *a Prob. rdg.*; Heb. adds and tumult of people.

thou makest morning and evening
sing aloud in triumph.

9 Thou dost visit the earth and give
it abundance,
as often as thou dost enrich it
with the waters of heaven, brimming in their channels,
providing rain[b] for men.
For this is thy provision for it,
10 watering its furrows, levelling its
ridges,
softening it with showers and blessing
its growth.
11 Thou dost crown the year with thy
good gifts
and the palm-trees drip with sweet
juice;
12 the pastures in the wild are rich
with blessing
and the hills wreathed in happiness,
13 the meadows are clothed with sheep
and the valleys mantled in corn,
so that they shout, they break into
song.

66

Answered prayer

1 Acclaim our God, all men on earth;
2 let psalms declare the glory of his
name,
make glorious his praise.
3 Say unto God, 'How fearful are thy
works!
Thy foes cower before the greatness of
thy strength.
4 All men on earth fall prostrate in
thy presence,
and sing to thee, sing psalms in honour of thy name.'
5 Come and see all that God has done,
tremendous in his dealings with
mankind.
6 He turned the waters into dry land
so that his people passed through
the sea on foot;
there did we rejoice in him.[c]

7 He rules for ever by his power,
his eye rests on the nations;
let no rebel rise in defiance.

8 Bless our God, all nations;
let his praise be heard far and near.
9 He set us in the land of the living;
he keeps our feet from stumbling.
10 For thou, O God, hast put us to the
proof
and refined us like silver.
11 Thou hast caught us in a net,
thou hast bound our bodies fast;
12 thou hast let men ride over our
heads.

We went through fire and water,
but thou hast brought us out into
liberty.

I will bring sacrifices into thy 13
temple
and fulfil my vows to thee,
vows which I made with my own 14
lips
and swore with my own mouth
when in distress.
I will offer thee fat beasts as sacri- 15
fices
and burn rams as a savoury offering;
I will make ready oxen and he-
goats.

Come, listen, all who fear God, 16
and I will tell you all that he has done
for me;
I lifted up my voice in prayer, 17
his high praise was on my lips.
If I had cherished evil thoughts, 18
the Lord would not have heard me;
but in truth God has heard 19
and given heed to my prayer.
Blessed is God 20
who has not withdrawn his love and
care from me.

67

Let all peoples praise thee

God be gracious to us and bless us, 1
God make his face shine upon us,
that his ways may be known on 2
earth
and his saving power among all the
nations.
Let the peoples praise thee, O God; 3
let all peoples praise thee.
Let all nations rejoice and shout in 4
triumph;
for thou dost judge the peoples
with justice
and guidest the nations of the earth.
Let the peoples praise thee, O God; 5
let all peoples praise thee.
The earth has given its increase 6
and God, our God, will bless us.

God grant us his blessing, 7
that all the ends of the earth may
fear him.

68

Song of triumph

God arises and his enemies are scat- 1
tered;
those who hate him flee before him,
driven away like smoke in the wind; 2

b Or corn.   *c* there . . . him: *or* where we see this, we will rejoice in him.

like wax melting at the fire,
the wicked perish at the presence of
God.

3 But the righteous are joyful, they
exult before God,
they are jubilant and shout for joy.

4 Sing the praises of God, raise a psalm
to his name,
extol him who rides over the desert
plains.*d*
Be joyful*e* and exult before him,

5 father of the fatherless, the widow's
champion—
God in his holy dwelling-place.

6 God gives the friendless a home
and brings out the prisoner safe and
sound;
but rebels must live in the scorching
desert.

7 O God, when thou didst go forth
before thy people,
marching across the wilderness,

8 earth trembled, the very heavens
quaked
before God the lord of Sinai, before
God the God of Israel.

9 Of thy bounty, O God, thou dost
refresh with rain
thy own land in its weariness,
the land which thou thyself didst
provide,

10 where thy own people made their
home,
which thou, O God, in thy goodness
providest for the poor.

13 The Lord proclaims good news:*f*
'Kings with their armies have fled
headlong.'
O mighty host, will you linger among
the sheepfolds
while the women in your tents
divide the spoil—
an image of a dove, its wings
sheathed in silver
and its pinions in yellow gold—

14 while the Almighty scatters kings
far and wide
like snowflakes falling on Zalmon?

15 The hill of Bashan is a hill of God
indeed,
a hill of many peaks is Bashan's hill.

16 But, O hill of many peaks, why gaze
in envy
at the hill where the LORD delights to
dwell,

where the LORD himself will live for
ever?

17 Twice ten thousand were God's chariots, thousands upon thousands,
when the Lord came in holiness from
Sinai.*g*

18 Thou didst go up to thy lofty home
with captives in thy train,
having received tribute from men;
in the presence of the LORD God no
rebel could live.

19 Blessed is the Lord:
he carries us day by day,
God our salvation.

20 Our God is a God who saves us,
in the LORD God's hand lies escape
from death.*h*

21 God himself will smite*i* the head of his
enemies,
those proud sinners with their flowing locks.

22 The Lord says, 'I will return from the
Dragon,*j*
I will return from the depths of the
sea,

23 that you may dabble your feet in
blood,
while the tongues of your dogs are
eager*k* for it.'

24 Thy procession, O God, comes into
view,
the procession of my God and King
into the sanctuary:

25 at its head the singers, next come
minstrels,
girls among them playing on tambourines.

26 In the great concourse they bless
God,
all Israel assembled*l* bless the LORD.

27 There is the little tribe of Benjamin
leading them,
there the company of Judah's princes,
the princes of Zebulun and of Naphtali.

28 O God, in virtue of thy power*m*—
that godlike power which has acted
for us—

29 command kings to bring gifts to thee
for the honour of thy temple in
Jerusalem.

30 Rebuke those wild beasts of the reeds,
that herd of bulls,
the bull-calf warriors of the nations;*n*
scatter these nations which revel in
war;

d over the desert plains: *or* on the plains.   *e* Be joyful: *prob. rdg.; Heb.* In the LORD is his name.
f proclaims good news: *or* gives the word, women bearing good news.   *g* came . . . from Sinai:
prob. rdg.; Heb. obscure.   *h* in the LORD God's hand . . . death: *or* death is expelled by the LORD
God.   *i* will smite: *or* smites.   *j* the Dragon: *or* Bashan.   *k* are eager: *prob. rdg.; Heb.* from
enemies.   *l* assembled: *prob. rdg.; Heb.* obscure.   *m* O God . . . power: *prob. rdg.; Heb.* Your
God your power.   *n* See first note on verse 31.

31 make them bring tribute from
    Egypt,
    precious stones and silver from
    Pathros;[o]
    let Nubia stretch out[p] her hands to
    God.

32 All you kingdoms of the world, sing
    praises to God,
    sing psalms to the Lord,
33 to him who rides on the heavens,
    the ancient heavens.
    Hark! he speaks in the mighty thun-
    der.
34 Ascribe all might to God, Israel's High
    God,
    Israel's pride and might throned in
    the skies.
35 Terrible is God as he comes from
    his sanctuary;
    he is Israel's own God,
    who gives to his people might and
    abundant power.

    Blessed be God.

69

A cry of distress

1   Save me, O God;
    for the waters have risen up to my
    neck.
2   I sink in muddy depths and have no
    foothold;
    I am swept into deep water, and the
    flood carries me away.
3   I am wearied with crying out, my
    throat is sore,
    my eyes grow dim as I wait for God to
    help me.
4   Those who hate me without reason
    are more than the hairs of my head;
    they outnumber my hairs, those who
    accuse me falsely.
    How can I give back what I have not
    stolen?
5   O God, thou knowest how foolish I
    am,
    and my guilty deeds are not hidden
    from thee.
6   Let none of those who look to thee be
    shamed on my account,
    O Lord GOD of Hosts;
    let none who seek thee be humbled
    through my fault,
    O God of Israel.
7   For in thy service I have suffered
    reproach;
    I dare not show my face for shame.
8   I have become a stranger to my
    brothers,

an alien to my own mother's sons;
bitter enemies of thy temple tear 9
    me in pieces;[q]
those who reproach thee reproach
    me.
I have broken my spirit with fasting, 10
only to lay myself open to many
    reproaches.
I have made sackcloth my clothing 11
and have become a byword among
    them.
Those who sit by the town gate 12
    talk about me;
drunkards sing songs about me in
    their cups.
But I lift up this prayer to thee, O 13
    LORD:
accept me[r] now in thy great love,
answer me with thy sure deliver-
    ance, O God.
Rescue me from the mire, do not 14
    let me sink;
let me be rescued from the muddy
    depths,[s]
so that no flood may carry me 15
    away,
no abyss swallow me up,
no deep close over me.
Answer me, O LORD, in the goodness of 16
    thy unfailing love,
turn towards me in thy great
    affection.
I am thy servant, do not hide thy 17
    face from me.
Make haste to answer me, for I am
    in distress.
Come near to me and redeem me; 18
ransom me, for I have many ene-
    mies.

Thou knowest what reproaches I 19
    bear,
all my anguish is seen by thee.
Reproach has broken my heart, 20
my shame and my dishonour[t] are
    past hope;
I looked for consolation and re-
    ceived none,
for comfort and did not find any.
They put poison in my food 21
and gave me vinegar when I was
    thirsty.
May their own table be a snare to 22
    them
and their sacred feasts lure them to
    their ruin;
may their eyes be darkened so that 23
    they do not see,
let a continual ague shake their
    loins.

---

o precious. . . Pathros: *prob. rdg., transposed from verse 30 and slightly altered.*   p stretch out:
prob. rdg.; Heb. obscure.   q bitter . . . pieces: *or zeal for thy temple has eaten me up (cp. John 2.
17).*   r *Prob. rdg.; Heb. acceptance.*   s from . . . depths: *prob. rdg.; Heb. from my haters and
from the depths.*   t my shame and my dishonour: *transposed from after* reproaches *in verse 19.*

24 Pour out thine indignation upon them
and let thy burning anger overtake them.
25 May their settlements be desolate, and no one living in their tents;
26 for they pursue him whom thou hast struck down
and multiply the torments of those whom thou hast wounded.
27 Give them the punishment their sin deserves;[u]
exclude them from thy righteous mercy;
28 let them be blotted out from the book of life
and not be enrolled among the righteous.

29 But by thy saving power, O God, lift me high
above my pain and my distress,
30 then I will praise God's name in song and glorify him with thanksgiving;
31 that will please the LORD more than the offering of a bull,
a young bull with horn and cloven hoof.

32 See and rejoice, you humble folk, take heart, you seekers after God;
33 for the LORD listens to the poor and does not despise those bound to his service.
34 Let sky and earth praise him, the seas and all that move in them,
5-6 for God will deliver Zion and rebuild the cities of Judah.
His servants' children shall inherit them;
they shall dwell there in their own possession
and all who love his name shall live in them.

70

Prayer for help

1[v] Show me favour,[w] O God, and save me;
hasten to help me, O LORD.
2 Let all who seek my life be brought to shame and dismay,
let all who love to hurt me shrink back disgraced;
3 let those who cry 'Hurrah!' at my downfall
turn back at the shame they incur,
4 but let all who seek thee
be jubilant and rejoice in thee,

and let those who long for thy saving help ever cry,
'All glory to God!'

But I am poor and needy; 5
O God, hasten to my aid.
Thou art my help, my salvation;
O LORD, make no delay.

71

Prayer in old age

In thee, O LORD, I have taken refuge; 1
never let me be put to shame.
As thou art righteous rescue me and 2
save my life;
hear me and set me free,
be a rock of refuge for me, 3
where I may ever find safety at thy call;
for thou art my towering crag and stronghold.
O God, keep my life safe from the 4
wicked,
from the clutches of unjust and cruel men.

Thou art my hope, O Lord, 5
my trust, O LORD, since boyhood.
From birth I have leaned upon thee, 6
my protector since I left[x] my mother's womb.[y]
To many I seem a solemn warning; 7
but I have thee for my strong refuge.
My mouth shall be full of thy 8
praises,
I shall tell of thy splendour all day long.
Do not cast me off when old age 9
comes,
nor forsake me when my strength fails,
when my enemies' rancour bursts 10
upon me[z]
and those who watch me whisper together,
saying, 'God has forsaken him; 11
after him! seize him; no one will rescue him.'
O God, do not stand aloof from me; 12
O my God, hasten to my help.
Let all my traducers be shamed and 13
dishonoured,
let all who seek my hurt be covered with scorn.
But I will wait in continual hope, 14
I will praise thee again and yet again;
all day long thy righteousness, 15

u Give them . . . deserves: *or* Add punishment to punishment.   v Verses 1–5: cp. Ps. 40. 13–17.
w Show me favour: *prob. rdg.; cp. Ps. 40. 13; Heb. om.   x my . . . left: *or* who didst bring me out
from.   y See note on verse 15.   z enemies' . . . me: *prob. rdg.; Heb.* enemies say of me.

thy saving acts, shall be upon my
lips.
Thou shalt ever be the theme of
my praise,[a]
although I have not the skill of a
poet.
16 I will begin with a tale of great deeds,
O Lord God,
and sing of thy righteousness, thine
alone.
17 O God, thou hast taught me from
boyhood,
all my life I have proclaimed thy
marvellous works;
18 and now that I am old and my
hairs are grey,
forsake me not, O God,
when I extol thy mighty arm to future
generations,
19 thy power and righteousness, O God,
to highest heaven;
for thou hast done great things.
Who is like thee, O God?
20 Thou hast made me pass through
bitter and deep distress,
yet dost revive me once again
and lift me again from earth's
watery depths.
21 Restore me to honour, turn and comfort me,
22 then I will praise thee on the lute
for thy faithfulness, O God;
I will sing psalms to thee with the
harp,
thou Holy One of Israel;
23 songs of joy shall be on my lips;
I will sing thee psalms, because thou
hast redeemed me.
24 All day long my tongue shall tell of
thy righteousness;
shame and disgrace await those who
seek my hurt.

72

Prayer for the king

1 O God, endow the king with thy own
justice,
and give thy righteousness to a
king's son,
2 that he may judge thy people
rightly
and deal out justice to the poor
and suffering.
3 May hills and mountains afford thy
people
peace and prosperity in righteousness.
4 He shall give judgement for the
suffering
and help those of the people that
are needy;

he shall crush the oppressor.
5 He shall live as long as the sun
endures,
long as the moon, age after age.
6 He shall be like rain falling on
early crops,
like showers watering[b] the earth.
7 In his days righteousness shall
flourish,
prosperity abound until the moon
is no more.
8 May he hold sway from sea to sea,
from the River to the ends of the
earth.
9 Ethiopians shall crouch low before
him;
his enemies shall lick the dust.
10 The kings of Tarshish and the islands
shall bring gifts,
the kings of Sheba and Seba shall
present their tribute,
11 and all kings shall pay him homage,
all nations shall serve him.
12 For he shall rescue the needy from their
rich oppressors,
the distressed who have no protector.
13 May he have pity on the needy and
the poor,
deliver the poor from death;
14 may he redeem them from oppression and violence
and may their blood be precious in
his eyes.

15 May the king live long
and receive gifts of gold[c] from
Sheba;
prayer be made for him continually,
blessings be his all the day long.
16 May there be abundance of corn in
the land,
growing in plenty to the tops of the
hills;
may the crops flourish like Lebanon,
and the sheaves[d] be numberless as
blades of grass.
17 Long may the king's name endure,
may it live for ever like the sun;
so shall all peoples pray to be blessed
as he was,
all nations tell of his happiness.

18 Blessed be the Lord God, the God of
Israel,
who alone does marvellous things;
19 blessed be his glorious name for ever,
and may his glory fill all the earth.
Amen, Amen.

20 Here end the prayers of David son of
Jesse.

---

a Line transposed from verse 6.   *b like showers watering: prob. rdg.; Heb. unintelligible.*   *c Or frankincense.*   *d the sheaves: prob. rdg.; Heb. from a city.*

BOOK 3

73

A true assessment of life

1 How good God is to the upright![e]
　How good to those who are pure in
　　heart!

2 My feet had almost slipped,
　my foothold had all but given way,
3 because the boasts of sinners roused
　　my envy
　when I saw how they prosper.
4 No pain, no suffering is theirs;
　they are sleek and sound in limb;
5 they are not plunged in trouble as
　　other men are,
　nor do they suffer the torments of
　　mortal men.
6 Therefore pride is their collar of
　　jewels
　and violence the robe that wraps
　　them round.
7 Their eyes gleam through folds of
　　fat;
　while vain fancies pass through
　　their minds.
8 Their talk is all sneers and malice;
　scornfully they spread their calum-
　　nies.
9 Their slanders reach up to heaven,
　while their tongues ply to and fro
　　on earth.
10 And so my people follow their lead[f]
　and find nothing to blame in them,[g]
11 even though they say, 'What does
　　God know?
　The Most High neither knows nor
　　cares.'
12 So wicked men talk, yet still they
　　prosper,
　and rogues[h] amass great wealth.

13 So it was all in vain that I kept my
　　heart pure
　and washed my hands in innocence.
14 For all day long I suffer torment
　and am punished every morning.
15 Yet had I let myself talk on in this
　　fashion,
　I should have betrayed the family of
　　God.
16 So I set myself to think this out
　but I found it too hard for me,
17 until I went into God's sacred
　　courts;
　there I saw clearly what their end
　　would be.

18 How often thou dost set them on
　　slippery ground
　and drive them headlong into ruin!
19 Then in a moment how dreadful their
　　end,
　cut off root and branch by death
　　with all its terrors,
20 like a dream when a man rouses
　　himself, O Lord,
　like images in sleep which are dis-
　　missed on waking!

21 When my heart was embittered
　I felt the pangs of envy,
22 I would not understand, so brutish
　　was I,
　I was a mere beast in thy sight, O
　　God.
23 Yet I am always with thee,
　thou holdest my right hand;
24 thou dost guide me by thy counsel
　and afterwards wilt receive me with
　　glory.
25 Whom have I in heaven but thee?
　And having thee,[i] I desire nothing
　　else on earth.
26 Though heart and body fail,
　yet God is my possession for ever.
27 They who are far from thee are lost;
　thou dost destroy all who wantonly
　　forsake thee.
28 But my chief good is to be near
　　thee, O God;
　I have chosen thee, Lord GOD, to be
　　my refuge.[j]

74

In time of national humiliation

1 Why hast thou cast us off, O God? Is
　　it for ever?
　Why art thou so stern, so angry with
　　the sheep of thy flock?
2 Remember the assembly of thy peo-
　　ple,
　taken long since for thy own,[k]
　and Mount Zion, which was thy home.
3 Now at last[l] restore what was ruined
　　beyond repair,
　the wreck that the foe has made of thy
　　sanctuary.

4 The shouts of thy enemies filled the
　　holy place,[m]
　they planted their standards there
　　as tokens of victory.
5 They brought it crashing down,[n]
　like woodmen plying their axes in
　　the forest;

e How . . . upright: *prob. rdg.*; *Heb.* How good it is to Israel!   *f* their lead: *prob. rdg.*; *Heb.* hither.
g and find . . . in them: *prob. rdg.*; *Heb.* obscure.   *h* yet . . . rogues: *prob. rdg.*; *Heb.* those at ease
for ever.   *i* Or And compared with thee.   *j* *Prob. rdg.*; *Heb. adds* to tell all thy works.
k *Prob. rdg.*; *Heb. adds* thou didst redeem the tribe of thy possession.   *l* Now at last: *prob. rdg.*;
Heb. Thy steps.   *m* the holy place: *or* thy meeting place.   ↳*n* They . . . down: *prob. rdg.*; *Heb.*
unintelligible.

6 they ripped the carvings clean out,
they smashed them with hatchet
and pick.
7 They set fire to thy sanctuary,
tore down and polluted the shrine
sacred to thy name.
8 They said to themselves, 'We will
sweep them away',
and all over the land they burnt
God's holy places.[o]

9 We cannot see what lies before us,[p]
we have no prophet now;
we have no one who knows how
long this is to last.
10 How long, O God, will the enemy
taunt thee?
Will the adversary pour scorn on thy
name for ever?
11 Why dost thou hold back thy hand,
why keep thy right hand within thy
bosom?

12 But thou, O God, thou king from
of old,
thou mighty conqueror all the
world over,
13 by thy power thou didst cleave the
sea-monster in two
and break the sea-serpent's heads
above the waters;
14 thou didst crush Leviathan's many
heads
and throw him to the sharks[q] for
food.
15 Thou didst open channels for spring
and torrent;
thou didst dry up rivers never
known to fail.
16 The day is thine, and the night is
thine also,
thou didst ordain the light of moon
and sun;
17 thou hast fixed all the regions of the
earth;
summer and winter, thou didst create
them both.

18 Remember, O Lord, the taunts of the
enemy,
the scorn a savage nation pours on
thy name.
19 Cast not to the beasts the soul that
confesses thee;
forget not for ever the sufferings of
thy servants.
20 Look upon thy creatures:[r] they are
filled with hatred,
and earth is the haunt of violence.
21 Let not the oppressed be shamed
and turned away;
let the poor and the downtrodden
praise thy name.
Rise up, O God, maintain thy own 22
cause;
remember how brutal men taunt
thee all day long.
Ignore no longer the cries of thy 23
assailants,
the mounting clamour of those who
defy thee.

75

God is judge

We give thee thanks, O God, we give 1
thee thanks;
thy name is brought very near to us
in the story of thy wonderful deeds.

I seize the appointed time 2
and then I judge mankind with
justice.
When the earth rocks, with all who 3
live on it,
I make its pillars firm.
To the boastful I say, 'Boast no 4
more',
and to the wicked, 'Do not toss
your proud horns:
toss not your horns against high 5
heaven
nor speak arrogantly against your
Creator.'
No power from the east nor from 6
the west,
no power from the wilderness, can
raise a man up.
For God is judge; 7
he puts one man down and raises up
another.
The Lord holds a cup in his hand, 8
and the wine foams in it, hot with
spice;
he offers it to every man for drink,
and all the wicked on earth must drain
it to the dregs.
But I will glorify him for ever; 9
I will sing praises to the God of
Jacob.

I will break off the horns of the 10
wicked,
but the horns of the righteous shall
be lifted high.

76

The greatness of Israel's God

In Judah God is known, 1
his name is great in Israel;

o holy places: *or* meeting places. p what . . . us: *prob. rdg.; Heb.* our signs. q to the sharks: *prob. rdg.; Heb.* to a people, desert-dwellers. r thy creatures: *prob. rdg.; Heb.* the covenant, because.

2 his tent is pitched in Salem,
   in Zion his battle-quarters are set
   up.[8]
3 He has broken the flashing arrows,
   shield and sword and weapons of
   war.

4 Thou art terrible, O Lord, and
   mighty:
5 men that lust for plunder stand
   aghast,
   the boldest swoon away,
   and the strongest cannot lift a
   hand.
6 At thy rebuke, O God of Jacob,
   rider and horse fall senseless.
7 Terrible art thou, O Lord;
   who can stand in thy presence when
   thou art angry?
8 Thou didst give sentence out of
   heaven;
   the earth was afraid and kept
   silence.
9 O God, at thy rising[t] in judgement
   to deliver all humble men on the
   earth,
10 for all her fury Edom shall confess
   thee,
   and the remnant left in Hamath
   shall dance in worship.

11 Make vows to the LORD your God,
   and pay them duly;
   let the peoples all around him bring
   their tribute;[u]
12 for he breaks the spirit of princes,
   he is the terror of the kings on
   earth.

77

Musings on Israel's history

1 I cried aloud to God,
   I cried to God, and he heard me.
2 In the day of my distress I sought the
   Lord,
   and by night I lifted[v] my outspread
   hands in prayer.
   I lay sweating and nothing would cool
   me;
   I refused all comfort.
3 When I called God to mind, I groaned;
   as I lay thinking, darkness came over
   my spirit.
4 My eyelids were tightly closed;
   I was dazed and I could not speak.
5 My thoughts went back to times long
   past,
   I remembered forgotten years;
6 all night long I was in deep distress,

as I lay thinking, my spirit was sunk
   in despair.

7 Will the Lord reject us for evermore
   and never again show favour?
8 Has his unfailing love now failed us
   utterly,
   must his promise time and again be
   unfulfilled?
9 Has God forgotten to be gracious,
   has he in anger withheld his mercies?
10 'Has his right hand', I said, 'lost its
   grasp?
   Does it hang powerless,[w] the arm
   of the Most High?'

11 But then, O LORD, I call to mind thy
   deeds;[x]
   I recall thy wonderful acts in times
   gone by.
12 I meditate upon thy works
   and muse on all that thou hast done.
13 O God, thy way is holy;
   what god is so great as our God?
14 Thou art the God who workest
   miracles;
   thou hast shown the nations thy
   power.
15 With thy strong arm thou didst
   redeem thy people,
   the sons of Jacob and Joseph.

16 The waters saw thee, O God,
   they saw thee and writhed in
   anguish;
   the ocean was troubled to its depths.
17 The clouds poured water, the skies
   thundered,
   thy arrows flashed hither and
   thither.
18 The sound of thy thunder was in the
   whirlwind,[y]
   thy lightnings lit up the world,
   earth shook and quaked.
19 Thy path was through the sea, thy
   way through mighty waters,
   and no man marked thy footsteps.
20 Thou didst guide thy people like a
   flock of sheep,
   under the hand of Moses and Aaron.

78

Lessons from Israel's history

1 Mark my teaching, O my people,
   listen to the words I am to speak.
2 I will tell you a story with a meaning,
   I will expound the riddle of things
   past,

s are set up: *prob. rdg.; Heb.* thither (*at beginning of verse 3*).   t O God . . . rising: *prob. rdg.;*
Heb. When God rises.   u *Prob. rdg.; Heb.* adds for the terror (*cp. verse 12*).   v I lifted: *prob.*
rdg.; Heb. om.   w lost . . . powerless: *prob. rdg.; Heb.* unintelligible.   x *Prob. rdg.; Heb.* then
I call to mind the deeds of the LORD, for.   y Or in the chariot-wheels.

3 things that we have heard and
know,
and our fathers have repeated to us.
4 From their sons we will not hide
the praises of the LORD and his
might
nor the wonderful acts he has performed;
then they shall repeat them to the
next generation.
5 He laid on Jacob a solemn charge
and established a law in Israel,
which he commanded our fathers
to teach their sons,
6 that it might be known to a future
generation,
to children yet unborn,
and these would repeat it to their
sons in turn.
7 He charged them to put their trust
in God,
to hold his great acts ever in mind
and to keep all his commandments;
8 not to do as their fathers did,
a disobedient and rebellious race,
a generation with no firm purpose,
with hearts not fixed steadfastly on
God.

9 The men of Ephraim, bowmen all
and marksmen,
turned and ran in the hour of battle.
10 They had not kept God's covenant
and had refused to live by his law;
11 they forgot all that he had done
and the wonderful acts which he
had shown them.

12 He did wonders in their fathers'
sight
in the land of Egypt, the country of
Zoan:
13 he divided the sea and took them
through it,
making the water stand up like
banks on either side.
14 He led them with a cloud by day
and all night long with a glowing fire.
15 He cleft the rock in the wilderness
and gave them water to drink,
abundant as the sea;
16 he brought streams out of the cliff
and made water run down like
rivers.
17 But they sinned against him yet
again:
in the desert they defied the Most
High,
18 they tried God's patience wilfully,
demanding food to satisfy their
hunger.
19 They vented their grievance against
God and said,

'Can God spread a table in the
wilderness?'
When he struck a rock, water
gushed out
until the gullies overflowed;
they said, 'Can he give bread as
well,
can he provide meat for his people?'
21 When he heard this, the LORD was
filled with fury:
fire raged against Jacob,
anger blazed up against Israel,
22 because they put no trust in God
and had no faith in his power to
save.
23 Then he gave orders to the skies
above
and threw open heaven's doors,
he rained down manna for them to eat
and gave them the grain of heaven.
25 So men ate the bread of angels;
he sent them food to their heart's
desire.
26 He let loose the east wind from
heaven
and drove the south wind by his
power;
27 he rained meat like a dust-storm
upon them,
flying birds like the sand of the
sea-shore,
28 which he made settle all over the
camp
round the tents where they lived.
29 So the people ate and were well
filled,
for he had given them what they
craved.
30 Yet they did not abandon their
complaints.ᶻ
even while the food was in their
mouths.
31 Then the anger of God blazed up
against them;
he spread death among their
stoutest men
and brought the young men of Israel
to the ground.

32 In spite of all, they persisted in their
sin
and had no faith in his wonderful acts.
33 So in one moment he snuffed out their
lives
and ended their years in calamity.
34 When he struck them, they began to
seek him,
they would turn and look eagerly for
God;
35 they remembered that God was their
Creator,
that God Most High was their
deliverer.

ᶻ Or craving.

36 But still they beguiled him with
words
and deceived him with fine speeches;
37 they were not loyal to him in their
hearts
nor were they faithful to his covenant.
38 Yet he wiped out their guilt
and did not smother his own^a natural
affection;
often he restrained his wrath
and did not rouse his anger to its
height.
39 He remembered that they were only
mortal men,
who pass by like a wind and never
return.

40 How often they rebelled against him
in the wilderness
and grieved him in the desert!
41 Again and again they tried God's
patience
and provoked the Holy One of
Israel.
42 They did not remember his prowess
on the day when he saved them from
the enemy,
43 how he set his signs in Egypt,
his portents in the land of Zoan.
44 He turned their streams into blood,
and they could not drink the running
water.
45 He sent swarms of flies which devoured
them,
and frogs which brought devastation;
46 he gave their harvest over to locusts
and their produce to the grubs;
47 he killed their vines with hailstones
and their figs with torrents of rain;
48 he abandoned their cattle to the
plague
and their beasts to the arrows of
pestilence.
49 He loosed upon them the violence of
his anger,
wrath and enmity and rage,
launching those messengers of evil
50-1 to open a way for his fury.
He struck down all the first-born in
Egypt,
the flower of their manhood in the
tents of Ham,
not shielding their lives from death
but abandoning their bodies to the
plague.
52 But he led out his own people like
sheep
and guided them like a flock in the
wilderness.
53 He led them in safety and they were
not afraid,

and the sea closed over their enemies.
He brought them to his holy mount- 54
ain,
the hill which his right hand had
won;
he drove out nations before them, 55
he allotted their lands to Israel as a
possession
and settled his tribes in their dwellings.
Yet they tried God's patience and 56
rebelled against him;
they did not keep the commands of
the Most High;
they were renegades, traitors like their 57
fathers,
they changed, they went slack like a
bow.
They provoked him to anger with 58
their hill-shrines
and roused his jealousy with their
carved images.
When God heard this, he put them 59
out of mind
and utterly rejected Israel.
He forsook his home at Shiloh, 60
the tabernacle in which he dwelt
among men;
he surrendered the symbol of his 61
strength into captivity
and his pride into enemy hands;
he gave his people over to the sword 62
and put his own possession out of
mind.
Fire devoured his young men, 63
and his maidens could raise no lament
for them;
his priests fell by the sword, 64
and his widows could not weep.

Then the Lord awoke as a sleeper 65
awakes,
like a warrior heated with wine;
he struck his foes in the back parts 66
and brought perpetual shame upon
them.
He despised the clan of Joseph 67
and did not choose the tribe of
Ephraim;
he chose the tribe of Judah 68
and Mount Zion which he loved;
he built his sanctuary high as the 69
heavens,
founded like the earth to last for ever.
He chose David to be his servant 70
and took him from the sheepfolds;
he brought him from minding the 71
ewes
to be the shepherd of his people
Jacob;^b
and he shepherded them in singleness 72
of heart
and guided them with skilful hand.

a his own: prob. rdg.; Heb. om.   b Prob. rdg.; Heb. adds and Israel his possession.

79

A lament over the destruction of Jerusalem

1 O God, the heathen have set foot in thy domain,
   defiled thy holy temple
   and laid Jerusalem in ruins.
2 They have thrown out the dead bodies of thy servants
   to feed the birds of the air;
   they have made thy loyal servants carrion for wild beasts.
3 Their blood is spilled all round Jerusalem like water,
   and there they lie unburied.
4 We suffer the contempt of our neighbours,
   the gibes and mockery of all around us.

5 How long, O LORD, wilt thou be roused to such fury?
   Must thy jealousy rage like a fire?
6 Pour out thy wrath over nations which do not know thee
   and over kingdoms which do not invoke thee by name;
7 see how they have devoured Jacob and laid waste his homesteads.
8 Do not remember against us the guilt of past generations
   but let thy compassion come swiftly to meet us,
   we have been brought so low.

9 Help us, O God our saviour, for the honour of thy name;
   for thy name's sake deliver us and wipe out our sins.
10 Why should the nations ask, 'Where is their God?'
   Let thy vengeance for the bloody slaughter of thy servants
   fall on those nations before our very eyes.

11 Let the groaning of the captives reach thy presence
   and in thy great might set free death's prisoners.
12 As for the contempt our neighbours pour on thee, O Lord,
   turn it back sevenfold on their own heads.
13 Then we thy people, the flock which thou dost shepherd,
   will give thee thanks for ever
   and repeat thy praise to every generation.

c *from slumber:* prob. rdg.; Heb. *and Manasseh.*
thou hast made strong for thy service (cp. verse 17).

80

The vine: an allegory

1 Hear us, O shepherd of Israel,
who leadest Joseph like a flock of sheep.
   Show thyself, thou that art throned on the cherubim,
2 to Ephraim and to Benjamin.
   Rouse thy victorious might from slumber,[c]
   come to our rescue.
3 Restore us, O God,
and make thy face shine upon us that we may be saved.
4 O LORD God of Hosts,
how long wilt thou resist thy people's prayer?
5 Thou hast made sorrow their daily bread
   and tears of threefold grief their drink.
6 Thou hast humbled us before our neighbours,
   and our enemies mock us to their hearts' content.
7 O God of Hosts, restore us;
   make thy face shine upon us that we may be saved.

8 Thou didst bring a vine out of Egypt;
   thou didst drive out nations and plant it;
9 thou didst clear the ground before it,
so that it made good roots and filled the land.
10 The mountains were covered with its shade,
   and its branches were like those of mighty cedars.
11 It put out boughs all the way to the Sea
   and its shoots as far as the River.
12 Why hast thou broken down the wall round it
   so that every passer-by can pluck its fruit?
13 The wild boar from the thickets gnaws it,
   and swarming insects from the fields feed on it.
14 O God of Hosts, once more look down from heaven,
take thought for this vine and tend it,
15 this stock that thy right hand has planted.[d]
16 Let them that set fire to it or cut it down
perish before thy angry face.

d *Prob. rdg.;* Heb. *adds* and on the son whom

7 Let thy hand rest upon the man at
thy right side,
the man whom thou hast made
strong for thy service.
8 We have not turned back from thee,
so grant us new life, and we will
invoke thee by name.
9 LORD God of Hosts, restore us;
make thy face shine upon us that
we may be saved.

81

God appeals to Israel

1 Sing out in praise of God our refuge,[e]
acclaim the God of Jacob.
2 Take pipe and tabor,
take tuneful harp and lute.
3 Blow the horn for the new month,
for the full moon on the day of our
pilgrim-feast.
4 This is a law for Israel,
an ordinance of the God of Jacob,
5 laid as a solemn charge on Joseph
when he came out of Egypt.[f]

6 When I lifted the load from his
shoulders,
his hands let go the builder's basket.
7 When you cried to me in distress,
I rescued you;
unseen, I answered you in thunder.
I tested you at the waters of Meribah,
where I opened your mouths and
filled them.[g]
h I fed Israel[i] with the finest wheat-
flour
and satisfied him with honey from
the rocks.

8 Listen, my people, while I give you
a solemn charge—
do but listen to me, O Israel:
9 you shall have no strange god
nor bow down to any foreign god;
10 I am the LORD your God
who brought you up from Egypt.[j]
11 But my people did not listen to my
words
and Israel would have none of me;
12 so I sent them off, stubborn as they
were,
to follow their own devices.

13 If my people would but listen to me,
if Israel would only conform to my
ways,
14 I would soon bring their enemies to
their knees
and lay a heavy hand upon their
persecutors.

Let those who hate them[k] come 15
cringing to them,
and meet with everlasting troubles.[l]

82

In the court of heaven

God takes his stand in the court of 1
heaven
to deliver judgement among the
gods themselves.

How long will you judge unjustly 2
and show favour to the wicked?
You ought to give judgement for 3
the weak and the orphan,
and see right done to the destitute
and downtrodden,
you ought to rescue the weak and 4
the poor,
and save them from the clutches of
wicked men.
But you know nothing, you under- 5
stand nothing,
you walk in the dark
while earth's foundations are giving
way.
This is my sentence: Gods you may 6
be,
sons all of you of a high god,[m]
yet you shall die as men die;[n]   7
princes fall, every one of them, and
so shall you.

Arise, O God, and judge the earth;   8
for thou dost pass all nations through
thy sieve.

83

Prayer during national distress

Rest not, O God;   1
O God, be neither silent nor still,
for thy enemies are making a 2
tumult,
and those that hate thee carry their
heads high.
They devise cunning schemes a- 3
gainst thy people
and conspire against those thou
hast made thy treasure:
'Come, away with them,' they cry, 4
'let them be a nation no longer,
let Israel's name be remembered no
more.'
With one mind they have agreed 5
together
to make a league against thee:
the families of Edom, the Ishmael- 6
ites,

e Or strength.   f Prob. rdg.; Heb. adds I hear an unfamiliar language.   g Line transposed from
end of verse 10.   h Verse transposed.   i I fed Israel: prob. rdg.; Heb. He fed him.   j See note
on verse 7.   k those . . . them: prob. rdg.; Heb. those who hate the LORD.   l Verse 16 transposed
to follow verse 7.   m Or of the Most High.   n Or as Adam died.

Moabites and Hagarenes,

7 Gebal, Ammon and Amalek,
Philistia and the citizens of Tyre,

8 Asshur too their ally,
all of them lending aid to the descendants of Lot.

9 Deal with them as with Sisera,
as with Jabin by the torrent of Kishon,

10 who fell vanquished as Midian*o* fell at En-harod,*p*
and were spread on the battlefield like dung.

11 Make their princes like Oreb and Zeeb,
make all their nobles like Zebah and Zalmunna;

12 for they said, 'We will seize for ourselves
all the pastures of God's people.'

13 Scatter them, O God, like thistledown,
like chaff before the wind.

14 Like fire raging through the forest or flames which blaze across the hills,

15 hunt them down with thy tempest,
and dismay them with thy stormwind.

16 Heap shame upon their heads, O LORD,
until they confess the greatness of thy name.

17 Let them be abashed, and live in perpetual dismay;
let them feel their shame and perish.

18 So let them learn that thou alone art LORD,
God Most High over all the earth.

84

Praise of God's house

1 How dear is thy dwelling-place,
thou LORD of Hosts!

2 I pine, I faint with longing
for the courts of the LORD's temple;
my whole being cries out with joy to the living God.

3 Even the sparrow finds a home,
and the swallow has her nest,
where she rears her brood beside thy altars,
O LORD of Hosts, my King and my God.

4 Happy are those who dwell in thy house;
they never cease from praising thee.

5 Happy the men whose refuge is in thee,

whose hearts are set on the pilgrim ways*q*!

6 As they pass through the thirsty valley
they find water from a spring;
and the LORD provides even men who lose their way
with pools to quench their thirst.*r*

7 So they pass on from outer wall to inner,
and the God of gods shows himself in Zion.

8 O LORD God of Hosts, hear my prayer;
listen, O God of Jacob.

9 O God, look upon our lord the king
and accept thy anointed prince with favour.

Better one day in thy courts 1
than a thousand days at home;
better to linger by the threshold of God's house
than to live in the dwellings of the wicked.

The LORD God is a battlement and a shield; 1
grace and honour are his to give.
The LORD will hold back no good thing
from those whose life is blameless.

O LORD of Hosts, 1
happy the man who trusts in thee!

85

Words of peace

1 LORD, thou hast been gracious to thy land
and turned the tide of Jacob's fortunes.

2 Thou hast forgiven the guilt of thy people
and put away all their sins.

3 Thou hast taken back all thy anger
and turned from thy bitter wrath.

4 Turn back to us, O God our saviour,
and cancel thy displeasure.

5 Wilt thou be angry with us for ever?
Must thy wrath last for all generations?

6 Wilt thou not give us new life
that thy people may rejoice in thee?

7 O LORD, show us thy true love
and grant us thy deliverance.

8 Let me hear the words of the LORD:
are they not*8* words of peace,
peace to his people and his loyal servants

o as Midian: transposed from previous verse.
q are set . . . ways: or high praises fill.
s of the LORD: are they not: prob. rdg.; Heb. of God the LORD.
p En-harod: prob. rdg., cp. Judg. 7. 1; Heb. Endor.
r they find . . . thirst: prob. rdg.; Heb. obscure.

and to all who turn and trust in
him?

9 Deliverance is near to those who
worship him,
so that glory may dwell in our land.

10 Love and fidelity have come together;
justice and peace join hands.

11 Fidelity springs up from earth
and justice looks down from heaven.

2 The LORD will add prosperity,
and our land shall yield its harvest.

3 Justice shall go in front of him
and the path before his feet shall be
peace.[t]

86

Prayer for protection and guidance

1 Turn to me, LORD, and answer;
I am downtrodden and poor.

2 Guard me, for I am constant and true;
save thy servant who puts his trust in
thee.

3 O Lord my God,[u] show me thy favour;
I call to thee all day long.

4 Fill thy servant's heart with joy,
O Lord,
for I lift up my heart to thee.

5 Thou, O Lord, art kind and forgiving,
full of true love for all who cry to
thee.

6 Listen, O LORD, to my prayer
and hear my pleading.

7 In the day of my distress I call on
thee;
for thou wilt answer me.

8 Among the gods not one is like thee,
O Lord,
no deeds are like thine.

9 All the nations thou hast made, O
Lord, will come,
will bow down before thee and honour
thy name;

10 for thou art great, thy works are
wonderful,
thou alone art God.

Guide me, O LORD,

11 that I may be true to thee and follow
thy path;
let me be one in heart
with those who revere thy name.

12 I will praise thee, O Lord my God,
with all my heart
and honour thy name for ever.

13 For thy true love stands high above
me;

thou hast rescued my soul from the
depths of Sheol.

14 O God, proud men attack me;
a mob of ruffians seek my life
and give no thought to thee.

15 Thou, Lord, art God, compassionate
and gracious,
forbearing, ever constant and true.

16 Turn towards me and show me thy
favour;
grant thy slave protection
and rescue thy slave-girl's son.

17 Give me proof of thy kindness;
let those who hate thee see to their
shame
that thou, O LORD, hast been my help
and comfort.

87[v]

Praise of Zion

1–2 The LORD loves the gates of Zion
more than all the dwellings of
Jacob;
her[w] foundations are laid upon holy
hills,

4–5 and he has made her his home.[x]
I will count Egypt and Babylon
among my friends;
Philistine, Tyrian and Nubian shall
be[y] there;
and Zion shall be called a mother
in whom men of every race are born.

6 The LORD shall write against each
in the roll of nations:
'This one was born in her.'

7 Singers and dancers alike all chant[z]
your praises,

3 proclaiming glorious things of you,
O city of God.

88

Face to face with death

1 O LORD, my God, by day I call for
help,[a]
by night I cry aloud in thy presence.

2 Let my prayer come before thee,
hear my loud lament;

3 for I have had my fill of woes,
and they have brought me to the
threshold of Sheol.

4 I am numbered with those who go
down to the abyss
and have become like a man beyond
help,

5 like a man who lies dead[b]
or the slain who sleep in the grave,
whom thou rememberest no more

---

t and the path . . . peace: prob. rdg.; Heb. so that he may put his feet to the way.   *u my God: transposed from previous verse.*   *v The text of this psalm is disordered, and several verses have been re-arranged.*   *w Prob. rdg.; Heb. his.*   *x his home: prob. rdg.; Heb. most high.*   *y Prob. rdg.; Heb. adds this one was born (cp. verse 6).*   *z all chant: prob. rdg.; Heb. all my springs.*   *a I call for help: prob. rdg.; Heb. my deliverance.*   *b who lies dead: prob. rdg.; Heb. obscure.*

because they are cut off from thy care.

6 Thou hast plunged me into the lowest abyss,
in dark places, in the depths.

7 Thy wrath rises against me,
thou hast turned on me the full force of thy anger.[c]

8 Thou hast taken all my friends far from me,
and made me loathsome to them.
I am in prison and cannot escape;

9 my eyes are failing and dim with anguish.
I have called upon thee, O LORD, every day
and spread out my hands in prayer to thee.

10 Dost thou work wonders for the dead?
Shall their company rise up and praise thee?

11 Will they speak of thy faithful love in the grave,
of thy sure help in the place of Destruction?

12 Will thy wonders be known in the dark,
thy victories in the land of oblivion?

13 But, LORD, I cry to thee,
my prayer comes before thee in the morning.

14 Why hast thou cast me off, O LORD,
why dost thou hide thy face from me?

15 I have suffered from boyhood and come near to death;
I have borne thy terrors, I cower beneath thy blows.

16 Thy burning fury has swept over me,
thy onslaughts have put me to silence;

17 all the day long they surge round me like a flood,
they engulf me in a moment.

18 Thou hast taken lover and friend far from me,
and parted me from my companions.

<h1 style="text-align:center">89</h1>

The LORD's covenant with David

1 I will sing the story of thy love, O LORD, for ever;
I will proclaim thy faithfulness to all generations.

2 Thy true love is firm as the ancient earth,[d]
thy faithfulness fixed as the heavens.

5 The heavens praise thy wonders, O LORD,
and the council of the holy ones exalts thy faithfulness.

6 In the skies who is there like the LORD,
who like the LORD in the court of heaven,

7 like God who is dreaded among the assembled holy ones,
great and terrible above all who stand about him?

8 O LORD God of Hosts, who is like thee?
Thy strength[f] and faithfulness, O LORD, surround thee.

9 Thou rulest the surging sea,
calming the turmoil[g] of its waves.

10 Thou didst crush the monster Rahab with a mortal blow
and scatter thy enemies with thy strong arm.

11 Thine are the heavens, the earth is thine also;
the world with all that is in it is of thy foundation.

12 Thou didst create Zaphon and Amanus;[h]
Tabor and Hermon echo thy name.

13 Strength of arm and valour are thine;
thy hand is mighty, thy right hand lifted high;

14 thy throne is built upon righteousness and justice,
true love and faithfulness herald thy coming.

15 Happy the people who have learnt to acclaim thee,
who walk, O LORD, in the light of thy presence!

16 In thy name they shall rejoice all day long;
thy righteousness shall lift them up.

17 Thou art thyself the strength in which they glory;
through thy favour we hold our heads high.

18 The LORD, he is our shield;
the Holy One of Israel, he is our king.

19 Then didst thou announce in a vision
and declare to thy faithful servants:

3 I have made a covenant with him I have chosen,

c anger: *or* waves.   d Thy . . . earth: *prob. rdg.*; *Heb.* Thou hast said for ever true love shall be made firm.   e Verses 3 and 4 transposed to follow servants in verse 19.   f Thy strength: *prob. rdg.*; *Heb.* obscure.   g turmoil: *prob. rdg.*; *Heb.* obscure.   h Amanus: *prob. rdg.*; *Heb.* right hand or south.

I have sworn to my servant David:
4 'I will establish your posterity for
ever,
I will make your throne endure for
all generations.'
I have endowed a warrior with
princely gifts,
so that the youth I have chosen towers
over his people.
20 I have discovered David my servant;
I have anointed him with my holy
oil.
21 My hand shall be ready to help him
and my arm to give him strength.
22 No enemy shall strike at him
and no rebel bring him low;
23 I will shatter his foes before him
and vanquish those who hate him.
24 My faithfulness and true love shall
be with him
and through my name he shall hold
his head high.
25 I will extend his rule over the Sea
and his dominion as far as the
River.
26 He will say to me, 'Thou art my
father,
my God, my rock and my safe
refuge.'
27 And I will name him my first-born,
highest among the kings of the
earth.
28 I will maintain my love for him for
ever
and be faithful in my covenant with
him.
29 I will establish his posterity for ever
and his throne as long as the
heavens endure.
30 If his sons forsake my law
and do not conform to my judgements,
31 if they renounce my statutes
and do not observe my commands,
32 I will punish their disobedience with
the rod
and their iniquity with lashes.
33 Yet I will not deprive him of my
true love
nor let my faithfulness prove false;
34 I will not renounce my covenant
nor change my promised purpose.
35 I have sworn by my holiness once
and for all,
I will not break my word to David:
36 his posterity shall continue for ever,
his throne before me like the sun;
37 it shall be sure for ever as the
moon's return,
faithful so long as the skies remain.[i]

Yet thou hast rejected thy anointed 38
king,
thou hast spurned him and raged
against him,[j]
thou hast denounced the covenant 39
with thy servant,
defiled his crown and flung it to the
ground.
Thou hast breached his walls   40
and laid his fortresses in ruin;
all who pass by plunder him,   41
and he suffers the taunts of his
neighbours.
Thou hast increased the power of 42
his enemies
and brought joy to all his foes;
thou hast let his sharp sword be 43
driven back
and left him without help in the
battle.
Thou hast put an end to his glorious 44
rule[k]
and hurled his throne to the ground;
thou hast cut short the days of his 45
youth and vigour
and covered him with shame.

How long, O LORD, wilt thou hide thy- 46
self from sight?
How long must thy wrath blaze
like fire?
Remember that I shall not live for 47
ever;[l]
hast thou created man in vain?
What man shall live and not see death 48
or save himself from the power of
Sheol?
Where are those former acts of thy 49
love, O Lord,
those faithful promises given to
David?
Remember, O Lord, the taunts 50
hurled at thy servant,
how I have borne in my heart the
calumnies of the nations;[m]
so have thy enemies taunted us, 51
O LORD,
taunted the successors of thy
anointed king.

Blessed is the LORD for ever.   52

Amen, Amen.

BOOK 4
90

The everlasting God and mortal man

Lord, thou hast been our refuge   1
from generation to generation.

---

i so long . . . remain: prob. rdg.; Heb. a witness in the skies.   *j raged against him: or* put him
out of mind.   *k* his glorious rule: *prob. rdg.; Heb.* from his purity.   *l* live for ever: *prob. rdg.;*
Heb. obscure.   *m* the calumnies . . . nations: *prob. rdg.; Heb.* all of many peoples.

2 Before the mountains were brought
     forth,
     or earth and world were born in
     travail,
   from age to age everlasting thou art
     God.
3 Thou turnest man back into dust;
     'Turn back,' thou sayest, 'you sons
     of men';
4 for in thy sight a thousand years
     are as yesterday;
5 a night-watch passes, and thou hast
     cut them off;
   they are like a dream at daybreak,
6 they fade like grass which springs
     up[n] with the morning
   but when evening comes is parched
     and withered.
7 So we are brought to an end by thy
     anger
   and silenced by thy wrath.
8 Thou dost lay bare our iniquities
     before thee
   and our lusts in the full light of thy
     presence.
9 All our days go by under the
     shadow of thy wrath;
   our years die away like a murmur.
10 Seventy years is the span of our life,
     eighty if our strength holds;[o]
   the hurrying years are labour and
     sorrow,
   so quickly they pass and are forgot-
     ten.
11 Who feels the power of thy anger,
   who feels thy wrath like those that
     fear thee?
12 Teach us to order our days rightly,
     that we may enter the gate of
     wisdom.
13 How long, O LORD?
   Relent, and take pity on thy
     servants.
14 Satisfy us with thy love when
     morning breaks,
   that we may sing for joy and be
     glad all our days.
15 Repay us days of gladness for our
     days of suffering,
   for the years thou hast humbled us.
16 Show thy servants thy deeds
   and their children thy majesty.
17 May all delightful things be ours, O
     Lord our God;
   establish firmly all we do.

and lodge under the shadow of the
  Almighty,
who say, 'The LORD is my safe 2
  retreat,
my God the fastness in which I
  trust';
he himself will snatch you away   3
from fowler's snare or raging
  tempest.
He will cover you with his pinions, 4
and you shall find safety beneath
  his wings;
you shall not fear the hunters' trap 5
  by night
or the arrow that flies by day,
the pestilence that stalks in dark- 6
  ness
or the plague raging at noonday.
A thousand may fall at your side, 7
ten thousand close at hand,
but you it shall not touch;
his truth[p] will be your shield and
  your rampart.[q]
With your own eyes you shall see 8
  all this;
you shall watch the punishment of
  the wicked.
For you, the LORD is a[r] safe retreat; 9
you have made the Most High your
  refuge.
No disaster shall befall you,   10
no calamity shall come upon your
  home.
For he has charged his angels   11
to guard you wherever you go,
to lift you on their hands   12
for fear you should strike your foot
  against a stone.
You shall step on asp and cobra,   13
you shall tread safely on snake and
  serpent.

Because his love is set on me, I will 14
  deliver him;
I will lift him beyond danger, for he
  knows me by my name.
When he calls upon me, I will 15
  answer;
I will be with him in time of
  trouble;
I will rescue him and bring him to
  honour.
I will satisfy him with long life   16
to enjoy the fullness of my salvation.

91

Trust in God

1   You that live in the shelter of the
    Most High

92

The LORD's goodness and righteousness

O LORD, it is good to give thee 1
  thanks,

n *Prob. rdg.; Heb. adds* and passes away.   o *Or* eighty at the most.   p *Or* his arm.   q his
truth . . . rampart: *transposed from end of verse 4.*   r *Prob. rdg.; Heb.* my.

to sing psalms to thy name, O Most
   High,
2 to declare thy love in the morning
   and thy constancy every night,
3 to the music of a ten-stringed lute,
   to the sounding chords of the harp.
4 Thy acts, O LORD, fill me with
   exultation;
    I shout in triumph at thy mighty
     deeds.
5 How great are thy deeds, O LORD!
   How fathomless thy thoughts!

6 He who does not know this is a brute,
   a fool is he who does not understand
    this:
7 that though the wicked grow like
    grass
   and every evildoer prospers,
   they will be destroyed for ever.
8 While thou, LORD, dost reign on high
   eternally,
9 thy foes will surely perish,
   all evildoers will be scattered.

10 I lift my head high, like a wild ox
   tossing its horn;
   I am anointed richly with oil.
11   I gloat over all who speak ill of me,
  I listen for the downfall of my cruel
   foes.
12 The righteous flourish like a palm-
   tree,
   they grow tall as a cedar on Leb-
    anon;
13 planted as they are in the house of
   the LORD,
   they flourish in the courts of our
    God,
14 vigorous in old age like trees full of
   sap,
   luxuriant, wide-spreading,
15 eager to declare that the LORD is
   just,
   the LORD my rock,^{s} in whom there
    is no unrighteousness.

93

The LORD is king

1 The LORD is king; he is clothed in
   majesty;
   the LORD clothes himself with might
   and fastens on his belt of wrath.

   Thou hast fixed the earth immovable and firm,
2 thy throne firm from of old;
   from all eternity thou art God.
3 O LORD, the ocean lifts up, the ocean
   lifts up its clamour;

the ocean lifts up^t its pounding
   waves.
The LORD on high is mightier far 4
than the noise of great waters,
mightier than the breakers of the
   sea.

Thy law stands firm, and holiness is 5
   the beauty of thy temple,
while time shall last, O LORD.

94

The teacher of mankind

O LORD, thou God of vengeance, 1
thou God of vengeance, show thyself.
Rise up, judge of the earth;   2
punish the arrogant as they deserve.
How long shall the wicked, O LORD, 3
how long shall the wicked exult?
Evildoers are full of bluster,   4
boasting and swaggering;
they beat down thy people, O LORD, 5
and oppress thy chosen nation;
they murder the widow and the 6
   stranger
and do the fatherless to death;
they say, 'The LORD does not see, 7
the God of Jacob pays no heed.'
Pay heed yourselves, most brutish 8
   of the people;
you fools, when will you be wise?
Does he that planted the ear not 9
   hear,
he that moulded the eye not see?
Shall not he that instructs the 10
   nations correct them?
The teacher of mankind, has he no^u
   knowledge?
The LORD knows the thoughts of man, 11
that they are but a puff of wind.

Happy the man whom thou dost 12
   instruct, O LORD,
and teach out of thy law,
giving him respite from adversity 13
until a pit is dug for the wicked.
The LORD will not abandon his people 14
nor forsake his chosen nation;
for righteousness still informs his 15
   judgement,^{v}
and all upright men follow it.

Who is on my side against these 16
   sinful men?
Who will stand up for me against
   these evildoers?
If the LORD had not been my helper, 17
I should soon have slept in the silent
   grave.
When I felt that my foot was slip- 18
   ping,

*s Or creator.   t the ocean lifts up: or let the ocean lift up.   u no: prob. rdg.; Heb. om.   v for
. . . judgement: prob. rdg.; Heb. for judgement will return as far as righteousness.*

thy love, O LORD, held me up.
19 Anxious thoughts may fill my
   heart,
   but thy presence is my joy and my
   consolation.
20 Shall sanctimonious calumny call
   thee partner,
   or he that contrives a mischief under
   cover of law?
21 For they put the righteous on trial[w]
   for his life
   and condemn to death innocent
   men.
22 But the LORD has been my strong
   tower,
   and God my rock of refuge;
23 our God requites the wicked for their
   injustice,
   the LORD puts them to silence for
   their misdeeds.

95

Call to worship

1 Come! Let us raise a joyful song to
   the LORD,
   a shout of triumph to the Rock of
   our salvation.
2 Let us come into his presence with
   thanksgiving,
   and sing him psalms of triumph.
3 For the LORD is a great God,
   a great king over all gods;
4 the farthest places of the earth are
   in his hands,
   and the folds of the hills are his;
5 the sea is his, he made it;
   the dry land fashioned by his hands
   is his.
6 Come! Let us throw ourselves at
   his feet in homage,
   let us kneel before the LORD who
   made us;
7 for he is our God,
   we are his people, we the flock he
   shepherds.
   You shall know[x] his power today
   if you will listen to his voice.

8 Do not grow stubborn, as you were
   at Meribah,[y]
   as at the time of Massah[z] in the
   wilderness,
9 when your forefathers challenged
   me,
   tested me and saw for themselves
   all that I did.
10 For forty years I was indignant
   with that generation, and I said:
   They are a people whose hearts are
   astray,

and they will not discern my ways.
As I swore in my anger: 11
They shall never enter my rest.

96

A new song

Sing a new song to the LORD;   1[a]
sing to the LORD, all men on earth.
Sing to the LORD and bless his name, 2
proclaim his triumph day by day.
Declare his glory among the nations, 3
his marvellous deeds among all
peoples.
Great is the LORD and worthy of all 4
praise;
he is more to be feared than all gods.
For the gods of the nations are 5
idols every one;
but the LORD made the heavens.
Majesty and splendour attend him, 6
might and beauty are in his sanctuary.

Ascribe to the LORD, you families 7
of nations,
ascribe to the LORD glory and might;
ascribe to the LORD the glory due 8
to his name,
bring a gift and come into his courts.
Bow down to the LORD in the 9
splendour of holiness,[b]
and dance in his honour, all men on
earth.
Declare among the nations, 'The 10
LORD is king.
He has fixed the earth firm, immovable;
he will judge the peoples justly.'
Let the heavens rejoice and the earth 11
exult,
let the sea roar and all the creatures
in it,
let the fields exult and all that is in 12
them;
then let all the trees of the forest
shout for joy
before the LORD when he comes to 13
judge the earth.
He will judge the earth with
righteousness
and the peoples in good faith.

97

The LORD is king

The LORD is king, let the earth be glad, 1
let coasts and islands all rejoice.
Cloud and mist enfold him,   2
righteousness and justice
are the foundation of his throne.

---

w they put . . . trial: *prob. rdg.*; Heb. they cut the righteous.   *x* You shall know: *prob. rdg.*; Heb.
om.   *y* *That is* Dispute.   *z* *That is* Challenge.   *a* Verses 1–13: *cp. 1 Chr. 16. 23–33.*   *b* the
splendour of holiness: *or* holy vestments.

3 Fire goes before him
  and burns up his enemies all around.
4 The world is lit up beneath his
  lightning-flash;
  the earth sees it and writhes in pain.
5 The mountains melt like wax as the
  LORD approaches,
  the Lord of all the earth.
6 The heavens proclaim his righteousness,
  and all peoples see his glory.
7 Let all who worship images, who
  vaunt their idols,
  be put to shame;
  bow down, all gods,*c* before him.

8 Zion heard and rejoiced, the cities of
  Judah were glad
  at thy judgements, O LORD.
9 For thou, LORD, art most high over
  all the earth,
  far exalted above all gods.

10 The LORD loves*d* those who hate
   evil;
   he keeps his loyal servants safe
   and rescues them from the wicked.
11 A harvest of light is sown for the
   righteous,
   and joy for all good men.
12 You that are righteous, rejoice in
   the LORD
   and praise his holy name.

98

When the LORD comes

1 Sing a new song to the LORD,
  for he has done marvellous deeds;
  his right hand and holy arm have won
  him victory.
2 The LORD has made his victory
  known;
  he has displayed his righteousness
  to all the nations.
3 He has remembered his constancy,
  his love for the house of Israel.
  All the ends of the earth have seen
  the victory of our God.

4 Acclaim the LORD, all men on earth,
  break into songs of joy, sing psalms.
5 Sing psalms in the LORD's honour
  with the harp,
  with the harp and with the music of
  the psaltery.
6 With trumpet and echoing horn
  acclaim the presence of the LORD
  our king.
7 Let the sea roar and all its creatures,
  the world and those who dwell in it.
8 Let the rivers clap their hands,

let the hills sing aloud together
before the LORD; for he comes   9
to judge the earth.
He will judge the world with righteousness
and the peoples in justice.

99

The LORD is king

The LORD is king, the peoples are 1
  perturbed;
he is throned on the cherubim, earth
  quivers.
The LORD is great in Zion;   2
he is exalted above all the peoples.
They extol his*e* name as great and 3
  terrible;
he is holy, he is mighty,   4
a king who loves justice.

Thou hast established justice and
  equity;
thou hast dealt righteously in Jacob.
Exalt the LORD our God,   5
bow down before his footstool;
he is holy.

Moses and Aaron among his priests, 6
and Samuel among those who call
  on his name,
called to the LORD, and he answered.
He spoke to them in a pillar of 7
  cloud;
they followed his teaching and kept
  the law he gave them.
Thou, O LORD our God, thou didst 8
  answer them;
thou wast a God who forgave all
  their misdeeds
and held them innocent.
Exalt the LORD our God,   9
bow down towards his holy hill;
for the LORD our God is holy.

100

The LORD is God

Acclaim the LORD, all men on 1
  earth,
worship the LORD in gladness;   2
enter his presence with songs of
  exultation.
Know that the LORD is God;   3
he has made us and we are his own,
his people, the flock which he
  shepherds.
Enter his gates with thanksgiving 4
and his courts with praise.
Give thanks to him and bless his
  name;

c bow . . . gods: *or* all gods bow down . . .
LORD.   e *Prob. rdg.; Heb.* thy.

d The LORD loves: *prob. rdg.; Heb.* Lovers of the

5 for the LORD is good and his love is
   everlasting,
   his constancy endures to all generations.

101

Character of a righteous ruler

1 I sing of loyalty and justice;
   I will raise a psalm to thee, O LORD.*f*

2 I will follow a wise and blameless
   course,
   whatever may befall me.*g*
   I will go about my house in purity
   of heart.
3 I will set before myself no sordid aim;
   I will hate disloyalty, I will have none
   of it.
4 I will reject all crooked thoughts;
   I will have no dealings with evil.
5 I will silence those who spread tales
   behind men's backs,
   I will not sit at table with proud,
   pompous men,
6 I will choose the most loyal for my
   companions;
   my servants shall be men whose lives
   are blameless.
7 No scandal-monger shall live in my
   household;
   no liar shall set himself up where I can
   see him.
8 Morning after morning I will put all
   wicked men to silence
   and will rid the LORD's city of all
   evildoers.

102

Prayer for restoration

1 LORD, hear my prayer
   and let my cry for help reach thee.
2 Hide not thy face from me
   when I am in distress.
   Listen to my prayer
   and, when I call, answer me soon;
3 for my days vanish like smoke,
   my body is burnt up as in an oven.
4 I am stricken, withered like grass;
   I cannot find the strength to eat.
5 Wasted away,*h* I groan aloud
   and my skin hangs on my bones.
6 I am like a desert-owl in the wilderness,
   an owl that lives among ruins.
7 Thin and meagre, I wail in solitude,
   like a bird that flutters on the roof-
   top.
8 My enemies insult me all the day
   long;

mad with rage, they conspire
against me.
I have eaten ashes for bread   9
and mingled tears with my drink.
In thy wrath and fury   10
thou hast taken me up and flung me
aside.
My days decline as the shadows   11
lengthen,
and like grass I wither away.

But thou, LORD, art enthroned for   12
ever
and thy fame shall be known to all
generations,
Thou wilt arise and have mercy on   13
Zion;
for the time is come*i* to pity her.
Her very stones are dear to thy   14
servants,
and even her dust moves them with
pity.
Then shall the nations revere thy   15
name, O LORD,
and all the kings of the earth thy
glory,
when the LORD builds up Zion   16
again
and shows himself in his glory.
He turns to hear the prayer of the 17
destitute
and does not scorn them when they
pray.
This shall be written down for future 18
generations,
and a people yet unborn shall praise
the LORD.
The LORD looks down from his   19
sanctuary on high,
from heaven he surveys the earth
to listen to the groaning of the   20
prisoners
and set free men under sentence of
death;
so shall the LORD's name be on men's 21
lips in Zion
and his praise shall be told in
Jerusalem,
when peoples are assembled to-   22
gether,
peoples and kingdoms, to serve the
LORD.

My strength is broken in mid   23
course;
the time allotted me is short.   24
Snatch me not away before half my
days are done,
for thy years last through all
generations.

f I sing . . . O LORD: *or* I will follow a course of justice and loyalty; *i* I will hold thee in awe, O
LORD.   *g* whatever may befall me: *prob. rdg.; Heb.* when comest thou to me?   *h* Wasted away:
transposed from previous verse.   *i* *Prob. rdg.; Heb. adds* season.

25 Long ago thou didst lay the foundations of the earth,
and the heavens were thy handiwork.
26 They shall pass away, but thou endurest;
like clothes they shall all grow old;
thou shalt cast them off like a cloak,
and they shall vanish;
27 but thou art the same and thy years shall have no end;
28 thy servants' children shall continue,
and their posterity shall be established in thy presence.

103

Meditating on the LORD's goodness

1 Bless the LORD, my soul;
my innermost heart, bless his holy name.
2 Bless the LORD, my soul,
and forget none of his benefits.
3 He pardons all my guilt
and heals all my suffering.
4 He rescues me from the pit of death
and surrounds me with constant love,
with tender affection;
5 he contents me with all good in the prime of life,
and my youth is ever new like an eagle's.
6 The LORD is righteous in his acts;
he brings justice to all who have been wronged.
7 He taught Moses to know his way
and showed the Israelites what he could do.
8 The LORD is compassionate and gracious,
long-suffering and for ever constant;
9 he will not always be the accuser
or nurse his anger for all time.
10 He has not treated us as our sins deserve
or requited us for our misdeeds.
11 For as the heaven stands high above the earth,
so his strong love stands high over all who fear him.
12 Far as east is from west,
so far has he put our offences away from us.
13 As a father has compassion on his children,
so has the LORD compassion on all who fear him.
14 For he knows how we were made,
he knows full well that we are dust.

Man's days are like the grass; 15
he blossoms like the flowers of the field:
a wind passes over them, and they 16
cease to be,
and their place knows them no more.
But the LORD's love never fails those 17
who fear him;
his righteousness never fails their sons and their grandsons
who listen to his voice[j] and keep 18
his covenant,
who remember his commandments and obey them.

The LORD has established his throne 19
in heaven,
his kingly power over the whole world.
Bless the LORD, all his angels, 20
creatures of might who do his bidding.
Bless the LORD, all his hosts, 21
his ministers who serve his will.
Bless the LORD, all created things, 22
in every place where he has dominion.

Bless the LORD, my soul.

104

Meditating on nature

Bless the LORD, my soul: 1
O LORD my God, thou art great indeed,
clothed in majesty and splendour,
and wrapped in a robe of light. 2
Thou hast spread out the heavens like a tent
and on their waters laid the beams 3
of thy pavilion;
who takest the clouds for thy chariot,
riding on the wings of the wind;
who makest the winds thy mes- 4
sengers
and flames of fire thy servants;
thou didst fix the earth on its 5
foundation
so that it never can be shaken;
the deep overspread it like a cloak, 6
and the waters lay above the mountains.
At thy rebuke they ran, 7
at the sound of thy thunder they rushed away,
flowing over the hills, 8
pouring down into the valleys
to the place appointed for them.
Thou didst fix a boundary which they 9
might not pass;
they shall not return to cover the earth.

j who listen to his voice: *transposed from end of verse 20.*

10 Thou dost make springs break out in
    the gullies,
    so that their water runs between
    the hills.
11 The wild beasts all drink from them,
    the wild asses quench their thirst;
12 the birds of the air nest on their
    banks
    and sing among the leaves.

13 From thy high pavilion thou dost
    water the hills;
    the earth is enriched by thy pro-
    vision.
14 Thou makest grass grow for the
    cattle
    and green things for those who toil
    for man,
    bringing bread out of the earth
15 and wine to gladden men's hearts,
    oil to make their faces shine
    and bread to sustain their strength.
16 The trees of the LORD are green and
    leafy,
    the cedars of Lebanon which he
    planted;
17 the birds build their nests in them,
    the stork makes her home in their
    tops.[k]
18 High hills are the haunt of the
    mountain-goat,
    and boulders a refuge for the rock-
    badger.

19 Thou hast made the moon to
    measure the year
    and taught the sun where to set.
20 When thou makest darkness and it is
    night,
    all the beasts of the forest come forth;
21 the young lions roar for prey,
    seeking their food from God.
22 When thou makest the sun rise,
    they slink away
    and go to rest in their lairs;
23 but man comes out to his work
    and to his labours until evening.
24 Countless are the things thou hast
    made, O LORD.
    Thou hast made all by thy wisdom;
    and the earth is full of thy creatures,
25 beasts great and small.

    Here is the great immeasurable sea,
    in which move creatures beyond
    number.
26 Here ships sail to and fro,
    here is Leviathan whom thou hast
    made thy plaything.[l]

27 All of them look expectantly to thee
    to give them their food at the
    proper time;

what thou givest them they gather 28
    up;
when thou openest thy hand, they
    eat their fill.
Then thou hidest thy face, and they 29
    are restless and troubled;
when thou takest away their breath,
    they fail
[and they return to the dust from
    which they came];
but when thou breathest into them, 30
    they recover;
thou givest new life to the earth.

May the glory of the LORD stand 31
    for ever
and may he rejoice in his works!
When he looks at the earth, it 32
    quakes;
when he touches the hills, they pour
    forth smoke.

I will sing to the LORD as long as 33
    I live,
all my life I will sing psalms to my
    God.
May my meditation please the LORD, 34
    as I show my joy in him!
Away with all sinners from the 35
    earth
and may the wicked be no more!

Bless the LORD, my soul.

O praise the LORD.

105

How the LORD led Israel

Give the LORD thanks and invoke him 1[m]
    by name,
make his deeds known in the world
    around.
Pay him honour with song and psalm 2
    and think upon all his wonders.
Exult in his hallowed name; 3
    let those who seek the LORD be joy-
    ful in heart.
Turn to the LORD, your strength, 4
    seek his presence always.
Remember the wonders that he has 5
    wrought,
    his portents and the judgements he
    has given,
O offspring of Abraham his servant, 6
    O chosen sons of Jacob.

He is the LORD our God; 7
    his judgements fill the earth.
He called to mind his covenant 8
    from long ago,[n]
    the promise he extended to a
    thousand generations—

---

k in their tops: *prob. rdg.*; *Heb.* the pine-trees.   l thy plaything: *or* that it may sport in it.
m *Verses 1–15: cp. 1 Chr. 16. 8–22.*   n from long ago: *or* for ever.

9 the covenant made with Abraham,
his oath given to Isaac,
10 the decree by which he bound himself for Jacob,
his everlasting covenant with Israel:
11 'I will give you the land of Canaan',
he said,
'to be your possession, your patrimony.'
12 A small company it was,
few in number, strangers in that
land,
13 roaming from nation to nation,
from one kingdom to another;
14 but he let no one ill-treat them,
for their sake he admonished kings:
15 'Touch not my anointed servants,
do my prophets no harm.'

16 He called down famine on the land
and cut short their daily bread.
17 But he had sent on a man before
them,
Joseph, who was sold into slavery;
18 he was kept a prisoner with fetters
on his feet
and an iron collar clamped on his
neck.
19 He was tested by the LORD's command
until what he foretold came true.
20 Then the king sent and set him
free,
the ruler of nations released him;
21 he made him master of his household
and ruler over all his possessions,
22 to correct his officers at will
and teach his counsellors wisdom.
23 Then Israel too went down into
Egypt
and Jacob came to live in the land
of Ham.
24 There God made his people very
fruitful,
he made them stronger than their
enemies,
25 whose hearts he turned to hatred of
his people
and double-dealing with his servants.
26 He sent his servant Moses
and Aaron whom he had chosen.
27 They were his mouthpiece to
announce his signs,
his portents in the land of Ham.
28 He sent darkness, and all was dark,
but still they resisted his commands.
29 He turned their waters into blood
and killed all their fish.
30 Their country swarmed with frogs,
even their princes' inner chambers.
31 At his command came swarms of
flies
and maggots the whole land through.

32 He changed their rain into hail
and flashed fire over their country.
33 He blasted their vines and their
fig-trees
and splintered the trees throughout
the land.
34 At his command came locusts,
hoppers past all number,
35 they consumed every green thing
in the land,
consumed all the produce of the
soil.
36 Then he struck down all the first-
born in Egypt,
the firstfruits of their manhood;
37 he led Israel out, laden with silver
and gold,
and among all their tribes no man
fell.
38 The Egyptians were glad when they
went,
for fear of Israel had taken hold of
them.
39 He spread a cloud as a screen,
and fire to light up the night.
40 They asked, and he sent them
quails,
he gave them bread from heaven in
plenty.
41 He opened a rock and water gushed
out,
a river flowing in a parched land;
42 for he had remembered his solemn
promise
given to his servant Abraham.
43 So he led out his people rejoicing,
his chosen ones in triumph.
44 He gave them the lands of heathen
nations
and they took possession where others
had toiled,
45 so that they might keep his statutes
and obey his laws.

O praise the LORD.

106

Israel's persistent disobedience

1 O praise the LORD.

It is good to give thanks to the
LORD;
for his love endures for ever.
2 Who will tell of the LORD's mighty
acts
and make his praises heard?
3 Happy are they who act justly
and do right at all times!
4 Remember me, LORD, when thou
showest favour to thy people,
look upon me when thou savest
them,
5 that I may see the prosperity of
thy chosen,

I

rejoice in thy nation's joy and exult
with thy own people.

6 We have sinned like our forefathers,
   we have erred and done wrong.
7 Our fathers in Egypt took no account
   of thy marvels,
   they did not remember thy many
      acts of faithful love,
   but in spite of all[o] they rebelled by
      the Red Sea,[p]
8 Yet the LORD delivered them for
   his name's sake
   and so made known his mighty
      power.
9 He rebuked the Red Sea and it
   dried up,
   he led his people through the deeps
      as through the wilderness.
10 So he delivered them from those
   who hated them,
   and claimed them back from the
      enemy's hand.
11 The waters closed over their adversaries,
   not one of them survived.
12 Then they believed his promises and
   sang praises to him.

13 But they quickly forgot all he had
   done
   and would not wait to hear his
      counsel;
14 their greed was insatiable in the
   wilderness,
   they tried God's patience in the
      desert.
15 He gave them what they asked
   but sent a wasting sickness among
      them.[q]

16 They were envious of Moses in the
   camp,
   and of Aaron, who was consecrated
      to the LORD.
17 The earth opened and swallowed
   Dathan,
   it closed over the company of
      Abiram;
18 fire raged through their company,
   the wicked perished in flames.

19 At Horeb they made a calf
   and bowed down to an image;
20 they exchanged their Glory[r]
   for the image of a bull that feeds
      on grass.
21 They forgot God their deliverer,
   who had done great deeds in Egypt,
22 marvels in the land of Ham,
   terrible things at the Red Sea.
23 So his purpose was to destroy them,
   but Moses, the man he had chosen,

threw himself into the breach
to turn back his wrath lest it
   destroy them.

They made light of the pleasant 24
   land,
disbelieving his promise;
they muttered treason in their 25
   tents
and would not obey the LORD.
So with uplifted hand he swore 26
to strike them down in the wilderness,
to scatter their descendants among 27
   the nations
and disperse them throughout the
   world.

They joined in worshipping the 28
   Baal of Peor
and ate meat sacrificed to lifeless
   gods.
Their deeds provoked the LORD to 29
   anger,
and plague broke out amongst them;
but Phinehas stood up and inter- 30
   ceded,
so the plague was stopped.
This was counted to him as right- 31
   eousness
throughout all generations for ever.

They roused the LORD to anger at 32
   the waters of Meribah,
and Moses suffered because of
   them;
for they had embittered his spirit 33
and he had spoken rashly.

They did not destroy the peoples 34
   round about,
as the LORD had commanded them
   to do,
but they mingled with the nations, 35
learning their ways;
they worshipped their idols 36
and were ensnared by them.
Their sons and their daughters 37
they sacrificed to foreign demons;
they shed innocent blood, 38
the blood of sons and daughters
offered to the gods of Canaan,
and the land was polluted with
   blood.
Thus they defiled themselves by 39
   their conduct
and they followed their lusts and
   broke faith with God.
Then the LORD grew angry with his 40
   people
and loathed them, his own chosen
   nation;

o in spite of all: *prob. rdg.*; Heb. obscure.   p Or the Sea of Reeds.   q among them: *or* in their
throats.   r their Glory: *or* the glory of God (*cp. Jer. 2. 11; Romans 1. 23*).

41 so he gave them into the hands of
the nations,
and they were ruled by their foes;
42 their enemies oppressed them
and made them subject to their
power.
43 Many times he came to their
rescue,
but they were disobedient and
rebellious still.[s]
44 And yet, when he heard them wail
and cry aloud,
he looked with pity on their distress;
45 he called to mind his covenant with
them
and, in his boundless love, relented;
46 he roused compassion for them
in the hearts of all their captors.

47 Deliver us, O LORD our God,
and gather us in from among the
nations
that we may give thanks to thy
holy name
and make thy praise our pride.

48 Blessed be the LORD the God of
Israel
from everlasting to everlasting;
and let all the people say 'Amen.'

O praise the LORD.

BOOK 5
107

The LORD's enduring love

1 It is good to give thanks to the LORD,
for his love endures for ever.
2 So let them say who were redeemed
by the LORD,
redeemed by him from the power
of the enemy
3 and gathered out of every land,
from east and west, from north and
south.

4 Some lost their way in desert wastes;
they found no road to a city to live
in;
5 hungry and thirsty,
their spirit sank within them.
6 So they cried to the LORD in their
trouble,
and he rescued them from their
distress;
7 he led them by a straight and easy
way
until they came to a city to live in.
8 Let them thank the LORD for his
enduring love

and for the marvellous things he
has done for men:
he has satisfied the thirsty   9
and filled the hungry with good
things.

Some sat in darkness, dark as death, 10
prisoners bound fast in iron,
because they had rebelled against 11
God's commands
and flouted the purpose of the
Most High.
Their spirit was subdued by hard 12
labour;
they stumbled and fell with none to
help them.
So they cried to the LORD in their 13
trouble,
and he saved them from their distress;
he brought them out of darkness, dark 14
as death,
and broke their chains.
Let them thank the LORD for his 15
enduring love
and for the marvellous things he
has done for men:
he has shattered doors of bronze,   16
bars of iron he has snapped in two.

Some were fools, they took to rebel- 17
lious ways,
and for their transgression they
suffered punishment.
They sickened at the sight of food   18
and drew near to the very gates of
death.
So they cried to the LORD in their 19
trouble,
and he saved them from their
distress;
he sent his word to heal them   20
and bring them alive out of the pit
of death.[t]
Let them thank the LORD for his 21
enduring love
and for the marvellous things he
has done for men.
Let them offer sacrifices of thanks- 22
giving
and recite his deeds with shouts of
joy.

Others there are who go to sea in ships 23
and make their living on the wide
waters.
These men have seen the acts of the 24
LORD
and his marvellous doings in the
deep.
At his command the storm-wind rose 25
and lifted the waves high.

s *Prob. rdg.*; *Heb. adds* and were brought low by their guilt.   t alive . . . death: *prob. rdg.*; *Heb.*
from their corruption.

26 Carried up to heaven, plunged down
       to the depths,
    tossed to and fro in peril,
27 they reeled and staggered like drun-
       ken men,
    and their seamanship was all in
       vain.
28 So they cried to the LORD in their
       trouble,
    and he brought them out of their
       distress.
29 The storm sank to a murmur
    and the waves of the sea were
       stilled.
30 They were glad then that all was calm,
    as he guided them to the harbour
       they desired.
31 Let them thank the LORD for his
       enduring love
    and for the marvellous things he has
       done for men.
32 Let them exalt him in the assembly
       of the people
    and praise him in the council of the
       elders.

33 He turns rivers into desert
    and springs of water into thirsty
       ground;
34 he turns fruitful land into salt waste,
    because the men who dwell there
       are so wicked.
35 Desert he changes into standing pools,
    and parched land into springs of
       water.
36 There he gives the hungry a home,
    and they build themselves a city to
       live in;
37 they sow fields and plant vineyards
    and reap a fruitful harvest.
38 He blesses them and their numbers
       increase,
    and he does not let their herds lose
       strength.
39 Tyrants[u] lose their strength and are
       brought low
    in the grip of misfortune and sorrow;
40 he brings princes into contempt
    and leaves them wandering in a
       trackless waste.
41 But the poor man he lifts clear of his
       troubles
    and makes families increase like
       flocks of sheep.
42 The upright see it and are glad,
    while evildoers are filled with dis-
       gust.
43 Let the wise man lay these things to
       heart,
    and ponder the record of the LORD's
       enduring love.

108

Prayer for God's help

My heart is steadfast, O God,   1[v]
    my heart is steadfast.
I will sing and raise a psalm;
    awake,[w] my spirit,
awake, lute and harp,   2
I will awake at dawn of day.[x]
I will confess thee, O LORD, among   3
    the peoples,
among the nations I will raise a
    psalm to thee;
for thy unfailing love is wider than   4
    the heavens
and thy truth reaches to the skies.
Show thyself, O God, high above   5
    the heavens;
let thy glory shine over all the
    earth.
Deliver those that are dear to thee;   6[y]
save with thy right hand and
    answer.

God has spoken from his sanctuary:[z] 7
    'I will go up now and measure out
       Shechem;
    I will divide the valley of Succoth
       into plots;
Gilead and Manasseh are mine;   8
Ephraim is my helmet, Judah my
    sceptre;
Moab is my wash-bowl, I fling my   9
    shoes at Edom;
    Philistia is the target of my anger.'

Who can bring me to the impregnable   10
    city,
    who can guide me to Edom,
since thou, O God, hast abandoned us   11
    and goest not forth with our armies?
Grant us help against the enemy,   12
    for deliverance by man is a vain
       hope.
    With God's help we shall do vali-   13
       antly,
    and God himself will tread our
       enemies under foot.

109

A cry for vengeance

O God of my praise, be silent no   1
    longer,
    for wicked men heap calumnies   2
       upon me.
They have lied to my face
    and ringed me round with words of   3
       hate.
They have attacked me without a
    cause[a]

u *Prob. rdg.; Heb. om.*   v *Verses 1–5: cp. Ps. 57. 7–11.*   w *awake: prob. rdg.; Heb. also.*
x *at dawn of day: or the dawn.*   y *Verses 6–13: cp. Ps. 60. 5–12.*   z *from his sanctuary: or in
his holiness.*   a *Prob. rdg.; Heb. adds in return for my love.*

4 and accused me though I have done nothing unseemly.[b]

5 They have repaid me evil for good and hatred in return for my love.

6 They say, 'Put up some rascal to denounce him,
an accuser to stand at his right side.'

7 But when judgement is given, that rascal will be exposed
and his follies accounted a sin.

8 May his days be few;
may his hoarded wealth[c] fall to another!

9 May his children be fatherless,
his wife a widow!

10 May his children be vagabonds and beggars,
driven from their homes!

11 May the money-lender distrain on all his goods
and strangers seize his earnings!

12 May none remain loyal to him,
and none have mercy on his fatherless children!

13 May his line be doomed to extinction,
may their name be wiped out within a generation!

14 May the sins of his forefathers be remembered
and his mother's wickedness never be wiped out!

15 May they remain on record before the LORD,
but may he extinguish their name from the earth!

16 For that man never set himself
to be loyal to his friend
but persecuted the downtrodden and the poor
and hounded the broken-hearted to their death.

17 Curses he loved: may the curse fall on him!
He took no pleasure in blessing: may no blessing be his!

18 He clothed himself in cursing like a garment:
may it seep into his body like water and into his bones like oil!

19 May it wrap him round like the clothes he puts on,
like the belt which he wears every day!

20 May the LORD so requite my accusers
and those who speak evil against me!

21 But thou, O LORD God,
deal with me as befits thy honour;
in the goodness of thy unfailing love deliver me,

22 for I am downtrodden and poor,
and my heart within me is distracted.

23 I fade like a passing shadow,
I am shaken off like a locust.

24 My knees are weak with fasting
and my flesh wastes away, so meagre is my fare.

25 I have become the victim of their taunts;
when they see me they toss their heads.

26 Help me, O LORD my God;
save me, by thy unfailing love,

27 that men may know this is thy doing
and thou alone, O LORD, hast done it.

28 They may curse, but thou dost bless;
may my opponents be put to shame,
but may thy servant rejoice!

29 May my accusers be clothed with dishonour,
wrapped in their shame as in a cloak!

30 I will lift up my voice to extol the LORD,
and before a great company I will praise him.

31 For he stands at the poor man's right side
to save him from his adversaries.[d]

110

The LORD's king and priest

1 The LORD said to my lord,
'You shall sit[e] at my right hand
when[f] I make your enemies the footstool under your feet.'

2 When the LORD from Zion hands you
the sceptre, the symbol of your power,
march forth through the ranks of[g] your enemies.

3 At birth[h] you were endowed with princely gifts
and[i] resplendent[j] in holiness.
You have shone with the dew of youth
since your mother bore you.

4 The LORD has sworn and will not change his purpose:
'You are a priest for ever,
in the succession of Melchizedek.'

5 The Lord at your right hand
has broken kings in the day of his anger.

b though . . . unseemly: *prob. rdg.; Heb. obscure.*   c hoarded wealth: *or* charge, *cp. Acts 1. 20.*
d *Prob. rdg.; Heb.* his judges.   e You shall sit: *or* Sit.   f *Or* until *or* while.   g *Or* reign in the
midst of.   h At birth: *or* On the day of your power.   i you were . . . and: *or* your people
offered themselves willingly; *mng. of Heb. uncertain.*   j *Or* apparelled.

6 So the king in his majesty,[k] sovereign
of a mighty land,
will punish nations;[l]
7 he will drink from the torrent beside the path
and therefore will hold his head high.

111

Praise of the LORD's goodness

1 O praise the LORD.

With all my heart will I praise the
LORD
in the company of good men, in the
whole congregation.
2 Great are the doings of the LORD;
all men study them for their delight.
3 His acts are full of majesty and
splendour;
righteousness is his for ever.
4 He has won a name by his marvellous
deeds;
the LORD is gracious and compassionate.
5 He gives food to those who fear him,
he keeps his covenant always in
mind.
6 He showed his people what his strength
could do,
bestowing on them the lands of
other nations.
7 His works are truth and justice;
his precepts all stand on firm
foundations,
8 strongly based to endure for ever,
their fabric goodness and truth.
9 He sent and redeemed his people;
he decreed that his covenant should
always endure.
Holy is his name, inspiring awe.
10 The fear of the LORD is the beginning[m]
of wisdom,
and they who live by it grow in understanding.
Praise will be his for ever.

112

Happiness of the God-fearing man

1 O praise the LORD.

Happy is the man who fears the LORD
and finds great joy in his commandments.
2 His descendants shall be the mightiest
in the land,
a blessed generation of good men.
3 His house shall be full of wealth and
riches;
righteousness shall be his for ever.

He is gracious, compassionate, good, 4
a beacon in darkness for honest men.
It is right for a man to be gracious in 5
his lending,
to order his affairs with judgement.
Nothing shall ever shake him; 6
his goodness shall be remembered
for all time.
Bad news shall have no terrors for him, 7
because his heart is steadfast,
trusting in the LORD.
His confidence is strongly based, he 8
will have no fear;
and in the end he will gloat over
his enemies.
He gives freely to the poor; 9
righteousness shall be his for ever;
in honour he carries his head high.
The wicked man shall see it with 10
rising anger
and grind his teeth in despair;
the hopes of wicked men shall come
to nothing.

113

The LORD's power and goodness

O praise the LORD.   1

Praise the LORD, you that are his
servants,
praise the name of the LORD.
Blessed be the name of the LORD   2
now and evermore.
From the rising of the sun to its setting 3
may the LORD's name be praised.
High is the LORD above all nations, 4
his glory above the heavens.
There is none like the LORD our God 5–6
in heaven or on earth,
who sets his throne so high
but deigns to look down so low;
who lifts the weak out of the dust 7
and raises the poor from the dunghill,
giving them a place among princes, 8
among the princes of his people;
who makes the woman in a child- 9
less house
a happy mother of children.[n]

114

The wonders of the Exodus

O praise the LORD.[o]   1

When Israel came out of Egypt,
Jacob from a people of outlandish
speech,
Judah became his sanctuary, 2
Israel his dominion.
The sea looked and ran away; 3

---

k So . . . majesty: *poss. rdg.; Heb.* full of corpses, he crushed.   l So . . . nations: *or* He
shall punish the nations—heaps of corpses, broken heads—over a wide expanse.   m *Or* chief part.
n O praise the LORD *transposed to the beginning of Ps. 114.*   o *See note on Ps. 113. 9.*

Jordan turned back.
4 The mountains skipped like rams,
    the hills like young sheep.
5 What was it, sea? Why did you run?
    Jordan, why did you turn back?
6 Why, mountains, did you skip like
      rams,
    and you, hills, like young sheep?
7 Dance, O earth, at the presence of
      the Lord,
    at the presence of the God of Jacob,
8 who turned the rock into a pool of
      water,
    the granite cliff into a fountain.

115

False gods and God

1 Not to us, O LORD, not to us,
    but to thy name ascribe the glory,
    for thy true love and for thy con-
      stancy.
2 Why do the nations ask,
    'Where then is their God?'
3 Our God is in high heaven;
    he does whatever pleases him.
4 Their idols are silver and gold,
    made by the hands of men.
5 They have mouths that cannot
      speak,
    and eyes that cannot see;
6 they have ears that cannot hear,
    nostrils, and cannot smell;
7 with their hands they cannot feel,
    with their feet they cannot walk,
    and no sound comes from their
      throats.
8 Their makers grow to be like them,
    and so do all who trust in them.

9 But Israel trusts in the LORD;
    he is their helper and their shield.
10 The house of Aaron trusts in the
      LORD;
    he is their helper and their shield.
11 Those who fear the LORD trust in
      the LORD;
    he is their helper and their shield.
12 The LORD remembers us, and he will
      bless us;
    he will bless the house of Israel,
    he will bless the house of Aaron.
13 The LORD will bless all who fear
      him,
    high and low alike.

14 May the LORD give you increase,
    both you and your sons.
15 You are blessed by the LORD,
    the LORD who made heaven and
      earth.
16 The heavens, they are the LORD's;

the earth he has given to all mankind.
17 It is not the dead who praise the
    LORD,
    not those who go down into silence;
18 but we, the living, bless the LORD,
    now and for evermore.

O praise the LORD.

116

*Thanksgiving for deliverance from
  death*

1 I love the LORD, for he has heard
    me
    and listens to my prayer;
2 for he has given me a hearing
    whenever I have cried to him.
3 The cords of death bound me,
    Sheol held me in its grip.
    Anguish and torment held me fast;
4 so I invoked the LORD by name,
    'Deliver me, O LORD, I beseech
      thee;
    for I am thy slave.'*p*
5 Gracious is the LORD and righteous,
    our God is full of compassion.
6 The LORD preserves the simple-
      hearted;
    I was brought low and he saved me.
7 Be at rest once more, my heart,
    for the LORD has showered gifts
      upon you.
8 He has rescued me from death
    and my feet from stumbling.
9 I will walk in the presence of the
      LORD
    in the land of the living.

10 I was sure that I should be swept
      away,
    and my distress was bitter.
11 In panic I cried,
    'How faithless all men are!'
12 How can I repay the LORD
    for all his gifts to me?
13 I will take in my hands the cup of
      salvation
    and invoke the LORD by name.
14 I will pay my vows to the LORD
    in the presence of all his people.
15 A precious thing in the LORD's
      sight
    is the death of those who die faithful
      to him.
16 *q*I am thy slave, thy slave-girl's son;
    thou hast undone the bonds that
      bound me.
17 To thee will I bring a thank-offering
    and invoke the LORD by name.
18 I will pay my vows to the LORD

p for . . . slave: *transposed from the beginning of verse 16; Heb. adds* O LORD.   *q Prob. rdg.; Heb.*
prefixes For I am thy slave, O LORD; *see note on verse 4.*

in the presence of all his people,
19　in the courts of the LORD's house,
in the midst of you, Jerusalem.

O praise the LORD.

117

Call to praise God

1　Praise the LORD, all nations,
extol him, all you peoples;
2　for his love protecting us is strong,
the LORD's constancy is everlasting.

O praise the LORD.

118

His love endures for ever

1　It is good to give thanks to the
LORD,
for his love endures for ever.
2　Declare it, house of Israel:
his love endures for ever.
3　Declare it, house of Aaron:
his love endures for ever.
4　Declare it, you that fear the LORD:
his love endures for ever.
5　When in my distress I called to the
LORD,
his answer was to set me free.
6　The LORD is on my side, I have no
fear;
what can man do to me?
7　The LORD is on my side, he is my
helper,
and I shall gloat over my enemies.
8　It is better to find refuge in the
LORD
than to trust in men.
9　It is better to find refuge in the
LORD
than to trust in princes.
10　All nations surround me,
but in the LORD's name I will drive
them away.
11　They surround me on this side and
on that,
but in the LORD's name I will drive
them away.
12　They surround me like bees at the
honey;
they attack me, as fire attacks
brushwood,
but in the LORD's name I will drive
them away.
13　They thrust hard against me so that
I nearly fall;
but the LORD has helped me.
14　The LORD is my refuge and defence,
and he has become my deliverer.
15　Hark! Shouts of deliverance
in the camp of the victors[r]!

r Or righteous.　s Or righteousness.

With his right hand the LORD does
mighty deeds,
the right hand of the LORD raises 16
up.
I shall not die but live 17
to proclaim the works of the LORD.
The LORD did indeed chasten me, 18
but he did not surrender me to
Death.

Open to me the gates of victory;[s] 19
I will enter by them and praise the
LORD.
This is the gate of the LORD; 20
the victors[r] shall make their entry
through it.
I will praise thee, for thou hast 21
answered me
and hast become my deliverer.
The stone which the builders re- 22
jected
has become the chief corner-stone.
This is the LORD's doing; 23
it is marvellous in our eyes.
This is the day on which the LORD 24
has acted:[t]
let us exult and rejoice in it.
We pray thee, O LORD, deliver us; 25
we pray thee, O LORD, send us
prosperity.
Blessed in the name of the LORD 26
are all who come;
we bless you from the house of the
LORD.
The LORD is God; he has given light 27
to us,
the ordered line of pilgrims by the
horns of the altar.
Thou art my God and I will praise 28
thee;
my God, I will exalt thee.
It is good to give thanks to the 29
LORD,
for his love endures for ever.

119

Meditations on the law of the LORD

Happy are they whose life is blame- 1
less,
who conform to the law of the LORD.
Happy are they who obey his 2
instruction,
who set their heart on finding him;
who have done no wrong 3
and have lived according to his will.
Thou, Lord, hast laid down thy 4
precepts
for men to keep them faithfully.
If only I might hold a steady course, 5
keeping thy statutes!
I shall never be put to shame 6

t Or which the LORD has made.

if I fix my eyes on thy commandments.

7 I will praise thee in sincerity of heart
as I learn thy just decrees.

8 Thy statutes will I keep faithfully;
O do not leave me forsaken.

9 How shall a young man steer an honest course?
By holding to thy word.

10 With all my heart I strive to find thee;
let me not stray from thy commandments.

11 I treasure thy promise in my heart,
for fear that I might sin against thee.

12 Blessed art thou, O LORD;
teach me thy statutes.

13 I say them over, one by one,
the decrees that thou hast proclaimed.

14 I have found more joy along the path of thy instruction
than in any kind of wealth.

15 I will meditate on thy precepts
and keep thy paths ever before my eyes.

16 In thy statutes I find continual delight;
I will not forget thy word.

17 Grant this to me, thy servant: let me live
and, living, keep thy word.

18 Take the veil from my eyes, that I may see
the marvels that spring from thy law.

19 I am but a stranger here on earth,[u]
do not hide thy commandments from me.

20 My heart pines with longing
day and night for thy decrees.

21 The proud have felt thy rebuke;
cursed are those who turn from thy commandments.

22 Set me free from scorn and insult,
for I have obeyed thy instruction.

23 The powers that be sit scheming together against me;
but I, thy servant, will study thy statutes.

24 Thy instruction is my continual delight;
I turn to it for counsel.

25 I lie prone in the dust;
grant me life according to thy word.

26 I tell thee all I have done and thou dost answer me;
teach me thy statutes.

27 Show me the way set out in thy precepts,
and I will meditate on thy wonders.

28 I cannot rest for misery;
renew my strength in accordance with thy word.

29 Keep falsehood far from me
and grant me the grace of living by thy law.

30 I have chosen the path of truth
and have set thy decrees before me.

31 I hold fast to thy instruction;
O LORD, let me not be put to shame.

32 I will run the course set out in thy commandments,
for they gladden my heart.

33 Teach me, O LORD, the way set out in thy statutes,
and in keeping them I shall find my reward.

34 Give me the insight to obey thy law
and to keep it with all my heart;

35 make me walk in the path of thy commandments,
for that is my desire.

36 Dispose my heart toward thy instruction
and not toward ill-gotten gains;

37 turn away my eyes from all that is vile,
grant me life by thy word.

38 Fulfil thy promise for thy servant,
the promise made to those who fear thee.

39 Turn away the censure which I dread,
for thy decrees are good.

40 How I long for thy precepts!
In thy righteousness grant me life.

41 Thy love never fails; let it light on me, O LORD,
and thy deliverance, for that was thy promise;

42 then I shall have my answer to the man who taunts me,
because I trust in thy word.

43 Rob me not of my power to speak the truth,
for I put my hope in thy decrees.

44 I will heed thy law continually,
for ever and ever;

45 I walk in freedom wherever I will,
because I have studied thy precepts.

46 I will speak of thy instruction before kings
and will not be ashamed;

47 in thy commandments I find continuing delight;
I love them with all my heart.

48 I will welcome thy commandments[v]
and will meditate on thy statutes.

u Or in the land.   v Prob. rdg.; Heb. adds which I love.

49 Remember the word spoken to me,
      thy servant,
   on which thou hast taught me to
      fix my hope.
50 In time of trouble my consolation
      is this,
   that thy promise has given me life.
51 Proud men treat me with insolent
      scorn,
   but I do not swerve from thy law.
52 I have cherished thy decrees all my
      life long,
   and in them I find consolation, O
      LORD.
53 Gusts of anger seize me as I think
      of evil men
   who forsake thy law.
54 Thy statutes are the theme of my
      song[w]
   wherever I make my home.
55 In the night I remember thy name,
      O LORD,
   and dwell upon thy law.
56 This is true of me,
   that I have kept thy precepts.

57 Thou, LORD, art all I have;
   I have promised to keep thy word.
58 With all my heart I have tried to
      please thee;
   fulfil thy promise and be gracious
      to me.
59 I have thought much about the
      course of my life
   and always turned back to thy in-
      struction;
60 I have never delayed but always
      made haste
   to keep thy commandments.
61 Bands of evil men close round me,
   but I do not forget thy law.
62 At midnight I rise to give thee
      thanks
   for the justice of thy decrees.
63 I keep company with all who fear
      thee,
   with all who follow thy precepts.
64 The earth is full of thy never-
      failing love;
   O LORD, teach me thy statutes.

65 Thou hast shown thy servant much
      kindness,
   fulfilling thy word, O LORD.
66 Give me insight, give me knowledge,
   for I put my trust in thy com-
      mandments.
67 I went astray before I was punished;
   but now I pay heed to thy promise.
68 Thou art good and thou doest good;
   teach me thy statutes.
69 Proud men blacken my name with
      lies,

yet I follow thy precepts with all
   my heart;
their hearts are thick and gross;   70
but I continually delight in thy law.
How good it is for me to have been 71
   punished,
to school me in thy statutes!
The law thou hast ordained means 72
   more to me
than a fortune in gold and silver.

Thy hands moulded me and made 73
   me what I am;
show me how I may learn thy commandments.
Let all who fear thee be glad when 74
   they see me,
because I hope for the fulfilment of
   thy word.
I know, O LORD, that thy decrees 75
   are just
and even in punishing thou keepest
   faith with me.
Let thy never-failing love console 76
   me,
as thou hast promised me, thy servant.
Extend thy compassion to me, that 77
   I may live;
for thy law is my continual delight.
Put the proud to shame, for with 78
   their lies they wrong me;
but I will meditate on thy precepts.
Let all who fear thee turn to me,   79
all who cherish thy instruction.
Let me give my whole heart to thy 80
   statutes,
so that I am not put to shame.

I long with all my heart for thy 81
   deliverance,
hoping for the fulfilment of thy
   word;
my sight grows dim with looking 82
   for thy promise
and still I cry, 'When wilt thou
   comfort me?'
Though I shrivel like a wine-skin 83
   in the smoke,
I do not forget thy statutes.
How long has thy servant to wait   84
for thee to fulfil thy decree against
   my persecutors?
Proud men who flout thy law   85
spread tales about me.
Help me, for they hound me with 86
   their lies,
but thy commandments all stand
   for ever.
They had almost swept me from 87
   the earth,
but I did not forsake thy precepts;
grant me life, as thy love is un- 88
   changing,

w the theme of my song: *or* wonderful to me.

that I may follow all thy instruction.

89 Eternal is thy word, O Lord,
planted firm in heaven.
90 Thy promise[x] endures for all time,
stable as the earth which thou hast fixed.
91 This day, as ever, thy decrees stand fast;
for all things serve thee.
92 If thy law had not been my continual delight,
I should have perished in all my troubles;
93 never will I forget thy precepts,
for through them thou hast given me life.
94 I am thine; O save me,
for I have pondered thy precepts.
95 Evil men lie in wait to destroy me;
but I will give thought to thy instruction.
96 I see that all things come to an end,
but thy commandment has no limit.

97 O how I love thy law!
It is my study all day long.
98 Thy commandments are mine for ever;
through them I am wiser than my enemies.
99 I have more insight than all my teachers,
for thy instruction is my study;
100 I have more wisdom than the old,
because I have kept thy precepts.
101 I set no foot on any evil path
in my obedience to thy word;
102 I do not swerve from thy decrees,
for thou thyself hast been my teacher.
103 How sweet is thy promise in my mouth,
sweeter on my tongue than honey!
104 From thy precepts I learn wisdom;
therefore I hate the paths of falsehood.

105 Thy word is a lamp to guide my feet
and a light on my path;
106 I have bound myself by oath and solemn vow
to keep thy just decrees.
107 I am cruelly afflicted;
O Lord, revive me and make good thy word.
108 Accept, O Lord, the willing tribute of my lips
and teach me thy decrees.
109 Every day I take my life in my hands,

yet I never forget thy law.
110 Evil men have set traps for me,
but I do not stray from thy precepts.
111 Thy instruction is my everlasting inheritance;
it is the joy of my heart.
112 I am resolved to fulfil thy statutes;
they are a reward that never fails.

113 I hate men who are not single-minded,
but I love thy law.
114 Thou art my shield and hiding-place;
I hope for the fulfilment of thy word.
115 Go, you evildoers, and leave me to myself,
that I may keep the commandments of my God.
116 Support me as thou hast promised, that I may live;
do not disappoint my hope.
117 Sustain me, that I may see deliverance;
so shall I always be occupied with thy statutes.
118 Thou dost reject those who stray from thy statutes,
for their talk is all malice and lies.
119 In thy sight all the wicked on earth are scum;
therefore I love thy instruction.
120 The dread of thee makes my flesh creep,
and I stand in awe of thy decrees.

121 I have done what is just and right;
thou wilt not abandon me to my oppressors.
122 Stand surety for the welfare of thy servant;
let not the proud oppress me.[y]
123 My sight grows dim with looking for thy deliverance
and waiting for thy righteous promise.
124 In all thy dealings with me, Lord, show thy true love
and teach me thy statutes.
125 I am thy servant; give me insight to understand thy instruction.
126 It is time to act, O Lord;
for men have broken thy law.
127 Truly I love thy commandments more than the finest gold.
128 It is by thy precepts that I find the right way;
I hate the paths of falsehood.

129 Thy instruction is wonderful;
therefore I gladly keep it.

x Prob. rdg.; Heb. Thy constancy.   y oppress me: or charge me falsely.

130 Thy word is revealed, and all is light;
it gives understanding even to the untaught.
131 I pant, I thirst,
longing for thy commandments.
132 Turn to me and be gracious,
as thou hast decreed for those who love thy name.
133 Make my step firm according to thy promise,
and let no wrong have the mastery over me.
134 Set me free from man's oppression,
that I may observe thy precepts.
135 Let thy face shine upon thy servant
and teach me thy statutes.
136 My eyes stream with tears
because men do not heed thy law.

137 How just thou art, O Lord!
How straight and true are thy decrees!
138 How just is the instruction thou givest!
It is fixed firm and sure.
139 I am speechless with resentment,
for my enemies have forgotten thy words.
140 Thy promise has been tested through and through,
and thy servant loves it.
141 I may be despised and of little account,
but I do not forget thy precepts.
142 Thy justice is an everlasting justice,
and thy law is truth.
143 Though I am oppressed by trouble and anxiety,
thy commandments are my continual delight.
144 Thy instruction is ever just;
give me understanding that I may live.

145 I call with my whole heart; answer me, Lord.
I will keep thy statutes.
146 I call to thee; O save me
that I may heed thy instruction.
147 I rise before dawn and cry for help;
I hope for the fulfilment of thy word.
148 Before the midnight watch also my eyes are open
for meditation on thy promise.
149 Hear me, as thy love is unchanging,
and give me life, O Lord, by thy decree.
150 My pursuers in their malice are close behind me,
but they are far from thy law.
151 Yet thou art near, O Lord,

and all thy commandments are true.
152 I have long known from thy instruction
that thou hast given it eternal foundations.

153 See in what trouble I am and set me free,
for I do not forget thy law.
154 Be thou my advocate and win release for me;
true to thy promise, give me life.
155 Such deliverance is beyond the reach of wicked men,
because they do not ponder thy statutes.
156 Great is thy compassion, O Lord;
grant me life by thy decree.
157 Many are my persecutors and enemies,
but I have not swerved from thy instruction.
158 I was cut to the quick when I saw traitors
who had no regard for thy promise.
159 See how I love thy precepts, O Lord!
Grant me life, as thy love is unchanging.
160 Thy word is founded in truth,
and thy just decrees are everlasting.

161 The powers that be persecute me without cause,
yet my heart thrills at thy word.
162 I am jubilant over thy promise,
like a man carrying off much booty.
163 Falsehood I detest and loathe,
but I love thy law.
164 Seven times a day I praise thee
for the justice of thy decrees.
165 Peace is the reward of those who love thy law;
no pitfalls beset their path.
166 I hope for thy deliverance, O Lord,
and I fulfil thy commandments;
167 gladly I heed thy instruction
and love it greatly.
168 I heed thy precepts and thy instruction,
for all my life lies open before thee.

169 Let my cry of joy reach thee, O Lord;
give me understanding of thy word.
170 Let my supplication reach thee;
be true to thy promise and save me.
171 Let thy praise pour from my lips,
because thou teachest me thy statutes;
172 let the music of thy promises be on my tongue,
for thy commandments are justice itself.

173 Let thy hand be prompt to help me,
    for I have chosen thy precepts;
174 I long for thy deliverance, O LORD,
    and thy law is my continual delight.
175 Let me live and I will praise thee;
    let thy decrees be my support.
176 I have strayed like a lost sheep;
    come, search for thy servant,
    for I have not forgotten thy com-
        mandments.

120

Prayer of an exile

1 I called to the LORD in my distress,
    and he answered me.
2 'O LORD,' I cried, 'save me from
    lying lips
    and from the tongue of slander.'
3 What has he in store for you,
    slanderous tongue?
    What more has he for you?
4 Nothing but a warrior's sharp
        arrows
    or red-hot charcoal.
5 Hard is my lot, exiled in Meshech,
    dwelling by the tents of Kedar.
6 All the time that I dwelt
    among men who hated peace,
7 I sought peace; but whenever I
    spoke of it,
    they were for war.

121

The only source of help

1 If I lift up my eyes to the hills,
    where shall I find help?
2 Help comes only from the LORD,
    maker of heaven and earth.
3 How could he let your foot stumble?
    How could he, your guardian,
    sleep?
4 The guardian of Israel
    never slumbers, never sleeps.
5 The LORD is your guardian,
    your defence at your right hand;
6 the sun will not strike you by day
    nor the moon by night.
7 The LORD will guard you against
    all evil;
    he will guard you, body and soul.
8 The LORD will guard your going and
    your coming,
    now and for evermore.

122

Jerusalem, the city of peace

1 I rejoiced when they said to me,
    'Let us go to the house of the LORD.'
2 Now we stand within your gates,
    O Jerusalem;
3 Jerusalem that is built to be a city

where people come together in
    unity;
to which the tribes resort, the tribes 4
    of the LORD,
to give thanks to the LORD himself,
the bounden duty of Israel.
For in her are set the thrones of 5
    justice,
the thrones of the house of David.
Pray for the peace of Jerusalem: 6
'May those who love you prosper;
peace be within your ramparts   7
and prosperity in your palaces.'
For the sake of these my brothers 8
    and my friends,
I will say, 'Peace be within you.'
For the sake of the house of the 9
    LORD our God
I will pray for your good.

123

Looking to the LORD

I lift my eyes to thee   1
whose throne is in heaven.
As the eyes of a slave follow his 2
    master's hand
or the eyes of a slave-girl her mis-
    tress,
so our eyes are turned to the LORD
    our God
waiting for kindness from him.
Deal kindly with us, O LORD, deal 3
    kindly,
for we have suffered insult enough;
too long have we had to suffer   4
the insults of the wealthy,
the scorn of proud men.

124

A merciful escape

If the LORD had not been on our 1
    side,
Israel may now say,
if the LORD had not been on our 2
    side
when they assailed us,
they would have swallowed us alive 3
when their anger was roused against
    us.
The waters would have carried us 4
    away
and the torrent swept over us;
over us would have swept   5
the seething waters.
Blessed be the LORD, who did not 6
    leave us
to be the prey between their teeth.
We have escaped like a bird   7
from the fowler's trap;
the trap broke, and so we escaped.
Our help is in the name of the LORD, 8
maker of heaven and earth.

125

Stability and security

1 Those who trust in the LORD are
    like Mount Zion,
  which cannot be shaken but stands
    fast for ever.
2 As the hills enfold Jerusalem,
  so the LORD enfolds his people, now
    and evermore.
3 The sceptre of wickedness shall
    surely find no home
  in the land allotted to the righteous,
  so that the righteous shall not set
    their hands to injustice.
4 Do good, O LORD, to those who are
    good
  and to those who are upright in heart.
5 But those who turn aside into
    crooked ways,
  may the LORD destroy them, as he
    destroys all evildoers!

  Peace be upon Israel!

126

Recalling past blessings

1 When the LORD turned the tide of
    Zion's fortune,
  we were like men who had found
    new health.[a]
2 Our mouths were full of laughter
  and our tongues sang aloud for joy.
  Then word went round among the
    nations,
  'The LORD has done great things
    for them.'
3 Great things indeed the LORD then
    did for us,
  and we rejoiced.

4 Turn once again our fortune, LORD,
  as streams return in the dry south.
5 Those who sow in tears
  shall reap with songs of joy.
6 A man may go out weeping,
  carrying his bag of seed;
  but he will come back with songs of
    joy,
  carrying home his sheaves.

127

Success depends on the LORD

1 Unless the LORD builds the house,
  its builders will have toiled in vain.
  Unless the LORD keeps watch over
    a city,
  in vain the watchman stands on
    guard.
2 In vain you rise up early
  and go late to rest,

toiling for the bread you eat;
he supplies the need of those he
    loves.[b]
Sons are a gift from the LORD   3
and children a reward from him.
Like arrows in the hand of a 4
    fighting man
are the sons of a man's youth.
Happy is the man   5
who has his quiver full of them;
such men shall not be put to shame
when they confront their enemies
    in court.

128

Long life and prosperity

Happy are all who fear the LORD, 1
who live according to his will.
You shall eat the fruit of your own 2
    labours,
you shall be happy and you shall
    prosper.
Your wife shall be like a fruitful 3
    vine
in the heart of your house;
your sons shall be like olive-shoots
round about your table.
This is the blessing in store for the 4
    man
who fears the LORD.
May the LORD bless you from Zion; 5
may you share the prosperity of
    Jerusalem
all the days of your life,
and live to see your children's 6
    children!

  Peace be upon Israel!

129

Prayer against Zion's enemies

Often since I was young have men 1
    attacked me—
let Israel now say—
often since I was young have men 2
    attacked me,
but never have they prevailed.
They scored my back with scourges, 3
like ploughmen driving long fur-
    rows.
Yet the LORD in his justice   4
has cut me loose from the bonds of
    the wicked.
Let all enemies of Zion   5
be thrown back in shame;
let them be like grass growing on 6
    the roof,
which withers before it can shoot,
which will never fill a mower's 7
    hand

a like . . . health: or like dreamers.   *b Prob. rdg.; Heb. adds an unintelligible word.*

nor yield an armful for the harvester,

8 so that passers-by will never say to them,
'The blessing of the LORD be upon you!
We bless you in the name of the LORD.'

130

Out of the depths

1 Out of the depths have I called to thee, O LORD;

2 Lord, hear my cry.
Let thy ears be attentive
to my plea for mercy.

3 If thou, LORD, shouldest keep account of sins,
who, O Lord, could hold up his head?

4 But in thee is forgiveness,
and therefore thou art revered.

5 I wait for the LORD with all my soul,
I hope for the fulfilment of his word.

6 My soul waits[c] for the Lord
more eagerly than watchmen for the morning.
Like men who watch for the morning,

7 O Israel, look for the LORD.
For in the LORD is love unfailing,
and great is his power to set men free.

8 He alone will set Israel free
from all their sins.

131

Humble submission

1 O LORD, my heart is not proud,
nor are my eyes haughty;
I do not busy myself with great matters
or things too marvellous for me.

2 No; I submit myself, I account myself lowly,
as a weaned child clinging to its mother.[d]

3 O Israel, look for the LORD
now and evermore.

132

The LORD's covenant with David

1 O LORD, remember David
in the time of his adversity,

2 how he swore to the LORD
and made a vow to the Mighty One of Jacob:

3 'I will not enter my house

nor will I mount my bed,
I will not close my eyes in sleep　4
or my eyelids in slumber,
until I find a sanctuary for the　5
LORD,
a dwelling for the Mighty One of Jacob.'
We heard of it in Ephrathah;　6
we came upon it in the region of Jaar.
Let us enter his dwelling,　7
let us fall in worship at his footstool.
Arise, O LORD, and come to thy　8
resting-place,
thou and the ark of thy power.
Let thy priests be clothed in　9
righteousness
and let thy loyal servants shout for joy.
For thy servant David's sake　10
reject not thy anointed king.
The LORD swore to David　11
an oath which he will not break:
'A prince of your own line
will I set upon your throne.
If your sons keep my covenant　12
and heed the teaching that I give them,
their sons in turn for all time
shall sit upon your throne.'
For the LORD has chosen Zion　13
and desired it for his home:
'This is my resting-place for ever;　14
here will I make my home, for such is my desire.
I will richly bless her destitute[e]　15
and satisfy her needy with bread.
With salvation will I clothe her　16
priests;
her loyal servants shall shout for joy.
There will I renew the line of　17
David's house
and light a lamp for my anointed king;
his enemies will I clothe with　18
shame,
but on his head shall be a shining crown.'

133

Blessing on brotherly unity

How good it is and how pleasant　1
for brothers to live[f] together!
It is fragrant as oil poured upon　2
the head
and falling over the beard,
Aaron's beard, when the oil runs down
over the collar of his vestments.
It is like the dew of Hermon falling　3

---

c waits: *transposed from after* the LORD *in verse 5.*　　d Prob. rdg.; Heb. adds as a weaned child
clinging to me.　e her destitute: *prob. rdg.; Heb.* her provisions.　f Or to worship.

upon the hills of Zion.
There the LORD bestows his blessing,
life for evermore.

134

An evening blessing

1   Come, bless the LORD,
all you servants of the LORD,
who stand night after night
in the house of the LORD.
2   Lift up your hands in the sanctuary
and bless the LORD.
3   The LORD, maker of heaven and
earth,
bless you from Zion!

135

Extolling the LORD's greatness

1   O praise the LORD.

Praise the name of the LORD;
praise him, you servants of the LORD,
2   who stand in the house of the LORD,
in the temple courts of our God.
3   Praise the LORD, for that is good;
honour his name with psalms, for
that is pleasant.
4   The LORD has chosen Jacob to be
his own
and Israel as his special treasure.
5   I know that the LORD is great,
that our Lord is above all gods.
6   Whatever the LORD pleases,
that he does, in heaven and on earth,
in the sea, in the depths of ocean.
7   He brings up the mist from the ends
of the earth,
he opens rifts*g* for the rain,
and brings the wind out of his
storehouses.
8   He struck down all the first-born in
Egypt,
both man and beast.
9   In Egypt he sent signs and portents
against Pharaoh and all his subjects.
10   He struck down mighty nations
and slew great kings,
11   Sihon king of the Amorites, Og the
king of Bashan,
and all the princes of Canaan,
12   and gave their land to Israel,
to Israel his people as their patrimony.
13   O LORD, thy name endures for ever;
thy renown, O LORD, shall last for
all generations.
14   The LORD will give his people
justice

g Prob. rdg.; Heb. lightnings.

and have compassion on his servants.
15   The gods of the nations are idols of
silver and gold,
made by the hands of men.
16   They have mouths that cannot
speak
and eyes that cannot see;
17   they have ears that do not hear,
and there is no breath in their
nostrils.*h*
18   Their makers grow like them,
and so do all who trust in them.
19   O house of Israel, bless the LORD;
O house of Aaron, bless the LORD.
20   O house of Levi, bless the LORD;
you who fear the LORD, bless the
LORD.
21   Blessed from Zion be the LORD
who dwells in Jerusalem.

O praise the LORD.

136

His love endures for ever

1   It is good to give thanks to the
LORD,
for his love endures for ever.
2   Give thanks to the God of gods;
his love endures for ever.
3   Give thanks to the Lord of lords;
his love endures for ever.
4   Alone he works great marvels;
his love endures for ever.
5   In wisdom he made the heavens;
his love endures for ever.
6   He laid the earth upon the waters;
his love endures for ever.
7   He made the great lights,
his love endures for ever,
8   the sun to rule by day,
his love endures for ever,
9   the moon and the stars to rule by
night;
his love endures for ever.
10   He struck down the first-born of
the Egyptians,
his love endures for ever,
11   and brought Israel from among
them;
his love endures for ever.
12   With strong hand and outstretched
arm,
his love endures for ever,
13   he divided the Red Sea in two,
his love endures for ever,
14   and made Israel pass through it,
his love endures for ever;
15   but Pharaoh and his host he swept
into the sea;
his love endures for ever.

h Prob. rdg.; Heb. mouths.

16 He led his people through the
    wilderness;
    his love endures for ever.
17 He struck down great kings;
    his love endures for ever.
18 He slew mighty kings,
    his love endures for ever,
19 Sihon king of the Amorites,
    his love endures for ever,
20 and Og the king of Bashan;
    his love endures for ever.
21 He gave their land to Israel,
    his love endures for ever,
22 to Israel his servant as their patri-
    mony;
    his love endures for ever.
23 He remembered us when we were
    cast down,
    his love endures for ever,
24 and rescued us from our enemies;
    his love endures for ever.
25 He gives food to all his creatures;
    his love endures for ever.
26 Give thanks to the God of heaven,
    for his love endures for ever.

137

An exile's longings for Jerusalem

1 By the rivers of Babylon we sat
    down and wept
    when we remembered Zion.
2 There on the willow-trees[i]
    we hung up our harps,
3 for there those who carried us off
    demanded music and singing,
    and our captors called on us to be
    merry:
    'Sing us one of the songs of Zion.'
4 How could we sing the LORD's song
    in a foreign land?

5 If I forget you, O Jerusalem,
    let my right hand wither away;
6 let my tongue cling to the roof of
    my mouth
    if I do not remember you,
    if I do not set Jerusalem
    above my highest joy.
7 Remember, O LORD, against the
    people of Edom
    the day of Jerusalem's fall,
    when they said, 'Down with it,
    down with it,
    down to its very foundations!'
8 O Babylon, Babylon the destroyer,
    happy the man who repays you
    for all that you did to us!
9 Happy is he who shall seize your
    children
    and dash them against the rock.

138

Confidence in the LORD's purpose

I will praise thee, O LORD, with all 1
    my heart;
boldly, O God, will I sing psalms to
    thee.[j]
I will bow down towards thy holy 2
    temple,
for thy love and faithfulness I will
    praise thy name;
for thou hast made thy promise wide
    as the heavens.
When I called to thee thou didst 3
    answer me
and make me bold and valiant-
    hearted.
Let all the kings of the earth praise[k] 4
    thee, O LORD,
when they hear the words thou
    hast spoken;
and let them sing of[l] the LORD's 5
    ways,
for great is the glory of the LORD.
For the LORD, high as he is, cares 6
    for the lowly,
and from afar he humbles the
    proud.
Though I walk among foes thou dost 7
    preserve my life,
exerting thy power against the rage
    of my enemies,
and with thy right hand thou savest
    me.
The LORD will accomplish his pur- 8
    pose for me.
Thy true love, O LORD, endures for
    ever;
leave not thy work unfinished.

139

God's knowledge of man

LORD, thou hast examined me and 1
    knowest me.
Thou knowest all, whether I sit 2
    down or rise up;
thou hast discerned my thoughts
    from afar.
Thou hast traced my journey and 3
    my resting places,
and art familiar with all my paths.
For there is not a word on my 4
    tongue
but thou, LORD, knowest them all.[m]
Thou hast kept close guard before 5
    me and behind
and hast spread thy hand over me.
Such knowledge is beyond my 6
    understanding,

i Or poplars.   *j boldly . . . thee: or* I will sing psalms to thee before the gods.   *k Or confess.*
l Or walk in.   *m For . . . them all: or* If there is any offence on my tongue, thou, LORD, knowest
it all.

I*

7 so high that I cannot reach it.
Where can I escape from thy spirit?
Where can I flee from thy presence?
8 If I climb up to heaven, thou art
there;
if I make my bed in Sheol, again I
find thee.
9 If I take my flight to the frontiers
of the morning
or dwell at the limit of the western
sea,
10 even there thy hand will meet me
and thy right hand will hold me fast.
11 If I say, 'Surely darkness will steal
over me,
night will close around me',
12 darkness is no darkness for thee
and night is luminous as day;
to thee both dark and light are one.

13 Thou it was who didst fashion my
inward parts;
thou didst knit me together in my
mother's womb.
14 I will praise thee, for thou dost fill
me with awe;
wonderful thou art, and wonderful
thy works.
Thou knowest me through and
through:
15 my body is no mystery to thee,
how I was secretly kneaded into
shape
and patterned in the depths of the
earth.
16 Thou didst see my limbs unformed
in the womb,
and in thy book they are all recorded;
day by day they were fashioned,
not one of them was late in growing.[n]
17 How deep I find thy thoughts, O
God,
how inexhaustible their themes!
18 Can I count them? They outnumber
the grains of sand;
to finish the count, my years must
equal thine.

19 O God, if only thou wouldst slay
the wicked!
If those men of blood would but
leave me in peace—
20 those who provoke thee with deliberate evil
and rise in vicious rebellion against
thee!
21 How I hate them, O Lord, that
hate thee!
I am cut to the quick when they
oppose thee;
22 I hate them with undying hatred;
I hold them all my enemies.

23 Examine me, O God, and know my
thoughts;
test me, and understand my mis-
givings.
24 Watch lest I follow any path that
grieves thee;
guide me in the ancient[o] ways.

140

Prayer for the Lord's protection

1 Rescue me, O Lord, from evil men;
keep me safe from violent men,
2 whose heads are full of wicked
schemes,
who stir up contention day after
day.
3 Their tongues are sharp as serpents'
fangs;
on their lips is spiders' poison.
4 Guard me, O Lord, from wicked
men;
keep me safe from violent men,
who plan to thrust me out of the
way.
5 Arrogant men set hidden traps for
me,
rogues spread their nets
and lay snares for me along the
path.
6 I said, 'O Lord, thou art my God;
O Lord, hear my plea for mercy.
7 O Lord God, stronghold of my
safety,
thou hast shielded my head in the
day of battle.
8–9 Frustrate, O Lord, their designs
against me;
never let the wicked gain their
purpose.
If any of those at my table rise
against me,
let their own conspiracies be their
undoing.
10 Let burning coals be tipped upon
them;
let them be plunged into the miry
depths,
never to rise again.
11 Slander shall find no home in the
land;
evil and violence shall be hounded
to destruction.'

12 I know that the Lord will give their
due to the needy
and justice to the downtrodden.
13 Righteous men will surely give
thanks to thy name;
the upright will worship in thy
presence.

n was late in growing: *prob. rdg.; Heb. om.*　　*o* Or everlasting.

141

Prayer for preservation from sin

1 O LORD, I call to thee, come quickly
to my aid;
listen to my cry when I call to thee.
2 Let my prayer be like incense duly
set before thee
and my raised hands like the
evening sacrifice.
3 Set a guard, O LORD, over my
mouth;
keep watch at the door of my lips.
4 Turn not my heart to sinful
thoughts
nor to any pursuit of evil courses.
The evildoers appal me;[p]
not for me the delights of their
table.
5 I would rather be buffeted by the
righteous
and reproved by good men.
My head shall not be anointed with
the oil of wicked men,
for that would make me a party to
their crimes.
6 They shall founder on the rock of
justice
and shall learn how acceptable my
words are.
7 Their bones shall be scattered at the
mouth of Sheol,
like splinters of wood or stone on
the ground.
8 But my eyes are fixed on thee, O
LORD God;
thou art my refuge; leave me not
unprotected.
9 Keep me from the trap which they
have set for me,
from the snares of evildoers.
10 Let the wicked fall into their own
nets,
whilst I pass in safety, all alone.

142

When no way of escape is in sight

1 I cry aloud to the LORD;
to the LORD I plead aloud for mercy.
2 I pour out my complaint before him
and tell over my troubles in his
presence.
3 When my spirit is faint within me,
thou art there to watch over my
steps.
In the path that I should take
they have hidden a snare.
4 I look to my right hand,
I find no friend by my side;
no way of escape is in sight,
no one comes to rescue me.
5 I cry to thee, O LORD,

[p] appal me: *prob. rdg.; Heb.* with men.

and say, 'Thou art my refuge;
thou art all I have
in the land of the living.
Give me a hearing when I cry, 6
for I am brought very low;
save me from my pursuers,
for they are too strong for me.
Set me free from my prison, 7
so that I may praise thy name.'
The righteous shall crown me with
garlands,[q]
when thou givest me my due reward.

143

Prayer for mercy and help

LORD, hear my prayer; 1
be true to thyself, and listen to my
pleading;
then in thy righteousness answer
me.
Bring not thy servant to trial before 2
thee;
against thee no man on earth can be
right.
An enemy has hunted me down, 3
has ground my living body under
foot
and plunged me into darkness like
a man long dead,
so that my spirit fails me 4
and my heart is dazed with despair.
I dwell upon the years long past, 5
upon the memory of all that thou
hast done;
the wonders of thy creation fill my
mind.
To thee I lift my outspread hands, 6
athirst for thee in a thirsty land.
LORD, make haste to answer, 7
for my spirit faints.
Do not hide thy face from me
or I shall be like those who go down
to the abyss.
In the morning let me know thy 8
true love;
I have put my trust in thee.
Show me the way that I must take;
to thee I offer all my heart.
Deliver me, LORD, from my ene- 9
mies,
for with thee have I sought refuge.
Teach me to do thy will, for thou 10
art my God;
in thy gracious kindness, show me
the level road.
Keep me safe, O LORD, for the 11
honour of thy name
and, as thou art just, release me
from my distress.
In thy love for me, reduce my 12
enemies to silence

[q] crown me with garlands: *or* crowd round me.

and bring destruction on all who oppress me;
for I am thy servant.

144

God in nature, history and providence

1 Blessed is the LORD, my rock,
who trains my hands for war,
my fingers for battle;
2 my help that never fails, my fortress,
my strong tower and my refuge,
my shield in which I trust,
he who puts nations under my feet.

3 O LORD, what is man that thou
carest for him?
What is mankind? Why give a
thought to them?
4 Man is no more than a puff of wind,
his days a passing shadow.
5 If thou, LORD, but tilt the heavens,
down they come;
touch the mountains, and they
smoke.
6 Shoot forth thy lightning flashes,
far and wide,
and send thy arrows whistling.
7 Stretch out thy hands from on high
to rescue me
and snatch me from great waters.[r]

9 I will sing a new song to thee, O
God,
psalms to the music of a ten-
stringed lute.
10 O God who gavest victory to kings
and deliverance to thy servant David,
rescue me from the cruel sword;
11 snatch me from the power of
foreign foes,
whose every word is false
and all their oaths are perjury.

12 Happy[s] are we whose sons in their
early prime
stand like tall towers,
our daughters like sculptured pillars
at the corners of a palace.
13 Our barns are full and furnish
plentiful provision;
our sheep bear lambs in thousands
upon thousands;
14 the oxen in our fields are fat and
sleek;
there is no miscarriage or untimely
birth,
no cries of distress in our public
places.
15 Happy are the people in such a case
as ours;

happy the people who have the
LORD for their God.

145

The LORD's unfathomable greatness

1 I will extol thee, O God my king,
and bless thy name for ever and
ever.
2 Every day will I bless thee
and praise thy name for ever and
ever.
3 Great is the LORD and worthy of all
praise;
his greatness is unfathomable.
4 One generation shall commend thy
works to another
and set forth thy mighty deeds.
5 My theme shall be thy marvellous
works,
the glorious splendour of thy
majesty.
6 Men shall declare thy mighty acts
with awe
and tell of thy great deeds.
7 They shall recite the story of thy
abounding goodness
and sing of thy righteousness with
joy.

8 The LORD is gracious and compassionate,
forbearing, and constant in his love.
9 The LORD is good to all men,
and his tender care rests upon all
his creatures.

10 All thy creatures praise thee, LORD,
and thy servants bless thee.
11 They talk of the glory of thy kingdom
and tell of thy might,
12 they proclaim to their fellows how
mighty are thy deeds,
how glorious the majesty of thy
kingdom.
13 Thy kingdom is an everlasting
kingdom,
and thy dominion stands for all
generations.

14 In all his promises the LORD keeps
faith,
he is unchanging in all his works;
the LORD holds up those who
stumble
and straightens backs which are bent.
15 The eyes of all are lifted to thee
in hope,
and thou givest them their food
when it is due;
16 with open and bountiful hand

---

[r] *Prob. rdg.; Heb. adds* from the power of foreign foes, (8) whose every word is false and all their oaths are perjury (*cp. verse 11*).   [s] *Prob. rdg.; Heb.* Who.

thou givest what they desire[t] to every living creature.

17 The LORD is righteous in all his ways,
and unchanging in all that he does;

18 very near is the LORD to those who call to him,
who call to him in singleness of heart.

19 He fulfils their desire if only they fear him;
he hears their cry and saves them.

20 The LORD watches over all who love him
but sends the wicked to their doom.

21 My tongue shall speak out the praises of the LORD,
and all creatures shall bless his holy name
for ever and ever.

146

The LORD, the only saviour

1 O praise the LORD.

Praise the LORD, my soul.

2 As long as I live I will praise the LORD;
I will sing psalms to my God all my life long.

3 Put no faith in princes,
in any man, who has no power to save.

4 He breathes his last breath,
he returns to the dust;
and in that same hour all his thinking ends.

5 Happy the man whose helper is the God of Jacob,
whose hopes are in the LORD his God,

6 maker of heaven and earth,
the sea, and all that is in them;
who serves wrongdoers as he has sworn

7 and deals out justice to the oppressed.
The LORD feeds the hungry
and sets the prisoner free.

8 The LORD restores sight to the blind
and straightens backs which are bent;
the LORD loves the righteous

9 and watches over the stranger;
the LORD gives heart to the orphan and widow
but turns the course of the wicked to their ruin.

10 The LORD shall reign for ever,
thy God, O Zion, for all generations.

O praise the LORD.

147

The LORD's care for Israel

O praise the LORD.   1

How good it is to sing psalms to our God!
How pleasant to praise him!
The LORD is rebuilding Jerusalem; 2
he gathers in the scattered sons of Israel.
It is he who heals the broken in 3 spirit
and binds up their wounds,
he who numbers the stars one by 4 one
and names them one and all.
Mighty is our Lord and great his 5 power,
and his wisdom beyond all telling.
The LORD gives new heart to the 6 humble
and brings evildoers down to the dust.
Sing to the LORD a song of thanks- 7 giving,
sing psalms to the harp in honour of our God.
He veils the sky in clouds   8
and prepares rain for the earth;
he clothes the hills with grass
and green plants for the use of man.
He gives the cattle their food   9
and the young ravens all that they gather.
The LORD sets no store by the 10 strength of a horse
and takes no pleasure in a runner's legs;
his pleasure is in those who fear 11 him,
who wait for his true love.

Sing to the LORD, Jerusalem;   12
O Zion, praise your God,
for he has put new bars in your 13 gates;
he has blessed your children within them.
He has brought peace to your realm 14
and given you fine wheat in plenty.
He sends his command to the ends 15 of the earth,
and his word runs swiftly.
He showers down snow, white as 16 wool,
and sprinkles hoar-frost thick as ashes;
crystals of ice he scatters like bread- 17 crumbs;
he sends the cold, and the water stands frozen;

t they desire: *or* thou wilt.

18 he utters his word, and the ice is
melted;
he blows with his wind and the
waters flow.
19 To Jacob he makes his word known,
his statutes and decrees to Israel;
20 he has not done this for any other
nation,
nor taught them his decrees.

O praise the LORD.

148

Praise from the whole creation

1 O praise the LORD.

Praise the LORD out of heaven;
praise him in the heights.
2 Praise him, all his angels;
praise him, all his host.
3 Praise him, sun and moon;
praise him, all you shining stars;
4 praise him, heaven of heavens,
and you waters above the heavens.
5 Let them all praise the name of the
LORD,
for he spoke the word and they
were created;
6 he established them for ever and
ever
by an ordinance which shall never
pass away.

7 Praise the LORD from the earth,
you water-spouts and ocean depths;
8 fire and hail, snow and ice,
gales of wind obeying his voice;
9 all mountains and hills;
all fruit-trees and all cedars;
10 wild beasts and cattle,
creeping things and winged birds;
11 kings and all earthly rulers,
princes and judges over the whole
earth;
12 young men and maidens,
old men and young together.
13 Let all praise the name of the LORD,
for his name is high above all others,
and his majesty above earth and
heaven;
14 he has exalted his people in the
pride of power
and crowned with praise his loyal
servants,
all Israel, the people nearest him.

O praise the LORD.

149

Israel to praise the LORD

O praise the LORD.   1

Sing to the LORD a new song,
sing his praise in the assembly of
the faithful;
let Israel rejoice in his maker   2
and the sons of Zion exult in their
king.
Let them praise his name in the 3
dance,
and sing him psalms with tambourine and harp.
For the LORD accepts the service of 4
his people;
he crowns his humble folk with
victory.
Let his faithful servants exult in 5
triumph;
let them shout for joy as they kneel
before him.
Let the high praises of God be on 6
their lips
and a two-edged sword in their
hand,
to wreak vengeance on the nations 7
and to chastise the heathen;
to load their kings with chains   8
and put their nobles in irons;
to execute the judgement decreed 9
against them—
this is the glory of all his faithful
servants.

O praise the LORD.

150

Universal praise

O praise the LORD.   1

O praise God in his holy place,
praise him in the vault of heaven,
the vault of his power;
praise him for his mighty works,   2
praise him for his immeasurable
greatness.
Praise him with fanfares on the 3
trumpet,
praise him upon lute and harp;
praise him with tambourines and 4
dancing,
praise him with flute and strings;
praise him with the clash of cym- 5
bals,
praise him with triumphant cymbals;
let everything that has breath 6
praise the LORD!

O praise the LORD.

PROVERBS

The value of proverbs

1 The proverbs of Solomon son of David, king of Israel,

2 by which men will come to wisdom and instruction
and will understand words that bring understanding,

3 and by which they will gain a well-instructed intelligence,
righteousness, justice, and probity.

4 The simple will be endowed with shrewdness
and the young with knowledge and prudence.

5 If the wise man listens, he will increase his learning,
and the man of understanding will acquire skill

6 to understand proverbs and parables,
the sayings of wise men and their riddles.

7 The fear of the LORD is the beginning[a] of knowledge,
but fools scorn wisdom and discipline.

8 Attend, my son, to your father's instruction
and do not reject the teaching of your mother;

9 for they are a garland of grace on your head
and a chain of honour round your neck.

Exhortation and warning

10 11 My son, bad men may tempt you[b] and say,
'Come with us; let us lie in wait for someone's blood;
let us waylay[c] an innocent man who has done us no harm.

12 Like Sheol we will swallow them alive;
though blameless, they shall be like men who go down to the abyss.

13 We shall take rich treasure of every sort
and fill our homes with booty;

14 throw in your lot with us,
and we will have a common purse.'

15 My son, do not go along with them,
keep clear of their ways;
they hasten hot-foot into crime, **16** impatient to shed blood.

In vain is a net spread wide **17** if any bird that flies can see it.

These men lie in wait for their own **18** blood
and waylay[c] no one but themselves.
This is the fate[d] of men eager for **19** ill-gotten gain:
it robs those who get it of their lives.

Wisdom's appeal

Wisdom cries aloud in the open air, **20** she raises her voice in public places;
she calls at the top of the busy street **21** and proclaims at the open gates of the city:
'Simple fools, how long will you be **22** content with your simplicity?[e]
If only you would respond to my **23** reproof,
I would give you my counsel
and teach you my precepts.
But because you refused to listen **24** when I called,
because no one attended when I stretched out my hand,
because you spurned all my advice **25** and would have nothing to do with my reproof,
I in my turn will laugh at your **26** doom
and deride you when terror comes upon you,
when terror comes upon you like a **27** hurricane
and your doom descends like a whirlwind.[f]
Insolent men delight in their insolence;
stupid men hate knowledge.[g]
When they call upon me, I will not **28** answer them;
when they search for me, they shall not find me.
Because they hate knowledge **29** and have not chosen to fear the LORD,
because they have not accepted my **30** counsel

---

a Or chief part.   *b* Prob. rdg.; Heb. adds do not come, or, with some MSS., do not consent.
c Prob. rdg.; Heb. store up.   *d* This . . . fate: prob. rdg.; Heb. Such are the courses.   *e* The rest of verse 22 transposed to follow verse 27.   *f* Prob. rdg.; Heb. adds when anguish and distress come upon you.   *g* Insolent . . . knowledge: transposed from end of verse 22.

31 and have spurned all my reproof,
they shall eat the fruits of their behaviour
and have a surfeit of their own devices;
32 for the simpleton turns a deaf ear and comes to grief,
and the stupid are ruined by their own complacency.
33 But whoever listens to me shall live without a care,
undisturbed by fear of misfortune.'

Reward of seeking wisdom

2 My son, if you take my words to heart and lay up my commands in your mind,
2 giving your attention to wisdom and your mind to understanding,
3 if you summon discernment to your aid
and invoke understanding,
4 if you seek her out like silver and dig for her like buried treasure,
5 then you will understand the fear of the LORD
and attain to the knowledge of God;
6 for the LORD bestows wisdom
and teaches knowledge and understanding.
7 Out of his store he endows the upright with ability
as a shield for those who live blameless lives;
8 for he guards the course of justice and keeps watch over the way of his loyal servants.

9 Then you will understand what is right and just
and keep[h] only to the good man's path;
10 for wisdom will sink into your mind, and knowledge will be your heart's delight.
11 Prudence will keep watch over you, understanding will guard you,
12 it will save you from evil ways and from men whose talk is subversive,
13 who forsake the honest course to walk in ways of darkness,
14 who rejoice in doing evil and exult in evil and subversive acts,
15 whose own ways are crooked, whose tracks are devious.
16 It will save you from the adulteress, from the loose woman with her seductive words,
17 who forsakes the teaching of her childhood

and has forgotten the covenant of her God;
18 for her path[i] runs downhill towards death,
and her course is set for the land of the dead.
19 No one who resorts to her[j] finds his way back
or regains the path to life.

20 See then that you follow the footsteps of good men
and keep to the course of the righteous;
21 for the upright shall dwell on earth and blameless men remain there;
22 but the wicked shall be uprooted from it
and traitors weeded out.

Advice to a young man

3 My son, do not forget my teaching, but guard my commands in your heart;
2 for long life and years in plenty will they bring you, and prosperity as well.
3 Let your good faith and loyalty never fail,
but bind them about your neck.
4 Thus will you win favour and success
in the sight of God and man.

5 Put all your trust in the LORD and do not rely on your own understanding.
6 Think of him in all your ways, and he will smooth your path.
7 Do not think how wise you are, but fear the LORD and turn from evil.
8 Let that be the medicine to keep you in health,
the liniment for your limbs.
9 Honour the LORD with your wealth as the first charge on all your earnings;
10 then your granaries will be filled with corn[k]
and your vats bursting with new wine.
11 My son, do not spurn the LORD's correction
or take offence at his reproof;
12 for those whom he loves the LORD reproves,
and he punishes a favourite son.

13 Happy he who has found wisdom, and the man who has acquired understanding;

h keep: *prob. rdg.*; *Heb.* uprightness. *i Prob. rdg.*; *Heb.* house. *j* resorts to her: *or* takes to them. *k* with corn: *or* to overflowing.

14 for wisdom is more profitable than
    silver,
and the gain she brings is better
    than gold.
15 She is more precious than red coral,
and all your jewels are no match
    for her.
16 Long life is in her right hand,
in her left hand are riches and
    honour.
17 Her ways are pleasant ways
and all her paths lead to prosperity.
18 She is a staff of life to all who grasp
    her,
and those who hold her fast are safe.

19 In wisdom the LORD founded the
    earth
and by understanding he set the
    heavens in their place;
20 by his knowledge the depths burst
    forth
and the clouds dropped dew.

21 My son, keep watch over your ability
    and prudence,
do not let them slip from sight;
22 they shall be a charm hung about
    your neck
and an ornament on your breast.
23 Then you will go your way without
    a care,
and your feet will not stumble.
24 When you sit, you need have no
    fear;
when you lie down, your sleep will
    be pleasant.
25 Do not be afraid when fools are
    frightened
or when ruin comes upon the wicked;
26 for the LORD will be at your side,
and he will keep your feet clear of
    the trap.
27 Refuse no man any favour that you
    owe him
when it lies in your power to pay it.
28 Do not say to your friend, 'Come
    back again;
you shall have it tomorrow'—when
    you have it already.
29 Plot no evil against your friend,
your unsuspecting neighbour.
30 Do not pick a quarrel with a man
    for no reason,
if he has not done you a bad turn.
31 Do not emulate a lawless man,
do not choose to follow his footsteps;
32 for one who is not straight is detest-
    able to the LORD,
but upright men are in God's confi-
    dence.

The LORD's curse rests on the house 33
    of the evildoer,
while he blesses the home of the
    righteous.
Though God himself meets the 34
    arrogant with arrogance,
yet he bestows his favour on the
    meek.[l]
Wise men are adorned with[m] honour, 35
but the coat[n] on a fool's back is
    contempt.

Listen, my sons, to a father's instruc- 4
    tion,
consider attentively how to gain
    understanding;
for it is sound learning I give you; 2
so do not forsake my teaching.
I too have been a father's son,   3
tender in years, my mother's only
    child.
He taught me and said to me: 4
Hold fast to my words with all your
    heart,
keep my commands and you will
    have life.
Do not forget or turn a deaf ear to 5
    what I say.

The first thing[o] is to acquire wisdom; 7
gain understanding though it cost
    you all you have.
Do not forsake her, and she will 6
    keep you safe;
love her, and she will guard you;
cherish her, and she will lift you high; 8
if only you embrace her, she will
    bring you to honour.
She will set a garland of grace on 9
    your head
and bestow on you a crown of glory.

Listen, my son, take my words to 10
    heart,
and the years of your life shall be
    multiplied.
I will guide you in the paths of 11
    wisdom
and lead you in honest ways.
As you walk you will not slip,   12
and, if you run, nothing will bring
    you down.
Cling to instruction and never let it 13
    go;
observe it well, for it is your life.
Do not take to the course of the 14
    wicked
or follow the way of evil men;
do not set foot on it, but avoid it; 15
turn aside and go on your way.
For they cannot sleep unless they 16
    have done some wrong;

l Or wretched.   *m* are adorned with: *prob. rdg.*; *Heb.* shall inherit.   *n* the coat: *prob. rdg.*; *Heb.* obscure.   *o* *Prob. rdg.*; *Heb. adds* wisdom.

unless they have been someone's
downfall they lose their sleep.

17 The bread they eat is the fruit of
crime
and they drink wine got by violence.

18 The course of the righteous is like
morning light,
growing brighter till it is broad day;

19 but the ways of the wicked are like
darkness at night,
and they do not know what has
been their downfall.

20 My son, attend to my speech,
pay heed to my words;

21 do not let them slip out of your
mind,
keep them close in your heart;

22 for they are life to him who finds
them,
and health to his whole body.

23 Guard your heart more than any
treasure,
for it is the source of all life.

24 Keep your mouth from crooked
speech
and your lips from deceitful talk.

25 Let your eyes look straight before
you,
fix your gaze upon what lies ahead.

26 Look out for the path that your feet
must take,
and your ways will be secure.

27 Swerve neither to right nor left,
and keep clear of every evil thing.

Faithfulness in marriage

5 My son, attend to my wisdom
and listen to my good counsel,

2 so that you may observe proper
prudence
and your speech be informed with
knowledge.

3 For though the lips of an adulteress
drip honey
and her tongue is smoother than
oil,

4 yet in the end she is more bitter
than wormwood,
and sharp as a two-edged sword.

5 Her feet go downwards on the path
to death,
her course is set for Sheol.

6 She does not watch for the road
that leads to life;
her course turns this way and that,
and what does she care?[p]

7 Now, my son, listen to me
and do not ignore what I say:

8 keep well away from her
and do not go near the door of her
house;

or you will lose your dignity in the 9
eyes of others
and your honour before strangers;
strangers will batten on your wealth, 10
and your hard-won gains pass to
another man's family.
The end will be that you will starve, 11
you will shrink to mere skin and
bones.
Then you will say, 'Why did I hate 12
correction
and set my heart against reproof?
I did not listen to the voice of my 13
teachers
or pay attention to my masters.
I soon earned[q] a bad name   14
and was despised in the public
assembly.'

Drink water from your own cistern 15
and running water from your own
spring;
do not let your[r] well overflow into 16
the road,
your runnels of water pour into the
street;
let them be yours alone,   17
not shared with strangers.
Let your fountain, the wife of your 18
youth,
be blessed, rejoice in her,
a lovely doe, a graceful hind, let 19
her be your companion;
you will at all times be bathed in
her love,
and her love will continually wrap
you round.
Wherever you turn, she will guide
you;
when you lie in bed, she will watch
over you,
and when you wake she will talk
with you.[s]
Why, my son, are you wrapped up 20
in the love of an adulteress?
Why do you embrace a loose woman?
For a man's ways are always in the 21
LORD's sight
who watches for every path that he
must take.
The wicked man is caught in his 22
own iniquities
and held fast in the toils of his own
sin;
he will perish for want of discipline, 23
wrapped in the shroud of his boundless folly.

On pledges

My son, if you pledge yourself to 6
another man
and stand surety for a stranger,

p what ... care?: or she is restless.   q Or I almost earned.   r do not let your: prob. rdg.; Heb.
shall your.   s Wherever ... with you: transposed from ch. 6 (verse 22).

2 if you are caught by your promise,
trapped by some promise you have
made,
3 do what I now tell you
and save yourself, my son:
when you fall into another man's
power,
bestir yourself, go and pester the
man,
4 give yourself no rest,
allow yourself no sleep.
5 Save yourself like a gazelle from
the toils,
like a bird from the grasp of the
fowler.

On idleness

6 Go to the ant, you sluggard,
watch her ways and get wisdom.
7 She has no overseer,
no governor or ruler;
8 but in summer she prepares her
store of food
and lays in her supplies at harvest.
9 How long, you sluggard, will you
lie abed?
When will you rouse yourself from
sleep?
10 A little sleep, a little slumber,
a little folding of the hands in rest,
11 and poverty will come upon you
like a robber,
want like a ruffian.

A troublemaker

12 A scoundrel, a mischievous man, is
he
who prowls about with crooked
talk—
13 a wink of the eye,
a touch with the foot,
a sign with the fingers.
14 Subversion is the evil that he is
plotting,
he stirs up quarrels all the time.
15 Down comes disaster suddenly upon
him;
suddenly he is broken beyond all
remedy.

What the LORD hates

16 Six things the LORD hates,
seven things are detestable to him:
17 a proud eye, a false tongue,
hands that shed innocent blood,
18 a heart that forges thoughts of
mischief,
and feet that run swiftly to do evil,
19 a false witness telling a pack of lies,
and one who stirs up quarrels
between brothers.

Warnings against adultery

My son, observe your father's com- 20
mands
and do not reject the teaching of
your mother;
wear them always next your heart 21
and bind them close about your
neck;
for a command is a lamp, and teach- 23[t]
ing a light,
reproof and correction point the
way of life,
to keep you from the wife of an- 24
other man,
from the seductive tongue of the
loose woman.
Do not desire her beauty in your 25
heart
or let her glance provoke you;
for a prostitute can be had for the 26
price of a loaf,
but a married woman is out for
bigger game.

Can a man kindle fire in his bosom 27
without burning his clothes?
If a man walks on hot coals,   28
will his feet not be scorched?
So is he who sleeps with his neigh- 29
bour's wife;
no one can touch such a woman and
go free.
Is not a thief contemptible when he 30
steals
to satisfy his appetite, even if he is
hungry?
And, if he is caught, must he not 31
pay seven times over
and surrender all that his house
contains?
So one who commits adultery is a 32
senseless fool:
he dishonours the woman and ruins
himself;
he will get nothing but blows and 33
contumely
and will never live down the disgrace;
for a husband's anger is a jealous 34
anger
and in the day of vengeance he will
show no mercy;
compensation will not buy his 35
forgiveness;[u]
no bribe, however large, will purchase his connivance.

My son, keep my words,   7
store up my commands in your
mind.
Keep my commands if you would 2
live,

t Verse 22 transposed to follow wrap you round in 5. 19.
rdg.; Heb. obscure.   u compensation . . . forgiveness: prob.

and treasure my teaching as the apple of your eye.

3 Wear them like a ring on your finger;
write them on the tablet of your memory.

4 Call Wisdom your sister,
greet Understanding as a familiar friend;

5 then they will save you from the adulteress,
from the loose woman with her seductive words.

6 I glanced*v* out of the window of my house,
I looked down through the lattice,

7 and I saw among simple youths,
there amongst the boys I noticed a lad, a foolish lad,

8 passing along the street, at the corner,
stepping out in the direction of her house

9 at twilight, as the day faded,
at dusk as the night grew dark;

10 suddenly a woman came to meet him,
dressed like a prostitute, full of wiles,

11 flighty and inconstant,
a woman never content to stay at home,

12 lying in wait at every corner,
now in the street, now in the public squares.

13 She caught hold of him and kissed him;
brazenly she accosted him and said,

14 'I have had a sacrifice, an offering, to make
and I have paid my vows today;

15 that is why I have come out to meet you,
to watch for you and find you.

16 I have spread coverings on my bed of coloured linen from Egypt.

17 I have sprinkled my bed with myrrh,
my clothes*w* with aloes and cassia.

18 Come! Let us drown ourselves in pleasure,
let us spend a whole night of love;

19 for the man of the house is away,
he has gone on a long journey,

20 he has taken a bag of silver with him;
until the moon is full he will not be home.'

21 Persuasively she led him on,
she pressed him with seductive words.

22 Like a simple fool he followed her,
like an ox on its way to the slaughter-house,
like an antelope bounding into the noose,

23 like a bird hurrying into the trap;
he did not know that he was risking his life
until the arrow pierced his vitals.

24 But now, my son, listen to me,
attend to what I say.

25 Do not let your heart entice you into her ways,
do not stray down her paths;

26 many has she pierced and laid low,
and her victims are without number.

27 Her house is the entrance to Sheol,
which leads down to the halls of death.

Wisdom and folly contrasted

8 Hear how Wisdom lifts her voice
and Understanding cries out.

2 She stands at the cross-roads,
by the wayside, at the top of the hill;

3 beside the gate, at the entrance to the city,
at the entry by the open gate she calls aloud:

4 'Men, it is to you I call,
I appeal to every man:

5 understand, you simple fools, what it is to be shrewd;
you stupid people, understand what sense means.

6 Listen! For I will speak clearly,
you will have plain speech from me;

7 for I speak nothing but truth
and my lips detest wicked talk.

8 All that I say is right,
not a word is twisted or crooked.

9 All is straightforward to him who can understand,
all is plain to the man who has knowledge.

10 Accept instruction and not silver,
knowledge rather than pure gold;

11 for wisdom is better than red coral,
no jewels can match her.

12 I am Wisdom, I bestow shrewdness
and show the way to knowledge and prudence.

13 *x*Pride, presumption, evil courses,
subversive talk, all these I hate.

14 I have force, I also have ability;
understanding and power are mine.

15 Through me kings are sovereign
and governors make just laws.

16 Through me princes act like princes,

v I glanced: *prob. rdg.*; *Heb. om.*　　　*w* my clothes: *prob. rdg.*; *Heb. om.*　　　*x* *Prob. rdg.*; *Heb. prefixes* The fear of the LORD is to hate evil.

from me all rulers on earth derive
their nobility.

17 Those who love me I love,
those who search for me find me.

18 In my hands are riches and honour,
boundless wealth and the rewards
of virtue.

19 My harvest is better than gold, fine
gold,
and my revenue better than pure
silver.

20 I follow the course of virtue,
my path is the path of justice;

21 I endow with riches those who love
me
and I will fill their treasuries.

22 'The LORD created me the beginning
of his works,
before all else that he made, long
ago.

23 Alone, I was fashioned in times
long past,
at the beginning, long before earth
itself.

24 When there was yet no ocean I was
born,
no springs brimming with water.

25 Before the mountains were settled
in their place,
long before the hills I was born,

26 when as yet he had made neither
land nor lake
nor the first clod*y* of earth.

27 When he set the heavens in their
place I was there,
when he girdled the ocean with the
horizon,

28 when he fixed the canopy of clouds
overhead
and set the springs of ocean firm in
their place,

29 when he prescribed its limits for the
sea*z*
and knit together earth's foundations.

30 Then I was at his side each day,
his darling and delight,
playing in his presence continually,

31 playing on the earth, when he had
finished it,
while my delight was in mankind.

2–3 'Now, my sons, listen to me,
listen to instruction and grow wise,
do not reject it.
Happy is the man who keeps to my
ways,

34 happy the man who listens to me,
watching daily at my threshold
with his eyes on the doorway;

35 for he who finds me finds life

and wins favour with the LORD,
while he who finds me not, hurts 36
himself,
and all who hate me are in love with
death.'

Wisdom has built her house,   9
she has hewn her seven pillars;
she has killed a beast and spiced 2
her wine,
and she has spread her table.
She has sent out her maidens to 3
proclaim
from the highest part of the town,
'Come in, you simpletons.'   4
She says also to the fool,
'Come, dine with me   5
and taste the wine that I have
spiced.
Cease to be silly, and you will live, 6
you will grow in understanding.'

Correct an insolent man, and be 7
sneered at for your pains;
correct a bad man, and you will put
yourself in the wrong.
Do not correct the insolent or they 8
will hate you;
correct a wise man, and he will be
your friend.
Lecture a wise man, and he will 9
grow wiser;
teach a righteous man, and his
learning will increase.

The first step to wisdom is the fear of 10
the LORD,
and knowledge of the Holy One is
understanding;
for through me your days will be 11
multiplied
and years will be added to your life.
If you are wise, it will be to your 12
own advantage;
if you are haughty, you alone are
to blame.
The Lady Stupidity is a flighty 13
creature;
the simpleton, she cares for nothing.
She sits at the door of her house, 14
on a seat in the highest part of the
town,
to invite the passers-by indoors 15
as they hurry on their way:
'Come in, you simpletons', she says. 16
She says also to the fool,
'Stolen water is sweet   17
and bread got by stealth tastes
good.'
Little does he know that death 18
lurks there,
that her guests are in the depths of
Sheol.

y the first clod: *or* the sum of the clods.
his command.   *z Prob. rdg.; Heb. adds* and the water shall not disobey

A collection of wise sayings

10 The proverbs of Solomon:

A wise son brings joy to his father;
a foolish son is his mother's bane.

2 Ill-gotten wealth brings no profit;
uprightness is a safeguard against
death.

3 The LORD does not let the righteous
go hungry,[a]
but he disappoints the cravings[b] of
the wicked.

4 Idle hands make a man poor;
busy hands grow rich.

5 A thoughtful son puts by in summer;
a son who sleeps at harvest is a
disgrace.

6 Blessings are showered on the
righteous;
the wicked are choked by their own
violence.

7 The righteous are remembered in
blessings;
the name of the wicked turns rotten.

8 A wise man takes a command to
heart;
a foolish talker comes to grief.

9 A blameless life makes for security;
crooked ways bring a man down.

10 To wink at a fault causes trouble;
a frank rebuke leads to peace.

11 The words of good men are a fountain of life;
the wicked are choked by their own
violence.

12 Hate is always picking a quarrel,
but love turns a blind eye to every
fault.

13 The man of understanding has
wisdom on his lips;
a rod is in store for the back of the
fool.

14 Wise men lay up knowledge;
when a fool speaks, ruin is near.

15 A rich man's wealth is his strong
city,
but poverty is the undoing of the
helpless.

16 The good man's labour is his livelihood;
the wicked man's earnings bring
him to a bad end.

17 Correction is the high road to life;
neglect reproof and you miss the
way.

18 There is no spite in a just man's
talk;
it is the stupid who are fluent with
calumny.

19 When men talk too much, sin is
never far away;
common sense holds its tongue.

A good man's tongue is pure silver; 20
the heart of the wicked is trash.

The lips of a good man teach many, 21
but fools perish for want of sense.

The blessing of the LORD brings 22
riches
and he sends no sorrow with them.

Lewdness is sport for the stupid; 23
wisdom a delight to men of understanding.

The fears of the wicked will over- 24
take them;
the desire of the righteous will be
granted.

When the whirlwind has passed by, 25
the wicked are gone;
the foundations of the righteous are
eternal.

Like vinegar on the teeth or smoke 26
in the eyes,
so is the lazy servant to his master.

The fear of the LORD brings length 27
of days;
the years of the wicked are few.

The hope of the righteous blossoms; 28
the expectation of the wicked
withers away.

The way of the LORD gives refuge 29
to the honest man,
but dismays those who do evil.

The righteous man will never be 30
shaken;
the wicked shall not remain on
earth.

Wisdom flows from the mouth of 31
the righteous;
the subversive tongue will be rooted
out.

The righteous man can suit his 32
words to the occasion;
the wicked know only subversive
talk.

False scales are the LORD's abo- **11**
mination;
correct weights are dear to his heart.

When presumption comes in, in 2
comes contempt,
but wisdom goes with sagacity.

Honesty is a guide to the upright, 3
but rogues are balked by their own
perversity.

Wealth is worth nothing in the day 4
of wrath,
but uprightness is a safeguard
against death.

By uprightness the blameless keep 5
their course,
but the wicked are brought down
by their wickedness.

Uprightness saves the righteous, 6
but rogues are trapped in their own
greed.

a Or be afraid.   *b Or* the clamour.

7 When a man dies, his thread of life ends,
and with it ends the hope of affluence.

8 A righteous man is rescued from disaster,
and the wicked man plunges into it.

9 By his words a godless man tries to ruin others,
but they are saved when the righteous plead for them.

10 A city rejoices in the prosperity of the righteous;
there is jubilation when the wicked perish.

11 By the blessing of the upright a city is built up;
the words of the wicked tear it down.

12 A man without sense despises others,
but a man of understanding holds his peace.

13 A gossip gives away secrets,
but a trusty man keeps his own counsel.

14 For want of skilful strategy an army is lost;
victory is the fruit of long planning.

15 Give a pledge for a stranger and know no peace;
refuse to stand surety and be safe.

16 Grace in a woman wins honour,
but she who hates virtue makes a home for dishonour.
Be timid in business and come to beggary;
be bold and make a fortune.

17 Loyalty brings its own reward;
a cruel man makes trouble for his kin.

18 A wicked man earns a fallacious[c] profit;
he who sows goodness reaps a sure reward.[d]

19 A man set on righteousness finds life,
but the pursuit of evil leads to death.

20 The LORD detests the crooked heart,
but honesty is dear to him.

21 Depend upon it: an evil man shall not escape punishment;
the righteous and all their offspring shall go free.

22 Like a gold ring in a pig's snout is a beautiful woman without good sense.

23 The righteous desire only what is good;
the hope of the wicked comes to nothing.

24 A man may spend freely and yet grow richer;
another is sparing beyond measure, yet ends in poverty.

25 A generous man grows fat and prosperous,
and he who refreshes others will himself be refreshed.

26 He who withholds his grain is cursed by the people,
but he who sells his corn is blessed.

27 He who eagerly seeks what is good finds much favour,
but if a man pursues evil it turns upon him.

28 Whoever relies on his wealth is riding for a fall,
but the righteous flourish like the green leaf.

29 He who brings trouble on his family inherits the wind,
and a fool becomes slave to a wise man.

30 The fruit of righteousness is a tree of life,
but violence means the taking away of life.

31 If the righteous in the land get their deserts,
how much more the wicked man and the sinner!

He who loves correction loves **12** knowledge;
he who hates reproof is a mere brute.

2 A good man earns favour from the LORD;
the schemer is condemned.

3 No man can establish himself by wickedness,
but good men have roots that cannot be dislodged.

4 A capable wife is her husband's crown;
one who disgraces him is like rot in his bones.

5 The purposes of the righteous are lawful;
the designs of the wicked are full of deceit.

6 The wicked are destroyed[e] by their own words;
the words of the good man are his salvation.

7 Once the wicked are down, that is the end of them,
but the good man's line continues.

8 A man is commended for his intelligence,
but a warped mind is despised.

c Or fraudulent.   d a sure reward: or the reward of honesty.   e Prob. rdg.; Heb. are an ambush for blood.

9 It is better to be modest[f] and earn one's living
than to be conceited[g] and go hungry.

10 A righteous man cares for his beast, but a wicked man is cruel at heart.

11 He who tills his land has enough to eat,
but to follow idle pursuits is foolishness.

12 The stronghold of the wicked crumbles like clay,[h]
but the righteous take lasting root.

13 The wicked man is trapped by his own falsehoods,
but the righteous comes safe through trouble.

14 One man wins success by his words;
another gets his due reward by the work of his hands.

15 A fool thinks that he is always right;
wise is the man who listens to advice.

16 A fool shows his ill humour at once;
a clever man slighted conceals his feelings.

17 An honest speaker comes out with the truth,
but the false witness is full of deceit.

18 Gossip can be sharp as a sword,
but the tongue of the wise heals.

19 Truth spoken stands firm for ever,
but lies live only for a moment.

20 Those who plot evil delude themselves,
but there is joy for those who seek the common good.

21 No mischief will befall the righteous,
but wicked men get their fill of adversity.

22 The LORD detests a liar
but delights in the honest man.

23 A clever man conceals his knowledge,
but a stupid man broadcasts his folly.

24 Diligence brings a man to power,
but laziness to forced labour.

25 An anxious heart dispirits a man,
and a kind word fills him with joy.

26 A righteous man recoils from evil,[i]
but the wicked take a path that leads them astray.

27 The lazy hunter puts up no game,
but the industrious man reaps a rich harvest.[j]

28 The way of honesty leads to life,
but there is a well-worn path to death.

A wise man sees the reason for his **13** father's correction;
an arrogant man will not listen to rebuke.

A good man enjoys the fruit of 2 righteousness,
but violence is meat and drink for the treacherous.

He who minds his words preserves 3 his life;
he who talks too much comes to grief.

A lazy man is torn by appetite unsatisfied, 4
but the diligent grow fat and prosperous.

The righteous hate falsehood; 5
the doings of the wicked are foul and deceitful.

To do right is the protection of an 6 honest man,
but wickedness brings sinners to grief.[k]

One man pretends to be rich, 7 although he has nothing;
another has great wealth but goes in rags.[l]

A rich man must buy himself off, 8
but a poor man is immune from threats.

The light of the righteous burns 9 brightly;
the embers of the wicked will be put out.

A brainless fool causes strife by his 10 presumption;
wisdom is found among friends in council.

Wealth quickly come by dwindles 11 away,
but if it comes little by little, it multiplies.

Hope deferred makes the heart 12 sick;
a wish come true is a staff of life.

To despise a word of advice is to ask 13 for trouble;
mind what you are told, and you will be rewarded.

A wise man's teaching is a fountain 14 of life
for one who would escape the snares of death.

Good intelligence wins favour, 15
but treachery leads to disaster.

A clever man is wise and conceals 16 everything,
but the stupid parade their folly.

An evil messenger causes trouble,[m] 17

---

f Or scorned.   g Or honoured.   h Prob. rdg.; Heb. A wicked man covets a stronghold of crumbling earth.   i recoils from evil: prob. rdg.; Heb. let him spy out his friend.   j but . . . harvest: prob. rdg.; Heb. obscure.   k brings . . . grief: or plays havoc with a man.   l One man . . . rags: or One man may grow rich though he has nothing; another may grow poor though he has great wealth.   m causes trouble: or is unsuccessful.

but a trusty envoy makes all go well again.

18 To refuse correction brings poverty and contempt;
one who takes a reproof to heart comes to honour.

19 Lust indulged sickens a man;[n]
stupid people loathe to mend their ways.

20 Walk with the wise and be wise;
mix with the stupid and be misled.

21 Ill fortune follows the sinner close behind,
but good rewards the righteous.

22 A good man leaves an inheritance to his descendants,
but the sinner's hoard passes to the righteous.

23 Untilled land might yield food enough for the poor,
but even that may be lost through injustice.

24 A father who spares the rod hates his son,
but one who loves him keeps him in order.

25 A righteous man eats his fill,
but the wicked go hungry.

14 The wisest women build up their homes;
the foolish pull them down with their own hands.

2 A straightforward man fears the LORD;
the double-dealer scorns him.

3 The speech of a fool is a rod for his back;[o]
a wise man's words are his safeguard.

4 Where there are no oxen the barn is empty,
but the strength of a great ox ensures rich crops.

5 A truthful witness is no liar;
a false witness tells a pack of lies.

6 A conceited man seeks wisdom, yet finds none;
to one of understanding, knowledge comes easily.

7 Avoid a stupid man,
you will hear not a word of sense from him.

8 A clever man has the wit to find the right way;
the folly of stupid men misleads them.

9 A fool is too arrogant to make amends;
upright men know what reconciliation means.

10 The heart knows its own bitterness,

and a stranger has no part in its joy.

The house of the wicked will be 11 torn down,
but the home of the upright flourishes.

A road may seem straightforward 12 to a man,
yet may end as the way to death.

Even in laughter the heart may 13 grieve,
and mirth may end in sorrow.

The renegade reaps the fruit of his 14 conduct,
a good man the fruit of his own achievements.

A simple man believes every word 15 he hears;
a clever man understands the need for proof.

A wise man is cautious and turns 16 his back on evil;
the stupid is heedless and falls headlong.

Impatience runs into folly;   17
distinction comes by careful thought.[p]

The simple wear the trappings of 18 folly;
the clever are crowned with knowledge.

Evil men cringe before the good, 19
wicked men at the righteous man's door.

A poor man is odious even to his 20 friend;
the rich have friends in plenty.

He who despises a hungry man does 21 wrong,
but he who is generous to the poor is happy.

Do not those who intend evil go 22 astray,
while those with good intentions are loyal and faithful?

The pains of toil bring gain,   23
but mere talk brings nothing but poverty.

Insight is the crown of the wise; 24
folly the chief ornament of the stupid.

A truthful witness saves life;   25
the false accuser utters nothing but lies.

A strong man who trusts in the 26 fear of the LORD
will be a refuge for his sons.

The fear of the LORD is the 27 fountain of life
for the man who would escape the snares of death.

Many subjects make a famous king; 28
with none to rule, a prince is ruined.

n Lust . . . a man: or Desire fulfilled is pleasant to the appetite.   o his back: prob. rdg.; Heb. pride.   p distinction . . . thought: prob. rdg.; Heb. a man of careful thought is hated.

29 To be patient shows great understanding;
quick temper is the height of folly.

30 A tranquil mind puts flesh on a man,
but passion rots his bones.

31 He who oppresses[q] the poor insults his Maker;
he who is generous to the needy honours him.

32 An evil man is brought down by his wickedness;
the upright man is secure in his own honesty.

33 Wisdom is at home in a discerning mind,
but is ill at ease in the heart of a fool.

34 Righteousness raises a people to honour;
to do wrong is a disgrace to any nation.

35 A king shows favour to an intelligent servant,
but his displeasure strikes down those who fail him.

15 A soft answer turns away anger,
but a sharp word makes tempers hot.

2 A wise man's tongue spreads knowledge;
stupid men talk nonsense.

3 The eyes of the LORD are everywhere,
surveying evil and good men alike.

4 A soothing word is a staff of life,
but a mischievous tongue breaks the spirit.

5 A fool spurns his father's correction,
but to take a reproof to heart shows good sense.

6 In the righteous man's house there is ample wealth;
the gains of the wicked bring trouble.

7 The lips of a wise man promote knowledge;
the hearts of the stupid are dishonest.

8 The wicked man's sacrifice is abominable to the LORD;
the good man's prayer is his delight.

9 The conduct of the wicked is abominable to the LORD,
but he loves the seeker after righteousness.

10 A man who leaves the main road resents correction,
and he who hates reproof will die.

11 Sheol and Abaddon lie open before the LORD,
how much more the hearts of men!

12 The conceited man does not take kindly to reproof
and he will not consult the wise.

13 A merry heart makes a cheerful face;
heartache crushes the spirit.

14 A discerning mind seeks knowledge,
but the stupid man feeds on folly.

15 In the life of the downtrodden every day is wretched,
but to have a glad heart is a perpetual feast.

16 Better a pittance with the fear of the LORD
than great treasure and trouble in its train.

17 Better a dish of vegetables if love go with it
than a fat ox eaten in hatred.

18 Bad temper provokes a quarrel,
but patience heals discords.

19 The path of the sluggard is a tangle of weeds,
but the road of the diligent is a highway.

20 A wise son brings joy to his father;
a young fool despises his mother.

21 Folly may amuse the empty-headed;
a man of understanding makes straight for his goal.

22 Schemes lightly made come to nothing,
but with long planning they succeed.

23 A man may be pleased with his own retort;
how much better is a word in season!

24 For men of intelligence the path of life leads upwards
and keeps them clear of Sheol below.

25 The LORD pulls down the proud man's home
but fixes the widow's boundary-stones.

26 A bad man's thoughts are the LORD's abomination,
but the words of the pure are a delight.[r]

27 A grasping man brings trouble on his family,
but he who spurns a bribe will enjoy long life.

28 The righteous think before they answer;
a bad man's ready tongue is full of mischief.

29 The LORD stands aloof from the wicked,
he listens to the righteous man's prayer.

q Or slanders.   r the words . . . delight: or gracious words are pure.

30 A bright look brings joy to the heart,
and good news warms a man's marrow.
31 Whoever listens to wholesome reproof
shall enjoy the society of the wise.
32 He who refuses correction is his own worst enemy,
but he who listens to reproof learns sense.
33 The fear of the LORD is a training in wisdom,
and the way to honour is humility.

16 A man may order his thoughts,
but the LORD inspires the words he utters.
2 A man's whole conduct may be pure in his own eyes,
but the LORD fixes a standard for the spirit of man.
3 Commit to the LORD all that you do,
and your plans will be fulfilled.
4 The LORD has made each thing for its own end;
he made even the wicked for a day of disaster.
5 Proud men, one and all, are abominable to the LORD;
depend upon it: they will not escape punishment.
6 Guilt is wiped out by faith and loyalty,
and the fear of the LORD makes men turn from evil.
7 When the LORD is pleased with a man and his ways,
he makes even his enemies live at peace with him.
8 Better a pittance honestly earned than great gains ill gotten.
9 Man plans his journey by his own wit,
but it is the LORD who guides his steps.
10 The king's mouth is an oracle,
he cannot err when he passes sentence.
11 Scales[s] and balances[t] are the LORD's concern;
all the weights in the bag are his business.
12 Wickedness is abhorrent to kings,
for a throne rests firm on righteousness.
13 Honest speech is the desire of kings,
they love a man who speaks the truth.

A king's anger is a messenger of 14 death,
and a wise man will appease it.
In the light of the king's countenance is life, 15
his favour is like a rain-cloud in the spring.
How much better than gold it is to 16 gain wisdom,
and to gain discernment is better than pure silver.
To turn from evil is the highway of 17 the upright;
watch your step and save your life.
Pride comes before disaster, 18
and arrogance before a fall.
Better sit humbly with those in 19 need
than divide the spoil with the proud.
The shrewd man of business will 20 succeed well,
but the happy man is he who trusts in the LORD.
The sensible man seeks advice from 21 the wise,
he drinks it in and increases his knowledge.[u]
Intelligence is a fountain of life to 22 its possessors,
but a fool is punished by his own folly.
The wise man's mind guides his 23 speech,
and what his lips impart increases learning.[v]
Kind words are like dripping honey, 24
sweetness on the tongue and health for the body.
A road may seem straightforward 25 to a man,
yet may end as the way to death.
The labourer's appetite is always 26 plaguing him,
his hunger spurs him on.
A scoundrel repeats evil gossip; 27
it is like a scorching fire on his lips.
Disaffection stirs up quarrels, 28
and tale-bearing breaks up friendship.
A man of violence draws others on 29
and leads them into lawless ways.
The man who narrows his eyes is 30 disaffected at heart,
and a close-lipped man is bent on mischief.
Grey hair is a crown of glory, 31
and it is won by a virtuous life.
Better be slow to anger than a 32 fighter,
better govern one's temper than capture a city.

s Or Pointer.   t Prob. rdg.; Heb. balances of justice.   u he drinks . . . knowledge: or and he whose speech is persuasive increases learning.   v and what . . . learning: or and increases the learning of his utterance.

33 The lots may be cast into the lap,
but the issue depends wholly on the
LORD.

17 Better a dry crust and concord with
it
than a house full of feasting and
strife.

2 A wise slave may give orders to a
disappointing son
and share the inheritance with the
brothers.

3 The melting-pot is for silver and
the crucible for gold,
but it is the LORD who assays the
hearts of men.

4 A rogue gives a ready ear to mischievous talk,
and a liar listens to slander.

5 A man who sneers at the poor insults his Maker,
and he who gloats over another's
ruin will answer for it.

6 Grandchildren are the crown of old
age,
and sons are proud of their fathers.

7 Fine talk is out of place in a boor,
how much more is falsehood in the
noble!

8 He who offers a bribe finds it work
like a charm,
he prospers in all he undertakes.

9 He who conceals another's offence
seeks his goodwill,
but he who harps on something
breaks up friendship.

10 A reproof is felt by a man of discernment
more than a hundred blows by a
stupid man.

11 An evil man is set only on disobedience,
but a messenger without mercy will
be sent against him.

12 Better face a she-bear robbed of her
cubs
than a stupid man in his folly.

13 If a man repays evil for good,
evil will never quit his house.

14 Stealing water starts a quarrel;
drop a dispute before you bare your
teeth.

15 To acquit the wicked and condemn
the righteous,
both are abominable in the LORD's
sight.

16 What use is money in the hands of
a stupid man?
Can he buy wisdom if he has no
sense?

17 A friend is a loving companion at
all times,
and a brother is born to share
troubles.

18 A man is without sense who gives
a guarantee
and surrenders himself to another
as surety.

19 He who loves strife loves sin.
He who builds a lofty entrance invites thieves.

20 A crooked heart will come to no
good,
and a mischievous tongue will end
in disaster.

21 A stupid man is the bane of his
parent,
and his father has no joy in a boor-
ish son.

22 A merry heart makes a cheerful
countenance,
but low spirits sap a man's strength.

23 A wicked man accepts a bribe
under his cloak
to pervert the course of justice.

24 Wisdom is never out of sight of a
discerning man,
but a stupid man's eyes are roving
everywhere.

25 A stupid son exasperates his father
and is a bitter sorrow to the mother
who bore him.

26 Again, to punish the righteous is
not good
and it is wrong to inflict blows on
men of noble mind.

27 Experience uses few words;
discernment keeps a cool head.

28 Even a fool, if he holds his peace, is
thought wise;
keep your mouth shut and show
your good sense.

18 The man who holds aloof seeks
every pretext
to bare his teeth in scorn at competent people.

2 The foolish have no interest in
seeking to understand,
but prefer to display their wit.

3 When wickedness comes in, in
comes contempt;
with loss of honour comes reproach.

4 The words of a man's mouth are a
gushing torrent,
but deep is the water in the well of
wisdom.*w*

5 It is not good to show favour to the
wicked
or to deprive the righteous of
justice.

6 When the stupid man talks, contention follows;
his words provoke blows.

w The words ... wisdom: prob. rdg., inverting phrases.

7 The stupid man's tongue is his undoing;
his lips put his life in jeopardy.
8 A gossip's whispers are savoury
morsels,
gulped down into the inner man.
9 Again, the lazy worker is own
brother
to the man who enjoys destruction.
10 The name of the LORD is a tower of
strength,
where the righteous may run for
refuge.
11 A rich man's wealth is his strong
city,
a towering wall, so he supposes.
12 Before disaster comes, a man is
proud,
but the way to honour is humility.
13 To answer a question before you
have heard it out
is both stupid and insulting.
14 A man's spirit may sustain him in
sickness,
but if the spirit is wounded, who
can mend it?
15 Knowledge comes to the discerning
mind;
the wise ear listens to get knowledge.
16 A gift opens the door to the giver
and gains access to the great.
17 In a lawsuit the first speaker seems
right,
until another steps forward and
cross-questions him.
18 Cast lots, and settle a quarrel,
and so keep litigants apart.
19 A reluctant brother is more un-
yielding than a fortress,
and quarrels are stubborn as the
bars of a castle.
20 A man may live by the fruit of his
tongue,
his lips may earn him a livelihood.
21 The tongue has power of life and
death;
make friends with it and enjoy its
fruits.
22 Find a wife, and you find a good
thing;
so you will earn the favour of the
LORD.
23 The poor man speaks in a tone of
entreaty,
and the rich man gives a harsh
answer.
24 Some companions are good only for
idle talk,
but a friend may stick closer than
a brother.

9 Better be poor and above reproach
than rich and crooked in speech.

Again, desire without knowledge is 2
not good;
the man in a hurry misses the way.
A man's own folly wrecks his life, 3
and then he bears a grudge against
the LORD.
Wealth makes many friends, 4
but a man without means loses the
friend he has.
A false witness will not escape 5
punishment,
and one who utters nothing but lies
will not go free.
Many curry favour with the great; 6
a lavish giver has the world for his
friend.
A poor man's brothers all dislike 7
him,
how much more is he shunned by
his friends!
Practice in evil makes the perfect
scoundrel;
the man who talks too much meets
his deserts.
To learn sense is true self-love; 8
cherish discernment and make sure
of success.
A false witness will not escape 9
punishment,
and one who utters nothing but lies
will perish.
A fool at the helm is out of place, 10
how much worse a slave in command of men of rank!
To be patient shows intelligence; 11
to overlook faults is a man's glory.
A king's rage is like a lion's roar, 12
his favour like dew on the grass.
A stupid son is a calamity to his 13
father;
a nagging wife is like water dripping
endlessly.
Home and wealth may come down 14
from ancestors,
but an intelligent wife is a gift from
the LORD.
Laziness is the undoing of the 15
worthless;
idlers must starve.
To keep the commandments keeps 16
a man safe,
but scorning the way of the LORD
brings death.
He who is generous to the poor lends 17
to the LORD;
he will repay him in full measure.
Chastise your son while there is 18
hope for him,
but be careful not to flog him to
death.
A man's ill temper brings its own 19
punishment;
try to save him, and you make
matters worse.

20 Listen to advice and accept instruction,
and you will die a wise man.

21 A man's heart may be full of schemes,
but the LORD's purpose will prevail.

22 Greed is a disgrace to a man;
better be a poor man than a liar.

23 The fear of the LORD is life;
he who is full of it will rest untouched by evil.

24 The sluggard plunges his hand in the dish
but will not so much as lift it to his mouth.

25 Strike an arrogant man, and he resents it like a fool;
reprove an understanding man, and he understands what you mean.

26 He who talks his father down vexes his mother;
he is a son to bring shame and disgrace on them.

27 A son who ceases to accept correction
is sure to turn his back on the teachings of knowledge.

28 A rascally witness perverts justice,
and the talk of the wicked fosters mischief.

29 There is a rod in pickle for the arrogant,
and blows ready for the stupid man's back.

20 Wine is an insolent fellow, and strong drink makes an uproar;
no one addicted to their company grows wise.

2 A king's threat is like a lion's roar;
one who ignores it is his own worst enemy.

3 To draw back from a dispute is honourable;
it is the fool who bares his teeth.

4 The sluggard who does not plough in autumn
goes begging at harvest and gets nothing.

5 Counsel in another's heart is like deep water,
but a discerning man will draw it up.

6 Many a man protests his loyalty,
but where will you find one to keep faith?

7 If a man leads a good and upright life,
happy are the sons who come after him!

8 A king seated on the judgement-throne
has an eye to sift all that is evil.

9 Who can say, 'I have a clear conscience;
I am purged from my sin'?

10 A double standard in weights and measures
is an abomination to the LORD.

11 Again, a young man is known by his actions,
whether his conduct is innocent or guilty.^{x}

12 The ear that hears, the eye that sees,
the LORD made them both.

13 Love sleep, and you will end in poverty;
keep your eyes open, and you will eat your fill.

14 'A bad bargain!' says the buyer to the seller,
but off he goes to brag about it.

15 There is gold in plenty and coral too,
but a wise word is a rare jewel.

16 Take a man's garment when he pledges his word for a stranger
and hold that as a pledge for the unknown person.

17 Bread got by fraud tastes good,
but afterwards it fills the mouth with grit.

18 Care is the secret of good planning;
wars are won by skilful strategy.

19 A gossip will betray secrets;^{y}
have nothing to do with a tattler.

20 If a man reviles father and mother,
his lamp will go out when darkness comes.

21 If you begin by piling up property in haste,
it will bring you no blessing in the end.

22 Do not think to repay evil for evil,
wait for the LORD to deliver you.

23 A double standard in weights is an abomination to the LORD,
and false scales are not good in his sight.

24 It is the LORD who directs a man's steps;
how can mortal man understand the road he travels?

25 It is dangerous to dedicate a gift rashly
or to make a vow and have second thoughts.

26 A wise king sifts out the wicked
and turns back for them the wheel of fortune.

27 The LORD shines into a man's very soul,
searching out his inmost being.

x Prob. rdg.; Heb. upright.   *y Or* He who betrays secrets is a gossip.

28 A king's guards are loyalty and good faith,
his throne is upheld by righteousness.

29 The glory of young men is their strength,
the dignity of old men their grey hairs.

30 A good beating purges the mind,
and blows chasten the inmost being.

21 The king's heart is under the LORD's hand;
like runnels of water, he turns it wherever he will.

2 A man may think that he is always right,
but the LORD fixes a standard for the heart.

3 Do what is right and just;
that is more pleasing to the LORD than sacrifice.

4 Haughty looks and a proud heart—
these sins mark a wicked man.

5 Forethought and diligence are sure of profit;
the man in a hurry is as sure of poverty.

6 He who makes a fortune by telling lies
runs needlessly into the toils of death.

7 The wicked are caught up in their own violence,
because they refuse to do what is just.

8 The criminal's conduct is tortuous;
straight dealing is a sign of integrity.

9 Better to live in a corner of the house-top
than have a nagging wife and a brawling household.

10 The wicked man is set on evil;
he has no pity to spare for his friend.

11 The simple man is made wise when he sees the insolent punished,
and learns his lesson when the wise man prospers.

12 The just God[z] makes the wicked man's home childless;[a]
he overturns the wicked and ruins them.

13 If a man shuts his ears to the cry of the helpless,
he will cry for help himself and not be heard.

14 A gift in secret placates an angry man;
a bribe slipped under the cloak pacifies great wrath.

15 When justice is done, all good men rejoice,
but it brings ruin to evildoers.

16 A man who takes leave of common sense
comes to rest in the company of the dead.

17 Love pleasure and you will beg your bread;
a man who loves wine and oil will never grow rich.

18 The wicked man serves as a ransom for the righteous,
so does a traitor for the upright.

19 Better to live alone in the desert
than with a nagging and ill-tempered wife.

20 The wise man has his home full of fine and costly treasures;
the stupid man is a mere spendthrift.

21 Persevere in right conduct and loyalty
and you shall find life and honour.

22 A wise man climbs into a city full of armed men
and undermines its strength and its confidence.

23 Keep a guard over your lips and tongue
and keep yourself out of trouble.

24 The conceited man is haughty, his name is insolence;
conceit and impatience are in all he does.

25 The sluggard's cravings will be the death of him,
because his hands refuse to work;

26 all day long his cravings go unsatisfied,
while the righteous man gives without stint.

27 The wicked man's sacrifice is an abomination to the LORD;
how much more when he offers it with vileness at heart!

28 A lying witness will perish,
but he whose words ring true will leave children behind him.

29 A wicked man puts a bold face on it,
whereas the upright man secures his line of retreat.

30 Face to face with the LORD,
wisdom, understanding, counsel go for nothing.

31 A horse may be made ready for the day of battle,
but victory comes from the LORD.

22 A good name is more to be desired than great riches;
esteem is better than silver or gold.

z Or The just man.   a makes . . . childless: *prob. rdg.*; *Heb.* considers the wicked man's home.

2   Rich and poor have this in common:
the LORD made them both.

3   A shrewd man sees trouble coming
and lies low;
the simple walk into it and pay the
penalty.

4   The fruit of humility is the fear of
God
with riches and honour and life.

5   The crooked man's path is set with
snares and pitfalls;
the cautious man will steer clear of
them.

6   Start a boy on the right road,
and even in old age he will not
leave it.

7   The rich lord it over the poor;
the borrower becomes the lender's
slave.

8   The man who sows injustice reaps
trouble,
and the end of his work will be the
rod.[b]

9   The kindly man will be blessed,
for he shares his food with the poor.

10   Drive out the insolent man, and
strife goes with him;
if he sits on the bench, he makes a
mockery of justice.

11   The LORD loves a sincere man;
but you will make a king your
friend with your fine phrases.

12   The LORD keeps watch over every
claim at law,
and overturns the scoundrel's case.

13   The sluggard protests, 'There's a
lion outside;
I shall get myself killed in the
street.'

14   The words of an adulteress are like
a deep pit;
those whom the LORD has cursed
will fall into it.

15   Folly is deep-rooted in the heart of
a boy;
a good beating will drive it right
out of him.

16   Oppression of the poor may bring
gain to a man,
but giving to the rich leads only to
penury.

Thirty wise sayings

17   The sayings of the wise:

Pay heed and listen to my words,
open your mind to the knowledge I
impart;

18   to keep them in your heart will be a
pleasure,
and then you will always have them
ready on your lips.

I would have you trust in the LORD   19
and so I tell you these things this
day for your own good.
Here I have written out for you   20
thirty sayings,
full of knowledge and wise advice,
to impart to you a knowledge of   21
the truth,
that you may take back a true
report[c] to him who sent you.

Never rob a helpless man because   22
he is helpless,
nor ill-treat a poor wretch in court;
for the LORD will take up their   23
cause
and rob him who robs them of their
livelihood.
Never make friends with an angry   24
man
nor keep company with a bad-
tempered one;
be careful not to learn his ways,   25
or you will find yourself caught in
a trap.
Never be one to give guarantees,   26
or to pledge yourself as surety for
another;
for if you cannot pay, beware: 27
your bed will be taken from under
you.
Do not move the ancient boundary-   28
stone
which your forefathers set up.
You see a man skilful at his craft: 29
he will serve kings, he will not serve
common men.

When you sit down to eat with a   2
ruling prince,
be sure to keep your mind on what
is before you,
and if you are a greedy man,   2
cut your throat first.
Do not be greedy for his dainties,   3
for they are not what they seem.
Do not slave to get wealth;[d]   4
be a sensible man, and give up.
Before you can look round, it will   5
be gone;
it will surely grow wings
like an eagle, like a bird in the sky.
Do not go to dinner with a miser,[e]   6
do not be greedy for his dainties;
for they will stick in your[f] throat   7
like a hair.
He will bid you eat and drink,
but his heart is not with you;
you will bring up the mouthful you   8
have eaten,
and your winning words will have
been wasted.

---

b the rod: *or* the threshing.   *c* Prob. rdg.; Heb. *adds* words of truth.   *d* to get wealth: *or* for an
invitation to a feast.   *e* Or a man with an evil eye.   *f* Prob. rdg.; Heb. his.

9   Hold your tongue in the hearing of
    a stupid man;
    for he will despise your words of
    wisdom.

10 Do not move the ancient boundary-
    stone
    or encroach on the land of orphans:

11 they have a powerful guardian
    who will take up their cause against
    you.

12 Apply your mind to instruction
    and open your ears to knowledge
    when it speaks.

13 Do not withhold discipline from a
    boy;
    take the stick to him, and save him
    from death.

14 If you take the stick to him your-
    self,
    you will preserve him from the jaws
    of death.

15 My son, if you are wise at heart,
    my heart in its turn will be glad;

16 I shall rejoice with all my soul
    when you speak plain truth.

17 Do not try to emulate sinners;
    envy only those who fear the LORD
    day by day;

18 do this, and you may look forward
    to the future,
    and your thread of life will not be
    cut short.

19 Listen, my son, listen, and become
    wise;
    set your mind on the right course.

20 Do not keep company with drunk-
    ards
    or those who are greedy for the
    fleshpots;

21 for drink and greed will end in
    poverty,
    and drunken stupor goes in rags.

22 Listen to your father, who gave you
    life,
    and do not despise your mother
    when she is old.

23 Buy truth, never sell it;
    buy wisdom, instruction, and under-
    standing.

24 A good man's father will rejoice
    and he who has a wise son will
    delight in him.

25 Give your father and your mother
    cause for delight,
    let her who bore you rejoice.

26 My son, mark my words,
    and accept my guidance with a will.

27 A prostitute is a deep pit,

a loose woman a narrow well;
she lies in wait like a robber   28
and betrays her husband with man
    after man.

Whose is the misery? whose the 29
    remorse?
Whose are the quarrels and the
    anxiety?
Who gets the bruises without
    knowing why?
Whose eyes are bloodshot?
Those who linger late over their 30
    wine,
those who are always trying some
    new spiced liquor.
Do not gulp down the wine, the 31
    strong red wine,
when the droplets form on the side
    of the cup;[g]
in the end it will bite like a snake 32
and sting like a cobra.
Then your eyes see strange sights, 33
your wits and your speech are con-
    fused;
you become like a man tossing out 34
    at sea,
like one who clings to[h] the top of
    the rigging;
you say, 'If it lays me flat, what do 35
    I care?
If it brings me to the ground, what
    of it?
As soon as I wake up,
I shall turn to it again.'

Do not emulate wicked men   **24**
or long to make friends with them;
for violence is all they think of,   2
and all they say means mischief.

Wisdom builds the house,   3
good judgement makes it secure,
knowledge furnishes the rooms   4
with all the precious and pleasant
    things that wealth can buy.

Wisdom prevails over strength,   5
knowledge over brute force;
for wars are won by skilful strategy, 6
and victory is the fruit of long plan-
    ning.

Wisdom is too high for a fool;   7
he dare not open his mouth in court.

A man who is bent on mischief   8
gets a name for intrigue;
the intrigues of foolish men misfire, 9
and the insolent man is odious to
    his fellows.

If your strength fails on a lucky[i] 10
    day,

g Prob. rdg.; Heb. adds it runs smoothly to and fro.
i lucky: prob. rdg.; Heb. om.

h clings to: prob. rdg.; Heb. lies on.

how helpless will you be on a day of disaster!

11 When you see a man being dragged
    to be killed, go to his rescue,
    and save those being hurried away
    to their death.
12 If you say, 'But I do not know this
    man',
    God, who fixes a standard for the
    heart, will take note.
    God who watches you—be sure he
    will know;
    he will requite every man for what
    he does.

13 Eat honey, my son, for it is good,
    and the honeycomb so sweet upon
    the tongue.
14 Make wisdom too your own;
    if you find it, you may look forward
    to the future,
    and your thread of life will not be
    cut short.

15 Do not lie in wait like a felon at the
    good man's house,
    or raid his farm.
16 Though the good man may fall
    seven times, he is soon up again,
    but the rascal is brought down by
    misfortune.
17 Do not rejoice when your enemy
    falls,
    do not gloat when he is brought
    down;
18 or the LORD will see and be dis-
    pleased with you,
    and he will cease to be angry with
    him.

19 Do not vie with evildoers
    or emulate the wicked;
20 for wicked men have no future to
    look forward to;
    their embers will be put out.

21 My son, fear the LORD and grow
    rich,
    but have nothing to do with men
    of rank,
22 they will bring about disaster with-
    out warning;
    who knows what ruin such men
    may cause[j]?

23 More sayings of wise men:

    Partiality in dispensing justice is
    not good.
24 A judge who pronounces a guilty
    man innocent
    is cursed by all nations, all peoples
    execrate him;

but for those who convict the 25
guilty all will go well,
they will be blessed with prosperity.
A straightforward answer 26
is as good as a kiss of friendship.

First put all in order out of doors 27
and make everything ready on the
land;
then establish your house and home.

Do not be a witness against your 28
neighbour without good reason
nor misrepresent him in your evidence.
Do not say, 29
'I will do to him what he has done
to me;
I will requite him for what he has
done.'

I passed by the field of an idle man, 30
by the vineyard of a man with no
sense.
I looked, and it was all dried up, 31
it was overgrown with thistles
and covered with weeds,
and the stones of its walls had been
torn down.
I saw and I took good note, 32
I considered and learnt the lesson:
a little sleep, a little slumber, 33
a little folding of the hands in rest,
and poverty will come upon you 34
like a robber,
want like a ruffian.

Proverbs transcribed under Hezekiah

More proverbs of Solomon transcribed 25
by the men of Hezekiah king of Judah:

The glory of God is to keep things 2
hidden
but the glory of kings is to fathom
them.
The heavens for height, the earth[k] 3
for depth:
unfathomable is the heart of a king.
Rid silver of its impurities, 4
then it may go to[l] the silversmith;
rid the king's presence of wicked 5
men,
and his throne will rest firmly on
righteousness.
Do not put yourself forward in the 6
king's presence
or take your place among the great;
for it is better that he should say 7
to you, 'Come up here',
than move you down to make room
for a nobleman.

---

j they ... cause: *or* they will come to sudden disaster; who knows what the ruin of such men will be. *k* Or the underworld. *l* then it may go to: *or* and it will come out bright for.

8 Be in no hurry to tell everyone
    what you have seen,
  or it will end in bitter reproaches
    from your friend.
9 Argue your own case with your
    neighbour,
  but do not reveal another man's
    secrets,
10 or he will reproach you when he
    hears of it
  and your indiscretion will then be
    beyond recall.
11 Like apples of gold set in silver
    filigree
  is a word spoken in season.
12 Like a golden earring or a necklace
    of Nubian gold
  is a wise man whose reproof finds
    attentive ears.
13 Like the coolness of snow in har-
    vest
  is a trusty messenger to those who
    send him.[m]
14 Like clouds and wind that bring no
    rain
  is the man who boasts of gifts he
    never gives.
15 A prince may be persuaded by
    patience,
  and a soft tongue may break down
    solid bone.[n]
16 If you find honey, eat only what
    you need,
  too much of it will make you sick;
17 be sparing in visits to your neigh-
    bour's house,
  if he sees too much of you, he will
    dislike you.
18 Like a club or a sword or a sharp
    arrow
  is a false witness who denounces
    his friend.
19 Like a tooth decayed or a foot
    limping
  is a traitor relied on in the day of
    trouble.
20 Like one who dresses[o] a wound with
    vinegar,
  so is the sweetest of singers to the
    heavy-hearted.
21 If your enemy is hungry, give him
    bread to eat;
  if he is thirsty, give him water to
    drink;
22 so you will heap glowing coals on
    his head,
  and the LORD will reward you.
23 As the north wind holds back the
    rain,
  so an angry glance holds back
    slander.

24 Better to live in a corner of the
    house-top
  than have a nagging wife and a
    brawling household.
25 Like cold water to the throat when
    it is dry
  is good news from a distant land.
26 Like a muddied spring or a tainted
    well
  is a righteous man who gives way
    to a wicked one.
27 A surfeit of honey is bad for a man,
  and the quest for honour is burden-
    some.
28 Like a city that has burst out of its
    confining walls[p]
  is a man who cannot control his
    temper.

26 Like snow in summer or rain at
    harvest,
  honour is unseasonable in a stupid
    man.
2 Like a fluttering sparrow or a
    darting swallow,
  groundless abuse gets nowhere.
3 The whip for a horse, the bridle for
    an ass,
  the rod for the back of a fool!
4 Do not answer a stupid man in the
    language of his folly,
  or you will grow like him;
5 answer a stupid man as his folly
    deserves,
  or he will think himself a wise man.
6 He who sends a fool on an errand
  cuts his own leg off and displays the
    stump.
7 A proverb in the mouth of stupid
    men
  dangles helpless as a lame man's
    legs.
8 Like one who gets the stone caught
    in his sling
  is he who bestows honour on a fool.
9 Like a thorn that pierces a drunk-
    ard's hand
  is a proverb in a stupid man's
    mouth.
10 Like an archer who shoots at any
    passer-by[q]
  is one who hires a stupid man or a
    drunkard.
11 Like a dog returning to its vomit
  is a stupid man who repeats his
    folly.
12 Do you see that man who thinks
    himself so wise?
  There is more hope for a fool than
    for him.

m Prob. rdg.; Heb. adds refreshing his master.   n solid bone: or authority.   o Prob. rdg.; Heb.
adds a garment on a cold day.   p Or that is breached and left unwalled.   q passer-by: transposed from end of verse.

13 The sluggard protests, 'There is a lion[r] in the highway,
a lion at large in the streets.'

14 A door turns on its hinges,
a sluggard on his bed.

15 A sluggard plunges his hand in the dish
but is too lazy to lift it to his mouth.

16 A sluggard is wiser in his own eyes than seven men who answer sensibly.

17 Like a man who seizes a passing cur by the ears
is he who meddles in another's quarrel.

19[s] A man who deceives another
and then says, 'It was only a joke',

18 is like a madman shooting at random
his deadly darts and arrows.

20 For lack of fuel a fire dies down
and for want of a tale-bearer a quarrel subsides.

21 Like bellows for the coal and fuel for the fire
is a quarrelsome man for kindling strife.

22 A gossip's whispers are savoury morsels
gulped down into the inner man.

23 Glib speech that covers a spiteful heart
is like glaze spread on earthenware.

24 With his lips an enemy may speak you fair
but inwardly he harbours deceit;

25 when his words are gracious, do not trust him,
for seven abominations fill his heart;

26 he may cloak his enmity in dissimulation,
but his wickedness is shown up before the assembly.

27 If he digs a pit, he will fall into it;
if he rolls a stone, it will roll back upon him.

28 A lying tongue makes innocence seem guilty,
and smooth words conceal their sting.

27 Do not flatter yourself about to-morrow,
for you never know what a day will bring forth.

2 Let flattery come from a stranger, not from yourself,
from the lips of an outsider and not from your own.

Stone is a burden and sand a dead 3 weight,
but to be vexed by a fool is more burdensome than either.

Wrath is cruel and anger is a 4 deluge;
but who can stand up to jealousy?

Open reproof is better 5
than love concealed.

The blows a friend gives are well 6 meant,
but the kisses of an enemy are perfidious.

A man well-fed refuses honey, 7
but even bitter food tastes sweet to a hungry man.

Like a bird that strays far from its 8 nest
is a man far from his home.

Oil and perfume bring joy to the 9 heart,
but cares torment a man's very soul.

Do not neglect your own friend or 10 your father's;[t]
a neighbour at hand is better than a brother far away.

Be wise, my son, then you will 11 bring joy to my heart,
and I shall be able to forestall my critics.

A shrewd man sees trouble coming 12 and lies low;
the simple walk into it and pay the penalty.

Take a man's garment when he 13 pledges his word for a stranger
and hold that as a pledge for the unknown person.

If one man greets another too 14 heartily,
he may give great offence.

Endless dripping on a rainy day— 15
that is what a nagging wife is like.

As well try to control the wind as to 16 control her!
As well try to pick up oil in one's fingers!

As iron sharpens iron, 17
so one man sharpens the wits of another.

He who guards the fig-tree will eat 18 its fruit,
and he who watches his master's interests will come to honour.

As face answers face reflected in the 19 water,
so one man's heart answers another's.

Sheol and Abaddon are insatiable; 20
a man's eyes too are never satisfied.

The melting-pot is for silver and 21 the crucible for gold,
but praise is the test of character.

---

r Or snake.   s Verses 18 and 19 transposed.
t Prob. rdg.; Heb. adds or how should you enter
your brother's house in the day of your ruin?

22 Pound a fool with pestle and mortar,[u]
    his folly will never be knocked out
    of him.

23 Be careful to know your own sheep
    and take good care of your flocks;
24 for possessions do not last for ever,
    nor will a crown endure to endless
    generations.
25 The grass disappears, new shoots
    are seen
    and the green growth on the hills is
    gathered in;
26 the lambs clothe you,
    the he-goats are worth the price of
    a field,
27 while the goats' milk is enough for
    your food
    and nourishment for your maidens.

28 The wicked man runs away with no
    one in pursuit,
    but the righteous is like a young
    lion in repose.
2   It is the fault of a violent man that
    quarrels start,
    but they are settled by a man of
    discernment.
3   A tyrant oppressing the poor
    is like driving rain which ruins the
    crop.
4   The lawless praise wicked men;
    the law-abiding contend with them.
5   Bad men do not know what justice
    is,
    but those who seek the LORD know
    everything good.
6   Better be poor and above reproach
    than rich and crooked.
7   A discerning son observes the law,
    but one who keeps riotous company
    wounds his father.
8   He who grows rich by lending at
    discount or at interest
    is saving for another who will be
    generous to the poor.
9   If a man turns a deaf ear to the law,
    even his prayers are an abomina-
    tion.
10 He who tempts the upright into
    evil courses
    will himself fall into the pit he has
    dug.
    The honest shall inherit a fortune,
    but the wicked shall inherit nothing.
11 The rich man may think himself
    wise,
    but a poor man of discernment sees
    through him.
12 When the just are in power, there
    are great celebrations,[v]

but when the wicked come to the
top, others are downtrodden.
Conceal your faults, and you will 13
not prosper;
confess and give them up, and you
will find mercy.
Happy the man who is scrupulous 14
in conduct,
but he who hardens his heart falls
into misfortune.
Like a starving lion or a thirsty 15
bear
is a wicked man ruling a helpless
people.
The man who is stupid and grasping 16
will perish,
but he who hates ill-gotten gain will
live long.
A man charged with bloodshed   17
will jump into a well to escape
arrest.
Whoever leads an honest life will be 18
safe,
but a rogue will fail, one way or
another.
One who cultivates his land has 19
plenty to eat;
idle pursuits lead to poverty.
A man of steady character will 20
enjoy many blessings,
but one in a hurry to grow rich will
not go unpunished.
To show favour is not good;   21
but men will do wrong for a mere
crust of bread.
The miser[w] is in a hurry to grow rich, 22
never dreaming that want will overtake him.
Take a man to task and in the end 23
win more thanks
than the man with a flattering
tongue.
To rob your father or mother and 24
say you do no wrong
is no better than wanton destruction.
A self-important[x] man provokes 25
quarrels,
but he who trusts in the LORD
grows fat and prosperous.
It is plain stupidity to trust in one's 26
own wits,
but he who walks the path of
wisdom will come safely through.
He who gives to the poor will never 27
want,
but he who turns a blind eye gets
nothing but curses.
When the wicked come to the top, 28
others are pulled down;[y]
but, when they perish, the righteous come into power.

u *Prob. rdg.; Heb. adds* with groats.   v *Or* there is great pageantry.   w *Or* The man with the
evil eye.   x *Or* grasping.   y *are pulled down: or* hide themselves.

29 A man who is still stubborn after much reproof
will suddenly be broken past mending.

2 When the righteous are in power the people rejoice,
but they groan when the wicked hold office.

3 A lover of wisdom brings joy to his father,
but one who keeps company with harlots squanders his wealth.

4 By just government a king gives his country stability,
but by forced contributions he reduces it to ruin.

5 A man who flatters his neighbour is spreading a net for his feet.

6 An evil man is ensnared by his sin,[z]
but a righteous man lives and flourishes.

7 The righteous man is concerned for the cause of the helpless,
but the wicked understand no such concern.

8 Arrogance can inflame a city,
but wisdom averts the people's anger.

9 If a wise man goes to law with a fool,
he will meet abuse or derision, but get no remedy.

10 Men who have tasted blood hate an honest man,
but the upright set much store by his life.

11 A stupid man gives free rein to his anger;
a wise man waits and lets it grow cool.

12 If a prince listens to falsehood,
all his servants will be wicked.

13 Poor man and oppressor have this in common:
what happiness each has comes from the LORD.

14 A king who steadfastly deals out justice to the weak
will be secure for ever on his throne.

15 Rod and reprimand impart wisdom,
but a boy who runs wild brings shame on his mother.

16 When the wicked are in power, sin is in power,
but the righteous will gloat over their downfall.

17 Correct your son, and he will be a comfort to you
and bring you delights of every kind.

18 Where there is no one in authority,[a] the people break loose,
but a guardian of the law keeps them on the straight path.

19 Mere words will not keep a slave in order;
he may understand, but he will not respond.

20 When you see someone over-eager to speak,[b]
there will be more hope for a fool than for him.

21 Pamper a slave from boyhood,
and in the end he will prove ungrateful.

22 A man prone to anger provokes a quarrel
and a hot-head is always doing wrong.

23 Pride will bring a man low;
a man lowly in spirit wins honour.

24 He who goes shares with a thief is his own enemy:
he hears himself put on oath and dare not give evidence.

25 A man's fears will prove a snare to him,
but he who trusts in the LORD has a high tower of refuge.

26 Many seek audience of a prince,
but in every case the LORD decides.

27 The righteous cannot abide an unjust man,
nor the wicked a man whose conduct is upright.

Sayings of Agur

Sayings of Agur son of Jakeh from **30** Massa:[c]

This is the great man's very word:
I am weary, O God,
I am weary and worn out;
2 I am a dumb brute, scarcely a man, without a man's powers of understanding;
3 I have not learnt wisdom
nor have I received knowledge from the Holy One.
4 Who has ever gone up to heaven and come down again?
Who has cupped the wind in the hollow of his hands?
Who has bound up the waters in the fold of his garment?
Who has fixed the boundaries of the earth?
What is his name or his son's name, if you know it?

5 God's every promise has stood the test:
he is a shield to all who seek refuge with him.

z *An evil . . . sin: or* When an evil man steps out a trap awaits him.　　*a Or* no vision.　　*b Or* someone hasty in business.　　*c* from Massa: *prob. rdg. (cp. 31. 1);* Heb. the oracle.

6 Add nothing to his words,
or he will expose you for a liar.
7 Two things I ask of thee;
do not withhold them from me
before I die.
8 Put fraud and lying far from me;
give me neither poverty nor wealth,
provide me only with the food I
need.
9 If I have too much, I shall deny
thee
and say, 'Who is the LORD?'
If I am reduced to poverty, I shall
steal
and blacken the name of my God.

10 Never disparage a slave to his
master,
or he will speak ill of you, and you
will pay for it.

11 There is a sort of people who defame their fathers
and do not speak well of their own
mothers;
12 a sort who are pure in their own
eyes
and yet are not cleansed of their
filth;
13 a sort—how haughty are their looks,
how disdainful their glances!
14 A sort whose teeth are swords,
their jaws are set with knives,
they eat the wretched out of the
country
and the needy out of house and
home.*d*

15 The leech has two daughters;
'Give', says one, and 'Give', says
the other.

Three things there are which will
never be satisfied,
four which never say, 'Enough!'
16 The grave and a barren womb,*e*
a land thirsty for water
and fire that never says, 'Enough!'

17 The eye that mocks a father or
scorns a mother's old age*f*
will be plucked out by magpies
or eaten by the vulture's young.

18 Three things there are which are too
wonderful for me,
four which I do not understand:
19 the way of a vulture in the sky,
the way of a serpent on the rock,
the way of a ship out at sea,
and the way of a man with a girl.

The way of an unfaithful wife is this: 20
she eats, then she wipes her mouth
and says, 'I have done no harm.'

At three things the earth shakes,   21
four things it cannot bear:
a slave turned king,   22
a churl gorging himself,
a woman unloved when she is 23
married,
and a slave-girl displacing her
mistress.

Four things there are which are 24
smallest on earth
yet wise beyond the wisest:
ants, a people with no strength,   25
yet they prepare their store of food
in the summer;
rock-badgers, a feeble folk,   26
yet they make their home among the
rocks;
locusts, which have no king,   27
yet they all sally forth in detach-
ments;
the lizard, which can be grasped in 28
the hand,
yet is found in the palaces of kings.

Three things there are which are 29
stately in their stride,
four which are stately as they move:
the lion, a hero among beasts,   30
which will not turn tail for anyone;
the strutting cock and the he-goat; 31
and a king going forth to lead his
army.*g*

If you are churlish and arrogant   32
and fond of filthy talk, hold your
tongue;
for wringing out the milk produces 33
curd
and wringing the nose produces
blood,
so provocation leads to strife.

Sayings of Lemuel

Sayings of Lemuel king of Massa, 31
which his mother taught him:

What, O my son, what shall I say 2
to you,
you, the child of my womb and
answer to my prayers?
Do not give the vigour of your man- 3
hood to women
nor consort with those who make
eyes at*h* kings.
It is not for kings, O Lemuel, not 4
for kings to drink wine

d house and home: *prob. rdg.; Heb.* man.   *e* Or a woman's desire.   *f* old age: *prob. rdg.; Heb.*
unintelligible.   *g* going forth to lead his army: *prob. rdg.; Heb. unintelligible.*   *h* who make
eyes at: *prob. rdg.; Heb. unintelligible.*

nor for princes to crave strong drink;

5 if they drink, they will forget rights and customs
and twist the law against their wretched victims.

6 Give strong drink to the desperate and wine to the embittered;

7 such men will drink and forget their poverty
and remember their trouble no longer.

8 Open your mouth and speak up for the dumb,
against the suit of any that oppose them;

9 open your mouth and pronounce just sentence
and give judgement for the wretched and the poor.

A capable wife

10 Who can find a capable wife?
Her worth is far beyond coral.

11 Her husband's whole trust is in her, and children are not lacking.

12 She repays him with good, not evil, all her life long.

13 She chooses wool and flax and toils at her work.

14 Like a ship laden with merchandise, she brings home food from far off.

15 She rises while it is still night and sets meat before her household.[i]

16 After careful thought she buys a field
and plants a vineyard out of her earnings.

17 She sets about her duties with vigour
and braces herself for the work.

18 She sees that her business goes well, and never puts out her lamp at night.

19 She holds the distaff in her hand, and her fingers grasp the spindle.

20 She is open-handed to the wretched and generous to the poor.

21 She has no fear for her household when it snows,
for they are wrapped in two cloaks.

22 She makes her own coverings,
and clothing of fine linen and purple.

23 Her husband is well known in the city gate
when he takes his seat with the elders of the land.

24 She weaves linen and sells it,
and supplies merchants with their sashes.

25 She is clothed in dignity and power
and can afford to laugh at tomorrow.

26 When she opens her mouth, it is to speak wisely,
and loyalty is the theme of her teaching.

27 She keeps her eye on the doings of her household
and does not eat the bread of idleness.

28 Her sons with one accord call her happy;
her husband too, and he sings her praises:

29 'Many a woman shows how capable she is;[j]
but you excel them all.'

30 Charm is a delusion and beauty fleeting;
it is the God-fearing woman who is honoured.

31 Extol her for the fruit of all her toil,
and let her labours bring her honour in the city gate.

i Prob. rdg.; Heb. adds and a prescribed portion for her maidens.   *j Or Many daughters show how capable they are.*

ECCLESIASTES

Preface

1 THE WORDS of the speaker, the son of David, king in Jerusalem.

2 Emptiness, emptiness, says the Speaker, emptiness, all is empty.

3 What does man gain from all his labour and his toil here under the sun? Generations come and generations go, while the earth endures for ever. 4

5 The sun rises and the sun goes down; back it returns to its place[a] and rises there again. The wind blows south, 6 the wind blows north, round and round it goes and returns full circle.

a back . . . place: prob. rdg.; Heb. to its place panting.

7 All streams run into the sea, yet the sea never overflows; back to the place from which the streams ran they return to run again.

8 All things are wearisome;[b] no man can speak of them all. Is not the eye surfeited with seeing, and the ear

9 sated with hearing? What has happened will happen again, and what has been done will be done again, and there is nothing new under the sun.

10 Is there anything of which one can say, 'Look, this is new'? No, it has already existed, long ago before our

11 time. The men of old are not remembered, and those who follow will not be remembered by those who follow them.

12 I, the Speaker, ruled as king over

13 Israel in Jerusalem; and in wisdom I applied my mind to study and explore all that is done under heaven. It is a sorry business that God has given

14 men to busy themselves with. I have seen all the deeds that are done here under the sun; they are all empti-

15 ness and chasing the wind. What is crooked cannot become straight; what is not there cannot be counted.

16 I said to myself, 'I have amassed great wisdom, more than all my predecessors on the throne in Jerusalem; I have become familiar with wisdom and

17 knowledge.' So I applied my mind to understand wisdom and knowledge, madness and folly, and I came to see

18 that this too is chasing the wind. For in much wisdom is much vexation, and the more a man knows, the more he has to suffer.

The emptiness of pleasures

2 I said to myself, 'Come, I will plunge into pleasures and enjoy myself'; but

2 this too was emptiness. Of laughter I said, 'It is madness!' And of pleasure,

3 'What is the good of that?' So I sought to stimulate myself with wine, in the hope of finding out what was good for men to do under heaven throughout the brief span of their lives. But my mind was guided by wisdom, not blinded by[c] folly.

The emptiness of amassing wealth

4 I undertook great works; I built my-

5 self houses and planted vineyards; made myself gardens and parks and planted all kinds of fruit-trees in them;

6 I made myself pools of water to irri-

gate a grove of growing trees; I 7 bought slaves, male and female, and I had my home-born slaves as well; I had possessions, more cattle and flocks than any of my predecessors in Jerusalem; I amassed silver and 8 gold also, the treasure of kings and provinces; I acquired singers, men and women, and all that man delights in.[d] I was great, greater than all my 9 predecessors in Jerusalem; and my wisdom stood me in good stead. Whatever my eyes coveted, I refused 10 them nothing, nor did I deny myself any pleasure. Yes indeed, I got pleasure from all my labour, and for all my labour this was my reward. Then 11 I turned and reviewed all my handiwork, all my labour and toil, and I saw that everything was emptiness and chasing the wind, of no profit under the sun.

The emptiness of both wisdom and folly

I set myself to look at wisdom and at 12 madness and folly.[e] Then I perceived 13 that wisdom is more profitable than folly, as light is more profitable than darkness: the wise man has eyes in 14 his head, but the fool walks in the dark. Yet I saw also that one and the same fate overtakes them both. So I 15 said to myself, 'I too shall suffer the fate of the fool. To what purpose have I been wise? What[f] is the profit of it? Even this', I said to myself, 'is emptiness. The wise man is remembered 16 no longer than the fool, for, as the passing days multiply,[g] all will be forgotten. Alas, wise man and fool die the same death!' So I came to hate 17 life, since everything that was done here under the sun was a trouble to me; for all is emptiness and chasing the wind. So I came to hate all my 18 labour and toil here under the sun, since I should have to leave its fruits to my successor. What sort of a man will he be who succeeds me, who inherits what others have acquired?[h] Who knows whether he will be a wise 19 man or a fool? Yet he will be master of all the fruits of my labour and skill here under the sun. This too is emptiness.

Despair

Then I turned and gave myself up to 20 despair, reflecting upon all my labour and toil here under the sun. For anyone 21

---

b Prob. rdg.; Heb. weary.   c not blinded by: prob. rdg.; Heb. to grasp.   d Prob. rdg.; Heb. adds two unintelligible words.   e The rest of verse 12 transposed to follow verse 18.   f Prob. rdg.; Heb. Then.   g for . . . multiply: prob. rdg.; Heb. because already.   h What sort . . . acquired: see note on verse 12.

who toils with wisdom, knowledge, and skill must leave it all to a man who has spent no labour on it. This too is emptiness and utterly wrong. 22 What reward has a man for all his labour, his scheming, and his toil here 23 under the sun? All his life long his business is pain and vexation to him; even at night his mind knows no rest. 24 This too is emptiness. There is nothing better for a man to do than to eat and drink and enjoy himself in return for his labours. And yet I saw that this comes from the hand of God. 25 For without him who can enjoy his 26 food, or who can be anxious? God gives wisdom and knowledge and joy to the man who pleases him, while to the sinner is given the trouble of gathering and amassing wealth only to hand it over to someone else who pleases God. This too is emptiness and chasing the wind.

A time for everything

3 For everything its season, and for every activity under heaven its time:

2 a time to be born and a time to die;
a time to plant and a time to uproot;
3 a time to kill and a time to heal;
a time to pull down and a time to build up;
4 a time to weep and a time to laugh;
a time for mourning and a time for dancing;
5 a time to scatter stones and a time to gather them;
a time to embrace and a time to refrain from embracing;
6 a time to seek and a time to lose;
a time to keep and a time to throw away;
7 a time to tear and a time to mend;
a time for silence and a time for speech;
8 a time to love and a time to hate;
a time for war and a time for peace.

9 What profit does one who works get 10 from all his labour? I have seen the business that God has given men to 11 keep them busy. He has made everything to suit its time; moreover he has given men a sense of time past and future, but no comprehension of God's 12 work from beginning to end. I know that there is nothing good for man[i] except to be happy and live the best 13 life he can while he is alive. Moreover, that a man should eat and drink and enjoy himself, in return for all his 14 labours, is a gift of God. I know that

whatever God does lasts for ever; to add to it or subtract from it is impossible. And he has done it all in such a way that men must feel awe in his presence. Whatever is has been 15 already,[j] and whatever is to come has been already, and God summons each event back in its turn.

Creatures of chance

Moreover I saw here under the sun 16 that, where justice ought to be, there was wickedness, and where righteousness ought to be, there was wickedness. I said to myself, 'God will judge 17 the just man and the wicked equally; every activity and[k] every purpose has its proper time.' I said to myself, 18 'In dealing with men it is God's purpose[l] to test them and to see what they truly are.[m] For man is a creature 19 of chance and the beasts are creatures of chance, and one mischance awaits them all: death comes to both alike. They all draw the same breath. Men have no advantage over beasts; for everything is emptiness. All go to the 20 same place: all came from the dust, and to the dust all return. Who knows 21 whether the spirit[n] of man goes upward or whether the spirit[n] of the beast goes downward to the earth?' So I saw that there is nothing better 22 than that a man should enjoy his work, since that is his lot. For who can bring him through to see what will happen next?

On injustice and on human achievement

Again, I considered all the acts of **4** oppression here under the sun; I saw the tears of the oppressed, and I saw that there was no one to comfort them. Strength was on the side of their oppressors, and there was no one to avenge them. I counted the 2 dead happy because they were dead, happier than the living who are still in life. More fortunate than either I 3 reckoned the man yet unborn, who had not witnessed the wicked deeds done here under the sun. I considered 4 all toil and all achievement and saw that it comes from rivalry between man and man. This too is emptiness and chasing the wind. The fool folds 5 his arms and wastes away. Better one 6 hand full and peace of mind, than both fists full and toil that is chasing the wind.

i for man: prob. rdg.[']* cp. 2. 24: Heb.* in them.   *j Or* Whatever has been already is.   *k Prob. rdg.; Heb.* and upon.   *l it is God's purpose: prob. rdg.; Heb.* obscure.   *m Prob. rdg.; Heb. adds* they to them.   *n Or* breath.

Rich but lonely

7 Here again, I saw emptiness under
8 the sun: a lonely man without a
friend, without son or brother, toiling
endlessly yet never satisfied with his
wealth—'For whom', he asks, 'am I
toiling and denying myself the good
things of life?' This too is emptiness,
9 a sorry business. Two are better than
one; they receive a good reward for
10 their toil, because, if one falls, the
other[o] can help his companion up
again; but alas for the man who falls
alone with no partner to help him up.
11 And, if two lie side by side, they keep
each other warm; but how can one
12 keep warm by himself? If a man is
alone, an assailant may overpower
him, but two can resist; and a cord
of three strands is not quickly snapped.

The emptiness of greatness

13 Better a young man poor and wise
than a king old and foolish who will
14 listen to advice no longer. A man who
leaves prison may well come to be
king, though born a pauper in his
15 future kingdom. But I have studied
all life here under the sun, and I saw
his place taken by yet another young
16 man, and no limit set to the number
of the subjects whose master he
became. And he in turn will be no hero
to those who come after him. This
too is emptiness and chasing the wind.

Reverence for God

5 Go carefully when you visit the house
of God. Better draw near in obedience
than offer the sacrifice of fools, who
2 sin without a thought. Do not rush
into speech, let there be no hasty utterance in God's presence. God is in
heaven, you are on earth; so let your
3 words be few. The sensible man has
much business in his hands; the fool
4 talks and it is so much chatter. When
you make a vow to God, do not be
slow to pay it, for he has no use for
5 fools; pay whatever you vow. Better
not vow at all than vow and fail to
6 pay. Do not let your tongue lead you
into sin, and then say before the
angel of God that it was a mistake; or
God will be angry at your words, and
all your achievements will be brought
7 to nothing.[p] You must fear God.

On injustice

If you witness in some province the 8
oppression of the poor and the denial
of right and justice, do not be surprised at what goes on, for every official has a higher one set over him, and
the highest[q] keeps watch over them
all. The best thing for a country is a 9
king whose[r] own lands are well tilled.

The problems wealth brings

The man who loves money can never 10
have enough, and the man who is in
love with great wealth enjoys no
return from it. This too is emptiness.
When riches multiply, so do those 11
who live off them; and what advantage has the owner, except to look at
them? Sweet is the sleep of the labour- 12
er whether he eats little or much; but
the rich man owns too much and cannot sleep. There is a singular evil here 13
under the sun which I have seen: a
man hoards wealth to his own hurt,
and then that wealth is lost through 14
an unlucky venture, and the owner's
son left with nothing. As he came 15
from the womb of mother earth, so
must he return, naked as he came; all
his toil produces nothing which he
can take away with him. This too 16
is a singular evil: exactly as he came,
so shall he go, and what profit does
he get when his labour is all for the
wind? What is more, all his days are 17
overshadowed; gnawing anxiety and
great vexation are his lot, sickness[s]
and resentment. What I have seen is 18
this: that it is good and proper for a
man to eat and drink and enjoy himself in return for his labours here under
the sun, throughout the brief span
of life which God has allotted him.
Moreover, it is a gift of God that every 19
man to whom he has granted wealth
and riches and the power to enjoy
them should accept his lot and rejoice
in his labour. He will not dwell over- 20
much upon the passing years; for God
fills his[t] time with joy of heart.
Here is an evil under the sun which 6
I have seen, and it weighs heavy upon
men. Consider the man to whom God 2
grants wealth, riches, and substance,[u]
and who lacks nothing that he has
set his heart on: if God has not given
him the power to enjoy these things,
but a stranger enjoys them instead,
that is emptiness and a grave disorder.

---

o if one falls, the other: *prob. rdg.*; *Heb. obscure.*
dreams and empty things and many words.
over him, the Highest . . .   r whose: *prob. rdg.*; *Heb. for.*
sickness.   t his: *prob. rdg.*; *Heb. om.*   u Or honour.

p *Prob. rdg.*; *Heb. adds* for in a multitude of
q for every . . . the highest: or though every . . .
s sickness: *prob. rdg.*; *Heb.* and his

3 A man may have a hundred children and live a long life; but however many his days may be, if he does not get satisfaction from the good things of life and in the end receives no burial, then I maintain that the still-born 4 child is in better case than he. Its coming is an empty thing, it departs into darkness, and in darkness its 5 name is hidden; it has never seen the sun or known anything, *v* yet its state 6 is better than his. What if a man should live a thousand years twice over, and never prosper? Do not both go to one place?

This brief span

7 The end of all man's toil is but to fill his belly, yet his appetite is never 8 satisfied. What advantage then in facing life has the wise man over the fool, or the poor man for all his 9 experience? It is better to be satisfied with what is before your eyes than give rein to desire; this too is empti-10 ness and chasing the wind. Whatever has already existed has been given a name, its nature is known; a man cannot contend with what is stronger 11 than he. The more words one uses the greater is the emptiness of it all; and 12 where is the advantage to a man? For who can know what is good for a man in this life, this brief span of empty existence through which he passes like a shadow? Who can tell a man what is to happen next here under the sun?

Wisdom and folly compared

7 A good name smells sweeter than the finest ointment, and the day of death 2 is better than the day of birth. Better to visit the house of mourning than the house of feasting; for to be mourned is the lot of every man, and the 3 living should take this to heart. Grief is better than laughter: a sad face 4 may go with a cheerful heart. Wise men's thoughts are at home in the house of mourning, but a fool's 5 thoughts in the house of mirth. It is better to listen to a wise man's rebuke 6 than to the praise of fools. For the laughter of a fool is like the crackling of thorns under a pot. This too is 7 emptiness. Slander drives a wise man crazy and breaks a strong man's*w* 8 spirit. Better the end of anything than its beginning; better patience 9 than pride. Do not be quick to show

resentment; for resentment is nursed by fools. Do not ask why the old days 10 were better than these; for that is a foolish question. Wisdom is better than 11 possessions and an advantage to all who see the sun. Better have wisdom 12 behind you than money; wisdom profits men by giving life to those who know her.

Consider God's handiwork; who 13 can straighten what he has made crooked? When things go well, be 14 glad; but when things go ill, consider this: God has set the one alongside the other in such a way that no one can find out what is to happen next.*x* In my empty existence I have seen it 15 all, from a righteous man perishing in his righteousness to a wicked man growing old in his wickedness. Do not 16 be over-righteous and do not be over-wise. Why make yourself a laughing-stock? Do not be over-wicked and do 17 not be a fool. Why should you die before your time? It is good to hold 18 on to the one thing and not lose hold of the other; for a man who fears God will succeed both ways. Wisdom 19 makes the wise man stronger than the ten rulers of a city. The world con-20 tains no man so righteous that he can do right always and never do wrong.*y* Moreover, do not pay attention to 21 everything men say, or you may hear your servant disparage you; for you 22 know very well how many times you yourself have disparaged others. All 23 this I have put to the test of wisdom. I said, 'I am resolved to be wise', but wisdom was beyond my grasp— whatever has happened lies beyond 24 our grasp, deep down, deeper than man can fathom.

I went on to reflect, I set my mind*z* 25 to inquire and search for wisdom and for the reason in things, only to dis-cover that it is folly to be wicked and madness to act like a fool. The wiles 26 of a woman I find mightier*a* than death; her heart is a trap to catch you and her arms are fetters. The man who is pleasing to God may escape her, but she will catch a sinner. 'See,' says 27 the Speaker, 'this is what I have found, reasoning things out one by one, after searching long without 28 success: I have found one man in a thousand worth the name, but I have not found one woman among them all. This alone I have found, that 29 God, when he made man, made him

---

v Or it.   w strong man's: prob. rdg.; Heb. obscure.   x find out . . . next: or hold him responsible.
y can do . . . wrong: or prospers without ever making a mistake.   z Prob. rdg.; Heb. adds to
know and.   a Or more bitter.

straightforward, but man invents endless subtleties of his own.'

The unknown future

8 Who is wise enough for all this? Who knows the meaning of anything? Wisdom lights up a man's face, but **2** grim looks make a man hated.[b] Do as the king commands you, and if you have to swear by God, do not be pre- **3** cipitate. Leave the king's presence and do not persist in a thing which displeases him; he does what he **4** chooses. For the king's word carries authority. Who can question what he **5** does? Whoever obeys a command will come to no harm. A wise man knows in his heart the right time and **6** method for action. There is a time and a method for every enterprise, although **7** man is greatly troubled by ignorance of the future; who can tell him what **8** it will bring? It is not in man's power to restrain the wind,[c] and no one has power over the day of death. In war no one can lay aside his arms, no **9** wealth will save its possessor. All this I have seen, having applied my mind to everything done under the sun. There was a time when one man had power over another and could make **10** him suffer. It was then that I saw wicked men approaching and even entering[d] the holy place; and they went about the city priding themselves on having done right. This too **11** is emptiness. It is because sentence upon a wicked act is not promptly carried out that men do evil so boldly. **12** A sinner may do wrong[e] and live to old age, yet I know that it will be well with those who fear God: their fear **13** of him ensures this, but it will not be well with a wicked man nor will he live long; the man who does not fear **14** God is a mere shadow. There is an empty thing found on earth: when the just man gets what is due to the unjust, and the unjust what is due to the just. I maintain that this too is **15** emptiness. So I commend enjoyment, since there is nothing good for a man to do here under the sun but to eat and drink and enjoy himself; this is all that will remain with him to reward his toil throughout the span of life which God grants him here under the **16** sun. I applied my mind to acquire wisdom and to observe the business which goes on upon earth, when man never closes an eye in sleep day or

night; and always I perceived that **17** God has so ordered it that man should not be able to discover what is happening here under the sun. However hard a man may try, he will not find out; the wise man may think that he knows, but he will be unable to find the truth of it.

Good man and sinner fare alike

I applied my mind to all this, and I **9** understood that the righteous and the wise and all their doings are under God's control; but is it love or hatred? No man knows. Everything that con- **2** fronts him, everything is empty, since one and the same fate befalls every one, just and unjust alike, good and bad, clean and unclean, the man who offers sacrifice and the man who does not. Good man and sinner fare alike, the man who can take an oath and the man who dares not. This is what is **3** wrong in all that is done here under the sun: that one and the same fate befalls every man. The hearts of men are full of evil; madness fills their hearts all through their lives, and after that they go down to join the dead. But for a man who is counted among **4** the living there is still hope: remember, a live dog is better than a dead lion. True, the living know that they will **5** die; but the dead know nothing. There are no more rewards for them; they are utterly forgotten. For them **6** love, hate, ambition,[f] all are now over. Never again will they have any part in what is done here under the sun.

Time and chance govern all

Go to it then, eat your food and enjoy **7** it, and drink your wine with a cheerful heart; for already God has accepted what you have done. Always be **8** dressed in white and never fail to anoint your head. Enjoy life with a **9** woman you love all the days of your allotted span here under the sun, empty as they are;[g] for that is your lot while you live and labour here under the sun. Whatever task lies to **10** your hand, do it with all your might; because in Sheol, for which you are bound, there is neither doing nor thinking, neither understanding nor wisdom. One more thing I have **11** observed here under the sun: speed does not win the race nor strength the battle. Bread does not belong to

---

b make . . . hated: *prob. rdg.; Heb. obscure.*   c Or *to retain the breath of life.*   d *approaching* . . . *entering: prob. rdg.; Heb. obscure.*   e *Prob. rdg.; Heb. adds an unintelligible word.*   f *Or* passion.   g *Prob. rdg.; Heb. adds* all your days, empty as they are.

the wise, nor wealth to the intelligent, nor success to the skilful; time and 12 chance govern all. Moreover, no man knows when his hour will come; like fish caught in a net, like a bird taken in a snare, so men are trapped when bad times come suddenly.

Wisdom better than strength

13 This too is an example of wisdom as I have observed it here under the sun, 14 and notable I find it. There was a small town with few inhabitants, and a great king came to attack it; he besieged it and constructed great 15 siege-works against it. There was in it a poor wise man, and he alone might have saved the town by his wisdom, but no one remembered that poor 16 wise man. 'Surely', I said to myself, 'wisdom is better than strength.' But the poor man's wisdom was despised, 17 and his words went unheeded. A wise man who speaks his mind calmly is more to be heeded than a commander 18 shouting orders among fools. Wisdom is better than weapons of war, and one mistake can undo many things done well.

On rulers and subjects

10 Dead flies make the perfumer's sweet ointment turn rancid and ferment; so can a little folly make wisdom lose its 2 worth. The mind of the wise man faces right, but the mind of the fool faces 3 left. Even when he walks along the road, the fool shows no sense and calls 4 everyone else[h] a fool. If your ruler breaks out in anger against you, do not resign your post; submission makes amends for great mistakes. 5 There is an evil that I have observed here under the sun, an error for which 6 a ruler is responsible: the fool given high office, but[i] the great and the rich 7 in humble posts. I have seen slaves on horseback and men of high rank going 8 on foot like slaves. The man who digs a pit may fall into it, and he who pulls down a wall may be bitten by a snake. 9 The man who quarries stones may strain himself, and the woodcutter 10 runs a risk of injury. When the axe is blunt and has not first[j] been sharpened, then one must use more force; the wise man has a better chance of suc- 11 cess. If a snake bites before it is charmed, the snake-charmer loses his fee.

12 A wise man's words win him favour, 13 but a fool's tongue is his undoing. He begins by talking nonsense and ends in mischief run mad. The fool talks on 14 and on; but no man knows what is coming, and who can tell him what will come after that? The fool wearies 15 himself to death[k] with all his labour, for he does not know the way to town.

Woe betide the land when a slave 16 has become its king, and its princes feast in the morning. Happy the land 17 when its king is nobly born, and its princes feast at the right time of day, with self-control, and not as drunkards. If the owner is negligent the rafters 18 collapse, and if he is idle the house crumbles away. The table has its plea- 19 sures, and wine makes a cheerful life; and money is behind it all. Do not speak 20 ill of the king in your ease, or of a rich man in your bedroom; for a bird may carry your voice, and a winged messenger may repeat what you say.

Actions, not speculation

Send your grain across the seas, and in **11** time you will get a return. Divide 2 your merchandise among seven ven- tures, eight maybe, since you do not know what disasters may occur on earth.[l] If the clouds are heavy with 3 rain, they will discharge it on the earth; whether a tree falls south or north, it must lie as it falls. He who 4 watches the wind will never sow, and he who keeps an eye on the clouds will never reap. You do not know how a 5 pregnant woman comes to have a body and a living spirit in her womb; nor do you know how God, the maker of all things, works. In the morning 6 sow your seed betimes, and do not stop work until evening, for you do not know whether this or that sowing will be successful, or whether both alike will do well.

Advice to a young man

The light of day is sweet, and pleasant 7 to the eye is the sight of the sun; if a 8 man lives for many years, he should rejoice in all of them. But let him remember that the days of darkness will be many. Everything that is to come will be emptiness. Delight in 9 your boyhood, young man, make the most of the days of your youth; let your heart and your eyes show you the way; but remember that for all these things God will call you to account. Banish discontent from 10 your mind, and shake off the troubles

---

h calls everyone else: *or* tells everyone he is.   *i* but: *prob. rdg.*; *Heb. om.*   *j* first: *prob. rdg.*;
Heb. face.   *k* fool . . . death: *prob. rdg.*; *Heb. obscure.*   *l* Or on land.

of the body; boyhood and the prime of life are mere emptiness.

12 Remember your Creator in the days of your youth, before the time of trouble comes and the years draw near when you will say, 'I see no pur-

2 pose in them.'[m] Remember him before the sun and the light of day give place to darkness, before the moon and the stars grow dim, and the

3 clouds return with the rain—when the guardians of the house tremble, and the strong men stoop, when the women grinding the meal cease work because they are few, and those who look through the windows look no

4 longer, when the street-doors are shut, when the noise of the mill is low, when the chirping of the sparrow grows faint[n] and the song-birds fall

5 silent;[o] when men are afraid of a steep place and the street is full of terrors, when the blossom whitens on the almond-tree and the locust's paunch is swollen and caper-buds have no more zest. For man goes to his everlasting home, and the mour-

6 ners go about the streets. Remember him before the silver cord is snapped[p]

and the golden bowl is broken, before the pitcher is shattered at the spring and the wheel broken at the well, before the dust returns to the earth 7 as it began and the spirit[q] returns to God who gave it. Emptiness, empti- 8 ness, says the Speaker, all is empty.

Conclusion

So the Speaker, in his wisdom, con- 9 tinued to teach the people what he knew. He turned over many maxims in his mind and sought how best to set them out. He chose his words to give 10 pleasure, but what he wrote was the honest truth. The sayings of the wise 11 are sharp as goads, like nails driven home; they lead the assembled people, for they come from one shepherd. One 12 further warning, my son: the use of books is endless, and much study is wearisome.

This is the end of the matter: you 13 have heard it all. Fear God and obey his commands; there is no more to man than this. For God brings every- 14 thing we do to judgement, and every secret, whether good or bad.

m *Or* I have no pleasure in them.   n *grows faint:* prob. rdg.; Heb. obscure.   o *Prob. rdg.; Heb.* sink low.   p *is snapped:* prob. rdg.; Heb. unintelligible.   q *Or* breath.

THE SONG OF SONGS

Bride[a]

1 I will sing the song of all songs to Solomon

2 that he may[b] smother me with kisses.

Your love is more fragrant than wine,
3 fragrant is[c] the scent of your perfume,
and your name like perfume poured
out;[d]
for this the maidens love you.
4 Take me with you, and we will run
together;
bring me into your chamber, O king.

Companions

Let us rejoice and be glad for you;
let us praise your love more than
wine,

and your caresses more than any
song.

Bride

I am dark but lovely, daughters of 5
Jerusalem,
like the tents of Kedar
or the tent-curtains of Shalmah.
Do not look down on me; a little 6
dark I may be
because I am scorched by the sun.
My mother's sons were displeased
with me,
they sent me to watch over the
vineyards;
so I did not watch over my own
vineyard.
Tell me, my true love,   7
where you mind your flocks,

a *The Hebrew text implies, by its pronouns, different speakers, but does not indicate them; they are given, however, in two MSS. of Sept.*   b *I will . . . that he may: or* The song of all songs which was Sol-omon's; may he . . .   c *Or* more fragrant than.   d *poured out:* prob. rdg.; Heb. word uncertain.

where you rest them at midday,
that I may not be left picking lice
as I sit among your companions'
herds.

Bridegroom

8   If you yourself do not know,
O fairest of women,
go, follow the tracks of the sheep
and mind your kids by the shepherds'
huts.

9   I would compare you, my dearest,
to Pharaoh's chariot-horses.
10   Your cheeks are lovely between
plaited tresses,
your neck with its jewelled chains.

Companions

11   We will make you braided plaits of
gold
set with beads of silver.

Bride

12   While the king reclines on his couch,
my spikenard gives forth its scent.
13   My beloved is for me a bunch of
myrrh
as he lies on my breast,
14   my beloved is for me a cluster of
henna-blossom
from the vineyards of En-gedi.

Bridegroom

15   How beautiful you are, my dearest,
O how beautiful,
your eyes are like doves!

Bride

16   How beautiful you are, O my love,
and how pleasant!

Bridegroom

Our couch is shaded with branches;
17   the beams of our house are of cedar,
our ceilings are all of fir.

Bride

2 I am an asphodel in Sharon,
a lily growing in the valley.

Bridegroom

2   No, a lily among thorns
is my dearest among girls.

Bride

3   Like an apricot-tree among the
trees of the wood,
so is my beloved among boys.
To sit in its shadow was my delight,

and its fruit was sweet to my taste.
He took me into the wine-garden 4
and gave me loving glances.
He refreshed me with raisins, he re- 5
vived me with apricots;
for I was faint with love.
His left arm was under my head, his 6
right arm was round me.

Bridegroom

I charge you, daughters of Jeru- 7
salem,
by the spirits and the goddesses[e] of
the field:
Do not rouse her, do not disturb my
love
until she is ready.[f]

Bride

Hark! My beloved! Here he comes, 8
bounding over the mountains, leaping
over the hills.
My beloved is like a gazelle   9
or a young wild goat:
there he stands outside our wall,
peeping in at the windows, glancing
through the lattice.

My beloved answered, he said to me: 10
Rise up, my darling;
my fairest, come away.
For now the winter is past,   11
the rains are over and gone;
the flowers appear in the country- 12
side;
the time is coming when the birds
will sing,
and the turtle-dove's cooing will be
heard in our land;
when the green figs will ripen on the 13
fig-trees
and the vines[g] give forth their fragrance.
Rise up, my darling;
my fairest, come away.

Bridegroom

My dove, that hides in holes in the 14
cliffs
or in crannies on the high ledges,
let me see your face, let me hear
your voice;
for your voice is pleasant, your
face is lovely.

Companions

Catch for us the jackals, the little 15
jackals,[h]
that spoil our vineyards, when the
vines are in flower.

e by . . . goddesses: *or* by the gazelles and the hinds.
g Prob. rdg.; Heb. adds blossom.   *h Or* fruit-bats.

f until . . . ready: *or* while she is resting.

Bride

16 My beloved is mine and I am his;
   he delights in the lilies.
17 While the day is cool and the shadows
      are dispersing,
   turn, my beloved, and show yourself
   a gazelle or a young wild goat
   on the hills where cinnamon grows.*i*

3 Night after night on my bed
   I have sought my true love;
   I have sought him but not found
      him,
   I have called him but he has not
      answered.
2 I said, 'I will rise and go the rounds of
      the city,
   through the streets and the squares,
      seeking my true love.'
   I sought him but I did not find him,
   I called him but he did not answer.
3 The watchmen, going the rounds of
      the city, met me,
   and I asked, 'Have you seen my
      true love?'
4 Scarcely had I left them behind me
   when I met my true love.
   I seized him and would not let him go
   until I had brought him to my
      mother's house,
   to the room of her who conceived
      me.

Bridegroom

5 I charge you, daughters of Jeru-
      salem,
   by the spirits and the goddesses*j* of
      the field:
   Do not rouse her, do not disturb my
      love
   until she is ready.*k*

Companions

6 What is this coming up from the
      wilderness
   like a column of smoke
   from burning myrrh or frankin-
      cense,
   from all the powdered spices that
      merchants bring?
7 Look; it is Solomon carried in his
      litter;
   sixty of Israel's chosen warriors
   are his escort,
8 all of them skilled swordsmen,
   all trained to handle arms,
   each with his sword ready at his
      side
   to ward off the demon of the night.

The palanquin which King Solomon 9
   had made for himself
   was of wood from Lebanon.
   Its poles he had made of silver, 10
   its head-rest of gold;
   its seat was of purple stuff,
   and its lining was of leather.

Come out, daughters of Jerusalem; 11
   you daughters of Zion, come out and
      welcome King Solomon,
   wearing the crown with which his
      mother has crowned him,
   on his wedding day, on his day of
      joy.

Bridegroom

   How beautiful you are, my dearest, 4
      how beautiful!
Your eyes behind your veil are like
      doves,
   your hair like a flock of goats stream-
      ing down Mount Gilead.
   Your teeth are like a flock of ewes 2
      just shorn
   which have come up fresh from the
      dipping;
each ewe has twins and none has cast
      a lamb.
   Your lips are like a scarlet thread, 3
   and your words are delightful;*l*
   your parted lips behind your veil
   are like a pomegranate cut open.
   Your neck is like David's tower, 4
   which is built with winding courses;
   a thousand bucklers hang upon it,
   and all are warriors' shields.
   Your two breasts are like two 5
      fawns,
   twin fawns of a gazelle.*m*
While the day is cool and the shadows 6
      are dispersing,
   I will go to the mountains of myrrh
   and to the hills of frankincense.
   You are beautiful, my dearest, 7
   beautiful without a flaw.

Come from Lebanon, my bride; 8
   come with me from Lebanon.
   Hurry down from the top of Amana,
   from Senir's top and Hermon's,
   from the lions' lairs, and the hills
      the leopards haunt.

   You have stolen my heart,*n* my 9
      sister,
   you have stolen it,*o* my bride,
   with one of your eyes, with one
      jewel of your necklace.
How beautiful are your breasts, my 10
   sister, my bride!

*i on . . . grows: or on the rugged hills or on the hills of Bether.   j by . . . goddesses: or by the
gazelles and the hinds.   k until . . . ready: or while she is resting.   l Or and your mouth is
lovely.   m Prob. rdg.; Heb. adds which delight in the lilies.   n stolen my heart: or put heart
into me.   o stolen it: or put heart into me.*

Your love is more fragrant than wine,
and your perfumes sweeter than any spices.

11 Your lips drop sweetness like the honeycomb, my bride,
syrup and milk are under your tongue,
and your dress has the scent of Lebanon.

13[p] Your two cheeks[q] are an orchard of pomegranates,
an orchard full of rare fruits:[r]

14 spikenard and saffron, sweet-cane and cinnamon
with every incense-bearing tree,
myrrh and aloes
with all the choicest spices.

12 My sister, my bride, is a garden close-locked,
a garden close-locked, a fountain sealed.

Bride

15 The fountain in my garden[s] is a spring of running water
pouring down from Lebanon.

16 Awake, north wind, and come, south wind;
blow upon my garden that its perfumes may pour forth,
that my beloved may come to his garden
and enjoy its rare fruits.

Bridegroom

5 I have come to my garden, my sister and bride,
and have plucked my myrrh with my spices;
I have eaten my honey and my syrup,
I have drunk my wine and my milk.
Eat, friends, and drink,
until you are drunk with love.

Bride

2 I sleep but my heart is awake.
Listen! My beloved is knocking:

'Open to me, my sister, my dearest, my dove, my perfect one;
for my head is drenched with dew, my locks with the moisture of the night.'

3 'I have stripped off my dress; must I put it on again?
I have washed my feet; must I soil them again?'

When my beloved slipped his hand 4 through the latch-hole,
my bowels stirred within me.

When I arose to open for my beloved, 5 my hands dripped with myrrh;
the liquid myrrh from my fingers
ran over the knobs of the bolt.

With my own hands I opened to my 6 love,
but my love had turned away and gone by;
my heart sank when he turned his back.
I sought him but I did not find him,
I called him but he did not answer.

The watchmen, going the rounds of 7 the city, met me;
they struck me and wounded me;
the watchmen on the walls took away my cloak.

I charge you, daughters of Jeru- 8 salem,
if you find my beloved, will you not tell him[t]
that I am faint with love?

Companions

What is your beloved more than any 9 other,
O fairest of women?
What is your beloved more than any other,
that you give us this charge?

Bride

My beloved is fair and ruddy,   10
a paragon among ten thousand.
His head is gold, finest gold;   11
his locks are like palm-fronds.[u]
His eyes are like doves beside brooks 12 of water,
splashed by the milky water
as they sit where it is drawn.
His cheeks are like beds of spices or 13 chests full of perfumes;
his lips are lilies, and drop liquid myrrh;
his hands are golden rods set in 14 topaz;
his belly a plaque of ivory overlaid with lapis lazuli.
His legs are pillars of marble in 15 sockets of finest gold;
his aspect is like Lebanon, noble as cedars.
His whispers are[v] sweetness itself, 16 wholly desirable.
Such is my beloved, such is my darling,
daughters of Jerusalem.

---

p Verse 12 transposed to follow verse 14.
r Prob. rdg.; Heb. adds henna with spikenard.
you . . . him: or what will you tell him?
nature is.

q Your two cheeks: prob. rdg.; Heb. Your shoots.
s my garden: prob. rdg.; Heb. gardens.   *t* will
u Prob. rdg.; Heb. adds black as the raven.   *v Or* His

Companions

6 Where has your beloved gone,
O fairest of women?
Which way did your beloved go,
that we may help you to seek him?

Bride

2 My beloved has gone down to his
garden,
to the beds where balsam grows,
to delight in the garden[w] and to pick
the lilies.

3 I am my beloved's, and my beloved is
mine,
he who delights in the lilies.

Bridegroom

4 You are beautiful, my dearest, as
Tirzah,
lovely as Jerusalem.[x]

5 Turn your eyes away from me;
they dazzle me.
Your hair is like a flock of goats
streaming down Mount Gilead;

6 your teeth are like a flock of ewes
come up fresh from the dipping,
each ewe has twins and none has cast
a lamb.

7 Your parted lips behind your veil
are like a pomegranate cut open.

8 There may be sixty princesses,
eighty concubines, and young women
past counting,

9 but there is one alone, my dove, my
perfect one,
her mother's only child,
devoted to the mother who bore
her;
young girls see her and call her
happy,
princesses and concubines praise
her.

10 Who is this that looks out like the
dawn,
beautiful as the moon, bright as the
sun,
majestic as the starry heavens?

11 I went down to a garden of nut-
trees
to look at the rushes by the stream,
to see if the vine had budded
or the pomegranates were in
flower.

12 I did not know myself;
she made me feel more than a
prince
reigning over the myriads[y] of his
people.

Companions

Come back, come back, Shulam- **13**
mite maiden,
come back, that we may gaze upon
you.

Bridegroom

How you love to gaze on the Shu-
lammite maiden,
as she moves between the lines of
dancers!

How beautiful are your sandalled feet, **7**
O prince's daughter!
The curves of your thighs are like
jewels,
the work of a skilled craftsman.
Your navel is a rounded goblet **2**
that never shall want for spiced
wine.
Your belly is a heap of wheat
fenced in by lilies.
Your two breasts are like two **3**
fawns,
twin fawns of a gazelle.
Your neck is like a tower of ivory. **4**
Your eyes are the pools in Heshbon,
beside the gate of the crowded
city.[z]
Your nose is like towering Lebanon
that looks towards Damascus.
You carry your head like Carmel; **5**
the flowing hair on your head is
lustrous black,
your tresses are braided with ribbons.
How beautiful, how entrancing you **6**
are,
my loved one, daughter of delights!
You are stately as a palm-tree, **7**
and your breasts are the clusters of
dates.
I said, 'I will climb up into the palm **8**
to grasp its fronds.'
May I find your breasts like clusters of
grapes on the vine,
the scent of your breath like apricots,
and your whispers like spiced wine **9**
flowing smoothly to welcome my
caresses,
gliding down through lips and
teeth.

Bride

I am my beloved's, his longing is all **10**
for me.
Come, my beloved, let us go out into **11**
the fields
to lie among the henna-bushes;
let us go early to the vineyards **12**

---

w *Prob. rdg.; Heb.* gardens.   x *Prob. rdg.; Heb. adds* majestic as the starry heavens (*see verse 10*).
y *Prob. rdg.; Heb.* chariots.   z *Or the gate of Beth-rabbim.*

and see if the vine has budded or its
  blossom opened,
if the pomegranates are in flower.
There will I give you my love,

13 when the mandrakes give their
    perfume,
and all rare fruits are ready at our
  door,
fruits new and old
which I have in store for you, my
  love.

8 If only you were my own true
    brother
that sucked my mother's breasts!
Then, if I found you outside, I
  would kiss you,
and no man would despise me.

2 I would lead you to the room of the
    mother who bore me,
bring you to her house for you to
  embrace me;[a]
I would give you mulled wine to
  drink
and the fresh juice of pomegranates,

3 your[b] left arm under my head and
  your[b] right arm round me.

Bridegroom

4 I charge you, daughters of Jeru-
    salem:
Do not rouse her, do not disturb my
  love
until she is ready.[c]

Companions

5 Who is this coming up from the
    wilderness
leaning on her beloved?

Bridegroom

Under the apricot-trees I roused you,
  there where your mother was in
    labour with you,
there where she who bore you was
  in labour.

6 Wear me as a seal upon your heart,
  as a seal upon your arm;
for love is strong as death,

passion cruel as the grave;
it blazes up like blazing fire,
fiercer than any flame.

Many waters cannot quench love,   7
no flood can sweep it away;
if a man were to offer for love
the whole wealth of his house,
it would be utterly scorned.

Companions

We have a little sister   8
who has no breasts;
what shall we do for our sister
when she is asked in marriage?
If she is a wall,   9
we will build on it a silver parapet,
but[d] if she is a door,
we will close it up with planks of
  cedar.

Bride

I am a wall and my breasts are like 10
  towers;
so in his eyes I am as one who brings
  contentment.
Solomon has a vineyard at Baal- 11
  hamon;
he has let out his vineyard to
  guardians,
and each is to bring for its fruit
a thousand pieces of silver.
But my vineyard is mine to give;   12
the thousand pieces are yours, O
  Solomon,
and the guardians of the fruit shall
  have two hundred.

Bridegroom

My bride, you who sit in my garden, 13
what is it that my friends[e] are listening to?
Let me also hear your voice.

Bride

Come into the open, my beloved,   14
and show yourself like a gazelle or a
  young wild goat
on the spice-bearing mountains.

a for you to embrace me: *or* to teach me how to love you.   *b* *Prob. rdg.*; *Heb.* his.   *c* until . . .
ready: *or* while she is resting.   *d* *Or* and.   *e* my garden . . . friends: *prob. rdg.*; *Heb.* the
gardens, friends.

THE BOOK OF THE PROPHET
ISAIAH

The case against Judah

1 THE VISION received by Isaiah son of Amoz concerning Judah and Jerusalem during the reigns of Uzziah, Jotham, Ahaz, and Hezekiah, kings of Judah.

2 Hark you heavens, and earth give ear,
  for the LORD has spoken:
  I have sons whom I reared and brought up,
  but they have rebelled against me.
3   The ox knows its owner
  and the ass its master's stall;
  but Israel, my own people,
  has no knowledge, no discernment.

4 O sinful nation, people loaded with iniquity,
race of evildoers, wanton destructive children
  who have deserted the LORD,
  spurned the Holy One of Israel
  and turned your backs on him.
5   Where can you still be struck
  if you will be disloyal still?
  Your head is covered with sores,
  your body diseased;
6 from head to foot there is not a sound spot in you—
nothing but bruises and weals and raw wounds
  which have not felt compress or bandage
  or soothing oil.
7 Your country is desolate, your cities lie in ashes.
Strangers devour your land before your eyes;
  it is desolate as Sodom[a] in its overthrow.
8   Only Zion is left,
  like a watchman's shelter in a vineyard,
  a shed in a field of cucumbers,
  a city well guarded.
9 If the LORD of Hosts had not left us a remnant,
  we should soon have been like Sodom,
  no better than Gomorrah.

Empty religious observances

Hear the word of the LORD, you rulers 10
  of Sodom;
attend, you people of Gomorrah, to the instruction of our God:
  Your countless sacrifices, what are 11
  they to me?
says the LORD.
I am sated with whole-offerings of rams
and the fat of buffaloes;
I have no desire for the blood of bulls,
of sheep and of he-goats.
Whenever you come to enter my 12–13 presence—
who asked you for this?
No more shall you trample my courts.
The offer of your gifts is useless,
the reek of sacrifice is abhorrent to me.
New moons and sabbaths and assemblies,
sacred seasons and ceremonies, I cannot endure.
I cannot tolerate your new moons and 14 your festivals;
they have become a burden to me,
and I can put up with them no longer.
When you lift your hands out- 15 spread in prayer,
I will hide my eyes from you.
Though you offer countless prayers,
I will not listen.
There is blood on your hands;
wash yourselves and be clean.   16
Put away the evil of your deeds,
away out of my sight.
Cease to do evil and learn to do right, 17
pursue justice and champion the oppressed;
give the orphan his rights, plead the widow's cause.

The LORD's answer

Come now, let us argue it out,   18
says the LORD.
Though your sins are scarlet,

---

a Sodom: *prob. rdg.; Heb.* strangers.

they may become white as snow;
though they are dyed crimson,
they may yet be like wool.

19 Obey with a will,
and you shall eat the best that earth
yields;

20 but, if you refuse and rebel,
locust-beans shall be your only
food.[b]
The LORD himself has spoken.

Verdict on social corruption

21 How the faithful city has played the
whore,
once the home of justice where
righteousness dwelt—
but now murderers!

22 Your silver has turned into base
metal
and your liquor is diluted with
water.

23 Your very rulers are rebels, confederate with thieves;
every man of them loves a bribe
and itches for a gift;
they do not give the orphan his
rights,
and the widow's cause never comes
before them.

The LORD will discipline Judah

24 This therefore is the word of the Lord,
the LORD of Hosts, the Mighty One of
Israel:

Enough! I will secure a respite
from my foes
and take vengeance on my enemies.

25 Once again I will act against you
to refine away your base metal as
with potash
and purge all your impurities;

26 I will again make your judges what
once they were
and your counsellors like those of
old.
Then at length you shall be called
the home of righteousness, the
faithful city.

27 Justice shall redeem Zion
and righteousness her repentant
people.

28 Rebels and sinners shall be broken
together
and those who forsake the LORD
shall cease to be.

29 For the sacred oaks in which you
delighted shall fail you,
the garden-shrines of your fancy shall
disappoint you.

30 You shall be like a terebinth whose
leaves have withered,

like a garden without water;
the strongest tree[c] shall become 31
like tow,
and what is made of it[d] shall go up
in sparks,
and the two shall burst into flames
together
with no one to quench them.

Zion's glorious future

This is the word which Isaiah son of 2
Amoz received in a vision concerning
Judah and Jerusalem.

In days to come   2
the mountain of the LORD's house
shall be set over all other mountains,
lifted high above the hills.
All the nations shall come streaming to it,
and many peoples shall come and say, 3
'Come, let us climb up on to the mountain of the LORD,
to the house of the God of Jacob,
that he may teach us his ways
and we may walk in his paths.'
For instruction issues from Zion,
and out of Jerusalem comes the
word of the LORD;
he will be judge between nations, 4
arbiter among many peoples.
They shall beat their swords into
mattocks
and their spears into pruning-
knives;[f]
nation shall not lift sword against
nation
nor ever again be trained for war.

Worldliness and idolatry

O people of Jacob, come,   5
let us walk in the light of the LORD.
Thou hast abandoned thy people the 6
house of Jacob;
for they are crowded with traders[g]
and barbarians like the Philistines,
and with the children of foreigners
everywhere.
Their land is filled with silver and gold, 7
and there is no end to their treasure;
their land is filled with horses,
and there is no end to their chariots;
their land is filled with idols,   8
and they bow down to the work of
their own hands,
to what their fingers have made.
Mankind shall be brought low,   9
all men shall be humbled;
and how can they raise themselves?[h]

---

b *locust-beans . . . food:* or, *with Scroll,* you shall be eaten by the sword.   c *Or* the strong man.
d *Or* what he makes.   e *Verses 2–4: cp. Mic. 4. 1–3.*   f *They shall beat . . . pruning-knives: cp.*
Joel 3. 9–12.   g *Or* hawkers.   h *Prob. rdg.; Heb.* and do not forgive them.

10 Get you into the rocks and hide yourselves in the ground
from the dread of the LORD and the
splendour of his majesty.
11 Man's proud eyes shall be humbled,
the loftiness of men brought low,
and the LORD alone shall be exalted
on that day.

The day of the LORD

12 For the LORD of Hosts has a day of
doom waiting
for all that is proud and lofty,
for all that is high and lifted up,
13 for all the cedars of Lebanon, lofty
and high,
and for all the oaks of Bashan,
14 for all lofty mountains and for all high
hills,
15 for every high tower and for every
sheer wall,
16 for all ships of Tarshish and all the
dhows of Arabia.
17 Then man's pride shall be brought
low,
and the loftiness of man shall be
humbled,
and the LORD alone shall be
exalted
on that day,
18 while the idols shall pass away
utterly.
19 Get you into caves in the rocks
and crevices in the ground
from the dread of the LORD and the
splendour of his majesty,
when he rises to inspire the earth
with fear.
20 On that day a man shall fling away
his idols of silver and his idols of gold
which he has made for himself to
worship;
he shall fling them to the dung-beetles
and the bats,
21 and creep into clefts in the rocks and
crannies in the cliffs
from the dread of the LORD and the
splendour of his majesty,
when he rises to inspire the earth
with fear.
22 Have no more to do with man, for
what is he worth?
He is no more than the breath in
his nostrils.

*The LORD will undermine Judah's
stability*

3 Be warned: the Lord, the LORD of
Hosts,
is stripping Jerusalem and Judah
of every prop and stay,[i]
2 warrior and soldier,

judge and prophet, diviner and elder,
captains of companies and men of 3
rank,
counsellor, magician, and cunning
enchanter.
Then I will appoint mere boys to be 4
their captains,
who shall govern as the fancy takes
them;
the people shall deal harshly   5
each man with his fellow and with his
neighbour;
children shall break out against
their elders,
and nobodies against men of substance.
If a man takes hold of his brother in 6
his father's house,
saying, 'You have a cloak, you shall
be our chief;
our stricken family shall be under
you',
he will cry out that day and say,   7
'I will not be your master;
there is neither bread nor cloak in
my house,
and you shall not make me head of
the clan.'

Disaster on Judah

Jerusalem is stricken and Judah fallen 8
because they have spoken and acted
against the LORD,
rebelling against the glance of his
glorious eye.
The look on their faces testifies 9
against them;
like Sodom they proclaim their sins
and do not conceal them.[j]
Woe upon them! they have earned
their own disaster.
Happy[k] the righteous man! all goes 10
well with him,
for such men enjoy the fruit of their
actions.
Woe betide the wicked! with him 11
all goes ill,
for he reaps the reward that he has
earned.
Money-lenders strip my people bare, 12
and usurers lord it over them.
O my people! your guides lead you
astray
and confuse the path that you
should take.
The LORD comes forward to argue 13
his case
and stands to judge his people.
The LORD opens the indictment   14
against the elders of his people and
their officers:
You have ravaged the vineyard,

i *Prob. rdg.; Heb. adds* all stay of bread and all stay of water.
like those of Sodom, denounce them; they do not deny them.

j *like . . . them: or* and their sins,
k *Prob. rdg.; Heb.* Say.

and the spoils of the poor are in your houses.

15 Is it nothing to you that you crush my people
and grind the faces of the poor?
This is the very word of the Lord, the LORD of Hosts.

The fate of the women of Zion

16 Then the LORD said:
Because the women of Zion hold themselves high
and walk with necks outstretched and wanton glances,
moving with mincing gait
and jingling feet,

17 the Lord will give the women of Zion bald heads,
the LORD will strip the hair from their foreheads.

18 In that day the Lord will take away all finery: anklets, discs, crescents,
19 20 pendants, bangles, coronets, head-bands, armlets, necklaces, lockets,
21 22 charms, signets, nose-rings, fine dress-es, mantles, cloaks, flounced skirts,
23 scarves of gauze, kerchiefs of linen, turbans, and flowing veils.

24 So instead of perfume you shall have the stench of decay,
and a rope in place of a girdle,
baldness instead of hair elegantly coiled,
a loin-cloth of sacking instead of a mantle,
and branding instead of beauty.

25 Your men shall fall by the sword, and your warriors in battle;

26 then Zion's gates shall mourn and lament,
and she shall sit on the ground stripped bare.

4 Then on that day
seven women shall take hold of one man and say,
'We will eat our own bread and wear our own clothes
if only we may be called by your name;
take away our disgrace.'

The future glory of Zion

2 On that day the plant that the LORD has grown
shall become glorious in its beauty,
and the fruit of the land shall be
the pride and splendour
of the survivors of Israel.

3 Then those who are left in Zion, who remain in Jerusalem, every one enrolled in the book of life, shall be called holy. If the Lord washes away 4 the filth of the women of Zion and cleanses Jerusalem from the blood that is in it by a spirit of judgement, a consuming spirit, then over every 5 building on Mount Zion and on all her places of assembly the LORD will create a cloud of smoke by day and a bright flame of fire by night; for glory shall be spread over all as a covering and a canopy, a shade from the heat 6 by day, a refuge and a shelter from rain and tempest.

The vineyard: an allegory

I will sing for my beloved   5
my love-song about his vineyard:
My beloved had a vineyard
high up on a fertile hill-side.
He trenched it and cleared it of 2 stones
and planted it with red vines;
he built a watch-tower in the middle
and then hewed out a winepress in it.
He looked for it to yield grapes,
but it yielded wild grapes.
Now, you who live in Jerusalem,   3
and you men of Judah,
judge between me and my vineyard.
What more could have been done 4
for my vineyard
that I did not do in it?
Why, when I looked for it to yield grapes,
did it yield wild grapes?
Now listen while I tell you   5
what I will do to my vineyard:
I will take away its fences and let it be burnt,
I will break down its walls and let it be trampled underfoot,
and so I will leave it derelict;   6
it shall be neither pruned nor hoed,
but shall grow thorns and briars.
Then I will command the clouds
to send no more rain upon it.
The vineyard of the LORD of Hosts is 7 Israel,
and the men of Judah are the plant he cherished.
He looked for justice and found it denied,
for righteousness but heard cries of distress.

Judah's complacency and hypocrisy

Shame on you! you who add house to 8 house
and join field to field,
until not an acre remains,
and you are left to dwell alone in the land.

9 The LORD of Hosts has sworn[l] in my
   hearing:
   Many houses shall go to ruin,
   fine large houses shall be uninhabited.
10 Five acres of vineyard shall yield only
   a gallon,
   and ten bushels of seed return only a
   peck.
11 Shame on you! you who rise early
   in the morning
   to go in pursuit of liquor
   and draw out the evening inflamed
   with wine,
12 at whose feasts there are harp and
   lute,
   tabor and pipe and wine,
   who have no eyes for the work of the
   LORD,
   and never see the things that he has
   done.
13 Therefore my people are dwindling
   away
   all unawares;
   the nobles are starving to death,
   and the common folk die of thirst.
14 Therefore Sheol gapes with straining
   throat
   and has opened her measureless
   jaws:
   down go nobility and common
   people,
   their noisy bustling mob.[m]
15 Mankind is brought low, men are
   humbled,
   humbled are haughty looks.
16 But the LORD of Hosts sits high in
   judgement,
   and by righteousness the holy God
   shows himself holy.
17 Young rams shall feed where fat
   bullocks once pastured,
   and kids shall graze broad acres where
   cattle grew fat.[n]
18 Shame on you! you who drag wickedness along like a tethered sheep
   and sin like a heifer on a rope,
19 who say, 'Let the LORD make haste,
   let him speed up his work for us to
   see it,
   let the purpose of the Holy One of
   Israel
   be soon fulfilled, so that we may
   know it.'
20 Shame on you! you who call evil good
   and good evil,
   who turn darkness into light and light
   into darkness,
   who make bitter sweet and sweet
   bitter.
21 Shame on you! you who are wise in
   your own eyes

and prudent in your own esteem.
22 Shame on you! you mighty topers,
   valiant mixers of drink,
23 who for a bribe acquit the guilty
   and deny justice to those in the
   right.

Foreign invasion

26[o] So he will hoist a signal to a nation far
   away,
   he will whistle to call them from
   the end of the earth;
   and see, they come, speedy and
   swift;
27 none is weary, not one of them
   stumbles,
   not one slumbers or sleeps.
   None has his belt loose about his
   waist
   or a broken thong to his sandals.
28 Their arrows are sharpened and their
   bows all strung,
   their horses' hooves flash like shooting stars,
   their chariot-wheels are like the
   whirlwind.
29 Their growling is the growling of a
   lioness,
   they growl like young lions,
   which roar as they seize the prey
   and carry it beyond reach of
   rescue.
30 They shall roar over it on that day
   like the roaring of the sea.
   If a man looks over the earth, behold,
   darkness closing in,
   and the light darkened on the hill-
   tops[p]!

The call of Isaiah

6 In the year of King Uzziah's death I
   saw the Lord seated on a throne, high
   and exalted, and the skirt of his robe
2 filled the temple. About him were
   attendant seraphim, and each had six
   wings; one pair covered his face and
   one pair his feet, and one pair was
3 spread in flight. They were calling
   ceaselessly to one another,

   Holy, holy, holy is the LORD of Hosts:
   the whole earth is full of his glory.

4 And, as each one called, the threshold
   shook to its foundations, while the
   house was filled with smoke. Then I
5 cried,

   Woe is me! I am lost,
   for I am a man of unclean lips
   and I dwell among a people of unclean lips;

l has sworn: *prob. rdg.; Heb. om.*   *m* nobility ... mob: *or* nobility, common people and noisy
mob, and are restless there.   *n* Young ... grew fat: *prob. rdg.; Heb. unintelligible.*   *o Verses
24 and 25 transposed to follow 10. 4.*   *p* hill-tops: *or clouds.*

K

yet with these eyes I have seen the King, the LORD of Hosts.

6 Then one of the seraphim flew to me carrying in his hand a glowing coal which he had taken from the altar 7 with a pair of tongs. He touched my mouth with it and said,

See, this has touched your lips;
your iniquity is removed,
and your sin is wiped away.

8 Then I heard the Lord saying, Whom shall I send? Who will go for me? And 9 I answered, Here am I; send me. He said, Go and tell this people:

You may listen and listen, but you
will not understand.[q]
You may look and look again, but
you will never know.[r]
10 This people's wits are dulled,
their ears are deafened and their eyes
blinded,
so that they cannot see with their
eyes
nor listen with their ears
nor understand with their wits,
so that they may turn and be
healed.

11 Then I asked, How long, O Lord? And he answered,

Until cities fall in ruins and are deserted,
houses are left without people,
and the land goes to ruin and lies
waste,
12 until the LORD has sent all mankind
far away,
and the whole country is one vast
desolation.
13 Even if a tenth part of its people
remain there,
they too will be exterminated
[like an oak or a terebinth,
a sacred pole thrown out from its
place in a hill-shrine[s]].

News of the Aramaean–Ephraimite alliance

7 While Ahaz son of Jotham and grand-son of Uzziah was king of Judah, Rezin king of Aram with Pekah son of Remaliah, king of Israel, marched on Jerusalem, but could not force a 2 battle. When the house of David heard that the Aramaeans had come to terms with the Ephraimites, king

and people were shaken like forest trees in the wind. Then the LORD 3 said to Isaiah, Go out with your son Shear-jashub[t] to meet Ahaz at the end of the conduit of the Upper Pool by the causeway leading to the Fuller's Field, and say to him, Be 4 on your guard, keep calm; do not be frightened or unmanned by these two smouldering stumps of firewood, be-cause Rezin and his Aramaeans with Remaliah's son are burning with rage. The Aramaeans with Ephraim and 5 Remaliah's son have laid their plans against you, saying, Let us invade 6 Judah and break her spirit;[u] let us make her join with us, and set the son of Tabeal on the throne. Therefore 7 the Lord GOD has said:

This shall not happen now, and
never shall,
for all that the chief city of Aram is 8
Damascus,
and Rezin is the chief of Damascus;
within sixty-five years
Ephraim shall cease to be a nation,
for all that Samaria is the chief city 9
of Ephraim,
and Remaliah's son the chief of
Samaria.
Have firm faith, or you will not stand
firm.

The sign Immanuel

Once again the LORD spoke to Ahaz 10 and said, Ask the LORD your God for 11 a sign, from lowest Sheol or from highest heaven. But Ahaz said, No, I 12 will not put the LORD to the test by asking for a sign. Then the answer 13 came: Listen, house of David. Are you not content to wear out men's patience? Must you also wear out the patience of my God? Therefore the 14 Lord himself shall give you a sign: A young woman is with child, and she will bear a son, and will[v] call him Im-manuel.[w] By the time that he has 15 learnt to reject evil and choose good, he will be eating curds and honey;[x] before that child has learnt to reject 16 evil and choose good, desolation will come upon the land before whose two kings you cower now. The LORD will 17 bring on you, your people, and your house, a time the like of which has not been seen since Ephraim broke away from Judah.[y]

q Or but how will you understand?   r Or but how will you know?   s a sacred pole . . . hill-
shrine: prob. rdg.; Heb. obscure.   t That is A remnant shall return.   u Or and parley with her.
v Or you will.   w That is God is with us.   x he will . . . honey: or curds and honey will be
eaten.   y Prob. rdg.; Heb. adds the king of Assyria.

Assyrian devastation

18 On that day the LORD will whistle for the fly from the distant streams of Egypt and for the bee from Assyria.
19 They shall all come and settle in the precipitous ravines and in the clefts of the rock; camel-thorn and stink-
20 wood shall be black with them. On that day the Lord shall shave the head and body with a razor hired on the banks of the Euphrates,[z] and it
21 shall remove the beard as well. On that day a man shall save alive a
22 young cow and two ewes; and he shall get so much milk that he eats curds; for all who are left in the land shall eat
23 curds and honey. On that day every place where there used to be a thousand vines worth a thousand pieces of silver shall be given over to thorns
24 and briars. A man shall go there only to hunt with bow and arrows, for thorns and briars cover the whole land;
25 and no one who fears thorns and briars shall set foot on any of those hills once worked with the hoe. Oxen shall be turned loose on them, and sheep shall trample them.

8 The LORD said to me, Take a large tablet and write on it in common
2 writing,[a] Maher-shalal-hash-baz;[b] and fetch Uriah the priest and Zechariah son of Jeberechiah for me as trust-
3 worthy witnesses. Then I lay with the prophetess, and she conceived and bore a son; and the LORD said to me,
4 Call him Maher-shalal-hash-baz. Before the boy can say Father or Mother, the wealth of Damascus and the spoils of Samaria shall be carried off and presented to the king of Assyria.
5 Once again the LORD said to me:

6 Because this nation has rejected the waters of Shiloah, which run so softly and gently,[c]
7 therefore the Lord will bring up against it
    the strong, flooding waters of the Euphrates,
    the king of Assyria and all his glory;
    it shall run up all its channels
    and overflow all its banks;
8 it shall sweep through Judah in a flood,
    pouring over it and rising shoulder-high.
    The whole expanse of the land shall be filled,

so wide he spreads his wings; for God is with us.[d]
9 Take note, you nations, and be dismayed.
    Listen, all you distant parts of the earth:
    you may arm yourselves but will be dismayed;
    you may arm yourselves but will be dismayed.
10 Make your plans, but they will be foiled,
    propose what you please, but it shall not stand;
    for God is with us.[d]

A personal word to Isaiah

11 These were the words of the LORD to me, for his hand was strong upon me; and he warned me not to follow[e] the ways of this people: You shall not say 'too
12 hard' of everything that this people calls hard; you shall neither dread nor
13 fear that which they fear. It is the LORD of Hosts whom you must count 'hard';[f] he it is whom you must fear
14 and dread. He shall become your 'hardship',[f] a boulder and a rock which the two houses of Israel shall run against and over which they shall stumble, a trap and a snare to those
15 who live in Jerusalem; and many shall stumble over them, many shall fall and be broken, many shall be snared and caught.

Apostasy, anarchy and gloom

    Fasten up the message,   16
seal the oracle with my teaching;[g]
    and I will wait for the LORD   17
    who hides his face from the house of Jacob;
    I will watch for him.
See, I and the sons whom the LORD 18
    has given me
    are to be signs and portents in Israel,
sent by the LORD of Hosts who dwells on Mount Zion.
    But men will say to you,   19
    'Seek guidance of ghosts and familiar spirits
    who squeak and gibber;
    a nation may surely seek guidance of its gods,
    of the dead on behalf of the living,
    for an oracle or a message?'   20
    They will surely say some such thing as this;
    but what they say is futile.

---

[z] Prob. rdg.; Heb. adds with the king of Assyria.
[stylus.]   [b] That is Speed-spoil-hasten-plunder.
Remaliah.   [d] God is with us: Heb. Immanuel.
[f] 'hard' and 'hardship': prob. rdg.; Heb. unintelligible in this context.

[a] in common writing: or with an ordinary
[c] Prob. rdg.; Heb. adds Rezin and the son of
[e] Or and he turned me from following . . .
[g] Or among my disciples.

21 So despondency and fear will come
    over them,
    and then, when they are afraid and
      fearful,
    they will turn against their king
      and their gods.
22 Then, whether they turn their gaze up-
      wards or look down,
    everywhere is distress and darkness
      inescapable,
    constraint and gloom that cannot
      be avoided;
9 for there is no escape for an oppressed
    people.

For, while the first invader has
dealt lightly with the land of Zebulun and the land of Naphtali, the
second has dealt heavily with Galilee
of the Nations on the road beyond
Jordan to the sea.

The Prince of peace

2   The people who walked in darkness
     have seen a great light:
     light has dawned upon them,
     dwellers in a land as dark as death.
3 Thou hast increased their joy and[h]
     given them great gladness;
   they rejoice in thy presence as men
     rejoice at harvest,
   or as they are glad when they share out
     the spoil;
4   for thou hast shattered the yoke
     that burdened them,
     the collar that lay heavy on their
       shoulders,
     the driver's goad, as on the day of
       Midian's defeat.
5   All the boots of trampling soldiers
     and the garments fouled with blood
   shall become a burning mass, fuel for
     fire.
6 For a boy has been born for us, a son
     given to us
     to bear the symbol of dominion on
       his shoulder;
     and he shall be called
     in purpose wonderful, in battle God-
       like,
     Father for all time,[i] Prince of
       peace.
▼   Great shall the dominion be,
     and boundless the peace
     bestowed on David's throne and on
       his kingdom,
     to establish it and sustain it
     with justice and righteousness
     from now and for evermore.
     The zeal of the LORD of Hosts shall
       do this.

Israel's futile efforts at rebuilding

The Lord has sent forth his word 8
    against Jacob
    and it shall fall on Israel;
    all the people shall be humbled,   9
    Ephraim and the dwellers in
      Samaria,
    though in their pride and arrogance
      they say,
The bricks are fallen, but we will 10
    build in hewn stone;
    the sycomores are hacked down,
    but we will use cedars instead.
The LORD has raised their foes[j] high 11
    against them
    and spurred on their enemies,
Aramaeans from the east and Philis- 12
    tines from the west,
    and they have swallowed Israel in
      one mouthful.
    For all this his anger has not turned
      back,
    and his hand is stretched out still.
    Yet the people did not come back 13
      to him who struck them,
    or seek guidance of the LORD of
      Hosts;
therefore on one day the LORD cut off 14
    from Israel
head and tail, palm and reed.[k]
This people's guides have led them 16
    astray;
    those who should have been guided
      are in confusion.
Therefore the Lord showed no mercy 17
    to their young men,
    no tenderness to their orphans and
      widows;
    all were godless and evildoers,
    every one speaking profanity.
    For all this his anger has not turned
      back,
    and his hand is stretched out still.

Social injustices

    Wicked men have been set ablaze 18
      like a fire
    fed with briars and thorns,
    kindled in the forest thickets;
    they are wrapped in a murky pall
      of smoke.
The land is scorched by the fury of 19
    the LORD of Hosts,
    and the people have become fuel
      for the fire.[l]
On the right, one man eats his fill 20
    but yet is hungry;
    on the left, another devours but is
      not satisfied;
    each feeds on his own children's flesh,

---

*h their joy and: prob. rdg.; Heb. the nation, not.   i Or of a wide realm.   j their foes: prob.
rdg.; Heb. the foes of Rezin.   k Prob. rdg.; Heb. adds (15) The aged and honoured are the head,
and the prophet who gives false instruction is the tail.   l See note on verse 20.*

and neither spares his own brother.[m]

21 [n]For all this his anger has not
turned back,
and his hand is stretched out still.

10 Shame on you! you who make unjust laws
and publish burdensome decrees,
2 depriving the poor of justice,
robbing the weakest of my people
of their rights,
despoiling the widow and plundering
the orphan.
3 What will you do when called to
account,
when ruin from afar confronts you?
To whom will you flee for help
and where will you leave your children,
4 so that they do not cower before the
gaoler
or fall by the executioner's hand?
For all this his anger has not turned
back,
and his hand is stretched out still.

[o] So, as tongues of fire lick up the
stubble
and the heat of the flame dies down,
their root shall moulder away,
and their shoots vanish like dust;
for they have spurned the instruction
of the LORD of Hosts
and have rejected the word of the
Holy One of Israel.
[o] So the anger of the LORD is roused
against his people,
he has stretched out his hand against
them and struck them down;
the mountains trembled,
and their corpses lay like offal in
the streets.
For all this his anger has not
turned back,
and his hand is stretched out still.

How the LORD uses Assyria

5 The Assyrian! He is the rod that
I wield in my anger,
and the staff of my wrath is in his
hand.[p]
6 I send him against a godless nation,
I bid him march against a people
who rouse my wrath,
to spoil and plunder at will
and trample them down like mud in
the streets.
7 But this man's purpose is lawless,
lawless are the plans in his mind;
for his thought is only to destroy

and to wipe out nation after nation.
8 'Are not my officers all kings?' he says;
9 'see how Calno has suffered the fate
of Carchemish.
Is not Hamath like Arpad, and Samaria like Damascus?
10 Before now I have found kingdoms
full of idols,
with more images than Jerusalem
and Samaria,
11 and now, what I have done to Samaria and her worthless gods,
I will do also to Jerusalem and her
idols.'

The king of Assyria's fall

12 When the LORD has finished all that
he means to do on Mount Zion and in
Jerusalem, he will punish the king of
Assyria for this fruit of his pride and
13 for his arrogance and vainglory, because he said:

By my own might I have acted
and in my own wisdom I have laid
my schemes;
I have removed the frontiers of
nations
and plundered their treasures,
like a bull I have trampled on their
inhabitants.
14 My hand has found its way to the
wealth of nations,
and, as a man takes the eggs from
a deserted nest,
so have I taken every land;
not a wing fluttered,
not a beak gaped, no chirp was
heard.

15 Shall the axe set itself up against
the hewer,
or the saw claim mastery over the
sawyer,
as if a stick were to brandish him
who wields it,
or a staff of wood to wield one who
is not wood?

16 Therefore the Lord, the LORD of Hosts,
will send disease
on his sturdy frame, from head to
toe,[q]
and within his flesh[r] a fever like fire
shall burn.
17 The light of Israel shall become a
fire
and his Holy One a flame,
which in one day shall burn up and
consume
his thorns and his briars;

m and neither . . . brother: *transposed from end of verse 19.*   n *Prob. rdg.; Heb. prefixes* Manasseh
devours Ephraim, and Ephraim Manasseh; together they are against Judah.   o *These are verses
24 and 25 of ch. 5, transposed to this point.*   p and . . . hand: *prob. rdg.; Heb. obscure.*   q from
. . . toe: *transposed from verse 18.*   r within his flesh: *or* in his strong body.

18 the glory of forest and meadow shall
    be destroyed
      as when a man falls in a fit;
19 and the remnant of trees in the
    forest shall be so few
      that a child may count them one
      by one.

A remnant will repent

20 On that day the remnant of Israel, the
    survivors of Jacob, shall cease to lean
    on him that proved their destroyer,
    but shall loyally lean on the LORD,
    the Holy One of Israel.

21 A remnant shall turn again, a remnant
    of Jacob,
      to God their champion.
22 Your people, Israel, may be many as
    the sands of the sea,
      but only a remnant shall turn
      again,
      the instrument of final destruction,
      justice in full flood;[s]
23 for the Lord, the LORD of Hosts, will
    bring final destruction
      upon all the earth.

Relief from oppression promised

24 Therefore these are the words of the
    Lord, the LORD of Hosts: My people
    who live in Zion, you must not be
    afraid of the Assyrians, though they
    beat you with their rod and lift their
    staff against you as the Egyptians
25 did; for soon, very soon, my anger will
    come to an end, and my wrath will all
26 be spent.[t] Then the LORD of Hosts will
    brandish his whip over them as he did
    when he struck Midian at the Rock of
    Oreb, and will lift his staff against the
    River as he did against Egypt.

27   On that day
      the burden they laid on your shoul-
      der shall be removed
      and their yoke shall be broken from
      your neck.
28 An invader from Rimmon[u] has come
    to Aiath,
      has passed by Migron,
      and left his baggage-train at Mich-
      mash;
29 he has passed by Maabarah
      and camped for the night at Geba.
    Ramah is anxious, Gibeah of Saul is
      in panic.
30 Raise a shrill cry, Bath-gallim;
      hear it, Laish, and answer her, Anath-
      oth:

'Madmenah is in flight; take refuge, 31
    people of Gebim.'
Today he is due to pitch his camp in 32
    Nob;
      he gives the signal to advance
      against the mount of the daughter
      of Zion,
      the hill of Jerusalem.

The LORD's reign of righteousness and peace

Look, the Lord, the LORD of Hosts, 33
    cleaves the trees with a flash of
    lightning,
the tallest are hewn down, the lofty
    laid low,
      the heart of the forest is felled with 34
      the axe,
      and Lebanon with its noble trees
      has fallen.
Then a shoot shall grow from the **11**
    stock of Jesse,
      and a branch shall spring from his
      roots.
The spirit of the LORD shall rest 2
    upon him,
a spirit of wisdom and understanding,
a spirit of counsel[v] and power,
a spirit of knowledge and the fear
    of the LORD.[w]
He shall not judge by what he sees 3
    nor decide by what he hears;
he shall judge the poor with justice 4
    and defend the humble in the land
    with equity;
his mouth shall be a rod to strike
    down the ruthless,[x]
and with a word he shall slay the
    wicked.
Round his waist he shall wear the belt 5
    of justice,
      and good faith shall be the girdle
      round his body.
Then the wolf shall live with the 6
    sheep,
      and the leopard lie down with the
      kid;
the calf and the young lion shall grow
    up together,
and a little child shall lead them;
      the cow and the bear shall be 7
      friends,
      and their young shall lie down to-
      gether.
The lion shall eat straw like cattle;
the infant shall play over the hole of 8
    the cobra,
and the young child dance over the
    viper's nest.

---

s the instrument . . . flood: or wasting with sickness, yet overflowing with righteousness.   t will
. . . spent: prob. rdg.; Heb. obscure.   u and their yoke . . . Rimmon: prob. rdg.; Heb. and their yoke
from upon your neck, and a yoke shall be broken because of oil. He . . .   v Or force.   w Prob.
rdg.; Heb. adds and his delight shall be in the fear of the LORD.   x Prob. rdg.; Heb. land.

9 They shall not hurt or destroy in all
  my holy mountain;
    for as the waters fill the sea,
  so shall the land be filled with the
    knowledge of the LORD.

10 On that day a scion from the root
   of Jesse
     shall be set up as a signal to the
       peoples;
     the nations shall rally to it,
     and its resting-place shall be
       glorious.

When Judah and Israel reunite

11 On that day the Lord will make his
   power more glorious by recovering the
   remnant of his people, those who are
   still left, from Assyria and Egypt,
   from Pathros, from Cush and Elam,
   from Shinar, Hamath and the islands
   of the sea.

12 Then he will raise a signal to the
   nations
     and gather together those driven
       out of Israel;
   he will assemble Judah's scattered
     people
   from the four corners of the earth.
13 Ephraim's jealousy shall vanish,
     and Judah's enmity shall be done
       away.
   Ephraim shall not be jealous of
     Judah,
   nor Judah the enemy of Ephraim.
14 They shall swoop down on the Philistine flank in the west
     and together they shall plunder the
       tribes of the east;
   Edom and Moab shall be within
     their grasp,
   and Ammon shall obey them.
15 The LORD will divide the tongue of
   the Egyptian sea
     and wave his hand over the River
     to bring a scorching wind;
   he shall split it into seven channels
     and let men go across dry-shod.
16 So there shall be a causeway for the
   remnant of his people,
     for the remnant rescued from
       Assyria,
   as there was for Israel when they came
     up out of Egypt.

Songs of praise

12 You shall say on that day:
     I will praise thee, O LORD,
       though thou hast been angry with
         me;
     thy anger has turned back,
     and thou hast comforted me.
 2   God is indeed my deliverer.

   I am confident and unafraid;
     for the LORD is my refuge and defence
     and has shown himself my deliverer.
   And so you shall draw water with 3
     joy
   from the springs of deliverance.

   You shall all say on that day: 4
   Give thanks to the LORD and invoke
     him by name,
   make his deeds known in the world
     around;
   declare that his name is supreme.
   Sing psalms to the LORD, for he has 5
     triumphed,
     and this must be made known in all
       the world.
   Cry out, shout aloud, you that dwell 6
     in Zion,
   for the Holy One of Israel is among
     you in majesty.

Destruction of Babylon

Babylon: an oracle which Isaiah son **13**
of Amoz received in a vision.

   Raise the standard on a windy 2
     height,
   roar out your summons,
   beckon with arm upraised to the
     advance,
   draw your swords, you nobles.
   I have given my warriors their 3
     orders
   and summoned my fighting men to
     launch my anger;
   they are eager for my triumph.
   Hark, a tumult in the mountains, the 4
     sound of a vast multitude;
   hark, the roar of kingdoms, of nations
     gathering!
   The LORD of Hosts is mustering a host
     for war,
   men from a far country, from beyond 5
     the horizon.
   It is the LORD with the weapons of
     his wrath
   coming to lay the whole land waste.
   Howl, for the Day of the LORD is at 6
     hand;
   it comes, a mighty blow from Al-
     mighty God.
   Thereat shall every hand hang limp, 7
   every man's courage shall melt
     away,
   his stomach hollow with fear;   8
   anguish shall grip them, like a woman
     in labour.
   One man shall look aghast at an-
     other,
   and their faces shall burn with
     shame.
   The Day of the LORD is coming 9
     indeed,

that cruel day of wrath and fury,
to make the land a desolation
and exterminate its wicked people.

10 The stars of heaven in their constellations shall give no light,
the sun shall be darkened at its rising,
and the moon refuse to shine.

11 I will bring disaster upon the world
and their due punishment upon the wicked.
I will check the pride of the haughty
and bring low the arrogance of ruthless men.

12 I will make men scarcer than fine gold,
rarer than gold of Ophir.

13 Then the heavens shall shudder,[y]
and the earth shall be shaken from its place
at the fury of the LORD of Hosts, on the day of his anger.

14 Then, like a gazelle before the hunter
or a flock with no man to round it up,
each man will go back to his own people,
every one will flee to his own land.

15 All who are found will be stabbed,
all who are taken will fall by the sword;

16 their infants will be dashed to the ground before their eyes,
their houses rifled and their wives ravished.

17 I will stir up against them the Medes,
who care nothing for silver and are not tempted by gold,[z]

18 who have no pity on little children
and spare no mother's son;

19 and Babylon, fairest of kingdoms,
proud beauty of the Chaldaeans,
shall be like Sodom and Gomorrah when God overthrew them.

20 Never again shall she be inhabited,
no man shall dwell in her through all the ages;
there no Arab shall pitch his tent,
no shepherds fold their flocks.

21 There marmots shall have their lairs,
and porcupines shall overrun her houses;
there desert owls shall dwell,
and there he-goats shall gambol;

22 jackals shall occupy her mansions,[a]
and wolves her gorgeous palaces.
Her time draws very near,
and her days have not long to run.

When Israel is restored

The LORD will show compassion for 1
Jacob and will once again make Israel
his choice. He will settle them on their
own soil, and strangers will come to
join them and attach themselves to
Jacob. Many nations shall escort Israel 2
to her place, and she shall employ
them as slaves and slave-girls on the
land of the LORD; she shall take her
captors captive and rule over her task-
masters.

The fall of the king of Babylon

When the LORD gives you relief from 3
your pain and your fears and from the
cruel slavery laid upon you, you will 4
take up this song of derision over the
king of Babylon:

See how the oppressor has met his end
and his frenzy ceased!
The LORD has broken the rod of the 5
wicked,
the sceptre of the ruler
who struck down peoples in his rage 6
with unerring blows,
who crushed nations in anger
and persecuted them unceasingly.
The whole world has rest and is at 7
peace;
it breaks into cries of joy.
The pines themselves and the cedars 8
of Lebanon exult over you:
Since you have been laid low, they say,
no man comes up to fell us.

Sheol below was all astir   9
to meet you at your coming;
she roused the ancient dead to meet you,
all who had been leaders on earth;
she made all who had been kings of the nations
rise from their thrones.
One and all they greet you with these 10
words:
So you too are weak as we are,
and have become one of us!
Your pride and all the music of 11
your lutes
have been brought down to Sheol;[b]
maggots are the pallet beneath you,
and worms your coverlet.

How you have fallen from heaven, 12
bright morning star,
felled to the earth, sprawling helpless
across the nations!
You thought in your own mind,   13

---

y *Prob. rdg.; Heb.* Then I will make the heavens shudder.   z *Prob. rdg.; Heb. adds* bows shall dash
young men to the ground.   a *Prob. rdg.; Heb.* her widows.   b *Or* Your pride has been brought
down to Sheol to the crowding throng of your dead.

I will scale the heavens;
I will set my throne high above the
stars of God,
I will sit on the mountain where the
gods meet
in the far recesses of the north.

14 I will rise high above the cloud-banks
and make myself like the Most
High.

15 Yet you shall be brought down to
Sheol,
to the depths of the abyss.

16 Those who see you will stare at you,
they will look at you and ponder:
Is this, they will say, the man who
shook the earth,
who made kingdoms quake,

17 who turned the world into a desert
and laid its cities in ruins,
who never let his prisoners go free
to their homes,

18 the kings of every land?
Now they lie all of them in honour,
each in his last home.

19 But you have been flung out unburied,
mere loathsome carrion,
a companion to the slain pierced by
the sword
who have gone down to the stony
abyss.
And you, a corpse trampled underfoot,

20 shall not share burial with them,
for you have ruined your land and
slaughtered your people.
Such a brood of evildoers shall never
be seen again.

21 Make the shambles ready for his
sons
butchered for their fathers' sin;
they shall not rise up and possess
the world
nor cover the face of the earth with
cities.

22 I will rise against them, says the
LORD of Hosts; I will destroy the
name of Babylon and what remains
of her, her offspring and posterity,

23 says the LORD; I will make her a
haunt of the bustard, a waste of fen,
and sweep her with the besom of
destruction. This is the very word of
the LORD of Hosts.

The LORD's plan for the whole earth

24 The LORD of Hosts has sworn:
In very truth, as I planned, so shall it
be;
as I designed, so shall it fall out:

25 I will break the Assyrian in my
own land

and trample him underfoot upon
my mountains;
his yoke shall be lifted from you,
his burden taken from your shoulders.

26 This is the plan prepared for the
whole earth,
this the hand stretched out over all
the nations.

27 For the LORD of Hosts has prepared his plan:
who shall frustrate it?
His is the hand stretched out, and who
shall turn it back?

Philistia

28 In the year that King Ahaz died this
oracle came from God:

29 Let none of you rejoice, you Philistines,
because the rod that chastised you
is broken;
for a viper shall be born of a snake as
a plant from the root,
and its fruit shall be a flying serpent.

30 But the poor shall graze their flocks
in my meadows,
and the destitute shall lie down in
peace;
but the offspring of your roots I will
kill by starvation,
and put the remnant of you to
death.

31 Howl in the gate, cry for help in the
city,
let all Philistia be in turmoil;
for a great enemy is coming from
the north,
not a man straying from his ranks.

32 What answer is there for the envoys
of the nation?
This, that the LORD has fixed Zion
in her place,
and the afflicted among his people
shall take refuge there.

Moab

Moab: an oracle. **15**

On the night when Ar is sacked, Moab
meets her doom;
on the night when Kir is sacked, Moab
meets her doom.

2 The people of Dibon go up*c* to the hill-
shrines to weep;
Moab howls over Nebo and over
Medeba.
The hair is torn from every head, and
every beard shaved off.

3 In the streets men go clothed with
sackcloth,
they cry out on the roofs;

c The people ... go up: prob. rdg.; Heb. He has gone up to the house and Dibon.

in the public squares every man howls,
weeping as he goes through them.

4 Heshbon and Elealeh cry for help,
their voices are heard as far as Jahaz.
Thus Moab's stoutest warriors become cowards,
and her courage ebbs away.

5 My heart cries out for Moab,
whose nobles have fled[d] as far as Zoar.[e]
On the ascent to Luhith men go up weeping;
on the road to Horonaim there are cries of 'Disaster!'

6 The waters of Nimrim are desolate indeed;
the grass is parched, the herbage dead,
not a green thing is left;

7 and so the people carry off across the gorge of the Arabim
their hard-earned wealth and all their savings.

8 The cry for help echoes round the frontiers of Moab,
their howling reaches Eglaim and Beer-elim.

9 The waters of Dimon already run with blood;
yet I have more troubles in store for Dimon,
for I have a vision[f] of the survivors of Moab,
of the remnant of Admah.

16 The rulers of the country send a present of lambs
from Sela in the wilderness
to the hill of the daughter of Zion;

2 the daughters of Moab at the fords of the Arnon
shall be like fluttering birds, like scattered nestlings.

3 'Take up our cause with all your might;
let your shadow shield us at high noon, dark as night.
Shelter the homeless, do not betray the fugitive;

4 let the homeless people of Moab find refuge with you;
hide them from the despoiler.'

When extortion has done its work and the looting is over,
when the heel of the oppressor has vanished from the land,

5 a throne shall be set up in mutual trust in David's tent,
and on it there shall sit a true judge,
one who seeks justice and is swift to do right.

We have heard tell of Moab's pride, 6
how great it is,
we have heard of his pride, his overweening pride;
his talk is full of lies.
For this all Moab shall howl; 7
Moab shall howl indeed;
he[g] shall mourn for the prosperous farmers of Kir-hareseth,
utterly ruined;
the orchards of Heshbon, 8
the vines of Sibmah languish,
though their red grapes once laid low the lords of the nations,
though they reached as far as Jazer
and trailed out to the wilderness,
though their branches spread abroad
and crossed the sea.
Therefore I will weep for Sibmah's 9
vines as I weep for Jazer.
I will drench you with my tears, Heshbon and Elealeh;
for over your summer-fruits and your harvest
the shouts of the harvesters are ended.
Joy and gladness shall be banished 10
from the meadows,
no more shall men shout and sing in the vineyards,
no more shall they tread wine in the winepresses;
I have silenced the shouting of the harvesters.
Therefore my heart throbs 11
like a harp for Moab,
and my very soul for Kir-hareseth.[h]
When Moab comes to worship 12
and wearies himself at the hill-shrines,
when he enters his sanctuary to pray,
he will gain nothing.

These are the words which the 13
LORD spoke long ago about Moab; and 14
now he says, In three years, as a hired labourer counts them off, the glory of Moab shall become contemptible for all his vast numbers; a handful shall be left and those of no account.

Damascus

Damascus: an oracle. **17**

Damascus shall be a city no longer,
she shall be but a heap of ruins.
For ever desolate, flocks shall have 2
her for their own,
and lie there undisturbed.

---

d have fled: prob. rdg.; Heb. om.   e Prob. rdg.; Heb. adds Eglath Shelishiya.   f I have a vision: prob. rdg.; Heb. a lion.   g Prob. rdg.; Heb. you.   h Prob. rdg.; Heb. Kir-hares.

3 No longer shall Ephraim boast a
     fortified city,
     or Damascus a kingdom;
the remnant of Aram and the glory of
     Israel, their fate is one.
     This is the very word of the LORD
     of Hosts.

Israel

4 On that day Jacob's weight shall
     dwindle
and the fat on his limbs waste away,
5 as when the harvester gathers up the
     standing corn
     and reaps the ears in armfuls,
or as when a man gleans the ears in
     the Vale of Rephaim,
6 or as when one beats an olive-tree
     and only gleanings are left on it,
two or three berries on the top of a
     branch,
     four or five on the boughs of the
     fruiting tree.
This is the very word of the LORD the
     God of Israel.

7 On that day men shall look to their
     Maker and turn their eyes to the Holy
8 One of Israel; they shall not look to
     the altars made by their own hands
     nor to anything that their fingers
     have made, sacred poles or incense-
     altars.
9 On that day their strong cities shall
     be deserted like the cities of the
     Hivites and the Amorites, which they
     abandoned when Israel came in; all
     shall be desolate.

10 For you forgot the God who de-
     livered you,
     and did not remember the rock,
     your stronghold.
Plant then, if you will, your gardens
     in honour of Adonis,
     strike your cuttings for a foreign
     god;
11 protect your gardens on the day
     you plant them,
     and next day make the seed sprout.
     But the crop will be scorched when
     wasting disease comes
     in the day of incurable pain.

12 Listen! it is the thunder of many
     peoples,
     they thunder with the thunder of
     the sea.
     Listen! it is the roar of nations
     roaring with the roar of mighty
     waters.
13 When he rebukes them, away they
     fly,
     driven like chaff on the hills before
     the wind,

like thistledown before the storm.
At evening all is confusion, 14
and before morning they are gone.
Such is the fate of our plunderers,
the lot of those who despoil us.

Cush

There is a land of sailing ships, 18
a land beyond the rivers of Cush
which sends its envoys by the Nile, 2
journeying on the waters in vessels
     of reed.
Go, swift messengers,
go to a people tall and smooth-
     skinned,
to a people dreaded near and far,
a nation strong and proud,
whose land is scoured by rivers.
All you who dwell in the world, in- 3
     habitants of earth,
shall see when the signal is hoisted on
     the mountains
     and shall hear when the trumpet
     sounds.

These were the words of the LORD to 4
me:

From my dwelling-place I will look
     quietly down
when the heat shimmers in the sum-
     mer sun,
when the dew is heavy at harvest
     time.
Before the vintage, when the bud- 5
     ding is over
and the flower ripens into a berry,
     the shoots shall be cut down with
     knives,
     the branches struck off and cleared
     away.
All shall be left to birds of prey on 6
     the hills
     and to beasts of the earth;
     in summer the birds shall make their
     home there,
in winter every beast of the earth.

At that time tribute shall be 7
brought to the LORD of Hosts from
a people tall and smooth-skinned,
dreaded near and far, a nation strong
and proud, whose land is scoured by
rivers. They shall bring it to Mount
Zion, the place where men invoke the
name of the LORD of Hosts.

Egypt

Egypt: an oracle. 19

See how the LORD comes riding swiftly
     upon a cloud,
     he shall descend upon Egypt;
     the idols of Egypt quail before him,
     Egypt's courage melts within her.

2 I will set Egyptian against Egyptian,
and they shall fight one against another,
neighbour against neighbour,
city against city and kingdom against kingdom.

3 Egypt's spirit shall sink within her,
and I will throw her counsels into confusion.
They may resort to idols and oracle-mongers,
to ghosts and spirits,

4 but I will hand Egypt over to a hard master,
and a cruel king shall rule over them.
This is the very word of the Lord, the LORD of Hosts.

5 The waters of the Nile shall drain away,
the river shall be parched and run dry;

6 its channels shall stink,
the streams of Egypt shall be parched and dry up;
reeds and rushes shall wither away;

7 the lotus too beside the Nile*i*
and all that is sown along the Nile shall dry up,
shall be blown away and vanish.

8 The fishermen shall groan and lament,
all who cast their hooks into the Nile
and those who spread nets on the water shall lose heart.

9 The flax-dressers shall hang their heads,
the women carding and the weavers shall grow pale,

10 Egypt's spinners shall be downcast,
and all her artisans sick at heart.

11 Fools that you are, you princes of Zoan!
Wisest of Pharaoh's counsellors you may be,
but stupid counsellors you are.
How can you say to Pharaoh,
'I am the heir of wise men and spring from ancient kings'?

12 Where are your wise men, Pharaoh,
to teach you and make known to you
what the LORD of Hosts has planned for Egypt?

13 Zoan's princes are fools, the princes of Noph are dupes;
the chieftains of her clans have led Egypt astray.

14 The LORD has infused into them

---

a spirit that warps their judgement;
they make Egypt miss her way in all she does,
as a drunkard will miss his footing as he vomits.
There shall be nothing in Egypt that 15
any man can do,
head or tail, palm or rush.

When that day comes the Egyptians 16
shall become weak as women; they
shall fear and tremble when they see
the LORD of Hosts raise his hand
against them, as raise it he will. The 17
land of Judah shall strike terror into
Egypt; its very name shall cause dismay, because of the plans that the
LORD of Hosts has laid against them.
When that day comes there shall 18
be five cities in Egypt speaking the
language of Canaan and swearing
allegiance to the LORD of Hosts, and
one of them shall be called the City
of the Sun.*j*
When that day comes there shall be 19
an altar to the LORD in the heart of
Egypt, and a sacred pillar set up for
the LORD upon her frontier. It shall 20
stand as a token and a reminder
to the LORD of Hosts in Egypt,
so that when they appeal to him
against their oppressors, he may send
a deliverer to champion their cause,
and he shall rescue them. The LORD 21
will make himself known to the
Egyptians; on that day they shall
acknowledge the LORD and do him
service with sacrifice and grain-offering, make vows to him and pay them.
The LORD will strike down Egypt, 22
healing as he strikes; then they will
turn back to him and he will hear
their prayers and heal them.
When that day comes there shall 23
be a highway between Egypt and
Assyria; Assyrians shall come to
Egypt and Egyptians to Assyria; then
Egyptians shall worship with*k* Assyrians.
When that day comes Israel shall 24
rank with Egypt and Assyria, those
three, and shall be a blessing in the
centre of the world. So the LORD of 25
Hosts will bless them: A blessing be
upon Egypt my people, upon Assyria
the work of my hands, and upon
Israel my possession.

Assyria's conquest of Egypt and Cush
Sargon King of Assyria sent his com- 20
mander-in-chief*l* to Ashdod, and he
took it by storm. At that time the 2

---

i Prob. rdg.; Heb. adds on the mouth of the Nile.
shall be slaves to.   *l Or sent Tartan.*

j the City of the Sun: or Heliopolis.   *k Or*

LORD said to Isaiah son of Amoz, Come, strip the sackcloth from your waist and take your sandals off. He did so, and went about naked and 3 barefoot. The LORD said, My servant Isaiah has gone naked and barefoot for three years as a sign and a warning 4 to Egypt and Cush; just so shall the king of Assyria lead the captives of Egypt and the exiles of Cush naked and barefoot, their buttocks shamefully exposed, young and old alike. 5 All men shall be dismayed, their hopes in Cush and their pride in 6 Egypt humbled. On that day those who dwell along this coast will say, So much for all our hopes on which we relied for help and deliverance from the king of Assyria; what escape have we now?

Babylon

21 A wilderness: an oracle.

Rough weather, advancing like a storm in the south,
coming from the wilderness, from a land of terror!
2 Grim is the vision shown to me:
the traitor betrayed, the spoiler himself despoiled.
Up, Elam; up, Medes, to the siege,
no time for weariness!
3 At this my limbs writhe in anguish,
I am gripped by pangs like a woman in labour.
I am distraught past hearing, dazed past seeing,
4 my mind reels, sudden convulsions seize me.

The cool twilight I longed for has become a terror:
5 the banquet is set out, the rugs are spread;
they are eating and drinking—
rise, princes, burnish your shields.
6 For these were the words of the Lord to me:
Go, post a watchman to report what he sees.
7 He sees chariots, two-horsed chariots,
riders on asses, riders on camels.
He is alert, alert, always on the alert.
8 Then the look-out cried:
All day long I stand on the Lord's watch-tower
and night after night I keep my station.
9 See, there come men in a chariot, a two-horsed chariot.
And a voice calls back:
Fallen, fallen is Babylon,

and all the images of her gods lie shattered on the ground.
O my people, 10
once trodden out and winnowed on the threshing-floor,
what I have heard from the LORD of Hosts,
from the God of Israel, I have told you.

Dumah

Dumah: an oracle. 11

One calls to me from Seir:
Watchman, what is left of the night?
Watchman, what is left?
The watchman answered: 12
Morning comes, and also night.^{m}
Ask if you must; then come back again.

The Arabs

With the Arabs: an oracle. 13

You caravans of Dedan, that camp in the scrub with the Arabs,
bring water to meet the thirsty. 14
You dwellers in Tema, meet the fugitives with food,
for they flee from the sword, the 15 sharp edge of the sword,
from the bent bow, and from the press of battle.

For these are the words of the 16 Lord to me: Within a year, as a hired labourer counts off the years, all the glory of Kedar shall come to an end; few shall be the bows left to the war- 17 riors of Kedar.
The LORD the God of Israel has spoken.

Jerusalem in ferment

The Valley of Vision:^{n} an oracle. **22**
Tell me, what is amiss
that you have all climbed on to the roofs,
O city full of tumult, town in ferment 2
and filled with uproar,
whose slain were not slain with the sword
and did not die in battle?
Your commanders are all in flight, 3
huddled together out of bowshot;
all your stoutest warriors are huddled together,
they have taken to their heels.
Then I said, Turn your eyes away 4 from me;
leave me to weep in misery.
Do not thrust consolation on me
for the ruin of my own people.

m and also night: or and the night is full spent.   n Or of Calamity.

5 For the Lord, the LORD of Hosts,
has ordained a day of tumult, a day
of trampling and turmoil in the Valley
of Vision,[n] rousing cries for help that
echo among the mountains.

6 Elam took up his quiver,
horses were harnessed to the chariots of Aram,[o]
Kir took the cover from his shield.
7 Your fairest valleys were overrun by
chariots and horsemen,
the gates were hard beset,
8 the heart of Judah's defence was
laid open.

On that day you looked to the
weapons stored in the House of the
9 Forest; you filled all the many pools
in the City of David, collecting water
10 from the Lower Pool.[p] Then you
surveyed the houses in Jerusalem,
tearing some down to make the wall
11 inaccessible, and between the two walls
you made a cistern for the Waters of
the Old Pool;
but you did not look to the Maker
of it all
or consider him who fashioned it
long ago.
12 On that day the Lord, the LORD of
Hosts,
called for weeping and beating the
breast,
for shaving the head and putting on
sackcloth;
13 but instead there was joy and merrymaking,
slaughtering of cattle and killing of
sheep,
eating of meat and drinking of wine,
as you thought,
Let us eat and drink; for tomorrow
we die.

14 The LORD of Hosts has revealed
himself to me; in my hearing he
swore:

Your wickedness shall never be
purged
until you die.
This is the word of the Lord, the
LORD of Hosts.

Words to Shebna the steward

15 These were the words of the Lord, the
LORD of Hosts:

Go to this steward,
to Shebna, comptroller of the household, and say:

What right, what business, have you 16
here,
that you have dug yourself a grave
here,
cutting out your grave on a height
and carving yourself a resting-place
in the rock?
The LORD will shake you out, 17
shake you as a garment[q] is shaken
out
to rid it of lice;
then he will bundle you tightly and 18
throw you
like a ball into a great wide land.
There you shall die,
and there shall lie your chariot of
honour,
an object of contempt to your
master's household.
I will remove you from office and 19
drive you from your post.

On that day I will send for my 20
servant Eliakim son of Hilkiah; I will 21
invest him with your robe, gird him
with your sash; and hand over your
authority to him. He shall be a father
to the inhabitants of Jerusalem and
the people of Judah. I will lay the key 22
of the house of David on his shoulder;
what he opens no man shall shut, and
what he shuts no man shall open. He 23
shall be a seat of honour for his
father's family; I will fasten him
firmly in place like a peg. On him shall 24
hang all the weight of the family,
down to the lowest dregs—all the
little vessels, both bowls and pots. On 25
that day, says the LORD of Hosts, the
peg which was firmly fastened in its
place shall be removed; it shall be
hacked out and shall fall, and the
load of things hanging on it shall be
destroyed. The LORD has spoken.

Tyre

Tyre: an oracle. **23**

The ships of Tarshish howl, for the
harbour is sacked;
the port of entry from Kittim is swept
away.
The people of the sea-coast, the 2-3
merchants of Sidon, wail,
people whose agents cross the great
waters,
whose harvest[r] is the grain of the
Shihor
and their revenue the trade of
nations.

n Or of Calamity.   o Prob. rdg.; Heb. man.   p you filled . . . Lower Pool: or you took note of the
cracks, many as they were, in the wall of the City of David, and you collected water from the Lower
Pool.   q Prob. rdg.; Heb. man.   r whose harvest: prob. rdg.; Heb. the harvest of the Nile.

4 Sidon, the sea-fortress,[s] cries in her disappointment,[t]

I no longer feel the anguish of labour or bear children;

I have no young sons to rear, no daughters to bring up.

5 When the news is confirmed in Egypt

her people sway in anguish at the fate of Tyre.

6 Make your way to Tarshish, they say,

howl, you who dwell by the sea-coast.

7 Is this your busy city, ancient in story,

on whose voyages you were carried to settle far away?

8 Whose plan was this against Tyre, the city of battlements,

whose merchants were princes and her traders the most honoured men on earth?

9 The LORD of Hosts planned it to prick every noble's pride

and bring all the most honoured men on earth into contempt.

10 Take to the tillage of your fields, you people of Tarshish;

for your market[u] is lost.

11 The LORD has stretched out his hand over the sea

and shaken kingdoms,

he has given his command to destroy the marts of Canaan;

12 and he has said, You shall busy yourselves no more,

you, the sorely oppressed virgin city of Sidon.

Though you arise and cross over to Kittim,

even there you shall find no rest.

13 Look at this land, the destined home of ships[v]! The Chaldaeans[w] erected their[x] siege-towers, dismantled its palaces and laid it in ruins.

14 Howl, you ships of Tarshish; for your haven is sacked.

15 From that day Tyre shall be forgotten for seventy years, the span of one king's life. At the end of the seventy years her plight shall be that of the harlot in the song:

16 Take your harp, go round the city, poor forgotten harlot;

touch the strings sweetly, sing all your songs,

make men remember you again.

At the end of seventy years, the LORD 17 will turn again to Tyre; she shall go back to her old trade and hire herself out to every kingdom on earth. The 18 profits of her trading will be dedicated to the LORD; they shall not be hoarded or stored up, but shall be given to those who worship the LORD, to purchase food in plenty and fine attire.

The LORD's judgement on the earth

Beware, the LORD will empty the 24 earth,

split it open and turn it upside down, and scatter its inhabitants.

Then it will be the same for priest 2 and people,

the same for master and slave, mistress and slave-girl,

seller and buyer,

borrower and lender, debtor and creditor.

The earth is emptied clean away 3 and stripped clean bare.

For this is the word that the LORD has spoken.

The earth dries up and withers, 4 the whole world withers and grows sick;

the earth's high places sicken,

and earth itself is desecrated by the 5 feet of those who live in it,

because they have broken the laws, disobeyed the statutes

and violated the eternal covenant.

For this a curse has devoured the 6 earth

and its inhabitants stand aghast.

For this those who inhabit the earth dwindle

and only a few men are left.

The new wine dries up, the vines 7 sicken,

and all the revellers turn to sorrow.

Silent the merry beat of tam- 8 bourines,

hushed the shouts of revelry,

the merry harp is silent.

No one shall drink wine to the sound 9 of song;

the liquor will be bitter to the man who drinks it.

The city of chaos is a broken city, 10 every house barred, that no one may enter.

Men call for wine in the streets; 11 all revelry is darkened,

and mirth is banished from the land.

Desolation alone is left in the city 12 and the gate is broken into pieces.

s the sea-fortress: *prob. rdg.*; *Heb.* the sea, sea-fortress, saying.   t in her disappointment: *prob. rdg.*; *Heb.* be disappointed.   u *Prob. rdg.*; *Heb.* girdle.   v *Or* marmots.   w *Prob. rdg.*; *Heb. adds* this was the people; it was not Assyria.   x *Prob. rdg.*; *Heb.* his.

13 So shall it be in all the world, in every
nation,
    as when an olive-tree is beaten and
stripped,
    as when the vintage is ended.

14 Men raise their voices and cry aloud,
    they shout in the west,[y] so great is
the LORD's majesty.
15 Therefore let the LORD be glorified
in the regions of the east,
    and the name of the LORD the God
of Israel
    in the coasts and islands of the
west.

16 From the ends of the earth we have
heard them sing,
    How lovely is righteousness!
    But I thought, Villainy, villainy!
    Woe to the traitors and their
treachery!
    Traitors double-dyed they are
indeed!
17 The hunter's scare, the pit, and the
trap
    threaten all who dwell in the land;
18 if a man runs from the rattle of the
scare
    he will fall into the pit;
    if he climbs out of the pit
    he will be caught in the trap.
    When the windows of heaven above
are opened
    and earth's foundations shake,
19 the earth is utterly shattered,
    it is convulsed and reels wildly.
20 The earth reels to and fro like a
drunken man
    and sways like a watchman's
shelter;
    the sins of men weigh heavy upon it,
    and it falls to rise no more.

21 On that day the LORD will punish
the host of heaven in heaven, and on
earth the kings of the earth,
22 herded together, close packed like
prisoners in a dungeon;
    shut up in gaol, after a long time they
shall be punished.
23 The moon shall grow pale and the
sun hide its face in shame;
    for the LORD of Hosts has become
king
    on Mount Zion and in Jerusalem,
    and shows his glory before their
elders.

A song of thanksgiving

25 O LORD, thou art my God;
    I will exalt thee and praise thy
name;

for thou hast accomplished a wonderful purpose,
    certain and sure, from of old.
For thou hast turned cities into 2
heaps of ruin,
    and fortified towns into rubble;
    every mansion in the cities is swept
away,
    never to be rebuilt.
For this a cruel nation holds thee 3
in honour,
    the cities of ruthless nations fear
thee.
Truly thou hast been a refuge to the 4
poor,
  a refuge to the needy in his trouble,
shelter from the tempest and shade
from the heat.
For the blast of the ruthless is
like an icy storm
    or a scorching drought;   5
    thou subduest the roar of the foe,[z]
    and the song of the ruthless dies
away.

The LORD's care and kindness

On this mountain the LORD of Hosts 6
will prepare
    a banquet of rich fare for all the
peoples,
    a banquet of wines well matured
and richest fare,
    well-matured wines strained clear.
On this mountain the LORD will 7
swallow up
    that veil that shrouds all the peoples,
    the pall thrown over all the nations;
    he will swallow up death for ever.   8
Then the Lord GOD will wipe away
the tears
    from every face
and remove the reproach of his
people from the whole earth.
    The LORD has spoken.

Deliverance for the oppressed

On that day men will say,   9
    See, this is our God
    for whom we have waited to deliver
us;
    this is the LORD for whom we have
waited;
    let us rejoice and exult in his
deliverance.
For the hand of the LORD will rest on 10
this mountain,
    but Moab shall be trampled under
his feet
    as straw is trampled into a midden.
In it Moab shall spread out his 11
hands
    as a swimmer spreads his hands to
swim,

[y] in the west: *or* more loudly than the sea.   [z] *Prob. rdg.; Heb. adds* heat in the shadow of a cloud.

but he shall sink his pride with every stroke of his hands.

12 The LORD has thrown down the high defences of your walls, has levelled them to the earth and brought them down to the dust.

Jerusalem: a city of righteousness and peace

26 On that day this song shall be sung in Judah:

We have a strong city whose walls and ramparts are our deliverance.

2 Open the gates to let a righteous nation in,
a nation that keeps faith.

3 Thou dost keep in peace men of constant mind,
in peace because they trust in thee.

4 Trust in the LORD for ever;
for the LORD himself is an everlasting rock.

5 He has brought low all who dwell high in a towering city;
he levels it to the ground and lays it in the dust,

6 that the oppressed and the poor may tread it underfoot.

7 The path of the righteous is level,
and thou markest out the right way for the upright.

8 We too look to the path prescribed in thy laws, O LORD;
thy name and thy memory are our heart's desire.

9 With all my heart I long for thee in the night,
I seek thee eagerly when dawn breaks;
for, when thy laws prevail in the land,
the inhabitants of the world learn justice.

10 The wicked are destroyed, they have never learnt justice;
corrupt in a land of honest ways,
they do not regard the majesty of the LORD.

Death and resurrection

11 O LORD, thy hand is lifted high,
but the bitter enemies of thy people do not see it;[a]
let the fire of thy enmity destroy them.

12 O LORD, thou wilt bestow prosperity on us;
for in truth all our works are thy doing.

13 O LORD our God,

---

other lords than thou have been our masters,
but thee alone do we invoke by name.

14 The dead will not live again,
those long in their graves will not rise;
to this end thou hast punished them and destroyed them,
and made all memory of them perish.

15 Thou hast enlarged the nation, O LORD,
enlarged it and won thyself honour,
thou hast extended all the frontiers of the land.

16 In our distress, O LORD, we[b] sought thee out,
chastened by the mere whisper of thy rebuke.

17 As a woman with child, when her time is near,
is in labour and cries out in her pains,
so were we in thy presence, O LORD.

18 We have been with child, we have been in labour,
but have brought forth wind.
We have won no success for the land,
and no one will be born to inhabit the world.

19 But thy dead live, their bodies will rise again.
They that sleep in the earth will awake and shout for joy;
for thy dew is a dew of sparkling light,
and the earth will bring those long dead to birth again.

The coming judgement

20 Go, my people, enter your rooms and shut your doors behind you;
withdraw for a brief while, until wrath has gone by.

21 For see, the LORD is coming from his place
to punish the inhabitants of the earth for their sins;
then the earth shall uncover her blood-stains
and hide her slain no more.

Allegories of the LORD's judgements

27 On that day the LORD will punish with his cruel sword, his mighty and powerful sword,
Leviathan that twisting[c] sea-serpent,
that writhing serpent Leviathan,
and slay the monster of the deep.

---

a Prob. rdg.; Heb. adds let them see and be ashamed.   *b Prob. rdg.; Heb.* they.   *c Or* primeval.

K*

2 On that day sing to the pleasant vineyard,
3 I the LORD am its keeper,
moment by moment I water it for fear its green leaves fail.
Night and day I tend it,
4 but I get no wine;
I would as soon have briars and thorns,
then I would wage war upon it and burn it all up,
5 unless it grasps me as its refuge and makes peace with me—
unless it makes peace with me.

6 In time to come Jacob's offspring shall take root
and Israel shall bud and blossom,
and they shall fill the whole earth with fruit.

7 Has God struck him down as he struck others down?
Has the slayer been slain as he slew others?
8-10[d] This then purges Jacob's iniquity,
this[e] has removed his sin:
that he grinds all altar stones to powder like chalk;
no sacred poles and incense-altars are left standing.

The fortified city is left solitary,
and his quarrel with her ends in brushing her away,[f]
removing her by a cruel blast when the east wind blows;
it is a homestead stripped bare, deserted like a wilderness;
there the calf grazes and there lies down,
and crops every twig.
11 Its boughs snap off when they grow dry,
and women come and light their fires with them.
For they are a people without sense;
therefore their maker will show them no mercy,
he who formed them will show them no favour.

The ingathering of dispersed Israelites

12 On that day the LORD will beat out the grain,
from the streams of the Euphrates to the Torrent of Egypt;
but you Israelites will be gleaned one by one.
13 On that day

a blast shall be blown on a great trumpet,
and those who are lost in Assyria
and those dispersed in Egypt will come in
and worship the LORD on the holy mountain, in Jerusalem.

The LORD's purpose for Ephraim

Oh, the proud garlands of the 28 drunkards of Ephraim
and the flowering sprays, so lovely in their beauty,
on the heads of revellers dripping with perfumes,
overcome with wine!
See, the Lord has one at his bidding, 2 mighty and strong,
whom he sets to work with violence against the land,
like a sweeping storm of hail, like a destroying tempest,
like a torrent of water in overwhelming flood.
The proud garlands of Ephraim's 3 drunkards
shall be trampled underfoot,
and the flowering sprays, so lovely 4 in their beauty
on the heads dripping with perfumes,
shall be like early figs ripe before summer;
he who sees them plucks them,
and their bloom is gone while they lie in his hand.
On that day the LORD of Hosts shall 5 be a lovely garland,
a beautiful diadem for the remnant of his people,
a spirit of justice for one who presides 6 in a court of justice,
and of valour for[g] those who repel the enemy at the gate.

Corruption of priests and prophets

These too are addicted to wine, 7 clamouring in their cups:
priest and prophet are addicted to strong drink
and bemused with wine;
clamouring in their cups, confirmed topers,[h]
hiccuping in drunken stupor;
every table is covered with vomit, 8 filth that leaves no clean spot.
Who is it that the prophet hopes to 9 teach,

d *Verses 8–10 re-arranged thus: 9, 10a, 8, 10b.*   e *Prob. rdg.; Heb. adds all fruit.*   f *Prob rdg.; Heb. adds by dismissing her.*   g *for: prob. rdg.; Heb. om.*   h *These too ... topers: or These too lose their way through wine and are set wandering by strong drink: priest and prophet lose their way through strong drink and are fuddled with wine; are set wandering by strong drink, lose their way through tippling.*

to whom will what they hear make
sense?
Are they babes newly weaned, just
taken from the breast?
10 It is all harsh cries and raucous
shouts,
'A little more here, a little there!'
11 So it will be with barbarous speech
and strange tongue
that this people will hear God
speaking,
12 this people to whom he once said,
'This is true rest; let the exhausted
have rest.
This is repose', and they refused to
listen.
13 Now to them the word of the LORD
will be
harsh cries and raucous shouts,
'A little more here, a little there!'—
and so, as they walk, they will
stumble backwards,
they will be injured, trapped and
caught.
14 Listen then to the word of the LORD,
you arrogant men
who rule this people in Jerusalem.
15 You say, 'We have made a treaty
with Death
and signed a pact with Sheol:
so that, when the raging flood sweeps
by, it shall not touch us;
for we have taken refuge in lies
and sheltered behind falsehood.'
16 These then are the words of the Lord
GOD:
Look, I am laying a stone in Zion,
a block of granite,
a precious corner-stone for a firm
foundation;
he who has faith shall not waver.
17 I will use justice as a plumb-line
and righteousness as a plummet;
hail shall sweep away your refuge
of lies,
and flood-waters carry away your
shelter.
18 Then your treaty with Death shall
be annulled
and your pact with Sheol shall not
stand;
the raging waters will sweep by,
and you will be like land swept by
the flood.
19 As often as it sweeps by, it will take
you;
morning after morning it will sweep
by,
day and night.
The very thought of such tidings
will bring nothing but dismay;
20 for 'The bed is too short for a man
to stretch,

and the blanket too narrow to
cover him.'
21 But the LORD shall arise as he rose on
Mount Perazim
and storm with rage as he did in the
Vale of Gibeon
to do what he must do—how strange
a deed!
to perform his work—how outlandish
a work!
22 But now have done with your arrogance,
lest your bonds grow tighter;
for I have heard destruction decreed
by the Lord GOD of Hosts for the
whole land.

The parable of the ploughman
23 Listen and hear what I say,
attend and hear my words.
24 Will the ploughman continually
plough for the sowing,
breaking his ground and harrowing
it?
25 Does he not, once he has levelled it,
broadcast the dill and scatter the
cummin?
Does he not plant the wheat in
rows
with barley[i] and spelt along the
edge?
26 Does not his God instruct him and
train him aright?
27 Dill is not threshed with a sledge,
and the cartwheel is not rolled over
cummin;
dill is beaten with a rod,
and cummin with a flail.
28 Corn is crushed, but not to the utter-
most,
not with a final crushing;
his cartwheels rumble over it and
break it up,
but they do not grind it fine.
29 This message, too, comes from the
LORD of Hosts,
whose purposes are wonderful
and his power great.

Judgement and mercy for Judah
29 Alas for Ariel! Ariel,
the city where David encamped.
Add year to year,
let the pilgrim-feasts run their
round,
2 and I will bring Ariel to sore straits,
when there shall be moaning and
lamentation.
I will make her my Ariel indeed, my
fiery altar.
3 I will throw my army round you
like a wall;

---

i Prob. rdg.; Heb. adds an unintelligible word.

I will set a ring of outposts all round
 you
and erect siege-works against you.
4 You shall be brought low, you will
 speak out of the ground
and your words will issue from the
 earth;
your voice will come like a ghost's
 from the ground,
and your words will squeak out of
 the earth.
5 Yet the horde of your enemies shall
 crumble into dust,
the horde of ruthless foes shall fly
 like chaff.
Then suddenly, all in an instant,
6 punishment shall come from the
 LORD of Hosts
with thunder and earthquake and
 a great noise,
with storm and tempest and a flame
 of devouring fire;
7 and the horde of all the nations war-
 ring against Ariel,
all their baggage-trains and siege-
 works,
and all her oppressors themselves,
shall fade as a dream, a vision of
 the night.
8 Like a starving man who dreams
 and thinks that he is eating,
but wakes up to find himself empty,
or a thirsty man who dreams
 and thinks that he is drinking,
but wakes up to find himself thirsty
 and dry,
so shall the horde of all the nations
 be
that war against Mount Zion.

Judah's religion and politics condemned
9 Loiter and be dazed, enjoy yourselves
 and be blinded,
be drunk but not with wine, reel
 but not with strong drink;
10 for the LORD has poured upon you a
 spirit of deep stupor;
he has closed your eyes, the prophets,
and muffled your heads, the seers.

11 All prophetic vision has become for
 you like a sealed book. Give such a
 book to one who can read and say,
 'Come, read this'; he will answer, 'I
12 cannot', because it is sealed. Give it to
 one who cannot read and say, 'Come,
 read this'; he will answer, 'I cannot
 read.'
13 Then the Lord said:

Because this people approach me with
 their mouths
and honour me with their lips

while their hearts are far from me,
and their religion is but a precept of
 men, learnt by rote,
therefore I will yet again shock this 14
 people,
adding shock to shock:
the wisdom of their wise men shall
 vanish
and the discernment of the discerning shall be lost.

Shame upon those who seek to 15
 hide their purpose
too deep for the LORD to see,
and who, when their deeds are done
 in the dark,
say, 'Who sees us? Who knows of
 us?'
How you turn things upside down, 16
as if the potter ranked no higher
 than the clay!
Shall the thing made say of its maker,
 'He did not make me'?
Shall the pot say of the potter, 'He
 has no skill'?
The time is but short 17
before Lebanon goes back to grassland
and the grassland is no better than
 scrub.

Future revival and restoration
On that day deaf men shall hear 18
 when a book is read,
and the eyes of the blind shall see
 out of impenetrable darkness.
The lowly shall once again rejoice in 19
 the LORD,
and the poorest of men exult in the
 Holy One of Israel.
The ruthless shall be no more, the 20
 arrogant shall cease to be;
those who are quick to see mischief,
those who charge others with a sin 21
or lay traps for him who brings the
 wrongdoer into court
or by falsehood deny justice to the
 righteous—
all these shall be exterminated.

Therefore these are the words of 22
the LORD the God of the house of
Jacob, the God who ransomed Abraham:

This is no time for Jacob to be
 shamed,
no time for his face to grow pale;
for his descendants will hallow my 23
 name
when they see what I have done in
 their nation.
They will hallow the Holy One of
 Jacob

and hold the God of Israel in awe;
24 those whose minds are confused will
gain understanding,
and the obstinate will receive instruction.

Egypt's help is worthless

30 Oh, rebel sons! says the LORD,
you make plans, but not of my
devising,
you weave schemes, but not inspired by me,
piling sin upon sin;
2 you hurry down to Egypt without
consulting me,
to seek protection under Pharaoh's
shelter
and take refuge under Egypt's wing.
3 Pharaoh's protection will bring you
disappointment
and refuge under Egypt's wing
humiliation;
4 for, though his officers are at Zoan
and his envoys reach as far as Hanes,
5 all are left in sorry plight by that unprofitable nation,
no help they find, no profit, only
disappointment and disgrace.

6 The Beasts of the South: an oracle.

Through a land of hardship and distress
the tribes of lioness and roaring lion,
sand-viper and venomous flying
serpent,
carry their wealth on the backs of
asses
and their treasures on camels'
humps
to an unprofitable people.
7 Vain and worthless is the help of
Egypt;
therefore have I given her this
name,
Rahab Quelled.
8 Now come and write it on a tablet,
engrave it as an inscription before
their eyes,
that it may be there in future days,
a testimony for all time.
9 For they are a race of rebels, disloyal
sons,
sons who will not listen to the LORD's
instruction;
10 they say to the seers, 'You shall not
see',
and to the visionaries, 'You shall
have no true visions;
give us smooth words and seductive
visions.
11 Turn aside, leave the straight path,
and rid us for ever of the Holy One of
Israel.'

The LORD is waiting to show his favour

These are the words of the Holy One 12
of Israel:

Because you have rejected this
warning
and trust in devious and dishonest
practices,
resting on them for support,
therefore you shall find this iniquity 13
will be
like a crack running down
a high wall, which bulges
and suddenly, all in an instant, comes
crashing down,
as an earthen jar is broken with a 14
crash,
mercilessly shattered,
so that not a shard is found among
the fragments
to take fire from the glowing embers,
or to scoop up water from a pool.

These are the words of the Lord GOD 15
the Holy One of Israel:

Come back, keep peace, and you
will be safe;
in stillness and in staying quiet, there
lies your strength.
But you would have none of it; you 16
said, No,
we will take horse and flee;
therefore you shall be put to flight:
We will ride apace;
therefore swift shall be the pace of
your pursuers.
When a thousand flee at the chal- 17
lenge of one,
you shall all flee at the challenge of
five, until you are left
like a pole on a mountain-top, a
signal post on a hill.
Yet the LORD is waiting to show you 18
his favour,
yet he yearns to have pity on you;
for the LORD is a God of justice.
Happy are all who wait for him!

A future day of blessing promised

O people of Zion who dwell in 19
Jerusalem, you shall weep no more.
The LORD will show you favour and
answer you when he hears your cry
for help. The Lord may give you 20
bread of adversity and water of
affliction, but he who teaches you
shall no longer be hidden out of sight,
but with your own eyes you shall see
him always. If you stray from the 21
road to right or left you shall hear
with your own ears a voice behind
you saying, This is the way; follow it.
You will reject, as things unclean, 22

your silvered images and your idols
sheathed in gold; you will loathe
them like a foul discharge and call
23 them ordure.[j] The Lord will give you
rain for the seed you sow, and as the
produce of your soil he will give you
heavy crops of corn in plenty. When
that day comes the cattle shall graze
24 in broad pastures; the oxen and asses
that work your land shall be fed with
well-seasoned fodder, winnowed with
25 shovel and fork. On each high mountain and each lofty hill shall be streams
of running water, on the day of massacre when the highest in the land fall.
26 The moon shall shine with a brightness like the sun's, and the sun with
seven times his wonted brightness,
seven days' light in one, on the day
when the LORD binds up the broken
limbs of his people and heals their
wounds.

The LORD will afflict Assyria

27   See, the name of the LORD comes
from afar,
his anger blazing and his doom
heavy.
His lips are charged with wrath
and his tongue is a devouring fire.
28   His breath is like a torrent in spate,
rising neck-high,
a yoke to force the nations to their
ruin,
a bit in the mouth to guide the peoples
astray.
29   But for you there shall be songs,
as on a night of sacred pilgrimage,
your hearts glad, as the hearts of men
who walk to the sound of the pipe
on their way to the LORD's hill, to the
rock of Israel.
30   Then the LORD shall make his voice
heard in majesty
and show his arm sweeping down in
fierce anger
with devouring flames of fire,
with cloudburst and tempests of rain
and hailstones;
31   for at the voice of the LORD
Assyria's heart fails her,
as she feels the stroke of his rod.
32 Tambourines and harps and shaking
sistrums
shall keep time
with every stroke of his rod,
of the chastisement which the LORD
inflicts on her.
33   Long ago was Topheth made ready,[k]
made deep and broad,
its fire-pit a blazing mass of logs,

and the breath of the LORD like a
stream of brimstone
blazing in it.

Deliverance is from the LORD, not Egypt

Shame upon those who go down to **31**
Egypt for help
and rely on horses,
putting their trust in chariots many
in number
and in horsemen in their thousands,
but do not look to the Holy One of
Israel
or seek guidance of the LORD!
Yet the LORD too in his wisdom can **2**
bring about trouble
and he does not take back his words;
he will rise up against the league of
evildoers,
against all who help those who do
wrong.
The Egyptians are men, not God,[l] **3**
their horses are flesh, not spirit;
and, when the LORD stretches out
his hand,
the helper will stumble and he who is
helped will fall,
and they will all vanish together.

This is what the LORD has said to me: **4**

As a lion or a young lion growls over
its prey
when the muster of shepherds is
called out against it,
and is not scared at their noise
or cowed by their clamour,
so shall the LORD of Hosts come down
to do battle
for Mount Zion and her high summit.
Thus the LORD of Hosts, like a bird **5**
hovering over its young,
will be a shield over Jerusalem;
he will shield her and deliver her,
standing over her and delivering
her.
O Israel, come back to him whom you **6**
have so deeply offended,
for on that day when you spurn, **7**
one and all,
the idols of silver and the idols of
gold
which your own sinful hands have
made,
Assyria shall fall by the sword, but **8**
by no sword of man;
a sword that no man wields shall
devour him.
He shall flee before the sword,
and his young warriors shall be put
to forced labour,

---

[j] call them ordure: *or* say to them, Be off.
king?   [l] *Or* gods.

[k] *Prob. rdg.; Heb. adds* is that prepared also for the

9 his officers shall be helpless from
  terror
  and his captains too dismayed to
    flee.
  This is the very word of the LORD
  whose fire blazes in Zion,
  and whose furnace is set up in
    Jerusalem.

When righteousness prevails

32 Behold, a king shall reign in righteous-
    ness
  and his rulers rule with justice,
2 and a man shall be a refuge from
    the wind
  and a shelter from the tempest,
  or like runnels of water in dry
    ground,
  like the shadow of a great rock in a
    thirsty land.
3 The eyes that can see will not be
    clouded,
  and the ears that can hear will
    listen;
4 the anxious heart will understand
    and know,
  and the man who stammers will at
    once speak plain.
5 The scoundrel will no longer be
    thought noble,
  nor the villain called a prince;
6 for the scoundrel will speak like a
    scoundrel
  and will hatch evil in his heart;
  he is an impostor in all his actions,
  and in his words a liar even to the
    LORD;
  he starves the hungry of their food
  and refuses drink to the thirsty.
7 The villain's ways are villainous
  and he devises infamous plans
  to ruin the poor with his lies
  and deny justice to the needy.
8 But the man of noble mind forms
    noble designs
  and stands firm in his nobility.

Times of dearth and times of plenty

9 You women that live at ease, stand
    up
  and hear what I have to say.
  You young women without a care,
    mark my words.
10 You have no cares now, but when the
    year is out, you will tremble,
  for the vintage will be over and no
    produce gathered in.
11 You who are now at ease, be anxious;
  tremble, you who have no cares.
  Strip yourselves bare;
  put a cloth round your waists
12 and beat your breasts

for the pleasant fields and fruitful
  vines.
On the soil of my people shall spring 13
  up thorns and briars,
in every happy home and in the busy
  town,
for the palace is forsaken and the 14
  crowded streets deserted;
citadel[m] and watch-tower are turned
  into open heath,
the joy of wild asses ever after and
  pasture for the flocks,
until a spirit from on high is lavished 15
  upon us.
  Then the wilderness will become
    grassland
  and grassland will be cheap as scrub;
  then justice shall make its home in 16
    the wilderness,
  and righteousness dwell in the
    grassland;
  when righteousness shall yield peace 17
and its fruit be quietness and confidence for ever.
  Then my people shall live in a tran- 18
    quil country,
dwelling in peace, in houses full of
  ease;
  it will be cool on the slopes of the 19
    forest then,
  and cities shall lie peaceful in the
    plain.
  Happy shall you be, sowing every 20
    man by the water-side,
  and letting ox and ass run free.

The LORD, the mainstay of the age

Ah! you destroyer, yourself un- 33
  destroyed,
betrayer still unbetrayed,
when you cease to destroy you will
  be destroyed,
after all your betrayals, you will be
  betrayed yourself.

O LORD, show us thy favour; we hope 2
  in thee.
Uphold us every morning,
save us when troubles come.
At the roar of the thunder the 3
  peoples flee,
at thy rumbling nations are scattered;
their spoil is swept up as if young 4
  locusts had swept it,
like a swarm of locusts men swarm
  upon it.

The LORD is supreme, for he dwells on 5
  high;
if you fill Zion with justice and with
  righteousness,

m Or hill; *Heb.* Ophel.

6 then he will be the mainstay of the age:[n]
wisdom and knowledge are the assurance of salvation;
the fear of the LORD is her[o] treasure.

Righteousness amidst moral decay

7 Hark, how the valiant cry aloud for help,
and those sent to sue for peace weep bitterly!
8 The highways are deserted, no travellers tread the roads.
Covenants are broken, treaties are flouted;
man is of no account.
9 The land is parched and wilting, Lebanon is eaten away and crumbling;
Sharon has become a desert, Bashan and Carmel are stripped bare.
10 Now, says the LORD, I will rise up. Now I will exalt myself, now lift myself up.
11 What you conceive and bring to birth is chaff and stubble;
a wind like fire shall devour you.
12 Whole nations shall be heaps of white ash,
or like thorns cut down and set on fire.
13 You who dwell far away, hear what I have done;
acknowledge my might, you who are near.
14 In Zion sinners quake with terror, the godless are seized with trembling and ask,
Can any of us live with a devouring fire?
Can any live in endless burning?
15 The man who lives an upright life and speaks the truth,
who scorns to enrich himself by extortion,
who snaps his fingers at a bribe, who stops his ears to hear nothing of bloodshed,
who closes his eyes to the sight of evil—
16 that is the man who shall dwell on the heights,
his refuge a fastness in the cliffs, his bread secure and his water never failing.

17 Your eyes shall see a king in his splendour
and will look upon a land of far distances.

You will call to mind what once you 18 feared:
'Where then is he that counted, where is he that weighed,
where is he that counted the treasures?'
You will no longer see that bar-19 barous people,
that people whose speech was so hard to catch,
whose stuttering speech you could not understand.

The LORD our king

Look upon Zion, city of our solemn 20 feasts,
let your eyes rest on Jerusalem,
a land of comfort, a tent that shall never be shifted,
whose pegs shall never be pulled up, not one of its ropes cast loose.
There we have the LORD's majesty;[p] 21
it will be a place[q] of rivers and broad streams;
but[r] no galleys shall be rowed there, no stately ship sail by.
For the LORD our judge, the LORD our 22 law-giver,
the LORD our king—he himself will save us.
[Men may say, Your rigging is slack; 23 it will not hold the mast firm in its socket,
nor can the sails be spread.]
Then the blind man shall have a full share of the spoil
and the lame shall take part in the pillage;
no man who dwells there shall say, 24 'I am sick';
and the sins of the people who live there shall be pardoned.

Desolation

Approach, you nations, to listen, 34
and attend, you peoples;
let the earth listen and everything in it,
the world and all that it yields;
for the LORD's anger is turned 2 against all the nations
and his wrath against all the host of them:
he gives them over to slaughter and destruction.
Their slain shall be flung out, 3
the stench shall rise from their corpses,
and the mountains shall stream with their blood.

n the age: *prob. rdg.; Heb.* your times.   o *Prob. rdg.; Heb.* his.   p *Or* threshing-floor.   q it
... place: *or* instead.   r *Or* and.

4 All the host of heaven shall crumble
   into nothing,
   the heavens shall be rolled up like
   a scroll,
   and the starry host fade away,
   as the leaf withers from the vine
   and the ripening fruit from the fig-
   tree;
5 for the sword of the LORD[s] appears
   in heaven.
   See how it descends in judgement
   on Edom,
   on the people whom he dooms[t] to
   destruction.
6 The LORD has a sword steeped in
   blood,
   it is gorged with fat,
   the fat of rams' kidneys, and the
   blood of lambs and goats;
   for he has a sacrifice in Bozrah,
   a great slaughter in Edom.
7 Wild oxen shall come down and
   buffaloes[u] with them,
   bull and bison together,
   and the land shall drink deep of
   blood
   and the soil be sated with fat.
8 For the LORD has a day of vengeance,
   the champion of Zion has a year
   when he will requite.
9 Edom's torrents shall be turned
   into pitch
   and its soil into brimstone,
   and the land shall become blazing
   pitch,
10 which night and day shall never be
   quenched,
   and its smoke shall go up for ever.
   From generation to generation it
   shall lie waste,
   and no man shall pass through it
   ever again.
11 Horned owl and bustard shall make
   their home in it,
   screech-owl and raven shall haunt
   it.
   He has stretched across it a
   measuring-line of chaos,
12 and its frontiers shall be a jumble
   of stones.
   No king shall be acclaimed there,
   and all its princes shall come to
   nought.
13 Thorns shall sprout in its palaces;
   nettles and briars shall cover its
   walled towns.
   It shall be rough land fit for wolves,
   a haunt of desert-owls.
14 Marmots shall consort with jackals,
   and he-goat shall encounter he-goat.
   There too the nightjar shall rest

and find herself a place for repose.
There the sand-partridge shall make 15
   her nest,
lay her eggs and hatch them
and gather her brood under her
   wings;
there shall the kites gather,
one after another.
Consult the book of the LORD and 16
   read it:
not one of these shall be lacking,
not one miss its fellow,
for with his own mouth he has
   ordered it
and with his own breath he has
   brought them together.
He it is who has allotted each its place, 17
and his hand has measured out
   their portions;
they shall occupy it for ever
and dwell there from generation to
   generation.

Restoration

Let the wilderness and the thirsty 35
   land be glad,
let the desert rejoice and burst into
   flower.
Let it flower with fields of asphodel, 2
let it rejoice and shout for joy.
The glory of Lebanon is given to it,
the splendour too of Carmel and
   Sharon;
these shall see the glory of the LORD,
the splendour of our God.
Strengthen the feeble arms, 3
steady the tottering knees;
say to the anxious, Be strong and 4
   fear not.
See, your God comes with vengeance,
with dread retribution he comes to
   save you.
Then shall blind men's eyes be 5
   opened,
and the ears of the deaf unstopped.
Then shall the lame man leap like 6
   a deer,
and the tongue of the dumb shout
   aloud;
for water springs up in the wilderness,
and torrents flow in dry land.
The mirage becomes a pool, 7
the thirsty land bubbling springs;
instead of reeds and rushes, grass
   shall grow
in the rough land where wolves now
   lurk.
And there shall be a causeway there 8
which shall be called the Way of
   Holiness,

---

s the sword of the LORD: *prob. rdg.; Heb.* my sword.
loes: *prob. rdg.; Heb. om.*   t *Prob. rdg.; Heb.* I doom.   u and buffa-

and the unclean shall not pass along
it;
it shall become a pilgrim's way,[v]
no fool shall trespass on it.

9 No lion shall come there,
no savage beast climb on to it;
not one shall be found there.
By it those he has ransomed shall
return

10 and the LORD's redeemed come
home;
they shall enter Zion with shouts of
triumph,
crowned with everlasting gladness.
Gladness and joy shall be their
escort,
and suffering and weariness shall
flee away.

Sennacherib invades Judah

36 1[w] In the fourteenth year of the reign of
Hezekiah, Sennacherib king of Assyria
attacked and took all the fortified
2 cities of Judah. From Lachish he sent
the chief officer[x] with a strong force
to King Hezekiah at Jerusalem; and
he halted by the conduit of the Upper
Pool on the causeway which leads
3 to the Fuller's Field. There Eliakim
son of Hilkiah, the comptroller of
the household, came out to him,
with Shebna the adjutant-general and
Joah son of Asaph, the secretary of
4 state. The chief officer said to them,
'Tell Hezekiah that this is the message
of the Great King, the king of Assyria:
"What ground have you for this con-
5 fidence of yours? Do you think fine
words can take the place of skill and
numbers? On whom then do you rely
for support in your rebellion against
6 me? On Egypt? Egypt is a splintered
cane that will run into a man's hand
and pierce it if he leans on it. That is
what Pharaoh king of Egypt proves
7 to all who rely on him. And if you tell
me that you are relying on the LORD
your God, is he not the god whose hill-
shrines and altars Hezekiah has suppressed, telling Judah and Jerusalem
that they must prostrate themselves
before this altar alone?"'

Sennacherib presses for surrender

8 'Now, make a bargain with my master
the king of Assyria: I will give you
two thousand horses if you can find
9 riders for them. Will you reject the
authority of even the least of my
master's servants and rely on Egypt
10 for chariots and horsemen? Do you
think that I have come to attack this

land and destroy it without the consent of the LORD? No; the LORD himself said to me, "Attack this land and
destroy it."'

Eliakim, Shebna, and Joah said to 11
the chief officer, 'Please speak to us
in Aramaic, for we understand it; do
not speak Hebrew to us within earshot of the people on the city wall.'
The chief officer answered, 'Is it to 12
your master and to you that my
master has sent me to say this? Is it
not to the people sitting on the wall
who, like you, will have to eat their
own dung and drink their own urine?'
Then he stood and shouted in Hebrew, 13
'Hear the message of the Great King,
the king of Assyria. These are the 14
king's words: "Do not be taken in by
Hezekiah. He cannot save you. Do not 15
let him persuade you to rely on the
LORD, and tell you that the LORD will
save you and that this city will never
be surrendered to the king of Assyria."
Do not listen to Hezekiah; these are 16
the words of the king of Assyria:
"Make peace with me. Come out to
me, and then you shall each eat the
fruit of his own vine and his own fig-
tree, and drink the water of his own
cistern, until I come and take you to 17
a land like your own, a land of grain
and new wine, of corn and vineyards.
Beware lest Hezekiah mislead you by 18
telling you that the LORD will save
you. Did the god of any of these
nations save his land from the king
of Assyria? Where are the gods of 19
Hamath and Arpad? Where are the
gods of Sepharvaim? Where are the
gods of Samaria? Did they save
Samaria from me? Among all the 20
gods of these nations is there one who
saved his land from me? And how is
the LORD to save Jerusalem?"'

The people were silent and answered 21
not a word, for the king had given
orders that no one was to answer him.
Eliakim son of Hilkiah, comptroller of 22
the household, Shebna the adjutant-
general, and Joah son of Asaph,
secretary of state, came to Hezekiah
with their clothes rent and reported
what the chief officer had said.

Hezekiah seeks Isaiah's advice

When King Hezekiah heard their 37 1
report, he rent his clothes and wrapped himself in sackcloth, and went
into the house of the LORD. He sent 2
Eliakim comptroller of the household,
Shebna the adjutant-general, and the

---

[v] a pilgrim's way: *prob. rdg.; Heb. unintelligible.*
1–19.   [x] Or sent Rab-shakeh.   [y] Verses 1–38: cp. 2 Kgs. 19. 1–37; 2 Chr. 32. 20–2.
[w] Verses 1–22: cp. 2 Kgs. 18. 13–37; 2 Chr. 32.

senior priests, all covered in sackcloth,
3 to the prophet Isaiah son of Amoz, to
give him this message from the king:
'This day is a day of trouble for us,
a day of reproof and contempt. We
are like a woman who has no strength
to bear the child that is coming to the
4 birth. It may be that the LORD your
God heard the words of the chief
officer whom his master the king of
Assyria sent to taunt the living God,
and will confute what he, the LORD
your God, heard. Offer a prayer for
5 those who still survive.' King Hez-
6 ekiah's servants came to Isaiah, and
he told them to say this to their
master: 'This is the word of the LORD:
"Do not be alarmed at what you
heard when the lackeys of the king of
7 Assyria blasphemed me. I will put
a spirit in him, and he shall hear a
rumour and withdraw to his own
country; and there I will make him
fall by the sword."'

Hezekiah prays to the LORD

8 So the chief officer withdrew. He
heard that the king of Assyria had
left Lachish, and he found him
9 attacking Libnah. But when the king
learnt that Tirhakah king of Cush
was on the way to make war on him,
he sent messengers again[z] to Hezekiah
10 king of Judah, to say to him, 'How
can you be deluded by your god on
whom you rely when he promises that
Jerusalem shall not fall into the hands
11 of the king of Assyria? Surely you
have heard what the kings of Assyria
have done to all countries, exterminating their people; can you then
12 hope to escape? Did their gods save
the nations which my forefathers
destroyed, Gozan, Harran, Rezeph,
and the people of Beth-eden living
13 in Telassar? Where are the kings
of Hamath, of Arpad, of Lahir,
Sepharvaim, Hena, and Ivvah?'
14 Hezekiah took the letter from the
messengers and read it; then he went
up into the house of the LORD, spread
15 it out before the LORD and offered
16 this prayer: 'O LORD of Hosts, God
of Israel, enthroned on the cherubim,
thou alone art God of all the kingdoms of the earth; thou hast made
17 heaven and earth. Turn thy ear to me,
O LORD, and listen; open thine eyes,
O LORD, and see; hear the message
that Sennacherib has sent to taunt
18 the living God. It is true, O LORD,
that the kings of Assyria have laid

waste every country, that they have 19
consigned their gods to the fire and
destroyed them; for they were no
gods but the work of men's hands,
mere wood and stone. But now, O 20
LORD our God, save us from his
power, so that all the kingdoms of the
earth may know that thou, O LORD,
alone art God.'

The LORD answers Hezekiah

Isaiah son of Amoz sent to Hezekiah 21
and said, 'This is the word of the
LORD the God of Israel: I have heard
your prayer to me concerning Sennacherib king of Assyria. This is the 22
word which the LORD has spoken concerning him:

The virgin daughter of Zion disdains
    you,
  she laughs you to scorn;
the daughter of Jerusalem tosses her
    head
  as you retreat.
  Whom have you taunted and 23
    blasphemed?
  Against whom have you clamoured,
casting haughty glances at the Holy
    One of Israel?
  You have sent your servants to 24
    taunt the Lord,
  and said:
With my countless chariots I have
    gone up
  high in the mountains, into the
    recesses of Lebanon.
I have cut down its tallest cedars,
  the best of its pines,
I have reached its highest limit of
    forest and meadow.[a]
  I have dug wells   25
  and drunk the waters of a foreign
    land,
and with the soles of my feet I have
    dried up
  all the streams of Egypt.

Have you not heard long ago?   26
  I did it all.
In days gone by I planned it
  and now I have brought it about,
making fortified cities tumble down
  into heaps of rubble.
Their citizens, shorn of strength,   27
  disheartened and ashamed,
  were but as plants in the field, as
    green herbs,
  as grass on the roof-tops blasted
    before the east wind.
  I know your rising up and your 28
    sitting down,
  your going out and your coming in.

z again: *prob. rdg., cp. 2 Kgs. 19. 9; Heb. and he heard.*
meadow.

a and meadow: *prob. rdg.; Heb.* its

29 The frenzy of your rage against me
and your arrogance
have come to my ears.
I will put a ring in your nose
and a hook in your lips,
and I will take you back by the
road
on which you have come.

30 This shall be the sign for you: this
year you shall eat shed grain and in the
second year what is self-sown; but in
the third year sow and reap, plant
31 vineyards and eat their fruit. The
survivors left in Judah shall strike
fresh root under ground and yield
32 fruit above ground, for a remnant
shall come out of Jerusalem and
survivors from Mount Zion. The zeal
of the LORD of Hosts will perform this.
33 'Therefore, this is the word of the
LORD concerning the king of Assyria:

He shall not enter this city
nor shoot an arrow there,
he shall not advance against it with
shield
nor cast up a siege-ramp against it.
34 By the way on which he came he shall
go back;
this city he shall not enter.
This is the very word of the LORD.
35 I will shield this city to deliver it,
for my own sake and for the sake of
my servant David.'

The LORD strikes down the Assyrians

36 The angel of the LORD went out and
struck down a hundred and eighty-
five thousand men in the Assyrian
camp; when morning dawned, they
37 all lay dead. So Sennacherib king of
Assyria broke camp, went back to
38 Nineveh and stayed there. One day,
while he was worshipping in the
temple of his god Nisroch, Adrammelech and Sharezer his sons murdered
him and escaped to the land of Ararat.
He was succeeded by his son Esarhaddon.

Hezekiah falls ill, and recovers

38 1[b] At this time Hezekiah fell dangerously ill and the prophet Isaiah son of
Amoz came to him and said, 'This is
the word of the LORD: Give your last
instructions to your household, for
you are a dying man and will not
2 recover.' Hezekiah turned his face to
the wall and offered this prayer to the
3 LORD: 'O LORD, remember how I have
lived before thee, faithful and loyal
in thy service, always doing what was

good in thine eyes.' And he wept
bitterly. Then the word of the LORD 4
came to Isaiah: 'Go and say to 5
Hezekiah: "This is the word of the
LORD the God of your father David:
I have heard your prayer and seen
your tears; I will add fifteen years to
your life. I will deliver you and this 6
city from the king of Assyria and will
protect this city."' Then Isaiah told 21[c]
them to apply a fig-plaster; so they
made one and applied it to the boil,
and he recovered. Then Hezekiah said, 22
'By what sign shall I know that I shall
go up into the house of the LORD?'
And Isaiah said,[d] 'This shall be your 7
sign from the LORD that he will do what
he has promised. Watch the shadow 8
cast by the sun on the stairway of
Ahaz: I will bring backwards ten steps
the shadow which has gone down on
the stairway.' And the sun went back
ten steps on the stairway down which
it had gone.

Hezekiah's poem

A poem of Hezekiah king of Judah 9
after his recovery from his illness, as
it was written down:

I thought: In the prime of life I must 10
pass away;
for the rest of my years I am consigned to the gates of Sheol.
I said: I shall no longer see the 11
LORD
in the land of the living;
never again, like those who live in
the world,
shall I look on a man.
My dwelling is taken from me, 12
pulled up like a shepherd's tent;
thou hast cut short my life like
a weaver
who severs the web from the thrum.
From morning to night thou tor-
mentest me,
then I am racked with pain till the 13
morning.
All my bones are broken, as a lion
would break them;
from morning to night thou tor-
mentest me.
I twitter as if I were a swallow, 14
I moan like a dove.
My eyes falter as I look up to the
heights;
O Lord, pay heed, stand surety for me.
How can I complain, what can I say 15
to the LORD
when he himself has done this?

b *Verses 1–8, 21, 22: cp. 2 Kgs. 20. 1–11.*   c *Verses 21, 22 transposed.*   d And Isaiah said: *prob.*
rdg., cp. 2 Kgs. 20. 9; Heb. om.

I wander to and fro all my life long
in the bitterness of my soul.
16 Yet, O Lord, my soul shall live with
thee;
do thou give my spirit rest.[e]
Restore me and give me life.
17 Bitterness had indeed been my lot
in place of prosperity;
but thou by thy love hast brought
me back
from the pit of destruction;
for thou hast cast all my sins
behind thee.
18 Sheol cannot confess thee,
Death cannot praise thee,
nor can they who go down to the
abyss
hope for thy truth.
19 The living, the living alone can
confess thee
as I do this day,
as a father makes thy truth known,
O God, to his sons.
20 The LORD is at hand to save me;
so let us sound the music of our
praises
all our life long in the house of the
LORD.[f]

Hezekiah receives Babylonian envoys

39 1[g] At this time Merodach-baladan son of
Baladan king of Babylon sent envoys
with a gift to Hezekiah; for he had
heard that he had been ill and was
2 well again. Hezekiah welcomed them
and showed them all his treasury,
silver and gold, spices and fragrant
oil, his entire armoury and everything
to be found among his treasures;
there was nothing in his house and in
all his realm that Hezekiah did not
3 show them. Then the prophet Isaiah
came to King Hezekiah and asked
him, 'What did these men say and
where have they come from?' 'They
have come from a far-off country,'
Hezekiah answered, 'from Babylon.'
4 Then Isaiah asked, 'What did they
see in your house?' 'They saw everything,' Hezekiah replied; 'there was
nothing among my treasures that I
5 did not show them.' Then Isaiah said
to Hezekiah, 'Hear the word of the
6 LORD of Hosts: The time is coming,
says the LORD, when everything in
your house, and all that your forefathers have amassed till the present
day, will be carried away to Babylon;
7 not a thing shall be left. And some

of the sons who will be born to you,
sons of your own begetting, shall be
taken and shall be made eunuchs in
the palace of the king of Babylon.'
8 Hezekiah answered, 'The word of the
LORD which you have spoken is good';
thinking to himself that peace and
security would last out his lifetime.

Good news for Zion

40 Comfort, comfort my people;[h]
—it is the voice of your God;
2 speak tenderly to Jerusalem[i]
and tell her this,
that she has fulfilled her term of
bondage,
that her penalty is paid;
she has received at the LORD's hand
double[j] measure for all her sins.

3 There is a voice that cries:
Prepare a road for the LORD through
the wilderness,
clear a highway across the desert for
our God.
4 Every valley shall be lifted up,
every mountain and hill brought down;
rugged places shall be made smooth
and mountain-ranges become a
plain.
5 Thus shall the glory of the LORD be
revealed,
and all mankind together shall see it;
for the LORD himself has spoken.

6 A voice says, 'Cry',
and another asks, 'What shall I cry?'
'That all mankind is grass,
they last no longer than a flower of the
field.
7 The grass withers, the flower fades,
when the breath of[k] the LORD blows
upon them;[l]
8 the grass withers, the flowers fade,
but the word of our God endures
for evermore.'

9 You who bring Zion good news,[m] up
with you to the mountain-top;
lift up your voice and shout,
you who bring good news to
Jerusalem,[n]
lift it up fearlessly;
cry to the cities of Judah, 'Your God
is here.'
10 Here is the Lord GOD coming in
might,
coming to rule with his right arm.
His recompense comes with him,

---

e Yet . . . rest: *prob. rdg.; Heb. unintelligible.*   *f Verses 21, 22 transposed to follow verse 6.*
g Verses 1–8: cp. 2 Kgs. 20. 12–19.   *h* Comfort . . . people: *or* Comfort, O my people, comfort.
i speak . . . Jerusalem: *or* bid Jerusalem be of good heart.   *j* double: *or* full.   *k* the breath of:
or a wind from.   *l Prob. rdg.; Heb. adds* surely the people are grass.   *m* You . . . news: *or* O
Zion, bringer of good news.   *n* you . . . Jerusalem: *or* O Jerusalem, bringer of good news.

he carries his reward before him.

11 He will tend his flock like a shepherd
and gather them together with his
arm;
he will carry the lambs in his bosom
and lead the ewes to water.

None can compare with the LORD

12 Who has gauged the waters in the
palm of his hand,
or with its span set limits to the
heavens?
Who has held all the soil of earth in
a bushel,
or weighed the mountains on a
balance
and the hills on a pair of scales?
13 Who has set limits to the spirit of
the LORD?
What counsellor stood at his side
to instruct him?
14 With whom did he confer to gain
discernment?
Who taught him how to do justice
or gave him lessons in wisdom?
15 Why, to him nations are but drops
from a bucket,
no more than moisture on the scales;
coasts and islands weigh as light as
specks of dust.
16 All Lebanon does not yield wood
enough for fuel
or beasts enough for a sacrifice.
17 All nations dwindle to nothing
before him,
he reckons them mere nothings, less
than nought.

18 What likeness will you find for God
or what form to resemble his?
19 Is it an image which a craftsman
sets up,
and a goldsmith covers with plate
and fits with studs of silver as a
costly gift?
20 Or is it mulberry-wood that will not
rot which a man chooses,
seeking out a skilful craftsman for
it,
to mount an image that will not
fall?

[6⁰] Each workman helps the others,
each man encourages his fellow.
[7⁰] The craftsman urges on the goldsmith,
the gilder urges the man who beats
the anvil,
he declares the soldering to be
sound;
he fastens the image with nails
so that it will not fall down.

Just cause for confidence in God

Do you not know, have you not heard, 21
were you not told long ago,
have you not perceived ever since the
world began,
that God sits throned on the vaulted 22
roof of earth,
whose inhabitants are like grasshoppers*p*?
He stretches out the skies like a
curtain,
he spreads them out like a tent to
live in;
he reduces the great to nothing 23
and makes all earth's princes less
than nothing.
Scarcely are they planted, scarcely 24
sown,
scarcely have they taken root in the
earth,
before he blows upon them and
they wither away,
and a whirlwind carries them off
like chaff.
To whom then will you liken me, 25
whom set up as my equal?
asks the Holy One.
Lift up your eyes to the heavens; 26
consider who created it all,
led out their host one by one
and called them all by their names;
through his great might, his might
and power,
not one is missing.
Why do you complain, O Jacob, 27
and you, Israel, why do you say,
'My plight is hidden from the LORD
and my cause has passed out of
God's notice'?
Do you not know, have you not 28
heard?
The LORD, the everlasting God, creator of the wide world,
grows neither weary nor faint;
no man can fathom his understanding.
He gives vigour to the weary, 29
new strength to the exhausted.
Young men may grow weary and 30
faint,
even in their prime they may
stumble and fall;
but those who look to the LORD will 31
win new strength,
they will grow wings like eagles;
they will run and not be weary,
they will march on and never grow
faint.

The LORD *addresses the nations*

Keep silence before me, all you **41**
coasts and islands;

o These are verses 6 and 7 of ch. 41, transposed to this point.　　　*p Or locusts.*

let the peoples come to meet me.*q*
Let them come near, then let them speak;
we will meet at the place of judgement, I and they.

2 Tell me, who raised up that one from the east,
one greeted by victory wherever he goes?
Who is it that puts nations into his power
and makes kings go down before him,*r*
he scatters them with his sword like dust
and with his bow like chaff before the wind;

3 he puts them to flight and passes on unscathed,
swifter than any traveller on foot?

4 Whose work is this, I ask, who has brought it to pass?
Who has summoned the generations from the beginning?
It is I, the LORD, I am the first,
and to the last of them I am He.

5 Coasts and islands saw it and were afraid,
the world trembled from end to end.*s*

The LORD addresses Israel

8*t* But you, Israel my servant,
you, Jacob whom I have chosen,
race of Abraham my friend,

9 I have taken you up,
have fetched you from the ends of the earth,
and summoned you from its farthest corners,
I have called you my servant,
have chosen you and not cast you off:

10 fear nothing, for I am with you;
be not afraid, for I am your God.
I strengthen you, I help you,
I support you with my victorious right hand.

11 Now shall all who defy you
be disappointed and put to shame;
all who set themselves against you
shall be as nothing; they shall vanish.

12 You will look for your assailants but not find them;
all who take up arms against you
shall be as nothing, nothing at all.

13 For I, the LORD your God,
take you by the right hand;
I say to you, Do not fear;
it is I who help you,

14 fear not, Jacob you worm and Israel poor louse.
It is I who help you, says the LORD,
your ransomer, the Holy One of Israel.

15 See, I will make of you a sharp threshing-sledge,
new and studded with teeth;
you shall thresh the mountains and crush them
and reduce the hills to chaff;

16 you shall winnow them, the wind shall carry them away
and a great gale shall scatter them.
Then shall you rejoice in the LORD
and glory in the Holy One of Israel.

Provision for the wilderness journey

17 The wretched and the poor look for water and find none,
their tongues are parched with thirst;
but I the LORD will give them an answer,
I, the God of Israel, will not forsake them.

18 I will open rivers among the sand-dunes
and wells in the valleys;
I will turn the wilderness into pools
and dry land into springs of water;

19 I will plant cedars in the wastes,
and acacia and myrtle and wild olive;
the pine shall grow on the barren heath
side by side with fir and box,

20 that men may see and know,
may once for all give heed and understand
that the LORD himself has done this,
that the Holy One of Israel has performed it.

A challenge to the idols of the nations

21 Come, open your plea, says the LORD,
present your case, says Jacob's King;

22 let them come forward, these idols,
let them foretell the future.
Let them declare the meaning of past events
that we may give our minds to it;
let them predict things that are to be
that we may know their outcome.

23 Declare what will happen hereafter;
then we shall know you are gods.
Do what you can, good or ill,
anything that may grip us with fear and awe.

q come to meet me: *prob. rdg., transposing, with slight change, from end of verse 5; Heb.* win new strength *(repeated from 40. 31).*   *r* before him: *prob. rdg.; Heb. om.*   *s* See note on verse 1.
t Verses 6 and 7 transposed to follow 40. 20.

24 You cannot! You are sprung from
      nothing,
   your works are rotten;
   whoever chooses you is vile as you
      are.
25 I roused one from the north, and he
      obeyed;
   I called one from the east, sum-
      moned him in*u* my name,
   he marches over viceroys as if they
      were mud,
   like a potter treading his clay.
26 Tell us, who declared this from the
      beginning, that we might know it,
   or told us beforehand so that we
      could say, 'He was right'?
   Not one declared, not one foretold,
   not one heard a sound from you.
27 Here is one who will speak first as
      advocate for Zion,
   here I appoint defending counsel
      for Jerusalem;
28 but from the other side no advocate
      steps forward
   and, when I look, there is no one
      there.
   I ask a question and no one answers;
29 see what empty things they are!
   Nothing that they do has any
      worth,
   their effigies are wind, mere noth-
      ings.

The LORD's chosen servant

42 Here is my servant, whom I uphold,
   my chosen one in whom I delight,
   I have bestowed my spirit upon
      him,
   and he will make justice shine on
      the nations.
2 He will not call out or lift his voice
      high,
   or*v* make himself heard in the open
      street.
3 He will not break a bruised reed,
   or snuff out a smouldering wick;
   he will make justice shine on every
      race,*w*
4 never faltering, never breaking
      down,*x*
   he will plant justice on earth,
   while coasts and islands wait for
      his teaching.
5 Thus speaks the LORD who is God,
   he who created the skies and stret-
      ched them out,
   who fashioned the earth and all
      that grows in it,
   who gave breath to its people,

the breath of life to all who walk
   upon it:
I, the LORD, have called you with 6
   righteous purpose
and taken you by the hand;
I have formed you, and appointed
   you
to be a light*v* to all peoples,
a beacon for the nations,
to open eyes that are blind,   7
to bring captives out of prison,
out of the dungeons where they lie
   in darkness.
I am the LORD; the LORD*z* is my name; 8
I will not give my glory to another
   god,
nor my praise to any idol.
See how the first prophecies have 9
   come to pass,
and now I declare new things;
before they break from the bud I announce them to you.

A new song to the LORD

Sing a new song to the LORD,   10
sing his praise throughout the earth,
you that sail the sea, and all sea-
   creatures,
and you that inhabit the coasts and
   islands.
Let the wilderness and its towns 11
   rejoice,
and the villages of the tribe of
   Kedar.
Let those who live in Sela shout for
   joy
and cry out from the hill-tops.
You coasts and islands, all uplift 12
   his praises;
let all ascribe glory to the LORD.
The LORD will go forth as a warrior, 13
he will rouse the frenzy of battle
   like a hero;
he will shout, he will raise the battle-
   cry
and triumph over his foes.
Long have I lain still,   14
I kept silence and held myself in
   check;
now I will cry like a woman in
   labour,
whimpering, panting and gasping.
I will lay waste mountains and hills 15
and shrivel all their green herbs;
I will turn rivers into desert wastes*a*
and dry up all the pools.
Then will I lead blind men on their 16
   way*b*
and guide them by paths they do
   not know;

---

u summoned him in: *or* who will call on.   *v* He will not . . . or: *or* In very truth he will call out
and lift his voice high, and . . .   *w* on every race: *or* in truth.   *x* never faltering . . . down: *or*
he will neither rebuke nor wound.   *y* Or a covenant.   *z* the LORD: *or* He.   *a* desert wastes:
prob. rdg.; Heb. coasts and islands.   *b* *Prob. rdg.; Heb. adds* which they do not know.

I will turn darkness into light before
them
and straighten their twisting roads.
All this I will do and leave nothing
undone.

17 Those who trust in an image,
those who take idols for their gods
turn tail in bitter shame.

Israel's persistent disobedience

18 Hear now, you that are deaf;
you blind men, look and see:

19 yet who is blind but my servant,
who so deaf as the messenger whom
I send?
Who so blind as the one who holds
my commission,
so deaf as the servant of the LORD?

20 You have seen much but remembered little,
your ears are wide open but nothing
is heard.

21 It pleased the LORD, for the further-
ance of his justice,
to make his law a law of surpassing
majesty;

22 yet here is a people plundered and
taken as prey,
all of them ensnared, trapped in
holes,
lost to sight in dungeons,
carried off as spoil without hope of
rescue,
as plunder with no one to say, 'Give
it back.'

23 Hear this, all of you who will,
listen henceforward and give me a
hearing:

24 who gave away Jacob for plunder,
who gave Israel away for spoil?
Was it not the LORD? They sinned
against him,
they would not follow his ways
and refused obedience to his law;

25 so in his anger he poured out upon
Jacob
his wrath and the fury of battle.
It wrapped him in flames, yet still
he did not learn the lesson,
scorched him, yet he did not lay it
to heart.

Israel ransomed

43 But now this is the word of the
LORD,
the word of your creator, O Jacob,
of him who fashioned you, Israel:
Have no fear; for I have paid your
ransom;
I have called you by name and you
are my own.

2 When you pass through deep waters,
I am with you,
when you pass through rivers,

they will not sweep you away;
walk through fire and you will not
be scorched,
through flames and they will not
burn you.

3 For I am the LORD your God,
the Holy One of Israel, your deliverer;
for your ransom I give Egypt,
Nubia and Seba are your price.

4 You are more precious to me than the
Assyrians,
you are honoured and I have loved
you,
I would give the Edomites in exchange for you,
and the Leummim for your life.

The LORD's absolute power to redeem

Have no fear; for I am with you;

5 I will bring your children from the
east
and gather you all from the west.

6 I will say to the north, 'Give them
up',
and to the south, 'Do not hold them
back.
Bring my sons and daughters from
afar,
bring them from the ends of the
earth;

7 bring every one who is called by
my name,
all whom I have created, whom I
have formed,
all whom I have made for my glory.'

8 Bring out this people,
a people who have eyes but are
blind,
who have ears but are deaf.

9 All the nations are gathered together
and the peoples assembled.
Who amongst them can expound
this thing
and interpret for us all that has
gone before?
Let them produce witnesses to
prove their case,
or let them listen and say, 'That is
the truth.'

10 My witnesses, says the LORD, are you,
my servants,
you whom I have chosen
to know me and put your faith in
me
and understand that I am He.
Before me there was no god
fashioned
nor ever shall be after me.

11 I am the LORD, I myself,
and none but I can deliver.

12 I myself have made it known in full,
and declared it,

I and no alien god amongst you,
and you are my witnesses, says the
LORD.

13 I am God; from this very day I am
He.
What my hand holds, none can
snatch away;
what I do, none can undo.

14 Thus says the LORD your ransomer,
the Holy One of Israel:
For your sakes I have sent to
Babylon;
I will lay the Chaldaeans prostrate
as they flee,
and their cry of triumph will turn
to groaning.

15 I am the LORD, your Holy One,
your creator, Israel, and your King.

The LORD appeals to Israel

16 Thus says the LORD,
who opened a way in the sea
and a path through mighty waters,

17 who drew on chariot and horse to
their destruction,
a whole army, men of valour;
there they lay, never to rise again;
they were crushed, snuffed out like a
wick:

18 Cease to dwell on days gone by
and to brood over past history.

19 Here and now I will do a new thing;
this moment it will break from the
bud.
Can you not perceive it?
I will make a way even through the
wilderness
and paths in the barren desert;

20 the wild beasts shall do me honour,
the wolf and the ostrich;
for I will provide water in the
wilderness
and rivers in the barren desert,
where my chosen people may drink.

21 I have formed this people for myself
and they shall proclaim my praises.

22 Yet you did not call upon me, O
Jacob;
much less did you weary yourself in
my service, O Israel.

23 You did not bring me sheep as
whole-offerings
or honour me with sacrifices;
I asked you for no burdensome
offerings
and wearied you with no demands
for incense.

24 You did not buy me sweet-cane with
your money

or glut me with the fat of your
sacrifices;
rather you burdened me with your
sins
and wearied me with your iniquities.

25 I alone, I am He,
who for his own sake wipes out your
transgressions,
who will remember your sins no
more.

26 Cite me by name, let us argue it
out;
set forth your pleading and justify
yourselves.

27 Your first father transgressed,
your spokesmen rebelled against
me,

28 and your princes profaned my
sanctuary;
so I sent Jacob to his doom
and left Israel to execration.

4 Hear me now, Jacob my servant,
hear me, my chosen Israel.

2 Thus says the LORD your maker,
your helper, who fashioned you
from birth:
have no fear, Jacob my servant,
Jeshurun whom I have chosen,

3 for I will pour down rain on a
thirsty land,
showers on the dry ground.
I will pour out my spirit on your
offspring
and my blessing on your children.

4 They shall spring up like a green
tamarisk,
like poplars by a flowing stream.

5 This man shall say, 'I am the LORD's
man',
that one shall call himself a son of
Jacob,
another shall write the LORD's name
on his hand
and shall add the name of Israel to
his own.

There is no god but the LORD

6 Thus says the LORD, Israel's King,
the LORD of Hosts, his ransomer:
I am the first and I am the last,
and there is no god but me.

7 Who is like me? Let him stand up,
let him declare himself and speak
and show me his evidence,
let him announce beforehand[c]
things to come,
let him[d] declare what is yet to
happen.

8 Take heart, do not be afraid.
Did I not foretell this long ago?

c let him announce beforehand: *prob. rdg.*; *Heb.* since my appointing an ancient people and . . .
d *Prob. rdg.*; *Heb.* them.

I declared it, and you are my witnesses.

Is there any god beside me,
or any creator, even one that I do not know?

9 Those who make idols are less than nothing;
all their cherished images profit nobody;
their worshippers are blind,
sheer ignorance makes fools of them.

10 If a man makes a god or casts an image,
his labour is wasted.

11 Why! its votaries show their folly;
the craftsmen too are but men.
Let them all gather together and confront me,
all will be afraid and look the fools they are.

The foolishness of idolatry

12 The blacksmith sharpens a graving tool and hammers out his work[e] hot from the coals and shapes it with his strong arm; when he grows hungry his strength fails, if he has no water
13 to drink he tires. The woodworker draws his line taut and marks out a figure with a scriber; he planes the wood and measures it with callipers, and he carves it to the shape of a man, comely as the human form, to be set up presently in a house.[f]

14 A man plants a cedar and the rain makes it grow, so that later on he will have cedars to cut down; or he chooses an ilex or an oak to raise a stout tree
15 for himself in the forest. It becomes fuel for his fire: some of it he takes and warms himself, some he kindles and bakes bread on it, and some he makes into a god and prostrates himself, shaping it into an idol and
16 bowing down before it. The one half of it he burns in the fire and on this he roasts meat, so that he may eat his roast and be satisfied; he also warms himself at it and he says, 'Good! I can feel the heat, I am growing warm.'
17 Then what is left of the wood he makes into a god by carving it into shape; he bows down to it and prostrates himself and prays to it, saying,
18 'Save me; for thou art my god.' Such people neither know nor understand, their eyes made too blind to see, their
19 minds too narrow to discern. Such a man will not use his reason, he has neither the wit nor the sense to say, 'Half of it I have burnt, yes, and used its embers to bake bread; I have roasted meat on them too and eaten it;

but the rest of it I turn into this abominable thing and so I am worshipping a log of wood.' He feeds on 20 ashes indeed! His own deluded mind has misled him, he cannot recollect himself so far as to say, 'Why! this thing in my hand is a sham.'

A reminder to Israel

Remember all this, Jacob, 21
remember, Israel, for you are my servant,
I have fashioned you, and you are to serve me;
you shall not forget me, Israel.
I have swept away your sins like a 22 dissolving mist,
and your transgressions are dispersed like clouds;
turn back to me; for I have ransomed you.
Shout in triumph, you heavens, for it 23 is the LORD's doing;
cry out for joy, you lowest depths of the earth;
break into songs of triumph, you mountains,
you forest and all your trees;
for the LORD has ransomed Jacob
and made Israel his masterpiece.

The LORD's purpose for Jerusalem

Thus says the LORD, your ransomer, 24 who fashioned you from birth:
I am the LORD who made all things,
by myself I stretched out the skies,
alone I hammered out the floor of the earth.
I frustrate false prophets and their 25 signs
and make fools of diviners;
I reverse what wise men say
and make nonsense of their wisdom.
I make my servants' prophecies 26 come true
and give effect to my messengers' designs.
I say of Jerusalem,
'She shall be inhabited once more',
and of the cities of Judah, 'They shall be rebuilt;
all their ruins I will restore.'
I say to the deep waters, 'Be dried 27 up;
I will make your streams run dry.'
I say to Cyrus, 'You shall be my 28 shepherd
to carry out all my purpose,
so that Jerusalem may be rebuilt
and the foundations of the temple may be laid.'

e his work: *prob. rdg.*; *Heb.* he works.   f Or a shrine.

Cyrus used by the LORD

45 Thus says the LORD to Cyrus his
anointed,
Cyrus whom he has taken by the
hand
to subdue nations before him
and undo the might of kings;
before whom gates shall be opened
and no doors be shut:
2 I will go before you
and level the swelling hills;
I will break down gates of bronze
and hack through iron bars.
3 I will give you treasures from dark
vaults,
hoarded in secret places,
that you may know that I am the
LORD,
Israel's God who calls you by name.
4 For the sake of Jacob my servant and
Israel my chosen
I have called you by name
and given you your title, though you
have not known me.
5 I am the LORD, there is no other;
there is no god beside me.
I will strengthen you though you
have not known me,
6 so that men from the rising and the
setting sun
may know that there is none but I:
I am the LORD, there is no other;
7 I make the light, I create darkness,
author alike of prosperity and
trouble.

I, the LORD, do all these things.

8 Rain righteousness, you heavens,
let the skies above pour down;
let the earth open to receive it,
that it may bear the fruit of salvation
with righteousness in blossom at its
side.
All this I, the LORD, have created.

The LORD answers Israel's objection

9 Will the pot contend[g] with the
potter,
or the earthenware[h] with the hand
that shapes it?
Will the clay ask the potter what he
is making?
or his[i] handiwork say to him, 'You
have no skill'?
10 Will the babe say[j] to his father, 'What
are you begetting?',
or to his mother, 'What are you
bringing to birth?'
11 Thus says the LORD, Israel's Holy
One, his maker:

Would you dare question me concerning my children,
or instruct me in my handiwork?
I alone, I made the earth   12
and created man upon it;
I, with my own hands, stretched out
the heavens
and caused all their host to shine.
I alone have roused this man in   13
righteousness,
and I will smooth his path before
him;
he shall rebuild my city
and let my exiles go free—
not for a price nor for a bribe,
says the LORD of Hosts.

The nations will acknowledge the LORD

Thus says the LORD: 14
Toilers of Egypt and Nubian mer-
chants
and Sabaeans bearing tribute[k]
shall come into your power and be
your slaves,
shall come and march behind you in
chains;
they shall bow down before you in
supplication, saying,
'Surely God is among you and there is
no other,
no other god.
How then canst thou be a god that   15
hidest thyself,
O God of Israel, the deliverer?'

Those who defy him are confounded   16
and brought to shame,
those who make idols perish in confusion.
But Israel has been delivered by   17
the LORD,
delivered for all time to come;
they shall not be confounded or put
to shame for all eternity.

The only God

Thus says the LORD, the creator of   18
the heavens,
he who is God,
who made the earth and fashioned
it
and himself fixed it fast,
who created it no empty void,
but made it for a place to dwell in:
I am the LORD, there is no other.
I do not speak in secret, in realms of 19
darkness,
I do not say to the sons of Jacob,
'Look for me in the empty void.'
I the LORD speak what is right, declare
what is just.

g Will . . . contend: *prob. rdg.*; *Heb.* Ho! he has contended.   h *Or* shard.   i *Prob. rdg.*; *Heb.*
your.   j Will . . . say: *prob. rdg.*; *Heb.* Ho! you that say.   k bearing tribute: *or* men of stature.

20 Gather together, come, draw near,
all you survivors of the nations,
you fools, who carry your wooden
idols in procession
and pray to a god that cannot save
you.
21 Come forward and urge your case,
consult together:
who foretold this in days of old,
who stated it long ago?
Was it not I the LORD?
There is no god but me;
there is no god other than I, victorious
and able to save.
22 Look to me and be saved,
you peoples from all corners of the
earth;
for I am God, there is no other.
23 By my life I have sworn,
I have given a promise of victory,
a promise that will not be broken,
that to me every knee shall bend
and by me every tongue shall
swear.
24 In the LORD alone, men shall say,
are victory and might;
and all who defy him
shall stand ashamed in his presence,
25 but all the sons of Israel shall stand
victorious
and find their glory in the LORD.

The impotence of idols

46 Bel has crouched down, Nebo has
stooped low:
their images, once carried in your
processions,
have been loaded on to beasts and
cattle,
a burden for the weary creatures;
2 they stoop and they crouch;
not for them to bring the burden to
safety;
the gods themselves go into captivity.
3 Listen to me, house of Jacob
and all the remnant of the house of
Israel,
a load on me from your birth, carried
by me from the womb:
4 till you grow old I am He,
and when white hairs come, I will
carry you still;
I have made you and I will bear the
burden,
I will carry you and bring you to
safety.
5 To whom will you liken me? Who is
my equal?
With whom can you compare me?
Where is my like?
6 Those who squander their bags of
gold

and weigh out their silver with a
balance
hire a goldsmith to fashion them into
a god;
then they worship it and fall prostrate before it;
they hoist it shoulder-high and carry 7
it home;
they set it down on its base;
there it must stand, it cannot stir
from its place.
Let a man cry to it as he will, it
never answers him;
it cannot deliver him from his
troubles.

God will carry out his plan

Remember this, you rebels,   8
consider it well, and abandon hope,
remember all that happened long 9
ago;
for I am God, there is no other,
I am God, and there is no one like
me;
I reveal the end from the beginning, 10
from ancient times I reveal what is
to be;
I say, 'My purpose shall take effect,
I will accomplish all that I please.'
I summon a bird of prey*l* from the 11
east,
one from a distant land to fulfil my
purpose.
Mark this; I have spoken, and I will
bring it about,
I have a plan to carry out, and
carry it out I will.
Listen to me, all you stubborn 12
hearts,
for whom victory is far off:
I bring my victory near, it is not far 13
off,
and my deliverance shall not be
delayed;
I will grant deliverance in Zion
and give my glory to Israel.*m*

Disaster befalling Babylon

Down with you, sit in the dust,   47
virgin daughter of Babylon.
Down from your throne, sit on the
ground,
daughter of the Chaldaeans;
never again shall men call you
soft-skinned and delicate.
Take up the millstone, grind meal, un- 2
cover your tresses;
strip off your skirt, bare your thighs,
wade through rivers,
so that your nakedness may be 3
plain to see
and your shame exposed.

l a bird of prey: *or* a massed host.   *m* and give my glory to Israel: *or* for Israel my glory.

I will take vengeance, I will treat with
    none of you,
4 says the Holy One of Israel, our
    ransomer,
    whose name is the LORD of Hosts.

5 Sit silent,
    be off into the shadows, daughter of
        the Chaldaeans;
    for never again shall men call you
        queen of many kingdoms.
6 When I was angry with my people,
    I dishonoured my own possession
    and gave them into your power.
    You showed them no mercy,
    you made your yoke weigh heavy on
        the aged.
7 You said then, 'I shall reign a queen
        for ever',
    while[n] you gave no thought to this
    and did not consider how it would
        end.
8 Now therefore listen to this,
    you lover of luxury, carefree on your
        throne.
    You say to yourself,
    'I am, and who but I?
    No widow's weeds for me, no deaths
        of children.'
9 Yet suddenly, in a single day,
    these two things shall come upon
        you;
    they shall both come upon you in full
        measure:[o]
    children's deaths and widowhood,
    for all your monstrous sorceries,
    your countless spells.
10 Secure in your wicked ways you
        thought, 'No one is looking.'
    Your wisdom betrayed you, omniscient
        as you were,
    and you said to yourself,
    'I am, and who but I?'
11 Therefore evil shall come upon you,
    and you will not know how to
        master it;
    disaster shall befall you,
    and you will not be able to charm it
        away;
    ruin all unforeseen
    shall come suddenly upon you.
12 Persist in your spells and your
        monstrous sorceries,[p]
    maybe you can get help from them,
    maybe you will yet inspire awe.
13 But no! in spite of your many wiles
        you are powerless.
    Let your astrologers, your star-
        gazers
    who foretell your future month by
        month,
    persist, and save you!

But look, they are gone like chaff; 14
    fire burns them up;
    they cannot snatch themselves from
        the flames;
    this is no glowing coal to warm
        them,
    no fire for them to sit by.
    So much for your magicians   15
    with whom you have trafficked all
        your life:
    they have stumbled off, each his
        own way,
    and there is no one to save you.

God reveals the future   **48**

Hear this, you house of Jacob,
    you who are called by the name of
        Israel,
    you who spring from the seed of
        Judah;
    who swear by the name of the
        LORD
    and boast in the God of Israel,
    but not in honesty or sincerity,
    although you call yourselves citi- 2
        zens of a holy city
    and lean for support on the God of
        Israel;
    his name is the LORD of Hosts.
    Long ago I announced what would 3
        first happen,
    I revealed it with my own mouth;
    suddenly I acted and it came about.
    I knew that you were stubborn,   4
    your neck stiff as iron, your brow
        like bronze,
    therefore I told you of these things 5
        long ago,
    and declared them before they came
        about,
    so that you could not say, 'This was
        my idol's doing;
    my image, the god that I fashioned,
        he ordained them.'
    You have heard what I said; con- 6
        sider it well,
    and you must admit the truth of it.
    Now I show you new things,
    hidden things which you did not
        know before.
    They were not created long ago, but 7
        in this very hour;
    you had never heard of them before
        today.
    You cannot say, 'I know them
        already.'
    You neither heard nor knew,   8
    long ago your ears were closed;
    for I knew that you were untrust-
        worthy, treacherous,
    a notorious rebel from your birth.

n for ever', while: *or* of a wide realm, for all time'; *but*.   o in full measure: *or* at random.
p Prob. rdg.; Heb. adds with which you have trafficked all your life (*cp. verse 15*).

9 For the sake of my own name I was
   patient,[q]
   rather than destroy you I held myself in check.
10 See how I tested you, not as silver is
   tested,
   but in the furnace of affliction; there
   I purified you.
11 For my honour, for my own honour
   I did it;
   let them disparage my past triumphs[r] if they will:
   I will not give my glory to any
   other god.
12 Hear me, Jacob,
   and Israel whom I called:
   I am He; I am the first,
   I am the last also.
13 With my own hands I founded the
   earth,
   with my right hand I formed the
   expanse of sky;
   when I summoned them,
   they sprang at once into being.
14 Assemble, all of you, and listen to
   me;
   which of you has declared what is
   coming,
   that he whom I love shall wreak
   my[s] will on Babylon
   and the Chaldaeans shall be scattered?
15 I, I myself, have spoken, I have called
   him,
   I have made him appear, and wherever he goes he shall prosper.
16 Draw near to me and hear this:
   from the beginning I have never
   spoken in secret;
   from the moment of its first happening I was there.[t]

'Come out of Babylon'

17 Thus says the LORD your ransomer,
   the Holy One of Israel:
   I am the LORD your God:
   I teach you for your own advantage
   and lead you in the way you must
   go.
18 If only you had listened to my commands,
   your prosperity would have rolled on
   like a river in flood
   and your just success like the
   waves of the sea;
19 in number your children would
   have been like the sand
   and your descendants countless as
   its grains;

their name would never be erased or
   blotted from my sight.
Come out of Babylon, hasten away 20
   from the Chaldaeans;
proclaim it with loud songs of triumph,
   crying the news to the ends of the
   earth;
tell them, 'The LORD has ransomed
   his servant Jacob.'
Though he led them through desert 21
   places they suffered no thirst,
for them he made water run from the
   rock,
for them he cleft the rock and streams
   gushed forth.

   There is no peace for the wicked,   22
      says the LORD.

The mission of the LORD's servant

   Listen to me, you coasts and islands, **49**
   pay heed, you peoples far away:
   from birth the LORD called me,
   he named me from my mother's
      womb.
He made my tongue his sharp sword 2
   and concealed me under cover of
      his hand;
   he made me a polished arrow
   and hid me out of sight in his quiver.
He said to me, 'You are my servant, 3
   Israel through whom I shall win
      glory';
   so I rose to honour in the LORD's
      sight
   and my God became my strength.[u]
Once I said, 'I have laboured in vain; 4
I have spent my strength for nothing,
   to no purpose';
   yet in truth my cause is with the
      LORD
   and my reward is in God's hands.
And now the LORD who formed me in 5
   the womb to be his servant,
   to bring Jacob back to him
   that Israel should be gathered to
      him,[v]
   now the LORD calls me again:[w]
it is too slight a task for you, as my 6
      servant,
   to restore the tribes of Jacob,
   to bring back the descendants of
      Israel:
   I will make you a light to the na-
      tions,
   to be my salvation[x] to earth's
      farthest bounds.
Thus says the Holy One, the LORD 7
   who ransoms Israel,
   to one who thinks little of himself,

q See note on verse 11.   r my past triumphs: *transposed from verse 9.*   s Or his.   t Prob. rdg.;
Heb. adds and now the Lord GOD has sent me, and his spirit.   u so I rose . . . strength: *transposed
from end of verse 5.*   v be gathered to him: *or* not be swept away.   w See note on verse 3.
x to be my salvation: *or* that my salvation may reach.

whom every nation abhors,
the slave of tyrants:
When they see you kings shall rise,
princes shall rise and bow down,
because of the LORD who is faithful,
because of the Holy One of Israel who
has chosen you.

The LORD's care for the returning exiles

8 Thus says the LORD:
In the hour of my favour I answered you,
and I helped you on the day of
deliverance,[y]
putting the land to rights
and sharing out afresh its desolate
fields;
9 I said to the prisoners, 'Go free',
and to those in darkness, 'Come
out and be seen.'
They shall find pasture in the
desert sands[z]
and grazing on all the dunes.
10 They shall neither hunger nor
thirst,
no scorching heat or sun shall distress them;
for one who loves them shall lead
them
and take them to water at bubbling
springs.
11 I will make every hill a path
and build embankments for my
highways.
12 See, they come; some from far away,
these from the north and these from
the west
and those from the land of Syene.
13 Shout for joy, you heavens, rejoice,
O earth,
you mountains, break into songs of
triumph,
for the LORD has comforted his
people
and has had pity on his own in their
distress.

Zion's vast population

14 But Zion says,
'The LORD has forsaken me; my God
has forgotten me.'
15 Can a woman forget the infant at
her breast,
or a loving mother the child of her
womb?
Even these forget, yet I will not forget
you.
16 Your walls are always before my
eyes,

I have engraved them on the palms
of my hands.
Those who are to rebuild you make 17
better speed
than those who pulled you down,
while those who laid you waste
depart.
Raise your eyes and look around 18
you:
see how they assemble, how they are
flocking back to you.
By my life I, the LORD, swear it,
you shall wear them proudly as
your jewels,
and adorn yourself with them like
a bride;
I did indeed make you waste and 19
desolate,
I razed you to the ground,
but your boundaries[a] shall now be
too narrow
for your inhabitants—
and those who laid you in ruins are
far away.
The children born in your bereave- 20
ment shall yet say in your hearing,
'This place is too narrow; make room
for me to live in.'
Then you will say to yourself, 21
'All these children, how did I come
by them,
bereaved and barren as I was?
Who reared them
when I was left alone, left by myself;
where did I get them all?'

The Lord GOD says, 22
Now is the time: I will beckon to the
nations
and hoist a signal to the peoples,
and they shall bring your sons in
their arms
and carry your daughters on their
shoulders;
kings shall be your foster-fathers 23
and their princesses shall be your
nurses.
They shall bow to the earth before
you
and lick the dust from your feet;
and you shall know that I am the
LORD
and that none who look to me will
be disappointed.
Can his prey be taken from the 24
strong man,
or the captive be rescued from the
ruthless?
And the LORD answers, 25

y *Prob. rdg.; Heb. adds* I have formed you, and appointed you to be a light to all peoples (*cp. 42. 6*).
z desert sands: *prob. rdg.; Heb.* ways.   a I did . . . boundaries: *or* your wasted and desolate land,
your ruined countryside.

The captive shall be taken even
from the strong,
and the prey of the ruthless shall be
rescued;
I will contend with all who contend
against you
and save your children from them.
26 I will force your oppressors to feed on
their own flesh
and make them drunk with their own
blood as if with fresh wine,
and all mankind shall know
that it is I, the LORD, who save you,
I your ransomer, the Mighty One of
Jacob.

Israel's unresponsiveness

50 The LORD says,
Is there anywhere a deed of divorce
by which I have put your mother
away?
Was there some creditor of mine
to whom I sold you?
No; it was through your own
wickedness that you were sold
and for your own misconduct that
your mother was put away.
2 Why, then, did I find no one when
I came?
Why, when I called, did no one
answer?
Did you think my arm too short to
redeem,
did you think I had no power to
save?
Not so. By my rebuke I dried up the
sea
and turned rivers into desert;
their fish perished for lack of water
and died on the thirsty ground;
3 I clothed the skies in mourning
and covered them with sackcloth.

The LORD's obedient servant

4 The Lord GOD has given me
the tongue of a teacher
and skill to console the weary
with a word in the morning;
he sharpened my hearing
that I might listen like one who is
taught.
5 The Lord GOD opened my ears
and I did not disobey or turn back in
defiance.
6 I offered my back to the lash,
and let my beard be plucked from
my chin,
I did not hide my face from spitting
and insult;
7 but the Lord GOD stands by to help
me;
therefore no insult can wound me.

I have set my face like flint,
for I know that I shall not be put to
shame,
because one who will clear my name 8
is at my side.
Who dare argue against me? Let us
confront one another.
Who will dispute my cause? Let him
come forward.
The Lord GOD will help me;   9
who then can prove me guilty?
They will all wear out like a garment,
the moths will eat them up.

Torment for the godless

Which of you fears the LORD and 10
obeys his servant's commands?
The man who walks in dark places with
no light,
yet trusts in the name of the LORD
and leans on his God.
But you who kindle a fire and set 11
fire-brands alight,
go, walk into your own fire
and among the fire-brands you have
set ablaze.
This is your fate at my hands:
you shall lie down in torment.

A lesson from history

Listen to me, all who follow the right 51
and seek the LORD:
look to the rock from which you
were hewn,
to the quarry from which you were
dug;
look to your father Abraham   2
and to Sarah who gave you birth:
when I called him he was but one,
I blessed him and made him many.
The LORD has indeed comforted 3
Zion,
comforted all her ruined homes,
turning her wilderness into an Eden,
her thirsty plains into a garden of
the LORD.
Joy and gladness shall be found in her,
thanksgiving and melody.
Pay heed to me, my people,   4
and hear me, O my nation;
for my law shall shine forth
and I will flash the light of my judgement over the nations.
My victory is near, my deliverance 5
has gone*b* forth
and my arm shall rule the nations;
for me coasts and islands shall wait
and they shall look to me for protection.
Lift your eyes to the heavens,   6
look at the earth beneath:
the heavens grow murky as smoke;

b Or shone.

the earth wears into tatters like a garment,
and those who live on it die like maggots;
but my deliverance is everlasting
and my saving power shall never wane.

⁷ Listen to me, my people who know what is right,
you who lay my law to heart:
do not fear the taunts of men,
let no reproaches dismay you;
8 for the grub will devour them like a garment
and the moth as if they were wool,
but my saving power shall last for ever
and my deliverance to all generations.

Encouragement for the exiles

9 Awake, awake, put on your strength, O arm of the LORD,
awake as you did long ago, in days gone by.
Was it not you
who hacked the Rahab in pieces and ran the dragon through?
10 Was it not you
who dried up the sea, the waters of the great abyss,
and made the ocean depths a path for the ransomed?
11 So the LORD's people shall come back, set free,
and enter Zion with shouts of triumph,
crowned with everlasting joy;
joy and gladness shall overtake them as they come,
and sorrow and sighing shall flee away.
12 I, I myself, am he that comforts you.
Why then fear man, man who must die,
man frail as grass?
13 Why have you forgotten the LORD your maker,
who stretched out the skies and founded the earth?
Why are you continually afraid, all the day long,
why dread the fury of oppressors ready to destroy you?
Where is that fury?
14 He that cowers under it shall soon stand upright and not die,
he shall soon reap the early crop and not lack bread.

15 I am the LORD your God, the LORD of Hosts is my name. I cleft the sea and its waves roared, that I might fix **16** the heavens in place and form the earth and say to Zion, 'You are my people.' I have put my words in your mouth and kept you safe under the shelter of my hand.

'Awake; rise up, Jerusalem'

Awake, awake; rise up, Jerusalem. **17**
You have drunk from the LORD's hand
the cup of his wrath,
drained to its dregs the bowl of drunkenness;
of all the sons you have borne there is **18** not one to guide you,
of all you have reared, not one to take you by the hand.
These two disasters have overtaken **19** you;
who can console you?—
havoc and ruin, famine and the sword;
who can comfort you?
Your sons are in stupor, they lie at **20** the head of every street,
like antelopes caught in the net,
glutted with the wrath of the LORD,
the rebuke of your God.
Therefore listen to this, in your **21** affliction,
drunk that you are, but not with wine:
thus says the LORD, your Lord and **22** your God,
who will plead his people's cause:
Look, I take from your hand
the cup of drunkenness;
you shall never again drink from the bowl of my wrath,
I will give it instead to your tor- **23** mentors and oppressors,
those who said to you, 'Lie down and we will walk over you';
and you made your backs like the ground beneath them,
like a roadway for passers-by.

Awake, awake, put on your strength, **52**
O Zion,
put on your loveliest garments, holy city of Jerusalem;
for never shall the uncircumcised and the unclean enter you again.
Rise up, captive Jerusalem, shake off **2** the dust;
loose your neck from the collar that binds it,
O captive daughter of Zion.

Good news for Zion

The LORD says, You were sold but no **3** price was paid, and without payment you shall be ransomed. The Lord GOD **4** says, At the beginning my people

went down into Egypt to live there,
and at the end it was the Assyrians who
5 oppressed them; but now what do I
find here? says the LORD. My people
carried off and no price paid, their
rulers derided, and my name reviled
6 all day long, says the LORD. But on
that day my people shall know my
name; they shall know that it is I
who speak; here I am.

7 How lovely on the mountains are the
  feet of the herald
who comes to proclaim prosperity and
  bring good news,
  the news of deliverance,
calling to Zion, 'Your God is king.'
8 Hark, your watchmen raise their
  voices
  and shout together in triumph;
  for with their own eyes they shall
  see
  the LORD returning in pity to Zion.
9 Break forth together in shouts of
  triumph,
  you ruins of Jerusalem;
for the LORD has taken pity on his
  people
  and has ransomed Jerusalem.
10 The LORD has bared his holy arm
  in the sight of all nations,
  and the whole world from end to end
  shall see the deliverance of our God.
11 Away from Babylon; come out, come
  out,
  touch nothing unclean.
  Come out from Babylon, keep
  yourselves pure,
  you who carry the vessels of the
  LORD.
12 But you shall not come out in urgent haste
  nor leave like fugitives;
  for the LORD will march at your
  head,
  your rearguard will be Israel's God.

The LORD's suffering servant

13 Behold, my servant shall prosper,
  he shall be lifted up, exalted to the
  heights.

14 Time was when many[c] were aghast at
  you, my people;[d]
15 so now many nations[e] recoil at sight
  of him,
and kings curl their lips in disgust.
For they see what they had never
  been told
  and things unheard before fill their
  thoughts.

Who could have believed what we 53
  have heard,
and to whom has the power of the
  LORD been revealed?

He grew up before the LORD like a 2
  young plant
  whose roots are in parched ground;
he had no beauty, no majesty to draw
  our eyes,
  no grace to make us delight in him;
his form, disfigured, lost all the likeness
  of a man,
  his beauty changed beyond human
  semblance.[f]
He was despised, he shrank from 3
  the sight of men,
  tormented and humbled by suffering;
we despised him, we held him of no
  account,
  a thing from which men turn away
  their eyes.
Yet on himself he bore our sufferings, 4
  our torments he endured,
  while we counted him smitten by
  God,
  struck down by disease and misery;
but he was pierced for our trans- 5
  gressions,
  tortured for our iniquities;
the chastisement he bore is health
  for us
  and by his scourging we are healed.
We had all strayed like sheep,   6
each of us had gone his own way;
  but the LORD laid upon him
  the guilt of us all.
He was afflicted, he submitted to be 7
  struck down
  and did not open his mouth;
he was led like a sheep to the
  slaughter,
  like a ewe that is dumb before the
  shearers.[g]
Without protection, without justice,[h] 8
  he was taken away;
  and who gave a thought to his fate,
  how he was cut off from the world
  of living men,
  stricken to the death for my people's
  transgression?
He was assigned a grave with the 9
  wicked,
  a burial-place among the refuse of
  mankind,
  though he had done no violence
  and spoken no word of treachery.
Yet the LORD took thought for his 10
  tortured servant

c Or the great.   d See note on 53. 2.   e Or great nations.   f his form . . . semblance: *transposed from end of 52. 14.*   g Prob. rdg.; Heb. *adds* and he would not open his mouth.   h Without protection, without justice: *or* After arrest and sentence.

and healed him who had made himself[i] a sacrifice for sin;
so shall he enjoy long life and see his
children's children,
and in his hand the LORD's cause
shall prosper.

11 After all his pains he shall be bathed
in light,
after his disgrace he shall be fully
vindicated;
so shall he, my servant, vindicate
many,
himself bearing the penalty of their
guilt.

12 Therefore I will allot him a portion
with the great,
and he shall share the spoil with the
mighty,
because he exposed himself to face
death[j]
and was reckoned among transgressors,
because he bore the sin of many
and interceded for their transgressions.

The LORD's affection for Israel

54 Sing aloud, O barren woman who
never bore a child,
break into cries of joy, you who
have never been in labour;
for the deserted wife has more sons
than she who lives in wedlock,
says the LORD.

2 Enlarge the limits of your home,
spread wide the curtains of your
tent;
let out its ropes to the full
and drive the pegs home;

3 for you shall break out of your
confines right and left,
your descendants shall dispossess
wide regions,[k]
and re-people cities now desolate.

4 Fear not; you shall not be put to
shame,
you shall suffer no insult, have no
cause to blush.
It is time to forget the shame of
your younger days
and remember no more the reproach
of your widowhood;

5 for your husband is your maker, whose
name is the LORD of Hosts;
your ransomer is the Holy One of
Israel
who is called God of all the earth.

6 The LORD has acknowledged you a
wife again,
once deserted and heart-broken,

your God has called you a bride still
young
though once rejected.
On the impulse of a moment I for- 7
sook you,
but with tender affection I will bring
you home again.
In sudden anger 8
I hid my face from you for a
moment;
but now have I pitied you with a love
which never fails,
says the LORD who ransoms you.
These days recall for me the days 9
of Noah:
as I swore that the waters of Noah's
flood
should never again pour over the
earth,
so now I swear to you
never again to be angry with you or
reproach you.
Though the mountains move and 10
the hills shake,
my love shall be immovable and
never fail,
and my covenant of peace shall not
be shaken.
So says the LORD who takes pity on
you.

The LORD will rebuild Zion

O storm-battered city, distressed 11
and disconsolate,
now I will set your stones in the finest
mortar
and your foundations in lapis
lazuli;
I will make your battlements of red 12
jasper[l]
and your gates of garnet;[m]
all your boundary-stones shall be
jewels.
Your masons shall all be instructed 13
by the LORD,
and your sons shall enjoy great
prosperity;
and in triumph[n] shall you be re- 14
stored.
You shall be free from oppression and
have no fears,
free from terror, and it shall not come
near you;
should any attack you, it will not be 15
my doing,
the aggressor, whoever he be, shall
perish for his attempt.
It was I who created the smith 16
to fan the coals in the furnace
and forge weapons each for its
purpose,

i healed . . . himself: prob. rdg.; Heb. he made sick, if you make.   j Or because he poured out his
life to the death.   k wide regions: or the nations.   l Or carbuncle.   m Or firestone.   n Or
in righteousness.

and I who created the destroyer to lay
waste;
17 but now no weapon made to harm you
shall prevail,
and you shall rebut every charge
brought against you.
Such is the fortune of the servants
of the LORD;
their vindication comes from me.
This is the very word of the LORD.

The LORD's invitation

55 Come, all who are thirsty, come,
fetch water;
come, you who have no food, buy
corn and eat;
come and buy, not for money, not for
a price.*o*
2 Why spend money and get what is not
bread,
why give the price of your labour
and go unsatisfied?
Only listen to me and you will have
good food to eat,
and you will enjoy the fat of the
land.
3 Come to me and listen to my words,
hear me, and you shall have life:
I will make a covenant with you,
this time for ever,
to love you faithfully as I loved
David.
4 I made him a witness to all races,
a prince and instructor of peoples;
5 and you in turn shall summon nations
you do not know,
and nations that do not know you
shall come running to you,
because the LORD your God,
the Holy One of Israel, has glorified
you.
6 Inquire of the LORD while he is
present,
call upon him when he is close at
hand.
7 Let the wicked abandon their ways
and evil men their thoughts:
let them return to the LORD, who will
have pity on them,
return to our God, for he will freely
forgive.
8 For my thoughts are not your
thoughts,
and your ways are not my ways.
This is the very word of the LORD.
9 For as the heavens are higher than
the earth,
so are my ways higher than your ways
and my thoughts than your
thoughts;
10 and as the rain and the snow come
down from heaven

and do not return until they have
watered the earth,
making it blossom and bear fruit,
and give seed for sowing and bread to
eat,
so shall the word which comes from 11
my mouth prevail;
it shall not return to me fruitless
without accomplishing my purpose
or succeeding in the task I gave it.
You shall indeed go out with joy 12
and be led forth in peace.
Before you mountains and hills shall
break into cries of joy,
and all the trees of the wild shall clap
their hands,
pine-trees shall shoot up in place of 13
camel-thorn,
myrtles instead of briars;
all this shall win the LORD a great
name,
imperishable, a sign for all time.

'A house of prayer for all nations'

These are the words of the LORD: 56
Maintain justice, do the right;
for my deliverance is close at hand,
and my righteousness will show
itself victorious.
Happy is the man who follows these 2
precepts,
happy the mortal who holds them
fast,
who keeps the sabbath undefiled,
who refrains from all wrong-doing!
The foreigner who has given his 3
allegiance to the LORD must not
say,
'The LORD will keep me separate from
his people for ever';
and the eunuch must not say,
'I am nothing but a barren tree.'
For these are the words of the LORD: 4
The eunuchs who keep my sabbaths,
who choose to do my will and hold
fast to my covenant,
shall receive from me something 5
better than sons and daughters,
a memorial and a name in my own
house and within my walls;
I will give them an everlasting
name,
a name imperishable for all time.
So too with the foreigners who give 6
their allegiance to me, the LORD,
to minister to me and love my name
and to become my servants,
all who keep the sabbath undefiled
and hold fast to my covenant:
them will I bring to my holy hill 7
and give them joy in my house of
prayer.

o Prob. rdg.; Heb. adds wine and milk.

Their offerings and sacrifices shall be
    acceptable on my altar;
for my house shall be called
a house of prayer for all nations.
8 This is the very word of the Lord
        God,
    who brings home the outcasts of
        Israel:
I will yet bring home all that remain
    to be brought in.

Failure of Israel's leaders

9 Come, beasts of the plain, beasts of the
        forest, come, eat your fill,
10 for Israel's watchmen are blind, all of
        them unaware.
    They are all dumb dogs who cannot
        bark,
    stretched on the ground, dreaming,
        lovers of sleep,
11 greedy dogs that can never have
        enough.
    They are shepherds who understand
        nothing,
        absent each of them on his own
            pursuits,
        each intent on his own gain wherever
            he can find it.
12 'Come,' says each of them, 'let me
        fetch wine,
    strong drink, and we will drain it
        down;
    let us make tomorrow like today,
        or greater far!'

57 The righteous perish,
    and no one takes it to heart;
    men of good faith are swept away, but
        no one cares,
    the righteous are swept away before
        the onset of evil,
2 but they enter into peace;
    they have run a straight course
    and rest in their last beds.

Immoral religious practices

3 Come, stand forth, you sons of a
        soothsayer.
    You spawn of an adulterer and a
        harlot,
4 who is the target of your jests?
    Against whom do you open your
        mouths
        and wag your tongues,
    children of sin that you are, spawn of
        a lie,
5 burning with lust under the tere-
        binths,
    under every spreading tree,
    and sacrificing children in the gorges,
        under the rocky clefts?
6 And you, woman,
    your place is with the creatures of
        the gorge;

that is where you belong.
To them you have dared to pour a
    libation
and present an offering of grain.[p]
On a high mountain-top   7
    you have made your bed;
    there too you have gone up to offer
        sacrifice.
In spite of all this am I to relent?[q]
Beside door and door-post you have 8
    put up your sign.
Deserting me, you have stripped and
    lain down
on the wide bed which you have
    made,
and you drove bargains with men
for the pleasure of sleeping together,
and you have committed countless
    acts of fornication
in the heat of your lust.
You drenched your tresses in oil   9
    blended with many perfumes;
you sent out your procurers far and
    wide
even down to the gates of Sheol.
Worn out by your unending ex- 10
    cesses,
even so you never said, 'I am past
    hope.'
You earned a livelihood
and so you had no anxiety.
Whom do you fear so much, that you 11
    should be false,
that you never remembered me or gave
    me a thought?
Did I not hold my peace and seem not
    to see
while you showed no fear of me?
Now I will denounce your conduct 12
    that you think so righteous.
These idols of yours shall not help 13
    when you cry;
    no idol shall save you.
The wind shall carry them off, one
    and all,
a puff of air shall blow them away;
but he who makes me his refuge shall
    possess the earth
    and inherit my holy hill.

The Lord's care for wilful Israel

Then a voice shall be heard: 14
Build up a highway, build it and clear
    the track,
    sweep away all that blocks my
        people's path.
Thus speaks the high and exalted one, 15
whose name is holy, who lives for
    ever:
I dwell in a high and holy place
    with him who is broken and humble
        in spirit,
    to revive the spirit of the humble,

p See note on verse 7.   *q Line transposed from end of verse 6.*

to revive the courage of the broken.

16 I will not be always accusing,
I will not continually nurse my
wrath.
For a breath of life passed out from
me,
and by my own act I created living
creatures.

17 For a time I was angry at the guilt
of Israel;
I smote him in my anger and withdrew my favour.
But he ran wild and went his wilful
way.

18 Then I considered his ways,
I cured him and gave him relief,
and I brought him comfort in full
measure,

19 brought peace to those who mourned
for him,
by the words that issue from my
lips,
peace for all men, both near and far,
and so I cured him, says the LORD.

20 But the wicked are like a troubled
sea,
a sea that cannot rest,
whose troubled waters cast up mud
and filth.

21 There is no peace for the wicked,
says the LORD.

True and false fasting

58 Shout aloud without restraint;
lift up your voice like a trumpet.
Call my people to account for their
transgression
and the house of Jacob for their
sins,

2 although they ask counsel of me
day by day
and say they delight in knowing my
ways,
although, like nations which have
acted rightly
and not forsaken the just laws of
their gods,
they ask me for righteous laws
and say they delight in approaching
God.

3 Why do we fast, if thou dost not
see it?
Why mortify ourselves, if thou
payest no heed?
Since you serve your own interest
only on your fast-day
and make all your men work the
harder,

4 since your fasting leads only to
wrangling and strife
and dealing vicious blows with the
fist,

on such a day you are keeping no
fast
that will carry your cry to heaven.

5 Is it a fast like this that I require,
a day of mortification such as this,
that a man should bow his head
like a bulrush
and make his bed on sackcloth and
ashes?
Is this what you call a fast,
a day acceptable to the LORD?

6 Is not this what I require of you as a
fast:
to loose the fetters of injustice,
to untie the knots of the yoke,
to snap every yoke
and set free those who have been
crushed?

7 Is it not sharing your food with the
hungry,
taking the homeless poor into your
house,
clothing the naked when you meet
them
and never evading a duty to your
kinsfolk?

8 Then shall your light break forth like
the dawn
and soon you will grow healthy like
a wound newly healed;
your own righteousness shall be
your vanguard
and the glory of the LORD your
rearguard.

9 Then, if you call, the LORD will
answer;
if you cry to him, he will say, 'Here
I am.'
If you cease to pervert justice,
to point the accusing finger and lay
false charges,

10 if you feed the hungry from your
own plenty
and satisfy the needs of the wretched,
then your light will rise like dawn
out of darkness
and your dusk be like noonday;

11 the LORD will be your guide continually
and will satisfy your needs in the
shimmering heat;
he will give you strength of limb;
you will be like a well-watered
garden,
like a spring whose waters never
fail.

12 The ancient ruins will be restored by
your own kindred
and you will build once more on
ancestral foundations;
you shall be called Rebuilder of
broken walls,
Restorer of houses in ruins.

The reward for honouring the sabbath

13 If you cease to tread the sabbath
     underfoot,
   and keep my holy day free from
     your own affairs,
   if you call the sabbath a day of joy
   and the LORD's holy day a day to
     be honoured,
   if you honour it by not plying your
     trade,
   not seeking your own interest
   or attending to your own affairs,
14 then you shall find your joy in the
     LORD,
   and I will set you riding on the
     heights of the earth,
   and your father Jacob's patrimony
     shall be yours to enjoy;
   the LORD himself has spoken it.

Iniquities—a barrier

59 The LORD's arm is not so short that
     he cannot save
   nor his ear too dull to hear;
2 it is your iniquities that raise a
     barrier
   between you and your God,
   because of your sins he has hidden
     his face
   so that he does not hear you.
3 Your hands are stained with blood
   and your fingers with crime;
   your lips speak lies
   and your tongues utter injustice.
4 No man sues with just cause,
   no man goes honestly to law;
   all trust in empty words, all tell lies,
   conceive mischief and give birth to
     trouble.
5 They hatch snakes' eggs, they weave
     cobwebs;
   eat their eggs and you will die,
   for rotten eggs hatch only rotten-
     ness.
6 As for their webs, they will never
     make cloth,
   no one can use them for clothing;
   their works breed trouble
   and their hands are busy with deeds
     of violence.
7 They rush headlong into crime
   in furious haste to shed innocent
     blood;
   their schemes are schemes of mis-
     chief
   and leave a trail of ruin and devasta-
     tion.
8 They do not know the way to peace,
   no justice guides their steps;
   all the paths they follow are crook-
     ed;
   no one who walks in them enjoys true
     peace.

Confession of sinfulness

Therefore justice is far away from us, 9
   right does not reach us;
we look for light but all is darkness,
   for the light of dawn, but we walk
     in deep gloom.
We grope like blind men along a 10
   wall,
   feeling our way like men without
     eyes;
   we stumble at noonday as if it
     were twilight,
   like dead men in the ghostly under-
     world.
We growl like bears,   11
   like doves we moan incessantly,
   waiting for justice, and there is
     none;
   for deliverance, but it is still far
     away.

Our acts of rebellion against thee 12
   are past counting
   and our sins bear witness against
     us;
we remember our many rebellions, we
   know well our guilt:
   we have rebelled and broken faith 13
     with the LORD,
   we have relapsed and forsaken our
     God;
we have conceived lies in our hearts
   and repeated them
   in slanderous and treacherous
     words.
Justice is rebuffed and flouted   14
   while righteousness stands aloof;
   truth stumbles in the market-place
   and honesty is kept out of court,
   so truth is lost to sight,   15
   and whoever shuns evil is thought
     a madman.

The LORD intervenes

The LORD saw, and in his eyes it was
     an evil thing,
   that there was no justice;
   he saw that there was no man to 16
     help
   and was outraged that no one
     intervened;
so his own arm brought him victory
   and his own integrity upheld him.
He put on integrity as a coat of 17
     mail
   and the helmet of salvation on his
     head;
   he put on garments of vengeance
   and wrapped himself in a cloak of
     jealous anger.
High God of retribution that he is, 18
   he pays in full measure,
wreaking his anger on his foes,
   retribution on his enemies.

19 So from the west men shall fear his
     name,
   fear his glory from the rising of the
     sun;
   for it shall come like a shining
     river,
   the spirit of the LORD hovering
     over it,
20 come as the ransomer of Zion
   and of all in Jacob who repent of
     their rebellion.
   This is the very word of the LORD.

21 This, says the LORD, is my covenant, which I make with them: My
   spirit which rests on you and my
   words which I have put into your
   mouth shall never fail you from
   generation to generation of your
   descendants from now onward for
   ever. The LORD has said it.

Jerusalem's glorious future

60 Arise, Jerusalem,
   rise clothed in light; your light has
     come
   and the glory of the LORD shines
     over you.
2 For, though darkness covers the earth
   and dark night the nations,
   the LORD shall shine upon you
   and over you shall his glory appear;
3 and the nations shall march towards
     your light
   and their kings to your sunrise.

4 Lift up your eyes and look all around:
   they flock together, all of them, and
     come to you;
   your sons also shall come from afar,
   your daughters walking beside them
     leading the way.
5 Then shall you see, and shine with
     joy,
   then your heart shall thrill with
     pride:
   the riches of the sea shall be lavi-
     shed upon you
   and you shall possess the wealth of
     nations.

6 Camels in droves shall cover the
     land,
   dromedaries of Midian and Ephah,
   all coming from Sheba
   laden with golden spice*r* and frank-
     incense,
   heralds of the LORD's praise.
7 All Kedar's flocks shall be gathered
     for you,
   rams of Nebaioth shall serve your
     need,

acceptable offerings on my altar,
and glory shall be added to glory in
   my temple.

Who are these that sail along like **8**
   clouds,
that fly like doves to their dovecotes?
They are vessels assembling from the **9**
   coasts and islands,
ships from Tarshish leading the
   convoy;
they bring your sons from afar,
   their gold and their silver with them,
to the honour of the LORD your God,
the Holy One of Israel;
for he has made you glorious.

Foreigners shall rebuild your walls **10**
and their kings shall be your
   servants;
for though in my wrath I struck
   you down,
now I have shown you pity and
   favour.
Your gates shall be open continually, **11**
they shall never be shut day or night,
that through them may be brought
   the wealth of nations
and their kings under escort.

For the nation or kingdom which **12**
refuses to serve you shall perish, and
wide regions shall be laid utterly
waste.

The wealth of Lebanon shall come **13**
   to you,
pine, fir,*s* and boxwood,*t* all together,
   to bring glory to my holy sanctuary,
   to honour the place where my feet
     rest.
The sons of your oppressors shall **14**
   come forward to do homage,
all who reviled you shall bow low at
   your feet;
   they shall call you the City of the
     LORD,
   the Zion of the Holy One of Israel.

No longer will you be deserted,   **15**
a wife hated and unvisited;*u*
I will make you an eternal pride
and a never-ending joy.
You shall suck the milk of nations **16**
and be suckled at the breasts of kings.
So you shall know that I the LORD am
   your deliverer,
   your ransomer the Mighty One of
     Jacob.

For bronze*v* I will bring you gold   **17**
and for iron I will bring silver,
bronze*v* for timber and iron for stone;

r golden spice: *or gold.*   *s Or elm.*   *t Or cypress.*   *u Or divorced and unmated.*   *v Or*
copper.

and I will make your government
be peace
and righteousness rule over you.
18 The sound of violence shall be heard
no longer in your land,
or ruin and devastation within your
borders;
but you shall call your walls
Deliverance
and your gates Praise.

19 The sun shall no longer be your light
by day,
nor the moon shine on you when
evening falls;
the LORD shall be your everlasting
light,
your God shall be your glory.
20 Never again shall your sun set
nor your moon withdraw her light;
but the LORD shall be your everlasting
light
and the days of your mourning
shall be ended.

21 Your people shall all be righteous
and shall for ever possess the land,
a shoot of my own planting,
a work of my own hands to bring
me glory.
22 The few shall become ten thousand,
the little nation great.
I am the LORD;
soon, in the fullness of time, I will
bring this to pass.

Good news proclaimed

61 The spirit of the Lord GOD is upon
me
because the LORD has anointed me;
he has sent me to bring good news
to the humble,
to bind up the broken-hearted,
to proclaim liberty to captives
and release to those in prison;
2 to proclaim a year of the LORD's
favour
and a day of the vengeance of our
God;
to comfort all who mourn,[w]
3 to give them garlands instead of
ashes,
oil of gladness instead of mourners'
tears,
a garment of splendour for the
heavy heart.
They shall be called Trees of Righteousness,
planted by the LORD for his glory.
4 Ancient ruins shall be rebuilt
and sites long desolate restored;
they shall repair the ruined cities

and restore what has long lain
desolate.
Foreigners shall serve as shepherds of 5
your flocks,
and aliens shall till your land and
tend your vines;
but you shall be called priests of the 6
LORD
and be named ministers of our God;
you shall enjoy the wealth of other
nations
and be furnished[x] with their riches.
And so, because shame in double 7
measure
and jeers and insults[y] have been
my people's lot,
they shall receive in their own land a
double measure of wealth,
and everlasting joy shall be theirs.
For I, the LORD, love justice 8
and hate robbery and wrong-doing;
I will grant them a sure reward
and make an everlasting covenant
with them;
their posterity will be renowned 9
among the nations
and their offspring among the
peoples;
all who see them will acknowledge
in them
a race whom the LORD has blessed.

A hymn of praise

Let me rejoice in the LORD with all 10
my heart,
let me exult in my God;
for he has robed me in salvation as
a garment
and clothed me in integrity as a
cloak,
like a bridegroom with his priestly
garland,
or a bride decked in her jewels.
For, as the earth puts forth her 11
blossom
or bushes in the garden burst into
flower,
so shall the Lord GOD make righteousness and praise
blossom before all the nations.

Prayer for Jerusalem, and its answer

For Zion's sake I will not keep 62
silence,
for Jerusalem's sake I will speak
out,
until her right shines forth like the
sunrise,
her deliverance like a blazing torch,
until the nations see the triumph of 2
your right
and all kings see your glory.

w Prob. rdg.; Heb. adds to appoint to Zion's mourners.   x be furnished: prob. rdg.; Heb. unintelligible.   y and insults: prob. rdg.; Heb. they shout in triumph.

Then you shall be called by a new
     name
which the LORD shall pronounce
     with his own lips;
3 you will be a glorious crown in the
     LORD's hand,
a kingly diadem in the hand of your
     God.
4 No more shall men call you Forsaken,
     no more shall your land be called
     Desolate,
but you shall be named Hephzi-bah*²*
     and your land Beulah;*ᵃ*
for the LORD delights in you
and to him your land is wedded.
5 For, as a young man weds a maiden,
     so you shall wed him who rebuilds
     you,
and your God shall rejoice over you
     as a bridegroom rejoices over the
     bride.
6 I have posted watchmen on your walls,
     Jerusalem,
who shall not keep silence day or
     night:
'You who invoke the LORD's name,
7 take no rest, give him no rest
     until he makes Jerusalem
     a theme of endless praise on earth.'

The LORD's proclamation

8 The LORD has sworn with raised
     right hand and mighty arm:
Never again will I give your grain to
     feed your foes
or let foreigners drink the new wine
     for which you have toiled;
9 but those who bring in the corn shall
     eat and praise the LORD,
and those who gather the grapes shall
     drink in my holy courts.

10 Go out of the gates, go out,
     prepare a road for my people;
build a highway, build it up,
     clear away the boulders;
     raise a signal to the peoples.
11 This is the LORD's proclamation
     to earth's farthest bounds:
Tell the daughter of Zion,
Behold, your deliverance has come.
His recompense comes with him;
he carries his reward before him;
12 and they shall be called a Holy
     People,
     the Ransomed of the LORD,
a People long-sought, a City not for-
     saken.

The LORD's day of vengeance

63 'Who is this coming from Edom,
     coming from Bozrah, his garments
     stained red?

Under his clothes his muscles stand
     out,
and he strides, stooping in his
     might.'
It is I, who announce that right
     has won the day,
I, who am strong to save.
'Why is your clothing all red,   2
like the garments of one who treads
     grapes in the vat?'
I have trodden the winepress alone; 3
no man, no nation was with me.
I trod them down in my rage,
I trampled them in my fury;
and their life-blood spurted over my
     garments
and stained all my clothing.
For I resolved on a day of vengeance; 4
the year for ransoming my own had
     come.
I looked for a helper but found no 5
     one,
I was amazed that there was no one
     to support me;
yet my own arm brought me victory,
     alone my anger supported me.
I stamped on nations in my fury,   6
I pierced them in my rage
and let their life-blood run out
     upon the ground.

Recalling past mercies

I will recount the LORD's acts of 7
     unfailing love
and the LORD's praises as High God,
all that the LORD has done for us
and his great goodness to the house
     of Israel,
all that he has done for them in his
     tenderness
and by his many acts of love.
He said, 'Surely they are my people, 8
my sons who will not play me false';
and he became their deliverer in all 9
     their troubles.
It was no envoy, no angel, but he him-
     self that delivered them;
he himself ransomed them by his love
     and pity,
lifted them up and carried them
through all the years gone by.
Yet they rebelled and grieved his holy 10
     spirit;
only then was he changed into their
     enemy
and himself fought against them.
Then men remembered days long 11
     past
and him who drew out*ᵇ* his people:
Where is he who brought them up
     from the Nile
with the shepherd*ᶜ* of his flock?

---

z That is My delight is in her.   *a That is* Wedded.   *b That is* Moses *whose name resembles the*
Heb. *verb meaning* draw out, *cp.* Exod. 2. 10 *and the note there.*   c Or shepherds.

Where is he who put within him
his holy spirit,
12 who made his glorious power march
at the right hand of Moses,
dividing the waters before them,
to win for himself an everlasting
name,
13 causing them to go through the
depths
sure-footed as horses in the wilderness,
14 like cattle moving down into a
valley without stumbling,
guided by the spirit of the LORD?
So didst thou lead thy people
to win thyself a glorious name.

Prayer to the LORD as father

15 Look down from heaven and behold
from the heights where thou dwellest
holy and glorious.
Where is thy zeal, thy valour,
thy burning and tender love?
16 Stand not aloof;[d] for thou art our
father,
though Abraham does not know us
nor Israel acknowledge us.
Thou, LORD, art our father;
thy name is our Ransomer[e] from of
old.
17 Why, LORD, dost thou let us wander
from thy ways
and harden our hearts until we
cease to fear thee?
turn again for the sake of thy
servants,
the tribes of thy patrimony.
18 Why have wicked men trodden down
thy sanctuary,[f]
why have our enemies trampled on
thy shrine?
19 We have long been reckoned as beyond
thy sway,
as if we had not been named thy
own.

64 Why didst thou not rend the heavens
and come down,
and make the mountains shudder
before thee
2 as when fire blazes up in brushwood
or fire makes water boil?
then would thy name be known to
thy enemies
and nations tremble at thy coming.
3 When thou didst terrible things that
we did not look for,
the mountains shuddered before
thee.
4 Never has ear heard[g] or eye seen

any other god taking the part of those
who wait for him.
Thou dost welcome him who rejoices 5
to do what is right,
who remembers thee in thy ways.
Though thou wast angry, yet we
sinned,
in spite of it we have done evil from
of old,
we all became like a man who is un- 6
clean
and all our righteous deeds like a
filthy rag;
we have all withered[h] like leaves
and our iniquities sweep us away
like the wind.
There is no one who invokes thee 7
by name
or rouses himself to cling to thee;
for thou hast hidden thy face from
us
and abandoned us to our iniquities.
But now, LORD, thou art our 8
father;
we are the clay, thou the potter,
and all of us are thy handiwork.
Do not be angry beyond measure, 9
O LORD,
and do not remember iniquity for
ever;
look on us all, look on thy people.
Thy holy cities are a wilderness, 10
Zion a wilderness, Jerusalem desolate;
our sanctuary, holy and glorious, 11
where our fathers praised thee,
has been burnt to the ground
and all that we cherish is a ruin.
After this, O LORD, wilt thou hold 12
back,
wilt thou keep silence and punish
us beyond measure?

The LORD appeals to an unruly people

65 I was there to be sought by a people
who did not ask,
to be found by men who did not
seek me.
I said, 'Here am I, here am I',
to a nation that did not invoke me
by name.
2 I spread out my hands all day
appealing to an unruly people
who went their evil way,
following their own devices,
3 a people who provoked me
continually to my face,
offering sacrifice in gardens, burning
incense on brick altars,
4 crouching among graves, keeping vigil
all night long,

d Stand not aloof: *prob. rdg.*; Heb. *obscure in context.*   e Or our Kinsman.   f Why . . . sanctuary:
prob. rdg.; Heb. For a little while they possessed thy holy people.   g Never . . . heard: *prob. rdg.*;
Heb. They have never heard or listened.   h have all withered: *or* are all carried away.

eating swine's flesh, their cauldrons
full of a tainted brew.
5 'Stay where you are,' they cry,
'do not dare touch me; for I am too
sacred for you.'
Such people are a smouldering fire,
smoking in my nostrils all day long.
6 All is on record before me; I will not
keep silence;
7 I will repay[i] your iniquities,
yours and your fathers', all at once,
says the LORD,
because they burnt incense[j] on the
mountains
and defied me on the hills;
I will first measure out their reward
and then pay them in full.

New heavens and a new earth

8   These are the words of the LORD:
As there is new wine in a cluster of
grapes
and men say, 'Do not destroy it; there
is a blessing in it',
so will I do for my servants' sake:
I will not destroy the whole nation.
9   I will give Jacob children to come
after him
and Judah heirs who shall possess
my mountains;
my chosen shall inherit them
and my servants shall live there.
10   Flocks shall range over Sharon,
and the Vale of Achor be a pasture
for cattle;
they shall belong to my people who
seek me.
11 But you that forsake the LORD and
forget my holy mountain,
who spread a table for the god of
Fate,
and fill bowls of spiced wine in
honour of Fortune,
12   I will deliver you to your fate, to
execution,
and you shall all bend the neck to
the sword,
because I called and you did not
answer,
I spoke and you did not listen;
and you did what was wrong in my
eyes
and you chose what was against
my will.
13 Therefore these are the words of the
Lord GOD:
My servants shall eat but you shall
starve;
my servants shall drink but you shall
go thirsty;
my servants shall rejoice but you shall
be put to shame;

my servants shall shout in triumph 14
in the gladness of their hearts,
but you shall cry from sorrow
and wail from anguish of spirit;
your name shall be used as an oath by 15
my chosen,
and the Lord GOD shall give you
over to death;
but his servants he shall call by
another name.
He who invokes a blessing on him- 16
self in the land
shall do so by the God whose name
is Amen,
and he who utters an oath in the
land
shall do so by the God of Amen;
the former troubles are forgotten
and they are hidden from my sight.
For behold, I create   17
new heavens and a new earth.
Former things shall no more be
remembered
nor shall they be called to mind.
Rejoice and be filled with delight, 18
you boundless realms which I
create;
for I create Jerusalem to be a delight
and her people a joy;
I will take delight in Jerusalem and 19
rejoice in my people;
weeping and cries for help
shall never again be heard in her.
There no child shall ever again die an 20
infant,
no old man fail to live out his life;
every boy shall live his hundred
years before he dies,
whoever falls short of a hundred shall
be despised.[k]
Men shall build houses and live to 21
inhabit them,
plant vineyards and eat their fruit;
they shall not build for others to 22
inhabit
nor plant for others to eat.
My people shall live the long life of
a tree,
and my chosen shall enjoy the fruit
of their labour.
They shall not toil in vain or raise 23
children for misfortune.
For they are the offspring of the
blessed of the LORD
and their issue after them;
before they call to me, I will answer, 24
and while they are still speaking I will
listen.
The wolf and the lamb shall feed 25
together
and the lion shall eat straw like
cattle.[l]

i Prob. rdg., transposing and then pay *to follow* reward.   [j Or sacrifices.   k Or cursed.   l Prob.
rdg.; Heb. adds* and the food of the snake shall be dust.

They shall not hurt or destroy in all
  my holy mountain,
says the LORD.

Reverence for the LORD

66 These are the words of the LORD:
Heaven is my throne and earth my
  footstool.
Where will you build a house for me,
  where shall my resting-place be?
2 All these are of my own making
and all these are mine.
This is the very word of the LORD.

The man I look to is a man downtrodden and distressed,
  one who reveres my words.
3 But to sacrifice an ox or to[m] kill a man,
slaughter a sheep or break a dog's
  neck,
offer grain or offer pigs' blood,
burn incense as a token and worship
  an idol—
all these are the chosen practices of
  men
  who[n] revel in their own loathsome
    rites.
4 I too will practise those wanton rites
  of theirs
  and bring down on them the very
    things they dread;
for I called and no one answered,
I spoke and no one listened.
They did what was wrong in my
  eyes
  and chose practices not to my
    liking.

5 Hear the word of the LORD, you who
  revere his word:
  Your fellow-countrymen who hate
    you,
  who spurn you because you bear
    my name, have said,
  'Let the LORD show his glory,
  then we shall see you rejoice';
  but they shall be put to shame.
6 That roar from the city, that uproar
  in the temple,
  is the sound of the LORD dealing
    retribution to his foes.

Jerusalem, a mother of children

7 Shall a woman bear a child without
  pains?
  give birth to a son before the onset
    of labour?
8 Who has heard of anything like this?
Who has seen any such thing?
Shall a country be born after one
  day's labour,

shall a nation be brought to birth all
  in a moment?
But Zion, at the onset of her pangs,
  bore her sons.
  Shall I bring to the point of birth 9
    and not deliver?
  the LORD says;
  shall I who deliver close the womb?
  your God has spoken.

Rejoice with Jerusalem and exult in 10
  her,
  all you who love her;
  share her joy with all your heart,
  all you who mourn over her.
Then you may suck and be fed from 11
  the breasts that give comfort,
delighting in her plentiful milk.
  For thus says the LORD: 12
I will send peace flowing over her like
  a river,
and the wealth of nations like a stream
  in flood;
  it shall suckle you,
  and you shall be carried in their
    arms
  and dandled on their knees.
  As a mother comforts her son,   13
  so will I myself comfort you,
  and you shall find comfort in Jeru-
    salem.
  This you shall see and be glad at 14
    heart,
  your limbs shall be as fresh as grass
    in spring;
the LORD shall make his power known
  among his servants
  and his indignation felt among his
    foes.
For see, the LORD is coming in fire,   15
  with his chariots like a whirlwind,
  to strike home with his furious
    anger
  and with the flaming fire of his re-
    proof.
The LORD will judge by fire,   16
  with fire he will test all living men,
and many will be slain by the LORD;
  those who hallow and purify them- 17
    selves in garden-rites,
  one after another in a magic ring,
those who eat the flesh of pigs and
  rats[o] and all vile vermin,
  shall meet their end, one and all,
  says the LORD,
for I know their deeds and their 18
  thoughts.

Universal praise

Then I myself will come to gather all
  nations and races,

---

m *to sacrifice an ox or to: or* those who sacrifice an ox and . . .   n *are the chosen practices of*
men who: *or* have chosen their own devices and . . .   o *Or* jerboas.

and they shall come and see my glory;

19 and I will perform a sign among them.

I will spare some of them and send them to the nations,
to Tarshish, Put, and Lud,[p]
to Meshek, Rosh,[q] Tubal, and Javan,[r]

distant coasts and islands which have never yet heard of me
and have not seen my glory;
these shall announce that glory among the nations.

20 From every nation they shall bring your countrymen
on horses, in chariots and wagons,
on mules and dromedaries,
as an offering to the LORD,
on my holy mountain Jerusalem,
says the LORD,

as the Israelites bring offerings in pure vessels to the LORD's house;

and some of them I will take for 21 priests, for Levites,
says the LORD.

For, as the new heavens and the new 22 earth
which I am making shall endure in my sight,
says the LORD,
so shall your race and your name endure;
and month by month at the new 23 moon,
week by week on the sabbath,
all mankind shall come to bow down before me,
says the LORD;
and they shall come out and see 24
the dead bodies of those who have rebelled against me;
their worm shall not die nor their fire be quenched,
and they shall be abhorred by all mankind.

p Or Lydia.   *q* Meshek, Rosh: *prob. rdg.; Heb.* those who draw the bow.   *r* Or Greece.

THE BOOK OF THE PROPHET
JEREMIAH

Jeremiah's call and two visions

1 THE WORDS of Jeremiah son of Hilkiah, one of the priests at Anathoth
2 in Benjamin. The word of the LORD came to him in the thirteenth year of the reign of Josiah son of Amon, king
3 of Judah; also during the reign of Jehoiakim son of Josiah, king of Judah, until the eleventh year of Zedekiah son of Josiah, king of Judah, was completed. In the fifth month the people of Jerusalem were carried away into exile.

4 The word of the LORD came to me:
5 'Before I formed you in the womb I knew you for my own; before you were born I consecrated you, I appointed you a prophet to the nations.'
6 'Ah! Lord GOD,' I answered, 'I do not know how to speak; I am only a
7 child.' But the LORD said, 'Do not call yourself a child; for you shall go to whatever people I send you and say

whatever I tell you to say. Fear none of 8 them, for I am with you and will keep you safe.' This was the very word of the LORD. Then the LORD stretched 9 out his hand and touched my mouth, and said to me, 'I put my words into your mouth. This day I give you 10 authority over nations and over kingdoms, to pull down and to uproot, to destroy and to demolish, to build and to plant.'

The word of the LORD came to me: 11 'What is it that you see, Jeremiah?' 'An almond in early bloom',[a] I answered. 'You are right,' said the 12 LORD to me, 'for I am early on the watch[b] to carry out my purpose.' The word of the LORD came to me a 13 second time: 'What is it that you see?' 'A cauldron', I said, 'on a fire, fanned by the wind; it is tilted away from the north.' The LORD said: 14

From the north disaster shall flare up
against all who live in this land;

a Heb. shaked.   *b Heb.* shoked.

15 for now I summon all peoples and
    kingdoms of the north,
  says the LORD.
Their kings shall come and each shall
    set up his throne
  before the gates of Jerusalem,
  against her walls on every side,
  and against all the cities of Judah.
16 I will state my case against my
    people
  for all the wrong they have done in
    forsaking me,
  in burning sacrifices to other gods,
  worshipping the work of their own
    hands.
17 Brace yourself, Jeremiah;
  stand up and speak to them.
  Tell them everything I bid you,
  do not let your spirit break at sight of
    them,
  or I will break you before their eyes.
18 This day I make you a fortified city,
  a pillar of iron, a wall of bronze,
  to stand fast against the whole land,
  against the kings and princes of
    Judah,
  its priests and its people.
19 They will make war on you but
    shall not overcome you,
  for I am with you and will keep you
    safe.
  This is the very word of the LORD.

When Israel was faithful

2 1 2 The word of the LORD came to me: Go,
  make a proclamation that all Jerusalem shall hear: These are the words
  of the LORD:

I remember the unfailing devotion of
    your youth,
  the love of your bridal days,
when you followed me in the wilder-
    ness,
  through a land unsown.
3 Israel then was holy to the LORD,
  the firstfruits of his harvest;
  no one who devoured her went un-
    punished,
  evil always overtook them.
  This is the very word of the LORD.

Israel's apostasy

4 Listen to the word of the LORD, people
  of Jacob, families of Israel, one and
5 all. These are the words of the LORD:

What fault did your forefathers find
    in me,
  that they wandered far from me,
  pursuing empty phantoms and them-
    selves becoming empty;
6 that they did not ask, 'Where is the
    LORD,

who brought us up from Egypt,
  and led us through the wilderness,
  through a country of deserts and
    shifting sands,
  a country barren and ill-omened,
    where no man ever trod,
  no man made his home?'
I brought you into a fruitful land   7
  to enjoy its fruit and the goodness
    of it;
  but when you entered upon it you
    defiled it
  and made the home I gave you
    loathsome.
The priests no longer asked, 'Where is 8
    the LORD?'
Those who handled the law had no
    thought of me,
  the shepherds of the people rebelled
    against me;
  the prophets prophesied in the
    name of Baal
  and followed gods powerless to help.
Therefore I will bring a charge against 9
    you once more,
  says the LORD,
  against you and against your de-
    scendants.
  Cross to the coasts and islands of 10
    Kittim and see,
  send to Kedar and consider well,
  see whether there has been any-
    thing like this:
has a nation ever changed its gods,   11
  although they were no gods?
But my people have exchanged their
    Glory
  for a god altogether powerless.
  Stand aghast at this, you heavens,   12
  tremble in utter despair,
  says the LORD.
Two sins have my people committed: 13
  they have forsaken me,
  a spring of living water,
and they have hewn out for them-
    selves cisterns,
  cracked cisterns that can hold no
    water.

Desperate pursuit of foreign gods

Is Israel a slave? Was he born in 14
    slavery?
If not, why has he been despoiled?
Why do lions roar and growl at him? 15
Why has his land been laid waste,
  why are his cities razed to the ground
    and abandoned?
Men of Noph and Tahpanhes   16
  will break your heads.
Is it not your desertion of the LORD 17
    your God
  that brings all this upon you?
And now, why should you make off to 18
    Egypt

to drink the waters of the Shihor?
Or why make off to Assyria
to drink the waters of the River?
19 It is your own wickedness that will
punish you,
your own apostasy that will condemn you.
See for yourselves how bitter a thing
it is and how evil,
to forsake the LORD your God and
revere me no longer.
This is the very word of the Lord
GOD of Hosts.
20 Ages ago you broke your yoke and
snapped your traces,
crying, 'I will not be your slave';
and you sprawled in promiscuous
vice
on all the hill-tops, under every
spreading tree.
21 I planted you as a choice red vine,
true stock all of you,
yet now you are turned into a vine
debased and worthless!
22 The stain of your sin is still there and
I see it,
though you wash with soda and do
not stint the soap.
This is the very word of the Lord
GOD.
23 How can you say, 'I am not polluted,
not I!
I have not followed the Baalim'?
Look how you conducted yourself in
the valley;
remember what you have done.
You have been like a she-camel,
twisting and turning as she runs,
24 rushing alone into^c the wilderness,
snuffing the wind in her lust;
who can restrain her in her heat?
No one need tire himself out in pursuit of her;
she is easily found at mating time.
25 Why not save your feet from stony
ground
and your throats from thirst?
But you said, 'No; I am desperate.
I love foreign gods and I must go
after them.'
26 As a thief is ashamed when he is
found out,
so the people of Israel feel ashamed,
they, their kings, their princes,
their priests and their prophets;
27 they say, 'You are our father' to a
block of wood
and cry 'Mother' to a stone.
But on me they have turned their
backs
and averted their faces from me.

And now on the day of disaster they
say,
'Rise up and save us.'
Where are they, those gods you made 28
for yourselves?
Let them come and save you in the
day of disaster.
For you, Judah, have as many gods
as you have towns.^{d}
The LORD answers,   29
Why argue your case with me?
You are rebels, every one of you.
In vain I struck down your sons,   30
the lesson was not learnt;
still your own sword devoured your
prophets
like a ravening lion.
^{e}Have I shown myself inhospitable to 31
Israel
like some wilderness or waterless
land?
Why do my people say, 'We have
broken away;
we will never come back to thee'?

Captivity foretold

Will a girl forget her finery   32
or a bride her ribbons?
Yet my people have forgotten me
over and over again.
How well you pick your way in search 33
of lovers!
Why! even the worst of women can
learn from you.
Yes, and there is blood on the corners 34
of your robe—
the life-blood of the innocent poor.
You did not get it by housebreaking
but by your sacrifices under every
oak.
You say, 'I am innocent;   35
surely his anger has passed away.'
But I will challenge your claim
to have done no sin.
Why do you so lightly change your 36
course?
Egypt will fail you as Assyria did;
you shall go out from here,   37
each of you with his hands above
his head,
for the LORD repudiates those in
whom you trusted,
and from them you shall gain nothing.

Israel's adultery

If a man puts away his wife   3
and she leaves him,
and if she then becomes another's,
may he go back to her again?
Is not that woman defiled,

c rushing alone into: *prob. rdg.; Heb.* a wild-ass taught in.   d towns: *or* blood-spattered altars.
e *Prob. rdg.; Heb. prefixes* You, O generation, see the word of the LORD.

a forbidden thing?
You have played the harlot with
  many lovers;
can you come back to me?
says the LORD.

2 Look up to the high bare places
    and see:
where have you not been ravished?
You sat by the wayside to catch
  lovers,
like an Arab lurking in the desert,
and defiled the land
with your fornication and your
  wickedness.

3 Therefore the showers were with-
    held
and the spring rain failed.
But yours was a harlot's brow,
and you were resolved to show no
  shame.

4 Not so long since, you called me
    'Father,
dear friend of my youth',

5 thinking, 'Will he be angry for ever?
Will he rage eternally?'
This is how you spoke; you have
  done evil
and gone unchallenged.

The LORD pleads with Israel

6 In the reign of King Josiah, the LORD
said to me, Do you see what apostate
Israel did? She went up to every hill-
top and under every spreading tree,
7 and there she played the whore. Even
after she had done all this, I said to
her, Come back to me, but she would
not. That faithless woman, her sister
8 Judah, saw it all; she saw too that I
had put apostate Israel away and
given her a note of divorce because
she had committed adultery. Yet that
faithless woman, her sister Judah,
was not afraid; she too has gone and
9 played the whore. She defiled the
land with her thoughtless harlotry
and her adulterous worship of stone
10 and wood. In spite of all this that
faithless woman, her sister Judah, has
not come back to me in good faith, but
only in pretence. This is the very
word of the LORD.

11   The LORD said to me, Apostate
Israel is less to blame than that faith-
12 less woman Judah. Go and proclaim
this message to the north:

Come back to me, apostate Israel,
says the LORD,
I will no longer frown on you.
For my love is unfailing, says the
  LORD,
I will not be angry for ever.

Only you must acknowledge your 13
  wrongdoing,
confess your rebellion against the
  LORD your God.
Confess your promiscuous traffic
  with foreign gods
under every spreading tree,
confess that you have not obeyed
  me.
This is the very word of the LORD.

Jerusalem's glorious future

Come back to me, apostate children, 14
says the LORD, for I am patient with
you, and I will take you, one from a
city and two from a clan, and bring
you to Zion. There will I give you 15
shepherds after my own heart, and
they shall lead you with knowledge
and understanding. In those days, 16
when you have increased and become
fruitful in the land, says the LORD,
men shall speak no more of the Ark of
the Covenant of the LORD; they shall
not think of it nor remember it nor
resort to it; it will be needed no more.
At that time Jerusalem shall be called 17
the Throne of the LORD. All nations
shall gather in Jerusalem to honour
the LORD's name; never again shall
they follow the promptings of their
evil and stubborn hearts. In those days 18
Judah shall join Israel, and together
they shall come from a northern land
into the land I gave their fathers as
their patrimony.

Repentance

I said, How gladly would I treat you 19
  as a son,
giving you a pleasant land,
a patrimony fairer than that of any
  nation!
I said, You shall call me Father
and never cease to follow me.
But like a woman who is unfaithful 20
  to her lover,
so you, Israel, were unfaithful to
  me.
This is the very word of the LORD.
Hark, a sound of weeping on the 21
  bare places,
Israel's people pleading for mercy!
For they have taken to crooked
  ways
and ignored the LORD their God.
Come back to me, wayward*f* sons; 22
I will heal your apostasy.

O LORD, we come! We come to thee;
for thou art our God.
There is no help in worship on the 23
  hill-tops,

f Or apostate.

no help from clamour on the heights;
truly in the LORD our God
is Israel's only salvation.
24 From our early days
Baal, god of shame, has devoured
the fruits of our fathers' labours,
their flocks and herds, their sons and daughters.
25 Let us lie down in shame, wrapped round by our dishonour,
for we have sinned against the LORD our God,
both we and our fathers,
from our early days till now,
and we have not obeyed the LORD our God.

4 If you will but come back, O Israel,
if you will but come back to me,
says the LORD,
if you will banish your loathsome idols from my sight,
and stray no more,
2 if you swear by the life of the LORD,
in truth, in justice and uprightness,
then shall the nations pray to be blessed like you*g*
and in you*g* shall they boast.

Threat of invasion

3 These are the words of the LORD to the men of Judah and Jerusalem:

Break up your fallow ground,
do not sow among thorns,
4 circumcise yourselves to the service of the LORD,
circumcise your hearts,
men of Judah and dwellers in Jerusalem,
lest the fire of my fury blaze up and burn unquenched,
because of your evil doings.
5 Tell this in Judah,
proclaim it in Jerusalem,
blow the trumpet throughout the land,
sound the muster,
give the command, Stand to!—and let us fall back
on the fortified cities.
6 Raise the signal—To Zion!
make for safety, lose no time,
for I bring disaster out of the north,
and dire destruction.
7 A lion has come out from his lair,
the destroyer of nations;
he has struck his tents, he has broken camp,
to harry your land
and lay your cities waste and unpeopled.

Well may you put on sackcloth, 8
beat the breast and wail,
for the anger of the LORD
is not averted from us.
On that day, says the LORD, 9
the hearts of the king and his officers shall fail them,
priests shall be struck with horror and prophets dumbfounded.

And I said, O Lord GOD, thou surely 10
didst deceive this people and Jerusalem in saying, 'You shall have peace',
while the sword is at our throats.

The enemy advances

At that time this people and Jerusalem 11
shall be told:

A scorching wind from the high bare places in the wilderness
sweeps down upon my people,
no breeze for winnowing or for cleansing;
a wind too strong for these 12
will come at my bidding,
and now I will state my case against them.

Like clouds the enemy advances 13
with a whirlwind of chariots;
his horses are swifter than eagles—
alas, we are overwhelmed!
O Jerusalem, wash the wrongdoing 14
from your heart
and you may yet be saved;
how long will you cherish
your evil schemes?
Hark, a runner from Dan, 15
tidings of evil from Mount Ephraim!
Tell all this to the nations, 16
proclaim the doom of Jerusalem:
hordes of invaders come from a distant land,
howling against the cities of Judah.
Their pickets are closing in all 17
round her,
because she has rebelled against me.
This is the very word of the LORD.
Your own ways, your own deeds 18
have brought all this upon you;
this is your punishment,
and all this comes of your rebellion.*h*
Oh, the writing of my bowels 19
and the throbbing of my heart!
I cannot keep silence.
I hear the sound of the trumpet,
the sound of the battle-cry.
Crash upon crash, 20
the land goes down in ruin,
my tents are thrown down,
their coverings torn to shreds.
How long must I see the standard 21
raised

g Prob. rdg.; Heb. him.   *h your* rebellion: *prob. rdg.; Heb. obscure.*

and hear the trumpet call?

22 My people are fools, they know
   nothing of me;
   silly children, with no understanding,
   they are clever only in wrongdoing,
   and of doing right they know
   nothing.

Universal chaos

22 I saw the earth, and it was without
   form and void;
   the heavens, and their light was
   gone.

24 I saw the mountains, and they
   reeled;
   all the hills rocked to and fro.

25 I saw, and there was no man,
   and the very birds had taken
   flight.

26 I saw, and the farm-land was wilderness,
   and the towns all razed to the
   ground,
   before the LORD in his anger.

27 These are the words of the LORD:
   The whole land shall be desolate,
   though I will not make an end of it.

28 Therefore the earth will mourn
   and the heavens above turn black.
   For I have made known my purpose;
   I will not relent or change my mind.

29 At the sound of the horsemen and
   archers
   the whole country is in flight;
   they creep into caves, they hide in
   thickets,
   they scramble up the crags.
   Every town is forsaken,
   no one dwells there.

Zion spurned

30 And you, what are you doing?
   When you dress yourself in scarlet,
   deck yourself out with golden ornaments,
   and make your eyes big with an-
   timony,
   you are beautifying yourself to no
   purpose.
   Your lovers spurn you
   and are out for your life.

31 I hear a sound as of a woman in
   labour,
   the sharp cry of one bearing her
   first child.
   It is Zion, gasping for breath,
   clenching her fists.
   Ah me! I am weary,
   weary of slaughter.

Rebellion and false security

Go up and down the streets of 5
   Jerusalem
and see for yourselves;
search her wide squares:
can you find any man who acts
   justly,
who seeks the truth,
that I may forgive that city?
Men may swear by the life of the 2
   LORD,
but they only perjure themselves.
O LORD, are thine eyes not set upon 3
   the truth?
Thou didst strike them down,
but they took no heed;
didst pierce them to the heart,
but they refused to learn.
They set their faces harder than
   flint
and refused to come back.
I said, 'After all, these are the poor, 4
these are stupid folk,
who do not know the way of the
   LORD,
the ordinances of their God.
I will go to the great   5
and speak with them;
for they will know the way of the
   LORD,
the ordinances of their God.'
But they too have broken the yoke
and snapped their traces.
Therefore a lion out of the scrub 6
   shall strike them down,
a wolf from the plains shall ravage
   them;
a leopard shall prowl about their
   cities
and maul any who venture out.
For their rebellious deeds are many,
their apostasies past counting.
How can I forgive you for all this? 7
Your sons have forsaken me and
   sworn by gods
that are no gods.
I gave them all they needed, yet
   they preferred adultery,
and haunted the brothels;
each neighs after another man's 8
   wife,
like a well-fed and lusty stallion.
Shall I not punish them for this? 9
the LORD asks.
Shall I not take vengeance
on such a people?
Go along her rows of vines and slash 10
   them,
yet do not make an end of them.
Hack away her green branches,
for they are not the LORD's.
Faithless are Israel and Judah,   11
both faithless to me.

This is the very word of the LORD.
12 They have denied the LORD,
saying, 'He does not exist.
No evil shall come upon us;
13 we shall never see sword or famine.
The prophets will prove mere wind,
the word not in them.'

The coming invader

14 And so, because you talk in this way,
these are the words of the LORD the
God of Hosts to me:

I will make my words a fire in your
mouth;
and it shall burn up this people like
brushwood.

15 I bring against you, Israel, a nation
from afar,
an ancient people established long
ago,
says the LORD.
A people whose language you do not
know,
whose speech you will not understand;
16 they are all mighty warriors,
their jaws are a grave, wide open,
17 to devour your harvest and your
bread,
to devour your sons and your
daughters,
to devour your flocks and your herds,
to devour your vines and your fig-
trees.
They shall batter down the cities in
which you trust,[i]
walled though they are.

18 But in those days, the LORD declares, I will still not make an end of
19 you. When you ask, 'Why has the
LORD our God done all this to us?' I
shall answer, 'As you have forsaken
me and served alien gods in your own
land, so shall you serve foreigners[j] in
a land that is not yours.'

Corruption and complacency

20 Tell this to the people of Jacob,
proclaim it in Judah:
21 Listen, you foolish and senseless
people,
who have eyes and see nothing,
ears and hear nothing.
22 Have you no fear of me? says the
LORD;
will you not shiver before me,
before me, who made the shivering
sand to bound the sea,
a barrier it never can pass?

Its waves heave and toss but they
are powerless;
roar as they may, they cannot pass.
But this people has a rebellious and 23
defiant heart,
rebels they have been and now they
are clean gone.
They did not say to themselves, 24
'Let us fear the LORD our God,
who gives us the rains of autumn
and spring showers in their turn,
who brings us unfailingly
fixed seasons of harvest.'
But your wrongdoing has upset 25
nature's order,
and your sins have kept from you her
kindly gifts.
For among my people there are 26
wicked men,
who lay snares like a fowler's net[k]
and set deadly traps to catch men.
Their houses are full of fraud, 27
as a cage is full of birds.
They grow rich and grand,
bloated and rancorous; 28
their thoughts are all of evil,
and they refuse to do justice,
the claims of the orphan they do not
put right
nor do they grant justice to the poor.
Shall I not punish them for this? 29
says the LORD;
shall I not take vengeance
on such a people?

An appalling thing, an outrage, 30
has appeared in this land:
prophets prophesy lies and priests go 31
hand in hand with them,
and my people love to have it so.
How will you fare at the end of it all?

Warning to Jerusalem

Save yourselves, men of Benjamin, 6
come out of Jerusalem,
blow the trumpet in Tekoa,
fire the beacon on Beth-hakkerem,
for calamity looms from the north
and great disaster.
Zion, delightful and lovely: 2
her end is near—
she to whom the shepherds come 3
and bring their flocks with them.
There they pitch their tents all
round her,
each grazing his own strip of
pasture.
Declare war solemnly against her; 4
come, let us attack her at noon.
Too late! the day declines
and the shadows lengthen.

i Prob. rdg.; Heb. adds with the sword. *j Or* foreign gods. *k* who . . . net: *prob. rdg.; Heb.*
unintelligible.

5 Come then, let us attack her by
    night
  and destroy her palaces.
6 These are the words of the LORD of
    Hosts:
  Cut down the trees of Jerusalem
  and raise siege-ramps against her,
  the city whose name is Licence,
  oppression is rampant in her.
7 As a well keeps its water fresh,
  so she keeps her evil fresh.
  Violence and outrage echo in her
    streets;
  sickness and wounds stare me in the
    face.
8 Learn your lesson, Jerusalem,
  lest my love for you be torn from my
    heart,
  and I leave you desolate,
  a land where no one can live.
9 These are the words of the LORD of
    Hosts:
  Glean the remnant of Israel
  like a vine,
  pass your hand like a vintager one
    last time
  over the branches.
10 To whom can I address myself,
   to whom give solemn warning? Who
     will hear me?
   Their ears are uncircumcised;
   they cannot listen;
   they treat the LORD's word as a re-
     proach;
   they show no concern with it.
11 But I am full of the anger of the
     LORD,
   I cannot hold it in.
   I must pour it out on the children
     in the street
   and on the young men in their gangs.
   Man and wife alike shall be caught
     in it,
   the greybeard and the very old.
12 Their houses shall be turned over to
     others,
   their fields and their women alike.
   For I will raise my hand, says the
     LORD,
   against the people of the country.
13 For all, high and low,
   are out for ill-gotten gain;
   prophets and priests are frauds,
   every one of them;
14 they dress my people's wound,
     but skin-deep only,
   with their saying, 'All is well.'
   All well? Nothing is well!
15 Are they ashamed when they prac-
     tise their abominations?
   Ashamed? Not they!
   They can never be put out of
     countenance.

Therefore they shall fall with a great
    crash,[l]
and be brought to the ground on the
    day of my reckoning.
  The LORD has said it.

The LORD rejects his people

These are the words of the LORD: Stop 16
at the cross-roads; look for the ancient
paths; ask, 'Where is the way that
leads to what is good?' Then take
that way, and you will find rest for
yourselves. But they said, 'We will
not.' Then I will appoint watchmen 17
to direct you; listen for their trumpet-
call. But they said, 'We will not.'
Therefore hear, you nations, and take 18
note, all you who witness it, of the
plight of this people. Listen, O earth, 19
I bring ruin on them, the harvest of
all their scheming; for they have
given no thought to my words and
have spurned my instruction. What 20
good is it to me if frankincense is
brought from Sheba and fragrant
spices from distant lands? I will not
accept your whole-offerings, your sacrifices do not please me. Therefore 21
these are the words of the LORD:

I will set obstacles before this people
    which shall bring them to the
    ground;
fathers and sons, friends and neigh-
    bours
  shall all perish together.

Terror let loose

These are the words of the LORD: 22

See, a people is coming from a nor-
    thern land,
a great nation rouses itself from
    earth's farthest corners.
They come with bow and sabre, cruel 23
    men and pitiless,
bestriding their horses, they sound
    like the thunder of the sea,
they are like men arrayed for battle
    against you, Zion.
  We have heard tell of them   24
  and our hands hang limp,
agony grips us, the anguish of a
    woman in labour.
  Do not go out into the country,   25
  do not walk by the high road;
  for the foe, sword in hand,
  is a terror let loose.
Daughter of my people, wrap your- 26
    self in sackcloth,
  sprinkle ashes over yourself, wail
    bitterly,
  as one who mourns an only son;

l with a great crash: *or* where they fall *or* among the fallen.

in an instant shall the marauder be upon us.

27 I have appointed you an assayer of my people;
you will know how to test them and will assay their conduct;
28 arch-rebels all of them,
mischief-makers, corrupt to a man.
29 The bellows puff and blow, the furnace glows;
in vain does the refiner smelt the ore,
lead, copper and iron[m] are not separated out.
30 Call them spurious silver;
for the LORD has spurned them.

Proclamation in the temple

7 This word came from the LORD to
2 Jeremiah. Stand at the gate of the LORD's house and there make your proclamation: Listen to the words of the LORD, all you men of Judah who come in through these gates to wor-
3 ship him. These are the words of the LORD of Hosts the God of Israel: Mend your ways and your doings, that I
4 may let you live in this place. You keep saying, 'This place[n] is the temple of the LORD, the temple of the LORD, the temple of the LORD!' This catchword of yours is a lie; put no trust in
5 it. Mend your ways and your doings,
6 deal fairly with one another, do not oppress the alien, the orphan, and the widow, shed no innocent blood in this place, do not run after other gods to
7 your own ruin. Then will I let you live in this place, in the land which I gave long ago to your forefathers for all
8 time. You gain nothing by putting
9 your trust in this lie. You steal, you murder, you commit adultery and perjury, you burn sacrifices to Baal, you run after other gods whom you
10 have not known; then you come and stand before me in this house, which bears my name, and say, 'We are safe'; safe, you think, to indulge in all these
11 abominations. Do you think that this house, this house which bears my name, is a robbers' cave? I myself
12 have seen all this, says the LORD. Go to my shrine at Shiloh, which once I made a dwelling for my Name, and see what I did to it because of the
13 wickedness of my people Israel. And now you have done all these things, says the LORD; though I took pains to speak to you, you did not listen, and though I called, you gave no answer.

Therefore what I did to Shiloh I will 14 do to this house which bears my name, the house in which you put your trust, the place I gave to you and your fore-fathers; I will fling you away out of 15 my sight, as I flung away all your kinsfolk, the whole brood of Ephraim.

No prayer for Jerusalem

Offer up no prayer, Jeremiah, for this 16 people, raise no plea or prayer on their behalf, and do not intercede with me; for I will not listen to you. Do you not 17 see what is going on in the cities of Judah and in the streets of Jerusalem? Children are gathering wood, fathers 18 lighting fires, women kneading dough to make crescent-cakes in honour of the queen of heaven; and drink-offerings are poured out to other gods than me—all to provoke and hurt me. But is it I, says the LORD, whom they 19 hurt? No; it is themselves, covering their own selves with shame. There- 20 fore, says the Lord GOD, my anger and my fury shall fall on this place, on man and beast, on trees and crops, and it shall burn unquenched.

Israel's stubbornness

These are the words of the LORD of 21 Hosts the God of Israel: Add whole-offerings to sacrifices and eat the flesh if you will. But when I brought 22 your forefathers out of Egypt, I gave them no commands about whole-offering and sacrifice; I said not a word about them. What I did com- 23 mand them was this: If you obey me, I will be your God and you shall be my people. You must conform to all my commands, if you would prosper. But they did not listen; they paid no 24 heed, and persisted in disobedience with evil and stubborn hearts; they looked backwards and not forwards, from the day when your forefathers 25 left Egypt until now. I took pains to send to them all my servants the prophets; they did not listen to me, 26 they paid no heed, but were obstinate and proved even more wicked than their forefathers. When you tell them 27 this, they will not listen to you; if you call them, they will not answer. Then 28 you shall say to them, This is the nation that did not obey the LORD its God nor accept correction; truth has perished, it is heard no more on their lips.

m copper and iron: *transposed from after* mischief-makers *in verse 28.*
Heb. Those.   n This place: *prob. rdg.;*

Idolatrous practices

29 O Jerusalem, cut off your hair,
the symbol of your dedication, and
throw it away;
raise up a lament on the high bare
places.

For the LORD has spurned the generation which has roused his wrath, and
30 has abandoned them. For the men of
Judah have done what is wrong in my
eyes, says the LORD. They have defiled
with their loathsome idols the house
31 that bears my name, they have built
a shrine of Topheth in the Valley of
Ben-hinnom, at which to burn their
sons and daughters; that was no command of mine, nor did it ever enter
32 my thought. Therefore a time is
coming, says the LORD, when it shall
no longer be called Topheth or the
Valley of Ben-hinnom, but the Valley
of Slaughter; for the dead shall be
buried in Topheth because there is no
33 room elsewhere. So the bodies of this
people shall become food for the birds
of the air and the wild beasts, and
there will be no one to scare them
34 away. From the cities of Judah and
the streets of Jerusalem I will banish
all sounds of joy and gladness, the
voice of the bridegroom and the
bride; for the land shall become
desert.

8 At that time, says the LORD, men
shall bring out from their graves the
bones of the kings of Judah, of the
officers, priests, and prophets, and of
2 all who lived in Jerusalem. They shall
expose them to the sun, the moon, and
all the host of heaven, whom they
loved and served and adored, to whom
they resorted and bowed in worship.
Those bones shall not be gathered up
nor buried but shall become dung on
3 the ground. All the survivors of this
wicked race, wherever I have banished them, would rather die than
live. This is the very word of the LORD
of Hosts.

Headlong to ruin

4 You shall say to them, These are
the words of the LORD:

If men fall, can they not also rise?
If a man breaks away, can he not
return?
5 Then why are this people so wayward,
incurable in their waywardness?
Why have they clung to their
treachery

o breaks away: or is wayward.

and refused to return to their
obedience?
I have listened to them   6
and heard not one word of truth,
not one sinner crying remorsefully,
'Oh, what have I done?'
Each one breaks away*o* in headlong
career
as a war-horse plunges in battle.

The stork in the sky   7
knows the time to migrate,
the dove and the swift and the wry-
neck
know the season of return;
but my people do not know the
ordinances of the LORD.
How can you say, 'We are wise,   8
we have the law of the LORD',
when scribes with their lying pens
have falsified it?
The wise are put to shame, they are 9
dismayed and have lost their wits.
They have spurned the word of the
LORD,
and what sort of wisdom is theirs?
Therefore will I give their wives to 10
other men
and their lands to new owners.
For all, high and low,
are out for ill-gotten gain;
prophets and priests are frauds,
every one of them;
they dress my people's wound, but 11
skin-deep only,
with their saying, 'All is well.'
All well? Nothing is well!
Are they ashamed when they prac- 12
tise their abominations?
Ashamed? Not they!
They can never be put out of countenance.
Therefore they shall fall with a great
crash,*p*
and be brought to the ground on the
day of my reckoning.
The LORD has said it.
I would gather their harvest, says 13
the LORD,
but there are no grapes on the vine,
no figs on the fig-tree;
even their leaves are withered.
Why do we sit idle? Up, all of you 14
together,
let us go into our walled cities and
there meet our doom.
For the LORD our God has struck
us down,
he has given us a draught of bitter
poison;
for we have sinned against the LORD.
Can we hope to prosper when 15
nothing goes well?

p with a great crash: or where they fall or among the fallen.

Can we hope for respite when the
terror falls suddenly?

16 The snorting of his horses is heard
from Dan;
at the neighing of his stallions the
whole land trembles.
The enemy come; they devour the
land and all its store,
city and citizens alike.

17 Beware, I am sending snakes against
you,
vipers, such as no man can charm,
and they shall bite you.
This is the very word of the LORD.

The prophet's lament

18 How can I bear my sorrow?[q]
I am sick at heart.

19 Hark, the cry of my people
from a distant land:
'Is the LORD not in Zion?
Is her King no longer there?'
Why do they provoke me with their
images
and foreign gods?

20 Harvest is past, summer is over,
and we are not saved.

21 I am wounded at the sight of my
people's wound;
I go like a mourner, overcome with
horror.

22 Is there no balm in Gilead,
no physician there?
Why has no new skin grown over
their wound?

Deceit and disloyalty

9 Would that my head were all water,
my eyes a fountain of tears,
that I might weep day and night
for my people's dead!

2 Oh that I could find in the wilderness
a shelter by the wayside,
that I might leave my people and
depart!
Adulterers are they all, a mob of
traitors.

3 The tongue is their weapon, a bow
ready bent.
Lying, not truth, is master in the land.
They run from one sin to another,
and for me they care nothing.
This is the very word of the LORD.

4 Be on your guard, each man against
his friend;
put no trust even in a brother.
Brother supplants brother,[r]

and friend slanders friend.

5 They make game of their friends
but never speak the truth;
they have trained their tongues to
lies;
deep in their sin, they cannot retrace
their steps.

6 Wrong follows wrong, deceit follows
deceit;
they refuse to acknowledge me.
This is the very word of the LORD.

7 Therefore these are the words of the
LORD of Hosts:
I am their refiner and will assay
them.
How can I disregard my people?

8 Their tongue is a cruel arrow,
their mouths speak lies.
One speaks amicably to another,
while inwardly he plans a trap for
him.

9 Shall I not punish them for this?
says the LORD;
shall I not take vengeance
on such a people?

10 Over the mountains will I raise weeping and wailing,
and over the desert pastures will I
chant a dirge.
They are scorched and untrodden,
they hear no lowing of cattle;
birds of the air and beasts have fled
and are gone.

Devastation of Judah

11 I will make Jerusalem a heap of ruins,
a haunt of wolves,
and the cities of Judah an unpeopled
waste.

12 What man is wise enough to understand this, to understand what the
LORD has said and to proclaim it? Why
has the land become a dead land,
scorched like the desert and untrodden? 13 The LORD said, It is because
they forsook my law which I set before them; they neither obeyed me
nor conformed to it. 14 They followed
the promptings of their own stubborn
hearts, they followed the Baalim as
their forefathers had taught them.
15 Therefore these are the words of the
LORD of Hosts the God of Israel: I will
feed this people with wormwood and
give them bitter poison to drink. 16 I will
scatter them among nations whom
neither they nor their forefathers have
known; I will harry them with the
sword until I have made an end of
them.

q How . . . sorrow?: *prob. rdg.; Heb. unintelligible.*
is a supplanter like Jacob (*cp. Gen. 27. 35 and note*).

r Brother supplants brother: *or* Every brother

L

Lamentation in Zion

17 These are the words of the LORD of Hosts:

Summon the wailing women to come, send for the women skilled in keening

18 to come quickly and raise a lament for us,
that our eyes may run with tears and our eyelids be wet with weeping.

19 Hark, hark, lamentation is heard in Zion:
How fearful is our ruin! How great our shame!
We have left our lands, our houses have been pulled down.

20 Listen, you women, to the words of the LORD,
that your ears may catch what he says.
Teach your daughters the lament, let them teach one another this dirge:

21 Death has climbed in through our windows,
it has entered our palaces,
it sweeps off the children in the open air
and drives young men from the streets.

22 This is the word of the LORD:

The corpses of men shall fall and lie like dung in the fields,
like swathes behind the reaper, but no one shall gather them.

If a man must boast . . .

23 These are the words of the LORD:

Let not the wise man boast of his wisdom
nor the valiant of his valour;
let not the rich man boast of his riches;

24 but if any man would boast, let him boast of this,
that he understands and knows me.
For I am the LORD, I show unfailing love,
I do justice and right upon the earth;
for on these I have set my heart.
This is the very word of the LORD.

25 The time is coming, says the LORD, when I will punish all the circumcised,

26 Egypt and Judah, Edom and Ammon, Moab, and all who haunt the fringes of the desert;[s] for all alike, the nations and Israel, are uncircumcised in heart.

Lifeless gods and the living God

Listen, Israel, to this word that the 1 LORD has spoken against you:

Do not fall into the ways of the 2 nations,
do not be awed by signs in the heavens;
it is the nations who go in awe of these.

For the carved images of the 3 nations are a sham,
they are nothing but timber cut from the forest,
worked with his chisel by a craftsman;

he adorns it with silver and gold, 4 fastening them on with hammer and nails
so that they do not fall apart.

They can no more speak than a 5 scarecrow in a plot of cucumbers;
they must be carried, for they cannot walk.

Do not be afraid of them: they can do no harm,
and they have no power to do good.

Where can one be found like thee, 6 O LORD?
Great thou art and great the might of thy name.

Who shall not fear thee, king of the 7 nations?
for fear is thy fitting tribute.

Where among the wisest of the nations and all their royalty
can one be found like thee?

They are fools and blockheads one 8 and all,
learning their nonsense from a log of wood.

The beaten silver is brought from 9 Tarshish
and the gold from Ophir;
all are the work of craftsmen and goldsmiths.

They are draped in violet and purple,
all the work of skilled men.

But the LORD is God in truth, 1
a living god, an eternal king.
The earth quakes under his wrath, nations cannot endure his fury.

[You shall say this to them: The 1 gods who did not make heaven and earth shall perish from the earth and from under these heavens.]

God made the earth by his power, 1
fixed the world in place by his wisdom,

s who . . . desert: *or* the dwellers in the desert who clip the hair on their temples.   t Verses 12–16: cp. 51. 15–19.

unfurled the skies by his understanding.

13 At the thunder of his voice the waters
in heaven are amazed;[u]
he brings up the mist from the ends
of the earth,
he opens rifts[v] for the rain
and brings the wind out of his
storehouses.

14 All men are brutish and ignorant;
every goldsmith is discredited by his
idol;
for the figures he casts are a sham,
there is no breath in them.

15 They are worth nothing, mere
mockeries,
which perish when their day of
reckoning comes.

16 God, Jacob's creator, is not like
these;
for he is the maker of all.
Israel is the people he claims as his
own;
the LORD of Hosts is his name.

Exile at hand

17 Put your goods together and carry
them out of the country,
living as you are under siege.

18 For these are the words of the LORD:
This time I will uproot
the whole population of the land,
and I will press them hard and
squeeze them dry.

19 O the pain of my wounds!
Cruel are the blows I suffer.
But this is my plight, I said, and I
must endure it.

20 My home is ruined, my tent-ropes all
severed,
my sons have left me and are gone,
there is no one to pitch my tent
again,
no one to put up its curtains.

21 The shepherds of the people are
mere brutes;
they never consult the LORD,
and so they do not prosper,
and all their flocks at pasture are
scattered.

22 Hark, a rumour comes flying,
then a mounting uproar from the
land of the north,
an army to make Judah's cities
desolate, a haunt of wolves.

23 I know, O LORD,
that man's ways are not of his own
choosing;
nor is it for a man to determine his
course in life.

24 Correct us, O LORD, but with justice,
not in anger,
lest thou bring us almost to nothing.

25 Pour out thy fury on nations
that have not acknowledged thee,
on tribes that have not invoked
thee by name;
for they have devoured Jacob and
made an end of him
and have left his home a waste.

The covenant broken

11 The word which came to Jeremiah
from the LORD: Listen to the terms of 2
this covenant and repeat them to the
men of Judah and the inhabitants of
Jerusalem. Tell them, These are the 3
words of the LORD the God of Israel:
A curse on the man who does not 4
observe the terms of this covenant by
which I bound your forefathers when
I brought them out of Egypt, from
the smelting-furnace. I said, If you
obey me and do all that I tell you,
you shall become my people and I will
become your God. And I will thus 5
make good the oath I swore to your
forefathers, that I would give them
a land flowing with milk and honey,
the land you now possess. I answered,
'Amen, LORD.' Then the LORD said: 6
Proclaim all these terms in the cities
of Judah and in the streets of Jerusalem. Say, Listen to the terms of this 7
covenant and carry them out. I have
protested to your forefathers since I
brought them out of Egypt, till this
day; I took pains to warn them: Obey
me, I said. But they did not obey; 8
they paid no attention to me, but
each followed the promptings of his
own stubborn and wicked heart. So I
brought on them all the penalties laid
down in this covenant by which I had
bound them, whose terms they did
not observe.

The LORD said to me, The men of 9
Judah and the inhabitants of Jerusalem have entered into a conspiracy:
they have gone back to the sins of 10
their earliest forefathers and refused
to listen to me. They have followed
other gods and worshipped them; Israel and Judah have broken the covenant which I made with their fathers.
Therefore these are the words of the 11
LORD: I now bring on them disaster from which they cannot escape;
though they cry to me for help I will
not listen. The inhabitants of the 12
cities of Judah and of Jerusalem may
go and cry for help to the gods to

---

u At the thunder . . . amazed: *prob. rdg.*; *Heb.* At the sound of his giving tumult of waters in heaven.
v rifts: *prob. rdg.*; *Heb.* lightnings.

whom they have burnt sacrifices; they will not save them in the hour of
13 disaster. For you, Judah, have as many gods as you have towns; you have set up as many altars to burn sacrifices to Baal as there are streets
14 in Jerusalem. So offer up no prayer for this people; raise no cry or prayer on their behalf, for I will not listen when they call to me in the hour of disaster.

15 What right has my beloved in my house
with her shameless ways?
Can the flesh of fat offerings on the altar
ward off the disaster that threatens you?
16 Once the LORD called you an olive-tree,
leafy and fair;
but now with a great roaring noise you will feel sharp anguish;[w]
fire sets its leaves alight
and consumes[x] its branches.

17 The LORD of Hosts who planted you has threatened you with disaster, because of the harm Israel and Judah brought on themselves when they provoked me to anger by burning sacrifices to Baal.

Plots to kill Jeremiah

18 It was the LORD who showed me, and
19 so I knew; he opened my eyes to what they were doing. I had been like a sheep led obedient to the slaughter; I did not know that they were hatching plots against me and saying, 'Let us cut down the tree while the sap is in it; let us destroy him out of the living, so that his very name shall be forgotten.'

20 O LORD of Hosts who art a righteous judge,
testing the heart and mind,
I have committed my cause to thee;
let me see thy vengeance upon them.

21 Therefore these are the words of the LORD about the men of Anathoth who seek to take my life, and say, 'Pro-
22 phesy no more in the name of the LORD or we will kill you'—these are his words: I will punish them: their young men shall die by the sword, their sons and daughters shall die by
23 famine. Not one of them shall survive; for in the year of their reckoning I will bring ruin on the men of Anathoth.

The prophet's problem

O LORD, I will dispute with thee, for 12
thou art just;
yes, I will plead my case before thee.
Why do the wicked prosper
and traitors live at ease?
Thou hast planted them and their 2
roots strike deep,
they grow up and bear fruit.
Thou art ever on their lips,
yet far from their hearts.
But thou knowest me, O LORD, thou 3
seest me;
thou dost test my devotion to thyself.
Drag them away like sheep to the shambles;
set them apart for the day of slaughter.

How long must the country lie 4
parched
and its green grass wither?
No birds and beasts are left, because its people are so wicked,
because they say, 'God will not see what we are doing.'

If you have raced with men and the 5
runners have worn you down,
how then can you hope to vie with horses?
If you fall headlong in easy country,
how will you fare in Jordan's dense thickets?

All men, your brothers and kinsmen, 6
are traitors to you,
they are in full cry after you;
trust them not, for all the fine words they give you.

I have forsaken the house of Israel, 7
I have cast off my own people.
I have given my beloved into the power of her foes.
My own people have turned on me like 8
a lion from the scrub,
roaring against me; therefore I hate them.
Is this land of mine a hyena's lair, 9
with birds of prey hovering all around it?
Come, you wild beasts; come, all of you, flock to the feast.
Many shepherds have ravaged my 10
vineyard
and trampled down my field,
they have made my pleasant field a desolate wilderness,
made it a waste land, waste and 11
waterless, to my sorrow.
The whole land is waste, and no one cares.

w you will feel sharp anguish: transposed from end of verse 15.   x consumes: prob. rdg.; Heb. they consume.

12 Plunderers have swarmed across the high bare places in the wilderness, a sword of the LORD devouring the land from end to end; no creature can find peace.

13 Men sow wheat and reap thistles; they sift but get no grain. They are disappointed of their[y] harvest because of the anger of the LORD.

14 These are the words of the LORD about all those evil neighbours who are laying hands on the land which I gave to my people Israel as their patrimony: I will uproot them from
16[z] that[a] soil. Yet, if they will learn the ways of my people, swearing by my name, 'By the life of the LORD', as they taught my people to swear by the Baal, they shall form families among
17 my people. But if they will not listen, I will uproot that people, uproot and destroy them. Also I will uproot Ju-
15 dah from among them; but after I have uprooted them, I will have pity on them again and will bring each man back to his patrimony and his land. This is the very word of the LORD.

The linen girdle

13 These were the words of the LORD to me: Go and buy yourself a linen girdle and put it round your waist,
2 but do not let it come near water. So I bought it as the LORD had told me
3 and put it round my waist. The LORD
4 spoke to me a second time: Take the girdle which you bought and put round your waist; go at once to Perath and hide it in a crevice among the
5 rocks. So I went and hid the girdle at[b] Perath, as the LORD had told me.
6 After a long time the LORD said to me: Go at once to Perath and fetch the girdle which I told you to hide
7 there. So I went to Perath and looked for the place where I had hidden it, but when I picked it up, I saw that it was spoilt, and no good for anything.
8 9 Again the LORD spoke to me and these were his words: Thus will I spoil the gross pride of Judah, the gross pride
10 of Jerusalem. This wicked nation has refused to listen to my words; they have followed other gods, serving them and bowing down to them. So it shall be[c] like this girdle, no good for

anything. For, just as a girdle is bound 11 close to a man's waist, so I bound all Israel and all Judah to myself, says the LORD, so that they should become my people to win a name for me, and praise and glory; but they did not listen.

The wine-jars

You shall say this to them: These are 12 the words of the LORD the God of Israel: Wine-jars should be filled with wine. They will answer, 'We know quite well that wine-jars should be filled with wine.' Then you shall say to 13 them, These are the words of the LORD: I will fill all the inhabitants of this land with wine until they are drunk—kings of David's line who sit on his throne, priests, prophets, and all who live in Jerusalem. I will dash 14 them to pieces one against another, fathers and sons alike, says the LORD, I will show them no compassion or pity or tenderness; nor refrain from destroying them.[d]

The LORD appeals to Judah

Hear and attend. Be not too proud 15 to listen, for it is the LORD who speaks. Ascribe glory to the LORD your God 16 before the darkness falls, before your feet stumble on the twilit hill-sides, before he turns the light you look for to deep gloom and thick darkness. If in those depths of gloom you will 17 not listen, then for very anguish I can only weep and shed tears,[e] my eyes must stream with tears; for the LORD's flock is carried away into captivity. Say to the king and the queen 18 mother:[f] Down, take a humble seat, for your proud crowns are fallen from your heads. Your cities in the Negeb are be- 19 sieged, and no one can relieve them; all Judah has been swept into exile, swept clean away. Lift up your eyes and see 20 those who are coming from the north. Where is the flock that was en- trusted to you,

y Prob. rdg.; Heb. your.   z The rest of verse 14 and verse 15 transposed to follow destroy them in verse 17.   a Prob. rdg.; Heb. their.   b Or by.   c Prob. rdg.; Heb. And let it be.   d nor refrain ... them: or so corrupt are they.   e If ... shed tears: or If you will not listen to this, for very an- guish I must weep in secret.   f Or queen.

the flock you were so proud of?

21 What will you say when you suffer
 because your leaders*g* cannot be
 found,
 though it was you who trained them
 to be your head?
 Will not pangs seize you,
 like the pangs of a woman in
 labour,

22 when you wonder,
 'Why has this come upon me?'
 For your many sins your skirts are
 torn off you,
 your limbs uncovered.

23 Can the Nubian change his skin,
 or the leopard its spots?
 And you? Can you do good,
 you who are schooled in evil?

24 Therefore I will scatter you*h* like
 chaff
 driven by the desert wind.

25 This is your lot, the portion of the
 rebel,
 measured out by me, says the LORD,
 because you have forsaken me
 and trusted in false gods.

26 So I myself have stripped off your
 skirts
 and laid bare your shame.

27 Your adulteries, your lustful neighing,
 your wanton lewdness, are an offence to me.*i*
 On the hills and in the open country
 I have seen your foul deeds.
 Alas, Jerusalem, unclean that you
 are!
 How long, how long will you delay?*j*

Drought

14 This came to Jeremiah as the word of
 the LORD concerning the drought:

2 Judah droops, her cities languish,
 her men sink to the ground;
 Jerusalem's cry goes up.

3 Their flock-masters send their boys
 for water;
 they come to the pools but find no
 water there.
 Back they go, with empty vessels;

4 the produce*k* of the land has failed,
 because there is no rain.
 The farmers' hopes are wrecked,
 they uncover their heads for grief.

5 The hind calves in the open country
 and forsakes her young
 because there is no grass;

6 for lack of herbage, wild asses stand
 on the high bare places
 and snuff the wind for moisture,

as wolves do, and their eyes begin
 to fail.

Though our sins testify against us, 7
 yet act,*l* O LORD, for thy own name's
 sake.
 Our disloyalties indeed are many; we
 have sinned against thee.

O hope of Israel, their saviour in 8
 time of trouble,
 must thou be a stranger in the land,
 a traveller pitching his tent for a
 night?

Must thou be like a man suddenly 9
 overcome,
 like a man powerless to save himself?
 Thou art in our midst, O LORD,
 and thou hast named us thine; do not
 forsake us.

Jeremiah pleads with the LORD

The LORD speaks thus of this people: 10
 They love to stray from my ways,
 they wander where they will. Therefore he has no more pleasure in them;
 he remembers their guilt now, and
 punishes their sins. Then the LORD 11
 said to me, Do not pray for the well-
 being of this people. When they fast, 12
 I will not listen to their cry; when
 they sacrifice whole-offering and grain-
 offering, I will not accept them. I will
 make an end of them with sword, with
 famine and pestilence. But I said, O 13
 Lord GOD, the prophets tell them
 that they shall see no sword and suffer
 no famine; for thou wilt give them
 lasting prosperity in this place. The 14
 LORD answered me, The prophets are
 prophesying lies in my name. I have
 not sent them; I have given them no
 charge; I have not spoken to them.
 The prophets offer them false visions,
 worthless augury, and their own deluding fancies. Therefore these are 15
 the words of the LORD about the
 prophets who, though not sent by
 me, prophesy in my name and say
 that neither sword nor famine shall
 touch this land: By sword and by
 famine shall those prophets meet
 their end. The people to whom they 16
 prophesy shall be flung out into
 the streets of Jerusalem, victims of
 famine and sword; they, their wives,
 their sons, and their daughters, with
 no one to bury them: I will pour down
 upon them the evil they deserve.

So this is what you shall say to 17
 them:
 Let my eyes stream with tears,

g leaders: *transposed from next line.* h *Prob. rdg.;* Heb. them. *i* an offence to me (Heb. you):
transposed from verse 26. j How ... delay?: *prob. rdg.;* Heb. *unintelligible.* k the produce:
prob. rdg.; Heb. *obscure.* l *Or* turn away.

ceaselessly, day and night.
For the virgin daughter of my people
has been broken in pieces,
struck by a cruel blow.
18 If I go out into the country,
I see men slain by the sword;
if I enter the city, I see the ravages
of famine;
prophet and priest alike
go begging round the land and are
never at rest.
19 Hast thou spurned Judah utterly?
Dost thou loathe Zion?
Why hast thou wounded us, and there
is no remedy;
why let us hope for better days, and
we find nothing good,
for a time of healing, and all is
disaster?
20 We acknowledge our wickedness,
the guilt of our forefathers;
O LORD, we have sinned against
thee.
21 Do not despise the place where thy
name dwells
nor bring contempt on the throne
of thy glory.
Remember thy covenant with us
and do not make it void.
22 Can any of the false gods of the
nations give rain?
Or do the heavens send showers of
themselves?
Art thou not God, O LORD,
that we may hope in thee?
It is thou only who doest*m* all these
things.

The LORD answers Jeremiah

15 The LORD said to me, Even if Moses
and Samuel stood before me, I would
not be moved to pity this people.
Banish them from my presence; let
2 them be gone. When they ask where
they are to go, you shall say to them,
These are the words of the LORD:

Those who are for death shall go to
their death,
and those for the sword to the sword;
those who are for famine to famine,
and those for captivity to captivity.

3 Four kinds of doom do I ordain for
them, says the LORD: the sword to
kill, dogs to tear, birds of prey from
the skies and beasts from their lairs
4 to devour and destroy. I will make
them repugnant to all the kingdoms
of the earth, because of the crimes of

Manasseh son of Hezekiah, king of
Judah, in Jerusalem.

Who will take pity on you, Jeru- 5
salem,
who will offer you consolation?
Who will turn aside to wish you well?
You cast me off, says the LORD, 6
you turned your backs on me.
So I stretched out my hand and
ruined you;
I was weary of relenting.
I winnowed them and scattered 7
them
through the cities of the land;
I brought bereavement on them, I
destroyed my people,
for they would not abandon their
ways.
I made widows among them more 8
in number
than the sands of the sea;
I brought upon them a horde of
raiders*n*
to plunder at high noon.
I made the terror of invasion fall
upon them
all in a moment.
The mother of seven sons grew faint, 9
she sank into a swoon;
her light was quenched while it was
yet day;
she was left humbled and shamed.
All the remnant I gave to perish by
the sword
at the hand of their enemies.
This is the very word of the LORD.

The LORD's care for Jeremiah

Alas, alas, my mother, that you 10
ever gave me birth!
a man doomed to strife, with the
whole world against me.
I have borrowed from no one, I have
lent to no one,
yet all men abuse me.

The LORD answered,   11

But I will greatly strengthen you;
in time of distress and in time of
disaster
I will bring the enemy to your feet.
Can iron break steel from the north?*o* 12
LORD, thou knowest;   15
remember me, LORD, and come to
visit me,
take vengeance for me on my
persecutors.
Be patient with me and take me not
away,

---

m Or madest.   *n* I brought . . . raiders: *prob. rdg.*; *Heb. obscure*.   *o Prob. rdg.*; *Heb. adds* and
bronze. *Heb. also adds* (13) I will give away your wealth as spoil, and your treasure for no payment,
because of your sin throughout your country. (14) I will make your enemies pass through a land you
do not know; for my anger is a blazing fire and it shall burn for ever (*cp. 17. 3, 4*).

see what reproaches I endure for thy
sake.

16 I have to suffer those who despise
thy words,
but thy word is joy and happiness to
me,
for thou hast named me thine,
O LORD, God of Hosts.

17 I have never kept company with
any gang of roisterers,
or made merry with them;
because I felt thy hand upon me I
have sat alone;
for thou hast filled me with indignation.

18 Why then is my pain unending,
my wound desperate and incurable?
Thou art to me like a brook that is not
to be trusted,
whose waters fail.

19 This was the LORD's answer:

If you will turn back to me, I will
take you back
and you shall stand before me.
If you choose noble utterance and
reject the base,
you shall be my spokesman.
This people will turn again to you,
but you will not turn to them.

20 To withstand them I will make you
impregnable,
a wall of bronze.
They will attack you but they will not
prevail,
for I am with you to deliver you
and save you, says the LORD;

21 I will deliver you from the wicked,
I will rescue you from the ruthless.

Exile and after

16 The word of the LORD came to me:
2 You shall not marry a wife; you shall
have neither son nor daughter in this
3 place. For these are the words of the
LORD concerning sons and daughters
born in this place, the mothers who
bear them and the fathers who beget
4 them in this land: When men die,
struck down by deadly ulcers, there
shall be no wailing for them and no
burial; they shall be like dung lying
upon the ground. When men perish by
sword or famine, their corpses shall
become food for birds and for beasts.
5 For these are the words of the
LORD: Enter no house where there is
a mourning-feast; do not go in to wail
or to bring comfort, for I have withdrawn my peace from this people,
says the LORD, my love and affection.
6 High and low shall die in this land,
but there shall be no burial, no wailing

for them; no one shall gash himself,
or shave his head. No one shall give 7
the mourner a portion of bread to
console him for the dead, nor give him
the cup of consolation, even for his
father or mother. Nor shall you enter 8
a house where there is feasting, to sit
eating and drinking there. For these 9
are the words of the LORD of Hosts,
the God of Israel: In your own days,
in the sight of you all, and in this
very place, I will silence all sounds of
joy and gladness, and the voice of
bridegroom and bride.

When you tell this people all these 10
things they will ask you, 'Why has
the LORD decreed that this great
disaster is to come upon us? What
wrong have we done? What sin have
we committed against the LORD our
God?' You shall answer, Because your 11
forefathers forsook me, says the LORD,
and followed other gods, serving them
and bowing down to them. They forsook me and did not keep my law.
And you yourselves have done worse 12
than your forefathers; for each of you
follows the promptings of his wicked
and stubborn heart instead of obeying
me. So I will fling you headlong out of 13
this land into a country unknown to
you and to your forefathers; there
you can serve other gods day and
night, for I will show you no favour.
Therefore, says the LORD, the time is 14
coming when men shall no longer
swear, 'By the life of the LORD who
brought the Israelites up from Egypt',
but, 'By the life of the LORD who 15
brought the Israelites back from a
northern land and from all the lands
to which he had dispersed them'; and
I will bring them back to the soil
which I gave to their forefathers.

I will send for many fishermen, says 16
the LORD, and they shall fish for them.
After that I will send for many hunters,
and they shall hunt them out from
every mountain and hill and from the
crevices in the rocks. For my eyes are 17
on all their ways; they are not hidden
from my sight, nor is their wrongdoing
concealed from me. I will first make 18
them pay in full*p* for the wrong they
have done and the sin they have
committed by defiling with the dead
lumber of their idols the land which
belongs to me, and by filling it with
their abominations.

O LORD, my strength and my strong- 19
hold,
my refuge in time of trouble,

p in full: or double.

to thee shall the nations come
from the ends of the earth and say,
Our forefathers inherited only a
  sham,
an idol vain and useless.

20 Can man make gods for himself?
  They would be no gods.
21 Therefore I am teaching them,
  once for all will I teach them
  my power and my might,
  and they shall learn that my name
  is the LORD.

Judah's sin recorded

17 The sin of Judah is recorded with an
  iron tool, engraved on the tablet of
  their heart with a point of adamant
  and carved on the horns of their altars
2 to bear witness against them.*q* Their
  altars and their sacred poles stand by
  every spreading tree, on the heights
3 and the hills in the mountain country.
  I will give away your wealth as spoil,
  and all your treasure for no payment,*r*
  because of your*s* sin throughout your
4 country. You will lose possession*t* of
  the patrimony which I gave you. I will
  make you serve your enemies as slaves
  in a land you do not know; for my
  anger is a blazing fire*u* and it shall
  burn for ever.

A curse and a blessing

5 These are the words of the LORD:

A curse on the man who trusts in man
  and leans for support on human
  kind,
  while his heart is far from the LORD!
6 He shall be like a juniper in the
  desert;
  when good comes he shall not see it.
  He shall dwell among the rocks in
  the wilderness,
  in a salt land where no man can
  live.
7 Blessed is the man who trusts in the
  LORD,
  and rests his confidence upon him.
8 He shall be like a tree planted by the
  waterside,
  that stretches its roots along the
  stream.
When the heat comes it has nothing
  to fear;
  its spreading foliage stays green.
  In a year of drought it feels no care,
  and does not cease to bear fruit.

The heart is deceitful

The heart is the most deceitful of 9
all things, desperately sick;*v* who can
fathom it?
I, the LORD, search the mind   10
  and test the heart,
  requiting man for his conduct,
  and as his deeds deserve.
Like a partridge which gathers into 11
  its nest
  eggs which it has not laid,
  so is the man who amasses wealth
  unjustly.
Before his days are half done he
  must leave it,
  and prove but a fool at the last.

Prayer for deliverance

O throne of glory, exalted from the 12
  beginning,
  the place of our sanctuary,
O LORD on whom Israel's hope is 13
  fixed,
  all who reject thee shall be put to
  shame;
  all in this land who forsake thee
  shall be humbled,*w*
for they have rejected the fountain of
  living water.*x*
Heal me, O LORD, and I shall be 14
  healed,
  save me and I shall be saved;
  for thou art my praise.
They say to me, 'Where is the word of 15
  the LORD?
  Let it come if it can!'
It is not the thought of disaster that 16
  makes me press after thee;
  never did I desire this day of despair.
  Thou knowest all that has passed
  my lips;
  it was approved by thee.
Do not become a terror to me;   17
  thou art my only refuge on the day
  of disaster.
May my persecutors be foiled, not I; 18
may they be terrified, not I.
  Bring on them the day of disaster;
  destroy them, destroy them utterly.

On keeping the sabbath

These were the words of the LORD to 19
me: Go and stand in the Benjamin*y*
Gate, through which the kings of
Judah go in and out, and in all the
gates of Jerusalem. Say, Hear the 20
words of the LORD, you princes of
Judah, all you men of Judah, and all

q to bear . . . them: *prob. rdg.*; *Heb.* as their sons remember.   *r* for no payment: *prob. rdg.*, *cp. 15. 13*; *Heb.* your hill-shrines.   *s* your: *prob. rdg.*, *cp. 15. 13*; *Heb. om.*   *t* You . . . possession: *prob. rdg.*; *Heb. obscure.*   *u* for . . . fire: *prob. rdg.*, *cp. 15. 14*; *Heb.* for you have kindled a fire in my anger.   *v* the most . . . sick: *or* too deceitful for any man.   *w* humbled: *prob. rdg.*; *Heb.* written.   *x* *Prob. rdg.*; *Heb. adds* the LORD.   *y* Benjamin: *prob. rdg.*; *Heb.* sons of the people.

you inhabitants of Jerusalem who
21 come in through these gates. These
are the words of the LORD: Observe
this with care, that you do not carry
any load on the sabbath or bring it
22 through the gates of Jerusalem. You
shall not bring any load out of your
houses or do any work on the sabbath,
but you shall keep the sabbath day
holy as I commanded your forefathers.
23 Yet they did not obey or pay attention, but obstinately refused to hear
24 or learn their lesson. Now if you will
obey me, says the LORD, and refrain
from bringing any load through the
gates of this city on the sabbath, and
keep that day holy by doing no work
25 on it, then kings shall come through
the gates of this city, kings^z who shall
sit on David's throne. They shall come
riding in chariots or on horseback,
escorted by their captains, by the
men of Judah and the inhabitants
of Jerusalem; and this city shall be
26 inhabited for ever. People shall come
from the cities of Judah, the country
round Jerusalem, the land of Benjamin, the Shephelah, the hill-country
and the Negeb, bringing whole-offerings, sacrifices, grain-offerings, and
frankincense, bringing also thank-
offerings to the house of the LORD.
27 But if you do not obey me by keeping
the sabbath day holy and by not
carrying any load as you come through
the gates of Jerusalem on the sabbath,
then I will set fire to those gates; it
shall consume the palaces of Jerusalem and shall not be put out.

At the potter's house

18 These are the words which came to
2 Jeremiah from the LORD: Go down
at once to the potter's house, and
there I will tell you what I have to
3 say. So I went down to the potter's
house and found him working at the
4 wheel. Now and then a vessel he was
making out of the clay would be spoilt
in his hands, and then he would
start again and mould it into another
5 vessel to his liking. Then the word of
6 the LORD came to me: Can I not deal
with you, Israel, says the LORD, as the
potter deals with his clay? You are
clay in my hands like the clay in his,
7 O house of Israel. At any moment I
may threaten to uproot a nation or a
kingdom, to pull it down and destroy
8 it. But if the nation which I have
threatened turns back from its wicked ways, then I shall think better

of the evil I had in mind to bring on
it. Or at any moment I may decide 9
to build or to plant a nation or a kingdom. But if it does evil in my sight 10
and does not obey me, I shall think
better of the good I had in mind for
it. Go now and tell the men of Judah 11
and the inhabitants of Jerusalem that
these are the words of the LORD: I am
the potter; I am preparing evil for
you and perfecting my designs against
you. Turn back, every one of you,
from his evil course; mend your ways
and your doings. But they answer, 12
'Things are past hope. We will do as
we like, and each of us will follow the
promptings of his own wicked and
stubborn heart.' Therefore these are 13
the words of the LORD:

Inquire among the nations: who ever
heard the like of this?
The virgin Israel has done a thing
most horrible.
Will the snow cease to fall on the 14
rocky slopes of Lebanon?
Will the cool rain streaming in torrents
ever fail?
No, but my people have forgotten me; 15
they burn sacrifices to a mere idol,
so they stumble in their paths, the
ancient ways,
and they take to byways and un-
made roads;
their own land they lay waste, 16
and men will jeer at it for ever in
contempt.
All who go by will be horror-struck
and shake their heads.
Like a wind from the east 17
I will scatter them before their
enemies.
In the hour of their downfall
I will turn my back towards them
and not my face.

Jeremiah prays for vindication

'Come, let us decide what to do with 18
Jeremiah', men say. 'There will still
be priests to guide us, still wise men
to advise, still prophets to proclaim
the word. Come, let us invent some
charges against him; let us pay no
attention to his message.'

But do thou, O LORD, pay atten- 19
tion,
and hear what my opponents are
saying against me.
Is good to be repaid with evil?^{a} 20
Remember how I stood before thee,
pleading on their behalf
to avert thy wrath from them.

z *Prob. rdg.; Heb. adds* and officers.   *a Prob. rdg.; Heb. adds* they have dug a pit for me (*cp.*
verse 22).

21 Therefore give their sons over to famine,
leave them at the mercy of the sword.
Let their women be childless and widowed,
let death carry off their men,
let their young men be cut down in battle.

22 Bring raiders upon them without warning,
and let screams of terror ring out from their houses.
For they have dug a pit to catch me and have hidden snares for my feet.

23 Well thou knowest, O LORD,
all their murderous plots against me.
Do not blot out their wrongdoing or annul their sin;
when they are brought stumbling into thy presence,
deal with them on the day of thy anger.

The broken jar

19 These are the words of the LORD: Go and buy an earthenware jar. Then take with you some of the elders of 2 the people and of the priests, and go out to the Valley of Ben-hinnom, on which the Gate of the Potsherds opens, and there proclaim what I tell you. 3 Say, Hear the word of the LORD, you princes of Judah and inhabitants of Jerusalem. These are the words of the LORD of Hosts the God of Israel: I will bring on this place a disaster which shall ring in the ears of all who 4 hear of it. For they have forsaken me, and treated this place as if it were not mine, burning sacrifices to other gods whom neither they nor their fathers nor the kings of Judah have known, and filling this place with the blood 5 of the innocent. They have built shrines to Baal, where they burn their sons as whole-offerings to Baal. It was no command of mine; I never spoke of it; it never entered my thought. 6 Therefore, says the LORD, the time is coming when this place shall no longer be called Topheth or the Valley of Ben-hinnom, but the Valley of 7 Slaughter. In this place I will shatter the plans of Judah and Jerusalem as a jar is shattered; I will make the people fall by the sword before their enemies, at the hands of those who would kill them, and I will give their corpses to the birds and beasts 8 to devour. I will make this city a scene of horror and contempt, so that every passer-by will be horror-struck and jeer in contempt at the sight of its wounds. I will compel men to eat the 9 flesh of their sons and their daughters; they shall devour one another's flesh in the dire straits to which their enemies and those who would kill them will reduce them in the siege. Then you must shatter the jar before 10 the eyes of the men who have come with you and say to them, These are 11 the words of the LORD of Hosts: Thus will I shatter this people and this city as one shatters an earthen vessel so that it cannot be mended, and the dead shall be buried in Topheth because there is no room elsewhere to bury them. This is what I will do to 12 this place, says the LORD, and to those who live there: I will make this city like Topheth. Because of their defile- 13 ment, the houses of Jerusalem and those of the kings of Judah shall be like Topheth, every one of the houses on whose roofs men have burnt sacrifices to the host of heaven and poured drink-offerings to other gods.

Jeremiah came in from Topheth, 14 where the LORD had sent him to prophesy, and stood in the court of the LORD's house. He said to all the people, These are the words of the 15 LORD of Hosts the God of Israel: I am bringing on this city and on all its blood-spattered altars every disaster with which I have threatened it, for its people have remained obstinate and refused to listen to me.

Jeremiah arrested and released

When Pashhur son of Immer the priest, **20** the chief officer in the house of the LORD, heard Jeremiah prophesying these things, he had him flogged[b] and 2 put him into the stocks at the Upper Gate of Benjamin, in the house of the LORD. The next morning he released 3 him, and Jeremiah said to him, The LORD has called you not Pashhur but Magor-missabib.[c] For these are the 4 words of the LORD: I will make you a terror to yourself and to all your friends; they shall fall by the sword of the enemy before your very eyes. I will hand over all Judah to the king of Babylon, and he will deport them to Babylon and put them to the sword. I will give all this city's store 5 of wealth and riches and all the treasures of the kings of Judah to their enemies; they shall seize them as spoil and carry them off to Bab-ylon. You, Pashhur, and all your 6

---

b had him flogged: or struck him.   c That is Terror let loose.

household shall go into captivity and
come to Babylon. There shall you die
and there shall you be buried, you and
all your friends to whom you have
been a false prophet.

The prophet's inner conflict

7 O LORD, thou hast duped me, and
I have been thy dupe;
thou hast outwitted me and hast
prevailed.
I have been made a laughing-stock
all the day long,
everyone mocks me.

8 Whenever I speak I must needs cry
out
and proclaim violence and destruction.
I am reproached and mocked all
the time
for uttering the word of the LORD.

9 Whenever I said, 'I will call him to
mind no more,
nor speak in his name again',
then his word was imprisoned in
my body,
like a fire blazing in my heart,
and I was weary with holding it
under,
and could endure no more.

10 For I heard many whispering,*d*
'Denounce him! we will denounce
him.'
All my friends were on the watch for
a false step,
saying, 'Perhaps he may be tricked,
then we can catch him
and take our revenge.'

11 But the LORD is on my side, strong
and ruthless,
therefore my persecutors shall stumble
and fall powerless.
Bitter shall be their abasement when
they fail,
and their shame shall long be remembered.

12 O LORD of Hosts, thou dost test the
righteous
and search the depths of the heart;
to thee have I committed my cause,
let me see thee take vengeance on
them.

13 Sing to the LORD, praise the LORD;
for he rescues the poor from those who
would do them wrong.

14 A curse on the day when I was born!
Be it for ever unblessed,
the day when my mother bore me!

15 A curse on the man who brought
word to my father,
'A child is born to you, a son',
and gladdened his heart!

16 That man shall fare like the cities
which the LORD overthrew without
mercy.
He shall hear cries of alarm in the
morning
and uproar at noon,

17 because death did not claim me
before birth,
and my mother did not become my
grave,
her womb great with me for ever.

18 Why did I come forth from the
womb
to know only sorrow and toil,
to end my days in shame?

Life or death

21 The word which came from the LORD
to Jeremiah when King Zedekiah sent
to him Pashhur son of Malchiah and
Zephaniah the priest, son of Maaseiah,
2 with this request: 'Nebuchadrezzar
king of Babylon is making war on us;
inquire of the LORD on our behalf.
Perhaps the LORD will perform a
miracle as he has done in past times,
so that Nebuchadrezzar may raise the
3 siege.' But Jeremiah answered them,
4 Tell Zedekiah, these are the words of
the LORD the God of Israel: I will turn
back upon you your own weapons
with which you are fighting the king
of Babylon and the Chaldaeans besieging you outside the wall; and I
will bring them into the heart of this
5 city. I myself will fight against you
in burning rage and great fury, with
an outstretched hand and a strong
6 arm. I will strike down those who live
in this city, men and cattle alike; they
shall die of a great pestilence. After
7 that, says the LORD, I will take Zedekiah king of Judah, his courtiers and
the people, all in this city who survive
pestilence, sword, and famine, and
hand them over to Nebuchadrezzar
the king of Babylon, to their enemies
and those who would kill them. He
shall put them to the sword and shall
show no pity, no mercy or compassion.

8 You shall say further to this people,
These are the words of the LORD: I
offer you now a choice between the
way of life and the way of death.
9 Whoever remains in this city shall die
by sword, by famine, or by pestilence,
but whoever goes out to surrender to
the Chaldaeans, who are now besieging you, shall survive; he shall take
home his life, and nothing more. I
10 have set my face against this city,
meaning to do them harm, not good,
says the LORD. It shall be handed over

d Prob. rdg.; Heb. adds Terror let loose.

to the king of Babylon, and he shall burn it to the ground.

Judah's covenant with the LORD

11 To the royal house of Judah.
Listen to the word of the LORD:

12 O house of David, these are the words of the LORD:
Administer justice betimes,
rescue the victim from his oppressor,
lest the fire of my fury blaze up and burn unquenched
because of your evil doings.

13 The LORD says,
I am against you who lie in the valley,
you, the rock in the plain,
you who say, 'Who can come down upon us?
Who can penetrate our lairs?'

14 I will punish you as you deserve, says the LORD,
I will kindle fire on the heathland around you,
and it shall consume everything round about.

22 These were the words of the LORD:
Go down to the house of the king of
2 Judah and say this: Listen to the words of the LORD, O king of Judah, you who sit on David's throne, you and your courtiers and your people
3 who come in at these gates. These are the words of the LORD: Deal justly and fairly, rescue the victim from his oppressor, do not ill-treat or do violence to the alien, the orphan or the widow, do not shed innocent
4 blood in this place. If you obey, and only if you obey, kings who sit on David's throne shall yet come riding through these gates in chariots and on horses, with their retinue of court-
5 iers and people. But if you do not listen to my words, then by myself I swear, says the LORD, this house shall
6 become a desolate ruin. For these are the words of the LORD about the royal house of Judah:

Though you are dear to me as Gilead
or as the heights of Lebanon,
I swear that I will make you a wilderness,
a land of unpeopled cities.

7 I will dedicate an armed host to fight against you,
a ravening horde;
they shall cut your choicest cedars down
and fling them on the fire.

Men of many nations shall pass by 8 this city and say to one another, 'Why has the LORD done this to such a great city?' The answer will be, 'Because they 9 forsook their covenant with the LORD their God; they worshipped other gods and served them.'

Concerning Shallum

Weep not for the dead nor brood over 10 his loss.
Weep rather for him who has gone away,
for he shall never return,
never again see the land of his birth.

For these are the words of the LORD 11 concerning Shallum son of Josiah, king of Judah, who succeeded his father on the throne and has gone away: He shall never return; he shall die in the place 12 of his exile and never see this land again.

Concerning Jehoiakim

Shame on the man who builds his 13 house by unjust means
and completes its roof-chambers by fraud,
making his countrymen work without payment,
giving them no wage for their labour!
Shame on the man who says, 'I will 14 build a spacious house
with airy roof-chambers,
set windows in it, panel it with cedar
and paint it with vermilion'!
If your cedar is more splendid,   15
does that prove you a king?
Think of your father: he ate and drank,
dealt justly and fairly; all went well with him.
He dispensed justice to the lowly 16 and poor;[e]
did not this show he knew me? says the LORD.
But you have no eyes, no thought for 17 anything but gain,
set only on the innocent blood you can shed,
on cruel acts of tyranny.

Therefore these are the words of 18 the LORD concerning Jehoiakim son of Josiah, king of Judah:
For him no mourner shall say, 'Alas, brother, dear brother!'
no one say, 'Alas, lord and master!'
He shall be buried like a dead ass, 19

e Prob. rdg.; Heb. adds all went well (repeated from verse 15).

dragged along and flung out
beyond the gates of Jerusalem.

Concerning Jerusalem

20 Get up into Lebanon and cry aloud,
    make your voice heard in Bashan,
cry aloud from Abarim, for all who
    befriend you are broken.

21 I spoke to you in your days of
    prosperous ease,
    but you said, 'I will not listen.'
This is how you behaved since your
    youth;
    never have you obeyed me.

22 The wind shall carry away all your
    friends,[f]
your lovers shall depart into exile.
Then you will be put to shame and
    abashed
for all your evil deeds.[g]

23 You dwellers in Lebanon, who make
    your nests among the cedars,
how you will groan when the pains
    come upon you,
like the pangs of a woman in
    labour!

Concerning Coniah

24 By my life, says the LORD, Coniah
son of Jehoiakim, king of Judah, shall
be the signet-ring on my right hand
no longer. Yes, Coniah, I will pull you
25 off. I will hand you over to those who
seek your life, to those you fear, to
Nebuchadrezzar king of Babylon and
26 to the Chaldaeans. I will fling you
headlong, you and the mother who
gave you birth, into another land, a
land where you were not born; and
27 there shall you both die. They shall
never come back to their own land,
the land for which they long.
28   This man, Coniah, then, is he a mere
puppet, contemptible and broken,
only a thing unwanted? Why else are
he and his children flung out headlong
and hurled into a country they do not
know?
29   O land, land, land, hear the words
30 of the LORD: These are the words of
the LORD: Write this man down as
stripped of all honour, one who in his
own life shall not prosper, nor shall he
leave descendants to sit in prosperity
on David's throne or rule again in
Judah.

The remnant returns

23 Shame on the shepherds who let the
sheep of my flock scatter and be lost!
2 says the LORD. Therefore these are
the words of the LORD the God of

Israel about the shepherds who tend
my people: You have scattered and
dispersed my flock. You have not
watched over them; but I am watching
you to punish you for your evil doings,
says the LORD. I will myself gather 3
the remnant of my sheep from all the
lands to which I have dispersed them.
I will bring them back to their homes,
and they shall be fruitful and increase.
I will appoint shepherds to tend them; 4
they shall never again know fear or
dismay or punishment. This is the
very word of the LORD.

    The days are now coming, says the 5
    LORD,
when I will make a righteous Branch
    spring from David's line,
a king who shall rule wisely,
maintaining law and justice in the
    land.
    In his days Judah shall be kept safe, 6
    and Israel shall live undisturbed.
    This is the name to be given to him:
    The LORD is our Righteousness.

    Therefore the days are coming, says 7
the LORD, when men shall no longer
swear, 'By the life of the LORD who
brought Israel up from Egypt', but, 8
'By the life of the LORD who brought
the descendants of the Israelites back
from a northern land and from all the
lands to which he had dispersed them,
to live again on their own soil.'

Against the prophets

On the prophets.   9

    Deep within me my heart is broken,
    there is no strength in my bones;
    because of the LORD, because of his
        dread words
    I have become like a drunken man,
    like a man overcome with wine.
    For the land is full of adulterers,   10
    and because of them the earth lies
        parched,
    the wild pastures have dried up.
    The course that they run is evil,
    and their powers are misused.
    For prophet and priest alike are 11
        godless;
I have come upon the evil they are
    doing even in my own house.
    This is the very word of the LORD.

Therefore the path shall turn slippery 12
    beneath their feet;
they shall be dispersed in the dark and
    shall fall there.
For I will bring disaster on them when
    their day of reckoning comes.
    This is the very word of the LORD.

f Or shepherds.   g Or calamities.

13 I found the prophets of Samaria
men of no sense:
they prophesied in Baal's name and
led my people Israel astray.
14 In the prophets of Jerusalem I see a
thing most horrible:
adulterers and hypocrites that they
are,
they encourage evildoers,
so that no man turns back from his
sin;
to me all her inhabitants are like
Sodom and Gomorrah.

15 These then are the words of the LORD
of Hosts concerning the prophets:

I will give them wormwood to eat
and a bitter poison to drink;
for a godless spirit has spread over
all the land
from the prophets of Jerusalem.

16 These are the words of the LORD of
Hosts:

Do not listen to what the prophets
say,
who buoy you up with false hopes;
the vision they report springs from
their own imagination,
it is not from the mouth of the
LORD.

17 They say to those who spurn the
word of the LORD,
'Prosperity shall be yours';
and to all who follow the promptings
of their own stubborn heart they
say,
'No disaster shall befall you.'

18 But which of them has stood in the
council of the LORD,
seen him and heard his word?
Which of them has listened to his
word and obeyed?

19 See what a scorching wind has gone
out from the LORD,
a furious whirlwind;
it whirls round the heads of the
wicked.

20 The LORD's anger is not to be
turned aside,
until he has accomplished and fulfilled his deep designs.
In days to come you will fully understand.

21 I did not send these prophets, yet
they went in haste;
I did not speak to them, yet they
prophesied.

22 If they have stood in my council,
let them proclaim my words to my
people
and turn them from their evil course
and their evil doings.

Am I a god only near at hand, not far 23
away?
Can a man hide in any secret place 24
and I not see him?
Do I not fill heaven and earth?
This is the very word of the LORD.

I have heard what the prophets say, 25
the prophets who speak lies in my
name and cry, 'I have had a dream,
a dream!' How long will it be till they 26
change their tune, these prophets who
prophesy lies and give voice to their
own inventions? By these dreams 27
which they tell one another these men
think they will make my people forget my name, as their fathers forgot
my name for the name of[h] Baal. If a 28
prophet has a dream, let him tell his
dream; if he has my word, let him
speak my word in truth. What has
chaff to do with grain? says the LORD.
Do not my words scorch[i] like fire? 29
says the LORD. Are they not like a
hammer that splinters rock? I am 30
against the prophets, says the LORD,
who steal my words from one another
for their own use. I am against the 31
prophets, says the LORD, who concoct
words of their own and then say, 'This
is his very word.' I am against the 32
prophets, says the LORD, who dream
lies and retail them, misleading my
people with wild and reckless falsehoods. It was not I who sent them or
commissioned them, and they will do
this people no good. This is the very
word of the LORD.

'The LORD's burden'

When you are asked by this people or 33
by a prophet or priest what the burden of the LORD's message is, you
shall answer, You are his burden, and
I shall throw you down, says the
LORD. If prophet or priest or layman 34
uses the term 'the LORD's burden', I
will punish that man and his family.
The form of words you shall use in 35
speaking amongst yourselves is: 'What
answer has the LORD given?' or,
'What has the LORD said?' You shall 36
never again mention 'the burden of
the LORD'; that is reserved for the
man to whom he entrusts his message.
If you do, you will make nonsense of
the words of the living God, the LORD
of Hosts our God. This is the form you 37
shall use in speaking to a prophet:
'What answer has the LORD given?'
or, 'What has the LORD said?' But to 38
any of you who do say, 'the burden of
the LORD', the LORD speaks thus:

h for the name of: or by their worship of.   i scorch: prob. rdg.; Heb. thus.

Because you say, 'the burden of the LORD', though I sent to tell you not 39 to say it, therefore I myself will carry you like a burden and throw you down, casting out of my sight both you and the city which I gave to you 40 and to your forefathers. I will inflict on you endless reproach, endless shame which shall never be forgotten.

Good and bad figs

24 This is what the LORD showed me: I saw two baskets of figs set out in front of the sanctuary of the LORD. This was after Nebuchadrezzar king of Babylon had deported from Jerusalem Jeconiah son of Jehoiakim, king of Judah, with the officers of Judah, the craftsmen and the smiths,[j] 2 and taken them to Babylon. In one basket the figs were very good, like the figs that are first ripe; in the other the figs were very bad, so bad that 3 they were not fit to eat. The LORD said to me, 'What are you looking at, Jeremiah?' 'Figs,' I answered, 'the good very good, and the bad so bad 4 that they are not fit to eat.' Then this word came to me from the LORD: 5 These are the words of the LORD the God of Israel: I count the exiles of Judah whom I sent away from this place to the land of the Chaldaeans 6 as good as these good figs. I will look upon them meaning to do them good, and I will restore them to their land; I will build them up and not pull them down, plant them and not uproot 7 them. I will give them the wit to know me, for I am the LORD; they shall become my people and I will become their God, for they will come 8 back to me with all their heart. But Zedekiah king of Judah, his officers and the survivors of Jerusalem, whether they remain in this land or live in Egypt—all these I will treat as bad figs, says the LORD, so bad that 9 they are not fit to eat. I will make them repugnant to all the kingdoms of the earth, a reproach, a by-word, an object-lesson and a thing of ridicule 10 wherever I drive them. I will send against them sword, famine, and pestilence until they have vanished from the land which I gave to them and to their forefathers.

The years of Babylonian rule

25 This came to Jeremiah as the word concerning all the people of Judah in the fourth year of Jehoiakim son of Josiah, king of Judah (that is the first year of Nebuchadrezzar king of Babylon). This is what the prophet Jere- 2 miah said to all Judah and all the inhabitants of Jerusalem: For twenty- 3 three years, from the thirteenth year of Josiah son of Amon, king of Judah, to the present day, I have been receiving the words of the LORD and taking pains to speak to you, but you have not listened. The LORD has 4 taken pains to send you his servants the prophets, but you have not listened or shown any inclination to listen. If each of you will turn from 5 his wicked ways and evil courses, he has said, then you shall for ever live on the soil which the LORD gave to you and to your forefathers. You 6 must not follow other gods, serving and worshipping them, nor must you provoke me to anger with the idols your hands have made; then I will not do you harm. But you did not 7 listen to me, says the LORD; you provoked me to anger with the idols your hands have made and so brought harm upon yourselves.

Therefore these are the words of the 8 LORD of Hosts: Because you have not listened to my words, I will summon 9 all the tribes of the north, says the LORD: I will send for my servant Nebuchadrezzar king of Babylon. I will bring them against this land and all its inhabitants and all these nations round it; I will exterminate them and make them a thing of horror and derision, a scandal for ever. I will 10 silence all sounds of joy and gladness among them, the voices of bridegroom and bride, and the sound of the handmill; I will quench the light of every lamp. For seventy years this 11 whole country shall be a scandal and a horror; these nations shall be in subjection to the king of Babylon. When those seventy years are com- 12 pleted, I will punish the king of Babylon and his people, says the LORD, for all their misdeeds and make the land of the Chaldaeans a waste for ever. I will bring upon that country 13 all I have said, all that is written in this book, all that Jeremiah has prophesied against these peoples. They 14 will be the victims[k] of mighty nations and great kings, and thus I will repay them for their actions and their deeds.

Punishment for the nations

These were the words of the LORD the 15 God of Israel to me: Take from my

j the smiths: or the harem.   *k They . . . victims: prob. rdg.; Heb. They were the victims.*

hand this cup of fiery wine and make all the nations to whom I send you 16 drink it. When they have drunk it they will vomit and go mad; such is the sword which I am sending 17 among them. Then I took the cup from the LORD's hand, gave it to all the nations to whom he sent me and 18 made them drink it: to Jerusalem, the cities of Judah, its kings and officers, making them a scandal, a thing of horror and derision and an object of 19 ridicule, as they still are: to Pharaoh king of Egypt, his courtiers, his 20 officers, all his people, and all his rabble of followers, all the kings of the land of Uz, all the kings of the Philistines: to Ashkelon, Gaza, Ekron, 21 and the remnant of Ashdod: also to 22 Edom, Moab, and the Ammonites, all the kings of Tyre, all the kings of Sidon, and the kings of the coasts 23 and islands: to Dedan, Tema, Buz, and all who roam the fringes of the 24 desert,*l* all the kings of Arabia living 25 in the wilderness, all the kings of Zamri, all the kings of Elam, and all 26 the kings of the Medes, all the kings of the north, neighbours or far apart, and all the kingdoms on the face of the earth. Last of all the king of 27 Sheshak*m* shall drink. You shall say to them, These are the words of the LORD of Hosts the God of Israel: Drink this, get drunk and be sick; fall, to rise no more, before the sword 28 which I am sending among you. If they refuse to take the cup from you and to drink, say to them, These are the words of the LORD of Hosts: You 29 must and shall drink. I will first punish the city which bears my name; do you think that you can be exempt? No, you cannot be exempt, for I am invoking the sword against all that inhabit the earth. This is the very word of the LORD of Hosts.

30 Prophesy to them and tell them all I have said:

The LORD roars from Zion on high
and thunders from his holy dwelling-
place.
Yes, he roars across the heavens,
his home;
an echo comes back like the shout of
men treading grapes.
31 The great noise reaches to the ends
of the earth
and all its inhabitants.
For the LORD brings a charge
against the nations,
he goes to law with all mankind

and has handed the wicked over to
the sword.
This is the very word of the LORD.

These are the words of the LORD of 32
Hosts:
Ruin spreads from nation to nation,
a mighty tempest is blowing up from
the ends of the earth.

In that day those whom the LORD 33 has slain shall lie like dung on the ground from one end of the earth to the other; no one shall wail for them, they shall not be taken up and buried.

The plight of the shepherds

Howl, shepherds, cry aloud,   34
sprinkle yourselves with ashes,
you masters of the flock.
It is your turn to go to the slaughter,
and you shall fall like fine rams.
The shepherds shall have nowhere 35
to flee,
the flockmasters no way of escape.
Hark, the shepherds cry out, the 36
flockmasters howl,
for the LORD is ravaging their
pasture,
and their peaceful homesteads lie in 37
ruins beneath his anger.
They flee like a young lion aban- 38
doning his lair,
for their land has become a waste,
wasted by the cruel sword and by his
anger.

Proclamation in the temple

At the beginning of the reign of 26 Jehoiakim son of Josiah, king of Judah, this word came to Jeremiah from the LORD: These are the words 2 of the LORD: Stand in the court of the LORD's house and speak to the inhabitants of all the cities of Judah who come to worship there. You shall tell them everything that I command you to say to them, keeping nothing back. Perhaps they may 3 listen, and every man may turn back from his evil courses. Then I will relent, and give up my purpose to bring disaster on them for their evil deeds. You shall say to them, These 4 are the words of the LORD: If you do not obey me, if you do not follow the law I have set before you, and listen 5 to the words of my servants the prophets whom I have taken pains to send to you, but you have never listened to them, then I will 6 make this house like Shiloh and this

l who roam . . . desert: or who clip the hair on their temples.   m A name for Babylon.

L*

city an object of ridicule to all nations on earth.

7 The priests, the prophets, and all the people heard Jeremiah say this in 8 the LORD's house and, when he came to the end of what the LORD had commanded him to say to them, priests, prophets, and people seized him and 9 threatened him with death. 'Why', they demanded, 'have you prophesied in the LORD's name that this house shall become like Shiloh and this city waste and uninhabited?' The people all gathered against Jeremiah in the 10 LORD's house. The officers of Judah heard what was happening, and they went up from the royal palace to the LORD's house and took their places there at the entrance of the new gate. 11 Then the priests and the prophets said to the officers and all the people, 'Condemn this fellow to death. He has prophesied against this city: you have 12 heard it with your own ears.' Then Jeremiah said to the officers and the people, 'The LORD sent me to prophesy against this house and this city 13 all that you have heard. If you now mend your ways and your doings and obey the LORD your God, then he may relent and revoke the disaster with 14 which he has threatened you. But I am in your hands; do with me what- 15 ever you think right and proper. Only you may be certain that, if you put me to death, you and this city and all who live in it will be guilty of murdering an innocent man; for in very truth the LORD has sent me to you to say all this in your hearing.'

Jeremiah saved from death

16 Then the officers and all the people said to the priests and the prophets, 'This man ought not to be condemned to death, for he has spoken to us in the 17 name of the LORD our God.' Some of the elders of the land also stood up 18 and said to the assembled people, 'In the time of Hezekiah king of Judah, Micah of Moresheth was prophesying and said to all the people of Judah: "These are the words of the LORD of Hosts:

Zion shall become a ploughed field,
Jerusalem a heap of ruins,
and the temple-hill rough heath."

19 Did King Hezekiah and all Judah put him to death? Did not the king show reverence for the LORD and seek to placate him? Then the LORD re-

lented and revoked the disaster with which he had threatened them. Are we to bring disaster on ourselves?'

20 There was another man who prophesied in the name of the LORD, Uriah son of Shemaiah, from Kiriath-jearim. He also prophesied against this city and this land, just as Jere-21 miah had done. King Jehoiakim with all his officers and his bodyguard heard what he said and sought to put him to death. When Uriah heard of it, he was afraid and fled to Egypt. 22 King Jehoiakim sent Elnathan son 23 of Akbor with others to fetch Uriah from Egypt, and they brought him to the king. He had him put to death by the sword, and his body flung into the burial-place of the common peo-24 ple. But Ahikam son of Shaphan used his influence on Jeremiah's behalf to save him from death at the hands of the people.

The yoke of Babylon

27 At the beginning of the reign of Zedekiah son of Josiah, king of Judah, this word came from the LORD to 2 Jeremiah: These are the words of the LORD to me: Take the cords and bars of a yoke and put them on your neck. 3 Then send to the kings of Edom, Moab, Ammon, Tyre, and Sidon by the envoys who have come from them to Zedekiah king of Judah in Jerusalem, and give them the following 4 message for their masters: These are the words of the LORD of Hosts the God of Israel: Say to your masters: 5 I made the earth with my great strength and with outstretched arm, I made man and beast on the face of the earth, and I give it to whom I see 6 fit. I now give all these lands to my servant Nebuchadrezzar king of Babylon, and I give him also all the beasts of the field to serve him. All nations 7 shall serve him, and his son and his grandson, until the destined hour of his own land comes, and then mighty nations and great kings shall use him as they please. If any nation or king-8 dom will not serve Nebuchadrezzar king of Babylon or submit to his yoke, I will punish them with sword, famine, and pestilence, says the LORD, until I leave them entirely in his power. Therefore do not listen to your pro-9 phets, your diviners, your wise women, your soothsayers, and your sorcerers when they tell you not to serve the king of Babylon. They are prophesy-10 ing falsely to you; and so you will be

carried far from your own land, and I shall banish you and you will perish.

11 But if any nation submits to the yoke of the king of Babylon and serves him, I will leave them on their own soil, says the LORD; they shall cultivate it and live there.

Judah must submit to Babylon

12 I have said all this to Zedekiah king of Judah: If you will submit to the yoke of the king of Babylon and serve him and his people, then you shall 13 save your lives. Why should you and your people die by sword, famine, and pestilence, the fate with which the LORD has threatened any nation which does not serve the king of 14 Babylon? Do not listen to the prophets who tell you not to become subject to the king of Babylon; they 15 are prophesying falsely to you. I have not sent them, says the LORD; they are prophesying falsely in my name, and so I shall banish you and you will perish, you and these prophets who prophesy to you.

16 I said to the priests and all the people, These are the words of the LORD: Do not listen to your prophets who tell you that the vessels of the LORD's house will very soon be brought back from Babylon; they are only 17 prophesying falsely to you. Do not listen to them; serve the king of Babylon, and save your lives. Why 18 should this city become a ruin? If they are prophets, and if they have the word of the LORD, let them intercede with the LORD of Hosts to grant that the vessels still left in the LORD's house, in the royal palace, and in Jerusalem, may not be carried off to 19 Babylon. For these are the words of the LORD of Hosts concerning the pillars, the sea, the trolleys, and all the other vessels still left in this city, 20 which Nebuchadrezzar king of Babylon did not take when he deported Jeconiah son of Jehoiakim, king of Judah, from Jerusalem to Babylon, together with all the nobles of Judah 21 and Jerusalem. These indeed are the words of the LORD of Hosts the God of Israel concerning the vessels still left in the LORD's house, in the royal 22 palace, and in Jerusalem: They shall be taken to Babylon and stay there until I recall them, says the LORD; then I will bring them back and restore them to this place.

Hananiah's false prophecy

That same year,[n] in the fifth month of 28 the first[o] year of the reign of Zedekiah king of Judah, Hananiah son of Azzur, the prophet from Gibeon, said to me in the house of the LORD, in the presence of the priests and all the people, 'These are the words of 2 the LORD of Hosts the God of Israel: I have broken the yoke of the king of Babylon. Within two years I will 3 bring back to this place all the vessels of the LORD's house which Nebuchadrezzar king of Babylon took from here and carried off to Babylon. I will also 4 bring back to this place, says the LORD, Jeconiah son of Jehoiakim, king of Judah, and all the exiles of Judah who went to Babylon; for I will break the yoke of the king of Babylon.' The prophet Jeremiah said 5 to Hananiah the prophet in the presence of the priests and all the people standing in the LORD's house: 'May it be so! May the LORD indeed 6 do this: may he fulfil all that you have prophesied, by bringing back the vessels of the LORD's house and all the exiles from Babylon to this place! Only hear what I have to say to you 7 and to all the people: the prophets 8 who preceded you and me from earliest times have foretold war, famine, and pestilence for many lands and for great kingdoms. If a prophet foretells pros- 9 perity, when his words come true it will be known that the LORD has sent him.'

Then the prophet Hananiah took 10 the yoke from the neck of the prophet Jeremiah and broke it, saying before 11 all the people,['These are the words of the LORD: Thus will I break the yoke of Nebuchadrezzar king of Babylon; I will break it off the necks of all nations within two years';[p] and the prophet Jeremiah went his way. After Hananiah had broken the yoke 12 which had been on Jeremiah's neck, the word of the LORD came to Jeremiah: Go and say to Hananiah, These 13 are the words of the LORD: You have broken bars of wood; in their place you shall get bars of iron. For these 14 are the words of the LORD of Hosts the God of Israel: I have put a yoke of iron on the necks of all these nations, making them serve Nebuchadrezzar king of Babylon. They shall serve him, and I have given him even the beasts of the field. Then 15

---

n Prob. rdg.; Heb. adds at the beginning of the reign.   *o Prob. rdg.; Heb. fourth.*   *p within two years: or* while there are still two full years to run.

Jeremiah said to Hananiah, 'Listen, Hananiah. The LORD has not sent you, and you have led this nation to trust 16 in false prophecies. Therefore these are the words of the LORD: Beware, I will remove you from the face of the earth; you shall die within the year, because you have preached rebellion 17 against the LORD.' The prophet Hananiah died that same year, in the seventh month.

Letter to the exiles

29 Jeremiah sent a letter from Jerusalem to the remaining elders among the exiles, to the priests and prophets, and to all the people whom Nebuchadrezzar had deported from Jeru- 2 salem to Babylon, after King Jeconiah had left Jerusalem with the queen mother and the eunuchs, the officers of Judah and Jerusalem, the crafts- 3 men and the smiths.*q* The prophet entrusted the letter to Elasah son of Shaphan and Gemariah son of Hilkiah, whom Zedekiah king of Judah had sent to Babylon to King Nebuchad- 4 rezzar. This is what he wrote: These are the words of the LORD of Hosts the God of Israel: To all the exiles whom I have carried off from Jeru- 5 salem to Babylon: Build houses and live in them; plant gardens and eat 6 their produce. Marry wives and beget sons and daughters; take wives for your sons and give your daughters to husbands, so that they may bear sons and daughters and you may increase 7 there and not dwindle away. Seek the welfare of any city to which I have carried you off, and pray to the LORD for it; on its welfare your welfare will 8 depend. For these are the words of the LORD of Hosts the God of Israel: Do not be deceived by the prophets or the diviners among you, and do not listen to the wise women whom you 9 set to dream dreams. They prophesy falsely to you in my name; I did not send them. This is the very word of the LORD.

10   These are the words of the LORD: When a full seventy years has passed over Babylon, I will take up your cause and fulfil the promise of good things I made you, by bringing you 11 back to this place. I alone know my purpose for you, says the LORD: prosperity and not misfortune, and a long 12 line of children after you. If you invoke me and pray to me, I will listen to 13 you: when you seek me, you shall find me; if you search with all your heart,

I will let you find me, says the LORD. 14 I will restore your fortunes and gather you again from all the nations and all the places to which I have banished you, says the LORD, and bring you back to the place from which I have carried you into exile.

You say that the LORD has raised 15 up prophets for you in Babylon. These are the words of the LORD con- 16 cerning the king who sits on the throne of David and all the people who live in this city, your fellow-countrymen who have not gone into exile with you. These are the words of the LORD 17 of Hosts: I bring upon them sword, famine, and pestilence, and make them like rotten figs, too bad to be eaten. I 18 pursue them with sword, famine, and pestilence, and make them repugnant to all the kingdoms of the earth, an object of execration and horror, of derision and reproach, among all the nations to which I have banished them. Just as they did not listen to 19 my words, says the LORD, when I took pains to send them my servants the prophets, so you did not listen, says the LORD. But now, you exiles whom 20 I have sent from Jerusalem to Babylon, listen to the words of the LORD. These are the words of the LORD of 21 Hosts the God of Israel concerning Ahab son of Kolaiah and Zedekiah son of Maaseiah, who prophesy falsely to you in my name. I will hand them over to Nebuchadrezzar king of Babylon, and he will put them to death before your eyes. Their names shall 22 be used by all the exiles of Judah in Babylon when they curse a man; they shall say, May the LORD treat you like Zedekiah and Ahab, whom the king of Babylon roasted in the fire! For their conduct in Israel was an 23 outrage: they committed adultery with other men's wives, and without my authority prophesied in my name, and what they prophesied was false. I know; I can testify. This is the very word of the LORD.

Reaction to Jeremiah's letter

To Shemaiah the Nehelamite.*r* These 24 25 are the words of the LORD of Hosts the God of Israel: You have sent a letter in your own name to Zephaniah son of Maaseiah the priest, in which you say: 'The LORD has appointed 26 you to be priest in place of Jehoiada the priest, and it is your duty, as officer in charge of the LORD's house, to put every madman who sets up as

q the smiths: or the harem.   r Prob. rdg.; Heb. adds you shall say, saying.

a prophet into the stocks and the
27 pillory. Why, then, have you not
reprimanded Jeremiah of Anathoth,
who poses as a prophet before you?
28 On the strength of this he has sent to
us in Babylon and said, "Your exile
will be long; build houses and live in
them, plant gardens and eat their
29 produce."' Zephaniah the priest read
this letter to Jeremiah the prophet,
30 and the word of the LORD came to
31 Jeremiah: Send and tell all the exiles
that these are the words of the LORD
concerning Shemaiah the Nehelamite:
Because Shemaiah has prophesied to
you, though I did not send him, and
has led you to trust in false prophecies,
32 these are now the words of the LORD:
I will punish Shemaiah and his children. He shall have no one to take
his place in this nation and enjoy the
prosperity which I will bestow on my
people, says the LORD, because he has
preached rebellion against me.

Deliverance and restoration

30 The word which came to Jeremiah
2 from the LORD. These are the words
of the LORD the God of Israel: Write
in a book all that I have said to you,
3 for this is the very word of the LORD:
The time is coming when I will restore the fortunes of my people Israel
and Judah, says the LORD, and bring
them back to the land which I gave
to their forefathers; and it shall be
their possession.
4   This is what the LORD has said to
5 Israel and Judah. These are the words
of the LORD:

You shall hear a cry of terror, of fear
without relief.
6 Ask and see: can a man bear a child?
Why then do I see every man
gripping his sides like a woman in
labour,
every face changed, all turned pale?
7   Awful is that day:
when has there been its like?
A time of anguish for Jacob,
yet he shall come through it safely.

8   In that day, says the LORD of Hosts,
I will break their yoke off their necks
and snap their cords; foreigners shall
no longer use them as they please;
9 they shall serve the LORD their God
and David their king, whom I will
raise up for them.

10 And you, Jacob my servant, have no
fear;
despair not, O Israel, says the LORD.

---

s *Prob. rdg.; Heb. adds* one judging your case.
injury. Your sore cannot be healed.

For I will bring you back safe from
afar
and your offspring from the land
where they are captives;
and Jacob shall be at rest once more,
prosperous and unafraid.
For I am with you and will save you, 11
says the LORD.
I will make an end of all the nations
amongst whom I have scattered
you,
but I will not make an end of you;
though I punish you as you deserve,
I will not sweep you clean away.

For these are the words of the LORD 12
to Zion:

Your injury is past healing,
cruel was the blow you suffered.
There can be no^s remedy for your 13
sore,
the new skin cannot grow.
All your lovers have forgotten you; 14
they look for you no longer.
I have struck you down
as an enemy strikes, and punished
you cruelly;
for your wickedness is great and your
sins are many.
Why complain of your injury,   15
that your sore cannot be healed?^{t}
I have done this to you,
because your wickedness is great and
your sins are many.

Yet all who devoured you shall them- 16
selves be devoured,
all your oppressors shall go into
captivity.
Those who plunder you shall be
plundered,
and those who despoil you I will
give up to be spoiled.
I will cause the new skin to grow   17
and heal your wounds, says the
LORD,
although men call you the Outcast,
Zion, nobody's friend.

These are the words of the LORD: 18

Watch; I will restore the fortunes of
Jacob's clans
and show my love for all his dwellings.
Every city shall be rebuilt on its
mound of ruins,
every mansion shall have its familiar household.
From them praise shall be heard   19
and sounds of merrymaking.
I will increase them, they shall not
diminish,

---

t *Why . . . healed?: or* Cry not for help in your

I will raise them to honour, they shall
no longer be despised.
20   Their sons shall be what they once
were,
and their community shall be established in my sight.
I will punish all their oppressors;
21   a ruler shall appear, one of themselves,
a governor shall arise from their
own number.
I will myself bring him[u] near and
so he[v] shall approach me;
for no one ventures of himself to
approach me,
says the LORD.
22   So you shall be my people,
and I will be your God.
23 See what a scorching wind has gone
out from the LORD,
a sweeping whirlwind.
It whirls round the heads of the
wicked;
24   the LORD's anger is not to be turned
aside,
till he has finished and achieved his
heart's desire.
In days to come you will understand.

The LORD's love for Israel

31 At that time, says the LORD, I will
become God of all the families of
Israel, and they shall become my peo-
2 ple. These are the words of the LORD:

A people that survived the sword
found favour in the wilderness;
Israel journeyed to find rest;
3   long ago[w] the LORD appeared to
them:
I have dearly loved you from of old,
and still I maintain my unfailing care
for you.
4 I will build you up again, O virgin
Israel,
and you shall be rebuilt.
Again you shall adorn yourself with
jingles,
and go forth with the merry throng
of dancers.
5 Again you shall plant vineyards on
the hills of Samaria,
vineyards which those who planted
them defiled;
6 for a day will come when the watchmen on Ephraim's hills cry out,
Come, let us go up to Zion, to the
LORD our God.

Israel's home-coming

7 For these are the words of the LORD:
Break into shouts of joy for Jacob's
sake,

lead the nations, crying loud and
clear,
sing out your praises and say,
The LORD has saved his people,
and preserved a remnant of Israel.
See how I bring them from the land 8
of the north;
I will gather them from the ends of
the earth,
their blind and lame among them,
women with child and women in
labour,
a great company.
They come home, weeping as they 9
come,
but I will comfort them and be
their escort.
I will lead them to flowing streams;
they shall not stumble, their path will
be so smooth.
For I have become a father to
Israel,
and Ephraim is my eldest son.

Listen to the word of the LORD, you 10
nations,
announce it, make it known to coasts
and islands far away:
He who scattered Israel shall gather
them again
and watch over them as a shepherd
watches his flock.
For the LORD has ransomed Jacob 11
and redeemed him from a foe too
strong for him.
They shall come with shouts of joy 12
to Zion's height,
shining with happiness at the
bounty of the LORD,
the corn, the new wine, and the oil,
the young of flock and herd.
They shall become like a watered
garden
and they shall never want again.
Then shall the girl show her joy in the 13
dance,
young men and old shall rejoice;
I will turn their mourning into gladness,
I will relent and give them joy to outdo their sorrow.
I will satisfy the priests with the fat 14
of the land
and fill my people with my bounty.
This is the very word of the LORD.

Israel's repentance

These are the words of the LORD: 15

Hark, lamentation is heard in Ramah,
and bitter weeping,
Rachel weeping for her sons.
She refuses to be comforted: they
are no more.

---

u Or them.   v Or they.

w long ago: or from afar.

16 These are the words of the LORD:

Cease your loud weeping,
shed no more tears;
for there shall be a reward for your
toil,
they shall return from the land of
the enemy.

17 You shall leave descendants after
you;[x]
your sons shall return to their own
land.

18 I listened; Ephraim was rocking in
his grief:
'Thou hast trained me to the yoke like
an unbroken calf,
and now I am trained;
restore me, let me return,
for thou, LORD, art my God.

19 Though I broke loose I have repented:
now that I am tamed I beat my
breast;
in shame and remorse
I reproach myself for the sins of my
youth.'

20 Is Ephraim still my dear son,
a child in whom I delight?
As often as I turn my back on him
I still remember him;
and so my heart yearns for him,
I am filled with tenderness towards
him.
This is the very word of the LORD.

21 Build cairns to mark your way,
set up sign-posts;
make sure of the road,
the path which you will tread.
Come back, virgin Israel,
come back to your cities.

22 How long will you twist and turn, my
wayward child?
For the LORD has created a new thing
in the earth:
a woman turned into a man.

When Judah's fortunes are restored

23 These are the words of the LORD of
Hosts the God of Israel: Once more
shall these words be heard in the land
of Judah and in her cities, when I
restore their fortunes:

The LORD bless you,
the LORD, your true goal,[y] your
holy mountain.

24 Ploughmen and shepherds who wander with their flocks
shall live together there.[z]

25 For I have given deep draughts to
the thirsty,
and satisfied those who were faint
with hunger.

Thereupon I woke and looked about 26
me, and my dream[a] had been pleasant.

The time is coming, says the LORD, 27
when I will sow Israel and Judah with
the seed of man and the seed of cattle.
As I watched over them with intent to 28
pull down and to uproot, to demolish
and destroy and harm, so now will I
watch over them to build and to plant.
This is the very word of the LORD.

In those days it shall no longer be 29
said,

'The fathers have eaten sour grapes
and the children's teeth are set on
edge';

for a man shall die for his own wrong- 30
doing; the man who eats sour grapes
shall have his own teeth set on edge.

A new covenant

The time is coming, says the LORD, 31
when I will make a new covenant with
Israel and Judah. It will not be like 32
the covenant I made with their forefathers when I took them by the
hand and led them out of Egypt.
Although they broke my covenant,
I was patient with them, says the
LORD. But this is the covenant which 33
I will make with Israel after those
days, says the LORD; I will set my
law within them and write it on their
hearts; I will become their God and
they shall become my people. No 34
longer need they teach one another
to know the LORD; all of them, high
and low alike, shall know me, says the
LORD, for I will forgive their wrongdoing and remember their sin no more.

These are the words of the LORD, 35
who gave the sun for a light by day
and the moon and stars for a light
by night, who cleft the sea and its
waves roared; the LORD of Hosts is
his name:

If this fixed order could vanish out of 36
my sight,
says the LORD,
then the race of Israel too could cease
for evermore
to be a nation in my sight.

These are the words of the LORD: If 37
any man could measure the heaven
above or fathom the depths of the
earth beneath, then I could spurn the
whole race of Israel because of all they
have done. This is the very word of
the LORD.

The time is coming, says the LORD, 38
when the city shall be rebuilt in the

x You shall . . . you: or There shall be hope for your posterity.   y the LORD . . . goal: or O
home of righteousness.   z Prob. rdg.; Heb. adds Judah and all his cities.   a Or sleep.

LORD's honour from the Tower of
39 Hananel to the Corner Gate. The
measuring line shall then be laid
straight out over the hill of Gareb
40 and round Goath.[b] All the valley and
every field as far as the gorge of the
Kidron to the corner by the Horse
Gate eastwards shall be holy to the
LORD. It shall never again be pulled
down or demolished.

Jeremiah imprisoned

32 The word which came to Jeremiah
from the LORD in the tenth year of
Zedekiah king of Judah (the eigh-
2 teenth year of Nebuchadrezzar). At
that time the forces of the Babylonian king were besieging Jerusalem, and
the prophet Jeremiah was imprisoned
in the court of the guard-house at-
3 tached to the royal palace. Zedekiah
king of Judah had imprisoned him
after demanding what he meant by
this prophecy: 'These are the words
of the LORD: I will deliver this city
into the hands of the king of Babylon,
4 and he shall take it. Zedekiah king
of Judah will not escape from the
Chaldaeans but will be surrendered to
the king of Babylon; he will speak
with him face to face and see him with
5 his own eyes. Zedekiah will be taken
to Babylon and will remain there until I turn my thoughts to him, says
the LORD. However much you fight
against the Chaldaeans you will have
no success.'

Jeremiah and the field

6 Jeremiah said, The word of the LORD
7 came to me: Hanamel son of your
uncle Shallum is coming to see you
and will say, 'Buy my field at Anathoth; you have the right of redemp-
8 tion, as next of kin, to buy it.' As the
LORD had foretold, my cousin Hanamel came to the court of the guard-
house and said, 'Buy my field at
Anathoth in Benjamin. You have
the right of redemption and possession as next of kin; buy it.' I knew
9 that this was the LORD's message; so I
bought the field at Anathoth from my
cousin Hanamel and weighed out the
10 price, seventeen shekels of silver. I
signed and sealed the deed and had it
witnessed; then I weighed out the
11 money on the scales. I took my copies
of the deed of purchase, both the
12 sealed and the unsealed, and gave
them to Baruch son of Neriah, son of
Mahseiah, in the presence of Hanamel
my cousin, of the witnesses whose

names were on the deed of purchase,
and of the Judaeans sitting in the
court of the guard-house. In the 13
presence of them all I gave my instructions to Baruch: These are the 14
words of the LORD of Hosts the God
of Israel: Take these copies of the
deed of purchase, the sealed and the
unsealed, and deposit them in an
earthenware jar so that they may be
preserved for a long time. For these 15
are the words of the LORD of Hosts
the God of Israel: The time will come
when houses, fields, and vineyards
will again be bought and sold in this
land. After I had given the deed of 16
purchase to Baruch son of Neriah, I
prayed to the LORD: O Lord GOD, thou 17
hast made the heavens and the earth
by thy great strength and with thy
outstretched arm; nothing is impossible for thee. Thou keepest faith with 18
thousands and thou dost requite the
sins of fathers on to the heads of their
sons. O great and mighty God whose
name is the LORD of Hosts, great are 19
thy purposes and mighty thy actions.
Thine eyes watch all the ways of men,
and thou rewardest each according to
his ways and as his deeds deserve.
Thou didst work signs and portents 20
in Egypt and hast continued them to
this day, both in Israel and amongst
all men, and hast won for thyself a
name that lives on to this day. Thou 21
didst bring thy people Israel out of
Egypt with signs and portents, with
a strong hand and an outstretched
arm, and with terrible power. Thou 22
didst give them this land which thou
didst promise with an oath to their
forefathers, a land flowing with milk
and honey. They came and took pos- 23
session of it, but they did not obey
thee or follow thy law, they disobeyed
all thy commands; and so thou hast
brought this disaster upon them.
Look at the siege-ramps, the men who 24
are advancing to take the city, and
the city given over to its assailants
from Chaldaea, the victim of sword,
famine, and pestilence. The word thou
hast spoken is fulfilled and thou dost
see it. And yet thou hast bidden me 25
buy the field, O Lord GOD, and have
the deed witnessed, even though the
city is given to the Chaldaeans.

The LORD's plan for Judah

These are the words of the LORD to 26
Jeremiah: I am the LORD, the God of 27
all flesh; is anything impossible for
me? Therefore these are the words of 28

b Or Goah.

the LORD: I will deliver this city into the hands of the Chaldaeans and of Nebuchadrezzar king of Babylon, and 9 he shall take it. The Chaldaeans who are fighting against this city will enter it, set it on fire and burn it down, with the houses on whose roofs sacrifices have been burnt to Baal and drink-offerings poured out to other gods, by which I was provoked to anger.

30 From their earliest days Israel and Judah have been doing what is wrong in my eyes, provoking me to anger by 31 their actions, says the LORD. For this city has so roused my anger and my fury, from the time it was built down to this day, that I would rid myself 32 of it. Israel and Judah, their kings, officers, priests, prophets, and every-one living in Jerusalem and Judah have provoked me to anger by their 33 wrongdoing. They have turned their backs on me and averted their faces; though I took pains to teach them, they would not hear or learn their 34 lesson. They set up their loathsome idols in the house which bears my 35 name and so defiled it. They built shrines to Baal in the Valley of Ben-hinnom, to surrender their sons and daughters to Molech. It was no com-mand of mine, nor did it ever enter my thought to do this abominable thing and lead Judah into sin.

36 Now, therefore, these are the words of the LORD the God of Israel to this city of which you say, 'It is being given over to the king of Babylon, with sword, famine, and pestilence': 37 I will gather them from all the lands to which I banished them in my anger, rage, and fury, and I will bring them back to this place and let them dwell 38 there undisturbed. They shall become my people and I will become their 39 God. I will give them one heart and one way of life so that they shall fear me at all times, for their own good and the good of their children after 40 them. I will enter into an eternal cove-nant with them, to follow them un-failingly with my bounty; I will fill their hearts with fear of me, and so 41 they will not turn away from me. I will rejoice over them, rejoice to do them good, and faithfully with all my heart and soul I will plant them in 42 this land. For these are the words of the LORD: As I brought on this people such great disaster, so will I bring them all the prosperity which I now 43 promise them. Fields shall again be bought and sold in this land of which

you now say, 'It is desolate, without man or beast; it is given over to the Chaldaeans.' Fields shall be bought 44 and sold, deeds signed, sealed, and witnessed, in Benjamin, in the neigh-bourhood of Jerusalem, in the cities of Judah, of the hill-country, of the Shephelah, and of the Negeb; for I will restore their fortunes. This is the very word of the LORD.

Future blessings

The word of the LORD came to Jere- 33 miah a second time while he was still imprisoned in the court of the guard-house: These are the words of the 2 LORD who made the earth, who formed it and established it; the LORD is his name: If you call to me I will answer 3 you, and tell you great and mysterious things which you do not understand. These are the words of the LORD the 4 God of Israel concerning the houses in this city and the royal palace, which are to be razed to the ground, concerning siege-ramp and sword, and 5 attackers[c] who fill the houses with the corpses of those whom he struck down in his furious rage: I hid my face from this city because of their wicked ways, but now I will bring her healing; 6 I will heal and cure Judah and Israel, and will let my people see an age of peace and security. I will restore their 7 fortunes and build them again as once they were. I will cleanse them of 8 all the wickedness and sin that they have committed; I will forgive all the evil deeds they have done in rebellion against me. This city will win me a 9 name[d] and praise and glory before all the nations on earth, when they hear of all the blessings I bestow on her; and they shall be moved and filled with awe because of the blessings and the peace which I have brought upon her.

These are the words of the LORD: 10 You say of this place, 'It is in ruins, and neither man nor beast lives in the cities of Judah or in the streets of Jerusalem. It is all a waste, inhabited by neither man nor beast.' Yet in this place shall be heard once again the 11 sounds of joy and gladness, the voice of the bridegroom and the bride; here too shall be heard voices shouting, 'Praise the LORD of Hosts, for he is good, for his love endures for ever', as they offer praise and thanksgiving in the house of the LORD. For I will restore the fortunes of the land as

c *Prob. rdg.; Heb. adds* the Chaldaeans.　　　d *Prob. rdg.; Heb. adds* of joy.

once they were. This is the word of the LORD.

12 These are the words of the LORD of Hosts: In this place and in all its cities, now ruined and inhabited by neither man nor beast, there shall once more be a refuge where shepherds

13 may fold their flocks. In the cities of the hill-country, of the Shephelah, of the Negeb, in Benjamin, in the neighbourhood of Jerusalem and the cities of Judah, flocks will once more pass under the shepherd's hand as he counts them. This is the word of the LORD.

14 Wait, says the LORD, the days are coming when I will bestow on Israel and Judah all the blessings I have

15 promised them. In those days, at that time, I will make a righteous Branch of David spring up; he shall maintain

16 law and justice in the land. In those days Judah shall be kept safe and Jerusalem shall live undisturbed; and this shall be her name: The LORD is our Righteousness.

The covenant with David confirmed

17 For these are the words of the LORD: David will never lack a successor on

18 the throne of Israel, nor will the levitical priests lack a man who shall come before me continually to present whole-offerings, to burn grain-offerings and to make other offerings.

19 This word came from the LORD to

20 Jeremiah: These are the words of the LORD: If the law that I made for the day and the night could be annulled so that they fell out of their proper

21 order, then my covenant with my servant David could be annulled so that none of his line should sit upon his throne; so also could my covenant with the levitical priests who minister

22 to me. Like the innumerable host of heaven or the countless sands of the sea, I will increase the descendants of my servant David and the Levites who minister to me.

23 The word of the LORD came to

24 Jeremiah: Have you not observed how this people have said, 'It is the two families whom he chose that the LORD has spurned'? So others will despise my people and no longer

25 regard them as a nation. These are the words of the LORD: If I had not made my law for day and night nor established a fixed order in heaven

26 and earth, then I would spurn the descendants of Jacob and of my servant David, and would not take any of David's line to be rulers over the

descendants of Abraham, Isaac and Jacob. But now I will restore their fortunes and have compassion upon them.

The LORD's word to Zedekiah

The word which came to Jeremiah 34 from the LORD when Nebuchadrezzar king of Babylon and his army, with all his vassal kingdoms and nations, were fighting against Jerusalem and all her towns: These are the words of 2 the LORD the God of Israel: Go and say to Zedekiah king of Judah, These are the words of the LORD: I will give this city into the hands of the king of Babylon and he will burn it down. You shall not escape, you will be 3 captured and handed over to him. You will see him face to face, and he will speak to you in person; and you shall go to Babylon. But listen to the LORD's 4 word to you, Zedekiah king of Judah. This is his word: You shall not die by the sword; you will die a peaceful 5 death, and they will kindle fires in your honour like the fires kindled in former times for the kings your ancestors who preceded you. 'Alas, my lord!' they will say as they beat their breasts in mourning for you. This I have spoken. This is the very word of the LORD. The prophet Jere- 6 miah repeated all this to Zedekiah king of Judah in Jerusalem when the 7 army of the king of Babylon was attacking Jerusalem and the remaining cities of Judah, namely Lachish and Azekah. These were the only fortified cities left in Judah.

Israel goes back on the covenant

The word that came to Jeremiah from 8 the LORD after Zedekiah had made a covenant with all the people in Jerusalem to proclaim an act of freedom for the slaves. All who had 9 Hebrew slaves, male or female, were to set them free; they were not to keep their fellow Judaeans in servitude. All 10 the officers and people, having made this covenant to set free their slaves, both male and female, and not to keep them in servitude any longer, fulfilled its terms and let them go. Afterwards, 11 however, they changed their minds and forced back again into slavery the men and women whom they had freed. Then this word came from the 12 LORD to Jeremiah: These are the 13 words of the LORD the God of Israel: I made a covenant with your forefathers on the day that I brought them out of Egypt, out of the land of

14 slavery. These were its terms: 'Within seven years each of you shall set free any Hebrew who has sold himself to you as a slave and has served you for six years; you shall set him free.' Your forefathers did not listen to me or obey 15 me. You, on the contrary, recently proclaimed an act of freedom for the slaves and made a covenant in my presence, in the house that bears my name, and so have done what is right 16 in my eyes. But you too have profaned my name. You have all taken back the slaves you had set free and you have forced them, both male and 17 female, to be your slaves again. Therefore these are the words of the LORD: After you had proclaimed an act of freedom, a deliverance for your kinsmen and your neighbours, you did not obey me; so I will proclaim a deliverance for you, says the LORD, a deliverance over to sword, to pestilence, and to famine, and I will make you repugnant to all the kingdoms of the 18 earth. You have disregarded my covenant and have not fulfilled the terms to which you yourselves had agreed; so I will make you like the calf of the covenant when they cut it into two and passed between the pieces. 19 Those who passed between the pieces of the calf were the officers of Judah and Jerusalem, the eunuchs and priests 20 and all the people of the land. I will give them up to their enemies who seek their lives, and their bodies shall be food for birds of prey and wild 21 beasts. I will deliver Zedekiah king of Judah and his officers to their enemies who seek their lives and to the army of the king of Babylon, which 22 is now raising the siege. I will give the command, says the LORD, and will bring them back to this city. They shall attack it and take it and burn it down, and I will make the cities of Judah desolate and unpeopled.

Jeremiah and the Rechabites

35 The word which came to Jeremiah from the LORD in the days of Jehoia-2 kim son of Josiah, king of Judah: Go and speak to the Rechabites, bring them to one of the rooms in the house of the LORD and offer them 3 wine to drink. So I fetched Jaazaniah son of Jeremiah, son of Habaziniah, with his brothers and all his sons and all the family of the Rechabites. 4 I brought them into the house of the LORD to the room of the sons of Hanan son of Igdaliah, the man of God;

this adjoins the officers' room above that of Maaseiah son of Shallum, the keeper of the threshold. I set bowls 5 full of wine and drinking-cups before the Rechabites and invited them to drink wine; but they said, 'We will 6 not drink wine, for our forefather Jonadab son of Rechab laid this command on us: "You shall never drink wine, neither you nor your children. You shall not build houses or sow seed 7 or plant vineyards; you shall have none of these things. Instead, you shall remain tent-dwellers all your lives, so that you may live long in the land where you are sojourners." We 8 have honoured all the commands of our forefather Jonadab son of Rechab and have drunk no wine all our lives, neither we nor our wives, nor our sons, nor our daughters. We have not built 9 houses to live in, nor have we possessed vineyards or sown fields. We have 10 lived in tents, obeying and observing all the commands of our forefather Jonadab. But when Nebuchadrezzar 11 king of Babylon invaded the land we said, "Come, let us go to Jerusalem before the advancing Chaldaean and Aramaean armies." And we have stayed in Jerusalem.'

Then the word of the LORD came 12 to Jeremiah: These are the words of 13 the LORD of Hosts the God of Israel: Go and say to the men of Judah and the inhabitants of Jerusalem, You must accept correction and obey my words, says the LORD. The command 14 of Jonadab son of Rechab to his descendants not to drink wine has been honoured; they have not drunk wine to this day, for they have obeyed their ancestor's command. But I have taken especial pains to warn you and yet you have not obeyed me. I sent 15 my servants the prophets especially to say to you, 'Turn back every one of you from his evil course, mend your ways and cease to follow other gods and worship them; then you shall remain on the land that I have given to you and to your forefathers.' Yet you did not obey or listen to me. The 16 sons of Jonadab son of Rechab have honoured their ancestor's command laid on them, but this people have not listened to me. Therefore, these are the 17 words of the LORD the God of Hosts, the God of Israel: Because they did not listen when I spoke to them, nor answer when I called them, I will bring upon Judah and upon all the inhabitants of Jerusalem the disaster with which I threatened them. To the 18

Rechabites Jeremiah said, These are the words of the LORD of Hosts the God of Israel: Because you have kept the command of Jonadab your ancestor and obeyed all his instructions and carried out all that he told you to 19 do, therefore these are the words of the LORD of Hosts the God of Israel: Jonadab son of Rechab shall not want a descendant to stand before me for all time.

Jeremiah dictates his message

36 In the fourth year of Jehoiakim son of Josiah, king of Judah, this word came to Jeremiah from the LORD: 2 Take a scroll and write on it every word that I have spoken to you about Jerusalem and Judah and all the nations, from the day that I first spoke to you in the reign of Josiah 3 down to the present day. Perhaps the house of Judah will be warned of the calamity that I am planning to bring on them, and every man will abandon his evil course; then I will forgive 4 their wrongdoing and their sin. So Jeremiah called Baruch son of Neriah, and he wrote on the scroll at Jeremiah's dictation all the words which 5 the LORD had spoken to him. He gave Baruch this instruction: 'I am prevented from going to the LORD's 6 house. You must go there in my place on a fast-day and read the words of the LORD in the hearing of the people from the scroll you have written at my dictation. You shall read them in the hearing of all the men of Judah who 7 come in from their cities. Then perhaps they will present a petition to the LORD and every man will abandon his evil course; for the LORD has spoken against this people in great anger and 8 wrath.' Baruch son of Neriah did all that the prophet Jeremiah had told him to do, and read the words of the LORD in the LORD's house out of the book.

The king burns the scroll

9 In the ninth month of the fifth year of the reign of Jehoiakim son of Josiah, king of Judah, all the people in Jerusalem and all who came there from the cities of Judah proclaimed 10 a fast before the LORD. Then Baruch read Jeremiah's words in the house of the LORD out of the book in the hearing of all the people; he read them from the room of Gemariah son of the adjutant-general Shaphan in the upper

court at the entrance to the new gate of the LORD's house. Micaiah son of 11 Gemariah, son of Shaphan, heard all the words of the LORD out of the book and went down to the palace, to 12 the adjutant-general's room where all the officers were gathered—Elishama the adjutant-general, Delaiah son of Shemaiah, Elnathan son of Akbor, Gemariah son of Shaphan, Zedekiah son of Hananiah and all the other officers. There Micaiah repeated all 13 the words he had heard when Baruch read out of the book in the people's hearing. Then the officers sent Jehudi 14 son of Nethaniah, son of Shelemiah, son of Cushi, to Baruch with this message: 'Come here and bring the scroll from which you read in the people's hearing.' So Baruch son of Neriah brought the scroll to them, and they 15 said, 'Sit down and[e] read it to us.' When they heard what he read, they 16 turned to each other trembling and said, 'We must report this to the king.' They asked Baruch to tell them how 17 he had come to write all this. He said 18 to them, 'Jeremiah dictated every word of it to me, and I wrote it down in ink in the book.' The officers said 19 to Baruch, 'You and Jeremiah must go into hiding so that no one may know where you are.' When they had 20 deposited the scroll in the room of Elishama the adjutant-general, they went to the court and reported everything to the king.

The king sent Jehudi to fetch the 21 scroll. When he had fetched it from the room of Elishama the adjutant-general, he read it to the king and to all the officers in attendance. It was 22 the ninth month of the year, and the king was sitting in his winter apartments with a fire burning in a brazier in front of him. When Jehudi had 23 read three or four columns of the scroll, the king cut them off with a penknife and threw them into the fire in the brazier. He went on doing so until the whole scroll had been thrown on the fire. Neither the king 24 nor any of his courtiers who heard these words showed any fear or rent their clothes; and though Elnathan, 25 Delaiah, and Gemariah begged the king not to burn the scroll, he would not listen to them. The king then 26 ordered Jerahmeel, a royal prince,[f] Seraiah son of Azriel, and Shelemiah son of Abdeel to fetch the scribe Baruch and the prophet Jeremiah; but the LORD had hidden them.

e Sit down and: or This time.   f a royal prince: or the king's deputy.

Another scroll is prepared

27 After the king had burnt the scroll with all that Baruch had written on it at Jeremiah's dictation, the word
28 of the LORD came to Jeremiah: Now take another scroll and write on it all the words that were on the first scroll which Jehoiakim king of Judah
29 burnt. You shall say to Jehoiakim king of Judah, These are the words of the LORD: You burnt this scroll and said, Why have you written here that the king of Babylon shall come and destroy this land and exterminate
30 both men and beasts? Therefore these are the words of the LORD about Jehoiakim king of Judah: He shall have no one to succeed him on the throne of David, and his dead body shall be exposed to scorching heat by
31 day and frost by night. I will punish him and also his offspring and his courtiers for their wickedness, and I will bring down on them and on the inhabitants of Jerusalem and on the men of Judah all the calamities with which I threatened them, and to
32 which they turned a deaf ear. Then Jeremiah took another scroll and gave it to the scribe Baruch son of Neriah, who wrote on it at Jeremiah's dictation all the words of the book which Jehoiakim king of Judah had burnt; and much else was added to the same effect.

Jerusalem's fate foretold

37 King Zedekiah son of Josiah was set on the throne of Judah by Nebuchadrezzar king of Babylon, in succession
2 to Coniah son of Jehoiakim. Neither he nor his courtiers nor the people of the land listened to the words which the LORD spoke through the prophet Jeremiah.
3 King Zedekiah sent Jehucal son of Shelemiah and the priest Zephaniah son of Maaseiah to the prophet Jeremiah to say to him, 'Pray for us to
4 the LORD our God.' At the time Jeremiah was free to come and go among the people; he had not yet been
5 thrown into prison. Meanwhile, Pharaoh's army had marched out of Egypt, and when the Chaldaeans who were besieging Jerusalem heard of it
6 they raised the siege. Then this word came from the LORD to the prophet
7 Jeremiah: These are the words of the LORD the God of Israel: Say to the king of Judah who sent you to consult me, Pharaoh's army which marched out to help you is on its way back to Egypt, its own land, and the Chal- 8 daeans will return to the attack. They will capture this city and burn it to the ground. These are the words of the 9 LORD: Do not deceive yourselves, do not imagine that the Chaldaeans will go away and leave you alone. They will not go; for even if you defeated 10 the whole Chaldaean force with which you are now fighting, and only the wounded were left lying in their tents, they would rise and burn down the city.

Jeremiah imprisoned

When the Chaldaean army had raised 11 the siege of Jerusalem because of the advance of Pharaoh's army, Jeremiah 12 was on the point of leaving Jerusalem to go into Benjamite territory and take possession of his patrimony in the presence of the people there. Iri- 13 jah son of Shelemiah, son of Hananiah, the officer of the guard, was in the Benjamin Gate when Jeremiah reached it, and he arrested the prophet, accusing him of going over to the Chaldaeans. 'It is a lie,' said Jere- 14 miah; 'I am not going over to the Chaldaeans.' Irijah would not listen to him but arrested him and brought him before the officers. The officers 15 were indignant with Jeremiah; they flogged him and imprisoned him in the house of Jonathan the scribe, which they had converted into a prison; for Jeremiah had been put 16 into a vaulted pit beneath the house, and here he remained for a long time.

King Zedekiah had Jeremiah brought 17 to him and consulted him privately in the palace, asking him if there was a word from the LORD. 'Indeed there is,' said Jeremiah; 'you shall fall into the hands of the king of Babylon.' Then Jeremiah said to King Zedekiah, 18 'What wrong have I done to you or your courtiers or this people? Why have you thrown me into prison? Where are your prophets who pro- 19 phesied that the king of Babylon would not attack you or your country? I pray you now, my lord king, 20 give me a hearing and let my petition be presented: do not send me back to the house of Jonathan the scribe, or I shall die there.' Then King 21 Zedekiah gave the order and Jeremiah was committed to the court of the guard-house and was granted a daily ration of one loaf from the Street of the Bakers, until the bread in the city was all gone. So Jeremiah remained in the court of the guard-house.

Ebed-melech rescues Jeremiah

38 Shephatiah son of Mattan, Gedaliah son of Pashhur, Jucal son of Shelemiah, and Pashhur son of Malchiah heard what Jeremiah was saying to 2 all the people: These are the words of the LORD: Whoever remains in this city shall die by sword, by famine, or by pestilence, but whoever goes out to surrender to the Chaldaeans shall survive; he shall survive, he shall take 3 home his life and nothing more. These are the words of the LORD: This city will fall into the hands of the king of Babylon's army, and they will cap- 4 ture it. Then the officers said to the king, 'The man must be put to death. By talking in this way he is discouraging the soldiers and the rest of the people left in the city. He is pursuing not the people's welfare but their ruin.' 5 King Zedekiah said, 'He is in your hands; the king is powerless against 6 you.' So they took Jeremiah and threw him into the pit,^{g} in the court of the guard-house, letting him down with ropes. There was no water in the pit, only mud, and Jeremiah sank 7-8 in the mud. Now Ebed-melech the Cushite, a eunuch, who was in the palace, heard that they had thrown Jeremiah into the pit and went to tell the king, who was seated in the Ben- 9 jamin Gate. 'Your majesty,' he said, 'these men have shown great wickedness in their treatment of the prophet Jeremiah. They have thrown him into the pit, and when there is no more bread in the city he will die of hunger 10 where he lies.' Thereupon the king told Ebed-melech the Cushite to take three men with him and hoist Jere- 11 miah out of the pit before he died. So Ebed-melech went to the palace with the men and took some tattered, cast-off clothes from the wardrobe^h and let them down with ropes to Jeremiah in 12 the pit. Ebed-melech the Cushite said to Jeremiah, 'Put these old clothes under your armpits to ease the ropes.' 13 Jeremiah did this, and they pulled him up out of the pit with the ropes; and he remained in the court of the guard-house.

Zedekiah's dilemma

14 King Zedekiah had the prophet Jeremiah brought to him by the third entrance to the LORD's house and said to him, 'I want to ask you some- 15 thing; hide nothing from me.' Jere-

miah answered, 'If I speak out, you will certainly put me to death; if I offer you any advice, you will not take it.' But King Zedekiah swore to 16 Jeremiah privately, 'By the life of the LORD who gave us our lives, I will not put you to death, nor will I hand you over to these men who are seeking to take your life.' Jeremiah said to 17 Zedekiah, 'These are the words of the LORD the God of Hosts, the God of Israel: If you go out and surrender to the officers of the king of Babylon, you shall live and this city shall not be burnt down; you and your family shall live. But if you do not surrender 18 to the officers of the king of Babylon, the city shall fall into the hands of the Chaldaeans, and they shall burn it down, and you will not escape them.' King Zedekiah said to Jere- 19 miah, 'I am afraid of the Judaeans who have gone over to the enemy. I fear the Chaldaeans will give me up to them and I shall be roughly handled.' Jeremiah answered, 'They will not 20 give you up. If you obey the LORD in everything I tell you, all will be well with you and you shall live. But if 21 you refuse to go out and surrender, this is what the LORD has shown me: all the women left in the king of 22 Judah's palace will be led out to the officers of the king of Babylon and they will say:

Your own friends have misled you
    and have been too strong for you;
they have let your feet sink in the mud
    and have turned away and left you.

All your women and children will be 23 led out to the Chaldaeans, and you will not escape; you will be seized by the king of Babylon and this city will be burnt down.' Zedekiah said 24 to Jeremiah, 'Let no one know about this, and you shall not be put to death. If the officers hear that I have 25 been speaking with you and they come to you and say, "Tell us what you said to the king and what he said to you; hide nothing from us, and we will not put you to death", then 26 answer, "I was presenting a petition to the king not to send me back to the house of Jonathan to die there."' The officers all came to Jeremiah and 27 questioned him, and he said to them just what the king had told him to say; so their talk came to an end and they were none the wiser. Jeremiah 28

---

g Prob. rdg.; Heb. adds Malchiah son (*or* deputy) of the king. *h the wardrobe: prob. rdg.; Heb.* underneath the treasury.

remained in the court of the guard-house till the day Jerusalem fell.

Jerusalem taken

1[i] In the tenth month of the ninth year of the reign of Zedekiah king of Judah, Nebuchadrezzar advanced with all his army against Jerusalem, 2 and they laid siege to it. In the fourth month of the eleventh year of Zedekiah, on the ninth day of the month, the city was thrown open. 3 All the officers of the king of Babylon came in and took their seats in the middle gate: Nergalsarezer of Simma-gir, Nebusarsekim[j] the chief eunuch,[k] Nergalsarezer the commander of the frontier troops,[l] and all the other 4 officers of the king of Babylon. When Zedekiah king of Judah saw them, he and all his armed escort left the city and fled by night by way of the king's garden through the gate called Be-tween the Two Walls. They escaped 5 towards the Arabah, but the Chal-daean army pursued them and over-took Zedekiah in the lowlands of Jericho. The king was seized and brought before Nebuchadrezzar king of Babylon at Riblah in the land of Hamath, and he pleaded his case 6 before him. The king of Babylon slew Zedekiah's sons before his eyes at Riblah; he also put to death the 7 nobles of Judah. Then Zedekiah's eyes were put out, and he was bound in fetters of bronze to be brought to 8 Babylon. The Chaldaeans burnt the royal palace and the house of the LORD and the houses[m] of the people, and pulled down the walls of Jeru-9 salem. Nebuzaradan captain of the bodyguard deported to Babylon the rest of the people left in the city, those who had deserted to him and 10 any remaining artisans.[n] At the same time the captain of the guard left behind the weakest class of the peo-ple, those who owned nothing at all, and made them vine-dressers and labourers.

Jeremiah and Ebed-melech kept safe

11 Nebuchadrezzar king of Babylon sent orders about Jeremiah to Nebuzar-12 adan captain of the guard. 'Take him,' he said; 'take special care of him, and do him no harm of any kind, but 13 do for him whatever he says.' So

Nebuzaradan captain of the guard sent Nebushazban the chief eunuch, Nergalsarezer the commander of the frontier troops, and all the chief officers of the king of Babylon, and 14 they fetched Jeremiah from the court of the guard-house and handed him over to Gedaliah son of Ahikam, son of Shaphan, to take him out to the Residence. So he stayed with his own people.

The word of the LORD had come 15 to Jeremiah while he was under arrest in the court of the guard-house: Go 16 and say to Ebed-melech the Cushite, These are the words of the LORD of Hosts the God of Israel: I will make good the words I have spoken against this city, foretelling ruin and not prosperity, and when that day comes you will be there to see it. But I will 17 preserve you on that day, says the LORD, and you shall not be handed over to the men you fear. I will keep 18 you safe and you shall not fall a victim to the sword; because you trusted in me you shall escape, you shall take home your life and nothing more. This is the very word of the LORD.

Jeremiah stays in Jerusalem

The word which came from the LORD 40 concerning Jeremiah: Nebuzaradan captain of the guard had taken him in chains to Ramah along with the other exiles from Jerusalem and Judah who were being deported to Babylon; and there he set him free, and took it 2 upon himself to say to Jeremiah, 'The LORD your God threatened this place with disaster, and has duly carried 3 out his threat that this should happen to all of you because you have sinned against the LORD and not obeyed him. But as for you, Jeremiah, today I 4 remove the fetters from your wrists. Come with me to Babylon if you wish, and I will take special care of you; but if you prefer not to come, well and good. The whole country lies before you; go wherever you think best.' Jeremiah had not yet answered 5 when Nebuzaradan went on,[o] 'Go back to Gedaliah son of Ahikam, son of Shaphan, whom the king of Babylon has appointed governor of the cities of Judah, and stay with him openly; or else go wherever you choose.' Then the captain of the guard granted him

---

i Verses 1–10: cp. 52. 4–16 and 2 Kgs. 25. 1–12. 13).   k the chief eunuch: or Rab-saris. the LORD and the houses: prob. rdg.; Heb. om. were left.   o Jeremiah . . . went on: prob. rdg.; Heb. unintelligible in context.

j Probably a different form of Nebushazban (verse l the commander . . . troops: or Rab-mag.   m of n artisans: prob. rdg., cp. 52. 15; Heb. people who

an allowance of food, and gave him a present, and so took leave of him. 6 Jeremiah then came to Gedaliah son of Ahikam at Mizpah and stayed with him among the people left in the land.

Gedaliah made governor

7 When all the captains of the armed bands in the country-side and their men heard that the king of Babylon had appointed Gedaliah son of Ahikam governor of the land, and had put him in charge of the weakest class of the population, men, women, and children, who had not been deported to 8 Babylon, they came to him at Mizpah; Ishmael son of Nethaniah came, and Johanan and Jonathan sons of Kareah, Seraiah son of Tanhumeth, the sons of Ephai[p] from Netophah, and Jezaniah of Beth-maacah, with their 9 men. Gedaliah son of Ahikam, son of Shaphan, gave them all this assurance: 'Have no fear of the Chaldaean officers. Settle down in the land and serve the king of Babylon; and then 10 all will be well with you. I am to stay in Mizpah and attend upon the Chaldaeans whenever they come, and you are to gather in the summer-fruits, wine, and oil, store them in jars, and settle in the towns you 11 have taken over.' The Judaeans also, in Moab, Ammon, Edom and other countries, heard that the king of Babylon had left a remnant in Judah and that he had set over them Gedaliah son of Ahikam, son of Shaphan. 12 The Judaeans, therefore, from all the places where they were scattered, came back to Judah and presented themselves before Gedaliah at Mizpah; and they gathered in a considerable store of fruit and wine.

13 Johanan son of Kareah and all the captains of the armed bands from the country-side came to Gedaliah at 14 Mizpah and said to him, 'Do you know that Baalis king of the Ammonites has sent Ishmael son of Nethaniah to assassinate you?' But Gedaliah son 15 of Ahikam did not believe them. Then Johanan son of Kareah said in private to Gedaliah, 'Let me go, unknown to anyone else, and kill Ishmael son of Nethaniah. Why allow him to assassinate you, and so let all the Judaeans who have rallied round you be scattered and the remnant of Judah lost?' 16 Gedaliah son of Ahikam answered him, 'Do no such thing. Your story about Ishmael is a lie.'

Gedaliah assassinated

In the seventh month Ishmael son of 4 Nethaniah, son of Elishama, who was a member of the royal house, came with ten men to Gedaliah son of Ahikam at Mizpah. While they were at table with him there, Ishmael son 2 of Nethaniah and the ten men with him rose to their feet and assassinated Gedaliah son of Ahikam, son of Shaphan, whom the king of Babylon had appointed governor of the land. They also murdered the Judaeans 3 with him in Mizpah and the Chaldaeans who happened to be there. The second day after the murder of 4 Gedaliah, while it was not yet common knowledge, there came eighty 5 men from Shechem, Shiloh, and Samaria. They had shaved off their beards, their clothes were rent and their bodies gashed, and they were carrying grain-offerings and frankincense to take to the house of the LORD. Ishmael son of Nethaniah came out 6 weeping from Mizpah to meet them and, when he met them, he said, 'Come to Gedaliah son of Ahikam.' But as soon as they reached the centre 7 of the town, Ishmael son of Nethaniah and his men murdered them and threw their bodies into a pit, all 8 except ten of them who said to Ishmael, 'Do not kill us, for we have a secret hoard in the country, wheat and barley, oil and honey.' So he held his hand and did not kill them with the others. The pit into which he threw 9 the bodies of those whose death he had caused by using Gedaliah's name was the pit which King Asa had made when threatened by Baasha king of Israel; and the dead bodies filled it. He rounded up the rest of the people 10 in Mizpah, that is the king's daughters and all who remained in Mizpah when Nebuzaradan captain of the guard appointed Gedaliah son of Ahikam governor; and with these he set out to cross over into Ammon. When 11 Johanan son of Kareah and all the captains of the armed bands heard of the crimes committed by Ishmael son of Nethaniah, they took all the men 12 they had and went to attack him. They found him by the great pool in Gibeon. The people with Ishmael 13 were glad when they saw Johanan son of Kareah and the captains of the armed bands with him; and all whom 14 Ishmael had taken prisoner at Mizpah turned and joined Johanan son of

[p] Or Ophai.

15 Kareah. But Ishmael son of Nethaniah escaped from Johanan with eight men, and they made their way to the Ammonites.

Johanan's request to Jeremiah

16 Johanan son of Kareah and all the captains of the armed bands took from Mizpah the survivors whom he had rescued from Ishmael son of Nethaniah after the murder of Gedaliah son of Ahikam—men, armed and unarmed, women, children, and eunuchs, whom he had brought back 17 from Gibeon. They started out and broke their journey at Kimham's holding near Bethlehem, on their way 18 into Egypt to escape the Chaldaeans. They were afraid because Ishmael son of Nethaniah had assassinated Gedaliah son of Ahikam, whom the king of Babylon had appointed governor of the country.

42 All the captains of the armed bands, including Johanan son of Kareah and Azariah son of Hoshaiah, together with the people, high and low, came 2 to the prophet Jeremiah and said to him, 'May our petition be acceptable to you: Pray to the LORD your God on our behalf and on behalf of this remnant; for, as you see for yourself, only a few of us remain out of many. 3 Pray that the LORD your God may tell us which way we ought to go and 4 what we ought to do.' Then the prophet Jeremiah said to them, 'I have heard your request and will pray to the LORD your God as you desire, and whatever answer the LORD gives I will tell you; I will keep 5 nothing back.' They said to Jeremiah, 'May the LORD be a true and faithful witness against us if we do not keep our oath! We swear that we will do whatever the LORD your God sends 6 you to tell us. Whether we like it or not, we will obey the LORD our God to whom we send you, in order that it may be well with us; we will obey the LORD our God.'

Warning against settling in Egypt

7 Within ten days the word of the LORD 8 came to Jeremiah; so he summoned Johanan son of Kareah, all the captains of the armed bands with him, and all the people, both high and low. 9 He said to them, These are the words of the LORD the God of Israel, to whom you sent me to present your 10 petition: If you will stay in this land,

then I will build you up and not pull you down, I will plant you and not uproot you; I grieve for the disaster which I have brought upon you. Do 11 not be afraid of the king of Babylon whom you now fear. Do not be afraid of him, says the LORD; for I am with you, to save you and deliver you from his power. I will show 12 you compassion, and he too will have compassion on you; he will let you stay on your own soil. But it may 13 be that you will disobey the LORD your God and say, 'We will not stay in this land. No, we will go to Egypt, 14 where we shall see no sign of war, never hear the sound of the trumpet, and not starve for want of bread; and there we will live.' Then hear 15 the word of the LORD, you remnant of Judah. These are the words of the LORD of Hosts the God of Israel: If you are bent on going to Egypt, if you do settle there, then the sword 16 you fear will overtake you in Egypt, and the famine you dread will still be with you, even in Egypt, and there you will die. All the men who are bent 17 on going to Egypt and settling there will die by sword, by famine, or by pestilence; not one shall escape or survive the calamity which I will bring upon them. These are the words 18 of the LORD of Hosts the God of Israel: As my anger and my wrath were poured out upon the inhabitants of Jerusalem, so will my wrath be poured out upon you when you go to Egypt; you will become an object of execration and horror, of ridicule and reproach; you will never see this place again. To you, then, remnant of 19 Judah, the LORD says, Do not go to Egypt. Make no mistake, I can bear witness against you this day. You 20 deceived yourselves when you sent me to the LORD your God and said, 'Pray for us to the LORD our God; tell us all that the LORD our God says and we will do it.' I have told you every- 21 thing today; but you have not obeyed the LORD your God in what he sent me to tell you. So now be sure of this: 22 you will die by sword, by famine, and by pestilence in the place where you desire to go and make your home.

Journey to Egypt

When Jeremiah had finished reciting 43 to the people all that the LORD their God had sent him to say, Azariah 2 son of Hoshaiah and Johanan son of Kareah and their party had the effrontery to say to[q] Jeremiah, 'You are lying; the LORD our God has not sent you to forbid us to go and make 3 our home in Egypt. Baruch son of Neriah has incited you against us in order to put us in the power of the Chaldaeans, so that they may kill us 4 or deport us to Babylon.' Johanan son of Kareah and the captains of the armed bands and all the people refused to obey the LORD and stay in 5 Judah. So Johanan son of Kareah and the captains collected the remnant of Judah, all who had returned from the countries among which they had been scattered to make their home 6 in Judah—men, women and children, including the king's daughters, all the people whom Nebuzaradan captain of the guard had left with Gedaliah son of Ahikam, son of Shaphan, as well as the prophet Jeremiah and 7 Baruch son of Neriah; these all went to Egypt and came to Tahpanhes, disobeying the LORD.

Jeremiah prophesies to the remnant

8 The word of the LORD came to Jere-9 miah at Tahpanhes: Take some large stones and set them in cement in the pavement at the entrance to Pharaoh's palace in Tahpanhes. Let the Judaeans 10 see you do it and say to them, These are the words of the LORD of Hosts the God of Israel: I will send for my servant Nebuchadrezzar king of Babylon, and he will place his throne on these stones that I have set there, 11 and spread his canopy over them. He will then proceed to strike Egypt down, killing those doomed to death, taking captive those who are for captivity, and putting to the sword 12 those who are for the sword. He will set fire to the temples of the Egyptian gods, burning the buildings and carrying the gods into captivity. He will scour the land of Egypt as a shepherd scours his clothes to rid them of lice. He will leave Egypt with 13 his purpose achieved. He will smash the sacred pillars of Beth-shemesh in Egypt and burn down the temples of the Egyptian gods.

44   The word that came to Jeremiah for all the Judaeans who were living in Egypt, in Migdol, Tahpanhes, Noph, 2 and the district of Pathros: These are the words of the LORD of Hosts the God of Israel: You have seen the calamity that I brought upon Jerusalem and all the cities of Judah: today they are laid waste and left un-

ness of those who provoked me to 3 anger by going after other gods, gods unknown to them, by burning sacrifices to them. It was you and your 4 fathers who did this. I took pains to send all my servants the prophets to you with this warning: 'Do not do this abominable thing which I hate.' But your fathers would not listen; 5 they paid no heed. They did not give up their wickedness or cease to burn sacrifices to other gods; so my anger 6 and wrath raged like a fire through the cities of Judah and the streets of Jerusalem, and they became the desolate ruin that they are today.

Now these are the words of the 7 LORD the God of Hosts, the God of Israel: Why bring so great a disaster upon yourselves? Why bring destruction upon Judaeans, men and women, children and babes, and leave yourselves without a survivor? This is 8 what comes of your provoking me by all your idolatry in burning sacrifices to other gods in Egypt where you have made your home. You will destroy yourselves and become an object of ridicule and reproach to all the nations of the earth. Have you 9 forgotten all the wickedness committed by your forefathers, by the kings of Judah and their wives, by yourselves and your wives in the land of Judah and in the streets of Jerusalem? To this day you have 10 shown no remorse, no reverence; you have not conformed to the law and the statutes which I set before you and your forefathers. These, therefore, 11 are the words of the LORD of Hosts the God of Israel: I have made up my mind to bring calamity upon you and exterminate the people of Judah. I will deal with the remnant of Judah 12 who were bent on going to make their home in Egypt; in Egypt they shall all meet their end. Some shall fall by the sword, others will meet their end by famine. High and low alike will die by sword or by famine and will be an object of execration and horror, of ridicule and reproach. I will punish 13 those who live in Egypt as I punished those in Jerusalem, by sword, famine, and pestilence. Those who had re- 14 mained in Judah came to make their home in Egypt, confident that they would return and live once more in Judah. But they shall not return;[r] not one of them shall survive, not one escape.

inhabited, all because of the wicked- 3

q *to say to: or* to say: It is being said to.

r *Prob. rdg.; Heb. adds* except fugitives.

Sacrificing to the queen of heaven

15 Then all the men who knew that their wives were burning sacrifices to other gods and the crowds of women stand-
16 ing by[s] answered Jeremiah, 'We will not listen to what you tell us in the
17 name of the LORD. We intend to fulfil all the promises by which we have bound ourselves: we will burn sacrifices to the queen of heaven and pour drink-offerings to her as we used to do, we and our fathers, our kings and our princes, in the cities of Judah and in the streets of Jerusalem. We then had food in plenty and were content;
18 no calamity touched us. But from the time we left off burning sacrifices to the queen of heaven and pouring drink-offerings to her, we have been in great want, and in the end we have fallen victims to sword and famine.'
19 And the women said, 'When we burnt sacrifices to the queen of heaven and poured drink-offerings to her, our husbands knew full well that we were making crescent-cakes marked with her image and pouring drink-offerings
20 to her.' When Jeremiah received this answer from these men and women
21 and all the people, he said, 'The LORD did not forget those sacrifices which you and your fathers, your kings and princes and the people of the land burnt in the cities of Judah and in the streets of Jerusalem, and they moun-
22 ted up in his mind until he could no longer tolerate them, so wicked were your deeds and so abominable the things you did. Your land became a desolate waste, an object of horror and ridicule, with no inhabitants, as
23 it still is. This calamity has come upon you because you burnt these sacrifices and sinned against the LORD and did not obey the LORD or conform to his laws, statutes, and teachings.'
24 Jeremiah further said to all the people and to the women, Listen to the word of the LORD, all you from
25 Judah who live in Egypt. These are the words of the LORD of Hosts the God of Israel: You women have made your actions match your words. 'We will carry out our vows', you said, 'to burn sacrifices to the queen of heaven and to pour drink-offerings to her.' Well then, fulfil your vows by all means, and make your words good.
26 But listen to the word of the LORD, all you from Judah who live in Egypt. I have sworn by my great name, says

the LORD, that my name shall never again be on the lips of the men of Judah; they shall no longer swear in Egypt, 'By the life of the Lord GOD.'
27 I am on the watch to bring you evil and not good, and all the men of Judah who are in Egypt shall meet their end by sword and by famine until not one is left.[t] It is then that all
28 the survivors of Judah who have made their home in Egypt shall know whose word prevails, theirs or mine.

29 This is the sign I give you, says the LORD, that I intend to punish you in this place, so that you may learn that my words against you will prevail to bring evil upon you: These are
30 the words of the LORD: I will hand over Pharaoh Hophra king of Egypt to his enemies and to those who seek his life, just as I handed over Zedekiah king of Judah to his enemy Nebuchadrezzar king of Babylon who was seeking to take his life.

The LORD's word to Baruch

45 The word which the prophet Jeremiah spoke to Baruch son of Neriah when he wrote these words in a book at Jeremiah's dictation in the fourth year of Jehoiakim son of Josiah, king
2 of Judah: These are the words of the LORD the God of Israel concerning
3 you, Baruch: You said, 'Woe is me, for the LORD has added grief to all my trials. I have worn myself out with my labours and have had no respite.' This
4 is what you shall say to Baruch, These are the words of the LORD: What I have built, I demolish; what I have planted, I uproot. So it will be with
5 the whole earth. You seek great things for yourself. Leave off seeking them; for I will bring disaster upon all mankind, says the LORD, and I will let you live wherever you go, but you shall save your life and nothing more.

Against the nations

46 This came to the prophet Jeremiah as the word of the LORD concerning the nations.

Egypt

2 Of Egypt: concerning the army of Pharaoh Necho king of Egypt at Carchemish on the river Euphrates, which Nebuchadrezzar king of Babylon defeated in the fourth year of

s *Prob. rdg.; Heb. adds* and all the people who lived in Egypt, in Pathros.   t *Prob. rdg.; Heb. adds* Few will escape the sword in Egypt and return to Judah.

Jehoiakim son of Josiah, king of Judah.

3   Hold shield and buckler ready
    and advance to battle;
4 harness the horses, let the riders
    mount;
form up, your helmets on, your lances
    burnished;
on with your coats of mail!
5   But now, what sight is this?
They are broken and routed,
    their warriors beaten down;
they have turned to flight and do not
    look behind them.
Terror let loose!
This is the very word of the LORD.

6 Can the swift escape, can the warrior
    save himself?
    In the north, by the river Eu-
      phrates,
    they stumble and fall.

7   Who is this rising like the Nile,
    like its streams turbulent in flood?
8   Egypt is rising like the Nile,
    like its streams turbulent in flood.

He[u] says:

I will rise and cover the earth,
I will destroy both city and people.

9 Charge, horsemen! On, you flashing
    chariots, on!
    Forward, the warriors,
    Cushites and men of Put carrying
      shields,
    Lydians grasping their bent bows!
10 This is the day of the Lord, the GOD
    of Hosts,
    a day of vengeance, vengeance on
      his enemies;
    the sword shall devour and be sated,
    drunk with their blood.
For the GOD of Hosts, the Lord, holds
    sacrifice
    in a northern land, by the river
      Euphrates.
11 Go up into Gilead and fetch balm,
    O virgin people of Egypt.
    You have tried many remedies, all
      in vain;
no skin shall grow over your wounds.
12 The nations have heard your cry,
    and the earth echoes with your
      screams;
    warrior stumbles against warrior
    and both fall together.

13   The word which the LORD spoke to
    the prophet Jeremiah when Nebu-

chadrezzar king of Babylon was
coming to harry the land of Egypt:

Announce it in Egypt, proclaim it in 14
    Migdol,
    proclaim it in Noph and Tahpan-
      hes.
    Say, Stand to! Be ready!
    for a sword devours all around you.
Why does Apis flee, why does your 15
    bull-god not[v] stand fast?
    The LORD has thrust him out.
The rabble of Egypt stumbles and 16
    falls,
    man against man;
    each says, 'Quick, back to our
      people,
to the land of our birth, far from the
    cruel sword!'
Give Pharaoh of Egypt the title King 17
    Bombast,
    the man who missed his moment.
    By my life, says the King   18
    whose name is the LORD of Hosts,
    one shall come mighty as Tabor
      among the hills,
    as Carmel by the sea.
Make ready your baggage for exile, 19
    you native people of Egypt;
    for Noph shall become a waste,
    ruined and unpeopled.

Egypt was a lovely heifer,   20
but a gadfly from the north descended
    on her.
The mercenaries in her land were like 21
    stall-fed calves;
but they too turned and fled,
    not one of them stood his ground.
    The hour of their downfall has
      come upon them,
    their day of reckoning.
Hark, she is hissing like a snake,   22
    for the enemy has come in all his
      force.
They fall upon her with axes
    like woodcutters at their work.
They cut down her forest, says the 23
    LORD,
    and it flaunts itself no more;
for they are many as locusts and past
    counting.
The Egyptians are put to shame, en- 24
    slaved to a northern race.
The LORD of Hosts the God of Israel 25
    has spoken:
    I will punish Amon god of No,[w]
Egypt with her gods and her princes,
Pharaoh and all who trust in him.
I will deliver them to those bent on 26
    their destruction,
to Nebuchadrezzar king of Babylon
    and his troops;

[u] Or It.   [v] Why does Apis . . . not: or Why is your bull-god routed, why does he not . . .
[w] Prob. rdg.; Heb. adds and Pharaoh.

yet in after time the land shall be peopled as of old.
This is the very word of the LORD.

Israel

27 But you, Jacob my servant, have no fear,
despair not, O Israel;
for I will bring you back safe from afar
and your offspring from the land where they are captives;
and Jacob shall be at rest once more, prosperous and unafraid.

28 O Jacob my servant, have no fear, says the LORD; for I am with you.
I will make an end of all the nations amongst whom I have banished you;
but I will not make an end of you; though I punish you as you deserve,
I will not sweep you clean away.

The Philistines

47 This came to the prophet Jeremiah as the word of the LORD concerning the Philistines before Pharaoh's harrying

2 of Gaza: The LORD has spoken:

See how waters are rising from the north
and swelling to a torrent in spate,
flooding the land and all that is in it,
cities and all who live in them.
Men shall shriek in alarm
and all who live in the land shall howl.

3 Hark, the pounding of his chargers' hooves,
the rattle of his chariots and their rumbling wheels!
Fathers spare no thought for their children;
their hands hang powerless,

4 because the day is upon them when Philistia will be despoiled,
and Tyre and Sidon destroyed to the last defender;
for the LORD will despoil the Philistines,
that remnant of the isle of Caphtor.

5 Gaza is shorn bare, Ashkelon ruined.
Poor remnant of their strength,
how long will you gash yourselves and cry:

6 Ah, sword in the hand of the LORD,
how long will it be before you rest?
Sheathe yourself, rest and be quiet.

7 How can it rest? for the LORD has given it work to do
against Ashkelon and the plain by the sea;

there he has assigned the sword its task.

Moab

Of Moab. The LORD of Hosts the God 48 of Israel has spoken:

Alas for Nebo! it is laid waste;
Kiriathaim is put to shame and captured,
Misgab reduced to shame and dismay;
Moab is renowned no longer.   2

In Heshbon they plot evil against her:
Come, destroy her, and leave her no longer a nation.
And you who live in Madmen shall be struck down,
your people pursued by the sword.
Hark to the cries of anguish from 3 Horonaim:
great havoc and disaster!
Moab is broken.   4
Their cries are heard as far as Zoar.
On the ascent of Luhith   5
men go up weeping bitterly;
on the descent of Horonaim
cries of 'Disaster!' are heard.
Flee, flee for your lives   6
like a sand-grouse in the wilderness.
Because you have trusted in your 7 defences and your arsenals,
you too will be captured,
and Kemosh will go into exile,
his priests and his captains with him;
and a spoiler shall descend on every 8 city.
No city shall escape,
valley and tableland will be laid waste and plundered;
the LORD has spoken.

Let a warning flash to Moab,^x   9
for she shall be laid in ruins^y
and her cities shall become waste places
with no inhabitant.

A curse on him who is slack in doing 10 the LORD's work!
A curse on him who withholds his sword from bloodshed!

All his life long, Moab has lain un- 11 disturbed
like wine settled on its lees,
not emptied from vessel to vessel;
he has not gone into exile.
Therefore the taste of him is unaltered,
and the flavour stays unchanged.
Therefore the days are coming, says 12 the LORD,
when I will send men to tilt the jars; they shall tilt them

x Let . . . Moab: or Doom Moab to become saltings.   y laid in ruins: prob. rdg.; Heb. obscure.

and empty his vessels and smash his jars;

13 and Moab shall be betrayed by Kemosh,
as Israel was betrayed by Bethel,
a god in whom he trusted.

14 How can you say, 'We are warriors and men valiant in battle'?

15 The spoiler of Moab and her cities has come up,
and the flower of her army goes down to the slaughter.

This is the very word of the King whose name is the LORD of Hosts.

16 The downfall of Moab is near at hand,
disaster rushes swiftly upon him.

17 Grieve for him, all you his neighbours
and all you who acknowledge him,
and say, 'Alas! The commander's staff is broken,
broken is the baton of honour.'

18 Come down from your place of honour,
sit on the thirsty ground, you natives of Dibon;
for the spoiler of Moab has come upon you
and destroyed your citadels.

19 You that live in Aroer, stand on the roadside and watch,
ask the fugitives, the man running, the woman escaping,
ask them, 'What has happened?'

20 Moab is reduced to shame and dismay:
howl and shriek,
proclaim by the Arnon that Moab is despoiled,

21 and that judgement has come to the tableland, to Holon and Jahazah,

22 Mephaath and Dibon, Nebo and

23 Beth-diblathaim and Kiriathaim,

24 Beth-gamul, Beth-meon, Kirioth and Bozrah, and to all the cities of Moab far and near.

25 Moab's horn is hacked off
and his strong arm is broken,
says the LORD.

26 Make Moab drunk—he has defied the LORD—
until he overflows with his vomit
and even he becomes a butt for derision.

27 But was Israel ever your butt?
Was he ever in company with thieves,
that whenever you spoke of him you should shake your head?

z and: *prob. rdg.*, *cp. Isa. 15. 4*; *Heb. as far as.*

28 Leave your cities, you inhabitants of Moab,
and find a home among the crags;
become like a dove which nests
in the rock-face at the mouth of a cavern.

29 We have heard of Moab's pride, and proud indeed he is,
proud, presumptuous, overbearing, insolent.

30 I know his arrogance, says the LORD;
his boasting is false, false are his deeds.

31 Therefore I will howl over Moab
and cry in anguish at the fate of every soul in Moab;
I will moan over the men of Kirheres.

32 I will weep for you more than I wept for Jazer,
O vine of Sibmah
whose branches spread out to the sea
and stretch as far as Jazer.
The despoiler has fallen on your fruit and on your vintage,

33 gladness and joy are taken away from the meadows of Moab,
and I have stopped the flow of wine from the vats;
nor shall shout follow shout from the harvesters—not one shout.

34 Heshbon and[z] Elealeh utter cries of anguish which are heard in Jahaz; the sound carries from Zoar to Horonaim and Eglath-shelishiyah; for the waters of Nimrim have become a desolate waste.

35 In Moab I will stop their sacrificing at hill-shrines and burning of offerings to their gods, says the LORD.

36 Therefore my heart wails for Moab like a reed-pipe, wails like a pipe for the men of Kir-heres. Their hard-earned wealth has vanished.

37 Every man's head is shorn in mourning, every beard shaved, every hand gashed, and every waist girded with sackcloth.

38 On Moab's roofs and in her broad streets nothing is heard but lamentation; for I have broken Moab like a useless thing.[a]

39 Moab in her dismay has shamefully turned to flight. Moab has become a butt of derision and a cause of dismay to all her neighbours.

For the LORD has spoken:

40 A vulture shall swoop down
and spread out his wings over Moab.

41 The towns are captured, the strongholds taken;
on that day the spirit of Moab's warriors shall fail

a *Prob. rdg.*; *Heb. adds* says the LORD.

like the spirit of a woman in childbirth.
42 Then Moab shall be destroyed, no
    more to be a nation;
for he defied the LORD.
43 The hunter's scare, the pit, and the
    trap
threaten all who dwell in Moab,
    says the LORD.
44 If a man runs from the scare
he will fall into the pit;
if he climbs out of the pit
he will be caught in the trap.
All this will I bring on Moab in the
    year of their reckoning.
This is the very word of the LORD.
45 In the shadow of Heshbon the fugi-
    tives stand helpless;
for fire has blazed out from Hesh-
    bon,
flames have shot out from the
    palace of Sihon;
they devour the homeland of Moab
and the country of the sons of tu-
    mult.
46 Alas for you, Moab! the people of
    Kemosh have vanished,
for your sons are taken into cap-
    tivity
and your daughters led away cap-
    tive.
47 Yet in days to come I will restore
    Moab's fortunes.
This is the very word of the LORD.

Here ends the sentence on Moab.

Ammon

49 Of the people of Ammon. Thus says
the LORD:

Has Israel no sons? Has he no heir?
Why has Milcom inherited the land of
    Gad,
and why do his people live in the
    cities of Gad?
2 Look, therefore, a time is coming,
    says the LORD,
when I will make Rabbath Ammon
    hear the battle-cry,
when it will become a desolate
    mound of ruins
and its villages will be burnt to
    ashes,
and Israel shall disinherit those who
    disinherited him,
    says the LORD.

3 Howl, Heshbon, for Ai is despoiled.
Cry aloud, you villages round Rab-
    bath Ammon,
put on sackcloth and beat your
    breast,

and score your bodies with gashes.
For Milcom will go into exile,
and with him his priests and officers.
4 Why do you boast of your resources,
you whose resources are melting
    away,
you wayward people who trust in your
    arsenals,
and say, 'Who will dare attack me?'
5 Beware, I am bringing fear upon you
    from every side,[b]
and every one of you shall be driven
    headlong
with no man to round up the strag-
    glers.
6 Yet after this I will restore the for-
    tunes of Ammon.
This is the very word of the LORD.

Edom

7 Of Edom. The LORD of Hosts has said:

Is wisdom no longer to be found
    in Teman?
Have her sages no skill in counsel?
Has their wisdom decayed?
8 The people of Dedan have turned
    and fled
and taken refuge in remote places;
for I will bring Esau's calamity
    upon him
when his day of reckoning comes.
9[c] When the vintagers come to you
they will surely leave gleanings;
and if thieves raid your early crop
    in the night,
they will take only as much as they
    want.
10 But I have ransacked Esau's treas-
    ure,
I have uncovered his hiding-places,
and he has nowhere to conceal him-
    self;
his children, his kinsfolk and his
    neighbours are despoiled;
there is no one to help him.
11 What! am I to save alive your
    fatherless children?
Are your widows to trust in me?

12 For the LORD has spoken: Those
who were not doomed to drink the
cup shall drink it none the less. Are
you alone to go unpunished? You
shall not go unpunished; you shall
13 drink it. For by my life, says the
LORD, Bozrah shall become a horror
and reproach, a byword and a thing
of ridicule; and all her towns shall be
a byword for ever.

14[d] When a herald was sent among the
    nations, crying,

b Prob. rdg.; Heb. adds says the Lord GOD of Hosts.   *c Verses 9 and 10: cp. Obad. 5, 6.*   *d Verses 14–16: cp. Obad. 1–4.*

'Gather together and march against her,
rouse yourselves for battle',
I heard this message from the LORD:

15 Look, I make you the least of all nations,
an object of all men's contempt.
16 Your overbearing arrogance and your insolent heart
have led you astray,
you who haunt the crannies among the rocks
and keep your hold on the heights of the hills.
Though you build your nest high as a vulture,
thence I will bring you down.
This is the very word of the LORD.
17 Edom shall become a scene of horror,
all who pass that way shall be horror-struck
and shall jeer in derision at the blows she has borne,
18 overthrown like Sodom and Gomorrah and their neighbours,[e]
says the LORD.
No man shall live there,
no mortal make a home in her.
19 Look, like a lion coming up
from Jordan's dense thickets to the perennial pastures,
in a moment I will chase every one away
and round up the choicest of[f] her rams.
For who is like me? Who is my equal?
What shepherd can stand his ground before me?
20 Therefore listen to the LORD's whole purpose against Edom and all his plans against the people of Teman:

The young ones of the flock shall be carried off,
and their pasture shall be horrified at their fate.
21 At the sound of their fall the land quakes;
it cries out, and the cry is heard at the Red Sea.[g]
22 A vulture shall soar and swoop down
and spread out his wings over Bozrah,
and on that day the spirit of Edom's warriors shall fail
like the spirit of a woman in labour.

Damascus

Of Damascus.   23

Hamath and Arpad are in confusion,
for they have heard news of disaster;
they are tossed up and down in anxiety
like the unresting sea.
Damascus has lost heart and turns 24 to flight;
trembling has seized her,
the pangs of childbirth have gripped her.
How forlorn is the town of joyful 25 song,
the city of gladness!
Therefore her young men shall fall in 26 her streets
and all her warriors lie still in death that day.
This is the very word of the LORD of Hosts.
Then will I kindle a fire against the 27 wall of Damascus
and it shall consume the palaces of Ben-hadad.

The Arabs

Of Kedar and the royal princes[h] of 28 Hazer which Nebuchadrezzar king of Babylon subdued. The LORD has said:

Come, attack Kedar,
despoil the Arabs of the east.
Carry off their tents and their 29 flocks,
their tent-hangings and all their vessels,
drive off their camels too,
and a cry shall go up: 'Terror let loose!'
Flee, flee; make haste,   30
take refuge in remote places, O people of Hazer,
for the king of Babylon has laid his plans
and formed a design against you,
says the LORD.
Come, let us attack a nation living at 31 peace,
in fancied security,
with neither gates nor bars.
sufficient to themselves.
Their camels shall be carried off as 32 booty,
their vast herds of cattle as plunder;
I will scatter them before the wind to roam
the fringes of the desert,[i]

e Or inhabitants.   f the choicest of: *prob. rdg.*; *Heb.* who is chosen?   g Or the Sea of Reeds.
h royal princes: *or* kingdom.   i them ... desert: *or* to the wind those who clip the hair on their temples.

and bring ruin upon them from
every side.
Hazer shall become a haunt of
wolves,
for ever desolate;
no man shall live there,
no mortal make a home in her.
This is the very word of the LORD.

Elam

This came to the prophet Jeremiah
as the word of the LORD concerning
Elam, at the beginning of the reign of
Zedekiah king of Judah: Thus says
the LORD of Hosts:

Listen, I will break the bow of Elam,
the chief weapon of their might;
I will bring four winds against
Elam
from the four quarters of heaven;
I will scatter them before these four
winds,
and there shall be no nation
to which the exiles from Elam shall
not come.
I will break Elam before their foes,
before those who are bent on their
destruction;
I will vent my anger upon them in
disaster;
I will harry them with the sword
until I make an end of them.
Then I will set my throne in Elam,
and there I will destroy the king and
his officers.
This is the very word of the LORD.
Yet in days to come I will restore the
fortunes of Elam.
This is the very word of the LORD.

Babylon

The word which the LORD spoke concerning Babylon, concerning the land
of the Chaldaeans, through the prophet Jeremiah:

Declare and proclaim among the
nations,
keep nothing back, spread the news:
Babylon is taken,
Bel is put to shame, Marduk is in
despair;
the idols of Babylon are put to
shame,
her false gods are in despair.
For a nation out of the north has
fallen upon her;
they will make her land a desolate
waste
where neither man nor beast shall
live.

In those days, at that time, says
the LORD, the people of Israel and the
people of Judah shall come together
and go in tears to seek the LORD their
God; they shall ask after Zion, turn- 5
ing their faces towards her, and they
shall come and join themselves to the
LORD in an everlasting covenant which
shall not be forgotten.

My people were lost sheep, whose 6
shepherds let them stray and run
wild on the mountains; they went
from mountain to hill and forgot their
fold. Whoever found them devoured 7
them, and their enemies said, 'We incur no guilt, because they have sinned
against the LORD, the LORD who is
the true goal and the hope of all their
fathers.'

Flee from Babylon, from the land of 8
the Chaldaeans;
go forth, and be like he-goats leading
the flock.
For I will stir up a host of mighty 9
nations
and bring them against Babylon,
marshalled against her from a
northern land;
and from the north she shall be
captured.
Their arrows shall be like a practised warrior
who never comes back empty-
handed;
the Chaldaeans shall be plundered, 10
and all who plunder them shall take
their fill.
This is the very word of the LORD.
You ravaged my patrimony; but 11
though you rejoice and exult,
though you run free like a heifer
after threshing,
though you neigh like a stallion,
your mother shall be cruelly disgraced, 12
she who bore you shall be put to
shame.
Look at her, the mere rump of the
nations,
a wilderness, parched and desert,
unpeopled through the wrath of the 13
LORD,
nothing but a desolate waste;
all who pass by Babylon shall be
horror-struck
and jeer in derision at the sight of
her wounds.

Marshal your forces against Babylon, 14
on every side,
you whose bows are ready strung;
shoot at her, spare no arrows.
Shout in triumph over her, she has 15
thrown up her hands,
her bastions are down, her walls demolished;
this is the vengeance of the LORD.

Take vengeance on her;
as she has done, so do to her.
16 Destroy every sower in Babylon,
every reaper with his sickle at
harvest-time.
Before the cruel sword every man will
go back to his people,
every man flee to his own land.

17 Israel is a scattered flock
harried and chased by lions:
as the king of Assyria was the first
to feed on him,
so the king of Babylon was the last
to gnaw his bones.

18 Therefore the Lord of Hosts the God
of Israel says this:

I will punish the king of Babylon
and his country
as I have punished the king of
Assyria.
19 I will bring Israel back to his
pasture,
and he shall graze on Carmel and
Bashan;
in the hills of Ephraim and Gilead he
shall eat his fill.

20 In those days, says the Lord, when
that time comes, search shall be
made for the iniquity of Israel but
there shall be none, and for the sin of
Judah but it shall not be found; for
those whom I leave as a remnant I
will forgive.

21 Attack the land of Merathaim;
attack it and the inhabitants of
Pekod;
put all to the sword and destroy
them,
and do whatever I bid you.
This is the very word of the Lord.

22 Hark, the sound of war in the land
and great destruction!
23 See how the hammer of all the earth
is hacked and broken in pieces,
how Babylon has become
a horror among the nations.
24 O Babylon, you have laid a snare
to be your own undoing;
you have been trapped, all unawares;
there you are, you are caught,
because you have challenged the
Lord.
25 The Lord has opened his arsenal
and brought out the weapons of his
wrath;
for this is work for the Lord the God
of Hosts
in the land of the Chaldaeans.
26 Her harvest-time has come:

throw open her granaries,[j] pile her in
heaps;
destroy her, let no survivor be left.
Put all her warriors to the sword;
let them be led to the slaughter.
Woe upon them! for their time has
come,
their day of reckoning.
I hear the fugitives escaping from the
land of Babylon
to proclaim in Zion the vengeance of
the Lord our God.

Let your arrows be heard whistling
against Babylon,
all you whose bows are ready
strung.
Pitch your tents all around her
so that no one escapes.
Pay her back for all her misdeeds;
as she has done, so do to her,
for she has insulted the Lord the
Holy One of Israel.
Therefore her young men shall fall in
her streets,
and all her warriors shall lie still in
death that day.
This is the very word of the Lord.

I am against you, insolent city;
for your time has come, your day of
reckoning.
This is the very word of the Lord
God of Hosts.
Insolence shall stumble and fall
and no one shall lift her up,
and I will kindle fire in the heath
around her
and it shall consume everything
round about.

The Lord of Hosts has said this:

The peoples of Israel and Judah together are oppressed;
their captors hold them firmly and
refuse to release them.
But they have a powerful advocate,
whose name is the Lord of Hosts;
he himself will plead their cause,
bringing distress on Babylon and turmoil on its people.

A sword hangs over the Chaldaeans,
over the people of Babylon, her officers
and her wise men,
says the Lord.
A sword over the false prophets, and
they are made fools,
a sword over her warriors, and they
despair,
a sword over her horses and her
chariots
and over all the rabble within her,
and they shall become like women;

j Or cattle-pens.

a sword over her treasures, and they
   shall be plundered,
38 a sword over her waters, and they
   shall dry up;
  for it is a land of idols
   that glories in its dreaded gods.[k]

39 Therefore marmots and jackals shall
skulk in it, desert-owls shall haunt it,
nevermore shall it be inhabited by
men and no one shall dwell in it
40 through all the ages. As when God
overthrew Sodom and Gomorrah and
their neighbours,[l] says the LORD, no
man shall live there, no mortal make
a home in her.

41 See, a people is coming from the north,
   a great nation,
mighty[m] kings rouse themselves from
   earth's farthest corners;
42 armed with bow and sabre, they are
   cruel and pitiless;
bestriding horses, they sound like the
   thunder of the sea;
they are like men arrayed for battle
   against you, Babylon.
43 The king of Babylon has heard news
   of them
  and his hands hang limp;
agony grips him, anguish as of a
   woman in labour.
44 Look, like a lion coming up
from Jordan's dense thickets to the
   perennial pastures,
in a moment I will chase every one
   away
and round up the choicest of[n] the
   rams.
For who is like me? Who is my
   equal?
What shepherd can stand his ground
   before me?

45 Therefore listen to the LORD's whole
purpose against Babylon and all his
plans against the land of the Chaldaeans:

   The young ones of the flock shall
   be carried off
and their pasture shall be horrified at
   their fate.
46 At the sound of the capture of
   Babylon
the land quakes and her cry is heard
   among the nations.

51 For thus says the LORD:

I will raise a destroying wind
   against Babylon and those who live
   in Kambul,[o]

and I will send winnowers to Bab- 2
   ylon,
who shall winnow her and empty
   her land;
for they shall assail her on all sides on
   the day of disaster.
How shall the archer then string 3
   his bow
or put on his coat of mail?

Spare none of her young men, destroy
   all her host,
and let them fall dead in the land 4
   of the Chaldaeans,
pierced through in her streets.
Israel and Judah are not left widowed 5
   by their God, by the LORD of Hosts;
but the land of the Chaldaeans is
   full of guilt,
condemned by the Holy One of
   Israel.

Flee out of Babylon, every man for 6
   himself,
or you will be struck down for her
   sin;
for this is the LORD's day of vengeance,
and he is paying her full recompense.
Babylon has been a gold cup in the 7
   LORD's hand
to make all the earth drunk;
the nations have drunk of her wine,
and that has made them mad.
Babylon falls suddenly and is broken. 8
Howl over her,
fetch balm for her wound;
perhaps she will be healed.
We would have healed Babylon, but 9
   she would not be[p] healed.
Leave her and let us be off, each to his
   own country;
for her doom reaches to heaven
and mounts up to the skies.
The LORD has made our innocence 10
   plain to see;
come, let us proclaim in Zion
what the LORD our God has done.

Sharpen the arrows, fill the quivers. 11
The LORD has roused the spirit of the
   king of the Medes;
for the LORD's purpose against
   Babylon is to destroy it,
and his vengeance is the avenging
   of his temple.
Raise the standard against Bab- 12
   ylon's walls,
mount a strong guard, post a watch,
   set an ambush;

---

k dreaded gods: or dire portents.   l Or inhabitants.   m Or many.   n the choicest of: prob.
rdg.; Heb. who is chosen?   o Kambul: prob. rdg.; Heb. the heart of my opponents.   p would
not be: or was not.

for the LORD has both planned and
    carried out
what he threatened to do to the people
    of Babylon.
13 O opulent city, standing beside great
        waters,
    your end has come, your destiny is
        certain.
14 The LORD of Hosts has sworn by him-
        self, saying,
    Once I filled you with men, countless
        as locusts,
        yet a song of triumph shall be
            chanted over you.

The maker of all

15*q*   God made the earth by his power,
        fixed the world in place by his
            wisdom,
        unfurled the skies by his under-
            standing.
16 At the thunder of his voice the waters
        in heaven are amazed;*r*
    he brings up the mist from the ends
        of the earth,
    he opens rifts*s* for the rain
    and brings the wind out of his
        storehouses.
17 All men are brutish and ignorant,
    every goldsmith is discredited by
        his idol;
    for the figures he casts are a sham,
        there is no breath in them.
18 They are worth nothing, mere
        mockeries,
    which perish when their day of
        reckoning comes.
19 God, Jacob's creator, is not like
        these;
    for he is the maker of all.
    Israel is the people he claims as his
        own;
    the LORD of Hosts is his name.

Babylon taken

20 You are my battle-axe, my weapon of
        war;
    with you I will break nations in
        pieces,
    and with you I will destroy kingdoms.
21 With you I will break horse and rider,
    with you I will break chariot and
        rider,
22 with you I will break man and woman,
    with you I will break young and old,
    with you I will break young man and
        maiden,
23 with you I will break shepherd and
        flock,

with you I will break ploughman and
        team,
with you I will break viceroys and
        governors.
So will I repay Babylon and the 2
        people of Chaldaea
for all the wrong which they did in
        Zion in your sight.
    This is the very word of the LORD.

    I am against you, O destroying 2
        mountain,*t*
    you who destroy the whole earth,
    and I will stretch out my hand
        against you
    and send you tumbling from your
        terraces
    and make you a burnt-out mount-
        ain.
No stone of yours shall be used as a 2
        corner-stone,
    no stone for a foundation;
    but you shall be desolate, for ever
        waste.
    This is the very word of the LORD.

    Raise a standard in the land,*u*   2
    blow the trumpet among the nations,
    hallow the nations for war against
        her,
summon the kingdoms of Ararat,
        Minni, and Ashkenaz,
    appoint a commander-in-chief a-
        gainst her,
bring up the horses like a dark swarm
        of locusts;*v*
    hallow the nations for war against 2
        her,
    the king of the Medes, his viceroys
        and governors,
    and all the lands of his realm.
    The earth quakes and writhes;   2
    for the LORD's designs against Bab-
        ylon are fulfilled,
to make the land of Babylon desolate
        and unpeopled.
    Babylon's warriors have given up 3
        the fight,
    they skulk in the forts;
    their courage has failed, they have
        become like women.
Her buildings are set on fire, the bars
        of her gates broken.
    Runner speeds to meet runner,   3
    messenger to meet messenger,
    bringing news to the king of Bab-
        ylon
that every quarter of his city is taken,
    the river-crossings are seized,   3
the guard-towers set on fire
    and the garrison stricken with
        panic.

*q Verses 15–19: cp. 10. 12–16.   r At the thunder ... amazed: prob. rdg.; Heb. At the sound of
his giving tumult of waters in heaven.   s rifts: prob. rdg.; Heb. lightnings.   t Or O Mount of
the Destroyer.   u Or earth.   v Or hoppers.*

Judgement on Babylon

3 For the LORD of Hosts the God of
Israel has spoken:

Babylon is like a threshing-floor when
it is trodden;
soon, very soon, harvest-time will
come.

4 'Nebuchadrezzar king of Babylon
has devoured me
and sucked me dry,
he has set me aside like an empty
jar.
Like a dragon he has gulped me
down;
he has filled his maw with my delicate flesh
and spewed me up.
5 On Babylon be the violence done
to me,
the vengeance taken upon me!',
Zion's people shall say.
'My blood be upon the Chaldaeans!',
Jerusalem shall say.

6 Therefore the LORD says:

I will plead your cause, I will avenge
you;
I will dry up her sea[w] and make her
waters fail;
7 and Babylon shall become a heap of
ruins, a haunt of wolves,
a scene of horror and derision, with
no inhabitant.

8 Together they roar like young lions,
they growl like the whelps of a
lioness.
9 I will cause their drinking bouts to
end in fever
and make them so drunk that they
will writhe and toss,
then sink into unending sleep, never
to wake.
This is the very word of the LORD.
40 I will bring them like lambs to the
slaughter,
rams and he-goats together.
41 Sheshak[x] is captured,
the pride of the whole earth taken;
Babylon has become a horror amongst
the nations!
42 The sea has surged over Babylon,
she is covered by its roaring waves.
43 Her cities have become waste places,
a land dried up and desert,
a land in whose cities no man lives
and through which no mortal travels.
44 I will punish Bel in Babylon
and make him bring up what he has
swallowed;
nations shall never again come streaming to him.

The wall of Babylon has fallen;
come out of her, O my people,   45
and let every man save himself
from the anger of the LORD.
Then beware of losing heart,   46
fear no rumours spread abroad in the
land,
as rumour follows rumour,
each year a new one:
violence on earth and ruler against
ruler.
Therefore a time is coming   47
when I will punish Babylon's idols,
and all her land shall be put to
shame,
and all her slain shall lie fallen in
her midst.
Heaven and earth and all that is in   48
them
shall sing in triumph over Babylon;
for marauders from the north shall
overrun her.
This is the very word of the LORD.
Babylon must fall for the sake of[y]   49
Israel's slain,
as the slain of all the world fell for the
sake of Babylon.
You who have escaped from her sword,   50
off with you, do not linger.
Remember the LORD from afar
and call Jerusalem to mind.
We are put to shame by the re-   51
proaches we have heard,
and our faces are covered with confusion:
strangers have entered the sacred
courts of the LORD's house.

A time is coming therefore, says the   52
LORD,
when I will punish her idols,
and all through the land there shall
be the groaning of the wounded.
Though Babylon should reach to the   53
skies
and make her high towers inaccessible,
I will send marauders to overrun her.
This is the very word of the LORD.
Hark, cries of agony from Babylon!   54
Sounds of destruction from the land
of the Chaldaeans!
For the LORD is despoiling Babylon   55
and will silence the hum of the city,
before the advancing wave that booms
and roars
like mighty waters.
For marauders march on Babylon   56
herself,
her warriors are captured and their
bows are broken;
for the LORD, a God of retribution,
will repay in full.

w Possibly the Euphrates.   x A name for Babylon.   y for the sake of: prob. rdg.; Heb. om.

57 I will make her princes and her
  wise men drunk,
  her viceroys and governors and
  warriors,
  and they shall sink into unending
  sleep, never to wake.
  This is the very word of the King,
  whose name is the LORD of Hosts.

58 The LORD of Hosts says:

  The walls of broad Babylon shall be
  razed to the ground,
  her lofty gates shall be set on fire.
  Worthless now is the thing for which
  the nations toiled;
  the peoples wore themselves out for
  a mere nothing.

Jeremiah and Seraiah

59 The instructions given by the prophet
  Jeremiah to the quartermaster Seraiah son of Neriah and grandson of
  Mahseiah, when he went to Babylon
  with Zedekiah king of Judah in the
  fourth year of his reign.
60   Jeremiah, having written down in
  a^z book^a a full description of the disaster which would come upon Bab-
61 ylon, said to Seraiah, 'When you
  come to Babylon, look at this, read it
62 all and then say, "Thou, O LORD, hast
  declared thy purpose to destroy this
  place and leave it with no one living
  in it, man or beast; it shall be deso-
63 late, for ever waste." When you have
  finished reading the book, tie a stone
  to it and throw it into the Euphrates,
64 and then say, "So shall Babylon sink,
  never to rise again after the disaster
  which I shall bring upon her."'

  Thus far are the collected sayings of
  Jeremiah.

Zedekiah's reign

52 1^b Zedekiah was twenty-one years old
  when he came to the throne, and he
  reigned in Jerusalem for eleven years;
  his mother was Hamutal daughter of
2 Jeremiah of Libnah. He did what was
  wrong in the eyes of the LORD, as
3 Jehoiakim had done. Jerusalem and
  Judah so angered the LORD that in
  the end he banished them from his
  sight; and Zedekiah rebelled against
  the king of Babylon.

Zedekiah taken captive

In the ninth year of his reign, in the
tenth month, on the tenth day of the
month, Nebuchadrezzar king of Babylon advanced with all his army
against Jerusalem, invested it and
erected watch-towers against it on
every side; the siege lasted till the
eleventh year of King Zedekiah. In
the fourth month of that year, on the
ninth day of the month, when famine
was severe in the city and there was
no food for the common people, the
city was thrown open. When Zedekiah king of Judah saw this, he and^c
all his armed escort left the city and
fled by night through the gate called
Between the Two Walls, near the
king's garden. They escaped towards
the Arabah, although the Chaldaeans
were surrounding the city. But the
Chaldaean army pursued the king
and overtook him in the lowlands of
Jericho; and all his company was
dispersed. The king was seized and
brought before the king of Babylon
at Riblah in the land of Hamath,
where he pleaded his case before him.
The king of Babylon slew Zedekiah's
sons before his eyes; he also put to
death all the princes of Judah in Riblah. Then the king of Babylon put
Zedekiah's eyes out, bound him with
fetters of bronze, brought him to Babylon and committed him to prison till
the day of his death.

Jerusalem destroyed

In the fifth month, on the tenth day
of the month, in the nineteenth year
of Nebuchadrezzar king of Babylon,
Nebuzaradan, captain of the king's
bodyguard,^{d} came to Jerusalem and
set fire to the house of the LORD and
the royal palace; all the houses in the
city, including the mansion of Gedaliah,^{e} were burnt down. The Chaldaean
forces with the captain of the guard
pulled down the walls all round Jerusalem. ^{f}Nebuzaradan captain of the
guard deported the rest of the people left in the city, those who had deserted to the king of Babylon and
any remaining artisans. The captain
of the guard left only the weakest
class of people to be vine-dressers
and labourers.
The Chaldaeans broke up the pillars

z Or one. a Prob. rdg.; Heb. adds all these things which are written concerning Babylon.
b Verses 1–27: cp. 39. 1–10 and 2 Kgs. 24. 18—25. 21. c When Zedekiah . . . and: prob. rdg., cp.
39. 4; Heb. om. d captain . . . bodyguard: prob. rdg., cp. 2 Kgs. 25. 8; Heb. captain of the bodyguard stood before the king of Babylon. e Gedaliah: prob. rdg.; Heb. the great man. f Prob.
rdg., cp. 39. 9 and 2 Kgs. 25. 11; Heb. prefixes The weakest class of the people (cp. verse 16).

of bronze in the house of the LORD, the trolleys, and the sea of bronze, and took the metal to Babylon. They took also the pots, shovels, snuffers, tossing-bowls, saucers, and all the vessels of bronze used in the service of the temple. The captain of the guard took away the precious metal, whether gold or silver, of which the cups, firepans, tossing-bowls, pots, lamp-stands, saucers, and flagons were made. The bronze of the two pillars, of the one sea and of the twelve oxen supporting it, which King Solomon had made for the house of the LORD, was beyond weighing. The one pillar was eighteen cubits high and twelve cubits in circumference; it was hollow and the metal was four fingers thick. It had a capital of bronze, five cubits high, and a decoration of network and pomegranates ran all round it, wholly of bronze. The other pillar with its pomegranates, was exactly like it. Ninety-six pomegranates were exposed to view and there were a hundred in all on the network all round.

The captain of the guard took Seraiah the chief priest and Zephaniah the deputy chief priest and the three on duty at the entrance; he took also from the city a eunuch who was in charge of the fighting men, seven of those with right of access to the king who were still in the city, the adjutant-general*g* whose duty was to muster the people for war, and sixty men of the people who were still there.

These Nebuzaradan captain of the guard brought to the king of Babylon at Riblah. There, in the land of Hamath, the king of Babylon had them flogged and put to death. So Judah went into exile from their own land.

Total number of exiles

These were the people deported by Nebuchadrezzar in the seventeenth*h* year: three thousand and twenty-three Judaeans. In his eighteenth year, eight hundred and thirty-two people from Jerusalem; in his twenty-third year, seven hundred and forty-five Judaeans were deported by Nebuzaradan the captain of the bodyguard: all together four thousand six hundred people.

Jehoiachin honoured in Babylon

In the thirty-seventh year of the exile *i* of Jehoiachin king of Judah, on the twenty-fifth day of the twelfth month, Evil-merodach king of Babylon in the year of his accession showed favour to Jehoiachin king of Judah. He brought him out of prison, treated him kindly and gave him a seat at table above the kings with him in Babylon. So Jehoiachin discarded his prison clothes and lived as a pensioner of the king for the rest of his life. For his maintenance a regular daily allowance was given him by the king of Babylon as long as he lived, to the day of his death.

g Prob. rdg.; Heb. adds commander-in-chief. *2 Kgs. 25. 27–30.*   *h Prob. rdg.; Heb.* seventh.   *i Verses 31–4: cp.*

LAMENTATIONS

Sorrows of captive Zion

1 How solitary lies the city, once so full
     of people!
   Once great among nations, now become a widow;
   once queen among provinces, now put to forced labour!
2 Bitterly she weeps in the night,
     tears run down her cheeks;
   she has no one to bring her comfort
     among all that love her;
   all her friends turned traitor

     and became her enemies.
   Judah went into the misery of exile 3
     and endless servitude.
   Settled among the nations,
     she found no resting-place;
   all her persecutors fell upon her
     in her sore straits.
   The paths to Zion mourn,   4
     for none attend her sacred feasts;
   all her gates are desolate.
   Her priests groan and sigh,
     her virgins are cruelly treated.
   How bitter is her fate!

5 Her adversaries have become her
    masters,
  her enemies take their ease,
  for the LORD has cruelly punished
    her
  because of misdeeds without num-
    ber;
  her young children have gone,
  driven away captive by the enemy.
6 All majesty has vanished
  from the daughter of Zion.
  Her princes have become like deer
  that can find no pasture
  and run on, their strength all spent,
  pursued by the hunter.
7 Jerusalem has remembered
  her days of misery and wandering,[a]
  when her people fell into the power
    of the adversary
  and there was no one to help her.
  The adversary saw and mocked
  at her fallen state.
8 Jerusalem had sinned greatly,
  and so she was treated like a filthy
    rag;
  all those who had honoured her
    held her cheap,
  for they had seen her nakedness.
  What could she do but sigh
  and turn away?
9 Uncleanness clung to her skirts,
  and she gave no thought to her fate.
  Her fall was beyond belief
  and there was no one to comfort
    her.
  Look, LORD, upon her misery,
  see how the enemy has triumphed.
10 The adversary stretched out his
    hand
  to seize all her treasures;
  then it was that she saw Gentiles
  entering her sanctuary,
  Gentiles forbidden by thee to enter
  the assembly, for it was thine.
11 All her people groaned,
  they begged for bread;
  they sold their treasures for food
  to give them strength again.

  Look, O LORD, and see
  how cheap I am accounted.
12 Is it of no concern to you who pass by?
  If only you would look and see:
  is there any agony like mine,
  like these my torments
  with which the LORD has cruelly
    punished me
  in the day of his anger?
13 He sent down fire from heaven,
  it ran through my bones;
  he spread out a net to catch my
    feet,

and turned me back;
he made me an example of desolation,
racked with sickness all day long.
My transgressions were bound[b] upon 14
  me,
his own hand knotted them round
  me;
his yoke was lifted on to my neck,
my strength failed beneath its
  weight;
the Lord abandoned me to its hold,[c]
and I could not stand.
The Lord treated with scorn 15
all the mighty men within my walls;
he marshalled rank on rank against
  me
to crush my young warriors.
The Lord trod down, like grapes in
  the press,
the virgin daughter of Judah.
For these things I weep over my 16
  plight,[d]
my eyes run with tears;
for any to comfort me and renew
  my strength
are far to seek;
my sons are an example of desolation,
for the enemy is victorious.

Prayer and confession

Zion lifted her hands in prayer, 17
but there was no one to comfort
  her;
the LORD gave Jacob's enemies the
  order
to beset him on every side.
Jerusalem became a filthy rag in their
  midst.
The LORD was in the right; 18
it was I who rebelled against his
  commands.
Listen, O listen, all you nations,
and look on my agony:
my virgins and my young men are
  gone into captivity.
I called to my lovers, they broke 19
  faith with me;
my priests and my elders in the
  city
went hungry and could find nothing,
although they sought food for
  themselves
to renew their strength.
See, LORD, how sorely I am distres- 20
  sed.
My bowels writhe in anguish
and my stomach turns within me,
because I wantonly rebelled.

a *Prob. rdg.; Heb. adds* all her treasures which have been from days of old.   b bound: *prob. rdg.;*
Heb. word unknown.   c its hold: *prob. rdg.; Heb. obscure.*   d my plight: *prob. rdg.; Heb.* my eye.

The sword makes orphans in the streets,
as plague does within doors.
21 Hear me when I groan
with no one to comfort me.
All my enemies, when they heard of my calamity,
rejoiced at what thou hadst done;
but hasten the day thou hast promised
when they shall become like me.
22 Let all their evil deeds come before thee;
torment them in their turn,
as thou hast tormented me
for all my transgressions;
for my sighs are many and my heart is faint.

The Lord punishes Zion

2 What darkness the Lord in his anger
has brought upon the daughter of Zion!
He hurled down from heaven to earth
the glory of Israel,
and did not remember in the day of his anger
that Zion was his footstool.
2 The Lord overwhelmed without pity
all the dwellings of Jacob.
In his wrath he tore down
the strongholds of the daughter of Judah;
he levelled with the ground and desecrated
the kingdom and its rulers.
3 In his anger he hacked down
the horn of Israel's pride,
he withdrew his helping hand
when the enemy came on;
and he blazed in Jacob like flaming fire
that rages far and wide.
4 In enmity he strung his bow;
he took his stand like an adversary
and with his strong arm he slew
all those who had been his delight;
he poured his fury out like fire
on the tent of the daughter of Zion.
5 The Lord played an enemy's part
and overwhelmed Israel.
He overwhelmed all their towered mansions
and brought down their strongholds in ruins;
sorrow upon sorrow he brought
to the daughter of Judah.
6 He stripped his tabernacle as a vine is stripped,

and made the place of assembly a ruin.
In Zion the Lord blotted out all memory
of festal assembly[e] and of sabbath;
king and priest alike he scorned
in the grimness of his anger.
The Lord spurned his own altar   7
and laid a curse upon his sanctuary.
He delivered the walls of her mansions
into the power of the enemy;
in the Lord's very house they raised shouts of victory
as on a day of festival.
The Lord was minded to bring 8
down in ruins
the walls of the daughter of Zion;
he took their measure with his line
and did not scruple to demolish her;
he made rampart and wall lament,
and both together lay dejected.
Her gates are sunk into the earth, 9
he has shattered and broken their bars;
her king and her rulers are among the Gentiles,
and there is no law;
her prophets too have received
no vision from the Lord.
The elders of the daughter of Zion 10
sit on the ground and sigh;
they have cast dust on their heads
and clothed themselves in sackcloth;
the virgins of Jerusalem
bow their heads to the ground.
My eyes are blinded with tears,   11
my bowels writhe in anguish.
In my bitterness my bile is spilt on the earth
because of my people's wound,
when children and infants faint
in the streets of the town
and cry to their mothers,   12
'Where can we get corn and wine?'—
when they faint like wounded things
in the streets of the city,
gasping out their lives
in their mothers' bosom.

How can I cheer you? Whose plight 13
is like yours,
daughter of Jerusalem?
To what can I compare you for your comfort,
virgin daughter of Zion?
For your wound gapes wide as the ocean;
who can heal you?
The visions that your prophets saw 14
for you

e festal assembly: *or* appointed seasons.

were false and painted shams;
they did not bring home to you
    your guilt
and so reverse your fortunes.
The visions that they saw for you
    were delusions,
false and fraudulent.*f*

15 All those who pass by
snap their fingers at you;
they hiss and wag their heads at you,
    daughter of Jerusalem:
'Is this the city once called Perfect in
    beauty,
Joy of the whole earth?'

16 All your enemies
make mouths and jeer at you;
they hiss and grind their teeth,
    saying, 'Here we are,
this is the day we have waited for;
we have lived to see it.'

17 The LORD has done what he planned
    to do,
he has fulfilled his threat,
all that he ordained from days of
    old.
He has demolished without pity
and let the enemy rejoice over you,
filling your adversaries with pride.

18 Cry with a full heart*g* to the Lord,
O wall of the daughter of Zion;
let your tears run down like a tor-
    rent
by day and by night.
Give yourself not a moment's rest,
let your tears never cease.

19 Arise and cry aloud in the night;
at the beginning of every watch
pour out your heart like water
in the Lord's very presence.
Lift up your hands to him
for the lives of your children.*h*

20 Look, LORD, and see:
who is it that thou hast thus tor-
    mented?
Must women eat the fruit of their
    wombs,
the children they have brought
    safely to birth?
Shall priest and prophet be slain
in the sanctuary of the Lord?

21 There in the streets young men and
    old
lie on the ground.
My virgins and my young men have
    fallen
by sword and by famine;
thou hast slain them in the day of
    thy anger,
slaughtered them without pity.

22 Thou didst summon my enemies
against me from every side,

like men assembling for a festival;
not a man escaped, not one survived
in the day of the LORD's anger.
All whom I brought safely to birth
    and reared
were destroyed by my enemies.

Despair

I am the man who has known afflic- 3
    tion,
I have felt the rod of his wrath.
It was I whom he led away and left 2
    to walk
in darkness, where no light is.
Against me alone he has turned his 3
    hand,
and so it is all day long.
He has wasted away my flesh and 4
    my skin
and broken all my bones;
he has built up walls around me,   5
    behind and before,
and has cast me into a place of 6
    darkness
like a man long dead.
He has walled me in so that I can- 7
    not escape,
and weighed me down with fetters;
even when I cry out and call for 8
    help,
he rejects my prayer.
He has barred my road with blocks 9
    of stone
and tangled up my way.
He lies in wait for me like a bear 10
or a lion lurking in a covert.
He has made my way refractory 11
    and lamed me
and left me desolate.
He has strung his bow   12
and made me the target for his
    arrows;
he has pierced my kidneys with 13
    shafts
drawn from his quiver.
I have become a laughing-stock to 14
    all nations,
the target of their mocking songs
    all day.
He has given me my fill of bitter 15
    herbs
and made me drunk with worm-
    wood.
He has broken my teeth on gravel; 16
    fed on ashes, I am racked with pain;
peace has gone out of my life,   17
and I have forgotten what pros-
    perity means.
Then I cry out that my strength 18
    has gone
and so has my hope in the LORD.

---

f fraudulent: *or* causing banishment.   *g* Cry . . . heart: *prob. rdg.; Heb.* Their heart cried.
h *Prob. rdg.; Heb. adds* who faint with hunger at every street-corner.

Hope

9 The memory of my distress and my
     wanderings
    is[i] wormwood and gall.
10 Remember, O remember,
    and stoop down to me.[jk]
11 All this I take to heart
    and therefore I will wait patiently:
12 the LORD's true love is surely not
     spent,[l]
    nor has his compassion failed;
13 they are new every morning,
    so great is his constancy.
14 The LORD, I say, is all that I have;
    therefore I will wait for him pa-
     tiently.
15 The LORD is good to those who look
    for him,
    to all who seek him;
16 it is good to wait in patience and
    sigh
    for deliverance by the LORD.
17 It is good, too, for a man
    to carry the yoke in his youth.
18 Let him sit alone and sigh
    if it is heavy upon him;
19 let him lay his face in the dust,
    and there may yet be hope.
20 Let him turn his cheek to the
    smiter
    and endure full measure of abuse;
21 for the Lord will not cast off
    his servants[m] for ever.
22 He may punish cruelly, yet he will
    have compassion
    in the fullness of his love;
23 he does not willingly afflict
    or punish any mortal man.

Repentance

24 To trample underfoot
    any prisoner in the land,
25 to deprive a man of his rights
    in defiance of the Most High,
26 to pervert justice in the courts—
    such things the Lord has never
    approved.
27 Who can command and it is done,
    if the Lord has forbidden it?
28 Do not both bad and good proceed
    from the mouth of the Most High?
29 Why should any man living com-
    plain,
    any mortal who has sinned?
30 Let us examine our ways and put
    them to the test
    and turn back to the LORD;

41 let us lift up our hearts, not our
    hands,
    to God in heaven.
42 We ourselves have sinned and rebel-
    led,
    and thou hast not forgiven.
43 In anger thou hast turned[n] and
    pursued us
    and slain without pity;
44 thou hast hidden thyself behind the
    clouds
    beyond reach of our prayers;
45 thou hast treated us as offscouring
    and refuse
    among the nations.
46 All our enemies make mouths
    and jeer at us.
47 Before us lie hunter's scare and pit,
    devastation and ruin.
48 My eyes run with streams of water
    because of my people's wound.
49 My eyes stream with unceasing
    tears
    and refuse all comfort,
50 while the LORD in heaven looks
    down
    and watches my affliction,[o]
51 while the LORD torments[p] me
    with the fate of all the daughters
    of my city.

Prayer for vindication

52 Those who for no reason were my
    enemies
    drove me cruelly like a bird;
53 they thrust me alive into the silent
    pit,
    and they closed it over me with a
    stone;
54 the waters rose high above my head,
    and I said, 'My end has come.'
55 But I called on thy name, O LORD,
    from the depths of the pit;
56 thou heardest my voice; do not turn
    a deaf ear
    when I cry, 'Come to my relief.'
57 Thou wast near when I called to
    thee;
    thou didst say, 'Have no fear.'
58 Lord, thou didst plead my cause
    and ransom my life;
59 thou sawest, LORD, the injustice
    done to me
    and gavest judgement in my favour;
60 thou sawest their vengeance,
    all their plots against me.
61 Thou didst hear their bitter taunts,
    O LORD,
    their many plots against me,

---

i The memory . . . is: *or* Remember my distress and my wanderings, the . . .   *j* stoop down to
me: *prob. original rdg., altered in Heb. to* I sink down.   *k* Remember . . . me: *or* I remember, I
remember them and sink down.   *l* spent: *prob. rdg.; Heb. unintelligible.*   *m* his servants: *prob.
rdg.; Heb. om.*   *n* Prob. rdg.; Heb. hidden.*   *o* my affliction: *prob. rdg.; Heb. my eye.*   *p* the
LORD torments: *prob. rdg.; Heb. tormenting.*

62 the whispering, the murmurs of my
    enemies
    all the day long.
63 See how, whether they sit or stand,
    they taunt me bitterly.
64 Pay them back for their deeds, O
    LORD,
    pay them back what they deserve.
65 Show them how hard thy heart can
    be,
    how little concern thou hast for
    them.
66 Pursue them in anger and exter-
    minate them
    from beneath thy heavens, O LORD.

Zion's wretched condition

4   How dulled is the gold,
    how tarnished the fine gold!
    The stones of the sanctuary[q] lie strewn
    at every street-corner.
2   See Zion's precious sons,
    once worth their weight in finest
    gold,
    now counted as pitchers of earthen-
    ware
    made by any potter's hand.
3   Even whales[r] uncover the teat
    and suckle their young;
    but the daughters of my people are
    cruel
    as ostriches in the desert.
4   The sucking infant's tongue
    cleaves to its palate from thirst;
    young children beg for bread
    but no one offers them a crumb.
5   Those who once fed delicately
    are desolate in the streets,
    and those nurtured in purple
    now grovel on dunghills.
6   The punishment[s] of my people is
    worse
    than the penalty[t] of Sodom,
    which was overthrown in a moment
    and no one wrung his hands.
7   Her crowned princes[u] were once
    purer than snow,
    whiter than milk;
    they were ruddier than branching
    coral,[v]
    and their limbs were lapis lazuli.
8   But their faces turned blacker than
    soot,
    and no one knew them in the streets;
    the skin was drawn tight over their
    bones,
    dry as touchwood.
9   Those who died by the sword were
    more fortunate

than those who died of hunger;
these wasted away, deprived
of the produce of the field.
Tender-hearted women with their 10
    own hands
boiled their own children;
their children became their food
in the day of my people's wounding.
The LORD glutted his rage 11
and poured forth his anger;
he kindled a fire in Zion,
and it consumed her foundations.
This no one believed, neither the 12
    kings of the earth
nor anyone that dwelt in the world:
that enemy or invader would enter
the gates of Jerusalem.
It was for the sins of her prophets 13
and for the iniquities of her priests,
who shed within her walls
the blood of the righteous.
They wandered blindly in the 14
    streets,
so stained with blood
that men would not touch
even their garments.
'Away, away; unclean!' men cried 15
to them.
'Away, do not come near.'
They hastened away, they wandered
    among the nations,[w]
unable to find any resting-place.
The LORD himself scattered them, 16
he thought of them no more;
he showed no favour to priests,
no pity for elders.

When Zion's punishment is complete

Still we strain our eyes, 17
looking in vain for help.
We have watched and watched
for a nation powerless to save us.
When we go out, we take to by-ways 18
to avoid the public streets;
our days are all but finished,[x]
our end has come.
Our pursuers have shown them- 19
    selves swifter
than vultures in the sky;
they are hot on our trail over the
    hills,
they lurk to catch us in the wilder-
    ness.
The LORD's anointed, the breath of 20
    life to us,
was caught in their machinations,
although we had thought to live
among the nations, save under his
    protection.

---

q The stones of the sanctuary: or Bright gems.
t Or sin.   u crowned princes: or Nazirites.
coral.   w Prob. rdg.; Heb. adds they said.
drawn near, our days are complete.

r Prob. rdg.; Heb. jackals.   s Or iniquity.
v than . . . coral: prob. rdg.; Heb. branch than
x our . . . finished: prob. rdg.; Heb. our end has

21 Rejoice and be glad, daughter of Edom,
you who live in the land of Uz.
Yet the cup shall pass to you in your turn,
and when you are drunk you will expose yourself to shame.
22 The punishment for your sin, daughter of Zion, is now complete,
and never again shall you be carried into exile.
But you, daughter of Edom, your sin shall be punished,
and your guilt revealed.

Prayer for restoration

5 Remember, O LORD, what has befallen us;
look, and see how we are scorned.
2 Our patrimony is turned over to strangers
and our homes to foreigners.
3 We are like orphans, without a father;
our mothers are like widows.
4 We must buy our own water to drink,
our own wood can only be had at a price.
5 The yoke is on our necks, we are overdriven;
we are weary and are given no rest.
6 We come to terms, now with the Egyptians,
now with the Assyrians, to provide us with food.
7 Our fathers sinned and are no more,
and we bear the burden of their guilt.
8 Slaves have become our rulers,
and there is no one to rescue us from them.

We must bring in our food from the 9 wilderness,
risking our lives in the scorching heat,[y]
Our skins are blackened as in a 10 furnace
by the ravages of starvation.
Women were raped in Zion, 11
virgins raped in the cities of Judah.
Princes were hung up by their 12 hands,
and elders received no honour.
Young men toil to grind corn, 13
and boys stumble under loads of wood.
Elders have left off their sessions in 14 the gate,
and young men no longer pluck the strings.
Joy has fled from our hearts, 15
and our dances are turned to mourning.
The garlands have fallen from our 16 heads;
woe betide us, sinners that we are.
For this we are sick at heart, 17
for all this our eyes grow dim:
because Mount Zion is desolate 18
and over it the jackals run wild.
O LORD, thou art enthroned for ever, 19
thy throne endures from one generation to another.
Why wilt thou quite forget us 20
and forsake us these many days?
O LORD, turn us back to thyself, and 21
we will come back;
renew our days as in times long past.
For if thou hast utterly rejected 22 us,
then great indeed has been thy anger against us.

[y] in the scorching heat: *or* by the sword.

THE BOOK OF THE PROPHET
EZEKIEL

A vision of God

1 ON THE FIFTH DAY of the fourth month in the thirtieth year, while I was among the exiles by the river Kebar,[a] the heavens were 2 opened and I saw a vision of God. On the fifth day of the month in the fifth year of the exile of King Jehoiachin, the word of the LORD came to Ezekiel 3 son of Buzi the priest, in Chaldaea, by the river Kebar, and there the hand of the LORD came upon him.

I saw a storm wind coming from the 4

[a] Or the Kebar canal.

north, a vast cloud with flashes of fire and brilliant light about it; and within was a radiance like brass, glowing
5 in the heart of the flames. In the fire was the semblance of four living
6 creatures in human form. Each had
7 four faces and each four wings; their legs were straight, and their hooves were like the hooves of a calf, glitter-
8 ing like a disc of bronze. Under the wings on each of the four sides were human hands; all four creatures had
9 faces and wings, and their wings touched one another. They did not turn as they moved; each creature
10 went straight forward. Their faces were like this: all four had the face of a man and the face of a lion on the right, on the left the face of an ox and
11 the face of an eagle. Their wings were spread; each living creature had one pair touching its neighbours',[b] while
12 one pair covered its body. They moved straight forward in whatever direction the spirit[c] would go; they
13 never swerved in their course. The appearance of the creatures was as if fire from burning coals or torches were darting to and fro among them; the fire was radiant, and out of the fire came lightning.[d]
15 As I looked at the living creatures, I saw wheels on the ground, one
16 beside each of the four.[e] The wheels sparkled like topaz, and they were all alike: in form and working they were
17 like a wheel inside a wheel, and when they moved in any of the four directions they never swerved in their
18 course. All four had hubs and each hub had a projection which had the power of sight,[f] and the rims of the wheels were full of eyes all round.
19 When the living creatures moved, the wheels moved beside them; when the creatures rose from the ground,
20 the wheels rose; they moved in whatever direction the spirit[e] would go; and the wheels rose together with them, for the spirit of the living creatures
21 was in the wheels. When the one moved, the other moved; when the one halted, the other halted; when the creatures rose from the ground, the wheels rose together with them, for the spirit of the creatures was in the wheels.
22 Above the heads of the living creatures was, as it were, a vault glittering like a sheet of ice, awe-inspiring,

stretched over their heads above them. Under the vault their wings were spread straight out, touching one another, while one pair covered the body of each. I heard, too, the noise of their wings; when they moved it was like the noise of a great torrent or of a cloud-burst,[g] like the noise of a crowd or of an armed camp; when they halted their wings dropped. A sound was heard above the vault over their heads, as they halted with drooping wings. Above the vault over their heads there appeared, as it were, a sapphire[h] in the shape of a throne, and high above all, upon the throne, a form in human likeness. I saw what might have been brass glowing like fire in a furnace from the waist upwards; and from the waist downwards I saw what looked like fire with encircling radiance. Like a rainbow in the clouds on a rainy day was the sight of that encircling radiance; it was like the appearance of the glory of the LORD.

Mission and message

When I saw this I threw myself on my face, and heard a voice speaking to me: Man, he said, stand up, and let me talk with you. As he spoke, a spirit came into me and stood me on my feet, and I listened to him speaking. He said to me, Man, I am sending you to the Israelites, a nation of rebels who have rebelled against me. Past generations of them have been in revolt against me to this very day, and this generation to which I am sending you is stubborn and obstinate. When you say to them, 'These are the words of the Lord GOD', they will know that they have a prophet among them, whether they listen or whether they refuse to listen, because they are rebels. But you, man, must not be afraid of them or of what they say, though they are rebels against you and renegades, and you find yourself sitting on scorpions. There is nothing to fear in what they say, and nothing in their looks to terrify you, rebels though they are. You must speak my words to them, whether they listen or whether they refuse to listen, rebels that they are. But you, man, must listen to what I say and not be rebellious like them. Open your mouth and eat what I give you.

---

b its neighbours': *prob. rdg.*; *Heb. unintelligible.*   c *Or* wind.   d *Prob. rdg.*, *cp. Sept.*; *Heb. adds* (14) and the living creatures went out (*prob. rdg.*) *Heb. obscure*) and in like rays of light.   e one . . . four: *prob. rdg.*; *Heb. obscure.*   f the power of sight: *prob. rdg.*; *Heb. fear.*   g *Or* of the Almighty.   h *Or* lapis lazuli.

9 Then I saw a hand stretched out to
10 me, holding a scroll. He unrolled it
before me, and it was written all over
on both sides with dirges and laments
3 and words of woe. Then he said to me,
'Man, eat what is in front of you, eat
this scroll; then go and speak to the
2 Israelites.' So I opened my mouth and
3 he gave me the scroll to eat. Then he
said, 'Man, swallow this scroll I give
you, and fill yourself full.' So I ate it,
and it tasted as sweet as honey.

4 Man, he said to me, go and tell the
Israelites what I have to say to them.
5 You are sent not to people whose
speech is thick and difficult, but to
6 Israelites. No; I am not sending you
to great nations whose speech is so
thick and so difficult that you cannot
make out what they say; if however I
had sent you to them they would have
7 listened to you. But the Israelites will
refuse to listen to you, for they refuse
to listen to me, so brazen are they all
8 and stubborn. But I will make you a
match for them. I will make you as
brazen as they are and as stubborn as
9 they are. I will make your brow like
adamant, harder than flint. Never
fear them, never be terrified by them,
0 rebels though they are. And he said
to me, Listen carefully, man, to all
that I have to say to you, and take it
1 to heart. Go to your fellow-countrymen in exile and speak to them.
Whether they listen or refuse to listen,
say, 'These are the words of the Lord
GOD.'

12 Then a spirit[i] lifted me up, and I
heard behind me a fierce rushing
sound as the glory of the LORD rose[j]
13 from his place. I heard the sound of
the living creatures' wings brushing
against one another, the sound of the
wheels beside them, and a fierce
14 rushing sound. A spirit[i] lifted me and
carried me along, and I went full of
exaltation, the hand of the LORD
15 strong upon me. So I came to the
exiles at Tel-abib who were settled
by the river Kebar. For seven days I
stayed with them, dumbfounded.

16 At the end of seven days the word
17 of the LORD came to me: Man, I have
made you a watchman for the Israelites; you will take messages from me
18 and carry my warnings to them. It
may be that I pronounce sentence of
death on a wicked man:[k] if you do not
warn him to give up his wicked ways
and so save his life, the guilt is his;
because of his wickedness he shall die,
but I will hold you answerable for his

death. But if you have warned him 19
and he still continues in his wicked and
evil ways, he shall die because of his
wickedness, but you will have saved
yourself. Or it may be that a right- 20
eous man turns away and does wrong,
and I let that be the cause of his
downfall; he will die because you have
not warned him. He will die for his
sin; the righteous deeds he has done
will not be taken into account, and I
will hold you answerable for his death.
But if you have warned the righteous 21
man not to sin and he has not sinned,
then he will have saved his life because
he has been warned, and you will have
saved yourself.

The LORD speaks to Ezekiel

The hand of the LORD came upon me 22
there, and he said to me, Rise up; go
out into the plain, and there I will
speak to you. So I rose and went out 23
into the plain; the glory of the LORD
was there, like the glory which I had
seen by the river Kebar; and I threw
myself down on my face. Then a spirit 24
came into me and stood me on my
feet, and spoke to me: Go, he said,
and shut yourself up in your house.
You shall be tied and bound with ropes, 25
man, so that you cannot go out among
the people. I will fasten your tongue 26
to the roof of your mouth and you will
be unable to speak; you will not be
the one to rebuke them, rebels though
they are. But when I have something 27
to say to you, I will give you back the
power of speech. Then you will say to
them, 'These are the words of the
Lord GOD.' If anyone will listen, he
may listen, and, if he refuses to listen,
he may refuse; for they are rebels.

The siege of Jerusalem portrayed

Man, take a tile and set it before you. 4
Draw a city on it, the city of Jerusalem: lay siege to it, erect watch- 2
towers against it, raise a siege-ramp,
put mantelets in position, and bring
battering-rams against it all round.
Then take an iron griddle, and put it 3
as a wall of iron between you and the
city. Keep your face turned towards
the city; it will be the besieged and
you the besieger. This will be a sign to
the Israelites.

Now lie on your left side, and I will 4
lay Israel's iniquity on you; you shall
bear their iniquity for as many days
as you lie on that side. Allowing one 5

i Or wind.   j rose: prob. rdg.; Heb. obscure.
k Prob. rdg.; Heb. adds if you do not warn him.

day for every year of their iniquity, I ordain that you bear it for one hundred and ninety days; thus you shall
6 bear Israel's iniquity. When you have completed all this, lie down a second time on your right side, and bear Judah's iniquity for forty days; I
7 count one day for every year. Then turn your face towards the siege of Jerusalem and bare your arm, and
8 prophesy against it. See how I tie you with ropes so that you cannot turn over from one side to the other until you complete the days of your distress.
9 Then take wheat and barley, beans and lentils, millet and spelt. Mix them all in one bowl and make your bread out of them. You are to eat it during the one hundred and ninety days you
10 spend lying on your side. And you must weigh out your food; you may eat twenty shekels' weight a day,
11 taking it from time to time. Measure out your drinking water too; you may drink a sixth of a hin a day,
12 taking it from time to time. You are to eat your bread baked like barley cakes, using human dung as fuel, and you must bake it where people can see
13 you. Then the LORD said, 'This is the kind of bread, unclean bread, that the Israelites will eat in the foreign lands
14 into which I shall drive them.' But I said, 'O Lord GOD, I have never been made unclean, never in my life have I eaten what has died naturally or been killed by wild beasts; no tainted meat has ever passed my lips.'
15 So he allowed me to use cow-dung instead of human dung to bake my bread.
16 Then he said to me, Man, I am cutting short their daily bread in Jerusalem; people will weigh out anxiously the bread they eat, and measure with
17 dismay the water they drink. So their food and their water will run short until they are dismayed at the sight of one another; they will waste away because of their iniquity.

5 Man, take a sharp sword, take it like a barber's razor and run it over your head and your chin. Then take scales and divide the hair into three.
2 When the siege comes to an end, burn one third of the hair in a fire in the centre of the city; cut up one third with the sword all round the city; scatter one third to the wind, and I
3 will follow it with drawn sword. Take a few of these hairs and tie them up in
4 a fold of your robe. Then take others of them, throw them into the fire and burn them, and out of them fire will come upon all Israel.

The reason for Jerusalem's fall

These are the words of the Lord GOD: 5 This city of Jerusalem I have set among the nations, with other countries around her, and she has rebelled 6 against my laws and my statutes more wickedly than those nations and countries; for her people have rejected my laws and refused to conform to my statutes.

Therefore the Lord GOD says: Since 7 you have been more ungrateful than the nations around you and have not conformed to my statutes and have not kept my laws or even the laws of the nations around you, therefore, 8 says the Lord GOD, I, in my turn, will be against you; I will execute judgements in your midst for the nations to see, such judgements as I have never 9 executed before nor ever will again, so abominable have your offences been. Therefore, O Jerusalem, fathers 10 will eat their children and children their fathers in your midst; I will execute judgements on you, and any who are left in you I will scatter to the four winds. As I live, says the Lord 11 GOD, because you have defiled my holy place with all your vile and abominable rites, I in my turn will consume you without pity; I in my turn will not spare you. One third of 12 your people shall die by pestilence and perish by famine in your midst; one third shall fall by the sword in the country round about; and one third I will scatter to the four winds and follow with drawn sword. Then my 13 anger will be spent, I will abate my fury against them and be calm; when my fury is spent they will know that it is I, the LORD, who spoke in jealous passion. I have made you a scandal[l] 14 and a reproach to the nations around you, and all who pass by will see it. You will be an object of reproach and 15 abuse, a terrible lesson to the nations around you, when I pass sentence on you and do judgement in anger and fury. I, the LORD, have spoken. When 16 I shoot the deadly arrows of famine against you,[m] arrows of destruction, I will shoot to destroy you. I will bring famine upon you and cut short your daily bread; I will unleash famine and 17 beasts of prey upon you, and they will leave you childless. Pestilence and slaughter will sweep through you, and

l Or desolation.   m Prob. rdg.; Heb. them.

I will bring the sword upon you. I, the LORD, have spoken.

Israel a desolate waste

6 These were the words of the LORD to me: Man, look towards the mountains of Israel, and prophesy to them: Mountains of Israel, hear the word of the Lord GOD. This is his word to mountains and hills, watercourses and valleys: I am bringing a sword against you, and I will destroy your hill-shrines. Your altars will be made desolate, your incense-altars shattered, and I will fling down your slain before your idols. I will strew the corpses of the Israelites before their idols, and I will scatter your bones about your altars. In all your settlements the blood-spattered altars[n] shall be laid waste and the hill-shrines made desolate. Your altars will be waste and desolate and your idols shattered and useless, your incense-altars hewn down, and all your works wiped out; with the slain falling about you, you shall know that I am the LORD. But when they fall,[o] I will leave you, among the nations, some who survive the sword. When you are scattered in foreign lands, these survivors, in captivity among the nations, will remember how I was grieved because their hearts had turned wantonly from me and their eyes had gone roving wantonly after idols. Then they will loathe themselves for all the evil they have done with their abominations. So they will know that I am the LORD, that I was uttering no vain threat when I said that I would bring this evil upon them.

These are the words of the Lord GOD: Beat your hands together, stamp with your foot, bemoan your vile abominations, people of Israel. Men will fall by sword, famine, and pestilence. Far away they will die by pestilence; at home they will fall by the sword; any who survive or are spared will die by famine, and so at last my anger will be spent. You will know that I am the LORD when their slain fall among the idols round their altars, on every high hill, on all mountain-tops, under every spreading tree, under every leafy terebinth, wherever they have brought offerings of soothing odour for their idols one and all. So I will stretch out my hand over them and make the land a desolate waste in all their settlements, more desolate than the desert of Riblah.[p] They shall know that I am the LORD.

Impending ruin

The word of the LORD came to me: **7** Man, the Lord GOD says this to the land of Israel: An end is coming, the end is coming upon the four corners of the land.[q] The end is now upon you; I will unleash my anger against you; I will call you to account for your doings and bring your abominations upon your own heads. I will neither pity nor spare you: I will make you suffer for your doings and the abominations that continue in your midst. So you shall know that I am the LORD.

These are the words of the Lord GOD: Behold, it comes, disasters one upon another; the end, the end, it comes, it comes.[r] Doom is coming upon you, dweller in the land; the time is coming, the day is near, with confusion and the crash of thunder.[s] Now, in an instant, I will vent my rage upon you and let my anger spend itself. I will call you to account for your doings and bring your abominations upon your own heads. I will neither pity nor spare; I will make you suffer for your doings and the abominations that continue in your midst. So you shall know that it is I, the LORD, who strike the blow.

Behold, the day! the doom is here, it has burst upon them. Injustice buds, insolence blossoms, violence shoots up into injustice and wickedness. And it is all their fault, the fault of their turmoil and tumult and all their restless ways. The time has come, the day has arrived; the buyer has no reason to be glad, and the seller none for regret, for I am angry at all their turmoil. The seller will never go back on his bargain while either of them lives; for the bargain will never be reversed because of the turmoil, and no man will exert himself, even in his iniquity, as long as he lives. The trumpet has sounded and all is ready, but no one goes out to war.

Outside is the sword, inside are pestilence and famine; in the country men will die by the sword, in the city famine and pestilence will carry them off. If any escape and take to the mountains, like moaning doves, there will I slay them, each for his iniquity,

n blood-spattered altars: or cities.   o when they fall: prob. rdg.; Heb. obscure.   p Prob. rdg.; Heb. Diblah.   q Or earth.   r Prob. rdg.; Heb. adds it wakes up, behold it comes.   s and the crash of thunder: prob. rdg.; Heb. unintelligible.

17 while their hands hang limp and their
18 knees run with urine. They will go in
sackcloth, shuddering from head to
foot, with faces downcast and heads
19 close shaved. They shall fling their
silver into the streets and cast aside
their gold like filth; their silver and
their gold will be powerless to save
them on the day of the LORD's fury.
Their hunger will not be satisfied nor
their bellies filled; for their iniquity
will be the cause of their downfall.
20 They have fed their pride on their
beautiful jewels, which they made
into vile and abominable images.
Therefore I will treat their jewels like
21 filth, I will hand them over as plunder
to foreigners and as booty to the most
evil people on earth, and these will
22 defile them. I will turn my face from
them and let my treasured land be
profaned; brigands will come in and
defile it.
23 Clench your fists, for the land is
full of bloodshed[t] and the city full
24 of violence. I will let in the scum of
nations to take possession of their
houses; I will quell the pride of the
strong, and their sanctuaries shall be
25 profaned. Shuddering will come over
them, and they will look in vain for
26 peace. Tempest shall follow upon
tempest and rumour upon rumour.
Men will go seeking a vision from
a prophet; there will be no more
guidance from a priest, no counsel
27 from elders. The king will mourn, the
prince will be clothed with horror, the
hands of the common people will
shake with fright. I will deal with
them as they deserve, and call them
to account for their doings; and so
they shall know that I am the LORD.

Ezekiel's vision of Jerusalem

8 On the fifth day of the sixth month in
the sixth year, I was sitting at home
and the elders of Judah were with me.
2 Suddenly the hand of the Lord GOD
came upon me, and I saw what looked
like a man. He seemed to be all fire
from the waist down and to shine and
glitter like brass from the waist up.
3 He stretched out what seemed a hand
and seized me by the forelock. A
spirit[u] lifted me up between heaven
and earth, carried me to Jerusalem in
a vision of God and put me down at
the entrance to the inner gate facing
north, where stands the image of Lust
4 to rouse lustful passion. The glory of
the God of Israel was there, like the
5 vision I had seen in the plain. The

LORD said to me, 'Man, look north- 6
wards.' I did so, and there to the north
of the altar gate, at the entrance, was
that image of Lust. 'Man,' he said, 'do
you see what they are doing? The
monstrous abominations which the
Israelites practise here are driving me
far from my sanctuary, and you will
see even more such abominations.'
Then he brought me to the entrance 7
of the court, and I looked and found
a hole in the wall. 'Man,' he said to 8
me, 'dig through the wall.' I did so,
and it became an opening. 'Go in,' he 9
said, 'and see the vile abominations
they practise here.' So I went in and 10
saw figures of reptiles, beasts, and
vermin, and all the idols of the Israelites, carved round the walls. Seventy 11
elders of Israel were standing in front
of them, with Jaazaniah son of Shaphan in the middle, and each held
a censer from which rose the fragrant
smoke of incense. 'Man,' he said to me, 12
'do you see what the elders of Israel
are doing in darkness, each at the
shrine of his own carved image? They
think that the LORD does not see
them, or that he has forsaken the
country. You will see', he said, 'yet 13
more monstrous abominations which
they practise.'
Then he brought me to that gate- 14
way of the LORD's house which faces
north; and there I saw women sitting
and wailing for Tammuz. 'Man, do 15
you see that?' he asked me. 'But you
will see abominations more monstrous
than these.' So he took me to the 16
inner court of the LORD's house, and
there, by the entrance to the sanctuary of the LORD, between porch
and altar, were some twenty-five men
with their backs to the sanctuary and
their faces to the east, prostrating
themselves to the rising sun. He said 17
to me, 'Man, do you see that? Is it
because they think these abominations a trifle, that the Jews have filled
the country with violence? They provoke me further to anger, even while
they seek to appease me; I will turn 18
upon them in my rage; I will neither
pity nor spare. Loudly as they may
cry to me, I will not listen.'

Godfearing Israelites marked

A loud voice rang in my ears: 'Here 9
they come, those appointed to punish
the city, each carrying his weapon of
destruction.' Then I saw six men ap- 2
proaching from the road that leads to
the upper northern gate, each carrying

t bloodshed: *prob. rdg.*; *Heb.* the judgement of bloodshed.   u Or wind.

a battle-axe, one man among them dressed in linen, with pen and ink at his waist; and they halted by the altar 3 of bronze. Then the glory of the God of Israel rose from above the cherubim. He came to the terrace of the temple and called to the man dressed in linen with pen and ink at his waist. 4 'Go through the city, through Jerusalem,' said the LORD, 'and put a mark on the foreheads of those who groan and lament over the abomina- 5 tions practised there.' Then I heard him say to the others, 'Follow him through the city and kill without pity; 6 spare no one. Kill and destroy them all, old men and young, girls, little children and women, but touch no one who bears the mark. Begin at my sanctuary.' So they began with the 7 elders in front of the temple. 'Defile the temple,' he said, 'and fill the courts with dead bodies; then go out into the city and kill.'

Ezekiel pleads for Jerusalem

8 While they did their work, I was left alone; and I threw myself upon my face, crying out, 'O Lord GOD, must thou destroy all the Israelites who are left, pouring out thy anger on Jeru- 9 salem?' He answered, 'The iniquity of Israel and Judah is great indeed; the land is full of murder, the city is filled with injustice. They think the LORD has forsaken this country; they 10 think he sees nothing. But I will neither pity nor spare them; I will make them answer for all they have done.' 11 Then the man dressed in linen with pen and ink at his waist came and made his report: 'I have done what thou hast commanded.'

The cherubim

10 Then I saw, above the vault over the heads of the cherubim, as it were a throne of sapphire*v* visible above 2 them. The LORD said to the man dressed in linen, 'Come in between the circling wheels under the cherubim, and take a handful of the burning embers lying among the cherubim; then toss them over the city.' So he went in before my eyes.

3 The cherubim stood on the right side of the temple as a man enters, 4 and a cloud filled the inner court. The glory of the LORD rose high from above the cherubim and moved on to the terrace; and the temple was filled with the cloud, while the radiance of the glory of the LORD filled

the court. The sound of the wings of 5 the cherubim could be heard as far as the outer court, as loud as if God Almighty were speaking. Then he told 6 the man dressed in linen to take fire from between the circling wheels and among the cherubim; the man came and stood by a wheel, and a cherub 7 from among the cherubim put its hand into the fire that lay among them, and, taking some fire, gave it to the man dressed in linen; and he received it and went out.

Under the wings of the cherubim 8 there appeared what seemed a human hand. And I saw four wheels beside 9 the cherubim, one wheel beside each cherub. They had the sparkle of topaz, and all four were alike, like a wheel 10 inside a wheel. When the cherubim 11 moved in any of the four directions, they never swerved in their course; they went straight on in the direction in which their heads were turned, never swerving in their course. Their 12 whole bodies, their backs and hands and wings, as well as the wheels, were full of eyes all round the four of them.*w* The whirring of the wheels sounded 13 in my ears. Each had four faces: the 14 first was that of a cherub, the second that of a man, the third that of a lion, and the fourth that of an eagle.

Then the cherubim raised them- 15 selves up, those same living creatures I had seen by the river Kebar. When 16 the cherubim moved, the wheels moved beside them; when the cherubim lifted their wings and rose from the ground, the wheels did not turn away from them. When the one halted, 17 the other halted; when the one rose, the other rose; for the spirit of the creatures was in the wheels. Then the 18 glory of the LORD left the temple terrace and halted above the cherubim. The cherubim lifted their wings and 19 raised themselves from the ground; I watched them go with the wheels beside them. They halted at the eastern gateway of the LORD's house, and the glory of the God of Israel was over them.

These were the living creatures I 20 had seen beneath the God of Israel at the river Kebar; I knew that they were cherubim. Each had four faces 21 and four wings and the semblance of human hands under their wings. Their faces were like those I had seen 22 in vision by the river Kebar;*x* they moved, each one of them, straight forward.

v Or lapis lazuli.   *w* Prob. rdg.; Heb. adds their wheels.   *x* Prob. rdg.; Heb. adds and them.

Judgement on the rulers

11 A spirit[v] lifted me up and brought me to the eastern gate of the LORD's house, the gate that faces east. By the doorway were twenty-five men, and I saw among them two of high office, Jaazaniah son of Azzur and 2 Pelatiah son of Benaiah. The LORD said to me, Man, it is these who are planning mischief and plotting trouble 3 in this city, saying to themselves, 'There will be no building of houses yet awhile; the city is a stewpot and 4 we are the meat in it.' Therefore, said he, prophesy against them, prophesy, 5 O man. Then the spirit of the LORD came suddenly upon me, and he told me to say, These are the words of the LORD: This is what you are saying to yourselves, you men of Israel; well do I know the thoughts that rise in your 6 mind. You have killed and killed in this city and heaped the streets with 7 the slain. These, therefore, are the words of the Lord GOD: The bodies of the slain that you have put there, it is they that are the meat. The city is indeed the stewpot, but I will take 8 you out of it. It is a sword that you fear, and a sword I will bring upon 9 you, says the Lord GOD. I will take you out of it; I will give you over to a foreign power; I will bring you to 10 justice. You too shall fall by the sword when I judge you on the frontier of Israel; thus you shall know 11 that I am the LORD. So the city will not be your stewpot, nor you the meat in it. On the frontier of Israel I will 12 judge you; thus you shall know that I am the LORD. You have not conformed to my statutes nor kept my laws, but you have followed the laws of the nations around you.

13 While I was prophesying, Pelatiah son of Benaiah fell dead; and I threw myself upon my face, crying aloud, 'O Lord GOD, must thou make an end of all the Israelites who are left?'

Promise of restoration and renewal

14 The word of the LORD came to me: 15 Man, they are your brothers, your brothers and your kinsmen, this whole people of Israel, to whom the men who now live in Jerusalem have said, 'Keep your distance from the LORD; the land has been made over 16 to us as our property.' Say therefore, These are the words of the Lord GOD: When I sent them far away among the nations and scattered them in

many lands, for a while I became their sanctuary in the countries to which they had gone. Say therefore, 17 These are the words of the Lord GOD: I will gather them from among the nations and assemble them from the countries over which I have scattered them, and I will give them the soil of Israel. When they come into it, they 18 will do away with all their vile and abominable practices. I will give them 19 a different heart and put a new spirit into them; I will take the heart of stone out of their bodies and give them a heart of flesh. Then they will 20 conform to my statutes and keep my laws. They will become my people, and I will become their God. But as 21 for those whose heart is set upon[z] their vile and abominable practices, I will make them answer for all they have done. This is the very word of the Lord GOD.

The Glory leaves Jerusalem

Then the cherubim lifted their wings, 22 with the wheels beside them and the glory of the God of Israel above them. The glory of the LORD rose up and 23 left the city, and halted on the mountain to the east of it. And a spirit[a] 24 lifted me up and brought me to the exiles in Chaldaea. All this came in a vision sent by the spirit of God, and then the vision that I had seen left me. I told the exiles all that the LORD 25 had revealed to me.

Ezekiel, a sign

The word of the LORD came to me: **12** Man, you live among a rebellious 2 people. Though they have eyes they will not see, though they have ears they will not hear, because they are a rebellious people. Therefore, man, 3 pack up what you need for a journey into exile, by day before their eyes; then set off on your journey. When you leave home and go off into exile before their eyes, it may be they will see that they are rebels. Bring out 4 your belongings, packed as for exile; do it by day, before their eyes, and then at evening, still before their eyes, leave home, as if you were going into exile. Next, before their eyes, break 5 a hole through the wall, and carry your belongings out through it. When 6 dusk falls, take your pack on your shoulder, before their eyes, and carry it out, with your face covered so that you cannot see the ground. I am

y Or wind.   z Prob. rdg.; Heb. adds the heart of.   a Or wind.

making you a warning sign for the Israelites.

7 I did exactly as I had been told. By day I brought out my belongings, packed as for exile, and at evening I broke through the wall with my hands. When dusk fell, I shouldered my pack and carried it out before their eyes.

8 Next morning, the word of the 9 LORD came to me: Man, he said, have not the Israelites, that rebellious people, asked you what you are doing? 10 Tell them that these are the words of the Lord GOD: This oracle concerns the prince in Jerusalem, and 11 all the Israelites therein.*b* Tell them that you are a sign to warn them; what you have done will be done to them; they will go into exile and 12 captivity. Their prince will shoulder his pack in the dusk and go through a hole made to let him out, with his face covered so that he cannot be seen 13 nor himself see the ground. But I will cast my net over him, and he will be caught in the meshes. I will bring him to Babylon, the land of the Chaldaeans, though he will not see it; and 14 there he will die. I will scatter his bodyguard and drive all his squadrons to the four winds; I will follow them 15 with drawn sword. Then they shall know that I am the LORD, when I disperse them among the nations and scatter them through many lands. 16 But I will leave a few of them who will escape sword, famine, and pestilence, to tell the whole story of their abominations to the peoples among whom they go; and they shall know that I am the LORD.

A warning to the people

17 And the word of the LORD came to 18 me: Man, he said, as you eat you must tremble, and as you drink you 19 must shudder with dread. Say to the common people, These are the words of the Lord GOD about those who live in Jerusalem and about the land of Israel: They will eat with dread and be filled with horror as they drink; the land shall be filled with horror because it is sated with the 20 violence of all who live there. Inhabited cities shall be deserted, and the land shall become a waste. Thus you shall know that I am the LORD.

Mistaken beliefs corrected

21 The word of the LORD came to me: 22 Man, he said, what is this proverb current in the land of Israel: 'Time runs on, visions die away'? Say to them, 23 These are the words of the Lord GOD: I have put an end to this proverb; it shall never be heard in Israel again. Say rather to them, The time, with all the vision means, is near. There will 24 be no more false visions, no specious divination among the Israelites, for I, 25 the LORD, will say what I will, and it shall be done. It shall be put off no longer: in your lifetime, you rebellious people, I will speak, I will act. This is the very word of the Lord GOD.

The word of the LORD came to me: 26 Man, he said, the Israelites say that 27 the vision you now see is not to be fulfilled for many years: you are prophesying of a time far off. Say to 28 them, These are the words of the Lord GOD: No word of mine shall be delayed; even as I speak it shall be done. This is the very word of the Lord GOD.

Condemnation of false prophets

The LORD said to me, Man, prophesy 13 1 2 of the prophets of Israel; prophesy, and say to those who prophesy out of their own hearts, Hear what the LORD says: These are the words of the 3 Lord GOD: Oh, the wicked folly of the prophets! Their inspiration comes from themselves; they have seen no vision. Your prophets, Israel, have 4 been like jackals among ruins. They 5 have not gone up into the breach to repair the broken wall round the Israelites, that they may stand firm in battle on the day of the LORD. Oh, 6 false vision and lying divination! Oh, those prophets who say, 'It is the very word of the LORD', when it is not the LORD who has sent them; yet they expect their words to control the event. Is it not a false vision that you 7 prophets have seen? Is not your divination a lie? You call it the very word of the LORD, but it is not I who have spoken.

These, then, are the words of the 8 Lord GOD: Because your words are false and your visions a lie, I am against you, says the Lord GOD. I will 9 raise my hand against the prophets whose visions are false, whose divinations are a lie. They shall have no place in the counsels of my people; they shall not be entered in the roll of Israel nor set foot upon its soil. Thus you shall know that I am the Lord GOD. Rightly, for they have misled 10 my people by saying that all is well when all is not well. It is as if they

b therein: prob. rdg.; Heb. among them.

were building a wall and used white-
11 wash for the daubing. Tell these
daubers that it will fall; rain will pour
down in torrents, and I will send hailstones hard as rock streaming down
and I will unleash a stormy wind.
12 When the building falls, men will ask,
'Where is the plaster you should have
13 used?' So these are the words of the
Lord GOD: In my rage I will unleash
a stormy wind; rain will come in torrents in my anger, hailstones hard as
rock in my fury, until all is destroyed.
14 I will demolish the building which
you have daubed with whitewash and
level it to the ground, so that its
foundations are laid bare. It shall fall,
and you shall be destroyed within it;
thus you shall know that I am the
15 LORD. I will spend my rage on the
building and on those who daubed it
with wash; and people[c] will say, 'The
building is gone and the men who
16 daubed it are gone, those prophets of
Israel who prophesied to Jerusalem,
who saw visions of prosperity when
there was no prosperity.' This is the
very word of the Lord GOD.
17   Now turn, man, to the women of
your people who prophesy out of their
own hearts, and prophesy to them.
18 Say to them, These are the words of
the Lord GOD: I loathe you, you
women who hunt men's lives by
sewing magic bands upon the wrists
and putting veils over the heads of
persons of every age; are you to hunt
the lives of my people and keep your
19 own lives safe? You have violated
my sanctity before my people with
handfuls of barley and scraps of
bread. You bring death to those who
should not die, and life to those who
should not live, by lying to this people
20 of mine who listen to lies. So these
are the words of the Lord GOD: I am
against your magic bands with which
you hunt men's lives for the excite-
21 ment of it. I will tear them from your
arms and set those lives at liberty,
lives that you hunt for the excitement
of it. I will tear up your long veils and
save my people from you; you shall
no longer have power to hunt them.
Thus you shall know that I am the
22 LORD. You discouraged the righteous
man with lies, when I meant him no
hurt; you so strengthened the wicked
that he would not abandon his evil
23 ways and be saved; and therefore you
shall never see your false visions again
nor practise your divination any more.
I will rescue my people from your

power; and thus you shall know that
I am the LORD.

Insincerity and hypocrisy cursed

Some of the elders of Israel came to 14
visit me, and while they sat with me 23
the LORD said to me, Man, these
people have set their hearts on their
idols and keep their eyes fixed on the
sinful things that cause their downfall. Am I to let such men consult me?
Speak to them and tell them that 4
these are the words of the Lord GOD:
If any Israelite, with his heart set on
his idols and his eyes fixed on the
sinful things that cause his downfall,
comes to a prophet, I, the LORD, in
my own person, shall be constrained
to answer him, despite his many idols.
My answer will grip the hearts of the 5
Israelites, estranged from me as they
are, one and all, through their idols.
So tell the Israelites that these are 6
the words of the Lord GOD: Turn
away, turn away from your idols;
turn your backs on all your abominations. If any man, Israelite or alien, 7
renounces me, sets his heart upon
idols and fixes his eyes upon the vile
thing that is his downfall—if such
a man comes to consult me through
a prophet, I, the LORD, in my own
person, shall be constrained to answer
him. I will set my face against that 8
man; I will make him an example and
a byword; I will rid my people of
him. Thus you shall know that I am
the LORD. If a prophet is seduced into 9
making a prophecy, it is I the LORD
who have seduced him; I will stretch
out my hand and rid my people Israel
of him. Both shall be punished; the 10
prophet and the man who consults
him alike are guilty. And never again 11
will the Israelites stray from their
allegiance, never again defy my will
and bring pollution upon themselves;
they will become my people, and I will
become their God. This is the very
word of the Lord GOD.

Righteous survivors

These were the words of the LORD to 12
me: Man, when a country sins by 13
breaking faith with me, I will stretch
out my hand and cut short its daily
bread. I will send famine upon it and
destroy both men and cattle. Even if 14
those three men were living there,
Noah, Danel[d] and Job, they would
save none but themselves by their
righteousness. This is the very word of

c Prob. rdg.; Heb. I.   d Or, as otherwise read, Daniel.

15 the Lord GOD. If I should turn wild beasts loose in a country to destroy its inhabitants, until it became a waste through which no man would 16 pass for fear of the beasts, then, if those three men were living there, as I live, says the Lord GOD, they would not save even their own sons and daughters; they would save themselves alone, and the country would 17 become a waste. Or if I should bring the sword upon that country and command it to go through the land and should destroy men and cattle, 18 then, if those three men were living there, as I live, says the Lord GOD, they could save neither son nor daughter; they would save themselves alone. 19 Or if I should send pestilence on that land and pour out my fury upon it in blood, to destroy men and 20 cattle, then, if Noah, Danel and Job were living there, as I live, says the Lord GOD, they would save neither son nor daughter; they would save themselves alone by their righteousness.

21   These were the words of the Lord GOD: How much less hope is there for Jerusalem when I inflict on her these four punishments of mine, sword and famine, wild beasts and pestilence, to 22 destroy both men and cattle! Some will be left in her, some survivors to be brought out, both sons and daughters. Look at them as they come out to you, and see how they have behaved and what they have done. This will be some comfort to you for all the harm I have done to Jerusalem and 23 all I have inflicted upon her. It will bring you comfort when you see how they have behaved and what they have done; for you will know that it was not without reason that I dealt thus with her. This is the very word of the Lord GOD.

The useless vine

15 These were the words of the LORD to me:

2 Man, how is the vine better than any other tree,
  than a branch from a tree in the forest?
3   Is wood got from it
    fit to make anything useful?
    Can men make it into a peg
    and hang things on it?
4   If it is put on the fire for fuel,
    if its two ends are burnt by the fire
    and the middle is charred,
    is it fit for anything useful?

Nothing useful could be made of it 5
  even when whole;
how much less, when it is burnt by
  the fire and charred,
  can it be made into anything useful!

So these are the words of the Lord 6
GOD:

I treat the vine, as against forest-
  trees,
  only as fuel for the fire,
even so I treat the people of Jerusalem;
  I set my face against them.   7
Though they escape from the fire, fire
  shall burn them up.
  Thus you shall know that I am the
  LORD
  when I set my face against them,
  making the land a waste   8
  because they have broken faith.
  This is the very word of the Lord
  GOD.

Jerusalem's unfaithfulness

The word of the LORD came to me: 16
Man, he said, make Jerusalem see her 2
abominable conduct. Tell her that 3
these are the words of the Lord GOD
to her: Canaan is the land of your
ancestry and there you were born;
an Amorite was your father and a
Hittite your mother. This is how you 4
were treated at birth: when you were
born, your navel-string was not tied,
you were not bathed in water ready
for the rubbing, you were not salted
as you should have been nor wrapped
in swaddling clothes. No one cared 5
for you enough to do any of these
things or, indeed, to have any pity
for you; you were thrown out on the
bare ground in your own filth on the
day of your birth. Then I came by and 6
saw you kicking helplessly in your
own blood; I spoke to you, there in
your blood, and bade you live. I ten- 7
ded you like an evergreen plant, like
something growing in the fields; you
throve and grew. You came to full
womanhood; your breasts became firm
and your hair grew, but still you were
naked and exposed.

Again I came by and saw that you 8
were ripe for love. I spread the skirt
of my robe over you and covered your
naked body. Then I plighted my troth
and entered into a covenant with you,
says the Lord GOD, and you became
mine. Then I bathed you in water and 9
washed off the blood and anointed
you with oil. I gave you robes of bro- 10
cade and sandals of stout hide; I

11 fastened a linen girdle round you and
dressed you in lawn. For jewellery I
put bracelets on your arms and a
12 chain round your neck; I gave you
a nose-ring, I put pendants in your
ears and a beautiful coronet on your
13 head. You had ornaments of gold and
silver, your dresses were of linen, lawn,
and brocade. You had flour and honey
and olive oil for food, and you grew
very beautiful, you grew into a queen.
14 The fame of your beauty went all over
the world, for the splendour with
which I decked you made it perfect.
This is the very word of the Lord GOD.
15   But you trusted to your beauty and
prostituted your fame; you committed fornication, offering yourself freely
to any passer-by for your beauty to
16 become his. You took some of your
clothes and decked a platform for yourself in gay colours and there you
committed fornication; you had intercourse with him for your beauty to
17 become his.[e] You took the splendid
ornaments of gold and silver which
I had given you, and made for yourself male images with which you com-
18 mitted fornication. You covered them
with your robes of brocade and offered
up my oil and my incense before
19 them. You took the food I had given
you, the flour, the oil, and the honey,
with which I had fed you, and set it
before them as an offering of soothing
odour. This is the very word of the
Lord GOD.
20   You took the sons and daughters
whom you had borne to me, and sacrificed them to these images for their
food. Was this of less account than
21 your fornication? No! you slaughtered
my children and handed them over,
you surrendered them to your images.
22 With all your abominable fornication
you forgot those early days when you
lay naked and exposed, kicking helplessly in your own blood.
23   After all the evil you had done (Oh!
24 the pity of it, says the Lord GOD), you
built yourself a couch and constructed
25 a high-stool in every open place. You
built up your high-stools at the top
of every street and disgraced your
beauty, offering your body to any
passer-by in countless acts of fornica-
26 tion. You committed fornication with
your gross neighbours, the Egyptians,
and you provoked me to anger by
your countless acts of fornication.
27   I stretched out my hand against
you and cut down your portion. Then

I gave you up to women who hated
you, Philistine women, who were so
disgusted by your lewd ways. Not 28
content with this, you committed
fornication with the Assyrians, led
them into fornication and still were
not content. You committed countless 29
acts of fornication in Chaldaea, the
land of commerce, and even with this
you were not content.
   How you anger me! says the Lord 30
GOD. You have done all this like the
imperious whore you are. You have 31
built your couch at the top of every
street and constructed your stool in
every open place, but, unlike the
common prostitute, you have scorned
a fee. An adulterous wife who owes 32
obedience to her husband takes a fee
from[f] strangers. The prostitute also 33
takes her fee; but you give presents
to all your lovers, you bribe them to
come from all quarters to commit
fornication with you. You are the 34
very opposite of other women in your
fornication: no one runs after you,
you do not receive a fee, you give it.
You are the very opposite.
   Listen to the words of the LORD, 35
whore that you are. These are the 36
words of the Lord GOD: You have
been prodigal in your excesses, you
have exposed your naked body in
fornication with your lovers. In return
for your abominable idols and for the
slaughter of the children you have
given them, I will gather all those 37
lovers to whom you made advances,[g]
all whom you loved and all whom you
hated. I will gather them in from all
quarters against you; I will strip you
naked before them, and they shall see
your whole body naked. I will put you 38
on trial for adultery and murder, and
I will charge you with[h] blood shed
in jealousy and fury. Then I will hand 39
you over to them. They will demolish
your couch and pull down your high-
stool; they will strip your clothes
off, take away your splendid ornaments, and leave you naked and exposed. They will bring up the mob 40
against you and stone you, they will
hack you to pieces with their swords.
They will burn down your houses and 41
execute judgement on you, and many
women shall see it. I will put an end
to your fornication, and you shall
never again give a fee to your lovers.
Then I will abate my fury, and my 42
jealousy will turn away from you. I
will be calm and will no longer be

e you had intercourse . . . his: prob. rdg.; Heb. obscure.   f a fee from: prob. rdg.; Heb. om.   g to
whom . . . advances: or whom you charmed.   h charge you with: prob. mng.; Heb. give you.

53 provoked to anger. For you had forgotten the days of your youth and exasperated me with all your doings: so I in my turn brought retribution upon you for your deeds. This is the very word of the Lord GOD.

Jerusalem and her sisters

Did you not commit these obscenities, as well as all your other abo- **44** minations? Dealers in proverbs will say of you, 'Like mother, like daughter.' **45** You are a true daughter of a mother who loathed her husband and children. You are a true sister of your sisters who loathed their husbands and children. You are all daughters of a Hittite **46** mother and an Amorite father. Your elder sister was Samaria, who lived with her daughters to the north of you; your younger sister, who lived with her daughters to the south of **47** you, was Sodom. Did you not behave as they did and commit the same abominations? You came very near **48** to doing even worse than they. As I live, says the Lord GOD, your sister Sodom and her daughters never behaved as you and your daughters **49** have done. This was the iniquity of your sister Sodom: she and her daughters had pride of wealth and food in plenty, comfort and ease, and yet she never helped the poor and wretched. **50** They grew haughty and did deeds abominable in my sight, and I made away with them, as you have seen. **51** Samaria was never half the sinner you have been; you have committed more abominations than she, abominations which have made your sis- **52** ter seem innocent. You must bear the humiliation which you thought your sisters deserved. Your sins are so much more abominable than theirs that they appear innocent in comparison with you; and now you must bear your shame and humiliation and make your sisters seem innocent. **53** But I will restore the fortunes of Sodom and her daughters and I will restore yours at the same time. **54** Even though you bring them comfort, you will bear your shame, you will be disgraced for all you have done; **55** but when your sister Sodom and her daughters become what they were of old, and when your sister Samaria and her daughters become what they were of old, then you and your daugh- **56** ters will be restored. Did you not hear and talk much of your sister Sodom

in the days of your pride, before your **57** wickedness was exposed, in the days when the daughters of Aram with those about her were disgraced, and the daughters of the Philistines round about, who so despised you? Now you **58** too must bear the consequences of your lewd and abominable conduct. This is the very word of the LORD.

These are the words of the Lord **59** GOD: I will treat you as you have deserved, because you violated a covenant and made light of a solemn oath. But I will remember the covenant I **60** made with you when you were young, and I will establish with you a covenant which shall last for ever. And **61** you will remember your past ways and feel ashamed when you receive your sisters, the elder and the younger. For I will give them to you as daughters, and they shall not be outside your covenant.[i] Thus I will establish **62** my covenant with you, and you shall know that I am the LORD. You will **63** remember, and will be so ashamed and humiliated that you will never open your mouth again once I have accepted expiation for all you have done. This is the very word of the Lord GOD.

The eagles and the vine

These were the words of the LORD to **17** me: Man, speak to the Israelites in **2** allegory and parable. Tell them that **3** these are the words of the Lord GOD:

A great eagle
with broad wings and long pinions,
in full plumage, richly patterned,
    came to Lebanon.
He took the very top of a cedar-
    tree,
he plucked its highest twig;   **4**
he carried it off to a land of com-
    merce,
and planted it in a city of merchants.
Then he took a native seed   **5**
and put it in nursery-ground;
he set it like a willow,
    a shoot beside abundant water.
It sprouted and became a vine,   **6**
sprawling low along the ground
and bending its trailing boughs to-
    wards him[j]
with its roots growing beneath him.
So it became a vine, it branched out
    and put forth shoots.
But there was another great eagle   **7**
with broad wings and thick plumage;
and this vine gave its roots
    a twist towards him;[j]

i and they . . . covenant: *or* though not on the ground of your covenant.   *j* Or inwards.

M

it pushed out its trailing boughs
   towards him,
seeking drink from the bed where it
   was planted,
8   though it had been set
in good ground beside abundant water
that it might bear shoots and be
   fruitful
   and become a noble vine.

9 Tell them that these are the words of
the Lord GOD:

Can such a vine flourish?   ·
Will not its roots be broken off
   and its fruit be stripped,
and all its fresh sprouting leaves
   wither,
until it is uprooted and carried away
   with little effort and few hands?
10 If it is transplanted, can it flourish?
Will it not be utterly shrivelled,
   as though by the touch of the east
   wind,
   on the bed where it ought to sprout?

The parable explained

11 These were the words of the LORD to
12 me: Say to that rebellious people, Do
you not know what this means? The
king of Babylon came to Jerusalem,
took its king and its officers and had
13 them brought to him at Babylon. He
took a prince of the royal line and
made a treaty with him, putting him
on his oath. He took away the chief
14 men of the country, so that it should
become a humble kingdom unable to
raise itself but ready to observe the
15 treaty and keep it in force. But the
prince rebelled against him and sent
messengers to Egypt, asking for horses
and men in plenty. Can such a man
prosper? Can he escape destruction if
he acts in this way? Can he violate a
16 covenant and escape? As I live, says
the Lord GOD, I swear that he shall
die in the land of the king who put
him on the throne; he made light of
his oath and violated the covenant
he made with him. He shall die in
17 Babylon. Pharaoh will send no large
army, no great host, to protect him
in battle; no siege-ramp will be raised,
no watch-tower put up, nor will the
18 lives of many men be lost. He has
violated a covenant and made
light of his oath. He had submitted,
and yet he did all these things; he
shall not escape.
19   These then are the words of the
Lord GOD: As I live, he has made light
of the oath he took by me and has

violated the covenant I made with
him. I will bring retribution upon
him; I will cast my net over him, 2
and he shall be caught in its meshes. I
will carry him to Babylon and bring
him to judgement there, because he
has broken faith with me. In all his 2
squadrons every commander shall fall
by the sword; those who are left will
be scattered to the four winds. Thus
you shall know that it is I, the LORD,
who have spoken.

The noble cedar

These are the words of the Lord GOD: 2

I, too, will take a slip
   from the lofty crown of the cedar
   and set it in the soil;
I will pluck a tender shoot from the
   topmost branch
   and plant it.
I will plant it high on a lofty mount- 2
   ain,
   the highest mountain in Israel.
It will put out branches, bear its fruit,
   and become a noble cedar.
Winged birds of every kind will roost
   under it,
   they will roost in the shelter of its
   sweeping boughs.
All the trees of the country-side will 2
   know
   that it is I, the LORD,
   who bring low the tall tree
   and raise the low tree high,
   who dry up the green tree
   and make the dry tree put forth
   buds.
I, the LORD, have spoken and will do
   it.

Personal responsibility

These were the words of the LORD to 1
me: What do you all mean by repeat- 2
ing this proverb in the land of Israel:

'The fathers have eaten sour grapes,
   and the children's teeth are set on
   edge'?

As I live, says the Lord GOD, this 3
proverb shall never again be used in
Israel. Every living soul belongs to 4
me; father and son alike are mine.
The soul that sins shall die.
   Consider the man who is righteous 5
and does what is just and right.
He never feasts at mountain-shrines, 6
never lifts his eyes to the idols of
Israel, never dishonours another man's
wife, never approaches a woman during her periods. He oppresses no man, 7
he returns the debtor's pledge, he
never robs. He gives bread to the

hungry and clothes to those who have
8 none. He never lends either at discount or at interest. He shuns injustice
and deals fairly between man and
9 man. He conforms to my statutes and
loyally observes my laws. Such a man
is righteous: he shall live, says the
Lord God.

10 He may have a son who is a man of
violence and a cut-throat who turns
11 his back on these rules.[k] He obeys
none of them, he feasts at mountain-
shrines, he dishonours another man's
12 wife, he oppresses the unfortunate and
the poor, he is a robber, he does not
return the debtor's pledge, he lifts his
eyes to idols and joins in abominable
13 rites; he lends both at discount and at
interest. Such a man shall not live.
Because he has committed all these
abominations he shall die, and his
blood will be on his own head.

14 This man in turn may have a son
who sees all his father's sins; he
sees, but he commits none of them.
15 He never feasts at mountain-shrines,
never lifts his eyes to the idols of
Israel, never dishonours another man's
16 wife. He oppresses no man, takes no
pledge, does not rob. He gives bread
to the hungry and clothes to those
17 who have none. He shuns injustice,
he never lends either at discount or at
interest. He keeps my laws and conforms to my statutes. Such a man
shall not die for his father's wrongdoing; he shall live.

18 His father may have been guilty of
oppression and robbery and may have
lived an evil life among his kinsfolk,
and so has died because of his iniquity.
19 You may ask, 'Why is the son not
punished for his father's iniquity?'
Because he has always done what is
just and right and has been careful to
obey all my laws, therefore he shall
20 live. It is the soul that sins, and no
other, that shall die; a son shall not
share a father's guilt, nor a father his
son's. The righteous man shall reap
the fruit of his own righteousness, and
the wicked man the fruit of his own
wickedness.
21 It may be that a wicked man gives
up his sinful ways and keeps all my
laws, doing what is just and right.
That man shall live; he shall not die.
22 None of the offences he has committed
shall be remembered against him; he
shall live because of his righteous
23 deeds. Have I any desire, says the
Lord God, for the death of a wicked

man? Would I not rather that he
should mend his ways and live?

24 It may be that a righteous man
turns back from his righteous ways
and commits every kind of abomination that the wicked practise; shall he
do this and live? No, none of his former righteousness will be remembered
in his favour; he has broken his faith,
he has sinned, and he shall die. You say
25 that the Lord acts without principle?
Listen, you Israelites, it is you who
act without principle, not I. If a
26 righteous man turns from his righteousness, takes to evil ways and dies,[l]
it is because of these evil ways that
he dies. Again, if a wicked man turns
27 from his wicked ways and does what
is just and right, he will save his life.
If he sees his offences as they are and
28 turns his back on them all, then he
shall live; he shall not die.

29 'The Lord acts without principle',
say the Israelites. No, Israelites, it is
you who act without principle, not I.
30 Therefore, Israelites, says the Lord
God, I will judge every man of you on
his deeds. Turn, turn from your offences, or your iniquity will be your
31 downfall. Throw off the load of your
past misdeeds; get yourselves a new
heart and a new spirit. Why should
32 you die, you men of Israel? I have
no desire for any man's death. This
is the very word of the Lord God.

The lioness and her cubs

19 Raise a lament over the princes of
2 Israel and say:

Your mother was a lioness
  among the lions!
She made her lair among the young
  lions
and many were the cubs she bore.
3 One of her cubs she raised,
and he grew into a young lion.
He learnt to tear his prey,
he devoured men.
4 Then the nations shouted at[m] him
and he was caught in their pit,
and they dragged him with hooks to
  the land of Egypt.
5 His case, she saw, was desperate, her
  hope was lost;
so she took another of her cubs
and made him a young lion.
6 He prowled among the lions
and acted like a young lion.
He learnt to tear his prey,
he devoured men;

k who turns . . . rules: *prob. rdg.; Heb. unintelligible.*
m shouted at: *or* heard a report about.

l *Prob. rdg.; Heb. adds* because of them.

7 he broke down their palaces, laid their
    cities in ruins.
  The land and all that was in it
    was aghast at the noise of his roar-
    ing.
8 From the provinces all round
    the nations raised the hue and cry;
  they cast their net over him
  and he was caught in their pit.
9 With hooks they drew him into a
    cage
  and brought him to the king of
    Babylon,
  who flung him into prison,
that his voice might never again be
    heard
    on the mountains of Israel.

The vine

10 Your mother was a vine in a vine-
    yard[n]
    planted by the waterside.
  It grew fruitful and luxuriant,
  for there was water in plenty.
11 It had stout branches,
    fit to make sceptres for those who
    bear rule.
  It grew tall, finding its way through
    the foliage,
  and conspicuous for its height and
    many trailing boughs.
12 But it was torn up in anger and thrown
    to the ground;
    the east wind blighted it,
    its fruit was blown off,
    its strong branches were blighted,
    and fire burnt it.
13 Now it is replanted in the wilder-
    ness,
    in a dry and thirsty land;
14 and fire bursts forth from its own
    branches
    and burns up its shoots.[o]
  It has no strong branch any more
    to make a sceptre for those who
    bear rule.

This is the lament and as a lament it
passed into use.

From Egypt to Canaan

20 On the tenth day of the fifth month in
the seventh year, some of the elders of
Israel came to consult the LORD and
2 were sitting with me. Then this word
3 came to me from the LORD: Man, say
to the elders of Israel, This is the word
of the Lord GOD: Do you come to
consult me? As I live, I will not be
consulted by you. This is the very
word of the Lord GOD.
4   Will you judge them? Will you
judge them, O man? Then tell them of

the abominations of their forefathers
and say to them, These are the words 5
of the Lord GOD: When I chose Israel,
with uplifted hand I bound myself by
oath to the race of Jacob and revealed
myself to them in Egypt; I lifted up
my hand and declared: I am the
LORD your God. On that day I swore 6
with hand uplifted that I would bring
them out of Egypt into the land I had
sought out for them, a land flowing
with milk and honey, fairest of all
lands. I told them, every one, to cast 7
away the loathsome things on which
they feasted their eyes and not to
defile themselves with the idols of
Egypt. I am the LORD your God, I
said.

But they rebelled against me, they 8
refused to listen to me, and not one of
them cast away the loathsome things
on which he feasted his eyes or forsook the idols of Egypt. I had thought
to pour out my wrath and exhaust my
anger on them in Egypt. I acted for 9
the honour of my name, that it might
not be profaned in the sight of the
nations among whom Israel was living:
I revealed myself to them by bringing Israel out of Egypt. I brought 10
them out of Egypt and led them into
the wilderness. There I gave my sta- 11
tutes to them and taught them my
laws, so that by keeping them men
might have life. Further, I gave them 12
my sabbaths as a sign between us, so
that they should know that I, the
LORD, was hallowing them for my-
self. But the Israelites rebelled against 13
me in the wilderness; they did not
conform to my statutes, they rejected my laws, though by keeping
them men might have life, and they
utterly desecrated my sabbaths. So
again I thought to pour out my wrath
on them in the wilderness to destroy
them. I acted for the honour of my 14
name, that it might not be profaned
in the sight of the nations who had
seen me bring them out.

Further, I swore to them in the 15
wilderness with uplifted hand that I
would not bring them into the land
I had given them, that land flowing
with milk and honey, fairest of all
lands. For they had rejected my laws, 16
they would not conform to my statutes and they desecrated my sabbaths,
because they loved to follow idols of
their own. Yet I pitied them too much 17
to destroy them and did not make an
end of them in the wilderness. I com- 18
manded their sons in the wilderness

---

n in a vineyard: *prob. rdg.; Heb. obscure in context.*   *o Prob. rdg.; Heb. adds* its fruit.

not to conform to their fathers' statutes, nor observe their laws, nor defile themselves with their idols. 19 I said, I am the LORD your God, you must conform to my statutes; you must observe my laws and act according to them. You must keep my 20 sabbaths holy, and they will become a sign between us; so you will know that I am the LORD your God.

21 But the sons too rebelled against me. They did not conform to my statutes or observe my laws, though any who had done so would have had life through them, and they desecrated my sabbaths. Again I thought to pour out my wrath and exhaust my anger on them in the wilderness. 22 I acted for the honour of my name, that it might not be profaned in the sight of the nations who had seen me 23 bring them out. Yes, and in the wilderness I swore to them with uplifted hand that I would disperse them among the nations and scatter them abroad, 24 because they had disobeyed my laws, rejected my statutes, desecrated my sabbaths, and turned longing eyes toward 25 the idols of their forefathers. I did more; I imposed on them statutes that were not good statutes, and laws by which 26 they could not win life. I let them defile themselves with gifts to idols; I made them surrender their eldest sons to them so that I might fill them with horror. Thus they would know that I am the LORD.

27 Speak then, O man, to the Israelites and say to them, These are the words of the Lord GOD: Once again your forefathers insulted me and broke faith 28 with me: when I brought them into the land which I had sworn with uplifted hand to give them, they marked down every hill-top and every leafy tree, and there they offered their sacrifices, they made the gifts which roused my anger, they set out their offerings of soothing odour and poured 29 out their drink-offerings. I asked them, What is this hill-shrine to which you are going up? And 'hill-shrine' has been its name ever since.

The LORD reasons with Israel

30 So tell the Israelites, These are the words of the Lord GOD. Are you defiling yourselves as your forefathers did? Are you wantonly giving your- 31 selves to their loathsome gods? When you bring your gifts, when you pass your sons through the fire, you are still defiling yourselves in the service of your crowd of idols. How can I let you consult me, men of Israel? As I live, says the Lord GOD, I will not be consulted by you. When you say to your- 32 selves, 'Let us become like the nations and tribes of other lands and worship wood and stone', you are thinking of something that can never be. As I live, 33 says the Lord GOD, I will reign over you with a strong hand, with arm outstretched and wrath outpoured. I will 34 bring you out from the peoples and gather you from the lands over which you have been scattered by my strong hand, my outstretched arm and outpoured wrath. I will bring you into the 35 wilderness of the peoples; there will I confront you, and there will I state my case against you. Even as I did in 36 the wilderness of Egypt against your forefathers, so will I state my case against you. This is the very word of the Lord GOD.

I will pass you under the rod and 37 bring you within the bond^p of the covenant. I will rid you of those who 38 revolt and rebel against me. I will take them out of the land where they are now living, but they shall not set foot on the soil of Israel. Thus shall you know that I am the LORD.

Now, men of Israel, these are the 39 words of the Lord GOD: Go, sweep away your idols, every man of you. So in days to come you will never be disobedient to me or desecrate my holy name with your gifts and your idolatries. But on my holy hill, the lofty 40 hill of Israel, says the Lord GOD, there shall the Israelites serve me in the land, every one of them. There will I receive them with favour; there will I demand your contribution and the best of your offerings, with all your consecrated gifts. I will receive your 41 offerings of soothing odour, when I have brought you out from the peoples and gathered you from the lands where you have been scattered. I, and only I, will have your worship, for all the nations to see.

You will know that I am the LORD, 42 when I bring you home to the soil of Israel, to the land which I swore with uplifted hand to give your forefathers. There you will remember your past 43 ways and all the wanton deeds with which you have defiled yourselves, and will loathe yourselves for all the evils you have done. You will know 44 that I am the LORD, when I have dealt with you, O men of Israel, not as your wicked ways and your vicious

p Or muster.

deeds deserve but for the honour of my name. This is the very word of the Lord God.

A forest fire

45,46 These were the words of the Lord to me: Man, turn and face towards Teman*q* and pour out your words to the south; prophesy to the rough country 47 of the Negeb. Say to it, Listen to the words of the Lord. These are the words of the Lord God: I will set fire to you, and the fire will consume all the wood, green and dry alike. Its fiery flame shall not be put out, but from the Negeb northwards every 48 face will be scorched by it. All men will see that it is I, the Lord, who have set it ablaze; it shall not be put 49 out. 'Ah no! O Lord God,' I cried; 'they say of me, "He deals only in parables." '

The sword of slaughter

21 These were the words of the Lord 2 to me: Man, turn and face towards Jerusalem, and pour out your words against her sanctuary;*r* prophesy a- 3 gainst the land of Israel. Say to the land of Israel, These are the words of the Lord: I am against you; I will draw my sword from the scabbard and cut off from you both righteous 4 and wicked. It is because I would cut off your righteous and your wicked equally that my sword will be drawn from the scabbard against all men, 5 from the Negeb northwards. All men shall know that I the Lord have drawn my sword; it shall never again 6 be sheathed. Groan in their presence, man, groan bitterly until your lungs 7 are bursting. When they ask you why you are groaning, say to them, 'I groan at the thing I have heard; when it comes, all hearts melt, all courage fails, all hands fall limp, all men's knees run with urine. It is coming. It is here.' This is the very word of the Lord God.

8 These were the words of the Lord 9 to me: Prophesy, man, and say, This is the word of the Lord:

A sword, a sword is sharpened and burnished,
10　sharpened to kill and kill again, burnished to flash*s* like lightning.
Ah! the club is brandished, my son, to defy all wooden idols!

The sword is given to be burnished 11 ready for the hand to grasp.
The sword—it is sharpened,
it is burnished,
ready to be put into the slayer's hand.

Cry, man, and howl; for all this 12 falls on my people, it falls on Israel's princes who are delivered over to the sword and are slain with my people. Therefore beat your breast in remorse, for it is the test—and what if it is not 13 in truth the club of defiance? This is the very word of the Lord God.

But you, man, prophesy and clap 1 your hands together;
swing the sword twice, thrice:
it is the sword of slaughter,
the great sword of slaughter whirling about them.
That their hearts may be troubled 15 and many stumble and fall,
I have set the threat of the sword at all their gates,
the threat of the sword*t* made to flash like lightning
and drawn to kill.
Be sharpened, turn right; be un- 16 sheathed, turn left,
wherever your point is aimed.

I, too, will clap my hands together 17 and abate my anger. I, the Lord, have spoken.

The king of Babylon advances

These were the words of the Lord to 18 me: Man, trace out two roads by 19 which the sword of the king of Babylon may come, starting both of them from the same land. Then carve a signpost, carve it at the point where the highway forks. Mark out a road 20 for the sword to come to the Ammonite city of Rabbah, to Judah, and to Jerusalem at the heart of it. For the 21 king of Babylon halts to take the omens at the parting of the ways, where the road divides. He casts lots with arrows, consults teraphim*u* and inspects the livers of beasts. The 22 augur's arrow marked 'Jerusalem' falls at his right hand: here, then,*v* he must raise a shout and sound the battle-cry, set battering-rams against the gates, pile siege-ramps and build watch-towers. It may well seem to the 23 people that the auguries are false, whereas they will put me in mind of their wrongdoing, and they will fall

---

q Or face southward.　　*r* her sanctuary: *prob. rdg.*; *Heb.* sanctuaries.　　*s* to flash: *prob. rdg.*; *Heb. unintelligible.*　　*t* the threat of the sword: *prob. rdg.*; *Heb. obscure in context.*　　*u* Or household gods.　　*v* *Prob. rdg.*; *Heb. adds* he must set battering-rams.

24 into the enemies' hand. These therefore are the words of the Lord GOD: Because you have kept me mindful of your wrongdoing by your open rebellion, and your sins have been revealed in all your acts, because you have kept yourselves in my mind, you will fall into the enemies' hand by force.

25 You, too, you impious and wicked prince of Israel, your fate has come upon you in the hour of final punish-
26 ment. These are the words of the Lord GOD: Put off your diadem, lay aside your crown. All is changed; raise the
27 low and bring down the high. Ruin! Ruin! I will bring about such ruin as never was before, until the rightful sovereign comes. Then I will give him all.

Prophecy to Ammon

28 Man, prophesy and say, These are the words of the Lord GOD to the Ammonites and to their shameful god:

A sword, a sword drawn for slaughter,
    burnished for destruction,[w]
    to flash like lightning!
29 Your visions are false, your auguries a lie,
    which bid you bring it[x] down
    upon the necks of impious and wicked men,
    whose fate has come upon them
    in the hour of final punishment.
30 Sheathe it again.
I will judge you in the place where you were born,
    the land of your origin.
31 I will pour out my rage upon you;
I will breathe out my blazing wrath over you.
    I will hand you over to brutal men, skilled in destruction.
32 You shall become fuel for fire,
    your blood shall be shed within the land
    and you shall leave no memory behind.

For I, the LORD, have spoken.

Corruption in Jerusalem

22 These were the words of the LORD to
2 me: Man, will you judge her, will you judge the murderous city and bring home to her all her abominable deeds?
3 Say to her, These are the words of the Lord GOD: Alas for the city that sheds blood within her walls and brings her fate upon herself, the city that makes herself idols and is defiled thereby:

The guilt is yours for the blood you 4 have shed, the pollution is on you for the idols you have made. You have shortened your days by this and brought the end of your years nearer. This is why I exposed you to the contempt of the nations and the mockery of every country. Lands far 5 and near will taunt you with your infamy and gross disorder. In you the 6 princes of Israel, one and all, have used their power to shed blood; men 7 have treated their fathers and mothers with contempt, they have oppressed the alien and ill-treated the orphan and the widow. You have 8 disdained what is sacred to me and desecrated my sabbaths. In you, Jeru-9 salem, informers have worked to procure bloodshed; in you are men who have feasted at mountain-shrines and have committed lewdness. In you 10 men have exposed their fathers' nakedness; they have violated women during their periods; they have committed an 11 outrage with their neighbours' wives and have lewdly defiled their daughters-in-law; they have ravished their sisters, their own fathers' daughters. In you men have accepted bribes to 12 shed blood, and they have exacted discount and interest on their loans. You have oppressed your fellows for gain, and you have forgotten me. This is the very word of the Lord GOD.

See, I strike with my clenched fist 13 in anger at your ill-gotten gains and at the bloodshed within your walls. Will your strength or courage stand 14 when I deal with you? I, the LORD, have spoken and I will act. I will dis-15 perse you among the nations and scatter you abroad; thus will I rid you altogether of your defilement. I will 16 sift you[y] in the sight of the nations, and you will know that I am the LORD.

The crucible

These were the words of the LORD to 17 me: Man, to me all Israelites are an 18 alloy, their silver alloyed with copper, tin, iron, and lead.[z] Therefore, these are 19 the words of the Lord GOD: Because you have all become alloyed, I will gather you together into Jerusalem, as a mass of silver, copper, iron, lead, 20 and tin is gathered into a crucible for the fire to be blown to full heat to melt them. So will I gather you in my

---

w for destruction: *prob. rdg.*; *Heb. obscure.*   x *Prob. rdg.*; *Heb. you.*   y I will sift you: *or* You will be profaned.   z their silver . . . lead: *prob. rdg.*; *Heb.* copper, tin, iron, and lead inside a crucible; they are an alloy, silver.

anger and wrath, set you there and
21 melt you; I will collect you and blow
up the fire of my anger until you are
22 melted within it. You will be melted
as silver is melted in a crucible, and
you will know that I, the LORD, have
poured out my anger upon you.

The whole society corrupt

23 These were the words of the LORD to
24 me: Man, say to Jerusalem, You are
like a land on which no rain has fallen;
no shower has come down upon you[a]
25 in the days of indignation. The princes
within her are like lions growling as
they tear their prey. They have devoured men, and seized their treasure and all their wealth; they have
widowed many women within her
26 walls. Her priests have done violence to
my law[b] and profaned what is sacred
to me. They make no distinction between sacred and common, and lead
men to see no difference between
clean and unclean. They have disregarded my sabbaths, and I am dis-
27 honoured among them. Her officers
within her are like wolves tearing their
prey, shedding blood and destroying men's lives to acquire ill-gotten
28 gain. Her prophets use whitewash
instead of plaster;[c] their vision is
false and their divination a lie. They
say, 'This is the word of the Lord
GOD', when the LORD has not spoken.
29 The common people are bullies and
robbers; they ill-treat the unfortunate and the poor, they are unjust
30 and cruel to the alien. I looked for
a man among them who could build
up a barricade, who could stand before me in the breach to defend the
land from ruin; but I found no such
31 man. I poured out my indignation
upon them and utterly destroyed
them in the fire of my wrath. Thus I
brought on them the punishment they
had deserved. This is the very word
of the Lord GOD.

Two sisters

23 The word of the LORD came to me:
2 Man, he said, there were once two
women, daughters of the same mother.
3 They played the whore in Egypt,
played the whore while they were
still girls; for there they let their
breasts be fondled and their virgin
4 bosoms pressed. The elder was named
Oholah, her sister Oholibah. They
became mine and bore me sons and
daughters. 'Oholah' is Samaria, 'Ohol-

ibah' Jerusalem. While she owed me 5
obedience Oholah played the whore
and was infatuated with her Assyrian lovers, staff officers in blue,[d] 6
viceroys and governors, handsome
young cavaliers all of them, riding
on horseback. She played the whore 7
with all of them, the flower of the
Assyrian youth; and she let herself
be defiled with all their idols, wherever
her lust led her. She never gave up the 8
whorish ways she had learnt in Egypt,
where men had lain with her when
young, had pressed her virgin bosom
and overwhelmed her with their fornication. So I abandoned her to her 9
lovers, the Assyrians, with whom she
was infatuated. They ravished her, 10
they took her sons and daughters,
and they killed her with the sword.
She became a byword among women, and judgement was passed upon
her.

Oholibah, her sister, had watched 11
her, and she gave herself up to lust
and played the whore worse than her
sister. She, too, was infatuated with 12
Assyrians, viceroys, governors and
staff officers, all handsome young
cavaliers, in full dress, riding on
horseback. I found that she too had 13
let herself be defiled; both had gone
the same way; but she carried her 14
fornication to greater lengths: she
saw male figures carved on the wall,
sculptured forms of Chaldaeans, picked
out in vermilion. Belts were round 15
their waists, and on their heads turbans with dangling ends. All seemed
to be high officers and looked like
Babylonians, natives of Chaldaea. As 16
she looked she was infatuated with
them, so she sent messengers to Chaldaea for them. And the Babylonians 17
came to her to share her bed, and
defiled her with fornication; she was
defiled by them until she was filled
with revulsion. She made no secret 18
that she was a whore but let herself
be ravished until I was filled with revulsion against her as I was against
her sister. She played the whore again 19
and again, remembering how in her
youth she had played the whore in
Egypt. She was infatuated with their 20
male prostitutes, whose members were
like those of asses and whose seed
came in floods like that of horses. So, 21
Oholibah, you relived the lewdness of
your girlhood in Egypt when you let
your bosom be pressed and your
breasts fondled.[e]

a Prob. rdg.; Heb. it.   b Or instruction.   c Cp. 13. 8–16.   d Or violet.   e fondled: prob.
rdg.; Heb. unintelligible.

22 Therefore these are the words of the Lord GOD: I will rouse them against you, Oholibah, those lovers of yours who have filled you with revulsion, and bring them upon you from every side, 23 the Babylonians and all those Chaldaeans, men of Pekod, Shoa, and Koa, and all the Assyrians with them. Handsome young men they are, viceroys and governors, commanders and staff 24 officers,[f] riding on horseback. They will come against you with war-horses, with chariots and wagons, with a host drawn from the nations, armed with shield, buckler, and helmet; they will beset you on every side. I will give them authority to judge, and they will use that authority to 25 judge you. I will turn my jealous wrath loose on you, and they will make you feel their fury. They will cut off your nose and your ears, and in the end you[g] will fall by the sword.[h] 26 They will strip you of your clothes 27 and take away all your finery. So I will put a stop to your lewdness and the way in which you learnt to play the whore in Egypt. You will never cast longing eyes on such things again, never remember Egypt any more.

28 These are the words of the Lord GOD: I am handing you over to those whom you hate, those who have filled 29 you with revulsion; and they will make you feel their hatred. They will take all you have earned and leave you naked and exposed; that body with which you have played the whore will be ravished. It is your lewdness and 30 your fornication that have brought this upon you, it is because you have followed alien peoples and played the whore and have allowed yourself to 31 be defiled with their idols. You have followed in your sister's footsteps, and I will put her cup into your hand. 32 These are the words of the Lord GOD:

You shall drink from your sister's cup,
    a cup deep and wide,
charged with mockery and scorn,
    more than ever cup can hold.
33 It[i] will be full of drunkenness and
        grief,
    a cup of ruin and desolation,
the cup of your sister Samaria;
34 and you shall drink it to the dregs.
    Then you will chew[j] it in pieces
    and tear out your breasts.
This is my verdict, says the Lord GOD.

Therefore, these are the words of the Lord GOD: Because you have forgotten me and flung me behind your back, you must bear the guilt of your lewdness and your fornication.

The LORD said to me, Man, will you 36 judge Oholah and Oholibah? Then tax them with their vile offences. They have committed adultery, and 37 there is blood on their hands. They have committed adultery with their idols and offered my children to them for food, the children they had borne me. This too they have done to me: 38 they have polluted my sanctuary and desecrated my sabbaths. They came 39 into my sanctuary and desecrated it by slaughtering their sons as an offering to their idols; this they did in my own house. They would send for men 40 from a far-off country; and the men came at the messenger's bidding. You bathed your body for these men, you painted your eyes, decked yourself in your finery, you sat yourself upon 41 a bed of state and had a table put ready before it and laid my own incense and my own oil on it. Loud 42 were the voices of the light-hearted crowd; and besides ordinary folk Sabaeans were there, brought from the wilderness; they put bracelets on the women's hands and beautiful garlands on their heads. I thought: Ah 43 that woman, grown old in adultery! Now they will commit fornication with her—with her of all women! They 44 resorted to her as a prostitute; they resorted to Oholah and Oholibah, those lewd women. Upright men will 45 condemn them for their adultery and bloodshed; for adulterous they are, and blood is on their hands.

These are the words of the Lord 46 GOD: Summon the invading host; abandon them to terror and rapine. Let the host stone them and hack 47 them to pieces with their swords, kill their sons and daughters and burn down their houses. Thus I will put an 48 end to lewdness in the land, and other women shall be taught not to be as lewd as they. You shall pay the 49 penalty for your lewd conduct and be punished for your idolatries, and you will know that I am the Lord GOD.

The corroded cauldron

These were the words of the LORD, 24 spoken to me on the tenth day of the tenth month in the ninth year: Man, 2

---

f staff officers: *prob. rdg.*, *cp. verses 5 and 12*; *Heb. obscure.*   g in the end you: *or* your successors.
h *Prob. rdg.*; *Heb. adds* They will take your sons and daughters, and in the end you will be burnt.
i *Prob. rdg.*; *Heb.* You.   j *Or* dash.

write down a name for this day, this very day: This is the day the king
3 of Babylon invested Jerusalem. Sing a song of derision to this people of rebels; say to them, These are the words of the Lord GOD:

Set a cauldron on the fire,
set it on and pour water into it.
4 Into it collect the pieces,
all the choice pieces,
cram it with leg and shoulder and the best of the bones;
5 take the best of the flock.
Pack the logs[k] round it underneath;
seethe the stew
and boil the bones in it.

6 O city running with blood,
O pot green with corrosion,
corrosion that will never be clean!

Therefore these are the words of the Lord GOD:

Empty it, piece after piece,
though no lot is cast for any of them.
7 The city had blood in her midst
and she poured it out on the gleaming rock,
not on the ground: she did not pour it there
for the dust to cover it.
8 But I too have spilt blood on the gleaming white rock
so that it cannot be covered,
to make anger flare up and to call down vengeance.

9 Therefore these are the words of the Lord GOD:

O city running with blood,
I too will make a great fire-pit.
10 Fill it with logs, light the fire;
make an end of the meat,
pour out all the broth[l] and the bones with it.[m]
11 Then set the pot empty on the coals
so that its copper may be heated red-hot,
and then the impurities in it may be melted
and its corrosion burnt off.
12 Try as you may,[n]
the corrosion is so deep that it will not come off;
only fire will rid it of corrosion for you.
13 Even so, when I cleansed you in your filthy lewdness,
you did not become clean from it,

and therefore you shall never again be clean
until I have satisfied my anger against you.

I, the LORD, have spoken; the time 14 is coming, I will act. I will not refrain nor pity nor relent; I will judge you for your conduct and for all that you have done. This is the very word of the Lord GOD.

Ezekiel's wife dies

These were the words of the LORD to 15 me: Man, I am taking from you at one 16 blow the dearest thing you have, but you must not wail or weep or give way to tears. Keep in good heart; be 17 quiet, and make no mourning for the dead; cover your head as usual and put sandals on your feet. You shall not cover your upper lip in mourning nor eat the bread of despair.

I spoke to the people in the morning; 18 and that very evening my wife died. Next morning I did as I was told. The 19 people asked me to say what meaning my behaviour had for them. I an- 20 swered, These were the words of the LORD to me: Tell the Israelites, This 21 is the word of the Lord GOD: I will desecrate my sanctuary, which has been the pride of your strength, the delight of your eyes and your heart's desire; and the sons and daughters whom you have left behind shall fall by the sword. But, I said, you shall do 22 as I have done: you shall not cover your upper lip in mourning nor eat the bread of despair. You shall cover 23 your head and put sandals on your feet; you shall not wail nor weep. Because of your wickedness you will pine away and will lament to[o] one another. The LORD says, Ezekiel will 24 be a sign to warn you, and when it happens you will do as he has done, and you will know that I am the Lord GOD.

And now, man, a word for you: I 25 am taking from them that fortress whose beauty so gladdened them, the delight of their eyes, their heart's desire; I am taking their sons and their daughters. Soon fugitives will 26 come and tell you their news by word of mouth. At once you will recover the 27 power of speech and speak with the fugitives; you will no longer be dumb. So will you be a portent to them, and they shall know that I am the LORD.

---

k Prob. rdg., cp. verse 10; Heb. bones.   l pour . . . broth: prob. rdg.; Heb. mix ointment.   m with
it: prob. rdg.; Heb. will be scorched.   n Try as you may: prob. rdg.; Heb. obscure.   o Or for.

Ammon

25 These were the words of the LORD to
2 me: Man, look towards the Ammonites
3 and prophesy against them. Say to
the Ammonites, Listen to the word of
the Lord GOD. These are his words:
Because you cried 'Aha!' when you
saw my holy place desecrated, the
soil of Israel laid waste and the people
4 of Judah sent into exile, I will hand
you over as a possession to the tribes
of the east. They shall pitch their
camps and put up their dwellings
among you; they shall eat your crops;
5 they shall drink your milk. I will make
Rabbah a camel-pasture and Ammon
a sheep-walk. Thus you shall know
6 that I am the LORD. These are the
words of the Lord GOD: Because you
clapped your hands and stamped
your feet, and exulted over the land
7 of Israel with single-minded scorn, I
will stretch out my hand over you and
make you the prey of the nations and
cut you off from all other peoples; in
every land I will exterminate you and
bring you to utter ruin. Thus you
shall know that I am the LORD.

Moab

8 These are the words of the Lord GOD:
Because Moab said, 'Judah is like all
9 the rest', I will expose the flank of
Moab and lay open its cities,*p* from
one end to the other—the fairest of
its cities: Beth-jeshimoth, Baal-meon
10 and Kiriathaim. I will hand over
Moab and Ammon together to the
tribes of the east to be their possession, so that the Ammonites shall not
be remembered among the nations,
11 and so that I may execute judgement
upon Moab. Thus they shall know
that I am the LORD.

Edom

12 These are the words of the Lord GOD:
Because Edom took deliberate revenge on Judah and by so doing
13 incurred lasting guilt, I will stretch
my hand out over Edom, says the
Lord GOD, and destroy both man and
beast in it, laying waste the land from
Teman as far as Dedan; they shall
14 fall by the sword. I will wreak my
vengeance upon Edom through my
people Israel. They will deal with
Edom as my anger and fury demand,
and it shall feel my vengeance. This is
the very word of the Lord GOD.

Philistia

These are the words of the Lord GOD: 15
Because the Philistines have taken
deliberate revenge and have avenged
themselves with single-minded scorn,
giving vent to their age-long enmity
in destruction, I will stretch out my 16
hand over the Philistines, says the
Lord GOD, I will wipe out the Kerethites and destroy all the rest of the
dwellers by the sea. I will take fearful 17
vengeance upon them and punish
them in my fury. When I take my
vengeance, they shall know that I am
the LORD.

Tyre

These were the words of the LORD to 26
me on the first day of the first month
in the eleventh year: Man, Tyre has 2
said of Jerusalem,

Aha! she that was the gateway of
    the nations
is broken,
her gates swing open to me;
I grow rich, she lies in ruins.

Therefore these are the words of the 3
Lord GOD:

I am against you, Tyre,
and will bring up many nations against
    you
    as the sea brings up its waves;
they will destroy the walls of Tyre 4
    and pull down her towers.
I will scrape the soil off her
and make her a gleaming rock,
she shall be an islet where men spread 5
    their nets;
I have spoken, says the Lord GOD.
She shall become the prey of na-
    tions,
and her daughters*q* shall be slain by 6
    the sword in the open country.

Thus they shall know that I am the
LORD.
    These are the words of the Lord 7
GOD: I am bringing against Tyre from
the north Nebuchadrezzar king of
Babylon, king of kings. He will come
with horses and chariots, with cavalry
and a great army.

Your daughters in the open country 8
    he will put to the sword.
He will set up watch-towers against
    you,
pile up siege-ramps against you
and raise against you a screen of
    shields.
He will launch his battering-rams on 9
    your walls

p and lay . . . cities: prob. rdg.; Heb. from the cities, from its cities.   *q Or daughter-towns.*

and break down your towers with
his axes.
10 He will cover you with dust from the
thousands of his cavalry;
at the thunder of his horses
and of his chariot-wheels
your walls will quake when he enters
your gates
as men enter a city that is breached.
11 He will trample all your streets
with the hooves of his horses
and put your people to the sword,
and your strong pillars will fall to
the ground.
12 Your wealth will become spoil,
your merchandise will be plundered,
your walls levelled,
your pleasant houses pulled down,
your stones, your timber and your
rubble
will be dumped into the sea.
13 So I will silence the clamour of your
songs,
and the sound of your harps shall be
heard no more.
14 I will make you a gleaming rock,
a place for fishermen to spread their
nets,
and you shall never be rebuilt.
I, the LORD, have spoken.
This is the very word of the Lord
GOD.

15 These are the words of the Lord
GOD to Tyre: How the coasts and
islands will shake at the sound of
your downfall, while the wounded
groan, and the slaughter goes on in
16 your midst! Then all the sea-kings
will come down from their thrones,
and lay aside their cloaks, and strip
off their brocaded robes. They will
wear coarse loin-cloths; they will sit
on the ground, shuddering at every
moment, horror-struck at your fate.
17 Then they will raise this dirge over
you:

How you are undone, swept from
the sea,
O famous city!
You whose strength lay in the sea,
you and your inhabitants,
who spread their terror throughout
the mainland.ʳ
18 Now the coast-lands tremble on the
day of your downfall,
and the isles of the sea are appalled at
your passing.

19 For these are the words of the Lord
GOD: When I make you a desolate
city, like a city where no man can

live, when I bring up the primeval
ocean against you and the great waters cover you, I will thrust you down 20
with those that descend to the abyss,
to the dead of all the ages. I will make
you dwell in the underworld as in
places long desolate, with those that
go down to the abyss. So you will
never again be inhabited or take your
place in the land of the living. I will 21
bring you to a fearful end, and you
shall be no more; men may look for
you but will never find you again.
This is the very word of the Lord GOD.

Dirge over Tyre

These were the words of the LORD to 27
me: Man, raise a dirge over Tyre and 2 3
say, Tyre, throned above your harbours, you who carry the trade of the
nations to many coasts and islands,
these are the words of the Lord GOD:

O Tyre, you said,
'I am perfect in beauty.'
Your frontiers are on the high seas, 4
your builders made your beauty
perfect;
they fashioned all your timbers 5
of pine from Senir;
they took a cedar from Lebanon
to raise up a mast over you.
They made your oars of oaks from 6
Bashan;
they made your deck strongˢ with
box-wood
from the coasts of Kittim.
Your canvas was linen, 7
patterned linen from Egypt
to make your sails;
your awnings were violet and purple
from the coasts of Elishah.
Men of Sidon and Arvad became your 8
oarsmen;
you had skilled men within you,
O Tyre,
who served as your helmsmen.
You had skilled veterans from 9
Gebal
caulking your seams.
You had all sea-going ships and their
sailors
to market your wares;
men of Pharas,ᵗ Lud,ᵘ and Put, 10
served
as warriors in your army;
they hung shield and helmet around
you,
and it was they who gave you your
glory.
Men of Arvad and Cilicia manned all 11
your walls,

r the mainland: *prob. rdg.; Heb.* her inhabitants.
u Or Lydia.   s strong: *prob. rdg.; Heb.* ivory.   t Or Persia.

men of Gammad were posted on
    your towers
and hung their shields around your
    battlements;
it was they who made your beauty
    perfect.

12 Tarshish was a source of your commerce, from its abundant resources
offering silver and iron, tin and lead,
13 as your staple wares. Javan,*v* Tubal,
and Meshech dealt with you, offering
slaves and vessels of bronze as your
14 imports. Men from Togarmah offered
horses, mares, and mules as your
15 staple wares. Rhodians dealt with
you, great islands were a source of
your commerce, paying what was due
16 to you in ivory and ebony. Edom was
a source of your commerce, so many
were your undertakings, and offered
purple garnets, brocade and fine
linen, black coral and red jasper,*w* for
17 your staple wares. Judah and Israel
dealt with you, offering wheat from
Minnith, and meal, syrup, oil, and
18 balsam, as your imports. Damascus
was a source of your commerce, so
many were your undertakings, from
its abundant resources offering wine
19 of Helbon and wool of Suhar, and
casks of wine from Izalla,*x* for your
staple wares; wrought iron, cassia,
and sweet cane were among your
20 imports. Dedan dealt with you in
21 coarse woollens for saddle-cloths. Arabia and all the chiefs of Kedar were
the source of your commerce in lambs,
rams, and he-goats; this was your
22 trade with them. Dealers from Sheba
and Raamah dealt with you, offering the choicest spices, every kind
of precious stone and gold, as your
23 staple wares. Harran, Kanneh, and
Eden, dealers from Asshur and all
24 Media, dealt with you; they were your
dealers in gorgeous stuffs, violet cloths
and brocades, in stores of coloured
fabric rolled up and tied with cords;
your dealings with them were in these.

25 Ships of Tarshish were the caravans
for your imports;
    you were deeply laden with full
        cargoes
    on the high seas.
26 Your oarsmen brought you into many
    waters,
    but on the high seas an east wind
        wrecked you.
27 Your wealth, your staple wares,
    your imports,
    your sailors and your helmsmen,

your caulkers, your merchants, and
    your warriors,
all your ship's company,
    all who were with you,
were flung into the sea on the day of
    your disaster;
at the cries of your helmsmen the 28
    troubled waters tossed.

When all the rowers disembark from 29
    their ships,
when the sailors, the helmsmen all
    together, go ashore,
    they exclaim over your fate,   30
    they cry out bitterly;
    they throw dust on their heads
    and sprinkle themselves with ashes.
They tear out their hair at your 31
    plight
    and put on sackcloth;
    they weep bitterly over you,
    bitterly wailing.
In their lamentation they raise a 32
    dirge over you,
    and this is their dirge:
    Who was like Tyre,
    with her buildings piled*y* off shore?
When your wares were unloaded off 33
    the sea
    you met the needs of many nations;
    with your vast resources and your
        imports
    you enriched the kings of the earth.
    Now you are broken by the sea   34
    in deep water;
your wares and all your company are
    gone overboard.
    All who dwell on the coasts and 35
        islands
    are aghast at your fate;
    horror is written on the faces of
        their kings
    and their hair stands on end.
Among the nations the merchants 36
    jeer in derision at you;
you have come to a fearful end and
    shall be no more for ever.

To the prince of Tyre

These were the words of the LORD to 28
me: Man, say to the prince of Tyre, 2
This is the word of the Lord GOD:

    In your arrogance you say,
    'I am a god;
    I sit throned like a god on the high
        seas.'
    Though you are a man and no god,
    you try to think the thoughts of a
        god.
What? are you wiser than Danel*z*? 3
    Is no secret too dark for you?

v Or Ionia.   *w* Or and carbuncles.   *x* casks . . . Izalla: *prob. rdg.; Heb. obscure.*   *y* with her
buildings piled: *prob. rdg.; Heb. obscure.*   *z* Or, *as otherwise read,* Daniel; *cp.* 14. 14, 20.

4 Clever and shrewd as you are,
   you have amassed wealth for your-
     self,
   you have amassed gold and silver in
     your treasuries;
5 by great cleverness in your trading
   you have heaped up riches,
   and with your riches your arro-
     gance has grown.

6 Therefore these are the words of the
   Lord GOD:

   Because you try to think the thoughts
     of a god
7 I will bring strangers against you,
   the most ruthless of nations,
   who will draw their swords against
     your fine wisdom
   and lay your pride in the dust,
8 sending you down to the pit[a] to die
   a death of disgrace on the high seas.
9 Will you dare to say that you are a
     god
   when you face your assailants,
   though you are a man and no god
   in the hands of those who lay you
     low?
10 You will die strengthless
   at the hands of strangers.

For I have spoken. This is the very
word of the Lord GOD.

Dirge over the king of Tyre

11 These were the words of the LORD to
12 me: Man, raise this dirge over the
king of Tyre, and say to him, This is
the word of the Lord GOD:

   You set the seal on perfection;
   full of wisdom you were and alto-
     gether beautiful.
13 You were in an Eden, a garden of
     God,
   adorned with gems of every kind:
   sardin and chrysolite and jade,
   topaz, cornelian and green jasper,
   lapis lazuli,[b] purple garnet and
     green felspar.
   Your jingling beads were of gold,
   and the spangles you wore were
     made for you
   on the day of your birth.
14 I set you with a towering cherub[c]
     as guardian;
   you were on God's holy hill
   and you walked proudly among
     stones that flashed with fire.
15 You were blameless in all your ways
   from the day of your birth
   until your iniquity came to light.
16 Your commerce grew so great,

lawlessness filled your heart and you
     went wrong,
so I brought you down in disgrace
   from the mountain of God,
   and the guardian cherub banished
     you[d]
   from among the stones that flashed
     like fire.
   Your beauty made you arrogant, 17
you misused your wisdom to increase
     your dignity.
   I flung you to the ground,
I left you there, a sight for kings to
     see.
So great was your sin in your wicked 18
     trading
   that you desecrated your sanctu-
     aries.
   So I kindled a fire within you,
   and it devoured you.
   I left you as ashes on the ground
   for all to see.
All among the nations who knew you 19
     were aghast:
you came to a fearful end and shall be
   no more for ever.

Sidon

These were the words of the LORD to 20
me: Man, look towards Sidon and 21
prophesy against her. These are the 22
words of the Lord GOD:

   Sidon, I am against you
   and I will show my glory in your
     midst.

   Men will know that I am the LORD
   when I execute judgement upon
     her
   and thereby prove my holiness.
   I will let loose pestilence upon her 23
   and bloodshed in her streets;
   the slain will fall in her streets,
   beset on all sides by the sword;
   then men will know that I am the
     LORD.

   No longer shall the Israelites suffer 24
from the scorn of their neighbours,
the pricking of briars and scratching
of thorns, and they shall know that I
am the Lord GOD.

When the Israelites return

These are the words of the Lord GOD: 25
When I gather the Israelites from the
peoples among whom they are scattered, I shall thereby prove my holiness in the sight of all nations. They
shall live on their native soil, which
I gave to my servant Jacob. They 26
shall live there in peace of mind,

---

a Or to destruction.   b Or sapphire.   c I set ... cherub: prob. rdg.; Heb. You were a towering
cherub whom I set.   d and the ... you: or and I parted you, O guardian cherub, ...

build houses and plant vineyards; they shall live there in peace of mind when I execute judgement on all their scornful neighbours. Thus they shall know that I am the LORD their God.

Egypt, Israel and Babylon

29 These were the words of the LORD to me on the twelfth day of the tenth 2 month in the tenth year: Man, look towards Pharaoh king of Egypt and prophesy against him and all his 3 country. Say, These are the words of the Lord GOD:

I am against you,
Pharaoh king of Egypt,
you great monster,
lurking in the streams of the Nile.
You have said, 'My Nile is my own;
it was I who made it.'
4 I will put hooks in your jaws
and make them cling[e] to your scales.
I will hoist you out of its streams
with all its fish clinging to your scales.
5 I will fling you into the wilderness,
you and all the fish in your streams;
you will fall on the bare ground
with none to pick you up and bury
you;
I will make you food
for beasts and for birds.
6 So all who live in Egypt will know
that I am the LORD,
for the support that you gave to the
Israelites
was no better than a reed,
7 which splintered in the hand when
they grasped you,
and tore their armpits;
when they leaned upon you, you
snapped
and their limbs gave way.

8 This therefore is the word of the Lord GOD: I am bringing a sword upon you to destroy both man and 9 beast. The land of Egypt shall become a desolate waste, and they shall know that I am the LORD, because you said, 'The Nile is mine; it was 10 I who made it.' I am against you therefore, you and your Nile, and I will make Egypt desolate, wasted by drought, from Migdol to Syene and 11 up to the very frontier of Cush. No foot of man shall pass through it, no foot of beast; it shall lie uninhabited 12 for forty years. I will make the land of Egypt the most desolate of desolate lands; her cities shall lie derelict among the ruined cities. For forty years shall they lie derelict, and I will

scatter the Egyptians among the nations and disperse them among the lands.

These are the words of the Lord 13 GOD: At the end of forty years I will gather the Egyptians from the peoples among whom they are scattered. I will turn the fortunes of Egypt 14 and bring them back to Pathros, the land of their origin, where they shall become a petty kingdom. She shall 15 be the most paltry of kingdoms and never again exalt herself over the nations, for I will make the Egyptians too few to rule over them. The Israel- 16 ites will never trust Egypt again; this will be a reminder to them of their sin in turning to Egypt for help. They shall know that I am the Lord GOD.

These were the words of the LORD 17 to me on the first day of the first month in the twenty-seventh year: Man, long did Nebuchadrezzar king 18 of Babylon keep his army in the field against Tyre, until every head was rubbed bare and every shoulder chafed. But neither he nor his army gained anything from Tyre for their long service against her. This, there- 19 fore, is the word of the Lord GOD: I am giving the land of Egypt to Nebuchadrezzar king of Babylon. He shall carry off its wealth, he shall spoil and plunder it, and so his army will be paid. I have given him the land of 20 Egypt as the wages for his service because they have disregarded me. This is the very word of the Lord GOD.

At that time I will make Israel put 21 out fresh shoots, and give you back the power to speak among them, and they will know that I am the LORD.

Day of reckoning for the nations

These were the words of the LORD to 30 me: Man, prophesy and say, These 2 are the words of the Lord GOD:

Woe, woe for the day!
for a day is near,   3
a day of the LORD is near,
a day of cloud, a day of reckoning
for the nations.
Then a sword will come upon 4
Egypt,
and there will be anguish in Cush,
when the slain fall in Egypt,
when its wealth is taken and its
foundations are torn up.
Cush and Put and Lud,[f]   5
all the Arabs and Libyans and the
peoples of allied lands,
shall fall with them by the sword.

---

e make them cling: *prob. rdg.*; *Heb.* make the fish of your streams cling.   f Or Lydia.

6 These are the words of the LORD:

All who support Egypt shall fall
and her boasted might be brought
low;
from Migdol to Syene men shall fall
by the sword.
This is the very word of the Lord
GOD.

7 They shall be the most desolate of
desolate lands, and their cities shall
lie derelict among the ruined cities.
8 When I set Egypt on fire and all her
helpers are broken, they will know
9 that I am the LORD. When that time
comes messengers shall go out in
haste from my presence to alarm
Cush, still without a care, and anguish
shall come upon her in Egypt's hour.
Even now it is on the way.
10 These are the words of the Lord
GOD:

I will make an end of Egypt's
hordes
by the hands of Nebuchadrezzar
king of Babylon.
11 He and his people with him, the most
ruthless of nations,
will be brought to ravage the land.
They will draw their swords against
Egypt
and fill the land with the slain.
12 I will make the streams of the Nile
dry land
and sell Egypt to evil men;
I will lay waste the land and everything in it by foreign hands.
I, the LORD, have spoken.

13 These are the words of the Lord GOD:

I will make an end of the lordlings*g*
and wipe out the princelings*h* of
Noph;
and never again shall a prince arise in
Egypt.
Then I will put fear in that land,
14 I will lay Pathros waste and set fire to
Zoan
and execute judgement on No.
15 I will pour out my rage upon Sin,
the bastion of Egypt,
and destroy the horde of Noph.
16 I will set Egypt on fire,
and Syene shall writhe in anguish;
the walls of No shall be breached
and flood-waters shall burst into it.
17 The young men of On and Pi-beseth*i*
shall fall by the sword
and the cities themselves go into
captivity.
18 Daylight shall fail in Tahpanhes
when I break the yoke of Egypt
there;

then her boasted might shall be
subdued;
a cloud shall cover her,
and her daughters*j* shall go into
captivity.
19 Thus I will execute judgement on
Egypt,
and they shall know that I am the
LORD.

20 This was the word of the LORD to
me on the seventh day of the first
21 month in the eleventh year: Man, I
have broken the arm of Pharaoh king
of Egypt. See, it has not been bound
up with dressings and bandage to give
22 it strength to wield a sword. These,
therefore, are the words of the Lord
GOD: I am against Pharaoh king of
Egypt; I will break both his arms,
the sound and the broken, and make
23 the sword drop from his hand. I will
scatter the Egyptians among the
nations and disperse them over many
24 lands. Then I will strengthen the arms
of the king of Babylon and put my
sword in his hand; but I will break
Pharaoh's arms, and he shall lie
25 wounded and groaning before him. I
will give strength to the arms of the
king of Babylon, but the arms of
Pharaoh will fall. Men will know that
I am the LORD, when I put my sword
in the hand of the king of Babylon,
and he stretches it out over the land
26 of Egypt. I will scatter the Egyptians
among the nations and disperse them
over many lands, and they shall know
that I am the LORD.

The great cedar

On the first day of the third month **31**
in the eleventh year this word came
to me from the LORD: Man, say to 2
Pharaoh king of Egypt and all his
horde:

What are you like in your greatness?

Look at Assyria: it was a cedar in 3
Lebanon,
whose fair branches overshadowed
the forest,
towering high with its crown finding
a way through the foliage.
Springs nourished it, underground 4
waters gave it height,
their streams washed the soil all round
it
and sent forth their rills to every tree
in the country.
So it grew taller than every other tree. 5
Its boughs were many, its branches
spread far;

g Or idols.   *h* Or false gods.   *i* Or Bubastis.   *j* Or daughter-towns.

for water was abundant in the channels.

6 In its boughs all the birds of the air had their nests,
under its branches all wild creatures bore their young,
and in its shadow all great nations made their home.

7 A splendid great tree it was, with its long spreading boughs,
for its roots were beside abundant waters.

8 No cedar in God's garden over-shadowed it,
no fir could compare with its boughs,
and no plane-tree had such branches;
not a tree in God's garden could rival its beauty.

9 I, the LORD, gave it beauty with its mass of spreading boughs,
the envy of all the tress in Eden, the garden of God.

The cedar's fall

0 Therefore these are the words of the Lord GOD: Because it grew so high and pushed its crown up through the foliage, and its pride mounted as it 1 grew, therefore I handed it over to a prince of the nations to deal with it; I made an example of it as its wicked-2 ness deserved. Strangers from the most ruthless of nations hewed it down and flung it away. Its sweeping boughs fell on the mountains and in all the valleys, and its branches lay broken beside all the streams in the land. All nations of the earth came out from under its shade and left it. 3 All the birds of the air settled on its fallen trunk; the wild creatures all 4 stood by its branches. Never again, therefore, shall the well-watered trees grow so high or push their crowns up through the foliage. Nor shall the strongest of them, well watered though they be, stand erect in their full height; for all have been given over to death, to the world below, to share the common doom and go down to the abyss.
5 These are the words of the Lord GOD: When he went down to Sheol, I closed the deep over him as a gate, I dammed its rivers, the great waters were held back. I put Lebanon in mourning for him, and all the trees 6 of the country-side wilted. I made nations shake with the crash of his fall, when I brought him down to Sheol with those who go down to the

abyss. From this all the trees of Eden, all the choicest and best of Lebanon, all the well-watered trees, drew comfort in the world below. They too like him 17 had gone down to Sheol, to those slain with the sword; and those who had lived in his shadow were scattered among the nations. Which among the 18 trees of Eden was like you in glory and greatness? Yet you will be brought down with the trees of Eden to the world below; you will lie with those who have been slain by the sword, in the company of the strengthless dead. This stands for Pharaoh and all his horde. This is the very word of the Lord GOD.

Dirge over Pharaoh

On the first day of the twelfth month 32 in the twelfth year the word of the LORD came to me: Man, raise a dirge 2 over Pharaoh king of Egypt and say to him:

Young lion of the nations, you are undone.
You were like a monster in the waters of the Nile
scattering[k] the water with its snout,[k l]
churning the water with its feet and fouling the streams.

These are the words of the Lord 3 GOD: When many nations are gathered together I will spread my net over you, and you will be dragged up in its meshes. I will fling you on land, 4 dashing you down on the bare ground. I will let all the birds of the air settle upon you and all the wild beasts gorge themselves on your flesh. Your 5 flesh I will lay on the mountains, and fill the valleys with the worms that feed on it. I will drench the land 6 with your discharge, drench it with your blood to the very mountain-tops, and the watercourses shall be full of you. When I put out your light I will 7 veil the sky and blacken its stars; I will veil the sun with a cloud, and the moon shall not give its light. I will 8 darken all the shining lights of the sky above you and bring darkness over your land. This is the very word of the Lord GOD.

I will disquiet many peoples when 9 I bring your broken army among the nations into lands you have never known. I will appal many peoples with 10 your fate; when I brandish my sword in the faces of their kings, their hair shall stand on end. In the day of

k snout: prob. rdg.; Heb. streams.   _l scattering . . . snout: or heaving itself up in the streams._

M*

your downfall each shall tremble for his own fate from moment to mo-
11 ment. For these are the words of the Lord GOD: The sword of the king
12 of Babylon shall come upon you. I will make the whole horde of you fall by the sword of warriors who are of all men the most ruthless. They shall make havoc of the pride of Egypt, and all its horde shall be wiped out.
13 I will destroy all their cattle beside many waters. No foot of man, no hoof of beast, shall ever churn them
14 up again. Then will I let their waters settle and their streams run smooth as oil. This is the very word of the
15 Lord GOD. When I have laid Egypt waste, and the whole land is devastated, when I strike down all who dwell there, they shall know that I am the
16 LORD. This is a dirge, and the women of the nations shall sing it as a dirge. They shall sing it as a dirge, as a dirge over Egypt and all its horde. This is the very word of the Lord GOD.

A lesson from history

17 On the fifteenth day of the first month in the twelfth year, the word of the LORD came to me:

18 Man, raise a lament, you and the daughters of the nations,
over the hordes of Egypt and her nobles,
whom I will bring down[m] to the world below
with those that go down to the abyss.

19 Are you better favoured than others?
Go down and be laid to rest with the strengthless dead.

20 A sword stands ready. Those who marched with her, and all her horde, shall fall into the midst of those slain
21 by the sword. Warrior chieftains in Sheol speak to Pharaoh and those who aided him:
The strengthless dead, slain by the sword, have come down and are laid
22 to rest. There is Assyria with all her company, her buried around her, all of them slain and fallen by the sword.
23 Her graves are set in the recesses of the abyss, with her company buried around her, all of them slain, fallen by the sword, men who once filled the land
24 of the living with terror. There is Elam, with all her hordes buried around her,

all of them slain, fallen by the sword; they have gone down strengthless to the world below, men who struck terror into the land of the living but now share the disgrace of those
2 that go down to the abyss. In the midst of the slain a resting-place has been made for her, with all her hordes buried around her; all of them strengthless, slain by the sword. For they who once struck terror into the land of the living now share the disgrace of those that go down to the abyss; they are assigned a place in the midst of the slain. There are Meshech
2 and Tubal with all their hordes, with their buried around them, all of them strengthless and slain by the sword, men who once struck terror into the
2 land of the living. Do they not rest with warriors fallen strengthless,[n] who have gone down to Sheol with their weapons, their swords under their heads and their shields over their bones,[o] though the terror of their prowess once lay on the land of the living? You also,
2 Pharaoh, shall lie broken in the company of the strengthless dead, resting with those slain by the sword. There is
29 Edom, her kings and all her princes, who, for all their prowess, have been lodged with those slain by the sword; they shall rest with the strengthless dead and with those that go down to the abyss. There are all the princes of
30 the North and all the Sidonians, who have gone down in shame with the slain, for all the terror they inspired by their prowess. They rest strengthless with those slain by the sword, and they share the disgrace of those that go down to the abyss.

Pharaoh will see them and will take
31 comfort for his lost hordes—Pharaoh who, with all his army, is slain by the sword, says the Lord GOD; though he
32 spread[p] terror throughout all the land of the living, yet he with all his horde is laid to rest with those that are slain by the sword, in the company of the strengthless dead. This is the very word of the Lord GOD.

A watchman for the people

These were the words of the LORD to
33 me: Man, say to your fellow-country-
2 men, When I set armies in motion against a land, its people choose one of themselves to be a watchman.
When he sees the enemy approaching
3 and blows his trumpet to warn the people, then if anyone does not heed
4

m her nobles . . . down: *prob. rdg.; Heb. obscure.*
o and . . . bones: *prob. rdg.; Heb. unintelligible.*

n *Prob. rdg.; Heb.* from strengthless ones.
p *Prob. rdg.; Heb.* I have spread.

the warning and is overtaken by the enemy, he is responsible for his own 5 fate. He is responsible because, when he heard the alarm, he paid no heed to it; if he had heeded it, he would 6 have escaped. But if the watchman does not blow his trumpet or warn the people when he sees the enemy approaching, then any man who is killed is caught with all his sins upon him; but I will hold the watchman answerable for his death.

7 Man, I have appointed you a watchman for the Israelites. You will take messages from me and carry my 8 warnings to them. It may be that I pronounce sentence of death on a man because he is wicked; if you do not warn him to give up his ways, the guilt is his and because of his wickedness he shall die, but I will hold you 9 answerable for his death. But if you have warned him to give up his ways, and he has not given them up, he will die because of his wickedness, but you will have saved yourself.

10 Man, say to the Israelites, You complain, 'We are burdened by our sins and offences; we are pining away because of them; we despair of life.' 11 So tell them: As I live, says the Lord GOD, I have no desire for the death of the wicked. I would rather that a wicked man should mend his ways and live. Give up your evil ways, give them up; O Israelites, why should you die?

Personal responsibility

12 Man, say to your fellow-countrymen, When a righteous man goes wrong, his righteousness shall not save him. When a wicked man mends his ways, his former wickedness shall not bring him down. When a righteous man sins, all his righteousness cannot save 13 his life. It may be that, when I tell the righteous man that he will save his life, he presumes on his righteousness and does wrong; then none of his righteous acts will be remembered: he will die for the wrong he has done. 14 It may be that when I pronounce sentence of death on the wicked, he mends his ways and does what is just 15 and right: if he then restores the pledges he has taken, repays what he has stolen, and, doing no more wrong, follows the rules that ensure life, he 16 shall live and not die. None of the sins he has committed shall be remembered against him; he shall live, because he does what is just and right.

Your fellow-countrymen are saying, 17 'The Lord acts without principle', but it is their ways that are unprincipled. When a righteous man gives 18 up his righteousness and does wrong, he shall die because of it; and when 19 a wicked man gives up his wickedness and does what is just and right, he shall live. How, Israel, can you say 20 that the Lord acts without principle, when I judge every man of you on his deeds?

Jerusalem has fallen!

On the fifth day of the tenth month 21 in the twelfth year of our captivity, fugitives came to me from Jerusalem and told me that the city had fallen. The evening before they arrived, the 22 hand of the LORD had come upon me, and by the time they reached me in the morning the LORD had given me back my speech. My speech was restored and I was no longer dumb.

Israel's hypocrisy

These were the words of the LORD to 23 me: Man, the inhabitants of these 24 wastes on the soil of Israel say, 'When Abraham took possession of the land he was but one; now we are many, and the land has been granted to us in possession.' Tell them, therefore, that 25 these are the words of the Lord GOD: You eat meat with the blood in it, you lift up your eyes to idols, you shed*q* blood; and yet you expect to possess the land! You trust to the sword, you 26 commit abominations, you defile one another's wives; and you expect to possess the land! Tell them that these 27 are the words of the Lord GOD: As I live, among the ruins they shall fall by the sword; in the open country I will give them for food to beasts; in dens and caves they shall die by pestilence. I will make the land a deso- 28 late waste; her boasted might shall be brought to nothing, and the mountains of Israel shall be an untrodden desert. When I make the land a deso- 29 late waste because of all the abominations they have committed, they will know that I am the LORD.

Man, your fellow-countrymen ga- 30 ther in groups and talk of you under walls and in doorways and say to one another, 'Let us go and see what message there is from the LORD.' So 31 my people will come crowding in, as people do, and sit down in front of you. They will hear what you have to

q Or pour out.

say, but they will not do it. 'Fine words[r]!' they will say, but their
32 hearts are set on selfish gain. You are no more to them than a singer of fine songs[s] with a lovely voice, or a clever harpist; they will listen to what you
33 say but will certainly not do it. But when it comes, as come it will, they will know that there has been a prophet in their midst.

Careless shepherds

34 These were the words of the LORD to
2 me: Prophesy, man, against the shepherds of Israel; prophesy and say to them, You shepherds, these are the words of the Lord GOD: How I hate the shepherds of Israel who care only for themselves! Should not the shep-
3 herd care for the sheep? You consume the milk, wear the wool, and slaughter the fat beasts, but you do not feed the
4 sheep. You have not encouraged the weary, tended the sick, bandaged the hurt, recovered the straggler, or searched for the lost; and even the strong you have driven with ruthless
5 severity. They are scattered, they have no shepherd, they have become
6 the prey of wild beasts. My sheep go straying over the mountains and on every high hill, my flock is dispersed over the whole country, with no one to ask after them or search for them.
7 Therefore, you shepherds, hear the
8 words of the LORD. As surely as I live, says the Lord GOD, because my sheep are ravaged by wild beasts and have become their prey for lack of a shepherd, because my shepherds have not asked after the sheep but have cared only for themselves and not for the
9 sheep—therefore, you shepherds, hear
10 the words of the LORD. These are the words of the Lord GOD: I am against the shepherds and will demand my sheep from them. I will dismiss those shepherds: they shall care only for themselves no longer; I will rescue my sheep from their jaws, and they shall feed on them no more.

The LORD as shepherd

11 For these are the words of the Lord GOD: Now I myself will ask after my
12 sheep and go in search of them. As a shepherd goes in search of his sheep when his flock is dispersed all around him, so I will go in search of my sheep and rescue them, no matter where they were scattered in dark and
13 cloudy days. I will bring them out

from every nation, gather them in from other lands, and lead them home to their own soil. I will graze them on the mountains of Israel, by her streams and in all her green fields.
14 I will feed them on good grazing-ground, and their pasture shall be the high mountains of Israel. There they will rest, there in good pasture, and find rich grazing on the mountains of
15 Israel. I myself will tend my flock, I myself pen them in their fold, says
16 the Lord GOD. I will search for the lost, recover the straggler, bandage the hurt, strengthen the sick, leave the healthy and strong to play, and give them their proper food.

Reign of peace

17 As for you, my flock, these are the words of the Lord GOD: I will judge between one sheep and another. You
18 rams and he-goats! Are you not satisfied with grazing on good herbage, that you must trample down the rest with your feet? Or with drinking clear water, that you must churn up the rest with your feet?
19 My flock has to eat what you have trampled and drink what you have
20 churned up. These, therefore, are the words of the Lord GOD to them: Now I myself will judge between the fat
21 sheep and the lean. You hustle the weary with flank and shoulder, you butt them with your horns until you have driven them away and scattered
22 them abroad. Therefore I will save my flock, and they shall be ravaged no more; I will judge between one sheep
23 and another. Then I will set over them one shepherd to take care of them, my servant David; he shall care for them and become their shep-
24 herd. I, the LORD, will become their God, and my servant David shall be a prince among them. I, the LORD,
25 have spoken. I will make a covenant with them to ensure prosperity; I will rid the land of wild beasts, and men shall live in peace of mind on the
26 open pastures and sleep in the woods. I will settle them in the neighbourhood of my hill and send them rain in
27 due season, blessed rain. Trees in the country-side shall bear their fruit, the land shall yield its produce, and men shall live in peace of mind on their own soil. They shall know that I am the LORD when I break the bars of their yokes and rescue them from
28 those who have enslaved them. They shall never be ravaged by the nations

---

r Fine words: or Love songs.

s fine songs: or love songs.

again nor shall wild beasts devour them; they shall live in peace of mind,
19 with no one to alarm them. I will give prosperity to their plantations; they shall never again be victims of famine in the land nor any longer
30 bear the taunts of the nations. They shall know that I, the LORD their God, am with them, and that they are my people Israel, says the Lord
31 GOD. You are my flock, my people, the flock I feed, and I am your God. This is the very word of the Lord GOD.

Prophecy to Seir

5 These were the words of the LORD
2 to me: Man, look towards the hill-country of Seir and prophesy against
3 it. Say, These are the words of the Lord GOD:

O hill-country of Seir, I am against you:
I will stretch out my hand over you and make you a desolate waste.
4 I will lay your cities in ruins and you shall be made desolate; thus you shall know that I am the LORD.
5 For you have maintained an immemorial feud
and handed over the Israelites to the sword
in the hour of their doom,
at the time of their final punishment.
6 Therefore, as I live, says the Lord GOD,
I make blood your destiny, and blood shall pursue you;
you are most surely guilty of blood, and blood shall pursue you.
7 I will make the hill-country of Seir a desolate waste
and put an end to all in it who pass to and fro;
8 I will fill your hills and your valleys with its slain,
and those slain by the sword shall fall into your streams.
9 I will make you desolate for ever, and your cities shall not be inhabited;
thus you shall know that I am the LORD.

10 You say, The two nations and the two countries shall be mine and I will take possession of them, though the
11 LORD is[t] there. Therefore, as I live, says the Lord GOD, your anger and jealousy shall be requited, for I will do to you what you have done in your hatred against them. I shall be

known among you when I judge you; you shall know that I am the LORD. 12 I have heard all your blasphemies; you have said, 'The mountains of Israel are desolate and have been given to us to devour.' You have set 13 yourselves up against me and spoken recklessly against me. I myself have heard you. These are the words of 14 the Lord GOD: I will make you so desolate that the whole world will gloat over you. I will do to you as you did 15 to Israel my own possession when you gloated over its desolation. O hill-country of Seir, you will be desolate, and it will be the end of all Edom. Thus men will know that I am the LORD.

Prophecy to Israel

And do you, man, prophesy to the 36 mountains of Israel and say, Mountains of Israel, hear the words of the LORD. These are the words of the 2 Lord GOD: The enemy has said, 'Aha! now the everlasting highlands are ours.' Therefore prophesy and say, 3 These are the words of the Lord GOD: You mountains of Israel, all round you men gloated over you and trampled you down when you were seized and occupied by the rest of the nations; your name was bandied about in the common talk of men. Therefore, 4 listen to the words of the Lord GOD when he speaks to the mountains and hills, to the streams and valleys, to the desolate palaces and deserted cities, all plundered and despised by the rest of the nations round you. These are the words of the Lord GOD: 5 In the fire of my jealousy I have spoken plainly against the rest of the nations, and against Edom above all. For Edom, swollen with triumphant scorn, seized on my land to hold it up to public contempt. Therefore 6 prophesy over the soil of Israel and say to the mountains and hills, the streams and valleys, These are the words of the Lord GOD: I have spoken my mind in jealousy and anger because you have had to endure the taunts of all nations. Therefore, says 7 the Lord GOD, I have sworn with uplifted hand that the nations round about shall be punished for[u] their taunts. But you, mountains of Israel, 8 you shall put forth your branches and yield your fruit for my people Israel, for their home-coming is near. See now, I am for you, I will turn to 9 you, and you shall be tilled and sown.

t Or has been.　　*u* be punished for: *or* bear.

10 I will plant many men upon you—the whole house of Israel. The cities shall again be inhabited and the palaces 11 rebuilt. I will plant many men and beasts upon you; they shall increase and be fruitful. I will make you populous as in days of old and more prosperous than you were at first. Thus you will 12 know that I am the LORD. I will make men—my people Israel—tread your paths again. They shall settle in you, and you shall be their possession; but you shall never again rob them of their children.

13 These are the words of the Lord GOD: People say that you are a land that devours men and robs your tribes 14 of their children. But you shall never devour men any more nor rob your tribes of their children, says the Lord 15 GOD. I will never let you hear the taunts of the nations again nor shall you have to endure the reproaches of the peoples. This is the very word of the Lord GOD.

His holy name

16 These were the words of the LORD to 17 me: Man, when the Israelites lived on their own soil they defiled it with their ways and deeds; their ways were foul 18 and disgusting in my sight. I poured out my fury upon them because of the blood they had poured out upon the land, and the idols with which they 19 had defiled it. I scattered them among the nations, and they were dispersed among different countries; I passed on them the sentence which their 20 ways and deeds deserved. When they came among those nations, they caused my holy name to be profaned wherever they came: men said of them, 'These are the people of the LORD, and it is from his land that they 21 have come.' And I spared them for the sake of my holy name which the Israelites had profaned among the nations to whom they had gone. 22 Therefore tell the Israelites that these are the words of the Lord GOD: It is not for your sake, you Israelites, that I am acting, but for the sake of my holy name, which you have pro-faned among the peoples where you 23 have gone. I will hallow my great name, which has been profaned among those nations. When they see that I reveal my holiness through you, the nations will know that I am the LORD, 24 says the Lord GOD. I will take you out of the nations and gather you from every land and bring you to 25 your own soil. I will sprinkle clean

water over you, and you shall be cleansed from all that defiles you; I will cleanse you from the taint of all your idols. I will give you a new heart 26 and put a new spirit within you; I will take the heart of stone from your body and give you a heart of flesh. I will 27 put my spirit into you and make you conform to my statutes, keep my laws and live by them. You shall live 28 in the land which I gave to your ancestors; you shall become my peo-ple, and I will become your God. I will save you from all that defiles 29 you; I will call to the corn and make it plentiful; I will bring no more famine upon you. I will make the 30 trees bear abundant fruit and the ground yield heavy crops, so that you will never again have to bear the reproach of famine among the nations. You will recall your wicked ways and 31 evil deeds, and you will loathe your-selves because of your wickedness and your abominations. It is not for 32 your sake that I am acting; be sure of that, says the Lord GOD. Feel, then, the shame and disgrace of your ways, men of Israel.

Restoring the land

These are the words of the Lord GOD: 33 When I cleanse you of all your wicked-ness, I will re-people the cities, and the palaces shall be rebuilt. The land 34 now desolate shall be tilled, instead of lying waste for every passer-by to see. Men will say that this same land 35 which was waste has become like a garden of Eden, and people will make their homes in the cities once ruined, wasted, and shattered, but now well fortified. The nations still left around 36 you will know that it is I, the LORD, who have rebuilt the shattered cities and planted anew the waste land; I, the LORD, have spoken and will do it.

These are the words of the Lord 37 GOD: Yet again will I let the Israelites ask me to act in their behalf. I will make their men numerous as sheep, like the sheep offered as holy-gifts, 38 like the sheep in Jerusalem at times of festival. So shall their ruined cities be filled with human flocks, and they shall know that I am the LORD.

The dry bones

The hand of the LORD came upon me, 37 and he carried me out by his spirit and put me down in a plain full of bones. He made me go to and fro 2 across them until I had been round them all;[v] they covered the plain, countless numbers of them, and they 3 were very dry. He said to me, 'Man, can these bones live again?' I answered, 'Only thou knowest that, 4 Lord GOD.' He said to me, 'Prophesy over these bones and say to them, O dry bones, hear the word of the 5 LORD. This is the word of the Lord GOD to these bones: I will put breath[w] 6 into you, and you shall live. I will fasten sinews on you, bring flesh upon you, overlay you with skin, and put breath in you, and you shall live; and you shall know that I am the LORD.' 7 I began to prophesy as he had bidden me, and as I prophesied there was a rustling sound and the bones fitted 8 themselves together. As I looked, sinews appeared upon them, flesh covered them, and they were overlaid with skin, but there was no breath in 9 them. Then he said to me, 'Prophesy to the wind, prophesy, man, and say to it, These are the words of the Lord GOD: Come, O wind, come from every quarter and breathe into these slain, 10 that they may come to life.' I began to prophesy as he had bidden me: breath came into them; they came to life and rose to their feet, a mighty 11 host. He said to me, 'Man, these bones are the whole people of Israel. They say, "Our bones are dry, our thread of life is snapped, our web is severed 12 from the loom."[x] Prophesy, therefore, and say to them, These are the words of the Lord GOD: O my people, I will open your graves and bring you up from them, and restore you to the 13 land of Israel. You shall know that I am the LORD when I open your graves and bring you up from them, 14 O my people. Then I will put my spirit[y] into you and you shall live, and I will settle you on your own soil, and you shall know that I the LORD have spoken and will act. This is the very word of the LORD.'

The kingdom united

15 These were the words of the LORD to 16 me: Man, take one leaf of a wooden tablet and write on it, 'Judah and his associates of Israel.' Then take another leaf and write on it, 'Joseph, the leaf of Ephraim and all his 17 associates of Israel.' Now bring the two together to form one tablet; then they will be a folding tablet in your

hand. When your fellow-countrymen 18 ask you to tell them what you mean by this, say to them, These are the 19 words of the Lord GOD: I am taking the leaf of Joseph, which belongs to Ephraim and his associate tribes of Israel, and joining[z] to it the leaf of Judah. Thus I shall make them one tablet, and they shall be one in my hand. The leaves on which you write 20 shall be visible in your hand for all to see.

Then say to them, These are the 21 words of the Lord GOD: I am gathering up the Israelites from their places of exile among the nations; I will assemble them from every quarter and restore them to their own soil. I will 22 make them one single nation in the land, on the mountains of Israel, and they shall have one king; they shall no longer be two nations or divided into two kingdoms. They shall never 23 again be defiled with their idols, their loathsome ways and all their disloyal acts; I will rescue them from all their sinful backsliding and purify them. Thus they shall become my people, and I will become their God. My ser- 24 vant David shall become king over them, and they shall have one shepherd. They shall conform to my laws, they shall observe and carry out my statutes. They shall live in the land 25 which I gave my servant Jacob, the land where your fathers lived. They and their descendants shall live there for ever, and my servant David shall for ever be their prince. I will make a 26 covenant with them to bring them prosperity; this covenant shall be theirs for ever.[a] I will greatly increase their numbers, and I will put my sanctuary for ever in their midst. They shall live under the shelter of 27 my dwelling; I will become their God and they shall become my people. The nations shall know that I the 28 LORD am keeping Israel sacred to myself, because my sanctuary is in the midst of them for ever.

Gog's plan to attack Israel

These were the words of the LORD to **38** me: Man, look towards Gog, the 2 prince of Rosh, Meshech, and Tubal, in the land of Magog, and prophesy against him. Say, These are the words 3 of the Lord GOD: I am against you, Gog, prince of Rosh, Meshech, and

v He made . . . all: or He made me pass all round them.   w Or wind or spirit.   x our web . . . loom: prob. rdg.; Heb. we are completely cut off.   y Or breath.   z Prob. rdg.; Heb. adds them.
a Prob. rdg.; Heb. adds and I will put them.

4 Tubal. I will turn you about, I will put hooks in your jaws. I will lead you out, you and your whole army, horses and horsemen, all fully equipped, a great host with shield and buckler, every man wielding a sword,
5 and with them the men of Pharas, Cush, and Put, all with shield and
6 helmet; Gomer and all its squadrons, Beth-togarmah with its squadrons from the far recesses of the north—a great
7 concourse of peoples with you. Be prepared; make ready, you and all the host which has gathered to join you, and hold yourselves in reserve for
8 me.[b] After many days you will be summoned; in years to come you will enter a land restored from ruin, whose people are gathered from many nations upon the mountains of Israel that have been desolate so long. The Israelites, brought out from the nations, will all be living undisturbed;
9 and you will come up, driving in like a hurricane; you will cover the land like a cloud, you and all your squadrons, a great concourse of peoples.
10 This is the word of the Lord GOD: At that time a thought will enter your
11 head and you will plan evil. You will say, 'I will attack a land of open villages, I will fall upon a people living quiet and undisturbed, un-defended by walls, with neither gates
12 nor bars.' You will expect to come plundering, spoiling, and stripping bare the ruins where men now live again, a people gathered out of the nations, a people acquiring cattle and goods, and making their home at the
13 very centre of the world. Sheba and Dedan, the traders of Tarshish and her leading merchants, will say to you, 'Is it for plunder that you have come? Have you gathered your host to get spoil, to carry off silver and gold, to seize cattle and goods, to collect rich spoil?'
14 Therefore, prophesy, man, and say to Gog, These are the words of the Lord GOD: In that day when my people Israel is living undisturbed,
15 will you not awake and come with many nations from your home in the far recesses of the north, all riding on horses, a great host, a mighty army?
16 You will come up against my people Israel; and in those future days you will be like a cloud covering the earth. I will bring you against my land, that the nations may know me, when they see me prove my holiness at your expense, O Gog.

Universal terror against Gog

17 This is the word of the Lord GOD: When I spoke in days of old through my servants the prophets, who pro-phesied in those days unceasingly, it was you whom I threatened to bring
18 against Israel. On that day, when at length Gog comes against the land of Israel, says the Lord GOD, my wrath
19 will boil over. In my jealousy and in the heat of my anger I swear that on that day there shall be a great earth-quake throughout the land of Israel.
20 The fish in the sea and the birds in the air, the wild animals and all reptiles that move on the ground, all mankind on the face of the earth, all shall be shaken before me. Mountains shall be torn up, the terraced hills collapse,
21 and every wall crash to the ground. I will summon universal terror against Gog, says the Lord GOD, and his men shall turn their swords against one
22 another. I will bring him to judgement with pestilence and bloodshed; I will pour down teeming rain, hailstones hard as rock, and fire and brimstone, upon him, upon his squadrons, upon the whole concourse of peoples with
23 him. Thus will I prove myself great and holy and make myself known to many nations; they shall know that I am the LORD.

Destruction of Gog and his horde

39 And you, man, prophesy against Gog and say, These are the words of the Lord GOD: I am against you, Gog, prince of Rosh, Meshech, and Tubal.
2 I will turn you about and drive you, I will fetch you up from the far recesses of the north and bring you to the mount-
3 ains of Israel. I will strike the bow from your left hand and dash the arrows
4 from your right hand. There on the mountains of Israel you shall fall, you, all your squadrons, and your allies;
5 I will give you as food to the birds of prey and the wild beasts. You shall fall on the bare ground, for it is I who have spoken. This is the very word
6 of the Lord GOD. I will send fire on Magog and on those who live un-disturbed in the coasts and islands, and they shall know that I am the
7 LORD. My holy name I will make known in the midst of my people Israel and will no longer let it be pro-faned; the nations shall know that in Israel I, the LORD, am holy.
8 Behold, it comes; it shall be, says the Lord GOD, the day of which I have

b *and hold . . . me: or* and you shall be their rallying-point.

spoken. The dwellers in the cities of Israel shall come out and gather weapons to light their fires, buckler and shield, bow and arrows, throwing-stick and lance, and they shall kindle fires with them for seven years. They shall take no wood from the fields nor cut it from the forests but shall light their fires with the weapons. Thus they will plunder their plunderers and spoil their spoilers. This is the very word of the Lord GOD.

In that day I will give to Gog, instead of[c] a burial-ground in Israel, the valley of Abarim east of the Sea.[d] There they shall bury Gog and all his horde, and all Abarim will be blocked; and they shall call it the Valley of Gog's Horde. For seven months the Israelites shall bury them and purify the land; all the people shall take their share in the burying. The day that I win myself honour shall be a memorable day for them. This is the very word of the Lord GOD. Men shall be picked for the regular duty of going through the country and searching for[e] any left above ground, to purify the land; they shall begin their search at the end of the seven months. They shall go through the country, and whenever one of them sees a human bone he shall put a marker beside it, until it has been buried in the Valley of Gog's Horde. So no more shall be heard of that great horde,[f] and the land will be purified.

Israel's fortunes restored

17 Man, these are the words of the Lord GOD: Cry to every bird that flies and to all the wild beasts: Come, assemble, gather from every side to my sacrifice, the great sacrifice I am making for you on the mountains of Israel; eat 18 flesh and drink blood, eat the flesh of warriors and drink the blood of princes of the earth; all these are your rams and sheep, he-goats and bulls, 19 and buffaloes of Bashan. You shall cram yourselves with fat and drink yourselves drunk on blood at the sacrifice which I am preparing for you. 20 At my table you shall eat your fill of horses and riders, of warriors and all manner of fighting men. This is the very word of the Lord GOD.

21 I will show my glory among the nations; all shall see the judgement that I execute and the heavy hand 22 that I lay upon them. From that day forwards the Israelites shall know

that I am the LORD their God. The 23 nations shall know that the Israelites went into exile for their iniquity, because they were faithless to me. So I hid my face from them and handed them over to their enemies, and they fell, every one of them, by the sword. I dealt with them as they deserved, 24 defiled and rebellious as they were, and hid my face from them.

These, therefore, are the words of 25 the Lord GOD: Now I will restore the fortunes of Jacob and show my affection for all Israel, and I will be jealous for my holy name. They shall forget 26 their shame and all their unfaithfulness to me, when they are at home again on their own soil, undisturbed, with no one to alarm them. When I 27 bring them home out of the nations and gather them from the lands of their enemies, I will make them an example of my holiness, for many nations to see. They will know that 28 I am the LORD their God, because I who sent them into exile among the nations will bring them together again on the soil of their own land and leave none of them behind. No longer will 29 I hide my face from them, I who have poured out my spirit upon Israel. This is the very word of the Lord GOD.

A vision: the temple buildings

At the beginning of the year, on the 40 tenth day of the month, in the twenty-fifth year of our exile, that is fourteen years after the destruction of the city, on that very day, the hand of the LORD came upon me and he brought me there. In a vision God 2 brought me to the land of Israel and set me on a very high mountain, where I saw what seemed the buildings of a city facing me. He led me 3 towards it, and I saw a man like a figure of bronze holding a cord of linen thread and a measuring-rod, and standing at the gate. 'Man,' he 4 said to me, 'look closely and listen carefully; mark well all that I show you, for this is why you have been brought here. Tell the Israelites all that you see.'

Round the outside of the temple 5 ran a wall. The length of the rod which the man was holding was six cubits, reckoning by the long cubit which was one cubit and a hand's breadth. He measured the thickness and the height of the wall; each was one rod. He came to a gate which 6

c Prob. rdg.; Heb. adds there.   d That is the Dead Sea.   e searching for: prob. rdg.; Heb. burying those who are passing through.   f So . . . horde: prob. rdg.; Heb. obscure.

faced eastwards, went up its steps and measured the threshold of the 7 gateway; its depth was one rod. Each cell was one rod long and one rod wide; the space between the cells five cubits, and the threshold of the gateway at the end of the vestibule on 8 the side facing the temple one rod. He measured the vestibule of the gate 9 and found it eight cubits, with pilasters two cubits thick; the vestibule of the gateway lay at the end near 10 the temple. Now the cells of the gateway, looking back eastwards, were three in number on each side; all three of the same size, and their pilasters on each side of the same size 11 also. He measured the entrance into the gateway; it was ten cubits wide, and the gateway itself throughout its 12 length thirteen cubits wide. In front of the cells on each side lay a kerb, one cubit wide; each cell was six 13 cubits by six. He measured the width of the gateway through the cell doors which faced one another, from the back of one cell to the back of the opposite cell; he made it twenty-five 14 cubits, and the vestibule twenty cubits, across; the gateway on every 15 side projected into*g* the court. From the front of the entrance-gate to the outer face of the vestibule of the inner gate the distance was fifty cubits. 16 Both cells and pilasters had loopholes all round inside the gateway, and the vestibule had windows all round within and palms carved on each pilaster.

The outer court

17 He brought me to the outer court, and I saw rooms and a pavement all round the court: in all, thirty rooms 18 on the pavement. The pavement ran up to the side of the gateways, as wide as they were long; this was the 19 lower pavement. He measured the width of the court from the front of the lower gateway to the outside of the inner gateway; it was a hundred cubits. He led me round to the north 20 and I saw a gateway facing northwards, belonging to the outer court, and he measured its length and its 21 breadth. Its cells, three on each side, together with its pilasters and its vestibule, were the same size as those of the first gateway, fifty cubits long 22 by twenty-five wide. So too its windows, and those of*h* its vestibule, and its palms were the same size as those

of the gateway which faced east; it was approached by seven steps with its vestibule facing them. A gate like 2₃ that on the east side led to the inner court opposite the northern gateway; he measured from gateway to gateway, and it was a hundred cubits. Then he led me round to the south, 2₄ and I found a gateway facing southwards. He measured its cells, its pilasters, and its vestibule, and found it the same size as the others, fifty cubits 2₅ long by twenty-five wide. Both gateway and vestibule had windows all round like the others. It was ap- 2₆ proached by seven steps with a vestibule facing them and palms carved on each pilaster. The inner court had a 2₇ gateway facing southwards, and he measured from gateway to gateway; it was a hundred cubits.

The inner court

He brought me into the inner court 28 through the southern gateway, measured it and found it the same size as the others. So were its cells, pilasters, 29 and vestibule, fifty cubits long by twenty-five wide. It and its vestibule had windows all round.*i* Its vestibule 31 faced the outer court; it had palms carved on its pilasters; and eight steps led up to it.

Then he brought me into the inner 32 court, towards the east, and measured the gateway and found it the same size as the others. So too were 33 its cells, pilasters, and vestibule; it and its vestibule had windows all round, and it was fifty cubits long by twenty-five wide. Its vestibule faced 34 the outer court and had a palm carved on each pilaster; eight steps led up to it. Then he brought me to the north 35 gateway and measured it and found it the same size as the others. So were 36 its cells, pilasters, and vestibule, and it had windows all round; it was fifty cubits long by twenty-five wide. Its 37 vestibule faced the outer court and had palms carved on the pilaster at each side; eight steps led up to it.

There was a room opening out 38 from the vestibule of the gateway;*j* here the whole-offerings were washed. In the vestibule of the gateway were 39 two tables on each side, at which to slaughter the whole-offering, the sin-offering, and the guilt-offering. At 40 the corner on the outside, as one goes up ‖to the opening of the northern

g Prob. rdg.; Heb. adds pilaster.   *h those of: prob. rdg.; Heb. om.*   *i So some MSS.; others add* (30) It had vestibules all round, and it was twenty-five cubits long by five wide.   *j the vestibule of the gateway: prob. rdg.; Heb.* pilasters, the gates.

gateway, stood two tables, and two more at the other corner of the vestibule
41 of the gateway. Another four stood on each side at the corner of the gateway, eight tables in all at which slaughter-
42 ing was done. Four tables used for the whole-offering were of hewn stone, each a cubit and a half long by a cubit and a half wide and a cubit high; and on them they put the instruments used for the whole-offering and other
43 sacrifices. The flesh of the offerings was on the tables, and ledges a hand's breadth in width were fixed all round facing inwards.
44   Then he brought me right into the inner court, and I saw two rooms in the inner court, one at the corner of the northern gateway, facing south, and one at the corner of the south-
45 ern gateway, facing north. This room facing south, he told me, is for the priests who have charge of the temple.
46 The room facing north is for the priests who have charge of the altar; these are the sons of Zadok, who alone of the Levites may come near
47 to serve the LORD. He measured the court; it was square, a hundred cubits each way, and the altar lay in front of the temple.
48   Then he brought me into the vesti-bule of the temple, and measured a pilaster of the vestibule; it was five cubits on each side, the width of the gateway fourteen cubits and that of the corners of the gateway three
49 cubits in each direction. The vestibule was twenty cubits long by twelve wide; ten steps led up to it, and by the pilasters rose pillars, one on each side.

The Holy of Holies

41 Then he brought me into the sanc-tuary and measured the pilasters; they were six cubits wide on each
2 side. The opening was ten cubits wide and its corners five cubits wide in each direction. He measured its length; it was forty cubits, and its
3 width twenty. He went inside and measured the pilasters at the opening: they were two cubits; the opening itself was six cubits, and the corners of the opening were seven cubits in
4 each direction. Then he measured the room at the far end of the sanctuary; its length and its breadth were each twenty cubits. He said to me, 'This is the Holy of Holies.'

Exterior of the temple

He measured the wall of the temple; 5 it was six cubits high, and each arcade all round the house was four cubits wide. The arcades were arranged in 6 three tiers, each tier in thirty sections. In the wall all round the temple there were intakes for the arcades, so that they could be supported without being fastened into the wall of the temple. The higher up the arcades were, the 7 broader they were all round by the addition of the intakes, one above the other all round the temple; the temple itself had a ramp running up-wards on a base, and in this way one went up from the lowest to the highest tier by way of the middle tier.

Then I saw a raised pavement all 8 round the temple, and the founda-tions of the arcades were flush with it and measured a full rod, six cubits high. The outer wall of the arcades 9 was five cubits thick. There was an unoccupied area beside the terrace[k] which was adjacent to the temple, and the arcades opened on to this area, 11[l] one opening facing northwards and one southwards; the unoccupied area was five cubits wide on all sides. There was a free space[m] twenty cubits 10 wide all round the temple. On the 12 western side, at the far end of the free space, stood a building seventy cubits wide; its wall was five cubits thick all round, and its length ninety cubits.

He measured the temple; it was a 13 hundred cubits long; and the free space, the building, and its walls, a hundred cubits in all. The eastern 14 front of the temple and the free space was a hundred cubits wide. He 15 measured the length of the building at the far end of the free space to the west of the temple, and its corridors on each side: a hundred cubits.

Interior of the temple

The sanctuary, the inner shrine and the outer vestibule were panelled; the 16 embrasures all round the three of them were framed with wood all round. From the ground up to the 17 windows and above the door, both in the inner and outer chambers, round all the walls, inside and out, were carved 18 figures,[n] cherubim and palm-trees, a palm between every pair of cheru-bim. Each cherub had two faces: one 19

---

k *beside the terrace: prob. rdg.; Heb.* between the arcades.
m *There . . . space: prob. rdg.; Heb.* Between the rooms. measures and carving.

l *Verses 10 and 11 transposed.*
n *carved figures: prob. rdg.; Heb.*

the face of a man, looking towards one palm-tree, and the other the face of a lion, looking towards another palm-tree. Such was the carving round 20 the whole of the temple. The cherubim and the palm-trees were carved from the ground up to the top of the doorway and on the wall of the sanc- 21 tuary. The door-posts of the sanctuary were square.[o]

In front of[p] the Holy Place was 22 what seemed an altar of wood, three cubits high and two cubits long; it was fitted with corner-posts, and its base and sides also were of wood. He told me that this was the table which 23 stood before the LORD. The sanctuary had a double door, and the Holy Place also had a double door: 24 the double doors had swinging leaves, 25 a pair for each door. Cherubim and palm-trees like those on the walls were carved on them.[q] Outside there was a wooden cornice over the vesti- 26 bule; on both sides of the vestibule were loopholes, with palm-trees carved at the corners.[r]

42 Then he took me to the outer court round by the north and brought me to the rooms facing the free space and facing the buildings to the north. 2 The length along the northern side was a hundred cubits, and the breadth 3 fifty. Facing the free space measuring twenty cubits, which adjoined the inner court, and facing the pavement of the outer court, were corridors at three levels corresponding to each 4 other. In front of the rooms a passage, ten cubits wide and a hundred cubits long, ran towards the inner court; 5 their entrances faced northwards. The upper rooms were shorter than the lower and middle rooms, because the corridors took building space from 6 them. For they were all at three levels and had no pillars as the courts had, so that the lower and middle levels were recessed from the ground up- 7 wards. An outside wall, fifty cubits long, ran parallel to the rooms and in front of them, on the side of the outer 8 court. The rooms adjacent to the outer court were fifty cubits long, and those facing the sanctuary a hundred 9 cubits. Below these rooms was an entry from the east as one entered 10 them from the outer court where the wall of the court began.[s] On the south side, passing by the free space

and the building, were other rooms with a passage in front of them. These 11 rooms corresponded, in length and breadth and in general character, to those facing north, whose exits and 12 entrances were the same as those of the rooms on the south. As one[t] went eastwards, where the passages began, there was an entrance in the face of the inner[u] wall. Then he said 13 to me, 'The northern and southern rooms facing the free space are the consecrated rooms where the priests who approach the LORD may eat the most sacred offerings. There they shall put these offerings as well as the grain-offering, the sin-offering, and the guilt-offering; for the place is holy. When the priests have entered 14 the Holy Place they shall not go into the outer court again without leaving here the garments they have worn while performing their duties, for these are holy. They shall put on other garments when they approach the place assigned to the people.'

The temple area

When he had finished measuring the 15 inner temple, he brought me out towards the gateway which faces eastwards and measured the whole area. He measured the east side with the 16 measuring-rod, and it was five hundred cubits. He turned and measured 17 the north side with his rod, and it was five hundred cubits. He turned to the 18 south side and measured it with his rod; it was five hundred cubits. He 19 turned to the west and measured it with his rod; it was five hundred cubits. So he measured all four sides; 20 in each direction the surrounding wall measured five hundred cubits. This marked off the sacred area from the profane.

The Glory fills the temple

He led me to the gate, the gate facing **43** eastwards, and I beheld the glory of 2 the God of Israel coming from the east. His voice was like the sound of a mighty torrent, and the earth shone with his glory. The form that I saw 3 was the same as that which I had seen when he came to destroy the city, and as that which I had seen by the river Kebar,[v] and I fell on my face. The glory of the LORD came up 4

o The door-posts . . . square: *prob. rdg.; Heb. unintelligible.*   p In front of: *prob. rdg.; Heb.* The face of.   q *Prob. rdg.; Heb. adds* on the doors of the sanctuary.   r *Prob. rdg.; Heb. adds and* the arcades of the temple and the cornices.   s began: *prob. rdg.; Heb.* breadth.   t *Prob. rdg.; Heb.* they.   u *Prob. rdg.; Heb. word unknown.*   v Or the Kebar canal.

to the temple towards the gate which
5 faced eastwards. A spirit[w] lifted me up
and brought me into the inner court,
and the glory of the LORD filled the
6 temple. Then I heard one speaking to
me from the temple, and the man was
7 standing at my side. He said, Man,
do you see the place of my throne,
the place where I set my feet, where
I will dwell among the Israelites for
ever? Neither they nor their kings
shall ever defile my holy name again
with their wanton disloyalty, and
with the corpses[x] of their kings when
8 they die. They set their threshold by
mine and their door-post beside mine,
with a wall between me and them,
and they defiled my holy name with
the abominations they committed,
and I destroyed them in my anger.
9 But now they shall abandon their
wanton disloyalty and remove the
corpses[x] of their kings far from me,
and I will dwell among them for ever.
10 So tell the Israelites, man, about this
temple, its appearance and propor-
tions, that they may be ashamed of
11 their iniquities. If they are ashamed
of all they have done, you shall describe to them the temple and its fittings, its exits and entrances, all the
details and particulars of its ele-
vation and plan; explain them and
draw them before their eyes, so that
they may keep them in mind and
12 carry them out. This is the plan of the
temple to be built on the top of the
mountain; all its precincts on every
side shall be most holy.

Altar and sacrifices

13 These were the dimensions of the
altar in cubits (the cubit that is a
cubit and a hand's breadth). This was
the height of the altar: the base was
a cubit high[y] and projected a cubit;
on its edge was a rim one span deep.
14 From the base to the cubit-wide ridge
of the lower pedestal-block was two
cubits, and from this shorter pedestal-
block to the cubit-wide ridge of the
taller pedestal-block was four cubits.
15 The altar-hearth was four cubits high
and was surmounted by four horns
16 a cubit high. The hearth was twelve
cubits long and twelve cubits wide,
17 being a perfect square. The upper
pedestal-block was fourteen cubits
long and fourteen cubits wide along
its four sides, and the rim round it
was half a cubit deep. The base of
the altar projected a cubit, and there
were steps facing eastwards.

He said to me, Man, these are the 18
words of the Lord GOD: These are
the regulations for the altar when it
has been made, for sacrificing whole-
offerings on it and flinging the blood
against it. The levitical priests of the 19
family of Zadok, and they alone, may
come near to me to serve me, says the
Lord GOD. You shall assign them a
young bull for a sin-offering; you 20
shall take some of the blood and put
it on the four horns of the altar, on
the four corners of the upper pedestal
and all round the rim, and so purify
it and make expiation for it. Then 21
take the bull assigned as the sin-
offering, and they shall destroy it by
fire in the proper place within the
precincts but outside the Holy Place.
On the second day you shall present 22
a he-goat without blemish as a sin-
offering, and with it they shall purify
the altar as they did with the bull.
When you have completely purified 23
the altar, you shall present a young
bull without blemish and a ram without blemish from the flock. You shall 24
present them before the LORD; the
priests shall throw salt on them and
sacrifice them as a whole-offering to
the LORD. For seven days you shall 25
provide as a daily sin-offering a goat,
a young bull, and a ram from the
flock; all of them shall be provided
free from blemish. For seven days 26
they shall make expiation for the
altar, and pronounce it ritually clean,
and consecrate it. At the end of that 27
time, on the eighth day and onwards,
the priests shall sacrifice on the altar your whole-offerings and your
shared-offerings, and I will accept you.
This is the very word of the Lord
GOD.

The east gate

He again brought me round to the 44
outer gate of the sanctuary facing
eastwards, and it was shut. The LORD 2
said to me, This gate shall be kept
shut; it must not be opened. No man
may enter by it, for the LORD the
God of Israel has entered by it. It
shall be kept shut. The prince, how- 3
ever, when he is here as prince, may
sit there to eat food in the presence
of the LORD; he shall come in and
go out by the vestibule of the gate.

Priests and Levites

He brought me round to the nor- 4
thern gate facing the temple, and I

w Or wind.   *x Or* effigies.   *y* the base . . . high: *prob. rdg.; Heb.* the base of the cubit.

saw the glory of the LORD filling the LORD's house, and I fell on my face.

5 The LORD said to me, Mark well, man, look closely, and listen carefully to all that I say to you, to all the rules and regulations for the house of the LORD. Mark well the entrance to the house of the LORD and all the exits 6 from the sanctuary. Say to that rebel people of Israel, These are the words of the Lord GOD: Enough of all these abominations of yours, you Israelites! 7 You have added to them by bringing foreigners, uncircumcised in mind and body, to stand in my sanctuary and defile my house when you present my food to me, both fat and blood, and they have made my covenant void. 8 Instead of keeping charge of my holy things yourselves, you have chosen to put these men in charge of my sanctuary. 9 These are the words of the Lord GOD: No foreigner, uncircumcised in mind and body, shall enter my sanctuary, not even a foreigner living 10 among the Israelites. But the Levites, though they deserted me when the Israelites went astray after their idols and had to bear the punishment of 11 their iniquity, shall yet do service in my sanctuary. They shall take charge of the gates of the temple and do service there. They shall slaughter the whole-offering and the sacrifice for the people and shall be in attendance 12 to serve them. Because they served them in the presence of their idols and brought Israel to the ground by their iniquity, says the Lord GOD, I have sworn with uplifted hand that they shall bear the punishment of their 13 iniquity. They shall not have access to me, to serve me as priests; they shall not come near to my holy things or to the Holy of Holies; they shall bear the shame of the abominable 14 deeds they have done. I will put them in charge of the temple with all the service which must be performed there.

15 But the levitical priests of the family of Zadok remained in charge of my sanctuary when the Israelites went astray from me; these shall approach me to serve me. They shall be in attendance on me, presenting the fat and the blood, says the Lord 16 GOD. It is they who shall enter my sanctuary and approach my table to serve me and observe my charge. 17 When they come to the gates of the inner court they shall dress in linen;

they shall wear no wool when they serve me at the gates of the inner court and within. They shall wear 1 linen turbans, and linen drawers on their loins; they shall not fasten their clothes with a belt so that they sweat. When they go out to the people in the 1 outer court, they shall take off the clothes they have worn while serving, leave them in the sacred rooms and put on other clothes; otherwise they will transmit the sacred influence to the people through their clothing.

They shall neither shave their 2 heads nor let their hair grow long; they shall only clip their hair. No 2 priest shall drink wine when he is to enter the inner court. He may not 2 marry a widow or a divorced woman; he may marry a virgin of Israelite birth. He may, however, marry the widow of a priest.

They shall teach my people to dis- 2 tinguish the sacred from the profane, and show them the difference between clean and unclean. When dis- 2 putes break out, they shall take their place in court, and settle the case according to my rules. At all my appointed seasons they shall observe my laws and statutes. They shall keep my sabbaths holy.

They shall not defile themselves by 2 contact with any dead person, except[z] father or mother, son or daughter, brother or unmarried sister. After 2 purification, they shall count seven days and then be clean. When they 2 enter the inner court to serve in the Holy Place, they shall present their sin-offering, says the Lord GOD.

They shall own no patrimony in 2 Israel; I am their patrimony. You shall grant them no holding in Israel; I am their holding. The grain-offering, 2 the sin-offering, and the guilt-offering shall be eaten by them, and everything in Israel devoted to God shall be theirs. The first of all the first- 3 fruits and all your contributions of every kind shall belong wholly to the priests. You shall give the first lump of your dough to the priests, that a blessing may rest upon your home. The priests shall eat no carrion, bird 3 or beast, whether it has died naturally or been killed by a wild animal.

Dividing the land

When you divide the land by lot 4 among the tribes for their possession, you shall set apart from it a sacred reserve for the LORD, twenty-five

z any . . . except: *or* anyone else's dead, but only their own . . .

thousand cubits in length and twenty thousand in width; the whole en-² closure shall be sacred. Of this a square plot, five hundred cubits each way, shall be devoted to the sanctuary, with fifty cubits of open land ³ round it. From this area you shall measure out a space twenty-five thousand by ten thousand cubits, in which the sanctuary, the holiest place ⁴ of all, shall stand. This space is for the priests who serve in the sanctuary and who come nearest in serving the LORD. It shall include space for their houses and a sacred plot for the sanc-⁵ tuary. An area of twenty-five thousand by ten thousand cubits shall belong to the Levites, the temple servants; on this shall stand the towns ⁶ in which they live. You shall give to each town an area of five thousand by twenty-five thousand cubits alongside the sacred reserve; this shall ⁷ belong to all Israel. On either side of the sacred reserve and of the city's holding the prince shall have a holding facing the sacred reserve and the city's holding, running westwards on the west and eastwards on the east. It shall run alongside one of the tribal portions, and stretch to the western ⁸ limit of the land and to the eastern. It shall be his holding in Israel; the princes of Israel shall never oppress my people again but shall give the land to Israel, tribe by tribe.

Fair weights and measures

⁹ These are the words of the Lord GOD: Enough, princes of Israel! Put an end to lawlessness and robbery; maintain law and justice; relieve my people and stop your evictions, says the ¹⁰ Lord GOD. Your scales shall be honest, your bushel and your gallon shall be ¹¹ honest. There shall be one standard for each, taking each as the tenth of a homer, and the homer shall have ¹² its fixed standard. Your shekel weight shall contain twenty gerahs; your mina shall contain weights of ten[a] and twenty-five and fifteen shekels.

Contributions

¹³ These are the contributions you shall set aside: out of every homer of wheat or of barley, one sixth of an ¹⁴ ephah. For oil the rule is[b] one tenth of a bath from every kor (at ten ¹⁵ bath to the kor); one sheep in every

flock of two hundred is to be reserved by every Israelite clan. For a grain-offering, a whole-offering, and a shared-offering, to make expiation for them, says the Lord GOD, all the ¹⁶ people of the land shall bring[c] this contribution to the prince in Israel; ¹⁷ and the prince shall be responsible for the whole-offering, the grain-offering, and the drink-offering, at pilgrim-feasts, new moons, sabbaths, and every sacred season observed by Israel. He himself is to provide the sin-offering and the grain-offering, the whole-offering and the shared-offering, needed to make expiation for Israel.

Purifying the sanctuary

These are the words of the Lord GOD: ¹⁸ On the first day of the first month you shall take a young bull without blemish, and purify the sanctuary. The priest shall take some of the ¹⁹ blood from the sin-offering and put it on the door-posts of the temple, on the four corners of the altar pedestal and on the gate-posts of the inner court. You shall do the same on the ²⁰ seventh day of the month;[d] in this way you shall make expiation for the temple.

The Passover

On the fourteenth day of the first ²¹ month you shall hold the Passover, the pilgrim-feast of seven days; bread must be eaten unleavened. On that ²² day the prince shall provide a bull as a sin-offering for himself and for all the people. During the seven days ²³ of the feast he shall offer daily as a whole-offering to the LORD seven bulls and seven rams without blemish, and a he-goat as a daily sin-offering. With ²⁴ every bull and ram he shall provide a grain-offering of one ephah, together with a hin of oil for each ephah. He ²⁵ shall do the same thing also on the fifteenth day of the seventh month at the pilgrim-feast; this also shall last seven days, and he shall provide the same sin-offering and whole-offering and the same quantity of grain and oil.

Rules and regulations

These are the words of the Lord GOD: **46** The eastern gate of the inner court shall remain closed for the six working

---

a Prob. rdg.; Heb. twenty. *b* Prob. rdg.; Heb. adds the bath, the oil. *c* All ... bring: prob. rdg.; Heb. unintelligible. *d* Prob. rdg.; Heb. adds This comes from a man who is wrong and foolish. Cp. Lev. 23. 24; Num. 29. 1.

days; it may be opened only on the
2 sabbath and at new moon. When the
prince comes through the porch of
the gate from the outside, he shall
halt at the door-post, and the priests
shall sacrifice his whole-offering and
shared-offerings. On the terrace he
shall bow down at the gate and then
go out, but the gate shall not be shut
3 till the evening. On sabbaths and
at new moons the people also shall
bow down before the LORD at the
entrance to that gate.

4   The whole-offering which the prince
sacrifices to the LORD shall be as
follows: on the sabbath, six sheep
without blemish and a ram without
5 blemish; the grain-offering shall be an
ephah with the ram and as much as
he likes with the sheep, together with
6 a hin of oil for every ephah. At the
new moon it shall be a young bull
without blemish, six sheep and a
7 ram, all without blemish. He shall
provide as the grain-offering to go
with the bull one ephah and with the
ram one ephah, with the sheep as
much as he can afford, adding a hin
of oil for every ephah.

8   When the prince comes in, he shall
enter through the porch of the gate
9 and come out by the same way. But
on festal days when the people come
before the LORD, a man who enters by
the northern gate to bow down shall
leave by the southern gate, and a man
who enters by the southern gate shall
leave by the northern gate. He shall
not turn back and go out through the
gate by which he came in but shall
10 go straight on. The prince shall then
be among them, going in when they
go in and coming out when they come
out.

11   At pilgrim-feasts and on festal days
the grain-offering shall be an ephah
with a bull, an ephah with a ram and
as much as he likes with a sheep,
together with a hin of oil for every
ephah.

12   When the prince provides a whole-
offering or shared-offerings as a voluntary sacrifice to the LORD, the eastern gate shall be opened for him,[e]
and he shall make his whole-offering
and his shared-offerings as he does on
the sabbath; when he goes out the
gate shall be closed[f] behind him.

13   You shall provide a yearling sheep
without blemish daily as a whole-
offering to the LORD; you shall pro-
14 vide it morning by morning. With it

every morning you shall provide as a
grain-offering one sixth of an ephah
with a third of a hin of oil to moisten
the flour; the LORD's grain-offering is
an observance prescribed for all time.
Morning by morning, as a regular 15
whole-offering, they shall offer a sheep
with the grain-offering and the oil.

These are the words of the Lord 16
GOD: When the prince makes a gift
out of his property to any of his sons,
it shall belong to his sons, since it is
part of the family property. But when 17
he makes such a gift to one of his
slaves, it shall be his only till the year
of manumission, when it shall revert
to the prince; it is the property of his
sons and shall belong to them.

The prince shall not oppress the 18
people by taking part of their holdings; he shall give his sons an inheritance from his own holding of
land, so that my people may not be
scattered and separated from their
holdings.

Then he brought me through the 19
entrance by the side of the gate to
the rooms which face north (the
sacred rooms reserved for the priests),
and, pointing to a place on their
western side, he said to me, 'This is 20
the place where the priests shall boil
the guilt-offering and the sin-offering
and bake the grain-offering; they
shall not take it into the outer court
for fear they transmit the sacred influence to the people.' Then he brought 21
me into the outer court and took me
across to the four corners of the court,
at each of which there was a further
court. These four courts were vaul- 22
ted and were the same size, forty
cubits long by thirty cubits wide.
Round each of the four was a row of 23
stones, with fire-places constructed
close up against the rows. He said 24
to me, 'These are the kitchens where
the attendants shall boil the people's
sacrifices.'

The river of life

He brought me back to the gate of **47**
the temple, and I saw a spring of
water issuing from under the terrace
of the temple towards the east; for
the temple faced east. The water was
running down along the right side, to
the south of the altar. He took me 2
out through the northern gate and
brought me round by an outside path
to the eastern gate of the court, and

e the eastern . . . him: or he shall open the gate facing east.   f the gate . . . closed: or he shall
close the gate.

water was trickling from the right
3 side. When the man went out eastwards he had a line in his hand. He
measured a thousand cubits and made
me walk through the water; it came
4 up to my ankles. He measured another
thousand and made me walk through
the water; it came up to my knees.
He measured another thousand and
made me walk through the water; it
5 was up to my waist. Another thousand, and it was a torrent I could not
cross, for the water had risen and
was now deep enough to swim in; it
had become a torrent that could not
6 be crossed. 'Mark this, man', he said,
and led me back to the bank of the
7 torrent. When we came back to the
bank I saw a great number of trees
8 on each side. He said to me, 'This
water flows out to the region lying
east, and down to the Arabah; at last
it will reach that sea whose waters
are foul, and they will be sweetened.
9 When any one of the living creatures
that swarm upon the earth comes
where the torrent flows, it shall draw
life from it. The fish shall be innumerable; for these waters come
here so that the others may be
sweetened, and where the torrent
10 flows everything shall live. From En-
gedi as far as En-eglaim fishermen
shall stand on its shores, for nets shall
be spread there. Every kind of fish
shall be there in shoals, like the fish of
11 the Great Sea; but its swamps and
pools shall not have their waters
sweetened but shall be left as salt-
12 pans. Beside the torrent on either
bank all trees good for food shall
spring up. Their leaves shall not
wither, their fruit shall not cease; they
shall bear early every month. For
their water comes from the sanctuary;
their fruit is for food and their foliage
for enjoyment.'

Boundary lines

13 These are the words of the Lord GOD:
These are the boundary lines within
which the twelve tribes of Israel shall
enter into possession of the land,
14 Joseph receiving two portions. The
land which I swore with hand uplifted to give to your fathers you shall
divide with each other; it shall be
assigned to you by lot as your patri-
15 mony. This is the frontier: on its
northern side, from the Great Sea
through Hethlon, Lebo-hamath, Ze-
16 dad, Berutha, and Sibraim, which are
between the frontiers of Damascus
and Hamath, to Hazar-enan, near the

frontier of Hauran. So the frontier 17
shall run from the sea to Hazar-enan
on the frontier of Damascus and
northwards; this is its northern side.
The eastern side runs alongside the 18
territories of Hauran, Damascus, and
Gilead, and alongside the territory
of Israel; Jordan sets the boundary
to the eastern sea, to Tamar. This is
the eastern side. The southern side runs 19
from Tamar to the waters of Meribah-
by-Kadesh; the region assigned to
you reaches the Great Sea. This is the
southern side towards the Negeb. The 20
western side is the Great Sea, which
forms a boundary as far as a point
opposite Lebo-hamath. This is the
western side. You shall distribute this 21
land among the tribes of Israel and 22
assign it by lot as a patrimony for
yourselves and for any aliens living in
your midst who leave sons among you.
They shall be treated as native-born
in Israel and with you shall receive
a patrimony by lot among the tribes
of Israel. You shall give the alien his 23
patrimony with the tribe in which he
is living. This is the very word of the
Lord GOD.

Tribal allotments

These are the names of the tribes: In **48**
the extreme north, in the direction of
Hethlon, to Lebo-hamath and Hazar-
enan, with Damascus on the northern
frontier in the direction of Hamath,
and so from the eastern side to the
western, shall be Dan: one portion.
Bordering on Dan, from the eastern 2
side to the western, shall be Asher:
one portion.
Bordering on Asher, from the 3
eastern side to the western, shall be
Naphtali: one portion.
Bordering on Naphtali, from the 4
eastern side to the western, shall be
Manasseh: one portion.
Bordering on Manasseh, from the 5
eastern side to the western, shall be
Ephraim: one portion.
Bordering on Ephraim, from the 6
eastern side to the western, shall be
Reuben: one portion.
Bordering on Reuben, from the 7
eastern side to the western, shall be
Judah: one portion.
Bordering on Judah, from the 8
eastern side to the western, shall be
the reserve which you shall set apart.
Its breadth shall be twenty-five thousand cubits and its length the same as
that of the other portions, from the
eastern side to the western, and the
sanctuary shall be in the middle of it.

9 The reserve which you shall set apart for the LORD shall measure twenty-five thousand cubits by twen-
10 ty[g] thousand. The reserve shall be apportioned thus: the priests shall have an area measuring twenty-five thousand cubits on the north side, ten thousand on the west, ten thousand on the east, and twenty-five thousand on the south side; the sanctuary of the LORD shall be in the
11 middle of it. It shall be for the consecrated priests, the sons of Zadok, who kept my charge and did not follow the Israelites when they went
12 astray, as the Levites did. The area set apart for the priests from the reserved territory shall be most sacred, reaching the frontier of the Levites.
13 The Levites shall have a portion running parallel to the border of the priests. It shall be twenty-five thousand cubits long by ten thousand wide; altogether, the length shall be twenty-five thousand cubits and the
14 breadth ten thousand. They shall neither sell nor exchange any part of it, nor shall the best of the land be alienated; for it is holy to the LORD.
15 The strip which is left, five thousand cubits in width by twenty-five thousand, is the city's secular land for dwellings and common land, and the city shall be in the middle of
16 it. These shall be its dimensions: on the northern side four thousand five hundred cubits, on the southern side four thousand five hundred cubits, on the eastern side four thousand five hundred cubits, on the western side four thousand five hundred cubits.
17 The common land belonging to the city shall be two hundred and fifty cubits to the north, two hundred and fifty to the south, two hundred and fifty to the east, and two hundred
18 and fifty to the west. What is left parallel to the reserve, ten thousand cubits to the east and ten thousand to the west,[h] shall provide food for
19 those who work in the city. Those who work in the city shall cultivate it; they may be drawn from any of the tribes of Israel.
20 You shall set apart the whole reserve, twenty-five thousand cubits square, as sacred, as far as the holding of the
21 city. What is left over on each side of the sacred reserve and the holding of the city shall be assigned to the prince. Eastwards, what lies over against the reserved twenty-five thousand cubits, as far as the eastern side, and westwards, what lies over against the twenty-five thousand cubits to the western side, parallel to the tribal portions, shall be assigned to the prince; the sacred reserve and the sanctuary itself shall be in the centre. The[i] holding of the Levites and the[i] 22 holding of the city shall be in the middle of that which is assigned to the prince; it shall be between the frontiers of Judah and Benjamin.

The rest of the tribes: from the 23 eastern side to the western shall be Benjamin: one portion.

Bordering on Benjamin, from the 24 eastern side to the western, shall be Simeon: one portion.

Bordering on Simeon, from the 25 eastern side to the western, shall be Issachar: one portion.

Bordering on Issachar, from the 26 eastern side to the western, shall be Zebulun: one portion.

Bordering on Zebulun, from the 27 eastern side to the western, shall be Gad: one portion.

Bordering on Gad, on the side of 28 the Negeb, the border on the south stretches from Tamar to the waters of Meribah-by-Kadesh, to the Brook as far as the Great Sea.

This is the land which you shall 29 allot as a patrimony to the tribes of Israel, and these shall be their lots. This is the very word of the Lord GOD.

The city gates

These are to be the ways out of the 30 city, and they are to be named after the tribes of Israel. The northern side, four thousand five hundred cubits long, shall have three gates, those of Reuben, Judah, and Levi; the 32 eastern side, four thousand five hundred cubits long, three gates, of Joseph, Benjamin, and Dan; the 33 southern side, four thousand five hundred cubits long, three gates, of Simeon, Issachar, and Zebulun; the western side, four thousand 34 five hundred cubits long, three gates, those of Gad, Asher, and Naphtali. The perimeter of the city shall be 35 eighteen thousand cubits, and the city's name for ever after shall be Jehovah-shammah.[j]

g Prob. rdg.; Heb. ten.   h Prob. rdg.; Heb. adds and it shall be parallel to the sacred reserve.
i Prob. rdg.; Heb. Some of the.   j That is the LORD is there.

THE BOOK OF
DANIEL

The Jews in Babylon

1 IN THE THIRD YEAR of the reign of Jehoiakim king of Judah, Nebuchadnezzar king of Babylon came to Jerusalem and laid siege to it. 2 The Lord delivered Jehoiakim king of Judah into his power, together with all that was left of the vessels of the house of God; and he carried them off to the land of Shinar, to the temple of his god, where he deposited the vessels 3 in the treasury. Then the king ordered Ashpenaz, his chief eunuch, to take certain of the Israelite exiles, of the 4 blood royal and of the nobility, who were to be young men of good looks and bodily without fault, at home in all branches of knowledge, well-informed, intelligent, and fit for service in the royal court; and he was to instruct them in the literature and 5 language of the Chaldaeans. The king assigned them a daily allowance of food and wine from the royal table. Their training was to last for three years, and at the end of that time they would*a* enter the royal service.

Four young men refuse the king's food

6 Among them there were certain young men from Judah called Daniel, Han-7 aniah, Mishael and Azariah; but the master of the eunuchs gave them new names: Daniel he called Belteshazzar, Hananiah Shadrach, Mishael Meshach and Azariah Abed-nego. 8 Now Daniel determined not to contaminate himself by touching the food and wine assigned to him by the king, and he begged the master of the eunuchs not to make him do so. 9 God made the master show kindness 10 and goodwill to Daniel, and he said to him, 'I am afraid of my lord the king: he has assigned you your food and drink, and if he sees you looking dejected, unlike the other young men of your own age, it will cost me my 11 head.' Then Daniel said to the guard whom the master of the eunuchs had put in charge of Hananiah, Mishael,

Azariah and himself, 'Submit us to 12 this test for ten days. Give us only vegetables to eat and water to drink; then compare our looks with those 13 of the young men who have lived on the food assigned by the king, and be guided in your treatment of us by what you see.'*b* The guard listened 14 to what they said and tested them for ten days. At the end of ten days 15 they looked healthier and were better nourished than all the young men who had lived on the food assigned them by the king. So the guard took 16 away the assignment of food and the wine they were to drink, and gave them only the vegetables.

The young men presented to the king

To all four of these young men God 17 had given knowledge and understanding of books and learning of every kind, while Daniel had a gift for interpreting visions and dreams of every kind. The time came which 18 the king had fixed for introducing the young men to court, and the master of the eunuchs brought them into the presence of Nebuchadnezzar. The 19 king talked with them and found none of them to compare with Daniel, Hananiah, Mishael and Azariah; so they entered the royal service. When-20 ever the king consulted them on any matter calling for insight and judgement, he found them ten times better than all the magicians and exorcists in his whole kingdom.¦Now Daniel was 21 there till the first year of King Cyrus.

Nebuchadnezzar's dream

In the second year of his reign Nebu- **2** chadnezzar had dreams, and his mind was so troubled that he could not sleep. Then the king gave orders to 2 summon the magicians, exorcists, sorcerers, and Chaldaeans to tell him what he had dreamt. They came in and stood in the royal presence, and 3 the king said to them, 'I have had a dream and my mind has been troubled to know what my dream was.' The 4

a at the end . . . would: or all of them were to.

b be guided . . . see: or treat us as you see fit.

Chaldaeans, speaking in Aramaic, said, ^c'Long live the king! Tell us what you dreamt and we will tell you the in-
5 terpretation.' The king answered, 'This is my declared intention. If you do not tell me both dream and interpretation, you shall be torn in pieces
6 and your houses shall be forfeit.^d But if you can tell me the dream and the interpretation, you will be richly rewarded and loaded with honours. Tell me, therefore, the dream and
7 its interpretation.' They answered a second time, 'Let the king tell his servants the dream, and we will tell
8 him the interpretation.' The king answered, 'It is clear to me that you are trying to gain time, because you see that my intention has been de-
9 clared. If you do not make known to me the dream, there is one law that applies to you, and one only. What is more, you have agreed among yourselves to tell me a pack of lies to my face in the hope that with time things may alter. Tell me the dream, therefore, and I shall know that you can
10 give me the interpretation.' The Chaldaeans answered in the presence of the king, 'Nobody on earth can tell your majesty what you wish to know; no great king or prince has ever made such a demand of magician, exorcist,
11 or Chaldaean. What your majesty requires of us is too hard; there is no one but the gods, who dwell remote from mortal men, who can give you
12 the answer.' At this the king lost his temper and in a great rage ordered the death of all the wise men of Bab-
13 ylon. A decree was issued that the wise men were to be executed, and accordingly men were sent to fetch Daniel and his companions for execution.

Daniel before the king

14 When Arioch, the captain of the king's bodyguard, was setting out to execute the wise men of Babylon, Daniel approached him cautiously and with
15 discretion and said, 'Sir, you represent the king; why has his majesty issued such a peremptory decree?'
16 Arioch explained everything; so Daniel went in to the king's presence and begged for a certain time by which he would give the king the
17 interpretation. Then Daniel went home and told the whole story to his companions, Hananiah, Mishael and
18 Azariah. They should ask the God of heaven in his mercy, he said, to dis-

close this secret, so that they and he with the rest of the wise men of Bab-
ylon should not be put to death. Then 19 in a vision by night the secret was revealed to Daniel, and he blessed the God of heaven in these words: 20

Blessed be God's name from age to age,
for all wisdom and power are his.
He changes seasons and times; 21
he deposes kings and sets them up;
he gives wisdom to the wise
and all their store of knowledge to the men who know;
he reveals deep mysteries; 22
he knows what lies in darkness,
and light has its dwelling with him.
To thee, God of my fathers, I give 23 thanks and praise,
for thou hast given me wisdom and power;
thou hast now revealed to me what we asked,
and told us what the king is concerned to know.

Daniel therefore went to Arioch 24 who had been charged by the king to put to death the wise men of Babylon and said to him, 'Do not put the wise men of Babylon to death. Take me into the king's presence, and I will now tell him the interpretation of the dream.' Arioch in great trepidation 25 brought Daniel before the king and said to him, 'I have found among the Jewish exiles a man who will make known to your majesty the interpretation of your dream.' Thereupon 26 the king said to Daniel (who was also called Belteshazzar), 'Can you tell me what I saw in my dream and interpret it?' Daniel answered in the king's 27 presence, 'The secret about which your majesty inquires no wise man, exorcist, magician, or diviner can disclose to you. But there is in heaven 28 a god who reveals secrets, and he has told King Nebuchadnezzar what is to be at the end of this age. This is the dream and these the visions that came into your head: the thoughts that 29 came to you, O king, as you lay on your bed, were thoughts of things to come, and the revealer of secrets has made known to you what is to be. This secret has been revealed to me 30 not because I am wise beyond all living men, but because your majesty is to know the interpretation and understand the thoughts which have entered your mind.'

c *The Aramaic text begins here and continues to the end of ch. 7.*   d *Or made into a dunghill (mng. of Aram. word uncertain).*

Daniel interprets the king's dream

31 'As you watched, O king, you saw a great image. This image, huge and dazzling, towered before you, fearful 32 to behold. The head of the image was of fine gold, its breast and arms of silver, its belly and thighs of bronze,[e] 33 its legs of iron, its feet part iron and 34 part clay. While you looked, a stone was hewn from a mountain, not by human hands; it struck the image on its feet of iron and clay and shattered 35 them. Then the iron, the clay, the bronze, the silver, and the gold, were all shattered to fragments and were swept away like chaff before the wind from a threshing-floor in summer, until no trace of them remained. But the stone which struck the image grew into a great mountain filling the 36 whole earth. That was the dream. We shall now tell your majesty the inter- 37 pretation. You, O king, king of kings, to whom the God of heaven has given the kingdom with all its power, au- 38 thority, and honour; in whose hands he has placed men and beasts and birds of the air, wherever they dwell, granting you sovereignty over them all— 39 you are that head of gold. After you there shall arise another kingdom, inferior to yours, and yet a third kingdom, of bronze, which shall have sovereignty over the whole world. 40 And there shall be a fourth kingdom, strong as iron; as iron shatters and destroys all things, it shall break and 41 shatter the whole earth.[f] As, in your vision, the feet and toes were part potter's clay and part iron, it shall be a divided kingdom. Its core shall be partly of iron just as you saw iron 42 mixed with the common clay; as the toes were part iron and part clay, the kingdom shall be partly strong and 43 partly brittle. As, in your vision, the iron was mixed with common clay, so shall men mix with each other by intermarriage, but such alliances shall not be stable: iron does not mix with 44 clay. In the period of those kings the God of heaven will establish a kingdom which shall never be destroyed; that kingdom shall never pass to another people; it shall shatter and make an end of all these kingdoms, while it shall itself endure for ever. 45 This is the meaning of your vision of the stone being hewn from a mountain, not by human hands, and then shattering the iron, the bronze, the clay, the silver, and the gold. The mighty God has made known to your majesty what is to be hereafter. The dream is sure and the interpretation to be trusted.'

Daniel and his friends promoted

Then King Nebuchadnezzar pros- 46 trated himself and worshipped Daniel, and gave orders that sacrifices and soothing offerings should be made to him. 'Truly,' he said, 'your god is in- 47 deed God of gods and Lord over kings, a revealer of secrets, since you have been able to reveal this secret.' Then 48 the king promoted Daniel, bestowed on him many rich gifts, and made him regent over the whole province of Babylon and chief prefect over all the wise men of Babylon. Moreover at 49 Daniel's request the king put Shadrach, Meshach and Abed-nego in charge of the administration of the province of Babylon. Daniel himself, however, remained at court.

The golden image

King Nebuchadnezzar made an image **3** of gold, ninety feet high and nine feet broad. He had it set up in the plain of Dura in the province of Babylon. Then 2 he sent out a summons to assemble the satraps, prefects, viceroys, counsellors, treasurers, judges, chief constables, and all governors of provinces to attend the dedication of the image which he had set up. So they assembled—the satraps, 3 prefects, viceroys, counsellors, treasurers, judges, chief constables, and all governors of provinces—for the dedication of the image which King Nebuchadnezzar had set up; and they stood before the image which Nebuchadnezzar had set up. Then 4 the herald loudly proclaimed, 'O peoples and nations of every language, you are commanded, when you hear 5 the sound of horn, pipe, zither, triangle, dulcimer, music, and singing of every kind, to prostrate yourselves and worship the golden image which King Nebuchadnezzar has set up. Whoever does not prostrate himself 6 and worship shall forthwith be thrown into a blazing furnace.' Accordingly, 7 no sooner did all the peoples hear the sound of horn, pipe, zither, triangle, dulcimer, music, and singing of every kind, than all the peoples and nations of every language prostrated themselves and worshipped the golden image which King Nebuchadnezzar had set up.

e Or copper.   f the whole earth: prob. rdg.; Aram. and like iron which shatters all these.

The three Jews refuse to worship the image

8 It was then that certain Chaldaeans came forward and brought a charge
9 against the Jews. They said to King Nebuchadnezzar, 'Long live the king!
10 Your majesty has issued an order that every man who hears the sound of horn, pipe, zither, triangle, dulcimer, music, and singing of every kind shall fall down and worship the image of
11 gold. Whoever does not do so shall be
12 thrown into a blazing furnace. There are certain Jews, Shadrach, Meshach and Abed-nego, whom you have put in charge of the administration of the province of Babylon. These men, your majesty, have taken no notice of your command; they do not serve your god, nor do they worship the golden image which you have set up.'
13 Then in rage and fury Nebuchadnezzar ordered Shadrach, Meshach and Abed-nego to be fetched, and they were brought into the king's presence.
14 Nebuchadnezzar said to them, 'Is it true, Shadrach, Meshach and Abednego, that you do not serve my god or worship the golden image which I
15 have set up? If you are ready at once to prostrate yourselves when you hear the sound of horn, pipe, zither, triangle, dulcimer, music, and singing of every kind, and to worship the image that I have set up, well and good. But if you do not worship it, you shall forthwith be thrown into the blazing furnace; and what god is there that
16 can save you from my power?' Shadrach, Meshach and Abed-nego said to King Nebuchadnezzar, 'We have no
17 need to answer you on this matter. If there is a god who is able to save us from the blazing furnace, it is our God whom we serve, and he will save us
18 from your power, O king; but if not, be it known to your majesty that we will neither serve your god nor worship the golden image that you have set up.'

Deliverance from the furnace

19 Then Nebuchadnezzar flew into a rage with Shadrach, Meshach and Abednego, and his face was distorted with anger. He gave orders that the furnace should be heated up to seven times
20 its usual heat, and commanded some of the strongest men in his army to bind Shadrach, Meshach and Abednego and throw them into the blaz-
21 ing furnace. Then those men in their trousers, their shirts, and their hats and all their other clothes, were bound and thrown into the blazing furnace. Because the king's order 22 was urgent and the furnace exceedingly hot, the men who were carrying Shadrach, Meshach and Abed-nego were killed by the flames that leapt out; and those three men, Shadrach, 23 Meshach and Abed-nego, fell bound into the blazing furnace.

Then King Nebuchadnezzar was 24 amazed and sprang to his feet in great trepidation. He said to his courtiers, 'Was it not three men whom we threw bound into the fire?' They answered the king, 'Assuredly, your majesty.' He answered, 'Yet I 25 see four men walking about in the fire free and unharmed; and the fourth looks like a god.' Nebuchadnezzar 26 approached the door of the blazing furnace and said to the men, 'Shadrach, Meshach and Abed-nego, servants of the Most High God, come out, come here.' Then Shadrach, Meshach and Abed-nego came out from the fire. And the satraps, prefects, 27 viceroys, and the king's courtiers gathered round and saw how the fire had had no power to harm the bodies of these men; the hair of their heads had not been singed, their trousers were untouched, and no smell of fire lingered about them.

Nebuchadnezzar blesses God

Then Nebuchadnezzar spoke out, 28 'Blessed is the God of Shadrach, Meshach and Abed-nego. He has sent his angel to save his servants who put their trust in him, who disobeyed the royal command and were willing to yield themselves to the fire rather than to serve or worship any god other than their own God. I therefore 29 issue a decree that any man, to whatever people or nation he belongs, whatever his language, if he speaks blasphemy against the God of Shadrach, Meshach and Abed-nego, shall be torn to pieces and his house shall be forfeit;[g] for there is no other god who can save men in this way.' Then the 30 king advanced the fortunes of Shadrach, Meshach and Abed-nego in the province of Babylon.

The king's proclamation

King Nebuchadnezzar to all peoples 4 and nations of every language living in the whole world: May all prosperity

g Or made into a dunghill (mng. of Aram. word uncertain).

2 be yours! It is my pleasure to recount the signs and marvels which the Most High God has worked for me:

3   How great are his signs,
   and his marvels overwhelming!
   His kingdom is an everlasting kingdom,
   his sovereignty stands to all generations.

The king's two visions

4 I, Nebuchadnezzar, was living peacefully at home in the luxury of my
5 palace. As I lay on my bed, I saw a dream which terrified me; and fantasies and visions which came into my
6 head dismayed me. So I issued an order summoning into my presence all the wise men of Babylon to make known to me the interpretation of
7 the dream. Then the magicians, exorcists, Chaldaeans, and diviners came in, and in their presence I related my dream. But they could not interpret
8 it. And yet another came into my presence, Daniel, who is called Belteshazzar after the name of my god, a man possessed by the spirit of the holy gods. To him, too, I related the dream:
9 'Belteshazzar, chief of the magicians, whom I myself know to be possessed by the spirit of the holy gods, and whom no secret baffles, listen to the vision I saw in a dream, and tell me its interpretation.
10 'Here is the vision which came into my head as I was lying upon my bed:

   As I was looking,
   I saw a tree of great height at the centre of the earth;
11   the tree grew and became strong,
   reaching with its top to the sky
   and visible to earth's farthest bounds.
12   Its foliage was lovely,
   and its fruit abundant;
   and it yielded food for all.
   Beneath it the wild beasts found shelter,
   the birds lodged in its branches,
   and from it all living creatures fed.

13 'Here is another vision which came into my head as I was lying upon my bed:

   As I was watching, there was a Watcher,
   a Holy One coming down from heaven.
14 He cried aloud and said,
   "Hew down the tree, lop off the branches,

   strip away the foliage, scatter the fruit.
   Let the wild beasts flee from its shelter
   and the birds from its branches,
   but leave the stump with its roots in 15 the ground.
   So, tethered with an iron ring,
   let him eat his fill of the lush grass;
   let him be drenched with the dew of heaven
   and share the lot of the beasts in their pasture;
   let his mind cease to be a man's 16 mind,
   and let him be given the mind of a beast.
   Let seven times pass over him.
   The issue has been determined by 17 the Watchers
   and the sentence pronounced by the Holy Ones.

Thereby the living will know that the Most High is sovereign in the kingdom of men: he gives the kingdom to whom he will and he may set over it the humblest of mankind."

Daniel's interpretation

'This is the dream which I, King 18 Nebuchadnezzar, have dreamed; now, Belteshazzar, tell me its interpretation; for, though all the wise men of my kingdom are unable to tell me what it means, you can tell me, since the spirit of the holy gods is in you.'

Daniel, who was called Belteshaz- 19 zar, was dumbfounded for a moment, dismayed by his thoughts; but the king said, 'Do not let the dream and its interpretation dismay you.' Belteshazzar answered, 'My lord, if only the dream were for those who hate you and its interpretation for your enemies! The tree which you saw 20 grow and become strong, reaching with its top to the sky and visible to earth's farthest bounds, its foliage 21 lovely and its fruit abundant, a tree which yielded food for all, beneath which the wild beasts dwelt and in whose branches the birds lodged, that 22 tree, O king, is you. You have grown and become strong. Your power has grown and reaches the sky; your sovereignty stretches to the ends of the earth. Also, O king, you saw a 23 Watcher, a Holy One, coming down from heaven and saying, "Hew down the tree and destroy it, but leave its stump with its roots in the ground. So, tethered with an iron ring, let him eat his fill of the lush grass; let him be drenched with the dew of heaven and share the lot of the beasts until seven 24 times pass over him." This is the interpretation, O king—it is a decree of the Most High which touches my 25 lord the king. You will be banished from the society of men; you will have to live with the wild beasts; you will feed on grass like oxen and you will be drenched with the dew of heaven. Seven times will pass over you until you have learnt that the Most High is sovereign over the kingdom of men 26 and gives it to whom he will. The command was given to leave the stump of the tree with its roots. By this you may know that from the time you acknowledge the sovereignty of heaven your 27 rule will endure. Be advised by me, O king: redeem your sins by charity and your iniquities by generosity to the wretched. So may you long enjoy peace of mind.'

Nebuchadnezzar's madness

28 All this befell King Nebuchadnezzar.
29 At the end of twelve months the king was walking on the roof of the royal 30 palace at Babylon, and he exclaimed, 'Is not this Babylon the great which I have built as a royal residence by my own mighty power and for the 31 honour of my majesty?' The words were still on his lips, when a voice came down from heaven: 'To you, King Nebuchadnezzar, the word is spoken: the kingdom has passed from 32 you. You are banished from the society of men and you shall live with the wild beasts; you shall feed on grass like oxen, and seven times will pass over you until you have learnt that the Most High is sovereign over the kingdom of men and gives it to 33 whom he will.' At that very moment this judgement came upon Nebuchadnezzar. He was banished from the society of men and ate grass like oxen; his body was drenched by the dew of heaven, until his hair grew long like goats' hair and his nails like eagles' talons.[h]

Nebuchadnezzar's sanity restored

34 At the end of the appointed time, I, Nebuchadnezzar, raised my eyes to heaven and I returned to my right mind. I blessed the Most High, praising and glorifying the Ever-living One:

His sovereignty is never-ending and his rule endures through all generations;
all dwellers upon earth count for 35 nothing
and he deals as he wishes with the host of heaven;[i]
no one may lay hand upon him and ask him what he does.

At that very time I returned to my 36 right mind and my majesty and royal splendour were restored to me for the glory of my kingdom. My courtiers and my nobles sought audience of me. I was established in my kingdom and my power was greatly increased. Now 37 I, Nebuchadnezzar, praise and exalt and glorify the King of heaven; for all his acts are right and his ways are just and those whose conduct is arrogant he can bring low.

Belshazzar's feast

Belshazzar the king gave a banquet 5 for a thousand of his nobles and was drinking wine in the presence of the thousand. Warmed by the wine, he gave 2 orders to fetch the vessels of gold and silver which his father Nebuchadnezzar had taken from the sanctuary at Jerusalem, that he and his nobles, his concubines and his courtesans, might drink from them. So the vessels of 3 gold and silver from the sanctuary in the house of God at Jerusalem were brought in, and the king and his nobles, his concubines and his courtesans, drank from them. They drank 4 wine and praised the gods of gold and silver, of bronze and iron, and of wood and stone. Suddenly there appeared 5 the fingers of a human hand writing on the plaster of the palace wall opposite the lamp, and the king could see the back of the hand as it wrote. At this the king's mind was filled with 6 dismay and he turned pale, he became limp in every limb and his knees knocked together. He called loudly 7 for the exorcists, Chaldaeans, and diviners to be brought in; then, addressing the wise men of Babylon, he said, 'Whoever can read this writing and tell me its interpretation shall be robed in purple and honoured with a chain of gold round his neck and shall rank as third in the kingdom.' Then all the king's wise men 8 came in, but they could not read the writing or interpret it to the king. King Belshazzar sat there pale and 9

h goats' hair . . . eagles' talons: prob. rdg.; Aram. eagles' and his nails like birds'.   i Prob. rdg.; Aram. adds and the dwellers upon earth.

utterly dismayed, while his nobles were perplexed.

Daniel and the writing on the wall

10 The king and his nobles were talking when the queen entered the banqueting-hall: 'Long live the king!' she said. 'Why this dismay, and why do 11 you look so pale? There is a man in your kingdom who has in him the spirit of the holy gods, a man who was known in your father's time to have a clear understanding and godlike wisdom. King Nebuchadnezzar, your father, appointed him chief of the magicians, exorcists, Chaldaeans, and 12 diviners. This same Daniel, whom the king named Belteshazzar, is known to have a notable spirit, with knowledge and understanding, and the gift of interpreting dreams, explaining riddles and unbinding spells;[j] let him be summoned now and he will give 13 the interpretation.' Daniel was then brought into the king's presence and the king said to him, 'So you are Daniel, one of the Jewish exiles whom the king my father brought from 14 Judah. I have heard that you possess the spirit of the holy gods and that you are a man of clear understanding 15 and peculiar wisdom. The wise men, the exorcists, have just been brought into my presence to read this writing and tell me its interpretation, and they have been unable to interpret it. 16 But I have heard it said of you that you are able to give interpretations and to unbind spells.[k] So now, if you are able to read the words and tell me what they mean, you shall be robed in purple and honoured with a chain of gold round your neck and shall rank 17 as third in the kingdom.' Then Daniel answered in the king's presence, 'Your gifts you may keep for yourself; or else give your rewards to another. Nevertheless I will read the writing to your majesty and tell you its inter-18 pretation. My lord king, the Most High God gave your father Nebuchadnezzar a kingdom and power and 19 glory and majesty; and, because of this power which he gave him, all peoples and nations of every language trembled before him and were afraid. He put to death whom he would and spared whom he would, he promoted them at will and at will degraded 20 them. But, when he became haughty, stubborn and presumptuous, he was

deposed from his royal throne and his glory was taken from him. He was 21 banished from the society of men, his mind became like that of a beast, he had to live with the wild asses and to eat grass like oxen, and his body was drenched with the dew of heaven, until he came to know that the Most High God is sovereign over the kingdom of men and sets up over it whom he will. But you, his son Belshazzar, 22 did not humble your heart, although you knew all this. You have set your-23 self up against the Lord of heaven. The vessels of his temple have been brought to your table; and you, your nobles, your concubines, and your courtesans have drunk from them. You have praised the gods of silver and gold, of bronze and iron, of wood and stone, which neither see nor hear nor know, and you have not given glory to God, in whose charge is your very breath and in whose hands are all your ways. This is why that hand 24 was sent from his very presence and why it wrote this inscription. And 25 these are the words of the writing which was inscribed: *Mene mene tekel u-pharsin.* Here is the interpretation: 26 *mene:*[l] God has numbered the days of your kingdom and brought it to an end; *tekel:*[m] you have been weighed in 27 the balance and found wanting; *u-*28 *pharsin:*[n] and your kingdom has been divided and given to the Medes and Persians.' Then Belshazzar gave the 29 order and Daniel was robed in purple and honoured with a chain of gold round his neck, and proclamation was made that he should rank as third in the kingdom.

That very night Belshazzar king of 30 the Chaldaeans was slain, and Darius 31 the Mede took the kingdom, being then sixty-two years old.

Scheme to depose Daniel

It pleased Darius to appoint satraps **6** over the kingdom, a hundred and twenty in number in charge of the whole kingdom, and over them three 2 chief ministers, to whom the satraps should send reports so that the king's interests might not suffer; of these three, Daniel was one. In the event 3 Daniel outshone the other ministers and the satraps because of his ability, and the king had it in mind to appoint him over the whole kingdom. Then 4 the chief ministers and the satraps

---

j Or and solving problems.   *k Or and to solve problems.*   *l That is numbered.*   *m That is shekel or weight.*   *n Prob. rdg.; Aram.* pheres. *There is a play on three possible meanings* halves *or* divisions *or* Persians.

began to look round for some pretext to attack Daniel's administration of the kingdom, but they failed to find any malpractice on his part; for he 5 was faithful to his trust. Since they could discover no neglect of duty or malpractice, they said, 'There will be no charge to bring against this Daniel unless we find one in his religion.' 6 These chief ministers and satraps watched for an opportunity to approach the king, and said to him, 7 'Long live King Darius! All we, the ministers of the kingdom, prefects, satraps, courtiers, and viceroys, have taken counsel and agree that the king should issue a decree and bring an ordinance into force, that whoever within the next thirty days shall present a petition to any god or man other than the king shall be thrown 8 into the lions' pit. Now, O king, issue the ordinance and have it put in writing, so that it may be unalterable, for the law of the Medes and Persians 9 stands for ever.' Accordingly King Darius issued the ordinance in written form.

Daniel is thrown to the lions

10 When Daniel learnt that this decree had been issued, he went into his house. He had had windows made in his roof-chamber looking towards Jerusalem; and there he knelt down three times a day and offered prayers and praises to his God as his custom 11 had always been. His enemies watched for an opportunity to catch Daniel and found him at his prayers making 12 supplication to his God. Then they came into the king's presence and reminded him of the ordinance. 'Your majesty,' they said, 'have you not issued an ordinance that any person who, within the next thirty days, shall present a petition to any god or man other than your majesty shall be thrown into the lions' pit?' The king answered, 'Yes, it is fixed. The law of the Medes and Persians stands for 13 ever.' So in the king's presence they said, 'Daniel, one of the Jewish exiles, has ignored the ordinance issued by your majesty, and is making petition 14 to his god three times a day.' When the king heard this, he was greatly distressed. He tried to think of a way to save Daniel, and continued his 15 efforts till sunset; then those same men watched for an opportunity to approach the king, and said to him, 'Your majesty must know that by the

law of the Medes and Persians no ordinance or decree issued by the king may be altered.' So the king gave 1 orders and Daniel was brought and thrown into the lions' pit; but he said to Daniel, 'Your own God, whom you serve continually, will save you.' A stone was brought and put over the mouth of the pit, and the king sealed it with his signet and with the signets of his nobles, so that no one might intervene to rescue Daniel.

The angel delivers Daniel

The king went back to his palace and 1 spent the night fasting; no woman was brought to him and sleep eluded him. At dawn, as soon as it was light, 1 he rose and went in fear and trembling to the pit. When the king reached 2 it, he called anxiously to Daniel, 'Daniel, servant of the living God, has your God whom you serve continually been able to save you from the lions?' Then Daniel answered, 'Long live the 2 king! My God sent his angel to shut 2 the lions' mouths so that they have done me no injury, because in his judgement I was found innocent;[o] and moreover, O king, I had done you no injury.' The king was overjoyed 2 and gave orders that Daniel should be lifted out of the pit. So Daniel was lifted out and no trace of injury was found on him, because he had put his faith in his God. By order of the 2 king Daniel's accusers were brought and thrown into the lions' pit with their wives and children, and before they reached the floor of the pit the lions were upon them and crunched them up, bones and all.

Darius issues a decree

Then King Darius wrote to all peo- 2 ples and nations of every language throughout the whole world: 'May your prosperity increase! I have issued 2 a decree that in all my royal domains men shall fear and reverence the God of Daniel;

for he is the living God, the ever-
    lasting,
whose kingly power shall not be
    weakened;
    whose sovereignty shall have no
        end—
a saviour, a deliverer, a worker of 2
    signs and wonders
    in heaven and on earth,
who has delivered Daniel from the
    power of the lions.'

o in his judgement . . . innocent: or before him success was granted me.

28 So this Daniel prospered during the reigns of Darius and Cyrus the Persian.

Daniel's vision of the beasts

7 In the first year of Belshazzar king of Babylon, as Daniel lay on his bed, dreams and visions came into his head. Then he wrote down the dream, and here his account begins:

2 In my visions of the night I, Daniel, was gazing intently and I saw a great sea churned up by the four winds of 3 heaven, and four huge beasts coming up out of the sea, each one different 4 from the others. The first was like a lion but had an eagle's wings. I watched until its wings were plucked off and it was lifted from the ground and made to stand on two feet like a man; it was also given the mind of 5 a man. Then I saw another, a second beast, like a bear. It was half crouching and had three ribs in its mouth, between its teeth. The command was given: 'Up, gorge yourself with flesh.' 6 After this as I gazed I saw another, a beast like a leopard with four bird's wings on its back; this creature had four heads, and it was invested with 7 sovereign power. Next in my visions of the night I saw a fourth beast, dreadful and grisly, exceedingly strong, with great iron teeth and bronze claws.[p] It crunched and devoured, and trampled underfoot all that was left. It differed from all the beasts which preceded it in having 8 ten horns. While I was considering the horns I saw another horn, a little one, springing up among them, and three of the first horns were uprooted to make room for it. And in that horn were eyes like the eyes of a man, and 9 a mouth that spoke proud words. I kept looking, and then

> thrones were set in place and one ancient in years took his seat,
> his robe was white as snow and the hair of his head like cleanest wool.
> Flames of fire were his throne and its wheels blazing fire;
10 a flowing river of fire streamed out before him.[q]
> Thousands upon thousands served him
> and myriads upon myriads attended his presence.
> The court sat, and the books were opened.

11 Then because of the proud words that the horn was speaking, I went on watching until the beast was killed and its carcass destroyed: it 12 was given to the flames. The rest of the beasts, though deprived of their sovereignty, were allowed to remain 13 alive for a time and a season. I was still watching in visions of the night and I saw one like a man coming with the clouds of heaven; he approached the Ancient in Years and was present-14 ed to him. Sovereignty and glory and kingly power were given to him, so that all people and nations of every language should serve him; his sovereignty was to be an everlasting sovereignty which should not pass away, and his kingly power such as should never be impaired.

Interpretation of the vision

15 My spirit within me was troubled, and, dismayed by the visions which 16 came into my head, I, Daniel, approached one of those who stood there and inquired from him what all this meant; and he told me the inter-17 pretation. 'These great beasts, four in number,' he said, 'are four kingdoms which shall rise from the ground. 18 But the saints[r] of the Most High shall receive the kingly power and shall retain it for ever, for ever and 19 ever.' Then I desired to know what the fourth beast meant, the beast that was different from all the others, very dreadful with its iron teeth and bronze claws, crunching and devouring and trampling underfoot all that 20 was left. I desired also to know about the ten horns on its head and the other horn which sprang up and at whose coming three of them fell—the horn that had eyes and a mouth speaking proud words and appeared 21 larger than the others. As I still watched, that horn was waging war with the saints and overcoming them 22 until the Ancient in Years came. Then judgement was given in favour of the saints of the Most High, and the time came when the saints gained possession of the kingly power. He 23 gave me this answer: 'The fourth beast signifies a fourth kingdom which shall appear upon earth. It shall differ from the other kingdoms and shall devour the whole earth, tread it down and crush it. The ten 24 horns signify the appearance of ten kings in this kingdom, after whom another king shall arise, differing from his predecessors; and he shall bring low three kings. He shall hurl defiance 25

p and bronze claws: *prob. rdg., cp. verse 19; Aram. om.*   q *Or it.*   r *Or holy ones.*

at the Most High and shall wear down the saints of the Most High. He shall plan to alter the customary times and law; and the saints shall be delivered into his power for a time and times 26 and half a time. Then the court shall sit, and he shall be deprived of his sovereignty, so that in the end it 27 may be destroyed and abolished. The kingly power, sovereignty, and greatness of all the kingdoms under heaven shall be given to the people of the saints of the Most High. Their kingly power is an everlasting power and all sovereignties shall serve them and obey them.'

28 Here the account ends. As for me, Daniel, my thoughts dismayed me greatly and I turned pale; and I kept these things in my mind.

The ram and the he-goat

8 1-2 *8*In the third year of the reign of King Belshazzar, while I was in Susa the capital city of the province of Elam, a vision appeared to me, Daniel, similar to my former vision. In this vision I was watching beside the 3 stream of the Ulai. I raised my eyes and there I saw a ram with two horns standing between me and the stream. The two horns were long, the one longer than the other, growing up 4 behind. I watched the ram butting west and north and south. No beasts could stand before it, no one could rescue from its power. It did what it liked, making a display of its strength. 5 While I pondered this, suddenly a he-goat came from the west skimming over the whole earth without touching the ground; it had a prominent 6 horn between its eyes. It approached the two-horned ram which I had seen standing between me and the stream and rushed at it with impetuous force. 7 I saw it advance on the ram, working itself into a fury against it, then strike the ram and break its two horns; the ram had no strength to resist. The he-goat flung it to the ground and trampled on it, and there was no one to save the ram. 8 Then the he-goat made a great display of its strength. Powerful as it was, its great horn snapped and in its place there sprang out towards the four quarters of heaven four prominent 9 horns. Out of one of them there issued one small horn, which made a prodigious show of strength south and

east and towards the fairest of all lands. It aspired to be as great as the 10 host of heaven, and it cast down to the earth some of the host and some of the stars and trod them underfoot. It aspired to be as great as the Prince 11 of the host, suppressed his regular offering and even threw down his sanctuary. The heavenly hosts were 12 delivered up, and it raised itself*t* impiously against the regular offering and threw true religion to the ground; in all that it did it succeeded. I heard 13 a holy one speaking and another holy one answering him, whoever he was. The one said, 'For how long will the period of this vision last? How long will the regular offering be suppressed, how long will impiety cause desolation,*u* and both the Holy Place and the fairest of all lands*v* be given over to be trodden down?' The an- 14 swer came, 'For two thousand three hundred evenings and mornings; then the Holy Place shall emerge victorious.'

Interpretation of the vision

All the while that I, Daniel, was see- 15 ing the vision, I was trying to understand it. Suddenly I saw standing before me one with the semblance of a man; at the same time I heard a 16 human voice calling to him across the bend of the Ulai, 'Gabriel, explain the vision to this man.' He came up to 17 where I was standing; I was seized with terror at his approach and threw myself on my face. But he said to me, 'Understand, O man: the vision points to the time of the end.' When he 18 spoke to me, I fell to the ground in a trance; but he grasped me and made me stand up where I was. And he said, 19 'I shall make known to you what is to happen at the end of the wrath; for there is an end to the appointed time. The two-horned ram which you saw 20 signifies the kings of Media and Persia, the he-goat is the kingdom*w* of the 21 Greeks and the great horn on his forehead is the first king. As for the horn 22 which was snapped off and replaced by four horns: four kingdoms shall rise out of that nation, but not with power comparable to his.

In the last days of those kingdoms, 23
when their sin is at its height,
a king shall appear, harsh and grim,
a master of stratagem.

---

s Here the Hebrew text resumes (see note at 2. 4).
u will impiety cause desolation: *prob. rdg.*; *Heb. obscure.*
verse 9; *Heb. host.*   *w* *Prob. rdg.*; *Heb. king.*
t and it raised itself: *prob. rdg.*; *Heb. om.*
v fairest of all lands: *prob. rdg., cp.*

24 His power shall be great, he shall
    work havoc untold;
  he shall succeed in whatever he
    does.
He shall work havoc among great
    nations and upon a holy people.
25 His mind shall be ever active,
  and he shall succeed in his crafty
    designs;
  he shall conjure up great plans
  and, when they least expect it, work
    havoc on many.
  He shall challenge even the Prince
    of princes
  and be broken, but not by human
    hands.
26 This revelation which has been
    given
  of the evenings and the mornings is
    true;
  but you must keep the vision secret,
    for it points to days far ahead.'

27 As for me, Daniel, my strength
failed me and I lay sick for a while.
Then I rose and attended to the king's
business. But I was perplexed by the
revelation and no one could explain
it.

Daniel's prayer for exiled Judah

9 In the first year of the reign of Darius
son of Ahasuerus (a Mede by birth,
who was appointed king over the
2 kingdom of the Chaldaeans) I, Daniel,
was reading the scriptures and reflecting on the seventy years which,
according to the word of the LORD to
the prophet Jeremiah, were to pass
3 while Jerusalem lay in ruins. Then I
turned to the Lord God in earnest
prayer and supplication with fasting
4 and sackcloth and ashes. I prayed to
the LORD my God, making confession
thus:
    'Lord, thou great and terrible God
who faithfully keepest the covenant
with those who love thee and observe
5 thy commandments, we have sinned,
we have done what was wrong and
wicked; we have rebelled, we have
turned our backs on thy command-
6 ments and thy decrees. We have not
listened to thy servants the prophets,
who spoke in thy name to our kings
and princes, to our forefathers and to
7 all the people of the land. O Lord, the
right is on thy side; the shame, now
as ever, belongs to us, the men of
Judah and the citizens of Jerusalem,
and to all the Israelites near and far
in every land to which thou hast
banished them for their treachery to-
8 wards thee. O LORD, the shame falls on

us as on our kings, our princes and
our forefathers; we have all sinned
against thee. Compassion and for- 9
giveness belong to the Lord our God,
though we have rebelled against him.
We have not obeyed the LORD our 10
God, we have not conformed to the
laws which he laid down for us through
his servants the prophets. All Israel 11
has broken thy law and not obeyed
thee, so that the curses set out in the
law of Moses thy servant in the
adjuration and the oath have rained
down upon us; for we have sinned
against him. He has fulfilled all that 12
he said about us and about our rulers,
by bringing upon us and upon Jerusalem a calamity greater than has
ever happened in all the world. It was 13
all foreshadowed in the law of Moses,
this calamity which has come upon
us; yet we have done nothing to
propitiate the LORD our God; we
have neither repented of our wrong-
ful deeds nor remembered that thou
art true to thy word. The LORD has 14
been biding his time and has now
brought this calamity upon us. In all
that he has done the LORD our God has
been right; yet we have not obeyed
him.

'And now, O Lord our God who 15
didst bring thy people out of Egypt
by a strong hand, winning for thyself
a name that lives on to this day, we
have sinned, we have done wrong.
O Lord, by all thy saving deeds we 16
beg that thy wrath and anger may
depart from Jerusalem, thy city, thy
holy hill; through our own sins and
our fathers' guilty deeds Jerusalem
and thy people have become a byword among all our neighbours. And 17
now, our God, listen to thy servant's
prayer and supplication; for thy own
sake, O Lord, make thy face shine
upon thy desolate sanctuary. Lend 18
thy ear, O God, and hear, open thine
eyes and look upon our desolation
and upon the city that bears thy
name; it is not by virtue of our own
saving acts but by thy great mercy
that we present our supplications
before thee. O Lord, hear; O Lord, 19
forgive; O Lord, listen and act; for
thy own sake do not delay, O God,
for thy city and thy people bear thy
name.'

Gabriel's message to Daniel

Thus I was speaking and praying, 20
confessing my own sin and my people Israel's sin, and presenting my

supplication before the LORD my God
21 on behalf of his holy hill. While I was
praying, the man Gabriel, whom I
had already seen in the vision, came
close to^x me at the hour of the even-
22 ing sacrifice, flying swiftly.^{y} He spoke
clearly to me and said, 'Daniel, I have
now come to enlighten your under-
23 standing. As you were beginning your
supplications a word went forth; this
I have come to pass on to you,
for you are a man greatly beloved.
Consider well the word, consider the
24 vision: Seventy weeks are marked out
for your people and your holy city;
then rebellion shall be stopped,^{z} sin
brought to an end,^{a} iniquity expiated,
everlasting right ushered in, vision
and prophecy sealed, and the Most
25 Holy Place anointed. Know then and
understand: from the time that the
word went forth that Jerusalem should
be restored and rebuilt, seven weeks
shall pass till the appearance of one
anointed, a prince; then for sixty-
two weeks it shall remain restored,
26 rebuilt with streets and conduits. At
the critical time, after the sixty-two
weeks, one who is anointed shall be
removed with no one to take his part;
and the horde of an invading prince
shall work havoc on city and sanctuary. The end of it shall be a deluge,
inevitable war with all its horrors.
27 He shall make a firm league with
the mighty^b for one week; and, the
week half spent, he shall put a stop to
sacrifice and offering. And in the
train of these abominations shall
come an author of desolation; then,
in the end, what has been decreed
concerning the desolation will be
poured out.'

Daniel's vision by the river Tigris

10 In the third year of Cyrus king of
Persia a word was revealed to Daniel
who had been given the name Belteshazzar. Though this word was true,
it cost him^c much toil to understand
it; nevertheless understanding came
to him in the course of the vision.
2   In those days I, Daniel, mourned
3 for three whole weeks. I refrained
from all choice food; no meat or wine
passed my lips, and I did not anoint
myself until the three weeks had
4 gone by. On the twenty-fourth day of
the first month, I found myself on the
bank of the great river, that is the
5 Tigris; I looked up and saw a man

clothed in linen with a belt of gold
from Ophir round his waist. His body 6
gleamed like topaz, his face shone like
lightning, his eyes flamed like torches,
his arms and feet sparkled like a disc
of bronze; and when he spoke his
voice sounded like the voice of a
multitude. I, Daniel, alone saw the 7
vision, while those who were near me
did not see it, but great fear fell upon
them and they stole away, and I was 8
left alone gazing at this great vision.
But my strength left me; I became a
sorry figure of a man, and retained
no strength. I heard the sound of his 9
words and, when I did so, I fell prone
on the ground in a trance. Suddenly 10
a hand grasped me and pulled me up
on to my hands and knees. He said to 11
me, 'Daniel, man greatly beloved,
attend to the words I am speaking
to you and stand up where you are,
for I am now sent to you.' When he
addressed me, I stood up trembling
and he said, 'Do not be afraid, Daniel, 12
for from the very first day that you
applied your mind to understand and
to mortify yourself before your God,
your prayers have been heard, and I
have come in answer to them. But 13
the angel prince of the kingdom of
Persia resisted me for twenty-one
days, and then, seeing that I had
held out there, Michael, one of the
chief princes, came to help me against
the prince of the kingdom of Persia.
And I have come to explain to you 14
what will happen to your people in
days to come; for this too is a vision
for those days.'

Interpretation of the vision

While he spoke to me I hung my head 15
and was struck dumb. Suddenly one 16
like a man touched my lips. Then I
opened my mouth to speak and
addressed him as he stood before me:
'Sir, this has pierced me to the heart,
and I retain no strength. How can my 17
lord's servant presume to talk with
such as my lord, since my strength
has failed me and no breath is left in
me?' Then the figure touched me 18
again and restored my strength. He 19
said, 'Do not be afraid, man greatly
beloved; all will be well with you. Be
strong, be strong.' When he had
spoken to me, I recovered strength
and said, 'Speak, sir, for you have
given me strength.' He said, 'Do you 20
know why I have come to you? I am

---

x Or touched. y flying swiftly: *prob. rdg.*; Heb. thoroughly wearied. z Or restrained.
a Or sealed. b Or many. c him: *prob. rdg.*; Heb. om.

first going back to fight with the prince of Persia, and, as soon as I have left, the prince of Greece will appear: I have no ally on my side to help and support me, except Michael your prince.[d] However I will tell you what is written in the Book of Truth. Here and now I will tell you what is true: 'Three more kings will appear in Persia, and the fourth will far surpass all the others in wealth; and when he has extended his power through his wealth, he will rouse the whole world against the kingdom of Greece. Then there will appear a warrior king. He will rule a vast kingdom and will do what he chooses. But as soon as he is established, his kingdom will be shattered and split up north, south, east and west. It will not pass to his descendants, nor will any of his successors have an empire like his; his kingdom will be torn up by the roots and given to others as well as to them. Then the king of the south will become strong; but another of the captains will surpass him in strength and win a greater kingdom. In due course the two will enter into a friendly alliance; to redress the balance the daughter of the king of the south will be given in marriage to the king of the north, but she will not maintain her influence and their line will not last. She and her escort, her child, and also her lord and master, will all be the victims of foul play. Then another shoot from the same stock as hers will appear in his father's place, will penetrate the defences of the king of the north and enter his fortress, and will win a decisive victory over his people. He will take back as booty to Egypt even the images of their gods cast in metal and their precious vessels of silver and gold. Then for some years he will refrain from attacking the king of the north. After that the king of the north will overrun the southern kingdom but will retreat to his own land. 'His sons will press on to assemble a great armed horde. One of them will sweep on and on like an irresistible flood. And after that he will press on as far as his enemy's stronghold. The king of the south, his anger roused, will march out to do battle with the king of the north who, in turn, will raise a great horde, but it will be delivered into the hands of his enemy.

When this horde has been captured, 12 the victor will be elated and he will slaughter tens of thousands, yet he will not maintain his advantage. Then 13 the king of the north will once more raise a horde even greater than the last and, when the years come round, will advance with a great army and a large baggage-train. During these 14 times many will resist the king of the south, but some hotheads among your own people will rashly attempt to give substance to a vision and will come to disaster. Then the king of the 15 north will come and throw up siege-ramps and capture a fortified town, and the forces of the south will not stand up to him; even the flower of their army will not be able to hold their ground. And so his adversary 16 will do as he pleases and meet with no opposition. He will establish himself in the fairest of all lands and it will come wholly into his power. He 17 will resolve to subjugate all the dominions of the king of the south; and he will come to fair terms with him,[e] and he will give him a young woman in marriage, for the destruction of the kingdom; but she will not persist nor serve his purpose. Then he will turn 18 to the coasts and islands and take many prisoners, but a foreign commander[f] will put an end to his challenge by wearing him down;[g] thus he will throw back his challenge on to him. He will fall back upon his own 19 strongholds; there he will come to disaster and be overthrown and be seen no more.

'He will be succeeded by one who 20 will send out an officer with a royal escort to extort tribute; after a short time this king too will meet his end, yet neither openly nor in battle.

'A contemptible creature will suc- 21 ceed but will not be given recognition as king; yet he will seize the kingdom by dissimulation and intrigue in time of peace. He will sweep away all 22 forces of opposition as he advances, and even the Prince of the Covenant will be broken. He will enter into 23 fraudulent alliances and, although the people behind him are but few, he will rise to power and establish himself in time of peace. He will overrun 24 the richest districts of the province and succeed in doing what his fathers and forefathers failed to do, distributing spoil, booty, and property to

d *Prob. rdg.; Heb. adds* and as for me, in the first year of Darius the Mede.   e and he . . . with him: *prob. rdg.; Heb. obscure.*   f *Or consul or legate.*   g by wearing him down: *prob. rdg.; Heb. obscure.*

his followers. He will lay his plans against fortresses, but only for a time.

25 'He will rouse himself in all his strength and courage and lead a great army against the king of the south, but the king of the south will press the campaign against him with a very great and numerous army; yet the king of the south will not persist, for

26 traitors will lay their plots. Those who eat at his board will be his undoing; his army will be swept away, and many will fall on the field of battle.

27 The two kings will be bent on mischief and, sitting at the same table, they will lie to each other with advantage to neither. Yet there will still be

28 an end to the appointed time. Then one will return home with a long baggage-train, and with anger in his heart against the Holy Covenant; he will work his will and return to his own land.

29 'At the appointed time he will once more overrun the south, but he will

30 not succeed as he did before. Ships from the west will sail against him, and he will receive a rebuff. He will turn and vent his fury against the Holy Covenant; on his way back he will take due note of those who have

31 forsaken it. Armed forces dispatched by him will desecrate the sanctuary and the citadel and do away with the regular offering. And there they will set up "the abominable thing that

32 causes desolation". He will win over by plausible promises those who are ready to condemn the covenant, but the people who are faithful to their God will hold firm and fight back.

33 Wise leaders of the nation will give guidance to the common people; yet for a while they will fall victims to fire and sword, to captivity and pillage.

34 But these victims will not want for help, though small, even if many who

35 join them are insincere. Some of these leaders will themselves fall victims for a time so that they may be tested, refined and made shining white. Yet there will still be an end[h] to the

36 appointed time. The king will do what he chooses; he will exalt and magnify himself above every god and against the God of gods he will utter monstrous blasphemies. All will go well for him until the time of wrath ends, for what is determined must be done.

37 He will ignore his ancestral gods, and the god beloved of women; to no god will he pay heed but will exalt him-

38 self above them all. Instead he will honour the god of the citadel, a god unknown to his ancestors, with gold

39 and silver, gems and costly gifts. He will garrison his strongest fortresses with aliens, the people of a foreign god. Those whom he favours he will load with honour, putting them in office over the common people and distributing land at a price.

40 'At the time of the end, he and the king of the south will make feints at one another, and the king of the north will come storming against him with chariots and cavalry and many ships. He will overrun land after land, sweeping over them like a flood,

41 amongst them the fairest of all lands, and tens of thousands shall fall victims. Yet all these lands [including Edom and Moab and the remnant of the Ammonites] will survive his

42 attack. He will reach out to land after land, and Egypt will not escape. He

43 will gain control of her hidden stores of gold and silver and of all her treasures; Libyans and Cushites will fol-

44 low in his train. Then rumours from east and north will alarm him, and he will depart in a great rage to destroy

45 and to exterminate many. He will pitch his royal pavilion between the sea and the holy hill, the fairest of all hills; and he will meet his end with no one to help him.

At that moment Michael shall **12**
appear,
Michael the great captain,
who stands guard over your fellow-countrymen;
and there will be a time of distress
such as has never been
since they became a nation till that moment.
But at that moment your people will be delivered,[i]
every one who is written in the book:

2 many of those who sleep in the dust of the earth will wake,
some to everlasting life
and some to the reproach of eternal abhorrence.

3 The wise leaders shall shine like the bright vault of heaven,
and those who have guided the people in the true path
shall be like the stars for ever and ever.

4 But you, Daniel, keep the words secret and seal the book till the time of the end. Many will be at their wits' end, and punishment will be heavy.'

h Yet ... end: *prob. rdg.*; Heb. *has different word order.*   i Or will escape.

Conclusion

5 And I, Daniel, looked and saw two others standing, one on this bank of the river and the other on the opposite bank.
6 And I said to the man clothed in linen who was above the waters of the river, 'How long will it be before these portents cease?'
7 The man clothed in linen above the waters lifted to heaven his right hand and his left, and I heard him swear by him who lives for ever: 'It shall be for a time, times, and a half. When the power of the holy people ceases to be dispersed, all these things
8 shall come to an end.' I heard but I did not understand, and so I said, 'Sir, what will the issue of these things

be?' He replied, 'Go your way, Daniel, 9 for the words are kept secret and sealed till the time of the end. Many 10 shall purify themselves and be refined, making themselves shining white, but the wicked shall continue in wickedness and none of them shall understand; only the wise leaders shall understand. From the time when the 11 regular offering is abolished and "the abomination of desolation" is set up, there shall be an interval of one thousand two hundred and ninety days. Happy the man who waits and lives 12 to see the completion of one thousand three hundred and thirty-five days! But go your way to the end and rest, 13 and you shall arise to your destiny at the end of the age.'

THE TWELVE PROPHETS

HOSEA

1 THE WORD of the LORD which came to Hosea son of Beeri during the reigns of Uzziah, Jotham, Ahaz, and Hezekiah, kings of Judah, and during the reign of Jeroboam son of Jehoash king of Israel.

Hosea's wife and children

2 This is the beginning of the LORD's message by Hosea. He said, Go, take a wanton for your wife and get children of her wantonness; for like a wanton this land is unfaithful to the LORD.
3 So he went and took Gomer, a worthless woman;[a] and she conceived and
4 bore him a son. And the LORD said to him,

Call him Jezreel;[b] for in a little while I will punish the line of Jehu for the blood shed in Jezreel
and put an end to the kingdom of Israel.
5 On that day
I will break Israel's bow in the Vale of Jezreel.
6 She conceived again and bore a daughter, and the LORD said to him,

Call her Lo-ruhamah;[c]
for I will never again show love to Israel,
never again forgive them.[d]

After weaning Lo-ruhamah, she con- 8 ceived and bore a son; and the LORD 9 said,

Call him Lo-ammi;[e]
for you are not my people,
and I will not be your God.
The Israelites shall become countless 10 as the sands of the sea
which can neither be measured nor numbered;
it shall no longer be said, 'They are not my people',
they shall be called Sons of the Living God.
Then the people of Judah and of 11 Israel shall be reunited
and shall choose for themselves a single head,
and they shall become masters of the earth;
for great shall be the day of Jezreel.

a a worthless woman: *or* daughter of Diblaim.   *b That is* God shall sow.   *c That is* Not loved.
d Prob. rdg.; Heb. adds (7) Then I will love Judah and will save them. I will save them not by bow or sword or weapon of war, by horses or by horsemen, but by the LORD their God.   *e That is* Not my people.

An unfaithful wife

2 Then you will say to your brothers,
'You are my people',
and to your sisters, 'You are loved.'

2　Plead my cause with your mother;
is she not my wife and I her husband?[f]
Plead with her to forswear those
wanton looks,
to banish the lovers from her bosom.

3　Or I will strip her and expose her
naked as the day she was born;
I will make her bare as the wilderness,
parched as the desert,
and leave her to die of thirst.

4　I will show no love for her children;
they are the offspring of wantonness,

5　and their mother is a wanton.
She who conceived them is shameless;
she says, 'I will go after my lovers;
they give me my food and drink,
my wool and flax, my oil and my
perfumes.'

6 Therefore I will block her road with
thorn-bushes
and obstruct her path with a wall,
so that she can no longer follow her
old ways.

7 When she pursues her lovers she will
not overtake them,
when she looks for them she will
not find them;
then she will say,
'I will go back to my husband again;
I was better off with him than I am
now.'

8 For she does not know that it is I who
gave her
corn, new wine, and oil,
I who lavished upon her silver and
gold
which they spent on the Baal.

9　Therefore I will take back
my corn at the harvest and my new
wine at the vintage,
and I will take away the wool and
the flax
which I gave her to cover her naked
body;

10　so I will show her up for the lewd
thing she is,
and no lover will want to steal her
from me.

12[g]　I will ravage the vines and the fig-
trees,
which she says are the fee
with which her lovers have hired her,

and turn them into jungle where wild
beasts shall feed.
I will put a stop to her merry- 11
making,
her pilgrimages and new moons, her
sabbaths[h] and festivals.
I will punish her for the holy days 13
when she burnt sacrifices to the
Baalim,
when she decked herself with earrings and necklaces,
ran after her lovers and forgot me.
This is the very word of the LORD.

Restored to her husband

But now listen, 14
I will woo her, I will go with her into
the wilderness
and comfort her:
there I will restore her vineyards, 15
turning the Vale of Trouble into
the Gate of Hope,[i]
and there she will answer as in her
youth,
when she came up out of Egypt.
On that day she shall call me 'My 16
husband'
and shall no more call me 'My
Baal';[j]
and I will wipe from her lips the very 17
names of the Baalim;
never again shall their names be
heard.
This is the very word of the LORD.[k]

'You are my people'

Then I will make a covenant on be- 18
half of Israel with the wild beasts, the
birds of the air, and the things that
creep on the earth, and I will break
bow and sword and weapon of war
and sweep them off the earth, so that
all living creatures may lie down
without fear. I will betroth you to 19
myself for ever, betroth you in lawful
wedlock with unfailing devotion and
love; I will betroth you to myself to 20
have and to hold, and you shall know
the LORD. At that time I will give 21
answer, says the LORD, I will answer
for the heavens and they will answer
for the earth, and the earth will 22
answer for the corn, the new wine,
and the oil, and they will answer for
Jezreel. Israel shall be my new sowing 23
in the land, and I will show love to
Lo-ruhamah and say to Lo-ammi,
'You are my people', and he will say,
'Thou art my God.'

---

f is she . . . husband?: *or* for she is no longer my wife nor I her husband.　*g* Verses 11 and 12 transposed.　*h* Or her full moons.　*i* turning . . . Hope: *or* Emek-achor to Pethah-tikvah.　*j* Also
means My husband.　*k* This . . . LORD: transposed from after On that day in verse 16.

Hosea buys back his wife

3 The LORD said to me,

Go again and love a woman
 loved by another man, an adulteress,
and love her as I, the LORD, love the
   Israelites
although they resort to other gods
 and love the raisin-cakes offered to
   their idols.

2 So I got her back[l] for fifteen pieces of
silver, a homer of barley and a mea-
3 sure of wine; and I said to her,

Many a long day you shall live in
   my house
 and not play the wanton,
and have no intercourse with a man,
 nor I with you.

4 For the Israelites shall live many a
   long day
 without king or prince,
 without sacrifice or sacred pillar,
 without image or household gods;
5 but after that they will again seek
the LORD their God and David their
   king,
and turn anxiously to the LORD for
   his bounty in days to come.

The LORD's charge against Israel

4 Hear the word of the LORD, O
   Israel;
for the LORD has a charge to bring
   against the people of the land:
 There is no good faith or mutual
   trust,
 no knowledge of God in the land,
2 oaths are imposed and broken, they
   kill and rob;
 there is nothing but adultery and
   licence,[m]
 one deed of blood after another.
3 Therefore the land shall be dried
   up,
 and all who live in it shall pine
   away,
 and with them the wild beasts and
   the birds of the air;
 even the fish shall be swept from
   the sea.
4 But it is not for any man to bring
   a charge,
 it is not for him to prove a case;
 the quarrel with you, false priest, is
   mine.

Priest?[n] By day and by night you 5
   blunder on,
you and the prophet with you.
My people are ruined for lack of 6
   knowledge;
your own countrymen are brought
   to ruin.[o]
You have rejected knowledge,
and I will reject you from serving
   me as priest.
You have forgotten the teaching of
   God,
and I, your God, will forget your
   sons.

The more priests there are, the 7
   more they sin against me;
their dignity I will turn into dishonour.
They feed on the sin of my people 8
and batten on their iniquity.
But people and priest shall be 9
   treated alike.
I will punish them for their conduct
and repay them for their deeds:
they shall eat but never be satisfied, 10
behave wantonly but their lust will
   never be overtaxed,
for they have forsaken the LORD
to give themselves to sacred prosti- 11
   tution.
New wine and old steal my people's 12
   wits:[p]
they ask advice from a block of
   wood
and take their orders from a fetish;
for a spirit of wantonness has led
   them astray
and in their lusts they are unfaithful
   to their God.
Your men sacrifice on mountain- 13
   tops
and burn offerings on the hills,
under oak and poplar
and the terebinth's pleasant shade.
Therefore your daughters play the
   wanton
and your sons' brides commit adultery.
I will not punish your daughters 14
   for playing the wanton
nor your sons' brides for their
   adultery,
because your men resort to wanton
   women
and sacrifice with temple-prosti-
   tutes.
A people without understanding
   comes to grief;

---

l got her back: *or* bought her.   *m* and licence: *prob. rdg.; Heb.* they exceed.   *n* the quarrel ...
Priest?: *prob. rdg.; Heb.* and your people are like those who quarrel with a priest.   *o* My people ...
ruin: *or* Your mother (Israel) is destroyed, my people destroyed for lack of knowledge.   *p* steal ...
wits: *or* embolden my people.

15 they are a mother turned wanton.
    Bring no guilt-offering,*q* Israel;
  do not come to Gilgal, Judah,
do not go up to Beth-aven to swear
  by the life of the LORD,
16 since Israel has run wild, wild as a
    heifer;
    and will the LORD now feed this
      people
    like lambs in a broad meadow?
17 Ephraim, keeping company with
      idols,
18 has held a drunken orgy,*r*
    they have practised sacred prosti-
      tution,
    they have preferred dishonour to
      glory.
19 The wind shall sweep them away,
    wrapped in its wings,
    and they will find their sacrifices
      a delusion.

Unalterable doom

5   Hear this, you priests,
  and listen, all Israel; let the royal
    house mark my words.
    Sentence is passed on you;
    for you have been a snare at Miz-
      pah,
    and a net spread out on Tabor.
2   The rebels! they have shown base
      ingratitude,
    but I will punish them all.
3   I have cared for Ephraim
    and I have not neglected Israel;
    but now Ephraim has played the
      wanton
    and Israel has defiled himself.
4 Their misdeeds have barred their way
    back to their God;
    for a wanton spirit is in them,
    and they care nothing for the LORD.
5   Israel's arrogance cries out against
      him;
    *s*Ephraim's guilt is his undoing,
    and Judah no less is undone.
6   They go with sacrifices of sheep and
      cattle
    to seek the LORD, but do not find
      him.
    He has withdrawn himself from
      them;
7   for they have been unfaithful to
      him,
    and their sons are bastards.
  Now an invader shall devour their
    fields.
8   Blow the trumpet in Gibeah,
    the horn in Ramah,
    raise the battle-cry in Beth-aven:
    'Benjamin, we are with you!'

On the tribes of Israel I have pro- 9
  claimed this unalterable doom:
on the day of punishment Ephraim
  shall be laid waste.
The rulers of Judah act like men who 10
  move their neighbour's bound-
    ary;
on them will I pour out my wrath like
  a flood.
    Ephraim is an oppressor trampling 11
      on justice,
    doggedly pursuing what is worth-
      less.
    But I am a festering sore to 12
      Ephraim,
    a canker to the house of Judah.
    So when Ephraim found that he 13
      was sick,
    Judah that he was covered with
      sores,
    Ephraim went to Assyria,
    he went in haste to the Great King;
    but he has no power to cure you
    or to heal your sores.
    Yes indeed, I will be fierce as a 14
      panther to Ephraim,
    fierce as a lion to Judah—
    I will maul the prey and go,
    carry it off beyond hope of rescue—
      I, the LORD.
    I will go away and return to my 15
      place
until in their horror they seek me,
  and look earnestly for me in their
    distress.

Call to repentance

Come, let us return to the LORD; 6
  for he has torn us and will heal us,
  he has struck us and he will bind up
    our wounds;
  after two days he will revive us, 2
  on the third day he will restore us,
  that in his presence we may live.
Let us humble ourselves, let us strive 3
  to know the LORD,
  whose justice dawns like morning
    light,*t*
  and its dawning is as sure as the
    sunrise.
  It will come to us like a shower,
  like spring rains that water the
    earth.

Loyalty, not sacrifice

O Ephraim, how shall I deal with 4
  you?
How shall I deal with you, Judah?
Your loyalty to me is like the morning mist,
like dew that vanishes early.

q Bring no guilt-offering: *prob. rdg.; Heb.* Let him not be guilty.   *r* a drunken orgy: *prob. rdg.;
Heb. unintelligible.*   *s Prob. rdg.; Heb. prefixes* Israel.   *t Line transposed from end of verse 5.*

5 Therefore have I lashed you through the prophets
and torn you[u] to shreds with my words;
6 loyalty is my desire, not sacrifice,
not whole-offerings but the knowledge of God.

Corruption of Ephraim

7 At Admah[v] they have broken my covenant,
there they have played me false.
8 Gilead is a haunt of evildoers,
marked by a trail of blood;
9 like robbers lying in wait for a man,
priests are banded together
to do murder on the road to Shechem;
their deeds are outrageous.
10 At Israel's sanctuary I have seen a horrible thing:
there Ephraim played the wanton
and Israel defiled himself.
11 And for you, too, Judah, comes a harvest of reckoning.

When I would reverse the fortunes of my people,
7 when I would heal Israel,
then the guilt of Ephraim stands revealed,
and all the wickedness of Samaria;
they have not kept faith.
They are thieves, they break into houses;[w]
they are robbers, they strip people in the street,
2 little thinking that I have their wickedness ever in mind.
Now their misdeeds beset them
and stare me in the face.
3 They win over the king with their wickedness
and princes with their treachery,
4 lecherous all of them, hot as an oven
over the fire
which the baker does not stir
after kneading the dough until it is proved.
5 On their king's festal day the officers
begin to be inflamed with wine,
and he joins in the orgies of arrogant men;
6 for their hearts are heated by it[x]
like an oven.
While they are relaxed all night long
their passion slumbers,
but in the morning it flares up
like a blazing fire;

they all grow feverish, hot as an 7 oven,
and devour their rulers.
King after king falls from power,
but not one of them calls upon me.
Ephraim and his aliens make a sorry 8 mixture;
Ephraim has become a cake half-baked.
Foreigners fed on his strength, 9
but he was unaware,
even his grey hairs turned white,
but he was unaware.
So Israel's arrogance cries out 10 against them;
but they do not return to the LORD their God
nor seek him, in spite of it all.
Ephraim is a silly senseless pigeon, 11
now calling upon Egypt, now turning to Assyria for help.
Wherever they turn, I will cast my 12 net over them
and will bring them down like birds on the wing;
I will take them captive as soon as I hear them flocking.
Woe betide them, for they have strayed 13 from me!
May disaster befall them for rebelling against me!
I long to deliver them,
but they tell lies about me.
There is no sincerity in their cry to 14 me;
for all their howling on their pallets
and gashing of themselves over corn and new wine,
they are turning away from me.
Though I support them, though I give 15 them strength of arm,
they plot evil against me.
Like a bow gone slack, 16
they relapse into the worship of their high god;[y]
their talk is all lies,[z]
and so their princes shall fall by the sword.

Israel sows the wind

Put the trumpet to your lips! 8
A[a] vulture hovers over the sanctuary of the LORD:
they have broken my covenant
and rebelled against my instruction.
They cry to me for help: 2
'We know thee, God of Israel.'[b]
But Israel is utterly loathsome; 3
and therefore he shall run before the enemy.

u Prob. rdg.; Heb. them.   v At Admah: prob. rdg.; Heb. Like Adam.   w houses: prob. rdg.; Heb. om.   x are heated by it: prob. rdg.; Heb. draw near.   y they relapse . . . god: prob. rdg.; Heb. obscure.   z Prob. rdg.; Heb. adds that is their stammering speech in Egypt.   a Prob. rdg.; Heb. Like a.   b We . . . Israel: prob. rdg.; Heb. O my God, we know thee, Israel.

4 They make kings, but not by my will;
   they set up officers, but without my
      knowledge;
   they have made themselves idols of
      their silver and gold.[c]

5 Your calf-gods stink, O Samaria;
   my anger flares up against them.
   Long will it be before they prove
      innocent.

6 For what sort of a god is this bull?
   It is no god,
   a craftsman made it;
   the calf of Samaria will be broken
      in fragments.

7 Israel sows the wind and reaps the
      whirlwind;
   there are no heads on the standing
      corn, it yields no grain;
   and, if it yielded any, strangers would
      swallow it up.

8 Israel is now swallowed up,
   lost among the nations,
   a worthless nothing.

9 For, like a wild ass that has left the
      herd,
   they have run to Assyria.
   Ephraim has bargained for lovers;

10 and, because they have bargained
      among the nations,
   I will now round them up,
   and then they will soon abandon
   this setting up of kings and princes.

11 For Ephraim in his sin has multi-
      plied altars,
   altars have become his sin.

12 Though I give him countless rules
      in writing,
   they are treated as invalid.

13 Though they sacrifice flesh as offerings
      to me and eat them,
   I,[d] the LORD, will not accept them.
   Their guilt will be remembered
   and their sins punished.
   They shall go back to Egypt,
   or in Assyria they shall eat un-
      clean food.

14 Israel has forgotten his Maker
   and built palaces,
   Judah has multiplied walled cities;
   but I will set fire to his cities,
   and it shall devour his castles.

Days of punishment

9 Do not rejoice, Israel, do not exult
      like other peoples;
   for like a wanton you have forsaken
      your God,
   you have loved an idol[e]
   on every threshing-floor heaped
      with corn.

Threshing-floor and winepress shall 2
      know them no more,
new wine shall disown[f] them.
They shall not dwell in the LORD's 3
      land;
Ephraim shall go back to Egypt,
   or in Assyria they shall eat unclean
      food.
They shall pour out no wine to the 4
      LORD,
   they shall not bring their sacrifices
      to him;
   that would be mourners' fare for
      them,
   and all who ate it would be polluted.
   For their food shall only stay their
      hunger;
   it shall not be offered in the house
      of the LORD.
What will you do for the festal day, 5
   the day of the LORD's pilgrim-
      feast?
For look, they have fled from a 6
      scene of devastation:
Egypt shall receive them,
Memphis shall be their grave;
   the sands of Syrtes shall wreck
      them,
   weeds shall inherit their land,
   thorns shall grow in their dwellings.
The days of punishment are come, 7
   the days of vengeance are come
   when Israel shall be humbled.
Then the prophet shall be made a
      fool
   and the inspired seer a madman
   by your great guilt.
With great enmity Ephraim lies in 8
      wait for God's people
while the prophet is a fowler's trap by
      all their paths.
   a snare in the very temple of God.
   They lead them deep into sin as at 9
      the time of Gibeah.
Their guilt will be remembered and
      their sins punished.

Israel rejected by God

I came upon Israel like grapes in the 10
      wilderness,
   I looked on their forefathers
   with joy like the first ripe figs;
   but they resorted to Baal-peor
   and consecrated themselves to a
      thing of shame,
and Ephraim became as loathsome as 11
      the thing he loved.
   Their honour shall fly away like a
      bird:
   no childbirth, no fruitful womb, no
      conceiving;

c *Prob. rdg.; Heb. adds* so that he may be cut off.
lot's fee.   f *Or* fail.

d *Prob. rdg.; Heb.* he.   e *an idol: or* a har-

12 even if they rear their children,
I will make them childless, without posterity.
Woe to them indeed when I turn away from them!

13 As lion-cubs emerge only to be hunted,*g*
so must Ephraim bring out his children for slaughter.

14 Give them, O LORD—what wilt thou give them?
Give them a womb that miscarries and dry breasts.

15 All their wickedness was seen at Gilgal; there did I hate them.
For their evil deeds I will drive them from my house,
I will love them no more: all their princes are in revolt.

16 Ephraim is struck down:
their root is withered, and they yield no fruit;
if ever they give birth,
I will slay the dearest offspring of their womb.

17 My God shall reject them,
because they have not listened to him,
and they shall become wanderers among the nations.

God's judgement on Israel

10 Israel is like a rank vine ripening its fruit:
his fruit grows more and more, and more and more his altars;
the fairer his land becomes, the fairer he makes his sacred pillars.

2 They are crazy now, they are mad.
God himself will hack down their altars
and wreck their sacred pillars.

3 Well may they say, 'We have no king,
for we do not fear the LORD;
and what can the king do for us?'

4 There is nothing but talk,
imposing of oaths and making of treaties, all to no purpose;
and litigation spreads like a poisonous weed
along the furrows of the fields.

5 The inhabitants of Samaria tremble for the calf-god of Beth-aven;
the people mourn over it*h* and its priestlings howl,
distressed for their image, their glory,
which is carried away into exile.

6 It shall be carried to Assyria

as tribute to the Great King;
disgrace shall overtake Ephraim
and Israel shall feel the shame of their disobedience.
Samaria and her king are swept 7 away
like flotsam on the water;
the hill-shrines of Aven are wiped 8 out,
the shrines where Israel sinned;
thorns and thistles grow over her altars.
So they will say to the mountains, 'Cover us',
and to the hills, 'Fall on us.'

It is time to seek the LORD

Since the day of Gibeah Israel has 9 sinned;
there they took their stand in rebellion.
Shall not war overtake them in Gibeah?
I have come against the rebels to 10 chastise them,
and the peoples shall mass against them
in hordes for their two deeds of shame.
Ephraim is like a heifer broken in, 11
which loves to thresh corn,
across whose fair neck I have laid a yoke;*i*
I have harnessed Ephraim to the pole that he*j* may plough,
that Jacob may harrow his land.
Sow for yourselves in justice,   12
and you will reap what loyalty deserves.
Break up your fallow;
for it is time to seek the LORD,
seeking him till he comes and gives you just measure of rain.
You have ploughed wickedness into 13 your soil,
and the crop is mischief;
you have eaten the fruit of treachery.

Destruction of Bethel

Because you have trusted in your chariots,
in the number of your warriors,
the tumult of war shall arise against 14 your people,
and all your fortresses shall be razed
as Shalman razed Beth-arbel in the day of battle,
dashing the mother to the ground with her babes.

g As lion-cubs . . . hunted: *prob. rdg.; Heb. unintelligible.*   h the people mourn over it: *or* the high god and his people mourn.   i a yoke: *prob. rdg.; Heb. om.*   j he: *prob. rdg.; Heb.* Judah.

15 So it shall be done to you, Bethel,
because of your evil scheming;
as sure as day dawns, the king of
Israel shall be swept away.

God's love for Israel

11 When Israel was a boy, I loved him;
I called my son out of Egypt;
2 but the more I called, the further they
went from me;
they must needs sacrifice to the
Baalim
and burn offerings before carved
images.
3 It was I who taught Ephraim to
walk,
I who had taken them in my arms;
4 but they did not know that I harnessed them in leading-strings[k]
and led them with bonds of love[l]—
that I had lifted them like a little
child[m] to my cheek,
that I had bent down to feed them.
5 Back they shall go to Egypt,
the Assyrian shall be their king;
for they have refused to return to
me.
6 The sword shall be swung over their
blood-spattered altars
and put an end to their prattling
priests
7 and devour my people in return for
all their schemings,
bent on rebellion as they are.
Though they call on their high god,
even then he will not reinstate
them.
8 How can I give you up, Ephraim,
how surrender you, Israel?
How can I make you like Admah
or treat you as Zeboyim?
My heart is changed within me,
my remorse kindles already.
9 I will not let loose my fury,
I will not turn round and destroy
Ephraim;
for I am God and not a man,
the Holy One in your midst;
10 I will not come with threats[n] like a
roaring lion.
No; when I roar, I who am God,
my sons shall come with speed out
of the west.
11 They will come speedily, flying like
birds out of Egypt,
like pigeons from Assyria,
and I will settle them in their own
homes.

This is the very word of the LORD.
Ephraim besets me with treachery, 12
the house of Israel besets me with
deceit;
and Judah is still restive under
God,
still loyal to the idols he counts
holy.
Ephraim is a shepherd whose flock **12**
is but[o] wind,
a hunter chasing the east wind all
day;[p]
he makes a treaty with Assyria
and carries tribute of oil to Egypt.

Israel's past misdeeds

The LORD has a charge to bring 2
against Judah
and is resolved to punish Jacob for
his conduct;
he will requite him for his misdeeds.
Even in the womb Jacob over- 3
reached his brother,
and in manhood he strove with
God.
The divine angel stood firm and 4
held his own;[q]
Jacob wept and begged favour for
himself.
Then God met him at Bethel
and there spoke with him.
The LORD the God of Hosts, the LORD 5
is his name.

Turn back all of you by God's help; 6
practise loyalty and justice
and wait always upon your God.
False scales are in merchants' 7
hands,
and they love to cheat;
so Ephraim says, 8
'Surely I have become a rich man, I
have made my fortune';
but all his gains will not pay
for the guilt[r] of his sins.
Yet I have been the LORD your God 9
since your days in Egypt;
I will make you live in tents yet
again, as in the old days.

I spoke to the prophets, 10
it was I who gave vision after
vision;
I spoke through the prophets in
parables.
Was there idolatry in Gilead? 11
Yes: they were worthless
and sacrificed to bull-gods in Gilgal;

---

k leading-strings: or cords of leather.   l bonds of love: or reins of hide.   m I had ... child:
prob. rdg.; Heb. like those who lift up a yoke.   n Prob. rdg.; Heb. adds they shall go after the
LORD.   o is a ... but: or feeds on.   p Prob. rdg.; Heb. adds piling up treachery and havoc.
q The divine ... own: or He stood firm against an angel, but flagged.   r for the guilt: prob. rdg.;
Heb. for me, guilt.

their altars were common as heaps of
stones beside a ploughed field.

12 Jacob fled to the land of Aram;
Israel did service to win a wife,
to win a wife he tended sheep.

13 By a prophet the LORD brought up
Israel out of Egypt
and by a prophet he was tended.

14 Ephraim has given bitter provocation;
therefore his Lord will make him
answerable
for his own death
and bring down upon his own head
the blame
for all that he has done.

13 When the Ephraimites mumbled
their prayers,
God himself denounced Israel;
they were guilty of Baal-worship
and died.

2 Yet now they sin more and more;
they have made themselves an
image of cast metal,
they have fashioned their silver
into idols,
nothing but the work of craftsmen;
men say of them,
'Those who kiss calf-images offer
human sacrifice.'

God's care for Israel

3 Therefore they shall be like the
morning mist
or like dew that vanishes early,
like chaff blown from the threshing-
floor
or smoke from a chimney.

4 But I have been the LORD your God
since your days in Egypt,
when you knew no other saviour
than me,
no god but me.

5 I cared for you in the wilderness,
6 in a land of burning heat, as if you
were in pasture.
So they were filled,
and, being filled, grew proud;
and so they forgot me.

7 So now I will be like a panther to
them,
I will prowl like a leopard by the
wayside;

8 I will meet them like a she-bear
robbed of her cubs
and tear their ribs apart,
like a lioness I will devour them on
the spot,
I will rip them up like a wild beast.

I have destroyed you, O Israel; who 9
is there to help you?
Where now is your king that he 10
may save you,
or the rulers in all your cities
for whom you asked me,
begging for king and princes?
I gave you a king in my anger, 11
and in my fury took him away.

Judgement on Ephraim

Ephraim's guilt is tied up in a 12
scroll,
his sins are kept on record.
When the pangs of his birth came 13
over his mother,
he showed himself a senseless child;
for at the proper time he could not
present himself
at the mouth of the womb.
Shall I redeem him from Sheol? 14
Shall I ransom him from death?
Oh, for your plagues, O death! Oh,
for your sting, Sheol!
I will put compassion out of my
sight.
Though he flourishes among the 15
reeds,[s]
an east wind shall come, a blast
from the LORD,
rising over the desert;
Ephraim's spring will fail and his
fountain run dry.
It will carry away as spoil
his whole store of costly treasures.
Samaria will become desolate be- 16
cause she has rebelled against her
God;
her babes will fall by the sword and
be dashed to the ground,
her women with child shall be
ripped up.

Repentance and restoration

Return, O Israel, to the LORD your 14
God;
for you have stumbled in your evil
courses.
Come with your words ready, 2
come back to the LORD;
say to him, 'Thou dost not endure
iniquity.[t]
Accept our plea,
and we will pay our vows with
cattle from our pens.
Assyria shall not save us, nor will we 3
seek horses to ride;
what we have made with our own
hands
we will never again call gods;
for in thee the fatherless find a
father's love.'

*s among the reeds: prob. rdg.; Heb. between (or a son of) brothers.   t Thou . . . iniquity: or Thou
wilt surely take away iniquity.*

4 I will heal their apostasy; of my own
   bounty will I love them;
   for my anger is turned away from
   them.
5 I will be as dew to Israel
   that he may flower like the lily,
   strike root like the poplar[u]
6 and put out fresh shoots,
   that he may be as fair as the olive
   and fragrant as Lebanon.
7 Israel shall again dwell in my[v]
   shadow
   and grow corn in abundance;
   they shall flourish like a vine

and be famous as the wine of Lebanon.
What has Ephraim any more to do 8
   with idols?
I have spoken and I affirm it:
I am the pine-tree that shelters
   you;
to me you owe your fruit.

Let the wise consider these things 9
and let him who considers take note;
for the LORD's ways are straight and
the righteous walk in them, while
sinners stumble.

u Prob. rdg.; Heb. like Lebanon.   v Prob. rdg.; Heb. its.

JOEL

1 The word of the LORD which came to
Joel son of Pethuel.

A mighty horde

2 Listen, you elders;
   hear me, all you who live in the
     land:
   has the like of this happened in all
     your days
   or in your fathers' days?
3 Tell it to your sons and they may tell
     theirs;
   let them pass it on from generation
     to generation.
4 What the locust has left the swarm
     eats,
   what the swarm has left the hopper
     eats,
   and what the hopper has left the
     grub eats.
5 Wake up, you drunkards, and
     lament your fate;
   mourn for the fresh wine, all you
     wine-drinkers,
   because it is lost to you.
6 For a horde has overrun my land,
   mighty and past counting;
   their teeth are a lion's teeth;
   they have the fangs of a lioness.
7 They have ruined my vines
   and left my fig-trees broken and
     leafless,
   they have plucked them bare
   and stripped them of their bark;
   they have left the branches white.

Cry to the LORD

8 Wail like a virgin wife in sackcloth,

wailing over the bridegroom of her
     youth:
the drink-offering and grain- 9
   offering are lost
to the house of the LORD.
Mourn, you priests, ministers of the
   LORD,
the fields are ruined, the parched 10
   earth mourns;
for the corn is ruined, the new wine is
   desperate,
   the oil has failed.
Despair, you husbandmen; you vine- 11
   dressers, lament,
because the wheat and the barley,
   the harvest of the field, is lost.
The vintage is desperate, and the fig- 12
   tree has failed;
   pomegranate, palm, and apple,
   all the trees of the country-side are
     parched,
   and none make merry over harvest.

Priests, put on sackcloth and beat 13
   your breasts;
lament, you ministers of the altar;
come, lie in sackcloth all night long,
   you ministers of my God;
for grain-offering and drink-
   offering
are withheld from the house of your
   God.
Proclaim a solemn fast, appoint a day 14
   of abstinence.
   You elders, summon all that live in
     the land
   to come together in the house of
     your God,
   and cry to the LORD.

15 Alas! the day is near,
the day of the LORD: it comes,
a mighty destruction from the Almighty.
16 Look! it stares us in the face;
the house of our God has lost its
food,
lost all its joy and gladness.
17 The soil is parched,
the dykes are dry,
the granaries are deserted,
the barns ruinous;
for the rains have failed.
18 The cattle are exhausted,
the herds of oxen distressed
because they have no pasture;
the flocks of sheep waste away.
19 To thee I cry, O LORD;
for fire has devoured the open
pastures
and the flames have burnt up all the
trees of the country-side.
20 The very cattle in the field look up to
thee;
for the water-channels are dried up,
and fire has devoured the open
pastures.

Call to repentance

2 Blow the trumpet in Zion,
sound the alarm upon my holy hill;
let all that live in the land tremble,
for the day of the LORD has come,
2 surely a day of darkness and gloom
is upon us,
a day of cloud and dense fog;
like a blackness spread over the
mountains
a mighty, countless host appears;
their like has never been known,
nor ever shall be in ages to come;
3 their vanguard a devouring fire,
their reguard leaping flame;
before them the land is a garden of
Eden,
behind them a wasted wilderness;
nothing survives their march.
4 On they come, like squadrons of
horse,
like war-horses they charge;
5 bounding over the peaks they advance with the rattle of chariots,
like flames of fire burning up the
stubble,
like a countless host in battle array.
6 Before them nations tremble,
every face turns pale.
7 Like warriors they charge,
they mount the walls like men at
arms,
each marching in line,
no confusion in the ranks,
8 none jostling his neighbour,
none breaking line.

They plunge through streams without
halting their advance;
they burst into the city, leap on to 9
the wall,
climb into the houses,
entering like thieves through the
windows.
Before them the earth shakes, 10
the heavens shudder,
sun and moon are darkened,
and the stars forbear to shine.
The LORD thunders before his host; 11
his is a mighty army,
countless are those who do his
bidding.
Great is the day of the LORD and
terrible,
who can endure it?
And yet, the LORD says, even now 12
turn back to me with your whole
heart,
fast, and weep, and beat your
breasts.
Rend your hearts and not your 13
garments;
turn back to the LORD your God;
for he is gracious and compassionate,
long-suffering and ever constant,
always ready to repent of the
threatened evil.
It may be he will turn back and 14
repent
and leave a blessing behind him,
blessing enough for grain-offering
and drink-offering
for the LORD your God.

Blow the trumpet in Zion, 15
proclaim a solemn fast, appoint a day
of abstinence;
gather the people together, proclaim a 16
solemn assembly;
summon the elders,
gather the children, yes, babes at the
breast;
bid the bridegroom leave his chamber
and the bride her bower.
Let the priests, the ministers of the 17
LORD,
stand weeping between the porch
and the altar
and say, 'Spare thy people, O LORD,
thy own people,
expose them not to reproach,
lest other nations make them a byword
and everywhere men ask,
"Where is their God?"'

Israel forgiven and restored

Then the LORD's love burned with 18
zeal for his land,

and he was moved with compassion for his people.

19 He answered their appeal and said,
I will send you corn, and new wine, and oil,
and you shall have your fill;
I will expose you no longer
to the reproach of other nations.

20 I will remove the northern peril far away from you
and banish them into a land parched and waste,
their vanguard into the eastern sea
and their rear into the western,
and the stench shall rise from their rotting corpses
because of their proud deeds!

21 Earth, be not afraid, rejoice and be glad;
for the LORD himself has done a proud deed.

22 Be not afraid, you cattle in the field;
for the pastures shall be green,
the trees shall bear fruit,
the fig and the vine yield their harvest.

23 O people of Zion,
rejoice and be glad in the LORD your God,
who gives you good food in due measure^a
and sends down rain^b as of old.

24 The threshing-floors shall be heaped with grain,
the vats shall overflow with new wine and oil.

25 So I will make good the years
that the swarm has eaten,
hopper and grub and locust,
my great army which I sent against you;

26 and you shall eat, you shall eat your fill
and praise the name of the LORD your God
who has done wonders for you,^{c}

27 and you shall know that I am present in Israel,
that I and no other am the LORD your God;
and my people shall not again be brought to shame.

28 Thereafter the day shall come
when I will pour out my spirit on all mankind;
your sons and your daughters shall prophesy,
your old men shall dream dreams
and your young men see visions;

29 I will pour out my spirit in those days

even upon slaves and slave-girls.

30 I will show portents in the sky and on earth,
blood and fire and columns of smoke;

31 the sun shall be turned into darkness
and the moon into blood
before the great and terrible day of the LORD comes.

32 Then everyone who invokes the LORD by name
shall be saved:
for when the LORD gives the word
there shall yet be survivors on Mount Zion
and in Jerusalem a remnant^d
whom the LORD will call.^{e}

3 When that time comes, on that day
when I reverse the fortunes of Judah and Jerusalem,

2 I will gather all the nations together
and lead them down to the Valley of the LORD's Judgement
and there bring them to judgement
on behalf of Israel, my own possession;
for they have scattered my people throughout their own countries,
have taken each their portion of my land

3 and shared out my people by lot,
bartered a boy for a whore,
and sold a girl for wine and drunk it down.

Tyre, Sidon and Philistia

4 What are you to me, Tyre and Sidon and all the districts of Philistia? Can you pay me back for anything I have done? Is there anything that you can do to me? Swiftly and speedily I will make your deeds recoil upon your own heads; for you have taken my 5 silver and my gold and carried off my costly treasures into your temples; you have sold the people of Judah 6 and Jerusalem to the Greeks, and removed them far beyond their own frontiers. But I will rouse them to 7 leave the places to which you have sold them. I will make your deeds recoil upon your own heads: I will sell 8 your sons and your daughters to the people of Judah, and they shall sell them to the Sabaeans, a nation far away. The LORD has spoken.

a Or gives you a sign pointing to prosperity.   *b Prob. rdg.; Heb. adds* spring rain and autumn rain.   *c Prob. rdg.; Heb. adds* and my people shall not again be brought to shame (*cp. verse 27*). *d* a remnant: *prob. rdg.; Heb.* among the remnant.   *e* Or when the LORD calls.

In the Valley of Decision

2*f* Proclaim this amongst the nations:
Declare a holy war, call your troops
    to arms!
    Beat your mattocks into swords
    and your pruning-hooks into spears.*g*
Rally to each other's help, all you
    nations round about.
Let the weakling say, 'I am strong',
    and let the coward show himself
    brave.*h*
    Let all the nations hear the call to
    arms
    and come to the Valley of the
    LORD's Judgement;
let all the warriors come and draw near
    and muster there;
    for there I will take my seat
    and judge all the nations round
    about.

13 Ply the sickle, for the harvest is ripe;
    come, tread the grapes,
    for the press is full and the vats over-
    flow;
    great is the wickedness of the
    nations.
14 The roar of multitudes, multitudes,
    in the Valley of Decision!
    The day of the LORD is at hand
    in the Valley of Decision;
15   sun and moon are darkened
    and the stars forbear to shine.
16   The LORD roars from Zion
    and thunders from Jerusalem;

heaven and earth shudder,
but the LORD is a refuge for his
    people
and the defence of Israel.

When the LORD dwells in Zion

Thus you shall know that I am the 17
    LORD your God,
    dwelling in Zion my holy mount-
    ain;
    Jerusalem shall be holy,
and no one without the right shall
    pass through her again.
    When that day comes,   18
    the mountains shall run with fresh
    wine
    and the hills flow with milk.
All the streams of Judah shall be full
    of water,
    and a fountain shall spring from
    the LORD's house
    and water the gorge of Shittim,
but Egypt shall become a desert   19
    and Edom a deserted waste,
    because of the violence done to
    Judah
    and the innocent blood shed in her
    land;
    and I will spill their blood,   20-1
    the blood I have not yet spilt.
Then there shall be people living in
    Judah for ever,
    in Jerusalem generation after genera-
    tion;
and the LORD will dwell in Zion.

*f The order of lines in verses 9–12 has been re-arranged in several places.   g Beat . . . spears: cp.
Isa. 2. 4; Mic. 4. 3.   h and let . . . brave: prob. rdg.; Heb. O LORD bring down thy warriors.*

AMOS

1 THE WORDS OF AMOS, one of
the sheep-farmers of Tekoa, which he
received in visions concerning Israel
during the reigns of Uzziah king of
Judah and Jeroboam son of Jehoash
king of Israel, two years before the
2 earthquake. He said,

    The LORD roars from Zion
    and thunders from Jerusalem;
    the shepherds' pastures are scor-
    ched
    and the top of Carmel*a* is dried up.

Damascus

These are the words of the LORD: 3

    For crime after crime of Damascus
    I will grant them no reprieve,
because they threshed Gilead under
    threshing-sledges spiked with
    iron.
    Therefore will I send fire upon the 4
    house of Hazael,
    fire that shall eat up Ben-hadad's
    palaces;

a top of Carmel: or choicest farmland.

5 I will crush the great men of Damascus
and wipe out those who live in the Vale of Aven
and the sceptred ruler of Betheden;
the people of Aram shall be exiled to Kir.
It is the word of the LORD.

Gaza

6 These are the words of the LORD:

For crime after crime of Gaza
I will grant them no reprieve,
because they deported a whole band of exiles
and delivered them up to Edom.
7 Therefore will I send fire upon the walls of Gaza,
fire that shall consume its palaces.
8 I will wipe out those who live in Ashdod
and the sceptred ruler of Ashkelon;
I will turn my hand against Ekron,
and the remnant of the Philistines shall perish.
It is the word of the Lord GOD.

Tyre

9 These are the words of the LORD:

For crime after crime of Tyre
I will grant them no reprieve,
because, forgetting the ties of kinship,
they delivered a whole band of exiles to Edom.
10 Therefore will I send fire upon the walls of Tyre,
fire that shall consume its palaces.

Edom

11 These are the words of the LORD:

For crime after crime of Edom
I will grant them no reprieve,
because, sword in hand, they hunted their kinsmen down,
stifling their natural affections.
Their anger raged unceasing,
their fury stormed unchecked.
12 Therefore will I send fire upon Teman,
fire that shall consume the palaces of Bozrah.

Ammon

13 These are the words of the LORD:

For crime after crime of the Ammonites
I will grant them no reprieve,
because in their greed for land

they invaded the ploughlands of Gilead.
Therefore will I set fire to the walls 14 of Rabbah,
fire that shall consume its palaces amid war-cries on the day of battle,
with a whirlwind on the day of tempest;
then their king shall be carried into 15 exile,
he and his officers with him.
It is the word of the LORD.

Moab

These are the words of the LORD: 2

For crime after crime of Moab
I will grant them no reprieve,
because they burnt the bones of the king of Edom to ash.[b]
Therefore will I send fire upon 2 Moab,
fire that shall consume the palaces in their towns;
Moab shall perish in uproar,
with war-cries and the sound of trumpets,
and I will cut off the ruler from 3 among them
and kill all their officers with him.
It is the word of the LORD.

Judah

These are the words of the LORD: 4

For crime after crime of Judah
I will grant them no reprieve,
because they have spurned the law of the LORD
and have not observed his decrees,
and have been led astray by the false gods
that their fathers followed.
Therefore will I send fire upon 5 Judah,
fire that shall consume the palaces of Jerusalem.

Israel

These are the words of the LORD: 6

For crime after crime of Israel
I will grant them no reprieve,
because they sell the innocent for silver
and the destitute for a pair of shoes.
They grind the heads of the poor into 7 the earth
and thrust the humble out of their way.
Father and son resort to the same girl,
to the profanation of my holy name.

b to ash: or for lime.

8 Men lie down beside every altar
   on garments seized in pledge,
   and in the house of their God*c* they
       drink liquor
   got by way of fines.

Israel's ingratitude

9 Yet it was I who destroyed the Am-
       orites before them,
   though they were tall as cedars,
   though they were sturdy as oaks,
   I who destroyed their fruit above
       and their roots below.
10 It was I who brought you up from
       the land of Egypt,
   I who led you in the wilderness forty
       years,
       to take possession of the land of
           the Amorites;
11 I raised up prophets from your
       sons,
   Nazirites from your young men.
   Was it not so indeed, you men of
       Israel?
   says the LORD.
12 But you made the Nazirites drink
       wine,
   and said to the prophets, 'You shall
       not prophesy.'
13 Listen, I groan under the burden of
       you,
   as a wagon creaks under a full load.
14 Flight shall not save the swift,
   the strong man shall not rally his
       strength.
   The warrior shall not save himself,
15   the archer shall not stand his
           ground;
   the swift of foot shall not be saved,
   nor the horseman escape;
16 on that day the bravest of warriors
   shall be stripped of his arms and
       run away.
   This is the very word of the LORD.

The LORD's care for Israel

3 Listen, Israelites, to these words that
   the LORD addresses to you, to the
   whole nation which he brought up
   from Egypt:

2 For you alone have I cared
   among all the nations of the world;
       therefore will I punish you
   for all your iniquities.
3 Do two men travel together
   unless they have agreed?
4 Does a lion roar in the forest
   if he has no prey?
   Does a young lion growl in his den
   if he has caught nothing?

Does a bird fall into a trap on the 5
    ground
if the striker is not set for it?
Does a trap spring from the ground
and take nothing?
If a trumpet sounds the alarm,   6
are not the people scared?
If disaster falls on a city,
has not the LORD been at work?*d*
For the Lord GOD does nothing   7
without giving to his servants the
    prophets knowledge of his plans.
The lion has roared; who is not 8
    terrified?
The Lord GOD has spoken; who will
    not prophesy?

Overthrow of Samaria

Stand upon the palaces in Ashdod 9
and upon the palaces of Egypt,
and proclaim aloud:
'Assemble on the hills of Samaria,
look at the tumult seething among
    her people
and at the oppression in her midst;
what do they care for honesty   10
who hoard in their palaces the gains
    of crime and violence?'
This is the very word of the LORD.

Therefore these are the words of the 11
Lord GOD:

An enemy shall surround*e* the land;
your stronghold shall be thrown
    down
and your palaces sacked.

A remnant saved

These are the words of the LORD: 12

As a shepherd rescues out of the jaws
    of a lion
two shin bones or the tip of an ear,
so shall the Israelites who live in
    Samaria be rescued
like a corner of a couch or a chip from
    the leg of a bed.*f*
Listen and testify against the family 13
    of Jacob.
This is the very word of the Lord
    GOD, the God of Hosts.

Israel's empty religion

On the day when I deal with Israel   14
    for all their crimes,
    I will most surely deal with the
        altars of Bethel:
    the horns of the altar shall be
        hacked off
    and shall fall to the ground.
I will break down both winter-house 15
    and summer-house;

*c Or gods. d If disaster . . . work?: or If there is evil in a city, will not the LORD act? e shall
surround: prob. rdg.; Heb. and round. f or a chip . . . bed: prob. rdg.; Heb. obscure.*

houses of ivory shall perish,
and great houses be demolished.
This is the very word of the LORD.

4 Listen to this,
you cows of Bashan who live on the
hill of Samaria,
you who oppress the poor and crush
the destitute,
who say to your lords, 'Bring us
drink':
2 the Lord GOD has sworn by his holiness
that your time is coming
when men shall carry you away on
their shields*g*
and your children in fish-baskets.
3 You shall each be carried straight
out
through the breaches in the walls
and pitched on a dunghill.*h*
This is the very word of the LORD.

4 Come to Bethel—and rebel!
Come to Gilgal—and rebel the
more!
Bring your sacrifices for the morning,
your tithes within three days.
5 Burn your thank-offering without
leaven;
announce, proclaim your freewill
offerings;
for you love to do what is proper,
you men of Israel!
This is the very word of the Lord
GOD.

Failure to heed correction

6 It was I who kept teeth idle
in all your cities,
who brought famine on all your
settlements;
yet you did not come back to me.
This is the very word of the LORD.

7 It was I who withheld the showers
from you
while there were still three months to
harvest.
I would send rain on one city
and no rain on another;
rain would fall on one field,
and another would be parched for
lack of it.
8 From this city and that, men would
stagger to another
for water to drink, but would not
find enough;
yet you did not come back to me.
This is the very word of the LORD.

9 I blasted you with black blight and
red;

I laid waste*i* your gardens and
vineyards;
the locust devoured your fig-trees
and your olives;
yet you did not come back to me.
This is the very word of the LORD.

I sent plague upon you like the 10
plagues of Egypt;
I killed with the sword
your young men and your troops
of horses.
I made your camps stink in your
nostrils;
yet you did not come back to me.
This is the very word of the LORD.

I brought destruction amongst you 11
as God destroyed Sodom and Gomorrah;
you were like a brand snatched from
the fire;
yet you did not come back to me.
This is the very word of the LORD.

Therefore, Israel, this is what I will 12
do to you;
and, because this is what I will do to
you,
Israel, prepare to meet your God.
It is he who forges the thunder and 13
creates the wind,
who showers abundant rain on the
earth,*j*
who darkens the dawn with thick
clouds
and marches over the heights of
the earth—
his name is the LORD the God of
Hosts.

Call to repentance

Listen to these words; I raise a dirge 5
over you, O Israel:

She has fallen to rise no more, 2
the virgin Israel,
prostrate on her own soil, with no
one to lift her up.

These are the words of the Lord GOD: 3

The city that marched out to war
a thousand strong
shall have but a hundred left,
that which marched out a hundred
strong
shall have but ten men of Israel left.

These are the words of the LORD to 4
the people of Israel:

Resort to me, if you would live, not 5
to Bethel;
go not to Gilgal, nor pass on to Beersheba;

g Or baskets.   *h* a dunghill: *prob. rdg.*; Heb. the Harmon.   *i* I laid waste: *prob. rdg.*; Heb. to
increase.   *j* who showers . . . earth: *prob. rdg.*; Heb. who tells his thoughts to mankind.

for Gilgal shall be swept away
and Bethel brought to nothing.

6 If you would live, resort to the
LORD,
or he will break out against Joseph
like fire,
fire which will devour Israel with
no one to quench it;

8[h] he who made the Pleiades and
Orion,
who turned darkness into morning
and darkened day into night,
who summoned the waters of the
sea
and poured them over the earth,

9 who makes Taurus rise after Cap-
ella
and Taurus set hard on the rising
of the Vintager[l]—
he who does this, his name is the
LORD.[m]

7 You that turn justice upside down[n]
and bring righteousness to the
ground,

10 you that hate a man who brings the
wrongdoer to court
and loathe him who speaks the
whole truth:

11 for all this, because you levy taxes
on the poor
and extort a tribute of grain from
them,
though you have built houses of
hewn stone,
you shall not live in them,
though you have planted pleasant
vineyards,
you shall not drink wine from them.

12 For I know how many your crimes
are
and how countless your sins,
you who persecute the guiltless, hold
men to ransom
and thrust the destitute out of
court.

13 At that time, therefore, a prudent
man will stay quiet,
for it will be an evil time.

14 Seek good and not evil,
that you may live,
that the LORD the God of Hosts may
be firmly on your side,
as you say he is.

15 Hate evil and love good;
enthrone justice in the courts;
it may be that the LORD the God of
Hosts
will be gracious to the survivors of
Joseph.

A day of gloom

16 Therefore these are the words of the
LORD the God of Hosts:

There shall be wailing in every
street,
and in all open places cries of woe.
The farmer shall be called to mourning,
and those skilled in the dirge to[o]
wailing;

17 there shall be lamentation in every
vineyard;
for I will pass through the midst of
you,
says the LORD.

18 Fools who long for the day of the
LORD,
what will the day of the LORD mean
to you?
It will be darkness, not light.

19 It will be as when a man runs from
a lion,
and a bear meets him,
or turns into a house and leans his
hand on the wall,
and a snake bites him.

20 The day of the LORD is indeed
darkness, not light,
a day of gloom with no dawn.

God spurns Israel's sacrifices

21 I hate, I spurn your pilgrim-feasts;
I will not delight in your sacred
ceremonies.

22 When you present your sacrifices and
offerings
I will not accept them,
nor look on the buffaloes of your
shared-offerings.

23 Spare me the sound of your songs;
I cannot endure the music of your
lutes.

24 Let justice roll on like a river
and righteousness like an ever-
flowing stream.

25 Did you bring me sacrifices and
gifts,
you people of Israel, those forty years
in the wilderness?

26 No! but now you shall take up
the shrine of your idol king
and the pedestals of your images,[p]
which you have made for yourselves,

27 and I will drive you into exile beyond
Damascus.

So says the LORD; the God of Hosts
is his name.

k *Verse 7 transposed to follow verse 9.*   l *who makes . . . Vintager: prob. rdg.; Heb. who smiles destruction on the strong, and destruction comes on the fortified city.*   m *his . . . LORD: transposed
from end of verse 8.*   n *upside down: prob. rdg.; Heb. poison.*   o *Prob. rdg.; Heb. places to before
those skilled.*   p *Prob. rdg.; Heb. adds the star of your gods.*

N

Selfish indulgence of Zion's leaders

6 Shame on you who live at ease in Zion,
and you, untroubled on the hill of Samaria,
men of mark in the first of nations,
you to whom the people of Israel resort!

2 Go, look at Calneh,
travel on to Hamath the great,
then go down to Gath of the Philistines—
are you better than these kingdoms?
Or is your*q* territory greater than theirs*r*?

3 You who thrust the evil day aside
and make haste to establish violence.*s*

4 You who loll on beds inlaid with ivory
and sprawl over your couches,
feasting on lambs from the flock
and fatted calves,

5 you who pluck the strings of the lute
and invent musical instruments like David,

6 you who drink wine by the bowlful
and lard yourselves with the richest of oils,
but are not grieved at the ruin of Joseph—

7 now, therefore,
you shall head the column of exiles;
that will be the end of sprawling and revelry.

Judgement for arrogance

8 The Lord GOD has sworn by himself:

I loathe the arrogance of Jacob,
I loathe his palaces;
city and all in it I will abandon to their fate.

9 If ten men are left in one house,
they shall die,

10 and a man's uncle and the embalmer shall take him up
to carry his body out of the house for burial,
and they shall call to someone in a corner of the house,
'Any more there?', and he shall answer, 'No.'
Then he will add, 'Hush!'—
for the name of the LORD must not be mentioned.

11 For the LORD will command,
and at the shock the great house will be rubble
and the cottage matchwood.

12 Can horses gallop over rocks?
Can the sea be ploughed with oxen?
Yet you have turned into venom the process of law
and justice itself into poison,
13 you who are jubilant over a nothing*t*
and boast,
'Have we not won power*t* by our own strength?'

14 O Israel, I am raising a nation against you,
and they shall harry your land
from Lebo-hamath to the gorge of the Arabah.
This is the very word of the LORD the God of Hosts.

Three visions

7 This was what the Lord GOD showed me: a swarm of locusts hatched out when the late corn, which comes after the king's early crop, was beginning 2 to sprout. As they were devouring the last of the herbage in the land, I said, 'O Lord GOD, forgive; what will Jacob be after this? He is so small.' Then 3 the LORD relented and said, 'This shall not happen.'

4 This was what the Lord GOD showed me: the Lord GOD was summoning a flame of fire*u* to devour the great abyss, and to devour all creation. I said, 5 'O Lord GOD, I pray thee, cease; what will Jacob be after this? He is so small.' The LORD relented and said, 6 'This also shall not happen.'

7 This was what the LORD showed me: there was a man standing by a wall*v* with a plumb-line in his hand. The LORD said to me, 'What do you 8 see, Amos?' 'A plumb-line', I answered, and the Lord said, 'I am setting a plumb-line to the heart of my people Israel; never again will I pass them by. The hill-shrines of 9 Isaac shall be desolated and the sanctuaries of Israel laid waste; I will rise, sword in hand, against the house of Jeroboam.'

Amos and Amaziah

10 Amaziah, the priest of Bethel, reported to Jeroboam king of Israel: 'Amos is conspiring against you in Israel; the country cannot tolerate what he is saying. He says, "Jero-11 boam shall die by the sword, and

---

q Prob. rdg.; Heb. their.   *r Prob. rdg.; Heb. yours.*   *s You . . . violence: or You who invoke the day of wrongdoing and bring near the sabbath of violence.*   *t a nothing and power: Heb. Lo-debar and Karnaim, making a word-play on the two place-names.*   *u a flame of fire: prob. rdg.; Heb. to contend with fire.*   *v Prob. rdg.; Heb. adds of a plumb-line.*

Israel shall be deported far from their
12 native land." ' To Amos himself
Amaziah said, 'Be off, you seer! Off
with you to Judah! You can earn
your living and do your prophesying
13 there. But never prophesy again at
Bethel, for this is the king's sanc-
14 tuary, a royal palace.' 'I am[w] no
prophet,' Amos replied to Amaziah,
'nor am I a prophet's son; I am[w] a
herdsman and a dresser of sycomore-
15 figs. But the LORD took me as I followed the flock and said to me, "Go
and prophesy to my people Israel."
16 So now listen to the word of the LORD.
You tell me I am not to prophesy
against Israel or go drivelling on
17 against the people of Isaac. Now
these are the words of the LORD:
Your wife shall become a city strumpet[x] and your sons and daughters
shall fall by the sword. Your land
shall be divided up with a measuring-
line, you yourself shall die in a heathen
country, and Israel shall be deported
far from their native land and go into
exile.'

A basket of summer fruit

8 This was what the Lord GOD showed
me: there was a basket of summer
2 fruit, and he said, 'What are you
looking at, Amos?' I answered, 'A
basket of ripe summer[y] fruit.' Then
the LORD said to me, 'The time is ripe[y]
for my people Israel. Never again
3 will I pass them by. In that day, says
the Lord GOD, the singing women in
the palace shall howl, "So many dead
men, flung out everywhere! Silence!"'

Spiritual famine

4 Listen to this, you who grind the
destitute and plunder[z] the humble,
5 you who say, 'When will the new
moon be over so that we may sell
corn? When will the sabbath be past
so that we may open our wheat again,
giving short measure in the bushel
and taking overweight in the silver,
6 tilting the scales fraudulently, and
selling the dust of the wheat; that we
may buy the poor for silver and the
7 destitute for a pair of shoes?' The
LORD has sworn by the pride of Jacob:
I will never forget any of their doings.

8 Shall not the earth shake for this?
Shall not all who live on it grieve?

All earth shall surge and seethe like
the Nile
and subside like the river of Egypt.

On that day, says the Lord GOD, 9
I will make the sun go down at
noon
and darken the earth in broad daylight.
I will turn your pilgrim-feasts into 10
mourning
and all your songs into lamentation.
I will make you all put sackcloth
round your waists
and have all your heads shaved.
I will make it like mourning for an
only son
and the end of it a bitter day.

The time is coming, says the Lord 11
GOD,
when I will send famine on the land,
not hunger for bread or thirst for
water,
but for hearing the word of the
LORD.
Men shall stagger from north to 12
south,[a]
they shall range from east to west,
seeking the word of the LORD,
but they shall not find it.
On that day fair maidens and young 13
men
shall faint from thirst;
all who take their oath by Ashimah, 14
goddess of Samaria,
all who swear, 'By the life of your
god, O Dan',
and, 'By the sacred way to Beersheba',
shall fall to rise no more.

Judgement inescapable

I saw the LORD standing by the altar, 9
and he said:

Strike the capitals so that the whole
porch is shaken;
I will smash them all into pieces[b]
and I will kill them to the last man[c]
with the sword.
No fugitive shall escape,
no survivor find safety;
if they dig down to Sheol, 2
thence shall my hand take them;
if they climb up to heaven,
thence will I bring them down.
If they hide on the top of Carmel, 3
there will I search out and take
them;

w Or was.   x become . . . strumpet: or be carried off as a prostitute in a raid.   y ripe summer
and ripe: a play on the Heb. qais (summer) and qes (end).   z and plunder: prob. rdg.; Heb. to destroy.   a south: prob. rdg.; Heb. west.   b I will . . . pieces: prob. rdg.; Heb. I will hack them on
the heads of them all.   c them to the last man: or their children.

if they conceal themselves from me in
the depths of the sea,
there will I bid the sea-serpent bite
them.
4 If they are herded into captivity by
their enemies,
there will I bid the sword slay them,
and I will fix my eye on them
for evil and not for good.
5 The Lord the God of Hosts,
at whose touch the earth heaves,
and all who dwell on it wither,[d]
it surges like the Nile,
and subsides like the river of Egypt,
6 who builds his stair up to the
heavens
and arches his ceiling over the
earth,
who summons the waters of the sea
and pours them over the land—
his name is the Lord.
7 Are not you Israelites like Cushites to
me?
says the Lord.
Did I not bring Israel up from Egypt,
the Philistines from Caphtor, the
Aramaeans from Kir?
8 Behold, I, the Lord God,
have my eyes on this sinful kingdom,
and I will wipe if off the face of the
earth.

A remnant restored
Yet I will not wipe out the family of
Jacob root and branch,
says the Lord.
9 No; I will give my orders,
I will shake Israel to and fro through
all the nations

as a sieve is shaken to and fro
and not one pebble falls to the
ground.
They shall die by the sword, all the 10
sinners of my people,
who say, 'Thou wilt not let disaster
come near us
or overtake us.'
On that day I will restore 11
David's fallen house;
I will repair its gaping walls and restore its ruins;
I will rebuild it as it was long ago,
that they may possess what is left of 12
Edom
and all the nations who were once
named mine.

This is the very word of the Lord,
who will do this.

A time is coming, says the Lord, 13
when the ploughman shall follow
hard on the vintager,[e]
and he who treads the grapes after
him who sows the seed.
The mountains shall run with fresh
wine,
and every hill shall wave with corn.
I will restore the fortunes of my 14
people Israel;
they shall rebuild deserted cities and
live in them,
they shall plant vineyards and drink
their wine,
make gardens and eat the fruit.
Once more I will plant them on 15
their own soil,
and they shall never again be uprooted
from the soil I have given them.
It is the word of the Lord your God.

d Or mourn.   e Or reaper.

OBADIAH

Edom's pride and downfall
1[a] The vision of Obadiah: what the Lord
God has said concerning Edom.

When a herald was sent out among
the nations, crying,
'Rouse yourselves;
let us rouse ourselves to battle
against Edom',
I heard this message from the Lord:

Look, I make you the least of all 2
nations,
an object of contempt.
Your proud, insolent heart has led 3
you astray;
you who haunt the crannies among
the rocks,
making your home on the heights,
you say to yourself, 'Who can bring
me to the ground?'

a Verses 1–4: cp. Jer. 49. 14–16.

4 Though you soar as high as a vulture
and your nest is set among the stars,
thence I will bring you down.
This is the very word of the LORD.

5[b] If thieves or robbers come to you by night,
though your loss be heavy,
they will steal only what they want;
if vintagers come to you,
will they not leave gleanings?

6 But see how Esau's treasure is ransacked,
his secret wealth hunted out!

7 All your former allies march you to the frontier,
your confederates mislead you and bring you low,
your own kith and kin lay a snare for your feet,
a snare that works blindly, without wisdom.

8 And on that very day
I will destroy all the sages of Edom
and leave no wisdom on the mount of Esau.
This is the very word of the LORD.

9 Then shall your warriors, O Teman, be so enfeebled,
that every man shall be cut down on the mount of Esau.

10 For the murderous violence done to your brother Jacob
you shall be covered with shame and cut off for ever.

11 On the day when you stood aloof,
on the day when strangers carried off his wealth,
when foreigners trooped in by his gates
and parcelled out Jerusalem by lot,
you yourselves were of one mind with them.

12 Do not gloat over your brother on the day of his misfortune,
nor rejoice over Judah on his day of ruin;
do not boast on the day of distress,

13 nor enter my people's gates on the day of his downfall.
Do not gloat over his fall on the day of his downfall

nor seize his treasure on the day of his downfall.

14 Do not wait at the cross-roads to cut off his fugitives
nor betray the survivors on the day of distress.

The LORD's dominion

15 For soon the day of the LORD will come on all the nations:
you shall be treated as you have treated others,
and your deeds will recoil on your own head.

16 The draught that you have drunk on my holy mountain
all the nations shall drink continually;
they shall drink and gulp down
and shall be as though they had never been;

17 but on Mount Zion there shall be those that escape,
and it shall be holy,
and Jacob shall dispossess those that dispossessed them.

18 Then shall the house of Jacob be fire,
the house of Joseph flame,
and the house of Esau shall be chaff;
they shall blaze through it and consume it,
and the house of Esau shall have no survivor.
The LORD has spoken.

19 Then they shall possess the Negeb, the mount of Esau,
and the Shephelah of the Philistines;
they shall possess the country-side of Ephraim and Samaria,
and Benjamin shall possess Gilead.

20 Exiles of Israel[c] shall possess[d] Canaan as far as Zarephath,
exiles of Jerusalem[e] shall possess the cities of the Negeb.

21 Those who find safety on Mount Zion shall go up
to hold sway over the mount of Esau,
and dominion shall belong to the LORD.

---

b Verses 5 and 6: cp. Jer. 49. 9, 10.   *c Prob. rdg.; Heb. adds this army.*   *d shall possess: prob. rdg.; Heb. which.*   *e Prob. rdg.; Heb. adds who are in Sepharad.*

JONAH

Jonah bound for Tarshish

1 THE WORD OF THE LORD
2 came to Jonah son of Amittai: 'Go to
the great city of Nineveh, go now and
denounce it, for its wickedness stares
3 me in the face.' But Jonah set out for
Tarshish to escape from the LORD. He
went down to Joppa, where he found
a ship bound for Tarshish. He paid
his fare and went on board, meaning
to travel by it to Tarshish out of reach
4 of the LORD. But the LORD let loose a
hurricane, and the sea ran so high in
the storm that the ship threatened to
5 break up. The sailors were afraid, and
each cried out to his god for help.
Then they threw things overboard to
lighten the ship. Jonah had gone down
into a corner of the ship and was lying
6 sound asleep when the captain came
upon him. 'What, sound asleep?' he
said. 'Get up, and call on your god;
perhaps he will spare us a thought
and we shall not perish.'

Jonah thrown overboard

7 At last the sailors said to each other,
'Come and let us cast lots to find out
who is to blame for this bad luck.' So
they cast lots, and the lot fell on
8 Jonah. 'Now then,' they said to him,
'what is your business? Where do you
come from? What is your country? Of
9 what nation are you?' 'I am a Hebrew,'
he answered, 'and I worship the LORD
the God of heaven, who made both
10 sea and land.' At this the sailors were
even more afraid. 'What can you have
done wrong?' they asked. They already knew that he was trying to escape from the LORD, for he had told
11 them so. 'What shall we do with you',
they asked, 'to make the sea go down?'
For the storm grew worse and worse.
12 'Take me and throw me overboard,'
he said, 'and the sea will go down.
I know it is my fault that this great
13 storm has struck you.' The crew
rowed hard to put back to land but in
vain, for the sea ran higher and higher.
14 At last they called on the LORD and
said, 'O LORD, do not let us perish at
the price of this man's life; do not
charge us with the death of an innocent man. All this, O LORD, is thy set

purpose.' Then they took Jonah and 15
threw him overboard, and the sea
stopped raging. So the crew were 16
filled with the fear of the LORD and
offered sacrifice and made vows to
him. But the LORD ordained that a 17
great fish should swallow Jonah, and
for three days and three nights he
remained in its belly.

Jonah's prayer

Jonah prayed to the LORD his God **2**
from the belly of the fish:

I called to the LORD in my distress, 2
and he answered me;
out of the belly of Sheol I cried for
help,
and thou hast heard my cry.
Thou didst cast me into the depths, 3
far out at sea,
and the flood closed round me;
all thy waves, all thy billows, passed
over me.
I thought I was banished from thy 4
sight
and should never see thy holy temple
again.
The water about me rose up to my 5
neck;
the ocean was closing over me.
Weeds twined about my head
in the troughs of the mountains; 6
I was sinking into a world
whose bars would hold me fast for
ever.
But thou didst bring me up alive from
the pit, O LORD my God.
As my senses failed me I remembered 7
the LORD,
and my prayer reached thee in thy
holy temple.
Men who worship false gods may 8
abandon their loyalty,
but I will offer thee sacrifice with words 9
of praise;
I will pay my vows; victory is the
LORD's.

Then the LORD spoke to the fish 10
and it spewed Jonah out on to the
dry land.

Nineveh repents

The word of the LORD came to Jonah **3**
a second time: 'Go to the great city of 2
Nineveh, go now and denounce it in
the words I give you.' Jonah obeyed 3-4

at once and went to Nineveh. He began by going a day's journey into the city, a vast city, three days' journey across, and then proclaimed: 'In forty days Nineveh shall be over-5 thrown!' The people of Nineveh believed God's word. They ordered a public fast and put on sackcloth, high 6 and low alike. When the news reached the king of Nineveh he rose from his throne, stripped off his robes of state, put on sackcloth and sat in ashes. 7 Then he had a proclamation made in Nineveh: 'This is a decree of the king and his nobles. No man or beast, herd or flock, is to taste food, to graze or to 8 drink water. They are to clothe themselves in sackcloth and call on God with all their might. Let every man abandon his wicked ways and his 9 habitual violence. It may be that God will repent and turn away from his anger: and so we shall not perish.' 10 God saw what they did, and how they abandoned their wicked ways, and he repented and did not bring upon them the disaster he had threatened.

Jonah and the gourd

4 Jonah was greatly displeased and 2 angry, and he prayed to the LORD: 'This, O LORD, is what I feared when I was in my own country, and to forestall it I tried to escape to Tarshish;

I knew that thou art "a god gracious and compassionate, long-suffering and ever constant, and always willing to repent of the disaster".[a] And now, 3 LORD, take my life: I should be better dead than alive.' 'Are you so angry?' 4 said the LORD. Jonah went out and 5 sat down on the east of the city. There he made himself a shelter and sat in its shade, waiting to see what would happen in the city. Then the LORD 6 God ordained that a climbing gourd[b] should grow up over his head to throw its shade over him and relieve his distress, and Jonah was grateful for the gourd. But at dawn the next day God 7 ordained that a worm should attack the gourd, and it withered; and at 8 sunrise God ordained that a scorching wind should blow up from the east. The sun beat down on Jonah's head till he grew faint. Then he prayed for death and said, 'I should be better dead than alive.' At this God said to 9 Jonah, 'Are you so angry over the gourd?' 'Yes,' he answered, 'mortally angry.' The LORD said, 'You are sorry 10 for the gourd, though you did not have the trouble of growing it, a plant which came up in a night and withered in a night. And should not I be sorry 11 for the great city of Nineveh, with its hundred and twenty thousand who cannot tell their right hand from their left, and cattle without number?'

a a god . . . disaster: *cp.* Exod. *34. 6.*   *b* a climbing gourd: *or* a castor-oil plant.

MICAH

1 THIS IS THE WORD of the LORD which came to Micah of Moresheth during the reigns of Jotham, Ahaz, and Hezekiah, kings of Judah; which he received in visions concerning Samaria and Jerusalem.

Israel and Judah denounced

2 Listen, you peoples, all together;
attend, O earth and all who are in it,
that the Lord GOD, the Lord from his
holy temple,
may bear witness against you.
3 For look, the LORD is leaving his
dwelling-place;
down he comes and walks on the
heights of the earth.

Beneath him mountains dissolve 4
like wax before the fire,
valleys are torn open,
as when torrents pour down the hill-
side—
and all for the crime of Jacob and the 5
sin of Israel.
What is the crime of Jacob? Is it not
Samaria?
What is the hill-shrine of Judah? Is it
not Jerusalem?
So I will make Samaria 6
a heap of ruins in open country,
a place for planting vines;
I will pour her stones down into the
valley
and lay her foundations bare.

7 All her carved figures shall be shattered,
her images burnt one and all;
I will make a waste heap of all her
idols.
She amassed them out of fees for
harlotry,
and a harlot's fee shall they become
once more.

8 Therefore I must howl and wail,
go naked and distraught;
I must howl like a wolf, mourn like a
desert-owl.

9 Her wound cannot be healed;
for the stroke has bitten deep into
Judah,
it has fallen on the gate of my people,
upon Jerusalem itself.

10 Will you not weep your fill, weep your
eyes out in Gath?
In Beth-aphrah sprinkle yourselves
with dust;

11 take the road, you that dwell in
Shaphir;
have not the people of Zaanan gone
out in shame from their city?
Beth-ezel is a place of lamentation,
she can lend you support no longer.

12 The people of Maroth are greatly
alarmed,
for disaster has come down from
the LORD
to the very gate of Jerusalem.

13 Harness the steeds to the chariot, O
people of Lachish,
for you first led the daughter of Zion
into sin;
to you must the crimes of Israel be
traced.

14 Let Moresheth-gath be given her dismissal.
Beth-achzib has*a* disappointed*b* the
kings of Israel.

15 And you too, O people of Mareshah,
I will send others to take your place;
and the glory of Israel shall hide in
the cave of Adullam.

16 Shave the hair from your head in
mourning
for the children of your delight;
make yourself bald as a vulture,
for they have left you and gone into
exile.

Judgement for injustice

2 Shame on those who lie in bed planning evil and wicked deeds
and rise at daybreak to do them,
knowing that they have the power!

They covet land and take it by 2
force;
if they want a house they seize it;
they rob a man of his home
and steal every man's inheritance.

Therefore these are the words of the 3
LORD:

Listen, for this whole brood I am planning disaster,
whose yoke you cannot shake from
your necks
and walk upright; it shall be your
hour of disaster.

On that day   4
they shall take up a poem about
you
and raise a lament thrice told,
saying, 'We are utterly despoiled:
the land of the LORD's*c* people changes
hands.
How shall a man have power*d*
to restore our fields, now parcelled
out*e*?'

Therefore there shall be no one to 5
assign to you
any portion by lot in the LORD's
assembly.

How they rant! They may say, 'Do 6
not rant';
but this ranting is all their own,
these insults are their*f* own invention.

The upright man's best friend

Can one ask, O house of Jacob,   7
'Is the LORD's patience truly at an
end?
Are these his deeds?
Does not good come of the LORD's
words?
He is the upright man's best
friend.'
But you are no*g* people for me,   8
rising up as my enemy to my*h* face,
to strip the cloak from him that was
safe*i*
and take away the confidence of
returning warriors,
to drive the women of my people from 9
their pleasant homes
and rob the children of my glory
for ever.
Up and be gone; this is no resting- 10
place for you,
you that to defile yourselves would
commit any mischief,
mischief however cruel,

a Beth-achzib has: *prob. rdg.*; *Heb.* The houses of Achzib have.   b *Heb.* achzab.   c the LORD's:
prob. rdg.; *Heb.* my.   d have power: *prob. rdg.*; *Heb.* remove from me.   e now parcelled out:
prob. rdg.; *Heb.* he will parcel out.   f *Prob. rdg.*; *Heb.* his.   g But . . . no: *prob. rdg.*; *Heb.* But
yesterday.   h my: *prob. rdg.*; *Heb. om.*   i the cloak . . . safe: *prob. rdg.*; *Heb.* mantle, cloak.

11 If anyone had gone about in a spirit of falsehood and lies, saying, 'I will rant to you of wine and strong drink', his ranting would be what this people like.

Promise of restoration

12 I will assemble you, the whole house of Jacob;
I will gather together those that are left in Israel.
I will herd them like sheep in a fold,
like a grazing flock which stampedes at the sight of a man.

13 So their leader breaks out before them,
and they all break through the gate and escape,
and their king goes before them,
and the LORD leads the way.

To the rulers of Israel

3 And I said:

Listen, you leaders of Jacob, rulers of Israel,
should you not know what is right?

2 You hate good and love evil,
you flay men alive and tear the very flesh from their bones;

3 you devour the flesh of my people,
strip off their skin,
splinter their bones;
you shred them like flesh into a pot,
like meat into a cauldron.

4 Then they will call to the LORD, and he will give them no answer;
when that time comes he will hide his face from them,
so wicked are their deeds.

5 These are the words of the LORD concerning the prophets who lead my people astray, who promise prosperity in return for a morsel of food, who proclaim a holy war against them if they put nothing into their mouths:

6 Therefore night shall bring you no vision,
darkness no divination;
the sun shall go down on the prophets,
the day itself shall be black above them.

7 Seers and diviners alike shall blush for shame;
they shall all put their hands over their mouths,
because there is no answer from God.

8 But I am full of strength,[j] of justice and power,

to denounce his crime to Jacob and his sin to Israel.

9 Listen to this, leaders of Jacob, rulers of Israel,
you who make justice hateful
and wrest it from its straight course,

10 building Zion in bloodshed
and Jerusalem in iniquity.

11 Her rulers sell justice,
her priests give direction in return for a bribe,
her prophets take money for their divination,
and yet men rely on the LORD.
'Is not the LORD among us?' they say;
'then no disaster can befall us.'

12 Therefore, on your account
Zion shall become a ploughed field,
Jerusalem a heap of ruins,
and the temple hill rough heath.

A remnant in an age of peace

4 1[k] In days to come
the mountain of the LORD's house
shall be set over all other mountains,
lifted high above the hills.
Peoples shall come streaming to it,

2 and many nations shall come and say,
'Come, let us climb up on to the mountain of the LORD,
to the house of the God of Jacob,
that he may teach us his ways
and we may walk in his paths.'
For instruction issues from Zion,
and out of Jerusalem comes the word of the LORD;

3 he will be judge between many peoples
and arbiter among mighty nations afar.
They shall beat their swords into mattocks
and their spears into pruning-knives;
nation shall not lift sword against nation
nor ever again be trained for war,

4 and each man shall dwell under his own vine,
under his own fig-tree, undisturbed.
For the LORD of Hosts himself has spoken.

5 All peoples may walk, each in the name of his god,
but we will walk in the name of the LORD our God
for ever and ever.

6 On that day, says the LORD,
I will gather those who are lost;

[j] *Prob. rdg.; Heb. adds* the spirit of the LORD.   [k] *Verses 1–3: cp. Isa. 2. 2–4.*

I will assemble the exiles and I will
    strengthen the weaklings.
7 I will preserve the lost as a remnant
    and turn the derelict into a mighty
    nation.
The LORD shall be their king on Mount
    Zion
    now and for ever.
8 And you, rocky bastion, hill of Zion's
    daughter,
    the promises to you shall be ful-
    filled;
    and your former sovereignty shall
    come again,
    the dominion of the daughter of
    Jerusalem.

Purpose in Israel's captivity

9   Why are you now filled with alarm?
    Have you no king?
    Have you no counsellor left,
    that you are seized with writhing
    like a woman in labour?
10 Lie writhing on the ground like a
    woman in childbirth,
    O daughter of Zion;
    for now you must leave the city
    and camp in the open country;
    and so you will come to Babylon.
    There you shall be saved,
    there the LORD will deliver you from
    your enemies.
11 But now many nations are massed
    against you;
    they say, 'Let her suffer outrage,
    let us gloat over Zion.'
12   But they do not know the LORD's
    thoughts
    nor understand his purpose;
    for he has gathered them like
    sheaves to the threshing-floor.
13   Start your threshing, daughter of
    Zion;
    for I will make your horns of iron,
    your hooves will I make of bronze,
    and you shall crush many peoples.
    You shall devote their ill-gotten
    gain to the LORD,
    their wealth to the Lord of all the
    earth.

A governor for Israel

5   Get you behind your walls, you
    people of a walled city;
    the siege is pressed home against
    you:
Israel's ruler shall be struck on the
    cheek with a rod.
2   But you, Bethlehem in Ephrathah,
    small as you are to be among
    Judah's clans,
    out of you shall come forth a governor
    for Israel,

one whose roots are far back in the
    past, in days gone by.
Therefore only so long as a woman 3
    is in labour
shall he give up Israel;
and then those that survive of his
    race
shall rejoin their brethren.
He shall appear and be their shep- 4
    herd
in the strength of the LORD,
in the majesty of the name of the
    LORD his God.
And they shall continue, for now his
    greatness shall reach
to the ends of the earth;
and he shall be a man of peace.   5

Defence against Assyria

When the Assyrian comes into our
    land,
when he tramples our castles,
we will raise against him seven men
    or eight
to be shepherds and princes.
They shall shepherd Assyria with 6
    the sword
and the land of Nimrod with bare
    blades;
they shall deliver us from the As-
    syrians
when they come into our land,
when they trample our frontiers.

The remnant

All that are left of Jacob, surrounded 7
    by many peoples,
shall be like dew from the LORD,
like copious showers on the grass,
which do not wait for man's com-
    mand
or linger for any man's bidding.
All that are left of Jacob among the 8
    nations,
surrounded by many peoples,
shall be like a lion among the beasts
    of the forest,
like a young lion loose in a flock of
    sheep;
as he prowls he will trample and
    tear them,
with no rescuer in sight.
Your hand shall be raised high over 9
    your foes,
and all who hate you shall be de-
    stroyed.

On that day, says the LORD,   10
I will destroy all your horses among
    you
and make away with your chariots.
I will destroy the cities of your land 11
and raze your fortresses.
I will destroy all your sorcerers,   12

and there shall be no more soothsayers among you.

3 I will destroy your images and all the
sacred pillars in your land;
you shall no longer bow in reverence
before things your own hands
made.

4 I will pull down the sacred poles in
your land,
and demolish your blood-spattered
altars.

5 In anger and fury will I take vengeance
on all nations who disobey me.

Israel denounced for her sins

6 Hear now what the LORD is saying:

Up, state your case to the mountains;
let the hills hear your plea.

2 Hear the LORD's case, you mountains,
you everlasting pillars that bear up
the earth;
for the LORD has a case against his
people,
and will argue it with Israel.

3 O my people, what have I done to
you?
Tell me how I have wearied you;
answer me this.

4 I brought you up from Egypt,
I ransomed you from the land of
slavery,
I sent Moses and Aaron and Miriam
to lead you.

5 Remember, my people,
what Balak king of Moab schemed
against you,
and how Balaam son of Beor answered him;
consider the journey[l] from Shittim
to Gilgal,
in order that you may know the
triumph of the LORD.

6 What shall I bring when I approach
the LORD?
How shall I stoop before God on
high?
Am I to approach him with whole-
offerings or yearling calves?

7 Will the LORD accept thousands of
rams
or ten thousand rivers of oil?
Shall I offer my eldest son for my
own wrongdoing,
my children for my own sin?

8 God[m] has told you what is good;

and what is it that the LORD asks of
you?
Only to act justly, to love loyalty,
to walk wisely before your God.

Hark, the LORD, the fear of whose 9
name brings success,
the LORD calls to the city.
Listen, O tribe of Judah and citi- 10
zens in assembly,[n]
can I overlook[o] the infamous false
measure,[p]
the accursed short bushel?
Can I connive at false scales or a bag 11
of light weights?
Your rich men are steeped in vio- 12
lence,
your townsmen are all liars,
and their tongues frame deceit.
But now I will inflict a signal punish- 13
ment on you
to lay you waste for your sins:
you shall eat but not be satisfied, 14
your food shall lie heavy on your
stomach;
you shall come to labour but not
bring forth,
and even if you bear a child
I will give it to the sword;
you shall sow but not reap, 15
you shall press the olives but not use
the oil,
you shall tread the grapes but not
drink the wine.
You have kept the precepts of 16
Omri;
what the house of Ahab did, you
have done;
you have followed all their ways.
So I will lay you utterly waste;
the nations shall jeer at your citizens,
and their insults you shall bear.

Disappointment turned to hope

Alas! I am now like the last gather- 7
ings of summer fruit,
the last gleanings of the vintage,
when there are no grapes left to eat,
none of those early figs that I love.
Loyal men have vanished from the 2
earth,
there is not one upright man.
All lie in wait to do murder,
each man drives his own kinsman
like a hunter into the net.
They are bent eagerly on wrong- 3
doing,
the officer who presents the requests,[q]

---

l consider the journey: prob. rdg.; Heb. om.   m God: prob. rdg.; Heb. obscure.   n citizens in
assembly: prob. rdg.; Heb. unintelligible.   o can I overlook: prob. rdg.; Heb. obscure.   p Prob.
rdg.; Heb. adds infamous treasures.   q the requests: prob. rdg.; Heb. om.

the judge who gives judgement[r] for
reward,
and the nobleman who harps on his
desires.

4 Thus their goodness is twisted[s] like
rank weeds
and their honesty like briars.[t]
As soon as thine eye sees, thy
punishment falls;
at that moment bewilderment seizes
them.

5 Trust no neighbour, put no confidence
in your closest friend;
seal your lips even from the wife of
your bosom.

6 For son maligns father,
daughter rebels against mother,
daughter-in-law against mother-in-
law,
and a man's enemies are his own
household.

7 But I will look for the LORD,
I will wait for God my saviour; my
God will hear me.

8 O my enemies, do not exult over
me;
I have fallen, but shall rise again;
though I dwell in darkness, the LORD
is my light.

9 I will bear the anger of the LORD, for
I have sinned against him,
until he takes up my cause and gives
judgement for me,
until he brings me out into light, and
I see his justice.

10 Then may my enemies see and be
abashed,
those who said to me, 'Where is he,
the LORD your God?'
Then shall they be trampled like mud
in the streets;
I shall gloat over them;

11 that will be a day for rebuilding
your walls,
a day when your frontiers will be
extended,

12 a day when men will come seeking
you
from Assyria to Egypt
and from Egypt to the Euphrates,
from every sea and every mountain;

13 and the earth with its inhabitants
shall be waste.
This shall be the fruit of their deeds.

A prayer

14 Shepherd thy people with thy crook,
the flock that is thy very own,
that dwells by itself on the heath and
in the meadows;
let them graze in Bashan and Gilead,
as in days gone by.

15 Show us[u] miracles as in the days when
thou camest out of Egypt;

16 let the nations see and be taken aback
for all their might,
let them keep their mouths shut,
make their ears deaf,

17 let them lick the dust like snakes,
like creatures that crawl upon the
ground.
Let them come trembling and fearful
from their strongholds,
let them fear thee, O LORD our God.

18 Who is a god like thee? Thou takest
away guilt,
thou passest over the sin of the remnant of thy own people,
thou dost not let thy anger rage for
ever
but delightest in love that will not
change.

19 Once more thou wilt show us tender
affection
and wash out our guilt,
casting all our sins into the depths
of the sea.

20 Thou wilt show good faith to Jacob,
unchanging love to Abraham,
as thou didst swear to our fathers in
days gone by.

r who gives judgement: *prob. rdg.; Heb. om.*   *s* twisted: *prob. rdg.; Heb. obscure.*   *t* their
honesty like briars: *prob. rdg.; Heb. obscure.*
u Prob. rdg.; Heb. I will show him.

NAHUM

1 An oracle about Nineveh: the book of the vision of Nahum the Elkoshite.

The Lord's vengeance on his enemies

2*a* The Lord is a jealous god, a god of vengeance;
the Lord takes vengeance and is quick to anger.*b*
3 *c*In whirlwind and storm he goes on his way,
and the clouds are the dust beneath his feet.
4 He rebukes the sea and dries it up
and makes all the streams fail.
Bashan and Carmel languish,
and on Lebanon the young shoots wither.
5 The mountains quake before him,
the hills heave and swell,
and the earth, the world and all that lives in it,
are in tumult at his presence.
6 Who can stand before his wrath?
Who can resist his fury?
His anger pours out*d* like a stream of fire,
and the rocks melt*e* before him.
7 The Lord is a sure refuge
for those who look to him in time of distress;
he cares for all who seek his protection
8 and brings them safely*f* through the sweeping flood;
he makes a final end of all who oppose him
and pursues his enemies into darkness.
-11 No adversaries dare oppose him twice;
all are burnt up*g* like tangled briars.
Why do you make plots against the Lord?
He himself will make an end of you all.
From you has come forth a wicked counsellor,
plotting evil against the Lord.
The Lord takes vengeance on his adversaries,
against his enemies he directs his wrath;
with skin scorched black, they are consumed
like stubble that is parched and dry.

Israel and Judah rid of the invaders

These are the words of the Lord:

Now I will break his yoke from 13 your necks
and snap the cords that bind you.
Image and idol will I hew down in the 14 house of your God.
This is what the Lord has ordained for you:
never again shall your offspring be scattered;
and I will grant you burial, fickle though you have been.
Has the punishment been so great? 12
Yes, but it has passed away and is gone.
I have afflicted you, but I will not afflict you again.

See on the mountains the feet of 15 the herald
who brings good news.
Make your pilgrimages, O Judah,
and pay your vows.
For wicked men shall never again overrun you;
they are totally destroyed.
The Lord will restore the pride of 2 2*h* Jacob and Israel alike,
although plundering hordes have stripped them bare
and pillaged their vines.

Nineveh's enemies triumphant

The battering-ram is mounted 1 against your bastions,
the siege is closing in.
Watch the road and brace yourselves;
put forth all your strength.
The shields of their warriors are 3 gleaming red,
their soldiers are all in scarlet;
their chariots, when the line is formed,
are like flickering*i* fire;
squadrons of horse advance on the 4 city in mad frenzy;*j*
they jostle one another in the outskirts, like waving torches;
the leaders display their prowess*k* 5

---

a Verses 2–14 are an incomplete alphabetic acrostic poem; some parts have been re-arranged accordingly.
b The rest of verse 2, The Lord takes . . . wrath, transposed to verse 11.   *c Prob. rdg.; Heb. inserts two lines The Lord is long-suffering and of great might, but the Lord does not sweep clean away.*
d pours out: or fuses or melts.   *e Prob. rdg.; Heb. are torn down.*   *f brings them safely: prob. rdg.; Heb. om.*   *g all are burnt up: prob. rdg.; Heb. for until.*   *h Verses 1 and 2 transposed.*
i flickering: prob. rdg.; Heb. obscure.   *j Prob. rdg.; Heb. adds chariots.*   *k display their prowess: or shout their own names.*

as they dash to and fro like lightning,
rushing[l] in headlong career;
they hasten to the wall, and mantelets
are set in position.
6 The sluices of the rivers are opened,
the palace topples down;
7 the train of captives goes into exile,
their slave-girls are carried off,
moaning like doves and beating
their breasts;
8 and Nineveh has become like a
pool of water,
like the waters round her, which are
ebbing away.
'Stop! Stop!' they cry; but none turns
back.

9 Spoil is taken, spoil of silver and gold;
there is no end to the store,
treasure beyond the costliest that
man can desire.
10 Plundered, pillaged, stripped bare!
Courage melting and knees giving
way,
writhing limbs, and faces drained of
colour!
11 Where now is the lions' den,
the cave[m] where the lion cubs lurked,
where the lion and[n] lioness and
young cubs
went unafraid,
12 the lion which killed to satisfy its
whelps
and for its mate broke the neck of
the kill,
mauling its prey to fill its lair,
filling its den with the mauled prey?

Fall of Nineveh

13 I am against you, says the LORD of
Hosts,
I will smoke out your pride,[o]
and a sword shall devour your cubs.
I will leave you no more prey on
the earth,
and the sound of your feeding[p]
shall no more be heard.

3 Ah! blood-stained city, steeped in
deceit,
full of pillage, never empty of prey!
2 Hark to the crack of the whip,
the rattle of wheels and stamping of
horses,
3 bounding chariots, chargers rearing,
swords gleaming, flash of spears!
The dead are past counting, their
bodies lie in heaps,
corpses innumerable, men stumbling
over corpses—

all for a wanton's monstrous wanton- 4
ness,
fair-seeming, a mistress of sorcery,
who beguiled nations and tribes
by her wantonness and her sorceries.
I am against you, says the LORD of 5
Hosts,
I will uncover your breasts to your
disgrace
and expose your naked body to
every nation,
to every kingdom your shame.
I will cast loathsome filth over you, 6
I will count you obscene and treat
you like excrement.

Futile defence

Then all who see you will shrink from 7
you and say,
'Nineveh is laid waste; who will console her?'
Where shall I look for anyone to
comfort you?
Will you fare better than No- 8
amon?—
she that lay by the streams of the
Nile,
surrounded by water,
whose rampart was the Nile, waters
her wall;
Cush and Egypt were her strength, 9
and it was boundless,
Put and the Libyans brought her help.
She too became an exile and went into 10
captivity,
her infants too were dashed to the
ground at every street-corner,
her nobles were shared out by lot,
all her great men were thrown into
chains.
You too shall hire yourself out, flaunt- 11
ing your sex;
you too shall seek refuge from the
enemy.
Your fortifications are like figs when 12
they ripen:
if they are shaken, they fall into the
mouth of the eater.
The troops[q] in your midst are a pack 13
of women,
the gates of your country stand open
to the enemy,
and fire consumes their bars.
Draw yourselves water for the siege, 14
strengthen your fortifications;
down into the clay, trample the mortar,
repair the brickwork.
Even then the fire will consume you, 15
and the sword will cut you down.[r]

l *Prob. rdg.; Heb. stumbling.*   m *Prob. rdg.; Heb. pasture.*   n *and: prob. rdg.; Heb. om.*
o *your pride: prob. rdg.; Heb. her chariot.*   p *your feeding: prob. rdg.; Heb. your messenger.*
q *Or people.*   r *Prob. rdg.; Heb. adds and consume you like the locust (or hopper).*

Make yourselves many as the locusts,
make yourselves many as the hoppers,

16 a swarm which spreads out and then flies away.
You have spies as numerous as the stars in the sky;

17 your secret agents are like locusts, your commanders like the hoppers
which lie dormant in the walls on a cold day;
but when the sun rises, they scurry off,

and no one knows where they have gone.
Your shepherds slumber, O king of 18 Assyria,
your flock-masters lie down to rest;
your troops[s] are scattered over the hills,
and no one rounds them up.
Your wounds cannot be assuaged, 19 your injury is mortal;
all who have heard of your fate clap their hands in joy.
Are there any whom your ceaseless cruelty has not borne down?

s Or people.

HABAKKUK

1 An oracle which the prophet Habakkuk received in a vision.

An unanswered prayer

2 How long, O Lord, have I cried to thee, unanswered?
I cry, 'Violence!', but thou dost not save.

3 Why dost thou let me see such misery,
why countenance[a] wrongdoing?

Devastation and violence confront me;
strife breaks out, discord raises its head,

4 and so law grows effete;
justice does not come forth victorious;
for the wicked outwit the righteous,
and so justice comes out perverted.

The mighty Chaldaeans

5 Look, you treacherous people, look:
here is what will astonish you and stun you,
for there is work afoot in your days
which you will not believe when it is told you.

6 It is this: I am raising up the Chaldaeans,
that savage and impetuous nation,
who cross the wide tracts of the earth
to take possession of homes not theirs.

7 Terror and awe go with them;
their justice and judgement are of their own making.

Their horses are swifter than hunting- 8 leopards,
keener than wolves of the plain;[b]
their cavalry wait ready, they spring forward,
they come flying from afar
like vultures swooping to devour the prey.
Their whole army advances, violence 9 in their hearts;
a sea of faces rolls on;
they bring in captives countless as the sand.
Kings they hold in derision, 10
rulers they despise;
they despise every fortress,
they raise siege-works and capture it.
Then they pass on like the wind and 11 are gone;
and dismayed are all those whose strength was their god.

Questioning God's methods

Art thou not from of old, O Lord?— 12
my God, the holy, the immortal.[c]
O Lord, it is thou who hast appointed them to execute judgement;
O mighty God, thou who hast destined them to chastise,
thou whose eyes are too pure to 13 look upon evil,
and who canst not countenance wrongdoing,
why dost thou countenance the treachery of the wicked?
Why keep silent when they devour men more righteous than they?

a Or dost thou let me see.   b Or evening.   c the immortal: prob. original rdg., altered in Heb. to we shall not die.

14 Why dost thou make men like the
    fish of the sea,
    like gliding creatures that obey no
    ruler?
15 They haul them up with hooks, one
    and all,
    they catch them in nets
    and drag them in their trawls;
    then they make merry and rejoice,
16 sacrificing to their nets
    and burning offerings[d] to their
    trawls;
    for by these they live sumptuously
    and enjoy rich fare.
17 Are they then to unsheathe the sword
    every day,
    to slaughter the nations without
    pity?

The watch-tower

2   I will stand at my post,
    I will take up my position on the
    watch-tower,
    I will watch to learn what he will
    say through me,
    and what I shall reply when I am
    challenged.[e]
2   Then the LORD made answer:
    Write down the vision, inscribe it on
    tablets,
    ready for a herald to carry it with
    speed;[f]
3 for there is still a vision for the ap-
    pointed time.
    At the destined hour it will come in
    breathless haste,
    it will not fail.
    If it delays, wait for it;
    for when it comes will be no time to
    linger.

Five woes

4 The reckless will be unsure of himself,
    while the righteous man will live
    by being faithful;[g]
5 as for the traitor in his over-
    confidence,
    still less will he ride out the storm,
    for all his bragging.
    Though he opens his mouth as wide
    as Sheol
    and is insatiable as Death,
    gathering in all the nations,
    making all peoples his own harvest,
6 surely they will all turn upon him
    with insults and abuse, and say,
    'Woe betide you who heap up
    wealth that is not yours[h]
    and enrich yourself with goods
    taken in pledge!'

Will not your creditors suddenly 7
    start up,
will not all awake who would shake
    you till you are empty,
and will you not fall a victim to
    them?
Because you yourself have plundered 8
    mighty[i] nations,
all the rest of the world will plunder
    you,
because of bloodshed and violence
    done in the land,
to the city and all its inhabitants.

Woe betide you who seek unjust 9
    gain for your house,
to build your nest on a height,
to save yourself from the grasp of
    wicked men!
Your schemes to overthrow mighty[i] 10
    nations
will bring dishonour to your house
and put your own life in jeopardy.
The very stones will cry out from 11
    the wall,
and from the timbers a beam will
    answer them.

Woe betide you who have built a 12
    town with bloodshed
and founded a city on fraud,
so that nations toil for a pittance, 13
and peoples weary themselves for
    a mere nothing!
Is not all this the doing of the LORD
    of Hosts?
For the earth shall be full of the 14
    knowledge of the glory of the
    LORD
as the waters fill the sea.

Woe betide you who make your[j] com- 15
    panions drink the outpouring of
    your wrath,
making them drunk, that you may
    watch their naked orgies!
Drink deep draughts of shame, not 16
    of glory;
you too shall drink until you stag-
    ger.
The cup in the LORD's right hand is
    passed to you,
and your shame will exceed[k] your
    glory.
The violence done to Lebanon shall 17
    sweep over you,
the havoc done to its beasts shall
    break your own spirit,
because of bloodshed and violence
    done in the land,
to the city and all its inhabitants.

---

d Or incense.   e when I am challenged: or concerning my complaint.   f ready . . . speed: or so
that a man may read it easily.   g Or by his faithfulness (*cp.* Romans. *1. 17; Galatians 3. 11*).
h *Prob. rdg.; Heb. adds* till when.   i Or many.   j *Prob. rdg.; Heb.* his.   k will exceed: *prob.*
rdg.; Heb. unintelligible.

18 What use is an idol when its maker
      has shaped it?—
   it is only an image, a source of lies;
   or when the maker trusts what he has
      made?—
   he is only making dumb idols.
19   Woe betide him who says to the
      wood, 'Wake up',
   to the dead stone, 'Bestir yourself'!*l*
   Why, it is firmly encased in gold and
      silver
   and has no breath in it.
20   But the LORD is in his holy temple;
   let all the earth be hushed in his
      presence.

Prayer for mercy

3 A prayer of the prophet Habakkuk.

2   O LORD, I have heard tell of thy
      deeds;
   I have seen, O LORD, thy work.*m*
   In the midst of the years thou didst
      make thyself known,
   and in thy wrath thou didst remem-
      ber mercy.

3   God comes from Teman,
   the Holy One from Mount Paran;
   his radiance overspreads the skies,
   and his splendour fills the earth.
4   He rises like the dawn,
   with twin rays starting forth at his
      side;
   the skies are*n* the hiding-place of
      his majesty,
   and the everlasting*o* ways are for*p*
      his swift flight.*q*
5   Pestilence stalks before him,
   and plague comes forth behind.
6   He stands still and shakes the
      earth,
   he looks and makes the nations
      tremble;
   the eternal mountains are riven,
   the everlasting*r* hills subside,
7   the tents of Cushan are snatched
      away,*s*
   the tent-curtains of Midian flutter.
8   Art thou angry with the streams?
   Is thy wrath against the sea, O
      LORD?
   When thou dost mount thy horses,
   thy riding is to victory.

Thou dost draw thy bow from its 9
   case*t*
and charge thy quiver with shafts.
Thou cleavest the earth with rivers;
the mountains see thee and writhe 10-11
   with fear.
The torrent of water rushes by,
and the deep sea thunders aloud.
The sun forgets to turn in his course,*u*
   and the moon stands still at her
      zenith,
at the gleam of thy speeding arrows
and the glance of thy flashing spear.
With threats thou dost bestride the 12
   earth
and trample down the nations in
   anger.
Thou goest forth to save thy people, 13
   thou comest to save thy anointed;
thou dost shatter the wicked man's
   house from the roof down,*v*
uncovering its foundations to the
   bare rock.*w*
Thou piercest their*x* chiefs with thy*y* 14
   shafts,
and their leaders are torn from
   them by the whirlwind,
as they open*z* their jaws
to devour their wretched victims in
   secret.

When thou dost tread the sea with 15
   thy horses
the mighty waters boil.
I hear, and my belly quakes;   16
my lips quiver at the sound;
trembling comes over my bones,
and my feet totter in their tracks;
I sigh for the day of distress
to dawn over my assailants.
Although the fig-tree does not bur- 17
   geon,
the vines bear no fruit,
the olive-crop fails,
the orchards yield no food,
the fold is bereft of its flock
and there are no cattle in the stalls,
yet I will exult in the LORD   18
and rejoice in the God of my
   deliverance.
The LORD God is my strength,   19
who makes my feet nimble as a
   hind's
and sets me to range the heights.

---

l Prob. rdg.; Heb. adds he will teach.   *m Prob. rdg.; Heb. adds* in the midst of the years quicken it.
n the skies are: *prob. rdg.; Heb.* there is.   *o Or* ancient.   *p* and . . . are for: *transposed from
end of verse 6.*   *q* his swift flight: *transposed, with slight change, from verse 7.*   *r Or* ancient.
s are snatched away: *prob. rdg.; Heb.* under wickedness.   *t* Thou . . . case: *prob. rdg.; Heb.* Thy
bow was quite bared.   *u* The sun . . . course: *prob. rdg.; Heb.* The sun raised the height of his
hands.   *v* the wicked . . . down: *prob. rdg.; Heb.* a head from the house of the wicked.   *w* bare
rock: *prob. rdg.; Heb.* neck.   *x* their: *prob. rdg.; Heb. om.*   *y Prob. rdg.; Heb.* his.   *z* from
them . . . open: *prob. rdg.; Heb.* obscure.

N*

ZEPHANIAH

1 THIS IS THE WORD of the LORD which came to Zephaniah son of Cushi, son of Gedaliah, son of A-mariah, son of Hezekiah, in the time of Josiah son of Amon king of Judah.

Universal devastation

2 I will sweep the earth clean of all that is on it,
> says the LORD.

3 I will sweep away both man and beast,
> I will sweep the birds from the air and the fish from the sea,
> and I will bring the wicked to their knees[a]
> and wipe out mankind from the earth.
> This is the very word of the LORD.

Judah's end

4 I will stretch my hand over Judah and all who live in Jerusalem;
> I will wipe out from this place the last remnant of Baal
> and the very name of the heathen priests,

5 those who bow down upon the house-tops
> to worship the host of heaven
> and who swear by Milcom,

6 those who have turned their backs on the LORD,
> who have not sought the LORD or consulted him.

7 Silence before the Lord GOD!
> for the day of the LORD is near.
> The LORD has prepared a sacrifice and has hallowed his guests.

8 On the day of the LORD's sacrifice
> I will punish the royal house and its chief officers
> and all who ape outlandish fashions.

9 On that day
> I will punish all who dance on the temple terrace,
> who fill their master's[b] house with crimes of violence and fraud.

10 On that day, says the LORD,
> an outcry shall be heard from the Fish Gate,
> wailing from the second quarter of the city,
> a loud crash from the hills;
> and[c] those who live in the Lower Town shall wail. 11
> For it is all over with the merchants,
> and all the dealers in silver are wiped out.

Day of wrath

At that time 12
I will search Jerusalem with a lantern
and punish all who sit in stupor over the dregs of their wine,
> who say to themselves,
> 'The LORD will do nothing, good or bad.'
> Their wealth shall be plundered, 13
> their houses laid waste;
> they shall build houses but not live in them,
they shall plant vineyards but not drink the wine from them.
> The great day of the LORD is near, 14
> it comes with speed;
> no runner so fast as that day,
> no raiding band so swift.[d]
> That day is a day of wrath, 15
> a day of anguish and affliction,
> a day of destruction and devastation,
> a day of murk and gloom,
> a day of cloud and dense fog,
> a day of trumpet and battle-cry 16
over fortified cities and lofty battlements.

I will bring dire distress upon men; 17
they shall walk like blind men for their sin against the LORD.
> Their blood shall be spilt like dust and their bowels like dung;
> neither their silver nor their gold 18
> shall avail to save them.
On the day of the LORD's wrath, by the fire of his jealousy
> the whole land shall be consumed;
for he will make an end, a swift end, of all who live in the land.

Shelter from distress

Gather together, you unruly nation, **2**
> gather together,
before you are sent far away and **2**
> vanish[e] like chaff,

---

a I will bring . . . knees: *prob. rdg.; Heb.* the ruins with the wicked.   *b Or* their Lord's.   *c and*: *prob. rdg.; Heb. om.*   *d* no runner . . . swift: *prob. rdg.; Heb.* hark, the day of the LORD is bitter, there the warrior cries aloud.   *e* you are . . . vanish: *prob. rdg.; Heb. obscure.*

before the burning anger of the LORD
  comes upon you,
before the day of the LORD's anger
  comes upon you.
3 Seek the LORD,
all in the land who live humbly by
  his laws,
seek righteousness, seek a humble
  heart;
  it may be that you will find shelter
    in the day of the LORD's anger.
4 For Gaza shall be deserted,
Ashkelon left desolate,
the people of Ashdod shall be driven
  out[f] at noonday
and Ekron uprooted.

Philistia

5 Listen, you who live by the coast, you
  Kerethite settlers.
  The word of the LORD is spoken
    against you;
  I will subdue you,[g] land of the
    Philistines,
  I will lay you waste and leave you
    without inhabitants,
6 and you, Kereth, shall be all shepherds' huts[h] and sheepfolds;
7 and the coastland shall belong to the
  survivors of Judah.
  They shall pasture their flocks by
    the sea[i]
  and lie down at evening in the
    houses of Ashkelon,
  for the LORD their God will turn to
    them
  and restore their fortunes.

Moab and Ammon

8 I have heard the insults of Moab, the
  taunts of Ammon,
  how they have insulted my people
  and encroached on their frontiers.
9 Therefore, by my life,
says the LORD of Hosts, the God of
  Israel,
Moab shall be like Sodom,
  Ammon like Gomorrah,
a pile of weeds, a rotting heap of saltwort,
  waste land for evermore.
The survivors of my people shall
  plunder them,
the remnant of my nation shall possess
  their land.
10 This will be retribution for their
pride, because they have insulted the
people of the LORD of Hosts and en-

croached upon their rights. The LORD 11
will appear against them with all his
terrors; for he will reduce to beggary
all the gods of the earth, and all the
coasts and islands of the nations will
worship him, every man in his own
home.

Cush and Assyria

  You Cushites also shall be killed   12
  by the sword of the LORD.[j]
  So let him stretch out his hand over 13
    the north
  and destroy Assyria,
  make Nineveh desolate,
  arid as the wilderness.
  Flocks shall couch there,   14
  and all the beasts of the wild.
Horned owl and ruffed bustard shall
    roost on her capitals;
  the tawny owl shall hoot in the
    window,
  and the bustard stand in the porch.[k]
This is the city that exulted in fancied 15
    security,
saying to herself, 'I am, and I alone.'
And what is she now? A waste, a
    haunt for wild beasts,
at which every passer-by shall hiss
    and shake his fist.

Jerusalem laid waste

Shame on the tyrant city, filthy and 3
  foul!
No warning voice did she heed, she 2
    took no rebuke to heart,
she did not trust in the LORD or come
    near to her God.
Her officers were lions roaring in her 3
    midst,
  her rulers wolves of the plain[l]
  that did not wait[m] till morning,
  her prophets were reckless, no true 4
    prophets.
  Her priests profaned the sanctuary
    and did violence to the law.
But the LORD in her midst is just; 5
he does no wrong;
morning by morning he gives judge-
    ment,
  without fail at daybreak.[n]

I have wiped out the proud;   6
  their battlements are laid in ruin.
I have made their streets a desert
    where no one passes.
Their cities are laid waste, deserted,
    unpeopled.

---

f the people . . . out: or Ashdod shall be made an example.   g I . . . you: prob. rdg.; Heb. Canaan.
h you . . . huts: Heb. has these words in a different order.   i by the sea: prob. rdg.; Heb. upon
them.   j the sword of the LORD: prob. rdg.; Heb. my sword.   k Prob. rdg.; Heb. adds an unintelligible phrase.   l Or evening.   m Or carry off.   n Prob. rdg.; Heb. adds but the wrongdoer
knows no shame.

7 In the hope that she would remember
    all my instructions,
  I said, 'Do but fear me
  and take my rebuke to heart';
but they were up betimes and went
    about their evil deeds.

8   Wait for me, therefore, says the
    LORD,
  wait for the day when I stand up to
    accuse you;
  for mine it is to gather nations
  and assemble kingdoms,
  to pour out on them my indigna-
    tion,
  all the heat of my anger;
the whole earth shall be consumed by
    the fire of my jealousy.
9   I will give all peoples once again
    pure lips,
  that they may invoke the LORD by
    name
  and serve him with one consent.
10   From beyond the rivers of Cush
  my suppliants of the Dispersion shall
    bring me tribute.

A remnant preserved

11   On that day, Jerusalem,
  you shall not be put to shame for
    all your deeds
  by which you have rebelled against
    me;
  for then I will rid you
  of your proud and arrogant citizens,
  and never again shall you flaunt
    your pride
  on my holy hill.
12   But I will leave in you a people
  afflicted and poor.
13 The survivors in Israel shall find refuge
    in the name of the LORD;
  they shall no longer do wrong or
    speak lies,
  no words of deceit shall pass their
    lips;

for they shall feed and lie down
  with no one to terrify them.

When the LORD reigns

Zion, cry out for joy;   14
  raise the shout of triumph, Israel;
  be glad, rejoice with all your heart,
    daughter of Jerusalem.
The LORD has rid you of your adver- 15
    saries,
  he has swept away your foes;
the LORD is among you as king, O
    Israel;
  never again shall you fear disaster.

On that day this shall be the message 16
    to Jerusalem:
Fear not, O Zion; let not your hands
    fall slack.
The LORD your God is in your midst, 17
  like a warrior, to keep you safe;
  he will rejoice over you and be glad;
  he will show you his love once more;
  he will exult over you with a shout
    of joy
  as in days long ago.*o*   18

I will take your cries of woe*p* away
    from you;
  and you shall no longer endure re-
    proach for her.
When that time comes, see,   19
  I will deal with all your oppressors.
  I will rescue the lost and gather the
    dispersed;
  I will win my people praise and
    renown
  in all the world where once they
    were despised.
When the time comes for me to 20
    gather you,*q*
  I will bring you home.
I will win you renown and praise
  among all the peoples of the earth,
  when I bring back your prosperity;
    and you shall see it.
It is the LORD who speaks.

o as . . . ago: prob. rdg.; Heb. obscure.   *p cries of woe: prob. rdg.; Heb. obscure.*   *q When . . .*
you: prob. rdg.; Heb. and in the time, my gathering you.

HAGGAI

Rebuilding of the temple begins

1 IN THE SECOND YEAR of King
Darius, on the first day of the sixth
month, the word of the LORD came
through the prophet Haggai to Zerub-

babel son of Shealtiel, governor of
Judah, and to Joshua son of Jehozadak,
the high priest: These are the words 2
of the LORD of Hosts: This nation
says to itself that it is not yet time for
the house of the LORD to be rebuilt.

3 Then this word came through Haggai
4 the prophet: Is it a time for you to live
in your own well-roofed houses, while
5 this house lies in ruins? Now these
are the words of the LORD of Hosts:
6 Consider your way of life. You have
sown much but reaped little; you eat
but never as much as you wish, you
drink but never more than you need,
you are clothed but never warm, and
the labourer puts his wages into a purse
7 with a hole in it. These are the words
of the LORD of Hosts: Consider your
8 way of life. Go up into the hills, fetch
timber, and build a house acceptable
to me, where I can show my glory,[a]
9 says the LORD. You look for much and
get little. At the moment when you
would bring home the harvest, I blast
it. Why? says the LORD of Hosts.
Because my house lies in ruins, while
each of you has a house that he can
10 run to. It is your fault that the heavens withhold their dew and the earth
11 its produce. So I have proclaimed a
drought against land and mountain,
against corn, new wine, and oil, and all
that the ground yields, against man
and cattle and all the products of man's
labour.
12 Zerubbabel son of Shealtiel, Joshua
son of Jehozadak, the high priest, and
the rest of the people listened to what
the LORD their God had said and
what the prophet Haggai said when
the LORD their God sent him, and they
were filled with fear because of the
13 LORD. So Haggai the LORD's messenger, as the LORD had commissioned
him, said to the people: I am with
14 you, says the LORD. Then the LORD
stirred up the spirit of Zerubbabel
son of Shealtiel, governor of Judah, of
Joshua son of Jehozadak, the high
priest, and of the rest of the people;
they came and began work on the
house of the LORD of Hosts their God
15 on the twenty-fourth day of the sixth
month.

The temple's future glory

2 In the second year of King Darius,
on the twenty-first day of the seventh
month, these words came from the
LORD through the prophet Haggai:
2 Say to Zerubbabel son of Shealtiel,
governor of Judah, to Joshua son of
Jehozadak, the high priest, and to the
3 rest of the people: Is there anyone
still among you who saw this house
in its former glory? How does it appear
to you now? Does it not seem to you
4 as if it were not there? But now,

Zerubbabel, take heart, says the LORD;
take heart, Joshua son of Jehozadak,
high priest. Take heart, all you people,
says the LORD. Begin the work, for
I am with you, says the LORD of Hosts,
and my spirit is present among you. 5
Have no fear. For these are the words 6
of the LORD of Hosts: One thing
more: I will shake heaven and earth,
sea and land, I will shake all nations; 7
the treasure of all nations shall come
hither, and I will fill this house with
glory;[b] so says the LORD of Hosts.
Mine is the silver and mine the gold, 8
says the LORD of Hosts, and the 9
glory[b] of this latter house shall surpass the glory[b] of the former, says the
LORD of Hosts. In this place will I
grant prosperity and peace. This is
the very word of the LORD of Hosts.

A lesson from the law

In the second year of Darius, on the 10
twenty-fourth day of the ninth month,
this word came from the LORD to the
prophet Haggai: These are the words 11
of the LORD of Hosts: Ask the priests
to give their ruling: If a man is carry- 12
ing consecrated flesh in a fold of his
robe, and he lets the fold touch bread
or broth or wine or oil or any other
kind of food, will that also become
consecrated? And the priests answered, 'No.' Haggai went on, But if 13
a person defiled by contact with a
corpse touches any one of these
things, will that also become defiled?
'It will', answered the priests. Haggai 14
replied, So it is with this people and
nation and all that they do, says the
LORD; whatever offering they make
here is defiled in my sight. And now 15
look back over recent times down to
this day: before one stone was laid
on another in the LORD's temple,
what was your plight? If a man came 16
to a heap of corn expecting twenty
measures, he found but ten; if he
came to a wine-vat to draw fifty
measures, he found but twenty. I 17
blasted you and all your harvest with
black blight and red and with hail,
and yet you had no mind to return
to me, says the LORD. Consider, from 18
this day onwards, from this twenty-
fourth day of the ninth month, the
day when the foundations of the
temple of the LORD are laid, consider:
will the seed still be diminished[c] in 19
the barn? Will the vine and the fig,
the pomegranate and the olive, still
bear no fruit? Not so, from this day I
will bless you.

a show my glory: or be honoured.   b Or wealth.   c diminished: prob. rdg.; Heb. om.

A word to Zerubbabel

20 On that day, the twenty-fourth day of the month, the word of the LORD 21 came to Haggai a second time: Tell Zerubbabel, governor of Judah, I will 22 shake heaven and earth; I will overthrow the thrones of kings, break the power of heathen realms, overturn chariots and their riders; horses and riders shall fall by the sword of their comrades. On that day, says the 23 LORD of Hosts, I will take you, Zerubbabel son of Shealtiel, my servant, and will wear you as a signet-ring; for you it is that I have chosen. This is the very word of the LORD of Hosts.

ZECHARIAH

Zechariah's commission

1 IN THE EIGHTH MONTH of the second year of Darius, the word of the LORD came to the prophet Zechariah son of Berechiah, son of Iddo. 2 The LORD was very angry with your 3 forefathers. Say to the people, These are the words of the LORD of Hosts: Come back to me, and I will come back to you, says the LORD of Hosts. 4 Do not be like your forefathers. They heard the prophets of old proclaim, 'These are the words of the LORD of Hosts: Turn back from your evil ways and your evil deeds.' But they did not listen or pay heed to me, says the 5 LORD. And where are your forefathers now? And the prophets, do they live 6 for ever? But the warnings and the decrees with which I charged my servants the prophets—did not these overtake your forefathers? Did they not then repent and say, 'The LORD of Hosts has treated us as he purposed; as our lives and as our deeds deserved, so has he treated us'?

Zechariah's vision of the horses

7 On the twenty-fourth day of the eleventh month, the month Shebat, in the second year of Darius, the word of the LORD came to the prophet Zechariah son of Berechiah, son of Iddo. 8 Last night I had a vision. I saw a man on a bay horse standing among the myrtles in a hollow; and behind him were other horses, black, dappled, 9 and white. 'What are these, sir?' I asked, and the angel who talked with me answered, 'I will show you what 10 they are.' Then the man standing among the myrtles said, 'They are those whom the LORD has sent to range through the world.' They re- 11 ported to the angel of the LORD as he stood among the myrtles: 'We have ranged through the world; the whole world is still and at peace.' Thereupon 12 the angel of the LORD said, 'How long, O LORD of Hosts, wilt thou withhold thy compassion from Jerusalem and the cities of Judah, upon whom thou hast vented thy wrath these seventy years?' Then the LORD spoke kind 13 and comforting words to the angel who talked with me, and the angel 14 said to me, Proclaim, These are the words of the LORD of Hosts: I am very jealous for Jerusalem and Zion. I am full of anger against the nations 15 that enjoy their ease, because, while my anger was but mild, they heaped evil on evil. Therefore these are the 16 words of the LORD: I have come back to Jerusalem with compassion, and my house shall be rebuilt in her, says the LORD of Hosts, and the measuring-line shall be stretched over Jerusalem. Proclaim once more, These are the 17 words of the LORD of Hosts: My cities shall again overflow with good things; once again the LORD will comfort Zion, once again he will make Jerusalem the city of his choice.

The horns and the smiths

I lifted my eyes and there I saw four 18 horns. I asked the angel who talked 19 with me what they were, and he answered, 'These are the horns which scattered Judah[a] and Jerusalem.' Then 20 the LORD showed me four smiths. I 21 asked what they were coming to do, and he said, 'Those horns scattered Judah and Jerusalem so completely that no man could lift his head. But

a Prob. rdg.; Heb. adds Israel.

these smiths have come to reunite them and to throw down the horns of the nations which had raised them against the land of Judah and scattered its people.'

The man with the measuring-line

2 I lifted my eyes and there I saw a man carrying a measuring-line. I asked him where he was going, and he said, 'To measure Jerusalem and see what should be its breadth and length.' 3 Then, as the angel who talked with me was going away, another angel came 4 out to meet him and said to him, Run to the young man there and tell him that Jerusalem shall be a city without walls, so numerous shall be the men 5 and cattle within it. I will be a wall of fire round her, says the LORD, and a glory in the midst of her.

Zion, a place of blessing

6 Away, away; flee from the land of the north, says the LORD, for I will make you spread your wings like the four 7 winds of heaven, says the LORD. Away, escape, you people of Zion who live in Babylon.

8   For these are the words of the LORD of Hosts, spoken when he sent me on a glorious mission[b] to the nations who have plundered you, for whoever touches you touches the apple of his 9 eye: I raise[c] my hand against them; they shall be plunder for their own slaves. So you shall know that the 10 LORD of Hosts has sent me. Shout aloud and rejoice, daughter of Zion; I am coming, I will make my dwelling 11 among you, says the LORD. Many nations shall come over to the LORD on that day and become his people, and he will make his dwelling with you. Then you shall know that the 12 LORD of Hosts has sent me to you. The LORD will once again claim Judah as his own possession in the holy land, and make Jerusalem the city of his choice.

13   Silence, all mankind, in the presence of the LORD! For he has bestirred himself out of his holy dwelling-place.

The lamp-stand and the olive-trees

4 1[d] The angel who talked with me came back and roused me as a man is roused 2 from sleep. He asked me what I saw,

and I answered, 'A lamp-stand all of gold with a bowl on it; it holds seven lamps, and there are seven pipes for the lamps on top of it, with two olive- 3 trees standing by it, one on the right of the bowl and another on the left.' I asked him, 'What are these two 11[e] olive-trees, the one on the right and the other on the left of the lamp-stand?' I asked also another question, 12 'What are the two sprays of olive beside the golden pipes which discharge the golden oil from their bowls?' He said, 'Do you not know 13 what these mean?' 'No, sir', I answered. 'These two', he said, 'are the 14 two consecrated with oil who attend the Lord of all the earth.'

Joshua the high priest

Then he showed me Joshua the high **3** priest standing before the angel of the LORD, with the Adversary[f] standing at his right hand to accuse him. The 2 LORD said to the Adversary, 'The LORD rebuke you, Satan, the LORD rebuke you who are venting your spite on Jerusalem.[g] Is not this man a brand snatched from the fire?' Now 3 Joshua was wearing filthy clothes as he stood before the angel; and the 4 angel turned and said to those in attendance on him, 'Take off his filthy clothes.' Then he turned to him and said, 'See how I have taken away your guilt from you; I will clothe you in fine vestments'; and he added, 'Let 5 a clean turban be put on his head.' So they put a clean turban on his head and clothed him in clean garments, while the angel of the LORD stood by. Then the angel of the 6 LORD gave Joshua this solemn charge: These are the words of the LORD of 7 Hosts: If you will conform to my ways and carry out your duties, you shall administer my house and be in control of my courts, and I grant you the right to come and go amongst these in attendance here. Listen, Josh- 8 ua the high priest, you and your colleagues seated here before you, all you who are an omen of things to come: I will now bring my servant, the Branch. In one day I will wipe 9–10 away the guilt of the land. On that day, says the LORD of Hosts, you shall all of you invite one another to come and sit each under his vine and his fig-tree.

b on a glorious mission: prob. rdg.; Heb. after glory.   c Or wave.   d 3. 1–10 transposed to follow
4. 14.   e 4. 4–10 transposed to follow 3. 10.   f Heb. the Satan.   g the LORD . . . Jerusalem:
or the LORD who has chosen Jerusalem rebuke you.

The stone with seven eyes

Here is the stone that I set before Joshua, a stone in which are seven eyes. I will reveal its meaning to you, **4** 4[h] says the LORD of Hosts. Then I asked the angel of the LORD who talked **5** with me, 'Sir, what are these?' And he answered, 'Do you not know what these mean?' 'No, sir', I answered. 'These seven', he said, 'are the eyes of the LORD ranging over the whole earth.'[i]

Zerubbabel will finish the building

6 Then he turned and said to me, This is the word of the LORD concerning Zerubbabel: Neither by force of arms nor by brute strength, but by my **7** spirit! says the LORD of Hosts. How does a mountain, the greatest mountain, compare with Zerubbabel? It is no higher than a plain. He shall bring out the stone called Possession[j] while **8** men acclaim its beauty. This word **9** came to me from the LORD: Zerubbabel with his own hands laid the foundation of this house and with his own hands he shall finish it. So shall you know that the LORD of Hosts has **10** sent me to you. Who has despised the day of small things? He shall rejoice when he sees Zerubbabel holding the stone called Separation.[j]

The flying scroll

5 I looked up again and saw a flying **2** scroll. He asked me what I saw, and I answered, 'A flying scroll, twenty **3** cubits long and ten cubits wide.' This, he told me, is the curse which goes out over the whole land; for by the writing on one side every thief shall be swept clean away, and by the writing on the other every perjurer shall be swept **4** clean away. I have sent it out, the LORD of Hosts has said, and it shall enter the house of the thief and the house of the man who has perjured himself in my name; it shall stay inside that house and demolish it, timbers and stones and all.

The woman in the barrel

5 The angel who talked with me came out and said to me, 'Raise your eyes and look at this thing that comes **6** forth.' I asked what it was, and he said, 'It is a great barrel coming forth,'

and he added, 'so great is their guilt **7** in all the land.' Then a round slab of lead was lifted, and a woman was **8** sitting there inside the barrel. He said, 'This is Wickedness', and he thrust her down into the barrel and rammed the leaden weight upon its mouth. I looked up again and saw two women **9** coming forth with the wind in their wings (for they had wings like a stork's), and they carried the barrel between earth and sky. I asked the **10** angel who talked with me where they were taking the barrel, and he an- **11** swered, 'To build a house for it[k] in the land of Shinar; when the house is ready, it[l] shall be set on the place prepared for it[k] there.'

The four chariots

I looked up again and saw four chariots **6** coming out between two mountains, and the mountains were made of copper.[m] The first chariot had bay horses, **2** the second black, the third white, and **3** the fourth dappled. I asked the angel **4** who talked with me, 'Sir, what are these?' He answered, 'These are the **5** four winds of heaven which have been attending the Lord of the whole earth, and they are now going forth. The chariot with the black horses is **6** going to the land of the north, that with the white to the far west,[n] that **7** with the dappled to the south, and that with the roan to the land of the east.'[o] They were eager to go and range over the whole earth; so he said, 'Go and range over the earth', and the chariots did so. Then he called **8** me to look and said, 'Those going to the land of the north have given my spirit rest in the land of the north.'

The man named the Branch

The word of the LORD came to me: **9** Take silver and gold from the exiles, **10** from Heldai, Tobiah, Jedaiah, and[p] Josiah son of Zephaniah, who have come back from Babylon. Take it and **11** make a crown; put the crown on the head of Joshua son of Jehozadak, the high priest,[q] and say to him, These **12** are the words of the LORD of Hosts: Here is a man named the Branch; he will shoot up from the ground where he is and will build the temple of the LORD. It is he who will build the **13**

---

h *See note on 4. 11 above (p. 775).*   i *These seven . . . earth: transposed from verse 10.*   j *Cp. Lev. 20.* 24–6.   k *Or her.*   l *Or she.*   m *Or bronze.*   n *to the far west: prob. rdg.; Heb. behind them.* o *to the land of the east: prob. rdg.; Heb. om.*   p *and: prob. rdg.; Heb. and go on that day your-* self and go to the house of . . .   q *Joshua . . . priest: possibly an error for Zerubbabel son of* Shealtiel, cp. 3. 5; 4. 9.

temple of the LORD, he who will assume royal dignity, will be seated on his throne and govern, with a priest at his right side, and concord shall 4 prevail between them. The crown shall be in the charge of Heldai, Tobiah, Jedaiah, and Josiah son of Zephaniah, as a memorial in the temple of the LORD.

5 Men from far away shall come and work on the building of the temple of the LORD; so shall you know that the LORD of Hosts has sent me to you. If only you will obey the LORD your God!

What the LORD requires

7 The word of the LORD came to Zechariah in the fourth year of the reign of King Darius, on the fourth day 2 of Kislev, the ninth month. Bethelsharezer sent Regem-melech with his men to seek the favour of the LORD. 3 They were to say to the priests in the house of the LORD and to the prophets, 'Am I to lament and abstain in the fifth month as I have done for so many years?' Then the word of 5 the LORD of Hosts came to me: Say to all the people of the land and to the priests, When you fasted and lamented in the fifth and seventh months these seventy years, was it indeed in 6 my honour that you fasted? And when you ate and drank, was it not to please 7 yourselves? Was it not this that the LORD proclaimed through the prophets of old, while Jerusalem was populous and peaceful, as were the cities round her, and the Negeb and the Shephelah?

8 The word of the LORD came to 9 Zechariah: These are the words of the LORD of Hosts: Administer true justice, show loyalty and compassion 10 to one another, do not oppress the orphan and the widow, the alien and the poor, do not contrive any evil one 11 against another. But they refused to listen, they turned their backs on me in defiance, they stopped their ears 12 and would not hear. Their hearts were adamant; they refused to accept instruction and all that the LORD of Hosts had taught them by his spirit through the prophets of old; and they suffered under the anger of the LORD 13 of Hosts. As they did not listen when I[r] called, so I did not listen when they 14 called, says the LORD of Hosts, and I drove them out among all the nations to whom they were strangers, leaving their land a waste behind them, so

that no one came and went. Thus they made their pleasant land a waste.

Jerusalem restored

The word of the LORD of Hosts came 8 to me: These are the words of the 2 LORD of Hosts: I have been very jealous for Zion, fiercely jealous for her. Now, says the LORD, I have come 3 back to Zion and I will dwell in Jerusalem. Jerusalem shall be called the City of Truth, and the mountain of the LORD of Hosts shall be called the Holy Mountain. These are the words 4 of the LORD of Hosts: Once again shall old men and old women sit in the streets of Jerusalem, each leaning on a stick because of their great age; and the streets of the city shall be full 5 of boys and girls, playing in the streets. These are the words of the 6 LORD of Hosts: Even if it may seem impossible[s] to the survivors of this nation on that day, will it also seem impossible to me?[t] This is the very word of the LORD of Hosts. These are 7 the words of the LORD of Hosts: See, I will rescue my people from the countries of the east and the west, and 8 bring them back to live in Jerusalem. They shall be my people, and I will be their God, in truth and justice.

Symbol of blessing

These are the words of the LORD of 9 Hosts: Take courage, you who in these days hear, from the prophets who were present when the foundations were laid for the house of the LORD of Hosts, their promise that the temple is to be rebuilt. Till that time 10 there was no hiring either of man or of beast, no one could safely go about his business because of his enemies, and I set all men one against another. But now I am not the same towards 11 the survivors of this people as I was in former days, says the LORD of Hosts. For they shall sow in safety; 12 the vine shall yield its fruit and the soil its produce, the heavens shall give their dew; with all these things I will endow the survivors of this people. You, house of Judah and house of 13 Israel, have been the very symbol of a curse to all the nations; and now I will save you, and you shall become the symbol of a blessing. Courage! Do not be afraid.

Love truth and peace

For these are the words of the LORD 14 of Hosts: Whereas I resolved to ruin

r Prob. rdg.; Heb. he.　　s Or wonderful.　　t will . . . me?: or it will seem wonderful also to me.

you because your ancestors roused me to anger, says the LORD of Hosts, and
15 I did not relent, so in these days I have once more[u] resolved to do good to Jerusalem and to the house of
16 Judah; do not be afraid. This is what you shall do: speak the truth to each other, administer true and sound jus-
17 tice in the city gate. Do not contrive any evil one against another, and do not keep perjury, for all this I hate. This is the very word of the LORD.

18 The word of the LORD of Hosts
19 came to me: These are the words of the LORD of Hosts: The fasts of the fourth month and of the fifth, the seventh, and the tenth, shall become festivals of joy and gladness for the house of Judah. Love truth and peace.

The LORD of hosts in Jerusalem

20 These are the words of the LORD of Hosts: Nations and dwellers in great
21 cities shall yet come; people of one city shall come to those of another and say, 'Let us go and entreat the favour of the LORD, and resort to the LORD of Hosts; and I will come too.'
22 So great nations and mighty peoples shall resort to the LORD of Hosts in Jerusalem and entreat his favour.
23 These are the words of the LORD of Hosts: In those days, when ten men from nations of every language pluck up courage, they shall pluck the robe of a Jew and say, 'We will go with you because we have heard that God is with you.'

Judah's triumph over her enemies

9 An oracle: the word of the LORD.

He has come to the land of Hadrach and[v] established himself in Damascus;
for the capital city[w] of Aram is the LORD's,
as are all the tribes of Israel.
2 [x]Sidon has closed her frontier against Hamath,
for she is very wary.
3 Tyre has built herself a rampart;
she has heaped up silver like dust and gold like mud in the streets.
4 But wait, the Lord will dispossess her
and strike down the power of her ships,

and the city itself will be destroyed by fire.
Let Ashkelon see it and be afraid; 5
Gaza shall writhe in terror,
and Ekron's hope shall be extinguished;
kings shall vanish from Gaza,
and Ashkelon shall be unpeopled;
half-breeds shall settle in Ashdod, 6
and I will uproot the pride of the Philistine.
I will dash the blood of sacrifices 7
from his mouth
and his loathsome offerings from his teeth;
and his survivors shall belong[y] to our God
and become like a clan in Judah,
and Ekron like a Jebusite.
And I will post a garrison for my 8 house
so that no one may pass in or out,
and no oppressor shall ever overrun them.
[This I have lived to see with my own eyes.]

Zion's king

Rejoice, rejoice, daughter of Zion, 9
shout aloud, daughter of Jerusalem;
for see, your king is coming to you,
his cause won, his victory gained,
humble and mounted on an ass,
on a foal, the young of a she-ass.
He shall banish chariots from Eph- 10 raim
and war-horses from Jerusalem;
the warrior's bow shall be banished.
He shall speak peaceably to every nation,
and his rule shall extend from sea to sea,
from the River to the ends of the earth.

Zion restored

And as for you, by your covenant 11 with me sealed in blood
I release your prisoners from the dungeon.[z]
(Come back to the stronghold, you 12 prisoners who wait in hope.)
Now is the day announced
when I will grant you twofold[a] reparation.
For my bow is strung, O Judah; 13
I have laid the arrow to it, O Ephraim;
I have roused your sons, O Zion,[b]

---

u once more: or changed my mind and.   v He has come . . . and: prob. rdg.; Heb. In the land of
Hadrach he has . . .   w capital city: or chief part.   x Prob. rdg.; Heb. prefixes Tyre and.
y his survivors shall belong: or he shall become kin.   z Prob. rdg.; Heb. adds no water in it.
a Or equal.   b Prob. rdg.; Heb. adds against your sons, O Javan (or Greece).

and made you into the sword of a
warrior.
14 The LORD shall appear above them,
and his arrow shall flash like lightning;
the Lord GOD shall blow a blast on
the horn
and march with the storm-winds of
the south.
15 The LORD of Hosts will be their
shield;
they shall prevail, they shall trample on the sling-stones;
they shall be roaring drunk as if
with wine,
brimful as a bowl, drenched like the
corners of the altar.
16 So on that day the LORD their God
will save them, his own people,
like sheep,
setting them all about his land,
like[c] jewels set to sparkle in a crown.
17 What wealth, what beauty, is theirs:
corn to strengthen young men,
and new wine for maidens!
10 Ask of the LORD rain in the autumn,
ask him for rain in the spring,
the LORD who makes the storm-
clouds,
and he will give you showers of rain
and to every man grass in his field;
2 for the household gods make mischievous promises;
diviners see false signs,
they tell lying dreams[d]
and talk raving nonsense.
Men wander about like sheep
in distress for lack of a shepherd.
3 My anger is turned against the
shepherds,
and I will visit with punishment
the leaders of the flock;
but the LORD of Hosts will visit his
flock,
the house of Judah,
and make them his royal war-horses.
4 They shall be corner-stone and tent-
peg,
they shall be the bow ready for
battle,
and from them shall come every
commander.
5 Together they shall be like warriors
who tramp the muddy ways in
battle,
and they will fight because the
LORD is with them;
they will put horsemen shamefully
to rout.
6 And I will give strength to the
house of Judah

and grant victory to[e] the house of
Joseph;
I will restore them, for I have
pitied them,
and they shall be as though I had
never cast them off;
for I am the LORD their God and I will
answer them.
So Ephraim shall be like warriors, 7
glad like men cheerful with wine,
and their sons shall see and be glad;
so let their hearts exult in the LORD.
I will whistle to call them in, for I 8
have redeemed them;
and they shall be as many as once
they were.
If I disperse them[f] among the 9
nations,
in far-off lands they will remember
me
and will rear their sons and then
return.
Then will I fetch them home from 10
Egypt
and gather them in from Assyria;
I will lead them into Gilead and
Lebanon
until there is no more room for them.
Dire distress[g] shall come upon the 11
Euphrates
and shall beat down its turbulent
waters;
all the depths of the Nile shall run
dry.
The pride of Assyria shall be
brought down,
and the sceptre of Egypt shall pass
away;
but Israel's strength shall be in the 12
LORD,
and they shall march proudly in his
name.
This is the very word of the LORD.

Throw open your gates, O Lebanon, 11
that fire may feed on your cedars.
Howl, every pine-tree; for the cedars 2
have fallen,
mighty trees are ravaged.
Howl, every oak of Bashan;
for the impenetrable forest is laid
low.
Hark to the howling of the shep- 3
herds,
for their rich pastures are ravaged.
Hark to the roar of the young lions,
for Jordan's dense thickets are
ravaged.

The shepherd allegory

These were the words of the LORD my 4
God: Fatten the flock for slaughter.

c *like*: *prob. rdg.*; *Heb. for.*   d *they . . . dreams*: *or* dreaming women make empty promises.
e *grant victory to*: *or* expand.   f *Or* scatter them like seed.   g *Dire distress*: *or* An enemy.

5 Those who buy will slaughter it and incur no guilt; those who sell will say, 'Blessed be the LORD, I am rich!' Its
6 shepherds will have no pity for it. For I will never again pity the inhabitants of the earth, says the LORD. I will put every man in the power of his neighbour and his king, and as each country is crushed I will not rescue him from their hands.

7 So I fattened the flock for slaughter for the dealers. I took two staves: one I called Favour and the other Union,
8 and so I fattened the flock. In one month I got rid of the three shepherds, for I had lost patience with them and
9 they had come to abhor me. Then I said to the flock, 'I will not fatten you any more. Any that are to die, let them die; any that stray, let them stray; and the rest can devour one
10 another.' I took my staff called Favour and snapped it in two, annulling the covenant which the LORD[h] had
11 made with all nations. So it was annulled that day, and the dealers who were watching me knew that all this
12 was the word of the LORD. I said to them, 'If it suits you, give me my wages; otherwise keep them.' Then they weighed out my wages, thirty
13 pieces of silver. The LORD said to me, 'Throw it into the treasury.' I took the thirty pieces of silver—that noble sum at which I was valued and rejected by them!—and threw them into the house of the LORD, into the
14 treasury. Then I snapped in two my second staff called Union, annulling the brotherhood between Judah and Israel.

15 Then the LORD said to me, Equip yourself again as a shepherd, a worth-
16 less one; for I am about to install a shepherd in the land who will neither miss any that are lost nor search for those that have gone astray nor heal the injured nor nurse the sickly, but will eat the flesh of the fat beasts and throw away their broken bones.

The shepherd prophecy

17 Alas for the worthless shepherd who abandons the sheep!
A sword shall fall on his arm and on his right eye;
his arm shall be shrivelled
and his right eye blinded.
13 7[i] This is the very word of the LORD of Hosts:
O sword, awake against my shepherd

and against him who works with me.
Strike the shepherd, and the sheep will be scattered,
and I will turn my hand against the shepherd boys.
8 This also is the very word of the LORD:
It shall happen throughout the land that two thirds of the people shall be struck down and die,
while one third of them shall be left there.
9 Then I will pass this third through the fire
and I will refine them as silver is refined,
and assay them as gold is assayed.
Then they will invoke me by my name,
and I myself will answer them;
I will say, 'They are my people',
and they shall say, 'The LORD is our God.'

Jerusalem, a rock

1 An oracle. This is the word of the LORD concerning Israel, the very word of the LORD who stretched out the heavens and founded the earth, and who formed the spirit of man
2 within him: I am making the steep approaches to Jerusalem slippery for all the nations pressing round her; and Judah will be caught up in the
3 siege of Jerusalem. On that day, when all the nations of the earth will be gathered against her, I will make Jerusalem a rock too heavy for any people to remove, and all who try to
4 lift it shall injure themselves. On that day, says the LORD, I will strike every horse with panic and its rider with madness; I will keep watch over Judah, but I will strike all the horses of the other nations with blindness.
5 Then the clans of Judah shall say to themselves, 'The inhabitants of Jerusalem find their strength[j] in the LORD of Hosts their God.'
6 On that day I will make the clans of Judah like a brazier in woodland, like a torch blazing among sheaves of corn. They shall devour all the nations round them, right and left, while the people of Jerusalem remain safe in their city. The LORD will first
7 set free all the families[k] of Judah, so that the glory of David's line and of the inhabitants of Jerusalem may not surpass that of Judah.
8 On that day the LORD will shield

---

h the LORD: *prob. rdg.; Heb.* I.   *i 13. 7–9 transposed to this point.*   *j* The . . . strength: *prob.*
rdg.; Heb. O inhabitants of Jerusalem, I am strong.   *k Or* tents.

the inhabitants of Jerusalem; on that day the very weakest of them shall be like David, and the line of David like God, like the angel of the Lord going 9 before them.

On that day I will set about de- 10 stroying all the nations that come against Jerusalem, but I will pour a spirit of pity and compassion into the line of David and the inhabitants of Jerusalem. Then

They shall look on me, on him whom
    they have pierced,

and shall wail over him as over an only child, and shall grieve for him 11 bitterly as for a first-born son.

On that day the mourning in Jeru- salem shall be as great as the mourning 12 over Hadad-rimmon in the vale of Megiddo. The land shall wail, each family by itself: the family of David by itself and its women by them- 13 selves; the family of Nathan by itself and its women by themselves; the family of Levi by itself and its women by themselves; the family of Shimei 14 by itself and its women by themselves; all the remaining families by them- selves and their women by themselves.

A cleansing fountain

13 On that day a fountain shall be opened for the line of David and for the inhabitants of Jerusalem, to remove all sin and impurity.

2   On that day, says the Lord of Hosts, I will erase the names of the idols from the land, and they shall be remembered no longer; I will also re- move the prophets and the spirit of 3 uncleanness from the land. Thereafter, if a man continues to prophesy, his parents, his own father and mother, will say to him, 'You shall live no longer, for you have spoken falsely in the name of the Lord.' His own father and mother will pierce him through because he has prophesied. 4 On that day every prophet shall be ashamed of his vision when he pro- phesies, nor shall he wear a robe of 5 coarse hair in order to deceive. He will say, 'I am no prophet, I am a tiller of the soil who has been schooled 6 in lust from boyhood.' 'What', some- one will ask, 'are these scars on your chest?' And he will answer, 'I got them in the house of my lovers.'[l]

The Lord will fight for Jerusalem

14 A day is coming for the Lord to act, and the plunder taken from you shall be shared out while you stand by. I 2 will gather all the peoples to fight against Jerusalem; the city shall be taken, the houses plundered and the women raped. Half the city shall go into exile, but the rest of the nation in the city shall not be wiped out. The Lord will come out and fight 3 against those peoples, as in the days of his prowess on the field of battle. On 4 that day his feet shall stand on the Mount of Olives, which is opposite Jerusalem to the east, and the mount- ain shall be cleft in two by an im- mense valley running east and west; half the mountain shall move north- wards and half southwards. The valley 5 between the hills[m] shall be blocked, for the new valley between them will reach as far as Asal. Blocked it shall be as it was blocked by the earth- quake in the time of Uzziah king of Judah, and the Lord my God will appear with all the holy ones.

The Lord will reign

On that day there shall be neither 6 heat nor cold nor frost. It shall be all 7 one day, whose coming is known only to the Lord, without distinction of day or night, and at evening-time there shall be light.

On that day living water shall 8 issue from Jerusalem, half flowing to the eastern sea and half to the western, in summer and winter alike. Then the 9 Lord shall become king over all the earth; on that day the Lord shall be one Lord and his name the one name. The whole land shall be levelled, flat 10 as the Arabah from Geba to Rim- mon southwards; but Jerusalem shall stand high in her place, and shall be full of people from the Benjamin Gate [to the point where the former gate stood,] to the Corner Gate, and from the Tower of Hananel to the king's wine-vats. Men shall live in 11 Jerusalem, and never again shall a solemn ban be laid upon her; men shall live there in peace. The Lord 12 will strike down all the nations who warred against Jerusalem, and the plague shall be this: their flesh shall rot while they stand on their feet, their eyes shall rot in their sockets, and their tongues shall rot in their mouths.

On that day a great panic, sent by 13 the Lord, shall fall on them. At the very moment when a man would en- courage his comrade his hand shall be raised to strike him down. Judah too 14

l Verses 7–9 transposed to follow 11. 17.   m *Prob. rdg.; Heb.* my hills.

shall join in the fray in Jerusalem, and the wealth of the surrounding nations will be swept away—gold and silver 15 and apparel in great abundance. And slaughter shall be the fate of horse and mule, camel and ass, the fate of every beast in those armies.

Jerusalem, centre of worship

16 All who survive of the nations which attacked Jerusalem shall come up year by year to worship the King, the LORD of Hosts, and to keep the pilgrim- 17 feast of Tabernacles. If any of the families of the earth do not go up to Jerusalem to worship the King, the LORD of Hosts, no rain shall fall upon 18 them. If any family of Egypt does not go up and enter the city, then the same disaster shall overtake it as that which the LORD will inflict on any nation which does not go up to keep the feast. This shall be the punish- 19 ment of Egypt and of any nation which does not go up to keep the feast of Tabernacles.

On that day, not a bell on a war- 20 horse but shall be inscribed 'Holy to the LORD', and the pots in the house of the LORD shall be like the bowls before the altar. Every pot in Jeru- 21 salem and Judah shall be holy to the LORD of Hosts, and all who sacrifice shall come and shall take some of them and boil the flesh in them. So when that time comes, no trader shall again be seen in the house of the LORD of Hosts.

MALACHI

1 An oracle. The word of the LORD to Israel through Malachi.[a]

The LORD's love for Jacob

2 I love you, says the LORD. You ask, 'How hast thou shown love to us?' Is not Esau Jacob's brother? the 3 LORD answers. I love Jacob, but I hate Esau; I have turned his mountains into a waste and his ancestral home 4 into a lodging in the wilderness. When Edom says, 'We are beaten down; let us rebuild our ruined homes', these are the words of the LORD of Hosts: If they rebuild, I will pull down. They shall be called a realm of wickedness, a people whom the LORD has cursed for 5 ever. You yourselves will see it with your own eyes; you yourselves will say, 'The LORD's greatness reaches beyond the realm of Israel.'

Unacceptable gifts

6 A son honours his father, and a slave goes in fear of his master. If I am a father, where is the honour due to me? If I am a master, where is the fear due to me? So says the LORD of Hosts to you, you priests who despise my name. You ask, 'How have we de- 7 spised thy name?' Because you have offered defiled food on my altar. You ask, 'How have we defiled thee?' Because you have thought that the table of the LORD may be despised, that if you offer a blind victim, there is 8 nothing wrong, and if you offer a victim lame or diseased, there is nothing wrong. If you brought such a gift to the governor, would he receive you or show you favour? says the LORD of Hosts. But now, if you 9 placate God, he may show you mercy; if you do this, will he withhold his favour from you? So the LORD of Hosts has spoken. Better far that one 10 of you should close the great door altogether, so that the light might not fall thus all in vain upon my altar! I have no pleasure in you, says the LORD of Hosts; I will accept no offering from you. From furthest east to 11 furthest west my name is great among the nations. Everywhere fragrant sacrifice and pure gifts are offered in my name; for my name is great among the nations, says the LORD of Hosts. But you profane it by 12 thinking that the table of the LORD may be defiled, and that you can offer on it food you yourselves despise. You sniff at it, says the LORD of Hosts, 13 and say, 'How irksome!' If you bring as your offering victims that are mutilated, lame, or diseased, shall I accept them from you? says the LORD. A curse on the cheat who pays 14

a Malachi: or my messenger.

his vows by sacrificing a damaged victim to the Lord, though he has a sound ram in his flock! I am the great king, says the LORD of Hosts, and my name is held in awe among the nations.

Unacceptable teaching

2 And now, you priests, this decree is for you: if you will not listen to me and pay heed to the honouring of my name, says the LORD of Hosts, then I will lay a curse upon you. I will turn your blessings into a curse; yes, into a curse, because you pay no heed. I will cut off your arm,[b] fling offal in your faces, the offal of your pilgrim-feasts, and I will banish you from my presence. Then you will know that I have issued this decree against you: my covenant with Levi falls to the ground, says the LORD of Hosts. My covenant was with him: I bestowed life and prosperity on him; I laid on him the duty of reverence, he revered me and lived in awe of my name. The instruction he gave was true, and no word of injustice fell from his lips; he walked in harmony with me and in uprightness, and he turned many back from sin. For men hang upon the words of the priest and seek knowledge and instruction from him, because he is the messenger of the LORD of Hosts. But you have turned away from that course; you have made many stumble with your instruction; you have set at nought the covenant with the Levites, says the LORD of Hosts. So I, in my turn, have made you despicable and mean in the eyes of the people, in so far as you disregard my ways and show partiality in your instruction.

Forbidden marriages

10 Have we not all one father? Did not one God create us? Why do we violate the covenant of our forefathers by being faithless to one another? Judah is faithless, and abominable things are done in Israel and in Jerusalem; Judah has violated the holiness of the LORD by loving and marrying daughters of a foreign god. May the LORD banish any who do this from the dwellings of Jacob, nomads or settlers, even though they bring offerings to the LORD of Hosts.

Marriage and divorce

13 Here is another thing that you do: you weep and moan, and you drown the altar of the LORD with tears, but he still refuses to look at the offering or receive an acceptable gift from you. You ask why. It is because the LORD has borne witness against you on behalf of the wife of your youth. You have been unfaithful to her, though she is your partner and your wife by solemn covenant. Did not the one God make her, both flesh and spirit? And what does the one God require but godly children? Keep watch on your spirit, and do not be unfaithful to the wife of your youth. If a man divorces or puts away his spouse, he overwhelms her with cruelty, says the LORD of Hosts the God of Israel. Keep watch on your spirit, and do not be unfaithful.

The LORD is coming

You have wearied the LORD with your talk. You ask, 'How have we wearied him?' By saying that all evildoers are good in the eyes of the LORD, that he is pleased with them, or by asking, 'Where is the God of justice?' Look, **3** I am sending my messenger[c] who will clear a path before me. Suddenly the Lord whom you seek will come to his temple; the messenger of the covenant in whom you delight is here, here already, says the LORD of Hosts. Who can endure the day of his coming? Who can stand firm when he appears? He is like a refiner's fire, like fuller's soap; he will take his seat, refining and purifying;[d] he will purify the Levites and cleanse them like gold and silver, and so they shall be fit to bring offerings to the LORD. Thus the offerings of Judah and Jerusalem shall be pleasing to the LORD as they were in days of old, in years long past. I will appear before you in court, prompt to testify against sorcerers, adulterers, and perjurers, against those who wrong[e] the hired labourer, the widow, and the orphan, who thrust the alien aside and have no fear of me, says the LORD of Hosts.

Defrauding God

I am the LORD, unchanging; and you, too, have not ceased to be sons of Jacob. From the days of your forefathers you have been wayward and have not kept my laws. If you will return to me, I will return to you, says the LORD of Hosts. You ask, 'How can we return?' May man defraud God, that you defraud me? You ask,

b Or posterity.   c my messenger: Heb. Malachi.
rdg.; Heb. adds the wages of.   d Prob. rdg.; Heb. adds silver.   e Prob.

'How have we defrauded thee?' Why,
9 in tithes and contributions. There is
a curse, a curse on you all, the whole
nation of you, because you defraud
10 me. Bring the tithes into the treasury,
all of them; let there be food in my
house. Put me to the proof, says the
LORD of Hosts, and see if I do not
open windows in the sky and pour a
blessing on you as long as there is
11 need. I will forbid pests to destroy
the produce of your soil or make your
vines barren, says the LORD of Hosts.
12 All nations shall count you happy, for
yours shall be a favoured land, says
the LORD of Hosts.

Hard words

13 You have used hard words about me,
says the LORD, and then you ask,
'How have we spoken against thee?'
14 You have said, 'It is useless to serve
God; what do we gain from the LORD
of Hosts by observing his rules and
15 behaving with deference? We ourselves count the arrogant happy; it
is evildoers who are successful; they
have put God to the proof and come
to no harm.'

The LORD's possession

16 Then those who feared the LORD
talked together, and the LORD paid
heed and listened. A record was written before him of those who feared

him and kept his name in mind. They 17
shall be mine, says the LORD of Hosts,
my own possession against the day
that I appoint, and I will spare them
as a man spares the son who serves
him. You will again tell good men 18
from bad, the servant of God from
the man who does not serve him.

The triumph of the righteous

The day comes, glowing like a furnace; 4
all the arrogant and the evildoers
shall be chaff, and that day when it
comes shall set them ablaze, says the
LORD of Hosts, it shall leave them
neither root nor branch. But for you 2
who fear my name, the sun of righteousness shall rise with healing in his
wings, and you shall break loose like
calves released from the stall. On the 3
day that I act, you shall trample
down the wicked, for they will be
ashes under the soles of your feet,
says the LORD of Hosts.

Remember the law of Moses my 4
servant, the rules and precepts which
I bade him deliver to all Israel at
Horeb.

Look, I will send you the prophet 5
Elijah before the great and terrible
day of the LORD comes. He will re- 6
concile fathers to sons and sons to
fathers, lest I come and put the land
under a ban to destroy it.

APPENDIX

MEASURES OF LENGTH

	span	cubit	rod[a]
span	1	..	..
cubit	2	1	..
rod[a]	12	6	1

The 'short cubit' was traditionally the measure from the elbow to the knuckles of the closed fist; and what seems to be intended as a 'long cubit' measured a 'cubit and a hand-breadth', i.e. 7 instead of 6 hand-breadths (Ezek. 40. 5). What is meant by cubits 'according to the old standard of measurement' (2 Chr. 3. 3) is presumably this pre-exilic cubit of 7 hand-breadths. Modern estimates of the Hebrew cubit range from 12 to 25·2 inches, without allowing for varying local standards.

MEASURES OF CAPACITY

liquid measures	equivalences	dry measures
'log'	1 'log'	..
..	4 'log'	'kab'
..	7½ 'log'	'omer'
'hin'	12 'log'	..
'bath'	72 'log'	'ephah'
'kor'	720 'log'	'homer' or 'kor'

According to ancient authorities the Hebrew 'log' was of the same capacity as the Roman *sextarius*; this according to the best available evidence was equivalent to 0·99 pint of the English standard.

WEIGHTS AND COINS

	heavy (Phoenician) standard			light (Babylonian) standard		
	shekel	mina	talent	shekel	mina	talent
shekel	1	..	..	1	..	..
mina	50	1	..	60	1	..
talent	3,000	60	1	3,600	60	1

The 'gerah' was 1/20 of the sacred or heavy shekel and probably 1/24 of the light shekel.

The 'sacred shekel' according to tradition was identical with the heavy shekel; while the 'shekel of the standard recognized by merchants' (Gen. 23. 16) was perhaps a weight stamped with its value as distinct from one not so stamped and requiring to be weighed on the spot.

The weight and value of the shekel varied so greatly according to the district and with the passing centuries that its evaluation in modern terms is impossible. Recent discoveries suggest that it may have weighed approximately 11·5 grammes.

Coins are not mentioned before the Exile. Only the 'daric' (1 Chr. 29. 7) and the 'drachma' (Ezra 2. 69; Neh. 7. 70–2), if this is a distinct coin, are found in the Old Testament; the former is said to have been a month's pay for a soldier in the Persian army, while the latter will have been the Greek silver drachma, estimated at approximately 4·4 grammes. The 'shekel' of this period (Neh. 5. 15) as a coin was probably the Graeco-Persian *siglos* weighing 5·6 grammes.

a Hebrew literally 'reed', the length of Ezekiel's measuring-rod.

THE NEW TESTAMENT

THE GOSPEL ACCORDING TO
MATTHEW

Family tree of Jesus Christ

1 A TABLE of the descent of Jesus Christ, son of David, son of Abraham.

2 Abraham was the father of Isaac, Isaac of Jacob, Jacob of Judah and 3 his brothers, Judah of Perez and Zarah (their mother was Tamar), Perez 4 of Hezron, Hezron of Ram, Ram of Amminadab, Amminadab of Nah-5 shon, Nahshon of Salma, Salma of Boaz (his mother was Rahab), Boaz of Obed (his mother was Ruth), Obed 6 of Jesse; and Jesse was the father of King David.

David was the father of Solomon (his mother had been the wife of 7 Uriah), Solomon of Rehoboam, Rehoboam of Abijah, Abijah of Asa, 8 Asa of Jehoshaphat, Jehoshaphat of 9 Joram, Joram of Azariah, Azariah of Jotham, Jotham of Ahaz, Ahaz 10 of Hezekiah, Hezekiah of Manasseh, Manasseh of Amon, Amon of Josiah; 11 and Josiah was the father of Jeconiah and his brothers at the time of the deportation to Babylon.

12 After the deportation Jeconiah was the father of Shealtiel, Shealtiel of 13 Zerubbabel, Zerubbabel of Abiud, Abiud of Eliakim, Eliakim of Azor, 14 Azor of Zadok, Zadok of Achim, 15 Achim of Eliud, Eliud of Eleazar, Eleazar of Matthan, Matthan of Ja-16 cob, Jacob of Joseph, the husband of Mary, who gave birth to[a] Jesus called Messiah.

17 There were thus fourteen generations in all from Abraham to David, fourteen from David until the deportation to Babylon, and fourteen from the deportation until the Messiah.

Birth of Jesus Christ

18 This is the story of the birth of the Messiah. Mary his mother was betrothed to Joseph; before their marriage she found that she was with 19 child by the Holy Spirit. Being a man of principle, and at the same time wanting to save her from exposure, Joseph desired to have the marriage contract set aside quietly. He had 20 resolved on this, when an angel of the Lord appeared to him in a dream. 'Joseph son of David,' said the angel, 'do not be afraid to take Mary home with you as your wife. It is by the Holy Spirit that she has conceived this child. She will bear a son; and 21 you shall give him the name Jesus (Saviour), for he will save his people from their sins.' All this happened in 22 order to fulfil what the Lord declared through the prophet: 'The virgin 23 will conceive and bear a son, and he shall be called Emmanuel', a name which means 'God is with us'. Rising 24 from sleep Joseph did as the angel had directed him; he took Mary home to be his wife, but had no intercourse 25 with her until her son was born. And he named the child Jesus.

Visitors from the east

Jesus was born at Bethlehem in **2** Judaea during the reign of Herod. After his birth astrologers from the 2 east arrived in Jerusalem, asking, 'Where is the child who is born to be king of the Jews?[b] We observed the rising of his star, and we have come to pay him homage.' King Herod was 3 greatly perturbed when he heard this; and so was the whole of Jerusalem. He called a meeting of the chief 4 priests and lawyers of the Jewish people, and put before them the question: 'Where is it that the Messiah is to be born?' 'At Bethlehem in 5 Judaea', they replied; and they referred him to the prophecy which reads: 'Bethlehem in the land of Judah, you 6 are far from least in the eyes of[c] the rulers of Judah; for out of you shall come a leader to be the shepherd of my people Israel.'

Herod next called the astrologers to 7 meet him in private, and ascertained from them the time when the star had appeared. He then sent them on to 8 Bethlehem, and said, 'Go and make

a Some witnesses read Joseph, to whom was betrothed Mary, a virgin, who gave birth to . . .; one witness has Joseph, and Joseph, to whom Mary, a virgin, was betrothed, was the father of . . .
b Or Where is the king of the Jews who has just been born? c Or least among.

a careful inquiry for the child. When you have found him, report to me, so that I may go myself and pay him homage.'

9 They set out at the king's bidding; and the star which they had seen at its rising went ahead of them until it
10 stopped above the place where the
11 child lay. At the sight of the star they were overjoyed. Entering the house, they saw the child with Mary his mother, and bowed to the ground in homage to him; then they opened their treasures and offered him gifts:
12 gold, frankincense, and myrrh. And being warned in a dream not to go back to Herod, they returned home another way.

Escape to Egypt

13 After they had gone, an angel of the Lord appeared to Joseph in a dream, and said to him, 'Rise up, take the child and his mother and escape with them to Egypt, and stay there until I tell you; for Herod is going to search for the child to do away with him.'
14 So Joseph rose from sleep, and taking mother and child by night he went
15 away with them to Egypt, and there he stayed till Herod's death. This was to fulfil what the Lord had declared through the prophet: 'I called my son out of Egypt.'
16 When Herod saw how the astrologers had tricked him he fell into a passion, and gave orders for the massacre of all children in Bethlehem and its neighbourhood, of the age of two years or less, corresponding with the time he had ascertained from
17 the astrologers. So the words spoken through Jeremiah the prophet were
18 fulfilled: 'A voice was heard in Rama, wailing and loud laments; it was Rachel weeping for her children, and refusing all consolation, because they were no more.'

Return to Palestine

19 The time came that Herod died; and an angel of the Lord appeared in a
20 dream to Joseph in Egypt and said to him, 'Rise up, take the child and his mother, and go with them to the land of Israel, for the men who threat-
21 ened the child's life are dead.' So he rose, took mother and child with him,
22 and came to the land of Israel. Hearing, however, that Archelaus had succeeded his father Herod as king of Judaea, he was afraid to go there. And being warned by a dream, he withdrew to the region of Galilee;

23 there he settled in a town called Nazareth. This was to fulfil the words spoken through the prophets: 'He shall be called a Nazarene.'

John the Baptist preaches repentance

About that time John the Baptist appeared as a preacher in the Judaean wilderness; his theme was: 'Repent;
2 for the kingdom of Heaven is upon you!' It is of him that the prophet
3 Isaiah spoke when he said, 'A voice crying aloud in the wilderness, "Prepare a way for the Lord; clear a straight path for him."'

4 John's clothing was a rough coat of camel's hair, with a leather belt round his waist, and his food was locusts and wild honey. They flocked
5 to him from Jerusalem, from all Judaea, and the whole Jordan valley,
6 and were baptized by him in the River Jordan, confessing their sins.
7 When he saw many of the Pharisees and Sadducees coming for baptism he said to them: 'You vipers' brood! Who warned you to escape
8 from the coming retribution? Then prove your repentance by the fruit it bears; and do not presume to say to
9 yourselves, "We have Abraham for our father." I tell you that God can make children for Abraham out of
10 these stones here. Already the axe is laid to the roots of the trees; and every tree that fails to produce good fruit is cut down and thrown on the
11 fire. I baptize you with water, for repentance; but the one who comes after me is mightier than I. I am not fit to take off his shoes. He will baptize you with the Holy Spirit and with
12 fire. His shovel is ready in his hand and he will winnow his threshing-floor; the wheat he will gather into his granary, but he will burn the chaff on a fire that can never go out.'

Jesus is baptized

13 Then Jesus arrived at the Jordan from Galilee, and came to John to be
14 baptized by him. John tried to dissuade him. 'Do you come to me?' he said; 'I need rather to be baptized by
15 you.' Jesus replied, 'Let it be so for the present; we do well to conform in this way with all that God requires.'
16 John then allowed him to come. After baptism Jesus came up out of the water at once, and at that moment heaven opened; he saw the Spirit of God descending like a dove to alight

7 upon him; and a voice from heaven was heard saying, 'This is my Son, my Beloved,[d] on whom my favour rests.'

The temptation of Jesus

1 Jesus was then led away by the Spirit into the wilderness, to be tempted by the devil.

2 For forty days and nights he fasted, and at the end of them he was fa-

3 mished. The tempter approached him and said, 'If you are the Son of God, tell these stones to become bread.'

4 Jesus answered, 'Scripture says, "Man cannot live on bread alone; he lives on every word that God utters."'

5 The devil then took him to the Holy City and set him on the parapet

6 of the temple. 'If you are the Son of God,' he said, 'throw yourself down; for Scripture says, "He will put his angels in charge of you, and they will support you in their arms, for fear you should strike your foot against a

7 stone."' Jesus answered him, 'Scripture says again, "You are not to put the Lord your God to the test."'

8 Once again, the devil took him to a very high mountain, and showed him all the kingdoms of the world in

9 their glory. 'All these', he said, 'I will give you, if you will only fall down

10 and do me homage.' But Jesus said, 'Begone, Satan! Scripture says, "You shall do homage to the Lord your God and worship him alone."'

11 Then the devil left him; and angels appeared and waited on him.

Jesus starts work in Galilee

12 When he heard that John had been arrested, Jesus withdrew to Galilee;

13 and leaving Nazareth he went and settled at Capernaum on the Sea of Galilee, in the district of Zebulun

14 and Naphtali. This was to fulfil the passage in the prophet Isaiah which

15 tells of 'the land of Zebulun, the land of Naphtali, the Way of the Sea, the land beyond Jordan, heathen Galilee', and says:

16 'The people that lived in darkness saw a great light; light dawned on the dwellers in the land of death's dark shadow.'

17 From that day Jesus began to proclaim the message: 'Repent; for[e] the kingdom of Heaven is upon you.'

Jesus calls four fishermen

18 Jesus was walking by the Sea of Galilee when he saw two brothers, Simon called Peter and his brother Andrew, casting a net into the lake; for they were fishermen. Jesus said to

19 them, 'Come with me, and I will make you fishers of men.' And at once they

20 left their nets and followed him.

21 He went on, and saw another pair of brothers, James son of Zebedee and his brother John; they were in the boat with their father Zebedee, overhauling their nets. He called them,

22 and at once they left the boat and their father, and followed him.

Teaching, preaching, and healing

23 He went round the whole of Galilee, teaching in the synagogues, preaching the gospel of the Kingdom, and curing whatever illness or infirmity there was

24 among the people. His fame reached the whole of Syria; and sufferers from every kind of illness, racked with pain, possessed by devils, epileptic, or paralysed, were all brought to him,

25 and he cured them. Great crowds also followed him, from Galilee and the Ten Towns,[f] from Jerusalem and Judaea, and from Transjordan.

The Sermon on the Mount

5 When he saw the crowds he went up the hill. There he took his seat, and when his disciples had gathered round

2 him he began to address them. And this is the teaching he gave:

Who is truly blest?

3 'How blest are those who know their need of God; the kingdom of Heaven is theirs.

4 How blest are the sorrowful; they shall find consolation.

5 How blest are those of a gentle spirit; they shall have the earth for their possession.

6 How blest are those who hunger and thirst to see right prevail;[g] they shall be satisfied.

7 How blest are those who show mercy; mercy shall be shown to them.

8 How blest are those whose hearts are pure; they shall see God.

9 How blest are the peacemakers; God shall call them his sons.

---

d Or This is my only Son.   e Some witnesses omit Repent; for.   f Greek Decapolis.   g Or to do what is right.

10 How blest are those who have suffered
persecution for the cause of right;
the kingdom of Heaven is theirs.

11 'How blest you are, when you suffer
insults and persecution and every
12 kind of calumny for my sake. Accept
it with gladness and exultation, for
you have a rich reward in heaven; in
the same way they persecuted the
prophets before you.'

Salt and light

13 'You are salt to the world. And if
salt becomes tasteless, how is its saltness to be restored? It is now good
for nothing but to be thrown away
and trodden underfoot.
14   'You are light for all the world. A
town that stands on a hill cannot be
15 hidden. When a lamp is lit, it is not
put under the meal-tub, but on the
lamp-stand, where it gives light to
16 everyone in the house. And you, like
the lamp, must shed light among your
fellows, so that, when they see the
good you do, they may give praise to
your Father in heaven.'

Jesus and the Law

17 'Do not suppose that I have come to
abolish the Law and the prophets; I
did not come to abolish, but to com-
18 plete. I tell you this: so long as heaven
and earth endure, not a letter, not a
stroke, will disappear from the Law
until all that must happen has hap-
19 pened.[h] If any man therefore sets
aside even the least of the Law's demands, and teaches others to do the
same, he will have the lowest place in
the kingdom of Heaven, whereas anyone who keeps the Law, and teaches
others so, will stand high in the
20 kingdom of Heaven. I tell you, unless
you show yourselves far better men
than the Pharisees and the doctors of
the law, you can never enter the kingdom of Heaven.'

About anger and grievances

21 'You have learned that our forefathers
were told, "Do not commit murder;
anyone who commits murder must
22 be brought to judgement." But what
I tell you is this: Anyone who nurses
anger against his brother[i] must be
brought to judgement. If he abuses
his brother he must answer for it to
the court; if he sneers at him he will
have to answer for it in the fires of
hell.

h Or before all that it stands for is achieved.

'If, when you are bringing your 23
gift to the altar, you suddenly remember that your brother has a
grievance against you, leave your gift 24
where it is before the altar. First go
and make your peace with your brother, and only then come back and
offer your gift.
'If someone sues you, come to terms 25
with him promptly while you are
both on your way to court; otherwise
he may hand you over to the judge,
and the judge to the constable, and
you will be put in jail. I tell you, once 26
you are there you will not be let out
till you have paid the last farthing.'

About lust and adultery

'You have learned that they were 27
told, "Do not commit adultery." But 28
what I tell you is this: If a man looks
on a woman with a lustful eye, he
has already committed adultery with
her in his heart.
'If your right eye is your undoing, 29
tear it out and fling it away; it is
better for you to lose one part of your
body than for the whole of it to be
thrown into hell. And if your right 30
hand is your undoing, cut it off and
fling it away; it is better for you to
lose one part of your body than for
the whole of it to go to hell.'

About divorce

'They were told, "A man who divorces 31
his wife must give her a note of dismissal." But what I tell you is this: If 32
a man divorces his wife for any cause
other than unchastity he involves her
in adultery; and anyone who marries
a divorced woman commits adultery.'

About oaths

'Again, you have learned that our 33
forefathers were told, "Do not break
your oath", and, "Oaths sworn to the
Lord must be kept." But what I tell 34
you is this: You are not to swear at
all—not by heaven, for it is God's
throne, nor by earth, for it is his foot- 35
stool, nor by Jerusalem, for it is the
city of the great King, nor by your 36
own head, because you cannot turn
one hair of it white or black. Plain 37
"Yes" or "No" is all you need to say;
anything beyond that comes from the
devil.'

About personal wrongs

'You have learned that they were told, 38
"Eye for eye, tooth for tooth." But 39

i Some witnesses insert without good cause.

what I tell you is this: Do not set yourself against the man who wrongs you. If someone slaps you on the right cheek, turn and offer him your left. If a man wants to sue you for your shirt, let him have your coat as well. If a man in authority makes you go one mile, go with him two. Give when you are asked to give; and do not turn your back on a man who wants to borrow.'

'Love your enemies'

'You have learned that they were told, "Love your neighbour, hate your enemy." But what I tell you is this: Love your enemies[j] and pray for your persecutors;[k] only so can you be children of your heavenly Father, who makes his sun rise on good and bad alike, and sends the rain on the honest and the dishonest. If you love only those who love you, what reward can you expect? Surely the tax-gatherers do as much as that. And if you greet only your brothers, what is there extraordinary about that? Even the heathen do as much. There must be no limit to your goodness, as your heavenly Father's goodness knows no bounds.'

Pretence and sincerity

'Be careful not to make a show of your religion before men; if you do, no reward awaits you in your Father's house in heaven.

'Thus, when you do some act of charity, do not announce it with a flourish of trumpets, as the hypocrites do in synagogue and in the streets to win admiration from men. I tell you this: they have their reward already. No; when you do some act of charity, do not let your left hand know what your right is doing; your good deed must be secret, and your Father who sees what is done in secret will reward you.'[l]

About prayer

'Again, when you pray, do not be like the hypocrites; they love to say their prayers standing up in synagogue and at the street-corners, for everyone to see them. I tell you this: they have their reward already. But when you pray, go into a room by yourself, shut the door, and pray to your Father who is there in the secret place; and your Father who sees what is secret will reward you.[l]

'In your prayers do not go babbling 7 on like the heathen, who imagine that the more they say the more likely they are to be heard. Do not imitate 8 them. Your Father knows what your needs are before you ask him.

'This is how you should pray: 9

"Our Father in heaven,
thy name be hallowed;
thy kingdom come, 10
thy will be done,
on earth as in heaven.
Give us today our daily bread.[m] 11
Forgive us the wrong we have done, 12
as we have forgiven those who have
wronged us.
And do not bring us to the test, 13
but save us from the evil one."[n] [o]

For if you forgive others the wrongs 14 they have done, your heavenly Father will also forgive you; but if you do 15 not forgive others, then the wrongs you have done will not be forgiven by your Father.'

About fasting

'So too when you fast, do not look 16 gloomy like the hypocrites: they make their faces unsightly so that other people may see that they are fasting. I tell you this: they have their reward already. But when you 17 fast, anoint your head and wash your face, so that men may not see that 18 you are fasting, but only your Father who is in the secret place; and your Father who sees what is secret will give you your reward.'

Cure for anxiety

'Do not store up for yourselves trea- 19 sure on earth, where it grows rusty and moth-eaten, and thieves break in to steal it. Store up treasure in 20 heaven, where there is no moth and no rust to spoil it, no thieves to break in and steal. For where your treasure 21 is, there will your heart be also.

'The lamp of the body is the eye. If 22 your eyes are sound, you will have light for your whole body; if the eyes 23 are bad, your whole body will be in darkness. If then the only light you have is darkness, the darkness is doubly dark.

j Some witnesses insert bless those who curse you, do good to those who hate you. *k Some witnesses insert* and those who treat you spitefully. *l Some witnesses add* openly. *m Or* our bread for the morrow. *n Or from evil.* *o Some witnesses add* For thine is the kingdom and the power and the glory, for ever. Amen.

24 'No servant can be the slave of two masters; for either he will hate the first and love the second, or he will be devoted to the first and think nothing of the second. You cannot serve God and Money.

25 'Therefore I bid you put away anxious thoughts about food and drink to keep you alive, and clothes to cover your body. Surely life is more than food, the body more than clothes.

26 Look at the birds of the air; they do not sow and reap and store in barns, yet your heavenly Father feeds them. You are worth more than the birds!

27 Is there a man of you who by anxious thought can add a foot to his height[p]?

28 And why be anxious about clothes? Consider how the lilies grow in the fields; they do not work, they do not

29 spin;[q] and yet, I tell you, even Sol-

30 omon in all his splendour was not attired like one of these. But if that is how God clothes the grass in the fields, which is there today, and tomorrow is thrown on the stove, will he not all the more clothe you? How little faith

31 you have! No, do not ask anxiously, "What are we to eat? What are we

32 to drink? What shall we wear?" All these are things that the heathen to run after, not for you, because your heavenly Father knows that you need

33 them all. Set your mind on God's kingdom and his justice before everything else, and all the rest will come

34 to you as well. So do not be anxious about tomorrow; tomorrow will look after itself. Each day has troubles enough of its own.'

Judging others

7 'Pass no judgement, and you will not

2 be judged. For as you judge others, so you will yourselves be judged, and whatever measure you deal out to

3 others will be dealt back to you. Why do you look at the speck of sawdust in your brother's eye, with never a thought for the great plank in your own? Or how can you say to your

4 brother, "Let me take the speck out of your eye", when all the time there is that plank in your own? You hypo-

5 crite! First take the plank out of your own eye, and then you will see clearly to take the speck out of your brother's.

'Do not give dogs what is holy; do

6 not throw your pearls to the pigs: they will only trample on them, and turn and tear you to pieces.'

Ask; seek; knock

'Ask, and you will receive; seek, and you will find; knock, and the door will be opened. For everyone who asks receives, he who seeks finds, and to him who knocks, the door will be opened.

'Is there a man among you who will offer his son a stone when he asks for bread, or a snake when he asks for fish? If you, then, bad as you are, know how to give your children what is good for them, how much more will your heavenly Father give good things to those who ask him!

'Always treat others as you would like them to treat you: that is the Law and the prophets.'

The gate to life

'Enter by the narrow gate. The gate is wide that leads to perdition, there is plenty of room on the road,[r] and many go that way; but the gate that leads to life is small and the road is narrow,[s] and those who find it are few.'

A tree and its fruit

'Beware of false prophets, men who come to you dressed up as sheep while underneath they are savage wolves. You will recognize them by the fruits they bear. Can grapes be picked from briars, or figs from thistles? In the same way, a good tree always yields good fruit, and a poor tree bad fruit. A good tree cannot bear bad fruit, or a poor tree good fruit. And when a tree does not yield good fruit it is cut down and burnt. That is why I say you will recognize them by their fruits.

'Not everyone who calls me "Lord, Lord" will enter the kingdom of Heaven, but only those who do the will of my heavenly Father. When that day comes, many will say to me, "Lord, Lord, did we not prophesy in your name, cast out devils in your name, and in your name perform many miracles?" Then I will tell them to their face, "I never knew you; out of my sight, you and your wicked ways!"'

A firm foundation

'What then of the man who hears these words of mine and acts upon them? He is like a man who had the sense to build his house on rock. The rain came down, the floods rose, the

---

p Or a day to his life.   q One witness reads Consider the lilies: they neither card nor spin, nor labour.   r Some witnesses read The road that leads to perdition is wide with plenty of room. s Some witnesses read but the road that leads to life is small and narrow.

wind blew, and beat upon that house; but it did not fall, because its founda-
5 tions were on rock. But what of the man who hears these words of mine and does not act upon them? He is like a man who was foolish enough
7 to build his house on sand. The rain came down, the floods rose, the wind blew, and beat upon that house; down it fell with a great crash.'
8 When Jesus had finished this discourse the people were astounded at
9 his teaching; unlike their own teachers he taught with a note of authority.

Jesus cleanses a leper

8 After he had come down from the hill
2 he was followed by a great crowd. And now a leper[t] approached him, bowed low, and said, 'Sir, if only you will,
3 you can cleanse me.' Jesus stretched out his hand, touched him, and said, 'Indeed I will; be clean again.' And his leprosy was cured immediately.
4 Then Jesus said to him, 'Be sure you tell nobody; but go and show yourself to the priest, and make the offering laid down by Moses for your cleansing; that will certify the cure.'

The faith of a soldier

5 When he had entered Capernaum a centurion came up to ask his help.
6 'Sir,' he said, 'a boy of mine lies at home paralysed and racked with pain.'
7 Jesus said, 'I will come and cure
8 him.'[u] But the centurion replied, 'Sir, who am I to have you under my roof? You need only say the word and the
9 boy will be cured. I know, for I am myself under orders, with soldiers under me. I say to one, "Go", and he goes; to another, "Come here", and he comes; and to my servant, "Do
10 this", and he does it.' Jesus heard him with astonishment, and said to the people who were following him, 'I tell you this: nowhere, even in Israel, have I found such faith.
11 'Many, I tell you, will come from east and west to feast with Abraham, Isaac, and Jacob in the kingdom of
12 Heaven. But those who were born to the kingdom will be driven out into the dark, the place of wailing and grinding of teeth.'
13 Then Jesus said to the centurion, 'Go home now; because of your faith, so let it be.' At that moment the boy recovered.

Acts of healing

Jesus then went to Peter's house and 14 found Peter's mother-in-law in bed with fever. So he took her by the 15 hand; the fever left her, and she got up and waited on him.

When evening fell, they brought to 16 him many who were possessed by devils; and he drove the spirits out with a word and healed all who were sick, to fulfil the prophecy of Isaiah: 17 'He took away our illnesses and lifted our diseases from us.'[v]

The cost of discipleship

At the sight of the crowds surround- 18 ing him Jesus gave word to cross to the other shore. A doctor of the law 19 came up, and said, 'Master, I will follow you wherever you go.' Jesus 20 replied, 'Foxes have their holes, the birds their roosts; but the Son of Man has nowhere to lay his head.' Another man, one of his disciples, 21 said to him, 'Lord, let me go and bury my father first.' Jesus replied, 'Follow 22 me, and leave the dead to bury their dead.'

Jesus calms a storm

Jesus then got into the boat, and his 23 disciples followed. All at once a great 24 storm arose on the lake, till the waves were breaking right over the boat; but he went on sleeping. So they came 25 and woke him up, crying: 'Save us, Lord; we are sinking!' 'Why are you 26 such cowards?' he said; 'how little faith you have!' Then he stood up and rebuked the wind and the sea, and there was a dead calm. The men were 27 astonished at what had happened, and exclaimed, 'What sort of man is this? Even the wind and the sea obey him.'

Jesus cures two madmen

When he reached the other side, in 28 the country of the Gadarenes, he was met by two men who came out from the tombs; they were possessed by devils, and so violent that no one dared pass that way. 'You son of God,' 29 they shouted, 'what do you want with us? Have you come here to torment us before our time?' In the distance 30 a large herd of pigs was feeding; and 31 the devils begged him: 'If you drive us out, send us into that herd of pigs.' 'Begone!' he said. Then they came 32

---

t *The words* leper, leprosy, *as used in this translation, refer to some disfiguring skin disease which entailed ceremonial defilement. It is different from what is now called leprosy.*   u *Or* Am I to come and cure him?   v *Or and bore the burden of our diseases.*

out and went into the pigs; the whole herd rushed over the edge into the lake, and perished in the water.

83 The men in charge of them took to their heels, and made for the town, where they told the whole story, and what had happened to the madmen.

34 Thereupon all the town came out to meet Jesus; and when they saw him they begged him to leave the district

9 and go. So he got into the boat and crossed over, and came to his own town.

Authority to forgive sins

2 And now some men brought him a paralysed man lying on a bed. Seeing their faith Jesus said to the man, 'Take heart, my son; your sins are

3 forgiven.' At this some of the lawyers said to themselves, 'This is blasphe-

4 mous talk.' Jesus knew what they were thinking, and said, 'Why do you

5 harbour these evil thoughts? Is it easier to say, "Your sins are forgiven",

6 or to say, "Stand up and walk"? But to convince you that the Son of Man has the right on earth to forgive sins' —he turned to the paralysed man— 'stand up, take your bed, and go home.'

7 Thereupon the man got up, and went

8 off home. The people were filled with awe at the sight, and praised God for granting such authority to men.

Jesus and the tax-gatherers

9 As he passed on from there Jesus saw a man named Matthew at his seat in the custom-house, and said to him, 'Follow me'; and Matthew rose and followed him.

10 When Jesus was at table in the house, many bad characters—tax-gatherers and others—were seated

11 with him and his disciples. The Pharisees noticed this, and said to his disciples, 'Why is it that your master eats with tax-gatherers and sinners?'

12 Jesus heard it and said, 'It is not the healthy that need a doctor, but the

13 sick. Go and learn what that text means, "I require mercy, not sacrifice." I did not come to invite virtuous people, but sinners.'

About fasting

14 Then John's disciples came to him with the question: 'Why do we and the Pharisees fast, but your disciples do

15 not?' Jesus replied, 'Can you expect the bridegroom's friends to go mourning while the bridegroom is with them? The time will come when the

bridegroom will be taken away from them; that will be the time for them to fast.'

Patched clothes and old wine-skins

'No one sews a patch of unshrunk cloth on to an old coat; for then the patch tears away from the coat, and leaves a bigger hole. Neither do you put new wine into old wine-skins; if you do, the skins burst, and then the wine runs out and the skins are spoilt. No, you put new wine into fresh skins; then both are preserved.'

Healing and restoration to life

Even as he spoke, there came a president of the synagogue, who bowed low before him and said, 'My daughter has just died; but come and lay your hand on her, and she will live.' Jesus rose and went with him, and so did his disciples.

Then a woman who had suffered from haemorrhages for twelve years came up from behind, and touched the edge of his cloak; for she said to herself, 'If I can only touch his cloak, I shall be cured.' But Jesus turned and saw her, and said, 'Take heart, my daughter; your faith has cured you.' And from that moment she recovered.

When Jesus arrived at the president's house and saw the flute-players and the general commotion, he said, 'Be off! The girl is not dead: she is asleep'; and they only laughed at him. But, when everyone had been turned out, he went into the room and took the girl by the hand, and she got up. This story became the talk of all the country round.

Sight restored to two blind men

As he passed on Jesus was followed by two blind men, who cried out, 'Son of David, have pity on us!' And when he had gone indoors they came to him. Jesus asked, 'Do you believe that I have the power to do what you want?' 'Yes, sir', they said. Then he touched their eyes, and said, 'As you have believed, so let it be'; and their sight was restored. Jesus said to them sternly, 'See that no one hears about this.' But as soon as they had gone out they talked about him all over the country-side.

A dumb man recovers his speech

They were on their way out when a man was brought to him, who was dumb and possessed by a devil; the devil was cast out and the patient recovered his speech. Filled with amazement the onlookers said, 'Nothing like this has ever been seen in Israel.'[w]

'Sheep without a shepherd'

So Jesus went round all the towns and villages teaching in their synagogues, announcing the good news of the Kingdom, and curing every kind of ailment and disease. The sight of the people moved him to pity: they were like sheep without a shepherd, harassed and helpless; and he said to his disciples, 'The crop is heavy, but labourers are scarce; you must therefore beg the owner to send labourers to harvest his crop.'

The twelve apostles and their mission

Then he called his twelve disciples to him and gave them authority to cast out unclean spirits and to cure every kind of ailment and disease.

These are the names of the twelve apostles: first Simon, also called Peter, and his brother Andrew; James son of Zebedee, and his brother John; Philip and Bartholomew, Thomas and Matthew the tax-gatherer, James son of Alphaeus, Lebbaeus,[x] Simon, a member of the Zealot party, and Judas Iscariot, the man who betrayed him.

These twelve Jesus sent out with the following instructions: 'Do not take the road to gentile lands, and do not enter any Samaritan town; but go rather to the lost sheep of the house of Israel. And as you go proclaim the message: "The kingdom of Heaven is upon you." Heal the sick, raise the dead, cleanse lepers, cast out devils. You received without cost; give without charge.

'Provide no gold, silver, or copper to fill your purse, no pack for the road, no second coat, no shoes, no stick; the worker earns his keep.

'When you come to any town or village, look for some worthy person in it, and make your home there until you leave. Wish the house peace as you enter it, so that, if it is worthy, your peace may descend on it; if it is not worthy, your peace can come back to you. If anyone will not receive you or listen to what you say, then as

you leave that house or that town shake the dust of it off your feet. I tell 15 you this: on the day of judgement it will be more bearable for the land of Sodom and Gomorrah than for that town.'

Coming persecutions

'Look, I send you out like sheep 16 among wolves; be wary as serpents, innocent as doves.

'And be on your guard, for men will 17 hand you over to their courts, they will flog you in the synagogues, and 18 you will be brought before governors and kings, for my sake, to testify before them and the heathen. But 19 when you are arrested, do not worry about what you are to say; when the time comes, the words you need will be given you; for it is not you who 20 will be speaking: it will be the Spirit of your Father speaking in you.

'Brother will betray brother to 21 death, and the father his child; children will turn against their parents and send them to their death. All will 22 hate you for your allegiance to me; but the man who holds out to the end will be saved. When you are 23 persecuted in one town, take refuge in another; I tell you this: before you have gone through all the towns of Israel the Son of Man will have come.

'A pupil does not rank above his 24 teacher, or a servant above his master. The pupil should be content to share 25 his teacher's lot, the servant to share his master's. If the master has been called Beelzebub, how much more his household!'

Freedom from fear

'So do not be afraid of them. There is 26 nothing covered up that will not be uncovered, nothing hidden that will not be made known. What I say to 27 you in the dark you must repeat in broad daylight; what you hear whispered you must shout from the house-tops. Do not fear those who 28 kill the body, but cannot kill the soul. Fear him rather who is able to destroy both soul and body in hell.

'Are not sparrows two a penny? 29 Yet without your Father's leave not one of them can fall to the ground. As 30 for you, even the hairs of your head have all been counted. So have no 31 fear; you are worth more than any number of sparrows.'

w Some witnesses add (34) But the Pharisees said, 'He casts out devils by the prince of devils.'
x Some witnesses read Thaddaeus.

Acknowledging and disowning Jesus

32 'Whoever then will acknowledge me
33 before men, I will acknowledge him
before my Father in heaven; and
whoever disowns me before men, I
will disown him before my Father in
heaven.'

Conflicting loyalties

34 'You must not think that I have come
to bring peace to the earth; I have
not come to bring peace, but a sword.
35 I have come to set a man against his
father, a daughter against her mother,
a son's wife against her mother-in-law;
36 and a man will find his enemies under
his own roof.
37   'No man is worthy of me who cares
more for father or mother than for
me; no man is worthy of me who cares
38 more for son or daughter; no man is
worthy of me who does not take up
his cross and walk in my footsteps.
39 By gaining his life a man will lose it;
by losing his life for my sake, he will
gain it.'

About rewards

40 'To receive you is to receive me, and
to receive me is to receive the One
41 who sent me. Whoever receives a
prophet as a prophet will be given a
prophet's reward, and whoever receives a good man because he is a
good man will be given a good man's
42 reward. And if anyone gives so much
as a cup of cold water to one of these
little ones, because he is a disciple of
mine, I tell you this: that man will
assuredly not go unrewarded.'

11   When Jesus had finished giving his
twelve disciples their instructions, he
left that place and went to teach and
preach in the neighbouring towns.

A message for John the Baptist

2 John, who was in prison, heard what
Christ was doing, and sent his own
3 disciples to him with this message:
'Are you the one who is to come, or
4 are we to expect some other?' Jesus
answered, 'Go and tell John what you
5 hear and see: the blind recover their
sight, the lame walk, the lepers are
made clean, the deaf hear, the dead
are raised to life, the poor are hearing
6 the good news—and happy is the
man who does not find me a stumbling-
block.'

About John the Baptist

When the messengers were on their
way back, Jesus began to speak to
the people about John: 'What was
the spectacle that drew you to the
wilderness? A reed-bed swept by the
wind? No? Then what did you go
out to see? A man dressed in silks
and satins? Surely you must look in
palaces for that. But why did you go
out? To see a prophet? Yes indeed,
and far more than a prophet. He is
the man of whom Scripture says,

"Here is my herald, whom I send on
     ahead of you,
and he will prepare your way before
     you."

I tell you this: never has there appeared on earth a mother's son greater
than John the Baptist, and yet the
least in the kingdom of Heaven is
greater than he.
    'Ever since the coming of John the
Baptist the kingdom of Heaven has
been subjected to violence and violent
men[y] are seizing it. For all the prophets and the Law foretold things to
come until John appeared, and John
is the destined Elijah, if you will but
accept it. If you have ears, then hear.
    'How can I describe this generation?
They are like children sitting in the
market-place and shouting at each
other,

"We piped for you and you would
     not dance."
"We wept and wailed, and you would
     not mourn."

For John came, neither eating nor
drinking, and they say, "He is possessed." The Son of Man came eating
and drinking, and they say, "Look at
him! a glutton and a drinker, a friend
of tax-gatherers and sinners!" And
yet God's wisdom is proved right by
its results.'

Jesus faces unbelief

Then he spoke of the towns in which
most of his miracles had been performed, and denounced them for their
impenitence. 'Alas for you, Chorazin!'
he said; 'alas for you, Bethsaida! If
the miracles that were performed in
you had been performed in Tyre and
Sidon, they would have repented long
ago in sackcloth and ashes. But it
will be more bearable, I tell you, for
Tyre and Sidon on the day of judgement than for you. And as for you,

y Or has been forcing its way forward, and men of force . . .

Capernaum, will you be exalted to the skies? No, brought down to the depths! For if the miracles had been performed in Sodom which were performed in you, Sodom would be standing to this day. But it will be more bearable, I tell you, for the land of Sodom on the day of judgement than for you.'

The Father and the Son

At that time Jesus spoke these words: 'I thank thee, Father, Lord of heaven and earth, for hiding these things from the learned and wise, and revealing them to the simple. Yes, Father, such[z] was thy choice. Everything is entrusted to me by my Father; and no one knows the Son but the Father, and no one knows the Father but the Son and those to whom the Son may choose to reveal him.

'Come to me'

'Come to me, all whose work is hard, whose load is heavy; and I will give you relief. Bend your necks to my yoke, and learn from me, for I am gentle and humble-hearted; and your souls will find relief. For my yoke is good to bear, my load is light.'

About the Sabbath

Once about that time Jesus went through the cornfields on the Sabbath; and his disciples, feeling hungry, began to pluck some ears of corn and eat them. The Pharisees noticed this, and said to him, 'Look, your disciples are doing something which is forbidden on the Sabbath.' He answered, 'Have you not read what David did when he and his men were hungry? He went into the House of God and ate the sacred bread, though neither he nor his men had a right to eat it, but only the priests. Or have you not read in the Law that on the Sabbath the priests in the temple break the Sabbath and it is not held against them? I tell you, there is something greater than the temple here. If you had known what that text means, "I require mercy, not sacrifice", you would not have condemned the innocent. For the Son of Man is sovereign over the Sabbath.'

A man with a withered arm

He went on to another place, and entered their synagogue. A man was there with a withered arm, and they asked Jesus, 'Is it permitted to heal on the Sabbath?' (They wanted to frame a charge against him.) But he said to them, 'Suppose you had one sheep, which fell into a ditch on the Sabbath; is there one of you who would not catch hold of it and lift it out? And surely a man is worth far more than a sheep! It is therefore permitted to do good on the Sabbath.' Turning to the man he said, 'Stretch out your arm.' He stretched it out, and it was made sound again like the other. But the Pharisees, on leaving the synagogue, laid a plot to do away with him.

The Servant of God

Jesus was aware of it and withdrew. Many followed, and he cured all who were ill; and he gave strict injunctions that they were not to make him known. This was to fulfil Isaiah's prophecy:

'Here is my servant, whom I have chosen,
my beloved, on whom my favour rests;
I will put my Spirit upon him,
and he will proclaim judgement among the nations.
He will not strive, he will not shout, nor will his voice be heard in the streets.
He will not snap off the broken reed, nor snuff out the smouldering wick, until he leads justice on to victory.
In him the nations shall place their hope.'

Controversy with the Pharisees

Then they brought him a man who was possessed; he was blind and dumb; and Jesus cured him, restoring both speech and sight. The bystanders were all amazed, and the word went round: 'Can this be the Son of David?' But when the Pharisees heard it they said, 'It is only by Beelzebub prince of devils that this man drives the devils out.'

He knew what was in their minds; so he said to them, 'Every kingdom divided against itself goes to ruin; and no town, no household, that is divided against itself can stand. And if it is Satan who casts out Satan, Satan is divided against himself; how then can his kingdom stand? And if it is by Beelzebub that I cast out devils, by whom do your own people drive them out? If this is your argument, they themselves will refute you. But if it is by the Spirit of God that

z Or Yes, I thank thee, Father, that such . . .

I drive out the devils, then be sure the kingdom of God has already come upon you.

29 'Or again, how can anyone break into a strong man's house and make off with his goods, unless he has first tied the strong man up before ransacking the house?

30 'He who is not with me is against me, and he who does not gather with me scatters.

31 'And so I tell you this: no sin, no slander, is beyond forgiveness for men, except slander spoken against the Spirit, and that will not be forgiven.

32 Any man who speaks a word against the Son of Man will be forgiven; but if anyone speaks against the Holy Spirit, for him there is no forgiveness, either in this age or in the age to come.

33 'Either make the tree good and its fruit good, or make the tree bad and its fruit bad; you can tell a tree by its fruit. You vipers' brood! How can

34 your words be good when you yourselves are evil? For the words that the mouth utters come from the over-

35 flowing of the heart. A good man produces good from the store of good within himself; and an evil man from evil within produces evil.

36 'I tell you this: there is not a thoughtless word that comes from men's lips but they will have to account for it on the day of judgement.

37 For out of your own mouth you will be acquitted; out of your own mouth you will be condemned.'

The sign of Jonah

38 At this some of the doctors of the law and the Pharisees said, 'Master, we should like you to show us a sign.'

39 He answered: 'It is a wicked, godless generation that asks for a sign; and the only sign that will be given it is

40 the sign of the prophet Jonah. Jonah was in the sea-monster's belly for three days and three nights, and in the same way the Son of Man will be three days and three nights in the

41 bowels of the earth. At the Judgement, when this generation is on trial, the men of Nineveh will appear against it[a] and ensure its condemnation, for they repented at the preaching of Jonah; and what is here is

42 greater than Jonah. The Queen of the South will appear at the Judgement when this generation is on trial,[b] and ensure its condemnation, for she came from the ends of the earth to hear the wisdom of Solomon; and what is here is greater than Solomon.

43 'When an unclean spirit comes out of a man it wanders over the deserts seeking a resting-place, and finds none.

44 Then it says, "I will go back to the home I left." So it returns and finds the house

45 unoccupied, swept clean, and tidy. Off it goes and collects seven other spirits more wicked than itself, and they all come in and settle down; and in the end the man's plight is worse than before. That is how it will be with this wicked generation.'

Jesus's relatives

46 He was still speaking to the crowd when his mother and brothers appeared; they stood outside, wanting to speak to him. Someone said, 'Your

47 mother and your brothers are here outside; they want to speak to you.'

48 Jesus turned to the man who brought the message, and said, 'Who is my

49 mother? Who are my brothers?'; and pointing to the disciples, he said, 'Here are my mother and my brothers.

50 Whoever does the will of my heavenly Father is my brother, my sister, my mother.'

Parables

That same day Jesus went out and 1 sat by the lake-side, where so many 2 people gathered round him that he had to get into a boat. He sat there, and all the people stood on the shore. He spoke to them in parables, at 3 some length.

A sower

He said: 'A sower went out to sow. And as he sowed, some seed fell along 4 the footpath; and the birds came and ate it up. Some seed fell on rocky 5 ground, where it had little soil, and it sprouted quickly because it had no depth of earth; but when the sun rose 6 the young corn was scorched, and as it had no root it withered away. Some 7 seed fell among thistles; and the thistles shot up, and choked the corn. And some of the seed fell into good 8 soil, where it bore fruit, yielding a hundredfold or, it might be, sixtyfold or thirtyfold. If you have ears, then 9 hear.'

Why Jesus told parables

The disciples went up to him and 10 asked, 'Why do you speak to them

---

a Or will rise again together with it.   b Or At the Judgement the Queen of the South will be raised to life together with this generation.

in parables?' He replied, 'It has been granted to you to know the secrets of the kingdom of Heaven; but to those others it has not been granted. For the man who has will be given more, till he has enough and to spare; and the man who has not will forfeit even what he has. That is why I speak to them in parables; for they look without seeing, and listen without hearing or understanding. There is a prophecy of Isaiah which is being fulfilled for them: "You may hear and hear, but you will never understand; you may look and look, but you will never see. For this people's mind has become gross; their ears are dulled, and their eyes are closed. Otherwise, their eyes might see, their ears hear, and their mind understand, and then they might turn again, and I would heal them."

16 'But happy are your eyes because they see, and your ears because they 17 hear! Many prophets and saints, I tell you, desired to see what you now see, yet never saw it; to hear what you hear, yet never heard it.'

The parable of the sower explained

18 'You then, may hear the parable of 19 the sower. When a man hears the word that tells of the Kingdom but fails to understand it, the evil one comes and carries off what has been sown in his heart. There you have 20 the seed sown along the footpath. The seed sown on rocky ground stands for the man who, on hearing the word, 21 accepts it at once with joy; but as it strikes no root in him he has no staying-power, and when there is trouble or persecution on account of the word 22 he falls away at once. The seed sown among thistles represents the man who hears the word, but worldly cares and the false glamour of wealth choke 23 it, and it proves barren. But the seed that fell into good soil is the man who hears the word and understands it, who accordingly bears fruit, and yields a hundredfold or, it may be, sixtyfold or thirtyfold.'

Wheat and darnel

24 Here is another parable that he put before them: 'The kingdom of Heaven is like this. A man sowed his field with 25 good seed; but while everyone was asleep his enemy came, sowed darnel 26 among the wheat, and made off. When the corn sprouted and began to fill out, the darnel could be seen among

it. The farmer's men went to their 27 master and said, "Sir, was it not good seed that you sowed in your field? Then where has the darnel come from?" "This is an enemy's doing", he replied. 28 "Well then," they said, "shall we go and gather the darnel?" "No," he 29 answered; "in gathering it you might pull up the wheat at the same time. Let them both grow together till har- 30 vest; and at harvest-time I will tell the reapers, 'Gather the darnel first, and tie it in bundles for burning; then collect the wheat into my barn.'"'

A mustard-seed

And this is another parable that he 31 put before them: 'The kingdom of Heaven is like a mustard-seed, which a man took and sowed in his field. As a seed, mustard is smaller than 32 any other; but when it has grown it is bigger than any garden-plant; it becomes a tree, big enough for the birds to come and roost among its branches.'

Yeast

He told them also this parable: 'The 33 kingdom of Heaven is like yeast, which a woman took and mixed with half a hundredweight of flour till it was all leavened.'

Jesus's way of teaching

In all this teaching to the crowds 34 Jesus spoke in parables; in fact he never spoke to them without a parable. This was to fulfil the prophecy of 35 Isaiah:[c]

'I will open my mouth in parables;
I will utter things kept secret since
the world was made.'

The wheat and darnel parable explained

He then dismissed the people, and 36 went into the house, where his disciples came to him and said, 'Explain to us the parable of the darnel in the field.' And this was his answer: 'The 37 sower of the good seed is the Son of Man. The field is the world; the good 38 seed stands for the children of the Kingdom, the darnel for the children of the evil one. The enemy who sowed 39 the darnel is the devil. The harvest is the end of time. The reapers are angels. As the darnel, then, is gathered up 40 and burnt, so at the end of time the 41 Son of Man will send out his angels, who will gather out of his kingdom

c Some witnesses omit of Isaiah.

whatever makes men stumble, and all 42 whose deeds are evil, and these will be thrown into the blazing furnace, the place of wailing and grinding of 43 teeth. And then the righteous will shine as brightly as the sun in the kingdom of their Father. If you have ears, then hear.'

Buried treasure

44 'The kingdom of Heaven is like treasure lying buried in a field. The man who found it, buried it again; and for sheer joy went and sold everything he had, and bought that field.'

The finest pearl

45 'Here is another picture of the kingdom of Heaven. A merchant looking 46 out for fine pearls found one of very special value; so he went and sold everything he had, and bought it.'

A net full of fish

47 'Again the kingdom of Heaven is like a net let down into the sea, where fish 48 of every kind were caught in it. When it was full, it was dragged ashore. Then the men sat down and collected the good fish into pails and threw the 49 worthless away. That is how it will be at the end of time. The angels will go forth, and they will separate the 50 wicked from the good, and throw them into the blazing furnace, the place of wailing and grinding of teeth.

51 'Have you understood all this?' he asked; and they answered, 'Yes.' 52 He said to them, 'When, therefore, a teacher of the law has become a learner in the kingdom of Heaven, he is like a householder who can produce from his store both the new and the old.'

Unbelief in Nazareth

53 When he had finished these parables 54 Jesus left that place, and came to his home town, where he taught the people in their synagogue. In amazement they asked, 'Where does he get this wisdom from, and these miracu- 55 lous powers? Is he not the carpenter's son? Is not his mother called Mary, his brothers James, Joseph, Simon, 56 and Judas? And are not all his sisters here with us? Where then has he got 57 all this from?' So they fell foul of him, and this led him to say, 'A prophet will always be held in honour, except in his home town, and in his own 58 family.' And he did not work many

miracles there: such was their want of faith.

Disturbing news for Herod

It was at that time that reports about **14** Jesus reached the ears of Prince Herod. 'This is John the Baptist,' he 2 said to his attendants; 'John has been raised to life, and that is why these miraculous powers are at work in him.'

The death of John the Baptist

Now Herod had arrested John, put 3 him in chains, and thrown him into prison, on account of Herodias, his brother Philip's wife; for John had 4 told him: 'You have no right to her.' Herod would have liked to put him to 5 death, but he was afraid of the people, in whose eyes John was a prophet. But at his birthday celebrations the 6 daughter of Herodias danced before the guests, and Herod was so delighted that he took an oath to give her any- 7 thing she cared to ask. Prompted by 8 her mother, she said, 'Give me here on a dish the head of John the Baptist.' The king was distressed when 9 he heard it; but out of regard for his oath and for his guests, he ordered the request to be granted, and had 10 John beheaded in prison. The head 11 was brought in on a dish and given to the girl; and she carried it to her mother. Then John's disciples came 12 and took away the body, and buried it; and they went and told Jesus.

Feeding five thousand

When he heard what had happened 13 Jesus withdrew privately by boat to a lonely place; but people heard of it, and came after him in crowds by land from the towns. When he came ashore, 14 he saw a great crowd; his heart went out to them, and he cured those of them who were sick. When it grew 15 late the disciples came up to him and said, 'This is a lonely place, and the day has gone; send the people off to the villages to buy themselves food.' He answered, 'There is no need for 16 them to go; give them something to eat yourselves.' 'All we have here', 17 they said, 'is five loaves and two fishes.' 'Let me have them', he replied. 18 So he told the people to sit down on 19 the grass; then, taking the five loaves and the two fishes, he looked up to heaven, said the blessing, broke the loaves, and gave them to the disciples; and the disciples gave them to the

20 people. They all ate to their hearts'
content; and the scraps left over,
which they picked up, were enough to
21 fill twelve great baskets. Some five
thousand men shared in this meal, to
say nothing of women and children.

Jesus walks on the water

22 Then he made the disciples embark
and go on ahead to the other side,
23 while he sent the people away; after
doing that, he went up the hill-side
to pray alone. It grew late, and he
24 was there by himself. The boat was
already some furlongs from the shore,*d*
battling with a head-wind and a
25 rough sea. Between three and six in
the morning he came to them, walk-
26 ing over the lake. When the disciples
saw him walking on the lake they
were so shaken that they cried out in
27 terror: 'It is a ghost!' But at once he
spoke to them: 'Take heart! It is I;
do not be afraid.'
28   Peter called to him: 'Lord, if it
is you, tell me to come to you over
29 the water.' 'Come', said Jesus. Peter
stepped down from the boat, and
walked over the water towards Jesus.
30 But when he saw the strength of the
gale he was seized with fear; and
beginning to sink, he cried, 'Save me,
31 Lord.' Jesus at once reached out and
caught hold of him, and said, 'Why
did you hesitate? How little faith you
32 have!' They then climbed into the
33 boat; and the wind dropped. And the
men in the boat fell at his feet,
exclaiming, 'Truly you are the Son of
God.'

Jesus heals in Gennesaret

34 So they finished the crossing and
35 came to land at Gennesaret. There
Jesus was recognized by the people of
the place, who sent out word to all the
country round. And all who were ill
36 were brought to him, and he was begged to allow them simply to touch the
edge of his cloak. And everyone who
touched it was completely cured.

About traditions

15 Then Jesus was approached by a
group of Pharisees and lawyers from
2 Jerusalem, with the question: 'Why
do your disciples break the ancient
tradition? They do not wash their
3 hands before meals.' He answered
them: 'And what of you? Why do you
break God's commandment in the
4 interest of your tradition? For God

said, "Honour your father and mother", and, "The man who curses his
father or mother must suffer death."
But you say, "If a man says to his 5
father or mother, 'Anything of mine
which might have been used for your
benefit is set apart for God', then he 6
must not honour his father or his
mother." You have made God's law
null and void out of respect for your
tradition. What hypocrisy! Isaiah was 7
right when he prophesied about you:
"This people pays me lip-service, but 8
their heart is far from me; their wor- 9
ship of me is in vain, for they teach
as doctrines the commandments of
men."'
    He called the crowd and said to 10
them, 'Listen to me, and understand
this: a man is not defiled by what 11
goes into his mouth, but by what
comes out of it.'

What defiles a man

Then the disciples came to him and 12
said, 'Do you know that the Pharisees
have taken great offence at what you
have been saying?' His answer was: 13
'Any plant that is not of my heavenly
Father's planting will be rooted up.
Leave them alone; they are blind 14
guides,*e* and if one blind man guides
another they will both fall into the
ditch.'
    Then Peter said, 'Tell us what that 15
parable means.' Jesus answered, 'Are 16
you still as dull as the rest? Do you 17
not see that whatever goes in by the
mouth passes into the stomach and
so is discharged into the drain? But 18
what comes out of the mouth has
its origins in the heart; and that is
what defiles a man. Wicked thoughts, 19
murder, adultery, fornication, theft,
perjury, slander—these all proceed
from the heart; and these are the 20
things that defile a man; but to eat
without first washing his hands, that
cannot defile him.'

A woman's faith

Jesus then left that place and with- 21
drew to the region of Tyre and Sidon.
And a Canaanite woman from those 22
parts came crying out, 'Sir! have pity
on me, Son of David; my daughter is
tormented by a devil.' But he said not 23
a word in reply. His disciples came
and urged him: 'Send her away; see
how she comes shouting after us.' Jesus 24
replied, 'I was sent to the lost sheep
of the house of Israel, and to them

d Some witnesses read already well out on the water.   *e Some witnesses insert* of blind men.

25 alone.' But the woman came and fell at his feet and cried, 'Help me, sir.'
26 To this Jesus replied, 'It is not right to take the children's bread and throw
27 it to the dogs.' 'True, sir,' she answered; 'and yet the dogs eat the scraps that fall from their masters' table.'
28 Hearing this Jesus replied, 'Woman, what faith you have! Be it as you wish!' And from that moment her daughter was restored to health.
29   After leaving that region Jesus took the road by the Sea of Galilee and went up to the hills. When he was
30 seated there, crowds flocked to him, bringing with them the lame, blind, dumb, and crippled, and many other sufferers; they threw them down at
31 his feet, and he healed them. Great was the amazement of the people when they saw the dumb speaking, the crippled strong, the lame walking, and sight restored to the blind; and they gave praise to the God of Israel.

Feeding four thousand

32 Jesus called his disciples and said to them, 'I feel sorry for all these people; they have been with me now for three days and have nothing to eat. I do not want to send them away
33 unfed; they might turn faint on the way.' The disciples replied, 'Where in this lonely place can we find bread
34 enough to feed such a crowd?' 'How many loaves have you?' Jesus asked. 'Seven,' they replied; 'and there are
35 a few small fishes.' So he ordered the people to sit down on the ground;
36 then he took the seven loaves and the fishes, and after giving thanks to God he broke them and gave to the disciples, and the disciples gave to the
37 people. They all ate to their hearts' content; and the scraps left over, which they picked up, were enough
38 to fill seven baskets. Four thousand men shared in this meal, to say noth-
39 ing of women and children. He then dismissed the crowds, got into a boat, and went to the neighbourhood of Magadan.

Demand for a sign

16 The Pharisees and Sadducees came, and to test him they asked him to
2 show them a sign from heaven. His
4 answer was:[f] 'It is a wicked genera-

tion that asks for a sign; and the only sign that will be given it is the sign of Jonah.' So he went off and left them.

A warning to the disciples

5 In crossing to the other side the disciples had forgotten to take bread
6 with them. So, when Jesus said to them, 'Beware, be on your guard against the leaven of the Pharisees
7 and Sadducees', they began to say among themselves, 'It is because we
8 have brought no bread!' Knowing what was in their minds, Jesus said to them: 'Why do you talk about bringing no bread? Where is your
9 faith? Do you not understand even yet? Do you not remember the five loaves for the five thousand, and how
10 many basketfuls you picked up? Or the seven loaves for the four thousand, and how many basketfuls you picked
11 up? How can you fail to see that I was not speaking about bread? Be on your guard, I said, against the leaven of the Pharisees and Sadducees.' Then
12 they understood: they were to be on their guard, not against baker's leaven, but against the teaching of the Pharisees and Sadducees.

Peter's confession of faith

13 When he came to the territory of Caesarea Philippi, Jesus asked his disciples, 'Who do men say that the Son of Man is[g]?' They answered,
14 'Some say John the Baptist, others Elijah, others Jeremiah, or one of the prophets.' 'And you,' he asked,
15 'who do you say I am?' Simon Peter
16 answered: 'You are the Messiah, the Son of the living God.' Then Jesus
17 said: 'Simon son of Jonah, you are favoured indeed! You did not learn that from mortal man; it was revealed
18 to you by my heavenly Father. And I say this to you: You are Peter, the Rock; and on this rock I will build my church, and the powers of death
19 shall never conquer it.[h] I will give you the keys of the kingdom of Heaven; what you forbid on earth shall be forbidden in heaven, and what you allow on earth shall be allowed in
20 heaven.' He then gave his disciples strict orders not to tell anyone that he was the Messiah.

f Some witnesses here insert 'In the evening you say, "It will be fine weather, for the sky is red"; (3) and in the morning you say, "It will be stormy today; the sky is red and lowering." You know how to interpret the appearance of the sky; can you not interpret the signs of the times?'   g Some witnesses read that I, the Son of Man, am.   h Or the gates of death shall never close upon it.

Jesus speaks of his death

21 From that time Jesus began to make it clear to his disciples that he had to go to Jerusalem, and there to suffer much from the elders, chief priests, and doctors of the law; to be put to death and to be raised again on the 22 third day. At this Peter took him by the arm and began to rebuke him: 'Heaven forbid!' he said. 'No, Lord, 23 this shall never happen to you.' Then Jesus turned and said to Peter, 'Away with you, Satan; you are a stumbling-block to me. You think as men think, not as God thinks.'

On following Jesus

24 Jesus then said to his disciples, 'If anyone wishes to be a follower of mine, he must leave self behind; he must take up his cross and come with 25 me. Whoever cares for his own safety is lost; but if a man will let himself be lost for my sake, he will find his true 26 self. What will a man gain by winning the whole world, at the cost of his true self? Or what can he give that 27 will buy that self back? For the Son of Man is to come in the glory of his Father with his angels, and then he will give each man the due reward for 28 what he has done. I tell you this: there are some of those standing here who will not taste death before they have seen the Son of Man coming in his kingdom.'

Jesus is transfigured

17 Six days later Jesus took Peter, James, and John the brother of James, and led them up a high mountain where 2 they were alone; and in their presence he was transfigured; his face shone like the sun, and his clothes became 3 white as the light. And they saw Moses and Elijah appear, conversing 4 with him. Then Peter spoke: 'Lord,' he said, 'how good it is that we are here! If you wish it, I will make three shelters here, one for you, one for 5 Moses, and one for Elijah.' While he was still speaking, a bright cloud suddenly overshadowed them, and a voice called from the cloud: 'This is my Son, my Beloved,[i] on whom my favour 6 rests; listen to him.' At the sound of the voice the disciples fell on their faces 7 in terror. Jesus then came up to them, touched them, and said, 'Stand up; do 8 not be afraid.' And when they raised

their eyes they saw no one, but only Jesus.

More about John the Baptist

On their way down the mountain, 9 Jesus enjoined them not to tell anyone of the vision until the Son of Man had been raised from the dead. The 10 disciples put a question to him: 'Why then do our teachers say that Elijah must come first?' He replied, 'Yes, 11 Elijah will come and set everything right. But I tell you that Elijah has 12 already come, and they failed to recognize him, and worked their will upon him; and in the same way the Son of Man is to suffer at their hands.' Then the disciples understood that he 13 meant John the Baptist.

Jesus heals an epileptic boy

When they returned to the crowd, a 14 man came up to Jesus, fell on his knees before him, and said, 'Have pity, 15 sir, on my son: he is an epileptic and has bad fits, and he keeps falling about, often into the fire, often into water. I brought him to your disciples, 16 but they could not cure him.' Jesus 17 answered, 'What an unbelieving and perverse generation! How long shall I be with you? How long must I endure you? Bring him here to me.' Jesus then spoke sternly to the boy; 18 the devil left him, and from that moment he was cured.

The power of faith

Afterwards the disciples came to 19 Jesus and asked him privately, 'Why could not we cast it out?' He answered, 20 'Your faith is too small. I tell you this: if you have faith no bigger even than a mustard-seed, you will say to this mountain, "Move from here to there!", and it will move; nothing will prove impossible for you.'[j]

Jesus again speaks of his death

They were going about together in 22 Galilee when Jesus said to them, 'The Son of Man is to be given up into the power of men, and they will kill him; 23 then on the third day he will be raised again.' And they were filled with grief.

Paying a tax

On their arrival at Capernaum the 24 collectors of the temple-tax came up to Peter and asked, 'Does your master

i Or This is my only Son.   j Some witnesses add (21) But there is no means of casting out this sort but prayer and fasting.

25 not pay temple-tax?' 'He does', said Peter. When he went indoors Jesus forestalled him by asking, 'What do you think about this, Simon? From whom do earthly monarchs collect tax or toll? From their own people, 26 or from aliens?' 'From aliens', said Peter. 'Why then,' said Jesus, 'their 27 own people are exempt! But as we do not want to cause offence, go and cast a line in the lake; take the first fish that comes to the hook, open its mouth, and you will find a silver coin; take that and pay it in; it will meet the tax for us both.'

A lesson from a child

18 At that time the disciples came to Jesus and asked, 'Who is the greatest 2 in the kingdom of Heaven?' He called a child, set him in front of them, 3 and said, 'I tell you this: unless you turn round and become like children, you will never enter the kingdom of 4 Heaven. Let a man humble himself till he is like this child, and he will be the greatest in the kingdom of Heaven, 5 Whoever receives one such child in my 6 name receives me. But if a man is a cause of stumbling to one of these little ones who have faith in me, it would be better for him to have a millstone hung round his neck and be drowned in the depths of the sea. 7 Alas for the world that such causes of stumbling arise! Come they must, but woe betide the man through whom they come! 8 'If your hand or your foot is your undoing, cut it off and fling it away; it is better for you to enter into life maimed or lame, than to keep two hands or two feet and be thrown into 9 the eternal fire. If it is your eye that is your undoing, tear it out and fling it away; it is better to enter into life with one eye than to keep both eyes and be thrown into the fires of hell. 10 'Never despise one of these little ones; I tell you, they have their guardian angels in heaven, who look continually on the face of my heavenly Father.'[k]

The sheep that strayed

12 'What do you think? Suppose a man has a hundred sheep. If one of them strays, does he not leave the other ninety-nine on the hillside and go in 13 search of the one that strayed? And if he should find it, I tell you this: he is more delighted over that sheep than over the ninety-nine that never strayed. In the same way, it is not 14 your heavenly Father's will that one of these little ones should be lost.'

On settling grievances

'If your brother commits a sin,[l] go 15 and take the matter up with him, strictly between yourselves, and if he listens to you, you have won your brother over. If he will not listen, 16 take one or two others with you, so that all facts may be duly established on the evidence of two or three witnesses. If he refuses to listen to them, 17 report the matter to the congregation; and if he will not listen even to the congregation, you must then treat him as you would a pagan or a tax-gatherer.

'I tell you this: whatever you for- 18 bid on earth shall be forbidden in heaven, and whatever you allow on earth shall be allowed in heaven.'

About prayer

'Again I tell you this: if two of you 19 agree on earth about any request you have to make, that request will be granted by my heavenly Father. For 20 where two or three have met together in my name, I am there among them.'

About forgiveness

Then Peter came up and asked him, 21 'Lord, how often am I to forgive my brother if he goes on wronging me? As many as seven times?' Jesus re- 22 plied, 'I do not say seven times; I say seventy times seven.'[m]

'The kingdom of Heaven, therefore, 23 should be thought of in this way: There was once a king who decided to settle accounts with the men who served him. At the outset there ap- 24 peared before him a man whose debt ran into millions.[n] Since he had no 25 means of paying, his master ordered him to be sold to meet the debt, with his wife, his children, and everything he had. The man fell prostrate at his 26 master's feet. "Be patient with me," he said, "and I will pay in full"; and 27 the master was so moved with pity that he let the man go and remitted the debt. But no sooner had the man 28 gone out than he met a fellow-servant who owed him a few pounds;[o] and

k Some witnesses add (11) For the Son of Man came to save the lost.   *l Some witnesses insert* against you.   *m Or* seventy-seven times.   *n Literally* who owed 10,000 talents.   *o Literally* owed him 100 denarii.

catching hold of him he gripped him by the throat and said, "Pay me what 29 you owe." The man fell at his fellow-servant's feet, and begged him, "Be patient with me, and I will pay you"; 30 but he refused, and had him jailed 31 until he should pay the debt. The other servants were deeply distressed when they saw what had happened, and they went to their master and 32 told him the whole story. He accordingly sent for the man. "You scoundrel!" he said to him; "I remitted the whole of your debt when you ap-33 pealed to me; were you not bound to show your fellow-servant the same 34 pity as I showed you?" And so angry was the master that he condemned the man to torture until he should 35 pay the debt in full. And that is how my heavenly Father will deal with you, unless you each forgive your brother from your hearts.'

About marriage and divorce

19 When Jesus had finished this discourse he left Galilee and came into the region of Judaea across Jordan. 2 Great crowds followed him, and he healed them there.

3 Some Pharisees came and tested him by asking, 'Is it lawful for a man to divorce his wife on any and every 4 ground?'[p] He asked in return, 'Have you never read that the Creator made them from the beginning male 5 and female?'; and he added, 'For this reason a man shall leave his father and mother, and be made one with his wife; and the two shall become 6 one flesh. It follows that they are no longer two individuals: they are one flesh. What God has joined together, 7 man must not separate.' 'Why then', they objected, 'did Moses lay it down that a man might divorce his wife by 8 note of dismissal?' He answered, 'It was because your minds were closed that Moses gave you permission to divorce your wives; but it was not 9 like that when all began. I tell you, if a man divorces his wife for any cause other than unchastity, and marries another, he commits adultery.'[q]

10 The disciples said to him, 'If that is the position with husband and wife, 11 it is better not to marry.' To this he replied, 'That is something which not everyone can accept, but only those 12 for whom God has appointed it. For while some are incapable of marriage because they are born so, or were

made so by men, there are others who have themselves renounced marriage for the sake of the kingdom of Heaven. Let those accept it who can.'

Jesus welcomes children

They brought children for him to lay 13 his hands on them with prayer. The disciples rebuked them, but Jesus 14 said to them, 'Let the children come to me; do not try to stop them; for the kingdom of Heaven belongs to such as these.' And he laid his hands 15 on the children, and went his way.

A rich man's question

And now a man came up and asked 16 him, 'Master, what good must I do to gain eternal life?' 'Good?' said Jesus. 17 'Why do you ask me about that? One alone is good. But if you wish to enter into life, keep the commandments.' 'Which commandments?' he asked. 18 Jesus answered, 'Do not murder; do not commit adultery; do not steal; do not give false evidence; honour your 19 father and mother; and love your neighbour as yourself.' The young 20 man answered, 'I have kept all these. Where do I still fall short?' Jesus said 21 to him, 'If you wish to go the whole way, go, sell your possessions, and give to the poor, and then you will have riches in heaven; and come, follow me.' When the young man 22 heard this, he went away with a heavy heart; for he was a man of great wealth.

Jesus said to his disciples, 'I tell 23 you this: a rich man will find it hard to enter the kingdom of Heaven. I 24 repeat, it is easier for a camel to pass through the eye of a needle than for a rich man to enter the kingdom of God.' The disciples were amazed to 25 hear this. 'Then who can be saved?' they asked. Jesus looked at them, and 26 said, 'For men this is impossible; but everything is possible for God.'

About rewards

At this Peter said, 'We here have left 27 everything to become your followers. What will there be for us?' Jesus 28 replied, 'I tell you this: in the world that is to be, when the Son of Man is seated on his throne in heavenly splendour, you my followers will have thrones of your own, where you will sit as judges of the twelve tribes of Israel. And anyone who has left 29

---

[p] Or Is there any ground on which it is lawful for a man to divorce his wife? [q] Some witnesses add And the man who marries a woman so divorced commits adultery.

brothers or sisters, father, mother, or children, land or houses for the sake of my name will be repaid many times 30 over, and gain eternal life. But many who are first will be last, and the last first.'

Labourers in the vineyard

20 'The kingdom of Heaven is like this. There was once a landowner who went out early one morning to hire 2 labourers for his vineyard; and after agreeing to pay them the usual day's wage[r] he sent them off to work. 3 Going out three hours later he saw some more men standing idle in the 4 market-place. "Go and join the others in the vineyard," he said, "and I will pay you a fair wage"; so off they went. 5 At midday he went out again, and at three in the afternoon, and made 6 the same arrangement as before. An hour before sunset he went out and found another group standing there; so he said to them, "Why are you standing about like this all day with 7 nothing to do?" "Because no one has hired us", they replied; so he told them, "Go and join the others 8 in the vineyard." When evening fell, the owner of the vineyard said to his steward, "Call the labourers and give them their pay, beginning with those who came last and ending with 9 the first." Those who had started work an hour before sunset came forward, and were paid the full day's 10 wage.[8] When it was the turn of the men who had come first, they expected something extra, but were paid 11 the same amount as the others. As they took it, they grumbled at their 12 employer: "These late-comers have done only one hour's work, yet you have put them on a level with us, who have sweated the whole day long in 13 the blazing sun!" The owner turned to one of them and said, "My friend, I am not being unfair to you. You agreed on the usual wage for the day,[t] 14 did you not? Take your pay and go home. I choose to pay the last man 15 the same as you. Surely I am free to do what I like with my own money. Why be jealous because I am kind?" 16 Thus will the last be first, and the first last.'

Jesus again speaks of his death

17 Jesus was journeying towards Jerusalem, and on the way he took the Twelve aside, and said to them, 'We 18 are now going to Jerusalem, and the Son of Man will be given up to the chief priests and the doctors of the law; they will condemn him to death and 19 hand him over to the foreign power, to be mocked and flogged and crucified, and on the third day he will be raised to life again.'

True greatness

The mother of Zebedee's sons then 20 came before him, with her sons. She bowed low and begged a favour. 'What is it you wish?' asked Jesus. 'I 21 want you', she said, 'to give orders that in your kingdom my two sons here may sit next to you, one at your right, and the other at your left.' Jesus turned to the brothers and said, 22 'You do not understand what you are asking. Can you drink the cup that I am to drink?' 'We can', they replied. Then he said to them, 'You shall in- 23 deed share my cup; but to sit at my right or left is not for me to grant; it is for those to whom it has already been assigned by my Father.'

When the other ten heard this, they 24 were indignant with the two brothers. So Jesus called them to him and said, 25 'You know that in the world, rulers lord it over their subjects, and their great men make them feel the weight of authority; but it shall not be so 26 with you. Among you, whoever wants to be great must be your servant, and 27 whoever wants to be first must be the willing slave of all—like the Son of 28 Man; he did not come to be served, but to serve, and to give up his life as a ransom for many.'

Sight restored to two blind men

As they were leaving Jericho he was 29 followed by a great crowd of people. At the roadside sat two blind men. 30 When they heard it said that Jesus was passing they shouted, 'Have pity on us, Son of David.' The people told 31 them sharply to be quiet. But they shouted all the more, 'Sir, have pity on us; have pity on us, Son of David.' Jesus stopped and called the men. 32 'What do you want me to do for you?' he asked. 'Sir,' they answered, 'we 33 want our sight.' Jesus was deeply 34 moved, and touched their eyes. At once their sight came back, and they followed him.

r Literally one denarius for the day.　　　s Literally one denarius each.　　　t Literally You agreed on a denarius.

Jesus rides into Jerusalem

They were now nearing Jerusalem; and when they reached Bethphage at the Mount of Olives, Jesus sent two disciples with these instructions: 'Go to the village opposite, where you will at once find a donkey tethered with her foal beside her; untie them, and bring them to me. If anyone speaks to you, say, "Our Master needs them"; and he will let you take them at once.'*u* This was to fulfil the prophecy which says, 'Tell the daughter of Zion, "Here is your king, who comes to you in gentleness, riding on an ass, riding on the foal of a beast of burden."'

The disciples went and did as Jesus had directed, and brought the donkey and her foal; they laid their cloaks on them and Jesus mounted. Crowds of people carpeted the road with their cloaks, and some cut branches from the trees to spread in his path. Then the crowd that went ahead and the others that came behind raised the shout: 'Hosanna to the Son of David! Blessings on him who comes in the name of the Lord! Hosanna in the heavens!'

When he entered Jerusalem the whole city went wild with excitement. 'Who is this?' people asked, and the crowd replied, 'This is the prophet Jesus, from Nazareth in Galilee.'

Jesus drives traders from the temple

Jesus then went into the temple and drove out all who were buying and selling in the temple precincts; he upset the tables of the money-changers and the seats of the dealers in pigeons; and said to them, 'Scripture says, "My house shall be called a house of prayer"; but you are making it a robbers' cave.'

Applause and opposition in the temple

In the temple blind men and cripples came to him, and he healed them. The chief priests and doctors of the law saw the wonderful things he did, and heard the boys in the temple shouting, 'Hosanna to the Son of David!', and they asked him indignantly, 'Do you hear what they are saying?' Jesus answered, 'I do; have you never read that text, "Thou hast made children and babes at the breast sound aloud thy praise"?' Then he left them and went out of the city to Bethany, where he spent the night.

A lesson from a fig-tree

Next morning on his way to the city he felt hungry; and seeing a fig-tree at the roadside he went up to it, but found nothing on it but leaves. He said to the tree, 'You shall never bear fruit any more!'; and the tree withered away at once. The disciples were amazed at the sight. 'How is it', they asked, 'that the tree has withered so suddenly?' Jesus answered them, 'I tell you this: if only you have faith and have no doubts, you will do what has been done to the fig-tree; and more than that, you need only say to this mountain, "Be lifted from your place and hurled into the sea", and what you say will be done. And whatever you pray for in faith you will receive.'

About the authority of Jesus

He entered the temple, and the chief priests and elders of the nation came to him with the question: 'By what authority are you acting like this? Who gave you this authority?' Jesus replied, 'I have a question to ask you too; answer it, and I will tell you by what authority I act. The baptism of John: was it from God, or from men?' This set them arguing among themselves: 'If we say, "from God", he will say, "Then why did you not believe him?" But if we say, "from men", we are afraid of the people, for they all take John for a prophet.' So they answered, 'We do not know.' And Jesus said: 'Then neither will I tell you by what authority I act.'

Two sons and their father

'But what do you think about this? A man had two sons. He went to the first, and said, "My boy, go and work today in the vineyard." "I will, sir", the boy replied; but he never went. The father came to the second and said the same. "I will not", he replied, but afterwards he changed his mind and went. Which of these two did as his father wished?' 'The second', they said. Then Jesus answered, 'I tell you this: tax-gatherers and prostitutes are entering the kingdom of God ahead of you. For when John came to show you the right way to live, you did not believe him, but the tax-gatherers and prostitutes did; and even when you had seen that, you did not change your minds and believe him.'

u Or "Our Master needs them and will send them back straight away."

Tenants in a vineyard

33 'Listen to another parable. There was a landowner who planted a vineyard: he put a wall round it, hewed out a winepress, and built a watch-tower; then he let it out to vine-growers
34 and went abroad. When the vintage season approached, he sent his servants to the tenants to collect the
35 produce due to him. But they took his servants and thrashed one, killed
36 another, and stoned a third. Again, he sent other servants, this time a larger number; and they did the same to
37 them. At last he sent to them his son. "They will respect my son", he said.
38 But when they saw the son the tenants said to one another, "This is the heir; come on, let us kill him, and get
39 his inheritance." And they took him, flung him out of the vineyard, and
40 killed him. When the owner of the vineyard comes, how do you think
41 he will deal with those tenants?' 'He will bring those bad men to a bad end', they answered, 'and hand the vineyard over to other tenants, who will let him have his share of the crop
42 when the season comes.' Then Jesus said to them, 'Have you never read in the scriptures: "The stone which the builders rejected has become the main corner-stone. This is the Lord's doing, and it is wonderful in our eyes"?
43 Therefore, I tell you, the kingdom of God will be taken away from you, and given to a nation that yields the proper fruit.'*v*
45 When the chief priests and Pharisees heard his parables, they saw that
46 he was referring to them; they wanted to arrest him, but they were afraid of the people, who looked on Jesus as a prophet.

A wedding-feast

22 Then Jesus spoke to them again in
2 parables: 'The kingdom of Heaven is like this. There was a king who prepared a feast for his son's wedding;
3 but when he sent his servants to summon the guests he had invited, they
4 would not come. He sent others again, telling them to say to the guests, "See now! I have prepared this feast for you. I have had my bullocks and fatted beasts slaughtered; everything is ready; come to the wedding at
5 once." But they took no notice; one went off to his farm, another to his
6 business, and the others seized the

servants, attacked them brutally, and killed them. The king was furious; he 7 sent troops to kill those murderers and set their town on fire. Then he 8 said to his servants, "The wedding-feast is ready; but the guests I invited did not deserve the honour. Go out to 9 the main thoroughfares, and invite everyone you can find to the wedding." The servants went out into the 10 streets, and collected all they could find, good and bad alike. So the hall was packed with guests.
'When the king came in to see the 11 company at table, he observed one man who was not dressed for a wedding. "My friend," said the king, 12 "how do you come to be here without your wedding clothes?" He had nothing to say. The king then said to 13 his attendants, "Bind him hand and foot; turn him out into the dark, the place of wailing and grinding of teeth." For though many are invited, 14 few are chosen.'

Paying tax to the Emperor

Then the Pharisees went away and 15 agreed on a plan to trap him in his own words. Some of their followers 16 were sent to him in company with men of Herod's party. They said, 'Master, you are an honest man, we know; you teach in all honesty the way of life that God requires, truckling to no man, whoever he may be. Give us your ruling on this: are we 17 or are we not permitted to pay taxes to the Roman Emperor?' Jesus was 18 aware of their malicious intention and said to them, 'You hypocrites! Why are you trying to catch me out? Show 19 me the money in which the tax is paid.' They handed him a silver piece. Jesus asked, 'Whose head is this, and 20 whose inscription?' 'Caesar's', they 21 replied. He said to them, 'Then pay Caesar what is due to Caesar, and pay God what is due to God.' This answer 22 took them by surprise, and they went away and left him alone.

About resurrection

The same day Sadducees came to him, 23 maintaining that there is no resurrection. Their question was this: 'Master, 24 Moses said, "If a man should die childless, his brother shall marry the widow and carry on his brother's family." Now we knew of seven 25 brothers. The first married and died,

v Some witnesses add (44) Any man who falls on this stone will be dashed to pieces; and if it falls on a man he will be crushed by it.

and as he was without issue his wife
6 was left to his brother. The same
thing happened with the second, and
the third, and so on with all seven.
8 Last of all the woman died. At the
resurrection, then, whose wife will she
be, for they had all married her?'
9 Jesus answered: 'You are mistaken,
because you know neither the scrip-
10 tures nor the power of God. At the
resurrection men and women do not
marry; they are like angels in heaven.
11 'But about the resurrection of the
dead, have you never read what God
12 himself said to you: "I am the God
of Abraham, the God of Isaac, and
the God of Jacob"? He is not God of
13 the dead but of the living.' The people heard what he said, and were
astounded at his teaching.

The greatest commandment

34 Hearing that he had silenced the Sadducees, the Pharisees met together;
35 and one of their number[w] tested him
36 with this question:'Master,which is the
greatest commandment in the Law?'
37 He answered, '"Love the Lord your
God with all your heart, with all your
38 soul, with all your mind." That is the
greatest commandment. It comes first.
39 The second is like it: "Love your neigh-
40 bour as yourself." Everything in the
Law and the prophets hangs on these
two commandments.'

About the Messiah

41 Turning to the assembled Pharisees
42 Jesus asked them, 'What is your
opinion about the Messiah? Whose
son is he?' 'The son of David', they
43 replied. 'How then is it', he asked,
'that David by inspiration calls him
44 "Lord"? For he says, "The Lord said
to my Lord, 'Sit at my right hand
until I put your enemies under your
45 feet.'" If David calls him "Lord",
46 how can he be David's son?' Not a
man could say a word in reply; and
from that day forward no one dared
ask him another question.

Pride and pretence

23 Jesus then addressed the people and
2 his disciples in these words: 'The
doctors of the law and the Pharisees
3 sit in the chair of Moses; therefore do
what they tell you; pay attention to
their words. But do not follow their
practice; for they say one thing and
do another. They make up heavy 4
packs and pile them on men's shoulders, but will not raise a finger to lift
the load themselves. Whatever they 5
do is done for show. They go about
with broad phylacteries[x] and with
large tassels on their robes; they like 6
to have places of honour at feasts and
the chief seats in synagogues, to be 7
greeted respectfully in the street, and
to be addressed as "rabbi".'

Real humility

'But you must not be called "rabbi"; 8
for you have one Rabbi, and you
are all brothers. Do not call any man 9
on earth "father"; for you have one
Father, and he is in heaven. Nor must 10
you be called "teacher"; you have
one Teacher, the Messiah. The great- 11
est among you must be your servant.
For whoever exalts himself will be 12
humbled; and whoever humbles himself will be exalted.'

Teachers who mislead

'Alas, alas for you, lawyers and Phari- 13
sees, hypocrites that you are! You shut
the door of the kingdom of Heaven in
men's faces; you do not enter yourselves, and when others are entering,
you stop them.[y]

'Alas for you, lawyers and Phari- 15
sees, hypocrites! You travel over sea
and land to win one convert; and
when you have won him you make
him twice as fit for hell as you are
yourselves.

'Alas for you, blind guides! You say, 16
"If a man swears by the sanctuary,
that is nothing; but if he swears by
the gold in the sanctuary, he is bound
by his oath." Blind fools! Which is 17
the more important, the gold, or the
sanctuary which sanctifies the gold?
Or you say, "If a man swears by the 18
altar, that is nothing; but if he swears
by the offering that lies on the altar,
he is bound by his oath." What 19
blindness! Which is the more important, the offering, or the altar which
sanctifies it? To swear by the altar, 20
then, is to swear both by the altar and
by whatever lies on it; to swear by 21
the sanctuary is to swear both by the
sanctuary and by him who dwells
there; and to swear by heaven is to 22
swear both by the throne of God and
by him who sits upon it.'

---

w *Some witnesses insert* a lawyer.   x *See Deuteronomy 6. 8–9 and Exodus 13. 9.*   y *Some witnesses add* (14) Alas for you, lawyers and Pharisees, hypocrites! You eat up the property of widows,
while you say long prayers for appearance' sake. You will receive the severest sentence.

The outside and the inside

23 'Alas for you, lawyers and Pharisees, hypocrites! You pay tithes of mint and dill and cummin; but you have overlooked the weightier demands of the Law, justice, mercy, and good faith. It is these you should have practised, without neglecting the others.
24 Blind guides! You strain off a midge, yet gulp down a camel!
25   'Alas for you, lawyers and Pharisees, hypocrites! You clean the outside of cup and dish, which you have filled inside by robbery and self-indulgence!
26 Blind Pharisee! Clean the inside of the cup first; then the outside will be clean also.
27   'Alas for you, lawyers and Pharisees, hypocrites! You are like tombs covered with whitewash; they look well from outside, but inside they are full of dead men's bones and all kinds
28 of filth. So it is with you: outside you look like honest men, but inside you are brim-full of hypocrisy and crime.'

A heritage of crime

29 'Alas for you, lawyers and Pharisees, hypocrites! You build up the tombs of the prophets and embellish the
30 monuments of the saints, and you say, "If we had been alive in our fathers' time, we should never have taken part with them in the murder of the pro-
31 phets." So you acknowledge that you are the sons of the men who killed the
32 prophets. Go on then, finish off what your fathers began!*z*
33   'You snakes, you vipers' brood, how can you escape being condemned
34 to hell? I send you therefore prophets, sages, and teachers; some of them you will kill and crucify, others you will flog in your synagogues and hound
35 from city to city. And so, on you will fall the guilt of all the innocent blood spilt on the ground, from innocent Abel to Zechariah son of Berachiah, whom you murdered between the
36 sanctuary and the altar. Believe me, this generation will bear the guilt of it all.

Jerusalem the doomed city

37 'O Jerusalem, Jerusalem, the city that murders the prophets and stones the messengers sent to her! How often have I longed to gather your children, as a hen gathers her brood under her wings; but you would
38 not let me. Look, look! there is your

temple, forsaken by God.*a b* And I tell 3 you, you shall never see me until the time when you say, "Blessings on him who comes in the name of the Lord."'

Destruction of the temple foretold

Jesus was leaving the temple when 2 his disciples came and pointed to the temple buildings. He answered, 'Yes, 2 look at it all. I tell you this: not one stone will be left upon another; all will be thrown down.'

Troubles and persecutions

When he was sitting on the Mount of 3 Olives the disciples came to speak to him privately. 'Tell us,' they said, 'when will this happen? And what will be the signal for your coming and the end of the age?'
    Jesus replied: 'Take care that no 4 one misleads you. For many will 5 come claiming my name and saying, "I am the Messiah"; and many will be misled by them. The time is coming 6 when you will hear the noise of battle near at hand and the news of battles far away; see that you are not alarmed. Such things are bound to happen; but the end is still to come. For nation will 7 make war upon nation, kingdom upon kingdom; there will be famines and earthquakes in many places. With all 8 these things the birth-pangs of the new age begin.
    'You will then be handed over for 9 punishment and execution; and men of all nations will hate you for your allegiance to me. Many will fall from 1 their faith; they will betray one another and hate one another. Many 1 false prophets will arise, and will mislead many; and as lawlessness 1 spreads, men's love for one another will grow cold. But the man who holds 1 out to the end will be saved. And this 1 gospel of the Kingdom will be proclaimed throughout the earth as a testimony to all nations; and then the end will come.'

'The abomination of desolation'

'So when you see "the abomination 1 of desolation", of which the prophet Daniel spoke, standing in the holy place (let the reader understand), then those who are in Judaea must 1 take to the hills. If a man is on the 1 roof, he must not come down to fetch his goods from the house; if in the ▶ field, he must not turn back for his

z Or You too must come up to your fathers' standards.   *a* Or Look, your home is desolate.
b Some witnesses add and laid waste.

9 coat. Alas for women with child in those days, and for those who have 0 children at the breast! Pray that it may not be winter when you have to 1 make your escape, or Sabbath. It will be a time of great distress; there has never been such a time from the beginning of the world until now, and 2 will never be again. If that time of troubles were not cut short, no living thing could survive; but for the sake of God's chosen it will be cut short.'

The coming of the Son of Man

3 'Then, if anyone says to you, "Look, here is the Messiah", or, "There he is", 4 do not believe it. Impostors will come claiming to be messiahs or prophets, and they will produce great signs and wonders to mislead even God's chosen, 5 if such a thing were possible. See, I 6 have forewarned you. If they tell you, "He is there in the wilderness", do not go out; or if they say, "He is there in the inner room", do not 7 believe it. Like lightning from the east, flashing as far as the west, will be the coming of the Son of Man.

8 'Wherever the corpse is, there the vultures will gather.

9 'As soon as the distress of those days has passed, the sun will be darkened, the moon will not give her light, the stars will fall from the sky, the 0 celestial powers will be shaken. Then will appear in heaven the sign that heralds the Son of Man. All the peoples of the world will make lamentation, and they will see the Son of Man coming on the clouds of heaven 1 with great power and glory. With a trumpet blast he will send out his angels, and they will gather his chosen from the four winds, from the farthest bounds of heaven on every side.

2 'Learn a lesson from the fig-tree. When its tender shoots appear and are breaking into leaf, you know that 3 summer is near. In the same way, when you see all these things, you may know that the end is near,*c* at 4 the very door. I tell you this: the present generation will live to see it 5 all. Heaven and earth will pass away; my words will never pass away.'

No one knows the day or hour: 'keep awake'

6 'But about that day and hour no one knows, not even the angels in heaven, not even the Son; only the Father.

'As things were in Noah's days, so 37 will they be when the Son of Man comes. In the days before the flood 38 they ate and drank and married, until the day that Noah went into the ark, and they knew nothing until the 39 flood came and swept them all away. That is how it will be when the Son of Man comes. Then there will be two 40 men in the field; one will be taken, the other left; two women grinding 41 at the mill; one will be taken, the other left.

'Keep awake, then; for you do not 42 know on what day your Lord is to come. Remember, if the householder 43 had known at what time of night the burglar was coming, he would have kept awake and not have let his house be broken into. Hold your- 44 selves ready, therefore, because the Son of Man will come at the time you least expect him.'

The trusty servant

'Who is the trusty servant, the sen- 45 sible man charged by his master to manage his household staff and issue their rations at the proper time? Happy that servant who is found at 46 his task when his master comes! I tell 47 you this: he will be put in charge of all his master's property. But if he is 48 a bad servant and says to himself, "The master is a long time coming", and begins to bully the other servants 49 and to eat and drink with his drunken friends, then the master will arrive on 50 a day that servant does not expect, at a time he does not know, and will cut 51 him in pieces. Thus he will find his place among the hypocrites, where there is wailing and grinding of teeth.'

Ten girls and their lamps

'When that day comes, the kingdom 25 of Heaven will be like this. There were ten girls, who took their lamps and went out to meet the bridegroom. Five of them were foolish, and five 2 prudent; when the foolish ones took 3 their lamps, they took no oil with them, but the others took flasks of oil 4 with their lamps. As the bridegroom 5 was late in coming they all dozed off to sleep. But at midnight a cry 6 was heard: "Here is the bridegroom! Come out to meet him." With that 7 the girls all got up and trimmed their lamps. The foolish said to the prudent, 8 "Our lamps are going out; give us some of your oil." "No," they said; 9

c Or that he is near.

"there will never be enough for all of us. You had better go to the shop and 10 buy some for yourselves." While they were away the bridegroom arrived; those who were ready went in with him to the wedding; and the door was 11 shut. And then the other five came back. "Sir, sir," they cried, "open the 12 door for us." But he answered, "I 13 declare, I do not know you." Keep awake then; for you never know the day or the hour.'

Three servants

14 'It is like a man going abroad, who called his servants and put his capi- 15 tal in their hands; to one he gave five bags of gold, to another two, to another one, each according to his capacity. Then he left the country. 16 The man who had the five bags went at once and employed them in busi- ness, and made a profit of five bags, 17 and the man who had the two bags 18 made two. But the man who had been given one bag of gold went off and dug a hole in the ground, and hid his 19 master's money. A long time after- wards their master returned, and pro- ceeded to settle accounts with them. 20 The man who had been given the five bags of gold came and produced the five he had made: "Master," he said, "you left five bags with me; 21 look, I have made five more." "Well done, my good and trusty servant!" said the master. "You have proved trustworthy in a small way; I will now put you in charge of something big. Come and share your master's 22 delight." The man with the two bags then came and said, "Master, you left two bags with me; look, I have made 23 two more." "Well done, my good and trusty servant!" said the master. "You have proved trustworthy in a small way; I will now put you in charge of something big. Come and 24 share your master's delight." Then the man who had been given one bag came and said, "Master, I knew you to be a hard man: you reap where you have not sown, you gather where 25 you have not scattered; so I was afraid, and I went and hid your gold in the ground. Here it is—you have 26 what belongs to you." "You lazy ras- cal!" said the master. "You knew that I reap where I have not sown, and gather where I have not scattered? 27 Then you ought to have put my money on deposit, and on my return I should 28 have got it back with interest. Take the bag of gold from him, and give

it to the one with the ten bags. For 2 the man who has will always be given more, till he has enough and to spare; and the man who has not will forfeit even what he has. Fling the useless 3 servant out into the dark, the place of wailing and grinding of teeth!"'

Judging the nations

'When the Son of Man comes in his 3 glory and all the angels with him, he will sit in state on his throne, with all 3 the nations gathered before him. He will separate men into two groups, as a shepherd separates the sheep from the goats, and he will place the sheep 3 on his right hand and the goats on his left. Then the king will say to those 3 on his right hand, "You have my Father's blessing; come, enter and possess the kingdom that has been ready for you since the world was made. For when I was hungry, you 3 gave me food; when thirsty, you gave me drink; when I was a stranger you took me into your home, when naked 3 you clothed me; when I was ill you came to my help, when in prison you visited me." Then the righteous will 3 reply, "Lord, when was it that we saw you hungry and fed you, or thirsty and gave you drink, a stranger and 3 took you home, or naked and clothed you? When did we see you ill or in 3 prison, and come to visit you?" And 4 the king will answer, "I tell you this: anything you did for one of my bro- thers here, however humble, you did for me." Then he will say to those on 4 his left hand, "The curse is upon you; go from my sight to the eternal fire that is ready for the devil and his angels. For when I was hungry you 4 gave me nothing to eat, when thirsty nothing to drink; when I was a stran- 4 ger you gave me no home, when naked you did not clothe me; when I was ill and in prison you did not come to my help." And they too will reply, "Lord, 4 when was it that we saw you hungry or thirsty or a stranger or naked or ill or in prison, and did nothing for you?" And he will answer, "I tell you 4 this: anything you did not do for one of these, however humble, you did not do for me." And they will go away to 4 eternal punishment, but the righteous will enter eternal life.'

A plot to kill Jesus

When Jesus had finished this dis- 2 course he said to his disciples, 'You 2 know that in two days' time it will be

Passover, and the Son of Man is to be handed over for crucifixion.'

3 Then the chief priests and the elders of the nation met in the palace 4 of the High Priest, Caiaphas; and there they conferred together on a scheme to have Jesus arrested by 5 some trick and put to death. 'It must not be during the festival,' they said, 'or there may be rioting among the people.'

A woman anoints Jesus

6 Jesus was at Bethany in the house of 7 Simon the leper, when a woman came to him with a small bottle of fragrant oil, very costly; and as he sat at table she began to pour it over his head. 8 The disciples were indignant when they saw it. 'Why this waste?' they 9 said; 'it could have been sold for a good sum and the money given to the 10 poor.' Jesus was aware of this, and said to them, 'Why must you make trouble for the woman? It is a fine 11 thing she has done for me. You have the poor among you always; but you 12 will not always have me. When she poured this oil on my body it was her 13 way of preparing me for burial. I tell you this: wherever in all the world this gospel is proclaimed, what she has done will be told as her memorial.'

Judas Iscariot plans to betray Jesus

14 Then one of the Twelve, the man called Judas Iscariot, went to the 15 chief priests and said, 'What will you give me to betray him to you?' They weighed him out[d] thirty silver pieces. 16 From that moment he began to look out for an opportunity to betray him.

Preparation for the Passover

17 On the first day of Unleavened Bread the disciples came to ask Jesus, 'Where would you like us to prepare 18 for your Passover supper?' He answered, 'Go to a certain man in the city, and tell him, "The Master says, 'My appointed time is near; I am to keep Passover with my disciples at 19 your house.'"' The disciples did as Jesus directed them and prepared for Passover.

The Last Supper

20 In the evening he sat down with the 21 twelve disciples; and during supper he said, 'I tell you this: one of you 22 will betray me.' In great distress they exclaimed one after the other, 'Can you

mean me, Lord?' He answered, 'One 23 who has dipped his hand into this bowl with me will betray me. The Son 24 of Man is going the way appointed for him in the scriptures; but alas for that man by whom the Son of Man is betrayed! It would be better for that man if he had never been born.' Then Judas spoke, the one who was 25 to betray him: 'Rabbi, can you mean me?' Jesus replied, 'The words are yours.'[e]

During supper Jesus took bread, 26 and having said the blessing he broke it and gave it to the disciples with the words: 'Take this and eat; this is my body.' Then he took a cup, and having 27 offered thanks to God he gave it to them with the words: 'Drink from it, all of you. For this is my blood, the 28 blood of the covenant, shed for many for the forgiveness of sins. I tell you, 29 never again shall I drink from the fruit of the vine until that day when I drink it new with you in the kingdom of my Father.'

Jesus foretells Peter's denial

After singing the Passover Hymn, 30 they went out to the Mount of Olives. Then Jesus said to them, 'Tonight 31 you will all fall from your faith on my account; for it stands written: "I will strike the shepherd down and the sheep of his flock will be scattered." But after I am raised again, I will go 32 on before you into Galilee.' Peter 33 replied, 'Everyone else may fall away on your account, but I never will.' Jesus said to him, 'I tell you, tonight 34 before the cock crows you will disown me three times.' Peter said, 'Even if I 35 must die with you, I will never disown you.' And all the disciples said the same.

Jesus prays in Gethsemane

Jesus then came with his disciples to 36 a place called Gethsemane. He said to them, 'Sit here while I go over there to pray.' He took with him 37 Peter and the two sons of Zebedee. Anguish and dismay came over him, and he said to them, 'My heart is 38 ready to break with grief. Stop here, and stay awake with me.' He went on 39 a little, fell on his face in prayer, and said, 'My Father, if it is possible, let this cup pass me by. Yet not as I will, but as thou wilt.'

He came to the disciples and found 40 them asleep; and he said to Peter,

d Or agreed to pay him . . .   e Or It is as you say.

'What! Could none of you stay awake
41 with me one hour? Stay awake, and
pray that you may be spared the test.
The spirit is willing, but the flesh is
weak.'
42 He went away a second time, and
prayed: 'My Father, if it is not possible for this cup to pass me by without my drinking it, thy will be done.'
43 He came again and found them asleep,
44 for their eyes were heavy. So he left
them and went away again; and he
prayed the third time, using the same
words as before.

Jesus is arrested

45 Then he came to the disciples and said
to them, 'Still sleeping? Still taking
your ease? The hour has come! The
Son of Man is betrayed to sinful men.
46 Up, let us go forward; the traitor is
upon us.'
47 While he was still speaking, Judas,
one of the Twelve, appeared; with
him was a great crowd armed with
swords and cudgels, sent by the chief
priests and the elders of the nation.
48 The traitor gave them this sign: 'The
49 one I kiss is your man; seize him'; and
stepping forward at once, he said,
50 'Hail, Rabbi!', and kissed him. Jesus
replied, 'Friend, do what you are
here to do.'f They then came forward,
seized Jesus, and held him fast.
51 At that moment one of those with
Jesus reached for his sword and drew
it, and he struck at the High Priest's
52 servant and cut off his ear. But Jesus
said to him, 'Put up your sword. All
who take the sword die by the sword.
53 Do you suppose that I cannot appeal
to my Father, who would at once send
to my aid more than twelve legions
54 of angels? But how then could the
scriptures be fulfilled, which say that
this must be?'
55 At the same time Jesus spoke to
the crowd: 'Do you take me for a
bandit, that you have come out with
swords and cudgels to arrest me? Day
after day I sat teaching in the temple,
56 and you did not lay hands on me. But
this has all happened to fulfil what
the prophets wrote.'
Then the disciples all deserted him
and ran away.

Jesus is charged with blasphemy

57 Jesus was led off under arrest to the
house of Caiaphas the High Priest,
where the lawyers and elders were
58 assembled. Peter followed him at a
distance till he came to the High

Priest's courtyard, and going in he sat
down there among the attendants,
meaning to see the end of it all.
The chief priests and the whole 59
Council tried to find some allegation
against Jesus on which a death-
sentence could be based; but they 60
failed to find one, though many came
forward with false evidence. Finally
two men alleged that he had said, 'I 61
can pull down the temple of God, and
rebuild it in three days.' At this the 62
High Priest rose and said to him,
'Have you no answer to the charge
that these witnesses bring against
you?' But Jesus kept silence. The 63
High Priest then said, 'By the living
God I charge you to tell us: Are you
the Messiah, the Son of God?' Jesus 64
replied, 'The words are yours.g But
I tell you this: from now on, you will
see the Son of Man seated at the right
hand of Godh and coming on the
clouds of heaven.' At these words the 65
High Priest tore his robes and exclaimed, 'Blasphemy! Need we call
further witnesses? You have heard
the blasphemy. What is your opinion?' 66
'He is guilty,' they answered; 'he
should die.'
Then they spat in his face and struck 67
him with their fists; and others said,
as they beat him, 'Now, Messiah, if 68
you are a prophet, tell us who hit you.'

Peter disowns Jesus

Meanwhile Peter was sitting outside 69
in the courtyard when a serving-maid
accosted him and said, 'You were
there too with Jesus the Galilean.'
Peter denied it in face of them all. 'I 70
do not know what you mean', he said.
He then went out to the gateway, 71
where another girl, seeing him, said
to the people there, 'This fellow was
with Jesus of Nazareth.' Once again 72
he denied it, saying with an oath, 'I do
not know the man.' Shortly after- 73
wards the bystanders came up and
said to Peter, 'Surely you are another
of them; your accent gives you away!'
At this he broke into curses and de- 74
clared with an oath: 'I do not know
the man.' At that moment a cock
crew; and Peter remembered how 75
Jesus had said, 'Before the cock crows
you will disown me three times.' He
went outside, and wept bitterly.

Jesus is handed over to the Romans

When morning came, the chief priests 27
and the elders of the nation met in
conference to plan the death of Jesus.

f Or Friend, what are you here for?   g Or It is as you say.   h Literally of the Power.

2 They then put him in chains and led him away, to hand him over to Pilate, the Roman Governor.

Judas hangs himself

3 When Judas the traitor saw that Jesus had been condemned, he was seized with remorse, and returned the thirty silver pieces to the chief priests 4 and elders. 'I have sinned,' he said; 'I have brought an innocent man to his death.' But they said, 'What is 5 that to us? See to that yourself.' So he threw the money down in the temple and left them, and went and hanged himself.

6 Taking up the money, the chief priests argued: 'This cannot be put into the temple fund; it is blood-7 money.' So after conferring they used it to buy the Potter's Field, as a 8 burial-place for foreigners. This explains the name 'Blood Acre', by which that field has been known ever 9 since; and in this way fulfilment was given to the prophetic utterance of Jeremiah: 'They took[i] the thirty silver pieces, the price set on a man's head (for that was his price among 10 the Israelites), and gave the money for the potter's field, as the Lord directed me.'

Pilate questions Jesus

11 Jesus was now brought before the Governor; and as he stood there the Governor asked him, 'Are you the king of the Jews?' 'The words are 12 yours',[j] said Jesus; and to the charges laid against him by the chief priests 13 and elders he made no reply. Then Pilate said to him, 'Do you not hear all this evidence that is brought 14 against you?'; but he still refused to answer one word, to the Governor's great astonishment.

Jesus is sentenced to death

15 At the festival season it was the Governor's custom to release one 16 prisoner chosen by the people. There was then in custody a man of some notoriety, called Jesus[k] Bar-Abbas. 17 When they were assembled Pilate said to them, 'Which would you like me to release to you—Jesus[k] Bar-18 Abbas, or Jesus called Messiah?' For he knew that it was out of malice that they had brought Jesus before him.

19 While Pilate was sitting in court a message came to him from his wife: 'Have nothing to do with that innocent man; I was much troubled on his account in my dreams last night.'

Meanwhile the chief priests and 20 elders had persuaded the crowd to ask for the release of Bar-Abbas and to have Jesus put to death. So when the 21 Governor asked, 'Which of the two do you wish me to release to you?', they said, 'Bar-Abbas.' 'Then what 22 am I to do with Jesus called Messiah?' asked Pilate; and with one voice they answered, 'Crucify him!' 'Why, what 23 harm has he done?' Pilate asked; but they shouted all the louder, 'Crucify him!'

Pilate could see that nothing was 24 being gained, and a riot was starting; so he took water and washed his hands in full view of the people, saying, 'My hands are clean of this man's blood; see to that yourselves.' And 25 with one voice the people cried, 'His blood be on us, and on our children.' He then released Bar-Abbas to them; 26 but he had Jesus flogged, and handed him over to be crucified.

Soldiers jeer at Jesus

Pilate's soldiers then took Jesus into 27 the Governor's headquarters, where they collected the whole company round him. They stripped him and 28 dressed him in a scarlet mantle; and 29 plaiting a crown of thorns they placed it on his head, with a cane in his right hand. Falling on their knees before him they jeered at him: 'Hail, King of the Jews!' They spat on him, 30 and used the cane to beat him about the head. When they had finished 31 their mockery, they took off the mantle and dressed him in his own clothes.

Jesus is crucified

Then they led him away to be crucified. On their way out they met a man 32 from Cyrene, Simon by name, and pressed him into service to carry his cross.

So they came to a place called Gol-33 gotha (which means 'Place of a skull') and there he was offered a draught 34 of wine mixed with gall; but when he had tasted it he would not drink.

After fastening him to the cross 35 they divided his clothes among them by casting lots, and then sat down 36 there to keep watch. Over his head 37 was placed the inscription giving the charge: 'This is Jesus the king of the Jews.'

i Or I took.   *j* Or It is as you say.   *k* Some witnesses omit Jesus.

38 Two bandits were crucified with him, one on his right and the other on his left.

39 The passers-by hurled abuse at him: 40 they wagged their heads and cried, 'You would pull the temple down, would you, and build it in three days? Come down from the cross and save yourself, if you are indeed the Son of 41 God.' So too the chief priests with the lawyers and elders mocked at him: 42 'He saved others,' they said, 'but he cannot save himself. King of Israel, indeed! Let him come down now from the cross, and then we will believe 43 him. Did he trust in God? Let God rescue him, if he wants him—for he 44 said he was God's Son.' Even the bandits who were crucified with him taunted him in the same way.

The death of Jesus

45 From midday a darkness fell over the whole land, which lasted until three 46 in the afternoon; and about three Jesus cried aloud, '*Eli, Eli, lema sabachthani?*', which means, 'My God, my God, why hast thou forsaken me?' 47 Some of the bystanders, on hearing 48 this, said, 'He is calling Elijah.' One of them ran at once and fetched a sponge, which he soaked in sour wine, and held it to his lips on the end of a cane. 49 But the others said, 'Let us see if Elijah will come to save him.'

50 Jesus again gave a loud cry, and 51 breathed his last. At that moment the curtain of the temple was torn in two from top to bottom. There was an 52 earthquake, the rocks split and the graves opened, and many of God's 53 saints were raised from sleep; and coming out of their graves after his resurrection they entered the Holy 54 City, where many saw them. And when the centurion and his men who were keeping watch over Jesus saw the earthquake and all that was happening, they were filled with awe, and they said, 'Truly this man was a son of God.'[l]

The burial of Jesus

55 A number of women were also present, watching from a distance; they had followed Jesus from Galilee and waited 56 on him. Among them were Mary of Magdala, Mary the mother of James and Joseph, and the mother of the sons of Zebedee.

57 When evening fell, there came a man of Arimathaea, Joseph by name, who was a man of means, and had himself become a disciple of Jesus. He 58 approached Pilate, and asked for the body of Jesus; and Pilate gave orders that he should have it. Joseph took 59 the body, wrapped it in a clean linen sheet, and laid it in his own unused 60 tomb, which he had cut out of the rock; he then rolled a large stone against the entrance, and went away. Mary of Magdala was there, and the 61 other Mary, sitting opposite the grave.

The grave is secured

Next day, the morning after that 62 Friday, the chief priests and the Pharisees came in a body to Pilate. 'Your Excellency,' they said, 'we re- 63 call how that impostor said while he was still alive, "I am to be raised again after three days." So will you 64 give orders for the grave to be made secure until the third day? Otherwise his disciples may come, steal the body, and then tell the people that he has been raised from the dead; and the final deception will be worse than the first.' 'You may have your guard,' 65 said Pilate; 'go and make it secure as best you can.' So they went and made 66 the grave secure; they sealed the stone, and left the guard in charge.

The resurrection

The Sabbath was over, and it was **28** about daybreak on Sunday, when Mary of Magdala and the other Mary came to look at the grave. Suddenly 2 there was a violent earthquake; an angel of the Lord descended from heaven; he came to the stone and rolled it away, and sat himself down on it. His face shone like lightning; 3 his garments were white as snow. At 4 the sight of him the guards shook with fear and lay like the dead.

The angel then addressed the wo- 5 men: 'You', he said, 'have nothing to fear. I know you are looking for Jesus who was crucified. He is not 6 here; he has been raised again, as he said he would be. Come and see the place where he was laid, and then go 7 quickly and tell his disciples: "He has been raised from the dead and is going on before you into Galilee; there you will see him." That is what I had to tell you.'

They hurried away from the tomb 8 in awe and great joy, and ran to tell the disciples. Suddenly Jesus was there 9

l Or the Son of God.

in their path. He gave them his greeting, and they came up and clasped his
10 feet, falling prostrate before him. Then Jesus said to them, 'Do not be afraid. Go and take word to my brothers that they are to leave for Galilee. They will see me there.'

Attempts to suppress the facts

11 The women had started on their way when some of the guard went into the city and reported to the chief priests
12 everything that had happened. After meeting with the elders and conferring together, the chief priests offered the
13 soldiers a substantial bribe and told them to say, 'His disciples came by night and stole the body while we
14 were asleep.' They added, 'If this should reach the Governor's ears, we will put matters right with him and
15 see that you do not suffer.' So they

took the money and did as they were told. This story became widely known, and is current in Jewish circles to this day.

Jesus commissions his eleven disciples

The eleven disciples made their way 16 to Galilee, to the mountain where Jesus had told them to meet him. When they saw him, they fell pros- 17 trate before him, though some were doubtful. Jesus then came up and 18 spoke to them. He said: 'Full authority in heaven and on earth has been committed to me. Go forth therefore 19 and make all nations my disciples; baptize men everywhere in the name of the Father and the Son and the Holy Spirit, and teach them to observe 20 all that I have commanded you. And be assured, I am with you always, to the end of time.'

THE GOSPEL ACCORDING TO
MARK

John preaches repentance

1 HERE BEGINS the Gospel of Jesus Christ the Son of God.[a]
2   In the prophet Isaiah it stands written: 'Here is my herald whom I send on ahead of you, and he will
3 prepare your way. A voice crying aloud in the wilderness, "Prepare a way for the Lord; clear a straight
4 path for him."' And so it was that John the Baptist appeared in the wilderness proclaiming a baptism in token of repentance, for the forgive-
5 ness of sins; and they flocked to him from the whole Judaean country-side and the city of Jerusalem, and were baptized by him in the River Jordan, confessing their sins.
6   John was dressed in a rough coat of camel's hair, with a leather belt round his waist, and he fed on locusts
7 and wild honey. His proclamation ran: 'After me comes one who is mightier than I. I am not fit to un-
8 fasten his shoes. I have baptized you with water; he will baptize you with the Holy Spirit.'

The baptism and temptation of Jesus

It happened at this time that Jesus 9 came from Nazareth in Galilee and was baptized in the Jordan by John. At the moment when he came up out 10 of the water, he saw the heavens torn open and the Spirit, like a dove, descending upon him. And a voice 11 spoke from heaven: 'Thou art my Son, my Beloved;[b] on thee my favour rests.'
  Thereupon the Spirit sent him 12 away into the wilderness, and there 13 he remained for forty days tempted by Satan. He was among the wild beasts; and the angels waited on him.

Jesus proclaims the kingdom of God

After John had been arrested, Jesus 14 came into Galilee proclaiming the Gospel of God: 'The time has come; 15 the kingdom of God is upon you; repent, and believe the Gospel.'

Jesus calls four fishermen

Jesus was walking by the Sea of 16 Galilee when he saw Simon and his

a Some witnesses omit the Son of God.   b Or Thou art my only Son.

brother Andrew on the lake at work
with a casting-net; for they were
17 fishermen. Jesus said to them, 'Come
with me, and I will make you fishers
18 of men.' And at once they left their
nets and followed him.
19   When he had gone a little further
he saw James son of Zebedee and his
brother John, who were in the boat
20 overhauling their nets. He called them;
and, leaving their father Zebedee in the
boat with the hired men, they went off
to follow him.

The authority of Jesus in word and deed

21 They came to Capernaum, and on the
Sabbath he went to synagogue and
22 began to teach. The people were
astounded at his teaching, for, unlike
the doctors of the law, he taught with
23 a note of authority. Now there was a
man in the synagogue possessed by an
24 unclean spirit. He shrieked: 'What do
you want with us, Jesus of Nazareth?
Have you[c] come to destroy us? I
25 know who you are—the Holy One of
God.' Jesus rebuked him: 'Be silent',
26 he said, 'and come out of him.' And
the unclean spirit threw the man into
convulsions and with a loud cry left
27 him. They were all dumbfounded and
began to ask one another, 'What is
this? A new kind of teaching! He
speaks with authority. When he gives
orders, even the unclean spirits sub-
28 mit.' The news spread rapidly, and
he was soon spoken of all over the
district of Galilee.

Acts of healing

29 On leaving the synagogue they went
straight to the house of Simon and
Andrew; and James and John went
30 with them. Simon's mother-in-law
was ill in bed with fever. They told
31 him about her at once. He came forward, took her by the hand, and
helped her to her feet. The fever left
her and she waited upon them.
32   That evening after sunset they
brought to him all who were ill or
33 possessed by devils; and the whole
town was there, gathered at the door.
34 He healed many who suffered from
various diseases, and drove out many
devils. He would not let the devils
speak, because they knew who he was.

Jesus preaches all through Galilee

35 Very early next morning he got up
and went out. He went away to a
lonely spot and remained there in
prayer. But Simon and his compan- 36
ions searched him out, found him, and 37
said, 'They are all looking for you.'
He answered, 'Let us move on to the 38
country towns in the neighbourhood;
I have to proclaim my message there
also; that is what I came out to do.'
So all through Galilee he went, preach- 39
ing in the synagogues and casting out
the devils.

Jesus cleanses a leper

Once he was approached by a leper, 40
who knelt before him begging his
help. 'If only you will,' said the man,
'you can cleanse me.' In warm indig- 41
nation Jesus stretched out his hand,[d]
touched him, and said, 'Indeed I will;
be clean again.' The leprosy left him 42
immediately, and he was clean. Then 43
he dismissed him with this stern
warning: 'Be sure you say nothing to 44
anybody. Go and show yourself to the
priest, and make the offering laid
down by Moses for your cleansing;
that will certify the cure.' But the 45
man went out and made the whole
story public; he spread it far and wide,
until Jesus could no longer show himself in any town, but stayed outside
in the open country. Even so, people
kept coming to him from all quarters.

Authority to forgive sins

When after some days he returned to 2
Capernaum, the news went round
that he was at home; and such a crowd 2
collected that the space in front of
the door was not big enough to hold
them. And while he was proclaiming
the message to them, a man was 3
brought who was paralysed. Four men
were carrying him, but because of 4
the crowd they could not get him near.
So they opened up the roof over the
place where Jesus was, and when they
had broken through they lowered the
stretcher on which the paralysed man
was lying. When Jesus saw their faith, 5
he said to the paralysed man, 'My
son, your sins are forgiven.'
    Now there were some lawyers sit- 6
ting there and they thought to themselves, 'Why does the fellow talk like 7
that? This is blasphemy! Who but
God alone can forgive sins?' Jesus 8
knew in his own mind that this was
what they were thinking, and said to
them: 'Why do you harbour thoughts
like these? Is it easier to say to this 9

c Or You have.   d Some witnesses read Jesus was sorry for him and stretched out his hand; one
witness has simply He stretched out his hand.

paralysed man, "Your sins are forgiven", or to say, "Stand up, take 10 your bed, and walk"? But to convince you that the Son of Man has the right on earth to forgive sins'—he turned 11 to the paralysed man—'I say to you, stand up, take your bed, and go home.' 12 And he got up, and at once took his stretcher and went out in full view of them all, so that they were astounded and praised God. 'Never before', they said, 'have we seen the like.'

Jesus and the tax-gatherers

13 Once more he went away to the lakeside. All the crowd came to him, and 14 he taught them there. As he went along, he saw Levi son of Alphaeus at his seat in the custom-house, and said to him, 'Follow me'; and Levi rose and followed him.

15   When Jesus was at table in his house, many bad characters—taxgatherers and others—were seated with him and his disciples; for there 16 were many who followed him. Some doctors of the law who were Pharisees noticed him eating in this bad company, and said to his disciples, 'He eats with tax-gatherers and sinners!' 17 Jesus heard it and said to them, 'It is not the healthy that need a doctor, but the sick; I did not come to invite virtuous people, but sinners.'

About fasting

18 Once, when John's disciples and the Pharisees were keeping a fast, some people came to him and said, 'Why is it that John's disciples and the disciples of the Pharisees are fasting, 19 but yours are not?' Jesus said to them, 'Can you expect the bridegroom's friends to fast while the bridegroom is with them? As long as they have the bridegroom with them, there can 20 be no fasting. But the time will come when the bridegroom will be taken away from them, and on that day they will fast.

Patched clothes and old wine-skins

21 'No one sews a patch of unshrunk cloth on to an old coat; if he does, the patch tears away from it, the new from the old, and leaves a bigger hole. 22 No one puts new wine into old wineskins; if he does, the wine will burst the skins, and then wine and skins are both lost. Fresh skins for new wine!'

About the Sabbath

One Sabbath he was going through 23 the cornfields; and his disciples, as they went, began to pluck ears of corn. The Pharisees said to him, 'Look, 24 why are they doing what is forbidden on the Sabbath?' He answered, 'Have 25 you never read what David did when he and his men were hungry and had nothing to eat? He went into the 26 House of God, in the time of Abiathar the High Priest, and ate the sacred bread, though no one but a priest is allowed to eat it, and even gave it to his men.'

He also said to them, 'The Sabbath 27 was made for the sake of man and not man for the Sabbath: therefore the 28 Son of Man is sovereign even over the Sabbath.'

A man with a withered arm

On another occasion when he went to 3 synagogue, there was a man in the congregation who had a withered arm; and they were watching to see 2 whether Jesus would cure him on the Sabbath, so that they could bring a charge against him. He said to the 3 man with the withered arm, 'Come and stand out here.' Then he turned 4 to them: 'Is it permitted to do good or to do evil on the Sabbath, to save life or to kill?' They had nothing to say; and, looking round at them 5 with anger and sorrow at their obstinate stupidity, he said to the man, 'Stretch out your arm.' He stretched it out and his arm was restored. But 6 the Pharisees, on leaving the synagogue, began plotting against him with the partisans of Herod to see how they could make away with him.

A crowd by the lake

Jesus went away to the lake-side with 7 his disciples. Great numbers from Galilee, Judaea and Jerusalem, Idu- 8 maea and Transjordan, and the neighbourhood of Tyre and Sidon, heard what he was doing and came to see him. So he told his disciples to have 9 a boat ready for him, to save him from being crushed by the crowd. For he cured so many that sick people 10 of all kinds came crowding in upon him to touch him. The unclean spirits 11 too, when they saw him, would fall at his feet and cry aloud, 'You are the Son of God'; but he insisted that they 12 should not make him known.

The twelve apostles

13 He then went up into the hill-country
and called the men he wanted; and
14 they went and joined him. He appointed twelve as his companions,
whom he would send out to proclaim
15 the Gospel, with a commission to
16 drive out devils. So he appointed the
Twelve: to Simon he gave the name
17 Peter; then came the sons of Zebedee,
James and his brother John, to whom
he gave the name Boanerges, Sons of
18 Thunder; then Andrew and Philip
and Bartholomew and Matthew and
Thomas and James the son of Alphaeus and Thaddaeus and Simon,
19 a member of the Zealot party, and
Judas Iscariot, the man who betrayed
him.

Controversy with the doctors of the law

20 He entered a house; and once more
such a crowd collected round them
21 that they had no chance to eat. When
his family heard of this, they set out
to take charge of him; for people
were saying that he was out of his
mind.*e*

22 The doctors of the law, too, who
had come down from Jerusalem, said,
'He is possessed by Beelzebub', and,
'He drives out devils by the prince of
23 devils.' So he called them to come
forward, and spoke to them in para-
24 bles: 'How can Satan drive out Satan? If a kingdom is divided against
25 itself, that kingdom cannot stand; if
a household is divided against itself,
26 that house will never stand; and if
Satan is in rebellion against himself,
he is divided and cannot stand; and
that is the end of him.

27 'On the other hand, no one can
break into a strong man's house and
make off with his goods unless he has
first tied the strong man up; then he
can ransack the house.

28 'I tell you this: no sin, no slander,
29 is beyond forgiveness for men; but
whoever slanders the Holy Spirit can
never be forgiven; he is guilty of
30 eternal sin.' He said this because they
had declared that he was possessed
by an unclean spirit.

Jesus's relatives

31 Then his mother and his brothers
arrived, and remaining outside sent
in a message asking him to come out
32 to them. A crowd was sitting round
and word was brought to him: 'Your
mother and your brothers are outside

asking for you.' He replied, 'Who is 33
my mother? Who are my brothers?'
And looking round at those who were 34
sitting in the circle about him he said,
'Here are my mother and my brothers.
Whoever does the will of God is my 35
brother, my sister, my mother.'

Parables

On another occasion he began to 4
teach by the lake-side. The crowd that
gathered round him was so large that
he had to get into a boat on the lake,
and there he sat, with the whole
crowd on the beach right down to the
water's edge. And he taught them 2
many things by parables.

A sower

As he taught he said:
'Listen! A sower went out to sow. 3
And it happened that as he sowed, 4
some seed fell along the footpath; and
the birds came and ate it up. Some 5
seed fell on rocky ground, where it
had little soil, and it sprouted quickly
because it had no depth of earth; but 6
when the sun rose the young corn was
scorched, and as it had no root it
withered away. Some seed fell among 7
thistles; and the thistles shot up and
choked the corn, and it yielded no
crop. And some of the seed fell into 8
good soil, where it came up and grew,
and bore fruit; and the yield was
thirtyfold, sixtyfold, even a hundredfold.' He added, 'If you have ears to 9
hear, then hear.'

Why Jesus told parables

When he was alone, the Twelve and 10
others who were round him questioned
him about the parables. He replied, 11
'To you the secret of the kingdom of
God has been given; but to those who
are outside everything comes by way
of parables, so that (as Scripture says) 12
they may look and look, but see
nothing; they may hear and hear, but
understand nothing; otherwise they
might turn to God and be forgiven.'

The parable of the sower explained

So he said, 'You do not understand 13
this parable? How then are you to
understand any parable? The sower 14
sows the word. Those along the foot- 15
path are people in whom the word is
sown, but no sooner have they heard
it than Satan comes and carries off
the word which has been sown in
them. It is the same with those who 16

e Or of him. 'He is out of his mind', they said.

receive the seed on rocky ground; as soon as they hear the word, they accept
17 it with joy, but it strikes no root in them; they have no staying-power; then, when there is trouble or persecution on account of the word, they
18 fall away at once. Others again receive the seed among thistles; they
19 hear the word, but worldly cares and the false glamour of wealth and all kinds of evil desire come in and choke
20 the word, and it proves barren. And there are those who receive the seed in good soil; they hear the word and welcome it; and they bear fruit thirty-fold, sixtyfold, or a hundredfold.'

A lesson from a lamp

21 He said to them, 'Do you bring in the lamp to put it under the meal-tub, or under the bed? Surely it is brought
22 to be set on the lamp-stand. For nothing is hidden unless it is to be disclosed, and nothing put under cover unless it is to come into the
23 open. If you have ears to hear, then hear.'
24 He also said, 'Take note of what you hear; the measure you give is the measure you will receive, with some-
25 thing more besides. For the man who has will be given more, and the man who has not will forfeit even what he has.'

From sowing to harvest

26 He said, 'The kingdom of God is like this. A man scatters seed on the land;
27 he goes to bed at night and gets up in the morning, and the seed sprouts and grows—how, he does not know.
28 The ground produces a crop by itself, first the blade, then the ear, then full-
29 grown corn in the ear; but as soon as the crop is ripe, he plies the sickle, because harvest-time has come.'

A mustard-seed

30 He said also, 'How shall we picture the kingdom of God, or by what para-
31 ble shall we describe it? It is like the mustard-seed, which is smaller than any seed in the ground at its sowing.
32 But once sown, it springs up and grows taller than any other plant, and forms branches so large that the birds can settle in its shade.'
33 With many such parables he would give his message, so far as they
34 were able to receive it. He never spoke to them except in parables; but privately to his disciples he explained everything.

Jesus calms a storm

That day, in the evening, he said to 35 them, 'Let us cross over to the other side of the lake.' So they left the 36 crowd and took him with them in the boat where he had been sitting; and there were other boats accompanying him. A heavy squall came on and the 37 waves broke over the boat until it was all but swamped. Now he was in 38 the stern asleep on a cushion; they roused him and said, 'Master, we are sinking! Do you not care?' He awoke, 39 rebuked the wind, and said to the sea, 'Hush! Be still!' The wind dropped and there was a dead calm. He said to 40 them, 'Why are you such cowards? Have you no faith even now?' They 41 were awestruck and said to one another, 'Who can this be? Even the wind and the sea obey him.'

Jesus cures a madman

So they came to the other side of the 5 lake, into the country of the Gerasenes. As he stepped ashore, a man possessed 2 by an unclean spirit came up to him from among the tombs where he had 3 his dwelling. He could no longer be controlled; even chains were useless; he had often been fettered and chained 4 up, but he had snapped his chains and broken the fetters. No one was strong enough to master him. And so, un- 5 ceasingly, night and day, he would cry aloud among the tombs and on the hill-sides and cut himself with stones. When he saw Jesus in the distance, 6 he ran and flung himself down before him, shouting loudly, 'What do 7 you want with me, Jesus, son of the Most High God? In God's name do not torment me.' (For Jesus was 8 already saying to him, 'Out, unclean spirit, come out of this man!') Jesus 9 asked him, 'What is your name?' 'My name is Legion,' he said, 'there are so many of us.' And he begged 10 hard that Jesus would not send them out of the country.

Now there happened to be a large 11 herd of pigs feeding on the hill-side, and the spirits begged him, 'Send us 12 among the pigs and let us go into them.' He gave them leave; and the 13 unclean spirits came out and went into the pigs; and the herd, of about two thousand, rushed over the edge into the lake and were drowned.

The men in charge of them took 14 to their heels and carried the news to the town and country-side; and the people came out to see what had

15 happened. They came to Jesus and saw the madman who had been possessed by the legion of devils, sitting there clothed and in his right mind;
16 and they were afraid. The spectators told them how the madman had been cured and what had happened to the
17 pigs. Then they begged Jesus to leave the district.

18 As he was stepping into the boat, the man who had been possessed
19 begged to go with him. Jesus would not allow it, but said to him, 'Go home to your own folk and tell them what the Lord in his mercy has done for
20 you.' The man went off and spread the news in the Ten Towns*f* of all that Jesus had done for him; and they were all amazed.

Jairus's plea

21 As soon as Jesus had returned by boat to the other shore, a great crowd once more gathered round him. While he
22 was by the lake-side, the president of one of the synagogues came up, Jairus by name, and, when he saw him,
23 threw himself down at his feet and pleaded with him. 'My little daughter', he said, 'is at death's door. I beg you to come and lay your hands on her to cure her and save her life.'
24 So Jesus went with him, accompanied by a great crowd which pressed upon him.

A woman healed of haemorrhages

25 Among them was a woman who had suffered from haemorrhages for twelve
26 years; and in spite of long treatment by many doctors, on which she had spent all she had, there had been no improvement; on the contrary, she
27 had grown worse. She had heard what people were saying about Jesus, so she came up from behind in the crowd
28 and touched his cloak; for she said to herself, 'If I touch even his clothes,
29 I shall be cured.' And there and then the source of her haemorrhages dried up and she knew in herself that she
30 was cured of her trouble. At the same time Jesus, aware that power had gone out of him, turned round in the crowd and asked, 'Who touched my
31 clothes?' His disciples said to him, 'You see the crowd pressing upon you and yet you ask, "Who touched me?"'
32 Meanwhile he was looking round to
33 see who had done it. And the woman, trembling with fear when she grasped

what had happened to her, came and fell at his feet and told him the whole truth. He said to her, 'My daughter, 34 your faith has cured you. Go in peace, free for ever from this trouble.'

Jairus's daughter restored to life

While he was still speaking, a mes- 35 sage came from the president's house, 'Your daughter is dead; why trouble the Rabbi further?' But Jesus, over- 36 hearing the message as it was delivered, said to the president of the synagogue, 'Do not be afraid; only have faith.' After this he allowed no one 37 to accompany him except Peter and James and James's brother John. They came to the president's house, 38 where he found a great commotion, with loud crying and wailing. So he 39 went in and said to them, 'Why this crying and commotion? The child is not dead: she is asleep'; and they only 40 laughed at him. But after turning all the others out, he took the child's father and mother and his own companions and went in where the child was lying. Then, taking hold of her 41 hand, he said to her, '*Talitha cum*', which means, 'Get up, my child.' Immediately the girl got up and 42 walked about—she was twelve years old. At that they were beside themselves with amazement. He gave them 43 strict orders to let no one hear about it, and told them to give her something to eat.

Unbelief in Nazareth

He left that place and went to his **6** home town accompanied by his disciples. When the Sabbath came he be- 2 gan to teach in the synagogue; and the large congregation who heard him were amazed and said, 'Where does he get it from?', and, 'What wisdom is this that has been given him?', and, 'How does he work such miracles? Is not this the carpenter, the 3 son of Mary,*g* the brother of James and Joseph and Judas and Simon? And are not his sisters here with us?' So they fell foul of him. Jesus said to 4 them, 'A prophet will always be held in honour except in his home town, and among his kinsmen and family.' He could work no miracle there, ex- 5 cept that he put his hands on a few sick people and healed them; and he 6 was taken aback by their want of faith.

f Greek Decapolis.   *g* Some *witnesses read* Is not this the son of the carpenter and Mary . . .

Mission of the twelve apostles

On one of his teaching journeys round 7 the villages he summoned the Twelve and sent them out in pairs on a mission. He gave them authority over 8 unclean spirits, and instructed them to take nothing for the journey beyond a stick: no bread, no pack, no money 9 in their belts. They might wear sandals, 10 but not a second coat. 'When you are admitted to a house', he added, 'stay 11 there until you leave those parts. At any place where they will not receive you or listen to you, shake the dust off your feet as you leave, as a warn-12 ing to them.' So they set out and 13 called publicly for repentance. They drove out many devils, and many sick people they anointed with oil and cured.

Disturbing news for Herod

14 Now King Herod heard of it, for the fame of Jesus had spread; and people were saying,[h] 'John the Baptist has been raised to life, and that is why these miraculous powers are at work 15 in him.' Others said, 'It is Elijah.' Others again, 'He is a prophet like 16 one of the old prophets.' But Herod, when he heard of it, said, 'This is John, whom I beheaded, raised from the dead.'

The death of John the Baptist

17 For this same Herod had sent and arrested John and put him in prison on account of his brother Philip's wife, Herodias, whom he had married. 18 John had told Herod, 'You have no 19 right to your brother's wife.' Thus Herodias nursed a grudge against him and would willingly have killed him, 20 but she could not; for Herod went in awe of John, knowing him to be a good and holy man; so he kept him in custody. He liked to listen to him, although the listening left him greatly perplexed.

21   Herodias found her opportunity when Herod on his birthday gave a banquet to his chief officials and commanders and the leading men of 22 Galilee. Her daughter came in[i] and danced, and so delighted Herod and his guests that the king said to the girl, 'Ask what you like and I will 23 give it you.' And he swore an oath to her: 'Whatever you ask I will give 24 you, up to half my kingdom.' She went out and said to her mother,

'What shall I ask for?' She replied, 'The head of John the Baptist.' The 25 girl hastened back at once to the king with her request: 'I want you to give me here and now, on a dish, the head of John the Baptist.' The king was 26 greatly distressed, but out of regard for his oath and for his guests he could not bring himself to refuse her. So the king sent a soldier of the guard 27 with orders to bring John's head. The soldier went off and beheaded him in the prison, brought the head on a 28 dish, and gave it to the girl; and she gave it to her mother.

When John's disciples heard the 29 news, they came and took his body away and laid it in a tomb.

Feeding five thousand

The apostles now rejoined Jesus and 30 reported to him all that they had done and taught. He said to them, 31 'Come with me, by yourselves, to some lonely place where you can rest quietly.' (For they had no leisure even to eat, so many were coming and going.) Accordingly, they set off 32 privately by boat for a lonely place. But many saw them leave and re-33 cognized them, and came round by land, hurrying from all the towns towards the place, and arrived there first. When he came ashore, he saw 34 a great crowd; and his heart went out to them, because they were like sheep without a shepherd; and he had much to teach them. As the day 35 wore on, his disciples came up to him and said, 'This is a lonely place and it is getting very late; send the people 36 off to the farms and villages round about, to buy themselves something to eat.' 'Give them something to eat 37 yourselves', he answered. They replied, 'Are we to go and spend twenty pounds[j] on bread to give them a meal?' 'How many loaves have you?' he 38 asked; 'go and see.' They found out and told him, 'Five, and two fishes also.' He ordered them to make the 39 people sit down in groups on the green grass, and they sat down in 40 rows, a hundred rows of fifty each. Then, taking the five loaves and the 41 two fishes, he looked up to heaven, said the blessing, broke the loaves, and gave them to the disciples to distribute. He also divided the two 42 fishes among them. They all ate to their hearts' content; and twelve great 43 basketfuls of scraps were picked up,

h Some witnesses read and he said . . .   i Or A festive occasion came when Herod on his birthday gave . . . of Galilee. The daughter of Herodias came in . . .   j Literally 200 denarii.

44 with what was left of the fish. Those who ate the loaves numbered five thousand men.

Jesus walks on the water

45 As soon as it was over he made his disciples embark and cross to Bethsaida ahead of him, while he himself 46 sent the people away. After taking leave of them, he went up the hill-side 47 to pray. It grew late and the boat was already well out on the water, 48 while he was alone on the land. Somewhere between three and six in the morning, seeing them labouring at the oars against a head-wind, he came towards them, walking on the lake. 49 He was going to pass them by; but when they saw him walking on the lake, they thought it was a ghost and 50 cried out; for they all saw him and were terrified. But at once he spoke to them: 'Take heart! It is I; do not 51 be afraid.' Then he climbed into the boat beside them, and the wind dropped. At this they were completely 52 dumbfounded, for they had not understood the incident of the loaves; their minds were closed.

Jesus heals in Gennesaret

53 So they finished the crossing and came to land at Gennesaret, where 54 they made fast. When they came ashore, he was immediately recog- 55 nized; and the people scoured that whole country-side and brought the sick on stretchers to any place where 56 he was reported to be. Wherever he went, to farmsteads, villages, or towns, they laid out the sick in the market-places and begged him to let them simply touch the edge of his cloak; and all who touched him were cured.

About traditions

7 A group of Pharisees, with some doctors of the law who had come from 2 Jerusalem, met him and noticed that some of his disciples were eating their food with 'defiled' hands—in other 3 words, without washing them. (For the Pharisees and the Jews in general never eat without washing the hands,[k] in obedience to an old-established 4 tradition; and on coming from the market-place they never eat without first washing. And there are many other points on which they have a

traditional rule to maintain, for example, washing of cups and jugs and copper bowls.) Accordingly, these 5 Pharisees and the lawyers asked him, 'Why do your disciples not conform to the ancient tradition, but eat their food with defiled hands?' He answered, 6 'Isaiah was right when he prophesied about you hypocrites in these words: "This people pays me lip-service, but their heart is far from me: their 7 worship of me is in vain, for they teach as doctrines the commandments of men." You neglect the command- 8 ment of God, in order to maintain the tradition of men.'

He also said to them, 'How well 9 you set aside the commandment of God in order to maintain[l] your tradition! Moses said, "Honour your father 10 and your mother", and, "The man who curses his father or mother must suffer death." But you hold that if a 11 man says to his father or mother, "Anything of mine which might have been used for your benefit is Corban"' (meaning, set apart for God), 'he is 12 no longer permitted to do anything for his father or mother. Thus by 13 your own tradition, handed down among you, you make God's word null and void. And many other things that you do are just like that.'

What defiles a man

On another occasion he called the 14 people and said to them, 'Listen to me, all of you, and understand this: nothing that goes into a man from 15 outside can defile him; no, it is the things that come out of him that defile a man.'[m]

When he had left the people and 17 gone indoors, his disciples questioned him about the parable. He said to 18 them, 'Are you as dull as the rest? Do you not see that nothing that goes from outside into a man can defile him, because it does not enter 19 into his heart but into his stomach, and so passes out into the drain?' Thus he declared all foods clean. He 20 went on, 'It is what comes out of a man that defiles him. For from inside, 21 out of a man's heart, come evil thoughts, acts of fornication, of theft, murder, adultery, ruthless greed, and 22 malice; fraud, indecency, envy, slander, arrogance, and folly; these evil 23 things all come from inside, and they defile the man.'

k Some witnesses insert with the fist; others insert frequently, or thoroughly.   l Some witnesses read establish.   m Some witnesses here add (16) If you have ears to hear, then hear.

A woman's faith

24 Then he left that place and went away into the territory of Tyre. He found a house to stay in, and he would have liked to remain unrecognized, but this was impossible.
25 Almost at once a woman whose young daughter was possessed by an unclean spirit heard of him, came in, and
26 fell at his feet. (She was a Gentile, a Phoenician of Syria by nationality.) She begged him to drive the spirit
27 out of her daughter. He said to her, 'Let the children be satisfied first; it is not fair to take the children's
28 bread and throw it to the dogs.' 'Sir,' she answered, 'even the dogs under the table eat the children's scraps.'
29 He said to her, 'For saying that, you may go home content; the unclean spirit has gone out of your daughter.'
30 And when she returned home, she found the child lying in bed; the spirit had left her.

A deaf man healed

31 On his return journey from Tyrian territory he went by way of Sidon to the Sea of Galilee through the terri-
32 tory of the Ten Towns.[n] They brought to him a man who was deaf and had an impediment in his speech, with the request that he would lay his hand
33 on him. He took the man aside, away from the crowd, put his fingers into his ears, spat, and touched his tongue.
34 Then, looking up to heaven, he sighed, and said to him, '*Ephphatha*', which
35 means 'Be opened'. With that his ears were opened, and at the same time the impediment was removed and he
36 spoke plainly. Jesus forbade them to tell anyone; but the more they forbade them, the more they published it.
37 Their astonishment knew no bounds: 'All that he does, he does well,' they said; 'he even makes the deaf hear and the dumb speak.'

Feeding four thousand

8 There was another occasion about this time when a huge crowd had collected, and, as they had no food, Jesus called his disciples and said to
2 them, 'I feel sorry for all these people; they have been with me now for
3 three days and have nothing to eat. If I send them home unfed, they will turn faint on the way; some of them
4 have come from a distance.' The disciples answered, 'How can anyone provide all these people with bread

in this lonely place?' 'How many 5 loaves have you?' he asked; and they answered, 'Seven.' So he ordered the 6 people to sit down on the ground; then he took the seven loaves, and, after giving thanks to God, he broke the bread and gave it to his disciples to distribute; and they served it out to the people. They had also a few 7 small fishes, which he blessed and ordered them to distribute. They all 8 ate to their hearts' content, and seven baskets were filled with the scraps that were left. The people 9 numbered about four thousand. Then he dismissed them; and, without 10 delay, got into the boat with his disciples and went to the district of Dalmanutha.[o]

Demand for a sign

Then the Pharisees came out and 11 engaged him in discussion. To test him they asked him for a sign from heaven. He sighed deeply to himself 12 and said, 'Why does this generation ask for a sign? I tell you this: no sign shall be given to this generation.' With that he left them, re-embarked, 13 and went off to the other side of the lake.

A warning to the disciples

Now they had forgotten to take 14 bread with them; they had no more than one loaf in the boat. He began to 15 warn them: 'Beware,' he said, 'be on your guard against the leaven of the Pharisees and the leaven of Herod.' They said among themselves, 'It is 16 because we have no bread.' Knowing 17 what was in their minds, he asked them, 'Why do you talk about having no bread? Have you no inkling yet? Do you still not understand? Are your minds closed? You have eyes: can you 18 not see? You have ears: can you not hear? Have you forgotten? When I 19 broke the five loaves among five thousand, how many basketfuls of scraps did you pick up?' 'Twelve', they said. 'And how many when I 20 broke the seven loaves among four thousand?' They answered, 'Seven.' He said, 'Do you still not understand?' 21

A blind man healed at Bethsaida

They arrived at Bethsaida. There the 22 people brought a blind man to Jesus and begged him to touch him. He 23 took the blind man by the hand and led him away out of the village. Then

---

n *Greek* Decapolis.   o *Some witnesses give* Magedan; *others give* Magdala.

he spat on his eyes, laid his hands
upon him, and asked whether he
24 could see anything. The man's sight
began to come back, and he said, 'I
see men; they look like trees, but they
25 are walking about.' Jesus laid his
hands on his eyes again; he looked
hard, and now he was cured so that
26 he saw everything clearly. Then Jesus
sent him home, saying, 'Do not tell
anyone in the village.'[p]

Peter's confession of faith

27 Jesus and his disciples set out for the
villages of Caesarea Philippi. On the
way he asked his disciples, 'Who do
28 men say I am?' They answered, 'Some
say John the Baptist, others Elijah,
29 others one of the prophets.' 'And you,'
he asked, 'who do you say I am?'
Peter replied: 'You are the Messiah.'
30 Then he gave them strict orders not
31 to tell anyone about him; and he
began to teach them that the Son of
Man had to undergo great sufferings,
and to be rejected by the elders, chief
priests, and doctors of the law; to
be put to death, and to rise again
32 three days afterwards. He spoke
about it plainly. At this Peter took
him by the arm and began to rebuke
33 him. But Jesus turned round, and,
looking at his disciples, rebuked Peter.
'Away with you, Satan,' he said;
'you think as men think, not as God
thinks.'

On following Jesus

34 Then he called the people to him, as
well as his disciples, and said to them,
'Anyone who wishes to be a follower
of mine must leave self behind; he
must take up his cross, and come with
35 me. Whoever cares for his own safety
is lost; but if a man will let himself
be lost for my sake and for the Gospel,
36 that man is safe. What does a man
gain by winning the whole world at
37 the cost of his true self? What can he
38 give to buy that self back? If anyone
is ashamed of me and mine[q] in this
wicked and godless age, the Son of
Man will be ashamed of him, when he
comes in the glory of his Father and
of the holy angels.'[r]

9 He also said, 'I tell you this: there
are some of those standing here who
will not taste death before they have
seen the kingdom of God already
come in power.'

Jesus is transfigured

Six days later Jesus took Peter, 2
James, and John with him and led
them up a high mountain where they
were alone; and in their presence he
was transfigured; his clothes became 3
dazzling white, with a whiteness no
bleacher on earth could equal. They 4
saw Elijah appear, and Moses with
him, and there they were, conversing
with Jesus. Then Peter spoke: 'Rabbi,' 5
he said, 'how good it is that we are
here! Shall we make three shelters,
one for you, one for Moses, and one
for Elijah?' (For he did not know what 6
to say; they were so terrified.) Then 7
a cloud appeared, casting its shadow
over them, and out of the cloud came
a voice: 'This is my Son, my Beloved;[s]
listen to him.' And now suddenly, 8
when they looked around, there was
nobody to be seen but Jesus alone
with themselves.

On their way down the mountain, 9
he enjoined them not to tell anyone
what they had seen until the Son of
Man had risen from the dead. They 10
seized upon those words, and discussed among themselves what this
'rising from the dead' could mean.
And they put a question to him: 11
'Why do our teachers say that Elijah
must come first?' He replied, 'Yes, 12
Elijah does come first to set everything right. Yet how is it[t] that the
scriptures say of the Son of Man that
he is to endure great sufferings and
to be treated with contempt? How- 13
ever, I tell you, Elijah has already
come and they have worked their will
upon him, as the scriptures say of
him.'

Jesus heals an epileptic boy

When they came back to the disciples 14
they saw a large crowd surrounding
them and lawyers arguing with them.
As soon as they saw Jesus the whole 15
crowd were overcome with awe, and
they ran forward to welcome him.
He asked them, 'What is this argu- 16
ment about?' A man in the crowd 17
spoke up: 'Master, I brought my son
to you. He is possessed by a spirit
which makes him speechless. When- 18
ever it attacks him, it dashes him
to the ground, and he foams at the
mouth, grinds his teeth, and goes rigid.
I asked your disciples to cast it out, but
they failed.' Jesus answered: 'What 19

p Some witnesses read Do not go into the village. *q Some witnesses read* me and my words.
r Some witnesses read Father with the holy angels. *s Or* This is my only Son. *t Or* Elijah, you say, comes first to set everything right: then how is it . . .

an unbelieving and perverse generation! How long shall I be with you? How long must I endure you? Bring
20 him to me.' So they brought the boy to him; and as soon as the spirit saw him it threw the boy into convulsions, and he fell on the ground and rolled
21 about foaming at the mouth. Jesus asked his father, 'How long has he been like this?' 'From childhood,' he
22 replied; 'often it has tried to make an end of him by throwing him into the fire or into water. But if it is at all possible for you, take pity upon us
23 and help us.' 'If it is possible!' said Jesus. 'Everything is possible to one
24 who has faith.' 'I have faith,' cried the boy's father; 'help me where
25 faith falls short.' Jesus saw then that the crowd was closing in upon them, so he rebuked the unclean spirit. 'Deaf and dumb spirit,' he said, 'I command you, come out of him and
26 never go back!' After crying aloud and racking him fiercely, it came out; and the boy looked like a corpse; in
27 fact, many said, 'He is dead.' But Jesus took his hand and raised him to his feet, and he stood up.
28 Then Jesus went indoors, and his disciples asked him privately, 'Why
29 could not we cast it out?' He said, 'There is no means of casting out this sort but prayer.'[u]

Jesus again speaks of his death

30 They now left that district and made a journey through Galilee. Jesus wished
31 it to be kept secret; for he was teaching his disciples, and telling them, 'The Son of Man is now to be given up into the power of men, and they will kill him, and three days after being killed,
32 he will rise again.' But they did not understand what he said, and were afraid to ask.

A lesson from a child

33 So they came to Capernaum; and when he was indoors, he asked them, 'What were you arguing about on the
34 way?' They were silent, because on the way they had been discussing
35 who was the greatest. He sat down, called the Twelve, and said to them, 'If anyone wants to be first, he must make himself last of all and servant
36 of all.' Then he took a child, set him

in front of them, and put his arm round him. 'Whoever receives one 37 of these children in my name', he said, 'receives me; and whoever receives me, receives not me but the One who sent me.'

He who is not against us is on our side

John said to him, 'Master, we saw a 38 man driving out devils in your name, and as he was not one of us, we tried to stop him.' Jesus said, 'Do not stop 39 him; no one who does a work of divine power in my name will be able the next moment to speak evil of me. For he who is not against us is on 40 our side. I tell you this: if anyone 41 gives you a cup of water to drink because you are followers of the Messiah, that man assuredly will not go unrewarded.'

Responsibility to others

'As for the man who is a cause of 42 stumbling to one of these little ones who have faith, it would be better for him to be thrown into the sea with a millstone round his neck. If your hand 43 is your undoing, cut it off; it is better for you to enter into life maimed than to keep both hands and go to hell and the unquenchable fire.[v] And if your 45 foot is your undoing, cut it off; it is better to enter into life a cripple than to keep both your feet and be thrown into hell.[w] And if it is your eye, tear 47 it out; it is better to enter into the kingdom of God with one eye than to keep both eyes and be thrown into hell, where the devouring worm never 48 dies and the fire is not quenched.
'For everyone will be salted with 49 fire.
'Salt is a good thing; but if the salt 50 loses its saltness, what will you season it with?
'Have salt in yourselves; and be[x] at peace with one another.'

About marriage and divorce

On leaving those parts he came into 10 the regions of Judaea and Transjordan; and when a crowd gathered round him once again, he followed his usual practice and taught them. The 2 question was put to him:[y] 'Is it lawful for a man to divorce his wife?'

---

u Some witnesses add and fasting.   v Some witnesses add (44) where the devouring worm never dies
and the fire is not quenched.   w Some witnesses add (46) where the devouring worm never dies
and the fire is not quenched.   x Or Have the salt of fellowship and be . . .; or You have the salt
of fellowship between you; then be . . .   y Some witnesses read The Pharisees came forward and
asked him the question . . .

3 This was to test him. He asked in
return, 'What did Moses command
4 you?' They answered, 'Moses permitted a man to divorce his wife by note
5 of dismissal.' Jesus said to them, 'It
was because your minds were closed
6 that he made this rule for you; but in
the beginning, at the creation, God
7 made them male and female. For this
reason a man shall leave his father
and mother, and be made one with
8 his wife;[z] and the two shall become
one flesh. It follows that they are
no longer two individuals: they are
9 one flesh. What God has joined together, man must not separate.'
10   When they were indoors again the
disciples questioned him about this
11 matter; he said to them, 'Whoever
divorces his wife and marries another
12 commits adultery against her: so too,
if she divorces her husband and marries another, she commits adultery.'

Jesus welcomes children

13 They brought children for him to
touch. The disciples rebuked them,
14 but when Jesus saw this he was indignant, and said to them, 'Let the
children come to me; do not try to
stop them; for the kingdom of God
15 belongs to such as these. I tell you,
whoever does not accept the kingdom
of God like a child will never enter
16 it.' And he put his arms round them,
laid his hands upon them, and blessed
them.

A rich man's question

17 As he was starting out on a journey, a stranger ran up, and, kneeling before him, asked, 'Good Master,
what must I do to win eternal life?'
18 Jesus said to him, 'Why do you call
me good? No one is good except
19 God alone. You know the commandments: "Do not murder; do not commit adultery; do not steal; do not
give false evidence; do not defraud;
honour your father and mother."'
20 'But, Master,' he replied, 'I have kept
21 all these since I was a boy.' Jesus
looked straight at him; his heart
warmed to him, and he said, 'One
thing you lack: go, sell everything
you have, and give to the poor, and
you will have riches in heaven; and
22 come, follow me.' At these words his
face fell and he went away with a
heavy heart; for he was a man of
great wealth.

Everything is possible for God

Jesus looked round at his disciples 23
and said to them, 'How hard it will
be for the wealthy to enter the kingdom of God!' They were amazed that 24
he should say this, but Jesus insisted,
'Children, how hard it is[a] to enter the
kingdom of God! It is easier for a 25
camel to pass through the eye of a
needle than for a rich man to enter
the kingdom of God.' They were more 26
astonished than ever, and said to one
another, 'Then who can be saved?'
Jesus looked at them and said, 'For 27
men it is impossible, but not for God;
everything is possible for God.'

About rewards

At this Peter spoke. 'We here', he 28
said, 'have left everything to become
your followers.' Jesus said, 'I tell you 29
this: there is no one who has given
up home, brothers or sisters, mother,
father or children, or land, for my
sake and for the Gospel, who will not 30
receive in this age a hundred times as
much—houses, brothers and sisters,
mothers and children, and land—and
persecutions besides; and in the age
to come eternal life. But many who 31
are first will be last and the last first.'

Jesus again speaks of his death

They were on the road, going up to 32
Jerusalem, Jesus leading the way;
and the disciples were filled with awe,
while those who followed behind were
afraid. He took the Twelve aside and
began to tell them what was to happen to him. 'We are now going to 33
Jerusalem,' he said; 'and the Son of
Man will be given up to the chief
priests and the doctors of the law;
they will condemn him to death and
hand him over to the foreign power.
He will be mocked and spat upon, 34
flogged and killed; and three days
afterwards, he will rise again.'

James and John ask a favour

James and John, the sons of Zebedee, 35
approached him and said, 'Master,
we should like you to do us a favour.'
'What is it you want me to do?' he 36
asked. They answered, 'Grant us the 37
right to sit in state with you, one
at your right and the other at your
left.' Jesus said to them, 'You do not 38
understand what you are asking. Can
you drink the cup that I drink, or be
baptized with the baptism I am baptized with?' 'We can', they answered. 39

z *Some witnesses omit* and be made ... wife.   a *Some witnesses insert* for those who trust in riches

Jesus said, 'The cup that I drink you shall drink, and the baptism I am bap-
40 tized with shall be your baptism; but to sit at my right or left is not for me to grant; it is for those to whom it has already been assigned.'[b]
41 When the other ten heard this, they were indignant with James and John.
42 Jesus called them to him and said, 'You know that in the world the recognized rulers lord it over their subjects, and their great men make them feel the
43 weight of authority. That is not the way with you; among you, whoever wants to be great must be your servant,
44 and whoever wants to be first must be
45 the willing slave of all. For even the Son of Man did not come to be served but to serve, and to give up his life as a ransom for many.'

Bartimaeus recovers his sight

46 They came to Jericho; and as he was leaving the town, with his disciples and a large crowd, Bartimaeus son of Timaeus, a blind beggar, was seated
47 at the roadside. Hearing that it was Jesus of Nazareth, he began to shout, 'Son of David, Jesus, have pity on
48 me!' Many of the people told him to hold his tongue; but he shouted all the more, 'Son of David, have pity
49 on me.' Jesus stopped and said, 'Call him'; so they called the blind man and said, 'Take heart; stand up; he is
50 calling you.' At that he threw off his cloak, sprang up, and came to Jesus.
51 Jesus said to him, 'What do you want me to do for you?' 'Master,' the blind man answered, 'I want my sight back.'
52 Jesus said to him, 'Go; your faith has cured you.' And at once he re-covered his sight and followed him on the road.

Jesus rides into Jerusalem

11 They were now approaching Jeru-salem, and when they reached Beth-phage and Bethany, at the Mount of Olives, he sent two of his disciples
2 with these instructions: 'Go to the village opposite, and, just as you enter, you will find tethered there a colt which no one has yet ridden. Untie
3 it and bring it here. If anyone asks, "Why are you doing that?", say, "Our Master[c] needs it, and will send
4 it back here without delay."' So they went off, and found the colt tethered at a door outside in the street. They
5 were untying it when some of the bystanders asked, 'What are you

doing, untying that colt?' They an- 6 swered as Jesus had told them, and were then allowed to take it. So they 7 brought the colt to Jesus and spread their cloaks on it, and he mounted. And people carpeted the road with 8 their cloaks, while others spread brush-wood which they had cut in the fields; and those who went ahead and 9 the others who came behind shouted, 'Hosanna! Blessings on him who comes in the name of the Lord! Blessings 10 on the coming kingdom of our father David! Hosanna in the heavens!'

He entered Jerusalem and went 11 into the temple, where he looked at the whole scene; but, as it was now late, he went out to Bethany with the Twelve.

A fig-tree without fruit

On the following day, after they had 12 left Bethany, he felt hungry, and, 13 noticing in the distance a fig-tree in leaf, he went to see if he could find anything on it. But when he came there he found nothing but leaves; for it was not the season for figs. He 14 said to the tree, 'May no one ever again eat fruit from you!' And his disciples were listening.

Jesus drives traders from the temple

So they came to Jerusalem, and he 15 went into the temple and began driving out those who bought and sold in the temple. He upset the tables of the money-changers and the seats of the dealers in pigeons; and 16 he would not allow anyone to use the temple court as a thoroughfare for carrying goods. Then he began 17 to teach them, and said, 'Does not Scripture say, "My house shall be called a house of prayer for all the nations"? But you have made it a robbers' cave.' The chief priests and 18 the doctors of the law heard of this and sought some means of making away with him; for they were afraid of him, because the whole crowd was spellbound by his teaching. And when 19 evening came he went out of the city.

A lesson from the fig-tree

Early next morning, as they passed 20 by, they saw that the fig-tree had withered from the roots up; and 21 Peter, recalling what had happened, said to him, 'Rabbi, look, the fig-tree which you cursed has withered.' Jesus 22 answered them, 'Have faith in God.

b *Some witnesses add* by my Father.   c *Or* Its owner.

23 I tell you this: if anyone says to this mountain, "Be lifted from your place and hurled into the sea", and has no inward doubts, but believes that what he says is happening, it will be done 24 for him. I tell you, then, whatever you ask for in prayer, believe that you have received it and it will be yours. 25 'And when you stand praying, if you have a grievance against anyone, forgive him, so that your Father in heaven may forgive you the wrongs you have done.'[d]

About the authority of Jesus

27 They came once more to Jerusalem. And as he was walking in the temple court the chief priests, lawyers, and 28 elders came to him and said, 'By what authority are you acting like this? Who gave you authority to act 29 in this way?' Jesus said to them, 'I have a question to ask you too; and if you give me an answer, I will tell 30 you by what authority I act. The baptism of John: was it from God, or 31 from men? Answer me.' This set them arguing among themselves: 'What shall we say? If we say, "from God", he will say, "Then why did you not 32 believe him?" Shall we say, "from men"?'—but they were afraid of the people, for all held that John was in 33 fact a prophet. So they answered, 'We do not know.' And Jesus said to them, 'Then neither will I tell you by what authority I act.'

Tenants in a vineyard

12 He went on to speak to them in parables: 'A man planted a vineyard and put a wall round it, hewed out a winepress, and built a watch-tower; then he let it out to vine-growers and 2 went abroad. When the season came, he sent a servant to the tenants to collect from them his share of the 3 produce. But they took him, thrashed him, and sent him away empty-4 handed. Again, he sent them another servant, whom they beat about the 5 head and treated outrageously. So he sent another, and that one they killed; and many more besides, of whom they 6 beat some, and killed others. He had now only one left to send, his own dear son.[e] In the end he sent him. "They will respect my son", he said. 7 But the tenants said to one another, "This is the heir; come on, let us kill him, and the property will be ours."

So they seized him and killed him, 8 and flung his body out of the vineyard. What will the owner of the vineyard 9 do? He will come and put the tenants to death and give the vineyard to others.

'Can it be that you have never 10 read this text: "The stone which the builders rejected has become the main corner-stone. This is the Lord's 11 doing, and it is wonderful in our eyes"?'

Then they began to look for a way 12 to arrest him, for they saw that the parable was aimed at them; but they were afraid of the people, so they left him alone and went away.

Paying tax to the Emperor

A number of Pharisees and men of 13 Herod's party were sent to trap him with a question. They came and said, 14 'Master, you are an honest man, we know, and truckle to no one, whoever he may be; you teach in all honesty the way of life that God requires. Are we or are we not permitted to pay taxes to the Roman Emperor? Shall we 15 pay or not?' He saw how crafty their question was, and said, 'Why are you trying to catch me out? Fetch me a silver piece, and let me look at it.' They brought one, and he said to 16 them, 'Whose head is this, and whose inscription?' 'Caesar's', they replied. Then Jesus said, 'Pay Caesar what is 17 due to Caesar, and pay God what is due to God.' And they heard him with astonishment.

About resurrection

Next Sadducees came to him. (It is 18 they who say that there is no resurrection.) Their question was this: 'Mas-19 ter, Moses laid it down for us that if there are brothers, and one dies leaving a wife but no child, then the next should marry the widow and carry on his brother's family. Now there 20 were seven brothers. The first took a wife and died without issue. Then 21 the second married her, and he too died without issue. So did the third. Eventually the seven of them died, 22 all without issue. Finally the woman died. At the resurrection, when they 23 come back to life, whose wife will she be, since all seven had married her?' Jesus said to them, 'You are mistaken, 24 and surely this is the reason: you do not know either the scriptures or the

---

d Some witnesses add (26) But if you do not forgive others, then the wrongs you have done will not be forgiven by your Father in heaven.   e Or his only son.

power of God. When they rise from the dead, men and women do not marry; they are like angels in heaven.

'But about the resurrection of the dead, have you never read in the Book of Moses, in the story of the burning bush, how God spoke to him and said, "I am the God of Abraham, the God of Isaac, and the God of Jacob"? God is not God of the dead but of the living. You are greatly mistaken.'

The greatest commandment

Then one of the lawyers, who had been listening to these discussions and had noted how well he answered, came forward and asked him, 'Which commandment is first of all?' Jesus answered, 'The first is, "Hear, O Israel: the Lord our God is the only Lord; love the Lord your God with all your heart, with all your soul, with all your mind, and with all your strength." The second is this: "Love your neighbour as yourself." There is no other commandment greater than these.' The lawyer said to him, 'Well said, Master. You are right in saying that God is one and beside him there is no other. And to love him with all your heart, all your understanding, and all your strength, and to love your neighbour as yourself—that is far more than any burnt offerings or sacrifices.' When Jesus saw how sensibly he answered, he said to him, 'You are not far from the kingdom of God.'

About the Messiah

After that nobody ventured to put any more questions to him; and Jesus went on to say, as he taught in the temple, 'How can the teachers of the law maintain that the Messiah is "Son of David"? David himself said, when inspired by the Holy Spirit, "The Lord said to my Lord, 'Sit at my right hand until I put your enemies under your feet.'" David himself calls him "Lord"; how can he also be David's son?'

There was a great crowd and they listened eagerly.[f] He said as he taught them, 'Beware of the doctors of the law, who love to walk up and down in long robes, receiving respectful greetings in the street; and to have the chief seats in synagogues, and places of honour at feasts. These are the men who eat up the property of widows, while they say long prayers for appearance' sake, and they will receive the severest sentence.'[g]

A poor widow's offering

Once he was standing opposite the temple treasury, watching as people dropped their money into the chest. Many rich people were giving large sums. Presently there came a poor widow who dropped in two tiny coins, together worth a farthing. He called his disciples to him. 'I tell you this,' he said: 'this poor widow has given more than any of the others; for those others who have given had more than enough, but she, with less than enough, has given all that she had to live on.'

Destruction of the temple foretold

As he was leaving the temple, one of his disciples exclaimed, 'Look, Master, what huge stones! What fine buildings!' Jesus said to him, 'You see these great buildings? Not one stone will be left upon another; all will be thrown down.'

Troubles and persecutions

When he was sitting on the Mount of Olives facing the temple he was questioned privately by Peter, James, John, and Andrew. 'Tell us,' they said, 'when will this happen? What will be the sign when the fulfilment of all this is at hand?'

Jesus began: 'Take care that no one misleads you. Many will come claiming my name, and saying, "I am he"; and many will be misled by them.

'When you hear the noise of battle near at hand and the news of battles far away, do not be alarmed. Such things are bound to happen; but the end is still to come. For nation will make war upon nation, kingdom upon kingdom; there will be earthquakes in many places; there will be famines. With these things the birth-pangs of the new age begin.

'As for you, be on your guard. You will be handed over to the courts. You will be flogged in synagogues. You will be summoned to appear before governors and kings on my account to testify in their presence. But before the end the Gospel must be proclaimed

---

f Or The mass of the people listened eagerly.

g Or As for those who eat up the property of widows, while they say long prayers for appearance' sake, they will have an even sterner judgement to face.

O*

11 to all nations. So when you are arrested and taken away, do not worry beforehand about what you will say, but when the time comes say whatever is given you to say; for it is not you who will be speaking, but the
12 Holy Spirit. Brother will betray brother to death, and the father his child; children will turn against their parents and send them to their death.
13 All will hate you for your allegiance to me; but the man who holds out to the end will be saved.'

'The abomination of desolation'

14 'But when you see "the abomination of desolation" usurping a place which is not his (let the reader understand), then those who are in Judaea must
15 take to the hills. If a man is on the roof, he must not come down into the
16 house to fetch anything out; if in the field, he must not turn back for
17 his coat. Alas for women with child in those days, and for those who have
18 children at the breast! Pray that it
19 may not come in winter. For those days will bring distress such as never has been until now since the beginning of the world which God created
20 —and will never be again. If the Lord had not cut short that time of troubles, no living thing could survive. However, for the sake of his own, whom he has chosen, he has cut short the time.
21 'Then, if anyone says to you, "Look, here is the Messiah", or, "Look, there he is", do not believe it.
22 Impostors will come claiming to be messiahs or prophets, and they will produce signs and wonders to mislead God's chosen, if such a thing were
23 possible. But you be on your guard; I have forewarned you of it all.'

The coming of the Son of Man

24 'But in those days, after that distress, the sun will be darkened, the moon
25 will not give her light; the stars will come falling from the sky, the celes-
26 tial powers will be shaken. Then they will see the Son of Man coming in the clouds with great power and glory,
27 and he will send out the angels and gather his chosen from the four winds, from the farthest bounds of earth to the farthest bounds of heaven.
28 'Learn a lesson from the fig-tree. When its tender shoots appear and

are breaking into leaf, you know that summer is near. In the same way, when you see all this happening, you may know that the end is near,[h] at the very door. I tell you this: the present generation will live to see it all. Heaven and earth will pass away; my words will never pass away.'

No one knows the day or hour: 'be alert'

'But about that day or that hour no one knows, not even the angels in heaven, not even the Son; only the Father.
'Be alert, be wakeful.[i] You do not know when the moment comes. It is like a man away from home: he has left his house and put his servants in charge, each with his own work to do, and he has ordered the door-keeper to stay awake. Keep awake, then, for you do not know when the master of the house is coming. Evening or midnight, cock-crow or early dawn—if he comes suddenly, he must not find you asleep. And what I say to you, I say to everyone: Keep awake.'

A plot to kill Jesus

Now the festival of Passover and Unleavened Bread was only two days off; and the chief priests and the doctors of the law were trying to devise some cunning plan to seize him and put him to death. 'It must not be during the festival,' they said, 'or we should have rioting among the people.'

A woman anoints Jesus

Jesus was at Bethany, in the house of Simon the leper. As he sat at table, a woman came in carrying a small bottle of very costly perfume, pure oil of nard. She broke it open and poured the oil over his head. Some of those present said to one another angrily, 'Why this waste? The perfume might have been sold for thirty pounds[j] and the money given to the poor'; and they turned upon her with fury. But Jesus said, 'Let her alone. Why must you make trouble for her? It is a fine thing she has done for me. You have the poor among you always, and you can help them whenever you like; but you will not always have me. She has done what lay in her power; she is beforehand with anointing

h Or that he is near.   i Some witnesses add and pray.   j Literally 300 denarii; some witnesses
read more than 300 denarii.

9 my body for burial. I tell you this: wherever in all the world the Gospel is proclaimed, what she has done will be told as her memorial.'

Judas Iscariot plans to betray Jesus

10 Then Judas Iscariot, one of the Twelve, went to the chief priests to
11 betray him to them. When they heard what he had come for, they were greatly pleased, and promised him money; and he began to look for a good opportunity to betray him.

Preparation for the Passover

12 Now on the first day of Unleavened Bread, when the Passover lambs were being slaughtered, his disciples said to him, 'Where would you like us to go and prepare for your Passover
13 supper?' So he sent out two of his disciples with these instructions: 'Go into the city, and a man will meet you carrying a jar of water. Follow him,
14 and when he enters a house give this message to the householder: "The Master says, 'Where is the room reserved for me to eat the Passover with
15 my disciples?'" He will show you a large room upstairs, set out in readiness. Make the preparations for us
16 there.' Then the disciples went off, and when they came into the city they found everything just as he had told them. So they prepared for Passover.

The Last Supper

17 In the evening he came to the house
18 with the Twelve. As they sat at supper Jesus said, 'I tell you this: one of you will betray me—one who is eating
19 with me.' At this they were dismayed; and one by one they said to him, 'Not
20 I, surely?' 'It is one of the Twelve', he said, 'who is dipping into the same
21 bowl with me. The Son of Man is going the way appointed for him in the scriptures; but alas for that man by whom the Son of Man is betrayed! It would be better for that man if he had never been born.'

22   During supper he took bread, and having said the blessing he broke it and gave it to them, with the words:
23 'Take this; this is my body.' Then he took a cup, and having offered thanks to God he gave it to them; and they
24 all drank from it. And he said, 'This is my blood, the blood of the covenant,
25 shed for many. I tell you this: never

k Some witnesses add using the same words. money has been paid', 'The account is settled.'

again shall I drink from the fruit of the vine until that day when I drink it new in the kingdom of God.'

Jesus foretells Peter's denial

After singing the Passover Hymn, 26 they went out to the Mount of Olives. And Jesus said, 'You will all fall from 27 your faith; for it stands written: "I will strike the shepherd down and the sheep will be scattered." Neverthe- 28 less, after I am raised again I will go on before you into Galilee.' Peter an- 29 swered, 'Everyone else may fall away, but I will not.' Jesus said, 'I tell you 30 this: today, this very night, before the cock crows twice, you yourself will disown me three times.' But he insis- 31 ted and repeated: 'Even if I must die with you, I will never disown you.' And they all said the same.

Jesus prays in Gethsemane

When they reached a place called 32 Gethsemane, he said to his disciples, 'Sit here while I pray.' And he took 33 Peter and James and John with him. Horror and dismay came over him, and he said to them, 'My heart is 34 ready to break with grief; stop here, and stay awake.' Then he went for- 35 ward a little, threw himself on the ground, and prayed that, if it were possible, this hour might pass him by. 'Abba, Father,' he said, 'all things are 36 possible to thee; take this cup away from me. Yet not what I will, but what thou wilt.'

He came back and found them 37 asleep; and he said to Peter, 'Asleep, Simon? Were you not able to stay awake for one hour? Stay awake, all 38 of you; and pray that you may be spared the test. The spirit is willing, but the flesh is weak.' Once more he 39 went away and prayed.[k] On his return 40 he found them asleep again, for their eyes were heavy; and they did not know how to answer him.

The third time he came and said 41 to them, 'Still sleeping? Still taking your ease? Enough![l] The hour has come. The Son of Man is betrayed to sinful men. Up, let us go forward! My 42 betrayer is upon us.'

Jesus is arrested

Suddenly, while he was still speaking, 43 Judas, one of the Twelve, appeared, and with him was a crowd armed with swords and cudgels, sent by the chief

l The Greek is obscure; a possible meaning is 'The

44 priests, lawyers, and elders. Now the traitor had agreed with them upon a signal: 'The one I kiss is your man; seize him and get him safely away.'
45 When he reached the spot, he stepped forward at once and said to Jesus,
46 'Rabbi', and kissed him. Then they seized him and held him fast.
47 One of the party[m] drew his sword, and struck at the High Priest's ser-
48 vant, cutting off his ear. Then Jesus spoke: 'Do you take me for a bandit, that you have come out with swords
49 and cudgels to arrest me? Day after day I was within your reach as I taught in the temple, and you did not lay hands on me. But let the scrip-
50 tures be fulfilled.' Then the disciples all deserted him and ran away.
51 Among those following was a young man with nothing on but a linen cloth.
52 They tried to seize him; but he slipped out of the linen cloth and ran away naked.

Jesus is charged with blasphemy

53 Then they led Jesus away to the High Priest's house, where the chief priests, elders, and doctors of the law were
54 all assembling. Peter followed him at a distance right into the High Priest's courtyard; and there he remained, sitting among the attendants, warming himself at the fire.
55 The chief priests and the whole Council tried to find some evidence against Jesus to warrant a death-
56 sentence, but failed to find any. Many gave false evidence against him, but
57 their statements did not tally. Some stood up and gave false evidence
58 against him to this effect: 'We heard him say, "I will pull down this temple, made with human hands, and in three days I will build another, not made
59 with hands."' But even on this point their evidence did not agree.
60 Then the High Priest stood up in his place and questioned Jesus: 'Have you no answer to the charges that these
61 witnesses bring against you?' But he kept silence; he made no reply.
Again the High Priest questioned him: 'Are you the Messiah, the Son of
62 the Blessed One?' Jesus said, 'I am; and you will see the Son of Man seated at the right hand of God[n] and coming
63 with the clouds of heaven.' Then the High Priest tore his robes and said,
64 'Need we call further witnesses? What is we have heard the blasphemy. What is

your opinion?' Their judgement was unanimous: that he was guilty and should be put to death.
Some began to spit on him, blind- 6
folded him, and struck him with their fists, crying out, 'Prophesy!'[o] And the High Priest's men set upon him with blows.

Peter disowns Jesus

Meanwhile Peter was still below in 6
the courtyard. One of the High Priest's serving-maids came by and saw him 6
there warming himself. She looked into his face and said, 'You were there too, with this man from Nazareth, this Jesus.' But he denied it: 6
'I know nothing,' he said; 'I do not understand what you mean.' Then he
went outside into the porch;[p] and the 6
maid saw him there again and began to say to the bystanders, 'He is one of them'; and again he denied it. 7
Again, a little later, the bystanders said to Peter, 'Surely you are one of them. You must be; you are a Galilean.' At this he broke out into curses, 7
and with an oath he said, 'I do not know this man you speak of.' Then the 7
cock crew a second time; and Peter re-
membered how Jesus had said to him, 'Before the cock crows twice you will disown me three times.' And he burst into tears.

Jesus before Pilate

As soon as morning came, the chief 1
priests, having made their plan with the elders and lawyers in full council, put Jesus in chains; then they led him away and handed him over to Pilate. Pilate asked him, 'Are you the king 2
of the Jews?' He replied, 'The words are yours.'[q] And the chief priests 3
brought many charges against him. Pilate questioned him again: 'Have 4
you nothing to say in your defence? You see how many charges they are bringing against you.' But, to Pilate's 5
astonishment, Jesus made no further reply.

Jesus is sentenced to death

At the festival season the Governor 6
used to release one prisoner at the people's request. As it happened, the 7
man known as Barabbas was then in custody with the rebels who had committed murder in the rising. When 8
the crowd appeared[r] asking for the

m *Or* of the bystanders. n *Literally* of the Power. o *Some witnesses add* Who hit you? *as in Matthew and Luke.* p *Some witnesses insert* and a cock crew. q *Or* It is as you say. r *Some witnesses read* shouted.

9 usual favour, Pilate replied, 'Do you
10 wish me to release for you the king
of the Jews?' For he knew it was out
of malice that they had brought Jesus
1 before him. But the chief priests incited the crowd to ask him to release
2 Barabbas rather than Jesus. Pilate
spoke to them again: 'Then what shall
I do with the man you call king of
3 the Jews?' They shouted back, 'Crucify
4 him!' 'Why, what harm has he done?'
Pilate asked; but they shouted all the
5 louder, 'Crucify him!' So Pilate, in
his desire to satisfy the mob, released
Barabbas to them; and he had Jesus
flogged and handed him over to be
crucified.

Soldiers jeer at Jesus

16 Then the soldiers took him inside
the courtyard (the Governor's headquarters[s]) and called together the
7 whole company. They dressed him in
purple, and plaiting a crown of thorns,
18 placed it on his head. Then they began to salute him with, 'Hail, King of
19 the Jews!' They beat him about the
head with a cane and spat upon him,
and then knelt and paid mock hom-
20 age to him. When they had finished
their mockery, they stripped him of
the purple and dressed him in his own
clothes.

Jesus is crucified

Then they took him out to crucify
21 him. A man called Simon, from Cyrene, the father of Alexander and
Rufus, was passing by on his way in
from the country, and they pressed
him into service to carry his cross.
22 They brought him to the place
called Golgotha, which means 'Place
23 of a skull'. He was offered drugged
24 wine, but he would not take it. Then
they fastened him to the cross. They
divided his clothes among them, casting lots to decide what each should
have.
25 The hour of the crucifixion was
26 nine in the morning, and the inscription giving the charge against him
27 read, 'The king of the Jews.' Two
bandits were crucified with him, one
on his right and the other on his left.[t]
29 The passers-by hurled abuse at
him: 'Aha!' they cried, wagging their
heads, 'you would pull the temple
down, would you, and build it in
30 three days? Come down from the

cross and save yourself!' So too the 31
chief priests and lawyers jested with
one another: 'He saved others,' they
said, 'but he cannot save himself. Let 32
the Messiah, the king of Israel, come
down now from the cross. If we see
that, we shall believe.' Even those
who were crucified with him taunted
him.

The death of Jesus

At midday a darkness fell over the 33
whole land, which lasted till three
in the afternoon; and at three Jesus 34
cried aloud, 'Eli, Eli, lema sabachthani?', which means, 'My God, my
God, why hast thou forsaken me?'[u]
Some of the bystanders, on hearing 35
this, said, 'Hark, he is calling Elijah.'
A man ran and soaked a sponge in 36
sour wine and held it to his lips on
the end of a cane. 'Let us see', he said,
'if Elijah will come to take him down.'
Then Jesus gave a loud cry and died. 37
And the curtain of the temple was 38
torn in two from top to bottom. And 39
when the centurion who was standing
opposite him saw how he died,[v] he
said, 'Truly this man was a son of
God.'[w]

The burial of Jesus

A number of women were also present, 40
watching from a distance. Among
them were Mary of Magdala, Mary the
mother of James the younger and of
Joseph, and Salome, who had all 41
followed him and waited on him when
he was in Galilee, and there were
several others who had come up to
Jerusalem with him.
By this time evening had come; 42
and as it was Preparation-day (that
is, the day before the Sabbath),
Joseph of Arimathaea, a respected 43
member of the Council, a man who
looked forward to the kingdom of
God, bravely went in to Pilate and
asked for the body of Jesus. Pilate 44
was surprised to hear that he was
already dead; so he sent for the
centurion and asked him whether it
was long since he died. And when he 45
heard the centurion's report, he gave
Joseph leave to take the dead body.
So Joseph bought a linen sheet, took 46
him down from the cross, and wrapped him in the sheet. Then he laid him
in a tomb cut out of the rock, and
rolled a stone against the entrance.

---

s Greek praetorium.   t Some witnesses add (28) Thus that text of Scripture came true which says,
'He was reckoned among criminals.'   u Some witnesses read My God, my God, why hast thou
shamed me?   v Some witnesses read saw that he died with a cry.   w Or the Son of God.

47 And Mary of Magdala and Mary the mother of Joseph were watching and saw where he was laid.

The resurrection

16 When the Sabbath was over, Mary of Magdala, Mary the mother of James, and Salome bought*x* aromatic oils 2 intending to go and anoint him; and very early on the Sunday morning, just after sunrise, they came to the 3 tomb. They were wondering among themselves who would roll away the stone for them from the entrance to 4 the tomb, when they looked up and saw that the stone, huge as it was, 5 had been rolled back already. They went into the tomb, where they saw a youth sitting on the right-hand side, wearing a white robe; and they were 6 dumbfounded. But he said to them, 'Fear nothing; you are looking for Jesus of Nazareth, who was crucified. He has been raised again; he is not here; look, there is the place where 7 they laid him. But go and give this message to his disciples and Peter: "He is going on before you into Galilee; there you will see him, as he told 8 you."' Then they went out and ran away from the tomb, beside themselves with terror. They said nothing to anybody, for they were afraid.*y*

Those who saw the risen Jesus

9 When he had risen from the dead early on Sunday morning he appeared first to Mary of Magdala, from whom he had formerly cast out seven devils. 10 She went and carried the news to his mourning and sorrowful followers, 11 but when they were told that he was alive and that she had seen him they did not believe it.

Later he appeared in a different 1 guise to two of them as they were walking, on their way into the country. These also went and took the news to 1 the others, but again no one believed them.

Afterwards while the Eleven were 1 at table he appeared to them and reproached them for their incredulity and dullness, because they had not believed those who had seen him after he was raised from the dead. Then he 1 said to them: 'Go forth to every part of the world, and proclaim the Good News to the whole creation. Those 1 who believe it and receive baptism will find salvation; those who do not believe will be condemned. Faith will 1 bring with it these miracles: believers will cast out devils in my name and speak in strange tongues; if they 1 handle snakes or drink any deadly poison, they will come to no harm; and the sick on whom they lay their hands will recover.'

So after talking with them the Lord 1 Jesus was taken up into heaven, and he took his seat at the right hand of God; but they went out to make their pro- 2 clamation everywhere, and the Lord worked with them and confirmed their words by the miracles that followed.

The message of eternal salvation

And they delivered all these instructions briefly to Peter and his companions. Afterwards Jesus himself sent out by them from east to west the sacred and imperishable message of eternal salvation.*z*

x Some witnesses omit When the Sabbath . . . Salome, reading And they went and bought . . .
y At this point some of the most ancient witnesses bring the book to a close; others continue with verses 9–20, as printed here, or in some cases expanded with additional matter; yet others insert here the paragraph And they delivered . . . eternal salvation (here printed below verse 20), and in one of them this is the conclusion of the book; in the remainder, verses 9–20 follow it.   z See note to verse 8.

THE GOSPEL ACCORDING TO
LUKE

Introduction

1 THE AUTHOR to Theophilus: Many writers have undertaken to draw up an account of the events 2 that have happened among us, following the traditions handed down to us by the original eyewitnesses and 3 servants of the Gospel. And so I in my turn, your Excellency, as one who has gone over the whole course of these events in detail, have decided to write a connected narrative for you, 4 so as to give you authentic knowledge about the matters of which you have been informed.

A son is promised to Zechariah

5 In the days of Herod king of Judaea there was a priest named Zechariah, of the division of the priesthood called after Abijah. His wife also was of priestly descent; her name was Elizabeth. 6 Both of them were upright and devout, blamelessly observing all the commandments and ordinances of the 7 Lord. But they had no children, for Elizabeth was barren, and both were well on in years.

8 Once, when it was the turn of his division and he was there to take part 9 in divine service, it fell to his lot, by priestly custom, to enter the sanctuary of the Lord and offer the incense; 10 and the whole congregation was at prayer outside. It was the hour of the 11 incense-offering. There appeared to him an angel of the Lord, standing on the right of the altar of incense. 12 At this sight, Zechariah was startled, 13 and fear overcame him. But the angel said to him, 'Do not be afraid, Zechariah; your prayer has been heard: your wife Elizabeth will bear you a son, and you shall name him John. 14 Your heart will thrill with joy and many will be glad that he was born; 15 for he will be great in the eyes of the Lord. He shall never touch wine or strong drink. From his very birth he 16 will be filled with the Holy Spirit; and he will bring back many Israelites to the Lord their God. He will go before 17 him as forerunner,[a] possessed by the spirit and power of Elijah, to reconcile father and child, to convert the rebellious to the ways of the righteous, to prepare a people that shall be fit for the Lord.'

Zechariah said to the angel, 'How 18 can I be sure of this? I am an old man and my wife is well on in years.'

The angel replied, 'I am Gabriel; I 19 stand in attendance upon God, and I have been sent to speak to you and bring you this good news. But now 20 listen: you will lose your power of speech, and remain silent until the day when these things happen to you, because you have not believed me, though at their proper time my words will be proved true.'

Meanwhile the people were waiting 21 for Zechariah, surprised that he was staying so long inside. When he did 22 come out he could not speak to them, and they realized that he had had a vision in the sanctuary. He stood there making signs to them, and remained dumb.

When his period of duty was com- 23 pleted Zechariah returned home. After 24 this his wife Elizabeth conceived, and for five months she lived in seclusion, thinking, 'This is the Lord's doing; 25 now at last he has deigned to take away my reproach among men.'

Mary is promised a son

In the sixth month the angel Gabriel 26 was sent from God to a town in Galilee called Nazareth, with a mes- 27 sage for a girl betrothed to a man named Joseph, a descendant of David; the girl's name was Mary. The angel 28 went in and said to her, 'Greetings, most favoured one! The Lord is with you.' But she was deeply troubled by 29 what he said and wondered what this greeting might mean. Then the angel 30 said to her, 'Do not be afraid, Mary, for God has been gracious to you; you 31 shall conceive and bear a son, and you shall give him the name Jesus. He 32 will be great; he will bear the title

a Or In his sight he will go forth.

"Son of the Most High"; the Lord God will give him the throne of his
33 ancestor David, and he will be king over Israel[b] for ever; his reign shall
34 never end.' 'How can this be?' said
35 Mary; 'I am still a virgin.' The angel answered, 'The Holy Spirit will come upon you, and the power of the Most High will overshadow you; and for that reason the holy child to be born
36 will be called "Son of God".[c] Moreover your kinswoman Elizabeth has herself conceived a son in her old age; and she who is reputed barren is now
37 in her sixth month, for God's promises
38 can never fail.'[d] 'Here am I,' said Mary; 'I am the Lord's servant; as you have spoken, so be it.' Then the angel left her.

Mary visits Elizabeth

39 About this time Mary set out and went straight to a town in the uplands
40 of Judah. She went into Zechariah's
41 house and greeted Elizabeth. And when Elizabeth heard Mary's greeting, the baby stirred in her womb. Then Elizabeth was filled with the Holy
42 Spirit and cried aloud, 'God's blessing is on you above all women, and his blessing is on the fruit of your womb.
43 Who am I, that the mother of my
44 Lord should visit me? I tell you, when your greeting sounded in my ears, the baby in my womb leapt for
45 joy. How happy is she who has had faith that the Lord's promise would be fulfilled!'

Mary praises God for his wonderful works

46 And Mary[e] said:

'Tell out, my soul, the greatness of the Lord,
47 rejoice, rejoice, my spirit, in God my saviour;
48 so tenderly has he looked upon his servant,
      humble as she is.
For, from this day forth,
   all generations will count me blessed,
49 so wonderfully has he dealt with me, the Lord, the Mighty One.

His name is Holy;
50 his mercy sure from generation to generation
      toward those who fear him;

the deeds his own right arm has done 51
   disclose his might:
the arrogant of heart and mind he has
      put to rout,
he has brought down monarchs from 52
      their thrones,
   but the humble have been lifted
      high.
The hungry he has satisfied with good 53
      things,
   the rich sent empty away.

He has ranged himself at the side of 54
      Israel his servant;
   firm in his promise to our fore- 55
      fathers,
he has not forgotten to show mercy
      to Abraham
   and his children's children, for
      ever.'

Mary stayed with her about three 56
months and then returned home.

Elizabeth's child is born, and named

Now the time came for Elizabeth's 57
child to be born, and she gave birth
to a son. When her neighbours and 58
relatives heard what great favour the
Lord had shown her, they were as
delighted as she was. Then on the 59
eighth day they came to circumcise
the child; and they were going to
name him Zechariah after his father.
But his mother spoke up and said, 60
'No! he is to be called John.' 'But', 61
they said, 'there is nobody in your
family who has that name.' They 62
inquired of his father by signs what
he would like him to be called. He 63
asked for a writing-tablet and to the
astonishment of all wrote down, 'His
name is John.' Immediately his lips 64
and tongue were freed and he began
to speak, praising God. All the neigh- 65
bours were struck with awe, and everywhere in the uplands of Judaea the
whole story became common talk.
All who heard it were deeply impres- 66
sed and said, 'What will this child
become?' For indeed the hand of the
Lord was upon him.[f]

Zechariah's prophecy

And Zechariah his father was filled 67
with the Holy Spirit and uttered this
prophecy:

   'Praise to the God of Israel!   68
For he has turned to his people, saved
      them and set them free,

---

b Literally the house of Jacob.   c Or the child to be born will be called holy, "Son of God".
d Some witnesses read for with God nothing will prove impossible.   e So the majority of witnesses;
some read Elizabeth; the original may have had no name.   f Some witnesses read 'What will this
child become, for indeed the hand of the Lord is upon him?'

69 and has raised up a deliverer of victorious power
from the house of his servant David.

70 So he promised: age after age he proclaimed
by the lips of his holy prophets,

71 that he would deliver us from our enemies,
out of the hands of all who hate us;

72 that he would deal mercifully with our fathers,
calling to mind his solemn covenant.

73 Such was the oath he swore to our father Abraham,

74 to rescue us from enemy hands,
and grant us, free from fear, to worship him

75 with a holy worship, with uprightness of heart,
in his presence, our whole life long.

76 And you, my child, you shall be called Prophet of the Highest,
for you will be the Lord's forerunner,
to prepare his way

77 and lead his people to salvation through knowledge of him,
by the forgiveness of their sins:

78 for in the tender compassion of our God
the morning sun from heaven will rise[g] upon us,

79 to shine on those who live in darkness, under the cloud of death,
and to guide our feet into the way of peace.'

80 As the child grew up he became strong in spirit; he lived out in the wilds until the day when he appeared publicly before Israel.

Mary gives birth to a son

2 In those days a decree was issued by the Emperor Augustus for a registration to be made throughout 2 the Roman world. This was the first registration of its kind; it took place when Quirinius[h] was governor of Syria. 3 For this purpose everyone made his 4 way to his own town; and so Joseph went up to Judaea from the town 5 of Nazareth in Galilee, to register at the city of David, called Bethlehem, because he was of the house of David by descent; and with him went Mary who was betrothed to him. She 6 was expecting a child, and while they were there the time came for her baby 7 to be born, and she gave birth to a son, her first-born. She wrapped him in his swaddling clothes, and laid him in a manger, because there was no room for them to lodge in the house.

The shepherds and the angels

Now in this same district there were 8 shepherds out in the fields, keeping watch through the night over their flock, when suddenly there stood be- 9 fore them an angel of the Lord, and the splendour of the Lord shone round them. They were terror-stricken, but 10 the angel said, 'Do not be afraid; I have good news for you: there is great joy coming to the whole people. To- 11 day in the city of David a deliverer has been born to you—the Messiah, the Lord.[i] And this is your sign: you 12 will find a baby lying wrapped in his swaddling clothes, in a manger.' All 13 at once there was with the angel a great company of the heavenly host, singing the praises of God:

'Glory to God in highest heaven,   14
and on earth his peace for men on whom his favour rests.'[j]

After the angels had left them and 15 gone into heaven the shepherds said to one another, 'Come, we must go straight to Bethlehem and see this thing that has happened, which the Lord has made known to us.' So they 16 went with all speed and found their way to Mary and Joseph; and the baby was lying in the manger. When 17 they saw him, they recounted what they had been told about this child; and all who heard were astonished at 18 what the shepherds said. But Mary 19 treasured up all these things and pondered over them. Meanwhile the 20 shepherds returned glorifying and praising God for what they had heard and seen; it had all happened as they had been told.

The child Jesus presented in the temple

Eight days later the time came to 21 circumcise him, and he was given the name Jesus, the name given by the angel before he was conceived.

Then, after their purification had 22 been completed in accordance with the Law of Moses, they brought him up to Jerusalem to present him to the Lord (as prescribed in the law of the 23 Lord: 'Every first-born male shall be

g Some witnesses read has risen.   *h Or* This was the first registration carried out while Quirinius ...
i Some witnesses read to you—the Lord's Messiah.   *j Some witnesses read* and on earth his peace,
his favour towards men.

24 deemed to belong to the Lord'), and also to make the offering as stated in the law: 'A pair of turtle doves or two young pigeons.'

Simeon's response

25 There was at that time in Jerusalem a man called Simeon. This man was upright and devout, one who watched and waited for the restoration of Israel, and the Holy Spirit was upon
26 him. It had been disclosed to him by the Holy Spirit that he would not see death until he had seen the Lord's
27 Messiah. Guided by the Spirit he came into the temple; and when the parents brought in the child Jesus to do for him what was customary under the
28 Law, he took him in his arms, praised God, and said:

29 'This day, Master, thou givest thy
    servant his discharge in peace;
    now thy promise is fulfilled.
30 For I have seen with my own eyes
31 the deliverance which thou hast made
    ready in full view of all the
    nations:
32 a light that will be a revelation to the
    heathen,
    and glory to thy people Israel.'

33 The child's father and mother were full of wonder at what was being said
34 about him. Simeon blessed them and said to Mary his mother, 'This child is destined to be a sign which men reject;
35 and you too shall be pierced to the heart. Many in Israel will stand or fall[k] because of him, and thus the secret thoughts of many will be laid bare.'

Anna's response

36 There was also a prophetess, Anna the daughter of Phanuel, of the tribe of Asher. She was a very old woman, who had lived seven years with her husband after she was first mar-
37 ried, and then alone as a widow to the age of eighty-four.[l] She never left the temple, but worshipped day and
38 night, fasting and praying. Coming up at that very moment, she returned thanks to God; and she talked about the child to all who were looking for the liberation of Jerusalem.

Return to Nazareth

39 When they had done everything prescribed in the law of the Lord, they returned to Galilee to their own town
40 of Nazareth. The child grew big and

strong and full of wisdom; and God's favour was upon him.

The boy Jesus in the temple

Now it was the practice of his parents 41 to go to Jerusalem every year for the Passover festival; and when he was 42 twelve, they made the pilgrimage as usual. When the festive season was 43 over and they started for home, the boy Jesus stayed behind in Jerusalem. His parents did not know of this; but 44 thinking that he was with the party they journeyed on for a whole day, and only then did they begin looking for him among their friends and relations. As they could not find him they 45 returned to Jerusalem to look for him; and after three days they found him 46 sitting in the temple surrounded by the teachers, listening to them and putting questions; and all who heard 47 him were amazed at his intelligence and the answers he gave. His parents 48 were astonished to see him there, and his mother said to him, 'My son, why have you treated us like this? Your father and I have been searching for you in great anxiety.' 'What made 49 you search?' he said. 'Did you not know that I was bound to be in my Father's house?' But they did not 50 understand what he meant. Then he 51 went back with them to Nazareth, and continued to be under their authority; his mother treasured up all these things in her heart. As Jesus 52 grew up he advanced in wisdom and in favour with God and men.

John preaches and baptizes

In the fifteenth year of the Emperor 3 Tiberius, when Pontius Pilate was governor of Judaea, when Herod was prince of Galilee, his brother Philip prince of Ituraea and Trachonitis, and Lysanias prince of Abilene, during 2 the high-priesthood of Annas and Caiaphas, the word of God came to John son of Zechariah in the wilderness. And he went all over the Jordan 3 valley proclaiming a baptism in token of repentance for the forgiveness of sins, as it is written in the book of 4 the prophecies of Isaiah:

'A voice crying aloud in the wilderness,
"Prepare a way for the Lord;
clear a straight path for him.
Every ravine shall be filled in,   5
and every mountain and hill levelled;
the corners shall be straightened,

---

k Or Many in Israel will fall and rise again . . .

l Or widow for another eighty-four years.

and the rugged ways made smooth;
6 and all mankind shall see God's deliverance."'

7 Crowds of people came out to be
baptized by him, and he said to them:
'You vipers' brood! Who warned you
to escape from the coming retribu-
8 tion? Then prove your repentance by
the fruit it bears; and do not begin
saying to yourselves, "We have Abraham for our father." I tell you that
God can make children for Abraham
9 out of these stones here. Already the
axe is laid to the roots of the trees;
and every tree that fails to produce
good fruit is cut down and thrown on
the fire.'

10 The people asked him, 'Then what
11 are we to do?' He replied, 'The man
with two shirts must share with him
who has none, and anyone who has
12 food must do the same.' Among those
who came to be baptized were tax-
gatherers, and they said to him,
13 'Master, what are we to do?' He told
them, 'Exact no more than the assess-
14 ment.' Soldiers on service also asked
him, 'And what of us?' To them he
said, 'No bullying; no blackmail;
make do with your pay!'

15 The people were on the tiptoe
of expectation, all wondering about
John, whether perhaps he was the
16 Messiah, but he spoke out and said to
them all: 'I baptize you with water;
but there is one to come who is
mightier than I. I am not fit to unfasten his shoes. He will baptize you
with the Holy Spirit and with fire.
17 His shovel is ready in his hand, to
winnow his threshing-floor and gather
the wheat into his granary; but he will
burn the chaff on a fire that can never
go out.'

Herod puts John in prison

18 In this and many other ways he made
his appeal to the people and announ-
19 ced the good news. But Prince Herod,
when he was rebuked by him over the
affair of his brother's wife Herodias
20 and for his other misdeeds, crowned
them all by shutting John up in
prison.

The baptism of Jesus

21 During a general baptism of the people, when Jesus too had been baptized
22 and was praying, heaven opened and
the Holy Spirit descended on him in

bodily form like a dove; and there
came a voice from heaven, 'Thou art
my Son, my Beloved;[m] on thee my
favour rests.'[n]

Family tree of Jesus

When Jesus began his work he was 23
about thirty years old, the son, as
people thought, of Joseph, son of Heli,
son of Matthat, son of Levi, son of 24
Melchi, son of Jannai, son of Joseph,
son of Mattathiah, son of Amos, son 25
of Nahum, son of Esli, son of Naggai,
son of Maath, son of Mattathiah, son 26
of Semein, son of Josech, son of Joda,
son of Johanan, son of Rhesa, son of 27
Zerubbabel, son of Shealtiel, son of
Neri, son of Melchi, son of Addi, son 28
of Cosam, son of Elmadam, son of Er,
son of Joshua, son of Eliezer, son of 29
Jorim, son of Matthat, son of Levi,
son of Symeon, son of Judah, son of 30
Joseph, son of Jonam, son of Eliakim,
son of Melea, son of Menna, son of 31
Mattatha, son of Nathan, son of
David, son of Jesse, son of Obed, son 32
of Boaz, son of Salmon, son of Nahshon, son of Amminadab,[o] son of 33
Arni,[p] son of Hezron, son of Perez,
son of Judah, son of Jacob, son of 34
Isaac, son of Abraham, son of Terah,
son of Nahor, son of Serug, son of 35
Reu, son of Peleg, son of Eber, son of
Shelah, son of Cainan, son of Arpach- 36
shad, son of Shem, son of Noah, son
of Lamech, son of Methuselah, son of 37
Enoch, son of Jared, son of Mahala-
leel, son of Cainan, son of Enosh, son 38
of Seth, son of Adam, son of God.

The temptation of Jesus

Full of the Holy Spirit, Jesus returned 4
from the Jordan, and for forty days 2
was led by the Spirit up and down the
wilderness and tempted by the devil.

All that time he had nothing to eat,
and at the end of it he was famished.
The devil said to him, 'If you are the 3
Son of God, tell this stone to become
bread.' Jesus answered, 'Scripture says, 4
"Man cannot live on bread alone."'

Next the devil led him up and 5
showed him in a flash all the kingdoms of the world. 'All this dominion 6
will I give to you,' he said, 'and the
glory that goes with it; for it has been
put in my hands and I can give it to
anyone I choose. You have only to do 7
homage to me and it shall all be
yours.' Jesus answered him, 'Scripture 8

---

m Or Thou art my only Son.   *n* *Some witnesses read* My Son art thou; this day I have begotten
thee.   *o* *Some witnesses add* son of Admin.   *p* *Some witnesses read* Aram; *Ruth 4. 19 and*
1 Chronicles 2. 9 have Ram.

says, "You shall do homage to the Lord your God and worship him alone.'''

9 The devil took him to Jerusalem and set him on the parapet of the temple. 'If you are the Son of God,' he
10 said, 'throw yourself down; for Scripture says, "He will give his angels
11 orders to take care of you", and again, "They will support you in their arms for fear you should strike your foot
12 against a stone."' Jesus answered him, 'It has been said, "You are not to put the Lord your God to the test."'
13 So, having come to the end of all his temptations, the devil departed, biding his time.

Jesus rejected at Nazareth

14 Then Jesus, armed with the power of the Spirit, returned to Galilee; and reports about him spread through the
15 whole country-side. He taught in their synagogues and all men sang his praises.
16 So he came to Nazareth, where he had been brought up, and went to synagogue on the Sabbath day as he regularly did. He stood up to read the
17 lesson and was handed the scroll of the prophet Isaiah. He opened the scroll and found the passage which says,

18 'The spirit of the Lord is upon me
　　because he has anointed me;
　he has sent me to announce good news
　　to the poor,
　to proclaim release for prisoners and
　　recovery of sight for the blind;
　to let the broken victims go free,
19 to proclaim the year of the Lord's
　　favour.'

20 He rolled up the scroll, gave it back to the attendant, and sat down; and all eyes in the synagogue were fixed on him.
21 He began to speak: 'Today', he said, 'in your very hearing this text
22 has come true.'*q* There was a general stir of admiration; they were surprised that words of such grace should fall from his lips. 'Is not this Joseph's
23 son?' they asked. Then Jesus said, 'No doubt you will quote the proverb to me, "Physician, heal yourself!", and say, "We have heard of all your doings at Capernaum; do the same
24 here in your own home town." I tell you this,' he went on: 'no prophet is
25 recognized in his own country. There were many widows in Israel, you may be sure, in Elijah's time, when for

three years and six months the skies never opened, and famine lay hard over the whole country; yet it was 26 to none of those that Elijah was sent, but to a widow at Sarepta in the territory of Sidon. Again, in the time 27 of the prophet Elisha there were many lepers in Israel, and not one of them was healed, but only Naaman, the 28 Syrian.' At these words the whole congregation were infuriated. They 29 leapt up, threw him out of the town, and took him to the brow of the hill on which it was built, meaning to hurl him over the edge. But he walked 30 straight through them all, and went away.

The authority of Jesus in word and deed

Coming down to Capernaum, a town 31 in Galilee, he taught the people on the Sabbath, and they were astounded at 32 his teaching, for what he said had the note of authority. Now there was 33 a man in the synagogue possessed by a devil, an unclean spirit. He shrieked at the top of his voice, 'What do you 34 want with us, Jesus of Nazareth? Have you*r* come to destroy us? I know who you are—the Holy One of God.' Jesus rebuked him: 'Be silent', 35 he said, 'and come out of him.' Then the devil, after throwing the man down in front of the people, left him without doing him any injury. Amaze- 36 ment fell on them all and they said to one another: 'What is there in this man's words? He gives orders to the unclean spirits with authority and power, and out they go.' So the news 37 spread, and he was the talk of the whole district.

Acts of healing

On leaving the synagogue he went to 38 Simon's house. Simon's mother-in-law was in the grip of a high fever; and they asked him to help her. He came 39 and stood over her and rebuked the fever. It left her, and she got up at once and waited on them.

At sunset all who had friends suffer- 40 ing from one disease or another brought them to him; and he laid his hands on them one by one and cured them. Devils also came out of many 41 of them, shouting, 'You are the Son of God.' But he rebuked them and forbade them to speak, because they knew that he was the Messiah.

q Or 'Today', he said, 'this text which you have just heard has come true.'　　*r* Or You have.

Jesus proclaims the Gospel in Judaea

42 When day broke he went out and made his way to a lonely spot. But the people went in search of him, and when they came to where he was they 43 pressed him not to leave them. But he said, 'I must give the good news of the kingdom of God to the other towns also, for that is what I was sent 44 to do.' So he proclaimed the Gospel in the synagogues of Judaea.[s]

Jesus calls Simon and his companions

5 One day as he stood by the Lake of Gennesaret, and the people crowded upon him to listen to the word of God, 2 he noticed two boats lying at the water's edge; the fishermen had come ashore and were washing their nets. 3 He got into one of the boats, which belonged to Simon, and asked him to put out a little way from the shore; then he went on teaching the crowds 4 from his seat in the boat. When he had finished speaking, he said to Simon, 'Put out into deep water and 5 let down your nets for a catch.' Simon answered, 'Master, we were hard at work all night and caught nothing at all; but if you say so, I will let down 6 the nets.' They did so and made a big haul of fish; and their nets began 7 to split. So they signalled to their partners in the other boat to come and help them. This they did, and loaded both boats to the point of 8 sinking. When Simon saw what had happened he fell at Jesus's knees and said, 'Go, Lord, leave me, sinner that 9 I am!' For he and all his companions were amazed at the catch they had 10 made; so too were his partners James and John, Zebedee's sons. 'Do not be afraid,' said Jesus to Simon; 'from 11 now on you will be catching men.' As soon as they had brought the boats to land, they left everything and followed him.

Jesus cleanses a leper]

12 He was once in a certain town where there happened to be a man covered with leprosy; seeing Jesus, he bowed to the ground and begged his help. 'Sir,' he said, 'if only you will, you can 13 cleanse me.' Jesus stretched out his hand, touched him, and said, 'Indeed I will; be clean again.' The leprosy 14 left him immediately. Jesus then ordered him not to tell anybody. 'But go,' he said, 'show yourself to the priest, and make the offering laid down by Moses for your cleansing; that will certify the cure.' But the 15 talk about him spread all the more; great crowds gathered to hear him and to be cured of their ailments. And 16 from time to time he would withdraw to lonely places for prayer.

Authority to forgive sins

One day he was teaching, and Pha- 17 risees and teachers of the law were sitting round. People had come from every village of Galilee and from Judaea and Jerusalem,[t] and the power of the Lord was with him to heal the sick. Some men appeared carrying a 18 paralysed man on a bed. They tried to bring him in and set him down in front of Jesus, but finding no way to 19 do so because of the crowd, they went up on to the roof and let him down through the tiling, bed and all, into the middle of the company in front of Jesus. When Jesus saw their faith, he 20 said, 'Man, your sins are forgiven you.'

The lawyers and the Pharisees 21 began saying to themselves, 'Who is this fellow with his blasphemous talk? Who but God alone can forgive sins?' But Jesus knew what they were 22 thinking and answered them: 'Why do you harbour thoughts like these? Is it easier to say, "Your sins are for- 23 given you", or to say, "Stand up and walk"? But to convince you that the 24 Son of Man has the right on earth to forgive sins'—he turned to the para- lysed man—'I say to you, stand up, take your bed, and go home.' And at 25 once he rose to his feet before their eyes, took up the bed he had been ly- ing on, and went home praising God. They were all lost in amazement and 26 praised God; filled with awe they said, 'You would never believe the things we have seen today.'

Jesus and the tax-gatherers

Later, when he went out, he saw a tax- 27 gatherer, Levi by name, at his seat in the custom-house, and said to him, 'Follow me'; and he rose to his feet, 28 left everything behind, and followed him.

Afterwards Levi held a big recep- 29 tion in his house for Jesus; among the guests was a large party of tax- gatherers and others. The Pharisees 30

s Or the Jewish synagogues; some witnesses read the synagogues of Galilee.   t Some witnesses read and Pharisees and teachers of the law, who had come from every village of Galilee and from Judaea and Jerusalem, were sitting round.

and the lawyers of their sect complained to his disciples: 'Why do you eat and drink', they said, 'with tax-31 gatherers and sinners?' Jesus answered them: 'It is not the healthy 32 that need a doctor, but the sick; I have not come to invite virtuous people, but to call sinners to repentance.'

About fasting

33 Then they said to him, 'John's disciples are much given to fasting and the practice of prayer, and so are the disciples of the Pharisees; but yours 34 eat and drink.' Jesus replied, 'Can you make the bridegroom's friends fast while the bridegroom is with 35 them? But a time will come: the bridegroom will be taken away from them, and that will be the time for them to fast.'

Patched clothes and old wine-skins

36 He told them this parable also: 'No one tears a piece from a new cloak to patch an old one; if he does, he will have made a hole in the new cloak, and the patch from the new will not 37 match the old. Nor does anyone put new wine into old wine-skins; if he does, the new wine will burst the skins, the wine will be wasted, and 38 the skins ruined. Fresh skins for new 39 wine! And no one after drinking old wine wants new; for he says, "The old wine is good."'

About the Sabbath

6 One Sabbath he was going through the cornfields, and his disciples were plucking the ears of corn, rubbing them in their hands, and eating them. 2 Some of the Pharisees said, 'Why are you doing what is forbidden on the 3 Sabbath?' Jesus answered, 'So you have not read what David did when 4 he and his men were hungry? He went into the House of God and took the sacred bread to eat and gave it to his men, though priests alone are allowed 5 to eat it, and no one else.' He also said, 'The Son of Man is sovereign even over the Sabbath.'

A man with a withered arm

6 On another Sabbath he had gone to synagogue and was teaching. There happened to be a man in the congregation whose right arm was withered; 7 and the lawyers and the Pharisees were on the watch to see whether Jesus would cure him on the Sabbath,

so that they could find a charge to bring against him. But he knew what 8 was in their minds and said to the man with the withered arm, 'Get up and stand out here.' So he got up and stood there. Then Jesus said to 9 them, 'I put the question to you: is it permitted to do good or to do evil on the Sabbath, to save life or to destroy it?' He looked round at them all and 10 then said to the man, 'Stretch out your arm.' He did so, and his arm was restored. But they were beside them- 11 selves with anger, and began to discuss among themselves what they could do to Jesus.

The twelve apostles

During this time he went out one day 12 into the hills to pray, and spent the night in prayer to God. When day 13 broke he called his disciples to him, and from among them he chose twelve and named them Apostles: Simon, to whom he gave the name 14 of Peter, and Andrew his brother, James and John, Philip and Bartholomew, Matthew and Thomas, James 15 son of Alphaeus, and Simon who was called the Zealot, Judas son of James, 16 and Judas Iscariot who turned traitor.

Jesus teaches and heals

He came down the hill with them and 17 took his stand on level ground. There was a large concourse of his disciples and great numbers of people from Jerusalem and Judaea and from the seaboard of Tyre and Sidon, who had come to listen to him, and to be cured of their diseases. Those who were 18 troubled with unclean spirits were cured; and everyone in the crowd was 19 trying to touch him, because power went out from him and cured them all.

True blessedness and its opposite

Then turning to his disciples he began 20 to speak:

'How blest are you who are in need; the kingdom of God is yours.

'How blest are you who now go 21 hungry; your hunger shall be satisfied.

'How blest are you who weep now; you shall laugh.

'How blest you are when men hate 22 you, when they outlaw you and insult you, and ban your very name as infamous, because of the Son of Man. On that day be glad and dance for joy; 23 for assuredly you have a rich reward in heaven; in just the same way did their fathers treat the prophets.

24 'But alas for you who are rich; you have had your time of happiness.

25 'Alas for you who are well-fed now; you shall go hungry.

'Alas for you who laugh now; you shall mourn and weep.

26 'Alas for you when all speak well of you; just so did their fathers treat the false prophets.'

Personal wrongs

27 'But to you who hear me I say:

'Love your enemies; do good to
28 those who hate you; bless those who curse you; pray for those who treat
29 you spitefully. When a man hits you on the cheek, offer him the other cheek too; when a man takes your coat, let him have your shirt as well.
30 Give to everyone who asks you; when a man takes what is yours, do not
31 demand it back. Treat others as you would like them to treat you.

32 'If you love only those who love you, what credit is that to you? Even sinners love those who love them.
33 Again, if you do good only to those who do good to you, what credit is that to you? Even sinners do as
34 much. And if you lend only where you expect to be repaid, what credit is that to you? Even sinners lend to
35 each other to be repaid in full. But you must love your enemies and do good; and lend without expecting any return;[u] and you will have a rich reward: you will be sons of the Most High, because he himself is kind to
36 the ungrateful and wicked. Be compassionate as your Father is compassionate.'

Judging others

37 'Pass no judgement, and you will not be judged; do not condemn, and you will not be condemned; acquit, and
38 you will be acquitted; give, and gifts will be given you. Good measure, pressed down, shaken together, and running over, will be poured into your lap; for whatever measure you deal out to others will be dealt to you in return.'

39 He also offered them a parable: 'Can one blind man be guide to another? Will they not both fall into the
40 ditch? A pupil is not superior to his teacher; but everyone, when his training is complete, will reach his teacher's level.

'Why do you look at the speck of 41 sawdust in your brother's eye, with never a thought for the great plank in your own? How can you say to 42 your brother, "My dear brother, let me take the speck out of your eye", when you are blind to the plank in your own? You hypocrite! First take the plank out of your own eye, and then you will see clearly to take the speck out of your brother's.'

A tree and its fruit

'There is no such thing as a good tree 43 producing worthless fruit, nor yet a worthless tree producing good fruit. For each tree is known by its own 44 fruit: you do not gather figs from thistles, and you do not pick grapes from brambles. A good man produces 45 good from the store of good within himself; and an evil man from evil within produces evil. For the words that the mouth utters come from the overflowing of the heart.'

A firm foundation

'Why do you keep calling me "Lord, 46 Lord"—and never do what I tell you? Everyone who comes to me and hears 47 what I say, and acts upon it—I will show you what he is like. He is like a 48 man who, in building his house, dug deep and laid the foundations on rock. When the flood came, the river burst upon that house, but could not shift it, because it had been soundly built. But he who hears and does not 49 act is like a man who built his house on the soil without foundations. As soon as the river burst upon it, the house collapsed, and fell with a great crash.'

The faith of a soldier

When he had finished addressing the 7 people, he went to Capernaum. A cen- 2 turion there had a servant whom he valued highly; this servant was ill and near to death. Hearing about 3 Jesus, he sent some Jewish elders with the request that he would come and save his servant's life. They 4 approached Jesus and pressed their petition earnestly: 'He deserves this favour from you,' they said, 'for he is 5 a friend of our nation and it is he who built us our synagogue.' Jesus went 6 with them; but when he was not far from the house, the centurion sent friends with this message: 'Do not trouble further, sir; it is not for me

u Or without ever giving up hope; some witnesses read without giving up hope of anyone.

7 to have you under my roof, and that is why I did not presume to approach you in person. But say the word and 8 my servant will be cured. I know, for in my position I am myself under orders, with soldiers under me. I say to one, "Go", and he goes; to another, "Come here", and he comes; and to my servant, "Do this", and he does 9 it.' When Jesus heard this, he admired the man, and, turning to the crowd that was following him, he said, 'I tell you, nowhere, even in Israel, have I 10 found faith like this.' And the messengers returned to the house and found the servant in good health.

Jesus raises a widow's son to life

11 Afterwards[v] Jesus went to a town called Nain, accompanied by his dis-12 ciples and a large crowd. As he approached the gate of the town he met a funeral. The dead man was the only son of his widowed mother; and many of the townspeople were there 13 with her. When the Lord saw her his heart went out to her, and he said, 14 'Weep no more.' With that he stepped forward and laid his hand on the bier; and the bearers halted. Then he spoke: 15 'Young man, rise up!' The dead man sat up and began to speak; and Jesus 16 gave him back to his mother. Deep awe fell upon them all, and they praised God. 'A great prophet has arisen among us', they said, and again, 'God has shown his care for his people.' 17 The story of what he had done ran through all parts of Judaea and the whole neighbourhood.

A message for John the Baptist

18 John too was informed of all this by 19 his disciples. Summoning two of their number he sent them to the Lord with this message: 'Are you the one who is to come, or are we to expect some 20 other?' The messengers made their way to Jesus and said, 'John the Baptist has sent us to you: he asks, "Are you the one who is to come, or 21 are we to expect some other?"' There and then he cured many sufferers from diseases, plagues, and evil spirits; and on many blind people he be-22 stowed sight. Then he gave them his answer: 'Go', he said, 'and tell John what you have seen and heard: how the blind recover their sight, the lame walk, the lepers are made clean,

the deaf hear, the dead are raised to life, the poor are hearing the good news—and happy is the man who 23 does not find me a stumbling-block.'

About John the Baptist

After John's messengers had left, 24 Jesus began to speak about him to the crowds: 'What was the spectacle that drew you to the wilderness? A reed-bed swept by the wind? 25 Then what did you go out to see? A man dressed in silks and satins? Surely you must look in palaces for grand clothes and luxury. But what 26 did you go out to see? A prophet? Yes indeed, and far more than a prophet. He is the man of whom Scripture says, 27

"Here is my herald, whom I send on
      ahead of you,
and he will prepare your way before
      you."

I tell you, there is not a mother's son 28 greater than John, and yet the least in the kingdom of God is greater than he.'

When they heard him, all the people, 29 including the tax-gatherers, praised God, for they had accepted John's baptism; but the Pharisees and law-30 yers, who refused his baptism, had rejected[w] God's purpose for themselves.

'How can I describe the people of 31 this generation? What are they like? They are like children sitting in the 32 market-place and shouting at each other,

"We piped for you and you would not
      dance."
"We wept and wailed, and you would
      not mourn."

For John the Baptist came neither 33 eating bread nor drinking wine, and you say, "He is possessed." The Son 34 of Man came eating and drinking, and you say, "Look at him! a glutton and a drinker, a friend of tax-gatherers and sinners!" And yet God's wisdom 35 is proved right by all who are her children.'

At the house of Simon the Pharisee

One of the Pharisees invited him to 36 eat with him; he went to the Pharisee's house and took his place at table. A woman who was living an 37 immoral life in the town had learned that Jesus was at table in the Pharisee's house and had brought oil of

v Some witnesses read On the next day.   w Or '. . . greater than he. And all the people, including the tax-gatherers, when they heard him, accepted John's baptism and acknowledged the righteous dealing of God; but the Pharisees and lawyers, by refusing his baptism, rejected . . .'

myrrh in a small flask. She took her place behind him, by his feet, weeping. His feet were wetted with her tears and she wiped them with her hair, kissing them and anointing them with the myrrh. When his host the Pharisee saw this he said to himself, 'If this fellow were a real prophet, he would know who this woman is that touches him, and what sort of woman she is, a sinner.' Jesus took him up and said, 'Simon, I have something to say to you.' 'Speak on, Master', said he. 'Two men were in debt to a money-lender: one owed him five hundred silver pieces, the other fifty. As neither had anything to pay with he let them both off. Now, which will love him most?' Simon replied, 'I should think the one that was let off most.' 'You are right', said Jesus. Then turning to the woman, he said to Simon, 'You see this woman? I came to your house: you provided no water for my feet; but this woman has made my feet wet with her tears and wiped them with her hair. You gave me no kiss; but she has been kissing my feet ever since I came in. You did not anoint my head with oil; but she has anointed my feet with myrrh. And so, I tell you, her great love proves that her many sins have been forgiven; where little has been forgiven, little love is shown.' Then he said to her, 'Your sins are forgiven.' The other guests began to ask themselves, 'Who is this, that he can forgive sins?' But he said to the woman, 'Your faith has saved you; go in peace.'

Women who accompanied Jesus

After this he went journeying from town to town and village to village, proclaiming the good news of the kingdom of God. With him were the Twelve and a number of women who had been set free from evil spirits and infirmities: Mary, known as Mary of Magdala, from whom seven devils had come out, Joanna, the wife of Chuza a steward of Herod's, Susanna, and many others. These women provided for them out of their own resources.

The parable of a sower

People were now gathering in large numbers, and as they made their way to him from one town after another, he said in a parable: 'A sower went out to sow his seed. And as he sowed, some seed fell along the footpath, where it was trampled on, and the birds ate it up. Some seed fell on rock 6 and, after coming up, withered for lack of moisture. Some seed fell in 7 among thistles, and the thistles grew up with it and choked it. And some 8 of the seed fell into good soil, and grew, and yielded a hundredfold.' As he said this he called out, 'If you have ears to hear, then hear.'

Why Jesus told parables

His disciples asked him what this 9 parable meant, and he said, 'It has 10 been granted to you to know the secrets of the kingdom of God; but the others have only parables, so that they may look but see nothing, hear but understand nothing.

The parable of the sower explained

'This is what the parable means. The 11 seed is the word of God. Those along 12 the footpath are the men who hear it, and then the devil comes and carries off the word from their hearts for fear they should believe and be saved. The 13 seed sown on rock stands for those who receive the word with joy when they hear it, but have no root; they are believers for a while, but in the time of testing they desert. That which 14 fell among thistles represents those who hear, but their further growth is choked by cares and wealth and the pleasures of life, and they bring nothing to maturity. But the seed in good 15 soil represents those who bring a good and honest heart to the hearing of the word, hold it fast, and by their perseverance yield a harvest.'

A lesson from a lamp

'Nobody lights a lamp and then covers 16 it with a basin or puts it under the bed. On the contrary, he puts it on a lampstand so that those who come in may see the light. For there is nothing 17 hidden that will not become public, nothing under cover that will not be made known and brought into the open.

'Take care, then, how you listen; 18 for the man who has will be given more, and the man who has not will forfeit even what he thinks he has.'

Jesus's relatives

His mother and his brothers arrived 19 but could not get to him for the crowd. He was told, 'Your mother and bro- 20 thers are standing outside, and they

21 want to see you.' He replied, 'My mother and my brothers—they are those who hear the word of God and act upon it.'

Jesus calms a storm

22 One day he got into a boat with his disciples and said to them, 'Let us cross over to the other side of the 23 lake.' So they put out; and as they sailed along he went to sleep. Then a heavy squall struck the lake; they began to ship water and were in grave 24 danger. They went to him, and roused him, crying, 'Master, Master, we are sinking!' He awoke, and rebuked the wind and the turbulent waters. The storm subsided and all was calm. 25 'Where is your faith?' he asked. In fear and astonishment they said to one another, 'Who can this be? He gives his orders to wind and waves, and they obey him.'

Jesus cures a madman

26 So they landed in the country of the Gergesenes,[x] which is opposite Galilee. 27 As he stepped ashore he was met by a man from the town who was possessed by devils. For a long time he had neither worn clothes nor lived in a house, but stayed among the tombs. 28 When he saw Jesus he cried out, and fell at his feet shouting, 'What do you want with me, Jesus, son of the Most High God? I implore you, do not torment me.' 29 For Jesus was already ordering the unclean spirit to come out of the man. Many a time it had seized him, and then, for safety's sake, they would secure him with chains and fetters; but each time he broke loose, and with the devil in charge made off to the solitary places. 30 Jesus asked him, 'What is your name?' 'Legion', he replied. This was because so many devils had taken 31 possession of him. And they begged him not to banish them to the Abyss. 32 There happened to be a large herd of pigs nearby, feeding on the hill; and the spirits begged him to let them go into these pigs. He gave them leave; 33 the devils came out of the man and went into the pigs, and the herd rushed over the edge into the lake and were drowned. 34 The men in charge of them saw what had happened, and, taking to

their heels, they carried the news to the town and country-side; and the 35 people came out to see for themselves. When they came to Jesus, and found the man from whom the devils had gone out sitting at his feet clothed and in his right mind, they were afraid. The spectators told them how 36 the madman had been cured. Then 37 the whole population of the Gerges-ene[y] district asked him to go, for they were in the grip of a great fear. So he got into the boat and returned. The 38 man from whom the devils had gone out begged leave to go with him; but Jesus sent him away: 'Go back home,' 39 he said, 'and tell them everything that God has done for you.' The man went all over the town spreading the news of what Jesus had done for him.

Jairus's plea

When Jesus returned, the people wel- 40 comed him, for they were all ex-pecting him. Then a man appeared 41 —Jairus was his name and he was president of the synagogue. Throwing himself down at Jesus's feet he begged him to come to his house, because he had an only daughter, about twelve years old, who was dying. And while 42 Jesus was on his way he could hardly breathe for the crowds.

A woman healed of haemorrhages

Among them was a woman who had 43 suffered from haemorrhages for twelve years; and[z] nobody had been able to cure her. She came up from behind 44 and touched the edge of[a] his cloak, and at once her haemorrhage stopped. Jesus said, 'Who was it that touched 45 me?' All disclaimed it, and Peter and his companions said, 'Master, the crowds are hemming you in and pres-sing upon you!' But Jesus said, 'Some- 46 one did touch me, for I felt that power had gone out from me.' Then the 47 woman, seeing that she was detected, came trembling and fell at his feet. Before all the people she explained why she had touched him and how she had been instantly cured. He said to her, 'My daughter, your faith has 48 cured you. Go in peace.'

Jairus's daughter restored to life

While he was still speaking, a man came from the president's house with the message, 'Your daughter is dead;

x Some witnesses read Gerasenes; others read Gadarenes.   y Some witnesses read Gerasene; others read Gadarene.   z Some witnesses add though she had spent all she had on doctors.   a Some witnesses omit the edge of.

trouble the Rabbi no further.' But Jesus heard, and interposed. 'Do not be afraid,' he said; 'only show faith and she will be well again.' On arrival at the house he allowed no one to go in with him except Peter, John, and James, and the child's father and mother. And all were weeping and lamenting for her. He said, 'Weep no more; she is not dead: she is asleep'; and they only laughed at him, well knowing that she was dead. But Jesus took hold of her hand and called her: 'Get up, my child.' Her spirit returned, she stood up immediately, and he told them to give her something to eat. Her parents were astounded; but he forbade them to tell anyone what had happened.

The twelve apostles

He now called the Twelve together and gave them power and authority to overcome all the devils and to cure diseases, and sent them to proclaim the kingdom of God and to heal. 'Take nothing for the journey,' he told them, 'neither stick nor pack, neither bread nor money; nor are you each to have a second coat. When you are admitted to a house, stay there, and go on from there. As for those who will not receive you, when you leave their town shake the dust off your feet as a warning to them.' So they set out and travelled from village to village, and everywhere they told the good news and healed the sick.

Disturbing news for Herod

Now Prince Herod heard of all that was happening, and did not know what to make of it; for some were saying that John had been raised from the dead, others that Elijah had appeared, others again that one of the old prophets had come back to life. Herod said, 'As for John, I beheaded him myself; but who is this I hear such talk about?' And he was anxious to see him.

Feeding five thousand

On their return the apostles told Jesus all they had done; and he took them with him and withdrew privately to a town called Bethsaida. But the crowds found out and followed him. He welcomed them, and spoke to them about the kingdom of God, and cured those who were in need of healing.

When evening was drawing on, the 12 Twelve came up to him and said, 'Send these people away; then they can go into the villages and farms round about to find food and lodging; for we are in a lonely place here.' 'Give them something to eat your- 13 selves', he replied. But they said, 'All we have is five loaves and two fishes, nothing more—unless perhaps we ourselves are to go and buy provisions for all this company.' (There were 14 about five thousand men.) He said to his disciples, 'Make them sit down in groups of fifty or so.' They did so and 15 got them all seated. Then, taking the 16 five loaves and the two fishes, he looked up to heaven, said the blessing over them, broke them, and gave them to the disciples to distribute to the people. They all ate to their 17 hearts' content; and when the scraps they left were picked up, they filled twelve great baskets.

Peter's confession of faith

One day when he was praying alone 18 in the presence of his disciples, he asked them, 'Who do the people say I am?' They answered, 'Some say 19 John the Baptist, others Elijah, others that one of the old prophets has come back to life.' 'And you,' he 20 said, 'who do you say I am?' Peter answered, 'God's Messiah.' Then he 21 gave them strict orders not to tell this to anyone. And he said, 'The Son of 22 Man has to undergo great sufferings, and to be rejected by the elders, chief priests, and doctors of the law, to be put to death and to be raised again on the third day.'

On following Jesus

And to all he said, 'If anyone wishes 23 to be a follower of mine, he must leave self behind; day after day he must take up his cross, and come with me. Whoever cares for his own safety is 24 lost; but if a man will let himself be lost for my sake, that man is safe. What will a man gain by winning 25 the whole world, at the cost of his true self? For whoever is ashamed of 26 me and mine,[b] the Son of Man will be ashamed of him, when he comes in his glory and the glory of the Father and the holy angels. And I tell you this: 27 there are some of those standing here who will not taste death before they have seen the kingdom of God.'

b Some witnesses read me and my words.

Jesus is transfigured

28 About eight days after this conversation he took Peter, John, and James with him and went up into the hills to
29 pray. And while he was praying the appearance of his face changed and his clothes became dazzling white.
30 Suddenly there were two men talking with him; these were Moses and Elijah,
31 who appeared in glory and spoke of his departure, the destiny he was to
32 fulfil in Jerusalem. Meanwhile Peter and his companions had been in a deep sleep; but when they awoke, they saw his glory and the two men
33 who stood beside him. And as these were moving away from Jesus, Peter said to him, 'Master, how good it is that we are here! Shall we make three shelters, one for you, one for Moses, and one for Elijah?'; but he spoke without knowing what he was
34 saying. The words were still on his lips, when there came a cloud which cast a shadow over them; they were
35 afraid as they entered the cloud, and from it came a voice: 'This is my Son,
36 my Chosen; listen to him.' When the voice had spoken, Jesus was seen to be alone. The disciples kept silence and at that time told nobody anything of what they had seen.

Jesus heals an epileptic boy

37 Next day when they came down from the hills he was met by a large crowd.
38 All at once there was a shout from a man in the crowd: 'Master, look at my son, I implore you, my only child.
39 From time to time a spirit seizes him, gives a sudden scream, and throws him into convulsions with foaming at the mouth, and it keeps on mauling
40 him and will hardly let him go. I asked your disciples to cast it out,
41 but they could not.' Jesus answered, 'What un unbelieving and perverse generation! How long shall I be with you and endure you all? Bring your
42 son here.' But before the boy could reach him the devil dashed him to the ground and threw him into convulsions. Jesus rebuked the unclean spirit, cured the boy, and gave him
43 back to his father. And they were all struck with awe at the majesty of God.

Jesus again speaks of his death

Amid the general wonder and admiration at all he was doing, Jesus said to his disciples, 'What I now say is for you: ponder my words. The Son of Man is to be given up into the power of men.' But they did not understand this saying; it had been hidden from them, so that they should not[c] grasp its meaning, and they were afraid to ask him about it.

A lesson from a child

A dispute arose among them: which of them was the greatest? Jesus knew what was passing in their minds, so he took a child by the hand and stood him at his side, and said, 'Whoever receives this child in my name receives me; and whoever receives me receives the One who sent me. For the least among you all—he is the greatest.'

'He who is not against you is on your side'

'Master,' said John, 'we saw a man driving out devils in your name, but as he is not one of us we tried to stop him.' Jesus said to him, 'Do not stop him, for he who is not against you is on your side.'

A Samaritan village rejects Jesus

As the time approached when he was to be taken up to heaven, he set his face resolutely towards Jerusalem, and sent messengers ahead. They set out and went into a Samaritan village to make arrangements for him; but the villagers would not have him because he was making for Jerusalem. When the disciples James and John saw this they said, 'Lord, may we call down fire from heaven to burn them up[d]?' But he turned and rebuked them,[e] and they went on to another village.

The cost of discipleship

As they were going along the road a man said to him, 'I will follow you wherever you go.' Jesus answered, 'Foxes have their holes, the birds their roosts; but the Son of Man has nowhere to lay his head.' To another he said, 'Follow me', but the man replied, 'Let me go and bury my father first.' Jesus said, 'Leave the dead to bury their dead; you must go and announce the kingdom of God.'

Yet another said, 'I will follow you, sir; but let me first say good-bye to

---

c Or it was so obscure to them that they could not . . .   d Some witnesses add as Elijah did.
e Some witnesses insert 'You do not know', he said, 'to what spirit you belong; (56) for the Son of Man did not come to destroy men's lives but to save them.'

my people at home.' To him Jesus said, 'No one who sets his hand to the plough and then keeps looking back[f] is fit for the kingdom of God.'

The Lord appoints a further seventy-two

After this the Lord appointed a further seventy-two[g] and sent them on ahead in pairs to every town and place he was going to visit himself. He said to them: 'The crop is heavy, but labourers are scarce; you must therefore beg the owner to send labourers to harvest his crop. Be on your way. And look, I am sending you like lambs among wolves. Carry no purse or pack, and travel barefoot. Exchange no greetings on the road. When you go into a house, let your first words be, "Peace to this house." If there is a man of peace there, your peace will rest upon him; if not, it will return and rest upon you. Stay in that one house, sharing their food and drink; for the worker earns his pay. Do not move from house to house. When you come into a town and they make you welcome, eat the food provided for you; heal the sick there, and say, "The kingdom of God has come close to you." When you enter a town and they do not make you welcome, go out into its streets and say, "The very dust of your town that clings to our feet we wipe off to your shame. Only take note of this: the kingdom of God has come close." I tell you, it will be more bearable for Sodom on the great Day than for that town.

'Alas for you, Chorazin! Alas for you, Bethsaida! If the miracles that were performed in you had been performed in Tyre and Sidon, they would have repented long ago, sitting in sackcloth and ashes. But it will be more bearable for Tyre and Sidon at the Judgement than for you. And as for you, Capernaum, will you be exalted to the skies? No, brought down to the depths!

'Whoever listens to you listens to me; whoever rejects you rejects me. And whoever rejects me rejects the One who sent me.'

The return of the seventy-two

The seventy-two[g] came back jubilant. 'In your name, Lord,' they said, 'even the devils submit to us.' He replied,

'I watched how Satan fell, like lightning, out of the sky. And now you see that I have given you the power to tread underfoot snakes and scorpions and all the forces of the enemy, and nothing will ever harm you.[h] Nevertheless, what you should rejoice over is not that the spirits submit to you, but that your names are enrolled in heaven.'

The Father and the Son

At that moment Jesus exulted in the Holy[i] Spirit and said, 'I thank thee, Father, Lord of heaven and earth, for hiding these things from the learned and wise, and revealing them to the simple. Yes, Father, such[j] was thy choice.' Then turning to his disciples he said,[k] 'Everything is entrusted to me by my Father; and no one knows who the Son is but the Father, or who the Father is but the Son, and those to whom the Son may choose to reveal him.'

Turning to his disciples in private he said, 'Happy the eyes that see what you are seeing! I tell you, many prophets and kings wished to see what you now see, yet never saw it; to hear what you hear, yet never heard it.'

'Who is my neighbour?'

On one occasion a lawyer came forward to put this test question to him: 'Master, what must I do to inherit eternal life?' Jesus said, 'What is written in the Law? What is your reading of it?' He replied, 'Love the Lord your God with all your heart, with all your soul, with all your strength, and with all your mind; and your neighbour as yourself.' 'That is the right answer,' said Jesus; 'do that and you will live.'

But he wanted to vindicate himself, so he said to Jesus, 'And who is my neighbour?' Jesus replied, 'A man was on his way from Jerusalem down to Jericho when he fell in with robbers, who stripped him, beat him, and went off leaving him half dead. It so happened that a priest was going down by the same road; but when he saw him, he went past on the other side. So too a Levite came to the place, and when he saw him went past on the other side. But a Samaritan who was making the journey came upon him, and when he saw him was moved

---

f *Some witnesses read* No one who looks back as he sets hand to the plough . . .   g *Some witnesses read* seventy.   h Or and he will have no way at all to harm you.   i *Some witnesses omit* Holy.   j Or Yes, I thank thee, Father, that such . . .   k *Some witnesses omit* Then . . . he said.

34 to pity. He went up and bandaged his wounds, bathing them with oil and wine. Then he lifted him on to his own beast, brought him to an inn, and 35 looked after him there. Next day he produced two silver pieces and gave them to the innkeeper, and said, "Look after him; and if you spend any more, I will repay you on my way 36 back." Which of these three do you think was neighbour to the man who fell into the hands of the robbers?' 37 He answered, 'The one who showed him kindness.' Jesus said, 'Go and do as he did.'

At the home of Martha and Mary

38 While they were on their way Jesus came to a village where a woman named Martha made him welcome in 39 her home. She had a sister, Mary, who seated herself at the Lord's feet and stayed there listening to his words. 40 Now Martha was distracted by her many tasks, so she came to him and said, 'Lord, do you not care that my sister has left me to get on with the work by myself? Tell her to come 41 and lend a hand.' But the Lord answered, 'Martha, Martha, you are fretting and fussing about so many 42 things; but one thing is necessary.[l] The part that Mary has chosen is best; and it shall not be taken away from her.'

About prayer

11 Once, in a certain place, Jesus was at prayer. When he ceased, one of his disciples said, 'Lord, teach us to pray, 2 as John taught his disciples.' He answered, 'When you pray, say,

"Father,[m] thy name be hallowed; thy kingdom come.[n]
3 Give us each day our daily bread.[o]
4 And forgive us our sins,
   for we too forgive all who have done us wrong.
And do not bring us to the test."'[p]

5 Then he said to them, 'Suppose one of you has a friend who comes to him in the middle of the night and says, 6 "My friend, lend me three loaves, for a friend of mine on a journey has turned up at my house, and I have 7 nothing to offer him"; and he replies

from inside, "Do not bother me. The door is shut for the night; my children and I have gone to bed; and I cannot get up and give you what you want." I tell you that even if he will not provide for him out of friendship, the very shamelessness of the request will make him get up and give him all he needs. And so I say to you, ask, and you will receive; seek, and you will find; knock, and the door will be opened. For everyone who asks receives, he who seeks finds, and to him who knocks, the door will be opened.

'Is there a father among you who will offer his son[q] a snake when he asks for fish, or a scorpion when he asks for an egg? If you, then, bad as you are, know how to give your children what is good for them, how much more will the heavenly Father give the Holy Spirit[r] to those who ask him!'

Controversy with the Jews

He was driving out a devil which was dumb; and when the devil had come out, the dumb man began to speak. The people were astonished, but some of them said, 'It is by Beelzebub prince of devils that he drives the devils out.' Others, by way of a test, demanded of him a sign from heaven. But he knew what was in their minds, and said, 'Every kingdom divided against itself goes to ruin, and a divided household falls. Equally if Satan is divided against himself, how can his kingdom stand?—since, as you would have it, I drive out the devils by Beelzebub. If it is by Beelzebub that I cast out devils, by whom do your own people drive them out? If this is your argument, they themselves will refute you. But if it is by the finger of God that I drive out the devils, then be sure the kingdom of God has already come upon you.

'When a strong man fully armed is on guard over his castle his possessions are safe. But when someone stronger comes upon him and overpowers him, he carries off the arms and armour on which the man had relied and divides the plunder.

'He who is not with me is against me, and he who does not gather with me scatters.[s]

---

l Some witnesses read but few things are necessary, or rather, one alone; others omit you are fretting . . . necessary.   m Some witnesses read Our Father in heaven.   n One witness reads thy kingdom come upon us; some others have thy Holy Spirit come upon us and cleanse us; some insert thy will be done, on earth as in heaven.   o Or our bread for the morrow.   p Some witnesses add but save us from the evil one (or from evil).   q Some witnesses insert a stone when he asks for bread, or . . . r Some witnesses read a good gift; some others read good things.   s Some witnesses add me.

'When an unclean spirit comes out of a man it wanders over the deserts seeking a resting-place; and if it finds none, it says, "I will go back to the home I left." So it returns and finds the house[t] swept clean, and tidy. Off it goes and collects seven other spirits more wicked than itself, and they all come in and settle down; and in the end the man's plight is worse than before.'

True happiness

While he was speaking thus, a woman in the crowd called out, 'Happy the womb that carried you and the breasts that suckled you!' He rejoined, 'No, happy are those who hear the word of God and keep it.'

The sign of Jonah

With the crowds swarming round him he went on to say: 'This is a wicked generation. It demands a sign, and the only sign that will be given it is the sign of Jonah. For just as Jonah was a sign to the Ninevites, so will the Son of Man be to this generation. At the Judgement, when the men of this generation are on trial, the Queen of the South will appear against[u] them and ensure their condemnation, for she came from the ends of the earth to hear the wisdom of Solomon; and what is here is greater than Solomon. The men of Nineveh will appear at the Judgement when this generation is on trial, and ensure[v] its condemnation, for they repented at the preaching of Jonah; and what is here is greater than Jonah.'

The lamp of the body

'No one lights a lamp and puts it in a cellar,[w] but rather on the lamp-stand so that those who enter may see the light. The lamp of your body is the eye. When your eyes are sound, you have light for your whole body; but when the eyes are bad, you are in darkness. See to it then that the light you have is not darkness. If you have light for your whole body with no trace of darkness, it will all be as bright as when a lamp flashes its rays upon you.'

The Lord denounces Pharisees and lawyers

When he had finished speaking, a 37 Pharisee invited him to a meal. He 38 came in and sat down. The Pharisee noticed with surprise that he had not begun by washing before the meal. But the Lord said to him, 'You 39 Pharisees! You clean the outside of cup and plate; but inside you there is nothing but greed and wickedness. You fools! Did not he who made the 40 outside make the inside too? But let 41 what is in the cup[x] be given in charity, and all is clean.

'Alas for you Pharisees! You pay 42 tithes of mint and rue and every garden-herb, but have no care for justice and the love of God. It is these you should have practised, without neglecting the others.[y]

'Alas for you Pharisees! You love 43 the seats of honour in synagogues, and salutations in the market-places.

'Alas, alas, you are like unmarked 44 graves over which men may walk without knowing it.'

In reply to this one of the lawyers 45 said, 'Master, when you say things like this you are insulting us too.' Jesus rejoined: 'Yes, you lawyers, it 46 is no better with you! For you load men with intolerable burdens, and will not put a single finger to the load.

'Alas, you build the tombs of the 47 prophets whom your fathers murdered, and so testify that you approve of the 48 deeds your fathers did; they committed the murders and you provide the tombs.

'This is why the Wisdom of God 49 said, "I will send them prophets and messengers; and some of these they will persecute and kill"; so that this 50 generation will have to answer for the blood of all the prophets shed since the foundation of the world; from the 51 blood of Abel to the blood of Zechariah who perished between the altar and the sanctuary. I tell you, this generation will have to answer for it all.

'Alas for you lawyers! You have 52 taken away the key of knowledge. You did not go in yourselves, and those who were on their way in, you stopped.'

After he had left the house, the 53 lawyers and Pharisees began to assail

---

t Some witnesses insert unoccupied.   *u Or* will be raised to life together with . . .   *v Or* At the Judgement the men of Nineveh will rise again together with this generation and will ensure . . .   *w Some witnesses insert* or under the meal-tub.   *x Or* what you can afford.   *y Some witnesses omit* It is . . . others.

him fiercely and to ply him with a
54 host of questions, laying snares to
catch him with his own words.

Warning against hypocrisy

12 Meanwhile, when a crowd of many
thousands had gathered, packed so
close that they were treading on one
another, he began to speak first to his
disciples: 'Beware of the leaven of the
Pharisees; I mean their hypocrisy.
2 There is nothing covered up that will
not be uncovered, nothing hidden
3 that will not be made known. You
may take it, then, that everything
you have said in the dark will be
heard in broad daylight, and what
you have whispered behind closed
doors will be shouted from the house-
tops.'

Freedom from fear

4 'To you who are my friends I say:
Do not fear those who kill the body
and after that have nothing more
5 they can do. I will warn you whom to
fear: fear him who, after he has killed,
has authority to cast into hell. Believe
me, he is the one to fear.
6   'Are not sparrows five for twopence?
And yet not one of them is overlooked
7 by God. More than that, even the
hairs of your head have all been
counted. Have no fear; you are worth
more than any number of sparrows.'

Acknowledging and disowning Christ

8 'I tell you this: everyone who acknowledges me before men, the Son
of Man will acknowledge before the
9 angels of God; but he who disowns
me before men will be disowned before the angels of God.
10   'Anyone who speaks a word against
the Son of Man will receive forgiveness; but for him who slanders the
Holy Spirit there will be no forgiveness.
11   'When you are brought before synagogues and state authorities, do not
begin worrying about how you will
conduct your defence or what you
12 will say. For when the time comes
the Holy Spirit will instruct you what
to say.'

On amassing wealth

13 A man in the crowd said to him,
'Master, tell my brother to divide the
14 family property with me.' He replied,

'My good man, who set me over you
to judge or arbitrate?'[z] Then he said
to the people, 'Beware! Be on your
guard against greed of every kind, for
even when a man has more than
enough, his wealth does not give him
life.' And he told them this parable:
'There was a rich man whose land
yielded heavy crops. He debated with
himself: "What am I to do? I have
not the space to store my produce.
This is what I will do," said he: "I
will pull down my storehouses and
build them bigger. I will collect in
them all my corn and other goods,
and then say to myself, 'Man, you
have plenty of good things laid by,
enough for many years: take life
easy, eat, drink, and enjoy yourself.'"
But God said to him, "You fool, this
very night you must surrender your
life; you have amassed your money—
who will get it now?" That is how it
is with the man who amasses wealth
for himself and remains a pauper in
the sight of God.'[a]

Cure for worry

'Therefore', he said to his disciples, 'I
bid you put away anxious thoughts
about food to keep you alive and
clothes to cover your body. Life is
more than food, the body more than
clothes. Think of the ravens: they
neither sow nor reap; they have no
storehouse or barn; yet God feeds
them. You are worth far more than
the birds! Is there a man among you
who by anxious thought can add a
foot to his height[b]? If, then, you
cannot do even a very little thing,
why are you anxious about the rest?
'Think of the lilies: they neither
spin nor weave;[c] yet I tell you, even
Solomon in all his splendour was not
attired like one of these. But if that
is how God clothes the grass, which
is growing in the field today, and
tomorrow is thrown on the stove, how
much more will he clothe you! How
little faith you have! And so you are
not to set your mind on food and
drink; you are not to worry. For all
these are things for the heathen to
run after; but you have a Father who
knows that you need them. No, set
your mind upon his kingdom, and all
the rest will come to you as well.
'Have no fear, little flock; for your
Father has chosen to give you the
Kingdom. Sell your possessions and

z Some witnesses omit or arbitrate.   a Some witnesses omit That . . . God; others add at the end
When he said this he cried out, 'If you have ears to hear, then hear.'   b Or a day to his life.
c Some witnesses read they grow, they do not toil or spin.

give in charity. Provide for yourselves purses that do not wear out, and never-failing treasure in heaven, where no thief can get near it, no moth destroy
34 it. For where your treasure is, there will your heart be also.'

'Be ready'

35 'Be ready for action, with belts fas-
36 tened and lamps alight. Be like men who wait for their master's return from a wedding-party, ready to let him in the moment he arrives and
37 knocks. Happy are those servants whom the master finds on the alert when he comes. I tell you this: he will fasten his belt, seat them at table,
38 and come and wait on them. Even if it is the middle of the night or before dawn when he comes, happy they if
39 he finds them alert. And remember, if the householder had known what time the burglar was coming he would not have let his house be broken into.
40 Hold yourselves ready, then, because the Son of Man will come at the time you least expect him.'

The trusty and sensible man

41 Peter said, 'Lord, do you intend this parable specially for us or is it for
42 everyone?' The Lord said, 'Well, who is the trusty and sensible man whom his master will appoint as his steward, to manage his servants and issue their
43 rations at the proper time? Happy that servant who is found at his task
44 when his master comes! I tell you this: he will be put in charge of all his
45 master's property. But if that servant says to himself, "The master is a long time coming", and begins to bully the menservants and maids, and eat and
46 drink and get drunk; then the master will arrive on a day that servant does not expect, at a time he does not know, and will cut him in pieces. Thus he will find his place among the faithless.
47 'The servant who knew his master's wishes, yet made no attempt to carry them out, will be flogged severely.
48 But one who did not know them and earned a beating will be flogged less severely. Where a man has been given much, much will be expected of him; and the more a man has had entrusted to him the more he will be required to repay.'

Conflicting loyalties

49 'I have come to set fire to the earth, and how I wish it were already kindled!

50 I have a baptism to undergo, and what constraint I am under until
51 the ordeal is over! Do you suppose I came to establish peace on earth? No indeed, I have come to bring
52 division. For from now on, five members of a family will be divided, three against two and two against three;
53 father against son and son against father, mother against daughter and daughter against mother, mother against son's wife and son's wife against her mother-in-law.'

'This fateful hour'

54 He also said to the people, 'When you see cloud banking up in the west, you say at once, "It is going to rain",
55 and rain it does. And when the wind is from the south, you say, "There will be a heat-wave", and there is.
56 What hypocrites you are! You know how to interpret the appearance of earth and sky; how is it you cannot interpret this fateful hour?
57 'And why can you not judge for yourselves what is the right course?
58 When you are going with your opponent to court, make an effort to settle with him while you are still on the way; otherwise he may drag you before the judge, and the judge hand you over to the constable, and the constable put you in jail. I tell you,
59 you will not come out till you have paid the last farthing.'

The need for repentance

13 At that very time there were some people present who told him about the Galileans whose blood Pilate had mixed with their sacrifices. He an-
2 swered them: 'Do you imagine that, because these Galileans suffered this fate, they must have been greater sinners than anyone else in Galilee?
3 I tell you they were not; but unless you repent, you will all of you come to the same end. Or the eighteen
4 people who were killed when the tower fell on them at Siloam—do you imagine they were more guilty than all the other people living in Jeru-
5 salem? I tell you they were not; but unless you repent, you will all of you come to the same end.'

The fig-tree without fruit

6 He told them this parable: 'A man had a fig-tree growing in his vineyard; and he came looking for fruit on it,
7 but found none. So he said to the vine-dresser, "Look here! For the last

three years I have come looking for fruit on this fig-tree without finding any. Cut it down. Why should it go 8 on using up the soil?" But he replied, "Leave it, sir, this one year while I 9 dig round it and manure it. And if it bears next season, well and good; if not, you shall have it down."'

Jesus heals a crippled woman

10 One Sabbath he was teaching in a 11 synagogue, and there was a woman there possessed by a spirit that had crippled her for eighteen years. She was bent double and quite unable to 12 stand up straight. When Jesus saw her he called her and said, 'You are 13 rid of your trouble.' Then he laid his hands on her, and at once she straightened up and began to praise God. 14 But the president of the synagogue, indignant with Jesus for healing on the Sabbath, intervened and said to the congregation, 'There are six working-days: come and be cured on one of them, and not on the Sabbath.' 15 The Lord gave him his answer: 'What hypocrites you are!' he said. 'Is there a single one of you who does not loose his ox or his donkey from the manger and take it out to water on the Sab- 16 bath? And here is this woman, a daughter of Abraham, who has been kept prisoner by Satan for eighteen long years: was it wrong for her to be freed from her bonds on the Sab- 17 bath?' At these words all his opponents were covered with confusion, while the mass of the people were delighted at all the wonderful things he was doing.

A mustard-seed

18 'What is the kingdom of God like?' he continued. 'What shall I compare it 19 with? It is like a mustard-seed which a man took and sowed in his garden; and it grew to be a tree and the birds came to roost among its branches.'

Yeast

20 Again he said, 'The kingdom of God, 21 what shall I compare it with? It is like yeast which a woman took and mixed with half a hundredweight of flour till it was all leavened.'

The narrow door

22 He continued his journey through towns and villages, teaching as he made his way towards Jerusalem. 23 Someone asked him, 'Sir, are only a few to be saved?' His answer was: 'Struggle to get in through the narrow 24 door; for I tell you that many will try to enter and not be able.

'When once the master of the house 25 has got up and locked the door, you may stand outside and knock, and say, "Sir, let us in!", but he will only answer, "I do not know where you come from." Then you will begin to 26 say, "We sat at table with you and you taught in our streets." But he 27 will repeat, "I tell you, I do not know where you come from. Out of my sight, all of you, you and your wicked ways!" There will be wailing and 28 grinding of teeth there, when you see Abraham, Isaac, and Jacob, and all the prophets, in the kingdom of God, and yourselves thrown out. From 29 east and west people will come, from north and south, for the feast in the kingdom of God. Yes, and some who 30 are now last will be first, and some who are first will be last.'

Jerusalem the doomed city

At that time a number of Pharisees 31 came to him and said, 'You should leave this place and go on your way; Herod is out to kill you.' He replied, 32 'Go and tell that fox, "Listen: today and tomorrow I shall be casting out devils and working cures; on the third day I reach my goal." However, 33 I must be on my way today and tomorrow and the next day, because it is unthinkable for a prophet to meet his death anywhere but in Jerusalem.

'O Jerusalem, Jerusalem, the city 34 that murders the prophets and stones the messengers sent to her! How often have I longed to gather your children, as a hen gathers her brood under her wings; but you would not let me. Look, look! there is your temple, for- 35 saken by God. And I tell you, you shall never see me until the time comes when you say, "Blessings on him who comes in the name of the Lord!"'

Jesus heals a man of dropsy

One Sabbath he went to have a meal 1 in the house of a leading Pharisee; and they were watching him closely. There, in front of him, was a man 2 suffering from dropsy. Jesus asked 3 the lawyers and the Pharisees: 'Is it permitted to cure people on the Sabbath or not?' They said nothing. 4 So he took the man, cured him, and sent him away. Then he turned to 5 them and said, 'If one of you has a donkey[d] or an ox and it falls into a well, will he hesitate to haul it up on 6 the Sabbath day?' To this they could find no reply.

Humility and hospitality

7 When he noticed how the guests were trying to secure the places of honour, he spoke to them in a parable: 8 'When you are asked by someone to a wedding-feast, do not sit down in the place of honour. It may be that some person more distinguished than 9 yourself has been invited; and the host will come and say to you, "Give this man your seat." Then you will look foolish as you begin to take the 10 lowest place. No, when you receive an invitation, go and sit down in the lowest place, so that when your host comes he will say, "Come up higher, my friend." Then all your fellow-guests will see the respect in 11 which you are held. For everyone who exalts himself will be humbled; and whoever humbles himself will be exalted.'
12 Then he said to his host, 'When you are having a party for lunch or supper, do not invite your friends, your brothers or other relations, or your rich neighbours; they will only ask you back again and so you will be 13 repaid. But when you give a party, ask the poor, the crippled, the lame, 14 and the blind; and so find happiness. For they have no means of repaying you; but you will be repaid on the day when good men rise from the dead.'

A big dinner party

15 One of the company, after hearing all this, said to him, 'Happy the man who shall sit at the feast in the king-16 dom of God!' Jesus answered, 'A man was giving a big dinner party and had sent out many invitations. 17 At dinner-time he sent his servant with a message for his guests, "Please come, everything is now ready." 18 They began one and all to excuse themselves. The first said, "I have bought a piece of land, and I must go and look over it; please accept my 19 apologies." The second said, "I have bought five yoke of oxen, and I am on my way to try them out; please 20 accept my apologies." The next said, "I have just got married and for that 21 reason I cannot come." When the servant came back he reported this to his master. The master of the house

was angry and said to him, "Go out quickly into the streets and alleys of the town, and bring me in the poor, the crippled, the blind, and the lame." The servant said, "Sir, your orders 22 have been carried out and there is still room." The master replied, "Go 23 out on to the highways and along the hedgerows and make them come in; I want my house to be full. I tell you 24 that not one of those who were invited shall taste my banquet."'

The cost of discipleship

Once when great crowds were accom- 25 panying him, he turned to them and said: 'If anyone comes to me and 26 does not hate his father and mother, wife and children, brothers and sisters, even his own life, he cannot be a disciple of mine. No one who does not 27 carry his cross and come with me can be a disciple of mine. Would any of 28 you think of building a tower without first sitting down and calculating the cost, to see whether he could afford to finish it? Otherwise, if he has laid its 29 foundation and then is not able to complete it, all the onlookers will laugh at him. "There is the man", 30 they will say, "who started to build and could not finish." Or what king 31 will march to battle against another king, without first sitting down to consider whether with ten thousand men he can face an enemy coming to meet him with twenty thousand? If he cannot, then, long before the 32 enemy approaches, he sends envoys, and asks for terms. So also none of 33 you can be a disciple of mine without parting with all his possessions.
'Salt is a good thing; but if salt 34 itself becomes tasteless, what will you use to season it? It is useless either 35 on the land or on the dung-heap: it can only be thrown away. If you have ears to hear, then hear.'

The lost sheep

Another time, the tax-gatherers and 15 other bad characters were all crowding in to listen to him; and the Pha- 2 risees and the doctors of the law began grumbling among themselves: 'This fellow', they said, 'welcomes sinners and eats with them.' He answered 3 them with this parable: 'If one of you 4 has a hundred sheep and loses one of them, does he not leave the ninety-nine in the open pasture and go after the missing one until he has found it?

d Some witnesses read son.

5 How delighted he is then! He lifts
6 it on to his shoulders, and home he
goes to call his friends and neighbours together. "Rejoice with me!"
he cries. "I have found my lost sheep."
7 In the same way, I tell you, there will
be greater joy in heaven over one
sinner who repents than over ninety-
nine righteous people who do not need
to repent.'

The lost silver

8 'Or again, if a woman has ten silver
pieces and loses one of them, does she
not light the lamp, sweep out the
house, and look in every corner till
9 she has found it? And when she has,
she calls her friends and neighbours
together, and says, "Rejoice with me!
10 I have found the piece that I lost." In
the same way, I tell you, there is joy
among the angels of God over one
sinner who repents.'

The lost son

11 Again he said: 'There was once a man
12 who had two sons; and the younger
said to his father, "Father, give me
my share of the property." So he
13 divided his estate between them. A
few days later the younger son turned
the whole of his share into cash and
left home for a distant country, where
14 he squandered it in reckless living. He
had spent it all, when a severe famine
fell upon that country and he began
15 to feel the pinch. So he went and attached himself to one of the local
landowners, who sent him on to his
16 farm to mind the pigs. He would have
been glad to fill his belly with[e] the
pods that the pigs were eating; and
17 no one gave him anything. Then he
came to his senses and said, "How
many of my father's paid servants
have more food than they can eat,
18 and here am I, starving to death! I
will set off and go to my father, and
say to him, 'Father, I have sinned,
19 against God and against you; I am no
longer fit to be called your son; treat
20 me as one of your paid servants.'" So
he set out for his father's house. But
while he was still a long way off his
father saw him, and his heart went
out to him. He ran to meet him, flung
his arms round him, and kissed him.
21 The son said, "Father, I have sinned,
against God and against you; I am
no longer fit to be called your son."[f]
22 But the father said to his servants,

"Quick! fetch a robe, my best one,
and put it on him; put a ring on his
finger and shoes on his feet. Bring 23
the fatted calf and kill it, and let us have
a feast to celebrate the day. For this 24
son of mine was dead and has come
back to life; he was lost and is found."
And the festivities began.

'Now the elder son was out on 25
the farm; and on his way back, as
he approached the house, he heard
music and dancing. He called one of 26
the servants and asked what it meant.
The servant told him, "Your brother 27
has come home, and your father has
killed the fatted calf because he has
him back safe and sound." But he was 28
angry and refused to go in. His father
came out and pleaded with him; but 29
he retorted, "You know how I have
slaved for you all these years; I never
once disobeyed your orders; and you
never gave me so much as a kid, to
feast with my friends. But now that 30
this son of yours turns up, after running through your money with his
women, you kill the fatted calf for
him." "My boy," said the father, "you 31
are always with me, and everything
I have is yours. How could we help 32
celebrating this happy day? Your
brother here was dead and has come
back to life, was lost and is found."'

A dishonest steward

He said to his disciples, 'There was 16
a rich man who had a steward, and he
received complaints that this man
was squandering the property. So he 2
sent for him, and said, "What is this
that I hear? Produce your accounts,
for you cannot be manager here any
longer." The steward said to himself, 3
"What am I to do now that my employer is dismissing me? I am not
strong enough to dig, and too proud
to beg. I know what I must do, to 4
make sure that, when I have to leave,
there will be people to give me house
and home." He summoned his mas- 5
ter's debtors one by one. To the first
he said, "How much do you owe
my master?" He replied, "A thou- 6
sand gallons of olive oil." He said,
"Here is your account. Sit down and
make it five hundred; and be quick
about it." Then he said to another, 7
"And you, how much do you owe?"
He said, "A thousand bushels of
wheat", and was told, "Take your account and make it eight hundred." And 8
the master applauded the dishonest

e Some witnesses read to have his fill of . . .
servants.

f Some witnesses add treat me as one of your paid

steward for acting so astutely. For the worldly are more astute than the other-worldly in dealing with their own kind.

9 'So I say to you, use your worldly wealth to win friends for yourselves, so that when money is a thing of the past you may be received into an eternal home.

10 'The man who can be trusted in little things can be trusted also in great; and the man who is dishonest in little things is dishonest also in 11 great things. If, then, you have not proved trustworthy with the wealth of this world, who will trust you with 12 the wealth that is real? And if you have proved untrustworthy with what belongs to another, who will give you what is your own?

13 'No servant can be the slave of two masters; for either he will hate the first and love the second, or he will be devoted to the first and think nothing of the second. You cannot serve God and Money.'

Some sayings of Jesus

4 The Pharisees, who loved money,
5 heard all this and scoffed at him. He said to them, 'You are the people who impress your fellow-men with your righteousness; but God sees through you; for what sets itself up to be admired by men is detestable in the sight of God.

6 'Until John, it was the Law and the prophets: since then, there is the good news of the kingdom of God, and everyone forces his way in.

7 'It is easier for heaven and earth to come to an end than for one dot or stroke of the Law to lose its force.

8 'A man who divorces his wife and marries another commits adultery; and anyone who marries a woman divorced from her husband commits adultery.'

The rich man and Lazarus

9 'There was once a rich man, who dressed in purple and the finest linen, and feasted in great magnificence every 10 day. At his gate, covered with sores, 11 lay a poor man named Lazarus, who would have been glad to satisfy his hunger with the scraps from the rich man's table. Even the dogs used to 12 come and lick his sores. One day the poor man died and was carried away by the angels to be with Abraham. The rich man also died and was buried, 13 and in Hades, where he was in torment,

he looked up; and there, far away, was Abraham with Lazarus close beside him. "Abraham, my father," 24 he called out, "take pity on me! Send Lazarus to dip the tip of his finger in water, to cool my tongue, for I am in agony in this fire." But Abraham 25 said, "Remember, my child, that all the good things fell to you while you were alive, and all the bad to Lazarus; now he has his consolation here and it is you who are in agony. But that is 26 not all: there is a great chasm fixed between us; no one from our side who wants to reach you can cross it, and none may pass from your side to us." "Then, father," he replied, "will you 27 send him to my father's house, where 28 I have five brothers, to warn them, so that they too may not come to this place of torment?" But Abraham 29 said, "They have Moses and the prophets; let them listen to them." "No, 30 father Abraham," he replied, "but if someone from the dead visits them, they will repent." Abraham answered, 31 "If they do not listen to Moses and the prophets they will pay no heed even if someone should rise from the dead."'

Responsibility to others

He said to his disciples, 'Causes of 17 stumbling are bound to arise; but woe betide the man through whom they come. It would be better for him 2 to be thrown into the sea with a millstone round his neck than to cause one of these little ones to stumble. Keep watch on yourselves. 3

'If your brother wrongs you, reprove him; and if he repents, forgive him. Even if he wrongs you seven times 4 in a day and comes back to you seven times saying, "I am sorry", you are to forgive him.'

About faith

The apostles said to the Lord, 'In- 5 crease our faith'; and the Lord replied, 6 'If you had faith no bigger even than a mustard-seed, you could say to this mulberry-tree, "Be rooted up and replanted in the sea"; and it would at once obey you.'

The right attitude of service

'Suppose one of you has a servant 7 ploughing or minding sheep. When he comes back from the fields, will the master say, "Come along at once and sit down"? Will he not rather say, 8 "Prepare my supper, fasten your belt, and then wait on me while I have my meal; you can have yours afterwards"?

9 Is he grateful to the servant for carry-
10 ing out his orders? So with you: when you have carried out all your orders, you should say, "We are servants and deserve no credit; we have only done our duty."'

The thankful leper

11 In the course of his journey to Jeru-salem he was travelling through the borderlands of Samaria and Galilee.
12 As he was entering a village he was met by ten men with leprosy. They
13 stood some way off and called out to him, 'Jesus, Master, take pity on us.'
14 When he saw them he said, 'Go and show yourselves to the priests'; and while they were on their way, they
15 were made clean. One of them, finding himself cured, turned back praising
16 God aloud. He threw himself down at Jesus's feet and thanked him. And
17 he was a Samaritan. At this Jesus said: 'Were not all ten cleansed? The
18 other nine, where are they? Could none be found to come back and give praise to God except this foreigner?'
19 And he said to the man, 'Stand up and go on your way; your faith has cured you.'

About the kingdom of God

20 The Pharisees asked him, 'When will the kingdom of God come?' He said, 'You cannot tell by observation when
21 the kingdom of God comes. There will be no saying, "Look, here it is!" or "there it is!"; for in fact the kingdom of God is among you.'g

The day of the Son of Man

22 He said to the disciples, 'The time will come when you will long to see one of the days of the Son of Man, but
23 you will not see it. They will say to you, "Look! There!" and "Look! Here!" Do not go running off in
24 pursuit. For like the lightning-flash that lights up the earth from end to end, will the Son of Man be when his
25 day comes. But first he must endure much suffering and be repudiated by this generation.
26 'As things were in Noah's days, so will they be in the days of the Son of
27 Man. They ate and drank and married, until the day that Noah went into the

ark and the flood came and made an
2 end of them all. As things were in Lot's days, also: they ate and drank; they bought and sold; they planted
2 and built; but the day that Lot went out from Sodom, it rained fire and sulphur from the sky and made an
3 end of them all—it will be like that on the day when the Son of Man is revealed.

31 'On that day the man who is on the roof and his belongings in the house must not come down to pick them up; he, too, who is in the fields must not
32 go back. Remember Lot's wife. Who-ever seeks to save his life will lose it; and whoever loses it will save it, and live.

34 'I tell you, on that night there will be two men in one bed: one will be
35 taken, the other left. There will be two women together grinding corn: one will be taken, the other left.'h
37 When they heard this they asked, 'Where, Lord?' He said, 'Where the corpse is, there the vultures will gather.'

The persistent widow

18 He spoke to them in a parable to show that they should keep on pray-ing and never lose heart: 'There was
2 once a judge who cared nothing for God or man, and in the same town
3 there was a widow who constantly came before him demanding justice against her opponent. For a long time
4 he refused; but in the end he said to himself, "True, I care nothing for God or man; but this widow is so
5 great a nuisance that I will see her righted before she wears me out with her persistence."' The Lord said, 'You
6 hear what the unjust judge says; and
7 will not God vindicate his chosen, who cry out to him day and night, while he listens patiently to them'i? I tell you, he will vindicate them soon
8 enough. But when the Son of Man comes, will he find faith on earth?'

The Pharisee and the tax-gatherer

9 And here is another parable that he told. It was aimed at those who were sure of their own goodness and looked down on everyone else. 'Two men
10 went up to the temple to pray, one a Pharisee and the other a tax-gatherer. The Pharisee stood up and prayed
11 thus:j "I thank thee, O God, that I

---

g Or for in fact the kingdom of God is within you, or for in fact the kingdom of God is within your grasp, or for suddenly the kingdom of God will be among you.   h Some witnesses add (36) two men in the fields: one will be taken, the other left.   i Or delays to help them.   j Some witnesses read stood up by himself and prayed thus; others read stood up and prayed thus privately.

am not like the rest of men, greedy, dishonest, adulterous; or, for that 12 matter, like this tax-gatherer. I fast twice a week; I pay tithes on all that 13 I get." But the other kept his distance and would not even raise his eyes to heaven, but beat upon his breast, saying, "O God, have mercy on me, sin- 14 ner that I am." It was this man, I tell you, and not the other, who went home acquitted of his sins. For every-one who exalts himself will be humbled; and whoever humbles himself will be exalted.'

Jesus welcomes children

15 They even brought babies for him to touch. When the disciples saw them 16 they rebuked them, but Jesus called for the children and said, 'Let the little ones come to me; do not try to stop them; for the kingdom of God 17 belongs to such as these. I tell you that whoever does not accept the kingdom of God like a child will never enter it.'

A rich man's question

18 A man of the ruling class put this question to him: 'Good Master, what 19 must I do to win eternal life?' Jesus said to him, 'Why do you call me good? 20 No one is good except God alone. You know the commandments: "Do not commit adultery; do not murder; do not steal; do not give false evidence; honour your father and mother."' 21 The man answered, 'I have kept all 22 these since I was a boy.' On hearing this Jesus said, 'There is still one thing lacking: sell everything you have and distribute to the poor, and you will have riches in heaven; and 23 come, follow me.' At these words his heart sank; for he was a very rich 24 man. When Jesus saw it he said, 'How hard it is for the wealthy to enter the 25 kingdom of God! It is easier for a camel to go through the eye of a needle than for a rich man to enter 26 the kingdom of God.' Those who heard asked, 'Then who can be saved?' 27 He answered, 'What is impossible for men is possible for God.' 28 Peter said, 'We here have left our belongings to become your followers.' 29 Jesus said, 'I tell you this: there is no one who has given up home, or wife, brothers, parents, or children, for the 30 sake of the kingdom of God, who will not be repaid many times over in this age, and in the age to come have eternal life.'

Jesus again speaks of his death

He took the Twelve aside and said, 31 'We are now going up to Jerusalem; and all that was written by the pro-phets will come true for the Son of Man. He will be handed over to the 32 foreign power. He will be mocked, maltreated, and spat upon. They will 33 flog him and kill him. And on the third day he will rise again.' But they 34 understood nothing of all this; they did not grasp what he was talking about; its meaning was concealed from them.

Jesus restores a blind beggar's sight

As he approached Jericho a blind man 35 sat at the roadside begging. Hearing 36 a crowd going past, he asked what was happening. They told him, 'Jesus of 37 Nazareth is passing by.' Then he 38 shouted out, 'Jesus, Son of David, have pity on me.' The people in front 39 told him to hold his tongue; but he called out all the more, 'Son of David, have pity on me.' Jesus stopped and 40 ordered the man to be brought to him. When he came up he asked him, 'What 41 do you want me to do for you?' 'Sir, I want my sight back', he answered. Jesus said to him, 'Have back your 42 sight; your faith has cured you.' He 43 recovered his sight instantly; and he followed Jesus, praising God. And all the people gave praise to God for what they had seen.

Jesus and Zacchaeus

Entering Jericho he made his way 19 through the city. There was a man 2 there named Zacchaeus; he was super-intendent of taxes and very rich. He 3 was eager to see what Jesus looked like; but, being a little man, he could not see him for the crowd. So he ran 4 on ahead and climbed a sycomore-tree in order to see him, for he was to pass that way. When Jesus came 5 to the place, he looked up and said, 'Zacchaeus, be quick and come down; I must come and stay with you to-day.' He climbed down as fast as he 6 could and welcomed him gladly. At 7 this there was a general murmur of disapproval. 'He has gone in', they said, 'to be the guest of a sinner.' But Zacchaeus stood there and said 8 to the Lord, 'Here and now, sir, I give half my possessions to charity; and if I have cheated anyone, I am ready to repay him four times over.' Jesus said to him, 'Salvation has 9 come to this house today!—for this

10 man too is a son of Abraham, and the Son of Man has come to seek and save what is lost.'

Three servants

11 While they were listening to this, he went on to tell them a parable, because he was now close to Jerusalem and they thought the reign of God
12 might dawn at any moment. He said, 'A man of noble birth went on a long journey abroad, to be appointed king
13 and then return. But first he called ten of his servants and gave them a pound each, saying, "Trade with this
14 while I am away." His fellow-citizens hated him, and they sent a delegation on his heels to say, "We do not want
15 this man as our king." However, back he came as king, and sent for the servants to whom he had given the money, to see what profit each had
16 made. The first came and said, "Your
17 pound, sir, has made ten more." "Well done," he replied; "you are a good servant. You have shown yourself trustworthy in a very small matter, and you shall have charge of ten
18 cities." The second came and said, "Your pound, sir, has made five more";
19 and he also was told, "You too, take
20 charge of five cities." The third came and said, "Here is your pound, sir; I kept it put away in a handkerchief.
21 I was afraid of you, because you are a hard man: you draw out what you never put in and reap what you did
22 not sow." "You rascal!" he replied; "I will judge you by your own words. You knew, did you, that I am a hard man, that I draw out what I never put in, and reap what I did not sow?
23 Then why did you not put my money on deposit, and I could have claimed it with interest when I came back?"
24 Turning to his attendants he said, "Take the pound from him and give
25 it to the man with ten." "But, sir," they replied, "he has ten already."
26 "I tell you," he went on, "the man who has will always be given more; but the man who has not will forfeit
27 even what he has. But as for those enemies of mine who did not want me for their king, bring them here and slaughter them in my presence."'

Jesus rides into Jerusalem

28 With that Jesus went forward and
29 began the ascent to Jerusalem. As he approached Bethphage and Bethany at the hill called Olivet, he sent two of
30 the disciples with these instructions:

'Go to the village opposite; as you enter it you will find tethered there a colt which no one has yet ridden. Untie it and bring it here. If anyone 31 asks why you are untying it, say, "Our Master needs it."' The two went on 32 their errand and found it as he had told them; and while they were unty- 33 ing the colt, its owners asked, 'Why are you untying that colt?' They 34 answered, 'Our Master needs it.' So 35 they brought the colt to Jesus.

Then they threw their cloaks on the colt, for Jesus to mount, and they 36 carpeted the road with them as he went on his way. And now, as he 37 approached the descent from the Mount of Olives, the whole company of his disciples in their joy began to sing aloud the praises of God for all the great things they had seen:

'Blessings on him who comes as king 38 in the name of the Lord!
Peace in heaven, glory in highest heaven!'

Some Pharisees who were in the 39 crowd said to him, 'Master, reprimand your disciples.' He answered, 'I tell 40 you, if my disciples keep silence the stones will shout aloud.'

When he came in sight of the city, 41 he wept over it and said, 'If only you 42 had known, on this great day, the way that leads to peace! But no; it is hidden from your sight. For a time will 43 come upon you, when your enemies will set up siege-works against you; they will encircle you and hem you in at every point; they will bring you to 44 the ground, you and your children within your walls, and not leave you one stone standing on another, because you did not recognize God's moment when it came.'

Jesus drives traders from the temple

Then he went into the temple and 45 began driving out the traders, with 46 these words: 'Scripture says, "My house shall be a house of prayer"; but you have made it a robbers' cave.'

Day by day he taught in the temple. 47 And the chief priests and lawyers were bent on making an end of him, with the support of the leading citizens, but found they were helpless, 48 because the people all hung upon his words.

About the authority of Jesus

One day, as he was teaching the people 20 in the temple and telling them the good news, the priests and lawyers, and the elders with them, came upon 2 him and accosted him. 'Tell us', they said, 'by what authority you are acting like this; who gave you this 3 authority?' He answered them, 'I have a question to ask you too: tell 4 me, was the baptism of John from 5 God or from men?' This set them arguing among themselves: 'If we say, "from God", he will say, "Why did 6 you not believe him?" And if we say, "from men", the people will all stone us, for they are convinced that John 7 was a prophet.' So they replied that 8 they could not tell. And Jesus said to them, 'Then neither will I tell you by what authority I act.'

Tenants in a vineyard

9 He went on to tell the people this parable: 'A man planted a vineyard, let it out to vine-growers, and went 10 abroad for a long time. When the season came, he sent a servant to the tenants to collect from them his share of the produce; but the tenants thrashed him and sent him away 11 empty-handed. He tried again and sent a second servant; but he also was thrashed, outrageously treated, 12 and sent away empty-handed. He tried once more with a third; this one too 13 they wounded and flung out. Then the owner of the vineyard said, "What am I to do? I will send my own dear son;[k] perhaps they will respect him." 14 But when the tenants saw him they talked it over together. "This is the heir," they said; "let us kill him so that the property may come to us." 15 So they flung him out of the vineyard and killed him. What then will the owner of the vineyard do to them? 16 He will come and put these tenants to death and let the vineyard to others.'

When they heard this, they said, 17 'God forbid!' But he looked straight at them and said, 'Then what does this text of Scripture mean: "The stone which the builders rejected has 18 become the main corner-stone"? Any man who falls on that stone will be dashed to pieces; and if it falls on a man he will be crushed by it.'

Paying tax to the Emperor

19 The lawyers and chief priests wanted to lay hands on him there and then, for they saw that this parable was aimed at them; but they were afraid 20 of the people. So they watched their

opportunity and sent secret agents in the guise of honest men, to seize upon some word of his as a pretext for handing him over to the authority and jurisdiction of the Governor. They 21 put a question to him: 'Master,' they said, 'we know that what you speak and teach is sound; you pay deference to no one, but teach in all honesty the way of life that God requires. Are we 22 or are we not permitted to pay taxes to the Roman Emperor?' He saw through 23 their trick and said, 'Show me a silver 24 piece. Whose head does it bear, and whose inscription?' 'Caesar's', they replied. 'Very well then,' he said, 'pay 25 Caesar what is due to Caesar, and pay God what is due to God.' Thus their 26 attempt to catch him out in public failed, and, astonished by his reply, they fell silent.

About resurrection

Then some Sadducees came forward. 27 They are the people who deny that there is a resurrection. Their question was this: 'Master, Moses laid it down 28 for us that if there are brothers, and one dies leaving a wife but no child, then the next should marry the widow and carry on his brother's family. Now, there were seven brothers: the 29 first took a wife and died childless; then the second married her, then the 30 31 third. In this way the seven of them died leaving no children. Afterwards 32 the woman also died. At the resurrec- 33 tion whose wife is she to be, since all seven had married her?' Jesus said to 34 them, 'The men and women of this world marry; but those who have been 35 judged worthy of a place in the other world and of the resurrection from the dead, do not marry, for they are not 36 subject to death any longer. They are like angels; they are sons of God, because they share in the resurrection. That the dead are raised to life again 37 is shown by Moses himself in the story of the burning bush, when he calls the Lord, "the God of Abraham, Isaac, and Jacob". God is not God of 38 the dead but of the living; for him all are[l] alive.'

At this some of the lawyers said, 39 'Well spoken, Master.' For there was 40 no further question that they ventured to put to him.

About the Messiah

He said to them, 'How can they say 41 that the Messiah is son of David? For 42

k Or my only son.

l Or they are all.

David himself says in the Book of
Psalms: "The Lord said to my Lord,
43 'Sit at my right hand until I make
44 your enemies your footstool.'" Thus
David calls him "Lord"; how then
can he be David's son?'

Warning against doctors of the law

45 In the hearing of all the people Jesus
46 said to his disciples: 'Beware of the
doctors of the law who love to walk up
and down in long robes, and have
a great liking for respectful greetings
in the street, the chief seats in our
synagogues, and places of honour at
47 feasts. These are the men who eat up
the property of widows, while they say
long prayers for appearance' sake;
and they will receive the severest
sentence.'

A poor widow's offering

21 He looked up and saw the rich people
dropping their gifts into the chest of
2 the temple treasury; and he noticed a
poor widow putting in two tiny coins.
3 'I tell you this,' he said: 'this poor
widow has given more than any of
4 them; for those others who have
given had more than enough, but she,
with less than enough, has given all
she had to live on.'

Destruction of the temple foretold

5 Some people were talking about the
temple and the fine stones and votive
offerings with which it was adorned.
6 He said, 'These things which you are
gazing at—the time will come when
not one stone of them will be left upon
another; all will be thrown down.'
7 'Master,' they asked, 'when will it all
come about? What will be the sign
when it is due to happen?'

Troubles and persecutions

8 He said, 'Take care that you are not
misled. For many will come claiming
my name and saying, "I am he", and,
"The Day is upon us." Do not follow
9 them. And when you hear of wars and
insurrections, do not fall into a panic.
These things are bound to happen
first; but the end does not follow im-
10 mediately.' Then he added, 'Nation
will make war upon nation, kingdom
11 upon kingdom; there will be great
earthquakes, and famines and plagues
in many places; in the sky terrors and
great portents.
12   'But before all this happens they
will set upon you and persecute you.
You will be brought before syna-

gogues and put in prison; you will be
haled before kings and governors for
your allegiance to me. This will be 13
your opportunity to testify; so make 14
up your minds not to prepare your
defence beforehand, because I myself 15
will give you power of utterance and
a wisdom which no opponent will be
able to resist or refute. Even your 16
parents and brothers, your relations
and friends, will betray you. Some of
you will be put to death; and all will 17
hate you for your allegiance to me.
But not a hair of your head shall be 18
lost. By standing firm you will win 19
true life for yourselves.'

Jerusalem will be trampled down

'But when you see Jerusalem en- 20
circled by armies, then you may be
sure that her destruction is near. Then 21
those who are in Judaea must take to
the hills; those who are in the city itself must leave it, and those who are
out in the country must not enter;
because this is the time of retribution, 22
when all that stands written is to be
fulfilled. Alas for women who are with 23
child in those days, or have children
at the breast! For there will be great
distress in the land and a terrible
judgement upon this people. They 24
will fall at the sword's point; they
will be carried captive into all countries; and Jerusalem will be trampled
down by foreigners until their day
has run its course.'

The coming of the Son of Man

'Portents will appear in sun, moon, 25
and stars. On earth nations will stand
helpless, not knowing which way to
turn from the roar and surge of the
sea; men will faint with terror at the 26
thought of all that is coming upon
the world; for the celestial powers will
be shaken. And then they will see the 27
Son of Man coming on a cloud with
great power and glory. When all this 28
begins to happen, stand upright and
hold your heads high, because your
liberation is near.'

He told them this parable: 'Look 29
at the fig-tree, or any other tree. As 30
soon as it buds, you can see for yourselves that summer is near. In the 31
same way, when you see all this
happening, you may know that the
kingdom of God is near.
'I tell you this: the present genera- 32
tion will live to see it all. Heaven and 33
earth will pass away; my words will
never pass away.

34 'Keep a watch on yourselves; do not let your minds be dulled by dissipation and drunkenness and worldly cares so that the great Day closes
35 upon you suddenly like a trap; for that day will come on all men, wherever they are, the whole world over.
36 Be on the alert, praying at all times for strength to pass safely through all these imminent troubles and to stand in the presence of the Son of Man.'
37 His days were given to teaching in the temple; and then he would leave the city and spend the night on the
38 hill called Olivet. And in the early morning the people flocked to listen to him in the temple.[m]

A plot to kill Jesus

22 Now the festival of Unleavened Bread, known as Passover, was approach-
2 ing, and the chief priests and the doctors of the law were trying to devise some means of doing away with him; for they were afraid of the people.

Judas Iscariot plans to betray Jesus

3 Then Satan entered into Judas Iscariot, who was one of the Twelve;
4 and Judas went to the chief priests and officers of the temple police to discuss ways and means of putting Jesus
5 into their power. They were greatly pleased and undertook to pay him a
6 sum of money. He agreed, and began to look out for an opportunity to betray him to them without collecting a crowd.

Preparations for the Passover

7 Then came the day of Unleavened Bread, on which the Passover victim
8 had to be slaughtered, and Jesus sent Peter and John with these instruc-
9 tions: 'Go and prepare for our Passover supper.' 'Where would you like us to make the preparations?' they
10 asked. He replied, 'As soon as you set foot in the city a man will meet you carrying a jar of water. Follow him
11 into the house that he enters and give this message to the householder: "The Master says, 'Where is the room in which I may eat the Passover with
12 my disciples?'"' He will show you a large room upstairs all set out: make
13 the preparations there.' They went

and found everything as he had said. So they prepared for Passover.

The Last Supper

14 When the time came he took his place at table, and the apostles with him;
15 and he said to them, 'How I have longed[n] to eat this Passover with you
16 before my death! For I tell you, never again shall I[o] eat it until the time when it finds its fulfilment in the kingdom of God.'
17 Then he took a cup, and after giving thanks he said, 'Take this and share it among yourselves; for I tell
18 you, from this moment I shall drink from the fruit of the vine no more until the time when the kingdom of God comes.' And he took bread, gave
19 thanks, and broke it; and he gave it to them, with the words: 'This is my body.'[p]
21 'But mark this—my betrayer is here, his hand with mine on the table.
22 For the Son of Man is going his appointed way; but alas for that man
23 by whom he is betrayed!' At this they began to ask among themselves which of them it could possibly be who was to do this thing.

A jealous dispute

24 Then a jealous dispute broke out: who among them should rank high-
25 est? But he said, 'In the world, kings lord it over their subjects; and those in authority are called their country's
26 "Benefactors". Not so with you: on the contrary, the highest among you must bear himself like the youngest,
27 the chief of you like a servant. For who is greater—the one who sits at table or the servant who waits on him? Surely the one who sits at table. Yet here am I among you like a servant.
28 'You are the men who have stood firmly by me in my times of trial; and
29 now I vest in you the kingship which my Father vested in me; you shall
30 eat and drink at my table in my kingdom and sit[q] on thrones as judges of the twelve tribes of Israel.

Jesus foretells Peter's denial

31 'Simon, Simon, take heed: Satan has been given leave to sift all of you like
32 wheat; but for you I have prayed that your faith may not fail; and when you

---

m Some witnesses here insert the passage printed on pp. 895-6.   n Or said to them, 'I longed . . .'
o Some witnesses read For I tell you, I shall not . . .   p Some witnesses add, in whole or in part, and
with various arrangements, the following: 'which is given for you; do this as a memorial of me.' (20) In
the same way he took the cup after supper, and said, 'This cup, poured out for you, is the new covenant sealed by my blood.'   q Or trial; and as my Father gave me the right to reign, so I give you
the right to eat and to drink . . . and to sit . . .

have come to yourself, you must lend
33 strength to your brothers.' 'Lord,' he
replied, 'I am ready to go with you to
34 prison and death.' Jesus said, 'I tell
you, Peter, the cock will not crow
tonight until you have three times
over denied that you know me.'

Purse, pack, and sword

35 He said to them, 'When I sent you
out barefoot without purse or pack,
were you ever short of anything?' 'No',
36 they answered. 'It is different now,'
he said; 'whoever has a purse had
better take it with him, and his pack
too; and if he has no sword, let him
37 sell his cloak to buy one. For Scripture says, "And he was counted a-
mong the outlaws", and these words,
I tell you, must find fulfilment in
me; indeed, all that is written of me
38 is being fulfilled.' 'Look, Lord,' they
said, 'we have two swords here.'
'Enough, enough!' he replied.

Jesus prays on the Mount of Olives

39 Then he went out and made his way
as usual to the Mount of Olives, ac-
40 companied by the disciples. When he
reached the place he said to them,
'Pray that you may be spared the
41 hour of testing.' He himself withdrew
from them about a stone's throw,
knelt down, and began to pray:
42 'Father, if it be thy will, take this cup
away from me. Yet not my will but
thine be done.'
43   And now there appeared to him
an angel from heaven bringing him
44 strength, and in anguish of spirit he
prayed the more urgently; and his
sweat was like clots of blood falling to
the ground.[r]
45   When he rose from prayer and came
to the disciples he found them asleep,
46 worn out by grief. 'Why are you sleeping?' he said. 'Rise and pray that you
may be spared the test.'

Jesus is arrested

47 While he was still speaking a crowd
appeared with the man called Judas,
one of the Twelve, at their head. He
48 came up to Jesus to kiss him; but
Jesus said, 'Judas, would you betray
the Son of Man with a kiss?'
49   When his followers saw what was
coming, they said, 'Lord, shall we use
50 our swords?' And one of them struck
at the High Priest's servant, cutting

off his right ear. But Jesus answered, 51
'Let them have their way.' Then he
touched the man's ear and healed
him.[s]
Turning to the chief priests, the 52
officers of the temple police, and the
elders, who had come to seize him, he
said, 'Do you take me for a bandit,
that you have come out with swords
and cudgels to arrest me? Day after 53
day, when I was in the temple with
you, you kept your hands off me. But
this is your moment—the hour when
darkness reigns.'

Peter disowns Jesus

Then they arrested him and led him 54
away. They brought him to the High
Priest's house, and Peter followed at a
distance. They lit a fire in the middle 55
of the courtyard and sat round it, and
Peter sat among them. A serving- 56
maid who saw him sitting in the fire-
light stared at him and said, 'This
man was with him too.' But he 57
denied it: 'Woman,' he said, 'I do not
know him.' A little later someone else 58
noticed him and said, 'You also are
one of them.' But Peter said to him,
'No, I am not.' About an hour passed 59
and another spoke more strongly still:
'Of course this fellow was with him.
He must have been; he is a Galilean.'
But Peter said, 'Man, I do not know 60
what you are talking about.' At that
moment, while he was still speaking,
a cock crew; and the Lord turned and 61
looked at Peter. And Peter remembered the Lord's words, 'Tonight
before the cock crows you will disown
me three times.'[t]

Jesus mocked and beaten

The men who were guarding Jesus 63
mocked at him. They beat him, they 64
blindfolded him, and they kept asking
him, 'Now, prophet, who hit you?
Tell us that.' And so they went on 65
heaping insults upon him.

Jesus is charged with blasphemy

When day broke, the elders of the 66
nation, chief priests, and doctors of
the law assembled, and he was
brought before their Council. 'Tell us,' 67
they said, 'are you the Messiah?' 'If
I tell you,' he replied, 'you will not
believe me; and if I ask questions, 68
you will not answer. But from now on, 69
the Son of Man will be seated at the

r *Some witnesses omit* And now . . . ground.   s *Or* 'Let me do as much as this', *and touching the*
man's ear. he healed him.   t *Some witnesses add* (62) He went outside, and wept bitterly, *as in*
Matthew 26. 75.

70 right hand of Almighty God.'[u] 'You are the Son of God, then?' they all said, and he replied, 'It is you who 71 say I am.'[v] They said, 'Need we call further witnesses? We have heard it ourselves from his own lips.'

Jesus before Pilate

23 With that the whole assembly rose, and they brought him before Pilate. 2 They opened the case against him by saying, 'We found this man subverting our nation, opposing the payment of taxes to Caesar, and claiming to be 3 Messiah, a king.'[w] Pilate asked him, 'Are you the king of the Jews?' He 4 replied, 'The words are yours.'[x] Pilate then said to the chief priests and the crowd, 'I find no case for this man 5 to answer.' But they insisted: 'His teaching is causing disaffection among the people all through Judaea. It started from Galilee and has spread as far as this city.'

Herod questions Jesus

6 When Pilate heard this, he asked if 7 the man was a Galilean, and on learning that he belonged to Herod's jurisdiction he remitted the case to him, for Herod was also in Jerusalem 8 at that time. When Herod saw Jesus he was greatly pleased; having heard about him, he had long been wanting to see him, and had been hoping to see some miracle performed by him. 9 He questioned him at some length 10 without getting any reply; but the chief priests and lawyers appeared and pressed the case against him vigorous- 11 ly. Then Herod and his troops treated him with contempt and ridicule, and sent him back to Pilate dressed in a 12 gorgeous robe. That same day Herod and Pilate became friends; till then there had been a standing feud between them.

Jesus is sentenced to death

13 Pilate now called together the chief 14 priests, councillors, and people, and said to them, 'You brought this man before me on a charge of subversion. But, as you see, I have myself examined him in your presence and found nothing in him to support your 15 charges. No more did Herod, for he has referred him back to us. Clearly he has done nothing to deserve death.

I therefore propose to let him off with 16 a flogging.' But[y] there was a general 18 outcry, 'Away with him! Give us Barabbas.' (This man had been put in 19 prison for a rising that had taken place in the city, and for murder.) Pilate 20 addressed them again, in his desire to release Jesus, but they shouted back, 21 'Crucify him, crucify him!' For the 22 third time he spoke to them: 'Why, what wrong has he done? I have not found him guilty of any capital offence. I will therefore let him off with a flogging.' But they insisted on 23 their demand, shouting that Jesus should be crucified. Their shouts prevailed and Pilate decided that they 24 should have their way. He released 25 the man they asked for, the man who had been put in prison for insurrection and murder, and gave Jesus up to their will.

Jesus is crucified

As they led him away to execution 26 they seized upon a man called Simon, from Cyrene, on his way in from the country, put the cross on his back, and made him walk behind Jesus carrying it.

Great numbers of people followed, 27 many women among them, who mourned and lamented over him. Jesus turned to them and said, 28 'Daughters of Jerusalem, do not weep for me; no, weep for yourselves and your children. For the days are surely 29 coming when they will say, "Happy are the barren, the wombs that never bore a child, the breasts that never fed one." Then they will start saying 30 to the mountains, "Fall on us", and to the hills, "Cover us." For if these 31 things are done when the wood is green, what will happen when it is dry?'

There were two others with him, 32 criminals who were being led away to execution; and when they reached 33 the place called The Skull, they crucified him there, and the criminals with him, one on his right and the other on his left. Jesus said, 'Father, 34 forgive them; they do not know what they are doing.'[z]

They divided his clothes among them by casting lots. The people stood 35 looking on, and their rulers jeered at him: 'He saved others: now let him save himself, if this is God's Messiah,

---

u Literally of the Power of God.   v Or You are right, for I am.   w Or to be an anointed king.
x Or It is as you say.   y Some witnesses read (17) At festival time he was obliged to release one person for them; (18) and now . . .   z Some witnesses omit Jesus said, 'Father . . . doing.'

36 his Chosen.' The soldiers joined in the mockery and came forward offer-
37 ing him their sour wine. 'If you are the king of the Jews,' they said, 'save
38 yourself.' There was an inscription above his head which ran: 'This is the king of the Jews.'
39 One of the criminals who hung there with him taunted him: 'Are not you the Messiah? Save yourself, and us.'
40 But the other rebuked him: 'Have you no fear of God? You are under the
41 same sentence as he. For us it is plain justice; we are paying the price for our misdeeds; but this man has done
42 nothing wrong.' And he said, 'Jesus, remember me when you come to your
43 throne.'[a] He answered, 'I tell you this: today you shall be with me in Para-dise.'

The death of Jesus

44 By now it was about midday and a darkness fell over the whole land, which lasted until three in the after-
45 noon; the sun's light failed. And the curtain of the temple was torn in two.
46 Then Jesus gave a loud cry and said, 'Father, into thy hands I commit my spirit'; and with these words he died.
47 The centurion saw it all, and gave praise to God. 'Beyond all doubt', he said, 'this man was innocent.'
48 The crowd who had assembled for the spectacle, when they saw what had happened, went home beating their breasts.

The burial of Jesus

49 His friends had all been standing at a distance; the women who had ac-companied him from Galilee stood with them and watched it all.
50 Now there was a man called Joseph, a member of the Council, a good,
51 upright man, who had dissented from their policy and the action they had taken. He came from the Judaean town of Arimathaea, and he was one who looked forward to the kingdom
52 of God. This man now approached Pilate and asked for the body of Jesus.
53 Taking it down from the cross, he wrapped it in a linen sheet, and laid it in a tomb cut out of the rock, in
53 which no one had been laid before. It was Friday, and the Sabbath was about to begin.

News of the resurrection

55 The women who had accompanied him from Galilee followed; they took note of the tomb and observed how
56 his body was laid. Then they went home and prepared spices and per-fumes; and on the Sabbath they rest-ed in obedience to the commandment.
2 But on the Sunday morning very early they came to the tomb bringing
2 the spices they had prepared. Finding
3 that the stone had been rolled away from the tomb, they went inside; but
4 the body was not to be found. While they stood utterly at a loss, all of a sudden two men in dazzling garments
5 were at their side. They were terrified, and stood with eyes cast down, but the men said, 'Why search among the
6 dead for one who lives?[b] Remember
7 what he told you while he was still in Galilee, about the Son of Man: how he must be given up into the power of sinful men and be crucified, and must rise again on the third day.'
8,9 Then they recalled his words and, returning from the tomb, they re-ported all this to the Eleven and all the others.
10 The women were Mary of Magdala, Joanna, and Mary the mother[c] of James, and they, with the other
11 women, told the apostles. But the story appeared to them to be nonsense, and they would not believe them.[d]

The encounter on the road to Emmaus

13 That same day two of them were on their way to a village called Emmaus, which lay about seven miles from
14 Jerusalem, and they were talking to-
15 gether about all these happenings. As they talked and discussed it with one another, Jesus himself came up and
16 walked along with them; but some-thing kept them from seeing who it
17 was. He asked them, 'What is it you are debating as you walk?' They
18 halted, their faces full of gloom, and one, called Cleopas, answered, 'Are you the only person staying in Jeru-salem not to know[e] what has hap-pened there in the last few days?'
19 'What do you mean?' he said. 'All this about Jesus of Nazareth,' they replied, 'a prophet powerful in speech and ac-tion before God and the whole peo-ple; how our chief priests and rulers handed him over to be sentenced to

---

a Some witnesses read come in royal power.   b Some witnesses insert He is not here: he has been raised.   c Or wife, or daughter.   d Some witnesses add (12) Peter, however, got up and ran to the tomb, and, peering in, saw the wrappings and nothing more; and he went home amazed at what had happened.   e Or Have you been staying by yourself in Jerusalem, that you do not know ...

21 death, and crucified him. But we had been hoping that he was the man to liberate Israel. What is more, this is 22 the third day since it happened, and now some women of our company have astounded us: they went early 23 to the tomb, but failed to find his body, and returned with a story that they had seen a vision of angels who 24 told them he was alive. So some of our people went to the tomb and found things just as the women had said; but him they did not see.'

25 'How dull you are!' he answered. 'How slow to believe all that the 26 prophets said! Was the Messiah not bound to suffer thus before entering 27 upon his glory?' Then he began with Moses and all the prophets, and explained to them the passages which referred to himself in every part of the scriptures.

28 By this time they had reached the village to which they were going, and he made as if to continue his journey, 29 but they pressed him: 'Stay with us, for evening draws on, and the day is almost over.' So he went in to stay 30 with them. And when he had sat down with them at table, he took bread and said the blessing; he broke the bread, and offered it to them. 31 Then their eyes were opened, and they recognized him; and he vanished 32 from their sight. They said to one another, 'Did we not feel our hearts on fire as he talked with us on the road and explained the scriptures to us?' 33 Without a moment's delay they set out and returned to Jerusalem. There they found that the Eleven and the rest of the company had assembled, 34 and were saying, 'It is true: the Lord has risen; he has appeared to Simon.' 35 Then they gave their account of the events of their journey and told how he had been recognized by them at the breaking of the bread.

Jesus appears to his disciples

36 As they were talking about all this, there he was, standing among them.[j] 37 Startled and terrified, they thought they were seeing a ghost. But he said, 38 'Why are you so perturbed? Why do questionings arise in your minds? 39 Look at my hands and feet. It is I myself. Touch me and see; no ghost has flesh and bones as you can see that I have.'[g] They were still unconvinced, 41 still wondering, for it seemed too good to be true. So he asked them, 'Have 42 you anything here to eat?' They offered him a piece of fish they had cooked, 43 which he took and ate before their eyes.

Jesus commissions his disciples

44 And he said to them, 'This is what I meant by saying, while I was still with you, that everything written about me in the Law of Moses and in the prophets and psalms was bound to be fulfilled.' Then he opened their 45 minds to understand the scriptures. 'This', he said, 'is what is written: 46 that the Messiah is to suffer death and to rise from the dead on the third day, and that in his name repentance bring- 47 ing the forgiveness of sins is to be proclaimed to all nations. Begin from Jerusalem; it is you who are the wit- 48 nesses to it all. And mark this: I am 49 sending upon you my Father's promised gift; so stay here in this city until you are armed with the power from above.'

The parting at Bethany

50 Then he led them out as far as Bethany, and blessed them with uplifted hands; and in the act of blessing he 51 parted from them.[h] And they[i] re- 52 turned to Jerusalem with great joy, and spent all their time in the temple 53 praising God.

f Some witnesses insert And he said to them, 'Peace be with you!' g Some witnesses insert (40) After saying this he showed them his hands and feet. h Some witnesses add and was carried up into heaven. i Some witnesses insert worshipped him and ...

THE GOSPEL ACCORDING TO
JOHN

The Word became flesh

1 WHEN ALL THINGS began, the Word already was.[a] The Word dwelt with God, and what God was, the
2 Word was. The Word, then, was with
3 God at the beginning, and through him all things came to be; no single thing was created without him. All
4 that came to be was alive with his life,[b]
5 and that life was the light of men. The light shines on in the dark, and the darkness has never mastered it.

6 There appeared a man named John,
7 sent from God; he came as a witness to testify to the light, that all might
8 become believers through him. He was not himself the light; he came to bear
9 witness to the light. The real light which enlightens every man was even then coming into the world.[c]
10 He was in the world;[d] but the world, though it owed its being to him,
11 did not recognize him. He entered his own realm, and his own would not
12 receive him. But to all who did receive him, to those who have yielded him their allegiance, he gave the
13 right to become children of God, not born of any human stock, or by the fleshly desire of a human father, but
14 the offspring of God himself. So the Word became flesh; he came to dwell among us, and we saw his glory, such glory as befits the Father's only Son, full of grace and truth.

15 Here is John's testimony to him: he cried aloud, 'This is the man I meant when I said, "He comes after me, but takes rank before me"; for before I was born, he already was.'
16 Out of his full store we have all
17 received grace upon grace; for while the Law was given through Moses, grace and truth came through Jesus
18 Christ. No one has ever seen God; but God's only Son, he who is nearest to the Father's heart, he has made him known.[e]

The testimony of John

19 This is the testimony which John gave when the Jews of Jerusalem sent a deputation of priests and Levites to
20 ask him who he was. He confessed without reserve and avowed, 'I am
21 not the Messiah.' 'What then? Are you Elijah?' 'No', he replied. 'Are you the prophet we await?' He answered 'No.'
22 'Then who are you?' they asked. 'We must give an answer to those who sent us. What account do you give of your-
23 self?' He answered in the words of the prophet Isaiah: 'I am a voice crying aloud in the wilderness, "Make the Lord's highway straight."'

24 Some Pharisees who were in the
25 deputation asked him, 'If you are not the Messiah, nor Elijah, nor the prophet, why then are you baptizing?'
26 'I baptize in water,' John replied, 'but among you, though you do not know
27 him, stands the one who is to come after me. I am not good enough to un-
28 fasten his shoes.' This took place at Bethany beyond Jordan, where John was baptizing.

The Lamb of God

29 The next day he saw Jesus coming towards him. 'Look,' he said, 'there is the Lamb of God; it is he who takes
30 away the sin of the world. This is he of whom I spoke when I said, "After me a man is coming who takes rank before me"; for before I was born, he
31 already was. I myself did not know who he was; but the very reason why I came, baptizing in water, was that he might be revealed to Israel.'

32 John testified further: 'I saw the Spirit coming down from heaven like a dove and resting upon him. I did not
33 know him, but he who sent me to baptize in water had told me, "When you see the Spirit coming down upon someone and resting upon him, you will know that this is he who is

---

a Or The Word was at the creation.   b Or no single created thing came into being without him. There was life in him ...   c Or The light was in being, light absolute, enlightening every man born into the world.   d Or The Word, then, was in the world.   e Some witnesses read but the only one, the one nearest to the Father's heart, has made him known; others read but the only one, himself God, the nearest to the Father's heart, has made him known.

to baptize in Holy Spirit." I saw it myself, and I have borne witness. This is God's Chosen One.'*f*

The first disciples

The next day again John was standing with two of his disciples when Jesus passed by. John looked towards him and said, 'There is the Lamb of God.' The two disciples heard him say this, and followed Jesus. When he turned and saw them following him, he asked, 'What are you looking for?' They said, 'Rabbi' (which means a teacher), 'where are you staying?' 'Come and see', he replied. So they went and saw where he was staying, and spent the rest of the day with him. It was then about four in the afternoon.

One of the two who followed Jesus after hearing what John said was Andrew, Simon Peter's brother. The first thing he did was to find*g* his brother Simon. He said to him, 'We have found the Messiah' (which is the Hebrew for 'Christ'). He brought Simon to Jesus, who looked at him and said, 'You are Simon son of John. You shall be called Cephas' (that is, Peter, the Rock).

Philip and Nathanael

The next day Jesus decided to leave for Galilee. He met Philip, who, like Andrew and Peter, came from Bethsaida, and said to him, 'Follow me.' Philip went to find Nathanael, and told him, 'We have met the man spoken of by Moses in the Law, and by the prophets: it is Jesus son of Joseph, from Nazareth.' 'Nazareth!' Nathanael exclaimed; 'can anything good come from Nazareth?' Philip said, 'Come and see.' When Jesus saw Nathanael coming, he said, 'Here is an Israelite worthy of the name; there is nothing false in him.' Nathanael asked him, 'How do you come to know me?' Jesus replied, 'I saw you under the fig-tree before Philip spoke to you.' 'Rabbi,' said Nathanael, 'you are the Son of God; you are king of Israel.' Jesus answered, 'Is this the ground of your faith, that I told you I saw you under the fig-tree? You shall see greater things than that.' Then he added, 'In truth, in very truth I tell you all, you shall see heaven wide open, and God's angels ascending and descending upon the Son of Man.'

The wedding at Cana-in-Galilee

On the third day there was a wedding at Cana-in-Galilee. The mother of Jesus was there, and Jesus and his disciples were guests also. The wine gave out, so Jesus's mother said to him, 'They have no wine left.' He answered, 'Your concern, mother, is not mine. My hour has not yet come.' His mother said to the servants, 'Do whatever he tells you.' There were six stone water-jars standing near, of the kind used for Jewish rites of purification; each held from twenty to thirty gallons. Jesus said to the servants, 'Fill the jars with water', and they filled them to the brim. 'Now draw some off', he ordered, 'and take it to the steward of the feast'; and they did so. The steward tasted the water now turned into wine, not knowing its source; though the servants who had drawn the water knew. He hailed the bridegroom and said, 'Everyone serves the best wine first, and waits until the guests have drunk freely before serving the poorer sort; but you have kept the best wine till now.'

This deed at Cana-in-Galilee is the first of the signs by which Jesus revealed his glory and led his disciples to believe in him.

Jesus drives traders from the temple

After this he went down to Capernaum in company with his mother, his brothers, and his disciples, but they did not stay there long. As it was near the time of the Jewish Passover, Jesus went up to Jerusalem. There he found in the temple the dealers in cattle, sheep, and pigeons, and the money-changers seated at their tables. Jesus made a whip of cords and drove them out of the temple, sheep, cattle, and all. He upset the tables of the money-changers, scattering their coins. Then he turned on the dealers in pigeons: 'Take them out,' he said; 'you must not turn my Father's house into a market.' His disciples recalled the words of Scripture, 'Zeal for thy house will destroy me.' The Jews challenged Jesus: 'What sign', they asked, 'can you show as authority for your action?' 'Destroy this temple,' Jesus replied, 'and in three days I will raise it again.' They said, 'It has taken forty-six years to build this temple. Are you going to raise it again in three days?' But the temple he was speaking of was his body. After

f Some witnesses read This is the Son of God.   *g Some witnesses read* In the morning he found . . .

his resurrection his disciples recalled what he had said, and they believed the Scripture and the words that Jesus had spoken.

Jesus knows what is in a man

23 While he was in Jerusalem for Passover many gave their allegiance to him when they saw the signs that he 24 performed. But Jesus for his part would not trust himself to them. He 25 knew men so well, all of them, that he needed no evidence from others about a man, for he himself could tell what was in a man.

Jesus and Nicodemus

3 There was one of the Pharisees named Nicodemus, a member of the Jewish 2 Council, who came to Jesus by night. 'Rabbi,' he said, 'we know that you are a teacher sent by God; no one could perform these signs of yours un- 3 less God were with him.' Jesus answered, 'In truth, in very truth I tell you, unless a man has been born over again he cannot see the kingdom of 4 God.' 'But how is it possible', said Nicodemus, 'for a man to be born when he is old? Can he enter his mother's womb a second time and be 5 born?' Jesus answered, 'In truth I tell you, no one can enter the kingdom of God without being born from water 6 and spirit. Flesh can give birth only to flesh; it is spirit that gives birth to 7 spirit. You ought not to be astonished, then, when I tell you that you must 8 be born over again. The wind[h] blows where it wills; you hear the sound of it, but you do not know where it comes from, or where it is going. So with everyone who is born from spirit[h].'

9 Nicodemus replied, 'How is this 10 possible?' 'What!' said Jesus. 'Is this famous teacher of Israel ignorant of 11 such things? In very truth I tell you, we speak of what we know, and testify to what we have seen, and yet you all 12 reject our testimony. If you disbelieve me when I talk to you about things on earth, how are you to believe if I should talk about the things of heaven?

13 'No one ever went up into heaven except the one who came down from heaven, the Son of Man whose home 14 is in heaven.[i] This Son of Man must be lifted up as the serpent was lifted 15 up by Moses in the wilderness, so that

everyone who has faith in him may in him possess eternal life.'

God's love for the world

'God loved the world so much that he 16 gave his only Son, that everyone who has faith in him may not die but have eternal life. It was not to judge the 17 world that God sent his Son into the world, but that through him the world might be saved.'

How men are judged

'The man who puts his faith in him 18 does not come under judgement; but the unbeliever has already been judged in that he has not given his allegiance to God's only Son. Here lies 19 the test: the light has come into the world, but men preferred darkness to light because their deeds were evil. Bad men all hate the light and avoid 20 it, for fear their practices should be shown up. The honest man comes to 21 the light so that it may be clearly seen that God is in all he does.'

Jesus and John the Baptist

After this, Jesus went into Judaea 22 with his disciples, stayed there with them, and baptized. John too was 23 baptizing at Aenon, near to Salim, because water was plentiful in that region; and people were constantly coming for baptism. This was before 24 John's imprisonment.

Some of John's disciples had fallen 25 into a dispute with Jews about purification; so they came to him and said, 26 'Rabbi, there was a man with you on the other side of the Jordan, to whom you bore your witness. Here he is, baptizing, and crowds are flocking to him.' John's answer was: 'A man can 27 have only what God gives him. You 28 yourselves can testify that I said, "I am not the Messiah; I have been sent as his forerunner." It is the bride- 29 groom to whom the bride belongs. The bridegroom's friend, who stands by and listens to him, is overjoyed at hearing the bridegroom's voice. This joy, this perfect joy, is now mine. As 30 he grows greater, I must grow less.'

The heavenly and the earthly

He who comes from above is above 31 all others; he who is from the earth belongs to the earth and uses earthly speech. He who comes from heaven[j] bears witness to what he has seen and 32

---

h wind and spirit are translations of the same Greek word, which has both meanings. i Some witnesses omit whose home is in heaven. j Some witnesses insert is above all and ...

heard, yet no one accepts his witness.
33 To accept his witness is to attest that
34 God speaks the truth; for he whom
God sent utters the words of God, so
measureless is God's gift of the Spirit.
35 The Father loves the Son and has en-
36 trusted him with all authority. He who
puts his faith in the Son has hold of
eternal life, but he who disobeys the
Son shall not see that life; God's wrath
rests upon him.

Jesus and a Samaritan woman

4 A report now reached the Pharisees:
'Jesus is winning and baptizing more
2 disciples than John'; although, in fact,
it was only the disciples who were baptizing and not Jesus himself. When
3 Jesus learned this, he left Judaea
and set out once more for Galilee.
4 5 He had to pass through Samaria, and
on his way came to a Samaritan town
called Sychar, near the plot of ground
which Jacob gave to his son Joseph
6 and the spring called Jacob's well.
It was about noon, and Jesus, tired
after his journey, sat down by the well.
8 The disciples had gone away to the
7 town to buy food. Meanwhile a Samaritan woman came to draw water.
Jesus said to her, 'Give me a drink.'
9 The Samaritan woman said, 'What!
You, a Jew, ask a drink of me, a
Samaritan woman?' (Jews and Samaritans, it should be noted, do not use
10 vessels in common.*k*) Jesus answered
her, 'If only you knew what God gives,
and who it is that is asking you for a
drink, you would have asked him and
he would have given you living water.'
11 'Sir,' the woman said, 'you have no
bucket and this well is deep. How can
12 you give me "living water"? Are you
a greater man than Jacob our ancestor, who gave us the well, and drank
from it himself, he and his sons, and
13 his cattle too?' Jesus said, 'Everyone
who drinks this water will be thirsty
14 again, but whoever drinks the water
that I shall give him will never suffer
thirst any more. The water that I
shall give him will be an inner spring
always welling up for eternal life.'
15 'Sir,' said the woman, 'give me that
water, and then I shall not be thirsty,
nor have to come all this way to draw.'
16 Jesus replied, 'Go home, call your
17 husband and come back.' She answered, 'I have no husband.' 'You are right',
said Jesus, 'in saying that you have
18 no husband, for, although the man with

whom you are now living is not your
husband; you told me the truth
there.' 'Sir,' she replied, 'I can see 19
that you are a prophet. Our fathers 20
worshipped on this mountain, but you
Jews say that the temple where God
should be worshipped is in Jerusalem.'
'Believe me,' said Jesus, 'the time is 21
coming when you will worship the
Father neither on this mountain, nor
in Jerusalem. You Samaritans wor- 22
ship without knowing what you worship, while we worship what we know.
It is from the Jews that salvation
comes. But the time approaches, 23
indeed it is already here, when those
who are real worshippers will worship
the Father in spirit and in truth. Such
are the worshippers whom the Father
wants. God is spirit, and those who 24
worship him must worship in spirit
and in truth.' The woman answered, 25
'I know that Messiah' (that is Christ)
'is coming. When he comes he will tell
us everything.' Jesus said, 'I am he, 26
I who am speaking to you now.'

At that moment his disciples re- 27
turned, and were astonished to find
him talking with a woman; but none
of them said, 'What do you want?'
or, 'Why are you talking with her?'
The woman put down her water-jar 28
and went away to the town, where
she said to the people, 'Come and see 29
a man who has told me everything
I ever did. Could this be the Messiah?'
They came out of the town and made 30
their way towards him.

Harvesting the crop

Meanwhile the disciples were urging 31
him, 'Rabbi, have something to eat.'
But he said, 'I have food to eat of 32
which you know nothing.' At this the 33
disciples said to one another, 'Can
someone have brought him food?' But 34
Jesus said, 'It is meat and drink for
me to do the will of him who sent me
until I have finished his work.
'Do you not say, "Four months 35
more and then comes harvest"? But
look, I tell you, look round on the
fields; they are already white, ripe for
harvest. The reaper is drawing his 36
pay and gathering a crop for eternal
life, so that sower and reaper may
rejoice together. That is how the say- 37
ing comes true: "One sows, and another reaps." I sent you to reap a 38
crop for which you have not toiled.
Others toiled and you have come in
for the harvest of their toil.'

k Or Jews, it should be noted, are not on familiar terms with Samaritans; *some witnesses omit these words.*

Samaritan believers

39 Many Samaritans of that town came to believe in him because of the woman's testimony: 'He told me 40 everything I ever did.' So when these Samaritans had come to him they pressed him to stay with them; and 41 he stayed there two days. Many more became believers because of what they 42 heard from his own lips. They told the woman, 'It is no longer because of what you said that we believe, for we have heard him ourselves; and we know that this is in truth the Saviour of the world.'

An officer's son is cured

43 When the two days were over he set 44 out for Galilee; for Jesus himself declared that a prophet is without 45 honour in his own country. On his arrival in Galilee the Galileans gave him a welcome, because they had seen all that he did at the festival in Jerusalem; they had been at the festival themselves.

46 Once again he visited Cana-in-Galilee, where he had turned the water into wine. An officer in the royal service was there, whose son 47 was lying ill at Capernaum. When he heard that Jesus had come from Judaea into Galilee, he came to him and begged him to go down and cure his son, who was at the point of death. 48 Jesus said to him, 'Will none of you ever believe without seeing signs and 49 portents?' The officer pleaded with him, 'Sir, come down before my boy 50 dies.' Then Jesus said, 'Return home; your son will live.' The man believed what Jesus said and started for home. 51 When he was on his way down his servants met him with the news, 'Your 52 boy is going to live.' So he asked them what time it was when he began to recover. They said, 'Yesterday at one in the afternoon the fever left him.' 53 The father noted that this was the exact time when Jesus had said to him, 'Your son will live,' and he and all his household became believers. 54 This was now the second sign which Jesus performed after coming down from Judaea into Galilee.

A cripple at the sheep-pool

5 Later on Jesus went up to Jerusalem 2 for one of the Jewish festivals.[l] Now at the Sheep-Pool in Jerusalem there is a place with five colonnades. Its name in the language of the Jews is Bethesda. In these colonnades there 3 lay a crowd of sick people, blind, lame, and paralysed.[m] Among them was a 5 man who had been crippled for thirty-eight years. When Jesus saw him 6 lying there and was aware that he had been ill a long time, he asked him, 'Do you want to recover?' 'Sir,' 7 he replied, 'I have no one to put me in the pool when the water is disturbed, but while I am moving, someone else is in the pool before me.' Jesus answered, 'Rise to your 8 feet, take up your bed and walk.' The 9 man recovered instantly, took up his stretcher, and began to walk.

That day was a Sabbath. So the 10 Jews said to the man who had been cured, 'It is the Sabbath. You are not allowed to carry your bed on the Sabbath.' He answered, 'The man 11 who cured me said, "Take up your bed and walk."' They asked him, 12 'Who is the man who told you to take up your bed and walk?' But the 13 cripple who had been cured did not know; for the place was crowded and Jesus had slipped away. A little later 14 Jesus found him in the temple and said to him, 'Now that you are well again, leave your sinful ways, or you may suffer something worse.' The 15 man went away and told the Jews that it was Jesus who had cured him.

Jesus answers a charge

It was works of this kind done on 16 the Sabbath that stirred the Jews to persecute Jesus. He defended himself 17 by saying, 'My Father has never yet ceased his work, and I am working too.' This made the Jews still more 18 determined to kill him, because he was not only breaking the Sabbath, but, by calling God his own Father, he claimed equality with God.

The Father and the Son

To this charge Jesus replied, 'In truth, 19 in very truth I tell you, the Son can do nothing by himself; he does only what he sees the Father doing: what the Father does, the Son does. For 20 the Father loves the Son and shows him all his works, and will show greater yet, to fill you with wonder.

l Some witnesses read for the Jewish festival.   m Some witnesses add waiting for the disturbance of the water; some further insert (4) for from time to time an angel came down into the pool and stirred up the water. The first to plunge in after this disturbance recovered from whatever disease had afflicted him.

21 As the Father raises the dead and gives them life, so the Son gives life 22 to men, as he determines. And again, the Father does not judge anyone, but has given full jurisdiction to the 23 Son; it is his will that all should pay the same honour to the Son as to the Father. To deny honour to the Son is to deny it to the Father who sent him.

24 'In very truth, anyone who gives heed to what I say and puts his trust in him who sent me has hold of eternal life, and does not come up for judgement, but has already passed 5 from death to life. In truth, in very truth I tell you, a time is coming, indeed it is already here, when the dead shall hear the voice of the Son of God, and all who hear shall come to life. 6 For as the Father has life-giving power in himself, so has the Son, by the Father's gift.

7 'As Son of Man, he has also been given the right to pass judgement. 8 Do not wonder at this, because the time is coming when all who are in the 9 grave shall hear his voice and come out: those who have done right will rise to life; those who have done wrong will rise to hear their doom. 10 I cannot act by myself; I judge as I am bidden, and my sentence is just, because my aim is not my own will, but the will of him who sent me.'

The testimony to Jesus

1 'If I testify on my own behalf, that 2 testimony does not hold good. There is another who bears witness for me, and I know that his testimony holds. 3 Your messengers have been to John; you have his testimony to the truth. 4 Not that I rely on human testimony, but I remind you of it for your own 5 salvation. John was a lamp, burning brightly, and for a time you were 6 ready to exult in his light. But I rely on a testimony higher than John's. There is enough to testify that the Father has sent me, in the works my Father gave me to do and to finish— 7 the very works I have in hand. This testimony to me was given by the Father who sent me, although you never heard his voice, or saw his 8 form. But his word has found no home in you, for you do not believe the one 9 whom he sent. You study the scriptures diligently, supposing that in having them you have eternal life; yet, although their testimony points 10 to me, you refuse to come to me for that life.

'I do not look to men for honour. 41 But with you it is different, as I know 42 well, for you have no love for God in you. I have come accredited by my 43 Father, and you have no welcome for me; if another comes self-accredited you will welcome him. How can you 44 have faith so long as you receive honour from one another, and care nothing for the honour that comes from him who alone is God? Do not 45 imagine that I shall be your accuser at the Father's tribunal. Your accuser is Moses, the very Moses on whom you have set your hope. If you be- 46 lieved Moses you would believe what I tell you, for it was about me that he wrote. But if you do not believe 47 what he wrote, how are you to believe what I say?'

Feeding five thousand

Some time later Jesus withdrew to 6 the farther shore of the Sea of Galilee (or Tiberias), and a large crowd of 2 people followed who had seen the signs he performed in healing the sick. Then Jesus went up the hill-side and 3 sat down with his disciples. It was 4 near the time of Passover, the great Jewish festival. Raising his eyes and 5 seeing a large crowd coming towards him, Jesus said to Philip, 'Where are we to buy bread to feed these people?' This he said to test him; Jesus himself 6 knew what he meant to do. Philip re- 7 plied, 'Twenty pounds[n] would not buy enough bread for every one of them to have a little.' One of his disciples, 8 Andrew, the brother of Simon Peter, said to him, 'There is a boy here who 9 has five barley loaves and two fishes; but what is that among so many?' Jesus said, 'Make the people sit down.' 10 There was plenty of grass there, so the men sat down, about five thousand of them. Then Jesus took the 11 loaves, gave thanks, and distributed them to the people as they sat there. He did the same with the fishes, and they had as much as they wanted. When everyone had had enough, he 12 said to his disciples, 'Collect the pieces left over, so that nothing may be lost.' This they did, and filled 13 twelve baskets with the pieces left uneaten of the five barley loaves.

When the people saw the sign 14 Jesus had performed, the word went round, 'Surely this must be the prophet that was to come into the world.' Jesus, aware that they meant 15 to come and seize him to proclaim

n *Literally* 200 denarii.

him king, withdrew again to the hills by himself.

Jesus walks on the water

16 At nightfall his disciples went down
17 to the sea, got into their boat, and pushed off to cross the water to Capernaum. Darkness had already fallen, and Jesus had not yet joined
18 them. By now a strong wind was blowing and the sea grew rough.
19 When they had rowed about three or four miles they saw Jesus walking on the sea and approaching the boat.
20 They were terrified, but he called out,
21 'It is I; do not be afraid.' Then they were ready to take him aboard, and immediately the boat reached the land they were making for.

The food of eternal life

22 Next morning the crowd was standing on the opposite shore. They had seen only one boat there, and Jesus, they knew, had not embarked with his disciples, who had gone away
23 without him. Boats from Tiberias, however, came ashore[o] near the place where the people had eaten the bread over which the Lord gave thanks.[p]
24 When the people saw that neither Jesus nor his disciples were any longer there, they themselves went aboard these boats and made for
25 Capernaum in search of Jesus. They found him on the other side. 'Rabbi,' they said, 'when did you come here?'
26 Jesus replied, 'In very truth I know that you have not come looking for me because you saw signs, but because you ate the bread and your
27 hunger was satisfied. You must work, not for this perishable food, but for the food that lasts, the food of eternal life.

'This food the Son of Man will give you, for he it is upon whom God the Father has set the seal of his autho-
28 rity.' 'Then what must we do', they asked him, 'if we are to work as God
29 would have us work?' Jesus replied, 'This is the work that God requires: believe in the one whom he has sent.'

Jesus the bread of life

30 They said, 'What sign can you give us to see, so that we may believe you?
31 What is the work you do? Our ancestors had manna to eat in the desert; as Scripture says, "He gave them
32 bread from heaven to eat."' Jesus

answered, 'I tell you this: the truth is, not that Moses gave you the bread from heaven, but that my Father gives you the real bread from heaven.
33 The bread that God gives comes down[q] from heaven and brings life to the
34 world.' They said to him, 'Sir, give us
35 this bread now and always.' Jesus said to them, 'I am the bread of life. Whoever comes to me shall never be hungry, and whoever believes in me shall never be thirsty. But you, as I
36 said, do not believe although you have seen.[r] All that the Father gives me
37 will come to me, and the man who comes to me I will never turn away.
38 I have come down from heaven, not to do my own will, but the will of
39 him who sent me. It is his will that I should not lose even one of all that he has given me, but raise them all up
40 on the last day. For it is my Father's will that everyone who looks upon the Son and puts his faith in him shall possess eternal life; and I will raise him up on the last day.'

41 At this the Jews began to murmur disapprovingly because he said, 'I am the bread which came down
42 from heaven.' They said, 'Surely this is Jesus son of Joseph; we know his father and mother. How can he now say, "I have come down from
43 heaven"?' Jesus answered, 'Stop murmuring among yourselves. No man
44 can come to me unless he is drawn by the Father who sent me; and I will raise him up on the last day. It is written in the prophets: "And they shall all be taught by God." Everyone who has listened to the Father and learned from him comes to me.

45 'I do not mean that anyone has seen the Father. He who has come from God has seen the Father, and
46 he alone. In truth, in very truth I tell
47 you, the believer possesses eternal life. I am the bread of life. Your fore-
48 fathers ate the manna in the desert
49 and they are dead. I am speaking of the bread that comes down from heaven, which a man may eat, and
50 never die. I am that living bread which has come down from heaven; if anyone eats this bread he shall live for ever. Moreover, the bread which I will give is my own flesh; I give it for the life of the world.'

51 This led to a fierce dispute among the Jews. 'How can this man give us his flesh to eat?' they said. Jesus
52 replied, 'In truth, in very truth I tell

---

o Some witnesses read Other boats from Tiberias came ashore . . .   p Some witnesses omit over which . . . thanks.   q Or is he who comes down . . .   r Some witnesses add me.

you, unless you eat the flesh of the Son of Man and drink his blood you can have no life in you. Whoever eats my flesh and drinks my blood possesses eternal life, and I will raise him up on the last day. My flesh is real food; my blood is real drink. Whoever eats my flesh and drinks my blood dwells continually in me and I dwell in him. As the living Father sent me, and I live because of the Father, so he who eats me shall live because of me. This is the bread which came down from heaven; and it is not like the bread which our fathers ate: they are dead, but whoever eats this bread shall live for ever.'

A challenge to the disciples' faith

This was spoken in synagogue when Jesus was teaching in Capernaum. Many of his disciples on hearing it exclaimed, 'This is more than we can stomach! Why listen to such talk?' Jesus was aware that his disciples were murmuring about it and asked them, 'Does this shock you? What if you see the Son of Man ascending to the place where he was before? The spirit alone gives life; the flesh is of no avail; the words which I have spoken to you are both spirit and life. And yet there are some of you who have no faith.' For Jesus knew all along who were without faith and who was to betray him. So he said, 'This is why I told you that no one can come to me unless it has been granted to him by the Father.'

From that time on, many of his disciples withdrew and no longer went about with him. So Jesus asked the Twelve, 'Do you also want to leave me?' Simon Peter answered him, 'Lord, to whom shall we go? Your words are words of eternal life. We have faith, and we know that you are the Holy One of God.' Jesus answered, 'Have I not chosen you, all twelve? Yet one of you is a devil.' He meant Judas, son of Simon Iscariot. He it was who would betray him, and he was one of the Twelve.

A challenge from Jesus's brothers

Afterwards Jesus went about in Galilee. He wished to avoid Judaea because the Jews were looking for a chance to kill him. As the Jewish Feast of Tabernacles was close at hand, his brothers said to him, 'You should leave this district and go into Judaea, so that your disciples there may see the great things you are doing. Surely no one can hope to be in the public eye if he works in seclusion. If you really are doing such things as these, show yourself to the world.' For even his brothers had no faith in him. Jesus said to them, 'The right time for me has not yet come, but any time is right for you. The world cannot hate you; but it hates me for exposing the wickedness of its ways. Go to the festival yourselves. I am not[s] going up to this festival because the right time for me has not yet come.' With this answer he stayed behind in Galilee.

Later, when his brothers had gone to the festival, he went up himself, not publicly, but almost in secret. The Jews were looking for him at the festival and asking, 'Where is he?', and there was much whispering about him in the crowds. 'He is a good man', said some. 'No,' said others, 'he is leading the people astray.' However, no one talked about him openly, for fear of the Jews.

At the festival

When the festival was already half over, Jesus went up to the temple and began to teach. The Jews were astonished: 'How is it', they said, 'that this untrained man has such learning?' Jesus replied, 'The teaching that I give is not my own; it is the teaching of him who sent me. Whoever has the will to do the will of God shall know whether my teaching comes from him or is merely my own. Anyone whose teaching is merely his own, aims at honour for himself. But if a man aims at the honour of him who sent him he is sincere, and there is nothing false in him.

'Did not Moses give you the Law? Yet you all break it. Why are you trying to kill me?' The crowd answered, 'You are possessed! Who wants to kill you?' Jesus replied, 'Once only have I done work on the Sabbath, and you are all taken aback. But consider: Moses gave you the law of circumcision (not that it originated with Moses but with the patriarchs) and you circumcise on the Sabbath. Well then, if a child is circumcised on the Sabbath to avoid breaking the Law of Moses, why are you indignant with me for giving health on the Sabbath to the whole of a man's

s *Some witnesses read* not yet.

24 body? Do not judge superficially, but be just in your judgements.'

Reactions to Jesus in Jerusalem

25 At this some of the people of Jerusalem began to say, 'Is not this the
26 man they want to put to death? And
here he is, speaking openly, and they
have not a word to say to him. Can
it be that our rulers have actually
27 decided that this is the Messiah? And
yet we know where this man comes
from, but when the Messiah appears
no one is to know where he comes
28 from.' Thereupon Jesus cried aloud as
he taught in the temple, 'No doubt
you know me; no doubt you know
where I come from.[t] Yet I have not
come of my own accord. I was sent by
the One who truly is, and him you do
29 not know. I know him because I come
from him and he it is who sent me.'
30 At this they tried to seize him, but no
one laid a hand on him because his
appointed hour had not yet come.
31 Yet among the people many believed
in him. 'When the Messiah comes,'
they said, 'is it likely that he will
perform more signs than this man?'
32   The Pharisees overheard these mut-
terings of the people about him, so
the chief priests and the Pharisees
33 sent temple police to arrest him. Then
Jesus said, 'For a little longer I shall
be with you; then I am going away to
34 him who sent me. You will look for
me, but you will not find me. Where
35 I am, you cannot come.' So the Jews
said to one another, 'Where does he
intend to go, that we should not be
able to find him? Will he go to the
Dispersion among the Greeks, and
36 teach the Greeks? What did he mean
by saying, "You will look for me, but
you will not find me. Where I am,
you cannot come"?'[u]

Living water

37 On the last and greatest day of the
festival Jesus stood and cried aloud,
'If anyone is thirsty let him come to
38 me; whoever believes in me, let him
drink.' As Scripture says, 'Streams of
living water shall flow out from with-
39 in him.'[v] He was speaking of the Spirit
which believers in him would receive
later; for the Spirit had not yet been
given, because Jesus had not yet been
glorified.

Divided opinion

40 On hearing this some of the people
said, 'This must certainly be the
41 expected prophet.' Others said, 'This
is the Messiah.' Others again, 'Surely
the Messiah is not to come from Gali-
42 lee? Does not Scripture say that the
Messiah is to be of the family of
David, from David's village of Beth-
43 lehem?' Thus he caused a split among
44 the people. Some were for seizing him,
but no one laid hands on him.

The unbelief of the rulers

The temple police came back to the
chief priests and Pharisees, who asked,
'Why have you not brought him?'
'No man', they answered, 'ever spoke
as this man speaks.' The Pharisees
retorted, 'Have you too been misled?
Is there a single one of our rulers who
has believed in him, or of the Pharisees? As for this rabble, which cares
nothing for the Law, a curse is on
them.' Then one of their number,
Nicodemus (the man who had once
visited Jesus), intervened. 'Does our
law', he asked them, 'permit us to
pass judgement on a man unless we
have first given him a hearing and
learned the facts?' 'Are you a Galilean too?' they retorted. 'Study the
scriptures and you will find that
prophets do not come from Galilee.'[w]

Jesus the light of the world

Once again Jesus addressed the people: 'I am the light of the world. No
follower of mine shall wander in the
dark; he shall have the light of life.'
The Pharisees said to him, 'You are
witness in your own cause; your testimony is not valid.' Jesus replied, 'My
testimony is valid, even though I do
bear witness about myself; because
I know where I come from, and where
I am going. You do not know either
where I come from or where I am going. You judge by worldly standards. I
pass judgement on no man, but if I do
judge, my judgement is valid because
it is not I alone who judge, but I and
he who sent me. In your own law it
is written that the testimony of two
witnesses is valid. Here am I, a witness in my own cause, and my other
witness is the Father who sent me.'
They asked, 'Where is your father?'
Jesus replied, 'You know neither me

---

t Or Do you know me? And do you know where I come from?   u Some witnesses here insert the
passage printed on pp. 895–6.   v Or 'If any man is thirsty let him come to me and drink. He who
believes in me, as Scripture says, streams of living water shall flow out from within him.'   w Some
witnesses here insert the passage 7. 53—8. 11, which is printed on pp. 895–6.

nor my Father; if you knew me you would know my Father as well.'

20 These words were spoken by Jesus in the treasury as he taught in the temple. Yet no one arrested him, because his hour had not yet come.

Further questions about Jesus

21 Again he said to them, 'I am going away. You will look for me, but you will die in your sin; where I am going 22 you cannot come.' The Jews then said, 'Perhaps he will kill himself: is that what he means when he says, "Where 23 I am going you cannot come"?' So Jesus continued, 'You belong to this world below, I to the world above. Your home is in this world, mine is 24 not. That is why I told you that you would die in your sins. If you do not believe that I am what I am, you will 25 die in your sins.' They asked him, 'Who are you?' Jesus answered, 'Why 26 should I speak to you at all?^{x} I have much to say about you—and in judgement. But he who sent me speaks the truth, and what I heard from him I report to the world.'

27 They did not understand that he was speaking to them about the 28 Father. So Jesus said to them, 'When you have lifted up the Son of Man you will know that I am what I am. I do nothing on my own authority, but in all that I say, I have been taught by my Father. He who sent me is present with me, and has not left me alone; for I always do what is acceptable to 30 him.' As he said this, many put their faith in him.

God's children and the devil's children

31 Turning to the Jews who had believed him, Jesus said, 'If you dwell within the revelation I have brought, you are 32 indeed my disciples; you shall know the truth, and the truth will set you 33 free.' They replied, 'We are Abraham's descendants; we have never been in slavery to any man. What do you mean by saying, "You will become free 34 men"?' 'In very truth I tell you', said Jesus, 'that everyone who commits 35 sin is a slave. The slave has no permanent standing in the household, but 36 the son belongs to it for ever. If then the Son sets you free, you will indeed be free.

37 'I know that you are descended from Abraham, but you are bent on killing me because my teaching makes

no headway with you. I am revealing 38 in words what I saw in my Father's presence; and you are revealing in action what you learned from your father.' They retorted, 'Abraham is 39 our father.' 'If you were Abraham's children', Jesus replied, 'you would do as Abraham did.^{y} As it is, you are 40 bent on killing me, a man who told you the truth, as I heard it from God. That is not how Abraham acted. You 41 are doing your own father's work.'

They said, 'We are not base-born; God is our father, and God alone.' Jesus said, 'If God were your father, 42 you would love me, for God is the source of my being, and from him I come. I have not come of my own accord; he sent me. Why do you not 43 understand my language? It is because my revelation is beyond your grasp.

'Your father is the devil and you 44 choose to carry out your father's desires. He was a murderer from the beginning, and is not rooted in the truth; there is no truth in him. When he tells a lie he is speaking his own language, for he is a liar and the father of lies. But I speak the truth and therefore 45 you do not believe me. Which of you 46 can prove me in the wrong?^{z} If what I say is true, why do you not believe me? He who has God for his father 47 listens to the words of God. You are not God's children; that is why you do not listen.'

Abraham and Jesus

The Jews answered, 'Are we not right 48 in saying that you are a Samaritan, and that you are possessed?' 'I am 49 not possessed,' said Jesus; 'I am honouring my Father, but you dishonour me. I do not care about my 50 own glory; there is one who does care, and he is judge. In very truth I tell 51 you, if anyone obeys my teaching he shall never know what it is to die.'

The Jews said, 'Now we are certain 52 that you are possessed. Abraham is dead; the prophets are dead; and yet you say, "If anyone obeys my teaching he shall not know what it is to die." Are you greater than our father 53 Abraham, who is dead? The prophets are dead too. What do you claim to be?'

Jesus replied, 'If I glorify myself, 54 that glory of mine is worthless. It is the Father who glorifies me, he of

---

x Or What I have told you all along. Jesus replied, 'do as Abraham did.' y Some witnesses read 'If you are Abraham's children', Jesus replied, 'do as Abraham did.' z Or Which of you convicts me of sin?

P

whom you say, "He is our God", though you do not know him. But I know him; if I said that I did not know him I should be a liar like you. But in truth I know him and obey his word.

56 'Your father Abraham was overjoyed to see my day; he saw it and 57 was glad.' The Jews protested, 'You are not yet fifty years old. How can 58 you have seen Abraham?'[a] Jesus said, 'In very truth I tell you, before Abraham was born, I am.'

59 They picked up stones to throw at him, but Jesus was not to be seen; and he left the temple.[b]

Jesus gives sight to a man born blind

9 As he went on his way Jesus saw a 2 man blind from his birth. His disciples put the question, 'Rabbi, who sinned, this man or his parents? Why was he 3 born blind?' 'It is not that this man or his parents sinned,' Jesus answered; 'he was born blind so that God's power might be displayed in curing 4 him. While daylight lasts we[c] must carry on the work of him who sent me; night comes, when no one can 5 work. While I am in the world I am the light of the world.'

6 With these words he spat on the ground and made a paste with the spittle; he spread it on the man's eyes, 7 and said to him, 'Go and wash in the pool of Siloam.' (The name means 'sent'.) The man went away and washed, and when he returned he could see.

8 His neighbours and those who were accustomed to see him begging said, 'Is not this the man who used to sit 9 and beg?' Others said, 'Yes, this is the man.' Others again said, 'No, but it is someone like him.' The man him- 10 self said, 'I am the man.' They asked him, 'How were your eyes opened?' 11 He replied, 'The man called Jesus made a paste and smeared my eyes with it, and told me to go to Siloam and wash. I went and washed, and 12 gained my sight.' 'Where is he?' they asked. He answered, 'I do not know.'

The healing investigated

13 The man who had been blind was 14 brought before the Pharisees. As it was a Sabbath day when Jesus made 15 the paste and opened his eyes, the Pharisees now asked him by what means he had gained his sight. The man told them, 'He spread a paste on my eyes; then I washed, and now I can see.' Some of the Pharisees said, 16 'This fellow is no man of God; he does not keep the Sabbath.' Others said, 'How could such signs come from a sinful man?' So they took different sides. Then they continued to question 17 him: 'What have you to say about him? It was your eyes he opened.' He answered, 'He is a prophet.'

The Jews would not believe that the 18 man had been blind and had gained his sight, until they had summoned his parents and questioned them: 'Is 19 this man your son? Do you say that he was born blind? How is it that he can see now?' The parents replied, 20 'We know that he is our son, and that he was born blind. But how it is that 21 he can now see, or who opened his eyes, we do not know. Ask him; he is of age; he will speak for himself.' His 22 parents gave this answer because they were afraid of the Jews; for the Jewish authorities had already agreed that anyone who acknowledged Jesus as Messiah should be banned from the synagogue. That is why the parents 23 said, 'He is of age; ask him.'

So for the second time they sum- 24 moned the man who had been blind, and said, 'Speak the truth before God. We know that this fellow is a sinner.' 'Whether or not he is a sinner, I do 25 not know', the man replied. 'All I know is this: once I was blind, now I can see.' 'What did he do to you?' 26 they asked. 'How did he open your eyes?' 'I have told you already,' he 27 retorted, 'but you took no notice. Why do you want to hear it again? Do you also want to become his disciples?' Then they became abusive. 28 'You are that man's disciple,' they said, 'but we are disciples of Moses. We know that God spoke to Moses, 29 but as for this fellow, we do not know where he comes from.'

The man replied, 'What an extra- 30 ordinary thing! Here is a man who has opened my eyes, yet you do not know where he comes from! It is common 31 knowledge that God does not listen to sinners; he listens to anyone who is devout and obeys his will. To open 32 the eyes of a man born blind—it is unheard of since time began. If that 33 man had not come from God he could have done nothing.' 'Who are you to 34

---

a Some witnesses read How can Abraham have seen you? *b Or the division may be made after the words* was not to be seen; *the paragraph following would then begin* Then Jesus left the temple, and as he went . . . *c Some witnesses read* I.

give us lessons,' they retorted, 'born and bred in sin as you are?' Then they expelled him from the synagogue.

35 Jesus heard that they had expelled him. When he found him he asked, 'Have you faith in the Son of Man[d]?'
36 The man answered, 'Tell me who he is, sir, that I should put my faith in him.'
37 'You have seen him,' said Jesus; 'indeed, it is he who is speaking to you.'
38 'Lord, I believe', he said, and bowed before him.

Blindness and judgement

39 Jesus said, 'It is for judgement that I have come into this world—to give sight to the sightless and to make
40 blind those who see.' Some Pharisees in his company asked, 'Do you mean
41 that we are blind?' 'If you were blind,' said Jesus, 'you would not be guilty, but because you say "We see", your guilt remains.'

The sheepfold

10 'In truth I tell you, in very truth, the man who does not enter the sheepfold by the door, but climbs in some other way, is nothing but a thief or a robber.
2 The man who enters by the door is the
3 shepherd in charge of the sheep. The door-keeper admits him, and the sheep hear his voice; he calls his own sheep
4 by name, and leads them out. When he has brought them all out, he goes ahead and the sheep follow, because
5 they know his voice. They will not follow a stranger; they will run away from him, because they do not recognize the voice of strangers.'
6 This was a parable that Jesus told them, but they did not understand what he meant by it.

Jesus the good shepherd

7 So Jesus spoke again: 'In truth, in very truth I tell you, I am the door of
8 the sheepfold. The sheep paid no heed to any who came before me, for these
9 were all thieves and robbers. I am the door; anyone who comes into the fold through me shall be safe. He shall go in and out and shall find pasturage.
10 'The thief comes only to steal, to kill, to destroy; I have come that men may have life, and may have it in all
11 its fullness. I am the good shepherd; the good shepherd lays down his life
12 for the sheep. The hireling, when he

sees the wolf coming, abandons the sheep and runs away, because he is no shepherd and the sheep are not his. Then the wolf harries the flock and scatters the sheep. The man runs 13 away because he is a hireling and cares nothing for the sheep.

'I am the good shepherd; I know 14 my own sheep and my sheep know me —as the Father knows me and I know 15 the Father—and I lay down my life for the sheep. But there are other 16 sheep of mine, not belonging to this fold, whom I must bring in; and they too will listen to my voice. There will then be one flock, one shepherd. The 17 Father loves me because I lay down my life, to receive it back again. No 18 one has robbed me of it; I am laying it down of my own free will. I have the right to lay it down, and I have the right to receive it back again; this charge I have received from my Father.'

These words once again caused a 19 split among the Jews. Many of them 20 said, 'He is possessed, he is raving. Why listen to him?' Others said, 'No 21 one possessed by an evil spirit could speak like this. Could an evil spirit open blind men's eyes?'

Jesus claims to be God's son

It was winter, and the festival of the 22 Dedication was being held in Jerusalem. Jesus was walking in the temple 23 precincts, in Solomon's Portico. The 24 Jews gathered round him and asked: 'How long must you keep us in suspense? If you are the Messiah say so plainly.' 'I have told you,' said Jesus, 25 'but you do not believe. My deeds done in my Father's name are my credentials, but because you are not 26 sheep of my flock you do not believe. My own sheep listen to my voice; I 27 know them and they follow me. I give 28 them eternal life and they shall never perish; no one shall snatch them from my care. My Father who has given 29 them to me is greater than all, and no one can snatch them[e] out of the Father's care. My Father and I are 30 one.'

Once again the Jews picked up 31 stones to stone him. At this Jesus 32 said to them, 'I have set before you many good deeds, done by my Father's power; for which of these would you stone me?' The Jews replied, 'We are 33

d *Some witnesses read* Son of God.   e *Some witnesses read* My Father is greater than all, and that which he has given me no one can snatch . . . ; *others read* That which my Father has given me is greater than all, and no one can snatch it . . .

not going to stone you for any good deed, but for your blasphemy. You, 34 a mere man, claim to be a god.'*f* Jesus answered, 'Is it not written in your own Law, "I said: You are gods"? 35 Those are called gods to whom the word of God was delivered—and Scrip- 36 ture cannot be set aside. Then why do you charge me with blasphemy because I, consecrated and sent into the world by the Father, said, "I am God's son"?

37 'If I am not acting as my Father 38 would, do not believe me. But if I am, accept the evidence of my deeds, even if you do not believe me, so that you may recognize and know that the Father is in me, and I in the Father.' 39 This provoked them to one more attempt to seize him. But he escaped from their clutches.

Jesus is told of the death of Lazarus

40 Jesus withdrew again across the Jordan, to the place where John had been baptizing earlier. There he stayed, 41 while crowds came to him. They said, 'John gave us no miraculous sign, but all that he said about this man 42 was true.' Many came to believe in him there.

11 There was a man named Lazarus who had fallen ill. His home was at Bethany, the village of Mary and her 2 sister Martha. (This Mary, whose brother Lazarus had fallen ill, was the woman who anointed the Lord with ointment and wiped his feet with her 3 hair.) The sisters sent a message to him: 'Sir, you should know that your 4 friend lies ill.' When Jesus heard this he said, 'This illness will not end in death; it has come for the glory of God, to bring glory to the Son of God.' 5 And therefore, though he loved Martha 6 and her sister and Lazarus, after hearing of his illness Jesus waited for two days in the place where he was.

7 After this, he said to his disciples, 8 'Let us go back to Judaea.' 'Rabbi,' his disciples said, 'it is not long since the Jews there were wanting to stone you. Are you going there again?' 9 Jesus replied, 'Are there not twelve hours of daylight? Anyone can walk in day-time without stumbling, because he sees the light of this world. 10 But if he walks after nightfall he stumbles, because the light fails him.' 11 After saying this he added, 'Our friend Lazarus has fallen asleep, but 12 I shall go and wake him.' The dis-

ciples said, 'Master, if he has fallen asleep he will recover.' Jesus, however, 13 had been speaking of his death, but they thought that he meant natural sleep. Then Jesus spoke out plainly: 14 'Lazarus is dead. I am glad not to have 15 been there; it will be for your good and for the good of your faith. But let us go to him.' Thomas, called 'the 16 Twin', said to his fellow-disciples, 'Let us also go, that we may die with him.'

Jesus is resurrection and life

On his arrival Jesus found that 17 Lazarus had already been four days in the tomb. Bethany was just under 18 two miles from Jerusalem, and many 19 of the people had come from the city to Martha and Mary to condole with them on their brother's death. As soon 20 as she heard that Jesus was on his way, Martha went to meet him, while Mary stayed at home.

Martha said to Jesus, 'If you had 21 been here, sir, my brother would not have died. Even now I know that 22 whatever you ask of God, God will grant you.' Jesus said, 'Your brother 23 will rise again.' 'I know that he will 24 rise again', said Martha, 'at the resurrection on the last day.' Jesus 25 said, 'I am the resurrection and I am life.*g* If a man has faith in me, even though he die, he shall come to life; and no one who is alive and has faith 26 shall ever die. Do you believe this?' 'Lord, I do,' she answered; 'I now 27 believe that you are the Messiah, the Son of God who was to come into the world.'

With these words she went to call 28 her sister Mary, and taking her aside, she said, 'The Master is here; he is asking for you.' When Mary heard 29 this she rose up quickly and went to him. Jesus had not yet reached the 30 village, but was still at the place where Martha had met him. The Jews 31 who were in the house condoling with Mary, when they saw her start up and leave the house, went after her, for they supposed that she was going to the tomb to weep there.

Jesus weeps at the tomb

So Mary came to the place where 32 Jesus was. As soon as she caught sight of him she fell at his feet and said, 'O sir, if you had only been here my brother would not have died.' When Jesus saw her weeping and the 33 Jews her companions weeping, he

f Or claim to be God.   g Some witnesses omit and I am life.

sighed heavily and was deeply moved.
34 'Where have you laid him?' he asked.
They replied, 'Come and see, sir.'
35 36 Jesus wept. The Jews said, 'How
37 dearly he must have loved him!' But
some of them said, 'Could not this
man, who opened the blind man's
eyes, have done something to keep
Lazarus from dying?'

Lazarus is raised from the dead

38 Jesus again sighed deeply; then he
went over to the tomb. It was a cave,
39 with a stone placed against it. Jesus
said, 'Take away the stone.' Martha,
the dead man's sister, said to him,
'Sir, by now there will be a stench;
40 he has been there four days.' Jesus
said, 'Did I not tell you that if you
have faith you will see the glory of
41 God?' So they removed the stone.
Then Jesus looked upwards and
said, 'Father, I thank thee; thou hast
42 heard me. I knew already that thou
always hearest me, but I spoke for
the sake of the people standing round,
that they might believe that thou
didst send me.'
43 Then he raised his voice in a great
44 cry: 'Lazarus, come forth.' The dead
man came out, his hands and feet
swathed in linen bands, his face wrapped in a cloth. Jesus said, 'Loose him;
let him go.'

A plot to kill Jesus

45 Now many of the Jews who had come
to visit Mary and had seen what Jesus
46 did, put their faith in him. But some
of them went off to the Pharisees and
reported what he had done.
47 Thereupon the chief priests and the
Pharisees convened a meeting of the
Council. 'What action are we taking?'
they said. 'This man is performing
48 many signs. If we leave him alone like
this the whole populace will believe
in him. Then the Romans will come
and sweep away our temple and our
49 nation.' But one of them, Caiaphas,
who was High Priest that year, said,
50 'You know nothing whatever; you do
not use your judgement; it is more
to your interest that one man should
die for the people, than that the whole
51 nation should be destroyed.' He did
not say this of his own accord, but as
the High Priest in office that year, he
was prophesying that Jesus would die
52 for the nation—would die not for the
nation alone but to gather together

the scattered children of God. So from 53
that day on they plotted his death.
Accordingly Jesus no longer went 54
about publicly in Judaea, but left
that region for the country bordering
on the desert, and came to a town
called Ephraim, where he stayed with
his disciples.
The Jewish Passover was now at 55
hand, and many people went up from
the country to Jerusalem to purify
themselves before the festival. They 56
looked out for Jesus, and as they stood
in the temple they asked one another,
'What do you think? Perhaps he is
not coming to the festival.' Now the 57
chief priests and the Pharisees had
given orders that anyone who knew
where he was should give information,
so that they might arrest him.

Mary anoints Jesus's feet

Six days before the Passover festival 12
Jesus came to Bethany, where Lazarus lived whom he had raised from
the dead. There a supper was given 2
in his honour, at which Martha served,
and Lazarus sat among the guests
with Jesus. Then Mary brought a 3
pound of very costly perfume, pure
oil of nard, and anointed the feet
of Jesus and wiped them with her
hair, till the house was filled with
the fragrance. At this, Judas Iscariot, 4
a disciple of his—the one who was
to betray him—said, 'Why was this 5
perfume not sold for thirty pounds[h]
and given to the poor?' He said this, 6
not out of any care for the poor, but
because he was a thief; he used to
pilfer the money put into the common purse, which was in his charge.
'Leave her alone', said Jesus. 'Let her 7
keep it till the day when she prepares
for my burial; for you have the poor 8
among you always, but you will not
always have me.'[i]

A plot to kill Lazarus also

A great number of the Jews heard that 9
he was there, and came not only to
see Jesus but also Lazarus whom he
had raised from the dead. The chief 10
priests then resolved to do away with
Lazarus as well, since on his account 11
many Jews were going over to Jesus
and putting their faith in him.

Jesus rides into Jerusalem

The next day the great body of pil- 12
grims who had come to the festival,
hearing that Jesus was on the way to

h Literally for 300 denarii.   i Some witnesses omit for you have . . . have me.

13 Jerusalem, took palm branches and went out to meet him, shouting, 'Hosanna! Blessings on him who comes in the name of the Lord! God bless the
14 king of Israel!' Jesus found a donkey and mounted it, in accordance with
15 the text of Scripture: 'Fear no more, daughter of Zion; see, your king is coming, mounted on an ass's colt.'
16 At the time his disciples did not understand this, but after Jesus had been glorified they remembered that this had been written about him, and
17 that this had happened to him. The people who were present when he called Lazarus out of the tomb and raised him from the dead told what they had
18 seen and heard. That is why the crowd went to meet him; they had heard of
19 this sign that he had performed. The Pharisees said to one another, 'You see you are doing no good at all; why, all the world has gone after him!'

Jesus sought after by Greeks

20 Among those who went up to worship
21 at the festival were some Greeks. They came to Philip, who was from Bethsaida in Galilee, and said to him, 'Sir,
22 we should like to see Jesus.' So Philip went and told Andrew, and the two of
23 them went to tell Jesus. Then Jesus replied: 'The hour has come for the
24 Son of Man to be glorified. In truth, in very truth I tell you, a grain of wheat remains a solitary grain unless it falls into the ground and dies; but
25 if it dies, it bears a rich harvest. The man who loves himself is lost, but he who hates himself in this world will
26 be kept safe for eternal life. If anyone serves me, he must follow me; where I am, my servant will be. Whoever serves me will be honoured by my Father.'

A voice from heaven

27 'Now my soul is in turmoil, and what am I to say? Father, save me from this hour.[j] No, it was for this that
28 I came to this hour. Father, glorify thy name.' A voice sounded from heaven: 'I have glorified it, and I will
29 glorify it again.' The crowd standing by said it was thunder, while others said, 'An angel has spoken to him.'
30 Jesus replied, 'This voice spoke for
31 your sake, not mine. Now is the hour of judgement for this world; now shall the Prince of this world be
32 driven out. And I shall draw all men to myself, when I am lifted up from

the earth.' This he said to indicate the 33 kind of death he was to die.
The people answered, 'Our Law 34 teaches us that the Messiah continues for ever. What do you mean by saying that the Son of Man must be lifted up? What Son of Man is this?' Jesus 35 answered them: 'The light is among you still, but not for long. Go on your way while you have the light, so that darkness may not overtake you. He who journeys in the dark does not know where he is going. While you 36 have the light, trust to the light, so that you may become men of light.' After these words Jesus went away from them into hiding.

Prophecy fulfilled

In spite of the many signs which 37 Jesus had performed in their presence they would not believe in him, for the 38 prophet Isaiah's utterance had to be fulfilled: 'Lord, who has believed what we reported, and to whom has the Lord's power been revealed?' So it 39 was that they could not believe, for there is another saying of Isaiah's: 'He has blinded their eyes and dulled 40 their minds, lest they should see with their eyes, and perceive with their minds, and turn to me to heal them.' Isaiah said this because[k] he saw his 41 glory and spoke about him.
For all that, even among those in 42 authority a number believed in him, but would not acknowledge him on account of the Pharisees, for fear of being banned from the synagogue. For they valued their reputation with 43 men rather than the honour which comes from God.

Not to judge, but to save

So Jesus cried aloud: 'When a man 44 believes in me, he believes in him who sent me rather than in me; seeing me, 45 he sees him who sent me. I have come 46 into the world as light, so that no one who has faith in me should remain in darkness. But if anyone hears my 47 words and pays no regard to them, I am not his judge; I have not come to judge the world, but to save the world. There is a judge for the man who 48 rejects me and does not accept my words; the word that I spoke will be his judge on the last day. I do not 49 speak on my own authority, but the Father who sent me has himself commanded me what to say and how to speak. I know that his commands 50

j Or . . . turmoil. Shall I say, "Father, save me from this hour"?   k Some witnesses read when.

are eternal life. What the Father has said to me, therefore—that is what I speak.'

Jesus washes his disciples' feet

13 It was before the Passover festival. Jesus knew that his hour had come and he must leave this world and go to the Father. He had always loved his own who were in the world, and now he was to show the full extent of his love.

2 The devil had already put it into the mind of Judas son of Simon Iscariot to betray him. During supper, 3 Jesus, well aware that the Father had entrusted everything to him, and that he had come from God and was going 4 back to God, rose from table, laid aside his garments, and taking a towel, 5 tied it round him. Then he poured water into a basin, and began to wash his disciples' feet and to wipe them with the towel.

6 When it was Simon Peter's turn, Peter said to him, 'You, Lord, wash-7 ing my feet?' Jesus replied, 'You do not understand now what I am doing, 8 but one day you will.' Peter said, 'I will never let you wash my feet.' 'If I do not wash you, Jesus replied, 'you 9 are not in fellowship with me.' 'Then, Lord,' said Simon Peter, 'not my feet only; wash my hands and head as well!'

10 Jesus said, 'A man who has bathed needs no further washing;[l] he is altogether clean; and you are clean, 11 though not every one of you.' He added the words 'not every one of you' because he knew who was going to betray him.

12 After washing their feet and taking his garments again, he sat down. 'Do you understand what I have done for 13 you?' he asked. 'You call me "Master" and "Lord", and rightly so, for that 14 is what I am. Then if I, your Lord and Master, have washed your feet, you also ought to wash one another's feet. 15 I have set you an example: you are 16 to do as I have done for you. In very truth I tell you, a servant is not greater than his master, nor a messen-17 ger than the one who sent him. If you know this, happy are you if you act upon it.

18 'I am not speaking about all of you; I know whom I have chosen. But there is a text of Scripture to be fulfilled: "He who eats bread with me

l Some witnesses read needs only to wash his feet.
n Some witnesses omit If God . . . in him.

has turned against me."*[m]* I tell you 19 this now, before the event, so that when it happens you may believe that I am what I am. In very truth 20 I tell you, he who receives any messenger of mine receives me; receiving me, he receives the One who sent me.'

Treachery among the twelve

After saying this, Jesus exclaimed in 21 deep agitation of spirit, 'In truth, in very truth I tell you, one of you is going to betray me.' The disciples 22 looked at one another in bewilderment: whom could he be speaking of? One 23 of them, the disciple he loved, was reclining close beside Jesus. So Simon 24 Peter nodded to him and said, 'Ask who it is he means.' That disciple, as 25 he reclined, leaned back close to Jesus and asked, 'Lord, who is it?' Jesus 26 replied, 'It is the man to whom I give this piece of bread when I have dipped it in the dish.' Then, after dipping it in the dish, he took it out and gave it to Judas son of Simon Iscariot. As 27 soon as Judas had received it Satan entered him. Jesus said to him, 'Do quickly what you have to do.' No 28 one at the table understood what he meant by this. Some supposed that, 29 as Judas was in charge of the common purse, Jesus was telling him to buy what was needed for the festival, or to make some gift to the poor. As soon 30 as Judas had received the bread he went out. It was night.

A new commandment

When he had gone out Jesus said, 'Now 31 the Son of Man is glorified, and in him God is glorified. If God is glorified in 32 him,*[n]* God will also glorify him in himself; and he will glorify him now. My 33 children, for a little longer I am with you; then you will look for me, and, as I told the Jews, I tell you now, where I am going you cannot come. I 34 give you a new commandment: love one another; as I have loved you, so you are to love one another. If there 35 is this love among you, then all will know that you are my disciples.'

Jesus foretells Peter's denial

Simon Peter said to him, 'Lord, 36 where are you going?' Jesus replied, 'Where I am going you cannot follow me now, but one day you will.' Peter 37 said, 'Lord, why cannot I follow you now? I will lay down my life for you.'

m Literally has lifted his heel against me.

38 Jesus answered, 'Will you indeed lay down your life for me? I tell you in very truth, before the cock crows you will have denied me three times.'

Jesus the way to the Father

14 'Set your troubled hearts at rest. Trust in God always; trust also in me.
2 There are many dwelling-places in my Father's house; if it were not so I should have told you; for I am going there on purpose to prepare a place
3 for you.[o] And if I go and prepare a place for you, I shall come again and receive you to myself, so that where
4 I am you may be also; and my way
5 there is known to you.'[p] Thomas said, 'Lord, we do not know where you are going, so how can we know the way?'
6 Jesus replied, 'I am the way; I am the truth and I am life; no one comes to the Father except by me.
7 'If you knew me you would know my Father too.[q] From now on you do know him; you have seen him.'
8 Philip said to him, 'Lord, show us the
9 Father and we ask no more.' Jesus answered, 'Have I been all this time with you, Philip, and you still do not know me? Anyone who has seen me has seen the Father. Then how can
10 you say, "Show us the Father"? Do you not believe that I am in the Father, and the Father in me? I am not myself the source of the words I speak to you: it is the Father who dwells in me doing his own work.
11 Believe me when I say that I am in the Father and the Father in me; or else accept the evidence of the deeds
12 themselves. In truth, in very truth I tell you, he who has faith in me will do what I am doing; and he will do greater things still because I am going
13 to the Father. Indeed anything you ask in my name I will do, so that the
14 Father may be glorified in the Son. If you ask[r] anything in my name I will do it.'

The Holy Spirit promised

15 'If you love me you will obey my com-
16 mands; and I will ask the Father, and he will give you another to be your Advocate, who will be with you for
17 ever—the Spirit of truth. The world cannot receive him, because the world neither sees nor knows him; but you

know him, because he dwells with you and is[s] in you. I will not leave you 18 bereft; I am coming back to you. In a 19 little while the world will see me no longer, but you will see me; because I live, you too will live; then you will 20 know that I am in my Father, and you in me and I in you. The man who 21 has received my commands and obeys them—he it is who loves me; and he who loves me will be loved by my Father; and I will love him and dis- close myself to him.'

Judas asked him—the other Judas, 22 not Iscariot—'Lord, what can have happened, that you mean to disclose yourself to us alone and not to the world?' Jesus replied, 'Anyone who 23 loves me will heed what I say; then my Father will love him, and we will come to him and make our dwelling with him; but he who does not love 24 me does not heed what I say. And the word you hear is not mine: it is the word of the Father who sent me. I 25 have told you all this while I am still here with you; but your Advocate, 26 the Holy Spirit whom the Father will send in my name, will teach you every- thing, and will call to mind all that I have told you.'

The parting gift of peace

'Peace is my parting gift to you, my 27 own peace, such as the world cannot give. Set your troubled hearts at rest, and banish your fears. You heard 28 me say, "I am going away, and com- ing back to you." If you loved me you would have been glad to hear that I was going to the Father; for the Father is greater than I. I have told 29 you now, beforehand, so that when it happens you may have faith.

'I shall not talk much longer with 30 you, for the Prince of this world ap- proaches. He has no rights over me; but the world must be shown that I 31 love the Father, and do exactly as he commands; so up, let us go forward!'[t]

The vine and the branches

'I am the real vine, and my Father is 15 the gardener. Every barren branch of 2 mine he cuts away; and every fruiting branch he cleans, to make it more fruitful still. You have already been 3 cleansed by the word that I spoke to

o Or if it were not so, should I have told you that I am going to prepare a place for you?   p Some witnesses read also. You know where I am going and you know the way.   q Some witnesses read If you know me you will know my Father too.   r Some witnesses insert me.   s Some witnesses read shall be.   t Or for the Prince of this world is coming, though he has nothing in common with me. But he is coming so that the world may recognize that I love the Father, and do exactly as he com- mands. Up, and let us go forward to meet him!

4 you. Dwell in me, as I in you. No branch can bear fruit by itself, but only if it remains united with the vine; no more can you bear fruit, unless you remain united with me.

5 'I am the vine, and you the branches. He who dwells in me, as I dwell in him, bears much fruit; for apart

6 from me you can do nothing. He who does not dwell in me is thrown away like a withered branch. The withered branches are heaped together, thrown on the fire, and burnt.

7 'If you dwell in me, and my words dwell in you, ask what you will, and

8 you shall have it. This is my Father's glory, that you may bear fruit in

9 plenty and so be my disciples.[u] As the Father has loved me, so I have loved

10 you. Dwell in my love. If you heed my commands, you will dwell in my love, as I have heeded my Father's commands and dwell in his love.

11 'I have spoken thus to you, so that my joy may be in you, and your joy

12 complete.[v] This is my commandment: love one another, as I have loved you.

13 There is no greater love than this, that a man should lay down his life

14 for his friends. You are my friends, if

15 you do what I command you. I call you servants no longer; a servant does not know what his master is about. I have called you friends, because I have disclosed to you everything

16 that I heard from my Father. You did not choose me: I chose you. I appointed you to go on and bear fruit, fruit that shall last; so that the Father may give you all that you ask

17 in my name. This is my commandment to you: love one another.'

The world's hatred of Jesus

18 'If the world hates you, it hated me

19 first, as you know well.[w] If you belonged to the world, the world would love its own; but because you do not belong to the world, because I have chosen you out of the world, for that

20 reason the world hates you. Remember what I said: "A servant is not greater than his master." As they persecuted me, they will persecute you; they will follow your teaching as little as they have followed mine.

21 It is on my account that they will treat you thus, because they do not know the One who sent me.

'If I had not come and spoken to 22 them, they would not be guilty of sin; but now they have no excuse for their sin: he who hates me, hates my 23 Father. If I had not worked among 24 them and accomplished what no other man has done, they would not be guilty of sin; but now they have both seen and hated both me and my Father.[x] However, this text in their 25 Law had to come true:[y] "They hated me without reason."'

When the Holy Spirit comes

'But when your Advocate has come, 26 whom I will send you from the Father —the Spirit of truth that issues from the Father—he will bear witness to me. And you also are my witnesses, 27 because you have been with me from the first.

'I have told you all this to guard **16** you against the breakdown of your faith. They will ban you from the 2 synagogue; indeed, the time is coming when anyone who kills you will suppose that he is performing a religious duty. They will do these things be- 3 cause they do not know either the Father or me. I have told you all this 4 so that when the time comes for it to happen you may remember my warning. I did not tell you this at first, because then I was with you; but now 5 I am going away to him who sent me. None of you asks me "Where are you going?" Yet you are plunged into 6 grief because of what I have told you. Nevertheless I tell you the truth: it is 7 for your good that I am leaving you. If I do not go, your Advocate will not come, whereas if I go, I will send him to you. When he comes, he will confute 8 the world, and show where wrong and right and judgement lie. He will con- 9 vict them of wrong, by their refusal to believe in me; he will convince them 10 that right is on my side, by showing that I go to the Father when I pass from your sight; and he will convince 11 them of divine judgement, by showing that the Prince of this world stands condemned.

'There is still much that I could say 12 to you, but the burden would be too great for you now. However, when he 13 comes who is the Spirit of truth, he will guide you into all the truth; for he will not speak on his own authority,

---

[u] Some witnesses read that you may bear fruit in plenty. Thus you will be my disciples.　　[v] Or so that I may have joy in you and your joy may be complete.　　[w] Or bear in mind that it hated me first.　　[x] Or but now they have indeed seen my work and yet have hated both me and my Father.　　[y] Or let this text in their Law come true.

but will tell only what he hears; and he will make known to you the things 14 that are coming. He will glorify me, for everything that he makes known to you he will draw from what is mine. 15 All that the Father has is mine, and that is why I said, "Everything that he makes known to you he will draw from what is mine."

Grief turned to joy

16 'A little while, and you see me no more; again a little while, and you 17 will see me.' Some of his disciples said to one another, 'What does he mean by this: "A little while, and you will not see me, and again a little while, and you will see me", and by this: "Because I am going to my Father"?' 18 So they asked, 'What is this "little while" that he speaks of? We do not know what he means.'

19   Jesus knew that they were wanting to question him, and said, 'Are you discussing what I said: "A little while, and you will not see me, and again a 20 little while, and you will see me"? In very truth I tell you, you will weep and mourn, but the world will be glad. But though you will be plunged in grief, your grief will be turned to joy. 21 A woman in labour is in pain because her time has come; but when the child is born she forgets the anguish in her joy that a man has been born 22 into the world. So it is with you: for the moment you are sad at heart; but I shall see you again, and then you will be joyful, and no one shall rob 23 you of your joy. When that day comes you will ask nothing of me. In very truth I tell you, if you ask the Father for anything in my name, he will give 24 it you.[z] So far you have asked nothing in my name. Ask and you will receive, that your joy may be complete.'

Parting words to the disciples

25 'Till now I have been using figures of speech; a time is coming when I shall no longer use figures, but tell you of 26 the Father in plain words. When that day comes you will make your request in my name, and I do not say that I 27 shall pray to the Father for you, for the Father loves you himself, because you have loved me and believed that 28 I came from God. I came from the Father and have come into the world. Now I am leaving the world again and

going to the Father.' His disciples 29 said, 'Why, this is plain speaking; this is no figure of speech. We are certain 30 now that you know everything, and do not need to be questioned; because of this we believe that you have come from God.'

Jesus answered, 'Do you now be- 31 lieve? Look,[a] the hour is coming, 32 has indeed already come, when you are all to be scattered, each to his home, leaving me alone. Yet I am not alone, because the Father is with me. I have told you all this so that in 33 me you may find peace. In the world you will have trouble. But courage! The victory is mine; I have conquered the world.'

Jesus prays to his Father

After these words Jesus looked up to 17 heaven and said:

'Father, the hour has come. Glorify thy Son, that the Son may glorify thee. For thou hast made him sove- 2 reign over all mankind, to give eternal life to all whom thou hast given him. This is eternal life: to know thee who 3 alone art truly God, and Jesus Christ whom thou hast sent.

'I have glorified thee on earth by 4 completing the work which thou gavest me to do; and now, Father, 5 glorify me in thy own presence with the glory which I had with thee before the world began.

'I have made thy name known to 6 the men whom thou didst give me out of the world. They were thine, thou gavest them to me, and they have obeyed thy command. Now they 7 know that all thy gifts have come to me from thee; for I have taught them 8 all that I learned from thee, and they have received it: they know with certainty that I came from thee; they have had faith to believe that thou didst send me.

'I pray for them; I am not praying 9 for the world but for those whom thou hast given me, because they belong to thee. All that is mine is thine, and 10 what is thine is mine; and through them has my glory shone.

'I am to stay no longer in the world, 11 but they are still in the world, and I am on my way to thee. Holy Father, protect by the power of thy name those whom thou hast given me,[b] that they may be one, as we are one.

z Some witnesses read if you ask the Father for anything, he will give it you in my name.   a Or At the moment you believe; but look . . .   b Or keep in loyalty to thee those whom thou hast given me; some witnesses read protect them by the power of thy name which thou hast given me.

12 When I was with them, I protected by the power of thy name those whom thou hast given me,[c] and kept them safe. Not one of them is lost except the man who must be lost, for Scripture has to be fulfilled.

13 'And now I am coming to thee; but while I am still in the world I speak these words, so that they may have

14 my joy within them in full measure. I have delivered thy word to them, and the world hates them because they are strangers in the world, as I am.

15 I pray thee, not to take them out of the world, but to keep them from the

16 evil one. They are strangers in the

17 world, as I am. Consecrate them by

18 the truth;[d] thy word is truth. As thou hast sent me into the world, I have

19 sent them into the world, and for their sake I now consecrate myself, that they too may be consecrated by the truth.[d]

20 'But it is not for these alone that I pray, but for those also who through

21 their words put their faith in me; may they all be one: as thou, Father, art in me, and I in thee, so also may they be in us, that the world may believe

22 that thou didst send me. The glory which thou gavest me I have given to them, that they may be one, as we

23 are one; I in them and thou in me, may they be perfectly one. Then the world will learn that thou didst send me, that thou didst love them as thou didst me.

24 'Father, I desire that these men, who are thy gift to me, may be with me where I am, so that they may look upon my glory, which thou hast given me because thou didst love me before

25 the world began. O righteous Father, although the world does not know thee, I know thee, and these men

26 know that thou didst send me. I made thy name known to them, and will make it known, so that the love thou hadst for me may be in them, and I may be in them.'

Jesus gives himself up

18 After these words, Jesus went out with his disciples, and crossed the Kedron ravine. There was a garden there, and he and his disciples went

2 into it. The place was known to Judas, his betrayer, because Jesus had often

3 met there with his disciples. So Judas took a detachment of soldiers, and police provided by the chief priests and the Pharisees, equipped with lanterns, torches, and weapons, and

4 made his way to the garden. Jesus, knowing all that was coming upon him, went out to them and asked,

5 'Who is it you want?' 'Jesus of Nazareth', they answered. Jesus said, 'I am he.' And there stood Judas the traitor

6 with them. When he said, 'I am he', they drew back and fell to the ground.

7 Again Jesus asked, 'Who is it you want?' 'Jesus of Nazareth', they

8 answered. Then Jesus said, 'I have told you that I am he. If I am the man you want, let these others go.'

9 (This was to make good his words, 'I have not lost one of those whom thou gavest me.') Thereupon Simon Peter

10 drew the sword he was wearing and struck at the High Priest's servant, cutting off his right ear. (The servant's

11 name was Malchus.) Jesus said to Peter, 'Sheathe your sword. This is the cup the Father has given me; shall I not drink it?'

Peter disowns Jesus

12 The troops with their commander, and the Jewish police, now arrested

13 Jesus and secured him. They took him first to Annas.[e] Annas was

14 father-in-law of Caiaphas, the High Priest for that year[e]—the same Caiaphas who had advised the Jews that it would be to their interest if one man died for the whole people.

15 Jesus was followed by Simon Peter and another disciple. This disciple, who was acquainted with the High Priest, went with Jesus into the High

16 Priest's courtyard, but Peter halted at the door outside. So the other disciple, the High Priest's acquaintance, went out again and spoke to the woman at the door, and brought

17 Peter in. The maid on duty at the door said to Peter, 'Are you another of this man's disciples?' 'I am not', he said. The servants and the police

18 had made a charcoal fire, because it was cold, and were standing round it warming themselves. And Peter too was standing with them, sharing the warmth.

The High Priest questions Jesus

19 The High Priest questioned Jesus about his disciples and about what

c Or kept in loyalty to thee those whom thou hast given me; some witnesses read protected them by the power of thy name which thou hast given me.　　d Or in truth.　　e See note on verse 24 (p. 892).

20 he taught. Jesus replied, 'I have spoken openly to all the world; I have always taught in synagogue and in the temple, where all Jews congregate;
21 I have said nothing in secret. Why question me? Ask my hearers what I told them; they know what I said.'
22 When he said this, one of the police who was standing next to him struck him on the face, exclaiming, 'Is that the way to answer the High Priest?'
23 Jesus replied, 'If I spoke amiss, state it in evidence; if I spoke well, why strike me?'
24 So Annas sent him bound to Caiaphas the High Priest.*f*

Peter again disowns Jesus

25 Meanwhile Simon Peter stood warming himself. The others asked, 'Are you another of his disciples?' But he
26 denied it: 'I am not', he said. One of the High Priest's servants, a relation of the man whose ear Peter had cut off, insisted, 'Did I not see
27 you with him in the garden?' Peter denied again; and just then a cock crew.

Pilate questions Jesus

28 From Caiaphas Jesus was led into the Governor's headquarters. It was now early morning, and the Jews themselves stayed outside the headquarters to avoid defilement, so that they could
29 eat the Passover meal.*g* So Pilate went out to them and asked, 'What charge do you bring against this man?'
30 'If he were not a criminal,' they replied, 'we should not have brought
31 him before you.' Pilate said, 'Take him away and try him by your own law.' The Jews answered, 'We are not allowed to put any man to death.'
32 Thus they ensured the fulfilment of the words by which Jesus had indicated the manner of his death.
33 Pilate then went back into his headquarters and summoned Jesus. 'Are you the king of the Jews?' he
34 asked.*h* Jesus said, 'Is that your own idea, or have others suggested it to
35 you?' 'What! am I a Jew?' said Pilate. 'Your own nation and their chief priests have brought you before me.
36 What have you done?' Jesus replied, 'My kingdom does not belong to this world. If it did, my followers would be fighting to save me from arrest by the

Jews. My kingly authority comes from elsewhere.' 'You are a king, then?' 37 said Pilate. Jesus answered, '"King" is your word. My task is to bear witness to the truth. For this was I born; for this I came into the world, and all who are not deaf to truth listen to my voice.' Pilate said, 'What is truth?', 38 and with those words went out again to the Jews. 'For my part,' he said, 'I find no case against him. But you 39 have a custom that I release one prisoner for you at Passover. Would you like me to release the king of the Jews?' Again the clamour rose: 'Not 40 him; we want Barabbas!' (Barabbas was a bandit.)

Jesus is sentenced to death

Pilate now took Jesus and had him 19 flogged; and the soldiers plaited a 2 crown of thorns and placed it on his head, and robed him in a purple cloak. Then time after time they came up to 3 him, crying, 'Hail, King of the Jews!', and struck him on the face.

Once more Pilate came out and 4 said to the Jews, 'Here he is; I am bringing him out to let you know that I find no case against him'; and 5 Jesus came out, wearing the crown of thorns and the purple cloak. 'Behold the Man!' said Pilate. The chief 6 priests and their henchmen saw him and shouted, 'Crucify! crucify!' 'Take him and crucify him yourselves,' said Pilate; 'for my part I find no case against him'. The Jews answered, 'We 7 have a law; and by that law he ought to die, because he has claimed to be Son of God.'

When Pilate heard that, he was 8 more afraid than ever, and going 9 back into his headquarters he asked Jesus, 'Where have you come from?' But Jesus gave him no answer. 'Do 10 you refuse to speak to me?' said Pilate. 'Surely you know that I have authority to release you, and I have authority to crucify you?' 'You 11 would have no authority at all over me', Jesus replied, 'if it had not been granted you from above; and therefore the deeper guilt lies with the man who handed me over to you.'

From that moment Pilate tried 12 hard to release him; but the Jews kept shouting, 'If you let this man go, you are no friend to Caesar; any man

f Some witnesses give this verse after first to Annas in verse 13; others at the end of verse 13.   *g Or could share in the offerings of the Passover season.*   *h Or 'You are king of the Jews, I take it',* *he said.*

who claims to be a king is defying
13 Caesar.' When Pilate heard what they
were saying, he brought Jesus out
and took his seat on the tribunal at
the place known as 'The Pavement'
('Gabbatha' in the language of the
14 Jews). It was the eve of Passover,[i]
about noon. Pilate said to the Jews,
15 'Here is your king.' They shouted,
'Away with him! Away with him!
Crucify him!' 'Crucify your king?'
said Pilate. 'We have no king but
16 Caesar', the Jews replied. Then at
last, to satisfy them, he handed Jesus
over to be crucified.

Jesus is crucified

17 Jesus was now taken in charge and,
carrying his own cross, went out to
the Place of the Skull, as it is called
(or, in the Jews' language, 'Gol-
18 gotha'), where they crucified him, and
with him two others, one on the
right, one on the left, and Jesus between them.
19   And Pilate wrote an inscription to
be fastened to the cross; it read, 'Jesus
20 of Nazareth King of the Jews.' This
inscription was read by many Jews,
because the place where Jesus was
crucified was not far from the city,
and the inscription was in Hebrew,
21 Latin, and Greek. Then the Jewish
chief priests said to Pilate, 'You
should not write "King of the Jews";
write, "He claimed to be king of the
22 Jews."' Pilate replied, 'What I have
written, I have written.'
23   The soldiers, having crucified Jesus,
took possession of his clothes, and
divided them into four parts, one for
each soldier, leaving out the tunic.
The tunic was seamless, woven in one
24 piece throughout; so they said to one
another, 'We must not tear this; let
us toss for it'; and thus the text of
Scripture came true: 'They shared
my garments among them, and cast
lots for my clothing.'
25   That is what the soldiers did. But
meanwhile near the cross where Jesus
hung stood his mother, with her sister,
Mary wife of Clopas, and Mary of
26 Magdala. Jesus saw his mother, with
the disciple whom he loved standing
beside her. He said to her, 'Mother,
27 there is your son'; and to the disciple,
'There is your mother'; and from that
moment the disciple took her into his
home.

The death of Jesus

After that, Jesus, aware that all had 28
now come to its appointed end, said
in fulfilment of Scripture, 'I thirst.'
A jar stood there full of sour wine; so 29
they soaked a sponge with the wine,
fixed it on a javelin,[j] and held it up
to his lips. Having received the wine, 30
he said, 'It is accomplished!' He
bowed his head and gave up his
spirit.[k]

Jesus's side is pierced

Because it was the eve of Passover,[l] 31
the Jews were anxious that the bodies
should not remain on the cross for the
coming Sabbath, since that Sabbath
was a day of great solemnity; so they
requested Pilate to have the legs
broken and the bodies taken down.
The soldiers accordingly came to the 32
first of his fellow-victims and to the
second, and broke their legs; but 33
when they came to Jesus, they found
that he was already dead, so they did
not break his legs. But one of the 34
soldiers stabbed his side with a lance,
and at once there was a flow of blood
and water. This is vouched for by an 35
eyewitness, whose evidence is to be
trusted. He knows that he speaks the
truth, so that you too may believe;
for this happened in fulfilment of the 36
text of Scripture: 'No bone of his shall
be broken.' And another text says, 37
'They shall look on him whom they
pierced.'

The burial of Jesus

After that, Pilate was approached 38
by Joseph of Arimathaea, a disciple
of Jesus, but a secret disciple for fear
of the Jews, who[m] asked to be allowed
to remove the body of Jesus. Pilate
gave the permission; so Joseph came
and took the body away. He was 39
joined by Nicodemus (the man who
had first visited Jesus by night), who
brought with him a mixture of myrrh
and aloes, more than half a hundredweight. They took the body of Jesus 40
and wrapped it, with the spices, in
strips of linen cloth according to Jewish burial-customs. Now at the place 41
where he had been crucified there was
a garden, and in the garden a new
tomb, not yet used for burial. There, 42
because the tomb was near at hand
and it was the eve of the Jewish Sabbath, they laid Jesus.

---

i Or It was Friday in Passover.   *j* So one *witness; the others read* on marjoram.   *k* Or breathed
out his life.   *l* Or Because it was Friday in Passover . . .   *m* Or of Arimathaea. He was a
disciple of Jesus, but had gone into hiding for fear of the Jews. He now . . .

The empty tomb

20 Early on the Sunday morning, while it was still dark, Mary of Magdala came to the tomb. She saw that the stone had been moved away from **2** the entrance, and ran to Simon Peter and the other disciple, the one whom Jesus loved. 'They have taken the Lord out of his tomb,' she cried, 'and we do not know where they have **3** laid him.' So Peter and the other set out and made their way to the tomb. **4** They were running side by side, but the other disciple outran Peter and **5** reached the tomb first. He peered in and saw the linen wrappings lying **6** there, but did not enter. Then Simon Peter came up, following him, and he went into the tomb. He saw the **7** linen wrappings lying, and the napkin which had been over his head, not lying with the wrappings but rolled **8** together in a place by itself. Then the disciple who had reached the tomb first went in too, and he saw **9** and believed; until then they had not understood the scriptures, which showed that he must rise from the dead.

Jesus appears to Mary of Magdala

10 11 So the disciples went home again; but Mary stood at the tomb outside, weeping. As she wept, she peered into the **12** tomb; and she saw two angels in white sitting there, one at the head, and one at the feet, where the body of **13** Jesus had lain. They said to her, 'Why are you weeping?' She answered, 'They have taken my Lord away, and I do not know where they have laid **14** him.' With these words she turned round and saw Jesus standing there, **15** but did not recognize him. Jesus said to her, 'Why are you weeping? Who is it you are looking for?' Thinking it was the gardener, she said, 'If it is you, sir, who have removed him, tell me where you have laid him, and **16** I will take him away.' Jesus said, 'Mary!' She turned to him and said, 'Rabbuni!' (which is Hebrew for 'My **17** Master'). Jesus said, 'Do not cling to me,[n] for I have not yet ascended to the Father. But go to my brothers, and tell them that I am now ascending[o] to my Father and your Father, **18** my God and your God.' Mary of Magdala went to the disciples with her news: 'I have seen the Lord!' she said, and gave them his message.

Jesus appears to his disciples

Late that Sunday evening, when the **19** disciples were together behind locked doors, for fear of the Jews, Jesus came and stood among them. 'Peace be with you!' he said, and then showed **20** them his hands and his side. So when the disciples saw the Lord, they were filled with joy. Jesus repeated, 'Peace **21** be with you!', and said, 'As the Father sent me, so I send you.' Then **22** he breathed on them, saying, 'Receive the Holy Spirit! If you forgive any **23** man's sins, they stand forgiven; if you pronounce them unforgiven, unforgiven they remain.'

One of the Twelve, Thomas, that is **24** 'the Twin', was not with the rest when Jesus came. So the disciples told him, **25** 'We have seen the Lord.' He said, 'Unless I see the mark of the nails on his hands, unless I put my finger into the place where the nails were, and my hand into his side, I will not believe it.'

Jesus and Thomas

A week later his disciples were again **26** in the room, and Thomas was with them. Although the doors were locked, Jesus came and stood among them, saying, 'Peace be with you!' Then he **27** said to Thomas, 'Reach your finger here; see my hands. Reach your hand here and put it into my side. Be unbelieving no longer, but believe.' Thomas said, 'My Lord and my God!' **28** Jesus said, 'Because you have seen **29** me you have found faith. Happy are they who never saw me and yet have found faith.'

Why this book was written

There were indeed many other signs **30** that Jesus performed in the presence of his disciples, which are not recorded in this book. Those here written have **31** been recorded in order that you may hold the faith[p] that Jesus is the Christ, the Son of God, and that through this faith you may possess life by his name.

Jesus appears to his disciples again

Some time later, Jesus showed him- **21** self to his disciples once again, by the Sea of Tiberias; and in this way. Simon Peter and Thomas 'the Twin' **2** were together with Nathanael of Cana-in-Galilee. The sons of Zebedee and two other disciples were also

n Or Touch me no more.   *o Or* I am going to ascend . . .   *p Some witnesses read* that you may come to believe . . .

3 there. Simon Peter said, 'I am going out fishing.' 'We will go with you', said the others. So they started and got into the boat. But that night they caught nothing.

4 Morning came, and there stood Jesus on the beach, but the disciples 5 did not know that it was Jesus. He called out to them, 'Friends, have you caught anything?' They answered 6 'No.' He said, 'Shoot the net to starboard, and you will make a catch.' They did so, and found they could not haul the net aboard, there were so 7 many fish in it. Then the disciple whom Jesus loved said to Peter, 'It is the Lord!' When Simon Peter heard that, he wrapped his coat about him (for he had stripped) and plunged into 8 the sea. The rest of them came on in the boat, towing the net full of fish; for they were not far from land, only about a hundred yards.

9 When they came ashore, they saw a charcoal fire there, with fish laid on 10 it, and some bread. Jesus said, 'Bring 11 some of your catch.' Simon Peter went aboard and dragged the net to land, full of big fish, a hundred and fifty-three of them; and yet, many as they 12 were, the net was not torn. Jesus said, 'Come and have breakfast.' None of the disciples dared to ask 'Who are you?' 13 They knew it was the Lord. Jesus now came up, took the bread, and gave it to them, and the fish in the same way.

14 This makes the third time that Jesus appeared to his disciples after his resurrection from the dead.

Jesus and Peter

15 After breakfast, Jesus said to Simon Peter, 'Simon son of John, do you love me more than all else^q?' 'Yes, Lord,' he answered, 'you know that I love you.'^{r} 'Then feed my lambs,' he said. 16 A second time he asked, 'Simon son of John, do you love me?' 'Yes, Lord, you know I love you.'^{r} 'Then tend my 17 sheep.' A third time he said, 'Simon son of John, do you love me^s?' Peter was hurt that he asked him a third time, 'Do you love me?'^{t} 'Lord,' he said, 'you know everything; you know I love you.'^{r} Jesus said, 'Feed my sheep.

'And further, I tell you this in very 18 truth: when you were young you fastened your belt about you and walked where you chose; but when you are old you will stretch out your arms, and a stranger will bind you fast, and carry you where you have no wish to go.' He said this to indicate 19 the manner of death by which Peter was to glorify God. Then he added, 'Follow me.'

Peter looked round, and saw the 20 disciple whom Jesus loved following —the one who at supper had leaned back close to him to ask the question, 'Lord, who is it that will betray you?' When he caught sight of him, Peter 21 asked, 'Lord, what will happen to him?' Jesus said, 'If it should be my 22 will that he wait until I come, what is it to you? Follow me.'

That saying of Jesus became cur- 23 rent in the brotherhood, and was taken to mean that that disciple would not die. But in fact Jesus did not say that he would not die; he only said, 'If it should be my will that he wait until I come, what is it to you?'

Testimony, written and unwritten

It is this same disciple who attests 24 what has here been written. It is in fact he who wrote it, and we know that his testimony is true.^{u}

There is much else that Jesus did. 25 If it were all to be recorded in detail, I suppose the whole world could not hold the books that would be written.

An incident in the temple*

And they went each to his home, and 53 1* Jesus to the Mount of Olives. At 2 daybreak he appeared again in the temple, and all the people gathered round him. He had taken his seat and was engaged in teaching them when 3 the doctors of the law and the Pharisees brought in a woman caught committing adultery. Making her stand out in the middle they said to 4 him, 'Master, this woman was caught in the very act of adultery. In the 5 Law Moses has laid down that such women are to be stoned. What do you say about it?' They put the question as a test, hoping to frame a charge against him. Jesus bent down and

---

* This passage, which in the most widely received editions of the New Testament is printed in the text of John, 7. 53—8. 11, has no fixed place in our witnesses. Some of them do not contain it at all. Some place it after Luke 21. 38, others after John 7. 36, or 7. 52, or 21. 24.

q Or more than they do. r Or that I am your friend. s Or are you my friend. t Or that at the third asking he should have said, 'Are you my friend?' u Some witnesses here insert the passage printed on pp. 895–6.

wrote with his finger on the ground. When they continued to press their question he sat up straight and said, 'That one of you who is faultless shall throw the first stone.' Then once again he bent down and wrote on the ground. When they heard what he said, one by one they went away, [v] the eldest first; and Jesus was left alone, with the woman still standing there. Jesus again sat up and [w] said to the woman, 'Where are they? Has no one condemned you?' She answered, 'No one, sir.' Jesus said, 'Nor do I condemn you. You may go; do not sin again.'

7 When they continued to press their question he sat up straight and said, 'That one of you who is faultless shall

8 throw the first stone.' Then once again he bent down and wrote on the ground.

9 When they heard what he said, one by one they went away, [v] the eldest first;

1 and Jesus was left alone, with the woman still standing there. Jesus again sat up and [w] said to the woman, 'Where are they? Has no one con-

11 demned you?' She answered, 'No one, sir.' Jesus said, 'Nor do I condemn you. You may go; do not sin again.'

v Some witnesses insert convicted by their conscience. the woman.

w Some witnesses insert seeing no one but

ACTS OF THE APOSTLES

Introduction

1 IN THE FIRST PART of my work, Theophilus, I wrote of all that Jesus did and taught from the begin-
2 ning until the day when, after giving instructions through the Holy Spirit to the apostles whom he had chosen,
3 he was taken up to heaven. He showed himself to these men after his death, and gave ample proof that he was alive: over a period of forty days he appeared to them and taught them
4 about the kingdom of God. While he was in their company he told them not to leave Jerusalem. 'You must wait', he said, 'for the promise made by my Father, about which you have
5 heard me speak: John, as you know, baptized with water, but you will be baptized with the Holy Spirit, and within the next few days.'

Jesus is taken up to heaven

6 So, when they were all together, they asked him, 'Lord, is this the time when you are to establish once again the
7 sovereignty of Israel?' He answered, 'It is not for you to know about dates or times, which the Father has set
8 within his own control. But you will receive power when the Holy Spirit comes upon you; and you will bear witness for me in Jerusalem, and all over Judaea and Samaria, and away to the ends of the earth.'
9 When he had said this, as they watched, he was lifted up, and a cloud
10 removed him from their sight. As he was going, and as they were gazing intently into the sky, all at once there stood beside them two men in white who said, 'Men of Galilee, why stand
11 there looking up into the sky? This Jesus, who has been taken away from you up to heaven, will come in the same way as you have seen him go.'
12 Then they returned to Jerusalem from the hill called Olivet, which is near Jerusalem, no farther than a Sabbath day's journey. Entering the city
13 they went to the room upstairs where they were lodging: Peter and John and James and Andrew, Philip and Thomas, Bartholomew and Matthew, James son of Alphaeus and Simon the Zealot, and Judas son of James. All these were
14 constantly at prayer together, and with them a group of women, including Mary the mother of Jesus, and his brothers.

A successor to Judas

15 It was during this time that Peter stood up before the assembled brotherhood, about one hundred and twenty in all, and said: 'My friends, the
16 prophecy in Scripture was bound to come true, which the Holy Spirit, through the mouth of David, uttered about Judas who acted as guide to those who arrested Jesus. For he was
17 one of our number and had his place in this ministry.' (This Judas, be it
18 noted, after buying a plot of land with the price of his villainy, fell forward on the ground, and burst open, so that his entrails poured out. This became
19 known to everyone in Jerusalem, and

they named the property in their own language Akeldama, which means 'Blood Acre'.) 'The text I have in mind', Peter continued, 'is in the Book of Psalms: "Let his homestead fall desolate; let there be none to inhabit it"; and again, "Let another take over his charge." Therefore one of those who bore us company all the while we had the Lord Jesus with us, coming and going, from John's ministry of baptism until the day when he was taken up from us—one of those must now join us as a witness to his resurrection.'

23 Two names were put forward: Joseph, who was known as Barsabbas, and bore the added name of Justus; 24 and Matthias. Then they prayed and said, 'Thou, Lord, who knowest the hearts of all men, declare which of 25 these two thou hast chosen to receive this office of ministry and apostleship which Judas abandoned to go where 26 he belonged.' They drew lots and the lot fell on Matthias, who was then assigned a place among the twelve apostles.[a]

The Holy Spirit is given

2 While the day of Pentecost was running its course they were all together 2 in one place, when suddenly there came from the sky a noise like that of a strong driving wind, which filled the whole house where they were sit- 3 ting. And there appeared to them tongues like flames of fire, dispersed among them and resting on each one. 4 And they were all filled with the Holy Spirit and began to talk in other tongues, as the Spirit gave them power of utterance.

5 Now there were living in Jerusalem devout Jews[b] drawn from every na- 6 tion under heaven; and at this sound the crowd gathered, all bewildered because each one heard his own lan- 7 guage spoken. They were amazed and in their astonishment exclaimed, 'Why, they are all Galileans, are they not, these men who are speaking? 8 How is it then that we hear them, each of us in his own native language? 9 Parthians, Medes, Elamites; inhabitants of Mesopotamia, of Judaea and Cappadocia, of Pontus and Asia, 10 of Phrygia and Pamphylia, of Egypt and the districts of Libya around Cyrene; visitors from Rome, both 11 Jews and proselytes, Cretans and Arabs, we hear them telling us in our own tongues the great things God has done.' And they were all amazed and 12 perplexed, saying to one another, 'What can this mean?' Others said 13 contemptuously, 'They have been drinking!'

Peter explains what has happened

But Peter stood up with the Eleven, 14 raised his voice, and addressed them: 'Fellow Jews, and all you who live in Jerusalem, mark this and give me a hearing. These men are not drunk, 15 as you imagine; for it is only nine in the morning. No, this is what the 16 prophet spoke of: "God says, 'This 17 will happen in the last days: I will pour out upon everyone a portion of my spirit; and your sons and daughters shall prophesy; your young men shall see visions, and your old men shall dream dreams. Yes, I will endue even 18 my slaves, both men and women, with a portion of my spirit, and they shall prophesy. And I will show portents 19 in the sky above, and signs on the earth below—blood and fire and drifting smoke. The sun shall be turned to 20 darkness, and the moon to blood, before that great, resplendent day, the day of the Lord, shall come. And then, 21 everyone who invokes the name of the Lord shall be saved.'"

'Men of Israel, listen to me: I 22 speak of Jesus of Nazareth, a man singled out by God and made known to you through miracles, portents, and signs, which God worked among you through him, as you well know. When he had been given up to you, 23 by the deliberate will and plan of God, you used heathen men to crucify and kill him. But God raised him to life 24 again, setting him free from the pangs of death, because it could not be that death should keep him in its grip.

'For David says of him: 25

"I foresaw that the presence of the Lord would be with me always,
for he is at my right hand so that I may not be shaken;
therefore my heart was glad and my 26 tongue spoke my joy;
moreover, my flesh shall dwell in hope,
for thou wilt not abandon my soul 27 to death,
nor let thy loyal servant suffer corruption.
Thou hast shown me the ways of life, 28
thou wilt fill me with gladness by thy presence."

---

a Some witnesses read was then appointed a colleague of the eleven apostles.   *b Some witnesses read* devout men.

P*

29 'Let me tell you plainly, my friends, that the patriarch David died and was buried, and his tomb is here to
30 this very day. It is clear therefore that he spoke as a prophet, who knew that God had sworn to him that one of his own direct descendants should
31 sit on his throne; and when he said he was not abandoned to death, and his flesh never suffered corruption, he spoke with foreknowledge of the
32 resurrection of the Messiah. The Jesus we speak of has been raised by God,
33 as we can all bear witness. Exalted thus with[c] God's right hand, he received the Holy Spirit from the Father, as was promised, and all that you now
34 see and hear flows from him. For it was not David who went up to heaven; his own words are: "The Lord said to
35 my Lord, 'Sit at my right hand until I make your enemies your footstool.'"
36 Let all Israel then accept as certain that God has made this Jesus, whom you crucified, both Lord and Messiah.'

A call to repentance

37 When they heard this they were cut to the heart, and said to Peter and the apostles,[d] 'Friends, what are we to
38 do?' 'Repent,' said Peter, 'repent and be baptized, every one of you, in the name of Jesus the Messiah for the forgiveness of your sins; and you will receive the gift of the Holy Spirit.
39 For the promise is to you, and to your children, and to all who are far away, everyone whom the Lord our God may call.'
40 In these and many other words he pressed his case and pleaded with them: 'Save yourselves', he said,
41 'from this crooked age.' Then those who accepted his word were baptized, and some three thousand were added to their number that day.

Life among the believers

42 They met constantly to hear the apostles teach, and to share the common life, to break bread, and to pray.
43 A sense of awe was everywhere, and many marvels and signs were brought
44 about through the apostles. All whose faith had drawn them together held
45 everything in common:[e] they would sell their property and possessions and make a general distribution as
46 the need of each required. With one mind they kept up their daily attendance at the temple, and, breaking bread in private houses, shared their meals with unaffected joy, as they
47 praised God and enjoyed the favour of the whole people. And day by day the Lord added to their number those whom he was saving.

Cure of a crippled man

3 One day at three in the afternoon, the hour of prayer, Peter and John were on their way up to the temple.
2 Now a man who had been a cripple from birth used to be carried there and laid every day by the gate of the temple called 'Beautiful Gate', to beg
3 from people as they went in. When he saw Peter and John on their way into
4 the temple he asked for charity. But Peter fixed his eyes on him, as John did also, and said, 'Look at us.'
5 Expecting a gift from them, the man
6 was all attention. And Peter said, 'I have no silver or gold; but what I have I give you: in the name of Jesus Christ of Nazareth, walk.' Then he grasped
7 him by the right hand and pulled him up; and at once his feet and
8 ankles grew strong; he sprang up, stood on his feet, and started to walk. He entered the temple with them,
9 leaping and praising God as he went. Everyone saw him walking and prais-
10 ing God, and when they recognized him as the man who used to sit begging at Beautiful Gate, they were filled with wonder and amazement at what had happened to him.

What lay behind the cure

11 And as he was clutching Peter and John all the people came running in astonishment towards them in Solomon's Portico, as it is called. Peter
12 saw them coming and met them with these words: 'Men of Israel, why be surprised at this? Why stare at us as if we had made this man walk by some power or godliness of our own?
13 The God of Abraham, Isaac, and Jacob, the God of our fathers, has given the highest honour to his servant Jesus, whom you committed for trial and repudiated in Pilate's court
14 —repudiated the one who was holy and righteous when Pilate had decided to release him. You begged as a favour the release of a murderer, and
15 killed him who has led the way to life. But God raised him from the dead; of that we are witnesses. And the name
16 of Jesus, by awakening faith, has

c Or at.   d Some witnesses read the rest of the apostles.   e Or All who had become believers held everything together in common.

strengthened this man, whom you see and know, and this faith has made him completely well, as you can all see for yourselves.

17 'And now, my friends, I know quite well that you acted in ignorance, 18 and so did your rulers; but this is how God fulfilled what he had foretold in the utterances of all the prophets: 19 that his Messiah should suffer. Repent then and turn to God, so that your sins may be wiped out. Then the Lord may grant you a time of re- 20 covery and send you the Messiah he has already appointed, that is, Jesus. 21 He must be received into heaven until the time of universal restoration comes, of which God spoke by 22 his holy prophets.[f] Moses said, "The Lord God will raise up a prophet for you from among yourselves as he raised me;[g] you shall listen to every- 23 thing he says to you, and anyone who refuses to listen to that prophet must 24 be extirpated from Israel." And so said all the prophets, from Samuel onwards; with one voice they all predicted this present time.

25 'You are the heirs of the prophets; you are within the covenant which God made with your fathers, when he said to Abraham, "And in your offspring all the families on earth 26 shall find blessing." When God raised up his Servant, he sent him to you first, to bring you blessing by turning every one of you from your wicked ways.'

Peter and John called to account

4 They were still addressing the people when the chief[h] priests came upon them, together with the Controller of 2 the Temple and the Sadducees, exasperated at their teaching the people and proclaiming the resurrection from the dead—the resurrection of Jesus. 3 They were arrested and put in prison for the night, as it was already even- 4 ing. But many of those who had heard the message became believers. The number of men now reached about five thousand.

5 Next day the Jewish rulers, elders, and doctors of the law met in Jeru- 6 salem. There were present, Annas the High Priest, Caiaphas, Jonathan,[i] Alexander, and all who were of the 7 high-priestly family. They brought the apostles before the court and

began the examination. 'By what power', they asked, 'or by what name have such men as you done this?' Then Peter, filled with the Holy Spirit, 8 answered, 'Rulers of the people and elders, if the question put to us today 9 is about help given to a sick man, and we are asked by what means he was cured, here is the answer, for all of 10 you and for all the people of Israel: it was by the name of Jesus Christ of Nazareth, whom you crucified, whom God raised from the dead; it is by his name[j] that this man stands here before you fit and well. This Jesus is the 11 stone rejected by the builders which has become the keystone—and you are the builders. There is no salvation 12 in anyone else at all,[k] for there is no other name under heaven granted to men, by which we may receive salvation.'

Cautioned and discharged

Now as they observed the boldness of 13 Peter and John, and noted that they were untrained laymen, they began to wonder, then recognized them as former companions of Jesus. And when 14 they saw the man who had been cured standing with them, they had nothing to say in reply. So they ordered 15 them to leave the court, and then discussed the matter among themselves. 'What are we to do with these 16 men?' they said; 'for it is common knowledge in Jerusalem that a notable miracle has come about through them; and we cannot deny it. But to stop 17 this from spreading further among the people, we had better caution them never again to speak to anyone in this name.' They then called them 18 in and ordered them to refrain from all public speaking and teaching in the name of Jesus.

But Peter and John said to them 19 in reply: 'Is it right in God's eyes for us to obey you rather than God? Judge for yourselves. We cannot pos- 20 sibly give up speaking of things we have seen and heard.'

The court repeated the caution and 21 discharged them. They could not see how they were to punish them, because the people were all giving glory to God for what had happened. The 22 man upon whom this miracle of healing had been performed was over forty years old.

---

f Some witnesses add from the beginning of the world.   *g Or* like me.   *h Some witnesses omit* chief.   *i Some witnesses read* John.   *j Some witnesses insert* and no other.   *k Some witnesses omit* There is no . . . at all.

The church at prayer

23 As soon as they were discharged they went back to their friends and told them everything that the chief 24 priests and elders had said. When they heard it, they raised their voices as one man and called upon God:

'Sovereign Lord, maker of heaven and earth and sea and of everything 25 in them, who by the Holy Spirit,[l] through the mouth of David thy servant, didst say,

"Why did the Gentiles rage and the peoples lay their plots in vain? 26 The kings of the earth took their stand and the rulers made common cause against the Lord and against his Messiah."

27 They did indeed make common cause in this very city against thy holy servant Jesus whom thou didst anoint as Messiah. Herod and Pontius Pilate conspired with the Gentiles and peo- 28 ples of Israel to do all the things which, under thy hand and by thy decree, 29 were foreordained. And now, O Lord, mark their threats, and enable thy servants to speak thy word with all 30 boldness. Stretch out thy hand to heal and cause signs and wonders to be done through the name of thy holy servant Jesus.'

31 When they had ended their prayer, the building where they were assembled rocked, and all were filled with the Holy Spirit and spoke the word of God with boldness.

Sharing and witnessing

32 The whole body of believers was united in heart and soul. Not a man of them claimed any of his possessions as his own, but everything was held 33 in common, while the apostles bore witness with great power to the resurrection of the Lord Jesus. They were 34 all held in high esteem; for they had never a needy person among them, because all who had property in land or houses sold it, brought the proceeds 35 of the sale, and laid the money at the feet of the apostles; it was then distributed to any who stood in need.

36 For instance, Joseph, surnamed by the apostles Barnabas (which means 'Son of Exhortation'), a Levite, by 37 birth a Cypriot, owned an estate,

which he sold; he brought the money, and laid it at the apostles' feet.

Ananias and Sapphira

But there was another man, called 5 Ananias, with his wife Sapphira, who sold a property. With the full know- 2 ledge of his wife he kept back part of the purchase-money, and part he brought and laid at the apostles' feet. But Peter said, 'Ananias, how was it 3 that Satan so possessed your mind that you lied to the Holy Spirit, and kept back part of the price of the land? While it remained, did it not 4 remain yours? When it was turned into money, was it not still at your own disposal? What made you think of doing this thing? You have lied not to men but to God.' When Ananias 5 heard these words he dropped dead; and all the others who heard were awestruck. The younger men rose and 6 covered his body, then carried him out and buried him.

About three hours passed, and then 7 his wife came in, unaware of what had happened. Peter turned to her and 8 said, 'Tell me, were you paid such and such a price for the land?' 'Yes,' she said, 'that was the price.' Then Peter 9 said, 'Why did you both conspire to put the Spirit of the Lord to the test? Hark! there at the door are the footsteps of those who buried your husband; and they will carry you away.' And suddenly she dropped dead at 10 his feet. When the young men came in, they found her dead; and they carried her out and buried her beside her husband. And a great awe fell upon 11 the whole church, and upon all who heard of these events; and many 12 remarkable and wonderful things took place among the people at the hands of the apostles.

Conversions and cures

They used to meet by common consent in Solomon's Portico, no one 13 from outside their number venturing to join with them. But people in general spoke highly of them,[m] and 14 more than that, numbers of men and women were added to their ranks as believers in the Lord.[n] In the end the 15 sick were actually carried out into the streets and laid there on beds and stretchers, so that even the shadow

---

l *Some witnesses omit* by the Holy Spirit.   m *Or . . .* Portico. Although others did not venture to join them, the common people spoke highly of them.   n *Or* and an ever-increasing number of believers, both men and women, were added to the Lord.

of Peter might fall on one or another
16 as he passed by; and the people from
the towns round Jerusalem flocked in,
bringing those who were ill or harassed
by unclean spirits, and all of them
were cured.

A miraculous escape from prison

17 Then the High Priest and his colleagues, the Sadducean party as it
then was, were goaded into action
18 by jealousy. They proceeded to arrest
the apostles, and put them in official
19 custody. But an angel of the Lord
opened the prison doors during the
night, brought them out, and said,
20 'Go, take your place in the temple and
speak to the people, and tell them
about this new life and all it means.'
21 Accordingly they entered the temple
at daybreak and went on with their
teaching.
　　When the High Priest arrived with
his colleagues they summoned the
'Sanhedrin', that is, the full senate of
the Israelite nation, and sent to the
22 jail to fetch the prisoners. But the
police who went to the prison failed to
find them there, so they returned and
23 reported, 'We found the jail securely
locked at every point, with the war-
ders at their posts by the doors, but
when we opened them we found no
24 one inside.' When they heard this,
the Controller of the Temple and the
chief priests were wondering what
25 could have become of them,[o] and
then a man arrived with the report,
'Look! the men you put in prison are
there in the temple teaching the
26 people.' At that the Controller went
off with the police and fetched them,
but without using force for fear of
being stoned by the people.

Before the council again

27 So they brought them and stood them
before the Council; and the High
28 Priest began his examination. 'We
expressly ordered you', he said, 'to
desist from teaching in that name;
and what has happened? You have
filled Jerusalem with your teaching,
and you are trying to make us respon-
29 sible for that man's death.' Peter replied for himself and the apostles:
'We must obey God rather than men.
30 The God of our fathers raised up
Jesus whom you had done to death[p]
31 by hanging him on a gibbet. He it is

whom God has exalted with his own
right hand[q] as leader and saviour, to
grant Israel repentance and forgiveness of sins. And we are witnesses to 32
all this, and so is the Holy Spirit
given by God to those who are obedient to him.'
　　This touched them on the raw, and 33
they wanted to put them to death.
But a member of the Council rose to 34
his feet, a Pharisee called Gamaliel,
a teacher of the law held in high
regard by all the people. He moved
that the men be put outside for a
while. Then he said, 'Men of Israel, 35
be cautious in deciding what to do
with these men. Some time ago Theu- 36
das came forward, claiming to be
somebody, and a number of men,
about four hundred, joined him. But
he was killed and his whole following
was broken up and disappeared. After 37
him came Judas the Galilean at the
time of the census; he induced some
people to revolt under his leadership,
but he too perished and his whole
following was scattered. And so now: 38
keep clear of these men, I tell you;
leave them alone. For if this idea of
theirs or its execution is of human
origin, it will collapse; but if it is from 39
God, you will never be able to put
them down, and you risk finding
yourselves at war with God.'
　　They took his advice. They sent for 40
the apostles and had them flogged;
then they ordered them to give up
speaking in the name of Jesus, and
discharged them. So the apostles went 41
out from the Council rejoicing that
they had been found worthy to suffer
indignity for the sake of the Name.
And every day they went steadily on 42
with their teaching in the temple and
in private houses, telling the good
news of Jesus the Messiah.[r]

Sorting out business matters

During this period, when disciples **6**
were growing in number, there was
disagreement between those of them
who spoke Greek[s] and those who spoke
the language of the Jews.[t] The former
party complained that their widows
were being overlooked in the daily
distribution. So the Twelve called 2
the whole body of disciples together
and said, 'It would be a grave mistake for us to neglect the word of God
in order to wait at table. Therefore, 3

o Or wondering about them, what this could possibly mean. 　p Or ... Jesus, and you did him to
death ... 　q Or at his right hand. 　r Or the good news that the Messiah was Jesus. 　s Literally the Hellenists. 　t Literally the Hebrews.

friends, look out seven men of good reputation from your number, men full of the Spirit and of wisdom, and we will appoint them to deal with 4 these matters, while we devote ourselves to prayer and to the ministry 5 of the Word.' This proposal proved acceptable to the whole body. They elected Stephen, a man full of faith and of the Holy Spirit, Philip, Prochorus, Nicanor, Timon, Parmenas, and Nicolas of Antioch, a former convert 6 to Judaism. These they presented to the apostles, who prayed and laid their hands on them.

7   The word of God now spread more and more widely; the number of disciples in Jerusalem went on increasing rapidly, and very many of the priests adhered to the Faith.

Stephen accused before the Council

8 Stephen, who was full of grace and power, began to work great miracles 9 and signs among the people. But some members of the synagogue called the Synagogue of Freedmen, comprising Cyrenians and Alexandrians and people from Cilicia and Asia, came for- 10 ward and argued with Stephen, but could not hold their own against the inspired wisdom with which he spoke. 11 They then put up men who alleged that they had heard him make blasphemous statements against Moses 12 and against God. They stirred up the people and the elders and doctors of the law, set upon him and seized him, and brought him before the Council. 13 They produced false witnesses who said, 'This man is for ever saying things against this holy place and 14 against the Law. For we have heard him say that Jesus of Nazareth will destroy this place and alter the customs handed down to us by Moses.' 15 And all who were sitting in the Council fixed their eyes on him, and his face appeared to them like the face of an angel.

Stephen's defence

7 Then the High Priest asked, 'Is this 2 so?' And he said, 'My brothers, fathers of this nation, listen to me. The God of glory appeared to Abraham our ancestor while he was in Mesopotamia, 3 before he had settled in Harran, and said: "Leave your country and your kinsfolk and come away to a land 4 that I will show you." Thereupon he left the land of the Chaldaeans and settled in Harran. From there, after

his father's death, God led him to migrate to this land where you now live. He gave him nothing in it to call 5 his own, not one yard; but promised to give it in possession to him and his descendants after him, though he was then childless. God spoke in these 6 terms: "Abraham's descendants shall live as aliens in a foreign land, held in slavery and oppression for four hundred years. And I will pass judge- 7 ment", said God, "on the nation whose slaves they are; and after that they shall come out free, and worship me in this place." He then gave him 8 the covenant of circumcision, and so, after Isaac was born, he circumcised him on the eighth day; and Isaac begot Jacob, and Jacob the twelve patriarchs.

'The patriarchs out of jealousy sold 9 Joseph into slavery in Egypt, but God was with him and rescued him from 10 all his troubles. He also gave him a presence and powers of mind which so commended him to Pharaoh king of Egypt, that he appointed him chief administrator for Egypt and the whole of the royal household.

'But famine struck all Egypt and 11 Canaan, and caused great hardship; and our ancestors could find nothing to eat. But Jacob heard that there 12 was food in Egypt and sent our fathers there. This was their first visit. 13 On the second visit Joseph was recognized by his brothers, and his family connections were disclosed to Pharaoh. So Joseph sent an invitation to 14 his father Jacob and all his relatives, seventy-five persons altogether; and 15 Jacob went down into Egypt. There he ended his days, as also our forefathers did. Their remains were later 16 removed to Shechem and buried in the tomb which Abraham had bought and paid for from the clan of Emmor at Shechem.

'Now as the time approached for 17 God to fulfil the promise he had made to Abraham, our nation in Egypt grew and increased in numbers. At 18 length another king, who knew nothing of Joseph, ascended the throne of Egypt. He made a crafty attack on 19 our race, and cruelly forced our ancestors to expose their children so that they should not survive. At this time 20 Moses was born. He was a fine child, and pleasing to God. For three months he was nursed in his father's house, and when he was exposed, Pharaoh's 21 daughter herself adopted him and brought him up as her own son. So 22

Moses was trained in all the wisdom of the Egyptians, a powerful speaker and a man of action.

23 'He was approaching the age of forty, when it occurred to him to look into the conditions of his fellow-
24 countrymen the Israelites. He saw one of them being ill-treated, so he went to his aid, and avenged the victim by striking down the Egyptian.
25 He thought his fellow-countrymen would understand that God was offering them deliverance through him,
26 but they did not understand. The next day he came upon two of them fighting, and tried to bring them to make up their quarrel. "My men," he said, "you are brothers; why are you
27 ill-treating one another?" But the man who was at fault pushed him away. "Who set you up as a ruler and
28 judge over us?" he said. "Are you going to kill me as you killed the
29 Egyptian yesterday?" At this Moses fled the country and settled in Midianite territory. There two sons were born to him.

30 'After forty years had passed, an angel appeared to him in the flame of a burning bush in the desert near
31 Mount Sinai. Moses was amazed at the sight. But as he approached to look closely, the voice of the Lord was
32 heard: "I am the God of your fathers, the God of Abraham, Isaac, and Jacob." Moses was terrified and dared
33 not look. Then the Lord said to him, "Take off your shoes; the place where
34 you are standing is holy ground. I have indeed seen how my people are oppressed in Egypt and have heard their groans; and I have come down to rescue them. Up, then; let me send you to Egypt."

35 'This Moses, whom they had rejected with the words, "Who made you ruler and judge?"—this very man was commissioned as ruler and liberator by God himself, speaking through the angel who appeared to him in the
36 bush. It was Moses who led them out, working miracles and signs in Egypt, at the Red Sea, and for forty years in
37 the desert. It was he again who said to the Israelites, "God will raise up a prophet for you from among your-
38 selves as he raised me."[u] He it was who, when they were assembled there in the desert, conversed with the angel who spoke to him on Mount Sinai, and with our forefathers; he received the living utterances of God, to pass on to us.

39 'But our forefathers would not accept his leadership. They thrust him aside. They wished themselves back in Egypt, and said to Aaron, "Make 40 us gods to go before us. As for that Moses, who brought us out of Egypt, we do not know what has become of him." That was when they made 41 the bull-calf, and offered sacrifice to the idol, and held a feast in honour of the thing their hands had made. But 42 God turned away from them and gave them over to the worship of the host of heaven, as it stands written in the book of the prophets: "Did you bring me victims and offerings those forty years in the desert, you house of Israel? No, you carried aloft the 43 shrine of Moloch and the star of the god Rephan, the images which you had made for your adoration. I will banish you beyond Babylon."

44 'Our forefathers had the Tent of the Testimony in the desert, as God commanded when he told Moses to make it after the pattern which he had seen. Our fathers of the next 45 generation, with Joshua, brought it with them when they dispossessed the nations whom God drove out before them, and there it was until the time of David. David found favour 46 with God and asked to be allowed to provide a dwelling-place for the God of Jacob;[v] but it was Solomon who 47 built him a house. However, the Most 48 High does not live in houses made by men: as the prophet says, "Heaven is 49 my throne and earth my footstool. What kind of house will you build for me, says the Lord; where is my resting-place? Are not all these things 50 of my own making?"

51 'How stubborn you are, heathen still at heart and deaf to the truth! You always fight against the Holy Spirit. Like fathers, like sons. Was 52 there ever a prophet whom your fathers did not persecute? They killed those who foretold the coming of the Righteous One; and now you have betrayed him and murdered him, you 53 who received the Law as God's angels gave it to you, and yet have not kept it.'

Stephen stoned to death

This touched them on the raw and 54 they ground their teeth with fury. But Stephen, filled with the Holy 55 Spirit, and gazing intently up to heaven, saw the glory of God, and Jesus

u Or like me.   *v Some witnesses read* for the house of Jacob.

56 standing at God's right hand. 'Look,' he said, 'there is a rift in the sky; I can see the Son of Man standing at
57 God's right hand!' At this they gave a great shout and stopped their ears.
58 Then they made one rush at him and, flinging him out of the city, set about stoning him. The witnesses laid their coats at the feet of a young man
59 named Saul. So they stoned Stephen, and as they did so, he called out,
60 'Lord Jesus, receive my spirit.' Then he fell on his knees and cried aloud, 'Lord, do not hold this sin against
8 them', and with that he died. And Saul was among those who approved of his murder.

An outbreak of persecution in Jerusalem

This was the beginning of a time of violent persecution for the church in Jerusalem; and all except the apostles were scattered over the country districts of Judaea and Samaria.
2 Stephen was given burial by certain devout men, who made a great la-
3 mentation for him. Saul, meanwhile, was harrying the church; he entered house after house, seizing men and women, and sending them to prison.

Philip's mission in Samaria

4 As for those who had been scattered, they went through the country preach-
5 ing the Word. Philip came down to a city in Samaria and began pro-
6 claiming the Messiah to them. The crowds, to a man, listened eagerly to what Philip said, when they heard him and saw the miracles that he
7 performed. For in many cases of possession the unclean spirits came out with a loud cry; and many paralysed and crippled folk were cured;
8 and there was great joy in that city.
9 A man named Simon had been in the city for some time, and had swept the Samaritans off their feet with his magical arts, claiming to be someone
10 great. All of them, high and low, listened eagerly to him. 'This man', they said, 'is that power of God which
11 is called "The Great Power".' They listened because they had for so long
12 been carried away by his magic. But when they came to believe Philip with his good news about the kingdom of God and the name of Jesus Christ, they were baptized, men and
13 women alike. Even Simon himself believed, and was baptized, and there-

upon was constantly in Philip's company. He was carried away when he saw the powerful signs and miracles that were taking place.

The apostles in Jerusalem now 14 heard that Samaria had accepted the word of God. They sent off Peter and 15 John, who went down there and prayed for the converts, asking that they might receive the Holy Spirit. For until then the Spirit had not 16 come upon any of them. They had been baptized into the name of the Lord Jesus, that and nothing more. So Peter and John laid their hands on 17 them and they received the Holy Spirit.

When Simon saw that the Spirit 18 was bestowed through the laying on of the apostles' hands, he offered them money and said, 'Give me the 19 same power too, so that when I lay my hands on anyone, he will receive the Holy Spirit.' Peter replied, 'Your 20 money go with you to damnation, because you thought God's gift was for sale! You have no part nor lot in 21 this, for you are dishonest with God. Repent of this wickedness and pray 22 the Lord to forgive you for imagining such a thing. I can see that you are 23 doomed to taste the bitter fruit and wear the fetters of sin.'[w] Simon an- 24 swered, 'Pray to the Lord for me yourselves and ask that none of the things you have spoken of may fall upon me.'

So, after giving their testimony and 25 speaking the word of the Lord, they took the road back to Jerusalem, bringing the good news to many Samaritan villages on the way.

Philip and an Ethiopian official

Then the angel of the Lord said to 26 Philip, 'Start out and go south to the road that leads down from Jerusalem to Gaza.' (This is the desert road.) So 27 he set out and was on his way when he caught sight of an Ethiopian. This man was a eunuch, a high official of the Kandake, or Queen, of Ethiopia, in charge of all her treasure. He had been to Jerusalem on a pilgrimage and was now on his way home, sit- 28 ting in his carriage and reading aloud the prophet Isaiah. The Spirit said 29 to Philip, 'Go and join the carriage.' When Philip ran up he heard him 30 reading the prophet Isaiah and said, 'Do you understand what you are reading?' He said, 'How can I under- 31 stand unless someone will give me the

w Literally you are for gall of bitterness and a fetter of unrighteousness.

clue?' So he asked Philip to get in and sit beside him.

32 The passage he was reading was this: 'He was led like a sheep to be slaughtered; and like a lamb that is dumb before the shearer, he does not
33 open his mouth. He has been humiliated and has no redress. Who will be able to speak of his posterity? For he is cut off from the world of living men.'

34 'Now', said the eunuch to Philip, 'tell me, please, who it is that the prophet is speaking about here: him-
35 self or someone else?' Then Philip began. Starting from this passage, he
36 told him the good news of Jesus. As they were going along the road, they came to some water. 'Look,' said the eunuch, 'here is water: what is there
38 to prevent my being baptized?';^{x} and he ordered the carriage to stop. Then they both went down into the water, Philip and the eunuch; and he bap-
39 tized him. When they came up out of the water the Spirit snatched Philip away, and the eunuch saw no more of him, but went happily on his way.
40 Philip appeared at Azotus, and toured the country, preaching in all the towns till he reached Caesarea.

The conversion of Saul

9 Meanwhile Saul was still breathing murderous threats against the disciples of the Lord. He went to the
2 High Priest and applied for letters to the synagogues at Damascus authorizing him to arrest anyone he found, men or women, who followed the new way, and bring them to Jerusalem.
3 While he was still on the road and nearing Damascus, suddenly a light flashed from the sky all around him.
4 He fell to the ground and heard a voice saying, 'Saul, Saul, why do you
5 persecute me?' 'Tell me, Lord,' he said, 'who you are.' The voice answered, 'I am Jesus, whom you are
6 persecuting. But get up and go into the city, and you will be told what
7 you have to do.' Meanwhile the men who were travelling with him stood speechless; they heard the voice but
8 could see no one. Saul got up from the ground, but when he opened his eyes he could not see; so they led him by the hand and brought him into Da-
9 mascus. He was blind for three days, and took no food or drink.
10 There was a disciple in Damascus

named Ananias. He had a vision in which he heard the voice of the Lord: 'Ananias!' 'Here I am, Lord', he answered. The Lord said to him, 'Go 11 at once to Straight Street, to the house of Judas, and ask for a man from Tarsus named Saul. You will 12 find him at prayer; he has had a vision of a man named Ananias coming in and laying his hands on him to restore his sight.' Ananias an- 13 swered, 'Lord, I have often heard about this man and all the harm he has done to thy people in Jerusalem. And 14 he is here with authority from the chief priests to arrest all who invoke thy name.' But the Lord said to him, 15 'You must go, for this man is my chosen instrument to bring my name before the nations and their kings, and before the people of Israel. I my- 16 self will show him all that he must go through for my name's sake.'

So Ananias went. He entered the 17 house, laid his hands on him and said, 'Saul, my brother, the Lord Jesus, who appeared to you on your way here, has sent me to you so that you may recover your sight, and be filled with the Holy Spirit.' And immedi- 18 ately it seemed that scales fell from his eyes, and he regained his sight. Thereupon he was baptized, and after- 19 wards he took food and his strength returned.

Saul proclaims Christ in Damascus

He stayed some time with the disciples in Damascus. Soon he was 20 proclaiming Jesus publicly in the synagogues: 'This', he said, 'is the Son of God.' All who heard were astounded. 21 'Is not this the man', they said, 'who was in Jerusalem trying to destroy those who invoke this name? Did he not come here for the sole purpose of arresting them and taking them to the chief priests?' But Saul grew more 22 and more forceful, and silenced the Jews of Damascus with his cogent proofs that Jesus was the Messiah.

Saul in Jerusalem

As the days mounted up, the Jews 23 hatched a plot against his life; but 24 their plans became known to Saul. They kept watch on the city gates day and night so that they might murder him; but his converts took him one 25 night and let him down by the wall, lowering him in a basket.

---

x *Some witnesses insert* (37) Philip said, 'If you whole-heartedly believe, it is permitted.' He replied, 'I believe that Jesus Christ is the Son of God.'

26 When he reached Jerusalem he tried to join the body of disciples there; but they were all afraid of him, because they did not believe that he 27 was really a convert. Barnabas, however, took him by the hand and introduced him to the apostles. He described to them how Saul had seen the Lord on his journey, and heard his voice, and how he had spoken out boldly in the name of Jesus at Da-28 mascus. Saul now stayed with them, 29 moving about freely in Jerusalem. He spoke out boldly and openly in the name of the Lord, talking and debating with the Greek-speaking Jews.[y] 30 But they planned to murder him, and when the brethren learned of this they escorted him to Caesarea and saw him off to Tarsus.

Peter in Lydda and Joppa

31 Meanwhile the church, throughout Judaea, Galilee, and Samaria, was left in peace to build up its strength. In the fear of the Lord, upheld by the Holy Spirit, it held on its way and grew in numbers.
32 Peter was making a general tour, in the course of which he went down 33 to visit God's people at Lydda. There he found a man named Aeneas who had been bed-ridden with paralysis 34 for eight years. Peter said to him, 'Aeneas, Jesus Christ cures you; get up and make your bed', and imme-35 diately he stood up. All who lived in Lydda and Sharon saw him; and they turned to the Lord.
36 In Joppa there was a disciple named Tabitha (in Greek, Dorcas, meaning a gazelle), who filled her days 37 with acts of kindness and charity. At that time she fell ill and died; and they washed her body and laid it in 38 a room upstairs. As Lydda was near Joppa, the disciples, who had heard that Peter was there, sent two men to him with the urgent request, 'Please 39 come over to us without delay.' Peter thereupon went off with them. When he arrived they took him upstairs to the room, where all the widows came and stood round him in tears, showing him the shirts and coats that Dorcas used to make while she was with them. 40 Peter sent them all outside, and knelt down and prayed. Then, turning towards the body, he said, 'Get up, Tabitha.' She opened her eyes, saw 41 Peter, and sat up. He gave her his hand and helped her to her feet. Then

he called the members of the congregation and the widows and showed her to them alive. The news spread all 42 over Joppa, and many came to believe in the Lord. Peter stayed on in 43 Joppa for some time with one Simon, a tanner.

A divine message to Cornelius

At Caesarea there was a man named 10 Cornelius, a centurion in the Italian Cohort, as it was called. He was a 2 religious man, and he and his whole family joined in the worship of God. He gave generously to help the Jewish people, and was regular in his prayers to God. One day about three 3 in the afternoon he had a vision in which he clearly saw an angel of God, who came into his room and said, 'Cornelius!' He stared at him in 4 terror. 'What is it, my lord?' he asked. The angel said, 'Your prayers and acts of charity have gone up to heaven to speak for you before God. And now 5 send to Joppa for a man named Simon, also called Peter: he is lodging 6 with another Simon, a tanner, whose house is by the sea.' So when the 7 angel who was speaking to him had gone, he summoned two of his servants and a military orderly who was a religious man, told them the whole 8 story, and sent them to Joppa.

Peter's vision

Next day, while they were still on 9 their way and approaching the city, about noon Peter went up on the roof to pray. He grew hungry and wanted 10 something to eat. While they were getting it ready, he fell into a trance. He saw a rift in the sky, and a thing 11 coming down that looked like a great sheet of sail-cloth. It was slung by the four corners, and was being lowered to the ground. In it he saw creatures of 12 every kind, whatever walks or crawls or flies. Then there was a voice which 13 said to him, 'Up, Peter, kill and eat.' But Peter said, 'No, Lord, no: I have 14 never eaten anything profane or unclean.' The voice came again a second 15 time: 'It is not for you to call profane what God counts clean.' This happened 16 three times; and then the thing was taken up again into the sky.

While Peter was still puzzling over 17 the meaning of the vision he had seen, the messengers of Cornelius had been asking the way to Simon's house, and now arrived at the entrance. They 18

y Literally the Hellenists.

called out and asked if Simon Peter
19 was lodging there. But Peter was
thinking over the vision, when the
Spirit said to him, 'Some* men are
20 here looking for you; make haste and
go downstairs. You may go with them
without any misgiving, for it was I
21 who sent them.' Peter came down to
the men and said, 'You are looking
for me? Here I am. What brings you
22 here?' 'We are from the centurion
Cornelius,' they replied, 'a good and
religious man, acknowledged as such
by the whole Jewish nation. He was
directed by a holy angel to send for
you to his house and to listen to what
23 you have to say.' So Peter asked them
in and gave them a night's lodging.
Next day he set out with them, accompanied by some members of the
congregation at Joppa.

Peter and Cornelius

24 The day after that, he arrived at
Caesarea. Cornelius was expecting
them and had called together his rela-
25 tives and close friends. When Peter
arrived, Cornelius came to meet him,
and bowed to the ground in deep
26 reverence. But Peter raised him to his
feet and said, 'Stand up; I am a man
27 like anyone else.' Still talking with
him he went in and found a large
28 gathering. He said to them, 'I need
not tell you that a Jew is forbidden
by his religion to visit or associate
with a man of another race; yet God
has shown me clearly that I must not
29 call any man profane or unclean. That
is why I came here without demur
when you sent for me. May I ask what
was your reason for sending?'
30 Cornelius said, 'Four days ago, just
about this time, I was in the house
here saying the afternoon prayers,
when suddenly a man in shining robes
31 stood before me. He said: "Cornelius,
your prayer has been heard and your
acts of charity remembered before
32 God. Send to Joppa, then, to Simon
Peter, and ask him to come. He is
lodging in the house of Simon the
33 tanner, by the sea." So I sent to you
there and then; it was kind of you to
come. And now we are all met here
before God, to hear all that the Lord
has ordered you to say.'
34 Peter began: 'I now see how true it
35 is that God has no favourites, but that
in every nation the man who is god-
fearing and does what is right is ac-
36 ceptable to him. He sent his word to

the Israelites and gave the good news
of peace through Jesus Christ, who is
Lord of all. I need not tell you what 37
happened lately all over the land of
the Jews, starting from Galilee after
the baptism proclaimed by John. You 38
know about Jesus of Nazareth, how
God anointed him with the Holy
Spirit and with power. He went about
doing good and healing all who were
oppressed by the devil, for God was
with him. And we can bear witness to 39
all that he did in the Jewish country-
side and in Jerusalem. He was put to
death by hanging on a gibbet; but 40
God raised him to life on the third day,
and allowed him to appear, not to the 41
whole people, but to witnesses whom
God had chosen in advance—to us,
who ate and drank with him after he
rose from the dead. He commanded 42
us to proclaim him to the people,
and affirm that he is the one who has
been designated by God as judge of
the living and the dead. It is to him 43
that all the prophets testify, declaring that everyone who trusts in him
receives forgiveness of sins through
his name.'

Gentile converts receive the Spirit

Peter was still speaking when the 44
Holy Spirit came upon all who were
listening to the message. The believers 45
who had come with Peter, men of
Jewish birth, were astonished that
the gift of the Holy Spirit should have
been poured out even on Gentiles. For 46
they could hear them speaking in
tongues of ecstasy and acclaiming the
greatness of God. Then Peter spoke:
'Is anyone prepared to withhold the 47
water for baptism from these persons,
who have received the Holy Spirit
just as we did ourselves?' Then he 48
ordered them to be baptized in the
name of Jesus Christ. After that they
asked him to stay on with them for a
time.

Peter reports to the Jerusalem church

News came to the apostles and the **11**
members of the church in Judaea that
Gentiles too had accepted the word
of God; and when Peter came up to 2
Jerusalem those who were of Jewish
birth raised the question with him.
'You have been visiting men who are 3
uncircumcised,' they said, 'and sitting
at table with them!' Peter began by 4
laying before them the facts as they
had happened.

z One witness reads Two; *others read* Three.

5 'I was in the city of Joppa', he said, 'at prayer; and while in a trance I had a vision: a thing was coming down that looked like a great sheet of sail-cloth, slung by the four corners and lowered from the sky till it 6 reached me. I looked intently to make out what was in it and I saw four-footed creatures of the earth, wild beasts, and things that crawl or fly. 7 Then I heard a voice saying to me, 8 "Up, Peter, kill and eat." But I said, "No, Lord, no: nothing profane or unclean has ever entered my mouth." 9 A voice from heaven answered a second time, "It is not for you to call profane what God counts clean." 10 This happened three times, and then they were all drawn up again into the 11 sky. At that moment three men, who had been sent to me from Caesarea, arrived at the house where I was[a] 12 staying; and the Spirit told me to go with them.[b] My six companions here came with me and we went into the 13 man's house. He told us how he had seen an angel standing in his house who said, "Send to Joppa for Simon 14 also called Peter. He will speak words that will bring salvation to you and 15 all your household." Hardly had I begun speaking, when the Holy Spirit came upon them, just as upon us at 16 the beginning. Then I recalled what the Lord had said: "John baptized with water, but you will be baptized 17 with the Holy Spirit." God gave them no less a gift than he gave us when we put our trust in the Lord Jesus Christ; then how could I possibly stand in God's way?' 18 When they heard this their doubts were silenced. They gave praise to God and said, 'This means that God has granted life-giving repentance to the Gentiles also.'

Developments at Antioch

19 Meanwhile those who had been scattered after the persecution that arose over Stephen made their way to Phoenicia, Cyprus, and Antioch, bringing the message to Jews only 20 and to no others. But there were some natives of Cyprus and Cyrene among them, and these, when they arrived at Antioch, began to speak to Gentiles as well, telling them the good news of 21 the Lord Jesus. The power of the Lord was with them, and a great many became believers, and turned to the Lord.

22 The news reached the ears of the church in Jerusalem; and they sent Barnabas to Antioch. When he ar- 23 rived and saw the divine grace at work, he rejoiced, and encouraged them all to hold fast to the Lord with resolute hearts; for he was a good man, 24 full of the Holy Spirit and of faith. And large numbers were won over to the Lord.

He then went off to Tarsus to look 25 for Saul; and when he had found him, 26 he brought him to Antioch. For a whole year the two of them lived in fellowship with the congregation there, and gave instructions to large numbers. It was in Antioch that the disciples first got the name of Christians.

During this period some prophets 27 came down from Jerusalem to Antioch. One of them, Agabus by name, 28 was inspired to stand up and predict a severe and world-wide famine, which in fact occurred in the reign of Claudius. So the disciples agreed to 29 make a contribution, each according to his means, for the relief of their fellow-Christians in Judaea. This they 30 did, and sent if off to the elders, in the charge of Barnabas and Saul.

Herod attacks leaders of the church

It was about this time that King 12 Herod attacked certain members of the church. He beheaded James, the 2 brother of John, and then, when 3 he saw that the Jews approved, proceeded to arrest Peter also. This happened during the festival of Unleavened Bread. Having secured 4 him, he put him in prison under a military guard, four squads of four men each, meaning to produce him in public after Passover. So Peter was 5 kept in prison under constant watch, while the church kept praying fervently for him to God.

Peter's miraculous escape from prison

On the very night before Herod had 6 planned to bring him forward, Peter was asleep between two soldiers, secured by two chains, while outside the doors sentries kept guard over the prison. All at once an angel of the 7 Lord stood there, and the cell was ablaze with light. He tapped Peter on the shoulder and woke him. 'Quick! Get up', he said, and the chains fell away from his wrists. The angel then 8 said to him, 'Do up your belt and put

a Some witnesses read we were, b Some witnesses add making no distinctions; others add without any misgiving, as in 10. 20.

your sandals on.' He did so. 'Now wrap your cloak round you and follow
9 me.' He followed him out, with no idea that the angel's intervention was real: he thought it was just a vision.
10 But they passed the first guard-post, then the second, and reached the iron gate leading out into the city, which opened for them of its own accord. And so they came out and walked the length of one street; and the angel left him.

11 Then Peter came to himself. 'Now I know it is true,' he said; 'the Lord has sent his angel and rescued me from Herod's clutches and from all that the Jewish people were expect-
12 ing.' When he realized how things stood, he made for the house of Mary, the mother of John Mark, where a
13 large company was at prayer. He knocked at the outer door and a maid
14 called Rhoda came to answer it. She recognized Peter's voice and was so overjoyed that instead of opening the door she ran in and announced that
15 Peter was standing outside. 'You are crazy', they told her; but she insisted that it was so. Then they said, 'It must be his guardian angel.'
16 Meanwhile Peter went on knocking, and when they opened the door and
17 saw him, they were astounded. With a movement of the hand he signed to them to keep quiet, and told them how the Lord had brought him out of prison. 'Report this to James and the members of the church', he said. Then he left the house and went off else-where.
18 When morning came, there was consternation among the soldiers: what could have become of Peter?
19 Herod made close search, but failed to find him, so he interrogated the guards and ordered their execution.

Herod's pride and fall

Afterwards he left Judaea to reside
20 for a time at Caesarea. He had for some time been furiously angry with the people of Tyre and Sidon, who now by common agreement presented themselves at his court. There they won over Blastus the royal chamber-lain, and sued for peace, because their country drew its supplies from the
21 king's territory. So, on an appointed day, attired in his royal robes and seated on the rostrum, Herod haran-
22 gued them; and the populace shouted

back, 'It is a god speaking, not a man!'
23 Instantly an angel of the Lord struck him down, because he had usurped the honour due to God; he was eaten up with worms and died.
24 Meanwhile the word of God con-tinued to grow and spread.
25 Barnabas and Saul, their task ful-filled, returned from Jerusalem,[c] tak-ing John Mark with them.

Barnabas and Saul commissioned

13 There were at Antioch, in the congre-gation there, certain prophets and teachers: Barnabas, Simeon called Niger, Lucius of Cyrene, Manaen, who had been at the court of Prince Herod, and Saul. While they were keeping a
2 fast and offering worship to the Lord, the Holy Spirit said, 'Set Barnabas and Saul apart for me, to do the work to which I have called them.' Then,
3 after further fasting and prayer, they laid their hands on them and let them go.

In Cyprus: opposition and belief

4 So these two, sent out on their mis-sion by the Holy Spirit, came down to Seleucia, and from there sailed to
5 Cyprus. Arriving at Salamis, they de-clared the word of God in the Jew-ish synagogues. They had John with
6 them as their assistant. They went through the whole island as far as Paphos, and there they came upon a sorcerer, a Jew who posed as a pro-
7 phet, Bar-Jesus by name. He was in the retinue of the Governor, Sergius Paulus, an intelligent man, who had sent for Barnabas and Saul and wanted
8 to hear the word of God. This El-ymas the sorcerer (so his name may be translated) opposed them, trying to turn the Governor away from the
9 Faith. But Saul, also known as Paul, filled with the Holy Spirit, fixed his
10 eyes on him and said, 'You swindler, you rascal, son of the devil and enemy of all goodness, will you never stop falsifying the straight ways of the
11 Lord? Look now, the hand of the Lord strikes: you shall be blind, and for a time you shall not see the sun-light.' Instantly mist and darkness came over him and he groped about for someone to lead him by the hand.
12 When the Governor saw what had happened he became a believer, deep-ly impressed by what he learned about the Lord.

c *Some witnesses read* their task fulfilled, returned to Jerusalem; *or, as it might be rendered,* their task at Jerusalem fulfilled, returned.

Paul's speech at Pisidian Antioch

13 Leaving Paphos, Paul and his companions went by sea to Perga in Pamphylia; John, however, left them and
14 returned to Jerusalem. From Perga they continued their journey as far as Pisidian Antioch. On the Sabbath they went to synagogue and took
15 their seats; and after the readings from the Law and the prophets, the officials of the synagogue sent this message to them: 'Friends, if you have anything to say to the people by way of exhortation, let us hear it.'
16 Paul rose, made a gesture with his hand, and began:

'Men of Israel and you who wor-
17 ship our God, listen to me! The God of this people of Israel chose our fathers. When they were still living as aliens in Egypt he made them into a nation and brought them out of that country with arm outstretched.
18 For some forty years he bore with
19 their conduct[d] in the desert. Then in the Canaanite country he overthrew seven nations, whose lands he gave
20 them to be their heritage for some four hundred and fifty years, and afterwards appointed judges for them until the time of the prophet Samuel.
21 'Then they asked for a king and God gave them Saul the son of Kish, a man of the tribe of Benjamin, who
22 reigned for forty years. Then he removed him and set up David as their king, giving him his approval in these words: "I have found David son of Jesse to be a man after my own heart, who will carry out all my pur-
23 poses." This is the man from whose posterity God, as he promised, has
24 brought Israel a saviour, Jesus. John made ready for his coming by proclaiming baptism as a token of repentance to the whole people of Israel.
25 And when John was nearing the end of his course, he said, "I am not what you think I am. No, after me comes one whose shoes I am not fit to unfasten."
26 'My brothers, you who come of the stock of Abraham, and others among you who revere our God, we are the people to whom the message of this
27 salvation has been sent. The people of Jerusalem and their rulers did not recognize him, or understand the words of the prophets which are read Sabbath by Sabbath; indeed they fulfilled them by condemning him.
28 Though they failed to find grounds

for the sentence of death, they asked Pilate to have him executed. And 29 when they had carried out all that the scriptures said about him, they took him down from the gibbet and laid him in a tomb. But God raised 30 him from the dead; and there was a 31 period of many days during which he appeared to those who had come up with him from Galilee to Jerusalem.

'They are now his witnesses before our nation; and we are here to give 32 you the good news that God, who made the promise to the fathers, has 33 fulfilled it for the children[e] by raising Jesus from the dead, as indeed it stands written, in the second[f] Psalm: "You are my son; this day I have begotten you." Again, that he raised 34 him from the dead, never again to revert to corruption, he declares in these words: "I will give you the blessings promised to David, holy and sure." This is borne out by another 35 passage: "Thou wilt not let thy loyal servant suffer corruption." As for 36 David, when he had served the purpose of God in his own generation, he died, and was gathered to his fathers, and suffered corruption; but the one 37 whom God raised up did not suffer corruption; and you must understand, 38 my brothers, that it is through him that forgiveness of sins is now being proclaimed to you. It is through him 39 that everyone who has faith is acquitted of everything for which there was no acquittal under the Law of Moses. Beware, then, lest you bring down 40 upon yourselves the doom proclaimed by the prophets: "See this, you scoff- 41 ers, wonder, and begone; for I am doing a deed in your days, a deed which you will never believe when you are told of it."'

As they were leaving the synagogue 42 they were asked to come again and speak on these subjects next Sabbath; and after the congregation had dis- 43 persed, many Jews and gentile worshippers went along with Paul and Barnabas, who spoke to them and urged them to hold fast to the grace of God.

Paul turns to the Gentiles

On the following Sabbath almost the 44 whole city gathered to hear the word of God. When the Jews saw the crowds, 45 they were filled with jealous resentment, and contradicted what Paul said, with violent abuse. But Paul 46

---

d Some witnesses read he sustained them.
children.   f Some witnesses read first.
e Some witnesses read our children; others read us their

and Barnabas were outspoken in their reply. 'It was necessary', they said, 'that the word of God should be declared to you first. But since you reject it and thus condemn yourselves as unworthy of eternal life, we now turn 47 to the Gentiles. For these are our instructions from the Lord: "I have appointed you to be a light for the Gentiles, and a means of salvation to 48 earth's farthest bounds."' When the Gentiles heard this, they were overjoyed and thankfully acclaimed the word of the Lord, and those who were marked out for eternal life became 49 believers. So the word of the Lord spread far and wide through the 50 region. But the Jews stirred up feeling among the women of standing who were worshippers, and among the leading men of the city; a persecution was started against Paul and Barnabas, and they were expelled from the 51 district. So they shook the dust off their feet in protest against them and 52 went to Iconium. And the converts were filled with joy and with the Holy Spirit.

At Iconium: Jewish opposition

14 At Iconium similarly they went[g] into the Jewish synagogue and spoke to such purpose that a large body both of Jews and Gentiles became believers. 2 But the unconverted Jews stirred up the Gentiles and poisoned their minds 3 against the Christians. For some time Paul and Barnabas stayed on and spoke boldly and openly in reliance on the Lord; and he confirmed the message of his grace by causing signs and miracles to be worked at their 4 hands. The mass of the townspeople were divided, some siding with the 5 Jews, others with the apostles. But when a move was made by Gentiles and Jews together, with the connivance of the city authorities, to mal- 6 treat them and stone them, they got wind of it and made their escape to the Lycaonian cities of Lystra and Derbe and the surrounding country, 7 where they continued to spread the good news.

At Lystra: enthusiasm and hostility

8 At Lystra sat a crippled man, lame from birth, who had never walked in 9 his life. This man listened while Paul was speaking. Paul fixed his eyes on him and saw that he had the faith to 10 be cured, so he said to him in a loud

voice, 'Stand up straight on your feet'; and he sprang up and started to walk. When the crowds saw what Paul had 11 done, they shouted, in their native Lycaonian, 'The gods have come down to us in human form.' And they call- 12 ed Barnabas Jupiter, and Paul they called Mercury, because he was the spokesman. And the priest of Jupiter, 13 whose temple was just outside the city, brought oxen and garlands to the gates, and he and all the people were about to offer sacrifice.

But when the apostles Barnabas 14 and Paul heard of it, they tore their clothes and rushed into the crowd shouting, 'Men, what is this that you 15 are doing? We are only human beings, no less mortal than you. The good news we bring tells you to turn from these follies to the living God, who made heaven and earth and sea and everything in them. In past ages he 16 allowed all nations to go their own way; and yet he has not left you with- 17 out some clue to his nature, in the kindness he shows: he sends you rain from heaven and crops in their seasons, and gives you food and good cheer in plenty.'

With these words they barely man- 18 aged to prevent the crowd from offering sacrifice to them.

Then Jews from Antioch and Ico- 19 nium came on the scene and won over the crowds. They stoned Paul, and dragged him out of the city, thinking him dead. The converts formed a ring 20 round him, and he got to his feet and went into the city. Next day he left with Barnabas for Derbe.

The mission completed

After bringing the good news to that 21 town, where they gained many converts, they returned to Lystra, then to Iconium, and then to Antioch, heartening the converts and encour- 22 aging them to be true to their religion. They warned them that to enter the kingdom of God we must pass through many hardships. They also appointed 23 elders for them in each congregation, and with prayer and fasting committed them to the Lord in whom they had put their faith.

Then they passed through Pisidia 24 and came into Pamphylia. When they 25 had given the message at Perga, they went down to Attalia, and from there 26 set sail for Antioch, where they had originally been commended to the

g Or At Iconium they went together . . .

grace of God for the task which they 27 had now completed. When they arrived and had called the congregation together, they reported all that God had done through them, and how he had thrown open the gates of faith 28 to the Gentiles. And they stayed for some time with the disciples there.

A conference at Jerusalem

15 Now certain persons who had come down from Judaea began to teach the brotherhood that those who were not circumcised in accordance with Mosaic practice could not be saved. 2 That brought them into fierce dissension and controversy with Paul and Barnabas. And so it was arranged that these two and some others from Antioch should go up to Jerusalem to see the apostles and elders about this question. 3 They were sent on their way by the congregation, and travelled through Phoenicia and Samaria, telling the full story of the conversion of the Gentiles. The news caused great rejoicing among all the Christians there. 4 When they reached Jerusalem they were welcomed by the church and the apostles and elders, and reported all that God had done through them. 5 Then some of the Pharisaic party who had become believers came forward and said, 'They must be circumcised and told to keep the Law of Moses.'

6 The apostles and elders held a 7 meeting to look into this matter; and, after a long debate, Peter rose and addressed them. 'My friends,' he said, 'in the early days, as you yourselves know, God made his choice among you and ordained that from my lips the Gentiles should hear and believe 8 the message of the Gospel. And God, who can read men's minds, showed his approval of them by giving the Holy Spirit to them, as he did to us. 9 He made no difference between them and us; for he purified their hearts by 10 faith. Then why do you now provoke God by laying on the shoulders of these converts a yoke which neither we nor our fathers were able to bear? 11 No, we believe that it is by the grace of the Lord Jesus that we are saved, and so are they.'

12 At that the whole company fell silent and listened to Barnabas and Paul as they told of all the signs and miracles that God had worked among the Gentiles through them.

When they had finished speaking, 13 James summed up: 'My friends,' he said, 'listen to me. Simeon has told 14 how it first happened that God took notice of the Gentiles, to choose from among them a people to bear his name; and this agrees with the words of the 15 prophets, as Scripture has it:

"Thereafter I will return and rebuild 16
    the fallen house of David;
even from its ruins I will rebuild it,
    and set it up again,
that they may seek the Lord—all the 17
    rest of mankind,
and the Gentiles, whom I have
    claimed for my own.
Thus says the Lord, whose work it is,
made known long ago."
    18

'My judgement therefore is that we 19 should impose no irksome restrictions on those of the Gentiles who are turning to God, but instruct them by 20 letter to abstain from things polluted by contact with idols, from fornication, from anything that has been strangled, and from blood.[h] Moses, 21 after all, has never lacked spokesmen in every town for generations past; he is read in the synagogues Sabbath by Sabbath.'

A letter to gentile Christians

Then the apostles and elders, with 22 the agreement of the whole church, resolved to choose representatives and send them to Antioch with Paul and Barnabas. They chose two leading men in the community, Judas Barsabbas and Silas, and gave them this 23 letter to deliver:

'We, the apostles and elders, send greetings as brothers to our brothers of gentile origin in Antioch, Syria, and Cilicia. Forasmuch as we have heard 24 that some of our number, without any instructions from us, have[i] disturbed you with their talk and unsettled your minds, we have resolved unani- 25 mously to send to you our chosen representatives with our well-beloved Barnabas and Paul, who have devo- 26 ted themselves to the cause of our Lord Jesus Christ. We are therefore 27 sending Judas and Silas, who will themselves confirm this by word of mouth. It is the decision of the Holy 28 Spirit, and our decision, to lay no further burden upon you beyond

h Some witnesses omit from fornication; others omit from anything that has been strangled; some add (after blood) and to refrain from doing to others what they would not like done to themselves.
i Some witnesses read have gone out and . . .

29 these essentials: you are to abstain from meat that has been offered to idols, from blood, from anything that has been strangled,[j] and from fornication.[k] If you keep yourselves free from these things you will be doing right. Farewell.'

30 So they were sent off on their journey and travelled down to Antioch, where they called the congregation together, and delivered the letter. 31 When it was read, they all rejoiced at 32 the encouragement it brought. Judas and Silas, who were prophets themselves, said much to encourage and 33 strengthen the members, and, after spending some time there, were dismissed with the good wishes of the brethren, to return to those who had 35 sent them.[l] But Paul and Barnabas stayed on at Antioch, and there, along with many others, they taught and preached the word of the Lord.

Paul and Barnabas part company

36 After a while Paul said to Barnabas, 'Ought we not to go back now to see how our brothers are faring in the various towns where we proclaimed 37 the word of the Lord?' Barnabas wanted to take John Mark with them; 38 but Paul judged that the man who had deserted them in Pamphylia and had not gone on to share in their work was not the man to take with them 39 now. The dispute was so sharp that they parted company. Barnabas took Mark with him and sailed for Cyprus, 40 while Paul chose Silas. He started on his journey, commended by the bro- 41 thers to the grace of the Lord, and travelled through Syria and Cilicia bringing new strength to the congregations.

At Lystra: Paul meets Timothy

16 He went on to Derbe and to Lystra, and there he found a disciple named Timothy, the son of a Jewish Chris- 2 tian mother and a Gentile father. He was well spoken of by the Christians 3 at Lystra and Iconium, and Paul wanted to have him in his company when he left the place. So he took him and circumcised him, out of consideration for the Jews who lived in those parts; for they all knew that his 4 father was a Gentile. As they made

their way from town to town they handed on the decisions taken by the apostles and elders in Jerusalem and enjoined their observance. And so, 5 day by day, the congregations grew stronger in faith and increased in numbers.

At Troas: an appeal from Macedonia

They travelled through the Phrygian 6 and Galatian region,[m] because they were prevented by the Holy Spirit from delivering the message in the province of Asia; and when they ap- 7 proached the Mysian border they tried to enter Bithynia; but the Spirit of Jesus would not allow them, so they 8 skirted[n] Mysia and reached the coast at Troas. During the night a vision 9 came to Paul: a Macedonian stood there appealing to him and saying, 'Come across to Macedonia and help us.' After he had seen this vision we 10 at once set about getting a passage to Macedonia, concluding that God had called us to bring them the good news.

At Philippi: the conversion of Lydia

So we sailed from Troas and made a 11 straight run to Samothrace, the next day to Neapolis, and from there to 12 Philippi, a city of the first rank in that district of Macedonia, and a Roman colony. Here we stayed for some days, and on the Sabbath day we went out- 13 side the city gate by the river-side, where we thought there would be a place of prayer,[o] and sat down and talked to the women who had gathered there. One of them named Lydia, a 14 dealer in purple fabric from the city of Thyatira, who was a worshipper of God, was listening, and the Lord opened her heart to respond to what Paul said. She was baptized, and her 15 household with her, and then she said to us, 'If you have judged me to be a believer in the Lord, I beg you to come and stay in my house.' And she insisted on our going.

The fortune-teller of Philippi

Once, when we were on our way to the 16 place of prayer, we met a slave-girl who was possessed by an oracular spirit and brought large profits to

---

j Some witnesses omit from anything that has been strangled.   k Some witnesses omit and from fornication; and some add and refrain from doing to others what you would not like done to yourselves. l Some witnesses add (34) But Silas decided to remain there.   m Or through Phrygia and the Galatian region.   n Possibly traversed.   o Some witnesses read where there was a recognized place of prayer.

17 her owners by telling fortunes. She followed Paul and the rest of us, shouting, 'These men are servants of the Supreme God, and are declaring to you
18 a way of salvation.' She did this day after day, until Paul could bear it no longer. Rounding on the spirit he said, 'I command you in the name of Jesus Christ to come out of her', and it went out there and then.

19 When the girl's owners saw that their hope of gain had gone, they seized Paul and Silas and dragged them to the city authorities in the
20 main square; and bringing them before the magistrates, they said, 'These men are causing a disturbance in our
21 city; they are Jews; they are advocating customs which it is illegal for us
22 Romans to adopt and follow.' The mob joined in the attack; and the magistrates tore off the prisoners' clothes
23 and ordered them to be flogged. After giving them a severe beating they flung them into prison and ordered the jailer to keep them under close guard.
24 In view of these orders, he put them in the inner prison and secured their feet in the stocks.

Earthquake at Philippi

25 About midnight Paul and Silas, at their prayers, were singing praises to God, and the other prisoners were
26 listening, when suddenly there was such a violent earthquake that the foundations of the jail were shaken; all the doors burst open and all the prisoners found their fetters unfasten-
27 ed. The jailer woke up to see the prison doors wide open, and assuming that the prisoners had escaped, drew his
28 sword intending to kill himself. But Paul shouted, 'Do yourself no harm;
29 we are all here.' The jailer called for lights, rushed in and threw himself down before Paul and Silas, trembling
30 with fear. He then escorted them out and said, 'Masters, what must I do to
31 be saved?' They said, 'Put your trust in the Lord Jesus, and you will be
32 saved, you and your household.' Then they spoke the word of the Lord[p] to him and to everyone in his house.
33 At that late hour of the night he took them and washed their wounds; and immediately afterwards he and
34 his whole family were baptized. He brought them into his house, set out a meal, and rejoiced with his whole household in his new-found faith in God.

When daylight came the magis- 35 trates sent their officers with instructions to release the men. The jailer 36 reported the message to Paul: 'The magistrates have sent word that you are to be released. So now you may go free, and blessings on your journey.'[q] But 37 Paul said to the officers: 'They gave us a public flogging, though we are Roman citizens and have not been found guilty; they threw us into prison, and are they now to smuggle us out privately? No indeed! Let them come in person and escort us out.' The officers 38 reported his words. The magistrates were alarmed to hear that they were Roman citizens, and came and apolo- 39 gized to them. Then they escorted them out and requested them to go away from the city. On leaving the 40 prison, they went to Lydia's house, where they met their fellow-Christians, and spoke words of encouragement to them; then they departed.

At Thessalonica: success and opposition

They now travelled by way of Am- 17 phipolis and Apollonia and came to Thessalonica, where there was a Jewish synagogue. Following his usual 2 practice Paul went to their meetings; and for the next three Sabbaths he argued with them, quoting texts of 3 Scripture which he expounded and applied to show that the Messiah had to suffer and rise from the dead. 'And this Jesus,' he said, 'whom I am proclaiming to you, is the Messiah.' Some 4 of them were convinced and joined Paul and Silas; so did a great number of godfearing Gentiles and a good many influential women.[r]

But the Jews in their jealousy re- 5 cruited some low fellows from the dregs of the populace, roused the rabble, and had the city in an uproar. They mobbed Jason's house, with the intention of bringing Paul and Silas before the town assembly. Failing to 6 find them, they dragged Jason himself and some members of the congregation before the magistrates, shouting, 'The men who have made trouble all over the world have now come here; and Jason has harboured them. 7 They all flout the Emperor's laws, and assert that there is a rival king, Jesus.' These words caused a great 8 commotion in the mob, which affected the magistrates also. They bound 9

---

p Some witnesses read of God.   q Some witnesses read . . . free and take your journey.   r Some
witnesses read a good many wives of leading men.

over Jason and the others, and let them go.

Eager welcome at Beroea

10 As soon as darkness fell, the members of the congregation sent Paul and Silas off to Beroea. On arrival, they
11 made their way to the synagogue. The Jews here were more civil than those at Thessalonica: they received the message with great eagerness, studying the scriptures every day to see
12 whether it was as they said. Many of them therefore became believers, and so did a fair number of Gentiles,
13 women of standing as well as men. But when the Thessalonian Jews learned that the word of God had now been proclaimed by Paul in Beroea, they came on there to stir up trouble and
14 rouse the rabble. Thereupon the members of the congregation sent Paul off at once to go down to the coast, while Silas and Timothy both stayed behind.
15 Paul's escort brought him as far as Athens, and came away with instructions for Silas and Timothy to rejoin him with all speed.

At Athens: encounter with philosophers

16 Now while Paul was waiting for them at Athens he was exasperated to see
17 how the city was full of idols. So he argued in the synagogue with the Jews and gentile worshippers, and also in the city square every day
18 with casual passers-by. And some of the Epicurean and Stoic philosophers joined issue with him. Some said, 'What can this charlatan be trying to say?'; others, 'He would appear to be a propagandist for foreign deities'—this because he was preaching about
19 Jesus and Resurrection. So they took him and brought him before the Court of Areopagus[s] and said, 'May we know what this new doctrine is
20 that you propound? You are introducing ideas that sound strange to us, and we should like to know what they
21 mean.' (Now the Athenians in general and the foreigners there had no time for anything but talking or hearing about the latest novelty.)
22 Then Paul stood up before the Court of Areopagus[t] and said: 'Men of Athens, I see that in everything that concerns religion you are uncommonly scrupulous. For as I was
23 going round looking at the objects of

your worship, I noticed among other things an altar bearing the inscription "To an Unknown God". What you worship but do not know—this is what I now proclaim.

24 'The God who created the world and everything in it, and who is Lord of heaven and earth, does not live in shrines made by men. It is not
25 because he lacks anything that he accepts service at men's hands, for he is himself the universal giver of life and breath and all else. He created
26 every race of men of one stock, to inhabit the whole earth's surface. He fixed the epochs of their history[u] and the limits of their territory. They were
27 to seek God, and, it might be, touch and find him; though indeed he is not far from each one of us, for in him we
28 live and move, in him we exist; as some of your own poets[v] have said, "We are also his offspring." As God's
29 offspring, then, we ought not to suppose that the deity is like an image in gold or silver or stone, shaped by human craftsmanship and design. As
30 for the times of ignorance, God has overlooked them; but now he commands mankind, all men everywhere, to repent, because he has fixed the
31 day on which he will have the world judged, and justly judged, by a man of his choosing; of this he has given assurance to all by raising him from the dead.'
32 When they heard about the raising of the dead, some scoffed; and others said, 'We will hear you on this sub-
33 ject some other time.' And so Paul
34 left the assembly. However, some men joined him and became believers, including Dionysius, a member of the Court of Areopagus; also a woman named Damaris, and others besides.

Working and teaching at Corinth

18 After this he left Athens and went to Corinth. There he fell in with a Jew
2 named Aquila, a native of Pontus, and his wife Priscilla; he had recently arrived from Italy because Claudius had issued an edict that all Jews should leave Rome. Paul approached
3 them and, because he was of the same trade, he made his home with them, and they carried on business together; they were tent-makers. He
4 also held discussions in the synagogue Sabbath by Sabbath, trying to convince both Jews and Gentiles.

---

s Or brought him to Mars' Hill.   *t Or* in the middle of Mars' Hill.   *u Or* fixed the ordered seasons . . .   *v Some witnesses read* some among you.

5 Then Silas and Timothy came down from Macedonia, and Paul devoted himself entirely to preaching, affirming before the Jews that the Messiah 6 was Jesus. But when they opposed him and resorted to abuse, he shook out the skirts of his cloak and said to them, 'Your blood be on your own heads! My conscience is clear; now I 7 shall go to the Gentiles.' With that he left, and went to the house of a worshipper of God named Titius Justus, who lived next door to the synagogue. 8 Crispus, who held office in the synagogue, now became a believer in the Lord, with all his household; and a number of Corinthians listened and 9 believed, and were baptized. One night in a vision the Lord said to Paul, 'Have no fear: go on with your preach- 10 ing and do not be silenced, for I am with you and no one shall attempt to do you harm;[w] and there are many 11 in this city who are my people.' So he settled down for eighteen months, teaching the word of God among them.

Gallio dismisses the case against Paul

12 But when Gallio was proconsul of Achaia, the Jews set upon Paul in a body and brought him into court. 13 'This man', they said, 'is inducing people to worship God in ways that 14 are against the law.' Paul was just about to speak when Gallio said to them, 'If it had been a question of crime or grave misdemeanour, I should, of course, have given you 15 Jews a patient hearing, but if it is some bickering about words and names and your Jewish law, you may see to it yourselves; I have no mind 16 to be a judge of these matters.' And he had them ejected from the court. 17 Then there was a general attack on Sosthenes, who held office in the synagogue, and they gave him a beating in full view of the bench. But all this left Gallio quite unconcerned.

More journeys

18 Paul stayed on for some time, and then took leave of the brotherhood and set sail for Syria, accompanied by Priscilla and Aquila. At Cenchreae he had his hair cut off, because he was 19 under a vow. When they reached Ephesus he parted from them and went himself into the synagogue, where he held a discussion with the

Jews. He was asked to stay longer, but 20 declined and set out from Ephesus, 21 saying, as he took leave of them, 'I shall come back to you if it is God's will.' On landing at Caesarea, he went 22 up and paid his respects to the church, and then went down to Antioch. After 23 spending some time there, he set out again and made a journey through the Galatian country and on through Phrygia, bringing new strength to all the converts.

Apollos at Ephesus

Now there arrived at Ephesus a Jew 24 named Apollos, an Alexandrian by birth, an eloquent man,[x] powerful in his use of the scriptures. He had been 25 instructed in the way of the Lord and was full of spiritual fervour; and in his discourses he taught accurately the facts about Jesus,[y] though he knew only John's baptism. He now 26 began to speak boldly in the synagogue, where Priscilla and Aquila heard him; they took him in hand and expounded the new way[z] to him in greater detail. Finding that he wished 27 to go across to Achaia, the brotherhood gave him their support, and wrote to the congregation there to make him welcome. From the time of his arrival, he was very helpful to those who had by God's grace become believers; for he strenuously confuted 28 the Jews, demonstrating publicly from the scriptures that the Messiah is Jesus.

Paul's successful work at Ephesus

While Apollos was at Corinth, Paul 19 travelled through the inland regions till he came to Ephesus. There he found a number of converts, to whom 2 he said, 'Did you receive the Holy Spirit when you became believers?' 'No,' they replied, 'we have not even heard that there is a Holy Spirit.' He 3 said, 'Then what baptism were you given?' 'John's baptism', they answered. Paul then said, 'The baptism 4 that John gave was a baptism in token of repentance, and he told the people to put their trust in one who was to come after him, that is, in Jesus.' On hearing this they were 5 baptized into the name of the Lord Jesus; and when Paul had laid his 6 hands on them, the Holy Spirit came upon them and they spoke in tongues of ecstasy and prophesied. Altogether 7 they were about a dozen men.

w Or and you will not be harmed by anyone's attacks.   x Or a learned man.   y Some witnesses read about the Lord.   z Some witnesses read the way of God.

8 During the next three months he attended the synagogue and, using argument and persuasion, spoke boldly and freely about the kingdom of God. 9 But when some proved obdurate and would not believe, speaking evil of the new way before the whole congregation, he left them, withdrew his converts, and continued to hold discussions daily in the lecture-hall 10 of Tyrannus. This went on for two years, with the result that the whole population of the province of Asia, both Jews and Gentiles, heard the 11 word of the Lord. And through Paul 12 God worked singular miracles: when handkerchiefs and scarves which had been in contact with his skin were carried to the sick, they were rid of their diseases and the evil spirits came out of them.

13 But some strolling Jewish exorcists tried their hand at using the name of the Lord Jesus on those possessed by evil spirits; they would say, 'I adjure you by Jesus whom Paul proclaims.' 14 There were seven sons of Sceva, a Jewish chief priest, who were using 15 this method, when the evil spirit answered back and said, 'Jesus I acknowledge, and I know about Paul, 16 but who are you?' And the man with the evil spirit flew at them, overpowered them all, and handled them with such violence that they ran out of the house stripped and battered. 17 This became known to everybody in Ephesus, whether Jew or Gentile; they were all awestruck, and the name of 18 the Lord Jesus gained in honour. Moreover many of those who had become believers came and openly confessed that they had been using magical spells. 19 And a good many of those who formerly practised magic collected their books and burnt them publicly. The total value was reckoned up and it came to fifty thousand pieces of silver. 20 In such ways the word of the Lord showed its power, spreading more and more widely and effectively.

Disturbance in Ephesus

21 When things had reached this stage, Paul made up his mind[a] to visit Macedonia and Achaia and then go on to Jerusalem; and he said, 'After I have been there, I must see Rome 22 also.' So he sent two of his assistants, Timothy and Erastus, to Macedonia, while he himself stayed some time longer in the province of Asia.

23 Now about that time, the Christian movement gave rise to a serious disturbance. There was a man named 24 Demetrius, a silversmith who made silver shrines of Diana and provided a great deal of employment for the craftsmen. He called a meeting of 25 these men and the workers in allied trades, and addressed them. 'Men,' he said, 'you know that our high standard of living depends on this industry. And you see and hear how this fellow 26 Paul with his propaganda has perverted crowds of people, not only at Ephesus but also in practically the whole of the province of Asia. He is telling them that gods made by human hands are not gods at all. There 27 is danger for us here; it is not only that our line of business will be discredited, but also that the sanctuary of the great goddess Diana will cease to command respect; and then it will not be long before she who is worshipped by all Asia and the civilized world is brought down from her divine pre-eminence.'

When they heard this they were 28 roused to fury and shouted, 'Great is Diana of the Ephesians!' The whole 29 city was in confusion; they seized Paul's travelling-companions, the Macedonians Gaius and Aristarchus, and made a concerted rush with them into the theatre. Paul wanted to appear 30 before the assembly but the other Christians would not let him. Even 31 some of the dignitaries of the province, who were friendly towards him, sent and urged him not to venture into the theatre. Meanwhile some were 32 shouting one thing, some another; for the assembly was in confusion and most of them did not know what they had all come for. But some of the 33 crowd explained the trouble to Alexander, whom the Jews had pushed to the front, and he, motioning for silence, attempted to make a defence before the assembly. But when they recog- 34 nized that he was a Jew, a single cry arose from them all: for about two hours they kept on shouting, 'Great is Diana of the Ephesians!'

The town clerk, however, quieted 35 the crowd. 'Men of Ephesus,' he said, 'all the world knows that our city of Ephesus is temple-warden of the great Diana and of that symbol of her which fell from heaven. Since these 36 facts are beyond dispute, your proper course is to keep quiet and do nothing rash. These men whom you have 37

a Or Paul, led by the Spirit, resolved . . .

brought here as culprits have committed no sacrilege and uttered no 38 blasphemy against our goddess. If therefore Demetrius and his craftsmen have a case against anyone, assizes are held and there are such people as proconsuls; let the parties bring their charges and counter-39 charges. If, on the other hand, you have some further question to raise, it will be dealt with in the statutory 40 assembly. We certainly run the risk of being charged with riot for this day's work. There is no justification for it, and if the issue is raised we shall be unable to give any explanation of this 41 uproar.' With that he dismissed the assembly.

To Greece, Macedonia, and Troas

20 When the disturbance had ceased, Paul sent for the disciples and, after encouraging them, said good-bye and set out on his journey to Macedonia. 2 He travelled through those parts of the country, often speaking words of encouragement to the Christians 3 there, and so came into Greece. When he had spent three months there and was on the point of embarking for Syria, a plot was laid against him by the Jews, so he decided to return by 4 way of Macedonia. He was accompanied by Sopater son of Pyrrhus, from Beroea, the Thessalonians Aristarchus and Secundus, Gaius the Doberian[b] and Timothy, and the Asians 5 Tychicus and Trophimus. These went 6 ahead and waited for us at Troas; we ourselves set sail from Philippi after the Passover season,[c] and in five days reached them at Troas, where we spent a week.

An all-night meeting at Troas

7 On the Saturday night, in our assembly for the breaking of bread, Paul, who was to leave next day, addressed them, and went on speaking 8 until midnight. Now there were many lamps in the upper room where we 9 were assembled; and a youth named Eutychus, who was sitting on the window-ledge, grew more and more sleepy as Paul went on talking. At last he was completely overcome by sleep, fell from the third storey to the ground, and was picked up for dead. 10 Paul went down, threw himself upon him, seizing him in his arms, and said

to them, 'Stop this commotion; there is still life in him.' He then went up- 11 stairs, broke bread and ate, and after much conversation, which lasted until dawn, he departed. And they took the 12 boy away alive and were immensely comforted.

Paul's farewell to the Ephesian elders

We went ahead to the ship and sailed 13 for Assos, where we were to take Paul aboard. He had made this arrangement, as he was going to travel by road. When he met us at Assos, we 14 took him aboard and went on to Mitylene. Next day we sailed from 15 there and arrived opposite Chios, and on the second day we made Samos. On the following day[d] we reached Miletus. For Paul had decided to pass 16 by Ephesus and so avoid having to spend time in the province of Asia; he was eager to be in Jerusalem, if he possibly could, on the day of Pentecost. He did, however, send from 17 Miletus to Ephesus and summon the elders of the congregation; and when 18 they joined him, he spoke as follows:

'You know how, from the day that I first set foot in the province of Asia, for the whole time that I was with you, I served the Lord in all humility 19 amid the sorrows and trials that came upon me through the machinations of the Jews. You know that I kept back 20 nothing that was for your good: I delivered the message to you; I taught you, in public and in your homes; with Jews and Gentiles alike I insisted 21 on repentance before God and trust in our Lord Jesus. And now, as you see, 22 I am on my way to Jerusalem, under the constraint of the Spirit.[e] Of what will befall me there I know nothing, except that in city after city the 23 Holy Spirit assures me that imprisonment and hardships await me. For 24 myself, I set no store by life; I only want to finish the race, and complete the task which the Lord Jesus assigned to me, of bearing my testimony to the gospel of God's grace.

'One word more: I have gone about 25 among you proclaiming the Kingdom, but now I know that none of you will see my face again. That being so, I 26 here and now declare that no man's fate can be laid at my door; for I have 27 kept back nothing; I have disclosed to you the whole purpose of God.

b *Some witnesses read the Derbaean.*   c *Literally after the days of Unleavened Bread.*   d *Some* witnesses read . . . *Samos, and, after stopping at Trogyllium, on the following day* . . .   e *Or* under an inner compulsion.

28 Keep watch over yourselves and over all the flock of which the Holy Spirit has given you charge, as shepherds of the church of the Lord,[f] which he 29 won for himself by his own blood.[g] I know that when I am gone, savage wolves will come in among you and 30 will not spare the flock. Even from your own body there will be men coming forward who will distort the truth to induce the disciples to break away 31 and follow them. So be on the alert; remember how for three years, night and day, I never ceased to counsel each of you, and how I wept over you. 32 'And now I commend you to God and to his gracious word, which has power to build you up and give you your heritage among all who are 33 dedicated to him. I have not wanted anyone's money or clothes for myself; 34 you all know that these hands of mine earned enough for the needs of 35 myself and my companions. I showed you that it is our duty to help the weak in this way, by hard work, and that we should keep in mind the words of the Lord Jesus, who himself said, "Happiness lies more in giving than in receiving."'

36 As he finished speaking, he knelt 37 down with them all and prayed. Then there were loud cries of sorrow from them all, as they folded Paul in their 38 arms and kissed him. What distressed them most was his saying that they would never see his face again. So they escorted him to his ship.

Sails set for Palestine

21 When we had parted from them and set sail, we made a straight run and came to Cos; next day to Rhodes, 2 and thence to Patara.[h] There we found a ship bound for Phoenicia, so we 3 went aboard and sailed in her. We came in sight of Cyprus, and leaving it to port, we continued our voyage to Syria, and put in at Tyre, for there the ship was to unload her cargo. 4 We went and found the disciples and stayed there a week; and they, warned by the Spirit, urged Paul to 5 abandon his visit to Jerusalem. But when our time ashore was ended, we left and continued our journey; and they and their wives and children all escorted us out of the city. We knelt 6 down on the beach and prayed, and bade each other good-bye; we went aboard, and they returned home.

Prophetic warning to Paul

7 We made the passage from Tyre and reached Ptolemais, where we greeted the brotherhood and spent one day 8 with them. Next day we left and came to Caesarea. We went to the home of 9 Philip the evangelist, who was one of the Seven, and stayed with him. He had four unmarried daughters, who 10 possessed the gift of prophecy. When we had been there several days, a prophet named Agabus arrived from Judaea. He came to us, took Paul's 11 belt, bound his own feet and hands with it, and said, 'These are the words of the Holy Spirit: Thus will the Jews in Jerusalem bind the man to whom this belt belongs, and hand him over to the Gentiles.' When we heard this, 12 we and the local people begged and implored Paul to abandon his visit to Jerusalem. Then Paul gave his an- 13 swer: 'Why all these tears? Why are you trying to weaken my resolution? For my part I am ready not merely to be bound but even to die at Jerusalem for the name of the Lord Jesus.' So, as he would not be persuaded, we 14 gave up and said, 'The Lord's will be done.'

At the end of our stay we packed 15 our baggage and took the road up to Jerusalem. Some of the disciples from 16 Caesarea came along with us, bringing a certain Mnason of Cyprus, a Christian from the early days, with whom we were to lodge. So we reached 17 Jerusalem, where the brotherhood welcomed us gladly.

In Jerusalem: Paul and James

Next day Paul paid a visit to James; 18 we were with him, and all the elders attended. He greeted them, and then 19 described in detail all that God had done among the Gentiles through his ministry. When they heard this, they 20 gave praise to God. Then they said to Paul: 'You see, brother, how many thousands of converts we have among the Jews, all of them staunch upholders of the Law. Now they have 21 been given certain information about you: it is said that you teach all the Jews in the gentile world to turn their backs on Moses, telling them to give up circumcising their children and following our way of life. What is the 22 position, then? They are sure to hear that you have arrived. You must there- 23 fore do as we tell you. We have four

f Some witnesses read of God.   g Or, according to some witnesses, by the blood of his Own.
h Some witnesses add and Myra.

24 men here who are under a vow; take them with you and go through the ritual of purification with them, paying their expenses, after which they may shave their heads. Then everyone will know that there is nothing in the stories they were told about you, but that you are a practising Jew and
25 keep the Law yourself. As for the gentile converts, we sent them our decision that they must abstain from meat that has been offered to idols, from blood, from anything that has been strangled,[i] and from fornication.'
26 So Paul took the four men, and next day, after going through the ritual of purification with them, he went into the temple to give notice of the date when the period of purification would end and the offering be made for each one of them.

Paul in protective custody

27 But just before the seven days were up, the Jews from the province of Asia saw him in the temple. They stirred up the whole crowd, and seized
28 him, shouting, 'Men of Israel, help, help! This is the fellow who spreads his doctrine all over the world, attacking our people, our law, and this sanctuary. On top of all this he has brought Gentiles into the temple and
29 profaned this holy place.' For they had previously seen Trophimus the Ephesian with him in the city, and assumed that Paul had brought him into the temple.
30 The whole city was in a turmoil, and people came running from all directions. They seized Paul and dragged him out of the temple; and at
31 once the doors were shut. While they were clamouring for his death, a report reached the officer commanding the cohort, that all Jerusalem was
32 in an uproar. He immediately took a force of soldiers with their centurions and came down on the rioters at the double. As soon as they saw the commandant and his troops, they stopped
33 beating Paul. The commandant stepped forward, arrested him, and ordered him to be shackled with two chains; he then asked who the man was and
34 what he had been doing. Some in the crowd shouted one thing, some another. As he could not get at the truth because of the hubbub, he ordered
35 him to be taken into barracks. When Paul reached the steps, he had to be carried by the soldiers because of the violence of the mob. For the whole
36 crowd were at their heels yelling, 'Kill him!'

Paul defends himself

37 Just before Paul was taken into the barracks he said to the commandant, 'May I have a word with you?' The commandant said, 'So you speak
38 Greek, do you? Then you are not the Egyptian who started a revolt some time ago and led a force of four thousand terrorists out into the wilds?'
39 Paul replied, 'I am a Jew, a Tarsian from Cilicia, a citizen of no mean city. I ask your permission to speak to the people.' When permission had been
40 given, Paul stood on the steps and with a gesture called for the attention of the people. As soon as quiet was restored, he addressed them in the Jewish language:

22 'Brothers and fathers, give me a hearing while I make my defence be-
2 fore you.' When they heard him speaking to them in their own language, they listened the more quietly.
3 'I am a true-born Jew,' he said, 'a native of Tarsus in Cilicia. I was brought up in this city, and as a pupil of Gamaliel I was thoroughly trained in every point of our ancestral law. I have always been ardent in God's
4 service, as you all are today. And so I began to persecute this movement to the death, arresting its followers, men and women alike, and putting them
5 in chains. For this I have as witnesses the High Priest and the whole Council of Elders. I was given letters from them to our fellow-Jews at Damascus, and had started out to bring the Christians there to Jerusalem as prisoners for punishment; and this is
6 what happened. I was on the road and nearing Damascus, when suddenly about midday a great light flashed from the sky all around me, and I fell
7 to the ground. Then I heard a voice saying to me, "Saul, Saul, why do you
8 persecute me?" I answered, "Tell me, Lord, who you are." "I am Jesus of Nazareth," he said, "whom you are
9 persecuting." My companions saw the light, but did not hear the voice
10 that spoke to me. "What shall I do, Lord?" I said, and the Lord replied, "Get up and continue your journey to Damascus; there you will be told of all the tasks that are laid upon you."
11 As I had been blinded by the brilliance of that light, my companions led

i Some witnesses omit from anything that has been strangled.

me by the hand, and so I came to Damascus.

12 'There, a man called Ananias, a devout observer of the Law and well spoken of by all the Jews of that place, 13 came and stood beside me and said, "Saul, my brother, recover your sight." Instantly I recovered my sight and 14 saw him. He went on: "The God of our fathers appointed you to know his will and to see the Righteous One 15 and to hear his very voice, because you are to be his witness before the world, and testify to what you have 16 seen and heard. And now why delay? Be baptized at once, with invocation of his name, and wash away your sins."

17 'After my return to Jerusalem, I was praying in the temple when I fell 18 into a trance and saw him there, speaking to me. "Make haste", he said, "and leave Jerusalem without delay, for they will not accept your 19 testimony about me." "Lord," I said, "they know that I imprisoned those who believe in thee, and flogged them 20 in every synagogue; and when the blood of Stephen thy witness was shed I stood by, approving, and I looked after the 21 clothes of those who killed him." But he said to me, "Go, for I am sending you far away to the Gentiles."'

The rights of a Roman citizen

22 Up to this point they had given him a hearing; but now they began shouting, 'Down with him! A scoundrel 23 like that is better dead!' And as they were yelling and waving their cloaks 24 and flinging dust in the air, the commandant ordered him to be brought into the barracks and gave instructions to examine him by flogging, and find out what reason there was for 25 such an outcry against him. But when they tied him up for the lash,[j] Paul said to the centurion who was standing there, 'Can you legally flog a man who is a Roman citizen, and moreover 26 has not been found guilty?' When the centurion heard this, he went and reported it to the commandant. 'What do you mean to do?' he said. 'This 27 man is a Roman citizen.' The commandant came to Paul. 'Tell me, are you a Roman citizen?' he asked. 'Yes', 28 said he. The commandant rejoined, 'It cost me a large sum to acquire this citizenship.' Paul said, 'But it 29 was mine by birth.' Then those who were about to examine him withdrew

hastily, and the commandant himself was alarmed when he realized that Paul was a Roman citizen and that he had put him in irons.

Paul before the High Priest

The following day, wishing to be quite 30 sure what charge the Jews were bringing against Paul, he released him and ordered the chief priests and the entire Council to assemble. He then took Paul down and stood him before them.

Paul fixed his eyes on the Council 23 and said, 'My brothers, I have lived all my life, and still live today, with a perfectly clear conscience before God.' At this the High Priest Ananias 2 ordered his attendants to strike him on the mouth. Paul retorted, 'God 3 will strike you, you whitewashed wall! You sit there to judge me in accordance with the Law; and then in defiance of the Law you order me to be struck!' The attendants said, 4 'Would you insult God's High Priest?' 'My brothers,' said Paul, 'I had no 5 idea that he was High Priest; Scripture, I know, says: "You must not abuse the ruler of your people."'

A division in the Council

Now Paul was well aware that one 6 section of them were Sadducees and the other Pharisees, so he called out in the Council, 'My brothers, I am a Pharisee, a Pharisee born and bred; and the true issue in this trial is our hope of the resurrection of the dead.' At these words the Pharisees and 7 Sadducees fell out among themselves, and the assembly was divided. (The 8 Sadducees deny that there is any resurrection, or angel, or spirit, but the Pharisees accept them.) So a great 9 uproar broke out; and some of the doctors of the law belonging to the Pharisaic party openly took sides and declared, 'We can find no fault with this man; perhaps an angel or spirit has spoken to him.' The dissension 10 was mounting, and the commandant was afraid that Paul would be torn in pieces, so he ordered the troops to go down, pull him out of the crowd, and bring him into the barracks.

The following night the Lord ap- 11 peared to him and said, 'Keep up your courage; you have affirmed the truth about me in Jerusalem, and you must do the same in Rome.'

j Or tied him up with thongs.

A plot against Paul's life disclosed

12 When day broke, the Jews banded together and took an oath not to eat or drink until they had killed Paul.
13 There were more than forty in this
14 conspiracy. They came to the chief priests and elders and said, 'We have bound ourselves by a solemn oath not to taste food until we have killed
15 Paul. It is now for you, acting with the Council, to apply to the commandant to bring him down to you, on the pretext of a closer investigation of his case; and we have arranged to do away with him before he arrives.'
16 But the son of Paul's sister heard of the ambush; he went to the barracks, obtained entry, and reported
17 it to Paul. Paul called one of the centurions and said, 'Take this young man to the commandant; he has
18 something to report.' The centurion took him and brought him to the commandant. 'The prisoner Paul', he said, 'sent for me and asked me to bring this young man to you; he has
19 something to tell you.' The commandant took him by the arm, drew him aside, and asked him, 'What is it
20 you have to report?' He said, 'The Jews have made a plan among themselves and will request you to bring Paul down to the Council tomorrow, on the pretext of obtaining more
21 precise information about him. Do not listen to them; for a party more than forty strong are lying in wait for him. They have sworn not to eat or drink until they have done away with him; they are now ready, and wait
22 only for your consent.' So the commandant dismissed the young man, with orders not to let anyone know that he had given him this information.

The case remitted to the Governor

23 Then he called a couple of his centurions and issued these orders: 'Get ready two hundred infantry to proceed to Caesarea, together with seventy cavalrymen and two hundred light-armed troops;[k] parade three hours
24 after sunset. Provide also mounts for Paul so that he may ride through under safe escort to Felix the Gover-
25 nor.' And he wrote a letter to this effect:
26 'Claudius Lysias to His Excellency the Governor Felix. Your Excellency:
This man was seized by the Jews and 27 was on the point of being murdered when I intervened with the troops and removed him, because I discovered that he was a Roman citizen. As 28 I wished to ascertain the charge on which they were accusing him, I took him down to their Council. I found 29 that the accusation had to do with controversial matters in their law, but there was no charge against him meriting death or imprisonment. How- 30 ever, I have now been informed of an attempt to be made on the man's life, so I am sending him to you at once, and have also instructed his accusers to state their case against him before you.'[l]

Acting on their orders, the infantry 31 took Paul and brought him by night to Antipatris. Next day they returned 32 to their barracks, leaving the cavalry to escort him the rest of the way. The 33 cavalry entered Caesarea, delivered the letter to the Governor, and handed Paul over to him. He read the letter, 34 asked him what province he was from, and learned that he was from Cilicia. 'I will hear your case', he said, 'when 35 your accusers arrive.' He then ordered him to be held in custody at his headquarters in Herod's palace.

The case against Paul opened

Five days later the High Priest 24 Ananias came down, accompanied by some of the elders and an advocate named Tertullus, and they laid an information against Paul before the Governor. When the prisoner was 2 called, Tertullus opened the case.

'Your Excellency,' he said, 'we owe it to you that we enjoy unbroken peace. It is due to your provident care that, in all kinds of ways and in all sorts of places, improvements are being made for the good of this province. We welcome this, sir, most 3 gratefully. And now, not to take up 4 too much of your time, I crave your indulgence for a brief statement of our case. We have found this man to 5 be a perfect pest, a fomenter of discord among the Jews all over the world, a ringleader of the sect of the Nazarenes. He even made an attempt 6 to profane the temple; and then we arrested him.[m] If you will examine 8 him yourself you can ascertain from

---

k Or two hundred spearmen (*the meaning of the Greek word is uncertain*).   l *Some witnesses read*
'... before you. Farewell.'   m *Some witnesses insert* It was our intention to try him under our law;
(7) but Lysias the commandant intervened and took him by force out of our hands, (8) ordering his accusers to come before you.

him the truth of all the charges we
9 bring.' The Jews supported the attack, alleging that the facts were as he stated.

Paul's defence before Felix

10 Then the Governor motioned to Paul to speak, and he began his reply: 'Knowing as I do that for many years you have administered justice in this province, I make my defence with
11 confidence. You can ascertain the facts for yourself. It is not more than twelve days since I went up to Jeru-
12 salem on a pilgrimage. They did not find me arguing with anyone, or collecting a crowd, either in the temple or in the synagogues or up and down
13 the city; and they cannot make good the charges they bring against me.
14 But this much I will admit: I am a follower of the new way (the "sect" they speak of), and it is in that manner that I worship the God of our fathers; for I believe all that is written in the
15 Law and the prophets, and in reliance on God I hold the hope, which my accusers too accept, that there is to be a resurrection of good and wicked
16 alike. Accordingly I, no less than they, train myself to keep at all times a clear conscience before God and man.
17 'After an absence of several years I came to bring charitable gifts to my
18 nation and to offer sacrifices. They found me in the temple ritually purified and engaged in this service. I had no crowd with me, and there was no disturbance. But some Jews from the province of Asia were there,
19 and if they had any charge against me it is they who ought to have been
20 in court to state it. Failing that, it is for these persons here present to say what crime they discovered when I
21 was brought before the Council, apart from this one open assertion which I made as I stood there: "The true issue in my trial before you today is the resurrection of the dead."'
22 Then Felix, who happened to be well informed about the Christian movement, adjourned the hearing. 'When Lysias the commanding officer comes down', he said, 'I will go into
23 your case.' He gave orders to the centurion to keep Paul under open arrest and not to prevent any of his friends from making themselves useful to him.

Felix leaves Paul in custody

24 Some days later Felix came with his wife Drusilla, who was a Jewess, and sending for Paul he let him talk to him
25 about faith in Christ Jesus. But when the discourse turned to questions of morals, self-control, and the coming judgement, Felix became alarmed and exclaimed, 'That will do for the present; when I find it convenient
26 I will send for you again.' At the same time he had hopes of a bribe from Paul; and for this reason he sent for him very often and talked with him.
27 When two years had passed, Felix was succeeded by Porcius Festus. Wishing to curry favour with the Jews, Felix left Paul in custody.

Paul appeals to the Emperor

25 Three days after taking up his appointment Festus went up from Cae-
2 sarea to Jerusalem, where the chief priests and the Jewish leaders brought before him the case against Paul.
3 They asked Festus to favour them against him, and pressed for him to be brought up to Jerusalem, for they were planning an ambush to kill him
4 on the way. Festus, however, replied, 'Paul is in safe custody at Caesarea, and I shall be leaving Jerusalem
5 shortly myself; so let your leading men come down with me, and if there is anything wrong, let them prosecute him.'
6 After spending eight or ten days at most in Jerusalem, he went down to Caesarea, and next day he took his seat in court and ordered Paul to be
7 brought up. When he appeared, the Jews who had come down from Jerusalem stood round bringing many grave charges, which they were unable
8 to prove. Paul's plea was: 'I have committed no offence, either against the Jewish law, or against the temple, or against the Emperor.' Festus,
9 anxious to ingratiate himself with the Jews, turned to Paul and asked, 'Are you willing to go up to Jerusalem and stand trial on these charges before me
10 there?' But Paul said, 'I am now standing before the Emperor's tribunal, and that is where I must be tried. Against the Jews I have committed no offence, as you very well
11 know. If I am guilty of any capital crime, I do not ask to escape the death penalty; but if there is no substance in the charges which these men bring against me, it is not open to anyone to hand me over as a sop to them. I
12 appeal to Caesar!' Then Festus, after conferring with his advisers, replied, 'You have appealed to Caesar: to Caesar you shall go.'

Festus and Agrippa

13 After an interval of some days King Agrippa and Bernice arrived at Caesarea on a courtesy visit to Festus.

14 They spent several days there, and during this time Festus laid Paul's case before the king. 'We have a man', 15 he said, 'left in custody by Felix; and when I was in Jerusalem the chief priests and elders of the Jews laid an information against him, demanding 16 his condemnation. I answered them, "It is not Roman practice to hand over any accused man before he is confronted with his accusers and given an opportunity of answering 17 the charge." So when they had come here with me I lost no time; the very next day I took my seat in court and ordered the man to be brought up. 18 But when his accusers rose to speak, they brought none of the charges I 19 was expecting; they merely had certain points of disagreement with him about their peculiar religion, and about someone called Jesus, a dead man whom Paul alleged to be alive. 20 Finding myself out of my depth in such discussions, I asked if he was willing to go to Jerusalem and stand 21 his trial there on these issues. But Paul appealed to be remanded in custody for His Imperial Majesty's decision, and I ordered him to be detained until I could send him to the 22 Emperor.' Agrippa said to Festus, 'I should rather like to hear the man myself.' 'Tomorrow', he answered, 'you shall hear him.'

23 So next day Agrippa and Bernice came in full state and entered the audience-chamber accompanied by high-ranking officers and prominent citizens; and on the orders of Festus 24 Paul was brought up. Then Festus said, 'King Agrippa, and all you gentlemen here present with us, you see this man: the whole body of the Jews approached me both in Jerusalem and here, loudly insisting that he had 25 no right to remain alive. But it was clear to me that he had committed no capital crime, and when he himself appealed to His Imperial Majesty, I 26 decided to send him. But I have nothing definite about him to put in writing for our Sovereign. Accordingly I have brought him up before you all and particularly before you, King Agrippa, so that as a result of this preliminary inquiry I may have some- 27 thing to report. There is no sense, it seems to me, in sending on a prisoner without indicating the charges against him.'

Paul's defence before Agrippa

26 Agrippa said to Paul, 'You have our permission to speak for yourself.' Then Paul stretched out his hand and began his defence:

2 'I consider myself fortunate, King Agrippa, that it is before you that I am to make my defence today upon all the charges brought against me by the Jews, particularly as you are 3 expert in all Jewish matters, both our customs and our disputes. And therefore I beg you to give me a patient hearing.

4 'My life from my youth up, the life I led from the beginning among my people and in Jerusalem, is familiar to all Jews. Indeed they have known 5 me long enough and could testify, if they only would, that I belonged to the strictest group in our religion: I lived as a Pharisee. And it is for a 6 hope kindled by God's promise to our forefathers that I stand in the dock today. Our twelve tribes hope to 7 see the fulfilment of that promise, worshipping with intense devotion day and night; and for this very hope I am impeached, and impeached by Jews, Your Majesty. Why is it 8 considered incredible among you that God should raise dead men to life?

9 'I myself once thought it my duty to work actively against the name of Jesus of Nazareth; and I did so in 10 Jerusalem. It was I who imprisoned many of God's people by authority obtained from the chief priests; and when they were condemned to death, my vote was cast against them. In all 11 the synagogues I tried by repeated punishment to make them renounce their faith; indeed my fury rose to such a pitch that I extended my persecution to foreign cities.

12 'On one such occasion I was travelling to Damascus with authority and commission from the chief priests; and as I was on my way, Your Majesty, 13 in the middle of the day I saw a light from the sky, more brilliant than the sun, shining all around me and my travelling-companions. We all fell to 14 the ground, and then I heard a voice saying to me in the Jewish language, "Saul, Saul, why do you persecute me? It is hard for you, this kicking against the goad." I said, "Tell me, 15 Lord, who you are"; and the Lord

replied, "I am Jesus, whom you are persecuting. But now, rise to your feet and stand upright. I have appeared to you for a purpose: to appoint you my servant and witness, to testify both to what you have seen and to what you shall yet see of me. I will rescue you from this people and from the Gentiles to whom I am sending you. I send you to open their eyes and turn them from darkness to light, from the dominion of Satan to God, so that, by trust in me, they may obtain forgiveness of sins, and a place with those whom God has made his own."

'And so, King Agrippa, I did not disobey the heavenly vision. I turned first to the inhabitants of Damascus, and then to Jerusalem and all the country of Judaea, and to the Gentiles, and sounded the call to repent and turn to God, and to prove their repentance by deeds. That is why the Jews seized me in the temple and tried to do away with me. But I had God's help, and so to this very day I stand and testify to great and small alike. I assert nothing beyond what was foretold by the prophets and by Moses: that the Messiah must suffer, and that he, the first to rise from the dead, would announce the dawn to Israel and to the Gentiles.'

Paul reasons with Agrippa

While Paul was thus making his defence, Festus shouted at the top of his voice, 'Paul, you are raving; too much study is driving you mad.' 'I am not mad, Your Excellency,' said Paul; 'what I am saying is sober truth. The king is well versed in these matters, and to him I can speak freely. I do not believe that he can be unaware of any of these facts, for this has been no hole-and-corner business. King Agrippa, do you believe the prophets? I know you do.' Agrippa said to Paul, 'You think it will not take much to win me over and make a Christian of me.' 'Much or little,' said Paul, 'I wish to God that not only you, but all those also who are listening to me today, might become what I am, apart from these chains.'

With that the king rose, and with him the Governor, Bernice, and the rest of the company, and after they had withdrawn they talked it over. 'This man', they said, 'is doing nothing that deserves death or imprisonment.' Agrippa said to Festus, 'The

fellow could have been discharged, if he had not appealed to the Emperor.'

Sails set for Italy

When it was decided that we should sail for Italy, Paul and some other prisoners were handed over to a centurion named Julius, of the Augustan Cohort. We embarked in a ship of Adramyttium, bound for ports in the province of Asia, and put out to sea. In our party was Aristarchus, a Macedonian from Thessalonica. Next day we landed at Sidon; and Julius very considerately allowed Paul to go to his friends to be cared for. Leaving Sidon we sailed under the lee of Cyprus because of the head-winds, then across the open sea off the coast of Cilicia and Pamphylia, and so reached Myra in Lycia.

There the centurion found an Alexandrian vessel bound for Italy and put us aboard. For a good many days we made little headway, and we were hard put to it to reach Cnidus. Then, as the wind continued against us, off Salmone we began to sail under the lee of Crete, and, hugging the coast, struggled on to a place called Fair Havens, not far from the town of Lasea.

Storm at sea

By now much time had been lost, the Fast was already over, and it was risky to go on with the voyage. Paul therefore gave them this advice: 'I can see, gentlemen,' he said, 'that this voyage will be disastrous: it will mean grave loss, loss not only of ship and cargo but also of life.' But the centurion paid more attention to the captain and to the owner of the ship than to what Paul said; and as the harbour was unsuitable for wintering, the majority were in favour of putting out to sea, hoping, if they could get so far, to winter at Phoenix, a Cretan harbour exposed south-west and north-west. So when a southerly breeze sprang up, they thought that their purpose was as good as achieved, and, weighing anchor, they sailed along the coast of Crete hugging the land. But before very long a fierce wind, the 'North-easter' as they call it, tore down from the landward side. It caught the ship and, as it was impossible to keep head to wind, we had to give way and run before it. We ran under the lee of a small island called Cauda, and with a struggle

managed to get the ship's boat under
17 control. When they had hoisted it
aboard, they made use of tackle and
undergirded the ship. Then, because
they were afraid of running on to the
shallows of Syrtis, they lowered the
18 mainsail and let her drive. Next day,
as we were making very heavy weather,
19 they began to lighten the ship; and
on the third day they jettisoned the
20 ship's gear with their own hands. For
days on end there was no sign of
either sun or stars, a great storm was
raging, and our last hopes of coming
through alive began to fade.
21 When they had gone for a long
time without food, Paul stood up
among them and said, 'You should
have taken my advice, gentlemen, not
to sail from Crete; then you would
have avoided this damage and loss.
22 But now I urge you not to lose heart;
not a single life will be lost, only the
23 ship. For last night there stood by me
an angel of the God whose I am and
24 whom I worship. "Do not be afraid,
Paul," he said; "it is ordained that
you shall appear before the Emperor;
and, be assured, God has granted you
the lives of all who are sailing with
25 you." So keep up your courage: I
trust in God that it will turn out as I
26 have been told; though we have to
be cast ashore on some island.'
27 The fourteenth night came and we
were still drifting in the Sea of Adria.
In the middle of the night the sailors
felt that land was getting nearer.
28 They sounded and found twenty
fathoms. Sounding again after a short
interval they found fifteen fathoms;
29 and fearing that we might be cast
ashore on a rugged coast they dropped
four anchors from the stern and
30 prayed for daylight to come. The sailors
tried to abandon ship; they had already lowered the ship's boat, pre-
tending they were going to lay out
31 anchors from the bows, when Paul
said to the centurion and the soldiers,
'Unless these men stay on board you
32 can none of you come off safely.' So
the soldiers cut the ropes of the boat
and let her drop away.
33 Shortly before daybreak Paul urged
them all to take some food. 'For the
last fourteen days', he said, 'you have
lived in suspense and gone hungry;
34 you have eaten nothing whatever. So
I beg you to have something to eat;
your lives depend on it. Remember,
not a hair of your heads will be lost.'
35 With these words, he took bread,
gave thanks to God in front of them

all, broke it, and began eating. Then
they all plucked up courage, and took
food themselves. There were on board
two hundred and seventy-six of us in
all. When they had eaten as much as
they wanted they lightened the ship
by dumping the corn in the sea.

Shipwreck

When day broke they could not
recognize the land, but they noticed
a bay with a sandy beach, on which
they planned, if possible, to run the
ship ashore. So they slipped the anchors and let them go; at the same
time they loosened the lashings of
the steering-paddles, set the foresail
to the wind, and let her drive to the
beach. But they found themselves
caught between cross-currents and
ran the ship aground, so that the bow
stuck fast and remained immovable,
while the stern was being pounded to
pieces by the breakers. The soldiers
thought they had better kill the
prisoners for fear that any should
swim away and escape; but the centurion wanted to bring Paul safely
through and prevented them from
carrying out their plan. He gave
orders that those who could swim
should jump overboard first and get
to land; the rest were to follow, some
on planks, some on parts of the ship.
And thus it was that all came safely
to land.

Wintering in Malta

Once we had made our way to safety
we identified the island as Malta. The
rough islanders treated us with un-
common kindness: because it was
cold and had started to rain, they lit
a bonfire and made us all welcome.
Paul had got together an armful of
sticks and put them on the fire, when
a viper, driven out by the heat, fastened on his hand. The islanders, seeing the snake hanging on to his hand,
said to one another, 'The man must
be a murderer; he may have escaped
from the sea, but divine justice has
not let him live.' Paul, however, shook
off the snake into the fire and was
none the worse. They still expected
that any moment he would swell up or
drop down dead, but after waiting
a long time without seeing anything
extraordinary happen to him, they
changed their minds and now said,
'He is a god.'

In the neighbourhood of that place
there were lands belonging to the chief

magistrate of the island, whose name was Publius. He took us in and entertained us hospitably for three days. [8] It so happened that this man's father was in bed suffering from recurrent bouts of fever and dysentery. Paul visited him and, after prayer, laid his hands upon him and healed him; [9] whereupon the other sick people on the island came also and were cured. [10] They honoured us with many marks of respect, and when we were leaving they put on board provision for our needs.

Paul reaches Rome

[11] Three months had passed when we set sail in a ship which had wintered in the island; she was the *Castor and* [12] *Pollux* of Alexandria. We put in at Syracuse and spent three days there; [13] then we sailed round and arrived at Rhegium. After one day a south wind sprang up and we reached Puteoli in [14] two days. There we found fellow-Christians and were invited to stay a week with them. And so to Rome. [15] The Christians there had had news of us and came out to meet us as far as Appii Forum and Tres Tabernae, and when Paul saw them, he gave thanks to God and took courage.

Discussions with the Jews

[16] When we entered Rome Paul was allowed to lodge by himself with a [17] soldier in charge of him. Three days later he called together the local Jewish leaders; and when they were assembled, he said to them: 'My brothers, I, who never did anything against our people or the customs of our forefathers, am here as a prisoner; I was handed over to the Romans at [18] Jerusalem. They examined me and would have liked to release me because there was no capital charge against [19] me; but the Jews objected, and I had no option but to appeal to the Emper-

or; not that I had any accusation to bring against my own people. That is [20] why I have asked to see you and talk to you, because it is for the sake of the hope of Israel that I am in chains, as you see.' They replied, 'We have had [21] no communication from Judaea, nor has any countryman of ours arrived with any report or gossip to your discredit. We should like to hear from [22] you what your views are; all we know about this sect is that no one has a good word to say for it.'

[23] So they fixed a day, and came in large numbers as his guests. He dealt at length with the whole matter; he spoke urgently of the kingdom of God and sought to convince them about Jesus by appealing to the Law of Moses and the prophets. This went on from dawn to dusk. Some [24] were won over by his arguments; others remained sceptical. Without [25] reaching any agreement among themselves they began to disperse, but not before Paul had said one thing more: 'How well the Holy Spirit spoke to your fathers through the prophet Isaiah when he said, "Go to this [26] people and say: You may hear and hear, but you will never understand; you may look and look, but you will never see. For this people's mind has [27] become gross; their ears are dulled, and their eyes are closed. Otherwise, their eyes might see, their ears hear, and their mind understand, and then they might turn again, and I would heal them." Therefore take notice [28] that this salvation of God has been sent to the Gentiles; the Gentiles will listen.'[n]

Two years in Rome

He stayed there two full years at his [30] own expense, with a welcome for all who came to him, proclaiming the [31] kingdom of God and teaching the facts about the Lord Jesus Christ quite openly and without hindrance.

n Some witnesses add (29) After he had spoken, the Jews went away, arguing vigorously among themselves.

THE LETTER OF PAUL TO THE

ROMANS

The Gospel of Christ

1 FROM PAUL, servant of Christ Jesus, apostle by God's call, set apart for the service of the Gospel.

2 This gospel God announced beforehand in sacred scriptures through his **3** prophets. It is about his Son: on the human level he was born of David's **4** stock, but on the level of the spirit—the Holy Spirit—he was declared Son of God by a mighty act in that he rose from the dead:*a* it is about Jesus **5** Christ our Lord. Through him I received the privilege of a commission in his name to lead to faith and obedi-**6** ence men in all nations, yourselves among them, you who have heard the call and belong to Jesus Christ.

Greetings and thanksgiving

7 I send greetings to all of you in Rome whom God loves and has called to be his dedicated people. Grace and peace to you from God our Father and the Lord Jesus Christ.

8 Let me begin by thanking my God, through Jesus Christ, for you all, because all over the world they are tell-**9** ing the story of your faith. God is my witness, the God to whom I offer the humble service of my spirit by preaching the gospel of his Son: God knows how continually I make mention of **10** you in my prayers, and am always asking that by his will I may, somehow or other, succeed at long last in **11** coming to visit you. For I long to see you; I want to bring you some spirit-**12** ual gift to make you strong; or rather, I want to be among you to be myself encouraged by your faith as well as you by mine.

God's way of righting wrong

13 But I should like you to know,*b* my brothers, that I have often planned to come, though so far without success,

in the hope of achieving something among you, as I have in other parts of the world. I am under obligation to **14** Greek and non-Greek, to learned and simple; hence my eagerness to declare **15** the Gospel to you in Rome as well as to others. For I am not ashamed of **16** the Gospel. It is the saving power of God for everyone who has faith—the Jew first, but the Greek also—because **17** here is revealed God's way of righting wrong, a way that starts from faith and ends in faith;*c* as Scripture says, 'he shall gain life who is justified through faith'.

The godless wickedness of men

For we see divine retribution revealed **18** from heaven and falling upon all the godless wickedness of men. In their wickedness they are stifling the truth. For all that may be known of God by **19** men lies plain before their eyes; indeed God himself has disclosed it to them. His invisible attributes, that is **20** to say his everlasting power and deity, have been visible, ever since the world began, to the eye of reason, in the things he has made. There is therefore no possible defence for their conduct; knowing God, they have refused to **21** honour him as God, or to render him thanks. Hence all their thinking has ended in futility, and their misguided minds are plunged in darkness. They **22** boast of their wisdom, but they have made fools of themselves, exchanging **23** the splendour of immortal God for an image shaped like mortal man, even for images like birds, beasts, and creeping things.

God has given them up

For this reason God has given them **24** up to the vileness of their own desires, and the consequent degradation of their bodies, because they have **25**

a Or declared Son of God with full powers from the time when he rose from the dead.   *b* Some witnesses read I believe you know.   *c* Or . . . wrong. It is based on faith and addressed to faith.

bartered away the true God for a false one,[d] and have offered reverence and worship to created things instead of to the Creator, who is blessed for ever; amen.

26 In consequence, I say, God has given them up to shameful passions. Their women have exchanged natural 27 intercourse for unnatural, and their men in turn, giving up natural relations with women, burn with lust for one another; males behave indecently with males, and are paid in their own persons the fitting wage of such perversion.

28 Thus, because they have not seen fit to acknowledge God, he has given them up to their own depraved reason. This leads them to break all rules of 29 conduct. They are filled with every kind of injustice, mischief, rapacity, and malice; they are one mass of envy, murder, rivalry, treachery, and mal-30 evolence; whisperers and scandal-mongers, hateful to God, insolent, arrogant, and boastful; they invent new kinds of mischief, they show no 31 loyalty to parents, no conscience, no fidelity to their plighted word; they are without natural affection and 32 without pity. They know well enough the just decree of God, that those who behave like this deserve to die, and yet they do it; not only so, they actually applaud such practices.

The day of retribution

2 You therefore have no defence—you who sit in judgement, whoever you may be—for in judging your fellow-man you condemn yourself, since you, 2 the judge, are equally guilty. It is admitted that God's judgement is rightly passed upon all who commit 3 such crimes as these; and do you imagine—you who pass judgement on the guilty while committing the same crimes yourself—do you imagine that you, any more than they, will escape 4 the judgement of God? Or do you think lightly of his wealth of kindness, of tolerance, and of patience, without recognizing that God's kindness is meant to lead you to a change of 5 heart? In the rigid obstinacy of your heart you are laying up for yourself a store of retribution for the day of retribution, when God's just judge-6 ment will be revealed, and he will pay 7 every man for what he has done. To those who pursue glory, honour, and immortality by steady persistence in

well-doing, he will give eternal life; but for those who are governed by 8 selfish ambition, who refuse obedience to the truth and take the wrong for their guide, there will be the fury of retribution. There will be trouble and 9 distress for every human being who is an evil-doer, for the Jew first and for the Greek also; and for every well- 10 doer there will be glory, honour, and peace, for the Jew first and also for the Greek.

How God will judge

For God has no favourites: those who 11 12 have sinned outside the pale of the Law of Moses will perish outside its pale, and all who have sinned under that law will be judged by the law. It is not by hearing the law, but by 13 doing it, that men will be justified before God. When Gentiles who do not 14 possess the law carry out its precepts by the light of nature, then, although they have no law, they are their own law, for they display the effect of the 15 law inscribed on their hearts. Their conscience is called as witness, and their own thoughts argue the case on either side, against them or even for them, on the day when God judges 16 the secrets of human hearts through Christ Jesus. So my gospel declares.

But as for you—you may bear the 17 name of Jew; you rely upon the law and are proud of your God; you know 18 his will; instructed by the law, you know right from wrong; you are 19 confident that you are the one to guide the blind, to enlighten the benighted, to train the stupid, and 20 to teach the immature, because in the law you see the very shape of knowledge and truth. You, then, who teach 21 your fellow-man, do you fail to teach yourself? You proclaim, 'Do not steal'; but are you yourself a thief? You say, 'Do not commit adultery'; 22 but are you an adulterer? You abominate false gods; but do you rob their shrines? While you take pride in the 23 law, you dishonour God by breaking it. For, as Scripture says, 'Because of 24 you the name of God is dishonoured among the Gentiles.'

The true Jew

Circumcision has value, provided you 25 keep the law; but if you break the law, then your circumcision is as if it had never been. Equally, if an un- 26 circumcised man keeps the precepts

d Or the truth of God for the lie.

of the law, will he not count as cir-
27 cumcised? He may be uncircumcised
in his natural state, but by fulfilling
the law he will pass judgement on you
who break it, for all your written code
28 and your circumcision. The true Jew
is not he who is such in externals,
neither is the true circumcision the
29 external mark in the flesh. The true
Jew is he who is such inwardly, and
the true circumcision is of the heart,
directed not by written precepts but
by the Spirit; such a man receives his
commendation not from men but from
God.

3 Then what advantage has the Jew?
What is the value of circumcision?
2 Great, in every way. In the first place,
the Jews were entrusted with the
3 oracles of God. What if some of them
were unfaithful? Will their faithless-
ness cancel the faithfulness of God?
4 Certainly not! God must be true
though every man living were a liar;
for we read in Scripture, 'When thou
speakest thou shalt be vindicated, and
win the verdict when thou art on
trial.'

All under the power of sin

5 Another question: if our injustice
serves to bring out God's justice, what
are we to say? Is it unjust of God (I
speak of him in human terms) to
6 bring retribution upon us? Certainly
not! If God were unjust, how could
he judge the world?
7 Again, if the truth of God brings him
all the greater honour because of my
falsehood, why should I any longer
8 be condemned as a sinner? Why not
indeed 'do evil that good may come',
as some libellously report me as saying?
To condemn such men as these is surely
no injustice.
9 What then? Are we Jews any better
off?[e] No, not at all![f] For we have already drawn up the accusation that
Jews and Greeks alike are all under
10 the power of sin. This has scriptural
warrant:

'There is no just man, not one;
11 no one who understands, no one who
seeks God.
12 All have swerved aside, all alike have
become debased;
there is no one to show kindness; no,
not one.

13 Their throat is an open grave,
they use their tongues for treachery,
adders' venom is on their lips,
14 and their mouth is full of bitter curses.

Their feet hasten to shed blood, 15
ruin and misery lie along their paths, 16
they are strangers to the high-road of 17
peace,
and reverence for God does not enter 18
their thoughts.'

Now all the words of the law are 19
addressed, as we know, to those who
are within the pale of the law, so that
no one may have anything to say in
self-defence, but the whole world may
be exposed to the judgement of God.
For (again from Scripture) 'no human 20
being can be justified in the sight of
God' for having kept the law: law
brings only the consciousness of sin.

Justified by God's free grace

But now, quite independently of law, 21
God's justice has been brought to
light. The Law and the prophets both
bear witness to it: it is God's way 22
of righting wrong, effective through
faith in Christ for all who have such
faith—all, without distinction. For all 23
alike have sinned, and are deprived
of the divine splendour, and all are 24
justified by God's free grace alone,
through his act of liberation in the
person of Christ Jesus. For God de- 25
signed him to be the means of expiating
sin by his sacrificial death, effective
through faith. God meant by this to
demonstrate his justice, because in
his forbearance he had overlooked the
sins of the past—to demonstrate his 26
justice now in the present, showing
that he is himself just and also justi-
fies any man who puts his faith in
Jesus.
What room then is left for human 27
pride? It is excluded. And on what
principle? The keeping of the law
would not exclude it, but faith does.
For our argument is that a man is 28
justified by faith quite apart from
success in keeping the law.
Do you suppose God is the God of 29
the Jews alone? Is he not the God of
Gentiles also? Certainly, of Gentiles
also, if it be true that God is one. 30
And he will therefore justify both the
circumcised in virtue of their faith,
and the uncircumcised through their
faith. Does this mean that we are 31
using faith to undermine law? By no
means: we are placing law itself on a
firmer footing.

Abraham's faith

What, then, are we to say about 4
Abraham, our ancestor in the natural

---

e Or Are we Jews any worse off?   f Or Not in all respects.

2 line? If Abraham was justified by anything he had done, then he has a ground for pride. But he has no such 3 ground before God; for what does Scripture say? 'Abraham put his faith in God, and that faith was counted 4 to him as righteousness.' Now if a man does a piece of work, his wages are not 'counted' as a favour; they 5 are paid as debt. But if without any work to his credit he simply puts his faith in him who acquits the guilty, then his faith is indeed 'counted as 6 righteousness'. In the same sense David speaks of the happiness of the man whom God 'counts' as just, apart from any specific acts of justice: 7 'Happy are they', he says, 'whose lawless deeds are forgiven, whose sins 8 are buried away; happy is the man whose sins the Lord does not count 9 against him.' Is this happiness confined to the circumcised, or is it for the uncircumcised also? Consider: we say, 'Abraham's faith was counted as 10 righteousness'; in what circumstances was it so counted? Was he circumcised at the time, or not? He was not yet circumcised, but uncircumcised; 11 and he later received the symbolic rite of circumcision as the hall-mark of the righteousness which faith had given him when he was still uncircumcised. Consequently, he is the father of all who have faith when uncircumcised, so that righteousness is 'coun-12 ted' to them; and at the same time he is the father of such of the circumcised as do not rely upon their circumcision alone, but also walk in the footprints of the faith which our father Abraham had while he was yet uncircumcised.

13 For it was not through law that Abraham, or his posterity, was given the promise that the world should be his inheritance, but through the righteousness that came from faith. 14 For if those who hold by the law, and they alone, are heirs, then faith is empty and the promise goes for noth-15 ing, because law can bring only retribution; but where there is no law 16 there can be no breach of law. The promise was made on the ground of faith, in order that it might be a matter of sheer grace, and that it might be valid for all Abraham's posterity, not only for those who hold by the law, but for those also who have the faith of Abraham. For he is 17 the father of us all, as Scripture says:

'I have appointed you to be father of many nations.' This promise, then, was valid before God, the God in whom he put his faith, the God who makes the dead live and summons things that are not yet in existence as if they already were. When hope seemed 18 hopeless, his faith was such that he became 'father of many nations', in agreement with the words which had been spoken to him: 'Thus shall your descendants be.' Without any weak-19 ening of faith he contemplated his own body, as good as dead (for he was about a hundred years old), and the deadness of Sarah's womb, and never 20 doubted God's promise in unbelief, but, strong in faith, gave honour to God, in the firm conviction of his 21 power to do what he had promised. And that is why Abraham's faith was 22 'counted to him as righteousness'.

Those words were written, not for 23 Abraham's sake alone, but for our 24 sake too: it is to be 'counted' in the same way to us who have faith in the God who raised Jesus our Lord from the dead; for he was given up to death 25 for our misdeeds, and raised to life to justify us.*g*

At peace with God

Therefore, now that we have been 5 justified through faith, let us continue at peace*h* with God through our Lord Jesus Christ, through whom we have 2 been allowed to enter the sphere of God's grace, where we now stand. Let us exult*i* in the hope of the divine splendour that is to be ours. More 3 than this: let us even exult*j* in our present sufferings, because we know that suffering trains us to endure, and 4 endurance brings proof that we have stood the test, and this proof is the ground of hope. Such a hope is no 5 mockery, because God's love has flooded our inmost heart through the Holy Spirit he has given us.

Reconciliation through Christ

For at the very time when we were 6 still powerless, then Christ died for the wicked. Even for a just man one 7 of us would hardly die, though perhaps for a good man one might actually brave death; but Christ died for us 8 while we were yet sinners, and that is God's own proof of his love towards us. And so, since we have now been 9 justified by Christ's sacrificial death,

we shall all the more certainly be saved through him from final retribu-
10 tion. For if, when we were God's enemies, we were reconciled to him through the death of his Son, how much more, now that we are reconciled, shall we be saved by his life!
11 But that is not all: we also exult in God through our Lord Jesus, through whom we have now been granted reconciliation.

Adam and Christ

12 Mark what follows. It was through one man that sin entered the world, and through sin death, and thus death pervaded the whole human race, inasmuch as all men have sinned.
13 For sin was already in the world before there was law, though in the absence of law no reckoning is kept
14 of sin. But death held sway from Adam to Moses, even over those who had not sinned as Adam did, by disobeying a direct command—and Adam foreshadows the Man who was to come.
15 But God's act of grace is out of all proportion to Adam's wrongdoing. For if the wrongdoing of that one man brought death upon so many, its effect is vastly exceeded by the grace of God and the gift that came to so many by the grace of the one man,
16 Jesus Christ. And again, the gift of God is not to be compared in its effect with that one man's sin; for the judicial action, following upon the one offence, issued in a verdict of condemnation, but the act of grace, following upon so many misdeeds, issued in
17 a verdict of acquittal. For if by the wrongdoing of that one man death established its reign, through a single sinner, much more shall those who receive in far greater measure God's grace, and his gift of righteousness, live and reign through the one man, Jesus Christ.
18 It follows, then, that as the issue of one misdeed was condemnation for all men, so the issue of one just act is
19 acquittal and life for all men. For as through the disobedience of the one man the many were made sinners, so through the obedience of the one man the many will be made righteous.
20 Law intruded into this process to multiply law-breaking. But where sin was thus multiplied, grace immeasur-
21 ably exceeded it, in order that, as sin established its reign by way of death, so God's grace might establish its

reign in righteousness, and issue in eternal life through Jesus Christ our Lord.

Dead to sin and alive to God

What are we to say, then? Shall we 6 persist in sin, so that there may be all the more grace? No, no! We died to 2 sin: how can we live in it any longer? Have you forgotten that when we were 3 baptized into union with Christ Jesus we were baptized into his death? By 4 baptism we were buried with him, and lay dead, in order that, as Christ was raised from the dead in the splendour of the Father, so also we might set our feet upon the new path of life.

For if we have become incorporate 5 with him in a death like his, we shall also be one with him in a resurrection like his. We know that the man 6 we once were has been crucified with Christ, for the destruction of the sinful self, so that we may no longer be the slaves of sin, since a dead man 7 is no longer answerable for his sin. But if we thus died with Christ, we 8 believe that we shall also come to life with him. We know that Christ, 9 once raised from the dead, is never to die again: he is no longer under the dominion of death. For in dying as he 10 died, he died to sin, once for all, and in living as he lives, he lives to God. In the same way you must regard 11 yourselves as dead to sin and alive to God, in union with Christ Jesus.

So sin must no longer reign in your 12 mortal body, exacting obedience to the body's desires. You must no 13 longer put its several parts at sin's disposal, as implements for doing wrong. No: put yourselves at the disposal of God, as dead men raised to life; yield your bodies to him as implements for doing right; for sin shall no longer 14 be your master, because you are no longer under law, but under the grace of God.

Two ways of life

What then? Are we to sin, because we 15 are not under law but under grace? Of course not. You know well enough 16 that if you put yourselves at the disposal of a master, to obey him, you are slaves of the master whom you obey; and this is true whether you serve sin, with death as its result; or obedience, with righteousness as its result. But God be thanked, you, 17 who once were slaves of sin, have yielded whole-hearted obedience to the

pattern of teaching to which you
18 were made subject,[k] and, emanci-
pated from sin, have become slaves of
19 righteousness (to use words that suit
your human weakness)—I mean, as
you once yielded your bodies to the
service of impurity and lawlessness,
making for moral anarchy, so now
you must yield them to the service
of righteousness, making for a holy
life.
20   When you were slaves of sin, you
were free from the control of righteous-
21 ness; and what was the gain? Nothing
but what now makes you ashamed,
22 for the end of that is death. But now,
freed from the commands of sin, and
bound to the service of God, your
gains are such as make for holiness,
23 and the end is eternal life. For sin
pays a wage, and the wage is death,
but God gives freely, and his gift is
eternal life, in union with Christ
Jesus our Lord.

An illustration from marriage

7 You cannot be unaware, my friends
—I am speaking to those who have
some knowledge of law—that a person
is subject to the law so long as he is
2 alive, and no longer. For example, a
married woman is by law bound to
her husband while he lives; but if her
husband dies, she is discharged from
the obligations of the marriage-law.
3 If, therefore, in her husband's lifetime
she consorts with another man, she
will incur the charge of adultery; but
if her husband dies she is free of the
law, and she does not commit adultery by consorting with another man.
4 So you, my friends, have died to the
law by becoming identified with the
body of Christ, and accordingly you
have found another husband in him
who rose from the dead, so that we
5 may bear fruit for God. While we
lived on the level of our lower nature,
the sinful passions evoked by the law
worked in our bodies, to bear fruit
6 for death. But now, having died to
that which held us bound, we are
discharged from the law, to serve God
in a new way, the way of the spirit, in
contrast to the old way, the way of a
written code.

Law and sin

7 What follows? Is the law identical
with sin? Of course not. But except
through law I should never have

become acquainted with sin. For
example, I should never have known
what it was to covet, if the law
had not said, 'Thou shalt not covet.'
Through that commandment sin found 8
its opportunity, and produced in
me all kinds of wrong desires. In
the absence of law, sin is a dead
thing. There was a time when, in the 9
absence of law, I was fully alive; but
when the commandment came, sin
sprang to life and I died. The com- 10
mandment which should have led to
life proved in my experience to lead
to death, because sin found its oppor- 11
tunity in the commandment, seduced
me, and through the commandment
killed me.
    Therefore the law is in itself holy, 12
and the commandment is holy and
just and good. Are we to say then 13
that this good thing was the death of
me? By no means. It was sin that
killed me, and thereby sin exposed
its true character: it used a good
thing to bring about my death, and
so, through the commandment, sin
became more sinful than ever.

Inner conflict

We know that the law is spiritual; but 14
I am not: I am unspiritual, the pur-
chased slave of sin. I do not even 15
acknowledge my own actions as mine,
for what I do is not what I want to do,
but what I detest. But if what I do is 16
against my will, it means that I agree
with the law and hold it to be admirable. But as things are, it is no longer 17
I who perform the action, but sin that
lodges in me. For I know that noth- 18
ing good lodges in me—in my unspiritual nature, I mean—for though
the will to do good is there, the deed
is not. The good which I want to do, 19
I fail to do; but what I do is the
wrong which is against my will; and 20
if what I do is against my will, clearly
it is no longer I who am the agent, but
sin that has its lodging in me.
    I discover this principle, then: that 21
when I want to do the right, only the
wrong is within my reach. In my in- 22
most self I delight in the law of God,
but I perceive that there is in my 23
bodily members a different law, fighting against the law that my reason
approves and making me a prisoner
under the law[l] that is in my members,
the law of sin. Miserable creature that 24
I am, who is there to rescue me out of
this body doomed to death[m]? God 25

k Or which was handed on to you.   l Or by means of the law.   m Or out of the body doomed
to this death.

alone, through Jesus Christ our Lord!
Thanks be to God! In a word then,
I myself, subject to God's law as a
rational being, am yet,[n] in my unspiritual nature, a slave to the law
of sin.

The conflict resolved

8 The conclusion of the matter is this:
there is no condemnation for those
2 who are united with Christ Jesus, because in Christ Jesus the life-giving
law of the Spirit has set you free from
3 the law of sin and death. What the
law could never do, because our lower
nature robbed it of all potency, God
has done: by sending his own Son in a
form like that of our own sinful nature,
and as a sacrifice for sin,[o] he has passed
judgement against sin within that very
4 nature, so that the commandment of
the law may find fulfilment in us, whose
conduct, no longer under the control
of our lower nature, is directed by the
Spirit.

The new life

5 Those who live on the level of our
lower nature have their outlook form-
6 ed by it, and that spells death; but
those who live on the level of the
spirit have the spiritual outlook, and
7 that is life and peace. For the outlook
of the lower nature is enmity with
God; it is not subject to the law of
8 God; indeed it cannot be: those who
live on such a level cannot possibly
please God.
9 But that is not how you live. You
are on the spiritual level, if only God's
Spirit dwells within you; and if a
man does not possess the Spirit of
10 Christ, he is no Christian. But if
Christ is dwelling within you, then
although the body is a dead thing
because you sinned, yet the spirit is
life itself because you have been justi-
11 fied.[p] Moreover, if the Spirit of him
who raised Jesus from the dead
dwells within you, then the God who
raised Christ Jesus from the dead
will also give new life to your mortal
bodies through his indwelling Spirit.
12 It follows, my friends, that our
lower nature has no claim upon us;
we are not obliged to live on that
13 level. If you do so, you must die. But
if by the Spirit you put to death all

the base pursuits of the body, then
you will live.
14 For all who are moved by the Spirit
15 of God are sons of God. The Spirit
you have received is not a spirit of
slavery leading you back into a life of
fear, but a Spirit that makes us sons,
enabling us to cry 'Abba! Father!'
16 In that cry the Spirit of God joins with
our spirit in testifying that we are
17 God's children; and if children, then
heirs. We are God's heirs and Christ's
fellow-heirs, if we share his sufferings
now in order to share his splendour
hereafter.

Waiting for final deliverance

18 For I reckon that the sufferings we
now endure bear no comparison with
the splendour, as yet unrevealed,
19 which is in store for us. For the created
universe waits with eager expectation
20 for God's sons to be revealed. It was
made the victim of frustration, not by
its own choice, but because of him
who made it so;[q] yet always there was
21 hope, because[r] the universe itself is to
be freed from the shackles of mortality and enter upon the liberty and
22 splendour of the children of God. Up
to the present, we know, the whole
created universe groans in all its
parts as if in the pangs of childbirth.
23 Not only so, but even we, to whom
the Spirit is given as firstfruits of the
harvest to come, are groaning inwardly while we wait for God to make
us his sons and[s] set our whole body
24 free. For we have been saved, though
only in hope. Now to see is no longer
to hope: why should a man endure
and wait[t] for what he already sees?
25 But if we hope for something we do
not yet see, then, in waiting for it, we
show our endurance.

The help of the Spirit

26 In the same way the Spirit comes to
the aid of our weakness. We do not
even know how we ought to pray[u] but
through our inarticulate groans the
27 Spirit himself is pleading for us, and
God who searches our inmost being
knows what the Spirit means, because he pleads for God's people in
God's own way; and in everything,
28 as we know, he co-operates for good
with those who love God[v] and are

n Or Thus, left to myself, while subject . . . rational being, I am yet . . .   o Or and to deal with
sin.   p Or so that you may live rightly.   q Or because God subjected it.   r Or with the
hope that . . .   s Some witnesses omit make us his sons and.   t Some witnesses read why should
a man hope . . .   u Or what it is right to pray for.   v Or and, as we know, all things work together for good for those who love God; some witnesses read and we know God himself co-operates for
good with those who love God.

29 called according to his purpose. For God knew his own before ever they were, and also ordained that they should be shaped to the likeness of his Son, that he might be the eldest 30 among a large family of brothers; and it is these, so fore-ordained, whom he has also called. And those whom he called he has justified, and to those whom he justified he has also given his splendour.

The love of Christ

31 With all this in mind, what are we to say? If God is on our side, who is 32 against us? He did not spare his own Son, but gave him up for us all; and with this gift how can he fail to lavish 33 upon us all he has to give? Who will be the accuser of God's chosen ones? It is God who pronounces acquittal; 34 then who can condemn? It is Christ— Christ who died, and, more than that, was raised from the dead—who is at God's right hand, and indeed pleads 35 our cause.[w] Then what can separate us from the love of Christ? Can affliction or hardship? Can persecution, hunger, nakedness, peril, or the 36 sword? 'We are being done to death for thy sake all day long,' as Scripture says; 'we have been treated like sheep 37 for slaughter'—and yet, in spite of all, overwhelming victory is ours through 38 him who loved us. For I am convinced that there is nothing in death or life, in the realm of spirits or superhuman powers, in the world as it is or the world as it shall be, in the forces of 39 the universe, in heights or depths— nothing in all creation that can separate us from the love of God in Christ Jesus our Lord.

The privileges of the Israelites

9 I am speaking the truth as a Christian, and my own conscience, enlightened by the Holy Spirit, assures 2 me it is no lie: in my heart there is 3 great grief and unceasing sorrow. For I could even pray to be outcast from Christ myself for the sake of my bro- 4 thers, my natural kinsfolk. They are Israelites: theirs were made God's sons; theirs is the splendour of the divine presence, theirs the covenants, the law, the temple worship, and the 5 promises. Theirs are the patriarchs,

and from them, in natural descent, sprang the Messiah.[x] May God, supreme above all, be blessed for ever![y] Amen.

The true Israelites

6 It is impossible that the word of God should have proved false. For not all descendants of Israel are truly Israel, 7 nor, because they are Abraham's offspring, are they all his true children;[z] but, in the words of Scripture, 'Through the line of Isaac your descendants shall be traced.'[a] That is to 8 say, it is not those born in the course of nature who are children of God; it is the children born through God's promise who are reckoned as Abraham's 9 descendants. For the promise runs: 'At the time fixed I will come, and Sarah shall have a son.'

10 But that is not all, for Rebekah's children had one and the same father, our ancestor Isaac; and yet, in order 11 that God's selective purpose might stand, based not upon men's deeds 12 but upon the call of God, she was told, even before they were born, when they had as yet done nothing, good or ill, 'The elder shall be servant to the 13 younger'; and that accords with the text of Scripture, 'Jacob I loved and Esau I hated.'

Establishing God's justice

14 What shall we say to that? Is God to be charged with injustice? By no 15 means. For he says to Moses, 'Where I show mercy, I will show mercy, and 16 where I pity, I will pity.' Thus it does not depend on man's will or effort, but on God's mercy. For Scripture 17 says to Pharaoh, 'I have raised you up for this very purpose, to exhibit my power in my dealings with you, and to spread my fame over all the world.' 18 Thus he not only shows mercy as he chooses, but also makes men stubborn as he chooses.

19 You will say, 'Then why does God blame a man? For who can resist his 20 will?' Who are you, sir, to answer God back? Can the pot speak to the potter and say, 'Why did you make me like this?'? Surely the potter can 21 do what he likes with the clay. Is he not free to make out of the same lump two vessels, one to be treasured, the other for common use?

w Or Who will be the accuser of God's chosen ones? Will it be God himself? No, he it is who pronounces acquittal. Who will be the judge to condemn? Will it be Christ—he who died, and, more than that, . . . right hand? No, he it is who pleads our cause.   x Greek Christ.   y Or sprang the Messiah, supreme above all, God blessed for ever; or sprang the Messiah, who is supreme above all. Blessed be God for ever!   z Or all children of God.   a Or God's call shall be for your descendants in the line of Isaac.

22 But what if God, desiring to exhibit[b] his retribution at work and to make his power known, tolerated very patiently those vessels which were objects of retribution due for destruc-
23 tion, and did so in order to make known the full wealth of his splendour upon vessels which were objects of mercy, and which from the first had been prepared for this splendour?
24 Such vessels are we, whom he has called from among Gentiles as well as
25 Jews, as it says in the Book of Hosea: 'Those who were not my people I will call My People, and the unloved
26 nation I will call My Beloved. For in the very place where they were told "you are no people of mine", they shall be called Sons of the living
27 God.' But Isaiah makes this proclamation about Israel: 'Though the Israelites be countless as the sands of the sea, only a remnant shall be saved;
28 for the Lord's sentence on the land
29 will be summary and final'; as also he said previously, 'If the Lord of Hosts had not left us the mere germ of a nation, we should have become like Sodom, and no better than Gomorrah.'

Righteousness based on faith

30 Then what are we to say? That Gentiles, who made no effort after righteousness, nevertheless achieved it, a righteousness based on faith;
31 whereas Israel made great efforts after a law of righteousness, but never
32 attained to it. Why was this? Because their efforts were not based on faith, but (as they supposed) on deeds. They
33 fell over the 'stone' mentioned in Scripture: 'Here I lay in Zion a stone to trip over, a rock to stumble against; but he who has faith in him will not be put to shame.'

The salvation of the Gentiles

10 Brothers, my deepest desire and my prayer to God is for their salvation.
2 To their zeal for God I can testify;
3 but it is an ill-informed zeal. For they ignore God's way of righteousness, and try to set up their own, and therefore they have not submitted them-
4 selves to God's righteousness. For Christ ends the law and brings righteousness for everyone who has faith.[c]
5 Of legal righteousness Moses writes, 'The man who does this shall gain life
6 by it.' But the righteousness that comes by faith says, 'Do not say to

yourself, "Who can go up to heaven?"'
7 (that is to bring Christ down), 'or, "Who can go down to the abyss?"' (to bring Christ up from the dead). But what does it say? 'The word is
8 near you: it is upon your lips and in your heart.' This means the word of faith which we proclaim. If on your
9 lips is the confession, 'Jesus is Lord', and in your heart the faith that God raised him from the dead, then you will find salvation. For the faith that
10 leads to righteousness is in the heart, and the confession that leads to salvation is upon the lips.
Scripture says, 'Everyone who has
11 faith in him will be saved from shame' —everyone: there is no distinction
12 between Jew and Greek, because the same Lord is Lord of all, and is rich enough for the need of all who invoke him. For everyone, as it says again—
13 'everyone who invokes the name of the Lord will be saved'. How could
14 they invoke one in whom they had no faith? And how could they have faith in one they had never heard of? And how hear without someone to spread the news? And how could anyone
15 spread the news without a commission to do so? And that is what Scripture affirms: 'How welcome are the feet of the messengers of good news!'
But not all have responded to the
16 good news. For Isaiah says, 'Lord, who has believed our message?' We
17 conclude that faith is awakened by the message, and the message that awakens it comes through the word of Christ.
But, I ask, can it be that they never
18 heard it? Of course they did: 'Their voice has sounded all over the earth, and their words to the bounds of the inhabited world.' But, I ask again, can
19 it be that Israel failed to recognize the message? In reply, I first cite Moses, who says, 'I will use a nation that is no nation to stir your envy, and a foolish nation to rouse your anger.' But Isaiah is still more daring:
20 'I was found', he says, 'by those who were not looking for me; I was clearly shown to those who never asked about me'; while to Israel he says,
21 'All day long I have stretched out my hands to an unruly and defiant people.'

God's plan for Israel

I ask then, has God rejected his
11 people? I cannot believe it! I am an

b Or although he had the will to exhibit . . . righteousness for everyone who has faith.

c Or Christ is the end of the law as a way to

Israelite myself, of the stock of Abraham, of the tribe of Benjamin. No! God has not rejected the people which he acknowledged of old as his own. You know (do you not?) what Scripture says in the story of Elijah —how Elijah pleads with God against Israel: 'Lord, they have killed thy prophets, they have torn down thine altars, and I alone am left, and they are seeking my life.' But what does the divine voice say to him? 'I have left myself seven thousand men who have not knelt to Baal.' In just the same way at the present time a 'remnant' has come into being, selected by the grace of God. But if it is by grace, then it does not rest on deeds done, or grace would cease to be grace. What follows? What Israel sought, Israel has not achieved, but the selected few have achieved it. The rest were made blind to the truth, exactly as it stands written: 'God brought upon them a numbness of spirit; he gave them blind eyes and deaf ears, and so it is still.' Similarly David says:

'May their table be a snare and a trap, both stumbling-block and retribution! May their eyes become so dim that they lose their sight! Bow down their backs unceasingly!'

I now ask, did their failure mean complete downfall? Far from it! Because they offended, salvation has come to the Gentiles, to stir Israel to emulation. But if their offence means the enrichment of the world, and if their falling-off means the enrichment of the Gentiles, how much more their coming to full strength!

Illustration from the olive-tree

But I have something to say to you Gentiles. I am a missionary to the Gentiles, and as such I give all honour to that ministry when I try to stir emulation in the men of my own race, and so to save some of them. For if their rejection has meant the reconciliation of the world, what will their acceptance mean? Nothing less than life from the dead! If the first portion of dough is consecrated, so is the whole lump. If the root is consecrated, so are the branches. But if some of the branches have been lopped off, and you, a wild olive, have been grafted in among them, and have come to share the same root and sap as the olive, do not make yourself superior to the branches. If you do so, remember that it is not you who sustain the root: the root sustains you.

You will say, 'Branches were lopped off so that I might be grafted in.' Very well: they were lopped off for lack of faith, and by faith you hold your place. Put away your pride, and be on your guard; for if God did not spare the native branches, no more will he spare you. Observe the kindness and the severity of God—severity to those who fell away, divine kindness to you, if only you remain within its scope; otherwise you too will be cut off, whereas they, if they do not continue faithless, will be grafted in; for it is in God's power to graft them in again. For if you were cut from your native wild olive and against all nature grafted into the cultivated olive, how much more readily will they, the natural olive-branches, be grafted into their native stock!

The mystery of God's mercy

For there is a deep truth here, my brothers, of which I want you to take account, so that you may not be complacent about your own discernment: this partial blindness has come upon Israel only until the Gentiles have been admitted in full strength; when that has happened, the whole of Israel will be saved, in agreement with the text of Scripture:

'From Zion shall come the Deliverer; he shall remove wickedness from Jacob. And this is the covenant I will grant them, when I take away their sins.'

In the spreading of the Gospel they are treated as God's enemies for your sake; but God's choice stands, and they are his friends for the sake of the patriarchs. For the gracious gifts of God and his calling are irrevocable. Just as formerly you were disobedient to God, but now have received mercy in the time of their disobedience, so now, when you receive mercy, they have proved disobedient, but only in order that they too may receive mercy. For in making all mankind prisoners to disobedience, God's purpose was to show mercy to all mankind.

O depth of wealth, wisdom, and knowledge in God! How unsearchable his judgements, how untraceable his ways! Who knows the mind of the Lord? Who has been his counsellor? Who has ever made a gift to him, to

36 receive a gift in return? Source, Guide, and Goal of all that is—to him be glory for ever! Amen.

Unity and diversity in the body of Christ

12 Therefore, my brothers, I implore you by God's mercy to offer your very selves to him: a living sacrifice, dedicated and fit for his acceptance, the worship offered by mind and heart.[d]

2 Adapt yourselves no longer to the pattern of this present world, but let your minds be remade and your whole nature thus transformed. Then you will be able to discern the will of God, and to know what is good, acceptable, and perfect.

3 In virtue of the gift that God in his grace has given me I say to everyone among you: do not be conceited or think too highly of yourself; but think your way to a sober estimate based on the measure of faith that 4 God has dealt to each of you. For just as in a single human body there are many limbs and organs, all with 5 different functions, so all of us, united with Christ, form one body, serving individually as limbs and organs to one another.

6 The gifts we possess differ as they are allotted to us by God's grace, and must be exercised accordingly: the gift of inspired utterance, for example, 7 in proportion to a man's faith; or the gift of administration, in administration. A teacher should employ his 8 gift in teaching, and one who has the gift of stirring speech should use it to stir his hearers. If you give to charity, give with all your heart; if you are a leader, exert yourself to lead; if you are helping others in distress, do it cheerfully.

The Christian way of life

9 Love in all sincerity, loathing evil and 10 clinging to the good. Let love for our brotherhood breed warmth of mutual affection. Give pride of place to one another in esteem.

11 With unflagging energy, in ardour of spirit, serve the Lord.[e]

12 Let hope keep you joyful; in trouble stand firm; persist in prayer.

13 Contribute to the needs of God's people, and practise hospitality.

14 Call down blessings on your persecutors—blessings, not curses.

15 With the joyful be joyful, and mourn with the mourners.

Care as much about each other as about yourselves. Do not be haughty, but go about with humble folk. Do not keep thinking how wise you are.

Never pay back evil for evil. Let 1 your aims be such as all men count honourable. If possible, so far as it 1 lies with you, live at peace with all men. My dear friends, do not seek 1 revenge, but leave a place for divine retribution; for there is a text which reads, 'Justice is mine, says the Lord, I will repay.' But there is another 2 text: 'If your enemy is hungry, feed him; if he is thirsty, give him a drink; by doing this you will heap live coals on his head.' Do not let evil conquer 2 you, but use good to defeat evil.

Submission to authorities

Every person must submit to the 1 supreme authorities. There is no authority but by act of God, and the existing authorities are instituted by him; consequently anyone who rebels 2 against authority is resisting a divine institution, and those who so resist have themselves to thank for the punishment they will receive. For 3 government, a terror to crime, has no terrors for good behaviour. You wish to have no fear of the authorities? Then continue to do right and you will have their approval, for they are God's 4 agents working for your good. But if you are doing wrong, then you will have cause to fear them; it is not for nothing that they hold the power of the sword, for they are God's agents of punishment, for retribution on the offender. That is why you are obliged 5 to submit. It is an obligation imposed not merely by fear of retribution but by conscience. That is also why you 6 pay taxes. The authorities are in God's service and to these duties they devote their energies.

Obligations to all men

Discharge your obligations to all men; 7 pay tax and toll, reverence and respect, to those to whom they are due. Leave no claim outstanding against 8 you, except that of mutual love. He who loves his neighbour has satisfied every claim of the law. For the com- 9 mandments, 'Thou shalt not commit adultery, thou shalt not kill, thou shalt not steal, thou shalt not covet', and any other commandment there may be, are all summed up in the one rule, 'Love your neighbour as yourself.'

d Or . . . acceptance, for such is the worship which you, as rational creatures, should offer.
e Some witnesses read meet the demands of the hour.

Love cannot wrong a neighbour; therefore the whole law is summed up in love.[f]

In all this, remember how critical the moment is. It is time for you to wake out of sleep, for deliverance is nearer to us now than it was when 2 first we believed. It is far on in the night; day is near. Let us therefore throw off the deeds of darkness and put on our armour as soldiers of the 3 light. Let us behave with decency as befits the day: no revelling or drunkenness, no debauchery or vice, no quar- 4 rels or jealousies! Let Christ Jesus himself be the armour that you wear; give no more thought to satisfying the bodily appetites.

Mutual forbearance in the church

If a man is weak in his faith you must accept him without attempting to 2 settle doubtful points. For instance, one man will have faith enough to eat all kinds of food, while a weaker man 3 eats only vegetables. The man who eats must not hold in contempt the man who does not, and he who does not eat must not pass judgement on the one who does; for God has ac- 4 cepted him. Who are you to pass judgement on someone else's servant? Whether he stands or falls is his own Master's business; and stand he will, because his Master has power to enable him to stand.

5   Again, this man regards one day more highly than another, while that man regards all days alike. On such a point everyone should have reached 6 conviction in his own mind. He who respects the day has the Lord in mind in doing so, and he who eats meat has the Lord in mind when he eats, since he gives thanks to God; and he who abstains has the Lord in mind no less, since he too gives thanks to God.

7   For no one of us lives, and equally 8 no one of us dies, for himself alone. If we live, we live for the Lord; and if we die, we die for the Lord. Whether therefore we live or die, we belong 9 to the Lord. This is why Christ died and came to life again, to establish 10 his lordship over dead and living. You, sir, why do you pass judgement on your brother? And you, sir, why do you hold your brother in contempt? We shall all stand before God's tri- 11 bunal. For Scripture says, 'As I live,

says the Lord, to me every knee shall bow and every tongue acknowledge God.' So, you see, each of us will have 12 to answer for himself.

Conduct to be guided by love

Let us therefore cease judging one 13 another, but rather make this simple judgement: that no obstacle or stumbling-block be placed in a brother's way. I am absolutely con- 14 vinced, as a Christian,[g] that nothing is impure in itself; only, if a man considers a particular thing impure, then to him it is impure. If your bro- 15 ther is outraged by what you eat, then your conduct is no longer guided by love. Do not by your eating bring disaster to a man for whom Christ died! What for you is a good thing 16 must not become an occasion for slanderous talk; for the kingdom of 17 God is not eating and drinking, but justice, peace, and joy, inspired by the Holy Spirit. He who thus shows 18 himself a servant of Christ is acceptable to God and approved by men.

About scruples of conscience

Let us then pursue the things that 19 make for peace and build up the common life. Do not ruin the work of 20 God for the sake of food. Everything is pure in itself, but anything is bad for the man who by his eating causes another to fall. It is a fine thing to 21 abstain from eating meat or drinking wine, or doing anything which causes your brother's downfall. If you have 22 a clear conviction, apply it to yourself in the sight of God. Happy is the man who can make his decision with a clear conscience![h] But a man who 23 has doubts is guilty if he eats, because his action does not arise from his conviction, and anything which does not arise from conviction is sin.[i] Those of **15** us who have a robust conscience must accept as our own burden the tender scruples of weaker men, and not 2 consider ourselves. Each of us must consider his neighbour and think what is for his good and will build up the common life. For Christ too did 3 not consider himself, but might have said, in the words of Scripture, 'The reproaches of those who reproached thee fell upon me.' For all the ancient 4 scriptures were written for our own instruction, in order that through the encouragement they give us we may

f Or the whole law is fulfilled by love.   g Or on the authority of the Lord Jesus.   h Or who does not bring judgement upon himself by what he approves!   i See p. 941, note r.

5 maintain our hope with fortitude. And may God, the source of all fortitude and all encouragement, grant that you may agree with one another after 6 the manner of Christ Jesus, so that with one mind and one voice you may praise the God and Father of our Lord Jesus Christ.

Christ came for Jew and Gentile

7 In a word, accept one another as Christ accepted us, to the glory of 8 God. I mean that Christ became a servant of the Jewish people to maintain the truth of God by making good 9 his promises to the patriarchs, and at the same time to give the Gentiles cause to glorify God for his mercy. As Scripture says, 'Therefore I will praise thee among the Gentiles and 10 sing hymns to thy name'; and again, 'Gentiles, make merry together with 11 his own people'; and yet again, 'All Gentiles, praise the Lord; let all peo- 12 ples praise him.' Once again, Isaiah says, 'There shall be the Scion of Jesse, the one raised up to govern the Gentiles; on him the Gentiles 13 shall set their hope.' And may the God of hope fill you with all joy and peace by your faith in him, until, by the power of the Holy Spirit, you overflow with hope.

Paul's confidence and ambition

14 My friends, I have no doubt in my own mind that you yourselves are quite full of goodness and equipped with knowledge of every kind, well able to give advice to one another; 15 nevertheless I have written to refresh your memory, and written somewhat boldly at times, in virtue of the gift 16 I have from God. His grace has made me a minister of Christ Jesus to the Gentiles; my priestly service is the preaching of the gospel of God, and it falls to me to offer the Gentiles to him as[j] an acceptable sacrifice, consecrated by the Holy Spirit. 17 Thus in the fellowship of Christ Jesus I have ground for pride in the 18 service of God. I will venture to speak of those things alone in which I have been Christ's instrument to bring the Gentiles into his allegiance, by word 19 and deed, by the force of miraculous signs and by the power of the Holy Spirit. As a result I have completed the preaching of the gospel of Christ from Jerusalem as far round as Illyri- 20 cum. It is my ambition to bring the

Gospel to places where the very name of Christ has not been heard, for I do not want to build on another man's foundation; but, as Scripture says, 2

'They who had no news of him shall see,
and they who never heard of him shall understand.'

Paul's immediate plans

That is why I have been prevented all 2 this time from coming to you. But 2 now I have no further scope in these parts, and I have been longing for many years to visit you on my way 2 to Spain; for I hope to see you as I travel through, and to be sent there with your support after having enjoyed your company for a while. But at the moment I am on my way 2 to Jerusalem, on an errand to God's people there. For Macedonia and 2 Achaia have resolved to raise a common fund for the benefit of the poor among God's people at Jerusalem. They have resolved to do so, and in- 2 deed they are under an obligation to them. For if the Jewish Christians shared their spiritual treasures with the Gentiles, the Gentiles have a clear duty to contribute to their material needs. So when I have finished this 2 business and delivered the proceeds under my own seal, I shall set out for Spain by way of your city, and I am 2 sure that when I arrive I shall come to you with a full measure of the blessing of Christ.

I implore you by our Lord Jesus 3 Christ and by the love that the Spirit inspires, be my allies in the fight; pray to God for me that I may be 3 saved from unbelievers in Judaea and that my errand to Jerusalem may find acceptance with God's people, so 3 that by his will I may come to you in a happy frame of mind and enjoy a time of rest with you. The God of 3 peace be with you all. Amen.[k]

Personal messages

I commend to you Phoebe, a fellow- 1 Christian who holds office in the congregation at Cenchreae. Give her, in 2 the fellowship of the Lord, a welcome worthy of God's people, and stand by her in any business in which she may need your help, for she has herself been a good friend to many, including myself.

Give my greetings to Prisca and 3 Aquila, my fellow-workers in Christ

j Or ... of God, so that the worship which the Gentiles offer may be ... k See p. 941, note r.

4 Jesus. They risked their necks to save my life, and not I alone but all the gentile congregations are grateful 5 to them. Greet also the congregation at their house.

Give my greetings to my dear friend Epaenetus, the first convert to Christ in Asia, and to Mary, who toiled hard 7 for you. Greet Andronicus and Junias[l] my fellow-countrymen and comrades in captivity. They are eminent among the apostles, and they were Christians before I was.

8 Greetings to Ampliatus, my dear friend in the fellowship of the Lord, 9 to Urban my comrade in Christ, and 10 to my dear Stachys. My greetings to Apelles, well proved in Christ's service, to the household of Aristobulus, 11 and my countryman Herodion, and to those of the household of Narcissus who are in the Lord's fellowship. 12 Greet Tryphaena and Tryphosa, who toil in the Lord's service, and dear Persis who has toiled in his service 13 so long. Give my greetings to Rufus, an outstanding follower of the Lord, and to his mother, whom I call mother 14 too. Greet Asyncritus, Phlegon, Hermes, Patrobas, Hermas, and all friends 15 in their company. Greet Philologus and Julia,[m] Nereus and his sister, and Olympas, and all God's people associated with them.

16 Greet one another with the kiss of peace. All Christ's congregations send you their greetings.

17 I implore you, my friends, keep your eye on those who stir up quarrels and lead others astray, contrary to the teaching you received. Avoid them, 18 for such people are servants not of Christ our Lord but of their own appetites, and they seduce the minds of innocent people with smooth and specious words. The fame of your 19 obedience has spread everywhere. This makes me happy about you; yet I should wish you to be experts in goodness but simpletons in evil; and the 20 God of peace will soon crush Satan beneath your feet. The grace of our Lord Jesus be with you![n]

21 Greetings to you from my colleague Timothy, and from Lucius, Jason, and Sosipater my fellow-countrymen. (I Tertius, who took this letter down, 22 add my Christian greetings.) Greet- 23 ings also from Gaius, my host and host of the whole congregation, and from Erastus, treasurer of this city, and our brother Quartus.[o]

Glory to God!

25 To him who has power to make your standing sure, according to the Gospel I brought you and the proclamation of Jesus Christ, according to the revelation of that divine secret kept in silence for long ages but 26 now disclosed, and through prophetic scriptures by eternal God's command made known to all nations, to bring them to faith and obedience—to God 27 who alone is wise, through Jesus Christ,[p] be glory for endless ages! Amen.[q r]

---

l Or Junia; some witnesses read Julia, or Julias.   *m Or Julias; some witnesses read Junia, or Junias.*   *n The words The grace . . . with you are omitted at this point in some witnesses; in some, these or similar words are given as verse 24, and in some others after verse 27 (see note on verse 23). o Some witnesses add (24) The grace of our Lord Jesus Christ be with you all! Amen.*   *p Some witnesses insert to whom.*   *q Here some witnesses add The grace of our Lord Jesus Christ be with you! r Some witnesses place verses 25–7 at the end of chapter 14, one other places them at the end of chapter 15, and others omit them altogether.*

THE FIRST LETTER OF PAUL
TO THE
CORINTHIANS

Thanksgiving

1 FROM PAUL, apostle of Jesus Christ at God's call and by God's will, together with our colleague Sosthenes,
2 to the congregation of God's people at Corinth, dedicated to him in Christ Jesus, claimed by him as his own, along with all men everywhere who invoke the name of our Lord Jesus Christ—their Lord as well as ours.
3 Grace and peace to you from God our Father and the Lord Jesus Christ.
4 I am always thanking God for you.
5 I thank him for his grace given to you in Christ Jesus. I thank him for all the enrichment that has come to you in Christ. You possess full knowledge and you can give full expression to it,
6 because in you the evidence for the truth of Christ has found confirma-
7 tion. There is indeed no single gift you lack, while you wait expectantly for our Lord Jesus Christ to reveal him-
8 self. He will keep you firm to the end, without reproach on the Day of our
9 Lord Jesus. It is God himself who called you to share in the life of his Son Jesus Christ our Lord; and God keeps faith.

Divisions at Corinth condemned

10 I appeal to you, my brothers, in the name of our Lord Jesus Christ: agree among yourselves, and avoid divisions; be firmly joined in unity of
11 mind and thought. I have been told, my brothers, by Chloe's people that
12 there are quarrels among you. What I mean is this: each of you is saying, 'I am Paul's man', or 'I am for Apollos'; 'I follow Cephas', or 'I am
13 Christ's.' Surely Christ has not been divided among you! Was it Paul who was crucified for you? Was it in the name of Paul that you were baptized?
14 Thank God, I never baptized one of
15 you—except Crispus and Gaius. So no one can say you were baptized in
16 my name.—Yes, I did baptize the household of Stephanas; I cannot think of anyone else. Christ did not send me to baptize, but to proclaim the Gospel; and to do it without relying on the language of worldly wisdom, so that the fact of Christ on his cross might have its full weight.

God's wisdom and man's

This doctrine of the cross is sheer folly to those on their way to ruin, but to us who are on the way to salvation it is the power of God. Scripture says, 'I will destroy the wisdom of the wise, and bring to nothing the cleverness of the clever.' Where is your wise man now, your man of learning, or your subtle debater—limited, all of them, to this passing age? God has made the wisdom of this world look foolish. As God in his wisdom ordained, the world failed to find him by its wisdom, and he chose to save those who have faith by the folly of the Gospel. Jews call for miracles, Greeks look for wisdom; but we proclaim Christ—yes, Christ nailed to the cross; and though this is a stumbling-block to Jews and folly to Greeks, yet to those who have heard his call, Jews and Greeks alike, he is the power of God and the wisdom of God.

Divine folly is wiser than the wisdom of man, and divine weakness stronger than man's strength. My brothers, think what sort of people you are, whom God has called. Few of you are men of wisdom, by any human standard; few are powerful or highly born. Yet, to shame the wise, God has chosen what the world counts folly; and to shame what is strong, God has chosen what the world counts weakness. He has chosen things low and contemptible, mere nothings, to overthrow the existing order. And so there is no place for human pride in the presence of God. You are in Christ Jesus by God's act, for God has made him our wisdom; he is our righteousness; in him we are consecrated and set free. And so (in the words of Scripture), 'If a man must boast, let him boast of the Lord.'

Nothing but Jesus Christ

As for me, brothers, when I came to you, I declared the attested truth of God[a] without display of fine words or wisdom. I resolved that while I was with you I would think of nothing but Jesus Christ—Christ nailed to the cross. I came before you weak, nervous, and shaking with fear. The word I spoke, the gospel I proclaimed, did not sway you with subtle arguments; it carried conviction by spiritual power, so that your faith might be built not upon human wisdom but upon the power of God.

Revelations by the Spirit

And yet I do speak words of wisdom to those who are ripe for it, not a wisdom belonging to this passing age, nor to any of its governing powers, which are declining to their end; I speak God's hidden wisdom, his secret purpose framed from the very beginning to bring us to our full glory. The powers that rule the world have never known it; if they had, they would not have crucified the Lord of glory. But, in the words of Scripture, 'Things beyond our seeing, things beyond our hearing, things beyond our imagining, all prepared by God for those who love him', these it is that God has revealed to us through the Spirit.

For the Spirit explores everything, even the depths of God's own nature. Among men, who knows what a man is but the man's own spirit within him? In the same way, only the Spirit of God knows what God is. This is the Spirit that we have received from God, and not the spirit of the world, so that we may know all that God of his own grace has given us; and, because we are interpreting spiritual truths to those who have the Spirit, we speak of these gifts of God in words found for us not by our human wisdom but by the Spirit. A man who is unspiritual refuses what belongs to the Spirit of God; it is folly to him; he cannot grasp it, because it needs to be judged in the light of the Spirit. A man gifted with the Spirit can judge the worth of everything, but is not himself subject to judgement by his

fellow-men. For (in the words of Scripture) 'who knows the mind of the Lord? Who can advise him?' We, however, possess the mind of Christ.

All too human

For my part, my brothers, I could not speak to you as I should speak to people who have the Spirit. I had to deal with you on the merely natural plane, as infants in Christ. And so I gave you milk to drink, instead of solid food, for which you were not yet ready. Indeed, you are still not ready for it, for you are still on the merely natural plane. Can you not see that while there is jealousy and strife among you, you are living on the purely human level of your lower nature? When one says, 'I am Paul's man', and another, 'I am for Apollos', are you not all too human?

God's fellow-workers

After all, what is Apollos? What is Paul? We are simply God's agents in bringing you to the faith. Each of us performed the task which the Lord allotted to him: I planted the seed, and Apollos watered it; but God made it grow. Thus it is not the gardeners with their planting and watering who count, but God, who makes it grow. Whether they plant or water, they work as a team,[b] though each will get his own pay for his own labour. We are God's fellow-workers;[c] and you are God's garden.

Or again, you are God's building. I am like a skilled master-builder who by God's grace laid the foundation, and someone else is putting up the building. Let each take care how he builds. There can be no other foundation beyond that which is already laid; I mean Jesus Christ himself. If anyone builds on that foundation with gold, silver, and fine stone, or with wood, hay, and straw, the work that each man does will at last be brought to light; the day of judgement will expose it. For that day dawns in fire, and the fire will test the worth of each man's work. If a man's building stands, he will be rewarded; if it burns, he will have to bear the loss; and yet he will escape with his life, as one might from a fire. Surely you know that you are God's temple, where the Spirit of God dwells. Anyone who destroys God's temple will

---

a Some witnesses read I declared God's secret purpose . . .   b Or Whether they plant or water, it is all the same.   c Or We are fellow-workers in God's service.

himself be destroyed[d] by God, because the temple of God is holy; and that temple you are.

True wisdom

18 Make no mistake about this: if there is anyone among you who fancies himself wise—wise, I mean, by the standards of this passing age—he must 19 become a fool to gain true wisdom. For the wisdom of this world is folly in God's sight. Scripture says, 'He traps 20 the wise in their own cunning', and again, 'The Lord knows that the 21 arguments of the wise are futile.' So never make mere men a cause for pride. For though everything belongs 22 to you—Paul, Apollos, and Cephas, the world, life, and death, the present and the future, all of them belong to 23 you—yet you belong to Christ, and Christ to God.

'My judge is the Lord'

4 We must be regarded as Christ's subordinates and as stewards of the 2 secrets of God. Well then, stewards are expected to show themselves trust- 3 worthy. For my part, if I am called to account by you or by any human court of judgement, it does not matter to me in the least. Why, I do not even 4 pass judgement on myself, for I have nothing on my conscience; but that does not mean I stand acquitted. My 5 judge is the Lord. So pass no premature judgement; wait until the time comes. For he will bring to light what darkness hides, and disclose men's inward motives; then will be the time for each to receive from God such praise as he deserves.

'Keep within the rules'

6 Into this general picture, my friends, I have brought Apollos and myself on your account, so that you may take our case as an example, and learn to 'keep within the rules', as they say, and may not be inflated with pride as you patronize one and flout the other. 7 Who makes you, my friend, so important? What do you possess that was not given you? If then you really received it all as a gift, why take the credit to yourself? 8 All of you, no doubt, have everything you could desire. You have come into your fortune already. You have come into your kingdom—and left us out. How I wish you had indeed won your kingdom; then you might share it with us! For it seems 9 to me God has made us apostles the most abject of mankind. We are like men condemned to death in the arena, a spectacle to the whole universe—angels as well as men. We are fools 10 for Christ's sake, while you are such sensible Christians. We are weak; you are so powerful. We are in disgrace; you are honoured. To this day we go 11 hungry and thirsty and in rags; we are roughly handled; we wander from place to place; we wear ourselves out 12 working with our own hands. They curse us, and we bless; they persecute us, and we submit to it; they slander 13 us, and we humbly make our appeal. We are treated as the scum of the earth, the dregs of humanity, to this very day.

An appeal to reason

I am not writing thus to shame you, 14 but to bring you to reason; for you are my dear children. You may have 15 ten thousand tutors in Christ, but you have only one father. For in Christ Jesus you are my offspring, and mine alone, through the preaching of the Gospel. I appeal to you there- 16 fore to follow my example. That is 17 the very reason why I have sent Timothy, who is a dear son to me and a most trustworthy Christian; he will remind you of the way of life in Christ which I follow, and which I teach everywhere in all our congregations. There are certain persons who are 18 filled with self-importance because they think I am not coming to Corinth. I shall come very soon, if the 19 Lord will; and then I shall take the measure of these self-important people, not by what they say, but by what power is in them. The kingdom of God 20 is not a matter of talk, but of power. Choose, then: am I to come to you 21 with a rod in my hand, or in love and a gentle spirit?

About sexual immorality

I actually hear reports of sexual im- 5 morality among you, immorality such as even pagans do not tolerate: the union of a man with his father's wife. And you can still be proud of your- 2 selves! You ought to have gone into mourning; a man who has done such a deed should have been rooted out of your company. For my part, though 3 I am absent in body, I am present in

d Some witnesses read is himself destroyed.

spirit, and my judgement upon the man who did this thing is already 4 given, as if I were indeed present: you all being assembled in the name of our Lord Jesus, and I with you in spirit, with the power of our Lord Jesus 5 over us, this man is to be consigned to Satan for the destruction of the body, so that his spirit may be saved on the Day of the Lord.

Discipline within the fellowship

6 Your self-satisfaction ill becomes you. Have you never heard the saying, 'A little leaven leavens all the dough'? 7 The old leaven of corruption is working among you. Purge it out, and then you will be bread of a new baking. As Christians you are unleavened Passover bread; for indeed our Passover has begun; the sacrifice is offered 8 —Christ himself. So we who observe the festival must not use the old leaven, the leaven of corruption and wickedness, but only the unleavened bread which is sincerity and truth.

9 In my letter I wrote that you must have nothing to do with loose livers. 10 I was not, of course, referring to pagans who lead loose lives or are grabbers and swindlers or idolaters. To avoid them you would have to get 11 out of the world altogether. I now write that you must have nothing to do with any so-called Christian who leads a loose life, or is grasping, or idolatrous, a slanderer, a drunkard, or a swindler. You should not even 12 eat with any such person. What business of mine is it to judge outsiders? 13 God is their judge. You are judges within the fellowship. Root out the evil-doer from your community.

Law-suits in pagan courts condemned

6 If one of your number has a dispute with another, has he the face to take it to pagan law-courts instead of to 2 the community of God's people? It is God's people who are to judge the world; surely you know that. And if the world is to come before you for judgement, are you incompetent to 3 deal with these trifling cases? Are you not aware that we are to judge angels? How much more, mere matters of 4 business! If therefore you have such business disputes, how can you entrust jurisdiction to outsiders, men who count for nothing in our community? 5 I write this to shame you. Can it be that there is not a single wise man

among you able to give a decision in a brother-Christian's cause? Must 6 brother go to law with brother—and before unbelievers? Indeed, you al- 7 ready fall below your standard in going to law with one another at all. Why not rather suffer injury? Why not rather let yourself be robbed? So 8 far from this, you actually injure and rob—injure and rob your brothers! Surely you know that the unjust will 9 never come into possession of the kingdom of God. Make no mistake: no fornicator or idolater, none who are guilty either of adultery or of homosexual perversion, no thieves or 10 grabbers or drunkards or slanderers or swindlers, will possess the kingdom of God. Such were some of you. But 11 you have been through the purifying waters; you have been dedicated to God and justified through the name of the Lord Jesus and the Spirit of our God.

Lust and fornication

'I am free to do anything', you say. 12 Yes, but not everything is for my good. No doubt I am free to do anything, but I for one will not let anything make free with me. 'Food is for 13 the belly and the belly for food', you say. True; and one day God will put an end to both. But it is not true that the body is for lust; it is for the Lord —and the Lord for the body. God not 14 only raised our Lord from the dead; he will also raise us by his power. Do 15 you not know that your bodies are limbs and organs of Christ? Shall I then take from Christ his bodily parts and make them over to a harlot? Never! You surely know that anyone 16 who links himself with a harlot becomes physically one with her (for Scripture says, 'The pair shall become one flesh'); but he who links 17 himself with Christ is one with him, spiritually. Shun fornication. Every 18 other sin that a man can commit is outside the body; but the fornicator sins against his own body. Do you not 19 know that your body is a shrine of the indwelling Holy Spirit, and the Spirit is God's gift to you? You do not belong to yourselves; you were bought at a 20 price. Then honour God in your body.

About marital relationships

And now for the matters you wrote 7 about.

It is a good thing for a man to have

2 nothing to do with women;*e* but because there is so much immorality, let each man have his own wife and 3 each woman her own husband. The husband must give the wife what is due to her, and the wife equally must 4 give the husband his due. The wife cannot claim her body as her own; it is her husband's. Equally, the husband cannot claim his body as his own; 5 it is his wife's. Do not deny yourselves to one another, except when you agree upon a temporary abstinence in order to devote yourselves to prayer; afterwards you may come together again; otherwise, for lack of self-control, you may be tempted by Satan.

6 All this I say by way of concession, 7 not command. I should like you all to be as I am myself; but everyone has the gift God has granted him, one this gift and another that.

8 To the unmarried and to widows I say this: it is a good thing if they 9 stay as I am myself; but if they cannot control themselves, they should marry. Better be married than burn with vain desire.

About divorce

10 To the married I give this ruling, which is not mine but the Lord's: a wife must not separate herself from 11 her husband; if she does, she must either remain unmarried or be reconciled to her husband; and the husband must not divorce his wife.

Marriage between Christians and pagans

12 To the rest I say this, as my own word, not as the Lord's: if a Christian has a heathen wife, and she is willing to live with him, he must not divorce 13 her; and a woman who has a heathen husband willing to live with her must 14 not divorce her husband. For the heathen husband now belongs to God through his Christian wife, and the heathen wife through her Christian husband. Otherwise your children would not belong to God, whereas in 15 fact they do. If on the other hand the heathen partner wishes for a separation, let him have it. In such cases the Christian husband or wife is under no compulsion; but God's call is a call 16 to live in peace. Think of it: as a wife you may be your husband's salvation; as a husband you may be your wife's salvation.

Remain as you were called

However that may be, each one must 17 order his life according to the gift the Lord has granted him and his condition when God called him. That is what I teach in all our congregations. Was a man called with the marks of 18 circumcision on him? Let him not remove them. Was he uncircumcised when he was called? Let him not be circumcised. Circumcision or un- 19 circumcision is neither here nor there; what matters is to keep God's commands. Every man should remain in 20 the condition in which he was called. Were you a slave when you were 21 called? Do not let that trouble you; but if a chance of liberty should come, take it.*f* For the man who as a slave 22 received the call to be a Christian is the Lord's freedman, and, equally, the free man who received the call is a slave in the service of Christ. You 23 were bought at a price; do not become slaves of men. Thus each one, 24 my friends, is to remain before God in the condition in which he received his call.

Celibacy and marriage

On the question of celibacy, I have 25 no instructions from the Lord, but I give my judgement as one who by God's mercy is fit to be trusted.

It is my opinion, then, that in a 26 time of stress like the present this is the best way for a man to live—it is best for a man to be as he is. Are you 27 bound in marriage? Do not seek a dissolution. Has your marriage been dissolved? Do not seek a wife. If, how- 28 ever, you do marry, there is nothing wrong in it; and if a virgin marries, she has done no wrong. But those who marry will have pain and grief in this bodily life, and my aim is to spare you.

What I mean, my friends, is this. 29 The time we live in will not last long. While it lasts, married men should be as if they had no wives; mourners 30 should be as if they had nothing to grieve them, the joyful as if they did not rejoice; buyers must not count on keeping what they buy, nor those 31 who use the world's wealth on using it to the full. For the whole frame of this world is passing away.

I want you to be free from anxious 32 care. The unmarried man cares for the Lord's business; his aim is to please the Lord. But the married man 33

e Or You say, 'It is a good thing ... women': ...
come, choose rather to make good use of your servitude.

f Or but even if a chance of liberty should

cares for worldly things; his aim is
34 to please his wife; and he has a divided mind. The unmarried or celibate woman cares[g] for the Lord's business; her aim is to be dedicated to him in body as in spirit; but the married woman cares for worldly things; her aim is to please her husband.

35 In saying this I have no wish to keep you on a tight rein. I am thinking simply of your own good, of what is seemly, and of your freedom to wait upon the Lord without distraction.

36 But if a man has a partner in celibacy[h] and feels that he is not behaving properly towards her, if, that is, his instincts are too strong for him,[i] and something must be done, he may do as he pleases; there is nothing
37 wrong in it; let them marry.[j] But if a man is steadfast in his purpose, being under no compulsion, and has complete control of his own choice; and if he has decided in his own mind to preserve his partner[k] in her virgin-
38 ity, he will do well. Thus, he who marries his partner[l] does well, and he who does not will do better.

39 A wife is bound to her husband as long as he lives. But if the husband die, she is free to marry whom she will, provided the marriage is with-
40 in the Lord's fellowship. But she is better off as she is; that is my opinion, and I believe that I too have the Spirit of God.

Christians in a pagan society

8 Now about food consecrated to heathen deities.
Of course we all 'have knowledge', as you say. This 'knowledge' breeds
2 conceit; it is love that builds. If anyone fancies that he knows, he knows nothing yet, in the true sense of know-
3 ing. But if a man loves,[m] he is acknowledged by God.[n]
4 Well then, about eating this consecrated food: of course, as you say, 'a false god has no existence in the real world. There is no god but one.'
5 For indeed, if there be so-called gods, whether in heaven or on earth—as indeed there are many 'gods' and
6 many 'lords'—yet for us there is one God, the Father, from whom all being comes, towards whom we move; and there is one Lord, Jesus Christ, through

whom all things came to be, and we through him.

But not everyone knows this. There 7 are some who have been so accustomed to idolatry[o] that even now they eat this food with a sense of its heathen consecration, and their conscience, being weak, is polluted by the eating. Certainly food will not 8 bring us into God's presence: if we do not eat, we are none the worse, and if we eat, we are none the better. But 9 be careful that this liberty of yours does not become a pitfall for the weak. If a weak character sees you sitting 10 down to a meal in a heathen temple —you, who 'have knowledge'—will not his conscience be emboldened to eat food consecrated to the heathen deity? This 'knowledge' of yours is 11 utter disaster to the weak, the brother for whom Christ died. In thus sinning 12 against your brothers and wounding their conscience,[p] you sin against Christ. And therefore, if food be the 13 downfall of my brother, I will never eat meat any more, for I will not be the cause of my brother's downfall.

Rights and duties of an apostle

Am I not a free man? Am I not an 9 apostle? Did I not see Jesus our Lord? Are not you my own handiwork, in the Lord? If others do not accept me 2 as an apostle, you at least are bound to do so, for you are yourselves the very seal of my apostolate, in the Lord.

To those who put me in the dock 3 this is my answer: Have I no right to 4 eat and drink? Have I no right to 5 take a Christian wife about with me, like the rest of the apostles and the Lord's brothers, and Cephas? Or are 6 Barnabas and I alone bound to work for our living? Did you ever hear of 7 a man serving in the army at his own expense? or planting a vineyard without eating the fruit of it? or tending a flock without using its milk? Do 8 not suppose I rely on these human analogies, for the law says the same; in the Law of Moses we read, 'You 9 shall not muzzle a threshing ox.' Do you suppose God's concern is with oxen? Or is the reference clearly to 10 ourselves? Of course it refers to us, in the sense that the ploughman should

---

g *Some witnesses read* . . . his wife. And there is a difference between the wife and the virgin. The unmarried woman cares . . .   h Or a virgin daughter (or ward).   i Or if she is ripe for marriage.
j Or let the girl and her lover marry.   k Or his daughter.   l Or gives his daughter in marriage.
m *Some witnesses read* loves God.   n Or he is recognized.   o *Some witnesses read* in whom the consciousness of the false god is so persistent . . .   p *Some witnesses insert* weak as it is.

plough and the thresher thresh in the hope of getting some of the produce.

11 If we have sown a spiritual crop for you, is it too much to expect from you
12 a material harvest? If you allow others these rights, have not we a stronger claim?

But I have availed myself of no such right. On the contrary, I put up with all that comes my way rather than offer any hindrance to the gos-
13 pel of Christ. You know (do you not?) that those who perform the temple service eat the temple offerings, and those who wait upon the altar claim
14 their share of the sacrifice. In the same way the Lord gave instructions that those who preach the Gospel should earn their living by the Gospel.
15 But I have never taken advantage of any such right, nor do I intend to claim it in this letter. I had rather die! No one shall make my boast
16 an empty boast. Even if I preach the Gospel, I can claim no credit for it; I cannot help myself; it would be
17 misery to me not to preach. If I did it of my own choice, I should be earning my pay; but since I do it apart from my own choice, I am simply
18 discharging a trust.*q* Then what is my pay? The satisfaction of preaching the Gospel without expense to anyone; in other words, of waiving the rights which my preaching gives me.

How Paul proclaims the Gospel

19 I am a free man and own no master; but I have made myself every man's servant, to win over as many as pos-
20 sible. To Jews I became like a Jew, to win Jews; as they are subject to the Law of Moses, I put myself under that law to win them, although I am
21 not myself subject to it. To win Gentiles, who are outside the Law, I made myself like one of them, although I am not in truth outside God's law, being under the law of
22 Christ. To the weak I became weak, to win the weak. Indeed, I have become everything in turn to men of every sort, so that in one way or an-
23 other I may save some. All this I do for the sake of the Gospel, to bear my part in proclaiming it.

Illustrations from the world of sport

24 You know (do you not?) that at the sports all the runners run the race, though only one wins the prize. Like

them, run to win! But every athlete 25 goes into strict training. They do it to win a fading wreath; we, a wreath that never fades. For my part, I run 26 with a clear goal before me; I am like a boxer who does not beat the air; I bruise my own body and make it 27 know its master, for fear that after preaching to others I should find myself rejected.

Illustrations from history

10 You should understand, my brothers, that our ancestors were all under the pillar of cloud, and all of them passed through the Red Sea; and so they 2 all received baptism into the fellowship of Moses in cloud and sea. They 3 all ate the same supernatural food, and all drank the same supernatural 4 drink; I mean, they all drank from the supernatural rock that accompanied their travels—and that rock was Christ. And yet, most of them 5 were not accepted by God, for the desert was strewn with their corpses.

These events happened as symbols 6 to warn us not to set our desires on evil things, as they did. Do not be 7 idolaters, like some of them; as Scripture has it, 'the people sat down to feast and rose up to revel'. Let us not 8 commit fornication, as some of them did—and twenty-three thousand died in one day. Let us not put the power 9 of the Lord*r* to the test, as some of them did—and were destroyed by serpents. Do not grumble against God, 10 as some of them did—and were destroyed by the Destroyer.

All these things that happened to 11 them were symbolic, and were recorded for our benefit as a warning. For upon us the fulfilment of the ages has come. If you feel sure that you are 12 standing firm, beware! You may fall. So far you have faced no trial beyond 13 what man can bear. God keeps faith, and he will not allow you to be tested above your powers, but when the test comes he will at the same time provide a way out, by enabling you to sustain it.

Questions of conscience

So then, dear friends, shun idolatry. 14 I speak to you as men of sense. Form 15 your own judgement on what I say. When we bless 'the cup of blessing', 16 is it not a means of sharing in the blood of Christ? When we break the

q Or If I do it willingly I am earning my pay; if I did it unwillingly I should still have a trust laid upon me.   r Some witnesses read of Christ.

bread, is it not a means of sharing in the body of Christ? Because there is one loaf, we, many as we are, are one body;[s] for it is one loaf of which we all partake.

18 Look at the Jewish people. Are not those who partake in the sacrificial 19 meal sharers in the altar? What do I imply by this? that an idol is anything but an idol? or food offered to 20 it anything more than food? No; but the sacrifices the heathen offer are offered (in the words of Scripture) 'to demons and to that which is not God'; and I will not have you become part-21 ners with demons. You cannot drink the cup of the Lord and the cup of demons. You cannot partake of the Lord's table and the table of demons. 22 Can we defy the Lord? Are we stronger than he?

23 'We are free to do anything', you say. Yes, but is everything good for us? 'We are free to do anything', but does everything help the building of 24 the community? Each of you must regard, not his own interests, but the other man's.

25 You may eat anything sold in the meat-market without raising ques-26 tions of conscience; for the earth is the Lord's and everything in it.

27 If an unbeliever invites you to a meal and you care to go, eat whatever is put before you, without raising 28 questions of conscience. But if somebody says to you, 'This food has been offered in sacrifice', then, out of consideration for him, and for conscience' 29 sake, do not eat it—not your conscience, I mean, but the other man's. 'What?' you say, 'is my freedom to be called in question by another man's 30 conscience? If I partake with thankfulness, why am I blamed for eating food over which I have said grace?' 31 Well, whether you eat or drink, or whatever you are doing, do all for the 32 honour of God: give no offence to Jews, or Greeks, or to the church of 33 God. For my part I always try to meet everyone half-way, regarding not my own good but the good of the many, so that they may be saved. **11** Follow my example as I follow Christ's.

Men and women in the church

2 I commend you for always keeping me in mind, and maintaining the 3 tradition I handed on to you. But I wish you to understand that, while every man has Christ for his Head, woman's head is man,[t] as Christ's Head is God. A man who keeps his 4 head covered when he prays or prophesies brings shame on his head; a 5 woman, on the contrary, brings shame on her head if she prays or prophesies bare-headed; it is as bad as if her head were shaved. If a woman is not 6 to wear a veil she might as well have her hair cut off; but if it is a disgrace for her to be cropped and shaved, then she should wear a veil. A man 7 has no need to cover his head, because man is the image of God, and the mirror of his glory, whereas woman reflects the glory of man.[u] For 8 man did not originally spring from woman, but woman was made out of man; and man was not created for 9 woman's sake, but woman for the sake of man; and therefore it is woman's 10 duty to have a sign of authority[v] on her head, out of regard for the angels.[w] And yet, in Christ's fellowship woman 11 is as essential to man as man to woman. If woman was made out of man, 12 it is through woman that man now comes to be; and God is the source of all.

Judge for yourselves: is it fitting for 13 a woman to pray to God bare-headed? Does not Nature herself teach you 14 that while flowing locks disgrace a man, they are a woman's glory? For 15 her locks were given for covering.

However, if you insist on arguing, 16 let me tell you, there is no such custom among us, or in any of the congregations of God's people.

The Lord's Supper

In giving you these injunctions I must 17 mention a practice which I cannot commend: your meetings tend to do more harm than good. To begin with, 18 I am told that when you meet as a congregation you fall into sharply divided groups; and I believe there is some truth in it (for dissensions are 19 necessary if only to show which of your members are sound). The result 20 is that when you meet as a congregation, it is impossible for you to eat the Lord's Supper, because each of you 21 is in such a hurry to eat his own, and while one goes hungry another has too much to drink. Have you no homes of 22 your own to eat and drink in? Or are

---

[s] Or For we, many as we are, are one loaf, one body.   [t] Or a woman's head is her husband. [u] Or a woman reflects her husband's glory.   [v] Some witnesses read to have a veil.   [w] Or and therefore a woman should keep her dignity on her head, for fear of the angels.

you so contemptuous of the church of God that you shame its poorer members? What am I to say? Can I commend you? On this point, certainly not!

23 For the tradition which I handed on to you came to me from the Lord himself: that the Lord Jesus, on the 24 night of his arrest, took bread and, after giving thanks to God, broke it and said: 'This is my body, which is for you; do this as a memorial of me.' 25 In the same way, he took the cup after supper, and said: 'This cup is the new covenant sealed by my blood. Whenever you drink it, do this as a 26 memorial of me.' For every time you eat this bread and drink the cup, you proclaim the death of the Lord, until he comes.

27 It follows that anyone who eats the bread or drinks the cup of the Lord unworthily will be guilty of desecrating the body and blood of the Lord. 28 A man must test himself before eating his share of the bread and drinking 29 from the cup. For he who eats and drinks eats and drinks judgement on himself if he does not discern the Body. 30 That is why many of you are feeble and sick, and a number have died. 31 But if we examined ourselves, we should not thus fall under judgement. 32 When, however, we do fall under the Lord's judgement, he is disciplining us, to save us from being condemned with the rest of the world.

33 Therefore, my brothers, when you meet for a meal, wait for one another. 34 If you are hungry, eat at home, so that in meeting together you may not fall under judgement. The other matters I will arrange when I come.

About gifts of the Spirit

12 About gifts of the Spirit, there are some things of which I do not wish you to remain ignorant. 2 You know how, in the days when you were still pagan, you were swept off to those dumb heathen gods, how-3 ever you happened to be led.^{x} For this reason I must impress upon you that no one who says 'A curse on Jesus!' can be speaking under the influence of the Spirit of God. And no one can say 'Jesus is Lord!' except under the influence of the Holy Spirit.

4 There are varieties of gifts, but 5 the same Spirit. There are varieties of 6 service, but the same Lord. There are many forms of work, but all of them,

in all men, are the work of the same God. In each of us the Spirit is mani-7 fested in one particular way, for some useful purpose. One man, through the 8 Spirit, has the gift of wise speech, while another, by the power of the same Spirit, can put the deepest knowledge into words. Another, by 9 the same Spirit, is granted faith; another, by the one Spirit, gifts of healing, and another miraculous powers; 10 another has the gift of prophecy, and another ability to distinguish true spirits from false; yet another has the gift of ecstatic utterance of different kinds, and another the ability to interpret it. But all these gifts are the 11 work of one and the same Spirit, distributing them separately to each individual at will.

For Christ is like a single body with 12 its many limbs and organs, which, many as they are, together make up one body. For indeed we were all 13 brought into one body by baptism, in the one Spirit, whether we are Jews or Greeks, whether slaves or free men, and that one Holy Spirit was poured out for all of us to drink.

Illustration from the body

A body is not one single organ, but 14 many. Suppose the foot should say, 15 'Because I am not a hand, I do not belong to the body', it does belong to the body none the less. Suppose the 16 ear were to say, 'Because I am not an eye, I do not belong to the body', it does still belong to the body. If the 17 body were all eye, how could it hear? If the body were all ear, how could it smell? But, in fact, God appointed 18 each limb and organ to its own place in the body, as he chose. If the whole 19 were one single organ, there would not be a body at all; in fact, however, 20 there are many different organs, but one body. The eye cannot say to the 21 hand, 'I do not need you'; nor the head to the feet, 'I do not need you.' Quite the contrary: those organs of 22 the body which seem to be more frail than others are indispensable, and 23 those parts of the body which we regard as less honourable are treated with special honour. To our unseemly parts is given a more than ordinary seemliness, whereas our seemly parts 24 need no adorning. But God has combined the various parts of the body, giving special honour to the humbler parts, so that there might be no sense 25

x Or . . . pagan, you would be seized by some power which drove you to those dumb heathen gods.

of division in the body, but that all its organs might feel the same con-
26 cern for one another. If one organ suffers, they all suffer together. If one flourishes, they all rejoice together.
27 Now you are Christ's body, and each of you a limb or organ of it.
28 Within our community God has appointed, in the first place apostles, in the second place prophets, thirdly teachers; then miracle-workers, then those who have gifts of healing, or ability to help others or power to guide them, or the gift of ecstatic
29 utterance of various kinds. Are all apostles? all prophets? all teachers?
30 Do all work miracles? Have all gifts of healing? Do all speak in tongues of
31 ecstasy? Can all interpret them? The higher gifts are those you should aim at.

Love, the best way of all

And now I will show you the best way of all.
13 I may speak in tongues of men or of angels, but if I am without love, I am a sounding gong or a clanging
2 cymbal. I may have the gift of prophecy, and know every hidden truth; I may have faith strong enough to move mountains; but if I have no
3 love, I am nothing. I may dole out all I possess, or even give my body to be burnt,[y] but if I have no love, I am none the better.
4 Love is patient; love is kind and envies no one. Love is never boastful,
5 nor conceited, nor rude; never selfish, not quick to take offence. Love keeps
6 no score of wrongs; does not gloat over other men's sins, but delights in
7 the truth. There is nothing love cannot face; there is no limit to its faith, its hope, and its endurance.
8 Love will never come to an end. Are there prophets? their work will be over. Are there tongues of ecstasy? they will cease. Is there knowledge?
9 it will vanish away; for our knowledge and our prophecy alike are partial,
10 and the partial vanishes when whole-
11 ness comes. When I was a child, my speech, my outlook, and my thoughts were all childish. When I grew up, I
12 had finished with childish things. Now we see only puzzling reflections in a mirror, but then we shall see face to face. My knowledge now is partial; then it will be whole, like God's
13 knowledge of me. In a word, there are three things that last for ever: faith,

hope, and love; but the greatest of them all is love.

Building up the community

Put love first; but there are other **14** gifts of the Spirit at which you should aim also, and above all prophecy. When a man is using the language 2 of ecstasy he is talking with God, not with men, for no man understands him; he is no doubt inspired, but he speaks mysteries. On the other hand, 3 when a man prophesies, he is talking to men, and his words have power to build; they stimulate and they encourage. The language of ecstasy is 4 good for the speaker himself, but it is prophecy that builds up a Christian community. I should be pleased for 5 you all to use the tongues of ecstasy, but better pleased for you to prophesy. The prophet is worth more than the man of ecstatic speech—unless indeed he can explain its meaning, and so help to build up the community. Sup- 6 pose, my friends, that when I come to you I use ecstatic language: what good shall I do you, unless what I say contains something by way of revelation, or enlightenment, or prophecy, or instruction?

Even with inanimate things that 7 produce sounds—a flute, say, or a lyre—unless their notes mark definite intervals, how can you tell what tune is being played? Or again, if the trum- 8 pet-call is not clear, who will prepare for battle? In the same way if your 9 ecstatic utterance yields no precise meaning, how can anyone tell what you are saying? You will be talking into the air. How many different kinds 10 of sound there are, or may be, in the world! Nothing is altogether sound-less. Well then, if I do not know the 11 meaning of the sound the speaker makes, his words will be gibberish to me, and mine to him. You are, I know, 12 eager for gifts of the Spirit; then aspire above all to excel in those which build up the church.

I say, then, that the man who falls 13 into ecstatic utterance should pray for the ability to interpret. If I use 14 such language in my prayer, the Spirit in me prays, but my intellect lies fallow. What then? I will pray as 15 I am inspired to pray, but I will also pray intelligently. I will sing hymns as I am inspired to sing, but I will sing intelligently too. Suppose you 16 are praising God in the language of

y Some witnesses read even seek glory by self-sacrifice.

inspiration: how will the plain man who is present be able to say 'Amen' to your thanksgiving, when he does 17 not know what you are saying? Your prayer of thanksgiving may be all that could be desired, but it is no help to 18 the other man. Thank God, I am more gifted in ecstatic utterance than any 19 of you,[z] but in the congregation I would rather speak five intelligible words, for the benefit of others as well as myself, than thousands of words in the language of ecstasy.

Appeal for order

20 Do not be childish, my friends. Be as innocent of evil as babes, but at least 21 be grown-up in your thinking. We read in the Law: 'I will speak to this nation through men of strange tongues, and by the lips of foreigners; and even so they will not heed me, 22 says the Lord.' Clearly then these 'strange tongues' are not intended as a sign for believers, but for unbelievers, whereas prophecy is designed not for unbelievers but for those who hold 23 the faith. So if the whole congregation is assembled and all are using the 'strange tongues' of ecstasy, and some uninstructed persons or unbelievers should enter, will they not think you 24 are mad? But if all are uttering prophecies, the visitor, when he enters, hears from everyone something that searches his conscience and brings 25 conviction, and the secrets of his heart are laid bare. So he will fall down and worship God, crying, 'God is certainly among you!'

26   To sum up, my friends: when you meet for worship, each of you contributes a hymn, some instruction, a revelation, an ecstatic utterance, or the interpretation of such an utterance. All of these must aim at one thing: 27 to build up the church. If it is a matter of ecstatic utterance, only two should speak, or at most three, one at a time, and someone must interpret. 28 If there is no interpreter, the speaker had better not address the meeting at 29 all, but speak to himself and to God. Of the prophets, two or three may speak, while the rest exercise their judgement 30 upon what is said. If someone else, sitting in his place, receives a revela- 31 tion, let the first speaker stop. You can all prophesy, one at a time, so that

the whole congregation may receive instruction and encouragement. It is 32 for prophets to control prophetic inspiration, for the God who inspires 33 them is not a God of disorder but of peace.

As in all congregations of God's people, women[a] should not address 34 the meeting. They have no licence to speak, but should keep their place as the law directs. If there is something 35 they want to know, they can ask their own husbands at home. It is a shocking thing that a woman should address the congregation.

Paul's authority

Did the word of God originate with 36 you? Or are you the only people to whom it came? If anyone claims to be 37 inspired or a prophet, let him recognize that what I write has the Lord's authority. If he does not acknow- 38 ledge this, God does not acknowledge him.[b]

In short, my friends, be eager to 39 prophesy; do not forbid ecstatic utterance; but let all be done decently 40 and in order.

The resurrection of Christ

And now, my brothers, I must remind 15 you of the gospel that I preached to you; the gospel which you received, on which you have taken your stand, and which is now bringing you salva- 2 tion. Do you still hold fast the Gospel as I preached it to you? If not, your conversion was in vain.[c]

First and foremost, I handed on to 3 you the facts which had been imparted to me: that Christ died for our sins, in accordance with the scriptures; that he was buried; that he was raised 4 to life on the third day, according to the scriptures; and that he appeared 5 to Cephas, and afterwards to the Twelve. Then he appeared to over 6 five hundred of our brothers at once, most of whom are still alive, though some have died. Then he appeared 7 to James, and afterwards to all the apostles.

In the end he appeared even to me. 8 It was like an abnormal birth; I had 9 persecuted the church of God and am therefore inferior to all other apostles —indeed not fit to be called an apostle. However, by God's grace I am what I 10

---

z Or . . . man. I say the thanksgiving; I use ecstatic speech more than any of you.   a Or of peace, as in all communities of God's people. Women . . .   b Some witnesses read If he refuses to recognize this, let him refuse!   c Or Do you remember the terms in which I preached the Gospel to you?—for I assume you did not accept it thoughtlessly.

am, nor has his grace been given to me in vain; on the contrary, in my labours I have outdone them all—not I, indeed, but the grace of God work-
11 ing with me. But what matter, I or they? This is what we all proclaim, and this is what you believed.

The resurrection of believers

12 Now if this is what we proclaim, that Christ was raised from the dead, how can some of you say there is no re-
13 surrection of the dead? If there be no resurrection, then Christ was not
14 raised; and if Christ was not raised, then our gospel is null and void, and
15 so is your faith; and we turn out to be lying witnesses for God, because we bore witness that he raised Christ to life, whereas, if the dead are not raised,
16 he did not raise him. For if the dead are not raised, it follows that Christ
17 was not raised; and if Christ was not raised, your faith has nothing in it and you are still in your old state of
18 sin. It follows also that those who have died within Christ's fellowship
19 are utterly lost. If it is for this life only that Christ has given us hope,[d] we of all men are most to be pitied.
20 But the truth is, Christ was raised to life—the firstfruits of the harvest of
21 the dead. For since it was a man who brought death into the world, a man also brought resurrection of the dead.
22 As in Adam all men die, so in Christ
23 all will be brought to life; but each in his own proper place: Christ the first-fruits, and afterwards, at his coming,
24 those who belong to Christ. Then comes the end, when he delivers up the kingdom to God the Father, after abolishing every kind of domination,
25 authority, and power. For he is des-tined to reign until God has put all
26 enemies under his feet; and the last enemy to be abolished is death.[e]
27 Scripture says, 'He has put all things in subjection under his feet.' But in saying 'all things', it clearly means to exclude God who subordinates them;
28 and when all things are thus subject to him, then the Son himself will also be made subordinate to God who made all things subject to him, and thus God will be all in all.
29 Again, there are those who receive baptism on behalf of the dead. Why should they do this? If the dead are

not raised to life at all, what do they mean by being baptized on their behalf?
30 And we ourselves—why do we face
31 these dangers hour by hour? Every day I die: I swear it by my pride in you, my brothers—for in Christ Jesus
32 our Lord I am proud of you. If, as the saying is, I 'fought wild beasts' at Ephesus, what have I gained by it?[f] If the dead are never raised to life, 'let us eat and drink, for tomorrow we die'.
33 Make no mistake: 'Bad company is
34 the ruin of a good character.' Come back to a sober and upright life and leave your sinful ways. There are some who know nothing of God; to your shame I say it.

Animal body, spiritual body

35 But, you may ask, how are the dead
36 raised? In what kind of body? How foolish! The seed you sow does not come to life unless it has first died;
37 and what you sow is not the body that shall be, but a naked grain, perhaps
38 of wheat, or of some other kind; and God clothes it with the body of his choice, each seed with its own particu-
39 lar body. All flesh is not the same flesh: there is flesh of men, flesh of beasts, of birds, and of fishes—all
40 different. There are heavenly bodies and earthly bodies; and the splendour of the heavenly bodies is one thing, the splendour of the earthly, another.
41 The sun has a splendour of its own, the moon another splendour, and the stars another, for star differs from
42 star in brightness. So it is with the resurrection of the dead. What is sown in the earth as a perishable
43 thing is raised imperishable. Sown in humiliation, it is raised in glory; sown in weakness, it is raised in power;
44 sown as an animal body, it is raised as a spiritual body.

If there is such a thing as an animal body, there is also a spiritual body.
45 It is in this sense that Scripture says, 'The first man, Adam, became an animate being', whereas the last Adam has become a life-giving spirit.
46 Observe, the spiritual does not come first; the animal body comes first, and
47 then the spiritual. The first man was made 'of the dust of the earth': the
48 second man is from heaven. The man

---

d Or If it is only an uncertain hope that our life in Christ has given us . . .   e Or Then at the end, when . . . power (for he . . . feet), the last enemy, death, will be abolished.   f Or If, as men do, I had fought wild beasts at Ephesus, what good would it be to me? or If I had been in no better case than one fighting beasts in the arena at Ephesus, what good would it be to me?

made of dust is the pattern of all men of dust, and the heavenly man is the 49 pattern of all the heavenly. As we have worn the likeness of the man made of dust, so we shall wear the likeness of the heavenly man.

'O Death, where is your victory?'

50 What I mean, my brothers, is this: flesh and blood can never possess the kingdom of God, and the perishable 51 cannot possess immortality. Listen! I will unfold a mystery: we shall not 52 all die, but we shall all be changed in a flash, in the twinkling of an eye, at the last trumpet-call. For the trumpet will sound, and the dead will rise im- 53 mortal, and we shall be changed. This perishable being must be clothed with the imperishable, and what is mortal must be clothed with immortality. 54 And when^g our mortality has been clothed with immortality, then the saying of Scripture will come true: 'Death is swallowed up; victory is 55 won!' 'O Death, where is your victory? 56 O Death, where is your sting?' The sting of death is sin, and sin gains its 57 power from the law; but, God be praised, he gives us the victory through our Lord Jesus Christ.

58 Therefore, my beloved brothers, stand firm and immovable, and work for the Lord always, work without limit, since you know that in the Lord your labour cannot be lost.

A gift for Christians in Jerusalem

16 And now about the collection in aid of God's people: you should follow my directions to our congregations in 2 Galatia. Every Sunday each of you is to put aside and keep by him a sum in proportion to his gains, so that there may be no collecting when I 3 come. When I arrive, I will give letters of introduction to persons approved by you, and send them to carry your 4 gift to Jerusalem. If it should seem worth while for me to go as well, they shall go with me.

Paul's plans

5 I shall come to Corinth after passing through Macedonia—for I am travel- 6 ling by way of Macedonia—and I may stay with you, perhaps even for the whole winter, and then you can help me on my way wherever I go next. I 7 do not want this to be a flying visit; I hope to spend some time with you, if the Lord permits. But I shall re- 8 main at Ephesus until Whitsuntide, for a great opportunity has opened 9 for effective work, and there is much opposition.

If Timothy comes, see that you put 10 him at his ease; for it is the Lord's work that he is engaged upon, as I am myself; so no one must slight him. 11 Send him happily on his way to join me, since I am waiting for him with our friends. As for our friend Apollos, 12 I urged him strongly to go to Corinth with the others, but he was quite determined not to go^h at present; he will go when opportunity offers.

Be alert; stand firm in the faith; be 13 valiant and strong. Let all you do be 14 done in love.

A request and greetings

I have a request to make of you, my 15 brothers. You know that the Steph- anas family were the first converts in Achaia, and have laid themselves out to serve God's people. I wish you to 16 give their due position to such persons, and indeed to everyone who labours hard at our common task. It is a 17 great pleasure to me that Stephanas, Fortunatus, and Achaicus have ar- rived, because they have done what you had no chance to do; they have 18 relieved my mind—and no doubt yours too. Such men deserve recogni- tion.

Greetings from the congregations 19 in Asia. Many greetings in the Lord from Aquila and Prisca and the con- gregation at their house. Greetings 20 from all the brothers. Greet one an- other with the kiss of peace.

This greeting is in my own hand— 21 PAUL.

If anyone does not love the Lord, 22 let him be outcast.

Marana tha—Come, O Lord!

The grace of the Lord Jesus Christ 23 be with you.

My love to you all in Christ Jesus. 24 Amen.

---

g *Some witnesses insert* our perishable nature has been clothed with the imperishable, and ...
h *Or* but it was by no means the will of God that he should go ...

THE SECOND LETTER OF PAUL
TO THE
CORINTHIANS

Divine consolation

1 FROM PAUL, apostle of Christ Jesus by God's will, and our colleague Timothy, to the congregation of God's people at Corinth, together with all who are dedicated to him throughout the whole of Achaia. **2** Grace and peace to you from God our Father and the Lord Jesus Christ. **3** Praise be to the God and Father of our Lord Jesus Christ, the all-merciful Father, the God whose con- **4** solation never fails us! He comforts us in all our troubles, so that we in turn may be able to comfort others in any trouble of theirs and to share with them the consolation we our- **5** selves receive from God. As Christ's cup of suffering overflows, and we suffer with him, so also through **6** Christ our consolation overflows. If distress be our lot, it is the price we pay for your consolation, for your salvation; if our lot be consolation, it is to help us to bring you comfort, and strength to face with fortitude the **7** same sufferings we now endure. And our hope for you is firmly grounded;[a] for we know that if you have part in the suffering, you have part also in the divine consolation.

8 In saying this, we should like you to know, dear friends, how serious was the trouble that came upon us in the province of Asia. The burden of it was far too heavy for us to bear, so heavy that we even despaired of life. **9** Indeed, we felt in our hearts that we had received a death-sentence. This was meant to teach us not to place reliance on ourselves, but on God who **10** raises the dead. From such mortal peril God delivered us; and he will deliver us again,[b] he on whom our hope is fixed. Yes, he will continue to de- **11** liver us, if you will co-operate by praying for us. Then, with so many people praying for our deliverance, there will be many to give thanks on our behalf for the gracious favour God has shown towards us.

The one thing we are proud of

There is one thing we are proud of: **12** our conscience assures us that in our dealings with our fellow-men, and above all in our dealings with you, our conduct has been governed by a devout and godly sincerity,[c] by the grace of God and not by worldly wisdom. There is nothing in our letters **13** to you but what you can read for yourselves, and understand too. Par- **14** tial as your present knowledge of us is, you will I hope come to understand fully that you have as much reason to be proud of us, as we of you, on the Day of our Lord Jesus.

It was because I felt so confident **15** about all this that I had intended to come first of all to you[d] and give you the benefit of a double visit: I meant **16** to visit you on my way to Macedonia, and after leaving Macedonia, to return to you, and you would then send me on my way to Judaea. That was **17** my intention; did I lightly change my mind?[e] Or do I, when I frame my plans, frame them as a worldly man might, so that it should rest with me to say 'yes' and 'yes', or 'no' and 'no'? As God is true, the language in which **18** we address you is not an ambiguous blend of Yes and No. The Son of God, **19** Christ Jesus, proclaimed among you by us (by Silvanus and Timothy, I mean, as well as myself), was never a blend of Yes and No. With him it was, and is, Yes. He is the Yes pro- **20** nounced upon God's promises, every one of them. That is why, when we give glory to God, it is through Christ Jesus that we say 'Amen'. And if you **21** and we belong to Christ, guaranteed

---

a Some witnesses give these clauses If distress . . . firmly grounded in different sequence.   *b Some witnesses read and he still delivers us.*   *c Some witnesses read by sincere and godly singleness of mind.*   *d Or had originally intended to come to you . . .*   *e Or In forming this intention, did I act irresponsibly ?*

as his and anointed, it is all God's
22 doing; it is God also who has set his
seal upon us, and as a pledge of what
is to come has given the Spirit to dwell
in our hearts.

23 I appeal to God to witness what I
am going to say; I stake my life
upon it: it was out of consideration
for you that I did not after all come
24 to Corinth. Do not think we are dic-
tating the terms of your faith; your
hold on the faith is secure enough.
We are working with you for your
2 own happiness. So I made up my mind
that my next visit to you must not be
2 another painful one. If I cause pain
to you, who is left to cheer me up,
except you, whom I have offended?
3 This is precisely the point I made in
my letter: I did not want, I said, to
come and be made miserable by the
very people who ought to have made
me happy; and I had sufficient confidence in you all to know that for me
to be happy is for all of you to be
4 happy. That letter I sent you came
out of great distress and anxiety;
how many tears I shed as I wrote it!
But I never meant to cause you pain;
I wanted you rather to know the love,
the more than ordinary love, that I
have for you.

Forgiveness and restoration

5 Any injury that has been done, has
not been done to me; to some extent,
not to labour the point, it has been
6 done to you all. The penalty on which
the general meeting has agreed has
7 met the offence well enough. Something very different is called for now:
you must forgive the offender and put
heart into him; the man's sorrow
must not be made so severe as to
8 overwhelm him. I urge you therefore
to assure him of your love for him by
9 a formal act. I wrote, I may say, to
see how you stood the test, whether
10 you fully accepted my authority. But
anyone who has your forgiveness has
mine too; and when I speak of forgiving (so far as there is anything for me
to forgive), I mean that as the representative of Christ I have forgiven
11 him for your sake.ʲ For Satan must
not be allowed to get the better of us;
we know his wiles all too well.

In Christ's triumphal procession

12 Then when I came to Troas, where I
was to preach the gospel of Christ,
and where an opening awaited me for

the Lord's work, I still found no relief 13
of mind, for my colleague Titus was
not there to meet me; so I took leave
of the people there and went off to
Macedonia. But thanks be to God, 14
who continually leads us about, captives in Christ's triumphal procession,
and everywhere uses us to reveal and
spread abroad the fragrance of the
knowledge of himself! We are indeed 15
the incense offered by Christ to God,
both for those who are on the way to
salvation, and for those who are on
the way to perdition: to the latter it 16
is a deadly fume that kills, to the
former a vital fragrance that brings
life. Who is equal to such a calling?
At least we do not go hawking the 17
word of God about, as so many do;
when we declare the word we do it in
sincerity, as from God and in God's
sight, as members of Christ.

The old covenant and the new

Are we beginning all over again to 3
produce our credentials? Do we, like
some people, need letters of introduction to you, or from you? No, you are 2
all the letter we need, a letter written
on our heart; any man can see it for
what it is and read it for himself. And 3
as for you, it is plain that you are a
letter that has come from Christ,
given to us to deliver: a letter written
not with ink but with the Spirit of the
living God, written not on stone tablets
but on the pages of the human heart.

It is in full reliance upon God, 4
through Christ, that we make such
claims. There is no question of our 5
being qualified in ourselves: we cannot claim anything as our own. The
qualification we have comes from God;
it is he who has qualified us to dis- 6
pense his new covenant—a covenant
expressed not in a written document,
but in a spiritual bond; for the written
law condemns to death, but the Spirit
gives life.

The law, then, engraved letter by 7
letter upon stone, dispensed death,
and yet it was inaugurated with
divine splendour. That splendour,
though it was soon to fade, made the
face of Moses so bright that the
Israelites could not gaze steadily at
him. But if so, must not even greater 8
splendour rest upon the divine dispensation of the Spirit? If splendour 9
accompanied the dispensation under
which we are condemned, how much
richer in splendour must that one be

ʲ Or that I have forgiven him for your sake, in the presence of Christ.

10 under which we are acquitted! Indeed, the splendour that once was is now no splendour at all; it is outshone by a 11 splendour greater still. For if that which was soon to fade had its moment of splendour, how much greater is the splendour of that which endures! 12 With such a hope as this we speak 13 out boldly; it is not for us to do as Moses did: he put a veil over his face to keep the Israelites from gazing on that fading splendour until it was 14 gone. But in any case their minds had been made insensitive, for that same veil is there to this very day when the lesson is read from the old covenant; and it is never lifted, because only in Christ is the old covenant abrogated.[g] 15 But to this very day, every time the Law of Moses is read, a veil lies over 16 the minds of the hearers. However, as Scripture says of Moses, 'whenever he turns to the Lord the veil is removed'.[h] 17 Now the Lord of whom this passage speaks is the Spirit; and where the Spirit of the Lord is, there is liberty. 18 And because for us there is no veil over the face, we all reflect as in a mirror the splendour of the Lord; thus we are transfigured into his likeness, from splendour to splendour; such is the influence of the Lord who is Spirit.

Open declaration of truth

4 Seeing then that we have been entrusted with this commission, which we owe entirely to God's mercy, we 2 never lose heart. We have renounced the deeds that men hide for very shame; we neither practise cunning nor distort the word of God; only by declaring the truth openly do we recommend ourselves, and then it is to the common conscience of our fellow- 3 men and in the sight of God. And if indeed our gospel be found veiled, the only people who find it so are those on 4 the way to perdition. Their unbelieving minds are so blinded by the god of this passing age, that the gospel of the glory of Christ, who is the very image of God, cannot dawn upon 5 them and bring them light. It is not ourselves that we proclaim; we proclaim Christ Jesus as Lord, and ourselves as your servants, for Jesus' sake. 6 For the same God who said, 'Out of darkness let light shine', has caused his light to shine within us, to give the light of revelation—the revelation

of the glory of God in the face of Jesus Christ.

Treasure in earthenware pots

We are no better than pots of earthen- 7 ware to contain this treasure, and this proves that such transcendent power does not come from us, but is God's alone. Hard-pressed on every 8 side, we are never hemmed in; bewildered, we are never at our wits' end; hunted, we are never abandoned to 9 our fate; struck down, we are not left to die. Wherever we go we carry 10 death with us in our body, the death that Jesus died, that in this body also life may reveal itself, the life that Jesus lives. For continually, while still 11 alive, we are being surrendered into the hands of death, for Jesus' sake, so that the life of Jesus also may be revealed in this mortal body of ours. Thus 12 death is at work in us, and life in you.

But Scripture says, 'I believed, and 13 therefore I spoke out', and we too, in the same spirit of faith, believe and therefore speak out; for we know that 14 he who raised the Lord Jesus to life will with Jesus raise us too, and bring us to his presence, and you with us. Indeed, it is for your sake that all 15 things are ordered, so that, as the abounding grace of God is shared by more and more, the greater may be the chorus of thanksgiving that ascends to the glory of God.

Outward decay, inward renewal

No wonder we do not lose heart! 16 Though our outward humanity is in decay, yet day by day we are inwardly renewed. Our troubles are 17 slight and short-lived; and their outcome an eternal glory which outweighs them far. Meanwhile our eyes 18 are fixed, not on the things that are seen, but on the things that are unseen: for what is seen passes away; what is unseen is eternal. For we 5 know that if the earthly frame that houses us today should be demolished, we possess a building which God has provided—a house not made by human hands, eternal, and in heaven. In this present body we do indeed 2 groan; we yearn to have our heavenly habitation put on over this one—in 3 the hope that, being thus clothed, we shall not find ourselves naked. We 4 groan indeed, we who are enclosed

g Or in Christ is it abolished.
h Or as Scripture says, when one turns to the Lord the veil is removed.

within this earthly frame; we are oppressed because we do not want to have the old body stripped off. Rather our desire is to have the new body put on over it, so that our mortal part may be absorbed into life immortal. 5 God himself has shaped us for this very end; and as a pledge of it he has given us the Spirit.

Serving the unseen Lord

6 Therefore we never cease to be confident. We know that so long as we are at home in the body we are exiles 7 from the Lord; faith is our guide, we 8 do not see him.[i] We are confident, I repeat, and would rather leave our home in the body and go to live with 9 the Lord. We therefore make it our ambition, wherever we are, here or 10 there, to be acceptable to him. For we must all have our lives laid open before the tribunal of Christ, where each must receive what is due to him for his conduct in the body, good or bad.

A new world

11 With this fear of the Lord before our eyes we address our appeal to men. To God our lives lie open, as I hope they also lie open to you in your heart 12 of hearts. This is not another attempt to recommend ourselves to you: we are rather giving you a chance to show yourselves proud of us; then you will have something to say to those whose pride is all in outward 13 show and not in inward worth. It may be we are beside ourselves, but it is for God; if we are in our right 14 mind, it is for you. For the love of Christ leaves us no choice, when once we have reached the conclusion that one man died for all and there-15 fore all mankind has died. His purpose in dying for all was that men, while still in life, should cease to live for themselves, and should live for him who for their sake died and was raised 16 to life. With us therefore worldly standards have ceased to count in our estimate of any man; even if once they counted in our understanding of Christ, they do so now no longer. 17 When anyone is united to Christ, there is a new world;[j] the old order has gone, and a new order has already begun.[k]

Be reconciled to God!

From first to last this has been the 18 work of God. He has reconciled us men to himself through Christ, and he has enlisted us in this service of reconciliation. What I mean is, that 19 God was in Christ reconciling the world to himself,[l] no longer holding men's misdeeds against them, and that he has entrusted us with the message of reconciliation. We come 20 therefore as Christ's ambassadors. It is as if God were appealing to you through us: in Christ's name, we implore you, be reconciled to God! Christ was innocent of sin, and yet for 21 our sake God made him one with the sinfulness of men,[m] so that in him we might be made one with the goodness of God himself. Sharing in God's work, 6 we urge this appeal upon you: you have received the grace of God; do 2 not let it go for nothing. God's own words are:

'In the hour of my favour I gave heed to you;
on the day of deliverance I came to your aid.'

The hour of favour has now come; now, I say, has the day of deliverance dawned.

The apostle's sufferings

In order that our service may not be 3 brought into discredit, we avoid giving offence in anything. As God's ser-4 vants, we try to recommend ourselves in all circumstances by our steadfast endurance: in distress, hardships, and dire straits; flogged, imprisoned, 5 mobbed; overworked, sleepless, starving. We recommend ourselves by the 6 innocence of our behaviour, our grasp of truth, our patience and kindliness; by gifts of the Holy Spirit, by sincere love, by declaring the truth, by the 7 power of God. We wield the weapons of righteousness in right hand and left. Honour and dishonour, praise and 8 blame, are alike our lot: we are the impostors who speak the truth, the 9 unknown men whom all men know; dying we still live on; disciplined by suffering, we are not done to death; in our sorrows we have always cause 10 for joy; poor ourselves, we bring

---

i Or faith is our guide and not the things we see. one is united to Christ he is a new creature: his old life is over; a new life has already begun. l Or God was reconciling the world to himself by Christ. for us. *j* Or a new act of creation. *k* Or When anyone is united to Christ he is a new creature: his old life is over; a new life has already begun. *l* Or God was reconciling the world to himself by Christ. *m* Or and yet God made him a sin-offering

wealth to many; penniless, we own the world.

11 Men of Corinth, we have spoken very frankly to you; we have opened 12 our heart wide to you all. On our part there is no constraint; any constraint there may be is in yourselves. 13 In fair exchange then (may a father speak so to his children?) open wide your hearts to us.

Call to consecration

14 Do not unite yourselves with unbelievers; they are no fit mates for you. What has righteousness to do with wickedness? Can light consort 15 with darkness? Can Christ agree with Belial, or a believer join hands with 16 an unbeliever? Can there be a compact between the temple of God and the idols of the heathen? And the temple of the living God is what we are. God's own words are: 'I will live and move about among them; I will be their God, and they shall be my 17 people.' And therefore, 'come away and leave them, separate yourselves, says the Lord; touch nothing unclean. 18 Then I will accept you, says the Lord, the Ruler of all being; I will be a father to you, and you shall be my sons and 7 daughters.' Such are the promises that have been made to us, dear friends. Let us therefore cleanse ourselves from all that can defile flesh or spirit, and in the fear of God complete our consecration.

A quarrel healed

2 Do make a place for us in your hearts! We have wronged no one, ruined no 3 one, taken advantage of no one. I do not want to blame you. Why, as I have told you before, the place you have in our heart is such that, come death, come life, we meet it together. 4 I am perfectly frank with you. I have great pride in you. In all our many troubles my cup is full of consolation, and overflows with joy.

5 Even when we reached Macedonia there was still no relief for this poor body of ours; instead, there was trouble at every turn, quarrels all round 6 us, forebodings in our heart. But God, who brings comfort to the downcast, has comforted us by the arrival of 7 Titus, and not merely by his arrival, but by his being so greatly comforted about you. He has told us how you long for me, how sorry you are, and

how eager to take my side; and that has made me happier still.

8 Even if I did wound you by the letter I sent, I do not now regret it. I may have been sorry for it when I saw that the letter had caused you pain, 9 even if only for a time; but now I am happy, not that your feelings were wounded but that the wound led to a change of heart. You bore the smart as God would have you bear it, and so 10 you are no losers by what we did. For the wound which is borne in God's way brings a change of heart too salutary to regret; but the hurt which is borne in the world's way brings death. 11 You bore your hurt in God's way, and see what its results have been! It made you take the matter seriously and vindicate yourselves. How angered you were, how apprehensive! How your longing for me awoke, yes, and your devotion and your eagerness to see justice done! At every point you have cleared yourselves of blame in this 12 trouble. And so, although I did send you that letter, it was not the offender or his victim that most concerned me. My aim in writing was to help to make plain to you, in the sight of God, how truly you are devoted to us. 13 That is why we have been so encouraged.

The mission of Titus

But besides being encouraged ourselves we have also been delighted beyond everything by seeing how happy Titus is: you have all helped to set his mind completely at rest. 14 Anything I may have said to him to show my pride in you has been justified. Every word we ever addressed to you bore the mark of truth; and the same holds of the proud boast we made in the presence of Titus: that 15 also has proved true. His heart warms all the more to you as he recalls how ready you all were to do what he asked, meeting him as you did in fear and 16 trembling. How happy I am now to have complete confidence in you!

About giving to fellow-Christians

8 We must tell you, friends, about the grace of generosity which God has imparted to[n] our congregations in Macedonia. The troubles they have 2 been through have tried them hard, yet in all this they have been so exuberantly happy that from the depths of their poverty they have shown

n Or how gracious God has been to . . .

3 themselves lavishly open-handed. Going to the limit of their resources, as I can testify, and even beyond that 4 limit, they begged us most insistently, and on their own initiative, to be allowed to share in this generous 5 service to their fellow-Christians. And their giving surpassed our expectations; for they gave their very selves, offering them in the first instance to the Lord, but also, under God, 6 to us. The upshot is that we have asked Titus, who began it all, to visit you and bring this work of genero-7 sity also to completion. You are so rich in everything—in faith, speech, knowledge, and zeal of every kind, as well as in the loving regard you have for us*o*—surely you should show yourselves equally lavish in this ge-8 nerous service! This is not meant as an order; by telling you how keen others are I am putting your love to 9 the test. For you know how generous our Lord Jesus Christ has been: he was rich, yet for your sake he became poor, so that through his poverty you might become rich.

10   Here is my considered opinion on the matter. What I ask you to do is in your own interests. You made a good beginning last year both in the work you did and in your willingness to 11 undertake it. Now I want you to go on and finish it: be as eager to complete the scheme as you were to adopt it, and give according to your means. 12 Provided there is an eager desire to give, God accepts what a man has; he does not ask for what he has not. 13 There is no question of relieving others at the cost of hardship to your-14 selves; it is a question of equality. At the moment your surplus meets their need, but one day your need may be met from their surplus. The aim is 15 equality; as Scripture has it, 'The man who got much had no more than enough, and the man who got little did not go short.'

A delegation to Corinth

16 I thank God that he has made Titus 17 as keen on your behalf as we are! For Titus not only welcomed our request; he is so eager that by his own desire 18 he is now leaving to come to you. With him we are sending one of our company whose reputation is high among our congregations everywhere for his 19 services to the Gospel. Moreover they have duly appointed him to travel with us and help in this beneficent work, by which we do honour to the Lord himself and show our own eagerness to serve. We want to guard 20 against any criticism of our handling of this generous gift; for our aims 21 are entirely honourable, not only in the Lord's eyes, but also in the eyes of men.

With these men we are sending 22 another of our company whose enthusiasm we have had many opportunities of testing, and who is now all the more earnest because of the great confidence he has in you. If there is 23 any question about Titus, he is my partner and my associate in dealings with you; as for the others, they are delegates of our congregations, an honour to Christ.*p* Then give them 24 clear expression of your love and justify our pride in you; justify it to them, and through them to the congregations.

An incentive to giving

About the provision of aid for God's 9 people, it is superfluous for me to write to you. I know how eager you 2 are to help; I speak of it with pride to the Macedonians: I tell them that Achaia had everything ready last year; and most of them have been fired by your zeal. My purpose in 3 sending these friends is to ensure that what we have said about you in this matter should not prove to be an empty boast. By that I mean, I want you to be prepared, as I told them you were; for if I bring with me men from 4 Macedonia and they find you are not prepared, what a disgrace it will be to us, let alone to you, after all the confidence we have shown! I have 5 accordingly thought it necessary to ask these friends to go on ahead to Corinth, to see that your promised bounty is in order before I come; it will then be awaiting me as a bounty indeed, and not as an extortion.

God's care for the generous

Remember: sparse sowing, sparse 6 reaping; sow bountifully, and you will reap bountifully. Each person should 7 give as he has decided for himself; there should be no reluctance, no sense of compulsion; God loves a cheerful giver. And it is in God's 8 power to provide you richly with

o Some witnesses read the love we have for you, *or* the love which we have kindled in your hearts.
p Or they are . . . congregations; they reflect Christ.

every good gift; thus you will have ample means in yourselves to meet each and every situation, with enough and to spare for every good cause. 9 Scripture says of such a man: 'He has lavished his gifts on the needy, his benevolence stands fast for ever.' 10 Now he who provides seed for sowing and bread for food will provide the seed for you to sow; he will multiply it and swell the harvest of your bene- 11 volence, and you will always be rich enough to be generous. Through our action such generosity will issue in 12 thanksgiving to God, for as a piece of willing service this is not only a contri- bution towards the needs of God's people; more than that, it overflows 13 in a flood of thanksgiving to God. For through the proof which this affords, many will give honour to God when they see how humbly you obey him and how faithfully you confess the gospel of Christ; and will thank him for your liberal contribution to their 14 need and to the general good. And as they join in prayer on your behalf, their hearts will go out to you be- cause of the richness of the grace which God has imparted to you. 15 Thanks be to God for his gift beyond words!

Paul's weakness and strength

10 But I, Paul, appeal to you by the gentleness and magnanimity of Christ —I, so feeble (you say) when I am face to face with you, so brave when 2 I am away. Spare me, I beg you, the necessity of such bravery when I come, for I reckon I could put on as bold a face as you please against those who charge us with moral 3 weakness. Weak men we may be, but it is not as such that we fight our 4 battles. The weapons we wield are not merely human,[q] but divinely 5 potent to demolish strongholds; we demolish sophistries and all that rears its proud head against the knowledge of God; we compel every human thought to surrender in obedi- 6 ence to Christ; and we are prepared to punish all rebellion when once you have put yourselves in our hands.

The apostle's authority

7 Look facts in the face.[r] Someone is convinced, is he, that he belongs to Christ? Let him think again, and reflect that we belong to Christ as much as he does. Indeed, if I am some- 8 what over-boastful about our autho- rity—an authority given by the Lord to build you up, not pull you down— I shall make my boast good. So you 9 must not think of me as one who scares you by the letters he writes. 'His letters', so it is said, 'are weighty 10 and powerful; but when he appears he has no presence, and as a speaker he is beneath contempt.' People who 11 talk in that way should reckon with this: when I come, my actions will show the same man as my letters showed in my absence.

The apostle's discretion

We should not dare to class ourselves 12 or compare ourselves with any of those who put forward their own claims. What fools they are to measure themselves by themselves, to find in themselves their own standard of comparison![s] With us there will be no 13 attempt to boast beyond our proper sphere; and our sphere is determined by the limit God laid down for us, which permitted us to come as far as Corinth. We are not overstretching 14 our commission, as we should be if it did not extend to you, for we were the first to reach Corinth in preaching the gospel of Christ. And we do not 15 boast of work done where others have laboured, work beyond our proper sphere. Our hope is rather that, as your faith grows, we may attain a position among you greater than ever before, but still within the limits of our sphere. Then we can carry the 16 Gospel to lands that lie beyond you, never priding ourselves on work al- ready done in another man's sphere. If a man must boast, let him boast 17 of the Lord. Not the man who 18 recommends himself, but the man whom the Lord recommends—he and he alone is to be accepted.

Sham-apostles

I wish you would bear with me in a 11 little of my folly; please do bear with me. I am jealous for you, with a di- 2 vine jealousy; for I betrothed you to Christ, thinking to present you as a chaste virgin to her true and only husband. But as the serpent in his 3

---

q Or charge us with worldly standards. We live, no doubt, in the world; but it is not on that level that we fight our battles. The weapons we wield are not those of the world . . .   r Or You are looking only at what catches the eye.   s Some witnesses read On the contrary we measure ourselves by ourselves, by our own standard of comparison.

cunning seduced Eve, I am afraid that your thoughts may be corrupted and you may lose your[t] single-4 hearted devotion to Christ. For if someone comes who proclaims another Jesus, not the Jesus whom we proclaimed, or if you then receive a spirit different from the Spirit already given to you, or a gospel different from the gospel you have already accepted, you manage to put up with 5 that well enough. Have I in any way come short of those superlative 6 apostles? I think not. I may be no speaker, but knowledge I have; at all times we have made known to you the full truth.

7 Or was this my offence, that I made no charge for preaching the gospel of God, lowering myself to help in rais-8 ing you? It is true that I took toll of other congregations, accepting[u] sup-9 port from them to serve you. Then, while I was with you, if I ran short I sponged on no one; anything I needed was fully met by our friends who came from Macedonia; I made it a rule, as I always shall, never to be 10 a burden to you. As surely as the truth of Christ is in me, I will preserve my pride in this matter throughout Achaia, and nothing shall stop me. 11 Why? Is it that I do not love you? God knows I do.

12 And I shall go on doing as I am doing now, to cut the ground from under those who would seize any chance to put their vaunted apostle-13 ship on the same level as ours. Such men are sham-apostles, crooked in all their practices, masquerading as 14 apostles of Christ. There is nothing surprising about that; Satan himself 15 masquerades as an angel of light. It is therefore a simple thing for his agents to masquerade as agents of good. But they will meet the end their deeds deserve.

Paul's ground for boasting

16 I repeat: let no one take me for a fool; but if you must, then give me the privilege of a fool, and let me have 17 my little boast like others. I am not speaking here as a Christian, but like 18 a fool, if it comes to bragging. So many people brag of their earthly distinc-19 tions that I shall do so too. How gladly you bear with fools, being 20 yourselves so wise! If a man tyrannizes over you, exploits you, gets you

in his clutches, puts on airs, and hits you in the face, you put up with it. And we, you say, have been weak! 21 I admit the reproach.

But if there is to be bravado (and here I speak as a fool), I can indulge in it too. Are they Hebrews? So am I. 22 Israelites? So am I. Abraham's descendants? So am I. Are they ser-23 vants of Christ? I am mad to speak like this, but I can outdo them. More overworked than they, scourged more severely, more often imprisoned, many a time face to face with death. Five times the Jews have given me 24 the thirty-nine strokes; three times 25 I have been beaten with rods; once I was stoned; three times I have been shipwrecked, and for twenty-four hours I was adrift on the open sea. I have been constantly on the road; 26 I have met dangers from rivers, dangers from robbers, dangers from my fellow-countrymen, dangers from foreigners, dangers in towns, dangers in the country, dangers at sea, dangers from false friends. I have toiled and 27 drudged, I have often gone without sleep; hungry and thirsty, I have often gone fasting; and I have suffered from cold and exposure.

Apart from these external things,[v] 28 there is the responsibility that weighs on me every day, my anxious concern for all our congregations. If anyone 29 is weak, do I not share his weakness? If anyone is made to stumble, does my heart not blaze with indignation? If 30 boasting there must be, I will boast of the things that show up my weakness. The God and Father of the Lord 31 Jesus (blessed be his name for ever!) knows that what I say is true. When 32 I was in Damascus, the commissioner of King Aretas kept the city under observation so as to have me arrested; and I was let down in a basket, 33 through a window in the wall, and so escaped his clutches.

Paul's visions and revelations

I am obliged to boast. It does no good; 12 but I shall go on to tell of visions and revelations granted by the Lord. I 2 know a Christian man who fourteen years ago (whether in the body or out of it, I do not know—God knows) was caught up as far as the third heaven. And I know that this same man 3 (whether in the body or out of it, I do not know—God knows) was caught 4

t Some witnesses insert purity and . . .   u Or Did I take toll of other congregations by accepting . . . ?
v Or Apart from things which I omit.

up into paradise, and heard words so secret that human lips may not re-
5 peat them. About such a man as that I am ready to boast; but I will not boast on my own account, except of
6 my weaknesses. If I should choose to boast, it would not be the boast of a fool, for I should be speaking the truth. But I refrain, because I should not like anyone to form an estimate of me which goes beyond the evidence
7 of his own eyes and ears. And so, to keep me from being unduly elated by the magnificence of such revelations, I was given[w] a sharp physical pain[x] which came as Satan's messenger to bruise me; this was to save me from
8 being unduly elated. Three times I
9 begged the Lord to rid me of it, but his answer was: 'My grace is all you need; power comes to its full strength in weakness.' I shall therefore prefer to find my joy and pride in the very things that are my weakness; and then the power of Christ will come
10 and rest upon me. Hence I am well content, for Christ's sake, with weakness, contempt, persecution, hardship, and frustration; for when I am weak, then I am strong.

The marks of a true apostle

11 I am being very foolish, but it was you who drove me to it; my credentials should have come from you. In no respect did I fall short of these super-lative apostles, even if I am a nobody.
12 The marks of a true apostle were there, in the work I did among you, which called for such constant forti-tude, and was attended by signs,
13 marvels, and miracles. Is there any-thing in which you were treated worse than the other congregations— except this, that I never sponged upon you? How unfair of me! I crave forgiveness.

Paul's aim in his coming visit

14 Here am I preparing to pay you a third visit; and I am not going to sponge upon you. It is you I want, not your money; parents should make provision for their children, not chil-
15 dren for their parents. As for me, I will gladly spend what I have for you —yes, and spend myself to the limit. If I love you overmuch, am I to be

loved the less? But, granted that I 16 did not prove a burden to you, still I was unscrupulous enough, you say, to use a trick to catch you. Who, of 17 the men I have sent to you, was used by me to defraud you? I begged 18 Titus to visit you, and I sent our friend with him. Did Titus defraud you? Have we not both been guided by the same Spirit, and followed the same course?

Perhaps you think that all this 19 time we have been addressing our defence to you. No; we are speaking in God's sight, and as Christian men. Our whole aim, my own dear people, is to build you up. I fear that when 20 I come I may perhaps find you dif-ferent from what I wish you to be, and that you may find me also different from what you wish. I fear I may find quarrelling and jealousy, angry tem-pers and personal rivalries, backbiting and gossip, arrogance and general dis-order. I am afraid that, when I come 21 again, my God may humiliate me in your presence, that I may have tears to shed over many of those who have sinned in the past and have not repented of their unclean lives, their fornication and sensuality.

A warning

This will be my third visit to you; and 13 all facts must be established by the evidence of two or three witnesses. To 2 those who have sinned in the past, and to everyone else, I repeat the warning I gave before; I gave it in person on my second visit, and I give it now in absence. It is that when I come this time, I will show no leniency. Then you will have the proof you 3 seek of the Christ who speaks through me, the Christ who, far from being weak with you, makes his power felt among you. True, he died on the cross 4 in weakness, but he lives by the power of God; and we who share his weak-ness shall by the power of God live with him in your service.

Self-examination

Examine yourselves: are you living 5 the life of faith? Put yourselves to the test. Surely you recognize that Jesus Christ is among you?—unless of course you prove unequal to the test. I hope you will come to see that we 6

w *Some witnesses read . . . ears, and because of the magnificence of the revelations themselves. Therefore to keep me from being unduly elated I was given . . .*   x *Or a painful wound to my pride (literally a stake, or thorn, for the flesh).*

7 are not unequal to it. Our prayer to God is that you may do no wrong; we are not concerned to be vindicated ourselves; we want you to do what is right, even if we should seem to be 8 discredited. For we have no power to act against the truth, but only for it. 9 We are well content to be weak at any time if only you are strong. Indeed, my whole prayer is that all may be put 10 right with you. My purpose in writing this letter before I come, is to spare myself, when I come, any sharp exercise of authority—authority which the Lord gave me for building up and not for pulling down.

Farewell and greetings

And now, my friends, farewell. Mend 11 your ways; take our appeal to heart; agree with one another; live in peace; and the God of love and peace will be with you. Greet one another with the 12 kiss of peace. All God's people send 13 you greetings.

The grace of the Lord Jesus Christ, 14 and the love of God, and fellowship in the Holy Spirit, be with you all.

THE LETTER OF PAUL
TO THE
GALATIANS

1 FROM PAUL, an apostle, not by human appointment or human commission, but by commission from Jesus Christ and from God the Father who 2 raised him from the dead. I and the group of friends now with me send greetings to the Christian congregations of Galatia.

3 Grace and peace to you from God the Father and our Lord Jesus Christ,[a] 4 who sacrificed himself for our sins, to rescue us out of this present age of wickedness, as our God and Father 5 willed; to whom be glory for ever and ever. Amen.

Paul defends the gospel of Christ

6 I am astonished to find you turning so quickly away from him who called you by grace,[b] and following a differ- 7 ent gospel. Not that it is in fact another gospel; only there are persons who unsettle your minds by trying 8 to distort the gospel of Christ. But if anyone, if we ourselves or an angel from heaven, should preach a gospel at variance with the gospel we preached 9 to you, he shall be held outcast. I now repeat what I have said before: if anyone preaches a gospel at variance with the gospel which you received, let him be outcast!

Does my language now sound as if 10 I were canvassing for men's support? Whose support do I want but God's alone? Do you think I am currying favour with men? If I still sought men's favour, I should be no servant of Christ.

I must make it clear to you, my 11 friends, that the gospel you heard me preach is no human invention. I did 12 not take it over from any man; no man taught it me; I received it through a revelation of Jesus Christ.

Paul defends his apostleship

You have heard what my manner of 13 life was when I was still a practising Jew: how savagely I persecuted the church of God, and tried to destroy it; and how in the practice of our nation- 14 al religion I was outstripping many of my Jewish contemporaries in my boundless devotion to the traditions of my ancestors. But then in his good 15 pleasure God, who had set me apart from birth and called me through his grace, chose to reveal his Son to me 16 and through me, in order that I might

---

a Some witnesses read God our Father and the Lord Jesus Christ. Christ who called you by grace, *or from* him who called you by grace of Christ. *b Some witnesses read from*

proclaim him among the Gentiles. When that happened, without con-
17 sulting any human being, without going up to Jerusalem to see those who were apostles before me, I went off at once to Arabia, and afterwards returned to Damascus.
18 Three years later I did go up to Jerusalem to get to know Cephas. I stayed with him for a fortnight,
19 without seeing any other of the apostles, except[e] James the Lord's
20 brother. What I write is plain truth; before God I am not lying.
21 Next I went to the regions of Syria
22 and Cilicia, and remained unknown by sight[d] to Christ's congregations in
23 Judaea. They only heard it said, 'Our former persecutor is preaching the good news of the faith which once he
24 tried to destroy'; and they praised God for me.

Dispute and agreement in Jerusalem

2 Next, fourteen years later, I went again[e] to Jerusalem with Barnabas,
2 taking Titus with us. I went up because it had been revealed by God that I should do so. I laid before them —but at a private interview with the men of repute—the gospel which I am accustomed to preach to the Gentiles, to make sure that the race I had run, and was running, should not be run
3 in vain. Yet even my companion Titus, Greek though he is, was not
4 compelled to be circumcised. That course was urged only as a concession to certain[f] sham-Christians, interlopers who had stolen in to spy upon the liberty we enjoy in the fellowship of Christ Jesus. These men wanted to
5 bring us into bondage, but not for one moment did I yield to their dictation; I was determined that the full truth of the Gospel should be maintained for you.[g]
6 But as for the men of high reputation (not that their importance matters to me: God does not recognize these personal distinctions)—these men of repute, I say, did not prolong
7 the consultation,[h] but on the contrary acknowledged that I had been entrusted with the Gospel for Gentiles as surely as Peter had been entrusted
8 with the Gospel for Jews. For God

whose action made Peter an apostle to the Jews, also made me an apostle to the Gentiles.
9 Recognizing, then, the favour thus bestowed upon me, those reputed pillars of our society, James, Cephas, and John, accepted Barnabas and myself as partners, and shook hands upon it, agreeing that we should go to the Gentiles while they went to the
10 Jews. All they asked was that we should keep their poor in mind, which was the very thing I made[i] it my business to do.

Paul at odds with Peter

11 But when Cephas came to Antioch, I opposed him to his face, because he
12 was clearly in the wrong. For until certain persons[j] came from James he was taking his meals with gentile Christians; but when they[k] came he drew back and began to hold aloof, because he was afraid of the advocates
13 of circumcision. The other Jewish Christians showed the same lack of principle; even Barnabas was carried away and played false like the rest.
14 But when I saw that their conduct did not square with[l] the truth of the Gospel, I said to Cephas, before the whole congregation, 'If you, a Jew born and bred, live like a Gentile, and not like a Jew, how can you insist that Gentiles must live like Jews?'

Jews, like Gentiles, saved by faith

15 We ourselves are Jews by birth, not
16 Gentiles and sinners. But we know that no man is ever justified by doing what the law demands, but only through faith in Christ Jesus; so we too have put our faith in Jesus Christ, in order that we might be justified through this faith, and not through deeds dictated by law; for by such deeds, Scripture says, no mortal man shall be justified.
17 If now, in seeking to be justified in Christ, we ourselves no less than the Gentiles turn out to be sinners against the law,[m] does that mean that Christ
18 is an abettor of sin? No, never! No, if I start building up again a system which I have pulled down, then it is that I show myself up as a transgres-
19 sor of the law. For through the law

---

c Or but only.   d Or unknown personally.   e Some witnesses omit again.   f Or The question was later raised because of certain . . .   g Or, following the reading of some witnesses, Yet even . . . is, was under no absolute compulsion to be circumcised, but for the sake of certain . . . of Christ Jesus, with the intention of bringing us into bondage, I yielded to their demand for the moment, to ensure that gospel truth should not be prevented from reaching you.   h Or gave me no further instructions. i Or had made, or have made.   j Some witnesses read a certain person.   k Some witnesses read he. l Or I saw that they were not making progress towards . . .   m Or no less than the Gentiles have accepted the position of sinners against the law.

20 I died to law—to live for God. I have been crucified with Christ: the life I now live is not my life, but the life which Christ lives in me; and my present bodily life is lived by faith in the Son of God, who loved me and
21 gave himself up for me. I will not nullify the grace of God; if righteousness comes by law, then Christ died for nothing.

Appeal to experience

3 You stupid Galatians! You must have been bewitched—you before whose eyes Jesus Christ was openly dis-
2 played upon his cross! Answer me one question: did you receive the Spirit by keeping the law or by believing
3 the gospel message[n]? Can it be that you are so stupid? You started with the spiritual; do you now look to the
4 material to make you perfect? Have all your great experiences been in vain
5 —if vain indeed they should be? I ask then: when God gives you the Spirit and works miracles among you, why is this? Is it because you keep the law, or is it because you have faith in the
6 gospel message? Look at Abraham: he put his faith in God, and that faith was counted to him as righteousness.

Appeal to Scripture

7 You may take it, then, that it is the men of faith who are Abraham's sons.
8 And Scripture, foreseeing that God would justify the Gentiles through faith, declared the Gospel to Abraham beforehand: 'In you all nations
9 shall find blessing.' Thus it is the men of faith who share the blessing with faithful Abraham.
10 On the other hand those who rely on obedience to the law are under a curse; for Scripture says, 'A curse is on all who do not persevere in doing everything that is written in the
11 Book of the Law.' It is evident that no one is ever justified before God in terms of law; because we read, 'he shall gain life who is justified through
12 faith'. Now law is not at all a matter of having faith: we read, 'he who does this shall gain life by what he does'.
13 Christ bought us freedom from the curse of the law by becoming for our sake an accursed thing; for Scripture says, 'A curse is on everyone who is
14 hanged on a gibbet.' And the purpose of it all was that the blessing of Abra-

ham should in Jesus Christ be extended to the Gentiles, so that we might receive the promised Spirit through faith.

Illustration from ordinary life

15 My brothers, let me give you an illustration. Even in ordinary life, when a man's will and testament has been duly executed, no one else can set
16 it aside or add a codicil. Now the promises were pronounced to Abraham and to his 'issue'. It does not say 'issues' in the plural, but in the singular, 'and to your issue'; and the
17 'issue' intended is Christ. What I am saying is this: a testament, or covenant, had already been validated by God; it cannot be invalidated, and its promises rendered ineffective, by a law made four hundred and thirty
18 years later. If the inheritance is by legal right, then it is not by promise; but it was by promise that God bestowed it as a free gift on Abraham.

From law to faith

19 Then what of the law? It was added to make wrongdoing a legal offence.[o] It was a temporary measure pending the arrival of the 'issue' to whom the promise was made. It was promulgated through angels, and there was an
20 intermediary; but an intermediary is not needed for one party acting alone, and God is one.
21 Does the law, then, contradict the promises? No, never! If a law had been given which had power to bestow life, then indeed righteousness would have come from keeping the law.
22 But Scripture has declared the whole world to be prisoners in subjection to sin, so that faith in Jesus Christ may be the ground on which the promised blessing is given, and given to those who have such faith.
23 Before this faith came, we were close prisoners in the custody of law,
24 pending the revelation of faith. Thus the law was a kind of tutor in charge of us until Christ should come,[p] when we should be justified through faith;
25 and now that faith has come, the tutor's charge is at an end.
26 For through faith you are all sons of God in union with Christ Jesus.
27 Baptized into union with him, you have all put on Christ as a garment.
28 There is no such thing as Jew and Greek, slave and freeman, male and

n Or by the message of faith, or or by hearing and believing.   o Or added because of offences.
p Or a kind of tutor to conduct us to Christ.

female; for you are all one person in Christ Jesus. But if you thus belong to Christ, you are the 'issue' of Abraham, and so heirs by promise. 29

4 This is what I mean: so long as the heir is a minor, he is no better off than a slave, even though the whole estate 2 is his; he is under guardians and trustees until the date fixed by his father. 3 And so it was with us. During our minority we were slaves to the ele- 4 mental spirits of the universe,*q* but when the term was completed, God sent his own Son, born of a woman, 5 born under the law, to purchase freedom for the subjects of the law, in order that we might attain the status of sons.

6 To prove that you are sons, God has sent into our hearts the Spirit of his 7 Son, crying 'Abba! Father!' You are therefore no longer a slave but a son, and if a son, then also by God's own act an heir.

8 Formerly, when you did not acknowledge God, you were the slaves of beings which in their nature are no 9 gods.*r* But now that you do acknowledge God—or rather, now that he has acknowledged you—how can you turn back to the mean and beggarly spirits of the elements?*s* Why do you propose to enter their service all over 10 again? You keep special days and 11 months and seasons and years. You make me fear that all the pains I spent on you may prove to be labour lost.

A personal plea

12 Put yourselves in my place, my brothers, I beg you, for I have put myself in yours. It is not that you did 13 me any wrong. As you know, it was bodily illness that originally*t* led to 14 my bringing you the Gospel, and you resisted any temptation to show scorn or disgust at the state of my poor body;*u* you welcomed me as if I were an angel of God, as you might have 15 welcomed Christ Jesus himself. Have you forgotten how happy you thought yourselves in having me with you? I can say this for you: you would have torn out your very eyes, and given them to me, had that been 16 possible! And have I now made myself your enemy by being frank with you?

The persons I have referred to are 17 envious of you, but not with an honest envy:*v* what they really want is to bar the door to you so that you may come to envy*w* them. It is always a 18 fine thing to deserve an honest envy*x* —always, and not only when I am present with you, dear children. For 19 my children you are, and I am in travail with you over again until you take the shape of Christ. I wish I 20 could be with you now; then I could modify my tone;*y* as it is, I am at my wits' end about you.

Illustration from Scripture

Tell me now, you who are so anxious 21 to be under law, will you not listen to what the Law says? It is written 22 there that Abraham had two sons, one by his slave and the other by his free-born wife. The slave-woman's 23 son was born in the course of nature, the free woman's through God's promise. This is an allegory. The two 24 women stand for two covenants. The one bearing children into slavery is the covenant that comes from Mount Sinai: that is Hagar. Sinai is a mount- 25 ain in Arabia and it represents the Jerusalem of today, for she and her children are in slavery. But the hea- 26 venly Jerusalem is the free woman; she is our mother. For Scripture says, 27 'Rejoice, O barren woman who never bore child; break into a shout of joy, you who never knew a mother's pangs; for the deserted wife shall have more children than she who lives with her husband.'

And you, my brothers, like Isaac, 28 are children of God's promise. But just 29 as in those days the natural-born son persecuted the spiritual son, so it is today. But what does Scripture say? 30 'Drive out the slave-woman and her son, for the son of the slave shall not share the inheritance with the free woman's son.' You see, then, my 31 brothers, we are no slave-woman's children; our mother is the free woman. Christ set us free, to be free 5 men.*z* Stand firm, then, and refuse to be tied to the yoke of slavery again.

Either law or Christ

Mark my words: I, Paul, say to you 2 that if you receive circumcision Christ

q Or the elements of the natural world, or elementary ideas belonging to this world.   r Or were slaves to 'gods' which in reality do not exist.   s See note on 4. 3.   t Or formerly, or on the first of my two visits.   u Or you showed neither scorn nor disgust at the trial my poor body was enduring.   v Or paying court to you, but not with honest intentions.   w Or pay court to.   x Or to be honourably wooed.   y Or now, and could exchange words with you.   z Or What Christ has done is to set us free.

3 will do you no good at all. Once again, you can take it from me that every man who receives circumcision is under obligation to keep the entire 4 law. When you seek to be justified by way of law, your relation with Christ is completely severed: you have fallen out of the domain of God's 5 grace. For to us, our hope of attaining that righteousness which we eagerly await is the work of the Spirit 6 through faith. If we are in union with Christ Jesus circumcision makes no difference at all, nor does the want of it; the only thing that counts is faith active in love.[a]

7 You were running well; who was it hindered you from following the truth? 8 Whatever persuasion he used, it did not come from God who is calling you; 9 'a little leaven', remember, 'leavens 10 all the dough'. United with you in the Lord, I am confident that you will not take the wrong view; but the man who is unsettling your minds, whoever he may be, must bear 11 God's judgement. And I, my friends, if I am still advocating circumcision, why is it I am still persecuted? In that case, my preaching of the cross 12 is a stumbling-block no more. As for these agitators, they had better go the whole way and make eunuchs of themselves!

The work of the Spirit

13 You, my friends, were called to be free men; only do not turn your freedom into licence for your lower nature, but be servants to one another 14 in love. For the whole law can be summed up in a single commandment: 'Love your neighbour as yourself.' 15 But if you go on fighting one another, tooth and nail, all you can expect is mutual destruction.

16 I mean this: if you are guided by the Spirit you will not fulfil the desires 17 of your lower nature. That nature sets its desires against the Spirit, while the Spirit fights against it. They are in conflict with one another so that what you will to do you cannot do. 18 But if you are led by the Spirit, you are not under law.

19 Anyone can see the kind of behaviour that belongs to the lower nature: fornication, impurity, and in-20 decency; idolatry and sorcery; quarrels, a contentious temper, envy, fits of rage, selfish ambitions, dissensions, 21 party intrigues, and jealousies; drink-

ing bouts, orgies, and the like. I warn you, as I warned you before, that those who behave in such ways will never inherit the kingdom of God.

22 But the harvest of the Spirit is love, joy, peace, patience, kindness, 23 goodness, fidelity, gentleness, and self-control. There is no law dealing 24 with such things as these. And those who belong to Christ Jesus have crucified the lower nature with its 25 passions and desires. If the Spirit is the source of our life, let the Spirit also direct our course.

Fulfilling the law of Christ

26 We must not be conceited, challenging one another to rivalry, jealous of 6 one another. If a man should do something wrong, my brothers, on a sudden impulse,[b] you who are endowed with the Spirit must set him right again very gently. Look to yourself, each one of you: you may be tempted 2 too. Help one another to carry these heavy loads, and in this way you will fulfil the law of Christ.

3 For if a man imagines himself to be somebody, when he is nothing, he is deluding himself. Each man should 4 examine his own conduct for himself; then he can measure his achievement by comparing himself with himself and not with anyone else. For every-5 one has his own proper burden to bear.

6 When anyone is under instruction in the faith, he should give his teacher a share of all good things he has.

7 Make no mistake about this: God is not to be fooled; a man reaps what he 8 sows. If he sows seed in the field of his lower nature, he will reap from it a harvest of corruption, but if he sows in the field of the Spirit, the Spirit will bring a harvest of eternal life. 9 So let us never tire of doing good, for if we do not slacken our efforts we shall in due time reap our harvest. 10 Therefore, as opportunity offers, let us work for the good of all, especially members of the household of the faith.

Paul's one boast

11 You see these big letters? I am now 12 writing to you in my own hand. It is all those who want to make a fair outward and bodily show who are trying to force circumcision upon you; their sole object is to escape persecu-13 tion for the cross of Christ. For even

a Or inspired by love.   b Or If a man is caught doing something wrong, my brothers, . . .

those who do receive circumcision are not thoroughgoing observers of the law; they only want you to be circumcised in order to boast of your having submitted to that outward 14 rite. But God forbid that I should boast of anything but the cross of our Lord Jesus Christ, through which[c] the world is crucified to me and I to 15 the world! Circumcision is nothing; uncircumcision is nothing; the only

thing that counts is new creation! Whoever they are who take this 16 principle for their guide, peace and mercy be upon them, and upon the whole Israel of God!

In future let no one make trouble 17 for me, for I bear the marks of Jesus branded on my body.

The grace of our Lord Jesus Christ 18 be with your spirit, my brothers. Amen.

c Or whom.

THE LETTER OF PAUL
TO THE
EPHESIANS

Spiritual blessings in Christ

1 FROM PAUL, apostle of Christ Jesus, commissioned by the will of God, to God's people at Ephesus,[a] believers incorporate in Christ Jesus. 2 Grace to you and peace from God our Father and the Lord Jesus Christ. 3 Praise be to the God and Father of our Lord Jesus Christ, who has bestowed on us in Christ every spiritual blessing in the heavenly realms. 4 In Christ he chose us before the world was founded, to be dedicated, to be without blemish in his sight, to be 5 full of love; and he[b] destined us—such was his will and pleasure—to be accepted as his sons through Jesus 6 Christ, in order that the glory of his gracious gift, so graciously bestowed on us in his Beloved, might redound 7 to his praise. For in Christ our release is secured and our sins are forgiven through the shedding of his blood. Therein lies the richness of God's free 8 grace lavished upon us, imparting full 9 wisdom and insight. He has made known to us his hidden purpose—such was his will and pleasure determined 10 beforehand in Christ—to be put into effect when the time was ripe: namely, that the universe, all in heaven and on earth, might be brought into a unity in Christ.

The pledge of our heritage

In Christ indeed we have been given 11 our share in the heritage, as was decreed in his design whose purpose is everywhere at work. For it was his will that we, who were the first to set 12 our hope on Christ,[c] should cause his glory to be praised. And you too, when 13 you had heard the message of the truth, the good news of your salvation, and had believed it, became incorporate in Christ and received the seal of the promised Holy Spirit; and 14 that Spirit is the pledge that we shall enter upon our heritage, when God has redeemed what is his own, to his praise and glory.

Prayer for spiritual illumination

Because of all this, now that I have 15 heard of the faith you have in the Lord Jesus and of the love you bear towards all God's people, I never 16 cease to give thanks for you when I mention you in my prayers. I pray 17 that the God of our Lord Jesus Christ, the all-glorious Father, may give you the spiritual powers of wisdom and vision, by which there comes the knowledge of him. I pray that your 18 inward eyes may be illumined, so that you may know what is the hope

a Some witnesses omit at Ephesus.   b Or . . . sight. In his love he . . .   c Or who already enjoyed the hope of Christ, or whose expectation and hope are in Christ.

to which he calls you, what the wealth and glory of the share he offers you among his people in their heritage, 19 and how vast the resources of his power open to us who trust in him. They are measured by his strength 20 and the might which he exerted in Christ when he raised him from the dead, when he enthroned him at his 21 right hand in the heavenly realms, far above all government and authority, all power and dominion, and any title of sovereignty that can be named, not only in this age but in the age to 22 come. He put everything in subjection beneath his feet, and appointed him as supreme head to the church, 23 which is his body and as such holds within it the fullness of him who himself receives the entire fullness of God.[d]

From death to life

2 Time was when you were dead in 2 your sins and wickedness, when you followed the evil ways of this present age, when you obeyed the commander of the spiritual powers of the air, the spirit now at work among God's 3 rebel subjects. We too were once of their number: we all lived our lives in sensuality, and obeyed the promptings of our own instincts and notions. In our natural condition we, like the rest, lay under the dreadful judgement 4 of God. But God, rich in mercy, for 5 the great love he bore us, brought us to life with Christ even when we were dead in our sins; it is by his grace you 6 are saved. And in union with Christ Jesus he raised us up and enthroned us with him in the heavenly realms, 7 so that he might display in the ages to come how immense are the resources of his grace, and how great his 8 kindness to us in Christ Jesus. For it is by his grace you are saved, through trusting him; it is not your own doing. 9 It is God's gift, not a reward for work done. There is nothing for anyone to 10 boast of. For we are God's handiwork, created in Christ Jesus to devote ourselves to the good deeds for which God has designed us.

Two made one in Christ

11 Remember then your former condition: you, Gentiles as you are outwardly,[e] you, 'the uncircumcised' so called by those who are called 'the circumcised' (but only with reference to an outward rite)—you were at that 12 time separate from Christ, strangers to the community of Israel, outside God's covenants and the promise that goes with them. Your world was a world without hope and without God. But now in union with Christ Jesus 13 you who once were far off have been brought near through the shedding of Christ's blood. For he is himself our 14 peace. Gentiles and Jews, he has made the two one, and in his own body of flesh and blood has broken down the enmity which stood like a dividing wall between them; for he annulled 15 the law with its rules and regulations, so as to create out of the two a single new humanity in himself, thereby making peace. This was his purpose, 16 to reconcile the two in a single body to God through the cross, on which he killed the enmity.[f]

So he came and proclaimed the good 17 news: peace to you who were far off, and peace to those who were near by; for through him we both alike 18 have access to the Father in the one Spirit. Thus you are no longer aliens 19 in a foreign land, but fellow-citizens with God's people, members of God's household. You are built upon the 20 foundation laid by the apostles and prophets, and Christ Jesus himself is the foundation-stone.[g] In him the 21 whole building[h] is bonded together and grows into a holy temple in the Lord. In him you too are being built 22 with all the rest into a spiritual dwelling for God.

The unfathomable riches of Christ

With this in mind I make my prayer, **3** I, Paul, who in the cause of you Gentiles am now the prisoner of Christ Jesus—for surely you have 2 heard how God has assigned the gift of his grace to me for your benefit. It 3 was by a revelation that his secret was made known to me. I have already written a brief account of this, and by reading it you may perceive 4 that I understand the secret of Christ. In former generations this was not 5 disclosed to the human race; but now it has been revealed by inspiration to

d Or as supreme head to the church, which is his body and as such holds within it the fullness of him who fills the universe in all its parts; or as supreme head to the church which is his body, and to be all that he himself is who fills the universe in all its parts.　　e Or by birth.　　f Or . . . cross. Thus in his own person he put the enmity to death.　　g Or built upon the foundation of the apostles and prophets, and Christ Jesus himself is the keystone.　　h Or every structure.

his dedicated apostles and prophets,
6 that through the Gospel the Gentiles
are joint heirs with the Jews, part of
the same body, sharers together in
the promise made in Christ Jesus.
7 Such is the gospel of which I was made
a minister, by God's gift, bestowed
unmerited on me in the working of
8 his power. To me, who am less than
the least of all God's people, he has
granted of his grace the privilege of
proclaiming to the Gentiles the good
news of the unfathomable riches of
9 Christ, and of bringing to light how
this hidden purpose was to be put
into effect. It was hidden for long
ages in God the creator of the uni-
10 verse, in order that now, through the
church, the wisdom of God in all its
varied forms might be made known
to the rulers and authorities in the
11 realms of heaven. This is in accord
with this age-long purpose, which he
12 achieved in Christ Jesus our Lord. In
him we have access to God with freedom, in the confidence born of trust
13 in him. I beg you, then, not to lose
heart over my sufferings for you; indeed, they are your glory.

The love of Christ

14 With this in mind, then, I kneel in
15 prayer to the Father, from whom
every family[i] in heaven and on earth
16 takes its name, that out of the
treasures of his glory he may grant
you strength and power through his
17 Spirit in your inner being, that
through faith Christ may dwell in
your hearts in love. With deep roots
18 and firm foundations, may you be
strong to grasp, with all God's people, what is the breadth and length
19 and height and depth of the love of
Christ, and to know it, though it is
beyond knowledge. So may you attain
to fullness of being, the fullness of
God himself.[j]
20   Now to him who is able to do im-
measurably more than all we can ask
or conceive, by the power which is at
21 work among us, to him be glory in the
church and in Christ Jesus from
generation to generation evermore!
Amen.

The unity of the body

4 I entreat you, then—I, a prisoner for
the Lord's sake: as God has called
2 you, live up to your calling. Be humble always and gentle, and patient

too. Be forbearing with one another
and charitable. Spare no effort to 3
make fast with bonds of peace the
unity which the Spirit gives. There is 4
one body and one Spirit, as there is
also one hope held out in God's call
to you; one Lord, one faith, one bap- 5
tism; one God and Father of all, who 6
is over all and through all and in all.
   But each of us has been given his 7
gift, his due portion of Christ's bounty. Therefore Scripture says: 8

'He ascended into the heights
   with captives in his train;
he gave gifts to men.'

Now, the word 'ascended' implies 9
that he also descended to the lowest
level, down to the very earth.[k] He 10
who descended is no other than he
who ascended far above all heavens,
so that he might fill the universe. And 11
these were his gifts: some to be
apostles, some prophets, some evan-
gelists, some pastors and teachers, to 12
equip God's people for work in his
service, to the building up of the body
of Christ. So shall we all at last 13
attain to the unity inherent in our
faith and our knowledge of the Son of
God—to mature manhood, measured
by nothing less than the full stature of
Christ. We are no longer to be chil- 14
dren, tossed by the waves and whirled
about by every fresh gust of teaching, dupes of crafty rogues and their
deceitful schemes. No, let us speak 15
the truth in love; so shall we fully
grow up into Christ. He is the head,
and on him the whole body depends. 16
Bonded and knit together by every
constituent joint, the whole frame
grows through the due activity of
each part, and builds itself up in love.

Be made new in mind and spirit

This then is my word to you, and I 17
urge it upon you in the Lord's name.
Give up living like pagans with their
good-for-nothing notions. Their wits 18
are beclouded, they are strangers to
the life that is in God, because ignorance prevails among them and their
minds have grown hard as stone. Dead 19
to all feeling, they have abandoned
themselves to vice, and stop at nothing to satisfy their foul desires. But 20
that is not how you learned Christ.
For were you not told of him, were 21
you not as Christians taught the
truth as it is in Jesus?—that, leaving 22
your former way of life, you must

i Or his whole family.   _j Or the fullness which God requires._   _k Or descended to the regions_
beneath the earth.

lay aside that old human nature which, deluded by its lusts, is sinking
23 towards death. You must be made
24 new in mind and spirit, and put on the new nature of God's creating, which shows itself in the just and devout life called for by the truth.
25 Then throw off falsehood; speak the truth to each other, for all of us are the parts of one body.
26 If you are angry, do not let anger lead you into sin; do not let sunset
27 find you still nursing it; leave no loop-hole for the devil.
28 The thief must give up stealing, and instead work hard and honestly with his own hands, so that he may have something to share with the needy.
29 No bad language must pass your lips, but only what is good and help-ful to the occasion, so that it brings a
30 blessing to those who hear it. And do not grieve the Holy Spirit of God, for that Spirit is the seal with which you were marked for the day of our final
31 liberation. Have done with spite and passion, all angry shouting and curs-ing, and bad feeling of every kind.
32 Be generous to one another, tender-hearted, forgiving one another as God in Christ forgave you.
5 In a word, as God's dear children,
2 try to be like him, and live in love as Christ loved you, and gave himself up on your behalf as an offering and sacrifice whose fragrance is pleasing to God.
3 Fornication and indecency of any kind, or ruthless greed, must not be so much as mentioned among you, as
4 befits the people of God. No coarse, stupid, or flippant talk; these things are out of place; you should rather
5 be thanking God. For be very sure of this: no one given to fornication or indecency, or the greed which makes an idol of gain, has any share in the kingdom of Christ and of God.

Daylight and darkness

6 Let no one deceive you with shallow arguments; it is for all these things that God's dreadful judgement is
7 coming upon his rebel subjects. Have
8 no part or lot with them. For though you were once all darkness, now as Christians you are light. Live like men
9 who are at home in daylight, for where light is, there all goodness
10 springs up, all justice and truth. Try to find out what would please the

Lord; take no part in the barren deeds 11 of darkness, but show them up for what they are. The things they do in 12 secret it would be shameful even to mention. But everything, when once 13 the light has shown it up, is illumined, and everything thus illumined is all light. And so the hymn says: 14

'Awake, sleeper,
rise from the dead,
and Christ will shine upon you.'

Be most careful then how you 15 conduct yourselves: like sensible men, not like simpletons. Use the present 16 opportunity to the full, for these are evil days. So do not be fools, but try 17 to understand what the will of the Lord is. Do not give way to drunken- 18 ness and the dissipation that goes with it, but let the Holy Spirit fill you: speak to one another in psalms, 19 hymns, and *l* songs; sing and make music in your hearts to the Lord; and in the 20 name of our Lord Jesus Christ give thanks every day for everything to our God and Father.

To wives and husbands

Be subject to one another out of 21 reverence for Christ.

Wives, be subject to your husbands 22 as to the Lord; for the man is the 23 head of the woman, just as Christ also is the head of the church. Christ is, indeed, the Saviour of the body; but 24 just as the church is subject to Christ, so must women be to their husbands in everything.

Husbands, love your wives, as 25 Christ also loved the church and gave himself up for it, to consecrate it, 26 cleansing it by water and word, so 27 that he might present the church to himself all glorious, with no stain or wrinkle or anything of the sort, but holy and without blemish. In the 28 same way men also are bound to love their wives, as they love their own bodies. In loving his wife a man loves himself. For no one ever hated his 29 own body: on the contrary, he pro-vides and cares for it; and that is how Christ treats the church, because it is 30 his body, of which we are living parts. Thus it is that (in the words of Scrip- 31 ture) 'a man shall leave his father and mother and shall be joined to his wife, and the two shall become one flesh'. It is a great truth that is hidden 32 here. I for my part refer it to Christ and to the church, but it applies also 33 individually: each of you must love

l Some witnesses insert spiritual, *as in Colossians 3. 16.*

his wife as his very self; and the woman must see to it that she pays her husband all respect.

To children and parents

6 Children, obey your parents, for it is
2 right that you should. 'Honour your father and mother' is the first commandment with a promise attached,
3 in the words: 'that it may be well with you and that you may live long in the land'.
4 You fathers, again, must not goad your children to resentment, but give them the instruction, and the correction, which belong to a Christian upbringing.

To slaves and masters

5 Slaves, obey your earthly masters with fear and trembling, single-mindedly,
6 as serving Christ. Do not offer merely the outward show of service, to curry favour with men, but, as slaves of Christ, do whole-heartedly the will
7 of God. Give the cheerful service of those who serve the Lord, not men.
8 For you know that whatever good each man may do, slave or free, will be repaid him by the Lord.
9 You masters, also, must do the same by them. Give up using threats; remember you both have the same Master in heaven, and he has no favourites.

The armour which God provides

10 Finally then, find your strength in the
11 Lord, in his mighty power. Put on all the armour which God provides, so that you may be able to stand firm
12 against the devices of the devil. For our fight is not against human foes, but against cosmic powers, against the authorities and potentates of this dark world, against the superhuman forces of evil in the heavens. There- 13 fore, take up God's armour; then you will be able to stand your ground when things are at their worst, to complete every task and still to stand. Stand firm, I say. Fasten on the belt of 14 truth; for coat of mail put on integrity; let the shoes on your feet be the 15 gospel of peace, to give you firm footing; and, with all these, take up the 16 great shield of faith, with which you will be able to quench all the flaming arrows of the evil one. Take salvation 17 for helmet; for sword, take that which the Spirit gives you—the words that come from God. Give yourselves 18 wholly to prayer and entreaty; pray on every occasion in the power of the Spirit. To this end keep watch and persevere, always interceding for all God's people; and pray for me, that 19 I may be granted the right words when I open my mouth, and may boldly and freely make known his hidden purpose, for which I am an 20 ambassador—in chains. Pray that I may speak of it boldly, as it is my duty to speak.

A personal note

You will want to know about my 21 affairs, and how I am; Tychicus will give you all the news. He is our dear brother and trustworthy helper in the Lord's work. I am sending him to 22 you on purpose to let you know all about us, and to put fresh heart into you.

Peace to the brotherhood and love, 23 with faith, from God the Father and the Lord Jesus Christ. God's grace 24 be with all who love our Lord Jesus Christ, grace and immortality.*m*

m Or who love ... Christ with love imperishable.

THE LETTER OF PAUL TO THE
PHILIPPIANS

1 FROM PAUL and Timothy, servants of Christ Jesus, to all those of God's people, incorporate in Christ Jesus, who live at Philippi, including **2** their bishops and deacons. Grace to you and peace from God our Father and the Lord Jesus Christ.

Thanksgiving and prayer

3 I thank my God whenever I think of **4** you; and when I pray for you all, my **5** prayers are always joyful, because of the part you have taken in the work of the Gospel from the first day until **6** now. Of one thing I am certain: the One who started the good work in you will bring it to completion by the Day **7** of Christ Jesus. It is indeed only right that I should feel like this about you all, because you hold me in such affection, and because, when I lie in prison or appear in the dock to vouch for the truth of the Gospel, you all share in the privilege that is mine.[a] **8** God knows how I long for you all, with the deep yearning of Christ **9** Jesus himself. And this is my prayer, that your love may grow ever richer and richer in knowledge and insight **10** of every kind, and may thus bring you the gift of true discrimination.[b] Then on the Day of Christ you will be **11** flawless and without blame, reaping the full harvest of righteousness that comes through Jesus Christ, to the glory and praise of God.

Paul's imprisonment and its results

12 Friends, I want you to understand that the work of the Gospel has been helped on, rather than hindered, by **13** this business of mine. My imprisonment in Christ's cause has become common knowledge to all at headquarters[c] here, and indeed among the public at large; and it has given **14** confidence to most of our fellow-Christians to speak the word of God fearlessly and with extraordinary courage.

Some, indeed, proclaim Christ in **15** a jealous and quarrelsome spirit; others proclaim him in true goodwill, and these are moved by love for me; **16** they know that it is to defend the Gospel that I am where I am. But the **17** others, moved by personal rivalry, present Christ from mixed motives, meaning to stir up fresh trouble for me as I lie in prison.[d] What does it **18** matter? One way or another, in pretence or sincerity, Christ is set forth, and for that I rejoice.

A difficult choice

Yes, and rejoice I will, knowing well **19** that the issue of it all will be my deliverance, because you are praying for me and the Spirit of Jesus Christ is given me for support.[e] For, as I **20** passionately hope, I shall have no cause to be ashamed, but shall speak so boldly that now as always the greatness of Christ will shine out clearly in my person, whether through my life or through my death. For **21** to me life is Christ, and death gain; but what if my living on in the body **22** may serve some good purpose? Which then am I to choose? I cannot tell. I am torn two ways: what I should **23** like is to depart and be with Christ; that is better by far; but for your sake **24** there is greater need for me to stay on in the body. This indeed I know **25** for certain: I shall stay, and stand by you all to help you forward and to add joy to your faith, so that when I **26** am with you again, your pride in me may be unbounded in Christ Jesus.

a Or I am justified in taking this view about you all, because I hold you in closest union, as those who, when I lie . . . of the Gospel, all share in the privilege that is mine.   b Or may teach you by experience what things are most worth while.   c Or to all the imperial guard, or to all at the Residency (Greek Praetorium).   d Or meaning to make use of my imprisonment to stir up fresh trouble. e Or supplies me with all I need.

Standing firm

27 Only, let your conduct be worthy of the gospel of Christ, so that whether I come and see you for myself or hear about you from a distance, I may know that you are standing firm, one in spirit, one in mind, contending as 28 one man for the gospel faith, meeting your opponents without so much as a tremor. This is a sure sign to them that their doom is sealed, but a sign of your salvation, and one afforded 29 by God himself; for you have been granted the privilege not only of believing in Christ but also of suffer- 30 ing for him. You and I are engaged in the same contest; you saw me in it once, and, as you hear, I am in it still.

The example of Christ in becoming man

2 If then our common life in Christ yields anything to stir the heart, any loving consolation, any sharing of the Spirit, any warmth of affection or 2 compassion, fill up my cup of happiness by thinking and feeling alike, with the same love for one another, the same turn of mind, and a com- 3 mon care for unity. There must be no room for rivalry and personal vanity among you, but you must humbly reckon others better than yourselves. 4 Look to each other's interest and not merely to your own. 5 Let your bearing towards one another arise out of your life in Christ 6 Jesus.[f] For the divine nature was his from the first; yet he did not think 7 to snatch at equality with God,[g] but made himself nothing, assuming the nature of a slave. Bearing the human 8 likeness, revealed in human shape, he humbled himself, and in obedience accepted even death—death on a 9 cross. Therefore God raised him to the heights and bestowed on him the 10 name above all names, that at the name of Jesus every knee should bow—in heaven, on earth, and in the 11 depths—and every tongue confess, 'Jesus Christ is Lord', to the glory of God the Father.

Children of God

12 So you too, my friends, must be obedient, as always; even more, now that I am away, than when I was with you. You must work out your own salvation in fear and trembling; for it is God who works in you, inspir- 13 ing both the will and the deed, for his own chosen purpose.

Do all you have to do without 14 complaint or wrangling. Show your- 15 selves guileless and above reproach, faultless children of God in a warped and crooked generation, in which you shine[h] like stars in a dark world[i] and 16 proffer the word of life.[j] Thus you will be my pride on the Day of Christ, proof that I did not run my race in vain, or work in vain. But if my life- 17 blood is to crown that sacrifice which is the offering up of your faith, I am glad of it, and I share my gladness with you all. Rejoice, you no less than 18 I, and let us share our joy.

Timothy and Epaphroditus

I hope (under the Lord Jesus) to send 19 Timothy to you soon; it will cheer me to hear news of you. There is no one 20 else here who sees things as I do, and takes[k] a genuine interest in your concerns; they are all bent on their own 21 ends, not on the cause of Christ Jesus. But Timothy's record is known 22 to you: you know that he has been at my side in the service of the Gospel like a son working under his father. Timothy, then, I hope to send as soon 23 as ever I can see how things are going with me; and I am confident, under 24 the Lord, that I shall myself be coming before long.

I feel also I must send our brother 25 Epaphroditus, my fellow-worker and comrade, whom you commissioned to minister to my needs. He has been 26 missing all of you sadly, and has been distressed that you heard he was ill. (He was indeed dangerously ill, but 27 God was merciful to him, and merciful no less to me, to spare me sorrow upon sorrow.) For this reason I am 28 all the more eager to send him, to give you the happiness of seeing him again, and to relieve my sorrow. Welcome 29 him then in the fellowship of the Lord with whole-hearted delight. You should honour men like him; in Christ's 30 cause he came near to death, risking his life to render me the service you could not give.

And now, friends, farewell; I wish 3 you joy in the Lord.

---

f Or Have that bearing towards one another which was also found in Christ Jesus.   g Or yet he did not prize his equality with God.   h Or . . . generation. Shine out among them . . .   i Or in the firmament.   j Or as the very principle of its life.   k Or no one else here like him, who takes . . .

A personal confession

To repeat what I have written to you before is no trouble to me, and it is a 2 safeguard for you. Beware of those dogs and their malpractices. Beware of those who insist on mutilation— 3 'circumcision' I will not call it; we are the circumcised, we whose worship is spiritual,[l] whose pride is in Christ Jesus, and who put no confidence in 4 anything external. Not that I am without grounds myself even for confidence of that kind. If anyone thinks to base his claims on externals, I could make a stronger case for myself: 5 circumcised on my eighth day, Israelite by race, of the tribe of Benjamin, a Hebrew born and bred;[m] in my 6 attitude to the law, a Pharisee; in pious zeal, a persecutor of the church; 7 in legal rectitude, faultless. But all such assets I have written off because 8 of Christ. I would say more: I count everything sheer loss, because all is far outweighed by the gain of knowing Christ Jesus my Lord, for whose sake I did in fact lose everything. I count it so much garbage,[n] for the sake of 9 gaining Christ and finding myself incorporate in him, with no righteousness of my own, no legal rectitude, but the righteousness which comes[o] from faith in Christ, given by God in re-10 sponse to faith. All I care for is to know Christ, to experience the power of his resurrection, and to share his sufferings, in growing conformity with 11 his death, if only I may finally arrive at the resurrection from the dead.

12 It is not to be thought that I have already achieved all this. I have not yet reached perfection, but I press on, hoping to take hold of that for which 13 Christ once took hold of me. My friends, I do not reckon myself to have got hold of it yet. All I can say is this: forgetting what is behind me, and reaching out for that which lies ahead, 14 I press towards the goal to win the prize which is God's call to the life above, in Christ Jesus.

15 Let us then keep to this way of thinking, those of us who are mature. If there is any point on which you think differently, this also God will 16 make plain to you. Only let our conduct be consistent with the level we have already reached.

Citizens of heaven

Agree together, my friends, to follow 17 my example. You have us for a model; watch those whose way of life conforms to it. For, as I have often told 18 you, and now tell you with tears in my eyes, there are many whose way of life makes them enemies of the cross of Christ. They are heading for 19 destruction, appetite is their god, and they glory in their shame. Their minds are set on earthly things. We, by 20 contrast, are citizens of heaven, and from heaven we expect our deliverer to come, the Lord Jesus Christ. He 21 will transfigure the body belonging to our humble state, and give it a form like that of his own resplendent body, by the very power which enables him to make all things subject to himself. Therefore, my friends, beloved friends 4 whom I long for, my joy, my crown, stand thus firm in the Lord, my beloved!

I beg Euodia, and I beg Syntyche, 2 to agree together in the Lord's fellowship. Yes, and you too, my loyal com-3 rade, I ask you to help these women, who shared my struggles in the cause of the Gospel, with Clement and my other fellow-workers, whose[p] names are in the roll of the living.

The peace of God

Farewell; I wish you all joy in the 4 Lord. I will say it again: all joy be yours.

Let your magnanimity be manifest 5 to all.

The Lord is near; have no anxiety, 6 but in everything make your requests known to God in prayer and petition with thanksgiving. Then the peace of 7 God, which is beyond our utmost understanding,[q] will keep guard over your hearts and your thoughts, in Christ Jesus.

And now, my friends, all that is 8 true, all that is noble, all that is just and pure, all that is lovable and gracious,[r] whatever is excellent and admirable—fill all your thoughts with these things.

The lessons I taught you, the 9 tradition I have passed on, all that you heard me say or saw me do, put into practice; and the God of peace will be with you.

---

l Some witnesses read who worship God in the spirit; others read who worship by the Spirit of God. m Or a Hebrew-speaking Jew of a Hebrew-speaking family.   n Or dung.   o Or and in him finding that, though I have no righteousness of my own, no legal rectitude, I have the righteousness which comes . . .   p Some witnesses read my fellow-workers, and the others whose . . .   q Or of far more worth than human reasoning.   r Or of good repute.

Giving and receiving

10 It is a great joy to me, in the Lord, that after so long your care for me has now blossomed afresh. You did care about me before for that matter; it
11 was opportunity that you lacked. Not that I am alluding to want, for I have learned to find resources in myself
12 whatever my circumstances. I know what it is to be brought low, and I know what it is to have plenty. I have been very thoroughly initiated into the human lot with all its ups and downs—fullness and hunger, plenty
13 and want. I have strength for anything through him who gives me
14 power. But it was kind of you to share the burden of my troubles.
15 As you know yourselves, Philippians, in the early days of my mission, when I set out from Macedonia, you alone of all our congregations were my
16 partners in payments and receipts; for even at Thessalonica you contributed

to my needs, not once but twice over.
Do not think I set my heart upon the 17 gift; all I care for is the profit accruing to you. However, here I give you my 18 receipt for everything—for more than everything; I am paid in full, now that I have received from Epaphroditus what you sent. It is a fragrant offering, an acceptable sacrifice, pleasing to God. And my God will supply all your 19 wants out of the magnificence of his riches in Christ Jesus. To our God 20 and Father be glory for endless ages! Amen.

Final greetings

Give my greetings, in the fellowship 21 of Christ Jesus, to each one of God's people. The brothers who are now with me send their greetings to you, and so do all God's people here, 22 particularly those who belong to the imperial establishment.
The grace of our Lord Jesus Christ 23 be with your spirit.

THE LETTER OF PAUL
TO THE
COLOSSIANS

1 FROM PAUL, apostle of Christ Jesus commissioned by the will of
2 God, and our colleague Timothy, to God's people at Colossae, brothers in the faith, incorporate in Christ.
Grace to you and peace from God our Father.

Thanksgiving and prayer

3 In all our prayers to God, the Father of our Lord Jesus Christ, we thank
4 him for you, because we have heard of the faith you hold in Christ Jesus, and the love you bear towards all
5 God's people. Both spring from the hope stored up for you in heaven— that hope of which you learned when
6 the message of the true Gospel first came to you. In the same way it is coming to men the whole world over; everywhere it is growing and bearing

fruit as it does among you, and has done since the day when you heard of the graciousness of God and recognized it for what in truth it is. You 7 were taught this by Epaphras, our dear fellow-servant, a trusted worker for Christ on our[a] behalf, and it is he 8 who has brought us the news of your God-given love.[b]
For this reason, ever since the day 9 we heard of it, we have not ceased to pray for you. We ask God that you may receive from him all wisdom and spiritual understanding for full insight into his will, so that your manner 10 of life may be worthy of the Lord and entirely pleasing to him. We pray that you may bear fruit in active goodness of every kind, and grow in the knowledge of God. May he strengthen 11 you, in his glorious might, with ample power to meet whatever comes with

a Some witnesses read your.   *b Or* your love within the fellowship of the Spirit.

R

12 fortitude, patience, and joy; and to give thanks[c] to the Father who has made you fit to share the heritage of God's people in the realm of light.

The supremacy of the Son of God

13 He rescued us from the domain of darkness and brought us away into 14 the kingdom of his dear Son, in whom our release is secured and our sins 15 forgiven. He is the image of the invisible God; his is the primacy over[d] 16 all created things. In him everything in heaven and on earth was created, not only things visible but also the invisible orders of thrones, sovereignties, authorities, and powers: the whole universe has been created 17 through him and for him. And he exists before everything, and all 18 things are held together in him. He is, moreover, the head of the body, the church. He is its origin, the first to return from the dead, to be in all 19 things alone supreme. For in him the complete being of God, by God's own 20 choice, came to dwell. Through him God chose to reconcile the whole universe to himself, making peace through the shedding of his blood upon the cross—to reconcile all things, whether on earth or in heaven, through him alone.

Reconciliation by Christ's death

21 Formerly you were yourselves estranged from God; you were his enemies in heart and mind, and your 22 deeds were evil. But now by Christ's death in his body of flesh and blood God has reconciled you to himself, so that he may present you before himself as dedicated men, without blemish 23 and innocent in his sight. Only you must continue in your faith, firm on your foundations, never to be dislodged from the hope offered in the gospel which you heard. This is the gospel which has been proclaimed in the whole creation under heaven; and I, Paul, have become its minister.

Disclosing God's secret

24 It is now my happiness to suffer for you. This is my way of helping to complete, in my poor human flesh, the full tale of Christ's afflictions still to be endured, for the sake of his body

which is the church. I became its 25 servant by virtue of the task assigned to me by God for your benefit: to deliver his message in full; to announce 26 the secret hidden for long ages and through many generations, but now disclosed to God's people, to whom 27 it was his will to make it known—to make known how rich and glorious it is among all nations. The secret is this: Christ in[e] you, the hope of a glory to come.

He it is whom we proclaim. We 28 admonish everyone without distinction, we instruct everyone in all the ways of wisdom, so as to present each one of you as a mature member of Christ's body. To this end I am toiling 29 strenuously with all the energy and power of Christ at work in me. For I **2** want you to know how strenuous are my exertions for you and the Laodiceans and all who have never set eyes on me. I want them to continue in 2 good heart and in the unity of love, and to come to the full wealth of conviction which understanding brings, and grasp God's secret. That secret is 3 Christ himself; in him lie hidden all God's treasures of wisdom and knowledge. I tell you this to save you from 4 being talked[f] into error by specious arguments. For though absent in 5 body, I am with you in spirit, and rejoice to see your orderly array and the firm front which your faith in Christ presents.

Complete in Christ

Therefore, since Jesus was delivered 6 to you as Christ and Lord, live your lives in union with him. Be rooted 7 in him; be built in him; be consolidated in the faith you were taught;[g] let your hearts overflow with thankfulness. Be on your guard; do not let 8 your minds be captured by hollow and delusive speculations, based on traditions of man-made teaching and centred on the elemental spirits of the universe[h] and not on Christ.

For it is in Christ that the complete 9 being of the Godhead dwells embodied,[i] and in him you have been brought to 10 completion. Every power and authority in the universe is subject to him as Head. In him also you were circum- 11 cised, not in a physical sense, but by being divested of the lower nature;

c Or with fortitude and patience, and to give joyful thanks . . .   d Or image of the invisible God, born before . . .   e Or among.   f Or What I mean is this: no one must talk you . . .   g Or by your faith, as you were taught.   h Or the elements of the natural world, or elementary ideas belonging to this world.   i Or corporately.

this is Christ's way of circumcision.
12 For in baptism[j] you were buried with him, in baptism also you were raised to life with him through your faith in the active power of God who raised
13 him from the dead. And although you were dead because of your sins and because you were morally uncircumcised, he has made you alive with Christ. For he has forgiven us all our
14 sins; he has cancelled the bond which pledged us to the decrees of the law. It stood against us, but he has set it
15 aside, nailing it to the cross. On that cross he discarded the cosmic powers and authorities like a garment; he made a public spectacle of them and led them[k] as captives in his triumphal procession.

Warning against self-mortification

16 Allow no one therefore to take you to task about what you eat or drink, or over the observance of festival, new
17 moon, or sabbath. These are no more than a shadow of what was to come;
18 the solid reality is Christ's. You are not to be disqualified by the decision of people who go in for self-mortification and angel-worship, and try to enter into some vision of their own. Such people, bursting with the futile
19 conceit of worldly minds, lose hold upon the Head; yet it is from the Head that the whole body, with all its joints and ligaments, receives its supplies, and thus knit together grows according to God's design.
20 Did you not die with Christ and pass beyond reach of the elemental spirits of the universe[l]? Then why behave as though you were still living the life of the world? Why let
21 people dictate to you: 'Do not handle this, do not taste that, do not touch
22 the other'—all of them things that must perish as soon as they are used? That is to follow merely human in-
23 junctions and teaching. True, it has an air of wisdom, with its forced piety, its self-mortification, and its severity to the body; but it is of no use at all in combating sensuality.

The old life and the new

3 Were you not raised to life with Christ? Then aspire to the realm above, where Christ is, seated at the right hand of God, and let your 2 thoughts dwell on that higher realm, not on this earthly life. I repeat, you 3 died; and now your life lies hidden with Christ in God. When Christ, 4 who is our life, is manifested, then you too will be manifested with him in glory.

Then put to death those parts of 5 you which belong to the earth—fornication, indecency, lust, foul cravings, and the ruthless greed which is nothing less than idolatry. Because of 6 these, God's dreadful judgement is impending; and in the life you once 7 lived these are the ways you yourselves followed. But now you must 8 yourselves lay aside all anger, passion, malice, cursing, filthy talk—have done with them! Stop lying to one 9 another, now that you have discarded the old nature, with its deeds and have 10 put on the new nature, which is being constantly renewed in the image of its Creator and brought to know God. There is no question here of Greek 11 and Jew, circumcised and uncircumcised, barbarian, Scythian, slave and freeman; but Christ is all, and is in all.

Then put on the garments that suit 12 God's chosen people, his own, his beloved: compassion, kindness, humility, gentleness, patience. Be forbear- 13 ing with one another, and forgiving, where any of you has cause for complaint: you must forgive as the Lord forgave you. To crown all, there must 14 be love, to bind all together and complete the whole. Let Christ's peace be 15 arbiter in your hearts; to this peace you were called as members of a single body. And be filled with gratitude. Let the message of Christ dwell among 16 you in all its richness. Instruct and admonish each other with the utmost wisdom. Sing thankfully in your hearts to God,[m] with psalms and hymns and spiritual songs. Whatever 17 you are doing, whether you speak or act, do everything in the name of the Lord Jesus, giving thanks to God the Father through him.

Personal relationships

Wives, be subject to your husbands; 18 that is your Christian duty. Husbands, 19

---

j Or . . . nature, in the very circumcision of Christ himself; for in baptism . . .   k Or he stripped himself of his physical body, and thereby boldly made a spectacle of the cosmic powers and authorities, and led them . . .; or he despoiled the cosmic powers and authorities, and boldly made a spectacle of them, leading them . . .   l Or the elements of the natural world, or elementary ideas belonging to this world.   m Some witnesses read the Lord.

love your wives and do not be harsh
20 with them. Children, obey your parents
in everything, for that is pleasing to
21 God and is the Christian way. Fathers,
do not exasperate your children, for
22 fear they grow disheartened. Slaves,
give entire obedience to your earthly
masters, not merely with an outward
show of service, to curry favour with
men, but with single-mindedness, out
23 of reverence for the Lord. Whatever
you are doing, put your whole heart
into it, as if you were doing it for the
24 Lord and not for men, knowing that
there is a Master who will give you
your heritage as a reward for your
service. Christ is the Master whose
25 slaves you must be. Dishonesty will
be requited, and he has no favourites.
4 Masters, be just and fair to your
slaves, knowing that you too have
a Master in heaven.
2 Persevere in prayer, with mind
3 awake and thankful heart; and include a prayer for us, that God may
give us an opening for preaching, to
tell the secret of Christ; that indeed
4 is why I am now in prison. Pray that
I may make the secret plain, as it is
my duty to do.
5 Behave wisely towards those outside your own number; use the pre-
6 sent opportunity to the full. Let your
conversation be always gracious, and
never insipid; study how best to talk
with each person you meet.

Final greetings

7 You will hear all about my affairs
from Tychicus, our dear brother and
trustworthy helper and fellow-servant
in the Lord's work. I am sending him 8
to you on purpose to let you know all
about us and to put fresh heart into
you. With him comes Onesimus, our 9
trustworthy and dear brother, who is
one of yourselves. They will tell you
all the news here.
Aristarchus, Christ's captive like 10
myself, sends his greetings; so does
Mark, the cousin of Barnabas (you
have had instructions about him; if
he comes, make him welcome), and 11
Jesus Justus. Of the Jewish Christians, these are the only ones who
work with me for the kingdom of God,
and they have been a great comfort
to me. Greetings from Epaphras, 12
servant of Christ, who is one of yourselves. He prays hard for you all the
time, that you may stand fast, ripe
in conviction[n] and wholly devoted to
doing God's will. For I can vouch for 13
him, that he works tirelessly for you
and the people at Laodicea and
Hierapolis. Greetings to you from our 14
dear friend Luke, the doctor, and
from Demas. Give our greetings to the 15
brothers at Laodicea, and Nympha
and the congregation at her house.[o]
And when this letter is read among 16
you, see that it is also read to the
congregation at Laodicea, and that
you in return read the one from Laodicea. This special word to Archip- 17
pus: 'Attend to the duty entrusted to
you in the Lord's service, and discharge it to the full.'
This greeting is in my own hand— 18
PAUL. Remember I am in prison.
God's grace be with you.

n *Or* stand fast, mature and complete . . .
at his house.   o *Some witnesses read* Nymphas and the congregation

THE FIRST LETTER OF PAUL
TO THE
THESSALONIANS

1 FROM PAUL, Silvanus, and Timothy to the congregation of Thessalonians who belong to God the Father and the Lord Jesus Christ.

Grace to you and peace.

The Gospel at Thessalonica

2 We always thank God for you all, and mention you in our prayers continu- **3** ally. We call to mind, before our God and Father, how your faith has shown itself in action, your love in labour, and your hope of our Lord Jesus Christ **4** in fortitude. We are certain, brothers beloved by God, that he has chosen **5** you and that*a* when we brought you the Gospel, we brought it not in mere words but in the power of the Holy Spirit, and with strong conviction, as you know well. That is the kind of men we were at Thessalonica, and it was for your sake.

6 And you, in your turn, followed the example set by us and by the Lord; the welcome you gave the message meant grave suffering for you, yet **7** you rejoiced in the Holy Spirit; thus you have become a model for all believers in Macedonia and in Achaia. **8** From Thessalonica the word of the Lord rang out; and not in Macedonia and Achaia alone, but everywhere your faith in God has reached men's ears. No words of ours are needed, **9** for they themselves spread the news of our visit to you and its effect: how you turned from idols, to be servants **10** of the living and true God, and to wait expectantly for the appearance from heaven of his Son Jesus, whom he raised from the dead, Jesus our deliverer from the terrors of judgement to come.

The apostle's example

2 You know for yourselves, brothers, that our visit to you was not fruitless. **2** Far from it; after all the injury and outrage which to your knowledge we

had suffered at Philippi, we declared the gospel of God to you frankly and fearlessly, by the help of our God. A hard struggle it was. Indeed, the **3** appeal we make never springs from error or base motive; there is no attempt to deceive; but God has ap- **4** proved us as fit to be entrusted with the Gospel, and on those terms we speak. We do not curry favour with men; we seek only the favour of God, who is continually testing our hearts. Our words have never been flattering **5** words, as you have cause to know; nor, as God is our witness, have they ever been a cloak for greed. We have **6** never sought honour from men, from you or from anyone else, although as Christ's own envoys we might have made our weight felt; but we were **7** as gentle with you as a nurse caring fondly for her children. With such **8** yearning love we chose to impart to you not only the gospel of God but our very selves, so dear had you become to us. Remember, brothers, how **9** we toiled and drudged. We worked for a living night and day, rather than be a burden to anyone, while we proclaimed before you the good news of God.

We call you to witness, yes and God **10** himself, how devout and just and blameless was our behaviour towards you who are believers. As you well **11** know, we dealt with you one by one, as a father deals with his children, appealing to you by encouragement, as well as by solemn injunctions, to **12** live lives worthy of the God who calls you into his kingdom and glory.

The Thessalonians' sufferings

This is why we thank God continu- **13** ally, because when we handed on God's message, you received it, not as the word of men, but as what it truly is, the very word of God at*b* work in you who hold the faith. You have fared like **14** the congregations in Judaea, God's

a Or ... chosen you, because ...   *b Or word of God who is at ...*

people in Christ Jesus. You have been treated by your countrymen as they
15 are treated by the Jews, who killed the Lord Jesus and the prophets[c] and drove us out, the Jews who are heedless of God's will and enemies of their
16 fellow-men, hindering us from speaking to the Gentiles to lead them to salvation. All this time they have been making up the full measure of their guilt, and now retribution has overtaken them for good and all.[d]

Paul's concern for them

17 My friends, when for a short spell you were lost to us—lost to sight, not to our hearts—we were exceedingly
18 anxious to see you again. So we did propose to come to Thessalonica—I, Paul, more than once—but Satan
19 thwarted us. For after all, what hope or joy or crown of pride is there for us, what indeed but you, when we stand before our Lord Jesus at his
20 coming? It is you who are indeed our glory and our joy.

3   So when we could bear it no longer, we decided to remain alone at Athens,
2 and sent Timothy, our brother and God's fellow-worker[e] in the service of the gospel of Christ, to encourage you
3 to stand firm for the faith and, under all these hardships, not to be shaken;[f] for you know that this is our ap-
4 pointed lot. When we were with you we warned you that we were bound to suffer hardship; and so it has
5 turned out, as you know. And thus it was that when I could bear it no longer, I sent to find out about your faith, fearing that the tempter might have tempted you and my labour might be lost.

Timothy brings good news

6 But now Timothy has just arrived from Thessalonica, bringing good news of your faith and love. He tells us that you always think kindly of us, and are as anxious to see us as we
7 are to see you. And so in all our difficulties and hardships your faith
8 reassures us about you. It is the breath of life to us that you stand
9 firm in the Lord. What thanks can we return to God for you? What thanks for all the joy you have brought us, making us rejoice before our Lord
10 while we pray most earnestly night

and day to be allowed to see you again and to mend your faith where it falls short?

11 May our God and Father himself, and our Lord Jesus, bring us direct
12 to you; and may the Lord make your love mount and overflow towards one another and towards all, as our love
13 does towards you. May he make your hearts firm, so that you may stand before our God and Father holy and faultless when our Lord Jesus comes with all those who are his own.

Call to holiness

4 And now, my friends, we have one thing to beg and pray of you, by our fellowship with the Lord Jesus. We passed on to you the tradition of the way we must live to please God; you are indeed already following it, but we beg you to do so yet more thoroughly.
2 For you know what orders we gave you, in the name of the Lord Jesus.
3 This is the will of God, that you should be holy: you must abstain from
4 fornication; each one of you must learn to gain mastery over his body,
5 to hallow and honour it, not giving way to lust like the pagans who are
6 ignorant of God; and no man must do his brother wrong in this matter,[g] or invade his rights, because, as we told you before with all emphasis, the
7 Lord punishes all such offences. For God called us to holiness, not to im-
8 purity. Anyone therefore who flouts these rules is flouting, not man, but God who bestows upon you his Holy Spirit.
9 About love for our brotherhood you need no words of mine, for you are yourselves taught by God to love
10 one another, and you are in fact practising this rule of love towards all your fellow-Christians throughout Macedonia. Yet we appeal to you,
11 brothers, to do better still. Let it be your ambition to keep calm and look after your own business, and to work with your hands, as we ordered you,
12 so that you may command the respect of those outside your own number, and at the same time may never be in want.

About death and resurrection

13 We wish you not to remain in ignorance, brothers, about those who sleep in death; you should not grieve like

---

c *Some witnesses read* their own prophets.   d Or now at last retribution has overtaken them.
e Or and fellow-worker for God; *one witness has simply* and fellow-worker.   f Or beguiled away.
g Or must overreach his brother in his business (*or* in lawsuits).

the rest of men, who have no hope.
14 We believe that Jesus died and rose again; and so it will be for those who died as Christians; God will bring them to life with Jesus.[h]

15 For this we tell you as the Lord's word: we who are left alive until the Lord comes shall not forestall those
16 who have died; because at the word of command, at the sound of the archangel's voice and God's trumpet-call, the Lord himself will descend from heaven; first the Christian dead
17 will rise, then we who are left alive shall join them, caught up in clouds to meet the Lord in the air. Thus we
18 shall always be with the Lord. Console one another, then, with these words.

The Day of the Lord

5 About dates and times, my friends,
2 we need not write to you, for you know perfectly well that the Day of the Lord comes like a thief in the
3 night. While they are talking of peace and security, all at once calamity is upon them, sudden as the pangs that come upon a woman with child;
4 and there will be no escape. But you, my friends, are not in the dark, that the day should overtake you like a
5 thief.[i] You are all children of light, children of day. We do not belong to
6 night or darkness, and we must not sleep like the rest, but keep awake
7 and sober. Sleepers sleep at night, and drunkards are drunk at night,
8 but we, who belong to daylight, must keep sober, armed with faith and love for coat of mail, and the hope of salva-
9 tion for helmet. For God has not destined us to the terrors of judgement, but to the full attainment of salvation through our Lord Jesus Christ.
10 He died for us so that we, awake or asleep, might live in company with him. Therefore hearten one another,
11 fortify one another—as indeed you do.

Final instructions and greetings

We beg you, brothers, to acknow-
12 ledge those who are working so hard among you, and in the Lord's fellowship are your leaders and counsellors.
13 Hold them in the highest possible esteem and affection for the work they do.

You must live at peace among yourselves. And we would urge you,
14 brothers, to admonish the careless, encourage the faint-hearted, support the weak, and to be very patient with them all.

See to it that no one pays back
15 wrong for wrong, but always aim at doing the best you can for each other and for all men.

Be always joyful; pray continually;
16 17 give thanks whatever happens; for
18 this is what God in Christ wills for you.

Do not stifle inspiration, and do
19 20 not despise prophetic utterances, but
21 bring them all to the test and then keep what is good in them and avoid
22 the bad of whatever kind.[j]

May God himself, the God of peace,
23 make you holy in every part, and keep you sound in spirit, soul, and body, without fault when our Lord Jesus Christ comes. He who calls you is to
24 be trusted; he will do it.

Brothers, pray for us also.
25
Greet all our brothers with the kiss
26 of peace.

I adjure you by the Lord to have
27 this letter read to the whole brotherhood.

The grace of our Lord Jesus Christ
28 be with you!

h Or will bring them in company with Jesus.   i Some witnesses read thieves.   j Or . . . utterances. Put everything to the test; keep hold of what is good and avoid every kind of evil.

THE SECOND LETTER OF PAUL
TO THE
THESSALONIANS

1 FROM PAUL, Silvanus, and Timothy to the congregation of Thessalonians who belong to God our Father and the Lord Jesus Christ.
2 Grace to you and peace from God the Father and the Lord Jesus Christ.

Thanksgiving for steadfastness under trials

3 Our thanks are always due to God for you, brothers. It is right that we should thank him, because your faith increases mightily, and the love you have, each for all and all for each,
4 grows ever greater. Indeed we boast about you ourselves among the congregations of God's people, because your faith remains so steadfast under all your persecutions, and all the
5 troubles you endure. See how this brings out the justice of God's judgement. It will prove you worthy of the kingdom of God, for which indeed you are suffering.

Judgement Day

6 It is surely just that God should balance the account by sending trouble
7 to those who trouble you, and relief to you who are troubled, and to us as well, when our Lord Jesus Christ is revealed from heaven with his
8 mighty angels in blazing fire. Then he will do justice upon those who refuse to acknowledge God and upon those who will not obey[a] the gospel of
9 our Lord Jesus. They will suffer the punishment of eternal ruin, cut off from the presence of the Lord and the
10 splendour of his might, when on that great Day he comes to be glorified among his own and adored among all believers; for you did indeed believe the testimony we brought you.
11 With this in mind we pray for you always, that our God may count you worthy of his calling, and mightily bring to fulfilment every good purpose
12 and every act inspired by faith, so that the name of our Lord Jesus may be glorified in you, and you in him, according to the grace of our God and the Lord Jesus Christ.

About the coming of our Lord

And now, brothers, about the coming **2** of our Lord Jesus Christ and his gathering of us to himself: I beg you, 2 do not suddenly lose your heads or alarm yourselves, whether at some oracular utterance, or pronouncement, or some letter purporting to come from us, alleging that the Day of the Lord is already here. Let no one 3 deceive you in any way whatever. That day cannot come before the final rebellion against God, when wickedness will be revealed in human form, the man doomed to perdition. He is the Enemy. He rises in his 4 pride against every god, so called, every object of men's worship, and even takes his seat in the temple of God claiming to be a god himself.

You cannot but remember that I 5 told you this while I was still with you; you must now be aware of the 6 restraining hand which ensures that he shall be revealed only at the proper time. For already the secret power of 7 wickedness is at work, secret only for the present until the Restrainer disappears from the scene. And then he 8 will be revealed, that wicked man whom the Lord Jesus will destroy with the breath of his mouth, and annihilate by the radiance of his coming. But the coming of that wicked man is 9 the work of Satan. It will be attended by all the powerful signs and miracles of the Lie, and all the deception that 10 sinfulness can impose on those doomed to destruction. Destroyed they shall be, because they did not open their minds to love of the truth, so as to find salvation. Therefore God puts 11 them under a delusion, which works upon them to believe the lie, so that 12

---

a Or justice upon those who refuse . . . and will not obey . . .

they may all be brought to judgement, all who do not believe the truth but make sinfulness their deliberate choice.

Stand firm

13 But we are bound to thank God always for you, brothers beloved by the Lord, because from the beginning of time God chose you[b] to find salvation in the Spirit that consecrates you, and 14 in the truth that you believe. It was for this that he called you through the gospel we brought, so that you might possess for your own the splendour of our Lord Jesus Christ. 15 Stand firm, then, brothers, and hold fast to the traditions which you have learned from us by word or by letter. 16 And may our Lord Jesus Christ himself and God our Father, who has shown us such love, and in his grace has given us such unfailing encourage- 17 ment and such bright hopes, still encourage and fortify you in every good deed and word!

A request for prayer

3 And now, brothers, pray for us, that the word of the Lord may have everywhere the swift and glorious course 2 that it has had among you, and that we may be rescued from wrong-headed and wicked men; for it is not all who 3 have faith. But the Lord is to be trusted, and he will fortify you and 4 guard you from the evil one. We feel perfect confidence about you, in the Lord, that you are doing and will 5 continue to do what we order. May the Lord direct your hearts towards God's love and the steadfastness of Christ!

Earn your own living

These are our orders to you, brothers, 6 in the name of our Lord Jesus Christ: hold aloof from every Christian brother who falls into idle habits, and does not follow the tradition you received from us. You know your- 7 selves how you ought to copy our example: we were no idlers among you; we did not accept board and 8 lodging from anyone without paying for it; we toiled and drudged, we worked for a living night and day, rather than be a burden to any of you—not because we have not the 9 right to maintenance, but to set an example for you to imitate. For even 10 during our stay with you we laid down the rule: the man who will not work shall not eat. We mention this 11 because we hear that some of your number are idling their time away, minding everybody's business but their own. To all such we give these 12 orders, and we appeal to them in the name of the Lord Jesus Christ to work quietly for their living.

A word of warning

But you, my friends, must never tire 13 of doing right. If anyone disobeys 14 our instructions given by letter, mark him well, and have no dealings with him until he is ashamed of himself. I 15 do not mean treat him as an enemy, but give him friendly advice, as one of the family. May the Lord of peace 16 himself give you peace at all times and in all ways.[c] The Lord be with you all.

The greeting is in my own hand, 17 signed with my name, P A U L; this authenticates all my letters; this is how I write. The grace[d] of our Lord 18 Jesus Christ be with you all.

b *Some witnesses read* because God chose you as his firstfruits . . .   c *Some witnesses read* at all times, wherever you may be.   d *Or* . . . letters. My message is this: the grace . . .

THE FIRST LETTER OF PAUL TO

TIMOTHY

1 FROM PAUL, apostle of Christ Jesus by command of God our Saviour and Christ Jesus our hope, to Timothy his true-born son in the faith.

Grace, mercy, and peace to you from God the Father and Christ Jesus our Lord.

The law and its purpose

3 When I was starting for Macedonia, I urged you to stay on at Ephesus. You were to command certain persons to give up teaching erroneous doctrines and studying those interminable myths and genealogies, which issue in mere speculation and cannot make known God's plan for us, which works through faith.*a*

5 The aim and object of this command is the love which springs from a clean heart, from a good conscience, and from faith that is genuine. 6 Through falling short of these, some people have gone astray into a wilderness of words. They set out to be teachers of the moral law, without understanding either the words they use or the subjects about which they are so dogmatic. 8 We all know that the law is an excellent thing, provided we treat it as law, recognizing that it is not aimed at good citizens, but at the lawless and unruly, the impious and sinful, the irreligious and worldly; at parricides and matricides, murderers 10 and fornicators, perverts, kidnappers, liars, perjurers—in fact all whose behaviour flouts the wholesome teaching which conforms with the gospel entrusted to me, the gospel which tells of the glory of God in his eternal felicity.

Paul's gratitude to Christ

12 I thank him who has made me equal to the task, Christ Jesus our Lord; I thank him for judging me worthy of this trust and appointing me to his service—although in the past I had 13 met him with abuse and persecution and outrage. But because I acted ignorantly in unbelief I was dealt with mercifully; the grace of our Lord was 14 lavished upon me, with the faith and love which are ours in Christ Jesus.

Here are words you may trust, 15 words that merit full acceptance: 'Christ Jesus came into the world to save sinners'; and among them I stand first. But I was mercifully dealt 16 with for this very purpose, that Jesus Christ might find in me the first occasion for displaying all his patience, and that I might be typical of all who were in future to have faith in him and gain eternal life. Now to the 17 King of all worlds, immortal, invisible, the only God, be honour and glory for ever and ever! Amen.

A personal word to Timothy

This charge, son Timothy, I lay upon 18 you, following that prophetic utterance which first pointed you out to me. So fight gallantly, armed with 19 faith and a good conscience. It was through spurning conscience that certain persons made shipwreck of their faith, among them Hymenaeus 20 and Alexander, whom I consigned to Satan, in the hope that through this discipline they might learn not to be blasphemous.

The prayers of the church

First of all, then, I urge that petitions, **2** prayers, intercessions, and thanksgivings be offered for all men; for 2 sovereigns and all in high office, that we may lead a tranquil and quiet life in full observance of religion and high standards of morality. Such prayer 3 is right, and approved by God our Saviour, whose will it is that all men 4 should find salvation and come to know the truth. For there is one God, 5 and also one mediator between God

a Or cannot promote the faithful discharge of God's stewardship.

and men, Christ Jesus, himself man,
6 who sacrificed himself to win freedom for all mankind, so providing, at the fitting time, proof of the divine pur-
7 pose; of this I was appointed herald and apostle (this is no lie, but the truth), to instruct the nations in the true faith.

8 It is my desire, therefore, that everywhere prayers be said by the men of the congregation, who shall lift up their hands with a pure intention, excluding angry or quarrelsome
9 thoughts. Women again must dress in becoming manner, modestly and soberly, not with elaborate hair-styles, not decked out with gold or pearls, or
10 expensive clothes, but with good deeds, as befits women who claim to be
11 religious. A woman must be a learner, listening quietly and with due sub-
12 mission. I do not permit a woman to be a teacher, nor must woman domineer over man; she should be quiet.
13 For Adam was created first, and Eve
14 afterwards; and it was not Adam who was deceived; it was the woman who, yielding to deception, fell into
15 sin. Yet she will be saved through motherhood[b]—if only women continue in faith,[c] love, and holiness, with a sober mind.

Character of a church leader

3 There is a popular saying:[d] 'To aspire to leadership is an honourable ambi-
2 tion.' Our leader, therefore, or bishop, must be above reproach, faithful to his one wife,[e] sober, temperate, courteous, hospitable, and a good teacher;
3 he must not be given to drink, or a brawler, but of a forbearing disposition, avoiding quarrels, and no lover
4 of money. He must be one who manages his own household well and wins obedience from his children, and a
5 man of the highest principles. If a man does not know how to control his own family, how can he look after
6 a congregation of God's people? He must not be a convert newly baptized, for fear the sin of conceit should bring upon him a judgement con-
7 trived by the devil.[f] He must moreover have a good reputation with the non-Christian public, so that he may not be exposed to scandal and get caught in the devil's snare.

Character of a deacon

Deacons, likewise, must be men of 8 high principle, not indulging in double talk, given neither to excessive drinking nor to money-grubbing. They 9 must be men who combine a clear conscience with a firm hold on the deep truths of our faith. No less than 10 bishops, they must first undergo a scrutiny, and if there is no mark against them, they may serve. Their 11 wives,[g] equally, must be women of high principle, who will not talk scandal, sober and trustworthy in every way. A deacon must be faithful 12 to his one wife,[e] and good at managing his children and his own household. For deacons with a good record of 13 service may claim a high standing and the right to speak openly on matters of the Christian faith.

The mystery of our religion

I am hoping to come to you before 14 long, but I write this in case I am 15 delayed, to let you know how men ought to conduct themselves in God's household, that is, the church of the living God, the pillar and bulwark of the truth. And great beyond all ques- 16 tion is the mystery of our religion:

'He who was manifested in the
    body,
    vindicated in the spirit,
    seen by angels;
who was proclaimed among the
    nations,
    believed in throughout the world,
    glorified in high heaven.'

How to counter subversive doctrines

The Spirit says expressly that in after 4 times some will desert from the faith and give their minds to subversive doctrines inspired by devils, through 2 the specious falsehoods of men whose own conscience is branded with the devil's sign. They forbid marriage 3 and inculcate abstinence from certain foods, though God created them to be enjoyed with thanksgiving by believers who have inward knowledge of the truth. For everything that God crea- 4 ted is good, and nothing is to be rejected when it is taken with thanksgiving, since it is hallowed by God's 5 own word and by prayer.

b Or saved through the Birth of the Child, or brought safely through childbirth.   c Or if only husband and wife continue in mutual fidelity . . .   d Some witnesses read Here are words you may trust, which some interpreters attach to the end of the preceding paragraph.   e Or married to one wife, or married only once.   f Or the judgement once passed on the devil.   g Or . . . serve. Deaconesses . . .

Limitless benefits of religion

6 By offering such advice as this to the brotherhood you will prove a good servant of Christ Jesus, bred in the precepts of our faith and of the sound instruction which you have followed.
7 Have nothing to do with those godless myths, fit only for old women. Keep yourself in training for the practice
8 of religion. The training of the body does bring limited benefit, but the benefits of religion are without limit, since it holds promise not only for this
9 life but for the life to come. Here are words you may trust, words that
10 merit full acceptance: 'With this before us we labour and struggle,[h] because[i] we have set our hope on the living God, who is the Saviour of all men'—the Saviour, above all, of believers.

A further word for Timothy

11 Pass on these orders and these teach-
12 ings. Let no one slight you because you are young, but make yourself an example to believers in speech and behaviour, in love, fidelity, and purity.
13 Until I arrive devote your attention to the public reading of the scriptures,
14 to exhortation, and to teaching. Do not neglect the spiritual endowment you possess, which was given you, under the guidance of prophecy, through the laying on of the hands of the elders as a body.[j]
15 Make these matters your business and your absorbing interest, so that your progress may be plain to all.
16 Persevere in them, keeping close watch on yourself and your teaching; by doing so you will further the salvation of yourself and your hearers.
5 Never be harsh with an elder; appeal to him as if he were your father. Treat the younger men as
2 brothers, the older women as mothers, and the younger as your sisters, in all purity.

Providing for dependent relatives

3 The status of widow is to be granted only to widows who are such in the
4 full sense. But if a widow has children or grandchildren, then they should learn as their first duty to show loyalty to the family and to repay what they owe to their parents and grand-
5 parents; for this God approves. A widow, however, in the full sense, one who is alone in the world, has all her hope set on God, and regularly attends the meetings for prayer and worship night and day. But a widow 6 given over to self-indulgence is as good as dead. Add these orders to 7 the rest, so that the widows may be above reproach. But if anyone does 8 not make provision for his relations, and especially for members of his own household, he has denied the faith and is worse than an unbeliever.

A widow should not be put on the 9 roll under sixty years of age. She must have been faithful in marriage to one man, and must produce evi- 10 dence of good deeds performed, showing whether she has had the care of children, or given hospitality, or washed the feet of God's people, or supported those in distress—in short, whether she has taken every opportunity of doing good.

Younger widows may not be placed 11 on the roll. For when their passions draw them away from Christ, they hanker after marriage and stand con- 12 demned for breaking their troth with him. Moreover, in going round from 13 house to house they learn to be idle, and worse than idle, gossips and busybodies, speaking of things better left unspoken. It is my wish, therefore, 14 that young widows shall marry again, have children, and preside over a home; then they will give no opponent occasion for slander. For there have in 15 fact been some who have taken the wrong turning and gone to the devil.

If a Christian man or woman has 16 widows in the family, he must support them himself;[k] the congregation must be relieved of the burden, so that it may be free to support those who are widows in the full sense of the term.

Pastoral responsibility

Elders who do well as leaders should 17 be reckoned worthy of a double stipend, in particular those who labour at preaching and teaching. For Scrip- 18 ture says, 'You shall not muzzle a threshing ox'; and besides, 'the worker earns his pay'.

Do not entertain a charge against 19 an elder unless it is supported by two or three witnesses. Those who commit 20 sins you must expose publicly, to put

---

h *Some witnesses read* suffer reproach.   i *Or* since 'It holds promise . . . to come.' These are words . . . acceptance. For this is the aim of all our labour and struggle, since . . .   j *Or through your* ordination as an elder.   k *Some witnesses read* If a Christian woman has widows in her family, she must support them herself.

21 fear into the others. Before God and Christ Jesus and the angels who are his chosen, I solemnly charge you, maintain these rules, and never prejudge the issue, but act with strict 22 impartiality. Do not be over-hasty in laying on hands in ordination,[l] or you may find yourself responsible for other people's misdeeds; keep your own hands clean.

23 Stop drinking nothing but water; take a little wine for your digestion, for your frequent ailments.

24 While there are people whose offences are so obvious that they run before them into court, there are others whose offences have not yet over- 25 taken them. Similarly, good deeds are obvious, or even if they are not, they cannot be concealed for ever.

6 All who wear the yoke of slavery must count their own masters worthy of all respect, so that the name of God and the Christian teaching are not 2 brought into disrepute. If the masters are believers, the slaves must not respect them any less for being their Christian brothers. Quite the contrary; they must be all the better servants because those who receive the benefit of their service are one with them in faith and love.

Snares to be avoided

This is what you are to teach and 3 preach. If anyone is teaching otherwise, and will not give his mind to wholesome precepts—I mean those of our Lord Jesus Christ—and to 4 good religious teaching, I call him a pompous ignoramus. He is morbidly keen on mere verbal questions and quibbles, which give rise to jealousy, quarrelling, slander, base suspicions, 5 and endless wrangles: all typical of men who have let their reasoning powers become atrophied and have lost grip of the truth. They think 6 religion should yield dividends; and of course religion does yield high dividends, but only to the man whose 7 resources are within him. We brought nothing into the world; for that matter we cannot take anything with us 8 when we leave, but if we have food and covering we may rest content. 9 Those who want to be rich fall into

temptations and snares and many foolish harmful desires which plunge men into ruin and perdition. The love of 10 money is the root of all evil things, and there are some who in reaching for it have wandered from the faith and spiked themselves on many thorny griefs.

The great race of faith

But you, man of God, must shun all 11 this, and pursue justice, piety, fidelity, love, fortitude, and gentleness. Run 12 the great race of faith and take hold of eternal life. For to this you were called; and you confessed your faith nobly before many witnesses. Now in 13 the presence of God, who gives life to all things, and of Jesus Christ, who himself made the same noble confession and gave his testimony to it before Pontius Pilate, I charge you to 14 obey your orders irreproachably and without fault until our Lord Jesus Christ appears. That appearance God 15 will bring to pass in his own good time—God who in eternal felicity alone holds sway. He is King of kings and Lord of lords; he alone possesses 16 immortality, dwelling in unapproachable light. No man has ever seen or ever can see him. To him be honour and might for ever! Amen.

A word to the rich

Instruct those who are rich in this 17 world's goods not to be proud, and not to fix their hopes on so uncertain a thing as money, but upon God, who endows us richly with all things to enjoy. Tell them to do good and to 18 grow rich in noble actions, to be ready to give away and to share, and 19 so to lay up a treasure which will form a good foundation for the future. Thus they will grasp the life which is life indeed.

Conclusion

Timothy, keep safe that which has 20 been entrusted to you. Turn a deaf ear to empty and worldly chatter, and the contradictions of so-called 'knowledge', for many who lay claim 21 to it have shot far wide of the faith.

Grace be with you all!

---

l Or in restoring an offender by the laying on of hands.

THE SECOND LETTER OF PAUL TO

TIMOTHY

1 FROM PAUL, apostle of Jesus Christ by the will of God, whose promise of life is fulfilled in Christ Jesus, 2 to Timothy his dear son.

Grace, mercy, and peace to you from God the Father and our Lord Jesus Christ.

Thanksgiving

3 I thank God—whom I, like my forefathers, worship with a pure intention—when I mention you in my prayers; this I do constantly night 4 and day. And when I remember the tears you shed, I long to see you again 5 to make my happiness complete. I am reminded of the sincerity of your faith, a faith which was alive in Lois your grandmother and Eunice your mother before you, and which, I am confident, lives in you also.

A word of encouragement

6 That is why I now remind you to stir into flame the gift of God which is within you through the laying on of 7 my hands. For the spirit that God gave us is no craven spirit, but one to inspire strength, love, and self-8 discipline. So never be ashamed of your testimony to our Lord, nor of me his prisoner, but take your share of suffering for the sake of the Gospel, in 9 the strength that comes from God. It is he who brought us salvation and called us to a dedicated life, not for any merit of ours but of his own purpose and his own grace, which was granted to us in Christ Jesus from all 10 eternity, but has now at length been brought fully into view by the appearance on earth of our Saviour Jesus Christ. For he has broken the power of death and brought life and immortality to light through the Gospel.

Paul's plight

Of this Gospel I, by his appointment, 11 am herald, apostle, and teacher. That 12 is the reason for my present plight; but I am not ashamed of it, because I know who it is in whom*a* I have trusted, and am confident of his power to keep safe what he has put into my charge,*b* until the great Day. Keep before you an outline of the 13 sound teaching which*c* you heard from me, living by the faith and love which are ours in Christ Jesus. Guard 14 the treasure put into our charge, with the help of the Holy Spirit dwelling within us.

As you know, everyone in the pro- 15 vince of Asia deserted me, including Phygelus and Hermogenes. But may 16 the Lord's mercy rest on the house of Onesiphorus! He has often relieved me in my troubles. He was not ashamed to visit a prisoner, but took pains 17 to search me out when he came to Rome, and found me. I pray that the 18 Lord may grant him to find mercy from the Lord on the great Day. The many services he rendered at Ephesus you know better than I could tell you.

Facing hardship

Now therefore, my son, take strength 2 from the grace of God which is ours in Christ Jesus. You heard my teach- 2 ing in the presence of many witnesses; put that teaching into the charge of men you can trust, such men as will be competent to teach others.

Take your share of hardship, like 3 a good soldier of Christ Jesus. A 4 soldier on active service will not let himself be involved in civilian affairs; he must be wholly at his commanding officer's disposal. Again, no athlete 5 can win a prize unless he has kept the rules. The farmer who gives his 6 labour has first claim on the crop.

a Or I know the one whom . . .   *b Or what I have put into his charge.*   *c Or Keep before you as a model of sound teaching that which* . . .

7 Reflect on what I say, for the Lord will help you to full understanding.

8 Remember Jesus Christ, risen from the dead, born of David's line. This 9 is the theme of my gospel, in whose service I am exposed to hardship, even to the point of being shut up like a common criminal; but the word 10 of God is not shut up. And I endure it all for the sake of God's chosen ones, with this end in view, that they too may attain the glorious and eternal salvation which is in Christ Jesus.

11 Here are words you may trust:

'If we died with him, we shall live with him;
12 if we endure, we shall reign with him. If we deny him, he will deny us.
13 If we are faithless, he keeps faith, for he cannot deny himself.'

A firm foundation

14 Go on reminding people of this, and charge them solemnly before God to stop disputing about mere words; it does no good, and is the ruin of those 15 who listen. Try hard to show yourself worthy of God's approval, as a labourer who need not be ashamed; be straightforward in your proclamation 16 of the truth. Avoid empty and worldly chatter; those who indulge in it will stray further and further into godless 17 courses, and the infection of their teaching will spread like a gangrene. Such are Hymenaeus and Philetus; 18 they have shot wide of the truth in saying that our resurrection has already taken place, and are upsetting 19 people's faith. But God has laid a foundation, and it stands firm, with this inscription: 'The Lord knows his own', and, 'Everyone who takes the Lord's name upon his lips must for-20 sake wickedness.' Now in any great house there are not only utensils of gold and silver, but also others of wood or earthenware; the former are 21 valued, the latter held cheap. To be among those which are valued and dedicated, a thing of use to the Master of the house, a man must cleanse himself from all those evil things;*d* then he will be fit for any honourable purpose.

22 Turn from the wayward impulses of youth, and pursue justice, integrity, love, and peace with all who invoke 23 the Lord in singleness of mind. Have nothing to do with foolish and ignorant speculations. You know they

breed quarrels, and the servant of the 24 Lord must not be quarrelsome, but kindly towards all. He should be a good teacher, tolerant, and gentle 25 when discipline is needed for the refractory. The Lord may grant them a change of heart and show them the truth, and thus they may come to their 26 senses and escape from the devil's snare, in which they have been caught and held at his will.*e*

A time of troubles

You must face the fact: the final age 3 of this world is to be a time of troubles. Men will love nothing but money 2 and self; they will be arrogant, boastful, and abusive; with no respect for parents, no gratitude, no piety, no 3 natural affection; they will be implacable in their hatreds, scandalmongers, intemperate and fierce, strangers to all goodness, traitors, 4 adventurers, swollen with self-importance. They will be men who put pleasure in the place of God, men who 5 preserve the outward form of religion, but are a standing denial of its reality, Keep clear of men like these. They 6 are the sort that insinuate themselves into private houses and there get miserable women into their clutches, women burdened with a sinful past, and led on by all kinds of desires, who are always wanting to be taught, but are incapable of reaching a knowledge of the truth. As Jannes and Jambres 8 defied Moses, so these men defy the truth; they have lost the power to reason, and they cannot pass the tests of faith. But their successes will be 9 short-lived, for, like those opponents of Moses, they will come to be recognized by everyone for the fools they are.

Steadfastness under persecution

But you, my son, have followed, step 10 by step, my teaching and my manner of life, my resolution, my faith, patience, and spirit of love, and my fortitude under persecutions and sufferings— 11 all that I went through at Antioch, at Iconium, at Lystra, all the persecutions I endured; and the Lord rescued me out of them all. Yes, persecution 12 will come to all who want to live a godly life as Christians, whereas 13 wicked men and charlatans will make progress from bad to worse, deceiving and deceived. But for your part, 14

d Or must separate himself from these persons. by God and made subject to his will.

e Or escape from the devil's snare, caught now

stand by the truths you have learned and are assured of. Remember from 15 whom you learned them; remember that from early childhood you have been familiar with the sacred writings which have power to make you wise and lead you to salvation through 16 faith in Christ Jesus. Every inspired scripture has its use for teaching the truth and refuting error, or for reformation of manners and discipline in 17 right living, so that the man who belongs to God may be efficient and equipped for good work of every kind.

Proclaim the message, press it home

4 Before God, and before Christ Jesus who is to judge men living and dead, I charge you solemnly by his coming 2 appearance and his reign, proclaim the message, press it home on all occasions,*f* convenient or inconvenient, use argument, reproof, and appeal, with all the patience that the work 3 of teaching requires. For the time will come when they will not stand wholesome teaching, but will follow their own fancy and gather a crowd of 4 teachers to tickle their ears. They will stop their ears to the truth and turn 5 to mythology. But you yourself must keep calm and sane at all times; face hardship, work to spread the Gospel, and do all the duties of your calling.

Nearing the end

6 As for me, already my life is being poured out on the altar, and the hour 7 for my departure is upon me. I have run the great race, I have finished the 8 course, I have kept faith. And now the prize awaits me, the garland of righteousness which the Lord, the all-just Judge, will award me on that great Day; and it is not for me alone, but for all who have set their hearts on his coming appearance.

Personal requests

Do your best to join me soon; for 9 Demas has deserted me because his heart was set on this world; he has gone to Thessalonica, Crescens to Galatia,*g* Titus to Dalmatia; I have 11 no one with me but Luke. Pick up Mark and bring him with you, for I find him a useful assistant. Tychicus 12 I have sent to Ephesus. When you 13 come, bring the cloak I left with Carpus at Troas, and the books, above all my notebooks.

'The Lord stood by me'

Alexander the copper-smith did me a 14 great deal of harm. Retribution will fall upon him from the Lord. You had 15 better be on your guard against him too, for he violently opposed everything I said. At the first hearing of 16 my case no one came into court to support me; they all left me in the lurch; I pray that it may not be held against them. But the Lord stood by 17 me and lent me strength, so that I might be his instrument in making the full proclamation of the Gospel for the whole pagan world to hear; and thus I was rescued out of the lion's jaws. And the Lord will rescue me 18 from every attempt to do me harm, and keep me safe until his heavenly reign begins.*h* Glory to him for ever and ever! Amen.

Final greetings

Greetings to Prisca and Aquila, and 19 the household of Onesiphorus.

Erastus stayed behind at Corinth, 20 and I left Trophimus ill at Miletus. Do try to get here before winter.   21

Greetings from Eubulus, Pudens, Linus, and Claudia, and from all the brotherhood here.

The Lord be with your spirit. Grace 22 be with you all!

---

f Or be on duty at all times.   *g* Or Gaul; *some witnesses read* Gallia.   *h* Or from all that evil can do, and bring me safely into his heavenly kingdom.

THE LETTER OF PAUL TO
TITUS

1 FROM PAUL, servant of God and apostle of Jesus Christ, marked as such by faith and knowledge and hope—the faith of God's chosen people, knowledge of the truth as our religion **2** has it, and the hope of eternal life.[a] Yes, it is eternal life that God, who cannot lie, promised long ages ago, **3** and now in his own good time he has openly declared himself in the proclamation which was entrusted to me by ordinance of God our Saviour.

4 To Titus, my true-born son in the faith which we share, grace and peace from God our Father and Christ Jesus our Saviour.

Character of an elder

5 My intention in leaving you behind in Crete was that you should set in order what was left over, and in particular should institute elders in each town. In doing so, observe the **6** tests I prescribed: is he a man of unimpeachable character, faithful to his one wife,[b] the father of children who are believers, who are under no imputation of loose living, and are not **7** out of control? For as God's steward a bishop must be a man of unimpeachable character. He must not be overbearing or short-tempered; he must be no drinker, no brawler, no money-**8** grubber, but hospitable, right-minded, temperate, just, devout, and self-**9** controlled. He must adhere to the true doctrine, so that he may be well able both to move his hearers with wholesome teaching and to confute objectors.

Call for discipline

10 There are all too many, especially among Jewish converts, who are out of all control; they talk wildly and **11** lead men's minds astray. Such men must be curbed, because they are ruining whole families by teaching things they should not, and all for **12** sordid gain. It was a Cretan prophet, one of their own countrymen,

who said, 'Cretans were always liars, vicious brutes, lazy gluttons'—and he **13** told the truth! All the more reason why you should pull them up sharply, so that they may come to a sane belief, instead of lending their ears to Jewish **14** myths and commandments of merely human origin, the work of men who turn their backs upon the truth.

To the pure all things are pure; but **15** nothing is pure to the tainted minds of disbelievers, tainted alike in reason and conscience. They profess to **16** acknowledge God, but deny him by their actions. Their detestable obstinacy disqualifies them for any good work.

Older men and women

For your own part, what you say must **2** be in keeping with wholesome doctrine. Let the older men know that they **2** should be sober, high-principled, and temperate, sound in faith, in love, and in endurance. The older women, **3** similarly, should be reverent in their bearing, not scandal-mongers or slaves to strong drink; they must set a high standard, and school the younger **4** women to be loving wives and mothers, temperate, chaste, and kind, **5** busy at home, respecting the authority of their own husbands. Thus the Gospel will not be brought into disrepute.

Younger men

Urge the younger men, similarly, to **6** be temperate in all things, and set **7** them a good example yourself. In your teaching, you must show integrity and high principle, and use **8** wholesome speech to which none can take exception. This will shame any opponent, when he finds not a word to say to our discredit.

Slaves

Tell slaves to respect their masters' **9** authority in everything, and to comply with their demands without

---

a Or apostle of Jesus Christ, to bring God's chosen people to faith and to a knowledge of the truth as our religion has it, with its hope for eternal life.   *b* See note on *1 Timothy 3. 2.*

R*

10 answering back; not to pilfer, but to show themselves strictly honest and trustworthy; for in all such ways they will add lustre to the doctrine of God our Saviour.

The happy fulfilment of our hope

11 For the grace of God has dawned upon the world with healing for all
12 mankind; and by it we are disciplined to renounce godless ways and worldly desires, and to live a life of temperance, honesty, and godliness in the
13 present age, looking forward to the happy fulfilment of our hope when the splendour of our great God and
14 Saviour[c] Christ Jesus will appear. He it is who sacrificed himself for us, to set us free from all wickedness and to make us a pure people marked out for his own, eager to do good.
15 These, then, are your themes; urge them and argue them. And speak with authority: let no one slight you.

Practical directions

3 Remind them to be submissive to the government and the authorities, to obey them, and to be ready for any
2 honourable form of work;[d] to slander no one, not to pick quarrels, to show forbearance and a consistently gentle disposition towards all men.
3 For at one time we ourselves in our folly and obstinacy were all astray. We were slaves to passions and pleasures of every kind. Our days were passed in malice and envy; we were odious ourselves and we hated one
4 another. But when the kindness and generosity of God our Saviour dawned

upon the world, then, not for any 5 good deeds of our own, but because he was merciful, he saved us through the water of rebirth and the renewing power of[e] the Holy Spirit. For he sent 6 down the Spirit upon us plentifully through Jesus Christ our Saviour, so 7 that, justified by his grace, we might in hope become heirs to eternal life. These are words you may trust.   8

Such are the points I should wish you to insist on. Those who have come to believe in God should see that they engage in honourable occupations, which are not only honourable in themselves, but also useful to their fellow-men.[f] But steer clear of 9 foolish speculations, genealogies, quarrels, and controversies over the Law; they are unprofitable and pointless.

A heretic should be warned once, 10 and once again; after that, have done with him, recognizing that a 11 man of that sort has a distorted mind and stands self-condemned in his sin.

Final note and greeting

When I send Artemas to you, or 12 Tychicus, make haste to join me at Nicopolis, for that is where I have determined to spend the winter. Do 13 your utmost to help Zenas the lawyer and Apollos on their travels, and see that they are not short of anything. And our own people must be taught 14 to engage in honest employment to produce the necessities of life; they must not be unproductive.

All who are with me send you greet- 15 ings. My greetings to those who are our friends in truth.[g] Grace be with you all!

c *Or* of the great God and our Saviour . . .   d *Or* ready always to do good.   e *Or* the water of rebirth and of renewal by . . .   f *Or* should make it their business to practise virtue. These precepts are good in themselves and useful to society.   g *Or* our friends in the faith.

THE LETTER OF PAUL TO
PHILEMON

Slave into brother

1 FROM PAUL, a prisoner of Christ Jesus, and our colleague Timothy, to Philemon our dear friend and fellow-
2 worker, and Apphia our sister, and Archippus our comrade-in-arms, and the congregation at your house.

Grace to you and peace from God 3 our Father and the Lord Jesus Christ.

I thank my God always when I 4 mention you in my prayers, for I hear 5 of your love and faith towards the Lord Jesus and towards all God's people. My prayer is that your fellow- 6 ship with us in our common faith may deepen the understanding of all the blessings that our union with

7 Christ brings us.[a] For I am delighted and encouraged by your love; through you, my brother, God's people have been much refreshed.

8 Accordingly, although in Christ I might make bold to point out your **9** duty, yet, because of that same love, I would rather appeal to you. Yes, I, Paul, ambassador as I am of Christ **10** Jesus—and now his prisoner—appeal to you about my child, whose father I have become in this prison.

11 I mean Onesimus, once so little use to you, but now useful indeed, **12** both to you and to me. I am sending him back to you, and in doing so I am **13** sending a part of myself. I should have liked to keep him with me, to look after me as you would wish, here **14** in prison for the Gospel. But I would rather do nothing without your consent, so that your kindness may be a matter not of compulsion, but of your **15** own free will. For perhaps this is why you lost him for a time, that you **16** might have him back for good, no longer as a slave, but as more than a slave—as a dear brother, very dear indeed to me and how much dearer to you, both as man and as Christian.

17 If, then, you count me partner in the faith, welcome him as you would **18** welcome me. And if he has done you any wrong or is in your debt, put **19** that down to my account. Here is my signature, PAUL; I undertake to repay—not to mention that you owe **20** your very self to me as well. Now brother, as a Christian, be generous with me, and relieve my anxiety; we are both in Christ!

21 I write to you confident that you will meet my wishes; I know that you **22** will in fact do better than I ask. And one thing more: have a room ready for me, for I hope that, in answer to your prayers, God will grant me to you.

23 Epaphras, Christ's captive like myself, sends you greetings. So do Mark, **24** Aristarchus, Demas, and Luke, my fellow-workers.

25 The grace of the Lord Jesus Christ be with your spirit!

a Or that bring us to Christ.

A LETTER TO
HEBREWS

The Son of God

1 WHEN IN former times God spoke to our forefathers, he spoke in fragmentary and varied fashion through **2** the prophets. But in this the final age he has spoken to us in the Son whom he has made heir to the whole universe, and through whom he created all **3** orders of existence: the Son who is the effulgence of God's splendour and the stamp of God's very being, and sustains[a] the universe by his word of power. When he had brought about the purgation of sins, he took his seat at the right hand of Majesty on high, **4** raised as far above the angels, as the title he has inherited is superior to theirs.

5 For God never said to any angel, 'Thou art my Son; today I have begotten thee', or again, 'I will be father to him, and he shall be my son.' **6** Again, when he presents the first-born to the world, he says, 'Let all the angels of God pay him homage.' Of **7** the angels he says,

'He who makes his angels winds,
and his ministers a fiery flame';

but of the Son, **8**

'Thy throne, O God, is for ever and ever,
and the sceptre[b] of justice is the sceptre of his kingdom.
Thou hast loved right and hated **9** wrong;
therefore, O God, thy God[c] has set thee above thy fellows,

a Or bears along.   *b Or* God is thy throne for ever and ever, and thy sceptre . . .   *c Or* therefore God who is thy God . . .

by anointing with the oil of exultation.'

10 And again,

'By thee, Lord, were earth's foundations laid of old,
and the heavens are the work of thy
hands.
11 They shall pass away, but thou endurest;
like clothes they shall all grow old;
12 thou shalt fold them up like a cloak;
yes, they shall be changed like any
garment.
But thou art the same, and thy years
shall have no end.'

13 To which of the angels has he ever
said, 'Sit at my right hand until I
make thy enemies thy footstool'?
14 What are they all but ministrant
spirits, sent out to serve, for the sake
of those who are to inherit salvation?
2 Thus we are bound to pay all the
more heed to what we have been told,
for fear of drifting from our course.
2 For if the word spoken through
angels had such force that any transgression or disobedience met with due
3 retribution, what escape can there be
for us if we ignore a deliverance so
great? For this deliverance was first
announced through the lips of the
Lord himself; those who heard him
4 confirmed it to us, and God added
his testimony by signs, by miracles,
by manifold works of power, and by
distributing the gifts of the Holy
Spirit at his own will.

The son of man

5 For it is not to angels that he has
subjected the world to come, which is
6 our theme. But there is somewhere a
solemn assurance which runs:

'What is man, that thou rememberest
him,
or the son of man, that thou hast
regard to him?
7 Thou didst make him for a short
while lower than the angels;
thou didst crown him with glory and
honour;
8 thou didst put all things in subjection
beneath his feet.'

For in subjecting all things to him,
he left nothing that is not subject.
But in fact we do not yet see all
9 things in subjection to man. In Jesus,
however, we do see one who*d* for a
short while was made lower than the

angels, crowned now with glory and
honour because he suffered death, so
that, by God's gracious will, in tasting
death he should stand*e* for us all.

Christ and his brother-men

It was clearly fitting that God for 10
whom and through whom all things
exist should, in bringing many sons
to glory, make the leader who delivers
them perfect through sufferings. For 11
a consecrating priest and those whom
he consecrates are all of one stock; and
that is why the Son does not shrink
from calling men his brothers, when 12
he says, 'I will proclaim thy name to
my brothers; in full assembly I will
sing thy praise'; and again, 'I will 13
keep my trust fixed on him'; and
again, 'Here am I, and the children
whom God has given me.' The chil- 14
dren of a family share the same flesh
and blood; and so he too shared ours,
so that through death he might break
the power of him who had death at
his command, that is, the devil; and 15
might liberate those who, through
fear of death, had all their lifetime
been in servitude. It is not angels, 16
mark you, that he takes to himself,
but the sons of Abraham. And there- 17
fore he had to be made like these
brothers of his in every way, so that
he might be merciful and faithful as
their high priest before God, to ex-
piate the sins of the people. For since 18
he himself has passed through the
test of suffering, he is able to help
those who are meeting their test now.

Jesus and Moses

Therefore, brothers in the family of 3
God, who share a heavenly calling,
think of the Apostle and High Priest
of the religion we profess,*f* who was 2
faithful to God who appointed him.
Moses also was faithful in God's
household; and Jesus, of whom I 3
speak, has been deemed worthy of
greater honour than Moses, as the
founder of a house enjoys more honour
than his household. For every house 4
has its founder; and the founder of all
is God. Moses, then, was faithful as 5
a servitor in God's whole household;
his task was to bear witness to the
words that God would speak; but 6
Christ is faithful as a son, set over his
household. And we are that household of his, if only we are fearless and
keep our hope high.

d Or in subjection to him. But we see Jesus, who . . . *e* *Some witnesses read* so that apart from
God he should taste death . . . *f* Or of him whom we confess as God's Envoy and High Priest.

God's promised rest

7 'Today', therefore, as the Holy Spirit says—

'Today if you hear his voice,
8 do not grow stubborn as in those days of rebellion,
at that time of testing in the desert,
9 where your forefathers tried me and tested me,
and saw[g] the things I did for forty years.
10 And so, I was indignant with that generation
and I said, Their hearts are for ever astray;
they would not discern my ways;
11 as I vowed in my anger, they shall never enter my rest.'

12 See to it, brothers, that no one among you has the wicked, faithless heart of a deserter from the living 13 God; but day by day, while that word 'Today' still sounds in your ears, encourage one another, so that no one of you is made stubborn by the wiles 14 of sin. For we have become Christ's partners[h] if only we keep our original confidence firm to the end.

15 When Scripture says, 'Today if you hear his voice, do not grow stubborn 16 as in those days of rebellion', who, I ask, were those who heard and rebelled? All those, surely, whom Moses 17 had led out of Egypt. And with whom was God indignant for forty years? With those, surely, who had sinned, 18 whose bodies lay where they fell in the desert. And to whom did he vow that they should not enter his rest, if not to those who had refused to 19 believe? We perceive that it was unbelief which prevented their entering.

4 Therefore we must have before us the fear that while the promise of entering his rest remains open, one or 2 another among you should be found to have missed his chance. For indeed we have heard the good news, as they did. But in them the message they heard did no good, because it met with 3 no faith in those who heard it. It is we, who have become believers, who enter the rest referred to in the words, 'As I vowed in my anger, they shall never enter my rest.' Yet God's work has been finished ever since the 4 world was created; for does not Scripture somewhere speak thus of the seventh day: 'God rested from all his 5 work on the seventh day'?—and once

again in the passage above we read, 'They shall never enter my rest.' The 6 fact remains that someone must enter it, and since those who first heard the good news failed to enter through unbelief, God fixes another day. Speak- 7 ing through the lips of David after many long years, he uses the words already quoted: 'Today if you hear his voice, do not grow stubborn.' If 8 Joshua had given them rest, God would not thus have spoken of another day after that. Therefore, a sab- 9 bath rest still awaits the people of God; for anyone who enters God's rest, 10 rests from his own work as God did from his. Let us then make every 11 effort to enter that rest, so that no one may fall by following this evil example of unbelief.

For the word of God is alive and 12 active. It cuts more keenly than any two-edged sword, piercing as far as the place where life and spirit, joints and marrow, divide. It sifts the purposes and thoughts of the heart. There is nothing in creation that can 13 hide from him; everything lies naked and exposed to the eyes of the One with whom we have to reckon.

A great high priest

Since therefore we have a great high 14 priest who has passed through the heavens, Jesus the Son of God, let us hold fast to the religion we profess. For ours is not a high priest unable to 15 sympathize with our weaknesses, but one who, because of his likeness to us, has been tested every way,[i] only without sin. Let us therefore boldly 16 approach the throne of our gracious God, where we may receive mercy and in his grace find timely help.

Christ and Melchizedek

For every high priest is taken from 5 among men and appointed their representative before God, to offer gifts and sacrifices for sins. He is able 2 to bear patiently with the ignorant and erring, since he too is beset by weakness; and because of this he is 3 bound to make sin-offerings for himself no less than for the people. And 4 nobody arrogates the honour to himself: he is called by God, as indeed Aaron was. So it is with Christ: he did 5 not confer upon himself the glory of becoming high priest; it was granted by God, who said to him, 'Thou art my Son; today I have begotten thee';

g *Or though they saw . . .*   h *Or have been given a share in Christ.*   i *Or who has been tested every way, as we are.*

6 as also in another place he says, 'Thou
7 art a priest for ever, in the succession
of Melchizedek.' In the days of his
earthly life he offered up prayers and
petitions, with loud cries and tears,
to God who was able to deliver him
from the grave. Because of his humble
8 submission his prayer was heard: son
though he was, he learned obedience
9 in the school of suffering, and, once
perfected, became the source of eternal
10 salvation for all who obey him, named
by God high priest in the succession of
Melchizedek.

11   About Melchizedek we have much
to say, much that is difficult to explain, now that you have grown so dull
12 of hearing. For indeed, though by this
time you ought to be teachers, you
need someone to teach you the ABC
of God's oracles over again; it has
come to this, that you need milk in-
13 stead of solid food. Anyone who lives
on milk, being an infant, does not
14 know[j] what is right. But grown men
can take solid food; their perceptions
are trained by long use to discriminate
between good and evil.

Warning and encouragement

6 Let us then stop discussing the rudi-
ments of Christianity. We ought not
to be laying over again the foundations of faith in God and of repentance
from the deadness of our former ways,
2 by instruction[k] about cleansing rites
and the laying-on-of-hands, about the
resurrection of the dead and eternal
judgement. Instead, let us advance
3 towards maturity; and so we shall, if
God permits.

4   For when men have once been enlightened, when they have had a taste
of the heavenly gift and a share in the
5 Holy Spirit, when they have experienced the goodness of God's word
and the spiritual energies of the age
6 to come, and after all this have fallen
away, it is impossible to bring them
again to repentance; for with their
own hands they are crucifying[l] the
Son of God and making mock of his
7 death. When the earth drinks in the
rain that falls upon it from time to
time, and yields a useful crop to those
for whom it is cultivated, it is receiv-
8 ing its share of blessing from God; but
if it bears thorns and thistles, it is
worthless and God's curse hangs over
9 it; the end of that is burning. But

although we speak as we do, we are
convinced that you, my friends, are
in the better case, and this makes for
your salvation. For God would not be 10
so unjust as to forget all that you did
for love of his name, when you rendered service to his people, as you
still do. But we long for every one of 11
you to show the same eager concern,
until your hope is finally realized. We 12
want you not to become lazy, but to
imitate those who, through faith and
patience, are inheriting the promises.

The hope set before us

When God made his promise to 13
Abraham, he swore by himself, because he had no one greater to swear
by: 'I vow that I will bless you 14
abundantly and multiply your descendants.' Thus is was that Abraham, 15
after patient waiting, attained the
promise. Men swear by a greater than 16
themselves, and the oath provides a
confirmation to end all dispute; and 17
so God, desiring to show even more
clearly to the heirs of his promise how
unchanging was his purpose, guaranteed it by oath. Here, then, are two 18
irrevocable acts in which God could
not possibly play us false, to give
powerful encouragement to us, who
have claimed his protection by grasping[m] the hope set before us. That 19
hope we hold. It is like an anchor for
our lives, an anchor safe and sure.
It enters in through the veil, where 20
Jesus has entered on our behalf as
forerunner, having become a high
priest for ever in the succession of
Melchizedek.

Melchizedek and Abraham

This Melchizedek, king of Salem, **7**
priest of God Most High, met Abraham returning from the rout of the
kings and blessed him; and Abraham 2
gave him a tithe of everything as his
portion. His name, in the first place,
means 'king of righteousness'; next
he is king of Salem, that is, 'king of
peace'. He has no father, no mother, 3
no lineage; his years have no beginning, his life no end. He is like the Son
of God: he remains a priest for all
time.

Consider now how great he must be 4
for Abraham the patriarch to give him
a tithe of the finest of the spoil. The 5

---

j Or is incompetent to speak of . . .   *k Or, according to some witnesses,* laying the foundations over
again: repentance from the deadness of our former ways and faith in God, instruction . . .   *l Or*
crucifying again.   *m Or* to give to us, who have claimed his protection, a powerful incentive to
grasp . . .

descendants of Levi who take the priestly office are commanded by the Law to tithe the people, that is, their kinsmen, although they too are 6 descendants of Abraham. But Melchizedek, though he does not trace his descent from them, has tithed Abraham himself, and given his blessing to the man who received the pro-7 mises; and beyond all dispute the lesser is always blessed by the greater. 8 Again, in the one instance tithes are received by men who must die; but in the other, by one whom Scripture 9 affirms to be alive. It might even be said that Levi, who receives tithes, has himself been tithed through Abraham; 10 for he was still in his ancestor's loins when Melchizedek met him.

Limitations of the Levitical priesthood

11 Now if perfection had been attainable through the Levitical priesthood (for it is on this basis that the people were given the Law), what further need would there have been to speak of another priest arising, in the succession of Melchizedek, instead of the 12 succession of Aaron? For a change of priesthood must mean a change of law. 13 And the one here spoken of belongs to a different tribe, no member of which has ever had anything to do with the 14 altar. For it is very evident that our Lord is sprung from Judah, a tribe to which Moses made no reference in speaking of priests.

15   The argument becomes still clearer, if the new priest who arises is one like 16 Melchizedek, owing his priesthood not to a system of earth-bound rules but to the power of a life that cannot be 17 destroyed. For here is the testimony: 'Thou art a priest for ever, in the 18 succession of Melchizedek.' The earlier rules are cancelled as impotent and 19 useless, since the Law brought nothing to perfection; and a better hope is introduced, through which we draw near to God.

20   How great a difference it makes that 21 an oath was sworn! There was no oath sworn when those others were made priests; but for this priest an oath was sworn, as Scripture says of him: 'The Lord has sworn and will not go back on his word, "Thou art 22 a priest for ever."' How far superior must the covenant also be of which 23 Jesus is the guarantor! Those other priests are appointed in numerous succession, because they are prevented

by death from continuing in office; but 24 the priesthood which Jesus holds is perpetual, because he remains for ever. That is why he is also able to save 25 absolutely those who approach God through him; he is always living to plead on their behalf.

Jesus fits our condition

Such a high priest does indeed fit 26 our condition—devout, guileless, undefiled, separated from sinners, raised high above the heavens. He has no 27 need to offer sacrifices daily, as the high priests do, first for his own sins and then for those of the people; for this he did once and for all when he offered up himself. The high priests 28 made by the Law are men in all their frailty; but the priest appointed by the words of the oath which supersedes the Law is the Son, made perfect now for ever.

The two covenants

Now this is my main point: just such **8** a high priest we have, and he has taken his seat at the right hand of the throne of Majesty in the heavens, a 2 ministrant in the real sanctuary, the tent pitched by the Lord and not by man. Every high priest is appointed 3 to offer gifts and sacrifices; hence, this one too must have[n] something to offer. Now if he had been on earth, 4 he would not even have been a priest, since there are already priests who offer the gifts which the Law prescribes, though they minister in a sanctuary which is only a copy and shadow of the heavenly. This is implied when Moses, about to erect the tent, is instructed by God: 'See to it that you make everything according to the pattern shown you on the mountain.' But in fact the ministry 6 which has fallen to Jesus is as far superior to theirs as are the covenant he mediates and the promises upon which it is legally secured.

Had that first covenant been fault- 7 less, there would have been no need to look for a second in its place. But God, 8 finding fault with them, says, 'The days are coming, says the Lord, when I will conclude a new covenant with the house of Israel and the house of Judah. It will not be like the covenant I made with their forefathers when I took them by the hand to lead them out of Egypt; because they did not abide by the terms of that covenant,

n Or must have had.

and I abandoned them, says the Lord.
10 For the covenant I will make with the house of Israel after those days, says the Lord, is this: I will set my laws in their understanding and write them on their hearts; and I will be their God, and they shall be my people.
11 And they shall not teach one another, saying to brother and fellow-citizen,⁰ "Know the Lord!" For all of them,
12 high and low, shall know me; I will be merciful to their wicked deeds, and I will remember their sins no more.'
13 By speaking of a new covenant, he has pronounced the first one old; and anything that is growing old and ageing will shortly disappear.

The first covenant

9 The first covenant indeed had its ordinances of divine service and its sanc-
2 tuary, but a material sanctuary. For a tent was prepared—the first tent—in which was the lamp-stand, and the table with the bread of the Presence;
3 this is called the Holy Place. Beyond the second curtain was the tent called
4 the Most Holy Place. Here was a golden altar of incense, and the ark of the covenant plated all over with gold, in which were a golden jar containing the manna, and Aaron's staff which once budded, and the tablets of
5 the covenant; and above it the cherubim of God's glory, overshadowing the place of expiation. On these we cannot now enlarge.
6 Under this arrangement, the priests are always entering the first tent in
7 the discharge of their duties; but the second is entered only once a year, and by the high priest alone, and even then he must take with him the blood which he offers on his own behalf and
8 for the people's sins of ignorance. By this the Holy Spirit signifies that so long as the earlier tent still stands, the way into the sanctuary remains
9 unrevealed. All this is symbolic, pointing to the present time. The offerings and sacrifices there prescribed cannot give the worshipper inward per-
10 fection. It is only a matter of food and drink and various rites of cleansing—outward ordinances in force until the time of reformation.

The new covenant

11 But now Christ has come, high priest of good things already in being.ᵖ The tent of his priesthood is a greater and

more perfect one, not made by men's hands, that is, not belonging to this created world; the blood of his sacri- 12 fice is his own blood, not the blood of goats and calves; and thus he has entered the sanctuary once and for all and secured an eternal deliverance. For if the blood of goats and bulls 13 and the sprinkled ashes of a heifer have power to hallow those who have been defiled and restore their external purity, how much greater is 14 the power of the blood of Christ; he offered himself without blemish to God, a spiritual and eternal sacrifice; and his blood will cleanse our conscience from the deadness of our former ways and fit us for the service of the living God.

And therefore he is the mediator of 15 a new covenant, or testament, under which, now that there has been a death to bring deliverance from sins committed under the former covenant, those whom God has called may receive the promise of the eternal inheritance. For where there is a testa- 16 ment it is necessary for the death of the testator to be established. A 17 testament is operative only after a death: it cannot possibly have force while the testator is alive. Thus we 18 find that the former covenant itself was not inaugurated without blood. For when, as the Law directed, 19 Moses had recited all the commandments to the people, he took the blood of the calves, with water, scarlet wool, and marjoram, and sprinkled the lawbook itself and all the people, saying, 20 'This is the blood of the covenant which God has enjoined upon you.' In the same way he also sprinkled 21 the tent and all the vessels of divine service with blood. Indeed, according 22 to the Law, it might almost be said, everything is cleansed by blood and without the shedding of blood there is no forgiveness.

The once-and-for-all sacrifice of Christ

If, then, these sacrifices cleanse the 23 copies of heavenly things, those heavenly things themselves require better sacrifices to cleanse them. For 24 Christ has entered, not that sanctuary made by men's hands which is only a symbol of the reality, but heaven itself, to appear now before God on our behalf. Nor is he there to offer 25 himself again and again, as the high

---

⁰ *Some witnesses read* brother and neighbour. are) to be.

ᵖ *Some witnesses read* good things which were (or

priest enters the sanctuary year by
26 year with blood not his own. If that
were so, he would have had to suffer
many times since the world was made.
But as it is, he has appeared once
and for all at the climax of history to
abolish sin by the sacrifice of himself.
27 And as it is the lot of men to die once,
28 and after death comes judgement, so
Christ was offered once to bear the
burden of men's sins,[q] and will appear
a second time, sin done away, to bring
salvation to those who are watching
for him.

The new covenant replaces the old

10 For the law contains but a shadow,
and no true image,[r] of the good things
which were to come; it provides for
the same sacrifices year after year,
and with these it can never bring
the worshippers to perfection for all
2 time.[s] If it could, these sacrifices
would surely have ceased to be offered,
because the worshippers, cleansed
once for all, would no longer have any
3 sense of sin. But instead, in these
sacrifices year after year sins are
4 brought to mind, because sins can
never be removed by the blood of
bulls and goats.
5 That is why, at his coming into the
world, he says:

'Sacrifice and offering thou didst not
desire,
but thou hast prepared a body for me.
6 Whole-offerings and sin-offerings thou
didst not delight in.
7 Then I said, "Here am I: as it is
written of me in the scroll,
I have come, O God, to do thy will."'

8 First he says, 'Sacrifices and offerings,
whole-offerings and sin-offerings, thou
didst not desire nor delight in'—
although the Law prescribes them—
9 and then he says, 'I have come to do
thy will.' He thus annuls the former
10 to establish the latter. And it is by
the will of God that we have been
consecrated, through the offering of
the body of Jesus Christ once and for
all.
11 Every priest stands performing his
service daily and offering time after
time the same sacrifices, which can
12 never remove sins. But Christ offered
for all time one sacrifice for sins, and
took his seat at the right hand of
13 God, where he waits henceforth until
his enemies are made his footstool.
14 For by one offering he has perfected

for all time those who are thus consecrated. Here we have also the testi- 15
mony of the Holy Spirit: he first says,
'This is the covenant which I will 16
make with them after those days,
says the Lord: I will set my laws in
their hearts and write them on their
understanding'; then he adds, 'and 17
their sins and wicked deeds I will
remember no more at all.' And where 18
these have been forgiven, there are
offerings for sin no longer.

Encouragement and warning

So now, my friends, the blood of 19
Jesus makes us free to enter boldly
into the sanctuary by the new, living 20
way which he has opened for us
through the curtain, the way of his
flesh.[t] We have, moreover, a great 21
priest set over the household of God;
so let us make our approach in sin- 22
cerity of heart and full assurance of
faith, our guilty hearts sprinkled clean,
our bodies washed with pure water.
Let us be firm and unswerving in the 23
confession of our hope, for the Giver
of the promise may be trusted. We 24
ought to see how each of us may best
arouse others to love and active goodness, not staying away from our 25
meetings, as some do, but rather
encouraging one another, all the more
because you see the Day drawing
near.
For if we wilfully persist in sin after 26
receiving the knowledge of the truth,
no sacrifice for sins remains: only a 27
terrifying expectation of judgement
and a fierce fire which will consume
God's enemies. If a man disregards 28
the Law of Moses, he is put to death
without pity on the evidence of two
or three witnesses. Think how much 29
more severe a penalty that man will
deserve who has trampled under foot
the Son of God, profaned the blood
of the covenant by which he was
consecrated, and affronted God's gracious Spirit! For we know who it 30
is that has said, 'Justice is mine: I
will repay'; and again, 'The Lord will
judge his people.' It is a terrible 31
thing to fall into the hands of the
living God.

The need for endurance

Remember the days gone by, when, 32
newly enlightened, you met the challenge of great sufferings and held
firm. Some of you were abused and 33

---

q Or to remove men's sins.   r One witness reads a shadow and likeness . . .   s Or bring to perfection the worshippers who come continually.   t Or through the curtain of his flesh.

tormented to make a public show, while others stood loyally by those 34 who were so treated. For indeed you shared the sufferings of the prisoners, and you cheerfully accepted the seizure of your possessions, knowing that you possessed something better 35 and more lasting. Do not then throw away your confidence, for it carries a 36 great reward. You need endurance, if you are to do God's will and win what 37 he has promised. For 'soon, very soon' (in the words of Scripture), 'he who is to come will come; he will not delay; 38 and by faith my righteous servant shall find life; but if a man shrinks 39 back, I take no pleasure in him.' But we are not among those who shrink back and are lost; we have the faith to make life our own.

Men of faith through the ages

11 And what is faith? Faith gives substance[u] to our hopes, and makes us certain of realities we do not see.
2   It is for their faith that the men of old stand on record.
3   By faith we perceive that the universe was fashioned by the word of God, so that the visible came forth from the invisible.
4   By faith Abel offered a sacrifice greater than Cain's, and through faith his goodness was attested, for his offerings had God's approval; and through faith he continued to speak after his death.
5   By faith Enoch was carried away to another life without passing through death; he was not to be found, because God had taken him. For it is the testimony of Scripture that before he was taken he had pleased God, 6 and without faith it is impossible to please him; for anyone who comes to God must believe that he exists and that he rewards those who search for him.
7   By faith Noah, divinely warned about the unseen future, took good heed and built an ark to save his household. Through his faith he put the whole world in the wrong, and made good his own claim to the righteousness which comes of faith.
8   By faith Abraham obeyed the call to go out to a land destined for himself and his heirs, and left home without 9 knowing where he was to go. By faith he settled as an alien in the land promised him, living in tents, as did Isaac and Jacob, who were heirs to the

same promise. For he was looking 10 forward to the city with firm foundations, whose architect and builder is God.
   By faith even Sarah herself received 11 strength to conceive, though she was past the age, because she judged that he who had promised would keep faith; and therefore from one man, 12 and one as good as dead, there sprang descendants numerous as the stars or as the countless grains of sand on the sea-shore.
   All these persons died in faith. 13 They were not yet in possession of the things promised, but had seen them far ahead and hailed them, and confessed themselves no more than strangers or passing travellers on earth. Those who use such language 14 show plainly that they are looking for a country of their own. If their 15 hearts had been in the country they had left, they could have found opportunity to return. Instead, we find 16 them longing for a better country—I mean, the heavenly one. That is why God is not ashamed to be called their God; for he has a city ready for them.
   By faith Abraham, when the test 17 came, offered up Isaac: he had received the promises, and yet he was on the point of offering his only son, of 18 whom he had been told, 'Through the line of Isaac your descendants shall be traced.'[v] For he reckoned that God 19 had power even to raise from the dead—and from the dead, he did, in a sense, receive him back.
   By faith Isaac blessed Jacob and 20 Esau and spoke of things to come. By faith Jacob, as he was dying, 21 blessed each of Joseph's sons, and worshipped God, leaning on the top of his staff. By faith Joseph, at the 22 end of his life, spoke of the departure of Israel from Egypt, and instructed them what to do with his bones.
   By faith, when Moses was born, his 23 parents hid him for three months, because they saw what a fine child he was; they were not afraid of the king's edict. By faith Moses, when he grew 24 up, refused to be called the son of Pharaoh's daughter, preferring to 25 suffer hardship with the people of God rather than enjoy the transient pleasures of sin. He considered the 26 stigma that rests on God's Anointed greater wealth than the treasures of Egypt, for his eyes were fixed upon the coming day of recompense. By 27 faith he left Egypt, and not because

u Or assurance.   v Or God's call shall be for your descendants in the line of Isaac.

he feared the king's anger; for he was resolute, as one who saw the invisible God.

28 By faith he celebrated the Passover and sprinkled the blood, so that the destroying angel might not touch the
29 first-born of Israel. By faith they crossed the Red Sea as though it were dry land, whereas the Egyptians, when they attempted the crossing, were drowned.

30 By faith the walls of Jericho fell down after they had been encircled on
31 seven successive days. By faith the prostitute Rahab escaped the doom of the unbelievers, because she had given the spies a kindly welcome.

32 Need I say more? Time is too short for me to tell the stories of Gideon, Barak, Samson, and Jephthah, of David and Samuel and the prophets.
33 Through faith they overthrew kingdoms, established justice, saw God's promises fulfilled. They muzzled raven-
34 ing lions, quenched the fury of fire, escaped death by the sword. Their weakness was turned to strength, they grew powerful in war, they put
35 foreign armies to rout. Women received back their dead raised to life. Others were tortured to death, disdaining release, to win a better resur-
36 rection. Others, again, had to face jeers and flogging, even fetters and prison
37 bars. They were stoned,*w* they were sawn in two, they were put to the sword, they went about dressed in skins of sheep or goats, in poverty, distress,
38 and misery. They were too good for a world like this. They were refugees in deserts and on the hills, hiding in
39 caves and holes in the ground. These also, one and all, are commemorated for their faith; and yet they did not enter upon the promised inheritance,
40 because, with us in mind, God had made a better plan, that only in company with us should they reach their perfection.

With eyes fixed on Jesus

12 And what of ourselves? With all these witnesses to faith around us like a cloud, we must throw off every encumbrance, every sin to which we cling,*x* and run with resolution the
2 race for which we are entered, our eyes fixed on Jesus, on whom faith depends from start to finish: Jesus who, for the sake of the joy that lay ahead of him,*y* endured the cross,

making light of its disgrace, and has taken his seat at the right hand of the throne of God.

The discipline of sons

Think of him who submitted to such 3 opposition from sinners: that will help you not to lose heart and grow faint. In your struggle against sin, you 4 have not yet resisted to the point of shedding your blood. You have for- 5 gotten the text of Scripture which addresses you as sons and appeals to you in these words:

'My son, do not think lightly of the
    Lord's discipline,
nor lose heart when he corrects you;
for the Lord disciplines those whom 6
    he loves;
he lays the rod on every son whom he
    acknowledges.'

You must endure it as discipline: God 7 is treating you as sons. Can anyone be a son, who is not disciplined by his father? If you escape the discipline 8 in which all sons share, you must be bastards and no true sons. Again, we 9 paid due respect to the earthly fathers who disciplined us; should we not submit even more readily to our spiritual Father, and so attain life? They dis- 10 ciplined us for this short life according to their lights; but he does so for our true welfare, so that we may share his holiness. Discipline, no doubt, is 11 never pleasant; at the time it seems painful, but in the end it yields for those who have been trained by it the peaceful harvest of an honest life. Come, then, stiffen your drooping 12 arms and shaking knees, and keep 13 your steps from wavering. Then the disabled limb will not be put out of joint, but regain its former powers.

The man who sold his birthright

Aim at peace with all men, and a 14 holy life, for without that no one will see the Lord. Look to it that there 15 is no one among you who forfeits the grace of God, no bitter, noxious weed growing up to poison the whole, no immoral person, no one worldly- 16 minded like Esau. He sold his birthright for a single meal, and you know 17 that although he wanted afterwards to claim the blessing, he was rejected; though he begged for it to the point of tears, he found no way open for second thoughts.

w Some witnesses insert they were put to the question.   *x Or* every clinging sin; *one witness reads* the sin which all too readily distracts us.   *y Or* who, in place of the joy that was open to him, . . .

Sinai and Zion

18 Remember where you stand: not before the palpable, blazing fire of Sinai, with the darkness, gloom, and 19 whirlwind, the trumpet-blast and the oracular voice, which they heard, and 20 begged to hear no more; for they could not bear the command, 'If even an animal touches the mountain, it must 21 be stoned.' So appalling was the sight, that Moses said, 'I shudder with fear.'

22 No, you stand before Mount Zion and the city of the living God, heavenly Jerusalem, before myriads of 23 angels, the full concourse and assembly of the first-born citizens of heaven, and God the judge of all, and the 24 spirits of good men made perfect, and Jesus the mediator of a new covenant, whose sprinkled blood has better things to tell than the blood of Abel. 25 See that you do not refuse to hear the voice that speaks. Those who refused to hear the oracle speaking on earth found no escape; still less shall we escape if we refuse to hear the One 26 who speaks from heaven. Then indeed his voice shook the earth, but now he has promised, 'Yet once again I will shake not earth alone, but the 27 heavens also.' The words 'once again' —and only once—imply that the shaking of these created things means their removal, and then what is not 28 shaken will remain. The kingdom we are given is unshakable; let us therefore give thanks to God, and so worship him as he would be wor-29 shipped, with reverence and awe; for our God is a devouring fire.

Directions for Christian living

13 Never cease to love your fellow-Christians.

2 Remember to show hospitality. There are some who, by so doing, have entertained angels without knowing it.

3 Remember those in prison as if you were there with them; and those who are being maltreated, for you like them are still in the world.

4 Marriage is honourable; let us all keep it so, and the marriage-bond inviolate; for God's judgement will fall on fornicators and adulterers.

5 Do not live for money; be content with what you have; for God himself has said, 'I will never leave you or de-6 sert you'; and so we can take courage and say, 'The Lord is my helper, I will not fear; what can man do to me?'

Remember your leaders, those who 7 first spoke God's message to you; and reflecting upon the outcome of their life and work, follow the example of their faith.

Jesus Christ is the same yesterday, 8 today, and for ever. So do not be 9 swept off your course by all sorts of outlandish teachings; it is good that our souls should gain their strength from the grace of God, and not from scruples about what we eat, which have never done any good to those who were governed by them.

Our altar is one from which[z] the 10 priests of the sacred tent have no right to eat. As you know, those 11 animals whose blood is brought as a sin-offering by the high priest into the sanctuary, have their bodies burnt outside the camp, and therefore Jesus 12 also suffered outside the gate, to consecrate the people by his own blood. Let us then go to him outside the 13 camp, bearing the stigma that he bore. For here we have no permanent 14 home, but we are seekers after the city which is to come. Through Je-15 sus, then, let us continually offer up to God the sacrifice of praise, that is, the tribute of lips which acknowledge his name, and never forget to show 16 kindness and to share what you have with others; for such are the sacrifices which God approves.

Obey your leaders and defer to 17 them; for they are tireless in their concern for you, as men who must render an account. Let it be a happy task for them, and not pain and grief, for that would bring you no advantage.

Pray for us; for we are convinced 18 that our conscience is clear; our one desire is always to do what is right. All the more earnestly I ask for your 19 prayers, that I may be restored to you the sooner.

A prayer

May the God of peace, who brought 20 up from the dead our Lord Jesus, the great Shepherd of the sheep, by the blood of the eternal covenant, make 21 you perfect in all goodness so that you may do his will; and may he make of us what he would have us be through Jesus Christ, to whom be glory for ever and ever! Amen.

A personal note

I beg you, brothers, bear with this 22 exhortation; for it is after all a short

z *Or* one like that from which . . .

23 letter. I have news for you: our friend Timothy has been released; and if he comes in time he will be with me when I see you.

Greet all your leaders and all God's 24 people. Greetings to you from our Italian friends.

God's grace be with you all!   25

A LETTER OF
JAMES

1 FROM JAMES, a servant of God and the Lord Jesus Christ.

Greetings to the Twelve Tribes dispersed throughout the world.

Wisdom and faith

2 My brothers, whenever you have to face trials of many kinds, count your-
3 selves supremely happy, in the knowledge that such testing of your faith
4 breeds fortitude, and if you give fortitude full play you will go on to complete a balanced character that
5 will fall short in nothing. If any of you falls short in wisdom, he should ask God for it and it will be given him, for God is a generous giver who neither refuses nor reproaches anyone.
6 But he must ask in faith, without a doubt in his mind; for the doubter is like a heaving sea ruffled by the wind.
7 A man of that kind must not expect
8 the Lord to give him anything; he is double-minded, and never can keep[a] a steady course.

Poverty and wealth

9 The brother in humble circumstances may well be proud that God lifts him
10 up; and the wealthy brother must find his pride in being brought low. For the rich man will disappear like
11 the flower of the field; once the sun is up with its scorching heat the flower withers, its petals fall, and what was lovely to look at is lost for ever. So shall the rich man wither away as he goes about his business.

Trial and temptation

12 Happy the man who remains steadfast under trial, for having passed that test he will receive for his prize the gift of life promised to those who love God. No one under trial or temp- 13 tation should say, 'I am being tempted by God'; for God is untouched by evil,[b] and does not himself tempt any- one. Temptation arises when a man 14 is enticed and lured away by his own lust; then lust conceives, and gives 15 birth to sin; and sin full-grown breeds death.

Make no mistake, my friends. All 16 17 good giving, every perfect gift, comes[c] from above, from the Father of the lights of heaven. With him there is no variation, no play of passing shadows.[d] Of his set purpose, by declaring the 18 truth, he gave us birth to be a kind of firstfruits of his creatures.

Hearing and doing

Of that you may be certain, my 19 friends. But each of you must be quick to listen, slow to speak, and slow to be angry. For a man's anger 20 cannot promote the justice of God. Away then with all that is sordid, and 21 the malice that hurries to excess, and quietly accept the message planted in your hearts, which can bring you salvation.

Only be sure that you act on the 22 message and do not merely listen; for that would be to mislead yourselves. A man who listens to the message but 23 never acts upon it is like one who looks in a mirror at the face nature gave him. He glances at himself and 24 goes away, and at once forgets what he looked like. But the man who 25 looks closely into the perfect law, the law that makes us free, and who lives in its company, does not forget what he hears, but acts upon it; and that is the man who by acting will find happiness.

---

a Or anything; a double-minded man never keeps . . .
c Or All giving is good, and every perfect gift comes . . . shadow caused by change.

b Or God cannot be tempted by evil.
d Some witnesses read no variation, or

True religion

26 A man may think he is religious, but if he has no control over his tongue, he is deceiving himself; that man's 27 religion is futile. The kind of religion which is without stain or fault in the sight of God our Father is this: to go to the help of orphans and widows in their distress and keep oneself untarnished by the world.

About snobbery

2 My brothers, believing as you do in our Lord Jesus Christ, who reigns in glory, you must never show snobbery. 2 For instance, two visitors may enter your place of worship, one a well-dressed man with gold rings, and the other a poor man in shabby clothes. 3 Suppose you pay special attention to the well-dressed man and say to him, 'Please take this seat', while to the poor man you say, 'You can stand; or you may sit here*e* on the floor by my 4 footstool', do you not see that you are inconsistent and judge by false standards?

5 Listen, my friends. Has not God chosen those who are poor in the eyes of the world to be rich in faith and to inherit the kingdom he has 6 promised to those who love him? And yet you have insulted the poor man. Moreover, are not the rich your oppressors? Is it not they who drag you 7 into court and pour contempt on the honoured name by which God has claimed you?

8 If, however, you are observing the sovereign law laid down in Scripture, 'Love your neighbour as yourself', 9 that is excellent. But if you show snobbery, you are committing a sin and you stand convicted by that law 10 as transgressors. For if a man keeps the whole law apart from one single point, he is guilty of breaking all of 11 it. For the One who said, 'Thou shalt not commit adultery', said also, 'Thou shalt not commit murder.' You may not be an adulterer, but if you commit murder you are a law-breaker all the 12 same. Always speak and act as men who are to be judged under a law of 13 freedom. In that judgement there will be no mercy for the man who has shown no mercy. Mercy triumphs over judgement.

The evidence of faith

14 My brothers, what use is it for a man to say he has faith when he does noth-ing to show it? Can that faith save him? Suppose a brother or a sister is 15 in rags with not enough food for the day, and one of you says, 'Good luck 16 to you, keep yourselves warm, and have plenty to eat', but does nothing to supply their bodily needs, what is the good of that? So with faith; if it 17 does not lead to action, it is in itself a lifeless thing.

But someone may object: 'Here is 18 one who claims to have faith and another who points to his deeds.' To which I reply: 'Prove to me that this faith you speak of is real though not accompanied by deeds, and by my deeds I will prove to you my faith.' You have faith enough to believe that 19 there is one God. Excellent! The devils have faith like that, and it makes them tremble. But can you not see, you 20 quibbler, that faith divorced from deeds is barren? Was it not by his 21 action, in offering his son Isaac upon the altar, that our father Abraham was justified? Surely you can see that 23 faith was at work in his actions, and that by these actions the integrity of his faith was fully proved. Here was 23 fulfilment of the words of Scripture: 'Abraham put his faith in God, and that faith was counted to him as righteousness'; and elsewhere he is called 'God's friend'. You see then 24 that a man is justified by deeds and not by faith in itself. The same is true 25 of the prostitute Rahab also. Was not she justified by her action in welcom-ing the messengers into her house and sending them away by a different route? As the body is dead when 26 there is no breath left in it, so faith divorced from deeds is lifeless as a corpse.

The tongue, an intractable evil

My brothers, not many of you should **3** become teachers, for you may be cer-tain that we who teach shall ourselves be judged with greater strictness. All 2 of us often go wrong; the man who never says a wrong thing is a perfect character, able to bridle his whole being. If we put bits into horses' 3 mouths to make them obey our will, we can direct their whole body. Or 4 think of ships: large they may be, yet even when driven by strong gales they can be directed by a tiny rudder on whatever course the helmsman chooses. So with the tongue. It is a small 5 member but it can make huge claims.*f*

e Some witnesses read Stand where you are or sit here . . . ; *others read* Stand where you are or sit . . .
f Or it is a great boaster.

What an immense stack of timber[g] can be set ablaze by the tiniest spark! 6 And the tongue is in effect a fire. It represents among our members the world with all its wickedness; it pollutes our whole being; it keeps the wheel of our existence red-hot, and its 7 flames are fed by hell. Beasts and birds of every kind, creatures that crawl on the ground or swim in the sea, can be subdued and have been 8 subdued by mankind; but no man can subdue the tongue. It is an intractable evil, charged with deadly 9 venom. We use it to sing the praises of our Lord and Father, and we use it to invoke curses upon our fellow-men 10 who are made in God's likeness. Out of the same mouth come praises and curses. My brothers, this should 11 not be so. Does a fountain gush with both fresh and brackish water 12 from the same opening? Can a fig-tree, my brothers, yield olives, or a vine figs? No more does salt water yield fresh.

Earthly and heavenly wisdom contrasted

13 Who among you is wise or clever? Let his right conduct give practical proof of it, with the modesty that comes 14 of wisdom. But if you are harbouring bitter jealousy and selfish ambition in your hearts, consider whether your claims are not false, and a defiance of 15 the truth. This is not the wisdom that comes from above; it is earth-bound, 16 sensual, demonic. For with jealousy and ambition come disorder and evil 17 of every kind. But the wisdom from above is in the first place pure; and then peace-loving, considerate, and open to reason; it is straightforward and sincere, rich in mercy and in the 18 kindly deeds that are its fruit. True justice is the harvest reaped by peace-makers from seeds sown in a spirit of peace.

About envious desires

4 What causes conflicts and quarrels among you? Do they not spring from the aggressiveness of your bodily de- 2 sires? You want something which you cannot have, and so you are bent on murder; you are envious, and cannot attain your ambition, and so you quarrel and fight. You do not get what you want, because you do not pray 3 for it. Or, if you do, your requests are not granted because you pray from

wrong motives, to spend what you get on your pleasures. You false, un- 4 faithful creatures! Have you never learned that love of the world is enmity to God? Whoever chooses to be the world's friend makes himself God's enemy. Or do you suppose that 5 Scripture has no meaning when it says that the spirit which God implanted in man turns towards envious desires? And yet the grace he gives is stronger. 6 Thus Scripture says, 'God opposes the arrogant and gives grace to the humble.' Be submissive then to God. 7 Stand up to the devil and he will turn and run. Come close to God, and he 8 will come close to you. Sinners, make your hands clean; you who are double-minded, see that your motives are pure. Be sorrowful, mourn and weep. 9 Turn your laughter into mourning and your gaiety into gloom. Humble your- 10 selves before God and he will lift you high.

About judging your neighbour

Brothers, you must never disparage 11 one another. He who disparages a brother or passes judgement on his brother disparages the law and judges the law. But if you judge the law, you are not keeping it but sitting in judgement upon it. There is only one 12 lawgiver and judge, the One who is able to save life and destroy it. So who are you to judge your neighbour?

About planning without God's guidance

A word with you, you who say, 'Today 13 or tomorrow we will go off to such and such a town and spend a year there trading and making money.' Yet you have no idea what tomorrow 14 will bring. Your life, what is it? You are no more than a mist, seen for a little while and then dispersing. What 15 you ought to say is: 'If it be the Lord's will, we shall live to do this or that.' But instead, you boast and 16 brag, and all such boasting is wrong. Well then, the man who knows the 17 good he ought to do and does not do it is a sinner.

A word to the wealthy

Next a word to you who have great 5 possessions. Weep and wail over the miserable fate descending on you. Your riches have rotted; your fine 2 clothes are moth-eaten; your silver 3

g Or What a huge forest . . .

and gold have rusted away, and their very rust will be evidence against you and consume your flesh like fire. You have piled up wealth in an age 4 that is near its close. The wages you never paid to the men who mowed your fields are loud against you, and the outcry of the reapers has reached 5 the ears of the Lord of Hosts. You have lived on earth in wanton luxury, fattening yourselves like cattle—and 6 the day for slaughter has come. You have condemned the innocent and murdered him; he offers no resistance.

Be patient and stout-hearted

7 Be patient, my brothers, until the Lord comes. The farmer looking for the precious crop his land may yield can only wait in patience, until the autumn and spring rains have fallen. 8 You too must be patient and stout-hearted, for the coming of the Lord 9 is near. My brothers, do not blame your troubles on one another, or you will fall under judgement; and there 10 stands the Judge, at the door. If you want a pattern of patience under ill-treatment, take the prophets who 11 spoke in the name of the Lord; remember: 'We count those happy who stood firm.' You have all heard how Job stood firm, and you have seen how the Lord treated him in the end. For the Lord is full of pity and compassion.

The power of prayer

Above all things, my brothers, do not 12 use oaths, whether 'by heaven' or 'by earth' or by anything else. When you say yes or no, let it be plain 'Yes' or 'No', for fear that you expose yourselves to judgement.

Is anyone among you in trouble? 13 He should turn to prayer. Is anyone in good heart? He should sing praises. Is one of you ill? He should send for 14 the elders of the congregation to pray over him and anoint him with oil in the name of the Lord. The prayer 15 offered in faith will save the sick man, the Lord will raise him from his bed, and any sins he may have committed will be forgiven. Therefore 16 confess your sins to one another, and pray for one another, and then you will be healed. A good man's prayer is powerful and effective. Elijah was a 17 man with human frailties like our own; and when he prayed earnestly that there should be no rain, not a drop fell on the land for three years and a half; then he prayed again, and 18 down came the rain and the land bore crops once more.

My brothers, if one of your number 19 should stray from the truth and another succeed in bringing him back, be sure of this: any man who brings 20 a sinner back from his crooked ways will be rescuing his soul from death and cancelling innumerable sins.

THE FIRST LETTER OF
PETER

A living hope for a time of trial

1 FROM PETER, apostle of Jesus Christ, to those of God's scattered people who lodge for a while in Pontus, Galatia, Cappadocia, Asia, and 2 Bithynia—chosen of old in the purpose of God the Father, hallowed by his service by the Spirit, and consecrated with the sprinkled blood of Jesus Christ.

Grace and peace to you in fullest measure.

3 Praise be to the God and Father of our Lord Jesus Christ, who in his great mercy gave us new birth into a living hope by the resurrection of Jesus Christ from the dead! The inherit- 4 ance to which we are born is one that nothing can destroy or spoil or wither. It is kept for you in heaven, and you, 5 because you put your faith in God, are under the protection of his power until salvation comes—the salvation which is even now in readiness and will be revealed at the end of time.

This is cause for great joy, even 6 though now you smart for a little while, if need be, under trials of many kinds. Even gold passes through the 7 assayer's fire, and more precious than perishable gold is faith which has stood the test. These trials come so that your faith may prove itself worthy of all praise, glory, and honour when Jesus Christ is revealed.

The theme the prophets pondered

8 You have not seen him, yet you love him; and trusting in him now without seeing him, you are transported with 9 a joy too great for words, while you reap the harvest of your faith, that is, 10 salvation for your souls. This salvation was the theme which the prophets pondered and explored, those who prophesied about the grace of God 11 awaiting you. They tried to find out what was the time,[a] and what the circumstances, to which the spirit of Christ in them pointed, foretelling the sufferings in store for Christ and 12 the splendours to follow; and it was disclosed to them that the matter they treated of was not for their time but for yours. And now it has been openly announced to you through preachers who brought you the Gospel in the power of the Holy Spirit sent from heaven. These are things that angels long to see into.

A call to holy living

13 You must therefore be mentally stripped for action, perfectly self-controlled. Fix your hopes on the gift of grace which is to be yours when 14 Jesus Christ is revealed. As obedient children, do not let your characters be shaped any longer by the desires you cherished in your days of ignor- 15 ance. The One who called you is holy; like him, be holy in all your behaviour, 16 because Scripture says, 'You shall be holy, for I am holy.' 17 If you say 'our Father' to the One who judges every man impartially on the record of his deeds, you must stand in awe of him while you live 18 out your time on earth. Well you know that it was no perishable stuff, like gold or silver, that bought your freedom from the empty folly of your 19 traditional ways. The price was paid in precious blood, as it were of a lamb without mark or blemish—the blood 20 of Christ. Predestined before the foundation of the world, he was made manifest in this last period of time for 21 your sake. Through him you have come to trust in God who raised him

from the dead and gave him glory, and so your faith and hope are fixed on God.

Born anew

Now that by obedience to the truth 22 you have purified your souls until you feel sincere affection towards your brother Christians, love one another whole-heartedly with all your strength. You have been born anew, not of 23 mortal parentage but of immortal, through the living and enduring word of God.[b] For (as Scripture says) 24

'All mortals are like grass;
all their splendour like the flower of the field;
the grass withers, the flower falls;
but the word of the Lord endures for 25 evermore.'

And this 'word' is the word of the Gospel preached to you.

Spiritual appetites

Then away with all malice and deceit, 2 away with all pretence and jealousy and recrimination of every kind! Like the new-born infants you are, 2 you must crave for pure milk (spiritual milk, I mean), so that you may thrive upon it to your souls' health. Surely you have tasted that the Lord 3 is good.

A spiritual temple; a holy priesthood

So come to him, our living Stone— 4 the stone rejected by men but choice and precious in the sight of God. Come, and let yourselves be built, as 5 living stones, into a spiritual temple; become a holy priesthood,[c] to offer spiritual sacrifices acceptable to God through Jesus Christ. For it stands 6 written:

'I lay in Zion a choice corner-stone of great worth.
The man who has faith in it will not be put to shame.'

The great worth of which it speaks is 7 for you who have faith. For those who have no faith, the stone which the builders rejected has become not only the corner-stone,[d] but also 'a stone to 8 trip over, a rock to stumble against'. They fall when they disbelieve the Word. Such was their appointed lot!

But you are a chosen race, a royal 9 priesthood, a dedicated nation, and a people claimed by God for his own, to proclaim the triumphs of him who has called you out of darkness into 10 his marvellous light. You are now the people of God, who once were not his people; outside his mercy once, you have now received his mercy.

Christian behaviour

11 Dear friends, I beg you, as aliens in a foreign land, to abstain from the lusts of the flesh which are at war 12 with the soul. Let all your behaviour be such as even pagans can recognize as good, and then, whereas they malign you as criminals now, they will come to see for themselves that you live good lives, and will give glory to God on the day when he comes to hold assize.

13 Submit yourselves to every human institution for the sake of the Lord, whether to the sovereign as supreme, 14 or to the governor as his deputy for the punishment of criminals and the commendation of those who do right. 15 For it is the will of God that by your good conduct you should put ignorance and stupidity to silence. 16 Live as free men; not however as though your freedom were there to provide a screen for wrongdoing, but 17 as slaves in God's service. Give due honour to everyone: love to the brotherhood, reverence to God, honour to the sovereign.

To servants

18 Servants, accept the authority of your masters with all due submission, not only when they are kind and considerate, but even when they are perverse. 19 For it is a fine[e] thing if a man endure the pain of undeserved suffering be-20 cause God is in his thoughts. What credit is there in fortitude when you have done wrong and are beaten for it? But when you have behaved well and suffer for it, your fortitude is a 21 fine thing[f] in the sight of God. To that you were called, because Christ suffered[g] on your behalf, and thereby left you an example; it is for you to 22 follow in his steps. He committed no sin, he was convicted of no falsehood; 23 when he was abused he did not retort with abuse, when he suffered he uttered no threats, but committed his cause to the One who judges justly. 24 In his own person he carried our sins to[h] the gibbet, so that we might cease to live for sin and begin to live for

e Or creditable.   f Or is creditable.

righteousness. By his wounds you have been healed. You were straying 25 like sheep, but now you have turned towards the Shepherd and Guardian of your souls.

To wives

In the same way you women must 3 accept the authority of your husbands, so that if there are any of them who disbelieve the Gospel they may be won over, without a word being said, by observing the chaste and reverent 2 behaviour of their wives. Your beauty 3 should reside, not in outward adornment—the braiding of the hair, or jewellery, or dress—but in the inmost 4 centre of your being, with its imperishable ornament, a gentle, quiet spirit, which is of high value in the sight of God. Thus it was among God's people 5 in days of old: the women who fixed their hopes on him adorned themselves by submission to their husbands. Such was Sarah, who obeyed 6 Abraham and called him 'my master'. Her children you have now become, if you do good and show no fear.

To husbands

In the same way, you husbands must 7 conduct your married life with understanding: pay honour to the woman's body, not only because it is weaker, but also because you share together in the grace of God which gives you life. Then your prayers will not be hindered.

About personal wrongs

To sum up: be one in thought and 8 feeling, all of you; be full of brotherly affection, kindly and humble-minded. Do not repay wrong with wrong, or 9 abuse with abuse; on the contrary, retaliate with blessing, for a blessing is the inheritance to which you yourselves have been called.

'Whoever loves life and would see 10 good days
must restrain his tongue from evil
and his lips from deceit;
must turn from wrong and do good, 11
seek peace and pursue it.
For the Lord's eyes are turned to- 12
wards the righteous,
his ears are open to their prayers;
but the Lord's face is set against
wrong-doers.'

Who is going to do you wrong if you 13 are devoted to what is good? And yet 14

g Some witnesses read died.   h Or on.

if you should suffer for your virtues, you may count yourselves happy. Have no fear of them:[i] do not be
15 perturbed, but hold the Lord Christ in reverence in your hearts.[j] Be always ready with your defence whenever you are called to account for the hope that is in you, but make that defence
16 with modesty and respect. Keep your conscience clear, so that when you are abused, those who malign your Christian conduct may be put to
17 shame. It is better to suffer for well-doing, if such should be the will of
18 God, than for doing wrong. For Christ also died[k] for our sins[l] once and for all. He, the just, suffered for the unjust, to bring us to God.

Significance of baptism

In the body he was put to death; in
19 the spirit he was brought to life. And in the spirit he went and made his proclamation to the imprisoned spi-
20 rits. They had refused obedience long ago, while God waited patiently in the days of Noah and the building of the ark, and in the ark a few persons, eight in all, were brought to
21 safety through the water. This water prefigured the water of baptism through which you are now brought to safety. Baptism is not the washing away of bodily pollution, but the appeal made to God by a good conscience; and it brings salvation through the resurrection of Jesus
22 Christ, who entered heaven after receiving the submission of angelic authorities and powers, and is now at the right hand of God.

Changed lives

4 Remembering that Christ endured bodily suffering, you must arm yourselves with a temper of mind like his. When a man has thus endured bodily
2 suffering he has finished with sin, and for the rest of his days on earth he may live, not for the things that men
3 desire, but for what God wills. You had time enough in the past to do all the things that men want to do in the pagan world. Then you lived in licence and debauchery, drunkenness, revelry, and tippling, and the for-
4 bidden worship of idols. Now, when you no longer plunge with them into all this reckless dissipation, they cannot understand it, and they vilify you

accordingly; but they shall answer for 5 it to him who stands ready to pass judgement on the living and the dead. Why was the Gospel preached to 6 those who are dead? In order that, although in the body they received the sentence common to men, they might in the spirit be alive with the life of God.

Serving one another

The end of all things is upon us, so you 7 must lead an ordered and sober life, given to prayer. Above all, keep your 8 love for one another at full strength, because love cancels innumerable sins. Be hospitable to one another with- 9 out complaining. Whatever gift each 10 of you may have received, use it in service to one another, like good stewards dispensing the grace of God in its varied forms. Are you a speaker? 11 Speak as if you uttered oracles of God. Do you give service? Give it as in the strength which God supplies. In all things so act that the glory may be God's through Jesus Christ; to him belong glory and power for ever and ever. Amen.

Encouragement in time of persecution

My dear friends, do not be bewildered 12 by the fiery ordeal that is upon you, as though it were something extraordinary. It gives you a share in 13 Christ's sufferings, and that is cause for joy; and when his glory is revealed, your joy will be triumphant. If 14 Christ's name is flung in your teeth as an insult, count yourselves happy, because then that glorious Spirit which is the Spirit of God is resting upon you. If you suffer, it must not 15 be for murder, theft, or sorcery,[m] nor for infringing the rights of others. But 16 if anyone suffers as a Christian, he should feel it no disgrace, but confess that name to the honour of God.

The time has come for the judge- 17 ment to begin; it is beginning with God's own household. And if it is starting with you, how will it end for those who refuse to obey the gospel of God? It is hard enough for the 18 righteous to be saved; what then will become of the impious and sinful? So 19 even those who suffer, if it be according to God's will, should commit their souls to him—by doing good; their Maker will not fail them.

---

i *Or* Do not fear what they fear.   j *Or* hold Christ in reverence in your hearts, as Lord.   k *Some witnesses read* suffered.   l *Some witnesses read* for sins; *others read* for sins on our behalf.   m *Or* other crime.

To elders

5 And now I appeal to the elders of your community, as a fellow-elder and a witness of Christ's sufferings, and also a partaker in the splendour **2** that is to be revealed. Tend that flock of God whose shepherds you are, and do it, not under compulsion, but of your own free will, as God would have it; not for gain but out of sheer **3** devotion; not tyrannizing over those who are allotted to your care, but **4** setting an example to the flock. And then, when the Head Shepherd appears, you will receive for your own the unfading garland of glory.

To younger men

5 In the same way you younger men must be subordinate to your elders. Indeed, all of you should wrap yourselves in the garment of humility towards each other, because God sets his face against the arrogant but **6** favours the humble. Humble yourselves then under God's mighty hand, and he will lift you up in due time. **7** Cast all your cares on him, for you are his charge.

Awake! be on the alert!

Awake! be on the alert! Your enemy **8** the devil, like a roaring lion, prowls round looking for someone to devour. Stand up to him, firm in faith, and **9** remember that your brother Christians are going through the same kinds of suffering while they are in the world. And the God of all grace, **10** who called you into his eternal glory in Christ, will himself, after your brief suffering, restore, establish, and strengthen you on a firm foundation. He holds dominion for ever and ever. **11** Amen.

Final greetings

I write you this brief appeal through **12** Silvanus, our trusty brother as I hold him, adding my testimony that this is the true grace of God. In this stand fast.

Greetings from her who dwells in **13** Babylon, chosen by God like you, and from my son Mark. Greet one another **14** with the kiss of love.

Peace to you all who belong to Christ!

THE SECOND LETTER OF
PETER

1 FROM SIMEON PETER, servant and apostle of Jesus Christ, to those who through the justice of our God and Saviour Jesus Christ share our faith and enjoy equal privilege with ourselves. **2** Grace and peace be yours in fullest measure, through the knowledge of God and Jesus our Lord.

Life and true religion

3 His divine power has bestowed on us everything that makes for life and true religion, enabling us to know the One who called us by his own splen- **4** dour and might. Through this might and splendour he has given us his promises, great beyond all price, and through them you may escape the corruption with which lust has in-

fected the world, and come to share in the very being of God.

With all this in view, you should **5** try your hardest to supplement your faith with virtue, virtue with knowledge, knowledge with self-control, **6** self-control with fortitude, fortitude with piety, piety with brotherly kind- **7** ness, and brotherly kindness with love.

Gifts worth possessing

These are gifts which, if you possess **8** and foster them, will keep you from being either useless or barren in the knowledge of our Lord Jesus Christ. The man who lacks them is short- **9** sighted and blind; he has forgotten how he was cleansed from his former sins. All the more then, my friends, **10** exert yourselves to clinch God's choice and calling of you. If you behave so, 11 you will never come to grief. Thus you will be afforded full and free admission into the eternal kingdom of our Lord and Saviour Jesus Christ.

The message of the prophets confirmed

12 And so I will not hesitate to remind you of this again and again, although you know it and are well grounded in the truth that has already reached 13 you. Yet I think it right to keep refreshing your memory so long as I 14 still lodge in this body. I know that very soon I must leave it; indeed our Lord Jesus Christ has told me so.[a] 15 But I will see to it that after I am gone you will have means of remembering these things at all times.

16 It was not on tales artfully spun that we relied when we told you of the power of our Lord Jesus Christ and his coming; we saw him with our 17 own eyes in majesty, when at the hands of God the Father he was invested with honour and glory, and there came to him from the sublime Presence a voice which said: 'This is my Son, my Beloved,[b] on whom my 18 favour rests.' This voice from heaven we ourselves heard; when it came, we were with him on the sacred mountain.

19 All this only confirms for us the message of the prophets,[c] to which you will do well to attend, because it is like a lamp shining in a murky place, until the day breaks and the morning star rises to illuminate your minds.

False prophets, false teachers

20 But first note this: no one can interpret any prophecy of Scripture by 21 himself. For it was not through any human whim that men prophesied of old; men they were, but, impelled by the Holy Spirit, they spoke the words of God.

2 But Israel had false prophets as well as true; and you likewise will have false teachers among you. They will import disastrous heresies, disowning the very Master who bought them, and bringing swift disaster on 2 their own heads. They will gain many adherents to their dissolute practices, through whom the true way will be 3 brought into disrepute. In their greed

for money they will trade on your credulity with sheer fabrications.

God's judgements in the past

But the judgement long decreed for them has not been idle; perdition waits for them with unsleeping eyes. God did not spare the angels who 4 sinned, but consigned them to the dark pits of hell,[d] where they are reserved for judgement. He did not spare the 5 world of old (except for Noah, preacher of righteousness, whom he preserved with seven others), but brought the deluge upon that world of godless men. The cities of Sodom and Gomor- 6 rah God burned to ashes, and condemned them to total destruction, making them an object-lesson for godless men in future days. But he 7 rescued Lot, who was a good man, shocked by the dissolute habits of the lawless society in which he lived; day 8 after day every sight, every sound, of their evil courses tortured that good man's heart. Thus the Lord is 9 well able to rescue the godly out of trials, and to reserve the wicked under punishment until the day of judgement.

Character and destiny of false teachers

Above all he will punish those who 10 follow their abominable lusts. They flout authority; reckless and headstrong, they are not afraid to insult celestial beings, whereas angels, for 11 all their superior strength and might, employ no insults in seeking judgement against them before the Lord.

These men are like brute beasts, 12 born in the course of nature to be caught and killed. They pour abuse upon things they do not understand; like the beasts they will perish, suffer- 13 ing hurt for the hurt they have inflicted. To carouse in broad daylight is their idea of pleasure; while they sit with you at table they are an ugly blot on your company, because they revel in their own deceptions.[e]

They have eyes for nothing but 14 women, eyes never at rest from sin. They lure the unstable to their ruin; past masters in mercenary greed, God's curse is on them! They have 15 abandoned the straight road and lost their way. They have followed in the steps of Balaam son of Beor, who consented to take pay for doing wrong,

---

a Or I must leave it, as our Lord Jesus Christ told me.   b Or This is my only Son.   c Or And in the message of the prophets we have something still more certain.   d Some witnesses read consigned them to darkness and chains in hell.   e Some witnesses read in their love-feasts.

16 but had his offence brought home to him when the dumb beast spoke with a human voice and put a stop to the prophet's madness.

17 These men are springs that give no water, mists driven by a storm; the place reserved for them is black-
18 est darkness. They utter big, empty words, and make of sensual lusts and debauchery a bait to catch those who have barely begun to escape from
19 their heathen environment. They promise them freedom, but are themselves slaves of corruption; for a man is the slave of whatever has mastered
20 him. They had once escaped the world's defilements through the knowledge of our Lord and Saviour Jesus Christ; yet if they have entangled themselves in these all over again, and are mastered by them, their plight in the end is worse than before.
21 How much better never to have known the right way, than, having known it, to turn back and abandon the sacred commandments delivered
22 to them! For them the proverb has proved true: 'The dog returns to its own vomit', and, 'The sow after a wash rolls in the mud again.'

Why the Lord delays his return

3 This is now my second letter to you, my friends. In both of them I have been recalling to you what you already know, to rouse you to honest
2 thought. Remember the predictions made by God's own prophets, and the commands given by the Lord and Saviour through your apostles.
3 Note this first: in the last days there will come men who scoff at religion
4 and live self-indulgent lives, and they will say: 'Where now is the promise of his coming? Our fathers have been laid to their rest, but still everything continues exactly as it has always been since the world began.'
5 In taking this view they lose sight of the fact[f] that there were heavens and earth long ago, created by God's word out of water and with water;
6 and by water that first world was destroyed, the water of the deluge.
7 And the present heavens and earth, again by God's word, have been kept in store for burning; they are being

reserved until the day of judgement when the godless will be destroyed.

8 And here is one point, my friends, which you must not lose sight of: with the Lord one day is like a thousand years and a thousand years like one day. It is not that the Lord is slow in 9 fulfilling his promise, as some suppose, but that he is very patient with you, because it is not his will for any to be lost, but for all to come to repentance.

The Day of the Lord

But the Day of the Lord will come; it 10 will come, unexpected as a thief. On that day the heavens will disappear with a great rushing sound, the elements will disintegrate in flames, and the earth with all that is in it will be laid bare.[g]

Since the whole universe is to 11 break up in this way, think what sort of people you ought to be, what devout and dedicated lives you should live! Look eagerly for the coming of 12 the Day of God and work to hasten it on; that day will set the heavens ablaze until they fall apart, and will melt the elements in flames. But we 13 have his promise, and look forward to new heavens and a new earth, the home of justice.

Final words

With this to look forward to, do your 14 utmost to be found at peace with him, unblemished and above reproach in his sight. Bear in mind that our Lord's 15 patience with us is our salvation, as Paul, our friend and brother, said when he wrote to you with his inspired wisdom. And so he does in all his 16 other letters, wherever he speaks of this subject, though they contain some obscure passages, which the ignorant and unstable misinterpret to their own ruin, as they do the other scriptures.[h]

But you, my friends, are fore- 17 warned. Take care, then, not to let these unprincipled men seduce you with their errors; do not lose your own safe foothold. But grow in the 18 grace and in the knowledge of our Lord and Saviour Jesus Christ.[i] To him be glory now and for all eternity!

---

f Or They choose to overlook the fact . . .   g Some witnesses read will be burnt up.   h Or his other writings.   i Or But grow up, by the grace of our Lord and Saviour Jesus Christ, and by knowing him.

THE FIRST LETTER OF
JOHN

The word of life

1 IT WAS THERE from the beginning; we have heard it; we have seen it with our own eyes; we looked upon it, and felt it with our own hands; and it is of this we tell. Our theme is the **2** word of life. This life was made visible; we have seen it and bear our testimony; we here declare to you the eternal life which dwelt with the Father and was made visible to us. **3** What we have seen and heard we declare to you, so that you and we together may share in a common life, that life which we share with the **4** Father and his Son Jesus Christ. And we write this in order that the joy of us all may be complete.

God is light

5 Here is the message we heard from him and pass on to you: that God is light, and in him there is no darkness **6** at all. If we claim to be sharing in his life while we walk in the dark, our **7** words and our lives are a lie; but if we walk in the light as he himself is in the light, then we share together a common life, and we are being cleansed from every sin by the blood of Jesus his Son.

Sin and forgiveness

8 If we claim to be sinless, we are self-deceived and strangers to the truth. **9** If we confess our sins, he is just, and may be trusted to forgive our sins and cleanse us from every kind of **10** wrong; but if we say we have committed no sin, we make him out to be a liar, and then his word has no place in us.

2 My children, in writing thus to you my purpose is that you should not commit sin. But should anyone commit a sin, we have one to plead our cause*a* with the Father, Jesus Christ, **2** and he is just. He is himself the remedy for the defilement of our sins, not our sins only but the sins of all the world.

Knowing Christ and living in him

Here is the test by which we can **3** make sure that we know him: do we keep his commands? The man who **4** says, 'I know him', while he disobeys his commands, is a liar and a stranger to the truth; but in the man who is **5** obedient to his word, the divine love has indeed come to its perfection.

Here is the test by which we can make sure that we are in him: who-**6** ever claims to be dwelling in him, binds himself to live as Christ himself lived. Dear friends, I give you no new **7** command. It is the old command which you always had before you; the old command is the message which you heard at the beginning. And yet again it is a new command **8** that I am giving you—new in the sense that the darkness is passing and the real light already shines. Christ has made this true, and it is true in your own experience.

A man may say, 'I am in the light'; **9** but if he hates his brother, he is still in the dark. Only the man who loves **10** his brother dwells in light: there is nothing to make him stumble. But **11** one who hates his brother is in darkness; he walks in the dark and has no idea where he is going, because the darkness has made him blind.

Children; fathers; young men

I write to you, my children, because **12** your sins have been forgiven for his sake.*b*

I write to you, fathers, because you **13** know him who is and has been from the beginning.*c*

I write to you, young men, because you have mastered the evil one.

To you, children, I have written because you know the Father.

To you, fathers, I have written be-**14** cause you know him who is and has been from the beginning.*c*

To you, young men, I have written because you are strong; God's

---

a Literally we have an advocate . . . we have known from the beginning.   *b Or* forgiven, since you bear his name.   *c Or* him whom

word remains in you, and you have mastered the evil one.

The world, or the Father's love

15 Do not set your hearts on the godless world or anything in it. Anyone who loves the world is a stranger to the Father's love. 16 Everything the world affords, all that panders to the appetites or entices the eyes, all the glamour of its life, springs not from the Father but from the godless world. 17 And that world is passing away with all its allurements, but he who does God's will stands for evermore.

False teachers and the true

18 My children, this is the last hour! You were told that Antichrist was to come, and now many antichrists have appeared; which proves to us that this 19 is indeed the last hour. They went out from our company, but never really belonged to us; if they had, they would have stayed with us. They went out, so that it might be clear that not all in our company truly belong to it.[d]

20 You, no less than they, are among the initiated;[e] this is the gift of the Holy One, and by it you all have 21 knowledge.[f] It is not because you are ignorant of the truth that I have written to you, but because you know it, and because lies, one and all, are alien to the truth.

22 Who is the liar? Who but he that denies that Jesus is the Christ? He is Antichrist, for he denies both the 23 Father and the Son: to deny the Son is to be without the Father; to acknowledge the Son is to have the 24 Father too. You therefore must keep in your hearts that which you heard at the beginning; if what you heard then still dwells in you, you will yourselves dwell in the Son and also in the 25 Father. And this is the promise that he himself gave us, the promise of eternal life.

26 So much for those who would mis- 27 lead you. But as for you, the initiation[g] which you received from him stays with you; you need no other teacher, but learn all you need to know from his initiation, which is real and no illusion. As he taught you, then, dwell in him.

Children of God

Even now, my children, dwell in him, 28 so that when he appears we may be confident and unashamed before him at his coming. If you know that he is 29 righteous, you must recognize that every man who does right is his child. How great is the love that the Father 3 has shown to us! We were called God's children, and such we are;[h] and the reason why the godless world does not recognize us is that it has not known him. Here and now, dear 2 friends, we are God's children; what we shall be has not yet been disclosed, but we know that when it is disclosed[i] we shall be like him,[j] because we shall see him as he is. Everyone who has 3 this hope before him purifies himself, as Christ is pure.

To commit sin is to break God's 4 law: sin, in fact, is lawlessness. Christ 5 appeared, as you know, to do away with sins, and there is no sin in him. No man therefore who dwells in him 6 is a sinner; the sinner has not seen him and does not know him.

Two parents, two ways of life

My children, do not be misled: it is 7 the man who does right who is righteous, as God is righteous; the man 8 who sins is a child of the devil, for the devil has been a sinner from the first; and the Son of God appeared for the very purpose of undoing the devil's work.

A child of God does not commit sin, 9 because the divine seed remains in him; he cannot be a sinner, because he is God's child. That is the distinc- 10 tion between the children of God and the children of the devil: no one who does not do right is God's child, nor is anyone who does not love his brother. For the message you have heard from 11 the beginning is this: that we should love one another; unlike Cain, who 12 was a child of the evil one and murdered his brother. And why did he murder him? Because his own actions were wrong, and his brother's were right.

Loving like Christ

My brothers, do not be surprised if 13 the world hates you. We for our part 14

---

d Or that none of them truly belong to us.   e Literally have an anointing (Greek chrism).
f Some witnesses read you have all knowledge.   g Literally the anointing.   h Or We are called
children of God! Not only called, we really are his children.   i Or when he appears.   j Or we
ar_ God's children, though he has not yet appeared; what we shall be we know, for when he does
appear we shall be like him.

have crossed over from death to life;
this we know, because we love our brothers. The man who does not love is still
15 in the realm of death, for everyone
who hates his brother is a murderer,
and no murderer, as you know, has
16 eternal life dwelling within him. It is
by this that we know what love is:
that Christ laid down his life for us.
And we in our turn are bound to lay
17 down our lives for our brothers. But
if a man has enough to live on, and
yet when he sees his brother in need
shuts up his heart against him, how
can it be said that the divine love[k]
dwells in him?

Conscience and the commands of Christ

18 My children, love must not be a
matter of words or talk; it must be
genuine, and show itself in action.
19 This is how we may know that we
belong to the realm of truth, and con-
20 vince ourselves in his sight that even
if our conscience condemns us, God
is greater than our conscience[l] and
knows all.
21   Dear friends, if our conscience
does not condemn us, then we can
22 approach God with confidence, and
obtain from him whatever we ask,
because we are keeping his commands
23 and doing what he approves. This is
his command: to give our allegiance
to his Son Jesus Christ and love one
24 another as he commanded. When we
keep his commands we dwell in him
and he dwells in us. And this is how
we can make sure that he dwells
within us: we know it from the Spirit
he has given us.

How to distinguish truth from error

4 But do not trust any and every
spirit, my friends; test the spirits, to
see whether they are from God, for
among those who have gone out into
the world there are many prophets
2 falsely inspired. This is how we may
recognize the Spirit of God: every
spirit which acknowledges that Jesus
Christ has come in the flesh is from
3 God, and every spirit which does not
thus acknowledge Jesus is not from
God. This is what is meant by 'Antichrist';[m] you have been told that he
was to come, and here he is, in the
world already!
4   But you, my children, are of God's

family, and you have the mastery
over these false prophets, because he
who inspires you is greater than he
who inspires the godless world. They 5
are of that world, and so therefore is
their teaching; that is why the world
listens to them. But we belong to God, 6
and a man who knows God listens to
us, while he who does not belong to
God refuses us a hearing. That is how
we distinguish the spirit of truth from
the spirit of error.

The love God has for us

Dear friends, let us love one another, 7
because love is from God. Everyone
who loves is a child of God and knows
God, but the unloving know nothing 8
of God. For God is love; and his love 9
was disclosed to us in this, that he
sent his only Son into the world to
bring us life. The love I speak of is 10
not our love for God, but the love
he showed to us in sending his Son
as the remedy for the defilement of
our sins. If God thus loved us, dear 11
friends, we in turn are bound to love
one another. Though God has never 12
been seen by any man, God himself
dwells in us if we love one another;
his love is brought to perfection within us.
   Here is the proof that we dwell in 13
him and he dwells in us: he has imparted his Spirit to us. Moreover, we 14
have seen for ourselves, and we attest,
that the Father sent the Son to be the
saviour of the world, and if a man 15
acknowledges that Jesus is the Son of
God, God dwells in him and he dwells
in God. Thus we have come to know 16
and believe the love which God has
for us.

When love is brought to perfection

God is love; he who dwells in love is
dwelling in God, and God in him. This 17
is for us the perfection of love, to have
confidence on the day of judgement,
and this we can have, because even in
this world we are as he is. There is no 18
room for fear in love; perfect love
banishes fear. For fear brings with it
the pains of judgement, and anyone
who is afraid has not attained to love
in its perfection. We love because he 19
loved us first. But if a man says, 'I 20
love God', while hating his brother,
he is a liar. If he does not love the

k Or that love for God . . .   l Or and reassure ourselves in his sight in matters where our conscience condemns us, because God is greater than our conscience . . . ; or and yet we shall do well to convince ourselves that if even our own conscience condemns us, still more will God who is greater than
conscience . . .   m Or This is the spirit of Antichrist.

brother whom he has seen, it cannot be that he loves God whom he has not
21 seen. And indeed this command comes to us from Christ himself: that he who loves God must also love his brother.

Victory over the world

5 Everyone who believes that Jesus is the Christ is a child of God, and to love the parent means to love his
2 child; it follows that when we love God and obey his commands we love
3 his children too. For to love God is to keep his commands; and they are not
4 burdensome, because every child of God is victor over the godless world. The victory that defeats the world is
5 our faith, for who is victor over the world but he who believes that Jesus is the Son of God?

Divine witness

6 This is he who came with water and blood: Jesus Christ. He came, not by water alone, but by water and blood; and there is the Spirit to bear witness,
▽ 8 because the Spirit is truth. For there are three witnesses, the Spirit, the water, and the blood, and these three
9 are in agreement. We accept human testimony, but surely divine testimony is stronger, and this threefold testimony is indeed that of God himself, the witness he has borne to his
10 Son. He who believes in the Son of God has this testimony in his own heart, but he who disbelieves God, makes him out to be a liar, by refusing to accept God's own witness to his
11 Son. The witness is this: that God has

given us eternal life, and that this life is found in his Son. He who possesses 12 the Son has life indeed; he who does not possess the Son of God has not that life.

Summing up

This letter is to assure you that you 13 have eternal life. It is addressed to those who give their allegiance to the Son of God.

We can approach God with confi- 14 dence for this reason: if we make requests which accord with his will he listens to us; and if we know that our 15 requests are heard, we know also that the things we ask for are ours.

If a man sees his brother commit- 16 ting a sin which is not a deadly sin, he should pray to God for him, and he will grant him life—that is, when men are not guilty of deadly sin. There is such a thing as deadly sin, and I do not suggest that he should pray about that; but although all 17 wrongdoing is sin, not all sin is deadly sin.

We know that no child of God is a 18 sinner; it is the Son of God who keeps him safe, and the evil one cannot touch him.

We know that we are of God's 19 family, while the whole godless world lies in the power of the evil one.

We know that the Son of God has 20 come and given us understanding to know him who is real; indeed we are in him who is real, since we are in his Son Jesus Christ. This is the true God, this is eternal life. My children, 21 be on the watch against false gods.

THE SECOND LETTER OF
JOHN

Truth and love

1 THE ELDER to the Lady chosen by God, and her children, whom I love in truth—and not I alone but all who
2 know the truth—for the sake of the truth that dwells among us and will be with us for ever.
3 Grace, mercy, and peace shall be with us from God the Father and from

Jesus Christ the Son of the Father, in truth and love.

I was delighted to find that some 4 of your children are living by the truth, as we were commanded by the Father. And now I have a request to 5 make of you. Do not think I am giving a new command; I am recalling the one we have had before us from the beginning: let us love one another.

6 And love means following the commands of God. This is the command which was given you from the beginning, to be your rule of life.

7 Many deceivers have gone out into the world, who do not acknowledge Jesus Christ as coming in the flesh. These are the persons described as

8 the Antichrist, the arch-deceiver. Beware of them, so that you may not lose all that we worked for, but receive your reward in full.

9 Anyone who runs ahead too far, and does not stand by the doctrine of the Christ, is without God; he who stands by that doctrine possesses both the Father and the Son. If anyone 10 comes to you who does not bring this doctrine, do not welcome him into your house or give him a greeting; for 11 anyone who gives him a greeting is an accomplice in his wicked deeds.

12 I have much to write to you, but I do not care to put it down in black and white. But I hope to visit you and talk with you face to face, so that our joy may be complete. The children of 13 your Sister, chosen by God, send their greetings.

THE THIRD LETTER OF

JOHN

Loyalty and discord in the church

1 THE ELDER to dear Gaius, whom I love in truth.

2 My dear Gaius, I pray that you may enjoy good health, and that all may go well with you, as I know it goes

3 well with your soul. I was delighted when friends came and told me how true you have been; indeed you are

4 true in your whole life. Nothing gives me greater joy than to hear that my children are living by the truth.

5 My dear friend, you show a fine loyalty in everything that you do for these our fellow-Christians, strangers

6 though they are to you. They have spoken of your kindness before the congregation here. Please help them on their journey in a manner worthy

7 of the God they serve. It was on Christ's work that they went out; and they would accept nothing from pagans.

8 We are bound to support such men, and so play our part in spreading the truth.

9 I sent a letter to the congregation, but Diotrephes, their would-be leader,[a] will have nothing to do with us. If I 10 come, I will bring up the things he is doing. He lays baseless and spiteful charges against us; not satisfied with that, he refuses to receive our friends, and he interferes with those who would do so, and tries to expel them from the congregation.

11 My dear friend, do not imitate bad examples, but good ones. The well-doer is a child of God; the evil-doer has never seen God.

12 Demetrius gets a good testimonial from everybody—yes, and from the truth itself. I add my testimony, and you know that my testimony is true.

13 I have much to write to you, but I do not care to set it down with pen and ink. I hope to see you very soon, 14 and we will talk face to face. Peace be with you. Our friends send their greetings. Greet our friends one by one.

a Or who enjoys being their leader.

A LETTER OF

JUDE

1 FROM JUDE, servant of Jesus Christ and brother of James, to those whom God has called, who live in the love of God the Father and in the safe keeping of Jesus Christ.
2 Mercy, peace, and love be yours in fullest measure.

Urgent appeal to defend the faith

3 My friends, I was fully engaged in writing to you about our salvation—which is yours no less than ours—when it became urgently necessary to write at once and appeal to you to join the struggle in defence of the faith, the faith which God entrusted
4 to his people once and for all. It is in danger from certain persons who have wormed their way in, the very men whom Scripture long ago marked down for the doom they have incurred. They are the enemies of religion; they pervert the free favour of our God into licentiousness, disowning Jesus Christ, our only Master and Lord.*a*

A reminder from history

5 You already know it all, but let me remind you how the Lord,*b* having once delivered the people of Israel out of Egypt, next time destroyed those who
6 were guilty of unbelief. Remember too the angels, how some of them were not content to keep the dominion given to them but abandoned their proper home; and God has reserved them for judgement on the great Day, bound beneath the darkness in
7 everlasting chains. Remember Sodom and Gomorrah and the neighbouring towns; like the angels, they committed fornication and followed unnatural lusts; and they paid the penalty in eternal fire, an example for all to see.

Character and destiny of false teachers

8 So too with these men today. Their dreams lead them to defile the body, to flout authority, and to insult celes-
9 tial beings. In contrast, when the archangel Michael was in debate with the devil, disputing the possession of Moses's body, he did not presume to condemn him in insulting words,*c* but said, 'May the Lord rebuke you!'

10 But these men pour abuse upon things they do not understand; the things they do understand, by instinct like brute beasts, prove their undoing.
11 Alas for them! They have gone the way of Cain; they have plunged into Balaam's error for pay; they have rebelled like Korah, and they share his doom.

12 These men are a blot on your love-feasts, where they eat and drink without reverence. They are shepherds who take care only of themselves. They are clouds carried away by the wind without giving rain, trees that in season bear no fruit, dead twice
13 over and pulled up by the roots. They are fierce waves of the sea, foaming shameful deeds; they are stars that have wandered from their course, and the place for ever reserved for them is blackest darkness.

14 It was to them that Enoch, the seventh in descent from Adam, directed his prophecy when he said: 'I saw the Lord come with his myriads of angels, to bring all men to judgement
15 and to convict all the godless of all the godless deeds they had committed, and of all the defiant words which godless sinners had spoken against him.'

16 They are a set of grumblers and malcontents. They follow their lusts. Big words come rolling from their lips, and they court favour to gain
17 their ends. But you, my friends, should remember the predictions made by the apostles of our Lord Jesus
18 Christ. This was the warning they gave you: 'In the final age there will be men who pour scorn on religion, and follow their own godless lusts.'

Fortify yourselves

19 These men draw a line between spiritual and unspiritual persons,

a Or disowning our one and only Master, and Jesus Christ our Lord.   b Some witnesses read Jesus (which might be understood as Joshua).   c Or to charge him with blasphemy.

although they are themselves[d] wholly
20 unspiritual. But you, my friends,
must fortify yourselves in your most
sacred faith. Continue to pray in the
21 power of the Holy Spirit. Keep yourselves in the love of God, and look
forward to the day when our Lord
Jesus Christ in his mercy will give
eternal life.

Some doubters need pity

22 There are some doubting souls who
23 need your pity;[e] snatch them from
the flames and save them.[f] There

are others for whom your pity must
be mixed with fear; hate the very
clothing that is contaminated with
sensuality.

Glory to God!

Now to the One who can keep you 24
from falling and set you in the presence of his glory, jubilant and above
reproach, to the only God our Saviour, 25
be glory and majesty, might and
authority, through Jesus Christ our
Lord, before all time, now, and for
evermore. Amen.

d Or These men create divisions; they are . . .
disputes; these you should refute.   e Some witnesses read There are some who raise
the flames and save.   f So one witness; the rest read some you should snatch from

THE REVELATION
OF JOHN

1 T H I S I S the revelation given by God
to Jesus Christ. It was given to him
so that he might show his servants
what must shortly happen. He made
it known by sending his angel to his
2 servant John, who, in telling all that
he saw, has borne witness to the word
of God and to the testimony of Jesus
Christ.[a]
3   Happy is the man who reads, and
happy those who listen to the words
of this prophecy and heed what is
written in it. For the hour of fulfilment is near.

Greetings to the seven churches

4 John to the seven churches in the
province of Asia.
    Grace be to you and peace, from
him who is and who was and who is to
come, from the seven spirits before
5 his throne, and from Jesus Christ, the
faithful witness, the first-born from
the dead and ruler of the kings of the
earth.
    To him who loves us and freed us
from our sins with his life's blood,
6 who made of us a royal house, to
serve as the priests of his God and
Father—to him be glory and dominion for ever and ever! Amen.
7   Behold, he is coming with the
clouds! Every eye shall see him, and

among them those who pierced him;
and all the peoples of the world shall
lament in remorse. So it shall be.
Amen.
    'I am the Alpha and the Omega', 8
says the Lord God, who is and who
was and who is to come, the sovereign
Lord of all.

A vision of Christ

I, John, your brother, who share with 9
you in the suffering and the sovereignty and the endurance which is
ours in Jesus—I was on the island
called Patmos because I had preached
God's word and borne my testimony
to Jesus. It was on the Lord's day, 10
and I was caught up by the Spirit;
and behind me I heard a loud voice,
like the sound of a trumpet, which 11
said to me, 'Write down what you
see on a scroll and send it to the seven
churches: to Ephesus, Smyrna, Pergamum, Thyatira, Sardis, Philadelphia,
and Laodicea.' I turned to see whose 12
voice it was that spoke to me; and
when I turned I saw seven standing
lamps of gold, and among the lamps 13
one like a son of man, robed down to
his feet, with a golden girdle round his
breast. The hair of his head was white 14
as snow-white wool, and his eyes
flamed like fire; his feet gleamed like 15

a Or has borne his testimony to the word of God and to Jesus Christ.

burnished brass refined in a furnace, and his voice was like the sound of
16 rushing waters. In his right hand he held seven stars, and out of his mouth came a sharp two-edged sword; and his face shone like the sun in full strength.

17 When I saw him, I fell at his feet as though dead. But he laid his right hand upon me and said, 'Do not be
18 afraid. I am the first and the last, and I am the living one; for I was dead and now I am alive for evermore, and I hold the keys of Death and Death's
19 domain. Write down therefore what you have seen, what is now, and what will be hereafter.

20 'Here is the secret meaning of the seven stars which you saw in my right hand, and of the seven lamps of gold: the seven stars are the angels of the seven churches, and the seven lamps are the seven churches.'

A message to Ephesus

2 'To the angel of the church at Ephesus write:

'"These are the words of the One who holds the seven stars in his right hand and walks among the seven
2 lamps of gold: I know all your ways, your toil and your fortitude. I know you cannot endure evil men; you have put to the proof those who claim to be apostles but are not, and have
3 found them false. Fortitude you have; you have borne up in my cause and
4 never flagged. But I have this against you: you have lost your early love.
5 Think from what a height you have fallen; repent, and do as you once did. Otherwise, if you do not repent, I shall come to you and remove your
6 lamp from its place. Yet you have this in your favour: you hate the practices of the Nicolaitans, as I do.
7 Hear, you who have ears to hear, what the Spirit says to the churches! To him who is victorious I will give the right to eat from the tree of life that stands in the Garden of God."'

A message to Smyrna

8 'To the angel of the church at Smyrna write:

'"These are the words of the First and the Last, who was dead and came
9 to life again: I know how hard pressed you are, and poor—and yet you are rich; I know how you are slandered by those who claim to be Jews but are not—they are Satan's synagogue.
10 Do not be afraid of the suffering to

come. The Devil will throw some of you into prison, to put you to the test; and for ten days you will suffer cruelly. Only be faithful till death, and I will give you the crown of life. Hear, you who have ears to hear, what 11 the Spirit says to the churches! He who is victorious cannot be harmed by the second death."'

A message to Pergamum

'To the angel of the church at Perga- 12 mum write:

'"These are the words of the One who has the sharp two-edged sword: I know where you live; it is the place 13 where Satan has his throne. And yet you are holding fast to my cause. You did not deny your faith in me even at the time when Antipas, my faithful witness, was killed in your city, the home of Satan. But I have a few 14 matters to bring against you: you have in Pergamum some that hold to the teaching of Balaam, who taught Balak to put temptation in the way of the Israelites. He encouraged them to eat food sacrificed to idols and to commit fornication, and in the same way 15 you also have some who hold the doctrine of the Nicolaitans. So repent! 16 If you do not, I shall come to you soon and make war upon them with the sword that comes out of my mouth. Hear, you who have ears to 17 hear, what the Spirit says to the churches! To him who is victorious I will give some of the hidden manna; I will give him also a white stone, and on the stone will be written a new name, known to none but him that receives it."'

A message to Thyatira

'To the angel of the church at Thy- 18 atira write:

'"These are the words of the Son of God, whose eyes flame like fire and whose feet gleam like burnished brass: I know all your ways, your love and 19 faithfulness, your good service and your fortitude; and of late you have done even better than at first. Yet I 20 have this against you: you tolerate that Jezebel, the woman who claims to be a prophetess, who by her teaching lures my servants into fornication and into eating food sacrificed to idols. I have given her time to repent, 21 but she refuses to repent of her fornication. So I will throw her on to a 22 bed of pain,[b] and plunge her lovers into terrible suffering, unless they

b *One witness reads* into a furnace.

23 forswear what she is doing; and her children I will strike dead. This will teach all the churches that I am the searcher of men's hearts and thoughts, and that I will reward each one of you 24 according to his deeds. And now I speak to you others in Thyatira, who do not accept this teaching and have had no experience of what they like to call the deep secrets of Satan; on you I will impose no further burden. 25 Only hold fast to what you have, until 26 I come. To him who is victorious, to him who perseveres in doing my will to the end, I will give authority over 27 the nations—that same authority which I received from my Father— and he shall rule them with an iron rod, smashing them to bits like earth- 28 enware; and I will give him also the 29 star of dawn. Hear, you who have ears to hear, what the Spirit says to the churches!"'

A message to Sardis

3 'To the angel of the church at Sardis write:
'"These are the words of the One who holds the seven spirits of God, the seven stars: I know all your ways; that though you have a name for 2 being alive, you are dead. Wake up, and put some strength into what is left, which must otherwise die! For I have not found any work of yours 3 completed in the eyes of my God. So remember the teaching you received; observe it, and repent. If you do not wake up, I shall come upon you like a thief, and you will not know the 4 moment of my coming. Yet you have a few persons in Sardis who have not polluted their clothing. They shall walk with me in white, for so they 5 deserve. He who is victorious shall thus be robed all in white; his name I will never strike off the roll of the living, for in the presence of my Father and his angels I will acknowledge him 6 as mine. Hear, you who have ears to hear, what the Spirit says to the churches!"'

A message to Philadelphia

7 'To the angel of the church at Phila- delphia write:
'"These are the words of the holy one, the true one, who holds the key of David; when he opens none may shut, when he shuts none may open: 8 I know all your ways; and look, I have set before you an open door, which no one can shut. Your strength,

I know, is small, yet you have observed my commands and have not disowned my name. So this is what I will do: 9 I will make those of Satan's synagogue, who claim to be Jews but are lying frauds, come and fall down at your feet; and they shall know that you are my beloved people. Because you 10 have kept my command and stood fast, I will also keep you from the ordeal that is to fall upon the whole world and test its inhabitants. I am 11 coming soon; hold fast what you have, and let no one rob you of your crown. He who is victorious—I will make 12 him a pillar in the temple of my God; he shall never leave it. And I will write the name of my God upon him, and the name of the city of my God, that new Jerusalem which is coming down out of heaven from my God, and my own new name. Hear, you 13 who have ears to hear, what the Spirit says to the churches!"'

A message to Laodicea

'To the angel of the church at Laodi- 14 cea write:
'"These are the words of the Amen, the faithful and true witness, the prime source of all God's creation: I 15 know all your ways; you are neither hot nor cold. How I wish you were either hot or cold! But because you 16 are lukewarm, neither hot nor cold, I will spit you out of my mouth. You 17 say, 'How rich I am! And how well I have done! I have everything I want.' In fact, though you do not know it, you are the most pitiful wretch, poor, blind, and naked. So I advise you to 18 buy from me gold refined in the fire, to make you truly rich, and white clothes to put on to hide the shame of your nakedness, and ointment for your eyes so that you may see. All 19 whom I love I reprove and discipline. Be on your mettle therefore and repent. Here I stand knocking at the door; 20 if anyone hears my voice and opens the door, I will come in and sit down to supper with him and he with me. To him who is victorious I will grant 21 a place on my throne, as I myself was victorious and sat down with my Father on his throne. Hear, you who 22 have ears to hear, what the Spirit says to the churches!"'

A vision of a throne in heaven

After this I looked, and there before 4 my eyes was a door opened in heaven; and the voice that I had first heard speaking to me like a trumpet said, 'Come up here, and I will show you what must happen hereafter.' At once I was caught up by the Spirit. There in heaven stood a throne, and on the throne sat one whose appearance was like the gleam of jasper and cornelian; and round the throne was a rainbow, bright as an emerald. In a circle about this throne were twenty-four other thrones, and on them sat twenty-four elders, robed in white and wearing crowns of gold. From the throne went out flashes of lightning and peals of thunder. Burning before the throne were seven flaming torches, the seven spirits of God, and in front of it stretched what seemed a sea of glass, like a sheet of ice.

In the centre, round the throne itself, were four living creatures, covered with eyes, in front and behind. The first creature was like a lion, the second like an ox, the third had a human face, the fourth was like an eagle in flight. The four living creatures, each of them with six wings, had eyes all over, inside and out; and by day and by night without a pause they sang:

'Holy, holy, holy is God the sovereign Lord of all, who was, and is, and is to come!'

As often as the living creatures give glory and honour and thanks to the One who sits on the throne, who lives for ever and ever, the twenty-four elders fall down before the One who sits on the throne and worship him who lives for ever and ever; and as they lay their crowns before the throne they cry:

'Thou art worthy, O Lord our God, to receive glory and honour and power, because thou didst create all things; by thy will they were created, and have their being!'

The Lamb receives a sealed scroll

5 Then I saw in the right hand of the One who sat on the throne a scroll, with writing inside and out, and it was sealed up with seven seals. And I saw a mighty angel proclaiming in a loud voice, 'Who is worthy to open the scroll and to break its seals?' There was no one in heaven or on earth or under the earth able to open the scroll or to look inside it. I was in tears because no one was found who was

worthy to open the scroll or to look inside it. But one of the elders said to me: 'Do not weep; for the Lion from the tribe of Judah, the Scion of David, has won the right to open the scroll and break its seven seals.'

Then I saw standing in the very middle of the throne, inside the circle of living creatures and the circle of elders,[c] a Lamb with the marks of slaughter upon him. He had seven horns and seven eyes, the eyes which are the seven spirits of God sent out over all the world. And the Lamb went up and took the scroll from the right hand of the One who sat on the throne. When he took it, the four living creatures and the twenty-four elders fell down before the Lamb. Each of the elders had a harp, and they held golden bowls full of incense, the prayers of God's people, and they were singing a new song:

'Thou art worthy to take the scroll and to break its seals, for thou wast slain and by thy blood didst purchase for God men of every tribe and language, people and nation; thou hast made of them a royal house, to serve our God as priests; and they shall reign upon earth.'

Then as I looked I heard the voices of countless angels. These were all round the throne and the living creatures and the elders. Myriads upon myriads there were, thousands upon thousands, and they cried aloud:

'Worthy is the Lamb, the Lamb that was slain, to receive all power and wealth, wisdom and might, honour and glory and praise!'

Then I heard every created thing in heaven and on earth and under the earth and in the sea, all that is in them, crying:

'Praise and honour, glory and might, to him who sits on the throne and to the Lamb for ever and ever!'

And the four living creatures said, 'Amen', and the elders fell down and worshipped.

The breaking of the six seals

Then I watched as the Lamb broke the first of the seven seals; and I heard one of the four living creatures say in a voice like thunder, 'Come!' And there before my eyes was a white horse, and its rider held a bow. He

c Or standing between the throne, with the four living creatures, and the elders . . .

was given a crown, and he rode forth, conquering and to conquer.

3 When the Lamb broke the second seal, I heard the second creature say, 4 'Come!' And out came another horse, all red. To its rider was given power to take peace from the earth and make men slaughter one another; and he was given a great sword.

5 When he broke the third seal, I heard the third creature say, 'Come!' And there, as I looked, was a black horse; and its rider held in his hand 6 a pair of scales. And I heard what sounded like a voice from the midst of the living creatures, which said, 'A whole day's wage for a quart of flour, a whole day's wage for three quarts of barley-meal! But spare the olive and the vine.'

7 When he broke the fourth seal, I heard the voice of the fourth creature 8 say, 'Come!' And there, as I looked, was another horse, sickly pale; and its rider's name was Death, and Hades came close behind. To him was given power over a quarter of the earth, with the right to kill by sword and by famine, by pestilence and wild beasts.

9 When he broke the fifth seal, I saw underneath[d] the altar the souls of those who had been slaughtered for God's word and for the testimony they 10 bore. They gave a great cry: 'How long, sovereign Lord, holy and true, must it be before thou wilt vindicate us and avenge our blood on the in-11 habitants of the earth?' Each of them was given a white robe; and they were told to rest a little while longer, until the tally should be complete of all their brothers in Christ's service who were to be killed as they had been.

12 Then I watched as he broke the sixth seal. And there was a violent earthquake; the sun turned black as a funeral pall and the moon all red as 13 blood; the stars in the sky fell to the earth, like figs shaken down by a gale; 14 the sky vanished, as a scroll is rolled up, and every mountain and island 15 was moved from its place. Then the kings of the earth, magnates and marshals, the rich and the powerful, and all men, slave or free, hid themselves in caves and mountain crags; 16 and they called out to the mountains and the crags, 'Fall on us and hide us from the face of the One who sits on the throne and from the vengeance of 17 the Lamb.' For the great day of their vengeance has come, and who will be able to stand?

Israel's hundred and forty-four thousand

After this I saw four angels stationed 7 at the four corners of the earth, holding back the four winds so that no wind should blow on sea or land or on any tree. Then I saw another angel 2 rising out of the east, carrying the seal of the living God; and he called aloud to the four angels who had been given the power to ravage land and sea: 'Do no damage to sea or land or trees 3 until we have set the seal of our God upon the foreheads of his servants.' And I heard the number of those who 4 had received the seal. From all the tribes of Israel there were a hundred and forty-four thousand: twelve thou- 5 sand from the tribe of Judah, twelve thousand from the tribe of Reuben, twelve thousand from the tribe of Gad, twelve thousand from the tribe 6 of Asher, twelve thousand from the tribe of Naphtali, twelve thousand from the tribe of Manasseh, twelve 7 thousand from the tribe of Simeon, twelve thousand from the tribe of Levi, twelve thousand from the tribe of Issachar, twelve thousand from the 8 tribe of Zebulun, twelve thousand from the tribe of Joseph, and twelve thousand from the tribe of Benjamin.

A vast throng no one could count

After this I looked and saw a vast 9 throng, which no one could count, from every nation, of all tribes, peoples, and languages, standing in front of the throne and before the Lamb. They were robed in white and had palms in their hands, and they shouted 10 together:

'Victory to our God who sits on the throne, and to the Lamb!'

And all the angels stood round the 11 throne and the elders and the four living creatures, and they fell on their faces before the throne and worshipped God, crying: 12

'Amen! Praise and glory and wisdom, thanksgiving and honour, power and might, be to our God for ever and ever! Amen.'

Then one of the elders turned to me 13 and said, 'These men that are robed in white—who are they and from where do they come?' But I answered, 14 'My lord, you know, not I.' Then he said to me, 'These are the men who have passed through the great ordeal;

d Or at the foot of . . .

they have washed their robes and made them white in the blood of the 15 Lamb. That is why they stand before the throne of God and minister to him day and night in his temple; and he who sits on the throne will dwell with 16 them. They shall never again feel hunger or thirst, the sun shall not beat 17 on them nor any scorching heat, because the Lamb who is at the heart of the throne will be their shepherd and will guide them to the springs of the water of life; and God will wipe all tears from their eyes.'

The breaking of the seventh seal

8 Now when the Lamb broke the seventh seal, there was silence in heaven 2 for what seemed half an hour. Then I looked, and the seven angels that stand in the presence of God were given seven trumpets.

3 Then another angel came and stood at the altar, holding a golden censer; and he was given a great quantity of incense to offer with the prayers of all God's people upon the golden altar 4 in front of the throne. And from the angel's hand the smoke of the incense went up before God with the prayers 5 of his people. Then the angel took the censer, filled it from the altar fire, and threw it down upon the earth; and there were peals of thunder, lightning, and an earthquake.

The first four trumpets blown

6 Then the seven angels that held the seven trumpets prepared to blow them.

7 The first blew his trumpet; and there came hail and fire mingled with blood, and this was hurled upon the earth. A third of the earth was burnt, a third of the trees were burnt, all the green grass was burnt.

8 The second angel blew his trumpet; and what looked like a great blazing mountain was hurled into the sea. A third of the sea was turned to blood, 9 a third of the living creatures in it died, and a third of the ships on it foundered.

10 The third angel blew his trumpet; and a great star shot from the sky, flaming like a torch; and it fell on a 11 third of the rivers and springs. The name of the star was Wormwood; and a third of the water turned to wormwood, and men in great numbers died of the water because it had been poisoned.

12 The fourth angel blew his trumpet;

and a third part of the sun was struck, a third of the moon, and a third of the stars, so that the third part went dark and a third of the light of the day failed, and of the night.

Then I looked, and I heard an eagle 13 calling with a loud cry as it flew in mid-heaven: 'Woe, woe, woe to the inhabitants of the earth when the trumpets sound which the three last angels must now blow!'

The fifth trumpet; the first woe

Then the fifth angel blew his trumpet; 9 and I saw a star that had fallen from heaven to earth, and the star was given the key of the shaft of the abyss. With this he opened the shaft of the 2 abyss; and from the shaft smoke rose like smoke from a great furnace, and the sun and the air were darkened by the smoke from the shaft. Then 3 over the earth, out of the smoke, came locusts, and they were given the powers that earthly scorpions have. They were told to do no injury to the 4 grass or to any plant or tree, but only to those men who had not received the seal of God on their foreheads. These they were allowed to torment 5 for five months, with torment like a scorpion's sting; but they were not to kill them. During that time these 6 men will seek death, but they will not find it; they will long to die, but death will elude them.

In appearance the locusts were like 7 horses equipped for battle. On their heads were what looked like golden crowns; their faces were like human faces and their hair like women's hair; 8 they had teeth like lions' teeth, and 9 wore breastplates like iron; the sound of their wings was like the noise of horses and chariots rushing to battle; they had tails like scorpions, with 10 stings in them, and in their tails lay their power to plague mankind for five months. They had for their king 11 the angel of the abyss, whose name, in Hebrew, is Abaddon, and in Greek, Apollyon, or the Destroyer.

The first woe has now passed. But 12 there are still two more to come.

The sixth trumpet; the second woe

The sixth angel then blew his trumpet; 13 and I heard a voice coming from between the horns of the golden altar that stood in the presence of God. It 14 said to the sixth angel, who held the trumpet: 'Release the four angels held bound at the great river Euphrates!'

15 So the four angels were let loose, to kill a third of mankind. They had been held ready for this moment, for this very year and month, day and 16 hour. And their squadrons of cavalry, whose count I heard, numbered two hundred million.

17 This was how I saw the horses and their riders in my vision: They wore breastplates, fiery red, blue, and sulphur-yellow; the horses had heads like lions' heads, and out of their mouths came fire, smoke, and sulphur. 18 By these three plagues, that is, by the fire, the smoke, and the sulphur that came from their mouths, a third of 19 mankind was killed. The power of the horses lay in their mouths, and in their tails also; for their tails were like snakes, with heads, and with them too they dealt injuries.

20 The rest of mankind who survived these plagues still did not abjure the gods their hands had fashioned, nor cease their worship of devils and of idols made from gold, silver, bronze, stone, and wood, which cannot see or 21 hear or walk. Nor did they repent of their murders, their sorcery, their fornication, or their robberies.

The angel with a scroll

10 Then I saw another mighty angel coming down from heaven. He was wrapped in cloud, with the rainbow round his head; his face shone like the sun and his legs were like pillars of fire. 2 In his hand he held a little scroll unrolled. His right foot he planted on 3 the sea, and his left on the land. Then he gave a great shout, like the roar of a lion; and when he shouted, the 4 seven thunders spoke. I was about to write down what the seven thunders had said; but I heard a voice from heaven saying, 'Seal up what the seven thunders have said; do not 5 write it down.' Then the angel that I saw standing on the sea and the land raised his right hand to heaven 6 and swore by him who lives for ever and ever, who created heaven and earth and the sea and everything in them: 'There shall be no more delay; 7 but when the time comes for the seventh angel to sound his trumpet, the hidden purpose of God will have been fulfilled, as he promised to his servants the prophets.'

8 Then the voice which I heard from heaven was speaking to me again, and it said, 'Go and take the open scroll in the hand of the angel that stands on the sea and the land.' So I went to the 9 angel and asked him to give me the little scroll. He said to me, 'Take it, and eat it. It will turn your stomach sour, although in your mouth it will taste sweet as honey.' So I took the 10 little scroll from the angel's hand and ate it, and in my mouth it did taste sweet as honey; but when I swallowed it my stomach turned sour.

Then they said to me, 'Once again 11 you must utter prophecies over peoples and nations and languages and many kings.'

The temple and the two witnesses

I was given a long cane, a kind of 11 measuring-rod, and told: 'Now go and measure the temple of God, the altar, and the number of the worshippers. But have nothing to do with the outer 2 court of the temple; do not measure that; for it has been given over to the Gentiles, and they will trample the Holy City underfoot for forty-two months. And I have two witnesses, 3 whom I will appoint to prophesy, dressed in sackcloth, all through those twelve hundred and sixty days.' These 4 are the two olive-trees and the two lamps that stand in the presence of the Lord of the earth. If anyone 5 seeks to do them harm, fire pours from their mouths and consumes their enemies; and thus shall the man die who seeks to do them harm. These 6 two have the power to shut up the sky, so that no rain may fall during the time of their prophesying; and they have the power to turn water to blood and to strike the earth at will with every kind of plague. But when 7 they have completed their testimony, the beast that comes up from the abyss will wage war upon them and will defeat and kill them. Their 8 corpses will lie in the street of the great city, whose name in allegory is Sodom, or Egypt, where also their Lord was crucified. For three days 9 and a half men from every people and tribe, of every language and nation, gaze upon their corpses and refuse them burial. All men on earth gloat 10 over them, make merry, and exchange presents; for these two prophets were a torment to the whole earth. But at 11 the end of the three days and a half the breath of life from God came into them; and they stood up on their feet to the terror of all who saw it. Then a loud voice was heard speaking 12 to them from heaven, which said,

'Come up here!' And they went up to heaven in a cloud, in full view of their 13 enemies. At that same moment there was a violent earthquake, and a tenth of the city fell. Seven thousand people were killed in the earthquake; the rest in terror did homage to the God of heaven.

14 The second woe has now passed. But the third is soon to come.

The seventh trumpet; the third woe announced

15 Then the seventh angel blew his trumpet; and voices were heard in heaven shouting:

'The sovereignty of the world has passed to our Lord and his Christ, and he shall reign for ever and ever!'

16 And the twenty-four elders, seated on their thrones before God, fell on their 17 faces and worshipped God, saying:

'We give thee thanks, O Lord God, sovereign over all, who art and who wast, because thou hast taken thy great power into thy hands and 18 entered upon thy reign. The nations raged, but thy day of retribution has come. Now is the time for the dead to be judged; now is the time for recompense to thy servants the prophets, to thy dedicated people, and all who honour thy name, both great and small, the time to destroy those who destroy the earth.'

19 Then God's temple in heaven was laid open, and within the temple was seen the ark of his covenant. There came flashes of lightning and peals of thunder, an earthquake, and a storm of hail.

Enmity between the dragon and the woman

12 Next appeared a great portent in heaven, a woman robed with the sun, beneath her feet the moon, and on her 2 head a crown of twelve stars. She was pregnant, and in the anguish of her labour she cried out to be delivered. 3 Then a second portent appeared in heaven: a great red dragon with seven heads and ten horns; on his 4 heads were seven diadems, and with his tail he swept down a third of the stars in the sky and flung them to the earth. The dragon stood in front of the woman who was about to give birth, so that when her child was born

he might devour it. She gave birth to 5 a male child, who is destined to rule all nations with an iron rod. But her child was snatched up to God and his throne; and the woman herself fled 6 into the wilds, where she had a place prepared for her by God, there to be sustained for twelve hundred and sixty days.

War in heaven; the dragon overthrown

Then war broke out in heaven. Michael 7 and his angels waged war upon the dragon. The dragon and his angels fought, but they had not the strength 8 to win, and no foothold was left them in heaven. So the great dragon was 9 thrown down, that serpent of old that led the whole world astray, whose name is Satan, or the Devil—thrown down to the earth, and his angels with him.

Then I heard a voice in heaven 10 proclaiming aloud: 'This is the hour of victory for our God, the hour of his sovereignty and power, when his Christ comes to his rightful rule! For the accuser of our brothers is overthrown, who day and night accused them before our God. By the sacrifice 11 of the Lamb they have conquered him, and by the testimony which they uttered;*e* for they did not hold their lives too dear to lay them down. Rejoice then, you heavens and you 12 that dwell in them! But woe to you, earth and sea, for the Devil has come down to you in great fury, knowing that his time is short!'

The dragon wages war on earth

When the dragon found that he had 13 been thrown down to the earth, he went in pursuit of the woman who had given birth to the male child. But the woman was given two great 14 eagle's wings, to fly to the place in the wilds where for three years and a half she was to be sustained, out of reach of the serpent. From his mouth the 15 serpent spewed a flood of water after the woman to sweep her away with its spate. But the earth came to her 16 rescue and opened its mouth and swallowed the river which the dragon spewed from his mouth. At this the 17 dragon grew furious with the woman, and went off to wage war on the rest of her offspring, that is, on those who keep God's commandments and maintain their testimony to Jesus. He took 13 his stand on the sea-shore.

e Or the word of God to which they bore witness.

A beast out of the sea

Then[f] out of the sea I saw a beast rising. It had ten horns and seven heads. On its horns were ten diadems, and on each head a blasphemous 2 name. The beast I saw was like a leopard, but its feet were like a bear's and its mouth like a lion's mouth. The dragon conferred upon it his power and rule, and great authority. 3 One of its heads appeared to have received a death-blow; but the mortal wound was healed. The whole world went after the beast in wondering 4 admiration. Men worshipped the dragon because he had conferred his authority upon the beast; they worshipped the beast also, and chanted, 'Who is like the Beast? Who can fight against it?'

5 The beast was allowed to mouth bombast and blasphemy, and was given the right to reign for forty-two 6 months. It opened its mouth in blasphemy against God, reviling his 7 name and his heavenly dwelling.[g] It was also allowed to wage war on God's people and to defeat them, and was granted[h] authority over every tribe and people, language and nation. 8 All on earth will worship it, except those whose names the Lamb that was slain keeps in his roll of the living, written there since the world was made.

9 Hear, you who have ears to hear! 10 Whoever is to be made prisoner, a prisoner he shall be. Whoever takes the sword to kill, by the sword he is bound to be killed. This is where the fortitude and faithfulness of God's people have their place.

A beast out of the earth

11 Then I saw another beast, which came up out of the earth; it had two horns like a lamb's, but spoke like a dragon. 12 It wielded all the authority of the first beast in its presence, and made the earth and its inhabitants worship this first beast, whose mortal wound 13 had been healed. It worked great miracles, even making fire come down from heaven to earth before men's eyes. 14 By the miracles it was allowed to perform in the presence of the beast it deluded the inhabitants of the earth, and made them erect an image in honour of the beast that had been wounded by the sword and yet lived. It was allowed to give breath to the 15 image of the beast, so that it could speak, and could cause all who would not worship the image to be put to death. Moreover, it caused everyone, 16 great and small, rich and poor, slave and free, to be branded with a mark on his right hand or forehead, and no 17 one was allowed to buy or sell unless he bore this beast's mark, either name or number. (Here is the key; 18 and anyone who has intelligence may work out the number of the beast. The number represents a man's name, and the numerical value of its letters is six hundred and sixty-six.)

A new song; a ransomed people

Then I looked, and on Mount Zion 14 stood the Lamb, and with him were a hundred and forty-four thousand who had his name and the name of his Father written on their foreheads. I heard a sound from heaven like the 2 noise of rushing water and the deep roar of thunder; it was the sound of harpers playing on their harps. There 3 before the throne, and the four living creatures and the elders, they were singing a new song. That song no one could learn except the hundred and forty-four thousand, who alone from the whole world had been ransomed. These are men who did not 4 defile themselves with women, for they have kept themselves chaste, and they follow the Lamb wherever he goes. They have been ransomed as the firstfruits of humanity for God and the Lamb. No lie was found in 5 their lips; they are faultless.

An angel with the eternal Gospel

Then I saw an angel flying in mid- 6 heaven, with an eternal gospel to proclaim to those on earth, to every nation and tribe, language and people. He cried in a loud voice, 'Fear God 7 and pay him homage; for the hour of his judgement has come! Worship him who made heaven and earth, the sea and the water-springs!'

A second angel

Then another angel, a second, followed, 8 and he cried, 'Fallen, fallen is Babylon the great, she who has made all nations drink the fierce wine of[i] her fornication!'

f Some witnesses read . . . testimony to Jesus. Then I stood by the sea-shore and . . .   g Some witnesses read reviling his name and his dwelling-place, that is, those that live in heaven.   h Some witnesses read It was granted . . . (omitting the words was also . . . them, and).   i Or drink the wine of God's wrath upon . . .

A third angel

9 Yet a third angel followed, crying out loud, 'Whoever worships the beast and its image and receives its mark
10 on his forehead or hand, he shall drink the wine of God's wrath, poured undiluted into the cup of his vengeance. He shall be tormented in sulphurous flames before the holy
11 angels and before the Lamb. The smoke of their torment will rise for ever and ever, and there will be no respite day or night for those who worship the beast and its image or
12 receive the mark of its name.' This is where the fortitude of God's people has its place—in keeping God's commands and remaining loyal to Jesus.

Happy are those who die in the faith

13 Moreover, I heard a voice from heaven, saying, 'Write this: "Happy are the dead who die in the faith of Christ! Henceforth",*j* says the Spirit,*k* "they may rest from their labours; for they take with them the record of their deeds."'

The harvest of the earth

14 Then as I looked there appeared a white cloud, and on the cloud sat one like a son of man. He had on his head a crown of gold and in his hand a
15 sharp sickle. Another angel came out of the temple and called in a loud voice to him who sat on the cloud: 'Stretch out your sickle and reap; for harvest-time has come, and earth's
16 crop is over-ripe.' So he who sat on the cloud put his sickle to the earth and its harvest was reaped.
17 Then another angel came out of the heavenly temple, and he also had a
18 sharp sickle. Then from the altar came yet another, the angel who has authority over fire, and he shouted to the one with the sharp sickle: 'Stretch out your sickle, and gather in earth's grape-harvest, for its clusters are ripe.'
19 So the angel put his sickle to the earth and gathered in its grapes, and threw
20 them into the great winepress of God's wrath. The winepress was trodden outside the city, and for two hundred miles around blood flowed from the press to the height of the horses' bridles.

The seven last plagues announced

15 Then I saw another great and astonishing portent in heaven: seven angels with seven plagues, the last plagues of all, for with them the wrath of God is consummated.
2 I saw what seemed a sea of glass shot with fire, and beside the sea of glass, holding the harps which God had given them, were those who had won the victory over the beast and its image and the number of its name.
3 They were singing the song of Moses, the servant of God, and the song of the Lamb, as they chanted:

'Great and marvellous are thy deeds, O Lord God, sovereign over all; just and true are thy ways,
thou king of the ages.*l* Who shall 4 not revere thee, Lord, and do homage to thy name? For thou alone art holy. All nations shall come and worship in thy presence, for thy just dealings stand revealed.'

5 After this, as I looked, the sanctuary of the heavenly Tent of Testimony
6 was thrown open, and out of it came the seven angels with the seven plagues. They were robed in fine linen, clean and shining, and had golden girdles round their breasts.
7 Then one of the four living creatures gave the seven angels seven golden bowls full of the wrath of God who lives for ever and ever; and the
8 sanctuary was filled with smoke from the glory of God and his power, so that no one could enter it until the seven plagues of the seven angels were completed.
16 Then from the sanctuary I heard a loud voice, and it said to the seven angels, 'Go and pour out the seven bowls of God's wrath on the earth.'

The outpouring of the bowls of wrath

So the first angel went and poured his 2 bowl on the earth; and foul malignant sores appeared on those men that wore the mark of the beast and worshipped its image.
3 The second angel poured his bowl on the sea, and it turned to blood like the blood from a corpse; and every living thing in the sea died.
4 The third angel poured his bowl on the rivers and springs, and they turned to blood.
5 Then I heard the angel of the waters say, 'Just art thou in these thy judgements, thou Holy One who art and
6 wast; for they shed the blood of thy people and of thy prophets, and thou hast given them blood to drink. They

j Or Assuredly.   k Some witnesses read " . . . the dead who henceforth die in the faith of Christ!" "Yes," says the Spirit . . .   l Some witnesses read king of the nations.

7 have their deserts!' And I heard the altar cry, 'Yes, Lord God, sovereign over all, true and just are thy judgements!'

8 The fourth angel poured his bowl on the sun; and it was allowed to burn

9 men with its flames. They were fearfully burned; but they only cursed the name of God who had the power to inflict such plagues, and they refused to repent or do him homage.

10 The fifth angel poured his bowl on the throne of the beast; and its kingdom was plunged in darkness. Men

11 gnawed their tongues in agony, but they only cursed the God of heaven for their sores and pains, and would not repent of what they had done.

12 The sixth angel poured his bowl on the great river Euphrates; and its water was dried up, to prepare the way for the kings from the east.

13 Then I saw coming from the mouth of the dragon, the mouth of the beast, and the mouth of the false prophet,

14 three foul spirits like frogs. These spirits were devils, with power to work miracles. They were sent out to muster all the kings of the world for the great day of battle of God the

15 sovereign Lord. ('That is the day when I come like a thief! Happy the man who stays awake and keeps on his clothes, so that he will not have to go naked and ashamed for all to see!')

16 So they assembled the kings at the place called in Hebrew Armageddon.

17 Then the seventh angel poured his bowl on the air; and out of the sanctuary came a loud voice from the

18 throne, which said, 'It is over!' And there followed flashes of lightning and peals of thunder, and a violent earth-

19 quake, like none before it in human history, so violent it was. The great city was split in three; the cities of the world fell in ruin; and God did not forget Babylon the great, but made her drink the cup which was filled with the fierce wine of his

20 vengeance. Every island vanished; there was not a mountain to be seen.

21 Huge hailstones, weighing perhaps a hundredweight, fell on men from the sky; and they cursed God for the plague of hail, because that plague was so severe.

The great whore

17 Then one of the seven angels that held the seven bowls came and spoke to me and said, 'Come, and I will show you the judgement on the great whore, enthroned above the ocean.

2 The kings of the earth have committed fornication with her, and on the wine of her fornication men all over the world have made themselves drunk.'

3 In the Spirit he carried me away into the wilds, and there I saw a woman mounted on a scarlet beast which was covered with blasphemous names and

4 had seven heads and ten horns. The woman was clothed in purple and scarlet and bedizened with gold and jewels and pearls. In her hand she held a gold cup, full of obscenities and the foulness of her fornication; and

5 written on her forehead was a name with a secret meaning: 'Babylon the great, the mother of whores and of

6 every obscenity on earth.' The woman, I saw, was drunk with the blood of God's people and with the blood of those who had borne their testimony to Jesus.

7 As I looked at her I was greatly astonished. But the angel said to me, 'Why are you so astonished? I will tell you the secret of the woman and of the beast she rides, with the seven

8 heads and the ten horns. The beast you have seen is he who once was alive, and is alive no longer, but has yet to ascend out of the abyss before going to perdition. Those on earth whose names have not been inscribed in the roll of the living ever since the world was made will all be astonished to see the beast; for he once was alive, and is alive no longer, and has still to appear.

A clue to interpret the vision

9 'But here is the clue for those who can interpret it. The seven heads are seven

10 hills on which the woman sits. They represent also seven kings,[m] of whom five have already fallen, one is now reigning, and the other has yet to come; and when he does come he is

11 only to last for a little while. As for the beast that once was alive and is alive no longer, he is an eighth—and yet he is one of the seven, and he is

12 going to perdition. The ten horns you saw are ten kings who have not yet begun to reign, but who for one hour are to share with the beast the exer-

13 cise of royal authority; for they have but a single purpose among them and will confer their power and autho-

14 rity upon the beast. They will wage war upon the Lamb, but the Lamb

m *Or emperors.*

will defeat them, for he is Lord of lords and King of kings, and his victory will be shared by his followers, called and chosen and faithful.'[n]

15 Then he said to me, 'The ocean you saw, where the great whore sat, is an ocean of peoples and populations,
16 nations and languages. As for the ten horns you saw, they together with the beast will come to hate the whore; they will strip her naked and leave her desolate, they will batten on her
17 flesh and burn her to ashes. For God has put it into their heads to carry out his purpose, by making common cause and conferring their sovereignty upon the beast until all that God has
18 spoken is fulfilled. The woman you saw is the great city that holds sway over the kings of the earth.'

The fall of Babylon

18 After this I saw another angel coming down from heaven; he came with great authority and the earth was lit
2 up with his splendour. Then in a mighty voice he proclaimed, 'Fallen, fallen is Babylon the great! She has become a dwelling for demons, a haunt for every unclean spirit, for
3 every vile and loathsome bird. For all nations have drunk deep of[o] the fierce wine of her fornication; the kings of the earth have committed fornication with her, and merchants the world over have grown rich on her bloated wealth.'
4 Then I heard another voice from heaven that said: 'Come out of her, my people, lest you take part in her sins
5 and share in her plagues. For her sins are piled high as heaven, and God
6 has not forgotten her crimes. Pay her back in her own coin, repay her twice over for her deeds! Double for her the strength of the potion she mixed!
7 Mete out grief and torment to match her voluptuous pomp! She says in her heart, "I am a queen on my throne! No mourning for me, no widow's
8 weeds!" Because of this her plagues shall strike her in a single day— pestilence, bereavement, famine, and burning—for mighty is the Lord God who has pronounced her doom!'

Earth mourns, heaven exults

9 The kings of the earth who committed fornication with her and wallowed in her luxury will weep and wail over her, as they see the smoke of her conflagration. They will stand at a 10 distance, for horror at her torment, and will say, 'Alas, alas for the great city, the mighty city of Babylon! In a single hour your doom has struck!'

The merchants of the earth also will 11 weep and mourn for her, because no one any longer buys their cargoes, cargoes of gold and silver, jewels and 12 pearls, cloths of purple and scarlet, silks and fine linens; all kinds of scented woods, ivories, and every sort of thing made of costly woods, bronze, iron, or marble; cinnamon 13 and spice, incense, perfumes and frankincense; wine, oil, flour and wheat, sheep and cattle, horses, chariots, slaves, and the lives of men. 'The 14 fruit you longed for', they will say, 'is gone from you; all the glitter and the glamour are lost, never to be yours again!' The traders in all these 15 wares, who gained their wealth from her, will stand at a distance for horror at her torment, weeping and mourning and saying, 'Alas, alas for the great 16 city, that was clothed in fine linen and purple and scarlet, bedizened with gold and jewels and pearls! Alas 17 that in one hour so much wealth should be laid waste!'

Then all the sea-captains and voyagers, the sailors and those who traded by sea, stood at a distance and cried 18 out as they saw the smoke of her conflagration: 'Was there ever a city like the great city?' They threw dust on 19 their heads, weeping and mourning and saying, 'Alas, alas for the great city, where all who had ships at sea grew rich on her wealth! Alas that in a single hour she should be laid waste!'

But let heaven exult over her; 20 exult, apostles and prophets and people of God; for in the judgement against her he has vindicated your cause!

Then a mighty angel took up a 21 stone like a great millstone and hurled it into the sea and said, 'Thus shall Babylon, the great city, be sent hurtling down, never to be seen again! No more shall the sound of harpers 22 and minstrels, of flute-players and trumpeters, be heard in you; no more shall craftsmen of any trade be found in you; no more shall the sound of the mill be heard in you; no more shall 23 the light of the lamp be seen in you; no more shall the voice of the bride and bridegroom be heard in you!

n Or . . . kings, and his followers are faithful men, called and selected for service.   o Other witnesses read have been ruined by . . .

Your traders were once the merchant princes of the world, and with your sorcery you deceived all the nations.'

24 For the blood of the prophets and of God's people was found in her, and blood of all who had been done to death on earth.

The Lamb's wedding-day

19 After this I heard what sounded like the roar of a vast throng in heaven; and they were shouting:

2 'Alleluia! Victory and glory and power belong to our God, for true and just are his judgements! He has condemned the great whore who corrupted the earth with her fornication, and has avenged upon her the blood of his servants.'

3 Then once more they shouted:

'Alleluia! The smoke goes up from her for ever and ever!'

4 And the twenty-four elders and the four living creatures fell down and worshipped God as he sat on the throne, and they too cried:

'Amen, Alleluia!'

5 Then a voice came from the throne which said: 'Praise our God, all you his servants, you that fear him, both great and small!'

6 Again I heard what sounded like a vast crowd, like the noise of rushing water and deep roars of thunder, and they cried:

'Alleluia! The Lord our God, sove-
7 reign over all, has entered on his reign! Exult and shout for joy and do him homage, for the wedding-day of the Lamb has come! His
8 bride has made herself ready, and for her dress she has been given fine linen, clean and shining.'

(Now the fine linen signifies the righteous deeds of God's people.)

9 Then the angel said to me, 'Write this: "Happy are those who are invited to the wedding-supper of the Lamb!"' And he added, 'These are
10 the very words of God.' At this I fell at his feet to worship him. But he said to me, 'No, not that! I am but a fellow-servant with you and your brothers who bear their testimony to Jesus. It is God you must worship. Those who bear testimony to Jesus are inspired like the prophets.'[p]

The Rider on a white horse

11 Then I saw heaven wide open, and there before me was a white horse; and its rider's name was Faithful and True, for he is just in judgement and
12 just in war. His eyes flamed like fire, and on his head were many diadems. Written upon him was a name known
13 to none but himself, and he was robed in a garment drenched in blood.[q] He
14 was called the Word of God, and the armies of heaven followed him on white horses, clothed in fine linen,
15 clean and shining. From his mouth there went a sharp sword with which to smite the nations; for he it is who shall rule them with an iron rod, and tread the winepress of the wrath and retribution of God the sovereign Lord.
16 And on his robe and on his thigh there was written the name: 'King of kings and Lord of lords.'

17 Then I saw an angel standing in the sun, and he cried aloud to all the birds flying in mid-heaven: 'Come and
18 gather for God's great supper, to eat the flesh of kings and commanders and fighting men, the flesh of horses and their riders, the flesh of all men,
19 slave and free, great and small!' Then I saw the beast and the kings of the earth and their armies mustered to do battle with the Rider and his army.
20 The beast was taken prisoner, and so was the false prophet who had worked miracles in its presence and deluded those that had received the mark of the beast and worshipped its image. The two of them were thrown alive into the lake of fire with its sulphu-
21 rous flames. The rest were killed by the sword which went out of the Rider's mouth; and all the birds gorged themselves on their flesh.

The dragon chained

20 Then I saw an angel coming down from heaven with the key of the abyss
2 and a great chain in his hands. He seized the dragon, that serpent of old, the Devil or Satan, and chained him
3 up for a thousand years; he threw him into the abyss, shutting and seal-ing it over him, so that he might seduce the nations no more till the thousand years were over. After that he must be let loose for a short while.

Christ's thousand-year reign

4 Then I saw thrones, and upon them sat those to whom judgement was

p Or . . . worship. For testimony to Jesus is the spirit that inspires prophets.   q Some witnesses read spattered with blood.

committed. I could see the souls of those who had been beheaded for the sake of God's word and their testimony to Jesus, those who had not worshipped the beast and its image or received its mark on forehead or hand. These came to life again and reigned with Christ for a thousand years, 5 though the rest of the dead did not come to life until the thousand years were over. This is the first resurrection. 6 Happy indeed, and one of God's own people, is the man who shares in this first resurrection! Upon such the second death has no claim; but they shall be priests of God and of Christ, and shall reign with him for the thousand years.

Final overthrow of the Devil

7 When the thousand years are over, Satan will be let loose from his dun- 8 geon; and he will come out to seduce the nations in the four quarters of the earth and to muster them for battle, yes, the hosts of Gog and Magog, 9 countless as the sands of the sea. So they marched over the breadth of the land and laid siege to the camp of God's people and the city that he loves. But fire came down on them from heaven and consumed them; 10 and the Devil, their seducer, was flung into the lake of fire and sulphur, where the beast and the false prophet had been flung, there to be tormented day and night for ever.

The Day of Judgement

11 Then I saw a great white throne, and the One who sat upon it; from his presence earth and heaven vanished away, and no place was left for them. 12 I could see the dead, great and small, standing before the throne; and books were opened. Then another book was opened, the roll of the living. From what was written in these books the dead were judged upon the record of 13 their deeds. The sea gave up its dead, and Death and Hades gave up the dead in their keeping; they were judged, each man on the record of his 14 deeds. Then Death and Hades were flung into the lake of fire. This lake 15 of fire is the second death; and into it were flung any whose names were not to be found in the roll of the living.

A new heaven and a new earth

21 Then I saw a new heaven and a new earth, for the first heaven and the first earth had vanished, and there was no longer any sea. I saw the holy city, 2 new Jerusalem, coming down out of heaven from God, made ready like a bride adorned for her husband. I 3 heard a loud voice proclaiming from the throne: 'Now at last God has his dwelling among men! He will dwell among them and they shall be his people, and God himself will be with them.[r] He will wipe every tear from 4 their eyes; there shall be an end to death, and to mourning and crying and pain; for the old order has passed away!'

Then he who sat on the throne said, 5 'Behold! I am making all things new!' (And he said to me, 'Write this down; for these words are trustworthy and true. Indeed they are already ful- 6 filled.') 'I am the Alpha and the Omega, the beginning and the end. A draught from the water-springs of life will be my free gift to the thirsty. All this is 7 the victor's heritage; and I will be his God and he shall be my son. But as for 8 the cowardly, the faithless, and the vile, murderers, fornicators, sorcerers, idolaters, and liars of every kind, their lot will be the second death, in the lake that burns with sulphurous flames.'

The new Jerusalem

Then one of the seven angels that held 9 the seven bowls full of the seven last plagues came and spoke to me and said, 'Come, and I will show you the bride, the wife of the Lamb.' So in 10 the Spirit he carried me away to a great high mountain, and showed me the holy city of Jerusalem coming down out of heaven from God. It 11 shone with the glory of God; it had the radiance of some priceless jewel, like a jasper, clear as crystal. It had 12 a great high wall, with twelve gates, at which were twelve angels; and on the gates were inscribed the names of the twelve tribes of Israel. There were 13 three gates to the east, three to the north, three to the south, and three to the west. The city wall had twelve 14 foundation-stones, and on them were the names of the twelve apostles of the Lamb.

The angel who spoke with me carried 15 a gold measuring-rod, to measure the city, its wall, and its gates. The 16 city was built as a square, and was as wide as it was long. It measured by his rod twelve thousand furlongs, its length and breadth and height being equal. Its wall was one hundred and 17

r *Some witnesses read* God-with-them shall himself be their God (*see Isaiah 7. 14; 8. 8*).

forty-four cubits high, that is, by human measurements, which the angel 18 was using. The wall was built of jasper, while the city itself was of 19 pure gold, bright as clear glass. The foundations of the city wall were adorned with jewels of every kind, the first of the foundation-stones being jasper, the second lapis lazuli, the third chalcedony, the fourth emerald, 20 the fifth sardonyx, the sixth cornelian, the seventh chrysolite, the eighth beryl, the ninth topaz, the tenth chrysoprase, the eleventh turquoise, 21 and the twelfth amethyst. The twelve gates were twelve pearls, each gate being made from a single pearl. The streets of the city were of pure gold, like translucent glass.

Light and life

22 I saw no temple in the city; for its temple was the sovereign Lord God and 23 the Lamb. And the city had no need of sun or moon to shine upon it; for the glory of God gave it light, and its 24 lamp was the Lamb. By its light shall the nations walk, and the kings of the earth shall bring into it all their 25 splendour. The gates of the city shall never be shut by day—and there will 26 be no night. The wealth and splendour of the nations shall be brought into it; 27 but nothing unclean shall enter, nor anyone whose ways are false or foul, but only those who are inscribed in the Lamb's roll of the living.

22 Then he showed me the river of the water of life, sparkling like crystal, flowing from the throne of God and 2 of the Lamb down the middle of the city's street. On either side of the river stood a tree of life, which yields twelve crops of fruit, one for each month of the year; the leaves of the 3 trees serve for the healing of the nations. Every accursed thing shall disappear. The throne of God and of the Lamb will be there, and his ser-4 vants shall worship him; they shall see him face to face, and bear his 5 name on their foreheads. There shall be no more night, nor will they need the light of lamp or sun, for the Lord God will give them light; and they shall reign for evermore.

Jesus promises to return

6 Then he said to me, 'These words are trustworthy and true. The Lord God who inspires the prophets has sent his angel to show his servants what must shortly happen. And, remember, 7 I am coming soon!'

Happy is the man who heeds the words of prophecy contained in this book! It is I, John, who heard and 8 saw these things. And when I had heard and seen them, I fell in worship at the feet of the angel who had shown them to me. But he said to me, 'No, 9 not that! I am but a fellow-servant with you and your brothers the prophets and those who heed the words of this book. It is God you must worship.' Then he told me, 'Do not 10 seal up the words of prophecy in this book, for the hour of fulfilment is near. Meanwhile, let the evil-doer go 11 on doing evil and the filthy-minded wallow in his filth, but let the good man persevere in his goodness and the dedicated man be true to his dedication.'

'Yes, I am coming soon, and bring- 12 ing my recompense with me, to requite everyone according to his deeds! I am 13 the Alpha and the Omega, the first and the last, the beginning and the end.'

Happy are those who wash their 14 robes clean! They will have the right to the tree of life and will enter by the gates of the city. Outside are dogs, 15 sorcerers and fornicators, murderers and idolaters, and all who love and practise deceit.

'I, Jesus, have sent my angel to you 16 with this testimony for the churches. I am the scion and offspring of David, the bright star of dawn.'

'Come!' say the Spirit and the 17 bride.

'Come!' let each hearer reply.

Come forward, you who are thirsty; accept the water of life, a free gift to all who desire it.

A final word of warning

For my part, I give this warning to 18 everyone who is listening to the words of prophecy in this book: should anyone add to them, God will add to him the plagues described in this book; should anyone take away from the 19 words in this book of prophecy, God will take away from him his share in the tree of life and the Holy City, described in this book.

He who gives this testimony speaks: 20 'Yes, I am coming soon!'

Amen. Come, Lord Jesus!

The grace of the Lord Jesus be with 21 you all.[s]

s *Some witnesses read* with all; *others read* with all God's people; *others read* with God's people; *some add* Amen.

RT=
975